The ENCYCLOPEDIA of POPULAR MUSIC

3rd EDITION

Compiled & Edited by

COLIN LARKIN

VOLUME 4

HERBAL MIXTURE - LOUVIN BROTHERS

muze

MUSIC
VIDEO
BOOKS

First edition published 1992
Reprinted 1994
Second edition published 1995
Reprinted 1997
Third edition published November 1998 by
MUZE UK Ltd
Iron Bridge House, 3 Bridge Approach
Chalk Farm, London NW1 8BD
e-mail: colin@muze.co.uk

MUZE UK Ltd is a wholly owned subsidiary of **MUZE Inc**.
304 Hudson Street, New York, NY 10013, USA
http://www.muze.com

Exclusive distribution in the UK and Rest of World except USA by
Macmillan Reference Ltd
25 Ecclestone Place, London SW1W 9NF
e-mail: macref@macmillan.co.uk

Exclusive distribution in the USA by
Grove's Dictionaries Inc.
345 Park Avenue South, New York, NY 10010, USA
e-mail: grove@grovereference.com

British Library Cataloguing-in-Publication data
A catalogue record for this book is available from the British Library
ISBN 0-333-74134-X (UK)
Library of Congress Cataloging-in-Publication Data
A catalogue record for this book is available from the Library of Congress
1-56159-237-4 (USA)

Conceived, designed, compiled and edited by Colin Larkin for
MUZE UK Ltd
to whom all editorial enquiries should be sent

Editor In Chief: Colin Larkin
Production Editor: Susan Pipe
Research Editor: Nic Oliver
Editorial Assistant: Sarah Lavelle
Executive Editor: Trev Huxley
Special thanks: Roger Kohn, Ian Jacobs, Paul Zullo, Tony Laudico
and every single Klugette

Typeset by Tin Teardrop Studio
Printed and bound in the USA by World Color

CONTENTS

ALBUM RATINGS

Outstanding

Without fault in every way. A classic and therefore strongly recommended. No comprehensive record collection should be without this album.

Excellent.

A high standard album from this artist and therefore highly recommended.

Good.

By the artist's usual standards and therefore recommended.

Disappointing.

Flawed or lacking in some way.

Poor.

An album to avoid unless you are a completist.

Herbal Mixture

Formed in London, England in 1966, Herbal Mixture consisted of Tony McPhee (guitar/vocals), Pete Cruickshank (bass) - both ex-members of John Lee's Groundhogs - and Mike Meeham (drums). The new act's name was inspired by McPhee's interest in alternative medicine. Herbal Mixture secured a deal with **Columbia Records**, for whom they recorded two inventive singles. 'A Love That's Died' married pop and psychedelia through McPhee's fuzz guitar playing, while the atmospheric 'Machines' opens with startling effects, before progressing through contrasting moods heightened by further compelling guitar work. Herbal Mixture split up in 1967 having failed to achieve commercial success either on record or as a live attraction. In 1968 McPhee and Cruickshank were reunited in the **Groundhogs**. *Please Leave My Mind* compiles singles, demo versions and two previously unreleased tracks.

● COMPILATIONS: *Please Leave My Mind* (Distortions 1993)★★.

Herbaliser

The Herbaliser is led by Jake Wherry and DJ Ollie Teeba, who work from the former's TrainTrax studio in Twickenham. Wherry grew up in south London interested in jazz, funk, rare groove and hip-hop, and played the bass and guitar in several jazz, funk and rock bands. Teeba began DJing when he was 15 and later played hip-hop, electro and funk in clubs and warehouses around London. After Wherry had built his studio in 1992, the pair began working together; they later met **DJ Food** at a club and signed with **Ninja Tune Records**. Their first release, 'The Real Killer'/'Blowin' It' (1995), was recorded with keyboards, percussion and horns to produce an abstract blend of jazz instrumental sounds and hip-hop beats, created in a repetitive, sample-orientated manner. After a second single, their first album, *Remedies*, arrived in October 1995. During 1996 they performed live around the UK and Europe with a band that included drums, bass, keyboards, percussion and horns. The following year they toured again to promote further singles, including 'New and Improved'/'Control Centre', and a new album, *Blow Your Headphones*.

● ALBUMS: *Remedies* (Ninja Tune 1995)★★★, *Blow Your Headphones* (Ninja Tune 1997)★★★.

Herbeck, Ray

Formed in Los Angeles, California, USA, in 1935, the Ray Herbeck Orchestra soon relocated to Chicago to pursue the lucrative Midwest one-nighter circuit. With their theme song, 'Romance', Herbeck's was one of the most commercially orientated orchestras of the day. Having previously worked with Leighton Noble, Herbeck recruited musicians George Van, Whitney Boyd, George Winslow, Benny Stabler, Bob McReynolds, Jay Stanley, James Baker, Jim Hefit, Bunny Rang, Art Skolnick, Louis Math, Tom Clark, Al

Ciola, Chi Chi Crozza, Bob Hartzell and Leo Benson, alongside vocalists Betty Benson, Hal Munbar, Kirby Brooks, Ray Olson, Lorraine Benson, Roy Cordell and Irene Wilson. With a supporting tag of 'Ray Herbeck And His Music With Romance', they offered a steady stream of sentimental numbers cultivated to the specific requirements of slow dancing, including songs such as 'Time Stood Still'. The 40s saw the band take engagements at famous hotels such as the Peabody, New Yorker, Muehlbach and Brown Palace, and there were few major ballrooms who did not book the band during their extensive tours. With recordings issued by **Vocalion**, **Columbia** and **OKeh Records** among many others, further exposure arrived during World War II with Herbeck's band making over 300 USO camp show appearances to entertain the forces. They also appeared several times on *Coca Cola's Spotlight Bands* radio show during this time. After the war Herbeck returned to California to play a year's residency at the Riverside Hotel in Reno, then two years at the Last Frontier in Las Vegas. But by the early 50s he had given up music to concentrate on real estate businesses in California and Phoenix.

Herbert, Victor

b. 1 February 1859, Dublin, Eire, d. 26 May 1924, New York, USA. An important and influential composer during the transitional period in the early part of the century when the operetta form was overtaken by American musical comedy. Brought up in the south of England, Herbert studied classical music as a youngster. He played cello in various European symphony orchestras, all the while composing music for the concert platform. In 1885 he accepted a teaching post in Stuttgart where he married an opera singer. The following year he accompanied her on a visit to the USA where he also played, taught and studied. Among Herbert's compositions from his early days in the USA were 'An American Fantasy'. He then began writing operettas, and in 1898 one of the first of them, *The Fortune Teller*, became a great success in New York, establishing his reputation. Four years later Herbert became a US citizen. He continued writing classical music and operettas, and, over the next 20 years composed the music for some 30 Broadway shows, including *Babes In Toyland* (1903), *It Happened In Nordland* (1904), **Mlle. Modiste** (1906), *The Red Mill* (1906), *The Prima Donna* (1908), *Naughty Marietta* (1910), *Sweethearts* (1913), *Princess Pat* (1915), *Eileen* (1917), *The Velvet Lady* (1919), *Orange Blossoms* (1922), *The Dream Girl* (1924), and contributed to several editions of the *Ziegfeld Follies*. The shows contained some of the most memorable and popular songs of the day, including 'Gypsy Love', 'Tramp! Tramp! Tramp!', 'Every Day Is Ladies Day With Me', 'Eileen', 'Because You're You', 'Kiss In The Dark', 'Kiss Me Again', 'Italian Street Song', 'Neapolitan Love Song', 'Indian Summer', 'Romany Life', 'Ah, Sweet Mystery Of Life', 'Sweethearts', 'Moonbeams', 'Yesterthoughts', 'Thine Alone', and

'Rose Of The World'. His main lyricist collaborators included Rida Johnson Young, Henry Blossom, **Buddy De Sylva**, Harry B. Smith, Glen MacDonough, Gene Buck, and Robert Smith. Herbert also wrote musical scores for silent films (usually performed only in those motion picture theatres in main urban centres equipped to house a full orchestra) and grand operas. In February 1924 Herbert's 'A Suite For Serenades' was performed by **Paul Whiteman**'s orchestra at a New York concert which also saw the first public performance of **George Gershwin**'s 'Rhapsody In Blue'. The 1939 movie, the Great Victor Herbert, starred Walter Connolly, **Allan Jones** and **Mary Martin**. Herbert's prolific output was achieved despite ill health but he suffered a fatal heart attack in May 1924

● FURTHER READING: *Victor Herbert: American Music Master*, Claire Lee.

Herbolzheimer, Peter

b. 31 December 1935, Bucharest, Romania. After playing guitar early in his career, much of his subsequent playing was on trombone, although he is perhaps best known as a bandleader, composer and arranger. Throughout the 60s Herbolzheimer was frequently to be found playing in orchestras in theatres and recording and broadcasting studios. He also led his own big band in which he used many European jazzmen including **Dusko Goykovich**, **Palle Mikkelborg**, **Niels-Henning Ørsted Pedersen** and **Alex Riel**, and temporarily resident Americans such as **Art Farmer** and **Herb Geller**. In the 70s, he worked extensively in television and radio, played with **Dizzy Gillespie** and others, and won awards and was honoured in a number of ways, including being invited to contribute music for the 1972 Munich-based Olympic Games. Herbolzheimer's playing and writing is an intriguing mingling of jazz and rock which, while not truly classifiable as jazz-rock, contains many of the more attractive and swinging elements of both forms.

● ALBUMS: *My Kind Of Sunshine* (MPS 1971)★★, *Wide Open* (MPS 1973)★★★, *Jazz Gala Concert* (Atlantic 1976)★★★, *Jazz Gala '77 All Star Big Band* (Telefunken 1977)★★★, *Bandfire* (Panda 1981).★★★

Herd

This UK group originally formed in 1965 as a quintet featuring Terry Clark (vocals), Andy Bown (bass), Gary Taylor (guitar) and Tony Chapman (drums). After several line-up shuffles, Bown took over on lead vocals and organ, occasionally relieved by the new guitarist **Peter Frampton**. In 1967, however, songwriting managers **Ken Howard** and **Alan Blaikley** were taken on in place of **Billy Gaff** and immediately promoted the reluctant Frampton to centre stage. A near miss with the psychedelic 'I Can Fly' was followed by a portentous adaptation of *Orpheus In The Underworld* (retitled 'From The Underworld'), which became a UK Top 10 hit. Having translated Virgil into pop, **Howard And Blaikley** next tackled Milton with 'Paradise Lost'.

Despite their strange mix of literate pop and jazz rhythms, the Herd were marketed for teenzine consumption and Frampton was voted the 'Face of '68' by *Rave* magazine. Not surprisingly, a more straightforward hit followed with 'I Don't Want Our Loving To Die'. Ambivalent feelings about their pop star status convinced them to dump Howard and Blaikley in favour of the mercurial **Andrew Loog Oldham**, but their next single, the Frampton-composed 'Sunshine Cottage', missed by a mile. A brief tie-up with yet another manager, **Harvey Lisberg**, came to nothing and by this time Frampton had left to form **Humble Pie**. For a brief period, the remaining members struggled on, but to no avail. Bown later teamed up with **Andy Fairweather-Low** and appeared on the road with **Status Quo**, while Taylor and Steele guested on various sessions.

● ALBUMS: *Paradise Lost* (1968)★★★, *Lookin' Thru You* (Fontana 1968)★★★, *Nostalgia* (Bumble 1973)★★★.

Here Come The Warm Jets - Brian Eno

Having left Roxy Music, Eno began his solo career with this idiosyncratic album. Robert Fripp, Paul Thompson and Phil Manzanera are among those appearing on a set of songs exhibiting a mischievous love of pure pop music. Macabre lyrics constantly subvert the quirky melodies, a feature fully expressed on 'Baby's On Fire', while the singer's cheeky vocals exaggerate the ambiguity. Savage guitar lines, erratic synthesizer and pounding drums provide exciting textures on a collection as beguiling as it is invigorating.

● Tracks: *Needles In A Camel's Eye; The Paw Paw Negro Blowtorch; Baby's On Fire; Cindy Tells Me; Driving Me Backwards; On Some Faraway Beach; Blank Frank; Dead Finks Don't Talk; Some Of Them Are Old; Here Come The Warm Jets.*

● First released 1974

● UK peak chart position: 26

● USA peak chart position: 151

Here My Dear - Marvin Gaye

A concept album of some magnitude, although the subject matter could hardly have been comfortable listening for Anna, Marvin Gaye's ex-wife. She was the subject of Gaye's public 'divorce album'. The illustration on the sleeve depicts love, marriage, pain and divorce, in addition to the scales of justice (equal). This lengthy album (originally a double vinyl) was poorly received by the critics, although now it has grown in stature, and it really does have considerable depth and melody. Let's face it, if Gaye sang a gardening seed catalogue from cover to cover it would be brilliant.

● Tracks: *Here, My Dear; I Met A Little Girl; When Did You Stop Loving Me, When Did I Stop Loving You; Anger; Is That Enough; Everybody Needs Love; Time To Get It Together; Sparrow; Anna's Song; When Did You Stop Loving Me, When Did I Stop Loving You (Instrumental); A Funky Space Reincarnation; You Can Leave, But It's Going To Cost You; Falling In Love Again; When Did You Stop Loving Me, When Did I Stop Loving You (Reprise).*

- First released 1978
- UK peak chart position: did not chart
- USA peak chart position: 26

Here We Go Again! - The Kingston Trio

Admirers of left-wing, thinking songsters such as Woody Guthrie and the Weavers, the Kingston Trio - Nick Reynolds, Bob Shane and Dave Guard - were the alternative. They cared, but also laced concern with commercial appeal. There was an intelligent market just waiting to sympathize, and for some four years The Trio were top dogs as far as folk-singing was concerned. Successful with a campfire rendering of 'Tom Dooley' they rattled out albums at a hell of a lick. Have guitars will record? *Here We Go Again*, probably exactly how they felt in the liberal whirlwind that surrounded them, is not only a fine slice of 50s American folkloric sound but a document of a period when acoustic music began inching towards acceptance.

- Tracks: *Molly Dee; Across The Wide Missouri; Haul Away; The Wanderer; 'Round About The Mountain; Oleanna; The Unfortunate Miss Bailey; San Miguel (Inn Taton); Rollin' Stone; Goober Peas; A Worried Man.*
- First released 1959
- UK peak chart position: did not chart
- USA peak chart position: 1

Here We Go Round The Mulberry Bush

Based on **Beatles**' biographer Hunter Davies' novel of the same name, *Here We Go Round The Mulberry Bush* provided a very British view of sexual awakening. Barry Evans starred as the naive school-leaver determined to lose his virginity; Adrienne Posta and Judy Geeson featured as two objects of desire. Deemed daring at the time of its release (1967), the film's modish trappings have dated badly. Its myopic view of women is largely unacceptable and the screenplay fails to recreate the angst of adolescence. Indeed, if the film has a place in British cinema history, it is as a stepping-stone between the 'Carry-On' and 'Confessions' series. Chief interest in *Here We Go Round The Mulberry Bush* centres on its soundtrack, the bulk of which was provided by the **Spencer Davis Group**. The quartet even make a cameo appearance as the featured group at a church dance. Paradoxically, it was another act, **Traffic**, formed by ex-Spencer Davis singer **Steve Winwood**, which enjoyed greater success through their association with the film. Their self-penned theme song provided Traffic with their third UK Top 10 hit. It remains more memorable than the film inspiring it.

Here's Little Richard - Little Richard

The enigmatic Little Richard turned rock 'n' roll inside-out with a succession of highly expressive recordings during the mid-50s. Fuelled by an unfettered New Orleans backbeat, he combined gospel fervour and orgasmic delight in equal doses, singing without recourse to convention, hammering the piano keys with barely checked passion. *Here's Little Richard* abounds with essential performances that define an era and few collections offer such unremitting excitement. The pace barely relents, while almost every track has become an integral part of pop history, either in their own right, or through the countless cover versions they have inspired. It is an exceptional album from an exceptional talent.

- Tracks: *Tutti Frutti; True, Fine Mama; Ready Teddy; Baby; Slippin' And Slidin'; Long Tall Sally; Miss Ann; Oh Why?; Rip It Up; Jenny Jenny; She's Got It; Can't Believe You Wanna Leave.*
- First released 1957
- UK peak chart position: did not chart
- USA peak chart position: 13

Heretic

Formed in 1984 in Los Angeles, California, USA, the band's original line-up consisted of Julian Mendez (vocals), Brian Korban (guitar), Bobby Marquez (guitar), Dennis O'Hara (bass) and Rick Merrick (drums). Quickly gaining popularity on the club circuit in and around the Los Angeles area, the band attracted the attention of Metal Blade Records. Heretic's debut release for the label was a mini-album, *Torture Knows No Boundaries*, in 1987. This was a worthwhile serving of fast power metal, slightly marred because Julian Mendez's vocals were not ideally suited to the band's hard-hitting approach. To his credit, the singer realized this and left the band, to be replaced by Mike Howe later the same year. On their second outing, the full-length *Breaking Point*, they sounded much more confident. However, when Howe left the band later that year to join **Metal Church**, a series of vocal replacements could not prevent Heretic folding in 1989.

- ALBUMS: *Torture Knows No Boundaries* mini-album (Metal Blade 1987)★★★, *Breaking Point* (Metal Blade 1988)★★★.

Herfurt, Skeets

b. Arthur Herfurt, 28 May 1911, Cincinnati, Ohio, USA. As a young man Herfurt played various reed instruments, mostly in the south-west and especially in Colorado, where he grew up and was educated. His first name-band engagement was with **Smith Ballew**, the popular singer. This was in 1934 and in the same year he joined the Dorsey Brothers band, remaining in its ranks after the brothers split up, when the band continued under **Jimmy Dorsey**'s name. Later in the 30s, Herfurt played with bands led by **Ray Noble**, **George Stoll** and **Tommy Dorsey**. Tiring of travelling, he settled in the Los Angeles area, and was briefly with the mid-40s band led by **Alvino Rey** before military service towards the end of World War II. After the war Herfurt worked in film studios, but had a short spell with **Benny Goodman**. During the 50s and beyond, he worked in studios, led his own band, and played in numerous recording studio orchestras under many different leaders and backing numerous artists of note. He had a further spell with Goodman in the early 60s and again in the middle of the decade. Herfurt's tenor saxophone and clarinet playing was of a very high standard and he was one of countless unsung stalwarts of the swing era's big bands.

● COMPILATIONS: *The Dorsey Brothers Orchestra* (MCA 1934-35)★★★★, *The Uncollected Alvino Rey* (Hindsight 1944-45)★★★.

Heritage

One of the lesser lights of the **N.W.O.B.H.M.** explosion, this band from Yorkshire, England, featured Steve Johnson (vocals, guitar), Steve Barratt (vocals, guitar), Fasker Johnson (vocals, bass) and Pete Halliday (drums). Like fellow north England group **Gaskin**, Heritage signed to the predominantly punk-orientated Rondolet Records, releasing their debut album, *Remorse Code*, in 1982. With literally hundreds of bands attempting to break into the mainstream rock music scene at the same time, most of them located much closer to its epicentre in London, Heritage had neither the songs nor the vision to attach themselves to the bandwagon.

● ALBUMS: *Remorse Code* (Rondolet 1982)★★.

Herman's Hermits

Originally known as the Heartbeats, Herman's Hermits were discovered in 1963 by manager **Harvey Lisberg** and his partner Charlie Silverman. After restructuring the group, the line-up emerged as **Peter Noone** (b. 5 November 1947, Manchester, England; vocals), Karl Green (b. 31 July 1947, Salford, Manchester, England; bass), Keith Hopwood (b. 26 October 1946, Manchester, England; rhythm guitar), Lek Leckenby (b. Derek Leckenby, 14 May 1946, Leeds, England, d. 4 June 1994, Manchester, England; lead guitar) and Barry Whitwam (b. 21 July 1946, Manchester, England; drums - formerly a member of Leckenby's first group, the Wailers). A link with producer **Mickie Most** and an infectious cover of **Earl Jean**'s US hit, 'I'm Into Something Good' gave the quintet a UK number 1 in 1964. By early 1965, the group had settled into covering 50s songs such as the **Rays**' 'Silhouettes' and **Sam Cooke**'s 'Wonderful World', when an extraordinary invasion of America saw them challenge the **Beatles** as a chart act with over 10 million record sales in under 12 months. A stream of non-stop hits over the next two years, including the vaudevillian 'Mrs Brown You've Got A Lovely Daughter' and 'I'm Henry VIII, I Am', effectively transformed them into teen idols. Director Sam Katzman even cast them in a couple of movies, *When The Boys Meet The Girls* (co-starring **Connie Francis**) and *Hold On!* Although their music-hall-inspired US chart-toppers were not issued as singles in the UK, they enjoyed a run of hits penned by the leading commercial songwriters of the day. 'A Must To Avoid' and 'No Milk Today' were inventive as well as catchy, although by 1968/9 their repertoire had become more formulaic. The hits continued until as late as 1970 when Noone finally decided to pursue a solo career. Thereafter, Herman's Hermits drifted into cabaret.

Although a reunion concert did take place at Madison Square Garden in New York in 1973, stage replacements for Noone were later sought, including Peter Cowap, Karl Green, Garth Elliott and Rod Gerrard. Noone eventually settled in California, where he presented his own music show on television, and rekindled an acting career which had begun many years earlier on the top UK soap opera, *Coronation Street*. Leckenby died in 1994 following a long fight with cancer.

● ALBUMS: *Herman's Hermits* (Columbia 1965)★★★, *Introducing Herman's Hermits* (Columbia 1965)★★★, *Herman's Hermits On Tour* (Columbia 1965)★★★, *Hold On!* soundtrack (Columbia 1966)★★, *Both Sides Of Herman's Hermits* (Columbia 1966)★★★, *There's A Kind Of Hush* (Columbia 1967)★★★, *Mrs Brown You've Got A Lovely Daughter* (Columbia 1968)★★★, *Blaze* (Columbia 1967)★★★.

● COMPILATIONS: *The Best Of* (Columbia 1969)★★★, *The Most Of* (MFP 1971)★★★, *The Most Of Vol. 2* (MFP 1972)★★★, *Twenty Greatest Hits* (K-Tel 1977)★★★, *The Very Best Of* (MFP 1984)★★★, *The Collection* (Castle 1990)★★★, *The EP Collection* (See For Miles 1990)★★★★, *Best Of The EMI Years Vol. 1* (EMI 1991)★★★★, *Best Of The EMI Years Vol. 2* (EMI 1992)★★★.

● FILMS: *Hold On* (1965).

Herman, Jerry

b. 10 July 1933, New York City, New York, USA. One of the leading composers and lyricists for the American musical theatre during the past 30 years, Herman was playing piano by the age of six under the tuition of his mother, a professional piano teacher. After high school, he started to train as a designer, but had second thoughts, and studied drama at the University of Miami. By the mid-50s he was playing piano in New York clubs and writing material for several well-known entertainers. During the late 50s and early 60s, he worked on a number of Off-Broadway musical shows, the first of which was *I Feel Wonderful* (1954), and had several songs in the revue *Nightcap*, which ran for nearly a year. He also wrote the book, music and lyrics - and directed - *Parade* (1960), and in the same year contributed the opening number, 'Best Gold', to the short-lived *A To Z*. In 1961, after writing some songs for the 13-performance flop, *Madame Aphrodite*, he enjoyed his first real success with his score for the Broadway musical *Milk And Honey*, which ran for 543 performances. He had a smash hit three years later with **Hello, Dolly!** ('Before The Parade Passes By', 'It Only Takes A Moment', 'It Takes A Woman', 'Put On Your Sunday Clothes', 'Elegance'), which stayed at the St. James Theatre in New York for nearly seven years. The show - with it's Grammy-winning title number - gave **Carol Channing** her greatest role, and has been constantly revived ever since. In 1966, Herman had another triumph with **Mame**, which is generally considered to be his best score. Once again, there was a marvellous title song, which was accompanied by other delights such as 'If He Should Walk Into My Life', 'We Need A Little Christmas', 'Open A New Window', 'Bosom Buddies', and 'It's Today'. Since then, his infrequent, but classy scores, have included *Dear World* ('And I Was Beautiful', 'The Spring Of Next Year', 1969), *Mack And Mabel* ('I Won't Send Roses', 'When Mabel Comes In The Room', 'Movies Were Movies', 1974), *The Grand Tour* (1979), and *La Cage Aux Folles* ('Song On the Sand (La Da Da Da)', 'With You On My Arm', 'I Am What I Am'). The latter show opened in 1983, and ran for 1,176 performances in New York. Herman won a Grammy for the *Mame* cast album, and **Tony Awards** for his work on *Hello, Dolly!* and *La Cage Aux Folles*. There was some controversy when Herman's 'old fashioned' music and lyrics for the latter show, triumphed over **Stephen Sondheim**'s typically contemporary score for *Sunday In The Park With George*. Herman has been inducted into the Theatre Hall of Fame and the Songwriters Hall of Fame. The latter organization honoured him with their **Johnny Mercer** Award in 1987, and in 1996, he received a lifetime achievement award from the Hollywood Press Club. Herman occasionally presents an evening devoted to his own songs, and many shows have been staged in tribute to him over the years, including *Jerry's Girls*, which played on Broadway in 1986. In 1993, Herman left New York to live in Bel Air on the west coast, but denied rumours of retirement, explaining that his 10-year absence had been due to lack of inspiration: 'Nothing has come along that is fresh and interesting.' Revivals of his earlier works, with which he is usually closely involved, are constantly circulating. In the early 90s, these included US regional productions of *La Cage Aux Folles* and *Mame*, as well as a 30th anniversary international tour of *Hello, Dolly!*, complete with its original leading lady, Carol Channing, which reached Broadway in October 1995. Two months later, Herman's personal favourite of all his own shows, *Mack And Mabel*, made its West End debut. Herman's 'dry' spell finally came to an end in December 1996, when the two-hour musical, *Mrs. Santa Claus*, was transmitted on CBS television. The composer's first creative contribution to the medium, it starred the original Auntie Mame, Angela Lansbury. Among the highlights of Herman's score, were 'Almost Young', 'We Don't Go Together', 'He Needs Me', 'Avenue A', and 'Whistle'. Although a generation removed from the past masters of the American musical theatre - whom he admires so much - Herman's style adheres closely to the earlier formulae and he brings to his best work a richness sadly lacking in that of many of his contemporaries.

● ALBUMS: *An Evening With Jerry Herman* (1993)★★★.
● FURTHER READING: *Showtune-A Memoir*, Jerry Herman with Marilyn Stasio.

Herman, Lenny

Although largely uncelebrated during his career as a bandleader, Lenny Herman made a significant contribution to the dance band music of New York, USA, from the early 50s onwards. Based in hotels such as the Astor, Edison, Roosevelt, Waldorf-Astoria and New Yorker, his compact band, often dubbed 'The Mightiest Little Band In The Land', etched a definite impression on the evening dancers of those establishments with songs such as 'No Foolin''. Led by Herman's accordion playing, the band, which never numbered more than ten and frequently less than eight, also found engagements further afield in Philadelphia (the Warwick Hotel), Atlantic City (the Straymore Hotel), Virginia Beach (the Cavalier Hotel) and Dallas (the Baker Hotel). By the mid-60s the band had moved permanently to the Lake Tahoe area, where the now five or six strong ensemble earned its living playing to mixed audiences at the resort hotels. They continue to do so to this day.

Herman, Woody

b. Woodrow Charles Herman, 16 May 1913, Milwaukee, Wisconsin, USA, d. 29 October 1987. A child prodigy, Herman sang and tap-danced in local clubs before touring as a singer in vaudeville. To improve his act he took up the saxophone and later the clarinet, all by the age of 12. By his mid-teens he was sufficiently accomplished to play in a band, and he went on to work in a string of dance bands during the late 20s and early 30s. Last in this line was **Isham Jones**, Herman first being in Isham Jones's Juniors, with whom he recorded early in 1936. When Jones folded the band later that year, Herman was elected leader by a nucleus of musicians who wanted to continue. Initially a co-operative group, the band included flügelhorn player Joe Bishop, bassist Walt Yoder, drummer Frank Carlson and trombonist Neil Reid. With a positive if uncommercial view of what they wanted to achieve, they were billed as 'The Band That Plays The Blues' and gradually built a following during the swing era. The success of their recordings of 'Golden Wedding', a Jiggs Noble re-working of 'La Cinquantaine', and especially Bishop's 'At The Woodchoppers' Ball' helped the band's fortunes. During the early 40s numerous personnel changes took place, some dictated by the draft, others by a gradual shift in style. By 1944 Herman was leading the band which eventually became labelled as the First Herd. Included in this powerhouse were trumpeters Ray Wetzel, **Neal Hefti** and **Pete Candoli**, trombonist **Bill Harris**, tenor saxophonist **Joe 'Flip' Phillips** and the remarkable rhythm section of **Ralph Burns**, **Billy Bauer**, **Chubby Jackson** and **Dave Tough**, to which was added vibraphonist **Margie Hyams**. This band made several records which were not only musically excellent but were also big sellers, amongst them 'Apple Honey', 'Caldonia', 'Northwest Passage' and 'Goosey Gander'. During the next year or so the band's personnel remained fairly stable, although the brilliant if unreliable Tough was replaced in late 1945 by **Don Lamond**, and they continued to make good records, including 'Bijou', 'Your Father's Mustache', 'Wild Root' and 'Blowin' Up A Storm'. In 1946 the band still included Candoli, Harris, Phillips, Bauer, Jackson and Lamond and amongst the newcomers were trumpeters **Sonny Berman**, **Shorty Rogers** and **Conrad Gozzo** and vibraphonist **Red Norvo**. The First Herd played a concert at Carnegie Hall to great acclaim but, despite the band's continuing popularity, at the end of this same year, 1946, Herman temporarily disbanded because of economic difficulties. The following year he was back with his Second Herd, known to posterity as the 'Four Brothers' band. This band represented a particularly modern approach to big band music, playing bop-influenced charts by **Jimmy Giuffre** and others. Most striking, however, and the source of the band's name, was the saxophone section. With Sam Marowitz and **Herbie Steward** on altos, **Stan Getz** and **Zoot Sims**, tenors, and **Serge Chaloff**, baritone, the section was thrustingly modern; and when Steward doubled on tenor, they created a deeper-toned sound that was utterly different to any other band of the time. The concept of the reed section had originated with **Gene Roland**, whose rehearsal band had included Getz, Sims, Steward and Giuffre. Heard by Burns and hired by Herman, these musicians helped create a new excitement and this band was another enormously successful group. Although the modern concepts took precedence, there was still room for straight ahead swingers. The brass section at this time included Rogers, Marky Markowitz and **Ernie Royal** and trombonist Earl Swope. The rhythm section included Lamond and vibraphonist **Terry Gibbs**. The reed section was dominant, however, and when Steward was replaced by **Al Cohn**, it was by far the best in the land. Apart from 'Four Brothers' the band had other successful records, including 'Keen And Peachy', 'The Goof And I' and 'Early Autumn'. This last piece was written by Burns to round out a three-part suite, 'Summer Sequence', he had composed earlier and which had already been recorded. The extra part allowed the record company to release a four-sided set, and Getz's solo on 'Early Autumn' was the first example of the saxophonist's lyrical depths to make an impression upon the jazz world. Unfortunately, despite its successes, the band wasn't quite popular enough, perhaps being a little ahead of its time. Once again Herman folded, only to re-form almost at once. Numbering the Herman Herds was never easy but the leader himself named his early 50s group as the Third Herd. Although lacking the precision of the Four Brothers band and the raw excitement of the First Herd, the new band was capable of swinging superbly. As before, Herman had no difficulty in attracting top-flight musicians, including **Red Rodney**, **Urbie Green**, **Kai Winding**, **Richie Kamuca**, **Bill Perkins**, **Monty Budwig** and **Jake Hanna**. Of particular importance to the band at this time (and for the next few years) was **Nat Pierce**, who not only played piano but also wrote many fine arrangements and acted as straw boss. The times were hostile to big bands, however, and by the mid-50s Herman was working in comparative obscurity. Members of the band, who then included **Bill Berry**, Bobby Lamb, Kamuca, Budwig and Harris, wryly described this particular Herman group as the 'un-Herd'. Towards the end of the decade Herman was still fighting against the tide, but was doing it with some of the best available musicians: Cohn, Sims, **Don Lanphere**, **Bob Brookmeyer**, Pierce, Kamuca, Perkins and **Med Flory**. During the 60s and 70s Herman's bands were given various informal tags; the Swinging Herd, the Thundering Herd. Mostly they did as these names suggested, thundering and swinging through some excellent charts and with many fine sidemen many of whom were culled from the universities. Other leaders did this, of course, but Herman always ensured that he was far from being the solitary veteran on a bandstand full of beginners. He kept many older hands on board to ensure the youngsters had experienced models from whom they could draw inspiration.

Among the sidemen during these years were Pierce, Hanna, **Bill Chase**, baritone saxophonist Nick Brignola, **Sal Nistico**, tenor saxophonist Carmen Leggio, **John Von Ohlen**, **Cecil Payne**, **Carl Fontana**, **Dusko Goykovich** and trombonists Henry Southall and Phil Wilson. In the late 60s Herman dabbled with jazz-rock but, although he subsequently kept a few such numbers in the band's book, it was not an area in which he was comfortable. In 1976 Herman played a major concert at Carnegie Hall, celebrating the 40th anniversary of his first appearance there. As the 80s began, Herman's health was poor and he might have had thoughts of retirement; he had, after all, been performing for a little over 60 years. Unfortunately, this was the time he discovered that his manager for many years had systematically embezzled funds set aside for taxes. Now Herman was not only flat broke and in danger of eviction from his home in the Hollywood Hills, but he also owed the IRS millions of dollars. Forced to play on, he continued to lead bands on punishing tours around the world, tours which were hugely successful but were simultaneously exacerbating his poor physical condition. In 1986 he celebrated 50 years as a bandleader with a tour that featured long-standing sideman **Frank Tiberi**, baritone saxophonist Mike Brignola, trumpeter Bill Byrne and bassist Lynn Seaton. The following year he was still on the road - and also on the sidewalk, when a gold star in his name was laid along Hollywood Boulevard's Walk of Fame. In March of that same year the Herman Herd, whatever number this one might be, was still thundering away at concerts, some of which fortunately, were recorded. But it could not, of course, go on forever, and Herman died in October 1987. As a clarinettist and saxophonist, sometimes playing alto, latterly soprano, Herman was never a virtuoso player in the manner of swing era contemporaries such as **Benny Goodman** or **Artie Shaw**. Unlike theirs, his playing was deeply rooted in the blues, and he brought to his music an unshakeable commitment to jazz. Despite the inevitable ups and downs of his career as a big band leader, he stuck to his principles and if he ever compromised it was always, somehow, on his own terms. He composed little, although many of the First Herd's greatest successes were head arrangements conceived and developed on the bandstand or in rehearsal. Herman's real skills lay in his ability to pick the right people for his band, to enthuse them, and to ensure that they never lost that enthusiasm. In selecting for his band he had patience and an excellent ear. He knew what he wanted and he nearly always got it. Over the many years he led a band, scores of musicians passed through the ranks, many of them amongst the finest in jazz. No one ever had a bad word to say about him.

● ALBUMS: *Sequence In Jazz* (Columbia 1949)★★★, *Dance Parade* (Columbia 1949)★★★, *And His Woodchoppers* (Columbia 1950)★★★★, *Swinging With The Woodchoppers* (Dial 1950)★★★★, *Blue Prelude* (Coral 1950)★★★★, *Souvenirs* (Coral 1950)★★★, *Live At The Hollywood Palladium* (1951)★★★★, with Charlie Parker *Bird With The Herd* (1951)★★★★, *Dance Date On Mars* (Mars 1952)★★★, *Woody Herman Goes Native* (Mars 1952)★★★, *At Carnegie Hall Vol 1 & 2* (MGM 1952)★★★★, *Classics In Jazz* (Capitol 1952)★★★, *Thundering Herd* (1953)★★★★, *The Third Herd* (MGM 1953)★★★★, *Woody's Best* (Coral 1953)★★★, *The Three Herds* (Columbia 1954)★★★★, *Woody Herman With The Erroll Garner Trio* (1954)★★★, *The Third Herd Live In Stockholm Vols 1 & 2* (1954)★★★★, *Jackpot* (1955)★★★, *Blue Flame* (MGM 1955)★★★, *The Woody Herman Band* (Capitol 1955)★★★, *Road Band* (Capitol 1955)★★★, *Music For Tired Lovers* (Columbia 1955)★★★, *12 Shades Of Blue* (Columbia 1955)★★★, *Woodchoppers Ball* (Decca 1955)★★★★, *Ridin' Herd* (Columbia 1955)★★★, *Woody* (Columbia 1956)★★★, *Hi-Fi-ing Herd* (MGM 1956)★★★★, *Jackpot* (Capitol 1956)★★★, *Blues Groove* (Capitol 1956)★★★, *Jazz The Utmost* (Clef 1956)★★★, *Woody Herman With Barney Kessel And His Orchestra* (1957)★★★, *Woody Herman And His Orchestra i* (1957)★★★, *Woody Herman Live Featuring Bill Harris Vols 1 & 2* (1957)★★★, *Bijou* (Harmony 1957)★★★, *Early Autumn* (Verve 1957)★★★★, *Songs For Hip Lovers* (Verve 1957)★★★, *The Swinging Herman Herd* (Brunswick 1957)★★★, *Love is The Sweetest Thing Sometimes* (Verve 1958)★★★, *Live At Peacock Lake, Hollywood* (1958)★★★★, *The Herd Rides Again In Stereo* (Verve 1958)★★★, *Summer Sequence* (Harmony 1958)★★★, *Men From Mars* (Verve 1958)★★★, *58'* (Verve 1958)★★★, *Herman's Beat And Puentes Beat* (Everest 1958)★★★, *Moody Woody* (Everest 1958)★★★, *The Fourth Herd* (Jazzland 1959)★★★★, *Woody Herman's New Big Band At The Monterey Jazz Festival* (1959)★★★★, *Woody Herman Sextet At the Round Table* (Roulette 1959)★★★★, *At The Monterey Jazz Festival* (Atlantic 1960)★★★, *1960* (1960)★★★, *The Woody Herman Quartet* (1962)★★★★, *Swing Low Sweet Chariot* (Philips 1962)★★★, *Woody Herman And His Orchestra ii* (1962)★★★★, *1963* (Philips 1963)★★★, *Encore Woody Herman 1963* (Philips 1963)★★★, *Live At Basin Street West* (1963)★★★, *Encore* (1963)★★★, *The New World Of Woody Herman* (1963)★★★, *Hey! Heard The Herd* (Verve 1963)★★★, *Woody Herman At Harrah's Club* (1964)★★★, *The Swinging Herman Herd Recorded Live* (Philips 1964)★★★★, *Woody Herman 1964* (Philips 1964)★★★, *Woody's Winners* (Columbia 1965)★★★, *Woody's Big Band Goodies* (Philips 1965)★★★, *My Kind Of Broadway* (Columbia 1965)★★★, *The Jazz Swinger* (Columbia 1966)★★★, *Blowing Up A Storm* (Sunset 1966)★★★, *Woody Live East And West* (Columbia 1967)★★★, *Live In Seattle* (1967)★★★, *Light My Fire* (1968)★★★, *Heavy Exposure* (1969)★★★, *Light My Fire* (Cadet 1969)★★, *Woody* (1970)★★, *Brand New* (1971)★★★, *The Raven Speaks* (1972)★★★, *Giant Steps* (1973)★★★, *Woody Herman And His Orchestra iii* (1974)★★★★, *Herd At Montreux* (1974)★★★★, *Woody Herman With Frank Sinatra* (1974)★★★, *Children Of Lima* (1974)★★★, *King Cobra* (1975)★★★, *Woody Herman In Warsaw* (1976)★★★★, *40th Anniversary: Carnegie Hall Concert* (1976)★★★★, *Lionel Hampton Presents Woody Herman* (1977)★★★, *Road Father* (1978)★★★, *Together: Flip & Woody* (1978)★★★, *Chick, Donald, Walter & Woodrow* (1978) *Woody Herman And Friends At The Monterey Jazz Festival* (1979)★★★★, *Woody Herman Presents A Concord Jam Vol. 1* (1980)★★★, *Woody Herman Presents Four Others Vol. 2* (1981)★★★, *Live At The Concord Jazz Festival* (1981)★★★★, *Live In Chicago* (1981)★★★, *Aurex Jazz Festival '82* (1982)★★★, *Woody Herman Presents A Great American Evening* (1983)★★★, *50th Anniversary Tour* (1986)★★★, *Woody's Gold Star* (1987).

● COMPILATIONS: *The Hits Of Woody Herman* (Capitol 1961)★★★, *The Thundering Herds Vols 1-3* 3-LP box set (Columbia 1963)★★★★, *Golden Hits* (Decca 1964)★★★, *Greatest Hits* (Columbia 1966)★★★★, *The Turning Point 1943-44* (Decca 1967)★★★★, *The Band That Plays The Blues* (1937-42 recordings)★★★, *The V-Disc Years Vol. 1* (1944-45 recordings)★★★★, *The First Herd* (1945 recordings)★★★★, *The Best Of Woody Herman* (1945-47 recordings)★★★, *The V Disc Years 1944 - 46* (Hep Jazz 1993)★★★, *The Fourth Herd & The New World Of Woody Herman* (Mobile Fidelity 1995)★★★★.

● FURTHER READING: *Woody Herman*, Steve Voce. *The Woodchopper's Ball*, Woody Herman with Stuart Troup. *Woody Herman: A Guide To The Big Band Recordings, 1936-87*, Dexter Morrill.

Hermeljin, Dylan

Dutchman Hermeljin was still studying business economics part-time when his first brace of 2000 And One records were released on Fierce Ruling Diva's Lower East Side label in 1989 preceding 1992's 'Focus', which arrived on fellow countryman Stefan Robber's Eevolute imprint. It was a typical slice of passionate techno. Much of his output remains mysterious, though 100% Pure is him and Sandy, his partner at the Black Beat Record Store. Their tribal techno opus 'My Life In The Bush' arrived on his own 100% Pure label. Other monikers include Planet Gong ('Planet Gong', a **Djax Up Beats** dose of Detroit techno, actually recorded two years before release in 1994), Babies From Gong and Edge Of Motion. After just four releases 100% Pure were rewarded with an installment on Beechwood's New Electronica series, an album entitled *The Lowlands* emerging.

● ALBUMS: *New Electronica Presents: The Lowlands* (Beechwood 1994)★★★.

Herndon, James

b. Durham, North Carolina, USA. Herndon grew up with gospel singing legend **Shirley Caesar** in North Carolina before enrolling at Hillside High School. He remained good friends with Caesar, and she soon asked him to join the Caravans as singer and pianist when she joined that group in the late 50s. From 1959-67 he travelled and recorded with the Caravans during a period many consider to be their peak. As a part-time diversion he also established his own gospel group, the Wright Special, in Detroit, and worked with **Motown Records** artist **Kim Weston**, serving as her bandleader, pianist and arranger. More infrequently, he also collaborated with **Aretha Franklin**. Through the late 60s and early 70s he likewise embarked on his own solo career, releasing a succession of high quality albums for Light Records, the best of which many contend to be *Nobody But You*.

● ALBUMS: *Nobody But You* (Light 1978)★★★.

Herndon, Ty

b. Butler, Alabama, USA. 90s country singer Ty Herndon grew up with a background of family singing, both at home and in church. He went to Nashville to seek his fortune, but through bad management agreements, he made no progress and his mother lost her house. 'Hat Full Of Rain' summarizes his problems: 'I've been ridin' through the storm, feelin' weary and worn.' He kept plugging away at his music and in 1993, he became the Texas Entertainer of the Year. Nashville has now welcomed him back and his debut album included guest vocals from **Joe Diffie** and **Patty Loveless**. The title track, a dramatic ballad, was a US country hit, while he dipped into the **Jim Croce** songbook for 'You Don't Mess Around With Jim'. The 1996 follow-up was a disappointment, suffering from a shortage of standout material.

● ALBUMS: *What Mattered Most* (Epic 1995)★★★★, *Living In A Moment* (Epic 1996)★★, *Big Hopes* (Epic 1998)★★★.

Heroes - David Bowie

The Germanic feel of this album is not surprising, as Bowie recorded it in Berlin during his infatuation with the city. It was a much more lively affair than *Low* and has the benefit of a title track that remains one of his best ever songs (in addition to excellent contributions from Fripp and Eno). 'Beauty And The Beast' was difficult to accept as a single, yet it works as the album's opener. 'Sense Of Doubt' is the opposite of 'Heroes' - dark and moody, as is 'Neukoln'. Even through the doom and gloom, this is an important Bowie album, and one to which critics return time and time again.

● Tracks: *Beauty And The Beast; Joe The Lion; Heroes; Sons Of The Silent Age; Blackout; V-2 Schneider; Sense Of Doubt; Moss Garden; Neukoln; The Secret Life Of Arabia.*
● First released 1977
● UK peak chart position: 3
● USA peak chart position: 35

Heron

Folk-rock attraction Heron were one of several groups signed to both the Red Bus agency and Dawn label, home of **Mungo Jerry** and **Mike Cooper**. The unit's grasp of melody was unveiled on *Heron*, released to coincide with the ambitious *Penny Concert Tour* on which the group shared a bill with progressive rock acts Comus and Titus Groan and afro-rock practitioners Demon Fuzz. Heron, whose line-up included Roy Apps (guitar/vocals), Steve Jones (keyboards), Tony Pook (vocals/percussion), Mike Finesilver (bass) and Terry Gittings (drums), then completed a second set, *Twice As Nice At Half The Price*, before disbanding.

● ALBUMS: *Heron* (Dawn 1970)★★★, *Twice As Nice At Half The Price* (Dawn 1972)★★.
● COMPILATIONS: *Best Of Heron* (1989)★★★.

Heron, Mike

b. 12 December 1942, Scotland. This multi-instrumentalist was a founder member of the **Incredible String Band**. Heron's first solo outing, on **Island**, included such names as the **Who**, and **John Cale** in the credits. After the band split, in 1974, Heron remained in the UK and formed Mike Heron's Reputation, following a more rock-orientated path. They released only *Mike Heron's Reputation*, this time on Neighbourhood Records. Although Heron recorded a number of albums, albeit on a different label every time, none of these achieved the degree of success that his former association with **Robin Williamson** had brought. *The Glenrow Tapes* was a set of remastered demo recordings that had not previously been released.

● ALBUMS: *Smiling Men With Bad Reputations* (Island 1971)★★, *Mike Heron's Reputation* (1975)★★★, *Diamond Of Dreams* (1977)★★, *Mike Heron* (1980)★★, *The Glenrow Tapes, Volume 1* (1987)★★, *The Glenrow Tapes, Volume 2* (1987)★★, *The Glenrow Tapes, Volume 3* (1987)★★, *Where The Mystics Swim* (Demon 1996)★★.
● COMPILATIONS: *The Glen Row Tapes* (1993)★★★.

Herring, Vincent

b. 19 November, 1964, California, USA. One of the most exciting alto saxophone players working in the hard bop idiom, he idolizes **Cannonball Adderley** and was chosen by Cannonball's brother **Nat Adderley** to play in the Cannonball Adderley Legacy Band. In July 1984, when his band was playing in the Manhattan streets, Herring was approached by record-label proprietor Sam Parkins with the offer of a recording date. Since then he has gigged or recorded with many distinguished figures, including **Horace Silver**, **Cedar Walton**, **Art Blakey**, **McCoy Tyner**, **Larry Coryell**, **Jack DeJohnette**, **Beaver Harris**, **Lionel Hampton**, and **David Murray**. In 1988 in Paris he took part in an alto summit with **Phil Woods**, **Frank Morgan**, Bob Mover, C. Sharps and McLean. In 1990 he toured Europe with his own quintet.

● ALBUMS: *Scene One* (1989)★★★★, *American Experience* (S&R 1990)★★★, with Nat Adderley: *Talkin' About You*

(1991)★★★, with Adderley *We Remember Cannon* (1991)★★★, *Evidence* (Landmark 1991)★★★, *Dawnbird* (Landmark 1994)★★★, Folklore, *Live At The Village Vanguard* (MusicMasters 1995)★★★★, *Don't Let It Go* (MusicMasters 1995)★★★.

Herrmann, Bernard

b. 29 June 1911, New York, USA, d. 24 December 1975, Los Angeles, USA. One of the most highly regarded composers and arrangers of background music for films, from the early 40s through to the 70s. Herrmann studied at New York University and the Juilliard School of Music, before joining **CBS** broadcasting in 1933. While serving as a composer conductor for radio documentaries and dramas he became associated with Orson Welles, and began his film career by scoring Welles' legendary *Citizen Kane*, for which he was nominated for an Academy Award in 1941. He did win the Oscar that year, not for *Citizen Kane*, but for his music to *All That Money Can Buy* (also known as *The Devil And Danny Webster* amongst other titles), generally thought of as among his best work. His other early scores included another Welles classic, *The Magnificent Ambersons*, *Jane Eyre*, *Hangover Square*, *Anna And The King Of Siam*, *The Ghost And Mrs Muir*, *The Day The Earth Stood Still*, *Five Fingers*, *Beneath The 12 Mile Reef*, *King Of The Khyber Rifles*, *Garden* Of *Evil*, *The Egyptian* (with **Alfred Newman**), *The Man In The Grey Flannel Suit*, *Prince Of Players* and *The Kentuckian* (1955). Herrmann then proceeded to make several films with Alfred Hitchcock - he became known as the director's favourite movie composer. They included thrillers such as *The Man Who Knew Too Much*, *The Wrong Man*, *Vertigo*, *North By Northwest*, *Psycho* and *Marnie*. He was also a consultant on Hitchcock's sinister *The Birds*. Herrmann was 'gravely wounded' when Hitchcock rejected his score for *Torn Curtain* in favour of one by **John Addison**; this decision terminated their relationship.

His other dramatic scores included *A Hatful Of Rain*, *The Naked And The Dead*, *Journey To The Centre Of The Earth*, *The Three Worlds Of Gulliver*, *Mysterious Island*, *Cape Fear*, *Tender Is The Night*, *Joy In The Morning*, *Sisters*, *It's Alive*. Between 1965 and 1975, Herrmann spent much of his time based in Britain, and composed the background music for a good many European productions, such as *Jason And The Argonauts*, *Fahrenheit 451*, *The Bride Wore Black*, *Twisted Nerve*, *The Battle Of Nereveta*, *The Night Digger* and *Endless Night*. At the end of his career, as at the beginning, Herrmann was nominated for an Academy Award twice in the same year. This time, however, neither *Taxi Driver* nor *Obsession* won the Oscar for Original Score, and Herrmann died, the day after he completed recording the music for Martin Scorsese's *Taxi Driver* in 1975. The many recordings of his vast output include *Classic Fantasy Film Scores* conducted by Herrmann, *Citizen Kane - Classic Film Scores Of Bernard Herrmann* with the National Philharmonic Orchestra, and *From Citizen Kane To Taxi Driver* (1993) on which Elmer Bernstein conducts the Royal Philharmonic Orchestra. In 1992, an hour-long, analytical documentary, *Music For The Movies: Bernard Herrmann*, which included home movies, interviews, and a scene from Hitchcock's *Torn Curtain* accompanied by Herrmann's original, rejected music, was shown on US television.
● FURTHER READING: *Bernard Herrmann*, E. Johnson. *A Heart At Fire's Center: The Life And Music Of Bernard Herrmann*, Steven C. Smith.

Hersh, Kristin

b. *c.*1966, Atlanta, Georgia, USA. As the lead singer of **Throwing Muses**, one of alternative US rock music's most influential and enduring groups, Hersh elected to pursue a simultaneous solo career after the parent band nearly dissolved in 1992. With her step-sister and bandmate Tanya Donelly setting out to form the commercially successful **Belly**, Hersh kept the name Throwing Muses but also began to write songs destined for self-accompaniment. She had already explored some disconcerting mental and psychological imagery on previous Muses albums, not least the loss of custody of her son Dylan (she now has a younger son, Ryder, five years Dylan's junior). It had resulted in Hersh relocating to her son's home-town of Newport, Rhode Island, where she herself grew up, sheltered from a stormy adolescence by her **X** and **Violent Femmes** records. Though her own parents were free-thinking liberals, she was equally influenced by her Baptist grandparents. She moved to Newport from Atlanta when she was six years old, and her father taught courses in Zen Buddhism and American Indian mythology. Her parents divorced at the age of 11, but this offered an unexpected boon: the father of her best friend, Tanya Donelly, marrying her mother. It was Hersh who was primarily behind the formation of Throwing Muses with Donelly, allowing her an outlet for the songs she had been writing from childhood. Some of these made extremely uncomfortable listening, and with the Muses' rise she found her new-found celebrity difficult to handle. By the advent of her solo career Hersh had partially conquered her psychological battle with the aid of lithium, and by the mid-90s she felt able to continue without any recourse to pharmaceuticals. Some of this turbulence was captured in the fibre of *Hips And Makers*, but so was a great deal more, the artist herself describing it as 'a real life record. It's personal, literally so; full of skin and coffee, shoes and sweat and babies and sex and food and stores - just stupid stuff that's a really big deal.' Michael Stipe of **R.E.M.** guested on backing vocals for promotional single 'Your Ghost', though elsewhere just Hersh's voice, guitar and intermittent cello carried the songs, produced by Lenny Kaye (**Patti Smith**). By now she had become wary of being characterized as the mad woman with a guitar, and the collection reflected her resentment with female creativity being so unobjectively linked with mental instability. After returning to the Throwing Muses format with palpable enthusiasm for *University* in 1995, she also revealed news of a first film project, *Guess What's Coming To Dinner*, written with husband and manager Billy O'Connell. Electing to leave Throwing Muses in 1997 Hersh released *Strange Angels*, a more confident and accessible collection.

● ALBUMS: *Hips And Makers* (Warners/4AD 1993)★★★, *Strange Angels* (4AD 1998)★★★.

Hession, Paul

b. 19 September 1956, Leeds, England. Although Hession's grandfather had played the drums in a cavalry regiment, his own first musical exposure was to the guitar, a gift from his parents when he was seven years old. About the same time he started singing in a church choir, and credits choir-leader and improvising organist William Isles-Pulford with instilling in him a love of music. He began playing drums himself in 1971, a new departure which involved the usual apprenticeship in Working Men's Club rock bands. Seeing **Elvin Jones** at **Ronnie Scott**'s Club in 1975 gave him 'food for thought for years'. In 1979 he formed a partnership with alto saxophonist **Alan Wilkinson**, which has carried on into the 90s. In 1983 they (together with guitarist Paul Buckton and live electronics improviser John McMillan) founded the Leeds Termite Club, both performing free improvised music and promoting players from the UK, Europe and the USA. In 1987 Hession proved his bop credentials by backing west coast bebop tenor saxophonist **Teddy Edwards**. Word of the quality of the Leeds improvisation scene reached London, and Hession played at **Derek Bailey**'s Company Week in 1988. A partnership with Wuppertal-based tenor Hans-Peter Hiby resulted in *The Real Case* in 1988. In a trio format with Wilkinson and bassist **Simon Fell**, Hession toured in 1991 under the title 'October Onslaught'. His torrential polyrhythmic style and his ability to raise the stakes in formidable company establish him as a prime mover in the attempt to inject excitement and power back into total improvisation - a return to its roots in free jazz.

● ALBUMS: with Hans-Peter Hiby *The Real Case* (1988)★★★, with Simon Fell *Compilation 2* (1991)★★★.

Hester, Carolyn

b. 1936, Waco, Texas, USA. Hester spent her childhood in Austin and Dallas (her grandparents had been folk singers) and then she relocated to New York in 1956 to study acting with the American Theater Wing. In 1958 Hester left to sing in clubs in Cleveland and Detroit. Her first album was released for **Decca Records**' Coral subsidiary in 1958 when Hester was 21. It was produced by **Norman Petty**, **Buddy Holly**'s manager, and Hester soon befriended both Petty and his charge. The record, containing purely traditional material, served as a springboard for performances on the New York folk network, as Hester became part of a new wave of acoustic talent who would dominate the 60s (**Joan Baez**

attended an early concert, and Hester met **Bob Dylan** at an early show at the famed Gerde's Folk City). Tradition Records hosted her second album, the first of several to be titled simply *Carolyn Hester*, which was produced with label owners the **Clancy Brothers**. In the UK it was renamed *Thursday's Child* and released on Ember Records. It included several folk club staples of the period such as 'House Of The Rising Sun' and 'Go Away From My Window'. After passing an audition at **Columbia Records** for **John Hammond** her second self-titled collection followed, featuring subsequent fellow Hammond signing Bob Dylan on harmonica, as well as guitarist Bruce Langhorne and **Odetta** bass player Bill Lee (father of film maker Spike Lee). To promote it she came to England, playing her first UK concerts at the Troubador. Taking a flat in Tregunter Road alongside new husband **Richard Farina**, they became the first of a wave of American folk emigrates to base themselves in London. Rory McEwan then booked both for the Edinburgh Festival, but the marital relationship was already failing, despite the fact that Hester was concurrently helping type Farina's celebrated book, *Been Down So Long, It Looks Like Up To Me*. Back in the USA she became a regular on the *Hullaballoo* television series, and renewed acquaintances with Norman Petty following a second, less successful album for Columbia. She subsequently recorded two live albums for Petty's **Dot Records**, and in the 90s these remain the only Hester material still in print thanks to reissues by Bear Family Records. She continued to appear regularly at the Edinburgh Festival and by the late 60s her popularity in the UK outstripped domestic sales. This situation was exacerbated by her noble organisation of a singers' boycott of ABC television's *Hootenanny* show, following its refusal to allow **Pete Seeger** to perform after he was blacklisted as a communist. A second contract was then signed with Columbia but no releases were forthcoming, aside from a 'best of' compilation. Although Hester remained a popular live attraction, her position in folk's heirarchy was gradually over-run by Joan Baez and **Judy Collins**. In the late 60s Hester embraced a rock-orientated direction with a group, the Carolyn Hester Coalition, but it was a largely unremarkable flirtation. She then abandoned music for a full decade while she brought up her children, though she continued to perform sporadically. She returned to a more active profile in 1982. In the 90s many were drawn to her back-catalogue via the testimony of long-term fan **Nanci Griffith**, who featured Hester on her *Other Voices* album and invited her to join her for her appearance at the Royal Albert Hall in London. Her recent albums for the Road Goes On Forever label have been well received.

● ALBUMS: *Carolyn Hester* (Coral 1957)★★★, *Scarlet Ribbons* (Coral 1958)★★★, *Carolyn Hester* (Tradition 1960)★★★, *Carolyn Hester* (Columbia 1961)★★★, *This Life I'm Living* (Columbia 1963)★★★, *That's My Song* (Dot 1964)★★★, *Carolyn Hester At The Town Hall* (Dot 1965)★★,

The Carolyn Hester Coalition (Pye 1969)★★★, *Thursday's Child Has Far To Go* (1971)★★★, *Carolyn Hester* (1974)★★★, *Music Medicine* (80s)★★★, *Warriors Of The Rainbow* (80s)★★, *Texas Songbird* (Road Goes On Forever 1994)★★★, *From These Hills* (Road Goes On Forever 1996)★★★.

Hewerdine, Boo

b. 1961, London, England. Singer-songwriter Hewerdine is a proud resident of Cambridge, England, where he moved with his parents aged 12 and which he likes because 'nothing ever happens here. You can get on with things.' However, at age 18 he returned to London to live in his late grandmother's house in Edgware, London, which set about a downward personal spiral. He suffered from agoraphobia and was (unjustly) accused of theft and fired from his job at a record shop. However, he found a friend with similar experiences and together they began to explore music as an outlet for their traumas. He returned to Cambridge to form Placebo Thing, then the marginally more successful The Great Divide. The latter released two singles for **Enigma Records** after being recommended to the label by Mike Scott of the **Waterboys**. These attracted a fair degree of attention within the UK's minor press, but more mainstream media support was not forthcoming. In January 1985 Hewerdine once again returned to Cambridge to work in a record shop, and set up a third band, the **Bible**. Working with jazz drummer Tony Shepherd he wrote an album of songs, *Walking The Ghost Back Home*, released through Norwich independent Backs Records in 1987. Two singles drawn from the set, 'Gracelands' and 'Mahalia', achieved slight success, with the album also earning extensive critical support. With the band having expanded to a quartet the Bible signed with **Chrysalis Records** and just missed the UK Top 40 with a re-recorded 'Gracelands' and 'Honey Be Good'. After the disappointing commercial performance of 1988's *Eureka*, Hewerdine grew unhappy about the band's direction: 'I thought we were turning into an ordinary group.' He began playing his first solo gigs as a result, while the rest of the Bible became Liberty Horses. Hewerdine then made the acquaintance of American 'new country' artist Darden Smith. Together they spent four days writing songs that later formed the collaborative *Evidence* album (they would also work together on Darden's solo album). Hewerdine's own solo debut came as a result of sessions spent recording nearly 30 songs at Church Studio in north London in 1990. These songs were whittled down and augmented with the help of co-producer Rob Peters (formerly of Birmingham's **Dangerous Girls**) to produce *Ignorance*. The lyrics addressed the period during the late 70s when the artist was slowly falling apart in north London, but escaped the morbidity that might have been triggered by those events with some bright, uplifting instrumentation. With support slots to **Tori Amos** and another widely applauded single, 'History', the album did just enough

commercially to sustain Hewerdine's status. He also wrote songs for **Eddi Reader** (notably 'Patience of Angels') and **Clive Gregson** and did production work with Laurie Freelove. *Baptist Hospital* failed to match the anticipation, the results being somewhat lacklustre.

● ALBUMS: with Darden Smith *Evidence* (Ensign 1989)★★★, *Ignorance* (Ensign 1992)★★★, *Baptist Hospital* (Blanco y Negro 1996)★★.

Hex

Hex started as the multi-media side of **Ninja Tune Records**, firstly with Rob Pepperell in charge and later Stuart Warren Hall. Working closely with Jonathan Moore and Matt Black, Hex has created a number of projects aimed at developing the role of the DJ and evolved into a 'multi-armed posse manipuLating multiple sound and vision sources'. Some of their software applications are based around sampling and remixing ideas, while two installations, 'Synopticon' (TRADE-MARK) at the Barbican and 'Generator' (TRADE-MARK) at the Glasgow Gallery of Modern Art, allowed visitors to create and mix sounds and visuals simultaneously. As a live attraction Hex has become an exciting VJ team working at Ninja Tune's club nights, Stealth and Kungfusion. Attempting to expand the established formats Hex created a scratch video *Natural Rhythm* to accompany **Coldcut**'s 'Atomic Moog' (1998). It was the first in a trilogy of collaboration that also included 'More Bits And Pieces' and 'Timber' (as Hexstatic). They also contributed a number of games, creative tools and videos to Coldcut's album *Let Us Play*. By 1998 Hex were signed to Ninja Tune as an artist, no longer just the multi-media arm of the label.

Hex Enduction Hour - Fall

To use the word challenging seems patronising when describing the Fall's work. Leader Mark E Smith does not tolerate fools gladly and he would verbally lash such pompous observations. However, it is a difficult album to love as it is lyrically uncompromising and musically spartan. This was the first of many Fall albums to chart, thanks to regular plugs from Fall-father John Peel, and as such it remains a favourite. 'Just Step S'Ways' is the track that remains in the head, although 'Who Makes The Nazis?' is a disturbingly accurate dialogue of what was to come throughout the 80s in the UK with right-wing factions.

● Tracks: *The Classical; Jawbone And The Air-Rifle; Hip Priest; Fortress/Deer Park; Mere Pseud Mag. Ed; Winter (Hostel Maxi); Winter 2; Just Step S'Ways; Who Makes The Nazis?; Iceland; And This Day.*

● First released 1982

● UK peak chart position: 71

● USA peak chart position: did not chart

Hey Boy! Hey Girl!

This slight 1959 feature starred husband and wife team **Keely Smith** and **Louis Prima**. The latter was renowned as a jazz vocalist, trumpeter, composer and bandleader, whose rhythmic style provided a stepping-stone towards rock 'n' roll. After their marriage, the pair embraced Smith's MOR inclinations, enjoying residencies in Las Vegas clubs where they were backed by Sam Butera And The Witnesses. The group appeared with the couple in *Hey Boy! Hey Girl!*, in which Smith plays Dorothy Spencer, a singer who joins Prima and the Witnesses on the understanding that the band will help her with a church bazaar. The film featured such numbers as 'Autumn Leaves', 'Fever', 'When The Saints Go Marching In' and 'Lazy River', although it does not include the duo's 1959 US hit, 'That Old Black Magic'. The couple separated in 1961; Smith later enjoyed a UK hit with 'You're Breaking My Heart' (1965), while Prima enjoyed greater acclaim by providing the voice for King Louis in the **Walt Disney** cartoon *The Jungle Book*.

Hey Let's Twist

Few imagined that when R&B troupe **Hank Ballard And The Midnighters** placed 'The Twist' on the b-side of 'Teardrops On Your Letter', that the song would inspire an early 60s dance craze. **Chubby Checker** gained the plaudits for popularizing the craze on record, but the Twist initially sprang from relative obscurity when it was showcased at Manhattan's chic club The Peppermint Lounge. The club's houseband, **Joey Dee And The Starlighters**, starred in this 1960 film alongside singers Jo-Ann Campbell and **Teddy Randazzo**. *Hey Let's Twist* offered little in the way of plot; rather it featured the venue and acts performing while clientele swivelled across the dancefloor in 'twisting' fashion. Decried at the time as 'lewd' by the moral majority, the Twist, now looks quaint and faintly ridiculous, adjectives also applicable to this film. However, Dee enjoyed brief success in the US charts with several songs from the soundtrack including the number 1 hit, 'Peppermint Twist', 'Shout', which reached number 6, and 'Hey Let's Twist', which peaked at number 20. 'Peppermint Twist' also entered the UK Top 40, inspiring a British release for the *Hey Let's Twist* soundtrack, as well as a less distinguished follow-up movie, *Two Tickets To Paris*. However, by the time this was achieved the first rumblings of Mersey Beat could be heard. The Twist and its propagators were about to be eclipsed by something of a less transitory nature.

Heyman, Edward

b. 14 March 1907, New York, USA. A prolific lyricist, whose output during the 30s and 40s included several enduring standards, Heyman studied at the University of Michigan, before collaborating with Ken Smith on 'I'll Be Reminded Of You' for the 1929 **Rudy Vallee** movie *The Vagabond Lover*. He had his first big hit a year later with the magnificent 'Body And Soul', written with **Johnny** (later John) **Green**, Robert Sour and Frank Eyton, which was introduced by **Libby Holman** in the sophisticated revue *Three's A Crowd*. Green was

to compose the music for many of Heyman's songs during the early 30s, including 'Hello, My Lover, Goodbye', 'My Sweetheart 'Tis Of Thee' and 'One Second Of Sex' (all three from the 1931 stage musical *Here Goes The Bride*), 'Out Of Nowhere' (a US number 1 for **Bing Crosby**), 'I Cover The Waterfront', 'Weep No More My Baby' (from the 1933 stage musical *Murder At The Vanities*), 'You're Mine You', 'Easy Come, Easy Go', and 'I Wanna Be Loved' (with **Billy Rose**). The latter number was revived in 1950 when it became a US number 1 for the **Andrews Sisters**. Heyman's other songs during the 30s and 40s included 'Ho Hum' (with **Dana Suesse** for the Marx Brothers film *Monkey Business*), 'It's Every Girl's Ambition', 'Kinda Like You', 'Kathleen Mine', 'You're Everywhere', 'Drums In My Heart' and 'Through The Years' (all with **Vincent Youmans** for the 1932 stage show *Through The Years*), 'My Darling' (with Richard Myers for the 1932 *Earl Carroll Vanities*), 'My Silent Love' (with Dana Suesse), 'Blame It On My Youth' (with **Oscar Levant**), 'You Oughta Be In Pictures' (with Dana Suesse, sung by **Jane Froman** in the *Zeigfeld Follies* of 1934), 'You're One In A Million', 'Dream Kingdom' and 'Silver Sails' (all three with Harden Church for the stage show *Caviar* (1934), several songs with Suesse for the 1935 film musical *Sweet Surrender*, 'Moonburn' (with **Hoagy Carmichael**, sung by Bing Crosby in the 1936 film *Anything Goes*), 'Boo-Hoo!' (with Carmen Lombardo and John Jacob Loeb), 'Bluebird Of Happiness' (with Harry Parr Davis and Sandor Harmati), 'Love Letters' (with **Victor Young**), and 'If I Steal A Kiss' and 'What's Wrong With Me?' (both with **Nacio Herb Brown**), which were featured, along with others, in the **Frank Sinatra-Kathryn Grayson** film *The Kissing Bandit* (1948). In the 50s Heyman worked again with Victor Young on the songs for the unsuccessful Olsen and Johnson stage show *Pardon Our French* (1950). They also collaborated on the exquisite ballad 'When I Fall In Love' (1951), which is usually associated with **Nat King Cole,** and on 'Blue Star' (1955), the theme from the popular *Medic* television series. After that Heyman worked only occasionally, but his old songs continued to be featured in musical films such as *The Five Pennies* and *The Helen Morgan Story* (UK title: *Both Ends Of The Candle*), and in 1963 he adapted composer Mark Lawrence's theme from the movie *David And Lisa*, for 'David And Lisa's Love Song'.

Heyward, Nick

b. 20 May 1961, Beckenham, Kent, England. The original lead vocalist in UK chart group **Haircut 100**, Heyward left for a solo career in late 1982. Early the following year he returned with a couple of chart hits, 'Whistle Down The Wind' and 'Take That Situation', both close to the 'boy next door blue-eyed soul' style developed by his former group. His debut solo album, *North Of A Miracle*, which included the up-tempo 'Blue Hat For A Blue Day', was a solid effort that won critical approval and sold well. It featured **Beatles** engineer

Geff Emerick as co-producer. An uneasy move away from his teenage audience was completed with the funk-influenced 'Warning Sign' but like many former teenage pin-ups the transition brought only limited commercial success. In 1988 he moved to **Warner Brothers Records**, but both the single, 'You're My World', and accompanying album, *I Love You Avenue*, failed to re-establish him in the mainstream. For the next four years Heyward concentrated on his second career as a graphic artist, until returning in 1992 with a new album for Epic Records and tour dates alongside **Squeeze**. Over the next two years he toured regularly, particularly in the USA, where he supported such alternative luminaries as **Belly**, **Lemonheads**, **Mazzy Star** and **Therapy?** (arguably the most unlikely coupling, given Heyward's reputation for gentle, pastoral songs). Much effort was put into *Tangled*; resulting in an outstanding album full of great melodies and fascinating lyrics. Released at the height of renewed interest in the Beatles, Heyward's album identifies him with the fab four and much of the late 60s quality pop song era. Neither the album nor the singles taken from it found much commercial favour, and it was difficult to imagine what he would have to do in the future, as on this showing Heyward had reached a creative peak. He worked on **Edward Ball**'s 1996 solo album, and signed to **Creation Records** in 1997. The album that followed was perplexing; all the regular Heyward trademarks were present, catchy hooks and vocals were up to standard yet the overall impression was strangely disappointing. It would appear that Heyward had been listening to the Beatles' *Revolver* prior to entering the recording studio. Stand out tracks were 'My Heavy Head', 'The Man You Used To Be' and 'Stars In Her Eyes', but the next classic Heyward pop song was not on this album. Creation released him from his contract in 1998.

● ALBUMS: *North Of A Miracle* (Arista 1983)★★★, *Postcards From Home* (Arista 1986)★★, *I Love You Avenue* (Warners 1988)★★, *From Monday To Sunday* (Epic 1992)★★, *Tangled* (Epic 1995)★★★★, *The Apple Bed* (Creation 1998)★★★.

● COMPILATIONS: *Best Of Nick Heyward And Haircut 100* (Ariola 1989)★★★★, *The Greatest Hits Of Nick Heyward & Haircut 100* (RCA Camden 1996)★★★★.

● FURTHER READING: *The Haircut 100 Catalogue*, Sally Payne. *Haircut 100: Not A Trace Of Brylcreem*, no editor listed.

Heywood, Eddie

b. 4 December 1915, Atlanta, Georgia, USA, d. 2 January 1989, North Miami, Florida, USA. Heywood received his first piano lessons from his father, also named Eddie, who was a well-known bandleader in the 20s. Heywood joined his father, playing piano in the pit band at an Atlanta theatre. He also accompanied singers, including **Bessie Smith**, and thereafter worked in various small jazz groups, including those led by **Wayman Carver**, **Benny Carter** and **Don Redman**. His gift for accompanying singers was displayed by his recordings with **Billie Holiday** and **Alberta Hunter**. In 1943 he took a sextet into the Cafe Society Downtown, being billed as the 'Biggest Little Band in the Land'. The type of music they played, and their billing, placed them in direct competition with **John Kirby** but, thanks to the presence of **Doc Cheatham** and **Vic Dickenson**, they held their own. Heywood had a hit record in 1944 with an unusual arrangement of 'Begin The Beguine' but his career was soon plagued by ill-health. Suffering partial paralysis in his hands, he worked less yet continued to write and had successes in the mid-50s with 'Canadian Sunset', 'Soft Summer Breeze' and other delightful songs. Further paralysis developed in the 60s; however he persevered and was still writing and occasionally performing throughout the 70s and into the early 80s. By this time he was working in the field of light music rather than jazz; indeed, close examination of his work, even from early in his career, shows him to have been a skilled musician with jazz associations and associates rather than a committed jazzman in his own right.

● ALBUMS: *The Eddie Heywood Trio* i (1951)★★★, *The Eddie Heywood Trio* ii (c.1954)★★★, *The Eddie Heywood Trio* iii (1956)★★, *Canadian Sunset* (1958)★★★.

● COMPILATIONS: *Biggest Little Band Of The 40* (1944)★★★★, *Eddie Heywood And The Blues Singers* (Document 1996)★★★★.

Heywood, Heather

b. Heather Williamson, 26 December 1950, Crosshouse, Kilmarnock, Ayrshire, Scotland. A Scottish ballad singer with a fine, clear voice and a growing reputation. Williamson had always experienced singing around her home, but it was not until hearing an album by **Martin Carthy** that she started to broaden her musical horizons. She first went to a folk club around 1968, in Irvine, and soon after performed her first floor spot. By now she had also come into contact with the singing of **Lizzie Higgins** and other Scottish singers. It was to be quite a few years, however, before she started doing bookings in her own right. Initially this was mainly the local clubs of Scotland while in 1970 she married Pete Heywood. As a singer, and interpreter of song, her main inspiration is **Dick Gaughan**. With her first release, Heywood was able to add to her growing reputation, but it was the follow-up, *By Yon Castle Wa'*, that started to awaken interest further afield in this highly talented singer. Equally at home with traditional or contemporary material, the album included contributions from, among others, Brian McNeill (fiddle/guitar/concertina/bouzouki), Dougie Pincock from the **Battlefield Band** (highland pipes/whistle/flute/low whistle/soprano saxophone) and Colin Matheson from **Ceolbeg** (piano). Heywood also sings with the group Quadrille, and in 1993 was was voted Artist Of The Year by Glasgow's Star Club.

● ALBUMS: *Some Kind Of Love* (1988)★★, *By Yon Castle Wa'* (Greentrax 1992)★★★★.

Hi Records

Formed in Memphis, Tennessee, USA, in 1957 by Ray Harris, a rockabilly singer, Hi Records - the letters originally stood for Hit Instrumentals - became a key black music label in the 70s, primarily as the home of soul/gospel giant **Al Green**. Harris launched the company for an investment of $3.50. Hi's first major hit came in late 1959 with 'Smokie Part 2' by the **Bill Black** Combo and crystallized the following year with Black's Top 10 'White Silver Sands'. In 1961 Black's saxophonist, **Ace Cannon**, began a short string of Hi hits with the US Top 20 single 'Tuff'. The mid-60s found soul singer **Willie Mitchell**, leader of Hi's house band, as the label's biggest seller with nine chart hits, none of which made the Top 20. Mitchell purchased Hi in 1970, the same year he brought Green to the label. Green eventually placed 16 Hi singles on the charts, seven of which were US Top 10 hits (including the 1972 number 1 hit 'Let's Stay Together'). **Ann Peebles** was the last notable Hi artist, best known for the 1973 Top 10 single 'I Can't Stand The Rain'. Hi was sold to Cream Records in the late 70s but failed to survive the disco era. Today Hi records are being reissued by **Demon Records** in the UK and MCA in the USA.

● COMPILATIONS: *The Greatest Hits From Memphis* (1969)★★★, *Hi Records - The Early Years* (1987)★★★, *Hi Records - The Early Years, Volume Two* (1988)★★★, *Hi Rhythm & Blues* (1988)★★★, *The Soul Years* (1988)★★★★, *Hi Records - The Blues Sessions* (1988)★★★, *The Hi Records Story* (1989)★★★★.

Hi-Bias Records

A dance label based in Toronto, Canada, Hi-Bias Records was widely proclaimed as 'the DJ's label' in the early 90s. The imprint grew out of the collapse of Big Shot Records (which had released material by Index, Dionne, Amy Jackson, **Dream Warriors**, etc.) in 1990, with producer and co-founder Nick Anthony Fiorucci describing his new label as 'the next progression to the Big Shot sound'. Fiorucci's partner was Michael Ova. The term Hi-Bias was first used by an artist title on Big Shot for the single, 'Wanna Take You Home'. Hi-Bias began with three releases in 1990 which were later accredited by *Record Mirror* as 'putting Canadian dance music on the map'. The label's high profile releases, which were often extravagantly packaged, included Z Formation's *Brutal* EP in 1991, a typically collaborative project which featured remixes from Ova, Fiorucci, Jason 'Deko' Steele and Nicky Holder. The 'Rhythm Formula Team' which formed the production basis for the label also produced material by artists such as Red Light (*Rhythm Formula* EP), Oval Emotion ('Do It', sung by Cissy Goodridge and created by her producer brother Kenny Moran and Fiorucci) and DJs Rule. Fiorucci's influence was celebrated in the 90s when he was invited to the UK to play sets at the **Ministry Of Sound**. 1992 releases included Syndicate 305's 'I Promise' and Groove Sector's 'The Love I Lost', but, following the death of Ova, the label endured a period

of reduced activity. However, the label signed a distribution deal with BMG Canada and concentrated on building their profile there rather than on export markets. That situation changed again in the mid-90s when Hi-Bias was invited to perform at the Ministry Of Sound to celebrate five years of activity in December 1995. As well as Fiorucci the label's major acts - Oval Emotions, DJ Rules, Shauna Davis, Furry Freaks and Temperance took part. By this time the label had released nearly 60s records, with 34 more on its Toronto Underground subsidiary. It also distributes seven other labels.

Hi-C

b. Louisiana, USA. From Compton, California, Hi-C is some way short of the in-yer-face gangsta rap made famous by that area: 'I'm into music first, messages later. I'm not hardcore and I don't constantly say "black this" or "black that"'. Hi-C introduced his pleasant, personable fare to a national audience in 1990 when singles like 'I'm Not Your Puppet' rose high in the Billboard charts. He also took roles in movies, including *Encino Man*, *CB4* and *South Central*. In *CB4* it was Hi-C who provided the voice and lyrics for the Chris Rock character's on-screen raps. He is backed on record by DJ Tony A from Wilmington, California.

● ALBUMS: *Skanless* (Skanless 1991)★★★, *Swing'n* (Skanless 1993)★★.

Hi-Life International

One of the most prominent London-based bands during the UK's mid-80s African music explosion, Hi-Life were founded by the Ghanaian guitarist Kwabena Oduro Kwarteng in 1982, playing a roots **highlife** style infused by touches of Zairois and Congolese soukous. After a few months of fluctuating line-ups, the personnel stabilized in late 1982 to include fellow Ghanaians Sam Ashalley Ashley (percussion), Herman Asafo-Agyei (bass guitar) and Kofi Adu (drums), together with South African Frank Williams (tenor saxophone) and Liverpudlian Stu Hamer (trumpet). Between them, the Ghanaian contingent had played with practically every major Ghanaian highlife band active between 1965 and 1975, and had come to the UK more or less independently in the mid-70s, hoping to make their mark on the international music scene. For a while, with Hi-Life, it looked as though these ambitions would be fulfilled, as the group released two superb albums for London-based specialist label Sterns, the debut *Travel And See* (accurately subtitled *Music To Wake The Dead*) and its follow-up, *Na Wa For You*. Between 1983 and 1985 they toured almost continuously in the UK and Europe, and in 1984 *Travel And See* was released in the USA. Hi-Life's critical and specialist market success did not lead to mainstream acceptance and in 1986, in common with several other UK-based African outfits, accelerating personnel changes led to their break-up.

● ALBUMS: *Travel And See* (Stern's 1983)★★★, *Na Wa For You* (Stern's 1985)★★★.

Hi-Lo's

The name of this outstanding North American vocal unit derived from the contrast in height between its tallest members - leader/arranger Eugene Thomas Puerling (b. 31 March 1929, Milwaukee, Wisconsin) and Robert Morse (b. 27 July 1927, Pasadena, Texas) - and diminutive Clark Burroughs (b. 3 March 1930, Los Angeles, California) and Robert Strasen (b. 1 April 1928, Strasbourg, France). While developing their sophisticated close-harmony style, they lived in the same Chicago house, making ends meet with menial jobs and engagements at weekends and evenings. Through the offices of bandleader **Jerry Fielding**, they recorded for several labels while building a reputation as a versatile, technically accomplished act via a Las Vegas hotel season, a tour supporting **Judy Garland** and replacing the **Four Esquires** as resident musical turn on comedian Red Skelton's networked television series. Before Strasen was replaced by Dan Shelton in 1958, the four teamed up on disc with the **Marty Paich** Dektette - and **Rosemary Clooney** with whom they notched up a US hit with 1957's 'Ring Around Rosie' (with Morse's counter-tenor prominent). This breakthrough assisted the passage of *Now Hear This* into the album Top 20. Further collections - some devoted to specific stylistic genres - sold steadily if less remarkably. After the Hi-Lo's disbanded in 1964, Puerling and Shelton found employment producing advertising jingles with vocalists Len Dresslar and Bonnie Herman with whom they formed **Singers Unlimited** in 1966. An impressed **Oscar Peterson** recommended them to Germany's BASF/MPS company, which released several Singers albums including *Sentimental Journey* and, accompanied by **Robert Farnon**'s orchestra, 1978's *Eventide*. That same year, the Shelton line-up of the Hi-Lo's re-formed as a recording entity and were affectionately welcomed at performances in nostalgia revues. The Hi-Lo's had a profound influence on the harmony sound of the **Four Freshmen** and the **Beach Boys**.

● ALBUMS: *Listen!* (Starlite 1955/56)★★★, *The Hi-Lo's, I Presume* (Starlite 1955/56)★★★, *The Hi-Lo's Under Glass* (Starlite 1956)★★★, *The Hi-Lo's On Hand* (Starlite 1956)★★★, *The Hi-Lo's And The Jerry Fielding Band* (Kapp 1956)★★★, *The Hi-Lo's In Stereo* (Omega 50s)★★★★, *Suddenly It's The Hi-Lo's* (Columbia 1957)★★★, *Now Hear This* (Columbia 1957)★★★, with Rosemary Clooney *Ring A Round Rosie* (Columbia 1957)★★★★, *The Hi-Lo's And All That Jazz,* (Columbia 1959)★★★, *Broadway Playbill* (Columbia 1959)★★, *All Over The Place* (Columbia 1960)★★★, *The Hi-Lo's Happen To Folk* (Columbia 1962)★★★, *This Time It's Love* (Columbia 1962)★★★, *The Hi-Lo's Happen To Bossa Nova* (Reprise 1963)★★, *Back Again* (1978)★★.

Hiatt, John

b. 1952, Indianapolis, Indiana, USA. The archetypal musicians' musician, John Hiatt is a powerful singer, guitarist and talented songwriter whose material has been recorded by various acts, including **Dr. Feelgood**,

Searchers, **Iggy Pop**, **Three Dog Night**, **Desert Rose Band**, **Bonnie Raitt**, **Bob Dylan**, **Nick Lowe**, **Rick Nelson** and the **Neville Brothers**. Hiatt started out in local R&B bands in the late 60s, most notably the White Ducks. Moving to Nashville in 1970 he signed to Epic and recorded two highly acclaimed albums. After the second album he left the label and toured for a spell as a solo performer before being offered a new contract by MCA at the end of the decade. This resulted in two further albums. In 1980, guitarist **Ry Cooder** was looking for some new songs and was recommended Hiatt's material. Cooder received a tape of demos from Hiatt's publisher, and although he was not convinced the material was suitable for him, he decided he could use the talented guitarist in his own band. Hiatt duly accepted Cooder's offer and played with him on *Borderline* and on several subsequent albums and tours. His first solo album after his engagements with Cooder was 1982's *All Of A Sudden* and it was followed by almost one new album every year produced by **Tony Visconti** and **Nick Lowe**. Lowe regularly forms part of Hiatt's band both in the studio and on tour. Lowe and Hiatt later became half of a new 'supergroup' when they teamed up with Cooder and Jim Keltner (veteran journeyman drummer) to form **Little Village**, who released their first disappointing self-titled album in 1992. Since then Hiatt's reputation as a songwriter has grown and his own recent recorded output has included two of his best albums; the title tracks to both *Perfectly Good Guitar* and *Walk On* are two of his most infectious songs.

● ALBUMS: *Hanging Around The Observatory* (Epic 1974)★★★, *Overcoats* (Epic 1975)★★★, *Slug Line* (Epic 1979)★★★, *Two Bit Monsters* (MCA 1980)★★★, *All Of A Sudden* (MCA 1982)★★, *Riding With The King* (Geffen 1983)★★★★, *Warming Up To The Ice Age* (Geffen 1985)★★★, *Bring The Family* (A&M 1987)★★★★, *Slow Turning* (A&M 1988)★★★, *Stolen Moments* (A&M 1990)★★★, *Perfectly Good Guitar* (A&M 1993)★★★★, with The Guilty Dogs *Hiatt Comes Alive At Budokan?* (A&M 1994)★★★, *Walk On* (Capitol 1995)★★★, *Little Head* (Capitol 1997)★★★.

● COMPILATIONS: *Y'All Caught? - The Ones That Got Away 1979-1985* (Geffen 1991)★★★.

Hibbard, Bruce

b. USA. Gospel singer Bruce Hibbard's musical apprenticeship began in local church choirs and led to spells playing in contemporary Christian rock bands such as Amplified Version and Sonlight. He also spent time as a church choir director before electing to concentrate on pursuing a solo career. His thoughtful, musically polished material was greeted with little enthusiasm by secular record companies, until Paul Clark signed him to Seed Records in the late 70s. However, *A Light Within* proved to be a disappointing selection of uninspired tribute songs without the passion or artistry to bring Hibbard's concepts alive.

● ALBUMS: *A Light Within* (Seed 1978)★★.

Hibbert, Toots
(see **Maytals**)

Hibbler, Al
b. 16 August 1915, Little Rock, Arkansas, USA. Blind from birth, Hibbler attended the Conservatory for the Blind in Little Rock, becoming a member of the school choir. After winning an amateur talent contest in Memphis, he worked with local bands and his own outfit before joining **Jay McShann** in 1942. In the following year he joined the **Duke Ellington** Orchestra, proving to be one of the best singers the Duke ever employed. In the 40s he sang on Ellington records such as 'Ain't Got Nothin' But The Blues', 'I'm Just a Lucky So And So', 'Pretty Woman', 'Don't Be so Mean To Baby', 'Good Woman Blues', and 'Build That Railroad' (1950). During his eight year stay with Ellington, Hibbler won the Esquire New Star Award and *Downbeat* Best Band Vocalist. He subsequently recorded with several well-known jazz musicans in his backing groups, among them **Harry Carney**, **Billy Kyle**, **Count Basie** and **Gerald Wilson**. In the 50s his recordings of songs such as 'It Shouldn't Happen To A Dream', which he had recorded with Ellington, 'The Very Thought Of You' and 'Stardust' proved popular, while his version of 'Unchained Melody' (a million-seller) was outstanding. In the 50s he also made the US Top 30 with 'He', '11th Hour Melody', 'Never Turn Back' and 'After The Lights Go Down Low'. A powerful, rich-toned baritone, Hibbler cannot be regarded as a jazz singer but as an exceptionally good interpreter of 20th-century popular songs who happened to work with some of the best jazz musicians of the time.

● ALBUMS: *Al Hibbler Sings Love Songs* (1952)★★★, *Al Hibbler Favorites* (Norgran 1954)★★★, *Sings Duke Ellington* (Norgran 1954)★★★, *Melodies By Al Hibbler* (Marterry 1956)★★★, *After The Lights Go Down Low* (Atlantic 1956)★★★, *Sings Love Songs* (Verve 1956)★★★, *Starring Al Hibbler* (Decca 1956)★★★, *Here's Hibbler* (Decca 1957)★★★, *I Surrender Dear* (Score 1957)★★★, *With The Ellingtonians* (Brunswick 1957)★★★, *Torchy And Blue* (Decca 1958)★★★, *Hits By Hibbler* (Decca 1958)★★★, *Remembers The Big Songs Of The Big Bands* (Decca 1958)★★★, *Monday Every Day* (Atlantic 1961)★★★, *Early One Morning* (LMI 1964)★★★, with Rahsaan Roland Kirk *A Meeting Of The Times* (1972)★★★, *For Sentimental Reasons* (1982)★★★, *Golden Greats* (MCA 1986)★★★, *Dedicated To You* (Starline 1988)★★★.

Hickey, Chris
Based in Los Angeles, California, Hickey was a member of the late 70s punk group, the Spoilers. In 1985 he released *Frames Of Mind, Boundaries Of Time*, an outstanding, semi-political acoustic album, which had been recorded at home. It recalled the sparse arrangements of Nick Drake and Suzanne Vega. Unfortunately, Hickey's melancholic neo-folk was out of step during this period, and little has been heard of him since.

● ALBUMS: *Frames Of Mind, Boundaries Of Time* (1985)★★.

Hickman, Art
Hickman has been noted in many histories as the first musician to assemble a dance band in its presently perceived format, though this remains a subject of some dispute. Though many groups had previously organised for impromptu performances, for example at weddings and other social functions, before Hickman's time none had done so on anything approaching a professional footing. Originally a sextet, Hickman's band was formed in San Francisco, California, USA, in or around 1913, with their first engagement accompanying the San Francisco Seals baseball team at their training camp. After that they were booked into the St. Francis Hotel for a six nights a week residency. This proved so popular that the engagement was extended, allowing Hickman to expand the number of musicians he employed. The line-up now included Fred Coffman, Walt Rosener, Bert Ralton, Clyde Doerr, Vic King, Mark Moica, Ben Black, Steve Douglas, Bela Spiller, Frank Ellis, Jess Fitzpatrick, Juan Ramos, **Roy Fox**, Forrest Ray, Ed Fitzpatrick, Dick Winfree, **Earl Burtnett**, Dick Noolan, Hank Miller, Lou Marcasie and Ray Hoback. Their most prestigious booking came in 1915, when San Francisco played host to the 1915 World's Fair, with Hickman's orchestra providing much of the musical accompaniment. Having heard them play at the St. Moritz Hotel **Florenz Ziegfeld** invited the group to New York in 1919, booking them into the Biltmore Hotel Roof and his own Ziegfeld Roof. Six months of further engagements kept them in New York, where they proved just as popular as they had been in front of Californian audiences. In 1920 Ziegfeld again commissioned them, this time to provide music for the theatre run of *Ziegfeld Follies*. They finally returned to the west coast later in that year to appear at the St. Francis Hotel. After opening the Cocoanut Grove in 1921, the group moved to the Ambassador Hotel in Los Angeles. But by now Hickman had tired of the big band business he had helped to create, and handed his orchestra over to Frank Ellis. Ellis kept it active until the late 20s, while Hickman died in the mid-30s. Luckily, recordings of this pivotal group still survive, mainly on **Victor**, **HMV** and **Columbia Records**, and Hickman's theme song, 'Rose Room', continues as one of the dance band genre's great standards.

Hickory Wind
A down-home, American bluegrass band who decided that they loved British folk rock so much they recorded a whole album of it. They even imported Dave Mattacks to play on half of the tracks.

● ALBUMS: *Crossing Devils Bridge* (1978)★★★.

Hicks, Dan
b. 9 December 1941, Little Rock, Arkansas, USA. A former folk musician, Hicks joined the **Charlatans** in 1965, replacing original drummer Sam Linde. This trailblazing group is credited with pioneering the 60s

San Francisco sound, although they sadly failed to reap due commercial rewards. Frustrated with his limited role, Hicks emerged from behind the drumkit to play guitar, sing and compose before establishing a new group, Dan Hicks And His Hot Licks, with David LaFlamme (violin - later of **It's A Beautiful Day**) and Bill Douglas (bass). However, within months the leader had reshaped the venture around Sid Page (violin), Jaime Leopold (bass) John Webber (b. 1947; guitar) and singers Tina Gancher (b. 1945) and Sherri Snow. *Original Recordings* established Hicks' 'folk-swing' style, which drew on country, 30s vocal jazz and the singer's quirky, deadpan humour to create a nostalgic, yet thriving, music. It included the mesmerizing 'I Scare Myself', later revived successfully by **Thomas Dolby**. Webber then dropped out of the group, while Gancher and Snow were replaced by Maryanne Price and Naomi Ruth Eisenberg. *Where's The Money*, recorded live at the Los Angeles Troubadour, confirmed the promise of its predecessor, while *Striking It Rich*, which introduced newcomer John Girton (guitar), was arguably Hicks' strongest collection. *Last Train To Hicksville* completed this idiosyncratic unit's catalogue before Hicks decided to pursue a solo career. *It Happened One Bite* nonetheless drew support from Page, Girton and Price, but this disappointing set lacked the verve and interplay of earlier releases. During the 80s Hicks formed the Acoustic Warriors with James 'Fingers' Shupe (fiddle, mandolin) and Alex Baum (bass) with whom he continued his unique vision.

● ALBUMS: with the Hot Licks *The Original Recordings* (Epic 1969)★★★, *Where's The Money?* (Blue Thumb/MCA 1971)★★★, *Striking It Rich!* (Blue Thumb/MCA 1972)★★★, *Last Train To Hicksville...The Home Of Happy Feet* (Blue Thumb/MCA 1973)★★, *It Happened One Bite* (Warners 1978)★★★, with the Acoustic Warriors *Shootin' Straight* (Private Music 1994)★★★.

● COMPILATIONS: *Rich And Happy In Hicksville - Very Best Of Dan Hicks And His Hot Licks* (See For Miles 1986)★★★.

Hicks, Edna

b. 14 October 1895, New Orleans, Louisiana, USA, d. 16 August 1925, Chicago, Illinois, USA. Sister of Herb Morand, and step-sister of **Lizzie Miles**, Hicks was a light-voiced singer reminiscent of **Esther Bigeou**. In musical comedy from 1916, she recorded vaudeville blues for no fewer than eight companies in 1923-24. Her death, the result of burns after a domestic accident with gasoline, robbed the blues of a promising artist.

● COMPILATIONS: *Volume 1 1923* (Document 1996)★★★, shared with Hazel Meyers, Laura Smith *Volume 2 1923-27* (Document 1996)★★★.

Hicks, Jacqui

b. Featherstone, Yorkshire, England. As a child, Hicks began playing on the recorder before graduating to the clarinet on which she studied classical music. She also played tenor saxophone for a while. Her musical tastes inclined towards the jazzier end of the current pop spectrum, including musicians such as **George Benson** and **Earth, Wind And Fire**. At the age of 18 Hicks attended the Leeds College of Music where she was encouraged by Bill Charleson. She sang with the college band, with Brian Layton's funk band, and with John Brown's Student Bodies. After Leeds, she went to the Guildhall School of Music in London. In 1989 she sang occasionally with the **National Youth Jazz Orchestra** and the following year joined the band on a regular basis. In the mid-90s she began a solo career. She has composed songs, including 'Just A Breath Away', which she recorded with NYJO. Hicks is a skilled yet un-fussy singer with charm and intelligence.

● ALBUMS: *Looking Forward/Looking Back* (1991)★★★.

Hicks, Johnny

b. 19 May 1918, on a farm near Kansas City, Missouri, USA. While attending the University of Texas, in 1938, he was offered an announcing job on a local Austin station. It turned out to be with the country music programme of **Wilbert Lee O'Daniel**, then Governor of Texas. In 1941, he worked as a disc jockey and sang on KABC San Antonio and WBAP Fort Worth, where working with **Ernest Tubb** converted him completely to country music. He relocated to Dallas, in 1942 and worked with the **Callahan Brothers** and **Jim Boyd** on different stations. He later appeared with **Jimmy Heap** and **Adolph Hofner** at other venues. In 1946, he returned to KRLD Dallas, a powerful station whose transmissions could even be received in Canada and Mexico. Here he first presented the *Cornbread Matinee*, a daily live show before taking over the new *Big "D" Jamboree*. He compered and sang on this show for 10 years, first on radio and later when it moved to television. He also did four *Hillbilly Hit Parade* record shows weekly. He recorded for **Columbia** and wrote many songs including the patriotic story of the recalled soldier 'I Thought I Was Home To Stay', a sort of tribute to **Bob Wills** 'I Can't Get Enough Of That Ah-Ha' and the semi-weepy story of a blind man 'The Man On The Corner'. Hicks finally retired to California but even then he presented his *Johnny Hick's Country Gold* on KTOM Salinas.

● COMPILATIONS: *Star Of The Big "D" Jamboree* (Cattle 1988)★★★.

Hideaways

In 1963, inspired by the beat music in the city, three schoolfriends at Liverpool Institute decided to form a group. They were Ozzie Yue (b. Austin Yue, 12 August 1947, Liverpool, England; lead guitar), John Shell (b. 9 April 1947, Dallas, Texas, USA, d. 1 February 1968, Vietnam; bass) and John Donaldson (b. 31 August 1947, Liverpool, England; drums). They were joined by Frankie Connor (b. Frank O'Connor, 29 October 1946, Liverpool, England; rhythm guitar). They went to a Liverpool club called the Hideaway, said that they were called the Hideaways - and got a booking. The band were resident at the Hideaway for two months when disc jockey Bob Wooler poached them for the **Cavern**. They advertised in a local music shop for a saxophone player and Judd Lander (b. Malcolm Anthony McNiven, 1 March 1948) responded: he could not play the instrument but he persuaded them to take a harmonica player. All five members of the Hideaways could sing but they eschewed harmonies in favour of a tougher, bluesier sound. They performed **Bo Diddley**'s 'Mama, Keep Your Big Mouth Shut' as part of an EP included with the German book, *Beat Im Liverpool*, but a record contract proved elusive. They did, however, have national attention through the insidious 'tick-a-tick Timex' advertisement. John Shell was called to serve in Vietnam and he told the group that he would return to the Cavern for his twenty-first birthday. He was killed in Saigon on 1 February 1968. His replacement in the Hideaways was Chris Findley from the **Masterminds**, who switched from keyboards to bass. They also added Richie Routledge of the Cryin' Shames as an additional vocalist. In the late 60s, they recorded under the name of Confusius for **RCA Records** and spent three months in Germany. With over 400 appearances, the Hideaways played the Cavern more than any other group, and Ozzie Yue, who moved to Supercharge, holds the individual record. Frank Connor has become a local radio personality and author, also writing and producing a successful local CD by the Class Of 64, *Cavern Days*. Ozzie Yue works as an actor and plays in the soul band, Yue Who. Judd Lander is an industry figure, playing harmonica on hits by **Culture Club** and the **Spice Girls**. In 1997 the Hideaways reformed for the fortieth anniversary of the Cavern.

Higginbotham, J.C.

b. 11 May 1906, Social Circle, Georgia, USA, d. 26 May 1973. After playing trombone with J. Neal Montgomery, an Atlanta-based territory bandleader of the early 20s, Higginbotham worked outside music for a number of years. In the middle of the decade he tried his hand at bandleading and then was briefly with the bands of Wingie Carpenter, **Chick Webb** and Willie Lynch before joining **Luis Russell**. In 1931 he moved on to **Fletcher Henderson**'s band, worked for **Benny Carter**, the **Mills Blue Rhythm Band**, Henderson again and **Louis Armstrong**, who was then fronting the Russell band. Towards the end of 1940 Higginbotham shifted from big band work to play in a small group led by **Red Allen**, with whom he remained for about seven years. Thereafter, he played in or led small bands in New York, Boston and Cleveland, recorded extensively, appeared at the 1957 Great South Bay Jazz Festival as a member of the Fletcher Henderson reunion band, and visited Europe. In the 60s Higginbotham continued his established pattern of work, often playing in tandem with trumpeter **Joe Thomas**. Towards the end of the decade ill-health affected his career and he died in May 1973. A powerful, gutsy player with a solid traditional approach to his instrument overlaid with a keen appreciation of swing era styling, Higginbotham was one of the best trombone soloists in big band jazz.

● ALBUMS: with Henderson All Stars *Big Reunion* (1957)★★★, *J.C. Higginbotham All Stars* (1966)★★★.
● COMPILATIONS: with Fletcher Henderson *A Study In Frustration* (1923-38 recordings)★★★, *Higgy Comes Home* (Jazzology 1990)★★★.

Higginbottom, Geoff

b. 13 February 1959, Stockport, Cheshire, England. During his early career Higginbottom played the circuit of folk clubs and pubs in his native northwest. In August 1985, he was placed third in a competition at the Warwick Folk Festival. In the November of the same year, he released *Songs From The Levenshulme Triangle*. The following year, he performed at the Sidmouth International Festival Of Folk Arts, and was subsequently re-booked for 1987 and 1988. This gave Higginbottom a wider profile, and brought club and festival bookings all over England. He has since ventured further afield, playing Scotland, Wales and the Channel Islands. In addition to his musical career, Higginbottom has also made numerous appearances on UK television in bit parts, turning up in such soaps as *Coronation Street*, *Brookside* and *Emmerdale*, as well as a number of other productions. *Flowers Tomorrow* received a good response and brought Higginbottom to wider attention. The title track has been sung by a number of other performers, and the album as a whole mixed contemporary and traditional styles, with his guitar and bodhran to the fore. *More Than Pounds And Pence*, released in December 1990 has helped to establish Higginbottom as a highly-regarded performer and writer.

● ALBUMS: *Songs From The Levenshulme Triangle* (1985)★★★, *Flowers Tomorrow* (Dragon 1987)★★★, *More Than Pounds And Pence* (1990)★★★.

Higgins, Bertie

b. 1946, Tarpon Springs, Florida, USA. Bertie Higgins is best known for his 1981 soft-rock hit 'Key Largo', a Top 10 single. Higgins secured his first professional engagement playing drums in the back-up band of singer **Tommy Roe**, the Roemans, in 1964. He stayed with them for four years and toured widely. He first recorded with that band in 1964, for the **ABC**-Paramount label, but none of the group's singles charted. After the Roemans split up in 1968, Higgins returned to his home-town and began writing songs. It was not until the early 80s that he found success with 'Key Largo', inspired by the film starring Humphrey Bogart and Lauren Bacall. The single was recorded for the small Kat Family label and reached number 8 in April 1982, nearly six months after first charting. Higgins' follow-up single, 'Just Another Day In Paradise', missed the Top 40 and he has been absent from the charts since then.

● ALBUMS: *Just Another Day In Paradise* (1982)★★★.

Higgins, Billy

b. 11 October 1936, Los Angeles, California, USA. Higgins began playing drums at the age of 12 and early in his career played with R&B bands. He was soon involved in jazz, playing with other local musicians, including **Dexter Gordon**. In 1957 he was in the quartet led by **Red Mitchell** which also included pianist Lorraine Geller and tenor saxophonist **James Clay**. This band recorded for Lester Koenig's Contemporary label, on what was Higgins' first record date. In New York in 1959 he appeared with **Ornette Coleman** at the altoist's controversial Five Spot concerts, in a band which also included **Don Cherry** and **Charlie Haden**. Later that year he joined **Thelonious Monk** and in 1960 was with **John Coltrane**. Throughout the 60s Higgins was in demand for tours, club dates and a staggering number of recording sessions, many of them for the Blue Note label. Amongst the artists with whom he played were **Sonny Rollins**, **Steve Lacy**, **Donald Byrd**, Gordon, **Lee Morgan**, **Herbie Hancock** and **Hank Mobley**. His activities increased during the 70s and he worked extensively with **Cedar Walton** and was also on dates with **Milt Jackson** and **Art Pepper**. In the 80s his musical companions included Coleman, **Pat Metheny** and **Slide Hampton**. Although the musical styles of Higgins' associates have latterly ranged through freeform, jazz-rock and jazz-funk, he has readily established himself as one of the two or three leading exponents of each form of drumming. He brings to his playing a remarkable subtlety and lithe swing akin to that of the best bop drummers, while readily accommodating the complex needs of the styles in which he plays.

● ALBUMS: *Presenting Red Mitchell/Red Mitchell Quartet* (1957)★★★, *Something Else! The Music Of Ornette Coleman* (1958)★★★★, with Coleman *The Shape Of Jazz To Come* (1959)★★★★, with Coleman *Free Jazz* (1960)★★★★, with Sonny Rollins *Our Man In Jazz* (1962)★★★, with Dexter Gordon *Go!* (1962)★★★★, with Hank Mobley *Dippin'* (1965)★★★, *Soweto* (Red 1979)★★★, *The Soldier* (Timeless 1980)★★★, *Mr Billy Higgins* (Evidence 1985)★★★.

Higgins, Chuck

b. Charles Williams Higgins, 17 April 1924, Gary, Indiana, USA. Higgins was an R&B singer best known for his recording 'Pachuko Hop' in 1952. The son of a preacher who also played trombone, Higgins learned to play the trumpet at the age of 10. In 1940 he moved to Los Angeles, where he played the trumpet in his high-school band. While attending the Los Angeles Music Conservatory, Higgins formed a band with pianist Frank Dunn, saxophonist Johnny Parker and others on bass and drums. After a series of personnel changes, Higgins took over the saxophone position and wrote 'Pachuko Hop', featuring a squealing solo on that instrument. It became a highlight of his stage show and was heard by Vernon 'Jake' Porter, owner of Combo Records. Porter released the single ('pachuko' was a slang word denoting a Mexican-American dressed fashionably in baggy pants, with a long key chain), with the b-side 'Motorhead Baby', another raw R&B rocker (and later the inspiration for the nickname of **Frank Zappa** sideman James 'Motorhead' Sherwood, and subsequently, the heavy metal band **Motorhead**). Although the record was not a big seller outside the Los Angeles area, it made Higgins a local favourite and he secured concert bookings with **Charlie Parker**, **Nat 'King' Cole**, **Johnny Ace**, **Little Richard** and the Orioles. Among Higgins' band members at the time was **Johnny 'Guitar' Watson**, who then left for a successful blues solo career. Higgins never signed an exclusive recording contract, so his records were released on numerous labels, including Aladdin Records, Caddy, Lucky, Recorded in Hollywood, **Specialty Records** and Dootone. Primarily an instrumentalist, Higgins also recorded some music featuring singers. He retired from performing in the early 60s and went on to teach music at Los Angeles high schools and colleges. He attempted a comeback briefly in the mid-70s, performing in a disco style, but achieved no success. Two albums recorded in the late 70s returned him to his earlier style and attracted a small European following. In 1983 he toured the UK and later returned to performing in his original style at Los Angeles nightclubs during the 80s. A collection of his early rare singles, *Yak A Dak*, was released on the Swedish Saxophonograph label in 1990.

● ALBUMS: *Pachuko Hop* (Combo 1956)★★★, *Rock 'N' Roll Versus Rhythm And Blues* (Dootone 1959)★★★, *Motor Head Chuck* (1977)★★★, *Chuck Higgins Is A Ph.D.* (1979)★★.

● COMPILATIONS: *Yak A Dak* (Saxophonograph 1990)★★★, *Pachuko Hop* (Ace/Specialty 1992)★★★.

Higgins, Lizzie

b. Elizabeth Ann Youlden, 20 September 1929, Aberdeen, Scotland, d. 20 February 1993. Higgins is the only daughter of Scottish ballad singer **Jeannie Robertson** and piper Donald Higgins. She left school at the age of 15 and worked for a while as a fish filleter. After the 'discovery' of her mother by the song collector **Hamish Henderson**, she occasionally accompanied Robertson on her travels around Scotland and England, collecting and performing songs. In the wake of their growing reputation, Lizzie took up singing full-time. It was only after her mother's death in 1975 that she started to perform with regularity. Her technique included what she herself called 'the pipe singing'. In this she would embellish a tune in much the same way a piper might. She is often remembered for her contribution to the double album of ballad recordings made by the School of Scottish Studies, *The Muckle Sangs*, and is widely regarded as one of the greatest Scottish traditional singers. Although Higgins appeared on a number of recordings, she only made two albums in her own right. She died of cancer in 1993.

● ALBUMS: *Princess Of The Thistle* (Topic 1969)★★★, *Up And Awa' Wi' The Laverock* (Topic)★★★, with various artists *The Muckle Sangs* (1973)★★, *What A Voice!* (Lismor 1985)★★★.

● FURTHER READING: *Lizzie Higgins And The Oral*

Transmission Of Ten Child Ballads, Ailie Munro. *A Study Of Lizzie Higgins As A Transitional Figure In The Development Of The Oral Tradition In The Northeast Of Scotland*, Stephanie Perrin.

Higgins, Monk

b. Milton Bland, 17 October 1936, Menifee, Arkansas, USA, d. 3 July 1986, Los Angeles, California, USA. Higgins began his career as a highly successful producer and arranger in Chicago, first with the One-Derful label complex, then with St. Lawrence, and finally with **Chess Records**. While at St. Lawrence he recorded a number of appealing instrumentals, notably the national hit 'Who-Dun-It?' (number 30 R&B) and a double-sided local hit, 'Ceatrix Did It'/'Who-Dun-It?'. Higgins moved to Los Angeles in 1969, and arranged and produced acts on the United Artists/Imperial/Minit complex of labels, and recorded himself on a number of singles and albums. He hit the national charts again with 'Gotta Be Funky' (number 22 R&B) in 1972. During the 70s, with ex-**Stax** head Al Bell, he produced many successful records for **Bobby Bland**.

Higgs, Joe

b. 3 June 1940, Kingston, Jamaica, West Indies. In the late 50s Higgs joined Roy Wilson to form the duo Higgs And Wilson. In 1959 they recorded their first single, 'Mammy Oh', for politico Edward Seaga, and it became a massive hit. In the early 60s they worked for **Coxsone Dodd**, and had several further hits including 'How Can I Be Sure' and 'There's A Reward'. Higgs was also coaching a young group called the **Wailers**, and he subsequently introduced them to Dodd, who launched their career. In the mid-60s Higgs decided to pursue a solo career, and made further recordings for Dodd including 'Change Of Plans' and 'Neighbour Neighbour'. In the early 70s Higgs recorded for a variety of producers, and outstanding songs from this period include 'The Wave Of War' and 'The World Is Spinning Round' (1972) for **Harry J.**, 'Burning Fire' (1974) for **Rupie Edwards**, 'More Slavery' (1975) for Jack Ruby, and 'Creation' (1975), a self-production. In 1975, Higgs finally had an album released, the excellent *Life Of Contradiction*. The imaginatively arranged songs were given faultless jazz-tinged performances by a group that included jazz guitarist **Eric Gale**. Further albums followed, with 1979's *Unity Is Power* and 1985's *Triumph* particularly strong collections. Higgs' thoughtful lyrics and expressive voice have made him one of the most singular artists to come from Jamaica.
● ALBUMS: *Life Of Contradiction* (Grounation 1975)★★★★, *Unity Is Power* (One Stop/Island 1979)★★★, *Triumph* (Alligator 1985)★★★, *Family* (Blue Mountain 1988)★★, *Blackman Know Thyself* (Shanachie 1990)★★.

High

The High were instigated in Manchester, England, in October 1987 by Andy Couzens (b. 15 July 1965, Macclesfield, Cheshire, England; guitar), who had previously plied his trade in the yet-to-blossom **Stone Roses**. Joined by John Matthews (b. 23 September 1967, Torquay, Devon, England; vocals), Simon Davies (b. 24 January 1967, Manchester, England; bass) and Chris Goodwin (b. 10 August 1965, Oldham, Lancashire, England; drums), the High immediately eschewed the traditional paths open to small bands by avoiding the pitfalls of incessant touring. Instead, the quartet fabricated a set of unashamedly classic guitar/pop songs and signed to **London Records** after just one high-profile home-town show. Armed with such a simple musical formula, the High were able to work at an unusually brisk pace, releasing three singles in 1990, each of which gradually pushed the band further towards the brink of the public's consciousness. Eventually, at the turn of the year, a remixed version of their debut, 'Box Set Go', worked its way up to number 28 in the UK charts, allowing them to concentrate on creating new material throughout 1991. However, along with the less worthy **Northside**, the High soon topped critical assassination lists in the backlash against all things 'baggy'. The result was an almost total absence of publicity to accompany the aptly titled *Hype*.
● ALBUMS: *Somewhere Soon* (London 1990)★★★, *Hype* (London 1993)★★.

High Button Shoes

Having established themselves as popular songwriters for Tin Pan Alley, and movies such as *Step Lively* and *Anchors Aweigh*, **Sammy Cahn** and **Jule Styne** turned to Broadway, and wrote the music and lyrics for this show which opened at the Century Theatre, on 9 October 1947. In Styne's case, it was be the beginning of a long and glorious stage career during which he composed the music for such legendary shows as *Gentlemen Prefer Blondes*, *Bells Are Ringing*, *Gypsy*, *Do Re Mi*, and *Funny Girl*. Stephen Longstreet based the book for *High Button Shoes* on his novel, *The Sisters Liked Them Handsome*, and Phil Silvers, who had appeared on Broadway in *Yokel Boy* (1939), rocketed to stardom as Harrison Floy, a small-time con-man who sells off some of his neighbours' land which turns out to be a useless swamp. He escapes with the money, and throughout the rest of the story, loses it, wins it back, and then loses it again, in a series of hair-brained schemes. Silvers was ideally cast as the accident-prone loser, and the strong supporting cast included Nanette Fabray, Jack McCauley, Joey Faye, and Helen Gallagher. Cahn and Styne's score contained several numbers that became popular hits, such as 'I Still Get Jealous', which was recorded by the Three Suns, **Harry James**, and **Gordon MacRae**; 'Papa, Won't You Dance With Me?', **Doris Day**, **Skitch Henderson**; and 'You're My Girl', which **Frank Sinatra** took into the US Hit Parade. Sinatra also made an appealing recording of another song from the show, 'Can't You Just See Yourself?'. The rest of the engaging score included 'There's Nothing Like A Model 'T'', 'Get Away For A Day In The Country', and 'On A Sunday By The Sea'. One of the most spectacular sequences in the show was the 'Bathing Beauty Ballet', which was choreographed by a young **Jerome Robbins** who went on to a glittering future on Broadway and in Hollywood. *High Button Shoes* ran for a more than decent 727 performances in New York, and for a further 291 in London.

High Country

Formed in San Francisco, California, USA, High Country had their origins on the city's traditional music circuit. Butch Waller (guitar/bass/vocals) had been a founding member of the Pine Valley Boys, a bluegrass/folk ensemble that also included David Nelson, Jeff Levine and Herb Petersen. Active in 1962, the quartet broke up when Nelson left to form the Wildwood Boys with **Jerry Garcia** and **Robert Hunter**, before finding fame in the **New Riders Of The Purple Sage**. Petersen subsequently joined the **Dillards**, Levine formed the less well-known People, while Waller put together High Country with guitarists Bill Kirchen (ex-**Commander Cody**) and Mylos Sonka. The group was signed to the **Youngbloods**' Racoon label for which they recorded two superb country albums, before Kirchen and Sonka left for the Ozones. Waller meanwhile remained active in traditional music, both solo and as part of an ever-fluctuating High Country.
● ALBUMS: *High Country* (Raccoon 1970)★★★, *Dreams* (Raccoon 1971)★★.

High Inergy

Barbara Mitchell, Linda Howard, Michelle Rumph and Vernessa Mitchell formed High Energy in April 1976, when all four singers were accepted into the Bicentennial Performing Arts Program in Pasadena, California, USA. They were discovered by Gwen Gordy-Lupper, sister of **Motown Records** boss **Berry Gordy**, who signed them to his Gordy label in 1977. Renamed High Inergy and promoted as 'the new **Supremes**', the vocal combo found immediate success with 'You Can't Turn Me Off (In The Middle Of Turning Me On)', a Top 20 hit in the USA in September 1977. By 1983, they had notched up eight further soul hits, without crossing over into the pop market. Vernessa Mitchell left the group in 1979 to pursue a career in gospel. High Inergy disbanded in 1984 when lead singer Barbara Mitchell went solo. She had already duetted with **Smokey Robinson** on a minor hit single, 'Blame It On Love', in 1983, but her 1984 debut, *Get Me Through The Night*, provoked little public response.
● ALBUMS: *Turnin' On* (Gordy 1977)★★★, *Steppin' Out* (Gordy 1978)★★, *Shoulda Gone Dancin'* (Gordy 1979)★★★, *Frenzy* (Gordy 1979)★★★, *Hold On* (Gordy 1981)★★, *So Right* (Gordy 1982)★★, *Groove Patrol* (Gordy 1983)★★. Solo: Barbara Mitchell *Get Me Through The Night* (1984)★★.

High Land, Hard Rain - Aztec Camera

Aztec Camera emerged from the ruins of Glasgow's acclaimed Postcard label with this poignant, poetic collection. Group leader Roddy Frame possessed a precious talent, sculpting melodies and arrangements in the manner of 60s Californian pop. Rippling acoustic guitars emphasize the album's fresh spirit while Frame invests his songs with an insight belying his comparative youthfulness. His astute lyrics employ a wordplay that is knowing but never too clever, resulting in a collection that shows bite behind its aural sweetness.
● Tracks: *Oblivious; The Boy Wonders; Walk Out To Winter; We Could Send Letters; The Bugle Sounds Again; Pillar To Post; Release; Lost Outside The Tunnel; Back On Board; Down The Dip.*
● First released 1983
● UK peak chart position: 22
● USA peak chart position: 129

High Llamas

London, England's High Llamas are the 90s vehicle of former **Microdisney** co-founder Sean O'Hagan (b. Eire). After that group sundered in 1987, O'Hagan spent three years incubating the High Llamas' debut album, released on Demon Records in 1990. Though a low-profile release, it received several encouraging reviews, not least from long-standing Microdisney fans within the press. Afterwards O'Hagan divided his time between the High Llamas and several side projects. He appeared on three albums by **Stereolab** (and one by that band's spin-off project Turn On), and also remixed the **Boo Radleys**' 'Find The Answer Within'. A second High Llamas album, *Gideon Gaye*, was produced on a budget of just £4,000, and released on the small Brighton independent label Target Records. Again, the critical response was encouraging, the resulting comparisons to **Brian Wilson** and the **Beach Boys** enticing Sony Records to offer O'Hagan a contract. *Gideon Gaye* was subsequently re-released via the group's own Alpaca Park label, with its international release handled by Sony/Epic Records. A single take from it, 'Checking In, Checking Out', proved especially popular in Germany, becoming an unexpected chart hit. *Hawaii* was an extraordinary album in so far as it sounded closer to what **Brian Wilson** was trying to achieve in 1966/7 than anything the **Beach Boys** subsequently released. The album is a reincarnation of the Beach Boys' *Friends, Smiley Smile, Sunflower* and *Pet Sounds* combined, and is paradoxically, fresh-sounding.
● ALBUMS: as Sean O'Hagan *High Llamas* (Demon 1990)★★★, *Apricots* mini-album (Plastic 1992)★★, *Santa Barbara* (Vogue/Mute 1994)★★★, *Gideon Gaye* (Target 1994)★★★★, *Hawaii* (Alpaca Park 1996)★★★★, *Cold And Bouncy* (Alpaca Park 1997)★★★.

High Note Records
(see **Pottinger, Sonia**)

High Society

This enjoyable musical adaptation of Philip Barry's stylish play, *The Philadelphia Story*, which was filmed (without songs) in 1940 with Katharine Hepburn, Cary

Grant and James Stewart, was released by MGM in 1956. Apart from some changes in characterization and locales, John Patrick's screenplay, which was set in swanky Newport, Rhode Island, stayed fairly close to the original and concerns Tracey Lord (Grace Kelly), who is set to marry an insufferable snob, George Ketteridge (John Lund), when her former husband, C.K. Dexter Haven (**Bing Crosby**), returns to his house next door, ostensibly to organize a jazz festival. This situation is further complicated by the arrival of Mike Connor (**Frank Sinatra**) and Liz Imbrie (Celeste Holm), two reporters from *Spy* magazine, which has been allowed access to the wedding because it is in possession of certain information regarding the (alleged) philandering of Tracey's father, Seth Lord (Sidney Blackmer). Louis Calhern is especially amusing as Tracey's uncle, and also in the cast were Lydia Reed, Margalo Gillmore, Richard Keene, Hugh Boswell, and jazz giant **Louis Armstrong** who played - who else but himself? By the end of the film Tracey comes to her senses, sends George off in a huff, and remarries Dexter. It is obvious that Mike and Liz will be making their own arrangements soon. **Cole Porter**'s score contained several pleasing numbers such as 'High Society Calypso' (Armstrong), 'Now You Has Jazz' (Crosby-Armstrong), 'Little One' (Crosby), 'Who Wants to Be A Millionaire?' (Sinatra-Holm), 'You're Sensational' (Sinatra), 'I Love You, Samantha' (Crosby) and 'Well, Did You Evah?' (Crosby-Sinatra). Bing Crosby and Grace Kelly's record of 'True Love' made the Top 5 in both the UK and US charts, and Sinatra's version of 'Mind If I Make Love To You?' remains one of his most endearing recorded performances. The director-choreographer was **Charles Walters**, and, in a decade that produced a feast of film musicals, *High Society* grossed nearly six million dollars.

A 1987 UK stage adaptation of the movie, starring Trevor Eve (Dexter), Stephen Rea (Mike), Natasha Richardson (Tracey), Angela Richards (Liz), Ronald Fraser (Uncle Willie) and Robert Swales (George), had a revised book by Richard Eyre, and interpolated into the score some of Porter's other numbers, including 'Give Him The Oo-La-La', 'Hey, Good Lookin'', 'Most Gentlemen Don't Like Love' and 'In The Still Of The Night'. Another version, adapted by Carolyn Burns, dipped further into the Porter song catalogue, and toured the English provinces in 1996. A year later, an American *High Society* started out in San Francisco on its journey to Broadway, where it opened in April 1998. This staging, with Melissa Errico (Tracey), Daniel McDonald (Dexter), Stephen Bogardus (Mike), Randy Graff (Liz), Mark Kudish (George) and John McMartin (Uncle Willie), supplemented the original film score with Porter numbers such as 'I Love Paris', 'Just One Of Those Things', 'It's All Right With Me' and 'Let's Misbehave'. Additional lyrics were credited to Susan Birkenhead, and Arthur Kopit (*Phantom*) provided the book.

High Spirits

Yes, it most definitely was, as the subtitle suggested, 'An Improbable Musical Comedy'. Any show in which a zany spiritualist - in this case, the infamous Mme. Arcati (Beatrice Lillie) - arranges for the spectre of a man's first wife Elvira (Tammy Grimes), to return to earth for one last lap of honour, is surely nearer to farce than *Fiddler On The Roof*. The latter show, along with *Funny Girl*, *Hello, Dolly!*, and *She Loves Me*, was the kind of opposition that *High Spirits* was up against during its Broadway run which began at the Alvin Theatre on 7 April 1964. The show was based on **Noël Coward**'s 1941 play *Blithe Spirit*, and Coward himself directed at first, but is said to have been replaced at a later stage by **Gower Champion**. It was to be Coward's last connection with the New York musical theatre. The British actor, Edward Woodward, played Condomine, the poor unfortunate earthly soul whose second marriage to Ruth (Louise Troy), is terminated when she (Ruth) is accidentally killed by wife number 1 in the course of trying to take her husband back with her to the 'other side'. Woodward, one of the UK's most respected actors, and a more than competent singer, would eventually achieve world-wide renown on television as *The Equalizer*, following on from his earlier small-screen break in *Callan*. The men responsible for adapting *Blithe Spirit* for the stage were **Hugh Martin** and Timothy Gray, and they also contributed the pretty, though unexciting score, which included 'Forever And A Day', 'Was She Prettier Than I?', 'The Bicycle Song', 'I Know Your Heart', 'If I Gave You', 'Something Tells Me', 'Go Into Your Trance', 'Where Is The Man That I Married?', 'Faster Than Sound', 'Home Sweet Heaven', 'Something Is Coming To Tea', and 'You'd Better Love Me', which attained some sort of popularity, and is probably better known as 'You'd Better Love Me (While You May)'. No show-stoppers there, and the reason for the production's 375-run existence was no doubt due to the presence of the redoubtable and irrepressible Beatrice Lillie in what what was to be her final Broadway show. Coincidentally, **Cicely Courtneidge,** who played the role of Mme. Arcati in the London production of *High Spirits*, was also saying goodbye to theatre audiences there, following a glorious career which began more than 50 years before with *The Arcadians* in 1909.

High Tide

Heavy/psychedelic progressive British band formed in 1969 by Tony Hill (ex-**Misunderstood**; guitar/vocals/keyboards), Simon House (violin/piano), Roger Hadden (drums/organ) and Peter Pavli (ex-White Rabbit; bass). Signed to the Clearwater production agency they obtained a recording contract with **Liberty Records** who were eager to join the progressive rock bandwagon that had been milked dry by other record companies. High Tide was a more than credible debut, complete with Mervyn Peake-styled sleeve illustrations. 'Walking Down Their Outlook' features Hill's

Jim Morrison-like vocals although longer tracks such as 'Pushed But Not Forgotten' allowed House and Hill to stretch out and improvise - always a feature of their live performances - with lead guitar and violin competing with each other. They played their first live concert with fellow Clearwater band, **Hawkwind**. After two albums with Liberty they were dropped, and a poor second album sold badly. After numerous tours they became involved with **Arthur Brown**, **Magic Muscle**, and the post-Arthur Brown band, Rustic Hinge. By 1972 Hadden was suffering from mental problems and was placed in hospital where he remains to this day. Hill then went on to work with Drachen Theaker while Pavli and House joined the **Third Ear Band**. Pavli soon involved himself in a number of musical projects with **Robert Calvert** and Michael Moorcock, House meanwhile joined Hawkwind and later **David Bowie**'s band. In 1987 House and Pavli re-formed High Tide and have overseen various other related projects and releases. Hill released a solo album, *Playing For Time*, in 1991, while House again joined up with Hawkwind and Magic Muscle.

● ALBUMS: *Sea Shanties* (Liberty 1969)★★★★, *High Tide* (Liberty 1970)★★★, *Ancient Gates* (80s)★★, *Interesting Times* (High Tide 1987)★★, *Precious Cargo* (Cobra 1989)★★, *The Flood* (High Tide 1990)★★, *A Fierce Native* (High Tide 1990)★★. Solo: Tony Hill *Playing For Time* (1991)★★★.

High, Wide And Handsome

This film is usually mentioned in conjunction with two of the acknowledged masterpieces of the musical theatre, *Show Boat* and *Oklahoma!*. This is partly, although not solely, because **Oscar Hammerstein II** wrote the book (or in the case of the film, the screenplay) and lyrics for all three projects. The other common factor is that each, in its own way, succeeds in musicalizing a slice of cherished American history. In the case of *High, Wide And Handsome*, which is set in the state of Pennsylvania in the year 1859, the story concerns the efforts of a group of militants led by a crooked railway mogul (Alan Hale), to prevent a farmer (Randolph Scott) and his showgirl sweetheart (Irene Dunne) from setting up a pipeline to transport the newly discovered oil from their land to the refinery. Irene Dunne introduced two of **Jerome Kern** and Oscar Hammerstein's most enduring standards, 'The Folks Who Live On The Hill' and 'Can I Forget You?', and the score also included 'Will You Marry Me Tomorrow, Maria?, 'Allegheny Al', 'The Things I Want', and the spirited title song. **Dorothy Lamour** - just three years before she donned her sarong and joined **Bob Hope** and **Bing Crosby** on the *Road To Singapore* - was also in the cast, along with Akim Tamiroff, William Frawley, Charles Bickford, Raymond Walburn, Elizabeth Patterson, and Ben Blue. *High, Wide And Handsome*, which was choreographed by LeRoy Prinz and directed by **Rouben Mamoulian**, was released by Paramount in 1937. A sobering thought: neither 'The Folks Who Live On The Hill' or 'Can I Forget You?' was even nomi-

nated for an Academy Award in 1937. The Oscar for best song went to 'Sweet Leilani' from the film *Waikiki Wedding*.

Higher And Higher

Idol of the bobby-soxers **Frank Sinatra** made his acting debut - as himself - in this 1944 screen version of the Broadway show, which was released by RKO in 1944. The screenplay, by Jay Dratler and Ralph Spence, stayed close to Gladys Hurlbut and Joshua Logan's original stage book in which a group of servants, headed by butler Jack Haley, plan to turn one of their number, a kitchen maid (Michele Morgan), into a debutante in order to raise money for their bankrupt boss (Leon Errol), to whom they owe so much (and vice-versa). For probably the only time in his film life, Sinatra did not get the girl - Michele preferred Haley - but he did get to sing a bunch of marvellous songs by **Jimmy McHugh** and **Harold Adamson**, including 'I Couldn't Sleep A Wink Last Night', 'This Is A Lovely Way To Spend An Evening', 'The Music Stopped', 'You're On Your Own', and 'I Saw You First'. The rest of the numbers consisted of 'It's A Most Important Affair', 'Today I'm A Debutante', 'Minuet In Boogie'; and 'Disgustingly Rich', the only song retained from **Richard Rogers** and **Lorenz Hart**'s original stage score. Another fine singer, **Mel Tormé**, made the first of his infrequent screen appearances, and also in the sprightly cast were Victor Borge, Mary Wickes, Marcy McGuire, Elizabeth Risdon, Barbara Hale, Paul and Grace Hartman, Ivy Scott, and Dooley Wilson. Additional dialogue was provided by William Bowers and Howard Harris, and the lively dance sequences were choreographed by Ernest Matray. The producer-director was Tim Whelan.

Higher Intelligence Agency

Higher Intelligence Agency are Dave Wheels and Bobby Bird, part of the Birmingham Oscillate Collective, who first set up their own ambient/dub club in the back of a local pub in 1992. Next to London's Megadog, the Oscillate night soon emerged as one of the leading such establishments, with a strong reputation built on HIA's 'non-DJing' live sets plus appearances from **Autechre**, **Biosphere**, **Orbital**, **Banco De Gaia**, **Drum Club** and others, plus DJ sets from **Mixmaster Morris** and the **Orb**'s Alex Paterson. They released their debut album in 1993, and a remix EP, *Re-Form*, the following year. This featured the imprints of Autechre, The Irresistable Force, Pentatonik and label-mates, A Positive Life. However, playing live remained their forte, using an improvised set and state of the art equipment to produce a powerful fusion of dub and club music.

● ALBUMS: *Colourform* (Beyond 1993)★★★.

Higher State Records

London based record company formed in 1992 and run by Mark Dillon and Patrick Dickens, whose backgrounds were resolutely in the funk and soul traditions.

As such they played out live as DJs in these genres, before the upsurge of house finally swept them up. However, the twenty-odd releases in their first two years revealed a strong residual flare for digifunk aesthetics. They soon cut out a niche with releases by Disco Biscuit, Spacebase and Sound Environment. There was also evidence of wider listening tastes, including dub reggae, new wave experimentalism (early **Simple Minds**) and proto hip hop (**Mantronix**): 'I could never listen to one particular kind of music all night in a club - it'd get too monotonous'. By 1994 they were still going strong with releases like 'My Geetar Hertz' by Roller Coaster and Lafferty's 'Thinkin' Bout'.

Highlife

More conventional and conservative than either **juju** or **fuji**, highlife has been the continuous thread in West African popular music since its birth in Ghana and Sierra Leone in the 30s. An expressive, cultured music predominantly reliant on guitars, it combines a lightness of touch with rhythms suitable for dancing. Rather than encompassing Western ideas as it evolved, Christian influences in the form of hymns, dance band and regimental music were present at its inception. Its undisputed king is Ghanaian **E.T. Mensah**, who achieved huge popularity in the 50s. By touring widely Mensah converted thousands to the new, readily accessible style. In his wake came **Rex Lawson**, Bobby Benson and **Victor Olaiya** from Nigeria. Artists including **E.K. Nyame** added theatrical elements to produce full-scale concert parties that were much more than simply musical events. However, with the rise of juju in the 70s, highlife declined in popularity, particularly among the Yoruba tribe of Nigeria, though it remained the music of choice for the Igbo people in eastern Nigeria. **C.K. Mann** and the **Sweet Talks** continued to keep highlife at the forefront of domestic music in Ghana, eventually bringing about a revival by the 80s. However, nearly all traces of highlife as a dance band tradition had now gone, in favour of 'guitar band' formations who eschewed highlife's previous associations with westernised, ballroom-orientated music. Even so, long-standing artists such as Mensah benefited from the renaissance which produced a return to form in the shape of 1977's *The King Of Highlife Music*. The **Oriental Brothers** 70s recordings are among the best representations of the new meeting the old, while groups such as **Hi Life International** (based in London, England) and **Orchestre Jazira** exported the sound beyond Africa. In Germany, **George Darko** developed 'burgher highlife', while revered vocalist **Pat Thomas** also took an international route, setting out on a solo career after singing with many of Ghana's great dance bands in earlier decades. The most popular current practitioners are not modern interpreters but seasoned veterans, among them Nigerians Olaiya and **Stephen Osadebe**, and **Mustapha Tettey Addy**, based in Germany. Each of these artists has survived highlife's volatile popularity to record consistent bodies of work, varied in style but all deeply rooted in the highlife tradition.

Highlights

The Highlights had one US Top 20 single in 1956 and never again approached similar success. The group, formed in the Chicago area, comprised singers Frank Pizani, Frank Calzaretta, Tony Calzaretta, Jerry Oleski and Bill Melshimer. The group's first recording was of a song called 'Jingle-lo', which they took to the local Bally Records. The label liked the group but not the song, and gave them one called 'City Of Angels' instead. It reached number 19 in the USA but when it was time to record a follow-up, the group, unsatisfied at being merely a backing group for Pizani, wanted a more equitable arrangement, causing Pizani to leave. Bally issued one song they had recorded with Pizani before his exit, and it hit the lower regions of the charts. The group soon broke up when its only subsequent single failed to chart; Pizani, meanwhile, had one last minor chart hit, 'Indiana Style'. He spent the 80s acting as a **Tony Bennett** impersonator. The others retired from the entertainment business.

Hightower, Rosetta

b. 23 June 1944, USA. This vocalist achieved fame as a member of the **Orlons**, a Philadelphia-based vocal group which enjoyed success with 'The Wah Watusi' and 'Don't Hang Up'. The unit disbanded in 1968 when Hightower went to the UK to pursue a career as a session singer. She contributed to **Joe Cocker**'s international smash hit 'With A Little Help From My Friends', and her later appearances included **Muddy Waters**' *London Sessions* (1972), **Dana Gillespie**'s *Wasn't Born A Man* (1973), **Doris Troy**'s *Stretching Out* and **Kevin Ayers**' *Confessions Of Dr. Dream* (both 1974). During this period Hightower was also a member of Charge, a short-lived studio group that also featured former **Grease Band** stalwarts Neil Hubbard, Alan Spenner and Chris Stainton. Her only solo album was produced by **Ric Grech**.
● ALBUMS: *Hightower* (Columbia 1971)★★.

Highway 101

Like the **Monkees**, Highway 101 is a manufactured US group. Chuck Morris, the manager of the **Nitty Gritty Dirt Band** and **Lyle Lovett**, wanted to form a group that would play 'traditional country with a rock 'n' roll backbeat'. He recruited session man Scott 'Cactus' Moser to help him. He worked with bassist Curtis Stone, the son of **Cliffie Stone**, in the film *Back To School*, and then added session guitarist Jack Daniels. Morris then heard some demos by **Paulette Carlson**. She had had songs recorded by **Gail Davies** and **Tammy Wynette** and had a cameo role as a nightclub singer in the film *Twins*. Their first single, 'Some Find Love', was not successful, but in 1987, they had their first US country hits with 'The Bed You Made For Me' (number 4), which Carlson wrote, and 'Whiskey, If You

Were A Woman' (number 2). They topped the US country charts with 'Somewhere Tonight' with its song-writing credit of 'old' and 'new' country, Harlan Howard and **Rodney Crowell**. In 1988 they had further chart-toppers with 'Cry, Cry, Cry' (which was a new song and not a revival of the **Johnny Cash** hit), 'If You Love Me, Just Say Yes' (being based on the slogan of Nancy Reagan's anti-drugs campaign, 'Just say no') and 'Who's Lonely Now' in 1989. Paulette Carlson took a turn off the Highway in 1990, and Nikki Nelson was recruited for *Bing Bang Boom*. The title track was an infectious and successful single, but the album failed to sell in the same quantities as before. Daniels quit in 1992 and the group made a final album, *The New Frontier*, before disbanding. In 1995 Carlson initiated a reunion, missing only 'Cactus' from the line-up, and the band released a new album.

● ALBUMS: *Highway 101* (Warners 1987)★★★, *101 2* (Warners 1988)★★★, *Paint The Town* (Warners 1989)★★★, *Bing Bang Boom* (Warners 1991)★★★, *The New Frontier* (Liberty 1993)★★★, *Reunited* (Willow Tree 1996)★★★.

● COMPILATIONS: *Greatest Hits* (Warners 1990)★★★★.

Highway 61 Revisited - Bob Dylan

Dylan's first fully fledged electric album engendered considerable controversy. Folk purists had already waved goodbye to him, but rock had become the métier through which the singer could now best express his vision. Session organist Al Kooper and blues guitarist Michael Bloomfield were among those providing free-spirited accompaniment to a collection of songs that redefined pop music. Wrapped in a raw, driving sound, Dylan's poems - part beat, part symbolist, part concrete - ensured that contemporaries could no longer rely on traditional forms, an influence immediately apparent on recordings by the Beatles and the Rolling Stones.

● Tracks: *Like A Rolling Stone; Tombstone Blues; It Takes A Lot To Laugh, It Takes A Train To Cry; From A Buick Six; Ballad Of A Thin Man; Queen Jane Approximately; Highway 61 Revisited; Just Like Tom Thumb's Blues; Desolation Row.*

● First released 1965
● UK peak chart position: 4
● USA peak chart position: 3

Highway QC's

Manager Charles Copeland put together gospel group the Highway QC's in 1945 in Chicago, Illinois, USA. He enlisted Spencer Taylor Jnr. (lead), **Sam Cooke** (lead and first tenor), Lee Richardson (second tenor), Creadell Copeland (baritone) and Charles Richardson (bass). Their name was taken from the Q.C. High School they all attended and the Highway Baptist Church where they rehearsed. Cooke was then recruited by the **Soul Stirrers** and replaced by Johnnie Taylor, formerly singer with the Five Echoes. Their belated recording career began in 1955 after being placed on the local Vee Jay Records label. 'Somewhere To Lay My Head' was their debut single, followed by several further sides and an album. Most of these tracks

were recorded without the aid of Copeland or the Richardson brothers, who had been replaced by James Walker (bass), Ray Crume (tenor), James Davis (tenor and second lead) and Chris Flowers (baritone). Spencer Taylor Jnr. was now the sole lead following his name-sake Johnnie Taylor's 1956 departure to replace the solo-bound Cooke in the Soul Stirrers. Johnnie Taylor subsequently enjoyed a solo career himself, working primarily in the blues medium and scoring a number 1 hit with 'Who's Makin' Love' in 1968. The Highway QC's continued in the interim, with the addition of Will Rogers on second lead in 1961 (he, too, would go on to join the Soul Stirrers). One album for ABC Dunhill in 1973 preceded a long spell at **Savoy Records**, where they recorded seven albums between 1976 and 1983. This was their most fertile period in commercial terms, but into the 90s a touring version of the group was still active (and still fronted by Spencer Taylor Jnr.). In 1995 they celebrated 50 years in the music business.

● ALBUMS: *Somewhere To Lay My Head* (VeeJay 1963)★★★, *Be At Rest* (Peacock 1966)★★★, *Stay With God* (Savoy 1976)★★★.

● COMPILATIONS: *The Best Of The Highway QC's* (Capitol/Chameleon 1990)★★★★.

Highway Robbery

A US rock group comprising Don Fracisco (vocals, drums), Michael Stevens (guitar) and John Livingston Tunison (bass), Highway Robbery proved themselves adept musicians and songwriters with the arrival of their 1972 **RCA Records** debut, *For Love Or Money*. With the lyrics containing multitudinous references to the 60s, Highway Robbery balanced their hippie ideal-ism with thunderous arrangements redolent of early **Black Sabbath**. The combination was a winning one, but it served to confuse record purchasers and also their record company, who dropped them shortly after the album's release.

● ALBUMS: *For Love Or Money* (RCA 1972)★★.

Highway To Hell - AC/DC

It's a mystery how a grown man can spend his life wear-ing a school tie and short trousers and receive adulation from the heavy metal fraternity. Angus Young's riff-laden fills, combined with the tough vocals of the late Bon Scott, made AC/DC one of the genre's all-time leading lights. Bordering on the lighter side of metal, songs such as 'Love Hungry Man', 'Touch Too Much' and the title track will always delight.

● Tracks: *Highway To Hell; Girl's Got Rhythm; Walk All Over You; Touch Too Much; Beating Around The Bush; Shot Down In Flames; Get It Hot; If You Want Blood (You've Got It); Love Hungry Man; Night Prowler.*

● First released 1979
● UK peak chart position: 8
● USA peak chart position: 17

Highwaymen

This self-contained folk quintet comprised Dave Fisher (b. 1940, New Haven, Connecticut, USA), Steve Butts (b. 1940, New York, New York, USA), Chan Daniels (b. 1940, Buenos Aires, Brazil, d. 2 August 1975), Bobby Burnett (b. 1940, Mystic, Connecticut, USA) and Steve Trott (b. 1940, Mexico City, Mexico). The group recorded their self-titled album for **United Artists** in 1961 whilst still students at the Wesleyan University in Middletown, Connecticut, where they had first met. Their haunting version of an old slave song 'Michael', arranged by Fisher, took them to the top on both sides of the Atlantic in 1961, despite a UK cover version by **Lonnie Donegan**. They followed their gold record with another 19th-century folk song 'Cotton Fields'. It too made the US Top 20 but it was to be their last major success. The group, whose repertoire included folk songs from around the world, sang in English, French, Spanish and Hebrew. For them, music was never much more than a hobby and they continued their studies rather than pursuing full-time musical careers. They unsuccessfully re-recorded 'Michael' in 1965 before recording for a time on **ABC**.

● ALBUMS: *The Highwaymen* (United Artists 1961)★★★★, *Standing Room Only!* (United Artists 1962)★★★, *Hootenanny With The Highwaymen* (1963)★★★.

Highways & Heartaches - Ricky Skaggs

Multi-instrumentalist Skaggs played traditional bluegrass with the Stanley Brothers, new bluegrass with J.D. Crowe and the new south and contemporary country with Emmylou Harris' Hot Band. All these influences combine on his albums, of which the best is his second for Epic, *Highways & Heartaches*. Among this 1982 album's many delights are Guy Clark's 'Heartbroke', Bill Monroe's 'Can't You Hear Me Callin'?' and Rodney Crowell's 'One Way Rider'. A great bluegrass album for people who didn't think they liked bluegrass.

● Tracks: *Heartbroke; You've Got A Lover; Don't Think I'll Cry; Don't Let Your Sweet Love Die; Nothing Can Hurt You; I Wouldn't Change You If I Could; Can't You Hear Me Callin'?; Highway 40 Blues; Let's Love The Bad Times Away; One Way Rider.*

● First released 1982

● UK peak chart position: did not chart

● USA peak chart position: did not chart

Higsons

Formed at Norwich University, England, in 1980 by Charlie 'Switch' Higson (lead vocals), Terry Edwards (guitar, saxophone, trumpet), Stuart McGeachin (guitar), Simon Charterton (drums), Colin Williams (bass) and Dave Cummings (guitar), who left the line-up early on, the band originally appeared under a plethora of guises such as the Higson 5, the Higson Brothers and the Higson Experience. They had settled for the Higsons by the time their first single, 'I Don't Want To Live With Monkeys' (1981), on the independent label Romans In Britain, was released. The song typified the Higsons' brand of quirky, tongue-in-cheek funk/pop and was treated to extensive airplay by the influential BBC radio disc jockey **John Peel**, achieving a number 2 position in the UK independent chart. A new label, Waap, brought with it a second single, 'The Lost And The Lonely' (1981), followed by 'Conspiracy' (1982). A contract with **Chrysalis**/2-Tone ensued for two singles, 'Tear The Whole Thing Down' (1982) and 'Run Me Down' (1983). They returned to Waap for 'Push Out The Boat' in 1983 and yet another change of label (Uptight) for a cover version of **Andy Williams'** 'Music To Watch Girls By'. The single failed to provide that elusive hit and was followed by the album *The Curse Of The Higsons*, combining several single sides with new material. Another move, to **EMI**'s R4 label, yielded 'Take It' in 1985, but although Cummings had rejoined for the single, the Higsons played their final gig in March 1986. A posthumous release by Waap, *Attack Of The Cannibal Zombie Businessmen*, married both sides of the first three 45s with six unreleased cuts, including a cover version of the **Buddy Miles** track 'Them Changes'. By that time, Charlie Higson had turned his hand to writing comedy, notably with comedians Harry Enfield and Vic Reeves; he later became the co-writer and star of BBC Television's *The Fast Show*, and published a number of serious novels. Charterton formed the short-lived Eat My Bed, and then Brazilian Nightmare with ex-**Serious Drinking** pair Pete Saunders (ex-**Dexy's Midnight Runners**) and Jem Moore. Terry Edwards later performed with, and produced, **Yeah Jazz**, released a single as New York, New York ('Roger Wilson Said'), teamed up with **Madness**'s Mark 'Bedders' Bedford as the **Butterfield 8**, and worked with **Tindersticks** and **Gallon Drunk**. Dave Cummings, meanwhile, joined **Lloyd Cole**'s Commotions in 1986 and later joined **Del Amitri**.

● ALBUMS: *Live At The Jacquard Club, Norwich* (1982)★★★, *The Curse Of The Higsons* (Waap 1984)★★★, *Attack Of The Cannibal Zombie Businessmen* (Waap 1987)★★★.

● COMPILATIONS: *It's A Wonderful Life* (Hux 1998)★★★.

Hijack

British hip-hop crew who garnered attention via their debut, 'Style Wars', on Simon Harris' Music Of Life label, going on to record for **Ice-T**'s Rhyme Syndicate. Ice-T had been doing a interview for Capitol Radio when the band's 'Hold No Hostage' was played to him. Reactions to the voice of Kamanchi Sly, a powerful MC, have often been positive, and their stage show is very effective. They also earned themselves a little celebrity via their 'Don't Go With Strangers' warning to young children. DJ Supreme from the band (who also include DJ Undercover, Agent Clueso, Agent Fritz and Ulysees) also released superior breakbeat albums like 1992's *Stolen Beats And Ripped Off Samples*.

● ALBUMS: *The Horns Of Jericho* (Rhyme Syndicate 1993)★★★.

Hijas Del Sol

Hijas Del Sol's *Sibèba* is accredited with being the first commercial release by any artist from Bioko (an Equatorial Guinea island formerly known as Fernando Po when it was a Spanish colony). It featured two female singers, Piruchi Apo and Paloma Loribo, from the island's Bubi people. Many of the tracks rested solely on their unaccompanied singing and harmonies, with others featuring the addition of acoustic guitar and percussion. The result was an appealing traditional music which reminded several critics of the nearby music of Benin and Cameroon.

● ALBUMS: *Sibèba* (NubeNegra 1995)★★★.

Hildegarde

b. Hildegarde Loretta Sell, 1906, Adell, Wisconsin, USA. Raised in Milwaukee, Wisconsin, Sell began her career playing piano in silent movie theatres. Later, she began to sing, performing in clubs and bars. For a few years, she toured the vaudeville circuit, accompanying the popular black-face entertainer Gus Edwards. In 1933 she visited London, playing in cabaret and building a reputation as an international entertainer. Her real breakthrough to popularity came almost by chance. Her manager, Anna Sosenko, wrote a song especially for her, in which English and French words were skilfully mixed. The song, 'Darling, Je Vous Aime Beaucoup', became synonymous with Hildegarde; and the intriguing mixture of languages allied to both her faintly exotic-sounding name and her husky delivery led audiences to believe that she was of European origin. If she was aware of this misapprehension, Hildegarde was too smart to set the record straight, recognizing that as a slightly mysterious Continental *chanteuse* she would attract more attention than as a simple songstress from Wisconsin. During the 40s Hildegarde had her own radio show in the USA and late in the decade returned to tour Europe. By the 50s her career had petered out and she never regained the popularity of her early years. Even so, she was still attracting excellent reviews in the early 90s at venues such as the Russian Tea Room in New York and London's Pizza On The Park.

● COMPILATIONS: *So Rare* (30s-40s recordings)★★★.

Hilder, Tony

b. Anthony John Hilder. A mysterious and reclusive figure, refusing even to divulge his date of birth, Tony Hilder was an entrepreneur based in Los Angeles, California, USA. During the late 50s he worked in an A&R capacity at **Modern Records**, which helped furnish him with various contacts in the music business. These included Bob Morgan, co-owner of the studio at which the **Beach Boys** made their first recordings, and Robert Hafner, who co-wrote, performed and produced for Hilder. The rise of surf music inspired Hilder to pursue independent ventures. He formed his first label, CT Records, in 1959, while releases on **Del-Fi Records** and Challenge Records, among others, bear his name as writer, publisher or orchestra leader. A second company, Impact Records, was established as an outlet for masters Hilder could not place elsewhere. Its output largely consisted of local aspirants, the best of which was Dave Myers And The Surftones. Impact Records also allowed Hilder to air his right-wing political sympathies. Slogans such as 'Our Country Can Never Go Right By Going Left' and 'God Bless America' were often printed on their labels, and its releases included 'John Birch American' by the New Breed, 'Voice Of Liberty' by Bob Preston and 'Our Opinion Of Barry Goldwater - The Next President' which featured endorsements from Ronald Reagan, Robert Stack and Efrem Zimbalist Jnr. Hilder meanwhile continued to lease masters to a variety of outlets, but the defeat of Goldwater in the 1964 US election, coupled with the demise of surf music, marked then end of his active involvement in the industry. He later became a salesman for freeze-dried foods.

Hill, Andrew

b. 30 June 1937, Chicago, Illinois, USA. Port Au Prince, Haiti, is usually given as Hill's birthplace, but he actually hails from Chicago. He studied composition privately with Paul Hindemith and Bill Russo, and played accordion and tap-danced on the streets where **Earl Hines** heard him. In his teens he was in Paul Williams's R&B band, played with **Charlie Parker**, **Coleman Hawkins**, **Gene Ammons**, Von Freeman, **Johnny Griffin**, **Malachi Favors** and **John Gilmore**, and became virtually Chicago's 'house' pianist for visiting artists. Having spent some months in New York as **Dinah Washington**'s accompanist he relocated there in 1960 whilst working with **Johnny Hartman**. From 1962-63 he worked in Los Angeles with **Rahsaan Roland Kirk** and **Jimmy Woode** among others. In 1963 he returned to New York to work with **Joe Henderson**. During the 60s he made a number of excellent albums for **Blue Note** (under his own name and with **Bobby Hutcherson** and **Joe Henderson**), probably the best-known being *Black Fire* and the highly-acclaimed *Point Of Departure*, which featured Henderson, **Eric Dolphy** and **Kenny Dorham**. Later Blue Note sessions (several of which remain unissued) often show a dense, turbulent music that is both strikingly individual and intensely gripping; *Compulsion* has John Gilmore in ferocious form, while a set recorded with **Sam Rivers** (and later released under the tenorist's name as one half of the double-set *Involution*) has a moving, almost desperate, sombreness. When the contract ran out in 1970 Hill moved to upstate New York. His career during the 70s is rather a mystery and he has seemed reluctant to clarify it, but he did hold a number of academic posts, including composer-in-residence at Colgate University in New York (where he wrote pieces for string quartet and orchestra) and with the Smithsonian Institute, for whom he toured rural areas of the US, playing hospitals, prisons and introducing jazz to an entirely new audience. In 1977 he moved to

Pittsburgh, California (near San Francisco), and from the early 80s his career seemed to take off again, with more record releases (most notably 1986's *Shades*, with **Clifford Jordan**) and tours, including a season at New York's Knitting Factory, and a Contemporary Music Network tour of Britain with Howard Riley, **Joachim Kuhn** and **Jason Rebello** in 1990. Now re-signed to the new Blue Note, where he has been paired with the upcoming alto saxophonist **Greg Osby**, Hill is a highly individual pianist and composer who is often compared with **Thelonious Monk** and **Cecil Taylor**, if only by virtue of his uniqueness. This quality has persisted through the brooding power of his 60s music to the more celebratory feel of recent releases. 'I'd say interesting . . . happy . . . warm', is how Hill responded to a 1976 request to describe his style. 'There was an angry period, but you get tired of pounding the piano. It's too good an instrument.'

● ALBUMS: *So In Love With The Sound Of Andrew Hill* (1956)★★★, *Black Fire* (1964)★★★, *Judgement* (1964)★★, *Point Of Departure* (Blue Note 1965)★★★, *Smokestack* (1965)★★★, *Andrew!* (1966)★★, *Compulsion* (1966)★★★, *Grass Roots* (1968)v, *Lift Every Voice* (1969)★★★, *Invitation* (Steeplechase 1975)★★★, *Spiral* (Freedom 1975)v, *Blueblack* (1975)★★★, *Homage* (1975)★★, *Live At Montreux* (Freedom 1975)★★★, *One For One* (1975)★★★, With Sam Rivers *Involution* 1966 recording (1975)★★, *Divine Revelation* (1976)★★★, *Nefertiti* (1976)★★★★, *From California With Love* (1979)★★★, *Dance With Death* 1968 recording (1980)★★, *Strange Serenade* (Soul Note 1980)★★★, *Faces Of Hope* (Soul Note 1980)★★★, *Solo Piano* (Artists House 1981)★★★, *Shades* (Soul Note 1987)★★★, *Verona Rag* (Soul Note 1988)★★★, *Eternal Spirit* (Blue Note 1989)★★★, *Black Fire* (Blue Note 1989)★★★, *But Not Farewell* (Blue Note 1991)★★★.

● COMPILATIONS: *The Complete Blue Note Andrew Hill Sessions* (Mosaic 1963-66)★★★★.

Hill, Benny

b. Alfred Hawthorne Hill, 25 January 1925, England, d. 18 April 1992. Hill entered showbusiness at an early age and played the variety circuit, specializing in comedy and impressions. He was already a well-known comedian in Britain when he was signed to Pye as a recording artist in the early 60s. His whimsical tunes, 'Gather In The Mushrooms', 'Transistor Radio' and 'Harvest Of Love' were all minor hits during this period. Hill went on to star in one of the decade's most successful comedy television series, *The Benny Hill Show*. Amazingly, the series later became hugely popular in the USA and many other countries, despite its peculiarly English 'saucy seaside postcard' humour. Hill usually had musical guests on the show and a segment was reserved for his own stories in song, which were usually filled with mild innuendo and grinning puns. One such song was 'Ernie (The Fastest Milkman In The West)' which captured the public's imagination and became the UK's Christmas number 1 in 1971. His saucy narrative ballads are available on album. His death in April 1992 resulted in considerable media coverage, praising his talent and probing his considerable fortune.

● COMPILATIONS: *Benny Hill: The Best Of* (1992)★★★.

Hill, Bertha 'Chippie'

b. 15 March 1905, Charleston, South Carolina, USA, d. 7 May 1950, New York City, New York, USA. Bertha Hill was in showbusiness as a singer and dancer aged 14, when she claimed to have stolen the show from **Ethel Waters**. Nicknamed for her youth and small stature, she settled in Chicago in the 20s. Her dark, hard voice was especially suited to blues, and good trumpeters seemed to inspire her; her finest recordings are those with **Joe 'King' Oliver** and **Louis Armstrong**. She retired in the late 20s after marrying, but was persuaded to return to singing and recording for the growing white jazz audience in the mid-40s. Still a fine singer, she was a success at the 1948 Paris Jazz Festival, but a promising second career was ended by a hit-and-run driver.

● ALBUMS: *Sounds Of The Twenties Vol. 4* (c.1965)★★★, *The Great Blues Singers* (c.1965)★★★, *Ida Cox/Chippie Hill* (c.1975)★★★, *When Women Sang The Blues* (1976)★★★, *Montana Taylor* (1991)★★★.

Hill, Billy

b. 14 July 1899, Boston, Massachusetts, USA, d. 24 December 1940, Boston, Massachusetts, USA. A prolific composer and lyricist during the 30s, whose songs have a comfortable, country feeling about them. This is probably due to Hill spending a good deal of his early life travelling the American west, playing violin and piano in bars and dance halls. He wrote one of his first songs, 'Old Man Of The Mountain', with composer **Victor Young** in 1932, but from then on, apart from an occasional collaboration with Peter De Rose and one or two others, he generally provided both music and lyrics himself. He had his first hit in 1933 with 'The Last Round-Up', which was recorded by many artists including **Guy Lombardo**, George Olsen, Don Bestor, **Bing Crosby** and Victor Young. Among his many other songs in the 30s were 'Have You Ever Been Lonely (Have You Ever Been Blue?)', 'The Old Spinning Wheel' (US number 1 for **Ray Noble**), 'Oh Muki Muki Oh', 'Rain', 'Alone At A Table For Two', 'Down The Oregon Trail', 'Lights Out' (US number 1 for **Eddie Duchin**), 'Put On An Old Pair Of Shoes', 'Empty Saddles' (sung by **Bing Crosby** in the film *Rhythm On The Range*), 'In The Chapel In The Moonlight' (US number 1 for **Shep Fields**, and successfully revived by **Dean Martin** in 1967), and 'The Glory Of Love' (US number 1 for **Benny Goodman**). Two other Hill compositions to make it to the top of the US chart, 'The Last Round-Up' (Guy Lombardo) and 'Wagon Wheels' (**Paul Whiteman**) were both featured in the *Zeigfeld Follies* of 1934. Nothing substantial was forthcoming after 1940 when Hill produced 'On A Little Street In Singapore' and the **Gene Autrey** movie title song 'The

Call Of The Canyon'. The former was impressively revived in more recent times by the classy vocal quartet **Manhattan Transfer**.

Hill, Dan

b. Daniel Hill Jnr., 3 June 1954, Toronto, Ontario, Canada. Hill achieved success when a soft ballad co-written by Hill and **Barry Mann**, reached number 3 in 1977, and 'Can't We Try', a duet with Vonda Sheppard, climbed to number 6 in 1987. Hill and his parents moved to Canada during the 50s and he discovered music in his teens, gravitating toward vocalists such as **Frank Sinatra**. Hill became a professional musician at the age of 18, playing at clubs and trying to sell his demo tapes to uninterested record labels. He gradually became popular in Canada, and signed to 20th Century Fox Records in the USA. His self-titled debut album just missed the US Top 100 in 1975 and his first chart single in the US was 'Growin' Up', in 1976. But the follow-up introduced Hill to a larger audience. It was the president of the publishing company for which he worked who teamed him with Mann, resulting in the success of 'Sometimes When We Touch'. Hill's album, *Longer Fuse*, which included that single, was also his biggest seller, reaching number 21 in 1977. The Hill-Mann collaboration was followed by a few lesser chart singles for Hill and it seemed he had disappeared from the music scene in the early 80s after recording two albums for Epic Records. In 1987, however, he collaborated with female singer Vonda Sheppard and returned to the Top 10. Hill placed one further single in the chart in early 1988 and had Top 10 hits in *Billboard*'s 'Adult' chart that year with 'Carmelia' and in 1990 with 'Unborn Heart'.

● ALBUMS: *Dan Hill* i (20th Century 1975)★★, *Longer Fuse* (20th Century 1977)★★★, *Hold On* (20th Century 1978)★★, *Frozen In The Night* (20th Century 1978)★★, *If Dreams Had Wings* (Epic 1980)★★, *Partial Surrender* (Epic 1981)★★, *Dan Hill* ii (Columbia 1987)★★.

● COMPILATIONS: *The Best Of Dan Hill* (20th Century 1980)★★★.

Hill, Ernest

b 14 March 1900, Pittsburgh, Pennsylvania, USA, d. 16 September 1964. In his earlier years Hill played brass bass as well as string bass, eventually concentrating on the latter. In the early 20s he was with the orchestra led by **Claude Hopkins** that visited Europe as part of a show featuring **Joséphine Baker**. In New York he again played with Hopkins, then several other bands in the city, and in the early 30s was with **Chick Webb**, **Benny Carter**, **Willie Bryant** and **Rex Stewart**. Towards the end of the 30s he again travelled to Europe where he worked until the start of World War II. In 1940 he returned to New York, again spent time with Hopkins, then toured with **Zutty Singleton**, **Louis Armstrong**, Hopkins yet again, and **Cliff Jackson**. He also toured with the globe-trotting band Herbie Cowens took on USO tours. Towards the end of the 40s, Hill was again

in Europe, playing with **Bill Coleman**, **Frank 'Big Boy' Goudie** and others. In the early 50s he was back in the USA, performing with several bands including that led by **Happy Caldwell**. As his career suggests, Hill was not only footloose but also held in high regard by bandleaders who welcomed his presence in their bands for the solidity he brought to rhythm sections.

Hill, Faith

b. Audrey Faith Perry, 21 September, 1967, Jackson, Mississippi, USA. Raised in the small town of Star, Mississippi, USA, the 90s country singer Faith Hill was singing at family gatherings from the age of three. She was influenced by **Reba McEntire** and formed her first band when she was 17 years old, performing at local rodeos. She moved to Nashville in 1989 and her first job was selling T-shirts at the Country Music Fan Fair. Attempts to make a name for herself in Nashville were fruitless, and Hill eventually accepted a secretarial job with a music publisher. Legend has it that the publisher/singer Gary Morris urged her to leave the job and take up singing as a career. She befriended songwriter Gary Burr, who produced her demo tape, and suitably impressed Warner Brothers Records. Hill has subsequently recorded several of Burr's songs, including 'I Would Be Stronger Than That', 'Just Around The Eyes' and 'Just About Now'. Her first album was produced by Scott Hendricks, who had previously had some success with **Brooks And Dunn** and **Restless Heart**. Her sparkling debut US country single, the rocking 'Wild One', topped the country charts and she followed it with a version of **Janis Joplin**'s 'Piece Of My Heart', another cheerful country-rocker. *Take Me As I Am* was successful, but surgery on her vocal cords delayed the making of *It Matters To Me*. This included a song about wife-beating, 'A Man's Home Is His Castle', a duet with **Shelby Lynne**, 'Keep Walkin' On', and a song written for her by **Alan Jackson**, 'I Can't Do That Anymore'. Her regular band features Trey Grey (drums), Steve Hornbeak (keyboards), Tom Rutledge (guitar, fiddle), Anthony Joyner (bass), Lou Toomey (lead guitar), Karen Staley (guitar, vocals) and is masterminded by dobro and steel guitarist Gary Carter. Much of Hill's popularity has been fuelled by having one of the best touring bands in the business. 'It Matters To Me' was a further US country chart topper in 1996. In 1997 she recorded with her husband **Tim McGraw**, resulting in the number 1 hit and CMA Award-winning 'It's Your Love'.

● ALBUMS: *Take Me As I Am* (Warners 1993)★★★, *It Matters To Me* (Warners 1995)★★★★, *Faith* (Warner Bros 1998)★★★.

● VIDEOS: *Piece Of My Heart* (Deaton Flanigen 1994).

Hill, Goldie

b. Angolda Voncile Hill, 11 January 1933, Karnes City, Texas, USA. Hill's career was far too short in the opinion of many country music fans. It started in 1952 and basically ended when she retired from the music in

1957. In 1952, she went with elder brother Tommy to his recording session. A country band leader told Tommy he needed a girl singer who could play bass fiddle. Hill later recalled 'Tommy told him he knew just the girl and before I knew it, for the first time in my life, I was holding a bass fiddle'. Soon after she made her debut on the KWKH Shreveport's *Louisiana Hayride* and joined **Decca Records**. In January 1953, her recording of 'I Let The Stars Get In My Eyes' (the answer song to Slim Willett and **Skeets McDonald** hit 'Don't Let The Stars Get In Your Eyes') entered the *Billboard* charts and became her first and only number 1. The success of the recording saw her begin to appear on the *Grand Ole Opry*. In the next two years, she had Top 14 chart hits duetting with **Justin Tubb** ('Looking Back To See' and 'Sure Fire Kisses') and with **Red Sovine** ('Are You Mine'). By the time her name next appeared in the charts with 'Yankee Go Home' (which contained a narration by Sovine), in 1959, Hill had retired. (It was a case of Decca wanting to use the recording made earlier). She had toured extensively and became affectionately known as The Golden Hillbilly, when, in 1957, during a Philip Morris package tour, she met top country star **Carl Smith**. They married and moved to a ranch in Franklin, near Nashville. Hill, then, decided to retire to raise their family. (They subsequently had three children, Carl Jnr., Larry and Lori). In 1968, after some persuasion, and recording as Goldie Hill Smith, she recorded two albums for Epic and gained a minor chart hit with 'Lovable Fool', before once again retiring. Many country fans have regretted the fact that they never recorded an album together. In 1977, Smith still a major star, also retired and the couple became noted for raising horses on their ranch. Commenting years later about her retirement she replied 'I was never that ambitious. I never missed it a bit. I was never hooked on it'.

● ALBUMS: *Goldie Hill* (Decca 1960)★★★, *Lonely Heartaches* (Decca 1961)★★★, *According To My Heart* (Decca 1962)★★, *Country Hit Parade* (Decca 1964)★★★, *Country Songs* (Vocalion 1967)★★, *Goldie Sings Again* (Epic 1968)★★, *Goldie Hill Sings Country* (Vocalion 1969)★★★, *The Country Gentleman's Lady Sings Her Favorites* (Epic 1969)★★★.

Hill, Jessie

b. 9 December 1932, New Orleans, Louisiana, USA, d. 17 September 1996. Jessie Hill's primary claim to fame was the classic New Orleans R&B hit 'Ooh Poo Pah Doo - Part II' in 1960. His first musical experience was as a drummer at the age of seven. At 15 he played in a Dixieland band and at 20 formed an R&B group called the House Rockers. He briefly worked with **Professor Longhair** and **Huey Smith** in the mid-50s before re-forming the House Rockers in 1958, abandoning the drums to sing. After Hill performed 'Ooh Poo Pah Doo' as a joke at his gigs, Joe Banashak of Minit Records heard the song and agreed to record it. Arranged by **Allen Toussaint**, it eventually reached number 3 on the R&B charts and number 28 on the

national pop charts. Hill had only one other minor chart single before moving to Los Angeles, where he wrote songs performed by **Sonny And Cher**, **Ike And Tina Turner** and **Iron Butterfly**. He recorded one album later in his career and there is a collection of his Minit sides on Charly Records.

● ALBUMS: *Naturally* (1972)★★.

● COMPILATIONS: *Y'all Ready Now?* (Charly 1980)★★★, *Golden Classics* (Collectables)★★★.

Hill, Michael

b. 1952, South Bronx, New York, USA. Very much a modern bluesman, Hill took **Jimi Hendrix** and **Eric Clapton** as his early models, and through them, encountered the music of **B.B. King**, **Albert King** and **T-Bone Walker**. He also saw **Buddy Guy** opening for the **Mothers Of Invention** in Central Park. In the early 70s, he formed Brown Sugar, which included his brother Kevin on bass and sisters Kathy and Wynette singing backing vocals. Hill went on to play in Dadahdoodahda with Vernon Reid, who later formed **Living Color**, and became part of Black Rock Coalition, which Reid helped to form in 1985. In 1987, he started another band, the Blues Mob, with Kevin, Tony Lewis and Doug Booth, while also performing with Bluesland, a larger version of Brown Sugar. The latter recorded 'Bluestime In America' for *The History Of Our Future*. At the same time a demo of Blues Mob, with Fred McFarlane replacing Booth on keyboards, was sent to Alligator boss Bruce Iglauer, who signed them to the label in 1994. *Bloodlines* contained original songs, with the exception of Reid's 'Soldier's Blues', in which Hill commented perceptively, and not without humour, on the quality of black life in his country, its dangers and shortcomings. Though couched in a rock format, his music is very much the blues of today.

● ALBUMS: *Bloodlines* (Alligator 1994)★★★, *Have Mercy!* (Alligator 1996)★★★.

Hill, Rosa Lee

b. 25 September 1910, Como, Mississippi, USA, d. 22 October 1968, Senatobia, Mississippi, USA. The daughter of **Sid Hemphill**, Rosa Lee Hill grew up in a musical family, playing a broad repertoire for both whites and blacks. Her recordings are confined to blues, which she sang 'from my mouth, and not from the heart', feeling them to be incompatible with her religious faith. Her blues are typical of Panola County, where she spent her whole life: accompanied by a droning guitar, her songs have an inward-looking, brooding feel, comparable to those of **Fred McDowell**. Hill and her husband were sharecroppers and lived in dire poverty, particularly towards the end of their lives, when their house burned down and they had to move into a tumbledown shack.

● ALBUMS: *Blues Roll On* (1961)★★★, *Mississippi Delta Blues Vol. 2* (c.1970)★★★, *Roots Of The Blues* (1977)★★★.

Hill, Teddy

b. Theodore Hill, 7 December 1909, Birmingham, Alabama, USA, d. 19 May 1978. After playing drums and trumpet, Hill switched to reed instruments and toured theatre circuits. In 1928 he joined **Luis Russell** as both sideman and assistant manager. In the early 30s he worked with **James P. Johnson** and then led his own big band, which survived until 1940. Hill's band held an occasional residency at the Savoy in Harlem and in 1937 toured Europe and the UK. During its existence, the band was home at one time or another to several outstanding jazzmen, including **Chu Berry**, **Dicky Wells** and a succession of fine trumpeters, among whom were **Roy Eldridge**, **Bill Coleman**, **Shad Collins**, **Frankie Newton** and **Dizzy Gillespie**. In 1940, Hill became manager of Minton's Playhouse and thus presided benevolently over the emergence of bebop, as his former sideman Gillespie joined with other revolutionaries in experimentation. While this might seem far removed from Hill's earlier role in jazz, in fact it reflected his lifelong interest in new developments. After Minton's closed, Hill continued in club management elsewhere.

● COMPILATIONS: *Teddy Hill And Cab Calloway* (1935-36 recordings, one side only)★★, *Uptown Rhapsody* (Hep Jazz 1992)★★★.

Hill, Tiny

A heavyweight bandleader in every sense, the inappropriately titled Tiny Hill was a massive man (nearing 400 lbs in weight) who formed his first dance band in 1933 in Illinois, USA. He had begun experimenting with music as the drummer in a trio while attending Illinois State Normal College. This informal group enjoyed significant local success at a variety of night-clubs and halls, and encouraged him to form his own, expanded unit. With a line-up including Jack Alexander, Sterling Bose, Bob Anderson, Ralph Richards, Dick Coffeen, Russ Phillips, Bob Kramer, Nick Schreier, Bob Walters, Norman Maxwell, Pat Patterson, Lloyd McCahn, Monte Mountjoy, Rolly Carpenter, Al Larsen, Leroy Hendricks and others, the Tiny Hill Orchestra quickly found themselves prime bookings on the Midwest one-nighter circuit. Augmented by vocalists such as Allen De Witt, Bob Freeman, Irwin Bendell and Hill himself, the group's popularity soon extended to Nebraska, Missouri and Iowa, growing steadily throughout the 30s and 40s. Undeterred by the decline in the commercial appeal of the big band sound, Hill resolutely remained at the helm of the combo until his death in 1972. In that time the Tiny Hill Orchestra left behind several excellent recordings for **Vocalion**, **OKeh** and **Mercury Records**, including their theme song, 'Angry'.

Hill, Vince

b. 16 April 1937, Coventry, England. A popular ballad singer who has been an enduring favourite in the UK since the 60s, Hill trained as baker and worked as a soft drinks salesman and in a colliery, while singing at pubs and clubs in his spare time. He served in the Royal Signals during his period of National Service, and sang with the regimental band in Europe and the Far East. After demobilization he toured in Leslie Stuart's 19th-century musical comedy *Floradora*, later joining trumpeter Teddy Foster's band as vocalist. After forming the Raindrops vocal group with Len Beadle, Jackie Lee and Johnny Worth in 1958, Hill turned solo in 1962 and released 'The River's Run Dry'. He soon found himself in demand on top television and radio shows, and his big breakthrough arrived when he became the resident singer on ITV's *Stars And Garters* and radio's *Parade Of the Pops*. Signed to **Columbia Records**, he enjoyed some modest success with 'Take Me To Your Heart Again', 'Heartaches' and 'Merci Cheri', before hitting the jackpot in 1967 with 'Edelweiss', which went to number 2 in the UK chart. He continued to register in the late 60s with a mixture of old and new ballads, such as 'Roses Of Picardy', 'Love Letters In The Sand', 'Importance Of Your Love', 'Doesn't Anyone Know My Name', and 'Little Blue Bird'. In 1970 Hill gained the Most Popular Singer Award while representing Britain at the Rio Song Festival, and a year later had more chart success with 'Look Around' from the movie *Love Story*. After guesting on most of the top UK television variety shows, in 1973 he starred in his own television series, *They Sold A Million*, which was enthusiastically received and ran initially for 15 weeks. Since then, he has hosted a 26-week television series in Canada, and performed his highly accomplished and extremely entertaining cabaret act at venues such as The Talk Of The Town in London, and in several other countries around the world. He is also much in demand on cruise ships such as the QE2. In the late 80s and early 90s he produced and appeared in his own nostalgia shows which feature music from the stage and screen, and continues to broadcast frequently on BBC Radio 2. In addition to writing and starring as George Loveless, the leader of the Tolpuddle martyrs in the Radio 4 drama *Tolpuddle*, Hill has also played the leading role of **Ivor Novello** in the musical *My Dearest Ivor*, and, in collaboration with Johnny Worth and playwright Alan Plater, written his own stage musical, *Zodiac*, based on the life of the Champagne magnate, Charles Heidseck.

● ALBUMS: *Have You Met* (Columbia 1966)★★★, *Heartaches* (Columbia 1966)★★★, *At The Club* (Columbia 1967)★★★, *Edelweiss* (Columbia 1967)★★★, *Always You And Me* (Columbia 1968)★★★, *You Forgot To Remember* (Columbia 1969)★★★, *Look Around And You'll Find Me There* (1971)★★★, *In My Thoughts Of You* (1972)★★★, *They Sold A Million* (1973)★★★, *Mandy* (1975)★★★, *Wish You Were Here* (1975)★★★, *Midnight Blue* (1976)★★★, *This Is My Lovely Day* (1978)★★★, *While The Feeling's Good* (1980)★★★, *That Loving Feeling* (President 1982)★★★, *Sings The Great Songs Of Today* (1984)★★★, *I'm The Singer* (1985)★★★, *I Will Always Love You* (1987)★★★, *Sings The Ivor Novello Songbook* (1988).

● COMPILATIONS: *The Vince Hill Collection* (1976)★★★, *The Very Best Of Vince Hill* (1979)★★★★, *20 Golden*

Favourites (1980)★★★★, *Greatest Hits: Vince Hill, An Hour Of Hits* (1986)★★★★, *Best Of The EMI Years* (EMI 1992)★★★★.

Hill, Z.Z.

b. Arzel Hill, 30 September 1935, Naples, Texas, USA, d. 27 April 1984. A singer in the mould of **Bobby 'Blue' Bland**, Hill served his musical apprenticeship in Dallas lounge bars. He recorded for his brother Matt's MH label before signing to Kent Records in 1964. A string of mature, sophisticated singles followed, including 'Hey Little Girl' (1965) and 'I Found Love' (1966). More 'adult' than contemporaries at **Stax**, such records struggled for acceptance outside the south and failed to reach the R&B chart. Although Hill left Kent in 1968, the label continued to release his material and three years later secured a Top 30 R&B hit with his 1964 recording, 'I Need Someone (To Love Me)'. The artist enjoyed similar success with the engaging 'Don't Make Me Pay For His Mistakes', which peaked at number 17 (US R&B). Other releases were less fortunate, but the singer's work with Jerry **'Swamp Dogg'** Williams improved the situation. Later spells with Hill/United Artists and **Columbia** were marred by corporate indecision. In 1981, Hill signed with Malaco, a company devoted to classic southern soul. His albums there, including *Down Home*, *The Rhythm And The Blues* and *I'm A Blues Man*, proved his most artistically satisfying. Hill died of a heart attack in April 1984.

● ALBUMS: *A Whole Lot Of Soul* (Kent 1969)★★★, *The Brand New Z.Z. Hill* (Mankind 1972)★★★, *Dues Paid In Full* (Kent 1972)★★★, *The Best Thing That's Ever Happened To Me* (Mankind 1972)★★★★, *Keep On Loving You* (1975)★★★, *Let's Make A Deal* (Columbia 1978)★★★, *Mark Of Z.Z.* (1979)★★★, *Z.Z. Hill* (Malaco 1981)★★★, *Down Home* (Malaco 1982)★★★★, *The Rhythm And The Blues* (Malaco 1983)★★★★, *I'm A Blues Man* (Malaco 1984)★★★, *Bluesmaster* (Malaco 1984)★★★.

● COMPILATIONS: *Dues Paid In Full* (Kent 1984)★★★, *In Memorium 1935-1984* (Malaco 1985)★★★, *Whoever's Thrilling You (Is Killing Me)* (Stateside 1986)★★★, *Greatest Hits* (Malaco 1986)★★★★, *The Best Of Z.Z. Hill* (Malaco 1986)★★★, *The Down Home Soul Of Z.Z. Hill* recorded 1964-68 (1992)★★★.

Hillage, Steve

b. 2 August 1951, England. Guitarist Hillage played with Uriel in December 1967 alongside Mont Campbell (bass), Clive Brooks (drums) and **Dave Stewart** (organ). This trio carried on as **Egg** when Hillage went to college. He returned to music in April 1971, forming Khan with Nick Greenwood (bass), Eric Peachey (drums) and Dick Henningham. Dave Stewart also joined but they had little success and split in October 1972. Hillage then joined **Kevin Ayers'** touring band Decadence, before linking up with French-based hippies **Gong**, led by Ayers' ex-**Soft Machine** colleague Daevid Allen. Hillage injected much-needed musicianship into the band's blend of mysticism, humour and

downright weirdness. In 1975 he released his first solo album *Fish Rising*, recorded with members from Gong, which marked the start of his writing partnership with longtime girlfriend Miquette Giraudy.

On leaving Gong in 1976, Hillage developed his new age idealism on the successful *L*, produced by **Todd Rundgren**, and featuring Rundgren's **Utopia**. *Motivation Radio* utilized the synthesizer skills of Malcom Cecil, of synthesizer pioneer group **Tonto's Expanding Headband**, and included an inspired update of **Buddy Holly**'s 'Not Fade Away'. *Live Herald* featured one side of new studio material which developed a funkier feel, an avenue that was explored further on *Open* in 1979. *Rainbow Dome Musick* was an instrumental experiment in ambient atmospherics. In the 80s, Hillage moved into production work, including albums by **Robin Hitchcock** and **Simple Minds**. In 1991 Hillage returned to recording and live performance as the leader of **System 7**, a loose aggregation of luminaries including disc jockey **Paul Oakenfield**, Alex Paterson of the **Orb** and Mick MacNeil of Simple Minds. As the line-up would suggest, System 7 produce ambient dance music, combining house beats with progressive guitar riffs and healthy bursts of soul and disco.

● ALBUMS: *Fish Rising* (Virgin 1975)★★★, *L* (Virgin 1976)★★★, *Motivation Radio* (Virgin 1977)★★★, *Green* (Virgin 1978)★★★, *Live Herald* (Virgin 1979)★★★, *Open* (Virgin 1979)★★★, *Rainbow Dome Musick* (Virgin 1979)★★★, *For To Next/And Not Or* (Virgin 1983)★★★, *System 7* (Ten 1991)★★★★.

Hilliard, Bob

b. 21 January 1918, New York, USA, d. 1 February 1971, Hollywood, California, USA. A prolific lyricist from the mid-40s into the 60s, the first of many Hilliard hit songs came in 1946 when he collaborated with Dick Miles on 'The Coffee Song'. It became successful for **Frank Sinatra**, who remembered it again many years later, and included it on *Ring-A-Ding-Ding*, the first album for his own **Reprise** label. In 1947, Hilliard and Carl Sigman contributed 'The Big Brass Band From Brazil' and 'Civilization' to the Broadway musical *Angel With Wings*. 'Civilization' was sung by **Elaine Stritch** in the show, and became a massive hit for **Danny Kaye** and the **Andrews Sisters**, **Ray McKinley** and **Louis Prima**. Hilliard's other 40s successes included 'A Strawberry Moon', 'Careless Hands' (with Sigman - revived by **Des O'Connor** in 1967) and 'Dear Hearts And Gentle People' (with **Sammy Fain**), which was a hit for **Bing Crosby**, **Dennis Day**, **Gordon MacRae** and others. In the 50s Hilliard collaborated with **Jule Styne** on the scores for two Broadway musicals, *Michael Todd's Peep Show* ('Stay With The Happy People') and *Hazel Flagg* ('Every Street's A Boulevard In Old New York' and 'How Do You Speak To An Angel?'). His film work around this time included several songs, with Sammy Fain, for **Walt Disney**'s *Alice In Wonderland* (1952, 'It's Late', 'Very

Good Advice'). Among Hilliard's other 50s songs were 'Dearie' (with Dave Mann), 'Be My Life's Companion', 'Jealous Eyes', 'Bouquet Of Roses', 'Downhearted' (a hit for **Eddie Fisher**), 'Sweet Forgiveness', 'Somebody Bad Stole De Wedding Bells' (with Mann) and 'Moonlight Gambler' (with Phil Springer). In 1959 Hilliard had a hit with another novelty song, 'Seven Little Girls Sitting In The Back Seat' (with Lee Pockriss), recorded by **Paul Evans** in the US, and the **Avons** in the UK. In the early 60s, with the advent of the beat boom, his output declined, although he had some success with 'Tower Of Strength' (with **Burt Bacharach**), 'You're Following Me', 'My Summer Love', 'My Little Corner Of The World' (with Pockriss) and 'Our Day Will Come' (with Mort Garson), which was a US number 1 for **Ruby And The Romantics**. Hilliard's other songs included 'Don't You Believe It', 'Any Day Now', 'Red Silk Stockings And Green Perfume', 'The Thousand Islands Song', 'Chocolate Whiskey And Vanilla Gin', 'Castanets And Lace', and 'Baby Come Home'. Among his many collaborators were Dick Sanford and Sammy Mysels.

Hillman, Chris

b. 4 December 1942, Los Angeles, California, USA. Originally a mandolin player of some distinction, Hillman appeared in the Scottsville Squirrel Barkers, the Blue Diamond Boys and the Hillmen before Jim Dickson offered him the vacant role of bassist in the fledgling **Byrds** in late 1964. The last to join that illustrious group, he did not emerge as a real force until 1967's *Younger Than Yesterday*, which contained several of his compositions. His jazz-influenced, wandering basslines won him great respect among rock *cognoscenti*, but it soon became clear that he hankered after his country roots. After introducing **Gram Parsons** to the Byrds, he participated in the much-acclaimed *Sweetheart Of The Rodeo* and went on to form the highly respected **Flying Burrito Brothers**. A line-up with **Stephen Stills** in **Manassas** and an unproductive period in the ersatz supergroup **Souther Hillman Furay Band** was followed by two mid-70s solo albums of average quality. A reunion with **Roger McGuinn** and **Gene Clark** in the late 70s proved interesting but short-lived. During the 80s, Hillman recorded two low-budget traditional bluegrass albums, *Morning Sky* and *Desert Rose*, before forming the excellent and highly successful **Desert Rose Band**. They enjoyed considerable but diminishing success and the unit folded in 1993. Hillman and Herb Pedersen worked as a duo in the mid-90s and released a traditionally flavoured album, *Bakersfield Bound*, in 1996.
● ALBUMS: with the Hillmen *The Hillmen* (Together 1970)★★★, *Slippin' Away* (Asylum 1976)★★★, *Clear Sailin'* (Asylum 1977)★★, *Morning Sky* (Sugar Hill 1982)★★★, *Desert Rose* (Sugar Hill 1984)★★★, with Herb Pedersen *Bakersfield Bound* (Sugar Hill 1996)★★★★, with Pedersen, Tony Rice, Larry Rice *Out Of The Woodwork* (Rounder 1996)★★★★.

Hillside

A contemporary soul trio from Los Angeles, California, USA, Hillside launched their recording career in 1996 with a self-titled collection released on their own Organized Fun label. Comprising Anthony 'Rox' Brown, Wayne Cockerham and Eric 'Junx' Jenkins, their album highlighted the group's tasteful blend of traditional vocal R&B harmonies with rhythms and melodies inspired by the soul and funk traditions. They had initially found the music industry disinterested in what they described as 'the live, instrumental thing', so the group set up Organized Fun, distributed by Bellmark, and produced *Hillside* themselves. The accent on live drums rather than a drum machine helped distinguish the group's 'classicist' intentions from the plethora of male R&B groups, as did the absence of samples and their preference for their own musicianship (keyboards, bass and drums). The album was promoted by the release of a single, 'Pearl'.
● ALBUMS: *Hillside* (Organized Fun 1996)★★★.

Hillside Singers

The Hillside Singers were brought together in 1972 by USA record producer Al Ham and left their mark with one chart hit, 'I'd Like To Teach The World To Sing (In Perfect Harmony)', that year. Ham, a music business veteran who once played bass and arranged for big band artists such as **Glenn Miller** and **Artie Shaw**, later worked as a staff producer for **Columbia Records** during the 50s and produced the original cast recordings of *West Side Story*, *My Fair Lady* and other Broadway shows. The members of the Hillside Singers were chosen by Ham for the express purpose of recording the single which Ham believed had potential beyond the Coca-Cola commercial it accompanied. The group consisted of Mary Mayo, Ham's daughter Lori, brothers Ron and Rick Shaw and members of another group called Good Life. The single was recorded for the Metromedia label and reached number 13. A rival version by the **New Seekers** from the UK climbed even higher at number 7, as well as topping the UK charts. The Hillside Singers recorded two albums and other singles, one of which was adapted from a McDonald's commercial, but did not chart after 1972, when Metromedia folded.
● ALBUMS: *I'd Like To Teach The World To Sing* (1972)★★.

Hillsiders

The Hillsiders played country when country was not cool - as the UK's leading country band, they have now introduced thousands of people to the music. The group's origins go back to 1959 when lead singer/rhythm guitarist Kenny Johnson (b. 11 December 1939, Liverpool, England) formed the Country Three. Johnson, joined by guitarist Joe Butler (b. 12 January 1939, Liverpool, England), changed the group to Sonny Webb and the Country Four, taking his stage name from the American country stars **Sonny James** and **Webb Pierce**. In 1961, following an argument, Johnson regrouped as Sonny Webb And The Cascades. Butler played bass and they were joined by lead guitarist Frank Wan, who had been with **Clinton Ford**, and Brian 'Noddy' Redman, of the **Fourmost** and **Kingsize Taylor** And The Dominoes. Playing the beat venues frequented by Merseybeat groups, they brought their tough environment to country music and so pioneered country rock before the **Byrds**. Their publicity proclaimed, 'For that country flavour and the best in pops', and their repertoire can be gauged from their recordings at the Rialto Ballroom in Liverpool for Oriole's *This Is Merseybeat* albums. The songs included **George Jones**' 'Who Shot Sam?', **Bob Luman**'s 'You've Got Everything', **Hank Locklin**'s 'Border Of The Blues' and **Buck Owens**' 'Excuse Me'. At Ozzie Wade's country music club in Liverpool in May 1964, Sonny Webb and the Cascades became the Hillsiders. Brian Hilton from Group One joined as lead guitarist when Frank Wan switched to steel. Wan, who tired of life on the road, was subsequently replaced by Ronnie Bennett in 1966. The Hillsiders had a residency at the Black Cat club in Liverpool but they spent time touring, working in Germany with **Red Sovine** and often backing visiting American artists. **Bobby Bare** and **George Hamilton IV** both made albums with the group. The Hillsiders made numerous records in their own right, starting with an appearance on **Decca**'s album *Liverpool Goes Country*. They won numerous country awards and became well known through the radio programmes *Country Meets Folk* and *Up Country*. The packaging for their album *By Request* features genuine requests and shows their most popular stage numbers - 'Proud Mary', 'Crying In The Rain' and 'Me And Bobby McGee'. However, they were also writing more and more of their own material, leading to their self-penned album *Our Country*, which included the excellent 'Across The Mountain' and 'Blue Kentucky Morning', a song they had written for Patsy Powell. The promising Butler-Johnson partnership ceased when Johnson left the Hillsiders in January 1975 to be replaced by Kevin McGarry from another Liverpool band, the Westerners. As the Hillsiders sold more of their **Polydor** albums at shows than in the shops, they were encouraged to set up their own label, Stile. Ronnie Bennett left the Hillsiders to develop his own steel guitar company and he was replaced by Dave Rowlands. Both the Hillsiders and Kenny Johnson, with his new group Northwind, have moved towards a more powerful-sounding country music and both have developed strong, original material. The *15 - 25* album, their fifteenth in 25 years, included guest apperances by Kenny Johnson and Ronnie Bennett and featured a new version of their first single, Diggy Liggy Lo'. Butler left the Hillsiders in 1993, largely because of his commitments as a broadcaster on local radio. He was replaced by Mick Kinney from another Merseyside band, **Phil Brady And The Ranchers**. Butler now plays in a well-established part-time band, Hartford West. The Hillsiders were notable for being the first UK band to pick up on the potential of the **Mavericks**; says

McGarry, 'We were performing their songs long before anyone had heard of them and then they got known through CMT. People have said to us "That American act is doing your songs".'
● ALBUMS: *The Hillsiders Play The Country Hits* (60s)★★★, *The Hillsiders* (60s)★★★, with Bobby Bare *The English Countryside* (RCA Victor 1967)★★★, *The Leaving Of Liverpool* (1969)★★★, with George Hamilton IV *Heritage* (1971)★★★, *By Request* (1972)★★, *Our Country* (1973)★★★, *To Please You* (1975)★★★, *Goodbye Scottie Road* (1976)★★★, *On The Road* (70s)★★, *A Day In The Country* (LP 1979)★★★, *15 - 25* (1990)★★★.
Solo: Kenny Johnson *Let Me Love You Once* (1980)★★★, *The Best Of Kenny Johnson* (1982)★★★.

Hilltoppers

This vocal quartet formed at the Western Kentucky College in Bowling Green, Kentucky, USA, comprised lead Jimmy Sacca (b. Hazard, Kentucky, USA), baritone **Billy Vaughn** (b. 12 April 1931, Glasgow, Kentucky, USA), tenor Seymour Speigelman and bass Don McGuire. Sacca and Vaughn formed the group to record 'Trying' in 1952 and named it after their college nickname. **Dot Records** signed the band, re-recorded 'Trying' in the college auditorium, and it reached the US Top 10 (making the UK charts in 1956). Over the next five years the group, who wore college sweaters and beanies on stage, scored a further nine US Top 20 singles, the biggest being 'P.S. I Love You' in 1953, 'Only You' in 1955 and 'Marianne' in 1957. Vaughn left in 1955 and had a very successful career as musical director for Dot and as an orchestra leader. In the UK, where the **Platters**' original version of 'Only You' was not released until 1956, they reached number 3 with their recording and were in the Top 20 for six months. They were one of the most successful early 50s vocal groups, but like many other acts they could not survive in a rock 'n' roll world and disbanded in 1963. Since then Sacca has occasionally played dates with new sets of Hilltoppers.
● ALBUMS: *Tops In Pops* (London 1957)★★★, *The Towering Hilltoppers* (London 1957)★★★, *Love In Bloom* (Dot 1958)★★.
● COMPILATIONS: *P.S. I Love You - The Best Of* (Varese Vintage 1994)★★★.

Hilton, Ronnie

b. Adrian Hill, 26 January 1926, Hull, England. Hilton left school at the age of 14 and worked in an aircraft factory during the war before joining the Highland Light Infantry. He was demobilized in 1947 and returned to factory work in Leeds. He sang with the Johnny Addlestone band at the Starlight Roof in Leeds from 1950 and was heard by A&R manager Wally Ridley and signed to **HMV**. At this point he underwent surgery for a hair lip, changed his name, and in July 1954 made his debut as **Ronnie Hilton**. His first appearance on stage was at the Dudley Hippodrome in 1955, and soon afterwards he had his own radio series.

For the next 10 years he was one of the most popular vocalists in the UK and specialized in romantic ballads. His hits included 'I Still Believe', 'Veni Vidi Vici', 'A Blossom Fell', 'Stars Shine In Your Eyes', 'Yellow Rose Of Texas', 'Young And Foolish', 'No Other Love' (a UK number 1 in 1956), 'Who Are We', 'Two Different Worlds', 'Around The World', 'The World Outside', and the novelty, 'A Windmill In Old Amsterdam'. Since his last hit in 1965 he has remained in demand especially in the north of England. He still performs summer seasons and tours with nostalgia packages that include contemporaries such as **Russ Conway**, **Dennis Lotis** and **Rosemary Squires**. For several years he presented *Sounds Of The 50s* for BBC Radio Two.

● ALBUMS: *I'm Beginning To See The Light* (EMI 1959)★★★.

● COMPILATIONS: *The Very Best Of Ronnie Hilton - 16 Favourites Of The 50s* (MFP 1984)★★★, *The EMI Years: The Best Of Ronnie Hilton* (EMI 1989)★★★★, *Ronnie Hilton* (Hour Of Pleasure 1990)★★★.

Himber, Richard

b. 1907, USA, d. December 1966. Himber formed his first dance band in the early 30s in New York City, New York, USA, having previously worked as a sideman with **Rudy Vallee** and as manager for **Buddy Rogers'** Band. He had also been employed as a magician in vaudeville, and would use his magic skills to embellish the band's live act, giving them a distinctive edge over the competition. Throughout the 30s and 40s the Himber orchestra proved popular at the smaller New York hotels such as Essex House, the Hotel Pierre and the Ritz-Carlton, with a style that borrowed from both the sweet and swing traditions. Himber's sidemen included Jerry Colona, Joey Nash, Johnny McGee, Ruby Weinstein, Sam Persoff, Dave Levy, Ernie Capozzi, Jack Kimmel, Nat Levine, Jimmy Rosellie, Pete Pumiglio, Jess Carneol, Sam Amorose, Jack Lacey, Lloyd Turner, Lyle Bowen, Paul Rici, Lou Raderman, Eddie Steinberg, Henry Patton, Charlie Margulis, Russ Case, Will Bradley, Sam Weiss, George Mazza, Rolly Dupont, Milt Yaner, Al Evans, Frank Victor, John Cusumano, Mel Solomon, Wally Barron, Sid Stoneburn, Jimmy Smith, Haig Stevens, John Dilliard, Ruby Waltzer, Bill Gaham, **Hank d'Amico**, Milt Shutz, Jim Blake, **Adrian Rollini**, **Bunny Berigan** and, at one point, **Artie Shaw**. The featured vocalists were Guy Russell, Joey Nash, Stuart Allen and a separate vocal group, consisting of **Dolores Gray**, Johnny Johnston, Harry Stanton and Joseph Lilley. **Johnny Mercer** also occasionally joined the band in the studio. The Richard Himber Orchestra soon found radio exposure with a slot on *The Eddie Peabody Show*. Several others followed, including *The Melody Puzzle Show* and *The Studebaker Champion Show*. On the latter he changed his group's billing to Richard Himber And His Studebaker Champions. Later they were also known as the Rhythmic Pyramids Orchestra to accommodate a change of style which saw him expand the orchestra's

string section. With the advent of World War II the orchestra was disbanded briefly during the 40s but reconvened in 1945. It continued with Himber at the helm until the late 50s, with numerous record releases such as 'It Isn't Fair', 'Moments In The Moonlight', 'Haunting Memories', 'Day After Day', 'Time Will Tell' and 'I'm Getting Nowhere Fast With You'.

Hinds, Justin

b. 7 May 1942, Steertown, St. Anns, Jamaica, West Indies. Justin Hinds, together with backing vocalists the Dominoes (Dennis Sinclair and Junior Dixon), first recorded in late 1963 for producer **Duke Reid**. That first session produced an instant hit, 'Carry Go Bring Come', recorded in one take, and set a pattern from which Hinds rarely deviated - Hinds' expressive country/gospel tenor lead vocals, with empathetic support from the two Dominoes, backed by the Treasure Isle studio band led by **Tommy McCook** and Herman Marquis. Hinds was Reid's most successful artist in the period from 1964 to 1966, reputedly recording 70 singles. He stayed with Reid until 1972; the relationship produced some of the finest Jamaican music, through **ska**, **rocksteady** and reggae. In the former style, 'King Samuel', 'Botheration', 'Jump Out Of The Frying Pan' (all 1964), 'The Ark', 'Peace And Love' and the bawdy 'Rub Up Push Up' (all 1965) are exemplary. The transition to the rocksteady format during 1966-67 resulted in hits such as 'The Higher The Monkey Climbs', 'No Good Rudy', a new rocksteady version of 'Carry Go Bring Come', 'On A Saturday Night', 'Once A Man', an anguished cover version of the **Rip Chords'** 'Here I Stand' and the sublime 'Save A Bread', both in 1968. Lyrically, Hinds utilized the rich Jamaican tradition of proverb and parable to reflect the wide range of issues thrown up by a society in transition from country to city. After Reid's death in 1975, Hinds made two albums with **sound system** owner and producer Jack Ruby. In 1978 he also recorded a handful of discs for producer **Sonia Pottinger**. Titles such as 'What A Weeping', 'Rig-Ma'Roe Game' and 'Wipe Your Weeping Eyes' showcased Hind's beautiful and expressive voice, and highlighted his lyrical concerns. Since 1985, when he recorded the excellent album *Travel With Love* for Nighthawk Records of St. Louis, he has apparently preferred the rural lifestyle to the 'rat race' of Kingston. He is also part of the **Wingless Angels**, a group of Nyahbingi Rastafarian drummers.

● ALBUMS: *Best Of Justin Hinds & The Dominoes* (1968)★★★, *Jezebel* (Island 1976)★★★, *From Jamaica With Reggae* (High Note 1984)★★★, *Travel With Love* (Night Hawk 1985)★★★★, *Justin Hinds* (Jwyanza 1990)★★.

● COMPILATIONS: *Early Recordings* (Esoldun/Treasure Isle 1992)★★★, *Peace And Love* (Trojan 1998)★★★.

Hindu Love Gods

The Hindu Love Gods are of most interest to **R.E.M.** fans, since three quarters of that band, Peter Buck (b. 6 December 1956, Los Angeles, California, USA; guitar),

Mike Mills (b. 17 December 1958, Orange County, California, USA; bass) and Bill Berry (b. 31 July 1958, Duluth, Minnesota, USA; drums), were in attendance at the 1987 sessions at which the band was formed. The group's singer/guitarist is **Warren Zevon**. In fact, the R.E.M. axis had contributed to two previous solo albums for Zevon, before forming the Hindu Love Gods as an *ad hoc* offshoot in 1986. Following the release of singles 'Narrator' and 'Good Time Tonight', the full recording of their meeting was finally released in 1990. This, a collection of blues standards and an unlikely **Prince** cover version, was little more than an adequate bar-room blues session, and has not subsequently been repeated.

● ALBUMS: *Hindu Love Gods* (Giant/Reprise 1990)★★.

Hines, Deni

b. Australia. Deni Hines, the daughter of popular Australian singer **Marcia Hines**, first came to national prominence in 1991 when she was the featured vocalist on an Australian Top 5 hit by the Rockmelons, a version of 'Ain't No Sunshine'. It was a full five years before her debut solo album followed. In the interim, she had aborted a projected album release which had involved recording sessions in America, and taken part in a long and highly successful run of *Jesus Christ Superstar* in Australia, where she took the female lead as Mary Magdalene. Her debut solo single, 'It's Alright', followed at the end of 1995. Her first album was released early in 1996 and achieved gold status domestically and an impressive 100,000 unit sales profile in Japan, where she was regularly featured in the mainstream fashion press.

● ALBUMS: *Imagination* (Mushroom 1996)★★★, *Pay Attention* (Mushroom 1998)★★★.

Hines, Earl 'Fatha'

b. 28 December 1903, Dusquene, Pennsylvania, USA, d. 22 April 1983. An outstanding musician and a major figure in the evolution of jazz piano playing, Hines began his professional career in 1918. By that time he had already played cornet in brass bands in his home town. By 1923, the year in which he moved to Chicago, Hines had played in several bands around Pittsburgh and had been musical director for singer Lois Deppe. He performed in bands in Chicago and also toured theatre circuits based on the city. Among the bands with which he played were those led by **Carroll Dickerson** and Erskine Tate. In 1927 he teamed up with **Louis Armstrong**, playing piano, acting as musical director and, briefly, as Armstrong's partner in a nightclub (the third partner was **Zutty Singleton**). With Armstrong, Hines made a series of recordings in the late 20s which became and have remained classics: these were principally Hot Five, Hot Seven or Savoy Ballroom Five tracks but also included the acclaimed duet 'Weather Bird', one of the peaks of early jazz. Also in 1927 he was with **Jimmy Noone**'s band and the following year was invited to form a band for a resi-

dency at Chicago's Grand Terrace. Although enormously popular at this engagement, the long residency, which lasted throughout the 30s, had an adverse effect upon the band's standing in big band history. Less well-known than the bands that toured the USA during the swing era, it was only through records and occasional radio broadcasts from live venues that the majority of big band fans could hear what Hines was doing. With outstanding arrangers such as **Jimmy Mundy** and top-flight sectionmen including **Trummy Young**, **Darnell Howard** and **Omer Simeon**, the band was in fact advancing musically at a speed which outstripped many of its better-known contemporaries. This was particularly so after 1937 when arranger **Budd Johnson** arrived, bringing an advanced approach to big band styling which foreshadowed later developments in bebop. The reason why Hines stayed at the Grand Terrace for so long is open to question, but some who were there have suggested that he had little choice: the Grand Terrace was run by mobsters and, as **Jo Jones** remarked, 'Earl had to play with a knife at his throat and a gun at his back the whole time he was in Chicago'.

In the early 40s Hines hired several musicians who modernized the band's sound still further, including **Dizzy Gillespie**, **Charlie Parker** and **Wardell Gray**, which led to **Duke Ellington** dubbing the band 'the incubator of bebop'. Hines also hired singers **Billy Eckstine** and **Sarah Vaughan**; but he eventually folded the big band in 1947 and the following year joined Louis Armstrong's All Stars, where he remained until 1951. He then led his own small groups, holding a long residency at the Club Hangover in San Francisco. In 1957 he toured Europe as co-leader, with **Jack Teagarden**, of an all-star band modelled on the Armstrong All Stars. For all this activity, however, Hines's career in the 50s and early 60s was decidedly low-profile and many thought his great days were over. A series of concerts in New York in 1964, organized by writer Stanley Dance, changed all that. A succession of fine recording dates capitalized upon the enormous success of the concerts and from that point until his death Hines toured and recorded extensively.

Despite the heavy schedule he set himself the standard of his performances was seldom less than excellent and was often beyond praise. If, in later years, his accompanying musicians were of a very different calibre to their leader, his own inventiveness and command were at their peak and some of his performances from the 70s rank with his groundbreaking work from half a century before. A brilliant and dynamic player, Hines had an astonishing technique which employed a dramatic tremolo. As indicated, as a soloist his powers of invention were phenomenal. However, he was initially an ensemble player who later developed into a great solo artist, unlike many pianists who began as soloists and had to adapt their style to suit a role within a band. Hines adopted an innovative style for the piano in jazz in which he clearly articulated the melody, used single note lines played in octaves, and employed his distinctive tremolo in a manner that resembled that of a wind player's vibrato. All this helped to land his technique with the potentially misleading term, 'trumpet style'. The number of pianists Hines influenced is impossible to determine: it is not too extravagant to suggest that everyone who played jazz piano after 1927 was in some way following the paths he signposted. Certainly his playing was influential upon **Nat 'King' Cole**, **Mary Lou Williams**, **Billy Kyle** and even the much less flamboyant **Teddy Wilson**, who were themselves important innovators of the 30s. During this period, perhaps only **Art Tatum** can be cited as following his own star.

● ALBUMS: *Earl Hines And The All Stars* (Mercury 1950)★★★★, *Piano Moods* (Columbia 1951)★★★★, *Fats Waller Memorial Set* (Advance 1951)★★★, *Earl Hines QRS Solos* (Atlantic 1952)★★★, *Earl Hines Trio* (Dial 1952)★★★, *Earl Hines All Stars* (Dial 1953)★★★★, *Earl Hines With Billy Eckstine* (RCA Victor 1953)★★★, *Earl Hines And His New Sound Orchestra* (1954)★★★★, *Earl 'Fatha' Hines* (Nocturne 1954)★★★, *Piano Solos* (X-LVA 1954)★★★, *The Earl Hines Trio* i (1954)★★★★, *Earl Hines At Club Hangover* (1955)★★★, *Earl 'Fatha' Hines And His All Stars Vols 1 & 2* (1956)★★★★, *Earl 'Fatha' Hines Plays Fats Waller* (1956)★★★★, *After You've Gone* (1956)★★★, *'Fatha' Plays Fats* (Fantasy 1956)★★★★, *Earl 'Fatha' Hines Solo* (Fantasy 1956)★★★, *Oh Father* (Epic 1956)★★★, *Here Is Earl Hines* (1957)★★★, *The Earl Hines Trio* ii (1957)★★★, *The Earl Hines Trio* iii (1957)★★★, *The Jack Teagarden-Earl Hines All Stars In England* (1957)★★★★, *The Earl Hines Quartet* i (1958)★★★, *Earl 'Fatha' Hines* (Epic 1958)★★★, *'Fatha'* (Tops 1958)★★★, *The Earl Hines Quartet* ii (1960)★★★★, *Swingin' And Singin'* (Craftsmen 1960)★★★, *Earl's Pearls* (MGM 1960)★★★, *All Stars* (Jazz Panorama 1960)★★★, *A Monday Date* (Riverside 1961)★★★, *Earl Hines And His All Stars* i (1961)★★★★, *Earl Hines And His All Stars* ii (1961)★★★, *Earl Hines With Ralph Carmichael And His Orchestra* (1963)★★★, *Earl 'Fatha' Hines* (Capitol 1963)★★★★, *Spontaneous Explorations* (Contact 2 1964)★★★, *The Earl Hines Trio At The Little Theatre, New York* (1964)★★★★, *Fatha* (1964)★★★, *The Earl Hines Quartet* iii (1964)★★★, *The Earl Hines Trio* iv (1964)★★★, *The Earl Hines Trio With Roy Eldridge And Coleman Hawkins Live At The Village Vanguard* (1965)★★★★, *The Real Earl Hines In Concert* (Focus 1965)★★★, *The New Earl Hines Trio* (Columbia 1965)★★★, *The Grand Terrace Band* (RCA Victor 1965)★★★, *Up To Date* (RCA Victor 1965)★★★, *Earl Hines & Roy Eldridge At The Village Vanguard* (1965)★★★★, *Hines '65/Tea For Two* (1965)★★★★, *Blues In Thirds* (1965)★★★, *Paris Session* (1965)★★★, *Life With Fatha* (Verve 1965)★★★, *Father's Freeway* (1965)★★★, *Once Upon A Time* (Impulse 1966)★★★, *Hines' Tune* (1965)★★★, with Coleman Hawkins *Grand Reunion* (Limelight 1965)★★★, with Roy Eldridge *Grand Reunion Volume 2* (Limelight 1965)★★★★, *Earl Hines At The Scandiano Di Reggio, Emilia* (1966)★★★, *The Earl Hines Trio* v (1966)★★★, *Blues So Low (For Fats)* (1966)★★★★, *Dinah* (1966)★★★, *The Earl Hines Trio* vi (1966)★★★, *Blues And Things* (1967)★★★, *Fatha Blows Best* (1968)★★★, *A Night At Johnnie's* (1968)★★★, *Master Jazz Piano Vols 1 & 2* (1969)★★★★, *Earl Hines At Home* (1969)★★★, *Boogie Woogie On St Louis Blues* i (1969)★★★, *Quintessential Recording Session* (1970)★★★, *Fatha And His Flock On Tour* (1970)★★★, *Earl Hines And Maxine Sullivan Live At The Overseas Press Club, New York* (1970)★★★★, *Earl Hines In Paris* (1970)★★★★, *It Don't Mean A Thing If It Ain't Got That Swing* (1970)★★★, *Master Jazz Piano Vols 3 & 4* (1971)★★★, with Jaki Byard *Duet* (1972)★★★, *Earl Hines* i (1972)★★★, *Solo Walk In Tokyo* (1972)★★★, *Tour De Force* (1972)★★★, *Earl Hines Plays Duke Ellington Vols 1-3* (1972)★★★★, *My Tribute To Louis* (c.1972-73)★★★★, *Hines Does Hoagy* (c.1972-73)★★★★, *Hines Comes In Handy* (c.1972-73)★★★, *Back On The Street* (1973)★★★, *Live At The New School* (1973)★★★, *Quintessential Recording Session Continued* (1973)★★★, *An Evening With Earl Hines And His Quartet* (1973)★★★, *Earl Hines Plays George Gershwin* (1973)★★★, *The Earl Hines Quartet* iv (1973)★★★, *Swingin' Away* (1973)★★★, *Quintessential 1974* (c.1974)★★★, *Earl Hines* ii (1974)★★★, *One For My Baby* (1974)★★★, *Masters Of Jazz Vol. 2* (Storyville 1974)★★★, *Earl Hines At The New School Vol. 2* (1974)★★★, *West Side Story* (1974)★★★, *Live!* (1974)★★★, *Fireworks* (1974)★★★, *Hines '74* (1974)★★★, *At Sundown* (1974)★★★, *The Dirty Old Men* (1974)★★★, *Jazz Giants In Nice* (1974)★★★, *Piano Portraits Of Australia* (1974)★★★, *Concert In Argentina* (1974)★★★, *Earl Hines In New Orleans With Wallace Davenport And Orange Kellin Vols 1 & 2* (1975)★★★★, *Earl Hines Plays Duke Ellington Vol. 4* (1975)★★★, *Earl Hines At Saralee's* (1976)★★★, *Live At Buffalo* (1976)★★★, *Jazz Is His Old Lady And My Old Man* (c.1977)★★★, *Lionel Hampton Presents Earl 'Fatha' Hines* (1977)★★★★, *Giants Of Jazz Vol. 2* (Storyville 1977)★★★, *Earl Hines In New Orleans* (1977)★★★, *Father Of Modern Jazz Piano/Boogie Woogie On St Louis Blues* ii (1977)★★★★, *East Of The Sun* (1977)★★★, *Texas Ruby Red* (1977)★★★, *Deep Forest* i (1977)★★★, with Harry 'Sweets' Edison *Earl Meets Harry* (1978)★★★, with Edison, Eddie 'Lockjaw' Davis *Earl Meets Sweets And Jaws* (1978)★★★★, *Fatha's Birthday* (1981)★★★, *Deep Forest* ii (1982)★★★, *Earl Hines Live At The New School* (1983)★★★.

● COMPILATIONS: *Louis Armstrong Classics Vol. 3* (1928 recordings)★★★, *Swingin' Down* (1932-33 recordings)★★★, *Fatha Jumps* (1940-42 recordings)★★★, *The Indispensable Earl Hines* rec. 1944-66 (RCA 1983)★★★★, *Earl Hines Big Band* (1945-46 recordings)★★★, *Father Steps In* (Tring 1993)★★★, *Another Monday Date* (Prestige 1995)★★★.

● FURTHER READING: *The World Of Earl Hines*, Harold Courlander.

Hines, Marcia

b. 20 July 1953, Boston, Massachusetts, USA. Hines went to Australia in 1970 to work in the stage production of *Hair*, and later became the world's first black Mary Magdalene, in the stage production *Jesus Christ Superstar*. With a cover of **James Taylor**'s 'Fire And Rain' in 1975 she had immediate success. Propelled by manager Peter Rix and producer Robie Porter, she followed this with many hit singles including 'I Just Don't Know What To Do With Myself', 'What I Did For Love' and 'You', (the last single reaching number 1 in Australia). She became an established MOR performer, winning hosts of media and pop industry awards. She also toured internationally with the acclaimed Australian jazz group, the Daly Wilson Big Band. Hines has continued a divided career in acting and music.

● ALBUMS: *Marcia Shines* (1975)★★★, *Shining* (1976)★★, *Ladies & Gentlemen, Marcia Hines* (1977)★★★, *Live Across Australia* (1978)★★, *Ooh Child* (1979)★★★, *Take It From The Boys* (1982)★★★.

● COMPILATIONS: *Greatest Hits* (1982)★★★.

Hines, Simone

b. c.1975, New Jersey, USA. Another of a seemingly endless roll-call of female soul/R&B singers to emerge in the mid-90s, Simone Hines released her self-titled debut for Epic Records in 1997. Hines' career began as a club singer who graduated to sharing a stage with **Queen Latifah** and **Michael Bolton**. She also appeared alongside **Aretha Franklin** at New York's **Apollo** Theatre during a 1992 Democratic Party fund-raiser. The producers on her debut album included **Narada Michael Walden**, Harvey Mason Jnr. and Rodney Jerkins. A highly polished collection of sensual R&B ballads, three of the album's tracks were co-written by the artist. It also included a cover version of the **Emotions**' 'Best Of My Love'. In addition to the release of a single, 'Yeah! Yeah! Yeah!', Hines increased her profile by recording a track alongside **Foxy Brown** for **Puff Daddy**'s 1997 album, a huge international seller.

● ALBUMS: *Simone Hines* (Epic 1997)★★★.

Hinnen, Peter

b. 19 September 1941, Zurich, Switzerland. Hinnen displayed musical talent at an early age. He studied bass and piano at music school and at 14, he had also appeared in three films. He learned guitar and became interested in traditional Swiss folk music (Volksmusik) and especially in yodelling. His first record release, 'Columbus Boogie', was on a Polydor 78 in 1955. By 1959, he was working as a singer, yodeller and instrumentalist with a folk band but also visited the USA, where he appeared on New York's *Radio City Music Hall*. He made two further visits to America in 1961 (when he appeared on a show with **Judy Garland**) and 1962. He enjoyed country music success in German-speaking countries with 'Auf Meiner Ranch Bin Ich Konig' ('El Rancho Grande') and 'Siebentausend Rinder' ('Seven Thousand Cattle') and clearly demonstrated his yodelling skills with his own composition 'Mein Pferd Tonky' ('My Horse Tonky'), which he based on the melody of **Elton Britt**'s 'Chime Bells'. These numbers later appeared on a 16-track country album. During the mid-60s, he had 15 Top 10 hits. He toured extensively and appeared on television in Europe and even Japan. He recorded a live album of Swiss folk music at Zurich's famous Kindli venue, which gained a UK release through the World Record Club and clearly demonstrated his outstanding yodel-

ling ability. In 1967, tiring of the hectic life style, he decided to take things easier. Resisting offers to play in Las Vegas and the London Palladium, he became a band leader. In 1990, he was persuaded to record an album of yodelling songs. He re-recorded some of his old hits, including 'Siebentausend Rinder', with more modern backing and the resultant success of the recordings saw him coaxed back into the entertainment business. In 1991, he undertook a 54-concert tour that saw him play to large audiences at venues in Germany, Austria and Switzerland. On 9 February 1992, in Zurich, he gained a place in the *Guinness Book Of Records* as the World's most rapid yodeller, when he yodelled 22 tones (15 falsetto) in one second. (This may sound totally impossible but the event was seemingly officially witnessed by Norris McWhirter.) The success of the tour saw him return to the public appearance circuits and, at the time of writing, he continues to record. The material is mainly country but naturally the yodel is never far away.

● ALBUMS: *Souvenirs Of Switzerland (Live At Kindli)* (Ariola 1964)★★★, *Star Album* (Ariola 1964)★★★, *Jodel Echo* (Ariola 1968)★★★, *Auf Meiner Ranch Bin Ich Konig* (Baccarola 1969)★★★, *Yodel Feeling* (Schnoutz 1974)★★★, *16 Seiner Erfolgreichsten Hits* cassette (SR International mid-70s)★★★, *20 Jahre Peter Hinnen* (Ariola 1984)★★★, *Der Generation Jodler* (Baur 1990)★★★, *Country Music* (Gruezi 1991)★★★, *Volksmusik & Country Music* (Koch 1991)★★★, *Treu Wie Gold* (UHU 1994)★★★.

Hino, Motohiko

b. 3 January 1946, Tokyo, Japan. Hino's father was a musician and dancer and Motohiko was a tap dancer when he was eight before learning the drums when he was 10. He turned professional when he was 17 and from 1972 won, yearly, the *Swing Journal* polls as Japan's top drummer. He moved to New York in 1978. There he worked with **Joe Henderson**, **Chuck Rainey**, **Jean-Luc Ponty** and others before joining **Hugh Masekela**'s band in 1979. Since 1980 he has played in the trio of **JoAnne Brackeen**, his sharp, dynamic drumming reflecting the playing of his two favourites, **Tony Williams** and **Elvin Jones**.

● ALBUMS: *First Album* (1970)★★★, *Toko: The Motohiko Hino Quartet At Nemu Festival* (1975)★★★, *Flash* (1977)★★, *Sailing Stone* (1992)★★★.

Hino, Terumasa

b. 25 October 1942, Tokyo, Japan. Following, more or less literally, in the footsteps of his trumpet-playing, tap-dancing father, Hino learned to tap at the age of four, and took up the trumpet when he was nine years old. He taught himself the principles of jazz improvisation by transcribing solos by **Miles Davis** (from whom, no doubt, he learned his conviction about the importance of space), **Louis Armstrong**, **John Coltrane**, **Clifford Brown**, **Lee Morgan** and **Freddie Hubbard**. He began playing publicly in American army clubs in 1955 in Japan, then joined Hiroshi Watanabe and

Takao Kusagaya, but his first major job was with the Hideo Shiraki Quintet, where he stayed from 1965-69. During 1964-65 he had led his own group, and left Shiraki at the end of the decade in order to lead his own band full-time. In 1974 he worked with **Masabumi Kikuchi**, then in June 1975 he went to the USA and worked with **Joachim Kuhn** (1975), **Gil Evans**, **Jackie McLean** and **Ken McIntyre** (1976), **Hal Galper** (1977), Carlos Garnett (1977), **Sam Jones** (1978), **Elvin Jones** (1982) and **Dave Liebman**, as well as continuing to lead his own group, the band which **John Scofield** credits as moving him from fusion to jazz. By then Hino was dividing his time equally between the USA and Japan. He plays trumpet and flugelhorn with a mellow fire, and his fame in Europe continues to grow almost matching his reputation in Japan and the USA. He toured Europe with **Eddie Harris** in November 1990.

● ALBUMS: *Hi-Nology* (1965)★★, *Vibrations* (Enja 1971)★★★, *Taro's Mood* (Enja 1973)★★★, *Speak To Loneliness* (1975)★★★, *Live In Concert* (1975)★★, *Hoginta* (1976)★★★, *Maiden Dance* (1978)★★★, *Terumasa Hino* (Denon 1986)★★★, *Bluestruck* (Blue Note 1990)★★★★, *From The Heart* (Blue Note 1992)★★★, *Warsaw Jazz Festival 1991* (Jazzmen 1993)★★★.

Hinojosa, Tish

b. San Antonio, Texas, USA. Chicano/Tex Mex singer-songwriter Hinojosa, a professional musician since 1980, earned a reputation in both Spanish and English speaking circles with her first album, *From Taos To Tennessee*. It was followed by *Homeland*, produced by Steve Berlin of **Los Lobos**, an autobiographical collection of songs focusing on her Texas-Mexican roots, switching between country and Latin pop. **Linda Ronstadt**, an artist Hinojosa has frequently been compared to, recorded a version of the track 'Donde Voy (Where I Go)'. Hinojosa then released a live recording of all-Spanish language songs, *Aquella Noche (That Certain Night)*. *Culture Swing*, produced by **Booker T. Jones** and featuring **Flaco Jimenez**, was voted Folk Album Of The Year by the National Association of Independent Record Distributors. *Fronteias*, recorded before *Destiny's Gate*, was a collection of border songs, descriptive of ranch life and the 'Tejano' identity, taught to her by folklorist and researcher Dr. Americo Paredes. Others had been sung to her long ago by her mother. *Destiny's Gate* featured regular accomplices such as Marvin Dykhuis on guitar and Paul Pearcy on drums and also featured Nashville musicians Danny Lvevin (piano/strings), Tony Compisi (saxophone), Sonny Garryish (steel guitar) and **Bela Fleck** (banjo). All of the songs were written by Hinojosa, who commented: 'This record is a much broader painting from my paintbrush. I feel I have stretched myself to the farther reaches of the studio as a producer and my music remains real and natural.'

● ALBUMS: *From Taos To Tennessee* (Independent 1987)★★★, *Homeland* (A&M 1989)★★★, *Aquella Noche* (Watermelon 1991)★★★, *Culture Swing* (Rounder 1992)★★★, *Destiny's Gate* (Warners 1994)★★★, *Frontejas* (Rounder 1995)★★★, *Dreaming From The Labryrinth/Sonar Del Laberinto* (Warners 1996)★★★★.

Hinsons

A family group from Salinas, California, USA, made up of brothers Chris Hinson, Larry Hinson and Kenny Hinson plus sister Yvonne Hinson, the unit made a big impact on gospel music fans in the 70s. They had been professionally active since the late 60s prior to this breakthrough, making their name as guests on the **Florida Boys'** *The Gospel Singing Jubilee* television programme. Their numerous albums for Calvary Records drew increasingly strong gospel chart returns and critical approval as the decade progressed, their song 'The Lighthouse' winning both a *Singing News* magazine and Dove Award as Best Gospel Song. They were also among the 1975 nominees for the Dove Awards' Best Mixed Group category. In the late 70s Yvonne Hinson left the group, her role taken by Chris Hawkins.

● ALBUMS: *The Hinsons Sing About The Lighthouse* (Calvary 1970)★★, *He Pilots My Ship* (Calvary 1971)★★★, *We Promised You Gospel* (Calvary 1972)★★, *Touch Of Hinsons, Depths Of Glory* (Calvary 1973)★★★, *Harvest Of Hits* (Calvary 1974)★★★, *Live And On Stage* (Calvary 1975)★★, *High Voltage* (Calvary 1976)★★★, *The Group That God Built* (Calvary 1977)★★★, *On The Road* (Calvary 1978)★★★, *Prime* (Calvary 1979)★★★.

Hinton, Eddie

b. Edward Craig Hinton, 15 June 1944, Jacksonville, Florida, USA, d. 28 July 1995, Birmingham, Alabama, USA. Guitarist Eddie Hinton's professional reputation was largely built around his session work. Having originally played on the club circuit of the southern states of America, he moved to Muscle Shoals, Alabama, in the mid-60s. Between 1967 and 1971 he was a principal member of the **Muscle Shoals** Sound house band, performing with **Aretha Franklin**, **Wilson Pickett**, **Otis Redding**, **Elvis Presley**, **Percy Sledge**, **Joe Tex** and many more. Although best known for his skilful guitar playing, Hinton was also proficient on several other instruments, including bass, drums and keyboards. His studio expertise saw him work as a producer, and he also wrote songs for others. His compositions included 'Choo Choo Train' (**Box Tops**), 'Breakfast In Bed' (**Dusty Springfield** and **UB40**) and 'It's All Wrong, But It's All Right' (Percy Sledge). He released a debut solo album in 1978, but *Very Extremely Dangerous* failed to sell. Afterwards, Hinton, long considered by associates to be a troubled soul, experienced a period of depression that culminated in his admittance to the Alabama Rescue Mission. He returned to recording in the late 80s with an album for Swedish label Almathea, before signing a new contract with **Rounder Records**. Two albums followed, but in 1995 he was discovered dead in the locked bathroom of his parents' home.

● ALBUMS: *Very Extremely Dangerous* (Capricorn 1978)★★,

Letters From Mississippi (Almathea 1988)★★★, *Cry And Moan* (Rounder 1991)★★★, *Very Blue Highway* (Rounder 1993)★★★.

Hinton, Joe

b. 15 November 1929, Evansville, Indiana, USA, d. 13 August 1968, Boston, USA. Hinton recorded a string of R&B singles for the Texas-based Back Beat label in the late 50s and 60s, the best-known of which, a cover version of **Willie Nelson**'s 'Funny', reached the Top 20 in the USA in August 1964. Hinton first applied his falsetto to gospel music with the Blair Singers and the Spirit Of Memphis Quartet. He moved to Memphis, Tennessee, to work with the latter group, who recorded for the Peacock label. In 1958 Peacock president Don Robey convinced Hinton to switch to secular music and in 1958 signed him to the Back Beat subsidiary. Hinton's first single for the label was 'Ladder of Love', which did not sell well. It was not until the 1963 'You Know It Ain't Right' that Hinton reached the charts, at number 20. After one other minor chart single, 'Better To Give Than Receive', Hinton had his greatest success with the Nelson ballad, which rose to number 13 in 1964. There was one further single in the charts that year, 'I Want A Little Girl', but Hinton's career declined after that. He recorded for Backbeat until 1968, when he died of skin cancer.

● ALBUMS: *Funny (How Time Slips Away)* (Backbeat 1965)★★★, *Duke-Peacock Remembers Joe Hinton* (Duke 1969)★★★, *Joe Hinton* (1973)★★★.

Hinton, Milt

b. 23 June 1910, Vicksburg, Mississippi, USA. During the 20s Hinton played bass with artists such as Boyd Atkins, **Tiny Parham** and **Jabbo Smith**. In the early 30s he established his reputation as one of the most reliable and forward-thinking contemporary bass players during engagements with **Eddie South**, Erskine Tate, **Zutty Singleton** and Fate Marable. In 1936 he began a sustained period with **Cab Calloway**. Not only was he a stalwart of an excellent rhythm section but he was also a featured soloist.

He left Calloway in 1951, thereafter working as a free-lance session and studio musician, appearing on count-less record dates. Many of these recordings were with jazzmen but his skills were such that he was in demand for sessions by pop singers too. Nicknamed 'the Judge', Hinton also toured extensively in the 70s and 80s, including one stint with **Bing Crosby**, appeared at jazz festivals and clubs around the world and still found time to establish himself as a teacher and jazz photographer. An important transitional figure in jazz bass playing, Hinton's career comfortably spanned the change from swing to bop, whilst his versatility ensured that so long as popular songs were being recorded he could work anywhere.

● ALBUMS: *The Milt Hinton Quartet* (1955)★★★, *Milt Hinton With Manny Albam's Orchestra* (1955)★★, *Here Swings The Judge* (1964-75)★★★, *Basically With Blue*

(1976)★★, *The Trio* (1977)★★★, *Back To Bass-ics* (Progressive 1984)★★★, *We Three Live In New York* (1985)★★★, *The Judge's Decision* (Exposure 1995)★★★, *Old Man Time* (1989-90)★★★.

● COMPILATIONS: *Sixteen Cab Calloway Classics* (1939-41)★★★★.

● FURTHER READING: *Bass Line*, Milt Hinton and David G. Berger.

Hinze, Chris

b. 30 June 1938, Hilversum, The Netherlands. Hinze's father was a conductor and he learned the piano and flute as a child. He studied flute at the Royal Conservatory in The Hague and then learned arranging at the **Berklee College Of Music** in the USA. He won a prize for the best soloist at the **Montreux Jazz Festival** in 1970 and formed his jazz fusion group the Combination the following year. He founded his own record label Keytone and has often worked as a producer for other musicians. He moved to New York in 1976 but in the late 70s toured Europe with **Chris Hinze** And Friends and then in a duo with guitarist **Sigi Schwab**. In 1972 he won the Beethoven Award of the City of Bonn for a suite called *Live Music Now*. He continued to write and record symphonic works as well as presenting jazz versions of Baroque composers with his band. He recorded an album of flute solos in the Ellora Caves in India in 1979 and the following year recorded a reggae album with **Peter Tosh**. He has since included African and Indian musicians in the Combination.

● ALBUMS: *Stoned Flute* (1971)★★★, *Virgin Sacrifice* (1972)★★★, *Mange* (1974)★★, *Variations On Bach* (1976)★★★, *Silhouettes* (1977)★★★, *Flute And Mantras* (1979)★★★, with Peter Tosh *World Sound And Power* (1980)★★★★, *Chris Hinze/Sigi Schwab Duo* (1980)★★★, *Mirror Of Dreams* (1982)★★★, *Backstage* (1983)★★, *Saliah* (1985)★★★.

Hip-Hop

Although **rap** is the obvious focal point, the black urban culture of hip-hop manifested itself in terms of graffiti and break dancing as well as music. The term, originally denoted in the **Sugarhill Gang**'s 1979 release 'Rapper's Delight', was born in the Bronx district of New York, USA, in the 70s. At street parties DJs such as **Grandmaster Flash**, **Kool Herc** and **Afrika Bambaataa** spun an eclectic mix of records while encouraging their dancers to aspire to ever greater feats. Flash was responsible for the development of 'scratch-mixing', moving discs backwards and forwards under the stylus, and switching between two turntables. Like his fellow DJs he would improvise dialogue over the resultant sounds in the manner of Jamaican toasting DJs. The dancers developed innovative new steps to keep up with the quick changes, including break-dancing, body-popping and robotics (best depicted in the film *Wildstyle*). At the same time New York subway trains were decorated with spray-cans in elaborate graffiti murals - an explosion of creativity which took as much joy in outraging authorities as it did in its own expression. Hip-hop has continued to be viewed as the 'mother culture' behind the commercial explosion of rap music in the 80s and 90s - with microphone artists keen to announce their credentials in other related fields such as graffiti.

Hipgnosis

This innovative UK design group was founded in 1968 by Storm Thorgerson and Aubrey Powell. Their first credited piece of artwork graced **Pink Floyd**'s third album, *More*. Friendship with this respected act led to further collaborations, including *Ummagumma* and *Atom Heart Mother*, but the duo also provided graphics for many other releases. Their brilliantly surreal photograph of red toy balls in the desert graced the cover of *Elegy* by the **Nice**, while a clever photographic negative effect was used on *Doctor Dunbar's Prescription* by the **Aynsley Dunbar Retaliation**. Other notable works include *Technical Ecstasy* (**Black Sabbath**), *Jump On It* (**Montrose**), *On The Shore* (**Trees**), *House On the Hill* (**Audience**), *How Dare You* (**10cc**) and *The Madcap Laughs* (**Syd Barrett**). Hipgnosis specialized in visual puns best exemplified in their design for the album by **Quatermass** which featured flying pterodactyls superimposed against a skyscraper. Although their work was sometimes undertaken without a particular act in mind, Thorgerson and Powell were adept at tailoring specific images. One such creation was the 'teddy boy' sleeve undertaken for *To Mum From Aynsley And The Boys*, a tongue-in-cheek release, again, by the Aynsley Dunbar Retaliation.

Peter Christopherson joined the team in 1974, but by this point Hipgnosis had lost much of its panache. Their imaginative sleeves were ideal for the expansive progressive era, but their relevance faded with the genre's passing. Their memorable photographic images however are firmly implanted in most rock fans' minds; the famous cows on the cover of the Floyd's *Atom Heart Mother* and their most famous icon is Pink Floyd's multi-million selling *Dark Side Of The Moon*.

Hipp, Jutta

b. 4 February 1925, Leipzig, Germany. Although her musical career was quite brief, Hipp made a big impression in post-war Europe. She studied piano formally as a child, taking an interest in jazz in her mid-teens. At the end of the war she formed her own small band, mostly playing bop. After playing throughout Europe, in the mid-50s she visited the USA where she led a trio that was completed by **Peter Ind** and **Ed Thigpen**. By the late 50s, however, Hipp had decided to concentrate upon being a painter. On the evidence of her few recordings, Hipp's decision to abandon professional music was purely a matter of personal choice and by no means an indication of either technical inability or lack of imaginative talent.

● ALBUMS: *Jutta Hipp At The Hickory House* (Blue Note 1956)★★.

Hipsway

Hipsway emerged in the mid-80s onto a Scottish pop scene that had enjoyed a high profile, both commercially and critically, with acts such as **Orange Juice**, the **Associates**, **Simple Minds** and **Altered Images**. It was ex-Altered Images bassist Jon McElhone who teamed up with guitarist Pim Jones, drummer Harry Travers and vocalist Graham Skinner (previously in the White Savages) around 1984. As Hipsway, the band secured a contract with **Mercury Records** who were impressed enough to promote strongly both 'Broken Years' in June and the catchy 'Ask The Lord' later in 1985, although neither made much impact. However, the momentum led to a chart hit with their third single, 'Honey Thief', early in 1986, and in its wake came both Hipsway's self-titled album and a reissue of 'Ask The Lord' in April. Unfortunately, Graham Skinner's dramatic vocal style was the only distinctive feature aside from the previous promising singles. Drawn from the album came 'Long White Car' in August, but both fell quickly by the wayside after a modest chart run. It was three years before Hipsway returned but unfortunately they failed even to manage what their second album, *Scratch The Surface*, suggested. 'Young Love' disappeared without trace, the album followed suit, and Hipsway broke up soon afterwards. Skinner and Jones moved on to Witness.

● ALBUMS: *Hipsway* (Mercury 1986)★★★, *Scratch The Surface* (Mercury 1989)★★.

Hirax

Hirax first formed in Los Angeles, California, USA, in 1984 - the band's original line-up consisting of Katon W. De Pena (vocals), Scott Owen (guitar), Gary Monardo (bass) and John Tabares (drums). Their promising demos attracted the attention of Metal Blade who included one of the band's tracks on the *Metal Massacre VI* compilation album, released in 1985. A debut album, *Raging Violence*, was released for the same label in 1985. Full of short and ultra-fast thrash metal, it offered nothing very innovative. Shortly after its release, Tabares left the band to be replaced by ex-**DRI** percussionist Eric Brecht. Their next release was a mini-album, *Hate, Fear And Power*, released in 1986. The material on offer was in the same vein as before, but the production this time around had improved greatly. However, owing to internal band wrangles vocalist Katon W. De Pena left to be replaced by ex-**Exodus** vocalist Paul Baloff. He, in turn, did not stay long before being replaced himself by Billy Wedgeworth. Unable to maintain a stable line-up, the band folded after recording several more demos in 1988.

● ALBUMS: *Raging Violence* (Metal Blade 1985)★★, *Hate, Fear And Power* (Metal Blade 1986)★★★.

Hired Man, The

In Howard Goodall's marvellous adaptation of Melvyn Bragg's novel, *The Hired Man* brought to the musical stage a powerful story of mining and farming life around the Lake District in the early years of the century. Opening at the Astoria Theatre in London on 31 October 1984, and tracing one family's domestic tribulations against the disturbing background of World War I, pit disasters and the birth of trades unionism, the plot was strong meat. Appropriately, Goodall took his musical inspiration from a powerful English musical tradition. His absorption of the grandeur of the choral work of Edward Elgar gave the show an impressive undercurrent. Sweeping along plot and characterization, the music counterpointed major national and international events even as it highlighted such decidedly domestic affairs as work in the mines, and such day-to-day country life as experienced at the hiring fairs. Among the cast were Claire Burt, Paul Clarkson, Julia Hills, Gerald Doyle, and Richard Walsh. The songs included 'Song Of The Hired Men', 'Work Song', 'Men Of Stone (Union Song)', 'What A Fool I've Been', and 'When You Next See That Smile'. Despite high critical regard, the show, which was produced by **Andrew Lloyd Webber**, folded after 164 performances and lost money at the box-office. the show was seen Off-Off Broadway in 1988. In March 1992, the 'entire original cast' gave a concert performance of *The Hired Man* at the Palace Theatre in London in aid of the Cancer Relief Macmillan Fund. A live recording was later released on a 2-CD set.

Hirt, Al

b. 7 November 1922, New Orleans, Louisiana, USA. After studying classical music, trumpeter Hirt divided his professional career between symphony orchestras and dance bands and still found time to play dixieland jazz in New Orleans clubs. Among the bands with which he played were those led by **Tommy Dorsey** and **Ray McKinley**, and a sideman in one of his own first bands was **Pete Fountain**. In the 60s an important recording contract (which resulted in albums under his own name and as accompanist to some transiently popular singers) a successful residency at his own club and a spectacular technique all helped to turn him into one of the best-known trumpeters in jazz. In the 60s, Hirt had 17 albums in the US jazz charts. As often happens, commercial success brought a measure of condemnation from jazz hardliners but Hirt was unmoved. He continued to perform in clubs and to record throughout the 70s, shrugging off a lip injury, and was still playing his high-spirited, good-humoured jazz in the 80s.

● ALBUMS: *The Greatest Horn In The World* (1961),★★★ *Al (He's The King) Hirt And his Band* (1961)★★, *Bourbon Street* (1962)★★★, *Horn-A-Plenty* (1962)★★★★, *Trumpet And Strings* (1963)★★★, *Our Man In New Orleans* (Novus 1963)★★★★, *Honey In The Horn* (1963)★★★, *Beauty And The Band* (1964)★★★, *Cotton Candy* (1964)★★, *Sugar Lips* (1964)★★★, *Pops Goes The Trumpet* (1964), *That Honey Horn Sound* (1965)★★, *Live At Carnegie Hall* (1965)★★★, *They're Playing Our Song* (1966)★★★, *The Happy Trumpet* (1966)★★★, *Music To Watch Girls Go By* (1967)★★★, *Al*

Hirt Plays Bert Kaempfert (1968)★★, *Solid Gold Brass* (RCA 1982)★★★, *Al Hirt* (Audio Fidelity 1984)★★★, *Pops Goes The Trumpet* (1985)★★★.

● COMPILATIONS: *The Best Of Al Hirt* (1965)★★★★.

His 'N' Hers - Pulp

Pulp's breakthrough album arrived after an unbelievably long haul, and then Jarvis Cocker was suddenly sharing front pages of music magazines with Liam and Damon. Here, the songs explored now-familiar Pulp territory, social class, seedy sexual encounters, voyeurism ('Babies'), bad sex ('you bought a toy that can reach the places he never goes'), good sex, and lots more sex, all blessed with Cocker's humorous, touching and, conversely, often innocent lyrical observations. Capable of writing almost unbearably tender love songs and laments for wasted lives ('your hair is a mess and your eyes are just holes in your face'), Cocker's honesty and insight were distilled to perfection in the wonderful 'Do You Remember The First Time'.

● Tracks: *Joyriders; Lipgloss; Acrylic Afternoons; Have You Seen Her Lately?; Babies; She's A Lady; Happy Endings; Do You Remember The First Time?; Pink Glove; Someone Like The Moon; David's Last Summer.*

● First released 1994

● UK peak chart position: 9

● USA peak chart position: did not chart

His Name Is Alive

Formed in 1987 in Livonia, Michigan, USA, His Name Is Alive (an obscure reference to Abraham Lincoln) was established by Warren Defever (b. 1969; guitar, bass, vocals, samples) with high-school friends Angela Carozzo (vocals) and Karin Oliver (guitar, vocals). Their first single was the independently released cassette 'Riotousness And Postrophe' (1987), and was followed by the idiosyncratic 'His Name Is Alive' (1987), 'I Had Sex With God' (1988) and 'Eutectic' (1988 - a commissioned piece for the Harbinger Dance Company in Detroit). The group slotted in perfectly in the set-up at **4AD Records**, a label that provided a natural home for their brand of elegant, dreamlike songs. After the release of *Livonia*, titled after their home-town, the group expanded to a sextet, despite the departure of Carozzo, to comprise Defever, Oliver, Denise James (vocals), Melissa Elliott (guitar), Jymn Auge (guitar) and Damian Lang (drums). Often compared to the **Cocteau Twins** and **This Mortal Coil** (and other lazy references to bands on the 4AD roster), Defever's eclecticism took a perverse turn when a cover version of **Ritchie Blackmore**'s 'Man On The Silver Mountain', was included on the 1992 EP *Dirt Eaters*. He has since released an astonishing amount of music (on his own Time Stereo cassette label) through his involvement in outside projects, including Princess Dragonmom, ESP-Summer (with ex-**Pale Saints** vocalist Ian Masters), ESP-Beetles, ESP-Family and Mystic Moog Orchestra.

● ALBUMS: *Livonia* (4AD 1990)★★★, *Home Is In Your Head*

(4AD 1991)★★★, *Mouth By Mouth* (4AD 1993)★★★, *King Of Sweet* (Perdition Plastics 1994)★★, *Sound Of Mexico* cassette only (Time Stereo 1995)★★, *Stars On E.S.P.* (4AD 1996)★★★★.

Hiseman, Jon

b. 21 June 1944, Woolwich, London, England. Hiseman studied violin and piano from an early age, but only applied himself to drums when he was 13 years old. The skiffle craze resulted in Hiseman playing all kinds of blues, jazz and hokum in the early 60s. In 1964 he was a founder member of the New Jazz Orchestra. Between 1966 and 1967 he drummed for the **Graham Bond** Organisation and then left to join **Georgie Fame** in the Blue Flames. After six months with **John Mayall** he formed his own **Colosseum** in 1968, a celebrated jazz/rock band which included saxophonist **Dick Heckstall-Smith** and **Dave Greenslade** on electric piano. Colosseum attracted a lot of attention and was one of the leading jazz/rock combos of all time. Hiseman's drums were much in demand, and he recorded frequently with pianist Mike Taylor, **Jack Bruce** and **John Surman**. In 1970 Colosseum released *Daughter Of Time* with **Chris Farlowe** on vocals, and ambitious lyrics from Hiseman that were typical of the period. Farlowe then left to form **Atomic Rooster**. After a year of studio work Hiseman formed Tempest, which was not a success. In 1975 he helped to organize the United Jazz & Rock Ensemble, and also formed Colosseum II with **Gary Moore** of **Thin Lizzy**. In 1979 he joined his wife, saxophonist **Barbara Thompson**, in Paraphernalia, which has made sporadic tours and albums ever since. The impact of punk aligned the couple with the musical establishment; they recorded for **Andrew Lloyd Webber** on *Variations* and on 1982's hit musical, *Cats*. Hiseman now runs a record company, TM Records, a PA hire company and manages Thompson, plays in her band as well as maintaining a busy schedule of production and session work.

● ALBUMS: with Colosseum *Those Who Are About To Die Salute You* (Fontana 1969)★★★★, *Valentyne Suite* (Vertigo 1969)★★★★, *The Daughter Of Time* (Vertigo 1970)★★, *Live* (Bronze 1971)★★★, *Strange New Flesh* (1976)★★, *Electric Savage* (1977)★★, *Wardance* (1977)★★.
● COMPILATIONS: *The Grass Is Greener* (Vertigo 1969)★★★, *Collector's Colosseum* (1971)★★★, *Pop Chronik* (1974)★★★, *Epitaph* (1986), *The Golden Decade Of Colosseum* (1990)★★★, with Paraphernalia *Live In Concert* (1980)★★★.

Hissanol

Hissanol is the solo project inaugurated by former **No Means No** singer/guitarist Tim Kerr (b. Canada). His debut album was recorded in tandem with old friend Scott Henderson through the postal exchange of tapes between two continents. Sadly, the disjointed nature of the experiment shone through on *4th And Black*. Songs such as 'Angra' and 'Exterminal' lacked none of the imagination shown on previous No Means No records,

but much of their considerable musical artistry was missing.
● ALBUMS: *4th And Black* (Alternative Tentacles 1995)★★★, *The Making Of Him* (Alternative Tentacles 1998)★★.

HIStory Past Present And Future Book I - Michael Jackson

Jackson had a lot to do to regain his credibility at this point. He was canny in offering an irresistible greatest hits collection on disc one, so as to remind us how great he was. On disc two he gave us some new songs, many with lyrics that were more biting than usual. Jackson was angry in 'They Don't Really Care About Us' and 'Money', while in 'Earth Song' he attempts, and succeeds with the epic song of anti-pollution, anti-war. Quietly hidden on this disc is 'Stranger In Moscow', one of his best ever compositions. For all his quirks and failings, Jackson is still a major force.

● Tracks: *Billie Jean; The Way You Make Me Feel; Black Or White; Rock With You; She's Out Of My Life; Bad; I Just Can't Stop Loving You; Man In The Mirror; Thriller; Beat It; The Girl Is Mine; Remember The Time; Don't Stop Til You Get Enough; Wanna Be Startin' Somethin'; Heal The World; Scream; They Don't Care About Us; Stranger In Moscow; This Time Around; Earth Song; D.S.; Money; Come Together; You Are Not Alone; Childhood (Theme From Free Willy); Tabloid Junkie; Bad; History; Little Susie; Smile.*
● First released 1995
● UK peak chart position: 1
● USA peak chart position: 1

Hit The Deck (film musical)

Considering the wealth of talent on board, this 1955 screen adaptation of the 1927 Broadway musical proved to be a pretty disappointing affair, mainly owing to a lack-lustre screenplay by Sonya Levien and William Ludwig. It told the by now familiar story of three off-duty sailors, (**Tony Martin**, **Russ Tamblyn** and **Vic Damone**) and their search for three lovely gals (**Ann Miller**, **Debbie Reynolds** and **Jane Powell**) with whom to embark on the voyage of life. Fortunately, there were plenty of musical highlights in composer **Vincent Youmans**' score, such as the lovely 'More Than You Know' (Tony Martin) (lyric: **Billy Rose**-Edward Eliscu), 'Sometimes I'm Happy' (Vic Damone-Jane Powell) (lyric: Clifford Grey-**Irving Caesar**), 'Hallelujah' (Martin-Tamblyn-Damone) (lyric: Grey-Leo Robin), 'I Know that You Know' (Damone-Powell) (lyric: Anne Caldwell) and 'Keepin' Myself For You' (Martin-Ann Miller) (lyric: Sidney Clare). The other songs included 'Join The Navy', 'Why, Oh Why', and 'Lucky Bird' (all with lyrics by Robin and Grey), and 'Lady From The Bayou' and 'A Kiss Or Two' (lyrics: Robin), and 'Ciribiribin' (Albert Pestalozza). **Hermes Pan** staged the dance sequences with his usual imagination and flair (especially in the sequences which involved Ann Miller) and Roy Rowland directed a cast which also included Walter Pidgeon, Kay Armen, Gene Raymond, J Carrol Naish, and Allan King. *Hit The Deck* was photographed in Eastman Color and Cinemascope, and produced for MGM by Joe Pasternak. Hubert Osborne's play *Shore Leave*, which was the basis for this film and the original Broadway musical, had been filmed before in 1930 with Jack Oakie, Polly Walker and Roger Gray.

Hit The Deck (stage musical)

Herbert Fields's book for this 'Nautical Musical Comedy' was based on the 1922 play, *Shore Leave*, by Hubert Osborne. With music by **Vincent Youmans**, and lyrics by Clifford Grey and **Leo Robin**, it began the 'stage phase' of its existence on 25 April 1927 at the Belasco theatre in New York, and stayed around for 352 performances. Field's story turned out to be yet another reworking of that familiar musical comedy saga of a boy (or girl) discovering that his (or her) beloved is blessed with a big bundle of cash. The marriage is always immediately called off - true happiness, they always agree, is based on love, and not lucre. Of course, they also invariably have second thoughts. Looloo Martin (Louise Groody) owns a coffee shop in Newport, Rhode Island, USA, and a lot of her customers are sailors. She is completely besotted by one of them, Bilge Smith (Charles King), and, in an effort to tie the marriage knot, is perfectly prepared to follow him to the ends of the earth - in Bilge's case that means China. Even out there, the sailor is reluctant to restrict himself to just one girl (Looloo) in one port (Rhode Island), particularly when he finds out that Looloo is wealthy. Matters are resolved when the lady agrees to assuage his pride and assign all the money to their first offspring. Youmans' songs with Grey and Robin included 'Join The Navy', 'Loo-Loo', 'Harbour Of My Heart', 'Why, Oh Why?', 'Lucky Bird', and 'Hallelujah!' which became something of a hit through recordings by **Nat Shilkret**, the Revelers, and Cass Hagen. Another of Youmans's numbers for the show, 'Sometimes I'm Happy' (with a lyric by **Irving Caesar**), also became popular at the time via **Roger Wolfe Kahn**, and a recording by two members of the original cast, Louise Groody and Charles King. The song, which was not at all like the smart, sophisticated material that **Cole Porter**, for instance, was writing at the time, had a charming, artless lyric: 'Sometimes I'm happy, sometimes I'm blue/My disposition, depends on you/I'll never mind the rain from the sky/If I can see the sun in your eye'. It endured, and was included, along with 'Hallelujah', in the 1930 and 1955 screen versions of the show, but omitted from the 1936 film, *Follow The Fleet* (which was also based on the original concept), in favour of an **Irving Berlin** score. The 1927 London stage production, which starred **Stanley Holloway** and Ivy Tresmand, used more or less the same songs, and ran for 277 performances.

Hitchcock, Nicola

UK singer/songwriter Hitchcock began her career in 1993 with an album which inspired a *Folk Roots* journalist to recommend it as 'a remarkable debut album of old-fashioned qualities with modern attitude.' Though a self-evidently basic recording conducted in archetypal bedsit songwriter mode, it included several compositions of worth, including the taut lover's exorcism, 'Pick Up Your Coat' and the assertive, confessional narrative, 'What You See Is What You Get'. Despite the rudimentary guitar playing and limited range of her voice, the disarming honesty and wit of the lyrics made the album enjoyable.

● ALBUMS: *A Bowl Of Chalk* (Demon 1993)★★★.

Hitchcock, Robyn

The possessor of a lyrical vision of a latter-day **Syd Barrett**, UK-born Hitchcock made his early reputation with the post-punk psychedelic group the **Soft Boys**, having previously appeared in various groups including the Beetles and Maureen And The Meat Packers. After the Soft Boys split in 1981 he spent some time writing for **Captain Sensible**, then formed his own group, the Egyptians, around erstwhile colleagues Andy Metcalfe (bass), Morris Windsor (drums) and Roger Jackson (keyboards). Hitchcock's live performances were punctuated by epic, surreal monologues of comic invention capable of baffling the uninitiated and delighting the converted. His sharp mind and predilection for the bizarre has revealed itself in many titles, such as 'Man With The Light Bulb Head' ('. . . I turn myself on in the dark'), 'My Wife And My Dead Wife', a tragi-comedy of a man coming to accept the intrusion into his life of a deceased spouse, 'Trash', a well-aimed diatribe against hopeless rock star hangers-on, 'Trams Of Old London', a love and remembrance saga of an era long gone, and a guide to bringing up children in the **a cappella** 'Uncorrected Personality Traits'. A move to **A&M Records** saw the release of *Globe Of Frogs*, which included the 'Ballroom Man', a favourite on US college radio which went some way to breaking new ground and earning Hitchcock a fresh audience. As a result, and despite his devoted cult following in the UK, the artist has in the early 90s concentrated more on recording and performing in the United States (occasionally guesting with **R.E.M.**). He has also re-formed the Soft Boys and seen his back-catalogue repackaged with loving commitment by **Sequel Records**. It remains to be seen whether the oddball workings of this endearing eccentric's mind will find a way into anything other than the US collegiate consciousness. **Warner Brothers Records** were prepared to take the risk in 1996 when a revitalized Hitchcock released *Moss Elixir*.

● ALBUMS: *Black Snake Diamond Role* includes material recorded with the Soft Boys (Armageddon 1981)★★★, *Groovy Decay* (Albion 1982)★★, *I Often Dream Of Trains* (Midnight Music 1984)★★★, *Groovy Decoy* original demos of *Groovy Decay* (Glass Fish)★★★, with the Egyptians *Fegmania!* (Slash 1985)★★★★, with the Egyptians *Gotta Let This Hen Out!* (Relativity 1985)★★★★, with the Egyptians *Exploding In Silence* mini-album (Relativity 1986)★★★, *Invisible Hitchcock* (Glass Fish 1986)★★★, with the Egyptians *Element Of Light*

(Glass Fish 1986)★★★★, with the Egyptians *Globe Of Frogs* (A&M 1988)★★★, with the Egyptians *Queen Elvis* (A&M 1989)★★, *Eye* (Twin/Tone 1990)★★★, *Perspex Island* (A&M 1991)★★★, with the Egyptians *Respect* (A&M 1993)★★★, *Gravy Deco* (Rhino 1995)★★★, *You And Oblivion* (Rhino 1995)★★★, *Mossy Liquor (Outtakes And Prototypes)* vinyl-only release (Warners 1996)★★★, *Moss Elixir* (Warners 1996)★★★.

● COMPILATIONS: *The Kershaw Sessions* (ROOT 1994)★★★, *Uncorrected Personality Traits* (Sequel 1998)★★★.

Hite, Les

b. 13 February 1903, DuQuoin, Illinois, USA, d. 6 February 1962. One of the most important figures in the southern Californian jazz scene of the 20s and early 30s, alto saxophonist Hite worked in numerous bands, often taking on responsibilities above that of sideman. In 1930 he took over leadership of Paul Howard's Quality Serenaders, which included in its ranks **Lawrence Brown** and **Lionel Hampton**. Securing a residency at Frank Sebastian's Cotton Club in Los Angeles, Hite backed many top line jazz artists, notably **Fats Waller** and **Louis Armstrong**, with whom he made some excellent recordings, and also appeared in films. Hite continued leading bands into the 40s, hiring musicians such as **Dizzy Gillespie**, but left the jazz scene in 1945. Thereafter, he ran a booking agency in California. Hite always demonstrated an ability to attract first-class musicians. Apart from those named above he also had George Orendorff, Joe 'King' Porter and **Marshal Royal** in his bands. Much less well-known outside jazz circles was another Hite sideman, trumpeter Lloyd Reese, who taught **Dexter Gordon, Buddy Collette, Charles Mingus** and **Eric Dolphy** among many others. Hite died in February 1962.

● COMPILATIONS: with Louis Armstrong *Louis In Los Angeles* (1930-31 recordings)★★★★.

Hithouse

Label and studio, a subsidiary of ARS, founded by Dutch DJ and producer Peter Slaghuis, whose surname literally translated as Hithouse (hit as in 'strike' rather than in the pop chart sense). He used the same name to score a hit in 1988 with 'Jack To The Sound Of The Underground', one of a rash of such records utilising the 'jack' word following the breakthrough success of **Steve 'Silk' Hurley**. Hithouse would host a slew of Dutch and Belgian techno acts, including Global Insert Project, Problem House, Holy Noise and Meng Syndicate ('Artificial Fantasy'). Slaghuis died in a car crash on 5 September 1991.

Hittman

Comprising Dirk Kennedy (vocals), John Kristen (guitar), Jim Bachie (guitar), Mike Buccell (bass) and Chuck Kory (drums), Hittman formed in New York City, New York, USA, in the mid-80s. Though there was nothing wholly innovative about their debut album

for SPV Records, critics throughout the USA and Europe acclaimed it as an exceptional collection of songs in the power metal mould of **Savatage** or **Accept**. However, thereafter a series of inter-group squabbles overtook the band, fatally delaying the release of a follow-up collection.

● ALBUMS: *Hittman* (SPV 1988)★★★.

HMV Records

The beginnings of the name HMV came in 1899 when managing director William Owen bought Francis Barraud's famous painting of 'Nipper', a bull terrier cross, looking quizzically down the horn of a gramophone. The picture was registered as a trademark and later the title - His Master's Voice (HMV) - was used as a label name. When Emile Berliner sold the rights to the disc gramophone in 1898 to a group of English speculators, they formed the Gramophone Company operating out of Hanover. It quickly became the biggest record company in the world, specializing in opera artists like Enrico Caruso and Dame Nellie Melba, as well as the speeches of Winston Churchill. In 1931 the Gramophone Co. (HMV) merged with **Columbia** and several smaller companies to form **EMI**, but each company retained separate label identities. HMV became the first label to issue 45 rpm 7-inch singles in the UK. Their biggest scoop of the rock era came when they acquired the rights to release **Elvis Presley**'s early recordings in the UK but ended when **RCA** started their own UK outlet. Other best selling acts of the rock 'n' roll era included **Sam Cooke** (again only until RCA started their own label), and **Lloyd Price**. Two of HMV's biggest hits were **Manfred Mann**'s 'Do Wah Diddy Diddy' (1964) and **Louis Armstrong**'s 'What A Wonderful World' (1968). Soon afterwards it became established as a classical rather than rock label, and to the average rock fan the HMV name became more associated with the retail outlets than the label. However, **Morrissey** obviously felt more strongly about it as he insisted the label was resurrected for him when he embarked on his post-**Smiths** solo career. As for Nipper - he died in 1895 and although there are several theories as to his place of burial, no-one is certain. EMI once launched a competition to locate his body and although some bones were unearthed, it is not known for sure whether or not they belong to Nipper.

Ho'op'i'i Brothers

Both born in Kahakuloa on the Hawaiian island of Maui, Richard and Solomon Ho'op'i'i grew up in a family of 28, before starting singing in the local church and at school gatherings. While Solomon formed a professional singing group in Hana, Richard began his career playing alongside slack-guitar legend Sonny Chillingworth. The brothers reunited in the 60s to form the Ho'onanea Serenaders. They eventually became the Ho'op'i'i Brothers in 1975. From then on they have exported traditional Hawaiian songs and songcraft throughout the world, from Japan to America, where they appeared in the movie *Hawaiian Rainbow* - a film which took its title from one of the brothers' songs. There has also been a video documentary, *Ku'u Home*, while in 1989 they performed before a massed audience of two million at the Smithsonian Institute Festival of American Folklife in Washington, D.C. In October 1995 they toured Europe for the first time, playing alongside slack key guitarist and songwriter Ledward Kaapana. Though each brother retains a day-job (Richard as a golf course keeper, Solomon for the county public works), they have gradually achieved a semi-mythical status to roots music followers beyond their native shores. The brothers remain one of the few authentic examples of Hawaiian 'falsetto music', or 'Leo Ki'eki'e', which has recently benefitted from the establishment of the Hawaiian Music Foundation's falsetto singing concert.

Hoax

Comprising Hugh Coltman (vocals/harmonica), Jon Amor and Jess Davey (guitars), Robin Davey (bass guitar), and Dave Raeburn (drums), and already earmarked as the 'Great White Hope', the Hoax create original blues-based music with the brash arrogance of the innately talented. With the exception of drummer Raeburn, the band's members all grew up in Great Cheverell, Wiltshire, England. The Davey brothers investigated their parents' extensive blues album collection and teamed up with schoolfriends Coltman and Amor with the intention of forming a band. Enlisting the services of Raeburn, they rehearsed for three weeks and set off for their first gig, using the name suggested by a newspaper report on the recent appearances of crop circles in their area. Over the next two years, they built up a strong fanbase in Britain and Europe before determining to turn professional. They were spotted by Code Blue boss **Mike Vernon** while opening for the Texas bar band led by **Smokin' Joe Kubek**. *Sound Like This* was well received when issued in October 1994 and the band increased its work schedule, opening for the likes of **Robert Cray** and **Walter Trout**. Their first American tour began in July 1995, including six gigs with **Buddy Guy** and others with **Joe Ely** and **Chris Duarte**. Although their twin-guitar work is sometimes reminiscent of **Wishbone Ash**, their determination to avoid the clichés of their chosen musical genre makes the Hoax an intriguing prospect. Their second album gained them many new fans in the rock world, and lost them a number of blues purists. *Unpossible* was hard to fault as a heavy blues rock album but they are currently treading a fine line of two musical styles. The band left their blues label Code Blue in late 1997 and at the same time parted company with their drummer Dave Raeburn.
● ALBUMS: *Sound Like This* (Code Blue 1994)★★★★, *Unpossible* (Code Blue 1997)★★★, *Humdinger* (Credible 1998)★★★.

Hobbs, Becky

b. Rebecca A. Hobbs, 24 January 1950, Bartlesville, Oklahoma, USA. Hobbs' father loved big band music and her mother country, two strong influences on her later work. She was given a piano when she was nine years old, and began playing the piano parts on rock 'n' roll records, notably those of **Jerry Lee Lewis**. At the age of 15, she formed an all-girl group, the Four Faces Of Eve, and from 1971, she worked with a bar band, Swamp Fox, in Baton Rouge. The band went to Los Angeles in 1973, but soon broke up. Hobbs recorded what is now a highly obscure album for MCA (**Helen Reddy** recorded one of the songs, 'I'll Be Your Audience'), and then recorded for Tattoo, finally achieving some entries on the US country charts with 'Honky Tonk Saturday Night' and 'I Can't Say Goodbye To You'. Her duet with **Moe Bandy**, 'Let's Get Over Them Together', was a US country hit and then came a top-selling single, 'Hottest Ex In Texas'. Her compositions include 'I Want To Know Who You Are Before We Make Love' (**Alabama, Conway Twitty**), 'Still On A Roll' (Moe Bandy and **Joe Stampley, Kelvin Henderson**), 'I'll Dance A Two Step' (**Shelley West**) and 'Feedin' The Fire' (Zella Lehr). Her effervescent style is well to the fore on her honky tonk album *All Keyed Up*, which was co-produced by Richard Bennett, **Steve Earle**'s guitarist. She has also recorded what is arguably the best of all tributes to **George Jones**, 'Jones On The Jukebox'. There was a six-year gap between *All Keyed Up* and *The Boots I Came To Town With*, during which the impetus had left her career. The latter album, still a good one, included her version of 'Angels Among Us', an original song that Alabama had first recorded. During a hiatus between albums, she recorded briefly with Curb Records, which included an interesting version of the 1963 **Ernest Ashworth** hit (also a hit for **Johnny Tillotson** later that year), 'Talk Back Trembling Lips'.
● ALBUMS: *Becky Hobbs* (MCA 1974)★★★, *From The Heartland* (Tattoo 1975)★★★, *Everyday* (Tattoo 1977)★★★, *Becky Hobbs* (Liberty 1984)★★★, *All Keyed Up* (RCA 1988)★★★, *The Boots I Came To Town With* (Intersound 1994)★★★.

Hockridge, Edmund

b. 9 August 1923, Vancouver, British Columbia, Canada. One of the UK's most popular leading men in the imported US musicals of the 50s, with rugged looks, a sure manner, and a big, strong, baritone voice. Hockridge first visited the UK in 1941 with the Royal Canadian Air Force, and helped set up the Allied Expeditionary Forces Network which supplied entertainment and news for troops in Europe. He also sang on many of the broadcasts, several of them with fellow Canadian **Robert Farnon** who was leader of the Canadian Allied Expeditionary Force Band. After the war, he featured in his own coast-to-coast show for the CBC, playing leading roles in operas such as *La Bohème*, *Don Giovanni* and Gilbert And Sullivan operettas. After seeing some Broadway musical shows, such as **Brigadoon** and **Carousel**, on a visit to New York, he decided that there was more of a future for him in that direction. That was certainly the case, for on his return to the UK in 1951, he replaced Stephen Douglass as Billy Bigelow in *Carousel* at the Drury Lane Theatre, London, and, when the run ended, took over from Jerry Wayne as Sky Masterson in **Guys And Dolls** at the Coliseum. He stayed at that theatre for two more shows, playing Judge Aristide Forestier in **Can-Can** and Sid Sorokin in **The Pajama Game**. A song from *The Pajama Game*, 'Hey There', gave him one of his biggest record hits. His other 50s singles included 'Young And Foolish', 'No Other Love', 'The Fountains Of Rome', 'Sixteen Tons', 'The Man From Laramie', 'A Woman In Love', 'More Than Ever' and 'Tonight'. Extremely popular in theatres and on television, he played a six-month season at the London Palladium, appeared in six Royal Command Performances, and was Canada's representative in the Westminster Abbey Choir at the Queen's Coronation in 1953. He headlined the cabaret on the liner QE2's maiden voyage, and toured Europe extensively, both in revivals of musicals, and his own one-man show, which contained over 30 songs.

In the early 80s he toured the UK with successful revivals of **The Sound Of Music** and **South Pacific**, before returning to Canada in 1984 for a concert tour with Robert Farnon and the Vancouver Symphony Orchestra. In 1986, 35 years after he strode onto the Drury Lane stage as young, arrogant Billy Bigelow, he played the part of senior citizen, Buffalo Bill, in a major London revival of **Annie Get Your Gun**, with pop star, **Suzi Quatro**, in the role of Annie. In the early 90s, Hockridge toured regularly with *The Edmund Hockridge Family*, being joined onstage by his wife, Jackie, and their two sons, Murray and Stephen.

● ALBUMS: *Edmund Hockridge Sings* (Pye 1957)★★★, *In Romantic Mood* (Pye 1957)★★★, *Hooray For Love* (Pye 1958)★★★, *Hockridge Meets Hammond* (1975)★★★, *Make It Easy On Yourself* (1984)★★★, *Sings Hits From Various Musicals* (1985)★★★★, with Jackie Hockridge *Sings Favourites Of Yours* (1991)★★★.

Hodeir, André

b. 22 January 1921, Paris, France. Hodeir studied musical formally for many years but also developed a fascination for jazz. In the late 40s he frequently wrote jazz criticism, becoming chief editor of the French magazine *Jazz Hot*. He also wrote an important book, first published in the USA in 1956 under the title *Jazz: Its Evolution And Essence*. He played violin and recorded with various jazz groups, including musicians such as **Django Reinhardt** and **Kenny Clarke**. However, Hodeir was more interested in composing and writing about jazz and his playing days were thus numbered. From the mid-50s until the end of the 60s he co-led a band, Jazz Groupe De Paris, with **Bobby Jaspar**, a vehicle for his own compositions. In the 60s he took an interest in third stream music, composing in this

hybrid medium. He was also in demand as a composer of music for the soundtracks of motion pictures. By the 80s Hodeir had abandoned composing, channelling most of his energies into writing. From recordings of his work, Hodeir's composing and arranging talents are evident, although there is much about his composing, especially in third-stream mode, that makes his work less than readily accessible to the general listener. His criticism is also interesting and perceptive although often pugnaciously argumentative and sometimes slightly wrong-headed. Nevertheless, he is always thought-provoking and some of his in-depth analyses are incisive and informed.

● ALBUMS: *Autour D'un Récif, St-Tropez* (Swing 1952)★★★, *Essais* (Swing 1954)★★★, *Le Jazz Groupe De Paris Joue André Hodeir* (Vega 1956)★★★★, as arranger *The Kenny Clarke Sextet Plays André Hodeir* (Philips 1956)★★, *Jazz Et Jazz* (Fontana 1963)★★★, *Anna Livia Plurabelle* (Epic 1966)★★★, *Bitter Ending* (Epic 1972)★★★.

Hodes, Art

b. 14 November 1904, Nikoliev, Ukraine, d. 4 March 1993, Harvey, Illinois, USA. A few months after Hodes was born, his family emigrated from Russia and settled in Chicago, Illinois. He began playing piano and by his late teenage years was working in dance halls and clubs. He played with several local bands, including **Wingy Manone**'s, but also established himself as a solo performer. For the next 10 years he was active in Chicago, but in 1938 moved to New York, where he played with jazzmen including **Joe Marsala**, **Sidney Bechet** and **Mezz Mezzrow**, continuing into the early 40s. During this time he had his first experience as a radio broadcaster, presenting record shows. He also began to write, and for some years was editor of *Jazz Record* magazine. He led his own bands for engagements at many clubs and restaurants in and around New York, but at the end of the 40s decided to move back to Chicago. For the next four decades he led bands, played solo piano, taught, broadcast on radio and television, all in and around Chicago. In the 60s he recorded with Truck Parham and **Estelle 'Mama' Yancey**. Hodes made occasional tours, including trips to Denmark, Europe and Canada, where he worked with **Jim Galloway**, one of their concerts being recorded and released as *Live From Toronto*. In the early 80s he appeared again in New York, but he remained true to his adopted hometown. Stylistically, Hodes was strongly rooted in the blues. His knowledge of blues piano and stride, allied to his teaching, writing and demonstration, helped keep the forms alive. In 1977 some of his earlier and perceptive writings for *Jazz Record* were published in book form.

● ALBUMS: *Mama Yancey Sings, Art Hodes Plays Blues* (1965)★★★★, *Someone To Watch Over Me* (1981)★★★, *Art Hodes: South Side Memories* (1984)★★★, *Blues In The Night* (1987)★★, *Joy to The World - Yuletide Piano Solos* (1987)★★, with Wally Fawkes *Midnight Blue* (1987)★★★, *Live From Toronto* (1988)★★★, *The Music Of Lovie Austin* (1988)★★★,

Pagin' Mr Jelly (Candid 1988)★★★, with Volly DeFaut *Up In Volly's Room* 50s recordings (Delmark 1993)★★, *Sessions At Blue Note* (Dormouse 1991)★★★★, *Hode's Art* 1968-1972 recordings (Delmark 1995)★★★, *Keepin' Out Of Mischief Now* (Candid/Koch 1995)★★★.

● FURTHER READING: *Selections From The Gutter: Jazz Portraits From 'The Jazz Record'*, Art Hodes and Chadwick Hansen (ed.).

Hodges, Eddie

b. 5 March 1947, Hattiesburg, Mississippi, USA. In the mid-50s child star Hodges appeared in television programmes The **Jackie Gleason** *Show* and *Name That Tune* and was seen on Broadway 405 times in the hit musical *The Music Man*. In 1959 he starred alongside **Frank Sinatra** and Edward G. Robinson in the film *A Hole In The Head* and can be heard on Sinatra's hit from the film, 'High Hopes'. He also had a major role in the film of *Huckleberry Finn*, starred with Hayley Mills in *Summer Magic* and even had his own television show, *The Secret World of Eddie Hodges*. His youthful revival of the **Isley Brothers**' 'I'm Gonna Knock On Your Door' on Cadence, not only took him into the US Top 20 in 1961 but also gave the 14-year-old an Australian and Canadian chart-topper and a small UK hit. He returned to the US Top 20 with an endearing song written by **Phil Everly**, '(Girls, Girls, Girls) Made To Love' in 1962. He had releases on **Columbia** in 1963 and **MGM** in 1964 before 'New Orleans' on Aurora in 1965 gave him his last US chart entry. It seems that, for Hodges, maturity brought a halt to his recording career.

Hodges, Johnny

b. 25 July 1907, Cambridge, Massachusetts, USA, d. 11 May 1970. One of the greatest alto saxophonists in jazz, Hodges first tried other instruments before settling upon the one that would best serve his glorious romanticism. Largely self-taught, Hodges played in a number of minor bands in Boston and New York in the early 20s but also spent a little time with **Willie 'The Lion' Smith**, in whose band he replaced **Sidney Bechet** - who had given him some of the little instruction he ever received. In 1926 he joined **Chick Webb**, where his brother-in-law, Don Kirkpatrick, was pianist-arranger. Two years later Hodges began an association with **Duke Ellington** that would continue virtually uninterrupted for the rest of his life. Apart from playing on hundreds of records with Ellington, soloing magnificently on many, Hodges also originated several tunes that Ellington developed, among them 'Jeep's Blues' and 'The Jeep Is Jumpin'' ('Jeep' was one of Hodges' nicknames; others were 'Rabbit' and 'Squatty Roo'). From 1951-55 Hodges led his own band, which briefly included **John Coltrane** in its ranks, and had a hit record with 'Castle Rock'. In 1958 and again in 1961 he worked outside the Ellington orchestra but always in an Ellingtonian style. Although capable of playing lowdown blues, Hodges was in his true element as a balladeer. The lush beauty of his playing was perfectly exhibited on compositions created for his special talents by Ellington and by **Billy Strayhorn**. Among the many tunes on which he played, and frequently recorded, were 'I Let A Song Go Out Of My Heart', 'Warm Valley', 'Black Butterfly', 'Isfahan' (from the 'Far East Suite') and 'Empty Ballroom Blues'. Hodges recorded several albums for **Norman Granz**, including a 1952 jam session that teamed him with fellow altoists **Benny Carter** and **Charlie Parker** and organist **Wild Bill Davis**. Despite the excellence of all his other forays, however, it is for his work with Ellington that he will be remembered. The liquid beauty of Hodges' contribution to the sound of the Ellington band, and especially to the manner in which it played ballads, was so crucial that his death in May 1970 marked the end of an era: as Ellington himself observed, 'our band will never sound the same'. Throughout his long career Hodges was indisputably among the finest alto players in jazz. Even though, after the early 40s, Charlie Parker took the alto saxophone in other directions, Hodges remains one of the giants of the instrument.

● ALBUMS: *Johnny Hodges, Volume 1* 10-inch album (Mercer 1951)★★★, *Johnny Hodges, Volume 2* 10-inch album (Mercer 1951)★★★, with Benny Carter, Charlie Parker *Norman Granz Jam Session* (1952)★★★★, *Alto Sax* 10-inch album (RCA Victor 1952)★★★, *Johnny Hodges Collates* 10-inch album (Mercury 1952)★★★, *Swing With Johnny Hodges* 10-inch album (Norgran 1954)★★★, *Memories Of Ellington* reissued as *In A Mellow Tone* (Norgran 1954)★★★, *More Of Johnny Hodges* (Norgran 1954)★★★, *Johnny Hodges Dance Bash* reissued as *Perdido* (Norgran 1955)★★★, *Creamy* (Norgran 1955)★★★, *Castle Rock* (Norgran 1955)★★★, *Hodge Podge* (Epic 1955)★★★, *Ellingtonia '56* (Norgran 1956)★★★★, with Duke Ellington *Ellington At Newport '56* (Columbia 1956)★★★★★, *In A Tender Mood* (Norgran 1956)★★★★, *Used To Be Duke* (Norgran 1956)★★★, *The Blues* (Norgran 1956)★★★, *Duke's In Bed* (Verve 1957)★★★, *The Big Sound* (Verve 1958)★★★, *The Prettiest Gershwin* (Verve 1959)★★★, with Ellington *Back To Back: Duke Ellington And Johnny Hodges Play The Blues* (Verve 1959)★★★★, with Ellington *Side By Side* (Verve 1959)★★★, *The Smooth One* (Verve 1960)★★★, *Not So Dukish* (Verve 1960)★★★, with Ellington *The Nutcracker Suite* (Columbia 1960)★★★, *Master Of Jazz* (1960)★★★, *Blues-A-Plenty* (Verve 1960)★★★★, *The Johnny Hodges All Stars/The Johnny Hodges-Harry Carney Sextet* (1961)★★★, *Johnny Hodges At The Sportspalast, Berlin* (1961)★★★, *Johnny Hodges In Scandinavia* (1961)★★★, with Wild Bill Davis *Johnny Hodges And Wild Bill Davis* (Verve 1961)★★★, with Billy Strayhorn *Johnny Hodges With Billy Strayhorn And His Orchestra* (Verve 1962)★★★★, *Johnny Hodges With Claus Ogermann's Orchestra* (1963)★★★, with Davis *Mess Of Blues* (Verve 1964)★★★★, with Davis *Blue Rabbit* (Verve 1964)★★★, *Everybody Knows Johnny Hodges* (Impulse 1964)★★★, with Davis *Blue Pyramid* (Verve 1965)★★★★, with Davis *Wings And Things* (Verve 1965)★★★, with Lawrence Welk *Johnny Hodges With Lawrence Welk's Orchestra* (Dot 1965)★★★, *Johnny Hodges And All The Dukesmen* (Verve 1966)★★★, *Alto Blue* (Verve 1966)★★★, with Earl Hines *Stride Right* (Verve 1966)★★★,

In A Mellotone (Bluebird 1966)★★★, *Things Ain't What They Used To Be* (RCA Victor 1966)★★★, with Ellington *Far East Suite* (RCA Victor 1967)★★★★, *Triple Play* (RCA Victor 1967)★★★, *Don't Sleep In The Subway* (Verve 1967)★★★, with Hines *Swing's Our Thing* (Verve 1967)★★★★, *Rippin' And Runnin'* (Verve 1968)★★★, *3 Shades Of Blue* (1970)★★★.

● COMPILATIONS: *The Indispensable Duke Ellington Volumes 1-12* (RCA 1983-87)★★★, with Ellington *The Blanton-Webster Band* (RCA Bluebird 1987)★★★★★, *Love In Swingtime (1938-39)* (Tax 1988)★★★, *The Complete Johnny Hodges Sessions 1951-1955* 6-LP box set (1989)★★★★★, *Rarities And Private Recordings* (Suisa 1992)★★★.

Hodgkinson, Colin

b. 14 October 1945, Peterborough, England. Hodgkinson is a self-taught bass player who turned professional with a jazz trio in 1966. In 1969 he began a long association with **Alexis Korner**, during which time they played in everything from a duo to a big band. In 1972 Hodgkinson and Ron Aspery (reeds) took time off in Yorkshire to write music. The two were joined by drummer Tony Hicks in the trio **Back Door** in which Hodgkinson had an opportunity to display his amazing technical facility. The band toured Europe and the USA and played at the **Montreux Jazz Festival**. In 1978 he began another long association, this time with **Jan Hammer**. Though he had written a lot for Back Door, with Hammer he writes lyrics more than tunes. In the late 80s he also played with **Brian Auger**'s Blues Reunion and in the mid-90s was constantly working, touring at times with various versions of the **Spencer Davis Group**. Hodgkinson is one of the few people who can make the solo bass sound quite unlike any other instrument. His solo version of 'San Francisco Bay Blues' is breathtakingly original.

● ALBUMS: with Alexis Korner *New Church* (1970)★★★, with Jan Hammer *Black Sheep* (1979)★★★, *Hammer* (1980)★★★, *Here To Stay* (1982)★★★, *City Slicker* (1986)★★★.

Hoez With Attitude

Whilst taking gangsta rap's misogynist attitudes to task may be a positive move, adopting the latter's agenda to do so seems less well-advised. All in all Hoez With Attitude (HWA) ('Baby Girl' Kim Kenner, Goldie and Jazz) are a tragic concept stretched ever thinner over scuttling Miami-bass rhythms. Emigrating from Chicago to Los Angeles in the late 80s, within a year they had unveiled an album that would sell nearly 400,000 copies. A group destined to earn their notoriety off skimpy stage wear rather than anything constructive they might have to offer, musically or lyrically.

● ALBUMS: *Livin' In A Hoe House* (Ruthless 1990)★★★, *As Much Ass Azz U Want* mini-album (Ruthless 1994)★★.

Hoffman, Al

b. 25 September 1902, Minsk, Russia, d. 21 July 1960, New York, USA. An important composer, with a varied output of songs from the romantic ballads of the 30s to the novelty songs of the 40s and 50s, Hoffman was taken to the USA in 1908 and grew up in Seattle, where he later led his own band. After moving to New York in 1928, he played the drums in night-clubs, and started composing around 1930. In the early 30s Hoffman wrote the music for such songs as 'I Don't Mind Walking In The Rain', 'Heartaches' (with John Klenner), 'I Apologize' (with Ed Nelson and Al Goodhart), 'Who Walks In (When I Walk Out?)' and 'Fit As A Fiddle' (both with **Arthur Freed** and Goodhart), 'Little Man You've Had A Busy Day' (with Maurice Sigler and **Mabel Wayne**) and 'Meet Me In The Gloaming'.

In the late 30s, together with Goodhart and Sigler, Hoffman contributed songs to several British stage shows and films. These included the **Jack Buchanan** and Elsie Randolph hit musical at London's Palace Theatre, *This'll Make You Whistle* ('Crazy With Love' and 'I'm In A Dancing Mood'); and the films *She Shall Have Music* (title song and 'My First Thrill'); *First A Girl* ('Everything's In Rhythm With My Heart'); *Jack Of All Trades* ('Where There's You, There's Me'); *Come Out Of The Kitchen* ('Everything Stops for Tea') and *Gangway* ('Lord And Lady Woozis'). In 1938, Hoffman, Al Lewis and Murray Mencher also wrote 'On The Bumpy Road To Love' for the **Judy Garland** movie *Listen Darling*, and 'I Ups To Her, And She Ups To Me', which suited the dancebands of **Guy Lombardo** and **Lew Stone**. During the 40s and 50s Hoffman's output consisted of a mixture of ballads such as 'The Story Of A Starry Night' (adapted with Mann Curtis and **Jerry Livingston** from 'Symphony No. 6' by Tchaikovsky, and a big hit for the **Glenn Miller** Orchestra), 'Goodnight, Wherever You Are' (another Miller favourite), 'Allegheny Moon' and 'The Hawaiian Wedding Song', along with a string of novelty songs, including 'Mairzy Doats', 'Chi-Baba, Chi-Baba', 'If I Knew You Were Comin', I'd Have Baked A Cake', 'Takes Two To Tango', 'Papa Loves Mambo' and 'Hot Diggety'. In 1949, Hoffman, **Mack David** and Jerry Livingston collaborated on 'Bibbidi-Bobbidi-Boo', 'A Dream Is A Wish Your Heart Makes', 'The Work Song' and 'So This Is Love' for the **Walt Disney** cartoon feature *Cinderella*. Hoffman's many other songs included 'Oh, What A Thrill', 'Black-Eyed Susan Brown', 'There's Always A Happy Ending', 'What's The Good Word, Mr Bluebird?', 'There's No Tomorrow', 'I'm Gonna Live Till I Die' (with Mann Curtis and Walter Kent), 'One Finger Melody', 'I Saw Stars', 'When You Kiss Me', 'Mama, Teach Me To Dance', 'Secretly', 'Oh, Oh, I'm Falling In Love Again' and 'Le Plume De Ma Tante'. Among his other collaborators were Milton Drake, Leo Corday, Sammy Lerner, Ed Nelson, **Bob Merrill**, and **Dick Manning** who was also involved in the novelty 'Gilly-Gilly Ossenfeffer Katzen Ellen Bogen By The Sea', which was a big hit for UK entertainer **Max Bygraves** in 1954. Hoffman was still active as a writer until just before he died in 1960.

Hoffs, Susanna

b. 17 January 1962, Newport Beach, California, USA. The **Bangles** folded in 1989 partly because Susanna Hoffs was being touted as the 'star' in a previously egalitarian band. It is ironic, therefore, that her solo career proper has yet to come close to the success enjoyed by her old band. Her first offering, *When You're A Boy* (including an ill-advised cover version of **David Bowie**'s 'Boys Keep Swinging') failed to maintain the interest of the mainstream fans who had discovered the Bangles in the wake of the smash single 'Eternal Flame', while simultaneously alienating the Paisley Underground loyalists with its AOR clichés. She faded from view and had a baby in 1995, but returned to the studio the following year, this time with assistance from various members of **Sparklehorse**, **Cracker**, **Jellyfish** and **4 Non Blondes** as well as legendary drummers Jim Keltner and Mick Fleetwood and a fellow alumna of a troubled girl group, the **Go-Go's**' Charlotte Caffey. Her lyrics had grown more wry over the years ('and these boots are made for walking/I'm walking back to you') but only one track, 'King Of Tragedy', had the edgy pop fizz of the Bangles' best work. Still, at least her profile is higher than her former bandmates with an appearance in the film *Austin Powers* in 1997.

● ALBUMS: *When You're A Boy* (Columbia 1991) ★★, *Susanna Hoffs* (London 1996) ★★★.

Hofner, Adolph

b. 8 June 1916, Moulton, Lavaca County, Texas, USA. His father was part-German and his mother Czechoslovakian, and Hofner grew up initially speaking Czech and with a love of polka music. He and his brother Emil (b. 1918) both learned to play stringed instruments and by the early 30s, with Emil playing steel and Adolph standard guitar and aspiring to be a vocalist, the two played in a trio around the clubs of San Antonio, where the family had relocated in 1928. Adolph joined Jimmy Revard's Oklahoma Playboys in 1935 and made his first recordings with them. By 1939, Adolph was a popular vocalist with his own band, the San Antonians, although during the war his name caused some problems until he became Dolph Hofner. He recorded a mixture of country, Texan and Czech music and later claimed to be the first artist to record 'Cotton Eyed Joe'. When, in the late 40s, polka music again became popular in Texas, Hofner was quick to add it to his band's repertoire, and even recorded several polkas, including 'Julida Polka'. He was sponsored by Pearl Beer and with his band renamed the Pearl Wranglers, playing a mixture of country, Tex-Mex, western swing and German-style polka music, he commenced a regular programme that was carried by several radio stations, and also toured extensively. In 1994, still active, Adolph Hofner was honoured at a special show in his favourite San Antonio dancehall to commemorate his fifty-fifth anniversary in country music.

● ALBUMS: *Dance-O-Rama* 10-inch album (Decca 1955) ★★, *South Texas Swing (His Early Recordings 1935-1955)* (Arhoolie 1964) ★★★★.

Hogan, John

b. 31 August, Kilbeggan, County Westmeath, Eire. After completing his education, Hogan worked as a supervisor in a peat briquette factory in Croghan, County Offaly. Inspired by **Jim Reeves** and **Hank Williams**, he dreamed of a singing career. Early in 1988, using the money scheduled as the next instalment on his mortgage to finance the project in a local studio, he recorded a demo tape of an old song that his mother had sung as a child, called 'Brown Eyes'. Air play on local radio provoked considerable interest and led to him quitting his job to concentrate on a singing career. He formed a band and with the help of appearances on some major television shows and a great deal of hard work, he gradually built his reputation and gained successes in the Irish charts. He also began to write songs such as 'My Feelings For You' and 'Turn Back The Years' and made his first recordings for **K-Tel Records**. His appearances extended to the UK, where he became very popular around the country club circuit. In 1990, he joined the Ritz label and early in 1993, he achieved an ambition when the label decided that he should record an album in Nashville. He has also released an in-concert video, *My Kind Of Country*, which helped increase his popularity, not only in his native Ireland, where he lives in County Offaly (near to the factory where he used to work), but also in the UK. He continues to write some of his own material, such as the semi-autobiographical 'My Guitar' and 'Stepping Stone', while Foster And Allen recorded his song 'My Christmas'.

● ALBUMS: *My Feelings For You* (K-Tel 1988) ★★, *Turn Back The Years* (K-Tel 1989) ★★★, *Humble Man* (Ritz 1991) ★★★, *The Nashville Album* (Ritz 1993) ★★★★, *Loving You* (Ritz 1996) ★★★.

● VIDEOS: *My Kind Of Country* (1994).

Hogan, Silas

b. 15 September 1911, Westover, Louisiana, USA, d. 9 January 1994. Hogan learned guitar from his uncles, but also from records by artists such as **Kokomo Arnold** and **Blind Lemon Jefferson**. He moved to Baton Rouge during his late 20s and over the years established himself on the city's blues scene. His band first recorded in 1959, with a record issued under the name of drummer **Jimmy Dotson**. From 1962-65 Hogan made a series of fine blues singles with producer Jay Miller, issued on Excello Records. These included upbeat R&B as well as gloomy down-home blues, but their quality is consistently high - the band always tight, and Hogan singing with power and conviction. The influence of **Jimmy Reed** and **Lightnin' Slim** is occasionally evident, but Hogan always retains his own distinctive sound. During the blues revival of the late 60s and early 70s, a few recordings were made by Hogan in Baton Rouge and released on **Arhoolie** and **Blue Horizon**. Later, in the 80s, he became one of the resident artists at **Tabby Thomas**'s Blues Box, and recorded an album issued by Blues South West in the UK.

● ALBUMS: *Free Hearted Man* (1961-65)★★★, *Trouble At Home* (1962-65)★★★, *The Godfather* (1989)★★★, *So Long Blues* (Ace 1994)★★★.

● COMPILATIONS: *Trouble: The Best Of The Excello Masters* (Excello/AVI 1997)★★★.

Hogg, John

b. 1912, Westconnie, Texas, USA. John Hogg was the impetus behind **Smokey Hogg**'s (his cousin) decision to pursue a music career in Los Angeles in 1947. John had been there since 1942, after several years of roaming which took him as far from his Texas home of Greenville as Denver, Colorado and Oklahoma - where he worked as a rodeo performer. He was never a committed bluesman but did have the advantage of being taught some guitar by the Los Angeles-based **Pee Wee Crayton**. Hogg played occasional gigs, retaining his day job. He recorded for **Mercury** and Octive in 1951, probably on the strength of his relationship with Smokey, and proved himself a performer of some ability. His practice of treating music as a sideline continued, although he did record again for Advent Records in 1974, appearing that year at the San Diego Blues Festival.

● COMPILATIONS: *Texas Blues* (1965)★★★.

Hogg, Smokey

b. Andrew Hogg, 27 January 1914, Westconnie, Texas, USA, d. 1 May 1960, McKinney, Texas. USA. Born in north-east Texas, Smokey came from a clan that included blues singers **Lightnin' Hopkins** and **John Hogg**. He learned to play the guitar and piano early in life under the instruction of his father, Frank. One of seven children, he looked upon music as a means of escape from labour in the fields. He sang around Dallas and Greenville and was popular enough to be known as Little **Peetie Wheatstraw** after his idol. He played in clubs with men such as B.K. Turner (**Black Aces**) and **D.C. Bender**. In 1937 he recorded two tracks for **Decca Records**, which, although much valued by collectors, made no impression on the blues-buying public of the time. During World War II he was drafted and served in the US Army, but by 1947 he was in Los Angeles, where he recorded for the Exclusive label, again without much success. His breakthrough came after he had moved back to Texas where he recorded 'Too Many Drivers', released under the Modern label in 1947. Back in Los Angeles, but still for Modern, he recorded his biggest hit, 'Little School Girl'. Now established, he began, like many of his contemporaries, to hop from label to label, recording for **Specialty**, **Imperial**, SIW, **Mercury** and many smaller concerns. He enjoyed a good deal of popularity, especially with older fans, and this allowed him to survive the initial impact of rock 'n' roll. Hogg's work seems to be something of an acquired taste and collectors are divided quite violently when

judging its worth. He had no such problems with his black audience when his rural blues were sung to a small (often saxophone-led) band accompaniment and were appearing on labels from Texas to the coast.

● ALBUMS: including *Smokey Hogg* (1962)★★★, *I'm So Lonely* (1964)★★★, *Original Folk Blues* (1967)★★★, *Sings The Blues* (1971)★★★, with Earl Hooker, Lightnin' Hopkins *Hooker, Hopkins And Hogg* (Specialty 1973)★★★, *U Better Watch That Jive* (1974)★★, *Going Back Home* (Krazy Kat 1984)★★, *Everybody Needs Help* (1986)★★.

● COMPILATIONS: *Angels In Harlem* rec. 1949-58 (Ace 1992)★★★.

Hogg, Willie 'Smokey'

b. 19 November 1908, Centerville, Texas, USA. Poor recording, and the record company's half-hearted attempt to pass him off as the real (and long dead) **Smokey Hogg**, obscured the genuine abilities of this New York-based blues singer, who played good electric guitar in duet with Benny Jefferson, and sang traditionally based blues in a high voice. Stylistically, he was in the south-western mainstream, his music more reminiscent of **Lowell Fulson** than of the man he claimed to be, although, as might be expected, there are echoes of the real Smokey Hogg.

● COMPILATIONS: *The All Star Blues World Of Spivey Records* (1970)★★★.

Hoggard, Jay

b. 24 September 1954, New York, USA. After learning to play the piano and saxophone as a child Hoggard studied vibraphone with Lynn Oliver. He went to Wesleyan University to study philosophy but transferred to ethnomusicology. In 1973 he toured Europe in a band with **Jimmy Garrison** (bass) and **Clifford Thornton** (trumpet) who were members of the faculty. He joined a group at Yale which included **Anthony Davis** (piano) and **Leo Smith** (trumpet). During a summer study in Tanzania he learned to play the balo, a West African xylophone. He returned to the USA to teach at the Educational Centre for Arts in New Haven. He moved to New York in 1977 and worked regularly with **Chico Freeman**, Anthony Davis, **Sam Rivers**, **Cecil Taylor** and **James Newton** (flute). As well as his vibraphone playing, which some find a little too mellow, he is able to bring his knowledge of and interest in ethnic music to any group with which he plays.

● ALBUMS: with Chico Freeman *Kings Of Mali* (1977)★★★★, *The Search* (1983)★★★; solo *A Solo Vibes Concert* (1978)★★★★, *Days Like These* (1979)★★★, *Rain Forest* (1980)★★★, *Mystic Winds, Tropic Breezes* (1981)★★, *Love Survives* (1983)★★★, *The Little Tiger* (1991)★★★, with James Newton *Luella* (1983)★★★, *In The Spirit* (1993)★★.

Hokey Pokey - Richard and Linda Thompson

A brave follow-up to their masterful *I Want To See The Bright Lights Tonight*, this attempts to encapsulate various British working-class musical styles - folk, brass band, playground songs and pub singalongs - much as the Band did for indigenous American genres. The Thompsons do not always succeed; *Hokey Pokey* sometimes feels like a theoretical exercise. Nevertheless, the tension between the songs' jaunty surfaces and the neurotic undercurrent of Richard's blistering guitar is beguiling. The one undeniably great song (other than the jaunty title track) is 'A Heart Needs A Home', sung by Linda with grave beauty and authority.

● Tracks: *Hokey Pokey; I'll Regret It In The Morning; Smiffy's Glass Eye; The Egypt Room; Never Again; Georgie On A Spree; Old Man Inside A Young Man; The Sun Never Shines On The Poor; A Heart Needs A Home; Mole In A Hole.*

● First released 1975

● UK peak chart position: did not chart

● USA peak chart position: did not chart

Hokum Boys

'Hokum', with its connotations of verbal cleverness, was first applied to black music on record in the billing of 'Tampa Red's Hokum Jug Band' (performing 'It's Tight Like That', hokum's archetypal song). Tampa and his partner **Georgia Tom** were prominent in the hokum craze of the late 20s and early 30s. The Hokum Boys were varied in personnel, and appeared on various labels; besides Tampa and Tom, participants included **Big Bill Broonzy**, **Ikey Robinson**, **Jimmy Blythe**, **Blind Blake**, **Teddy Edwards**, **Casey Bill Weldon**, **Black Bob**, **Washboard Sam** and 'hokum girl' Jane Lucas. Also celebrating the spirit of hokum were Frankie Jaxon (vocalist with the Hokum Jug Band) and Kansas City Kitty. Hokum groups favoured danceable rhythms and skilful musicianship, but the 'hokum' part of the billing seems chiefly to refer to the verbal content, heavily reliant on *double entendres* that are often ingenious and sometimes witty, and which probably seemed less tedious in the pre-album era. It has been plausibly suggested that the appeal of the Hokum Boys, apart from their obvious entertainment value, was to a black audience newly migrated from the south, and keen to confirm its newly urbanized sophistication.

● ALBUMS: *You Can't Get Enough Of That Stuff* (1976)★★★, *The Remaining Titles* (1988)★★★, *The Famous Hokum Boys* (Matchbox 1989)★★★.

● COMPILATIONS: *Complete Recordings 1935-1937* (Document 1987)★★★.

Holcombe, Wendy

b. Wendy Lou Holcombe, 19 April 1963, Dogwood, near Alabaster, Alabama, USA, d. 14 February 1987. She grew up loving the country music that she heard on radio broadcasts from the *Grand Ole Opry* and taught herself to play her father's banjo at 11. When taken to Nashville to visit the *Opry* as a treat, the show was sold out and they had no tickets. Her father took her into a music shop to look at a banjo and her rendition of 'Foggy Mountain Breakdown' led to her being taken back stage at the *Opry* and invited to play with **Grandpa Jones**. **Roy Acuff** heard them and, amazed at

her ability, arranged for her to play on the *Midnight Jamboree*. She made her *Opry* debut at the age of 12. She began to appear regularly on a Birmingham television show and played local venues with her father and brother backing her on guitar and bass. At 13, she regularly made appearances in Nashville and soon after she began making tours with noted artists, including **Jim Ed Brown** and **Jerry Clower**. She began to sing and also proved herself to be a multi-instrumentalist by also using guitar, mandolin and fiddle on concert appearances. She toured all over the USA and even played London's Wembley Festival. In 1980, she began regular spots on *Nashville Swing*, made acting roles in various television programmes and recorded *Wendy Holcombe, U.S. Army* for NBC-TV in 1981. In 1981, she collapsed on stage at Fort Wayne, Indiana and tests found that she was suffering from an enlarged heart. She was instructed to cease performing and take things very easy. She did but on 14 February 1987, the short life of this talented performer came to an end.

Hold Everything!

College football having proved to be a winning formula for **De Sylva, Brown And Henderson** in their *Good News!* (1927), two years later they placed their collective fingers firmly on the pulse of the New York theatre-going public, and deduced - quite rightly - that the noble art of boxing would be good for a few rounds as the subject matter for another amusing musical comedy. The result, *Hold Everything!*, opened at the Broadhurst Theatre on 10 October 1929, with a book by De Sylva and John McGowan in which 'Sonny Jim' Brooks (Jack Wilding), a welterweight contender, is temporarily estranged from his girlfriend, Sue Burke (Ona Munson), when she discovers that he is being coached in various aspects of his technique by the young and extremely sociable Norine Lloyd (Betty Compton). Sue may be down, but she is not out, and when she is bad-mouthed by his opponent, the reigning champ, 'Sonny Jim' bounces off the ropes, clinches the title, and signs her to a long-term contract. Much of the show's humour was provided by Victor Moore and Bert Lahr, who made a big impact in the role of Gink Schiner, a punch-drunk fighter who rather carelessly floors himself instead of his opponent. As usual, De Sylva, Brown And Henderson's lively, carefree songs fitted the action like a glove. They included 'To Know You Is To Love You', 'Don't Hold Everything', 'Too Good To Be True', and one of the songwriters' all-time big ones, the zippy 'You're The Cream In My Coffee', which became popular for a great many artists and bands, particularly **Ben Selvin**, **Ted Weems**, and **Ruth Etting**. It all added up to a lot of fun, and America would soon be in need of a lot more of that particular commodity - the Wall Street Crash and the Depression were just around the corner. With the Roaring 20s rapidly running out of steam, *Hold Everything!* held on for 413 performances in New York, and added another 173 to that total in London. The 1930 film version, which starred Joe E. Brown, was considered to one of the best of the earlie talkie comedies.

Hold My Hand

Another in the series of comedy musicals starring the popular British funny-man **Stanley Lupino**. This one, which was released by the Associated British Picture Corporation in 1938, cast Lupino as Eddie Marston, a soft-hearted gentleman who secretly finances a newspaper which is run by his dependant, Paula (Polly Ward), who thinks he is after the profits. Further farcical complications ensue when Eddie's fiancée, Helen (Sally Gray), falls in love with Pop Currie (Jack Melford) the paper's editor; his friend Bob Crane (John Wood) is attracted by Polly; and his secretary, Jane (Barbara Blair) find it difficult to keep her hands off him! While all this is going on, Eddie gets involved in a bizarre cat burglary with Lord Milchester (Fred Emney), and the others joining in the fun and games included Bertha Belmore (as Lady Milchester), Syd Walker, Arthur Rigby, and Gibb McLaughlin. Polly Ward and John Wood handled most of the songs which included 'Turn On The Love-light', 'As Long As I Can Look At You', and 'Hold My Hand'. Clifford Grey, Bert Lee, William Freshman, adapted the screenplay from Stanley Lupino's original story. American Thornton Freeland, a leading exponent of this zany kind of musical entertainment in the US and UK, directed with flair.

Hold On!

The first of two films starring **Herman's Hermits**, this 1966 feature was funded and shot in the US where the group enjoyed considerable popularity. The plot was risible - an employee of NASA follows the quintet on tour to decide whether or not they merit having a space-ship named after them. The soundtrack was equally anodyne, featuring a version of the **George Formby** standard 'Leaning On A Lampost'. Herman's Hermits' interpretation reached number 9 in the US, but the single was not issued in the UK. *Hold On!* co-starred singer **Shelley Fabares**, who at that point was married to **Lou Adler**, owner of Dunhill Records. One of the label's major talents, **P.F. Sloan**, co-composed several songs featured on film, including 'Where Were You When I Needed You?' and 'A Must To Avoid'. The latter was a Top 10 hit in the US and UK.

Hold On, I'm Comin' - Sam And Dave

Sam Moore and Dave Prater began singing together in 1958 and commenced recording two years later. Their gospel-tinged work for the Roulette label made little commercial impact but, having switched to Atlantic in 1965, they proceeded to cut some of soul music's finest singles. *Hold On I'm Comin'* captures their searing vocal interplay. Songwriters Isaac Hayes and David Porter contribute material playing to the duo's strengths, resulting in a collection that encapsulates one of the genre's most exciting acts.

● Tracks: *Hold On, I'm Comin'; If You Got The Loving; I Take What I Want; Ease Me; I Got Everything I Need; Don't Make It So Hard On Me; It's A Wonder; Don't Help Me Out; Just Me; You Got It Made; You Don't Know Like I Know; Blame Me (Don't Blame My Heart)*.

● First released 1967

● UK peak chart position: 35

● USA peak chart position: 45

Holden, Ron

b. 7 August 1939, Seattle, Washington, USA, d. 22 January 1997. Holden's career had a unique beginning: he had been arrested for driving with alcohol and marijuana in his possession and was in the police station when a police officer heard him singing. The officer, Larry Nelson, told Holden that he was planning on quitting the police department for a career in music and gave Holden his phone number. The teenager called Nelson upon his release from jail and Nelson recorded Holden singing his own composition 'Love You So'. The ballad was issued on Nelson's Nite Owl label and then sold to the larger Donna label, reaching the US Top 10 in the summer of 1960. An album was released on Donna but further singles on that and other labels did not recapture the flavour of the hit and Holden retired from the music business.

● ALBUMS: *Love You So* (Donna 1960)★★★.

Holder, Terrence

b. c.1898. Holder's early background is extremely sketchy, but by the early 20s he was well-established as lead trumpet and principal soloist with **Alphonso Trent**'s important **territory band**. In the middle of the decade he formed his own band, the Dark Clouds Of Joy, which was based in Dallas, Texas. In 1929, while undergoing financial and domestic strain, Holder resigned and the band was taken over by one of his leading sidemen, **Andy Kirk**. Although Kirk retained most of the original name, calling the band the **Clouds Of Joy**, Holder was undeterred and formed a new band with the same name as before. He continued to play into the mid-30s, employing a number of outstanding musicians who used his and other territory bands as training grounds before gaining major success elsewhere. Among the artists who played with Holder at various times were **Don Byas**, **Budd Johnson**, **Herschel Evans**, **Earl Bostic**, Carl 'Tatti' Smith and **Buddy Tate**. After folding his band in the late 30s Holder drifted in and out of music, never making the breakthrough into national fame. Reputedly a fine player, Holder was still working intermittently into the 60s. It must be assumed that he is now dead, although like his music, his demise has gone unrecorded.

Holdsworth, Allan

b. 6 August 1946, Leeds, England. The professional regard for this Leeds guitarist is illustrated by the range of people with whom he has appeared, starting with **Ian Carr**'s **Nucleus** in 1972. The end of Holdsworth's time with Nucleus coincided with a spell in **Jon Hiseman**'s

Tempest (in which he also played the violin). In its turn this overlapped with membership of **Soft Machine**. 1977 brought a brief period with **Gong**, prior to forming the band UK with **Bill Bruford**, **John Wetton**, and Eddie Jobson. When Bruford left to form his own outfit, Holdsworth went with him. Typically Holdsworth soon left them, rejoining Soft Machine prior to going solo in the late 70s. After a fallow period Holdsworth seems to be more active and his work in the late 80s and 90s has shown has shown his former frantic sparkle.

● ALBUMS: *Road Games* (1983)★★★, *Metal Fatigue* (JMS 1985)★★★, *IOU* (1985)★★, *Atavachron* (JMS 1986)★★★★, *Sand* (JMS 1987)★★★, *With A Heart In My Song* (JMS 1989)★★★, *Secrets* (Cream 1989)★★★, *Wardenclyffe Tower* (Cream 1993)★★★, *Hard Hat Era* (Cream 1993)★★★, *None Too Soon* (Ah/Restless 1996)★★★.

Hole

US hardcore guitar band fronted by the effervescent Courtney Love (b. 9 July 1965, San Francisco, California, USA; vocals, guitar). An ex-stripper and actress, who had minor roles in Alex Cox's *Sid And Nancy* and *Straight To Hell*, she was born to hippie parents (**Grateful Dead** associate Hank Harrison and Oregon therapist Linda Carroll) and even attended **Woodstock** as a small child. She spent the rest of her childhood years at boarding schools in England and New Zealand, where her parents had bought a sheep farm, before travelling around the world in her teens. She spent some time in San Francisco, joining an ill-fated Sugar Baby Doll (with **L7**'s Jenifer Finch and Kat Bjelland), and also participated in a formative line-up of Bjelland's **Babes In Toyland**. In Los Angeles, Love appeared for a while as vocalist with **Faith No More** in an incarnation that only reached the rehearsal stage. Still in LA, she formed Hole with Caroline Rue (drums), Jill Emery (bass) and Eric Erlandson (b. 9 January 1963, Los Angeles, California, USA; guitar), following encouragement from **Sonic Youth**'s Kim Gordon. The band quickly produced a trio of fine singles; 'Retard Girl', 'Dicknail', and 'Teenage Whore', which were pointed and unsettling dirges, set in a grimly sexual lyrical environment. Favourable UK press coverage, in particular from the *Melody Maker*'s resident sycophant Everett True, helped make Hole one of the most promising new groups of 1991. Equally impressive was a debut album, produced by Don Fleming (**Gumball**, **B.A.L.L.**, etc.) and Kim Gordon (**Sonic Youth**), followed by massive exposure supporting **Mudhoney** throughout Europe. It was on this jaunt that Love achieved further notoriety by being the first woman musician to 'trash' her guitar on stage in the UK. In March 1992 Love married **Nirvana** singer/guitarist Kurt Cobain. That same month bassist Emery departed from the group line-up, with Rue following shortly afterwards. Love's domestic travails continued to dominate coverage of her musical project, with Cobain's death on the eve of the release of *Live*

Through This practically obliterating that album's impact. This served to do the much-maligned Love a genuine disservice, as the album contained another startling collection of songs, written with intellect as well as invective. It included 'I Think That I Would Die', co-written with old friend and sparring partner Kat Bjelland, as well as a cover version of the **Young Marble Giants**' 'Credit In The Straight World'. Replacements for Emery and Rue had been found in Kristen Pfaff (bass) and Patty Schemel (b. 24 April 1967, Seattle, Washington, USA; drums), though tragedy again followed Love when Pfaff was found dead from a heroin overdose in her bathtub shortly after the album's release, and just two months after Cobain's death. She was replaced by Melissa Auf Der Maur (b. 17 March 1972, Montreal, Canada) for Hole's 1994 tour, which extended into the following year with stays in Australasia and Europe. These dates again saw Love dominate headlines with violent and/or inflammatory stage behaviour. In 1997 she moved back into acting with a starring role in *The People Vs Larry Flynt*. *My Body The Hand Grenade* was a compilation of rare and unreleased material from the group's early days, compiled by Erlandson.

● ALBUMS: *Pretty On The Inside* (City Slang 1991)★★★, *Live Through This* (Geffen 1994)★★★★.

● COMPILATIONS: *My Body The Hand Grenade* (City Slang 1997)★★★.

● FURTHER READING: *Courtney Love*, Nick Wise. *Queen Of Noise: A Most Unauthorised Biography*, Melissa Rossi. *Look Through This*, Susan Wilson. *Courtney Love: The Real Story*, Poppy Z. Brite.

● FILMS: *The People Vs Larry Flynt* (1997), *Kurt And Courtney* (1998).

Hole, Dave

b. 30 March 1948, Heswall, Cheshire, England. Dave Hole's family moved to Perth, Western Australia, when Dave was four years old. The music of the **Rolling Stones** inspired him to pick up the guitar, and through them he discovered **Muddy Waters** and **Howlin' Wolf**. He had been playing for some 10 years before he took up slide guitar. A broken little finger caused him to play over the fretboard with the slide on his index finger, an unconventional method also adopted by Stan Webb. With various musicians, Hole led bands for some 20 years, playing the 'booze barns' around the Western Territory. A self-produced cassette that he sold at gigs found its way to Europe and America, where a *Guitar Player* article resulted in a contract with Alligator. The same album, *Short Fuse Blues*, prompted **Gary Moore** to add Hole to his 1992 European tour. Like many of his American counterparts, Hole is happy to play rousing, bar-band blues rock that is best heard live, but which remains entertaining on the albums that have followed.

● ALBUMS: *Short Fuse Blues* (Provogue 1992)★★★, *The Plumber* (Provogue 1993)★★★, *Working Overtime* (Provogue 1993)★★, *Steel On Steel* (Provogue 1995)★★★.

● COMPILATIONS: *Whole Lotta Blues* (Provogue 1996)★★★.

Holiday Inn

The cinema's favourite (male) singer and dancer of the 30s and 40s, **Bing Crosby** and **Fred Astaire**, co-starred for the first time in this Paramount release of 1942. **Irving Berlin** contributed a wonderful score, and he is also credited with the original idea for what turned out be a novel story, which was adapted for the screen by the distinguished playwright, Elmer Rice. Claude Binyon's screenplay concerned a couple of song and dance men, Jim Hardy (Crosby) and Ted Hanover (Astaire), who were doing all right before Jim gets tired of the nightly grind and takes up farming. That proves a little too taxing too, so he turns a large New England farmhouse into a night club that will only be open on holidays. The Holiday Inn has it's gala opening on New Year's Eve, and proves to be a tremendous success. Berlin celebrated that holiday by writing 'Let's Start The New Year Right', and each of the other seven important annual American vacations, such as Lincoln's Birthday and Valentine's Day, was allocated it's own song, with the Fourth of July getting two. Two of the numbers, 'Lazy' and 'Easter Parade', had been used before in other productions, but the rest of the score was new, and included 'I'll Capture Your Heart Singing', 'You're Easy To Dance With', 'Happy Holiday', 'Holiday Inn', 'Abraham', 'Be Careful, It's My Heart', 'I Can't Tell A Lie', 'Let's Say It With Firecrackers' (an explosive Astaire solo dance), 'Song Of Freedom', 'Plenty To Be Thankful For', and 'White Christmas'. The latter song won an Academy Award, was inducted into the NARAS Hall of Fame, and went on to become an enduring Christmas favourite. Crosby's recording is reputed to have sold in excess of 30 million copies. In the film, he and Astaire were perfect together - each with his own relaxed and easygoing style, and a mutual flair for comedy. Their characters, Jim and Ted, clash for a while - over a girl, naturally - but eventually Jim finds happiness with Linda (Marjorie Reynolds), and Ted settles for Lila (Virginia Dale). Also in the cast were Bing's brother Bob and his Bobcats, and Harry Barris, a former member, with Bing and Al Rinker, of the famous Rhythm Boys. The dance director was Danny Dare, and *Holiday Inn*, which took nearly $4 million at the US box-office, was produced and directed by Mark Sandrich, who had worked so successfully with Fred Astaire at RKO.

Holiday, Billie

b. Eleanora Harris, 7 April 1915, Philadelphia, Pennsylvania, USA, d. 17 July 1959. Billie 'Lady Day' taught herself to sing during her early teens in Baltimore, Maryland, where she was brought up until moving to New York in 1929. Factual inaccuracies and elements of myth and exaggeration have clouded the picture of her formative years despite the best efforts of researchers to present her career story in a properly ordered manner. Not until Stuart Nicholson's immaculately researched book appeared in 1995 was a detailed and reliable account of these years made available. Nicholson's research revealed that some of the statements made by the singer in her 1956 autobiography, *Lady Sings The Blues*, were true, despite having been dismissed as exaggeration by other writers. Holidays's teenage parents, Sadie Harris (aka Fagan) and probable father, Clarence Holiday, probably never married, and it seems unlikely that they lived together for any length of time. Holiday, a banjo and guitar player is remembered principally for his work with **Fletcher Henderson**'s band in the early 30s. He remains a somewhat shadowy figure who left his daughter in the care of Fagan or other relatives. As a musician with touring bands in the later 20s Holiday would often be away from home, and during the stay with Henderson, which lasted until 1932, the guitarist severed connections with the Fagans. However Billie proved hard to shake off after joining her mother in New York's Harlem district, and when rent on their apartment was overdue, she confronted Clarence at the Roseland Ballroom - where Henderson's orchestra enjoyed a lengthy 'residency' - and extorted money by threatening to show him up publicly.

Fragments of information about Holiday's deprived, cruelly exploited and extravagantly ill-fated early history prove she had learned how to survive extreme poverty, race prejudice and the injustice of black ghetto life by the time she was 15 or 16. Also, they hint at a more influential relationship between father and daughter (no matter how tenuous it might have been) than Holiday revealed in print. Clarence, a more than competent guitarist with a reputation for 'good time' in a rhythm section, seemed surrounded by paradox. Through the 30s, even after his barely noted death early in 1937, compilers of books which included record reviews and personnel listings employed the spellings Haliday or Halliday, and there is evidence that Billie used that name occasionally until persuaded to sing professionally as Billie Holiday. For jazz historians the interest lies in tracking down a link between her father's fine, relaxed sense of rhythm and her own astonishing command of time and swing: *laid-back* swing of a type not previously heard on records by singers. Since Holiday had very little schooling and no formal musical training, her extraordinary creative gifts were intuitive in the first place. She developed her singing in obscure New York speakeasies and Harlem nightclubs such as Pods' and Jerry's Log Cabin, the Yeah Man, Monette Moore's Supper Club, the Hot-Cha, Alabama Grill and Dickie Wells's place. She even sang at the local Elks club in order to pick up a few dollars in tips. Poverty was the spur, the initial incentive, but the dedication she then displayed to the mastering of jazz-craft is not easy to explain. No amount of theorizing will help to a real understanding of her seemingly instinctive gift for music-making. She was a perfectionist in her fashion, depending upon her excellent ear, innate taste and honesty of purpose to make up artistically for her small voice and range. This integrity, so far as vocal sound and style went, is the more baffling because of the insecurity and brutal ugliness of her early life. (She had already survived rape at age 11 and a period in care which followed this attack. In New York she endured a brief stint as a prostitute for which she and her mother were arrested in 1929. For this she served time on the notorious Ryker's Island).

It has frequently been stated that fame and success depend largely on an artist or performer being in the right place at the right time. In Holiday's case, the lucky break came when she found herself by sheer chance singing in front of the well-connected record producer and talent spotter **John Hammond Jnr**. Hammond had stopped off at the 133rd Street club with the intention of listening to singer Monette Moore. Instead of the blues singer, a performer who had been recording since 1923, he heard the unknown girl deputizing for Monette (absent, playing in a Broadway show) and was immediately impressed. 'She sang popular songs in a manner that made them completely her own', Hammond wrote later in his autobiography, praising her excellent memory for lyrics and sense of phrasing. He also gave Holiday the first press notice of her career. In April 1933 it appeared in the *Melody Maker*, and Hammond wrote: 'This month there has been a real find in the person of a singer called Billie Halliday' (she had by now adopted the first name of film actress Billie Dove, a childhood favourite whom she regarded as the epitome of glamour). Hammond represented a real break in Holiday's long run of bad luck because he had the power and willingness to forward the careers of those he thought worthy of special aid. The enthusiasm of his initial reaction to the promising youngster was shown in his description, 'She is incredibly beautiful and sings as well as anybody I ever heard', printed in the 1933 *Melody Maker*. Living up to his reputation, Hammond 'got into the habit of bringing people uptown to hear Billie'. Benny Goodman shared his opinion of Holiday and agreed to record with her. In the course of three sessions during November and December 1933, two songs were recorded with Goodman in charge of a nine-man studio group most of whom were strangers to the already nervous Holiday. 'Your Mother's Son-in-Law' was the first record she ever made; 'Riffin' The Scotch', a lightweight novelty concoction, was the second. Neither was successful as a showcase for her - nor, in truth, designed to be - because her role in the proceedings presented Holiday as band vocalist in a setting which stressed the instrumental prowess of Goodman, trombonist **Jack Teagarden** and other soloists. However, the singer managed to stamp her imprint on the vocal refrains and, for a young black performer with no experience of recording and, in her words, 'afraid to sing in the mike', came across as reasonably confident. For the Lady (she had earned that nickname on the Harlem club circuit for her regal sense of dignity, and it was amended by

Lester Young who added a typically personal touch, calling her Lady Day), expecting little she was not disappointed. Royalties were not routinely paid to recording artists in those days, and Holiday remembered receiving a flat fee of about 35 dollars for her work. Having a record on the market was no great deal; she placed little value on either song, not bothering to include them in her club or stage programmes or future recording repertoire.

Holiday continued her round of club dates, as well as being heard in the film *Symphony In Black*, made with **Duke Ellington** and released in 1935. Her career was given a boost when she won a week's engagement at the **Apollo** Theatre, Harlem's most famous and, for up-and-coming artists, formidable entertainment centre. Holiday, then just 20 years old, appeared with pianist Bobbie Henderson and her notices were, at best, mildly critical. Clearly, her relaxed, seemingly lazy, behind-the-beat style did not appeal to the Apollo's often vociferous patrons. Nevertheless, when the entire show was held over for a second week, at which time she appeared with Ralph Cooper's orchestra, her notices improved thanks to her capacity to adapt. By this time, Holiday had settled on the spelling of her name (earlier, her given name, Eleanora, was also subject to variation).

By mid-July the singer had returned to the record studio and used her real name on a session organized by Hammond and directed by **Teddy Wilson**. In Wilson, an accomplished musician and sensitive pianist, Holiday had found the sympathetic partner she needed to reveal the full range of her talents. The four songs picked for this groundbreaking record date were above average - 'I Wished On The Moon' and 'Miss Brown To You' were film numbers - and the easygoing jam-session atmosphere suited Holiday admirably. She responded to Wilson's masterly accompaniments and solo playing, and to the brilliance of Goodman, **Roy Eldridge** and **Ben Webster**, and similar jazz aces on subsequent recordings. They in turn seemed to be spurred by the rhythmic thrust and innovative magic of her singing. Here was a rising star (since 10 July 1936 she had achieved own-name status on the Vocalion label) who could invest ordinary popular songs with the emotional kick of a first-rate blues or ballad composition. The records also paid off sufficiently well to satisfy the market men.

Following appearances at a few slightly more prestigious venues than hitherto, Holiday sang with the bands of **Count Basie** (1937-38) and **Artie Shaw** (1938). She enjoyed the company of the bandsmen, and had an affair with Basie's guitarist **Freddie Green**. In spite of this rapport, the period with Basie was not a consistently happy one for Holiday, who encountered setbacks on the road and rejection by management people who disliked her 'way-out' style, or criticism from friends advising her to tailor her singing to the perceived requirements of the orchestra. As usual, Lady Day refused to compromise. She quit the Basie band, or was fired, in February of 1938 and, reservations about the touring life notwithstanding, joined Shaw almost at once and was on the road again, this time with a white band. She ran into trouble with racists, especially in the 'Jim Crow' Southern states, and before the end of the year had left Shaw. It was to be her final appearance as a band member: from now on she would be presented as a solo artist.

She continued making records and it seems likely that those closest to her heart were those recorded in association with Wilson, her beloved **Lester Young** and trumpeter Buck Clayton. And there is an emerging consensus that the inspirational partnership of Holiday and Young - musical and emotional - led to a batch of the finest vocal interpretations of her life. Undeniably, these discs and others made between 1935 and 1942 are among the finest in jazz. Early in 1939, Holiday's career took a giant step upwards. Again Hammond proffered a helping hand, as did Barney Josephson who dreamed of running a racially integrated nightclub in New York's Greenwich Village. Hammond was the one who invested in the project and, asked to advise on appropriate attractions for liberal patrons, recommended Holiday. She opened at Café Society with **Frankie Newton**'s band that January and had her first taste of stardom at the Café whose slogan read 'The wrong place for the right people'. Holiday stayed there for nearly nine months, during which time she was given a song-poem, 'Strange Fruit', Lewis Allen's anti-lynching protest, which led her to a real hit record and new and international fame as a purveyor of socially significant ballads. The song continued to be identified with Holiday who, on 20 April 1939, made a record of this controversial title for the Commodore label, her own having refused to release it. Opinion divided sharply on the merits of 'Strange Fruit' as a jazz vehicle, and the effect it had upon her instinctive taste and artistry. Critics feared it could lead to a self-consciousness which would destroy the strangely innocent qualities of earlier days.

Unfortunately as the sound of jazz progressed into the 40s and 50s Holiday responded positively, if unwisely, to some changes in the musical and social climate. Already an eager drinker, smoker of tobacco and marijuana, eater, dresser and shopper with a sexual appetite described as 'healthy-plus', she embraced the hard-drug culture of the 40s as to the manner born. She was having troublesome love affairs, nothing new to her, but on 25 August 1941 married **Jimmy Monroe**. It was a union that did nothing to ease her situation, being an on-off affair which lasted until their divorce in 1957. Nobody now can say when exactly, and by whom, but Holiday was turned on to opium and then heroin. The details are unimportant; the addiction hardly affected her singing at first, although her behaviour grew increasingly unpredictable, and she gained a reputation for unreliability. At last she was earning real money, as much as $1,000 weekly, it was reported, and about half that sum was going to pay for her 'habit'. Nevertheless, she now had the public recognition she craved. In the first *Esquire* magazine poll (1943) the critics voted her best vocalist, topping Mildred Bailey and **Ella Fitzgerald** in second and third places respectively. Holiday was a stellar act, in spite of drug problems, and one accompanist spoke years later of her 'phenomenal musicianship.' The series of 78s - 36 titles made for **Decca Records** with a wide variety of more commercially acceptable accompaniments, including strings on a dozen or so sides and a vocal group on two - rank with the mature Holiday's most accomplished performances, technically speaking, although the revolutionary approach had become more calculating and mannered. To compensate, she turned up the emotional heat, depending on her imagination to deliver the right touch. Among these 78s, recorded between October 1944 and March 1950, are a number of gems of jazz singing - among them 'Lover Man', 'Porgy', 'Good Morning Heartache', 'You Better Go Now' and, as a welcome example of Lady Day back to top form as a commanding, exuberant, mistress of swing phrasing, the mid-tempo blues-drenched 'Now Or Never'. To round off this set, assembled on three *The Lady Sings* albums, she exhibits another facet of her craft by duetting comfortably with Armstrong on 'My Sweet Hunk O' Trash' and sharing space on a second Armstrong track.

At this stage of her life Holiday experienced regular bouts of depression, pain and ill-health. In 1947 she was sentenced to a long term in the Federal Reformatory, West Virginia, her arraignment coming, surprisingly, at the behest of her manager, Joe Glaser. The attendant publicity disastrously affected her confidence while drugs slowly weakened her physique. Running her own big band with husband **Joe Guy** in 1945 had cost Holiday a sum reckoned to be $35,000, and that blow was followed by the death of her mother. Another disappointment to Holiday's professional aspirations was her failure to secure a film break, after pinning her hopes on the part she was offered in the jazz film, *New Orleans* (1946). Both Holiday and her idol, Armstrong, had roles involving a great deal of music-making - much of it left in the cutting room - but the purported jazz story turned out to be a nonsensical fantasy; and worse, Holiday and Armstrong were cast as servants. She was quoted later as saying: 'I fought my whole life to keep from being somebody's damn maid. It was a real drag . . . to end up as a make-believe maid'. The picture failed but gave her valuable international exposure, and jazz fanciers were pleased to see and hear sequences featuring Holiday Armstrong, **Kid Ory**, **Woody Herman** and other musicians. For Holiday it was goodbye to the movies.

From the 50s on, Holiday and trouble seemed often to be inseparable, and as a consequence of her criminal record on drugs, Holiday's cabaret card was withdrawn by the New York Police Department. This prevented her appearance at any venue where liquor was on sale, and effectively ruled out New York nightclubs. In her eyes it amounted to an absolute injustice and one that diminished her out-of-town earning capacity. She appeared in England during 1954 to great acclaim, and in 1956, her outspoken autobiography (written with William Dufty) brought increased fame, or notoriety. In 1957, Holiday was still making good money but by the following year the drink and drugs crucially influenced her vocal control, and the 'hoarsely eloquent voice' had increased in hoarseness at the expense of the eloquence. However, one further segment of the Holiday discography deserves attention: the body of work on the Clef-Verve label (produced or masterminded by **Norman Granz**) which placed her in a jazz setting and encouraged her to shine when she and the small-group accompaniment felt right. These recordings (1952-57) include a number of satisfying performances, and several worthy of high praise. As for the final albums with the Ray Ellis Orchestra, they are, for the majority of jazz fanciers, a painfully acquired taste, although certain tracks, most notably 'You've Changed' on *Lady In Satin* are immensely moving on their own terms.

Billie Holiday paid a second and last visit to Europe late in 1958, and came to London to make a television appearance on Granada's *Chelsea At Nine* show in February 1959. Back in America, however, her condition worsened and at the end of May she was taken to hospital suffering from heart and liver disease. Harried still by the police (she had been arrested twice already for possession, in 1949 and 1956), and placed under arrest in her private room, she was charged with 'possession' and put under police guard - the final cruelty the system could inflict upon her. Thus the greatest of jazz singers died in humiliating circumstances at 3.10 am on 17 July 1959 with $750 in notes taped to one leg - an advance on a series of promised articles. Even at the end squabbles had begun between a lawyer, virtually self-appointed, and her second husband, Louis McKay, whom she had married on 28 March 1957. She did not live to rejoice in the flood of books, biographical features, critical studies, magazine essays, album booklets, discographies, reference-book entries, chapters in innumerable jazz volumes, films and television documentaries which far exceed any form of recognition she experienced in her lifetime.

In defiance of her limited vocal range, Billie Holiday's use of tonal variation and vibrato, her skill at jazz phrasing, and her unique approach to the lyrics of popular songs, were but some of the elements in the work of a truly original artist. Her clear diction, methods of manipulating pitch, improvising on a theme, the variety of emotional moods ranging from the joyously optimistic, flirtatious even, to the tough, defiant, proud, disillusioned and buoyantly barrelhouse, were not plucked out of the air, acquired without practice. Holiday paid her dues in a demanding milieu. That she survived at all is incredible; that she should become the greatest jazz singer there has ever been - virtually without predecessor or successor - borders on the miracu-

lous. Today she is revered beyond her wildest imaginings in places which, in her lifetime, greeted her with painfully closed doors. Sadly, she would not have been surprised. As she wrote in her autobiography: 'There's no damn business like show business. You had to smile to keep from throwing up'.

● ALBUMS: *Lady In Satin* (Columbia 1958)★★★, *The Billie Holiday Story* (Decca 1972)★★★, *Strange Fruit* (Atlantic 1973)★★★, *Lady In Autumn* (Verve 1973)★★★★★, *The Original Recordings* (Columbia 1973)★★★, *Lady And The Legend Vols 1, 2* and *3.* (1984)★★★★, *Billie Holiday At Monterey 1958* (1986)★★★, *The Legendary Masters* (1988)★★★★, *Quintessential Vols 1-9* (Columbia 1987-1991)★★★★★, *Billie Holiday: The Voice Of Jazz* 8CD set (1992)★★★★★, *The Complete Recordings 1933-1940* (Charly 1993), *Fine And Mellow (1935-1941)* (Indigo 1995)★★★, *Love Songs* (Legacy 1996)★★★★, *Billie Holiday: This Is Jazz No. 15* (Legacy 1997)★★★★. *The Complete Commodore Recordings* (GRP 1997)★★★★★, *Priceless Jazz* (GRP 1997)★★★.

● FURTHER READING: *Billie's Blues*, John Chilton. *Lady Sings The Blues*, Billie Holiday with William Duffy, *Billie Holiday*, Stuart Nicholson.

Holiday, Jimmy

b. 24 July 1934, Durant, Mississippi, USA, d. 15 February 1987. This versatile singer first came to prominence in 1963 with the self-penned 'How Can I Forget?' which was covered at the same time by **Ben E. King**. Holiday later joined the Minit label where he made several excellent recordings, ranging from the 'Memphis'-influenced R&B of 'You Won't Get Away' to the urban soul of 'I'm Gonna Move To The City'. His biggest hit on Minit was 'Baby I Love You' (1966), a bigger hit for **Little Milton** in 1970. Holiday also recorded with former Raelette Clydie King, and later pursued a career as a songwriter on his departure from the label. A partnership with Randy Myers and **Jackie DeShannon** produced several excellent compositions, including the much-covered 'Put A Little Love In Your Heart', recorded successfully in 1989 by **Al Green** and **Annie Lennox**. Holiday died of heart failure in 1987.

● ALBUMS: *Turning Point* (1967)★★★, *Spread Your Love* (1968)★★.

● COMPILATIONS: *Everybody Needs Help* (Stateside 1986)★★★.

Holland

Despite the name, Holland was a UK heavy metal act from the early 80s who rode briefly on the crest of the **N.W.O.B.H.M.** Comprising Bob Henman (guitar), Graeme Hutchinson (bass), Kenny Nicholson (guitar) and Marty Day (drums), their name was initially made on the burgeoning demo tape scene, a reputation that eventually led to a recording contract with Ebony Records. However, poor production on *Early Warning* dissipated the critical buzz surrounding the band and they never recovered their footing. The same line-up changed the band's name to Hammer, recording the more impressive *Contract With Hell* two years later.

● ALBUMS: *Early Warning* (Ebony 1984)★★.

Holland - Beach Boys

Having finally rid themselves of a dated stripe-shirt image with the masterful *Surf's Up*, the Beach Boys continued the process with this ambitious album. The entire group had decamped to the Nederlands to record much of its content, a decision adding an emotional fission to its 'California Saga' trilogy. Although Brian Wilson's contribution was limited to two excellent songs, siblings Dennis and Carl rose to the occasion, with the latter's particularly impressive 'Trader'. The group's harmonies remain as distinctive as ever, while two recent additions to the line-up, Blondie Chaplin and Ricky Fataar, increased the vocal range and added new instrumental muscle. This became their best-selling album for six years, and *Holland* prepared the way for the Beach Boys' 70s comeback.

● Tracks: *Sail On Sailor; Steamboat; California Saga: - Big Surf, - The Beaks Of Eagles, - California ; Trader; Leaving This Town; Only With You; Funky Pretty.*

● First released 1973

● UK peak chart position: 20

● USA peak chart position: 36

Holland, Brian

b. 15 February 1941, Detroit, Michigan, USA. A mainstay of black music in Detroit since the mid-50s, Brian Holland emerged as the lead vocalist of the **Satintones**, before touring as pianist with **Barrett Strong** in 1960. He joined Strong at **Motown Records** in 1961, enjoying immediate success as the co-writer and producer of the label's biggest hit to date, the **Marvelettes**' 'Please Mr Postman'. In 1962 he formed a production team with **Lamont Dozier** and Freddy Gorman; a year later, Gorman was replaced by Holland's brother **Eddie**. Working as **Holland/Dozier/Holland**, the trio masterminded a remarkable series of hits for Motown during the remainder of the 60s. In 1967, they clashed with the label's head, **Berry Gordy**, and left to set up the Invictus and Hot Wax labels. Throughout this period, Brian Holland was the partnership's chief voice in the studio, while his colleagues were responsible for composing the majority of the trio's hits. Holland scored a rare solo hit himself in 1972, 'Don't Leave Me Starvin' For Your Love', plus two chart duets with Lamont Dozier. Since the demise of Invictus in the mid-70s, he has featured in periodic production projects with his brother.

Holland, Dave

b. 1 October 1946, Wolverhampton, Staffordshire, England. Holland plays guitar, piano, bass guitar and also composes, but it is as a bassist and cellist that he has made an international reputation. He studied at London's Guildhall School of Music and Drama from 1965-68 and was principal bassist in the college orchestra. On the London scene he worked with **John Surman, Kenny Wheeler, Evan Parker, Ronnie Scott**

and **Tubby Hayes** and deputized for **Johnny Mbizo Dyani** with **Chris McGregor**'s group. In 1968 **Miles Davis** heard him at Ronnie Scott's club and asked him to join his band in New York. Holland did so in September in time to appear on some of the tracks for *Les Filles De Kilimanjaro*. He stayed until autumn 1970, appearing on the seminal *In A Silent Way* and *Bitches Brew*, then he and **Chick Corea** (who had joined Davis at about the same time as Holland had) formed Circle with **Anthony Braxton** and **Barry Altschul**. Circle broke up in 1972 when Corea left, but Braxton, Altschul and **Sam Rivers** played on Holland's *Conference Of The Birds*. Holland also played in Rivers's and Braxton's groups in the 70s, as well as in the occasional trio **Gateway** (with **John Abercrombie** and **Jack DeJohnette**). The 1977 *Emerald Tears* was a solo bass album, and in 1980 Holland played at **Derek Bailey**'s **Company** Festival, recording *Fables* with Bailey, **George Lewis** and **Evan Parker**. Since the early 80s, following recovery from serious illness, he has lead his own much-admired group, which has included Kenny Wheeler, **Julian Priester**, **Marvin 'Smitty' Smith**, **Kevin Eubanks** and **Steve Coleman**, and in 1984 he began a series of fine records for ECM, perhaps most notably 1990's highly-acclaimed *Extensions*. In 1986 he toured Europe in a remarkable quartet with **Albert Mangelsdorff**, **John Surman** and **Elvin Jones** which, regrettably, did not issue any recordings; and in the late 80s also played with the **London Jazz Composers Orchestra**, recording on their Zurich Concerts collaboration with his longtime associate Anthony Braxton.

● ALBUMS: with Derek Bailey *Improvisation For Cello And Guitar* (ECM 1971)★★★, with Barre Phillips *Music From Two Basses* (1971)★★★, *Conference Of The Birds* (ECM 1973)★★★★, *Emerald Tears* (ECM 1978)★★★, with Company *Fables* (1980)★★★, *Life Cycle* (ECM 1983)★★★, *Jumpin' In* (ECM 1984)★★★, *Seeds Of Time* (ECM 1985)★★★, *The Razor's Edge* (ECM 1987)★★★, *Triplicate* (ECM 1988)★★★, *Extensions* (ECM 1990)★★★★, with Steve Coleman *Phase-Space* (1993)★★★, *Dream Of The Elders* (ECM 1996)★★★, *Points Of View* (ECM 1998)★★★★.

Holland, Eddie

b. 30 October 1939, Detroit, Michigan, USA. Like his brother **Brian Holland**, Eddie was active in the Detroit music scene from the mid-50s onwards, leading the Fideltones vocal group, and producing demo recordings for **Jackie Wilson**. In 1958, he met **Berry Gordy**, who produced a series of solo singles for Holland on **Mercury** and United Artists. Gordy signed Holland to his fledgling **Motown Records** concern in 1961, and was rewarded when Holland's 'Jamie', an affectionate parody of Jackie Wilson, became a US Top 30 hit. Holland achieved three further chart successes in 1964, among them 'Leaving Here', which proved popular among British R&B bands. That year he also helped to inaugurate the **Holland/Dozier/Holland** partnership, Motown's most successful writing and production team of all time. Working mostly as the trio's lyricist,

Holland was involved in a chain of hits for artists such as the **Supremes** and the **Four Tops**. He also collaborated with writer/producer **Norman Whitfield** on a series of singles by the **Temptations**, notably 'I'm Losing You' and 'Beauty Is Only Skin Deep'. The same pairing evolved 'He Was Really Saying Something' and 'Needle In A Haystack' for the **Velvelettes**, while Holland also co-wrote **Shorty Long**'s dancefloor classic, 'Function At The Junction'. Eddie Holland continued to compose and produce with his brother and **Lamont Dozier** when the trio formed the Invictus and Hot Wax labels in 1968. Since then he has continued to work periodically with both his former partners.

● ALBUMS: *Eddie Holland* (Motown 1962)★★★.

Holland, Jools

b. Julian Holland, 24 January 1958, London, England. An effervescent pianist, television host and model car collector, Holland learned the piano as a child and later came to the attention of fellow Deptford residents Glen Tilbrook and Chris Difford who invited him to join their new band **Squeeze** in 1974. Signed to Deptford Fun City in 1978, Squeeze began their aural assault of the pop charts at the same time as Holland had his first solo release, the *Boogie Woogie* EP. Holland left Squeeze in August 1980 after a farewell gig in their native Deptford, whereupon he was replaced by **Paul Carrack**. He then formed the Millionaires with Mike Paice (saxophone), Pino Palladino (bass) and Martin T. Deegan (drums). 'Bumble Boogie', their debut, trickled out in April 1981. After a few more singles with the Millionaires he went solo in 1983 with 'Crazy Over You'. Further singles followed at various junctures in his multi-media career. He can turn his hand to most styles, but would appear to favour New Orleans blues best. He became well known for his presentation of the UK television pop show *The Tube*, achieving infamy for his use of a four-letter word ('. . . all you groovy fuckers'). He rejoined Squeeze in 1985, and continued to play with them occasionally until 1990. Further television appearances with Roland Rivron preceded his return to pop presentation with the resurrected *Juke Box Jury* television programme. In 1992 he presented a BBC2 Television series, *Later*, and could be seen playing piano with his band on *Don't Forget Your Toothbrush*. In 1994 he undertook a tour with the ambitious, yet excellent, Jools Holland Rhythm And Blues Orchestra, in support of the album of the same name. *Later* has since become UK television's last hope for new and interesting music. For some, Holland's jokey persona clouds his extraordinary gift as an outstanding pianist.

● ALBUMS: *Jools Holland And His Millionaires* (A&M 1981)★★★, *Jools Holland Meets Rock 'A' Boogie Billy* (1984)★★★, *A World Of His Own* (IRS 1990)★★★, *The Full Complement* (IRS 1991)★★★, *The A-Z Geographer's Guide To The Piano* (1992)★★, *Jools Holland And The Rhythm And Blues Orchestra - Live Performance* (Beautiful 1994)★★★, *Sex And Jazz And Rock And Roll* (Coliseum 1996)★★★.

Holland, Maggie

b. 19 December 1949, Alton, Hampshire, England. Holland plays guitar/banjo/vocals/bass guitar, and her early career was spent performing in the folk clubs of Surrey, Bristol and Hampshire from 1967-72. In 1973, she formed the duo Hot Vultures with her then husband **Ian A. Anderson**. Recording a number of albums, she and Anderson then formed the English Country Blues Band in 1980 with **Rod Stradling**, formerly with Oak and the **Old Swan Band**, (melodeon), and either **Sue Harris** (formerly of the **Richard Thompson** Band - hammer dulcimer), or **Chris Coe** (formerly of the New Victory Band - hammer dulcimer). Despite the various group commitments, Holland found time to record *Still Pause*, her first solo album. She then became a member of the roots dance band Tiger Moth from 1984-89. Holland also supplied vocals and bass guitar on the Ian A. Anderson and **Mike Cooper** release *The Continuous Preaching Blues* in 1984. *A Short Cut*, recorded with Jon Moore (guitar), led to the formation of the trio Maggie's Farm which toured both in the UK and Bangladesh. Also during the period 1984-86, Holland worked occasionally as a duo with Chris Coe, touring the UK, Nepal, Thailand, the Phillipines and Ghana. In 1985, she had the role of lead singer in the National Theatre's production of *The Mysteries* at the Lyceum, London. Another solo simply called *The Cassette*, appeared in 1989. In 1992, she issued *Down To The Bone* and in 1995 *By Heart* which featured excellent covers of **Billy Bragg**'s 'Tank Park Salute' and **Michael Chapman**'s glorious 'Postcards From Scarborough'.

● ALBUMS: *Still Pause* (Rogue 1982)★★★, *The Cassette* (Rogue 1989)★★★, *Down To The Bone* (Rogue 1992)★★★, *By Heart* (Rhiannon 1995)★★★★.

● COMPILATIONS: *Vulturama* (Rogue 1983)★★★.

Holland, Peanuts

b. Herbert Lee Holland, 9 February 1910, Norfolk, Virginia, USA, d. 7 February 1979. Holland was one of several young boys to get his musical start in the Jenkins' Orphanage Band in Charleston, South Carolina, for which he played trumpet. In the late 20s and early 30s he was with **Alphonso Trent**'s famous **territory band** and also worked with the **Jeter-Pillars Orchestra**, **Willie Bryant** and **Jimmie Lunceford**. By the end of the 30s he was based in New York, where he played in bands led by **Coleman Hawkins** and **Fletcher Henderson** and then helped to break racial restraints by becoming one of a succession of black jazzmen hired by **Charlie Barnet**. In 1946 he joined **Don Redman** for a European tour and stayed behind, first in Stockholm and later in Paris, to attain great popularity.

● ALBUMS: *Peanuts Holland With Michel Attenoux In Concert At The Salle Pleyal, Paris* (1952)★★, *Peanuts Holland In Paris* (1954)★★★★, *Peanuts Holland In Finland* (1959)★★★.

● COMPILATIONS: with Alphonso Trent, included on *Sweet And Low Blues* (1933)★★★, *Charlie Barnet In Discographical Order Vol. 16* (1942-43)★★★.

Holland/Dozier/Holland

Brothers **Eddie Holland** (b. 30 October 1939, Detroit, Michigan, USA) and **Brian Holland** (b. 15 February 1941, Detroit, Michigan, USA), and **Lamont Dozier** (b. 16 June 1941, Detroit, Michigan, USA) formed one of the most successful composing and production teams in popular music history. Throughout the mid-60s, they almost single-handedly fashioned the classic **Motown** sound, creating a series of hit singles that revolutionized the development of black music. All three men were prominent in the Detroit R&B scene from the mid-50s, Brian Holland as lead singer with the **Satintones**, his brother Eddie with the Fideltones, and Dozier with the Romeos. By the early 60s, they had all become part of Berry Gordy's Motown concern, working both as performers and as writers/arrangers. After masterminding the **Marvelettes**' 1961 smash 'Please Mr Postman', Brian Holland formed a production team with his brother Eddie, and Freddy Gorman. In 1963, Gorman was replaced by Dozier, and the trio made their production debut with a disregarded record by the Marvelettes, 'Locking Up My Heart'. Over the next five years, the triumvirate wrote and produced scores of records by almost all the major Motown artists, among them a dozen US number 1 hits. Although **Smokey Robinson** can claim to have been the label's first true auteur, Holland/Dozier/Holland created the records that transformed Motown from an enthusiastic Detroit soul label into an international force. Their earliest successes came with **Marvin Gaye**, for whom they wrote 'Can I Get A Witness?', 'Little Darling', 'How Sweet It Is (To Be Loved By You)' and 'You're A Wonderful One', and **Martha And The Vandellas**, who had hits with the trio's 'Heatwave', 'Quicksand', 'Nowhere To Run' and 'Jimmy Mack'. Impressive although these achievements were, they paled alongside the team's run of success with the **Supremes**. Ordered by Berry Gordy to construct suitable vehicles for the wispy, feminine vocal talents of **Diana Ross**, they produced 'Where Did Our Love Go?', a simplistic but irresistible slice of lightweight pop-soul. The record reached number 1 in the USA, as did its successors, 'Baby Love', 'Come See About Me', 'Stop! In The Name Of Love' and 'Back In My Arms Again' - America's most convincing response to the otherwise overwhelming success of British beat groups in 1964 and 1965. These Supremes hits charted the partnership's growing command of the sweet soul idiom, combining unforgettable hooklines with a vibrant rhythm section that established a peerless dance groove. The same process was apparent - albeit with more sophistication - on the concurrent series of hits that Holland/Dozier/Holland produced and wrote for the **Four Tops**. 'Baby I Need Your Loving' and 'I Can't Help Myself' illustrated their stylish way with up-tempo material; '(It's The) Same Old Song' was a self-mocking riposte to critics of their sound, while 'Reach Out I'll Be There', a worldwide number 1 in 1966, pioneered what came to be known as 'symphonic soul', with a towering arrangement and a melodic flourish that was the peak of their work at Motown. Besides the Supremes and the Four Tops, the trio found success with the **Miracles** ('Mickey's Monkey' and 'I'm The One You Need'), **Kim Weston** ('Take Me In Your Arms'), and the **Isley Brothers** ('This Old Heart Of Mine', 'Put Yourself In My Place' and 'I Guess I'll Always Love'). Their long-standing commitments continued to bring them recognition in 1966 and 1967, however, as the Supremes reached the top of the US charts with 'You Can't Hurry Love', 'You Keep Me Hanging On', 'Love Is Here And Now You're Gone', and the mock-psychedelic 'The Happening', and the Four Tops extended their run of success with 'Bernadette' and 'Standing In The Shadows Of Love'.

In 1967, when Holland/Dozier/Holland effectively commanded the US pop charts, they split from Berry Gordy and Motown, having been denied more control over their work and more reward for their labours. Legal disputes officially kept them out of the studio for several years, robbing them of what might have been their most lucrative period as writers and producers. They were free, however, to launch their own rival to Motown, in the shape of the Invictus and Hot Wax labels. Neither concern flourished until 1970, and even then the names of the company's founders were absent from the credits of their records - although there were rumours that the trio were moonlighting under the names of their employees. On the evidence of Invictus hits by artists such as the **Chairmen Of The Board** and **Freda Payne**, the case was convincing, as their records successfully mined the familiar vein of the trio's Motown hits, at a time when their former label was unable to recapture that magic without them. Business difficulties and personal conflicts gradually wore down the partnership in the early 70s, and in 1973 Lamont Dozier left the Holland brothers to forge a solo career. Invictus and Hot Wax were dissolved a couple of years later, and since then there have been only occasional reunions by the trio, none of which have succeeded in rekindling their former artistic fires.

● COMPILATIONS: *The Very Best Of The Invictus Years* (Deep Beats 1997)★★★.

Holley, 'Lyin'' Joe

b. *c.*1915, USA. Holley was recorded in April 1977 by George Paulus of Barrelhouse Records, who estimated his age as 'early sixties'. Holley had travelled throughout the southern USA and played in St. Louis and Detroit before settling in Chicago. He reputedly played blues piano at house parties and at the Provident Barber Shop on Saturdays for many years, and his recordings reveal a traditionally based pianist with a large repertoire and an ability to improvise memorable lyrics over a tough piano accompaniment. Holley is important as 'one of the last of the house party entertainers' but remains a very obscure figure, although he is reportedly still living in the Chicago area.

● ALBUMS: *So Cold In The USA* 1977 recording (JSP 1982)★★★, *Piano Blues Legends* four tracks only (1983)★★.

Holley, Major

b. 10 July 1924, Detroit, Michigan, USA, d. 26 October 1990. After starting out on violin and occasionally doubling on tuba, Holley switched to bass while serving in the US Navy. In the 40s he worked with **Dexter Gordon**, **Earl Bostic**, **Coleman Hawkins** and **Charlie Parker** and in 1950 recorded with **Oscar Peterson**. In the 50s he was first resident in the UK, where he worked in the studios of the BBC, then toured with **Woody Herman** and was a member of a small group co-led by **Al Cohn** and **Zoot Sims**. Throughout the 60s he was in great demand as a session player, recording with many leading jazz artists. Late in the decade he also taught at **Berklee College Of Music**. In the 70s Holley recorded and toured with many jazzmen and became a familiar and popular figure on the international festival circuit. Affectionately known as 'Mule' (a name bestowed by **Clark Terry**, with whom he worked in navy bands), Holley is one of a small number of bass players to effectively adopt **Slam Stewart**'s habit of singing in unison with his own arco playing. Although strongly identified with the post-war bebop scene, Holley was happy to play in all kinds of company and while in the UK worked with traditionally-orientated musicians such as **Mick Mulligan** and **Chris Barber**. He also played classical music with the Westchester Symphony Orchestra.

● ALBUMS: *The Good Neighbors Jazz Quartet* (1958)★★★, *Woody Herman* (1958)★★★★, with Coleman Hawkins *Today And Now* (1962)★★★, *Mule!* (Black And Blue 1974)★★★, *Excuse Me, Ludwig* (1977)★★★, *Major Step* (Timeless 1990)★★.

Holliday, Jennifer

b. 19 October 1960, Houston, Texas, USA. This powerful vocalist first attracted attention as lead in the Broadway show ***Your Arm's Too Short To Box With God***. She is, however, better known for her **Tony**-winning role in the musical ***Dreamgirls***, a thinly disguised adaptation of the **Supremes**' story, which former member **Mary Wilson** took as the title of her autobiography. The show's undoubted highlight was Holliday's heart-stopping rendition of 'And I Am Telling You I'm Not Going', one of soul's most emotional, passionate performances. The single's success in 1982 prompted Holliday's solo career, but subsequent work was overshadowed by that first hit. She returned to the stage in 1985 in *Sing, Mahalia Sing* and has also acted in the television series *The Love Boat*. Holliday was also part of the backing choir on **Foreigner**'s 1984 UK number 1 hit single, 'I Wanna Know What Love Is'. *Say You Love Me* won her a second Grammy award in 1985. She appeared in the musical ***Grease*** in the 90s and has recorded only sporadically. Holliday possesses an outstandingly powerful and emotional voice, the range of which has seen her compared to **Aretha Franklin**.

● ALBUMS: with Loretta Devine, Cleavant Derricks *Dreamgirls* Original Broadway Cast (Geffen 1982)★★★, *Feel My Soul* (Geffen 1983)★★★, *Say You Love Me* (Geffen 1985)★★★, *Get Close To My Love* (Geffen 1987)★★★, *I'm On Your Side* (Arista 1991)★★★, *On And On* (Inter Sound 1994)★★★.

● COMPILATIONS: *The Best Of Jennifer Holliday* (Geffen 1996)★★★★.

Holliday, Judy

b. Judith Tuvim, 21 June 1922, New York, USA, d. 7 June 1965, New York, USA. An actress and singer with an endearing quality and a warm, unique comic style, Holliday's first attempt to break into showbusiness was with Orson Welles and John Houseman at the Mercury Theatre, but she only succeeded in getting a job there as a telephone operator - ironic considering her later memorable role in the musical theatre. Holliday joined some more young hopefuls, **Betty Comden**, **Adolph Green**, John Frank and Alvin Hammer, in a nightclub act called the Revuers, who attracted a good deal of attention. In 1945 she made her Broadway debut in the play *Kiss Them For Me*, and a year later was acclaimed for her performance in the Garson Kanin comedy *Born Yesterday*. She had taken over the dizzy blonde role after the producers' original choice, Jean Arthur, withdrew during the Philadelphia try-out. In 1950 Holliday won an Academy Award when she recreated her part for the Columbia film version. In the previous year she had almost stolen the glory from stars Katharine Hepburn and Spencer Tracey in *Adam's Rib*, which also had a screenplay by Kanin and his wife Ruth Gordon. In 1956 Holliday returned to Broadway in the musical ***Bells Are Ringing***. The book and lyrics were by her old friends, Comden and Green (music by **Jule Styne**), and Holliday played Ella Peterson, a telephone operator who cannot help becoming emotionally involved with the clients who subscribe to Susanswerphone, the answering service where she works. *Bells Are Ringing* was a smash hit, and Holliday introduced several of its delightful songs, including 'The Party's Over', 'Drop That Name', 'Just In Time' and 'Long Before I Knew You' (both with Sydney Chaplin), and the immortal 'I'm Goin' Back (To The Bonjour Tristesse Brassiere Company)'. Her unforgettable performance won her **Tony** and New York Drama Critics awards.

In 1948 she had married musician David Oppenheim, who became head of the classical division of **Columbia Records**, but they divorced in 1957. Holliday's subsequent partner was another musician, a giant of the jazz world, **Gerry Mulligan**. He played one of her boyfriends in the 1960 screen adaptation of *Bells Are Ringing*, in which she co-starred with **Dean Martin**, and they also wrote songs together. Four of the best of these, 'What's The Rush?', 'Loving You', 'It Must Be Christmas' and 'Summer's Over', were included among the standards on an album they recorded in 1961. In spite of its tender and poignant quality, and the presence of accompanying luminaries such as **Bob Brookmeyer**, **Mel Lewis** and **Al Klink**, Holliday was reported to be unhappy with the result, and the album was not released until 1980. In 1960 she was out of town with the play *Laurette*, based on the life of the former Broadway star Laurette Taylor, when she found that she was unable to project her voice properly. It was the first sign that she had cancer. After surgery, she returned to New York in 1963 with the musical *Hot Spot*, but it folded after only 43 performances. She died just two weeks before her forty-third birthday.

● ALBUMS: with Gerry Mulligan *Holliday With Mulligan* 1961 recording (DRG 1980)★★★★, and Original Cast and soundtrack recordings.

● FURTHER READING: *Judy Holliday*, W. Holtzman. *Judy Holliday*, G. Carey.

● FILMS: *Greenwich Village* (1944), *Something For The Boys* (1944), *Winged Victory* (1944), *Adam's Rib* (1949), *Born Yesterday* (1950), *The Marrying Kind* (1952), *It Should Happen To You* (1954), *Phffft* (1954), *The Solid Gold Cadillac* (1956), *Full Of Life* (1956), *Bells Are Ringing* (1960).

Holliday, Michael

b. Michael Milne, 26 November 1928, Liverpool, England, d. 29 October 1963, Croydon, Surrey, England. A popular singer in the UK during the 50s, influenced by, and very similar in style and tone to **Bing Crosby**. After entertaining his shipmates in the Merchant Navy, Holliday made his first public appearance as a singer when his ship docked in New York. He won a talent contest on the stage of Radio City Music Hall, one of the world's largest theatres. In the absence of offers to star in a big Broadway musical, he returned to the UK, was released from the navy, and obtained work as a singer-guitarist with the **Eric Winstone** Band, touring UK holiday camps. He was signed for Columbia by **Norrie Paramor** in 1955, and during the next couple of years, covered several US artists' hits such as 'The Yellow Rose Of Texas' (**Mitch Miller**), 'Sixteen Tons' (**Tennessee Ernie Ford**) and 'Hot Diggity' (**Perry Como**), while also reaching the UK Top 30 with 'Nothin' To Do', 'Ten Thousand Miles' and 'The Gal With The Yaller Shoes', from the 1956 movie *Meet Me In Las Vegas*. In 1958 he had some success with 'In Love', 'Stairway Of Love' and the 1929 number 'I'll Always Be In Love With You', and topped the UK chart with 'The Story Of My Life', an early composition by **Burt Bacharach** and **Hal David**. On the b-side of that record was one of Holliday's own compositions, 'Keep Your Heart'. Early in 1960 he had another number 1 with 'Starry Eyed', but after 'Skylark' and 'Little Boy Lost' later in the year, the singles hits dried up. On his albums such as *Mike* and *Holliday Mixture*, he ignored the contemporary music scene, and sang old standards - as he did on television. With his casual, easy-going style, he was a natural for the small screen, and had his own *Relax With Mike* series, on which he duetted with himself on a tape recorder, in the days when those machines were a domestic novelty in the UK. His only appearance on the larger screen was in the movie *Life Is A Circus* (1962), with one of Britain's best-loved comedy teams, the Crazy Gang. Unfortunately,

his relaxed image seems to have been a façade, concealing professional and personal problems. When Holliday died in a Croydon hospital the cause of death was reported to be have been an overdose of drugs.

● ALBUMS: *Hi!* (Columbia 1958)★★★, *Mike* (Columbia 1959)★★★, *Holliday Mixture* (Columbia 1960)★★★, *Happy Holiday* (Columbia 1961)★★, *To Bing From Mike* (Columbia 1962)★★★.

● COMPILATIONS: *The Best Of Michael Holliday* (Columbia 1964)★★★, *Story Of My Life* (One-Up 1973)★★★, *The Very Best Of Michael Holliday* (MFP 1984)★★★, with Edna Savage *A Sentimental Journey* (See For Miles 1988)★★★, *The EMI Years: The Best Of Michael Holliday* (EMI 1989)★★★★, *30th Anniversary Collection* (1994)★★★★.

Hollies

Formed in Manchester in 1962 by childhood friends **Allan Clarke** (b. 15 April 1942, Salford, Lancashire, England; vocals), and **Graham Nash** (b. 2 February 1942, Blackpool, Lancashire, England; vocals/guitar). They had already been singing together locally for a number of years as a semi-professional duo under a number of names such as the Guytones, the Two Teens and Ricky And Dane. They enlarged the group by adding Eric Haydock (b. 3 February 1943, Burnley, Lancashire, England; bass) and Don Rathbone (drums), to became the Fourtones and then the Deltas. Following the recruitment of local guitar hero Tony Hicks from the Dolphins (b. 16 December 1943, Nelson, Lancashire, England) they became the Hollies. Almost immediately they were signed to the same label as the **Beatles**, the prestigious **Parlophone**. Their first two singles were covers of the **Coasters**' '(Ain't That) Just Like Me' and 'Searchin''. Both made the UK charts and the group set about recording their first album. At the same time Rathbone left to become their road manager and was replaced by Bobby Elliott (b. 8 December 1942) from **Shane Fenton** (**Alvin Stardust**) And The **Fentones**. The group's excellent live performances throughout Britain had already seasoned them for what was to become one of the longest beat group success stories in popular music. Their first two albums contained the bulk of their live act and both albums became long-time residents in the UK charts. Meanwhile, the band was enjoying a train of singles hits that continued from 1963-74, and their popularity almost rivalled that of the Beatles and **Rolling Stones**. Infectious, well-produced hits such as **Doris Troy**'s 'Just One Look', 'Here I Go Again' and the sublime 'Yes I Will' all contained their trademark soaring harmonies. The voices of Clarke, Hicks and Nash combined to make one of the most distinctive sounds to be heard in popular music.

As their career progressed the aforementioned trio developed into a strong songwriting team, and wrote most of their own b-sides (under the pseudonym 'L. Ransford'). On their superb third collection, *Hollies* in 1965, their talents blossomed with 'Too Many People', an early song about over-population. Their first UK number 1 came in 1965 with 'I'm Alive' and was followed within weeks by **Graham Gouldman**'s uplifting yet simple take 'Look Through Any Window'. By Christmas 1965 the group experienced their first lapse when their recording of **George Harrison**'s 'If I Needed Someone' just scraped the UK Top 20 and brought with it some bad press. Both the Hollies and **John Lennon** took swipes at each other, venting frustration at the comparative failure of a Beatles song. Early in 1966, the group enjoyed their second number 1, 'I Can't Let Go', which topped the *New Musical Express* chart jointly with the **Walker Brothers**' 'The Sun Ain't Gonna Shine Anymore'. 'I Can't Let Go', co-written by **Chip Taylor**, had already appeared on the previous year's *The Hollies* and was one of their finest recordings, combining soaring harmonies with some exceptionally strong, driving guitar work.

The enigmatic and troublesome Eric Haydock was sacked in April 1966 and was replaced by Hick's former colleague in the Dolphins, Bernie Calvert (b. 16 September 1942, Brierfield, Lancashire, England). The Hollies success continued unabated with Graham Gouldman's 'Bus Stop', the exotic 'Stop! Stop! Stop!' and the poppier 'On A Carousel', all UK Top 5 hits, and (at last) became major hits in the US charts. The Hollies were quick to join the 'flower power' bandwagon, as a more progressive feel had already pervaded their recent album, *For Certain Because*, but with *Evolution*, their beads and kaftans were everywhere. That same year (1967) the release of the excellent *Butterfly* showed signs of discontent. Inexplicably, the album failed to make the charts in either the UK or the US. It marked two distinct types of songs from the previously united team of Nash/Clarke/Hicks. On one hand there was a Clarke-influenced song, 'Charley And Fred', and on the other an obvious Nash composition like 'Butterfly'. Nash took a more ambitious route. His style was perfectly highlighted with the exemplary 'King Midas In Reverse', an imaginative song complete with brass and strings. It was, by Hollies standards, a surprising failure (UK number 18). The following year during the proposals to make *Hollies Sing Dylan*, Nash announced his departure for **Crosby, Stills And Nash**. His replacement was Terry Sylvester of the **Escorts**. Clarke was devastated by the departure of his friend of more than 20 years and after seven further hits, including 'He Ain't Heavy He's My Brother', Clarke decided to leave for a solo career. The band soldiered on with the strange induction of Mickael Rickfors from Sweden. In the USA the million-selling 'Long Cool Woman (In A Black Dress)' narrowly missed the top spot, ironic also because Allan Clarke was the vocalist on this older number taken from the successful album *Distant Light*. Clarke returned after an abortive solo career which included two average albums, *My Real Name Is 'Arold* and *Headroom*. The return was celebrated with the worldwide hit, 'The Air That I Breathe', composed by **Albert Hammond**. Over the next five years the Hollies pursued the supper-club and cabaret circuit as their

chart appearances began to dwindle. Although their albums were well produced they were largely unexciting and sold poorly. In 1981 Sylvester and Calvert left the group. Sensing major problems ahead, **EMI** suggested they put together a **Stars On 45**-type segued single. The ensuing 'Holliedaze' was a hit, and Graham Nash was flown over for the television promotion. This reunion prompted the album *What Goes Around*, which included a minor hit with the **Supremes**' 'Stop In The Name Of Love'. The album was justifiably slammed by the critics, and only made the US charts because of Nash's name.

Following this, the Hollies went back to the oldies path, until in 1988 a television beer commercial used 'He Ain't Heavy', and once again they were at the top of the charts for the first time in over a dozen years. In 1993 they were given an **Ivor Novello** award in honour of their contribution to British music. The mid-90s lineup in addition to Clarke, Elliott and the youthful Hicks featured Alan Coates (guitar), Ray Stiles (bass) and Ian Parker (keyboards). Their longevity is assured as their expertly crafted, harmonic songs represent some of the greatest music of all mid-60s pop.

● ALBUMS: *Stay With The Hollies* (Parlophone 1964)★★★★, *In The Hollies' Style* (Parlophone 1964)★★★★, *Here I Go Again* (Imperial 1964)★★★, *Hear! Hear!* (Imperial 1965)★★★, *The Hollies* (Parlophone 1965)★★★★, *Would You Believe* (Parlophone 1966)★★★★, *For Certain Because* (Parlophone 1966)★★★★, *The Hollies - Beat Group* (Imperial 1966)★★★, *Bus Stop* (Imperial 1966)★★★, *Stop! Stop! Stop!* (Imperial 1966)★★★, *Evolution* (Parlophone 1967)★★★, *Butterfly* (Parlophone 1967)★★★, *The Hollies Sing Dylan* (Parlophone 1969)★★, *Hollies Sing Hollies* (Parlophone 1969)★★, *He Ain't Heavy He's My Brother* (Epic 1969)★★, *Reflection* reissue of *The Hollies* (Regal Starline 1969)★★★★, *Moving Finger* (Epic 1970)★★, *Confessions Of The Mind* (Parlophone 1970)★★, *Distant Light* (Parlophone 1971)★★, *The Hollies* reissue of *Evolution* (MFP 1972)★★★, *Romany* (Polydor 1972)★★, *Out On The Road* (Hansa 1973)★★, *The Hollies* (Polydor 1974)★★, *Another Night* (Polydor 1975)★★, *Write On* (Polydor 1976)★★, *Russian Roulette* (Polydor 1976)★★, *Hollies Live Hits* (Polydor 1977)★★, *A Crazy Steal* (Polydor 1978)★★, *The Other Side Of The Hollies* (Parlophone 1978)★★★, *Five Three One-Double Seven O Four* (Polydor 1979)★★, *Long Cool Woman In A Black Dress* (MFP 1979)★★★, *Buddy Holly* (Polydor 1980)★★, *What Goes Around* (Warners 1983)★★, *Rarities* (EMI 1988)★★★★.

● COMPILATIONS: *The Hollies' Greatest* (Parlophone 1968)★★★★, *The Hollies Greatest Hits Volume 2* (Parlophone 1972)★★★, *The History Of The Hollies* (1975)★★★★, *The Best Of The Hollies EPs* (1978)★★★★, *20 Golden Greats* (1978)★★★★, *The EP Collection* (See For Miles 1987)★★★★, *Not The Hits Again* (See For Miles 1987)★★★★, *All The Hits And More* (EMI 1988)★★★★, *The Air That I Breathe: Greatest Hits* (1993)★★★, *Singles A's And B's 1970-1979* (1993)★★★★, *Treasured Hits And Hidden Treasures* 3-CD box set (EMI 1993)★★★, *Four Hollies Originals* 4-CD set (EMI 1995)★★★, *Four More Hollies Originals* (EMI 1996)★★★★, *The Best Of ...* (EMI

1997)★★★, *Special Collection* 3-CD box set (Trio/EMI 1997)★★★, *At Abbey Road 1963-1966* (EMI 1997)★★★★, *At Abbey Road (1966-1970)* (EMI 1998)★★★★.
● FILMS: *It's All Over Town* (1964).

Holloway, Brenda

b. 21 June 1946, Atascadero, California, USA. Brenda Holloway began her recording career with three small Los Angeles labels, Donna, Catch and Minasa, in the early 60s, recording under the aegis of producer Hal Davis. In 1964, Holloway made an impromptu performance at a disc jockeys' convention in California, where she was spotted by a **Motown Records** talent scout. She signed to the label later that year, becoming its first west coast artist. Her initial Tamla single, 'Every Little Bit Hurts', established her bluesy soul style, and was quickly covered by the **Spencer Davis Group** in Britain. She enjoyed further success in 1964 with 'I'll Always Love You', and the following year with 'When I'm Gone' and 'Operator'. Her consistent record sales led to her winning a place on the **Beatles'** 1965 US tour, but subsequent Tamla singles proved less successful. Holloway began to devote increasing time to her songwriting, forming a regular writing partnership with her sister Patrice, and Motown staff producer **Frank Wilson**. This combination produced her 1968 single 'You've Made Me So Very Happy', a song that proved more successful via the million-selling cover version by the white jazz-rock group **Blood, Sweat And Tears**. In 1968, Holloway's contract with Motown was terminated. The label issued a press release stating that the singer wished to sing for God, although Holloway blamed business differences for the split. She released a gospel album in 1983 and worked with Ian Levine from 1987. She teamed with **Jimmy Ruffin** in 1989 for a duet, 'On The Rebound'.
● ALBUMS: *Every Little Bit Hurts* (Tamla 1964)★★★, *The Artistry Of Brenda Holloway* (Motown 1968)★★★, *All It Takes* (1991)★★★.
● COMPILATIONS: *Greatest Hits And Rare Classics* (1991)★★★.

Holloway, Ken

b. 1965, Lafayette, Louisiana, USA. Holloway was a promising country singer working in bars and hoping for a contract with a major label, but his career was changed when his wife, Connie, became a born-again Christian. He says, 'I woke up one night and Connie was praying for me. She thought I was asleep but I could hear her saying, "God, he's my best friend. I love him so much, I don't want to go to heaven without him. You do what you have to do to get him saved"' (this event is recorded in his song 'I Don't Wanna Go Alone'). Holloway attended church meetings and a few months later, after witnessing a fight at a honky tonk, he put down the microphone and walked out of the club, resolving never to sing in one again. He studied theology and became an ordained minister. At the same time, a new strand of religious music was developing

that sounded like state-of-the-art country. **Paul Overstreet** and Russ Taff led the way, but at the forefront of the new Christian Country videos on CMT was Ken Holloway. As energetic as **Alan Jackson** and Ken Diffie, his songs are full of moral dilemmas, Christian sentiments and the joys of family life. The analogies are forced - heaven is seen as an endless honky-tonk party in 'Hoedown', and in another he states that 'the old rugged cross became our family tree' - best is 'Unplug the jukebox/I won't need it anymore/No more lonely nights walking the floor/I've found a new love that's worth waiting for.' Most of Holloway's concerts take place in churches and he has never returned to honky tonks.
● ALBUMS: *Ken Holloway* (Ransom 1994)★★, *He Who Made The Rain* (Ransom 1995)★★★, *The Ordinary* (Ransom 1997)★★★.

Holloway, Laurie

b. 31 March 1938, Oldham, Lancashire, England. A pianist, musical director, arranger and composer, Holloway took piano lessons from the age of seven, and six years later was organist and choirmaster at his local church. During the 50s, he toured with various groups, spent some time as pianist with **Harry Roy**'s former drummer, **Joe Daniels**, and also played on cruise ships such as the QE2, with 'Geraldo's Navy'. In 1959, he joined **Cyril Stapleton** and became a regular session musician in UK record studios. Also in 1959, Holloway served as musical director for the popular Australian entertainer **Rolf Harris**'s BBC radio show. This led him to work in that capacity for a whole range of musical personalities such as **Judy Garland**, **Liza Minnelli**, **Anthony Newley** and **Cleo Laine**. In 1964, Holloway contributed the music to Bob Grant's West End musical, *Instant Marriage*, starring Grant and Joan Sims. In spite of some unfriendly notices, ('This show puts British musicals back twenty or thirty years'), it ran for a healthy 366 performances. In 1965, he married US singer **Marian Montgomery** and became her musical director. From then on, the couple made frequent appearances on television, radio and the concert stage. From 1969-75, Holloway toured, as musical director, with **Engelbert Humperdinck**, appearing on top-rated US television shows with such as Johnny Carson, **Bob Hope** and **Dean Martin**. Holloway's many compositions include '(Michael) Parkinson's Theme', The Russell Harty Theme', 'Punchlines', 'Game For A Laugh', 'Blind Date', 'Child's Play Themes', 'Pop Preludes (Novellos)', 'More Pop Preludes', and (with Montgomery), a musical play *A Dream Of Alice*, written in 1981 to commemorate the 150th anniversary of the birth of Lewis Carroll. Apart from accompanying numerous artists on record, including **Stéphane Grappelli** (*Norwegian Wood*), Holloway worked regularly on radio with his own small groups, including **Prism**, a rock-jazz combo which he formed in the 80s specifically to play his own compositions. In the 90s Holloway continued to perform and record with a variety of musicians and singers, and was also a familiar figure - as musical director - on television shows featuring Dame Edna Everage.

● ALBUMS: *Cumulus* (1979)★★★, *About Time* (1992)★★.

Holloway, Loleatta

b. November 1946, Chicago, Illinois, USA. With her full-bodied gospelized vocals, which lent tremendous energy to her disco recordings, Holloway, as one of the leading disco divas, epitomized like no other singer of her day the transition of African-American popular music from soul to disco in the late 70s. She started in the church singing gospel, and sang with the famed **Caravans** from 1967-71. She was first recorded by her manager/husband Floyd Smith in Chicago on his Apache label, releasing 'Rainbow 71'. In 1973 she signed with GRC's Aware label and achieved a double-sided chart record with 'Mother Of Shame'/'Our Love' (number 43 R&B). These songs came from her debut album, *Loleatta*, which was recorded in Chicago and Atlanta. 'Cry To Me' (number 10 R&B, number 68 pop), a 1975 remake of the **Solomon Burke** hit, was pure, heartfelt soul and her biggest hit, effectively launching her second album, *Cry To Me*. In 1976 she moved to Philadelphia producer Norman Harris's **Gold Mind** label and recorded *Loleatta*, which featured a healthy tension between her earthy, soulful, gospelized roots and the Philly rhythm section. It produced her first disco hit, 'Hit And Run' (number 56 R&B), in 1977. *Queen Of The Night*, one of her most successful albums, consolidated her position in the disco galaxy of stars, but at the expense of the soulful sides of her artistry. *Loleatta Holloway*, with production help from Smith, brought her back to a more balanced presentation of deep soul and disco, but was notable for her disco groove 'All About The Paper'. *Love Sensation*, under the production aegis of **Dan Hartman**, featured soulful workouts, such as the splendid remake of **Otis Redding**'s hit 'I've Been Loving You Too Long', and disco numbers such as 'Love Sensation', a dancehall classic that was much sampled by rappers years later. Holloway's last chart single was 'Crash Goes Love' for Streetwise in 1984. During the 80s she confined her recording to small independent labels such as DJ International and Saturday Records.

● ALBUMS: *Loleatta* (Aware 1973)★★★, *Cry To Me* (Aware 1975)★★★★, *Loleatta* (Gold Mind 1976)★★★, *Queen Of The Night* (Gold Mind 1978)★★★, *Loleatta Holloway* (Gold Mind 1979)★★★, *Love Sensation* (Gold Mind 1980)★★★.

Holloway, Red

b. James W. Holloway, 31 May 1927, Helena, Arkansas, USA. Holloway grew up in a musical family - his father and mother were both musicians - and he initially played piano. He grew up in Chicago where he attended DuSable High School and the Conservatory of Music. While still at school, where his classmates included **Von Freeman** and **Johnny Griffin**, he took up the baritone saxophone, later switching to tenor. He played in and

around Chicago, working with Gene Wright's big band for three years before entering the US Army. After his discharge he returned to Chicago, where he became deeply involved in the local jazz scene, playing with such artists as **Yusef Lateef** and **Dexter Gordon**. In 1948 he joined **Roosevelt Sykes** for a US tour. He remained based in Chicago throughout the 50s and early 60s, playing with many leading blues artists. In the early 60s he was resident in New York, then went back to Chicago for some time. In the mid-60s Holloway toured with **Lionel Hampton** and 'Brother' Jack **McDuff** and also led his own small groups. Towards the end of the decade he settled on the west coast. At first he worked in the studios, but eventually secured a lengthy club engagement in Los Angeles. In the early part of his career Holloway worked with many bluesmen, including **Willie Dixon**, **Junior Parker**, **Bobby Bland**, **Lloyd Price**, **John Mayall**, **Muddy Waters**, **Chuck Berry** and **B.B. King**. His jazz affiliations over the years include leading artists such as **Billie Holiday**, **Ben Webster**, **Jimmy Rushing**, **Sonny Rollins**, **Red Rodney**, **Lester Young** and **Wardell Gray**. He has worked with big bands, including **Juggernaut**, but became best known internationally after he teamed up with **Sonny Stitt** in 1977. During this partnership, Holloway began playing alto saxophone (at Stitt's insistence). After Stitt's death, Holloway resumed touring on his own, but occasionally worked with jazzmen such as **Jay McShann** and **Clark Terry** and jazz singer **Carmen McRae**.

● ALBUMS: *The Burner* (Prestige 1963)★★★, *Cookin' Together* (Prestige 1964)★★★, *Sax, Strings & Soul* (Prestige 1964)★★★, *Red Soul* (Prestige 1966)★★★, with Sonny Stitt *Just Friends* (1977)★★★, *Red Holloway And Company* (Concord 1986)★★★, with Carmen McRae *Fine And Mellow* (1987)★★★★, with Clark Terry *Locksmith Blues* (Concord 1988)★★, with Knut Riisnaes *The Gemini Twins* (1992)★★★.

Holloway, Stanley

b. Stanley Augustus Holloway, 1 October 1890, London, England, d. 30 January 1982, Littlehampton, Sussex, England. A much-loved comedian, actor, singer, at the age of 10 Holloway was performing professionally as Master Stanley Holloway-The Wonderful Boy Soprano. He then toured in concert parties before studying in Milan for a period in 1913 with the intention of becoming an opera singer. After serving in the Connaught Rangers during World War I, Holloway played the music halls and made his London stage musical debut as Captain Wentworth in *Kissing Time* at the Winter Garden Theatre in 1919. This was followed by roles in *A Night Out* (1920), ***Hit The Deck*** (1927), *Song Of The Sea* (1928) and *Coo-ee* (1929). During the 20s Holloway received much acclaim for his appearances in several editions of the renowned *Co-Optimists* shows which were produced at various London theatres, beginning with the Royalty in London in 1921, and toured the provinces. He also became extremely popular on radio, especially for his monologues which involved characters such as Albert, who is eventually eaten by a lion at a zoo; and soldier Sam, who refuses to participate in the Battle of Waterloo until he has been approached by the Duke of Wellington himself. Throughout the 30s and 40s he continued to appear in the West End in revues and musicals such as *Savoy Follies, Three Sisters, Here We Are Again, All Wave, London Rhapsody, Up And Doing* and *Fine And Dandy*. He also worked occasionally in the straight theatre, and it was while playing the role of Bottom in *A Midsummer Summer Night's Dream* in New York that Holloway was offered the role of philosophical dustman Alfred P. Doolittle in **Alan Jay Lerner** and **Frederick Loewe**'s musical, *My Fair Lady*, which opened on Broadway in March 1956. It proved to be the highlight of his career, and his ebullient performance of the show-stopping numbers 'Get Me To The Church On Time' and 'I'm Getting Married In The Morning' earned him a Tony nomination. He reprised his role in the 1958 London production, and again in the 1964 film for which he was nominated for an Oscar. Holloway's film career had begun in 1921 with *The Rotters*, a comedy, as were many of the other upwards of 60 films he made. He is particularly renowned for his outstanding work in the series of postwar Ealing comedies such as *Passport To Pimlico, The Lavender Hill Mob* and *The Titfield Thunderbolt*, but also shone in more serious pictures such as *This Happy Breed* and *The Way Ahead* (both 1944), *Brief Encounter* (1945), *No Love For Johnnie* (1961) and the musicals *Champagne Charlie* (1944) in which he co-starred with another top comic, Tommy Trinder, and *The Beggar's Opera* (1952) with Laurence Olivier. Holloway was awarded the OBE in 1960, and two years later found nationwide fame in the USA when he starred as an English butler trying to come to terms with the American way of life in the television situation comedy *Our Man Higgins*. From then on he continued to be active, making films and occasional stage appearances, and in 1977 toured Australia and the Far East in a tribute to **Noël Coward** entitled *The Pleasure Of His Company*. After a long and distinguished career, he is said to have told his actor son Julian that his only regret was that he had not been asked to do the voice-over for a television commercial extolling the virtues of Mr. Kipling's cakes.

● ALBUMS: *Famous Adventires With Old Sam And The Ramsbottoms* (Columbia 1956)★★★, *'Ere's 'Olloway* (Philips 1959)★★★, *Join In The Chorus* (Nixa 1961)★★★, *Stanley Holloway's Concert Party* (Riverside 1962)★★★, *Stanley, I Presume* (Columbia 60s).

● COMPILATIONS: *World Of* (Decca 1971)★★★, *Best Of* (Encore 1979)★★★, *More Monologues And Songs* (Encore 1980)★★★, *Brahn Boots* (Decca 1982)★★★, *Many Happy Returns* (Movie Stars 1989)★★★, *Nostalgic Memories* (Savage 1989)★★★.

● FURTHER READING: *Wiv A Little Bit O' Luck*, Stanley Holloway.

Holly And The Italians

Holly Beth Vincent (b. Chicago, Illinois, USA) formed the band in Los Angeles, California, in 1978 with herself on vocals and guitar, Mark Henry on bass, and New York-born Steve Young on drums. Feeling more affinity with the UK music scene, they flew to London shortly after their inauguration. There they met disc jockey Charlie Gillett and signed to his Oval label, releasing 'Tell That Girl To Shut Up', which was later covered by **Transvision Vamp**. They played around the pub and club circuit before coming to prominence as support to **Blondie**. Signed to **Virgin Records**, they recorded two fine new wave pop singles in 'Miles Away' and 'Youth Coup', with a debut album produced by Richard Gottehrer. However, soon after its release the group split, leaving behind just two further singles. Vincent moved on to pursue a solo career, with the confusingly titled album *Holly And The Italians*, which was credited solely to Holly Beth Vincent. She duetted with **Joey Ramone** on 'I Got You Babe', alongside further solo singles for Virgin. After a brief spell replacing Patty Donahue in the **Waitresses**, she appeared in an *ad hoc* combo called the Wild Things with Anthony Thistlethwaite of the **Waterboys**. They provided a track, 'Siberian Miles', for the fanzine *What A Nice Way To Turn 17*, with Vincent doing her best to sound like Peter Perrett (**Only Ones**). In 1995, she collaborated with Johnette Napolitano on the eclectic *Vowel Movement*.

● ALBUMS: *The Right To Be Italian* (Virgin 1981)★★★.
Solo: Holly Beth Vincent *Holly And The Italians* (Virgin 1982)★★★, *Vowel Movement* (1995)★★★.

Holly, Buddy

b. Charles Hardin Holley, 7 September 1936, Lubbock, Texas, USA, d. 3 February 1959. Holly was one of the first major rock 'n' roll groundbreakers, and one of its most influential artists. He wrote his own songs, recorded with a self-contained guitar-bass-drums combo, experimented in the studio and even changed the image of what a rock singer could look like: until he came along, the idea of a bespectacled rock idol was unthinkable. Holly's hiccupping vocal style and mature, melodic compositions inspired many of the rockers who would emerge in the 60s and 70s, from the **Beatles** and **Bob Dylan** to the **Hollies**. Later, British singer-songwriter **Elvis Costello** would emerge with an unabashed Holly-inspired physical appearance. Like many other early rock 'n' rollers, Holly's musical influences included both C&W music and 'race' music, or R&B. He made his first stage appearance at the age of five, joining with his brothers Larry and Travis in a talent contest; he won $5. During his childhood, Holly learned to play guitar, violin and piano, taking formal lessons but teaching himself boogie-woogie rhythms on the piano. At 12 years old he was entertaining friends with **Hank Williams** songs and in 1949 formed a bluegrass duo, Buddy And Bob, with friend Bob Montgomery. He learned to play banjo and mandolin during this period. Holly made his first recording on a home tape recorder in 1949, a song called 'My Two Timin' Woman'.

By 1952 Buddy And Bob had become popular around Lubbock; recording two songs together at Holly's home that year and another in 1953. In September of that year Buddy And Bob appeared on KDAV radio, performing two numbers. Adding Larry Welborn on bass, they were given their own programme, *The Buddy And Bob Show*. They performed country material primarily, but occasionally included an R&B song by artists such as **Hank Ballard**. KDAV disc jockey Hipockets Duncan became the trio's manager and secured work for them in the West Texas area. Further recording took place at KDAV but none of it was released. In 1954 the trio added fiddler **Sonny Curtis** and steel guitarist Don Guess to the group, and together made more recordings in Lubbock and at Nesman Recording Studio in Wichita Falls, Texas. That year the group, now including drummer Jerry Allison, opened concerts for **Bill Haley And His Comets** and **Elvis Presley** in Texas. Holly was impressed by Presley and began thinking about performing in the new rock 'n' roll style. However, in the meantime he continued to play country.

In December 1955 Nashville agent Eddie Crandall requested of KDAV disc jockey Dave Stone that Holly and his group record four demo songs, believing he could secure them a contract with **Decca Records**. The group, now minus Montgomery, sent five songs, and Decca brought them to Nashville where they recorded four songs produced by **Owen Bradley** at Bradley's Barn Studio on 26 January 1956. Decca issued 'Blue Days, Black Nights', backed with 'Love Me', under the name Buddy Holly And The Three Tunes (the Crickets were not contracted to Decca at this time), in April. Several other records were recorded in two sessions for Decca during the autumn of 1956, but Holly, dissatisfied with Decca's insistence that he continue to play country music, together with the loss of his group to insensitive sessionmen, left the label in September. Later that year, Holly, Allison and Welborn went to Clovis, New Mexico, where they recorded two songs with Norman Petty at his NorVaJak studio. Upon returning to Lubbock, Holly formed the **Crickets** with Allison and Niki Sullivan on rhythm guitar. On 25 February 1957 they went back to Clovis and recorded a rock 'n' roll version of Holly's 'That'll Be The Day', a song from their period in Nashville. The song was a revelation and contained one of the most gripping vocals and distinctive galloping riffs of any record released during the 50s. Joe B. Mauldin joined as the Crickets' bassist following those sessions. A number of record companies turned down the song until it was issued by **Brunswick Records** in May, ironically a division of Decca, of which Coral Records was another subsidiary, although artistically idependent. With Petty as manager, the single underwent heavy promotion until it reached number 1 in September 1957. It also reached number 1 in the UK. Just as the record was being released, the Crickets performed at such venues as the **Apollo** Theatre in New York and the Howard Theater in Washington, DC, winning over predominantly black audiences and helping to further break down racial barriers in rock. They spent the next three months touring the USA.

The group recorded prolifically in 1957, including such indisputable classics as 'Words Of Love', 'Maybe Baby', 'Not Fade Away', 'Everyday', 'Peggy Sue' (named after Allison's girlfriend) and 'Oh Boy'. Holly was innovative in the studio, making much use of newly available production techniques, such as overdubbing vocals and double-tracking guitar parts. The vocals on 'Peggy Sue' were a typical example of Holly's technique. Although simple in structure and execution, Holly somehow managed to recite the words 'Peggy Sue' differently in every line, as if fascinated by the very syllables of her name. A seemingly straightforward song like 'Everyday' is similarly transformed by the ingenious use of a celeste (played by Petty's wife, Vi) and the decision to include Jerry Allison slapping his knee, in place of drums. Brunswick continued to issue recordings under the Crickets name while Holly signed on as a solo artist to Coral Records. Despite this, most releases featured the entire group, often with other musicians (Vi Petty on piano) and a vocal group (the Picks). Of these releases, 'Peggy Sue' reached number 3 in the USA and 'Oh Boy' number 10 during 1957. Contrary to the legend, Holly and the Crickets only charted 11 times in the USA during their brief career. No albums charted during Holly's lifetime. The Crickets closed 1957 with an appearance on the influential *Ed Sullivan* Show and again in January 1958, by which time Holly had left the group. In late January the Crickets recorded 'Rave On' in New York and then toured Australia for six days. Further Clovis recording sessions, including 'Well...All Right' occupied February. This was followed by a UK tour beginning on 2 March at the Trocadero in London, which also included appearances on the UK television programmes *Sunday Night At The London Palladium* and *Off The Record*. The UK tour finished on 25 March at the Hammersmith Gaumont. Holly and the group enjoyed immense popularity in Britain, with nine top 10 singles. 'Maybe Baby' became the fourth Holly/Crickets single to chart in the USA in March, eventually peaking at number 17 (and number 4 in the UK). The group returned to the USA in late March and immediately embarked on a US tour instigated by disc jockey **Alan Freed**, also featuring such popular artists as **Jerry Lee Lewis** and **Chuck Berry**. Coral released the frantic 'Rave On' in May and although it reached only number 37 in the USA, it made number 5 in the UK. Following the tour, on 19 June, Holly recorded two songs written by **Bobby Darin** in New York without the Crickets; they remained unreleased but signalled an impending rift between Holly and the group. While in New York Holly met Maria Elena Santiago, whom he married two months later. During that summer Holly returned to Petty's studio in Clovis and recorded 'Heartbeat', 'Love's Made A Fool Of You' and 'Wishing'. Guitarist Tommy Allsup played on the latter two and was subsequently asked to join the Crickets. During September sessions in Clovis, extra musicians including saxophonist **King Curtis** and guitarist **Phil Everly** joined Holly. **Waylon Jennings**, then unknown, provided backing vocals on one track; during the same period, Holly produced Jennings' debut single. By September three more Holly/Crickets singles had charted in the USA, but none fared very well.

Holly and the Crickets toured the north-east and Canada during October, by which time there was apparently friction between the Hollys and the Pettys. Buddy and Maria Holly travelled separately from the group between dates. During the trip, Holly decided to try recording with strings, but prior to returning to New York for that session in October 1958, he announced to manager/producer Petty that he was leaving him. To Holly's surprise the other Crickets chose to leave Holly and remain with Petty; Holly allowed them use of the group's name and they continued to record without him (Sonny Curtis joined the group after Holly's death). Meanwhile, on 21 October, Holly, producer Dick Jacobs and studio musicians (including a string section) recorded 'True Love Ways', 'It Doesn't Matter Anymore' (written by **Paul Anka**), 'Raining In My Heart' and 'Moondreams'. They were held for later release while 'It's So Easy' was released; it failed to chart in the USA. 'Heartbeat' was issued in December and became the last Holly single to chart in the USA during his lifetime. The superb 'It Doesn't Matter Anymore' was released posthumously and its lyrics betrayed an unintended elegiac mood in light of the singer's fate. The song provided Holly with his only UK number 1 hit and served as a perfect memorial. The flip-side, 'Raining In My Heart', was equally inventive, with a touching melody reinforced by the orchestral arrangement in which strings were used to startling effect to suggest tearful raindrops.

In December 1958 Holly, now living in New York with his wife, recorded six songs at home on his tape recorder, presumably to be re-recorded in the studio at a later date. During Christmas Holly returned to Lubbock and appeared on radio station KLLL with Jennings. Back in New York during January 1959 he made other demos at home by himself. That month he began assembling a band to take on the 'Winter Dance Party' tour of the US Midwest. Allsup was hired on guitar, Jennings on bass and Carl Bunch on drums. They were billed as the Crickets despite the agreement to give Holly's former bandmates that name. Also starring **Ritchie Valens**, the **Big Bopper**, **Dion And The Belmonts** and the unknown Frankie Sardo, the tour began on 23 January 1959 in Milwaukee, Wisconsin. On the afternoon of 1 February the tour played in Green Bay, Wisconsin, but an evening show was cancelled owing to bad weather. The 2 February date at the Surf Ballroom in Clear Lake, Iowa, went ahead. It was following this show that Holly, Valens and the Big Bopper chartered a small plane to take them to the next date in Moorhead, Minnesota, rather than travel on the tour bus, which had a defective heater and had previously broken down several times. In the dark early hours of a freezing cold morning and as a result of the snowy weather, the plane crashed minutes after take-off, killing all three stars and the pilot. (The tour actually continued after their deaths, with **Bobby Vee**, **Jimmy Clanton** and **Frankie Avalon** filling in.)

Holly's popularity increased after his death, and his influence continues to this day. Even as late as the 80s unreleased material was still being released. Several of the posthumous releases fared particularly well in the UK. In 1962 Norman Petty took the demos Holly had recorded at home in 1958 and had the instrumental group the **Fireballs** play along to them, creating new Buddy Holly records from the unfinished tapes. In 1965, *Holly In The Hills*, comprised of the early Buddy and Bob radio station recordings, was released and charted in the UK. Compilation albums also charted in both the USA and the UK, as late as the 70s. During the 70s the publishing rights to Holly's song catalogue were purchased by **Paul McCartney**, who began sponsoring annual Buddy Holly Week celebrations. A Buddy Holly Memorial Society was also formed in the USA to commemorate the singer. In 1978, a film called *The Buddy Holly Story*, starring actor Gary Busey as Holly, premiered; members of the Crickets, in particular, denounced it as containing many inaccurate scenes. The following year, a six-record boxed set called *The Complete Buddy Holly* was released in the UK (it was issued in the USA two years later). A 1983 release, *For The First Time Anywhere*, contained original Holly recordings prior to overdubbing. As of the early 90s a group called the Crickets, which included at least one original member (and usually more), was still touring. In 1990, *Buddy*, a musical play that had previously been staged in London, opened on Broadway in New York. Buddy Holly's legacy lives on, not only with tributes such as these, but in the dozens of cover versions of his songs that have been recorded over the years. Holly was an initial inductee into the **Rock And Roll Hall of Fame** in 1986. To have a catalogue of songs of this calibre behind him at the age of 22 was remarkable. How would he have approached the 60s and subsequent decades? Such was the quality of his work that few could doubt that he would have lasted the course.

● ALBUMS: *The 'Chirping' Crickets* (Brunswick 1957)★★★★, *Buddy Holly* (Coral 1958)★★★★, *That'll Be The Day* (Decca 1958)★★★★, *The Buddy Holly Story* (Coral 1959)★★★★★, *The Buddy Holly Story, Volume 2* (Coral 1960)★★★★★, *Buddy Holly And The Crickets* (Coral 1963)★★★★, *Reminiscing* (Coral 1963)★★★★, *Showcase* (Coral 1964)★★★★, *Holly In The Hills* (Coral 1965)★★★★, *The Great Buddy Holly* (Vocalion 1967)★★★★, *Giant* (Coral 1969)★★★★, *Remember* (Coral 1971)★★★, *Good Rockin'* (Vocalion 1971)★★★, *A Rock And Roll Collection* (Decca 1972)★★★, *The Nashville Sessions* (MCA 1975)★★★★,

Western And Bop (Coral 1977)★★, *For The First Time Anywhere* (MCA 1983)★★★, *From The Original Master Tapes* (MCA 1985)★★★★★, *Something Special From Buddy Holly* (Rollercoaster 1986)★★★★, Buddy Holly And The Picks *Original Voices Of The Crickets* (1993)★★★★.

● COMPILATIONS: *The Best Of Buddy Holly* (Coral 1966)★★★★, *Buddy Holly's Greatest Hits* (Coral 1967)★★★★, *Rave On* (MFP 1975)★★★, *20 Golden Greats* (MCA 1978)★★★★★, *The Complete Buddy Holly* 6-LP box set (Coral 1979)★★★★★, *Love Songs* (MCA 1981)★★★, *Legend* (MCA 1985)★★★★, *Buddy Holly Rocks* (Charly 1985)★★★, *Buddy Holly* (Castle 1986)★★★, *True Love Ways* (Telstar 1989)★★★★, *Words Of Love* (Polygram 1993)★★★★, *The Singles Collection 1957-1960* (Pickwick 1994)★★★, *The Very Best Of Buddy Holly* (Dino 1996)★★★★.

● FURTHER READING: *Buddy Holly*, Dave Laing. *Buddy Holly: A Biography In Words Photographs And Music*, Elizabeth Peer and Ralph Peer. *Buddy Holly: His Life And Music*, John Goldrosen. *The Buddy I Knew*, Larry Holley. *The Buddy Holly Story*, John Goldrosen. *Buddy Holly And The Crickets*, Alan Clark. *Buddy Holly: 30th Anniversary Memorial Series No 1*, Alan Clark. *The Legend That Is Buddy Holly*, Richard Peters. *Buddy Holly, Alan Mann's A-Z*, Alan Mann. *Buddy Holly: A Biography*, Ellis Amburn. *Remembering Buddy*, John Goldrosen and John Beecher. *Buddy The Biography* (UK) *Rave On* (USA), Phillip Norman. *Memories Of Buddy Holly*, Jim Dawson and Spencer Leigh.

Holly, Doyle

b. Hoyle F. Hendricks, 30 June 1936, Perkins, Oklahoma, USA. Holly worked in oilfields in Kansas, Oklahoma and California and made some of his first musical appearances as a member of **Johnny Burnette**'s band. Between 1963 and 1970, a fine guitarist, he was a regular member of **Buck Owens**' Buckeroos, playing bass guitar and singing harmony as well as solo vocals. He also appeared on many of Owens' recordings. Holly sings a fine solo version of 'Streets Of Laredo' on Owens' 1965 *I've Got A Tiger By The Tail*. In 1970, he decided to form his own band, the Vanishing Breed. He signed to Barnaby Records and made his chart debut in 1972 with 'My Heart Cries For You'. The following year, he registered the first charted version of 'Queen Of The Silver Dollar' and his only Top 20 success, 'Lila', which reached number 17 in 1973. His last chart entries came in 1974, when he had three minor hits, including 'Just Another Cowboy Song'. Holly later played with other bands but nothing has been heard of him in recent years.

● ALBUMS: *Doyle Holly* (Barnaby 1973)★★★, *Just Another Cowboy Song* (Barnaby 1973)★★★.

Hollywood Argyles

The Hollywood Argyles was a group assembled after a record, 'Alley Oop', had already been released under that name. The song was written by **Dallas Frazier** and recorded by vocalist **Gary S. Paxton** and producer Bobby Rey while Paxton was a member of the Arizona-based duo **Skip And Flip**. Because that duo was contracted to Brent Records, and 'Alley Oop' was issued on Lute Records, the name Hollywood Argyles was created for the occasion, named after the intersection where the recording studio was located, Hollywood Boulevard and Argyle Street. When the **Coasters**-like novelty single made its way to number 1 in the US charts in May 1960, a group was created, including Paxton, Rey, Ted Marsh, Gary Webb, Deary Weaver and Ted Winters. Further singles by the Hollywood Argyles, on such labels as Paxley (co-owned by Paxton and producer **Kim Fowley**), Chattahoochie, Felsted and Kammy failed to reach the charts. Paxton later started the Garpax label, which released the number 1 'Monster Mash' by **Bobby 'Boris' Pickett**. More recently, as a born-again Christian, Paxton was rumoured to be romantically linked with fallen US evangelist Tammy Faye Bakker.

● ALBUMS: *The Hollywood Argyles* (Lute 1960)★★★.

Hollywood Beyond

Essentially the creation of Mark Rogers, this English artist made an immediate impression in 1986 with the release of the superior pop single, 'What's The Colour Of Money'. In the UK it reached number 7 in July and established Hollywood Beyond as one of the year's top newcomers. He was bullish about its charms. 'It's modern, it's 86, it's challenging. It's 'pop' but not 'pap'. It's artistic without being intellectual. It's vibrant without being blasé, it's unique without being original.' The song actually reflected Rogers' background, being brought up on his parents' reggae and jazz records before he became aware of rock music as a schoolboy. This musicality was reflected in his ability to play classical piano and guitar by the time he was a teenager. However, 'What's The Colour Of Money' proved hard to follow-up. Only one further single, 'No More Tears', reached the Top 50 in September 1986. A debut album followed, but neither *If* nor the singles 'After Midnight' and 'Save Me' secured any further chart reward.

● ALBUMS: *If* (WEA 1987)★★.

Hollywood Brats

In 1973 the Hollywood Brats came together in London and recorded an album that would later be cited as one of the most influential of the punk era, even though it was not released in the UK until 1980. The group was led by Canadian vocalist Andrew Matheson, but arguably their strength was Norwegian keyboard player Casino Steel. The rest of the band was Eunan Brady (guitar), Wayne Manor (bass) and Louis Sparks (drums). *Hollywood Brats* featured elements of the **Flamin' Groovies** and the **New York Dolls** welded to the ethos of the new wave, which endeared it to European fans and consequently some copies crept into the UK. However, by the time **Cherry Red Records** finally issued their 1979 single, the memorable 'Then He Kissed Me', and the album the following year, the band had gone their separate ways. Matheson was still recording with Brady, helping out in-between spells with the Tools and **Wreckless Eric**'s Last Orders. Steel joined the infamous **London SS** and played at a couple of rehearsals before Mat Dangerfield dragged him away to help form the **Boys** in June 1976.

● ALBUMS: *Hollywood Brats* (Cherry Red 1980)★★★.

Hollywood Fats

b. Michael Mann, 17 March 1954, d. December 1986, Los Angeles, California, USA. Hollywood Fats must be considered the father of the modern west-coast blues guitar. Having dropped out of school, he spent years on the road where he played with artists including **J.B. Hutto**, **John Lee Hooker**, **Albert King** and **Muddy Waters**. When Fats returned to Los Angeles he formed the Hollywood Fats Band in the mid-70s. In 1979 the group, which included Larry Taylor (ex-**Canned Heat**), Al Blake, Fred Kaplan and Richard Innes, recorded *Hollywood Fats*. Two years later Fats joined the band of his friend **James Harman** and recorded several albums, and later recorded with Smokey Wilson (*88th Street Blues* 1983), **Rod Piazza** (*Harpburn* 1986), and **William Clarke** (*Tip Of The Top* 1987). In 1986 Hollywood Fats was drafted into the **Blasters**, with whom he spent his final months before suffering a fatal heart attack at the age of 32.

● ALBUMS: *Hollywood Fats* (Stomp 1979)★★★, with James Harman Band *Those Dangerous Gentlemens* (Rhino 1987)★★★, with Harman *Extra Napkins* (Rivera 1988)★★★, with Harman *Strictly Live...In '85 Volume One* (Rivera 1990)★★★, *Rock This House* (Black Top 1993)★★★.

Hollywood Flames

Formed as the Flames in 1949, this R&B group went through a variety of name changes - Four Flames, Hollywood Four Flames, Jets, Ebbtides and Satellites - during its career. However, it was as the Hollywood Flames that they had their biggest success, the 1957 hit 'Buzz, Buzz, Buzz'. The song was written by founding member Bobby Byrd, who also had a solo career as **Bobby Day**. The vocal on the song was not by Day, however, but by group member Earl Nelson, who also recorded as **Jackie Lee** and as half of **Bob And Earl**. The other members of the group at the time of the hit, which reached number 11 in the US pop charts and number 5 in the R&B charts, were founding member David Ford and baritone Curtis Williams, co-writer of the hit 'Earth Angel' and a former member of the group that recorded it, the **Penguins**. 'Buzz, Buzz, Buzz' was released on Ebb Records, run by Lee Rupe, wife of **Specialty Records** owner Art Rupe. Released in November 1957, the single spent 17 weeks in the charts. Follow-up singles were issued under Day's name, but by 1959 Ebb had folded. The group continued to record with various personnel for several years.

● COMPILATIONS: *The Hollywood Flames* (Specialty 1992)★★★.

Hollywood Hotel

A slice of Hollywood hokum starring crooner **Dick Powell** and directed by **Busby Berkeley**. The film's wan plot is centred around a small-town boy's attempt to hit the bigtime via a radio show broadcast from the hotel of the title. The film's one virtue for the fans of big band swing (and quite a big virtue at that) is the appearance of the current sensation of the era, **Benny Goodman** And His Orchestra. The quartet of Goodman, **Teddy Wilson**, **Lionel Hampton** and **Gene Krupa** is featured. Showing an integrated group like this on screen in 1937 was as much a departure for Hollywood as it was for the music business when Goodman first presented Wilson a year earlier. The quartet plays 'I've Got A Heartful Of Music' and the big band, including **Harry James**, **Ziggy Elman**, **Chris Griffin**, **Murray McEachern**, Red Ballard, **Vido Musso**, **Hymie Schertzer** and **Jess Stacy**, performs several numbers including the film's title song and a short, breakneck version of the Goodman-Krupa showstopper, 'Sing, Sing, Sing'.

Holm, June

b. 14 June 1925, Brisbane, Queensland, Australia (but grew up on a farm by the Clarence River in New South Wales), d. 31 December 1966. One of the first female Australian country artists, and in spite of her relatively short career, she is held in very high esteem by followers of the music for her excellent guitar playing and exceptionally clear vocals and yodelling. Her mother played steel guitar and ukulele but it is claimed that June taught herself to play guitar while riding her pony to school, and only took up singing and yodelling in protest of the fact that all the popular country music singers were men. She made her first public appearance in 1935 and for a time sang with Beverley Thorn, mainly featuring Hawaiian-type music; however, Holm leaned more towards hillbilly music, and the duo split in 1939. She recorded some radio transcription discs that year and appeared on **ABC**. In the early 40s, she established herself and during the war years, working with a Red Cross entertainment unit, she was very popular with Australian servicemen. On 28 January 1942, she made her only six recordings, which included 'Happy Yodelling Cowgirl' and 'Daddy Was A Yodelling Cowboy'. In view of the popularity of her records and the fact that she remained active on stage and radio for several years after making them, it is strange that she made no further recordings. After the war, she toured all the Australian states with a Stage Spectacular show. In 1948, she married a man called Hayes (Leo or Tom), a government official, whose work took him to various overseas postings, and they spent some years in Nigeria and Suva. She appeared on Brisbane radio in 1958 but retired from entertaining two years later. Tragedy struck when her mother and father died and then, early in 1966, her husband died suddenly, leaving her three months pregnant with twins. She became very depressed and underwent medical treatment. She died on 31 December 1966, as a result of an overdose of barbiturates - whether accidental or deliberate is still open to conjecture. She was buried in an unmarked grave on 3 January 1967, the day before the twins celebrated their first birthday, leaving them and her other three children orphans. In 1980, an EP was released to raise funds to provide a memorial for her grave and in December 1981, her six recordings, plus a souvenir booklet and six songs by Zeta Burns (who had fronted the memorial campaign), were released. June Holm was known as Australia's Yodelling Cowgirl and the three Regal-Zonophone 78s of her recordings are now collectable records.

● COMPILATIONS: *Songs To Be Remembered* (Queensland Country Style 1981)★★★.

Holm, Michael

b. Lothar Walter 29 July 1943, Germany. Having gained some recognition as a songwriter in his native Germany, Holm decided that it would do no harm to try some records under his own name on Ariola Records. his most memorable hit came with a version of **Doug Sahm**'s 'Mendocino' to which he had added German lyrics. Released in autumn 1969, it climbed to number 3 to linger in the German national Top 10 for almost three months, selling a million copies within a year. In 1974 he reached the top of the German charts with 'Tränen Lügen Nicht' and now continues as a sucessful composer and producer.

Holman, Bill

b. 21 May 1927, Olive, California, USA. After studying at Westlake College, California, in the late 40s, tenor saxophonist Holman played in **Charlie Barnet**'s big band for three years, and then for four years with **Stan Kenton**. During this period Holman was not only playing but also contributing extensively to the Kenton band's book, his charts being amongst the most swinging Kenton ever played. In common with many other Kentonians of the time, Holman was also active in the various small groups experimenting on the west coast. Among the musicians with whom he worked, and sometimes recorded, were **Shorty Rogers**, **Conte Candoli**, **Art Pepper** and **Shelly Manne** (whose Blackhawk band used a Holman tune, 'A Gem From Tiffany', as their theme). He subsequently wrote for **Count Basie**, **Louie Bellson**, **Maynard Ferguson**, **Woody Herman** and **Gerry Mulligan**. His arrangements were also popular with the Boston-based band of **Herb Pomeroy**. During the late 50s he formed occasional big bands for record dates, but then came a 27-year spell during which Holman was active only in the studios. He still wrote jazz charts, however, notably for the Basie and **Buddy Rich** bands, and in these intervening years he often arranged for pop musicians too (e.g. 'Aquarius' by **Fifth Dimension**). It was not until 1975 that he reformed a big band specifically to play his own arrangements and compositions, and another 13 years elapsed before his band was eventually recorded. A

sometimes overlooked arranger, Holman's contribution to latterday big band music has nonetheless been considerable.

● ALBUMS: *The Bill Holman Octet* (1954)★★★, *The Fabulous Bill Holman* (1957)★★, *In A Jazz Orbit* (1958)★★★, *Bill Holman's Great Big Band* (Creative World 1960)★★★, *World Class Music* (1987)★★★, *Bill Holman Band* (Fresh Sounds 1988)★★★★, *Jive For Five* (VSOP 1988)★★, *A View From The Side* (JVC 1995)★★★, *Brilliant Corners: The Music Of Thelonious Monk* (JVC 1998)★★★★.

Holman, Eddie

b. 3 June 1946, Norfolk, Virginia, USA. Holman's claim to fame was the 1969 soul ballad 'Hey There Lonely Girl', sung in a piercing falsetto style. Holman began playing keyboards and guitar as a child and studied music at schools in New York City and Pennsylvania. He first recorded in 1962 for the small Leopard Records and later with the **Cameo/Parkway** company. He collected minor chart hits for that company and then signed with **ABC** in 1968. 'Hey There Lonely Girl' was a remake of a song originally recorded by **Ruby And The Romantics** as 'Hey There Lonely Boy'. Holman changed the gender and took the song to number 2 in the US charts in 1970. Four years later the song reached number 4 in the UK. He continued to have lesser R&B hits on the Parkway label with 'This Can't Be True' (1965) and 'I'm A Loser' (1966). Releases during the early 70s kept the singer in the US soul chart while his career enjoyed a brief revival in 1977 with 'This Will Be A Night To Remember' and 'You Make My Life Complete'. He recorded on such labels as **Polydor** and Salsoul in the 70s and recorded for his own label, Agape, as a Christian artist in the early 90s.

● ALBUMS: *I Love You* (ABC 1969)★★★, *Night To Remember* (1977)★★, *United* (New Cross 1985)★★.

Holman, Libby

b. Elsbeth Holzman, 23 May 1904, Cincinnati, Ohio, USA, d. 18 June 1971, Stamford, Connecticut, USA. Holman was regarded by some as the first great white torch singer, and by others as 'a dark purple menace', because of her tempestuous private life. She played minor roles in Broadway musicals such as **Richard Rodgers** and **Lorenz Hart**'s *The Garrick Gaieties* (1925), but became a featured star in *Merry-Go-Round* (1927), and *Rainbow* (1928), in which she gave a languorous performance of 'I Want A Man'. After making the US Top 10 in 1929 with 'Am I Blue?', she was acclaimed a major star following her performance in *The Little Show*, in which she sang 'Can't We Be Friends' and 'Moanin' Low'. Holman received rave reviews for her sultry renditions of 'Body And Soul' and 'Something To Remember Me By' in *Three's A Crowd* (1930). Her career declined following the shooting of her husband Zachary Smith Reynolds. She was accused of his murder but the case was declared *nolle prosequi*, and never came to court. Holman returned to Broadway in *Revenge With Music* (1934), in which she introduced **Arthur Schwartz** and **Howard Dietz**'s insinuating 'You And The Night And The Music', and subsequently appeared in **Cole Porter**'s *You Never Know* (1938). Sadly, she never achieved her former heights. During the early 40s she caused a furore by appearing as a double-act with black folk singer **Josh White**, playing clubs and concerts in an era when a black male and white female stage relationship was frowned upon by many bookers and critics. Holman continued touring during the 50s presenting a programme called *Blues, Ballads And Sin Songs*, but still controversy followed her when she befriended ill-fated screen idol, Montgomery Clift. Mainly inactive in her later years, Holman is said to have died of carbon monoxide poisoning.

● COMPILATIONS: *The Legendary Libby Holman* (Evergreen 1965)★★★, *Something To Remember Her By* (1979)★★★.

● FURTHER READING: *Libby*, Milt Machlin. *Dreams That Money Can Buy: The Tragic Life Of Libby Holman*, Jon Bradshaw.

Holmes Brothers

Sherman Holmes (b. 29 September 1939, Plainfield, New Jersey, USA), Wendell Holmes (b. 19 December 1943, Plainfield, New Jersey, USA), Popsy Dixon (b. 26 July 1942, Virginia Beach, Virginia, USA) and Gib Wharton (b. 15 September 1955, Mineral Wells, Texas, USA). The Holmes Brothers took almost three decades to become an overnight sensation. Both Sherman and Wendell sang in the church choir in Christchurch (now Salud), Virginia, where they grew up. Sherman studied clarinet and piano before taking up the bass he plays onstage, while Wendell learned trumpet, organ and guitar. In 1959, Sherman took a break from studying music theory and composition at Virginia State University to visit New York and never returned south. When Wendell graduated from high school in 1963, his brother brought him to New York.

After working with **Jimmy Jones** and **Charlie And Inez Foxx**, they formed their own band, the Sevilles, which lasted from 1963 to 1966, after which they worked in a variety of Top 40 bands. The Holmes Brothers band finally came together in 1980, when they were joined by drummer Popsy Dixon, who subsequently proved to be the possessor of a strong tenor voice. Steel guitarist Geb Wharton played in Texas country groups until he decided to move to New York in 1988. The band's albums reveal the breadth of their repertoire, which they have claimed contains some 250 songs. Their long experience of playing all forms of popular music has enabled them to fuse elements of gospel, C&W, R&B and soul and present them in an easily assimilable form.

● ALBUMS: *In The Spirit* (Rounder 1989)★★★, *Where It's At* (Rounder 1991)★★★★, *Soul Street* (Rounder 1993)★★★, *Lotto Land: Original Soundtrack Recording* (Stony Plain 1996)★★, *Promised Land* (Rounder 1997)★★★.

Holmes, Charlie

b. 27 January 1910, Boston, Massachusetts, USA, d. 12 September 1985. Holmes started out on oboe, and gained acceptance to the Boston Civic Symphony Orchestra. Later, influenced by his childhood friend and neighbour, **Johnny Hodges**, he switched to alto saxophone. In 1927, in company with another friend and neighbour, **Harry Carney**, he went to New York. Over the next year he played with several bands, including those led by **Chick Webb** and **Luis Russell**. He spent much of the next ten years with Russell, recording with many leading jazzmen, including **Joe 'King' Oliver**, **Red Allen** and **Louis Armstrong**. In the early 40s Holmes played with **Cootie Williams**'s band and later in the decade was with **John Kirby** and **Billy Kyle**. Early in the 50s he retired from music, but played occasional gigs in New York. In the 70s he was again active in music, playing with **Clyde Bernhardt** and the Harlem Blues And Jazz Band.

● ALBUMS: with Clyde Bernhardt *More Blues And Jazz From Harlem* (1973)★★★, with Bernhardt *Sittin' On Top Of The World* (1975)★★★.

● COMPILATIONS: *Luis Russell And His Orchestra, 1926-1930/1930-1934* (1926-34)★★★★.

Holmes, Clint

b. 9 May 1946, Bournemouth, Dorset, England. Holmes is best remembered for one major hit, 'Playground In My Mind', in 1973. He was raised in Farnham, New York, USA, and began singing and acting as a child. He led a high school rock group and also studied music in college. His professional music career began upon his discharge from the army, at clubs in the Bahamas. There he met songwriters Paul Vance and Lee Pockriss, who offered Holmes their newest composition, 'Playground In My Mind'. Holmes considered it a novelty song, likely due to the inclusion of a child's vocal (by Vance's son, Philip), but recorded it despite those reservations, and after its release on Epic Records, it reached number 2 in the US. None of Holmes's subsequent releases charted. Holmes was still performing in clubs at the end of the 80s.

● ALBUMS: *Playground In My Mind* (1973)★★★.

Holmes, David

b. Belfast, Northern Ireland. House mixer, DJ and recording artist David Holmes is a former member of the Disco Evangelists. After the latter group's successes for **Positiva Records** ('De Niro', 'A New Dawn'), he recorded his first solo effort, 'Johnny Favourite', for **Warp Records**. An enormously popular DJ, Holmes also found time to collaborate with former **Dub Federation** musicians Andy Ellison and Pete Latham as one third of the Scubadevils. The latter two met him while performing at the Sugarsweet night-club. Together they recorded 'Celestial Symphony' for the *Trance Europe Express* compilation, which was also remixed for a **Novamute Records** 12-inch release. This was backed by Holmes solo on 'Ministry' (credited to

Death Before Disco). He has also recorded as the Well Charged Latinos ('Latin Prayer') and 4 Boy 1 Girl Action ('The Hawaian Death Stomp'). Holmes' remixing projects include commissions for the **Sandals** ('We Want To Live'), Robotman ('Do Da Doo'), **Fortran 5** ('Persian Blues', 'Time To Dream'), **Freaky Realistic** ('Koochie Ryder'), **Secret Knowledge** ('Sugar Daddy'), Abfahrt ('Come Into My Life'), Bahia Black ('Capitao Do Asfolto') and **Sabres Of Paradise** ('Smokebelch'). He was also partially behind Sugarsweet Records, the Belfast dance label, run with Ian McCready and Jim McDonald. As Holmes explained at the time: 'It's more of a front to feed our obsession with music, to put out what we like, when we like.' Releases on the label included the Arabic house excursions of Wah Wah Warrior (essentially Ian McCready), plus Holmes' Death Before Disco. However, when it was clear that Sugarsweet was not going to take off it was replaced by the Exploding Plastic Inevitable imprint. In 1994 Holmes signed with **Sabres Of Paradise** as a solo artist, but when that label's **Andy Weatherall** decided to rethink his strategy, he found a new home at **Go! Discs**. His debut album emerged in 1995, with Sarah Cracknell (ex-**Saint Etienne**) contributing to the quasi-James Bond theme, 'Gone', while elsewhere Holmes luxuriated in the possibilities of the long playing format by incorporating cinematic elements, Celtic flavours and ambient guitar (provided by **Steve Hillage**).
● ALBUMS: *This Film's Crap, Let's Slash The Seats* (Go! Discs 1995)★★★, *Let's Get Killed* (Go! Beat 1997)★★★.

Holmes, Richard 'Groove'

b. 2 May 1931, Camden, New Jersey, USA, d. 29 June 1991, St. Louis, Missouri, USA. A self-taught organist, early in his career Holmes worked along the east coast. A 1961 recording session with **Les McCann** and **Ben Webster** resulted in widespread interest in his work. He toured and recorded throughout the 60s, achieving widespread acceptance among mainstream and post-bop jazz audiences. Customarily working in a small group format, Holmes developed a solid working relationship with **Gene Ammons**, and their playing exemplified the soul-heavy, organ-tenor pairings that proliferated in the early and mid-60s. Displaying his wide-ranging interests, Holmes also played with big bands including that led by **Gerald Wilson**, with whom he made a fine album, and recorded with singer **Dakota Staton**. His powerful playing style, with its thrusting swing and booming bass notes lent itself to soul music but his playing had much more than this to offer. Later in his career Holmes's appeal to crossover audiences sometimes led to the unjustified indifference of many jazz fans. He understood the power of a simple riff and like **Jimmy Smith** and **Jimmy McGriff**, 'he had soul'.
● ALBUMS: *Richard Groove Holmes* (Pacific Jazz 1961)★★★, with Gene Ammons *Groovin' With Jug* (1961)★★★★, *Something Special* (Pacific Jazz 1962)★★★, *The Groove Holmes Trio* (1962)★★★, *The Groove Holmes Quintet* (1962)★★★, *After Hours* (Pacific Jazz 1962)★★★, *Groove*

Holmes With Onzy Matthews And His Orchestra (1964)★★★, *Book Of The Blues* (Warners 1964)★★★, *Soul Message* (Prestige 1965)★★★, *Tell It Like It Is* (Pacific Jazz 1966)★★★, *Living Soul* (Prestige 1966)★★★, *Misty* (Prestige 1966)★★★, *Spicy* (Prestige 1966)★★★, *Super Cool* (Prestige 1967)★★★, *Soul Message* (Prestige 1967)★★★, *Get Up And Get It* (Prestige 1967)★★★, *The Groover* (Prestige 1968)★★★, *That Healin' Feelin'* (Pretige 1968)★★★, *Welcome Home* (1968)★★★, *Blues Groove* (Prestige 1968)★★★, *Workin' On A Groovy Thing* (1969)★★★, with Gerald Wilson *You Better Believe It!* (60s)★★★, *Dakota Staton* (60s)★★★, *X-77* (c.1970)★★★, *Night Glider* (c.1973)★★, *Comin' On Home* (c.1974)★★, *Six Million Dollar Man* (1975)★★, *I'm In The Mood For Love* (c.1975)★★★, *Slippin' Out* (Muse 1977)★★★, *Star Wars-Close Encounters* (1977)★★, *Good Vibrations* (Muse 1977)★★★, *Nobody Does It Better* (Manhattan 1980)★★, *Broadway* (Muse 1980)★★, *Swedish Lullaby* (1984)★★★, *Hot Tat* (Muse 1989)★, *Blues All Day Long* (Muse 1992)★★★.
● COMPILATIONS: *The Best Of Richard Groove Holmes* (Prestige 1969)★★★.

Holmes, Rupert

b. 24 February 1947, Northwich, Cheshire, England. This American-based singer-songwriter, and arranger was born in the UK where his father was serving in the USAF. However, Holmes was brought up in New York where he attended the Manhattan School Of Music before starting out as a songwriter. He also performed on sessions for the **Cuff Links** and arranged songs for **Gene Pitney**, the **Drifters** and the **Platters**. His first success was the song 'Timothy', recorded by the Buoys and a US hit in 1971. The song, about hungry, trapped pot-holers devouring one of their number, also featured Holmes on piano. He wrote next for the **Partridge Family** and the Drifters before launching his own singing career with an album in 1974. The follow-up album inspired **Barbra Streisand** to ask him to produce her, and he followed work on her *Lazy Afternoon* with credits on albums by **Sparks**, **Sailor**, and the **Strawbs** amongst others. He continued to record as well and was rewarded in 1980 when *Partners In Crime* yielded two big hits - 'Escape (The Pina Colada Song)' and 'Him' - on both sides of the Atlantic.
● ALBUMS: *Widescreen* (1974)★★, *Rupert Holmes* (1975)★★★, *The Singles* (1977)★★★, *Pursuit Of Happiness* (1978)★★, *Partners In Crime* (1979)★★★, *Adventure* (1980)★★, *Full Circle* (1981)★★.

Holmes, Winston, And Charlie Turner

Turner played rack harmonica and guitar, and was an accomplished player of blues and ragtime (and, on unissued titles, of Sousa marches); Holmes sang, but played no instrument, although he appears to play clarinet in a photograph promoting a record by Lottie Kimbrough on his Merritt label. Neither the clarinettist nor Kimbrough, who was sick, arrived for the session, so Holmes and Kimbrough's sister Estella sat in. As might be inferred, Holmes was an energetic and resourceful music promoter in Kansas City, arranging concerts and recording sessions on his own and other labels; he was responsible for the debut (on Merritt) of Rev. J.C. Burnett. Holmes's own recordings, both with Turner and with Kimbrough, reveal a surreal sense of humour, and possibly a medicine show background; along with the blues, he parodied sentimental ballads and black church services, throwing in yodelling, whistling and bird calls.

● ALBUMS: *Lottie Kimbrough And Winston Holmes* (*c*.1988)★★★.

Holmes, Wright

b. 4 July 1905, Hightower, Texas, USA. Apart from a spell of wartime defence work in the north, Holmes was based in Houston from 1930, by which time he was already a blues singer and guitarist, working in clubs on Dowling Street. His first recordings in 1947 were not issued because the producer felt he sounded too much like **Lightnin' Hopkins**, a judgment belied by three titles recorded the same year, and issued by Miltone and Gotham. Some of Holmes's lyrics come from **Texas Alexander** ('Alley Special' is based on two Alexander recordings), but both words and music (including vocal melodies) sound completely improvised; his guitar playing determinedly obscures its basic pulse with syncopations, changes of tempo, and explosive, random-sounding runs. Holmes gave up blues by 1950, and was last seen in 1967, by which time he had lost a leg and turned to religion.

● ALBUMS: *Alley Special* (1988)★★★.

Holness, Winston 'Niney'

b. 1951, Montego Bay, Jamaica, West Indies. Winston 'Niney' Holness, aka The Observer, is one of the great characters of reggae music. Nicknamed 'Niney' when he lost a thumb in a workshop accident, he has been a singer, producer, engineer, DJ, fixer, arranger, manager and virtually everything else in reggae. Although Holness had organized bands to play at school dances in the 50s, it was not until he came under the tutelage of producer **Bunny Lee** in the late 60s that he achieved his entry into the professional music business. In 1967/8 he worked with **Lee Perry** for **Joe Gibbs**, taking over when Perry left in mid-1968 to start his own label. By 1970 he had set up his own operation, with his first production entitled 'Mr Brown'/'Everybody Bawling' by DJs **Dennis Alcapone** and **Lizzy**. It sold modestly, but his next record, 'Blood & Fire', released in December 1970, was an immediate smash, eventually selling 30,000 copies in Jamaica alone. The tune propelled Holness into the front rank of the new 'rebel' vanguard, establishing him as a producer fully capable of building original rhythms. The record bore a slight resemblance to **Bob Marley**'s 'Duppy Conqueror' but far outsold it, and the pair clashed when Marley heard the record.

Holness productions of the early 70s are characterized by their sparse simplicity and heaviness, often cultural/political in sentiment, and frequently espousing Rasta themes.

During 1973 he began an association with **Dennis Brown**, with the results released initially by Joe Gibbs, but later that year records began appearing on Holness's 'Observer' label. Again Holness had changed the beat, and Brown became the hottest singer of 1974. The local hits of the period included 'Westbound Train' (1973), 'Cassandra', 'I Am The Conqueror', and 'No More Will I Roam' (all 1974). Brown's sessions with Holness constitute a high point in the development of reggae during the 70s. Holness also issued records by **Gregory Isaacs**, Michael Rose, **Junior Delgado**, Sang Hugh, **Horace Andy**, **Delroy Wilson**, **Leroy Smart**, **Junior Byles** and **Cornell Campbell**. He issued a dub album - *Dubbing With The Observer* - mixed by **King Tubby**'s, and DJ music by the likes of **U-Roy**, **Big Youth**, **I. Roy**, **Dillinger** and **Trinity**. At the end of the 70s Holness vanished from view, only to materialize in Paris in 1982. During the mid-80s he worked at Kingston's **Channel One** studio in an unspecified capacity, and issued a few singles and an album. He was next spotted in New York, apparently retired, although he went on to release his first new work in years, with recordings by **Frankie Paul** and **Andrew Tosh**.

● ALBUMS: *Dubbing With The Observer* (Attack 1975)★★★★, *Live At The Turntable Club* (1975)★★★, *Sledgehammer Dub* (1976)★★★, *Niney The Observer* (Charly 1990)★★★, *Turbo Charge* (Rounder 1991)★★★.

● COMPILATIONS: *Blood & Fire 1971-1972* (Trojan 1988)★★★★, *Bring The Couchie 1974-1976* (Trojan 1989)★★★.

Holocaust

Holocaust were formed in Edinburgh, Scotland, in 1978. The original line-up consisted of Gary Lettice (vocals), John Mortimer (guitar), Edward Dudley (guitar), Robin Begg (bass) and Paul Collins (drums). They were signed by Phoenix Records, who released the band's debut, 'Heavy Metal Mania', in 1980. The band's long-playing debut, *The Nightcomers*, arrived a year later. The material on offer was basic hard rock, fuelled by the enthusiasm that the **New Wave Of British Heavy Metal** had fired. It was to prove a very influential release, **Metallica** later covering one of the tracks on their *Garage Days Revisited* EP. By 1982 and the release of Holocaust's second single, 'Coming Through', the band was disintegrating. A posthumous live album appeared in 1983, again on Phoenix Records, entitled *Live, Hot Curry & Wine*. Guitarist Edward Dudley left to form Hologram (who recorded one album, also for Phoenix, entitled *Steal The Stars*, in 1982). Hologram, however, proved short-lived as Holocaust re-formed to release a third album, *No Mans Land*, in 1984. Soon after its release the band folded again. With the resurgence of interest in the N.W.O.B.H.M. bands (primarily owing to **Metallica** cover versions), the band started working together again in 1989.

● ALBUMS: *The Nightcomers* (Phoenix 1981)★★★★, *Live,*

Hot Curry & Wine (Phoenix 1983)★★★, *No Mans Land* (Phoenix 1984)★★★, *The Land Of Souls* (Chrome 1990)★★, *Hypnosis Of Birds* (1993),★★ *Covenant* (Neat 1997)★★★.

Holt, Errol

b. *c*.1959, Kingston, Jamaica, West Indies. Holt began recording in the mid-70s with **Prince Far I** and Ja Man. Early hits included 'Who Have Eyes To See', 'Gimme Gimme' and 'Shark Out Deh'. In 1976 he recorded 'A You Lick Me First', a **sound system** hit that provided the foundation to the **Jah Woosh** hit 'Lick Him With The Dustbin'. In the same year he was enrolled as part of Maurice Wellington's group the **Morwells**. He stayed with the group until its demise in the early 80s. While with the band he performed on the hits 'Kingston 12 Tuffy' and 'Africa We Want To Go'. With fellow band member **Bingi Bunny** he formed the **Roots Radics**, who became the most in-demand session band on the island. Holt also shared production credits with **Gregory Isaacs** for *Out Deh*. The band's performance with Isaacs on his UK tour led to their being in demand to support the island's top performers. In 1985 Roots Radics released 'Earsay', with Holt singing on the b-side a cover version of **Delroy Wilson**'s 'I'm Not A King'.
● ALBUMS: *Vision Of Africa* (Dread & Dread 1982)★★★★.

Holt, John

b. 1947, Kingston, Jamaica, West Indies. At the age of 12 Holt's voice was a regular feature of the talent contests run by Vere Johns at various Jamaican theatres, and by 1963 Holt had cut his first single, 'I Cried A Tear'/'Forever I'll Stay', for **Leslie Kong**'s **Beverley's** label. Holt also recorded duets with **Alton Ellis** for Randy's, including 'Rum Bumper' (1964). Between 1965 and 1970 he was lead singer with the **Paragons**, one of the smoothest, most accomplished vocal trios in reggae, and heavily dependent on Holt's precise, creamy tenor. The group's work with producer **Duke Reid** was impeccable, and they enjoyed a string of hits, 'Ali Baba', 'Tonight' and 'I See Your Face', among them. Holt, sometimes with the Paragons, also worked with **Studio One** on sides such as 'Fancy Make-Up', 'A Love I Can Feel', 'Let's Build Our Dreams' and 'OK Fred' (later a chart smash for **Errol Dunkley**), as well as **Prince Buster** ('Oh Girl', 'My Heart Is Gone').
By the early 70s Holt was one of reggae's biggest stars and ready to cross over into the pop market. His 'Stick By Me', one of dozens of songs he cut with producer **Bunny Lee**, was the biggest-selling Jamaican record of 1972. Just over a year later, his *Time Is The Master* set for producer **Harry Mudie** proved a masterpiece, and pointed the way ahead: fine songs (among them cover versions of Ivory Joe Hunter's 'It May Sound Silly' and **Brook Benton**'s 'Looking Back'), heavy rhythms, and a sweet addition of lush, orchestral arrangements recorded in London. **Trojan Records** issued a best-selling series of Bunny Lee-produced John Holt albums, including the *1,000/2,000/3,000 Volts* series, and brought him to London to work with Tony Ashfield,

who again used string arrangements. In December 1974 he achieved a huge pop hit across Europe with 'Help Me Make It Through The Night', but Holt was more than a balladeer, and by 1976 he was enjoying further Jamaican success with 'Up Park Camp', a massive roots hit for producer **Joseph 'Joe Joe' Hookim**. A brief experiment with disco (*Holt Goes Disco*) was virtually the only blot on his copybook during the 70s, and he has continued to work in a contemporary style to the present day, occasionally enjoying enormous roots reggae hits ('Police In Helicopter' in 1987) while still being willing to work in other styles, as demonstrated by the *Reggae, Hip House, R&B Flavor* album title he employed in 1993. He remains a unique talent, perhaps underrated among more élitist fans because of his flirtation with the pop world.
● ALBUMS: *A Love I Can Feel* (Studio One 1971)★★★, *Greatest Hits* (Studio One 1972)★★★★, *Presenting The Fabulous John Holt* (Trojan 1973)★★★★, *Holt* (Trojan 1973)★★★, *Still In Chains* (Trojan 1973)★★★, *1,000 Volts Of Holt* (Trojan 1973)★★★, *Time Is The Master* (Creole 1974)★★★★, *Dusty Roads* (Trojan 1974)★★★, *Sings For I* (Trojan 1974)★★, *Pledging My Love* (Trojan 1975)★★★, *Before The Next Teardrop Falls* (Klik 1976)★★★, *Up Park Camp* (Channel One 1977)★★★, *Holt Goes Disco* (Trojan 1977)★★, *2,000 Volts Of Holt* (Trojan 1979)★★★, *Just The Two Of Us* (CSA 1982)★★★, *Sweetie Come Brush Me* (Volcano 1982)★★★, *Police In Helicopter* (Greensleeves 1983)★★★, *Further You Look* (Trojan 1983)★★, *Let It Go On* (Trojan 1983)★★★, *For Lovers And Dancers* (Trojan 1984)★★★, *Live In London* (Very Good 1984)★★★, with Dennis Brown *Wild Fire* (Natty Congo 1986)★★★, *3,000 Volts Of Holt* (Trojan 1986)★★★, *Reggae Christmas Album* (Trojan 1986)★★, with Horace Andy *From One Extreme To Another* (Beta 1986)★★★, *OK Fred* (Spartan 1987)★★, *Time Is The Master* (Creole 1988)★★★, *Rock With Me Baby* (Trojan 1988)★★★, *If I Were A Carpenter* (1989)★★, *Why I Care* (Greensleeves 1989)★★★, *Reggae, Hip House, R&B Flavor* (1993)★★★, *Peacemaker* (1993).
● COMPILATIONS: *Roots Of Holt* (Trojan 1983)★★★, *Greatest Hits* (Prince Buster 1984)★★★, *Pure Gold* (Vista Sounds 1985)★★★, *16 Songs For Soulful Lovers* (Platinum 1986)★★★, *Living Legend* (Classic 1986)★★★, *20 Golden Love Songs* (Trojan 1986)★★★★, *Let Your Love Flow* (CSA 1988)★★★, *Best Of* (Action Replay 1990)★★★★, *Love Songs Volume 2* (Parish 1992)★★★.

Holts, Roosevelt

b. 15 January 1905, Tylertown, Mississippi, USA. Although he had been singing and playing blues guitar since his 20s, Holts was over 60 before he became known outside of his home area of southern Mississippi and Louisiana. A friend and companion of **Tommy Johnson** during the 30s, Holts learned to play many of that artist's pieces. In the 50s, he settled in Louisiana, and it was there he was discovered in the 60s. The Johnson connection seems to have rather preoccupied those who produced his records, but his repertoire was much wider and more substantial, and both his instrumental and vocal skills were remarkable for a performer of his age. For a short time around the end of the 60s, he issued some singles on his own label, Bluesman.

● ALBUMS: *Presenting The Country Blues* (Bluesman 1968)★★★.

Holy Barbarians

Although the **Cult** enjoyed huge commercial success after relocating to the west coast of America, by the mid-90s they were facing artistic stalemate. The Holy Barbarians, led by Cult singer Ian Astbury, were inaugurated because, 'I guess I just wanted to go home'. Keen to find fresh, enthusiastic musicians with which to work, he recruited Patrick Sugg (guitar, backing vocals) from Los Angeles punk band Lucifer Wong. Together they demoed songs in his Los Angeles garage amid Astbury's famed collection of **Beatles** and Everton Football Club memorabilia. The group was completed with the addition of former Cult drummer Scott Garrett, who in turn recruited his brother, bass player Matt Garrett. Astbury then elected to return home to Liverpool, England, where the band is now based. Their debut album, *Cream*, was released by **Beggars Banquet Records** in April 1996. While Astbury's voice remained distinctive, many ties with Cult records of the past had obviously been cut - in opposition to too many songs led by Billy Duffy's lead guitar work, the new material had a more rhythmic and contemporary edge. Fittingly, the album's title was inspired by Astbury's regular attendance at the famous Cream house venue in Liverpool.

● ALBUMS: *Cream* (Beggars Banquet 1996)★★.

Holy Ghost Inc

One of a number of groups picked up from the underground and hoisted on to a major in the early 90s, in this case **Island Records** subsidiary Blunted. Holy Ghost Inc were formed in 1989 and produced two EPS, *The Word*, and the widely praised *Mad Monks On Zinc*, prior to the move. *The Megawatt Messiah* EP, a slower techno piece continuing their religous themes, was their first release for Blunted in January 1994. Other associated projects run in conjunction with the group exist, under the titles Saucer Crew ('Andromeda' etc) and Ouija Board, though the participants continue to shroud their identities in mystery.

Holy Modal Rounders

Peter Stampfel (b. 1938, Wauwautosa, Wisconsin, USA) and Steve Weber (b. 1942, Philadelphia, Pennsylvania, USA). This on-off partnership was first established in New York's Greenwich Village. The two musicians shared a passion for old-time music and unconventional behaviour, and together they created some of the era's most distinctive records. The duo completed their debut album, *The Holy Modal Rounders* in 1963. It contained several of their finest moments, including the influential 'Blues In The Bottle', which the **Lovin' Spoonful**, among others, later

recorded. The Rounders' second collection, although less satisfying, continued the same cross-section of 20s/30s-styled country and blues. Having accompanied the **Fugs** on their early releases, Stampfel and Weber broke up; the former began writing for 'alternative' publications. The musicians were reunited in 1967 to complete the experimental, but flawed, *Indian War Whoop*. This often incoherent collection also featured drummer Sam Shepard, an off-Broadway playwright from a parallel Stampfel venture, the Moray Eels. The amalgamation of the two groups led to another album, *The Moray Eels Eat The Holy Modal Rounders*, which was a marked improvement on its predecessor. It featured the sweeping 'Bird Song', later immortalized in the film *Easy Rider*. Shepard left the Rounders in 1970, from where he became a successful writer and actor. Three albums of varying quality were then completed until the group, which suffered a plethora of comings and goings, ground to a halt in 1977. Weber and Stampfel were reunited five years later. *Goin' Nowhere Fast* was an excellent set, evocative of the duo's first recordings together, but their revitalized relationship proved temporary. The latter later worked with an all-new group, Pete Stampfel And The Bottlecaps. Another reunion took place in 1996.

● ALBUMS: *The Holy Modal Rounders* (Folklore 1964)★★★, *The Holy Modal Rounders 2* (Prestige 1965)★★, *Indian War Whoop* (ESP 1967)★★, *The Moray Eels Eat The Holy Modal Rounders* (Elektra 1968)★★, *Good Taste Is Timeless* (Metromedia 1971)★★, *Alleged In Their Own Time* (1975)★★, *Last Round* (1978)★★, *Goin' Nowhere Fast* (1982)★★★★ .

Holy Moses

This thrash metal group from Germany, formed in the mid-80s, comprised Andy Classen (guitar), Sabina Classen (vocals), Reiner Laws (guitar), Thomas Becker (bass) and Ulli Kusch (drums). Their early efforts for the independent domestic label Aaarrg Records saw the group hone its sound into one of the more powerful examples of the speed-metal genre, drawing obvious influence from **Slayer** and **Anthrax**. A series of excellent reviews and a growing live reputation led to a contract with **WEA Records**. Unfortunately, *The New Machine Of Lichenstein*, produced by Anthrax and **Testament** producer Alex Parialis, showcased a group confused as to whether to pursue the style with which they had earned their reputation, or to produce something more accessible to the mainstream. With the group unable to resolve their direction, it received mixed reviews and their association with WEA was discontinued. They persevered with a further album for an independent label, 1990's *World Chaos*, but by this time they had lost much of their initial momentum.

● ALBUMS: *Queen Of Siam* (Aaarrg 1986)★★★, *Finished With The Dogs* (Aaarrg 1987)★★, *The New Machine Of Lichenstein* (WEA 1989)★★★, *World Chaos* (Virginia 1990)★★★.

Holzman, Jac

b. 15 September 1931, New York City, New York, USA. Holzman, a trained engineer, founded **Elektra Records** in 1950 and remained its guiding light over the next 23 years. His label was renowned for traditional music, and early releases featured such artists as **Theodore Bikel**, **Ed McCurdy** and Cynthia Gooding. Elektra's foremost reputation was secured during the folk revival of the early 60s. Holzman provided a natural home for a new generation of committed performers, and **Judy Collins**, **Tom Paxton**, **Fred Neil** and **Phil Ochs** recorded their most lasting work for the label. The company began signing electric acts with the acquisition of the **Butterfield Blues Band**. Having failed to secure the **Lovin' Spoonful** and the embryonic **Byrds**, Holzman's long-term commitment to rock was established with **Love**. He produced their debut album, a release that paved the way for early seminal work by the **Doors** and **Tim Buckley**. Elektra's songwriter tradition was maintained through the work of **David Ackles**, Steve Noonan and **Carly Simon**, while **Bread**'s sweet pop achieved international commercial success. Holzman's direct involvement in Elektra's direction lessened as the 60s progressed, although he continued his role of production supervisor. However, in 1970 the label was acquired by the Kinney Corporation, who grouped it as WEA with the emergent **Asylum Records** roster three years later. By then Elektra had forsaken the quest for excellence that marked its epochal era, and Holzman, now senior vice president at Warner Communications, abandoned music for computer technology. In 1991, Holzman purchased the west coast-based Discovery/Trend conglomerate, specialists in jazz reissues, and continues to be very active in the music business.

● FURTHER READING: *Follow The Music: The Life And High Times Of Elektra Records*, Jaz Holzman and Gavan Daws.

Hombres

Formed in Memphis in 1966, the Hombres - Gary Wayne McEwen (guitar), B.B. Cunningham (organ) the brother of Bill Cunningham of the **Boxtops**, Jerry Lee Masters (bass) and John Will Hunter (d. 1976; drums) - originally served as a touring version of **Ronny And The Daytonas**, whose leader, John 'Bucky' Wilkin, did not like to tour. While in Houston, the group met Shelby Singleton who introduced them to producer **Huey P. Meaux**, who agreed to record them. They wrote 'Let It Out (Let It All Hang Out)', a rambling, funky shuffle, on the way to the session. Lyrically patterned after **Bob Dylan**'s 'Subterranean Homesick Blues', the single was issued on **Verve**/Forecast the following year and rose to number 12 in the US charts. The group had no further hits.

● ALBUMS: *Let It Out (Let It All Hang Out)* (Verve/Forecast 1967)★★.

Home Service

Formed in 1980 as the First Eleven, this UK group evolved from the ever changing **Albion Band**, which at the time included **John Kirkpatrick** in the line-up. Led by John Tams (vocals), the group featured **Bill Caddick** (b. June 1944, Wolverhampton, England; vocals/guitar/dobro), Graeme Taylor (b. 2 February 1954, Stockwell, London, England; vocals/guitar), Michael Gregory (b. 16 November 1949, Gower, South Wales; drums/percussion), Roger Williams (b. 30 July 1954, Cottingham, Yorkshire, England; trombone), Howard Evans (b. 29 February 1944, Chard, Somerset, England; trumpet) and Jonathan Davie (b. 6 September 1954, Twickenham, Middlesex, England; bass). Both Evans and Williams were concurrently members of Brass Monkey, and Caddick had already released a number of solo albums. The group was involved with work for the National Theatre, for which they provided the music for the York Mystery Plays. The resultant album appeared in 1985. This release included **Linda Thompson**, and covered both traditional and contemporary material. By 1985, Caddick had left the group, unhappy with the lack of live concert work. This situation was caused by the many commitments the group had to theatre, television and film work. The following year, 1986, Andy Findon (saxophone) and Steve King (keyboards) were added to the line-up. It was 1991 before the line-up played together again, on the Hokey Pokey charity compilation *All Through The Year*.

● ALBUMS: *The Home Service* (Jigsaw 1984)★★★, *The Mysteries* (Coda 1985)★★★, *Alright Jack* (Celtic Music 1986)★★★★, *Wild Life* 1992 live recording (Fledg'ling 1995)★★★.

● COMPILATIONS: *All Through The Year* (Hokey Pokey 1991)★★★.

Home T

b. Michael Bennet, *c.*1962, Kingston, Jamaica, West Indies. Bennet began his career as a vocalist in the quartet Home T4, and in 1980 had a hit with 'Irons In The Fire'. The group later became known for covering popular standards, including versions of **Bunny Wailer**'s 'Cool Runnings' and **Marvin Gaye**'s 'What's Going On'. They established their popularity with live performances at the Reggae Sunsplash Show in 1984 and were the only vocal group to appear on the Dancehall '84 stage show in Kingston alongside **Half Pint**, **Michael Palmer**, **Edi Fitzroy**, **Charlie Chaplin** and **Ini Kamoze**. The group's recorded output never reached the top of the charts despite working with **Sly Dunbar** and **Robbie Shakespeare**. They were, however, able to find some success on their collaborations with **Josie Wales** ('Changing'), **Yellowman** ('Mr Counsellor') and **Phillip Papa Levi** ('Dear Pastor') in the mid-80s, which brought them to the attention of a wider audience. Following the reduction of the group to a trio, Bennet continued recording as Home T, with Tony Anderson and Winston 'Diego' Tucker at **Gussie Clarke**'s Music Works Studio. They had hits with

'Rockers Don't Move You', 'Are You Going My Way', 'How Hot' and 'Same Friend'. In 1988 they recorded a version of 'Telephone Love' as 'Single Life', while also providing backing vocals and helping to arrange the original version for **J.C. Lodge**. In 1990 Gussie Clarke recorded the combined talents of **Shabba Ranks, Cocoa Tea** and Home T for 'Pirates Anthem'. When the London-based pirate radio station Kiss FM was granted a license the track was selected as the first tune to be played on the now legal transmission. Home T continued working with Clarke until the early 90s when he set up his Philadelphia-based Two Friends label with Patrick Lindsay. They continued to utilize the Music Works Recording Studio, producing hits for **Dennis Brown**, Cocoa Tea, Shabba Ranks and **Cutty Ranks**. With Brown, the duo produced 'No More Walls', which became a massive hit. The combined talents of Home T, Cocoa Tea and Shabba were also produced by the Two Friends crew in 1991 and they had a hit on the reggae charts with a version of the Philadelphia Sounds track 'Your Body's Here With Me'. Other hits for the duo included **Gregory Isaacs**' 'Loverman', **Brian and Tony Gold**'s, 'Ram Dance' and Daddy Lizard's 'Show Them The Way'. When Shabba was unavailable to record a follow-up to the successful combination single, Cutty Ranks took the DJ role. This coalition topped the reggae chart with 'The Going Is Rough' and the equally successful 'Another One For The Road'. By 1992 Mikey Melody had moved on to producing with Clifton 'Specialist' Dillon as Twin City productions, and enjoyed international success with a remake of 'Mr Loverman' by Shabba Ranks and **Chevelle Franklin** (originally a **Deborahe Glasgow** hit) and 'Housecall' with **Maxi Priest** and Shabba. Twin City enjoyed a number of hits but competition from **Steely And Clevie** overshadowed the duo's success.

● ALBUMS: *Sly & Robbie Present Home T4* (Taxi 1983)★★★★, with Cocoa Tea, Shabba Ranks *Holding On* (Greensleeves 1989)★★★, with Cocoa Tea, Cutty Ranks *Another One For The Road* (Greensleeves 1991)★★★, *Red Hot* (Two Friends 1992)★★★.

Homer And Jethro

Homer (b. Henry D. Haynes, 27 July 1920, d. 7 August 1971, Chicago, Illinois, USA) and Jethro (b. Kenneth C. Burns, 10 March 1920, d. 4 February 1989, Evanston, Illinois, USA) were both from Knoxville, Tennessee, USA. They went to the same school and learned to play stringed instruments as young children. In 1932, they began to work together as musicians on WNOX Knoxville, where they performed in a quartet known as the String Dusters. With Homer on guitar and Jethro on mandolin, they mainly played instrumental pop music and any vocals were usually performed as a trio. Somewhat bored with the regular format, they developed a comedy act that they used backstage. They began to present comedy versions of popular songs by maintaining the melody but changing the lyrics, and before long, they were encouraged to perform them live on the radio. They were given the names of Homer and Jethro by the programme director, Lowell Blanchard. The act quickly proved a popular part of the String Dusters' routine. In 1936, they left the group to work solely as Homer and Jethro but stayed at WNOX until 1939. They then became regulars on the *Renfro Valley Barn Dance* in Kentucky, but in 1941, they were both called up for military service. In 1945, they were back together as regulars on the *Midwestern Hayride* on WLW Cincinnati, and between 1946 and 1948, they recorded their humorous songs for the local King label. In 1949, after a move to **RCA Records**, they had Top 10 US country chart success with a recording with **June Carter** of 'Baby It's Cold Outside'. In the late 1940s, they toured with their own tent show but eventually joined **Red Foley** on KWTO Springfield. In 1949, they toured the USA as part of orchestra leader **Spike Jones**' show and in 1951, while in Chicago with Jones, they were invited to become regulars on the *National Barn Dance* on WLS, where they remained until 1958. During the 50s and 60s, they toured extensively, their humour proving very popular in many varied venues, including Las Vegas. Their biggest country chart hit came in 1953, when 'How Much Is That Hound Dog In The Window' reached number 2. In 1959, they had a US pop Top 20 hit with 'The Battle Of Kookamonga', their parody of Johnny Horton's hit 'Battle Of New Orleans'. Proving that no song was safe from the couple's attentions in 1964, they had their last chart entry with their version of the **Beatles**' 'I Want To Hold Your Hand'. They also made commercials for Kellogg's Cornflakes during the 60s, which made them household names in the USA, but might have prompted a drop in sales had they been shown in Britain. The zany comedy tended to overshadow the fact that the duo were fine musicians. They made instrumental albums and in 1970, they recorded with **Chet Atkins** (Jethro's brother-in-law) as the Nashville String Band (it was not until the album had reached the charts that RCA revealed the identities of the musicians). Atkins rated Homer as one of the best rhythm guitarists he ever knew. He was also a good enough vocalist to have pursued a singing career but had no interest in doing so. Jethro was also noted as an excellent mandolin player and one who, even in his early days, did much to make the instrument acceptable in jazz music. The partnership came to an end after 39 years on 7 August 1971, when Homer suffered a heart attack and died. Jethro was deeply affected by Homer's death but eventually returned to work as a musician. In the late 70s, he toured and recorded with **Steve Goodman**. Jethro died of cancer at his home in February 1989. Homer and Jethro's parodies included such titles as 'The Ballad Of Davy Crew-Cut' and 'Hart Brake Motel', and few could match album titles such as *Songs My Mother Never Sang, Ooh! That's Corny* (named after their catchphrase) or, bearing in mind they had been steadily turning out albums for 16 years, to suddenly decide to call one simply *Homer & Jethro's Next Album.* They never enjoyed success in the UK but were an institution in the USA.

● ALBUMS: *Homer & Jethro Fracture Frank Loesser* 10-inch album (RCA Victor 1953)★★★, *The Worst Of Homer & Jethro* (RCA Victor 1957)★★★★, *Barefoot Ballads* (RCA Victor 1957)★★★, *Life Can Be Miserable* (RCA Victor 1958)★★★★, *Musical Madness* (Audio Lab 1958)★★★, *They Sure Are Corny* (King 1959)★★★★, *At The Country Club* (RCA Victor 1960)★★★, *Songs My Mother Never Sang* (RCA Victor 1961)★★★, *Homer & Jethro At The Convention* (RCA Victor 1962)★★★, *Homer & Jethro Strike Back* (Camden 1962)★★★, *Playing It Straight* (RCA Victor 1962)★★★, *Cornier Than Corn* (King 1963)★★★★, *Zany Songs Of The 30s* (RCA Victor 1963)★★★, *Homer & Jethro Go West* (RCA Victor 1963)★★★, *Ooh, That's Corny!* (RCA Victor 1963)★★★, *The Humorous Side Of Country Music* (Camden 1963)★★★, *Cornfucius Say* (RCA Victor 1964)★★★, *Fractured Folk Songs* (RCA Victor 1964)★★★, *Homer & Jethro Sing Tenderly And Other Love Ballads* (RCA Victor 1965)★★★, *The Old Crusty Minstrels* (RCA Victor 1965)★★★, *Songs To Tickle Your Funny Bone* (Camden 1966)★★★, *Wanted For Murder* (RCA Victor 1966)★★★, *Any News From Nashville* (RCA Victor 1966)★★★, *It Ain't Necessarily Square* (RCA Victor 1967)★★★, *Nashville Cats* (RCA Victor 1967)★★★, *24 Great Songs In The Homer & Jethro Style* (King 1967)★★★, *Something Stupid* (RCA Victor 1967)★★★, *Songs For The 'Out' Crowd* (RCA Victor 1967)★★★, *The Playboy Song* (Camden 1968)★★★, *There's Nothing Like An Old Hippie* (RCA Victor 1968)★★, *Homer & Jethro Live At Vanderbilt University* (RCA Victor 1968)★★★, *Cool Crazy Christmas* (RCA Victor 1968)★★, *Homer & Jethro's Next Album* (RCA Victor 1969)★★★, *The Far Out World Of Homer & Jethro* (RCA Victor 1972)★★★. With The Nashville String Band *Down Home* (RCA Victor 1970)★★★, *Identified* (RCA Victor 1970)★★★, *Strung Up* (RCA Victor 1971)★★★.

By Jethro Burns: with Joe Venuti, Curly Chalker, Eldon Shamblin *S'Wonderful (4 Giants Of Swing)* (Flying Fish 1977)★★★, *Jethro Burns* (Flying Fish 1977)★★★, *Jethro Burns Live* (Flying Fish 1978)★★★, with Tiny Moore *Back To Back* (Flying Fish 1980)★★★, *Tea For One* (Flying Fish 1982)★★★, with Red Rector *Old Friends* (Flying Fish 1983)★★★.

● COMPILATIONS: *The Best Of Homer & Jethro* (RCA Victor 1966)★★★, *Country Comedy* (Camden 1971)★★★, *Assault On The Rock 'N' Roll Era* (Bear Family 1989)★★★, *The Best Of* (RCA 1992)★★★, *America's Favorite Song Butchers: The Weird World Of Homer & Jethro* (Razor & Tie 1997)★★★★.

Homesick James

b. James Williamson, 3 May 1914, Somerville, Tennessee, USA. Williamson's father was a drummer and by the age of 14, he was playing guitar at local dances and taverns. Williamson developed a 'bottleneck' style by sliding a pocket-knife up and down the strings. In 1932 he moved north to Chicago and by the end of the decade had formed a small band which toured the southern states during the 40s. Among its members were **Snooky Pryor** and Baby Face Leroy

Foster. His first recording was 'Lonesome Ole Train' (Chance 1952). From the mid-50s, Williamson worked regularly with his cousin **Elmore James**, playing second guitar on many of the latter's most famous records. Now known as Homesick James, he recorded his own most famous track for USA in 1962. An updated version of **Robert Johnson**'s 'Crossroads', its pounding rhythms and heavily amplified bottleneck made it a landmark in city blues. After the death of Elmore James in 1963, Homesick James saw himself as the standard-bearer of his cousin's powerful guitar style. He recorded for Prestige and toured Europe in 1973, where he made an album with Pryor for Jim Simpson's Birmingham, England-based label, Big Bear.

● ALBUMS: *Blues From The Southside* (1964)★★★, *Homesick James & Snooky Pryor* (Big Bear 1973)★★★★, *Ain't Sick No More* (1973)★★, *Home Sweet Homesick* (Big Bear 1976)★★★, *Goin' Back In The Times* (Earwig 1994)★★, *Juanita* (Appaloosa 1994)★★★, *Got To Move* (Trix 1994)★★, *Words Of Wisdom* (Icehouse 1997)★★★, *Last Of The Broomdusters* (Fedora 1998)★★★★.

Homo Liber

Vladimir Tolkachev (b. 17 June 1951, Serov, Sverdolvsk, Russia; reeds/percussion), Yuri Yukechev (b. 1954, Western Ukraine; piano/percussion). Based in Novosibirsk, Siberia, Homo Liber grew out of a trio formed in the 70s by Tolkachev, drummer Sergey Belichenko and bassist Sergey Panasenko. In 1980 Yukechev joined the group, but within a few years Homo Liber had settled into a duo of Tolkachev and Yukechev, although their first recording, *Siberian 4*, smuggled out of the USSR and released in Eurpoe and the USA by **Leo Records**, comprised one side by the quartet and one by the duo. The music's cool spaciousness and haunting beauty won critical acclaim around the world and was later voted one of the top 50 albums of the 80s by *Wire* magazine. A second release followed on Leo, plus three tracks on the label's eight-CD compilation *Document*, but recordings and biographical facts remain scarce. Tolkachev cites only Messaien and fellow-Sverdolvsk saxophonist **Vladimir Chekasin** as influences. He began to play music at the age of 12, studied accordion at the local music institute and took up the saxophone in 1969. In the early 70s he moved to the Siberian industrial centre of Novosibirsk and became involved in the contemporary jazz scene at the neighbouring 'university' town of Akademgorodok. He currently works in an orchestra. Playing music is, for him, 'an opportunity to go beyond the limits of everyday experience, to exist in another world'. Yukechev studied piano at Lutsk (1960-65) and composition at the Leningrad Conservatoire (1965-70). In addition to his improvisations in Homo Liber, he is a full-time 'classical' composer, whose works include a piano trio, a cantata for choir, a concerto for violin and 18 brass and wind instruments and an opera, *The Legend Of The People Of Taiga*. Though active in their home region, Homo Liber have rarely toured or played at festivals.

● ALBUMS: *Siberian 4* (1983)★★★★, *Untitled* (1986)★★★, with others *Document* (1990)★★★.

Hondells

The Hondells were a non-existent group when they released their Top 10 single 'Little Honda' in 1964. The mastermind behind the record was producer **Gary Usher**, a friend and songwriting partner of **Beach Boys** leader **Brian Wilson**. Usher had created a series of surf music records using a revolving team of musicians and singers and assigning different group names to the finished products. The Hondells were one such creation. Usher and his hired hands for the day recorded a version of the Brian Wilson song extolling the virtues of Honda motorcycles, which was released on **Mercury Records** and reached number 9 in the US. With the record a success, the company asked Usher to assemble a touring group of Hondells. He hired Ritchie Burns, one of the background singers on the record, to lead the group. Burns still had not left his job at a bank when the album cover photos were taken, and he had friends of his (who were not involved with the record) pose for its cover. The Hondells continued to make records, and appeared on popular television programmes and in a number of 'beach party' films, including *Beach Blanket Bingo*. Only two further singles charted, 'My Buddy Seat' in 1964-65, and a cover of the **Lovin' Spoonful**'s 'Younger Girl' in 1966. Following this release the group assembled to masquerade as the Hondells began to sing and play on the records, recording a version of **Bob Lind**'s 'Cheryl's Going Home'. Subsequent singles on **Columbia Records** and Amos did not chart and only the first of the Hondells' albums made the charts. The group and the Hondells name were retired in 1970.

● ALBUMS: *Go Little Honda* (Mercury 1964)★★★, *The Hondells* (Mercury 1965)★★★.

● FILMS: *Beach Ball* (1964), *Beach Blanket Bingo* (1965).

Honey Bane

b. Donna Tracy, England. Honey Bane was previously the young singer in the Fatal Microbes, who released an EP, *Violence Grows*, and shared a 12-inch single release with the **Poison Girls**. She started her solo career in 1979 after escaping from a reform centre where she had been admitted for alcohol abuse. 'You Can Be You', on the Crass label, was recorded in a single day. Her backing band was the Kebabs, actually a pseudonym for **Crass**, although the three 'anarcho-punk' songs still retained the spirit of Fatal Microbes. It was almost a year before the follow-up, 'Guilty', was released on Honey's own label, and it stirred up enough interest to secure a contract with **EMI** subsidiary Zonophone. With the help of Peter Godwin from Metro and Jimmy Pursey from **Sham 69**, they tried to manufacture a pop star. In January 1981 'Turn Me On, Turn Me Off' peaked at number 37. Her provocative 'naughty girl' image had short-lived appeal and after one further glimpse at the charts with a cover version of the

Supremes' 'Baby Love', her popularity saw a rapid decline. Successive singles 'Jimmy . . . (Listen To Me)', 'Wish I Could Be Me' and 'Dizzy Dreamers' passed unnoticed, prompting Honey to concentrate on her acting career.

Honey Boy

b. Keith Williams, *c.*1955, St. Elizabeth, Jamaica, West Indies. Williams moved to Britain in the late 60s and settled in Oxford before moving to London. He began his career working with **Laurel Aitken** on the session that resulted in 'Guilty' by **Tiger** (one of Aitken's pseudonyms) for the Palmer brothers. Honey Boy's first session as a vocalist came when working for Junior Lincoln, who had set up an independent label after leaving B&C Music. Lincoln's label Banana had been an outlet for **Coxsone Dodd**'s **Studio One** recordings in the UK, but also released Honey Boy's debut, 'Homeward Bound'. His alias was appropriate because his vocal cords were considered to be sweeter than honey. Although the single did not make a big impact, many releases followed, including 'I'm Not Going Down', 'Sweet Cherie' and 'Happiness Comes'. He also recorded under different guises, as Happy Junior on 'Sugar Dandy', and as Boy Wonder on 'All On The House'. His vocals also graced *Trojan Reggae Party Volume One* when he performed alongside the **Pioneers**, **Greyhound**, **Bruce Ruffin**, **Nicky Thomas**, **Delroy Wilson** and Count Prince Miller. By 1976 he had teamed up with Winston Curtis, a Studio One veteran who had taken up residence in the UK, and a number of releases followed, notably 'Rock Me' and 'Who Baby'. He was also a featured vocalist on *Winston's Greats*. In 1977 Honey Boy recorded for Count Shelley cover versions of **Derrick Harriott**'s 'Penny For Your Song' and **Jackie Edwards**' 'Keep On Running'. In 1980, Honey Boy returned to Curtis, and with the nucleus of **Aswad**, Angus 'Drummie Zeb' Gaye, Tony 'Gad' Robinson and George Oban, he released *Arise*. Although a major hit has eluded him, he has been involved in the UK reggae scene for many years and is considered to be one of the pioneers of **lovers rock**.

● ALBUMS: *Sweet Cherries Impossible Love* (Cactus 1974)★★★, *Taste Of Honey* (Cactus 1975)★★★, *This Is Honey Boy* (Third World 1975)★★★, *Strange Thoughts* (Trojan 1977)★★★, *Arise* (Diamond 1980)★★.

Honey Cone

The product of various Los Angeles female groups, Carolyn Willis (b. 1946, Los Angeles, USA), Edna Wright (b. 1944, Los Angeles, USA) and Shellie Clark (b. 1943, Brooklyn, New York, USA), first came together as Honey Cone to work on the **Andy Williams** television show. Each was an established singer: Willis in the Girlfriends, Clark in the **Ikettes**, while Wright had sung in the **Blossoms** alongside her sister, **Darlene Love**. Early Honey Cone singles, 'While You're Out Looking For Sugar' and 'Girls It Ain't Easy', were R&B

hits in 1969, before two 1971 soul chart-toppers, 'Want Ads' and 'Stick Up', established the trio. Stylistically, such songs invoked a saltier **Supremes**, and this gritty approach was confirmed on 'One Monkey Don't Stop No Show' and 'Sittin' On A Time Bomb (Waitin' On The Hurt To Come)'. The group broke up in 1973 when later singles were less successful, leaving Edna Wright free to resume her career as a session singer.

● ALBUMS: *Honey Cone* (Hot Wax 1969)★★★, *Take Me With You* (Hot Wax 1970)★★★, *Sweet Replies* (Hot Wax 1971)★★★, *Soulful Tapestry* (Hot Wax 1971)★★★, *Love, Peace And Soul* (Hot Wax 1972)★★★.

● COMPILATIONS: *Girls It Ain't Easy* (HDH 1984)★★★, *Are You Man Enough?* (HDH 1992)★★★★.

Honeybus

Originally managed by one-time **Them** drummer Terry Noon, Honeybus was a vehicle for minor hit songwriters Pete Dello and Ray Cane. Following the recruitment of Colin Hare (vocals/guitar) and Peter Kircher (drums), the group was signed to the hip **Decca** subsidiary **Deram Records**. Their second single, 'Do I Still Figure In Your Life', with its plaintive lyric and striking string arrangement, received extensive airplay but narrowly failed to reach the Top 50. The similarly paced 'I Can't Let Maggie Go' fared better, entering the charts in March 1968 and peaking at number 8. Rather than exploiting the group's success, however, Dello dramatically left Honeybus only months later. Deprived of their main songwriter and gifted arranger, the group failed to escape the one-hit-wonder trap, but almost broke through with 'Girl Of Independent Means'. After advice from their management they folded in 1969. The post-demise release, *Story* (1970), testifies to their fledgling talent. Their single moment of chart glory was later resurrected as the long-running theme for a UK television bread commercial.

● ALBUMS: *Story* (Deram 1970)★★★.

● COMPILATIONS: *At Their Best* (See For Miles 1989)★★★.

Honeycombs

Formed in north London in November 1963, the group was originally known as the Sherabons and comprised: Denis D'ell (b. Denis Dalziel, 10 October 1943, London, England; vocals), Anne 'Honey' Lantree (b. 28 August 1943, Hayes, Middlesex, England; drums), John Lantree (b. 20 August 1940, Newbury, Berkshire, England; bass), Alan Ward (b. 12 December 1945, Nottingham, England; lead guitar) and Martin Murray (rhythm guitar), later replaced by Peter Pye (b. 12 July 1946, London, England). Producer **Joe Meek** had selected one of their songs as a possible single and the group's chances were enhanced following a management agreement with **Ken Howard** and **Alan Blaikley**. Although several record companies passed on the quintet's debut, 'Have I The Right', Pye Records' managing director Louis Benjamin agreed to release the disc. First, however, there was the obligatory name change, with Benjamin selecting Honeycombs after a track by

Jimmie Rodgers. The fact that the focus of attention in the group was the red-haired drummer 'Honey' made the rechristening even more appropriate. When 'Have I The Right' hit number 1 in the UK in the summer of 1964, the group's pop star future seemed assured. However, a dramatic flop with the follow-up 'Is It Because' caused concern, and although Howard and Blaikley came to the rescue with 'That's The Way', the group faltered amid line-up changes and poor morale, before moving inexorably towards cabaret and the revivalist circuit.

● ALBUMS: *The Honeycombs* (Pye 1964)★★★, *All Systems Go* (Pye 1965)★★★, *Here Are The Honeycombs* (Vee Jay 1964)★★★.

● COMPILATIONS: *Meek And Honey* (PRT 1983)★★★, *It's The Honeycombs/All Systems Go* (Sequel 1990)★★★, *The Best Of The Honeycombs* (1993)★★★.

Honeycrack

Comprising Pete Clarke (bass), Hugo Degenhardt (drums), Mark McCrae (guitar, ex-**Rub Ultra**), Willie Dowling (keyboards, ex-Grip; **Wildhearts**) and CJ (b. Chris Jagdhar; vocals, guitar, ex-**Tattooed Love Boys**; Wildhearts), UK heavy rock band Honeycrack were formed with an agenda that stated 'we have no messages to convey, but we do want to change the world'. The group was conceived in August 1994 after both CJ and Dowling had been ejected from the Wildhearts. Honeycrack's debut single, 'King Of Misery', was released to accompany their first tour of 1995, and was followed by October's 'Sitting At Home'. 'Go Away' followed in February 1996 and became their most successful single to date, entering the UK Top 40 and coinciding with a headlining tour and a four-week residency at London's Splash Cub. The debut album was an exciting and assured set and contained a glut of strong songs in addition to the previous singles. The biggest problem the band experienced was not writing songs or recording them but in choosing a name: 'We busked around for weeks on end, we should be marrying up the notion of something sweet and something dreadfully hard' - hence their sweet harmonies with bone-crunching guitar. The band appeared to have broken up by spring 1997.

● ALBUMS: *Prozaic* (Epic 1996)★★★.

Honeydogs

Veterans of their local Minneapolis, Minnesota, USA alternative rock scene, by 1997 it appeared the Honeydogs might be about to forge a national reputation. By that time, the group had signed to Debris Records, a new label set up by **Mercury Records** employee Ed Eckstine. Led by singer and songwriter Adam Levy, the Honeydogs, who originally formed in 1994, additionally include bassist Trent Norton and Levy's brother Noah on drums (the latter also plays with **Golden Smog**). Rhythm guitarist Tommy Borscheid joined in time for 1996's *Everything, I Bet You*. Their debut album, released for independent label

October Records in 1995, featured a suite of songs built around the group's self-evident **Beatles/Rolling Stones** influences - although elements of the raw pop tradition pioneered by band favourites the **Replacements** were also much in evidence. The best moments on the follow-up included the relatively tender ballad 'Miriam', and the steely pop of 'Busy Man'. For their major label debut the group collaborated with producer Tom Herbers, with the final mix overseen by Nick DiDia, a veteran of work with grunge bands **Pearl Jam** and **Stone Temple Pilots**. *Seen A Ghost* saw the band stick to their strengths - formidable roots rock *a la* the **Jayhawks**, played with considerable skill and an endearing lack of pretence.

● ALBUMS: *The Honeydogs* (October 1995)★★★, *Everything, I Bet You* (October 1996)★★★★, *Seen A Ghost* (Debris/Mercury 1997)★★★.

Honeydrippers

Formed in 1984, the Honeydrippers included **Led Zeppelin** alumni **Robert Plant** (vocals) and **Jimmy Page** (guitar), former **Chic** bassist Nile Rodgers and guitarist **Jeff Beck**. Their affection for 50s R&B was made apparent on *Honeydrippers Volume 1*, a mini-album which featured, among others, a sterling interpretation of **Ray Charles**' 'I Got A Woman'. Their reading of Phil Phillips' 'Sea Of Love' gave the group a surprise US Top 10 hit single, but despite this success, the concept has not been followed up, in part because of continued commitment by the individuals to their separate careers.

● ALBUMS: *Honeydrippers Volume 1* (Es Paranza 1984)★★★.

Honeyman-Scott, James

b. 1956, Hereford, England, d. 16 June 1982, London, England. This flaxen-headed guitarist who doubled on keyboards was a founder member of the **Pretenders** in 1978. If less prominent onstage than Chrissie Hynde, he was solidly at the music's heart: loud enough for vocal harmonies, but quietly ministering to overall effect instrumentally. Remembered principally as a guitarist, his riffs and solos were constructed to integrate with melodic and lyrical intent, rather than a flashier reaction to underlying chord sequences. This style was commensurate with a personality that permitted Hynde to take increasing control of the band's destiny after Pretenders II in 1981 - the year he married Peggy Sue Fender. Weakened by a detoxification course for drug addiction, his death in June 1982 occurred shortly after snorting cocaine at a London party. The group found a replacement in Robert McIntosh, a Honeyman-Scott soundalike.

Honeymoon Suite

A Canadian hard rock quintet of Johnny Dee (guitar, vocals), Derry Grehan (lead guitar), Dave Betts (drums), Gary Lalonde (bass) and Ray Coburn (keyboards), Honeymoon Suite formed in 1982 and set about establishing the strong club following that accompanied them throughout their career. Their debut release was a self-financed single, 'New Girl Now', which sold in sufficient quantities locally to attract the interest of **Warner Brothers Records**. Their self-titled debut album for the major was a dextrous, committed example of contemporary Canadian rock music, though some critics considered the lyrics to be banal even by AOR standards. It was followed by two further collections, *The Big Prize* and *Racing After Midnight*, which sold well in Canada without giving the group the impetus to break through across the southern border.

● ALBUMS: *Honeymoon Suite* (Warners 1984)★★, *The Big Prize* (WEA 1986)★★, *Racing After Midnight* (WEA 1988)★★.

Honeys

Arguably the definitive female surf group, the Honeys were formed in Califonia, USA as the Rovell Sisters in 1961. Marilyn, Diane and Barbara Rovell initially appeared at amateur talent shows, but embarked on a more substantial career when a cousin, Sandra Glantz aka Ginger Blake, replaced Barbara. The newcomer, a budding songwriter, brought the trio to producer **Gary Usher**, who in turn introduced the group to **Beach Boys** svengali, **Brian Wilson**. Now dubbed the Honeys, a term for 'female surfer', the trio embarked on a series of exemplary singles, each of which featured Wilson as either producer, arranger or composer. They included a reworking of a **Stephen Foster** standard, retitled 'Surfin' Down The Swanee River' (a number 1 in Denmark), 'Pray For Surf' and 'The One You Can't Have', a superb attempt at emulating the **Phil Spector** 'wall-of-sound'. Such releases were commercially unsuccessful but the Honeys remained in demand as backing vocalists for the Beach Boys, **Jan And Dean** and **Bruce Johnston**. Their ties within this close-knit circle were enhanced in December 1964 when Brian Wilson and Marilyn Rovell were married. A 1969 single, 'Goodnight My Love', anticipated the style the Rovells then followed as (**American**) **Spring**. Ginger Blake, meanwhile, pursued a parallel career, singing back-up with several live acts before establishing her own song publishing company. The trio was reunited during the early 80s for *Ecstasy*.

● ALBUMS: *Ecstasy* (1983)★★.

Honeysmugglers

Formed in London at the end of the 80s by Chris Spence, Steve Dinsdale, Ged Murphy and Steve C., the Honeysmugglers struggled to loosen the retrogressive tag awarded to them by virtue of their bold, Hammond organ-infested sound. In reality, the quartet were far more contemporary than most people gave them credit for, fusing 60s melodic instincts with the fluent rhythms of the 90s to create a boisterously tuneful panorama. After singles on Non-Fiction and Ultimate Records, however, the Honeysmugglers split up acrimoniously in 1991, without ever releasing an album.

Honky

Honky were formed from the ashes of Club St Louis, a small time rap duo who attracted some music biz attention in the early 90s. That outfit signed to **East West Records**, releasing a solitary single. When they lost their contract in 1992 they returned home to Doncaster, Yorkshire, England, disillusioned. Matt, responsible for the group's music, soldiered on as a studio engineer, before teaming up once more with his old rapping partner, Kyle, the line-up completed by Stu, Joloise and Rosa. Together they wrote the song which would become the debut Honky release. 'KKK (Koffee Koloured Kids)' emerged on **ZTT** in 1993. It concerned Kyle's alienation at being the son of a white mother and black father, and his exclusion from both societies. A follow-up, 'The Whistler', proved similarly thoughtful. Again it concerned Kyle's parentage, this time discussing his father's temper, which could always be detected by his whistling before an impending act of violence.

● ALBUMS: *The Ego Has Landed* (ZTT 1994)★★★, *Kuljit* (Columbia 1996)★★★.

Honourable Apache

b. Richard Bailey, Kingston, Jamaica, West Indies. Bailey's academic achievements led to his initial aspiration to become a teacher. He may well have fulfilled his ambition had he not been drawn to the delights of the **dancehall** and remarkably emulated his DJ heroes. In the mid-80s he emigrated to Baltimore, USA. He soon found solace with a local **sound system**, where he nurtured his career. Although he proved a competent performer, his location in Baltimore offered little opportunity to sustain a career as a DJ. In 1988 he moved to Miami where his reputation quickly spread, and he attracted the attention of Willie Lindo who took him into the studio. The sessions resulted in 'Stamina Man', 'Hurricane' and 'Gangsta Roll' for Lindo's Heavy Beat label. The historic end to Nelson Mandela's incarceration was described in Apache's 1990 hit, 'Them Free Mandela'. In the same year, he recorded in combination with **Screwdriver** the local hit 'Long Time'. His success led to live appearances at the Jamaican Reggae Sunsplash Festival in 1992 and 1993, as well as the Miami Reggae Festival, previously known as the Jamaica Awareness Reggae Festival, for four consecutive years. In 1994 Honourable Apache produced his biggest hit, 'Yardie Anthem'. His prominence led to a signing with Clifton 'Specialist' Dillon, who, through his Shang production stable, successfully exposed works by **Shabba Ranks**, **Mad Cobra** and **Patra** to a global audience. By the mid-90s he became the Hono Rebel Apache, a name emphasizing his unwillingness to compromise his music for commercial purposes.

Hoodoo Gurus

An Australian rock band whose belief in the power of the bar chord has never diminished, Sydney's Hoodoo Gurus share links with that city's other major alternative rock attraction of the 80s, the **Scientists** (after both relocated from Perth). That connection was instigated by singer-songwriter Dave Faulkner, who had previously played in a band called the Gurus, before joining Scientists guitarist Rod Radalj (guitar) in an untitled band. Bolstered by the arrival of another ex-Scientist member, drummer Jim Baker, the trio named their new band Le Hoodoo Gurus. That group would eventually evolve into the tight, hypnotic garage rock machine which, under a slightly abbreviated title, became widely venerated in underground circles through their releases for a variety of American labels. Indeed, much of their popularity stemmed from the USA, where tours of the west coast made them as popular as the musically aligned **Fleshtones**. Led by the power-pop playing of Brad Sheperd (guitar, harmonica), with the rhythm section of Baker (drums) and Clyde Bramley (bass), their ceaseless exploration of the riff has seen them compared to everyone from the **Cramps** to the **Fall**, beginning with their influential *Stoneage Romeos* debut of 1983. Dedicated to US television sitcom legends Arnold Ziffel and Larry Storch, it included the stage favourite '(Let's All) Turn On' and the nonsensical 'I Was A Kamikaze Pilot'. *Mars Needs Guitars!*, with Mark Kingsmill taking over on drums, was slightly hampered by inferior production, but the tunes were still memorable and even adventurous given their limited musical range, which veered from country punk to booming, bass-driven sleaze rock. A rarer outbreak of melodicism was introduced on *Blow Your Cool!*, with the band joined by the **Bangles** on several selections, although elsewhere they retreated to pounding rhythms and tough rock 'n' roll. The gap between albums in 1988 saw Bramley replaced by Rick Grossman on bass. More feedback and heightened songwriting tension, together with improved production, produced the band's finest album to date in 1989's *Magnum Cum Louder*. *Kinky* mined a similar furrow, drawing lyrical targets from US and Australian pop culture, though there was little stylistic variation to the band's themes. *Crank* brought in **Ramones** producer Ed Stasium, but, like follow-up *Blue Cave*, was a weaker effort. It seems unlikely that the Hoodoo Gurus will rise above their current cult status.

● ALBUMS: *Stoneage Romeos* (Big Time/A&M 1983)★★★, *Mars Need Guitars!* (Big Time/Elektra 1985)★★★, *Blow Your Cool!* (Big Time/Elektra 1987)★★★, *Magnum Cum Louder* (RCA 1989)★★★★, *Kinky* (RCA 1991)★★★, *Crank* (RCA 1995)★★, *Blue Cave* (Zoo 1996)★★.

● COMPILATIONS: *Electric Soup - The Singles Collection* Australian release (RCA 1992)★★★★, *Gorilla Bisquit* Australian release (RCA 1992)★★★.

Hoodoo Rhythm Devils

Formed in San Francisco in 1970, this eclectic band featured several of the city's best-known musicians. They revolved around Joe Crane (guitar, vocals, keyboards), a veteran of Texas' thriving blues circuit, and Glenn 'Hambone' Walters (harmonica/vocals) while the original line-up was completed by John Rewind (ex-**Grootna**; guitar), Dexter C. Plates (bass) and Roger Clark (bass). Their early albums, although commercially moribund, contained several excellent songs, notably 'All Tore Down' (later recorded by **Johnny Winter**) and a rousing version of **Bobby Fuller**'s 'I Fought The Law', and featured cameos by the **Pointer Sisters** and **Tower Of Power**. The collapse of the Blue Thumb label undermined the Hoodoo's career, but in 1976 Crane and Walters re-emerged with a revised band of Bob Flurie (ex-**It's A Beautiful Day**; guitar), Boots Hughston (saxophone), MacCridlin (bass) and Scott Matthews (drums). Misfortune continued to dog their progress - the group's secretary was murdered in a frenzied axe-attack - and when Crane died of leukæmia in 1980, his partner then formed Glen Walters And The Neptunes. The vocalist resurrected the Hoodoos' name in 1982, but the 'new' group remained low-key, playing local clubs with an ever changing pool of musicians.

● ALBUMS: *Rack Jobbers Rule* (1971)★★★, *Bar Be Que Of Deville* (1972)★★★, *What The Kids Want* (1973)★★★, *Safe In Their Homes* (1976)★★, *All Kidding Aside* (1978)★★.

Hooj Toons

One of the more upfront UK house record labels, whose *esprit de corps* seems to rise from knowing how to spot a breaking tune - rather than veiling themselves in clique mystique. Among their many notable releases were Simon Sed's 'Wigged Criminal', **Felix**'s 'Don't You Want Me' (which made the UK Top 10), **Hyper Go Go**'s 'High', Dis-Cuss' 'Pissed Apache' (a gay anthem from DJ Malcolm Duffy, Jonothan Blanks and DJ Kenny Clarke), **Gloworm**'s 'I Lift My Cup', **Andronicus**' (Blanks again) 'Make You Whole' and DCO2's 'Do What You Feel', all of which were included on the listed sampler album. They were also the first to release JX's 'Son Of A Gun', before licensing it to the London-affiliated **Internal** Dance imprint. The label originally grew out of Greedy Beat Records, which was set up by an accountant, before A&R man Jerry Dickens joined after leaving college. Dissatisfied with the small returns on his imput, Dickens spent most of 1993 trying to disentangle himself from the relationship, eventually setting up his own studio and gaining his own publishing deal. With slightly more solid financial footing, 1994 saw Dickens sign his first act for more than a one-off deal, JX (Jake Williams and vocalist Billie Godfrey). He also set up a subsidiary operation, Prolekult.

● ALBUMS: Various: *Some Of These Were Hooj* (Hooj Toons 1994)★★.

Hook

Formed in Los Angeles, California, USA, in 1967 by former **Leaves** guitarist Bobby Arlin, Hook also consisted of Buddy Sklar (bass) and Craig Boyd (drums). *Will Grab You* showed little of the folk/rock style Arlin's previous group was noted for, offering instead power-trio heavy rock. The departure of Boyd in 1968 prompted a re-think which saw former **Grass Roots** keyboard player Danny Provisor and new drummer Dale Loyola drafted into the line-up. *Hook* offered a more polished style but, as neither release was a commercial success, Arlin folded the band the following year. He subsequently became a booking agent in Orange County, California.

● ALBUMS: *Will Grab You* (UNI 1967)★★, *Hook* (UNI 1968)★★★.

Hooker 'N' Heat - Canned Heat/John Lee Hooker

Over the course of a double album, the Boogie Man is joined by the members of Canned Heat, the only group to take the blues into the UK and US Top 20. When they weren't having hits like 'On The Road Again' or 'Goin' Up The Country', Canned Heat were boogin' up a storm. As Hooker had shown in his collaboration with Britain's John Lee and the Groundhogs, a vigorous rhythm section held no threat for him. When the full band weighed into 'Whiskey And Wimmen' and 'Let's Make It', he was just preparing for a marathon stomp-off on 'Boogie Chillen No. 2'. Within the next two decades, Alan Wilson and Bob Hite had died and John Lee just carried on with his endless boogie.

● Tracks: *Messin' With The Hook; Drifter; You Talk Too Much; Burning Hell; Bottle Up And Go; I Got My Eyes On You; The Feelin' Is Gone; Send Me Your Pillow; You Talk Too Much; I Got My Eyes On You; Whiskey And Wimmen; Just You And Me; Let's Make It; Peavine; Boogie Chillen No. 2.*

● First released 1971

● UK peak chart position: did not chart

● USA peak chart position: 77

Hooker, Earl

b. Earl Zebedee Hooker, 15 January 1930, Clarksdale, Mississippi, USA, d. 21 April 1970. Hooker's interest in music was kindled at an early age. A self-taught guitarist, he began his itinerant career as a teenager, and having toured America's southern states in the company of **Robert Nighthawk**, **Ike Turner** and many others, Earl made his first, rudimentary recordings in 1952. The artist followed a sporadic release schedule throughout the 50s, but by the end of the decade Hooker had settled in Chicago where he began a more consistent output. However, his early work was spread over several of the city's independent outlets, and although undeniably talented, the difficult search for success saw Hooker aping the styles of contemporaries rather than forging one of his own. The guitarist asserted his gifts more fully in the wake of the blues revival and became one of the city's most highly regarded talents. He made a rare UK television appearance on the pioneering music programme *Ready Steady Go*, performed in-concert at London's Royal Albert Hall and toured Europe with the American Folk-Blues festival. Hooker also completed albums for several specialist labels, and led his own band, Electric Dust, but the tuberculosis against which he had battled throughout his life finally took its toll. Earl Hooker died in a Chicago sanitarium in April 1970.

● ALBUMS: *Don't Have To Worry* (1969)★★★, *Sweet Black Angel* (1970)★★★, with Lightnin' Hopkins, Smokey Hogg *Hooker, Hopkins And Hogg* (Specialty 1973)★★★, *Do You Remember* (1973)★★★, with Steve Miller *Hooker And Steve* (Arhoolie 1975)★★★, *First And Last Recordings* (Arhoolie 1975)★★★, *Two Bugs And A Roach* (Arhoolie 1976)★★★, *Play Your Guitar, Mr. Hooker* (Black Magic 1985)★★★.

● COMPILATIONS: *There's A Fungus Amung Us* (1972)★★★, *The Leading Brand* (Red Lightnin' 1978)★★★, with Magic Sam *Calling All Blues* (Charly 1986)★★★.

Hooker, John Lee

b. 22 August 1917, Clarksdale, Mississippi, USA. Born into a large family of agricultural workers, Hooker's first musical experiences, like those of so many other blues singers, were in church. A contrivance made from an inner tube attached to a barn door represented his first makeshift attempts at playing an instrument, but he subsequently learned some guitar from his stepfather William Moore, and they played together at local dances. At the age of 14, he ran away to Memphis, Tennessee, where he met and played with **Robert Lockwood**. A couple of years later he moved to Cincinnatti, where he stayed for about 10 years and sang with a number of gospel quartets. In 1943, he moved to Detroit, which was to be his home for many years, and began playing in the blues clubs and bars around Hastings Street, at the heart of that city's black section. Over the years he had developed the unique guitar style that was to make his music so distinctive and compelling. In 1948 he was finally given the chance to record. Accompanied only by his own electric guitar and constantly tapping foot, 'Boogie Chillen', with its driving rhythm and hypnotic drone of an accompaniment, was a surprise commercial success for Modern Records. Over the next few years, they leased a large amount of his material first from Bernie Besman and later from legendary Detroit entrepreneur **Joe Von Battle** (both of whom also tried a few Hooker issues on their own Sensation and JVB labels, respectively). Most of these early recordings feature Hooker performing entirely solo; only a few are duets with Eddie Kirkland or another guitarist, and there are one or two with a band. It seems that this solo setting was not typical of his live work at the time, which would have used a small band, probably including piano, second guitar and drums, but his idiosyncratic sense of timing has always made him a difficult musician to accompany, and it may be that recording him solo was the most reliable way of ensuring a clean take. Nevertheless, his solo sound on these early records was remarkably self-sufficient. His unique open-tuned guitar enabled him to combine a steady rhythm with inspired lead picking, thereby making full use of his rich, very bluesy baritone vocals. Although this one-man-band format might suggest a throwback to a more down-home ambience,

there is a certain hipness and urbane sophistication about these performances that represent a significant departure from the rural background of Hooker's music and contribute very strongly to his characteristic sound. While a solo blues singer was something of an anachronism by this time, there is no doubt that the records sold consistently.

From the late 40s to the early 50s, Hooker recorded prolifically and enjoyed an enormously successful run with Modern, producing such classic records as 'Crawling King Snake', 'In The Mood', 'Rock House Boogie' and 'Shake Holler & Run'. As well as these successes under his own name, he saw records released on a wide variety of labels, under a deliberately bewildering array of different pseudonyms: Johnny Williams on Gotham, Birmingham Sam And His Magic Guitar on Savoy, John Lee Booker on **Chess**, Delta John on Regent, The Boogie Man on Acorn, Johnny Lee on DeLuxe and Texas Slim or John Lee Cooker on King. Most of these were also leased from Joe Von Battle. His recording success led to tours. He played the R&B circuit across the country and this further developed his popularity with the black American public. In 1955, he severed his connection with Modern and began a long association with **Vee Jay Records** of Chicago.

By this time, the solo format was finally deemed too old-fashioned for the contemporary R&B market and all of these recordings used a tight little band, often including **Eddie Taylor** on guitar, as well as piano and various combinations of horns. The association with Vee Jay proved very satisfactory, both artistically and commercially, producing a string of hits such as 'Dimples', 'Maudie' and 'Boom Boom' and promoting further extensive tours. In the late 50s, as the market for R&B was beginning to contract, a new direction opened up for Hooker and he began to appear regularly at folk clubs and folk festivals. He found himself lionized by a new audience consisting mainly of young, white listeners. The folk connection also resulted in new recordings, issued on album by Riverside. These reverted to the solo format, with an acoustic guitar. While these recordings lacked the hard edge of the best of his earlier commercial sides, they were fascinating for the fact that the producers encouraged him to dig back into his older repertoire. Several songs reflecting his rural Mississippi background, such as 'Bundle Up And Go' and 'Pea Vine Special' were given his distinctive treatment. These records spread his name more widely when they were released overseas. In the early 60s his reputation grew as he was often cited by younger pop and rock musicians, in particular the **Rolling Stones**, as a major influence. As a result international tours soon followed. Throughout this period, he continued to release singles and albums on Vee Jay, but records also appeared on other labels. Later in the 60s, he made a number of records for Bluesway, aimed at this younger market. The connection with a new generation of musicians led to various 'super sessions', predictably of varying quality, but it perhaps bore fruit most successfully in the early 70s with the release of *Hooker 'N' Heat*, in which he played with the American rock blues band **Canned Heat**. Their famous long improvised boogies clearly owed a great deal to the influence of the older man. Although the popular enthusiasm for blues waned for a while in the late 70s and early 80s, Hooker's standing has rarely faltered and he has continued to tour, latterly with the Coast To Coast Blues Band. His early recordings have been repackaged and re-released over and over again, with those companies who used him pseudonymously in the early days now proudly taking the opportunity to capitalize on his real name. He has also made many new records but few of these have been of outstanding quality. A remarkable transformation came in 1989 when he recorded *The Healer*. This superb album featured guests on most tracks including **Bonnie Raitt**, **Los Lobos** and, arguably the finest track, a duet with **Carlos Santana** on the title track. If such a thing as 'Latin blues' existed, this was it. This album has since become one of the biggest-selling blues albums of all time and has helped fuel a blues revival in prompting older statesmen to record again. *Mr Lucky* reached number 3 in the UK album charts, setting a record for Hooker, at 74, as the oldest artist to achieve that position. On this second guest album he was paired with **Ry Cooder**, **Van Morrison**, **Albert Collins**, and a gamut of other superstars. In his old age, Hooker has begun to fulfil the role of elder statesman of the blues, even appearing in an advertisement for a multinational chemical corporation, but this has not prevented him from touring and he continues to perform widely and often. Hooker is genuinely loved by fellow musicians; Bonnie Raitt stated in 1992 that his guitar sound was one of the most erotic things she had ever heard. The Hooker boom continued right through 1992 with the use of a new version of 'Boom Boom' for a Lee Jeans television advertisement. Both the single and the subsequent album were considerable hits. Following a hernia operation in 1994 the great man decided to slow down and enjoy his cars and houses. Another fine release, *Chill Out*, came in 1995, again produced by Roy Rogers. Shortly after its release it was announced that Hooker had retired from performing and was prepared to rest until they 'lowered his bones into the earth'. However, he was back on stage performing in 1996 and released a new album in 1997. *Don't Look Back* was a Van Morrison production and bore clear signs of his influence; Morrison's 'The Healing Game' and **Jimi Hendrix**'s 'Red House' were the highlights, and 'Don't Look Back' was beautifully understated, with some fine noodling organ and guitar from **Charles Brown** and Danny Caron respectively. Another reworking of 'Dimples' added nothing to the classic Vee Jay recording. This formidable man is the last surviving giant of the blues, and therefore, represents our final touchstone with a body of music that is both rich in history and unmatched in its importance.

● ALBUMS: *The Folk Blues Of John Lee Hooker* (Riverside 1959)★★★★, *I'm John Lee Hooker* (Vee Jay 1959)★★★★, *Travelin'* (Vee Jay 1960)★★★, *Sings The Blues* (King 1960)★★★★, *Thats My Story* (Riverside 1960)★★★★, *House Of The Blues* (Chess 1960)★★★★, *The Blues* (Crown 1960)★★★, *The Folk Lore Of John Lee Hooker* (Vee Jay 1961)★★★★, *Burnin'* (Vee Jay 1962)★★★, *John Lee Hooker On Campus* (1963)★★★, *The Big Soul Of John Lee Hooker* (Vee Jay 1963)★★★, *Don't Turn Me From Your Door* (Atco 1963)★★★, *John Lee Hooker At Newport* (Vee Jay 1964)★★★★, *I Want To Shout The Blues* (Stateside 1964)★★★, *And Seven Nights* (Verve/Folkways 1965)★★★, *Real Folk Blues* (Chess 1966)★★★★, *It Serves You Right To Suffer* (Impulse 1966)★★★, *Live At The Cafe Au Go Go* (Bluesway 1966)★★★, *Urban Blues* (Bluesway 1967)★★★, *Simply The Truth* (Bluesway 1968)★★★, *You're Leaving Me Baby* (1969)★★★, *If You Miss 'Im* (Bluesway 1969)★★★, *Tupelo Blues* (1969)★★★, *Alone* (1970)★★★, *Hooker 'N' Heat* (Specialty 1971)★★★★, *Endless Boogie* (ABC 1971)★★★, *Never Get Out Of These Blues Alive* (Crescendo 1972)★★★, *John Lee Hooker's Detroit* (1973)★★★, *Live At Kabuki Wuki* (Bluesway 1973)★★, *Mad Man's Blues* (Chess 1973)★★★, *Free Beer And Chicken* (1974)★★, *Blues Before Sunrise* (1976)★★★, *No Friend Around* (1979)★★, *This Is Hip* (1980)★★★, *Black Snake Blues* (1980)★★★, *Moanin' The Blues* (1982)★★★, *Lonesome Mood* (1983)★★★, *Solid Sender* (1984)★★, *Jealous* (Pointblank 1986)★★★, *The Healer* (Chameleon 1989)★★★★★, *The Detroit Lion* (1990)★★★, *Boogie Awhile* (1990)★★, *More Real Folk Blues: The Missing Album* (1991)★★★, *Mr. Lucky* (Charisma 1991)★★★★, *Boom Boom* (Point Blank 1992)★★★, *Chill Out* (Point Blank 1995)★★★★, with the Groundhogs *Hooker & The Hogs* rec. 1965 (Indigo 1996)★★, *The First Concert - Alone* 1976 recording (Blues Alliance 1996)★★★, *Don't Look Back* (Silvertone 1997)★★★.

● COMPILATIONS: *The Best Of John Lee Hooker* (Vee Jay 1962)★★★, *Collection: John Lee Hooker - 20 Blues Greats* (Déjà Vu 1985)★★★, *The Ultimate Collection 1948-1990* (1992)★★★★, *The Best Of John Lee Hooker 1965-1974* (1992)★★★★, *Blues Brother* (1992)★★★, *The Vee Jay Years 1955 - 1964* (1992)★★★★, *Gold Collection* (1993)★★★, *The Legendary Modern Recordings 1948-54* (1993)★★★★, *Helpless Blues* (Realisation 1994)★★★, *Original Folk Blues ... Plus* (Ace 1994)★★★★, *The Rising Sun Collection* (Just A Memory 1994)★★★, *Whiskey & Wimmen* (Charly 1994)★★★, *The EP Collection Plus* (See For Miles 1995)★★★★, *The Early Years* (Tomato 1995)★★★, *I Feel Good* (Jewel 1995)★★★, *Alternative Boogie: Early Studio Recordings 1948-1952* (Capitol 1996)★★★, *The Complete 50s Chess Recordings* (Chess 1998)★★★.

● VIDEOS: *Survivors - The Blues Today* (Hendring Video 1989), *John Lee Hooker/Lowell Fulson/Percy Mayfield* (1992), *John Lee Hooker And Friends 1984-1992* (Vestapol 1996), *Rare Performances 1960-1984* (Vestapol 1996).

● FURTHER READING: *Boogie Chillen: A Guide To John Lee Hooker On Disc*, Les Fancourt.

● FILMS: *The Blues Brothers* (1980).

Hookey Band

An unconvincing electric band that grew out of many Oxfordshire folk and dance groups, claiming lineage to

Dave Pegg (**Fairport Convention**) and Chris Leslie (**Whippersnapper**). One for completists only.

● ALBUMS: *Making A Song & Dance About It* (1983)★★★.

Hookfoot

Ian Duck (vocals/guitar), Dave Glover (bass) and Roger Pope (drums) formed the nucleus of this highly-proficient unit. The trio had already worked together in the Soul Agents and Loot before establishing their new act with guitarist Caleb Quaye. Hookfoot became the house band for music publisher **Dick James** and members appeared, individually or collectively, on numerous sessions, notably those for **Elton John**'s *Empty Sky*, *Elton John* and *Tumbleweed Connection*. *Hookfoot* and *Good Times A-Comin'* established the quartet as a unit in its own right, but whereas Quaye's guitar work was always meritorious, their material was largely unexceptional. Ex-**Fairies**' bassist Fred Gandy replaced Glover for *Communication*, but the alteration made little difference to the group's commercial fortunes. Pope and Quaye continued studio-based careers upon Hookfoot's disintegration.

● ALBUMS: *Hookfoot* (DJM 1971)★★★★, *Good Times A-Comin'* (DJM 1972)★★, *Communications* (DJM 1973)★★, *Roaring* (1974)★★.

● COMPILATIONS: *Headlines* (1975)★★★.

Hookim, Joseph 'Joe Joe'

b. Jamaica, West Indies. One of four brothers involved with music from an early age (the other brothers were Kenneth, Ernest and Paulie), Joe Joe and his brother Ernest started on the bottom rung of the entertainment industry ladder, controlling juke-boxes and one-armed bandits, but in 1970 the Jamaican government outlawed gaming machines. The brothers subsequently decided to branch out and build their own recording studio - **Channel One** - in the heart of the Kingston ghetto on Maxfield Avenue. At first, Joe Joe hired veteran Sid Bucknor as engineer, since none of his family were particularly adept at the technical side of the business, but before long, Ernest took over at the mixing desk. By this time, the Hookims also had their own pressing plant and label-printing workshop. Channel One slowly established a name for itself with releases on a variety of different labels from established singers such as **Leroy Smart**, **Junior Byles** and **Horace Andy**, but it was when the **Mighty Diamonds** started work for them that everything came together, particularly after the release of 'Right Time' in 1976. The Diamonds offered an exciting and different **rockers** rhythm, dominated by 'militant' double drumming courtesy of **Sly Dunbar** of the in-house **Revolutionaries** band. The sound influenced the entire Jamaican music business for the next two years, with every producer on the island formulating their own variation on the beat.

The bestsellers continued for the Diamonds, along with DJs **Dillinger** and **Trinity**, plus countless instrumental records from the Revolutionaries that appeared in the charts; Joe Joe professed embarrassment at seeing nine out of the Top 10 records on his own Well Charge label! Many of the rhythms were versions of **Studio One** classics, which caused some friction, and Joe Joe was the object of a great deal of criticism. He was, however, always open about the fact that he copied some of **Coxsone Dodd**'s rhythms. Throughout the 70s and on into the mid-80s, the Maxfield Avenue Studio was in constant demand by artists and producers, all hoping to capture a little of the magic, and in 1979 the set-up was upgraded to sixteen tracks to accommodate the demand. The Hookim brothers were the first to introduce 12-inch 45 rpm records to Jamaica with 'Truly' by the Jayes (a version of an old **Marcia Griffiths** Studio One hit), which was released with a DJ version by Ranking Trevor. The dynamic range of these 12-inch releases was a vast improvement on the 7-inch, and the 12-inch 'Disco-Mix' went on to become an integral part of reggae music, with vocal, DJ and instrumental cuts of the same rhythm all together on one release. Less successful were the 'Channel One Economic Packages' - 7-inch releases that played at 33 and a third rpm, but, sadly, the sound quality left much to be desired. Joe Joe founded a New York branch of Channel One and in the early 80s their future looked assured as he released a highly successful series of 'Clash' albums from the USA - featuring a different artist on each side. Even with hindsight it is difficult to see exactly what went wrong at Channel One, but the Kingston and New York operations were summarily shut down in the late 80s and the innovative Hookim brothers are no longer active in the music business.

● COMPILATIONS: Various Artists: *Jonkanoo Dub* (Cha Cha 1978)★★★, *General For All General - Dance Hall Style* (Hitbound 1984)★★★★, *Hit Bound! Revolutionary Sound Of Channel One* 1976-79 recordings (Heartbeat 1990)★★★★

Hooper, Les

b. 27 February 1940, Baton Rouge, Louisiana, USA. Although a self-taught pianist, Hooper studied composition at Louisiana State University before entering the advertising business as a writer of jingles. In Chicago in the mid-70s he formed a big band which made a fine album, *Look What They've Done*, and was beaten to a Grammy by **Woody Herman**. Examples of his assimilation of current musical thought can be heard on charts that he wrote for **Don Ellis**. Hooper's advertising career ran from the mid-60s until the late 70s, when he became a studio musician in Los Angeles. An occasional big band under Hooper's leadership has demonstrated his arranging skills with their blend of swing era principles and contemporary sounds. These charts have attracted the attention of many young musicians playing in college and university bands on both sides of the Atlantic, many of whom use Hooper's arrangements.

● ALBUMS: *Look What They've Done* (1974)★★★, *Dorian Blue* (c.1980)★★, *Hoopla* (1980)★★★, *Raisin' The Roof* (1982)★★★.

Hooray For What!

A toned-down political and anti-war musical satire, *Hooray For What!* opened at New York's Winter Garden Theatre on 1 December 1937, nearly two years before World War II itself opened - in Europe at least. The book by Howard Lindsay and Russel Crouse, told of Chuckles (Ed Wynn), a horticultural scientist who invents a gas that kills appleworms - unfortunately it also kill humans as well. The discovery sparks off a string of diplomatic and political incidents and high-level conferences, culminating in Chuckles's appearance at the Geneva Peace Convention. While he is there, agents from an 'unfriendly power' steal the formula with the aid of a mirror, and so get it backwards. The result is a harmess laughing gas, which enables the world to breath a sigh of relief. During the pre-Broadway tryout, the show's originally powerful messages were modified somewhat - **Agnes de Mille**'s anti-war ballet was cut - but with **E.Y. 'Yip' Harburg** providing the lyrics to **Harold Arlen**'s music, there was always going to be an irreverent, and more 'sideways' look at issues and songs. Not content with coming up with 'In The Shade Of The *New* Apple Tree' in place of the cosy 1905 number, 'In the Shade of The *Old* Apple Tree', he actually had the tongue-in-cheek effrontery to question the basic ingredient of popular music itself - love. His witty 'Down With Love' contained lines such as 'Down with songs that moan about night and day . . . give it back to the birds and bees - and the Viennese . . . down with songs romantic and stupid/Down with sighs, and down with Cupid/Brother, let's stuff that dove/Down with love'. The rest of the fine score included 'Moanin' In The Mornin'', 'I've Gone Romantic On You', 'Life's A Dance', and 'God's Country', which was featured in the 1939 **Judy Garland**-Mickey Rooney film *Babes In Arms*, and also became a hit in 1950 for both **Frank Sinatra** and **Vic Damone**. *Hooray For What!* stayed around for 200 performances - a reasonable run - and besides Ed Wynn, with his zany, crazy antics, the cast included Jack Whiting, Paul Haakon, June Clyde, Vivian Vance (who went on to become an important member of the 50s hit television show, *I Love Lucy*), and singers **Hugh Martin** and **Ralph Blane**, who were to make an impact on Broadway with their own songs in the 1941 show *Best Foot Forward*.

Hoosier Hot Shots

The group consisted of Hezzie Trietsch (drums, song whistle, alto horn, washboard), brother Kenny Triesch (guitar, bass, banjo, horn), Frank Kettering (bass, guitar, banjo, flute, piano, piccolo) and Gabe Ward (clarinet). After starting out as a dance band, they found comedy routines were more enjoyable to perform and consequently, by 1935, when they became regulars on the WLS *National Barn Dance* in Chicago, they had become a novelty act. Their rousing stage entrance, preceded by the cry 'Are you ready, Hezzie', inspired a national catchphrase, and for years they worked the NBC *Alka Seltzer Show* segment with Uncle Ezra. Songs that they made popular include 'Meet Me In The Icehouse Lizzie', 'Red Hot Fannie' and 'The Man With Whiskers'. They toured extensively and recorded for ARC, **Vocalion** and **Mercury Records**, but their comedy and zany behaviour firmly established their live appeal. They toured with the WLS tours and historian Bill C. Malone states in *Country Music USA* that they 'frequently grossed between $3,000 and $5,000 dollars for one-day stands'. They visited Hollywood and even made appearances in several films. Naturally, over the years, there were personnel changes and other artists who appeared as members included Nathan Harrison, Keith Milheim and Gil Taylor.

● ALBUMS: *The Hoosier Hot Shots* (Tops 1959)★★★★, *The Hoosier Hot Shots Hoop It Up (Wha Hoo)* (Golden Tone 1960)★★★★, *The Original Hoosier Hot Shots* (Dot 1964)★★★★, *It's The Hoosier Hot Shots (National Barn Dance)* (Sunbeam 1975)★★★, *Nashville's Original Hoosier Hot Shots - Country Kiddin'* (Spin-O-Rama 70s)★★★.

● COMPILATIONS: Rural Rhythm (Columbia/ Legacy 1992)★★★★.

Hooters

This long-running Philadelphia band the Hooters have become well versed in the fickle nature of fame since their formation in 1978. Originally a quintet fusing folk, rock and ska, they spent the early 80s building a formidable live reputation throughout surrounding states. Led by Rob Hyman and Eric Bazilian, the Hooters took their name from the distinctive keyboard and harmonica sound which dominated their early recordings. They had several US hits in the mid-80s as **MTV** exposure took 'All You Zombies' (number 58), 'And We Danced' (number 21), 'Day By Day' (number 18) and 'Where Do The Children Go' (number 38) into the *Billboard* charts. All four were included on their debut album, which received universally strong reviews. Two more singles, 'Johnny B' and 'Satellite', failed to break the Top 50, although the latter did become a strong international seller, topping several European lists. On *Zig Zag* they pursued a more sober direction, with songs such as 'Give The Music Back' and 'Don't Knock It 'Til You Try It' adding darker shades to their repertoire. However, when the sales of the album were only moderate, a dramatic self-appraisal was undertaken. 'We did talk about ending the band, but we came to the conclusion that we still have too much energy.' *Out Of Body* revealed plenty of the Hooters' customary catchy rock verve, but with a new focus on folk-rock (including the use of a mandolin, violin and accordion). They had also moved to a new label, following **Columbia Records**' purchase by Sony (which had upset the promotion of their previous album). They also changed producers (Richard Chertoff departing in favour of **Steve Earle** collaborator Joe Hardy). Multi-instrumentalist Mindy Jostyn (formerly part of **Donald Fagen**'s New Rock 'N' Soul Revue) was also added as a sixth member. Despite a revitalized sound, the Hooters failed to regain the commercial ground lost in the early 90s, and the band returned to session playing. Most in-demand was Hyman who had already worked with **Sophie B. Hawkins**, **Willie Nelson** and **Johnny Clegg**. He also continued to write for **Cyndi Lauper**.

● ALBUMS: *Nervous Night* (Columbia 1985)★★★, *One Way Home* (Columbia 1987)★★★, *Zig Zag* (Columbia 1989)★★★, *Out Of Body* (1993)★★★.

Hootie And The Blowfish

This South Carolina quartet were formed at the turn of the 90s and are led by Darius Rucker (Hootie), whose soulful vocals add sparkle to an otherwise fairly formu-laic rock sound. The quartet is completed by Mark Bryan (b. 1967; guitar, ex-Missing In Action), Dean Felber (b. 1967; bass) and Jim 'Soni' Sonefield (b. 1965; drums). Sonefield stated in *Rolling Stone*, 'Everyone says we're one black guy in an all-white band, but that's not true - we're actually three white guys in an all-black band'. Bryan and Rucker played together in a soft rock duo as the Wolf Brothers. Following an aborted contract with J.R.S. Records they put out a self-financed EP, which contained 'Hold My Hand'. They sold it at gigs and after a short time it had sold over 50,000 copies. Their spectacularly successful debut *Cracked Rear View* was a slow burner on the US charts, climbing into the Top 10 after over seven months on the chart. Rucker was a strong live performer on their vast 1994 tour (of more than 300 dates), presiding over a clutch of songs about emotional isolation and yearning. Part of the 'buzz' surrounding the band followed US televi-sion talk show host David Letterman's pronouncement that Hootie were 'my favourite new band'. *Cracked Rear View* took its title from a **John Hiatt** lyric and was produced by **R.E.M./John Cougar Mellencamp** associ-ate Don Gehman. It documented the band's career to date, and included the single 'Hold My Hand', one of several numbers to address ecological concerns and human frailty, which featured guest vocals from **David Crosby**. The album became one of the most successful rock debuts of all time, sales in its homeland having already surpassed 15 million (by February 1997). Similar sales over the rest of the world indicated that theirs would be the most 'difficult second album' in rock history. At the 1995 Grammy Awards, however, they picked up two statuettes, for Best New Artist and Best Pop Performance By A Group. It was inevitable that the follow-up proved to be anti-climatic. Having performed songs from *Fairweather Johnson* onstage they were now familiar to their loyal fans. Even though it debuted in the US chart at number 1, by the band's previous standards the album was seen as something of a flop; by anybody else's it was a massive success.

● ALBUMS: *Cracked Rear View* (East West 1994)★★★, *Fairweather Johnson* (Atlantic 1996)★★★.

● VIDEOS: *Summer Camp With Trucks* (Warners 1995), *A Series Of Short Trips* (Atlantic Video 1996).

Hope, Bob

b. Leslie Townes Hope, 26 May 1903, Eltham, England. One of the all-time great entertainers; an actor and comedian, whose singing ability has usually been sadly under-rated. Hope was taken to the USA at the age of four and grew up in Cleveland. As a teenager he tried his hand at various jobs including boxing, and toured in vaudeville as a song-and-dance-man for a time. In the late 20s and early 30s he had small parts and some chorus work in a few Broadway shows before making a big impression in *Roberta* in 1933. He had the amusing duet, 'Don't Tell Me It's Bad', with Linda Watkins in *Say When* (1934), and in 1936 introduced the lovely 'I Can't Get Started' in the *Ziegfeld Follies*, and (with **Ethel Merman**) **Cole Porter**'s amusing 'It's De-lovely' in *Red, Hot And Blue*. By this time he had broken into radio, and in 1938 he was given his own show. In the same year he made his first feature film, *The Big Broadcast Of 1938*, in which he introduced (with Shirley Ross) yet another durable song, **Leo Robin** and **Ralph Rainger**'s 'Thanks For The Memory', which won an Oscar and went on to become his life-long theme tune. In 1939 Hope was highly acclaimed for his perfor-mance in the comedy-thriller *The Cat And The Canary*, and he continued to appear in musicals such as *College Swing*, *Give Me A Sailor*, and *Some Like It Hot*. In 1940 he teamed up with **Bing Crosby** and **Dorothy Lamour** for *Road To Singapore*, the first of seven comedy musi-cals which took the trio to Zanzibar, Morocco, Utopia, Rio, Bali, and finally, in 1962, to Hong Kong. Over the years the comedy pictures far outweighed the musicals, but during the 40s and 50s Hope still appeared in a few, such as *Louisiana Purchase* (1941), *Star Spangled Rhythm* (1942), *Let's Face It* (1943), *My Favourite Spy* (1951), *Here Come The Girls* (1953), *The Seven Little Foys* (1955), and *Beau James* (1957). He also sang the occasional engaging number in other films, including two by **Jay Livingston** and **Ray Evans**: 'Buttons And Bows', another Oscar-winner, from *The Paleface* (1948), and 'Silver Bells' from *The Lemon Drop Kid* (1950). In 1958 he joined Crosby for one of their 'insulting' duets, 'Nothing In Common', which **Sammy Cahn** and **Jimmy Van Heusen** composed for the zany *Paris Holiday*. Hope's ongoing 'feud' with Crosby has been a permanent feature of his act since the 30s, and has featured prominently on the comedian's annual trips overseas to entertain US troops, events that were particularly newsworthy during the years of the Vietnam War. He also spent much of World War II in the South Pacific war zone, along with artists such as Jerry Colonna and **Frances Langford**. Hope has been with NBC radio and television since 1934, the year his first *Pepsodent* show was aired - his 1992 Christmas TV Special was his 43rd - and there was a good deal of speculation when, following the 1993 tribute *Bob Hope: The First 90 Years*, his annual contract was not immedi-ately renewed. During his career he has been showered with awards from many organizations and countries, including Emmys, a Peabody, 50 honorary academic degrees, and five special Academy Awards for humanitarianism and contributions to the film industry. He has also hosted the Academy Awards ceremony itself on numerous occasions. In 1994 he appeared at the Royal Albert Hall in London as part of the D-Day 50th Anniversary celebrations, and called in at the American Embassy to collect a Supreme Headquarters Allied Expeditionary Forces plaque to commemorate his wartime work. Two years later, he hosted *Bob Hope . . . Laughing With Presidents*, 'his 284th and final special for NBC television'.

Early in 1998, it was announced that Hope was to be given an honorary knighthood by the Queen in recognition of his long service as an entertainer, particularly for troops in wartime. He is supposed to be 'the most wealthy entertainer who has ever lived', a point which was touched on by fellow comedian Milton Berle at a Friar's Club Roast in Hope's honour in 1989. Berle noted: 'This guy owns so much property in America he should be Japanese.'

● FURTHER READING: *The Amazing Careers Of Bob Hope*, Joe Morelli, Edward Epstein, Eleanor Clarke. *The Secret Life Of Bob Hope*, Arthur Marx. *Have Tux Will Travel. I Owe Russia $1,200. They Got Me Covered. I Never Left Home. The Road To Hollywood* (autobiography), all by Bob Hope.

● FILMS: *Thanks For The Memory* (1938), *Give Me A Sailor* (1938), *The Big Broadcast Of 1938, College Swing* (1938), *The Cat And The Canary* (1939), *Some Like It Hot* (1939), *Never Say Die* (1939), *The Ghost Breakers* (1940), *Road To Singapore* (1940), *Louisiana Purchase* (1941), *Nothing But The Truth* (1941), *Caught In The Draft* (1941), *Road To Zanzibar* (1941), *They Got Me Covered* (1942), *Star Spangled Rhythm* (1942), *Road To Morocco* (1942), *My Favorite Blonde* (1942), *Let's Face It* (1943), *The Princess And The Pirate* (1944), *Road To Utopia* (1945), *Monsieur Beaucaire* (1946), *Variety Girl (cameo)* (1947), *Where There's Life* (1947), *My Favorite Brunette* (1947), *The Paleface* (1948), *Road To Rio* (1948), *The Great Lover* (1949), *Sorrowful Jones* (1949), *Fancy Pants* (1950), *My Favorite Spy* (1951), *The Lemon Drop Kid* (1951), *Road To Bali* (1952), *The Greatest Show On Earth* cameo (1952), *Son Of Paleface* (1952), *Here Come The Girls* (1953), *Off Limits* (1953), *Casanova's Big Night* (1954), *The Seven Little Foys* (1955), *The Iron Petticoat* (1956), *That Certain Feeling* (1956), *Beau James* (1957), *Paris Holiday* (1958), *Alias Jesse James* (1959), *The Facts Of Life* (1960), *Bachelor In Paradise* (1961), *The Road To Hong Kong* (1962), *Call Me Bwana* (1963), *Critics Choice* (1963), *A Global Affair* (1964), *I'll Take Sweden* (1965), *The Oscar* cameo (1966), *Boy Did I Get A Wrong Number* (1966), *Eight On The Lam* (1967), *The Private Navy Of Sgt O'Farrell* (1968), *How To Commit Marriage* (1969), *Cancel My Reservation* (1972), *The Muppet Movie* cameo (1979), *Spies Like Us* cameo (1985).

Hope, Elmo

b. 27 June 1923, New York City, New York, USA. Influenced by **Bud Powell**, Hope was regarded by some as a mere imitator. However he did develop his own highly individual piano style. His playing could be just as effective in the context of hard bop with **John** Coltrane and **Hank Mobley** on 'All Star Session', or in his trio work with drummer **Frank Butler**. Other collaborations include **Harold Land** 'The Fox' and the **Curtis Counce** Quintet 'Exploring The Future'.

● ALBUMS: *Meditation* (Original Jazz Classics 1958)★★★★, *Hope Meets Foster* (Original Jazz Classics 1956)★★★★, *Homecoming* (Original Jazz Classics 1962)★★★.*Elmo Hope Trio With Jimmy Bond And Frank Butler* (Fresh Sounds 1988)★★★, *Trio And Quartet* (Blue Note 1991)★★.

Hope, Lynn

b. 26 September 1926, Birmingham, Alabama, USA. Tenor saxophonist Hope joined King Kolax's band upon graduation before forming his own outfit with his sister and brothers and converting to the Moslem faith, which resulted in his changing his name to Al Hajji Abdullah Rasheed Ahmed and wearing either a fez or, more usually, a turban. Seeking a recording deal, he signed an invalid contract with Miracle in 1950 and, when no recording sessions resulted, went to Premium Records where he recorded his biggest hit, the standard 'Tenderly' which was picked up by **Chess Records**. He recorded prolifically for Aladdin between 1951 and 1957 during which he continued his policy of bringing standards up-to-date with instrumental readings of 'September Song', 'Summertime', 'She's Funny That Way' and a re-recording of 'Tenderly' amongst others. His straight, melodic saxophone playing was derided by the musically hip - who rechristened him 'No Hope' - but his modernization of old standards was loved by the general public (in person, if not on record), and his records often harboured an exciting blues or jump tune on the b-side. Hope's last recordings were made for King in 1960, after which he seems to have disappeared from the public eye

● COMPILATIONS: *Lynn Hope And His Tenor Sax* (1983)★★★, *Morocco* (1985)★★★.

Hopkin, Mary

b. 3 May 1950, Pontardawe, Glamorganshire, Wales. Hopkin's career began while she was still a schoolgirl. Briefly a member of a local folk rock band, she completed several Welsh-language releases before securing a slot on the televised talent show, *Opportunity Knocks*. Fashion model Twiggy was so impressed by Hopkin's performance she recommended the singer to **Paul McCartney** as a prospective signing for the newly formed Apple label. 'Those Were The Days', a traditional song popularized by Gene Raskin of the **Limelighters**, was selected as the artist's national debut and this haunting, melancholic recording, produced by McCartney, topped both the UK and US charts in 1968. Her follow-up single, 'Goodbye' reached number 2 the following year, but despite its excellent versions of Donovan's 'Happiness Runs' and 'Lord Of The Reedy River', the concurrent *Post Card* showed a singer constrained by often inappropriate material. Nevertheless, the **Mickie Most**-produced 'Temma Harbour' was another Top 10 hit, while 'Knock Knock

Who's There?', Britain's entry to the 1970 Eurovision Song Contest, peaked at number 2.

'Think About Your Children', penned by Most protégés **Hot Chocolate**, was Hopkin's last Top 20 entry, as the singer became increasingly unhappy over the style of her releases. However, a second album *Earth Song/Ocean Song*, was more representative of Hopkin's talent, and sympathetic contributions from **Ralph McTell** and **Danny Thompson** enhanced its enchanting atmosphere. Paradoxically, the set was issued as her contract with Apple expired and, having married producer **Tony Visconti**, she retired temporarily from recording.

Hopkin resumed her career in 1972 with 'Mary Had A Baby' and enjoyed a minor hit four years later with 'If You Love Me'. The singer also added backing vocals on several sessions, notably **David Bowie**'s *Sound And Vision*, before joining Mike Hurst (ex-**Springfields**) and Mike D'Albuquerque (ex-**Electric Light Orchestra**) in Sundance. Having left this short-lived aggregation, Hopkin resurfaced in 1983 as a member of Oasis (not the UK indie band). **Peter Skellern** and Julian Lloyd Webber were also members of this act which enjoyed a Top 30 album, but was brought to a premature end when Hopkin was struck by illness. Her subsequent work includes an appearance on **George Martin**'s production of *Under Milk Wood*, but she remains indelibly linked to her million-selling debut hit.

● ALBUMS: *Post Card* (Apple 1969)★★, *Earth Song/Ocean Song* (Apple 1971)★★, *Those Were The Days* (Apple 1972)★★, *The King Of Elfland's Daughter* (Chrysalis 1977)★★, with Oasis *Oasis* (WEA 1984)★★, with George Martin *Under Milk Wood* (EMI 1988)★★★.

● COMPILATIONS: *The Welsh World Of Mary Hopkin* (Decca 1979)★★, *Those Were The Days: The Best Of Mary Hopkin* (EMI 1995)★★.

Hopkins, Claude

b. 24 August 1903, Alexandria, Virginia, USA, d. 19 February 1984. Hopkins was born into a well-educated, middle-class family, both parents being members of the faculty of Howard University. He studied formally at Howard before starting a career as a dance band pianist. In the mid-20s he visited Europe as leader of a band accompanying **Joséphine Baker**. Later in the decade and into the early 30s he worked in and around New York, leading bands at many prestigious dancehalls, including the Savoy and Roseland. In 1934 he began a residency at the Cotton Club, sharing headline space with the **Jimmie Lunceford** band, which lasted until the club closed its Harlem premises in February 1936. In the late 30s and early 40s Hopkins toured extensively but folded the band in 1942. He regularly employed first-class musicians such as **Hilton Jefferson**, **Edmond Hall**, **Vic Dickenson** and **Jabbo Smith**. After a spell outside music he returned to the scene, fronting a band in New York in 1948, and continued to appear in the city and other east coast centres, with large and small

groups, into the 70s. Among the musicians with whom he performed during these years were **Red Allen**, **Wild Bill Davison** and **Roy Eldridge**. The bands which Hopkins led always had a relaxed, lightly swinging sound, eschewing powerhouse bravura performances.

● ALBUMS: *Yes, Indeed!* (1960)★★★, *Let's Jam* (1961)★★★, *Swing Time* (1963)★★★, with others *Master Jazz Piano Vol. 1* (1969)★★, with others *The Piano Jazz Masters* (1972)★★, *Crazy Fingers* (1972)★★★, *Soliloquy* (1972)★★★, *Safari Stomp* (1974)★★★, *Sophisticated Swing* (1974)★★.

● COMPILATIONS: *Harlem* (1935)★★★, *Claude Hopkins And His Orchestra* (1935)★★★★, *Singin' In The Rain* (1935)★★★, *Claude Hopkins 1932-34* (Original Jazz Classics 1993)★★★★, *Claude Hopkins 1934-35* (Original Jazz Classics 1993)★★★★, *Claude Hopkins 1937-40* (Original Jazz Classics 1994)★★★★.

Hopkins, Doc

b. 26 January 1900, Harlan County, Kentucky, USA, d. 3 January 1988, Chicago, Illinois, USA. Hopkins, who grew up in the Renfro Valley, is remembered as an old-time singer and guitarist, but he originally learned banjo from blind Kentucky player Dick Burnett. He saw army service during World War I and on his discharge, he spent 10 years working on medicine shows that saw him tour all over the USA, frequently playing Hawaiian music. In 1930, he moved to WLS Chicago, where he became a prominent member of the **Cumberland Ridge Runners**. He also worked with **Bradley Kincaid** and **Karl And Harty** and established himself as a regular on the *National Barn Dance*. Although he was more interested in working on the radio than in records, he did record for Broadway and ARC, and in March 1941, he cut six sides for **Decca**, including 'My Little Georgia Rose' and 'Wreck Of The Old Thirty-One'. He also made around 200 radio transcriptions for the MM Cole Company. He basically retired from performing in the 50s and became well known as a teacher of the banjo.

Hopkins, Fred

b. 11 October 1947, Chicago, Illinois, USA. Hopkins began to play double bass while a student at DuSable High School in Chicago. In the late 60s he became involved in the **AACM**. In 1970 he played and recorded with **Kalaparush Maurice McIntyre**. In 1971 he worked in a trio with altoist **Henry Threadgill** and drummer **Steve McCall**, which evolved into the group **Air** and remained active until the mid-80s. Gifted with a springy, propulsive rhythm and blues-drenched tone, Hopkins is the pre-eminent bass player of his generation. His scything, 'out' explorations using the bow combine folk and *avant garde* classical freedoms to devastating effect. He has contributed to the power of Threadgill's later Sextet in no small way and has supplied rhythmic bounce to the work of **Oliver Lake**, **David Murray** (recording on the seminal *Flowers For Albert* in 1977), **Hamiet Bluiett**, **Marion Brown**, **Muhal Richard Abrams**, and **Craig Harris**. In 1988 he toured in a trio with Murray and the founder of free drumming, **Sunny Murray**, showing that the spirit of leaderless free jazz is still alive.

● ALBUMS: with David Murray *Flowers For Albert* (1976)★★★, with Henry Threadgill *X-15 Vol I* (1979)★★★★, with Threadgill *Just The Facts And Pass The Bucket* (1983)★★★, with Craig Harris *Black Bone* (1983)★★★, with Hamiet Bluiett *Ebu* (1984)★★★★, with Threadgill *You Know The Number* (1986)★★★, with Muhal Richard Abrams *Colors In Thirty Third* (1987)★★★.

Hopkins, Joel

b. 3 January 1904, Centreville, Texas, USA, d. 15 February 1975, Galveston, Texas, USA. An elder brother of **Lightnin' Hopkins**, guitarist Joe learned his trade from **Blind Lemon Jefferson** when they travelled together during the 20s. Joel Hopkins spent most of his life working outside of music, but in 1947 he accompanied his brother Lightin' on his famous Gold Star recording of 'Short Haired Woman'. He resurfaced in 1959 to record a handful of archaic Texas blues for historian and folklorist Mack McCormick. The latter part of his life was spent in ill health, and he died from a heart attack in 1975.

● ALBUMS: including with Lightnin' Hopkins *Joel & Lightnin' Hopkins 1959* (1990)★★★.

Hopkins, Lightnin'

b. Sam Hopkins, 15 March 1912, Centreville, Texas, USA, d. 30 January 1982. One of the last great country blues singers, Hopkins' lengthy career began in the Texas bars and juke joints of the 20s. Towards the end of the decade he formed a duo with a cousin, Texas Alexander, while his Lightnin' epithet was derived from a subsequent partnership with barrelhouse pianist Thunder Smith, with whom he made his first recordings. Hopkins' early work unveiled a masterly performer. His work first came to prominence when, after being discovered by Sam Charters at the age of 47, *The Roots Of Lightnin' Hopkins* was released in 1959 and numerous sessions followed. His sparse acoustic guitar and narrated prose quickly made him an important discovery, appealing to the audience of the American folk boom of the early 60s. His harsh, emotive voice and compulsive, if irregular, guitarwork, conveyed an intensity enhanced by the often personal nature of his lyrics. He became one of post-war blues most prolific talents, completing hundreds of sessions for scores of major and independent labels. This inevitably diluted his initial power, but although Hopkins' popularity slumped in the face of Chicago's electric combos, by the early 60s he was re-established as a major force on the college and concert-hall circuit. In 1967 the artist was the subject of an autobiographical film, *The Blues Of Lightnin' Hopkins*, which subsequently won the Gold Hugo award at the Chicago Film Festival. Like many other bluesmen finding great success in the 60s (for example, **Muddy Waters** and **John Lee Hooker**), he too recorded a 'progressive' elec-

tric album: *The Great Electric Show And Dance*. During the 70s he toured the USA, Canada and, in 1977, Europe, until ill health forced him to reduce such commitments. Hopkins was a true folk poet, embracing social comments with pure blues. He died in 1982, his status as one of the major voices of the blues assured.

● ALBUMS: *Strums The Blues* (Score 1958)★★★★, *Lightnin' And The Blues* (Herald 1959)★★★, *The Roots Of Lightnin' Hopkins* (Folkways 1959)★★★, *Down South Summit Meeting* (1960)★★★★, *Mojo Hand* (Fire 1960)★★★★, *Country Blues* (Tradition 1960)★★★, *Lightnin' In New York* (Candid 1961)★★★, *Autobiography In Blues* (Tradition 1961)★★★, *Lightnin'* (Bluesville 1961)★★★, *Last Night Blues* (Bluesville 1961)★★★, *Blues In My Bottle* (Bluesville 1962)★★★★, *Lightnin' Strikes Again* (Dart 1962)★★★, *Sings The Blues* (Crown 1962)★★★, *Lightnin' Hopkins* (Folkways 1962)★★★★, *Fast Life Woman* (Verve 1962)★★★, *On Stage* (Imperial 1962)★★, *Walkin' This Street* (Bluesville 1962)★★★★, *Lightnin' And Co* (Bluesville 1963)★★★, *Smokes Like Lightnin'* (Bluesville 1963)★★★, *First Meetin'* (World Pacific 1963)★★★, *Lightnin' Hopkins And The Blues* (Imperial 1963)★★★, *Goin' Away* (Bluesville 1963)★★★, *Hootin' The Blues* (Folklore 1964)★★★, *Down Home Blues* (Bluesville 1964)★★★★, *The Roots Of Lightnin' Hopkins* (Verve/Folkways 1965)★★★★, *Soul Blues* (Prestige 1966)★★★, *Something Blue* (Verve/Folkways 1967)★★★, *The Great Electric Show And Dance* (1968)★★★, *Free Form Patterns* (International Artists 1968)★★★, *King Of Dowling Street* (1969)★★★, *California Mudslide* (Vault/Rhino 1969)★★★.

● COMPILATIONS: *Legacy Of The Blues Volume Twelve* (Sonet 1974)★★★★, *The Best Of Lightnin' Hopkins* (Tradition 1964)★★★, *The Gold Star Sessions - Volumes 1&2* (Arhoolie 1990)★★★★, *The Complete Prestige/Bluesville Recordings* 7CD set(Prestige/Bluesville 1992)★★★★, *The Complete Aladdin Recordings* (EMI 1992)★★★★, *Sittin' In With Lightnin' Hopkins* (Mainstream 1992)★★★, *Blues Is My Business* rec. 1971 (1993)★★★, *You're Gonna Miss Me* (1993)★★★, *Mojo Hand: The Lightnin' Hopkins Anthology* (Rhino 1993)★★★★, *It's A Sin To Be Rich* rec. 1973 (1993)★★★, *Coffee House Blues* rec. 1960-62 (1993)★★★★, *Po' Lightnin'* (Arhoolie 1995)★★★★, *Blue Lightnin'* (Jewel 1995)★★★, *Hootin' The Blues* (Prestige 1995)★★★★, *The Rising Sun Collection* (Just A Memory 1995)★★★★, *Autobiography In Blues* (Tradition 1996)★★★★, *Country Blues* (Tradition 1996)★★★★, *Shake It Baby* (Javelin 1996)★★★.

● VIDEOS: *Rare Performances 1960-1979* (Vestapol 1995).

● FURTHER READING: *Lightnin' Hopkins: Blues'*, M. McCormick.

Hopkins, Nicky

b. 24 February 1944, London, England, d. 6 September 1994, California, USA. A classically trained pianist at the Royal Academy Of Music, Hopkins embraced rock 'n' roll in 1960 when, inspired by **Chuck Berry**, he joined the Savages, a seminal pre-**Beatles** group led by **Screaming Lord Sutch**. In 1962 Hopkins accompanied singer **Cliff Bennett** and his Rebel Rousers during a residency at Hamburg's *Star Club*, before becoming a founder-member of **Cyril Davies**' R&B All Stars. The unit's debut release, 'Country Line Special', now regarded as a classic of British blues, owes much of its urgency to the pianist's compulsive technique. A lengthy spell in hospital undermined Hopkins' career, but he re-emerged in 1965 as one of the country's leading session musicians (although he was frequently referred to as the greatest unknown in popular music). His distinctive fills were prevalent on releases by the **Who**, **Dusty Springfield**, **Tom Jones** and the **Kinks**, the latter of whom paid tribute with 'Session Man' from *Face To Face*. Hopkins later released a version of that group's 'Mr. Pleasant', before completing the novelty-bound *Revolutionary Piano Of Nicky Hopkins*. Sterling contributions to *Their Satanic Majesties Request* established a rapport with the **Rolling Stones** which continued over successive releases including *Let It Bleed* (1969), *Exile On Main Street* (1972) and *Black And Blue* (1976). His distinctive piano opens the Stones' 'We Love You'.

Tired of unremitting studio work, the pianist joined the **Jeff Beck** Group in October 1968, but left the following year to augment the **Steve Miller Band**. After moving to California, Hopkins switched to the **Quicksilver Messenger Service** with whom he completed two albums, including *Shady Grove,* which featured his lengthy solo *tour de force*, 'Edward, The Mad Shirt Grinder'. This epithet reappeared on *Jammin' With Edward*, an informal session dating from the Stones' *Let It Bleed* sessions, belatedly issued in 1971. Hopkins was also a member of Sweet Thursday, a studio-based group that included guitarist Jon Mark, before completing a second solo album, *The Tin Man Was A Dreamer* with assistance from **George Harrison**, **Mick Taylor** and **Klaus Voorman**. He also sessioned on **John Lennon**'s *Imagine* and worked on countless albums by other rock stars of the 60s and 70s. His contribution to **Jefferson Airplane**'s *Volunteers* was among his finest sessions. In 1979 Hopkins joined Night, a group that also featured vocalist Chris Thompson (ex-**Manfred Mann's Earth Band**) and future **Pretenders** and **Paul McCartney** guitarist Robbie McIntosh. However, the pianist left the line-up following the release of their debut album, returning to session playing by contributing to **Ron Wood**'s 1981 release, *1,2,3,4*. As a resident of California his subsequent activities included informal work with local Bay Area musicians including fellow expatriate Pete Sears (former member of **Jefferson Starship**) and **Merrell Fankhauser**. Hopkins continued to be dogged by ill health in the 90s, his death coming on 6 September 1994 after complications following further stomach surgery.

● ALBUMS: *The Revolutionary Piano Of Nicky Hopkins* (CBS 1966)★★, *The Tin Man Was A Dreamer* (Columbia 1973)★★, *No More Changes* (1976)★★.

Hopper

Hopper made an impressive start within the UK indie scene in 1995, but they seemed to achieve more recog-

nition for their famous fans than for their own music. The band formed in 1992, when Rachel Morris (vocals) started working with Paul Shepperd (guitar). Once a rhythm section of Chris Bowers (bass) and Matt Alexander (drums) had joined, the band released two well-received singles on the indie Damaged Goods Records. Morris's impassioned, slightly folky vocals attracted the attention of **Factory Records** svengali Tony Wilson, who made the band the first signing to his new Factory Too operation and then recruited ex-**Suede** guitar deity **Bernard Butler** to produce their debut album. Two further singles, the punky 'Wasted' and the soaring 'Bad Kid', did well on the UK indie charts but did not achieve the mainstream breakthrough that other guitar bands seemed to be making. Butler (who described Morris as 'quite psychotic') laced their guitar-based sound with sweeping strings that echoed some of Suede's more epic moments, creating a somewhat bombastic, radio-friendly record that seemed to be partly targeted at the US market but *English And French* was dismissed as a second-rate **Sleeper**-clone by many critics, with *Melody Maker* rating it as 'a lot of shite' and 'foot-chewingly tedious'. It does remain to be seen whether, in the wake of the **Cranberries** and **Skunk Anansie**, there is room for another guitar band of slightly anonymous blokes fronted by a big female voice and personality.

● ALBUMS: *English And French* (Factory Too 1996)★★★.

Horizon 222

Horizon 222 are Ben and Andy, who keep their surnames a closely guarded secret. From Whitley Bay in Tyneside, England, they run their own Charm Records label, taking their neo-ambient music on the road via a camper-van: 'Never mind all this stuff about ambient music being designed to send you to sleep. As far as we're concerned, it should be a wake-up call.' The music employed on their 1994 debut album included samples which echo their interest in social justice and politics: Oliver North admitting he lied to Congress, and samples taken from news coverage of the release of the Guildford Four.

● ALBUMS: *The Three Of Swans* (Charm 1994)★★★.

Horler, John

b. John Douglas Horler, 26 February 1947, Lymington, Hampshire, England. Horler began playing piano as a very small child, and while still a young teenager he played in a band led by his trumpeter father Ronnie Horler. In the mid-60s he studied piano and also clarinet at London's Royal Academy of Music, then began a full-time professional career. He worked with many bands, some of them jazz-orientated, including those led by Bobby Lamb-Raymond Premru, Allan Littlejohns, Tony Milliner and Tony Faulkner. In the early 70s he began a long association with the BBC, playing in many groups and musical settings. From these years onwards he was also in great demand as a session musician and accompanied many fine visiting jazzmen at London club dates. During the 70s and 80s he worked with UK and US musicians such as **Art Farmer**, **Chet Baker**, **Zoot Sims**, **Maynard Ferguson**, **Tony Coe**, **Ronnie Ross**, **Pete King**, **Kenny Wheeler** and **Tommy Whittle**. In the mid-80s he also began a long-term musical relationship with **John Dankworth** and **Cleo Laine**. In the 90s, although Horler continued to work in similar settings, he became better known to jazz fans thanks to some exceptionally good albums. As an accompanist, Horler's gifts are self-evident from the list of musicians he has accompanied over the years. He has also often demonstrated a flair for accompanying singers with his work with Laine and **Elaine Delmar**. Away from the relative anonymity of his radio work, Horler's abiding love for the playing of **Bill Evans** is apparent, although he never descends to merely aping his idol's style. Oddly enough, Horler has declared that he never wanted to be a jazz pianist, having had as a youth a desire to 'blow something', in particular the trombone (his older brother, Dave Horler, is a trombonist). Horler's playing demonstrates his remarkable technical gifts, which he also uses in classical work, and he is an outstanding improvisatory jazz artist. His style and repertoire, while eclectic, display a thoughtful and deeply creative musician, and his late 90s work has rightfully gained him a new and enthusiastic following.

● ALBUMS: *Lost Keys* (Mastermix 1993)★★★, with Tony Coe *Blue Jersey* (AB 1993)★★★, *Gentle Piece* (Spotlite 1996).

Horn, Paul

b. 17 March 1930, New York, USA. Horn started to play the piano at the age of four and moved on to the saxophone when he was 12. He studied the flute at Oberlin College Conservatory during 1952 and went on to the Manhattan School of Music the following year. He played with the **Sauter-Finnegan Orchestra** as tenor soloist before joining **Chico Hamilton**'s Quintet (1956-58). Then he settled to work in Hollywood's film studios. He was the main soloist in **Lalo Schifrin**'s *Jazz Suite Of Mass Texts* in 1965 and worked with **Tony Bennett** the following year. During 1967 he went to India where he became a teacher of transcendental meditation. Later he toured China (1979) and the USSR (1983). In 1970 he had settled on an island near Victoria, British Colombia where he formed his own quintet, presented a weekly television show and founded his own record company called Golden Flute (1981). He wrote scores for the Canadian National Film Board and won an award for the score of *Island Eden*. His education and keen travelling encouraged and enabled him to expand his music beyond jazz into what he hoped would be 'universal music'. In 1968 he had recorded an album of solo flute pieces in the Taj Mahal making use of the half minute reverberation time; he later recorded at the Great Pyramid of Cheops near Cairo and even produced a record using the sound of whales as an accompaniment. For Horn, the term jazz merely describes the revival in this century of the art of improvisation and it is this that he continues to do either solo on a variety of flutes including the Chinese ti-tzi, or in a duo with David Friesen on bass.

● ALBUMS: *Inside Taj Mahal* (1968)★★★, *Inside The Great Pyramid* (Kickuck 1976)★★, with David Friesen *Heart To Heart* (1983)★★★, *Traveller* (1985)★★★, *China* (Kuckuck 1987)★★★, *Inside The Cathedral* (Kuckuck 1987)★★, *Something Blue* (Fresh Sounds 1988)★★★, *Peace Album* (Kickuck 1988)★★, *Paul Horn* (Cleo 1989)★★★★, *A Special Edition* (TM 1989)★★★, *Altitude Of The Sun* (TM 1989)★★★, *The Jazz Years* (Black Sun 1991)★★★, *Brazilian Images* (Black Sun 1992)★★★.

● FURTHER READING: *Inside Paul Horn: The Spiritual Odessey Of A Universal Traveller*, Paul Horn with Lee Underwood.

Horn, Shirley

b. 1 May 1934, Washington, DC, USA. After studying piano formally, Horn continued her musical education at university. She began leading her own group in the mid-50s and made several records, often in company with front-rank bop musicians. For some years Horn spent much of her time in Europe where her cabaret-oriented performances went down especially well. Nevertheless, this absence from the USA tended to conceal her talent, something her return to the recording studios in the 80s has begun to correct. Although her piano playing is of a high order most attention is centred upon her attractive singing. Interpreting the best of the Great American Song Book in a breathily personal manner, Horn continues to perform and record. She is strikingly adept at the especially difficult task of accompanying herself on the piano. Her 1996 album *The Main Ingredient* was an interesting concept of creating a relaxed jam session atmosphere by having the musicians drop by her home. Recorded over 5 days in between Horn preparing the food for her house guests it featured Charles Ables; bass/guitar), **Joe Henderson** (tenor saxophone), **Elvin Jones** (drums), Buck Hill (tenor saxophone), Steve Williams (drums), **Roy Hargrove** (trumpet) and **Billy Hart** (drums).

● ALBUMS: *Embers And Ashes* (1961)★★★, *Live At The Village Vanguard* (1961)★★★, *Loads Of Love* (Mercury 1963)★★★, *Shirley Horn With Horns* (Mercury 1963)★★★, *Shirley Horn* (1965)★★★, *Trav'lin Light* (Impulse 1965)★★★, *A Lazy Afternoon* (Steeplechase 1978)★★★, *All Night Long* (Syeeplechase 1981)★★★, *Violets For Your Furs* (Steeplechase 1981)★★★, *The Garden Of The Blues* (Steeplechase 1984)★★★, *Softly* (Audiophile 1987)★★★, *I Thought About You* (Verve 1987)★★★, *Close Enough For Love* (Verve 1988)★★★, *You Won't Forget Me* (Verve 1990)★★★, *Heres To Life* (Verve 1991)★★★, *Light Out Of Darkness (A Tribute To Ray Charles)* (1993)★★★, *I Love You Paris* (Verve 1994)★★★, *The Main Ingredient* (Verve 1996)★★★, *Loving You* (Verve 1997)★★★, *I Remember Miles* (Verve 1998)★★.

Horne, Lena

b. 30 June 1917, Brooklyn, New York, USA. A dynamic performer, of striking appearance and elegant style. The daughter of an actress and a hotel operator, she was brought up mainly by her paternal grandmother, Cora Calhoun Horne. She made her professional debut at the age of 16 as a singer in the chorus at Harlem's Cotton Club, learning from **Duke Ellington**, **Cab Calloway**, **Billie Holiday** and **Harold Arlen**, the composer of a future big hit, 'Stormy Weather'. From 1935-36 she was featured vocalist with the all-black **Noble Sissle**'s Society Orchestra (the same Noble Sissle who, with **Eubie Blake**, wrote several hit songs including 'Shuffle Along' and 'I'm Just Wild About Harry') and later toured with the top swing band of **Charlie Barnet**, singing numbers such as 'Good For Nothin' Joe' and 'You're My Thrill'. Sometimes, when Barnet's Band played the southern towns, Horne had to stay in the band bus. She made her Broadway debut in 1934 as 'A Quadroon Girl' in *Dance With Your Gods*, and also appeared in Lew Leslie's *Blackbirds Of 1939*, in which she sang **Mitchell Parish** and **Sammy Fain**'s 'You're So Indifferent' - but only for the show's run of nine performances.

After a spell at the Café Society Downtown in New York, she moved to Hollywood's Little Troc Club and was spotted by **Roger Edens**, musical supervisor for MGM Pictures, and former accompanist for **Ethel Merman**, who introduced her to producer **Arthur Freed**. In her first film for MGM, *Panama Hattie* (1942), which starred Merman, Horne sang **Cole Porter**'s 'Just One Of Those Things', and a rhumba number called 'The Sping'. To make her skin appear lighter on film, the studio used a special make-up called 'Light Egyptian'. Horne referred to herself as 'a sepia Hedy Lamarr'. Her next two films, *Cabin In The Sky* and *Stormy Weather*, both made in 1943, are generally regarded as her best. In the remainder of her 40s and 50s movie musicals (which included *Thousands Cheer*, *Swing Fever*, *Broadway Rhythm*, *Two Girls And A Sailor*, *Ziegfeld Follies*, *Till The Clouds Roll By*, *Words And Music*, *Duchess Of Idaho* and *Meet Me In Las Vegas*), she merely performed guest shots that were easily removable, without spoiling the plot, for the benefit of southern-state distributors.

Her 40s record hits included her theme song, 'Stormy Weather', and two other Arlen songs, '"Deed I Do' and 'As Long As I Live'. She also recorded with several big swing era names such as **Artie Shaw**, Cab Calloway and **Teddy Wilson**. During World War II, she became the pin-up girl for many thousands of black GIs and refused to appear on US tours unless black soldiers were admitted to the audience. In 1947 she married pianist, arranger and conductor **Lennie Hayton**, who also became her manager and mentor until his death in 1971. For a time during the 50s Lena Horne was black-listed, probably for her constant involvement with the Civil Rights movement, but particularly for her friend-ship with alleged Communist sympathizer **Paul Robeson**. Ironically, she was at the peak of her powers at that time, and although she was unable to appear much on television and in films, she continued to make records and appear in nightclubs, which were regarded as her special forte. Evidence of that was displayed on *Lena Horne At The Waldorf Astoria*. The material ranged from the sultry 'Mood Indigo', right through to the novelty 'New Fangled Tango' and *Lena At The Sands*, with its medleys of songs by **Richard Rodgers/Oscar Hammerstein II**, **Jule Styne** and **E.Y. 'Yip' Harburg**. Other US Top 30 chart albums included *Give The Lady What She Wants* and *Porgy And Bess*, with **Harry Belafonte**. Horne also made the US Top 20 singles charts in 1955 with 'Love Me Or Leave Me', written by **Gus Kahn** and **Walter Donaldson** for **Ruth Etting** to sing in the 1928 Broadway show *Whoopee*. In 1957 Horne had her first starring role on Broadway when she played Savannah, opposite Ricardo Montalban, in the Arlen/Harburg musical *Jamaica*. In the 60s, besides the usual round of television shows and records, she appeared in a dramatic role, with Richard Widmark, in *Death Of A Gunfighter* (1969). After Hayton's death in 1971 she worked less, but did feature in *The Wiz*, an all-black film version of *The Wizard Of Oz*, starring **Diana Ross** and **Michael Jackson**, and in 1979 she received an honorary doctorate degree from Harvard University. In May 1981, she opened on Broadway in her own autobiographical show, *Lena Horne: The Lady And Her Music*. It ran at the Nederland Theatre to full houses for 14 months, a Broadway record for a one-woman show. Horne received several awards including a special **Tony Award** for 'Distinguished Achievement In The Theatre', a Drama Desk Award, New York Drama Critics' Special Award, New York City's Handel Medallion, Dance Theatre of Harlem's Emergence Award, two Grammy Awards and the NAACP Springarn Award. She took the show to London in 1984, where it was also acclaimed. In 1993, after not having sung in public for several years, Lena Horne agreed to perform the songs of **Billy Strayhorn** at the US JVC Jazz Festival. She included several of the same composer's songs on her 1994 album *We'll Be Together Again*, and, in the same year, surprised and delighted her fans by appearing in concert at Carnegie Hall.

● ALBUMS: *Lena Horne Sings* 10-inch album (MGM 1952)★★★, *This Is Lena Horne* 10-inch album 10-inch album (RCA Victor 1952)★★★★, *Moanin' Low* 10-inch album (Tops 1954)★★, *It's Love* (RCA Victor 1955)★★★, *Stormy Weather* (RCA Victor 1956)★★★★, with Ivie Anderson *Lena And Ivie* (Jazztone 1956)★★★, *Lena Horne At The Waldorf Astoria* (RCA Victor 1957)★★★★, *Jamaica* film soundtrack (RCA Victor 1957)★★, *Give The Lady What She Wants* (RCA Victor 1958)★★★, with Harry Belafonte *Porgy And Bess* film soundtrack (RCA Victor 1959)★★★★, *Songs Of Burke And Van Heusen* (RCA Victor 1959)★★★, *Lena Horne At The Sands* (RCA Victor 1961)★★★★, *Lena On The Blue Side* (RCA Victor 1962)★★★, *Lena ... Lovely And Alive* (RCA Victor 1963)★★★, *Lena Goes Latin* (RCA Victor 1963)★★★, with Gabor Szabo *Lena And Gabor* (Skye 1970)★★★, *Lena* (1974)★★★, *Lena, A New Album* (RCA 1976)★★★, *Lena Horne: The Lady And Her Music* stage cast (Qwest 1981)★★★, *A Song For You* (1992)★★★, *We'll Be Together Again* (Blue

Note 1994)★★, *An Evening With Lena Horne* (Blue Note 1995)★★★, *Being Myself* (Blue Note 1998)★★★★.

● COMPILATIONS: *Twenty Golden Pieces Of Lena Horne* (Bulldog 1979)★★★, *Lena Horne* (Jazz Greats 1979)★★★, *Lena Horne And Pearl Bailey* (Jazz Greats 1979)★★★, shared with Billie Holiday, Ella Fitzgerald and Sarah Vaughan *Billie, Ella, Lena, Sarah!* (Columbia 1980)★★★★, *Lena Horne And Frank Sinatra* (Astan 1984)★★★, *The Fabulous Lena Horne* (Cambra 1985)★★★.

● FURTHER READING: *In Person*, Lena Horne. *Lena*, Lena Horne with Richard Schikel. *Lena: A Personal And Professional Biography*, J. Haskins and K. Benson.

● FILMS: *The Duke Is Tops* (1938), *Panama Hattie* (1942), *I Dood It* (1943), *Swing Fever* (1943), *Stormy Weather* (1943), *Thousands Cheer* (1943), *Cabin In The Sky* (1943), *Two Girls And A Sailor* (1944), *Broadway Rhythm* (1944), *Till The Clouds Roll By* (1946), *Ziegfeld Follies* (1946), *Words And Music* (1948), *Duchess Of Idaho* (1950), *Meet Me In Las Vegas* (1956), *Death Of A Gunfighter* (1969), *The Wiz* (1978).

Horner, James

b. 1953, Los Angeles, California, USA. A prolific composer, arranger and conductor for films from the late 70s through to the 90s, Horner studied at the Royal College Of Music in London, at USC Los Angeles, and UCLA. In the late 70s he worked on several films for Roger Corman's New World production company, including *Up From The Depths*, *The Lady In Red*, *Battle Beyond The Stars* and *Humanoids From The Deep* (1980); reminders of Corman's Z Grade movies of the 50s. During the 80s he scored some 35 feature films, mainly with recurring themes of grisly tales of horror, violence, science-fiction, fantasy, and sinister drama. These included *Deadly Blessing*, *The Hand*, *Wolfen*, *Star Trek II: 48 Hours* (Eddie Murphy's screen debut), *The Wrath Of Khan*; *Brainstorm*; *Krull*, *Testament*; *Gorky Park*, *Star Trek III: The Search For Spock*, *Cocoon*, *Commando*, *The Name Of The Rose*, *Project X*, *Batteries Not Included*, *Willow*, *Red Heat*, *Cocoon: The Return* and *Honey, I Shrunk The Kids* (1989). In 1986 Horner was nominated for an Academy Award for his *Aliens* score, and for the song 'Somewhere Out There' (written with **Barry Mann** and **Cynthia Weil**), for the animated feature *American Tail*. Both compositions gained **ASCAP** Awards. Horner was nominated again for an Oscar in 1989 for his music for another fantasy, *Field Of Dreams*, starring Kevin Costner, and, in the same year, won a Grammy for his score to *Glory*. Horner's 90s feature film credits include *Thunderheart*, *My Heroes Have Always Been Cowboys*, a tribute to the 'Wild West'; the live-action *Rocketeer*, two animated features, *An American Tail: Fievel Goes West* and *Fish Police* (1992), *Patriot Games*, *Unlawful Entry*, *Sneakers*, *House Of Cards*, *Jack The Bear*, *Swing Kids*, *A Far Off Place*, *Once Upon A Forest*, *The Man Without A Face*, *Innocent Moves*, *The Pelican Brief*, *Clear And Present Danger*, *Legends Of The Fall*, *Apollo 13* and *Braveheart*. In 1998, he won two Oscars for his work on *Titanic*, 'Best Original Dramatic Score', and 'Best Song' for 'My Heart Will Go On' (lyric: Will Jennings). Horner has also worked in television, composing music for such as *Angel Dusted*, *A Few Days In Weasel Creek*, *Rascals And Robbers - The Secret Adventures Of Tom Sawyer And Huck Finn*, *A Piano For Mrs Cimino*, *Between Friends* and *Surviving*.

Hornets Attack Victor Mature

Until the mid-80s, this American band was one of the most influential groups that never existed. During the late 70s, against the backdrop of new wave, legions of young rockers with thin ties and excessive safety-pins were congregating under increasingly strange names that eschewed the rakishness and romance of earlier eras (for example, the **Searchers**, the **Telstars**, the **Temptations**, the **Kinks**), using everything from body parts (the **Brains**) to *realpolitik* (**Gang Of Four**) to establish mystique. One afternoon two rock journalists, both neighbours and columnists for competing music weeklies, saw a perfect new name for a band in a headline in the *Los Angeles Times*: 'Hornets Attack Victor Mature'. The actor had been whisked off to the Encino burn centre. It is unknown whether he was still under observation several days later when both scribes faced Wednesday deadlines for their rather similar columns, both devoted to reporting the latest news in Hollywood music circles. What is known is that both reporters encountered a not uncommon problem, a surfeit of committed editorial space against a shortfall of compelling fact, and that both reporters arrived at the same solution. As many journalistic professionals know, a misstatement of fact is a gross miscarriage of the truth; a misstatement followed by a question mark is entirely legal. Thus, these resourceful members of the Fourth Estate wondered aloud: 'Will Hornets Attack Victor Mature be the next L.A. power pop band to snare big bucks in a record deal?' The following week, two respected industry journals both queried a heretofore disinterested collective readership about the fate of this group. A week thereafter, a rock radio newsletter not known for its exhaustive fact-checking protocols reprinted the information, *sans* question mark. Thus was the long and largely fruitless career of Hornets Attack Victor Mature launched, accumulating momentum and new copy lines without benefit of a single, album, video, tour or lawsuit. In 1980, *Musician* magazine named the band winner in both the Best Name For A New Band and Worst Name For A New Band categories. At the beginning of the 80s a buxom centrefold in *Oui* magazine was quoted as loving new wave and punk, naming Hornets Attack Victor Mature alongside the **Clash** as among her favourites (possibly the bio was ghosted by one of our former columnists). This virtual career might have gone on indefinitely, but in the mid-80s the members of **R.E.M.** actually booked themselves into an Athens club under this very name.

● ALBUMS: *The Underground Car Park Tapes* (Redmond West 1997)★★, *The Barnes Sutherland Expedition* (Redmond West 1998)★★★.

Hornsby, Bruce, And The Range

b. 23 November 1954, Williamsburg, Virginia, USA. After many years working in the music business as pianist and contract songwriter for 20th Century Fox, Hornsby burst onto the market in 1986 with a superb debut. The single 'The Way It Is', with its captivating piano introduction and infectious melody, was a transatlantic hit. The first album, part produced by **Huey Lewis**, contained a plethora of piano based southern American rock songs, with Hornsby's strong voice, reminiscent of **Bruce Springsteen**, making it one of the year's best rock albums. The line-up of the Range on the debut was: David Mansfield (violin, mandolin, guitar), Joe Puerta (bass), John Molo (drums) and George Marinelli (guitar). Hornsby followed the first album with *Scenes From The South Side*, an even stronger collection including the powerful 'The Valley Road' and 'Defenders Of The Flag'. The former song won him a composers' Grammy for the best bluegrass recording, as performed by the **Nitty Gritty Dirt Band**. Hornsby has a technique of hitting the piano keys hard, which still results in a clean melodic sound, reminiscent of **Floyd Cramer**. Many of the 'American heritage' songs on the albums are co-written with his brother John. The third collection *Night On The Town* in 1990 was a move away from the piano dominated sound and featured **Jerry Garcia** on guitar. Following the death of the **Grateful Dead**'s Brent Mydland on 26 July 1990, Hornsby joined as a temporary replacement. In addition to many session/guest appearances during the early 90s, Hornsby found time to record *Harbor Lights*, a satisfying and more acoustic sounding record. In forsaking an overtly commercial direction Hornsby sounded both confident and happy with his recent 'sound'. A new album in 1995 resorted back to the commercial sounding formula of his debut.

● ALBUMS: *The Way It Is* (RCA 1986)★★★, *Scenes From The South Side* (RCA 1988)★★★★, *Night On The Town* (RCA 1990)★★★. Solo: *Harbor Lights* (RCA 1993)★★★★, *Hot House* (RCA 1995)★★★.

Horsburgh, Wayne

b. 11 June 1955, Lima, near Benalla, Victoria, Australia. Horsburgh grew up on the family's dairy farm and was given his first guitar at the age of eight. His interest in country music began when he used to listen to his father's **Hank Snow** and **Wilf Carter** records. When he was aged 11, he sang with a local dance band and made the finals of a national television programme in Melbourne. After completing his high school studies in 1971, he spent four years working for the State Savings Bank, first in Benalla and later in Melbourne. However, in August 1973, after seeing **Slim Whitman** during an Australian tour, he decided upon a career in country music. Impressed by Whitman's clever use of falsetto, he practised and soon became a proficient yodeller, a talent that endeared him to his American audiences when, some years later, he made regular visits to the USA. He finally achieved his breakthrough in 1978,

when he was offered the opportunity to tour with the travelling show of Australian legend **Buddy Williams**. He benefited greatly from this experience and soon built up a popular stage act of his own. Now a household name in Australia thanks to major television shows such as **Reg Lindsay**'s *Country Homestead* and the *Midday Show* and countless country radio shows, he has already won many awards. He divides his time between Australia and the USA, where he has toured and appeared with such stars as **Roy Rogers**, **Riders In The Sky** and the **Sons Of The Pioneers**. His recordings have resulted in Australian hits such as 'Lover's Carousel', 'Shepherd's Farewell', 'September's Sweet Child' (released in the UK on *Yodelling Crazy* by **EMI** in 1992) and 'Give 'Em Another Encore'. In 1991, he recorded an album of songs of the singing cowboys, which, as a lover of the style of Rogers and **Gene Autry**, represented the fulfilment of a lifelong ambition. He made a brief visit to the UK in 1992, where his yodelling and country ballads endeared him to British country music audiences. In 1994, he recorded his first Nashville-based album. His all-round friendly and courteous manner, in addition to the fact that he always finds time to meet his fans, places Horsburgh as one of the most popular of the modern Australian artists.

● ALBUMS: with Desree Ilona Crawford *I Run Alone* (Country-City 1984)★★★, with Deniese Morrison *Sequins And Satins, Buckles And Britches* (Country-City 1984)★★★, *Yodelling For You* (Country-City 1985)★★★, *Now & Then & Again* (Country-City 1986)★★, *Where In The World* (Country-City 1989)★★★, *I've Always Wanted To Be A Singing Cowboy* (Rich River 1992)★★★, *In Every Stone There's A Diamond* (Country-City 1992)★★★, *From Nashville To You* (Rotation 1994)★★★.

Horse

Based in London, England, Horse combined heavy metal musicianship with some of the lyrical concerns of the punk movement. Comprising Gary Gene (vocals), Marc Perez (guitar), Damion Williams (bass) and Dave Hoyland (drums), after forming in 1988 they embarked on a gruelling circuit of support and club dates to establish their reputation. Their onstage behaviour won them immediate notoriety in London fanzines such as *House Of Dolls*, and by the turn of the 90s some critics were hailing them as the natural successors to the musical and visual excesses of early **Motörhead**. In truth, their sound owed more to the mysticism of the **Cult** and the unreconstructed attitude of **Guns N'Roses**. An American recording contract followed in 1990 with the MCA Records subsidiary Mechanic, **Atlantic Records** having turned them down for being 'too erratic'. However, the group's debut, *Diesel Power*, was strangely lacking in the feisty qualities that had made the group such an intimidating live spectacle.

● ALBUMS: *Diesel Power* (Mechanic 1990)★★.

Horses - Patti Smith

Poet/playwright Patti Smith embraced rock as a critic and performer during New York punk's formative era. These different elements gelled to startling effect on *Horses*, which attacked preconceptions and declared innovation to great effect. Her untutored voice provides raw realism while a refusal to compromise took music into uncharted territory. Smith's splicing together of her own 'Horses' to the standard 'Land Of 1000 Dances' simultaneously declared pop history and its future. John Cale's production inevitably suggests comparisons with the Velvet Underground, but despite a sense of shared commitment, Smith's music is powerful and exciting on its own terms. Few debut albums are as intense or as fully formed.

● Tracks: *Gloria (In Excelsis Deo); Redondo Beach; Birdland; Free Money; Kimberly; Break It Up; Land: Horses - Land Of A 1000 Dances - La Mer; Elegie.*

● First released 1975

● UK peak chart position: did not chart

● USA peak chart position: 47

Horslips

This innovative and much imitated Irish folk-rock band comprised Barry Devlin (bass/vocals), Declan Sinnott (lead guitar/vocals), Eamonn Carr (drums/vocals), Charles O'Connor (violin), and Jim Lockhart (flute/violin/keyboards). Sinnott, later joined **Moving Hearts** and was replaced by Gus Gueist and John Fean in turn. Horslips, formed in 1970 and took the theme of Irish legends for many of their songs. The group toured as support to **Steeleye Span** and featured a complete performance of *The Tain*, a more rock-based recording than their previous recordings. Feans guitar work could switch from the melodic style of 'Aliens', to the much heavier 'Man Who Built America'. They maintained a strong cult following, but, only one album, *The Book Of Invasions - A Celtic Symphony*, reached the UK Top 40. *The Man Who Built America* received a lot of air-play when it was released in 1979, but wider acceptance evaded them, and the group split. Fean, O'Connor and Carr later formed Host, with Chris Page (bass), and Peter Keen (keyboards), in order to pursue the folk path still further.

● ALBUMS: *Happy To Meet Sorry To Part* (Oats 1973)★★★, *The Tain* (Oats 1974)★★★, *Dancehall Sweethearts* (1974)★★★, *Unfortunate Cup Of Tea* (1975)★★★, *Drive The Cold Winter Away* (Oats 1976)★★★, *Horslips Live* (1976)★★★, *The Book Of Invasions - A Celtic Symphony* (1977)★★★, *Aliens* (1977)★★★, *Tracks From The Vaults* (1978)★★★, *The Man Who Built America* (1979)★★★, *Short Stories - Tall Tales* (1980)★★★, *The Belfast Gigs* (1980)★★.

● COMPILATIONS: *The Best Of Horslips* (1982)★★★★, *Folk Collection* (1984)★★★, *Horslips History 1972-75* (1983)★★★★, *Horslips History 1976-80* (1984)★★★★, *The Horslips Story; Straight From the Horse's Mouth* (1989)★★★★.

Horton, Johnny

b. 3 April 1925, Los Angeles, California, USA, d. 5 November 1960, Texas, USA. Horton was raised in Tyler, Texas, where his sharecropping family settled in search of work. He learned the guitar from his mother and, due to his athletic prowess, won scholarships at Baylor University and later the University of Seattle. For a time he worked in the fishing industry but began his singing career on KXLA Pasadena in 1950, quickly acquiring the nickname of 'The Singing Fisherman'. He recorded for Cormac in 1951 and then became the first artist on Fabor Robinson's Abbott label. In 1952 he moved to **Mercury Records** but was soon in conflict with the company about the choice of songs. He married **Hank Williams**' widow, Billie Jean, in September 1953, who encouraged him to better himself. With Tillman Franks as his manager, Horton moved to **Columbia Records**, and their co-written 'Honky Tonk Man' marked his debut in the US country charts. Horton recorded 'Honky Tonk Man' the day after **Elvis Presley** recorded 'Heartbreak Hotel' and Presley's bass player, **Bill Black**, was on the session. The song was successfully revived by **Dwight Yoakam** in 1986, while **George Jones** revived another song recorded that day, 'I'm A One Woman Man', in 1989. Other fine examples of Horton's rockabilly talents are 'All Grown Up' and the hard-hitting 'Honky Tonk Hardwood Floor'. In 1959, Horton switched direction and concentrated on story songs, often with an historical basis, and had his first US country number 1 with a **Tillman Franks** song, 'When It's Springtime In Alaska'. This was followed by his version of **Jimmie Driftwood**'s 'The Battle Of New Orleans', which became a number 1 pop and country hit in the USA. **Lonnie Donegan**'s 'Battle Of New Orleans' made number 2 in the UK, but Horton's number 16 was respectable, especially in view of the fact that his version was banned by the BBC for referring to 'the bloody British'. Horton's next record was another historical song, 'Johnny Reb', backed with the up-tempo novelty, 'Sal's Got A Sugar Lip'. Told simply to cover Horton's latest record, Donegan mistakenly covered 'Sal's Got A Sugar Lip' - and still managed to have a hit! Horton's 'Sink The Bismarck', inspired by the film, made number 3 in the US charts, while he sang the title song of the John Wayne film *North To Alaska* and took it to number 4 in the USA and number 23 in the UK. It also topped the US country charts for five weeks.

On 5 November 1960, Horton died on the way to hospital after a head-on collision with a pick-up truck near Milano, Texas. Tillman Franks received head and chest injuries that required hospital treatment and guitarist Tommy Tomlinson suffered a very serious leg injury which, because of his diabetes, failed to heal and a few months later the leg was amputated. He later played guitar for a time with **Claude King** but never really recovered from the crash (the driver of the other vehicle, James Davis, aged 19, also died). Billie Jean (who later stated that before he left for the last time, Horton kissed her on exactly the same place on the same cheek that Hank Williams had kissed her when he set off for his final trip) became a country star's widow for the second time in 10 years. Horton, who has been described as the last major star of the *Louisiana Hayride*, is buried in Hillcrest Cemetery, Bossier City, Louisiana. Much of his up-tempo material did not appeal to the traditionalists but somebody once wrote that 'he was ten years older than most of the rockabillies but with his cowboy hat hiding a receding hairline, he more or less looked the part'. However, his 'saga' songs have certainly guaranteed that he is not forgotten.

● ALBUMS: *Honky Tonk Man* (Columbia 1957)★★, *Done Rovin'* (Briar Internatonal 1958)★★, *Free And Easy Songs* (Sesac 1959)★★, *The Fantastic Johnny Horton* (Mercury 1959)★★★, *The Spectacular Johnny Horton* (Columbia 1960)★★★, *Johnny Horton Makes History* (Columbia 1960)★★★, *Honky Tonk Man* (Columbia 1962)★★★, *Johnny Horton* (Dot 1962)★★★, *I Can't Forget You* (Columbia 1965)★★★, *The Voice Of Johnny Horton* (Hilltop 1965)★★★, *Johnny Horton On The Louisiana Hayride* (Columbia 1966)★★★, *All For The Love Of A Girl* (Hilltop 1968)★★, *The Unforgettable Johnny Horton* (Harmony 1968)★★★, *Johnny Horton On The Road* (Columbia 1969)★★, *The Battle Of New Orleans* (Harmony 1971)★★★.

● COMPILATIONS: *Johnny Horton's Greatest Hits* (Columbia 1961)★★★, *America Remembers Johnny Horton* (Columbia Special Products 1980)★★★, *Rockin' Rollin' Johnny Horton* (Bear Family 1981)★★★★, *American Originals* (Columbia 1989)★★★, *The Early Years* 7-LP box set (Bear Family 1991)★★★, *Johnny Horton 1956-1960* 4-CD box set (Bear Family 1991)★★★★, *Honky Tonk Man: The Essential Johnny Horton 1956-1960* (Columbia/Legacy 1996)★★★★, *Somebody's Rockin'* (Bear Family 1996)★★★.

● FURTHER READING: *Johnny Horton: Your Singing Fisherman*, Michael LeVine.

Horton, Vaughan

b. 6 June 1911, Broad Top Mountain, Pennsylvania, USA, d. 1 March 1988. Although he sang and played steel guitar, guitar and mandolin, Horton is remembered as a songwriter. He played in college bands and with dance bands before his talented steel guitar playing led him to country music. In 1935, he and his brother Roy (bass) moved to New York City, where later with others including Ray Smith, Rusty Keefer and Johnny Browers, they formed the Pinetoppers and had their own show on NBC and CBS radio. The group's vocals were by the Beaver Valley Sweethearts (Trudy and Gloria Marlin). In 1950, they had a number 3 country and number 10 pop hit with Horton's song 'Mocking Bird Hill'. (The song was also a US country Top 10 for **Les Paul** And Mary Ford and a US pop hit for **Patti Page** in 1951. It later reappeared in the UK pop charts, in 1964, for the **Migil Five** and in the US country charts for **Donna Fargo** in 1977). Horton later claimed that the song, which he wrote on a train, was recorded more than 400 times and sold in excess of 20 million copies.

Other Horton songs to be successfully recorded by other artists include 'Address Unknown' (**Gene Autry**), 'Hillbilly Fever' (**Little Jimmy Dickens**), 'Sugarfoot Rag' (**Red Foley**), 'An Old Christmas Card' (**Jim Reeves**), 'Teardrops In My Heart' (**Marty Robbins** and **Rex Allen Jnr.**) and 'Choo Choo Ch'Boogie' (**Asleep At The Wheel**). Horton was inducted into the Nashville Songwriters Association, International Hall Of Fame in 1971. He retired to Florida where he died in 1988.

Horton, Walter 'Shakey'

b. 6 April 1918, Horn Lake, Mississippi, USA, d. 8 December 1981, Chicago, Illinois, USA. Horton, also aka 'Mumbles' and 'Big Walter', claimed to have taught himself harmonica by the time he was five years old, and certainly the extraordinary skill he achieved speaks of a very special affinity with the instrument. By his teens, he was in Memphis and beginning to make a living from music. He later claimed to have been on recordings by the Memphis Jug Band in 1927, but as he would have been only nine years old, this seems unlikely. More plausibly, he may have been the harmonica accompanist on **Buddy Doyle**'s 1939 records. Throughout the 40s, he continued to develop his skills on the instrument, but it was not until 1951 that he recorded in his own right, back in Memphis. Over the next two years he made a series of recordings, many of which were not issued until many years later, but which demonstrate Horton's remarkable talent, singing and playing his harmonica with great skill and imagination. One of the finest recordings was 'Easy', a slow instrumental solo, accompanied only by **Jimmy DeBerry**'s guitar, issued on **Sun** in 1953. Later that year, he was again in Chicago and issued two sides under **Johnny Shines**' name. With Horton's brilliant, soaring and swooping harmonica work and Shines' uniquely powerful, impassioned vocals, 'Evening Sun', with its flip-side 'Brutal Hearted Woman', was widely regarded as one of the finest blues records from post-war Chicago. Throughout the decade, he was playing regularly in Chicago, sometimes with Shines, or with **Muddy Waters**. He appeared on some of the latter's recordings, as well as others by **Jimmy Rogers**, **Arbee Stidham** and **Sunnyland Slim**. In the 60s, he reached a new audience, travelling widely in the USA and touring Europe with blues packages. As time went on, he demonstrated his versatility by adding pop and jazz themes to his repertoire, as well as showing a fondness for Latin tunes such as 'La Cucaracha' and 'La Paloma'. He was always primarily a blues player and the tough, electric sounds of Memphis and Chicago remained the essence of his music through many fine recordings in the 60s and 70s.

● ALBUMS: *Walter Horton And Carey Bell* (Alligator 1972)★★★, *Fine Cuts* (Blind Pig 1978)★★★★, *Little Boy Blue* (JSP 1980)★★★★, *Mouth Harp Maestro* (Ace 1988)★★★, with Joe Hill Louis, Mose Vinson *The Be-Bop Boy* (1993)★★★.

Host

Eamonn Carr, Johnny Fean, and Charles O'Connor regrouped with a couple of other friends post-Horslips to try to recapture the spirit of that band. It worked too; their sole album is dark and mystical, a rock concept written around the last witch burning in Eire. Sadly O'Connor left and though the others briefly carried on, the group fell apart.
● ALBUMS: *Tryal* (1982)★★★.

Hot Butter

This one-man band comprised US Moog synthesizer player Stan Free, who had performed on recordings by **John Denver**, **Arlo Guthrie** and the Boston Pops Orchestra. Hot Butter made one US Top 10 record and promptly disappeared. Having previously recorded some unsuccessful singles under his own name in the 60s, Free took on the name Hot Butter and recorded the cleverly titled 'Popcorn', an instrumental which reached the UK Top 5 in 1972. Subsequent singles attempted to update early rock instrumentals such as 'Pipeline' and 'Tequila' but they did not reach the charts.

Hot Buttered Soul - Isaac Hayes

A staff songwriter with the legendary Stax label, Isaac Hayes, with partner David Porter, composed material for many of the company's artists, including Sam And Dave, Carla Thomas and Johnnie Taylor. Frustrated with this backroom role, he began recording in his own right, and with *Hot Buttered Soul*, redefined the notion of soul music. Although the tracks were lengthy, there was no sense of self-indulgence, each one evolving over sensual rhythms and taut arrangements. Hayes' vocal anticipated the 'rap' genre of Barry White and Millie Jackson without slipping into self-parody.
● Tracks: *Walk On By; Hyperbolicsyllaciscesquedalymistic; One Woman; By The Time I Got To Phoenix.*
● First released 1969
● UK peak chart position: did not chart
● USA peak chart position: 8

Hot Chocolate

This highly commercial UK pop group was formed in Brixton, London, by percussionist Patrick Olive (b. 22 March 1947, Grenada), guitarist Franklyn De Allie and drummer Ian King. Songwriter/vocalist Errol Brown (b. 12 November 1948, Kingston, Jamaica) and bassist Tony Wilson (b. 8 October 1947, Trinidad, Jamaica) and pianist Larry Ferguson (b. 14 April 1948, Nassau, Bahamas) joined later in 1969. Following the departure of De Allie the group was signed to the **Beatles**' label **Apple** for an enterprising reggae version of the **Plastic Ono Band**'s 'Give Peace A Chance'. They also provided label-mate **Mary Hopkin** with the hit 'Think About Your Children'. The following year, Hot Chocolate signed to **Mickie Most**'s RAK label and again proved their songwriting worth by composing **Herman's Hermits** hit 'Bet Yer Life I Do'. In September 1970, Hot Chocolate enjoyed the first hit in their own right with the melodic 'Love Is Life'. Over the next year, they brought in former **Cliff Bennett** guitarist Harvey Hinsley (b. 19 January 1948, Northampton, England) and replacment drummer Tony Connor (b. 6 April 1948, Romford, Essex, England) to bolster the line-up. The Brown-Wilson songwriting team enabled Hot Chocolate to enjoy a formidable run of UK Top 10 hits including 'I Believe (In Love)', 'Brother Louie' (a US number 1 for **Stories**), 'Emma', 'A Child's Prayer', 'You Sexy Thing', 'Put Your Love In Me', 'No Doubt About It', 'Girl Crazy', 'It Started With A Kiss' and 'What Kinda Boy You Looking For (Girl)'. In the summer of 1987, they scored a number 1 UK hit with the **Russ Ballard** song 'So You Win Again'. Although Wilson had left in 1976, the group managed to sustain their incredible hit run. However, the departure of their shaven-headed vocalist and songwriter Errol Brown in 1987 was a much more difficult hurdle to overcome and it came as little surprise when Hot Chocolate's break-up was announced. Brown went on to register a hit with 'Personal Touch', and completed two albums.
● ALBUMS: *Cicero Park* (RAK 1974)★★, *Hot Chocolate* (RAK 1975)★★, *Man To Man* (RAK 1976)★★, *Every 1's A Winner* (RAK 1978)★★★, *Going Through The Motions* (RAK 1979)★★, *Class* (RAK1980)★★, *Mystery* (RAK 1982)★★, *Love Shot* (RAK 1983)★★.
Solo: Errol Brown *That's How Love Is* (Warners 1989)★★, *Secret Rendevous* (1992)★★.
● COMPILATIONS: *Hot Chocolate's Greatest Hits* (RAK 1976)★★, *20 Hottest Hits* (EMI 1979)★★★, *The Very Best Of Hot Chocolate* (EMI 1987)★★★, *Their Greatest Hits* (EMI 1993)★★★.
● VIDEOS: *Greatest Hits* (Video Collection 1985), *Very Best Of* (Video Collection 1987).

Hot Gossip

Ostensibly a risqué dance troupe, Hot Gossip also made it to number 6 in the UK charts in November 1978 with the preposterous space fantasy, 'I Lost My Heart To A Starship Trooper'. The follow-up single was credited to **Sarah Brightman** And The Starship Troopers. Hot Gossip were formed by dance teacher Arlene Phillips, and appeared regularly at Maunkbury's nightclub in London before being spotted by the director of the *Kenny Everett Television Show* who was looking for a 'racier version of Pan's People'. Hot Gossip were best known thereafter for the inclusion of future **Andrew Lloyd-Webber** wife Sarah Brightman. Other members of the group included Chrissie Wickham, Floyd, Roy Gayle, Richard Lloyd King, Jane Newman, Julia Redburn, Kim Leeson, Perry Lister, Debbie Ash, Virginia Hartley and Alison Hierlehy. That list includes members from several different line-ups, including the splinter group Spinooch. Most subsequently returned to careers as dancers in West End shows, though Gayle, a British aerobic champion, retained his involvement in music by singing with London soul band Frank The Cat. Lister was briefly married to **Billy Idol**.

Hot Knives

Hot Knives were formed in San Francisco, California, USA, in 1974 by two ex-members of the **Flamin' Groovies**. Tim Lynch (guitar) and Danny Mihm (drums) were joined by Debbie Houpt (vocals), Mike Houpt (guitar, vocals) and Ed Wilson (bass) in an act that replayed San Francisco's pop sound of the 60s. Two singles, 'I Hear The Wind Blow' and a version of **Moby Grape**'s 'Hey Grandma', appeared on the Hot Knives' own label. Both proved popular in Europe, where the Flamin' Groovies and its offshoots still enjoy a cult following, but the band was dissolved in 1977, leaving behind an unfinished album. Mihm joined **Roy Loney And The Phantom Movers** led by another ex-member of the Flamin' Groovies - before forming the Kingsnakes.

Hot Mikado

During the 30s, when President Roosevelt inaugurated his New Deal to help America emerge from its crippling Depression, the Federal Theatre Project became an important part of his plan to absorb the unemployed - in this case actors and technicians - in government-sponsored jobs. In 1938, the Federal Theatre in Chicago launched a particularly successful production, *The Swing Mikado*. It was a jazzy Negro version of what many consider to be the best of all W.S. Gilbert and Arthur Sullivan's operas, *The Mikado* or *The Town Of Titipu*, which was first presented at the Savoy Theatre in London on 14 March 1885. The flamboyant show-man Mike Todd offered to buy the project and take it to New York, but he was informed that it was public property, and not for sale. However, the Federal Theatre organization itself subsequently moved *The Swing Mikado* to Broadway, where it opened on 1 March 1939 at the New Yorker Theatre. Not to be outdone, Todd responded by assembling a cast of more than 100 African-American actors, including the renowned 60-year old tap dancer, **Bill 'Bojangles' Robinson**, and installing them in *The Hot Mikado* which moved into the nearby Broadhurst Theatre a few weeks later on 23 March. *The Hot Mikado* was directed by Hassard Short, who had previously staged such prominent musicals and revues as *Three's A Crowd*, *The Band Wagon*, *As Thousands Cheer*, *Roberta*, and **Irving Berlin**'s *Music Box Review* series. Garbed all in gold - even down to his cane - Robinson played the Mikado, the title given by foreigners to the Emperor of Japan, and scored a big hit with his version of 'The Punishment Fit The Crime'. Early each evening he performed at Harlem's famous Cotton Club, before donning his Emperor's robes to go on stage at the Broadhurst. Members of the press especially liked the Jitterbug Girls in their snazzy slacks, and reported that the creators of *The Hot Mikado* 'have done amazing and agreeably absurd things with Gilbert and Sullivan's score, leaving large chunks out entirely. Everything has been chucked overboard except the basic melodies, but it is very entertaining to have Katisha (an elderly lady in

love with the Emperor's son) sing to torch rhythms.' Both shows ran through the summer, but while *The Swing Mikado* faded, Todd shrewdly took *The Hot Mikado* to the New York World's Fair at Flushing Meadow, and then on tour until April 1940. By that time, it was considered the most successful black musical show since **Shuffle Along** (1921), although, ironically, all the members of the orchestra were white.

Towards the end of World War II, in May 1945, two more shows adapted from another Gilbert and Sullivan opera, *H.M.S. Pinafore* or *The Lass That Loved A Sailor*, made brief visits to Broadway. The first of them, *Memphis Bound!*, had Bill 'Bojangles' Robinson again, and stayed fairly close to its source material, but *Hollywood Pinafore*, which starred William Gaxton and Victor Moore, was more up to date, and had a witty book by **George S. Kaufman**. Neither of them lasted for very long.

Some 40 years after they both went down, David H. Bell, the Artistic Director of Ford's Theatre, Washington, decided to present *Hot Mikado* as its 1986 Spring Musical. Unable to track down any of the material from the 1939 show, he and his collaborator Rob Bowman decided to adapt the material themselves. Most of the titles of the songs they included seemed familiar, and Gilbert and Sullivan aficionados will be able to judge how close to the 1885 original this production was - as far as the score was concerned at least - by browsing the following list: 'We Are The Gentlemen Of Japan', 'A Wand'ring Minstrel I', 'I Am Right', 'The Brass Will Crash', 'The Lord High Executioner', 'A Little List', 'Three Little Maids', 'This I'll Never Do', 'A Cheap And Chippy Chopper', 'With Joyous Shout', 'Katisha's Warning', 'Braid The Raven Hair', 'The Sun And I', 'Swing A Merry Madrigal', 'A How-Dee-Doo', 'The Punishment Fit The Crime', 'The Criminal's End', 'Alone And Yet Alive', 'Tit Willow', and 'Beauty In The Bellow'. Prominent among the cast were Robin Baxter (Pitti-Sing), Raymond Bazemore (Pooh-Bah), Steve Blanchard (Nanki Poo), Merwin Foard (Pish-Tush), Lawrence Hamilton (Mikado), Frank Kopyc (Ko-Ko), Kathleen Mahony-Bennett (Yum-Yum), Val Scott (Peep-Bo), Helena-Joyce Wright (Katisha), and Gregg Hellems and Mona Wyatt (both Swing). *Hot Mikado* was well received in Washington, and had stagings in several other US locations (but not on Broadway) before venturing to England - the heartland of Gilbert and Sullivan - at London's Queen's Theatre on 18 May 1995. Lawrence Hamilton recreated his fine tap-dancing performance as Washington's *Mikado*, and also singled out for praise were Ross Lehman, as the reluctant executioner Ko-Ko, for his superb clowning in the style of American vaude-villians such as **Eddie Cantor** and Phil Silvers, as well as his compelling rendition of 'Tit Willow', and Sharon Benson, who transformed Katisha from an ageing battleaxe into 'a sensational vamp in an hourglass suit of pillar-box red, singing 'The Hour Of Gladness' with barely controlled sexual rage as a fierce blues number'.

Among the rest of a high class cast were Neil Couperthwaite (Junior), Veronica Hart (Peep-Bo), Paulette Ivory (Yum-Yum), Alison Jiear (Pitti-Sing), Richard Lloyd King (Pooh-Bah), Paul Manuel (Nanki-Poo), and Ben Richards (Pish-Tush). With the production set in the late 30s-early 40s, traditional Japanese costumes were eschewed in favour of 'snappy zoot suits and the skin tight skirts of jitterbuggers', modes of dress entirely suitable for performing a score consisting of elements of gospel, jazz, blues and swing, as well as the odd **Andrews Sisters** take-off. So, more than 50 years after its inception, *Hot Mikado* 1995-style was generally acclaimed as 'more fun than you can shake a chopstick at'. By now employing several white actors, its re-creators justified the 'brash attack' on this particular Savoy opera by claiming that even the original show was a Victorian, non-authentic interpretation of Japan. Sadly, it failed to secure an audience in the West End, and closed on the 19 August 1995.

Among the other attempts to up-date, jazz-up, or generally play around with *The Mikado* on stage, have been the highly successful *The Black Mikado*, which had a long run in London during 1975/6, a *Cool Mikado*, and a Berlin jazz *Mikado*, in which Nanki-Poo 'Charlestoned in Oxford Bags'.

Hot Rats - Frank Zappa

Having temporarily disbanded the Mothers Of Invention, Frank Zappa recorded this exceptional solo album. His group was renowned for musical satire, but here the artist opted to showcase his prowess on guitar. 'Willie The Pimp' apart, which features a cameo vocal by his old friend Captain Beefheart, the set is comprised of instrumentals. The players, who include Don 'Sugarcane' Harris, Jean-Luc Ponty and Ian Underwood, are uniformly excellent, combining to provide a solid jazz-rock platform for Zappa's always compulsive soloing. He relishes a freedom which, while acknowledging past achievements, prepared new territories for exploration. *Hot Rats* was a pivotal release in Zappa's misunderstood career.

● Tracks: *Peaches En Regalia; Willie The Pimp; Son Of Mr. Green Genes; Little Umbrellas; The Gumbo Variations; It Must Be A Camel.*

● First released 1969

● UK peak chart position: 9

● USA peak chart position: 173

Hot Rod Gang

Retitled *Fury Unleashed* for UK audiences, *Hot Rod Gang* was a low-budget film notable only for the appearance of **Gene Vincent** in its cast. This 1958 feature starred John Ashley as John Abernethy III, who is unable to inherit a considerable fortune in time to finance his entry to a hot-rod race. He attempts to secure the cash required to build a car by joining Vincent's group, the Blue Caps. Although not credited, rock singer **Eddie Cochran** also appears as a member of the band, cementing a friendship with Vincent that culminated in their joint 1960 UK tour. This fateful visit ended with the car crash in which Cochran was killed. Although both artists are seen to better effect in *The Girl Can't Help It*, *Hot Rod Gang* does at least afford another opportunity to see two of rock 'n' roll's seminal performers.

Hot Streak

Jazz-disco fusion quartet from New Jersey, USA, comprising Derrick Dupree (vocals), Al Tanner (lead guitar), Jacob Dixon (bass) and Ricci Burgess (drums). The group started in the gospel field and entered the R&B arena in 1982. They were originally called A Different Flavour and then became Special Forces and had a single, 'Stroke It', released on Salsoul. They worked with Curtis Hudson and his wife Lisa Stevens who, apart from being members of Pure Energy, had penned **Madonna**'s huge hit 'Holiday'. The duo renamed the foursome Hot Streak and wrote 'Body Work' for them. The New York disco label Easy Street snapped up the single and had it remixed by John 'Jellybean' Benitez. The record, which included a well-known US army chant, became a favourite in US discos, and perhaps not surprisingly, in health clubs. In the UK it shot to the top of the club charts and also went into the Top 20. Despite the good start, the group never continued their hot streak.

● FILMS: *Breakdance - The Movie* (1984).

Hot Tuna

This US group represented the combination of two members of the **Jefferson Airplane**, Jack Casady (b. 13 April 1944, Washington, DC, USA; bass) and **Jorma Kaukonen** (b. 23 December 1940, Washington, DC, USA; guitar/vocals). The group evolved as a part-time extension of the Airplane with Kaukonen and Casady utilizing the services of colleagues **Paul Kantner** (guitar) and Spencer Dryden (drums) and other guests, displaying their talents as blues musicians. Stage appearances were initially integrated within the Airplane's performances on the same bill. During one of the Airplane's rest periods, the duo began to appear in their own right, often as a rock trio with then Airplane drummer, Joey Covington. Having the name Hot Shit rejected, they settled on Hot Tuna and released a self-titled debut as a duo, with a guest appearance from harmonica player, Will Scarlet. Kaukonen has since rejected this stating that 'age-old rumors that we planned to call it Hot Shit are completely unfounded'. The set was drawn largely from traditional blues/ragtime material by **Jelly Roll Morton** and the **Rev. Gary Davis**, with Casady's booming and meandering bass lines interplaying superbly with Kaukonen's fluid acoustic guitar. By the time of their second album, another live set, they were a full-blown rock quartet with the addition of violinist **Papa John Creach** and Sammy Piazza on drums. This line-up displayed the perfect combination of electric and acoustic rock/blues for which Casady and Kaukonen had been looking. Creach had departed by the time *The Phosphorescent Rat* was recorded, and Piazza, who had left to join **Stoneground** was replaced by Bob Steeler in 1974. The music became progressively louder, so that by the time of their sixth album they sounded like a rumbling heavy rock traditional ragtime blues band. Kaukonen's limited vocal range added to this odd concoction, but throughout all this time the group maintained a hardcore following. In the late 70s the duo split, resulting in Casady embarking on an ill-advised excursion into what was perceived as 'punk' with SVT. Kaukonen continued with a solo career combining both electric and acoustic performances. At best Hot Tuna were excitingly different, at worst they were ponderous and loud. Selected stand-out tracks from their erratic repertoire were 'Mann's Fate' from *Hot Tuna*, 'Keep On Truckin'' and 'Sea Child' from *Burgers*, 'Song From The Stainless Cymbal' from *Hoppkorv*, and 'Hit Single #1' from *America's Choice*. Casady and Kaukonen reunited in 1991 with a workmanlike album that found little favour with the record-buying public.

● ALBUMS: *Hot Tuna* (RCA 1970)★★★, *First Pull Up Then Pull Down* (RCA 1971)★★★, *Burgers* (Grunt 1972)★★★★, *The Phosphorescent Rat* (Grunt 1973)★★, *America's Choice* (Grunt 1974)★★★, *Yellow Fever* (Grunt 1975)★★, *Hoppkorv* (Grunt 1976)★★★, *Double Dose* (Grunt 1978)★★★, *Final Vinyl* (Grunt 1980)★★★, *Splashdown* (Relix 1985)★★, *Pair A Dice Found* (Epic 1991)★★, *Live At Sweetwater* (1993), *Historic* (Relix 1993)★★, *Classic Electric* (Relix 1996)★★★★, *Acoustic Hot Tuna* (Relix 1996)★★★.

● COMPILATIONS: *Trimmed And Burning* (Edsel 1994)★★★★, *Hot Tuna In A Can* 5-CD tin (Rhino 1996)★★★★.

Hotel

This US rock band, formed in the late 70s, was frequently accused of 'taking a hammer to crack a nutshell', to quote one analogy. The assembled ranks of Hotel, who specialized in grandiloquent, multi-layered AOR, included Tommy Caton (guitar, vocals), Marc Phillips (keyboards, vocals), Michael Reid (guitar, vocals), George Creasman (bass, vocals), Lee Bargeon (keyboards, vocals) and Michael Cadenhead (drums, percussion). Their 1979 debut album, released on MCA Records, was a disappointing collection of songs where the focus on unnecessary musical embellishment detracted from the group's songwriting. *Half Moon Silver*, which followed a year later, was an improvement, but it, too, failed to elevate them into the AOR mainstream.

● ALBUMS: *Hotel* (MCA 1979)★★, *Half Moon Silver* (MCA 1980)★★★.

Hotel California - Eagles

A steady growth suddenly mushroomed into a monster as the Eagles, along with Fleetwood Mac, epitomized AOR in the early 70s. This record is supposedly a concept album but most of the purchasers merely enjoyed the accessible songs while driving down to the coast in their Volkswagen Caravanettes with 2.4 children. Joe Walsh was added to give gutsy guitar in the wake of the country flavour of Bernie Leaden, while Randy Meisner grew in stature as a writer with 'Try And Love Again' and 'New Kid In Town'. The title track still bites as Henley's voice blends with Walsh's epic solo.

● Tracks: *Hotel California; New Kid In Town; Life In The Fast Lane; Wasted Time; Wasted Time (Reprise); Victim Of Love; Pretty Maids All In A Row; Try And Love Again; The Last Resort*.

● First released 1976

● UK peak chart position: 2

● USA peak chart position: 1

Hothouse Flowers

This folk-inspired Irish rock group, who took their name from the title of a **Wynton Marsalis** album, are based around the nucleus of Liam O'Maonlai and Fiachna O'Broainain. O'Maonlai was formerly in a punk band called Congress that would later evolve into **My Bloody Valentine**. They started performing together as the Incomparable Benzini Brothers and busked in their native Dublin. In 1985 they won the Street Entertainers Of The Year Award. Recruiting Maria Doyle, they became the Hothouse Flowers and landed a regular gig at the Magic Carpet Club just outside Dublin. Their notoriety spreading, they were highly praised in **Rolling Stone** magazine before they had even secured a recording contract. An appearance on RTE's Saturday night chat programme *The Late Show* led to the issue of a single on **U2**'s Mother label. 'Love Don't Work That Way' came out in 1987 and though it was not a great success it brought them to the attention of **PolyGram Records** who signed them up. Their debut single for the major - 'Don't Go' - was a number 11 UK hit. Further hits followed, including a cover version of **Johnny Nash**'s 'I Can See Clearly Now', 'Give It Up', and 'Movies'. Their debut, *People*, reached number 2 in the UK charts. The band existed as part of a larger, looser 'Raggle Taggle' musical community, and members can be heard on material by the **Indigo Girls**, **Adventures**, **Michelle Shocked** and **Maria McKee**. In the early 90s they made their 'acting' debut in an episode of the UK television series *Lovejoy*. Further albums showed little musical progression from their debut, and in 1995 O'Maonlai formed a side project, Alt, with Andy White and Tim Finn. Hothouse Flowers returned in 1998 with the uninspiring *Born*.

● ALBUMS: *People* (London 1988)★★★, *Home* (London 1990)★★, *Songs From The Rain* (London 1993)★★★, *Born* (London 1998)★★.

Hotlegs

This UK studio group was formed in 1970 and featured Kevin Godley (b. 7 October 1945, Manchester, England; vocals/drums), Lol Creme (b. 19 September 1947, Manchester, England; vocals/guitar) and Eric

Stewart (b. 20 January 1945, Manchester, England; vocals/guitar). Godley had previously played in the **Mockingbirds**, while Stewart was a former member of both **Wayne Fontana And The Mindbenders** and the **Mindbenders**. While working at Stewart's Strawberry Studios, the group completed a track, which caught the attention of Philips Records managing director, **Dick Leahy**. The result was a highly original UK Top 10 single 'Neanderthal Man' and an album, *Thinks School Stinks*. The group then returned to the studio, where they formed the nucleus of **10cc**. **Godley And Creme** later enjoyed further success as a duo.

● ALBUMS: *Thinks School Stinks* (Fontana 1970)★★.

Houghton Weavers

This folk-based group from Lancashire, England was formed in 1975 by Tony Berry (b. Anthony Berry, 15 January 1950, Bolton, Lancashire, England; vocals), Norman Prince (b. Norman Anthony Prince, 26 April 1946, Eccles, Manchester, England; vocals/guitar), David Littler (b. David George Littler, 13 March 1949, Westhoughton, Lancashire, England; vocals/banjo/guitar/ukelele), and John Oliver (b. Appley Bridge, Wigan, Lancashire, England; vocals). They were the resident group at a number of venues in the north west of England, but within 12 months, Oliver left the group. He was replaced by Denis Littler (b. Westhoughton, Lancashire, England; bass/vocals), who himself left in February 1984. Jeff Hill (b. Jeffrey Martin Hill, 14 September 1958 Warrington, Lancashire, England; vocals/bass/guitar) joined the group the same month. A featured spot on a BBC television series, *We'll Call You*, in 1977, led to the group receiving their own television series, *Sit Thi Deawn*, which started in January 1978. In addition, the group's popularity on radio has enabled them to hold down five series of their own show on BBC Radio 2, with a new series being recorded early in 1992. As a result of success in pantomime, the Houghton Weavers now regularly tour at Christmas under the banner of the Christmas Cracker Tour, playing 20 dates in 24 nights. *Keep Folk Smiling* was released to coincide with the group's 10th anniversary. Given the depth of popularity that the group command, it is surprising that they are not better known nationally.

● ALBUMS: *Howfen Wakes* (1976)★★★, *Gone Are The Days* (1977)★★★, *Sit Thi Deawn* (1978)★★★, *In Concert* (1979)★★, *Up Your Way* (1980)★★★, *Alive And Kicking* (1981)★★, *In The Rare Old Times* (1983)★★★, *Keep Folk Smiling* (1985)★★★, *It's Good To See You* (1986)★★★, *Lancashire Lads* (1988)★★★, *When Granny Sang Me Songs* (1990)★★★, *Christmas Collection* (1991)★★.

Hound-Dog Man

Fabian was one of several 50s rock 'n' roll singers styled on **Elvis Presley**, but boasting only a slim resemblance to their role model. 'Turn Me Loose' and 'Tiger' were among his US Top 10 entries, but the sexual bravura of their titles was undermined by unconvincing vocals.

However, he was quickly plucked from the singles chart and presented in a series of blithe Hollywood films. Released in 1959, *Hound-Dog Man* provided Fabian's first starring role, in which he plays one of two teenagers star-struck by a wayward acquaintance. The light comedy feature was set in 1912, demanding that Fabian act rather than simply perform, while rising director Don Seigel, later famed for Clint Eastwood's *Dirty Harry* series, brought a sharper focus to the proceedings than many contemporary releases of its type. The title song became one of Fabian's five US Top 30 entries during 1959, but the appeal of his recordings waned as quickly as it arose.

Hounds

As predictable as the music of US heavy metal band the Hounds was, its lack of intelligence paled into insignificance compared to their record sleeves. On *Unleashed*, their 1978 debut for **Columbia Records**, John Hunter (vocals, keyboards), Jim Orkis (guitar), Glen Rupp (guitar), Joe Cuttone (bass) and John Horvath (drums) struck unpleasant macho poses behind salivating, chained dogs. The music contained within struck out aggressively, but with little substance, while the lyrics caused at least one bout of hilarity among the critics subjected to it. *Puttin' On The Dog* continued in the same vein, but by now, Columbia's initial confidence in the group had all but collapsed. Though **Spinal Tap** have acknowledged that their heavy metal satire was based on the real-life exploits of **Uriah Heep**, they could just as easily have been inspired by either of the Hounds' record sleeves.

● ALBUMS: *Unleashed* (Columbia 1978)★★, *Puttin' On The Dog* (Columbia 1979★★★.

Hounds Of Love - Kate Bush

Though not the most prolific of album artists, Bush's works make up in impact what they lack in frequency. Her style and material has always been unique, eccentric even, but *Hounds Of Love* is probably the strongest mix of controlled musical experimentation and lyrical expression. It deals with big issues - childhood fantasy and trauma, conflict, sexuality - but rarely lapses into pretension. The intense arrangements are perfectly matched to the subjects: 'Running Up That Hill' climactically erotic, 'Cloudbusting' broodingly triumphant, and 'The Big Sky' just… big.

● Tracks: *Running Up That Hill (A Deal With God); Hounds Of Love; The Big Sky; Mother Stands For Comfort; Cloudbusting; And Dream Of Sheep; Under Ice; Waking The Witch; Watching You Without Me; Jig Of Life; Hello Earth; The Morning Fog.*

● First released 1985

● UK peak chart position: 1

● USA peak chart position: 30

Hour Glass

Formed in Decatur, Alabama, USA, in 1967 from the ashes of the Allman Joys, the group was fronted by **Gregg Allman** (b. Gregory Lenoir Allman, 8 December

1947, Nashville, Tennessee, USA; vocals/organ) and his brother **Duane Allman** (b. 20 November 1946, Nashville, Tennessee, USA, d. 29 October 1971, Macon, Georgia, USA; guitar). Paul Hornsby (keyboards), Mabron McKinney (bass) and Johnny Sandlin completed the original line-up, 'discovered' playing juke-box favourites by the **Nitty Gritty Dirt Band** and their manager, Bill McEwan. The Hour Glass then moved to California, where they became a popular live attraction. Although their debut album consisted largely of pop/soul cover versions, it did include 'Cast Off All My Fears', an early **Jackson Browne** composition. However, the set was essentially a vehicle for Gregg's voice, and with session musicians replacing the group proper, the results bore no relation to the quintet's own ambitions. Jesse Willard Carr replaced McKinney for *Power Of Love*, in which several 'southern' soul songs vied with group originals. Once again the album failed to capture their full potential and in a final act of defiance, the Hour Glass booked themselves into the fabled Fame studios (see **Muscle Shoals**), where they completed a searing **B.B. King** medley. When their label rejected the master as unsuitable, the quintet decided to go their separate ways. Gregg and Duane later formed the **Allman Brothers Band**, an act later produced by Johnny Sandlin. Hornsby became manager of the group's Capricorn Sound studios while Carr enjoyed a lucrative session career.

● ALBUMS: *Hour Glass* (Liberty 1967)★★, *The Power Of Love* (Liberty 1968)★★.
● COMPILATIONS: *Hour Glass 1967-1969* (1973)★★, *The Soul Of Time* (1985)★★.

House

Chicago was the kindergarten of the warm, feel-good music in the late 80s that came to be known as house, although its actual birthplace was New York, and the Loft. House was built on the innovations of disco but with less of the 'flash' and even less of a reliance on lyrics. In 1983/1984 dance music was, indeed, essentially disco, although hybrids such as electro, go go and rare groove also existed. The term was invoked due to the warehouse parties it was to be heard at during its infancy. The music arrived in Chicago when DJ **Frankie Knuckles** relocated to the region and inaugurated the original Warehouse club. The scene was confined to the gay clubs until **Farley Jackmaster Funk** began to play it on the radio. As the house scene evolved its early were stages chronicled by records like Colonel Abram's 'Music Is The Answer' (the first to press a record was Jesse Saunders). The trickle became a river as Chicago releases like J.M. Silk's 'Music Is The Key' (an answer record to the aforementioned Colonel Abrams' release), Jack Master Funk's 'Aw Shucks' and **Jamie Principle**'s 'Waiting On My Angel' piled up. Many of these were housed on imprints like **Trax** and **DJ International**, which ably documented the era. Following Farley important early mixers and movers on Chicago radio included Julian Peruse, Frankie

Rodriguez, Mike 'Hitman' Wilson, Bad Boy Bill, Tim Shomer and Brian Middleton. It would be **Steve 'Silk' Hurley**'s 'Jack Your Body' which finally took the new music to commercial recognition and the number 1 slot in the UK charts. Variants like acid house were also given birth in Chicago via **DJ Pierre**, while Detroit took the electronic elements to forge techno. Frankie Rodriguez arguably has the best answer to a rigid definition of house: 'If I go out the country, the first thing anyone asks is 'What Is House?'. Who cares? Put the record on, enjoy it'.

House Band

Comprising Ged Foley (b. Gerard Foley, 24 February 1955, Peterlee, Co. Durham, England; vocals, guitar, Northumbrian pipes), Chris Parkinson (b. 31 March 1950, Rawtenstall, Lancashire, England; piano accordion, vocals, melodeon, synthesizer, harmonica) and John Skelton (b. 26 September 1954, Bromley, Kent, England; flute, whistle, bombarde, bodhran), the House Band have rapidly established themselves on the UK folk circuit, despite their relatively recent emergence. The group, formed in 1985, originally consisted of Parkinson and Foley with Iain MacLeod (mandolin), and Jimmy Young (flute, small pipes). With the departure of both MacLeod and Young, in February 1986, the House Band were joined, in the same month, by Skelton and Brian Brooks (bouzouki, keyboards, whistle, vocals). In January 1988, Brooks left the group due to family commitments. Combining traditional instruments, augmented by synthesizer and modern arrangements, the House Band have played to a wide range of audiences, and even supported **Status Quo** at a Swiss rock festival. The various members of the band have all been involved in performing in other capacities, in particular Foley in the **Battlefield Band**, and both Skelton and Brooks in Shegui. This has resulted in tours of the USA, Canada and New Zealand, in addition to Europe and the UK. Although Foley is now resident in the USA, the group are still performing at folk festivals and folk clubs in the UK, and released the excellent *Rockall* in 1996.

● ALBUMS: *The House Band* (Topic 1986)★★★, *Pacific* (Topic 1987)★★★, *Word Of Mouth* (Topic 1988)★★★, *Stonetown* (Harbourtown 1991)★★★, *Rockall* (Green Linnet 1996)★★★.
● COMPILATIONS: *Groundwork* (1993)★★★, *The Very Best Of* (Reactive 1998)★★★★.

House Of Flowers

Truman Capote is said to have got the idea for this show while visiting Port-au-Prince in Haiti in the late 40s. In an event, he wrote the libretto, and collaborated with composer **Harold Arlen** on the lyrics for what was a short-lived, but fondly remembered production. It opened at New York's Alvin Theatre on 30 December 1954, and told of the trials and tribulations of two brothels on an unidentified West Indies island. Madame Fleur (**Pearl Bailey**) tends the House of

Flowers, while Madame Tango (Juanita Hall) performs a similar service for a rival concern. One of Madame Fleur's young blooms, Ottilie (Diahann Carroll), turns down the opportunity of real career advancement in favour of an exclusive love contract with the young and innocent Royal (Rawn Spearman), and eventually, Madame Fleur corners the terra firma market franchise when Madame Tango's operation is floated (on a world cruise). However, it is the unusual, but somehow overwhelming score that makes this a memorable show. It contained the delightful calypso-styled 'Two Ladies In De Shade Of De Banana Tree', along with 'I Never Has Seen Snow', 'I'm Gonna Leave Off Wearin' My Shoes', 'Smellin' Of Vanilla', 'Has I Let You Down?', 'One Man Ain't Quite Enough', and 'A Sleepin' Bee' which was sung in the show by Ottilie and Royal, and received what was probably its definitive version from **Barbra Streisand** on her first album. There was another lovely ballad, 'Don't Like Goodbyes', which was given a smooth treatment by **Frank Sinatra** on his *Close To You*. During the pre-Broadway tryout there were rumours of backstage battles involving several of the principals, and, indeed, some particularly volatile personalities and egos assembled for this production. Diahann Carroll and Truman Capote both made highly impressive Broadway debuts, and Pearl Bailey was her usual dominating self. Oliver Messel's pastel-coloured sets, which somehow gave the whole affair a kind of etheral quality, were singled out for special praise. *House Of Flowers* had a disappointing run of 165 performances, and a 1968 Off Broadway revival was brief and to the point.

House Of Lords

This five-piece US heavy rock supergroup was put together by ex-**Angel** keyboardist Gregg Giuffria. Augmented by bassist Chuck Wright (ex-**Quiet Riot**), drummer Ken Mary (ex-**Alice Cooper**), vocalist James Christian (ex-Canata) and guitarist Lanny Cordola (ex-**Giuffria**), the line-up was impressive and promised much. With Giuffria in control, the band pursued an overstated melodic approach with swathes of keyboards, multi-phased harmonies and atmospheric arrangements redolent of mid-70s arena rock. Signing to **RCA Records**, their debut was recorded with the help of Andy Johns and long-time friend **Gene Simmons** (**Kiss** bassist) at the production desk. The result was well received, a state-of-the-art pomp-rock album with a powerful and sparkling sound. Apart from a few support slots on the **Scorpions'** European tour, the band did not commit themselves to touring in a way that was necessary to stimulate album sales. Lanny Cordola quit as a result, and was replaced by Michael Guy (ex-Fire) before the band entered the studio once more. *Sahara* continued in the same musical vein, but the interest it generated (the album went platinum) was once again allowed to ebb away as the band was still reluctant to tour. Guests included David Glen Eisley, the original Giuffria vocalist, whom

Simmons had advised they replace prior to them becoming House Of Lords. They split shortly thereafter, though they did re-form to record a new album for the Japanese market. After the band's dissolution, Christian eventually regrouped with both Cordola and Wright to pursue a solo career, releasing his debut album, *Rude Awakening*, on Now & Then Records in 1995. However, it lacked much of the sparkle that had once made the House Of Lords so vital.

● ALBUMS: *House Of Lords* (RCA 1988)★★★, *Sahara* (RCA 1990)★★★.
Solo: James Christian *Rude Awakening* (Now & Then 1995)★★.

House Of Love

After a short spell with the ill-fated, glam rock-inspired Kingdoms, UK-born vocalist and guitarist Guy Chadwick teamed up with drummer Pete Evans, guitarist Terry Bickers, bassist Chris Groothuizen and vocalist/guitarist Andrea Heukamp to form UK group the House Of Love. Throughout 1986, the quintet played at small pubs and despatched a demo tape to **Creation Records**, which, after constant play in the office, attracted the attention of label head Alan McGee. He financed the recording of their debut single, the sparkling 'Shine On', which was released in May 1987. A follow-up, 'Real Animal', was also issued, but sold relatively poorly. After touring extensively under tough conditions, Heukamp decided to leave the group. Continuing as a quartet, the House Of Love spent the spring of 1988 recording their debut album, which cost an astonishingly meagre £8,000 to complete. A pilot single, 'Christine', was rightly acclaimed as one of the best UK independent singles of the year. Its shimmering guitarwork was exemplary and indicated the enormous potential of the ensemble. The debut album did not disappoint and was included in many critics' nominations for the best record of 1988. Already, the House Of Love were being tipped as the group most likely to succeed in 1989 and the release of the excellent 'Destroy The Heart' reinforced that view. Speculation was rife that they would sign to a major label and eventually PhonoGram secured their signatures. In keeping with their 60s/guitar-based image the group's releases were subsequently issued on the newly revived **Fontana Records** label. A torturous period followed. The first two singles for the label, 'Never' and 'I Don't Know Why I Love You', both stalled at number 41, while the album suffered interminable delays. By Christmas 1989, guitarist Terry Bickers had quit over what was euphemistically termed a personality clash. He was immediately replaced by Simon Walker, and early the following year the group's long-awaited £400,000 second album, *Fontana*, appeared to mixed reviews. As Chadwick later acknowledged: 'We'd stated everything on the first album'. Extensive touring followed, ending with the departure of Walker, tentatively replaced by original member Andrea Heukamp, who returned from Germany. Thereafter, Chadwick suffered a long period of writer's block while the departing Bickers enjoyed acclaim in **Levitation**. Although the House Of Love lost ground to newly revered guitar groups such as the **Stone Roses**, they re-emerged in October 1991 with an acclaimed EP featuring the excellent 'The Girl With The Loneliest Eyes'. In 1992, the group's long-awaited new album, *Babe Rainbow*, was released to a degree of critical acclaim, but the impression of underachievement was hard to avoid. Following 1993's *Audience Of The Mind* the band collapsed, Chadwick re-emerging a year later with the Madonnas. By 1997 he was signed to Setanta as a solo artist, releasing the 'This Strength' single in November and *Lazy, Soft & Slow* the following year.

● ALBUMS: *House Of Love* (Creation 1988)★★★, *Fontana* (Fontana 1989)★★, *Babe Rainbow* (Fontana 1992)★★★, *Audience Of The Mind* (Fontana 1993)★★★.
Solo: Guy Chadwick *Lazy, Soft & Slow* (Setanta 1998)★★★.
● COMPILATIONS: *A Spy In The House Of Love* (Fontana 1990)★★★.

House Of Pain

Hardcore Irish American hip-hoppers whose origins can be traced to Taft High School in Los Angeles (former students of which include Ice Cube). The band comprise lead rapper **Everlast** (b. Eric Schrody, USA), his co-lyricist Danny Boy (b. Daniel O'Connor, USA), and DJ Lethal (b. Leor DiMant, c.1974, Latvia). Everlast was originally signed to **Warner Brothers**, and was often to be seen 'hanging' with **Ice-T** and his Rhythm Syndicate at that time. With House Of Pain he scored a debut Top 10 hit with the impressive 'Jump Around', a good example of the street poetry hybrid which they branded 'Fine malt lyricism'. 'Jump Around' seemed to offer the pinnacle in House Of Pain's career, however. Their debut album gloried in self-styled Gaelic dressing. 'Shamrocks And Shenanigans', an ode to their spurious links with the Emerald Isle, contained a novelty sample of **David Bowie**'s 'Fame'. Elsewhere the album's grooves were populated with familiar, dumb macho lines, delivered with a quite singular lack of dexterity: 'I feel blessed, I'm casually dressed, I wear a gun, But I don't wear a vest'. No strangers to controversy, House Of Pain were involved in two near riots on their 1993 tour with **Rage Against The Machine**; once in Baltimore when they refused to take the stage, and again when a member of the band's road crew was assaulted by security staff at a Manchester Academy gig. This was only a matter of days after the rapper had been arrested at JFK Airport in New York for illegal possession of a handgun. Such incidents led to his being subject to a tracking device and house arrest for three months in 1994. The press were also starting to ask awkward questions about Sinn Fein tattoos. Everlast has ventured in to the world of films, appearing in both the US rap movie, *Who's The Man* (alongside **Public Enemy, Heavy D** etc), and the Dennis Leary flick, *Judgement Day*, where, unsurprisingly, he played a gangster. House Of Pain also opened a pizza restaurant,

in partnership with Mickey Rourke (House Of Pizza). *Same As It Ever Was*, despite the title, proved to be a much more impressive outing, with Everlast unleashing his frustration with his 'imprisonment' and the media in tracks like 'Back From The Dead'

● ALBUMS: *House Of Pain* (Tommy Boy 1992)★★★★, *Same As It Ever Was* (Tommy Boy 1994)★★★, *Truth Crushed To Earth Shall Rise Again* (Tommy Boy 1996)★★★.

House, James

b. 21 March 1955, Sacramento, California, USA. His father and his uncles sang **a cappella** country music, but House was more interested in rock music as he grew up. He started performing as a solo acoustic act but then formed his own group, the House Band, which was signed to **Warner** and then moved to **Atlantic**. He started to write country music and, with the advent of more rock-based musicians in the genre such as **Steve Earle**, he was signed to **MCA**. House made the US country charts with 'Don't Quit Me Now', 'Hard Times For A Honest Man', 'You Just Get Better All The Time' and 'That'll Be The Last Thing'. He acted as vocal coach for Dustin Hoffman on the film *Ishtar*, and played a solo acoustic set when he came to the UK with **Randy Travis**.

● ALBUMS: *James House* (MCA 1989)★★★★, *Hard Times For A Honest Man* (MCA 1990)★★★, *Days Gone By* (Epic 1994)★★.
● VIDEOS: *A Real Good Way To Wind Up Lonesome* (Planet 1994).

Housemartins

Formed in 1984, this UK pop group comprised Paul Heaton (b. 9 May 1962, Birkenhead, Lancashire, England; vocals, guitar), Stan Collimore (b. 6 April 1962, Hull, Humberside, England; bass), Ted Key (guitar) and Hugh Whitaker (drums). After signing to Go! Discs, the group humorously promoted themselves as 'the fourth best band from Hull'. Their modesty and distinctly plain image disguised a genuine songwriting talent, which quickly emerged. During late 1985, Key departed and was replaced by **Norman Cook** (b. 31 July 1963, Brighton, Sussex, England). By 1986, the group achieved their first UK hit with their third release, the infectious 'Happy Hour', which climbed to number 3. Their UK Top 10 debut album *London 0 Hull 4* displayed a wit, freshness and verve that rapidly established them as one of Britain's most promising groups. In December 1986, their excellent a cappella version of 'Caravan Of Love' gave them a deserved UK number 1 hit. Early in 1987 the Housemartins received a coveted BPI award as the Best Newcomers of the year. In the summer, they underwent a line-up change, with David Hemmingway replacing drummer Hugh Whitaker. An acclaimed EP, *Five Get Over Excited* followed, after which the group displayed their left-wing political preferences by performing at the 'Red Wedge' concerts. After securing another Top 20 hit with the catchy 'Me And The Farmer', the group issued their final studio album, the self-mocking *The People Who Grinned Themselves To Death*. Although still at the peak of their powers, the group split in June 1988, annoucing that they had only intended the Housemartins to last for three years. The power of the original line-up was indicated by the subsequent successes of offshoot groups such as the **Beautiful South** and **Beats International**. In 1993 Hugh Whitaker was charged and sentenced to six years' imprisonment for wounding with intent and three arson attacks on a business acquaintance.

● ALBUMS: *London 0 Hull 4* (Go! Discs 1986)★★★★, *The People Who Grinned Themselves To Death* (Go! Discs 1987)★★.

● COMPILATIONS: *Now That's What I Call Quite Good!* (Go! Discs 1988)★★★★.

● FURTHER READING: *The Housemartins, Tales From Humberside*, Nick Swift.

Houses Of The Holy - Led Zeppelin

Led Zeppelin at their most wilfully inventive. Displaying an eclectic irreverence for their recent history, they struck out with an assured astuteness that let them play what they felt. Consequently, the results were so genuinely original that the idea that they had any real musical contemporaries suddenly seemed absurd. 'The Crunge', played at funk rock years before the popular press had discovered and christened it, 'D'yer Mak'er' tossed reggae around for fun, while 'No Quarter' went on to be lifted wholesale by Pearl Jam predecessors, Mother Love Bone. At the heart of, and yet still ahead of, their time.

● Tracks: *The Song Remains The Same; The Rain Song; Over The Hills And Far Away; The Crunge; Dancing Days; D'yer Mak'er; No Quarter; The Ocean.*

● First released 1973

● UK peak chart position: 1

● USA peak chart position: 1

Houston, Cisco

b. Gilbert Vandine Houston, 18 August 1918, Wilmington, Delaware, USA, d. 25 April 1961, San Bernadino, California, USA. Houston's family moved to California in 1919. Having spent his early years in a variety of simple jobs, he found himself, like many others in the 30s, unemployed. He wanted to become a comedian, but obtained only secondary roles in a few Hollywood movies. Houston subsequently became involved in theatre work and a number of folk festivals, as well as union meetings and political gatherings. He then travelled with **Woody Guthrie** and Will Geer. In 1940 Houston joined the US merchant marines with Guthrie and performed for the benefit of fellow seamen. It was after the war that the two returned to New York and Houston began touring, performing at concerts and recording. In 1959, the US State Department sent him, together with **Sonny Terry** and **Brownie McGhee**, to India on a cultural exchange. By this time Houston knew that cancer of the stomach was threatening his life. Despite this fact, he still performed

at the 1960 Newport Folk Festival and continued to record for **Vanguard**. He made his last appearance in Pasadena at a folk concert, in spite of his painful illness, and died in April 1961. **Tom Paxton** commemorated his memory in the song 'Fare Thee Well Cisco'.

● ALBUMS: *900 Miles And Other Railroad Ballads* (Folkways 1952)★★★, *Sings Cowboy Ballads* (Folkways 1952)★★★, *Hard Travelin'* (Folkways 1954)★★★, *Sings Folk Songs* (Folkways 1955)★★★, *The Cisco Special* (Vanguard 1961)★★★, *I Aint Got No Home* (Vanguard 1962)★★★, *Sings The Songs Of Woody Guthrie* (Vanguard 1963)★★★★, *Songs Of The Open Road* (Folkways 1964)★★★★, *Passing Through* (Verve/Folkways 1965)★★★.

● COMPILATIONS: *The Folkways Years 1944-1961* (Smithsonian/Folkways 1994)★★★★.

● FURTHER READING: *900 Miles - The Ballads, Blues And Folksongs Of Cisco Houston.*

Houston, Cissy

b. Emily Drinkard, 1933, Newark, New Jersey, USA. Houston's singing career began in a family gospel group, the Drinkard Singers, which also featured her nieces Dee Dee and **Dionne Warwick**. The trio was later employed as backing singers for many artists, including **Solomon Burke** and **Wilson Pickett**. While Dionne began recording as a solo artist, Houston continued this backroom work. Between 1967 and 1970 she was lead vocalist with the **Sweet Inspirations**, an impressive quartet who sang on countless releases, primarily for **Atlantic Records**. Houston's subsequent solo releases included 'I'll Be There' (1970), 'Be My Baby' (1971) and 'Think It Over' (1978), but her career failed to match expectations and was later eclipsed by the success of her daughter **Whitney Houston**. Cissy has now returned chiefly to the gospel fold, as a major figure in the New Hope Baptist Church Choir of Newark, New Jersey, although in 1992 she shared a secular Shanachie CD with **Chuck Jackson**.

● ALBUMS: *Presenting Cissy Houston* (Major Minor 1970)★★★, *The Long And Winding Road* (Pye 1971)★★, *Cissy Houston* (Private Stock 1977)★★★, *Think It Over* (Private Stock 1978)★★, *Warning - Danger* (Private Stock 1979)★★, *Step Aside For A Lady* (EMI 1980)★★, with Chuck Jackson *I'll Take Care Of You* (Shanachie 1992)★★, *Face To Face* (House Of Blues 1996)★★★.

● COMPILATIONS: *Mama's Cookin'* (Charly 1987)★★★, *Midnight Train To Georgia: The Janus Years* (Ichiban 1995)★★★.

Houston, David

b. 9 December 1938, Bossier City, Louisiana, USA, d. 30 November 1993, Bossier City, Louisiana, USA. Houston's forefathers included Sam Houston, who fought for Texas's independence from Mexico, and the Civil War general Robert E. Lee. His parents were friends of 20s singer **Gene Austin**, who was his godfather and encouraged his talent. Houston made his debut on *Louisiana Hayride* when aged only 12. He continued with his studies and, encouraged by his manager, Tillman Franks, made a one-off single for **Sun Records** in Memphis, 'Sherry's Lips'/'Miss Brown'. In 1963 he was signed to Epic Records, who wanted to break into the country market. His first release, 'Mountain Of Love', made number 2 in the US country charts, and was followed by further hits including 'Livin' In A House Of Love' and 'Sweet, Sweet Judy'. In 1966, a song partly written by his producer **Billy Sherrill**, 'Almost Persuaded', topped the US country charts and also made the Top 30. It established him as one of country music's top balladeers, and he had further country chart-toppers with 'With One Exception', 'My Elusive Dreams' (a duet with **Tammy Wynette**), 'You Mean The World To Me', 'Have A Little Faith', 'Already In Heaven' and 'Baby Baby (I Know You're A Lady)'. He also appeared in the 1967 country film *Cotton-Pickin' Chicken Pluckers*. He never repeated his success with Tammy Wynette and she says in her autobiography, *Stand By Your Man*, 'If he was the last singer on earth, I'd never record with him again'. However, Houston has recorded several successful duets with other singers, including 'I Love You, I Love You' and 'After Closing Time', with **Barbara Mandrell**. His last Top 10 country success was with 'Can't You Feel It?' in 1974, and when he left Epic, he recorded with seven other labels. During his career, Houston had seven number 1 country records and 61 chart entries, the last, 'A Penny For Your Thoughts Tonight Virginia', a minor hit on the Country International label in 1989. In 1991, he appeared in the UK at Wembley's International Festival of Country Music. Houston, who joined the *Grand Ole Opry* in 1972, made his last appearance on the show on 6 November 1993. He suffered a ruptured brain aneurism and remained in a coma until his death five days later. He is remembered by his country music associates for his knowledge of the music and its artists.

● ALBUMS: *David Houston (New Voice From Nashville)* (Epic 1964)★★★, *David Houston Sings Twelve Great Country Hits* (Epic 1965)★★★, *Almost Persuaded* (Epic 1966)★★★, *Golden Hymns* (Epic 1967)★★, *My Elusive Dreams with Tammy Wynette* (Epic 1967)★★★★, *You Mean The World To Me* (Epic 1967)★★★, *Already, It's Heaven* (Epic 1968)★★★, *Kiss Away* (Epic 1968)★★★, *David* (Epic 1969)★★★, *Baby Baby* (Epic 1970)★★★, *The Wonders Of The Wine* (Epic 1970)★★★, *A Woman Always Knows* (Epic 1971)★★★, *Gentle On My Mind* (Harmony 1972)★★★, *The Day Love Walked In* (Epic 1972)★★★, with Barbara Mandrell *A Perfect Match* (Epic 1972)★★★, *Good Things* (Epic 1973)★★★, *Old Time Religion* (Harmony 1973)★★★, *What A Night* (Epic 1976)★★★, *A Man Needs Love* (Epic 1975)★★★, *David Houston* (Starday 1977)★★, *From The Heart Of Houston* (Derrick 1979)★★, *Next Sunday I'm Gonna Be Saved* (Excelsior 1980)★★, *From Houston To You* (Excelsior 1981)★★, *David Houston Sings Texas Honky Tonk* (Delta 1982)★★, *Mountain Of Love* (51 West 1982)★★, with Mandrell *Back To Back* (51 West 1983)★★★, *Houston Country* (51 West 1984)★★.

● COMPILATIONS: *Greatest Hits* (Epic 1969)★★★★, *Greatest Hits, Vol. 2* (Epic 1972)★★★, *The Best Of David Houston* (Gusto 1978)★★★, *The Best Of David Houston* (First Base 1985)★★★, *American Originals* (Epic 1989)★★★★, *Almost Persuaded - 20 Greatest Hits* (Country Stars Collection 1994)★★★.

● FILMS: *Carnival Rock* (1957), *Cotton-Pickin' Chicken Pluckers* (1967).

Houston, Edward 'Bee'

b. 19 April 1938, San Antonio, Texas, USA, d. 19 March 1991, Los Angeles, California, USA. Houston ran a band in San Antonio and did back-up work for visiting artists such as **Brook Benton**, **Little Willie John**, **Junior Parker** and **Bobby Bland**. In 1961 he moved to the west coast, and played with **McKinley Mitchell**, **Little Johnny Taylor** and (his most enduring association) **Big Mama Thornton**. His playing was influenced by **Clarence 'Gatemouth' Brown** and **B.B. King**, but his album was both lacking in individuality and was too soul-influenced for the white blues audience at whom it was aimed. As a result he failed to become a name artist. Little was heard of Houston thereafter until it was reported that he had died from alcoholism in 1991.

● ALBUMS: *Bee Houston* (1970)★★.

Houston, Joe

b. 1927, Austin, Texas, USA. Joe Houston was inspired to take up the saxophone after seeing Count Hastings playing with **Tiny Bradshaw**'s Orchestra, and lists **Joe Thomas**, **Charlie Parker** and **Arnett Cobb** among his other influences. By 1949 he became associated with **Big Joe Turner**, and made his recording debut on Turner's sole release on the Rouge label and probably played on Turner's first Freedom session. Houston's own recording career began in 1949 with Freedom Records, although his biggest successes were with 'Worry-Worry-Worry' (recorded by **Bob Shad** for his Sittin In With label, but actually issued on **Mercury** in 1951), 'Cornbread And Cabbage Greens' and 'Blow, Joe, Blow' (both for Macy's Records, also in 1951), and with 'All Night Long' (recorded for both the Money and Caddy labels, after Houston relocated to Los Angeles in 1955). Other recordings were issued on a gamut of labels: Modern/RPM/Crown, Imperial/Bay'ou, Combo, Lucky, Recorded In Hollywood, Cas, Dooto and other independent Los Angeles labels. In recent years, Houston has made a comeback with numerous personal appearances.

● ALBUMS: *Kicking Back* (1983)★★★, *Rockin' At The Drive In* (Ace 1984)★★★, *Earthquake* (Pathe Marconi 1985)★★★, *Rockin' 'N' Boppin'* (Saxophonograph 1989)★★★, *Cornbread And Cabbage Greens* (Ace 1992)★★★, with Otis Grand *The Return Of Honk* (JSP 1994)★★★.

Houston, Thelma

Thelma Houston left her home-town of Leland, Mississippi, USA, in the late 60s to tour with the gospel group the Art Reynolds Singers. Her impassioned vocal style and innate mastery of phrasing brought her to the attention of the prodigal writer/arranger **Jimmy Webb** in 1969. He composed and produced *Sunshower*, a remarkable song cycle that also included an adaptation of the **Rolling Stones**' 'Jumpin' Jack Flash'. The album transcended musical barriers, mixing the fluency of jazz with the passion of soul, and offering Houston the chance to bite into a sophisticated, witty set of lyrics. *Sunshower* won great critical acclaim, and helped her to secure a contract with **Motown Records**. Initially, the company made inadequate use of her talents, failing to provide material that would stretch her vocal capacities to the full. The stasis was broken in 1976 when Houston reworked 'Don't Leave Me This Way', previously a hit for **Harold Melvin And The Bluenotes**. Her disco interpretation brought a refreshing touch of class to the genre, and achieved impressive sales on both sides of the Atlantic. Ever enthusiastic to repeat a winning formula, Motown made several attempts to reproduce the verve of the hit single. Houston issued a series of interesting, if slightly predictable, albums in the late 70s, and also collaborated on two efforts with **Jerry Butler**, in an attempt to echo Motown's great duets of the 60s. The results were consistent sellers among the black audience, without ever threatening to rival Houston's earlier pop success. A switch to **RCA** failed to alter her fortunes. Houston enjoyed wider exposure in the late 70s with film roles in *Death Scream, Norman ... Is That You?* and *The Seventh Dwarf*, and for a while it seemed as if acting would become her main source of employment. She retired from recording during the mid-80s, re-emerging in 1987 on MCA with a critically acclaimed but commercially disappointing album. An album for **Reprise** in 1990 suffered the same fate. Houston's inconsistent chart record over the last two decades belies the impressive calibre of her vocal talents.

● ALBUMS: *Sunshower* (Stateside 1969)★★, *Thelma Houston* (Mowest 1973)★★, *Anyway You Like It* (Tamla 1976)★★, with Jerry Butler *Thelma And Jerry* (Motown 1977)★★, *The Devil In Me* (Tamla 1977)★★, with Butler *Two To One* (Motown 1978)★★, *Ready To Roll* (Tamla 1978)★★, *Ride To The Rainbow* (Tamla 1979)★★, *Breakwater Cat* (RCA 1980)★★, *Never Gonna Be Another One* (RCA 1981)★★, *I've Got The Music In Me* (RCA 1981)★★, *Qualifying Heats* (MCA 1987)★★★, *Throw You Down* (Reprise 1990)★★★.

● COMPILATIONS: *Best Of Thelma Houston* (Motown 1991)★★★.

Houston, Whitney

b. 9 August 1963, Newark, New Jersey, USA. This pop and soul singer followed the traditions of her mother **Cissy** and cousin **Dionne Warwick** by beginning her vocal career in gospel. There was much diversity in her early performances, however. These included engagements as backing singer with established acts, such as **Chaka Khan**, as well as lead vocals on the Michael Zager Band's single 'Life's A Party'. She also appeared as a model in various magazines and as an actress in television shows such as *Give Me A Break*. By 1983 she

had entered a worldwide contract with **Arista Records**, and the following year had her first commercial success when 'Hold Me', a duet with **Teddy Pendergrass**, crept into the US Top 50. However, the rest of that year was taken up with the recording of a debut album. Clive Davis, the head of Arista, who had taken a strong personal interest in the vocalist, insisted on selecting the best songwriters and producers in search of the definitive debut album. *Whitney Houston* was finally released in March 1984, from which time it would begin its slow stalking of the album charts, topping them early the next year. Its steady climb was encouraged by the success of the singles 'You Give Good Love' and 'Saving All My Love For You', which hit numbers 3 and 1, respectively. The latter single also saw her on top of the charts in the UK and much of the rest of the world. The disco-influenced 'How Will I Know' and the more soul-flavoured 'Greatest Love Of All', both topped the US charts in rapid succession. Her domination was acknowledged by a series of prestigious awards, notably a Grammy for 'Saving All My Love For You' and an Emmy for Outstanding Individual Performance In A Variety Program On US TV. 'I Want To Dance With Somebody (Who Loves Me)', released in 1987, topped the charts on both sides of the Atlantic once more, paving the way for *Whitney* to become the first album by a female artist to debut at number 1 on the US album charts, a feat it also achieved in the UK. The album included a version of 'I Know Him So Well', sang as a duet with her mother Cissy, and the ballad 'Didn't We Almost Have It All' which became her fifth successive US number 1 shortly afterwards. However, even this was surpassed when 'So Emotional' and 'Where Do Broken Hearts Go' continued the sequence, breaking a record previously shared by the **Beatles** and the **Bee Gees**. In 1988 she made a controversial appearance at Nelson Mandela's 70th Birthday Party, where other acts accused her of behaving like a prima donna. By September 'Love Will Save The Day' had finally broken the winning sequence in the USA where it could only manage number 9. Another series of awards followed, including Pop Female Vocal and Soul/R&B Female Vocal categories in the American Music Awards, while rumours abounded of film offers alongside Robert De Niro and Eddie Murphy. Her recording of the title track to the 1988 Olympics tribute, *One Moment In Time*, restored her to prominence, while 'I'm Your Baby Tonight' put her back on top of the singles chart. Despite the relatively modest success of the album of the same name (number 3 in the US charts), 'All The Man That I Need' compensated by becoming her ninth number 1. She became permanently enshrined in the hearts of the American public, however, when she took the microphone to perform 'The Star Spangled Banner' at Super Bowl XXV in Miami. The public response ensured that the version emerged as a single shortly afterwards. She also performed the song at Houston as she welcomed back US troops returning from the Gulf War. Such open displays of patriotism have not endeared her to all, but her remarkably rich voice looks set to continue as a fixture of the charts in the 90s, although critics claim that her masterful vocal technique is not equalled by her emotional commitment to her music. In 1992, Houston married singer **Bobby Brown** (the relationship would prove tempestous). The same year she made a credible acting debut in the film *The Bodyguard*. Two songs recorded by her were lifted from the phenomenally successful soundtrack album - cover versions of **Dolly Parton**'s powerful 'I Will Always Love You', which topped the US chart for 12 weeks and the UK charts for nine, and Chaka Khan's 'I'm Every Woman'.

● ALBUMS: *Whitney Houston* (Arista 1985)★★★, *Whitney* (Arista 1987)★★★★, *I'm Your Baby Tonight* (Arista 1990)★★★, various artists *The Bodyguard* film soundtrack (Arista 1992)★★★, *The Preacher's Wife* film soundtrack (Arista 1996)★★.

Hovington, Frank

b. 9 January 1919, Reading, Pennsylvania, USA, d. 21 June 1982, Felton, Delaware, USA. Raised in Frederica, Delaware, Hovington was playing banjo and guitar by 1934, learning from Adam Greenfield and William Walker. From 1939-71, he played intermittently with Gene Young. Hovington's music and repertoire were influenced by the omnipresent **Blind Boy Fuller**, but he played with a firm thumb beat, and sometimes took considerable rhythmic liberties. Moving to Washington DC in 1948, Hovington occasionally went to Philadelphia, where he worked with **Doug Quattlebaum** and **Washboard Slim** (Robert Young); in Philadelphia. He also played with **Blind Connie Williams**, and this, together with his occasional work in jazz and gospel groups, probably accounts for the relative sophistication of his harmonies.

● ALBUMS: *Lonesome Road Blues* (1975)★★★, *Lonesome Home Blues* (1982)★★★.

How Dare You - 10CC

They gave it the ludicrous moniker, '70s art rock'. Over twenty years later it simply sounds like a very good pop album, which is what it was in the first place. Gouldman was already a polished veteran on catchy 60s pop songs and Eric Stewart was an early Mindbender. They gelled perfectly with Godley and Creme and produced some excellent hit singles. This is their best album, which features two of their huge hits, 'Art For Art's Sake' and 'I'm Mandy Fly Me' (nothing to do with the withdrawn drug Mandrax, of course). 10CC had lots of middle-eights, hooks, melodies and twiddly bits, and they still sound very, very good.

● Tracks: *How Dare You; Lazy Ways; I Wanna Rule The World; I'm Mandy Fly Me; Iceberg; Art For Art's Sake; Rock 'N' Roll Lullaby; Head Room; Don't Hang Up; Get It While You Can.*

● First released 1976
● UK peak chart position: 5
● USA peak chart position: 47

How To Stuff A Wild Bikini

Another in a string of 'beach' movies undertaken by the American International Pictures group in the wake of *Beach Party*, *How To Stuff A Wild Bikini* (1965) showed the genre was flagging badly. **Annette Funicello** took the lead role. The former Disney Mouseketeer starred as Dee Dee, whose boyfriend, played by Dwayne Hickman, is called up on naval reserve duty. Fearful of the attentions of predatory males, the Hickman character employs a witch-doctor to watch over her. Silent veteran Buster Keaton took the latter role in a film which also featured **Mickey Rooney**, and Harvey Lembeck, who portrayed the 'bad guy', Erich Von Zipper. **Beach Boys**' leader **Brian Wilson** enjoyed a non-singing cameo role, while guest act the **Kingsmen**, popularizers of 'Louie Louie', contributed the title song and 'Give Her Lovin''. The film was retitled *How To Fill A Wild Bikini* in the UK, but such machinations were unnecessary as this sorry featured failed to gain a British release.

How To Succeed In Business Without Really Trying

If *Guys And Dolls* is considered to be composer and lyricist **Frank Loesser**'s masterpiece, then this show must be right up there in second place. After its world première at the Shubert Theatre in Philadelphia on 4 September 1961, it opened on Broadway at the 46th Street Theatre just over a month later on 14 October. The libretto, by Abe Burrows, Jack Weinstock, and Willie Gilbert, based on a book of the same title by Shepheard Mead, was 'a witty satire on the methods and mores of Big Business in general, and in particular, on the wiles and ways of Big Business in new glass-enclosed office buildings on Park Avenue'. The story concerns a young man, J. Pierpont Finch (Robert Morse), who climbs from his position as a window-washer to the position of Chairman of the Board of the World Wide Wickets Company, Inc. His rapid rise is not due to diligence or hard work. He simply follows the rules in a book called *How To Succeed In Business Without Even Trying*, which he pauses to consult whenever he is faced with an obstacle to his success ('How To'). With its aid, he is able to defeat his main rival, Bud Frump (Charles Nelson Reilly), the boss's oily nephew, and avoid the usual traps such as the office wolf, the office party, the dangerous secretary, and the big boss himself, J.B. Biggley (**Rudy Vallee**). Finch's girlfriend and main supporter is the attractive secretary Rosemary Pilkington (Bonnie Harris), who makes it clear that she would be 'Happy To Keep His Dinner Warm', while he goes onward and upward. When stuck for a time in the mailroom ('Coffee Break'), he emphasises that he considers the best route to advancement is 'The Company Way', while always bearing in mind, of course, that 'A Secretary Is Not A Toy' - even if she is Biggley's mistress. Additionally, although he agrees with Rosemary and her best friend Smitty (Claudette Sutherland), that it has 'Been A Long Day', it does not prevent him from being slumped over his desk, looking as though he has been working all night, when Biggley calls into the office on a Sunday morning en route to his round of golf. With cries of 'Groundhog!', they unite in Biggley's hymn to his alma mata, 'Grand Old Ivy' (Rip the Chipmunks off the field!'). From then on, Finch's onward and upward progress is positively phenomenal, and his self-assurance is undisguised as he sings 'I Believe In You' to his reflection in the executive washroom mirror. There are still some awkward moments to survive, including a treasure hunt during which the company's offices are wrecked, but Finch surmounts them all to become the Chairman, to marry Rosemary, and to watch his ex-rival Frump washing the office windows while reading a book entitled *How To Succeed In Business Without Even Trying*. 'I Believe In You', sung as a love song and not a soliloquy, achieved some popularity outside the show, particularly in a recording by **Peggy Lee**. The rest of the outstanding score included 'Paris Original', 'Rosemary', 'Cinderella, Darling', 'Love From A Heart Of Gold', and 'Brotherhood Of Man'. Rudy Vallee, the enormously popular singing idol of the 30s, and Robert Morse, who had previously appeared on Broadway in *Say, Darling* and *Take Me Along*, were perfectly cast, and the show reunited Frank Loesser, Abe Burrows, and producers Cy Feuer and Ernest Martin, 11 years after their collective triumph with *Guys And Dolls*. It was to be Loesser's final Broadway score, and he could not have gone out on a higher note. The show ran in New York for 1,417 performances, and was showered with awards: the prestigious Pulitzer Prize for Drama (1962), the New York Drama Critics Award for best musical, and **Tony Awards** for best musical, actor (Morse), lyrics, librettists, and director (Burrows). The 1963 London production, starring Warren Berlinger and Billy De Wolfe, ran at the Shaftesbury Theatre for well over a year, and Rudy Vallee and Robert Morse reprised their original performances in the 1967 film version. In 1995, a 'wonderful' Broadway revival starred the popular film and stage actor Matthew Broderick, who won a Tony Award for best actor in a musical.

How Will The Wolf Survive - Los Lobos

The critical breakthrough album for a refreshing sound that created Tex-Mex rock 'n' roll. The band were already a highly efficient live band by the time of this release and their confidence flows as they tackle different styles, from straight rock 'n' roll on 'I Got Loaded' to traditional Mexican folk with 'Serenata Nortena'. 'Evangeline' and 'Don't Worry Baby' are also strong album tracks, with the latter featuring a piercingly good guitar solo over a furious drum beat. The title track is the peak - the best vocal performance that Steve Winwood never sang; the resemblance to Winwood on this track is uncanny.

● Tracks: *Don't Worry Baby; A Matter Of Time; Corrido No 1; Our Last Night; The Breakdown; I Got Loaded; Serenata Nortena; Evangeline; I Got To Let You Know; Lil King Of Everything; Will The Wolf Survive.*
● First released 1984
● UK peak chart position: 77
● USA peak chart position: 47

Howard And Blaikley

This highly successful UK songwriting and occasional management team was formed in 1964. Their first discoveries were the **Honeycombs**, then recording for producer **Joe Meek**. At the time, the songwriting duo was employed by the BBC so wrote songs under the transparent psedonym, Howard Blaikley. Soon, the Honeycombs reached number 1 in the UK with the duo's 'Have I The Right?' and 'Howard Blaikley' was exposed as two people: Ken Howard and Alan Blaikley. After leaving the BBC, the duo discovered another pop act for whom they would write a series of hits. **Dave Dee, Dozy, Beaky, Mick And Tich** perfectly exemplified the style of commerical pop in which Howard And Blaikley specialized. The duo extended their management roster to embrace such acts as the Wolves, Alan Dean And His Problems, **Gary Wright** and the **Herd**. After writing three major hits for the latter, including the classically-influenced 'From The Underworld' and 'Paradise Lost', the group left them for rival entrepreneur **Andrew Oldham**. Other clients included **Flaming Youth** (with **Phil Collins**), Dando Shaft, **Iain Matthews** and **Matthews' Southern Comfort**. Following their forays into the charts, they later enjoyed success writing musicals for London's West End stage.

Howard, Adina

b. Grand Rapids, Michigan, USA. With her 1995 debut, *Do You Wanna Ride?*, assertive soul singer Adina Howard managed to achieve commercial success as well as raising eyebrows with her volatile cocktail of sexually potent imagery and effusive R&B. The mainstream success of the attendant single, 'Freak Like Me', helped pave the way for other upfront female R&B singers, including **Foxy Brown** and **Lil' Kim**. Peaking at number 7 in the *Billboard* R&B charts, the debut album's sales profile of over half a million copies was encouraging. The follow-up, 1997's *Welcome To Fantasy Island*, opted for sensuality over sexuality: '(the lyrics) are not vulgar. I may say some things straight out, but for the most part, it's a pretty mature album.' Howard was also more closely involved in the creative process, writing four of the songs and co-producing two others. However, the promotional single, '(Freak) And U Know It', at least maintained some of the titular traditions of the previous album.

● ALBUMS: *Do You Wanna Ride?* (Mecca Don/Elektra 1995)★★★, *Welcome To Fantasy Island* (Mecca Don/Elektra 1997)★★★.

Howard, Bob

b. Howard Joyner, 20 June 1906, Newton, Massachusetts, USA, d. 3 December 1986. Howard had begun playing piano and singing in his home state but, at the end of his teenage years, he decided to move to New York where he quickly embarked on a successful career as a hotel and nightclub act and as a recording artist. He was briefly in Europe but the mid-30s found him consolidating his popularity in New York where he added a regular radio series to his roster of achievements (no mean thing for a black musician in these years). He continued to work throughout the 40s and into the 50s, by which time he was sufficiently popular to move into television. Although he favoured New York, Howard did occasionally travel to other parts of the USA, playing residencies in Los Angeles and Las Vegas. Howard's popularity with the general public came largely as a result of his following in the footsteps of **Fats Waller**, his lack of originality being cloaked in skilled musicianship and easygoing rapport with audiences. From time to time Howard played and sometimes recorded with jazzmen but it is as a jazz-tinged popular singer and player that he made his mark. His singing voice varied according to material and mood, ranging from tenor to baritone, from robustness to coy meanderings. During a period when he led a band that emulated **Cab Calloway**'s, Howard employed good musicians but habitually yelled encouragement at inappropriate moments, his exhortations getting in the way of their solos. This band is best remembered for **Benny Carter**'s arrangements.

● COMPILATIONS: *Bob Howard* (Rarities 1935)★★.

Howard, Camille

b. 29 March 1914, Galveston, Texas, USA. Howard took over the stool from Betty Hall Jones as pianist with Roy Milton's Solid Senders in the early 40s. She recorded with Milton on all his prime recordings for **Specialty Records** and his own Roy Milton/Miltone labels of the 40s and early 50s, and was occasionally featured singing her 'Groovy Blues', 'Mr Fine', 'Thrill Me' and 'Pack Your Sack, Jack', among others. Remaining with Milton, Howard simultaneously pursued her own recording career from 1946 when she recorded for the small Pan American label with **James Clifford**'s band and, more notably, with her own sessions for Specialty, which resulted in her successful instrumental boogies (including her biggest hit 'X-temperaneous Boogie') and small band R&B vocals (like the similarly successful 'Money Blues'). In 1953 Howard was signed to Federal for two west coast sessions and she went to Chicago and **Vee Jay** for her final single in 1956. Camille Howard still lives in Los Angeles, where her voice and keyboard skills are reserved only for spiritual performances. Her reissued material on **Ace Records** covers her most interesting work.

● COMPILATIONS: with Edith Mackey, Priscilla Bowman, Christine Kittrell *Rock 'N' Roll Mamas* (1985)★★★, with Lil Armstrong And Dorothy Donegan *Brown Gal 1946-1950* (Krazy Kat 1987)★★★, *X-Temperaneous Boogie* (1989)★★★, *Rock Me Daddy: Camille Howard Vol 1* (Ace 1993)★★★★, *X-Temporaneous Boogie: Camille Howard Vol 2* (Ace 1996)★★★★.

Howard, Chuck

b. Flat Fork, Kentucky, USA, d. 15 August 1983. In 1963, Howard produced the ridiculous pop hit 'Surfin' Bird', for the **Trashmen**. He wrote the mean-spirited 'Happy Birthday Darlin'' for **Conway Twitty** and in 1980 made the US country chart himself with 'I've Come Back (To Say I Love You One More Time)'.

Howard, Darnell

b. 25 July c.1900, Chicago, Illinois, USA, d. 2 September 1966. Combining studying with semi-professional playing, Howard was musically active in his home town, performing on clarinet, saxophones and violin, before he entered his teens. In 1917 he visited New York to make records as a member of **W.C. Handy**'s orchestra. In the early 20s he occasionally led his own bands and also played with Charlie Elgar, who had previously given him tuition. During the 20s Howard worked with several important bandleaders, including **James P. Johnson**, **Carroll Dickerson**, Erskine Tate and **Joe 'King' Oliver**. Mostly, these bands were based in and around Chicago, although the Johnson band toured Europe, playing in London, and Howard also performed in China and Japan. In the 30s he spent six years with **Earl Hines**, again in Chicago, and then towards the end of the decade and into the early 40s flitted through bands led by **Fletcher Henderson**, **Coleman Hawkins** and **Kid Ory**. Although his experience had broadened to encompass contemporary big band music, Howard's later career gravitated towards small groups that played more traditional forms of jazz. In the 50s he was with **Muggsy Spanier**, **Jimmy Archey**, **Don Ewell** and Hines again, but by the early 60s his health was poor. In 1966 he toured Europe but had a stroke in the middle of the year and died on 2 September. A sound saxophonist and fiddle player, Howard is perhaps best remembered for the clarinet playing of his later years when his warm, big-toned solos enhanced many club dates and record albums.

● ALBUMS: *Music To Listen To Don Ewell By* (1956)★★, with Earl Hines *A Monday Date* (1961)★★★.

Howard, Don

b. Donald Howard Koplow, 11 May 1935, Cleveland, Ohio, USA. Pop vocalist Don Howard was 17 years old when he first heard a particular folk song recited by a girlfriend. After playing it on his guitar he adjusted the lyrics and copyrighted it under the title 'Oh Happy Day'. With his booming voice and the song's slow, chanting rhythm, it was released in the USA in December 1952 and rose to number 4 in the charts without any promotion or plugging, selling over a million copies. Some time afterwards, Nancy Binns Reed (the girlfriend), an amateur songwriter, claimed ownership of the tune. Howard gave her a credit as co-writer and agreed to share the royalties. A cover version by vocal quartet the **Johnston Brothers** also reached number 4 in the UK in mid-1953.

Howard, Eddy

b. 12 September 1914, Woodland, California, USA, d. 23 May 1963, Palm Desert, California, USA. After attending San Jose State College and Stanford University Medical School, Howard sang on radio and worked with bands led by George Olsen, Tom Gerun and **Ben Bernie**, eventually becoming the resident crooner with the **Dick Jurgens** Orchestra in 1934. Howard spent nearly six years with Jurgens, and had hits with 'My Last Goodbye' and 'Careless', both his own compositions. In 1941, after a short spell as a solo act, he formed his own band, basing its style on the popular **Isham Jones** Orchestra. This brought him success with 'To Each His Own', 'My Adobe Haçienda', 'I Wonder, I Wonder', 'An Apple Blossom Wedding' and 'Now Is The Hour', all Top 20 recordings. In 1949 Howard signed to **Mercury Records**, and during the early 50s supplied the label with such major hits as 'Maybe It's Because', 'Be Anything, But Be Mine', 'Auf Wiederseh'n Sweetheart' and 'Sin'. Beset by ill health, Howard decided to go solo again, though he did re-form his band later and made a slight impression on a rapidly changing music scene with his final success, 'The Teenagers Waltz'.

● ALBUMS: *Paradise Isle* (1957)★★★, *Saturday Nite Dance Date* (1958)★★★, *Words Of Love* (1958)★★, *Great For Dancing* (1959)★★★, *Sleepy Serenade* (1960)★★, *Great Old Waltzes* (1962)★★★, *Great Band Hits* (1963)★★★, *The Velvet Voice Of Eddy Howard* (1963)★★★★, *Intimately Yours* (1964)★★★, *Sings The Great Ones* (1965)★★★, *Softly And Sincerely* (1965)★★★.

● COMPILATIONS *Golden Hits* (1961)★★★★, *Eddy Howard And His Orchestra 1949-53* (1986)★★★★, *His Top Hits* (1987)★★, *Eddy Howard 1946-51* (1988)★★★, *To Each His Own 1946-56* (1988)★★★.

Howard, Harlan

b. Harlan Perry Howard, 8 September 1929, Lexington, Harlan County, Kentucky, USA. Howard was raised in Detroit and began songwriting when he was 12. After graduation, he spent four years as a paratrooper and was able to spend weekends in Nashville. His talent was recognized by **Johnny Bond** and **Tex Ritter**, who published his early songs. **Wynn Stewart** recorded 'You Took Her Off My Hands' and Howard had his first US country hit in 1958 with 'Pick Me Up On Your Way Down' for Charlie Walker, which was followed by 'Mommy For A Day' by **Kitty Wells**. Many songs were recorded by **Buck Owens** including 'Above And Beyond', 'Excuse Me (I Think I've Got A Heartache)', 'Under The Influence Of Love', 'I've Got A Tiger By The Tail' (based on a campaign for Esso petrol) and 'Foolin' Around', most of them being co-written with Owens. In 1959 **Guy Mitchell** recorded **Ray Price**'s country hit 'Heartaches By The Number' for the pop market and went to number 1 in the USA and number 5 in the UK. He married country singer **Jan Howard** in 1960 and they moved to Nashville, where she recorded many of his demos. One of **Patsy Cline**'s best-known recordings, 'I Fall To Pieces', was written by Howard and **Hank Cochran**, and he also wrote her US country Top 10 single 'When I Get Through With You (You'll Love Me Too)'. Howard wrote two of **Jim Reeves**' best recordings, 'I Won't Forget You' and 'The Blizzard', as well as 'The Image Of Me', a Reeves demo discovered in the 80s. Other country successes include 'Don't Call Me From A Honky Tonk' (**Johnny And Jonie Mosby**), 'Still In Town' (**Johnny Cash**), 'Three Steps To The Phone' (**George Hamilton IV**), 'You Comb Her Hair' (with **Hank Cochran** for **George Jones**), 'Your Heart Turned Left (And Mine Was On The Right)' (George Jones) and 'Yours Love' (**Willie Nelson**). Other crossover hits were 'Too Many Rivers' (Kitty Wells and then **Brenda Lee**), 'Busted' (Johnny Cash and then **Ray Charles**) and 'The Chokin' Kind' (**Waylon Jennings** and then **Joe Simon**). He wrote numerous songs for folk singer **Burl Ives** when he started recording for the country market, including 'Call Me Mr. In-Between' and 'I'm The Boss'. **Bob Dylan** praised his song 'Ole Podner', Howard's tribute to a sick fishing buddy, producer Happy Wilson, while **Richard Thompson** has called 'Streets Of Baltimore', written by Howard and **Tompall Glaser**, 'a wonderfully succinct story told in three verses with every line a killer.' Howard touched a vein with his sentimental 'No Charge', which has been recorded by **Melba Montgomery** and **Tammy Wynette** and was a UK number 1 for **J.J. Barrie**. Howard has made several albums, and although he had a US country hit with 'Sunday Morning Christian' in 1971, the albums are little more than collections of demos for other artists. In 1975, a long-forgotten Howard song, 'She Called Me Baby', was revived very successfully by **Charlie Rich**. In 1977 the UK division of **RCA Records** released a 16-track compilation album, *The Songs Of Harlan Howard*. He spends his time pitching his songs at Tree Music in Nashville and he often works with younger writers. In 1984 he wrote a US country number 1 for **Conway Twitty**, 'I Don't Know A Thing About Love (The Moon Song)', and subsequent number 1s have included 'Why Not Me?' (with Sonny Throckmorton and Brent Maher for the **Judds**), 'Somebody Should Leave' (with Chick Rains for **Reba McEntire**) and 'Somewhere Tonight' (with **Rodney Crowell** for **Highway 101**). Other 80s compositions include 'You're A Hard Dog To Keep Under The Porch' (with Susanna Clark for **Gail Davies**), 'I Don't Remember You' (with Bobby Braddock for **John Conlee**) and 'Never Mind' for **Nanci Griffith**. Howard cites 'Another Bridge To Burn' (Ray Price, **Little Jimmy Dickens**) as his best song.

● ALBUMS: *Harlan Howard Sings Harlan Howard* (Capitol 1961)★★★★, *All Time Favourite Country Songwriter* (Monument 1965)★★★, *Mr. Songwriter* (RCA Victor 1967)★★★, *Down To Earth* (RCA Victor 1968)★★, *To The Silent Majority, With Love* (Nugget 1971)★★, *Singer And Songwriter* (1981)★★.

Howard, James Newton

b. USA. Although he is regarded as a prolific composer of film music, Howard began his musical career as a musician (keyboards, synthesizer, mellotron) during the 70s, and played on record sessions with rock artists such as **Ringo Starr**, **Neil Diamond**, **Melissa Manchester**, **Harry Nilsson**, **Neil Sedaka**, **Yvonne Elliman** and **Boz Scaggs**. From 1975-80, he was member of **Elton John**'s Band (Mark II), and served as his studio arranger. Howard, and another American, bassist Joe Passarelli, were part of the new John line-up which was introduced to the 75,000 crowd at Wembley Stadium in 1975. He was on Elton John's *Rock Of The Westies, Blue Moves, 21 At 33* and *The Fox* (1980) and, in the same year, played at John's free concert in New York's Central Park to an estimated audience of 400,000. Howard was also a member of the band, China, and John produced one of their albums. In the 80s Howard began composing music for films. His first feature credit, Ken Finkleman's comedy *Head Office*, was followed by *Wildcats* (co-composed with Hawk Wolinski), *Never Too Young To Die, 8 Million Ways To Die, Nobody's Fool, Tough Guys, Campus Man, Five Corners* ('an appropriately moody score'), *Russkies, Promised Land, Off Limits, Some Girls, Everybody's All-American, Tap*, a tribute to tap dancing, starring Gregory Hines and **Sammy Davis Jnr.** in the latter's last feature film; *Major League* and *The Package* (1989). In the 90s, Howard became known as 'hot' in Hollywood, with his scores for movies such as *Pretty Woman, Flatliners, King Ralph, Marked For Death, Guilty By Suspicion, Dying Young, Three Men And A Little Lady, Coupe De Ville, The Man In The Moon, My Girl, American Heart, A Private Matter* (television), *Grand Canyon, Diggstown, Glengarry Glen Ross, Night And The City, Alive, Falling Down, The Fugitive, Dave*, and *The Saint Of Fort Washington* (1993). His status was not diminished when **Barbra Streisand** chose him to replace UK composer **John Barry** on *The Prince Of Tides* (1991).
● ALBUMS: *James Newton Howard & Friends* (1988)★★.

Howard, Jan

b. Lula Grace Johnson, 13 March 1930, Kansas City, Missouri, USA. Howard, with a mixture of Cherokee and Irish blood, was raised in poverty, married at 15 and had three sons in quick succession. Her husband beat her and squandered what little money they had, and she divorced him in 1953. A few weeks later, she 'married' a serviceman, who was supposedly divorced, and when that relationship collapsed, she moved to Los Angeles in the hope of finding work as a singer. She met and married aspiring songwriter **Harlan Howard** within 30 days. She sang on his demonstration records and her version of 'Mommy For A Day' (for **Kitty Wells**) led to her own recording contract. Her first record was a duet with **Wynn Stewart**, 'Yankee Go Home', which was followed by her first US country hit, 'The One You Slip Around With', in 1960. The Howards moved to Nashville and she skilfully combined the roles of housewife and country star. Harlan Howard wrote several of her country hits including 'Evil On Your Mind', 'What Makes A Man Wander', 'Wrong Company' and 'I Don't Mind'. In 1968 she recorded her own personal song, 'My Son', for Jimmy in Vietnam. Before the record could be released, her son died in action. The marriage subsequently broke up and a second son committed suicide. Howard worked herself out of the crisis, touring with **Bill Anderson** and finding success with several duets: 'I Know You're Married', 'For Loving You' (a number 1 US country hit), 'If It's All The Same To You', 'Someday We'll Be Together' and 'Dissatisfied'. She also has long spells on the road with **Johnny Cash** and **Tammy Wynette**, and with the *Grand Ole Opry*. She published her best-selling autobiography in 1987.
● ALBUMS: with Wynn Stewart *Sweethearts Of Country Music* (Challenge 1961)★★★, *Jan Howard* (Dot 1962)★★★, with the Jordanaires *Sweet And Sentimental* (Capitol 1962)★★★★, *Bad Seed* (1966)★★★, *Jan Howard Sings 'Evil On Your Mind'* (1966)★★★, *This Is Jan Howard Country* (1967)★★★, *Lonely Country* (1967)★★★, with Bill Anderson *For Loving You* (Decca 1967)★★★, with Stewart *Wynn Stewart And Jan Howard Sing Their Hits* (Starday 1968)★★★★, *Count Your Blessings, Woman* (1968)★★★, *The Real Me* (1968)★★★, *Jan Howard* (1969)★★, *For God And Country* (1970)★★, *Rock Me Back To Little Rock* (1970)★★, with Anderson *If It's All The Same To You* (Decca 1971)★★★, *Love Is Like A Spinning Wheel* (1972)★★★, with Anderson *Bill And Jan (Or Jan And Bill)* (Decca 1972)★★★, with Anderson *Singing His Praise* (Decca 1972)★★, *Sincerely* (1976)★★, *Tainted Love* (1984)★★★, *The Life Of A Country Girl Singer* (1987)★★.
● FURTHER READING: *Sunshine And Shadow*, Jan Howard.

Howard, Johnny

b. 5 February 1931, Croydon, Surrey, England. Howard learned to play the saxophone at school and, after playing semi-professionally for several years, became a full-time professional musician in 1959. Two years later he followed **Lou Preager** as the resident leader at London's prestigious Lyceum Ballroom and, during the next few years, fronted bands at most of London's major dance venues. During the 60s he led his own band on popular UK radio shows such *Easy Beat* and *Saturday Club* and, through the years, has become a familiar name in BBC Radio's music programmes. He also formed and led the Capital Radio Big Band, and features in concerts, sometimes accompanying visiting star vocalists and musicians from the USA.
● ALBUMS: *The Velvet Touch Of Johnny Howard* (Deram 1967)★★★, *Domee Craze* (1975)★★★, *Johnny Howard Plays Cole Porter* (1980)★★★, *Irving Berlin Hit Parade* (1980)★★★.
● COMPILATIONS: *The World Of Johnny Howard* (Decca 1970)★★★.

Howard, Ken, And Alan Blaikley
(see **Howard And Blaikley**)

Howard, Kid

b. Avery Howard, 22 April 1908, New Orleans, Louisiana, USA, d. 28 March 1966. Howard played drums in bands in and around his home town for several years. He then switched to trumpet and by the late 20s was leading a popular local band. Although he occasionally played outside the city, New Orleans was where he was at ease and he remained there throughout the next two decades. In the 50s he ventured further afield, even visiting Europe with **George Lewis**. By the 60s he was back home, where he continued to play despite illness until shortly before his death, in 1966. Highly regarded by his fellow New Orleans musicians, Howard was reputed to have been a powerful player with a rich sound and fierce attack that revealed the influence of players such as **Chris Kelly** and **Louis Armstrong**. By the time of his appearances with Lewis, however, his lip was in poor shape and he was capable of only a few flashes of the power displayed on his scarce early recordings.
● ALBUMS: *George Lewis In Europe Vols. 1* and *2* (1959)★★★, *George Lewis In Europe Vol. 3/Pied Piper* (1959)★★★★, *Kid Howard And La Vida Jazzband* (Jazzology 1990)★★★★, *Heart And Bowels Of Jazz* (Jazzology 1990)★★★★, *Lavida* (American Music 1993)★★★.

Howard, Miki

The soul singer Miki Howard combines spiritual soul music with touches of jazz singing. Before turning solo, she was a jazz session singer, working with, among others, **Grover Washington Jnr.**, **Philip Bailey** and **Billy Cobham**. *Come Share My Love* attracted comparisons with Regina Belle, while *Love Confessions* introduced a slick R&B sound and included 'That's What Love Is', a duet with **Gerald LeVert**, as well as her familiar jazz stylings, best represented by her version of **Earth, Wind And Fire**'s 'Reasons'. On *Miki Howard*, the singer tackled a variety of styles, including a swing-beat reworking of **Aretha Franklin**'s 'Until You Come Back To Me (That's What I'm Gonna Do)'. Her ballads revealed an emotional depth to match her vocal range and technical abilities. *Femme Fatale* included versions of **Billie Holiday**'s 'Good Morning Heartache', **Dinah Washington**'s 'This Bitter Earth' and **Sly Stone**'s 'Thank You'. She also co-wrote three songs herself, and dueted with Christopher Williams on 'I Hope That We Can Be Together Soon'. Following the album she concentrated on pursuing an acting career, appearing in 1993's *Malcolm X* biopic (as Billie Holiday) and co-starring in John Singleton's *Poetic Justice*.
● ALBUMS: *Come Share My Love* (Atlantic 1986)★★, *Love Confessions* (Atlantic 1987)★★★, *Miki Howard* (Atlantic 1989)★★★, *Femme Fatale* (Giant 1992)★★★.
● FILMS: *Malcom X* (1993).

Howard, Noah

b. 6 April 1943, New Orleans, Louisiana, USA. Howard sang in a choir as a child, taking up trumpet and alto saxophone, his main instrument, only after his two years of national service (1960-62). After discharge from the forces he moved to California where he met Byron Allen, **Sonny Simmons** and Dewey Johnson. He became dissatisfied with his progress while taking trumpet lessons from Johnson and, meeting Allen at Johnson's house, he switched to taking alto saxophone lessons from him. Moving to New York City in 1965 he became involved with the *avant garde* movement, playing with **Donald Ayler**, **Archie Shepp**, **Bill Dixon**, Sunny Murray, and recorded a two albums for ESP. He began to lead his own groups, which included at various times **Dave Burrell, Sirone**, trumpeter Earl Cross and tenor saxophonist Arthur Durrell. At the end of the 60s he went to Europe for a while, recording for BYG, working with Bobby Few, Muhammad Ali (Robert Patterson) and Frank Wright, and, he has explained, being made to feel like a concert artist for the first time.
● ALBUMS: *Judson Hall Concert* (1965)★★★, *The Black Ark* (1969)★★★, *Space Dimension* (1972)★★, *Live In Europe I* (1975),★★ *Berlin Concert* (1975)★★★, *Live At The Village Vanguard* 1972 recording 1975)★★★★, *Schizophrenic Blues* (1977)★★★.

Howard, Paul

b. 10 July 1908, on a farm near Midland, Arkansas, USA, d. 18 June 1984, Little Rock, Arkansas, USA. He left home at the age of 15 and worked as a construction worker, a coal miner and a copper miner. Whilst working in Bisbee, Arizona, he acquired a guitar, taught himself to play and made his first radio appearance on KOY Phoenix in 1931. During the 30s, he eked a living in various ways including entertaining between films in Arkansas cinemas where, although adopting the **Jimmie Rodgers**' style dress of a railroad brakeman, he actually travelled between venues by bicycle. In 1940, he successfully auditioned for **George D. Hay** at the *Grand Ole Opry* and as a result became a regular both on the *Opry* and on WSM radio. He toured with *Opry* shows and in 1941, formed and toured with his own band, the Arkansas Cotton Pickers. It has been claimed that Howard's band was the first outfit playing western swing music to appear regularly on the *Opry* and that he was the first band leader to actually bring an electric guitar on to the *Opry* stage. By 1949, Howard realised that his music was no longer so popular in the Tennessee area but knowing the success of **Bob Wills** in Texas, he moved to Houston, where he played both the dancehall circuit and a daily show on KPRC. Later, at the invitation of his friend, **Zeke Clements**, he relocated to KTBS Shreveport and worked the circuits throughout Louisiana, Arkansas and Texas. He even played Jack Ruby's club in Dallas for a short time but left amicably because of differing tastes in music. In January 1952, Howard was involved in a serious road accident. His injuries prevented him travelling with his band and for a time, he worked as commercial manager at KAPK Minden, while Al Hobson ran the band. This bored him and in 1953, he rejoined the band and during 1954/5, they played the theatre circuit throughout the eastern and southeastern USA. In 1956, he took up promotional work but still worked with his band, using Shreveport as his base, until he disbanded it in 1973. After that date, he still booked and played shows but used 'pick-up' bands. During his career he recorded for **Columbia Records** and King. In 1981, he moved to Little Rock where he worked with the bluegrass gospel band, the Sullivan Family and was still involved with promotional work until his death in 1984. The legendary **Hank Garland** was the lead guitarist with the band on some of the recordings. In 1984, the German based Cattle label released an album containing some of his best 1946-48 recordings.

● ALBUMS: with Ralph Willis *Faded Picture Blues* (King 1970)★★★, *Western Swing At Its Best* (Cattle 1984)★★.

Howard, Randy (fiddle)

b. 1960, Georgia, USA. The fiddle player Randy Howard was encouraged by his father to play an instrument - first, the drums, then the electric guitar and then the fiddle. Howard developed an affinity with the fiddle and joined his father and cousin in a bluegrass band. In 1979, aged 18, Randy Howard became the youngest person to win the World Championship Fiddling Contest in Union Grove, North Carolina, and has won numerous fiddling - and mandolin - contests since. Howard's first sessions were with the southern rock bands **Charlie Daniels**, **Marshall Tucker** and the **Allman Brothers** Band. Howard had a minor US country hit with 'All American Redneck' in 1983 and had to wait until 1988 for another one, which was a revival of 'Ring Of Fire'. In 1990, encouraged by his friend **Mark O'Connor**, he moved to Nashville and has played on sessions with **Blackhawk**, **Vince Gill**, **Kennedy Rose**, **Shelby Lynne** and his namesake, **Randy Howard**. He often tours with **Kathy Chiavola**'s band. Howard says, 'I'd like to be remembered as a musician who was creative, who has never played mechanically and who always gave each song his best shot.'

● ALBUMS: *Survival Of The Fiddlist* (Survival Of The Fiddlist 1993)★★★.

Howard, Randy (singer-songwriter)

b. Randall Lamar Howard, 9 May 1950, Macon, Georgia, USA. After working in local clubs he made his name on the Bobby Lord television series, after which he had his own show. He wrote 'God Don't Live In Nashville, Tennessee' and 'She's A Lover' and had a minor US country hit with his 'All-American Redneck' in 1983. He had to wait until 1988 for another one, which was a revival of 'Ring Of Fire'. *Macon Music* is a mixture of southern rock and country with titles typical of the era - 'The Last Rebel Yell' and 'Heaven, Hell Or Macon'. The album includes some quickfire fiddling from the fiddle player also called **Randy Howard** (and also from Georgia).

● ALBUMS: *Randy Howard* (Atlantic 1988)★★★, *Macon Music* (Sweet Lake 1994)★★★.

Howard, Rosetta

b. *c*.1914, Chicago, Illinois, USA, d. 1974, Chicago, Illinois, USA. Initially a dancer, Rosetta Howard moved into singing by joining in with juke-box selections at the club where she worked, graduating to live work in Chicago with **Jimmie Noone**, **Eddie Smith** and **Sonny Thompson**. Her warm tones can be heard on a distinguished series of light-hearted, jazz-tinged blues recordings made with the **Harlem Hamfats** between 1937 and 1939, and she also recorded with **Henry 'Red' Allen**. In 1947 Howard recorded with **Willie Dixon**'s Big Three Trio, including a fine version of 'Ebony Rhapsody', but from the early 50s she devoted her time to church work at **Thomas A. Dorsey**'s Pilgrim Baptist Church.

● ALBUMS: *Rosetta Howard* (1989)★★★, *Harlem Hamfats (With Rosetta Howard)* (Earl Archives 1990)★★★.

Howe II

After recording a solo instrumental album in 1988, guitarist Greg Howe decided to expand his musical horizons and incorporate his talents within a band framework. Brother Al stepped in as vocalist, with Vern Parsons and Joe Nevolo taking on bass and drum duties, respectively. Released in 1989, their debut album was a highly accomplished work that combined elements of **Van Halen** and **Rising Force**; Al Howe's vocals were reminiscent of vintage **Dave Lee Roth**, while Greg's guitar style was not far removed from that of the Swedish guitarist **Yngwie Malmsteen**. Their second album built on these solid foundations, but featured more melodic compositions.

● ALBUMS: *High Gear* (Roadrunner 1989)★★★, *Now Hear This* (Roadrunner 1991)★★★★.

Howe, Steve

b. 8 April 1947, London, England. Best known as the guitarist with **Yes**, Howe began his career with the Syndicats in 1963. Playing R&B and **Chuck Berry** numbers, the group released three singles without much success before splitting in 1965. Howe then joined soul band the Incrowd. The group added John 'Twink' Adler (drums) and changed its name to **Tomorrow** in 1967, embracing psychedelia and flower-power. They became popular at London 'Underground' venues UFO and the Roundhouse alongside **Pink Floyd** and the **Soft Machine**. Their 'My White Bicycle' was a classic of the genre and was later a hit for heavy rockers **Nazareth**. After singer **Keith West**'s solo success with 'Excerpt From A Teanage Opera' on which Howe played, the group fell apart. Howe then teamed up with Bobby Woodman (drums) and Dave Curtiss (bass/vocals) in Bodast. Augmented by Clive Maldoon (guitar/vocals) and Bruce Thomas (bass), the group gigged sporadically but never lived up to its early promise. Their album, recorded in 1969, remained unissued until 1981. After Bodast's demise, Howe joined **P.P. Arnold**'s backing group but was seeking a greater musical challenge and an opportunity presented itself when Peter Banks left Yes in March 1970. Howe's adventurous playing, drawing on his love of jazz, ragtime and rock 'n' roll, was perfectly suited to the elaborately arranged, quasi-symphonic epics the group were striving to create. He first appeared on *The Yes Album* which was the first in a series of increasingly successful albums. During his 10-year stint with Yes, Howe recorded his first two solo albums and also played sessions for **Lou Reed**, **Rick Wakeman**, Alan White and **Frankie Goes To Hollywood**.

When Yes folded in 1980, Howard helped form **Asia** with **John Wetton** (bass/vocals), Geoff Downes (keyboards) and Carl Palmer (drums). This critically unfashionable supergroup proved remarkably successful, particularly in the USA, where their debut *Asia* was number 1 for nine weeks. Howe's next project was the short-lived group **GTR** with ex-Genesis guitarist **Steve Hackett**, after which he rejoined former Yes colleagues as Anderson, Bruford, Wakeman, Howe, rivalling the reformed Yes led by Chris Squire. After lengthy court battles, the two groups settled their differences and suprisingly merged into one megagroup, releasing *Union* and embarking on a mammoth tour in 1991. Howe has also recorded a third solo album, as well as contributing to Miles Copeland's Guitar Speak and Night Of The Guitar projects, and albums by ex-**Ultravox** violinist Billy Currie.

● ALBUMS: *Beginnings* (Atlantic 1975)★★★, *The Steve Howe Album* (Atlantic 1979)★★★, *The Bodast Tapes* (1981)★★, *Turbulance* (1991)★★★, *The Grand Scheme Of Things* (1993)★★★.
● COMPILATIONS with Bodast *The Early Years* (1993)★★★, *Mothballs* (RPM 1995)★★.

Howell, Peg Leg

b. Joshua Barnes Howel, 5 March 1888, Eatonton, Georgia, USA, d. 11 August 1966, Atlanta, Georgia, USA. Howell's music is a complex mixture of blues, street vendors' cries, gamblers' argot, fragments of narrative ballads and, in the company of his 'Gang' (usually guitarist Henry Williams and fiddler **Eddie Anthony**), white fiddle pieces, ragtime, and other dance music. As a soloist, he sang introspective pieces, with a plaintive delivery, accompanied by short melodic fragments on guitar. His work with his group was very different, the lyrics delivered in a low growl as part of perhaps the liveliest, and rowdiest, party music on record. Also a bootlegger (for which he served time in jail), Howell abandoned music in 1934 when Anthony died, and was very ill when found in 1963. An album was released that year, primarily to generate royalties.

● ALBUMS: *The Legendary Peg Leg Howell* (1963)★★, *Peg Leg Howell Volume 1, 1926-1927* (Matchbox 1983)★★★, *Peg Leg Howell Volume 2, 1928-1929* (Matchbox 1983)★★★, *Complete Recorded Works Vols. 1 & 2* (Matchbox 1994)★★★.

Howes, Bobby

b. Robert William Howes, 4 August 1895, Battersea, London, England, d. 27 April 1972. An actor, singer and dancer with a charming, disarming style, Howes was apprenticed to be an electrical engineer before realising his ambition to go on to the stage. While in his teens he performed at music halls and with concert parties, before spending three years in the Army during World War I. After the war he had difficulty getting work, but he made his West End debut in 1923 in *The Little Revue Starts At 9*, and from then on, for the next 25 years, his inimitable comic style allied to an appealing way of putting over a song and dance, ensured that he stayed at the top in the British musical theatre. Among the shows and revues he appeared in were *The Second Little Revue* (1924), *The Punch Bowl, The Blue Kitten, Vaudeville Vanities, The Blue Train, The Yellow Mask, Mr. Cinders* - the first of three in which he starred with **Binnie Hale** ('I'm A One-Man Girl' and 'Ev'ry Little Moment'), *Sons O' Guns, Song Of The Drum, For The Love Of Mike* ('Who Do You Love?' and 'Got A Date With An Angel'), *Tell Her The Truth, He Wanted Adventure, Yes, Madame?, Please, Teacher, Big Business, Hide And Seek* ('She's My Lovely'), *Bobby Get Your Gun, All Clear, Shephard's Pie, Lady Behave, Let's Face It!, Here Come The Boys, Four, Five, Six!, Roundabout,* and *Finian's Rainbow* (New York replacement 1960). In 1953 he starred with his daughter, Sally Ann Howes (b. 20 July 1930, London, England) in ***Paint Your Wagon***. She had made her first appearance on the London musical stage two years earlier in *Fancy Free*, and subsequently developed into an elegant and charming leading lady. Her principal appearances in musicals have included *Bet Your Life* (1952), *Romance In Candlelight, Summer Song,* ***My Fair Lady*** (1958 Broadway replacement), *Kwamina,* ***Brigadoon*** and ***Wonderful Town*** (both New York City Centre revivals), ***What Makes Sammy Run?*** (introducing 'A Room Without Windows'), ***The King And I*** (1973 London replacement), ***The Sound Of Music*** (US regional production 1973/4), and ***Robert And Elizabeth*** (1976 UK regional revival). She has toured consistently in shows throughout the world, both musicals and straight theatre, and has appeared extensively on television, especially in America. She was married for a time to the US composer **Richard Adler**. Like her father, Sally Ann Howes has made a number of films, including the musical, ***Chitty Chitty Bang Bang***. In the early 90s, her cabaret act was receiving enthusiastic reviews in London and New York.

● ALBUMS: with Binnie Hale, Sally Ann Howes *She's My Lovely* (World Records 60s)★★.

Howlin' Wilf

b. James Hunter, c.1962. As a youngster in Essex, England, Wilf was interested in 50s rock 'n' roll, leading to a later appreciation of Chicago blues, particularly the music of **Little Walter**, and he received his first electric guitar in 1977, when he was around 15 years of age. His first band, the DMFs, played at Colchester Labour Club in 1983. He initially recorded with a rockabilly band for a compilation issued by Lost Moment Records in 1984.

Two years later he moved to London, where he was touted as one of England's best young blues singers, and with his band the Vee-Jays he quickly established himself as one of the mainstays of the capital's blues scene. In 1989 he disbanded the Vee-Jays and took his music in more of an R&B direction. His scattered recordings bear witness to the fact that he is regarded primarily as a live entertainer.

Howlin' Wolf

b. Chester Arthur Burnett, 10 June 1910, West Point, Mississippi, USA, d. 10 January 1976, Hines, Illinois, USA. Howlin' Wolf was one of the most important of the southern expatriates who created the post-war blues out of their rural past and moulded it into the tough 'Chicago sound' of the 50s. He was one of six children born to farmer Dock Burnett and his wife Gertrude, and spent his earliest years around Aberdeen, Mississippi, where he sang in the local baptist church. In 1923 he relocated to Ruleville, Mississippi, and 10 years later moved again to work on Nat Phillips' plantation at Twist, Arkansas. By this time he was working in music, appearing at local parties and juke-joints. He had been inspired by performers such as **Charley Patton** and **Tommy Johnson**, both of whom he had met, and he took much of the showmanship of his act from them, although his hoarse, powerful voice and eerie 'howling' were peculiarly his own. Other seminal Mississippi figures, **Robert Johnson** and **Son House**, also proved influential. During this period he enjoyed many nicknames such as 'Big Foot' and 'Bull Cow' but it was as Howlin' Wolf that his fame grew. He was a huge man with a commanding presence and threatening aspect, whom contemporary **Johnny Shines** once likened to a wild animal, saying that he (Shines) was scared to lay his hand on him.

Throughout the 30s Wolf combined farming with working in music, sometimes travelling in the company of people such as Shines, **Robert Johnson**, and **Sonny Boy 'Rice Miller' Williamson**. Williamson, who courted and married Wolf's half-sister Mary, taught his new brother-in-law to play some harmonica and Wolf also experimented with the guitar. Wolf's first marriage had been to a sister of singer **Willie Brown** and it was during this time that he married his second wife, Lillie Handley. It was a union that lasted until his death. During 1941-44 Wolf was drafted into the army but once he had left, he formed his own group and gained sufficient fame to be approached by KWEM, a west Memphis radio station that was competing for local black listeners and recognized Wolf's potential. For KWEM, Wolf worked as a disc jockey as well as performing himself, and this brought him to the attention of **Sam Phillips**, who was recording material in Memphis and leasing it to others for sale in the black communities of the northern and western areas of the USA. Phillips, who considered Wolf to be one of the greatest talents he knew, originally made separate agreements with the Bihari Brothers in California and

the Chess Brothers of Chicago to issue Wolf's recordings. The success of the early recordings led to something of a war between these two camps, with each trying to attract him under their own aegis. On the evidence of some of the songs that he recorded at the time, it seems that Wolf was tempted to take a 'stroll out west', but in the event he went to Chicago, 'the onliest one who drove out of the south like a gentleman'.

In Memphis, Wolf, whose recording sessions were often under the direction of Ike Turner, had been lucky to employ the talents of guitarist Willie Johnson, who refused to move north, and in Chicago that good fortune continued as he worked first with **Jody Williams** and then the unique **Hubert Sumlin**. The raw delta sound of Wolf's earlier records assured him of a ready-made audience once he reached Chicago, and he quickly built a powerful reputation on the club circuit, extending it with such classic records as 'Smokestack Lightning' and 'Killing Floor'. Like his great rival **Muddy Waters**, he maintained his audience, and a **Chess** recording contract, through the lean times of rock 'n' roll and into the blues boom of the 60s. He came to Europe with the AFBF in 1964 and continued to return over the next ten years. The **Rolling Stones** and the **Yardbirds** did much to publicize Wolf's (and Waters') music, both in Europe and white America, and as the 60s progressed, the newer artists at Chess saw their target audience as the emerging white 'love and peace' culture and tried to influence their material to suit it. Wolf's music was a significant influence on rock and many of his best-known songs - 'Sitting On Top Of The World', 'I Ain't Superstitious', 'Killin' Floor', 'Back Door Man' and 'Little Red Rooster' - were recorded by acts as diverse as the **Doors**, **Cream**, the Rolling Stones, the Yardbirds and **Manfred Mann**. Few, however, rivalled the power or sexual bravura displayed on the originals and only Don Van Vliet (**Captain Beefheart**) came close to recapturing his aggressive, raucous voice. A compelling appearance on the teen-oriented *Shindig* television show (at the behest of the Rolling Stones) was a rare concession to commerciality. His label's desire for success, akin to the white acts he influenced, resulted in the lamentable *The Howlin' Wolf Album*, which the artist described as 'dog shit'. This ill-conceived attempt to update earlier songs was outshone by *The London Howlin' Wolf Sessions*, on which Wolf and long-serving guitarist Hubert Sumlin were joined by an array of guests, including **Eric Clapton**, **Steve Winwood**, and Rolling Stones members **Bill Wyman** and Charlie Watts. Wolf, along with others like Muddy Waters, resisted this move but were powerless to control it. They were, of course, men in their 50s, set in their ways but needing to maintain an audience outside the dwindling Chicago clubs. Fortunately, Wolf outlived this trend, along with that for piling well-known artists together into 'super bands'. Wolf continued to tour but his health was declining. After a protracted period of illness Howlin' Wolf died of cancer in the Veterans Administration Hospital in 1976. His influence has survived the excesses of the 'swinging 60s' and is to be seen today in the work of many of the emerging black bluesmen such as **Roosevelt 'Booba' Barnes**.

● ALBUMS: *Moaning In The Moonlight* (Chess 1959)★★★★, *Howlin' Wolf* aka *The Rocking Chair Album* (Chess 1962)★★★★, *Howlin' Wolf Sings The Blues* (Crown 1962)★★★, *The Real Folk Blues* (Chess 1966)★★★★, *Big City Blues* (Custom 1966)★★★, *Original Folk Blues* (Kent 1967)★★★, *More Real Folk Blues* (Chess 1967)★★★★, *This Is Howlin' Wolf's New Album* aka *The Dog Shit Album* (Cadet 1969)★★, *Evil* (Chess 1969)★★★, *Message To The Young* (Chess 1971)★★, *The London Sessions* (Chess 1971)★★★, *Live And Cookin' At Alice's Revisited* (Chess 1972)★★, *Howlin' Wolf AKA Chester Burnett* (Chess 1972)★★★, *The Back Door Wolf* (Chess 1973)★★★★, *Change My Way* (Chess 1975)★★★, *Ridin' In The Moonlight* (Ace 1982)★★★, *Live In Europe 1964* (Sundown 1988)★★★, *Memphis Days Volume 1* (Bear Family 1989)★★★, *Memphis Days Volume 2* (Bear Family 1990)★★★, *Howlin' Wolf Rides Again* (Ace 1991)★★★.

● COMPILATIONS: *Going Back Home* (1970)★★★, *Chess Blues Masters* (Chess 1976)★★★★, *The Legendary Sun Performers* (Charly 1977)★★★, *Chess Masters* (Chess 1981)★★★★, *Chess Masters 2* (Chess 1982)★★★★, *Chess Masters 3* (Chess 1983)★★★, *The Wolf* (Blue Moon 1984)★★★, *Golden Classics* (Astan 1984)★★★, *The Howlin' Wolf Collection* (Deja Vu 1985)★★★★, *His Greatest Hits* (Chess 1986)★★★, *Cadillac Daddy: Memphis Recordings, 1952* (Rounder 1987)★★★, *Howlin' For My Baby* (Sun 1987)★★★, *Shake For Me - The Red Rooster* (Vogue 1988)★★★, *Smokestack Lightnin'* (Vogue 1988)★★★, *Red Rooster* (Joker 1988)★★★, *Moanin' And Howlin'* (Charly 1988)★★★, *Howlin' Wolf* 5-LP box set (Chess 1991)★★★★, *Going Down Slow* 5-CD box set (Roots 1992)★★★★, *Gold Collection* (1993)★★★, *The Wolf Is At Your Door* (Fan 1994)★★★, *The Complete Recordings 1951-1969* 7-CD box set (Charly 1994)★★★★, *The Genuine Article - The Best Of* (MCA 1994)★★★★, *The Very Best Of Howlin' Wolf* 3-CD set (Charly 1995)★★★★, *His Best* (Chess 1997)★★★★.

Hoyle, Linda

Formerly lead vocalist with progressive act **Affinity**, Hoyle embarked on a brief solo career in 1971. *Pieces Of Me* is a superb showcase for the singer's dynamic style. Aided by guitarist **Chris Spedding** and Karl Jenkins (oboe), **Jeff Clyne** (bass) and **John Marshall** (drums) from **Nucleus**, Hoyle exhibits her grasp of a wide range of material, notably through interpretations of **Laura Nyro**'s 'Lonely Women' and **Nina Simone**'s 'Backlash Blues'. However, Hoyle opted to leave music following her marriage to Pete King, former musical director to saxophonist **Ronnie Scott**.

● ALBUMS: *Pieces Of Me* (Vertigo 1971)★★★.

HSAS

This US group was formed in the early part of 1984 by **Sammy Hagar** (vocals) and Neil Schon (guitar). Both were from the San Francisco area and had planned a collaboration for some time. When Hagar had finished promoting his latest solo record and Schon had completed touring with **Journey**, HSAS was formed. They brought in Peter Schrieve (drums) and Kenny Aaronson (bass), primarily because they shared the same management. They wrote approximately 15 songs during one month and then decided to tour with the set. It was while they were on the road that they recorded two dates in their home-town of San Francisco for their debut album, rather than in the studio. A deal was struck with Sammy Hagar's label, **Geffen**, and *Through The Fire* was prepared for release. However, American radio was resistant to live records, so most of the crowd noise was removed from the final mix, with the exception of two tracks where the audience actively participated in the songs. Never a permanent band, after the album's release, Hagar returned to his solo career and Schon went back to Journey.

● ALBUMS: *Through The Fire* (Geffen 1984)★★★.

Hubba Hubba Records

Falkirk, Scotland label, formed in late 1992, whose eclectic release schedule quickly established the name. Among their earliest releases were Ohm's 'Tribal Zone' and Sheffield-based techno crew the Forgemasters' *Quababa EP*. The latter outfit were picked up after spells at **Warp** and **Network**. Other signings included Scotland's Dub Commission ('Lost In House'), and Bamboo ('Coney Island'). Their product was licensed to Murk subsidiary, Vibe, while Hubba Hubba also housed material from US label MegaTrend (run by Photon Inc's **Roy Davies Jnr.**). The label is run by **Utah Saints**' manager John MacLennan.

Hubbard, Freddie

b. 7 April 1938, Indianapolis, Indiana, USA. Hubbard began playing trumpet as a child, and in his teens worked locally with **Wes** and **Monk Montgomery**. When he was 20 he moved to New York, immediately falling in with the best of contemporary jazzmen. Amongst the musicians with whom he worked in the late 50s were **Eric Dolphy** (his room-mate for 18 months), **Sonny Rollins**, **J.J. Johnson** and **Quincy Jones**. In 1961 he joined **Art Blakey**'s **Jazz Messengers**, quickly establishing himself as an important new voice in jazz. He remained with Blakey until 1966, leaving to form his own small groups, which over the next few years featured **Kenny Barron** and **Louis Hayes**. Throughout the 60s he also played in bands led by others, including **Max Roach** and **Herbie Hancock** and was featured on four classic 60s sessions: **Ornette Coleman**'s *Free Jazz*, **Oliver Nelson**'s *Blues And The Abstract Truth*, Eric Dolphy's *Out To Lunch* and **John Coltrane**'s *Ascension*. Although his early 70s jazz albums *First Light* and *Straight Life* were particularly well received, this period saw Hubbard emulating Herbie Hancock and moving into jazz fusions. However, he sounded much more at ease in the hard bop context of V.S.O.P., the band which retraced an earlier quintet led by **Miles Davis** and brought together ex-Davis sidemen Hancock, Hayes, **Wayne Shorter** and **Ron Carter**, with Hubbard taking the Davis role. In the 80s Hubbard was again leading his own jazz group, attracting very favourable notices for his playing at concerts and festivals in the USA and Europe. He played with **Woody Shaw**, recording with him in 1985, and two years later recorded *Stardust* with Benny Golson. In 1988 he teamed up once more with Blakey at an engagement in Holland, from which came *Feel The Wind*.

In 1990 he appeared in Japan headlining an American-Japanese concert package which also featured **Elvin Jones**, **Sonny Fortune**, pianists **George Duke** and Benny Green, bassists Carter and Rufus Reid and singer **Salena Jones**. An exceptionally talented virtuoso performer, Hubbard's rich full tone is never lost, even when he plays dazzlingly fast passages. As one of the greatest of hard bop trumpeters, he contrives to create impassioned blues lines without losing the contemporary context within which he plays. Although his periodic shifts into jazz-rock have widened his audience, he is at his best playing jazz. He continues to mature, gradually leaving behind the spectacular displays of his early years, replacing them with a more deeply committed jazz. *MMTC* highlights this maturity with new recordings of the music of four giants; **Thelonious Monk**, Miles, Coltrane and **Cannonball Adderly**.

● ALBUMS: *Open Sesame* (Blue Note 1960)★★★, *Minor Mishap* (Blue Note 1961)★★★, *Ready For Freddie* (Blue Note 1961)★★★, *Hub Cap* (Blue Note 1961)★★★, *The Artistry Of Freddie Hubbard* (Impulse 1962)★★★★, *Hub-Tones* (Blue Note 1962)★★★★, *Here To Stay* (Blue Note 1963)★★★, *The Body And Soul Of Freddie Hubbard* (Impulse 1963)★★★, *Breaking Point* (Blue Note 1966)★★★, *Blue Spirits* (Blue Note 1965)★★★, *The Night Of The Cookers* (Blue Note 1966)★★★, *Backlash* (Atlantic 1967)★★★, *High Pressure Blues* (Atlantic 1969)★★★, *The Hub Of Hubbard* (1969)★★★, *Straight Life* (1970)★★★, *First Light* (1972)★★★, *Keep Your Soul Together* (CTI 1973)★★★, *Sky Dive* (CTI 1973)★★★, *High Energy* (1974)★★★, *Liquid Love* (1975)★★★, *V.S.O.P.* (1976)★★★, *Super Blue* (1978)★★★, *Mistral* (1980)★★★, *At The Northsea Jazz Festival* (1980)★★★, *Back To Birdland* (c.1980)★★★, *Anthology* (1981)★★★, *Outpost* (Enja 1981)★★★, *Ride Like The Wind* (1981)★★★, *Splash* (1981)★★★, *A Little Night Music* (1981)★★★, *Born To Be Blue* (Original Jazz Classics 1981)★★★, *Face To Face* (Pablo 1982)★★★, *Sweet Return* (1983)★★★, with Woody Shaw *Double Take* (1985)★★, with Shaw *The Eternal Triangle* (1987)★★★, with Benny Golson *Stardust* (1987)★★, with Art Blakey *Feel The Wind* (Timeless 1988)★★★, *Minor Mishap* (Black Lion 1989)★★★, *Times 'Are Changin'* (Blue Note 1989)★★, *Bolivia* (Limelight 1991)★★★, *Live At Fat Tuesday's* (1992)★★, *Live At The Warsaw Jazz Festival* (Jazzmen 1992)★★★, *Topsy* (Enja 1993)★★, *MMTC* (Music Masters 1995)★★.

● COMPILATIONS: *The Best Of Freddie Hubbard* (Blue Note 1990)★★★★, *Ballads* (Blue Note 1997)★★★★.

Hubbard, Ray Wylie

b. 13 November 1946, Soper, Oklahoma, USA. Much of Hubbard's fame rests on his songwriting. **Jerry Jeff Walker** recorded his composition 'Up Against The Wall, Redneck Mother', turning it into a left-field country standard. He formed the Cowboy Twinkies who released a self-titled debut for **Warner Brother Records** in 1975, but the album's failure led to the band's break-up. Hubbard went on to record his solo debut, before performing with Walker's old back-up band as the Ray Wylie Hubbard Band. His solo work has attracted increasing critical and commercial success. His collection, *Lost Train Of Thought*, was self-released in 1992 and sold at shows throughout his home state of Texas. Despite its low-key origins, it introduced many to his intelligent, uncompromising songwriting. The contents included a moving duet with **Willie Nelson** ('These Eyes'), plus several further excellent Hubbard standards such as 'When She Sang Amazing Grace'. *Loco Gringo's Lament* followed two years later, earning rave reviews from several quarters including ***Rolling Stone*** magazine, who described it as 'the most welcome comeback by a Texas honky-tonker since **Billy Joe Shaver**'s'. *Dangerous Spirits* was another left-field classic that featured Hubbard backed by several guest artists, including **Tony Joe White** and **Lucinda Williams**.

● ALBUMS: *Off The Wall* (Lone Star 1978)★★★, *Lost Train Of Thought* (Misery Loves Company 1992)★★★, *Loco Gringo's Lament* (Deja 1994)★★★★, *Dangerous Spirits* (Continental Song City 1997)★★★★.

Hubble, Eddie

b. 6 April 1928, Santa Barbara, California, USA. Hubble's father played trombone, composed and arranged for a radio station staff band in Los Angeles. Hubble was thus encouraged to pursue a career in music and at the age of 12 was playing trombone in the LA County Band. In 1944 the family moved to New York, where he continued his schooling in company with **Bob Wilber**. Heavily influenced by **Jack Teagarden** and **Miff Mole**, Hubble's first full-time professional job was with **Red McKenzie** in 1947 and around this time he also made his first records, substituting for **George Brunis** on a **Doc Evans** date. After a brief spell with the **Alvino Rey** band Hubble joined **Buddy Rich**, with whom he remained for about three years. Throughout the 50s he worked steadily, sometimes leading his own group, and in 1966 joined the **Dukes Of Dixieland**. In 1968 he was a member of the newly-formed **World's Greatest Jazz Band** - led by **Bob Haggart** and **Yank Lawson**. In the early 70s Hubble worked with musicians such as **Flip Phillips**, **Pee Wee Erwin** and **Bernie Privin**. A road accident in 1979 interrupted his career, but he was soon back on the bandstand again. He worked with **Jim Cullum** in Texas and continued to tour into the 80.

● ALBUMS: with World's Greatest Jazz Band *Century Plaza* (1972)★★★★, *Pee Wee Erwin Memorial* (1981)★★★.

Hucko, Peanuts

b. Michael Andrew Hucko, 7 April 1918, Syracuse, New York, USA. Between his arrival in New York in 1939 and his induction into the US Army Air Force in 1942, Hucko had played in several bands, usually on tenor saxophone. They included outfits led by **Jack Jenney**, **Will Bradley**, **Joe Marsala**, **Charlie Spivak** and Bob Chester. In the army, Hucko switched over to clarinet as the tenor was not an easy instrument to play while marching. He was recommended to **Glenn Miller** by **Ray McKinley** and **Zeke Zarchy** and, after several delays resulting from typical military 'snafus', he finally made the AAF band. Eventually settled in with the band, as lead alto saxophonist doubling on clarinet, Hucko became noted for his version of 'Stealin' Apples', a tune with which he has subsequently remained associated. After the war Hucko worked with **Benny Goodman** (on tenor) and McKinley, spent time in radio bands, and also played dixieland with **Jack Teagarden**, **Eddie Condon** and others. He was a member of the Teagarden-**Earl Hines** band that toured Europe in 1957 and the following year he joined **Louis Armstrong**'s All Stars. In the 60s he was employed mostly in studio work at **CBS**, NBC and **ABC**, where, for 15 years, he played lead clarinet in their light orchestra and second clarinet in the classical orchestra. In between these engagements, he found time to play in jazz clubs with Condon and squeeze in solo tours around the world. In the 70s he played for **Lawrence Welk**, continued to tour, sometimes as leader of the Glenn Miller Orchestra, and also led his own band, which featured his wife, Louise Tobin, on vocals. In the 80s he was still touring, sometimes as a single, sometimes with his band, the **Pied Pipers**. Late in 1991 he toured Europe and the UK, leading a small band which included **Glenn Zottola** and **Roy Williams** in its Anglo-American ranks.

● ALBUMS: *Peanuts Hucko And His Orchestra* i (1953)★★★, *Peanuts Hucko And His Orchestra* ii (1956)★★★, *Peanuts Hucko And His Orchestra* iii (1957)★★★, *The Jack Teagarden Earl Hines All Stars In England* (1957)★★★, *Peanuts Hucko And His Roman New Orleans Jazz Band* (1959)★★★★, *Live At Eddie Condon's* (1960-61)★★★★, with Eddie Condon *Midnight In Moscow* (1962)★★★, with Red Norvo *Live In Pasadena* (1970-72)★★★, *Peanuts...* (1975)★★★, *Peanuts Hucko With His Pied Piper Quintet* (1978)★★★★ *Peanuts In Everybody's Bag* (c.1980)★★★, *Stealin' Apples* (c.1982)★★★, *Tribute To Louis Armstrong* (1983)★★★, *Tribute To Benny Goodman* (1983)★★★.

● COMPILATIONS: with Glenn Miller *Rare Performances* (1943-44)★★★★ *Jam With Peanuts* (1947-48)★★★★, *The Sounds Of The Jazz Greats* (Zodiac 1981)★★★, *Jam With Peanuts* (Swing House 1984)★★★★.

Hudson Brothers

Siblings Brent, Bill and Mark Hudson first performed together as members of the My Sirs, before forming another group, the New Yorkers, with a friend, Kent Fillmore. Based in Portland, Oregon, USA, the quartet recorded several singles between 1966 and 1969, including a commendable version of **Nilsson**'s song 'I Guess The Lord Must Be In New York City'. The group's name was changed to Everyday Hudson when Fillmore dropped out of the line-up, and the trio later switched between Hudson and the Hudson Brothers. Despite several strong power-pop styled releases, they did not secure a hit single until 'So You Are A Star' reached the US Top 30 in the mid-70s. Their subsequent releases for **Elton John**'s Rocket label, 'Rendezvous' (co-written with **Bruce Johnson**) and '(How Does It Feel To Be) Spinning The Wheel' were excellent **Beach Boys/Paul McCartney**-influenced performances and a 1976 album *Ba Fa*, is arguably the brothers' most consistent work. However the Hudsons then chose to pursue a US television career as 'all-round' entertainers which devalued their recorded work.

● ALBUMS: *Hudson* (1972)★★★, *Totally Out Of Control* (1974)★★★, *Hollywood Situation* (1974)★★★, *Ba Fa* (Rocket 1976)★★★★, *The Truth About Us* (Rocket 1978)★★★, *Damn Those Kids* (1980)★★★.

Hudson, Keith

b. 1946, Kingston, Jamaica, West Indies, d. 14 November 1984, New York, USA. As a youth, Hudson attended Boys Town School where his fellow pupils included **Bob Marley**, **Delroy Wilson**, **Ken Boothe** and the **Heptones**, with whom he organized school concerts. From an early age, he was a **sound system** fanatic, and became an ardent follower of **Coxsone Dodd**'s Downbeat. He also came to know members of the **Skatalites**, and gained entry to **Studio One** recording sessions by carrying **Don Drummond**'s trombone. He was only 14 years old when he produced his first recording, an instrumental featuring members of the Skatalites that eventually saw release with a blank label in 1968, and two years later was reused for **Dennis Alcapone**'s 'Shades Of Hudson'. After leaving school, he served an apprenticeship in dentistry, and subsidized his early recordings with money earned from these skills. In late 1967, he launched his Inbidimts label with Ken Boothe's 'Old Fashioned Way', which subsequently became a number 1 in Jamaica. Over the next two years he released hits by Delroy Wilson ('Run Run') and **John Holt** ('Never Will I Hurt My Baby'). In 1970 he began to feature himself as a vocalist with 'Working Like A Slave' and 'Don't Get Confused', which caused a sensation at the time. Over the next two years, he had hits with **U-Roy**'s 'Dynamic Fashion Way', **Alton Ellis**' 'Big Bad Boy', Dennis Alcapone's 'The Sky's The Limits', **Big Youth**'s 'S.90 Skank' and **Soul Syndicate**'s 'Riot', and released a host of other singles on his Imbidimts, Mafia, Rebind and other labels. His willingness to experiment was evident on U-Roy's 'Dynamic Fashion Way', on which he re-employed the 'Old Fashioned Way' rhythm, added a string bass to lay a new bassline, and overdubbed saxophone to transform the track completely. For 'S.90 Skank' he arranged for a motorcycle to be surreptitiously brought into **Byron**

Lee's recording studio so that he could record it being revved up. It created such an impact on motorcycle-mad Jamaica that Coxsone Dodd, **Lee Perry** and other producers were soon wheeling motorcycles into their recording sessions.

In 1972 Hudson released his first LP, *Furnace*, on his Imbidimts label, which featured four songs by himself, together with DJ, instrumental and dub tracks. He followed this with *Class And Subject*, and though he continued to record other artists, from this point in time he concentrated on his own career. In 1973 he emigrated to London, issuing *Entering The Dragon*, which showed him continuing to experiment and develop, even if the results at this stage were inconsistent. In particular, his practice of utilizing one rhythm track for two or more different songs on one album was an innovation that only fully entered the reggae mainstream some ten years later. In 1974 he released *Flesh Of My Skin, Blood Of My Blood*, which still stands as a masterpiece. Sandwiched between two atmospheric instrumentals was a series of uplifting laments set to bare, understated rhythms, which sounded like nothing that had preceded them and nothing that has followed them, forcefully conveying not only a feeling of pain and oppression, but also an iron resolve to endure and defeat those obstacles. There were two further stunning releases in 1975: *Torch of Freedom* and *Pick A Dub*. The latter is simply one of the greatest dub albums ever issued, featuring versions of his classic singles plus cover versions of the **Abyssinians**' 'Satta Massa Gana' and 'Declaration Of Rights'. It also included both the vocal and dub cuts of his cover version of the **Dramatics**' **Stax** hit, 'In The Rain', on which he makes the song wholly his own. *Torch Of Freedom* was another one-off stroke of genius, featuring an understated, introverted sound with a distinct soul influence, for a series of songs on the theme of love, before eventually changing its focus for the final song, the visionary title track.

In 1976 he moved to New York and signed a four-year contract with **Virgin Records**, who had followed **Island Records**' lead in signing reggae acts in response to increased interest in the music, primarily from a new, predominantly white audience. If Hudson had released a strong mainstream reggae album at this juncture, then he would probably have become at least as big a star as **Burning Spear** or **Dennis Brown**. However, Hudson's insatiable desire to keep moving artistically and try new things compelled him to follow his own course, and he duly delivered to Virgin a fully blown soul album, *Too Expensive*. Virgin marketed it along with their reggae releases, but it sounded so out of step with prevailing tastes and expectations that it received a savaging at the hands of the press, and generated poor sales. In truth, it is a strong album, let down only by two poor tracks and an irritating, thin saxophone sound. The reaction to the album severely strained Hudson's relationship with Virgin, and he released his next single, '(Jonah) Come Out Now', under the pseu-

donym of Lloyd Linberg on his wryly titled Tell A Tale label. Hudson had moved on again, returning to reggae and reusing the rhythm he had previously employed for 'The Betrayer' to build a classic track. Virgin were evidently underwhelmed by their artist's intention to make each album entirely different, and they terminated Hudson's contract. In October, he released another excellent single in Jamaica, 'Rasta Country', before starting Joint, his new label in New York.

In 1977 a dub album, *Brand* (aka *The Joint*) was issued, followed the next year by its companion vocal set, *Rasta Communication*, which included 'Rasta Country' and a remade 'Jonah'. The brilliant, militant songs, outstanding rhythms and inspired playing made both of these albums masterpieces. An unusual feature enhancing several tracks was the excellent slide guitar work of Willy Barratt, who added a ghostly shimmer to the sound. In 1979, he again preceded his new vocal album with its dub counterpart, but *Nuh Skin Up Dub* and *From One Extreme To Another* were less inspired than their predecessors and were marred by overuse of in-vogue synth-drums. Nevertheless, they still contained some fine music. That year, Hudson also issued a strong DJ album to back *Brand*, Militant Barry's *Green Valley*. *Playing It Cool* was an excellent set, featuring new songs built over six of his earlier rhythms. The following year *Steaming Jungle* was issued, but proved to be his most disappointing release.

In early 1984 rumours circulated that Hudson was recording with the **Wailers** in New York, but nothing was ever released. In August he was diagnosed as having lung cancer. He received radiation therapy, and appeared to be responding well to the treatment, but on the morning of 14 November he complained of stomach pains, collapsed and died. Very little of his music has remained on catalogue. Hopefully this situation will change, and allow his music to be appreciated by the wider audience it deserves.

● ALBUMS: *Furnace* (Imbidimts 1972)★★, *Class And Subject* (1972)★★★, *Entering The Dragon* (1973)★★★, *Flesh Of My Skin, Blood Of My Blood* (Mamba 1974)★★★★, *Torch Of Freedom* (Altra 1975)★★★★, *Pick A Dub* (1975)★★★★, *Too Expensive* (Virgin 1976)★★★, *Brand/The Joint* (Joint 1977)★★★★, *Rasta Communication* (Joint 1978)★★★★, *Nuh Skin Up Dub* (1979)★★, *From One Extreme To Another* (1979)★★, *Playing It Cool* (1981)★★★★, *Steaming Jungle* (Vista Sounds 1982)★★.

● COMPILATIONS: various artists *The Big J Of Reggae* covers 1970-75 (1978)★★★, various artists *Studio Kinda Cloudy* covers 1967-72 (Trojan 1988)★★★★.

Hudson, Lord Tim

b. Timothy Hudson, Manchester, England. One of the 60s many mercurial characters, Hudson first attracted attention as part of the 'Chelsea Set' centred on the Keyna Coffee House in London, alongside fellow aspirants Michael Caine, Julie Christie and Terence Stamp. Inspired by the success of the **Beatles**, Hudson began seeking out pop talent and was instrumental in introducing the **Moody Blues** to **Decca Records**. When a new management team saw no further use for his services, a piqued Hudson left the UK on the advice of New York disc jockey B. Mitch Reed. Denied a US work permit, Hudson moved to Canada where, as Lord Tim Hudson, he became a highly successful DJ in Montreal. In 1965 he switched to a leading radio station in San Diego, California, USA. In 1966 he made the **Seeds'** 'Pushin' Too Hard' his record of the week. Lead singer, **Sky Saxon**, was so impressed he invited Hudson to become the group's manager. It was a combination similar to that of the **Rolling Stones** and **Andrew Loog Oldham**, with Hudson writing liner notes for Seeds' releases. Despite an undoubted flair for publicity - he claims to have coined the term 'flower power' - Hudson was unable to break the Seeds nationally, although they remained popular in California. He later managed the equally fascinating **Lollipop Shoppe**, but left music in 1969, disillusioned at the direction it was following. 'Groups with no talent were rich and the Seeds were starving,' he later commented. Little was heard of Hudson until the mid-80s when he briefly emerged as business manager to the UK cricketer Ian Botham.

Hudson, Will

b. 1908, Barstow, California, USA. Hudson began his music studies in Detroit, becoming an accomplished arranger. Local group **McKinney's Cotton Pickers** enlisted his services, and by the mid-30s when he formed his first dance band, he had already worked as arranger with **Fletcher Henderson, Cab Calloway, Don Redman, Andy Kirk, Earl Hines, Louis Armstrong, Jimmie Lunceford** and **Ina Ray Hutton**. The Hudson-De Lange Orchestra was formed in 1936. Co-led with **Eddie De Lange**, this 12-piece aggregation occasionally included Nan Wynn as vocalist. When that group disbanded after two and a half years Hudson put together his own orchestra under his own billing, with sidemen Charles Mitchell, Rudy Novak, Joe Bauer, Jack Andrews, Edward Kolyer, George Bohn, Gus Bivona, Pete Brendel, Charlie Brosen, Mark Hyams, Doc Goldberg, Russ Etri, Billy Exner, Will Hutton, Mike Rosati, Max Herman, Frank Beraldi, George Siravo, Walter Burleson, George Berg, Bob Dukoff, Tommy Morgan and Ernie Matthias. The featured vocalists included Ruth Gaylor, Jane Dover, Elyse Cooper and Ray Kenny. Many of these musicians were kept on from the original Hudson-De Lange Orchestra. They were briefly popular in hotels and ballrooms in the late 30s and early 40s, but Hudson soon gave up bandleading to concentrate on his arranging career, which continued to blossom.

Hudson-Ford

With the follow-up to their **Ivor Novello** award-winning composition, 'Part Of The Union', only a minor hit, UK-born bass guitarist John Ford and drummer Richard Hudson left the **Strawbs** in 1973 to try their luck as a duo. Though each of their albums

spawned a UK Top 40 placing - 'Pick Up The Pieces', 'Burn Baby Burn' and 'Floating In The Wind' - each sold less than its predecessor, and lack of fan commitment to Hudson-Ford *per se* forced disbandment after a tour to promote *Worlds Collide* - on which Hudson played lead guitar. The pair were joined on stage by drummer Ken Laws and, on keyboards, Chris Parren who, with members of **If**, had assisted during the *Worlds Collide* sessions at **Ringo Starr**'s Ascot studio. 1979 brought Ford and Hudson's belated and cynical crack at punk as the Monks - and a royalty-earning chart run with 'Nice Legs Shame About Her Face'. In 1989, Hudson was heard on a re-formed Strawbs album, *Don't Say Goodbye*.

● ALBUMS: *Nickelodeon* (A&M 1973)★★★, *Free Spirit* (A&M 1974)★★★, *Worlds Collide* (A&M 1975)★★★.

Hue And Cry

Based in Coatbridge, Scotland, brothers Patrick (b. 10 March 1964, Coatbridge, Strathclyde, Scotland) and Gregory Kane (b. 11 September 1966, Coatbridge, Strathclyde, Scotland) started as a band in 1986. Patrick handles the lyrics and singing duties while his brother concentrates on writing music, and plays piano and keyboards. Although they use session players both on stage and in the studio, some of their most powerful work has been just voice and piano - including the 1989 *Bitter Suite*. Their first single, 'I Refuse', was released in 1986 and flopped, but the following year the soul-fired 'Labour Of Love' gave them a UK hit. They received much attention for the memorable single 'Looking For Linda' (the true story of a woman who left home to buy a packet of cigarettes and ended up on a southbound train heading away from her old life). Since then, only their work as a bare duo has attracted any attention. The *Violently* EP in 1989 contained a cover of **Kate Bush**'s 'The Man With The Child In His Eyes', and in 1991 they parted company with their long-term label Circa.

In early 1992 they were seeking a new deal, while Patrick remained prominent outside of music. Always one of the more articulate of personalities within the pop world, he has served as both an outspoken television presenter and music journalist. He is also the Rector of Glasgow University (narrowly edging out Tony Benn). A firm socialist, he has recently turned his back on the Labour Party and given very vocal support to the Scottish Nationalist Party. Certainly he refuses to accept the boundaries between music and politics, as the lyrics to the single 'Peaceful Face' demonstrate: 'The future I see, The century comes and it goes, And my child will be there to bear all its woes'. He has been instrumental in forming the Artists For An Independent Scotland organization which is supported by other Scottish 'celebrities' and rock stars such as **Fish**. *Stars Crash Down*, their most recent album, features contributions from fellow Scots **Eddi Reader** and Vernal and Prime from **Deacon Blue**. *Piano & Vocal* was a bold project that worked because of the strength of Pat Kane's voice, even when tackling syrupy standards such as 'Send In The Clowns'.

● ALBUMS: *Seduced And Abandoned* (Circa 1987)★★★, *Remote/The Bitter Suite* (Circa 1989)★★★, *Stars Crash Down* (Circa 1991)★★, *Truth And Love* (Fidelity 1992)★★, *Showtime!* (Permanent 1994)★★, *Piano & Voice* (Permanent 1995)★★★.

● COMPILATIONS: *Labours Of Love - The Very Best Of* (Circa 1993)★★★.

Hues Corporation

Formed in 1969 in Los Angeles, California, USA. Their name was taken as a pun on the Howard Hughes billion-dollar corporation. They had been performing for five years when their biggest hit, 'Rock The Boat', arrived. The vocal trio consisted of Hubert Ann Kelly (b. 24 April 1947, Fairchild, Alabama, USA; soprano), St. Clair Lee (b. Bernard St. Clair Lee Calhoun Henderson, 24 April 1944, San Francisco, California, USA; baritone) and Fleming Williams (b. Flint, Michigan, USA; tenor). Their first record, 'Goodfootin'', was recorded for **Liberty Records** in 1970 but failed to hit. They signed with **RCA Records** in 1973 and made the charts with a song called 'Freedom For The Stallion'. 'Rock The Boat', originally a forgotten album track, was released in 1974 as the next single and reached number 1 in the US pop charts and number 6 in the UK, becoming one of the first significant disco hits. Tommy Brown (b. Birmingham, Alabama, USA) replaced Williams after the single hit and their only other chart success came later that same year with 'Rockin' Soul', which peaked at number 18 in the US chart and reached the Top 30 in the UK. The group continued to record into the late 70s, but they were unable to repeat their earlier success. However, in 1983 'Rock The Boat' made another chart appearance when **Forrest** took the single to the UK Top 5 position.

● ALBUMS: *Freedom For The Stallion* (RCA 1974)★★, *Love Corporation* (RCA 1975)★★, *I Caught Your Act* (Warners 1977)★★, *Your Place Or Mine* (Warners 1978)★★.

● COMPILATIONS: *Best Of The Hues Corporation* (RCA 1976)★★★.

Huff, Luther

b. 5 December 1910, Fannin, Mississippi, USA, d. 18 November 1973, Detroit, Michigan, USA. Luther and younger brother Percy made only two records in 1951, but they cleaved so startlingly and entertainingly to the old traditions that they have been prized ever since. They learned guitar from older brother Willie and cousin Donnee Howard and, like them, played at fish fries and country picnics. One picnic, held at a plantation in Belzoni, lasted 13 days. Luther bought a mandolin in 1936 and taught himself to play. Drafted into the army in 1942, Luther saw service in England, France and Belgium, where, in 1944, he recorded two acetates, now lost. In 1947, he moved to Detroit and started what would be a large family of 12 children. Percy stayed in Jackson, Mississippi, driving a taxicab.

On a visit in 1950, Luther bumped into Sonny Boy Williamson (Rice Miller), who suggested that he and Percy record for Trumpet. Needing train fare home to Detroit, Huff contacted Lillian McMurry and, in January and February 1951, the pair recorded 'Dirty Disposition', '1951 Blues', 'Bull Dog Blues' and 'Rosalee', the latter pair featuring Luther's mandolin. Luther returned north to work at the Chrysler factory, and later, for Plymouth, making little effort to continue as a musician. In 1968, along with brothers Willie and Percy, he was recorded by Adelphi Records, but the results were never issued.

● ALBUMS: *Delta Blues - 1951* (1990)★★★.

Hufstetter, Steve

b. 7 February 1936, Monroe, Michigan, USA. Hufstetter began his musical career as a teenager, playing trumpet in Phoenix, Arizona, where he was raised. In 1959 he moved to Los Angeles, California, where he joined **Stan Kenton**'s orchestra. He remained with Kenton for a year, then in the early 60s played in bands led by **Si Zentner**, **Les Brown** and others. In the mid-60s he worked with the band led by **Louie Bellson** to accompany **Pearl Bailey** and was also briefly with **Ray Charles**. He then played in the band led by Preston Love for **Motown** shows. At the end of the decade he played with **Clare Fischer** and in the studio band for the Donald O'Connor television show. In 1970 he began a working relationship with **Willie Bobo** which lasted, on and off, for a decade. Another long-lasting musical relationship began in 1973, when he became an important member of the big band co-led by **Toshiko Akiyoshi** and **Lew Tabackin**. Also during the 70s, Hufstetter played with **Bob Florence**, whom he had first met in the Zentner band, making many concert and record dates. Throughout the 80s Hufstetter worked with Florence, **Gordon Brisker**, Bellson, **Dave Pell**, **Bill Berry** and Poncho Sanchez, all the while being much in demand for studio work. Towards the end of the decade and into the 90s his busy schedule included tours with Akiyoshi, **Benny Carter** and **Supersax**, and concert appearances with a Kenton reunion band formed for a 1991 engagement at Newport Beach, sponsored by KLON, which also featured **Bill Holman** and **Shorty Rogers**. Although comfortably at home with all kinds and sizes of bands, much of Hufstetter's best work comes when he is with a contemporary big band. Combining fiery, powerful trumpet playing with a warm and intimate ballad style on flügelhorn, Hufstetter is one of the outstanding talents of the day. The facts that much of his work has been concentrated in the Los Angeles area and that many of his recordings have been made as a sideman have tended to keep his name from the wider jazz audience.

● ALBUMS: with Stan Kenton *Two Much* (1960)★★★★, with Kenton *Stan Kenton's Christmas* (1961)★★, with Clare Fischer *Thesaurus* (1969)★★★, with Akiyoshi-Tabackin *Road Time* (1976)★★★, with A-T *Insights* (1976)★★, with A-T *Live At Newport '77* (1977)★★★, with Bob Florence *Live At*

Concerts By The Sea (1979)★★★, with Florence *Westlake* (1981)★★, with A-T *Tanuki's Night Out* (1981)★★★, with Florence *Trash Can City* (1986)★★★, with Gordon Brisker *New Beginning* (1987)★★★, with Florence *State Of The Art* (1989)★★★, *Circles* (1990)★★★.

Hug, Armand

b. 6 December 1910, New Orleans, Louisiana, USA, d. 19 March 1977. Taught to play piano by his mother, Hug worked for a while as a pianist in silent movie theatres before starting to play in a dance band. Still only in his early teens, he quickly built a solid reputation in his home town. In the mid-30s he recorded with **Sharkey Bonano** but by the end of the decade had decided upon a career as a soloist. He played several long club residencies in New Orleans culminating, in 1967, in a lifetime contract at a leading Cresent City hotel. In later years, Hug occasionally returned to playing in bands, including those led by Bonano and **Johnny Wiggs**, but was at his best as a single. His repertoire mixed traditional New Orleans music with the popular songs of his hey-days. Solid, reliable, with a stirring left hand, Hug was a thorough professional and throughout his career ably continued the great tradition of New Orleans jazz pianists.

● ALBUMS: *Armand Hug Plays Armand Piron* (1953)★★★, *Piano Solos* (Nola 1968)★★, *Armand Hug Of New Orleans: 1971* (Swaggie 1971)★★★, *Armand Hug Of New Orleans: 1974* (Swaggie 1974)★★★, *In New Orleans On Sunday Afternoon* (1974-75)★★★, *Armand Hug Plays Jelly Roll Morton* (Swaggie 1976)★★★★, *New Orleans Piano* (unk. date)★★★, *Huggin' The Keys* (Swaggie 1983)★★★, with Eddie Miller *New Orleans Dixielanders And Rhythm Pals* (Southland 1988)★★.

Hugg, Mike

b. b. 11 August 1942, Andover, Hampshire, England. In 1962 drummer Hugg became a founder member of the Mann Hugg Blues Brothers, a London-based club band making the transition from modern jazz to R&B. In 1963 they took the name **Manfred Mann**. Over the next six years they became one of Britain's most consistently successful pop attractions. During this period Hugg composed several songs for the group, notably much of the score to the film soundtrack of *Up The Junction*. He showed a knack for writing intelligent pop songs, a talent often overshadowed by his drumming skills. Hugg also produced material for other acts, including **Cherry Smash**, and wrote several advertising jingles, the best-known of which was for Ski yoghurt. In 1969 Hugg joined band leader Manfred Mann in **Manfred Mann's Chapter Three**, which fulfilled their ambitions to follow a less commercial musical path. When the group broke up in 1972 Hugg began a solo career with *Somewhere*. Unfortunately, the material on this and its successor *Stress And Strain*, lacked the charm of his 60s work. Nevertheless, a single, 'Blue Suede Shoes Again', garnered considerable airplay. Hugg also wrote and sang the theme tune to BBC Television's *Whatever*

Happened To The Likely Lads before forming a new group, Hug, with Marcus James, John Knightsbridge and Ron Telemacque. He eschewed drums in favour of keyboards on 1975's *Neon Dream*, released on **Polydor Records**, but, as with his previous solo offerings, this set was pleasant, but undemanding. A new act, the Mike Hugg Freeway, completed a single, 'Same Old Fantasy' in 1976, after which Hugg retired from recording.

● ALBUMS: *Somewhere* (Polydor 1972)★★★, *Stress And Strain* (Polydor 1973)★★.

Huggy Bear

Brighton, England-based three female/two male band at the forefront of the 'Riot Grrrl' collective philosophy on female emancipation in the music industry. Riot Grrrl had origins in America, a subversive counter-culture dedicated to 'cutting the tripwires of alienation that separate girls from boys'. In the UK, Huggy Bear were at the leading edge of this movement, their activities incorporating fanzine production (*Huggy Nation*) as well as the band. Their musical arm comprised Jo Johnson (vocals, bass), Nicki Elliot (vocals), Chris (vocals), Karen (drums) and John Slade (guitar), though their ethos had more to do with musical access than practice. Despite this, their stirring proto-punk anthems, particularly the rallying 'Her Jazz', helped stir considerable media interest in 1993, despite the fact that they still resisted attempts to be interviewed by the mainstream music press. Their antagonistic stance led to two significant incidents; after performing 'Her Jazz' on the television programme *The Word*, they were among a number of men and women to vocally object to an item on 'bimbos' being screened after their performance. The band were ejected from the building amid allegations and counter-allegations of physical violence. Shortly afterwards a gig at the Derby Warehouse on 15 March 1993 ended in chaos when, according to several press reports, the band were accosted by a male member of the audience and his girlfriend. The man in question had proved resistant to the band's 'girls only at the front' performance dictates. Their early releases included debut EP *Rubbing The Impossible To Burst* and a shared album with similarly confrontational US band **Bikini Kill**, which did much to bring the divisive nature of sexism in the music industry back into focus. *Taking The Rough With The Smooch* collects their early EPs, while *Weaponry Listens To Love* is a poorly recorded album released in 1995. Guitarist John Slade now plays with **Comet Gain**.

● ALBUMS: with Bikini Kill *Our Troubled Youth/Yeah! Yeah! Yeah!* (Catcall/Kill Rock Stars 1993)★★★, *Taking The Rough With The Smooch* (Kill Rock Stars 1993)★★★, *Weaponry Listens To Love* (Kill Rock Stars 1995)★★.

Hughes, David

b. 11 October 1929, Birmingham, England, d. 19 October 1972. A ballad singer with a fine tenor voice, who had success in the popular field in the UK during the 50s and early 60s, before he went on to become a star in opera. After studying at the Royal Academy, Hughes made his West End debut in the romantic musical *Belinda Fair* (1949). During the 50s, he was a regular on radio and television in programmes such as *The Passing Show, Come To Charlie, Henry Hall's Guest Night, Presenting David Hughes, TV Starlight, Sunday Night At The London Palladium, Spring Song, Boy Meets Girls* (from Paris), and his own series, *Make Mine Music*. He also appeared with **Ginger Rogers**, Lizabeth Webb and Brian Reece in a television version of the 1948 West End musical *Carissima*, and was back on the London stage himself in 1956 in *Summer Song*. Hughes was also popular on the UK variety circuit, and had several successful records, including 'By The Fountains Of Rome', which won an **Ivor Novello** Award as 'the most outstanding song of the year' in 1956, for its writers Matyas Seiber and **Norman Newell**. Around this time, with his good looks and romantic delivery, he was dubbed 'Mr. Hearthrob'. In 1962 he appeared in *Scapa*, a musical version of the 1950 hit comedy *Seagulls Over Sorrento*, and shortly afterwards decided to forsake the world of pop, for light music and opera. In 1964 he made an album of 16th-century songs, which led to appearances at Glyndebourne the following year, and eventually with the Sadler's Wells Company. From then on, encouraged by the legendary Sir John Barbarolli, he sang many leading roles in opera, including Lieutenant Pinkerton in *Madame Butterfly*, in the UK and abroad.

● ALBUMS: *Songs You Love* (1968)★★★, *Favourite Opera And Operetta Arias* (1970)★★★, *World Of Great Classic Love Songs* (1973)★★★.

Hughes, Glenn

b. 21 August 1952, Cannock, Staffordshire, England. Hughes left school at the age of 15 to follow his dream of becoming a musician. He began playing lead guitar with the News in 1967, where he also sang, emulating his heroes **Otis Redding** and **Wilson Pickett**. Later he switched to bass guitar, inspired by James Jamerson from the Tamla/**Motown Records** 'house band'. These influences, married to a love of rock 'n' roll, led him to form **Trapeze** with Dave Holland (drums) and Mel Galley (guitar). Trapeze signed to the **Moody Blues**' record label, Threshold, and released four albums up to 1973, when Hughes was offered a job with a new Birmingham band, **Electric Light Orchestra**. However, he declined and in June joined **Deep Purple** instead. It was with Purple that Hughes made his mark in the UK with his superb singing on *Burn*, where he joined with, and some believe outclassed, their new vocalist David Coverdale. Hughes' influence over the band became a major factor in **Ritchie Blackmore**'s decision to quit, and his association with the band continued until 1976 when he re-formed Trapeze with the original line-up, although this venture failed to tour or record. When they finally began a US tour, Hughes walked out halfway through. The band continued without him while their leader disappeared from public view. Two

years later he resurfaced with a solo album before again dropping out of sight. In 1982 he joined with Pat Thrall (guitar, ex-**Pat Travers Band**) and **Quiet Riot** drummer Frankie Banali to form Hughes/Thrall, who released one album to a poor reception (although this set went on to achieve 'legendary' status and became one of the most sought-after rock albums of the 80s). After the project fell apart, Hughes worked for a time with **Gary Moore**, but little came of the collaboration. In 1985 he reunited with Mel Galley and a host of stars to record the concept album *Phenomena*. Although considered obsolete by rock critics, it did serve to put Hughes back on the map, and Tony Iommi, looking for a replacement for **Ian Gillan** in **Black Sabbath**, contacted him. Hughes spent less than a year with the band but recorded some fine vocals for *Seventh Star*. He then returned to obscurity and suffered personal problems, but help from an unusual quarter was at hand. Bill Drummond of the **KLF** was keen to experiment with blending rock and dance music (he had already gained infamy in such matters with **Extreme Noise Terror**), and in 1991 he coaxed Hughes back into the limelight for the hit single 'America - What Time Is Love?'. This success reanimated the vocalist's efforts and he set about forming a new band that has since enjoyed a small degree of concert success. He has also renewed his partnership with Pat Thrall for a projected second album. A new band, World, was assembled in 1993, although his solo career continues. On *Feel*, he edged closer to AOR balladry.

● ALBUMS: *Play Me Out* (Safari 1978)★★★, as Hughes/Thrall *Hughes/Thrall* (Epic 1982)★★★, with Phenomena *Phenomena* (Bronze 1985)★★, *From Now On* (Roadrunner 1994)★★★, *Feel* (SPV 1995)★★, *Addiction* (Steamhammer 1996)★★★.

Hughes, Jimmy

b. 1938, Leighton, Alabama, USA, d. 4 January 1997. This former member of the Singing Clouds abandoned the gospel field following the success of **Arthur Alexander** and recorded a handful of secular songs. When his producer, Rick Hall, was unable to secure an outlet for one such master, 'Steal Away', he issued it himself, inaugurating the Fame label. The prototype country-soul ballad, it became a US Top 20 R&B hit in 1964. Hughes enjoyed even greater success with 'Neighbor Neighbor' (1966) and 'Why Not Tonight?' (1967), but was unable to sustain the momentum. Two 1968 singles on **Atlantic** and **Stax**/Volt, 'It Ain't What You Got' and 'I Like Everything About You', achieved only minor placings. He later retired from music altogether, dying of cancer in January 1997. *Why Not Tonight* is an excellent representation of his later Fame recordings, while *Soul Neighbors*, shared with **Joe Simon**, offers some of his earlier work.

● ALBUMS: *Steal Away* (Fame 1964)★★★, *Why Not Tonight* (Fame 1967)★★★★, *Something Special* (1969)★★★.

● COMPILATIONS: *A Shot Of Rhythm And Blues* (Charly 1980)★★★, with Joe Simon *Soul Neighbors* (Charly

1984)★★★, *Something Special* 13 tracks plus nine by Joe Hicks (1993)★★★.

Hughes, Joe 'Guitar'

b. 29 September 1937, Houston, Texas, USA. A product of Houston's third ward, Joe 'Guitar' Hughes turned to music at an early age under the influence of the work of **T-Bone Walker**. He claims to have used money earned washing dishes to buy his first electric guitar at the age of 14 and to have been appearing professionally by the time he was 16. His first band was the Dukes Of Rhythm, which included in its line-up Hughes' neighbour and friend **Johnny Copeland**. When this group disbanded in 1964 Hughes joined **Grady Gaines** working for **Little Richard**'s old group the Upsetters. His next job was working as a member of **Bobby Bland**'s band, which he left in the wake of Bland's supporting star Al 'TNT' Braggs. After three years with Braggs, Hughes moved on to playing lead with Julius Jones and the Rivieras and from there to various groups operating around the Houston area. An upsurge of interest in the post-war Texas blues brought Hughes to some prominence during the early 80s, since which time he has toured in Europe and recorded for Double Trouble Records of Holland. *Texas Guitar Slinger* was co-produced by Jerry Jenkins.

● ALBUMS: *Craftsman* (Double Trouble 1988)★★★, *Down & Depressed: Dangerous* (Munich 1993)★★★, *Live At Vrendenburg* (Double Trouble 1993)★★★, *Texas Guitar Slinger* (Bullseye 1996)★★★.

Hughes, Spike

b. Patrick C. Hughes, 19 October 1908, London, England, d. 2 February 1987. In the early and mid-30s bassist Hughes was active in UK dance band and light music circles, playing and composing in a wide range of musical styles. Some of his compositions attempted to blend jazz with classical music - for example, his 'A Harlem Symphony' and 'High Yellow', a jazz ballet. After making some jazz-oriented records in the UK, Hughes visited New York where he led a recording date with a band organized for him by **Benny Carter**, playing several of his own compositions and arrangements. These records, on which outstanding musicians such as **Coleman Hawkins**, **Red Allen**, **Chu Berry**, **Dicky Wells** and **Sid Catlett** appeared, proved that Hughes had fully assimilated what was still, for many Europeans, an alien musical concept. These 1933 recordings became, and remain, classics of big band music. As if aware that he had achieved a peak he could never surpass, Hughes played little after this, concentrating instead on journalism. He was for many years 'Mike' of *Melody Maker* and also wrote extensively on classical music as well as publishing two volumes of autobiography.

● COMPILATIONS: *Spike Hughes And His Decca-dents* (1930)★★★, *Spike Hughes And His All-American Orchestra* (1933)★★★.

● FURTHER READING: *Opening Bars*, Spike Hughes. *Second Movement*, Spike Hughes.

Hughes/Thrall

This was a short-lived collaboration between former **Deep Purple** and **Trapeze** bassist/vocalist Glenn Hughes and guitarist Pat Thrall, who had previously played with **Automatic Man** and **Pat Travers**. With the help of various session drummers, including Frankie Banali (later of **Quiet Riot**), they recorded an album that fused rock and funk through the use of synthesized guitar effects. Shortly after the album was released, Thrall went back to session work, while Hughes had stints with **Gary Moore**, **Black Sabbath** and **Phenomena**. In 1987 they worked together again, on the soundtrack of the film *Dragnet*.

● ALBUMS: *Hughes/Thrall* (1982)★★★.

Hughey, John

b. *c.*1935, Elaine, Arkansas, USA. The steel guitarist John Hughey was given a **Gene Autry** flat-top guitar when he was nine, but in his teens switched to steel guitar. He initially joined the Phillips County Ramblers and later joined Slim Rhodes And Mother's Best Mountaineers when their steel player was drafted to Vietnam and stayed with them for 15 years. In 1968 he met up with his childhood friend **Conway Twitty** and became a member of Twitty's backing band, the Lonely Blue Boys. His steel guitar playing was featured on Twitty's first US country number 1, 'Next In Line'. The Lonely Blue Boys evolved into the Twitty Birds and for a time, also included John's brother, Gene. His steel guitar with its 'crying' sound was featured on most of Conway's chart-topping singles, but by 1980 Hughey was becoming frustrated. Twitty had sold the franchise for his souvenirs to another company and so his backing musicians no longer received their percentage cut on the sales. Twitty was also moving away from the steel guitar and after several unhappy years, Hughey finally left in 1988. He worked for **Loretta Lynn** for a year and since then, has worked for **Vince Gill**. His session work has included two albums with **Elvis Presley** (*From Elvis In Memphis* and *Back In Memphis*) as well as albums with **Joe Diffie**, **Alan Jackson**, **Reba McEntire**, **Dean Martin** and **Dolly Parton**.

Hugill, Stan

b. 19 November 1906, in the coastguard cottages at Hoylake, Cheshire, England, to a seafaring family, d. 13 May 1992. A veritable encyclopaedia of songs nautical and shanties from the last great days of sail, Hugill went to sea with the Merchant Service during the early 20s. He served in Sail (square riggers and fore 'n' afters), of ships from the USA, Germany, and Britain, for 10 years. He then moved into steam (Blue Funnel Line), to China and Japan; and Hugill then spent over four years as a prisoner of war. After the war, Hugill studied for three years at the London University Oriental and African school of languages, and obtained a diploma in Japanese in 1949. From 1950, Hugill joined the Outward Bound movement, as an instructor, and later as bosun. He married Bronwen Irene Benbow in 1952, and both his sons later became folk musicians. When *Shanties From The Seven Seas* was published, Hugill went to the BBC in London to be interviewed, later turning up at the famous Singer's Club', then run by **Peggy Seeger** and Stan Kelly. It was here that he sang in public for the first time. He was later introduced to the Bluecoat School, in Liverpool, and met both the **Spinners** and **A.L. Lloyd**. For the next few years, while still working, Hugill sang at clubs and colleges all over Britain. He later limited himself to singing at festivals worldwide, after he retired in 1975. In addition to his recordings and books, Hugill also painted marine oils, as well as illustrating his own books. Hugill lived in Wales, but continued to travel giving lectures on shanty singing, and old sailing ships. He also made two videos, *Jack Tar*, in Poland in 1987 and *Stan Hugill* in Holland in 1991. He was probably the last of the British Shantymen.

● ALBUMS: *Shanties From The Seven Seas* (1961)★★★, *Men And The Sea* (70s)★★★★, *Reminisces* (1977)★★★, *Aboard The Cutty Sark* (1979)★★★★, with others *Songs Of The Sea* (1979)★★★, *Ratcliffe Highway* (80s)★★★, with others *Sea Songs* (1980)★★★, with others *Sea Music Of Many Lands* (1980)★★★, *Shantyman* (1987)★★★, *Salty Foretopman* (1988)★★★.

● FURTHER READING: *Shanties From The Seven Seas*, Stan Hugill. *Sailortown*, Stan Hugill. *Shanties And Sailor Songs*, Stan Hugill. *Songs Of The Sea - The Tales And Tunes Of Sailors And Sailing Ships*, Stan Hugill

Hula

Based in Sheffield, England, Hula were one of the city's most prominent exponents of the independent music scene, churning out numerous albums and 12-inch singles of funky, synthesized pop for Yorkshire's Red Rhino label. Hula hinged around Mark Albrow (keyboards, tapes), Alan Fish (drums, percussion; later replaced by Nort) and Ron Wright (vocals, guitar, tapes, clarinet), helped at first by Chakk's Mark Brydon (bass, percussion). Their debut EP, 1982's *Back Pop Workout*, was well received, but it was a year before their debut album, *Cut From Inside*, was released. 1984 brought perhaps their best-known single, 'The Fever Car', in September, alongside a second album, *Murmur In November*. 'Get The Habit' and 'Walk On Stalks Of Shattered Glass' (for which Hula was joined by John Avery) were followed early in the new year by *One Thousand Years* and then *Freeze Out*, taken from sessions for BBC Radio 1 disc jockey **John Peel**. For *Shadowland*, Hula were aided by Adam Barnes and sleeve designer Simon Crump. This preceded 'Black Wall Blue' in November and 'Poison' in March 1987, produced by Daniel Miller. In May, Hula unleashed *Voice*, again enlisting outside help from Alan Fisch, Justin Bennett and Darrell D'Silva, to add a wider instrumental range. 'Cut Me Loose' in August and *Threshold* in November meant that 1987 was Hula's busiest year; but strangely, it turned out to be their last. Red Rhino went bankrupt soon after and without the

freedom the label had given them, Hula as a band disappeared, although members continued to work within Sheffield's active music scene.

● ALBUMS: *Cut From Inside* (Red Rhino 1983)★★★, *Murmur* (Red Rhino 1984)★★★, *One Thousand Hours* (Red Rhino 1986)★★, *Shadowland* (Red Rhino 1986)★★, *Voice* (Red Rhino 1987)★★★.

Solo: John Avery *Jessica In The Room Of Lights* (Technical 1986)★★★.

● COMPILATIONS: *Threshold* (Red Rhino 1987)★★★.

Hulbert, Jack

b. 24 April 1892, Ely, England, d. 25 March 1978, London, England. A popular actor, singer, dancer, director, author choreographer, and producer, whose jaunty onstage image was of the 'terribly British, "I say, old chap"' variety. Hulbert began to develop his various skills in undergraduate productions while he was studying at Cambridge University. In 1913, while appearing in *The Pearl Girl* in the West End, he met **Cicely Courtneidge**, the daughter of producer Robert Courtneidge, and they were married in 1916. *The Pearl Girl* was the first of 13 musicals in which they appeared together. During the next few years Hulbert established himself in a mixture of musical comedies and revues such as *The Cinema Star*, **The Arcadians**, *The Light Blues* (for which he was also co-librettist), *See-Saw*, *Bubbly*, *Bran-Pie*, *A Little Dutch Girl*, *Ring Up*, *Pot Luck*, and *The Little Revue Starts At 9* (1923). From 1925 onwards he co-produced and/or directed (and sometimes choreographed) a range of productions, particularly those in which he also acted. These included *By The Way* (in London and New York), *Lido Lady*, *Clowns In Clover*, *The House That Jack Built*, **Follow A Star** (1930), **Under Your Hat**, *Full Swing*, and *Something In The Air* (1943). After World War II, with **Oklahoma!** and the other American blockbusters on the horizon, Hulbert's smart and sophisticated style of musical comedy was less in demand, although he directed Cicely Courtneidge in the highly successful **Gay's The Word** in 1951. Over the years he introduced several popular songs, including 'The Flies Crawled Up The Window', 'My Hat's On The Side Of My Head', 'She's Such A Comfort To Me', and 'I Was Anything But Sentimental', a duet with his wife from their film *Take My Tip* (1937). Hulbert made several other light comedy movies during the 30s, - he and Courtneidge were just as popular on the screen as on the stage - such as **Elstree Calling** (1930), *The Ghost Train*, *Jack's The Boy*, *Bulldog Jack*, *Paradise For Two*, and *Kate Plus Ten*. From then on there were only occasional releases which included **Under Your Hat** (1940), *Into The Blue* (1951) *Spider's Web* (1960), and *Not Now Darling* (1973).

● ALBUMS: *The Golden Age Of Cicely Courtneidge And Jack Hulbert* (1984)★★★.

● FURTHER READING: *The Little Woman's Always Right*, Jack Hulbert. *Cicely*, Cicely Courtneidge.

Hull, Alan

b. 20 February 1945, Newcastle-upon-Tyne, England, d. 17 November 1995. Alan Hull's career began as a founder-member of the Chosen Few, a Tyneside beat group which also included future **Ian Dury** pianist, Mickey Gallagher. Hull composed the four tracks constituting their output, before leaving to become a nurse and sometime folk singer. In 1967 Alan founded Downtown Faction, which evolved into **Lindisfarne**. This popular folk rock act had hit singles with 'Meet Me On The Corner' and the evocative latter-day classic 'Lady Eleanor', both of which Hull wrote (the latter for his wife). Their first two albums were critical and commercial successes. *Pipedream*, Hull's fine debut album, was recorded with assistance from many members of Lindisfarne, in 1973. Its content was more introspective than that of his group and partly reflected on the singer's previous employment in a mental hospital. Although Hull continued to lead his colleagues throughout the 70s and 80s, he pursued a solo career with later releases *Squire* and *Phantoms*, plus a one-off release on the Rocket label as Radiator, a group formed with the assistance of Lindisfarne drummer Ray Laidlaw. None of these albums were able to achieve the same degree of success as *Pipedream*, the second decade proved more low-key, including some time spent in local politics (he was a committed socialist), resulting in only one collection, *On The Other Side*. The live recording *Back To Basics* was a mixture of his great compositions such as the cruelly poignant 'Winter Song' and the previously mentioned 'Lady Eleanor' together with more recent material including the powerful yet beautiful ode to Mother Russia 'This Heart Of Mine'. Hull carved a small but solid niche as one of the UK's leading troubadours. He was still very active in the 90s performing his familiar catalogue to a small but loyal following throughout the UK. Known to be fond of a drink or three, he died when he had a heart attack on the way the back from his local pub. His final album was ironically one that could have seen his work re-appraised. The posthumous *Statues And Liberties* contained some excellent songs such as 'Statues & Liberties' and 'Treat Me Kindly'. His passionate voice was still intact. Hull never wasted a lyric, every line was meant to count, and even if we sometimes failed to understand, his intention was always honest and true, dark and humorous. His work deserves to endure.

● ALBUMS: *Pipedream* (Charisma 1973)★★★★, *Squire* (Warners 1975)★★★, with Radiator *Isn't It Strange* (Rocket 1977)★★★, *Phantoms* (Rocket 1979)★★★, *On The Other Side* (Black Crow 1983)★★★, *Another Little Adventure* (Black Crow 1988)★★★, *Back To Basics* (Mooncrest 1994)★★★, *Statues And Liberties* (Transatlantic 1996)★★★★.

● COMPILATIONS: *When War Is Over* (New Millenium 1998)★★★.

● FURTHER READING: *The Mocking Horse*, Alan Hull.

Hull, Papa Harvey, And Long Cleve Reed

Probably from northern Mississippi, Hull and Reed, together with guitarist Sunny Wilson, formed a small group of black songsters. Reed and Wilson's two-guitar accompaniment was a blend of parlour guitar and ragtime. They sang blues, but much of their repertoire was from the turn of the century, when blues was not yet the dominant black music, and included ballads, medicine show material, and coon songs; their harmony singing, too, was of an earlier age. Long Cleve Reed may also have been Big Boy Cleveland, who recorded shortly after Hull and Reed, playing a slide guitar blues and 'Quill Blues', a fife solo unparalleled on commercial race records.

● ALBUMS: *The Songster Tradition* (1991)★★★.

Hullaballoos

Formed in 1963 in Hull, England, and originally known as Ricky And The Crusaders, the Hullaballoos comprised Rick Knight, Andrew Woonton, Geoffrey Mortimer and Harold Dunn. The quartet made its recording debut the following year with a version of **Buddy Holly**'s 'I'm Gonna Love You Too', but although their singles made no commercial impression in Britain, the group became popular in the USA. Adopted by producers Hugo And Luigi, they enjoyed an association with the successful *Hullaballoo* USA television show, but by the end of 1965 the lustre of their now anachronistic brand of beat had faded. Guitarist Mick Wayne, later of **Juniors Eyes** and the **Pink Fairies**, joined the group towards the end of its career, but was not featured on any recordings.

● ALBUMS: *The Hullaballoo Show* (Columbia 1965)★, *The Hullaballoos On Hullaballoo* (1965)★.

Hum

Hum were formed in 1989 in Champaign, Illinois, USA, and consist of Jeff Dimpsey (b. 23 May 1967, Illinois, USA; bass), Tim Lash (b. 16 June 1974, Champaign, Illinois, USA; guitar), Bryan St. Pere (b. 2 April 1966, Evergreen Park, Illinois, USA; drums) and Matt Talbott (b. 27 June 1967, Geneseo, Illinois, USA; vocals, guitar). Adhering rigidly to the principles of self-booked touring dates and own-label releases, they have steadily built an international following for their intelligent but caustic musicality and Talbott's engaging, oblique lyrics. After a series of releases on their own 12-Inch Records label, the group signed to UK label Dedicated Records in 1996 in time for the release of their third album, *You'd Prefer An Astronaut*. Produced by Keith Cleversley (**Flaming Lips**, **Spiritualized**), it prompted a series of excellent reviews and confirmed Hum's rise as one of the more interesting and entertaining of the mid-90s alternative rock crop.

● ALBUMS: *You'd Prefer An Astronaut* (Dedicated 1996)★★★.

Humair, Daniel

b. 23 May 1938, Geneva, Switzerland. Humair played clarinet and drums from the age of seven and won a competition for jazz playing in his teens. Paris has traditionally provided a Mecca for exiled jazz musicians: by the time he was 20 Humair was accompanying these visiting heroes from the drums. Most celebrated was a season with tenor saxophonist **Lucky Thompson** at a club called Le Chat Qui Pêche. Humair became the drummer American musicians would ask to work with (despite a gig with the **Swingle Singers** in the early 60s). In 1967 he played on violinist **Jean-Luc Ponty**'s debut *Sunday Walk* (also contributing the title track). When alto saxophonist **Phil Woods** emigrated to Paris in 1968 it was natural that Humair should be the drummer in what Woods called the European Rhythm Machine.

In 1969 he won the *Downbeat* critics' poll as Talent Deserving Wider Recognition. Humair was so in demand that his job-sheet for the 70s reads like a list of the pre-eminent names in jazz: **Herbie Mann**, **Roy Eldridge**, **Stéphane Grappelli** and **Anthony Braxton** all availed themselves of his graceful, incisive drums. He played with **Gato Barbieri** on the soundtrack to *Last Tango In Paris* in 1972. *Welcome* on **Soul Note** in 1986, a record which listed all members of the quartet as leaders, was a perfect demonstration of his warmth and responsiveness as a drummer. Cited by Nat Hentoff as a European 'who long ago destroyed the notion that European drummers can't swing' and also active as a painter, Humair continued to top drum polls in France into the 90s. In 1991 *Surrounded* documented a selection of his work from 1964-87, including tracks with legends such as **Eric Dolphy**, **Gerry Mulligan** and **Johnny Griffin** - a neat way of giving Humair centre-stage and celebrating the breadth of his involvement with jazz history.

● ALBUMS: with Gordon Beck, Ron Mathewson *All In The Morning* (1971)★★★, with Claudio Fasoli, Kenny Wheeler, J-F Jenny Clarke *Welcome* (1986)★★★, *Surrounded* (1991)★★.

Human Beast

This short-lived psychedelic pop outfit was formed in the UK at the end of the 60s. Featuring Gillies Buchan (guitar/vocals), Edward Jones (bass/vocals), David McNiven (clarinet) and John Romsey (drums), the group was originally known as Skin but did not record as such. Human Beast signed to **Decca Records** in 1970 and made their debut with *Volume One (Instinct)*. Though it sold poorly at the time, it has subsequently become the subject of collector's interest. Typical of its contents were songs with expansive titles such as 'Brush With The Midnight Butterfly', 'Reality Presented As An Alternative' and 'Appearance Is Everything Style Is A Way Of Living'. Fittingly, each featured similarly ponderous lyrics. In common with other progressive bands of the period, there was also a degree of experimentation with Eastern melodies and rhythms, resulting in the best track, 'Maybe Someday'. However, the group never recorded again and disappeared from the music business thereafter.

● ALBUMS: *Volume One (Instinct)* (Decca 1970)★★.

Human Beinz

This Ohio-based quartet - Richard Belley (lead guitar), Ting Markulin (rhythm guitar), Mel Pachuta (bass) and Mike Tatman (drums) - made their recording debut on the local Gateway label. Their early releases featured spirited versions of **Bob Dylan**'s 'Times They Are A-Changin'' and **Them**'s 'Gloria' while other covers revealed an affection for the **Who** and **Yardbirds**. Signed to **Capitol Records** in 1967, the Beinz enjoyed a US Top 10 hit that year with an interpretation of 'Nobody But Me', originally recorded by the **Isley Brothers**. The quartet embraced a more original direction with the competent *Evolutions*, but disbanded when this brand of superior pop/rock proved unsuccessful.

● ALBUMS: *Nobody But Me* (Capitol 1967)★★, *Evolutions* (Capitol 1968)★★.

● COMPILATIONS: *The Human Beinz With The Mammals* (1968)★★.

Human League

The history of the Human League is essentially that of two radically different UK groups, one experimental and arcane, the other melodic and commercial. The first incarnation of the group formed in the summer of 1978 with a line-up comprising Ian Craig Marsh (b 11 November 1956, Sheffield, England; synthesizer), Martyn Ware (b. 19 May 1956, Sheffield, England; synthesizer), Phil Oakey (b. 2 October 1955, Sheffield, England; vocals) and Addy Newton. The latter left soon after the group was named Human League and was replaced by Adrian Wright (b. 30 June 1956, Sheffield, England), who was credited as 'visual director'. Early in 1978, the group was signed to Robert Last's Edinburgh-based independent label Fast Product. Their first single was the unusual 'Being Boiled', which sold 16,000 copies and resulted in them securing a tie-in deal with **Virgin Records**. Their debut, *Reproduction*, sold steadily, while the EP *Holiday, '80*, won them an appearance on the prestigious television show *Top Of The Pops*. By this point, Philip Oakey's pierced nipples and geometric haircut had made him the focal point of the group. This led to some friction within the Human League, which was not overcome by the chart success of their second album, *Travelogue*. Matters culminated at the end of 1980 with the shock departure of Marsh and Ware, who went on to found BEF and its offshoot group **Heaven 17**. In return for a percentage of royalties on future releases, Marsh and Ware allowed Oakey to retain the name Human League. Instead of recruiting experienced musicians as replacements Oakey, somewhat bizarrely, chose two teenage girls, whom he discovered at a Sheffield discotheque. Susanne Sulley (b. 22 March 1963, Sheffield, England) and Joanne Catherall (b. 16 September 1962, Sheffield, England) had absolutely no knowledge of the music business, had never sung professionally and were busy at school studying for A-levels when Oakey made his offer. The new line-up was completed by bassist Ian Burden (b. 24 December 1957, Sheffield, England) and former **Rezillos** guitarist Jo Callis (b. 2 May 1955, Glasgow, Scotland). The new group contrasted radically with the cold, remote image of the original Human League and pursued a pure pop Holy Grail, which delivered a series of UK hits during 1981. 'Boys And Girls', 'The Sound Of The Crowd', 'Love Action' and 'Open Your Heart' paved the way for the group's celebrated pop album, *Dare*, which sold over five million copies. An extraordinary year ended with the awesome Christmas chart-topper, 'Don't You Want Me', the biggest-selling UK single of 1981. The song was particularly notable for its use of a double point of view, which was brilliantly captured in the accompanying video with Oakey and Catherall trading perspectives on a fragmenting relationship. The track went on to become a number 1 in the USA, spearheading a British invasion of 'new pop' artists. The Human League then took a long sabbatical, interrupted only by a couple of further hits with 'Mirror Man' and '(Keep Feeling) Fascination' and a mini-album of dance remixes. The 1984 comeback album, *Hysteria*, met a mixed response, while the attendant singles, 'The Lebanon', 'Life On Your Own' and 'Louise', all reached the UK Top 20. Oakey ended 1984 by teaming up with disco producer **Giorgio Moroder** for a surprisingly successful single and album. A further two years passed before the next Human League album, *Crash*, and, along the way, Wright and Callis departed. Several of the tracks on the new album were composed by producers Jam and Lewis, among them a US number 1 'Human'. In 1990, the group returned with a new album, which met a cool response. Following a lengthy break from the public eye, and just when the world had seemingly buried them they returned five years later with *Octopus* and a series of sparkling hit singles. Much of the freshness and simplicity of *Dare* was present in the new collection. Singles such as 'Tell Me When' indicated a strong grasp of how repeated hooklines in pop songs can creep into the subconscious - and cannot be resisted. Despite their erratic career, the Human League have shown a remarkable ability to triumph commercially and aesthetically, and usually at the least predictable moments.

● ALBUMS: *Reproduction* (Virgin 1979)★★, *Travelogue* (Virgin 1980)★★, *Dare* (Virgin 1981)★★★★, *Love And Dancing* (Virgin 1982)★★★, *Hysteria* (Virgin 1984)★★, *Crash* (Virgin 1986)★★, *Romantic* (Virgin 1990)★★, *Octopus* (East West 1995)★★★.

● COMPILATIONS: *Human League's Greatest Hits* (Virgin 1988)★★★★, *Greatest Hits* (Virgin 1995)★★★★.

● VIDEOS: *Greatest Video Hits* (Warners 1995).

● FURTHER READING: *The Story Of A Band Called The Human League*, Alaska Ross and Jill Furmanovsky. *The Human League: Perfect Pop*, Peter Nash.

Human Nature

This Australian pop group, packaged and marketed in a manner reminiscent of England's **Take That**, has enjoyed huge success since forming in the mid-90s. However, much of that success has come not from Antipodean markets, but from Japan, where the group have been feted by the teenage press. The group was formed by brothers Andrew and Mike Tierney when they met Toby Allen and Phil Burton while attending high school in Sydney. After taking part in classical singing lessons, the group began rehearsing together as a quartet, practising an a cappella version of 'Earth Angel' for performance at a school concert. The group then approached Sony Music Australia, singing in the office of label president, Denis Handlin. Peddling a hybrid of balladeering pop, hallmarked by the group's beatific harmonies, with dance tunes, the group first reached the charts with 'Got It Goin' On'. The debut album, *Telling Everybody*, followed shortly thereafter, and was released in Japan, Germany and the UK by Epic Records.

● ALBUMS: *Telling Everybody* (Epic/Sony 1996)★★★.

Humble Pie

An early example of the 'supergroup', Humble Pie was formed in April 1969 by **Peter Frampton** (guitar/vocals, ex-**Herd**), **Steve Marriott** (guitar/vocals, ex-**Small Faces**) and Greg Ridley (b. 23 October 1943, Carlisle, Cumbria, England; bass, ex-**Spooky Tooth**). Drummer Jerry Shirley (b. 4 February 1952) completed the original line-up which had a UK Top 5 hit with its debut release, 'Natural Born Bugie'. The quartet's first two albums blended the single's hard-rock style with several acoustic tracks. Having failed to consolidate their early success, Humble Pie abandoned the latter, pastoral direction, precipitating Frampton's departure. He embarked on a prosperous solo career in October 1971, while his former colleagues, now bolstered by former **Colosseum** guitarist **Dave Clempson**, concentrated on wooing US audiences. This period was best captured on *Smokin'*, the group's highest ranking UK chart album. Humble Pie latterly ran out of inspiration and, unable to escape a musical rut, broke up in March 1975. Marriott then formed Steve Marriott's All Stars, which latterly included both Clempson and Ridley, while Shirley joined a new venture, Natural Gas. Tragically, Marriott died on 20 April 1991, following a fire at his Essex home.

● ALBUMS: *As Safe As Yesterday Is* (Immediate 1969)★★★, *Town And Country* (Immediate 1969)★★★, *Humble Pie* (A&M 1970)★★★, *Rock On* (A&M 1971)★★★, *Performance - Rockin' The Fillmore* (A&M 1972)★★, *Smokin'* (A&M 1972)★★, *Eat It* (A&M 1973)★★, *Thunderbox* (A&M 1974)★, *Street Rats* (A&M 1975)★, *On To Victory* (Jet 1980)★, *Go For The Throat* (Jet 1981)★.

● COMPILATIONS: *Crust Of Humble Pie* (EMI 1975)★★, *The Humble Pie Collection* (Castle 1994)★★★.

Humble, Derek

b. 1931, Livingston, Durham, England, d. 22 February 1971. Humble began playing alto saxophone as a child, becoming a professional musician in his mid-teens. In the early 50s he played in bands led by **Vic Lewis**, **Kathy Stobart** and others, working alongside **Peter King**. In 1953 he joined **Ronnie Scott** where he remained for the next few years during which he recorded extensively with **Vic Feldman**, **Jimmy Deuchar**, **Tony Crombie** and other leading British modernists. In 1957 he went to Germany where he began a long association with **Kurt Edelhagen** and, a few years later, with the **Clarke-Boland Big Band** with whom he made several records. In 1970 he began a stint with **Phil Seamen** but his health, never good owing to his lifestyle, deteriorated sharply following a mugging. A gifted player with a direct, passionate solo style, Humble was one of the outstanding alto saxophonists of his generation. His long periods in Europe kept him from attracting the international status he warranted and his early death has helped make him one of the forgotten men of UK jazz.

● ALBUMS: with Clarke-Boland *More Smiles* (1968)★★★.

Humblebums

This Scottish folk-singing duo originally consisted of Tam Harvey (guitar/mandolin) and **Billy Connolly** (b. 1942, Anderston, Glasgow, Scotland; guitar/banjo). Their debut, *First Collection of Merrie Melodies*, showcased a quirky sense of humour, but it was not until Harvey was replaced by **Gerry Rafferty** (b. 16 April 1946, Paisley, Scotland), that the group forged an individuality. Rafferty, a former member of the beat group, Fifth Column, introduced a gift for melody and the first release with Connolly, *The New Humblebums*, featured several excellent compositions, including 'Please Sing A Song For Us' and 'Her Father Didn't Like Me Anyway'. A further collection, *Open Up The Door*, confirmed Rafferty's skills but the contrast between his **Paul McCartney**-influenced compositions ('My Singing Bird') and his partner's lighter, more whimsical offerings was too great to hold under one banner. Connolly returned to the folk circuit, where his between-songs banter quickly became the focal point of his act and introduced a newfound role as a successful comedian. Meanwhile his erstwhile partner began his solo career in 1971 with *Can I Have My Money Back*, before forming a new group, **Stealers Wheel**.

● ALBUMS: *First Collection Of Merrie Melodies* (1968)★★★, *The New Humblebums* (1969)★★★, *Open Up The Door* (1970)★★★.

● COMPILATIONS: *The Humblebums* (1981)★★★, *Early Collection* (1987)★★★, *The New Humblebums/Open Up The Door* (Transatlantic 1997)★★★.

Humes, Helen

b. 23 June 1913, Louisville, Kentucky, USA, d. 13 September 1981. Coming from a happy, close-knit, musical family, Humes learned to play trumpet and piano. As a child she sang with the local Sunday school band, which boasted future jazz stars such as **Dicky Wells** and **Jonah Jones**. In 1927 she made her first records for the **OKeh** label in St. Louis. Humes then went to New York where she recorded again, this time accompanied by **James P. Johnson**, and worked for several years with the orchestra led by Vernon Andrade, star of Harlem's Renaissance Ballroom. She also recorded with **Harry James**. In 1937 she was offered a job by **Count Basie** but turned it down because the pay was too meagre. The following year she changed her mind and signed up, replacing **Billie Holiday**. Her recordings with Basie mixed attractive performances of poor-quality songs and marvellous versions of the better material she was given. She left Basie in 1941 to freelance, and by 1944 was working on the west coast; she had moved into the then popular R&B field. Humes had a big hit with 'Be-Baba-Leba', recorded with **Bill Doggett**. On a 1947 session in New York, supervised by **John Hammond Jnr.**, she made some excellent mainstream jazz records with **Buck Clayton** and **Teddy Wilson**. By the 50s, despite another big hit with 'Million Dollar Secret', her career was in the doldrums as the R&B tag she had acquired proved somewhat limiting. This hiatus continued into the late 60s, at which time she retired to care for ailing members of her family. In 1973 the writer and record producer Stanley Dance persuaded her out of retirement and into an appearance with Basie at the Newport Jazz Festival. This date was a great success and Humes returned to full-time singing. Equally at home with ballads, to which she brought faultless jazz phrasing, blues shouting and R&B rockers, Humes was one of the outstanding singers of her day. Her light, clear voice retained its youthful sound even into her 60s, and late-period recordings were among the best she ever made.

● ALBUMS: including *T'ain't Nobody's Biz-ness If I Do* (Contemporary 1959)★★★, *Helen Humes* (1959)★★★, *Songs I Like To Sing* (1960)★★★, *Swingin' With Humes* (1961)★★★, *Helen Comes Back* (1973)★★★, *Helen Humes* (1974)★★★, *On The Sunny Side Of The Street* (Black Lion 1974)★★★, with Gerard Badini *Sneaking Around* (Black And Blue 1974)★★★, *The Incomparable Helen Humes* (1974)★★★, *Talk Of The Town* (1975)★★★, *Helen Humes And The Muse All Stars* (Muse 1979)★★★, *Helen* (Muse 1980)★★★, *The New Years Eve* (Le Chant Du Monde 1980)★★★, *Live At The Aurex Jazz Festival, Tokyo, '81* (1980)★★★, *Let The Good Times Roll* (Black And Blue 1983)★★★, *Swing With Helen Humes And Wynton Kelly* (Contemporary 1983)★★★, *Helen Humes With The Connie Berry Trio* (Audiophile 1988)★★★, *New Million Dollar Secret* (Whiskey Women And Song 1988)★★★, *Deed I Do* (Contemporary 1995)★★★.

● COMPILATIONS: *Be-Baba-Leba* rec. 1944-52 (Whiskey Women And Song 1991)★★★.

Hummon, Marcus

b. Washington DC, USA. The country singer Marcus Hummon was the son of a US diplomat and grew up travelling the world, living in Africa, Italy and the Philippines. Hummon developed a love of country music but his influences also include **James Taylor** and **John Denver**. While at college, he played many clubs in the Washington area with his three sisters and built up a strong reputation. In 1986, he moved to Nashville and had his first success as a songwriter with 'Pilgrims On The Way (Mathew's Song)' for **Michael Martin Murphey**. He wrote 'Only Love', a Grammy-nominated hit for **Wynonna**, 'Cheap Seats' (**Alabama**), 'Over My Shoulder' (**Patty Loveless**), 'Every Little Word' (**Hal Ketchum**) and 'Honky Tonk Mona Lisa' (**Doug Stone**). He has also written 'The Pathway To The Moon' for the British group MN8. His band is called Red Wing, but he came to the UK with just his steel player, Darrell Scott, for dates supporting **Alison Krauss** in 1995.

● ALBUMS: *All In Good Time* (Columbia 1995)★★★.

Humperdinck, Engelbert

b. Arnold George Dorsey, 2 May 1936, Madras, India. Originally known as Gerry Dorsey, this singer had attempted to achieve mainstream success in the UK during the 50s. He was a featured artist on the television series *Oh Boy*, toured with **Marty Wilde** and recorded a failed single, 'I'll Never Fall In Love Again'. It was during this period that he first met **Gordon Mills**, a singer in the **Viscounts**, who later moved into songwriting and management. By 1963, Dorsey's career had hit rock bottom. The beat boom hampered his singing career and to make matters worse, he fell seriously ill with tuberculosis. Mills, meanwhile, was beginning to win international success for **Tom Jones** and in 1967 decided to help his old friend Gerry Dorsey. Soon after, the singer was rechristened Engelbert Humperdinck, a name inspired by the composer of Hansel And Gretel, and relaunched as a balladeer. His first single for **Decca Records**, 'Dommage Dommage', failed to chart, but received considerable airplay. There was no mistake with the follow-up, 'Release Me', which sold a million copies in the UK alone, dominated the number 1 spot for five weeks and, most remarkably, prevented the **Beatles** from reaching the top with the magnificent 'Penny Lane'/'Strawberry Fields Forever'. Humperdinck's follow-up, 'There Goes My Everything', climbed to number 2 in the UK and by the end of the summer he was back at the top for a further five weeks with 'The Last Waltz'. The latter once again sold in excess of a million copies in the UK alone. In a year dominated by psychedelia and experimentation in rock, Humperdinck was the biggest-selling artist in England. His strong vocal and romantic image ensured regular bookings and brought a further series of UK Top 10 hits including 'Am I That Easy To Forget', 'A Man Without Love', 'Les Bicyclettes De Belsize', 'The Way It Used To Be' and 'Winter World Of Love'. Although he faded as a hit-making artist after the early 70s, his career blossomed in America where he was a regular on the lucrative Las Vegas circuit. Like his stablemate Tom Jones he went through a long period without recording, which ended in 1987 with the release of a comeback album, *Remember I Love You*, which featured a duet with **Gloria Gaynor**. In 1990, it was estimated that he had earned 58 Gold records, 18 Platinum albums, and several Grammy Awards He was still selling plenty of albums, and filling venues such as London's Royal Albert Hall, well into the 90s.

● ALBUMS: *Release Me* (Decca 1967)★★★, *The Last Waltz* (Decca 1967)★★★, *A Man Without Love* (1968)★★★, *Engelbert* (1969)★★★, *Engelbert Humperdinck* (1969)★★★, *We Made It Happen* (1970)★★, *Another Time, Another Place* (1971)★★, *Live At The Riviera* (1972)★★★, *Getting Sentimental* (1975)★★, *Remember I Love You* (1987)★★★, *Hello Out There* (1992)★★★, with Tom Jones *Back To Back* (1993)★★★.

● COMPILATIONS: *Engelbert Humperdinck - His Greatest Hits* (1974)★★★, *The Engelbert Humperdinck Collection* (1987)★★★, *The Best Of ... Live* (Repertoire 1995)★★★, *The Collection* (Spectrum 1998).

● FURTHER READING: *Engelbert Humperdinck: The Authorized Biography*, Don Short.

Humphrey, Percy

b. 1905, New Orleans, Louisiana, USA, d. 22 July 1995, New Orleans, Louisiana, USA. Humphrey enjoyed a long career as a trumpeter and bandleader in the pre-war dixieland dance band scene. Having played in or around New Orleans with the Louisiana Jazz Hounds, Sweet Emma Barret, the Eureka Brass Band, George Lewis And The Crescent City Joy Makers, he founded his own band in 1925. In the 30s Humphrey toured with **Bessie Smith**, but turned down the chance of national fame to remain with his family in New Orleans. He remained active on the local scene there, and in 1961 he founded the Preservation Hall. He continued to appear with the Preservation Hall Jazz Band regularly, until his elder brother, Willie Humphrey, died in 1994. His last performance came as the closing act at the annual New Orleans Jazz and Heritage Festival jazz tent, an honour he had been afforded over several years for his contribution to the local music community. He was still an active musician when he died of heart failure in 1995, aged 90.

Humphrey, Willie

b. 29 December 1900, New Orleans, Louisiana, USA, d. 7 June 1994. A member of a highly musical family, Humphrey started out on violin before switching to clarinet. His brothers Earl and **Percy Humphrey** played trombone and trumpet respectively. After playing in local bands and on riverboats, Humphrey moved to Chicago in 1919, playing briefly in bands led by **Freddie Keppard** and **Joe 'King' Oliver**. Between 1920 and the early 30s he played in New Orleans and St Louis. After a short spell in **Lucky Millinder**'s big band, Humphrey settled in New Orleans where, war service and an occasional tour apart, he remained. Over the years he played in several bands including those led by **Paul Barbarin**,

Sweet Emma Barrett and De De Pierce. Playing in a forceful manner, deeply rooted in the New Orleans tradition, Humphrey remained a vigorous and enthusiastic performer into his old age.

● ALBUMS: *Billie And De De Pierce In Scandanavia* (1967)★★★, *New Orleans Clarinet* (1974)★★★★, *New Orleans Jazz* (GHB 1989)★★★, *Two Clarinets On The Porch* (GHB 1992)★★★.

Humphries, Tony

Legendary for his shows on New York's Kiss FM, New Jersey-born Humphries was a hugely influential figure in development of the east coast dance scene. His support for **Adeva**'s 'Respect', for instance, was the essential ingredient in her winning a record contract. Humphries gained access to the radio after meeting **Shep Pettibone** in 1981, who approved of his demo cassette. His break as a live DJ was offered in the same year by Larry Patterson. Previously he had been a mobile jock and worked for the *New York Daily* newspaper. Patterson gave him his opportunity at the Zanzibar club which became New Jersey's premier nightspot. Humphries has gone on to produce and remix for a huge variety of clients, just a smattering of which include **Mass Order** ('Lift Every Voice'), **Alison Limerick** ('Make It On My Own', 'Hear My Call'), **Bananarama** ('Movin' On'), **KLF** ('3AM Eternal'), **Cure** ('Love Cats'), **Jungle Brothers** ('What Are You Waiting For'), **Steel Pulse** ('Rollerskates') and **Evelyn King** ('Shakedown') - which represents a mere fraction of his client list. He moved to the UK in 1992 to start a residency at the **Ministry Of Sound**, while in 1994 Romanthony's 'In The Mix' (on **Azuli**) celebrated his status by building a song out of the repetition of Tony Humphries name.

Hunky Dory - David Bowie

David Bowie's most eclectic album acknowledged 60s mentors and prepared the artist for subsequent musical directions. Andy Warhol, Bob Dylan and the Velvet Underground were illiberally canonized, and a veneer of menace bubbled beneath the surface of several sweet pop songs, especially 'Life On Mars'. Is it Lennon or Lenin that is on sale again? The subject matter embraced transexuality, Nitszche and science fiction. Guitarist Mick Ronson proved a sympathetic foil amid a support cast that understood Bowie's chameleon-like qualities and reacted accordingly. The singer's eclectic interests have never been captured so confidently, even though he sings 'didn't know what I was looking for' in 'Changes'.

● Tracks: *Changes; Oh! You Pretty Thing; Eight Line Poem; Life On Mars?; Kooks; Quicksand; Fill Your Heart (Biff); Andy Warhol; Song For Bob Dylan; Queen Bitch; The Bewlay Brothers.*
● First released 1971
● UK peak chart position: 3
● USA peak chart position: 93

Hunley, Con

b. Conrad Logan Hunley, 9 April 1945, Luttrell, Knox County, Tennessee, USA. The Hunley family were known as a local gospel singing group and from an early age Con appeared with them. He grew up an admirer of **Chet Atkins** and for a time sought to emulate his idol; however, he quickly realized that the guitar was not to be his instrument and instead turned his attention to the piano. Influenced by **Ray Charles** and singing somewhat like **Charlie Rich**, he began to play in groups during his high school years and during his time in the US Air Force, played in various bands. After his discharge he returned to Knoxville, first working in a mill but soon found work in local country clubs. In 1976, he formed his own band and recorded five singles for the minor Prairie Dust label. Some were his own compositions and three of the recordings became minor hits in the US country charts, helping to build his reputation. He decided to move to Nashville in 1977 and as a result of appearances at **George Jones**' *Possum Holler*, he managed to secure a contract with **Warner Brothers**. His first release on that label was **Jimmy C. Newman**'s song 'Cry, Cry Darling' which went to number 34 in the charts. He followed this with 11 successive Top 20 hits, including 'Week End Friend', 'You've Still Got A Place In My Heart', 'I've Been Waiting For You All Of My Life' (a pop hit for **Paul Anka** two years later) and in 1982, 'Oh Girl', which had been a number 1 pop hit for the **Chi-Lites** 10 years earlier. During the 80s the hits became less frequent. He recorded a version of 'Satisfied Mind' that featured a guest vocal from **Porter Wagoner** (who had a hit with the song in 1955) and in 1986, he charted with 'Blue Suede Shoes'. Perhaps prophetically, his last successful record was in 1986 with a song called 'Quittin' Time' - whether it was remains to be seen.

● ALBUMS: *Con Hunley* (Warners 1979)★★, *I Don't Want To Lose You* (Warners 1980)★★★, *Don't It Break Your Heart* (Warners 1980)★★★, *Ask Any Woman* (Warners 1981)★★, *Oh Girl* (Warners 1982)★★.

Hunningale, Peter

b. *c.*1962, London, England. Hunningale, aka Mr Honey Vibes, established his reputation in the **lovers rock** idiom. He began his musical career playing bass as part of the Vibes Corner Collective, which also featured Barrington Levine, Jimmy Simpson, Ray Simpson and Fitzroy Blake. In 1982 he released his debut as a singer, 'Slipping Away'/'Swing And Dine', which sold respectably on LGR Records. 'Got To Know You'/'Money Money' was then issued on his own Street Vibes label, which he co-founded with long-term collaborator Blake (it is now run in association with **Tippa Irie** and Crucial Robbie). In 1987 he topped the UK reggae chart with 'Be My Lady', regarded by many as his debut. The success of this single and his debut album led to a prolific period that included the singles 'Falling', 'Its My Turn', 'If You Want It' and 'Mr Vibes'. The popularity of combination hits from Jamaica inspired Hunningale and Tippa Irie to team up for 'Ragamuffin Girl' in 1989, which went straight to number 1 in the UK reggae charts, and was voted Best British Reggae Record by *Echoes* newspaper at the close of the year; the single led to a long and fruitful partnership with Irie. With this success behind them they embarked on two album collaborations - *The New Decade* for **Island Records** and *Done Cook And Currie* for **Rebel MC**'s Tribal Base label. The former collection was produced by Hunningale himself and featured two songs popular on the UK sound system circuit, 'Shocking Out' and 'Dibi Dibi'. He also produced and played all the instruments on *Done Cook And Currie*, which produced another major domestic reggae hit with 'Inner City'. His second solo album, *Mr Vibes*, followed in the same year. Hunningale's next collaboration with Irie came in 1993, this time a single, 'Shouting For The Gunners', to celebrate their mutual fondness for the London football club Arsenal. The following year's *Mr Government* was a more roots-flavoured offering, released on the **Mad Professor**'s **Ariwa Sounds** label, after which Hunningale worked with Crucial Robbie once more on a version of **Desmond Dekker**'s '007'.

Throughout Hunningale's career awards have been bestowed upon him, including Best Newcomer in 1987, Best Reggae Vocalist Of The Year in 1989 and 1991 and in the mid-90s he made a rare television appearance after winning additional accolades in the Black Music Association Awards. Hunningale also demonstrated his versatility when he performed in the reggae musical *Johnny Dollar* and secured his independence with the inauguration of the Street Vibes label. As well as recording many hits in the UK, Hunningale also worked with legendary Jamaican producer **Gussie Clarke**, which resulted in 'Love Like This'.

Hunningale's outstanding achievements continued in 1995 when Lloyd 'Musclehead' Francis's production of his hit 'Baby Please' knocked his Gussie P production of 'Perfect Lady' from the number 1 position in the reggae chart. In 1995 Hunningale recorded a version of 'Declaration Of Rights' in a reunion with Tippa Irie, which featured on his *Nah Give Up* compilation, alongside such reggae chart hits as 'Trust Me' and 'Sorry'. Hunningale displayed his honeyed voice on songs including 'Out In The Country', 'Candy', 'Crazy Love', 'How Could I Leave' and 'Love Is Here To Stay'. A series of popular duets with **Dennis Brown**, Lloyd Brown and Janet Lee Davis, performing 'Cupid', 'Lonely Girl' and 'We Can Work It Out', respectively, all met with approval. His distinguished career has also seen him work with artists such as the Original Pioneers, **Maxi Priest** (writing the title track to his *Best Of Me* hit album), **Chosen Few**, **Trevor Hartley**, Double Trouble, Tinga Stewart and **B.B. Seaton**, as well as many others, either as musician, producer or writer. Late in 1996 Hunningale performed as part of the combination Passion, which also included **Glamma Kid** and **Nerious Joseph**, among others. 'Share Your Love', their version of **Teddy Riley**'s R&B hit, 'No Diggity', spent over eight weeks at number 1 on the reggae chart.

● ALBUMS: *In This Time* (Level Vibes 1987)★★★, with Tippa Irie *The New Decade* (Mango/Island 1991)★★★★, *Mr Vibes* (Street Vibes 1992)★★★, with Tippa Irie *Done Cook And Currie* (Tribal Base 1992)★★★, *Mr Government* (Ariwa Sounds 1994)★★★.

● COMPILATIONS: *Nah Give Up* (Kalymazoo 1995)★★★★, *Reggae Max* (Jet Star 1996)★★★.

Hunsecker, Ralph Blane
(see **Blane, Ralph**)

Hunt

A Canadian trio of Paul Dickinson (guitar/vocals), Carl Calvert (bass) and Paul Kersey (drums), the Hunt formed in the late 70s and set about establishing their reputation as a high quality pomp rock and AOR band. Recording three studio albums over a five year period for three different labels, the group never settled into an established pattern, which was both their chief failing and saving grace. After their more grandiose debut, 1980's *Back On The Hunt* was a mainstream blues-rock orientated effort, while *The Thrill Of The Kill* was close in conception to a **Ted Nugent** album, notwithstanding its title. Such eclecticism, which endeared them to some critics and the group's considerable fan base, nevertheless continued to confuse their record labels, and by the mid-80s the Hunt found themselves without a recording contract.

● ALBUMS: *The Hunt* (Daffodil 1978)★★★, *Back On The Hunt* (Visa 1980)★★★, *The Thrill Of The Kill* (Passport 1982)★★★.

Hunt, Clive

b. c.1955, Linstead, St. Catherine, Jamaica, West Indies. Hunt originally trained as a tailor and learnt to play the trumpet while at school. At the age of 17 he joined the Jamaican Military Band, where he honed his trumpeting skills. He was initially recruited by **Byron Lee** as part of the Dragonaires and joined them on their tour of North America. On his return, Hunt became involved in playing on a number of sessions in Jamaica, including **Culture**'s *Combolo*, which was produced by **Sonia Pottinger** at the reactivated Treasure Isle Studios in Bond Street. In the latter half of the 70s Hunt emigrated to New York, USA, where he teamed up with **Chalice** and co-wrote the hit for **Joe Gibbs**, 'Good To Be There', although there was subsequently some dispute regarding the origins of the song. Hunt's association with Gibbs also resulted in the composition 'Milk And Honey' for **Dennis Brown**; Hunt played trumpet on the sessions for Brown's *Spellbound* and co-produced his 1981 **A&M Records** debut, *Foul Play*. Hunt then began working with Wackies, where he played on sessions and performed as a soloist, recording 'Rockfort Rock' as Clive 'Azul' Hunt. He remained a US citizen until 1987 but then returned to Jamaica, where his career as a producer and arranger flourished. He produced a number of singles with **Beres Hammond**, including the perennial 'Putting Up Resistance'. Hunt's reputation grew and he worked on the internationally successful 'I Can See Clearly Now' for **Jimmy Cliff**, the **Steely And Clevie** remake of 'You Don't Love (No No No)' for **Dawn Penn**, and was employed by veteran rockers the **Rolling Stones**. In 1994 Hunt co-produced **Judy Mowatt**'s *Life* on her own Judy M label, later released by Pow Wow as *Rock Me*. Much of Hunt's production work was based at **Bob Marley**'s Tuff Gong studio where he worked with the **Abyssinians** remaking their classic hits, and also with **Tyrone Taylor**, the I-Threes, **Yvad**, Richie Spice and **Garnett Silk**.

Hunt, Fred

b. 21 September 1923, London, England, d. 25 April 1986. A self-taught pianist, Hunt began playing jazz in the 40s. In the next decade he emerged as a significant figure in traditional jazz when, after stints with **Mike Daniels** and **Cy Laurie**, he joined **Alex Welsh**. Throughout the 50s and 60s, Hunt could be heard with Welsh where he was a featured soloist as well as a stalwart member of the robustly swinging rhythm section. His work with Welsh did not prevent him from accompanying visiting Americans, including recording with the four-tenor group, Tenor Of Jazz, featuring **Ben Webster** and **Eddie 'Lockjaw' Davis**, which toured in the late 60s. In the mid-70s Hunt left the UK, residing successively in South Africa, Denmark and Germany. At the end of the decade he returned to the UK but soon afterwards retired through ill health. Although remembered primarily for his long association with Welsh, Hunt's eclectic, strong style made him a sought-after and thoroughly dependable player in both traditional and mainstream settings.

● ALBUMS: with Alex Welsh *The Melrose Folio* (1958)★★, with Welsh *Echoes Of Chicago* (1962)★★★, *Pearls On Velvet* (1968)★★★.

Hunt, Geraldine

b. Chicago, Illinois, USA. Hunt attended the same school as **Minnie Ripperton** and took time off from her studies to release her first single, 'I Let Myself Go', in 1962. Hunt's first US R&B chart entry came in 1970 with 'You & I', a duet with Charlie Hodges. She had two more small soul hits on Roulette in the early 70s. She relocated to Montreal, Canada, shortly after and by the late 70s had her first French language hit there with 'Ne Me Dis Pas Adieu'. In 1980 she signed to Canadian disco label Unidisc and her production of her own song 'Can't Fake The Feeling' returned her to the US R&B chart and became her only UK Top 40 entry. In 1982 her composition 'Murphy's Law', which she also produced, was a transatlantic hit for **Cheri**, a duo that included her daughter Rosalind.

Hunt, Marsha

b. 1946, Philadelphia, USA. Singer Hunt arrived in the UK during the mid-60s and emerged as a solo act following a spell in the chorus of the London production of *Hair*. A series of powerful live performances ensued, including the 1969 Isle Of Wight Festival, on which she was backed by Scottish group (White) **Trash**. Her debut single was a rousing version of 'Walk On Guilded Splinters', originally recorded by **Dr John**, but despite critical acclaim, the singer's fiery brand of rock had only limited appeal. Follow-up releases included **Paul Simon**'s 'Keep The Customer Satisfied' and **Marc Bolan**'s 'Hot Rod Poppa', while the latter artist contributed two further songs to *Woman Child*, which he also produced. Hunt then turned to acting, but resumed singing in 1973 with Marsha Hunt's 22. Her subsequent career included a period hosting a chat show on Capital Radio, and Hunt later drew publicity during a successful paternity suit against **Mick Jagger**. The artist's thespian ambitions were furthered as a member of both the Royal Shakespeare Company and the Royal National Theatre and in 1985 she published her autobiography, *Real Life*. Hunt's first novel, *Joy*, followed in 1990 and she has subsequently become established as a writer.

● ALBUMS: *Woman Child* (Track 1971)★★★.
● COMPILATIONS: *Walk On Guilded Splinters* (1987)★★★.
● FURTHER READING: *Real Life*, Marsha Hunt. *Joy*, Marsha Hunt.

Hunt, Pee Wee

b. Walter Hunt, 10 May 1907, Mt. Healthy, Ohio, USA, d. 22 June 1979, Plymouth, Massachusetts, USA. A bandleader since the mid-40s, Pee Wee Hunt came from a musical family, his father being a violinist and his mother a banjoist. Hunt also started playing banjo during his teen years and after graduating from Cincinnati Conservatory of Music and Ohio State University, he began playing with local bands. He played both banjo and trombone before becoming trombonist with **Jean Goldkette**'s Orchestra in 1928. A year later he joined **Glen Gray**'s Orange Blossoms, a Detroit band that eventually became known as the **Casa Loma Orchestra**, and remained a heavily featured member of that unit for many years, providing not only a solid line in trombone choruses but also a large portion of likeable vocals. Hunt eventually left the Casa Loma in 1943, and became a Hollywood radio disc jockey for a while before spending the closing period of the war as a member of the Merchant Marine. He returned to the west coast music scene again in 1946, forming his own dixieland outfit and playing the Hollywood Palladium, where audience reaction to his pure hokum version of '12th Street Rag' was so enthusiastic that Hunt decided to record the number at one of the band's **Capitol** sessions. The result was a hit that topped the US charts for eight weeks in 1948. Five years later, Hunt was in the charts again with a cornball version of 'Oh!', an evergreen song from 1919. Like

'12th Street Rag' it became a million-seller and charted for nearly six months. This proved to be Hunt's last major record and the trombonist dropped from the limelight, but still continued playing his happy music until his death in June 1979.

● ALBUMS: *Plays And Sings Dixie* (1958)★★★, *Cole Porter A La Dixie* (1958)★★★★, *Blues A La Dixie* (1959)★★★★, *Dixieland Kickoff!* (1959)★★★, *Dance Party* (1960)★★★, *Saturday Night Dancing Party* (1961)★★★.

● COMPILATIONS: *Masters Of Dixieland, Volume Six* (1975)★★★.

Hunt, Tommy

b. Charles Hunt, 18 June 1933, Pittsburgh, Pennsylvania, USA. Hunt's dramatic pop-soul vocals, on string-drenched ballads, perfectly represented the **Brill Building** sound of the early 60s. He had a long career in vocal groups prior to his solo career of the early 60s. In 1952 and 1953 he was a member of the Chicago-based Five Echoes along with future soul superstar **Johnnie Taylor**. He was a member of the **Flamingos** from 1958 to 1961. His biggest hit was 'Human' (number 5 R&B, number 48 pop) in 1961, recorded for Scepter Records. He recorded other top-notch material for the company, including 'I Am A Witness' (1963) and the original version of 'I Just Don't Know What To Do For Myself', which later became a hit for **Dusty Springfield**. His last hit was the wonderful Luther Dixon-produced hit 'The Biggest Man', for the Dynamo label in 1967. He moved to England in the 70s and recorded for **Polydor** in 1972 and Pye in 1974. In the late 70s he was a star on the northern soul circuit, and had a hit with a revival of **Roy Hamilton**'s 'Crackin' Up' on the Spark label, the first of three UK hits. He recorded two albums while in England, *Live At The Wigan Casino* (1975), a collection of 60s soul songs, and *A Sign Of The Times* (1976), a collection of songs that reflected the tastes of northern soul fans.

● ALBUMS: *I Just Don't Know What To Do With Myself* (Scepter 1962)★★★, *Live At The Wigan Casino* (Spark 1975)★★, *A Sign Of The Times* (Spark 1976)★★★.

● COMPILATIONS: *Tommy Hunt's Greatest Hits* (Dynamo 1967)★★★★, *Your Man* (Kent 1986)★★★, *Human: His Golden Classics* (Collectables 1991)★★★, *The Biggest Man* (Kent 1997)★★★★.

Hunter Muskett

A fine band of UK singer/songwriters, presenting a rich blend of pseudo ballads. The group was also notable for the inclusion of future **Magna Carta/Albion** guitarist Doug Morter.

● ALBUMS: *Every Time You Move* (Decca Nova 1970)★★★, *Hunter Muskett* (Bradleys 1973)★★.

Hunter, 'Long John'

b. John Thurman Hunter, 13 July 1931, Ringold, Louisiana, USA. The son of a sharecropper, Hunter was raised on a farm in Magnolia, Arkansas. Until his mid-20s, he heard little else but country music, only hearing

blues after moving to Beaumont, Texas, to work in a box factory. Attending a **B.B. King** gig, he was inspired to attempt to play the guitar after witnessing its effect on women. From 1955, he spent three years in Houston, having one record, 'Crazy Girl', released on the Duke label. On 7 August 1957, he moved with his band, The Hollywood Bearcats, to El Paso. Soon after his arrival, he was engaged to play the Lobby Club, a residence he held for more than a decade. Between 1961 and 1971, he made four rock-oriented singles, including 'El Paso Rock' and 'The Scratch', for Yucca Records in Alamogordo, New Mexico. In 1986, he recorded his first album for the Boss label. His second, *Ride With Me*, was recorded in Austin in 1992 with Texas veterans **T.D. Bell** and Erbie Bowser, and the Antones' rhythm section. Hunter's lean guitar style and characterful voice are evidence that there is more to Texas blues than **Albert Collins**.

● ALBUMS: *Texas Border Town Blues* (Boss 1986)★★★, *Ride With Me* (Antones 1992)★★★, *Border Town Legend* (Alligator 1996)★★★★, *Swinging From The Rafters* (Alligator 1997)★★★.

Hunter, Alberta

b. 1 April 1895, Memphis, Tennessee, USA, d. 17 October 1984. Growing up in Chicago, Hunter began her remarkable career singing at Dago Frank's, one of the city's least salubrious whorehouses. There she sang for the girls, the pimps and the customers, earning both their admiration and good money from tips. Later, she moved on and marginally upwards to a job singing in Hugh Hoskins' saloon. She continued to move through Chicago's saloons and bars, gradually developing a following. She entered the big time with an engagement at the Dreamland Cafe, where she sang with **Joe 'King' Oliver**'s band. Among the songs she sang was 'Down Hearted Blues', which she composed in collaboration with **Lovie Austin** and which was recorded in 1923 by **Bessie Smith**. Early in her career she sometimes performed and occasionally recorded under different names, including **May Alix** and Josephine Beaty. During the 20s and early 30s Hunter often worked in New York, singing and recording with many leading jazzmen of the day, among them **Louis Armstrong**, **Sidney Bechet**, **Eubie Blake**, **Fletcher Henderson** and **Fats Waller**. She also appeared in various shows on and off Broadway. A visit to London prompted so much interest that she was offered the role of Queenie in *Show Boat* at the Drury Lane Theatre, playing opposite **Paul Robeson** in the 1928/9 season. During the 30s she frequently returned to London to appear at hotels and restaurants, including an engagement at the Dorchester Hotel with Jack Jackson's popular band. She also appeared in the UK musical film *Radio Parade Of 1935*. The 30s saw her in Paris and Copenhagen too, consistently meeting with enormous success. In the 40s she continued to appear at New York clubs and to make records, notably with **Eddie Heywood**. These recordings include two of her own compositions, 'My Castle's

Rockin'' and 'The Love I Have For You'. In the war years she toured extensively to perform for US troops. In the early 50s she visited the UK with **Snub Mosley** and again toured with the USO, this time to Korea. She played a number of club dates, but, due to increasingly hard times, in 1954 she retired from showbusiness. At that time, aged 60, she began a new career as a nurse. In 1961 writer and record producer Chris Alberston persuaded her to record two albums, but she continued to concentrate on her new profession. Then, in 1977, her employers belatedly realized that diminutive Nurse Hunter was 82 and insisted that she should retire. Having already lived a remarkably full life she could have been forgiven for calling it a day, but she was a tough and spirited lady. She supplied the score for the film *Remember My Name* (1978) and, invited to sing at Barney Josephson's club, The Cookery in Greenwich Village, New York, she was a smash hit and began her singing career anew. She made numerous club and concert appearances, made more records and appeared on several television shows. Hunter sang with power and conviction, her contralto voice having a distinct but attractive vibrato. Inimitably interpreting every nuance of the lyrics, especially when they were her own, she made many fine recordings. Even late in her career, she ably controlled her audiences with a delicate but firm hand, all the time displaying a sparkling wit and a subtle way with a risqué lyric. It is hard to think of any singer who has improved upon her performances of certain songs, notably 'The Love I Have For You' and 'Someday, Sweetheart'.

● COMPILATIONS: including *Alberta Hunter With Lovie Austin And Her Blues Serenaders* (1961)★★★, *Amtrak Blues* (c.1980)★★★, *Classic Alberta Hunter: The Thirties* recorded 1935-40 (Stash 1981)★★★★, *The Legendary* (DRG 1983)★★★, *The Glory Of* (Columbia 1986)★★★, *Complete Works 1921-46, Volumes 1-4* 4-CD set(Document 1996)★★★.
● VIDEOS: *My Castle's Rockin'* (Virgin Vision 1992).

Hunter, Alfonzo

b. c.1973, USA. Despite starting his musical career as a jazz alto saxophonist, Alfonzo Hunter was subsequently driven to find work outside of a declining live scene in Chicago, Illinois. His determination was rewarded when he built a new audience for his singing capabilities. He auditioned as a back-up musician for R&B star **R. Kelly**, but Kelly opted to use him as a full-time backing singer instead of a saxophonist. His debut vocal set combined the spaciousness of hip hop grooves with more complex jazz songwriting conventions and ideas. Nine of the 13 tracks were produced by Erick Sermon (**EPMD**) in his role as founder of the label and production team, Def Squad. Much of the recording was tailored to Sermon's preference for spontaneous performances in the studio. This imbued *Blacka Da Berry* with an engaging freshness, accentuated by Hunter's evident talents as a vocalist.
● ALBUMS: *Blacka Da Berry* (Def Squad/EMI 1996)★★★.

Hunter, Chris

b. 21 February 1957, London, England. Hunter took up the saxophone at the age of 12 and later studied improvisation with **Don Rendell**. Between 1976 and 1978 he played with the New York Jazz Orchestra with whom he toured Europe and the USSR. During the late 70s he worked extensively with **Mike Westbrook**'s Brass Band and became involved in studio work where his excellent technique and committed soloing were much in demand. In 1983 he played with **Gil Evans**' British Orchestra and in the following year moved to New York where he continued to work and tour with Evans. He also worked with the **Michel Camilo** Sextet and then back in Europe as soloist on projects with the Metropole Orchestra, Holland and with **Mike Gibbs** and the Cologne Radio Orchestra.
● ALBUMS: with Mike Westbrook *Mama Chicago* (1979)★★★, *The Cortège* (1982)★★★★; *Early Days* (1980)★★★, *The Warriors* (1981)★★; with Gil Evans *The British Orchestra* (1983)★★★★, *Gil Evans And The Monday Night Orchestra Live At Sweet Basil* (1984)★★★★; with Michel Camilo *The Michel Camilo Sextet* (1985)★★★.

Hunter, Ian

b. 3 June 1946, Shrewsbury, Shropshire, England. Having served a musical apprenticeship in several contrasting groups, Hunter was employed as a contract songwriter when approached to audition for a new act recently signed by **Island Records**. Initially known as Silence, the band took the name **Mott The Hoople** on his installation and Hunter's gravelly vocals and image-conscious looks - omnipresent dark glasses framed by long Dylanesque curly hair - established the vocalist/pianist as the group's focal point. He remained their driving force until 1974 when, having collapsed from physical exhaustion, he left the now-fractious line-up to begin a career as a solo artist. Late-period Mott guitarist **Mick Ronson** quit at the same time and the pair agreed to pool resources for particular projects. Ronson produced and played on *Ian Hunter*, which contained the singer's sole UK hit, 'Once Bitten Twice Shy'. Having toured together as Hunter/Ronson with Peter Arnesen (keyboards), Jeff Appleby (bass) and Dennis Elliott (drums), the colleagues embarked on separate paths. *All American Alien Boy* contained contributions from **Aynsley Dunbar**, **David Sanborn** and several members of **Queen**, but despite several promising tracks, the set lacked the artist's erstwhile passion. *Overnight Angels* continued this trend towards musical conservatism, although following a period of seclusion, Hunter aligned himself with the punk movement by producing *Beyond The Valley Of The Dolls* for **Generation X**. *You're Never Alone With A Schizophrenic* marked his reunion with Ronson and subsequent live dates were commemorated on *Ian Hunter Live/Welcome To The Club*, which drew material from their respective careers. Hunter's output during the 80s was minimal, occasionally recording songs for film soundtracks, and in 1990 he resumed his partnership with Ronson on *YUI Orta*. He made an appearance at the 1992 **Freddie Mercury** AIDS benefit and in 1995 was once again tempted out of retirement to front the all-star band, Ian Hunter's Dirty Laundry, which featured ex-**Crybabys** Darrell Barth and Honest John Plain, plus Vom (ex-**Doctor And The Medics**), Casino Steele (ex-**Hollywood Brats**) and Glen Matlock (ex-**Sex Pistols**).

● ALBUMS: *Ian Hunter* (Columbia 1975)★★★, *All American Alien Boy* (Columbia 1976)★★, *Overnight Angels* (Columbia 1977)★★, *You're Never Alone With A Schizophrenic* (Chrysalis 1979)★★★, *Ian Hunter Live/Welcome To The Club* double album (Chrysalis 1980)★★★, *Short Back And Sides* (Chrysalis 1981)★★★, *All Of The Good Ones Are Taken* (Chrysalis 1983)★★★, with Mick Ronson *YUI Orta* (Mercury 1990)★★★, as Ian Hunter's Dirty Laundry *Ian Hunter's Dirty Laundry* (Norsk 1995)★★★, *The Artful Dodger* (Citadel 1997)★★★, as the Hunter Ronson Band *BBC Live In Concert* (Strange Fruit 1998)★★★.

● COMPILATIONS: *Shades Of Ian Hunter* (Columbia 1979)★★★★, *The Collection* (Castle 1991)★★★, *The Very Best Of* (Columbia 1991)★★★.

● FURTHER READING: *Diary Of A Rock 'N' Roll Star*, Ian Hunter.

Hunter, Ivory Joe

b. 10 October 1911, Kirbyville, Texas, USA, d. 8 November 1974. Although Hunter was a well-known figure in Texas through his radio shows, it was not until the 40s, when he moved to the west coast, that his career flourished. He established his own record companies, Ivory and Pacific, the latter of which provided the outlet for Hunter's first R&B chart-topper, 'Pretty Mama Blues'. Hunter continued his success with several singles recorded with sidemen from the **Duke Ellington** Orchestra before one of his most enduring compositions, 'I Almost Lost My Mind', became a second R&B number 1 in 1950. A re-recorded version also proved popular when the singer moved to the **Atlantic** label later in the decade, but **Pat Boone**'s opportunistic cover version was a greater commercial success. However, a further fine Hunter original, 'Since I Met You Baby', then swept to the top of the R&B chart in 1956 and to number 12 in the national pop chart. Unhappy at being labelled an R&B act, this talented and prolific artist was equally adept with pop, ballad and spiritual styles and in later years became a popular C&W attraction, so much so that a benefit concert was held for him at Nashville's *Grand Ole Opry* shortly before his death in 1974, as a result of lung cancer.

● ALBUMS: *I Get That Lonesome Feeling* (1957)★★★, *Ivory Joe Hunter* (Sound 1957)★★★, *Ivory Joe Hunter* (Atlantic 1958)★★★, *Ivory Joe Hunter Sings The Old And The New* (Atlantic 1958)★★★, *Ivory Jo Hunter* (Sage 1959)★★★, *The Fabulous Ivory Joe Hunter* (1961)★★★, *This Is Ivory Joe Hunter* (1964)★★★, *The Return Of Ivory Joe Hunter* (Epic 1971)★★★, *I've Always Been Country* (1974)★★★.

● COMPILATIONS: *Sixteen Of His Greatest Hits*

(1958)★★★, *Ivory Joe Hunter's Greatest Hits* (1963)★★★, *7th Street Boogie* (Route 66 1980)★★★, *The Artistry Of Ivory Joe Hunter* (Bulldog 1982)★★★, *This Is Ivory Joe* (Ace 1984)★★★★, *I Had A Girl* (Route 66 1987)★★★, *Jumping At The Dewdrop* (Route 66 1987)★★★, *Since I Met You Baby* (Mercury 1988)★★★, *I'm Coming Down With The Blues* (Home Cooking 1989)★★★, *Sings 16 Greatest Hits* (1992)★★★★.

Hunter, James

b. 1962. As a youngster in Essex, England, Hunter was interested in 50s rock 'n' roll, leading to a later appreciation of Chicago blues, particularly the music of **Little Walter**. He received his first electric guitar in 1977 when he was around 15 years of age, while his first band, the DMFs, played at Colchester Labour Club in 1983. He initially recorded with a rockabilly band for a compilation issued by Lost Moment Records in 1984. Two years later he moved to London, and began performing as **Howling Wilf**. With his band the Vee-Jays he quickly established himself as one of the mainstays of the capital's blues scene, and was touted as one of England's best young blues singers. In 1989 he disbanded the Vee-Jays and took his music in more of an R&B direction, assembling a band that at present includes Jonathan Lee (drums), Dave Lagnado (double bass), Nick Lunt (baritone saxophone) and Damian Hand (tenor saxophone). His biggest break came when he was invited to play guitar with **Van Morrison**'s Rhythm & Blues Revue, and he featured prominently on the Morrison albums *A Night In San Francisco* and *Days Like This*. Hunter has also worked with a diverse group of artists, including **Solomon Burke**, Mary Love and **Captain Sensible**, and briefly appeared in the West End musical *Buddy*. His debut album featured a winning mix of Hunter originals and choice cover versions, including duets with Van Morrison (on 'Turn On Your Lovelight' and 'Ain't Nothing You Can Do') and **Doris Troy** (on 'Hear Me Calling'). Central to the album's success were Hunter's vocals, with his powerful and expressive voice belying his comparatively young age.

● ALBUMS: *Believe What I Say* (Ace 1996)★★★★.

Hunter, Robert

b. c.1938, California, USA. Hunter is best known as the long-standing lyricist with **Jerry Garcia** of the **Grateful Dead**. His inventive and surreal stories have played a large part in the popularity of this legendary band. His work appears on all of the Grateful Dead's albums but he has also recorded his own solo work. As a lyricist his work is greatly underrated. Hunter never uses unnecessary words and couples his exemplary command of the English language with sometimes intricate and baffling story collages. *Jack O'Roses* is a fine example of Hunter at his lyrical best, accompanied by his solo guitar. He collaborated with **Bob Dylan** on the 1987 *Down In the Groove*, and continued to work with the Grateful Dead until their break-up following Garcia's death in 1995.

His standing as uncredited full member of the Dead and all it/they stood for would not be disputed by the legions of fans.

● ALBUMS: *Tales Of The Great Rum Runners* (Round 1974)★★★, *Tiger Rose* (Round 1975)★★★★, *Jack O'Roses* (Relix/Dark Star 1980)★★★★, *Promontory Rider* (1982)★★★, *Amagamalin St* (Relix 1984)★★★, *Live 85* (Relix 1985)★★, *The Flight Of The Marie Helena* (Relix 1985)★★★, *Rock Columbia* (Round 1986)★★★, *Liberty* (Relix 1988)★★, *A Box Of Rain* (Ryko 1991)★★★, *Sentinel* (Rykodisc 1994)★★★.

● FURTHER READING: *Sentinel*, Robert Hunter. *A Box Of Rain: Collected Lyrics Of Robert Hunter*, Robert Hunter. *Night Carde*, Robert Hunter.

Hunter, Tab

b. Arthur Andrew Kelm, 11 July 1931, New York City, New York, USA. This blond-haired, blue-eyed pop vocalist/actor used his mother's maiden name, Gelien, until he was spotted in 1948, working at a stable, by talent scout Dick Clayton. He introduced him to Rock Hudson's Hollywood agent Harry Wilson, who said 'We've got to tab you something', then named him Tab Hunter. He made his screen debut in the 1950 film *The Lawless* and two years later co-starred with Linda Darnell in the British film *Saturday Island* (US title: *Island Of Desire*). In late 1956 he received a phone call from Randy Wood, president of **Dot Records**, asking him to record a song recently cut by US country star **Sonny James**, the lilting ballad 'Young Love'. Both versions made the US charts, Hunter reaching number 1 and James peaking at number 2. Hunter also topped the UK chart, but James lagged behind at number 11. He continued recording for Dot and hit with the slightly up-tempo '99 Ways', which narrowly missed the US Top 10 but made the UK Top 5 (1957). In the following year he appeared in the film version of the Broadway show *Damn Yankees*, with **Gwen Verdon** and **Ray Walston**. As Warner Brothers had him under contract to make films, they resented him recording for Dot and established their own record label in 1958. He signed, with moderate success, and in 1960 starred in his own NBC US television series. He continued his acting and appeared opposite **Fabian** in the 1964 'beach party' film *Ride The Wild Surf*. He was still acting in the 80s, notably with the late Divine in *Polyester* and *Lust In The Dust*, and also in the *Grease* sequel, *Grease 2*. In the late 80s Hunter moved to Mexico to write, and set up a film production company, one of the fruits of which was the 'family' picture *Dark Horse* (1992).

● ALBUMS: *Tab Hunter* (Warners 1958)★★, *When I Fall In Love* (Warners 1959)★★, *R.F.D. Tab Hunter* (Warners 1960)★★, *Young Love* (Dot 1961)★★.

● FILMS: *The Lawless* (1950), *Saturday Island* (1952), *Damn Yankees* (1958), *Ride The Wild Surf* (1964).

Hunter, Tommy

b. Thomas James Hunter, 20 March 1937, London, Ontario, Canada. Hunter developed a keen interest in country music as a child, after seeing **Roy Acuff** during a Canadian tour, and by his early teens, he had mastered the guitar and was playing and singing locally. He played on CBC radio in 1952 and the following year, he left home to tour in Canada and the USA. In 1956, he became a regular on the Canadian television programme *Country Hoedown* (remaining on the show until 1965) and also presented the daily *Tommy Hunter Show* on radio. In 1962, it also became a very popular syndicated television programme which ran until 1989. He made his first recordings for **RCA/Victor Records** in 1956 and the first of many appearances on the **Grand Ole Opry** in 1965. He later recorded for **Capitol** and **Columbia Records**, and, in 1990, he formed his own Edith label. Curiously, he has never placed much emphasis on the recording aspect of his long association with country music. His recorded output includes many albums but unfortunately few appeared to be readily available outside his native Canada, and although a superstar there, he is far less known in other countries. He remained active into the 90s, regularly performing with his band. He has received several awards over the years, including Canada's highest civilian award, the Order Of Canada, in 1986.

● ALBUMS: *Tommy Hunter Readings* (Edith 90s)★★★, *Songs Of Inspiration* (Edith 90s)★★★, *Tommy Hunter Sings For You* (Edith 90s)★★★.

● FURTHER READING: *My Story*, Tommy Hunter.

Hunter, Willie

b. February 1933, Shetlands, Scotland, d. 27 January 1995. Hunter is widely regarded as one of the greats of Shetland fiddling, having done much to rejuvenate that tradition alongside the more celebrated **Aly Bain**. Distinctively, Shetland fiddling relies as much on the Scandinavian and Irish traditions as the Scottish, preferring fast reels and four-part bars to propel both improvised and ceremonial tunes - and Hunter was one of the best examples of this technique. His father, Willie senior, was also well versed in it, and was a fiddler of note in his own right (briefly recorded on **Greentrax Records**' *Shetland Fiddle Music* alongside his son). As well as his father Willie was instructed from an early age (he began playing at four and was stated to know a number of tunes competently by the age of five) by Gideon Stove from Lerwick and Geoffrey Di Mercado, who provided classical violin training. An early duo was formed with his sister Lorna before he joined a succession of country dance bands which eventually led him to the Hamefarers (one album in 1974). Though he rarely left the isles, his apprenticeship was completed by meeting peers such as Hector McAndrew and Angus Fitchet (an accompanist to **Jimmy Shand**) from the mainland, and later, Irish fiddler Sean Maguire. He went to London in 1958 to perform with 'Peerie' Willie Johnson at the Royal Festival Hall as part of a celebration of Britain's varied folk traditions, and the duo teamed up once more for a series of workshops and concerts in the 80s. By this time he had retired from his laundrette business and used much of his spare time to teach fiddle to Shetland children as well as playing weekend dances with friends such as the Yell Band and Culleyvoe Band. He also continued to work with pianist Violet Tulloch, with whom he recorded his only solo album in 1982.

● ALBUMS: *Willie Hunter 82* (Celtic Recordings 1982)★★★, with Hamefarers *A Breath o' Shetland* (Polydor 1974)★★, with Violet Tulloch *Leaving Lerwick Harbour* (Greentrax 1996)★★★★.

Hunters And Collectors

Formed in Melbourne, Australia, in 1981, Hunters And Collectors experimented with a punk/funk style, drawing comparisons in some quarters to **Talking Heads**, something that earned them a strong following on the Australian alternative music scene. The core members of the group have over the years comprised Mark Seymour (guitar, lead vocals), Jeremy Smith (keyboards, saxophone), Doug Falconer (drums), John Archer (bass), Martin Lubran (guitar), Geoff Crosbie (keyboards), Greg Perano (percussion), and trombonists Michael Waters and Jack Howard (trombone). The band recorded a single, two EPs and an album in 1982. Their debut album incorporated harsh brass instruments and their second album extended this further, but their experimentation failed to impress the public. Once the band began to focus on lead singer Mark Seymour's lyrics and songwriting about troubled relationships, his anguished voice propelled the band to new heights. The music took on a more solid, rock sound with dynamic arrangements, shifting the emphasis from horns to bass and drums. With each album honing and refining this sound, the band's audience expanded as it toured widely, eventually going to the USA and Europe. Given the high musicianship of the band, it is perhaps surprising that the emphasis of their latter albums has been on Seymour's lyrics and the band's macho image.

● ALBUMS: *Hunters & Collectors* Australia only double album (White Label 1982)★★★, *Hunters & Collectors* (Oz/A&M 1983)★★★, *Fireman's Curse* (Virgin 1983)★★★, *Jaws Of Life* (Slash 1984)★★★, *Way To Go Out* (White Label 1985)★★★, *Human Frailty* (IRS 1986)★★★, *What's A Few Men* (White Label 1987)★★★ re-released as *Fate* (IRS 1988)★★★, *Ghost Nation* (Atlantic 1990)★★, *Demon Flower* (Mushroom 1994)★★.

● COMPILATIONS: *Collected Works* (IRS 1990)★★★.

Hunting Of The Snark, The

Prior to 24 October 1991, **Mike Batt** was best-known in Britain as the arranger and producer of a highly successful series of children's novelty records (on which he also sang) involving the Wombles, a mythical group of small, furry, friendly creatures, who apparently lived on Wimbledon Common in south east London. Soon after that date he became renowned as an obstinate entrepreneur who had poured several years of his life, and a good deal of his own money, into a spectacular

flop musical called *The Hunting Of The Snark*. The project, which was based on Lewis Carroll's epic nonsense poem, first surfaced in 1987 as a concept album which was narrated by Sir John Gielgud and John Hurt, and performed by such luminaries as **Roger Daltrey**, **Art Garfunkel**, **Julian Lennon**, **Cliff Richard**, **Deniece Williams** *et al*. Four years later, a concert version was well-received at the State Theatre in Sydney, Australia, and the full West End production opened at the Prince Edward Theatre in October 1991. It was Mike Batt's baby all along; he wrote the book, music, and lyrics, staged the show with James Hayes, and was also credited with the design and the orchestrations. The story concerned the search for an 'improbable beast', and involved the Bellman (Philip Quast) and his crew which consisted of the Beaver (Veronica Hart), the Butcher (John Partridge), the Barrister (Allan Love), the Banker (David Firth), the Baker (Mark McGann), the Bandmaster (Jae Alexander), the Broker (Peter Leadbury), and the Bishop (Gary Martin). The disc jockey and television presenter, Kenny Everett, made his West End musical theatre debut as the Billiard Marker, and the role of the author-narrator was played by the film and television actor, David McCallum. Quast, McGann, John Partridge, and Veronica Hart, were all singled out by the critics for special praise. Most of the reputed £2.1 million investment was up there on the stage for all to see in the shape of a 50 piece orchestra and the high-tech computerized scenic projections. The score, with its 'prosaic music and portenteous lyrics', contained some 26 numbers including 'Children Of The Sky', 'Hymn To The Snark', 'Who'll Join Me On This Escapade?', 'Nursery Pictures', 'The Pig Must Die', 'As Long As The Moon Can Shine', and the prophetically titled 'Dancing Towards Disaster'. Audiences stayed away in their thousands (the Prince Edward is a medium-sized house with a capacity of 1,666), and, throughout November, Batt refused to bring the curtain down despite heavy losses. It was rumoured that **Andrew Lloyd Webber**, **Tim Rice**, and **Cameron Mackintosh** were contributing to the diminishing kitty. Some people loved what they regarded as 'one of the most unusual and intriguing musicals to be seen in the West End', and an angry exchange of opposing views raged in the letters column of *The Stage* newspaper. Finally, on 14 December, Batt could take no more and closed the show after only seven weeks, incurring personal losses that were estimated to be in excess of £600,000.

Hupfeld, Herman

b. 1 February 1894, Montclair, New Jersey, USA, d. 8 June 1951, Montclair, New Jersey, USA. A little-known songwriter, pianist and conductor, who, although he did not compose complete scores, was particularly adept in interpolating the occasional superior song into stage shows and films of the 20s and 30s. After being sent to Germany at the age of nine to study the violin, Hupfeld returned to the USA and completed his education at the local Montclair high school. After serving in the US Navy during World War I, he worked as a pianist-singer before contributing songs such as 'Baby's Blue', 'Sort Of Lonesome', and 'The Calinda' to the smart and fashionable Broadway revues of the day. In 1930 his 'Sing Something Simple' attracted some attention when it was introduced by Ruth Tester, with Arline Judge and Fay Brady, in *The Second Little Show*. A year later, as well as contributing the amusing 'When Yuba Plays The Rumba On His Tuba' to *The Third Little Show*, he wrote the song for which he will always be remembered - 'As Time Goes By'. It was first sung by the popular platinum blonde singer Frances Williams in the musical *Everybody's Welcome*, and subsequently recorded by Jacques Renard and **Rudy Vallee**, amongst others. However, it came to world-wide prominence in the 1943 film *Casablanca*, when it was memorably performed by Dooley Wilson. More than 50 years later, it still conjures up the bitter-sweet romance between Humphrey Bogart and Ingrid Bergman in the movie, and that magical moment when Bergman requests the pianist to 'Play it Sam. Play 'As Time Goes By''. In 1932 Hupfeld had another of his best-known numbers, 'Let's Put Out The Lights And Go To Sleep', featured in **George White**'s *Music Hall Varieties* stage show, and during the remainder of the 30s his other songs included 'Wouldn't That Be Wonderful' (*Hey Nonny Nonny!* revue), 'Savage Serenade' (**Earl Carroll**'s *Murder At The Vanities*), and 'Buy Yourself A Balloon' (*The **Show Is On*** revue). He also placed songs in movies such as *Moonlight And Pretzels* ('Gotta Get Up And Get To Work' and 'Are You Makin' Any Money ?') and *Take A Chance* ('Night Owl'). During World War II Hupfeld travelled widely, entertaining the troops in the USA and Europe. In 1950 he had one last fling at Broadway, contributing material to the musical *Dance Me A Song*. The show was notable only for an early appearance of dancer **Bob Fosse**, and was quickly withdrawn.

Hurley, Michael

b. 20 December 1941, Buck County, Pennsylvania, USA. Hurley began playing guitar at the age of 13 and subsequently led an itinerant lifestyle until gravitating to the folk enclave at New York's Greenwich Village. An accomplished performer and songwriter, he was about to secure a major recording deal when a combination of hepatitis and mononucleosis led to a lengthy spell in hospital. Hurley made his delayed debut in 1964 on the traditional outlet, **Folkways**. *First Songs* featured support from longtime friend and associate Robin Remaily and revealed an artist of quirky imagination and vocal delivery. The set included the singer's first version of 'The Werewolf', later popularized by the **Holy Modal Rounders**, and the piece for which its creator is best remembered. The same group recorded several other Hurley compositions, including 'Radar Blues' and 'Morning Glory', while the **Youngbloods** acknowleged their respect by signing Hurley to their

Raccoon label, thus ending a six-year hiatus. *Armchair Boogie* and *Hi-Fi Snock Uptown* maintained the singer's idiosyncratic style while offering muted instrumental support. During the 70s Hurley completed several releases for the traditional outlet Rounder, and was a major contributor to *Have Moicy*, a various artist's compendium declared 'best album of 1975' in the New York *Village Voice* and 'one of the Top 10 albums of the decade' in ***Rolling Stone***. By this point the singer had repaired to rural Vermont and although opportunities to record lessened, the enchanting *Watchtower* and subsequent albums in the 90s showed Hurley's gifts and wit intact.

● ALBUMS: *First Songs* (1964)★★★, *Armchair Boogie* (1970)★★★, *Hi-Fi Snock Uptown* (1972)★★★, with others *Have Moicy* (1975)★★★★, *Long Journey* (1977)★★★, *Snockgrass* (70s)★★★, *Blue Navigator* (1984)★★★, *The Watchtower* (1988)★★★, *Wolfways* (Veracity 1995)★★★, *Watertower* (Fundamental 1996)★★★.

Hurley, Steve 'Silk'

Formerly a DJ at Chicago station WBMX, Hurley's first recordings, like many of his peers, were originally cut specifically to augment his DJ repertoire. One such track, 'Music Is The Key', got a particularly warm reception, and Hurley borrowed money from his father and placed it on his friend Rocky Jones' **DJ International** label. It made number 9 in the US dance charts, though no royalties were forthcoming. He was similarly dismayed when his 'I Can't Turn Around' was hijacked by **Farley Jackmaster Funk**, and turned into 'Love Can't Turn Around', with new vocals by Daryl Pandy, in 1985. It became a hit without any of the credit being extended to Hurley. However, his reward was just around the corner. After recording the mighty 'Baby Wants To Ride' with **Jamie Principal** he scored the first house number 1 with 'Jack Your Body' on 24 January 1987. Later he would create **Kym Sims**' 'Too Blind To See', and was invited to remix **Roberta Flack**'s 'Uh Uh Ooh Ooh Look Out' - which he saw as a great personal achievement. Other remix projects came thick and fast, including **Paula Abdul** (*Vibeology* EP), Yasmin ('Sacrifice'), **Simply Red** ('Something Got Me Started'), **Ce Ce Peniston** ('We Got A Love Thang') and **Rodeo Jones** ('Get Wise'). At one time in the 90s it seemed that a dozen such remixes were appearing on the market at the same time, and in truth they were all relatively similar, albeit polished and accomplished. Hurley had few complaints, raking in the money at a reported $20,000 per throw, and working with heroes like **Stevie Wonder**. In addition he established his own production company ID (signed to Sony in the UK and Europe, its remix roster including Chicago DJ Ralphi Rosario and **Juan Atkins**). A previous such venture, JM Silk (formed with famous house vocalist Keith Nunnally) had proved ill-fated.

● ALBUMS: *Work It Out* (Atlantic 1989)★★★.

Hurrah!

Originally known as the Green-Eyed Children, Hurrah! consisted of Paul Handyside (b. 28 September 1960, Newcastle-upon-Tyne, Tyne And Wear, England; guitar, vocals), David 'Taffy' Hughes (b. 16 March 1961, Southmoor, Northumberland, England; guitar, vocals), David Porterhouse (b. 17 August 1961, Gateshead, Tyne And Wear, England; bass) and Mark Sim (drums). Switching to the moniker of Hurrah!, the quartet signed to the new Kitchenware Records label in 1982. Mark Sim soon departed to be replaced by Damien Mahoney, whereupon a series of acclaimed singles such as 'The Sun Shines Here' and 'Hip Hip' earned the band great respect from the British independent sector. Based upon the pivotal force of the singing, guitar-playing and songwriting partnership of Paul Handyside and David Hughes, Hurrah! mastered a jittery, urgent style rich in melodic content. By 1986, however, the band had pushed their sound towards a rockier terrain, replacing the initial charm with power and passion. Mahoney left to join the police force in the spring of that year, allowing Steve Price to fill the vacant drum-stool. Their debut album, *Tell God I'm Here*, saw the light of day in 1987, swiftly followed by a support date with U2 at London's Wembley stadium and, on a more bizarre note, live shows in Iraq, Egypt and Jordan after accepting an invitation from the British Council. In spite of the band's determination, commercial success remained elusive. When *The Beautiful* failed to have a significant impact on the marketplace Hurrah! parted company with the 'misunderstanding' **Arista Records** label and returned to the independent sector. Adrian Evans (b. 6 March 1963, County Durham, England) became the band's fourth drummer when Steve Price emigrated to America, but by then the band were in their death throes.

● ALBUMS: *Tell God I'm Here* (Kitchenware 1987)★★★, *The Beautiful* (Arista 1989)★★.
● COMPILATIONS: *Boxed* (Kitchenware 1985)★★★.

Hurricane

Formed in Los Angeles, California, USA, in 1983, this heavy metal band's original line-up consisted of Kelly Hanson (vocals), Robert Sarzo (guitar), Tony Cavazo (bass) and Jay Schellen (drums). Robert Sarzo is the brother of **Whitesnake** bassist Rudy Sarzo and Tony Cavazo is the brother of **Quiet Riot** guitarist Carlos Cavazo. Hurricane arrived via a mini-album released in 1986, entitled *Take What You Want*, on Roadrunner Records. It was a fine debut, featuring hard-edged melodic rockers. The band then switched labels, signing to Enigma Records and releasing *Over The Edge*. It failed to sell and during 1989 Robert Sarzo left the band to be replaced by ex-**Lion** guitarist Doug Aldrich. This line-up went on to record the much improved *Slave To The Thrill*, released in 1990 to critical acclaim.

● ALBUMS: *Take What You Want* mini-album (Roadrunner 1986)★★★, *Over The Edge* (Enigma 1988)★★, *Slave To The Thrill* (Enigma 1990)★★★★.

Hurricane #1

After the acromonious ending to his former band **Ride**, Andy Bell underwent a period of soul-searching that saw him performing occasional solo shows and writing new material at his wife **Idha**'s parents' home in Sweden. With the support of **Alan McGee** at **Creation Records**, Bell announced a new band, Hurricane #1, at the start of 1997. His new singer, Glaswegian ex-boxer Alex Lowe (b. *c*.1971), was recruited through an advert in the music press, and was joined by Gareth Farmer (b. *c*.1979; drums) and Will Pepper (ex-**Thee Hypnotics**; bass). Having laid down the material for their debut within three weeks of forming, the band quickly developed a reputation as an aggressive and truculent outfit, somewhat at odds with Bell's former reputation. However, the release of the singles 'Just Another Illusion' and 'Step Into My World' showed them in a better light, with Bell's melodic touch and Lowe's bluesy voice establishing themselves as the band's strong points. Their self-titled debut album, produced by **Kula Shaker** associate Steve Harris, suffered from a lack of variety, earning them mixed reviews in the music press.

● ALBUMS: *Hurricane #1* (Creation 1997)★★★.

Hurt, Mississippi John

b. John Smith Hurt, 3 July 1893, Teoc, Mississippi, USA, d. 2 November 1966. One of the major 'rediscoveries' during the 60s folk blues revival, Mississippi John Hurt began playing at informal gatherings and parties at the turn of the century, when guitars were still relatively uncommon. Although he worked within the idiom, Hurt did not regard himself as a blues singer and his relaxed, almost sweet, intonation contrasted with the aggressive approaches of many contemporaries. In 1928 he recorded two sessions for the **OKeh** label. These early masters included 'Candy Man Blues', 'Louis Collins' and 'Ain't No Tellin' (aka 'A Pallet On The Floor'), songs that were equally redolent of the ragtime tradition. For the ensuing three decades, Hurt worked as a farm-hand, reserving music for social occasions. His seclusion ended in 1963. Armed with those seminal OKeh recordings, a blues aficionado, Tom Hoskins, followed the autobiographical lyric of 'Avalon Blues' and travelled to the singer's home-town. He persuaded Hurt to undertake a series of concerts, which in turn resulted in several new recordings. Appearances at the Newport Folk Festival ensued, before the artist completed several sessions for the **Vanguard** label, supervised by folk-singer **Patrick Sky**. These included masterly reinterpretations of early compositions, as well as new, equally compelling pieces. Hurt's re-emergence was sadly brief. He died at Grenada County Hospital on 2 November 1966 following a heart attack, having inspired a new generation of country-blues performers.

● ALBUMS: *Mississippi John Hurt - Folk Songs And Blues* (Piedmont 1963)★★★, *Live* (Piedmont 1964)★★★, *Worried Blues* (Piedmont 1964)★★★, *Blues At Newport* (Vanguard 1965)★★★, *Last Sessions* (Vanguard 1966)★★, *Mississippi*

John Hurt - Today (Vanguard 1967)★★★.
● COMPILATIONS: *The Immortal Mississippi John Hurt* (Vanguard 1967)★★★, *Avalon Blues* (Heritage 1982)★★★, *Shake That Thing* (Blue Moon 1986)★★★, *Monday Morning Blues* (Flyright 1987)★★★, *Mississippi John Hurt, Sacred And Secular 1963* (Heritage 1988)★★★, *Memorial Anthology* (Edsel 1994)★★★, *Legend* (Rounder 1997)★★★, *Satisfied . . . Live* (Javelin 1996)★★★.

Husband, Gary

b. 14 June 1960, Leeds, England. A drummer who comes from a musical family (his father played flute and composed, his mother danced), Husband started on piano lessons at the age of seven, then took up drums in 1970. An infant prodigy, he created a stir in the local jazz clubs with his precision and fire. Drawn towards jazz-rock and its older protagonists, he gravitated to London in the late 70s, playing and recording with **Gordon Beck**, **Barbara Thompson** and **Allan Holdsworth**.
● ALBUMS: *Allan Holdsworth IOU* (1982)★★★, *Metal Fatigue* (1984)★★★, with John Themis *Ulysses & the Cyclops* (1984)★★.

Husik, Lida

b. *c.*1963, Washington, D.C., USA. Ambient musician Lida Husik lost her mother at a very young age, helping to foster both an independent spirit and a sense of loss which has permeated through a series of critically-acclaimed albums. She grew up with her English-teacher father, who encouraged her to study violin and piano. By the time she attended junior high school she had switched to guitar. In the early 80s she regularly attended shows run by Dischord Records' artists such as **Fugazi** - a band she still holds in high esteem for their positivity and morality. Her first musical employment came as drummer in Missing In Action - 'We really lived up to our name. We only had one gig.', she later advised. After being kicked out of the local American University after a year, she attended art school at the Corcoran before moving to San Francisco. There she worked in a library before being introduced to **Kramer** (of the **Shimmy-Disc** label) through producer Don Fleming. It was here she released her first records, which relied predominantly on ambient textures shot through with Husik's intimate, ever-personal vocals. Her growing reputation led to a collaboration with UK techno ambient guru **Beaumont Hannant** for the *Evening At The Grange* EP. That was followed by a more mainstream rock recording, *Joyride*, essentially a collection of demos with many of the songs inspired by the recent death of her father. She returned to ambient sound collages for her next collection, 1996's *Green Blue Fire*, an album written while on holiday in England, where the ancient city of York inspired many of the movements and textures.
● ALBUMS: *Joyride* (Shimmy-Disc 1994)★★★, *Green Blue Fire* (1996), *Fly Stereophonic* (Alias 1997)★★★.

Hüsker Dü

Formed in Minneapolis, Minnesota, USA, in 1979, Hüsker Dü were a punk trio consisting of guitarist/vocalist **Bob Mould**, bassist Greg Norton and drummer **Grant Hart**, whose melding of pop and punk influences inspired thousands of UK, US and European bands. Indeed, it is hard to think of a single other band who have had such a profound impact on modern alternative music than this trio. Taking their name, which means 'Do you remember?', from a Norwegian board game, they started out as an aggressive hardcore thrash band before challenging that genre's restrictions and expanding to other musical formats. Their primary strength, like so many other truly great groups, was in having two songwriting partners (Mould and Hart) who for the entirety of their career fully complemented each other. Their first single, 'Statues', was released on the small Reflex label in 1981. The following year, a debut album, *Land Speed Record*, arrived on New Alliance Records, followed by an EP, *In A Free Land*. *Everything Falls Apart* in 1983 saw them back on Reflex. By the advent of their second EP, *Metal Circus* (now on SST Records), Hüsker Dü had become a critics' favourite in the USA - a rapport that was soon to be exported to their UK brethren. *Zen Arcade* in 1984 brought about a stylistic turning point - a two-record set, it followed a single storyline about a young boy leaving home and finding life even more difficult on his own. A 14-minute closing song, 'Reoccurring Dreams', in which it was revealed that the boy's entire ordeal had been a dream, broke all the rules of punk. A non-album cover version of the **Byrds**' 'Eight Miles High' followed, and a 1985 album, *New Day Rising*, maintained the trio's reputation as a favourite of critics and college radio stations, with its irresistible quicksilver pop songs. After *Flip Your Wig* the band signed with **Warner Brothers Records** (there were several other interested parties), with whom they issued *Candy Apple Grey* in 1986 and *Warehouse: Songs And Stories*, another double set, the following year. In 1988 Hart was dismissed from the group (though there are many conflicting versions of events leading up to this juncture), which summarily disbanded. Mould and Hart continued as solo artists, before Mould formed the equally rumbustious **Sugar** in 1991.
● ALBUMS: *Land Speed Record* (New Alliance 1981)★★, *Everything Falls Apart* (Reflex 1982)★★, *Metal Circus* mini-album (Reflex/SST 1983)★★★, *Zen Arcade* (SST 1984)★★★★, *New Day Rising* (SST 1985)★★★, *Flip Your Wig* (SST 1985)★★★★, *Candy Apple Grey* (Warners 1986)★★★★, *Warehouse: Songs And Stories* (Warners 1987)★★★★, *The Living End* 1987 recording (Warners 1994)★★★.
● COMPILATIONS: *Everything Falls Apart And More* (Warners 1993)★★★★.

Husky, Ferlin

b. 3 December 1925, on a farm near Flat River, Missouri, USA. Husky learned to play guitar as a child and during World War II served in the US Merchant Navy. His mother wanted him to be a preacher and his father a farmer, but after discharge, he found radio work as an announcer and disc jockey but gradually turned to performing while at KXLW St. Louis. In the late 40s he moved to California, where he appeared on the Los Angeles *Hometown Jamboree* and played clubs in the Bakersfield area. Believing that Ferlin Husky, his real name, was unsuitable, he first called himself Tex Preston, then changed again to Terry Preston. He also developed an alter ego country philosopher character, Simon Crum, whom he introduced into his act. (A few years later, **Sheb Wooley** also adopted a similar practice with his character Ben Colder, who sought to entertain with his supposed humorous parodies on popular and country songs.) In the early 50s, he recorded for Capitol and worked with **Tennessee Ernie Ford**. In 1953, as Ferlin Huskey, he recorded 'A Dear John Letter' with **Jean Shepard**, which became a smash US country number 1, as well as reaching number 4 on the US pop charts. An answer version called 'Forgive Me John', also had success in both charts. Following success with his self-penned 'Hank's Song' (a tribute to **Hank Williams**), Huskey finally dropped the name of Terry Preston. In 1957, now minus the 'e' again, Husky joined the *Grand Ole Opry* and achieved another smash hit number 1 with his million-selling recording of 'Gone', which, ironically, he had first recorded unsuccessfully as Preston five years earlier. In 1960, he charted a further country number 1 with the gospel/country 'Wings Of A Dove', which also became a Top 20 pop hit. He recorded 'The Drunken Driver', a tear-jerking narrative about a father who runs over his son, which has been rated a classic by some and one of the worst recordings ever made by others. He became a popular entertainer on many network television shows, including hosting the *Arthur Godfrey Show* and appearing as a dramatic actor on *Kraft TV Theatre*. While not always singing traditional country material, he maintained his country popularity through the character of Simon Crum. In this guise, he demonstrated a great talent for impersonating other country stars, presenting rustic comedy, and even managed a number 2 country hit with 'Country Music's Here To Stay'. He recorded an album of pop songs called *Boulevard Of Broken Dreams* in 1957 and also recorded several rock 'n' roll singles such as 'Wang Dang Do'. Husky has appeared in several films including *Mr. Rock & Roll* and *Country Music Holiday*. From the 60s to the mid-70s, he toured extensively with his band, the Hush Puppies, and had regular country chart entries including 'Once', 'Just For You', 'True True Lovin'' and 'Freckles And Polliwog Days'. He moved to **ABC Records** in 1973 and achieved a country chart entry, 'An Old Memory Got In My Eye', in 1975. Husky has been married six times and has nine children, one of whom is called Terry Preston. In 1977 he had a heart operation but he recovered and continued to perform, and later recorded once more.

● ALBUMS: with Jean Shepard *Ferlin Husky And Jean Shepard*

(Capitol 1955)★★★, *Ferlin Husky's Songs Of The Home And Heart* (Capitol 1956)★★★, *Boulevard Of Broken Dreams* (Capitol 1957)★★, *Born To Lose* (Capitol 1959)★★★, *Ferlin Husky - Country Tunes From The Heart* (King 1959)★★★, *Sittin' On A Rainbow* (Capitol 1959)★★★, *Gone* (Capitol 1960)★★★, *Easy Livin'* (King 1960)★★★, *Ferlin's Favorites* (Capitol 1960)★★★, *Some Of My Favorites* (Capitol 1960)★★★, *Walkin' & Hummin'* (Capitol 1961)★★★, *Memories Of Home* (Capitol 1963)★★★, *The Heart & Soul Of Ferlin Husky* (Capitol 1963)★★★, *The Unpredictable Simon Crum* (Capitol 1963)★★, *By Request* (Capitol 1964)★★★, *True True Lovin'* (Capitol 1965)★★★, *I Could Sing All Night* (Capitol 1966)★★★, *Songs Of Music City, USA* (Capitol 1966)★★★, *Christmas All Year Long* (Capitol 1967)★★, *What Am I Gonna Do Now* (Capitol 1967)★★★, *Where No One Stands Alone* (Capitol 1968)★★★, *Just For You* (Capitol 1968)★★★, *White Fences And Evergreen Trees* (Capitol 1969)★★★, *That's Why I Love You So Much* (Capitol 1969)★★★, *Your Love Is Heavenly Sunshine* (Capitol 1970)★★★, *Your Sweet Love Lifted Me* (Capitol 1970)★★★, *One More Time* (Capitol 1971)★★★, *Just Plain Lonely* (Capitol 1972)★★★, *Sweet Honky Tonk* (1973)★★★, *True True Lovin'* (1973)★★★, *Champagne Ladies & Blue Ribbon Babies* (ABC 1974)★★★, *Freckles & Polliwog Days* (ABC 1974)★★★, *Mountain Of Everlasting Love* (ABC 1974)★★, *The Foster & Rice Songbook* (ABC 1975)★★, *Ferlin Husky* (1982)★★★, *Live* (1983)★★.

● COMPILATIONS: *Hits Of Ferlin Husky* (Capitol 1963)★★★★, *The Best Of Ferlin Husky* (Capitol 1969)★★★, *Collector's Series* (Capitol 1989)★★★★, *Greatest Hits* (Curb 1990)★★★★, *Vintage* (Capitol 1996)★★★★.

Hussain, Zakir

b. Zakir Hussain Allarakha Qureshi, 9 March 1951, Bombay, India. The son of virtuoso tabla player Ustad Alla Rakha, Hussain, predestined to uphold family traditions, began his initiation into the rhythmic complexities of Indian drumming as soon as he was able to sit. By the time he was 12 he had already accompanied many of the master musicians of north India, and has since played on literally hundreds of Indian classical sessions. He took over his father's job as tabla player for **Ravi Shankar** and made his American debut with Shankar at the Fillmore East in 1970. While in New York, he met **John McLaughlin**, and their friendship led to the formation of **Shakti** (featuring south Indian violinist **L. Shankar**) and, more recently, to McLaughlin's appearance on *Making Music*. Hussain has been a tireless campaigner for 'world music', working with the **Grateful Dead's Mickey Hart, Jefferson Starship, Van Morrison** and others and with his own Rhythm Experience, a pan-cultural percussion group. He also maintains a parallel career as a film actor and plays alongside Julie Christie in *Heat And Dust*.

● ALBUMS: *Making Music* (ECM 1987)★★★★, *Zakir Hussain And The Rhythm Experience* (Aspen 1987)★★★, with Ustad Alla Rakha *Tabla Duet* (1988)★★★, *Venu* 1972 recording (Rykodisc 1991)★★★.

Hustler

Among the early pioneers of UK hard rock, Hustler comprised Steve Haynes (vocals), Micky Llewellyn (guitar, vocals), Tigger Lyons (bass, vocals), Kenny Daughters (keyboards) and Tony Beard (drums, percussion). At a time when the UK music scene still related anything from the rock field with complex, multi-layered progressive recordings, Hustler seemed somewhat of place with their straightforward rock hooks and 'good-time boogie' style. Nevertheless, both *High Street* and *Play Loud* remain excellent examples of the back-to-basics British rock movement that eventually exploded into the **N.W.O.B.H.M.** After the group's collapse, Llewellyn joined **Mr. Big**.

● ALBUMS: *High Street* (Firefly/A&M 1974)★★★, *Play Loud* (Firefly/A&M 1975)★★★.

Hustlers Convention

A duo of Mike Gray and John Pearn. Mike had been a DJ for 14 years, spinning old school disco from labels such as **Prelude** and **Salsoul**, playing various gigs around Croydon, Surrey, England. He met Pearn when he was operating the lights at a local pub. They started to collaborate together, bringing samplers in for live mixes with drum machines and records. Although John did not at that time possess Mike's experience, he quickly became a self-taught engineer, and offered megamixes and remixes for DMC. Hustlers Convention is essentially 'Mike's baby', and is disco based, with samples culled from old disco records from **Chic** to more obscure Prelude 12-inches. A good example was the well-received *Groover's Delight* EP for Stress in 1992. They also record as Greed, for **Virgin**, as a more vocal orientated group. In addition to their own output the Hustlers have also remixed for mainstream star **Kenny Thomas** ('Trippin' On Your Love').

Hustlers HC

Three young Sikhs from west London, England, fronted by Hustler MC, who confront those factors relevant to their ethnic and geographical societies via a hip hop beta beat. Touted as part of the new 'Asian Cool' alongside **Trans-global Express** and **Fun-Da-Mental**, their debut single, 'Big Trouble In Little Asia', came out at the same time as Gurinder Chadha's groundbreaking film, *Bhaji On The Beach*. It was a similarly themed address to the cross-cultural problems facing the Asian community. They also run the Bombay Jungle nightclub, a mixed bhangra/hip-hop venue, in London. They are managed by Simon Underwood (ex-**Pop Group** and **Pigbag**).

Hutchence, Michael

(see **INXS**)

Hutchenrider, Clarence

b. Clarence Behrens Hutchenrider, 13 June 1908, Waco, Texas, USA. After playing clarinet and saxophones as a teenage schoolboy, Hutchenrider began playing profes-sionally with bands in south-eastern states. He contin-ued working in **territory bands** throughout the late 20s and into the 30s and then, in 1931, joined the **Casa Loma Orchestra**. Despite a sometimes shaky early tech-nique, Hutchenrider quickly became one of the band's most popular soloists, playing hot jazz clarinet on records such as 'Clarinet Marmalade' and 'Dixie Lee'. He also played good solos on tenor saxophone, 'No Name Jive', and on baritone, 'I Got Rhythm'. As the 30s advanced and **Benny Goodman**'s popularity grew, Hutchenrider adapted some aspects of his sound and style, finding a somewhat richer texture than the occa-sionally slightly reedy, but hard-swinging, sound of his earlier years. Hutchenrider remained with the Casa Lomans until 1943 when his career was interrupted by illness. He then joined a band led by fellow-clarinettist Jimmy Lytell which played mostly on radio in New York. Further illness with a lung condition followed, but he continued playing in the early 50s, sometimes leading a small group for club and hotel lounge work in New York. He continued to play into the late 70s, often with bands formed to recapture the musical sounds of the 20s and early 30s, Hutchenrider's glory days when his clarinet solos were an important feature in the success of the Casa Loma band.

● COMPILATIONS: *The Casa Loma Orchestra* (1930-36)★★★★.

Hutcherson, Bobby

b. 27 January 1941, Los Angeles, California, USA. After formal tuition on piano, Hutcherson switched to play-ing jazz vibraphone when he heard records by **Milt Jackson**. He worked briefly on the west coast then, in 1961, moved to New York, where he established himself as an inventive, forward-thinking musician. He played with many of the outstanding artists of the 60s, among them **Archie Shepp**, **Eric Dolphy**, **Herbie Hancock**, **Andrew Hill** and **McCoy Tyner**. Hutcherson made many records, sometimes as sideman (including the important *Out To Lunch* album with Dolphy), but regularly led his own groups, which often featured tenor saxophonist **Harold Land**, with whom he co-led a quintet from 1968-71. By now back on the west coast, Hutcherson played with **Gerald Wilson** and remained in San Francisco through the 70s, though he also toured around the world. In the late 80s, often playing in all-star bebop revival groups, Hutcherson continued to make numerous records, bringing his superb technique to bear upon an eclectic choice of material that demon-strated his awareness of his jazz roots. Despite this late flurry of activity, Hutcherson undeservedly remains one of the lesser-known of contemporary jazzmen.

● ALBUMS: with Eric Dolphy *Out To Lunch* (Blue Note 1964)★★★★★, *Dialogue* (Blue Note 1965)★★★, *Components* (1965)★★★, *Happenings* (Blue Note 1966)★★★, *Stick Up!* (1966)★★★★, *Total Eclipse* (Blue Note 1967)★★★, *Oblique* (Blue Note 1967)★★★, *Bobby Hutcherson* (1968)★★★, *Patterns* (1968)★★★, *Spiral* (1968)★★★, *Now* (1969)★★, *Medina* (1969)★★, *San Francisco* (1971)★★,

Head On (1971)★★★, *Natural Illusions* (1972)★★★, *Live At Montreux* (1973)★★★★, *Cirrus* (1974)★★★, *Linger Lane* (1974)★★, *Montara* (1975)★★★, *Waiting* (1976)★★★, *The View From The Inside* (1976)★★★★, *Knucklebean* (1977)★★★, *For Bobby Hutcherson/Blue Note Meets The Los Angeles Philharmonic* (1977)★★★, *Highway One* (1978)★★★, *Conception: The Gift Of Love* (1979)★★★, *Un Poco Loco* (1979)★★★, *Bobby Hutcherson Solo/Quartet* (Original Jazz Classics 1982)★★★★, *Farewell Keystone* (Theresa 1982)★★, *Four Seasons* (Timeless 1984)★★★, *Good Bait* (Landmark 1984)★★★, *Colour Schemes* (Landmark 1985)★★★, *In The Vanguard* (Landmark 1987)★★★, *Cruisin' The Bird* (Landmark 1988)★★★, *Ambos Mundos: Both Worlds* (Landmark 1989)★★★, *Mirage* (Landmark 1992)★★, *Farewell Keystone* (1993)★★★, *Components* (Connoisseur 1994)★★★, with McCoy Tyner *Moodswings* (Blue Note 1994)★★★.

Hutchings, Ashley

b. 26 January 1945, Southgate, Middlesex, England. Although largely remembered as the founder-member of **Fairport Convention**, where he was often afforded the nickname 'Tyger', Hutchings also went on to form **Steeleye Span** in 1970. He played on the first four Fairport Convention albums, ending with the classic *Liege And Lief*. Hutchings had grown unhappy with the increase in original material that the group was playing, at the expense of more traditional works. While with Fairport Convention he contributed to their one hit record, 'Si Tu Dois Partir', in 1969. After three albums with Steeleye Span, Hutchings formed the **Albion Country Band**, in 1971, and has led a succession of Albion Band line-ups ever since. The first of these line-ups was on *No Roses*, which included a total of 26 musicians, including himself and his then wife **Shirley Collins**. Many of the personnel involved have worked with Hutchings on other occasions, such as **John Kirkpatrick**, **Barry Dransfield**, **Nic Jones**, and the late Royston Wood, formerly of **Young Tradition**. With Hutchings the Albion Band became the first electric group to appear in plays at London's National Theatre. The group also 'electrified' Morris dancing, exemplified in *Morris On*, and *Son Of Morris On*. Hutchings has also done much work with former Fairport Convention members, **Richard Thompson**, and the late **Sandy Denny**. Hutchings has written and presented programmes on folk music for the BBC, and both he and the Albion Band were the subject of their own BBC television documentary in 1979. More recently, Hutchings wrote and acted in his own one-man show about song collector **Cecil Sharp**. The show has been performed nationwide since 1984. The presentation resulted in *An Evening With Cecil Sharp And Ashley Hutchings*. Hutchings continues to tour and record. It is not undeserved that he has been called the Father of Folk Rock in the UK.

● ALBUMS: with others *Morris On* (1972)★★★★, with John Kirkpatrick *The Compleat Dancing Master* (1974)★★★, *Kicking Up The Sawdust* (1977)★★★, *An Hour With Cecil Sharp And Ashley Hutchings* (1986)★★★, *By Gloucester Docks I Sat Down And Wept* (1987)★★★, the Ashley Hutchings All Stars *As You Like It* (Making Waves 1989)★★★, *A Word In Your Ear* (1991)★★★.

● COMPILATIONS: various artists *49 Greek Street* (1970)★★★, various artists *Clogs* (1971)★★★, with Shirley Collins *A Favourite Garland* (1974)★★★, with Richard Thompson *Guitar Vocal* (1976)★★★★, various artists *Buttons And Bows* (1984)★★★★, various artists *Buttons And Bows 2* (1985)★★★, with Sandy Denny *Who Knows Where The Time Goes?* (1985)★★★★, *The Guv'nor* 4-CD box set (HTD 1997)★★★★.

Hutchinson, Dolly

(see **Jones, Dolly**)

Hutchinson, Leslie 'Hutch'

b. c.1900, Grenada, West Indies, d. 18 August 1969. In his early teens Hutchinson was in New York where he studied law. In 1924 he was in Paris where he played piano and sang at various bars and restaurants, including Joselli's. He became friendly with many other ex-patriates and visitors including Bricktop and **Cole Porter**. In 1927 he was heard by UK impresario **C. B. Cochran** who invited him to London to appear in the **Richard Rodgers/Lorenz Hart** show, *One Dam Thing After Another*. Hutchinson remained in London, appearing at the best hotels and restaurants including long residencies at Quaglino's and Café De Paris, and making the occasional stage appearance in shows such as Porter's *Wake Up And Dream!* During the 30s and 40s he was frequently heard on radio, but in 1949 he retired, making a comeback in 1953, and playing at Quaglino's again in the following year. Although best known for his work in the UK, Hutchinson also appeared in Kenya where he was popular with the white Anglo-Kenyan community. In London his reputation extended outside the world of showbusiness and he had several affairs, some much-publicized, but one, with Lady Mountbatten, which was covered up for many years. Hutchinson played the piano simply and discreetly, singing in a huskily confidential manner which befitted the type of venue with which he was customarily associated. (This artist should not be confused with the trumpeter **Leslie 'Jiver' Hutchinson** who led and played in several dance bands in London during the same period.)

● ALBUMS: *Moonlight Cocktail* (30s-40s recordings)★★★, *Hutch At The Piano* (30s-40s recordings)★★★, *With A Song In My Heart* (30s-40s recordings)★★★, *The Magic Of Hutch* (30s-40s recordings)★★★.

Hutchinson, Leslie 'Jiver'

b. 18 March 1906, Crossroads, St. Andrews, Jamaica, d. 22 November 1959. Schooled on the trumpet in Jamaica's West India Regiment army band, Hutchinson appeared in London with them at the 1924 Empire Exhibition, Wembley. Fellow WIR bandsman Louis Stephenson had moved to England in 1935 with saxophonist Bertie King and pianist Yorke de Souza, and in 1936 Hutchinson followed, joining them in drummer Happy Blake's band at Soho's Cuba Club. He played with trumpeter **Leslie Thompson**'s Emperors Of Jazz, who were fronted by dancer **Ken 'Snakehips' Johnson**, then recorded and performed intermittently with Johnson's West Indian Dance Orchestra when the dancer took over the leadership. At Mayfair's Florida Club he played with Nigerian pianist Fela Sowande and led the same band in the Rialto film *Traitor Spy* (1939). During the war he played with leading dance bands, attaining prominence as star soloist with **Geraldo** and broadcasting frequently. He formed his own band with former Johnson sidemen and, until his death in a road accident in 1959, struggled to remain a bandleader and, in particular, to maintain a visible black presence on the UK jazz scene. His musicians included pre-war Jamaican settlers Joe Appleton (saxophone), **Coleridge Goode** (bass), Clinton Maxwell (drums), and later arrivals George Tyndale (saxophone), Peter Pitterson, Bushy Thompson and Frank Williams (trumpets) as well as UK-born black singers **Cab Kaye** and Marion Williams. He appeared in the film *The Captain's Paradise* (1953), worked with American pianist **Mary Lou Williams** during her extended London sojourn and recorded with his own band in Czechoslovakia ('I Can't Get Started', 1947) and accompanying Jamaican vocalists Tony Johnson (1958) and the distinguished folklorist Louise Bennett (1950). He was also the father of singer **Elaine Delmar**. (This artist should not be confused with the pianist **Leslie 'Hutch' Hutchinson** who played in London during the same period.)

Hutchison, Frank

b. 20 March 1897, Raleigh County, West Virginia, USA, d. 9 November 1945, Dayton, Ohio, USA. Hutchison grew up in Logan County, in an area where many black workers were constructing the railroad to serve the mines. He listened to their music and was taught to play the harmonica and guitar as a child. His main teachers were guitarists Henry Vaughan and Billy Hunt, from whom he learned to play country-blues in the bottleneck style; however, it seems that he used a penknife, rather than a bottleneck, to fret the strings. Hutchison worked in the mines as a teenager, but during the 20s he mostly made his living entertaining around the mining camps. His repertoire included blues numbers, which was highly unusual for a white musician in that area at the time. Between 1926 and 1929, he recorded 32 sides for **OKeh Records** and all but three were issued. Some were old ballads, and some, such as 'K.C. Blues', effectively displayed his harmonica and guitar playing talents. Among the songs associated with him is 'Coney Isle' which, with a few small variations and renamed 'Alabam', became a major hit for **Cowboy Copas** in 1961. The best remembered is 'The Train That Carried My Girl From Town', which **Doc Watson** later recorded. In the face of the Depression, Hutchison moved to Chesapeake, Ohio,

where he worked on steamboats, before he returned to Lake, West Virginia, to open a shop and post office. In April 1942, he lost everything in a fire and he returned to Ohio, where he died of liver cancer in 1945. Once known affectionately as the Pride Of West Virginia, he was, by then, almost forgotten. In 1974, **Rounder Records** released an album of his work, while some of his recordings appear on compilation albums by **CBS**, County, Old Homestead, Vetco and **Folkways Records**.
● COMPILATIONS: *The Train That Carries My Girl From Town* covers 20s (Rounder 1974)★★★.

Hutson, Leroy

b. 4 June 1945, Newark, New Jersey, USA. This African-American instrumentalist, composer, arranger, producer and multi-talented performer generated a host of affiliations, but never achieved a level of success commensurate with his talent. He first formed a vocal group in his native New Jersey, but emerged as a soul music talent while attending Howard University in 1970. There with his room-mate **Donny Hathaway**, he collaborated on 'The Ghetto', a hit for Hathaway in early 1970. Hutson and Hathaway also sang in the Mayfield Singers, who released one single for **Curtis Mayfield** in 1967. Later Hutson teamed up with Deborah Rollins to form Sugar And Spice, recording several singles with no success. In 1971 Hutson replaced Mayfield in the **Impressions** and recorded two unsatisfactory albums with the group. Hudson began his solo career on Curtom in 1973 and through 1980 established himself with a moderately successful recording career, recording seven albums and charting with some 13 singles in the USA. On most of his work, he wrote, produced, arranged and played multiple instruments, but Hutson never made a truly top-notch album. His best charted singles were 'All Because Of You' (1975), 'Feel The Spirit' (1976), 'I Do I Do' (1976), 'Where Did Love Go' (1978), and 'Right Or Wrong' (1979). When Curtom went out of business in 1980, Hutson's career was essentially behind him and he soon disappeared from the music world.
● ALBUMS: *Love O' Love* (Curtom 1973)★★★, *Leroy Hutson, The Man* (Curtom 1975)★★★, *Le Roy Hutson* (Curtom 1975)★★, *Feel The Spirit* (Curtom 1976)★★★, *Hutson II* (Curtom 1976)★★★, *Closer To The Source* (Curtom 1978)★★, *Unforgettable* (RSO/Curtom 1979)★★.
● COMPILATIONS: *The Very Best Of* (Deep Beats 1997)★★★, *More Where That Came From (Best Of Volume 2)* (Deep Beats 1998)★★★.

Hutto, J.B

b. Joseph Benjamin Hutto, 26 April 1926, Elko, near Blackville, South Carolina, USA, d. 12 June 1983, Chicago, Illinois, USA. Hutto's family moved to Augusta, Georgia when he was three years old, and he later sang in the Golden Crowns Gospel Singers, before moving to Chicago in 1949. While in Chicago he began to play drums and sing blues with Johnny Ferguson's Twisters, and during the intervals he taught himself to play Ferguson's guitar. In 1954 he recorded for the Chance label and these tracks are now considered to be classics of post-war blues. Hutto's slide guitar demonstrated that he was influenced by **Elmore James** but had utilized his style to create a unique, personal sound; however, at the time of release, the records met with little success. In 1965 J.B. and his unit the Hawks were the resident band at Turner's Blue Lounge (he worked there for over 10 years), when they recorded for the influential Vanguard series *Chicago/The Blues/Today*. Following this, Hutto recorded for many collector labels including Testament, Delmark, JSP, Amigo, Wolf, Baron, Black And Blue, and Varrick, with much of the later material, in particular, being licensed to different companies, and appearing on numerous anthologies. Hutto's music was raunchy, electric slide guitar blues that found great favour among young white blues enthusiasts. During live sets he would walk out into the audience and climb over tables in clubs, while continuing to play; 'party blues' was how one critic so aptly described it. Hutto died of cancer in June 1983. He was a major influence on his nephew **Lil' Ed Williams** who continued to perform some of Hutto's songs.

● ALBUMS: *Masters Of Modern Blues* (Testament 1966)★★★★, *Hawk Squat* (Delmark 1967)★★★, *Sidewinder* (Delmark 1972)★★★, *Slideslinger* (1982)★★★, *Slippin' And Slidin'* (1983)★★★, *High & Lonesome* (1993)★★★, with Sunnyland Slim *Hawk Squat* 1966-68 recordings (Delmark 1994)★★★.

Hutton, Betty

b. 26 February 1921, Battle Creek, Michigan, USA. A dynamic and vivacious singer and actress, while still a small child Hutton began singing in the streets to help support her impoverished family. By her early teens she was already beginning to make a name for herself when she was hired by **Vincent Lopez**, then leader of a popular radio band. In 1940, by then known as 'The Blonde Bombshell' in recognition of her fizzing vitality, Hutton appeared on Broadway in *Panama Hattie*, and the following year was snapped up by Hollywood. During the 40s she appeared in a string of popular musicals including *Star Spangled Rhythm*, *Happy Go Lucky*, *Let's Face It*, *And The Angels Sing*, *Here Comes The Waves*, *Incendiary Blonde*, *Duffy's Tavern*, *The Stork Club*, *Cross My Heart*, *The Perils Of Pauline*, *Dream Girl* and *Red Hot And Blue*. However, it was her sensational performance in the title role of *Annie Get Your Gun* in 1950 that established her as a major star. It gained her an international reputation, which she enhanced with roles in *Let's Dance* (1950), *The Greatest Show On Earth* and *Somebody Loves Me* (both 1952). Subsequent contractual difficulties with the studio resulted in her career coming to an abrupt halt, and although she made a brief appearance in the 1957 film *Spring Reunion*, she was declared bankrupt in 1967. In 1971, the last of her four marriages, to trumpeter **Pete Candoli**, ended in divorce, and after suffering a nervous breakdown and problems with drugs and alcohol, she worked for several years as a cook and housekeeper in a rectory in Portsmouth, Long Island. She made a triumphant comeback in 1980 when she took over the role of Miss Hannigan in the hit Broadway musical *Annie*. Later, she enrolled as a student at a New England college, before settling in Los Angeles. Her sister, Marion, two years her senior, was also a singer who worked with **Glenn Miller**'s civilian band. In 1994 **Capitol** issued a collection of some of her most entertaining tracks, and a year later ex-**Sugarcubes** lead singer **Björk** included one of Hutton's specialities, 'It's Oh So Quiet', on her *Post* album.

● ALBUMS: *Square In The Social Circle* 10-inch album (Capitol 1950)★★★, *Annie Get Your Gun* film soundtrack (MGM 1950/55)★★★, *Somebody Loves Me* film soundtrack (RCA 1952)★★★, *Satins And Spurs* TV soundtrack (Capitol 1954)★★, *At The Saints And Sinners Ball* (Warners 1959)★★★.

● COMPILATIONS: *Great Ladies Of Song: Spotlight On Betty Hutton* (Capitol 1994)★★★.

● FILMS: *The Fleet's In* (1942), *Star Spangled Rhythm* (1942), *The Miracle Of Morgan's Creek* (1943), *Let's Face It* (1943), *Here Comes The Waves* (1944), *And The Angels Sing* (1944), *Incendiary Blonde* (1945), *The Stork Club* (1946), *Cross My Heart* (1946), *The Perils Of Pauline* (1947), *Dream Girl* (1948) *Annie Get Your Gun* (1950), *Let's Dance* (1951), *Somebody Loves Me* (1952), *The Greatest Show On Earth* (1952), *Spring Reunion* (1957).

Hutton, Ina Ray

b. Odessa Cowan, 13 March 1916, Chicago, USA, d. 19 February 1984. As a child Hutton tap-danced in a Gus Edwards revue and later worked for other leading impresarios of the period, among them George White and Flo Ziegfeld. In 1934 Hutton was hired by **Irving Mills** to front an all-female band he was organizing. This was at a time when the concept of women playing big band music was briefly a commercial proposition and one which the astute Mills decided to exploit. The band, Ina Ray Hutton And Her Melodears, benefited from the Mills organization's publicity machine and became hugely popular. Hutton played no instrument but waved a baton colourfully. Dressed-to-kill, and labelled 'the Blonde Bombshell of Rhythm', Hutton exuded extravagant sex-appeal and her eye-catching outfits and on-stage antics helped the band's commercial success. The band had some fine musicians, notably multi-instrumentalist Alyse Wells, tenor saxophonist Betty Sattley and pianist Betty Roudebush. From 1936 the band's repertoire was in the hands of **Eddie Durham**, which greatly enhanced its musical qualities. Hutton led her band in several Hollywood films and they also made some records. By 1939, Hutton had severed her connection with Mills and led an all-male band but then drifted from the scene. In the late 40s and again in 1956 she appeared on television with an all-woman band and made another film but shortly afterwards went into married retirement from show business. Although by far the best known of the all-woman big bands, Hutton's Melodears were musically outclassed by the **International Sweethearts Of Rhythm**; they were, nevertheless, a far better outfit than their glitzy, showbiz trappings might suggest.

● COMPILATIONS: with others *Jazz Women: A Feminist Retrospective* (c.1936 recordings)★★★.

Hutton, Joe

b. *c*.1924, England, d. 17 July 1995, England. Northumbrian piper Joe Hutton worked as a shepherd in the Cheviot Hills throughout his life, also making occasional trips to folk festivals in Sidmouth, Shetland and Switzerland. A strongly lyrical musician, he never pursued music for profit, preferring instead to pass on the piping tradition to a number of students and through appearances on folk stages throughout the country. Alongside the better-known Billy Pigg, Hutton was partially responsible for the continuance of a unique tradition, which in the 90s reached a commercial peak with the emergence of **Kathryn Tickell**.

● ALBUMS: *Northumbrian Piper* (East Allen 1995)★★★.

Hutton, June

b. 11 August *c*.1920, Chicago, Illinois, USA, d. 2 May 1973, Encinio, California, USA. A popular band vocalist during the 40s swing era, Hutton was the half-sister of **Ina Ray Hutton**, and sang with her fine all-female band in the late 30s. From 1941-43 she was a member of **Charlie Spivak**'s vocal group, the Stardusters, and appeared with the Spivak outfit in the 1944 movie, *Pin Up Girl*, which starred **Betty Grable**. In that same year, Hutton replaced **Jo Stafford** in **Tommy Dorsey**'s renowned **Pied Pipers**, and stayed with the group after it left Dorsey. She was on Pipers hits such as 'Dream', 'Lily Belle', 'Aren't You Glad You're You?', 'Mam'selle', and 'Ok'l Baby Dok'l'. In 1950 she went solo, and during the next few years had US hits with 'Say You're Mine Again', 'No Stone Unturned' and 'For The First Time (In A Long Time)', all of which featured orchestral accompaniment by her husband, arranger-conductor **Axel Stordahl**. Along with other artists of her kind, she suffered with the arrival of rock 'n' roll, and by the end of the 50s her career was in decline.

● ALBUM: *Johnny Mercer And The Pied Pipers* (40s material)★★★.

Hutton, Marion

(see **Miller, Glenn**)

Hyams, Margie

b. 1923, New York City, New York, USA. Hyams's brother was the pianist Mike Hyams and she also played piano, but it was on vibraphone that she first attracted serious attention in the jazz world. While working in Atlantic City she was heard by **Woody Herman**, who hired her. From 1944 until 1945 she was a member of the First Herd, but left to play in the small group setting she favoured. Her trio was popular for the next few years and appeared regularly at the Hickory House on New York's 52nd Street. She also appeared in an all-woman trio led by **Mary Lou Williams** at a 1947 Carnegie Hall concert. In 1949 she joined **George Shearing**, appearing on several of his records, including the big hit 'September In The Rain'. In 1950 Hyams married **Rolf Ericson** and decided to leave a business which, while giving her pleasure and success, had brought more than its share of problems. Like so many women in jazz, she had grown tired of the pressures created by musicians who refused to take her very real talents seriously.

● COMPILATIONS: *Woody Herman's Greatest Hits* (1945)★★★, with others *Women In Jazz Vol. 1* (1948)★★★★, *The George Shearing Quintet: Lullaby Of Birdland* (1949-50)★★★.

Hyder, Ken

b. 29 June 1946, Dundee, Scotland. Hyder took up the drums at the age of 15 and began playing bebop in Edinburgh and Dundee. He soon switched to free jazz, inspired by the music of **John Coltrane** and **Albert Ayler** - and, in particular, by their drummers **Elvin Jones** and Sunny Murray. At the end of the 60s Hyder moved to London and in 1970 set up his group Talisker to explore and combine his interest in free jazz and Celtic folk musics. He guided Talisker through two decades and various personnel changes (though saxophonists John Rangecroft and Davie Webster play on most of the albums), and has provided a blueprint for the increasing number of European musicians who have been incorporating elements of folk music into their jazz. Hyder's own interest in Scottish and Irish traditional musics had led to collaborations with **Dick Gaughan**, Irish uillean piper Tomas Lynch and Scottish bagpipes player Dave Brooks. A more recent fascination with shamanic singing has taken him on research trips to Canada and Siberia and brought projects with vocalists Valentina Ponomareva, Sainkho Namchilak and Anatoly Kokov. Back in the 70s, Hyder played with **Julian Bahula**'s Jo'burg Hawk and in the 80s was busy on the UK improvised music scene, co-founding the occasional Orchestra Of Lights, recording *Under The Influence* with his octet, Big Team (which included **Chris Biscoe**, **Elton Dean** and **Paul Rogers**), and the duo Shams with ex-**Henry Cow** member Tim Hodgkinson. His latest group is the leftfield, 'polytempic' One Time, with members of B-Shops For The Poor and the Honkies.

● ALBUMS: with Talisker *Dreaming Of Glenisla* (1975)★★★, with Talisker *Land Of Stone* (1977)★★★, with Talisker *The Last Battle* (1978)★★★, with Talisker *The White Light* (1980)★★, *Under The Influence* (1984)★★★, with Dick Gaughan *Fanfare For Tomorrow* (1985)★★, with Talisker *Humanity* (1986)★★★, with Tim Hodgkinson *Shams* (1987)★★★, with Hodgkinson, Valentina Ponomareva *The Goose* (1992)★★.

Hydra

Based in the southern states of America, hard rock band Hydra formed in the early 70s around a line-up of Wayne Bruce (vocals, guitar), Spencer Kirkpatrick (guitar), Orville Davis (bass) and Steve Pace (drums). Signed to the **Allman Brothers** and **Marshall Tucker Band**'s record label, Capricorn Records, they made their debut in 1974 with a self-titled collection that drew heavily on **Lynyrd Skynyrd**'s southern boogie tradition, but also added elaborate pop hooks and disciplined rhythmic codas. Songs such as 'Glitter Queen' won them a fervent fanbase, though the subsequent *Land Of Money*, a more abrasive collection, was less successful. By the advent of *Rock The World* Davis had departed to join **Rex** and the resultant instability stalled the group's progress.

● ALBUMS: *Hydra* (Capricorn 1974)★★★, *Land Of Money* (Capricorn 1975)★★★, *Rock The World* (Polydor 1977)★★.

Hyland, Brian

b. 12 November 1943, Woodhaven, Queens, New York, USA. A demonstration disc, recorded with the artist's high school group the Delphis, alerted Kapp Records to Hyland's vocal talent. In 1960 he enjoyed a US chart-topper with 'Itsy Bitsy Teenie Weenie Yellow Polkadot Bikini', one of the era's best-known 'novelty' recordings which subsequently sold over one million copies. Having switched outlets to the larger **ABC** Paramount, the singer enjoyed further success with 'Let Me Belong To You (1961 - a US Top 20 hit) 'Ginny Come Lately' (1962 - a UK Top 10 hit), before securing a second gold award for 'Sealed With a Kiss'. Its theme of temporary parting was empathetic to the plight of many lovestruck teenagers and the song returned to the UK Top 10 in 1975 before being revived in 1990 by **Jason Donovan**. Hyland continued to enjoy US chart entries, notably with 'The Joker Went Wild' and 'Run, Run, Look And See' (both 1966), but reasserted his career in 1970 with a sympathetic version of the **Impressions**' 'Gypsy Woman'. This third million-seller was produced by long-time friend **Del Shannon**, who co-wrote several tracks on the attendant album, but this rekindled success proved shortlived and the artist later ceased recording.

● ALBUMS: *The Bashful Blonde* (Kapp 1960)★★, *Let Me Belong To You* (ABC 1961)★★, *Sealed With A Kiss* (ABC 1962)★★★, *Country Meets Folk* (ABC 1964)★, *Here's To Our Love* (Philips 1964)★★, *Rockin' Folk* (Philips 1965)★★, *The Joker Went Wild* (Philips 1966)★★★, *Tragedy* (1969)★★, *Stay And Love Me All Summer* (1969)★★, *Brian Hyland* (1970)★★.

● COMPILATIONS: *Golden Decade 1960-1970* (1988)★★★, *Ginny O Ginny* (1988)★★★.

Hylton, Jack

b. 2 July 1892, Lancashire, England, d. 29 January 1965, London, England. Hylton was the leader of an outstanding showband, often called 'Britain's answer to **Paul Whiteman**' because their repertoire included popular songs, novelties, light classical pieces and a few 'hot' jazz numbers. Hylton sang as a boy soprano in his father's bar before turning to the piano and organ. After playing in a small band at the Queen's Hall Roof in London, he took over, enlarged the group, and started recording in 1921. Although broadcasting occasionally, Hylton concentrated on 'live' performances, and built his showband into a major stage attraction. During the late 20s he toured Europe extensively, while still recording prolifically under several other names such as the Kit-Cat Band, the Hyltonians and the Rhythmagicians. He sold over three million records in 1929 alone, sometimes using gimmicks like flying low over Blackpool in an aircraft, to publicize Joe Gilbert's novelty song, 'Me And Jane In A Plane'. During the 30s his band became the first to broadcast directly to America. Subsequently, he toured the USA using local musicians, while still remaining the premier European showband. Hylton also made two films, *She Shall Have Music* (1935) and *Band Waggon* (1940) the movie version of the highly popular radio programme featuring Arthur Askey and Richard Murdoch. The band broke up in 1940, when several of the members were drafted into the forces. Hylton had used some of the best musicians, such as **Ted Heath**, Eric Pogson, **Jack Jackson**, Lew Davis, arranger **Billy Ternent**, jazzman **Coleman Hawkins**, and singers Jack Plant, Sam Browne and Peggy Dell. With his vast experience, Hylton then moved on to become an impresario, presenting countless West End productions such as *Annie Get Your Gun*, *Kiss Me, Kate*, *Call Me Madam*, *Camelot* and many more. One of his most endearing legacies was the legendary series of Crazy Gang shows at the Victoria Palace, London.

● COMPILATIONS: *Jack Hylton And His Orchestra* (1966)★★★, *Bands That Matter* (Eclipse 1970)★★★, *The Band That Jack Built* (Retrospect 1973)★★★, *Plays DeSylva, Brown & Henderson* (Retrospect 1974)★★★, *A Programme Light Orchestra Favour's* (1978)★★★, *From Berlin - 1927/31* (1979)★★★, *Jack's Back* (Living Era 1982)★★★, *Breakaway* (Joy 1982)★★★, *Swing* (Saville 1983)★★★, *The Talk Of The Town* (Saville 1984)★★★, *The Golden Age Of Jack Hylton* (Golden Age 1984)★★★, *I'm In A Dancing Mood* (Retrospect 1986)★★★, *Song Of Happiness 1931-33* (Saville 1987)★★★, *This'll Make You Whistle* (Burlington 1988)★★★, *Cream Of Jack Hylton* (Flapper 1992)★★★.

Hylton, Sheila

b. 1956, London, England. Hylton's family moved to Jamaica in 1959, and she later attended the Jamaica Commercial Institute. Her first association with the music business came when she worked as a secretary at Total Sounds. Uninspired by secretarial work, she later divided her time between working as an air hostess for Air Jamaica and singing under the guidance of **Harry J.** In 1979 her debut, 'Don't Ask My Neighbour', became a local chart hit and heralded the beginning of a fruitful partnership. In the early 70s Harry J. had produced a version of Jeanette Washington's 'Breakfast In Bed', which became an international hit for **Lorna Bennett**, and following Hylton's successful debut, Harry J. persuaded her to re-record the song; it entered the UK pop chart, and even surpassed his previous production. In 1980 she enjoyed a second foray into the pop charts with her interpretation of 'Bed's Too Big Without You', arranged by **Sly And Robbie** with Harry J. taking the production credits. Third I productions in the UK recorded an identical version of the Sly And Robbie cut with vocals supplied by Julie Roberts. The television documentary *Deep Roots Music* featured Hylton recording in the studio, with her proud mentor Harry J. producing. In 1983 she recorded 'Let's Dance', which was a minor hit in the reggae charts. Hylton left for the USA in 1984, where she found occasional employment and a husband. In 1995 she returned to Jamaica, where she signed a contract with **Tommy Cowan**'s Talent Corporation and recorded a version of **Diana Ross** And The **Supremes**' 'My World Is Empty Without You'.

● ALBUMS: *Sheila Hylton* (Harry J 1979)★★★.

Hyman, Dick

b. 8 March 1927, New York City, New York, USA. After studying classical music, Hyman broadened his interests to encompass jazz and many other areas of music. In the late 40s he played piano in and around his hometown, working with leading bop musicians, including founding fathers **Charlie Parker** and **Dizzy Gillespie**. Early in the 50s he began a long career as a studio musician, playing piano, arranging, composing and leading orchestras. His work in the studios did not keep him from actively participating in jazz dates, many of which he himself organized. He also became deeply interested in the history of jazz and especially the development of jazz piano. He demonstrated his interest in radio broadcasts and concert performances. His enormously eclectic taste allowed him to range from ragtime to freeform with complete confidence. Through performances and recordings with the New York Jazz Repertory Company, he encouraged interest in the music of **Jelly Roll Morton**, **Fats Waller**, **James P. Johnson** and **Louis Armstrong**. He also formed a small group, the Perfect Jazz Repertory Quintet. During his freeform period he played electric piano and later added the organ to the instruments at his command, recording *Cincinnati Fats*, *New School Concert* and other duo albums with **Ruby Braff**. Later still, Hyman recorded with Braff using, however improbably in a jazz context, a Wurlitzer organ. Unusual though it might have been, *A Pipe Organ Recital Plus One* was a critical and popular success. As a composer, Hyman has written for large and small ensembles and composed the score for the film *Scott Joplin* in 1976. A master of jazz piano, his performances not only display his extraordinary virtuoso technique but also demonstrate his deep understanding and abiding love for the great traditions of the music.

● ALBUMS: *60 Great All Time Songs, Volume 3* (MGM 1957)★★★, *Electrodynamics* (Command 1963)★★★, *Fabulous* (Command 1964)★★★, *Mirrors - Reflections Of*

Today (Command 1968)★★★, *Moog -The Electric Eclectics Of Dick Hyman* (Command 1969)★★★, *The Age Of Electronicus* (Command 1969)★★★, *The Happy Breed* (1972)★★★, *Genius At Play* (1973)★★★, *Some Rags, Some Stomps And A Little Blues* (1973)★★★★, with NYJRC *Satchmo Remembered* (1974)★★★, *Scott Joplin: The Complete Works For Piano* (1975)★★★★, *A Waltz Dressed In Blue* (1977)★★★, *Charleston* (1977)★★, *Sliding By* (1977)★★★, *Ragtime, Stomp And Stride* (1977)★★★, with NYJRC *The Music Of Jelly Roll Morton* (1978)★★★, *Dick Hyman And The Perfect Jazz Repertory Quintet Plays Irving Berlin* (World Jazz 1979)★★★, *Dick Hyman Piano Solos* (Monmouth 1979)★★★, with Ruby Braff *Cincinnati Fats* (1981)★★★★, with Braff *A Pipe Organ Recital Plus One* (1982)★★★, *The New School Concert 1983* (1983)★★★, *Kitten On The Keys: The Music Of Zez Confrey* (1983)★★, with Braff *The New School Concert 1983* (1983)★★★, *Eubie* (1984)★★★, *Manhattan Jazz* (Limelight 1985)★★★, *Music Of 1937* (Concord 1990)★★★, with Braff *Younger Than Swingtime* (1990)★★★.

Hyman, Phyllis

b. Pittsburgh, Pennsylvania, USA, d. 30 June 1995. A singer, actress and fashion model, Hyman was one of several acts nurtured by vocalist **Norman Connors**. Although she had already secured a minor R&B hit with 'Baby I'm Gonna Love You' in 1976, a duet with Connors the following year, covering the **Stylistics** hit 'Betcha By Golly Wow', brought the artist a wider audience. Although Hyman failed to reach the US pop Top 100, over the next 10 years she enjoyed 13 soul hits, including 'You Know How To Love Me' (1979) and 'Can't We Fall In Love Again' (1981). The latter release coincided with the singer's appearance in the Broadway musical *Sophisticated Ladies*.

● ALBUMS: *Phyllis Hyman* (Buddah 1977)★★, *Somewhere In My Lifetime* (Arista 1979)★★★, *Sing A Song* (Buddah 1979)★★★, *You Know How To Love Me* (Arista 1979)★★★★, *Can't We Fall In Love Again* (Arista 1981)★★★★, *Goddess Of Love* (Arista 1983)★★★, *Living All Alone* (Philadelphia International 1986)★★★, *Prime Of My Life* (Philadelphia International 1991)★★★.

● COMPILATIONS: *The Best Of Phyllis Hyman* (Arista 1986)★★★, *The Legacy Of Phyllis Hyman* (Arista 1996)★★★★, *Sweet Music* (Camden 1998)★★★.

Hymns To The Silence - Van Morrison

A double CD at this stage of his career came as a surprise, but a double CD this good, came as a shock. Morrison had a great deal to say in 1991 about his childhood and his faith; much of it came through on this record in a much less oblique way than we had been used to. The spoken dialogue on 'On Hyndford Street' is intensely personal and revealing. For once, we were hearing Morrison's thoughts. Morrison clearly has religion but on this riveting record he refused to preach. Georgie Fame continued to add familiarity to the sound and this was the best Morrison album for many, many years.

● Tracks: *Professional Jealousy; I'm Not Feeling It Anymore;*

Ordinary Life; Some Peace Of Mind; So Complicated; I Can't Stop Loving You; Why Must I Always Explain; Village Idiot; See Me Through Part II (Just A Closer Walk With Thee); Take Me Back; By His Grace; All Saints Day; Hymns To The Silence; On Hyndford Street; Be Thou My Vision; Carrying A Torch; Green Mansions; Pagan Streams; Quality Street; It Must Be You; I Need Your Kind Of Loving.
- First released 1991
- UK peak chart position: 5
- USA peak chart position: 99

Hype-A-Delics

Rap crew, based in the Templehof region of Berlin, though only DJ Derezon (b. Berlin) is a native German. The two MC's, Rodski (b. New York, USA) and BMG the Funky Funktioneer (b. Flint, Michigan, USA) are both relics of America's armed presence in West Germany, where their fathers were in the services. Both, however, are now married and settled in their adopted country. Derezon and Rodski had worked together under different names for several years, signing to Ariole as the Hype-A-Delics in 1991. After one single they departed and added BMG - who had formerly worked with his own crew back in Flint (Rodski had also been a friend of **Doctor Ice** in his Brooklyn days). They have subsequently inaugurated their own Juiceful Records, now home to several German hip hop crews including Cheeba Garden and Islamic Force. This imprint released their debut album in 1994, which reflected their concerns over the rise of the right wing in Europe, as well as dissing the police and praising the herb.
- ALBUMS: *More Funk For You Ass* (Juiceful 1994)★★★.

Hyper Go-Go

Never regarded as strikingly original, Hyper Go-Go are nevertheless one of the most commercially prominent UK house acts, a fact confirmed when their early singles, including 'High' (UK number 30) and 'Never Let Go' (number 45), both crossed over into the UK charts. The team, James Diplock and Alex Ball, have been working together since they left school in the mid-80s. They have their own studio, a converted warehouse in the middle of a disused airfield, in the heart of the Essex countryside. 'High' was originally released on **Hooj Toons** before being picked up by **DeConstruction**. For 'Never Let Go', a typical 'storming piano house tune', they switched to the **Positiva** label on a more permanent footing. 'Raise' used the familiar 'Raise Your Hands' vocal line as its core, with guest vocals from Brian Chambers. Other contributors have included Sally Anne Marsh, currently of **Hysterix**. Bell and Diplock are also one half of techno/rave sideline Electroset (whose 'How Does It Feel?' was their 'rave thing') and experimental electronic outfit Compufonic ('Ecstacy 0376' for Ocean Records in 1992, now signed to **Mute** for whom they debuted with the *Make It Move* EP).

Hyperhead

When the UK band **Gaye Bykers On Acid** folded, frontman Mary Mary (previously known as Mary Byker, though his real name is Ian Garfield Hoxley) began following a different musical path, working with the experimental industrial collective **Pigface**, before forming Hyperhead with a long-time friend, American bassist Karl Leiker. Pigface colleagues Martin Atkins (drums, ex-**PiL**; **Killing Joke**) and guitarist William Tucker (**My Life With The Thrill Kill Kult**; **Revolting Cocks**), along with guitarist Paul Dalloway, contributed to *Metaphasia*, showcasing an unpredictable hybrid style that drew from hard rock, soul, funk, indie pop and industrial for a diverse and interesting album. Mary, Leiker and Dalloway assembled a touring band with guitarist Oscar, drummer Chin and percussionist Keith, and this line-up recorded the *Terminal Fear* EP, which actually preceded *Metaphasia*'s release. Hyperhead established an excellent live reputation, boosted by Keith's sometimes crazed behaviour on stage, adding to the band's unpredictable air.
- ALBUMS: *Metaphasia* (Devotion 1993)★★★.

Hypnotics, (Thee)

Formed in High Wycombe, Buckinghamshire, England, this **MC5** and **Stooges**-influenced group was the product of James Jones (vocals), Ray Hanson (guitar), Will Pepper (bass) and Mark Thompson (drums). On the strength of 'Love In A Different Vein' (1988), their debut single on the Hipsville label, the band signed to **Beggars Banquet Records** offshoot Situation 2, and enjoyed independent chart success early the following year with the eight-minute 'Justice In Freedom'. Awash with loud, distorted, wah-wah guitars and blues riffs, the single had to be re-pressed due to popular demand. The powerful 'Soul Trader' followed later that year, and after supports to **Spacemen 3** and **Gaye Bykers On Acid** the band commemorated their first national tour with a live mini-album, *Live'r Than God!*. A tour of the USA with the **Cult** won them praise across the Atlantic, before the band's first studio album surfaced early in 1990. *Come Down Heavy* was more refined and showed a definite nod towards early **Santana**, with guest appearances from the **Pretty Things**' Dick Taylor and Phil May. Two singles followed, 'Half Man Half Boy' and 'Floatin' In My Hoodoo Dream', before the band appeared at the 1990 Reading Festival. However, in 1992 band member Craig Pike died of a heroin overdose. *The Very Crystal Speed Machine* (only released in the UK a year later) saw production from Chris Robinson and friends from the **Black Crowes**, and reflected on his passing with the mournful 'Goodbye'.
- ALBUMS: *Live'r Than God!* mini-album (Sub Pop 1989)★★★, *Come Down Heavy* (Beggars Banquet 1990)★★, *Soul, Glitter And Sin* (Beggars Banquet 1991)★★★, *The Very Crystal Speed Machine* (SPV/American 1994)★★★.

Hypnotised - Undertones

Often neglected next to the Undertones' debut, *Hypnotised* has huge merit of its own. Prior to the more ragged experimentalism of *Positive Touch*, *Hypnotised* saw the Undertones rampantly expanding on their favourite subjects (as declared by the self-explanatory title track, 'More Songs About Chocolate And Girls'). It was the latter that always proved a mystery to the Derry five-piece: practically every song makes mention of females either collectively or singularly, yet never mentions one by name. The feeling is one of schoolyard chaps bemused by the opposite sex, treating them with a reverence one would associate with an alien culture. Psychology aside, the tracks are without exception rip-roaring efforts, especially the mighty 'Tearproof'. However, you will have to buy the CD to pick up the superb 'You've Got My Number'.

● Tracks: *More Songs About Chocolate And Girls; There Goes Norman; Hypnotised; See That Girl; Whizz Kids; Under The Broadwalk; The Way Girls Talk; Hard Luck; My Perfect Cousin; Boys Will Be Boys; Tearproof; Wednesday Week; Nine Times Out Of Ten; Girls That Don't Talk; What's With Terry?; You've Got My Number (Why Don't You Use It); Hard Luck (Again); Let's Talk About Girls; I Told You So; I Don't Wanna See You Again.*

● First released 1980

● UK peak chart position: 6

● USA peak chart position: did not chart

Hypnotist, The

Comprising UK **Rising High Records**' owner Casper Pound (b. c.1970; once the 'hippie' in **A Homeboy, A Hippie And A Funki Dred**), and in the early stages Pete Smith. Pound rejoiced in statements like: 'I wanna scare people on the dancefloor. I wanna use sounds that are disturbing to the mind and really freak people out when they're tripping'. He seemed determined to prove his mettle with cuts like debut 12-inch 'Rainbows In The Sky' and 'This House Is Mine', the latter a Top 75 hit single in September 1991. More notorious was *The Hardcore* EP, which included the neo-legendary 'Hardcore U Know The Score'. Follow-ups included 'Live In Berlin' (The Hypnotist were celebrated as pop stars in Germany) and 'Pioneers Of The Universe'. Pound also works as part of **Rising High Collective** with former **Shamen** vocalist Plavka, and records under the name New London School Of Electronics and several more. He is also a distant relative of the US poet Ezra Pound.

● ALBUMS: *The Complete Hypnotist* (Rising High 1992)★★★.

Hypnotone

Hypnotone revolves around Tony Martin, who had previously worked with **Creation Records** with a different line-up featuring the vocals of **Denise Johnson** on releases such as 'Dream Beam' (remixed by **Danny Rampling** and Ben Champion). The modern Hypnotone included vocalist Cordelia Ruddock,

discovered by Martin at a fashion show, Lee Royle, whom he met through a computer bulletin board and Cormac Fultan, a pianist and organist, who met Martin in the more conventional environment of a bar.

Hypocrisy

One of Sweden's more extreme metal concerns, combining a musical intensity that borders on spite and unremittingly dark and violent lyrics. Comprising Peter Tägtgren (vocals, guitar, keyboards), Michael Hedlund (drums) and Lars Szöke (drums), Hypocrisy's reputation was established with *Osculum Obscenum* and European tours with labelmates **Brutality**. Forthright exponents of black metal, the group's exposition of the mystical and diabolical was conveyed in tracks such as 'Orgy In Blood' and 'The Arrival Of The Demons' on their 1994 opus, *Fourth Dimension*. This saw the trio concentrate on generating the maximum possible power from their riffs, sacrificing some velocity in the process. However, generally superior songwriting (particularly the title track and 'Apocalypse') ensured that they lost nothing in impact. *The Final Chapter*, their ninth release, was dominated by more of the same forceful riffing.

● ALBUMS: *Osculum Obscenum* (Nuclear Blast 1993)★★★, *Fourth Dimension* (Nuclear Blast 1994)★★★★ *The Final Chapter* (Nuclear Blast 1997)★★★.

Hypocrisy Is The Greatest Luxury - Disposable Heroes Of Hiphoprisy

Often berated as the group that it is OK for non-rap fans to like, the Disposable Heroes' solitary album proper represents much more than that might imply. Shades of Michael Franti and Rono Tse's previous incarnation, as part of the Beatnigs, resurface in the collision of samples, noise and breakbeats. Tse's technique is exemplary. However, it is Franti's fiercely intelligent narratives that carry the day. Where bombast and finger-pointing had been the order of the day in hip-hop, Franti includes his own inadequacies (notably calling himself a 'jerk' in 'Music And Politics') in his diagnosis of the problem.

● Tracks: *Satanic Reverses; Famous And Dandy (Like Amos 'N' Andy); Television, The Drug Of The Nation; Language Of Violence; The Winter Of The Long Hot Summer; Hypocrisy Is The Greatest Luxury; Everyday Life Has Become A Health Risk; Ins Greencard A-19 191 500; Socio-Genetic Experiment; Music And Politics; Financial Leprosy; California Über Alles; Water Pistol Man.*

● First released 1992

● UK peak chart position: 40

● USA peak chart position: did not chart

Hyskos

Formed in Los Angeles, California, USA, Hyskos drew much of their inspiration from the burgeoning fantasy role playing scene. Dungeons and dragons' styled mythological themes dotted their debut album, released on their own record label in 1982. Tony Gonzales (guitar), Art Gonzalez (guitar), Barry Benjamin (bass), Clay Guinaldo (drums) and Mark Bradley (vocals) found little favour among local critics. Even in 1982, such medieval sword and sorcery themes seemed passé, and their hoped for leap to a major label never took place.

● ALBUMS: *Hyskos* (Hyskos 1982)★★.

Hysteria - Def Leppard

Four years after *Pyromania*, Def Leppard were a comparative write-off. Dismissed by critics, seemingly dogged by bad luck, with drummer Rick Allen losing an arm in a car accident, *Hysteria* had to be an album to turn heads. In retrospect, it sounded like the first true hard rock record for the CD generation. Ambitious arrangements and remixes on songs such as 'Rocket' and 'Armaggedon It', a crisp single in 'Animal', and a dense paean to love with 'Love Bites', all bets were off. Def Leppard had created an intriguing language of ideas that still speaks volumes more than a decade on.

● Tracks: *Women; Rocket; Animal; Love Bites; Pour Some Sugar On Me; Armaggedon It; Gods Of War; Don't Shoot Shot Gun; Run Riot; Hysteria; Excitable; Love And Affection; I Can't Let You Be A Memory.*

● First released 1987

● UK peak chart position: 1

● USA peak chart position: 1

Hysterix

Formed when the principal members met up on the Tokyo dance music scene, where Tony Quinn was DJing at the Gold club for Yohji Yahamoto, Hysterix are not yet the most renowned of **DeConstruction**'s acts. However, they have not been absent through want of trying. A typical act of anarchy came in 1993 when, via a live pirate broadcast, they illegally interrupted terrestrial television to transmit the slogan 'You've been Hysterixed!'. Dance magazine columns regularly overflowed with tales of their clubland ligging. They blew their record advance on tequila during an all-expenses trip to Mexico to shoot a video, which never materialised. Another five day jaunt to Florida was arranged when they pretended to be a completely different band. They joined **Technotronic** on their Eastern European tour, demanding payment in champagne and caviar, and persuaded **Jean-Michel Jarre** to let them mix his work, staying at a hotel drinking Dom Perignon at his expense and completely forgetting to deliver the tape. They have also kidnapped their manager and booking agent and left them tied up at Skegness railway station, among many other pranks. Influenced by the original disco sounds of **T Connection** and **Earth, Wind And Fire** as much as late 80s house, they were signed to their label for a full three years before a debut single, 'Must Be The Magic', emerged. DeConstruction had originally been impressed by the 'Talk To Me' 12-inch, which later saw a tremendously popular, but elusive **Sasha** remix. The nucleus of the group is 'Tokyo' Tony Quinn, Darren Black and Richard Belgrave. Their numerous female vocalists have included ex-**KLF** singer Maxine, though from October 1993 the band chose Sally Anne Marsh and Marie Harper. Marsh had originally been part of Tom Watkins (manager of **Bros, East 17** etc) pop act Faith Hope And Charity when she was 14, alongside television 'presenter' Danni Behr. She also sang on Xpansions Top 10 hit, 'Move Your Body', in 1991, and has worked with **Hyper Go Go** and **Aerial**. Harper, meanwhile, formerly operated on the jazz circuit. Hysterix finally looked as though they were getting their house in order for 1994, supporting **D:Ream** on their UK tour and garnering good press for the single.

Hyts

While most AOR artists stand or fall by the ability of their vocalist to present the genre's emotional melodrama with conviction and empathy, that was not the case with California, USA group Hyts. While there was nothing amiss with vocalist Roland Little's delivery, the contributions of Stan Miller (bass), Tommy Thompson (keyboards/guitar) and Roy Garcia (drums) were less effective in animating his lovelorn lyrics. Following a self-titled debut collection for Gold Mountain Records, the group moved to **A&M Records** in 1985 for the improved *Looking From The Outside*. Despite this, Hyts faded from view as competition to gain space on the all-important AOR airwaves defeated them.

● ALBUMS: *Hyts* (Gold Mountain 1983)★★, *Looking From The Outside* (A&M 1985)★★★.

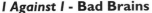

I Against I - Bad Brains

Some people just don't 'get' Bad Brains. To be fair, their early recordings can be intimidating, and it is only when you familiarize yourself with the musical dialectics of tracks such as 'Pay To Cum' that you can really appreciate their kinetic aesthetic. Abandoning the speed-freak punk cum dub reggae crossover of old, Bad Brains now employed funk and conventional rock stylings. What they lost in 'edge' they more than compensated for in power, allowing temperamental vocalist H.R. to make the most of his famously elastic vocal range over the album's 31 minutes. The exception was 'Sacred Love', where H.R.'s vocals were phoned in from jail during recording sessions after being busted for marijuana possession.

● Tracks: *Intro; I Against I; House Of Suffering; Re-Ignition; Secret 77; Let Me Help; She's Calling You; Sacred Love; Hired Gun; Return To Heaven.*

● First released 1986

● UK peak chart position: did not chart

● USA peak chart position: did not chart

I Am - Earth Wind And Fire

Very possibly one of the most uplifting albums ever released. The combination of brass and quite immaculate harmonies induce a feeling of warmth and big cheesy grins. Earth Wind And Fire sound like a family; they sound as if they know what they are doing, and mostly, they sound as if they like it. Every track is a rush of adrenalin, even the one weepie 'After The Love Has Gone' still manages to retain the atmosphere of overall happiness. Supported by the Emotions and a cast of hundreds of violins, trumpets, trombones, cellos and french horns, this is mainstream soul music at its very, very best.

● Tracks: *In The Stone; Can't Let Go; After The Love Has Gone; Let Your Feelings Show; Boogie Wonderland; Star; Wait; Rock That; You And I.*

● First released 1979

● UK peak chart position: 5

● USA peak chart position: 3

I Can Get It For You Wholesale

Notable mainly for the Broadway debut of the 19-year-old **Barbra Streisand**, who, in her role as an overworked secretary, stopped the show nightly with 'Miss Marmelstein', this production opened at the Shubert Theatre in New York on 22 March 1962. The 'wholesale' aspect referred to librettist Jerome Weidman's story, based on his own book, which was set in the 30s Depression days of the 'dog-eat-dog' world of New York's rag trade. Harry Bogen (Elliot Gould) is the tough small-time businessman, who will stop at nothing to get to the top, even though his mother, (Lillian Roth) and his girlfriend, Ruthie Rivkin (Marilyn Cooper) plead with him to change his ways. Ruthie is replaced by the flashy nightclub singer, Martha Mills (Sheree North), and, in the end, Harry gets his just deserts. Streisand was low down in the billing, but she was given another effective number, 'What Are They Doing To Us Now?', in a what was generally considered to be a lacklustre **Harold Rome** score that also included 'Have I Told You Lately?', 'Momma, Momma', 'The Sound Of Money', 'A Gift for Today', 'On My Way To Love', 'Too Soon', 'What's In It For Me?', and 'Who Knows'. Even during the show's run of 300 performances, the young, self-assured lady who married the leading man (Gould), was recording her breakthrough *The Barbra Streisand Album*, complete with its prophetic sleeve-note by no less a person than **Harold Arlen**, part of which ran: 'I advise you to watch Barbra Streisand's career. This young lady has a stunning future'. How right he was.

I Could Go On Singing

Nine years elapsed between **Judy Garland**'s critically acclaimed performance in *A Star Is Born* and this, her next musical film, which was released in 1963 and provoked an entirely different response. Mayo Simon's often poignant story was about a star American singer, Jenny Bowman (Garland), who travels to England for a concert tour and, while there, engineers a meeting with Harley Street surgeon David Donne (Dirk Bogarde), in an effort to get to know their illegitimate son, Matt (Gregory Phillips). Jenny's craving for the boy's affection, and his sudden realization that she is his mother, bordered on the maudlin and was generally unconvincing. Not so the musical sequences, however, in which Garland was at the top of her form. She pulled all the stops out on **E.Y. 'Yip' Harburg** and **Harold Arlen**'s highly appropriate title song, and on the other lovely numbers such as 'It Never Was You' (**Kurt Weill-Maxwell Anderson**), 'By Myself' (**Arthur Schwartz-Howard Dietz**), and 'Hello, Bluebird' (Cliff Friend). Dirk Bogarde himself provided some additional (and much-needed) extra dialogue, and gave his usually efficient performance. Also in the cast were Jack Klugman as George Kogan (Jenny's long-suffering manager), Aline MacMahon, Pauline Jameson, and Russell Waters. Ronald Neame directed what sadly proved to be Garland's last film. It was produced by Stuart Millar and Laurence Turman in Eastman Color and Panavision for Barbican Films in Great Britain, and released by United Artists.

I Do! I Do!

This musical opened at the 46th Street Theatre in New York on 5 December 1966 with a cast consisting of just two people. However, they were two extraordinary people - each of them a theatrical legend. **Robert Preston** had burst onto the Broadway scene some nine years previously as the conniving Professor Harold Hill in *The Music Man*, and **Mary Martin**'s glorious career in musicals such as *One Touch Of Venus*, *South Pacific*, *Peter Pan*, and *The Sound Of Music*, was destined to end with this unusual two-hander. **Tom Jones**'s book, which was adapted from the 1951 play *The Fourposter* by Jan de Hartog, told of a couple's 50 years of marriage, from their wedding day at the turn of the century, through the good times and bad, the arrival of the children, his affair, and finally, their exit from the large house to make way for a young couple with, no doubt, the same kind of aspirations that she (Agnes) and he (Michael) had all those years ago. Tom Jones and **Harvey Schmidt**'s score augmented the story with appropriate numbers such as 'I Love My Wife', 'My Cup Runneth Over', 'Love Isn't Everything', 'Nobody's Perfect', 'Together Forever', 'What Is A Woman?', 'The Honeymoon Is Over', 'Where Are The Snows?', 'When The Kids Get Married', 'Someone Needs Me', 'Roll Up the Ribbons', and the title song. Carol Lawrence and **Gordon MacRae** succeeded the two original stars during the New York production which ran for over a year, a total of 560 performances. Jones and Schmidt are familiar with long runs - their off-Broadway show, *The Fantasticks*, has reigned for over 30 years. The London production of *I Do! I Do!*, with Ian Carmichael and Ann Rogers, played for 166 performances in 1968, and a short-lived 1976 West End revival starred Rock Hudson and Juliet Prowse.

I Feel For You - Chaka Khan

Just as people were beginning to think she had peaked (after the less than great *Chaka Khan*), she bounced back with this excellent set. Using a glut of producers - Mardin, Titleman, Foster and more - she attempted, and achieved, the combination of a great choice of material with the ability to keep her fans dancing. The Bacharach/Bayer Sager/Roberts 'Stronger Than Before' is beautifully performed, and la-di-da, ex-Spooky Tooth Gary Wright wrote 'My Love Is Alive'. Prince's 'I Feel For You' is another strong track, featuring the distinctive harmonica sound of Stevie Wonder. A pretty joyous album for dusting away cobwebs.
● Tracks: *This Is My Night; Stronger Than Before; My Love Is Alive; Eye To Eye; La Flamme; I Feel For You; Hold Her; Through The Fire; Caught In The Act; Chinatown.*
● First released 1984
● UK peak chart position: 15
● USA peak chart position: 14

I Feel Like I'm Fixin' To Die - Country Joe And The Fish

Apart from the 'let's look weird' cover shot, this is merely a dressed-up folk rock album made unusual by some stinging guitar from the talented Barry Melton. It was his sound more than Country Joe's voice that gave them a unique psych sound. In fact, sometimes the guitar is so laid-back a non-stoned listener could doze off. This is the one with the famous Woodstock anthem and anti-war song rolled into one, 'The Fish Cheer & I Feel Like I'm Fixing To Die Rag'. Sadly, it all sounds just a little bit twee and dated, apart from the afore-mentioned Melton guitar.
● Tracks: *The Fish Cheer & I Feel Like I'm Fixing To Die Rag; Who Am I; Pat's Song; Rock Coast Blues; Magoo; Janis; Thought Dream; Thursday; Eastern Jam; Colours For Susan.*
● First released 1967
● UK peak chart position: did not chart
● USA peak chart position: 67

I Give My Heart

This film version of the celebrated 1931 German operetta *The Dubarry* by Paul Knepler and J.M. Welleminsky, with music by Carl Millöcker adapted by Theo Mackeben, was released by British International Pictures in 1935. The story is set in France in 1769, where the delightful Gitta Alpar, who starred in the original production, recreates her role as Jeanne, the little milliner who dispenses her favours rather freely to, among others, her compatriot René (Patrick Waddington), and husband Count Dubarry (Arthur Margetson), in an effort to achieve her ambition of becoming the mistress of Louis XV (Owen Nares). The Marechale de Luxembourg (Margaret Bannerman) and Choiseul (Hugh Miller) plot together to rouse the Paris mob against her, but they are overwhelmed by the majority of people who have come to love their little Jeanne. Other roles were taken by Gibb McClaughlin, Iris Ashley, and Hay Petrie. All the famous songs were retained, and Gitta Alpar excelled in a cast of all-round excellent vocal talents. A charming and appealing film, it had a screenplay by Frank Launder, Roger Burford, Kurt Siodmak, and Paul Perez, adapted from the original play. After this film, director Marcel Varnel left the world of operetta and devoted all his energies to creating classic comedy films starring Will Hay, **George Formby**, the Crazy Gang and Arthur Askey.

I Got A Name - Jim Croce

One of the most catastrophic stories in popular music. In the summer of 1973, Croce was somewhere on the road to stardom; his style was balladic and it fell between James Taylor and Gordon Lightfoot, with a down-to-earth quality that probably came from his direct blue-collar experience and which, despite the hits and exposure, he never lost. Croce had just hit the top when his life was taken in a plane crash. This set, completed before his demise but released posthumously, is ironically his most accomplished - what might have followed can only be guessed at; he was certainly stretching the accepted idea of folk singer-songwriters, and he was highly popular. In the afterglow, both the title track and 'Time In A Bottle', an aching love song, rocketed up the American charts. His removal was tragic and untimely.

● Tracks: *I Got A Name; Lover's Cross; Five Short Minutes; Age; Workin' At The Car Wash Blues; I'll Have To Say I Love You In A Song; Salon And Saloon; Thursday; Top Hat Bar And Grille; Recently; The Hard Way Every Time.*

● First released 1973

● UK peak chart position: did not chart

● USA peak chart position: 2

I Got My Mojo Workin' - Jimmy Smith

Nobody, but nobody, has ever made the Hammond organ work so hard as Smith. He is the undisputed king of jazz organ, and defined the sound of 'soul jazz' throughout the 60s. His work with arrangers such as *Oliver Nelson* represents the commercial peak of his long career. This album is one of many on the Verve label that it was cool to tuck under your arm and say that you owned. Smooth covers of 'C-Jam Blues', 'Satisfaction' and 'Hi Heel Sneakers' complement the originals as another entirely different way of playing them. The bargain CD reissue has the complete *Hoochie Coochie Man* as a fantastic bonus.

● Tracks: *Hi-Heel Sneakers; (I Can't Get No) Satisfaction; 1-2-3; Mustard Greens; Got My Mojo Working; Johnny Come Lately; C-Jam Blues; Hobson's Hop; I'm Your Hoochie Coochie Man; One Mint Julip; Ain't That Just Like A Woman; Boom Boom; Blues And The Abstract Truth; TNT; (I Can't Get No) Satisfaction (alternate take).*

● First released 1966

● UK peak chart position: 19 & did not chart

● USA peak chart position: 28 & 77

I Just Can't Stop It - The Beat

Along with Madness and the Specials, the Beat were the best of the late 70s two-tone movement. Left-of-centre politics were coupled to a sensitive grasp of ska and blue beat. Their debut is virtually a greatest hits package with the sparkling 'Mirror In The Bathroom', 'Hands Off She's Mine' and 'Twist And Crawl'. Additionally there are great covers of Andy Williams' smooth ballad 'Can't Get Used To Losing You' and a wonderful rude 'Rough Rider' first heard in 1968 from Prince Buster. Singer Dave Wakeling left in 1983 to form General Public and the band fell apart.

● Tracks: *Mirror In The Bathroom; Hands Off She's Mine; Two Swords; Twist & Crawl; Rough Rider; Click Click; Big Shot; Whine & Grine/Stand Down Margaret; Noise In This World; Can't Get Used To Losing You; Best Friend; Jackpot.*

● First released 1980

● UK peak chart position: 3

● USA peak chart position: did not chart

I Love My Wife

Wife-swapping in Trenton, New Jersey, USA (popula-tion a healthy 92,124), was the slightly old-fashioned subject of Michael Stewart's book for this show which opened at the Ethel Barrymore Theatre on Broadway on 17 April 1977. The two couples, initially intent on being 'Sexually Free', 'Lovers On A Christmas Eve', where 'Everybody Is Turning On' because they each feel there is 'Something Wonderful I've Missed', were Ileen Graff, Lenny Baker, Joanna Gleason, and James Naughton. Of course, being decent, upright citizens, they changed their minds at the last minute - one of the men takes an age to undress - and even then has to finish his dessert - with both husbands affirming: 'I Love My Wife'. Those songs, and the show's outstanding number, 'Hey There, Good Times', were the work of **Cy Coleman** (music) and Michael Stewart (lyrics). A small onstage orchestra dressed in various fancy clothing, comments on the action in the manner of a Greek chorus, a device that was also used by **Richard Rodgers** and **Oscar Hammerstein II** in *Allegro*. *I Love My Wife* caught on, and had a good run of 872 performances. The London production, which opened in October 1977, also did well. It starred Richard Beckinsale, an extremely popular actor in British television comedy programmes such as *Porridge*, who died so tragically young.

I Married An Angel

Originally intended for Hollywood, this adaptation by **Richard Rodgers** and **Lorenz Hart** of an Hungarian play by John Vaszary, changed course and flew into New York, and landed at the Shubert Theatre on 11 May 1938. It turned out to be a satirical, comic-fantasy concerning a banker in Budapest, Count Willy Palaffi (Dennis King), who breaks off his engagement to Audrey Christie (Ann Murphy), swearing that he will only ever marry an angel. Lo and behold, an apparition answering to the name of Angel (Vera Zorina), flies in through Willy's window. They are wed, but Angel's open and honest winning ways cause chaos and confusion until she is taken in hand by Willie's sister, Countess Palaffi (Vivienne Segal). Walter Slezak, the Austrian character actor who later had a successful Hollywood career, played the financial backer who bailed out Willie when he was in trouble. Vivienne Segal was a revelation. For more than 20 years she had valiantly hung on to her honour in operettas such as *The Desert Song* and *The Yankee Princess*, and yet, here she was in *I Married An Angel*, shining in a sophisticated comedy role. King, too, who was a classically trained singer, came from a similar background, and the two combined on one of Rodgers and Hart's loveliest ballads, the bleak 'Spring Is Here' ('Stars appear!/Why doesn't the night invite me?/Maybe it's because nobody loves me/Spring is here. I hear!'). King, of course, sang the title song, which also endured in the repertoires of several high-quality vocalists. The ex-ballet dancer, Vera Zorina, was graceful and charming, but Audrey Christie had the show-stopper, 'At The Roxy Music Hall', a hilarious send-up of that vast, venerable institution: 'Where they change the lights a million times a minute/Where the stage goes up and down when they begin in it/It's a wonder Mrs. Roosevelt isn't in it.' . . . 'Where the acrobats are whirling on their digits/Where the balcony's so high you get the fidgets/Where the actors seem to be a lot of midgets/At the Roxy Music Hall'. The rest of the composers' songs in a high-quality score included 'Did You Ever Get Stung?', 'I'll Tell The Man In The Street', 'How To Win Friends And Influence People', 'A Twinkle In Your Eye', 'I'm Ruined', and 'Angel Without Wings'. This was an unusual show in many ways, for instance, there was a full-scale ballet in each of the two acts, and some of the dialogue leading up to the songs was rhymed and sung. The production was also notable as the Broadway debut of director Joshua Logan, who was associated with subsequent Rodgers and Hart shows, and with Rodgers and **Oscar Hammerstein**'s *South Pacific*. Miss Segal's impact, too, earned her the plum role of Vera Simpson in *Pal Joey* in 1940. *I Married An Angel* enjoyed a good run of 338 performances, which was followed by a satisfying road tour. The 1942 film version starred **Jeanette MacDonald** and **Nelson Eddy**.

I Mother Earth

Alternative rock band I Mother Earth were formed in Toronto, Canada, in 1990. Within two years the group: Christian Tanna (drums), brother Jagori Tanna (bass), Luis Conte (drums) and Daniel Mansilla (guitar), had set off a major label bidding war. The eventual winners were **Capitol Records**. However, the ensuing debut set, *Dig*, was ineffectively marketed, falling, like so many records of the period, between the spheres of heavy metal and alternative rock. Despite selling some 70,000 copies in Canada, there was a long gap between the debut and the follow-up, *Scenery And Fish*, as the group concentrated on touring. This second set featured a slightly less harsh, more commercially orientated collection of songs. 'One More Astronaut', released as a single, proved that the absence had not dulled I Mother Earth's edge, and featured an innovative video coupled to the group's first truly convincing commercial song.

● ALBUMS: *Dig* (Capitol 1993)★★, *Scenery And Fish* (Capitol 1996)★★★.

I Never Loved A Man The Way I Love You - Aretha Franklin

Aretha Franklin emerged from years of often inappropriate recordings with Columbia with 'I Never Loved A Man', one of soul music's definitive performances. The song's simple, uncluttered arrangement allowed the singer free expression and her sense of artistic relief is palpable. The attendant album captured all of Franklin's gifts as she brings gospel fervour and individuality to a peerless collection of songs. Material drawn from Sam Cooke, Otis Redding and Ray Charles is infused with a rampant spirituality and given new perspectives when sung by this woman. The set also provides a showcase for Aretha's own compositional skills, as well as her propulsive piano playing which both employs and boosts the forcefulness of her singing. This album unleashed a major talent.

● Tracks: *Respect; Drown In My Own Tears; I Never Loved A Man (The Way I Love You); Soul Serenade; Don't Let Me Lose This Dream; Baby, Baby, Baby; Dr. Feelgood (Love Is A Serious Business); Good Times; Do Right Woman Do Right Man; Save Me; A Change Is Gonna Come.*

● First released 1967

● UK peak chart position: 36

● USA peak chart position: 2

I Still Believe In You - Vince Gill

Vince Gill wrote this album with eight songwriting partners, yet it still has a consistency and fluidity of its own. This is a truly great collection of love songs performed by a country singer with a beautiful tenor voice. Every track could make you weep but extra tissues are needed for 'One More Last Chance', I Still Believe In You' and 'Tryin' To Get Over You'. The care and attention lavished on this album is evident in every note, where nothing has been left to chance. The excellent musicians include Delbert McClinton, who played harmonica on Bruce Channel's 'Hey! Baby'.

● Tracks: *Don't Let Our Love Start Slipping Away; No Future In The Past; Nothing Like A Woman; Tryin' To Get Over You; Say Hello; One More Last Chance; Under These Conditions; Pretty Words; Love Never Broke Anyone's Heart; I Still Believe In You.*

● First released 1992

● UK peak chart position: did not chart

● USA peak chart position: 10

I Want To See The Bright Lights Tonight - Richard And Linda Thompson

The debut album from Richard and Linda started a career that has placed Thompson in the 'forever to be a huge cult figure' bracket. They did everything on this album, bar make the charts and sell records. Folk, rock, country and pop are brilliantly covered in a tasteful and controlled package that is a delight from beginning to end, with Linda singing beautifully. Concert favourites such as 'The Calvary Cross' and 'When I Get To The Border' are to be found here. It is not flippant to say that Richard Thompson is a world class songwriter and guitarist, albeit totally under-appreciated.

● Tracks: *When I Get To The Border; The Calvary Cross; Withered And Died; I Want To See The Bright Lights Tonight; Down Where The Drunkards Roll; We Sing Hallelujah; Has He Got A Friend For Me; The Little Beggar Girl; The End Of The Rainbow; The Great Valerio.*

● First released 1974

● UK peak chart position: did not chart

● USA peak chart position: did not chart

I Want You - Marvin Gaye

Another in a series of suberb wandering groove albums from the premier sweet soul singer. He took the standard three-minute pop soul song and expanded the format. It is Gaye that is responsible for today's smooching urban R&B; he was for much of his career many years ahead of the game. This has been described as his 'oral sex' album, not that the others were not; this has the erotic edge. Built around the title track, the album is a theme album and as such should be played as a whole. There are no 'Too Busy Thinking Bout My Baby's on this; it is a much more challenging but satisfying work.

● Tracks: *I Want You (Vocal); Come Live With Me Angel; After The Dance (Instrumental); Feel All My Love Inside; I Wanna Be Where You Are; I Want You (Intro Jam); All The Way Round; Since I Had You; Soon I'll Be Loving You Again; I Want You (Intro Jam); After The Dance (Vocal)*.

● First released 1976
● UK peak chart position: 22
● USA peak chart position: 4

I Was Warned - Robert Cray

With this album, Cray said farewell to bassist Richard Cousins, the last survivor of his original band. At this point, the Memphis Horns were a regular part of the organization. Inevitably, their presence had drawn the songwriting team into writing material that evoked the Stax era. Having previously kept a tight rein on both his singing and guitar playing, Cray was now becoming more adventurous, evinced by the rhumba beat that propelled the title track. Many of the songs, including 'I'm A Good Man' and 'The Price I Pay', were written by Cray and producer Dennis Walker, but the album's one poignant note was struck with 'He Don't Live Here Anymore', written by keyboard man Jim Pugh.

● Tracks: *Just A Loser; I'm A Good Man; I Was Warned; The Price I Pay; Won The Battle; On The Road Down; A Whole Lotta Pride; A Picture Of A Broken Heart; He Don't Live Here Anymore; Our Last Time*.

● First released 1993
● UK peak chart position: 29
● USA peak chart position: 103

I Wish My Brother George Was Here - Del Tha Funkee Homosapien

With its title a reference to George Clinton, something of a godhead figure to west coast rap squads, Del introduced himself properly to the record-buying public via this, his debut album. Previously he had played a minor role in his cousin Ice Cube's backing band, Da Lench Mob. A long way from the hardcore gang narratives of his better-known relation, Del offered a more detached viewpoint, and one that came laced with humour. Artistically, it was an unqualified success, providing a blueprint that Del's own Hieroglyphic crew would follow.

● Tracks: *What Is Booty; Mistadobalina; The Wacky World Of Rabid Transit; Pissin' On Your Steps; Dark Skin Girls; Money For Sex; Ahonetwo, Ahonetwo; Prelude; Dr. Bombay; Sunny Meadowz; Sleepin' On My Couch; Hoodz Come In Dozens; Same Ol' Thing; Ya Lil' Crumbsnatchers*.

● First released 1991
● UK peak chart position: did not chart
● USA peak chart position: did not chart

I'd Rather Be Right

Even before it opened, this eagerly awaited show, which marked **George M. Cohan**'s return to the Broadway musical stage after an absence of nearly 10 years, had more than the usual set of problems. The composer, **Richard Rodgers**, who wrote the score with lyricist **Lorenz Hart**, did not like Cohan (the loathing was mutual) - and he did not care much for the director **George S. Kaufman** (*he* did not like musicals) either, who co-authored the book with **Moss Hart**. Cohan, in turn, could not stand President Franklin D. Roosevelt, the somewhat controversial figure he had been chosen to play in his comeback vehicle. However, with the exception of Roosevelt, the rest of the combatants assembled on 2 November 1937 at the Alvin Theatre for the opening of what promised to be an historic event: it was the first time that a President had been portrayed in a book musical - as opposed to a revue - and a satirical one, at that. As the curtain rises, the setting is New York's Central Park on 4 July. Peggy (Joy Hodges) and Phil (Austin Marshall) are in love, but are waiting to get married until Phil gets an increase in salary - which his boss has refused to give him until Roosevelt balances the budget. Phil falls asleep, and in his dreams the two young people meet Roosevelt who promises to do what he can to help, but all his efforts, which include the introduction of hundred dollar postage stamps, come to nothing. Phil and Peggy decide to get married anyway. In spite of fears that the show might turn out to be an attack on the President, it was, in fact, a warm-hearted piece that poked fun at most of the prominent political figures of the day, with the notable exception of Eleanor Roosevelt (she was on holiday at the time). Initially, Cohan, who was appearing for the first time in a musical that he had not written himself, took some liberties with the material, particularly 'Off The Record', a song about Al Smith the Democratic candidate who had lost to Herbert Hoover in the 1928 election. In any event, Rodgers' music was not considered to be anywhere near his best, although Hart's lyrics were as sharp and witty as ever in songs such as 'We're Going To Balance The Budget', 'Sweet Sixty-Five', 'I'd Rather Be Right', 'Take And Take And Take', and the charming 'Have You Met Miss Jones?'. The latter number was the nearest the show came to having a love song, and it went on to become something of a minor standard. *I'd Rather Be Right* played for 290 performances in New York before undertaking a successful road tour.

I'll Be Your Sweetheart

This film was regarded at the time of its release in 1945 as Britain's answer to the highly popular 20th Century-Fox musicals. Set in London in 1900, it deals with the bitter struggle between the popular songwriters of the day and the pirates who copy their sheet music and sell it for a fraction of the true price. Screen newcomer Michael Rennie plays the young, idealistic song publisher Bob Fielding, who leads the fight for justice - that is when he is not vying with fellow songwriter Jim Knight (Peter Graves) for the hand of music-hall star Edie Storey, who is played by Margaret Lockwood (singing voice dubbed by Maudie Edwards). Vic Oliver and Moore Marriott, as songwriters Sammy Kahn and George Le Brunn, led a strong supporting cast that includes Frederick Burtwell, Maudie Edwards, Garry Marsh, and George Merritt. Several of the songs in the film were hits, such as 'I'll Be Your Sweetheart' (Harry Dacre), 'Oh! Mr. Porter' (Thomas Le Brunn-George Le Brunn), 'Honeysuckle And The Bee' (W.H. Penn-A.H. Fitz), 'I Wouldn't Leave My Little Wooden Hut For You' (Tom Mellor-Charles Collins), and 'Liza Johnson' (George Le Brunn-Edgar Bateman). These were supplemented by three compositions written by Manning Sherwin and Val Guest: 'I'm Banking Everything On You', 'Sooner Or Later', and 'Mary Anna'. The musical numbers were devised by Robert Nesbitt and choreographed by Wendy Toye. Director Val Guest, who wrote the screenplay with Val Valentine, captured the style of the period perfectly, and although not *quite* in the class of the Fox movies, *I'll Be Your Sweetheart* was certainly an extremely diverting film. The producer for Gainsborough Pictures was Louis Levy.

I'll Get By
(see *Tin Pan Alley*)

I'm Alive - Jackson Browne
An album that saw Browne return to high-quality songs brought about by the familiar chestnut 'relationship problems'. Much media attention was given to his break-up with actress Darryl Hannah, and Browne seemed to come off worse. However, he deserves the last laugh because it prompted stellar songs such as the title track, 'My Problem Is You' and the light reggae beat of 'Everywhere I Go'. Few contemporary songwriters can analyze and discuss their own problems and failings through songs as openly and, apparently honestly, as Jackson Browne. Anybody that wrote him off as one of 'those 70s singer songwriters' should lend an ear to this album, especially those with marital problems.
● Tracks: *I'm Alive; My Problem Is You; Everywhere I Go; I'll Do Anything; Miles Away; Too Many Angels; Take This Rain; Two Of Me, Two Of You; Sky Blue And Black; All Good Things.*
● First released 1993
● UK peak chart position: 35
● USA peak chart position: 40

I'm Getting My Act Together And Taking It On The Road
Produced by Joseph Papp at his New York Shakespeare Festival Public Theatre, the launchpad for several successful musical productions through the years,

including *A Chorus Line*, this show opened on 14 June 1978. Nancy Ford (music) and Gretchen Cryer (lyrics and libretto) were well known in the US feminist movement, and their work consistently reflected their beliefs. In this piece, Ford plays a divorced 39-year-old pop singer on the comeback trail, who, with the help of her manager, played by Joe Fabiani, discovers her true self, and becomes a completely liberated person through her songs. These included 'Happy Birthday', 'Dear Tom', 'Natural High', 'Old Friend', 'Miss America', and 'Strong Woman Number'. After six months, the show transferred to the Circle in the Square Theatre in Greenwich Village, and eventually ran for 1,165 performances. During that time, other well-known names such as **Betty Buckley**, Phyllis Newman, Carol Hall, and Virginia Vestoff played the leading role. In 1981, a London production starring Ben Cross, Nicky Croydon, Diane Langton, Greg Martyn, and Megg Nichol, played briefly at the Apollo Theatre.

I'm Stranded - The Saints
Formed in 1975 in Brisbane, Australia, the Saints were aspiring to punk glory before the Sex Pistols had even taken up their instruments. Fronted by the guttural sneer of vocalist Chris Bailey and the enigmatic guitarwork of Ed Kuepper, the Saints had a swagger that was pure Stooges, but a lyrical bent that was almost Dylan with a sneer. Ramshackle, but consistently profound, this, their first album, was full of high glories and damning asides, featuring the biting title track, the uproarious 'Demolition Girl', and the insistent and quite brilliant 'Erotic Neurotic'. Buy it.
● Tracks: *(I'm) Stranded; One Way Street; Wild About You; Messin' With The Kid; Erotic Neurotic; No Time; Kissin' Cousins; Story Of Love; Demolition Girl; Nights In Venice.*
● First released 1977
● UK peak chart position: did not chart
● USA peak chart position: did not chart

I'm Your Man - Leonard Cohen
A strange juxtaposition of biting lyrics, haunting melodies, world-weary vocals, and dinky production, *I'm Your Man* was Leonard Cohen's best-received album in years, making the UK Top 50 and earning kudos from critics across the globe. The lead-off track, 'First We Take Manhattan', immediately sets the mood, as Cohen intones sinisterly, 'They sentenced me to twenty years of boredom' but then, to borrow from Lou Reed, the coloured girls sing, and we're in Las Vegas. However, despite Cohen's dodgy self-production, the songs, and his unmistakable delivery, quickly take centre-stage. One stand-out is 'Everybody Knows', a love-gone-wrong tune full of angst.
● Tracks: *First We Take Manhattan; Ain't No Cure For Love; Everybody Knows; I'm Your Man; Take This Waltz; Jazz Police; I Can't Forget; Tower Of Song.*
● First released 1988
● UK peak chart position: 48
● USA peak chart position: did not chart

I've Gotta Horse

In 1964 pop singer **Billy Fury** purchased a racehorse, Anselmo. When it came fourth in that year's Derby race, the seeds were sewn for this anachronistic 1965 feature. Art mirrored life in the plot; Fury played a pop star distracted from his career by his devotion to animals, in particular his horse, Armitage, which emulates Anselmo in the cheery finale. Michael Medwin and Amanda Barrie co-starred with Fury in this largely forgettable film, which compounded a cosy view of pop by including passé vocal group the **Bachelors**. Mike Leander directed a score composed by David Heneker, who had previously written the music for **Tommy Steele**'s highly successful *Half A Sixpence*. The songs on *I've Gotta Horse* were, however, below par, reaching a nadir with 'I Like Animals (Much Better Than Human Beings)'. The film, unimaginatively retitled *Wonderful Day* for the USA, was a waste of Fury's talents. Arguably one of Britain's finest pop talents of the 50s and 60s, he cried out for a vehicle that would enhance his moody, vulnerable image, rather than blithe, inconsequential fare. The **Beatles**, **Rolling Stones** and **Byrds** were taking pop into new arenas. *I've Gotta Horse* ensured that Fury remained criminally trapped in the past.

I, Ludicrous

Offbeat indie band I, Ludicrous comprises Will Hung (b. David Rippingale, 4 November 1956, London, England; vocals) and John Procter (b. 9 May 1957, Epsom, England; instruments). The duo first met in 1981 while working for Finsbury Data Services in London. Their mutual passion for the **Fall** and Crystal Palace Football Club cemented the partnership. They had additionally been involved in various failed punk bands over the years, but only formed a group together in February 1985. After witnessing a performance by **John Cooper Clarke** and **Nico** at the Cricketers in Kensington, London, the duo decided they could do much better than the third support, a talentless comedian. Their debut gig was dreamed up as support to performance artist friend Max Couper, with Procter providing a musical soundtrack to Hung's off-the-cuff observations on the day he had endured. This intention soon metamorphosed into a songwriting partnership, which after just three gigs secured them a contract with Kaleidoscope Records. Armed only with a Casio keyboard and Littlewoods mail-order guitar, their central appeal lay in the monotone delivery of unlikely narratives about 'Lunch With The Geldofs' or 'Preposterous Tales In The Life Of John Mackenzie'. The latter was their first release, on a flexi-disc which accompanied *Blah Blah Blah* fanzine in April 1987. It was received warmly by disc jockey **John Peel**, who offered them a Radio 1 session, while his favourite band, the Fall, invited them to support at London's Astoria venue. Their debut album, *It's Like Everything Else*, duly emerged in September 1987 to glowing and/or confused reviews. 'Quite Extraordinary'

followed in 1988 as their first single, but then the band were hamstrung by a series of business problems. The collapse of Red Rhino distribution led to a contract with the tiny Rodney, Rodney! label, but this failed to give the requisite push to either *A Warning To The Curious* or *Light And Bitter*, their next two albums. Forced to finance their own output, the duo offered a new album in 1992, *Idiots Savants*, while the attendant single, 'We Stand Around', was Single Of The Week in the *New Musical Express* in September 1992. None of this was enough to allow the participants to give up their many and various day jobs, however, though the release of 'Hats Off To Eldorado' in 1994 confirmed their continued wry presence in the UK music industry's underbelly.
● ALBUMS: *It's Like Everything Else* (Kaleidoscope 1987)★★★, *A Warning To The Curious* (Rodney, Rodney! 1989)★★★, *Light And Bitter* (Rodney, Rodney! 1990)★★★, *Idiots Savants* (I, Ludicrous 1992)★★★.

I-Threes

The I-Threes were formed, at the instigation of **Bob Marley**, on the departure of **Peter Tosh** and **Bunny Wailer**. Having lost his two main backing vocalists, he recruited **Marcia Griffiths**, **Judy Mowatt** and **Rita Marley** to fill out the Wailers' sound. The trio's harmonies added substantially to many of Marley's most successful records, and they also added visual depth to live concerts, with dance steps choreographed by Mowatt. All three had recorded solo previously, and returned to those careers following the death of their band leader. They have not recorded as a trio outside of the Wailers' legacy, aside from the 'Music For The World' 12-inch, credited to Marley, Mowatt and Griffiths, in 1983, although there have been several reunion concerts.

I. Roy

b. Roy Reid, c.1949, Spanish Town, Jamaica, West Indies. I. Roy, aka Roy Reid, aka Roy Senior, is one of the great originals of Jamaican music. Always the most intellectual of his peers, he arrived at the start of the 70s as an accomplished DJ with a neat line in storytelling and the ability to ride a rhythm as if it was first recorded for him and not simply 'borrowed'. He drew his name from **U-Roy**, the first truly popular reggae star, and his first records were slightly derivative of the older man's style, and also owed a little to another DJ pioneer, **Dennis Alcapone**. However, I. Roy soon hit his stride and recorded a mighty series of singles for producer **Gussie Clarke**, including 'Black Man Time', 'Tripe Girl' and 'Magnificent Seven'. 'Brother Toby Is A Movie From London' emerged for **Glen Brown**; 'Dr Who' for **Lee Perry** and innumerable sides for **Bunny Lee**. His debut album *Presenting* was magnificent, collating most of his hits for **Gussie Clarke**. It remains a classic of its genre today. Further albums *Hell And Sorrow* and *Many Moods Of* were nearly as strong. In 1975 he became involved in an on-record slanging match with fellow DJ **Prince Jazzbo**, a bizarre name-calling affair that nonetheless presented the public with a new twist to such rivalries and helped to maintain sales. In 1976 a liaison with producer Prince Tony Robinson brought I. Roy a contract with **Virgin Records** and Roy's albums graced the label five times: *General, Musical Shark Attack, World On Fire, Crisis Time* and the excellent 1977 set *Heart Of A Lion*. By the early 80s I. Roy had burnt out his lyrical store and was overtaken by younger DJs. However, he is still to be found on the periphery of reggae today, sometimes, ironically, on Ujama, the label owned by his old rival, Prince Jazzbo.

● ALBUMS: *Presenting* (Gussie/Trojan 1973)★★★★★, *Hell And Sorrow* (Trojan 1974)★★★★, *Many Moods Of* (Trojan 1974)★★★★, *Truths & Rights* (Grounation 1975)★★★, with Prince Jazzbo *Step Forward Youth* (Live & Love 1975)★★★★, *Can't Conquer Rasta* (Justice 1976)★★, *Crisis Time* (Caroline/Virgin 1976)★★★, *Dread Baldhead* (Klik 1976)★★★, *Ten Commandments* (Micron 1977)★★★, *Heart Of A Lion* (Front Line 1977)★★★★, *Musical Shark Attack* (Front Line 1977)★★★, *The Best Of* (GG's 1977)★★★, *The Godfather* (Third World 1977)★★★, *The General* (Front Line 1977)★★★, *World On Fire* (Front Line 1978)★★★, *African Herbsman* (Joe Gibbs 1979)★★★, *Hotter Yatta* (Harry J 1980)★★★, *I. Roy's Doctor Fish* (Imperial 1981)★★★, *Outer Limits* (Intense/Hawkeye 1983)★★★, with Jah Woosh *We Chat You Rock* (Trojan 1987)★★★, *The Lyrics Man* (Witty 1990)★★★, with Prince Jazzbo *Head To Head Clash* (Ujama 1990)★★★, *Straight To The Heart* reissue of *Truths & Rights* with four non-I. Roy dub tracks (Esoldun 1991)★★★.

● COMPILATIONS: *Crucial Cuts* (Virgin 1983)★★★, *Classic I. Roy* (Mr. Tipsy 1986)★★★, *Crisis Time - Extra Version* (Front Line 1991)★★★, *Don't Check Me With No Lightweight Stuff (1972-75)* (Blood & Fire 1997)★★★.

Iam

One of the more impressive of a new wave of French hip-hop groups expanding throughout the 90s, Iam were formed in Marseilles at the beginning of the decade. After an independent debut that was not released internationally, they signed with **Virgin Records** for their second album. *Oembre Est Lumiére*, the title translating as 'Shadow Is Light', was a sprawling, 40-track package conducted over a double album, featuring a cocktail of American-derived, funk-based hip hop. Alongside the work of **MC Solaar**, it became the first French rap album to sell significantly outside of mainland Europe, aided by strong reviews in the USA and UK. These included a five-star rating from *H.H.C.* magazine, who described it as 'a colossal feast of a record. Open your mind and feed your ears.' Taken from the album, 'Je Danse Le Mia' won an award for Iam as the best band of the year during the Victoires De La Musique ceremony.

● ALBUMS: *Oembre Est Lumiére* (Virgin 1994)★★★★.

Ian And Sylvia

see (**Tyson, Ian And Sylvia**).

Ian And The Zodiacs

This pop group, formed in Crosby, Liverpool, England, in 1960, played a significant role in the development of the Hamburg beat scene, and initially comprised Ian Edwards (vocals, guitar), Peter Wallace (guitar), Charlie Flynn (bass; aka Charlie Wade and Wellington Wade), John Bethel (keyboards) and Cliff Roberts (drums). Oriole Records released two singles, before they switched to **Fontana Records** in 1964. After recording an album for the label's budget series, housed on the Wing subsidiary, they arrived in Hamburg, Germany, in May. By this time the group was a quartet, having left behind Bethel and found a new drummer, Geoff Bamford. They quickly became regulars at Hamburg's famed Star Club, mixing beat pop with soul, hallmarked by the group's outstanding harmonies. Although their progress was minor compared to that of the **Beatles**, they remained pillars of the venue and scene, and by the mid-60s specialized in covering the Fab Four's material to appreciative late-coming audiences. By this time there had been a series of line-up shuffles - new drummer Fred Smith (ex-Big Six) arrived in 1966, while later in the year Wallace was replaced by Arthur Ashton. Tony Coates became their fourth drummer in 1967, at which time the group recorded two albums of Beatles cover versions under the guise of the Koppycats. However, they disbanded in late 1967, remaining quiet for two decades before playing a reunion gig in Hamburg in 1988.

● ALBUMS: *Gear Again* (Wing 1964)★★, *Star-Club Show 7* (1965)★★, *Just Listen To ...* (1965)★★, *Locomotive* (1966)★★, *The Beatles Best Done By The Koppycats* (1966)★, *More Beatles Best Done By The Koppycats* (1967)★.

Ian, Janis

b. Janis Eddy Fink, 7 April 1951, New York, USA. A teenage prodigy, Ian first attracted attention when her early composition, 'Hair Of Spun Gold', was published in a 1964 issue of *Broadside* magazine. Performances at New York's Village Gate and Gaslight venues inspired a recording contract that began with the controversial 'Society's Child (Baby I've Been Thinking)'. Brought to national prominence following the singer's appearance on **Leonard Bernstein**'s television show, this chronicle of a doomed, interracial romance was astonishingly mature and inspired a series of equally virulent recordings attacking the perceived hypocrisy of an older generation. Ian's dissonant, almost detached delivery, enhanced the lyricism offered on a series of superior folk rock-styled albums, notably *For All The Seasons Of Your Mind*. Later relocated in California, Janis began writing songs for other artists, but re-embraced recording in 1971 with *Present Company*. *Stars* re-established her standing, reflecting a still personal, yet less embittered, perception. The title song was the subject of numerous cover versions, while 'Jesse' provided a US Top 10 hit for **Roberta Flack**. *Between The Lines* contained the evocatively simple 'At Seventeen', Ian's sole US chart topper, and subsequent releases continued to reflect a growing sophistication. *Night Rains* featured two film theme songs, 'The Foxes' and 'The Bell Jar', although critics began pointing at an increasingly maudlin self pity. The artist's impetus noticeably waned during the 80s and Janis Ian seemed to have retired from music altogether. However, she re-emerged in 1991 giving live performances and appearing on a British concert stage for the first time in 10 years. Her 1995 album *Revenge* moved firmly into smooth pop, but Ian's lyrics remained as personal, biting and original as ever.

● ALBUMS: *Janis Ian* (Verve 1967)★★, *For All The Seasons Of Your Mind* (Verve 1967)★★★, *The Secret Life Of J. Eddy Fink* (1968)★★, *Present Company* (Capitol 1971)★★, *Stars* (Columbia 1974)★★★, *Between The Lines* (Columbia 1975)★★★★, *Aftertones* (Columbia 1976)★★★, *Miracle Row* (Columbia 1977)★★, *Night Rains* (Columbia 1979)★★, *Restless Eyes* (Columbia 1981)★★, *Breaking Silence* (1993)★★★, *Revenge* (Grapevine 1995)★★★, *Hunger* (Windham Hill 1997)★★★.

● COMPILATIONS: *The Best Of Janis Ian* (Columbia 1980)★★, *Society's Child: The Anthology* (Polydor 1995)★★★, *Live On The Test 1976* (Nighttracks/Windsong 1995)★★.

● FURTHER READING: *Who Really Cares?*, Janis Ian.

Ibrahim, Abdullah

b. Adolph Johannes Brand, 9 October 1934, Cape Town, South Africa. Ibrahim began playing piano as a small child, learning church music and hearing many other forms, including jazz, from radio and records. Known initially by the name Dollar Brand, he began his professional career in the mid-50s playing popular music of the day, but by the end of the decade had formed a band that included **Hugh Masakela** and concentrated on jazz. In the early 60s his political activities drew the attention of the authorities and he embarked upon a protracted visit to Europe with singer **Sathima Bea Benjamin**, whom he married. In Switzerland they attracted the much more benign and welcome attention of **Duke Ellington**, who helped arrange a recording date and opened other doors that led to appearances in the USA in the mid-60s. Later resident in New York City, Ibrahim played with leading exponents of free-form music, amongst them **John Coltrane, Don Cherry** and **Ornette Coleman**. He also continued to develop his involvement in politics and religion and in the late 60s he converted to Islam, subsequently adopting the name by which he has since been known. The banning of the African National Congress made it difficult for Ibrahim to retain close personal ties with his homeland but he returned there occasionally for recording dates. Despite the enforced separation from his roots he continued to explore African music and the manner in which it could be blended with contemporary American jazz. As a consequence, his extensive performing and recording dates, often of his own compositions, are shot through with rare intensity. In the early 80s Ibrahim expanded his

musical horizons with the composition of an opera, *Kalahari Liberation*, which was performed throughout Europe to great acclaim. From the mid-80s his seven-piece band, Ekaya, has recorded and performed in concert and at festivals. As a performer, Ibrahim's playing of the piano (he also plays cello, flute and soprano saxophone) is vigorously rhythmic, intriguingly mixing bop with the music of his homeland and overlaid with touches of Ellington and **Thelonious Monk**. As a composer Ibrahim has ably and convincingly mixed the music of two cultures creating a distinctive style through which his highly motivated political and religious beliefs can be spread to a wide, mixed audience.

● ALBUMS: *Jazz Epistles: Verse I* (1960)★★★, *Duke Ellington Presents The Dollar Brand Trio* (1963)★★★★, *Anatomy Of A South African Village* (1965)★★★, *The Dream* (1965)★★, with Gato Barbieri *Hamba Khale* (1968 recording), *This Is Dollar Brand* 1965 recording (1973), *African Piano* 1969 recording (1973)★★★, *Sangoma* (1973)★★, *African Portraits* (1973)★★★, *Ode To Duke Ellington* (West Wind 1973)★★★, *African Sketchbook* (Enja 1974)★★★★, *African Space Program* (Enja 1974)★★★, with Johnny Dyani *Good News From Africa* (1974)★★★, *Ancient Africa* (1974)★★★★, *The Children Of Africa* (Enja 1976)★★★★, *African Herbs* (1976),★★★ *Blues For A Hip King* (1976)★★★, *Black Lightning* (1976)★★★, *The Journey* (1978)★★★, with Max Roach *Streams Of Consciousness* (1978)★★★, *Soweto* (Bellaphon 1978)★★★★, *Africa - Tears And Laughter* (1979),★★★ with Dyani *Echoes From Africa* (Enja 1980)★★★, *Memories* (1980)★★★, *African Market Place* (1980)★★★, *At Montreux* (Enja 1980)★★, *Matsidiso* (1981)★★★, *South African Sunshine* (1982)★★★, *Duke's Memories* (1982)★★★, *African Dawn* (Enja 1982)★★★, *Mannenberg - Is Where It's Happening* (1983)★★★, *Zimbabwe* (1983)★★★, *The Mountain* (Kaz 1983)★★, *Autobiography* 1978 recording (1983)★★★, *Ekaya* (Blackhawk 1984)★★★, with Carlos Ward *Live At Sweet Basil Vol. 1* (Blackhawk 1984)★★★, *Water From An Ancient Well* (Tiptoe 1986)★★★, *Mindiff* (Enja 1988)★★★, *Desert Flowers* (Enja 1993)★★★, *Fats, Duke & Monk* (Sackville 1993)★★★★, *S'En Fout La Mort* (1993)★★, *Knysna Blue* (Enja/Tip Toe 1994)★★★, *Yarona* (Enja/Tip Toe 1995)★★★, *Cape Town Flowers* (Enja 1997)★★★.

Ice

UK psychedelic pop quintet Ice were formed in the mid-60s while John Carter (bass), Glyn James (vocals), Lynton Naiff (organ), Grant Serpell (drums) and Steve Turner (guitar) were attending Sussex University in Brighton, Sussex, England. Their debut single, 'Anniversary (Of Love)', was released in 1967 after the group signed a recording contract with **Decca Records**. The single revealed a band clearly in the thralls of a **Procul Harum** fixation, with its layered keyboards and nostalgic lyrics. A second single followed a year later, but 'Whisper Her Name (Maria Laine)' also failed to impress commercially. As a result Ice returned to their studies/professional employment and have not recorded since, although both singles have been compiled on numerous psychedelic compilations.

Ice Cube

b. O'Shea Jackson, 15 June 1969, Crenshaw, South Central Los Angeles, California, USA. Controversial hardcore rapper who formerly worked with the equally inflammatory **NWA**. Following a relatively stable background, with both his mother and father working at UCLA, Cube entered the homeboy lifestyle: 'One day I was sitting in class with a friend called Kiddo and we had some time on our hands, so he said let's write a rap'. At the age of 16 he penned his first important rap, 'Boyz 'N The Hood', which was later recorded by **Eazy-E**. He subsequently spent time with CIA, an embryonic rap outfit produced by **Dr Dre**. As guest lyricist, he brought NWA '8 Ball' and 'Dopeman', which would comprise the opening salvo from the band. After studying architectural draughtsmanship in Phoenix, Arizona, he returned to the NWA fold in time for the groundbreaking *Straight Outta Compton*. He would leave the group at the tail-end of 1989, amid thinly veiled attacks on NWA's Jewish manager Jerry Heller. His debut album, recorded with **Public Enemy** producers the **Bomb Squad**, drew immediate mainstream attention with its controversial lyrical platform. As well as homophobia and the glamorization of violence, his work was attacked primarily for its overt sexism, raps about kicking a pregnant girlfriend ('You Can't Fade Me') notwithstanding. Conversely, Ice Cube overlooks a production empire (Street Knowledge) run for him by a woman, and he also fostered the career of female rapper **Yo Yo** (who appears alongside him defending her gender on *AmeriKKKa's Most Wanted*'s 'It's A Man's World'). The politicization of his solo work should also be noted; in his NWA days he had once written, 'Life ain't nothing but bitches and money', but his words since then have incorporated numerous references to black ideology that add up to something approaching a manifesto. His defence against critical discomfort with his rhymes, 'I put a mirror to black America', has been hijacked by many other, less worthy cases. To Ice Cube's credit, he went on to produce two excellent sets, *The Predator* and *Lethal Injection*. The former, in particular, boasted a much more discursive approach to the problems of the ghetto, including reflections on the Los Angeles riots and the Rodney King beating. Perhaps it was marred by the blunt sexism of tracks such as 'Cave Bitch', but it was certainly an advance. Musically it was typified by a stirring 'One Nation Under A Groove', with a lead vocal by the song's writer, **George Clinton**. In 1993 he also teamed up with fellow rapper **Ice-T**, with whom he shares more than a similarity in name, to launch a fashion range incorporating a gun logo. No stranger to controversy, Ice Cube became better acquainted with commerce too. His 1992 film *Trespass*, retitled after the LA Riots deemed original moniker *Looters* unsavoury, saw him team up with Ice-T once more. He had already starred in John Singleton's 1991 hit film, titled after his first rap, *Boyz 'N The Hood*, and later appeared in the same director's *Higher Learning*. Having completed four million-selling albums, Ice Cube's career attracted the attention of those outside the hip-hop fraternity. 'It Was A Good Day' gave him a massive profile via MTV. Like Ice-T, Cube was targeted on right wing assassination lists discovered by the police in 1993. However, his career has continued unabated. Street Knowledge has provided **Da Lench Mob** and **Kam** with successful albums on which Cube has acted as executive producer, and he has set up a second subsidiary, titled after his posse, Lench Mob, and written several screenplays. The soundtrack to his 1998 directorial debut, *The Player's Club*, was a Top 10 success in the USA. The film itself, set in a strip club, was one of the year's suprise successes, having grossed $20 million at the box office only six weeks after its April release.

● ALBUMS: *AmeriKKKa's Most Wanted* (Priority 1990)★★★★, *Kill At Will* mini-album (Priority 1990)★★★, *Death Certificate* (Priority 1991)★★★, *The Predator* (Lench Mob/Priority 1992)★★★, *Lethal Injection* (Lench Mob/Priority 1993)★★★, *Bootlegs & B-Sides* (Lench Mob/Priority 1994)★★.

Ice Pickin' - Albert Collins

The 70s were a frustrating time for Albert Collins. Canned Heat had discovered him in Houston in 1968 and arranged a contract with Imperial Records that resulted in three rather formulaic hot guitar albums. In 1972, he made an album (which few heard) for Tumbleweed some months before the label closed. It took another six years of unrewarding hard work before another label took an interest in him. Bruce Iglauer surrounded him with first-rate musicians and chose material sympathetic to Collins' slyly humorous vocal style. *Ice Pickin'* set the tone for all the albums that followed, with tracks such as 'Master Charge' and 'Cold, Cold Feeling', but they could not reproduce the hungry feeling an artist develops when he knows that success is just around the corner.

● Tracks: *Talking Woman Blues; When The Welfare Turns Its Back On You; Ice Pick; Cold, Cold Feeling; Too Tired; Master Charge; Conversation With Collins; Avalanche.*

● First released 1978

● UK peak chart position: did not chart

● USA peak chart position: did not chart

Ice-T

One of the most outspoken rappers on the west coast, Ice-T (b. Tracy Marrow, c.1958, Newark, New Jersey, USA) boasts (sometimes literally) a violent past in which he was shot twice - once whilst involved in an armed robbery. His name, fittingly, is taken from black exploitation author Iceberg Slim, and he is backed on record by Afrika Islam and DJ Aladdin's hardcore hip hop. His first record was actually 'The Coldest Rapper' in 1983, which was improvised over a **Jimmy Jam And Terry Lewis** rhythm, and made him the first Los Angeles hip-hop artist. Unfortunately, he was subsequently held under contract by mogul Willie Strong for several years. Disillusioned, he made his money from petty and not so petty crime, and also appeared in the breakdance film *Breakin'*, which included his 'Reckless' cut on the soundtrack. He followed it with the faddish 'Killers' single. The breakthrough, however, came with 'Ya Don't Know', which was widely credited with being the first west coast hip-hop artefact (although the honour was undoubtedly Ice-T's, the real beneficiary should have been the obscure 'The Coldest Rapper' cut). Four LPs in just three years created something of a stir in the USA, based as they were largely on his experiences as a gang member in Los Angeles. In 1989 he reached the lower end of the UK charts with 'High Rollers', but did better the following year teaming up with **Curtis Mayfield** on a remake of 'Superfly'. He is married to Darlene who normally appears semi-clad on his record sleeves, and owns a pit pull terrier affectionately titled Felony. For a time, too, he delighted in inviting journalists to his luxury Beverly Hills home to show them his personal armoury of semi-automatic weapons. Success has also enabled him to start his own record company, Rhyme Syndicate. His vision of the black man as sophisticated and articulate (being hard as nails is, of course, *de rigeur*) ranks him among the most potent forces in contemporary black culture. His refusal to engage in a white liberal agenda (he was the first rap artist to have warning stickers placed on his album sleeves) has irritated many, but helped to establish him as an authentic spokesperson for dispossessed black youth. His debut album, *Rhyme Pays*, with an Uzi emblazoned on the cover, served as a mission statement: hardcore raps on street violence and survival being the order of the day. By the time of its follow-up, there was demonstrably greater imagination displayed in terms of backing music. Like many of his west coast brethren, Ice-T had rediscovered funk. Notable tracks included 'Girls L.G.B.N.A.F., which the PMRC later discovered stood for 'Let's Get Butt Naked And Fuck'. Their reaction to this (arguably among the least offensive statements on Ice-T's records) was so overheated that the debate heavily informed his follow-up set. However, his crowning glory so far was *OG* (an acronym for Original Gangster that has passed into rap's lexicon) which ranks alongside the best work of **Ice Cube**, **Public Enemy** or **NWA** in terms of sustained intensity, yet managed to maintain a little more finesse than his previous work. In 1991, with appealing irony, he starred as a cop in the movie *New Jack City*. He had earlier contributed the title track to the LA gangster movie *Colors*, rapping the title song. He also appeared with former NWA and solo artist Ice Cube in the Walter Hill film *Looters*. (renamed *Trespassers* due to its release at the same time as the LA riots), as well as *Surviving The Game* and the cult comic hero movie, *Tank Girl*. His other soundtrack credits include *Dick Tracy*. Ice-T's hobbies include his own thrash metal outfit, **Body Count**, who released an album in 1992 and stirred up immeasurable controversy via one of its cuts, 'Cop Killer' (detailed under Body Count entry). Little wonder that he was targeted on right-wing assassina-

tion lists discovered by the police in 1993. His album from that year, *Home Invasion*, saw him take on the mantle of agent provocateur in the young white male's home, a theme reinforced in its cover and title - Ice-T was a threat in your neighbourhood, with another manifesto of spiteful intent ('I'm takin' your kids' brains, You ain't getting them back, I'm gonna fill 'em with hard drugs, big guns, bitches, hoes and death'). Then he went and spoiled all the good work by writing a book, the *Ice-T Opinion*, which was so full of dumb ideas that it largely discredited such achievements. On 22 March 1994 he introduced Channel 4's *Without Walls*, a documentary on the rise of the blaxploitation movies. His own life would make an excellent documentary subject. He continues to fascinate those on both sides of the rap lobby, and, as he notes in *Home Invasion*'s 'Ice Muthafuckin' T': 'Every fucking thing I write, Is going to be analysed by somebody white'.

● ALBUMS: *Rhyme Pays* (Sire 1987)★★★, *Power* (Sire 1988)★★, *The Iceberg/Freedom Of Speech . . . Just Watch What You Say* (Sire 1989)★★★, *OG: Original Gangster* (Syndicate/Sire 1991)★★★★, *Home Invasion* (Priority 1993)★★★, *Born Dead* (Priority 1994)★★★.
● VIDEOS: *O.G. - The Original Gangster Video* (1991).
● FURTHER READING: *The Ice Opinion*, Ice-T and Heidi Seigmund.

Icebreaker

A British band formed in 1988 by several young musicians with an interest in a diverse range of music, from Dutch minimalism, through rock to jazz, all directed by flautist James Poke. Icebreaker's main inspiration was **Louis Andriessen**: the band was put together specifically for a performance of Andriessen's 'Hoketus' and first played in public at the festival of new Dutch music in York, England during April 1988. Andriessen was very impressed and has subsequently given the band much encouragement. Their repertoire includes compositions by established figures like Andriessen, **Steve Reich** and **Michael Nyman** as well as new writers such as Peter Garvey and band members Poke and Damian Le Gassick. Their non-compartmentalized attitude, shared by others of Andriessen's followers, has led to an exciting and viable fusion of contemporary classical genres like minimalism, musique concrete and electro-acoustic music with their rock descendants, scratch, techno-pop and hip-hop. At the time of writing they have not issued any recordings but have made several enthusiastically received tours, including concerts at London's Purcell Room and Shaw Theatre, and a Contemporary Music Network tour at the end of 1991.

Icehouse

This Australian rock band was formed as Flowers in the late 70s by songwriter and multi-instrumentalist Iva Davies (b. Ivor Davies, 22 May 1955). Influenced by **Roxy Music** and **David Bowie**, Flowers' other members included Keith Welsh (bass), John Lloyd (drums) and Michael Hoste (keyboards). The first single, 'Can't Help

Myself' was a Top 10 hit in 1980. The following year the group signed to **Chrysalis Records**, touring the UK and North America. Its name was changed to Icehouse (the title of the debut album) to avoid confusion with a US group called Flowers. Despite further Australian success with 'Love In Motion' and 'Great Southern Land', Davies disbanded the group in 1982 to concentrate on the solo *Primitive Man*. However, he was persuaded to re-form Icehouse the next year with British musicians Andy Qunta (keyboards) and ex-**Killing Joke** member Guy Pratt (guitar). The new line-up also included Lloyd, Hoste and leading Australian guitarist Bob Kretshmer. Almost immediately, Icehouse had a British hit with 'Hey Little Girl', which was accompanied by a striking video directed by Russell Mulcahy. After touring Europe in support of David Bowie, Davies took the band off the road for a further two years. During this time he composed scores for Mulcahy's feature film *Razorback* and (with Kretshmer) for a ballet for the Sydney Dance Company. The group returned in 1986 with the tougher 'No Promises' and the glam-rock flavoured 'Baby You're So Strange' from *Measure For Measure*. In 1987 there were more Australian hits with 'Crazy' and 'Electric Blue', both of which reached the US Top 20 the following year.

● ALBUMS: *Icehouse* (Chrysalis 1981)★★★, *Primitive Man* (Chrysalis 1982)★★, *Sidewalk* (Chrysalis 1984)★★, *Measure For Measure* (Chrysalis 1986)★★★, *Man Of Colours* (Chrysalis 1987)★★, *Code Blue* (Diva 1990)★★★, *Big Wheel* (Diva 1993)★★★, *Full Circle* (Diva 1994)★★★, *The Berlin Tapes* (Diva 1995)★★★.

● COMPILATIONS: *Great Southern Land* (Diva 1989)★★★, *Masterfile* (Diva 1992)★★★, *Love In Motion* (Chrysalis 1996)★★.

● VIDEOS: *Icehouse: Live* (Video Collection 1988), *Icehouse* (Music Club Video 1989).

Iceman - Albert Collins

In what was to be his penultimate album, Albert Collins finally moved into the blues mainstream. In essence, the ingredients were no different from his Alligator albums, but better promotion ensured significant success. Collins was renowned for straight-ahead, jazz-oriented blues, his guitar solos sharp and piercing, evoking the imagery that inspired his nickname. He also became a sardonic and humorous vocalist, aided by his wife Gwendolyn's knowing lyrics. Having struggled in the wasteland of endless club circuits, in his last years Collins took to the high ground, providing credibility for Gary Moore's 'rediscovery' of his blues roots and guesting on albums by John Lee Hooker and B.B. King. Death robbed him of the rewards he deserved.

● Tracks: *Mr. Collins, Mr. Collins; Iceman; Don't Mistake Kindness For Weakness; Travelin' South; Put The Shoe On The Other Foot; I'm Beginning To Wonder; Head Rag; The Hawk; The Blues For Gabe; Mr. Collins, Mr. Collins (Reprise).*

● First released 1991

● UK peak chart position: did not chart

● USA peak chart position: did not chart

Ichiban

Ichiban is a Georgia corporation that was founded in Atlanta in 1985 by John E. Abbey (London-born former proprieter of *Blues & Soul* magazine) and his wife, Nina K. Easton, who took the company title from the Japanese for number one. Their goal of providing an outlet for black music, be it blues, gospel, jazz, R&B or rap, has remained constant. Since its inception Ichiban has grown to become the distributor of some 20 to 30 labels. The company first came into contact with rap music when approached to distribute **Vanilla Ice**'s *To The Extreme* album in 1990 (later picked up by SBK). As Abbey admitted, 'We literally stumbled into rap'. Their next project was **MC Breed**'s 'Ain't No Future In Yo' Frontin', via Swamp Dogg's SDEG label. Buoyed by these initial successes, Ichiban launched its primary rap stable, Wrap Records. Product included a second MC Breed album, plus music from **Success-N-Effect**, **Kilo** and **Gangsta Pat**. Other releases filtered through on subsidiary rap imprints such as 380 Recordings, Easylee and Mo' Money, and for a time the Nastymix operation was also distributed through Ichiban's offices. The company's catalogue has extended to a point at which over 60% of its releases are in the rap/hip hop field, and they possess one of the most talented rosters of new artists in the US. Apart from the aforementioned artists, some of these include **Detroit's Most Wanted**, **Kid Sensation**, **Kwamé**, **Menace To Society**, **95 South**, **Treacherous 3**, **Snoman** and **MC Shy D**.

Icho Candy

b. Winston Evans, Jamaica, West Indies. Probably the first the world heard of roots enigma Icho Candy was his anonymous appearance on Channel 4's *Deep Roots* programme in 1982, where he was seen twisting his tortured, **Horace Andy**-styled tonsils around 'Where Do The Children Play' in company with DJ Bobby Culture, singing live on the late Jack Ruby's **sound system**. His earliest vinyl outing, 'Little Children No Cry', was for Ruby, followed by 'Bandulu' for **Joe Gibbs**, finally achieving some prominence with titles such as 'Captain Selassie I', on the Jwyanza label, and 'Mr User' and 'Bloodsuckers' for **Prince Jazzbo**'s Ujama label, thereby establishing a small cult following for himself in the UK. Never the most prolific of singers, he embarked on, what was for him, a burst of recording activity during the latter part of the decade, with singles such as 'In Texas Town' (1987), a bizarre cowboy variation on the Cajun standard 'Jambalaya', the apocalyptic roots anthem 'Babylon' (1987) for **Augustus Pablo**'s Rockers label, 'Cool Down Sufferer' (1989) for Tesfa McDonald, and 'Jah Calling All Over The World' (1990) for Cashima Steel's Creation label, for whom he also recorded a (so far) unreleased album. He also provided an album's worth of material for Finnish producer Tero Kaski, of which only one track, 'Resign Babylon' (1994), has so far emerged. Another period of obscurity was broken in 1993 by the release of

Glory To The King, issued on **Jah Shaka**'s King Of The Zulu Tribe label.

● ALBUMS: *Glory To The King* (King Of The Zulu Tribe 1993)★★★.

Icicle Works

Emerging from the profligate network of Liverpudlian bands that existed during the punk rock and new wave era, the Icicle Works were formed by **Ian McNabb** (b. 3 November 1962; vocals, guitar), Chris Layhe (bass) and Chris Sharrock (drums). McNabb was formerly in City Limits with the near-legendary Edie Shit (Howie Mimms), and Sharrock played with the Cherry Boys (who also included Mimms at one point). Taking their name from a science fiction novel - *The Day The Icicle Works Closed Down* - they made their recording debut with a six-track cassette, *Ascending*, released on the local Probe Plus emporium in 1981. The band then founded their own Troll Kitchen label on which they prepared 'Nirvana', their premier single. Gaining support from BBC disc jockey **John Peel**, they came to the attention of **Beggars Banquet Records**, initially through their Situation 2 offshoot. Their second single, 'Birds Fly (Whisper To A Scream)', was an 'indie' hit but they had to wait for the next effort, 'Love Is A Wonderful Colour', to breach the UK Top 20. The subject matter was typically subverted by McNabb's irony and cynicism ('When love calls me, I shall be running swiftly, To find out, just what all the fuss is all about'). Teaming up with producer Ian Broudie (ex-**Big In Japan**; **Lightning Seeds**), he helped them to a string of singles successes over the ensuing years, including 'Hollow Horse' and 'Understanding Jane', with their sound gradually shifting from subtle pop to harder rock territory. In 1986 they recruited Dave Green on keyboards, but the following year the group was turned upside down when both Sharrock and Layhe left within a short space of time. Sharrock joined the **La's** and later drummed for **World Party**. Layhe's role was taken by former **Black** bassist Roy Corkhill, while the drummer's stool was claimed by Zak Starkey, whose father **Ringo Starr** formerly drummed for another Liverpool band. This line-up prospered for a short time but in 1989 McNabb assembled a new band. Retaining only Corkhill, he added Mark Revell on guitar, Dave Baldwin on keyboards, and Paul Burgess on drums. The band signed a new contract with Epic Records and released an album before McNabb left to go solo. One of England's most underrated natural lyricists, his cult status looks set to continue, while his time with the Icicle Works has left a rich legacy of songwriting.

● ALBUMS: *The Icicle Works* (Beggars Banquet 1984)★★★, *The Small Price Of A Bicycle* (Beggars Banquet 1985)★★★, *If You Want To Defeat Your Enemy Sing His Song* (Beggars Banquet 1987)★★★, *Blind* (Beggars Banquet 1988)★★★, *Permanent Damage* (Epic 1990)★★★, *BBC Radio One Live In Concert* 1987 recording (Windsong 1994)★★.

● COMPILATIONS: *Seven Singles Deep* (Beggars Banquet 1986)★★, *The Best Of* (Beggars Banquet 1992)★★★.

Icon

Icon were formed in Phoenix, Arizona, USA, in 1981, by schoolfriends Dan Wexler (guitar), Tracy Wallach (bass, backing vocals) and Stephen Clifford (lead vocals). Drummer Pat Dixon and John Aquilino (guitar) joined a couple of months later. Icon spent their first three years playing local bars and recording demo tapes, originally under the name of the Schoolboys. Mike Varney heard the band and subsequently signed them to his Shrapnel label, after which Icon recorded their first album with Varney and Dan Wexler producing. After the sessions were completed, Varney realized that he had a commercial record on his hands, and sold Icon's contract to **Capitol Records**. In late 1984 *Icon* was released, a dynamic record in the **Don Dokken** tradition of melodic heavy metal. Brushing aside poor sales, they returned to the studio in 1985 with producer Eddie Kramer to record the follow-up, *Night Of The Crime*. Capitol dropped them from their roster following further disappointing sales, and Icon returned to Phoenix. At this point, Clifford, who had become a born-again Christian, was replaced by Jerry Harrison. In 1987 Icon released a cassette album, *A More Perfect Union*, which was sold locally and was reissued in 1995 as *An Even More Perfect Union*, also featuring four unissued tracks from the same sessions. Two years later Johnny Zazula heard the tape and signed them to his Megaforce label, which had just negotiated a worldwide distribution agreement with **Atlantic Records**. In the middle of 1989 Icon were about to start recording when Aquilino left the band. His replacement was Drew Bollmann, a Phoenix native. With Dan Wexler again producing, *Right Between The Eyes* saw Icon deliver their best record to date - again in their familiar AOR/melodic heavy rock vein - it also featured **Alice Cooper** guesting on two tracks. However, this did not signal Icon's triumphant return. After a short UK tour, Wexler announced their break-up.

● ALBUMS: *Icon* (Capitol 1984)★★★, *Night Of The Crime* (Capitol 1985)★★★, *A More Perfect Union* cassette only (Icon 1987)★★★, *Right Between The Eyes* (Megaforce 1989)★★★, *An Even More Perfect Union* CD reissue of *A More Perfect Union* (Epilogue 1995)★★★.

Ideals

An R&B vocal group from Chicago, Illinois, USA. Formed in 1952, the outfit scuffled for many years with several personnel changes before recording in 1961 on the local Paso label. The Ideals at this time consisted of Reggie Jackson, Leonard Mitchell, Robert Tharp and Sam Steward (bass). In 1963 the group added a fifth member, lead Eddie Williams, and with his rough-hewn, soulful delivery they recorded their most successful record, 'The Gorilla'; its 'monkey dance' theme was designed to reap sales from the success of the dance fad. It never reached any national charts but nonetheless received national exposure, partly in the pop market, and earned the group its first national tour. In 1965 the

Ideals reorganized as a trio with Jackson, Mitchell and Steward, and they finally reached the R&B charts with 'Kissin'' in 1966, although the record did not, in fact, sell as well as 'The Gorilla'. A notable song in 1966 was 'You Lost And I Won', which neatly married the group's doo-wop past with the sound of soul. However, the group broke up a short time later. Most of the members did not join other acts after their Ideals association, except for Tharp and Mitchell. Tharp, under the name Tommy Dark, joined Jerry Murray in 1964 to form a dance duo called Tom And Jerrio, specializing in Boogaloo records. They had a hit with 'Boo-Ga-Loo' (number 10 R&B) in 1965. Leonard Mitchell continued to record by joining with Jerome Johnson and Robert Thomas to form the Channel 3, who released one single, to no great acclaim.

Ides Of March

Formed in Chicago, Illinois, USA, the Ides Of March began life as anglophiles, but quickly adopted prevailing American influences to create a series of excellent pop singles. Success eluded the group until 1970 when a brass-laden single, 'Vehicle', became an international hit in the wake of **Chicago** and **Blood, Sweat And Tears**. Despite further releases, the Ides Of March - James Peterik (vocals), Ray Herr (guitar), John Larson (trumpet), Larry Millas (guitar, flute), Bob Bergland (bass), Mike Borch (drums, vibes) and Chuck Soumar (percussion) - were unable to sustain their brief spell in the spotlight and Peterik subsequently formed the soul group, Essence.
● ALBUMS: *Vehicle* (Warners 1970)★★★, *Common Bond* (1971)★★, *World Woven* (1972)★★, *Midnight Oil* (1973)★★.

Idha

b. Idha Ovelius, 22 May 1972, Södertälje, Sweden. The wife of ex-**Ride** guitarist Andy Bell, Idha has released two accomplished albums characterized by their melodic but downbeat air. Eager to leave Sweden to establish a musical career, she moved to London and signed to leading independent label **Creation**. Recordings with a group of musicians including **Ian McLagan** of **The Faces**, ostensibly to lay down a single, led to the release of her 1993 debut, *Melody Inn*. A mixture of originals and cover versions, the album's country-styled sound was captured in a lush version of **Gram Parsons**' 'Hickory Wind', while the lyrics dealt with her personal experience of beginning a new life in a new country. The pointedly titled *A Woman In A Man's World* EP followed, featuring Evan Dando of the **Lemonheads**, before work began on a second album. Recorded during a troubled period in the singer's personal life, *Troublemaker* took shape over two years of sessions with musicians including Bell (now with **Hurricane #1**), Tony Barber (**Buzzcocks**) and Alan White (later-**Oasis**). Finally released in 1997, Idha's distinctive songwriting rose above the musical talent on offer, with the melancholy air of 'Sorry, Sorry' and 'Just Moved In' providing the key to the mood of the album,

although a more abrasive tone was readily apparent on 'Still Alive'.
● ALBUMS: *Melody Inn* (Creation 1993)★★★, *Troublemaker* (Creation 1997)★★★★.

Idle Cure

Christian music rarely achieves column inches in the mainstream rock press, and that fate also befell late 80s US rock group Idle Cure, despite their obvious musical talents. Comprising Steve Shannon (vocals, bass), Mark Ambrose (guitar) and Peter Lomakin (keyboards), the group produced two albums of splendid AOR for Frontline Records in 1987 and 1988. On both, Lomakin's multi-textured keyboard playing compensated for the lack of a regular drummer, and the quality of the songwriting was universally excellent, regardless of what critics thought of the subject matter. *Tough Love* was dedicated to the forthright parental control mechanisms advocated by a number of leading Christian evangelists, and in interview the group were candid about their endorsement of such methods. Nevertheless, the songs on the album were contrastingly dynamic and free of inhibitions, and would surely have attracted wider coverage had Idle Cure not been consigned to the Christian rock ghetto.
● ALBUMS: *Idle Cure* (Frontline 1987)★★★★, *Tough Love* (Frontline 1988)★★★.

Idle Moments - Grant Green

Guitarist Grant Green's bright but bluesy sound and infectious swing have been featured on a huge number of Blue Note albums. During the label's soul-jazz trend, Green was a true stalwart, touching each session with a certain spirited brilliance. Probably his best date, *Idle Moments* is marked by a more serious, introspective quality, and features vibraphone by Bobby Hutcherson, tenor saxophone by a young but already undeniably exceptional Joe Henderson and underrated pianist and composer Duke Pearson. The long, intimate title track is a particular highlight, and deserves to be played again and again.
● Tracks: *Idle Moments; Jean De Fleur; Django; Nomad.*
● First released 1963
● UK peak chart position: did not chart
● USA peak chart position: did not chart

Idle On Parade

Taking inspiration from **Elvis Presley**'s induction into the US Army, **Anthony Newley** starred as the drafted pop star Jeep Jones in this 1959 British feature. Comedy stalwarts Sid James and Lionel Jeffries were also cast, but this jaundiced film owed more to television's *The Army Game* than rock 'n' roll. The soundtrack material, including 'Idle Rock-A-Boogie' and 'Saturday Night Rock-A-Boogie', consisted of little more than poorly formed pastiches, lacking neither the charm of Newley's Goons-inspired hits, 'Strawberry Fair' and 'That Noise', nor the wistfulness of his two UK chart-toppers, 'Why' and 'Do You Mind'. The four-track *Idle On Parade* EP nonetheless reached number 13 in the UK singles chart, reflecting the singer's popularity rather than the success of the film itself. Newley later became a celebrated songwriter for West End and Broadway productions, having bade farewell to his pop-styled inclinations.

Idle Race

Dave Pritchard (guitar), Greg Masters (bass) and Roger Spencer (drums) spent several years in the Nightriders, backing Birmingham singer Mike Sheridan. Their frontman left for a solo career in 1966, but with the addition of guitarist/composer **Jeff Lynne** (b. 30 December 1947, Birmingham, West Midlands, England), the restructured group embarked on an enthralling, independent direction. The quartet took the name the Idle Race in the wake of an unsuccessful debut single released under their former appellation. By 1967 Lynne had become the group's focal point, contributing the bulk of their original material and shaping its sound and direction. *The Birthday Party* showcased his gift for melody and quirky sense of humour, facets prevalent in two of its undoubted highlights, 'Follow Me Follow' and 'The Skeleton And The Roundabout'. The guitarist's grasp on the group was strengthened with their second album, *Idle Race*, which he produced. This evocative selection featured some of Lynne's finest compositions, many of which bore a debt to the **Beatles**, but without seeming plagiaristic. Any potential, however, was bedevilled by public indifference. Repeated overtures to join the **Move** ultimately proved too strong for Lynne to ignore. Highly commercial pop songs such as 'Come With Me' and 'At The End Of The Road' surprisingly failed to become hits.

Lynne's departure in January 1970 to form the **Electric Light Orchestra** precipitated several changes. Pritchard, Masters and Spencer drafted Mike Hopkins and Roy Collum into the line-up, the latter of whom was then replaced by Dave Walker. This reshaped quintet was responsible for *Time Is*, a progressive rock collection at odds with the erstwhile group's simple pop. Walker then left for **Savoy Brown** and his place was taken by Birmingham veteran **Steve Gibbons**. Founder members Pritchard and Spencer abandoned their creation, Bob Lamb and Bob Wilson from **Tea And Symphony** joined, before a third member of that august ensemble, Dave Carroll, replaced Mike Hopkins. When Greg Masters left the Idle Race in 1971, their link with the past was finally severed and the group became known as the Steve Gibbons Band.

● ALBUMS: *The Birthday Party* (Liberty 1968)★★★, *Idle Race* (Liberty 1969)★★★, *Time Is* (Regal Zonophone 1971)★★.

● COMPILATIONS: *On With The Show* (Sunset 1973)★★★, *Imposters Of Life's Magazine* (1976)★★★, *Light At The End Of The Road* (1985)★★★, *Back To The Story* (Premier 1996)★★★.

Idlewild - Everything But The Girl

Through a sea of changes they moved, from sparse indie folk to jazz, and with this album, they slotted into the classy pop niche. Very much a cosy 80s album for those that had weathered the new wave of the late 70s, EBTG still have the Habitat/Ikea image in their front-room. This is unnecessary carping because the songs are quite excellent, from the romantic innocence of 'These Early Days' to the romantic experience of 'I Always Was Your Girl'. Thorn's voice is at last sounding fully in command and the choice of the late Danny Whitten's 'I Don't Want To Talk About It' is inspired.

● Tracks: *I Don't Want To Talk About It; Love Is Here Where I Live; These Early Days; I Always Was Your Girl; Oxford Street; The Night I Heard Caruso Sing; Goodbye Sunday; Shadow On A Harvest Moon; Blue Moon Rose; Tears All Over Town; Lonesome For A Place I Know; Apron Strings.*

● First released 1988

● UK peak chart position: 13

● USA peak chart position: did not chart

Idol, Billy

b. William Michael Albert Broad, 30 November 1955, Stanmore, Middlesex, England. While studying English Literature at Sussex University, Broad became involved with the 'Bromley contingent' followers of the **Sex Pistols**. Inspired by the energy of punk, he formed his own group, **Chelsea**, in 1976. The original outfit was short-lived and Billy Idol, as he was now known, next founded **Generation X**. The group lasted from 1976-81, after which Idol launched his solo career in New York and recorded *Don't Stop*, which featured a revival of **Tommy James And The Shondells'** UK number 1 'Mony Mony'. Through 1982-83, Idol's career blossomed and his acerbic vocal style and lively stage act brought a string of hits including 'Hot In The City', 'White Wedding', 'Rebel Yell' and 'Eyes Without A Face'. With his album sales increasing each year, Idol actually became an idol and turned an old hit to advantage by taking 'Mony Mony' to number 1 in the USA in 1987. Despite his legendarily excessive lifestyle, Idol has appeared in several charity shows. In 1988, he took part in **Neil Young**'s Bridge School Benefit concert and the following year guested in the charity performance of the **Who**'s *Tommy* in London. After being slated for a part in the Oliver Stone film of the **Doors**, Idol almost emulated its central character by suffering an early death. A serious motorcycle crash seriously damaged his leg, but he recovered remarkably quickly. However, he soon found himself back in trouble, this time with the Los Angeles courts when, in 1992, he was put on probation for two years and fined $2,700 for an assault on a 'fan'. This all added fuel to the rebel image and, in many respects, he has become more successful than most of the punk founders with whom he rubbed shoulders back in 1977. Idol's brand of heavy punk was perfectly honed and showcased on *Cyberpunk*.

● ALBUMS: *Billy Idol* (Chrysalis 1981)★★★, *Don't Stop* (Chrysalis 1981)★★★, *Rebel Yell* (Chrysalis 1984)★★★★, *Whiplash Smile* (Chrysalis 1986)★★★, *Charmed Life* (Chrysalis 1990)★★, *Cyberpunk* (Chrysalis 1993)★★.

● COMPILATIONS: *Vital Idol* (Chrysalis 1986)★★★, *Idol Sings - 11 Of The Best* (Chrysalis 1988)★★★.
● FURTHER READING: *Billy Idol: Visual Documentary*, Mike Wrenn.

If

This ambitious, multi-instrumentalist jazz-rock ensemble made its recording debut in 1970. Leader **Dick Morrissey** (saxophones, flute) was already a well-established figure in UK jazz circles, having led a quartet that included **Phil Seaman** and Harry South. Having flirted with pop and rock through an association with the **Animals** and **Georgie Fame**, Morrissey formed this new venture with guitarist Terry Smith, J.W. Hodgkinson (vocals), Dave Quincy (alto saxophone), John Mealing (keyboards), Jim Richardson (bass) and Dennis Elliott (drums) completing the initial line-up. They recorded four powerful, if commercially moribund, albums before internal pressures undermined progress. Mealing, Richardson and Elliott - the latter of whom later joined **Foreigner** - abandoned the group in 1972, while by the release of If's final album in 1975 only Morrissey remained from the founding septet. Although popular in Europe, the group was never able to achieve consistent commercial success, though the saxophonist subsequently enjoyed a fruitful partnership with guitarist **Jim Mullen** as **Morrissey/Mullen**.
● ALBUMS: *If* (Capitol 1970)★★★, *If2* (Capitol 1970)★★★, *If3* (Capitol 1971)★★★, *If4* aka *Waterfall* (Capitol 1972)★★, *Double Diamond* (Capitol 1973)★★★, *Not Just Another Bunch Of Pretty Faces* (Capitol 1974)★★★, *Tea Break Is Over, Back On Your Heads* (Gull 1975)★★★.
● COMPILATIONS: *This Is If* (Capitol 1973)★★, *God Rock* (1974)★★, *Forgotten Roads: The Best Of If* (Sequel 1995)★★★.

If Only I Could Remember My Name - David Crosby

Although this was a highly successful album, Crosby was later accused of being self-indulgent by some critics. In recent years that opinion has reversed, acknowledging that the amount of space he allowed to fellow musicians, makes this a wholly unselfish record. The cream of San Francisco assembled, and in no particular order, there are **Jerry Garcia**, Phil Lesh, Jack Casady, Paul Kantner, **Joni Mitchell** and Grace Slick. Crosby moves from the humour in his modern-day Jesse James story, 'Cowboy Movie', to wondrous spiritual voice excursions in 'I'd Swear There Was Somebody Here' and 'Tamalpais High'. The playing is faultless throughout and if you are not familiar with this wondrous record, please take the risk.
● Tracks: *Music Is Love; Cowboy Movie; Tamalpais High; Laughing; What Are Their Names; Traction In The Rain; Song With No Words; Tree With No Leaves; Orleans; I'd Swear There Was Somebody Here.*
● First released 1971
● UK peak chart position: 12
● USA peak chart position: 12

If There Was A Way - Dwight Yoakam

The packaging is clearly designer country - **Dwight Yoakam** attached to his large Stetson, torn jeans, lanky legs and James Dean posture. Packaging aside, the music is very good, hillbilly deluxe, and Dwight's solid country voice certainly makes no concessions to commerciality. Among the many excellent tracks are Dwight's duet with Patty Loveless, 'Send A Message To My Heart', a revival of Wilbert Harrison and **Bryan Ferry**'s 'Let's Work Together' and a joint composition with **Roger Miller**, 'It Only Hurts When I Cry'. Obviously, the best place to hear Yoakam is a crowded honky tonk.
● Tracks: *The Distance Between You And Me; The Heart That You Own; Takes A Lot To Rock You; Nothing's Changed Here; Sad, Sad Music; Since I Started Drinkin' Again; If There Was A Way; Turn It On, Turn It Up, Turn Me Loose; It Only Hurts When I Cry; Send A Message To My Heart; I Don't Need It Done; You're The One.*
● First released 1990
● UK peak chart position: did not chart
● USA peak chart position: 96

If You Feel Like Singing
(see **Summer Stock**)

If You Want Blood You've Got It - AC/DC

From the bloody artwork, vocalist Bon Scott forcing a guitar through Angus Young's midriff, this, AC/DC's truly bombastic live album, was an unrepentant amalgamation of attitude, boogie and rock 'n' roll, which combined to give this Australian outfit international notoriety. From Young's schoolboy outfit and antics to his elongated soloing, and an uproarious version, complete with full crowd backing, of 'Whole Lotta Rosie', Bon Scott's lurid retelling of his encounter with a somewhat overweight and overwrought lady friend, *If You Want Blood You've Got It* is a very live record indeed.
● Tracks: *Riff Raff; Hell Ain't A Bad Place To Be; Bad Boy Boogie; The Jack; Problem Child; Whole Lotta Rosie; Rock 'N' Roll Damnation; High Voltage; Let There Be Rock; Rocker.*
● First released 1978
● UK peak chart position: 13
● USA peak chart position: 113

If?

If? emerged in the UK during 1990's Summer Of Love, graduating from the backrooms of the Brain Club, which was co-managed by the group's Sean McLusky. They hit the rave scene in turn, before organizing a London Calling tour with **Airstream**, **Natural Life** and others. With vocals from Paul Wells, If? peddled a straightforward Balearic model of 90s dance culture. Member Lyndsay Edwards went on to join the **Disco Evangelists**.
● ALBUMS: *English Boys On The Love Ranch* (MCA 1992)★★.

Ifang Bondi

Though based in Senegal, Ifang Bondi (which translates as 'Be Yourself') are an offshoot of the acclaimed Gambian band, the **Super Eagles**. Following a two-year gap after their break-up, members of the Eagles reconvened as Ifang Bondi in 1974. A musical switch accompanied the new name, with traditional Senegalese music, instruments and rhythms dominating a sound which had once strayed far enough to allow the Super Eagles to record a cover version of the **Beatles**' 'Hey Jude'. Two albums followed, *Sanio* and *Mantra*, the latter recorded in Holland, where manager Oko Drammeh runs an annual African music festival. It offered an exemplary distillation of African jazz, kora and mbalax, with Paps Touray's distinctive vocals an evocative counter balance to the music's intricacy. The group christened their new sound 'mantra', a legacy of their days in London with the Super Eagles in the 60s.

● ALBUMS: *Sanio* (MAG 1982)★★★, *Mantra* (LPH 1983)★★★, *Sanyo* (D&K 1991)★★★.

Ifield, Frank

b. 30 November 1937, Coventry, Warwickshire, England. The most successful recording artist in the UK during the early 60s, Ifield is now also one of the most underrated. At the age of nine, his family emigrated to Australia, and Ifield entered show business during his teens. He first came to prominence in Australia during 1957 with 'Whiplash', a song about the 1851 Australian goldrush that was later used as the theme for a long-running television series. After returning to England in the late 50s, Ifield was signed to the **EMI** subsidiary **Columbia Records** and soon found success working with producer **Norrie Paramor**. After scoring minor hits with 'Lucky Devil' and 'Gotta Get A Date', he broke through spectacularly with the chart-topping 'I Remember You'. The song had a wonderfully elegiac feel, complemented by Ifield's relaxed vocal and a pleasing harmonica break. The track dominated the UK chart listings, staying at number 1 for a staggering seven weeks and was the first record ever to sell a million copies in England alone. The song also charted in America, a rare feat for a British-based singer in the early 60s. Late in 1962, Ifield was back at the top of the UK charts for a further five weeks with 'Lovesick Blues', which betrayed his love of C&W and emphasized his extraordinary ability as a yodeller. His engaging falsetto became something of a trademark, which differentiated him from other UK vocalists of the period. A revival of **Gogi Grant**'s 'The Wayward Wind' put Ifield into the record books. No artist in British pop history had previously logged three consecutive number 1 records, but during February 1963 Ifield achieved that honour. Ironically, he shared the number 1 spot jointly with the **Beatles**' 'Please Please Me', and it was their abrupt rise that year which tolled the death knell for Ifield as a regular chart contender. After stalling at number 4 with 'Nobody's Darlin' But Mine' Ifield experienced his fourth UK chart-topper with the breezy 'Confessin''.

His version of the perennial 'Mule Train' added little to the **Frankie Laine** version and Ifield's last Top 10 hit in the UK was almost an apology for his previous release; the beautifully arranged 'Don't Blame Me'. Thereafter, the material chosen for him seemed weaker and his chart career atrophied. He became the most celebrated victim of the beat boom that was sweeping the UK and never regained the seemingly unassailable position that he enjoyed in the early 60s. He continued his career, playing regularly in pantomime and in stage productions like *Up Jumped A Swagman*, before reverting to cabaret work. During the 80s Ifield concentrated singing his beloved country music, performing regularly in Australia and the USA. In the 90s following lengthy bouts of ill health, Ifield was residing in Australia, and in 1996 following further illness (an abcess on the lung) his singing was permanently impaired. He now works as a television presenter.

● ALBUMS: *I'll Remember You* (1963)★★★, *Portrait In Song* (Columbia 1965)★★★, *Blue Skies* (Columbia 1964), *Up Jumped A Swagman* soundtrack (Columbia 1965)★★, *Someone To Give My Love To* (Spark 1973)★★, *Barbary Coast* (Fir 1978)★★, *Sweet Vibrations* (Fir 1980)★★, *If Love Must Go* (Fir 1982)★★, *At The Sandcastle* (Fir 1983)★★.
● COMPILATIONS: *Greatest Hits* (1964)★★★, *Best Of The EMI Years* (1991)★★★★, *The EP Collection* (1991)★★★★.
● FILMS: *Up Jumped A Swagman* (1965).

Igginbottom

Comprising Dave Freeman (drums), Steve Robinson (guitar, vocals), **Allan Holdsworth** (guitar, vocals) and Mick Skelly (bass), 'Igginbottom was formed in the late 60s in an attempt to fuse rock and jazz traditions. Certainly there was nothing wrong with the musicianship on display on the group's debut, 1969's *Igginbottom's Wrench*, but a series of endless (seemingly improvised) solos revealed an absence of direction and forethought. However, the album, released on **Deram Records**, is notable for featuring the recorded debut of Alan Holdsworth, who later formed **Tempest** and recorded solo work in the late 80s before joining **Soft Machine** and later **Level 42**. 'Igginbottom never recorded a follow-up record and their sole album is now a treasured obscurity among collectors.

● ALBUMS: *Igginbottom's Wrench* (Deram 1969)★★.

Iggy Pop

b. James Jewel Osterburg, 21 April 1947, Ypsilanti, Michigan, USA. The sinewy 'Godfather Of Punk', Iggy Pop was born just west of Detroit to an English father and raised in nearby Ann Arbor. He first joined bands while at high school, initially as a drummer, most notably with the Iguanas in 1964 where he picked up the nickname Iggy. The following year he joined the Denver blues-styled Prime Movers, but a year later he dropped out of the University of Michigan to travel to Chicago and learn about the blues from former **Howlin' Wolf** and **Paul Butterfield Blues Band** drummer Sam Lay. On returning to Detroit as Iggy Stooge, and further inspired after seeing the **Doors**, he formed the Psychedelic Stooges with Ron Asheton of the Chosen Few. Iggy was vocalist and guitarist, Asheton initially played bass, and they later added Asheton's brother Scott on drums. Before the Chosen Few, Ron Asheton had also been in the Prime Movers with Iggy. The Psychedelic Stooges made their debut on Halloween night 1967, in Ann Arbor. The same year Iggy also made his acting debut in a long-forgotten Françoise De Monierre film that also featured **Nico**. Meanwhile, Dave Alexander joined on bass and the word 'Psychedelic' was dropped from their name. Ron switched to guitar leaving Iggy free to concentrate on singing and showmanship. The Stooges were signed to **Elektra Records** in 1968 by A&R man Danny Fields (later manager of the **Ramones**). They recorded two albums (the first produced by **John Cale**) for the label which sold moderately at the time but later became regarded as classics, featuring such quintessential Iggy numbers as 'No Fun' and 'I Wanna Be Your Dog'. Steven MacKay joined on saxophone in 1970 in-between the first and second albums, as did Bill Cheatham on second guitar. Cheatham and Alexander left in August 1970, with Zeke Zettner replacing Alexander and James Williamson replacing Cheatham - but the Stooges broke up not long afterwards as a result of Iggy's heroin problem. Stooge fan **David Bowie** tried to resurrect Iggy's career and helped him record *Raw Power* in London in the summer of 1972 (as Iggy and the Stooges, with Williamson on guitar, Scott Thurston on bass, and the Ashetons, who were flown in when no suitable British musicians could be found). The resultant album included the nihilistic anthem 'Search And Destroy'. Bowie's involvement continued (although his management company Mainman withdrew support because of constant drug allegations) as Iggy sailed through stormy seas (including self-admission to a mental hospital). The popular, but poor quality, live *Metallic KO* was released only in France at the time. Iggy Pop live events had long been a legend in the music industry, and it is doubtful whether any other artist has sustained such a high level of abject self-destruction on stage. It was his performance on the British television slot *So It Goes*, for example, that ensured the programme would never air again. After *Raw Power* there were sessions for *Kill City*, although it was not released until 1978, credited then to Iggy Pop and James Williamson. It also featured Thurston, Hunt and Tony Sales, Brian Glascock (ex-**Toe Fat** and later in the **Motels**), and others. The Stooges had folded again in 1974 with Ron Asheton forming New Order (not the same as the UK band) and then **Destroy All Monsters**. Steve MacKay later died from a drugs overdose and Dave Alexander from alcohol abuse. Thurston also joined the Motels. Interest was stirred in Iggy with the arrival of punk, on which his influence was evident (**Television** recorded the tribute 'Little Johnny Jewel'). In 1977 Bowie produced two studio albums - *The Idiot* and *Lust For Life* - using Hunt and Tony Sales, with

Bowie himself, unheralded, playing keyboards. Key tracks from these two seminal albums include 'Night Clubbin'', 'The Passenger' and 'China Girl' (co-written with and later recorded by Bowie). Iggy also returned one of the several favours he owed Bowie by guesting on backing vocals for *Low*. In the late 70s Iggy signed to **Arista Records** and released some rather average albums with occasional assistance from Glen Matlock (ex-**Sex Pistols**) and Ivan Kral. He went into (vinyl) exile after 1982's autobiography and the Chris Stein-produced *Zombie Birdhouse*. During his time out of the studio he cleaned up his drug problems and married. He started recording again in 1985, with **Steve Jones** (ex-Sex Pistols) featuring on the next series of albums. He also developed his acting career (even taking lessons), appearing in *Sid And Nancy*, *The Color Of Money*, *Hardware*, and on television in *Miami Vice*. His big return came in 1986 with the Bowie-produced *Blah Blah Blah* and his first ever UK hit single, 'Real Wild Child', a cover version of Australian **Johnny O'Keefe**'s 50s rocker. His rejuvenated *Brick By Brick* album featured **Guns N'Roses** guitarist Slash, who co-wrote four of the tracks, while his contribution to the *Red Hot And Blue* AIDS benefit was an endearing duet with **Debbie Harry** on 'Well Did You Evah?'. This was followed in 1991 by a duet with the **B-52**'s' Kate Pierson, who had also featured on *Brick By Brick*. *American Caesar* from its jokily self-aggrandising title onwards, revealed continued creative growth, with longer spaces between albums now producing more worthwhile end results than was the case with his 80s career. Throughout he has remained the consummate live performer, setting a benchmark for at least one generation of rock musicians.

● ALBUMS: *The Idiot* (RCA 1977)★★★★, *Lust For Life* (RCA 1977)★★★★, *TV Eye Live* (RCA 1978)★★, *New Values* (Arista 1979)★★, *Soldier* (Arista 1980)★★, *Party* (Arista 1981)★★, *Zombie Birdhouse* (Animal 1982)★★, *Blah Blah Blah* (A&M 1986)★★★, *Instinct* (A&M 1988)★★, *Brick By Brick* (Virgin 1990)★★★, *American Caesar* (Virgin 1993)★★★, *Naughty Little Doggie* (Virgin 1996)★★★, *Heroin Hates You* recorded 1979 (Other People's Music 1997)★★★, *Live On The King Biscuit Flower Hour* recorded 1988 (King Biscuit 1998)★★★.

● COMPILATIONS: *Choice Cuts* (RCA 1984)★★★, *Compact Hits* (A&M 1988)★★★, *Suck On This!* (Revenge 1993)★★, *Live NYC Ritz '86* (Revenge 1993)★★, *Best Of ... Live* (MCA 1996)★★, *Nude & Rude: The Best Of ...* (Virgin 1996)★★★★, *Pop Music* (BMG/Camden 1996)★★★.

● FURTHER READING: *The Lives And Crimes Of Iggy Pop*, Mike West. *I Need More: The Stooges And Other Stories*, Iggy Pop with Anne Wehrer. *Iggy Pop: The Wild One*, Per Nilsen and Dorothy Sherman. *Neighbourhood Threat: On Tour With Iggy Pop*, Alvin Gibbs.

Iglesias, Enrique

b. *c*.1976, Spain. The son of global superstar **Julio Iglesias**, Enrique recorded his self-titled debut album of Latin-influenced pop in 1995. The album's release saw him catapulted to superstar status in the Spanish-speaking music world. Assured of media exposure of similar intensity to the elder Iglesias, certain sections of the media also implied a rivalry between father and progeny - his parents having divorced when Enrique was seven. Certainly Enrique's statement to Spain's top-selling daily newspaper, *El Pais*, 'When I have children, I'll leave work to one side for a while - something my father never did', helped to fuel the conjecture. Although his anthemic love songs and ballads, such as 'Experiencia Religiosa' and 'No Llores Por Mi', placed him in the same stylistic area as his father, Enrique claims to have been influenced as much by rock acts such as **Journey**, **Foreigner** and **Roxy Music**, having spent much of his youth growing up in Miami, Florida. His follow-up collection, *Vivir*, won a Grammy award, and by 1997 the two albums were credited with global sales in excess of eight million. By that time he had also achieved a sequence of seven chart-topping singles on *Billboard*'s Latin Top 50 chart.

● ALBUMS: *Enrique Iglesias* (Fonovisa 1995)★★★, *Vivir* (Fonovisa 1997)★★★★.

Iglesias, Julio

b. 23 September 1943, Madrid, Spain. Iglesias trained as a lawyer and played football (goalkeeper) for Real Madrid before suffering severe injuries in a car accident. While recuperating, he learned guitar and began to write songs. After completing his studies at Cambridge University, he entered the 1968 Spanish Song Festival at Benidorm. Performing his own composition 'La Vida Sigue Igual' ('Life Continues All The Same'), he won first prize and soon afterwards signed a recording contract with the independent Discos Columbia where Ramon Arcusa became his producer. In 1970, Iglesias represented Spain in the Eurovision Song Contest, subsequently recording the song 'Gwendolyne' in French, Italian and English. During the next few years he toured widely in Europe and Latin America, scoring international hits with 'Manuela' (1975) and 'Hey' (1979). His global reach was increased in 1978 when he signed to **CBS** International and soon had hits in French and Italian. The first big English-language success came in 1981 when his version of 'Begin The Beguine' topped the UK charts. This was followed by the multi-language compilation album *Julio* which sold a million in America. Co-produced by Arcusa and **Richard Perry**, *1100 Bel Air Place* was aimed directly at American audiences and included duets with **Willie Nelson** ('To All The Girls I've Loved Before') and **Diana Ross** ('All Of You'). A later duet (and international hit) was 'My Love' with **Stevie Wonder** in 1988. By the end of the 80s Iglesias had sold in excess of 100 million albums in seven languages. He won the Billboard Latin album of the year award in 1996 for *La Carreterra*.

● ALBUMS: *Yo Canto* (Columbia 1968)★★★, *Todos Los Dias Un Dia* (Columbia 1969)★★★, *Soy* (Columbia 1970)★★, *Gwendolyne* (Columbia 1970)★★, *Como el Alamo al Camino* (Columbia 1971)★★, *Rio Rebelde* (Columbia 1972)★★, *Asi Nacemos* (Columbia 1973)★★, *A Flor de Piel* (Columbia 1974)★★, *El Amor* (Columbia 1975)★★, *A Mexico* (Columbia 1975)★★, *America* (Columbia 1976)★★, *En El Olympia* (Columbia 1976)★★, *A Mis 33 Anos* (Columbia 1977)★★, *Mi Vida en Canciones* (Columbia 1978)★★, *Emociones* (Columbia 1979)★★, *Hey* (Columbia 1980)★★, *De Nina A Mujer* (Columbia 1981)★★, *Begin The Beguine* (Columbia 1981)★★★, *Momentos* (Columbia 1981)★★, *En Concierto* (Columbia 1982)★★, *Amor* (Columbia 1982)★★, *Julio* (Columbia 1983)★★, *1100 Bel Air Place* (Columbia 1984)★★, *Libra* (Columbia 1985)★★, *Un Hombre Solo* (Columbia 1987)★★, *Non Stop* (Columbia 1988)★★, *Sentimental* (Columbia 1988)★★, *Raices* (Columbia 1989)★★, *Starry Night* (Columbia 1990)★★★, *Calor* (Columbia 1992)★★, *La Carreterra* (Columbia 1995)★★★, *Tango* (Columbia 1996)★★.

● FURTHER READING: *Julio!*, Jeff Rovin.

Ignorance

A London hip-hop duo comprising Mark Martin and Trevor, who formerly found fame and fortune as dancers for the **Pet Shop Boys**. They started off their own career at **Polydor** with the 'Phat Girls' 45, a politically correct attempt to redress hip-hop's attitudes to women. They also took a non-conventional approach to their music, choosing a ska mix over the more preferred funk/jazz stylings of their American neighbours. This was done primarily to reinstate the Black British experience, reflecting the sounds of reggae and calypso that were so evident where they grew up. And there was no cussing of bitches and ho's to be found on their debut album, either: 'I mean, when we went to school we never had rucksacks with Uzis in 'em! To me, all that infatuation with being a hard superhuman with a gun by your side is bollocks. It's just a weak excuse for people that are insecure.'

● ALBUMS: *The Epitome Of Ignorants* (Polydor 1994)★★★.

Ikettes

This female R&B trio was formed by Ike Turner as part of his revue and was used for chorusing. Throughout the 60s and 70s, there were several line-ups of Ikettes, each of which provided a stunning visual and aural complement on stage to the performances of **Ike And Tina Turner**. Ike Turner occasionally recorded the group, with results that emhasized their tough, soulful R&B sound, much like his work with Tina. The original group was formed from the Artettes - Robbie Montgomery, Frances Hodges and Sandra Harding - who were the backing vocalists for the St. Louis singer Art Lassiter. They provided the chorus sound to Ike And Tina Turner's first hit, 'A Fool In Love.' On the first recordings of the Ikettes in 1962, the group consisted of Delores Johnson (lead), Eloise Hester and **'Joshie' Jo Armstead** (b. Josephine Armstead, 8 October 1944, Yazoo City, Mississippi, USA). They recorded the hit 'I'm Blue (The Gong-Gong Song)' (number 3 R&B, number 19 pop) for **Atco** in 1962. The best-known group of Ikettes were Vanetta Fields, Robbie Montgomery and Jessie Smith, a line-up formed in the St. Louis area around 1963. They recorded for the Modern label, including the hits 'Peaches 'N' Cream' (number 28 R&B, number 36 pop) and 'I'm So Thankful' (number 12 R&B, number 74 pop), both in 1965. This group left Turner in 1968 and enjoyed a big hit as the Mirettes in 1968 with a remake of the **Wilson Pickett** hit, 'In The Midnight Hour' (number 18 R&B, number 45 pop). Later line-ups of Ikettes included several singers who developed careers of their own, notably **P.P. Arnold**, Claudia Lennear and Bonnie Bramlett (who formed the duo **Delany And Bramlett**).

● ALBUMS: *Soul Hits* (Modern 1965)★★, *Gold And New* (United Artists 1974)★★, as the Mirettes *In The Midnight Hour* (Revue 1968)★★, *Whirlpool* (Uni 1969)★★.
● COMPILATIONS: *Fine Fine Fine* (Kent 1992)★★.

Ill (Featuring Al Skratch)

aka Big Ill The Mack, who first came to prominence in his home-town of Brooklyn, New York, by appearing on a freestyle tape that was circulated after a performance at a **Big Daddy Kane** birthday party (where he successfully 'dissed' both the birthday boy and other 'sucker MCs'). He made an impressive debut, backed by DJ Al Skratch, with the anthemic 'Where My Homiez?' 12-inch for **Mercury**. The track was produced by LG, brother of Easy Mo Bee (**Rappin' Is Fundamental**).

● ALBUMS: *Creep Wit' Me* (Mercury 1994)★★★★.

Illegal

Illegal are two diminutive youngsters from the USA, Lil' Malik Edwards and Jamal Phillips. Far from the cutesy **Kriss Kross** school of teen-rappers, Illegal won a degree of notoriety when curtailing an interview with a US rap magazine and offering to 'smoke' the interviewer. Their debut album boasted production from heavyweights like **Erick Sermon**, **Diamond D**, **Lord Finesse**, **Biz Markie** and others. Having subsequently split, Malik featured as part of **Snoop Doggy Dogg**'s Dog Pound, appearing on albums by the latter and **Warren G**.

● ALBUMS: *The Untold Truth* (Rowdy 1993)★★★.
Solo: Jamal *Last Chance, No Breaks* (Arista 1995)★★★.

Illegal Substance

From New South Wales, Australia, this three-piece rap group comprises MCs Micke and Flip (both b. c.1976), alongside DJ/producer ESP. The trio met in a record store and each had a long history of activity in Sydney's fledgling hip-hop scene, including graffiti and break-dancing. They recorded their debut album, *Off Da Back Of A Truck*, in a bedroom in a single day, using live takes of music that reflected their devotion to the hard funk sounds of west coast American rappers such as **NWA** and **Dr Dre**.

● ALBUMS: *Off Da Back Of A Truck* (Illegal Substance 1994)★★★.

Illinois Speed Press

The Chicago-based Illinois Speed Press was originally known as the Gentrys. The quintet - Kal David (vocals, guitar), Paul Cotton (vocals, guitar), Mike Anthony (organ), Frank Bartoli (bass) and Fred Pappalardo (drums) - was later known as the Rovin' Kind and as such recorded several singles including covers of the **Who**'s 'My Generation' and **John Sebastian**'s 'Didn't Want To Have To Do It'. The group assumed the name Illinois Speed Press in February 1968. Rob Lewine replaced Bartoli prior to recording their first album. This debut showed a promising grasp of melody, but within a year, David and Cotton were the only remaining members. They completed *Duet* together before the latter guitarist accepted an offer to join **Poco**. His erstwhile colleague was later a founder-member of the Fabulous Rhinestones.

● ALBUMS: *The Illinois Speed Press* (Columbia 1969)★★, *Duet* (Columbia 1970)★★★.

Illusion

Formed in 1964 in Long Island, New York, USA, the Illusion were a locally popular band in the same 'blue-eyed soul' scene that also produced more world-famous bands as the **Rascals, Vanilla Fudge**, the **Vagrants** (featuring **Leslie West**) and the Hassles (featuring **Billy Joel**). The group originally consisted of John Vinci (vocals), Frank Carillo (guitar), Howie Bloom (bass), Mike Ricciardella (drums) and Steve Berg (saxophone, vocals). That line-up continued for nearly five years and built a large following in New York clubs, particularly on Long Island. In 1969 the group was signed to the small Steed label, run by songwriter **Jeff Barry**, who also produced them. While recording their debut album, all but Vinci and Ricciardella left the band. They were replaced by Richie Cerniglia (lead guitar), Mike Maniscalco (organ, rhythm guitar) and Chuck Adler (bass). (Adler was later replaced by Butch Poveromo.) The group's first and biggest single was the soul-rock song 'Did You See Her Eyes', which peaked at number 32 nationally in the summer of 1969 but was a large hit in the New York area clubs. The group's self-titled debut album was also released at that time, with Maniscalco going under the name Mike Coxton and Ricciardella using the name Mike Sylvester. Only the debut album charted (at number 69) but the Illusion released two more within a year, after which they disbanded. Several of the members later resurfaced in such groups as Network, Barnaby Bye and the **Blues Magoos**. Cerniglia briefly worked with **Hall And Oates**.

● ALBUMS: *The Illusion* (Dot 1969)★★★, *Together (As A Way Of Life)* (Dot 1969)★★, *If It's So* (Dot 1970)★★★.

Imagination

One of the most successful British funk bands of the early 80s, Imagination were formed by the idiosyncratically named Lee John (b. John Lesley McGregor, 23 June 1957, Hackney, London, England; vocals), Ashley Ingram (b. 27 November 1960, Northampton, England;

guitar) and Errol Kennedy (b. Montego Bay, West Indies). John (of St. Lucian descent) was educated in New York, where he also became a backing vocalist for the **Delfonics** and **Chairmen Of The Board**. He met Ingram, who played bass for both bands, and they formed a duo called Fizzz. Back in England, John, who had already appeared on *Junior Showtime* as a child, enrolled at the Anna Scher Theatre School where he studied drama. Kennedy was an experienced singer with Jamaican bands and learnt the drums through the Boys Brigade and later the Air Training Corps band. He had also spent some time in the soul group Midnight Express. Kennedy met John and Ingram in early 1981, after which they formed Imagination as a pop/soul three-piece. They made an immediate impact with their debut 'Body Talk', and further **Tony Swain**-produced hits followed, including UK Top 5 entries with 'Just An Illusion' and 'Music And Lights'. However, the run of hits dried up by 1984, when John returned to acting. He had already appeared in the *Dr Who* story *Enlightenment* in 1983. Having switched to **RCA Records** in 1986, Imagination made a minor comeback in 1988 with 'Instinctual'.
● ALBUMS: *Body Talk* (R&B 1981)★★★, *In The Heat Of The Night* (R&B 1982)★★, *Night Dubbing* (R&B 1983)★★, *Scandalous* (R&B 1983)★★, *Imagination* (RCA 1989)★★.
● COMPILATIONS: *Imagination Gold* (Stylus 1984)★★★.

Imaginations

Formed in Bellmore, Long Island, New York, USA, in 1961, doo-wop group the Imaginations consisted of Frank Mancuso (lead), **Bobby Bloom** (first tenor), Phil Agtuca (second tenor), Pete Agtuca (baritone) and Richard LeCausi (bass). In April 1961, Music Makers released the group's 'Goodnight Baby', which featured **King Curtis** on saxophone. The Imaginations' second studio engagement came as back-up singers for **Darlene Day**, and, with studio time remaining, they also recorded two of their own songs, 'Guardian Angel' and 'Hey You'. When the tracks formed their second single, both sides attracted airplay, and the record was licensed to Duel Records, although too late, apparently, to allow it a chance to reach the national charts. Despite this, 'Hey You', primarily through repeated radio plays, became established as one of the most popular vocal group records in the New York area throughout the early 60s. However, that impetus was stalled when Mancuso joined the air forces, and Music Makers closed down. Bobby Caupin took over on lead as the group switched to a new title, the Ebonaires. A single was recorded ('Chapel Bells') but never released. Still not dispirited, Bobby Bloom took over on lead as the group then reverted to their former name for 'Wait A Little Longer Son', issued on new label Ballad Records. Again a release of genuine quality, it too was picked up for extended distribution, this time by Laurie Records. By 1963 the group had broken up, but they re-formed when producers Pete Antell and John Linde took an interest in their careers. Bloom, Phil Agtuca and

LeCausi were then joined by John Governale (first tenor) and Pete Lanzetta (baritone) in the Expressions. As well as backing **Tommy Boyce** in the studio, the Expressions released a debut single in 1963, 'On The Corner' - a eulogy to the origins of doo-wop on street corners. However, it flopped, and the group broke up once again. Bloom, however, persevered as a solo artist, and was rewarded in 1970 when his 'Montego Bay' became a national Top 10 hit (number 3 in England). Despite further chart appearances he committed suicide on 28 February 1974.

Imagine

Between 1968 and 1972 **John Lennon** and **Yoko Ono** completed numerous *avant garde* films including *Smile*, *Self Portrait* and *Erection*. Shot largely at the couple's home in Ascot, England and released in 1972, *Imagine* was based around Lennon's album of the same title, his 'Power To The People' single, and portions of Ono's concurrent *Fly*. 'We're putting the picture to the sound, not the other way round', the former **Beatle** later explained and indeed there were several interludes where visual and aural impressions matched to perfection. This was especially true of 'Imagine' itself, which featured Lennon at a white piano while Ono gradually opened up shutters to allow light to penetrate the room. Indeed the entire *Imagine* project evolved from this particular sequence. Other notable moments include the pair's attempt at rowing a boat on the lake within their grounds and a game of chess where all the pieces are white, itself based on one of Ono's early art works. Newsreel footage was intercut into the free-flowing, dreamlike images and **George Harrison** and **Phil Spector** were among those momentarily appearing in the tableaux. A party scene featuring Andy Warhol was shot by Jonas Mekas, the director of *Guns Of The Trees* and a fellow member of the Fluxus Group with Ono during the early 60s.
The first print of *Imagine* lasted 81 minutes, although this represented only 20% of the actual footage shot. The film was not well received upon release and this first print was withdrawn and trimmed to 55 minutes. The bulk of Ono's contributions - 'Mind Train' and 'Midsummer New York' - were removed, but fortunately her haunting 'Mrs. Lennon' was retained. *Imagine* was edited further for video release during the 80s; clips and out-takes were also included in posthumous projects undertaken following Lennon's death.

Imagine (stage musical)

Devised by Keith Strachen and Ian Kellgren (who also directed) from an original idea by Bob Eaton, with additional material by Liam Lloyd, this tribute to **John Lennon** played the Liverpool Playhouse Theatre late in 1992. Mark McGann, who portrayed the late Beatle in the play *Lennon*, in the early 80s, and on film in *John And Yoko - A Love Story*, once again gave a performance that 'nurtures the the shrewd, enquiring mind of John behind his eyes, and masters not only his native arrogance, his comic manner, bearing and stance, but his grim lips in repose'. In *Imagine*, the direct narrative was shared by Cynthia Lennon (Caroline Dennis), **Yoko Ono** (Ava de Souza), and composite characters such as an American fan (Francine Brody). Some 40 **Beatles** numbers were played and sung 'live' by McGann, along with Karl Lorne (Paul), Peter Ferris (George), and Paul Case (Ringo). Andy Walmsley's setting varied between a New York skyline and a section of the Cavern Club, and the evening provided 'moments of glorious affirmation as John Lennon's career describes its meteoric curve from rock musician to freaked-out martyr - with some marvellous songs along the way'.

Imagine - **John Lennon**

Lennon's solo debut, although powerful, did not have the universal appeal of this album. Lennon veered from spitting anger in 'How Do You Sleep?', 'Give Me Some Truth' and cruel humour with 'Crippled Inside', yet the man was capable of intense romanticism as highlighted in 'Jealous Guy' and 'Oh My Love'. Those who resented John for being part of the Beatles break-up finally forgave him and began to love him again with this collection. The title track will stand as a classic of popular song and one that should be made part of the national curriculum, if not the new national anthem.

● Tracks: *Imagine; Crippled Inside; Jealous Guy; It's So Hard; I Don't Want To Be A Soldier; Give Me Some Truth; Oh My Love; How Do You Sleep?; How?; Oh Yoko!.*
● First released 1971
● UK peak chart position: 1
● USA peak chart position: 1

Imbruglia, Natalie

b. 4 February 1975, Sydney, Australia. One of 1998's surprise successes, Imbruglia's first brush with stardom came when she played Beth on the popular Australian soap opera *Neighbours*. She had originally started out as a singer, turning to acting later. Imbruglia spent two years on *Neighbours*, but after leaving struggled to find work in Australia. A move to England in 1996 offered little in the way of career progress, but she began turning her thoughts and experiences into songs. In 1997 she gained a contract with **RCA** Records in London, helped by her perceived affinity with the chart-topping 'feminine angst rock' of **Alanis Morissette** and **Meredith Brooks**. Recorded in London with Phil Thornalley (ex-**Cure**) and Nigel Godrich (**Radiohead**), in Los Angeles with Mark Goldenberg (**Eels**), and in New York with Mark Plati (**David Bowie**, **Dee-lite**), *Left Of The Middle* sold strongly on the back of the success of her debut single, 'Torn', a massive hit in Europe and America. Imbruglia subsequently ran into controversy when it was revealed that 'Torn' was actually the work of obscure Norwegian songwriter Trine Rein. Subsequent singles, 'Big Mistake' and 'Wishing I Was There', repeated the highly melodic indie-rock formula of her debut and were also chart successes.

● ALBUMS: *Left Of The Middle* (RCA 1997)★★★.

Imlach, Hamish

b. 10 February 1940, Calcutta, India, d. 1 January 1996, Motherwell, Scotland. Until his death, he was a larger-than-life singer, and humorist, who toured regularly up until his death. Meeting **Ralph Rinzler** in Glasgow in 1958, he was introduced to finger picking guitar technique. In 1959, Hamish played on the first night of the Glasgow Folk Club, at Corner House Cafe, Glasgow, eventually going on to run the club with the artists such as Archie Fisher, Ewan McVicar, and Jackie O'Conner. That same year, Imlach, along with **Josh MacRae** and Bobby Campbell recorded six tracks (released as three singles), of Irish Rebel songs for the **Decca** Beltona label. They made the recordings as the Emmettones, and one track, 'Bold Robert Emmett', made number 1 in the Irish charts. Through 1960-62, he was being booked to play Folk Clubs all over Scotland, and in 1962, he played his first bookings in England, in Coventry and Leicester. In 1961, Imlach was involved with other singers at the first Anti-Polaris demonstration, among them Josh MacRae, and Nigel Denver. The demonstrations were covered by Russian television, with the subsequent live recordings being issued on a Russian record label, and eventually on **Folkways** in the USA. In 1963, Imlach played four tracks on *Folksong At The Edinburgh Festival (Volumes 1 & 2)*, and became a resident performer at Scotland's first all-night folk club, Clive's Incredible Folk Club, with the **Incredible String Band**. On his first album, he was accompanied by Clive Palmer, **Robin Williamson**, and Maryanne Alburger. In 1978, in Dublin, he recorded a single, 'Sonny's Dream'/'Maryanne'. The recording was produced by **Christy Moore** and Donal Lunny, and he was accompanied by Keith Donald and Declan Sinnott, from **Moving Hearts**, and **Mary Black**. From 1989, he toured with partner Muriel Graves, who had originally sung backing vocals on some of his Transatlantic recordings from the 60s. Years of serious drinking and ill-health took their toll when he died at the beginning of 1996.

● ALBUMS: *Live At Rockfield* (Transatlantic 1966)★★, *Hamish Imlach* (Transatlantic 1966)★★★★, *Before And After* (Xtra 1967)★★★, *Two Sides Of Hamish Imlach* (Xtra 1968)★★★, *Ballads Of Booze* (Transatlantic 1969)★★★, *Hamish Imlach Sampler* (Transatlantic 1969)★★★, *Old Rarity* (Transatlantic 1971)★★★, *Fine Old English Tory Times* (Xtra 1972)★★★★, *Murdered Ballads* (Transatlantic 1973)★★★, *Scottish Sabbath* (Autogram 1974)★★★, *Hamish Imlach* (Autogram 1975)★★★, with Iain Mackintosh *Man's A Man* (Autogram 1975)★★, *Sportin' Life* (Kettle Records 1981)★★★, *Sonny's Dream* (Lismor 1981)★★★, with Mackintosh *Live In Hamburg* (Musikiste 1984)★★★, *Portrait* (Musikiste 1989)★★★, with Muriel Graves *Two's Company* (Vindaloo 1993)★★★, with Graves and Kate Kramer *More & Merrier* (Lochshore 1996)★★★.
● VIDEOS: *Keep Taking The Medicine* (Jamminpiece 1993).
● FURTHER READING: *Cod Liver Oil And The Orange Juice: Reminiscences Of A Fat Folk Singer*, Hamish Imlach and Ewan McVicar.

Immaculate Fools

UK pop band consisting of two sets of brothers from Kent, Kevin Weatherall (vocals), Paul Weatherall, Andy Ross and Peter Ross. They made their debut with 'Nothing Means Nothing' in September 1984, before hitting with 'Immaculate Fools' in January 1985. Afterwards they spent much time touring the continent where they enjoyed more popularity, especially in Spain. Further singles included 'Hearts Of Fortune' and 'Save It' in 1985. Their second album, *Dumb Poet*, was well received by critics (including a five-star review in *Sounds* magazine), though it did not recapture their earlier chart success. It spawned the singles 'Tragic Comedy' and 'Never Give Less Than Anything'. Barry Wickens (fiddle) joined in time for *Another Man's World*, but by then impetus had been lost, and the media proved less sympathetic to the group's summery, fey pop songs.

● ALBUMS: *Hearts Of Fortune* (A&M 1985)★★★★, *Dumb Poet* (A&M 1987)★★★, *Another Man's World* (A&M 1990)★★.
● VIDEOS: *Searching For Sparks* (Channel 5 1987).

Immature

Starting out as MCA Records' answer to the teenage R&B boy band boom, Immature have belied both these inauspicious beginnings and their own choice of moniker by prospering as a commercial act in the 90s. A trio comprising lead singer Marques 'Batman' Houston (b. *c.*1982, USA), Jerome 'Romeo' Jones (b. *c.*1982, USA) and Kelton 'LDB' Kessee (b. *c.*1981, USA), they became regulars on the pages of the American teen press from their inception in the late 80s. However, they enjoyed their biggest commercial success in 1994 with 'Never Lie', a number 5 hit on *Billboard*'s R&B chart. The attendant album, *We Got It*, peaked at number 14 in the equivalent album chart, and sold close to half a million copies. Their 1997 release, *The Journey*, was their most ambitious to date, and paired them with R&B songwriting/production veterans **Keith Sweat**, Rodney Jerkins and Marc Gordon of **Levert**. The up-tempo, party-orientated atmosphere was further embossed by the presence of rappers Bizzy Bones (**Bone Thugs N'Harmony**) and Daz (the **Dogg Pound**). In the same year the group also recorded a pilot for their own television show, entitled *Keepin' It Real*, said to be a 'funkier take on *The Wonder Years*'.

● ALBUMS: *We Got It* (MCA 1994)★★★, *The Journey* (MCA 1997)★★★.

Immediate Records

Rolling Stones manager **Andrew Loog Oldham** and publicist Tony Calder joined forces to found Immediate in 1965. The label enjoyed success when its first release, 'Hang On Sloopy' by the **McCoys**, reached number 5 in the UK charts. The single was licensed from USA outlet **Bang**, and other master purchases included recordings by the **Strangeloves** and **Turtles**. Early UK signings included the **Poets**, the **Mockingbirds** and comedian

Jimmy Tarbuck, who recorded an exclusive **Mick Jagger/Keith Richard** composition, '(We're) Wasting Time'. Gothic chanteuse **Nico** made her debut, 'I'm Not Saying', for Immediate. It featured stellar guitarist **Jimmy Page**, who enjoyed an association with the company during its early stages. Oldham's *laissez-faire* attitude helped to attract several acts seeking greater freedom of expression, notably the **Small Faces**. The quartet enjoyed chart success on the label with 'Here Comes The Nice', 'Itchycoo Park', 'Tin Soldier' and 'Lazy Sunday'. **Chris Farlowe** emerged from the R&B circuit under the tutelage of Mick Jagger, reaching the number 1 spot with 'Out Of Time'. **Amen Corner** reached the same position in 1969 with '(If Paradise Is) Half As Nice', but by this point Immediate was in considerable financial trouble. **Fleetwood Mac** remained on its books for a solitary single, the poignant 'Man Of The World', before departing for **Reprise**, and although enjoying success in the 'underground' market with the **Nice**, Immediate was unable to survive the crisis. In a last attempt to salvage the company, Oldham and Calder switched supergroup **Humble Pie** from the Instant subsidiary to the parent label, but it was too late. Immediate was wound up in 1970. It has nevertheless retained a fascination and its back-catalogue has been reactivated many times over the years. In 1994 the founding partners announced plans to relaunch the company with new signings but nothing transpired. It would appear to have been yet another publicity stunt, of which Calder and Oldham are past masters.

● COMPILATIONS: *The Best Of Immediate* (Renaissance/Castle 1997)★★★.

Impalas

With sweet-voiced lead singer Joe 'Speedo' Frazier (b. 5 September 1943, New York City, New York, USA), this New York doo-wop group had an overnight success with their first record, '(Sorry) I Ran All The Way Home'. From the Carnesie section of Brooklyn, the rest of the Impalas were Richard Wagner, Lenny Renda and Tony Calouchi. They were discovered by disc jockey **Alan Freed** and Artie Zwirn, who co-wrote the bright, brash novelty tune with Gino Giosasi (of the Gino and Gina vocal duo). With an arrangement by Ray Ellis, '(Sorry) I Ran All The Way Home' was released in 1959 on the **MGM** subsidiary label Cub, reaching number 2 in America and entering the UK Top 30. The follow-up, 'Oh What A Fool' was a smaller hit. The Impalas made later records for Hamilton and 20th Century Fox before splitting up. Frazier went on to sing with Love's Own in 1973.

● ALBUMS: *Sorry I Ran All The Way Home* (Cub 1959)★★★.

Impelliteri, Chris

Impelliteri is a new-age guitarist influenced by a combination of rock and classical music styles. Utilizing a high-speed fretboard technique, he is distinguished by his ability to fit as many notes as possible into the shortest time-span. Moving to Los Angeles in 1986, he first recorded a self-financed mini-album of up-tempo instrumentals. The following year, he formed Impelliteri, which also featured vocalist **Graham Bonnet** (ex-**MSG** and **Rainbow**), drummer Pat Torpey (ex-**Ted Nugent**), bassist Chuck Wright (ex-**Quiet Riot**) and keyboardist Phil Wolfe. Together they recorded the stunning hard rock album, *Stand In Line*. Although it provoked unjustified accusations of plagiarism from Rainbow devotees, the music was powerful, exciting and melodic. However, the band disintegrated shortly after the album's release; Chuck Wright joined **House Of Lords** and Pat Torpey teamed up with **Mr. Big**. Impelliteri himself joined forces with ex-**Dio** keyboard player Claude Schnell and vocalist Mark Weisz in 1990.

● ALBUMS: *Impelliteri* (Polytour 1986)★★★. As Impelliteri: *Stand In Line* (Music For Nations 1988)★★★★.

Imperial Bedroom - Elvis Costello

Elvis clearly had a lot to get off his chest on this album dealing with emotional turmoil. While much of its lyrical brilliance deals with his thoughts, a small percentage slipped through with which we mortals could empathize. Now, having shown us he can tackle humour, politics and romance like no other, *Imperial Bedroom* was his most substantial album, as the issues covered will always be relevant and important. Chris Difford pitched in with one composition, 'Boy With A Problem'; perhaps Elvis found it too painful to write so directly about himself? Every track is powerful, simply read the lyrics. A gigantic record.

● Tracks: *Beyond Belief; Tears Before Bedtime; Shabby Doll; The Long Honeymoon; Man Out Of Time; Almost Blue; And In Every Home; The Loved Ones; Human Hands; Kid About It; Little Savage; Boy With A Problem; Pidgin English; You Little Fool; Town Crier.*

● First released 1982

● UK peak chart position: 6

● USA peak chart position: 30

Imperial Records

Formed in Los Angeles, California, USA, by **Lew Chudd** in 1947, Imperial emerged as one of the most influential independent R&B labels of the 50s. Despite the company's devotion to the R&B market, for many years their only major hit was by the C&W artist **Slim Whitman**, with 'Indian Love Call' in 1952. Having secured the New Orleans R&B bandleader **Dave Bartholomew** as house producer, a former Bartholomew band member, **Fats Domino**, was signed to record for the label, and his first release, 'The Fat Man' became a US R&B chart hit. The subsequent and consistent success of Domino's career in the national US chart between 1955 and 1962 was, for some time, crucial to Imperial's ability to promote other R&B artists, such as **Roy Brown** ('Let The Four Winds Blow'), **Smiley Lewis** ('I Hear You Knockin''), **Chris Kenner** ('Sick And Tired') and **Ernie Freeman** ('Raunchy'). In 1957 Chudd found his new pop star in

Rick Nelson, who provided the label with a string of 16 hits up until 1962. An effort to cash in on **Phil Spector**'s **Teddy Bears** success with 'To Know Him Is To Love Him' (having been recorded on the Dore label) came to nought, except that the group did release their only (and very rare) album on the Imperial label. Other US hits during this period were supplied by **Garry Mills** (a 1960 Top 30 hit with 'Look For A Star - Part 1') and the rock 'n' roll drummer **Sandy Nelson**, with his instrumental hits 'Let There Be Drums' (1961) and 'Drums Are My Beat' (1962). Throughout this time the label was well served by the steady success of Slim Whitman, particularly in the UK, where the Imperial label was licensed to **London Records**.

In the early 60s Chudd acquired the New Orleans label Minit. He sold the company to **Liberty Records** in 1963, after which Imperial concentrated more on the mainstream pop market, releasing many British acts in the USA, including **Billy J. Kramer** (a Top 10 hit with 'Little Children'/'Bad To Me' in 1964), **Georgie Fame** (a Top 30 hit in 1965 with 'Yeh Yeh') and the **Hollies** (notably, two Top 10 hits in 1966 with 'Bus Stop' and 'Stop Stop Stop'). **Cher** had begun her solo career with Imperial, achieving five US Top 40 hits between 1965 and 1967, including 'Bang Bang (My Baby Shot Me Down)' (number 2) and 'You Better Sit Down Kids' (number 9), and former rock 'n' roll singer-turned-MOR act **Johnny Rivers** had an impressive string of 13 hit singles from 1964-67, including the number 1 'Poor Side Of Town' in 1966. A link with the R&B past was maintained with **Irma Thomas**'s Top 20 hit 'Wish Someone Would Care' (1964) and with **Mel Carter**'s three Top 40 hits during 1965-66, which included the Top 10 'Hold Me, Thrill Me, Kiss Me' (1965). Songwriter **Jackie DeShannon**'s occasional excursion into the recording studio rewarded Imperial with two Top 10 hits with the classic **Burt Bacharach** song 'What The World Needs Now Is Love' (1965) and 'Put A Little Love In Your Heart' (1969). **Classic IV** rounded off the label's list of Top 10 hits during 1968-69 with 'Spooky' (number 3), 'Stormy' (number 5) and 'Traces' (number 2). By the end of the 60s, the machinations of the corporate music industry had forced Liberty and Imperial to merge with the United Artists label who, in turn, were swallowed up by the giant **EMI** conglomerate by 1979. Chudd died on 15 June 1998.

● COMPILATIONS: *Imperial Rockabillies* (1977)★★★★, *Imperial Rockabillies Volume 2* (1979)★★★, *Imperial Rockabillies Volume 3* (1980)★★★, *Imperial Musicians 1951-1962: The Rhythm In Rhythm & Blues* (1987)★★★★.

Imperial Teen

Much of the attention initially surrounding San Francisco, California, USA rock band Imperial Teen focused on the fact that one of its members was concurrent **Faith No More** keyboard player Roddy Böttum. He put together the band in 1994 as a reaction to the death of two of his friends, his father's terminal cancer and his own heroin addiction. He took over guitar and vocal duties, while he enlisted friends Lynn Perko (drums, ex-Wrecks; Sister Double Happiness), Jone Stebbins (bass, also ex-Wrecks) and Will Schwarz (guitar, vocals). The group's debut album, *Seasick*, was produced by Steve McDonald of Red Kross and featured songs addressing the death of his friend Kurt Cobain ('Butch'), his father ('Luxury') and Courtney Love ('Copafeelia'). However, the emotional scar tissue was hidden deep within an upbeat blend of pop and rock riffs, many of the songs being characterized by the female backing vocals.

● ALBUMS: *Seasick* (Slash/London 1996)★★★.

Impressions

Formed in Chicago in 1957 and originally known as the Roosters, this group comprised **Jerry Butler** (b. 8 December 1939, Sunflower, Mississippi, USA), **Curtis Mayfield** (b. 3 June 1942, Chicago, Illinois, USA), Sam Gooden (b. 2 September 1939, Chattanooga, Tennessee, USA), and brothers Richard Brooks and Arthur Brooks (both born in Chattanooga, Tennessee, USA). Mayfield and Butler first met in the choir of the Travelling Soul Spiritualists Church, from where they formed the Modern Jubilaires and Northern Jubilee Singers. The two teenagers then drifted apart, and while Mayfield was involved in another group, the Alphatones, Butler joined Gooden and the Brooks brothers in the Roosters. Mayfield was subsequently installed as their guitarist. Dubbed the Impressions by their manager, the group's first single for Abner/Falcon, 'For Your Precious Love', was a gorgeous ballad and a substantial hit, reaching number 11 in the US pop chart in 1958. The label credit, which read 'Jerry Butler And The Impressions', caused internal friction and the two sides split after one more release. While Butler's solo career gradually prospered, that of his erstwhile colleagues floundered. He and Mayfield were later reconciled on Butler's 1960 single 'He Will Break Your Heart', the success of which (and of other Mayfield-penned songs) rekindled the Impressions' career. Signed to **ABC**-Paramount in 1961, they had a hit with the haunting 'Gypsy Woman'. Subsequent releases were less well received until 'It's All Right' (1963) soared to number 1 in the R&B chart and to number 4 in the pop chart. The group was now a trio of Mayfield, Gooden and Fred Cash, and their rhythmic harmonies were set against Johnny Pate's stylish arrangements. Magnificent records – including 'I'm So Proud', 'Keep On Pushing', 'You Must Believe Me' (all 1964) and 'People Get Ready' (1965) – showed how Mayfield was growing as an incisive composer, creating lyrical songs that were alternately poignant and dynamic. During this period the Impressions had what was to be their last US pop Top 10 hit, 'Amen', which was featured in the film *Lilies Of The Field*. Mayfield then set up two short-lived record companies, Windy C in 1966, and Mayfield in 1967. However, it was the singer's third venture, Curtom, that proved most durable. In the meantime, the Impressions had emerged from a period when

Motown had provided their prime influence. 'You Been Cheatin'' (1965) and 'You Always Hurt Me' (1967), however good in themselves, lacked the subtlety of their predecessors, but represented a transition in Mayfield's musical perceptions. Statements that had previously been implicit were granted a much more open forum. 'This Is My Country' (1968), 'Mighty Mighty Spade And Whitey' (1969) and 'Check Out Your Mind' (1970) were tougher, politically based performances, while his final album with the group, the quintessential *Young Mod's Forgotten Story*, set the framework for his solo work. Mayfield's replacement, Leroy Hutson, left in 1973. Reggie Torian and Ralph Johnson were subsequently added, and the new line-up topped the R&B chart in 1974 with 'Finally Got Myself Together (I'm A Changed Man)'. 'First Impressions' (1975) became their only British hit, but the following year Johnson left. Although Mayfield, Butler, Cash and Gooden have, on occasions, re-formed, the latter pair have also kept active their version of the Impressions.

● ALBUMS: *The Impressions* (ABC-Paramount 1963)★★★, *The Never Ending Impressions* (ABC-Paramount 1964)★★★, *Keep On Pushing* (ABC-Paramount 1964)★★★, *People Get Ready* (ABC-Paramount 1965)★★★, *One By One* (ABC-Paramount 1965)★★★, *Ridin' High* (ABC-Paramount 1966)★★★, *The Fabulous Impressions* (ABC 1967)★★★, *We're A Winner* (ABC 1968)★★, *This Is My Country* (ABC 1968)★★, *The Versatile Impressions* (1969)★★, *The Young Mod's Forgotten Story* (Curtom 1969)★★, *Check Out Your Mind* (Curtom 1970)★★, *Times Have Changed* (Curtom 1972)★★, *Preacher Man* (Curtom 1973)★★, *Finally Got Myself Together* (Curtom 1974)★★, *Three The Hard Way* (1974)★★, *First Impressions* (Curtom 1975)★★★, *It's About Time* (Cotillion 1976)★★, *Loving Power* (Curtom 1976)★★, *Come To My Party* (1979)★★, *Fan The Fire* (20th Century 1981)★★.

● COMPILATIONS: *The Impressions Greatest Hits* (ABC-Paramount 1965)★★★★, *The Best Of The Impressions* (ABC 1968)★★★★, *16 Greatest Hits* (ABC 1971)★★★★, *Curtis Mayfield/His Early Years With The Impressions* (ABC 1973)★★★, with Butler and Mayfield solo tracks *The Vintage Years - The Impressions Featuring Jerry Butler And Curtis Mayfield* (Sire 1977)★★★, *Your Precious Love* (Topline 1981)★★★★, *The Definitive Impressions* (Kent 1989)★★★★, *The Impressions Greatest Hits* (MCA 1989)★★★★, as Curtis Mayfield And The Impressions *The Anthology 1961 - 1977* (1992)★★★★, *All The Best* (Pickwick 1994)★★★★.

Impressions - John Coltrane

So this is the source of the Byrds' 'Eight Miles High'? (Yes, listen to 'India'.) Coltrane continued to influence and break barriers both within his own highly fickle cognoscenti and outside in the rock world during the mid-60s, as his contemporaries cited his massive influence. Four exquisite excursions with McCoy Tyner (piano), Jimmy Garrison and Reggie Workman (bass), Elvin Jones and Roy Haynes (drums) and Eric Dolphy playing some extraordinary bass clarinet on the afore-mentioned 'India'. The other *tour de force* is the similarly explorative 'Impressions'. Not easy, but absolutely worthwhile.

● Tracks: *India; Up Against The Wall; Impressions; After The Rain.*
● First released 1963
● UK peak chart position: did not chart
● USA peak chart position: did not chart

Imps

A trio of **Frank Soda** (vocals, guitar), Charles Towers (bass) and John Lechesseur (drums), Canadian rock band the Imps were always distinguished by Soda's esoteric songwriting and even more outlandish stage apparel. Live performances featuring exploding television sets and other garish visuals established the group's identity, though in truth their three albums lacked the musical ideas to substantiate the initial good impression they created on the Canadian rock scene (where Soda was credited with being the 'Canadian **Frank Zappa**'). Their final album, 1981's *Saturday Night Getaway*, is arguably the best representation of their frothy, **Cheap Trick**-inspired pop-rock style. Soda later went on to a solo career and collaborations with artists such as **Lee Aaron**.

● ALBUMS: *In The Tube* (Quality 1979)★★, *And The Imps* (Quality 1980)★★★, *Saturday Night Getaway* (Quality 1981)★★★★.

Impulse! Records

Founded in 1960 to record currently developing areas of jazz, the Impulse! label was a division of **ABC**-Paramount. Under the supervision first of Creed Taylor and later **Bob Thiele**, Impulse! rapidly became synonymous with the new wave. Amongst the artists recorded in the 60s were **Albert Ayler**, **John Coltrane**, **Pharoah Sanders** and **Archie Shepp**. The producers were, however, alert to the continuing interest in bop and recorded several major jazzmen including **Art Blakey**, **Freddie Hubbard** and **Max Roach**. Simultaneously, the company's catalogue was broadened and commercially strengthened by recordings of musicians playing in older traditions: **Benny Carter**, **Duke Ellington**, **Terry Gibbs**, **Paul Gonsalves** and **Coleman Hawkins**. Following Coltrane's death in 1967 Impulse! gradually adopted a more commercial approach. A major reissue programme in the 80s saw much of the company's back catalogue on the shelves again, sometimes under licence to other companies, at other times under the original label and using the original distinctive fold-out sleeve format.

In A Silent Way - Miles Davis

Miles Davis's hushed masterpiece *In A Silent Way* was pieced together in the studio from a series of long stretches of quiet and intense collective improvisation. Masterfully demonstrating to the jazz world that rock's electric instruments were not necessarily harsh and noisy creatures, he again proved his creative and conceptual genius, fashioning the sound of fusion with

the aid of Herbie Hancock, Chick Corea and Joe Zawinul on electric pianos and organ, John McLaughlin on electric guitar, Wayne Shorter on soprano saxophone, British bassist Dave Holland and drummer Tony Williams. This is a delicate and beautiful thing that has rarely been repeated.

● Tracks: *Shhh; Peaceful; In A Silent Way; It's About That Time.*
● First released 1969
● UK peak chart position: did not chart
● USA peak chart position: 134

In Concert Vol. 1 - Peter, Paul And Mary

Even though Bob Dylan and Joan Baez dominated the folk world and the album charts during 1964, there was still room for the gentle approach folkies. Peter Paul And Mary were able to appear regularly on peak television shows in the UK because they sounded harmless, and the bite in their lyrics was overshadowed by their overall pleasant sound. This album stayed in the charts for months on both sides of the Atlantic and contains two essential Dylan protest songs, 'Blowin' In The Wind' and The Times They Are A Changin'', in addition to the mass-market 'Puff The Magic Dragon'. Although important it now sounds dated.

● Tracks: *The Times They Are A Changin'; A 'Soalin'; 500 Miles; Blue; Three Ravens; One Kind Favour; Blowin' In The Wind; Car, Car; Puff; Jesus Met The Woman.*
● First released 1964
● UK peak chart position: 20
● USA peak chart position: 4

In Crowd

Formed in 1964, this London-based group was originally known as Four Plus One. They completed a single, 'Time Is On My Side', under this early name, before **Keith West** (vocals), Les Jones (lead guitar), John 'Junior' Wood (rhythm guitar), Simon 'Boots' Wood (bass) and Ken Lawrence (drums) adopted the In Crowd appellation in 1965. A sympathetic version of 'That's How Strong My Love Is' brought the quintet a minor hit, while its b-side, 'Things She Says', showed the group adopting a mod/pop art style. Les Jones was then replaced by ex-Syndicats' guitarist **Steve Howe**, but two subsequent singles failed to emulate the In Crowd's early success. Former **Pink Fairies'** drummer John 'Twink' Alder joined the group on Lawrence's departure. Simon Alcott dropped out in March 1967 which prompted an internal realignment. The quartet dropped their now anachronistic name and embraced the emergent underground scene as **Tomorrow**.

In Crowd (reggae)

The In Crowd was a popular showband in the late 70s led by Phil Callender (lead guitar, vocals, percussion), supported by Errol Walker (lead vocals), Clevie Browne (drums, vocals), Tony Lewis (bass guitar, vocals), Freddie Butler (keyboards) and Wigmore Francis (guitar), with a horn section featuring Egbert Evans

(tenor saxophone, alto saxophone, flute) and Barry Bailey (trombone). Browne had performed with his brothers as part of the Browne Bunch in the latter half of the 70s prior to joining the In Crowd. The band initially came to prominence with the chart-topping 'We Play Reggae', a laid-back tune that encapsulated the feeling of the summer of 1978. The success of the single prompted eager anticipation for the follow-up. The expectations were fulfilled with the sublime 'Back A Yard', which surpassed its predecessor and was regarded as an all-time classic of the genre, with its cheery celebration of Jamaican life. Encouraged by the achievements of the two singles, the band recorded their debut album, *His Majesty Is Coming*, which mingled various styles in contrast to the melodious single releases. The group performed in their ethereal style covering topics that demanded a heavier sound. 'Slave Ship', 'You Facety Whitey' and 'Beg You A Ten Cent' did not lend themselves to the sugar-coated harmonies of the group. The band enjoyed a further hit with the title track from their debut and signed to **Island Records**, who released *Man From New Guinea*, with less success. The album featured the three earlier single releases alongside six new tracks, notably 'Marcus Garvey's Back In Town' and the prophetic 'Time Is Running Out'. Despite the short history of the group, they provided reggae lovers with two classic hits, guaranteed to provoke much lighter-waving on the revival circuit. Following the group's demise, Callender pursued a solo career, notably with the celebratory 'Island Music', while Browne went on to become one half of the eminent duo **Steely And Clevie**.
● ALBUMS: *His Majesty Is Coming* (Cactus 1978)★★★, *Man From New Guinea* (Island 1979)★★★.

In Dahomey

A significant production in the history of the musical theatre on both sides of the Atlantic, *In Dahomey* is said to be the first full-length musical written and performed by black Americans to play a major Broadway theatre, and, perhaps rather less importantly, it introduced sophisticated New Yorkers to the current dance craze - a syncopated predecessor to ragtime - the cakewalk. In fact, one of the most popular moments in the show came when the audience was invited to judge a cakewalk competition by the level of its applause. *In Dahomey* opened on 18 February 1903 at the New York Theatre, with a book by Jesse A. Shipp that told of a gang of Boston con-men who plan to colonize Africa with the money they inveigle out of a geriatric millionaire. The popular ex-vaudeville team of Bert Williams and George. W. Walker supplied most of the comedy, and a lively score by Will Marion Cook (music) and Paul Lawrence Dubar (lyrics), included 'I'm A Jonah Now', 'I Want to Be A Real Lady', and 'On Emancipation Day'. *In Dahomey* only ran for 53 performances in New York, but, somewhat surprisingly, none of the expected racial tensions materialized, and the production was acclaimed for its verve and enthusiasm.

Those factors also took London by surprise. Audiences there were not used to that level of exuberance, but they liked it, and the show stayed at the Shaftesbury Theatre for 251 performances during 1903, with Williams and Walker in their original roles.

In Full Gear - Stetsasonic

Elder statesmen of rap who afforded De La Soul and the Jungle Brothers much of their 'Afrocentric' philosophical viewpoint. Rarely have two such talented individuals as Daddy-O and Prince Paul been housed in a single group, as they would prove in their subsequent solo/production careers. However, this set captures Stetsasonic at the height of their powers. It set other another huge precedent with 'Talkin' All That Jazz', which established the pattern for the jazz-rap boom, and captured the energy of their renowned stage act for posterity. Tracks such as the Floaters' cover 'Float On' and 'Miami Bass' remain enthralling in a musical environment in which shelf-life is notoriously short.
● Tracks: *This Is It, Y'all (Go Stetsa II); Sally; It's In My Song; The Odad; Rollin' Wit Rush; Miami Bass; In Full Gear; DBC Let The Music Play; Float On; Pen And Paper; Stet Troop '881.*
● First released 1988
● UK peak chart position: did not chart
● USA peak chart position: did not chart

In It For The Money - Supergrass

Eagerly awaited by both fans and critics, *In It For The Money* was an energetic and accomplished second album that inexplicably failed to make a great impact with the record-buying public. Like their debut, virtually every track was worthy of single release, and the singles themselves, notably the blistering punk of 'Richard III' and the classy brass arrangements of 'Going Out', were outstanding. Never afraid of slowing down the pace at the right moment, subdued ballads such as 'It's Not Me' were as impressive as the rockers. Humorous and imaginative throughout, revealing a remarkable grasp of melody and knack for hooklines, Supergrass promise much in the long haul of British pop music.
● Tracks: *In It For The Money; Richard III; Tonight; Late In The Day; G-Song; Sun Hits The Sky; Going Out; It's Not Me; Cheapskate; You Can See Me; Hollow Little Reign; Sometimes I Make You Sad.*
● First released 1997
● UK peak chart position: 1
● USA peak chart position: did not chart

In My Tribe - 10,000 Maniacs

Natalie Merchant is one of those writers with an uncanny ability to portray the minutiae of life with pinpoint accuracy and detached humour. The songs on *In My Tribe* cover the difficulty of getting up in the morning ('Like The Weather'), her sister's wedding ('My Sister Rose') and childhood holidays ('Verdi Cries'), as well as relationships, drinking, corporal punishment and soldiering. Merchant writes free-flowing prose songs and performs them impeccably, ably assisted by the other Maniacs and the production of Peter Asher. All slightly off-the-wall, but none the worse for that.

- Tracks: *What's The Matter Here?; Hey Jack Kerouac; Like The Weather; Cherry Tree; Painted Desert; Don't Talk; Peace Train; Gun Shy; My Sister Rose; A Campfire Song; City Of Angels; Verdi Cries.*
- First released 1987
- UK peak chart position: did not chart
- USA peak chart position: 37

In Pieces - Garth Brooks

The phenomenon that is **Garth Brooks** triumphed again on this 1993 album. This is irresistible popular country that reaches out beyond the C&W market. The press have tried to find something negative to say about Brooks, but other than the fact that he is a bit overweight and slightly religious they have no scam on him. He is as clean as his superb voice, which can tackle a country rocker such as 'The Night I Called The Old Man Out' as well as the tear-jerking ballad 'One Night A Day'.

- Tracks: *Standing Outside The Fire; The Night I Called The Old Man Out; American Honky-Tonk Bar Association; One Night A Day; Kickin' And Screamin'; Ain't Going Down (Til The Sun Comes Up); The Red Strokes; Callin' Baton Rouge; The Night Will Only Know; The Cowboy Song.*
- First released 1993
- UK peak chart position: 2
- USA peak chart position: 1

In Rock - Deep Purple

Formed by discontented pop musicians, Deep Purple embraced progressive rock through judicious cover versions that drew acclaim at the expense of original material. Sensing a stylistic blind alley, Jon Lord (keyboards) and **Ritchie Blackmore** (guitar) brought new vocalist **Ian Gillan** into the line-up, a decision that irrevocably changed their fortunes. *In Rock* is one of the genre's definitive albums, combining hard-edged riffs with virtuoso technique, topped by Gillan's full-throated roar. Few singers could survive the instrumental power beneath him, but this he does with room to spare, reacting to and emphasizing his colleagues' musical prowess. Chock-full of material destined to become Deep Purple anthems, later releases were evaluated against this trail-blazing, heavy rock collection.

- Tracks: *Speed King; Blood Sucker; Child In Time; Flight Of The Rat; Into The Fire; Living Wreck; Hard Lovin' Man.*
- First released 1970
- UK peak chart position: 4
- USA peak chart position: 143

In Search Of The Lost Chord - Moody Blues

After the success of *Days Of Future Passed*, the Mark II Moodies knew that they had hit upon a winning formula. Once again, mellotrons swirled around each member's contributions, a truly democratic band at this stage. 'Voices In The Sky' became a hit single, but here it is one part of a trilogy that includes 'Visions Of Paradise' and the hypnotic 'The Best Way To Travel'. Whatever 'beep' they created to simulate a spaceship travelling through the cosmos, it works. The throwaway 'Dr Livingstone I Presume' does not, but can be programmed out in the CD age. 'Ride My See-Saw' proved that they had not gone completely soft, and could still rock.

- Tracks: *Departure; Ride My See-Saw; Dr. Livingstone I Presume; House Of Four Doors; Legend Of A Mind; House Of Four Doors (Part Two); Voices In The Sky; The Best Way To Travel; Visions Of Paradise; The Actor; The Word; Om.*
- First released 1968
- UK peak chart position: 5
- USA peak chart position: 23

In Step - Stevie Ray Vaughan

The album opens with an unashamedly simple rock 'n' roll track, 'The House Is Rockin', well chosen, because it sets the tone for an album that you feel Mr Vaughan dusted off before breakfast, such is his fluidity. Most of the tracks maintain a lively R&B feel, although **Buddy Guy**'s 'Leave My Girl Alone' is a slow blues that Vaughan relishes and plays with sparing care. The final track is another of his brilliant solo instrumentals (as was his previous version of 'Little Wing'); this time 'Riviera Paradise' gets the nine-minute treatment. His guitar shimmers through a glorious, moody, romantic piece.

- Tracks: *The House Is Rockin'; Crossfire; Tightrope; Let Me Love You Baby; Leave My Girl Alone; Travis Walk; Wall Of Denial; Scratch-N-Sniff; Love Me Darlin'; Riviera Paradise.*
- First released 1989
- UK peak chart position: 63
- USA peak chart position: 33

In The City - The Jam

Although bracketed with punk, the **Jam** were, in many ways, its apotheosis. Their unashamed love of 60s Mod culture was fully exposed on this nerve-tingling collection that drew on style icons the Who and Tamla/**Motown**, yet articulated frustration for a different generation. Anger and alienation explode from Paul Weller's crisp, well-sculpted compositions, the group's tight playing contrasting with his barely checked emotion. Although unambiguous lyrically, it is on guitar that Weller really sets his ire free, in particular on 'Bricks And Mortar', which bursts into a pop-art frenzy. A highly charged debut album.

- Tracks: *Art School; I've Changed My Address; Slow Down; I Got By In Time; Away From The Numbers; Batman; In The City; Sounds From The Street; Non Stop Dancing; Time For Truth; Takin' My Love; Bricks And Mortar.*
- First released 1977
- UK peak chart position: 20
- USA peak chart position: did not chart

In The Court Of The Crimson King - King Crimson

One of the pioneering works of art-rock, and a musical and lyrical signpost for the pomposity of early 70s progressive rock music, *In The Court Of The Crimson King* is of lasting interest mainly thanks to the superb musicianship of **Greg Lake**, Ian McDonald and Michael Giles, and the wonderfully inventive guitarwork of the masterful **Robert Fripp.** Subtitled 'An Observation By King Crimson', the album flounders on Pete Sinfield's dreadful lyrics and the stilted dynamics of the multi-part arrangements. Anyone wishing to investigate the roots of **Yes** and **Emerson, Lake And Palmer**, however, should refer to this album.

- Tracks: *21st Century Schizoid Man; I Talk To The Wind; Epitaph; Moonchild; The Court Of The Crimson King.*
- First Released 1969
- UK peak chart position: 5
- USA peak chart position: 28

In The Dark - Grateful Dead

The great comeback album, or at least an album that no deadhead expected at this stage in their career. Garcia had been seriously ill for some time, and was not expected to recover. Suddenly, a new studio album was announced, as a seemingly fit Garcia started to tour and was reputedly appalled when they had a huge hit single with the autobiographical 'Touch Of Grey'. Other strong tracks are Weir's 'Hell In A Bucket' and the magnificent 'Black Muddy River' written by Garcia and Hunter. With such a strong bunch of songs it is amazing that the underwhelming 'Tons Of Steel', by the late Brent Mydland, was even considered.

- Tracks: *Touch Of Grey; Hell In A Bucket; When Push Comes To Shove; West L.A. Fadeaway; Tons Of Steel; Throwing Stones; Black Muddy River.*
- First released 1987
- UK peak chart position: 57
- USA peak chart position: 6

In The Dark - Toots And The Maytals

This album was released at a time when reggae was first making inroads on the 'rock' consciousness and was being viewed as 'serious' music by many who had previously scorned its 'monotony' and 'lack of variation'. 'Toots' Hibbert's voice had a power and strength achieved from over 10 years as lead singer in one of Jamaica's most popular vocal groups - the Maytals - along with 'Jerry' Mathias and 'Raleigh' Gordon, whose harmonies ensured that nothing was ever missing from this Jamaican wall of sound. **Toots And The Maytals** were poised for the big time. The clean, sharp rhythms from the Dynamic house band - the Dynamites - were the perfect setting for Toots' hoarse style and the team even managed to transform 'Take Me Home Country Roads' into a Jamaican *tour de force*. Sadly, the big break never came their way, although Toots demonstrated in some UK shows in the summer of 1994 that he never lost it and still had just what it takes.

- Tracks: *Got To Be There; In The Dark; Having A Party; Time Tough; I See You; Take A Look In The Mirror; Take Me Home Country Roads; Fever; Love Gonna Walk Out On Me; Revolution; 54-46 Was My Number; Sailing On.*
- First released 1974
- UK peak chart position: did not chart
- USA peak chart position: did not chart

In The Wee Small Hours - Frank Sinatra

As ever, Sinatra's collaboration with **Nelson Riddle** on this album is wholly successful, this time a magnificent statement in understated orchestration. Emotional and romantic Sinatra gently eases himself through another 16 classics of American popular song. Although he fails to swing he never ceases to move the listener, and images of comfy sofas, scotch on the rocks and radiograms spring to mind as we hear songs by Ellington, Rodgers and Hart, Van Heusen, Arlen and Harburg, and Porter. Mellow, rich and pure, and now universally acclaimed as one of the best albums Sinatra ever recorded.

- Tracks: *In the Wee Small Hours Of The Morning; Mood Indigo; Glad To Be Unhappy; I Get Along Without You Very Well; Deep In A Dream; I See Your Face Before Me; Can't We Be Friends?; When Your Lover Has Gone; What Is This Thing Called Love; Last Night When We Were Young; I'll Be Around; Ill Wind; It Never Entered My Mind; Dancing On The Ceiling; I'll Never Be The Same; This Love Of Mine.*
- First released 1955
- UK peak chart position: did not chart
- USA peak chart position: 2

In Tua Nua

This septet from Dublin, Eire combined traditional Irish instrumentation (pipes and whistles) with commercial instruments. Unlike the **Pogues** or the **Saw Doctors**, however, they used this musical platform to play in the style of a rock act. Led by vocalist Leslie Dowdall, other members included Brian O'Briaian, Martin Colncy, Vinnie Kilduf and Steve Wickham. 'Discovered' by Bono (**U2**) they were originally signed to **Island Records** but later moved to **Virgin Records**. Their singles included 'Comin' Thru', 'Take My Hand' (their Island debut in 1984), a version of **Jefferson Airplane**'s 'Somebody To Love' (1985), 'Seven Into The Sea' (1986), 'Heaven Can Wait' (1987) and 'The Long Acre' (1988). Only 'All I Wanted' (1989) gave them a hit, and a minor breakthrough at that. They gigged with **Bob Dylan** at the Irish Self Aid show, before Wickham left in 1986 to join the **Waterboys**. He was replaced on violin by Angela De Burca. *The Long Acre* was produced by Don Dixon of **R.E.M.** fame.

- ALBUMS: *Vaudeville* (Virgin 1987)★★★, *The Long Acre* (Virgin 1988)★★★.

In Utero - Nirvana

Following his final act of self-destruction, Cobain will probably assume Morrison-like status, which is a little out of balance since the band have only three proper albums under their belt compared with the Doors' output. Taken as a rock band, they were the phenomenon of the 90s, both important and successful. Their penchant for romanticizing death is being followed with Pied Piper regularity. Their ability to shock was far better than any of the new wave followers. It was only the troubled Cobain who could write songs such as 'Rape Me' (an anti-rape song!) and 'Heart-Shaped Box' with real conviction.

● Tracks: *Serve The Servants; Scentless Apprentice; Heart-Shaped Box; Rape Me; Frances Farmer Will Have Her Revenge On Seattle; Dumb; Very Ape; Milk It; Pennyroyal Tea; Radio Friendly Unit Shifter; Tourette's; All Apologies; Gallons Of Rubbing Alcohol Flow Through The Strip.*

● First released 1993
● UK peak chart position: 1
● USA peak chart position: 1

In-A-Gadda-Da-Vida - **Iron Butterfly**

For many years this late 60s heavyish extravaganza was the biggest-selling record in Atlantic's history. The reason was the title track, a meorable but ponderous 17-minute slice of self-indulgence. It is all here: drum solo (takka takka, ding ding, ba boom boom), guitar solo sounds like it's played with a tenon saw, and finally an overlong church organ solo, that needed the beef of a Hammond instead of a Vox Farfisa sound. The vocals are great, but in a strange sort of way so is the whole album. Often put down, but glorious stuff, especially the Rhino reissue with the extra tracks and the fluttering butterfly cover.

● Tracks: *Most Anything You Want; My Mirage; Termination; Are You Happy; In-A-Gadda-Da-Vida; Flowers And Beads; In-A-Gadda-Da-Vida (Live Version); In-A-Gadda-Da-Vida (Single Version).*

● First released 1968
● UK peak chart position: did not chart
● USA peak chart position: 4

In-Be-Tweens

The In-Be-Tweens were a group originating from Wolverhampton, Midlands, England, who eventually transmuted into the better-known **Slade**. The original line-up featured Dave Hill (guitar), Johnny Howells (vocals), Dave Jones (bass), Mickey Marston (guitar) and Don Powell (drums). They in turn had evolved out of an earlier Wolverhampton group known as the Vendors, who never released vinyl but did record a four-track demo in 1965. The In-Be-Tweens recorded two EPs for the French label Barclay in their original formation, but nothing was released in their home territory. In 1966 original members Hill and Powell were joined by former Steve Brett And The Mavericks frontman Noddy Holder (vocals) and Jim Lea (bass, piano, violin), and cut a single for **Columbia Records**. This was a cover of the **Young Rascals**' 'You Better Run', which was typical of the group's cover version-dominated set of the time. No further releases were forthcoming; the group subsequently changed its name

to Slade. However, 'You Better Run' was included on *The Perfumed Garden Vol II* compilation, while *Sixties Backbeat* (1985) unearthed two previously unissued tracks by the band that were recorded at the same session. As well as an energetic cover version of **Dave Dee, Dozy, Beaky, Mick And Tich**'s 'Hold Tight' hit, the other track was a co-composition between Noddy Holder and **Kim Fowley**, who produced the session, called 'Ugly Girl'.

Inbreds

Formed in Kingston, Ontario, Canada, in January 1992, the Inbreds are a duo of songwriter Mike O'Neill (bass, vocals) and Dave Ullrich (drums). Their unique sound utilizes fuzz pedals that extend the dynamic range of O'Neill's bass guitar, but the overriding impression of their sound remains one of distinctive sparsity. The duo decided to put the Inbreds on a professional footing after a jam session held in Ullrich's attic. They immediately recorded a tape, *Darn Foul Dog*, on their own four-track equipment, duplicated it and released it on their own PF Records. Selling 500 copies, it also served to launch PF as a label, which has since overseen 20 releases by neighbouring bands such as Los Seamonsters, the Hammertones, the Caspers and Yellowbelly. It is also host to the Inbreds' entire output. Their next release was the *Let's Get Together* EP, before renting an eight-track recorder for January 1993's *Egrog* EP. Their first full album, *Hilario*, which included selections from earlier releases alongside seven new songs, was released in June. It was followed by the group's first national tour, ending with an appearance at Toronto's Edgefest alongside the **Lemonheads**. A provisional date at New York's New Music Seminar in July was cancelled due to the lack of work visas. *Kombinator* was released in August 1994 and was followed by a European tour with **Buffalo Tom**. The newly established Tag Records, meanwhile, picked up *Kombinator* for international release in February 1996.

● ALBUMS: *Hilario* (PF 1993)★★★, *Kombinator* (PF 1994, Tag 1996)★★★.

Incantation

This UK instrumental group found success playing South American panpipe music and ethnic instruments such as whistles, armadillo shells, llama toenails, condor bones and nose flutes. Formed in 1982 and signed initially to **Beggars Banquet Records** subsidiary Coda Records, they are led by Mike Taylor (quena, zamponas, bombo, chajchas, vocals) and Tony Hinnigan (quena, zamponas, bombo, caja, guitar, tiple). The other members of the band include Forbes Henderson, Simon Rogers and Chris Swithinbank. Their distinctive sound earned them a surprise UK Top 20 hit in 1982 with 'Chacarpaya (Andes Pumpsa Daesi)' which was used in the popular BBC Television natural history programme, *Flight Of The Condor*. Afterwards, their commercial fortunes dwindled, though their albums continued to sell modestly to the folk/world community. Their innovative music can also be heard on the soundtracks of the films *The Mission* and *Patriot Games*.

● ALBUMS: *Cacharpaya (Panpipes Of The Andes)* (Coda 1982)★★★★, *Dance Of The Flames* (Coda 1983),★★★ *The Meeting* (Hiam 1987)★★★, *On Gentle Rocks* (1992)★★★, *The Mission* (Destiny 1993)★★★★, *Sergeant Early's Dream & Ghost Dance* (Cooking Vinyl 1994)★★★.

● COMPILATIONS: *Best Of Incantation - Music From The Andes* (Coda 1985)★★★★.

Incognito

Incognito were among the most prolific and popular of the 90s UK jazz funk generation, though their origins can be traced back to the previous decade's Brit Funk movement. The mainstay of the group is Jean Paul 'Bluey' Maunick, a veteran of Light Of The World. His original co-conspirator in Incognito was Paul 'Tubs' Williams, plus a loose collection of friends and associates including Ganiyu 'Gee' Bello, Ray Carless, Jef Dunn, Vin Gordon and Peter Hinds. Incognito made their debut when a demo single, 'Parisienne Girl', received such strong club and radio support that it was made an official release, peaking at number 73 in the UK charts in 1980. However, this early incarnation of the group was a brief one, and yielded just a single album for Ensign Records. Williams joined The Team, a funk group assembled by Bello, also working with Maunick on his Warriors side project. However, at the prompting of Gilles Peterson of **Talkin' Loud Records**, Incognito reconvened in the 90s with Maunick again at the helm. This time, a variety of guest singers were included in the package. 'Always There' (1991) featured the vocals of **Jocelyn Brown**, and was also remixed by **David Morales** (though Maunick was none too happy with the experiment). It reached number 6 in the UK charts. Maysa Leak, who had begun by guesting on their 1991 single 'Crazy For You', left the band amicably in June 1994. She was previously best known for her contribution to **Stock, Aitken And Waterman**'s 'Roadblock'. The highly rated *Positivity* sold 350,000 copies in the USA, a market where Maunick was also beginning to enjoy success as a producer (**Ray Simpson, Chaka Khan, George Benson**). For 1995's fifth album the new vocal recruits were Joy Malcolm (ex-**Young Disciples**) and Pamela Anderson (a relative of sisters **Carleen** and **Jhelisa Anderson**). This time the sound veered from jazz funk to include Philly soul-styled orchestral arrangements and more luxuriant vocal interplay.

● ALBUMS: *Jazz Funk* (Ensign 1981)★★, *Inside Life* (Talkin' Loud 1991)★★★, *Tribes Vibes And Scribes* (Talkin' Loud 1992)★★★, *Positivity* (Talkin' Loud 1993)★★★★, *100° And Rising* (Talkin' Loud 1995)★★★★, *Beneath The Surface* (Talkin' Loud 1996)★★★.

Incredible String Band

This UK folk group was formed in 1965 in Glasgow, Scotland, at 'Clive's Incredible Folk Club' by **Mike**

Heron (b. 12 December 1942, Glasgow, Scotland), **Robin Williamson** (b. 24 November 1943, Edinburgh, Scotland) and Clive Palmer (b. London, England). In 1966 the trio completed *The Incredible String Band*, a collection marked by an exceptional blend of traditional and original material, but they broke up upon its completion. Heron and Williamson regrouped the following year to record the exceptional *5000 Spirits Or The Layers Of The Onion*. On this the duo emerged as a unique and versatile talent, employing a variety of exotic instruments to enhance their global folk palate. Its several highlights included Mike's 'Painting Box' and two of Robin's most evocative compositions, 'Way Back In The 1960s' and 'First Girl I Loved'. The latter was later recorded by **Judy Collins**. A *de rigeur* psychedelic cover encapsulated the era and the pair were adopted by the emergent underground. Two further releases, *The Hangman's Beautiful Daughter* and *Wee Tam And The Big Huge*, consolidated their position and saw Williamson, in particular, contribute several lengthy, memorable compositions. *Changing Horses*, as its title implies, reflected a growing restlessness with the acoustic format and the promotion of two previously auxiliary members, Licorice McKechnie (vocals, keyboards, guitar, percussion) and Rose Simpson (vocals, bass, violin, percussion), indicated a move to a much fuller sound. The album polarized aficionados with many lamenting the loss of an erstwhile charm and idealism. *I Looked Up* continued the transformation to a rock-based perspective although *U*, the soundtrack to an ambitious ballet-cum-pantomime, reflected something of their earlier charm. *Liquid Acrobat As Regards The Air* in 1971, was stylistically diverse and elegiac in tone. Dancer-turned-musician Malcolm Le Maistre was introduced to the group's circle and, with the departure of both Rose and Licorice, a woodwinds/keyboard player, Gerald Dott, joined the String Band for *No Ruinous Feud*. By this point the group owed little to the style of the previous decade although Williamson's solo, *Myrrh*, invoked the atmosphere of *Wee Tam* rather than the apologetic rock of *No Ruinous Feud*. The two founding members were becoming estranged both musically and socially and in 1974 they announced the formal end of their partnership.

● ALBUMS: *The Incredible String Band* (Elektra 1966)★★★, *5000 Spirits Or The Layers Of The Onion* (Elektra 1967)★★★★, *The Hangman's Beautiful Daughter* (Elektra 1968)★★★★, *Wee Tam And The Big Huge* (Elektra 1968)★★★, *Changing Horses* (Elektra 1969), *I Looked Up* (Elektra 1970)★★, *U* (Elektra 1970)★★, *Be Glad For The Song Has No Ending* (Island 1971)★★, *Liquid Acrobat As Regards The Air* (Island 1971)★★, *Earthspan* (Island 1972)★★, *No Ruinous Feud* (Island 1973)★★, *Hard Rope And Silken Twine* (Island 1974)★★, *On Air* (1991)★★★, *In Concert* (Windsong 1992)★★★, *The Chelsea Sessions* (Pig's Whisker Music 1997).

● COMPILATIONS: *Relics Of The Incredible String Band* (1971)★★★, *Seasons They Change* (Island 1976)★★★.

● VIDEOS: *Be Glad For The Song Has No Ending* (1994).

Incredibles

The original members of this vocal group from Los Angeles, California, USA, were lead Cal Waymon (b. 1942, Houston, Texas, USA), Carl Gilbert (b. 1943, Toledo, Ohio, USA) and Jean Smith (b. 1945, Arkansas, USA), all graduates of Los Angeles' Jefferson High School. Waymon, the writer and producer of the group, had a background as a folk-singer, and had for a time lived in New York, where he played guitar and sang topical songs in Greenwich Village coffee-houses. On his return to Los Angeles in 1966, he formed the Incredibles, and within months had a moderate national R&B success with 'I'll Make It Easy (If You'll Come On Home)' (number 39 R&B). The group then added a fourth member, Alda Denise Erwin (b. St. Louis, Missouri, USA), and the following year achieved another moderate hit with a remake of the old standard 'Heart And Soul' (number 45 R&B). The Incredibles - featuring Waymon, Erwin, and new member Don Rae Simpson, from Montreal, Canada - were still recording and touring in 1969, when their only album was released, but their career was behind them. The Incredibles boasted a smooth, relaxed sound that had an enduring power.

● ALBUMS: *Heart & Soul* (Audio Arts 1969)★★★.

● COMPILATIONS: *Heart And Soul* (Collectables 1998)★★★.

Incubus Succubus

Incubus Succubus, from Cheltenham, Gloucestershire, England, are a rock band with strong English folk and gothic punk influences. Most of their lyrics revolve around either of two themes - vampirism and the pagan faith of Wicca. The vampiric strand accounts for much of their gothic feel. It is Wicca, however, that dominates their material, with its continuation of the Medieval witchcraft tradition of pre-Christian hunting gods and moon goddesses. Their Wiccan beliefs have attracted a strong following in the UK's pagan subculture, though this has yet to translate into mainstream success. The band (originally known as Children Of The Moon) has had a fluctuating line-up, but the core remains Tony McCormick (ex-**Screaming Dead**; guitars) and Candia (vocals).

● ALBUMS: *Beltaine* (Nightbreed 1992)★★★, *Belladonna And Aconite* (Nightbreed 1992)★★, *Wytches* (Pagan Media 1994)★★★.

Ind, Peter

b. 20 July 1928, Uxbridge, Middlesex, England. After studying piano and composition formally, Ind began playing bass at the age of 19 and was soon hired to play in a band working on transatlantic liners. In 1951 he settled in New York where over the next few years he played with many noted jazz artists, including **Lee Konitz**, **Warne Marsh** and **Buddy Rich**. He also continued his studies under **Lennie Tristano**. In the early 60s he relocated to California, then returned to the UK. By performing and recording unaccompanied, Ind has greatly extended acceptance of the bass as a solo instrument. He has also worked in bass duos with **Bernie Cash**. In addition to his playing, Ind operates his own record company, Wave, and until the mid-90s ran his own London club, The Bass Clef.

● ALBUMS: with Lennie Tristano *Descent Into The Maelstrom* (1951)★★★, with Lee Konitz *Timespan* (1954-76)★★★★, *Warne Marsh New York* (1960)★★★, *Looking Out* (Wave 1957-61)★★★, *Improvisation* (Wave 1968)★★★, with Sal Mosca *At The Den* 1959 recording (1969)★★★, *No Kidding* (1974)★★★, *Peter Ind Sextet* (Wave 1975)★★, with Bernie Cash *Contrabach* (1975)★★★★, with Konitz, Marsh *London Concert* (1976)★★★, *At The Den* (Wave 1979)★★★, with Martin Taylor *Triple Libra* (1981)★★★, with Taylor *Jazz Bass Baroque* (1987)★★★.

Independents

This Chicago-based group consisted of Charles 'Chuck' Jackson (22 March 1945, Greenville, South Carolina, USA), Maurice Jackson - no relation (b. 12 June 1944, Chicago, Illinois, USA), Eric Thomas (b. 1951, Chicago, Illinois, USA) and Helen Curry (b. Clarksdale, Mississippi, USA). Chuck Jackson (no relation to the 'Any Day Now' artist of the same name) was at one time an art director at *Playboy* magazine and also found time to write occasional sermons for his brother, the civil rights leader and politician Reverend Jesse Jackson. Fired with an ambition to put his words into song, Chuck joined **Jerry Butler**'s writers workshop and teamed up with Marvin Yancey. The duo's talents were recognized by Butler, who recorded two of their compositions for his 1971 album, *JB Sings Assorted Songs*. Encouraged by this, the duo recorded one of their own songs, 'Just As Long As You Need Me', and discovered that they had a moderate success on their hands, enough to prompt them to form a group as a vehicle for their talents. They recruited from the Chicago club scene Maurice Jackson and Helen Curry (who had previously worked together as a duo, and prior to which Maurice had recorded with the vocal group Mark 4), and finally, Eric Thomas. Yancey preferred to stay behind the scenes to write and produce, occasionally performing live and playing keyboards. Between 1972 and 1974 they had a run of eight R&B Top 40 entries, including 'Leaving You' (1973), a million-selling single that peaked at number 21 in the US pop chart. Despite this consistency, the quartet was unable to break into the Top 20 pop chart, a factor that precipitated their demise. Yancey and Chuck Jackson continued working together and subsequently guided the early career of singer **Natalie Cole**.

● ALBUMS: *The First Time We Met* (Wand 1973)★★★, *Helen, Eric, Chuck, Maurice* (Wand 1973)★★.

● COMPILATIONS: *Discs Of Gold* (1974)★★★, *The First Time We Met - The Greatest Hits* (Charly 1986)★★★.

Indigo Girls

This American duo comprises Amy Ray (b. 12 April 1964, Decatur, Georgia, USA; vocals, guitar) and Emily

Saliers (b. 22 July 1963, New Haven, Connecticut, USA; vocals, guitar) who had met aged 10 and 11 while at school in Decatur, Georgia, USA. Soon they started to perform together, initially as the B Band, then Saliers And Ray. Their first cassette, *Tuesday's Children*, mainly consisted of cover versions. They changed their name to Indigo Girls while at Emory University in Atlanta. Their early releases were on their own label, J. Ellis Records, named after an English teacher on whom they shared a crush. These commenced with a single, 'Crazy Game', in 1985, followed by an EP the following year, produced by Frank French of **Drivin' And Cryin'**. An album, *Strange Fire*, produced by John Keane, featured re-recorded versions of their strongest early songs, 'Crazy Game' and 'Land Of Canaan'. Ray And Saliers were then signed to Epic Records in 1988, and their first release for the label featured, among others, Michael Stipe of **R.E.M.** and the Irish group **Hothouse Flowers**. *Indigo Girls* was produced by Scott Litt, and included Saliers' composition 'Closer To Fine', later recorded by the **Wonderstuff**. The duo toured heavily throughout the USA to promote the album, in addition to playing support dates to **Neil Young** and R.E.M. *Indigo Girls* achieved gold status in September 1989, and the duo won a Grammy award as the Best Contemporary Folk Group of 1989. *Strange Fire* was reissued towards the end of that year, but with an additional track, 'Get Together', made famous by the **Youngbloods**. In addition to playing an AIDS research benefit in Atlanta, Georgia, in 1989, the duo were also asked by **Paul Simon** to perform at a fund-raising event in 1990 for the Children's Health Fund, a New York-based project founded by the singer. *Nomads, Indians, Saints* included the excellent Emily Saliers song 'Hammer And A Nail', which also featured **Mary-Chapin Carpenter** on backing vocals. Litt was once again recalled as producer, with R.E.M.'s Peter Buck also guesting, but the album lacked something of its predecessors' impact. As Ray would later admit: 'We stuck to a lot of patterns that were similar to the first album. We didn't grow hardly at all.' *Rites Of Passage* repaired much of the damage, with a full musical cast including guest vocals by **Jackson Browne**, the **Roches** and **David Crosby**, drums from Budgie (**Siouxsie And The Banshees**) and production by **Queensrÿche** veteran Peter Collins. Traditional songs such as 'The Water Is Wide' as well as a cover version of **Dire Straits**' 'Romeo And Juliet' made it the Indigo Girls' broadest and finest set to date. Touring and vacations preceded work on *Swamp Ophelia* at the end of 1993. The sessions saw the duo swap acoustic for electric guitars for the first time on 'Touch Me Fall', and while touring they took a break to appear in a new recording of **Andrew Lloyd Webber**'s musical, *Jesus Christ Superstar*, with Saliers as Mary Magdalene and Ray as Jesus Christ. *Shaming Of The Sun* broke no new ground, but the duo's songwriting was as dependable as ever.

● ALBUMS: as the B Band *Tuesday's Children* cassette only (Unicorn 1981)★★, *Blue Food* cassette only (J Ellis

1985)★★★, *Strange Fire* (Indigo 1987)★★, *Indigo Girls* (Epic 1989)★★★, *Nomads, Indians, Saints* (Epic 1990)★★★, *Back On The Bus Y'All* live mini-album (Epic 1991)★★, *Rites Of Passage* (Epic 1992)★★★, *Swamp Ophelia* (Epic 1994)★★★, *Shaming Of The Sun* (Epic 1997)★★★.

Solo: Amy Ray *Color Me Grey* cassette only (No Label 1985)★★.

● COMPILATIONS: *4.5 - The Best Of The Indigo Girls* (Epic 1995)★★★.

● VIDEOS: *Watershed* (Columbia Music Video 1995).

Industrial Music

Drawing on the legacy of the German art rock movement pioneered by **Can** and **Faust**, and the scrapping of the rule book engendered by punk rock, industrial music became a label of convenience in the late 70s to describe the emergence of a new breed of *avant garde*, anti-commercial artists. The most important of these was **Throbbing Gristle**, from Sheffield, England, who originally coined the term 'industrial' for use as their record label. Taking their name from a Yorkshire slang term for erection, Throbbing Gristle used distorted vocals, electronic noise and lyrics about torture, psychological control and mass murderers to attack conventional society. Industrial Records also issued work by local peers **Cabaret Voltaire** and **Clock DVA**, in turn inspiring disaffected, would-be intelligentsia throughout the UK and USA to experiment with sound in their bedrooms and campus common rooms. From the existing punk ideology industrial music borrowed both its willingness to use shock tactics as a means of engagement, and also its cavalier disregard for technical ability, favouring minimalist modes of expression. Indeed, some authors hailed industrial music as the legitimate extension of punk — bridging 'the gap caused by the failure of punk rock's apocalyptic rhetoric.' It was first discussed in the mainstream by the journalists of *Sounds* magazine, who initially called the movement 'New Musick'. Among pieces on established left field stars such as **Brian Eno**, the **Residents**, **Kraftwerk** and **Devo**, it contained the first report on Throbbing Gristle's activities. Tellingly, it also included a piece on **William Burroughs**, the author whose 'cut up theory' approach would influence industrial musicians for generations to come. Like Burroughs, both Throbbing Gristle and Cabaret Voltaire were motivated by the 'information war', and the struggle to control access to the media, reflected in the production of independent magazines and record labels. All this was similar to punk, albeit executed in a more disciplined, cerebral manner. As Throbbing Gristle's Genesis P-Orridge later recalled in liner notes which accompanied 1984's *The Industrial Records Story* compilation: 'Industrial Records began as an investigation to what extent you could mutate and collage sound, present complex non-entertainment noises to a popular culture situation and convince and convert. We wanted to re-invest Rock musick with content, motivation and risk.' Industrial music was set apart by its reliance on such 'anti-music', a veiled celebration of unconventional sounds and sources, in itself an implicit damnation of punk as having become merely the new rock 'n' roll. Throbbing Gristle dissolved in the early 80s (factions thereof forming **Psychic TV**, **Coil** and other groups) leaving Cabaret Voltaire as the elder statesmen of a burgeoning movement, though one rarely covered in the mainstream press. Monte Cazazza offered the most extreme example of the genre, a victim of child abuse who used these experiences as a platform for performance art and music which rigorously pushed at society's taboos. Non (later to record under his real name, Boyd Rice) combined fierce noise with pop art samples. **SPK** and, later, **Test Department**, experimented with tribal percussion played on relics of modern industry. **Einsturzende Neubaten** combined a cohesive rationale while also provoking debate (most famously in England by drilling a hole through a stage on one London performance). The most musical member of this generation was undoubtedly America's **Jim Thirlwell** (aka **Foetus**), a talented songwriter who first bridged the gap between extreme ideas and accessible music. The least palatable of the crop were Come/Whitehouse, whose dalliance with fascist imagery moved far beyond that initially used by impressionable punk rockers. In America the hardcore punk movement utilised industrial music's minimalism aggression as a starting point — the **Swans**' overbearing volume in live performance being one indicator of the shared heritage. **Wax Trax Records** documented the emergence of a new wave of bands, the most important of which was Al Jourgenson's **Ministry**, alongside **Nine Inch Nails** the figureheads of industrial music in the 90s. However, while those two groups have both enjoyed commercial approbation, informing several developments in hard rock such as doom and death metal, in reality true industrial music remains, by its own definitions and precedents, avowedly counter culture. Yet it continues to prosper, documented in magazines such as *Music For The Empty Quarter*, where thousands of small scale releases illuminate a musical genre which offers a unique space for the expression of new ideas.

● FURTHER READING: *Industrial Culture Handbook*, various authors (Re/Search).

Infascelli, Silvia

b. Italy. A gifted singer with an attractively tuneful voice, she studied vocal technique with **Maggie Nicols** and also studied and occasionally still plays the oboe. Her repertoire is built upon many of her own compositions, for which she also writes lyrics. Her name remains somewhat unknown outside her homeland but Infascelli has all the hallmarks of an international singer.

● ALBUMS: *Blue Tracks* (Lion 1994)★★★.

Infectious Grooves

This heavy Los Angeles, USA funk-rock band was founded by the **Suicidal Tendencies** duo of vocalist Mike Muir and hugely talented bassist Robert Trujillo, with guitarists Adam Siegel (from Excel) and Dean Pleasants and ex-**Jane's Addiction** drummer Stephen Perkins. The band was deemed more than a side project for Muir and Trujillo, given equal status with Suicidal Tendencies, and the two bands often toured together, necessitating two exhausting sets per night for the pair. The debut established an entirely different sound from the parent band, with a heavy, **Red Hot Chilli Peppers**-style funk attack, with Muir, for once, producing lighter lyrical fare. Stand-out track 'Therapy' featured guest backing vocals from **Ozzy Osbourne**, who punctuated Muir's vocals with gleeful, manic roars of the title over furious riffing and a potent Trujillo-Perkins rhythm. Perkins left for **Porno For Pyros** the following year, and Josh Freese stepped in on *Sarsippius' Ark*, an odd collection of previously unreleased songs, live takes, cover versions and new numbers, with spoken interjections from a 'Sarsippius' character. *Groove Family Cyco* was a more conventional set of new material in the same hard funk vein, with Muir taking a satirical lyrical swipe at **Rage Against The Machine** on 'Do What I Tell Ya!', while adopting his more customary serious lyrical slant. With the break-up of Suicidal in early 1995, it seems likely that more time may be devoted to Infectious Grooves, although the industrious Muir has also formed a punk band, My Head, with Siegel.

● ALBUMS: *The Plague That Makes Your Booty Move...It's The Infectious Grooves* (Epic 1991)★★★, *Sarsippius' Ark* (Epic 1993)★★, *Groove Family Cyco* (Epic 1994)★★★.

Infinite Wheel

North London-based ambient techno duo who consist of former **Pigbag** percussionist/guitarist James Johnstone and Mark Smith. Their first recording, 'Segun International', was unveiled on cult New York label **Nu Groove** in 1991 after the duo simply sent them a tape in the post. They followed it with the *Dharma Sunburst* EP in 1992 for Brainiak. They described the latter thus: 'We wanted to use sounds that had some sort of depth to them, rather than pure bleeps. So it's a mixture of deep and shallow'. They made an appearance on **Positiva**'s Ambient Collection ('Digi Out'), as well as releasing 'Gravity Attack' on **R&S**. Their other releases have graced imprints like **Tomato**, marking an effective sweep of the very best in international record labels.

● ALBUMS: *Blow* (Brainiak 1996)★★★.

Infinity Project, The

Raja Ram (Ron Rothfield), who had trained as a jazz flautist in the 50s and played in the band **Quintessence** in the 60s, began making music with Graham Wood as The Infinity Project in 1989. Over the next few years they experimented with a kind of abstract techno gradually forming a sound that became known as the psychedelic or 'Goa' trance, often in collaboration with Simon Posford (Hallucinogen), Nick Barber (**Doof**) and Martin Freeland (Man With No Name). After producing material on DATs and white labels, in 1992 they started to release their music via the labels Fabulous ('Freedom In The Flesh'), Spiritzone ('Telepathy/Binary Neuronaut') and **Dragonfly** ('Bizarro', 'Time And Space', 'Super Booster' and 'Feeling Very Wierd'). In 1994 with Ian St. Paul they formed **TIP Records** and launched the label with 'Stimuli/Uforica'. At the same time they worked on projects with Posford and others, including the *Mystery Of The Yeti* album (TIP 1996) and various releases as Total Eclipse. After an ambient album *Mystical Experiences* (1995) for **Blue Room**, they released 'Alien Airport/Hyperspaced' on TIP followed by the album *Feeling Wierd* which was mostly made up of their previous releases. In the spirit of the 'Goa' scene *Feeling Wierd* was steeped in psychedelic hippie/sci-fi imagery. While tracks such as 'Telepathy', 'Stimuli' and the Doof remix of 'Hyperspaced' successfully blend the rigid four-on-the-floor rhythms, modal riffs, mysterious dialogue and abstract electronic phasing and filter sweeps that characterize the early psy-trance sound, 'Noises From The Darkness' and the early track 'Freedom From The Flesh' (written 1992) sound rather limp in comparison. In 1997 the group released the single 'Overwind/Incandescence' and contributed the excellent, but rather dark 'Mindboggler' to the TIP compilation *3D* Wood also began recording as Excess Head for TIP's subsidiary 10 Kilo while Ram continued to work with Posford. By 1998 The Infinity Project had split up to concentrate on individual projects.

● ALBUMS: *Mystical Experiences* (Blue Room 1995), *Feeling Wierd* (TIP 1995)★★★.

Infonet Records

The dance label subsidiary of **Creation Records**, managed by Chris Abbott who enjoys total creative freedom in his selection of artists. This has resulted in a refreshing lack of 'house style' (in both senses), with Infonet regaling its followers with a variety of shades of electronic music. Their premier acts include **Bandulu** and **Reload**, while among their most significant releases were the *Thunderground* EP (Thunderground), 'Better Nation' and 'Guidance' (Bandulu), 'Terminus' (**Syzygy**), 'Liquid Poetry' (Subterfuge), 'Phase 4' (Reload) and 'I'm A Winner, Not A Loser' (**Eddie 'Flashin'' Fowlkes**). New signings in 1994 included Sons Of The Subway, Indika and Kohtao.

● COMPILATIONS: various artists *Beyond The Machines* (Infonet 1993).

Ingénue - k.d. lang

Emerging from her ambivalent affair with country music, lang assembled a solid collection of material for this, her most commercially successful album. The opening lines: 'Save me/Save me from you/But pave me/The way to you', introduce a recurring theme - the agonizing conflict between the pain and the ecstasy of love. This is serious stuff; anthems of introspection and cries for honesty illuminated with startling imagery.

There are lighter moments too, particularly in 'Miss Chatelaine', and the omnipresent Ben Mink ensures that the country influence is not totally abandoned. This will always be her best album, no matter how hard she tries.

● Tracks: *Save Me; The Mind Of Love; Miss Chatelaine; Wash Me Clean; So It Shall Be; Still Thrives This Love; Season Of Hollow Soul; Outside Myself; Tears Of Love Is Recall; Constant Craving.*

● First released 1992
● UK peak chart position: 3
● USA peak chart position: 18

Ingham, Keith

b. 5 February 1942, London, England. Ingham is a self-taught jazz pianist who turned professional in 1964. He played with artists including **Sandy Brown** and **Bruce Turner**. In 1974 he recorded in London with **Bob Wilber** and **Bud Freeman** and recorded two solo albums for **EMI**. In 1978 he moved to New York where he played with **Benny Goodman** and the **World's Greatest Jazz Band**. He became musical director and record producer for **Susannah McCorkle** as well as recording with **Maxine Sullivan**. He works with guitarist **Marty Grosz** in various bands including the Orphan Newsboys in which they perform some of the lesser-known music of the 30s and 40s.

● ALBUMS: with Bud Freeman *Superbud* (1977)★★, with Dick Sudhalter *Get Out And Get Under The Moon* (1989)★★★★, with Marty Grosz *Unsaturated Fats* (1990)★★★, with the Orphan Newsboys *Laughing At Life* (1990)★★★, *Out Of The Past* (Stomp Off 1992)★★★.

Ingle, Red

b. *c.*1907, Toledo, Ohio, USA, d. 7 September 1965. As a young man Ingle played saxophone in several dance-bands in and around his home-town. In 1932 he joined the popular band led by **Ted Weems** and by the end of the decade was an established studio musician. He became a founder member of **Spike Jones**'s famous novelty band and in 1947 decided to form a similar band of his own. He had a number of hit records, among them 'Tim-Tay-Shun', 'Cigareets And Whiskey And Wild, Wild Women', and also recorded with **Jo Stafford** in one of her many comedy guises.

Infascelli, Silvia

b. 16 February 1956, Akron, Ohio, USA. A singer, composer and multi-instrumentalist, Ingram moved to Los Angeles in the early 70s where he played keyboards for **Leon Haywood**, and formed his own group, Revelation Funk. He also served as demo singer for various publishing companies, an occupation that led to his meeting and working with **Quincy Jones**. Ingram's vocals were featured on 'Just Once' and 'One Hundred Ways' from *The Dude* (1981), one of Jones's last albums for **A&M Records**. Both tracks made the US Top 20. Signed to Jones's own Qwest label, Ingram had a US number 1 in 1982, duetting with **Patti Austin** on

'Baby, Come To Me', which became the theme for the popular television soap *General Hospital*. In the same year, he released *It's Your Night*, an album that eventually spawned the hit single 'Ya Mo B There' (1984), on which he was joined by singer-songwriter **Michael McDonald**, and made the US Top 20 again when he teamed with **Kenny Rogers** and **Kim Carnes** for 'What About Me?'. Ingram's subsequent albums, *Never Felt So Good*, produced by Keith Diamond, and *It's Real*, on which he worked with Michael Powell and Gene Griffin, failed to live up to the promise of his earlier work, although he continued to feature in the singles chart with 'Somewhere Out There', a duet with **Linda Ronstadt** from Steven Spielberg's animated movie *An American Tail*, and 'I Don't Have The Heart', which topped the US chart in 1990. Also in that year, Ingram was featured, along with Al B. Sure!, **El DeBarge** and **Barry White**, on 'The Secret Garden (Sweet Seduction Suite)', from Quincy Jones's album *Back On The Block*. Ingram has also served as a backing singer for several other big-name artists, such as **Luther Vandross** and the **Brothers Johnson**. His compositions include 'P.Y.T. (Pretty Young Thing)', which he wrote in collaboration with Quincy Jones for **Michael Jackson**'s 1982 smash hit album *Thriller*.

● ALBUMS: *It's Your Night* (Qwest 1983)★★, *Never Felt So Good* (Qwest 1986)★★, *It's Real* (Qwest 1989)★★, *Always You* (Qwest 1993)★★.

● COMPILATIONS: *The Power Of Great Music* (Qwest 1991)★★★.

Ingram, Luther

b. Luther Thomas Ingram, 30 November 1944, Jackson, Tennessee, USA. This singer-songwriter's professional career began in New York with work for producers **Jerry Leiber** and **Mike Stoller**. Several unsuccessful singles followed, including 'I Spy For The FBI', which failed in the wake of Jamo Thomas's 1966 hit version. Ingram then moved to Koko Records, a tiny independent label later marketed by **Stax**. Ingram's career flourished in the wake of this arrangement. With Mack Rice, he helped to compose 'Respect Yourself' for the **Staple Singers**, while several of his own releases were R&B hits. The singer's finest moment came with his 1972 recording of the classic **Homer Banks**, Raymond Jackson and Carl Hampton song, '(If Loving You Is Wrong) I Don't Want To Be Right'. This tale of infidelity was later recorded by **Rod Stewart**, **Millie Jackson** and **Barbara Mandrell**, but neither matched the heartbreaking intimacy Ingram brought to his superb original version. It went on to sell over a million copies and reached number 3 in the US pop charts. The haunting 'I'll Be Your Shelter (In Time Of Storm)' then followed as the artist proceeded to fashion a substantial body of work. His undoubted potential was undermined by Koko's financial problems, but after eight years in the commercial wilderness, Ingram returned to the R&B chart in 1986 with 'Baby Don't Go Too Far'.

● ALBUMS: *I've Been Here All The Time* (Koko 1972)★★, *(If Loving You Is Wrong) I Don't Want To Be Right* (Koko 1972)★★★, *Let's Steal Away To The Hideaway* (Koko 1976)★★★, *Do You Love Somebody* (Koko 1977)★★, *It's Your Night* (QWest 1983)★★, *Luther Ingram* (Profile 1986)★★.

● COMPILATIONS: *Greatest Hits* (The Right Stuff 1996)★★★.

Ink Spots

The original line-up consisted of Jerry Franklin Daniels (b. 1916, d. 7 November 1995, Indianapolis, Indiana, USA; lead tenor, guitar), Orville 'Hoppy' Jones (b. 17 February 1905, Chicago, Illinois, USA, d. 18 October 1944; bass), Charlie Fuqua (d. 1979; baritone, guitar) and Ivory 'Deek' Watson (d. 1967; second tenor). Most sources state that this enormously popular black vocal quartet was formed in the early 30s when they were working as porters at the Paramount Theatre in New York. Early in their career the Ink Spots played 'hot' numbers, and travelled to England in the mid-30s where they performed with the **Jack Hylton** Band. When they returned to the USA, Daniels became ill and was replaced by Bill Kenny (b. 1915, d. 23 March 1978). The new combination changed their style, slowed down the tempos, and had a big hit in 1939 with 'If I Didn't Care', which featured Kenny's impressive falsetto and a deep-voiced spoken chorus by bass singer Jones. This record set the pattern for their future success, mixed with only a few slightly more up-tempo items, such as 'Java Jive', 'Your Feet's Too Big', and two of several collaborations with **Ella Fitzgerald**, 'Cow-Cow-Boogie' and 'Into Each Life Some Rain Must Fall'. The latter sold more than a million copies. Throughout the 40s their US hits included 'Address Unknown' (number 1), 'My Prayer', 'Bless You', 'When The Swallows Come Back To Capistrano', 'Whispering Grass', 'We Three' (number 1), 'Do I Worry?', 'I Don't Want To Set The World On Fire', 'Don't Get Around Much Any More', 'I'll Get By', 'Someday I'll Meet You Again', 'I'm Making Believe' (number 1) and 'I'm Beginning To See The Light' (both with Ella Fitzgerald), 'The Gypsy' (number 1 and a million-seller), 'Prisoner Of Love', 'To Each His Own' (number 1 and another million-seller), 'It's A Sin To Tell A Lie', 'You Were Only Fooling (While I Was Falling In Love)' and 'You're Breaking My Heart' (1949). The group were also popular on radio, in theatres, and made guest appearances in movies such as *The Great American Broadcast* and *Pardon My Sarong*. Orville Jones died in 1944 and was replaced by Bill Kenny's twin brother Herb (b. Herbert Cornelius Kenny, 1915, d. 11 July 1992, Columbia, Maryland, USA). A year later, founder-member Watson recruited Jimmie Nabbie (b. 1920, Tampa, Florida, USA, d. 15 September 1992, Atlanta, Georgia, USA) as lead tenor, and then Watson himself was replaced by Billy Bowen. Subsequent personnel changes were many and varied. There was some confusion in 1952 when two different groups began using the Ink Spots' name, Charlie Fuqua and Bill Kenny each owning 50 per cent of the title. Fuqua's Inkspots consisted of himself, Watson, Harold Jackson, and high tenor Jimmy Holmes. Other members included Isaac Royal, Leon Antoine and Joseph Boatner (d. 8 May 1989, Laconia, New Hampshire, USA). In the early 50s the Ink Spots had further chart success with 'Echoes', 'Sometime' and 'If', and Bill Kenny also had US hits in his own name, including 'It Is No Secret' (with the Song Spinners) and '(That's Just My Way Of) Forgetting You'. It is said that, over the years, many other groups worked under the famous name, including one led by Al Rivers (d. 17 February 1993, aged 65) who sang with the Ink Spots in the late 40s and 50s, and another fronted by Stanley Morgan (d. 21 November 1989, aged 67), an occasional guitar player with the quartet in the 30s. In 1988 the original group's first hit, 'If I Didn't Care', was awarded a Grammy, and a year later the Inkspots were inducted into the **Rock And Roll Hall Of Fame**. Jimmie Nabbie's Inkspots appeared extensively worldwide for many years through to the early 90s, until Nabbie's death in 1992 following double bypass heart surgery. Gregory Lee took over as front-man when the group co-starred with **Eartha Kitt** in the UK tour of *A Night At The Cotton Club*, during which, according to one critic, 'they reproduced the sedate four-part harmonies with skill and just enough spontaneity to satisfy their long-term fans'. In 1995, when the Inkspots were in cabaret at London's Café Royal, the line-up was Grant Kitchings (lead tenor), Sonny Hatchett (second lead tenor), Ellis Smith (baritone and guitar) and Harold Winley (bass). The latter is said to have worked with the group for more than 40 years.

● ALBUMS: *Americas Favorite Music* 10-inch album (Waldorf Music 1950)★★★, *The Ink Spots Volume 1* 10-inch album (Decca 1950)★★★★, *The Ink Spots Volume 2* 10-inch album (Decca 1950)★★★★, *Precious Memories* 10-inch album (Decca 1951)★★★, *Street Of Dreams* 10-inch album (Decca 1954)★★★★, *The Ink Spots* (Decca 1955)★★★, *Time Out For Tears* (Decca 1956)★★★, *Torch Time* (Decca 1958)★★★, *Something Old, Something New* (King 1958)★★★, *Sincerely Yours* (1958)★★★, *Songs That Will Live Forever* (King 1959)★★★, *The Ink Spots Favorites* (Verve 1960)★★★, *Lost In A Dream* (1965)★★★, *Stanley Morgan's Ink Spots In London* (1977)★★★, *Just Like Old Times* (Open Sky 1982)★★★.

● COMPILATIONS: *Golden Favourites* (Decca 1962)★★★★, *The Best Of The Ink Spots* (Decca 1965)★★★★, *The Ink Spots Greatest, Volumes. 1 & 2* (Grand Award 1956)★★, *The Best Of The Ink Spots* (MCA 1980)★★★★, *Golden Greats: Ink Spots* (MCA 1986)★★★, *Swing High! Swing Low!* (Happy Days 1989)★★★. In addition, there are a great many compilations available under the title of *Greatest Hits* or *Best Of*.

Inky Blacknuss

A highly regarded new techno duo comprising Alex Knight, a DJ and proprietor of London's Fat Cat record store, fellow DJ Andrea Parker and engineer Ian Tregonim. The latter, who handles production, was for many years responsible for **Yello**'s engineering. Parker takes charge of mixing, while Knight looks after percussion. Together they made a strong impression on their debut 1993 release, 'Blacknuss', on the **Sabrettes** imprint, which was awarded the *New Musical Express'* hastily improvised 'Filthy, Dirty, Techno Thing Of The Week' award. Dark and foreboding, its menacing ambience was recreated by a follow-up release, 'Drumulator'. Utilizing backwards synthesizer sounds and 'natural noises', Parker described her interests as being 'anything that blows the speaker up'.

Inman, Autry

b. Robert Autry Inman, 6 January 1929, Florence, Alabama, USA, d. 6 September 1988. An early prodigy, Inman played guitar at the age of five and at 12, he formed his band, the Alabama Blue Boys. He played on various local radio stations and in the mid-40s, he began to appear on the WWVA *Wheeling Jamboree*. He appeared on the *Grand Ole Opry* in 1947, where he became friendly with **Cowboy Copas**. In 1949/50, he played bass for Copas's Oklahoma Cowboys, before spending the next two years playing with **George Morgan**. In 1953, recording for **Decca Records**, he enjoyed a number 4 country hit with 'That's All Right', but failed to achieve a follow-up hit with the label. He made further recordings for **RCA/Victor Records** (1958-60), **United Artists Records** (1960) and **Mercury Records** (1962), without finding chart success (in 1961, he formed his own Lakeside label and released a live album). In 1963, his Sims recording of 'The Volunteer' made the Top 25. He recorded two risqué live albums for Jubilee the following year and eventually returned to the charts in 1968, with 'The Ballad Of Two Brothers', a patriotic narrative delivered over strains of the 'Battle Hymn Of The Republic'. It reached number 14 in the country charts and also crossed over to become a Top 50 pop hit. He appeared in two films, *A Face In The Crowd* (1957) and *Music City USA* (1966), and released further albums, but achieved no further chart success.

● ALBUMS: *Autry Inman At The Frontier Club* (Lakeside 1961)★★★★, reissued on Sims 1964, *Autry Inman i* (Mountain Dew 1963)★★★, *Riscotheque-Saturday Night* (Jubilee 1964)★★, *Riscotheque Adult Comedy Volume 2 - New Year's Eve With Autry Inman* (Jubilee 1964)★★, *Ballad Of Two Brothers* (Epic 1968)★★, *Autry Inman ii* (Jubilee 1969)★★, *Autry Inman - Great Country & Western Singer* (Guest Star 70s)★★★ *Country Gospel* (Guest Star 70s)★★.

● COMPILATIONS: *12 Country Hits From Autry Inman* (Alshire 1969)★★★, *Country Love Songs* (CowgirlBoy 90s)★★★.

Inmates

The Inmates - Bill Hurley (vocals), Peter Gunn (b. Peter Staines; guitar), Tony Oliver (guitar), Ben Donnelly (bass) and Jim Russell (drums) - emerged in the late 70s as a UK R&B group in the style of **Dr. Feelgood**. Their adaptation of 'Dirty Water', a garage-band classic originally recorded by the **Standells**, led to the Inmates' debut album. In common with several similarly styled groups, the quintet was unable to transfer their live excitement onto record, and despite other promising collections, the band was restricted to a narrow, pub rock-influenced ghetto. Singer Bill Hurley recorded the solo *Double Agent* in 1985, but its gritty mixture of soul and R&B classics fared no better than those of the parent group. *Meet The Beatles, Live In Paris* is a set of **Beatles** songs performed in a hard R&B and Chicago blues vein.

● ALBUMS: *First Offence* (Polydor 1979)★★★, *Shot In The Dark* (Radar 1980)★★★, *Heatwave In Alaska* (1982)★★★, *True Live Stories* (1984)★★★, *Five* (Lolita 1984)★★★, *Meet The Beatles, Live In Paris* (1988)★★★, *Fast Forward* (Sonet 1989)★★★, *Inside Out* (New Rose 1991)★★★, *Wanted* (1993)★★★.

Inner Circle

Inner Circle first emerged in the early 70s, comprising brothers Ian and Roger Lewis (guitars) and three future members of **Third World**, Stephen 'Cat' Coore, Richard Daley and Michael 'Ibo' Cooper. As Third World reassembled, the Lewis brothers recruited drummer Calvin McKenzie, keyboard players Charles Farquharson and Bernard 'Touter' Harvey. Together they won the prestigious Best Band Contest on the *Johnny Golding Show*. Although they later enjoyed moderately successful album sales and a hit single, 'I See You', it was not until the brothers brought in singer **Jacob 'Killer' Miller** (b. c.1955, Jamaica, West Indies, d. 23 March, 1980) that they became a viable commercial proposition. Miller had been a child prodigy, and had created a series of classic roots records ('Tenement Yard', 'Forward Jah Jah Children') before joining Inner Circle. Miller and the Lewis brothers were all of fairly heavy build, and together, the trio made a formidable, imposing combination. Early albums showed the band fusing dancefloor rhythms and reggae with reasonable success. In 1976, however, they signed to **Capitol** Records, releasing two albums for the label, *Reggae Thing* and *Ready For The World*, rising rapidly up the reggae hierarchy in the process. At one point Miller was more popular in Jamaica than **Bob Marley**: at the now-legendary Peace Concert in 1978, the band appeared above him on the bill.

Everything Is Great, their first album for **Island Records** gave the band an overdue international hit with its title song, and its disco rhythms made it a huge seller in Europe. 'Stop Breaking My Heart' was also a hit single, and *New Age Music* consolidated their position. However, disaster struck in 1980 when Jacob Miller was killed in a car crash. The remainder of Inner Circle quit, with the Lewis brothers and Harvey eventually opening a studio in Miami. However, in 1987 the band recorded an album for RAS, *One Way*, with new singer Carlton Coffey. US dates were critically acclaimed, and the band, with the addition of Lance Hall (drums) and Lester Adderley (guitar), signed to WEA/Metronome. *Identified*, their first LP for the label, brought the band to wider recognition with 'Bad Boys', which was

employed as the theme to the US television series *Cops*. In 1993 pop success eventually returned with 'Sweat (A La La La La La Long)', a catchy, upbeat single from the *Bad To the Bone* album. Bright, unsentimental, and thoroughly professional, Inner Circle deserve their long-overdue success.

● ALBUMS: *Dread Reggae Hits* (Top Ranking 1973)★★★, *Heavy Reggae* (Top Ranking 1974)★★★, *Blame It On The Sun* (Trojan 1975)★★★, *Rock The Boat* (Trojan 1975)★★★, *Reggae Thing* (Capitol 1976)★★★, *Ready For The World* (Capitol 1977)★★★, *Everything Is Great* (Island 1978)★★★★, *New Age Music* (Island 1979)★★★, *One Way* (RAS 1987)★★★, *Identified* (Warners 1989)★★★★, *Bad To The Bone* (RAS 1993)★★★.

● COMPILATIONS: *Reggae Greats* (Island 1985)★★★.

Inner City

Dance team built around the prolific genius of **Kevin Saunderson** (b. Kevin Maurice Saunderson, 9 May 1964, Brooklyn, New York, USA; programming), and the vocals of Paris Grey (b. Shanna Jackson, 5 November 1965, Glencove, Illinois, USA). Kevin, who is also widely revered for his remix and recorded work under the title **Reese Project**, is brother to a member of **Brass Connection**, and his mother was a member of the **Marvelettes**. He went on to study telecommunications at university, firing an interest in technology that would quickly become obvious in his musical leanings. Saunderson is the creative powerhouse of the unit, a studio denizen who writes all the songs and plays all the instruments. Grey is responsible for writing her own melodies. Their first single together, 'Big Fun', was lying around unissued in Saunderson's home base of Detroit until a friend discovered it while looking for tracks for a compilation LP. The record-buying public homed in on the strength of the tune (arguably one of dance music's all-time top five anthems), and with its follow-up, 'Good Life', Inner City had discovered a commercial career, with their debut album going on to worldwide sales of six million. Further singles have included 'That Man (He's Mine)', while the album that housed it, *Fire*, even boasted a token effort at rap. Other notable singles included 'Back Together Again', a stylish 1993 cover of **Roberta Flack** and **Donnie Hathaway**'s standard. Saunderson runs his own label, **KMS**, through **Network**, whose Neil Rushton is his manager. This led to Network also picking up the Inner City name when **Virgin** allowed the group to run out of contract in the 90s.

● ALBUMS: *Paradise* (Ten 1989)★★★, *Paradise Remixed* (Ten 1990)★★★, *Fire* (Ten 1990)★★.

● VIDEOS: *Paradise Live* (1990).

Inner City Griots - Freestyle Fellowship

Although from South Central Los Angeles, Freestyle Fellowship are definitely not of the gangsta rap persuasion. Their superior old school rhyming abilities and dextrous wordplay (learned at the famed Good Life Center) dominate this set. Despite comparisons with

De La Soul and Dream Warriors (for their free-form word association), the Fellowship proved themselves unique by employing rhymes that consciously employed poetic devices, such as alliteration, to emphasize the effect. However, the dizzy speed of their delivery and appetite for innovation is the real key, notably on cuts such as 'Inner City Boundary', which carries as much weight as any territorial claim made by gangsta rap, but with a much greater sense of propriety and skill.

● Tracks: *Bully Of The Block; Everything's Everything; Shammy's; Six Tray; Danger; Inner City Boundaries; Corn Bread; Way Cool; Hot Potato; Mary; Park Bench People; Heavyweights; Respect Due; Pure Thought.*
● First released 1993
● UK peak chart position: did not chart
● USA peak chart position: did not chart

Inner City Unit

The weird and wonderful Inner City Unit were formed by Oxford-born English eccentric Nik Turner (saxophone, vocals) in 1979, along with Trev Thoms (guitar), Dead Fred Reeves (keyboards), Baz Magneto (bass) and Mick Stupp (drums). Turner's first non-**Hawkwind** album was with **Steve Hillage** in 1977, entitled *Sphynx (Xitintoday)* - a set far removed from the punk sound then prevalent, which became a major influence on Inner City Unit. A debut album, *Pass Out*, and two singles, 'Solitary Ashtray' and 'Paradise Beach', appeared on his own Riddle label. In 1981 he moved the band to Avatar for *The Maximum Effect*, which also featured **Captain Sensible** and comedian Max Wall. Magneto reverted to his real name of Barry Downes to join **Weapon** and was replaced by Reeves, who doubled up on bass and keyboards. The next album, *Punkadelic*, featured reworkings of earlier tracks, but soon afterwards, Turner rejoined Hawkwind. In 1984 Turner reformed Inner City Unit, with Steve Pond replacing Stupp. Their first album together, *New Anatomy*, produced two firsts: it was the first album on ex-Hawkwind bassist Dave Anderson's new record label, Demi-Monde, and it was also the first album to feature a computer programme on vinyl for the Spectrum system. Inner City Unit then recorded the *Blood And Bone* 12-inch EP and backed it with a video that included the surreal 'Little Black Egg' and a guest appearance from **Robert Calvert**. A final album, *The Presidents Tapes*, was received with mass indifference and the band folded. Thoms then formed the Atom Gods and Turner the Fantastic All Stars, before journeying to the USA in 1993 and recording with Pressurehead. He has since worked on new projects with members of **Psychic TV**.

● ALBUMS: *Pass Out* (Riddle 1980)★★★, *The Maximum Effect* (Avatar 1981)★★★, *Punkadelic* (Flicknife)★★, *New Anatomy* (Demi-Monde 1984)★★★, *The Presidents Tapes* (Flicknife 1985)★★.
● VIDEOS: *Blood And Bone* (1985).

Inner Sanctum

Formed in late 1979, Inner Sanctum surfaced at the time of the **N.W.O.B.H.M.** but also predated the rise of **Metallica**, **Anthrax** and thrash metal by combining traditional hard rock postures with the dark imagery of **Black Sabbath**. The group's early material, such as 'Streets And Alleys' and 'The Butcher', provided a discernible influence on prototype thrash metal bands **Hellhammer**, **Testament** and **Coroner**. Over the years the core membership of Inner Sanctum has remained two sets of brothers: Mick Pendergast (vocals), Rick Pendergast (guitar), Eric Barbasso (bass) and Adam Barbasso (guitar). The position of drummer has never been quite as secure, however. On the debut, Mike Portnoy, now of **Dream Theater**, was the drummer. Two further drummers have also recorded with the band, including Jed Hawkins, who together with fellow Inner Sanctum part-timer Dave Ray joined **Skyclad** in the mid-90s. *12 a.m.* comprised a selection of the 28 tracks the band had been perfecting since their formation, and was re-released as an 'undiscovered classic' by Rock The Nation Records in 1994.

● ALBUMS: *Revenge* (1986)★★★, *R.I.P. - Live* (1988)★★, *12 a.m.* (Rock The Nation 1994)★★★.

Innervisions - Stevie Wonder

Uplifting and rolling, continuing a sequence of outstanding albums, Stevie Wonder again stamped his seal of importance during the early 70s. More than twenty years later, 'Living For The City' does sound a bit crass, especially rhyming pollution with solution, but that is a small carp when placed against the magnificence of 'He's Misstra Know-It-All', the out-and-out cleverness of 'Too High' and the graceful 'Golden Lady'. Stevie has an amazing conception of what vision is, something we take for granted when listening to the lyrics of 'Golden Lady', for example. Quite uncanny.

● Tracks: *Too High; Visions; Living For The City; Golden Lady; Higher Ground; Jesus Children Of America; All In Love Is Fair; Don't You Worry 'Bout A Thing; He's Misstra Know-It-All.*
● First released 1973
● UK peak chart position: 8
● USA peak chart position: 4

Innes, Neil

Innes first attracted attention as one of the principal songwriters in the **Bonzo Dog Doo-Dah Band**. His affection for pop melody, evinced in the group's only hit, 'I'm The Urban Spaceman', was expanded with the World - Roger McKew (guitar), Roger Rowan (bass) and Ian Wallace (drums) - founded on the former act's collapse. Innes then embarked on a solo career with *How Sweet To Be An Idiot*, as well as fronting Grimms, an ambitious confluence of poetry, satire and rock. The artist's friendship with Eric Idle, formerly of comedy team Monty Python's Flying Circus, resulted in a short-lived though excellent BBC television series, *Rutland Weekend Television*. Its songs were later compiled on *Rutland Times*, while one of the sketches inspired the

Rutles, a full-length feature which parodied the rise of the **Beatles**. Innes skilfully encapsulated his subject's entire oeuvre on *Meet The Rutles* (1978), while the project was itself lampooned by maverick New York label, **Shimmy-Disc**, on *Rutles Highway Revisited*. Innes maintained his idiosyncratic career with *Taking Off* and *The Innes Book Of Records*, and he later contributed music to television commercials and children's television programmes, including *Raggy Dolls* and *Rosie And Jim*.

● ALBUMS: with World *Lucky Planet* (1970)★★★, *How Sweet To Be An Idiot* (United Artists 1973)★★★, *Rutland Times* (1976)★★★, *Taking Off* (1977)★★, *The Innes Book Of Records* (1979)★★★, *Neil Innes A Go Go* (1981)★★, *Off The Record* (MMC 1983)★★★.

● COMPILATIONS: *Re-Cycled Vinyl Blues* (EMI 1994)★★★.

Innocence

The Innocence was a studio-only creation of songwriters/producers **Anders And Poncia**. Peter Andreoli (b. 28 April 1941, New York, USA) and Vincent Poncia Jnr. (b. 29 April 1942) were former members of Rhode Island lounge group, the Videls prior to composing songs for several **Phil Spector** protégés, including the **Ronettes**, the **Crystals** and **Darlene Love**. In 1964 the pair founded the **Tradewinds**. This excellent harmony group initially recorded for **Red Bird**, but switched to **Kama Sutra** two year later. Label MD Artie Ripp encouraged Anders And Poncia to work with other songwriters, notably Don Ciccone of the **Critters**. One of his compositions, 'There's Got To Be A Word!', marked the debut of Innocence, a studio-only act featuring Pete and Vinnie. (Ripp cheekily included himself in attendant publicity photographs.) The single reached the US Top 40 in September 1966, inspiring four follow-up releases and an album. The Innocence ceased to exist in 1967 when Anders and Poncia began using their own names for recording purposes.

● ALBUMS: *The Innocence* (Kama Sutra 1967)★★.

Innocence (techno)

Comprising brother/sister combination Mark and Anna Jolley (guitar and vocals, respectively), plus Brian Harris (percussion), Mattie (synthesizer) and Phil Dane (production) - although Gee Morris also featured heavily on their debut album. Innocence scored a UK Top 20 hit in 1990 with 'Natural Thing', a good part of the notoriety surrounding the release caused by one of the mixes featuring a sample of **Pink Floyd**'s 'Shine On You Crazy Diamond'. Since then they have released 'Silent Voice', 'Let's Push It' and 'A Matter Of Fact' (all 1990), 'Remember The Day' (1991), 'I'll Be There', 'One Love In My Lifetime' and 'Build' (1992) all charting but none breaching the Top 20.

● ALBUMS: *Belief* (Cooltempo 1990)★★★.

Innocents

This smooth harmony vocal trio from Sun Valley, California, USA, consisted of Jim West (b. 7 January 1941), Al Candelaria (b. 7 March 1941) and Darron Stankey (b. 5 July 1942). Candelaria and Stankey originally performed as a duo before being joined by lead singer West. They first recorded as the Echoes on the west coast Andex label and after renaming themselves (after the car club they belonged to), they had their first chart success with the haunting and beautiful ballad 'Honest I Do', a **Gary Paxton** production that made the US Top 40 in 1960. Shortly afterwards, the group backed 14-year-old **Kathy Young** on a revival of the Revileers 'A Thousand Stars' which made the US Top 5. With Kathy they scored a further two US chart entries and their own revival of 'Gee Whiz' gave them their second and last Top 40 hit. They later recorded without chart success on **Reprise**, **Decca**, **Warner**, Canadian American, Transworld, Monogram and Starfire. West went on to greater success later as a member of hit group **Gary Lewis And The Playboys**.

● ALBUMS: *Innocently Yours* (1961)★★★.

Inoue, Tetsuo

b. Japan, but based in New York, USA, where he settled because of the greater opportunities for techno artists. Inoue has recorded for New York's Mik Mak and, more prolifically, Germany's Fax label. In 1993 he released two LPs for the latter, and has also collaborated with German producer **Atom Heart** on the acid-inspired 'Datacide' project.

● ALBUMS: *Shades Of Orion* (Fax 1993)★★★, *2351 Broadway* (Fax 1993)★★★, *Ambient Otaku* (Fax 1994)★★★.

Inoue, Yôsui

b. 30 August 1948, Fukuoka, Japan. After the failure of his **CBS** Sony debut single as Andre Kandre in 1970, Inoue, one of many male singer-songwriters under the musical and lyrical influence of contemporary American styles, relaunched himself in 1972 with 'Jinsei Ga Nido Areba' ('If I Had Two Lives'). This was followed by the Japanese hit single 'Yume No Naka E' ('Into A Dream') and a successful album, *Kôrino Sekai* in 1973. That same year also saw a hit in 'Kokoro Moyô ('A Mind Pattern'), the introspective lyricism of which, in both words and melody, had widespread appeal among an audience who were ready to hear something other than the traditionally socially-orientated songs. The image-conscious singer, who is always to be seen wearing sunglasses and who has consistently avoided appearing on television, has continued his run of success in later years with hit singles, 'Isso Serenade' ('Rather A Serenade') (1984) and 'Shônen Jidai' ('Boyhood') (1990).

● ALBUMS: *Danzetsu (Rapture)* (1972)★★★, *Yôsui II: Sentimental* (1972)★★★, *Inoue Yôsui Live* (1973)★★, *Kôrino Sekai (The World Of Ice)* (1973)★★★★, *Nishokuno Koma (Two-Coloured Top)* (1974)★★★, *Good Pages* (1975)★★★★, *Yôsui Seitan (The Birth Of Yôsui)* (1975)★★★, *Shôtaijônonai Show (A Show Without Invitations)* (1976)★★★, *Good Pages 2* (1976)★★★, *Tokyo Washington Club* (1976)★★★, *White* (1978)★★★★, *Your Sweet Yôsui* (1978)★★★, *Sneaker Dancer*

(1979)★★★, *Every Night* (1980)★★★, *Ayashii Yoruwo Matte (Waiting For An Uncanny Night)* (1981)★★, *Much* (1982)★★★★, *So* (1982)★★★, *Lion And Pelican* (1982)★★★, *Ballerina* (1983)★★★, *9.5 Carat* (1984)★★★, *Myôjô (The Morning Star)* (1985)★★★, *Heibon (Humdrum)* (1985)★★, *Clam Chowder* (1986)★★★, *Negative* (1987)★★★, *Handsome Boy* (1990)★★★.

● COMPILATIONS: *1975-1986* (1986)★★★★, *Single Collection* (1987)★★★★.

● FURTHER READING: *Otono Sotogawade (Outside The Sound)*, Yôsui Inoue. *Yôsuino Kairaku (The Pleasure Of Yôsui)*, Seiji Takeda.

Insane Clown Posse

Formed in Detroit, Michigan, USA. Insane Clown Posse's highly shocking rap/metal fusion and spectacular live performances had, by the time they were signed to a major label in 1997, earnt them both public notoriety and commercial success. Violent J. (b. Joseph Bruce) and Shaggy 2 Dope (b. Joey Ulster) originally performed as the Inner City Posse in the late 80s, releasing the hardcore gangsta rap *Dog Beats* in 1991. Following the underground success of this album, Bruce and Ulster changed their name to Insane Clown Posse and underwent a startling change of image, adopting **Kiss**-style clown make-up and rapping about the apocalypse. The duo released several albums on their own Psycopathic Records imprint (each claiming to contain a further revelation from the final judgement), and gained a sizeable underground following in the Midwest without the backing of any radio play. They also roused the public ire of several local politicians and moral and religious campaigners, who reacted with shock to the foul-mouthed lyrics, open fires, chainsaws and barely contained violence of the duo's live shows. Jive Records signed the duo and released *The Riddle Box* in 1995, but the album failed to sell. Disney's Hollywood Records signed the band a year later and poured nearly a million dollars into *The Great Milenko*, Insane Clown Posse's 1997 major label debut recorded with guest artists including Slash and **Alice Cooper**. The label recalled the album only six hours after it was released, however, with the duo's obscene lyrics placing Disney under further pressure from powerful Christian groups. **Island Records** bought out the Hollywood contract, and re-released the album later in the year with Insane Clown Posse still a permanent fixture in the media pages.

● ALBUMS: *Carnival Of Carnage* (Psychopathic 1992)★★★, *The Ringmaster* (Psychopathic 1994)★★, *The Riddle Box* (Battery 1995)★★, *The Great Milenko* (Hollywood 1997)★★★.

● COMPILATIONS: *Forgotten Freshness* (PSY 1995)★★.

Insect Trust

One of the most engaging groups to emerge from New York's folk and blues enclaves, the Insect Trust - Luke Faust (banjo, guitar), Bill Barth (guitars), Robert Palmer (woodwind, saxophones), Trevor Koehler (saxophone, upright bass, piano) and Nancy Jeffries (vocals) - were steeped in Greenwich Village heritage (members had played with the Solip Singers and Peter Stampfel of the **Holy Modal Rounders**). Their eponymous debut album included material from artists as diverse as **Gabor Szabo** and **Skip James**, while the quintet's own compositions offered glimpses of traditional American music, which echoed the experimentation found in early **Fairport Convention** material. A second Insect Trust album, *Hoboken Saturday Night*, was less purposeful; nevertheless, it offered its own share of excellent moments. The use of former **John Coltrane** drummer **Elvin Jones** provided an undeniable muscle, but overall the collection lacked the element of surprise which made the group's debut so spellbinding. The group broke up soon after its recording and Koehler's suicide. Palmer subsequently became a respected journalist but although Faust reappeared in the Holy Modal Rounders' circle, the rest of this excellent group failed to maintain a significant career in music.

● ALBUMS: *The Insect Trust* (Capitol 1969)★★★★, *Hoboken Saturday Night* (Atco 1970)★★★.

Inside U.S.A.

The last of the seven always entertaining revues with music and lyrics by **Arthur Schwartz** and **Howard Dietz** opened at the New Century Theatre in New York on 30 April 1948. The show, which was also produced by Schwartz, is said to have been 'suggested' by John Gunther's famous book, but that was not apparent in the sketches by Arnold Auerbach, Arnold B. Horwitt, and **Moss Hart**. The indomitable Beatrice Lillie skylarked around along with Jack Haley in a series of comical geographical situations in which they, as two Indians in Alberquerque, resolutely refuse the offer of the whole country ('We Won't Take It Back'), and become involved with members of a choral society who are intent on solving the problems of pollution in Pittsburgh. 'Haunted Heart' was the song that achieved some popularity outside the show in recordings by **Perry Como** and **Jo Stafford**, and another ballad, 'First Prize At The Fair', was also singled out for praise. However, the novelty show-stopper was a United States list song, 'Rhode Island Is Famous For You', which was performed in the show by Haley, and seemed fairly conventional early on: 'Old whiskey, comes from old Kentucky/Ain't the country lucky?/New Jersey gives us glue' . . . 'Grand Canyons, come from Colorada/Gold comes from Nevada/Divorces also do' . . . but then 'declined' into the amusingly excruciating: 'Pencils come from Pencilvania/Vests from Vest Virgina/And tents from Tentassee'. The composer himself gave the song a more than adequate reading nearly 30 years later on his *From The Pen Of Arthur Schwartz*. The show's other numbers were 'Blue Grass', 'My Gal Is Mine Once More', and 'At The Mardi Gras', and the chorus contained some famous names: Jack Cassidy, who went on to star in **Wish You Were Here** and **She Loves Me**, and become the father of pop star **David Cassidy** before marrying **Shirley Jones**; and Carl Reiner, who achieved fame in the 60s as the writer of television's *The Dick Van Dyke Show*. *Inside U.S.A.* enjoyed a run of 399 performances, and, shortly after it closed, Schwartz devised a television variety programme based on the idea, which used the same songs, and starred Peter Lind Hayes and Mary Healy.

Inspiral Carpets

During the late 80s UK music scene, the city of Manchester and its surrounds spawned a host of exciting new groups and the Inspiral Carpets were at the head of the pack alongside **Happy Mondays**, **James**, the **Stone Roses** and **808 State**. The group was formed in Oldham by schoolfriends Graham Lambert (guitar) and Stephen Holt (vocals). They were joined by drummer Craig Gill and performed in their home-town of Oldham with various other members until they were joined by organist Clint Boon and bassist David Swift. Boon met the group when they began rehearsing at his studio in Ashton-under-Lyne. His **Doors**-influenced playing later became the group's trademark. Their debut EP, *Planecrash*, was released by the independent label Playtime, and the group were consequently asked to record a **John Peel** session for BBC Radio 1. In 1988 there was an acrimonious split between the band and label and also between the group members. Holt and Swift were replaced by Tom Hingley and Martin Walsh, formerly with local bands Too Much Texas and the Next Step, respectively. The band formed their own label, Cow Records, and after a string of well-received singles they signed a worldwide contract with **Mute Records**. 'This Is How It Feels' was a hit and *Life* was critically acclaimed for its mixture of sparkling pop and occasional experimental flashes. Further singles had less impact and *The Beast Inside* received a mixed response, some critics claiming the band were becoming better known for their merchandise, like T-shirts and promotional milk bottles. The T-shirts bearing the immortal words 'Cool as Fuck!' inevitably aroused considerable controversy, particularly when a fan was arrested for causing offence by wearing such a garment. Afterwards the group journeyed onwards without ever arousing the same level of interest, though both *Revenge Of The Goldfish* and *Devil Hopping* had their moments. 'Bitch's Brew', from the former, stronger album, was a classy stab at **Rolling Stones**-styled sweeping pop revival, though elsewhere too many songs continued to be dominated by Boon's organ, which, once a powerful novelty, now tended to limit the band's songwriting range. The band were released from Mute Records in 1995 with their former company issuing an epitaph in the shape of *The Singles*.
- ALBUMS: *Life* (Mute 1990)★★★, *The Beast Inside* (Mute 1991)★★, *Revenge Of The Goldfish* (Mute 1992)★★★, *Devil Hopping* (Mute 1994)★★★.
- COMPILATIONS: *The Singles* (Mute 1995)★★★.

Instant Funk

Based in Philadelphia, USA, Instant Funk comprised James Carmichael (vocals), George Bell (guitar), Kim Miller (guitar), Scotty Miller (drums), Raymond Earl (bass), Dennis Richardson (keyboards), Charles Williams (percussion), Larry Davis (trumpet) and John Onderline (sax). They were ostensibly the musical vehicle for noted producer/writer **Bunny Sigler**, who used them for the instrumentation on his own albums and subsequently secured them a contract with T.S.O.P. Records. Their debut album, *Get Down With The Philly Jump*, received considerable attention, thanks to the success of the single, 'It Ain't Reggae (But It's Funky)'. Their biggest breakthrough was achieved through 'I Got My Mind Made Up', a number 20 US hit and gold disc for **Salsoul Records** in 1979. They recorded further albums for that label without coming close to repeating this success, and eventually surfaced in 1985, recording 'Tailspin' for the Pop Art label.
- ALBUMS: *Get Down With The Philly Jump* (T.S.O.P. 1976)★★★, *I Got My Mind Made Up* (Salsoul 1978)★★★, *Instant Funk* (Salsoul 1979)★★★, *Witch Doctor* (Salsoul 1979)★★, *The Funk Is On* (Salsoul 1980)★★, *Kinky* (Salsoul 1983)★★, *Instant Funk* (Salsoul 1983)★★.

Instigators

The Instigators were a north London-based reggae band formed in 1976, featuring the illustrious duo **Mafia And Fluxy**. Attributed to the original line-up were **Toyin** (b. Toyin Adekale, 21 December 1963, London, England; lead vocals), Leroy 'Mafia' Heywood (b. 1962, London, England; bass guitar), David 'Fluxy' Heywood (b. 1963, London, England; drums), Dingle Heywood (rhythm guitar), Conway Keeler (lead guitar), Tony Cooper (keyboards) and Oliver Robinson (percussion). The band recorded their debut, 'Let's Make Love', which was an instant hit but also marked the departure of Toyin, who embarked on a solo career. The group were employed to provide backing on the live circuit for a number of tours including the UK's **Pablo Gad**, as well as **Studio One**'s finest, **Johnny Osbourne**, **Delroy Wilson** and **Sugar Minott**. The band were also employed as session musicians, notably on the 1980 reggae chart-topper, 'Late Night Blues', for Roy Ranking and Raymond Naptali. In addition to their supportive role they continued to record their own material, having enrolled Courtney Bartlett to provide lead vocals. The group released 'Boom' for the Mighty Fatman, alongside 'Pretty Girl', 'Your Love', 'Five O' and 'Blessing From Above'. Leroy and David also performed as soloists, releasing 'Can't Get Enough Love' and 'Stranger In Love', respectively. While pursuing individual careers, the duo of Mafia And Fluxy concurrently performed with the Instigators, who were voted the best reggae band in 1989 and in the same year reached number 4 in the UK reggae chart with 'Aint Been Getting Along'. Due to Leroy and David's extensive commitments, the band dissolved, and the duo released further solo outings alongside production obligations, notably with the A Class Crew. By 1996 they recorded alongside **Peter Hunningale**, **Nerious Joseph** and **Glamma Kid**, performing in the revered supergroup Passion for the hit 'Share Your Love'. There are no Instigators albums, although Mafia And Fluxy have released a popular series of *Revival Hits*.

Intelligent Hoodlum

b. Percy Chapman, *c.*1968, Rikers Island, USA. The Hoodlum grew up on the same street as **Marley Marl**, whom he pestered every day to try and get a record out, after having picked up the rap bug from his cousin Kadiya. Finally Marl acquiesced, and Hoodlum had his first record released, 'Coke Is It'. It was later retitled 'Tragedy', after the Hoodlum's own sorry tale. He was only 14, but instead of further releases he pursued a life of crime to support his crack habit. Inevitably, he found himself in prison on a one- to three-year sentence. However, the prison term gave him the chance to cool off, and he spent his time reading avidly. Having got through black-consciousness standards by Malcolm X and Elijah Muhammed, he was paroled just as **Public Enemy** arrived on the scene. Chuck D's bleak messages struck a chord with Hoodlum, and although he returned to the drug trade to support himself, he also attended college to learn more about his new heroes, Marcus Garvey and Malcolm X. Eventually he met up with Marley Marl again, by now a major hip-hop talent, who invited him to perform some more raps. The eventual results were the improvised 'Party Pack' and 'Vitally Tragic'. The Intelligent Hoodlum moniker indicated a path for the future, renouncing his illegal activities but acknowledging the necessary part his criminal past had played in his development. The intelligent prefix inferred his desire to learn, and use his new-found wisdom for the benefit of himself and others. This attitude was clearly demonstrated on his debut album by the ferocious protest of 'Black And Proud' or 'Arrest The President'. Now a practising Muslim, and affiliated to the Nation of Islam, Hoodlum also set up his own organization, MAAPS - Movement Against the American Power Structure.

● ALBUMS: *Tragedy* (A&M 1990)★★★, *Saga Of A Hoodlum* (A&M 1993)★★★★.

Intelligent Hoodlum - Intelligent Hoodlum

The influence of Public Enemy is obvious, Percy Chapman (aka the Intelligent Hoodlum) having spent several months in jail listening to nothing else. However, his largely autobiographical, self-titled debut album is much more than a carbon copy. It saw him reunited with childhood friend Marley Marl who provided one of his most persuasive musical suites to bedeck the set. The ferocious protest of 'Black And Proud', or, more poignantly, 'Arrest The President', announced the Hoodlum as a major new talent.

● Tracks: *Intelligent Hoodlum; Back To Reality; Trag Invasion; No Justice, No Peace; Party Animal; Black And Proud; Game*

Type; Microphone; Keep Striving; Party Pack; Arrest The President; Your Tragedy.

● First released 1990
● UK peak chart position: did not chart
● USA peak chart position: did not chart

Internal Records

A connoisseurs' UK dance label formed in 1992 by Christian Tattersfield, the former Marketing Manager of **London Records**, with whom the label is financially linked. They struck immediately; their first signings were **Orbital**, whose second album, having moved over from sister label **ffrr**, went on to sell over a million copies. Zero B's *Reconnections* EP followed, before an album of **Yellow Magic Orchestra** remixes which featured the work of the **Orb**, **808 State**, **Shamen** and **Altern 8** among others. Vapourspace also recorded for the label, before the unexpected, runaway success of **Capella** on the Internal Dance subsidiary. On the same imprint JX's 'Son Of A Gun' also hit, though the Outthere Brothers' 'Fuk U In The Ass' was probably a little risqué even for underground dance punters. More recent signings include Cisco Ferreira and **Salt Tank**.

● ALBUMS: Orbital: *Untitled 2* (Internal 1993)★★★.

International Artists Records

Inaugurated in 1965 in Houston, Texas, USA, International Artists is one of the 60s most revered cult record labels. It was founded by Fred Carroll in partnership with two lawyers, Noble Ginther and Bill Dillard, and partly funded by a local oil company. Initial releases were inauspicious and many were simply master purchases from local, 'rival' outlets. In 1966 the board sent a package of their singles to Texan expatriate Lelan Rodgers, at that point working in California for **Reprise Records**. Rodgers, elder brother of singer **Kenny Rodgers**, was impressed with one release, 'You're Gonna Miss Me' by the **Thirteenth Floor Elevators**. He offered to promote it in return for a percentage, but within months had been persuaded to return to Houston and take up day-to-day running of International Artists itself. As such he oversaw the label's golden era. The Thirteenth Floor Elevators' brand of psychedelic R&B meshed with Texan-styled rock 'n' roll resulted in some of the finest records of the 60s. Inspired, Rodgers signed fellow mavericks the **Red Crayola**, **Golden Dawn** and **Lost And Found**, each of whom completed excellent albums for the label. However, Rodgers left the company in 1968 following disputes with the board. He moved to Nashville, Tennessee, USA, and set up Silver Fox Records in partnership with entrepreneur **Shelby Singleton**. International Artists nonetheless remained active, but once again their release schedule became erratic. They did enjoy a minor US hit in 1969 with **Bubble Puppy**'s 'Hot Smoke And Sasafrass' and recordings by Endle St. Cloud ensured their reputation for experimental albums remained intact. By 1970 the partners' interest had waned and the label was wound down. However, during the 70s Rodgers purchased the entire catalogue, and the rights to the name, to begin a reissue programme. Sadly, all master tapes have been mislaid and subsequent pressings have been dubbed from disc.

● COMPILATIONS: *The International Artists Singles Collection* (Decal 1989)★★★★.

International Foot Language

Comprising Noel McKoy (vocals) and Steve Spiro (keyboards), International Foot Language, based in London, England, came together in 1990 when the duo met and elected to join forces, though each was already heavily implicated in their own separate projects. McKoy is a veteran of his own band, McKoy, plus the **James Taylor Quartet**, co-writing most of their 1993 album *Supernatural Feeling* and singles such as 'Love The Life' and 'Brighter Day'. He has also worked with the **Pasadenas**, Snowboy and **Steve Williamson**. Spiro made his name in production and writing, working with artists including **East 17** and the **Pet Shop Boys**. His remixes include work for **MC Hammer**, the **Farm** and **Talk Talk**. He had previously been commissioned by BBC Television to provide music for its sports programmes, including the 1992 Olympics, Grand Prix coverage, *Ski Sunday* and *Match Of The Day*. This connection led to International Foot Language's first single, 'The Brave', being used as the theme to the BBC's coverage of the 1994 Commonwealth Games. 'The Brave' was written and produced by the duo with the use of Canadian Indian chants and recordings of tribal music form north-west Canada, where the Games were being held. Underpinning the vocals were western dance beats, sampling and production technology.

International Submarine Band

This country rock group was formed in New England, USA, in 1965 by **Gram Parsons** (vocals, keyboards, guitar), Ian Dunlop (bass, vocals), John Nuese (guitar, ex-Trolls) and Tom Snow (piano), who was later replaced by a drummer, Mickey Gauvin. It was Gauvin and Dunlop who suggested the group's new name - a reference to the 'International Silverstream Submarine Band' from the 'Our Gang' film series of the 1930s. They moved to New York where they backed former child actor Brandon De Wilde on a series of demos for **RCA Records** and also made two singles. The first, an instrumental version of the title song to the film *The Russians Are Coming, The Russians Are Coming*, was backed by a version of **Buck Owens**' 'Truck Driving Man' and was issued on Ascot Records in 1966. Later that year the quartet switched to **Columbia** for 'Sum Up Broke'/'One Day Week', the a-side of which was an impressive synthesis of folk rock and pop. When these singles were unsuccessful, the group followed De Wilde to Los Angeles where they supported several acts, including **Love** and **Iron Butterfly**, but their blend of R&B, C&W and rock 'n' roll was at odds with prevailing psychedelic trends. Footage of the ISB appeared in the film ***The Trip***. **Lee Hazlewood** showed interest in

the C&W element of their music but internal disputes broke apart the founding line-up. In 1967 Dunlop and Gauvin left to form the original **Flying Burrito Brothers** while Parsons and Nuese were joined in the International Submarine Band by Bob Buchanan (bass) and Jon Corneal (drums). *Safe At Home* was released on Hazlewood's LHI label. It featured material by **Johnny Cash** and **Merle Haggard**, alongside four Parsons originals, notably 'Luxury Liner' and 'Blue Eyes'. Both of these songs were completed prior to Buchanan's arrival and feature Chris Ethridge on bass. The album, however, was not a success and the band dissolved. Parsons briefly joined the **Byrds**, then formed a revamped **Flying Burrito Brothers**, initially including both Corneal and Ethridge. Gauvin formed Vegelava with two ex-members of the **Blues Magoos** before retiring from music. Dunlop returned to his native Cornwall where he formed the Muscletones, while Nuese fronted a version of the International Submarine Band during the early 70s. At the same time Parsons was enjoying an influential solo career.

● ALBUMS: *Safe At Home* (LHI 1967)★★★.

International Sweethearts Of Rhythm

In 1937, Laurence Clifton Jones, administrator of a school for poor and orphaned children at Piney Woods, Mississippi, USA, decided to form a band. At first his enterprise was only mildly successful, but by the end of the decade it had achieved a high standard of musicianship and was growing in reputation. In 1941 the band came under new management and hired **Eddie Durham** as arranger and musical director. Soon afterwards, Durham was replaced by Jesse Stone, a noted Kansas City bandleader and arranger. Although mostly using black female musicians, a few white women were hired but, given the existence of segregation, these often had to 'pass' for black. At the end of World War II the Sweethearts toured American bases in Europe, played the Olympia Theatre in Paris, and broadcast on the Armed Forces Radio service. In 1949 the band folded but their leader for many years, Ann Mae Winburn, formed a new group. By the mid-50s, however, this band too had ceased to exist. All but forgotten, memories of the band were revived largely through the efforts of record producer Rosetta Reitz, who released an album of the Sweethearts' AFRS broadcasts. Reminiscences by former members of the band were recorded in books on women jazz players by Sally Placksin (*Jazz Women*), Linda Dahl (*Stormy Weather*) and others, and in a television documentary which included footage of the band in performance. At its peak, in the early 40s, the Sweethearts were an excellent, swinging band with a style and power similar to that of bands such as **Lucky Millinder**'s. Although the band led by **Ina Ray Hutton** was more popular with the general public, the Sweethearts were more accomplished musicians; unfortunately they were ignored in certain important areas of showbusiness, such as the motion-picture industry, because they were black.

Among the long-serving members of the band were several excellent musicians, particularly trumpeter Ray Carter and alto saxophonist Roz Cron. The band's outstanding players were another trumpeter, **Ernestine 'Tiny' Davis**, Pauline Braddy and Vi Burnside. Davis was a fine jazz player who also sang; Braddy was a superb, driving drummer whose advisers and admirers included **Big Sid Catlett** and **Jo Jones**. The solo playing of Burnside, a tenor saxophonist (one of whose high-school classmates was **Sonny Rollins**) shows her to have been a player who, had she been male, would have been ranked alongside the best of the day. Her breathy sound resembled that of **Ben Webster**, but there was never any suggestion that she was merely a copyist. Burnside was a major jazz talent and the International Sweethearts Of Rhythm were one of the best big bands of the swing era. The fact that they are so often overlooked is a sad reflection on the male-dominated world in which they strove to make their mark.
● COMPILATIONS: *The International Sweethearts Of Rhythm* (Rosetta 1945-46)★★★, with others *Women In Jazz Vol. 1* (1945-46)★★★.

Interns
(see **Viceroys**)

Into Another
Proffering a melodic brand of intelligent east coast hard rock, Into Another were formed in New York, USA, in 1990, by Richie Birkenhead, formerly a member of hardcore legends Youth Of Today. Additionally comprising Peter Moses (guitar), Tony Bono (bass, ex-Whiplash) and Drew Thomas (drums), the group made its debut with a self-titled collection in 1991. This, and subsequent EPs such as *Creepy Eppy* and *Herbivore*, established a musical agenda that drew from the psychedelic metal crossover style of **Redd Kross** and **Urge Overkill**. By 1996 and the *Seamless* album, the group had been made a priority by their record company and enlisted the services of **Pearl Jam/Soundgarden** producer Rick Parashar in an attempt to develop a fuller, more polished rock sound. Certainly some of the tracks, such as opener 'Mutate Me', recalled the sound of grunge, but elsewhere Into Another adopted a more cerebral approach, with Birkenhead's lyrics in particular winning critical praise.
● ALBUMS: *Into Another* (Hollywood 1991)★★, *Ignaurus* (Hollywood 1994)★★★, *Seamless* (Hollywood 1996)★★★.

Into Paradise
This rock-pop outfit formed in Dublin, Eire, in 1986, as Backwards Into Paradise. By 1988 their line-up had stabilized as Dave Long (vocals, guitar), James Eadie (lead guitar, keyboards), Rachael Tighe (bass) and Ronan Clarke (drums). They gathered few second glances until the release of *Under The Water*, early in 1990. A capricious and deceptive album, it secured many plaudits and a predictably enthusiastic response from the media. Being from Dublin, they were auto-

matically and inaccurately compared to both **U2** and the **Hothouse Flowers**. Other critics noted the proliferation of drink-orientated songs, which placed them in a more definite Irish tradition. The follow-up, *Churchtown*, on their new Ensign Records home, was given an altogether more terse reception. Ultimately the accommodation with a major label went awry, and Into Paradise returned to original home Setanta Records, who in the meantime had enjoyed success with **A House** and **Frank And Walters**. This more sympathetic environment has seen Long continue to mine a strong creative furrow, though his lyrics may be a little too barbed for major success to come courting again.
● ALBUMS: *Under The Water* (Setanta 1990)★★★, *Churchtown* (Ensign 1991)★★, *Down All The Days* (Setanta 1992)★★★, *For No One* (Setanta 1993)★★★.

Into The Great Wide Open - Tom Petty And The Heartbreakers
Petty once represented the new wave of pop in the late 70s. There was an edge of punkiness to his music and that has served him well throughout his career. Very few stars as unassuming as Petty have courted all audiences and succeeded. This is a Jeff Lynne production, which would usually have had pundits making a heretic cross with their fingers. Fortunately, it was listened to for what it was: an excellent album of Petty songs played by the best support band in the world. 'Learning To Fly', for example, has a simple repeated four-chord pattern, F C Am G, and out of this Petty has woven the perfect pop song. One of many.
● Tracks: *Learning To Fly; Kings Highway; Into The Great Wide Open; Two Gunslingers; The Dark Of The Sun; All Or Nothing; All The Wrong Reasons; Too Good To Be True; Out In The Cold; You And I Will Meet Again; Makin' Some Noise; Built To Last.*
● First released 1991
● UK peak chart position: 3
● USA peak chart position: 13

Into The Purple Valley - Ry Cooder
Guitarist Cooder was a respected session musician prior to launching a solo career. His distinctive style blossomed fully on this, his second album, which is a brilliant compendium of American country/folk styles. Tight, but sparse accompaniment takes the artist through songs largely drawn from the Dustbowl Ballads of the Depression era. An unerring empathy is heard throughout, particularly on Woody Guthrie's 'Vigilante Man'. Cooder's ungainly voice captures the pervasive atmosphere, but it is his chilling slide guitarwork for which this album is renowned.
● Tracks: *How Can You Keep On Moving; Billy The Kid; Money Honey; FDR In Trinidad; Teardrops Will Fall; Denomination Blues; On A Monday; Hey Porter; Great Dreams Of Heaven; Taxes On The Farmer Feeds Us All; Vigilante Man.*
● First released 1971
● UK peak chart position: did not chart
● USA peak chart position: 113

Into The Woods

Once again **Stephen Sondheim** came up with something surprising and original for this show, which made its debut at the Martin Beck Theatre in New York on 5 November 1987. He and director-librettist James Lapine transformed a series of nursery rhyme characters, Cinderella (Kim Crosby), Red Riding Hood (Danielle Ferland), Jack (Ben Wright) And The Beanstalk, and Rapunzel (Pamela Winslow) into what one critic called 'a symbolic world of adulthood and self-discovery'. The tales are linked by the Baker (Chip Zien) and his wife (Joanna Gleason), who desperately want a child. A nearby Witch (**Bernadette Peters**) offers to solve their sterility problem if the baker will deliver to her within three days: Cinderella's slipper, Red Riding Hood's cape, Jack's cow, and Rapunzel's hair. The Baker obliges, and his wife duly becomes pregnant. Thereafter, the story takes on Freudian overtones, and becomes a 'timely moral allegory for adults'. Red Riding Hood is swallowed by the wolf but later emerges unscathed; Rapunzel goes mad; Jack's mother and Red Riding Hood's grandmother die suddenly; and the witch is transformed into her younger self. Sondheim's score was regarded as 'melodic and lyrically rich', and included such numbers as the recurring 'Into The Woods', 'Any Moment', 'Children Will Listen', 'It Takes Two', 'I Know Things Now', 'Moments In The Woods', and 'No More'. Another song that attracted some attention was 'Agony', a duet for two princes (Robert Westenberg and Chuck Wagner) who decide that adultery is more fun than fidelity. *Into The Woods* ran for 764 performances, slightly over-par for Sondheim, and won **Tony Awards** for the score, book, and best actress (Joanna Gleason), despite *The Phantom Of The Opera* running off with most of them in that year. It also gained the New York Drama Critics Circle and Drama Desk Awards for best musical. The 1990 London production, which ran for five months, starred **Julia McKenzie** as the Witch, and won **Laurence Olivier Awards** for the director (Richard Jones) and best actress (Imelda Staunton as the Baker's wife). An acclaimed revival was presented by the Long Beach Civic Light Opera in 1993.

Intrigue

An R&B vocal trio comprising Audley Wiggan Jnr., and brothers Jason and Anthony Harper, Intrigue piloted a new musical hybrid in the mid-90s that they themselves described as 'acoustic soul'. An attempt to stamp out a new musical identity in a crowded R&B marketplace, the same epithet served as the title of the group's 1995 debut album. Co-produced with **Ali Dee**, the album favoured traditional instrumentation - strings, keyboards, piano, horns and upright bass - to provide a sympathetic melodic backdrop to the vocalists' oscillating melodies. *Acoustic Soul* was promoted by a single, 'If You've Ever Been In Love', a typically lush, evocative example of the album's contents. Previous singles had included 'Dance With Me', a cover version of the **Drifters** hit, which gave a strong indication of the trio's influences. The group confirmed their commitment to a traditional style of vocal R&B by performing an all-acoustic tour of trade conventions, benefits and parades through the early months of 1997.
● ALBUMS: *Acoustic Soul* (GRV/Universal 1995)★★★.

Intrinsic

This power-metal quintet from California, USA, was formed in 1983 with guitarists Mike Mellinger and Ron Crawford settling on the rhythm section of Joel Stern (bass) and Chris Binns (drums) in late 1984, with vocalist Garrett Graupner joining the following year. The band refined their fast, **Iron Maiden**-influenced style on the club scene, playing support slots to the likes of **Megadeth** and **Armored Saint** in San Francisco while conversely opening for glam bands in Los Angeles, before releasing *Intrinsic* to enormous critical acclaim. However, the band were held back while they searched for a new vocalist, with Graupner having departed by mutual consent, as both parties felt that his bluesy tones were unsuited to Intrinsic's more aggressive material. David Wayne (ex-**Metal Church**) stepped in as the band signed a contract with Important Records, who re-released the debut, but was ousted after only five live shows, and the band's continuing search for a vocalist prevented them capitalizing on their good press. A self-financed EP followed, demonstrating again the band's sophisticated guitarwork, but failing to reach the heights of the debut; no new contract ensued, and Intrinsic continued to haul their power demos around record labels.
● ALBUMS: *Intrinsic* (No Wimp 1987)★★★, *Distortion Of Perspective* mini-album (Cheese Flag 1991)★★★.

Intro

From Brooklyn, New York, USA, Intro are led by songwriter/lead vocalist Kenny Greene, with Jeff Sanders and Buddy Wike his fellow singers. They made their initial impact in 1993, establishing themselves on the US R&B vocal scene with a self-titled debut album that reached number 11 on the *Billboard* R&B album chart. By the advent of a follow-up collection in 1995, the group had slowed the pace of their delivery to present a more reflective, melodic song suite dominated by ballads. Yet there was still an absence of the explicit lyrics favoured by other R&B practitioners: 'We're focusing on giving listeners a well-rounded album, but the important thing is that listeners feel that there's love out there in the music industry, and we're one of the groups around to help send it,' claimed Greene. Typical of this approach was 'There Is A Way', which addressed child abuse and wife battering. The album reunited Greene with his former production partner Dave Hall, with other contributions from David Cintron and Rodney Jherkins.
● ALBUMS: *Intro* (Atlantic 1993)★★★★, *New Life* (Atlantic 1995)★★★.

Intruders

Formed in Philadelphia in 1960, Eugene 'Bird' Daughtry (b. 29 October 1939, Kinston, North Carolina, USA, d. 25 December 1994), Phil Terry (b. 1 November 1943, Philadelphia, Pennsylvania, USA), Robert 'Big Sonny' Edwards (b. 22 February 1942, Philadelphia, Pennsylvania, USA) and Sam 'Little Sonny' Brown have enjoyed the benefit of a long-standing relationship with producers **Gamble And Huff**. Signed to the duo's Excel/Gamble outlet, the group achieved several minor hits, notably '(We'll Be) United' (1966) and 'Together' (1967). In 1968 'Cowboys To Girls', a prototype for the emergent Philly-soul sound, became their first million-seller, peaking at number 6 in the national US pop chart. The follow-up, '(Love Is Like A) Baseball Game', was another huge R&B smash, as well as one of soul's best sporting metaphors, **Mel And Tim**'s 'Backfield In Motion' notwithstanding. In 1970, the Intruders replaced lead Sam Brown with Bobby Starr (b. 19 January 1937, Baltimore, Maryland, USA), and subsequently reached the charts with 'When We Get Married' (1970), '(Win, Place Or Show) She's A Winner' (1971) and 'I'll Always Love My Mama' (1973). Despite an undeniable quality, the Intruders' releases were always overshadowed by those of stablemates the **O'Jays** and **Harold Melvin And The Blue Notes**.

● ALBUMS: *Cowboys To Girls* (Gamble 1968)★★★, *When We Get Married* (Gamble 1970)★★★, *Save The Children* (Gamble 1973)★★★★, *Energy Of Love* (Gamble 1974)★★★.
● COMPILATIONS: *The Intruders Greatest Hits* (Gamble 1969)★★★, *Cowboys To Girls: The Best Of The Intruders* (Sony/Legacy 1996)★★★★.

Intveld, James

b. Compton, California, USA. John Intveld and his brother Ricky grew up watching their father play with a local band. He was given a guitar when he was eight and he sang in the church choir. In 1981, after playing with various bands, he (vocals, guitar) and Ricky (drums) formed the Rockin' Shadows with Pat Woodward (double bass). In 1983 they opened for **Ricky Nelson** who was so impressed that he invited both Ricky and Pat Woodward to join his Stone Canyon Band. Two years later Nelson and his entire band were killed in a aeroplane crash. Intveld worked as a solo artist in Pasadena and enrolled at an acting school. He wrote a US country hit for **Rosie Flores**, 'Cryin' Over You', and found work as a session player, notably for rockabilly performer Ray Campi. He provided Johnny Depp's singing voice in the film *Cry Baby*, and later appeared in the film *Indian Runner*. He is part of the **Blasters** and also part of an occasional band with Harry Dean Stanton and **Billy Swan**, the Repo Men. His music is neo-rockabilly and it is no insult to say that it could have been made at any time since 1960.

● ALBUMS: *James Intveld* (Bear Family 1996)★★★.

Investigators

The Investigators were based in Battersea, south London, England, as a **lovers rock** band formed in 1975. The line-up included Lorenzo Hall (lead vocals), Michael Gordon (lead vocals), Ian Austin (bass guitar), Reg Graham (keyboards) and Martin Christie (percussion); the remaining instrumentalists were session players. The group were no strangers to the UK reggae scene, having performed as the Private I's, working alongside Chris Lane of **Fashion Records**. As the Private I's they recorded Otis Gayle's **Studio One** classic, 'I'll Be Around', although it was the b-side, 'Love Won't Let Me Wait', that secured a placing in the reggae chart, along with a version of **Black Uhuru**'s 'Folk Song'. The band recorded numerous melodies including 'Living In A World Of Magic', 'What Love Has Done' and 'Loving Feeling' on their Private Eye label, 'Love Is What You Make It, and the seductive 'Turn Out The Lights'. For Inner City they recorded their number 1 reggae hit, 'Baby I'm Yours', followed by 'Summertime Blues' and 'Close To You'. The line-up was also responsible for providing the foundation to **Dee Sharp**'s debut, 'Let's Dub It Up', which topped the reggae chart in 1980, closely followed by 'Its Too Late Baby'. The releases did much to acquaint reggae followers with the newly formed Fashion label. In 1981 the group toured the UK and USA supporting Black Uhuru, but to little acclaim. In 1984 the band gained recognition with 'Woman I Need Your Loving'. They continued to maintain a high profile releasing lovers hits, and in 1985 they performed as the opening act at the second Reggae Sunsplash festival in the UK. The showcase was a prelude to the European leg of the Sunsplash world tour, which has since flourished, although not in the UK. Following the demise of the Investigators, both Lorenzo Hall and Michael Gordon have pursued successful solo careers, Gordon having a notable chart hit with 'Don't Want No More', while Hall recorded the popular 'Don't Let Go'.

● ALBUMS: *First Case* (Investigator 1982)★★.
● COMPILATIONS: *Greatest Hits* (Jet Star 1990)★★★.

Invincibles

An R&B vocal trio from Los Angeles, California, USA. The falsetto lead in soul music was especially strong in the genre of stand-up vocal groups, and from the groups of the 60s, the Invincibles were perhaps one of the greatest practitioners of the falsetto-edged vocal harmony style. The group members were David Richardson, Lester Johnson and Clifton Knight. Richardson was originally from Louisiana and brought a background in gospel singing to the group, and Johnson and Knight both came from Texas. The Invincibles' best work was demonstrated on two superb hits, 'Heart Full Of Love' (number 31 R&B) from 1965, and 'Can't Win' (number 38 R&B) from 1966, both of which went beyond mere sweetness to exhibit deep, soulful feeling. However, the Invincibles faded after these two records.

Invisible Girls
(see **Murray, Pauline, And The Invisible Girls**)

Invisible Man's Band
(see **Five Stairsteps**)

Invitation To The Dance

Filming began on this ambitious **Gene Kelly** project in 1952, but the finished product was only presented to the public four years later. Produced by **Arthur Freed** for MGM, the picture was a gallant but unsuccessful attempt by Kelly to bring ballet to the cinema-going masses. There was no dialogue, and the film consisted of three individual ballet sequences (another, featuring several popular songs, had been cut prior to release). The first, 'Circus', in which Kelly plays a Pierrot character whose love for a ballerina (Claire Sombert) ends in tragedy, had music by Jacques Ibert. The second, 'Ring Around The Rosy', with music by **André Previn**, had overtones of La Ronde in its story of a bracelet which, after being presented by a husband to his wife, then passed through the hands of an artist, a nightclub singer, and a whore, among others, is finally returned to the husband. The final sequence, 'Sinbad The Sailor', composed by Rimsky-Korsakov, revived memories of Kelly's innovative dance with Jerry the cartoon mouse in *Anchors Aweigh* (1945). This time he was a sailor once more, involved with animated characters as well as the real-life Carol Haney and David Kasday. Other artists featured in the first two scenes were Igor Youskevitch, Claude Bessey, Tommy Rall, Tamara Toumanova, Belita, Irving Davies, Diana Adams and David Paltenghi. Gene Kelly was also the overall director-choreographer, and the film was beautifully photographed in Technicolor by Freddie Young and Joseph Ruttenberg, and shot mostly in England. Although it was critical and financial flop, the picture became something of a cult item, especially in Europe where it was awarded the Grand Prize in the 1958 West Berlin film festival. It is invariably included in Gene Kelly retrospectives.

INXS

Formed in 1977 as the Farriss Brothers in Sydney, Australia, INXS comprised the three Farriss brothers Tim (b. 16 August 1957; guitar), Jon (b. 18 August 1961; drums) and Andrew (b. 27 March 1959; keyboards); Michael Hutchence (b. 22 January 1960, Lain Cove, Sydney, Australia, d. 22 November 1997, Sydney, Australia; lead vocals), Kirk Pengilly (b. 4 July 1958; guitar, saxophone, vocals) and Garry Beers (b. 22 June 1957; bass, vocals). The group moved to Perth, Western Australia to develop their own distinctive rock sound which incorporated both black dance music and white soul influences. The band began its recording career in 1980 with a single, 'Simple Simon'/'We Are The Vegetables' on the independent Deluxe label. Over the next three years, half a dozen singles reached the lower Top 40 in Australia, but the second album,

Underneath The Colours sold well, and the next *Shabooh Shoobah* reached the Top 5. It was with the 'Original Sin' single of early 1985 and its accompanying album, *The Swing*, that the band finally hit the top of the charts in Australia. The album and single generated interest in the band from the USA, Europe and South America, and the follow-up album, *Listen Like Thieves*, consolidated their worldwide success, except in the UK where critics savaged the band, but it would not be long before sales finally took off there as well. In 1986 Hutchence made his acting debut in the film *Dogs In Space*. One song from the film, 'Rooms For The Memory', earned him a solo Australian Top 10 single. The band toured the USA and Europe constantly, and **MTV** aired their videos; as a result, *Kick* achieved over 1 million sales on advance orders in the USA alone and the band finally gained a number 1 US hit with 'Need You Tonight' in January 1988. The band's success could be attributed to many factors, including an unchanged line-up from the beginning, the sultry good looks of vocalist Hutchence, unstinting touring schedules, diverse songwriters in the band and consistently fres production with a new producer for each album. After *Kick* and before the release of *X*, all the members had a 12-month break and became involved with other projects - Hutchence with Max Q; Andrew Farriss in production work with **Jenny Morris**; and Garry Beers joined a loose collection of friends for a tour and recording as Absent Friends. *Live Baby Live* is a document of the INXS Wembley Stadium concert in July 1991. Hutchence's much publicized, fleeting romance with **Kylie Minogue** brought the group's name to the attention of a whole new generation of potential fans. Their 1993 set, *Full Moon, Dirty Hearts*, included a Hutchence/Chrissie Hynde (**Pretenders**) duet on 'Kill The Pain' and the single 'The Gift'. The video of the latter was banned by MTV, formerly INXS's greatest ally, due to its use of Holocaust and Gulf War footage. Hutchence embarked on a highly publicized relationship with Paula Yates, being cited in her divorce from **Bob Geldof**. Over the next few years, until his untimely suicide in 1997, Hutchence and Geldof were at loggerheads over the custody of the latter's children with Yates. Hutchence was found hanged in his hotel room in Sydney, Australia, on 22 November 1997.

● ALBUMS: *INXS* (Deluxe 1980)★★, *Underneath The Colours* (RCA 1981)★★, *Shabooh Shoobah* (Mercury 1982)★★, *The Swing* (Mercury 1984)★★★, *Listen Like Thieves* (Mercury 1985)★★★, *Kick* (Mercury 1987)★★★, *X* (Mercury 1990)★★, *Live Baby Live* (Mercury 1991)★★, *Welcome To Wherever You Are* (Mercury 1992)★★★, *Full Moon, Dirty Hearts* (Mercury 1993)★★★, *Elegantly Wasted* (Mercury 1997)★★.
Solo: Max Q *Max Q* (Mercury 1989)★★. Absent Friends *Here's Looking Up Your Address* (Roo Art 1990).
● COMPILATIONS: *Greatest Hits* (Mercury 1994)★★★★.
● VIDEOS: *Truism* (PMI 1991), *The Best Of INXS* (1994).
● FURTHER READING: *INXS: The Official Story Of A Band On The Road*, St John Yann Gamblin (ed.).

Iommi, Tony

b. Anthony Frank Iommi, 19 February 1948, Birmingham, England. A blues/jazz-influenced guitarist, Iommi was eager to escape the mundanity of industrial Birmingham and his job repairing typewriters. A number of small-time bands, including Polka Tulk and Earth, gradually led to the formation of **Black Sabbath** in 1969, with Iommi on guitar, John **'Ozzy' Osbourne** (vocals), Terence 'Geezer' Butler (bass) and Bill Ward (drums). It was with Black Sabbath that Iommi established his international reputation as a guitarist of skill and invention. The Black Sabbath sound was built on his devastating riffing, delivered with a fuzzy, distorted guitar tone that became his trademark. He was, and still is, the godfather of the heavy metal riff. Iommi has a unique soloing and rhythm style, and sports an unusual set of plastic finger extensions on his right hand as a result of an accident (he is left-handed). A tall, dark, moustachioed man, he is also famed for his lack of movement on stage. Personal differences between Iommi and Osbourne contributed to the latter's departure from Black Sabbath in 1978, to be replaced by American **Ronnie James Dio**. After Dio's own departure in 1982, Black Sabbath entered a highly unstable phase, and it was Iommi who held the band together and kept the Black Sabbath name alive. The album *Seventh Star* was released under the heading 'Black Sabbath Featuring Tony Iommi', according to record company wishes. Iommi, however, had intended it to be a solo efort, giving the songs a different emphasis to those from a pure Black Sabbath album.
● ALBUMS: See Black Sabbath.

Iona

This Christian Celtic band were formed by Nick Beggs (b. 15 December 1961; vocals, bass), an ex-member of UK pop group **Kajagoogoo**: He departed to take up a job as an A&R man with Phonogram Records, leaving the present line-up as Terl Bryant, Tim Harris, Joanne Hogg, Dave Bainbridge, Mike Haughton and Troy Donockley, They produce moody, atmospheric recordings, but live they retained a rockier edge. Iona may yet prove capable of following **Clannad** and **Capercaillie** on to bigger and better things. *Journey Into The Mourn* was inspired by an 8th century Irish hymn and featured guests were Maire Brennan of **Clannad** and guitarist **Robert Fripp**.
● ALBUMS: *Book Of Kells* (1990)★★★, *Beyond These Shores* (1994)★★★, *Journey Into The Mourn* (Forefront 1996)★★★.

Iona And Andy

Iona and Andy started performing together in 1980, the year they were married. They harmonize together and Iona plays guitar and Andy bass. One of their most-requested songs is 'An Old Cottage Home In The Country'. In 1994 they released what is possibly the first bilingual country music album, with half the tracks sung in Welsh. The success of this album has led to increased bookings and they also plan an unplugged show as a trio with Jim Donaldson.
● ALBUMS: including *Across The Mountain* (Barge 1987)★★★, *Spirit Of The Night* (Sain 1994)★★★, *Milltiroedd - 100 Miles* (Sain 1996)★★★.

Iovine, Jimmy

b. 11 March 1953, Brooklyn, New York, USA. One of the leading record producers of the 80s, Iovine found his first studio job through songwriter **Ellie Greenwich** in 1977, and by 1973 he was an engineer at the Record Plant in New York City. There he worked on tracks by **John Lennon**, **Southside Johnny** and **Bruce Springsteen**. His first assignment as producer was for New Jersey band Flame in 1977, but his first hit album was *Easter* by **Patti Smith**, which included the Top 40 single 'Because The Night'. Iovine was now established as a top-grade producer and during the 80s he worked with numerous major rock acts. In 1979 he began his association with **Tom Petty** for whom he produced three albums. There was later work with **Dire Straits** (*Making Movies*) and with **Stevie Nicks** on her first two solo albums. In 1983 he was called in for the **U2** live recording *Under A Blood Red Sky*, followed by the group's double-album *Rattle & Hum*. Often co-producing with the artist, Iovine's other credits include work with **Simple Minds** (*Once Upon A Time*), **Alison Moyet** (*Raindancing*), **Shakespears Sister**, the **Eurythmics** (*We Two Are One*) and **Gene Loves Jezebel**. He renewed his partnership with Patti Smith in 1988, co-producing her *Dream Of Life* with Fred Smith. In 1990, Iovine began a new career in A&R, setting up the Interscope label with Ted Fields. During its first year the company had hits from Marky Mark And The Funky Bunch, Primus and Gerardo.

IQ

A performance art-based assembly who formed in Southampton, England, in 1981, having previously existed as the Lens three years earlier. By the time of their debut album's release the line-up had stabilized with Pete Nicholls (vocals), Tim Esau (bass), Mike Holmes (guitar), Martin Orford (keyboards) and Mark Rideout (drums). Taking their influences from jazz, blues, rock and reggae, they also interspersed elements of theatre and drama. Nicholls had some acting experience, the highlight of his early career being an appearance on children's television show *Cheggers Plays Pop*. Following the cassette-only *Seven Stories Into Eight*, his band's debut album received excellent reviews in the music press including the late *Sounds*, which ensured a healthy cult following. Moving away from their early gothic leanings, later recordings became further associated with the progressive rock movement and bands such as Twelfth Night. However, productive over the ensuing mid-80s, they rapidly acquiesced to the law of diminishing returns.
● ALBUMS: *Seven Stories Into Eight* (private pressing

1982)★★★, *Tales From The Lush Attic* (Sahara 1984)★★★★, *The Wake* (Sahara 1985)★★★, *Nine In A Pond Is Here* (Stal Boxer 1985)★★★, *Living Proof* (Samurai 1986)★★, *Nomzamo* (Squark 1987)★★★, *Are You Sitting Comfortably* (Squark 1989)★★, *J'ai Pollette D'arnu* (1991)★★★, *Ever* (1993)★★★.

IQ Procedure

This London, England hip-hop trio specialize in mixing dub reggae with more conventional hip-hop rhythms. Rapper and programmer Baron Smith, the group's guiding hand and spokesman, was among the many discoveries of British rap svengali **MC Duke**. Alongside fellow rapper Mr Million and ragga disc jockey DJ Danger, IQ Procedure (a name they translate as a desire 'to constantly strive for and pursue new forms of intelligence') made their debut with the EP, *U Can Get With This*, in 1993. Like many of their UK rap peers, however, its potential audience was restricted by poor distribution and press coverage.

Irby, Jerry

b. Gerald Irby, 20 October 1917, New Braunfels, Texas, USA, d. 1983. Irby was raised by his wealthy grandmother, a fact that contradicted his claim to have struggled 'with just a cheap guitar and a few songs'. In 1933, he moved to Houston playing honky tonks, and in 1936 formed a duo with **Ted Daffan**. In 1938, they split when Daffan joined the Bar X Cowboys and Irby briefly fronted his Serenaders in Beaumont. In 1940, thanks to grandmother's finances, he opened Jerry's Country Palace, but in June 1941, it closed and he became the vocalist with the Bar X Cowboys (Daffan had by this time left to form his Texans). In 1945, although still with the Cowboys, Irby made solo recordings for Gulf, achieving local state success with his song 'Driving Nails In My Coffin'. He also made recordings with the Cowboys but when further solo recordings for Globe caused disagreements, he left the Cowboys to form his Texas Ranchers. He later recorded for **Mercury**, **Imperial** and 4 Star, before joining **MGM Records** in 1948. He achieved success with 'Roses Have Thorns' and his songs were recorded by **Bob Wills** and **Bill Boyd**. In 1948, he opened his *Texas Corral Nite Club* (with grandmother's backing) and played there until the early 50s, when, plagued by a drink problem and almost broke, he sold the club to go into farming. He was equally unsuccessful in this area and by 1955, he was back in Houston. In December 1955, his old friend Daffan recorded him singing 'Tangled Mind', for his Daffan label. It proved a hit and he formed a band and made further recordings, including 'A Man Is A Slave'. Sadly, he failed to make a return to the good times and left music for a time during the 60s, helping his wife to run a beauty salon. After they divorced, he returned to singing around 1971, even opening a club. He remarried and, in 1973, became an evangelist. He recorded albums of gospel music and even gave some of his old songs new religious lyrics. He was quoted as saying, 'I'm still in the country music business; it just has a

different message'. In 1977, he had a popular television programme in Houston. His recordings for the Daffan label were included on **Bear Family Records**' 2-CD *The Daffan Records*, released in 1995, but few others are available.

● ALBUMS: *Hot Line To Heaven* (Bagatelle 1975)★★, *Are You Ready* (World Witness 1976)★★.

Irene

Yet another show based on the familiar 'Cinderella' rags-to-riches story, this is, nevertheless, one of America's most treasured musical productions. It opened at the Vanderbilt Theatre in New York on 18 November 1919. James Montgomery's book, based on his own play, *Irene O'Dare*, told of a poor young girl (Edith Day), who works for an upholsterer, who is sent by her employer to do some work for Donald Marshall (Walter Regan) at his grand home in Long Island. Impressed by the personable girl, Donald arranges a job for her at an establishment belonging to a male fashion designer, Mme. Lucy (Bobby Watson). She charms everyone, including the extra-snobbish J.P. Bowden (Arthur Burckly), who gives a her a party, and becomes stricken with love for her, until he discovers that she is from 'the other side of the tracks'. Donald, however, has no such prejudice, and, after the usual trouble with his high-falutin' family, he and Irene eventually marry. The memorable score, by **Harry Tierney** (music), who was making his Broadway debut, and **Joseph McCarthy** (lyrics), produced one enormous hit, 'Alice Blue Gown', which was introduced by Edith Day, and later became popular through recordings by Day herself, and Frankie Masters, **Ozzie Nelson**, and **Glenn Miller**. There were some other good songs, too, such as 'Castle Of Dreams', 'The Talk Of The Town', 'Sky Rocket', 'To Be Worthy Of You', 'Irene', and the exuberant 'The Last Part Of Every Party'. During the show's run of 670 performances, a record for a Broadway musical, which it held for 18 years, Edith Day left to recreate her role in the London production which stayed at the Empire Theatre for almost a year. The show's incredible popularity continued via road companies which at one stage were estimated to be around 17 in number. In 1973, more than 50 years after it had first been produced, *Irene* was revived in New York with the popular film actress **Debbie Reynolds**, making her Broadway debut. In the revised book by Joseph Stein, Hugh Wheeler, and Harry Rigby, Irene O'Day's days as a model were long gone, and she was now - of all things - a piano tuner. Several changes were made to the score, including the addition of some songs by Charles Gaynor, **Fred Fisher**, and Otis Clements; and two others, both with lyrics by Joseph McCarthy, 'You Made Me Love You' (music by **Jimmy Monaco**), and 'I'm Always Chasing Rainbows' (music by Harry Carroll), which was originally used in the show *Oh Look!* (1918). Once again, the show endeared itself to the public, and stayed around for 604 performances. Two films of *Irene* were made, a silent version in 1926, with Colleen Moore, and another, in 1940, starring **Anna Neagle**, Ray Milland, and Roland Young.

Iris, Donnie, And The Cruisers

b. Dominic Ierace, Beaver Falls, Pennsylvania, USA. Iris is an accomplished songwriter and arguably one of the leading perfectionists in the American hard rock idiom - his first hit record, 1981's 'Ah! Leah!' was completed only after 80 vocal overdubs. Iris was formerly the lead singer, songwriter and guitarist for Pittsburgh rock group the **Jaggerz**, and had also toured with the funk group **Wild Cherry**. He formed the Cruisers at the turn of the 80s with Mark Avsec (keyboards), Marty Lee (guitar), Albritton McClain (bass) and Kevin Valentine (drums). 'Ah! Leah!' was included on the group's debut, *Back On The Streets*, in 1980. In 1982 he charted in the US Top 40 once more with 'Love Is Like A Rock' and for a final time later that year with 'My Girl'. Despite a reduced commercial profile in the rest of the decade, Iris's albums have continued to inspire his devoted American audience with their consummate musicianship and sharply observed lyrics.

● ALBUMS: *Back On The Streets* (MCA 1980)★★★, *King Cool* (MCA 1981)★★★, *The High And Mighty* (MCA 1982)★★, *Fortune 410* (MCA 1983)★★★, *No Muss No Fuss* (HME 1985)★★★.

Irma La Douce

This show originally opened at the tiny Theatre Gramont in Paris on 12 November 1956, and gave the city a new star - young Colette Renard - in the leading role. The book and lyrics were written by the ex-taxi driver and novelist Alexandre Breffort, and the music was provided by Marguerite Monnot, who had written several songs for **Edith Piaf**, including 'Poor People Of Paris', which became a big hit in France, and gave the personality pianist, **Winifred Atwell**, a UK number 1. Serious doubts were expressed as to whether this tender, typically French love story between a prostitute and her pimp, could weather the Channel crossing, and survive the trip to London's West End. In the event, it did so triumphantly. The production arrived at the Lyric Theatre, via the seaside town of Bournemouth, on 17 July 1958, with an English book and lyrics by three comparitive newcomers to the musical theatre, **Julian More**, **David Heneker**, and Monty Norman. Rather than 'Anglicize' the show completely, the writers inserted a glossary of terms in the theatre programme, a device which had also been found to be necessary in France. The list of 'translations' included, Milieu (underworld), Poule (tart), Mec (pimp), and Grisbi (money). The story is set in the the backstreets, off the Pigalle ('Valse Milieu'), with its small-time crooks ('Tres Tres Snob') and the poules, such as Irma-la-Douce (Elizabeth Seal). She falls in love with an impoverished law student, Nestor-le-Fripe (Keith Michell) ('The Bridge Of Caulaincourt'), and they live together ('Our Language Of Love') while Irma continues to work so that Nestor can continue his studies ('She's Got

The Lot'). Nestor disguises himself as Monsieur Oscar, and becomes her sole client ('Dis-Donc'), but he soon becomes disenchanted with the double life ('The Wreck Of A Mec'), and dispenses with his alter ego ('That's A Crime'). He is found guilty of murder ('Le Grisbi Is Le Root Of Le Evil In Man') and sent to Devil's Island ('From A Prison Cell'), but he escapes ('There Is Only One Paris For That'), and returns to Irma just in time for the birth of their baby ('Christmas Child'). The production was a triumph all round, with a particularly strong supporting cast which included Clive Revill (Bob-le-Hontu), John East (Polyte-le-Mou), Julian Orchard (Police Inspector), and Gary Raymond (Frangipane). It ran for more than three and half years in London, a total of 1,512 performances, and the New York edition, in which several of the principals recreated their roles, played for over a year. Elizabeth Seal won the **Tony Award** for best actress, and Elliot Gould, who was on the brink of a successful film career at the time, played an Usher, a Priest, and a Warder. The 1963 film of *Irma La Douce* starred Shirley MacLaine and Jack Lemmon, but deleted all the songs, and used some of the music as background themes.

Iron Butterfly

During the progressive music revolution in the late 60s, one of the most surprising successes was that of Iron Butterfly. The band was formed by Doug Ingle (b. 9 September 1946, Omaha, Nebraska, USA; organ, vocals), who added Ron Bushy (b. 23 September 1941, Washington, DC, USA; drums), Eric Brann (b. 10 August 1950, Boston, Massachusetts, USA; guitar), Lee Dorman (b. 19 September 1945, St. Louis, Missouri, USA; bass, vocals) and, briefly, Danny Weiss. Together, they were arguably the first to amalgamate the terms 'heavy' and 'rock', following the release of their debut in 1968. Their second effort, *In-A-Gadda-Da-Vida* ('In The Garden Of Eden'), became a multi-million-seller and was for a number of years the biggest-selling item in **Atlantic Records**' catalogue. The album also became the record industry's first platinum disc. The 17-minute title track contained everything a progressive rock fan could want - neo-classical organ with Far East undertones, a solid beat, screeching guitar parts, barbed-wire feedback and an overlong drum solo. Magnificently overwrought at the time, the intervening years have been less kind to its standing. The follow-up, *Ball*, was less of a success, despite being a better collection of songs, notably the invigorating 'It Must Be Love' and the more subtle 'Soul Experience'. Brann departed after a poor live album and was replaced by two guitarists: Larry 'Rhino' Rheinhart (b. 7 July 1948, Florida, USA) and Mike Pinera (b. 29 September 1948, Florida, USA; ex-**Cactus**; **Alice Cooper**). However, no further success ensued. *Metamorphosis* was a confused collection, recorded when the band was disintegrating. They reformed in the mid-70s, delivering two disappointing albums. Another re-formation, this time in 1992, was masterminded by Mike Pinera. A new version of 'In-A-

Gadda-Da-Vida' was recorded and Pinera recruited Dorman and Bushy for extensive touring in the USA. By 1993, their legendary second album had sold an astonishing 25 million copies and in 1995 the band reformed once more for an anniversary tour.

● ALBUMS: *Heavy* (Atco 1968)★★★, *In-A-Gadda-Da-Vida* (Atco 1968)★★★★, *Ball* (Atco 1969)★★★, *Iron Butterfly Live* (Atco 1970)★, *Metamorphosis* (Atco 1970)★★, *Scorching Beauty* (MCA 1975)★★, *Sun And Steel* (MCA 1976)★★★.

● COMPILATIONS: *Evolution* (Atco 1971)★★★, *Star Collection* (1973)★★★, *Light And Heavy: The Best Of* (1993)★★★.

Iron Fist - Motörhead

From the moment it begins right up to 'Bang To Rights', there is no let up whatsoever, the music breakneck fast and powerful. Lemmy will always be the figurehead of metal - both he and the band may not have invented the genre but they certainly define its style and attitude. Metal vocalists often have high voices (Robert Plant, Axl Rose and Bruce Dickinson, for instance), but Lemmy has a hoarse shout, sounding as if he should be emblazoned across the back of a Lewis leather astride a Harley Davison. Perhaps a lyric sheet should be included for those who actually want to know what he is singing; many others will just nod furiously to the breathtaking speed of the music. Have a lie down afterwards.

● Tracks: *Iron Fist; Heart Of Stone; I'm The Doctor; Go To Hell; Loser; Sex And Outrage; America; Shut It Down; Speedfreak; (Don't Let 'Em) Grind Ya Down; (Don't Need) Religion; Bang To Rights.*

● First released 1982

● UK peak chart position: 6

● USA peak chart position: 174

Iron Maiden

Formed in London, England, in 1976, Iron Maiden was from the start the brainchild of Steve Harris (b. 12 March 1957, Leytonstone, London, England; bass), formerly a member of pub rockers Smiler. Named after a medieval torture device, the music was suitably heavy and hard on the senses. The heavy metal scene of the late 70s was widely regarded as stagnant, with only a handful of bands proving their ability to survive and produce music of quality. It was at this time that a new breed of young British bands began to emerge. This movement, which began to break cover in 1979 and 1980, was known as the **New Wave Of British Heavy Metal**, or NWOBHM. Iron Maiden were one of the foremost bands in the genre, and many would say its definitive example. Younger and meaner, the NWOBHM bands dealt in faster, more energetic heavy metal than any of their forefathers (punk being an obvious influence). There were several line-up changes in the Iron Maiden ranks in the very early days, and come the release of their debut EP, the group featured Harris, Dave Murray (b. 23 December 1958, London, England; guitar), **Paul Di'Anno** (b. 17 May 1959,

Chingford, London, England; vocals) and Doug Sampson (drums). The group made its live debut at the Cart & Horses Pub in Stratford, east London, in 1977, before honing its sound on the local pub circuit over the ensuing two years. Unable to solicit a response from record companies, the group sent a three-track tape, featuring 'Iron Maiden', 'Prowler' and 'Strange World', to Neal Kay, DJ at north London's hard rock disco, the Kingsbury Bandwagon Soundhouse. Kay's patronage of Iron Maiden won them an instant welcome, which prompted the release of *The Soundhouse Tapes* on the band's own label. In November 1979 the group added second guitarist Tony Parsons to the line-up for two tracks on the *Metal For Muthas* compilation, but by the time the group embarked on sessions for their debut album, he had been replaced by Dennis Stratton (b. 9 November 1954, London, England), and Sampson by Clive Burr (b. 8 March 1957; drums). A promotional single, 'Running Free', reached number 34 on the UK charts and brought an appearance on BBC Television's *Top Of The Pops*. Refusing to mime, they became the first band since the **Who** in 1973 to play live on the show. *Iron Maiden* was a roughly produced album, but reached number 4 in the UK album listings on the back of touring stints with **Judas Priest** and enduringly popular material such as 'Phantom Of The Opera'. *Killers* boasted production superior to that of the first album, and saw Dennis Stratton replaced by guitarist Adrian Smith (b. 27 February 1957). In its wake, Iron Maiden became immensely popular among heavy metal fans, inspiring fanatical devotion, aided by blustering manager Rod Smallwood and apocalyptic mascot Eddie (the latter had been depicted on the cover of 'Sanctuary' standing over Prime Minister Margaret Thatcher's decapitated body).

The release of *Number Of The Beast* was crucial to the development of the band. Without it, Iron Maiden might never have gone on to be such a force in the heavy metal arena. The album was a spectacular success, the sound of a band on the crest of a wave. It was also the debut of former infantryman and new vocalist **Bruce Dickinson** (b. Paul Bruce Dickinson, 7 August 1958, Worksop, Nottinghamshire, England), replacing Paul Di'Anno (who went on to front **Lone Wolf**, **Battlezone** and **Killers**). Formerly of **Samson**, history graduate Dickinson made his live debut with Maiden on 15 November 1981. Singles such as 'Run To The Hills' and 'The Number Of The Beast' were big UK chart hits, Iron Maiden leaving behind their NWOBHM counterparts in terms of success, just as the movement itself was beginning to peter out. *Piece Of Mind* continued their success and was a major hit in the USA (number 14). Clive Burr was replaced by Nicko McBrain on the sessions, formerly drummer with French metal band **Trust**, who had supported Maiden on their 1981 UK tour (he had also played in Streetwalkers). *Piece Of Mind* was not dissimilar to the previous album, showcasing the strong twin-guitar bite of Murray and Smith, coupled with memorable vocal lines and a sound that perfectly suited their air-punching dynamic. Single offerings, 'Flight of Icarus' and 'The Trooper', were instant hits, as the group undertook two massive tours, the four-month *World Piece* jaunt in 1983, and a *World Slavery* retinue, which included four sell-out dates at London's Hammersmith Odeon a year later. With the arrival of *Powerslave* in November, some critics accused Iron Maiden of conforming to a self-imposed writing formula, and playing safe with tried and tested ideas. Certainly, there was no significant departure from the two previous albums, but it was nonetheless happily consumed by the band's core supporters, who also purchased in sufficient quantities to ensure UK chart hits for 'Aces High' and 'Two Minutes To Midnight'. *Live After Death* was a double-album package of all their best-loved material, recorded live on their gargantuan 11-month world tour. By this time, Iron Maiden had secured themselves an unassailable position within the metal hierachy, their vast popularity spanning all continents. *Somewhere In Time* was a slight departure: it featured more melody than previously, and heralded the use of guitar synthesizers. Their songwriting still shone through and the now obligatory hit singles were easily attained in the shape of 'Wasted Years' and 'Stranger In A Strange Land'. Reaching number 11 in the USA, this was another million-plus seller. Since the mid-80s Maiden had been staging increasingly spectacular live shows, with elaborate lighting effects and stage sets. The *Somewhere In Time* tour (seven months) was no exception, ensuring their continued fame as a live band, which had been the basis for much of their success. A period of comparative inactivity preceded the release of *Seventh Son Of A Seventh Son*, which was very much in the same vein as its predecessor. A concept album, it retained its commercial edge and yielded hit singles in 'Can I Play With Madness', the surprisingly sensitive 'Evil That Men Do' and 'The Clairvoyant'.

After another exhausting mammoth world trek, the band announced their intention to take a well-earned break of at least a year. Speculation abounded that this signalled the dissolution of the band, exacerbated by Dickinson's solo project, *Tattooed Millionaire*, his book, *The Adventures Of Lord Iffy Boatrace*, and **EMI Records'** policy of re-releasing Maiden's single catalogue in its entirety (on 12-inch). After a considerable hiatus, news of the band surfaced again. Steve Harris felt that the direction pursued on the last two albums had been taken as far as possible, and a return to the style of old was planned. Unhappy with this game plan, Adrian Smith left to be replaced by Janick Gers (b. Hartlepool, Lancashire, England), previously guitarist with **White Spirit** and **Gillan** (he had also contributed to Dickinson's solo release). The live show was also scaled down in a return to much smaller venues. *No Prayer For The Dying* was indeed much more like mid-period Iron Maiden, and was predictably well received, bringing enormous UK hit singles with 'Holy Smoke' and 'Bring Your Daughter To The Slaughter'. The latter,

previously released in 1989 on the soundtrack to *A Nightmare On Elm Street 5*, had already been awarded the Golden Raspberry Award for Worst Song that year. Nevertheless, it gave Iron Maiden their first ever UK number 1. The obligatory world tour followed. Despite being denounced as 'Satanists' in Chile, 1992 also saw the band debut at number 1 in the UK charts with *Fear Of The Dark*, which housed another major single success in 'Be Quick Or Be Dead' (number 2). However, it was Dickinson's swan-song with the band, who invited demo tapes from new vocalists following the lead singer's announcement that he would depart following current touring engagements. His eventual replacement was Blaze Bayley (b. 1963, Birmingham, West Midlands, England) from **Wolfsbane**. His debut album was *X-Factor*, and on this and at live gigs (which they only resumed in November 1995), he easily proved his worth. This was a daunting task, having had to learn Maiden's whole catalogue and win over patriotic Dickinson followers. Smith resurfaced in a new band, Psycho Motel, in 1996.

● ALBUMS: *Iron Maiden* (EMI 1980)★★★, *Killers* (EMI 1981)★★, *Number Of The Beast* (EMI 1982)★★★★, *Piece Of Mind* (EMI 1983)★★, *Powerslave* (EMI 1984)★★, *Live After Death* (EMI 1985)★★★, *Somewhere In Time* (EMI 1986)★★★, *Seventh Son Of A Seventh Son* (EMI 1988)★★★★, *No Prayer For The Dying* (EMI 1990)★★★, *Fear Of The Dark* (EMI 1992)★★★, *A Real Live One (Volume One)* (EMI 1993)★★★, *A Real Dead One* (EMI 1993)★★, *Live At Donington '92* (EMI 1993)★★, *The X Factor* (EMI 1995)★★★, *Virtual XI* (EMI 1998)★★★.

● COMPILATIONS: *Best Of The Beast* (EMI 1996)★★★.

● VIDEOS: *Live At The Rainbow* (1984), *Behind The Iron Curtain Video EP* (1986), *Live After Death* (1986), *Run To The Hills* (1987), *Twelve Wasted Years* (1987), *Maiden England* (1989), *First Ten Years (The Videos)* (1990), *Raising Hell* (1993), *Donington Live 1992* (1994).

● FURTHER READING: *Running Free: The Official Story Of Iron Maiden*, Garry Bushell and Ross Halfin. *A Photographic History*, Ross Halfin. *What Are We Doing This For?*, Ross Halfin. *Run To The Hills, Iron Maiden: The Official Biography*, Mick Wall.

Iron Maiden - Iron Maiden

The first appearance of the now infamous Eddie the 'Ead mascot for one of the most consistently successful British metal acts, it was this debut that set the tone for bassist Steve Harris's occasionally complex arrangements and the clever use of twin guitars, borrowed from Judas Priest and Thin Lizzy. However, it was Iron Maiden's distinct use of concise rhythm changes and clever switches in tempo that set them apart. From the punky 'Prowler', to 'Running Free', with its almost hypnotic hook, *Iron Maiden* contained all the elements that would soon elevate the band to Odeon status and ultimately further still.

● Tracks: *Prowler, Remember Tomorrow; Running Free; Phantom Of The Opera; Transylvania; Strange World; Charlotte The Harlot; Iron Maiden.*

- First released 1980
- UK peak chart position: 4
- USA peak chart position: did not chart

Iron Man, The

With the smash hit, razzle-dazzle production of the **Who**'s *Tommy* doing 101.1% business on Broadway, its creator, **Pete Townshend**, turned his hand to this much smaller project which opened for a three month season at the Young Vic in London on 25 November 1993. Together with the show's director David Thacker, he adapted Poet Laureate Ted Hughes' 1968 book of children's fairytales into a musical production 'which is pitched somewhere between a children's show with a strong ecological message and one of those hippy musicals which surfaced in the late 60s and early 70s'. On a set 'that makes the rubbish dump in *Cats* look like an assembly line in a Japanese car factory', there emerges from time to time a 12 feet-high figure with vast headlamps for eyes, spanners for hands, and huge cans for feet. In between all of that is another load of junk. Actually none of the critics went that far, but, with hardly any exceptions, they did not like the show much. One of the main quibbles was the 'watering down' of certain characters such as the Star Spirit (Josette Bushell-Mingo), who, in Hughes' book, is a giant male dragon, and in this production is 'prettified and turned into a female sex symbol'. As to the plot, for most of the time the huge metal giant, accompanied by the Spirit of the Iron Man (Trevor Michael Georges), eats every piece of metal he can find ('cannabalism', one reviewer called it) and threatens to dominate the earth until a young boy named Hogarth (Anthony Barclay), together with some of his friends, pacifies him by singing 'Let's Have A Ball-Bearing Ball'. Townshend's music was deemed to be a good deal stronger than his lyrics in a score which contained numbers such as 'Over The Top We Go', 'Man Makes Machines', 'Dig!', 'Every Young Kid Has To Train', 'When Eyes Meet In Silence', 'I Eat Heavy Metal', 'I Awake Deep In The Night', 'Fast Food', 'I'm Not Gonna Run Anymore', 'Was There Life Before This Love?', and a typical 60s 'flower-power' plea for love and understanding, 'What We Want Is A Brand New Year'. Not an auspicious event, but, following *Tommy*'s triumph, it may be wise not to bet against Townshend eventually getting it right.

Ironhorse

This US group was founded by Randy Bachman, formerly the leader of the Canadian rock group **Bachman Turner Overdrive**. The initial line-up comprised Bachman (b. 27 September 1943, Winnipeg, Manitoba, Canada; guitar, vocals), John Pierce (bass), Tom Sparks (guitar, vocals) and Mike Baird (drums). They enjoyed a US Top 40 hit in 1979 with 'Sweet Lui-Louise' and by the time the second album was recorded, the line-up had undergone several alterations, with Ron Foos and Chris Leighton replacing Pierce and Baird, respectively. This largely undistin-guished outfit recorded one further album, the title of which neatly summarized the attitude of their critics.

- ALBUMS: *Ironhorse* (Scotti Bros 1979)★★, *Everything Is Grey* (Scotti Bros 1980)★.

Ironing Board Sam

b. Sammie Moore, 1939, Rockfield, South Carolina, USA. Sam learned to play the organ as a youngster, concentrating on boogie-woogie and gospel music before turning to blues while playing in Miami, Florida. He formed his first band in 1959 and acquired his stage name while based in Memphis, when he mounted his keyboard on an ironing board. Initially he loathed the name but turned it to his advantage by giving away ironing boards at his shows! *Blues Unlimited* described Sam as having 'a really great voice and his songs have strong lyrics'. His music has appeared on several labels including Holiday Inn, Atlantic, Styletone and Board, and his live sets feature 'very fine, intense blues and jazz' (*Living Blues*). His onstage antics include playing in a tank of water! He is now based in New Orleans.

- COMPILATIONS: two tracks only *Blues Is Here To Stay* (1973), *The Human Touch* (Orleans 1995)★★★.

Irvine, Andy

This highly-regarded Irish singer-songwriter and guitarist has been involved in a number of highly influential groups. Having followed acting as a career in the late 50s, and learned classical guitar, Irvine then chanced upon the music of **Woody Guthrie**. Turning away from classical to folk guitar, and adding harmonica and mandolin, hurdy-gurdy, bouzouki and mandola, he moved into the Dublin folk scene, after travelling with **Derroll Adams** and **Ramblin' Jack Elliott**. Overseas trips widened his musical sphere and in 1966, he formed **Sweeney's Men** with Johnny Moynihan and **Joe Dolan**. After one album, a trip to the Balkans led him to discover new rhythms and musical styles to add to his acquisitive talent. In 1972, with **Christy Moore**, Donal Lunny and **Liam O'Flynn**, he formed **Planxty**. Drawing on the experiences of his Eastern trip, and adding to his earlier work with Sweeney's Men, Planxty, with Irvine, became one of the most innovative, and influential, groups to emerge from Ireland's folk scene. After the group split in 1975, Irvine teamed up with **Paul Brady**, and toured and recorded, receiving praise from the popular music press, and appearing at the Cambridge Folk Festival in 1977. He also performed and recorded with **De Dannan**. When Planxty re-formed in 1979, Andy divided his time between the group and solo performances, travelling to Australia and New Zealand, in addition to the USA and Europe. *Rainy Sundays...Windy Dreams* saw Irvine accommodate many varied influences from his travels, such as jazz and Eastern European music. When Planxty disbanded in 1983, Irvine formed Mosaic, a group featuring members from Ireland, Denmark, Hungary and Holland. Despite a successful British and European tour, the group split due to rehearsal problems. Irvine, continued to work solo, then formed Patrick Street in 1986 with Kevin Burke (fiddle), Jackie Daly (melodeon) and Gerry O'Beirne. Arty McGlynn (guitar) joined, replacing O'Beirne who was unable to commit himself to the group. Despite the success of Patrick Street, Irvine continues working in a solo capacity and his enthusiasm shows no sign of abating.

● ALBUMS: with Sweeney's Men *Sweeney's Men* (1968)★★★★, with Christy Moore *Prosperous* (1972)★★★, with Planxty *Planxty* (1972)★★★★, with Planxty *The Well Below The Valley* (1973)★★★, with Planxty *Cold Blow And The Rainy Night* (1974)★★★, *Andy Irvine/Paul Brady* (1976)★★★★, with Planxty *After The Break* (1979)★★★, *Rainy Sundays...Windy Dreams* (1980)★★★, with Planxty *The Woman I Loved So Well* (1980)★★★, with Dick Gaughan *Parallel Lines* (1982)★★★, with Planxty *Words And Music* (1983)★★★, *Rude Awakening* (1991)★★★, with Davy Spillane *East Wind* (1992)★★★.

● COMPILATIONS: *The Planxty Collection* (1976)★★★★.

Irvine, Weldon

b. *c.*1944, USA. Publisher Irvine Weldon rose to prominence in the 90s when his extensive catalogue became widely sampled by prominent rap and hip hop artists. **A Tribe Called Quest**, **Boogie Down Productions**, **Leaders Of The New School**, **Ice Cube**, **3rd Bass**, **Too Short** and **Snoop Doggy Dogg** are among those who have featured samples of Irvine's Nodlew Music catalogue in their work. However, music publishing is just one of his musical interests. Irvine was inspired into following a musical career by the rock, soul and jazz sounds that surrounded him in his youth. In the 50s he sang as leader of several big bands, and also worked as **Nina Simone**'s musical director. He also wrote musicals, the most famous of which was *Young, Gifted And Broke*, which won an Audelco Award for Achievement in Black Theater in 1977. He became immersed in hip hop in the 80s when one of his students asked where he saw its place in the continuum of black music. When he investigated rap, he quickly discovered that some of its participants had been borrowing liberally from his own catalogue. However, he was keen to take on a mediating role rather than simply pursue legal action. 'When sampling began, I thought it was viable and that its potential was unlimited in terms of the kinds of music that could be created that way. But I did have a concern about the matter of compensation to the creators and owners of the original works.' The first of his works to be widely sampled was 'Sister Sanctified'. This tune, which he originally wrote for saxophonist **Stanley Turrentine**, eventually turned up, in amended form, in songs by Ice Cube, 3rd Bass and Boogie Down Productions. Other popular samples of Irvine's authorship include the **Fatback Band**'s 'Fatbackin'' (sampled by Leaders Of The New School), Rhythm Combination And Brass's 'Mr. Clean' (sampled by **Casual**) and his own recording of 'We Gettin' Down' (sampled by A Tribe Called Quest on 'Award Tour').

Irvis, Charlie

b. *c.*1899, possibly New York City, New York, USA, d. *c.*1939. After playing in a youth band in which his companions included **Bubber Miley**, trombonist Irvis accompanied blues singer Lucille Hegamin and also worked with **Willie 'The Lion' Smith**. During the early and mid-20s he was with **Duke Ellington** and also appeared on numerous recording dates, often under the leadership of **Clarence Williams**. In the late 20s he played with bands led by **Charlie 'Fess' Johnson** and **Jelly Roll Morton** and in 1931 performed briefly with his old school friend Miley. Although he drifted into obscurity as the decade progressed, Irvis left a number of recordings on which his distinctive muted playing can be heard, notably those made with **Fats Waller**.

● COMPILATIONS: *The Real Fats Waller* (1929)★★★.

Irwin, Big Dee

b. Difosco Ervin, 4 August 1939, New York City, New York, USA, d. 27 August 1995, Las Vegas, Nevada, USA. The corpulent R&B singer first made his mark as lead for the doo-wop group the **Pastels**, who had successes with two sumptuous ballads, 'Been So Long' (1957) and 'So Far Away' (1958). As a solo artist, he is recalled for a series of tongue-in-cheek singles, the most successful of which was a version of the **Bing Crosby** hit 'Swingin' On A Star' in 1963, an irreverent performance on which he was joined by a perky **Little Eva**. Irwin's other releases included 'Everybody's Got A Dance But Me', on which he begrudged the dance-based releases of other artists, and 'Happy Being Fat', where Eva, once again, provided the spiky interjections. Irwin later enjoyed intermittent success as a songwriter, including 'What Kind Of Boy', recorded on the **Hollies**' debut album. He died in 1995 of heart failure.

● COMPILATIONS: *Another Night With Big Dee Irwin* (Westside 1997)★★★.

Isaac, Owen

Isaac began his career demonstrating his dextrous dance steps in bars in Kingston, Jamaica. He saved up the money earned through his dancing in order to pursue a career in music. His first experience in the business was as part of the Seven Seals band, whose line-up also included **Errol Dunkley**. Isaac concurrently began producing other artists and was responsible for the foundation of the Seven I's youth clubs in St. Mary and St. Elizabeth. The clubs exposed young Jamaicans to many opportunities that might otherwise have bypassed them, and the success of the organization led to expansion in London and Kingston. As a producer he had amassed a considerable collection of master tapes from his recording sessions, although the masters were never stamped. The tapes were apparently *en route* to the pressing plant when they mysteriously disappeared, a fate also experienced by the singer **Chris Wayne**. Both artists have suggested that they were the victims of subversive tactics. In Isaac's case, it resulted in the loss of his life savings, although his disillusionment with the music business was tempered by the collective support of friends such as **Dennis Brown** and **Gregory Isaacs**. In 1980 he formed an allegiance with Frankie Davis, founding the Natami Music label and releasing their DJ debut, 'Three Little Birds'. The single proved a hit both in Jamaica and abroad and was swiftly followed by the equally popular 'Girls'. Sounding relatively simple upon first hearing, the song in fact proved to be rather complex, and eventually provided the duo with a commercial success. In 1983 Isaac released the solo 'Heavy Load', which sadly faltered, and he returned to relative anonymity.

Isaacs, Barry

b. 23 August 1955, Portland, Jamaica, West Indies. In 1966 Isaacs joined his parents in the UK where he continued his education. He initially formed a band in the mid-70s known as Ras Isaacs And The Rasses, prior to the emergence of the **Royal Rasses**. The band enjoyed a strong local following in north London and the Midlands where they performed in the roots and culture style. The group disbanded in 1980 and Isaacs concentrated on a solo career, releasing 'Special King Of Love', which featured backing vocals from Trevor Walters. Isaacs' initial success led to the 1980 release of 'Come Turn Me On', followed by a combination with Eli Emmanuel, the inane 'Tickle Me Medley'. In 1985 with other artists he released 'One More Rub A Dub' for Three Kings. In the late 80s Isaacs formed the Reggae On Top label, working with the cream of UK roots performers. He continued to record his own songs, including the popular 90s hits 'Revelation Time' and 'Happiness', but concentrated his efforts on promoting his increasing roster of artists, including UK roots stalwart **Pablo Gad**, I Jah Man's former right-hand man Steven Wright, and the astute Hughie Izachaar. In 1997 Isaacs released his own 'Birthday Song' and embarked on a promotional tour.
● ALBUMS: *Revolutionary Man* (Reggae On Top 1995)★★, *Jah Mek I* (Reggae On Top 1997)★★★.

Isaacs, Bud

b. 26 March 1928, Bedford, Indiana, USA. Isaacs was playing steel guitar professionally at the age of 16 and after playing on some local stations, he relocated to Nashville. He began to play on the *Grand Ole Opry* in 1951 with Eddie Hill, later joining **Little Jimmy Dickens**. In 1953, he was responsible for the addition of foot and knee pedals to a steel guitar. By careful foot-work, he was able to vary the tension on individual strings and change the pitch of a single string so as to alter individual chords. His idea caused a sensation as it had previously been considered impossible to change anything less than an whole chord at one time. The first recording to feature his new invention was when Isaacs played it on **Webb Pierce**'s hit recording of 'Slowly' in 1954. (**Jimmy Day** had played steel on earlier versions by Pierce). His idea revolutionized the sound of steel guitars on country recordings and most of the leading exponents of the instrument soon followed his lead. He was much in demand for session work but he also made solo recordings that year for **RCA Records**, including his lilting 'The Waltz You Saved For Me'. In 1955, he became a member of the *Ozark Jubilee*, appearing on radio and television programmes with the star, **Red Foley**. It has been recorded that Isaacs played on the 11 top country hits of the year in 1955. In 1958, Isaacs, with **Chet Atkins**, Homer Haynes, Jethro Burns (**Homer And Jethro**) and Dale Potter, recording as the Country All-Stars, cut *String Dustin'*, a very up-tempo release. Isaacs married Geri Mapes, a yodeller, singer and bass player and they worked together with an act they called the Golden West Singers. He continued to play on countless recordings and was inducted into the Steel Guitar Hall Of Fame; they eventually retired to Arizona. Isaacs will always be remembered for his dazzling steel guitar playing, especially his catchy 'Bud's Bounce'. His 1955 **RCA/Victor Records** EP, *Crying Steel Guitar*, is now a highly prized collectable.

Isaacs, David

Isaacs' initial rise to prominence came with the 1966 hit, 'I'd Rather Be Lonely'. The song, produced by Ronnie Nasralla, introduced the singer's style to the Jamaican public and it gained a Top 10 placing. He maintained a steady profile through to 1968, when he joined **Lee Perry**, who had embarked on an independent career in production. His initial foray as an independent producer came to fruition with the Untouchables, the Inspirations, and Isaacs. With Perry, Isaacs recorded a version of the **Stevie Wonder** hit, 'Place In The Sun'. The song proved a hit locally and introduced the singer to a global audience. He remained with Perry through to the mid-70s; notable releases included a version of the **Chi-lites'** 'We Are Neighbours Whether We Want To Be Or Not' and the sublime 'Just Enough To Keep Me Hanging On'. His association with Perry culminated when Isaacs released a surprisingly successful version of **Acker Bilk**'s 'Stranger On The Shore'. The release also signalled the end of Perry licensing his Upsetter label (collectors may wish to note the matrix number US400) with **Trojan Records** in the UK. Isaacs continued to maintain notoriety with the hits 'Love And Devotion', 'Just Like A Song' and 'More Love'. By the mid-80s Isaacs joined forces with **Ronnie Davis** and Keith Porter in the **Itals**. Isaacs replaced singer Lloyd Ricketts, who left the line-up owing to personal problems. With the group, Isaacs recorded a series of successful albums, including the Grammy-nominated *Rasta Philosphy* in 1987. Isaacs has remained with the Itals through to the present day, where he currently performs alongside Keith Porter.
● ALBUMS: *Place In The Sun* (Vista 1977)★★★★, *Happy Ending* (Cartridge 1982)★★★.

Isaacs, Gregory

b. 1951, Kingston, Jamaica, West Indies. Reggae super-star Gregory Isaacs has seldom looked back during a three-decade career that has gone from strength to strength, and while many rock stars like to toy with an 'outlaw' image, Isaacs is the real thing - the ultimate rude boy reggae star - who shows no signs of slowing down in the 90s. Like so many other others before him, he began by doing the rounds of Kingston's producers and entering various talent competitions, before recording with **Rupie Edwards**' Success Records in the early 70s. He set up his own African Museum shop and label in 1973 with **Errol Dunkley**, in order to gain artistic and financial control of his own work. He continued to record for many other producers during the rest of the decade to finance his own label, notably **Winston 'Niney' Holness**, **Gussie Clarke**, Lloyd F. Campbell, **Glen Brown**, Alvin 'GG' Ranglin and Phil Pratt. His early recordings were romantic ballads crooned in the inimitable Isaacs style, cool, leisurely, and always sounding vulnerable or pained by his adventures in love. However, these translated effortlessly into social protest or 'reality' songs as the decade progressed and the preoccupations of reggae music shifted towards songs with a more cultural emphasis. By 1980 Gregory was the number one star in the reggae world, touring the UK and the USA extensively, and his live appearances resulted in frenzied crowd scenes, with audiences eating out of the palm of his hand. He had by this time signed with **Virgin Records**' Front Line label and was gaining a considerable name for himself outside of the confines of the traditional reggae music audience and, even though he had recorded many classic sides for outside producers, he still managed to release his best 45s on African Museum (and subsequently Front Line). His pre-eminence during this period was confirmed by the mantle of 'Cool Ruler', chosen for him by critics and fans after the title of the album.

A new contract with **Charisma Records**' Pre label led to the UK release of two further classic albums, though he was never less than prodigious even by Jamaican standards. He was, however, beset by personal and legal problems in the mid-80s and was even jailed in Kingston's notorious General Penitentiary. His release was celebrated with *Out Deh!*. His spell inside left him short of money and he proceeded to record for anyone and everyone who was prepared to pay him. Because of his name, he was inundated with offers of work and the market was soon flooded with Gregory Isaacs releases on any number of different labels. Incredibly, his standards did not drop, and he generally recorded original material that was still head and shoulders above the competition. In the latter half of the decade, virtually every week saw the release of yet more Isaacs material, voiced with current hot producers such as Jammys, Red Man, **Bobby Digital** and **Steely And Clevie**, among others; in so doing, he took on the youth of Jamaica at their own game and won. Rumours abound about Isaacs' rude boy lifestyle - but he would claim he has to be tough to maintain his position within Kingston's notorious musical industry. Certainly the reasons for his lofty seat in the reggae hierarchy are purely musical

- a combination of his boundless talent and his uncompromising attitude. Of all reggae's star performers, Isaacs alone has actually improved over the years. The anticipation of more high-quality releases is not merely wishful thinking, but a justifiable expectation, inspired by his high standards. It is very difficult to see how anyone could take away his crown - his legendary status and reputation in the reggae business are truly second to none.

● ALBUMS: *Gregory Isaacs Meets Ronnie Davis* (Plant 1970)★★★, *In Person* (Trojan 1975)★★★, *All I Have Is Love* (Trojan 1976)★★★, *Extra Classic* (Conflict 1977, Shanachie 1981)★★★, *Mr Isaacs* (Earthquake 1977)★★★, *Slum Dub* (Burning Sounds 1978)★★★★, *Best Of Volumes 1 & 2* not compilations (GG's 1976, 1981)★★★, *Cool Ruler* (Front Line 1978)★★★★, *Soon Forward* (Front Line 1979)★★★★, *Showcase* (Taxi 1980)★★★, *The Lonely Lover* (Pre 1980)★★★, *For Everyone* (Success 1980)★★★, *More Gregory* (Pre 1981)★★★, *Night Nurse* (Mango/Island 1982)★★★, *The Sensational Gregory Isaacs* (Vista 1982)★★★, *Out Deh!* (Mango/Island 1983)★★★★, *Reggae Greats (Live)* (Mango/Island 1984)★★★, *Live At The Academy Brixton* (Rough Trade 1984)★★★, with Dennis Brown *Two Bad Superstars Meet* (Burning Sounds 1984)★★★, *Judge Not* (Greensleeves 1984)★★★, with Jah Mel *Double Explosive* (Andys 1984)★★★, *Private Beach Party* (RAS 1985)★★★, *Easy* (Tad's 1985)★★★, *All I Have Is Love, Love Love* (Tad's 1986)★★★, with Sugar Minott *Double Dose* (Blue Mountain 1987)★★★, *Victim* (C&E 1987)★★★, *Watchman Of The City* (Rohit 1988)★★★, *Sly And Robbie Presents Gregory Isaacs* (RAS 1988)★★★, *Talk Don't Bother Me* (Skengdon 1988)★★★, *Come Along* (Live & Love 1988)★★★, *Encore* (Kingdom 1988)★★★, *Red Rose For Gregory* (Greensleeves 1988)★★★, *I.O.U.* (RAS 1989)★★★, *No Contest* (Music Works 1989)★★★, *Call Me Collect* (RAS 1990)★★★, *Dancing Floor* (Heartbeat 1990)★★★, *Come Again Dub* (ROIR 1991)★★★, *Can't Stay Away* (1992)★★★, *Pardon Me* (1992)★★★, *No Luck* (1993)★★★, *Absent* (Greensleeves 1993)★★★, *Over The Bridge* (Musidisc/I&I Sound 1994)★★★, *Reggae Greats - Live* 1982 recording (1994)★★★, *Midnight Confidential* (Greensleeves 1994)★★★, *Mr Love* (Virgin Front Line 1995)★★★, *Memories* (Musidisc 1995)★★★, *Dem Talk Too Much* (Trojan 1995)★★★.

● COMPILATIONS: *The Early Years* (Trojan 1981)★★★, *Lover's Rock* double album comprising *The Lonely Lover* and *More Gregory* (Pre 1982)★★★, *Crucial Cuts* (Virgin 1983)★★★, *My Number One* (Heartbeat 1990)★★★, *Love Is Overdue* (Network 1991)★★★, *The Cool Ruler Rides Again - 22 Classics From 1978-81* (Music Club 1993)★★★.

Isaacs, Ike

b. 1 December 1919, Rangoon, Burma. Until the end of World War II Isaacs lived in India and Burma, where he occasionally played guitar but mostly worked as a chemist. In the UK in the late 40s he freelanced, playing radio shows and leading his own small groups. Among the musicians with whom he played and sometimes recorded during the 40s and 50s were **Ted Heath**, **Ralph Sharon** and **George Chisholm**. A busy session musician, very active in studio work and playing in all manner of musical styles, Isaacs' first love was for jazz and through the 60s, 70s and 80s he played with leading jazz musicians, including **Barney Kessel**, **Stéphane Grappelli**, **Digby Fairweather** and **Martin Taylor**. A notable player on both acoustic and electric guitars, Isaacs has written extensively on his craft and in the 80s taught music at the Sydney Guitar School in Australia. This artist should not be confused with the similarly named American bass player, Charles Edward 'Ike' Isaacs.

● ALBUMS: *Ike Isaacs* (1966)★★★, *The Latin Guitars Of Ike Isaacs* (1978)★★★★, with Martin Taylor *After Hours* (1979)★★★.

Isaacs, Mark

b. 22 June 1958, London, England. Isaacs's family emigrated to Australia in 1963. He was taught harmony and theory by his jazz musician father and at the age of 12 Mark had written a woodwind suite. During his schooling he was an after-hours student at the Sydney Conservatorium, studying piano and theory with the eminent Peter Sculthorpe. By the age of 18, Isaacs was developing a simultaneous career as a classical and jazz musician. In 1979 his first jazz solo album was released containing original compositions. In the early 80s he went to America to play and continue his studies, where he completed his Master Of Music degree at the Eastman School of Music. His second album, *Preludes*, was recorded in Australia in 1988. Returning to America, Isaacs witnessed his work, *So It Does*, performed at Carnegie Hall by the Australian Ensemble. In New York in 1988, Isaacs, together with jazz veterans **Dave Holland** and **Roy Haynes**, recorded *Encounters*, an impromptu album of jazz originals. The album was a major breakthrough for Isaacs and heralded him as a major talent. He then formed a trio with Adam Armstrong (bass) and Andrew Gander (drums), which toured Europe. This unit captured Isaacs at his peak of creative flair and technical virtuosity and in 1993 they toured Russia playing 24 concerts in 17 cities. Isaacs also performed his own piano concerto with the St. Petersburg State Symphony Orchestra. 'Playing the same piano that Rachmaninov and Shostakovich played was quite an experience', says Isaacs, who completed his Russian tour with five trio concerts in Moscow. In 1995 ABC Music released a four-album set of originals, *Air*, *Earth*, *Fire* and *Water*, collectively entitled *The Elements*. The work featured an introspective Isaacs at the piano and his response to the transcendent and spiritual potential of music. In 1996 he was arranging for the Australian Art Orchestra, working with his trio and contemplating writing an opera. An admirable jazz piano player and composer, Isaacs personifies a fertile and creative period of Australian improvised music. His uncle is the guitarist **Ike Isaacs**.

● ALBUMS: *Originals* (ABC 1979)★★★, *Preludes* (1988)★★★★, *Encounters* (ABC 1988)★★★, *So It Does* (ABC 1989)★★★, *For Sure* (ABC 1993)★★★, *The Elements* (ABC 1995)★★★★.

Isaak, Chris

b. 26 June 1956, Stockton, California, USA. Isaak is a crooner in the **Roy Orbison** mould who had been active on the music scene a long time before he broke through in the late 80s. The son of a forklift truck driver, Isaak spent time participating in an exchange programme at university which led him to study in Japan. He also worked as a tour guide for a film studio and held teenage boxing ambitions, ultimately leading to his distinctive flattened nose. After graduating with a degree in English and Communication Arts, he put together his first band, Silvertone. The rockabilly outfit consisted of James Calvin Wilsey (guitar), Rowland Salley (bass) and Kenney Dale Johnson (drums), who would all remain with Isaak as his permanent backing band. After acquiring a contract with **Warner Brothers Records** in 1985, Isaak and the band moved through three years and two albums with little success, apart from 'Blue Hotel' which was a hit in France. The debut *Silvertone* was raw and diverse, with country blues mingling with conventional folk ballads. The self-titled follow-up saw him hone his style to sophisticated R&B. Throughout he was backed by the excellent moody guitar of Wilsey, whose mimicry of 50s styles is impeccable. After working with David Lynch on the film *Wild At Heart*, he finally had a major hit with 'Wicked Game', while a re-released 'Blue Hotel' made the chart in 1991. In a music scene frequently dominated by synthesized, frantic pop, his simple approach has proved refreshing: 'I just respond to music where the singer and melody are right up in the mix, whereas in most modern stuff the drum is usually the loudest thing'. His acting career has ploughed a parallel path to his singing career with cameo roles in *Married To The Mob* and *Silence Of The Lambs*. His music is strangely out of time - it is too well-recorded to be regarded as a recreation of the **Sun** or **Monument** sound - yet the influences are too apparent to make him wholly contemporary.

● ALBUMS: *Silvertone* (Warners 1985)★★, *Chris Isaak* (Warners 1987)★★★, *Heart Shaped World* reissued as *Wicked Game* (Reprise 1989)★★★, *San Francisco Days* (Reprise 1993)★★★, *Forever Blue* (Reprise 1995)★★, *Baja Sessions* (Reprise 1996)★★.

● VIDEOS: *Wicked Game* (Warner Music Video 1991).

Isham, Mark

b. c.50s, New York City, New York, USA. Born into a musical family that encouraged him to learn the piano, violin and trumpet at an early age, Mark Isham began studying the jazz trumpet while at high school and then explored electronic music while in his early 20s. For a time he pursued parallel careers as a classical, jazz and rock musician, performing, for instance, with the San Francisco Opera, the **Beach Boys** and **Pharoah Sanders**, but by he early 70s, he concentrated his efforts on jazz. As co-leader of pianist **Art Lande**'s Rubisa Patrol, he recorded two albums on **ECM Records** in the late 70s, continuing his partnership with Lande through to the late 80s. Together with guitarist Peter Mannu, Synthesizer player Patrick O'Hearn and drummer Terry Bozzio, he set up the Group 87 ensemble in 1979, releasing a self-titled debut album in 1981. At the same time, Isham continued his links with rock music, recording and touring as part of **Van Morrison**'s band, where his trumpet and flugelhorn set off the saxophone of Pee Wee Ellis to good effect. During the 80s, Isham developed his compositional skills, using a synthesis of brass, electronics and his own plaintive trumpet to produce a very visual, narrative form of music. He recalls that 'my mother once told me that, as a kid, even before I really played music, I tried to tell stories with music. So, whether it's in the vocabulary of heavy metal or Stravinsky, the thread has to do with images.' Isham has taken that thread into film music, scoring the Academy winning documentary *The Life and Times Of Harvey Milk*, the film *Mrs Soffel* (both recorded on *Film Music*), and writing music to accompany children's fairy tales. His feature credits include *Trouble In Mind, Everybody Wins, Reversal Of Fortune, Billy Bathgate, Little Man Tate, Cool World, Of Mice And Men, Sketch Artist, The Public Eye, A River Runs Through It, Nowhere To Run, Fire In The Sky, A Midnight Clear, Made In America, Romeo Is Bleeding, Short Cuts, Quiz Show, The Getaway, The Moderns, The Browning Version, Timecop, Mrs. Parker And The Vicious Circle, Nell, Quiz Show* (1994) and *Gotti* (1996). Throughout his career, Isham has remained a prolific session man, whose work encompasses recordings with artists as varied as saxophonist **David Liebman**, guitarist **David Torn**, and singers **Suzanne Vega, Tanita Tikaram** and **Marianne Faithfull**. Isham is blessed with an instantly memorable trumpet sound, one that is burnished, resonant, in places lush but which can, at times, be bleakly powerful, relying on minimalist fragments to achieve its subdued effect.

● ALBUMS: with Art Lande *Rubisia Patrol* (ECM 1976)★★, with Lande *Desert Marauders* (ECM 1978)★★★, *Group 87* (1981)★★, *Vapour Drawings* (Windham Hill 1983)★★★★, *A Career In Dada Processing* (1984)★★★, with Lande *We Begin* (1987)★★★, *Film Music* (Windham Hill 1987)★★★★, *Fire In The Sky* (1993)★★★, *Blue Sun* (Columbia 1995)★★★, *Afterglow* (Columbia 1998)★★★★.

Ishii, Ken

b. *c.*1970, Tokyo, Japan. Ishii's early infatuation with music arrived via the electonica of **Yellow Magic Orchestra, Kraftwerk** and **DAF**. It was a fixation he would follow until it led him to the work of **Derrick May**. Impressed and inspired, he subsequently immersed himself in what little dance culture and recordings made it over to Japan. His modern tastes include the **Black Dog** and **D-Jax Up Beats** empires, whose experimental edge is reflected in his own works. These began with 'Rising Sun' for Dutch label **ESP**,

before a double-pack **R&S** release, 'Garden On The Palm', and the *Utu* EP for **Richie Hawtin**'s **Plus 8** label. Nominally a daytime office worker, Ishii's wild and bracing material, often reflecting the keyboard undulations of his earliest influences, have made him Japan's first and biggest techno export.

● ALBUMS: *Innerelements* (R&S 1994)★★★, *Jelly Tones* (R&S 1995)★★★★.

Ishola, Haruna

b. 1919, Ibadan, Nigeria, d. 23 July 1983, Ijebu-Igbo, Nigeria. A bandleader and vocalist born into the Muslim Yoruba community, Ishola began recording in 1935, in the apala style that he would refine and to which he would remain faithful throughout his career. Using call and response vocals, together with choirs of talking drums and thumb pianos, the hypnotic, seemingly repetitive (to western ears) apala style is part Muslim religious music, part commentary on current affairs, part praise singing for local religious leaders, businessmen and politicians. By the 50s, Ishola and his Apala Group were leading exponents of the style, a position they retained until Ishola's death. During the 50s, Ishola released hundreds of 78s, and while his style did not change with the advent of the long-playing album, the longer track times the new format permitted meant that he was able to exploit apala's mesmeric power to the utmost. By the early 70s Ishola's prodigious output, and his pre-eminent position in apala, had made him a wealthy man. In 1979, he opened his own 24-track recording studio, Phonodisc, near his home at Ijebu-Igbo outside Ibadan.

● ALBUMS: *Ire Owo Pelu Omo* (Decca West Africa 1974)★★★, *Eyin Ti Nperi Wa* (Decca West Africa 1975)★★★★, *Oluwa Wikan Loba* (Decca West Africa 1979)★★★, *Oluwa Kii Binu* (Decca West Africa 1981)★★★, *Egbe Oredegbe* (Decca West Africa 1982)★★★★, *Gbobi Oloti Le* (Decca West Africa 1983)★★★.

Islam, Yusuf

(see **Cat Stevens**)

Island Records

Chris Blackwell, the son of a wealthy plantation owner and Crosse and Blackwell food family, founded this label in Jamaica in 1961. Its early, low-key singles were imported into Britain where several were subsequently issued by Starlite. Blackwell opened a UK office the following year, instigating the famed 'WI' (West Indian) prefix with Lord Creator's 'Independent Jamaica'. Island's ensuing releases included material by the **Maytals, Jackie Edwards** and the **Skatalites** and over the next four years they encompassed the shift in styles from jump R&B, through **ska**, to **rock steady**. In 1963 Island secured the UK rights to the New York-based Sue label and although the agreement was later rescinded, the appellation was kept as an outlet for material licensed from a variety of sources, including **Vee Jay, Ace** and Kent. Although most of its recordings were distributed independently, Island enjoyed a marketing agreement with Fontana. Thus, their first chart success - **Millie**'s 'My Boy Lollipop' (1964) - bore the latter's label, a feature also prevalent on their first pop signing, the **Spencer Davis Group**. Such diversification was later shown by releases on Island by **Wynder K. Frog**, the V.I.Ps (later **Spooky Tooth**) and **Kim Fowley**, but the company did not undertake a fully fledged switch to rock until 1967 and the formation of **Traffic**, which Blackwell also managed. The group achieved three UK Top 10 hits but, more importantly, also established Island as a force within the nascent album market. Having assigned its West Indian catalogue to **Trojan**, the label now welcomed many of the era's best-loved 'underground' acts, including **Jethro Tull**, **Fairport Convention** and **Free**, and by 1970 was firmly established as one of Britain's leading labels. Judicious production deals with companies including **Chrysalis**, Bronze and EG, brought further success with, among others, **Roxy Music, King Crimson** and **Uriah Heep**, but Island's eminent position was undermined later in the decade when several such enterprises themselves opted for independence. Blackwell developed a reputation for nurturing talent and persevering with his artists. **John Martyn** was with Island for many years, although major success eluded him. **Cat Stevens** by contrast became one of the most successful singer-songwriters of the 70s. By this point the company had exhumed its interest in Jamaican music with the **Wailers**' *Catch A Fire*. Island's relationship with group leader **Bob Marley**, which was maintained until his death, was largely responsible for introducing reggae into the rock mainstream. By the late 70s the company's diverse catalogue included the **Chieftains**, **Inner Circle** and **Eddie And The Hot Rods**, but a flirtation with punk act the **Slits** incurred the wrath of Blackwell, who returned from a recently founded US office to take charge of UK operations. **U2** became the label's most impressive signing of this period, but long-time artists **Robert Palmer** and **Stevie Winwood** also enjoyed considerable success, while Island was also responsible for transforming **Grace Jones** from cult act into international star. The departure of all three individuals was another major blow, but Island nonetheless boasted a roster including **Tom Waits**, the **Christians**, **Julian Cope** and **Anthrax** at the time of its 25th Anniversary celebrations in 1987. However, two years later, Blackwell sold his company to **A&M**, ending Island's tenure as an independent outlet. In the 90s Island continued to maintain its reggae and hip hop reputation although it was the **Cranberries** that became the label's strongest act. In 1996 **Wille Nelson** became the first ever country artist to sign to the label. In 1997 Blackwell walked out of **PolyGram Records** (A&M's new owners) after a protracted dispute with president and ceo Alain Levy. Plans for a new label were announced in 1998.

● COMPILATIONS: *Island Story* (Island 1987)★★★, *Island Life* (Island 1988)★★★.

Islanders

This instrumental duo of Randy Starr (guitar) and Frank Metis (accordion) came from New York, New York, USA. Starr (b. Warren Nadel, 2 July 1930, Bronx, New York, USA) and Metis (b. 8 August 1925, Gruenberg, Germany) met in 1959 when they collaborated on 'The Enchanted Sea', an exotic-sounding instrumental that evoked the romance of the South Pacific. The record went to number 15 on the *Billboard* pop chart in 1959. Metis was a composer/arranger who had previously worked with **George Shearing** and **Dave Brubeck**. Starr had earlier achieved one-hit-wonder status writing and singing the 1957 hit 'After School' (number 32 pop), a teen heart-throb number that vaguely sounded like **Sonny James**'s 'Young Love'. At the same time Starr was carrying on a dental practice, but managed to tour occasionally. In the 60s, collaborating mainly with Fred Wise, he wrote songs for **Elvis Presley** movies, notably 'Kissin' Cousins'.

Islandica

Islandica, their name deriving from the Latin form for 'Icelandic', emerged from that country in the 90s as one of a new wave of traditional/folk bands giving Scandinavia a new critical reputation. As the Reykjavik band's singer and bass player Hardis Hallvarosdottir elucidated, 'Three of us were in a loose grouping before Islandica, but a few years ago we decided to push into a market we'd identified for folk music.' Together the quartet devised a combination of folk rock akin to **Steeleye Span**, traditional melodies and 'quints' - songs where two voices co-exist in parallel, with one holding the melody and the other weaving beneath it. Their debut album was recorded in a Reykjavik church during a thunderstorm and included age-old cultural verses as well as ballads and Nordic drinking songs. Enormously popular, it led to solo albums by three of the quartet which were also major sellers in Iceland. Extensive touring engagements were also undertaken, with sponsorship by Icelandic air lines and the National Tourist Board.

● ALBUMS: *Rammislensk* (1992)★★★★.

Isle Of Wight Festivals

Although many remember the Isle of Wight festivals as the UK's answer to 1969's **Woodstock**, the first low-profile IoW event preceded its USA counterpart by a year. However, it was the publicity explosion resulting from Woodstock (15-17 August), together with the stimulus of a summer of free Hyde Park festivals (most notably by the **Rolling Stones**) that fuelled the success of the 1969 event (31 August - 2 September). The scoop headlining appearance of **Bob Dylan** (at that time a rare live performer) put a match to the fuel, and the small island off England's south coast was invaded by an 200,000-strong army of hippies. Other acts included **Fat Mattress**, the **Who**, **Richie Havens**, the **Moody Blues**, the **Nice**, **Joe Cocker**, and the **Band**. The 1969 IoW was marred by poor organization and primitive sanitation, but that did not stop the event being repeated the following August Bank Holiday. The 1970 line-up consisted of **Jimi Hendrix** (who died three weeks later), **Melanie, Procul Harum, Chicago, Taste, Family, Cactus, Emerson Lake And Palmer,** the **Doors, Joni Mitchell, Ten Years After,** the Who, **Sly And The Family Stone, Donovan, Leonard Cohen,** the Moody Blues, **Joan Baez, Miles Davis, Tiny Tim,** Richie Havens, **Free, Arrival** and **Jethro Tull.** The organizers (the Foulk brothers) were less than pleased as their losses mounted, and declared that there would be no more Isle of Wight festivals. Unlike the Woodstock organizers, they had failed to secure the movie rights to the event, and the footage had, until the 90s, laid in cans as a result of contractual difficulties.

Isley Brothers

Three brothers, O'Kelly (b. 25 December 1937, d. 31 March 1986), Rudolph (b. 1 April 1939) and Ronald Isley (b. 21 May 1941), began singing gospel in their home-town of Cincinnati, USA, in the early 50s, accompanied by their brother Vernon, who died in a car crash around 1957. Moving to New York the following year, the trio issued one-off singles before being signed by the **RCA Records** production team, Hugo And Luigi. The Isleys had already developed a tight vocal unit, with Rudolph and O'Kelly supporting Ronald's strident tenor leads in a call-and-response style taken directly from the church. The self-composed 'Shout' - with a chorus based on an ad-libbed refrain that had won an enthusiastic response in concert - epitomized this approach, building to a frantic crescendo as the brothers screamed out to each other across the simple chord changes. 'Shout' sold heavily in the black market, and has since become an R&B standard, but RCA's attempts to concoct a suitable follow-up were unsuccessful. The group switched labels to Wand in 1962, where they enjoyed a major hit with an equally dynamic cover version of the Top Notes' 'Twist And Shout', an arrangement that was subsequently copied by the **Beatles.** In the fashion of the times, the Isleys were forced to spend the next two years recording increasingly contrived rewrites of this hit, both on Wand and at United Artists. A brief spell with **Atlantic Records** in 1964 produced a classic R&B record, 'Who's That Lady?', but with little success. Tired of the lack of control over their recordings, the Isleys formed their own company, T-Neck Records, in 1964 - an unprecedented step for black performers. The first release on the label, 'Testify', showcased their young lead guitarist, **Jimi Hendrix,** and allowed him free rein to display his virtuosity and range of sonic effects. However, the record's experimental sound went unnoticed at the time, and the Isleys were forced to abandon both T-Neck and Hendrix, and sign a contract with **Motown Records.** They were allowed little involvement in the production of their records and the group were teamed with the **Holland/Dozier/Holland** partnership, who effectively treated them as an extension of the **Four**

Tops, and fashioned songs for them accordingly. This combination reached its zenith with 'This Old Heart Of Mine' in 1966, a major hit in the USA, and a belated chart success in Britain in 1968. UK listeners also reacted favourably to 'Behind A Painted Smile' and 'I Guess I'll Always Love You' when they were reissued at the end of the 60s. Such singles were definitive Motown: a driving beat, an immaculate house band and several impassioned voices; but although the Isleys' records always boasted a tougher edge than those by their stablemates, little of their work for Motown exploited their gospel and R&B heritage to the full.

Tired of the formula and company power games, the Isleys reactivated T-Neck in 1969, along with a change of image from the regulation mohair suits to a freer, funkier 'west coast' image, reflected in their choice of repertoire. At this point too, they became a sextet, adding two younger brothers, Ernie (b. 7 March 1952; guitar) and Marvin (bass), as well as a cousin, Chris Jasper (keyboards). While their mid-60s recordings were enjoying overdue success in Britain, the Isleys were scoring enormous US hits with their new releases, notably 'It's Your Thing' and 'I Turned You On'. These records sported a stripped-down funk sound, inspired by **James Brown** And The JBs, and topped with the brothers' soaring vocal harmonies. They issued a succession of ambitious albums in this vein between 1969 and 1972, among them a live double set that featured extended versions of their recent hits, and *In The Beginning*, a collection of their 1964 recordings with Jimi Hendrix. In the early 70s, the Isleys incorporated into their repertoire a variety of rock material by composers such as **Bob Dylan, Stephen Stills** and **Carole King.** Their dual role as composers and interpreters reached a peak in 1973 on *3+3*, the first album issued via a distribution agreement with **CBS Records.** The record's title reflected the make-up of the group at that time, with the three original vocalists supported by the new generation of the family. Ernie Isley's powerful, sustained guitarwork, strongly influenced by Jimi Hendrix, became a vital ingredient in the Isleys' sound, and was featured heavily on the album's lead single, 'That Lady', a revamped version of their unheralded 1964 single on Atlantic. *3+3* also contained soft soul interpretations of material by **Seals And Croft, James Taylor** and the **Doobie Brothers.** An important key track was the Isleys' own 'Highway Of My Life', which demonstrated Ronald's increasing mastery of the romantic ballad form. Having established a winning formula, the Isleys retained it throughout the rest of the 70s, issuing a succession of slick, impressive soul albums that were divided between startlingly tough funk numbers and subdued Ronald Isley ballads. *The Heat Is On* in 1975 represented the pinnacle of both genres; the angry lyrics of 'Fight The Power', a US Top 10 single, contrasted sharply with the suite of love songs on the album's second side, aptly summarized by the title of one of the tracks, 'Sensuality'. 'Harvest For The World' (1976) proved to be one of the Isleys' most popular recordings in Britain, with its stunning blend of dance rhythm, melody and social awareness (the song hit the charts in 1988 for the **Christians**). In the late 70s, the increasing polarization of the rock and disco markets ensured that while the Isleys continued to impress black record buyers, their work went largely unheard in the white mainstream. 'The Pride', 'Take Me To The Next Phase', 'I Wanna Be With You' and 'Don't Say Goodnight' all topped the specialist black music charts without registering in the US Top 30, and the group responded in kind, concentrating on dance-flavoured material to the exclusion of their ballads. 'It's A Disco Night', a UK hit in 1980, demonstrated their command of the idiom, but a growing sense of self-parody infected the Isleys' music in the early 80s. Conscious of this decline, Ernie and Marvin Isley and Chris Jasper left the group in 1984 to form the success-ful **Isley, Jasper, Isley** combination. The original trio soldiered on, but the sudden death of O'Kelly Isley from a heart attack on 31 March 1986 brought their 30-year partnership to an end. Ronald and Rudolph dedi-cated their next release, *Smooth Sailin'*, to him, and the album produced another black hit in Angela Wimbush's ballad, 'Smooth Sailin' Tonight'. Wimbush now assumed virtual artistic control over the group, and she wrote and produced their 1989 release *Spend The Night*, which was effectively a Ronald Isley solo album. The artistic innovations of the Isley Brothers, continued by the second generation of the family in Isley, Jasper, Isley, belie the conservatism of their releases since the late 70s. Their 1996 release *Mission To Please* attempted to move them into the same smooth urban soul territory as **Keith Sweat** and **Babyface**. The group represented the apogee of gospel-inspired soul on their early hits, they pioneered the ownership of record labels by black artists, and invented a new funk genre with their blend of dance rhythms and rock instrumentation in the early 70s. Their series of US hits from the 50s to the 90s is one of the major legacies of black American music.

● ALBUMS: *Shout* (RCA Victor 1959)★★★, *Twist And Shout* (Wand 1962)★★★★, *The Fabulous Isley Brothers-Twisting And Shouting* (Wand 1964)★★, *Take Some Time Out-The Famous Isley Brothers* (United Artists 1964)★★, *This Old Heart Of Mine* (Tamla 1966)★★, *Soul On The Rocks* (Tamla 1967)★★, *It's Our Thing* (T-Neck 1969)★★★, *Doin' Their Thing* (Tamla 1969)★★★, *The Brothers: Isley* (T-Neck 1969)★★★, with Brooklyn Bridge and Edwin Hawkins *Live At Yankee Stadium* (T-Neck 1969)★★, *Get Into Something* (T-Neck 1970)★★★, *Givin' It Back* (T-Neck 1971)★★★, *Brother Brother Brother* (T-Neck 1972)★★★, *The Isleys Live* (T-Neck 1973)★★★, *3+3* (T-Neck 1973)★★★★, *Live It Up* (T-Neck 1974)★★★, *The Heat Is On* (T-Neck 1975)★★★★, *Harvest For The World* (T-Neck 1976)★★★, *Go For Your Guns* (T-Neck 1977)★★★, *Showdown* (T-Neck 1978)★★★, *Winner Takes All* (T-Neck 1979)★★★, *Go All The Way* (T-Neck 1980)★★★, *Grand Slam* (T-Neck 1981)★★★, *Inside You* (T-Neck 1981)★★★, *The Real Deal* (T-Neck 1982)★★★, *Between The Sheets* (T-Neck 1983)★★★, *Masterpiece*

(Warners 1985)★★★, *Smooth Sailin'* (Warners 1987)★★★, as Isley Brothers Featuring Ronald Isley *Spend The Night* (Warners 1989)★★, *Tracks Of Life* (Warners 1992)★★★, *Live* (Elektra 1993)★★, *Mission To Please* (Island 1996)★★.

● COMPILATIONS: *In The Beginning: With Jimi Hendrix* (T-Neck 1970)★★, *Isleys' Greatest Hits* (T-Neck 1973)★★★★, *Rock Around The Clock* (Camden 1975)★★, *Super Hits* (Motown 1976)★★★, *Forever Gold* (T-Neck 1977)★★★★, *The Best Of The Isley Brothers* (United Artists 1978)★★★, *Timeless* (Epic 1979)★★★, *Let's Go* (Stateside 1986)★★, *Greatest Motown Hits* (Motown 1987)★★★, *The Complete UA Sessions* (EMI 1990)★★★, *The Isley Brothers Story/Volume 1: The Rockin' Years (1959-1968)* (Rhino 1991)★★★, *The Isley Brothers Story/Volume 2: T-Neck Years (1968-1985)* (Rhino 1991)★★★★, *Beautiful Ballads* (Epic Legacy 1995)★★, *Funky Family* (Epic Legacy 1995)★★, *Early Classics* (Spectrum 1996)★★★, *Shout!* (Camden 1998)★★★.

Isley, Jasper, Isley

This trio broke away from the **Isley Brothers** in 1984. Instrumentalists Ernie Isley, Chris Jasper and Marvin Isley had augmented the latter group during its highly successful 70s reign, but their own subsequent career confirmed their deft vocal abilities. The group's early releases were overshadowed by their former achieve-ments, but a soul chart topper, 'Caravan Of Love' (1985), successfully covered in the UK by the **Housemartins**, proclaimed their new identity. Later singles were, however, less popular, and two years later Jasper began recording as a solo act. His 'Superbad' single reached the R&B Top 3 in 1987.

● ALBUMS: *Broadway's Closer To Sunset Boulevard* (Columbia 1985)★★★, *Caravan Of Love* (Columbia 1985)★★★, *Different Drummer* (Columbia 1987)★★★. Solo: Chris Jasper *Superbad* (Epic 1988)★★.

Ismailov, Enver

b. Enver Serverovych Ismailov, Uzbekistan. Although not born in the Crimea due to ethnic dispersion, Ismailov is a Crimean Tartar by blood descent. His childhood among a number of ethnic groups such as Jews, Russians, Turks and Uzbekis helped inform his songwriting before he was able to move his family back to the Crimea. He originally worked as a gas welder in Ferghana, playing his first concerts in the evenings at weddings. He is a self-taught guitarist who was forced to adapt his technique to make the most of cheap imported electric instruments. Fundamental to this style is his own, highly sophisticated but simple-sound-ing method of repeatedly tapping the strings with both his left and right hands. His songs tell traditional tales of the Steppes, of the people and the mixed cultures, aided by inflections borrowed from Western jazz and rock. Something of a showman, he often plays up to three guitars at the same time by employing his feet to tap out rhythms. His delivery, too, is unique, incorpo-rating figurative humour and mime. In the 90s, follow-ing the break-up of the former Soviet Union, he found himself able to tour Europe more freely, though having rediscovered his home village in Crimea he was reluctant to completely abandon it for the demands of international touring.

● ALBUMS: *The Eastern Legend* (RDM 1995)★★★.

Isn't Anything - My Bloody Valentine

Where earlier recordings showed a group struggling to find its niche, *Isn't Anything* established My Bloody Valentine's uncompromising art. Layers of feedback and guitars laid a tapestry of sound into which they sank delicate harmonies. The final effect was not necessarily aggressive, although on '(When You Wake)' and 'Feed Me With Your Kiss' the quartet unveil a remarkable power. Elsewhere, the combination results in a hypnotic wash of sound, punctuated by fevered drumming, heavy bass and hooks that take unexpected twists and turns. *Isn't Anything* is a highly inventive release.

● Tracks: *Soft As Snow (But Warm Inside); Lose My Breath; Cupid Come; (When You Wake) You're Still In A Dream; No More Sorry; All I Need; Feed Me With Your Kiss; Several Girls Galore; You Never Should; Nothing Much To Lose; I Can See It (But I Can't Feel It)*.

● First released 1988

● UK peak chart position: did not chart

● USA peak chart position: did not chart

Isola, Frank

b. 20 February 1925, Detroit, Michigan, USA. When Isola was 11 years old he was taken to see the **Benny Goodman** band with **Gene Krupa** on drums and was inspired to take up drumming. Six years later he won a local heat of a national Gene Krupa Drum Contest but was later disqualified as being already technically a professional. (The eventual national winner was **Louie Bellson** whom he met a few years later when doing basic training following induction into the armed services during World War II.) After the war, Isola studied formally in California, then joined successively the bands of Earle Spencer and Johnny Bothwell. In the late 40s and on into the early 50s he gigged in New York and also sat in on countless informal jam sessions, playing with **Stan Getz**, **Charlie Parker**, **Warne Marsh** and many others. Some of the sessions with Parker were privately recorded and released many years later. In 1952 he joined Getz and for the next five years was a frequent member of his quintet. During this period Isola also played with **Gerry Mulligan**. When **Mose Allison** joined Getz the two hit if off and Isola was hired by the pianist when he recorded *Back Country Suite*. This was in 1957 and proved to be Isola's last recording date. By the time the 60s were over Isola's career as a jazz musician was virtually finished, although he continued to play occasionally in Detroit to where he returned. As Gordon Jack reported in *Jazz Journal International*, for many years Isola lived in a hotel from where he could see the building in which he first took drum lessons, then in 1992 he moved to an apartment from which he could see the Fox Theatre where he had seen Gene Krupa back in 1936. A self-effacing, undemonstrative drummer, Isola always regarded himself as 'just a time-keeper' but, as his recordings with Getz, **Bob Brookmeyer**, Mulligan and others clearly demonstrate, his understated skills were a major contribution to some outstanding jazz sessions.

● ALBUMS: with Charlie Parker *Apartment Sessions* (Spotlite 1950)★★★★, with Stan Getz *At The Shrine Auditorium* (1954)★★★, with Gerry Mulligan *Paris Concert* (Vogue 1954)★★★★, with Mose Allison *Back Country Suite* (Original Jazz Classics 1957)★★★.

Isotonik

UK-based Isotonik is essentially Chris Paul, helped out by DJ Hype and Grooverider, who claims to have remixed everyone from 'Mozart to **Yazz**'. He is also an efficient multi-instrument musician, especially adept at keyboards and saxophone. As well as working widely as a session musician he has DJed at venues like Camden Palace, and ran the Orange Club in North London. His first record came out in 1986 - 'Expansions '86'. However, there was a long gap before his next major success with 'Different Strokes', on **ffrr** in 1992, which sampled the **Ten City** song of the same name. This had been picked up following release on his own label, again titled Orange Records, in 1991. It was succeeded by an eponymous EP the following year.

Isotope

Led by former session guitarist Gary Boyle (b. 24 November 1941, Patna, India), Isotope was a highly-regarded UK jazz-rock band of the 70s. Boyle had previously played with **Brian Auger**, **Keith Tippett**, and **Stomu Yamash'ta** when he formed this progressive jazz/rock fusion band in 1974 with **Jeff Clyne** (b. 29 January 1947, London, England; bass), Brian Miller (b. 28 April 1947, St. Neots, Cambridgeshire, England; keyboards) and Nigel Norris (b. 20 June 1948, Dalston, London, England; drums). They signed to the newly formed Gull label but after a US tour in 1974 Clyne and Miller returned to the orthodox jazz scene. They were replaced for the second album with ex-**Soft Machine** stalwart Hugh Hopper (bass) and Lawrence Scott (keyboards). Vocalist Zoe Kronberger appeared on the final album and guested on *The Dancer* (1977), the first of two solo albums made by Boyle for Gull after Isotope disbanded in 1976.

● ALBUMS: *Isotope* (Gull 1974)★★★★, *Illusion* (Gull 1974)★★★, *Deep End* (1976)★★★.

● COMPILATIONS: *The Best Of Isotope* (1979)★★★★.

Israel Vibration

Comprising Cecil 'Skeleton' Spence, Albert 'Apple' Craig and Lascelles 'Wiss' Bulgrin, this vocal group was formed while the members, all crippled in infancy during the polio epidemic that swept the Jamaica in the 50s, were inmates at Kingston's Mona Rehabilitation Centre. Resident since childhood, they were expelled after they began to grow dreadlocks in accordance with their Rastafarian beliefs. For six years they lived rough, literally singing for their supper. Their attempts to survive on hand-outs from the institution in which they had lived for most of their lives were met with indifference, hostility, and sometimes brutality. Their first release, 'Why Worry' (1976), financed by the Twelve Tribes organization to whom they had become affiliated, and recorded at Treasure Isle Studio, was a big success, as were their live shows supporting **Dennis Brown** and **Bob Marley**. In 1978 they teamed up with **Inner Circle**'s Lewis Brothers, Ian and Roger aka the Fatman Riddim Section, to record their debut, *The Same Song*, for Tommy Cowan's Top Ranking label. It swiftly became hailed as an instant roots classic, as did its dub companion, *Israel Tafari*. *Same Song* and its follow-up, *Unconquered People* (1980), appeared through a licensing agreement with Harvest Records in the UK, as did the 12-inch 'Crisis', which featured a melodica version by **Augustus Pablo**. The group's unique brand of gentle, rural-sounding harmonies and sincere Rasta lyrics has sustained them across a number of albums - mostly released through RAS Records in the USA - over the years, especially in the international market, where they continue to flourish.

● ALBUMS: *The Same Song* (Top Ranking 1978)★★★★, *Same Song Dub* (Top Ranking 1978)★★★, *Israel Tafari* (Top Ranking 1978)★★★★, *Unconquered People* (Israel Vibes/Greensleeves 1980)★★★, *Strength Of My Life* (RAS 1988)★★★, *Praises* (RAS 1990)★★★, *Forever* (RAS 1991)★★★, *Israel Dub* remixed version of *Same Song Dub* (Greensleeves 1992)★★★, *Why You So Craven* (RAS 1992)★★★★, *Free To Move* (Ras 1996)★★★.

● COMPILATIONS: *Best Of* (Sonic Sounds 1988)★★★★.

Israels, Chuck

b. Charles H. Israels, 10 October 1936, New York City, New York, USA. After extensive studies in the USA and France, Israels began playing bass with various leading jazzmen in the mid-50s. He recorded with **Cecil Taylor**, **John Coltrane**, **George Russell** and **Eric Dolphy**. In 1961 he joined the **Bill Evans** trio, taking over from **Scott La Faro**. He remained with Evans for five years, concurrently recording with several other artists including **Herbie Hancock**, **Stan Getz** and **Hampton Hawes**. In the early 70s Israels was instrumental in establishing the **National Jazz Ensemble**, a big band which brought contemporary ideas and techniques to the music of early jazzmen, such as **Jelly Roll Morton** and **Louis Armstrong**, while simultaneously developing for big band the creations of **Thelonious Monk** and other leading bop musicians. After the dissolution of the NJE in 1978 Israels performed less, although he did make occasional record dates in the early 80s.

● ALBUMS: with Bill Evans *How My Heart Sings!* (1962)★★★★, with Evans *The Second Trio* (1962)★★★, *National Jazz Ensemble* (1975-76)★★★.

It Bites

Formed in Egremont, Cumbria, England in 1982, this rock/pop band had all played together in various guises

previously, usually in cover bands. Dunnery spent time with a punk outfit called Waving At Trains, having previously worked as an engineer. The rest of the band's *curriculum vitae* ranged from bricklayer to factory worker. The band's stable line-up has remained: Francis Dunnery (vocals and guitars), John Beck (keyboards), Dick Nolan (bass), Bob Dalton (drums). Their first release was the strictly amateur 'All In Red', but under the wing of **Virgin Records** they hit in 1986 with 'Calling All The Heroes'. Unjustly assumed to be strictly for teenagers, they were continually marketed as such by their record company. They demonstrated considerable talent with 'Whole New World', which surprisingly stalled outside the UK Top 50. It Bites, however, wanted to be a rock band. This fact was born out by some of their influences (**10cc** to **Led Zeppelin** to **Can**) and a tour with **Robert Plant**. Later albums were more blues-based, and included 'green' material such as 'Murder Of The Planet Earth'.

● ALBUMS: *Big Lad In The Windmill* (Virgin 1986)★★, *Once Around The World* (Virgin 1988)★★, *Eat Me In St Louis* (Virgin 1989)★★, *Thank You And Goodnight* (Virgin 1991)★★.

It Happened At The World's Fair

The second 1962 film to star **Elvis Presley**, *It Happened At The World's Fair* had a typically slight plot. Using the contemporaneous Seattle World's Fair as a backdrop, the singer falls in love, despite inevitable mix-ups, to provide a suitable happy last frame. A mere 10 songs were recorded for the accompanying soundtrack, described by one Presley biographer as 'the first in a string of albums that had fans despairing of him ever doing any decent material again'. Indeed, its playing time was barely 20 minutes. The track selected as a single, 'One Broken Heart For Sale', lasted a mere 1 minute 43 seconds, and failed to reach the Top 10 in either the USA or UK.

It Happened In Brooklyn

This pleasant MGM musical was released in 1947, and had a typically post-war story. Isobel Lennart's screenplay told of a shy ex-GI (**Frank Sinatra**) who returns to his beloved Brooklyn in New York, determined to make it to the top as a singer. As in the earlier *Anchors Aweigh*, he meets up with **Kathryn Grayson** (this time playing a music teacher) who, as usual, feels that she is destined for great things in the operatic vocal department. **Jimmy Durante** - the old scene stealer himself - is a kindly school caretaker who makes it his business to boost Sinatra's self confidence (!) in the film's high spot, 'The Song's Gotta Come From The Heart'. In this joyous hymn to sincerity and success, Sinatra spoofs Durante's straight-legged strut, and even manages to work in an excerpt from the traditional Russian folk song 'Orchi Chornya' ('Dark Eyes'). Apart from that piece, and the obligatory classical extracts from Grayson, the rest of the score was provided by **Sammy Cahn** and **Jule Styne**, and contained some lovely ballads for Sinatra such as 'Time After Time', 'It's The Same Old Dream', and 'The Brooklyn Bridge', as well as the livelier 'I Believe' and 'Whose Baby Are You?'. They did not do the singer much good, though, because his best friend, played by Peter Lawford, ended up with Grayson, and, when last seen, Sinatra was on the trail of a nurse (Gloria Grahame) he left behind in the US Army. Also in the cast were Aubrey Mather, Marcy McGuire, Tamara Shayne, Bobby Long and Billy Roy. Jack Donahue staged the dance sequences, and Richard Thorpe directed this unpretentious little film, which became quite a hit.

It Takes A Nation Of Millions To Hold Us Back - Public Enemy

The title says it all. In 1988, when this album was released, Public Enemy's music cut with a wholly revolutionary edge. Rarely has fear, anger, paranoia and anxiety been so masterfully compressed onto a record's grooves. The Bomb Squad's artistry is the keynote to the hard, lean delivery, while Chuck D's supremely pointed lyrics leave no stone of the black experience unturned. It is not comfortable listening, but on tracks such as 'Don't Believe The Hype', 'Night Of The Living Baseheads' and 'Rebel Without A Pause' the listener is left in no doubt that they are facing a fantastically potent force.

● Tracks: *Countdown To Armageddon; Bring The Noise; Don't Believe The Hype; Cold Lampin With Flavor; Terminator X To The Edge Of Panic; Mind Terrorist; Louder Than A Bomb; Caught, Can We Get A Witness?; Show Em Whatcha Got; She Watch Channel Zero?!; Night Of The Living Baseheads; Black Steel In The Hour Of Chaos; Security Of The First World; Rebel Without A Pause; Prophets Of Rage; Party For Your Right To Fight.*

● First released 1988
● UK peak chart position: 8
● USA peak chart position: 42

It's A Beautiful Day

This San Francisco-based unit centred on the virtuoso skills of violinist David LaFlamme, formerly of **Dan Hicks** And His Hot Licks. Patti Santos (b. 16 November 1949, d. 1989; vocals), Hal Wagenet (guitar), Linda LaFlamme (b. 5 April 1941: keyboards), Mitchell Holman (bass) and Val Fluentes (drums) completed the line-up which won a major recording contract in the wake of its appearance on **Cream**'s farewell concert bill. *It's A Beautiful Day* was marked by the inclusion of 'White Bird', the haunting opening track with which the act is inexorably linked. The instrumental 'Bombay Calling' and 'Wasted Union Blues' were other stand-out tracks. Elsewhere, a pot-pourri of musical styles revealed their undoubted versatility, a facet continued on *Marrying Maiden*. However, the appeal of the leader's extravagant soloing quickly paled as numerous departures undermined an early sense of purpose, rendering later releases, *Choice Quality Stuff* and *Live At Carnegie Hall* superfluous. LaFlamme later abandoned

his creation as a protracted lawsuit with former manager Matthew Katz destroyed any lingering enthusiasm. Late period members Bud Cockrell (bass) and David Jenkins (guitar) resurfaced in **Pablo Cruise**, while both LaFlamme and Santos enjoyed low-key solo careers. The violinist briefly resuscitated the band in 1978 under the sarcastic title It Was A Beautiful Day. Santos was killed in a car accident in 1989.

● ALBUMS: *It's A Beautiful Day* (Columbia 1969)★★★, *Marrying Maiden* (Columbia 1970)★★★, *Choice Quality Stuff/Anytime* (Columbia 1971)★★, *It's A Beautiful Day At Carnegie Hall* (Columbia 1972)★★, *It's A Beautiful Day ... Today* (Columbia 1973)★, *1001 Nights* (Columbia 1974)★★.

● COMPILATIONS: *It's A Beautiful Day* (Columbia 1979)★★★.

It's A Bird, It's A Plane, It's Superman

A camp version of the famous comic strip, with a book by David Newman and Robert Benton, this show zoomed into the Alvin Theatre in New York on 29 May 1966, and zoomed out again just four months later. In the stage musical phase of his varied and interesting life - as opposed to the film or printed page - Clark Kent (Bob Holiday), the meek and mild newspaper reporter on the *Daily Planet*, is still prepared to strip off to reveal that famous suit, complete with large letter 'S', at the merest hint of a national emergency. Surely Superman should have suspected foul play when the mad scientist, Dr. Sedgwick (Michael O'Sullivan), invites him to a dedication ceremony in his honour at the physics hall, while he (Sedgwick) sneaks away to blow up the Metropolis city hall? What a stroke of luck that he is in the power station to rescue Lois Lane (Patricia Marand), before streaking into the atmosphere to intercept a missile in mid-air that is destined for the city. Throw in an egotistical columnist, Max Mencken (Jack Cassidy), and an amusing score by **Charles Strouse** (music) and **Lee Adams** (lyrics), and somehow it is difficult to understand why the show did not run for more than 129 performances. One of the songs, 'You've Got Possibilities', received a much attention, and most of the other numbers were enjoyable, including 'It's Superman', 'We Don't Matter At All', 'The Woman For The Man', 'Ooh, Do You Love You!', 'What I've Always Wanted', 'You've Got What I Need', 'Pow! Bam! Zonk!', and 'It's Super Nice'. In the 80s there was the famous series of big blockbuster movies, starring Christopher Reeve, and then, in 1992, the stage show resurfaced in a production by the Godspeed Opera House, Connecticut, USA. The roles of Superman/Clark Kent and Lois were played by Gary Jackson and Kay McClelland, Strouse and Adams contributed several new songs, including 'Thanks To You', 'Karabitz!', and 'It's Up To Me', but the best notices went to 'Flying By Foy', 'the world's largest flying effects company', whose aerial manoeuvring of Superman over the heads of the audience was, by all accounts, sensational.

It's Alive

Formed in Stockholm, Sweden, in 1987, It's Alive are a hard rock sextet comprising Martin White (vocals), Per Aldeheim (guitar), Kim Björkegren (guitar), Peter Kahn (bass), John Rosth (keyboards) and Richard Eversand (drums). Describing their sound as 'rock with funk influences', the group grew up listening to dramatic bands such as **Kiss** and the **Sweet**. That influence was much in evidence on their breakthrough 1993 single, 'Sing This Blues', which, like other releases, arrived in packaging shot by internationally acclaimed photographer Lennart Nilsson. The concurrent debut album, *Earthquake Visions*, on Cheiron Records (later through Music For Nations in the UK), saw them garner further critical support, including nominations for a Swedish Grammy plus Album Of The Year and Best Breakthrough Act in the country's Zeppelin awards. In its wake, they commenced touring engagements with **Kingdom Come**. They remain one of the most genuinely innovative groups working on the Scandinavian hard rock circuit.

● ALBUMS: *Earthquake Visions* (Cheiron/Music For Nations 1993)★★★.

It's All Happening

British singer and all-round entertainer **Tommy Steele** starred in this 1963 feature. In a plot that even in 1963 inspired a sense of *déjà vu*, a talent scout gathers together acts signed to his record label in order to stage a fund-raising concert for a local orphanage. This weak storyline is hampered further by his uninspiring roster, which included anachronistic stalwarts the **George Mitchell** Minstrels, pianist **Russ Conway** and vocalist **Marion Ryan**, mother of pop-singing twins, **Paul And Barry Ryan**. **Shane Fenton And The Fentones**, **Carol Deen** and the Clyde Valley Stompers do nothing to enliven proceedings which are saved, albeit only momentarily, by the presence of **John Barry**. *It's All Happening* was renamed *The Dream Maker* in the US, a title derived from the insouciant song during which Steele is accompanied by a trilling children's chorale. Hopelessly out of date - this was, after all, the year of the **Beatles**' 'She Loves You' and 'I Want To Hold Your Hand' - *It's All Happening* is undoubtedly one of the most inappropriately titled films in cinema history.

It's All Over Town

This 1964 film was a homage to a pre-'Swinging' London that revolved around Lance Percival and Roy Kinnear, two members of the team responsible for UK television's *That Was The Week That Was*. Sadly, the satirical elements of that pivotal weekly revue were not on offer herein and the travelogue merely provided famous landmarks in which to feature a succession of 'family'-orientated acts. 50s heart-throb **Frankie Vaughan**, clarinettist **Acker Bilk** and harmony trio the **Bachelors** were among those on offer. Pulses were raised slightly by the appearance of the **Springfields**, paradoxically about to disband to facilitate **Dusty Springfield**'s solo career. **Wayne Gibson And The Dynamic Sounds** contributed a reading of **Richie Valens**' 'Come On Let's Go', but the film's real highlight came from the **Hollies**, who performed 'Now's The Time' to the backdrop of Covent Garden's fruit market. However, *It's All Over Town* neither captures a moment in time nor retains kitsch value.

It's Always Fair Weather

As the opening titles fade in this entertaining and somewhat satirical musical, released by MGM in 1955, three US soldier buddies, back home in New York after serving together in World War II, have a final drink and sing the poignant 'The Time For Parting' as they pledge to meet again 10 years later. However, when the threesome, played by **Gene Kelly**, **Dan Dailey** and **Michael Kidd**, reunite in their favourite bar after 10 years, things have changed. Dailey is conceited, continually stressed and hates his job in advertising; Kelly has turned into a tough city dweller with one eye on the fight scene and the other looking over his shoulder; and Kidd is the only one who seems reasonably content with his life as the owner of a provincial diner grandly named the Cordon Bleu. High-powered executive (and boxing fan) **Cyd Charisse** deviously manoeuvres them and their 'fascinating' story onto the tacky television show *The Throb Of Manhattan*, which is hosted by the gorgeously over-the-top **Dolores Gray**. When Kelly is threatened by some unsavoury colleagues in the fight racket and Dailey and Kidd jump in to defend him with all fists blazing, the years roll back and it is just like old times for the three pals again. Originally conceived by screenwriters **Betty Comden** and **Adolph Green** as a sequel to *On The Town* (1949), *It's Always Fair Weather* turned out to be quite different from that project, with a marked cynical edge, especially in regard to the burgeoning US television industry. The basic creative team remained the same, however, with **Arthur Freed** producing and Gene Kelly and **Stanley Donen** sharing the director-choreographer credit. The score, by composer **André Previn** and Comden and Green (lyrics), had some marvellous moments, such as 'Situation-Wise', Dailey's exposé of the advertising industry; Kelly's escape from a gang of hoodlums via a song, dance and a pair of roller skates in 'I Like Myself'; Gray's magnificently syrupy and effusive 'Thanks A Lot But No Thanks'; and Charisse boxing clever in 'Baby You Knock Me Out'. The three male stars come together for a split screen rendition of 'Once Upon A Time' (the Cinemascope effect is generally destroyed when shown on television), and for an exhilarating dance routine through the streets, at one point using dustbin lids as improvised tap shoes. The other numbers included 'March, March' (Kelly-Dailey-Kidd), 'Stillman's Gym' (Charisse and boxers), and 'Music Is Better Than Words' (lyric: Comden-Green-**Roger Edens**; ensemble). Also featured were Jay C. Flippen, David Burns, Hal March and Lou Lubin.

It's Everly Time! - The Everly Brothers

It's Everly Time! was the duo's first album under their million-dollar contract with Warner Brothers, the first in pop's history. Having repaid some of the company's faith with the riveting 'Cathy's Clown', the brothers continued to show an adventurous approach with this selection. Of the 12 songs, six were written by long-time associates Felice and Boudleaux Bryant, including the poignant 'Some Sweet Day'. The highlight, however, is Don Everly's 'So Sad', a haunting ballad tailor-made for the pair's woven harmonies that captures all that was special in their work. Released at a time when pop albums were largely an adjunct to hit singles, the consistency offered on *It's Everly Time!* helped establish the 12-inch long-player as an entity in its own right.
● Tracks: *So Sad (To Watch Good Love Go Bad); Just In Case; Memories Are Made Of This; That's What You Do To Me; Sleepless Nights; What Kind Of Girl Are You; Oh, True Love; Carol Jane; Some Sweet Day; Nashville Blues; You Thrill Me (Through And Through); I Want You To Know.*
● First released 1960
● UK peak chart position: 2
● USA peak chart position: 9

It's Great To Be Young

Although rock 'n' roll was gathering pace throughout the world in 1956, this engaging British musical, which was released by AB-Pathé-Marble Arch, showed no sign of any such influence. Set in a co-educational school, it concerns the charismatic Mr Dingle (John Mills), a teacher whose interest in the school orchestra leads to a clash with the newly appointed (and very square) headmaster Mr Frome (Cecil Parker). Dingle is eventually dismissed, and his infuriated pupils stage a massive sit-in in order to get him reinstated. All ends happily when the combatants realize that a bit of give and take is all that is needed to live and learn in harmony together. The most memorable song remains the pretty ballad, 'You Are My First Love' (**Paddy Roberts**-Lester Powell), which is sung over the opening titles by **Ruby Murray**, and reprised during the sit-in by Paulette (Dorothy Bromiley, dubbed by Edna Savage). She aims it straight at Nicky (Jeremy Spenser), the young man to whom she has decided to give her adolescent heart. Other songs include 'Rhythm Is Our Business' (**Sammy Cahn**-Saul Chaplin-**Jimmy Lunceford**), performed engagingly by a group of pupils, singing and dancing on the sidewalk (dubbed by the Coronets). John Mills was perfectly cast in the role of the trumpet-playing music master who 'moonlights' on the piano in the local pub. Jazzman **Humphrey Lyttelton** helped out on the trumpet, and it was pianist **Winifred Atwell**'s excellent version of 'The Original Dixieland One-Step' that was heard on the soundtrack. The film's musical director, **Ray Martin**, contributed the title song, the rousing 'Marching Strings', and the film's background score. In fact he also co-wrote the big ballad, 'You Are My First Love', because 'Lester Powell' was just one of his several aliases. *It's Great To Be Young* was directed by Cyril Frankel, produced by Victor Skutezky and had a screenplay by Ted Willis. Among the cast of this immensely enjoyable, unpretentious (and rare) British musical were Eleanor Summerfield, John Salew, Bryan Forbes, Brian Smith, Carole Shelley, Derek Blomfield, and a 13-year-old Richard O'Sullivan.

It's Great When You're Straight, Yeah! - Black Grape

Few could have been expecting great things from ex-Happy Monday Shaun Ryder, last seen drug-addled and artistically barren when that group fizzled out unceremoniously. However, his return was glorious - harnessing the remixing talents of Danny Saber and the croaky rapping of Kermit, *It's Great...* offered an instant high for party people. Ryder's slurred rantings and nonsense lyrics seemed more at home than ever: 'A Big Day In The North' most clearly recalled the Mondays sound, but the mighty 'Reverend Black Grape', 'Kelly's Heroes' and the irresistible invitation to 'Shake Your Money' defined the in-yer-face Black Grape sound.
● Tracks: *Reverend Black Grape; In The Name Of The Father; Tramazi Parti; Kelly's Heroes; Yeah Yeah Brother; A Big Day In The North; Shake Well Before Opening; Submarine; Shake Your Money; Little Bob.*
● First released 1995
● UK peak position: 1
● USA peak position: did not chart

It's Immaterial

This pop duo, based in Liverpool, England, enjoyed an unlikely UK chart hit with 1986's 'Driving Away From Home (Jim's Tune)', and an album with the enduring catchphrase title of *Life's Hard And Then You Die*. Following 'Eds Funky Diner' and the impeccably strange 'Space (He Called From The Kitchen)', they disappeared from view for some time, before principal duo John Campbell and Jarvis Whitehead re-emerged with a second album for Siren Records in 1990. As before, the music was of a subdued, understated nature, with wry wit in the manner of an indie **Pet Shop Boys**. Other members of the band have, at various times, included members of the **Christians** (Henry Priestman), plus Paul Barlow (drums), Julian Scott (bass), Mick Dempsey (percussion), Brenda Airturo (percussion), Brenda Kenny (percussion) and Gillian Miller (backing vocals).
● ALBUMS: *Life's Hard And Then You Die* (Siren/Virgin 1986)★★★, *Song* (Siren/Virgin 1990)★★.

It's In The Air

Another **George Formby** vehicle - and this time the vehicle is a motorcycle that George (wearing a friend's RAF uniform) borrows in order to post a letter. Mistaken for a dispatch rider, he is forced to drive around the Commanding Officer (Garry Marsh) of the RAF station, and eventually has to take an experimental aeroplane into the air and demonstrate it to a Government official, Sir Philip Bargrave (C. Denier

Warren). The slapstick fun is fast and furious, with George getting involved in many complicated adventures, one of which concerns certain nocturnal experiences in an NCO's bedroom. Throughout it all, he wears that endearing toothy grin and ingenuous expression, and pauses occasionally to pull out his ukulele and slip in the odd song, such as 'They Can't Fool Me', 'It's In The Air', and 'Our Sergeant Major' (George Formby-Fred E. Cliffe-Harry Gifford). Polly Ward was his long-suffering fiancée, and among the other familiar names were Julien Mitchell, Jack Hobbs, Jack Melford, Hal Gordon, Frank Leighton, Michael Shepley, Ilena Sylva, and O.B. Clarence. Anthony Kimmins wrote the story and directed, and Basil Dean produced the film for Associated Talking Pictures in Britain in 1938.

It's Love Again

Having captivated London theatre audiences with her enchanting dancing and singing during the 20s, in the next decade **Jessie Matthews** established herself as one of Britain's brightest film stars. In this picture, which was released by Gaumont in 1936, she plays Elaine Bradford, an ambitious but frustrated young performer who impersonates the alluring and mysterious Mrs. Smythe-Smythe, a dashing pilot, big-game hunter and friend of maharajahs, whose exciting exploits are constantly being revealed in the *Daily Record*. Unbeknown to her, Mrs. Smythe-Smythe does not in fact exist, and has been dreamed up by gossip columnist Peter Carlton (Robert Young) in an effort to boost the paper's circulation. Even when he acquaints her with the facts, Elaine still perpetuates the masquerade, and, after performing the sensational 'Temple Dance Of The East' at a party, she is engaged by impresario Archibald Raymond (Ernest Milton) for his new revue. Threatened with exposure by one of Peter's rival columnists (Cyril Raymond), she resigns, but is re-hired as Elaine Bradford, a name she changes soon enough to Mrs. Peter Carlton. Jessie Matthews' real-life husband. **Sonnie Hale**, led a supporting cast that also included lugubrious comedian Robb Wilton, Sara Allgood, Warren Jenkins, Glennis Lorimer, and Athene Seyler. Marion Dix and Lesser Samuels wrote the screenplay, and American songwriters Sam Coslow and **Harry Woods** came up with some snappy numbers, including 'Gotta Dance My Way To Heaven', 'I Nearly Let Love Go Slipping Through My Fingers', 'Tony's In Town', and 'It's Love Again'. The attractive musical score was written by Louis Levy and Bretton Byrd, and the dances were arranged by Buddy Bradley. This popular feature was directed by Victor Saville and produced by Michael Balcon.

It's Magic

(see *Romance On The High Seas*)

It's My Life - Talk Talk

An early band of New Romantics, they spent some time trying to shake off the image. Vocalist Mark Hollis has a problem in as much that his voice is very much of the New Romantic era, the pristine, pitch-perfect singing style similar to Tony Hadley (Spandau Ballet) and Martin Fry -. Hollis's distinctive voice made some good pop songs sound great. The title track, for example, has every synth gimmick under the sun but cannot fail in its infectious spirit. Some splendid old-timers are added to the proceedings; jazz trumpeter Henry Lowther wails beautifully and guitarist Robbie McIntosh excels. Splendid, unchallenging stuff.

● Tracks: *Dum Dum Girl; Such A Shame; Renée; It's My Life; Tomorrow Started; The Last Time; Call In The Night Boy; Does Caroline Know?; It's You.*
● First released 1984
● UK peak chart position: 35
● USA peak chart position: 42

It's My Life, Baby! - Junior Wells

It was Junior Wells' bad luck to be the second-best harmonica player in Chicago; the only thing that he shared in full measure with Little Walter was a volatile temper. In the late 50s, he made a series of pop-oriented singles for Mel London's Chief and Profile labels, finding success with 'Little By Little' and 'Messin' With The Kid'. During the early 60s, he formed a loose partnership with Buddy Guy and *It's My Life, Baby!* was their third album collaboration in two years. Four songs, including the title track, were recorded live at Chicago's Pepper's Lounge; the remainder was comprised of studio cuts that indulged Wells' growing penchant for soul-based performances, a tendency marring many of his later records. He is caught here on the cusp.

● Tracks: *It's My Life Baby; Country Girl; Stormy Monday Blues; Checking On My Baby; I Got A Stomach Ache; Slow, Slow; It's So Sad To Be Lonely; You Lied To Me; Shake It Baby; Early In The Morning; Look How Baby; Everything's Going To Be Alright.*
● First released 1964
● UK peak chart position: did not chart
● USA peak chart position: did not chart

It's Too Late To Stop Now - Van Morrison

Having completed a sequence of peerless studio albums, Van Morrison embarked on an expansive tour with this searing live set. Drawing sterling support from the Caledonia Soul Orchestra, the singer performs some of his most popular songs, acknowledges influences and even pays homage to his hit group, Them, with a medley of their two most successful singles. Not content with simply recreating material, Morrison uses his instinctive gifts to change inflections and bring new emphases, reshaping each piece according to the moment's mood, rather than relying on previously recorded versions. His sense of timing on tracks such as the penultimate 'Caravan', is amazing; just to snap your finger and know the band can follow must be a great feeling.

● Tracks: *Ain't Nothing You Can Do; Warm Love; Into The Mystic; These Dreams Of You; I Believe To My Soul; I've Been Working; Help Me; Wild Children; Domino; I Just Wanna Make Love To You; Bring It On Home; Saint Dominic's Preview; Take Your Hand Out Of My Pocket; Listen To The Lion; Here Comes The Night; Gloria; Caravan; Cypress Avenue.*
● First released 1974
● UK peak chart position: did not chart
● USA peak chart position: 53

It's Trad Dad

Clearly taking its cue from US films inspired by the **Twist** craze (*Twist Around The Clock, Hey, Let's Twist*), this 1962 feature drew upon the 'trad jazz' boom then gripping British pop. Its title came from a popular television show and, forsaking any notion of plot, *It's Trad Dad* (called *Ring A Ding Rhythm* in the USA) presented a succession of acts playing their current bestsellers. Although directed by Richard Lester, later to find fame for his work with the **Beatles**, the film is curiously reserved, lacking the spontaneity of its television counterpart. The cast included **Kenny Ball, Acker Bilk, Terry Lightfoot** and **Chris Barber**, each of whom was firmly in the New Orlean's revivalist camp, as well as the memorably eccentric **Temperance 7**. British pop acts featured included **Helen Shapiro** and **Craig Douglas**, but performances by US imports **Gene Vincent, Gary U.S. Bonds** and **Del Shannon** showed how staid their UK counterparts were. **John Leyton**, a protégé of iconoclast producer **Joe Meek**, was the sole British act offering something unique, largely through his mentor's bizarre fix on science-fiction pop. Meek, however, was an exception; a better measure of UK pop was emerging from Liverpool *It's Trad Dad* crossed the country.

It's Your Thing

Popularizers of the seminal 'Twist And Shout', the **Isley Brothers** subsequently spent a frustrating period signed to Tamla/**Motown** before leaving the label to found their own outlet, T-Neck. Their first release on the label, 'It's Your Thing', topped the US R&B charts and reached number 2 in the corresponding pop listing. Energized by this new-found success, the group produced this 1969 feature film the following year which features moments from a soul music concert held in New York's Yankee Stadium. **Ike And Tina Turner**, themselves enjoying an artistic rebirth at the time, contributed powerful versions of 'Proud Mary', 'Honky Tonk Woman' and '(I Want To Take You) Higher'. The **Edwin Hawkins Singers** perform a memorable rendition of their international hit, 'Oh Happy Day', while the **Five Stairsteps, Brooklyn Bridge** and **Patti Austin** display contrasting contemporary soul styles. The Isley Brothers close the event with an exhilarating performance. Buoyed by artistic freedom, their melange of gospel, pop, R&B and **Jimi Hendrix**-styled guitarwork, provides a suitably exciting finale to a film capturing a musical genre as it moved out of the shadows of Tamla/Motown and **Stax** to fully engage with rock.

Itals

The Itals were a vocal group that formed in 1976 and comprised Keith Porter, **Ronnie Davis** and Lloyd Ricketts. Porter began his career in 1967 at **Studio One** as part of the Westmorelites, who recorded 'Miss Hitie Titie'. Before joining the Itals, Porter also sang lead vocals for the Future Generation and the Soul Hermit. Davis and Ricketts had performed as part of the **rocksteady** group the Tennors and recorded with **Duke Reid** at Treasure Isle and **Coxsone Dodd** at Studio One. The trio enjoyed a number of hits, including 'Hopeful Village', 'Weather Report', 'Ride Your Donkey' and the powerful 'Pressure And Slide'. Davis pursued a successful solo career, enjoying hits such as 'Stop Yu Loafing', and a showcase album with **Gregory Isaacs**. Comparable to the **Mighty Diamonds** and **Tamlins**, the Itals were inspired by the late 60s/early 70s American R&B groups, although their themes were Rastafarian-orientated. Their debut was the popular 'In Dis A Time'. By 1977 the group established a distinguished reputation with the release of 'You Don't Care' and 'Brutal'; the US Nighthawk label signed the trio and the group enjoyed unprecedented success in America. 'Herbs Pirate' featured on a specially commissioned compilation, *Calling Rastafari*, and sessions and studio time were secured with **Harry J.** Through the Itals the record company recruited the Mighty Diamonds, the **Gladiators**, **Culture** and the **Wailing Souls** for a historic recording session, which is still widely available. Throughout the 80s and 90s the Itals maintained a high profile with a number of hits, including the Rastafarian-influenced 'Truth Must Reveal', 'Jah Glory' and 'Run Baldhead Run'.
● ALBUMS: *Brutal Out Deh* (Nighthawk 1978)★★★★, *Give Me Power* (Nighthawk 1980)★★★, *Easy To Catch* (Rhythm Safari 1985)★★★, *Cool And Dread* (Nighthawk 1989)★★, *Rasta Philosophy* (Nighthawk 1992)★★.
● COMPILATIONS: *The Early Recordings* (Nighthawk 1995)★★★★.

It's A Shame About Ray - Lemonheads

The band's leader Evan Dando received an immense amount of media coverage between this and their next album, *Come On Feel The Lemonheads*. The press saw another self-destructive rock 'n' roller in the making and hounded him about his drug habit. This album, however, is a delight and has the same feel as a Big Star record, or the rolling melody of the early Byrds, but much more sloppy and loose. Dando is a fine songwriter and the first 12 songs on this record feel like one great track. The unlucky 13th track is Paul Simon's 'Mrs Robinson', which you will either love or hate.
● Tracks: *Rockin Stroll; Confetti; It's A Shame About Ray; Rudderless; Buddy; The Turnpike Down; Bit Part; Alison's Starting To Happen; Hannah & Gabi; Kitchen; Ceiling Fan In My Spoon; Frank Mills; Mrs Robinson.*

- First released 1992
- UK peak chart position: 33
- USA peak chart position: 68

Ivanay

b. Rosalin Thompson, February 1972, St. Thomas, Jamaica, West Indies. Thompson was the youngest of 13 siblings, all reared in a Christian environment, and her initial vocal training was in the local church and school choirs. In 1994 she began singing professionally through Howlers International Music, performing as Rosie T. Although her initial recordings were all cover versions, they proved moderately successful, and she was invited to appear at the 1995 Reggae Sumfest in Montego Bay, where she gave a triumphant performance on the International Night alongside the likes of **Buju Banton**, Everton Blender and **Freddie McGregor**. This gained her a following, and prompted invitations to perform with other renowned artists. She recorded 'Empower Me' as Ivanay, a song co-written with Tony Rochester, combining a steadfast rhythm with masterful lyricism. Her name change emphasized her individuality, and she recorded self-compositions alongside the earlier cover versions for the long-awaited debut album, which demonstrated both her vocal and writing skills. The set featured guest vocals from Angie Angel on a ragga remix of 'Empower Me', Louie Culture on the **dancehall** mover 'Make Love To You', and a version of a **Peter Tosh** hit, retitled 'God Is My Keeper'.
- ALBUMS: *Empower Me* (Howlers 1997)★★★.

Ivers, Eileen

b. *c*.1964, USA. This Irish-American fiddler has been playing since she was eight, and by the 90s, her mastery of it was beginning to create interest throughout the roots and folk community. Playing rock, blues, jazz, classical and bluegrass, Ivers featured chiefly in two all-female groups, Cherish The Ladies and Chanting House. She has also been a guest on live performances and sessions by **Luka Bloom**, **Sharon Shannon** and **Hothouse Flowers**. Her solo work has largely been played with the African drummer Kimati Dinizulu and the guitarist John Doyle. Her debut additionally featured Cape Breton musicians Dave MacIsaac (guitar) and Natalie McMaster (fiddle), plus New York flautist Joanie Madden and several other renowned guests. Further jigs and reels appeared on her second album, buoyed with her success performing with *Riverdance*. Notable tracks on *Wild Blue* are a Latin reel, 'On Horseback', and the heavier 'Blue Grooves'. Ivers is highly talented and, even with the limitation of the violin's sound, refreshingly original.
- ALBUMS: *Eileen Ivers* (Green Linnet 1994)★★★, *Wild Blue* (Green Linnet 1996)★★★.
- COMPILATIONS: *So Far* (Green Linnet 1997)★★★.

Ives, Burl

b. Burl Icle Ivanhoe Ives, 14 June 1909, Hunt Township, Jasper County, Illinois, USA, d. 14 April 1995, Anacortes, Washington, USA. One of the world's most celebrated singers of folk ballads, with a gentle, intimate style, Ives was also an actor on the stage and screen, and an anthologist and editor of folk music. The son of tenant farmers in the 'Bible Belt' of Illinois, he was singing in public for money with his brothers and sisters when he was four years old. Many of the songs they sang originated in the British Isles, and were taught to them by their tobacco-chewing grandmother. After graduating from high school in 1927 Ives went to college with the aim of becoming a professional football coach. Instead, he left college early, in 1930, and hitchhiked throughout the USA, Canada and Mexico, supporting himself by doing odd jobs and singing to his own banjo accompaniment, picking up songs everywhere he went. After staying for a time in Terre Haute, Indiana, attending the State Teachers College, he moved to New York and studied with vocal coach Ekka Toedt, before enrolling for formal music training at New York University. Despite this classical education, he was determined to devote himself to folk songs. In 1938 he played character roles in several plays, and had a non-singing role on Broadway in the **Richard Rodgers** and **Lorenz Hart** musical *The Boys From Syracuse*, followed by a four-month singing engagement at New York's Village Vanguard nightclub. He then toured with another Rodgers and Hart show, *I Married An Angel*. In 1940 Ives performed on radio, singing his folk ballads to his own guitar accompaniment on programmes such as *Back Where I Come From*, and was soon given his own series entitled *Wayfaring Stranger*. The introductory 'Poor Wayfaring Stranger', one of America's favourite folk songs, and by then already over 100 years old, became his long-time theme. Drafted into the US Army in 1942, Ives sang in **Irving Berlin**'s military musical revue *This Is The Army*, both on Broadway and on tour. In 1944, after medical discharge from the forces, Ives played a long stint at New York's Cafe Society Uptown nightclub, and also appeared on Broadway with **Alfred Drake** in *Sing Out Sweet Land*, a 'Salute To American Folk And Popular Music'. For his performance, Ives received the Donaldson Award as Best Supporting Actor. During the following year, he made a concert appearance at New York's Town Hall, and played a return engagement in 1946. Also in that year he made his first film, *Smoky*, with Fred McMurray and Anne Baxter, and appeared with **Josh White** in a full-length feature about folk music. Ives' other movies, in which he played characters ranging from villainous to warmly sympathetic, included *So Dear To My Heart* (1948), *East Of Eden* (1955) and *Cat On A Hot Tin Roof* (1958), in which he played Big Daddy, recreating his highly acclaimed Broadway performance in the Tennessee Williams play; he also appeared in *Wind Across The Everglades* (1958), *Desire Under The Elms* (1958) and *The Big Country* (1958), for which he received an Oscar as the Best Supporting Actor; and *Our Man In Havana* (1960). In 1954 Ives appeared as Cap'n Andy Hawkes in a revival of **Jerome Kern** and **Oscar Hammerstein II**'s *Show Boat* at the New York City Center. In the 60s and 70s he appeared regularly on US television, sometimes in his dramatic series, such as *OK Crackerby* and *The Bold Ones*, and several musical specials. In the 80s, he continued to contribute character roles to feature films and television, and performed in concerts around the world. Back in 1948, his first chart record, 'Blue Tail Fly', teamed him with the **Andrews Sisters**. The song, written by Dan Emmett in 1846, had been in the Ives repertoire for some years. Other US Top 30 hits through to the early 60s included 'Lavender Blue (Dilly Dilly)', 'Riders In The Sky (Cowboy Legend)', 'On Top Of Old Smokey', 'The Wild Side Of Life', 'True Love Goes On And On', 'A Little Bitty Tear', 'Funny Way Of Laughin'' and 'Call Me Mr In-Between'. Many other songs became associated with him, such as 'Foggy Foggy Dew', 'Woolie Boogie Bee', 'Turtle Dove', 'Ten Thousand Miles', 'Big Rock Candy Mountain', 'I Know An Old Lady (Who Swallowed A Fly)', 'Aunt Rhody' and 'Ballad Of Davy Crockett'. Ives published several collections of folk ballads and tales, including *America's Musical Heritage - Song Of America*, *Burl Ives Song Book*, *Tales Of America*, *Burl Ives Book Of Irish Songs*, and for children, *Sailing On A Very Fine Day*. In 1993, in the distinguished company of **Tom Paxton**, **Pete Seeger**, **Theodore Bikel**, the **Chad Mitchell Trio**, **Oscar Brand** and Paul Robeson Jnr., Burl Ives performed in an emotional and nostalgic concert at the 92nd Street 'Y' Theatre in New York. Ives died in April 1995.

● ALBUMS: *The Wayfaring Stranger* 10-inch album (Stinson 1949)★★★, *Ballads And Folk Songs Volume 1* 10-inch album (Decca 1949)★★★, *Ballads And Folk Songs Volume 2* 10-inch album (Decca 1949)★★★★, *The Return Of The Wayfaring Stranger* 10-inch album (Columbia 1949)★★★★, *Ballads, Folk And Country Songs* 10-inch album (Decca 1949)★★★★, *More Folksongs* 10-inch album (Columbia 1950)★★★, *Christmas Day In The Morning* 10-inch album (Decca 1952)★★★, *Folk Songs Dramatic And Dangerous* 10-inch album (Decca 1953)★★★★, *Women: Folk Songs About The Fair* 10-inch album (Decca 1954)★★★, *Children's Favorites* 10-inch album (Columbia 1954)★★★, *Coronation Concert* (Decca 1956)★★★, *The Wild Side Of Life* (Decca 1956)★★★, *Men* (Decca 1956)★★★, *Down To The Sea In Ships* (Decca 1956)★★★★, *Women* (Decca 1956)★★, *In The Quiet Of Night* (Decca 1956)★★★, *Burl Ives Sings For Fun* (Decca 1956)★★, *Burl Ives Sings Songs For All Ages* (Columbia 1957)★★, *Christmas Eve With Ives* (Decca 1957)★★, *Songs Of Ireland* (Decca 1958)★★★, *Old Time Varieties* (Decca 1958)★★★, *Captain Burl Ives' Ark* (Decca 1958)★★★, *Australian Folk Songs* (Decca 1958)★★★, *Cheers* (Decca 1959)★★★, *Little White Duck* (Fontana 1960)★★, *Burl Ives Sings Irving Berlin* (1961)★★, *The Versatile Burl Ives!* (Decca 1962)★★, *It's Just My Funny Way Of Laughin'* (Decca 1962)★★★, *Songs Of The West* (Brunswick 1962)★★★, *Sunshine In My Soul* (Brunswick 1963)★★★, *Singin' Easy* (Brunswick 1963)★★★, *Walt Disney Presents Burl Ives - Animal Folk* (1964)★★, *Pearly Shells* (Decca 1964)★★★, *Rudolph The Red Nosed Reindeer* (Decca 1966)★, *Something*

Special (Brunswick 1966)★★★, *Times They Are A-Changin'* (Columbia 1968)★★, *Animal Folk* (Castle Music 1974)★, *Chim Chim Cheree* (Castle Music 1974)★, with the Korean Children Choir *Faith And Joy* (Sacred/Word 1974)★, *How Great Thou Art* (Word 1974)★★, *Songs I Sang In Sunday School* (Sacred/Word 1974)★★, *I Do Believe* (Word 1974)★★★, *Shall We Gather At The River* (Sacred/Word 1978)★★★, *Talented Man* (Bulldog 1978)★★★, *Live In Europe* (Polydor 1979)★★★, *Bright And Beautiful* (Word 1979)★★, *Christmas At The White House* (Caedmon 1979)★★, *Stepping In The Light* (Word 1984)★★★, *Love And Joy* (Word 1984)★★★, and the 50s film and audio series *Historical America In Song* for *Encyclopedia Britannica*.

● COMPILATIONS: *The Best Of Burl Ives* (MCA 1965)★★★, *Junior Choice* (MFP 1979)★★, *The Best Of Burl's For Boys And Girls* (MCA 1980)★★, *The Very Best Of* (1993)★★★, *A Little Bitty Tear: The Nashville Years 1961-65* (1993)★★★.

● FURTHER READING: *Wayfaring Stranger*, Burl Ives.

● FILMS: *Smoky* (1946), *So Dear To My Heart* (1948), *East Of Eden* (1955), *Cat On A Hot Tin Roof* (1958), *Wind Across The Everglades* (1958), *Desire Under The Elms* (1958), *The Big Country* (1958), *Our Man In Havana* (1960), *The Brass Bottle* (1964), *Rocket To The Moon* (1967).

Iveys

Originally an all-Welsh group, the Iveys played the legendary Cavern Club in the mid-60s with a line-up comprising Pete Ham (b. 27 April 1947, Swansea, Wales, d. 23 April 1975; vocals), Mike Gibbons (b. 12 March 1949, Swansea, Wales; drums), David Jenkins (guitar) and Ron Griffiths (bass). Not surprisingly, for a group who had taken their name in imitation of the **Hollies**, they were vocally tight and very melodic. During 1967, they became backing group to operatic pop singer **David Garrick**. An initial demo tape was sent to **Apple Records** and so impressed **Paul McCartney** that he immediately invited them to sign with the label. By this time, Jenkins had been replaced by Liverpudlian Tom Evans (b. 5 June 1947, Liverpool, England, d. 23 November 1983). They made their debut in 1968 with 'Maybe Tomorrow'/'And Her Daddy's A Millionaire', written by Evans and produced by **Tony Visconti**. Although it did not chart in the UK, it did reach number 67 in the US charts. A projected album of the same title was never issued in the UK, but was pressed in Europe and Japan. A second single, 'Dear Angie'/'No Escaping Your Love', was also released in Europe but not the UK, in 1969. They then set about recording a McCartney composition, 'Come And Get It', but by the time this was released they had changed their name to **Badfinger**. Frustrated by the lack of coverage for the band, Griffiths left in December 1969 to be replaced by guitarist Joey Molland (b. 21 June 1948, Liverpool, England). *Maybe Tomorrow* was belatedly released in the UK in 1992 on CD along with previously unissued tracks. Several of the songs it contained were later reprised by Badfinger on their *Magic Christian Music* album.

● ALBUMS: *Maybe Tomorrow* (Apple 1968)★★★.

Ivor Biggun

This was a late 70s/early 80s comedy musical group led by Doc Cox. Ivor Biggun became well known through the release of 'The Winker's Song (Misprint)', an ode to masturbation that was banned on every national radio and television service, but which nevertheless was frequently played by the more risqué mobile disc jockeys of the time. It eventually became a UK Top 30 hit, credited to Ivor Biggun And The Red Nosed Burglars. It was followed by the similarly titled 'I've Parted (Misprint)' and 'Bras On 45 (Family Version)'. His albums were also awash with seaside postcard humour, with titles that included 'Where Did The Lead In My Pencil Go?', 'Hide The Sausage' and 'I Can Be The Hot Dog And You Can Be The Bun'. Cox then became the 'funny man' on *That's Life*, a BBC Television consumer programme that also had an obsession with penis-shaped vegetables. Cox contributed several artless songs to the programme.

● ALBUMS: *The Winker's Album* (Beggars Banquet 1979)★★★, *More Filth Dirty Cheap* (Beggars Banquet 1981)★★★, *Partners In Grime* (Dead Badger 1987)★★.

Ivy

Comprising Dominique Durand (b. France), her husband Andy Chase and Adam Schlesinger, this offbeat US pop band's profile rose in the 90s as a consequence of Schlesinger's other musical project, **Fountains Of Wayne**. Schlesinger is also the joint founder of Scratchie Records with James Iha and D'Arcy Wretzky of **Smashing Pumpkins**. Ivy's sound proved to be slightly divorced from the lo-fi pop of Fountains Of Wayne; Durand's breathy vocals, in particular, added a touch of grandiloquence to a musical backing compared to artists including **Stereolab** and the **Cardigans**. The group's debut album, released prior to the success of Schlesinger's extracurricular activities, received strong reviews but disappointing sales. Their second effort, *Apartment Life*, was completed in a piecemeal fashion due to his increased workload and touring commitments with Fountains Of Wayne. However, as he conceded to ***Billboard*** magazine, 'A lot of the process of making a record for us involves experimentation in the studio. We're not the kind of band that just breaks in new songs on the road and runs into the studio to record them.' The better songs on *Apartment Life* included 'This Is The Day' and 'Baker', both featuring a prominent horn section. Chris Collingwood and Jody Porter of Fountains Of Wayne also contributed to the album, as did drummer Stanley Demeski (ex-**Luna** and **Feelies**). The producers were **Kolderie And Slade**. Durand also returned the compliment by singing backing vocals on Fountains Of Wayne's debut set. For touring purposes, Ivy were joined in late 1997 by Brian Young, also of the **Posies** and, inevitably, Fountains Of Wayne.

● ALBUMS: *Realistic* (Seed/Atlantic 1995)★★★, *Apartment Life* (Atlantic 1997)★★★.

Ivy League

Formed in 1964, the Ivy League was an outlet for songwriters John Carter (b. John Shakespeare, 20 October 1942, Birmingham, England) and Ken Lewis (b. James Hawker, 3 December 1942, Birmingham, England). The duo's talent had been established through compositions for several acts, including Mike Sarne's UK novelty hit, 'Will I What', and their own beat group, Carter-Lewis And The Southerners, which featured guitarist **Jimmy Page**. Perry Ford (b. Bryan Pugh, 1940, Lincoln, England), a former member of **Bert Weedon**'s backing band, completed the Ivy League line-up which had three UK hits in 1965 with 'Funny How Love Can Be' (number 8), 'That's Why I'm Crying' (number 22) and 'Tossing And Turning' (number 3). Their close harmony, falsetto style was modelled on that of the **Four Freshmen** and **Four Seasons** and while obviously competent, grew increasingly out-of-step as contemporary pop progressed. The trio reached a creative peak with the atmospheric 'My World Fell Down', but John Carter was now tiring of his creation. **Tony Burrows** replaced him in 1966 and although Ken Lewis left the group several months later, Perry Ford remained at its helm until the end of the decade, fronting an ever-changing line-up. By then, however, the Ivy League had been surpassed by newer Carter/Lewis projects including the **Flowerpot Men** and **White Plains**. Carter's original demos were released in 1998.

● ALBUMS: *This Is The Ivy League* (Pye 1965)★★★.
● COMPILATIONS: *Sounds Of The Ivy League* (Marble Arch 1967)★★★, *Tomorrow Is Another Day* (Marble Arch 1969)★★★, *The Best Of The Ivy League* (1988)★★★, *Major League* (Sequel 1997)★★★★.
Solo: John Carter *As You Like It Volume 1: The Denmark Street Demo's 1963-67* (Westside 1998)★★★.

Ivy, Quin

b. 1938, Oxford, Mississippi, USA. Although **Rick Hall** was perhaps chiefly responsible for putting **Muscle Shoals**-recorded soul music on the map with his fine 60s and early 70s productions at Fame Studios, Quin Ivy, who entered the business just after Hall, deserves credit, not only for the consistent run of hits he had with his mainstay artist **Percy Sledge**, but for the other fine southern-soul music he recorded with lesser-known musicians and singers at his Quinvy Studio in nearby Sheffield, Alabama. A white sharecropper's son, Ivy's first interest was country music, but he switched to R&B in the mid-50s after hearing records by artists such as **LaVern Baker** and **Ivory Joe Hunter**, as well as the Nashville 'black music' shows of Hoss Allen and John R. He began working in radio at the tiny local Oxford station, before moving to WMPS in Memphis, and several other stations, including WLAY in Muscle Shoals, Alabama, where **Sam Phillips** had been a DJ. In 1963, he used the name Tune Town (a previous Shoals-area record label owned by James Joiner) for his new record store in nearby Sheffield. Quin and Rick Hall began writing songs, including two for **Jimmy Hughes**:

his first a-side, 'I'm Qualified', leased to the Guyden label, and 'Lollipops, Lace And Lipstick', the b-side of his first hit 'Steal Away' (and the first ever single on the Fame label). In 1966 Ivy opened his first Quinvy Studio across the street from his Sheffield record store, using an old rewired console discarded by the WLAY radio station, an equally old Ampex recorder bought in Nashville and some dilapidated A7 speakers. He tried to persuade Fame regular **Dan Penn** to work as his engineer, but instead settled for Marlin Greene. Quin offered Greene 10% of the business, and besides engineering, he played guitar, arranged strings, and even designed the new company logo. The first ever session held at the Quinvy studio was for a local singer, Donna Thatcher (later a backing singer, as Donna Godchaux, with **Grateful Dead**), but it was the second session that propelled Ivy into the big time when he recorded a black male nurse who worked at the nearby Colbert County Hospital. The nurse was Percy Sledge and the record was 'When A Man Loves A Woman'. **Jerry Wexler** of **Atlantic Records** leased the track from Ivy (with some assistance from Rick Hall) and it became a US number 1 in 1966. The steady sales of Sledge's many records over the next few years financed several other fine soul artists on Ivy's own labels, Quinvy and South Camp (distributed by **Atco**/Atlantic). Quin Ivy's artists had the cream of the late 60s Shoals-based musicians to support them, including Roger Hawkins, Junior Lowe, **Spooner Oldham**, David Hood, Eddie Hinton, **Jimmy Johnson** and Marlin Greene. Stand-out tracks included Don Varner's UK northern dance favourite, the pulsating 'Tearstained Face', and the equally superb up-tempo soul of Tony Borders' 'What Kind Of Spell'. There were also many prime examples of southern deep soul, including Borders' 'Cheaters Never Win', the young **Z.Z. Hill**'s 'Faithful & True', and three tracks in particular by the outstanding Bill Brandon: 'Self Preservation', 'One Minute Woman' (unissued at the time), and the first, and arguably best, recording of a deep ballad called 'Rainbow Road', written by Dan Penn and Donnie Fritts for and about **Arthur Alexander**, who recorded it himself some years later for **Warner**. Most of these sides appeared on Quinvy or South Camp, but Ivy also leased product to other small labels (in addition to the Sledge material and one Z.Z. Hill single to Atlantic, and an Eddie Bradford single to **Chess**). These included Tower, Revue, Nugget, Diamond and Uni. Their relative lack of success, combined with an eventual decline in the sales of Percy Sledge records, caused Ivy to sell the studio to his engineer, David Johnson, in 1973. It was renamed Broadway Sound, and Percy Sledge recorded two further albums there in 1974 and 1983, and James Govan and Freddie North recorded in the studio during the 70s. Quin Ivy gained an MA degree at Mississippi University before returning to the Shoals area to teach accountancy. Virtually the complete Quinvy-South Camp soul output (excluding the Sledge material) was released in 1989 by the UK Charly label

on five separate albums, followed by a 27-track selective CD that also included four sides not on the albums.
● COMPILATIONS: *Tear Stained Soul* (Charly 1989)★★★, *High On the Hog* (Charly 1989)★★★, *You Better Believe It!* (Charly 1989)★★★, *More Power To Ya!* (Charly 1989)★★★, *Rainbow Road* (Charly 1989)★★★, *Rare Soul From Alabama - The South Camp Quinvy CD* (Charly 1989)★★★★.

Iwan, Dafydd

b. 24 August 1943, Brynaman, South Wales. Singer-songwriter Iwan was one of four sons born to a non-conformist preacher, who himself came from a family of Welsh poets. Iwan sang in chapel and learned from his mother how to read music. When he was 12, the family moved to the farming community of Llanuwchllyn, near Bala, in North Wales, a contrast to the mining village he had been brought up in. After trying to learn a variety of instruments, he finally settled for the guitar, before going on to study architecture in Cardiff, graduating in 1968. It was during this time that he started writing and singing his own songs, the main influences singer-songwriters such as **Pete Seeger** and **Bob Dylan**. It was also during the mid-60s that he started appearing on Welsh television, releasing his first EP, *Wrth Feddwl Am Fy Nghymru (When I Think Of My Wales)*, in 1966, on the Welsh Teldisc label. In all, between 1966 and 1969, he released eight EPs and two singles, before setting up **Sain** records in 1969 with fellow singer Huw Jones, and Brian Morgan Edwards. His 1969 release, 'Carlo' was a satire on the Investiture of Prince Charles as the Prince Of Wales. During the 60s and 70s, Iwan became very active in the non-violent Welsh language campaigns, leading to his imprisonment in 1970. In 1982, he collaborated for the first time with **Ar Log** to record *Rhwng Hwyl A Thaith*, an album combining traditional and new material. In 1988 the *Dafydd Iwan Yng Nghorwen* video was released, documenting a concert held in Corwen, Wales to celebrate Iwan's 25 years of singing. He is Vice-President of Plaid Cymru in North Wales with an ambition 'to see Wales free in a new Europe of the peoples, a world at peace, and to retire gracefully'. A volume of 152 of his songs was published in 1992, and he is listed in the International Who's Who. He has been honoured with a Gold Disc for his services to Welsh music, and he is an honorary member of the Gorsedd of Bards for his services to the Welsh language. Iwan has sung, both at home and overseas, for over 30 years; his songs reflect the aspirations of the Welsh people, and the Welsh language, and his empathy with the struggles for human rights in other parts of the world.
● ALBUMS: *Yma Mae 'Nghan* (Sain 1972)★★, *Mae'r Darnau Yn Disgyn I'w Lle* (Sain 1976)★★★, *Bod Yn Rhydd* (Sain 1979)★★★, *Dafydd Iwan Ar Dan* (Sain 1981)★★★, with Ar Log *Rhwng Hwyl A Thaith* (Sain 1982)★★★★, *Gwinllan A Roddwyd: I Gofio'r Tri* (Sain 1986)★★★, *Dal I Gredu* (Sain 1991)★★★, *Caneuon Gwerin (Folk Songs)* (Sain 1993)★★★.
● COMPILATIONS: *Carlo A Chaneuon Eraill* (Sain

1977)★★★, *I'r Gad* (Sain 1977)★★★, with Ar Log *Yma O Hyd* (Sain 1993)★★★★, *Can Celt* (Sain 1996)★★★.
● VIDEOS: *Dafydd Iwan Yng Nghorwen* (1988), *Dafydd Iwan Yn Fyw O'r Cnapan* (1992).
● FURTHER READING: *Dafydd Iwan*, Dafydd Iwan.

Izenzon, David

b. 17 May 1932, Pittsburgh, Pennsylvania, USA, d. 8 October 1979. Izenzon sang in the local synagogue as a child, and did not begin studying bass until 1956. After working with **Bill Dixon**, **Archie Shepp**, **Paul Bley** and **Sonny Rollins** he joined the **Ornette Coleman** trio from 1962-66, recording on important releases such as *Town Hall Concert*, *An Evening With Ornette Coleman*, the two volumes of *At The Golden Circle* and the film soundtracks *Chappaqua Suite* and *Who's Crazy?*. Izenzon was later re-united with Coleman for some gigs in 1968, 1972 and 1973 by a two bass quartet where he played in tandem with one of his predecessors, **Charlie Haden**. During Coleman's 1965-66 European tour Izenzon settled in London, recording a number of tracks which have never been publicly issued. Back in New York in 1967 he played with Coleman at the funeral of **John Coltrane**, and also worked with **Jaki Byard** (*Sunshine Of My Soul*) and **Perry Robinson**. From 1968-71 he taught at Bronx Community College, New York. After his second stint with Coleman he formed a quintet with **Carlos Ward**, **Gato Barbieri**, **Karl Berger** and Art Lewis, and an all-bass band called Bass Revolution. In 1972 Izenzon gave up performing to spend more time with his son, who was born with serious brain-damage, and to study for a PhD in psychotherapy at Indiana Northwestern University. He set up in practice as a therapist in New York and published a book, *Emotions*. Although he restricted his playing he continued to compose during this time, one piece being a jazz opera, *How Music Can Save The World*. He was a highly individual and influential player, especially because of his remarkable arco (bowed) playing.

Izit

Rare UK groove revivalists of the early 90s whose name stemmed from a technological mishap; when they were sampling the word 'music' their sequencer messed up and looped 'Izit' instead. They enjoyed breakthrough success with 'Stories', on their own Pig & Trumpet label in 1989, a version of the rare groove staple originally recorded by Chakachas. The group, who comprise former Tarzan-a-gram Tony Colman (guitar, keyboards; ex-Pulse, who once appeared on *Wogan*), Peter Shrubshall (flute, tenor saxophone) and sister Catherine Shrubshall (soprano, alto and baritone saxophone) were originally a studio-based enterprise. However, they added drummer Andrew Messingham and a bass player to the line-up for their first live shows. A huge hit in 1989, Messingham had actually scratched 'Acid Free Zone' onto the run-out grooves of 'Stories'. Despite their avowed wish to slow the pace of the summer's soundtrack, the single was widely adored by the acid crowd after the track was initially bought on import (Izit having licensed its release in Italy). Eventually it transferred to **Paul Oakenfold**'s Perfecto label where he produced a popular remix, before the group joined **Maze** on a tour of the UK and Europe. They eventually followed up with 'Make Way For The Originals', again on Pig & Trumpet, before electing to sign with the independent Optimism. However, when the latter neglected to pay the studio bill for Izit's debut album the tapes were retained, though the set did emerge under the name Main Street People in late 1993. Disillusioned, original members of the band drifted away, though Colman beavered away in the background, setting up a new Tongue & Groove imprint, which eventually saw Izit return on 'Don't Give Up Now' and 'One By One', featuring vocalist Sam Edwards. Later material introduced Nicola Bright, who co-wrote much of *The Whole Affair*. Other guests/semi-permanent members include Byron Wallen (trumpet), Andy Gangadeen (drums), Steven Lewinson (bass) and Haji Mike and **MC Mell 'O'** (rappers).
● ALBUMS: *The Whole Affair* (Tongue & Groove 1993).

J-Blast And The 100% Proof

One-off spoof merchants notable for their articulate 'dissing' of **De La Soul**. 'Break Ya Dawn' was a specific attack on Prince Be and his cohorts, released, tellingly enough, on the Geek St label, in 1992. It was introduced by a sample of UK disk jockey Bruno Brookes using entirely forced language such as 'peace' and 'respect', before the outfit waylay Prince Be and a host of other 'pseuds'. Alhough of UK origins, the protagonists identities remained hidden, until J Blast went on to join the **Scientists Of Sound**.

J., Harry

b. Harry Johnson, *c.*1945, Kingston, Jamaica, West Indies. After completing his education, Johnson joined a band called the Virtues, playing bass guitar. The group recorded a few tunes, notably a version of 'Amen'. Intrigued by the business side of music, he became the band's manager until his partners decided to disperse. Following the group's demise he concentrated on a career in insurance but was drawn back into the music business as a producer in 1968. His first sessions resulted in 'No More Heartaches' by the Beltones, which became a big local hit. The song was covered in the 80s by Keble Drummond of the **Cables** with Harry producing. His skilful negotiating with **Coxsone Dodd** won him the use of **Studio One**'s facilities, when he recorded **Lloyd Robinson** performing 'Cuss Cuss'. He employed some of the island's top session men, notably Hux Brown, **Winston Wright** and **Boris Gardiner**, collectively known as the Harry J. Allstars. The studio band enjoyed a UK number 9 crossover hit with 'The Liquidator' in October 1969, which re-entered the chart in March 1980. The success of the single led to a compilation of instrumentals taking its title from the hit, and featuring 'Jay Moon Walk', 'The Big Three' and a version of 'Je T'Aime (Moi Non Plus)'. In March 1970 his production of **Bob And Marcia**'s 'Young Gifted And Black', one of the first reggae records to use strings, reached the Top 5 in the UK. In July 1971 the duo enjoyed a second hit with 'Pied Piper' (number 11 UK pop chart) with **Bob Andy** in the producer's chair.

In 1972 Harry sold his record shop and invested the money, and the profits from his UK hits, into his 16-track studio at 10 Roosevelt Avenue. He later installed former Studio One engineer Sylvan Morris at the controls in place of Sid Bucknor, who moved to England. Harry J's became one of the most popular recording studios on the island, utilized by the likes of

Burning Spear, **Augustus Pablo**, and, prior to the advent of Tuff Gong, **Bob Marley**. Harry J. also produced work by the Cables, the **Heptones**, Busty Brown, Lloyd Robinson and Lorna Bennett. His production of Bennett's 'Breakfast In Bed', originally a Nashville country tune, was a financial success but failed to make an impression on the UK chart. Some of the pressings of her hit were released with a **Scotty** toast, 'Skank In Bed', on the b-side. The song was also covered by another of Harry's protégés, **Sheila Hylton**, who entered the UK chart in 1979, peaking at number 57. In the late 70s Harry moved down a gear and produced mainly DJ records for the local market. His studio remained popular, however, and in 1981 he was tempted back into the production seat to achieve another international hit with Hylton's 'The Bed's Too Big Without You', which reached number 35 in the UK chart in February of that year. Another substantial hit was the Heptones' 'Book Of Rules', which lost its appeal when **Island Records** inadvisably added strings. The version without strings can be found on *Night Food*.

Over the years, Harry J.'s studio facilities have been used by some of reggae's finest musicians, and **Bob Marley And The Wailers**' *Catch A Fire*, *Burning*, *Natty Dread* and *Rastaman Vibration*, and their collaborations with **Johnny Nash** (including 'Guava Jelly', 'Stir It Up' and 'Nice Time'), were all recorded there. By the 80s Harry had set up his own distribution network in Jamaica with Sunset, 10 Roosevelt Avenue, Junjo and, of course, the Harry J label. In 1996 the 'Cuss Cuss' rhythm resurfaced, providing hits for a number of DJs where a loop of the original recording was clearly audible.

● ALBUMS: *Liquidator* (Trojan 1970)★★★★.

J., Ollie

b. Oliver Jacobs, *c.*1975, London, England. One of techno's new breed of studio operators, who first locked horns with a control panel at the age of 13. After which his education went to the cleaners, as he spent every waking hour at the consoles, using school as a dormitory. The end would, however, justify the means. By the age of 19 he had remixed for **Adamski**, **Frankie Goes To Hollywood**, **D:Ream** and **Take That**, and provided full production for **Rozalla**, **East 17** and **Deja Vu**. As well as engineering for **Leftfield** and **Delta Lady**, he would help on sessions at Rollover Studios in Kilburn, owned by his father Phil Jacobs. The studio has seen notable works recorded by **Sure Is Pure**, **Paul Gotel**, **Qui 3**, the **Sandals** and the **Leftfield**/Lydon collaboration ('Open Up'). Jacobs has a big future ahead of him; judged on the terms of an age to output matrix there is nobody to touch him.

J.T. The Bigga Figga

b. San Francisco, California, USA. The most popular northern Californian to record in the hip hop vein patented as 'G-Funk', J.T. is also the owner of Get Low Records, his record label, and Paper Chase Management, run by his mother Pearl. His reputation was built on several small-scale releases for Get Low in the early 90s which achieved successively greater sales, particularly within San Francisco where his rise coincided with the breakthrough of fellow artist and friend E-40. Together with long-standing collaborators San Quinn and D-Moe, J.T.'s debut album, *Don't Stop 'Til We Major*, established his credibility as a street artist. It was followed by *Playaz N The Game*, a superior collection of ghetto recriminations and personality-enhancing boasts, the best track, 'Peep Game', featuring D-Moe. Better still was 1994's *Straight Out The Labb*, though by this time J.T. had converted to the Nation Of Islam and that new spiritual base reflected in his lyrics.

● ALBUMS: *Don't Stop 'Til We Major* (Get Low 1992)★★★, *Playaz N The Game* (Get Low 1993)★★★★, *Straight Out The Labb* (Get Low 1994)★★★★.

Jack

Anthony Reynolds formed this band at the age of 19 with fellow Cardiff, Wales native Matthew Scott (guitar), the two drawing on a shared love of the bleak humour of **Nick Cave** and the raddled prose of Charles Bukowski. By March 1995 the rest of the band was in place, with Richard Adderley (guitar), Patrick Pulzer (drums), Colin Williams (bass) and George Wright (keyboards) on board in time for their debut London gig, after which they were immediately snapped up by Too Pure Records. Their first release, the limited edition 'Kid Stardust', was single of the week in *Melody Maker*; this was followed by *Pioneer Soundtracks*, the bohemian ambience of which was accentuated by the work of ex-**Scott Walker** producer Peter Walsh and the string arrangements of seventh member, cellist Audrey Morse. The album was released at a point when the *cabaret noir* sound of Cave (almost parodied in 'I Didn't Mean It, Marie'), Walker, **Jacques Brel** and the **Tindersticks** was flavour of the month. Reynolds, however, took their black-clad moodiness to a new extreme: 'I don't believe in happiness,' he declared, 'do you?' He expressed the darkness more fully in Jacques, described as Jack's 'older, slightly eccentric brother', a spin-off collaboration with fellow Brel-obsessive **Momus** that resulted in 1997's *How To Make Love Volume 1*.

● ALBUMS: *Pioneer Soundtracks* (Too Pure 1996)★★★.

Jack Frost

A loose collaboration between two giants of Australian alternative rock, ex-**Go-Between** Grant McLennan (b.

12 February 1958, Rockhampton, Queensland, Australia; bass, guitar, vocals) and **Steven Kilbey** (b. *c*.1960, England; guitar, vocals) of the **Church** occasionally meet to write songs together and record. It sounds simple, but quite why the project is not taken more seriously is perplexing, as the quality of their work, particularly on the second album, is excellent. With a chiming 12-string **Rickenbacker** and glorious 60s harmonies there are less obvious evocations (for example, mid-period **Hollies**), all treated with slick 90s production. The opener, 'Jack Frost Blues, on *Jack Frost*, features a wondrous middle eight, and the remaining songs rarely fall below this high standard. With both artists involved with solo projects, however, it was five years before the equally accomplished follow-up, *Snow Job*, appeared.

● ALBUMS: *Jack Frost* (Arista 1991)★★★, *Snow Job* (Beggars Banquet 1996)★★★★.

Jack Orion - Bert Jansch

Where Jansch's previous albums were largely comprised of self-penned material, this third set was drawn from traditional songs, bar an instrumental reading of Ewan MacColl's 'First Time Ever I Saw Your Face'. The artist's highly original guitar style underpins the lengthy title track and the enthralling 'Black Water Side'. Jimmy Page is only one of many musicians expressing a debt to Jansch and the latter track provided the template for 'Black Mountain Side' on *Led Zeppelin I*. Bert's languid interpretation of 'Nottamun Town' inspired a later version by Fairport Convention, but they struggled to match the enthralling atmosphere created here. *Jack Orion* is a mesmerizing selection from a hugely influential performer.

● *The Waggoner's Lad; The First Time I Ever Saw Your Face; Jack Orion; The Gardener; Nottamun Town; Henry Martin; Blackwaterside; Pretty Polly.*
● First released 1966
● UK peak chart position: did not chart
● USA peak chart position: did not chart

Jack The Lad

This offshoot of Lindisfarne, comprising Billy Mitchell (guitar/vocals), Simon Cowe (guitar/vocals), Ray Laidlaw (drums) and Rod Clements (bass), was formed in 1973. The quartet recorded some rock 'n' jig material with Maddy Prior's vocals, before Clements left for session and production work. Ian Walter Fairburn (fiddle) and Phil Murray (bass) were recruited for *The Old Straight Track*, a song cycle of 'Geordie' electric folk songs. After the failure of this somewhat experimental project, the group returned to philosophical good time material, and, in 1976, signed for United Artists. Cowe assisted in the preparation of *Jackpot*, but had left before the band recorded the dense, commercial album which was produced by Tom Allom. Despite having a loyal cult following on the college and club circuit, Jack The Lad disbanded shortly after Laidlaw's departure to Radiator, playing a few farewell gigs with Eric Green on

drums. In 1993, after several CD releases, and **Lindisfarne**'s impending 25th anniversary, Jack The Lad re-formed in two forms: the original band, and as a festival act which included Mitchell, Fairburn and Murray.
● ALBUMS: *It's Jack The Lad* (Charisma 1974)★★, *The Old Straight Track* (Charisma 1974)★★★, *Rough Diamonds* (Charisma 1975)★★★, *Jackpot* (United Artists 1976)★★★, *Back On The Road Again* (Mah Mah 1994)★★.

Jackie And Roy
(see **Kral, Roy**)

Jackie And The Starlites
Jackie And The Starlites were perhaps the most extreme example of overt emotionalism in doo-wop, in which lead Jackie Rue would scream out the lyrics in the most anguished, heartbreaking voice, and in the middle of the songs break down sobbing. The members, besides Rue, were Alton Thomas, John Felix and Billy Montgomery. Rue began singing with the Five Wings, a group in Harlem, New York, in 1955, and made two haunting singles for the **King** label, most notably 'Teardrops Are Falling' (a stunning remake appeared in the 1990 John Waters film *Cry Baby*). In 1960 Rue surfaced again with the Starlights and signed with Bobby Robinson's Fury label. Their first record was 'Valerie', and it quickly became something of a phenomenon on the east coast. Their best follow-up, 'I Found Out Too Late', made the national charts in 1962, but later records for Robinson failed to find favour. The Starlites recorded unsuccessfully for the Hull label during 1962-63 before breaking up. With a scruffy and rough image, Rue and his group were not destined to attain middle-class respectability. In 1961 two members of the group killed a man in an armed robbery and received extensive jail sentences. Rue died of a drug overdose some time in the late 60s or early 70s.
● COMPILATIONS: *The Kodaks Versus The Starlites* (Sphere Sound 1965)★★★, *Valerie* (Relic 1991)★★★, *Jackie & The Starlites Meet The Bopchords* (Collectables 1991)★★★.

Jacks
(see **Cadets**)

Jacks, Terry
b. *c.*1953, Winnipeg, Canada. Jacks was a former member of the hit group **Poppy Family**, and a well-known session player. While working in the studio with the **Beach Boys**, he attempted to persuade them to record 'Le Moribund', a song about a dying man by French composer **Jacques Brel**. When the group declined, Jacks himself recorded the English translation by **Rod McKuen**, retitled 'Seasons In The Sun'. A smash hit in Canada, it subsequently reached number 1 in both the US and UK charts. Although Jacks enjoyed one further hit with a cover of Brel's 'If You Go Away', no other successes followed.
● ALBUMS: *Seasons In The Sun* (Bell 1974)★★.

Jackson Five
The Jackson Five comprised five brothers, **Jackie** (b. Sigmund Esco Jackson, 4 May 1951), Tito (b. Toriano Adaryll Jackson, 15 October 1953), **Jermaine** (b. Jermaine Lajuan Jackson, 11 December 1954), Marlon (b. 12 March 1957) and **Michael Jackson** (b. 29 August 1958). Raised in Gary, Indiana, USA, by their father Joe, a blues guitarist, they began playing local clubs in 1962, with youthful prodigy Michael as lead vocalist. Combining dance routines influenced by the **Temptations** with music inspired by **James Brown**, they first recorded for the Indiana-based Steeltown label before auditioning for **Motown Records** in 1968. **Bobby Taylor** recommended the group to Motown, although the company gave **Diana Ross** public credit for their discovery. A team of Motown writers known as the Corporation composed a series of songs for the group's early releases, all accentuating their youthful enthusiasm and vocal interplay. Their debut single for Motown, 'I Want You Back', became the fastest-selling record in the company's history in 1969, and three of their next five singles also topped the American chart. Michael Jackson was groomed for a concurrent solo recording career, which began in 1971, followed by similar excursions for Jermaine and elder brother Jackie. As the group's appeal broadened, they became the subjects of a cartoon series on American television, *The Jackson 5*, and hosted a television special, *Goin' Back To Indiana*. After the dissolution of the Corporation in 1971, the group recorded revivals of pop and R&B hits from the 50s, and cover versions of other Motown standards, before being allowed to branch out into more diverse material, such as **Jackson Browne**'s 'Doctor My Eyes'. They also began to record their own compositions in the early 70s, a trend that continued until 1975, by which time they were writing and producing most of the songs on their albums. The Jackson Five reached the peak of their popularity in Britain when they toured there in 1972, but after returning to America they suffered decreasing record sales as their music grew more sophisticated. By 1973, they had dropped the teenage stylings of their early hits, concentrating on a cabaret approach to their live performances, while on record they perfected a harder brand of funk. The group's recording contract with Motown expired in 1975. Feeling that the label had not been promoting their recent records, they signed to Epic Records. Jermaine Jackson, however, who was married to the daughter of Motown boss **Berry Gordy**, chose to leave the group and remain with the company as a solo artist. Gordy sued the Jackson Five for alleged breach of contract in 1976, and the group were forced to change their name to the Jacksons. The case was settled in 1980, with the brothers paying Gordy $600,000, and allowing Motown all rights to the 'Jackson Five' name.
● ALBUMS: *Diana Ross Presents The Jackson 5* (Motown 1970)★★★, *ABC* (Motown 1970)★★★★, *Third Album* (Motown 1970)★★★, *Christmas Album* (Motown 1970)★★,

Maybe Tomorrow (Motown 1971)★★, *Goin' Back To Indiana* (Motown 1971)★★, *Lookin' Through The Windows* (Motown 1972)★★★, *Skywriter* (Motown 1973)★★★, *Get It Together* (Motown 1973)★★★, *Dancing Machine* (Motown 1974)★★★, *Moving Violation* (Motown 1975)★★★, *Joyful Jukebox Music* (Motown 1976)★★★.

● COMPILATIONS: *Jackson 5 Greatest Hits* (Motown 1971)★★★★, *Jackson Five Anthology* 3-LP set (Motown 1976)★★★★, *Soulstation! - 25th Anniversary Collection* 4-CD box set (Motown 1995)★★★★, *Early Classics* (Spectrum 1996)★★★.

● FURTHER READING: *Jackson Five*, Charles Morse. *The Jacksons*, Steve Manning. *Pap Joe's Boys: The Jacksons' Story*, Leonard Pitts. *The Magic And The Madness*, J. Randy Taraborrelli. *The Record History: International Jackson Record Guide*, Ingmar Kuliha.

Jackson Heights

This group was formed in 1970 by bassist/vocalist Lee Jackson (b. 8 January 1943, Newcastle-upon-Tyne, Tyne And Wear, England) on the dissolution of the **Nice**. His new venture pursued a more pop-orientated path than its virtuoso-based predecessor, but despite prolific live work and four well-promoted albums, an unstable line-up hampered the group's ultimate progress. Early members Charlie Harcourt (guitar), Mario Tapia (guitar) and Tommy Sloane (drums) were replaced by a series of new inductees, none of whom was able to halt Jackson's ailing fortunes. However, having decided that recent addition **Patrick Moraz** (b. 24 June 1948, Morges, Switzerland) played a keyboard style unsuited to the primarily melodic group, Jackson left his creation in 1974 to shape **Refugee** around his new discovery's dexterous technique. His former colleagues briefly continued under the truncated name Heights before breaking up.

● ALBUMS: *King's Progress* (Charisma 1970)★★★★, *5th Avenue Bus* (Vertigo 1972)★★★, *Ragmuffin's Fool* (Vertigo 1973)★★, *Jackson Heights* (1973)★★, *Bump And Grind* (Vertigo 1973)★★.

Jackson, 'New Orleans' Willie

Jackson sang comic renditions of opera tunes in black-face at a New Orleans ice cream parlour. His mid-20s recordings are versatile and vaudevillian, with strong dance numbers, *double entendres*, and humorous vignettes of Darktown life, ranging from the church to politics and the judiciary. He also sang a number of traditionally based blues, covered contemporary hits such as 'Kansas City Blues', and made the first recording of 'T.B. Blues', generally associated with **Victoria Spivey**.

● ALBUMS: *New Orleans Willie Jackson* (1989)★★★.

Jackson, Alan

b. 17 October 1958, Newman, Georgia, USA. Jackson, the son of a motor mechanic, had a love of gospel music through church and his family. His roots can be heard in 'Home' (written for Mother's Day),

'Chattahoochee' and his tribute to **Hank Williams**, 'Midnight In Montgomery'. He has also revived several songs from his youth including **Eddie Cochran**'s 'Summertime Blues' and a joint composition from **Roger Miller** and **George Jones**, 'Tall Tall Trees'. He tried several jobs, but in 1986, he moved with his wife, Denise, to Nashville to try to succeed as a country performer. Through a chance meeting with **Glen Campbell**, he gained an audition with his publishing company, and he became the first artist to be signed to **Arista Records**' Nashville division. He wrote most of his debut album, *Here In The Real World*, which remained on the US country album chart for over a year. He had immediate success with 'Blue Blooded Woman' and then four more singles from the album topped the US country charts - 'Here In The Real World', 'Wanted', 'Chasin' That Neon Rainbow' and 'I'd Love You All Over Again'. The UK magazine *Country Music People* said of him, 'He's uncontroversial, stands for the flag, Mom and apple pie, looks like he washes every day and sings for middle America.' The lanky, quiet-spoken Georgian is one of the Hat brigade and he joined the *Grand Ole Opry* in 1991. *Don't Rock The Jukebox* confirmed that his initial success was no fluke and the album spawned five number 1 singles - 'Don't Rock The Jukebox', 'Someday', 'Midnight In Montgomery', 'Dallas' and 'Love's Got A Hold On You'. He also wrote songs with **Randy Travis**, including the latter's number 1 hit 'Forever Together', and his own 'She's Got The Rhythm And I Got The Blues', another number 1 from 1992. The album on which it featured, *A Lot About Livin'*, is Jackson's most successful to date, selling six million copies to the end of August 1995. Even his *Honky Tonk Christmas* has notched up a respectable 700,000. This album includes **Alison Krauss**, the **Chipmunks** and a duet with the deceased **Keith Whitley**. Other number 1s from *A Lot About Livin'* are 'Tonight I Climbed The Wall', 'Chattahoochee' and 'Who Says You Can't Have It All'. His next album, *Who I Am*, included four more country number 1s, 'Summertime Blues', 'Livin' On Love', 'Gone Country' and 'I Don't Even Know Your Name', giving him 16 chart-topping records to that time. 'Gone Country' wittily parodies people who turned to country music when it became fashionable: 'I heard down there, it's changed, you see/They're not as backward as they used to be.' He has contributed to tribute albums to the **Eagles** and **Merle Haggard** and displayed his traditional side by recording a duet of 'A Good Year For The Roses' with its originator, **George Jones**. Jackson wrote 'Job Description' to explain to his daughters, Mattie Denise and Alexandra Jane, why he was rarely home, and he has won a succession of industry awards, establishing himself as a top ranking country star, not too far behind **Garth Brooks**. He stands for simple truths in straightforward, well-crafted songs and he says, 'I don't dance, I don't swing from ropes, I just stand there.'

● ALBUMS: *Here In The Real World* (Arista 1990)★★★, *Don't Rock The Jukebox* (Arista 1991)★★★★, *A Lot About*

Livin' (And A Little 'Bout Lovin) (Arista 1992)★★★★, *Honky Tonk Christmas* (Arista 1993)★★, *Who I Am* (Arista 1994)★★★, *Everything I Love* (Arista 1996)★★★★.

● COMPILATIONS: *The Greatest Hits Collection* (Arista 1995)★★★★.

● VIDEOS: *Here In The Reel World* (1990), *Livin', Lovin', And Rockin' That Jukebox* (1994), *Who Says You Can't Have It All* (DNA 1994), *The Greatest Video Hits Collection* (6 West Home Video 1995).

Jackson, Armand 'Jump'

b. 25 March 1917, New Orleans, Louisiana, USA, d. 31 January 1985, Chicago, Illinois, USA. Jackson's forceful 'sock' rhythm was heard on many of the blues records made in Chicago in the late 40s and 50s. In 1946-47, he appeared as bandleader on sessions for **Columbia**, **Specialty** and Aristocrat; vocalists included St. Louis Jimmy, **Roosevelt Sykes**, **Sunnyland Slim** and **Baby Doo Caston**. As well as performing, Jackson was active as a booking agent, and in 1959 founded La Salle Records, recording himself, **Eddie Boyd**, **Eddy Clearwater**, **Little Mack Simmons** and Sunnyland Slim, among others. In 1962 he was the drummer for the inaugural American Folk Blues Festival tour of Europe, although by this date his swing era sound had largely been supplanted in Chicago blues by the 'back beat' of Fred Below.

● ALBUMS: *Chicago Rock With Jump Jackson And Friends* (Redita 1988)★★★, *Nothing Like The Rest* (Cold Wind 1995)★★★.

Jackson, Aunt Molly

b. Mary Magdalene Garland, 1880, Clay County, Kentucky, USA, d. 1 September 1960. Her mother died of starvation when she was six, at 10 she was imprisoned due to her family's unionist campaign for better conditions for miners, and she was married at 14. Her husband and son were both killed in mining accidents and her father and brother blinded. In the early 30s, she served as a nurse but consolidated her work for improving conditions in the mines. She acquired a considerable repertoire of local songs, some of which she adapted as her own protest songs, such as 'Kentucky Miner's Wife', which she recorded for **Columbia Records** in 1932. She also used the melody of 'Precious Memories' for her melancholy ballad of the death of a child from starvation, in her song 'Dreadful Memories'. In 1931, the authorities, because of her unionist activities, forced her to leave Kentucky. She settled in New York, where her work attracted the attention of both folk song collectors and historians. In 1939, she began to record some of her songs for the Library of Congress, although few actually gained a public release at the time. The folk music revival, in the late 50s, saw her songs gain popularity and in 1960, arrangements were made for her, at the age of 80, to record an album. When ill health rendered her incapable of singing, it was decided that she should introduce the songs and her friend John Greenway would

sing them. On 1 September 1960, a few days before the scheduled recording day, she died in poverty and relative obscurity. Greenway continued with the project and recorded *The Songs And Stories Of Aunt Molly Jackson* (Folkways 1961). In the 70s, Aunt Molly Jackson's 1939 recordings were finally released on an album by Rounder. Her half-sister, Sarah Ogan Gunning (b. Sarah Elizabeth Garland, 28 June 1910, Ely Branch, Knox County, Kentucky, USA), who had endured similar hardships, also moved to New York and in 1937 made recordings for the Library of Congress, including her popular 'I Am A Girl Of Constant Sorrow'. In 1963, she came out of retirement to appear at concerts, union meetings and even the Newport Folk Festival. She also recorded many of her songs on *Girl Of Constant Sorrow* (Folk-Legacy 1975).

● ALBUMS: *Aunt Molly Jackson Library Of Congress Recordings* (Rounder 1976)★★★.

Jackson, Bo Weavil

Bo Weavil Jackson presents another of those conundrums that are sent to frustrate researchers of early blues recordings. Virtually nothing is known of his life apart from the fact that he was discovered playing for tips on the streets of Birmingham, Alabama, USA, and on two occasions in 1926, he made recordings in Chicago. The first of these was for Paramount under the name Jackson and the second for Vocalion as Sam Butler. His real identity remains a mystery, as does his place of origin. Paramount publicity referred to his being from the Carolinas, although all references in his songs seem to point to a long familiarity with Alabama. Whoever he was, he was an outstanding performer whose high-pitched, expressive voice and chilling slide guitar can be enjoyed as much today as when first recorded. There are 13 known tracks attributed to Jackson; four are religious numbers and the remainder are early blues made up from individual traditional verses subjected to the singer's personal interpretation.

● ALBUMS: *Complete Recordings* (1982)★★★, *1926* (Matchbox 1983)★★★.

Jackson, Bullmoose

b. Benjamin Clarence Jackson, 1919, Cleveland, Ohio, USA, d. 31 July 1989, Cleveland, Ohio, USA. Jackson become interested in music at an early age, and received singing and violin lessons by the age of four. In high school he learned to play the saxophone, and upon his graduation in the late 30s he was hired by legendary trumpeter **Freddie Webster** to play alto and tenor with his Harlem Hotshots. Living briefly in Buffalo, New York, in the early 40s, Jackson returned to Cleveland to a job at the Cedar Gardens, where in 1944, he was discovered by bandleader **Lucky Millinder** who needed a musician to replace tenor saxophonist **Lucky Thompson**. Initially recording simply as a talented accompanist with Millinder's orchestra on **Decca** and as a guest musician with **Big Sid Catlett**'s band on **Capitol**, Jackson astounded his colleagues by substituting for blues shouter **Wynonie Harris** one night in Lubbock, Texas. He remained a part of the Millinder aggregation until June 1948 with the huge success of his R&B hit 'I Love You, Yes I Do'. He began making records under his own name from 1945 with King/Queen and Superdisc, as well as appearing on Millinder's Decca tracks. He also made an appearance in the 1948 musical film *Boarding House Blues*. Jackson enjoyed great success on King Records between 1947 and 1954 with ballads such as 'I Love You, Yes I Do' (which spawned innumerable cover versions for every conceivable market), 'All My Love Belongs To You' and 'Little Girl Don't Cry'. Bullmoose was also responsible for some of the hottest, most suggestive R&B ever recorded, and it is these titles - 'Big Ten-Inch (Record)', 'I Want A Bow-Legged Woman', 'Nosey Joe' and 'Oh John' - that found favour with the later crop of jump and R&B revival bands. Jackson moved to **Chess**'s short-lived Marterry subsidiary in 1955, switched to the tiny Encino label in 1956, and was reduced to making re-recordings of his old hits in the early 60s for Warwick and 7 Arts. By that time he had taken a job with a catering firm during the week and only played the occasional weekend gig. In 1974 he made a cameo appearance in the dramatic film *Sincerely The Blues*, led a jazz band at the Smithsonian Institute in 1976, and went on to tour France and North Africa with **Buck Clayton**'s Quartet. In 1983 Jackson was tracked down by the Pittsburgh-based band the Flashcats, who had been covering his risqué R&B songs, and after 35 years he was big news again with a sell-out tour, a new recording contract with Bogus Records, a celebrated show at Carnegie Hall and a European tour with the **Johnny Otis** Show in 1985.

● ALBUMS: *Big Fat Mamas Are Back In Style Again* (Route 66 1980)★★★, *Moosemania!* (Bogus 1985)★★★, *Moose On The Loose* (Bogus 1985)★★★.

● FILMS: *Sincerely The Blues* (1974).

Jackson, Carl

b. 18 September 1953, Louisville, Mississippi, USA. Carl Jackson started at the age of 13 by accompanying his father and his uncle on the banjo in a bluegrass band. One of his compositions, 'Banjo Man', describes how he learnt **Earl Scruggs**' licks by listening to his records. Jackson toured with **Jim And Jesse** and during that time made his first solo album, *Bluegrass Festival*. In 1972, he joined **Glen Campbell**'s band, and Campbell produced his **Capitol** album, *Banjo Player*. The interplay between Campbell and Jackson, particularly on 'Duellin' Banjos', has been much admired, but staying with Campbell prevented him from developing his own musical personality. He has now branched out on his own and his fine musicianship can be heard on his album with John Starling, *Spring Training*, which won a **Grammy** for Best Bluegrass Album.

● ALBUMS: *Bluegrass Festival* (Prize 1971)★★★ *Banjo Player* (Capitol 1973)★★★, *Old Friends* (Capitol 1978)★★, *Banjo Man* (Sugar Hill 1981)★★★★, *Song Of The South* (Sugar Hill

1982)★★★, *Banjo Hits* (Sugar Hill 1983)★★★, with John Starling and the Nash Ramblers *Spring Training* (Sugar Hill 1991)★★★, with Emmylou Harris *Nashville Country Duets* (1993)★★★.

Jackson, Carlton

b. *c.*1955, Greenwich Town, Jamaica, West Indies. Jackson began his musical career on the Ethiopian Hi Fi Sound System in the early 70s. To be a serious contender on the **sound system** circuit, the operators would secure unique dub plates, and this led Jackson to **Lee Perry**'s Black Ark studio in Washington Gardens. At the studio, Perry persuaded Jackson to record his debut, the timeless 'History'. The song related the history of Afro-Caribbeans from slavery to the awakening of Rastafari: 'I was bound in chains and taken to the Caribbean - The new faces that I met - Sayin' they are my master - to teach I to be like fools - Jah Jah'. The song surfaced in the UK on a limited-edition Upsetter disco mix, where it was snapped up by Perry enthusiasts, and it was later remixed and re-released in Jamaica on Jackson's own Ital International label. Jackson followed the song with 'Only Jah Can Do It', but elected to concentrate on working with other artists, including the **Soul Syndicate**, **Prince Allah**, Sammy Dread and **Bunny Wailer**. There was a brief return to performing in 1982 when he recorded 'Disarmament', ably supported by **Roots Radics**. By the mid-80s he returned to production and promotional work in the USA on behalf of reggae. While based in New York, Jackson worked with a variety of contemporary **dancehall** singers, including **Cocoa Tea**, **Pinchers** and **Sanchez**. In the late 80s Jackson toured Europe with Pinchers and settled in London, when the release of *Open The Gate*, featuring 'History', ensured the performer cult status.

● ALBUMS: with Lee Perry *Open The Gate* (Trojan 1988)★★★.

Jackson, Chad

Larger-than-life UK cult DJ who in 1987 won the World DJ Championships. Like so many others behind the decks in the house boom, Jackson's origins were in hip hop, though his other interests included reggae and punk. He scored a surprise number 3 in the UK charts with 'Hear The Drummer (Get Wicked)', before going on to remix for numerous clients including **Gang Of Four** ('Money Talks'), **De La Soul** ('Magic Number'), **Beats International** ('Dub Be Good To Me'), **Public Enemy** ('Bring The Noise'), **Prince** ('Sign Of The Times') and **Kraftwerk** ('Tour De France').

Jackson, Chubby

b. Greig Stewart Jackson, 25 October 1918, New York City, New York, USA. As a youth Jackson started out playing clarinet but switched to bass in the mid-30s. In 1937 he began playing professionally, working in a number of minor dance bands. In 1942 he joined the **Charlie Barnet** band and, the following year, was a member of **Woody Herman**'s First Herd, where he played alongside **Ralph Burns**, **Billy Bauer** and **Dave Tough** in one of the most exciting rhythm sections in the history of big band jazz. After leaving Herman in 1946 Jackson freelanced, playing with various bands for record dates, including those led by **Charlie Ventura** and Herman. He also led a bop-orientated small group, featuring **Conte Candoli**, **Terry Gibbs**, Frank Socolow, **Lou Levy**, **Denzil Best** and others, with which he toured Scandinavia. In the late 40s and early 50s Jackson was active in the studios, led his own big band and made numerous record dates with artists including **Bill Harris**, **Zoot Sims** and **Gerry Mulligan**. Jackson was also a member of the Charlie Ventura Big Four with **Marty Napoleon** and **Buddy Rich**. In the 60s Jackson worked in television, hosting a programme for children. He intermittently led bands during these years and also freelanced, playing in bands led by **Harold Baker** and **Bill Coleman**. To a great extent, however, Jackson was largely forgotten by the jazz world other than through his earlier records. Then, in the late 70s, he reappeared as a member of the all-star band which **Lionel Hampton** led on a tour of festivals in the USA, UK and Europe. One of the most overtly enthusiastic musicians in jazz, Jackson's forceful, attacking style was particularly suited to the bands of Herman, Ventura and Hampton. His son is Duffy Jackson, drummer with **Count Basie** and Hampton. In the late 80s Jackson was still around the jazz scene, lending his exhilarating support to a variety of bands.

● ALBUMS: with Charlie Ventura *The Big Four* (1951)★★★, *Chubby's Back!* (1957)★★★, with Lionel Hampton *All Star Band At Newport '78* (1978)★★★★.

● COMPILATIONS: *The Best Of Woody Herman* (1945-47)★★★★, with Woody Herman *Carnegie Hall Concert* (1946)★★★★, *Jam Session* (1947)★★★, *Choice Cuts* (Esquire 1986)★★★, *The Happy Monster* (Cool 'n' Blue 1993, recordings 1944-1947)★★★★.

Jackson, Chuck

b. 22 July 1937, Latta, South Carolina, USA. Jackson travelled the traditional 50s route into soul music via a spell in the gospel group the Raspberry Singers. In 1957, he joined the hit doo-wop group the **Del-Vikings**, taking a prominent role on their US Top 10 success 'Whispering Bells'. His strong baritone vocals enabled him to launch a solo career with Beltone Records in 1960, before signing to the more prestigious **Wand** label the following year. Jackson's early 60s singles for Wand epitomized the New York uptown soul style, with sophisticated arrangements - often crafted by **Burt Bacharach** - supporting his sturdy vocals with female vocalists and orchestras. He enjoyed enormous success in the R&B market for several years with a run of hits that have become soul classics, such as 'I Don't Want To Cry', 'I Wake Up Crying', 'Any Day Now' and 'Tell Him I'm Not Home', although only the majestic 'Any Day Now', co-written by Bacharach, crossed into the US Top 30. In 1965 he was teamed

with **Maxine Brown** on a revival of **Chris Kenner**'s R&B favourite, 'Something You Got', the first of three hit duets over the next two years. Their partnership was severed in 1967 when Jackson joined **Motown**, a decision he later described as 'one of the worst mistakes I ever made in my life'. Although he notched up a minor hit with **Freddie Scott**'s 'Are You Lonely For Me Baby?' in 1969, the majority of his Motown recordings found him pitched against unsympathetic backdrops in a vain attempt to force him into the label's formula. Jackson left Motown in 1971 for **ABC**, where again he could only muster one small hit, 'I Only Get This Feeling', in 1973. Another switch of labels, to All-Platinum in 1975, produced the chart entry 'I'm Wanting You, I'm Needing You' in his traditional style. In 1980, he joined **EMI** America, where his most prominent role was as guest vocalist on two hit albums by **Gary 'U.S.' Bonds**. In the late 80s Jackson was one of many ex-Motown artists signed to Ian Levine's Motor City label, with whom he released two singles. He released an album with **Cissy Houston** in 1992.

● ALBUMS: *I Don't Want To Cry* (Wand 1961)★★★, *Any Day Now* (Wand 1962)★★★★, *Encore* (Wand 1963)★★★, *Chuck Jackson On Tour* (Wand 1964)★★★, *Mr Everything* (Wand 1965)★★★, with Maxine Brown *Saying Something* (Wand 1965)★★★, *A Tribute To Rhythm And Blues* (Wand 1966)★★★, *A Tribute To Rhythm And Blues Vol. 2* (Wand 1966)★★★, with Brown *Hold On We're Coming* (Wand 1966)★★★, *Dedicated To The King* (Wand 1966)★★★, *The Early Show* (1967)★★★, *Chuck Jackson Arrives* (Motown 1968)★★★, *Goin' Back To Chuck Jackson* (Motown 1969)★★★, *Teardrops Keep Falling On My Heart* (Motown 1970)★★★, *Through All Times* (ABC 1974)★★★, *Needing You, Wanting You* (All Platinum 1975)★★★, *The Great Chuck Jackson* (Bulldog 1977)★★★, *I Wanna Give You Some Love* (EMI America 1980)★★★, *After You* (EMI America 1980)★★, with Cissy Houston *I'll Take Care Of You* (Shanachie 1992)★★.

● COMPILATIONS: *Chuck Jackson's Greatest Hits* (Wand 1967)★★★★, *Mr. Emotion* (Kent 1985)★★★, *A Powerful Soul* (Kent 1987)★★★, *Good Things* (Kent 1991)★★★, *I Don't Want To Cry/Any Day Now* (Ace 1993)★★★★, *Encore/Mr Everything* (Ace 1994)★★★, *The Great Recordings* (Tomato 1995)★★★, *Bing Bing Bing!* (Sequel 1998)★★.

Jackson, Cliff

b. 19 July 1902, Culpeper, Virginia, USA, d. 24 May 1970. After studying piano formally Jackson turned to jazz, working in various east coast cities before coming to New York in the early 20s. During the rest of the decade he played in several minor bands, eventually joining one led by **Elmer Snowden**. Jackson later formed his own small group for club engagements. In the 30s he worked mostly as a soloist but also accompanied singers. In the 40s he was with **Sidney Bechet**, **Eddie Condon** and others, appearing regularly throughout this and the following decade at New York's top jazz clubs, including Nick's Cafe Society (Downtown) and Jimmy Ryan's. Also in the 60s he worked with his wife, **Maxine Sullivan**. He was resident at the RX Room from 1968 until the night before his death in May 1970. His widow later turned their home into a museum, the 'House That Jazz Built'. A vigorous performer, early in his career Jackson was a leading stride pianist, greatly feared in cutting contests where he would happily take on much bigger names.

● ALBUMS: *Cliff Jackson's Washboard Wanderers* (1961)★★★, *Uptown And Lowdown* (1961)★★★, *Carolina Shout!* (Black Lion 1961-62)★★★★, *Hot Piano* (1965)★★★, *Parlor Social Call* (1968)★★★, Cliff Jackson And His Crazy Cats (Fountain 1981)★★, *Hot Piano* (Ri-Disc 1988)★★★, with Lil Armstrong *B&W Masters* (Storyville 1988)★★★.

Jackson, Dee D.

This UK vocalist attained success with a crossover dance track 'Automatic Lover', which reached the UK Top 5 in 1978 as well as topping the charts all over Europe. The song had a futuristic, space theme which was continued on her second single 'Meteor Man'. An album's worth of similar material was also released.

● ALBUMS: *Cosmic Curves* (1978)★★★.

Jackson, Deon

b. 26 January 1946, Ann Arbor, Michigan, USA. This versatile performer was discovered by producer Ollie McLaughlin, who also guided the careers of **Del Shannon** and **Barbara Lewis**. An accomplished drummer and clarinettist, Jackson established himself as a singer and composer with 'Love Makes The World Go Round', a smooth, melodic mid-tempo single which reached the US R&B Top 3 and peaked at number 11 in the US pop chart in 1966. Despite undoubted promise, Jackson was only able to secure two further chart entries when 'Love Takes A Long Time Growing' (1966) and 'Ooh Baby' (1967) only managed to scrape in at the lower regions of the charts. From there this musician's career faded and Jackson now makes a living playing cocktail lounge and nightclub piano spots.

● ALBUMS: *Love Makes The World Go Round* (Contempo 1966)★★★.

● COMPILATIONS: *His Greatest Recordings* (1984)★★★.

Jackson, Dewey

b. 21 June 1900, St. Louis, Missouri, USA. Jackson began playing trumpet as a child and was still only in his mid-teens when he was playing professionally with several bands in his home-town. In 1919 he became a regular on the Mississippi riverboats plying out of St. Louis, where his musical companions included **Charlie Creath** and, a few years later, Fate Marable. He continued to work the riverboats with Creath and Marable during the 20s and into the late 30s, although he spent a few months in New York playing in Andy Preer's band at the Cotton Club in 1926. In the early 40s he was still based in St. Louis, but now playing hotels, before he drifted from music for a while, returning in the 50s to play with fellow townsman Singleton Palmer's popular local orchestra. Jackson continued to play sporadically through the 50s and 60s but became steadily less active as the years passed. A sound player in an early jazz style, Jackson's career choices kept him from the big city limelight, but doubtless also offered him a more reliable career than the much more competitive New York scene. Although his rather ornamental style now sounds a little dated, he played with considerable command and fluency. His playing with his own Peacock Orchestra, a band he led on the riverboat *SS Capitol*, and which made a tiny handful of records, shows a fine sense of the polyphonic drive of post-New Orleans music.

Jackson, Freddie

b. 2 October 1956, Harlem, New York, USA. A singer-songwriter, who was especially successful in the late 80s, Jackson was brought up in Harlem, and sang at the White Rock Baptist church while he was still a young child. Later, he worked in a bank before joining the group LJE, along with the singer, songwriter and producer Paul Laurence. In the early 80s, Jackson moved to California and became lead singer with the R&B vocal/instrumental group Mystic Merlin. He sang on their *Full Moon*, which featured the popular soul/dance track 'Mr Magician'. In 1984, Jackson returned to the east coast where he was spotted singing in a New York club by **Melba Moore**. After serving as a backing vocalist for Moore, **Evelyn 'Champagne' King**, and others, Jackson signed a solo contract with **Capitol Records**, and issued *Rock Me Tonight* in 1985. Both the album, and its title track, 'Rock Me Tonight (For Old Times Sake)', which Jackson had written with Paul Laurence, made the US Top 20, and also did well in the UK. Subsequent singles from *Rock Me Tonight*, such as 'You Are My Lady' and 'He'll Never Love You (Like I Do)', proved to be ideally suited for the burgeoning soul club scene on both sides of the Atlantic. In 1986, Jackson duetted with Melba Moore on 'A Little Bit More' from her album *A Lot Of Love*, and issued his own *Just Like The First Time*, which included three more successful dance sides, 'Have You Ever Loved Somebody', 'Tasty Love', and 'Jam Tonight'. Jackson's subsequent albums did not fare so well, and were sometimes critized for their 'sameness'. Nevertheless, *Don't Let Love Slip Away* contained two UK hits, 'Nice 'N' Slow' and 'Crazy (For Me)', and *Time For Love* was given extra interest by the inclusion of guest artists such as Audrey Wheeler, **Will Downing** and Naje. *Here It Is* was released on **RCA Records**. Jackson's songwriting activities, mostly in collaboration with Paul Laurence, resulted in numbers such as 'Trust Me' for Lilo Thomas, 'Keepin' My Lover Satisfied' for Melba Moore, and 'Jam Song' for **Howard Johnson**.

● ALBUMS: *Rock Me Tonight* (Capitol 1985)★★★, *Just Like The First Time* (Capitol 1986)★★, *Don't Let Love Slip Away* (Capitol 1988)★★, *Do Me Again* (Capitol 1990)★★★, *Time For Love* (Capitol 1992)★★, *Here It Is* (RCA 1993)★★.

● COMPILATIONS: *The Greatest Hits Of ...* (Capitol 1993)★★★.

Jackson, George

b. 1946, Greenville, Mississippi, USA. Jackson has a quietly emotional country-soul delivery that could have made him a southern-soul singing star in his own right, but as he only recorded 15 singles over a 22-year period between 1963 and 1985 (and, more recently, a fine album), it is as a prolific and highly skilled songwriter that he is most respected. When Jackson was 14, he offered some of his songs to Ike Turner when Turners' Revue was playing Greenville, and went with him to Cosimo's famous studio in New Orleans to record 'Nobody Wants To Cha Cha With Me'/'Who Was That Guy' for Turner's Prann label. Later, Jackson travelled extensively, trying to promote himself and his songs. He was rejected by the fast-growing **Stax Records**, but in 1965, while in Memphis, Jackson linked up with the **Ovations** on the newly formed Goldwax label, penning their biggest hit, 'It's Wonderful To Be In Love'. Goldwax soon recognized Jackson's writing ability and he provided material for other artists on the label, including 'Old Friend' and 'He's Too Old' for **Spencer Wiggins**, and 'Coming Back To Me Baby' for **James Carr**. He also joined fellow singer-songwriter Dan Greer to cut the Goldwax single 'Good Times'/'You Didn't Know It But You Had Me' as George And Greer. By 1968, Jackson had left Goldwax for the nearby Hi label, where he initially recorded one single, 'I'm Gonna Wait'/'So Good To Me'. While still involved with Hi, Jackson appeared as Bart Jackson on a **Decca** release, 'Wonderful Dream'/'Dancing Man', and, shortly afterwards, moved across to **Muscle Shoals** and Rick Hall's Fame studio at the instigation of Nashville producer (and an old friend of Hall's) **Billy Sherrill**. This was Fame's peak soul period, and Hall engaged Jackson as a 'house' writer. He found immediate success with **Clarence Carter**'s 'Too Weak To Fight' and **Wilson Pickett**'s 'A Man And A Half'. Later Jackson songs for Fame included many of **Candi Staton**'s superb early recordings, such as 'I'm Just A Prisoner', 'I'd Rather Be An Old Man's Sweetheart (Than A Young Man's Fool)', the racy 'Get It When I Want It', 'Evidence', 'Too Hurt To Cry', 'Freedom Is Just Beyond The Door' and the beautiful 'How Can I Put Out The Flame'. These songs are widely regarded as examples of some of the finest southern soul ever recorded by a female artist, with lyrics that were full of meaning and innuendo, a hallmark of Jackson's best work. He wrote for other Fame artists, and recorded three singles himself, two appearing on Fame, and one later leased out to **Chess**. By the early 70s Rick Hall's Fame productions for 'out-of-town' artists were increasingly 'pop'-orientated. The **Osmonds** recorded there, and Jackson gave them their first ever hit on **MGM**, the massive-selling early 1971 US chart-topper, 'One Bad Apple', which he had originally written with the **Jackson Five** in mind. Meanwhile, Jackson 'the performer' fleetingly rejoined **Willie Mitchell** at Hi, and in 1972/3 released two more singles of his own, including the beautiful southern country/soul song 'Aretha, Sing One For Me', a paean

to the great female soul singer. It had little commercial impact, and Jackson soon linked up with MGM, for whom he had effectively launched the Osmonds pop act. While still writing for others, Jackson also recorded three singles for the label in 1973/4, the best being the punchy '(If I Could Get On That) Soul Train'. One more followed in 1976 for Er Music ('Talkin' About The Love I Have For You') and then, in 1979, Jackson cut 'Fast Young Lady' for Muscle Shoals Sounds. After **Bob Seger** had a big hit in 1979 with Jackson's 'Old Time Rock And Roll', the singer-songwriter formed his own publishing company, Happy Hooker Music, and gained further financial rewards in 1981 from another Seger success, 'Trying To Live My Life Without You', originally cut some years earlier by **Otis Clay** for Hi. Jackson then recorded several more obscure singles for his own Washataw and Happy Hooker labels in 1984/5, before joining the burgeoning southern blues and soul label Malaco as a staff writer. Jackson's successful compositions for the label included the huge seller for the late **Z.Z. Hill**, 'Down Home Blues', which he originally wrote some 10 years earlier. With the likes of **Bobby 'Blue' Bland**, **Johnnie Taylor**, **Latimore** and **Denise LaSalle** all recording for **Malaco**, Jackson's brand of southern soul songwriting has plenty of scope. In March 1991, he recorded an excellent album, *Heart To Heart Collect*, for Senator Jones' Hep' Me Records, and wrote all of the 10 tracks. Recorded at IRS studio in Pearl, Mississippi, it was released in the UK on CD in 1993 on Gary Cape's Black Grape label.

● ALBUMS: *Heart To Heart Collect* (Hep' Me 1991)★★★★.

● COMPILATIONS: *Hi Records The Blue Sessions* one track (1988)★★★★, *Hi Records The Soul Years* two tracks (1988)★★, *The History Of Hi Records Rhythm & Blues Volume 1* one track (1988)★★, *River Town Blues* one track (1988)★★, *The Hi Records Story* one track (1989)★★★, *Hi R&B And Soul* two tracks (1992)★★, *The Hi Records 45's Collection Volume 2* five tracks (1992)★★.

Jackson, J.J.

b. Bronx, New York City, New York, USA. Jackson first attracted attention as an arranger for jazz organist **Brother Jack McDuff** and blues singer **Jimmy Witherspoon**. He subsequently formed a songwriting partnership with Sid Barnes and enjoyed success with compositions for **Inez And Charlie Foxx** and **Mary Wells**. Jackson's performing career began in earnest in 1966. The ebullient 'But It's Alright' was recorded in London with a backing band which featured saxophonists **Dick Morrissey** and **John Marshall**. Subsequent releases included the energetic 'Come See Me', later recorded by the **Pretty Things**, as well as a version of **Robbie Robertson**'s 'The Stones I Throw'. Jackson continued recording into the 70s and his voice was featured in the soundtrack to the film *Car Wash*. He has since become a respected disc jockey and, more recently, a 'video jockey' on the **MTV** channel.

● ALBUMS: *J.J.* (1966)★★, *But It's Alright/I Dig Girls* (1967)★★★, *J.J. Jackson With The Greatest Little Soul Band*

(Strike 1967)★★★, *The Great J.J. Jackson* (1968)★★★, *The Greatest Little Soul Band In The World* (MCA 1969)★★★, *J.J.'s Dilemma* (RCA Victor 1970)★★.

Jackson, Jack

b. 20 February 1906, Belvedere, Kent, England, d. 15 January 1978, Jersey, Channel Islands. A trumpeter, bandleader, and disc jockey, Jackson was an accomplished musician and a dynamic character. The son of a brass bandsman, he was playing the cornet in local brass bands by the time he was 11. As a teenager, he played various instruments in dance bands before learning to play the trumpet at the Royal Academy of Music. He joined Bert Ralton's Band, and was with him on the 1926 South African tour during which Ralton was killed in a hunting accident. On his return in 1927, Jackson worked briefly for **Ambrose**, and then spent more than two years with **Jack Hylton**, during which time his spirited solos enlivened several of the band's excellent recordings. After leaving Hylton, be played with Howard Jacobs, Percival Mackey, and **Jack Payne**, before forming his own band which opened at the Dorchester Hotel in London in 1933. His opening theme was 'Make Those People Sway', and he ended the evening with the haunting 'Dancing In The Dark'. He began recording and broadcasting almost straight away, with ensembles which featured several top musicians, and vocalists such as **Al Bowlly**, Fred Latham, **Denny Dennis**, Peggy Cochran, Jack Cooper, Helen Clare, and **Alberta Hunter**. Early in 1939, he began to tour the music halls, but with the outbreak of World War II he ran an engineering shop and a drawing office. He returned to bandleading again after the war, but formally retired in 1947. His outgoing personality made him a natural for broadcasting, and he compered BBC programmes such as *Salute To Rhythm*, *Band Call*, and *Band Parade*, as well as working on **Decca** shows for **Radio Luxembourg**. In 1948, Jackson began his famous revolutionary late night hour-long record programme, *Record Roundup*, on the BBC Light Programme. It went out for some 20 years, and became the first radio show that was able to actually 'break' a new record. During that time, Jackson introduced British audiences to the delights of numerous American artists such as **Rose Murphy** and **Nellie Lutcher**. As recording tape became widely available, he cleverly intercut excerpts from comedy monologue discs by such as Shelley Berman and Bob Newhart, with his own voice and current popular records, to make a fast-moving, zany programme, which became compulsive listening. In the 50s, he also appeared frequently on television programmes such as *Rooftop Rendezvous* and *Cabaret Cruise*, and in variety theatres. In 1962 he went to live in Tenerife, where he continued to record his radio programmes, and fly them back to England. From 1973 he was plagued by ill-health, and retired to Rickmansworth on the outskirts of London, where his sons ran the Jackson Music Group, which consisted of a recording studio and a sound equipment business. He

managed to present a new record programme, *The Jack Jackson Show*, for a time in the mid-70s, before his health finally deteriorated.
● ALBUMS: with Alberta Hunter *The Legendary Alberta Hunter-The London Sessions* (DRG 1983)★★★, *Make Those People Sway* (World Records 80s)★★★, *Things Are Looking Up-Jack Jackson & His Orchestra At The Dorchester Hotel, London* (Saville 1985)★★.

Jackson, Jackie

b. Sigmund Esco Jackson, 4 May 1951, Gary, Indiana, USA. Jackie has spent his entire professional career as a member of the **Jackson Five** (later known as the **Jacksons**). He was a founder of the family troupe in 1962, and has remained a relatively sheltered figure within the group ever since. Like his brothers **Michael** and **Jermaine**, he was groomed for a solo career at the height of the group's American popularity in the early 70s. When his solitary album flopped, he resumed his place as a backing singer for his younger brothers. By the late 70s, he had won some measure of artistic involvement in the Jacksons' recordings, and he co-wrote the hit singles 'Destiny', 'Can You Feel It?', 'Walk Right Now' and 'Torture' between 1978 and 1982. Since then, he has surfaced only occasionally in the media, expressing his frustration at being overshadowed by the success of his brother Michael.
● ALBUMS: *Jackie Jackson* (Motown 1973)★★.

Jackson, Janet

b. Janet Damita Jackson, 16 May 1966, Gary, Indiana, USA. Jackson was the youngest of the nine children in the family that produced the **Jackson Five** (including **Michael Jackson**, **Jermaine Jackson** and **LaToya Jackson**). When Janet was four years old, the family moved to the Los Angeles area; three years later she made her performing debut in Las Vegas with her brothers. At the age of nine, she joined them on a television special. She was cast in the US television programmes *Good Times* from 1977-79 and *Diff'rent Strokes* from 1981-82. She signed to **A&M Records** in 1982 and recorded her self-titled debut album, followed by *Dream Street* in 1984. Both albums sold only moderately, although they each yielded one US Top 10 single. Jackson's breakthrough came in 1986 with *Control*, which reached number 1 and produced an astonishing five US Top 10 singles and three UK Top 10 singles. The album was ultimately certified quadruple platinum for sales of over four million copies in the USA. Jackson followed up in 1989 with *Janet Jackson's Rhythm Nation 1814*, another quadruple platinum album, which yielded chart-topping singles such as 'Miss You Much' and 'Rhythm Nation'. Jackson undertook her first concert tour in 1990. By the end of the year she had scooped eight **Billboard** awards, including Top R&B Albums and Singles Artist, Best Pop and R&B Album Award for *Rhythm Nation*, and Top Hot 100 Singles Artist. The success of the *Rhythm Nation* album continued into 1991 when, in January, Jackson became the first artist in history to have culled from one album seven Top 5 singles in the *Billboard* chart. Jackson's commercial peak continued into the 90s with the unprecedented performance of *Janet*, which entered the US album chart at number 1, beating brother Michael's sales record by selling 350,000 copies in its first week. The compilation album *Design Of A Decade* was another huge seller, and followed her collaboration with brother Michael on 'Scream'. Her first studio set in four years, *The Velvet Rope*, was a deeply personal album which dealt frankly with her much self-publicized emotional breakdown.

● ALBUMS: *Janet Jackson* (A&M 1982)★★, *Dream Street* (A&M 1984)★★★, *Control* (A&M 1986)★★★★, *Control: The Remixes* (A&M 1987)★★★, *Janet Jackson's Rhythm Nation 1814* (A&M 1989)★★★★, *Janet* (Virgin 1993)★★★★, *The Velvet Rope* (Virgin 1997)★★★.

● COMPILATIONS: *Janet Remixed* (Virgin 1995)★★★, *Design Of A Decade 1986/1996* (A&M 1995)★★★.

● VIDEOS: *Janet* (Virgin 1994), *Design Of A Decade 86-96* (VVL 1995).

● FURTHER READING: *Out Of The Madness (The Strictly Unauthorised Biography Of ...)*, Andrew Bart and J Randy Taraborrelli (eds.).

Jackson, Jermaine

b. Jermaine Lajuan Jackson, 11 December 1954, Gary, Indiana, USA. Jermaine was one of five brothers who made up the **Jackson Five** in 1962. Besides playing bass, he acted as vocal counterpoint to his younger brother **Michael Jackson**, a musical relationship that continued after the group were signed to **Motown Records** in 1968. Jermaine contributed occasional lead vocals to their albums in the early 70s, and his performance of 'I Found That Girl' on *Third Album* was one of their most affecting ballads. Like his brothers Michael and **Jackie**, Jermaine was singled out by Motown for a solo career, and he had an immediate US Top 10 hit with a revival of **Shep And The Limeliters**' doo-wop classic 'Daddy's Home', in 1972. Later releases were less favourably received, but he consolidated his position within the company in 1973 with his marriage to Hazel, the daughter of Motown boss **Berry Gordy**. His new family connections entailed a stark conflict of interest when the other members of the Jackson Five decided to leave the label in 1975. Given the choice of deserting either his brothers or his father-in-law, he elected to remain with Motown, where his solo releases were subsequently given a higher priority than before. Despite heavy promotion, Jermaine's late 70s recordings failed to establish him as a distinctive soul voice, and he faced constant critical comparisons with the **Jacksons**' work on Epic. His career was revitalized by the intervention of **Stevie Wonder**, who wrote and produced the 1979 hit 'Let's Get Serious' in 1979, which successfully echoed the joyous funk of Wonder's own recordings. The gentle soul of 'You Like Me Don't You' brought him another hit in 1981, while the US Top 20 single 'Let Me Tickle Your Fancy' the following year featured

an unlikely collaboration with new wave band **Devo**. Jackson's increased public profile won him a more generous contract with Motown in the early 80s. He formed his own production company, launching Michael Lovesmith as a recording artist and overseeing the career development of **Syreeta**. But this increased freedom was not enough to keep him at Motown, and in 1983 he signed with **Arista Records**. The following year, he was reconciled with his brothers: he joined the Jacksons on the *Victory* album and tour, and his own *Jermaine Jackson* featured a sparkling duet with Michael Jackson on 'Tell Me We're Not Dreaming'. He subsequently collaborated with Pia Zadora on the theme from the film *Voyage Of The Rock Aliens*, and with **Whitney Houston** on his 1986 project *Precious Memories*. In that same year, he formed his own label, WORK Records, and accepted an offer to portray the late **Marvin Gaye** in a biopic that was never completed. He has continued to work with the Jacksons and as a soloist since then, although his recent projects have been overshadowed by the media circus surrounding his brother Michael, a subject touched upon in Jermaine's 'Word To The Badd!!'.

● ALBUMS: *Jermaine* (Motown 1972)★★, *Come Into My Life* (Motown 1973)★★, *My Name Is Jermaine* (Motown 1976)★★, *Feel The Fire* (Motown 1977)★★, *Frontier* (Motown 1978)★★, *Let's Get Serious* (Motown 1980)★★★, *Jermaine* (Motown 1980)★★, *I Like Your Style* (Motown 1981)★★, *Let Me Tickle Your Fancy* (Motown 1982)★★, *Jermaine Jackson* (USA) *Dynamite* (UK) (Arista 1984)★★★, *Precious Moments* (Arista 1986)★★, *Don't Take It Personal* (Arista 1989)★★, *You Said* (La Face 1991)★★.

Jackson, Jim

b. *c.*1890, Hernando, Mississippi, USA, d. 1937, Hernando, Mississippi, USA. Emerging from the minstrel and medicine show circuit, Jackson was a well-known figure around the Memphis area where he worked with artists such as **Robert Wilkins**, **Furry Lewis** and **Gus Cannon**. His first record, 'Jim Jackson's Kansas City Blues, Parts 1 & 2', recorded for Vocalion in October 1927, became one of the first, and biggest, 'race' hits. He later recorded 'Parts 3 & 4' and many variations on its basic theme. He continued to record for various labels up until 1930, and some 40 tracks of his work are extant. Jackson was never an outstanding guitarist and his success was based on his humour; although it has not dated well, occasional numbers such as 'I Heard The Voice Of A Pork Chop' can still raise a smile.

● ALBUMS: *Best Of Jim Jackson 1928-1930* (Earl Archives 1987)★★, *Kansas City Blues* (Agram 1988)★★, *Jim Jackson 1927-1929* (Blues Document 1989)★★.

Jackson, Joe

b. 11 August 1955, Burton-upon-Trent, Staffordshire, England. Having learned violin and piano as a teenager, Jackson gained a place to study piano at London's Royal College of Music. After two years of finding his way in the music business, first through being in Arms And Legs and then as musical director to Coffee And Cream, he was signed up by **A&M Records** in the summer of 1978. His accomplished debut, 'Is She Really Going Out With Him?', was not an immediate hit; however, by the time *Look Sharp* was released, the song had become one of the stand-out numbers of his live shows, and reached the UK charts, albeit some months after first nudging the US Top 20. Jackson's first two albums revealed a confident writer of thoughtful lyrics, coupled with exciting new wave energy. 'Is She Really Going Out With Him?' has a classic opening line, containing humour, irony and jealousy: 'Pretty women out walking with gorillas down my street'. While *Look Sharp* and *I'm The Man* were power-pop, the subsequent *Beat Crazy* (containing some reggae) began a trend of changing musical direction, which Jackson relished. *Jumpin' Jive*, although superb, was a throwback to the music of the 40s; on this he covered classic songs by **Cab Calloway** and **Louis Jordan**. One of his most satisfying works came in 1982 with *Night And Day*. The album was recorded in New York, where Jackson settled following his marriage break-up. The songs are introspective but positive; the hauntingly hummable 'Steppin' Out', with its mantric bass line and crisp piano, is a superbly crafted pop song that won him many new admirers. *Body And Soul* came close to repeating the success, and Jackson was again critically acclaimed. *Big World*, minus the long-standing bass of Graham Maby, was a three-sided direct to two-track disc. However, the songs had less commercial appeal and Jackson's fortunes began to decline. The instrumental *Will Power*, although faultlessly recorded with a high standard of musicianship, put Jackson in a musical netherworld. He had come so far musically, in such a short time, that his followers found it hard to keep up with him. A live album and the film soundtrack to *Tucker* both arrived in 1988 and despite the critical plaudits, following the commercial failure of *Blaze Of Glory* in 1989, his contract with A&M was not renewed. It was inconceivable that a talent as great as Jackson's would be without a contract for long, and by early 1991 he was signed to **Virgin Records**, releasing *Laughter And Lust* to little commercial success. Jackson finds himself in the difficult position of still being viewed as part of the new wave pop movement, yet he has developed way beyond those realms. As a serious musician, he needs to be allowed to work without the constraints of commercial considerations. He has now left behind all remnants of power-punk, and shown that film scores and orchestral works are well within his boundaries. He was signed to Sony Classical in 1997.

● ALBUMS: *Look Sharp!* (A&M 1979)★★★★, *I'm The Man* (A&M 1979)★★★★, *Beat Crazy* (A&M 1980)★★, *Joe Jackson's Jumpin' Jive* (A&M 1981)★★★★, *Night And Day* (A&M 1982)★★★★, *Mike's Murder* film soundtrack (A&M 1983)★★, *Body And Soul* (A&M 1984)★★★★, *Big World* (A&M 1986)★★, *Will Power* (A&M 1987)★★★, *Joe Jackson - Live* (A&M 1988)★★★, *Tucker: Original Soundtrack* (A&M 1988)★★, *Blaze Of Glory* (A&M 1989)★★, *Laughter And Lust* (Virgin 1991)★★, *Night Music* (Virgin 1994)★★★, *Heaven And Hell* (Sony 1997)★★★★.

● COMPILATIONS: *Steppin' Out - The Very Best Of ...* (A&M 1990)★★★, *This Is It - The A&M Years* (A&M 1997)★★★★.

Jackson, John

b. 25 February 1924, Woodville, Virginia, USA. Born into a musical family, Jackson began to play guitar at around five years old, learning from a convict who worked on a chain gang. Jackson's music, at least some of which was learned from records, covers a wide range of traditional southern material, including blues, rags, country dance tunes and ballads (which have earned him the description of songster rather than blues singer), and he plays in a style related to other black guitarists from the eastern states, such as **Blind Blake** and **Blind Boy Fuller**. Since the 60s Jackson has made many records, including one where he played second guitar to **Buddy Moss**, as well as concert and festival appearances, both in the USA and overseas.

● ALBUMS: *Blues And Country Dance Tunes from Virginia* (Arhoolie 1965)★★★, *In Europe* (Arhoolie 1969)★★★.

● VIDEOS: *John Jackson* (Kay Jazz 1988).

Jackson, Larry

b. 15 June 1947, Gadsden, Alabama, USA. His father died in a car accident four months before he was born. He began playing guitar as a child and made his first performance at the age of 10 singing at a local theatre. He relocated to Columbus, Georgia, in 1957 where he lived with his two sisters until the mid-50s, when he moved to Atlanta. He began songwriting in 1962 and in later years, he formed his own publishing company, Mountain Water Publishing. He made his first recordings in 1986 in Nashville for the Columbus-based Trish label, owned by his sister Pat. In June 1986, the death of his mother saw him lose all interest in the music industry for almost two years and the recordings were never issued. He returned to the recording studios in 1988 and his recording of 'Country Music Never Let Me Down', recorded for JDS in Atlanta, had independent chart success. He subsequently moved to Nashville, where he hopes that his talent for writing on a wide range of subjects and his personal appearances will see him fulfil his ambition of country stardom. He formed his own Loree label and, in addition to his own recordings, works on producing other artists. His first album, which contained two of the unissued Trish tracks, namely 'Damn Those Memories' and 'Sarah', has received air play in America and Japan and also Eastern Europe.

● ALBUMS: *The Blue Highway* (Loree 1991)★★★.

Jackson, LaToya

b. 29 May 1956, Gary, Indiana, USA. As a member of the singing Jackson family, LaToya served her apprenticeship as a backing vocalist to the **Jacksons** group along with her sisters, Rebbie and **Janet Jackson**.

LaToya embarked on a solo career in 1980, signing to the Polydor label. Despite the family connection, LaToya's solo career found difficulty in emulating the success of her younger sister Janet; her highest single chart position was with the US number 56, 'Hearts Don't Lie' (1984) on her new label, Private I/Epic. A later label change to **RCA Records** did not alter her fortunes. She later exacerbated family relations with a somewhat scurrilous autobiography in 1991, and by refusing to sanction the 1992 ABC mini-series *The Jacksons: An American Dream*.

● ALBUMS: *LaToya Jackson* (Polydor 1980)★★, *My Special Love* (Polydor 1981)★★, *Heart Don't Lie* (Private Stock 1984)★★, *Imagination* (Private Stock 1985)★★, *You're Gonna Get Rocked* (RCA 1988)★★.

● FURTHER READING: *LaToya Jackson*, LaToya Jackson with Patricia Romanowski.

Jackson, Lee
(see **Jackson Heights**; **Nice**; **Refugee**)

Jackson, Li'l Son
b. Melvin Jackson, 16 (or 17) August 1915, Barry, Texas, USA, d. 30 May 1976, Dallas, Texas, USA. Having been raised in a sharecropping environment and taught to play guitar by his father, Johnny, Lil' Son ran away from home during the 30s. He has been described as a sincere man and religion seems to have played an important part in his life. He worked with the Blue Eagle Four Spiritual group before being drafted into the army. He served in the UK, France and Germany before returning to take up a career as a blues singer. Friends persuaded Melvin Jackson to send in a fairground recording to Bill Quinn, the owner of Gold Star Records, in the hope that it might lead to a recording contract. It did, and between 1948 and 1954 Jackson, who had moved on to the more prestigious Imperial label, made records in a style that combined his rural roots with currently acceptable R&B sounds. These sold well, particularly in his home state, Texas, and on the west coast, where many black Texans had settled. He toured extensively, but after a road accident retired from music to work in an automobile scrap yard; he was also employed by his local church. Fortunately Chris Strachwitz of **Arhoolie Records** traced and recorded him in 1960, in a more simple setting. Jackson died of cancer in 1976.

● ALBUMS: *Lil Son Jackson* (Arhoolie 1960)★★★, *Blues Come To Texas* (Arhoolie 1981)★★★, *Rockin' An' Rollin'* (Pathe Marconi 1984)★★★.

● COMPILATIONS: *Mississippi Delta Blues Vols. 1 & 2* (Arhoolie 1994)★★★, *Complete Imperial Recordings* 2-CD set (Capitol 1995)★★★.

Jackson, Mahalia
b. 26 October 1911, New Orleans, Louisiana, USA, d. 27 January 1972, Chicago, Illinois, USA. For many commentators, Mahalia Jackson remains the definitive exponent of gospel music. At the age of four she sang at the Plymouth Rock Baptist Church and later joined the Mount Moriah Baptist Church junior choir. She mixed the singing styles of the Baptists with the Sanctified Church, which produced a powerful rhythm and beat, and fell under the influence of gospel artists Roberta Martin and Willie Mae Ford Smith. Coupled with the expressions of **Bessie Smith** and **Ma Rainey**, which in her teens Jackson had begun to observe, she developed the beginnings of a deep soulful blues style. In 1927, Mahalia moved from New Orleans to Chicago; after her first Sunday church service, where she had given a impromptu performance of her favourite song, 'Hand Me Down My Favourite Trumpet, Gabriel', she was invited to join the Greater Salem Baptist Church Choir and began touring the city's churches and surrounding areas with the Johnson Singers.

After several years with the Johnsons, Mahalia began to forge a solo career. During this time, as well as singing in church, she sang at political rallies and in 1937 became a song demonstrator of the talents of gospel songwriter **Thomas A. Dorsey**. That same year she recorded four tracks for **Decca**, to little commercial success, and was dropped soon afterwards. Jackson then toured extensively - in the intervening time she qualified as a beautician to safeguard her future - and recorded again, this time for the Apollo label in 1946, which included the first use in gospel music of the Hammond organ rather than the usual lone piano. These recordings, most of which feature a simple backdrop, show a singer of peerless quality, whose prudent use of slow hymns allowed space for her voice to develop its seemingly effortless inflections. Pianist Mildred Falls, who remained with Jackson throughout her career, added a measured, complimentary background. The success of the Apollo pressings, in particular 'Move On Up A Little Higher', culminated in 1954 with Jackson hosting and starring in her own Sunday night radio show for **CBS**, bringing black gospel music to a mass white audience. That same year she began recording for CBS which resulted in a number of tight productions and a departure from the almost improvisational feel of previous sessions. Although these releases lacked the simplicity of earlier work, they became a huge success; in 1956 she brought the studio audience at the *Ed Sullivan Show* to its feet. She later triumphed at the rain-soaked **Newport Jazz Festival** in 1958. Jackson became an ambassador for gospel music, and embarked on several successful European tours. Despite endless entreaties, she resisted crossing over into jazz or blues and pop for many years, although she did perform with **Duke Ellington** in his 'Black, Brown And Beige Fantasy' suite. She sang at one of the inaugural balls for President John F. Kennedy in 1960, and often performed at Dr. Martin Luther King's rallies. In 1968 she sang at King's funeral, where she gave an emotional rendition of Dorsey's 'Precious Lord, Take My Hand'. Towards the end of her career Jackson did bow to pressure to record more secular songs and included, among others, 'What The World Needs Now' and **Dion**'s classic anthem, 'Abraham Martin And John'. Mahalia gave her last public performance in Germany in October 1971, and died of heart failure in 1972.

● ALBUMS: *Mahalia Jackson* (Vogue 1952)★★★, *Newport 1958* (1958)★★★★, *Great Gettin' Up Morning* (Columbia 1959)★★★, *Just As I Am* (Kenwood 1960)★★★★, *The Power And The Glory* (Columbia 1960)★★, *Come On Children Let's Sing* (1960)★★★, *I Believe* (Columbia 1961)★★★, *Sweet Little Jesus Boy* (Columbia 1961)★★★, *Every Time I Feel The Spirit* (1961)★★★, *Recorded Live In Europe* (1962)★★, *Great Songs Of Love And Faith* (1962)★★★, *Silent Night - Songs For Christmas* (1962)★★, *Make A Joyful Noise Unto The Lord* (1962)★★★, *Bless This House* (Columbia 1963)★★★, *Let's Pray Together* (1964)★★★, *In The Upper Room* (Kenwood 1965)★★★, *Mahalia* (1965)★★★★, *No Matter How You Pray* (1965)★★★, *Mahalia Sings* (1966)★★★★, *The Old Rugged Cross* (1966)★★★, *My Faith* (Columbia 1967)★★★, *In Concert* (Columbia 1968)★★★, *A Mighty Fortress* (Columbia 1968)★★★, *Sings The Best-Loved Hymns Of Dr. Martin Luther King, Jr.* (Columbia 1968)★★★, *You'll Never Walk Alone* (1968)★★★, *Christmas With Mahalia* (Columbia 1968)★★, *Sings America's Favorite Hymns* (Columbia 1971)★★★, *Right Out Of The Church* (Columbia 1976)★★★.

● COMPILATIONS: *Best Of Mahalia Jackson* (Kenwood)★★★★, *1911 - 1972* (Kenwood)★★★★, *Mahalia Jackson's Greatest Hits* (Columbia 1963)★★★, *The Great Mahalia Jackson* (Columbia 1972)★★, *The World's Greatest Gospel Singer* (Columbia 1975)★★★, *How I Got Over* (Columbia 1976)★★★★, *Gospel* (Vogue 1977)★★★, *The Warm And Tender Soul Of Mahalia Jackson* (Joker 1981)★★★, *20 Greatest Hits* (Astan 1984)★★★, *The Mahalia Jackson Collection* (Deja Vu 1985)★★★, *When The Saint's Go Marching In* (Columbia 1987)★★★★, *The Mahalia Jackson Story* (Deja Vu 1989)★★★, *Gospels, Spirituals And Hymns* (Columbia/ Legacy 1991)★★★.

● VIDEOS: *Mahalia* (Hendring Video 1990).

● FURTHER READING: *Just Mahalia, Baby*, Laurraine Goreau. *Got To Tell It: Mahalia Jackson Queen Of Gospel*, Jules Schwerin.

Jackson, Michael

b. Michael Joseph Jackson, 29 August 1958, Gary, Indiana, USA. Jackson has spent almost his entire life as a public performer. He was a founder-member of the **Jackson Five** at the age of four, soon becoming the group's lead vocalist and frontman. Onstage, he modelled his dance moves and vocal styling on **James Brown**, and portrayed an absolute self-confidence on stage that belied his shy, private personality. The Jackson Five were signed to **Motown Records** at the end of 1968; their early releases, including chart-toppers 'I Want You Back' and 'I'll Be There', illustrated his remarkable maturity. Although Michael was too young to have experienced the romantic situations that were the subject of his songs, he performed with total sincerity, showing all the hallmarks of a great soul artist. Ironically, his pre-adolescent vocal work carried a conviction that he often failed to recapture later in his

career. When **MGM Records** launched the **Osmonds** as rivals to the Jackson Five in 1970, and singled out their lead singer, 13-year-old **Donny Osmond**, for a solo career, Motown felt duty bound to reply in kind. Michael Jackson's first release as a solo performer was the aching ballad 'Got To Be There', a major US and UK hit. A revival of **Bobby Day**'s rock 'n' roll novelty 'Rockin' Robin' reached the top of the US charts in 1972, while the sentimental film theme 'Ben' repeated that achievement later in the year. Motown capitalized on Jackson's popularity with a series of hurried albums, which mixed material angled towards the teenage market with a selection of the label's standards. They also stockpiled scores of unissued tracks, which were released in the 80s to cash in on the success of his Epic recordings. As the Jackson Five's sales slipped in the mid-70s, Michael's solo career was put on hold, and he continued to reserve his talents for the group after they were reborn as the **Jacksons** in 1976. He re-entered the public eye with a starring role in the film musical *The Wiz*, collaborating on the soundtrack album with **Quincy Jones**. Their partnership was renewed in 1979 when Jones produced *Off The Wall*, a startlingly successful collection of contemporary soul material that introduced the world to the adult Michael Jackson. In his new incarnation, Jackson retained the vocal flexibility of old, but added a new element of sophistication and maturity. The album topped the charts in the UK and USA, and contained two number 1 singles, 'Don't Stop Till You Get Enough' (for which Jackson won a Grammy award) and 'Rock With You'. Meanwhile, Motown capitalized on his commercial status by reissuing a recording from the mid-70s, 'One Day In Your Life', which duly topped the UK charts. Jackson continued to tour and record with the Jacksons after this solo success, while media speculation grew about his private life. He was increasingly portrayed as a figure trapped in an eternal childhood, surrounded by toys and pet animals, and insulated from the traumas of the real world. This image was consolidated when he was chosen to narrate an album based on the 1982 fantasy film *ET - The Extra Terrestrial*. The record was quickly withdrawn because of legal complications, but still won Jackson another Grammy award. In 1982 *Thriller*, Jackson's second album with Quincy Jones, was released, and went on to become one of the most commercially successful albums of all time. It also produced a run of successful hit singles, each accompanied by a promotional video that widened the scope of the genre. 'The Girl Is Mine', a duet with **Paul McCartney**, began the sequence in relatively subdued style; it reached number 1 in the USA and UK, but merely set the scene for 'Billie Jean', an effortless mix of disco and pop that spawned a series of answer records from other artists. The accompanying video was equally spectacular, portraying Jackson as a master of dance, a magician who could transform lives, and a shadowy figure who lived outside the everyday world. Its successor, 'Beat It', established another precedent, with its determinedly rock-flavoured guitar solo by **Eddie Van Halen** making it the first black record to receive rotation airplay on the **MTV** video station. Its promo film involved Jackson at the centre of a choreographed street battle, a conscious throwback to the set pieces of *West Side Story*. However, even this was a modest effort compared to 'Thriller', a rather mannered piece of disco-funk accompanied by a stunning long-form video that placed Jackson in a parade of Halloween horrors. This promo clip spawned a follow-up, *The Making Of 'Thriller'*, which in turn sold more copies than any other home video to date.

The *Thriller* album and singles won Jackson a further seven Grammies; amidst this run of hits, Jackson slotted in 'Say Say Say', a second chart-topping duet with Paul McCartney. He accepted the largest individual sponsorship deal in history from Pepsi-Cola in 1983; the following year, his involvement in the Jacksons' 'Victory Tour' sparked the greatest demand for concert tickets in the history of popular music. Jackson had by now become an almost mythical figure, and like most myths he attracted hyperbole. A group of Jehovah's Witnesses announced that he was the Messiah; he was said to be taking drugs to change his skin colour to white; it was claimed that he had undergone extensive plastic surgery to alter his appearance; and photographs were published that suggested he slept in a special chamber to prevent himself ageing. More prosaically, Jackson began 1985 by co-writing and performing on the **USA For Africa** benefit single 'We Are The World', another international number 1. He then spent $47.5 million in purchasing the ATV Music company, who controlled the songs of **John Lennon** and Paul McCartney, thus effectively sabotaging his musical relationship with his erstwhile partner. Later that year he took part in *Captain Eo*, a short film laden with special effects that was only shown at the Disneyworld amusement park; he also announced plans to write his autobiography. The book was delayed while he recorded *Bad*, another collaboration with Quincy Jones that finally appeared in 1987. It produced seven Top 10 singles, among them the title track, which again set fresh standards with its promotional video. The album suffered by comparison with his previous work, however, and even its multi-million sales were deemed disappointing after the phenomenal success of *Thriller*. In musical terms, *Bad* certainly broke no fresh ground; appealing though its soft funk confections were, they lacked substance, and represented only a cosmetic advance over his two earlier albums with Jones. Unabashed, Jackson continued to work in large scale. He undertook a lengthy world concert tour to promote *Bad*, utilizing stunning visual effects to capture the atmosphere of his videos. At the same time, he published his autobiography, *Moonwalker*, which offered little personal or artistic insight; neither did the alarmingly expensive feature film that accompanied it, and which buttressed his otherworldly image. The long-awaited *Dangerous* arrived at the end of 1991 and justifiably scaled the charts. This was a *tour de force* of gutsy techno pop, with Teddy Riley contributing to a number of tracks. Although the customarily sweet pop was sharpened to a hard point, it still displayed the unmistakable Jackson sound. By maintaining a leisurely working schedule, Jackson had guaranteed that every new project was accompanied by frenzied public anticipation.

Until 1992, his refusal to undergo probing interviews had allowed the media to portray him as a fantasy figure, a hypochondriac who lived a twilight existence cut off from the rest of humanity. He attempted to dispel this image, and succeeded to a degree, with a carefully rehearsed interview with US chat show host Oprah Winfrey in 1992. The televised programme was shown all over world, during which viewers saw his personal funfair in the back garden, and watched as Jackson spoke of his domineering father. However, the unthinkable happened in 1993, just as Jackson's clean image was at its peak. Allegations of sexual abuse were made by one of Jackson's young friends and the media had a riotous time. Jackson's home was raided by police while he was on tour in the Far East and the artist, clearly disturbed, cancelled a number of performances due to dehydration. No charges were made, and things began to quieten down until November 1993, when Jackson left the USA and went into hiding. Additionally, he confessed to being addicted to painkillers and was seeking treatment. After this admission, Jackson's long-time sponsors Pepsi-Cola decided to pull out of their contract with the now damaged career of the world's most popular superstar. The media were handed more bait when he married Lisa Marie Presley on 26 May 1994, perhaps in an attempt to rebuild his image. The marriage collapsed nineteen months later, giving further rise to allegations that it was merely a set-up to improve his soiled image. He did, however, enhance his reputation with *HIStory Past, Present And Future, Book 1*. One half of the double set chronicled his past hits, but there was the equivalent of a new album forming the second half. Lyrically, the new material was strong, and Jackson very cleverly gave himself a forum to respond to his critics. Although not breaking any new ground musically, the sound was refreshingly varied and, as ever, highly polished. The downside of this return was a sickening display of self-aggrandizement at the 1996 BRIT Awards. Controversy surrounded Jarvis Cocker (of **Pulp**), who invaded the stage in protest while Jackson, dressed in Messiah-white, was surrounded by, among others, worshipping children and a rabbi. *Blood On The Dancefloor - HIStory In The Mix* was a collection of remixes and new material that spawned further hit singles. It appeared that, despite the allegations of child abuse and the constant media attacks, particularly surrounding his unexpected second marriage (to Debbie Rowe) and the birth of two children, Jackson's fans remained loyal to the 'King of Pop'.

● ALBUMS: *Got To Be There* (Motown 1971)★★★, *Ben* (Motown 1972)★★★, *Music And Me* (Motown 1973)★★★,

Forever, Michael (Motown 1975)★★★, *Off The Wall* (Epic 1979)★★★★, *One Day In Your Life* (Motown 1981)★★★, *Thriller* (Epic 1982)★★★★★, *ET - The Extra Terrestrial* (MCA 1983)★★, *Farewell My Summer Love* 1973 recording (Motown 1984)★★★, *Looking Back To Yesterday* (Motown 1986)★★★, *Bad* (Epic 1987)★★★★, *Dangerous* (Epic 1991)★★★, *HIStory Past, Present & Future, Book 1* (Epic 1995)★★★★, *Blood On The Dance Floor - HIStory In The Mix* (Epic 1997)★★★.

● COMPILATIONS: *The Best Of Michael Jackson* (Motown 1975)★★★, *Michael Jackson 9 Single Pack* (Epic 1983)★★★, *The Michael Jackson Mix* (Stylus 1987)★★★, *Souvenir Singles Pack* (1988)★★★, *Anthology* (Motown 1993)★★★★.

● VIDEOS: *The Making Of Thriller* (Vestron Music Video 1986), *The Legend Continues* (Video Collection 1988), *Moonwalker* (1992), *Dangerous - The Short Films* (1994), *HIStory Past, Present & Future, Book 1* (1995).

● FURTHER READING: *Michael Jackson*, Stewart Regan. *The Magic Of Michael Jackson*, no editor listed. *Michael Jackson*, Doug Magee. *The Michael Jackson Story*, Nelson George. *Michael In Concert*, Phyl Garland. *Michael Jackson: Body And Soul: An Illustrated Biography*, Geoff Brown. *Michael!: The Michael Jackson Story*, Mark Bego. *On The Road With Michael Jackson*, Mark Bego. *Sequins & Shades: The Michael Jackson Reference Guide*, Carol D. Terry. *Michael Jackson: Electrifying*, Greg Quill. *Moonwalk*, Michael Jackson, *Michael Jackson: The Magic And The Madness*, J. Randy Taraborrelli. *Michael Jackson : The Man In The Mirror*, Todd Gold. *Sequins And Shades*, Carol D. Terry. *Michael Jackson: The King Of Pop*, Lisa D. Campbell. *Michael Jackson: In His Own Words*, Michael Jackson. *The Visual Documentary*, Adrian Grant. *Michael Jackson Unauthorized*, Christopher Andersen. *The Many Faces Of Michael Jackson*, Lee Pinkerton.

Jackson, Millie

b. 15 July 1944, Thompson, Georgia, USA. A former model, Millie Jackson's controversial singing career began professionally in 1964 at a club in Hoboken, New Jersey, USA. Her first recordings followed in 1970; over the next three years she made several excellent, if traditional, soul singles, which included two US R&B Top 10 entries, with 'Ask Me What You Want' and 'My Man A Sweet Man'. 'Hurts So Good', a song from a pseudo-feminist 'blaxploitation' film, *Cleopatra Jones*, was Jackson's biggest hit to date, but her subsequent direction was more fully shaped in 1974 with the release of *Caught Up*. With backing from the **Muscle Shoals** rhythm section, the tracks included a fiery interpretation of '(If Lovin' You Is Wrong) I Don't Wanna Be Right'. The accompaniment intensified the sexual element in her work as Millie embraced either the pose of adultress or of wronged wife. A further collection, *Still Caught Up*, continued the saga, but Jackson's style later verged on self-parody as she progressed down an increasingly blind alley. The raps became longer and more explicit, and two later albums, *Feelin' Bitchy* and *Live And Uncensored*, required warning stickers for public broadcast. Despite excursions into C&W and a collaboration with **Isaac Hayes**, Jackson seemed unable

to abandon her 'bad mouth' role, exemplified in 80s titles such as 'Sexercise Pts 1 & 2' and 'Slow Tongue (Working Your Way Down)'. Despite her strong cult following, the only occasion on which Jackson has made any significant impact on the UK singles market was in 1985 when duetting with **Elton John** on 'Act Of War', which reached the Top 40. She possesses one of soul's outstanding voices, yet sadly chooses to limit its obvious potential. Nearly all of Jackson's Spring albums saw CD release in the 90s on UK Ace's Southbound label.

● ALBUMS: *Millie Jackson* (Spring 1972)★★★, *It Hurts So Good* (Spring 1973)★★★, *Caught Up* (Spring 1974)★★★★, *Soul Believer* (Spring 1974)★★★, *Still Caught Up* (Spring 1975)★★★, *Free And In Love* (Spring 1976)★★★, *Lovingly Yours* (Spring 1977)★★★, *Feelin' Bitchy* (Spring 1977)★★★★, *Get It Out 'Cha System* (Spring 1978)★★★, *A Moment's Pleasure* (Spring 1979)★★★, with Isaac Hayes *Royal Rappin's* (Polydor 1979)★★, *Live And Uncensored* (Spring 1979)★★★, *For Men Only* (Spring 1980)★★★, *I Had To Say It* (Spring 1981)★★, *Just A Lil' Bit Country* (1981)★★, *Live And Outrageous* (Spring 1982)★★, *Hard Times* (Spring 1982)★★, *E.S.P. (Extra Sexual Persuasion)* (Sire 1984)★★, *An Imitation Of Love* (Jive 1986)★★★, *The Tide Is Turning* (Jive 1988)★★★, *Back To The Sh.t* (Jive 1989)★★★.

● COMPILATIONS: *Best Of Millie Jackson* (Spring 1976)★★★★, *21 Of The Best* (Southbound/Ace 1994)★★★.

Jackson, Milt 'Bags'

b. 1 January 1923, Detroit, Michigan, USA. Jackson's first professional engagement, at the age of 16, was in his hometown, playing the vibraphone alongside tenor saxophonist **Lucky Thompson** (one year his junior). Jackson benefited from the 40s loose attitude towards band personnel, spending six years accompanying visiting musicians, as well as studying at Michigan State University. In 1945 **Dizzy Gillespie** heard him and invited him to join his band for a west coast tour. Later moving to New York, the brilliant young vibes player found himself much in demand, playing and recording with **Howard McGhee** and **Thelonious Monk** (including Monk's classic 1951 session for **Blue Note**). A spell with **Woody Herman** (1949-50) and more work with Gillespie established him as the pre-eminent player on his instrument. Jackson's recording debut as a leader was for Gillespie's Dee Gee label in 1951. He also had the depth of experience to play with both **Ben Webster** and **Charlie Parker**. In 1954 the Milt Jackson Quartet transformed itself into the **Modern Jazz Quartet**, with pianist **John Lewis** becoming musical director. For the next 20 years, Milt Jackson led a Dr Jeckyll and Mr Hyde existence, playing the consummately sophisticated music of the MJQ, all dressed in their famous tuxedoes, and leading his own dates in the swinging company of **Coleman Hawkins**, Lucky Thompson or **Horace Silver**. In 1961 Jackson accompanied **Ray Charles** on *Soul Meeting*, on which the soul singer restricted himself to electric piano and alto saxophone. Sleevenote writers loved to debate how happy Jackson could be with the MJQ's starchy charts. Certainly when he broke up the group in 1974, it was due to what he considered its financial exploitation rather than musical antagonism. Before Jackson, the vibes were an instrument associated with the hot, swinging proto-R&B of big band leaders **Lionel Hampton** and **Johnny Otis**. By slowing the vibrato and giving the right-hand mallet sweeping lines like a saxophone, Jackson gave the instrument sensuality and soul. Not until the appearance of **Bobby Hutcherson** in the mid-60s did anyone come up with an alternative modern approach to playing it. Jackson's harmonic sense was unerringly inventive and he also kept his ears open for new talent. He championed guitarist **Wes Montgomery** and recorded with him for the Riverside label (*Bags Meets Wes*, 1961). Jackson was a strong force in the reintegration of bebop with swing values and musicians, the very definition of what came to be known as 'mainstream' jazz. His own quintets included players such as **Cedar Walton**, **Jimmy Heath** and **James Moody**. The 70s were a hard period for jazz players, but even in the dated arrangements of **Bob James** on a record like *Olinga* (recorded in 1974 for CTI) his caressing, ebullient vibes playing shines through. The 80s jazz revival was reflected by the MJQ reforming and appearing at countless jazz festivals. In 1985 Jackson toured Europe under his own name. The Pablo record label continued to document his music into the 90s.

● ALBUMS: *In The Beginning* (Original Jazz Classics 1947-48 recordings)★★★★, *Milt Jackson Quartet* (1954)★★★★, *Opus De Jazz* (Savoy 1955)★★★, *Jackson's Ville* (Savoy 1956)★★★, *Meet Milt Jackson* (Savoy 1957)★★★★, *Roll 'Em Bags* (Savoy 1957)★★★, *The Jazz Skyline* (Savoy 1957)★★★, *Bluesology* (1957)★★★, *Plenty Plenty Soul* (1957)★★★, *Ballads & Blues* (1958)★★★★, *Bags' Opus* (Blue Note 1959)★★★, with John Coltrane *Bags Meets Trane* (Atlantic 1961)★★★, *Bags Meets Wes* (1961)★★, *Invitation* (Original Jazz Classics 1963)★★★★, *Big Bags* (Original Jazz Classics 1963)★★★★, with Ray Charles *Soul Meeting* (1964)★★★★, *Vibrations* (1964)★★★, *At The Village Gate* (Original Jazz Classics 1964)★★★★, *For Someone I Love* (Original Jazz Classics 1964)★★★, *Statements* (Impulse 1965)★★★, with Cannonball Adderley *Accent On Africa* (Capitol 1968)★★, *Olinga* (1974)★★, *Milt Jackson Big 4* (1975)★★, *Montreaux '77* (Original Jazz Classics 1978)★★★, *Feelings* (Original Jazz Classics 1978)★★★, *Soul Fusion* (Original Jazz Classics 1978)★★★★, *Milt Jackson + Count Basie + The Big Band Vols 1 and 2* (Original Jazz Classics 1978)★★★, *Soul Believer* (Original Jazz Classics 1979)★★★, *Night Mist* (1980)★★, *All Too Soon* (Original Jazz Classics 1981)★★★, *Soul Route* (Pablo 1984)★★★, *It Don't Mean A Thing If You Can't Tap Your Foot To It* (Original Jazz Classics 1985)★★★, *Brother Jim* (Pablo 1986)★★★, *A London Bridge* (Pablo 1986)★★, *Milt Jackson* (1987)★★★, *Bebop* (1988)★★★, *The Harum* (Limelight 1991)★★★, *Reverence And Compassion* (Qwest 1993)★★★, *Burnin' In The Woodhouse* (Qwest 1995)★★★.

● COMPILATIONS: *The Best Of Milt Jackson* (Pablo 1982)★★★★.

Jackson, Oliver

b. 28 April 1933, Detroit, Michigan, USA, d. 29 May 1994, New York, USA. In the mid-40s drummer Jackson was active among Detroit R&B and bebop musicians, picking up the nickname 'Bops Jnr.' in the process. Among the artists with whom he worked during his formative years were **Barry Harris**, **Donald Byrd** and **Tommy Flanagan**, as well as the equally young and inexperienced **John Coltrane**. Jackson established a reputation as a sensitive accompanist to pianists and later in the decade played in trios with Flanagan and **Dorothy Donegan**. Then, in collaboration with fellow drummer Eddie Locke, Jackson formed a tap-dancing duo, Bops And Locke, which met with considerable success. Throughout the 50s he played with a variety of jazzmen, shifting comfortably between exponents of traditional and of modern music such as **Red Allen** and **Yusef Lateef**. In the early 60s he worked with **Charlie Shavers**, **Buck Clayton**, **Benny Goodman** and **Lionel Hampton** and then spent the rest of the decade with **Earl Hines**. In 1969 he formed the JPJ Quartet (with **Budd Johnson**, Bill Pemberton and **Dill Jones**), which played extensively in the USA. In the 70s and 80s Jackson appeared with **Sy Oliver**, Hampton again, **Oscar Peterson**, **Doc Cheatham**, **Vic Dickenson**, **Buddy Tate**, a band he co-led with Haywood Henry, and with his own groups, which featured Irving Stokes, Norris Turney and his bass-playing brother, Ali Jackson (who died in 1987). During this period Oliver became a familiar and popular figure at jazz festivals in the USA and Europe. Jackson's playing ranged over the full spectrum of jazz and he made an important contribution to many excellent concert and recording sessions.

● ALBUMS: *The Oliver Jackson-Jack Sels Quartet* (1961)★★★, with Buck Clayton *Olympia Concert* (1961)★★★★, *Coleman Hawkins And The Earl Hines Trio* (1965)★★★, with Doc Cheatham *Jive At Five* (1975)★★★, with Haywood Henry *Real Jazz Express* (1977)★★, *The Oliver Jackson Trio* (1979)★★★, *Oliver Jackson Presents Le Quartet* (1982)★★, *Billie's Bounce* (Black And Blue 1984)★★★.

Jackson, Papa Charlie

b. c.1885, New Orleans, Louisiana, USA, d. 1938, Chicago, Illinois, USA. Papa Charlie Jackson belonged to the first generation of rural black singers to record. He was a banjo player who had toured the South in medicine shows and worked anywhere else where he thought he might make money. He became popular after his first records were issued by Paramount in 1924, by which time he seems to have already moved to Chicago, where he often performed for tips in the Maxwell Street market. Like numerous banjoists from the minstrel tradition, Jackson was something of a humorist and many of his 70 or more recordings were sanitized versions of bawdy songs. He recorded with **Freddie Keppard**'s Jazz Cardinals in 1926, taking the vocal on 'Salty Dog', a number he had already recorded under his own name with marked success. Despite providing support for artists such as **Ma Rainey**, **Lucille**

Bogan and **Ida Cox**, Jackson's recording activities suffered a hiatus between 1930 and 1934 owing to the onset of the Depression and the demise of Paramount. He recorded for Vocalion in 1934 and recorded an unreleased session with **Big Bill Broonzy** in 1935. He scuffled on Chicago's west side until his death in 1938.
● ALBUMS: *Fat Mouth 1924 - 1927* (Yazoo 1988)★★★.

Jackson, Peg Leg Sam

b. Arthur Jackson, 18 December 1911, Jonesville, South Carolina, USA, d. 27 October 1977, Jonesville, South Carolina, USA. Also known as Peg Pete, Jackson learned to play the harmonica when he was 10 years old by listening to local men, Butler Jennings and Biggar Mapps, who played in an older style known as 'accordion'. He had already learned many secular and spiritual songs from his mother, Emily. He left home about this time, spending much of his adult life travelling, and learned his blues style in the late 20s from Elmon 'Keg Shorty' Bell. He lost the lower part of his right leg under a freight train in Durham, North Carolina, in 1930. Seven years later, he teamed up with **Pink Anderson** on the medicine show circuit, which he worked for the next 30 years, mostly in partnership with Chief Thundercloud. He also played regularly in Rocky Mount, North Carolina, at Fenner's Warehouse, a focal point for musicians such as **Tarheel Slim**, **Willie Trice** and **Brownie McGhee**. In later years, the right side of his face was scarred while trying to break up a domestic argument. He was first recorded by Pete Lowry in August 1970, in the company of **Baby Tate** and Pink Anderson. Jackson became a favourite at folk festivals and also recorded in New York with **Louisiana Red**. He died on the family homestead he had left as a child.
● ALBUMS: *Medicine Show Man* (1973)★★★, *Joshua* (1975)★★★.

Jackson, Preston

b. 3 January 1902, New Orleans, Louisiana, USA, d. 12 November 1983. From his early teens Jackson lived in Chicago, where he learned the trombone in 1920. He played with several local bands throughout the 20s and in the early 30s was in demand by prominent local bandleaders such as Dave Peyton and Erskine Tate. In 1926 he recorded with **Luis Russell** and with a band led by clarinettist Arthur Sims; he also fronted his own pick-up group on a 1928 date. In 1931 he joined **Louis Armstrong**, then worked with **Frankie Jaxon**, recording with him in 1933, **Carroll Dickerson**, **Jimmie Noone**, Zilner Randolph, **Walter Barnes** and others, mostly touring the mid-western and south-west states by the end of the decade. However, Jackson was musically active only on a part-time basis. During the 40s and 50s he was involved in musicians' union work, but occasionally formed bands for club and record dates and also worked briefly with **Richard M. Jones**, **Johnny Dodds**, **Lillian Armstrong** and others. He continued this sporadic activity into the next decade, towards the end of which he worked with **Little Brother**

Montgomery. In the 70s he toured with **Kid Thomas** and, resident once more in New Orleans, played with the Preservation Hall Jazz Band. During his playing career Jackson's style moved with the times. Although his occupation began in Chicago, he based his early playing on that of other relocated New Orleans jazzmen. In mid-career he incorporated swing era developments into his repertoire, then late in life returned to his roots but with a sophisticated stylistic patina. Deeply interested in the history of jazz, Jackson wrote extensively for magazines over a 40-year period.
● ALBUMS: with Kid Thomas *The New Orleans Joymakers* (1973)★★★. ● COMPILATIONS: *Louis Armstrong And His Orchestra Vol. 9* (1931)★★★★.

Jackson, Quentin

b. 13 January 1909, Springfield, Ohio, USA, d. 2 October 1976. As a child Jackson had learned to play piano, organ and violin, but in his late teens he took up the trombone. He received tuition from his brother-in-law, **Claude Jones**, who played in **McKinney's Cotton Pickers**; after a couple of years of intensive touring with various **territory bands**, in 1930 Jackson, too, joined McKinney. Two years later he switched to the band formed by the McKinney band's musical director, **Don Redman**. During his long stay with Redman he picked up the nickname, 'Butter', and attracted considerable attention from other trombone players and bandleaders. In 1939 he joined **Cab Calloway**, with whom he remained for eight years, then moved on to the **Duke Ellington** orchestra for an even longer period, eventually leaving in 1959. In the early 60s Jackson was briefly with **Quincy Jones** and **Count Basie**, Ellington again, and recorded important albums with **Charles Mingus**. Jackson then settled into a combination of studio work and appearances with big bands led by **Louie Bellson** and **Gerald Wilson** and in the early 70s was in the **Thad Jones-Mel Lewis** Jazz Orchestra. A strong and reliable section player, Jackson was also an excellent soloist with a rich, emotional tone.
● ALBUMS: *Ellington '55* (1953-54)★★★★, with Ellington *Such Sweet Thunder* (1957)★★★, *Mingus, Mingus, Mingus, Mingus* (1963)★★★★, with Thad Jones-Mel Lewis *Suite For Pops* (1972)★★★.

Jackson, Ronald Shannon

b. 12 January 1940, Fort Worth, Texas, USA. Jackson studied piano at the age of five, taking up clarinet and drums at school. He began professional work when he was 15, gigging regularly in Dallas with James Clay and Leroy Cooper who were then in the **Ray Charles**'s band. He studied history and sociology before gaining a music scholarship in New York, where he worked with artists including **Albert Ayler**, **Charles Tyler**, **Betty Carter**, **Charles Mingus** and **Stanley Turrentine**. From 1975-79 Jackson played alongside **James 'Blood' Ulmer** in the **Ornette Coleman** Sextet which evolved into Prime Time, and also worked with **Cecil Taylor**. Jackson joined Ulmer's band until setting up his own innovative and highly acclaimed Decoding Society in 1981. Although continuing to be based in Coleman's theory of harmolodics, the music of the Decoding Society changed its sound and direction with each album during the late 80s, often radically changing its instrumental line-up too. However, the foundation was always Jackson's thunderous, supple percussion. In 1986 he set up Last Exit with **Peter Brötzmann, Sonny Sharrock** and **Bill Laswell**, and in 1987 formed the trio Power Tools with **Bill Frisell** and Melvin Gibbs. In the late 80s and early 90s Jackson was re-united with Ulmer on record and in tours with a blues/funk-based power trio.

● ALBUMS: *Eye On You* (1981)★★★, *Nasty* (1981)★★★★, *Man Dance* (1982)★★, *Barbecue Dog* (Antilles 1984)★★★, *Decode Yourself* (Island 1985)★★★, *When Colors Play* (1987)★★★, with Power Tools *Strange Meeting* (1987)★★★, *When Colours Play* (Caravan Of Dreams 1987)★★★, *Live At The Caravan Of Dreams* (1987)★★, *Texas* (1989)★★★, *Taboo* (Virgin 1990)★★★, *Red Warrior* (Axiom 1991)★★, *Raven Roc* (DIW 1992)★★★.

Jackson, Shot

b. Harold B. Jackson, 4 September 1920, Wilmington, North Carolina, USA, d. 24 January 1991. He grew up on a farm in Georgia, with a childhood nickname of 'Buckshot', which was curtailed in adulthood to 'Shot'. Impressed by the dobro playing of **Pete Kirby** (Bashful Brother Oswald), he learned to play and was proficient enough to start his career in 1941. He relocated to Nashville in 1944, where he played on the *Grand Ole Opry* with Cousin Wilbur (Westbrooks). After service in the US Navy, he became steel guitarist for the **Bailes Brothers**, with whom he recorded and played regularly on the *Louisiana Hayride*, until 1951. Between 1951 and 1957, he played dobro for **Johnnie And Jack** and electric steel guitar for **Kitty Wells**, appearing on numerous recordings. Jackson then played steel guitar for **Roy Acuff** for almost five years. In the early 60s, he, **Buddy Emmons** and **Jimmy Day** were responsible for the manufacture of Sho-Bud pedal steel guitars. It was a small project that started in their garage but quickly became a major business enterprise. He still played with Acuff but also managed **Melba Montgomery** and played on her recordings, including her noted duets with **George Jones**. He was critically injured and pinned in the wreckage following a car crash, while travelling with Acuff, on 10 July 1965. When he was eventually fit enough to work again, he toured for a time with his wife, Donna Darlene, a featured singer on *The Wheeling Jamboree*. He also produced a seven-string guitar which he named Sho-Bro. He continued to make appearances at various venues, including on *Hee Haw* and at special events, including reunion shows with his old friends, the Bailes Brothers. In the mid-70s, he cut down on his performing and worked at making and repairing instruments. He sold his Sho-Bud interest in 1980 and his repair business in 1983, when he decided to retire completely. Some eight weeks later, he

suffered a stroke. He survived but the lasting effect left him without speech and unable to play. In June 1990, a further stroke left him completely incapacitated, before his death on 24 January 1991. His old friend Walter Bailes conducted the funeral. Jackson made various solo recordings during his career and gained induction to the Steel Guitar Hall Of Fame in 1986.

● ALBUMS: *Singing Strings Of Steel Guitar And Dobro* (Starday 1962)★★, *Bluegrass Dobro* (Cumberland 1965)★★★, *The Hurtin' Side Of Country* (Arc 60s)★★★, *Steelin' With A Dobro* (Arc 60s)★★★, *Nashville Northwest* (Wasp 60s)★★★, with Merle Travis, Charlie Collins *Shot Jackson & Friends* (Vetco 1977)★★★.

Jackson, Stonewall

b. 6 November 1932, Tabor City, North Carolina, USA. Jackson's family tree does in fact extend to the famous Confederate general of the American Civil War - hence his name. After the death of his father when Stonewall was aged two, his mother relocated to Moultrie, Georgia, where, at the age of eight, he worked on his uncle's farm. When he was 10 he swapped his bicycle for a guitar and learned to play by watching others. He joined the army in 1948, lying about his age, but the error was soon discovered. The next year he joined the navy legally and began his singing career by entertaining his shipmates. After discharge in 1954, he spent two years working on a farm but in 1956, with no professional singing experience, he decided to try his luck in Nashville. He impressed **Wesley Rose** enough for him to record some demo discs of his songs; after auditioning for **George D. Hay**, Jackson became one of the few performers without a recording contract to become a member of the *Grand Ole Opry*. In fact, he recalled, 'I found out later it's the only time anybody's ever come and just was hired off the street'. He signed for **Columbia Records** in 1957 and first worked on **Ernest Tubb**'s roadshow. He made his US country chart debut in 1958 when his recording of **George Jones**'s prison saga, 'Life To Go', reached number 2. In 1959, Jackson's recording of **John D. Loudermilk**'s 'Waterloo' became a million-selling country number 1, also reaching number 4 in the US pop charts. Between 1959 and 1963 further successes followed, including 'Why, I'm Walking', 'A Wound Time Can't Erase', 'Leona' and 'Old Showboat', before he achieved another country number 1 with 'B.J. The D.J.' Throughout the mid-60s and early-70s he charted regularly, including his own songs 'Don't Be Angry' (a song he had initially recorded as a demo for Wesley Rose eight years earlier), 'I Washed My Face In Muddy Water' and 'Stamp Out Loneliness'. ('Don't Be Angry' was revived in 1987 by **Daniel O'Donnell** on his album *Don't Forget To Remember*). Jackson's style gradually went out of fashion but he did make the country Top 10 in 1971 with a country version of 'Me And You And A Dog Named Boo'. During the Vietnam War he recorded a patriotic single, 'The Minute Men Are Turning In Their Graves', and even renamed his band the Minute Men to emphasize the point. *The Great Old Songs* contains many folk ballads, including arguably his best track, 'The Black Sheep'. He also has the distinction of being the first artist to record a live in-concert album at the *Opry*. He still resides in Nashville and maintains his *Opry* appearances.

● ALBUMS: *The Dynamic Stonewall Jackson* (Columbia 1959)★★★, *Sadness In A Song* (Columbia 1963)★★, *I Love A Song* (Columbia 1963)★★★, *Trouble And Me* (Columbia 1964)★★★, *The Exciting Stonewall Jackson* (Columbia 1966)★★★, *All's Fair In Love 'N' War* (Columbia 1966)★★★, *Help Stamp Out Loneliness* (1967)★★★, *Stonewall Jackson Country* (1967)★★★, *The Great Old Songs* (1968)★★★★, *Thoughts Of A Lonely Man* (1968)★★★, *Nothing Takes The Place Of Loving You* (1968)★★★, *I Pawned My Past Today* (1969)★★★, *The Old Country Church* (1969)★★, *A Tribute To Hank Williams* (1969)★★, *The Real Thing* (1970)★★★, *The Lonesome In Me* (1970)★★★, *Stonewall Jackson Recorded Live At The Grand Ole Opry* (1971)★★★, *Waterloo* (1971)★★★★, *Me And You And A Dog Named Boo* (1971)★★★, *World Of Stonewall Jackson* (1972)★★★, *Nashville* (1974)★★★, *Stonewall (Platinum Country)* (1979)★★★, *My Favorite Sin* (1980)★★★, *Stonewall Jackson* (1982)★★★, *Solid Stonewall* (1982)★★, *Alive* (1984)★★, *Up Against The Wall* (Allegience 1984)★★.

● COMPILATIONS: *Stonewall Jackson's Greatest Hits* (Columbia 1965)★★★, *American Originals* (Columbia 1989)★★★.

● FURTHER READING: *From The Bottom Up: The Stonewall Jackson Story*, Billy Henson (ed.).

Jackson, Tommy

b. Thomas Lee Jackson Jnr., 31 March 1926, Birmingham, Alabama, USA, d. 9 December 1979. His parents relocated to Nashville when Jackson was a baby and he grew up listening to the *Grand Ole Opry*. Greatly influenced by **'Fiddlin'' Arthur Smith**, at the age of seven Jackson was playing in bars and on street corners. When he was 12, he toured with **Johnny And Jack**, before leading the Tennessee Mountaineers on Nashville radio. In the early 40s, he played regularly on the *Opry* with **Curley Williams** and **Paul Howard**, before serving as a rear gunner in Flying Fortress bombers during World War II, for which he received five decorations. In April 1946, he returned to Nashville and began to work with various *Opry* stars but played regularly in **Red Foley**'s Cumberland Valley Boys (the band, consisting of Jackson alongside Zeke Turner on electric guitar, **Jerry Byrd** on steel guitar, Louis Innis on rhythm guitar, were also perhaps Nashville's first real session musicians). His dislike of touring saw him increasingly seeking work as a session musician and it was in this capacity that, in 1947, he made his first recordings playing fiddle behind **Hank Williams** (Jackson provided the brilliant fiddlework on 'I Saw The Light', 'Lovesick Blues' and several other Williams hits). In 1948, after moving with Foley to Cincinnati, he also worked with **Cowboy Copas**, **Hawkshaw Hawkins** and **Grandpa Jones**, as well as playing on sessions for

King. He made his first solo recordings for **Mercury Records** in the early 50s, but in 1953, he joined **Dot Records**, where he recorded a whole series of albums and singles for square dancing. They not only popularized the dancing but also led to many new players becoming attracted to the fiddle. In 1954, having more session work than he could cope with, he ceased working with Foley or any specific artist.

He continued to play into the 70s, by which time he had worked with or played on recordings by almost every major star, including **Faron Young**, **Ray Price**, **George Jones**, **Bill Monroe**, **Jim And Jesse** and **Hank Snow**. Jackson died in December 1979 after a long period of poor health. Noted historian Charles. K. Wolfe accurately described Jackson as 'the first great Nashville session fiddler who virtually invented the standard country fiddle back-up style and in the early 50s, his string of albums both reflected and stimulated the square dance craze'.

● ALBUMS: *Popular Square Dance Music Without Calls* (Dot 1957)★★★, *Square Dance Tonight* (Dot 1958)★★★, *Square Dance Fiddle Favorites* (Mercury 1958)★★★, *Do-Si-Do* (Dot 1959)★★★, *Square Dances Without Calls* (Decca 1959)★★★, *Square Dance Festival Volumes 1 & 2* (Dot 1960)★★★, *Swing Your Partner* (Dot 1962)★★★, *Square Dance Festival Volume 3* (Dot 1963)★★★, *Let's Dance To Country Pops* (Somerset 1964)★★★, *Bluegrass Square Dance Jamboree* (Hamilton 1964)★★, *Square Dances* (Dot 1964)★★★, with Lloyd Ellis *Guitar & Fiddle Country Style* (Mercury 1965)★★★, with Pete Wade *Twin Fiddles Play Country's Greatest Waltzes* (Cumberland 1965)★★.

● COMPILATIONS: *Square Dance Music* 14 volumes EPs (Dot 1957)★★★, *Greatest Bluegrass Hits* (Dot 1962).

Jackson, Tony

b. 5 June 1876, New Orleans, Louisiana, USA, d. 20 April 1920. An entertainer of great repute, Jackson played piano and sang in New Orleans saloons and brothels in the early 1900s. His repertoire included popular songs of the day, emergent blues and operatic arias, but it was as a ragtime pianist that he had most influence upon his contemporaries. As with **Buddy Bolden** in the field of jazz, Jackson's fame rests on stories told about him by other musicians because, like Bolden, he never recorded. In 1912 Jackson moved to Chicago, where he played in the city's leading nightclubs, usually as a solo act. Billed as 'the 'world's greatest single-handed entertainer', Jackson's private life was troubled. He was an alcoholic and his sexual activities left him disease-ridden. However, his musical ability was such that **Jelly Roll Morton**, who rarely praised anyone but himself, spoke very highly of him. Jackson seldom bothered to have his own compositions published, believing that the pittance which music publishers of the day would pay him would not be worth the effort involved. Among his songs were such delights as 'Some Sweet Day' and 'Pretty Baby'.

Jackson, Walter

b. 19 March 1938, Pensacola, Florida, USA, d. 20 June 1983. Crippled by polio as a child, Jackson spent much of his life on crutches. This disability imbued his work with a greater pathos. Jackson recorded in 1959 as a member of the Velvetones, but his solo career unfolded on signing to the **OKeh** label. 'It's All Over' (1964), a **Curtis Mayfield**-penned ballad, was Jackson's first R&B hit. It was followed by exceptional performances such as 'Welcome Home' (1965) and 'It's An Uphill Climb To The Bottom' (1966), both of which reached the soul Top 20. However, the singer's definitive, towering version of 'My Ship is Comin' In' (first recorded by Jimmy Radcliffe and later by the **Walker Brothers**) sadly failed to chart. Walter later recorded for Cotillion and **Brunswick**, but between 1973 and 1976 he retired from active performing. Jackson returned with a series of minor hits, including an interpretation of **Morris Albert**'s 'Feelings', but his health was deteriorating. He died of a cerebral haemorrhage in 1983.

● ALBUMS: *It's All Over* (OKeh 1964)★★★, *Welcome Home: The Many Moods Of Walter Jackson* (OKeh 1965)★★★, *Speak Her Name* (OKeh 1967)★★, *Feeling Good* (Chi-Sound 1976)★★★, *I Want To Come Back As A Song* (Chi-Sound 1977)★★, *Good To See You* (Chi-Sound 1978)★★, *Send In The Clowns* (1979)★★, *Tell Me Where It Hurts* (1981)★★, *A Portrait Of Walter Jackson* (Bluebird 1984)★★★.

● COMPILATIONS: *Walter Jackson's Greatest Hits* compiles 12 of his OKeh recordings (Epic 1987)★★★.

Jackson, Wanda

b. Wanda Jean Jackson, 20 October 1937, Maud, Oklahoma, USA. Jackson started her career as one of the rawest of female rockabilly singers before going on to successful work in both country and gospel music. Her family moved to California when she was four, settling in the city of Bakersfield, but moved back to Oklahoma when she was 12. There Jackson won a talent contest that led to her own radio programme. Country singer **Hank Thompson** liked her style and hired her to tour with his band. In 1954 Jackson signed to **Decca Records**, recording 15 country tracks, one of which, 'You Can't Have My Love', a duet with Billy Gray, made the country Top 10. The following year Jackson joined **Red Foley**'s touring company and met **Elvis Presley**. He advised her to change her style to the new rock 'n' roll. When she signed with **Capitol Records** in 1956, she recorded a number of singles, one side of each a rocker, the other a honky-tonk country number. Only one of these rockabilly records, 'I Gotta Know', made the country charts, but her other recordings for Capitol, such as 'Honey Bop', 'Fujiyama Mama' and 'Hot Dog That Made Him Mad', are prized by collectors decades later. Only one, 'Let's Have A Party', earlier recorded by Elvis, made the US pop charts when Capitol belatedly released it in 1960. Backed by the Blue Caps, this song is delivered in raucous style and it remains an extraordinary vocal delivery. That same year, Jackson chose to stay with country and recorded her own composition, 'Right Or Wrong', which has since become a hit for both **Ronnie Dove** and **George Strait**. 'Right Or Wrong' and 'In The Middle Of a Heartache' became the last of Jackson's Top 10 country songs in 1961/2, although she placed 30 singles in that chart in total. She recorded nearly two dozen albums for Capitol in the 60s. By the early 70s Jackson began recording Christian music for Capitol and later the Word and Myrrh labels, returning to rock 'n' roll for one album, *Rock 'N' Roll Away Your Blues*, in 1984. In 1995 she duetted on **Rosie Flores**' *Rockabilly Filly* album, and supported the singer on her US tour.

● ALBUMS: *Wanda Jackson* (Capitol 1958)★★★, *Rockin' With Wanda* (Capitol 1960)★★★★, *There's A Party Goin' On* (Capitol 1961)★★★, *Right Or Wrong* (Capitol 1961)★★★, *Lovin' Country Style* (Decca 1962)★★★, *Wonderful Wanda* (Capitol 1962)★★★, *Love Me Forever* (Capitol 1963)★★★, *Two Sides Of Wanda Jackson* (Capitol 1964)★★★★, *Blues In My Heart* (Capitol 1964)★★★, *Wanda Jackson Sings Country Songs* (Capitol 1966)★★★, *Salutes The Country Music Hall Of Fame* (Capitol 1966)★★★, *Reckless Love Affair* (Capitol 1967)★★★, *You'll Always Have My Love* (Capitol 1967)★★★, *Cream Of The Crop* (Capitol 1968)★★★, *The Happy Side Of...* (Capitol 1969)★★★, *In Person At Mr. Lucky's In Phoenix, Arizona* (Capitol 1969)★★★, *The Many Moods Of...* (Capitol 1969)★★★, *Country!* (Capitol 1970)★★★, *Woman Lives For Love* (Capitol 1970)★★★, *I've Gotta Sing* (Capitol 1971)★★★, *I Wouldn't Want You Any Other Way* (Capitol 1972)★★★, *Praise The Lord* (Capitol 1972)★★★, *When It's Time To Fall In Love Again* (Myrrh 1973)★★★, *Country Keepsakes* (Myrrh 1973)★★★, *Now I Have Everything* (Myrrh 1974)★★★, *Closer To Jesus* (Word 1982)★★★, *Rock 'N' Roll Away Your Blues* (1984)★★★.

● COMPILATIONS: *The Best Of Wanda Jackson* (Capitol 1967)★★★★, *Her Greatest Country Hits* (EMI 1983)★★★★, *Early Wanda Jackson* (Bear Family 1984)★★★, *Rockin' In The Country: The Best Of ...* (Rhino 1990)★★★★, *Right Or Wrong 1954-62* (1993)★★★★, *16 Rock 'N' Roll Hits* (1993)★★★★, *Capitol Country Music Classics* (Capitol 1993)★★★★, *Vintage Collection Series* (Capitol 1996)★★★★.

Jacksons

Jackie (b. Sigmund Esco Jackson, 4 May 1951, Gary, Indiana, USA), **Tito** (b. Toriano Adaryll Jackson, 15 October 1953, Gary), **Marlon** (b. Marlon David Jackson, 12 March 1957, Gary), **Michael** (b. Michael Joseph Jackson, 29 August 1958, Gary) and **Randy** Jackson (b. Steven Randall Jackson, 29 October 1962, Gary) changed their collective name from the **Jackson Five** to the **Jacksons** in March 1976, following their departure from **Motown Records**. At the same time, Randy Jackson replaced his brother **Jermaine**, handling percussion and backing vocals. The group's new recording contract with Epic offered them a more lucrative agreement than they had enjoyed with Motown, although at first they seemed to have exchanged one artistic strait-jacket for another. Their initial releases were written, arranged and produced by **Gamble And Huff**, whose expertise ensured that the

Jacksons sounded professional, but slightly anonymous. 'Enjoy Yourself' and 'Show You The Way To Go' were both major hits in the US charts, and the latter also topped the UK sales listing. The group's second album with Gamble And Huff, *Goin' Places*, heralded a definite decline in popularity. *Destiny* saw the Jacksons reassert control over writing and production, and produced a string of worldwide hit singles. 'Blame It on The Boogie' caught the mood of the burgeoning disco market, while the group's self-composed 'Shake Your Body (Down To The Ground)' signalled Michael Jackson's growing artistic maturity. The success of Michael's first adult solo venture, *Off The Wall* in 1979, switched his attention away from the group. On *Triumph*, they merely repeated the glories of their previous album, although the commercial appeal of anything bearing Michael's voice helped singles such as 'Can You Feel It?', 'Heartbreak Hotel' and 'Lovely One' achieve success on both sides of the Atlantic. The Jacksons' 1981 US tour emphasized Michael's dominance over the group, and the resulting *Live* included many of his solo hits alongside the brothers' joint repertoire. Between 1981 and the release of *Victory* in 1984, Michael issued *Thriller*, until recently the best-selling album of all time. When the Jacksons' own effort was released, it became apparent that he had made only token contributions to the record, and its commercial fortune suffered accordingly. 'State Of Shock', which paired Michael with **Mick Jagger**, was a US hit, but sold in smaller quantities than expected. Hysteria surrounded the group's 'Victory Tour' in the summer of 1984; adverse press comment greeted the distribution of tickets, and the Jacksons were accused of pricing themselves out of the reach of their black fans. Although they were joined onstage by their brother Jermaine for the first time since 1975, media and public attention was focused firmly on Michael. Realizing that they were becoming increasingly irrelevant, the other members of the group began to voice their grievances in the press; as a result, Michael Jackson stated that he would not be working with his brothers in the future. The Jacksons struggled to come to terms with his departure, and it was five years before their next project was complete. *2300 Jackson Street* highlighted their dilemma: once the media realized that Michael was not involved, they effectively boycotted its release. Randy Jackson was sentenced to a one-month jail sentence in November 1990 for assaulting his wife. In 1992, ABC aired the five-hour mini-series *The Jacksons: An American Dream*.

● ALBUMS: *The Jacksons* (Epic 1976)★★★, *Goin' Places* (Epic 1977)★★★, *Destiny* (Epic 1978)★★★★, *Triumph* (Epic 1980)★★★, *The Jacksons Live* (Epic 1981)★★★, *Victory* (Epic 1984)★★★, *2300 Jackson Street* (Epic 1989)★★.

Jackyl

This Atlanta, Georgia-based band was formed in 1990 by larger-than-life frontman Jesse James Dupree, guitarists Jeff Worley and Jimmy Stiff, bassist Tom Bettini and drummer Chris Worley. The band created an enormous buzz, with a basic **AC/DC** style that transferred well to the live setting on a heavy touring schedule, and they were quickly signed by John Kalodner to **Geffen Records**. *Jackyl* courted controversy from the start, enraging feminists with the ludicrously titled 'She Loves My Cock', while Dupree's onstage antics kept the music press busy. During 'The Lumberjack', Dupree soloed on a chainsaw - his father had been so impressed by a club performance with a hired chainsaw that he bought his son a new one - and also regularly indulged his penchant for performing the latter part of the set naked, which resulted in an early departure from a **Lynyrd Skynyrd** support slot. However, tours with **Damn Yankees** and, in particular, **Aerosmith** proved more successful, and *Jackyl* achieved platinum status against the grunge-loaded odds. *Push Comes To Shove* continued in the vein of the debut, and added to the controversy when an advertising hoarding in Nashville was censored (Dupree was displaying his bare buttocks in the band photograph).

● ALBUMS: *Jackyl* (Geffen 1992)★★★, *Push Comes To Shove* (Geffen 1994)★★★, *Night Of The Living Dead* (Music For Nations 1996)★★, *Cut The Crap* (Epic 1997)★★★.

Jacob's Mouse

At the age of 11 identical twins Hugo (guitar) and Jebb (bass) Boothby met Sam Marsh (vocals, drums) at a swimming competition, when all three boys were wearing heavy metal band T-shirts. The band was formed and they soon graduated from **Status Quo** cover versions to writing their own material, drawing their primary influence from the noisier acts appearing on UK disc jockey **John Peel**'s radio show (Peel later sponsored the band's career, and is a close neighbour of theirs in Bury St Edmunds, Suffolk, England). Their name, hardly descriptive of their ferocious sound, was inspired by their cousin's pet, and was first used on a 7-inch EP, *The Dot*, released on the Liverish label in January 1991. It was Single Of The Week in the soon-to-be-defunct *Sounds* magazine, and heralded support slots with **Nirvana**, **Carter USM**, **Senseless Things** and others. Still without a recording contract, they released *No Fish Shop Parking* (a name taken from a road sign in Bury St Edmunds) on their own Blithering Idiot label, which was run by the father of their manager, Sam Marsh. This brought them acclaim from UK disc jockeys John Peel and Mark Goodier, and the band subsequently signed with Wiiija Records, whose Gary Walker had at first turned them down. After touring with **Babes In Toyland** they released the *Ton Up* EP in September 1992, and they also signed a US contract with **Frontier Records** to give them wider distribution. *I'm Scared* deserved the healthy amount of press it received, with its low-fi hardcore sound draped in feedback and metal riffs. The band were also highly playful, pushing their sound in varied and quite unexpected directions in a manner reminiscent of **Captain Beefheart**. Live, they were equally distinctive, with

Marsh's guttural, non-linear vocals used primarily as an instrument (the band humbly stated that, as they were so young, they would feel daft trying to impart wisdom to others), and the identical twins standing either side of the drum kit, flailing in unison. In the autumn of 1993 they released two further EPs, *Good* and *Group Of Seven*, after which the band took a break before releasing a third album, *Rubber Room*.

● ALBUMS: *No Fish Shop Parking* (Blithering Idiot 1992)★★★, *I'm Scared* (Wiiija 1992)★★★, *Rubber Room* (Wiiija 1994)★★★.

● COMPILATIONS: *Wryly Smiling* (Wiiija 1994)★★★.

Jacobites

British indie band formed by **Nikki Sudden** (b. 19 July 1956, London, England; guitar, vocals, ex-**Swell Maps**) and Dave Kusworth (b. 26 March 1960, Birmingham, England; guitar, vocals), alongside Sudden's brother and former Swell Maps drummer **Epic Soundtracks** (b. Kevin Paul Godley, 23 March 1959, d. 22 November 1997), and Mark Lemon (bass). The band released three albums on the Glass and What's So Funny About labels, with Tyla from **Dogs D'Amour** helping out on guitar. *Robespierre's Velvet Basement* was the most successful of these albums, but touring difficulties led to the demise of the band in 1986, with Sudden and Kusworth both resuming solo careers. However, the reissue of the band's first two albums in 1993 led to a reunion between the two founding members, who with Glenn Tranter (b. 7 July 1962, Dudley, England; acoustic guitar), Carl Eugene Picôt (b. 11 May 1964, Weymouth, England; bass) and Mark Williams (b. 30 October 1965, Birmingham, England; drums) have released four albums to date, all of which have proved more popular in Europe than their home country.

● ALBUMS: *Jacobites* (Glass 1984)★★★, *Robespierre's Velvet Basement* (Glass 1985)★★★, *Lost In A Sea Of Scarves* (What's So Funny About 1985)★★★, *Howling Good Times* (Regency Sound 1994)★★★, *Heart Of Hearts (The Spanish Album)* (Por Caridad Producciones 1995)★★, *Old Scarlett* (Glitterhouse 1995)★★★, *Kiss Of Life* (Swamp Room 1996)★★★.
Solo: Dave Kusworth *The Bounty Hunters* (Swordfish 1987)★★★, *Wives, Weddings And Roses* (Kaleidoscope 1988)★★★, *Threads (A Tear Stained Scar)* (Creation 1989)★★★, *All The Heartbreak Stories* (Creation 1991)★★★, *Princess Thousand Beauty* (Glitterhouse 1996)★★★.

● COMPILATIONS: *Fortune Of Fame (Big Hits And Stereo Landings)* (Glass 1988)★★★★, *Hawks Get Religion* (Regency Sound 1996)★★★. Dave Kusworth: *Champagne Eyes, Lemonade Pockets* (Creation 1992)★★★.

Jacobs, 'Boogie Jake'

b. Matthew Jacobs, *c.*1929, Marksville, Louisiana, USA. Like many blues artists with a small discography, Jacobs was a reluctant performer, even at the height of his (limited) popularity. Learning guitar from a neighbour, Ernest Barrow, Jacobs' first public performance was with his second cousin, **Little Walter Jacobs**, at the Golden Lantern Club in Marksville. Soon afterwards,

he moved to Baton Rouge, met drummer Joe Hudson, and played clubs such as the Apex & Rhythm. He came to the notice of **Jay Miller** and was invited to play on a **Slim Harpo** session, supposedly playing the distinctive guitar riff on 'King Bee'. Miller recorded Jacobs some time later, in company with **Lazy Lester** and **Katie Webster**; of several titles, only 'Early Morning Blues' and 'I Don't Know Why' were issued decades later on Flyright. In 1959, he was approached by New Orleans record distributor Joe Banashak, who proposed that Jacobs launch his Minit label. 'Early Morning Blues' and 'Bad Luck And Trouble' ('I Don't Know Why' in disguise) were recorded in June of that year. About a month later, a second single was recorded, 'Loaded Down', and the swamp-pop 'Chance For Your Love'. Jacobs' music had the flavour of the juke joint and his first single was picked up for national distribution by **Chess Records**. For a time, he toured with other Minit artists and alongside **Lightnin' Slim**, but disillusionment caused him to take his family west to California, remaining outside music throughout the 60s. His appearance at the 1974 San Francisco Blues Festival led to more regular work and a session for the Blues Connoisseur label in 1977. At this time, he had formed a partnership with another Louisiana migrant, 'Schoolboy' Cleve White.

● ALBUMS: *Loaded Down With The Blues* (1987)★★★.

Jacobs, Dick

b. 29 March 1918, New York, USA, d. 1988. A graduate from the city university, Jacobs was to be one of the few producers for a major US record company in the 50s who catered for rock 'n' roll consumers without finding the form personally objectionable. With his orchestra, he had a US Top 30 entry with **Elmer Bernstein**'s jazzy main theme to 1956's *The Man With The Golden Arm* (starring **Frank Sinatra**) but after serving as musical director for the nationally televised Hit Parade, he became recording manager for Coral, a **Decca** subsidiary. Among his clients were **Jackie Wilson**, **Bobby Darin** and **Buddy Holly**, for whom Jacobs cut corners by duplicating the Darin arrangement of 'Early In The Morning'. By contrast, 'the most unplanned thing I have ever written' was the pizzicato string section that embroidered Holly's posthumous smash, 'It Doesn't Matter Any More', taped in the New York's Pythian Temple studio. During the 60s, Jacobs functioned in a more administrative capacity in the music industry, working for New York's Springboard Records prior to his retirement in the late 70s.

Jacobsen, Erik

b. Chicago, Illinois, USA. Jacobsen attracted attention as a banjo player in the bluegrass trio, the Plum Creek Boys, who were later renamed the Knob Lick Upper 10,000. This unlikely-named group recorded two albums, but broke up when lead singer Dwain Story embarked on a solo career. The third member, Pete Childs, became a session guitarist and dobro player.

The **Beatles** inspired Jacobsen's switch to popular music and he scoured several Greenwich Village haunts for sympathetic musicians. **John Sebastian**, at that point a fixture on the folk scene, brought him an original composition, 'Rooty Toot', and together they began forming a group. Having completed several demos with bassist **Felix Pappalardi**, Sebastian was joined by Joe Butler, Steve Boone and **Zalman Yanovsky** to form **Lovin' Spoonful**. Jacobsen produced all of this excellent group's US Top 10 material, including 'Do You Believe In Magic?', 'Daydream' and 'Summer In The City'. This success paved the way for work with **Tim Hardin** and the **Sopwith Camel**. Erik was also responsible for guiding **Norman Greenbaum**'s solo career which was launched, spectacularly, with a million-selling single, 'Spirit In The Sky'. Despite this impressive roster, Jacobsen withdrew from active involvement in music for much of the 70s, although his publishing company, Faithful Virtue Music, through which all his artists' major compositions were assigned, would continue to reward him financially. He returned to studio work when he produced **Chris Isaak**'s 1985 debut *Silvertone*.

● ALBUMS: with the Knob Lick Upper 10,000 *The Introduction Of The Knob Lick Upper 10,000* (1963)★★★, *Workout!!!* (1964)★★★.

Jacques Brel Is Alive And Well And Living In Paris

This cabaret-style revue which celebrates the songs of the well-known Belgian composer, author, and performer, opened Off Broadway at the Village Gate on 22 January 1968, and ran for an incredible 1,847 performances. The show was conceived by Americans **Mort Shuman** and Eric Blau, who also wrote the lyrics and sundry other additional material. **Jacques Brel**'s original critical and satirical approach to his life and work was impressively reflected in the upwards of 20 numbers that were used in the piece. These included some tender ballads, 'Marieke', 'Old Folks', and 'You're Not Alone', along with an impressive variety of other songs, such as the exuberant 'Carousel' and 'Brussels'. Shuman himself was in the cast of four, along with Shawn Elliot, Alice Whitfield, and Elly Stone, who got to sing most of the best songs, and received all the best notices. She also starred in the London production, along with Shuman, Elliot, and June Gable, but that folded after only 41 performances. Some 20 years later, Stone's connection with the show was renewed when she directed a revival which ran briefly at the Town Hall, New York in 1988. The performers then were Karen Akers, Shelle Ackerman, Kenny Morris, and Elmore James. By then the title was an anachronism - Jacques Brel had died in 1978. Even so, the piece has become a cult item over the years, so it was fitting that, in 1993, a 25th anniversary production was mounted at its original birthplace, the Village Gate, directed of course, by Elly Stone. In 1995, the show returned to Britain and played theatres on the London Fringe.

Jacquet, Illinois

b. Jean Baptiste Jacquet, 31 October 1922, Broussard, Louisiana, USA. Raised in Texas, Jacquet started out on drums, later switching to alto and soprano saxophones. He worked in the popular **territory band** led by Milt Larkins and after stints with other units ended up on the west coast, where he was invited to join **Lionel Hampton**'s new band. In fact, Hampton had wanted Jacquet's section-mate in the Larkins band, tenor saxophonist **Arnett Cobb**, but when Cobb refused to leave, Hampton took Jacquet on condition he switch instruments. Jacquet took the plunge and his solo on Hampton's 1942 recording of 'Flying Home' established him as a major figure in jazz. Indeed, his solo was eventually integrated into subsequent performances of the tune. At the end of 1942, when Cobb finally agreed to leave Larkins and join Hampton, Jacquet moved on first to **Cab Calloway** and then to **Count Basie**. Also in the early 40s, he was involved with **Norman Granz**, appearing in the short film, *Jammin The Blues* (1944), and appearing with Granz's **Jazz At The Philharmonic**. From the mid-40s and on through the 50s Jacquet combined leading his own bands with JATP tours. In the 50s and 60s he became a popular figure at international festivals, leading his own groups, working in all-star ensembles and periodically appearing with Hampton. In the 80s Jacquet continued to record, and late in the decade formed a fine big band for occasional concerts and recording sessions. An important if often overlooked transitional figure in the development of the tenor saxophone, Jacquet has made a significant contribution to the mainstream of jazz while retaining a strong affinity for the blues of his adopted state. This blues feeling, superbly realized on his first recording of 'Flying Home', helped immeasurably in giving rise and substance to the Texas tenor style. His reputation as a wild man of the tenor, based in part upon his time with JATP, is ill-deserved. Indeed, although his high-note playing in the uptempo flagwavers was a demonstration of his incredible technical ability, almost any concert performance or recording date will attest that Jacquet is also a consummate interpreter of ballads.

● ALBUMS: *Jam Session* (Apollo 1951)★★★, *Illinois Jacquet Collates* (Mercury 1952)★★★, *Collates Number 2* (Clef 1953)★★★, *Tenor Sax* (Savoy 1953)★★★, *Illinois Jacquet And His Tenor Sax* (Aladdin 1954)★★★, *Jazz By Jacquet* (Clef 1954)★★★, *Illinois Jacquet Septet* (Clef 1955)★★★, with Ben Webster *The Kid And The Brute* (Clef 1955)★★★★, *Jazz Moods By Illinois Jacquet* (Clef 1956)★★★, *Port Of Rico* (Clef 1956)★★★, *Groovin' With Jacquet* (Clef 1956)★★★, *Swing's The Thing* (Clef 1956)★★★, *Illinois Flies Again* (Roulette/Argo 1959)★★★, *And His Orchestra* (Verve 1961)★★★, *Jazz Moods* (Verve 1961)★★★, *Illinois Jacquet* (Epic 1962)★★★, *Flying Home* (Imperial 1962)★★★, *Message* (Argo 1963)★★★, *Desert Winds* (1964)★★★, *Plays Cole Porter* (Argo 1964)★★, *Spectrum* (Argo 1965)★★★, *Go Power!* (Cadet 1965)★★★, *Bottoms Up* (Prestige 1968)★★★★, *The King* (Prestige 1968)★★★, *The Blues That's Me* (Prestige 1969)★★★, *The Soul Explosion* (Prestige

1970)★★★, *Genius At Work* (Black Lion 1971)★★★, *The Comeback* (Black Lion 1972)★★★, *The Blues For Louisiana* (1973)★★★, *Illinois Jacquet And Wild Bill Davis* (Black And Blue 1973)★★★★, *Jacquet's Street* (1974-76)★★★, with Buddy Tate *Texas Tenors* (1976)★★★★, with Howard McGhee *Here Comes Freddy* (1976)★★★, *Jacquet's Street* (Black And Blue 1977)★★★, *Midnight Slows Volume 8* (Black And Blue 1978)★★★, *God Bless My Solo* (1978)★★★, *Battle Of The Horns* (1980)★★★, *Illinois Jacquet With His All Star New York Band* (1980)★★, *Groovin'* (Verve 1981)★★★, *Illinois Jacquet And His Big Band* (1988)★★★.

● COMPILATIONS: *The Black Velvet Band* recorded 1947-67 (Bluebird 1988)★★★★, *Flying Home: The Best Of The Verve Years* (Bluebird 1992)★★★★, *The Complete Illinois Jacquet Sessions, 1945-50* (Mosiac 1996)★★★★.

Jade

The first working unit of Jade was formed in Winnipeg, Canada, in 1982. The original line-up consisted of Roxy Lyons (vocals), Pat Belrose (guitar), Terry Rudd (bass) and Dave Samson (drums). The band initially played on the local club circuit in the absence of a genuine rock scene. They decided to relocate to Ottawa where they quickly struck a one-off album contract with the small independent label Zaphia Records. Their debut, *Teasing Eyes*, released in 1984, was a mediocre collection of tired pop rock. Realizing their mistake in choice of locale, they relocated once again, this time to Toronto, where the rock community was much more active. Following disagreements on personal and professional matters, Lyons left the band to be replaced by ex-Aggressor vocalist Sweet Marie Black. The band worked hard on their songwriting, taking a more rock-based approach, and subsequent demos led to them being signed by the **Roadrunner** label, who released *If You're Man Enough* in 1985. With more rock and less pop, the album nevertheless failed to attract any interest and the band sank back into obscurity in 1986.

● ALBUMS: *Teasing Eyes* (Zaphia 1984)★★★, *If You're Man Enough* (Roadrunner 1985)★★.

Jade Warrior

Formed in 1970, USA rock band Jade Warrior centred on the multi-instrumental talents of Tony Duhig (d. November 1990; electric and acoustic guitar, bass, keyboards) and John Field (percussion, flute, guitar, keyboards), previously members of psychedelic-pop group July. Glyn Havard (bass, guitar, vocals) completed the pair's new venture, which, although inspired by oriental motifs, betrayed a greater debt to British progressive rock. Jade Warrior completed three albums for the renowned **Vertigo** label, the last of which, *Last Autumn's Dream*, introduced Duhig's brother David (guitar) into the line-up. Havard left the group when a fourth set, *Eclipse*, failed to secure a release, while the founding duo began a parallel career as session musicians. Jade Warrior's later releases, issued by **Island Records**, showed an even greater propensity for experimentation, but failed to elevate the

band above cult status. Following six years of inactivity, the group was reassembled for *Horizons*, but the reunion proved short-lived. Tony Duhig succumbed to a fatal heart attack in November 1990.

● ALBUMS: *Jade Warrior* (Vertigo 1971)★★★, *Released* (Vertigo 1971)★★★, *Last Autumn's Dream* (Vertigo 1972)★★, *Floating World* (Island 1974)★★★, *Waves* (Island 1975)★★★, *Kites* (Island 1976)★★★, *The Way Of The Sun* (Island 1978)★★, *Horizons* (1984)★★★.

● COMPILATIONS: *Reflections* (1980)★★★, *Breathing The Storm* (1993)★★★.

Jae, Jana

b. Jana Margaret Meyer, 30 August 1942, Great Falls, Montana, USA. Her parents both studied classical violin and she began playing at the age of three. However, her maternal grandfather, a country fiddler, influenced her musical direction. After her parents divorced, Jae grew up with her mother in Colorado and Idaho, gaining musical experience playing in school orchestras and talent contests. She qualified in classical music at a Denver college and gained a scholarship to study for a year at the Vienna Academy in Austria. Between 1967 and 1970, she was married, raised two children, was divorced and resumed a musical career, winning national fiddle championships in 1973 and 1974. In 1974, while playing in a bluegrass band, she was heard by **Buck Owens**. When, in 1975, Don Rich died in a motor cycle accident, she replaced him in Owens' Buckeroos and regularly played with them on tour and on *Hee Haw*. In 1977, after recording a solo album of Owens' songs without permission, she was sacked, but later, she and Owens married: it proved a stormy relationship. First, Owens divorced her; they then remarried, but soon afterwards she divorced Owens. She continued to play with him until 1979, when she became a solo artist and recorded for Lark Records. Apart from her country fiddling, with her trademark blue fiddle, she has a love of jazz music, which has even seen her play at the **Montreux Jazz Festival** in Switzerland. In the 80s, with her band Hotwire, she continued to perform and also worked on commercials and promotional work for a major chain store company. She gained the nickname of Fiddling Femme Fatale and stands as the first female musician to become a member of Owens' band.

● ALBUMS: *I Love Fiddling* (American Heritage 70s)★★★, *The Devil You Say* (Lark 80s)★★★, *Live* (Lark 80s)★★, *Symphony Pops* (Lark 80s)★, *By Request* (Lark 80s)★★, *Don't Rock The Bow* (Lark 80s)★★★.

Jaffa, Max

b. 28 December 1911, London, England, d. 30 July 1991, London, England. A classically trained violinist, inspired and influenced by Jascha Heifetz and Fritz Kreisler, who had a long and successful career in British popular music. Born into a non-musical family, Jaffa's father presented him with a violin on his sixth birthday. At the age of nine he made his first concert appearance at the Palace Pier Theatre, Brighton, and later studied at the Guildhall School Of Music. To supplement his income, he formed a trio to play for silent movies. When he was 17 years old, he worked at the Piccadilly Hotel in London and, during a five-year stay, formed his Salon Orchestra, which made its first broadcast from the hotel in August 1929. Later that year he was released for a season to become the youngest ever leader of the Scottish Symphony Orchestra, and went on a concert tour of Scotland with Joseph Hislop. During World War II, Jaffa flew with the Royal Air Force, and afterwards found that he was physically unable to play the violin. After reverting to the basics of the instrument, assisted by one of his original tutors, he joined the **Mantovani** Orchestra, eventually becoming its leader, and played on the original version of the 1951 multi-million-selling record of 'Charmaine'. Around this time, Jaffa's meeting with cellist Reginald Kilbey and pianist Jack Byfield led to the formation of the renowned Max Jaffa Trio. It was a professional association lasting over 30 years. For 27 years, from 1959-86, Max Jaffa served as musical director at Scarborough in Yorkshire, conducting the Spa Orchestra in two concerts a day, during the 17-week summer season. His wife, contralto Jean Grayston, was a regular guest artist. A prolific broadcaster, his radio and television programmes included *Music At Ten*, *Music For Your Pleasure*, *Melody On Strings*, *Max Jaffa Trio*, and the long-running, affectionately remembered *Grand Hotel*, in which he presided over the Palm Court Orchestra. A film he made in 1959, entitled *Music With Max Jaffa*, was billed intriguingly as: 'Musical: Violin, Songs and *Sword Dance*'. His honours included the Gold Medal and Principal's Prize from the Guildhall School of Music, the Freedom of Scarborough, and the OBE, which he received in 1982 for services to music. After a career lasting 70 years, he announced his retirement in 1990. A humorous and enlightened attitude to life and music was reflected in his autobiography, which was published in 1991.

● ALBUMS: *Palm Court Concert* (Columbia 1958)★★★, *Reflections In Gold* (1980)★★★, *Prelude To Romance* (Valentine 1983)★★★, *Music For A Grand Hotel* (Valentine 1986)★★★, *Relax With The Music Of Max Jaffa* (MFP 1987)★★★, *The Way You Look Tonight* (Warwick 1987)★★★, *Favourite Violin Melodies* (Pickwick 1992)★★★.
● FURTHER READING: *A Life On The Fiddle*, Max Jaffa.
● FILMS: *Music With Max Jaffa* (1959).

Jag Panzer

Formed in Colorado, USA, in 1981, the band's original line-up consisted of the curiously named The Tyrant (vocals), Mark Briody (guitar), John Tetley (bass) and Butch Carlson (drums). Quickly signing to the small independent Azra Records, their debut mini-album, *Jag Panzer*, was released in 1983. Basically a collection of demo tracks, it was a rough and ready affair of straight-ahead power metal-inspired rock. The band decided to add another guitarist to give them an extra dimension,

and with this in mind, they relocated to Los Angeles to seek young hopefuls. There they auditioned countless guitarists until Joey Tafolla was finally recruited. With Tafolla in place, they promptly headed back to Colorado to record their first full-length album, *Ample Destruction*, released in 1984 (it was later re-released in 1990 on the Metalcore label). Unfortunately, the album only served to establish the band as a strong underground act with minimal cult status. Dissatisfied with this lack of success, Tafolla left the outfit for a solo career and later went on to play in **Alice Cooper**'s touring band. Shortly after his departure, both The Tyrant and Carlson also left the band. The Tyrant joined **Riot**, albeit briefly, before forming his own band, Titan Force. This left Briody and Tetley to pick up the pieces and re-form the band. Joining them in this new incarnation of Jag Panzer were Bob Parduba (vocals), Christian Lasage (guitar) and Rikard Stjernqvist (drums). This line-up went on to record an impressive demo that secured them a new recording contract with Auburn Records in 1987, resulting in *Chain Of Command* being released the same year.

● ALBUMS: *Jag Panzer* mini-album (Iron Works 1983)★★, *Ample Destruction* (Iron Works 1984)★★, *Chain Of Command* (Auburn 1987)★★★, *The Fourth Judgement* (Century Media 1997)★★.

Jag Wire

Formed in Los Angeles, California, USA, Jag Wire's origins lay in a band named Sin, a popular attraction on the local rock club scene. Comprising Art Deresh (vocals), Howard Drossin (guitar), Vince Gilbert (keyboards), Joey Cristofanilli (bass) and Carl Elizondo (drums), their initial appearances brought comparisons with groups such as **Mötley Crüe** and **Legs Diamond**, leading to a recording contract with local independent Target Records. Their long-playing debut, *Made In Heaven*, followed in 1985. This featured songs rooted in the west-coast glam rock tradition, though the tidy harmonies and anthemic choruses were more forthright than many of their peers. However, it failed to bring the group to the attention of a major label and Jag Wire broke up within a year of its release.

● ALBUMS: *Made In Heaven* (Target 1985)★★★.

Jagged Edge

This UK-based quartet was formed in 1987 by guitarist Myke Gray. A series of personnel changes followed before Andy Robbins (bass), Fabio Del Rio (b. Italy; drums) and Matti Alfonzetti (b. Sweden; vocals, ex-Bam Bam Boys) became the full-time members. Having been picked up by **Polydor Records** before a singer was even recruited, their debut five-track mini-album was rushed out in 1990. Although it featured some fine guitarwork, complemented by Gray and Alfonzetti's vocals, the songs were weak. *Fuel For Your Soul*, released later the same year, was much better. Intricate solos, power-ballads and hard-driving rock 'n' roll were enhanced by Jeff Glixman's production. However,

Jagged Edge split a year later. Gray and Del Rio joined **Bruce Dickinson** (Jagged Edge had previously been signed to **Iron Maiden**'s management company, Sanctuary). Alfonzetti later led his own band, Skintrade, based in Sweden.

● ALBUMS: *Trouble* mini-album (Polydor 1990)★★, *Fuel For Your Soul* (Polydor 1990)★★★★.

Jagged Little Pill - Alanis Morissette

One wonders how on earth can she follow this remarkable debut. Morissette defined the independent rock chick genre started, but not completed, by Suzanne Vega and Sheryl Crow. They like men, but they don't need 'em. Most major record companies have now been signing up Morissette soundalikes for the past two years, but the popularity of this album is inflated because it caught the mood at the right time. There is no doubt that 'Ironic' and 'Hand in My Pocket' are great songs, but radio almost killed them off. Morissette is ballsy and this is a very fine rock album, but time will tell if its current popularity will endure.

● Tracks: *All I Really Want; You Oughta Know; Perfect; Hand In My Pocket; Right Through You; Forgiven; You Learn; Head Over Feet; Mary Jane; Ironic; Not The Doctor; Wake Up.*

● First released 1995

● UK peak chart position: 1

● USA peak chart position: 1

Jagger, Chris

b. 19 December 1947, Dartford, Kent, England. Writer, actor and occasional singer whose work has failed to overcome his familial burden: he is the brother of **Mick Jagger**. Chris first attended Manchester University to study drama, before becoming Assistant Stage Manager at Hampstead Theatre Club. Later he earned his crust designing clothes for fashionable London, including a jacket which appeared on the cover of one of **Jimi Hendrix**'s albums. He then departed for the hippie pilgrimage, visiting India and Nepal. On his return the was offered a touring role in *Hair*, and there was additionally a Kenneth Anger film shot in Egypt in 1972. The rest of the decade was spent living at and maintaining one of Mick's country houses in Newbury, where he would look after guests wishing to use the mobile studio there (**Led Zeppelin**, **Who**, **Faces** etc.). Brother Mick actually helped out on one of Chris' early 70s sets, which laced folk and country with a drawl highly reminiscent of his sibling. Other projects, including efforts to record a country album with the **Flying Burrito Brothers**, and work with Steve Cropper, were aborted. He turned instead to acting, working in repertory theatre after training under Stella Adler. After his guitar company folded in 1984 he turned to writing, first in music journalism but later tackling other subjects. The late 80s saw a return to music, working on sessions with French writer Franck Langolf (who penned many of **Vanessa Paradis**' hits), though these came to nothing. However, he did make small writing contributions to the **Rolling Stones**' albums *Dirty Work* and *Steel*

Wheels. In 1993 he released his first album for 20 years, which this time included Cajun, R&B and swing influences. Among the accompanying musicians featured were Charlie Hart (fiddle), Ed Dean (guitar), Malcolm Mortimore (drums) and Robbie McKidd (accordion). Other guests included **Leo Sayer**, **Dave Gilmour** (who had once played with McKidd in Cambridge band Jokers Wild) and brother Mick.

● ALBUMS: *You Know The Name But Not The Face* (GM 1973)★★, *The Adventures Of Valentine Fox* (Asylum 1974)★★, *Atcha* (Sequel 1993)★★★, *Rock The Zydeco* (Curb 1996)★★★.

Jagger, Mick

b. Michael Philip Jagger, 26 July 1943, Dartford, Kent, England. The celebrated singer of the **Rolling Stones**, Jagger has become less a pop star than a media icon. Initially a shy, middle-class student at the London School of Economics, his love of blues, distinctive vocal style and charismatic stage persona marked him out as an original. The image of Jagger is arguably as crucial to the ultimate long-term success of the Stones as the quality of their songwriting and musicianship. The antithesis of the pretty-boy lead vocalists of the era, Jagger's surly demeanour, rubber lips and scarecrow body were initially greeted with bemusement by the pin-up pop magazines of the time. What Jagger did was to reinforce those apparent pop star deficiencies and, with remarkable effect, transform them into commodities. The lascivious stage presence was emphasized to such a degree that Jagger became both an appealing and strikingly odd-looking pop star. His self-reconstruction even extended as far as completely altering his accent. In mid-60s television interviews Jagger came across as an urbane, well-spoken university student, but as the decade progressed pseudo-cockney inflexions infiltrated his speech, ultimately creating the multi-mouthed media monster of the present - a figure equally at home talking yobbish platitudes to the gutter press and high-brow after-dinner conversation to the quality monthlies. Jagger's capacity to outrage the elder members of the community in the 60s was perfected in his highly energetic dervish stage persona, anti-authoritarian stance and unromantic songwriting. In songs such as '(I Can't Get No) Satisfaction', 'Get Off Of My Cloud', '19th Nervous Breakdown' and 'Have You Seen Your Mother Baby, Standing In The Shadow?' Jagger gave short shrift to sex, women, religion and even life itself. He was, undoubtedly, one of rock's most underrated and nihilistic lyricists. The force of his negative catechism was, of course, complemented by the musical contribution of **Keith Richards**, the architect behind the Rolling Stones' most memorable melodies. Jagger was also assisted by the quality of his players, especially **Bill Wyman**, Charlie Watts, Brian Jones and later, **Mick Taylor**.

From the mid-60s onwards the rebellion implicit in Jagger's lyrics was reflected in increasingly bizarre real life situations. From urinating against an East London garage wall to saturnalian drug sessions and short-term imprisonment, Jagger came to embody the changing social values and bohemian recklessness that characterized the rock culture of the 60s. It must also be said that he performed a similar role in the 70s when his broken marriage, jet-set romances, cafe society fraternization and millionaire seclusion in exotic climes typified the bloated complacency of the musical elite of the period. The barometer of his time, Jagger yet resisted the temptation to branch out from the Stones into too many uncharted areas. A desultory appearance in the film *Ned Kelly* revealed that his powers of mimicry did not extend as far as a convincing Australian/Irish accent. By contrast, the extraordinary *Performance* captured the combined innocence and malevolence of Jagger's pop persona to striking effect in the guise of an east end gangster and decadent rock star The experiment was not repeated.

Jagger was even less concerned about expressing himself in a literary form, unlike **John Lennon**, **Pete Townshend** and others of his generation. The most articulate of the Stones frankly admitted that he could not even remember sufficient details of his life to pen a ghosted biography. That peculiar combination of indolence and disinterest may have kept the Rolling Stones together as a performing unit, for Jagger studiously avoided customary rock star solo outings for virtually 25 years. When he finally succumbed to the temptation in the late 80s, the results were insubstantial. Apart from a small handful of tracks, most notably the driving 'Just Another Night', the albums *She's The Boss* and *Primitive Cool* proved disappointing and no doubt contributed to his decision to take the Rolling Stones back on the road at the end of the decade. He has since teamed-up with **Tina Turner** for a **Live Aid** performance and with **David Bowie** for a charity cover of **Martha And The Vandella**'s 'Dancin' In The Street'. Jagger once stated that he would retire before middle-age for fear that the Rolling Stones might become an anachronistic parody of themselves. These days such fears appear to have been banished as the Stones are still recording and, in 1990/91, embarked upon a massive US and European stadium tour. Six years passed before Jagger made his third solo album, the critics were once again unmoved. The addition of **Courtney Pine** and **Billy Preston** could not produce a significant hit album.

● ALBUMS: *She's The Boss* (Columbia 1985)★★, *Primitive Cool* (Columbia 1987)★★, *Wandering Spirit* (Atlantic 1993)★★.

● FURTHER READING: *Mick Jagger: The Singer Not The Song*, J. Marks. *Mick Jagger*, Tony Scaduto. *Up And Down With The Rolling Stones*, Tony Sanchez. *The Stones*, Philip Norman. *The True Adventures Of The Rolling Stones*, Stanley Booth. *Jagger Unauthorised*, Christopher Andersen. *Mick Jagger: Primitive Cool*, Christopher Sandford.

Jaggerz

Formed in Pittsburgh, Pennsylvania, USA in the mid-60s, the Jaggerz comprised Dominic Ierace (b. Ellwood City, Pennsylvania, USA; lead vocals/guitar), Billy Maybray (drums/bass/vocals), Thom Davis (b. Duquesne, Pennsylvania, USA; keyboards/trumpet), Benny Faiella (b. Beaver Falls, Pennsylvania, USA; guitar/bass), Jimmy Ross (b. Aliquippa, Pennsylvania, USA; trombone/bass) and Jim Pugliano (drums). Pittsburgh entrepreneur Joe Rock introduced the group to producers **Gamble And Huff**, who signed them to their own Gamble label in 1969, with one album but no hits resulting. They next signed with Kama Sutra Records, and released 'The Rapper', a funky rocker written by Ierace under his stage name Donnie Iris. The song reached number 2 in the US charts. Follow-up singles failed although the group continued into the mid-70s. Iris joined the funk group **Wild Cherry** before going on to a moderately successful solo career in the early 80s.

● ALBUMS: *We Went To Different Schools Together* (Buddah 1970)★★★, *Come Again* (1975)★★.

Jags

One of the many so called UK power pop bands to emerge from the new wave, the Jags did so in style with their classic debut 'Back Of My Hand'. They came together when Nick Watkinson and his school friend, John Alder from Scarborough, Yorkshire, England, began writing songs together around 1977. Despite Watkinson leaving for Bournemouth College Of Art they remained in contact and in late 1978 formed the Jags together. Watkinson sang while Alder played guitar; the line-up was completed by Steve Prudence from Guildford, Surrey, England on bass and Alex Baird on drums. Baird from Glasgow, Scotland was the only member with any real previous experience, having once played alongside **Midge Ure** in Stumble (before Ure found fame in **Slik**) and also playing for a while in the Banned. Signed to **Island** they released 'Back Of My Hand' in 1979 which reached the Top 20. The follow up - 'Woman's World' - was their only other hit but their debut album was well received. Mainly produced by Jon Astley and Phil Chapman, production assistance was credited to **Buggles** who were just making their own breakthrough as recording artists. The follow-up album in 1981 was produced by Alex Sadkin and contained strong singles in 'The Sound Of G-O-O-D-B-Y-E' and 'I Never Was A Beachboy'.

● ALBUMS: *Evening Standards* (1980)★★★, *No Tie Like The Present* (1981)★★.

Jaguar

This band was formed in Bristol, England, in 1979, with an original line-up comprising Rob Reiss (vocals), Garry Pepperd (guitar), Jeff Cox (bass) and Chris Lovell (drums). Early demos led to the band having a track included on the *Heavy Metal Heroes* compilation album. The unit subsequently attracted the attention of

Neat Records, who released two Jaguar singles, 'Back Street Woman' and 'Axe Crazy', in 1981 and 1982, respectively. The band quickly gained popularity with their **New Wave Of British Heavy Metal**-rooted speed metal. 'Axe Crazy' was the first single release to feature new vocalist Paul Merrell, who replaced Reiss. Merrell's powerful melodic voice was in fine form for the band's debut album, *Powergames*, again released on Neat in 1983. This was well received, with excellent vocal and guitar work complementing the high-speed power-metal rhythms. The band quickly gained a strong following in Europe, especially in the Netherlands, where they toured extensively. However, this all changed with a drastic shift in musical style on their next album. After switching labels to **Roadrunner** Records, *This Time* was released in 1984. This saw the band slow down considerably, proffering instead melodic rock, accompanied by the guest keyboards of Larry Dawson. It was an ill-conceived gambit that lost the band many fans. Shortly after its release, drummer Lovell was replaced by Gary Davies. Owing to the adverse press reaction the album received, the band folded in 1985.

● ALBUMS: *Powergames* (Neat 1983)★★★★, *This Time* (Roadrunner 1984)★★.

Jaguars

An R&B vocal group from Los Angeles, California, USA. The Jaguars were one of the few Los Angeles groups that could sing standards in the spirit and style of pop music, but added a hard rock 'n' roll edge. The members of this black-white-Hispanic group were Sonny Chaney (lead), Val Poliuto (tenor), Manual Chavez (baritone) and Charles Middleton (bass). The group began recording for a small label in Los Angeles in 1955, and the following year found success with a doo-wop remake of the **Jerome Kern** standard 'The Way You Look Tonight'. The group lost Middleton in 1958, and the following year the remaining three, with freelance vocalists Tony Allen and **Richard Berry**, recorded as the Velvetones. The record was not a success and the group disbanded. Chavez and Chaney went on to record as a duo.

● COMPILATIONS: *The Way You Look Tonight* (Earth Angel 1988)★★★.

Jah Free

Jah Free began his musical career with the band Tallowah, who later evolved into Bushfire. The band built a solid reputation on the European live circuit until their premature demise. This was followed by the inauguration of Jah Free Music, set up to record, design and release Jah Free records. He released the favoured roots hit 'Wicked Can't Run', followed by the equally popular discomix, 'Lighting Clap'. Both hits proved to be especially popular on the **sound system** circuit, notably with **Jah Shaka**. Shaka's sound is notorious for its reverberating bass levels, and his releases and mixing works attracted the attention of **Zion Train**, who

enrolled Jah Free into the Universal Egg collective. With the organization he released his debut, *Breaking Out*, which featured his earlier releases and the disparaging 'Jacques Chirac'. Echoing the **Motown** Revues of the 60s, he was enrolled as a compere on the Egg Experience '97 tour, a showcase that featured various artists from the label. In addition to his collaboration with Zion Train, he also produced the classic 'Rich Man' for Martin Campbell of the Jah Works posse. At the close of 1997 he had completed an exhaustive schedule, having worked with the **Mad Professor**, Iration Steppas, Conscious Sounds, Armagideon (sic) and the Belgium dub heroes Bong Messages. He embarked on a series of sessions in 1998 with **Vibronics** that led to a series of Live 'Dub Conferences' across Europe, promoting the duo's album. Jah Free also released his solo plea that we should 'Love One And Other'.

● ALBUMS: *Breaking Out* (Universal Egg 1995)★★★, with Vibronics *Outernational Dub Conference Volume One* (Universal Egg 1998)★★★★.

Jah Lion

b. Pat Francis, *c.*1950, Kingston, Jamaica, West Indies. Pat Francis has recorded under a variety of aliases including Jah Lion, Jah Lloyd and the Black Lion Of Judah. In the mid-60s he sang alongside Fitzroy 'Bunny' Simpson as the Mediators and also as a soloist, notably with 'Soldier Round The Corner' and 'Know Yourself Blackman' for producer **Rupie Edwards**. In the early 70s he turned to production when he recorded his sparring partner Simpson alongside Donald 'Tabby' Shaw and Lloyd 'Judge' Ferguson, known collectively as the **Diamonds**. In 1976 he introduced the renamed **Mighty Diamonds** to **Joseph 'Joe Joe' Hookim** at **Channel One**, where they recorded the legendary *Right Time*, which proved to be the beginning of the vocal trio's lengthy career. As Jah Lloyd he turned to the art of the DJ, recording the hits 'Black Snowfall', 'World Class', and a comment on a report about a batch of poisoned flour discovered in Kingston, 'Beware Of The Flour'. With **Lee Perry** Francis recorded, as Jah Lion, *Columbia Collie*. The project was critically acclaimed and enjoyed a prolonged stay on the reggae album chart. 'Wisdom' was lifted from the album and featured in the film *Countryman*, and his version of **Junior Murvin**'s 'Police And Thieves', 'Soldier And Police War', topped the reggae charts. In 1978 he reverted to the pseudonym of Jah Lloyd and secured a two-album contract with **Virgin Records**' Front Line label. With Maurice 'Blacka' Wellington and **Bingi Bunny** producing, he recorded *The Humble One*, which included 'Jah Lion' and 'Cocaine'. The latter surfaced as a single through Front Line, although it failed to make a significant impact on the charts. In 1979 he returned to production, initially his own recordings at Channel One, assisted by **Sly And Robbie**; together, they recorded 'Green Bay Incident' and 'Dispenser', a return to lyrics relating to hard drugs. His final appearance as

Jah Lloyd came in 1982 when he recorded the unusual 'Shake And Flicker'. By the mid-80s he was promoting his latest protégé, Julie Charles, with her debut 'As Long As You Love Me', and reverted to the pseudonym of Jah Lion.

● ALBUMS: *Columbia Collie* (Island 1977)★★★, *The Humble One* (Front Line 1978)★★★, *Black Moses* (Front Line 1979)★★, *In Action With The Revolutionaries* (Vista 1983)★★★.

Jah Screw

b. Paul Love, *c.*1955, Kingston, Jamaica, West Indies. Love began his musical career as the operator for Echo Bell and later **U-Roy**'s Stur Gav **sound system** with DJ Little Joe, aka **Ranking Joe**. Love's period as Stur Gav's operator ended when the sound was destroyed during the 1980 elections in Jamaica. The duo then joined Ray Symbolics Hi Fi. The sound system toured the UK to rave reviews, but was marred by tragedy when Ray returned to Jamaica. Stories relating to Ray's death were plentiful, and varied from drink-driving to a shoot-out with the police. Ranking Joe and Love embarked on a production partnership with their own Sharp Axe label and had hits in 1982 with 'Ice Cream Style' and *Armageddon*. In 1984 Love produced **Barrington Levy**'s 'Under Mi Sensi', which led to a long and successful partnership. His production of 'Here I Come' was accompanied by national radio and television exposure when licensed to **London Records**. The label also released 'Money Moves', which flopped. Love also set up his own Time One production stable. In 1988 Love released his production of Levy's 'She's Mine', and 'Step Up In Life' with **Sassafras**. In the late 80s, as a performer he recorded 'Original Soundboy Killer' for Wildfire, although he found greater success in the role of producer. In 1991 'Dancehall Rock', a variation on **Bob Marley**'s 'Trenchtown Rock', topped the reggae charts when Love, now known as Jah Screw, teamed Levy with DJ **Cutty Ranks**. A year later Jah Screw produced a number of notable hits with artists including **Dennis Brown**, **Reggie Stepper** and **Chaka Demus**. In 1994 he produced DJ **Beenie Man** for the ragga remix of 'Under Mi Sensi 94 Spliff', resulting in another reggae chart-topper. Following Jah Screw's success in pairing up Levy with the DJs, he then recruited **Bounty Killer** for 1995's 'Living Dangerously'.

● ALBUMS: *Original Experience* (Time One 1991)★★★, *Jah Screw Presents Dancehall Glamity* (Time One 1994)★★★.

Jah Shaka

An enigmatic and highly individual performer on the UK **sound system** scene, Jah Shaka (his real name remains a mystery) came with his parents to the UK from Jamaica at the age of eight, settling in south-east London. Succumbing to his passion for music, he began his career a few years later in the late 60s, playing in a band and travelling around in an obscure local sound system named Freddie Cloudburst. Inspired spiritually by his interest in Rastafari, and consciously by the American Civil Rights movement (particularly such exponents of black awareness as Angela Davis and George Jackson), he began to assemble equipment for his own sound, named after the great eighteenth century Zulu, King Shaka, the 'Black Napoleon'. From quite modest beginnings in the early 70s, by the end of the decade Shaka's sound had become one of the top three in the country, alongside such luminaries as **Lloyd Coxsone** and the Mighty Fatman, specializing in heavyweight, dubwise steppers material, and exclusive cuts on **dub plates**. However, whereas these and other sounds usually supported a team of selectors and DJs, Shaka performed all these functions alone, assistance in setting up the sound coming from a team of devoted youths for whom Shaka's music was almost a way of life.

His dances became famous for their spiritually charged atmosphere and the acrobatic, stylized dancing of the participants. Shaka would operate his sound like a single instrument, the music played at ear-splitting distortion levels, the air torn by his trademark sirens and syndrums, the man himself caught up in the spirit, alternatively chanting, singing and dancing as furiously as many of those in the crowd. In 1980 Shaka inaugurated his Jah Shaka King Of The Zulu Tribe label with the release of 'Jah Children Cry' by African Princess, which sold well in the reggae market. This was followed by the first instalment in his long-running *Commandments Of Dub* series. Over the years the label has carried well over 50 releases by UK-based artists such as Junior Brown, Sgt Pepper, Vivian Jones, Sis Nya and the **Twinkle Brothers**, as well as dozens of releases by Shaka himself, and Jamaican artists such as **Horace Andy**, **Icho Candy** and **Max Romeo**. With the decline of interest in Rastafarianism in the 80s, Shaka's dances became more and more isolated affairs, the crowd thinning to a hardcore of older followers. However, Shaka's adherence to Rasta, and the particular type of heavy, spiritual reggae with which his name has become synonymous, remained unswerving. By the latter part of the decade a new, young, multiracial crowd of disaffected roots fans had begun to appear. Out of this crowd emerged a number of artists and sound systems who largely shunned contemporary reggae in favour of the revived sounds of the 70s and early 80s in which Shaka still specialised. Though seen by some observers as anachronistic and irrelevant, this 'new dub school', predominantly inspired by Shaka, has nevertheless gained much support over the last few years, nurturing and sustaining its own network of musicians, record labels, studios, sound systems, clubs and radio shows.

● ALBUMS: *Commandments Of Dub Chapters 1-10* (Jah Shaka 1980-1991)★★★★, *Revelation Songs* (Jah Shaka 1983)★★★, *Kings Music* (Jah Shaka 1984)★★★, with Mad Professor *Jah Shaka Meets Mad Professor At Ariwa Sounds* (Ariwa 1984)★★★, *Message From Africa* (Jah Shaka 1985)★★, *The Music Message* (Jah Shaka 1988)★★★, *My Prayer* (Jah Shaka 1990)★★, with Mad Professor *A New Decade Of Dub* (RAS 1996)★★★.

Jah Stitch

b. Melbourne James, 1949, Kingston, Jamaica, West Indies. Jah Stitch was one of the pioneering DJs. Although famed as a DJ, he began his career singing in a music yard alongside **Roy Shirley**, **Stranger Cole**, the **Wailers** and the **Heptones**. Jah Stitch soon became the leading DJ with the Lord Tippertone and Black Harmony **sound systems**. **Errol Holt** produced his debut, 'Danger Zone', and his vocals bore a resemblance to **Big Youth**, who was an influence on the young DJ. Many of Jah Stitch's early hits were DJ versions of **Johnny Clarke**'s extensive back catalogue, such as 'Legalise It' as 'Collie Bud', 'My Conversation' as 'How Long Jah Jah', and 'Roots Natty Roots Natty Congo' as 'True Born African'. Other hits included 'Crazy Joe', 'King In The Arena' and, with **Yabby You**, 'African Queen'. Prior to the One Love Peace Concert in Jamaica, organized in an attempt to thwart the escalating street violence and bring an end to the State Of Emergency, Jah Stitch was shot. Although scarred by the event, he returned to the recording studio, responding with 'No Dread Can't Dead'. By 1977 his hits included 'Militant Man' and 'Jah Jah Forgive You' and he successfully toured the UK. In 1985 he re-emerged as Major Stitch, selecting the tunes for **Sugar Minott**'s Youth Promotion sound system. A number of up-and-coming vocalists began their careers with the sound, including **Tenor Saw**, Jah Mikey, Dickie Ranking and **Yammie Bolo**. A prolonged period of anonymity came to an end when, in 1995, he recorded with Trevor Douglas and **Jah Woosh** and his career was documented on a compilation released through **Simply Red**'s Blood & Fire label.

● ALBUMS: *No Dread Can't Dead* (1976)★★★, *Watch Your Step Youthman* (Third World 1977)★★★, with Prince Jazzbo *Straight To Babylon Chest* (1979)★★★, *Moving Away* (Live And Love 1979)★★★, with Jah Woosh *Jah Woosh Meets Jah Stitch At Leggo Sounds* (Leggo 1995)★★.

● COMPILATIONS: *Jah Stitch, Original Ragga Muffin 1975 - 77* (Blood & Fire 1996)★★★★.

Jah Stone

b. Gladstone Fisher, c.1953, Jamaica, West Indies. After working as a DJ on a variety of **sound systems**, Fisher recorded as Jah Stone with **Bim Sherman**. In 1977 Sherman inaugurated his own Scorpio label and due to financial restraints, was forced to employ Jah Stone to deliver two separate chants over the same rhythm track. The association with Sherman led to the **dancehall** favourites 'Fat Ting' and 'Burning'. His notoriety led to work with producer Alvin 'GG' Ranglin, who featured the DJ in combination with **Freddie McKay** on his remake of 'Picture On The Wall' and the solo hit 'Ten Ton Woman'. He was also employed on the **Sonia Pottinger** production of 'Baby Love' by the reactivated vocal group the **Sensations**. In 1978 Jah Stone recorded for **Doctor Alimantado**, the sessions producing the assertive 'Militant Dread'. In 1979 Jah Stone recorded in session with **Winston Jarrett** of the Righteous

Flames, resulting in the release of 'War' and 'Kaya', both of which were later featured on *The Messiah*. Notable album tracks included the admonishing 'Sergeant Black', the bizarre 'Kung Fu Ballet' and the chauvinistic 'Irie Lickle Filly'. Sadly, the album signalled his swan-song, and in spite of this and his work with a number of Jamaican producers, Jah Stone is usually only recalled as the DJ who recorded with Bim Sherman. The 1997 release of a Freddie McKay compilation featuring Jah Stone demonstrated the latter's versatility and rekindled interest in the DJ's work.

● ALBUMS: *The Messiah* (Gorgon 1979)★★★.

● COMPILATIONS: with Freddie McKay *The Right Time 1977-78 recordings* (GG's 1997)★★★★.

Jah Warriors

Jah Warriors were a UK-based reggae band from Ipswich, Suffolk. The line-up included Lloyd 'Captain' Morgan (lead vocals), Ira Jones (vocals, lead guitar), Gordon Mulraine (bass guitar), Joseph White (drums), Aubrey Mulraine (keyboards), Lloyd Clarke (saxophone) and Trevor Jones (trombone). In 1982 the band released their debut, 'If Only You Knew'/'Can't Take It No More', which was met with critical acclaim but failed commercially. Undeterred, the group built a solid reputation touring, and in 1984 they were asked to support the legendary **Curtis Mayfield**. Although an R&B performer, Mayfield and the **Impressions** had influenced many of Jamaica's top performers, notably **Bob Marley**, **Black Uhuru**, **Pat Kelly**, the **Mighty Diamonds** and **Brown Sugar**. Conscious and respectful of the singer's eminence, the young group gave their all in support of the influential performer. The group performed 'Tribute To Bob Marley' alongside tracks from their forthcoming album, including 'Drug Squad', 'Can't Cook' and their earlier singles releases. Mayfield was impressed by the band's performance and predicted a bright future for the group. The experience proved beneficial and the band released *Poor Mans Story*, which covered a diversity of subjects including abortion ('Innocent Ones') and an interpretation of an advertising jingle, 'Liquor'. The album was recorded locally by the band at a studio owned by the 60s pop singer **Chris Andrews**, who had a Top 10 hit with 'Yesterday Man', later covered in a reggae version by **Nicky Thomas**.

The group continued to work with Andrews for their second album, which included the Bob Marley tribute. The track featured the playing skills of one-time **Wailer Al Anderson**, and has since become a standard for the group. The group also released the **lovers rock** hit 'What's This Feeling', followed by 'Love Has A Way'. While performing lovers rock tracks, they also continued in a roots vein for the haunting 'Apartheid' and still enjoy cult status. Their status as UK rockers was endorsed when they were invited to perform alongside the reggae élite as part of the British Reggae Artists Famine Appeal. In the 90s the group enjoyed a revival as dubmasters, releasing *Great Kings Of Israel In Dub* and *African Tribes Dub*.

● ALBUMS: *Poor Mans Story* (Vista 1984)★★★, *No Illusions* (A Records 1985)★★.

Jah Wobble

b. John Wardle, London, England. An innovative bass player, Wobble began his career with **Public Image Limited**. Previously he had been known as one of the 'four Johns' who hung around **Malcolm McLaren**'s 'Sex' boutique. Heavily influenced by the experimental rhythms of bands like **Can**, his input to PiL's *Metal Box* collection inspired in turn many novice post-punk bass players. By August 1980 he had become one of the many instrumentalists to fall foul of Lydon in PiL's turbulent career, and set about going solo. 1983 saw him joining with his hero **Holger Czukay** and U2's The Edge for *Snake Charmer*, before he put together the Human Condition, a group specializing in free-form jazz and dub improvisation. However, when they disbanded, the mid-80s quickly became wilderness years for Wobble: 'The biggest kickback I have had was from sweeping the platform at Tower Hill station. It was a scream. You felt like getting on the intercom and saying "The next train is the Upminster train, calling at all stations to Upminster and by the way, I USED TO BE SOMEONE!".' However, when he began listening to North African, Arabic and Romany music, he was inspired to pick up his bass once more. It was 1987 when he met guitarist Justin Adams, who had spent much of his early life in Arab countries. Their bonding resulted in Wobble putting together Invaders Of The Heart, with producer Mark Ferda on keyboards. After tentative live shows they released *Without Judgement* in the Netherlands, where Wobble had maintained cult popularity. As the late 80s saw a surge in the fortunes of dance and rhythmic expression, Invaders Of The Heart and Wobble suddenly achieved a surprise return to the mainstream. This was spearheaded by 1990's 'Bomba', remixed by **Andy Weatherall** on the fashionable **Boy's Own Records**. Wobble was in demand again, notably as collaborator on **Sinead O'Connor**'s *I Do Not Want What I Haven't Got* and **Primal Scream**'s 'Higher Than The Sun'. This was quickly followed by Invaders Of The Heart's *Rising Above Bedlam*, in turn featuring contributions from O'Connor (the dance hit, 'Visions Of You') and Natacha Atlas. Wobble's creative renaissance has continued into the 90s, with Invaders Of The Heart slowly building a formidable live reputation and releasing a series of infectious, upbeat albums for **Island Records**. He collaborated with **Brian Eno** on 1995's *Spanner*, and then released a series of concept albums exploring subjects as diverse as William Blake and Celtic poetry.

● ALBUMS: *The Legend Lives On ... Jah Wobble In 'Betrayal'* (Virgin 1980)★★, with Holger Czukay and The Edge *Snake Charmer* (Island 1983)★★★, *Jah Wobble's Bedroom Album* (Lago 1983)★★, with Ollie Morland *Neon Moon* (Island 1985)★★★, *Psalms* (Wob 1987)★★★, with Invaders Of The Heart *Without Judgement* (Island 1990)★★★, with Invaders Of The Heart *Rising Above Bedlam* (Island 1991)★★★★, *Take Me To God* (Island 1994)★★★★, *Heaven & Earth* (Island 1995)★★★, with Eno *Spanner* (All Saints 1995)★★★, *The Inspiration Of William Blake* (All Saints 1996)★★★, *The Celtic Poets* (30 Hertz 1997)★★★, *The Light Programme* (30 Hertz 1997)★★, *Umbra Sumus* (30 Hertz 1998)★★.

Jah Woosh

b. Neville Beckford, 1952, Kingston, Jamaica, West Indies. Before entering a recording studio, Beckford served an apprenticeship as a mechanic. He and his friend **Reggae George** attended auditions with the island's top producers under the name of Neville and George, but their partnership was short-lived and both went on to pursue solo careers. Beckford's career took off when he became resident DJ on Prince Lloyd's **sound system**, and producer George Bell liked what he heard. The result was 'Angela Davis', a tribute to the black freedom fighter credited under his new pseudonym, Jah Woosh. Despite the strong lyrics, it was not a hit, but he was able to impress producer **Rupie Edwards**. The sessions with Edwards led to the release of *Jah Woosh*, through Cactus in the UK. He subsequently enjoyed a brief spell of fame, recording for a number of producers, and enjoying hits with 'Psalm 121', 'Ital Feast' and 'Zion Sound'. Following his success, he recorded a self-production with The Mighty Clouds band, resulting in the release of *Dreadlocks Affair*, which featured the popular 'Natty Bal' Head', 'Shimi Skank' and the title track. Other records followed, but it was the release of *Religious Dread* that produced a successful run in the Jamaican reggae charts, including 'Marcus Say', 'Chant Freedom' and a tribute to the Four Aces club, a popular dance venue in the UK. With Sydney Crooks of the **Pioneers** in the production seat and a host of top sessioners assembled, *Loaded With TNT* was the follow-up. Despite excellent musicianship from **Lloyd Parks** and keyboard wizard **Ansell Collins**, the set was destined not to repeat the success of his earlier recordings.

● ALBUMS: *Jah Woosh* (Cactus 1974)★★, *Dreadlocks Affair* (Trojan 1974)★★★, *Rebellion* (1975)★★★, *Religious Dread* (Trojan 1976)★★★★, *Loaded With TNT* (Trenchtown 1976)★★★, with I-Roy *We Chat You Rock* (Trojan 1987)★★★, with Mixman *Fire In A Blackamix* (Blackamix 1993)★★, with Jah Stitch *Jah Woosh Meets Jah Stitch At Leggo Sounds* (Leggo 1995)★★.

Jahmali

b. Ryan Thomas, 5 April 1972, Vere, Clarendon, Jamaica, West Indies. Thomas was the ninth of 10 children and was raised among the sugar plantations in the Jamaican countryside. His love for the **dancehall** sounds of **Shabba Ranks**, **Pinchers**, **Red Dragon** and **Wayne Wonder** inspired a move to Kingston, where he embarked on his own musical career. He received encouragement from **King Jammy**, **Philip 'Fatis' Burrell** and **Tony Rebel**, although they remained hesitant about producing his work. Rebel subsequently introduced Thomas to the Rastafarian faith, which prompted a radical change in the young singer's approach. Performing as Jahmali, he began voicing hits for **Donovan Germain**, **Bobby Digital** and Roof International's Barry O'Hare. A string of hits followed, including the inspired 'Victory', 'Let Me Live', 'Wake Up' and 'El Shaddai'. Jahmali's association with O'Hare led to a collaboration with **Mikey Spice**, who had set up his own Ingredients label. Spice produced for Jahmali's 'Let Jah Be Praised' and 'Only Love', both of which demonstrated his new, conscientious stance. Jahmali's critically acclaimed debut album featured many top Jamaican performers, including Earl 'Chinna' Smith, **Sly Dunbar**, **Robbie Shakespeare**, Stephen 'Cat' Coore and Aston 'Familyman' Barrett. Jahmali's reputation was further enhanced when he recorded 'Mother's Cry' with **Buju Banton**, featured on the latter's accomplished *Inna Heights*. Following his combination success, Jahmali released his own 'Cry People' and the haunting 'Politics'.

● ALBUMS: *Jahmali* (High Times 1997)★★★.

Jahson, David

b. Everald Pickersgill, 4 November 1954, Kingston, Jamaica, West Indies. Jahson embarked on his recording career with his debut, 'For I', which peaked at number 7 on the JBC chart in Jamaica. His overnight success led to the release of a number of hits, including 'Ruff Neck Soldier', 'Give Thanks And Praise' and the melancholy 'People Bawling'. By 1977 he joined the line-up of the Well Pleased And Satisfied band who enjoyed a string of hits during their brief career, including 'Black On Black', 'West Man Rock', 'News Carrier Dem A Warrior', 'Barberman Bawling' and 'Open The Gates'. Following the band's demise, Jahson reactivated his solo career, working with brothers Ian and Roger Lewis of **Inner Circle**. The alliance led to Jahson's pivotal hit, 'Natty Chase The Barber', which reiterated his acrimonious attitude towards hairdressers. The song inspired a series of barber-related tunes in the late 70s, including **Doctor Alimantado** riding the same rhythm for 'I Killed The Barber'. Jahson simultaneously accompanied the Inner Circle band on their promotional tour for *Everything Is Great*, where he is credited as percussionist. He remained with the band under the guise of 'Black Spy' until **Jacob Miller**'s untimely demise in March 1980, which led to the band's temporary dissolution. He settled in the UK throughout the 80s, initially recording with fellow expatriate **Errol Dunkley**. Jahson's sporadic releases include 'True Believer', 'She Loves The Rub A Dub', 'Lips Of Wine', 'Stop Your Gun Shooting' and 'Zion Home'.

● ALBUMS: *Natty Chase The Barber* (Top Ranking 1978)★★★, *Past And Present* (Spy 1982)★★, *Come Again Showcase* (Top Ranking 1985)★★.

● COMPILATIONS: *Natty Chase* (Lagoon 1996)★★★, *Root Of David* (Pick A Skill 1997)★★★★.

Jai

b. Jason Roe, *c*.1973, Yeovil, Somerset, England. A contemporary pop singer-songwriter, Jai's first musical experience came as part of a Somerset band that featured **PJ Harvey** collaborators Rob Ellis and Steve Vaughan. He signed to the M&G subsidary label Wired Recordings in 1995. Despite a high media profile, including appearances on the *National Lottery Live* and features in both mainstream and teenage pop magazines, his first two singles, 'I Believe' and 'Don't Give Me Away', flopped. In truth, his record company were struggling to find the correct marketing formula for a young singer with a mature, soulful voice. After first targeting a younger pop audience, M&G attempted to build his profile on the club circuit by employing remixers including the Psychonauts, Carl Mackintosh and UNKLE. He also toured in support of **Olive** and **Gabrielle**, in an attempt to broaden his audience. As he told *Music Week* in 1997, 'I was uncomfortable with being promoted as a pop act. I understand it though, because I'm not doing anything majorly leftfield.' Despite minimal sales returns on his early recordings, his management decided to launch him in America, where his soul-based style was not restricted to such a niche audience. His blend of classic and contemporary soul (his influences include **Marvin Gaye**, **Stevie Wonder** and **Soul II Soul**) and the use of real instruments had by now earned him comparisons to **David McAlmont**. His debut album, *Heaven*, was co-written by producer Joel Bogen, who provided a series of sumptuous arrangements as a backdrop to Jai's arresting falsetto. The only cover version was a contemporary interpretation of the Arthur Hamilton standard, 'Cry Me A River'.

● ALBUMS: *Heaven* (Wired Recordings 1997)★★★.

Jailbreak - Thin Lizzy

Not true heavy metal perpetrators, more out-and-out rockers, with a feeling for pop. The late Phil Lynott has a growing core of younger fans, as word is passed down that even though he had his demons he was an outstanding performer. This is their best studio album and it contains two classics; 'The Boys Are Back In Town' and the title track. Both spit and crackle, bass and lead guitar burst out of the speaker at loud volume, and throughout, the gentle, laconic voice of Lynott delivers his poetry. Don't allow his death to see Thin Lizzy fade from the memory.

● Tracks: *Angel From The Coast; The Boys Are Back In Town; Cowboy Song; Emerald; Fight Or Jail; Jailbreak; Romeo And The Lonely Girl; Running Back; Warriors.*

● First released 1976

● UK peak chart position: 10

● USA peak chart position: 18

Jailhouse Rock

Although hamstrung by mediocre films throughout much of his Hollywood career, **Elvis Presley** did complete some outstanding early features. In *Jailhouse*

Rock he was aided by a superior plot in which the singer is taught to play guitar while serving in prison for manslaughter. Fame and egotism follow suit until his former cell-mate returns to haunt him and, eventually, prick his conscience. The film also provides an insight into record company practices during the 50s and has a visual impact many other contemporary works lacked. The highly choreographed scene that the title track accompanies has passed into pop cinema history. The **Leiber And Stoller** songwriting team, famed for their work with the **Coasters**, provided all of the soundtrack material, which ranges from the electric 'Baby I Don't Care' to the ballad-styled 'Young And Beautiful'. Taken together, the album and film represent a high-water mark in Presley's output.

Jakszyk, Jakko

b. 8 June 1958, Highgate, London, England. As a teenager Jaksyzk's intentions were to become a professional soccer player, but he failed his trial with Watford Football Club. Already playing guitar in his bedroom, he also enjoyed acting, and joined the National Youth Theatre at the age of 14. His first band, Soon After, was formed a year later. In 1975 this trio came third in a *Melody Maker* National Rock Competition. After various dead end jobs he eventually found acting work after leaving school, moving on to the 64 Spoons troupe, whose marriage of punk rock attitude with classical musicianship and bawdy, music hall humour were a memorable sight around the lesser venues of England. Through the Spoons Jakszyk met **Dave Stewart**, with whom toured England and Europe, before appearing on Stewart's recording with **Colin Blunstone** and **Barbara Gaskin**. He signed a solo deal with Chiswick Records in 1981. A series of singles ensued while an album, *Silesia*, was released only in Germany. Jakszyk then moved over to **Stiff Records** for more singles and a second album. By 1985 he had joined Mark Dean's Innervision/MDM record label for album number three. In 1987 he formed an all acoustic indo-fusion band titled Dizrhythmia, which included **Danny Thompson** on double bass and various Indian classical musicians. A self-titled album, for Antilles Records, found critical favour both in the UK and USA. Jakszyk then moved to New York to join *avant garde* band the Lodge, whose personnel included ex-**Henry Cow** members John Greaves and **Peter Blegvad**, plus Anton Fier of the **Golden Palominos** on drums. After contributing to and arranging material on **Sam Brown**'s *Stop* album, before joining with **Tom Robinson** to tour and co-write the album *We Never Had It So Good*. He joined **Level 42** as lead guitarist in 1991, by which time his session credits included **Swing Out Sister**, **Gary Moore** and **Mica Paris**. He has also produced several acts, appeared on television programmes including *French And Saunders* and *Birds Of A Feather*, and written about music widely in such organs as *Melody Maker* and *Musician's Only*. His television incidental music has been heard on the Bafta

nominated *Chef*, Jo Brand's *Through The Cakehole* and *Birds Of A Feather*. In June 1994, *Kingdom Of Dust*, was released as the result of collaborating with ex-members of **Japan**; Richard Barbieri, Steven Jansen and **Mick Karn**. It was followed by Jaksyzk's solo album, *Mustard Gas And Roses*.

● ALBUMS: with Dizrhythmia *Dizrhythmia* (Antilles 1988)★★★, with Tom Robinson *We Never Had It So Good* (Musidisc 1991)★★, *Kingdom Of Dust* mini-album (Resurgence 1994)★★, *Mustard Gas And Roses* (Resurgence 1994)★★★.

Jale

Canadian group Jale, from Halifax, Nova Scotia, arrived on the music scene during a period when that region was enjoying something of a renaissance in the fortunes of its groups, who at the time also included Sloan. Although Jale were signed to **Sub Pop Records** just when the label was beginning to enjoy huge success, they were immediately distinct from other members of the label's roster, opting for indie pop harmonies in preference to the repetitious riffs of grunge. The group originally comprised Jennifer Pierce (vocals/guitar), Alyson MacLeod (drums), Laura Stein (vocals/bass) and Eve Hartling (vocals/guitar), their title an acronym of their forename initials. They made their debut in 1991 with a single on the local Cinnamon Toast label, before joining Sub Pop because of that label's empathy with their low-key approach. Much of the attention initially focused on them concerned the fact that they were an all-female group. The band members found this category tiresome and limiting, and with the replacement of MacLeod by Mike Belitsky in 1995, they were happy to lay such stigmas to rest. Their first full-length release was *Dream Cake* in 1994, which performed well on alternative radio formats and sold respectably. The follow-up collection, *So Wound*, was produced by **Liz Phair** and **Veruca Salt** collaborator Brad Wood, and featured a delicate balance between power pop and entrancing harmonies on songs such as 'Mosquito' and 'Ali'.

● ALBUMS: *Dream Cake* (Sub Pop 1994)★★★★, *So Wound* (Sub Pop 1996)★★★.

Jam

This highly successful late 70s and early 80s group comprised **Paul Weller** (b. 25 May 1958, Woking, Surrey, England; vocals/guitar), **Bruce Foxton** (b. 1 September 1955, Woking, Surrey, England; bass/vocals) and Rick Buckler (b. Paul Richard Buckler, 6 December 1955, Woking, Surrey, England; drums). After gigging consistently throughout 1976, the group were signed to **Polydor Records** early the following year. Although emerging at the peak of punk, the Jam seemed oddly divorced from the movement. Their leader, Paul Weller, professed to voting Conservative (although he would later switch dramatically to support the Labour Party), and the group's musical influences were firmly entrenched in the early **Who**-influenced mod style.

Their debut, 'In The City', was a high energy outing, with Weller displaying his **Rickenbacker** guitar to the fore. With their next record, 'All Around The World' they infiltrated the UK Top 20 for the first time. For the next year, they registered only minor hits, including 'News Of The World' (their only single written by Foxton) and a cover of the **Kinks'** 'David Watts'. A turning point in the group's critical fortunes occurred towards the end of 1978 with the release of 'Down In The Tube Station At Midnight'. This taut, dramatic anti-racist song saw them emerge as social commentators par excellence. *All Mod Cons* was widely acclaimed and thereafter the group rose to extraordinary heights. With *Setting Sons*, a quasi-concept album, Weller fused visions of British colonialism with urban decay and a satirical thrust at suburban life. The tone and execution of the work recalled the style of the Kinks' **Ray Davies**, whose class-conscious vignettes of the 60s had clearly influenced Weller. The superbly constructed 'Eton Rifles', lifted from the album, gave the Jam their first UK Top 10 single in late 1979. Early the following year, they secured their first UK number 1 with 'Going Underground', indicating the enormous strength of the group's fan base. By now they were on their way to topping music paper polls with increasing regularity. Throughout 1982, the Jam were streets ahead of their nearest rivals but their parochial charm could not be translated into international success. While they continued to log number 1 hits with 'Start' and 'Town Called Malice', the US market remained untapped. In late 1982, the group's recent run of UK chart-toppers was interrupted by 'The Bitterest Pill (I Ever Had To Swallow)' which peaked at number 2. Weller then announced that the group were to break up, and that he intended to form a new band, the **Style Council**. It was a shock decision, as the group were still releasing some of the best music to come out of Britain and were most certainly at their peak. Their final single, the exuberant, anthemic 'Beat Surrender' entered the UK chart at number 1, an extraordinary conclusion to a remarkable but brief career. After the mixed fortunes of the Style Council Weller embarked on a solo career, a move Foxton made immediately after the Jam's dissolution. Buckler and Foxton worked together briefly in Time U.K., with Foxton then joining **Stiff Little Fingers** and Buckler retiring from the music industry as a furniture restorer. The latter two sued Weller for alleged unpaid royalties. This was resolved in 1996 when Weller purchased all remaining interests from Foxton and Buckler.

● ALBUMS: *In The City* (Polydor 1977)★★★★, *This Is The Modern World* (Polydor 1977)★★★, *All Mod Cons* (Polydor 1978)★★★★, *Setting Sons* (Polydor 1979)★★★★, *Sound Affects* (Polydor 1980)★★★★, *The Gift* (Polydor 1982)★★★, *Dig The New Breed* (Polydor 1982)★★★, *Live Jam* (Polydor 1993)★★★.

● COMPILATIONS: *Snap!* (Polydor 1983)★★★★, *Greatest Hits* (Polydor 1991)★★★★, *Extras* (Polydor 1992)★★★, *The Jam Collection* (Polydor 1996)★★★★, *Direction, Reaction, Creation* 4-CD box set (Polydor 1997)★★★★.

● VIDEOS: *Video Snap* (Polygram 1984)★★★, *Transglobal Unity Express* (Channel 5 1988)★★★, *Greatest Hits* (Polygram 1991)★★★, *Little Angels: Jam On Film* (1994)★★★. ●

FURTHER READING: *The Jam: The Modern World By Numbers*, Paul Honeyford. *Jam*, Miles. *The Jam: A Beat Concerto, The Authorized Biography*, Paolo Hewitt. *About The Young Idea: The Story Of The Jam 1972-1982*, Mike Nicholls. *Our Story*, Bruce Foxton and Rick Buckler with Alex Ogg. *Keeping The Flame*, Steve Brookes.

Jam And Spoon

Duo credited by some as the originators of the 'trance' style. Based in Frankfurt, Germany, the faces behind the team are producer Jam El Mar and DJ Mark Spoon. Their groundbreaking work on a remix of Alex Lee's 'The Age Of Love' was the first track to set the ball rolling, followed in quick succession by work with **Moby, Cosmic Baby** and **Frankie Goes To Hollywood**. The latter was a difficult but rewarding project, as it had been this band and the production work of Trevor Horn in general which had originally inspired Jam El Mar into music. Another key reference point are the soundtrack recordings of **Tangerine Dream**. Only one single under their own name, 'Stella', preceded the release of their debut double album in the early months of 1994. This time they had moved away from the fast, pumping backbeat and acid tones which had flavoured their remixes, opting instead for a much more commercial slant. A sleevenote written for **R&S** label boss Renaat wryly declares: 'I hope this is not too commercial for your uncommercial label". Perhaps not, but it did see them crossover into the pop charts proper. Other 45s like 'Follow Me' were considered to be bona-fide trance classics. Mark Spoon was also head of A&R for **Logic** and is boss of Frankfurt's XS Club.

● ALBUMS: *Tripomatic Fairytales 2001/2002* (1994)★★★, *Kaleidoscope* (Sony 1997)★★★.

Jamaica

Making her only appearance in a Broadway book musical, **Lena Horne** was the main attraction when this show opened at the Imperial Theatre in New York on 31 October 1957. Ironically, it is sometimes claimed that **Harry Belafonte** was first choice for the leading role until he became unwell (Horne herself says: 'There's always been talk of a slight resemblance!'). If that is so, then the book, by **E.Y. 'Yip' Harburg** and Fred Saidly, obviously underwent some radical changes to enable Savannah (Lena Horne), to become the object of affection for Koli (Ricardo Montalban), a fisherman who lives on a mythical, magical tropical paradise known as Pigeon Island. Savannah is dissatisfied with that particular island, and would much prefer to move to another one where there is a bit more action - like Manhattan, for instance. However, after briefly flirting with an example of the civilization from that area in the shape of Joe Nashua (Joe Adams), she thinks better of it, and decides to settle for what she has got. The show had a top-notch score by Harburg and composer **Harold Arlen**, which included the outstanding ballad, 'Cocoanut Sweet', along with 'I Don't Think I'll End It Today', 'Ain't It The Truth', 'Pretty To Walk With', 'Little Biscuit', 'Incompatibility', 'Take It Slow, Joe', 'Napoleon', an amusing 'list' song, and Savannah's hymn to Manhattan, 'Push De Button'. A few years later, another of the songs, 'What Good Does It Do?', received a sensitive reading from **Tony Bennett** on an album he recorded in concert at Carnegie Hall in New York. On the strength of Lena Horne's box-office appeal (she was at her peak around this time), the show ran for nearly a year and a half, a total of 559 performances.

Jamal, Ahmad

b. Fritz Jones, 2 July 1930, Pittsburgh, Pennsylvania, USA. A professional pianist from before his teenage years, Jamal (who changed his name in the early 50s) managed to break through to a wider audience than most jazz artists. His trio work produced many excellent recordings and his accompanists included **Israel Crosby**. The most influential of his advocates was **Miles Davis**, who recognized Jamal's interesting rhythmic concepts as being something which he could incorporate into his own work. Jamal worked extensively in the USA throughout the 60s, 70s and 80s, usually in trio format but occasionally with larger backing for record dates, and also appeared with **Gary Burton**. Jamal is an important figure among mainstream pianists and their post-bop successors, mainly as a result of the indirect influence he has had through Davis. A lyrical, gently swinging musician, Jamal's playing is a constant delight.
● ALBUMS: *Chamber Music Of The New Jazz* (1955)★★★, *The Ahmad Jamal Trio* i (1955)★★★, *Count 'Em* (1956)★★★, *But Not For Me* (1958)★★★, *Ahmad Jamal At The Pershing* (1958)★★, *Ahmad's Blues* (Impulse 1958)★★★★, *The Ahmad Jamal Trio* ii (1959)★★★, *Happy Moods* (1960)★★★, *Listen To The Ahmad Jamal Quartet* (1960)★★★, *Ahmad Jamal's Alhambra* (1961)★★★, *Ahmad Jamal At The Blackhawk* (1961)★★★★, *Macanudo* (1962)★★★, *Naked City Theme* (1963)★★, *The Roar Of The Greasepaint, The Smell Of The Crowd* (1965)★★, *Extensions* (1965)★★★, *Ahmad Jamal With String* (1965)★★★, *Heat Wave* (1966)★★★, *Cry Young* (1967)★★★, *The Bright, The Blue And The Beautiful* (1968)★★★, *Tranquillity* (1968)★★★, *Jamal At The Top/Poinciana Revisited* (1968)★★★, *The Awakening* (1970)★★, *Free Flight Vol. 1* (1971)★★★, *Outer Time Inner Space* (1971)★★★, *Jamal Plays Jamal* (1974)★★★ *Live At Oil Can Harry's* (1976)★★, *Prelude To A Kiss* (1976-8)★★★, *Steppin' Out With A Dream* (c.1977)★★★, *Genetic Walk* (c.1978)★★, *Intervals* (c.1979)★★★, *Ahmad Jamal Live At Bubba's* (Kingdom Jazz 1980)★★★, *Night Song* (Motown 1980)★★★, *Ahmad Jamal In Concert* (1981)★★, *American Classical Music* (1982)★★★, *Digital Works* (Atlantic 1985)★★★★, *Rossiter Road* (Atlantic 1985)★★★, *Live At The Montreaux Jazz Festival* (Atlantic 1986)★★★★, *Goodbye Mr Evans* (Black Lion 1988)★★★, *Crystal* (WEA 1993)★★★, *Chicago Revisited* (Telarc 1993)★★★, *Live In Paris 92* (Birdology 1993)★★★, *I Remember Duke, Hoagy & Strayhorn* (Telarc 1995)★★.

Jamal-Ski

b. Jamal Mitchell, New York, USA. By the time he released his debut solo album, Jamal-Ski's name had already cropped up on several high profile releases. Most notable among these were **Boogie Down Production**'s *Edutainment* and the **Brand New Heavies'** *Heavy Rhyme Experience Vol. 1*. Jamal-Ski grew up in Manhattan, and was a product of the hip hop cultural experience, from rapping through to **sound system** parties, graffiti and breakdancing. He originally hung around with the **Rocksteady Crew** and **Afrika Bambaataa**'s Zulu Nation. His chosen path mixes traditional, old school rap with the rhythms of reggae. His musical heritage is certainly impressive, his father a jazz drummer who appeared alongside **Stan Getz** and **Chet Baker**, which allowed him to meet luminaries such as **Thelonious Monk**, ensuring that music remained in his blood through adolescence. He attended New York university for a year before moving to Oregon to play with reggae and ska bands, eventually returning east to take up the hip hop cudgels.
● ALBUMS: *Rough Reality* (Columbia 1993)★★.

Jamaneh, Bubacar

b. 1948, Gambia. Jamaneh grew up in a secluded Gambian village where the main activities were farming, fishing and Islamic worship. He took up music full-time in 1963 despite the vociferous protests of his father. He initially joined Ambiance Jazz of Bakau before joining the Gambian Police Band in 1965. That group's tough discipline failed to satiate his appetite for adventure, though, and in 1967 he joined a Greek shipping crew. His travels then took him to Sierra Leone and Liberia (as a diamond miner) before Spain and finally Berlin, Germany, where he settled in 1975. It was while here that he reawakened his longstanding interest in music, joining a number of groups, including the Afro-Combo, Banjulos and Jajang Bands, as either electric or acoustic guitarist. Most achieved a competent fusion of African and Western pop, but without ever achieving an audience outside of Berlin's expatriate African community. Undeterred, Jamaneh entered the studio under his own auspices in 1982, recording his debut (and so far only) solo album with the aid of musicians drawn from Vedette Jazz and Gulewar.
● ALBUMS: *Manding Beats From The Gambia* (JR 1982)★★★.

Jamboree

(see *Disc Jockey Jamboree*)

Jamerson, James

b. James Lee Jamerson, 29 January 1936, Charleston, South Carolina, USA, d. 2 August 1983. Jamerson revolutionized bass session playing in R&B as the mainstay bassist for **Motown Records** during the 60s and early 70s. Using his jazz background, he expanded bass playing beyond holding the two-beat rhythm, to create complex basslines that made songs move with a great, propulsive force. He spent his formative years in Charleston, but in 1953 he moved to Detroit with his mother. The following year, Jamerson took up the upright bass, when he enrolled in Northwestern High. Before he finished high school, Jamerson was regularly playing in the jazz clubs. In 1958, he began playing sessions for Johnnie Mae Matthews' Northern Records, playing behind Timmy Shaw, **Betty Lavette**, and other Northern Records artists. In 1959, Jamerson joined the fledging Motown organization. By 1961, Jamerson had switched to an electric Fender bass, but he occasionally switched back to the upright. Jamerson's bass work was considered one of Motown's most valuable assets in creating hits for such artists as the **Miracles**, **Four Tops**, **Marvin Gaye**, **Martha And The Vandellas**, **Supremes**, **Temptations**, and many others. Besides playing in innumerable recording sessions, until 1964 Jamerson was also one of the crucial components of the band that accompanied Motown acts on the road (the rhythm section was called **Earl Van Dyke** And The Funk Brothers). He also played on many moonlighting sessions, notably with **Jackie Wilson** in Chicago. In 1973, Jamerson moved to Los Angeles to follow Motown's operations there, but continued alcoholism diminished his skills so severely that by the late 70s, he rarely worked for Motown or any other label.

James

Championed initially by **Morrissey** of the **Smiths**, James signed with their home-town record label, Manchester's **Factory Records**, in 1983. Their early singles, 'What's The World?' and 'Hymn From A Village', and the EPs *JimOne* and *James II*, were acclaimed for their unusual mixture of folk and new wave textures. The original line-up was Timothy Booth (4 February 1960; vocals), James Glennie (10 October 1963; bass), James Gott (guitar) and Gavan Whelan (drums). They signed to **Sire Records** in 1985 and began an unsettled three-year relationship with the company. *Stutter* was a collection of strange but striking songs, followed two years later by *Strip Mine*, which had a stronger melodic edge. *One Man Clapping*, a live set recorded in Bath, England, marked a return to independent status with **Rough Trade Records**. Dave Baynton-Power replaced Whelan and soon afterwards the group was augmented by Saul Davies (guitar, violin), Mark Hunter (keyboards) and Andy Diagram (trumpet). **Fontana Records**, with its policy of signing England's leading independent bands, re-released 'Come Home' and 'Sit Down', the latter single reaching number 2 in the UK charts. *Gold Mother* was more accessible than previous albums; the band writing in a more direct lyrical style, though there were still echoes of earlier eccentricities. The title track was a paean to mothers and the extreme physical pain they underwent

during childbirth, and drew from Booth's personal exposure to the birth of his own child. Although their recording career stretched back further than their contemporaries, they became part of an upsurge in talent from Manchester during the late 80s and early 90s, and the media attention on the city made the transition from independent to major league status that much easier. *Seven* saw the band digress further away from the immediacy of 'Sit Down', which up to that point was their most enduring and popular song. Instead, the emphasis was on atmosphere and multi-layered, unconventional song structures. The upshot of this was a fall-off in commercial viability, although the group maintained a loyal fanbase. *Laid*, meanwhile, was a title presumably inspired by Booth's return from a life of celibacy, and its hit single of the same title was the first to make an impression in the USA. The other contents were described as 'paranoid love songs, ecstatic laments and perverse lullabies' by *Select* magazine's reviewer. The heavily experimental *Wah Wah* was seen by some critics as an attempt to steal U2's *Zooropa* thunder. It was recorded with **Brian Eno** during sessions for *Laid*, for release as an 'alternative' album. The move into ambient electronics had, however, been signposted by the 1993 **Sabres Of Paradise** remix of 'Jam J'. Tim Booth recorded an album with American composer Angelo Badalamenti as **Booth And The Bad Angel** before, in 1997, the group broke a three-year silence with the well-received *Whiplash* and the hit single 'She's A Star'.

● ALBUMS: *Stutter* (Sire 1986)★★★, *Strip Mine* (Sire 1988)★★★, *One Man Clapping* (Rough Trade 1989)★★★, *Gold Mother* (Fontana 1990)★★★★, *Seven* (Fontana 1992)★★★★, *Laid* (Fontana 1993)★★★, *Wah Wah* (Fontana 1994)★★, *Whiplash* (Fontana 1997)★★★.
● COMPILATIONS: *The Best Of James* (Fontana 1998)★★★★.
● VIDEOS: *Come Home Live* (Polygram Video 1991), *Seven - The Live Video* (Polygram Video 1992).

James Gang

Formed in 1967 in Cleveland, Ohio, USA, the embryonic James Gang was comprised of Glenn Schwartz (guitar/vocals), Tom Kriss (bass/vocals) and Jim Fox (drums/vocals). Schwartz left in April 1969 to join **Pacific Gas And Electric**, but **Joe Walsh** proved a more than competent replacement. *Yer Album* blended group originals with excellent interpretations of material drawn from **Buffalo Springfield** ('Bluebird') and the **Yardbirds** ('Lost Women'). The group enjoyed the approbation of **Pete Townshend**, who admired their mature cross-section of British and 'west coast' rock. Kriss was replaced by Dale Peters for *The James Gang Rides Again*, an excellent, imaginative amalgamation of rock, melody and instrumental dexterity. Here Walsh emerged as the group's director, particularly on the second side which also marked his maturation as a songwriter. Keyboards were added to create a dense, yet more fluid sound as the group embraced themes drawn from country and classical music. *Thirds* was another highlight, including the excellent 'Walk Away', but when a retreat to hard rock proved unconvincing, Walsh quit to pursue solo ambitions. He later found fame as a member of the **Eagles**. Two Canadians - Roy Kenner (vocals) and Dom Troiano (guitar) - joined Fox and Peters for *Straight Shooter* and *Passin' Thru*, but both sets were viewed as disappointing. Troiano was then replaced by **Tommy Bolin**, formerly of Zephyr, whose exemplary technique provided new bite and purpose. *Bang*, which featured eight of the newcomer's songs, was a marked improvement, but still lacked the verve and conviction of the Walsh era. *Miami*, released in July 1974, coincided with Bolin's departure to **Deep Purple**, following which the James Gang was dissolved. The ever optimistic Fox and Peters resurrected the name the following year, adding Bubba Keith (vocals) and Richard Shack (guitar), but finally dropped the name following the undistinguished *Jesse Come Home*.

● ALBUMS: *Yer Album* (BluesWay 1969)★★★, *The James Gang Rides Again* (ABC 1970)★★★★, *Thirds* (ABC 1971)★★★, *James Gang Live In Concert* (ABC 1971)★★★, *Straight Shooter* (ABC 1972)★★, *Passin' Thru'* (ABC 1972)★★, *Bang* (Atco 1974)★★, *Miami* (Atco 1974)★★, *Newborn* (Atco 1975)★★, *Jesse Come Home* (1976)★★.

● COMPILATIONS: *The Best Of The James Gang Featuring Joe Walsh* (ABC 1973)★★★, *16 Greatest Hits* (ABC 1973)★★★, *The True Story Of The James Gang* (See For Miles 1987)★★★.

James, Bob

b. 23 December 1939, Marshall, Michigan, USA. James played the piano from the age of four and eventually gained an MA in Composition from the University of Michigan in 1962. He worked as musical director and accompanist with vocalist **Sarah Vaughan** until 1968. In 1973 **Quincy Jones** introduced him to Creed Taylor who was forming his CTI label. James became his arranger and producer working on albums with **Dionne Warwick**, **Roberta Flack**, **Eric Gale**, **Grover Washington** and Quincy Jones, as well as producing four solo works. In 1976 he moved to **CBS** as Director of Progressive A&R and worked with musicians as diverse as **Joanne Brackeen** and Santamaria. In 1986 James worked with saxophonist **David Sanborn** on *Double Vision*. James has also written musical scores for Broadway and for films including *The Selling Of The President* and *Serpico*. The television series *Taxi* used 'Angela' from the 1978 *Touchdown* as its theme.

● ALBUMS: *One* (CTI 1974)★★, *Two* (CTI 1975)★★, *Three* (CTI 1976)★★, *BJ4* (CTI 1977)★★, *Heads* (Tappan Zee 1977)★★, *Touchdown* (Tappan Zee 1978)★★★, *Lucky Seven* (Tappan Zee 1979)★★★, *One On One* (Tappan Zee 1979)★★★, *H* (Tappan Zee 1980)★★★, *All Around The Town* (Tappan Zee 1981)★★★, *Sign Of The Times* (Tappan Zee 1981)★★★, *Hands Down* (Tappan Zee 1982)★★★, *Two Of A Kind* (Capitol 1982)★★★, *The Genie* (Columbia 1983)★★★, *Foxie* (Tappan Zee 1983)★★★, *12* (Tappan Zee 1984)★★★, *Double Vision* (Warners 1986)★★★, *Obsession*

(Warners 1986)★★★, *Ivory Coast* (Warners 1988)★★★, *Cool* (Warners 1992)★★★, with Kirk Whalum *Joined At The Hip* (Warners 1996)★★★, *Straight Up* (Warners 1996)★★★, *Playin' Hooky* (Warners 1997)★★★★.

James, Calvin

b. George Underwood, London, England. Calvin James was the stage name adopted briefly by Underwood, founder member of the King Bees and Manish Boys with **David Bowie**. Underwood then came under the tutelage of **Mickie Most** and, as Calvin James, recorded 'Some Things You Never Get Used To' for **Columbia Records** in 1965. This emotive ballad was not a success and Underwood ceased recording. Instead he pursued a career as an artist, designing the sleeve of *My People Were Fair And Had Sky In Their Hair...*, the debut album by **Tyrannosaurus Rex**.

James, Colin, And The Little Big Band

b. Colin James Munn, 1964, Regina, Saskatchewan, Canada. The son of Quaker parents, James's first musical love was folk, but by his early teens he had developed a keen interest in the blues. His school work suffered as he proceeded to master blues guitar, and upon leaving school at the age of 16, he moved to Winnipeg and formed the HooDoo Men. In 1983 James befriended **Stevie Ray Vaughan** who became a mentor to the young Canadian. Having impressed a **Virgin Records** executive by literally dancing on his table at a gig, he was signed and released *Colin James* in 1988. His band at this time comprised John Ferreira (saxophone), Dennis Marenko (bass), Rick Hopkins (keyboards) and Darrel Mayes (drums). The debut, although competent, did not fully convey the excitement of his live gigs. Much more satisfying and gutsy was *Sudden Stop*, with a sound undoubtedly aided by **Z.Z. Top**'s producer Joe Hardy. 'Just Came Back' from the album became a major hit in Canada and he duetted with Bonnie Raitt on another track. James gigged solidly for 18 months promoting this successful album and it was not until the end of 1993 that he found enough time to issue a new release. *The Little Big Band* was a powerful and tasteful jump-blues and R&B excursion showcasing great brass and James's fluid guitar style. The line-up included Chuck Leavell on piano and utilized the Roomful Of Blues horn section in addition to the continuing presence of Ferreira on sax. In 1994 he signed to Elektra Records and the following year a much more mainstream rock album, *Bad Habits*, was released.

● ALBUMS: *Colin James* (Virgin 1988)★★★, *Sudden Stop* (Virgin 1990)★★★, *Colin James And The Little Big Band* (Pointblank 1993)★★★, *Bad Habits* (Elektra 1995)★★.

James, Dick

b. Isaac Vapnick, 1921, London, England, d. 1 February 1986, London, England. Originally a dance band singer under the name of Lee Sheridan, he sang with several of the major bandleaders of the 40s and 50s, including

Geraldo and **Cyril Stapleton**. After changing his name to Dick James he was signed to **EMI**'s **Parlophone** label and achieved a memorable UK Top 20 with 'Robin Hood'. The song was commissioned for a long-running television series, *The Adventures Of Robin Hood*, and a generation of children were entranced by James's lusty, barrel-voiced, perfectly enunciated vocal. The singer enjoyed a further hit with the much-covered 'Garden Of Eden' before retiring from recording, and going into music publishing with Sydney Bron, Eleanor Bron's father. In 1961, he launched his own firm, and in November 1962, to his lasting fortune, was visited by entrepreneur **Brian Epstein**, and acquired the most lucrative songwriting catalogue of modern times. With the **Beatles**, James changed irrevocably Tin Pan Alley music publishing in the UK. Instead of offering the group the traditional 10 per cent retail price of sheet music, he suggested that they form Northern Songs, a separate company that would deal exclusively with the songs of **John Lennon** and **Paul McCartney**. The offer was 50/50, half to James and his partner, 20 per cent each to Lennon/McCartney and 10 per cent to Epstein. The success of the Beatles' songwriting team eroded the power of the old Tin Pan Alley songsmiths, but James remained a prominent figure. He had the cream of the Merseybeat groups as part of his company, and also published Manchester's major pop act, the **Hollies**, and Birmingham's **Spencer Davis Group**. During the late 60s, he oversaw the publishing side of **Larry Page**'s record company, Page One. After many successful years with the Beatles, James eventually sold his major shareholding in Northern Songs to Lew Grade's ATV company in 1969. His major concern during the early 70s was the extension of Dick James Music into **DJM Records**, a company in which he was eventually joined by his son Stephen James. As a publisher and record company mogul, he rose to new heights after signing the songwriting team of **Elton John** and **Bernie Taupin**. Their catalogue proved one of the most valuable of the era. James finally retired from the business but was forced to return to the fray in 1985 when Elton John belatedly instituted successful legal proceedings to obtain an increased royalty in respect of his compositions from Dick James Music. Some three months after the court case ended, James died at his St John's Wood home.

James, Elmore

b. 27 January 1918, Richland, Mississippi, USA, d. 23 May 1963. Although his recording career spanned 10 years, Elmore James is chiefly recalled for his debut release, 'Dust My Broom'. This impassioned, exciting performance, based on a virulent composition by country blues singer **Robert Johnson**, was marked by the artist's unfettered vocals and his searing electric slide guitar. James's formative years were spent in Mississippi juke joints where he befriended Rice Miller (**Sonny Boy Williamson**), a regular performer on the US radio station KFFA's *King Biscuit Time* show.

Elmore accompanied Miller for several years, and through his influence secured his initial recording contract in 1951. James then moved to Chicago where he formed the first of several groups bearing the name 'the Broomdusters'. Subsequent recordings included different variations on that initial success - 'I Believe', 'Dust My Blues' - as well as a series of compositions that proved equally influential. 'Bleeding Heart' and 'Shake Your Moneymaker' were later adopted, respectively, by **Jimi Hendrix** and **Fleetwood Mac**, while the guitarist's distinctive 'bottleneck' style resurfaced in countless British blues bands. James's style was accurately copied by Jeremy Spencer of Fleetwood Mac - the band often had 'Elmore James' segments in their act during the late 60s. Another James devotee was Brian Jones of the **Rolling Stones**, whose early stage name of Elmo Lewis, and bottleneck guitar work paid tribute to James. **John Mayall**'s 'Mr. James' was a thoughtful tribute to this significant performer who sadly did not live to enjoy such acclaim. In May 1963, James suffered a fatal heart attack at the home of his cousin, **Homesick James**, who, along with **J.B. Hutto**, then assumed the late musician's mantle.

● COMPILATIONS: *Blues After Hours* (Crown 1961)★★★★, *Original Folk Blues* (Kent 1964)★★★★, *The Sky Is Crying* (Sphere Sound 1965)★★★, *The Best Of Elmore James* (Sue 1965)★★★★, *I Need You* (Sphere Sound 1966)★★★, *The Elmore James Memorial Album* (Sue 1966)★★★★, *Something Inside Of Me* (Bell 1968)★★★, *The Late Fantastically Great Elmore James* (Ember 1968)★★★, *To Know A Man* (Blue Horizon 1969)★★★, *Whose Muddy Shoes* (Chess 1969)★★★, *Elmore James* (Bell 1969)★★★, *Blues In My Heart, Rhythm In My Soul* (1969)★★★, *The Legend Of Elmore James* (United Artists 1970)★★★, *Tough* (Blue Horizon 1970)★★★, *Cotton Patch Hotfoots* (Polydor 1974)★★★, *All Them Blues* (DJM 1976)★★★, with Robert Nighthawk *Blues In D'Natural* (1979)★★★★, *The Best Of Elmore James* (Ace 1981)★★★, *Got To Move* (Charly 1981)★★★, *King Of The Slide Guitar* (Ace 1983)★★★★, *Red Hot Blues* (Blue Moon 1983)★★★, *The Original Meteor And Flair Sides* (Ace 1984)★★★★, *Come Go With Me* (Charly 1984)★★★, *One Way Out* (Charly 1985)★★★, *The Elmore James Collection* (Déjà Vu 1985)★★★★, *Let's Cut It* (Ace 1986)★★★, *King Of The Bottleneck Blues* (Crown 1986)★★★★, *Shake Your Moneymaker* (Charly 1986)★★★★, *Pickin' The Blues* (Castle 1986)★★★, *Greatest Hits* (Blue City 1988)★★★, *Chicago Golden Years* (Vogue 1988)★★★, *Dust My Broom* (Instant 1990)★★★★, *Rollin' And Tumblin' - The Best Of* (Relic 1992)★★★★, *Elmore James Box Set* (Charly 1992)★★★★, *The Classic Early Recordings 1951-56* 3-CD box set (Flair/Ace 1993)★★★★, *The Best Of Elmore James: The Early Years* (Ace 1995)★★★★.

James, Etta

b. Jamesetta Hawkins, 25 January 1938, Los Angeles, California, USA. James's introduction to performing followed an impromptu audition for **Johnny Otis** backstage at San Francisco's Fillmore Auditorium. 'Roll With Me Henry', her 'answer' to the **Hank Ballard** hit

'Work With Me Annie', was retitled 'The Wallflower' in an effort to disguise its risqué lyric and became an R&B number 1. 'Good Rockin' Daddy' provided another hit, but the singer's later releases failed to chart. Having secured a contract with the **Chess** group of labels, James, also known as Miss Peaches, unleashed a series of powerful songs, including 'All I Could Do Was Cry' (1960), 'At Last' (1961), 'Trust In Me' (1961), 'Don't Cry Baby' (1961), 'Something's Got A Hold On Me' (1962), 'Stop The Wedding' (1962) and 'Pushover' (1963). She also recorded several duets with **Harvey Fuqua**. Heroin addiction sadly blighted both her personal and professional life, but in 1967 Chess took her to the Fame studios. The resultant *Tell Mama* was a triumph, and pitted James's abrasive voice with the exemplary **Muscle Shoals** house band. Its highlights included the proclamatory title track, a pounding version of **Otis Redding**'s 'Security' (both of which reached the R&B Top 20) and the despairing 'I'd Rather Go Blind', which was later a UK Top 20 hit for **Chicken Shack**. The 1973 album *Etta James* earned her a US Grammy nomination, despite her continued drug problems, which she did not overcome until the mid-80s. A 1977 album, *Etta Is Betta Than Evah*, completed her Chess contract, and she moved to **Warner Brothers**. A renewed public profile followed her appearance at the opening ceremony of the Los Angeles Olympics in 1984. *Deep In The Night* was a critics' favourite. The live *Late Show* albums, released in 1986, featured **Shuggie Otis** and **Eddie 'Cleanhead' Vinson**, and were followed by *Seven Year Itch*, her first album for **Island Records**, in 1989. This, and the subsequent release, *Stickin' To My Guns*, found her back on form, aided and abetted once more by the Muscle Shoals team. She was inducted into the Rock And Roll Hall Of Fame in 1993. Her ability to take and shape a song demonstrates the depth of her great ability to 'feel' the essence of the lyric and melody. All her cover versions, from 'Need Your Love So Bad' to 'The Night Time Is The Right Time', are given her indelible stamp. Following the use in a television advertisement of her version of **Muddy Waters**' 'I Just Want To Make Love To You', she unexpectedly found herself near the top of the UK charts in 1996. She is both emotional and 'foxy', yet still remains painfully underexposed; this hit may open the door to her extraordinary voice, which was showcased to great effect on 1997's *Love's Been Rough On Me*.

● ALBUMS: *Miss Etta James* (Crown 1961)★★★, *At Last!* (Argo 1961)★★★★, *Second Time Around* (Argo 1961)★★★★, *Twist With Etta James* (Crown 1962)★★★★, *Etta James* (Argo 1962)★★★★, *Etta James Sings For Lovers* (Argo 1962)★★★★, *Etta James Top Ten* (Argo 1963)★★★, *Etta James Rocks The House* (Argo 1964)★★★, *The Queen Of Soul* (Argo 1965)★★★★, *Call My Name* (Cadet 1967)★★★, *Tell Mama* (Cadet 1968)★★★★★, *Etta James Sings Funk* (Cadet 1970)★★★, *Losers Weepers* (Cadet 1971)★★★, *Etta James* (Chess 1973)★★★, *Come A Little Closer* (Chess 1974)★★★, *Etta Is Betta Than Evah!* (Chess 1977)★★★, *Deep In The Night* (Warners 1978)★★★, *Changes* (MCA 1980)★★★, *Red, Hot And Live* (1982)★★★, *The Heart And Soul Of* (1982)★★★, with Eddie 'Cleanhead' Vinson *Blues In The Night: The Early Show* (Fantasy 1986)★★★, *Blues In The Night: The Late Show* (Fantasy 1986)★★★, *Seven Year Itch* (Island 1989)★★★, *Stickin' To My Guns* (Island 1990)★★★★, *Something's Gotta Hold On Me (Etta James Volume 2)* (Roots 1992)★★★, *The Right Time* (Elektra 1992)★★★, *Mystery Lady: Songs Of Billie Holiday* (Private Music 1994)★★★, *Love's Been Rough On Me* (Private Music 1997)★★★, *Life, Love & The Blues* (Private 1998)★★.

● COMPILATIONS: *The Best Of ...* (Crown 1962)★★★★, *The Soul Of Etta James* (Ember 1968)★★★★, *Golden Decade* (Chess 1972)★★★★, *Peaches* (Chess 1973)★★★★, *Good Rockin' Mama* (Ace 1981)★★★★, *Chess Masters* (Chess 1981)★★★, *Tuff Lover* (Ace 1983)★★★★, *Juicy Peaches* (Chess 1985)★★★, *R&B Queen* (Crown 1986)★★★, *Her Greatest Sides, Volume One* (Chess/MCA 1987)★★★★, *R&B Dynamite* reissued as *Hickory Dickory Dock* (Ace 1987)★★★★, *Rocks The House* (Charly 1987)★★★, *The Sweetest Peaches: The Chess Years, Volume 1 (1960-1966)* (Chess/MCA 1988)★★★★, *The Sweetest Peaches: The Chess Years, Volume 2 (1967-1975)* (Chess/MCA 1988)★★★★, *Tell Mama* (1988)★★★★, *Chicago Golden Years* (Vogue 1988)★★★, *Come A Little Closer* (Charly 1988)★★★, *Juicy Peaches* (Charly 1989)★★★★, *The Gospel Soul Of Etta James* (AJK 1990)★★★, *Legendary Hits* (Jazz Archives 1992)★★★, *Back In The Blues* (Zillion 1992)★★★, *The Soulful Miss Peaches* (Charly 1993)★★★★, *I'd Rather Go Blind - The World Of Etta James* (Trace 1993)★★★, *Something's Got A Hold* (Charly 1994)★★★, *Blues In The Night, The Early Show* (Fantasy 1994)★★★, *Blues In The Night, The Late Show* (Fantasy 1994)★★★, *Miss Peaches Sings The Soul* (That's Soul 1994)★★★, *Live From San Francisco '81* (Private Music 1994)★★★, *The Genuine Article: The Best Of* (MCA/Chess 1996)★★★★.

● VIDEOS: *Live At Montreux* (Island Visual Arts 1990), *Live At Montreux: Etta James* (Polygram Music Video 1992).

● FURTHER READING: *Rage To Survive*, Etta James with David Ritz.

James, Frank 'Springback'

James recorded his piano blues between 1934 and 1937. The first tracks, released in the depths of the Depression, sold in miserable quantities; they show a strong affinity with the styles of St. Louis. Later recordings mostly included **Willie Bee James** on guitar, and are influenced by the popular recording team of **Leroy Carr** and Scrapper Blackwell. James wrote strong, original lyrics, but was often a monotonous performer. Sometimes, however, he struck a more compelling stance, as on the erotic 'Snake Hip Blues' and the seemingly autobiographical 'Poor Coal Loader' and 'Will My Bad Luck Ever Change?'.

● ALBUMS: *Frank 'Springback' James* (Document 1988)★★★.

James, George

b. 7 December 1906, Beggs, Oklahoma, USA. After moving to St. Louis, Missouri, as a youth, James began playing clarinet and various saxophones with popular local bands, including some of those organized by band contractor Charlie Creath for work in hotels and on riverboats. In the late 20s James tried his luck in Chicago where he played with **Jimmie Noone** and also led his own small outfit. In 1931 he joined **Louis Armstrong** for several months, then played in a number of New York bands including the Savoy Bearcats, **Fats Waller**, **James P. Johnson**, **Benny Carter**, and **Teddy Wilson**. After a spell with **Lucky Millinder** he led his own bands in New York and other eastern cities during the early 40s. In the mid-40s he was with **Claude Hopkins**, **Noble Sissle** and others before forming a band of his own which he continued to lead intermittently during the next two decades. During the 70s and early 80s he became well known internationally through tours as a member of **Clyde Bernhardt**'s Harlem Blues And Jazz Band. James was a competent sideman and could also deliver good solos when the opportunity or need arose. Indeed, his alto playing is one of the highlights of Armstrong's 1931 recordings with what was otherwise a rather inferior band.

● ALBUMS: *Harlem Blues & Jazz Band 1973-1980* (Barron 1973-80)★★★.

● COMPILATIONS: *The Chronological Louis Armstrong 1931-1932* (Classics 1931-32)★★★★.

James, Harry

b. 15 March 1916, Albany, Georgia, USA, d. 5 July 1983, Las Vegas, Nevada, USA. Harry James's father played trumpet in the band of a touring circus, and at first Harry played the drums, but then he, too, took up the trumpet and at the age of nine was also playing in the circus band. He showed such enormous promise that his father had soon taught him everything he knew. Harry left the circus and played with various bands in Texas before joining **Ben Pollack** in 1935. Early in 1937 James was hired by **Benny Goodman**, an engagement which gave him maximum exposure to swing era audiences. Heavily featured with Goodman and, with **Ziggy Elman** and **Chris Griffin**, forming part of a powerful and exciting trumpet section, James quickly became a household name. He remained with Goodman a little under two years, leaving to form his own big band. James popularity increased and his public image, aided by his marriage to film star **Betty Grable**, reached remarkable heights for a musician. The band's popularity was achieved largely through James own solos, but a small part of its success may be attributed to his singers, Louise Tobin, to whom he was briefly married before Grable, **Frank Sinatra**, who soon left to join **Tommy Dorsey**, **Dick Haymes** and Kitty Kallen. James maintained his band throughout the 40s and into the early 50s, establishing a solid reputation thanks to distinguished sidemen such as **Willie Smith**,

Buddy Rich, Corky Corcoran and Juan Tizol. Owing chiefly to the recorded repertoire, much of which featured James playing florid trumpet solos on tunes such as 'The Flight Of The Bumble Bee', 'The Carnival of Venice', 'I Cried For You' and 'You Made Me Love You', his band was at times less than popular with hardcore jazz fans. This view should have altered when, in the mid-50s, after a period of re-evaluation, James formed a band to play charts by **Ernie Wilkins** and **Neal Hefti**. One of the outstanding big bands, this particular group is often and very unfairly regarded as a copy of **Count Basie**'s, a point of view which completely disregards chronology. In fact, James band can be seen to have pre-empted the slightly later but much more widely recognized middle-period band led by Basie, which also used Wilkins's and Hefti's charts. James continued leading into the 60s and 70s, dividing his time between extended residencies at major hotel and casino venues, mostly in Las Vegas, Nevada, and touring internationally. Amongst the first-rate musicians James used in these years were Willie Smith again, a succession of fine drummers (including Rich, **Sonny Payne** and **Louie Bellson**) and lead trumpeter Nick Buono, who had joined in December 1939 and showed no signs of relinquishing his chair and would, indeed, remain until the end. In his early years James was a brashly exciting player, attacking solos and abetting ensembles with a rich tone and what was at times an overwhelmingly powerful sound. With his own band he exploited his virtuoso technique, performing with great conviction the ballads and trumpet spectaculars that so disconcerted his jazz followers but which delighted the wider audience at whom they were aimed. Over the years James appeared in several movies - with his band in *Private Buckaroo* (1942), *Springtime In The Rockies*, *Best Foot Forward*, *Bathing Beauty*, *Two Girls And A Sailor*, *Do You Love Me?*, *If I'm Lucky*, *Carnegie Hall*, and *I'll Get By* (1950) - and as a solo artist in *Syncopation* (1942) and *The Benny Goodman Story* (1956). He also played trumpet on the soundtrack of *Young Man With A Horn* (1950). Later in his career, James work combined the best of both worlds - jazz and the more flashy style - and shed many of its excesses. He remained popular into the 80s and never lost his enthusiasm, despite suffering from cancer, which eventually claimed him in 1983.

● ALBUMS: *All Time Favorites* (Columbia 1950)★★★, *Trumpet Time* (Columbia 1950)★★★, *Dance Parade* 1950)★★★★, *Your Dance Date* (Columbia 1950)★★★★, *Soft Lights And Sweet Trumpet* (Columbia 1952)★★★, *One Night Stand* (Columbia 1953)★★★★, *At The Hollywood Palladium* (Columbia 1954)★★★★, *Trumpet After Midnight* (Columbia 1954)★★★, *Juke Box Jamboree* (Columbia 1955)★★★, *Man With The Horn* (Columbia 1995)★★★, *Harry James In Hi-Fi* (Capitol 1955)★★★★, *More Harry James In Hi-Fi* (Capitol 1956)★★, *Wild About Harry* (Capitol 1957)★★★, *The New James* (1958)★★★, *Harry's Choice!* (Capitol 1958)★★★, *Harry James And His New Swingin' Bands* (1959)★★★, *Harry James Today* (MGM 1960)★★★, *The Spectacular Sound Of*

Harry James (1961)★★★, *Harry James Plays Neal Hefti* (1961)★★★★, *The Solid Trumpet Of Harry James* (1962)★★★, *Double Dixie* (1962)★★, *On Tour In '64* (1964)★★★, *Harry James Live At The Riverboat* (1966)★★★, *Live From Clearwater, Florida Vols 1-3* (1970)★★★★, *Live In London* (1971)★★★, *King James Version* (1976)★★★, *Still Harry After All These Years* (1979)★★★.
● FILMS: *The Big Beat* (1957).

James, Jesse

It was once believed that James was a convict, brought to the studio under guard to make his four recordings in 1936, and that he broke down before they were completed. This romantic extrapolation from the lyrics of 'Lonesome Day Blues' - 'I'm goin' to the Big House, an' I don't even care . . . I might get four or five years, lord, an' I might get the chair' - seems to be untrue; James was probably Cincinnati-based, as he accompanied titles by Walter Coleman. James was a rough, two-fisted barrelhouse pianist, with a hoarse, declamatory vocal delivery, equally suited to the anguished 'Lonesome Day Blues', a robust version of 'Casey Jones' and the earthily obscene 'Sweet Patuni', which was issued much later on a bootleg 'party' single.
● ALBUMS: *Piano Blues Vol. 2 - The Thirties* (1987)★★.

James, Jimmy

b. Michael James, 13 September 1940, USA. James was raised in Jamaica where he began his career in the late 50s. His debut, 'Bewildered And Blue', appeared through Tip Top productions and topped the Jamaican charts. He followed this hit with the equally successful 'Come To Me Softly', which he re-recorded in the UK during the mid-60s. The latter version appeared on the *Billboard* Hot 100, an unprecedented achievement for a Jamaican performer. By 1960 he accepted the role of lead vocalist with the Vagabonds. The band performed around Jamaica, regarded as second only to **Byron Lee And The Dragonaires** as the island's top showband. The group performed prosaic refrains to the tourists, including 'Love Letters In The Sand', 'Anchors Aweigh' and 'Happy Wanderer', which featured on their debut album. In an attempt to promote their career, the group financed a trip to the UK, where, after supporting the **Who** at the Marquee club in London, they were enlisted to perform weekly at the venue. The shows were highly acclaimed and enhanced the band's reputation, notably through the stage antics of **Count Prince Miller**. His charismatic charm and unique style earned him a huge following, which led to his reggae hit 'Mule Train', in 1971. James and the Vagabonds released a number of singles that failed to cross over, but in 1968 the band recorded their most popular hit, **Neil Diamond**'s 'Red Red Wine', also their debut on the UK pop chart. It was James's interpretation that inspired Tony Tribe's reggae hit, later covered by **UB40**. By 1970, the original Vagabonds decided to relinquish the band although James retained the rights to the name. In 1970 he recorded the commercially successful 'A Man

Like Me' with producer Biddu. He released a few singles for **Trojan Records** before his breakthrough into the pop world with the classic 'Help Yourself'. Consolidating his association with Biddu, he released 'Dancing To The Music Of Love' and 'Whatever Happened To The Love We Knew'. The newly formed Vagabonds featured an all-white line-up who supported him through the 70s, touring and playing on the 1976 pop hits 'Now Is The Time' and 'I'll Go Where The Music Takes Me'. He remained in relative obscurity throughout the 80s, although in 1984 he released the effervescent but overlooked 'Love Fire', before returning to obscurity. In 1987 another bid for a pop hit arose when he reworked 'I'll Go Where The Music Takes Me' and 'Now Is The Time', but a return to the chart eluded the performer. He restored his credibility when he returned to his Jamaican roots in the 90s, performing alongside Winston Curtis on the Count Prince Miller-produced hit 'Muriel'.
● ALBUMS: as the Vagabonds: *Presenting The Fabulous Vagabonds* (Island 1964)★★, *The New Religion* (Picadilly 1967)★★, *Live At The Marquee* (Pye 1967)★★★, *Open Up Your Soul* (Pye 1968)★★.

James, Jimmy, And The Vagabonds

Jimmy James (b. September 1940, Jamaica), enjoyed local success with two self-composed singles, 'Bewildered And Blue' and 'Come Softly To Me', before arriving in England in 1964. He joined the multiracial Vagabonds - Wallace Wilson (lead guitar), Carl Noel (organ), Matt Fredericks (tenor saxophone), Milton James (baritone saxophone), Phillip Chen (bass), Rupert Balgobin (drums) and Count Prince Miller (vocals/MC) - and the new unit became a leading attraction at UK soul venues during the 60s. The group was managed and produced by the early **Who** mentor Peter Meaden. Although they failed to secure a substantial chart hit, the Vagabonds' early albums were impressive, infectious reinterpretations of contemporary releases, featuring material by the **Impressions**, the **Miracles** and **Bobby Bland**. Such a function, however enthusiastic, lost its impetus when the original artists gained popular acclaim. 'Red Red Wine' gave the group a belated, if minor, success in 1968, but the unit was latterly dubbed *passé*. Chen later enjoyed a fruitful association with **Rod Stewart**, while James enjoyed two hits in 1976 alongside another set of Vagabonds with 'I'll Go Where The Music Takes Me' and 'Now Is The Time', the latter of which reached the UK Top 5. The singer has since pursued a career as a cabaret attraction.
● ALBUMS: *The New Religion* (1966)★★★, *Open Up Your Soul* (1968)★★★, one side only *London Swings* (1968), *You Don't Stand A Chance If You Can't Dance* (Pye 1975)★★, *Now* (Pye 1976)★★, *Life* (Pye 1977)★★, *Dancin' Till Dawn* (PRT 1979)★★.
● COMPILATIONS: *This Is Jimmy James* (1968)★★★, *Golden Hour Of Jimmy James* (Golden Hour 1979)★★.

James, John

This guitarist from Wales is very well regarded, but lacks the high profile afforded to other, less talented, guitar players. His style defies categorization, as he plays through jazz, folk and blues forms with equal ease. His first release, *Morning Brings the Light*, for **Transatlantic Records**, highlighted his exceptional ability. Despite much television work, and tours with Eddie Walker as the duo Carolina Shout, James remains largely unknown to the British public. He has also recorded soundtrack music for television. *Carolina Shout* included such variations as **Bob Wills**' 'San Antone Rose', and **Sam Cooke**'s 'Another Saturday Night'.
● ALBUMS: *Morning Brings The Light* (Transatlantic 1970)★★★, *John James* (1971)★★★, with Pete Berryman *Sky In My Pie* (1971)★★★, *Guitar Jump* (Kicking Mule 1977)★★★, with Sam Mitchell *I Got Rhythm* (Kicking Mule 1978)★★★, *Acoustica Eclectica* (Stoptime 1984)★★★, *Guitar Music* (Stoptime 1988)★★★, with Eddie Walker *Carolina Shout* (1989)★★★.

James, Joni

b. Joan Carmello Babbo, 22 September 1930, Chicago, Illinois, USA. Growing up during the Depression years, James attended drama and dance lessons and organized a ballet club in high school. Following graduation, she worked as a dancer and began singing. In 1952 she recorded her first tracks for **MGM Records**, with the second single, 'Why Don't You Believe Me', becoming a million-seller and a number 1 hit on the US pop charts. The hit was later covered by both **Patti Page** and **Margaret Whiting**. James next two singles, the double-sided hit 'Have You Heard'/'Wishing Ring' and a cover of **Hank Williams**' 'Your Cheatin' Heart', were also major hits. James hit the Top 10 four more times up to 1955 with 'Almost Always', 'My Love, My Love', 'How Important Can It Be?' and 'You Are My Love'. Joni continued to record for MGM until 1964; when the hits stopped coming she retired from show business.
● ALBUMS: *Let There Be Love* (MGM 1953)★★★★, *The Joni James Award Winning Album* (1954)★★★, *Little Girl Blue* (1955)★★★, *When I Fall In Love* (1955)★★★, *In The Still Of The Night* (1956)★★★, *Among My Souvenirs* (1958)★★★, *Songs Of Hank Williams* (1959)★★, *Joni Sings Sweet* (1959)★★★, *At Carnegie Hall* (1960)★★, *I'm In The Mood for Love* (1960)★★★, *Sings Hollywood* (1960)★★★, *100 Strings And Joni* (1960)★★, *100 Voices, 100 Strings* (1961)★★, *Mood Is Blue* (1961)★★★, *Mood Is Romance* (1961)★★★, *Mood Is Swinging* (1961)★★★, *Sings Folk Songs* (1961)★, *After Hours* (1962)★★★, *I'm Your Girl* (1962)★★★, *Something For The Boys* (1963)★★★, *Beyond The Reef* (1964)★★★, *Sings The Gershwins* (1964)★★, *My Favourite Things* (1964)★★★, *Put On A Happy Face* (1964)★★★, *Italianissime* (1964)★★, *Bossa Nova Style* (MGM 1965)★★.

James, Nicky

Based in Birmingham, Midlands, England, Nicky James had previously led local band the Lawmen, and been a member of **Denny Laine**'s Diplomats, before embarking on a solo career. Signing to **Columbia Records**, he then added a suffix to his name to produce the Nicky James Movement. That group made its debut in 1965 with a version of 'Stagger Lee'. When the single did not sell he moved from Columbia to **Philips Records** and reverted to solo billing. As such he made his debut in 1967 with 'So Glad We Made It'. Four further singles, 'Would You Believe', 'Nobody But Me', 'Time' and 'Reaching For The Sun', ensued, but it was not until 1971 that he made his self-titled album debut. By now he had perfected a vocal technique which melded the blues with prevalent beat pop tendencies, although he found it difficult to make a commercial breakthrough. In 1972 he switched to **Threshold Records**, a label established by the **Moody Blues**, who were clearly a major influence on him. Two more albums followed alongside four further singles, which increasingly moved towards blues rock. The last of these, 'Maggie', was released in 1976, by which time he had also appeared on solo albums by Moody Blues members Graeme Edge and Ray Thomas. With the advent of punk, however, James's career declined and 'Maggie' proved to be his final recording.
● ALBUMS: *Nicky James* (Philips 1971)★★★, *Every Home Should Have One* (Threshold 1973)★★, *Thunderthroat* (Threshold 1976)★★.

James, Rick

b. James Johnson, 1 February 1948, Buffalo, New York, USA. The nephew of **Temptations** vocalist Melvin Franklin, James pioneered a crossover style between R&B and rock in the mid-60s. In 1965, he formed the Mynah Birds in New York with two future members of the **Buffalo Springfield**, **Neil Young** and Bruce Palmer, plus Goldie McJohn, later with **Steppenwolf**. **Motown Records** signed the band as a riposte to the British wave of R&B artists then dominating the charts, before their career was aborted when James was arrested for draft evasion. Resuming his career in Britain in the early 70s, James formed the funk combo Main Line. Returning to the USA, he assembled a like-minded group of musicians to perform a dense, brash brand of funk, influenced by **Sly Stone** and **George Clinton**. Signed to Motown in 1977, initially as a songwriter, he rapidly evolved a more individual style, which he labelled 'punk funk'. His first single, 'You And I', typified his approach, with its prominent bass riffs, heavy percussion, and sly, streetwise vocals. The record reached the US Top 20 and topped the specialist soul charts - a feat that its follow-up, 'Mary Jane', came close to repeating, though the song's blatant references to marijuana cut short any hopes of radio airplay. James chose to present himself as a social outlaw, with outspoken views on drugs and sex. In a move subsequently echoed by **Prince**, he amassed a stable of artists under his control at Motown, using the **Stone City Band** as his backing group, and the Mary Jane Girls as female pawns in his macho master-plan. James also produced records by actor Eddie Murphy, vocalist **Teena Marie**, **Val Young**, and Process and the Doo-Rags. His own recordings, predominantly in the funk vein, continued to corner the disco market, with 'Give It To Me Baby' and 'Super Freak', on which he was joined by the Temptations, achieving notable sales in 1981. Both tracks came from *Street Songs*, a Grammy-nominated record that catapulted James into the superstar bracket. Secure in his commercial standing, he revealed that he preferred recording ballads to the funk workouts that had made his name, and his drift towards a more conservative image was heightened when he duetted with **Smokey Robinson** on the hit single 'Ebony Eyes', and masterminded the Temptations' reunion project in 1983. James's flamboyant lifestyle took its toll on his health and he was hospitalized several times between 1979 and 1984. His career continued unabated, and he had major hits in 1984 and 1985 with the more relaxed '17' and 'The Glow'. The latter also provided the title for a highly acclaimed album, which reflected James's decision to abandon the use of drugs, and move towards a more laid-back soul style. He was angered by constant media comparisons of his work with that of Prince, and cancelled plans to star in an autobiographical film called *The Spice Of Life* in the wake of the overwhelming commercial impact of his rival's *Purple Rain*. After releasing *The Flag* in 1986, James ran into serious conflict with Motown over the status of his spin-off acts. When they refused to release any further albums by the Mary Jane Girls, James left the label, signing to **Reprise Records**, where he immediately achieved a soul number 1 with 'Loosey's Rap', a collaboration with **Roxanne Shante**. James's drug problems had not disappeared and following years of abuse he was jailed in 1991, together with his girlfriend Tanya Hijazi, for various offences including dealing cocaine, assault and torture. The King Of Funk confessed to *Rolling Stone* that at least by being in prison he 'could not do drugs'. He was released in 1996.

● ALBUMS: *Come Get It!* (Gordy 1978)★★★, *Bustin' Out Of L Seven* (Gordy 1979)★★★, *Fire It Up* (Gordy 1979)★★★, *In 'n' Out* (Gordy 1980)★★, *Garden Of Love* (Gordy 1980)★★, *Street Songs* (Gordy 1981)★★★★, *Throwin' Down* (Gordy 1982)★★★, *Cold Blooded* (Gordy 1983)★★, *Glow* (Gordy 1985)★★, *The Flag* (Gordy 1986)★★, *Wonderful* (Reprise 1988)★★, *Urban Rapsody* (Higher Source 1997)★★★.

● COMPILATIONS: *Reflections: All The Great Hits* (Gordy 1984)★★★★, *Greatest Hits* (Motown 1993)★★★, *Bustin' Out: The Best Of Rick James* (Motown 1994)★★★, *Greatest Hits* (Spectrum 1996)★★★.

James, Siân

b. 24 December 1961, Llanerfyl, Powys, Wales. James singing career began when she was put on the stage of a local musical competition at the age of four. She learned to play piano at six years old and, by 11, the harp. By the age of 16, James was touring with a harp trio, playing for music and Welsh societies in England and Wales. James then studied for a music degree at Bangor University, North Wales, and began to travel extensively, singing and playing harp. On 14 March 1981, the group Bwchadanas was formed, at Bangor University. The acoustic line-up featured, in addition to James; Geraint Cynan (b. 20 June 1961, Treorci, Rhondda, Mid-Glamorgan, Wales; piano), Rhys Harries (b. 6 January 1962, Newbridge, Gwent, Wales; guitar), Gareth Ioan, who left in 1986, (b. 19 September 1961, Aberynolwyn, Gwynedd, Wales; pipes), Lilio Rolant, who also left in 1986, (b. 3 May 1962, Cardiff, South Glamorgan, Wales; harp) and Rhodri Tomas (b. 15 April 1962, Llanelli, Dyfed, Wales; guitar). The group were gigging constantly, and were voted the Best Welsh Folk Band for 1983, 1984 and 1985. *Cariad Cywir*, released on Sain Records, gained the group a wider audience, but with the making of the album, a new electric line-up was formed. This included Marc Jones (bass), who was later replaced by Ray Jones (b. 11 October 1951, London, England; bass), Meredydd Morris (electric guitar), and Owen Huws (drums). Other musicians who have contributed to the band have included drummers Gwyn Jones, Graham Land, and Charlie Britten, as well as Dafydd Dafis (soprano and alto saxophone). The group represented Wales in the Pan-Celtic Festival in Killarney, Eire, in 1985, winning the folk song competition. Bwchadanas also supported **Moving Hearts** in 1985, and played one date with **Runrig**, in 1987. Owing to individual members' commitments, Bwchadanas now only play a handful of dates every year. Much television coverage has, however, enabled the group to become one of the most successful folk rock bands in Wales. Meanwhile, Siân James has continued to tour in her own right throughout Ireland, Scotland, Brittany and America, and *Cysgodion Karma*, released on Sain, attracted a good deal of interest in the artist. James is currently performing with Tich Gwilym (b. 10 September 1950, Pen y graig, Rhondda, South Wales; guitar, charango), and Geraint Cynan (keyboards), with herself on harp and vocals. She continues to sing traditional and contemporary Welsh folk songs, as well as fronting Bwchadanas as vocalist.

● ALBUMS: with Bwchadanas *Cariad Cywir* (Sain 1984)★★★★, *Cysgodion Karma* (Sain 1990)★★★, *Distaw* (Sain 1993)★★★.

● COMPILATIONS: *Cwlwm Pedwar* (Sain 1981)★★.

James, Skip

b. Nehemiah Curtis James, 9 June 1902, Bentonia, Mississippi, USA, d. 3 October 1969, Philadelphia, Pennsylvania, USA. A solitary figure, James was an emotional, lyrical performer whose talent as a guitar player and arranger enhanced an already impressive body of work. His early career included employment as a pianist in a Memphis whorehouse, as well as the customary appearances at local gatherings and roadhouses. In 1931 he successfully auditioned for the Paramount recording company, for whom he completed an estimated 26 masters. These exceptional performances included 'Devil Got My Woman', written when his brief marriage broke down, as well as 'Hard Time Killin' Floor Blues' and 'I'm So Glad', which was subsequently recorded by **Cream**. James abandoned music during the late 30s in favour of the church and was ordained as a Baptist minister in 1942. He briefly resumed more secular pursuits during the 50s, and was brought back to public attention by guitarists **John Fahey**, Bill Barth and **Canned Heat**'s Henry Vestine, who discovered the dispirited singer in a Mississippi hospital. James remained a reserved individual, but his accomplished talents were welcomed on the thriving folk and college circuit where he joined contemporaries such as **Mississippi John Hurt** and **Sleepy John Estes**. Two superb collections for the **Vanguard** label, *Skip James Today* and *Devil Got My Woman*, showcased James's remarkable skills. His high, poignant voice brought an air of vulnerability to an often declamatory genre and his albums remain among the finest of the country-blues canon. Recurring illness sadly forced James to retire and he died in 1969 following a prolonged battle with cancer.

● ALBUMS: *The Greatest Of The Delta Blues Singers* (Melodeon 1964)★★★, *Skip James Today!* (Vanguard 1965)★★★★, *Devil Got My Woman* (Vanguard 1968)★★★★, *Live At The 2nd Fret, Philadelphia, 1966* (Document 1988)★★.

● COMPILATIONS: *I'm So Glad* (Vanguard 1978)★★★★, *The Complete 1931 Session* (Yazoo 1986)★★★★, *The Complete 1931 Recordings* (Document 1992)★★★★, *The Complete Early Recordings* (Yazoo 1994)★★★★, *She Lyin'* (Edsel 1994)★★★★, *Skip's Piano Blues* (Edsel 1996)★★★.

● FURTHER READING: *I'd Rather Be The Devil*, Stephen Calt.

James, Sonny

b. James Loden, 1 May 1929, Hackleburg, Alabama, USA. The Country Music Hall Of Fame includes a guitar that Sonny James' father made for him when he was three years old. James has been performing since that time and has played fiddle and guitar with the Lodens' family revue. Sonny won several junior fiddle championships, although he was to play guitar on his records. He was signed by **Capitol Records** in 1953 and marketed as Sonny James by producer Ken Nelson. James had his first US country hits with 'That's Me Without You', 'She Done Give Her Heart To Me' and 'For Rent', and made the UK Top 30 with a record that is now a children's favourite, 'The Cat Came Back'. He had a number 1 record on the US pop charts with 'Young Love' in 1957, which was also a number 1 record for film star **Tab Hunter**. Hunter repeated his success in the UK charts, but James only reached number 11. (The original version of 'Young Love' by composer Rick Cartey is long-forgotten.) 'First Date, First Kiss, First Love' made number 25 in the US pop charts and James had 19 other records in the Hot 100. Because he was tall, quiet, respectable and good-looking, he became known as the Southern Gentleman. He

left Capitol and recorded for NRC and **RCA** but returned to Capitol and enjoyed numerous country hits between 1963 and 1971, including 16 consecutive number 1s. His hits included 'You're The Only World I Know', 'Behind The Tear', 'Take Good Care Of Her', 'The Minute You're Gone', which was covered by **Cliff Richard**, and 'A World Of Our Own' and 'I'll Never Find Another You', two of the **Seekers**' pop hits that he covered for the country market. He appeared in several low-budget country films - *Second Fiddle To An Old Guitar, Nashville Rebel, Las Vegas Hillbillies* (with Jayne Mansfield) and *Hillbilly In A Haunted House* (with Basil Rathbone and Lon Chaney). James has also revived pop songs for the country market including 'Only The Lonely', 'It's Just A Matter Of Time' and 'Running Bear', all three being number 1 records. His 1972 number 1, 'That's Why I Love You Like I Do', was a remade and retitled version of the b-side of 'Young Love', 'You're The Reason (I'm In Love)'. He switched to **Columbia** in 1972 and continued his success with 'When The Snow Is On The Roses', 'Is It Wrong (For Loving You)?' (both reaching number 1), 'Little Band Of Gold' and 'Come On In'. He produced **Marie Osmond**'s transatlantic Top 10 revival of 'Paper Roses' and made an album inside Tennessee State Prison. The 57-year-old singer recorded a new version of 'Young Love' for **Dot Records**, but the album, particularly the track 'You've Got Your Troubles', exposed some shaky vocals. In total, Sonny James has had 72 records in the US country charts including 23 number 1s, which makes him one of the most successful country artists in history.

● ALBUMS: *Sonny* (Capitol 1957)★★★, *The Southern Gentleman* (Capitol 1957)★★★, *Honey* (Capitol 1958)★★★★, *The Sonny Side* (Capitol 1959)★★★, *This Is Sonny James* (Capitol 1959)★★★★, *Young Love* (Dot 1962)★★★, *The Minute You're Gone* (Capitol 1964)★★★, *You're The Only World I Know* (Capitol 1965)★★★, *I'll Keep Holding On (Just To Your Love)* (Capitol 1965)★★★, *Behind The Tear* (Capitol 1965)★★★, *True Love's A Blessing* (Capitol 1966)★★★, *Till The Last Leaf Shall Fall* (Capitol 1966)★★★, *My Christmas Dream* (Capitol 1966)★★, *Young Love And Other Songs Of The Heart* (Capitol 1967)★★★, *I'll Never Find Another You* (Capitol 1967)★★★, *Born To Be With You* (Capitol 1968)★★★, *A World Of Our Own* (Capitol 1968)★★★, *Heaven Says Hello* (Capitol 1968)★★, *Need You* (Capitol 1968)★★★, *Close Up* (Capitol 1969)★★★, *The Astrodome Presents - In Person - Sonny James* (Capitol 1969)★★, *Only The Lonely* (Capitol 1969)★★★, *Traces* (Capitol 1970)★★★, *It's Just A Matter Of Time* (Capitol 1970)★★★, *My Love/Don't Keep Me Hanging On* (Capitol 1970)★★★, *Number One (The Biggest Hits In Country Music History)* (Capitol 1970)★★, *Empty Arms* (Capitol 1971)★★★, *Here Comes Honey Again* (Capitol 1971)★★★, *The Sensational Sonny James* (Capitol 1971)★★★, *That's Why I Love You Like I Do* (1972)★★, *When The Snow Is On The Roses* (Columbia 1972)★★★, *The Greatest Country Hits Of 1972* (Columbia 1973)★★, *The Gentleman From The South* (Columbia 1973)★★★, *If She Just Helps Me Get Over You*

(Columbia 1973)★★★, *Sonny James* (Columbia 1973)★★★, *Young Love* (Columbia 1973)★★★, *Is It Wrong?* (Columbia 1974)★★★, *Country Male Artist Of The Decade* (Columbia 1975)★★★, *A Little Bit South Of Saskatoon* (Columbia 1975)★★★, *The Guitars Of Sonny James* (Columbia 1975)★★★, *200 Years Of Country Music* (Columbia 1976)★★, *When Something Is Wrong With My Baby* (Columbia 1976)★★★, *A Mi Esposa Con Amor* (Columbia 1977)★★, *Sonny James In Prison - In Person* (Columbia 1977)★★, *You're Free To Go* (Columbia 1977)★★★, *This Is The Love* (Columbia 1978)★★★, *Favorites* (Columbia 1979)★★★, *Sonny's Side Of The Street* (Monument 1979)★★★, *I'm Lookin' Over The Rainbow* (Dimension 1982)★★★, *Sonny James* (Dot 1986)★★★.

● COMPILATIONS: *The Best Of Sonny James* (Capitol 1965)★★★, *American Originals* (Columbia 1989)★★★, *Capitol Collector's Series* (Capitol 1990)★★★, *Greatest Hits* (Columbia 1992)★★★.

James, Steve

b. 15 July 1950, New York City, New York, USA. James took up his father's guitar when he was 12 and a few years later was playing bass in a rock 'n' roll band. When the blues boom brought **Muddy Waters** and **Mississippi John Hurt** to town, he moved from Manhattan to the East Village, worked in a guitar factory and played for coins on the Bowery. He moved to Bristol, Tennessee, in 1973, where he played old-time music and wrote *Old Time Country Guitar*. Travelling through the south, he learned first-hand from **Bukka White**, **Walter 'Furry' Lewis** and **R.L. Burnside**. While living in Memphis he formed a band with Lum Guffin called the White Hots. In the late 70s, he moved to San Antonio, Texas, working in a museum, doing solo gigs and supporting saxophonist Clifford Scott. *Two Track Mind* was an enhanced reissue of a self-produced cassette, consisting of material by **Big Bill Broonzy**, Sylvester Weaver, **Mance Lipscomb** and others. *American Primitive* contained more original songs, at times featuring a small group that included harmonica player Gary Primich.

● ALBUMS: *Two Track Mind* (Antone's 1993)★★★, *American Primitive* (Antone's 1994)★★★, *Art And Grit* (Antone's 1996)★★★.

James, Tommy

b. 29 April 1947, Dayton, Ohio, USA. After the disbandment of **Tommy James And The Shondells**, James, the lead singer, produced New York group Alive And Kicking, whose 'Tighter And Tighter' reached the US Top 10. James himself then launched his solo career and after three minor hits, returned to the upper echelons of the chart with 'Draggin' The Line'. Although the follow-up, 'I'm Comin' Home' scraped into the *Billboard* Top 40, it was another nine years before he charted again with 'Three Times In Love'. In the meantime, he pursued a variety of club dates, trading on a healthy repertoire of past Shondells hits.

● ALBUMS: *Tommy James* (Roulette 1970)★★, *Christian Of*

The World (Roulette 1971)★★, *My Head, My Bed And My Red Guitar* (Roulette 1971)★★, *In Touch* (Fantasy 1976)★, *Midnight Rider* (Fantasy 1977)★, *Three Times In Love* (Milennium 1980)★★, *A Night In Big City* (Aura 1995)★★, *Tommy James Greatest Hits Live* (Aura 1996)★★.

● COMPILATIONS: *Tommy James : The Solo Years (1970-1981)* (Rhino 1991)★★★.

James, Tommy, And The Shondells

Tommy James formed his first group Tommy And The Tornadoes at the age of 13, by which time he had already recorded his debut single, 'Long Pony Tale'. The Shondells comprised James, Larry Coverdale (guitar), Craig Villeneuve (keyboards), Larry Wright (bass) and Jim Payne (drums) and were assembled to fulfil weekend engagements, but they secured a deal with the local Snap label in 1962. Their first release, 'Hanky Panky', was a regional success, but a chance discovery four years later by Pittsburg disc jockey Bob Mack led to its becoming a national smash, selling in excess of 1one million copies. Now signed to the Roulette label, James assembled a new Shondells which, following defections, settled around a nucleus of Eddie Gray (guitar), Ronnie Rossman (keyboards), Mike Vale (b. 17 July 1949; bass) and Pete Lucia (drums). The addition of producer/songwriting team Ritchie Cordell and Bo Gentry resulted in a string of classic, neo-bubblegum hits, including 'I Think We're Alone Now', 'Mirage' (both gold discs from 1967) and 'Out Of The Blue' (1968). The group's effortless grasp of hooklines and melody culminated with the pulsating 'Mony Mony' (1968), a UK number 1 which invoked the style of the classic garage band era. James then assumed complete artistic control of his work, writing, arranging and producing the psychedelic-influenced 'Crimson And Clover'. This haunting, atmospheric piece, described by the singer as 'our second renaissance', topped the US chart and garnered sales of over five million copies. This desire to experiment continued with two further gold-selling singles, 'Sweet Cherry Wine' and 'Crystal Blue Persuasion' (both 1969), and the album *Cellophane Symphony*. In 1970 the group and singer parted on amicable terms. The latter continued under the name Hog Heaven, while an exhausted James retired to a farm before launching a solo career. 'Draggin' The Line' (1971) provided a US Top 5 hit although subsequent releases from the early 70s failed to broach the Top 30. In 1980 the singer had another million-seller with 'Three Times In Love', since when he has continued to record, albeit with less success. Tommy James And The Shondells' power was encapsulated in their danceability and bracing fusion of soulful voices, garage group riffs, effervescent pop and occasional bubblegum appeal. This pop pourri legacy was picked up by younger artists over a decade on when **Joan Jett** charted with 'Crimson And Clover' and both **Billy Joel** and **Tiffany** took Shondells' covers back to number 1 in the US charts.

● ALBUMS: *Hanky Panky* (Roulette 1966)★★★, *It's Only*

Love (Roulette 1967)★★★, *I Think We're Alone Now* (Roulette 1967)★★★, *Gettin' Together* (Roulette 1968)★★, *Mony Mony* (Roulette 1968)★★★, *Crimson & Clover* (Roulette 1968)★★★, *Cellophane Symphony* (1969)★★, *Travelin'* (1970)★★, as the Shondells *Hog Heaven* (1971)★★.
● COMPILATIONS: *Something Special! The Best Of Tommy James And The Shondells* (Roulette 1968)★★★, *The Best Of Tommy James And The Shondells* (1969)★★★, *Anthology* (Rhino 1990)★★★★, *The Best Of ...* (Rhino 1994)★★★★, *It's A New Vibration - An Ultimate Anthology* (Westside 1997)★★★★.

James, Wendy

b. 21 January 1966, London, England. Something of a standing joke among UK music journalists, Wendy James's post-**Transvision Vamp** career had been greeted with even more vitriol and cynicism than her former band endured. Having challenged allcomer journalists to a million-pound bet that she would be an international star of the proportions of **Madonna** within a few years, James's blonde ambition had been severely dented by the collapse of Transvision Vamp. In a desperate attempt to reactivate her recording career she wrote to **Elvis Costello** in 1993 asking him to write her a song. He responded by sending her no less than 10 - enough for the album that would become *Now Ain't The Time For Tears*. Despite an extensive round of press interviews (James still gave good copy after all) and the associations with Costello, it did little to revive her career and did not give **MCA Records** the UK Top 40 placing they clearly envisaged. James has been ominously quiet since.
● ALBUMS: *Now Ain't The Time For Tears* (MCA 1993)★★★.

James, Willie Bee

Chicago-based James could sing blues to good effect - he issued a fine 78 on Vocalion Records - but the bulk of his recording was done as a studio guitarist for Bluebird Records during the 30s. James's light, swinging guitar was reminiscent of **Big Bill Broonzy**, but he was equally at home backing relatively unemotional northern singers such as **Bumble Bee Slim**, **Merline Johnson** and **Curtis Jones**, as well as duetting with Tennessee guitarist **John Henry Barbee** or the pianist **Frank James**, and as a member of **Tampa Red**'s pop-inflected Chicago Five.
● ALBUMS: including *Chicago Blues* (1985)★★★, *Mississippi Country Blues Vol. 2* (1987)★★, *The Yas Yas Girl* (1989)★★★.

Jamiroquai

Jason 'Jay' Kay's UK funk group Jamiroquai (named after the Iroquois tribe whose pantheism inspired him) made a rapid impact - they were signed to **Sony Records** for an eight-album contract on the strength of just one single for **Acid Jazz Records** - 'When You Gonna Learn?'. Kay (b. *c.*1969, London, England) was brought up in Ealing, London, England, by his jazz-singer mother, **Karen Kay**. Inspired by **Sly Stone**, **Gil**

Scott-Heron and **Roy Ayers**, he integrated those influences into a 90s pop format that also combined 'new age' mysticism and the growing urban funk movement, which took its name from the Acid Jazz label. However, as a former breakdancer, he had already recorded in a hip-hop style, releasing a single with a sampler and drum machine for Morgan Khan's Streetsounds label in 1986. His first major label single, 'Too Young To Die', immediately broke into the UK Top 10, while the debut album entered the chart at number 1 (it has since gone on to worldwide sales of over two million). However, a press backlash soon followed, not helped by Kay's naïve statements about the environment after he had blown his advance on petrol-guzzling cars. Despite the healthy sales, his case was not helped by a less than spectacular debut album, which came with an order form for his own brand clothing (seven per cent of profits going to Greenpeace), although there were strong compositions such as 'If I Like It, I Do It'. The second album was a considerable improvement, with the previous emphasis on his media relations now switched to his music. Songs such as 'Kids', 'Return' and 'Morning Glory' gave his obvious vocal talents better service, adding ghetto hip-hop rhythms to the previous acid jazz and funk backdrops. *Travelling Without Moving* confirmed Jamiroquai as a highly commercial act, selling to date over five and a half million copies worldwide, and winning four trophies at the 1997 MTV Awards.
● ALBUMS: *Emergency On Planet Earth* (Sony 1993)★★★, *The Return Of The Space Cowboy* (Sony 1994)★★★★, *Travelling Without Moving* (Sony 1996)★★★★.

Jammin' The Blues

Held by many to be the finest jazz short ever filmed, and with considerable justification. The film, released in 1944, features superbly evocative photography by Gjon Mili, who also directed, and was supervised by **Norman Granz**. The musicians include **Red Callender**, **Big Sid Catlett**, **Harry Edison**, **Illinois Jacquet**, **Jo Jones**, **Barney Kessel** and the magnificent **Lester Young**. Timeless music by these assembled giants, allied to moody, smoky chiaroscuro makes this a must for any self-respecting jazz fan.

Jan And Arnie

Jan Berry (b. 3 April 1941, Los Angeles, California, USA) and Arnie Ginsburg. Berry later went on to great success with **Jan And Dean**, one of the most popular duos in rock history. Before that pair's success, however, Berry and Ginsburg had one US Top 10 single together. Berry, Ginsburg and Dean Torrence were members of a group called the Barons (which at one point included drummer **Sandy Nelson** and future **Beach Boys** member **Bruce Johnston**). When that group split, the three friends recorded, in Berry's garage, 'Jennie Lee', a tribute to a stripper in a local club. While Torrence served briefly in the US Army Reserves, the tape of that song was brought to the attention of Arwin Records, (owned by Marty Melcher, the husband of actress **Doris Day**) by then-unknowns **Herb Alpert** and **Lou Adler**. Credited to Jan And Arnie, the record rose to number 8 nationally. Two more Jan And Arnie singles were released, one of which charted. By that time Torrence had returned and Ginsburg dropped out of the group, paving the way for Jan And Dean's quick rise to stardom.

Jan And Dean

Jan Berry (b. 3 April 1941, Los Angeles, California, USA) and Dean Torrence (b. 10 March 1940, Los Angeles, California, USA). Students at Emerson Junior High School, Berry and Torrence began singing together on an informal basis. They formed an embryonic group, the Barons, with **Bruce Johnston** and **Sandy Nelson**, but its members gradually drifted away, leaving Berry, Torrence and singer Arnie Ginsburg to plot a different course. The trio recorded 'Jennie Lee' in 1958. A homage to the subject of Ginsburg's affections, a local striptease artist, the single became a surprise hit, reaching number 8 in the US chart. Although featured on the song, Torrence was drafted prior to its success, and the pressing was credited to **Jan And Arnie**. Subsequent releases failed to achieve success and the pair split up. Berry and Torrence were reunited the following year. They completed several demos in Berry's makeshift studio and, having secured the production and management services of local entrepreneur **Lou Adler**, the reshaped duo enjoyed a Top 10 entry with 'Baby Talk'. Jan And Dean scored several minor hits over the ensuing four years until a 1963 release, 'Linda', heralded a departure in their style. Here the duo completed all the backing voices, while the lead was sung in falsetto. The sound was redolent of the **Beach Boys** and the two performers' immediate future became entwined.

Brian Wilson co-wrote 'Surf City', Jan And Dean's first number 1 hit; this glorious summer hit evokes fun, sunshine and 'two girls for every boy'. The Beach Boys' leader also made telling contributions to several other notable classics, including 'Drag City', 'Dead Man's Curve' and 'Ride The Wild Surf', although Berry's contribution as writer, and later producer, should not be underestimated. However, despite the promise of a television series, and a role in the film *Easy Come - Easy Go*, relations between he and Torrence became increasingly strained. Dean added fuel to the fire by singing lead on 'Barbara Ann', an international hit pulled from the informal *Beach Boys Party*. The exploitative 'Batman' single, released in January 1966, was the last session the pair recorded together. Within weeks Jan Berry had crashed his sports car receiving appalling injuries. He incurred severe brain damage, but although recovery was slow, the singer did complete a few singles during the early 70s. Torrence kept the Jan And Dean name alive, but failed to recapture the duo's success and subsequently found his true vocation with his highly respected design company, Kittyhawk Graphics. However, the pair were reunited in 1978 when they undertook the support slot for that year's Beach Boys tour.

● ALBUMS: *Jan And Dean* (Dore 1960)★★★, *Jan And Dean Take Linda Surfin'* (Liberty 1963)★★★, *Surf City (And Other Swinging Cities)* (Liberty 1963)★★★, *Drag City* (Liberty 1964)★★★, *Dead Man's Curve/New Girl In School* (Liberty 1964)★★★, *Ride The Wild Surf* (Liberty 1964)★★★, *The Little Old Lady From Pasadena* (Liberty 1964)★★★, *Command Performance - Live In Person* (Liberty 1965)★, *Folk 'N' Roll* (Liberty 1966)★★, *Filet Of Soul - A 'Live' One* (Liberty 1966)★, *Jan And Dean Meet Batman* (Liberty 1966)★★, *Popsicle* (1966)★★, *Save For A Rainy Day* (1967)★★.

● COMPILATIONS: *Jan And Dean's Golden Hits* (Liberty 1962)★★★, *Golden Hits Volume 2* (1965)★★★, *The Jan And Dean Anthology Album* (1971)★★★, *Gotta Take That One Last Ride* (1973)★★★, *Ride The Wild Surf (Hits From Surf City, USA)* (1976)★★★★, *Teen Suite 1958-1962* (1995)★★★★.

● FURTHER READING: *Jan And Dean*, Allan Clark.

Jan And Kjeld

Publicized as 'The Kids From Copenhagen', these Danish teenagers had only big hit after signing with Germany's Ariola label in 1959. Composed by Charles Niessen, the main theme from his *Kein Mann Zum Hieraten* movie soundtrack did well as a single in central Europe before the duo re-made it as 'Banjo Boy' with English lyrics by New Yorker Buddy Kaye. As such, it spread itself thinly enough to sell a purported million by 1962 without rising above number 36 in the UK and number 58 in the US charts.

Jan Dukes De Grey

Originally formed in Yorkshire, England, as a duo of Michael Bairstow (flute, clarinet, saxophone, trumpet, percussion, keyboards) and Derek Noy (vocals, guitar, keyboards, bass, percussion), Jan Dukes De Grey were among the least conventional folk musicians of their time. Their debut album, *Sorcerers*, was composed entirely of Noy originals, the 18 tracks varying wildly in tone and quality, but occasional compositions, with their unusual arrangements and Noy's highly mannered singing, did succeed. By the advent of a second album, the group had expanded with the inclusion of drummer Denis Conlan. For *Mice And Rats In The Loft* the trio had transferred to the better-distributed Transatlantic Records. Instead of the numerous short songs on their debut, this set comprised just three tracks, one of them a side long. The dissonant tones of its forerunner were given free reign over these expanded tracks, although again the quality of musicianship sometimes failed to match the imagination and invention displayed by Noy's songcraft.

● ALBUMS: *Sorcerers* (Decca Nova 1969)★★, *Mice And Rats In The Loft* (Transatlantic 1971)★★.

Jane's Addiction

This innovative, art-rock quartet was formed in Los Angeles, USA, in 1986, by vocalist Perry Farrell (b. 29 March 1959, Queens, New York, USA). He had formerly starred in the **Cure**-influenced Psi Com, from whose ranks would also emerge Dino Paredes, while it is rumoured that two other former members joined the Hare Krishna sect. With the addition of guitarist Dave Navarro, bassist Eric A. and drummer Stephen Perkins, Jane's Addiction incorporated elements of punk, rock, folk and funk into a unique and unpredictable soundscape. They debuted with a live album on the independent Triple X label, recorded at Hollywood's Roxy venue, which received widespread critical acclaim, despite a throwaway cover version of **Lou Reed**'s 'Rock 'n Roll' and Farrell's limited stage banter, largely consisting of profanities. Drawing inspiration from the **Doors**, **PiL**, **Velvet Underground** and **Faith No More**, they set about delivering a hypnotic and thought-provoking blend of intoxicating rhythms, jagged and off-beat guitar lines and high-pitched vocals of mesmeric intensity. *Ritual De Lo Habitual* was a work of depth and complexity that required repeated listening to reveal its hidden melodies, subtle nuances and enigmatic qualities. It included the video-friendly shoplifting narrative, 'Been Caught Stealing'. In the USA, because of censorship of the album's provocative front cover (as with earlier work, featuring a Farrell sculpture), it was released in a plain envelope with the text of the First Amendment written on it. Farrell, meanwhile, helmed the **Lollapalooza** concert series. Despite widespread media coverage, Jane's Addiction never achieved the commercial breakthrough that their talents deserved, and Farrell dissolved the band in 1992. On his decision to defect to **Porno For Pyros**, taking drummer Perkins and bass player Martyn Le Noble with him, Farrell concluded: 'What it really boiled down to was, I wasn't getting along with them. I'm not saying whose fault it was. Even though I *know* whose fault it was'. The subject of these slurs, Navarro, went on to join the **Red Hot Chili Peppers** in 1994. In the summer of 1997 the original band reunited to record together. Two new tracks appeared on a compilation of live material, demos and out-takes.

● ALBUMS: *Jane's Addiction* (Triple X 1987)★★★, *Nothing's Shocking* (Warners 1988)★★★★, *Ritual De Lo Habitual* (Warners 1991)★★★.
● COMPILATIONS: *Kettle Whistle* (Warners 1997)★★★.

Janet - Janet Jackson

Although Janet Jackson's sleeve note dedication to her fans, 'who made me what I am', might seem a little over the top, those fans responded by buying millions of copies. Although there are 27 listed tracks, many merely constitute a few-second segue. Nevertheless, the album showed increasing confidence aligned with a desire to explore a wider variety of styles, not always successfully - perfect production, good voice, but somehow lacking in heart and soul. Can 10 million fans be wrong? Perhaps the promise of an album is greater than the content. Oh, and Janet, the top button and zip on your Levis have inadvertently come undone.

● Tracks: *Morning; That's The Way Love Goes; You Know; You Want This; Be A Good Boy; If; Back; This Time; Go On Miss Janet; Throb; What'll I Do; The Lounge; Funky Big Band; Racism; New Agenda; Love pt 2; Because Of Love; Wind; Again; Another Lover; Where Are You Now; Hold On Baby; The Body That Loves You; Rain; Any Time Any Place; Are You Still Up; Sweet Dreams.*
● First released 1993
● UK peak chart position: 1
● USA peak chart position: 1

Janet Jackson's Rhythm Nation 1814 - Janet Jackson

Little did you know that the American national anthem, 'God Bless America', was written in 1814. Janet did, and she sets out in 'Rhythm Nation' to dish out a bit of 'let's all work together for a better world and improve our way of life type thing'. This vein continues for a number of tracks, and admirable though it is, she sounds so much more convincing singing a good old-fashioned love song. The Jacksons were meant to dance, not to sermonize. That said, 'Miss You Much', 'Lonely' and 'Come Back To Me' are fabulous. Slick, sweet soul sung and played perfectly.

● Tracks: *Interlude: Pledge; Rhythm Nation; Interlude: TV; State Of The World; Interlude: Race; The Knowledge; Interlude: Let's Dance; Miss You Much; Interlude: Come Back; Love Will Never Do (Without You); Livin' In A World (They Didn't Make); Alright; Interlude: Hey Baby; Escapade; Interlude: No Acid; Black Cat; Lonely; Come Back To Me; Someday Is Tonight; Interlude: Livin' In Complete Darkness.*
● First released 1989
● UK peak chart position: 4
● USA peak chart position: 1

Janis

Released in 1974 and directed by Howard Alk and Seaton Findlay, *Janis* is an entertaining documentary on rock singer **Janis Joplin**. However, the film was made with the co-operation of the Joplin family and, although not a hagiography, *Janis* avoids controversial aspects of the singer's life, notably her bisexuality and the heroin addiction which brought her life to a premature end. Nevertheless, *Janis* does excel as a musical biography with the bulk of the in-concert footage left intact. These include Joplin's dazzling performance at the 1967 **Monterey Pop Festival** as a member of **Big Brother And The Holding Company** and an exciting rendition of 'Move Over' with her final group, the apply-titled Full Tilt Boogie Band. Behind-the-scenes footage at the recording of *Cheap Thrills* - where the tension is almost tangible - is equally revealing.

Jankowski, Horst

b. 30 January 1936, Berlin, Germany. Jankowski's family was driven from the city and his father killed during World War II. He returned to Berlin to study at its Conservatory of Music while moonlighting as a multi-instrumental session player. From 1952-64, he was part of **Caterina Valente**'s touring band, an experience that began the gradual recognition of him as one of Germany's most polished mainstream jazz pianists. In 1960, he merged his 18-voice amateur choir with an orchestra to mine a similar easy-listening seam to that of **Lawrence Welk** and **Ray Conniff**. Issued as a single in 1965, the self-composed title track of *Eine Schwarzwaldfahrt* - translated as 'A Walk In The Black Forest' - was a huge global smash. He was also accorded the dubious attribute of 'genius' recorded and a tie-in album that sold a million in the USA. A precursor of sorts to **James Last**, he was, nonetheless, unable to recreate that 'Schwarzwaldfahrt' miracle by protracting a prolific recording career. Before his death, Jankowski reverted to the style in which he felt most comfortable through prestigious employment as an arranger for artists including **Benny Goodman**, **Oscar Peterson**, **Ella Fitzgerald** and **Miles Davis**. His extraordinary success in Germany resulted in being voted the top Jazz pianist for 11 consecutive years (1955-65).

● ALBUMS: *The Genius Of Jankowski!* (1965)★★★, *Horst Jankowski And His Orchestra* (1979)★★★, *Piano Interlude* (1979)★★★.

Jansch, Bert

b. 3 November 1943, Glasgow, Scotland. This highly gifted acoustic guitarist and influential performer learned his craft in Edinburgh's folk circle before being absorbed into London's burgeoning circuit, where he established a formidable reputation as an inventive guitar player. His debut, *Bert Jansch*, is a landmark in British folk music and includes 'Do You Hear Me Now', a Jansch original later covered by **Donovan**, the harrowing 'Needle Of Death', and an impressive version of **Davey Graham**'s 'Angie'. The artist befriended **John Renbourn**, who played supplementary guitar on Jansch's second selection, *It Don't Bother Me*. The two musicians then recorded the exemplary *Bert And John*, which was released alongside *Jack Orion*, Jansch's third solo album. This adventurous collection featured a nine-minute title track and a haunting version of 'Nottamun Town', the blueprint for a subsequent reading by **Fairport Convention**. Jansch continued to make exceptional records, but his own career was overshadowed by his participation in the **Pentangle** alongside Renbourn, Jacqui McShee (vocals), **Danny Thompson** (bass) and Terry Cox (drums). Between 1968 and 1973 this accomplished, if occasionally sterile, quintet was one of folk music's leading attractions, although the individual members continued to pursue their own direction during this time. The Danny Thompson-produced *Moonshine* marked the beginning of his creative renaissance with delightful sleeve notes from the artist: 'I hope that whoever listens to this record gets as much enjoyment as I did from helping me to make it'. *LA Turnaround*, released following the Pentangle's dissolution, was a promising collection and featured assistance from several American musicians including former member of the **Monkees**, **Michael Nesmith**. Although Jansch rightly remains a respected

figure, his later work lacks the invention of those early releases. It came to light that much of this lethargy was due to alcoholism, and by his own admission, it took six years to regain a stable condition. In the late 80s he took time out from solo folk club dates to join Jacqui McShee in a regenerated Pentangle line-up, with whom he continues to tour. In the mid-90s he was performing regularly once again with confidence and fresh application. This remarkable reversal after a number of years of indifference was welcomed by his loyal core of fans. *When The Circus Comes To Town* was an album that easily matched his early pivotal work. Not only does Jansch sing and play well but he brilliantly evokes the atmosphere and spirit of the decade in which he first came to prominence. *Live At The 12 Bar* is an excellent example of his sound in the mid-90s, following a successful residency at London's 12 Bar Club.

● ALBUMS: *Bert Jansch* (Transatlantic 1965)★★★★, *It Don't Bother Me* (Transatlantic 1965)★★★★, *Jack Orion* (Transatlantic 1966)★★★★, with John Renbourn *Bert And John* (1966)★★★★, *Nicola* (Transatlantic 1967)★★★, *Birthday Blues* (Transatlantic 1968)★★★, *Lucky Thirteen* (1969)★★★, with Renbourn *Stepping Stones* (Vanguard 1969)★★★, *Rosemary Lane* (Transatlantic 1971)★★★, *Moonshine* (Reprise 1973)★★★, *LA Turnaround* (Charisma 1974)★★, *Santa Barbara Honeymoon* (Charisma 1975)★★, *A Rare Conundrum* (Charisma 1978)★★, *Avocet* (Charisma 1979)★★, *Thirteen Down* (Sonet 1980)★★, *Heartbreak* (Logo 1982)★★, *From The Outside* (Konexion 1985)★★, *Leather Launderette* (Black Crow 1988)★★, *The Ornament Tree* (Run River 1990)★★, *When The Circus Comes To Town* (Cooking Vinyl 1995)★★★★, *Live At The 12 Bar* (Jansch 1996)★★★, *Toy Balloon* (Cooking Vinyl 1998).

● COMPILATIONS: *The Bert Jansch Sampler* (Transatlantic 1969)★★★★, *Box Of Love* (Transatlantic 1972)★★★, *The Essential Collection Volume 1 (Strolling Down The Highway)* (Transatlantic 1987)★★★★, *The Essential Collection Volume 2 (Black Water Side)* (Transatlantic 1987)★★★, *The Gardener: Essential Bert Jansch 1965-71* (1992)★★★★, *The Collection* (Castle 1995)★★★★, *Blackwater Slide* (Recall 1998)★★★ .

Jap, Philip

This UK vocalist found success after winning a BBC television talent show hosted by **David Essex**. Already signed to a major label, Jap went on to win the finals of the show and was awarded a 30-minute television special. This gave him a chance to showcase the tracks from his debut album which featured production work from **Trevor Horn** and Colin Thurston. Jap's second single 'Total Erasure' just missed out as did two further releases. Although the exposure was there, the record buying public were not and Jap disappeared just as quickly as he appeared.

● ALBUMS: *Philip Jap* (1983)★★.

Japan

Formed in London in early 1974, this group comprised **David Sylvian** (b. David Batt, 23 February 1958, Lewisham, London, England; vocals), his brother Steve

Jansen (b. Steven Batt, 1 December 1959, Lewisham, London, England; drums), Richard Barbieri (b. 30 November 1958; keyboards) and **Mick Karn** (b. Anthony Michaelides, 24 July 1958, London, England; saxophone). A second guitarist, Rob Dean, joined later and the group won a recording contract with the German record company Ariola-Hansa. During the same period, they signed to manager **Simon Napier-Bell**. The group's derivative pop style hampered their prospects during 1978, and they suffered a number of hostile reviews. Eminently unfashionable in the UK punk era, they first found success in Japan. After three albums with Ariola-Hansa, they switched to **Virgin Records** in 1980 and their fortunes improved a year later thanks to the surge of popularity in the new romantic movement. Japan's androgynous image made them suddenly fashionable and they registered UK Top 20 hits with 'Quiet Life', 'Ghosts' and a cover version of **Smokey Robinson And The Miracles**' 'I Second That Emotion'. Their album, *Tin Drum*, was also well received. Disagreements between Karn and Sylvian undermined the group's progress, just as they were achieving some long-overdue success and they split in late 1982. Sylvian and Karn went on to record solo.

● ALBUMS: *Adolescent Sex* (Ariola-Hansa 1978)★★, *Obscure* (Ariola-Hansa 1978)★★, *Quiet Life* (Ariola-Hansa 1979)★★★, *Gentlemen Take Polaroids* (Virgin 1980)★★★, *Tin Drum* (Virgin 1981)★★★, *Oil On Canvas* (Virgin 1983)★★.

● COMPILATIONS: *Assemblage* (Hansa 1981)★★★, *Exorcising Ghosts* (Virgin 1984)★★★, *In Vogue* (Camden 1997)★★★.

● FURTHER READING: *A Tourist's Guide To Japan*, Arthur A. Pitt.

Jaramillo, Jerry

b. 7 March 1954, Belen, New Mexico, USA. Jaramillo became interested in music as a child and his father gave him his first guitar when he was 12. He began performing locally and eventually formed his Brown River Road Band, with which he played a residency at an Albuquerque nightclub. He has acted as opener for several artists including **Loretta Lynn** and **Faron Young**. In 1988, he gained some indie chart successes with 'Face To The Wall', 'Jeanie Loved The Roses' and his self-penned 'Honky Tonk Cinderella'. His recordings generally feature a mixture of down-to-earth honky tonk, bar-room ballads and Tex-Mex, while his bilingual talent, like that of **Johnny Rodriguez**, sometimes gives rise to Spanish as well as English vocals.

● ALBUMS: *Jerry Jaramillo* (LRJ 1988)★★★, *Favorites* (LRJ 1989)★★.

Jarman, Joseph

b. 14 September 1937, Pine Bluff, Arkansas, USA. When he was a child Jarman's family moved to Chicago, where he studied drums at high school. While in the army he played saxophone and clarinet; after demobilisation he travelled until settling back in Chicago in 1961. He joined the **AACM** in 1965, leading various groups and playing in **Richard Muhal Abrams**'s The Experimental Band. During that year he also collaborated with controversial classical composer **John Cage** on a multi-media event. A poet himself, Jarman's concerts would often include poets or dancers, his taste for the theatrical having been developed when he studied drama at the Second City Theatre School and the Art Institute of Chicago School. In 1969, dispirited by the death of Charles Clark and Chris Gaddy, two of his regular sidemen, he disbanded his own group and joined the **Art Ensemble Of Chicago**, with whom the bulk of his work has been done since then. Like his partners in the Ensemble (**Lester Bowie**, **Roscoe Mitchell**, **Malachi Favors** and **Don Moye**) he plays a dazzling number of instruments, the primary ones being sopranino, soprano, alto, tenor and bass saxophones, bassoon, oboe, flutes and clarinets as well as various percussion and 'little instruments'. If Jarman is the dramatist of the Ensemble to Mitchell's purer musician, he has nonetheless written a number of rigorous compositions for large groups. Regrettably, little of his work away from the AEC has been recorded during the 70s and 80s; that which has is mostly in small groups which he co-leads with Moye, though he sometimes guests with other bands - playing, for example, with the **Reggie Workman** Ensemble in the late 80s and recording with **Leroy Jenkins**.

● ALBUMS: *Song For* (Delmark 1966)★★★★, *As If It Were The Seasons* (1968)★★★, *Sunbound* (1976)★★★, with Don Moye *Egwu-Anwu* (1978)★★★, *The Magic Triangle* (1979)★★★★, *Black Paladins* (1980)★★★, *Earth Passage - Density* (1981)★★★, with Leroy Jenkins *Out Of The Mist* (Ocean 1998)★★★.

Jarmels

The Jarmels were formed in Richmond, Virginia, USA, by Nathaniel Ruff (b. 1939), Ray Smith (b. 1941), Paul Burnett (b. 1942), Earl Christian (b. 1940) and Tom Eldridge (b. 1941). They scored a major chart entry in 1961 with 'A Little Bit Of Soap', a song that retained an enduring appeal when composer **Bert Berns** recorded further versions with the **Exciters** and deep soul singer **Garnet Mimms**. British rock 'n' roll revivalists **Showaddywaddy** later took this favoured composition into the UK Top 5 in 1978. Despite appearances to the contrary, the Jarmels continued to record, although they were never able to recapture that early success. A later version of the group featured singer **Major Harris**, who subsequently joined the **Delfonics** prior to launching his solo career.

● COMPILATIONS: *The Complete Jarmels* (Ace 1986)★★★, with the Mystics *The Mystics Meet The Jarmels* (Ace 1990)★★★.

Jarre, Jean-Michel

b. 24 August 1948, Lyon, France. This enigmatic composer and keyboard wizard has long been hailed as the premier exponent of European electronic music.

From the age of five he took up the piano, and studied harmony and structure at the Paris Conservatoire, before abandoning classical music and joining Pierre Schaeffer's Musical Research group. Becoming gradually more fascinated with the scope offered by electronics, his first release comprised the passages 'La Cage' and 'Eros Machine' on **EMI** Pathe in France. He then contributed 'Aor' for the Paris Opera ballet, and the soundtrack for the film *Les Granges Bruless*, among others. After marrying actress Charlotte Rampling, he set about composing his first full-scale opus, *Oxygene*. This reached number 2 in the UK charts, signalling Jarre's arrival as a commercial force. The subsequent *Equinoxe* continued in familiar style, exploring the emotive power of orchestrated electronic rhythms and melody. The first of several massive open air performances took place in Paris at the Place De La Concorde, with a world record attendance of over one million. However, it was not until 1981 and the release of *Magnetic Fields* that Jarre undertook his first tour, no small task considering the amount of stage equipment required. His destination was China where five concerts took place with the aid of 35 traditional Chinese musicians. A double album was released to document the event. 1983's *Music For Supermarkets* proved his most elusive release, recorded as background music for an art exhibition. Just one copy was pressed and sold at an auction for charity before the masters were destroyed. The *Essential Jean Michel Jarre*, compiled from earlier albums, proved more accessible for Jarre's legion of fans. *Zoolook* utilized a multitude of foreign language intonations in addition to the familiar electronic backdrop, but an unexpectedly lethargic reaction from the public prompted a two-year absence from recording. He returned with another outdoor extravaganza, this time celebrating NASA's 25th anniversary in Houston. Viewed by over one million people this time, it was also screened on worldwide television. The release of *Rendezvous* the following month was hardly coincidental. His first concerts in the UK, advertised as 'Destination Docklands', were also televised in October 1988. Whatever the size of audience he attracted, he was still unable to woo the critics. *Revolutions* appeared in the shops shortly afterwards, while one of its two singles, 'London Kid,' featured the **Shadows**' Hank B. Marvin on guitar. *Waiting For Cousteau* anticipated his most recent update on the world record for attendance at a music concert. This time two million crammed into Paris on Bastille Day to witness 'La Defence'. While Jarre continues to bewilder and infuriate music critics, statistical evidence shows he is far from short of advocates in the general public. The *Odyssey Through O2* album featured dance disciples, including DJ Cam, **Apollo 440** and Hani revisiting and remixing *Oxygene 7-13*.

● ALBUMS: *Oxygene* (Polydor 1977)★★★★, *Equinoxe* (Polydor 1978)★★★, *Magnetic Fields* (Polydor 1981)★★★, *Concerts In China* (Polydor 1982)★★★, *Zoolook* (Polydor 1984)★★★, *Rendezvous* (Polydor 1986)★★, *Houston/Lyon*

(Polydor 1987)★★, *Revolutions* (Polydor 1988)★★★, *Live* (Polydor 1989)★★, *Waiting For Cousteau* (Polydor 1990)★★, *Oxygene 7-13* (1997)★★.

● COMPILATIONS: *The Essential* (Polydor 1983)★★★, various artists *Odyssey Through O2* (Epic/Dreyfus 1998)★★★.

● FURTHER READING: *The Unofficial Jean-Michel Jarre Biography*, Graham Needham.

Jarre, Maurice

b. 13 September 1924, Lyons, France. An important composer for films for over 40 years, as a youngster Jarre intended to become an electrical engineer, but changed his mind and studied music at the Paris Conservatoire in 1944. He joined the orchestra of the Jean Louise Barrault Theatre, and in 1951, composed the music for Kleist's *Le Prince De Homburg*. Soon afterwards he moved into films, and during the 50s, wrote the scores for such French productions as *Hotel Des Invalides*, *Le Grand Silence*, *Le Tetre Contre Les Murs* and *Les Yeux Sans Visage* (*Eyes Without A Face*). During the early 60s, he began to score the occasional non-Gallic movie, such as *Crack In The Mirror*, starring Orson Welles, *The Big Gamble* and 'the last great epic of World War II', *The Longest Day* (1962). In the same year, Jarre won his first Academy Award for his memorable score for *Lawrence Of Arabia*, and was honoured again, three years later, for his music to *Doctor Zhivago*, featuring the haunting 'Lara's Theme' ('Somewhere, My Love'), which, with a lyric by **Paul Francis Webster**, became a Top 10 singles hit for the **Ray Conniff** Singers, and was the title track of one of their million-selling albums. Jarre's other 60s scores for English-speaking films included *Behold A Pale Horse*, *The Collector*, *Is Paris Burning?*, *The Professionals*, *Grand Prix*, *Gambit*, *The Night Of The Generals*, *Villa Rides!*, *Five Card Stud*, *The Fixer*, *Isadora*, *The Damned* and Alfred Hitchcock's *Topaz* (1969). He continued to write prolifically in the 70s for films such as director George Steven's swan-song, *The Only Game In Town*, one of Neil Simon's funniest comedies, *Plaza Suite*, and many others, such as *The Effect Of Gamma Rays On Man-In-The-Moon Marigolds*, *The Life And Times Of Judge Roy Bean*, in which **Andy Williams** sang Jarre's 'Marmalade, Molasses And Honey' (lyric by **Alan** and **Marilyn Bergman**), *The Mackintosh Man*, *Great Expectations*, *Posse*, *The Man Who Would Be King*, *The Last Tycoon*, *Mohammed, Messenger Of God*, *March Or Die* and *Winter Kills*. His third Oscar came in 1984 for his 'anachronistic' score for David Lean's *A Passage To India*, and he was nominated in the following year for his work on *Witness*, starring Harrison Ford. His other 80s scores included *Resurrection*, *Lion Of The Desert*, *Taps*, *The Year Of Living Dangerously*, *Dreamscape*, *The Bride*, *Mad Max And The Thunderdrome*, *Enemy Mine*, *The Mosquito Coast*, *No Way Out*, *Fatal Attraction*, *Distant Thunder*, *Gorillas In The Mist* (another Academy Award nomination for Jarre), *Moon Over Parador*, *Chances Are*, *Dead Poets Society* (BAFTA Award, 1989), *Prancer* and *Enemies, A Love Story*. In

1991, Jarre received an **ASCAP** Award as the composer of the music for *Ghost*, the 'top box office film of 1990'. His other early 90s work included *After Dark, My Sweet*, *School Ties*, *Shadow Of The Wolf* (aka *Agaguk*), *Only The Lonely*, *Fearless* and *Mr. Jones* (1994). Apart from feature films, Jarre also wrote extensively for television. His credits included *The Silence*, *Jesus Of Nazareth* (mini-series), *Ishi, The Last Of His Tribe*, *Shogun* (mini-series), *Enola Gay*, *Coming Out Of The Ice*, *The Sky's No Limit*, *Samson And Delilah*, *Apology*, *The Murder Of Mary Phagan* (mini-series) and *Robinson Crusoe And Man Friday*.

● ALBUMS: *Jarre By Jarre* (Silva Screen 1989)★★★, *Only The Lonely* (Colosseum 1991)★★.

Jarreau, Al

b. 12 March 1940, Milwaukee, Wisconsin, USA. Although Jarreau sang from childhood, it was many years before he decided to make singing his full-time occupation. Working outside music for most of the 60s, he began to sing in small west coast clubs and eventually achieved enough success to change careers. By the mid-70s he was becoming well known in the USA, and, via records and a European tour, greatly extended his audience. Singing a highly sophisticated form of vocalese, Jarreau's style displays many influences. Some of these come from within the world of jazz, notably the work of **Jon Hendricks**, while others are external. He customarily uses vocal sounds that include the clicks of African song and the plosives common in oriental speech and singing patterns. This range of influences makes him both hard to classify and more accessible to the wider audience for crossover music. More commercially successful than most jazz singers, Jarreau's work in the 70s and 80s consistently appealed to young audiences attuned to fusions in popular music. By the early 90s, when he was entering his 50s, his kinship with youth culture was clearly diminishing, but his reputation was by this time firmly established.

● ALBUMS: *1965* (1965)★★, *We Got By* (Reprise 1975)★★★, *Glow* (Reprise 1976)★★, *Look To The Rainbow: Live In Europe* (Warners 1977)★★, *All Fly Home* (Warners 1978)★★, *This Time* (Warners 1980)★★★, *Breakin' Away* (Warners 1981)★★★, *Jarreau* (Warners 1983)★★★, *Spirits And Feelings* (Happy Bird 1984)★★★, *Ain't No Sunshine* (Blue Moon 1984)★★★, *High Crime* (Warners 1984)★★, *Al Jarreau In London* (Warners 1984)★★, *You* (Platinum 1985)★★★, *L Is For Lover* (Warners 1986)★★★, *Hearts Horizon* (Reprise 1988)★★★, *Manifesto* (Masters 1988)★★★, *Heaven And Earth* (Reprise 1992)★★★, *Tenderness* (Warners 1994)★★★.

● FILMS: *Breakdance - The Movie* (1984).

Jarrell, Tommy

b. 1901, near Round Peak, Surry County, North Carolina, USA, d. 28 January 1985, Mount Airy, USA. Jarrell was an old-time fiddler, banjoist and singer, but never became a professional musician, nor was heard outside his home locale, until he was nearly 70 years old. The Jarrells were of Scots-Irish descent and he learned his fiddle playing and much of his vast repertoire of songs from his father, Ben Jarrell, a noted old-time fiddler who played and recorded with Da-Costa Woltzs Southern Broadcasters in the late 20s. Tommy was also influenced by Fred Cockerham, another fiddler. The family moved to Mount Airy in 1921 and from 1925 to his retirement in 1966, Jarrell worked for the State Highways Department. After his wife died in 1967, he began to play the fiddle again. He became recognized as an authority on old-time music and was much in demand for appearances at various folk festivals and colleges. Jarrell recorded several albums, both as a solo artist and also with Cockerham and Oscar Jenkins, and his versatility was showcased on his 1974 album *Come And Go With Me*, which featured all banjo tracks. Jarrell was invited to perform at President Reagan's inaugural ceremony but was not well enough to attend. Many of his best performances are available on record and a film, *Sprout Wings And Fly*, was made about him. Some of his last recordings were made in June 1984, when, along with Alice Gerrard, Andy Cahan and Verlen Clifton, he proved that, even at the age of 83, he was still a most competent fiddle performer. Jarrell died following an heart attack at his home in 1985.

● ALBUMS: *June Apple* (1972)★★★, *Joke On The Puppy* (1972)★★★, with Oscar Jenkins, Fred Cockerham *Down At The Cider Mill* (c.1973)★★★, Jenkins, Jarrell & Cockerham, *Vol. 2 (Back Home In Blue Ridge)* (c.1973)★★★, *Stay All Night* (1973)★★★, *Come And Go With Me* (1974)★★★★, *Sail Away Ladies* (1976)★★★, *Pickin' On Tommy's Porch* (1983)★★★, *Rainbow Sign* (1986)★★.

Jarrett, Art

Multi-instrumentalist Jarrett played the guitar, banjo and trombone in addition to his abilities as singer and bandleader. He also acted widely in the theatre and in film in the early 30s. His own dance band was inaugurated in January 1935, making its bow at the Blackhawk Restaurant in Chicago, Illinois, USA. The band included Jule Styne, Randy Brooks, James Fitzpatrick, Hal Sharff, Harold Dankers, Les Cooper, Jack Turner, Arthur Owen, Bruce Milligan, Rufus Smith, John Zellner, Floyd Sullivan, Babe Stuart, Ken La Bohn, Emery Kenyon, Sid Nierman and Ken Binford. There were several alternating vocalists: Jeri Sullivan, Gale Robbins, Eleanor Holm, Doris Singleton, Betty Barrett, Billy Blair and Jarrett himself. With the Blackhawk Restaurant their most regular venue, the orchestra concentrated on engagements in the Midwest and east coast, specialising in the smooth, sweet style of musical presentation which dominated the period. Their recordings included 'Everything's Been Done Before' and ''Neath The Silvery Moon', issued on **Brunswick**, **Columbia** and **Victor Records**. They also appeared widely on sponsored radio shows, including *The Florsheim Shoe Show*, *Dr. Pepper Show*, *Fitch Bandwagon* and *Coca Cola Spotlight Bands*. Eleanor

Holm, who was married to Jarrett during the early 30s, was also well known as a swimming star, and left the band in 1936 to take part in the Olympics of that year. By the early 40s Jarrett disbanded his own orchestra to take over the **Hal Kemp** dance band following their leader's death. He remained at their helm for many years, before retiring to Yonkers, New York, where he started his own orange juice business.

Jarrett, Keith

b. 8 May 1945, Allentown, Pennsylvania, USA. Growing up in a highly musical family, Jarrett displayed startling precocity and was playing piano from the age of three. From a very early age he also composed music and long before he entered his teens was touring as a professional musician, playing classical music and his own compositions. He continued with his studies at **Berklee College Of Music** in the early 60s but was soon leading his own small group. From the mid-60s he was based in New York where he was heard by **Art Blakey** who invited him to join his band. Jarrett stayed with Blakey for only a few months but it was enough to raise his previously low profile. In 1966 he joined **Charles Lloyd**'s quartet which made his name known internationally, thanks to extensive tours of Europe and visits to the Soviet Union and the Far East. It was with this quartet that he befriended **Jack DeJohnette**. During his childhood Jarrett had also played vibraphone, saxophone, flute and percussion instruments, and he resumed performing on some of these instruments in the late 60s. In 1969 he joined **Miles Davis**, playing organ for a while, before turning to electric piano. This was during the jazz/fusion period and although the best music from this group was never recorded they released *Live At The Fillmore* and *Live-Evil*. By now, word was out that Jarrett was one of the most exciting new talents in the history of jazz piano. During his two years with Davis he also found time to record under his own name, enhancing his reputation with a succession of fine albums with **Charlie Haden**, **Dewey Redman**, **Paul Motian** and others. After leaving Davis he resumed playing acoustic piano and established a substantial following for his music, which he has described as 'universal folk music'. *Facing You* in 1971 created a considerable response and was a brilliant demonstration of speed, dynamics and emotion. The now familiar Jarrett characteristic of brilliantly adding styles was first aired on this album. Country, folk, classical, blues and rock were given brief cameos, this was a remarkable solo debut.

Subsequently, Jarrett has become a major figure not only in furthering his own music but in 'showing the way' for contemporary jazz and in particular the growth of **ECM Records** and the work of Manfred Eicher. Eicher and Jarrett complement each other like no other business partnership. Jarrett's success with huge sales of his albums enabled ECM to expand. Eicher in turn will record and release anything Jarrett wishes, such is their trust in each other. He has often

worked and recorded with artists including **Jan Garbarek**, **Gary Burton**, Palle Danielsson and Jon Christensen. It is with DeJohnette and bassist **Gary Peacock**, he regularly returns to playing with. Known as the 'standards trio', there can be few units currently working that have such intuition and emotional feeling of each others musical talent. Albums such as *Changes*, *Standards Vol. 1* and *Vol. 2*, *Live Standards* and *The Cure* represent the finest possibilities of an acoustic jazz trio. Jarrett's greatest achievement, however, is as the master of improvised solo piano. It is in this role that Jarrett has arguably created a musical genre. His outstanding improvisational skills have led to his ability to present solo concerts during which he might play works of such a length that as few as two pieces will comprise an entire evening's music. His pivotal and often breathtaking *Solo Concerts: Bremen and Lausanne* released in 1973, received numerous accolades in the USA and Europe. Similarly in 1975 *The Koln Concert* was a huge success becoming a million plus seller. It remains his biggest selling work and is a must for any discerning music collection, even though it was recorded on a badly tuned piano. In **Ian Carr**'s biography, Jarrett explains that in addition to feeling unwell on the day of the concert the right piano did not arrive in time. Instead he had to make do by restricting his improvisation to the middle keys as the top end was shot and the bass end had no resonance. Additionally the ambitious multi-album set *The Sun Bear Concerts* are rich journeys into the improvisational unknown. Jarrett's solo improvised work has not resulted in his turning his back on composing and he has written and recorded music for piano and string orchestra resulting in albums such as *In The Light* and *The Celestial Hawk*. His interest in this form of music has added to his concert repertoire and during the 80s, in addition to solo and continuing small group jazz concerts he also played and recorded classical works. Jarrett's continuing association with ECM Records has helped advance his constantly maturing musical persona. Technically flawless, Jarrett's playing style draws upon many sources reaching into all areas of jazz while simultaneously displaying a thorough understanding of and deep feeling for the western classical form. Unquestionably one of the most dazzling improvising talents the world of music has ever known, Jarrett is also remarkable for having achieved recognition from the whole musical establishment as well as the jazz audience while also enjoying considerable commercial success.

● ALBUMS: *Life Between The Exit Signs* (Vortex 1967)★★, *Restoration Ruin* (Vortex 1968)★★, *Somewhere Before* (Atlantic 1968)★★, with Gary Burton *Gary Burton And Keith Jarrett* (Atlantic 1970)★★★, with Jack DeJohnette *Ruta And Daitya* (ECM 1971)★★★, *The Mourning Of A Star* (Atlantic 1971)★★, *Facing You* (ECM 1971)★★★★★, *Expectations* (Columbia 1972)★★★, *Fort Yawuh* (Impulse 1973)★★★, *In The Light* (ECM 1973)★★★, *Solo Concerts: Bremen And Lausanne* (ECM 1973)★★★★★, *Treasure Island* (Impulse 1974)★★★, with Jan Garbarek *Belonging* (ECM

1974)★★★★, with Garbarek *Luminessence* (ECM 1974)★★★, *Death And The Flower* (Impulse 1975)★★★, *Arbour Zena* (ECM 1975)★★★, *The Köln Concert* (ECM 1975)★★★★★, *Sun Bear Concerts* (ECM 1976)★★★★, *Mysteries* (Impulse 1976)★★★, *The Survivor's Suite* (ECM 1976)★★★★, *Silence* (Impulse 1976)★★★, *Shades* (Impulse 1976)★★★, *Byablue* (Impulse 1977)★★★, *My Song* (ECM 1977)★★★★, *Nude Ants* (ECM 1979)★★★★, *Personal Mountains* (ECM 1979)★★★, *Expectations* (Columbia 1979)★★★, *The Moth And The Flame* (ECM 1980)★★★, *The Celestial Hawk* (ECM 1980)★★★, *Invocations* (ECM 1980)★★★, *Concerts Bregenz And München* (ECM 1981)★★★★, *Concerts (Bregenz)* (ECM 1982)★★★★, *Bop-Be* (Impulse 1982)★★, *Standards Volume 1* (ECM 1983)★★★★, *Changes* (ECM 1983)★★★, *Backhand* (Impulse 1983)★★★, *Eyes Of The Heart* (ECM 1985)★★★, *Spirits* (ECM 1985)★★★, *Standards Live* (ECM 1985)★★★★, *Sacred Hymns* (ECM 1985)★★★, *Staircase* (1985)★★★★, *Still Live* (ECM 1986)★★★, *Book Of Ways* (ECM 1986)★★★, *Hymns Spheres* (ECM 1986)★★, *Dark Intervals* (ECM 1988)★★★, *Standards Volume 2* (ECM 1988)★★★★, *The Well Tempered Clavier Book* (ECM 1988)★★, *J.S. Bach Das Wohltemperierte Klavier Buch 1* (ECM 1988)★★★, *Changeless* (ECM 1989)★★★, *Treasure Island* (Impulse 1989)★★, *Paris Concert* (ECM 1990)★★★★, *J.S. Bach Das Wohltemperierte Klavier Buch 2* (ECM 1991)★★★★, *Tribute* (ECM 1991)★★★★, *The Cure* (ECM 1992)★★★★, *Vienna Concert* (ECM 1992)★★★★, *Bye Bye Blackbird* (ECM 1993)★★★★, with Gary Peacock, Paul Motian *At The Deer Head Inn* (ECM 1994)★★★, *Standards In Norway* (ECM 1995)★★★, *At The Blue Note* (ECM 1995)★★★★, with the Stuttgart Chamber Orchestra *W.A. Mozart Piano Concertos Nos. 21, 23, 17. Masonic Funeral Music* (ECM 1996)★★★, *La Scala* (ECM 1997)★★★, *Tokyo '96* (ECM 1998)★★★.

● COMPILATIONS: *Best Of Keith Jarrett* (Impulse 1979)★★, *Works* (ECM 1989)★★★, *The Impulse Years 1973-74* 5-CD box set (1997)★★★, *Keith Jarrett* (GRP 1998)★★★.

● FURTHER READING: *Keith Jarrett: The Man And His Music* Ian Carr.

Jarrett, Pigmeat

b. James Jarrett Jnr., 8 December 1899, Cordele, Georgia, USA, d. 5 September 1995. Barrelhouse blues pianist Pigmeat Jarrett moved to Kentucky as a child where his Geechee father worked as a coalminer, his mother being half-Geechee, half-Cherokee. Some years later the family settled in Cincinnati, the city with which he would become synonymous. Jarrett attended the local Beecher Stowe School: 'I got my nickname there from the teacher', he told *Living Blues* magazine, 'because every time she seen me I had a piece of hog.' His mother sang at church, but would have nothing to do with the nascent blues movement, considering it to be the 'devil's music'. Her son did not share her opinion, picking up the basics from local 'open house' gatherings. Later he helped run whiskey from Newport during prohibition. He also began to play alongside local musicians and visiting stars such as **Bessie Smith**. His first ventures out of town came courtesy of covert train rides in cattle trucks - a method of transport he shared with bluesmen such as **Blind Lemon Jefferson** and **Leroy Carr**. In the 30s he found employment on steam paddlers, operating on the Ohio and Illinois Rivers. The Depression and the subsequent introduction of juke-boxes curtailed his employment somewhat, and for a time he joined a 16-piece house band, moving progressively into jazz as opportunities for blues artists dwindled. Later he started a small electrical shop. Despite his long career, Jarrett was recorded only once, when blues scholar Steve Tracy produced his 1980 album *Look At The People*. He was later honoured at the Cincinnati Public Library with a Pigmeat Jarrett Day in 1992 and also performed at the Chicago Blues Festival that year.

● ALBUMS: *Look At The People* (June Appal 1980)★★★.

Jarrett, Winston

b. 1941, St. Ann, Jamaica, West Indies. Jarrett began his career with **Alton Ellis**'s group the Flames and is widely acknowledged as the writer of Ellis's classic 'Sunday Coming' and 'True Born African', although he is not always credited as such. The Flames shared in Ellis's fame during Jamaica's fleeting flirtation with **rock-steady**. By 1967 the newly emerging reggae beat had gained favour and the original Flames disbanded. Jarrett enrolled Junior Green and Egga Gardner, and they collectively embarked on a recording career, performing as the Righteous Flames. With **Coxsone Dodd** they released their debut, 'Born To Be Loved', followed by a string of credible hits including 'Ease Up', 'You Don't Know' and 'I Was Born To Be Loved'. In 1969 the group recorded sessions with **Lee Perry**, resulting in the excellent 'Zion I Love You'. Returning to **Studio One**, the group became known as Winston Jarrett And The Flames and released the bizarrely titled 'Peck Up A Pagan'. The group returned in 1978 with 'War'. By the early 80s, Jarrett concentrated on his solo career, enjoying a modicum of success throughout the decade. In the early 90s he re-formed the Flames to pay homage and acknowledge their debt to Bob Marley when he performed alongside **Peter Tosh** and **Bunny Wailer**. Some cynics suggested the motivation for the sessions was purely fiscal and the songs were greeted with indifference, sadly eclipsing Jarrett's virtuoso performance. The 10-track album featured five vocal cuts with their respective dub versions; notable tracks include 'Selassie Is The Chapel', 'African Herb Man' and 'Pound Get A Blow'.

● ALBUMS: *Wise Man* (Wambesi 1980)★★★, *Kingston Vibrations* (Ras 1994)★★★, *Solid Foundation* (Heartbeat 1995)★★★, *Too Many Boundaries* (Ras 1996)★★★★, with the Righteous Flames *Sings Tribute To Bob Marley* (Original 1994)★★★.

Jars Of Clay

Jars Of Clay rose to sudden prominence in May 1995 when their self-titled album became the first debut by a contemporary Christian act to achieve platinum status.

The group was formed in 1994 by four friends from Greenville College in Illinois, USA - Dan Heseltine (vocals), Stephen Mason, Matt Odmark and Charlie Lowell. They won a competition for unsigned bands sponsored by the Gospel Music Association, and were rewarded with a contract with Brentwood Music's Essential label. Buoyed by the success of the debut album's first single, 'Flood', Jars Of Clay became fixtures on **MTV** and played a series of support slots to **Sting** among 300 tour dates completed in 1996. Their second album, *Much Afraid*, was titled after one of the characters in Hannah Hurnard's book *Hind's Feet On High Places* - a Christian allegory in which each of the characters plays a human emotion. The album was completed in London and Nashville and was produced by Stephen Lipson (a former collaborator of Sting, **Whitney Houston** and **Simple Minds**).

● ALBUMS: *Jars Of Clay* (Essential/Silvertone 1995)★★★, *Much Afraid* (Essential/Silvertone 1997)★★★.

Jarvis, Clifford

b. Clifford Osbourne Jarvis, 26 August 1941, Boston, Massachusetts, USA. One of the most significant alumni of **Sun Ra**'s Arkestras, Jarvis was prominent for much of the 60s and periodically thereafter. **Barry Harris, Yusef Lateef** and **Grant Green** were among his other employers. Jarvis's hard-hitting, supportive drumming can be heard on several Sun Ra classics. *Nothing Is* and *Pictures Of Infinity* both contain several excellent examples of his playing. Jarvis has been less well-represented on record in recent years. During the 80s he moved to England.

● ALBUMS: with Jackie McLean *Right Now* (1965)★★★★, with Sun Ra *Nothing Is* (1966)★★★, with Pharoah Sanders *Deaf, Dumb, Blind* (1971)★★★.

Jarvis, J.D.

b. John Dill Jarvis, 21 April 1924, Manchester, Clay County, Kentucky, USA. He began to play guitar when he was seven and later also became highly competent on banjo, mandolin and bass. He developed an early love of traditional music being particularly keen on gospel numbers. He served in the US Army from 1942-48 and was seriously wounded during World War II. After recovering he became a dedicated Christian. He also worked with his friend, **Brother Claude Ely**, at his church in Cumberland, Kentucky and played on Ely's recording made at the church by King Records. He relocated to Hamilton, Ohio in 1959, where he made a living by forming a painting and decorating company. He began to write songs and played on local radio and television and at social gatherings. He was a most prolific recording artist in the 60s and 70s, making recordings for Jewel, Rural Rhythm, Vetco, Heart Warming, his own Down Home and Log Cabin labels and others. He mainly recorded with a bluegrass backing supplied by any of the genre's musicians who were available in the area at the time. These, on occasions, included Buck Graves, Harley Gabbard and even **Ralph**

Stanley's Clinch Mountain Boys. Later some of his gospel songs such as 'Take Your Shoes Off Moses' and 'Six Hours On The Cross' were recorded by noted gospel groups like the Lewis Family and by Ralph Stanley. He also wrote patriotic and saga songs such as 'Thank God For Old Glory' and 'The Hyden Mine Tragedy'. Jarvis remained active in a smaller way in Hamilton into the 90s; his decorating company was still operative but managed by his son.

● ALBUMS: *J.D Jarvis & The Rocky Mountain Boys* (Ark 1963)★★★★, *Bluegrass Hymn Time* (Jewel 1967)★★★, *Take Your Shoes Off Moses* (Jewel 1967)★★, *Walk The Streets Of Glory* (Harp 1967)★★, *Your Favorite Hymns Bluegrass Style* (Log Cabin 1967)★★★, *J.D. Says Everybody Sing Bluegrass* (Down Home 1968)★★★, *Bluegrass Style* (Down Home 1968)★★★, *Old Time Country Gospel* (Rural Rhythm 1968)★★★, *Down Home Gospel* (Rural Rhythm 1968)★★★, *Jubilee Gospel Songs* (Rural Rhythm 1968)★★, with Rusty York *Bluegrass Gospel Songs* (Rural Rhythm 1968)★★, *I Got Up With Heaven On My Mind* (Down Home 1968)★★★, *More Bluegrass Gospel Songs* (Rural Rhythm 1970)★★★, with Ralph Stanley band *More Country Gospel* (Rural Rhythm 1970)★★★, *The Old Crossroad* (Jewel 1971)★★★★, *Sings He Made Me Whole* (Artist c.1971)★★, *The Hyden Miners Tragedy* (Down Home 1971)★★★, *Mountain Music Bluegrass Style* (Jewel 1971)★★★, *Early One Day* (Down Home 1972)★★★, *Thank God For Old Glory* (Vetco 1974)★★.

● COMPILATIONS: *The Best Of J.D. Jarvis* (Sagegrass 1981)★★★.

Jason And The Scorchers

This country-rock 'n' roll styled US band was led by Jason Ringenberg (b. 22 November 1959; vocals, guitar, harmonica) who left his parents' farm in Sheffield, Illinois in 1981 to travel to Nashville. There he teamed up with Warner Hodges (b. 4 June 1959, Nashville, Tennessee, USA; guitar) and Jeff Johnson (b. Nashville, Tennessee, USA; bass). Another original member was Jack Emerson, who went on to become the band's manager. Hodges' parents provided the band's pedigree, having been country musicians who toured with **Johnny Cash**. The band recruited Perry Bags (b. 22 March 1962, Nashville, Tennessee, USA; drums) and became Jason And The Nashville Scorchers, with the prefix later dropped, playing fast country rock ('cow punk' was the description coined in the UK). Their first EP for the Praxis label was 1982's *Reckless Country Soul* (USA only), followed by the mini-album *Fervor* a year later. This brought them well-deserved attention in the press and was subsequently re-released in 1984 on **EMI**-America. It was notable for the inclusion of **Bob Dylan**'s 'Absolutely Sweet Marie', while a subsequent single tackled the **Rolling Stones**' '19th Nervous Breakdown'. *Lost And Found* included a cover of **Hank Williams**' 'Lost Highway'; the combination of these three covers gives a useful insight into the band's influences and sound.

After moving increasingly towards hard rock with *Thunder And Fire* in 1989, the Scorchers split up when that album failed to bring the expected commercial breakthrough. While guitarist Warner Hodges quit the music business in disgust, Jason Ringenberg took time to gather himself for an assault on the country market. His raunchy solo debut, *One Foot In The Honky Tonk* (released by **Liberty Records** and credited to 'Jason'), proved to be too traditional for country radio, but he remains an irrespresible live performer. They reformed and released *A Blazing Grace*, and under the name Jason And the Nashville Scorchers they released *Reckless Country Soul* in 1996.

● ALBUMS: *Fervor* (EMI 1983)★★★, *Lost And Found* (EMI 1985)★★★, *Still Standing* (EMI 1986)★★★, *Thunder And Fire* (A&M 1989)★★★, *A Blazing Grace* (Mammoth 1995)★★★, *Reckless Country Soul* (Mammoth 1996)★★★, *Clear Impetuous Morning* (Mammoth 1996)★★★, *Midnight Roads And Stages Seen* (Mammoth 1998)★★★.

● VIDEOS: *Midnight Roads And Stages Seen* (Mammoth 1998).

Jason Crest

Initially comprising Terry Clarke (vocals), Terry Dobson (guitar), Ron Fowler (bass), Roger Siggery (drums) and Derek Smallcombe (guitar), Jason Crest were formed in Tunbridge Wells, Kent, England, in the late 60s. After spending a few months working as the Spurlyweeves and then the Good Thing Brigade, in November 1967 they were spotted by Fritz Fryer, formerly bass player with the **Four Pennies** who was working in an A&R capacity for **Phillips Records**. They took their new name from an adjustment to one of the Spurlyweeves' original songs, 'The Collected Works Of Justin Crest'. Their debut single for Phillips, 'Turquoise Tandem Cycle', followed in 1968. As its title indicated, it was a classic example of late 60s pop-psyche, complete with organ-driven backing and self-consciously ridiculous lyrics. Neither it nor the follow-up single, 'Juliano The Bull', made the UK charts. Phillips were growing impatient with their lack of success, and **Roy Wood** was duly drafted in as producer for the group's third single, '(Here We Go Round) The Lemon Tree', a cover of the **Move** song which had originally appeared as the b-side to 'Flowers In The Rain'. It too flopped.

Increasingly alarmed, Phillips then ordered the group to record a Fritz Fryer song, 'Waterloo Road'. For their final single the group elected to record an original song, 'Black Mass', composed by Clarke and Dobson. This was probably their most effective release, a composite of progressive and blues rock which took the group far away from its whimsical pop-pschedelic origins. However, once that single again failed to produce anything but indifference from the critics and public alike, the group broke-up. Dobson left the music business while the other members of the band (who by the time of their demise also included bassist John Selley who had replaced Fowler) worked in progressive rock groups such as Orang Utan, High Broom and Samuel Prody. In 1983 Terry Clarke joined Vendetta as singer,

working alongside guitarist Brian Bennett (ex-**Mike Stuart Span**).

● COMPILATIONS: *The Black Mass* (Scanner Jots 1993)★★★.

Jaspar, Bobby

b. 20 February 1926, Liege, Belgium, d. 28 February 1963. Jaspar came from a family of musicians, and studied piano between the ages of 11 and 13. In 1939 he adopted the clarinet and played jazz at US army bases in Germany. In 1950 he relocated to Paris, where he played tenor sax and flute with Henri Renaud and Bernard Peiffer. In the mid-50s he led a quartet at the Club St. Germain, backing visiting Americans such as **Chet Baker** and **Jimmy Raney**. He married the singer **Blossom Dearie** and moved to New York in April 1956. Jaspar had no difficulty in making contacts, as he had been voted 'New Star' in the *Downbeat* critics' poll, and recorded some sterling hard bop with **Elvin Jones** and **Tommy Flanagan** in November of that year. A tour with **J.J. Johnson** followed, then a brief stint with **Miles Davis** in 1957 and six months with **Donald Byrd**. Returning to Paris he held court for five months at the Chat Qui Peche club in 1958, then went back to New York to work with pianist **Bill Evans** (1959) and singer **Chris Connor** (1960). In 1962 he toured Europe with guitarist **Rene Thomas**. Involvement with heroin took its toll. Hospitalized in September 1962, he died aged 37 after heart surgery. His relaxed, authentic version of the **Stan Getz** sound hardened up and became more individual after his move to New York. Jaspar remains one of a handful of Europeans who managed to feel at ease in straight-ahead jazz while creating their own individual niche.

● ALBUMS: with Hank Jones *Relaxin' At Camarillo* (1956)★★, *Bobby Jaspar Quintet* (1956)★★★, with Rene Thomas *Live At Ronnie Scott's* (1962)★★★, with Herbie Mann *Flute Souffle* (1993)★★★, *Bobby Jaspar* (1993)★★★.

Javells (featuring Nosmo King)

b. Stephen Jameson, 1949, London, England. This singer/songwriter's first success came with the duo **Truth**, who had a UK Top 40 hit with a cover of the **Beatles** 'Girl' on Pye in 1966. He recorded solo for Pye and its subsidiary Dawn in the early 70s, under his own name, and also as Nosmo King (No Smoking!). The record company felt that 'Goodbye Nothing To Say', the b-side of an old Nosmo King single 'Teenage Love', could be a northern soul hit and sent copies to clubs under the pseudonym the Javells to give the impression that it was a USA group. This ploy made Jameson an overnight star on the northern soul circuit and a trio was quickly put together to work as the Javells in the clubs. The record, which was produced by **Roger Greenaway**, just missed the UK Top 20. Similar sounding follow-ups failed and the fictitious group faded as fast as it had arrived. Jameson went back to his own name and recorded without success for **Decca** in 1977.

Jawara, Jali Musa

b. 1961, Kankan, Mali. Half-brother of Malian band-leader **Mory Kante**, Jawara is a lesser known but equally adept master of the kora (west African harp). His entire family were musical, being members of the Jali clan of hereditary musicians. His brother initially taught him the music, before Jali joined Mory's band in 1979, relocating to Abidjan, where music was less censored by the government. He also kept his own kora and balafon group operative simultaneously. His greatest solo album, *Fote Mogobon*, was released in Mali in 1983 and, fortunately for world music fans, was picked up for UK release by the London label Oval Records in 1986. It remains one of the most celebrated song collections to emerge from West Africa in the 80s, and has been reissued several times under different titles (*Yaismika* for Hannibal Records and *Direct From West Africa* for **Go! Discs**).

● ALBUMS: *Fote Mogobon* (Tangent 1983)★★★★, *Soubindoor* (World Circuit 1988)★★★.

Jaxon, Frankie

b. 3 February 1895, Montgomery, Alabama, USA. Nicknamed for his short stature, Frankie 'Half Pint' Jaxon entered showbusiness at the age of 15 as a singer, dancer, comedian and female impersonator, and was also active as a producer of revues. After singing and dancing in amateur shows and in the streets outside theatres and saloons, Jaxon became an actor with a tent show. By 1912 he had formed a double act with Gallie DeGaston, with which they toured the deep south. From then until the mid-40s Jaxon worked almost non-stop, singing, dancing, acting, sometimes straight, sometimes in blackface, and occasionally in drag. He appeared on radio and recorded in a variety of genres, and was at his most outrageous doing a lascivious drag vocal for **Tampa Red**'s Hokum Jug Band, changing the subject of 'How Long How Long' from passing time to penis size. Contrastingly, he also recorded gospel with the Cotton Top Mountain Sanctified Singers. More typical were his many titles recorded with small jazz groups, several of which were reworkings of his signature tune, 'Fan It'. He also worked in theatre administration on the black theatre circuit, was a frequent broadcaster and made numerous records with blues artists including **Cow Cow Davenport** and **Thomas A. Dorsey**. Jaxon also appeared on club and theatre dates with several noted jazzmen, **Bennie Moten** and **King Oliver**, and recorded with the **Harlem Hamfats, Lillian Armstrong, Red Allen**, and **Barney Bigard**. Jaxon's singing style was unusual in that he frequently used a shrill, high-pitched voice that matched his female impersonation act. Nothing is known of Jaxon after 1944, but he is believed to have entered government service, and by now it must be presumed that he is dead.

● COMPILATIONS: *Frankie Jaxon And Tampa Red's Hokum Jug Band* (1928)★★★, *Red Allen And The Blues Singers Vol. 1 and 2* (1940)★★★★, *Can't You Wait Till You Get Home* (Collectors Items 1986)★★★★, *Frankie Half Pint Jaxon, 1927-1940* (Blues Document 1989)★★★, *Frankie Half Pint Jaxon, 1937-1939* (Document 1989)★★★.

Jay And The Americans

This New York-based act was formed in 1961 when former **Mystics** vocalist John 'Jay' Traynor (b. 2 November 1938) joined ex-Harbor Lites duo Kenny Rosenberg, aka Kenny Vance, and Sandy Yaguda, aka Sandy Deane. Howie Kane (b. Howard Kerschenbaum) completed the line-up, which in turn secured a recording deal through the aegis of the songwriting and production team, **Leiber And Stoller**. Jay And The Americans scored a US Top 5 hit with their second single, the dramatic 'She Cried', but a series of misses exacerbated tension within the group and in 1962 Traynor left for a low-key solo career. Bereft of a lead vocalist, the remaining trio recruited David 'Jay' Black (b. 2 November 1941) from the Empires. Dubbed 'Jay' to infer continuity, Black introduced fifth member Marty Saunders (guitar) to the line-up, and the following year established his new role with the powerful 'Only In America'. Initially intended for the **Drifters**, the song's optimism was thought hypocritical for a black act and the Americans' vocal was superimposed over the original backing track. In 1964 Artie Ripp assumed the production reins for the quintet's 'Come A Little Bit Closer', a US Top 3 entry. The following year the group was assigned to **Gerry Granahan** who in turn secured a greater degree of consistency. 'Cara Mia', 'Some Enchanted Evening' and 'Sunday And Me' (the last-named penned by **Neil Diamond**) all reached the US Top 20, and although 'Livin' Above Your Head' was less successful, this enthralling performance is now recognized as one of the group's finest recordings. The quintet's brand of professional pop proved less popular as the 60s progressed, although revivals of 'This Magic Moment' (1968) and 'Walkin' In The Rain' (1969) were US Top 20 hits. The latter featured the musical talents of **Donald Fagen** and **Walter Becker**, later of **Steely Dan**, but at that point members of the Americans' studio band. By the turn of the decade the group's impetus was waning and with Vance embarking on solo recordings, Sanders writing and Deane producing, Jay Black was granted the rights to the group's name. Further recordings did ensue and he continues to perform on the nostalgia circuit.

● ALBUMS: *She Cried* (United Artists 1962)★★★, *Jay And The Americans At The Cafe Wha?* (United Artists 1963)★★, *Come A Little Bit Closer* (United Artists 1964)★★★, *Blockbusters* (United Artists 1965)★★, *Sunday And Me* (United Artists 1966)★★★, *Livin' Above Your Head* (United Artists 1966)★★★, *Wild, Wild Winter* soundtrack (1966)★★, *Try Some Of This* (United Artists 1967)★★, *Sands Of Time* (1969)★★, *Wax Museum* (1970)★★.

● COMPILATIONS: *Jay And The Americans' Greatest Hits* (United Artists 1965)★★★, *Very Best Of* (1979)★★★, *Jay And The Americans' Greatest Hits Volume Two* (United Artists 1966)★★★, *Come A Little Bit Closer* (1990)★★★.

Jay And The Techniques

Formed in Allentown, Pennsylvania, USA, in the mid-60s, Jay And The Techniques were an inter-racial pop group best known for the Top 10 debut single 'Apples, Peaches, Pumpkin Pie' in 1967. The group consisted of vocalist Jay Proctor and six other members: Karl Landis, Ronald Goosly, John Walsh, George Lloyd, Charles Crowl and Dante Dancho. The group built a following in the northeast and was discovered by producer Jerry Ross, who arranged to have them signed to Smash Records, a subsidiary of **Mercury Records**. 'Apples, Peaches, Pumpkin Pie', was their biggest hit, reaching number 6 in the US in 1967. 'Keep The Ball Rolling' was, like the first, based on a children's game, and it climbed to number 14. The formula held up for one further game-orientated single, 'Strawberry Shortcake', which scraped into the Top 40 in 1968. A final chart success, 'Baby Make Your Own Sweet Music', ended their run on the pop charts in 1968, but a revived Jay And The Techniques placed 'Number Onederful' on the R&B charts in 1976, on Event Records. This was the group's swan song.

● ALBUMS: *Apples, Peaches, Pumpkin Pie* (Smash 1967)★★, *Love, Lost & Found* (Smash 1968)★★.
● COMPILATIONS: *Apples, Peaches, Pumpkin Pie* (Collectables 1995)★★, *The Best Of Jay And The Techniques* (Mercury 1995)★★.

Jay, Barbara

b. England. Growing up in a jazz-loving family, her father playing trumpet in various bands, Jay began singing as a child. During the 60s she sang with many leading British jazz musicians, including **Ronnie Scott**, **George Chisholm** and **Tommy Whittle**. In 1970 she sang with the orchestra **Benny Goodman** led on a long European tour. She also sang in New York, appearing at the Carnegie Tavern where she was accompanied by **Ellis Larkins**. Jay has performed extensively on radio and television in the UK and at many European festivals including Nice and Cork. She sings with a true, clear voice, warmly interpreting the great standards of the popular and jazz repertoires. Her phrasing is elegant and her diction superb. Consistently working with outstanding British jazz musicians, she is married to Whittle with whom she regularly appears.

● ALBUMS: *The Nearness Of You* (Tee-Jay 80s)★★★, *Memories Of You* (Tee-Jay 90s)★★★★.

Jay, Peter, And The Jaywalkers

Originally based in East Anglia, England, the Jaywalkers - Peter Miller (lead guitar), Tony Webster (rhythm guitar), Mac McIntyre (tenor saxophone/flute), Lloyd Baker (piano/baritone saxophone), Geoff Moss (acoustic bass), Johnny Larke (electric bass), and Peter Jay (drums), pre-dated the British beat boom. They scored a minor hit in 1962 with 'Can Can 62', but despite an unquestioned competence, their rather stilted act became increasingly anachronistic. The group attempted a more contemporary image with several R&B-based releases, and in 1966 a restructured line-up emerged under the name Peter Jay And The New Jaywalkers. Now reduced to a quintet, the unit featured vocalist **Terry Reid**, but despite an impressive appearance on the **Rolling Stones**' UK tour, they disbanded by the end of that year.

Jaydee

b. Robin Alders, *c*.1958, Netherlands. Alders is a regular DJ at Utrecht, Holland's Vlanen venue. Jaydee's beautiful trance cut 'Plastic Dreams' crossed over massively on the Belgian **R&S** label in 1993, with its distinctive Hammond B3 organ signature. It was his first release; previously he had been three times winner of the Dutch arm-wrestling championship, and a member of the national baseball team. Since the early 80s he had worked on Dutch radio, proffering a critically lauded selection of house music. He turned to recording when his radio show was axed. After 'Plastic Dreams', the first release on the reactivated UK arm of R&S, he also released the 'Acceleration By Trance' 12-inch as Graylock on **Logic**'s Save The Vinyl imprint. Far from usual rave convention, this contained the ominous 'Everybody Feel Free' warning on the flip-side. This boasted a spoken word narrative on the dangers of E, which also plotted Alders' semi-autobiographical downfall through the drug. A second Graylock release, 'The Movement', emerged on Belgium's Mental Radio Records, before he returned as Jaydee for 'The Hunter' for Dutch label Clubstitute.

Jaye, Jerry

b. Gerald Jaye Hatley, 19 October 1937, Manila, Arkansas, USA. A singer/guitarist whose material sometimes leaned more towards rock than traditional country, Jaye made his first recordings for his own label in 1966, before gaining an album release on **Hi Records** the following year. In 1975, recording for **Columbia**, Jaye had a minor hit with his version of **Tommy Edwards**' 1958 pop number 1, 'It's All In The Game'. The following year, he returned to the Hi label and registered two minor hits, 'Honky Tonk Women Love Red Neck Men', being the highest placing at number 32. Since then he has been conspicuous by his absence from the country charts.

● ALBUMS: *My Girl Josephine* (Hi 1967)★★, *Honky Tonk Women Love Red Neck Men* (Hi 1976)★★★, *My Girl Josephine* UK release (Demon 1992)★★.

Jayhawks (R&B)

The R&B novelty song 'Stranded In The Jungle' was a hit in 1956 for two US groups. The **Cadets**' version remains the best-known (although the **New York Dolls**' 70s cover version is also highly regarded by some), but the Jayhawks actually beat them to the US charts by one week. The doo-wop quartet consisted of lead Jimmy Johnson, baritone Dave Govan, tenor Carl Fisher and bass Carver Bunkum. They formed while in high school in Los Angeles, USA, in the early 50s.

'Stranded In The Jungle' was co-written by Johnson and friend Ernest Smith. It reached number 18 while the Cadets' cover version landed three positions higher. Subsequent records by the group failed and by 1960, with a few personnel changes, they had metamorphosed into the **Vibrations**, who had success with the dance hit 'The Watusi' (1961) and 'My Girl Sloopy' (1964), the latter adapted by the **McCoys** as 'Hang On Sloopy'. The Vibrations also moonlighted in 1961 as the **Marathons**, another one-hit-wonder with the novelty tune 'Peanut Butter'.

Jayhawks (rock)

Def American Records producer George Drakoulias discovered the country/rock/R&B-influenced Jayhawks after they had made two low-key records. Legend has it that he phoned Dave Ayers of Twin/Tone Records and overheard a collection of the band's demos, and signed them up. The band, who come from Minneapolis, Minnesota, USA, boasted a core line-up of Mark Olson (vocals/guitar) and Gary Louris (vocals/guitar), joined by Ken Callahan (bass), and subsequently Karen Grotberg (keyboards) and Marc Perlman, who replaced Callahan. Together since 1985, until their induction to **Rick Rubin**'s eclectic label they had only sold approximately 10,000 records. Songs such as 'Waiting For The Sun' saw them compared to the **Black Crowes** (another Drakoulias discovery), combining rugged country imagery with harsh, rough hewn bar blues. Their second album, *The Blue Earth*, threw up another name; that of **Neil Young**. For their own part they cited the **Flying Burrito Brothers** and Charlie and Ira Louvin of the **Louvin Brothers** as their greatest influences. They also record widely as session musicians, including work for acts such as **Soul Asylum**, **Counting Crows** and **Maria McKee**. The group's rapid turnover of drummers continued on *Tomorrow The Green Grass*, with Don Heffington on hand in the studio and Tim O'Regan available for touring duties. Songs on this set included 'Miss Williams' Guitar', a tribute to Mark Olson's wife, **Victoria Williams**, and the exquisite single, 'Blue'. It saw them still playing simple, direct music, a traditional but never stultifying sound. Olson left the band in 1996 and the main songwriting was completed by Louris. *Sound of Lies* was a deep and often sad album with many of the songs relating to the break up of Louris' marriage. Similarities between **Richard Thompson**'s 'Calvary Cross' and 'Stick In The Mud' were purely coincidental, while 'Big Star' was one of their best songs in years.

● ALBUMS: *The Jayhawks* (Bunkhouse 1986)★★★, *The Blue Earth* (Twin/Tone 1989)★★★, *Hollywood Town Hall* (Def American 1992)★★★, *Tomorrow The Green Grass* (American 1995)★★★★, *Sound Of Lies* (American 1997)★★★★.

Jaynetts

Songwriter Zelma 'Zell' Sanders formed this New York-based act around her daughter, Johnnie Louise Richardson, previously half of hit duo **Johnnie And Joe**. Ethel Davis, Mary Sue Wells, Yvonne Bushnell and Ada Ray completed the line-up featured on 'Sally, Go Round The Roses', the quintet's debut single and sole US chart entry. This haunting performance reached number 2 in 1963, and has since become an early classic of the 'girl group' genre, but the Jaynetts' progress was undermined when Richardson left following its release. Ensuing singles, including 'Keep An Eye On Her' and 'Johnny Don't Cry', were not successful, and the group ceased recording in 1965. Johnnie Louise died in 1988.

● ALBUMS: *Sally, Go 'Round The Roses* (Tuff 1963)★★.

Jazz At The Philharmonic

In 1944 the tyro jazz impresario **Norman Granz** began a series of jazz concerts at the Philharmonic Auditorium in Los Angeles, USA. Reputedly, the name by which these concerts became known, JATP, arose from an abbreviation of the foregoing. The form, style and content of the concerts caught the jazz public's imagination and they continued through the rest of the decade and into the 50s, gradually becoming bigger and more spectacular musical packages. Fortunately, Granz had the foresight and acumen to record all his concerts. The release, on the new long-playing records, of these extended jam session performances proved commercially profitable and helped to establish Granz as a leading record producer. From 1957 onwards JATP tours were confined to Europe and in 1967, after a farewell tour of the USA, the concept was largely abandoned, although Granz continued to tour artists under the generic banner. Indeed, in some measure it might be claimed that his concept is mirrored in many latterday festival packages. Although often criticized for their showier aspects, JATP concerts included a wealth of fine playing by a succession of outstanding mainstream and bebop performers. Among the musicians who appeared with JATP over the years have been trumpeters **Joe Guy**, **Howard McGhee**, **Buck Clayton**, **Charlie Shavers**, **Dizzy Gillespie** and **Roy Eldridge**, trombonists **J.J. Johnson**, **Bill Harris** and Tommy Turk, saxophonists **Charlie Parker**, **Willie Smith**, **Benny Carter**, **Lester Young**, **Coleman Hawkins**, **Illinois Jacquet**, **Flip Phillips** and **Stan Getz**, pianists **Oscar Peterson**, **Nat 'King' Cole**, **Hank Jones** and Kenny Kersey, and drummers **Gene Krupa**, **Buddy Rich**, **J.C. Heard**, **Jo Jones** and **Louie Bellson**. Granz also included the entire **Count Basie** and **Duke Ellington** orchestras in some of his more ambitious packages, and **Ella Fitzgerald** too was a mainstay for many years.

● ALBUMS: *JATP* (1944)★★, *JATP: Vols 1 & 3* (1944-46)★★, *JATP: Vols 2 & 6/JATP: Bird And Pres* (1946)★★★★, *JATP: Vol. 14* (1946)★★★, *JATP: Vols 4 & 5* (1946)★★★, *JATP: Vol. 7* (1946)★★★, *JATP: Vol. 8* (1947)★★★, *JATP: Vols 9 & 10* (1947)★★★, *JATP: Vols 12 & 13* (1949)★★, *JATP: Vol. 15* (1953)★★★, *JATP: Live At The Nichigeki Theatre, Tokyo* (1953)★★★, *JATP: Hartford, Connecticut* (1954)★★, *JATP: The Exciting Battle, Stockholm '55* (1955)★★★, *JATP All Stars At The Opera House, Chicago*

(1957)★★★, *JATP: In London 1969* (1969)★★★, *JATP: At The Montreux Festival* (1975)★★★★.

Jazz Butcher

From Northampton and formed in 1982, Jazz Butcher served as a vehicle for the idiosyncratic, melodic song-writing talents of Pat Fish (b. Patrick Huntrods; guitar, vocals), otherwise known as the Jazz Butcher. Although early group line-ups were erratic - including Rolo McGinty and Alice Thompson (both later to emerge in the **Woodentops**), and ex-**Bauhaus** bassist David J. - the one constant member during most of the early years was lead guitarist Max Eider, whose light jazz/blues feel gave an eloquence to even the most heavy-handed of tunes. In terms of style, there was a large nod in the direction of **Lou Reed** and **Jonathan Richman**, while the songs' subject matter dealt with the diverse traumas of everyday life, taking in the joys and woes of small-town living ('Living In A Village'), drink ('Soul Happy Hour'), fear and paranoia ('Death Dentist'), love ('Only A Rumour'/'Angels'), the virtues of public transport ('Groovin' In The Bus Lane'), film noir and Vladimir Ilyich Lenin. The classic Jazz Butcher line-up, including Max Eider, Felix Ray (bass) and 'Mr' O.P. Jones (drums), underwent a major upheaval in 1987 with the departure of Eider, resulting in the unit's disintegration. By the time of *Fishcotheque*, Fish was working virtually alone, but for a new partner in guitarist Kizzy O'Callaghan. The Jazz Butcher (Conspiracy) model of the band was rebuilt to comprise Fish, O'Callaghan, Laurence O'Keefe (bass), Paul Mulreany (drums) and Alex Green (saxophone), and saw the group undergoing a change of label, moving from Glass to **Creation Records**. Subsequent albums saw an increasing use of cut-up film/television dialogue, and continued to garner encouraging reviews. *Illuminated* included the anti-Conservative government tract 'Sixteen Years'. It also saw some critics scoff at the way in which Creation's perseverance with the Jazz Butcher mirrored the British public's unwillingness to change administration. While the Jazz Butcher found a large audience in Europe, and America, substantial success in his homeland continued to elude him, and he decided to play his farewell concerts at the end of 1995. He subsequently drummeds with the Stranger Tractors.

● ALBUMS: *The Jazz Butcher In Bath Of Bacon* (Glass 1982)★★★, *A Scandal In Bohemia* (Glass 1984)★★★, *Sex And Travel* (Glass 1985)★★★, as Jazz Butcher And His Sikkorskis From Hell - *Hamburg - A Live Album* (Rebel 1985)★★★, as Jazz Butcher Conspiracy *Distressed Gentlefolk* (Glass 1986)★★★, *Fishcotheque* (Creation 1988)★★★, *Big Planet, Scarey Planet* (Genius 1989)★★★, *Cult Of The Basement* (Rough Trade 1990)★★★, *Condition Blue* (Creation 1991)★★★, *Western Family (Live)* (Creation 1993)★★★, *Waiting For The Love Bus* (Creation 1993)★★★, *Illuminated* (Creation 1995)★★★.

Solo: Max Eider *The Best Kisser In The World* (Big Time 1987)★★★.

● COMPILATIONS: *The Gift Of Music* (Glass 1984)★★★, *Bloody Nonsense* (Big Time 1986)★★★, *Big Questions - The Gift Of Music Vol 2* (Glass 1987)★★★, *Edward's Closet* (Creation 1991)★★★, *Draining The Glass 1982-86* (Nectar 1997)★★★.

Jazz Composer's Orchestra Association

The Jazz Composer's Orchestra grew out of the Jazz Composer's Guild, a co-operative formed in 1964 by **Cecil Taylor**, **Bill Dixon**, **Archie Shepp**, **Roswell Rudd**, **John Tchicai**, **Sun Ra**, **Paul Bley**, **Carla Bley**, **Michael Mantler** and Burton Greene, with the intention of finding new performance outlets for the New Jazz. In practice, Guild members spent as much time arguing with each other as with the powers that controlled the concert world and the airwaves, and the co-operative collapsed within a year - but not before Mantler and Carla Bley had initiated the Jazz Composer's Guild Orchestra. In 1966, Mantler, taking the idea further, established the Jazz Composer's Orchestra Association (JCOA) as a non-profit, tax-exempt organization to support an orchestra committed to New Jazz, release the orchestra's music on its own label, and operate the New Music Distribution Service, an alternative distribution network for independent labels. In the first decade JCOA gave many concerts and workshops, and released fine albums by Mantler, Bley, **Don Cherry**, Rudd, Clifford Thornton, **Grachan Moncur III**, and **Leroy Jenkins**, but funding was always problematic. By the late 70s, the orchestra folded. The New Music Distribution Service lasted until the early 90s.

Jazz Dance

In 1954 an excellent idea took director Roger Tilton and a film crew into New York City's Central Plaza Dance Hall. Without gimmickry, they filmed the dancers and the end result is a marvellous feeling for the occasion. The band on the stand features **Jimmy Archey**, **George 'Pops' Foster**, **Jimmy McPartland**, **Willie 'The Lion' Smith**, **Pee Wee Russell** and **George Wettling**.

Jazz Festivals

In its early years, jazz music was tightly bound to such social activities as drinking, dancing and 'goodtiming' of all kinds. Most jazz was heard in small, intimate clubs, and the larger venues were usually dance halls which still provided a kind of intimacy, even if it took a slightly different form. By the mid-50s, however, the mass audience for jazz frequently had to settle for somewhat strait-laced concert-hall performances. When they became a major feature of the jazz life, festivals sometimes managed to combine large-scale performances with a kind of intimacy, this became one of their great strengths. The intimacy came from the free and easy manner in which artists and customers might meet between sets at outdoor venues. This, together with the fact that they offer an unrivalled opportunity for many people to see and hear more jazz in a few tightly-packed days than they usually hear in the rest of the year, gave the festival scene an unrivalled attractiveness. Outdoor concerts had been given in the USA in the late 30s, notably at Randall's Island, New York City, but the palm for the first real festival goes to Australia and the 1946 Australian Jazz Convention which was founded by Harry Stein and band leader **Graeme Bell**. It was, however, the first Nice Jazz Festival, held in 1948 at which **Louis Armstrong** was the main attraction, that spread the word that a festival could work both artistically and financially. The following year, the French tried their hand again, this time with the Festival International de Jazz in Paris, featuring such strikingly different musical styles as those of **Sidney Bechet**, soon to make France his home, and **Charlie Parker** and **Miles Davis**. During the early 50s the notion that jazz festivals were a sound proposition prompted a string of such events and by the early 90s jazz festivals were the dominating force in live jazz around the world.

For all their worldwide popularity, the majority of festivals are held in the USA where the early starters included two which quickly established themselves amongst the most prestigious events on the jazz calendar: the Newport Jazz Festival and the **Monterey Jazz Festival**. Among the estimated 1,000 jazz festivals held annually around the word in the 90s are some which concentrate upon certain clearly-defined stylistic or thematic areas of jazz. For example, Sacramento, California holds an annual Dixieland Jubilee, the **Bix Beiderbecke** memorial festival takes place in his hometown of Davenport, Iowa. Jazz women, so often lightly regarded in jazz circles except as singers, were given their due at the Women's Jazz Festival, in Kansas City, Missouri, between 1978 and 1985. One of the most important impresarios in jazz, **George Wein**, has a hand in numerous festivals including those held at Saratoga Springs, New York; Jacksonville, Florida; Boston, Massachusetts, among many other venues throughout the USA and elsewhere around the world of jazz. Festivals can range from intimate affairs in small towns or quiet rural areas to major events in cities. Among the former are the annual Colorado Jazz Party held in Denver by Dick Gibson, and every April, in Oregon, high on cliffs overlooking the Pacific Ocean, jazz musicians and fans gather at the Inn at Otter Crest for a relaxed weekend during which audience and performers mingle on easy and equal terms. Important city festivals include that held in New Orleans. The annual Heritage festival, begun in the early 60s, brings in a flood of visitors eager to sample a wide range of music, from old-time marching bands to hard bop groups. Among UK festivals is another excellent city-based event, Peter Boizot's Soho Jazz Festival, held in London for 10 days at the end of September. Another increasingly important British festival, which 'takes over' a town as its venue, is that held at Brecon in Wales.

Among other important events around the world is the **Montreux International Jazz Festival**, the Aurex Jazz Festival in Japan and the International Jazz Festival of Japan, held over 15 days in February in eight cities. Every July since 1976 the North Sea Festival, at The Hague in The Netherlands, has offered a package to daunt even the most ardent fan. Ten stages are in simultaneous use for very nearly 24 hours on each of its three days, extended to four in 1991. In Eire, for four days every October, there is the Cork Jazz Festival. Begun in the late 70s, and sponsored by Guinness since 1982, this is rapidly rising in the estimation of audiences and performers, offering as it does an atmosphere befitting a nation which prides itself on greeting its visitors with a thousand welcomes. Other important, popular and musically excellent festivals include the JVC/Capital Radio Jazz Parade in London, Montauban in France and Kongsberg in Norway which began in the mid-60s. There are jazz festivals in Italy, Spain, Gemany, Poland and several other countries which formed what was once the eastern bloc. Then there are the floating festivals, jazz cruises of which the S.S. *Norway*, sailing out of Miami and Caribbean bound on a seven-day jaunt, is an outstanding example. The word 'festival' is commonly defined as 'a musical entertainment on a large scale, usually periodical', a definition which prompts the thought that not all organizers of jazz events have read their dictionaries lately. Some so-called festivals are little more than a series of concerts strung together but the jazz festival looks set to remain the means by which live jazz will continue to reach the biggest audiences. Importantly, many festivals are recorded and even filmed and, perhaps most significant of all, they have become the principal means by which many jazz fans have a chance to see and hear their idols - and, perhaps, discover new ones.

Jazz Giant - Benny Carter

One of a very small number of jazz musicians to have enjoyed successful careers playing both trumpet and saxophone, Benny Carter was already firmly established as an important swing name when, in 1958, he recorded this superb small-group album. Accompanied by tenor saxophone legend Ben Webster, Stan Kenton-trombonist Frank Rosolino, pianists André Previn and Jimmie Rowles, swinging west coast guitarist Barney Kessel, bassist Leroy Vinnegar and top west coast drummer Shelly Manne, Carter proves he was as great a jazz improviser as big band composer and arranger, on a selection of standards and two original compositions.

● Tracks: *Old Fashioned Love; I'm Coming Virginia; A Walkin' Thing; Blue Lou; Ain't She Sweet; How Can You Lose; Blues My Naughty Sweetie Gives To Me.*
● First released 1958
● UK peak chart position: did not chart
● USA peak chart position: did not chart

Jazz In Exile

American jazz musicians in Europe have been the cynosure of fascinated interest not only by audiences but also by jazz historians. Magazine articles abound and there have been several good books on the subject. There have also been a number of films but none as good or effective as this exceptional documentary directed by Chuck France released in 1978. There are many interviews with musicians such as **Gary Burton**, **Richard Davis**, **Dexter Gordon**, **Freddie Hubbard**, **Ben Sidran**, **McCoy Tyner** and **Phil Woods**. There is some fine music to be heard, notably from Davis and Woods.

Jazz In Silhouette - Sun Ra

This 1957 Sun Ra album is perhaps surprisingly orthodox for what we have come to expect of an Arkestra outing. Speaking a language grounded in bop, a superb 10-piece of Sun Ra's finest players work through some inspired tunes and arrangements with an unusual flair and consistency – baritone saxophonist Pat Patrick and tenor genius John Gilmore soloing with particular strength. Breaking the mould, and in many ways a glimpse of what was to come, 'Ancient Aiethopia' is a mesmerizing percussion-based composition with chanting, displaying an unusual freedom and featuring superbly compelling solo contributions by trumpeter Hobart Dotson and pianist Ra himself.

● Tracks: *Enlightenment; Saturn; Velvet; Ancient Aiethopia; Hours After; Horoscope; Images; Blues At Midnight.*
● First released 1959
● UK peak chart position: did not chart
● USA peak chart position: did not chart

Jazz Is Our Religion

Directed by John Jeremy, this excellent USA documentary released in 1972 features the idiosyncratic photography of Valerie Wilmer. There are numerous audio interviews with **Art Blakey**, **Bill Evans**, **Jimmy Garrison**, **Dizzy Gillespie**, **Johnny Griffin**, **Jo Jones**, **Blue Mitchell**, **Sunny Murray** and **Dewey Redman**, amongst many. Music by Griffin, **Dizzy Reece**, **Jon Hendricks**, **Lol Coxhill** and the **Clarke-Boland Big Band** and others fills the soundtrack. Altogether a satisfactory mixture that goes a long way to confirming the premise of the film's title and creating an understanding of its meaning.

Jazz Jamaica

Jazz Jamaica was the brainchild of **Gary Crosby**, who in 1991, inspired by the rhythms of traditional Jamaican music and the largely improvisational nature of jazz, turned his concept into a reality. He enrolled a number of talented young jazz musicians from the jazz and reggae circuits, including himself on double bass, Clifton 'Bigga' Morrison (keyboards), Alan Weekes (guitar), Kenrick Rowe (drums), Tony Uter (percussion) and a horn section featuring the legendary **Rico Rodriguez** (trombone), Eddie 'Tan Tan' Thornton (trumpet), and Michael 'Bammi' Rose (alto saxophone, flute). The group toured extensively, playing worldwide festivals from 1993 to the present day. In 1993 the Roots and Reminiscence Tour included performances

from Crosby's uncle, **Ernest Ranglin**, and Majorie Whylie, who played the piano, provided vocals and followed in the tradition of an African griot as the storyteller. Also featured on the tour was Lord Tanamo who performed in his own distinctive style. Following the tour the band set up workshops specifically for elderly Caribbean expatriates, although these were, in fact, attended by a cosmopolitan audience encompassing all ages and races. In 1994 the band played the St. Lucia Jazz Festival, where they proved so successful that the great **George Benson** had to wait in the wings until the band played an encore. The band also released *Skaravan*, initially through the Japanese Quattro label. Tracks included **ska** versions of 'Peanut Vendor', **Charlie Parker**'s 'Barbados', **Don Drummond**'s 'Don Cosmic' and 'Confucius', the **Skatalites**' 'Green Island' and Rodriguez's 'Africa'. By the autumn of 1994 the group secured a Japanese-based major label contract. The release of *The Jamaican Beat - Blue Note Blue Beat Volume One* found the musicians playing alongside **Courtney Pine**, Brian Edwards, **Cleveland Watkiss** and Julie Dexter. The album leant heavily towards jazz while remaining faithful to the initial concept of a ska fusion. In 1995, sponsored by the British Council, the group toured Senegal and Nigeria, featuring a performance at the British Embassy in Senegal, and a live jamming session with the Nigerian ensemble Fran And Tunde Kuboye And The Extended Family Band, who supported Jazz Jamaica on their UK tour in October. As well as the constant touring, the band's recording sessions included Dennis Rollins, Denys Baptiste, Tony Kofi, Byron Wallen, Kevin Robinson, and the sublime vocals of **lovers rock** singer **Carroll Thompson**. Despite their increasing touring schedule, the band has, ironically, never actually played together in Jamaica. In addition to his Jazz Jamaica commitments, Crosby also leads a jazz ensemble known as Gary Crosby's Nu Troop. In 1997 the group contributed a competent skazz version of 'Wrapped Around Your Finger' to the **Police** tribute album.

● ALBUMS: *Skaravan* (Skazz/Rykodisc 1994)★★★, *The Jamaican Beat - Blue Note Blue Beat Volume One* (Toshiba EMI 1994)★★★★, *The Jamaican Beat - Blue Note Blue Beat Volume Two* (Toshiba EMI 1995)★★★.

Jazz Messengers

In 1947 **Art Blakey** formed a short-lived big band which he named the 17 Messengers. He also recorded with a smaller group which he called the Jazz Messengers. In 1954 Blakey was a member of a co-operative band with **Kenny Dorham, Hank Mobley, Doug Watkins** and **Horace Silver**. This band recorded in 1955 as the Jazz Messengers with Silver as nominal leader. With minor personnel changes the group remained together until 1956. Subsequently, Blakey formed his own band, calling it the Jazz Messengers, a name he retained for all his bands until his death in 1990.

Jazz On A Summer's Day

From its opening moments, depicting reflected sail-boats while **Jimmy Giuffre**'s 'The Train And The River' bubbles on the soundtrack, this film sets out to create an unforgettable record of the 1958 **Newport Jazz Festival**. Directed by Bert Stern in 1960, repeated viewing might make some of the 60s photo-gimmickry a little trying and there are certainly too many audience cutaways during performances, but, overall, the concept is very well-realized. And the music is magnificent. Amongst the assembled giants are **Louis Armstrong**, **Bob Brookmeyer**, **Ben Webster**, **Thelonious Monk**, **Roy Haynes**, **Rex Stewart**, **Sonny Stitt**, **Dinah Washington** singing superbly and also clowning very musically on vibes with **Terry Gibbs**, **Max Roach**, **Gerry Mulligan**, **Art Farmer**, **Chico Hamilton** seen in rehearsal, **Eric Dolphy**, **George Shearing**, **Jack Teagarden**, **Buck Clayton** and **Jo Jones**. **Mahalia Jackson** brings the show to a sacred finale but for most people the outstanding moment is the considerably less-sacred sight of **Anita O'Day**, in high heels, cartwheel hat, gloves, and tight dress, struggling up onto the stage where she memorably recomposes 'Sweet Georgia Brown' and 'Tea For Two' in her own image. The video of this film should be on every jazz fan's shelf.

Jazz Passengers

Formed as an alternative to the more stoic traditions of jazz, this New York ensemble took influence instead from the music's renegades, be they **Thelonious Monk**, **Sun Ra** or **Charlie Mingus**. Evolving in 1987 out of the Knitting Factory in Lower Manhattan, a popular art scene, the group specialised in a free-flowing form of bop-inspired jazz. However, their range also took in Latin dance, jazz rap and film dialogue. The principals behind the Jazz Passengers were Roy Nathanson and Curtis Fowlkes, who first met when working in the pit band for the Big Apple Circus. They subsequently moved to **John Lurie**'s Lounge Lizards, with the intention of recording a duo album together. However, along the way they picked up a whole host of additional musicians who would make up the Jazz Passengers, in particular E.J. Rodriguez (percussion), Brad Jones (bass; also an accompanist to **Elvin Jones** and **Muhal Richard Abrams**), Bill Ware (vibraphone; has also worked with **Steely Dan**) and Marc Ribot (guitar; also recorded with **Tom Waits** and **Elvis Costello**). After releasing some five albums on small and obscure labels, including *Implement Yourself* using a grant from the Lila Wallace/Reader's Digest Fund, the group made its major label debut in 1994 with *Jazz Passengers In Love*, produced by Hal Willner. A collection of 12 originals, the guest vocalists featured included **Jimmy Scott**, **Debbie Harry**, **Mavis Staples**, **Freedy Johnston** and **Jeff Buckley**. Other personnel involved were lyricist **Arto Lindsay**, singer **Bob Dorough**, playwright Ray Dobbins and David Cale, a performance artist. They collaborated with 70s new wave icon **Deborah Harry** in 1997 for *Individually Twisted* which featured a new version of her **Blondie** hit 'The Tide Is high'.

● ALBUMS: *Broken Night/Red Light* (Crépescule 1987)★★★, *Deranged And Decomposed* (Crépescule 1988)★★★★, *Implement Yourself* (New World 1990)★★★, *Live At The Knitting Factory* (Knitting Factory 1991)★★, *Plain Old Joe* (Knitting Factory 1993)★★★, *Jazz Passengers In Love* (High Street 1994)★★, with Deborah Harry *Individually Twisted* (32 Records 1997)★★.

Jazz Samba - Stan Getz

The album that launched Jobim's now classic 'Desafinado', *Jazz Samba* was released in 1962, in the early days of America's bossa nova craze and before the music lost its charm to cliché. Joined by fellow Latin jazz pioneer Charlie Byrd on classical guitar, and a discreet bass and drums team, tenor saxophonist Getz makes light and elegant music out of a collection of catchy bossas and sambas. His virtuosity, bluesy drive and smooth, soft tone make the music cook like bossa jazz rarely has since. There are still enough surprises to make this record more than just a period piece, and it stands as a fine example of Getz's lyrical genius.

● Tracks: *Desafinado; Samba Dees Days; O Pato; Samba Triste; Samba De Uma Nota So; E Luxo So; Baia.*

● First released 1962

● UK peak chart position: 15

● USA peak chart position: 1

Jazz Singer, The

Al Jolson, one of the world's all-time great entertainers, spoke a few words and sang a few songs in this, the first feature length talking picture which was released by Warner Brothers in 1927, and the screen musical was born. Alfred A. Cohen's screenplay was adapted from the short story, *The Day Of Atonement*, by Samson Raphaelson, which had been produced as a play on Broadway in 1925. It told of Jakie Rabinowitz (Jolson), a cantor's son who breaks his parents' hearts when he gives up his life in the synagogue for a career as a popular singer. Of course it was all pure schmaltz, and cinema audiences wept when, after his father has died, he returns to his beloved mother and tries to explain to her his love of music and his need to perform. Jolson, who appeared in blackface for the theatre sequences, was sensational, especially on songs which he had previously introduced in various stage productions such as 'My Mammy' and 'Toot Toot Tootsie'. The rest of the numbers included 'Dirty Hands, Dirty Face', 'Blue Skies', 'Mother Of Mine, I Still Have You', 'My Gal Sal', and the traditional Jewish 'Yahrzeit'. Also in the cast were Warner Oland, May McAvoy, Otto Lederer, Eugenie Besserer, Bobby Gordon, and Myrna Loy. The sound, which was only heard on the musical sequences and some short pieces of dialogue -the rest of the film was silent - was recorded on the Vitaphone sound-on-disc system, and the film was directed by Alan Crosland and produced by Darryl F. Zanuck.

The exciting and extremely complicated changeover

from silents to talkies was brilliantly spoofed in one of the world's favourite musicals, **Singin' In The Rain**, which was made in 1952. A year later, Warner released a remake of *The Jazz Singer* starring Danny Thomas, **Peggy Lee**, and Mildred Dunnock. This time the sentimental screenplay dealt with the return of US soldier from the Korean war. The score consisted of a bunch of well-tried musical standards. A third version, with **Neil Diamond** as Jess Rabinovitch and Laurence Olivier as his father, was made in 1980. The story remained fairly true to the 1927 original, and the cast included Lucie Arnaz, Catlin Adams, and **Paul Nicholas** as a particularly unpleasant recording artist. Diamond took three of the film's songs, 'America', 'Love On The Rocks', and 'Hello Again', all co-written by him, into the US Top 10.

Jazz Warriors

Formed in London in the mid-80s, largely through the efforts of **Courtney Pine** and Gail Thompson, the Jazz Warriors drew musicians from the growing group of young black musicians who were active in the UK during the 80s. Initially the band was around 20 pieces and made extensive use of Afro-Caribbean percussive patterns overlaid with powerhouse brass. Many of the band's early soloists demonstrated their enthusiasm for **John Coltrane**, but in later years a wider range of influences was evident. The freedom from stylization that the Warriors displayed in their approach to big band music allowed the introduction of disparate musical forms, and proved a heady mixture which attracted many fans from the fringes of jazz. This freedom also extended into the band's public performances, which were sometimes undisciplined and disorganized. At their best, however, and with excellent soloists such as Pine, **Phillip Bent**, Orphy Robinson and singer **Cleveland Watkiss**, the Warriors offered an interesting concept of how big band music might evolve. In the late 80s, the Warriors worked with guest American leaders **Henry Threadgill** and **Craig Harris**, while another, home-grown, project was a suite in tribute to **Joe Harriott**. By the early 90s the lack of discipline and commitment displayed by some of its members allowed the band to drift and led to the defection of some elder statesmen, such as **Harry Beckett**. Sad though this was, several of the individual members retained a measure of their initial popularity and embarked upon successful solo careers.

● ALBUMS: *Out Of Many, One People* (Antilles 1987)★★★.

Jazz writing

Newspaper and magazine articles apart, and most of them ill-informed and derogatory, very little was written about jazz during the music's formative years. In the late 30s and early 40s, however, a more informed coterie of writers emerged, some of whom launched what was to become an ongoing list of formal histories. Amongst the earlier works were *Aux Frontières Du Jazz* (1932) and *Jazz From The Congo To The Metropolitan*

(1946) (alt. title: *Jazz: From Congo To Swing*) by Robert Goffin, *American Jazz Music* (1939) by Wilder Hobson, *Shining Trumpets: A History Of Jazz* (1946) by Rudi Blesh, *Jazz: A People's Music* (1948) by Sidney Finkelstein and *Introduction À La Musique De Jazz* (1948) and *Jazz: Its Evolution And Essence* (1956) by André Hodeir. Several of these histories were the work of Europeans, detached by time, distance and culture from their subject matter. For all such distancing, some of these early books provided an interesting, frequently perceptive and often undeniably worthy basis for an understanding of the music's origins. Unfortunately, by the 40s and 50s, when these books were written, many of the music's pioneers and early innovators were dead often leaving behind only sketchy evidence of their roles in jazz. Through this and other factors created by the passage of time misconceptions crept in to some of these histories and were given an aura of authenticity. In part, these frequently understandable errors resulted from the historians concerned having to form opinions upon the evidence of recorded jazz. Although this is a legitimate means of research, it can and did lead to misjudgements on such important matters as chains of influence. Later jazz historians were able to bring into their deliberations clearer views of the chronology of the music's development together with an understanding of the social context and the significance of jazz in the black experience and of black culture in American society. Nevertheless, only a small percentage of jazz writers and historians are of African-American origin and to some extent certain important aspects of jazz as a cultural phenomenon remain less than fully explored to this day. Among later jazz histories are James Lincoln Collier's *The Making Of Jazz: A Comprehensive History* (1978), John Chilton's *Jazz* (1979) and Joachim Berendt's *The Jazz Book: From Ragtime To Fusion And Beyond* (1982). Gunther Schuller's *Early Jazz: Its Roots And Musical Development* (1968) and *The Swing Era: The Development Of Jazz 1930-1945* (1989), two volumes which form part of a projected trilogy, already displays the qualities necessary to make this, on its completion, the most thorough and best-researched history of jazz.

Many other histories of jazz exist, of course, some dealing with the subject as a whole, others dealing in close detail with specific areas or periods or concise themes. Amongst these latter volumes are *Jazz Style In Kansas City And The Southwest* (1971) by Ross Russell, *Big Band Jazz* (1974) by Albert McCarthy, *Jazz: A History Of The New York Scene* (1981) by Samuel B. Charters and Leonard Kunstadt, *Swing To Bop: An Oral History* (1985) by Ira Gitler, *The Jazz Cataclysm* (1967) by Barry McRae, *The Freedom Principle: Jazz After 1958* (1985) by John Litweiler and *American Women In Jazz: 1900 To The Present* (1982) by Sally Placksin.

An important source of information on jazz lies in the many biographies and autobiographies of musicians. In some cases, these works need to be viewed with caution. Some biographers approach their subjects in awe, treating them almost as idols and taking for granted utterances that need an element of discernment. Some musicians, writing of their own lives - whether directly or through a 'ghost' - also require to be considered with a cautiously critical eye. This is not to suggest that any musician deliberately sets out to deceive but there are those who choose not to let accuracy hinder their love for a good story. Important artists who have attracted biographers include Louis Armstrong: *Louis: The Louis Armstrong Story 1900-1971* (1971) by **John Chilton** and Max Jones, the contentious *Louis Armstrong: An American Genius* (1983) by James Lincoln Collier, and Gary Giddins's *Satchmo* (1988). Books on **Duke Ellington** include *Duke* (1977) by Derek Jewell and *Duke Ellington* (1987), another contentious volume by James Lincoln Collier. Charlie Parker's life was explored by Robert Reisner in *Bird: The Legend Of Charlie Parker* (1962), Ross Russell in *Bird Lives!: The High Life And Hard Times Of Charlie 'Yardbird' Parker* (1973), and Gary Giddins in *Celebrating Bird: The Triumph Of Charlie Parker* (1986). John Chilton's books include several on noted jazz artists including *Billie's Blues: A Survey Of Billie Holiday's Career 1933-1959* (1975), *Sidney Bechet: The Wizard Of Jazz* (1987), and *Song Of The Hawk: The Life And Recordings Of Coleman Hawkins* (1990). Ian Carr is the author of *Miles Davis: A Critical Biography* (1982), Dave Gelly and Lewis Porter have both written books entitled *Lester Young* (respectively in 1984 and '85), and the story of Bessie Smith was told by Chris Albertson in *Bessie* (1972).

Musicians' autobiographies which also project a vivid picture of the jazz life include *A Life In Jazz* (1986) by Danny Barker, *Treat It Gentle* (1960) by Sidney Bechet, *Buck Clayton's Jazz World* (1986), *We Called It Music* (1948) by Eddie Condon, *Dizzy, To Be Or Not To Bop: The Autobiography Of Dizzy Gillespie* (1979), *Beneath The Underdog* (1971) by Charles Mingus and *Straight Life: The Story Of Art Pepper* (1979). Books by lesser musicians abound and some of these can often provide interesting reading and cast light on overlooked areas of jazz. Mezz Mezzrow's *Really The Blues* (1946) is an example of the workings of a particularly extravagant if highly entertaining imagination.

A very valuable source of information are interviews, sometimes conducted for magazines or radio shows, many of which have found their way into book form. Noted interviewers include Max Jones and Whitney Balliett. Both have an enviable ability to put their subjects at ease and to draw from them revealing and insightful commentaries upon their lives and music. For all such similarities, Jones and Balliett differ in their prose style, Jones opting for a spare yet discerning approach, Balliett for a sometimes lavish yet usually appropriate approach which includes a remarkable ability to convey through words striking visual and aural images. Jones's interviews have been collected in book form as *Talking Jazz* (1987) while Balliett's appear in several volumes including *The Sound Of Surprise*

(1959), *Dinosaurs In The Morning* (1962), *Such Sweet Thunder* (1966), *Improvising: Sixteen Jazz Musicians And Their Art* (1977) and *Jelly Roll, Jabbo And Fats* (1983). Other important volumes of interviews are *Hear Me Talkin' To Ya: The Story Of Jazz By The Men Who Made It* (1955) edited by Nat Shapiro and Nat Hentoff and *Notes And Tones* (1983) by Arthur Taylor.

Books that mingle interviews with essays on a wide range of topics and artists include Gary Giddins's *Riding On A Blue Note: Jazz And American Pop* (1981) and *Rhythm-a-ning: Jazz Tradition And Innovation In The '80s* (1985), Stanley Dance's *The World Of Duke Ellington* (1970), *The World Of Earl Hines* (1977) and *The World Of Count Basie* (1980), *Jam Session: An Anthology Of Jazz* (1958) edited by Ralph Gleason, *Jazzmen* (1958) edited by Frederic Ramsey Jnr. and Charles Edward Smith, *A Handbook Of Jazz* by Barry Ulanov, *Jazz* (1977) edited by Nat Hentoff and Albert McCarthy, and *The Art Of Jazz: Ragtime To Bebop* (1981) by Martin Williams.

Among many others who have written on jazz with wit, insight, a perceptive critical eye and ear, and occasionally with a touch of contentiousness, are Francis Davis, Richard Hadlock, Philip Larkin, Gene Lees, Humphrey Lyttelton, Leroy Ostransky and Valerie Wilmer.

Important vehicles for jazz writing are the jazz magazines. Amongst many magazines, some of which have proved impossible to keep afloat despite the determination of their editors and proprietors, are *Le Jazz Hot* (1935-), edited for several years by André Hodeir, *Jazz Journal International* (1948-), whose editors have included Sinclair Traill, Mike Hennessey and, currently, Eddie Cook, *Coda* (1958-), *Crescendo International* (1962-) and *Cadence* (1976-). These magazines may be broadly identified with mainstream to bop while traditional and New Orleans jazz has been served by *Storyville* (1965-) and *Footnote* (1969-). More recent developments in jazz have been closely followed by *Wire* (1986-), under the editorship of Richard Cook. At certain times, some popular music magazines have had strong leanings towards jazz. Amongst American magazines in this category are *Metronome* (1885-1961) which was strongly jazz-orientated between the mid-30s and the mid-50s, the period when George T. Simon held senior editorial posts, and *Down Beat* (1934-), especially during the late 30s, 40s and 50s. In the UK, ***Melody Maker*** (1926-) was an important jazz organ in the 40s and 50s, especially during the tenure as editor of Max Jones.

Other sources of often valuable comment which should not be overlooked are sleeve notes. Although the sleeve of a record album is customarily a part of the marketing package, the notes on jazz albums have often escaped becoming merely a part of the sales pitch. Writers with perception and style who frequently appear in this form include Alun Morgan, author of *Count Basie* (1984) and co-author of *Modern Jazz: 1945-1970 The Essential Records*, and Dan Morgenstern, who also edited *Metronome*, *Jazz* and *Down Beat* in the 60s, has been director of the Institute Of Jazz Studies at Rutgers University since the mid-70s, and whose books include *Jazz People* (1976).

Jazz encyclopedias which set out to provide in capsule form data on numerous artists have also become a familiar part of the literature of jazz. An early venture was Hugues Panassie's *Dictionary Of Jazz* (1954), a volume sometimes too readily maligned because of its author's dismissal of any of the music's developments after 1940 (Panassie chose to regard bop as being something other than jazz). For all such eccentricities, Panassie's book is frequently perceptive even if much of its content has been overtaken by later research. Later encyolpedias include Leonard Feather's *The Encyclopedia Of Jazz* (1955), *The Encyclopedia Of Jazz In The '60s* (1966) and *The Encyclopedia Of Jazz In The '70s* (1976), *The Illustrated Encyclopedia Of Jazz* (1986) by Brian Case, Stan Britt and Chrissie Murray, John Chilton's *Who's Who Of Jazz* (1985), *Jazz: The Essential Companion* by Ian Carr, Digby Fairweather and Brian Priestley (1987), and *The New Grove Dictionary of Jazz* (1988) by Barry Kernfeld and others.

Some of the most assiduous of the many researchers into jazz are the discographers. The sheer volume of work involved in accumulating the necessary data would daunt even the most dedicated enthusiasts and, indeed, some discographies have suddenly stopped in mid-alphabet, never to be resumed. There exist numerous discographies on individual artists with few major figures being without a volume. Comprehensive discographies (or at least those that seek to be comprehensive) include Charles Delauney's pathfinding *Hot Discography*, which first appeared in 1936, Dave Carey and Albert McCarthy's *Jazz Directory* (1949-1957), which fizzled out around the letter 'k', and Brian Rust's *Jazz Records: A-Z, 1897-1942* (1978). The major discograhies are those prepared by Jorgen Grunnet Jepsen and Walter Bruyninckx, both of which appear in multiple volumes.

Although not directly relevant to the subject of jazz writing, the work of many jazz photographers continually illuminate magazines, books and album sleeves, to say nothing of sometimes appearing in exhibitions. Amongst the best known in the field are K. Abé, *Jazz Giants: A Visual Retrospective* (1986), Ole Brask, in Morgenstern's *Jazz People*, and David Redfern, *David Redfern's Jazz Album* (1980). Other skilled photographers of jazz musicians include Ray Avery, William Claxton, William Gottlieb, Tim Motion, Bob Parent, Charles 'Chuck' Stewart, Val Wilmer and some, like Colin Priestley, Lee Richardson and Sue Storey, perhaps less well known but whose work is often at least on par with more noted figures.

Jazzamatazz - Guru

This jazz rap collision had been anticipated by earlier Gang Starr efforts such as 'Jazz Thing', a collaboration with Branford Marsalis that Spike Lee used to theme his film *Mo' Better Blues*.. This 'side-project' saw Guru

reproducing that winning formula, which others, notably Us3, have subsequently attempted to emulate. However, the latter's approach (that of ram-raiding the Blue Note vaults with a sampler) can hardly compare to the assembled cast that make up the Jazzamatazz ranks, the exponents including N'Dea Davenport (Brand New Heavies), Carleen Anderson, Courtney Pine, Marsalis, Roy Ayers, Donald Byrd, Lonnie Liston Smith and French rapper MC Solaar. Rap had many times been called the rock 'n' roll of the 90s, but this album saw critics retrace its heritage back to its own black traditions.

● Tracks: *Introduction; Loungin'; When You're Near; Transit Ride; No Time To Play; Down The Backstreets; Respectful Dedications; Take A Look (At Yourself); Trust Me; Slicker Than Most; Le Bien, Le Mal; Sights In The City.*
● First released 1993
● UK peak chart position: 58
● USA peak chart position: 3

Jazzie B.

b. Beresford Romeo, 26 January 1963, London, England. The larger-than-life svengali Jazzie B. began his musical apprenticeship on the London **sound system** circuit before helming the enormous international success of **Soul II Soul**. As such, Jazzie B. is widely credited with having pioneered a renaissance in British soul music in the late 80s - certainly his group were the first of their generation to make a serious impact on the US R&B charts. By the advent of Soul II Soul's fifth album, Jazzie B. had signed a new contract with **Island Records**' subsidiary 4th And Broadway, following six successful years with **Virgin Records**. Island also provided a home for his record label, production and publishing company, Soul II Soul Records, and an artist roster including Yorker, Backroom, the Funki Dreds and EFUA. Although his publishing agreement with EMI Publishing for the Jazzie B. Music, Soul II Soul and Mad Music catalogues also expired in 1996, his music remained omnipresent in the UK media, including advertisements for Renault and Levi's. Indeed, his only significant setback has been the clothes stores opened in the late 80s under the Soul II Soul banner, which have since closed. While waiting to conclude record company business and begin work on the new Soul II Soul album, Jazzie B. continued to occupy himself by running his studio complex in Camden, north London.

Jazzmatazz

A collaboration between seasoned jazz exponents and Guru (b. Keith Allam, Roxbury, Massachusetts, USA) of **Gang Starr**. Some of the names involved included **N'Dea Davenport** (**Brand New Heavies**), **Carleen Anderson**, **Courtney Pine**, **Branford Marsalis**, **Roy Ayers**, **Donald Byrd**, **Lonnie Liston Smith** and French rapper **MC Solaar**. An inventive combination, highlighted by a single, 'No Time To Play', featuring the vocals of **Paul Weller**'s missus **D.C. Lee**, which in turn helped relaunch the latter's career. The Jazzmatazz project's roots were undoubtedly laid in Gang Starr's 'Jazz Thing', a collaboration with Marsalis which Spike Lee has used to theme his film, *Mo' Better Blues*.

● ALBUMS: *Jazzmatazz* (Chrysalis 1993) ★★★.

Jazzy Jason

UK artist of the early 90s who first emerged with Epitome Of Hype's 'Ladies With An Attitude', which sampled **Madonna**, and was first released on his own Pure Bonhomie label before being licensed to **Big Life**. Further funky rave tunes, dominated by breakbeats, followed. As part of Blapps Posse! he was also behind 'Bus It'/'Don't Hold Back', which sold some 10,000 copies on white label before being picked up by **Rebel MC**'s Trible Bass label. He moved over to Essex's rave central HQ - **D-Zone Records,** for Turntable Symphony's 'Instructions Of Life', created with fellow Blaaps Posse! member Aston Harvey.

Jazzy Jay

b. *c*.1963, Bronx, New York, USA. Bronx studio-based DJ who was one of the early movers in **Afrika Bambaataa**'s Zulu Nation movement, travelling with his mentor from early park and block parties to the stadia of the Roxy and the *Planet Rock* tour. In a less-publicised role he was also Rick Rubin's original partner in **Def Jam**, and co-produced the label's first single, **T La Rock**'s 'It's Yours' (with lyrics written by his brother, **Special-K**). His own label (with Rocky Bucano) Strong City, would unveil records by Busy Bee, Ultimate Force, Ice Cream Tee, Don Baron and **Grand Puba**'s first outfit, **Masters Of Ceremony**. Regular visitors and pupils of his Bronx studio have included **Diamond D**, **Fat Joe Da Gangster**, **Showbiz and AG** and Skeff Anslem. Jazzy Jay grew up in the Bronx River region, and started DJing in his early teens. Kid Cassidy and Sundance were his first two MC recruits, playing together in the park by Soundview Houses, distributing tapes of the shows to other early hip hop fans. After working with the Chuck City Crew from Bronxdale he received the call from Bambaataa, and debuted with them in 1977. He was promoted to the head of the Jazzy 5 enclave, and was partially behind the 'Jazzy Sensation' cut. He had already hooked up with Rubin whom he had met at the Club Negril, before 'Planet Rock' took off. Though neither the liaison with Rubin nor his Strong City venture actually afforded him great finanical reward, Jay has gone on to maintain the respect afforded him by the hip hop community with a series of productions which have never been less than competent, and often much more.

Jazzy Jeff

A former member of the **Funky Four**, Jazzy Jeff should not be confused, as frequently and quite naturally happens, with **DJ Jazzy Jeff**. The latter, alongside The Fresh Prince, shares not only his name, but also his label and producer. Though the original Jazzy Jeff has

largely been eclipsed by the duo, he is a rapper of some historical note. His able, clear rhymes decorated a likeable album for **Jive** in the mid-80s, aided by Bryan 'Chuck' New and Phil Nicholas of the Willesden Dodgers. Eschewing the macho delivery and breast-beating more familiar at the time, *On Fire* included the vulnerable tribute 'My Mother (Yes I Love Her)' alongside material that frowned upon the ghetto's drug problems. 'King Heroin (Don't Mess With Heroin)' is actually one of rap's few lyrics about that drug in a subculture sadly obsessed with cannabis, crack and cocaine.

● ALBUMS: *On Fire* (Jive 1985) ★★★.
● COMPILATIONS: *Greatest Hits* (Jive 1998) ★★★★.

Jazzy M.

UK DJ who started out on that career's familiar route to stardom by working at a record shop counter, before appearing on the LWR pirate radio station, playing early Detroit techno and Chicago house on his *Jackin' Zone* shows. After DJing at his own Mania nights and varous club appearance he joined with Pete Tong to compile **ffrr**'s *The House Sound Of London Vol. 4*, which featured his first recording, 'Living In A World Of Fantasy', a collaboration with **Fingers Inc**. He ran his own shop, Vinyl Zone, and launched his first label, Oh Zone Records. The first release on which was **Orbital**'s 'Chime', lincensed to ffrr. It sold 66,000 copies after being passed to Jazzy M on a TDK cassette. His second label was Delphinus Delphis which dealt with more garage-house themes. It saw the release of the well-received 'Hold On' by Cuddles, before a third label was mooted, Spankin'. This produced several notable cuts, such as the *Rubberneck* EPs and Dub Nation's 'I Can't Help Myself', produced with partner Doug Martin. Jazzy continued to play out all the time, feeding back the results into his recordings and *vice versa*. Not surprising then that the Spankin' releases were held in high regard by the DJ fraternity in the early 90s, similar to **Tony Humphries** and **C+C**. He continues to play regular sets at Release The Pressure.

JC001

b. 16 June 1966. Rapper JC001 boasts one of the world's most fearsome, animated rap deliveries. His maniacal rants adorn a mixed hip-hop/ragga backing, with samples lifted from classic Jamaican fare (**Dave And Ansell Collins**' 'Double Barrel' on the 'Cupid' 45, etc). Born of part Indian/Catholic parentage, he first listened to ragga rhymes on David Rodigan's *Roots Rockers* radio programme, but he bought into rap with the advent of electro and 'Planet Rock'. After performing at blues parties and carnivals he joined the pirate radio stations. His first record emerged in 1987, 'I Diss Therefore I Am', built on the **Ethiopians**' 'Train To Skaville', before collaborating with others for 'Bad Place To Get Hit'. Though his press image is one of devilish intensity and spite, his lyrics trace strong anti-racism sentiments. He collaborated with the **Beatmasters** on

their 1991 comeback single, 'Boulevard of Broken Dreams'.
● ALBUMS: *Ride To The Break* (Anxious/East West 1993)★★★.

Jean, Cathy, And The Roommates

The vocal quartet the Roommates was formed in 1959 in Queens, New York, USA, by Steve Susskind (lead), Bob Minsky (bass), Felix Alvarez (second tenor) and Jack Carlson (first tenor and falsetto). Their debut was cover version of the **Kitty Wells** hit 'Making Believe'. Their manager, Jody Malis, was also looking after the career of the 14-year-old singer, Cathy Jean, who had just recorded a song called 'Please Love Me Forever'. Malis asked the Roommates to overdub vocal harmonies and the single went on to reach number 12 in the **Billboard** charts, despite the two parties credited on the record never having met. In March 1961 the Roommates version of 'Glory Of Love' reached number 49 in the USA chart. 'Band Of Gold' might have provided them with a third chart single, but a manufacturing defect meant that all copies jumped at a certain point and by the time this problem had been rectified, the momentum had gone. 'My Foolish Heart', their next single, flopped, and they joined Cathy Jean (this time uncredited) for her May 1961 single, 'Make Me Smile Again', which did not chart. A year later the group moved to Cameo Records where they covered the **Harptones**' 'Sunday Kind Of Love', then **Philips** for 'Gee' and 'The Nearness Of You'. None of these releases charted, aand neither did their final single, 'My Heart', on Canadian American Records. The group broke up in 1965 but Cathy Jean has continued to tour with a version of the Roommates into the 90s.

Jeannie And The Big Guys

Rita Hughes (b. *c*.1947, d. 1989) the daughter of a Chester, Cheshire, England publican, was the leader of a 1961 group, originally called themselves the Pacemakers. They were unaware of **Gerry And The Pacemakers**' existence until a curt letter from **Brian Epstein** put them in their place and they became Four Hits And A Miss. They included 'Lullaby Of Birdland' alongside rock 'n' roll favourites and became Chester's top group. When they signed to **Pye Records**, the name changed again - this time to Jeannie And The Big Guys. Then they were confused with another group, Jeannie And The Tall Boys. Their singles were 'Boys' and 'Sticks And Stones' and the newspaper, *Mersey Beat*, criticised her for her unladylike manners: she had brought fish and chips into a dressing-room. After the singles failed to connect, Jeannie worked with **Earl Royce And The Olympics** and then changed her name again, this time to Cindy Cole, and recorded two singles for **EMI Records**, 'A Love Like Yours' and 'Lonely City, Blue Boy'. She worked in cabaret, often doing prestige bookings until her unexpected death in 1989.

Jeeves

This show is the skeleton in the cupboard of **Andrew Lloyd Webber**, the most successful composer of stage musicals during the past 20 years. Most of the creative giants of Broadway and the West End have had their superflops - **Alan Jay Lerner** (*Dance A Little Closer*), **Lionel Bart** (*Twang!!*), and **Stephen Sondheim** (*Anyone Can Whistle*), to mention only a few - and *Jeeves* proved that Lloyd Webber is no exception. The débâcle occurred at Her Majesty's Theatre in London on 22 April 1975, and was despatched, 38 performances later, on 24 May. The composer had already tasted substantial success with *Jesus Christ Superstar* and *Joseph And The Amazing Technicolor Dreamcoat* - and another smash-hit, *Evita*, was only three years into the future. **Tim Rice**, his collaborator on all three of those productions, was conveniently unavailable for *Jeeves*, so Lloyd Webber turned for the book and lyrics to the celebrated comedy playwright Alan Ayckbourn. One critic claimed that the result was 'like a dream of all the **P.G. Wodehouse** novels combined in the ultimate ghastly weekend', although Ayckbourn maintained that he 'tried to 'narrow in'' on one book, *The Code Of The Woosters*, and adapt that, with a few references to other books'. Jeeves (Michael Aldridge) and Bertie Wooster (David Hemmings) were joined by the usual Drones Club crowd, along with a veritable gaggle of girlfriends, and various other comical characters. Members of the cast included **Betty Marsden**, Gordon Clyde, Christopher Good, John Turner, Bill Wallis, Angela Easterling, Graham Hamilton, and Gabrielle Drake. It was widely felt that Lloyd Webber's music failed to capture the lively, happy-go-lucky flavour of the 20 and 30s period with a score which contained such songs as 'Code Of The Woosters', 'Travel Hopefully', 'Today', 'S.P.O.D.E.', 'Eulalie', 'Banjo Boy', 'Female Of The Species', 'When Love Arrives', 'Half A Moment', 'Summer Day', and 'Jeeves Is Past His Peak'. It must have seemed such a good idea at the time, but this 'straggling, heavy-handed affair' - the book of which, all concerned admitted, was a 'huge dinosaur' and far too long - proved to be only a slight hiccup in the careers of both Andrew Lloyd Webber and Alan Ayckbourn.

Almost exactly 20 years later, the bruises had apparently healed sufficiently for the duo to take a look at the subject again, and consequently 'an almost entirely new musical' entitled *By Jeeves* made its debut at the recently converted Stephen Joseph Theatre-in-the-round in Scarborough, Yorkshire, on 1 May 1996. Reaction was generally enthusiastic, and the production transferred to the fairly intimate (654-seater) Duke Of York's Theatre on 2 July for a 12-week season, which was extended at the Lyric in Shaftesbury Avenue until February 1997. It featured a radically revised (and down-sized) book, with an entirely original plot by Ayckbourn, who also directed (much of the blame for *Jeeves*'s failure had been apportioned to director Eric Thompson, father of film actress Emma). This time round, in a classic mistaken identity plot, Bertie (Steven Pacey), is foiled in his commendable (but questionable) intention to entertain an expectant village hall audience with his banjo playing in aid of charity, when some music lover - Jeeves (Malcolm Sinclair) - hides the offending instrument. Undeterred, Bertie launches into a programme of 'this has been my life' anecdotes, which results in a series of hilarious escapades involving Gussie Fink-Nottle (Simon Day), Bingo Little (Nicholas Haverson), Harold 'Stinker' Pinker (Richard Long), the inevitable American house guest, jam millionaire Cyrus Budge III Junior (Nicolas Colicos), a grim magistrate, Sir Watkyn Bassett (Robert Austin), and female admirers Madeline Bassett (Diana Morrison), Stiffy Byng (Cathy Sara), and Honoria Glossop (Lucy Tregear). Regretfully, there was no sign of any of Bertie's eccentric aunts. However, whether impersonating a hatstand, being 'driven' through the countryside on an upturned table pulled by Jeeves, or burgling Madeline's home disguised in a pig's mask, Pacey's ebullient Wooster was a 'delightful mixture of silliness, charm, and bemusement'. He was aided and abetted by Sinclair's 'wonderfully supercilious Jeeves - sleek, calm, and ostentatiously unobtrusive', and the jolly choreography of Sheila Carter. The score, which gave a nod in the direction of **Sandy Wilson** and **Vivian Ellis**, amongst others, contained eight new songs, 'A False Start', 'That Was Nearly Us', 'Love's Maze', 'The Hallo Song', the jaunty second act opener, 'By Jeeves', 'What Have You Got To Say, Jeeves?', 'It's A Pig', and 'The Wizard Rainbow Finale'. Five numbers from the 1975 *Jeeves* were retained - some of which were re-lyricised by Ayckbourn - 'Code Of The Woosters', 'Travel Hopefully', 'When Love Arrives', 'Banjo Boy', and the appealing 'Half A Moment'. According to Lloyd Webber, the melody of another song from that earlier ill-fated production, 'Summer Day', was re-used by the composer in *Evita* as 'Another Suitcase In Another Hall'. After accomplishing 'one of the slickest comebacks since Lazarus', *By Jeeves* was nominated for three **Laurence Olivier Awards**, but failed to convert any. It had its American premiere at the Goodspeed Opera House, Connecticut, in November 1996.

Jefferson

b. Geoff Turton, 11 March 1944, Birmingham, England. A one-time toolmaker, Turton found fame in the mid-60s as singer in the **Rockin' Berries** before quitting for a solo career in the autumn of 1968. A self-confessed 'penniless bum', Turton relaunched himself as Jefferson and enjoyed a flurry of fame with the 1969 hit 'Colour Of My Love', written by **Paul Ryan**. The transition into a 70s star failed to materialize although Jefferson did enjoy some success in the USA where 'Baby Take Me In Your Arms' reached the Top 30. After playing on the USA college circuit, he returned to the UK in 1972 but failed to avoid the one-hit-wonder tag in his own country.

Jefferson Airhead
(see **Airhead**)

Jefferson Airplane

Along with the **Grateful Dead**, Jefferson Airplane are regarded as the most successful San Francisco band of the late 60s. The group were formed in 1965 by **Marty Balin** (b. Martyn Jerel Buchwald, 30 January 1942, Cincinnati, Ohio, USA; vocals/guitar). The other members in the original line-up were **Paul Kantner** (b. 17 March 1941, San Francisco, California, USA; guitar/vocals) and **Jorma Kaukonen** (b. 23 December 1940, Washington DC, USA; guitar/vocals). Bob Harvey and Jerry Peloquin gave way to **Alexander 'Skip' Spence** and Signe Anderson (b. Signe Toly Anderson, 15 September 1941, Seattle, Washington, USA). Their replacements; Spencer Dryden (b. 7 April 1938, New York, USA; drums) and Jack Casady (b. 13 April 1944, Washington, DC, USA), made up a seminal band that blended folk and rock into what became known as west coast rock. Kantner, already a familiar face on the local folk circuit and Balin, formerly of the Town Criers and co-owner of the Matrix club, soon became highly popular locally, playing gigs and benefits organized by promoter **Bill Graham**. Eventually they became regulars at the Fillmore Auditorium and the Carousel Ballroom, both a short distance from their communal home in the Haight Ashbury district. Anderson departed shortly after the release of their moderately successful debut *Takes Off* and was replaced by **Grace Slick** (b. Grace Barnett Wing, 30 October 1939, Evanston, Illinois, USA; vocals). Slick was already well known with her former band, the **Great Society**, and donated two of their songs, 'White Rabbit' and 'Somebody To Love' to the Airplane. Both titles were on their second influential collection, *Surrealistic Pillow*, and both became US Top 10 hits. They have now achieved classic status as definitive songs from that era. 'White Rabbit's' lyrics combined the harmless tale of *Alice In Wonderland* with an LSD trip. Their reputation was enhanced by a strong performance at the legendary **Monterey Pop Festival** in 1967. This national success continued with the erratic *After Bathing At Baxters* and the brilliant *Crown Of Creation*. The latter showed the various writers in the band maturing and developing their own styles. Balin's 'If You Feel', Kaukonen's 'Ice Cream Phoenix' and Slick's tragicomic 'Lather' gave the record great variety. This album also contained 'Triad', a song their friend **David Crosby** had been unable to include a **Byrds** album. They maintained a busy schedule and released a well-recorded live album, *Bless Its Pointed Little Head* in 1969. The same year they appeared at another milestone in musical history: the **Woodstock Festival**. Later that year they were present at the infamous **Altamont Festival**, where a group of Hells Angels killed a young spectator and attacked Balin.

Slick and Kantner had now become lovers and their hippie ideals and political views were a major influence on *Volunteers*. While it was an excellent album, it marked the decline of Balin's role in the band. Additionally, Dryden departed and the offshoot **Hot Tuna** began to take up more of Casady and Kaukonen's time. Wizened fiddler **Papa John Creach** (b. 28 May 1917, Beaver Falls, Pennsylvania, USA, d. 22 February 1994; violin) joined the band full-time in 1970, although he still continued to play with Hot Tuna. Kantner released a concept album, *Blows Against The Empire*, bearing the name Paul Kantner And The **Jefferson Starship**. The 'Starship' consisted of various Airplane members, plus **Jerry Garcia**, David Crosby, **Graham Nash**, *et al*. This majestic album was nominated for the science fiction Hugo Award. Slick meanwhile gave birth to a daughter, China, who later in the year graced the cover of Slick And Kantner's *Sunfighter*. Following a greatest hits selection, *Worst Of* and the departure of Balin, the band released the cleverly packaged *Bark*. Complete with brown paper bag, the album offered some odd moments, notably Slick's 'Never Argue With A German', sung in spoof German, and Covington's 50s-sounding acappella, 'Thunk'. It also marked the first release on their own Grunt label. The disappointing *Long John Silver* was followed by a gutsy live outing, *30 Seconds Over Winterland*. This was the last album to bear their name, although an interesting compilation consisting of single releases and studio out-takes later appeared as *Early Flight*. Hot Tuna became Casady and Kaukonen's main interest and Slick and Kantner released further 'solo' albums. The name change evolved without any fuss, and one of the most inventive bands in history prepared for a relaunch as the Jefferson Starship. Kantner, Balin and Casady regrouped briefly as the **KBC Band** in 1986. The Airplane title was resurrected in 1989 when Slick, Kaukonen, Casady, Balin and Kantner re-formed and released *Jefferson Airplane* to an indifferent audience. By the early 90s Hot Tuna had re-formed, Kantner was rebuilding his Jefferson Starship and Slick had apparently retired from the music business.

● ALBUMS: *Jefferson Airplane Takes Off* (RCA 1966)★★, *Surrealistic Pillow* (RCA 1967)★★★★, *After Bathing At Baxter's* (RCA 1967)★★★, *Crown Of Creation* (RCA 1968)★★★★, *Bless Its Pointed Little Head* (RCA 1969)★★★, *Volunteers* (RCA 1969)★★★★, *Bark* (Grunt 1971)★★★, *Long John Silver* (Grunt 1972)★★★, *30 Seconds Over Winterland* (Grunt 1973)★★★, *Early Flight* (Grunt 1974)★★★, *Jefferson Airplane* (Epic 1989)★.

● COMPILATIONS: *Worst Of Jefferson Airplane* (RCA 1970)★★★, featuring Jefferson Airplane and Starship *Flight Log (1966-1976)* (Grunt 1977)★★★★, *2400 Fulton Street* (RCA 1987)★★★★, *Journey ... Best Of* (Camden 1996)★★★.

● FURTHER READING: *The Jefferson Airplane And The San Francisco Sound*, Ralph J. Gleason. *Grace Slick - The Biography*, Barbara Rowe.

Jefferson Starship

Formerly the **Jefferson Airplane**, the band evolved into the Jefferson Starship after **Paul Kantner** (b. 17 March 1941, San Francisco, California, USA; guitar/vocals) had previously released *Blows Against The Empire* in 1970, billed as Paul Kantner And The Jefferson Starship. His fascination with science fiction no doubt led the Airplane to metamorphose into a Starship. The official debut was *Dragonfly* in 1974, which became an immediate success. The band played with a freshness and urgency that had been missing on recent Airplane releases. Joining Kantner on this album were **Grace Slick** (b. Grace Barnett Wing, 30 October 1939, Chicago, Illinois, USA; vocals), **Papa John Creach** (b. 28 May 1917, Beaver Falls, Pennsylvania, USA; violin), former **Quicksilver Messenger Service** bassist David Freiberg (b. 24 August 1938, Boston, Massachusetts, USA; vocals/keyboards), Craig Chaquico (b. 26 September 1954; lead guitar), ex-**Turtles** member John Barbata (drums) and Pete Sears (bass/keyboards). Among the tracks were 'Ride The Tiger', which was accompanied by an imaginatively graphic, early video and 'Hyperdrive', a Slick magnum opus featuring Chaquico's frantic screaming guitar. Old Airplane fans were delighted to hear **Marty Balin** guesting on one track with his own composition 'Caroline', and further cheered when he joined the band at the beginning of 1975. *Red Octopus* later that year became their most successful album and ended up selling several million copies and spending a month at the top of the US charts. The flagship track was Balin's beautiful and seemingly innocent 'Miracles'. This was the first known pop lyric to feature reference to cunnilingus with Balin singing 'I had a taste of the real world, when I went down on you' and Slick innocently responding in the background with 'Mmm, don't waste a drop of it, don't ever stop it'.

Soon afterwards, Kantner and Slick separated; she moved in with Skip Johnson, the band's lighting engineer, and eventually married him. Later that year Slick was regularly in the news when her drinking problems got out of control. *Spitfire* and *Earth* continued their success, although the band had now become a hard rock outfit. Balin's lighter 'Count On Me' was a US Top 10 hit in 1978. That year, Slick was asked to leave the band, to be allowed to return when she dried out. She was eventually dismissed in 1978, closely followed by Balin, who left towards the end of a turbulent year. He was replaced by Mickey Thomas and further changes were afoot when stalwart drummer **Aynsley Dunbar** (b. 1946, Liverpool, England) joined in place of Barbata. *Freedom From Point Zero* and the US Top 20 hit 'Jane', at the end of 1979, bore no resemblance to the musical style towards which remaining original member Kantner had attempted to steer them. He suffered a stroke during 1980, but returned the following spring together with a sober Grace Slick. Both *Modern Times* (1981) and *Winds Of Change* (1982), continued the success, although by now the formula was wearing thin. Kantner found his role had diminished and released a solo album later that year. He continued with them throughout the following year, although he was openly very unsettled. Towards the end of 1984 Kantner performed a nostalgic set of old Airplane songs with Balin's band, amid rumours of a Jefferson Airplane reunion.

The tension broke in 1985 when, following much acrimony over ownership of the band's name, Kantner was paid off and took with him half of the group's moniker. Kantner claimed the rights to the name, although he no longer wanted to use the title, as his reunion with Balin and Casady in the KBC Band demonstrated. In defiance his former band performed as Starship Jefferson, but shortly afterwards became Starship. Both Thomas and Freiberg left during these antagonistic times, leaving Slick the remaining original member after the incredible changes of the previous few years. The new line-up added Denny Baldwin on drums and recorded *Knee Deep In The Hoopla* in 1985, which became their most successful album since *Red Octopus*. Two singles from the album, 'We Built This City' (written by **Bernie Taupin**) and 'Jane', both reached number 1 in the USA. The following year they reached the top spot on both sides of the Atlantic with the theme from the film *Mannequin*, 'Nothing's Gonna Stop Us Now'. Their image is now of slick perpetrators of AOR, performing immaculate music for the **MTV** generation (on which China Kantner was a presenter). Now, having gone full circle, Grace Slick departed in 1989 to join Kaukonen, Casady, Balin and Kantner in . . . the Jefferson Airplane. Kantner still carries the Starship banner, and in the mid-90s still had Balin and Casady in tow. A new live album was issued in 1995.

● ALBUMS: *Dragonfly* (Grunt 1974)★★★, *Red Octopus* (Grunt 1975)★★★★, *Spitfire* (Grunt 1976)★★★, *Earth* (Grunt 1978)★★, *Freedom At Point Zero* (Grunt 1979)★★, *Modern Times* (RCA 1981)★★, *Winds Of Change* (Grunt 1982)★★, *Nuclear Furniture* (Grunt 1984)★★; as Starship *Knee Deep In The Hoopla* (RCA 1985)★★, *No Protection* (RCA 1987)★★, *Love Among The Cannibals* (RCA 1989)★, *Deep Space/Virgin Sky* (Intersound 1995)★.

● COMPILATIONS: featuring Jefferson Airplane and Starship *Flight Log (1966-1976)* (Grunt 1977)★★★★, *Gold* (Grunt 1979)★★★★, *Jefferson Starship: The Collection* (1992)★★★.

Jefferson, Blind Lemon

b. July 1897, Wortham (Couchman), Texas, USA, d. December 1929, Chicago, Illinois, USA. Jefferson was one of the earliest and most influential rural blues singers to record. He was one of seven children born to Alex Jefferson and Classie Banks (or Bates) and was either blind or partially blind from early childhood. As his handicap precluded his employment as a farm-hand he turned to music and sang at rural parties, on the streets of small towns, in cafes, juke joints and brothels. This mode of life turned him into a wanderer and he travelled far, although he always maintained his links with Texas. Like many 'blind' singers, stories are told of his ability to find his way around and read situations. He was usually armed and was even said to have been involved in shooting incidents. In late 1925 or early

1926, he was taken to Chicago by a Dallas record retailer to record for Paramount Records. His first offerings were two religious tracks that were issued under the pseudonym 'Reverend L.J. Bates'. Soon after this, he was to begin the long series of blues recordings that made him famous throughout black America and even affected the work of rural white musicians. Between 1926 and 1929 he had more than 90 tracks issued, all bar two appearing on Paramount. His only known photograph, taken from a Paramount publicity shot, shows a portly man of indeterminate age wearing clear glasses over closed eyes set in a 'baby' face. He was accorded the distinction (shared with **Ma Rainey**) of having a record issued with his picture on the label and described as 'Blind Lemon Jefferson's Birthday Record'. He had a good vocal range, honed by use in widely different venues, and a complicated, dense, free-form guitar style that became a nightmare for future analysts and copyists due to its disregard for time and bar structure; however, it suited his music perfectly and spoke directly to his black audience, both in the city and in the country. His success can be measured by the fact that he once owned two cars and could afford to hire a chauffeur to drive them. He is also said to have employed boys to lead him. **Lead Belly** and **T-Bone Walker** both claimed to have worked for him in this capacity during their youth. His later recordings seemed to lose some of the originality and impact of his earlier work but he remained popular until his sudden and somewhat mysterious death. Legend has it that he froze to death on the streets of Chicago, although a more likely story is that he died of a heart attack while in his car, possibly during a snowstorm, and was abandoned by his driver. At this late date it is unlikely that the truth will ever be established. His records continue to be issued after his death and some recorded tributes have been made. His body was transported back to Texas for burial.

● COMPILATIONS: *The Folk Blues Of Blind Lemon Jefferson* (Riverside 1953)★★★, *Penitentiary Blues* (Riverside 1955)★★★, *Classic Folk Blues* (Riverside 1957)★★★, *Blind Lemon Jefferson* (Riverside 1957)★★★, *Blind Lemon Jefferson Volume 2* (Riverside 1958)★★★, *The Immortal Blind Lemon Jefferson* (Milestone 1968)★★★, *The Immortal Blind Lemon Jefferson* (Milestone 1969)★★★, *Black Snake Moan* (Milestone 1970)★★★, *Collection* (Déjà Vu 1986)★★★, *King Of The Country Blues* (Yazoo 1988)★★★, *The Complete* (1991)★★★, *The Best Of Blind Lemon Jefferson* (Wolf 1994)★★★.

Jefferson, Eddie

b. 3 August 1918, Detroit, Michigan, USA, d. 9 May 1979, Detroit, Michigan, USA. Beginning his show business career as a dancer and occasional singer, Jefferson gradually concentrated on his latter talent. After achieving limited success, as a scat singer in the mid- to late 40s, Jefferson was largely responsible for the creation of so-called 'vocalese', devising lyrics to fit solos originally improvised by leading jazz musicians. Among the solos to which Jefferson wrote words was that played on 'Body And Soul' by **Coleman Hawkins** (with whom he had briefly worked in the early 40s), 'Parker's Mood' by **Charlie Parker** and **James Moody**'s version of 'I'm In The Mood For Love'. This tune, variously retitled but usually known as 'Moody's Mood For Love' was recorded by **King Pleasure**, and achieved considerable success, thus opening doors for its adaptor. Jefferson subsequently worked with Moody's small group as both singer and manager, an association which lasted for almost 20 years. He continued to adapt solos by important musicians, including **Miles Davis** and **Horace Silver**. In the early 70s Jefferson sang with **Richie Cole** but on 9 May 1979, during an engagement at the Showcase in Detroit and within days of being filmed in performance there, he was fatally shot in the street outside the club.

● ALBUMS: *The Jazz Singer* (Evidence 1962)★★★, *Hipper Than Thou* (Zu Zazz, 1959-61 recordings)★★★★, with James Moody *Letter From Home* (Original Jazz Classics 1962)★★★★, *Moody's Mood/Moody/Hi-Fi Party* (1962)★★★, *Body And Soul* (Original Jazz Classics 1968)★★★★, *Come Along With Me* (Original Jazz Classics 1969)★★★★, *Things Are Getting Better* (1974)★★★, *Still On The Planet* (1976)★★★, *The Live-liest* (1976)★★, *Godfather Of Vocalese* (Muse 1977)★★★, *The Main Man* (1977)★★★, *There I Go Again* (Prestige 1984)★★★.

Jefferson, Hilton

b. 30 July 1903, Danbury, Connecticut, USA, d. 14 November 1968. After playing banjo in various outfits in the north-eastern states, Jefferson switched to alto saxophone and by 1926 had graduated to the **Claude Hopkins** band in New York. During the next few years he played briefly with ensembles led by **King Oliver** (recording on 'Shake It And Break It'), **Benny Carter**, **McKinney's Cotton Pickers** and **Fletcher Henderson** ('You Can Take It' and 'Harlem Madness') but was mainly in the **Chick Webb** and Hopkins bands. After these years of restlessness he joined **Cab Calloway**, staying as lead alto saxophonist for nine years. With Calloway he was featured only occasionally but used such moments to great advantage, placing on record some of his gorgeously lyrical performances as, for example, on 'Willow Weep For Me'. He left Calloway in 1949, returned in 1951 and then worked with **Duke Ellington** and **Don Redman** (accompanying **Pearl Bailey**). In 1953 Jefferson left music to work as a bank guard, but frequently turned up at club sessions, reunions and on recording dates, including the magnificent *Big Reunion* by former members of the Fletcher Henderson orchestra.

● ALBUMS: with Fletcher Henderson All Stars *The Big Reunion* (1957)★★★. ● COMPILATIONS: with Henderson *A Study In Frustration* (1923-38)★★★, *Cab Calloway's Sixteen Classics* (1939-41)★★★★.

Jefferson, Marshall

One of the legends of USA acid house music, Jefferson claims to have invented the familiar 'squelch' of the Roland TR 303 (a claim hotly countered by **DJ Pierre**). Jefferson's reputation rests more squarely on records such as Reggie Hall's 'Music', Richard Rogers' mighty 'Can't Stop Loving You', and **Ce Ce Rogers**' epic 'Someday'. Afterwards he would move on to helm production for **Ten City**, but was criticised at the time of their arrival for what some critics observed to be a fixation with nostalgia in the latter's soulful house grooves. Jefferson preferred the description deep house, and was quick to proclaim the death knell for acid. Nevertheless, Ten City hit with singles like 'That's The Way Love Is' and 'Right Back To You', with Byron Stingily's distinctive vocals providing an excellent outlet for Jefferson's studio craft. He has also worked with **Tyrrel Corporation** and **Kym Mazelle** ('I'm A Lover') amongst many others, and recorded as Jungle Wonz ('Time Marches On') and Truth ('Open Your Eyes'). 1994 saw him record only the second track under his own name, 'I Found You', for Centrestage Records, as well as continuing to produce artists of the calibre of **Tom Jones**, **System 7** and **Keith Thompson**.

● ALBUMS: Ten City: *Foundation* (East West 1988)★★★.

Jeffery, Robert

b. 14 January 1915, Tulsa, Oklahoma, USA, d. 20 July 1976, San Diego, California, USA. A blues guitarist, influenced by **Blind Lemon Jefferson**, as well as a pianist, Jeffery worked with a carnival as a young man, snake-charming and boxing against allcomers. He moved to California 'with the rest of the Okies' in the Depression, working as a car mechanic and playing piano on weekends, often at a club owned by **Thomas Shaw**. After his retirement, he made some festival appearances and recordings on piano in the 70s, and was still a good guitarist, although he insisted he had given it up.

● ALBUMS: *San Diego Blues Jam* (1974)★★★, *Off Yonder Wall* (Fat Possum 1997)★★★.

Jeffes, Simon

(see **Penguin Café Orchestra**)

Jeffrey, Joe, Group

Although his one hit, 'My Pledge Of Love', can still be heard on American radio, Jeffrey and his group remain something of a mystery to music historians. Jeffrey is known to have emanated from the area of Buffalo, New York, USA and to have recorded both in Cleveland, Ohio and Memphis, Tennessee. His first single, the jaunty soul-dance number 'My Pledge Of Love' was a dynamic, horn-laden piece that indicated its singer had much promise. It was released on **Wand Records** and reached number 14 in the US pop charts in the summer of 1969. An album, titled after the single, followed, but Jeffrey disappeared from the recording scene after his sole success.

● ALBUMS: *My Pledge Of Love* (Wand 1969)★★.

Jeffrey, Paul H.

b. 8 April 1933, New York, USA. In the 50s Jeffrey had worked throughout the USA with R&B/Blues artists including **Wynonie Harris**, **Big Maybelle** and **B.B. King** before returning to New York to study music at Ithaca College. Jeffrey worked with **Illinois Jacquet**, **Sadik Hakim** and **Howard McGhee** before touring Europe in 1968 with **Dizzy Gillespie**. In the 70s, after a brief spell with the **Count Basie** Orchestra, Jeffrey worked on and off with **Thelonious Monk** as well as conducting a concert of his music at the Newport Jazz Festival in 1974. Later he arranged and conducted **Charles Mingus**'s music on his last albums. Jeffrey has also been head of Jazz Studies at Rutgers University since the early 80s.

● ALBUMS: *Electrifying Sounds* (1968)★★.

Jeffreys, Garland

b. 1944, Brooklyn, New York, USA. Singer/songwriter Jeffreys first gained attention in 1973 with a critically-acclaimed self-titled album that contained the anthemic 'Wild In The Streets'. Jeffreys, of mixed racial background, studied art in Italy before deciding to concentrate on music. He first performed solo around New York and in 1966 formed a band called Grinder's Switch (not the US southern rock band of a similar name that recorded in the 70s). Jeffreys spent the early 70s going back to performing solo and honed a sound that crossed elements of rock, folk, reggae, salsa and soul. His 1973 **Atlantic Records** debut album contained frank songs of New York street life and the struggle for acceptance and survival Jeffreys witnessed and experienced in his youth. It was not commercially successful, yet 'Wild In The Streets' became a staple on FM radio. Jeffreys re-recorded the song for his next album. *Ghost Writer*, his debut for **A&M Records** in 1977, another critical favourite, made a minor dent in the charts. That pattern continued throughout the late 70s and 80s; Jeffreys recorded two more albums for A&M before switching to Epic in 1981 and recording three more albums. Ironically, considering the critical praise he had gathered for his writing, his only chart single in the USA was a remake of **? And The Mysterians**' '96 Tears' in 1981. He has enjoyed success outside the USA, however, and the 1981 single 'Matador' reached the Top 10 in some European countries. That same year, Jeffreys employed the services of **Graham Parker**'s backing band, the **Rumour** on his *Rock And Roll Adult* album. This respected artist has, in the past, enjoyed the support of various illustrious musicians including **David Sanborn**, **Phoebe Snow**, **Herb Alpert**, **James Taylor**, **Luther Vandross**, **David Bromberg** and **Dr. John**.

● ALBUMS: *Grinder's Switch Featuring Garland Jeffreys* (1970)★★, *Garland Jeffreys* (Atlantic 1973)★★★, *Ghost Writer* (A&M 1977)★★★, *One-Eyed Jack* (A&M 1978)★★★, *American Boy And Girl* (A&M 1979)★★, *Escape Artist* (Epic 1981)★★★, *Rock And Roll Adult* (Epic 1981)★★★, *Guts For Love* (Epic 1983)★★★.

Jeffries, Herb

b. 24 September 1916, Detroit, Michigan, USA. Early in his career Jeffries sang with the Erskine Tate band, for many years one of the most popular bands residing in Chicago. In 1931 he joined **Earl Hines** and was then briefly with Blanche Calloway. A tall, striking-looking man, in the late 30s Jeffries appeared in a number of films made by black producer-director Oscar Micheaux. In *The Bronze Buckaroo* and similar tales, Jeffries appeared as a black equivalent to the then popular white singing cowboys such as **Gene Autry**. In the early 40s Jeffries sang with **Duke Ellington** and his recording of 'Flamingo' was hugely successful. In the 50s Jeffries sang in clubs, often on the west coast, recording with artists including **Lucky Thompson** and **Bobby Hackett**. A re-recording of 'Flamingo', this time with **Les Brown**, was also successful. In the 70s and 80s Jeffries continued performing as a singer and actor, operated his own record label, United National, and appeared, exuding charm, bonhomie and good humour, as singer and master of ceremonies at several of the Ellington reunion conventions in the USA and UK. At one such reunion in Los Angeles in the summer of 1991, Jeffries received excellent notices for his performance in a revival of Ellington's *Jump For Joy*, half a century after his first appearance in the show.

● ALBUMS: *Calypso Joe* (1957)★★★, *Flamingo* (c.1957)★★, *Say It Isn't So* (1957)★★★, *If I Were A King* (c.1960)★★★, *I Remember Bing* (c.1960)★★.

● COMPILATIONS: with Earl Hines *Swingin' Down* (1932-33)★★★, with Duke Ellington *The Blanton-Webster Band* (1940-42)★★★★★, *The Bronze Buckaroo Rides Again* (Warner Western 1995)★★★.

Jekyll & Hyde

This musicalization of Robert Louis Stevenson's famous 1886 novella, *The Strange Case Of Dr. Jekyll And Mr. Hyde*, first saw the light in the form of a concept album in 1990. It featured pop versions of the songs, performed by Colm Wilkinson as Jekyll/Hyde and Linda Eder as Lucy, the prostitute who has a love/hate relationship with the celebrated split personality. Soon after its release, in June 1990 the stage show had its world premiere at the Alley Theatre in Houston, Texas, but failed to generate enough interest to warrant a tour or Broadway transfer. However, boosted by a second (double) album, on which Eder was joined by Anthony Warlow, the Australian star of **The Phantom Of The Opera** and **Les Misérables**, as well as former Broadway legend **John Raitt**, a much-expanded production played Houston and Seattle in the spring of 1995, before touring extensively prior to Broadway. Robert Cuccioli assumed the dual roles of Jekyll/Hyde in December 1994, and he was still leading the cast when the show finally opened at New York's Plymouth Theatre on 28 April 1997. The show was conceived for the stage by Steve Cuden and Frank Wildhorn, with book and lyrics by **Leslie Bricusse**, and music by former pop composer Wildhorn. Although the original story had inevitably been reworked, Bricusse's book followed the familiar tale, set in Victorian London, of the upstanding Dr. Henry Jekyll (Cuccioli), who has developed a potion that, once and for all, will separate good from evil in humanity - and cure mental illness. After an asylum's board of governors refuses to test the brew on their patients, Jekyll swallows it (along with his pride), turns into Edward Hyde, and sets out to execute each member of the board. Fortunately, he omits to inform his fiancée, Emma Carew (Christiane Noll), of his intentions, and she continues to support him. Eder's 'stunning show-stopping voice', and considerable stage presence as the prostitute, attracted the best notices, and she was blessed with some of the best numbers, such as the soaring 'A New Life', 'Someone Like You' and 'In His Eyes' (with Noll). Cuccioli duetted with Noll on 'Take Me As I Am', and with himself for the dramatic 'Confrontation', as well as handling the impressive 'This Is The Moment'. Also included in the score, which was described by one critic as having a 'romantic pop-synth twist', were 'Lost In The Darkness', 'Facade', 'Jekyll's Plea', 'Emma's Reasons', 'Letting Go', 'No One Knows Who I Am', 'Good 'n' Evil', 'Alive', 'His Work And Nothing More', 'Murder, Murder', 'Once Upon A Dream', 'Obsession', 'Dangerous Game', 'The Way Back', 'Sympathy, Tenderness' and 'Dear Lord And Father Of Mankind'. Robin Phillips was the director, and Joey Pizzi the choreographer. The cast also featured George Merritt (John Utterson), Barrie Ingham (Sir Danvers Carew), Raymond Jaramillo McLeod (Mr. Simon Stride), Michael Ingam (Rupert, Bishop of Basingstoke), Brad Oscar (Archibald Proops), Martin Van Treuren (Lord Savage), Emily Zacharias (Lady Beaconsfield, Guinevere) and Geoffrey Blaisdell (General Lord Glossop). Bricusse received his usual generous dose of poison from the New York critics, and the show failed to win any of its four **Tony Award** nominations, although Cuccioli won FANY (Friends of New York Theatre), Drama Desk and Outer Critics Circle prizes for best actor in a musical. Two other musical adaptations of Stevenson's tale appeared in 1996: *Dr. Jekyll And Mr. Hyde*, with book and lyrics by David Levy and Leslie Eberhard and music by Phil Hall, played Beverly, Massachusetts, and *Jekyll*, with a score by Tony Rees and Gary Young toured the UK provinces with ex-Phantom **Dave Willetts** in the lead.

Jelly Beans

This New York-based group boasted a varied line-up and at different times was either a quintet - Alan Brewer, Diane Taylor, Charles Thomas and sisters Elyse and Maxine Herbert - a quartet, or an all-female trio. They were signed to the **Red Bird** label in 1964, completing two singles under the supervision of songwriters/producers **Jeff Barry** and **Ellie Greenwich**. The first, 'I Wanna Love Him So Bad', reached the US Top 10, but although their follow-up, 'Baby Be Mine', fared less well, it was an artistic triumph. This tender ballad

was one of the duo's finest songs and the Jelly Beans' reputation rests on their heartfelt performance. There was an attempt at recording an album for Red Bird but, it was aborted and subsequently the group's disbanded.
● COMPILATIONS: *Jelly Beans* (1976)★★.

Jelly's Last Jam

Although full to the brim with the music of the legendary pioneer jazz composer, pianist, and bandleader **Jelly Roll Morton**, this is an original book musical, and not just a run-down of a bunch of songs, most of which are over 60 years old. *Jelly's Last Jam* opened at the Virginia Theatre in New York on 26 April 1992. The book, by a newcomer to Broadway, George C. Wolfe who also directed the piece, opens with Morton (Gregory Hines) recently demised. Up (or down) there, in the anti-room in which the big decisions as to the eventual direction (eternity-wise) are made, the Chimney Man (Keith David), reviews the evidence as to Morton's earthly behaviour - from his early piano-playing days in Storyville brothels, through his self-appointed position as the 'inventor of jazz', to his controversial rejection of his African ancestry. Morton's own compositions are supplemented by some additional material from Luther Henderson, who also adapted and orchestrated the musical side of the whole production, and a set of sometimes saucy and sardonic lyrics by Susan Birkenhead. Naturally, with Hines on board, the tap dancing is sensational, but the entire cast, including Savion Glover as the young Morton, Stanley Wayne Mathis in the role of Jack the Bear, Morton's best friend, and Tonya Pinkins as his sexy girlfriend, were all outstanding. With the benefit of some memorable musical numbers such as 'Lovin' Is A Lowdown Blues', 'Play The Music For Me', 'The Last Chance Blues', 'The Chicago Stomp', 'Dr. Jazz', and many more, *Jelly's Last Jam* sang and danced its way into 1993, but after May of that year, when Hines was replaced by Brian Mitchell, things were never quite the same, although the highly popular Ben Vereen took over the role of the Chimney Man around the same time. However, the show still ran for a year and a half, closing in September 1993. Considering that it opened in the same season as *Falsettos*, along with *Crazy For You* and a revival of *Guys And Dolls*, the last two of which show-cased three of America's favourite composers, *Jelly's Last Jam* did remarkably well in the kudos stakes. In the Drama Desk Awards, Gregory Hines tied with Nathan Lane (*Guys And Dolls*) for best actor, and the show won outright for featured actress (Tonya Pinkins), lyrics, orchestrations-musical adaptations, and book. **Tony Awards** went to Hines, Pinkins, and lighting designer Jules Fisher. US television viewers were given a rare opportunity to see the creators and performers discussing the show's roots and relevance, in *Jammin': Jelly Roll Morton On Broadway*, which was transmitted in November 1992. Maurice Hines, brother of Gregory, headed the touring road company which rolled late in 1994.

Jellybean

John 'Jellybean' Benitez, a native of the Bronx and renowned Manhattan club DJ, made his mark in the early 80s as one of the post-disco dance scene's most favoured remixers/producers. Eventually he would earn his own record contract, though his *modus operandi* did not change; maintaining instead a largely supervisory role on his output. His debut release under his own name was the 1984 EP, *Wotupski!?!*, which carried two minor dance classics, 'The Mexican' and 'Sidewalk Talk', the latter penned by **Madonna** (he had significantly enhanced his own personal reputation by working on tracks for her earlier, including her breakthrough hit 'Holiday'). It wouldn't be until *Spillin' The Beans*, however, that Jellybean would actually record his own voice, alongside guest vocalists like Nikki Harris, who, ironically, had last been seen on Madonna's tour.
● ALBUMS: *Just Visiting This Planet* (Chrysalis 1987)★★★, *Jellybean Rocks The House* (Chrysalis 1988)★★★, *Spillin' The Beans* (Atlantic 1991)★★★.

Jellybread

Formed at England's Essex University by pianist **Pete Wingfield**, Jellybread was originally completed by Paul Butler (guitar/vocals) John Best (bass) and Chris Walters (drums). In 1969 the quartet secured a recording contract with the exemplary **Blue Horizon** label and although largely unadventurous, their albums offered a highly competent grasp of black music, including both blues and soul. They provided stellar accompaniment on **Lightnin' Slim**'s *London Gumbo* and *B.B. King In London*, but the unit dissolved in 1971 with the departure of Wingfield and Waters. Newcomers Rick Birkett (guitar) and Kenny Lamb (drums) joined for *Back To Beginning Again*, but Jellybread broke up when the set failed to make commercial headway. However, Wingfield enjoyed success as a solo artist, session pianist and member of Olympic Runners.
● ALBUMS: *First Slice* (Blue Horizon 1969)★★★, *65 Parkway* (Blue Horizon 1970)★★, *Back To Beginning Again* (Blue Horizon 1972)★★.

Jellyfish

This US band from San Francisco broke into the 90s by brilliantly repackaging the most gaudy elements of 60s and 70s pop with irresistible kitsch appeal. The band's dress sense was particularly colourful, one critic observing that it could have been drawn from the wardrobes of colour-blind charity shop consumers. The group was composed of Andy Sturmer (b. Pleasanton, San Francisco, California, USA; drums, vocals), **Jason Falkner** (guitar), along with brothers Chris Manning (b. Pleasanton, San Francisco, California, USA; bass) and Roger Manning (b. Pleasanton, San Francisco, California, USA; keyboards). This home-town they describe as '*Twin Peaks* without the Tree'. Members of the band were previously in Beatnik Beach, a short-lived funk pop outfit on **Atlantic Records**. Their debut single, 'The King Is Half Undressed', was a classy slice of retro-pop. Allied to their childlike dress sense, the formula guaranteed immediate television exposure. An album followed shortly after, which was assured and close to outright **Beatles** pastiche with strange overtones of **Earth Opera**. It was produced by Albhy Galuten, his first job since *Saturday Night Fever*. However, subsequent highly commercial singles, 'Baby's Coming Back', 'I Wanna Stay Home' and 'Now She Knows She's Wrong', failed to build on a strong chart platform. Jellyfish were more than happy to be able to play with at least two of their heroes, **Ringo Starr** and **Brian Wilson**, following introductions from Don Was from **Was (Not Was)**. Their debut album remains one of the more exciting debuts of the 90s and was followed in 1993 by the similarly crafted *Spilt Milk*. More complex arrangements and sometimes breathtaking harmonies showed definite influences of **10cc**, **Queen** and **Badfinger**. The line-up in 1993 included Eric Dover (guitar), who replaced Falkner, and Tim Smith (bass), who took over from Chris Manning. The band collapsed shortly afterwards. Falkner formed the Greys, who lasted for only one album, before working with **Eric Matthews** and releasing an excellent solo album. Manning and Dover formed Imperial Drag in 1996.
● ALBUMS: *Bellybutton* (Virgin 1991)★★★★, *Spilt Milk* (Virgin 1993)★★★★.

Jemini The Gifted One

b. *c*.1959, Brooklyn, New York, USA. Brooklyn-based **Mercury Records** recording artist Jemini made his mainstream debut with the *Scars And Pain* EP in 1995. Its title was taken from the artist's own struggle to gain recognition and a recording contract: 'I spent all of my formative years trying to get to where I am now. There were a whole lot of hard times, trials and tribulations. I made many sacrifices'. The EP, which was initially shipped on vinyl before emerging on CD, featured a variety of producers on its seven tracks, including Minesota, Prince Poetry (**Organized Konfusion**), Rah Boogie, Buckwild and Fatman. Prior to this release, there had been a single, 'Funk Soul Sensation', which married a booming reggae bassline with more traditional west coast sounds. It was backed by his hometown pride anthem, 'Brooklyn Kids'.

Jenkins, Andrew

b. 6 November 1885, Jenkinsburg, Georgia, USA, d. 1956. Jenkins, like **Riley Puckett**, was given incorrect medical treatment for eye disorders as a child. It took away almost all his vision and finally led to complete blindness. He took to religion as a boy and reputedly regularly preached to his friends. He developed a talent for playing musical instruments, becoming proficient on banjo, guitar, mandolin, piano, organ and French harp and began writing songs. He sold newspapers on the streets of Atlanta but in 1910, he became a Holiness preacher, which together with his songwriting and recording remained his main interest until his death. His first marriage failed but in 1919, he remarried and began to play local functions with his two newly acquired stepdaughters Irene (Spain) and Mary Lee (Eskew). In 1922, when WSB commenced broadcasting the Jenkins Family began regular programmes. When they first recorded, on 29 August 1924, they probably became the first country music family to do so and certainly one of the first to record both country and gospel music. They recorded sessions for several years sometimes under differing names including the Jenkins Sacred Singers and the Irene Spain Family. He also recorded as Blind Andy (a nickname he acquired early in his career) and with **Carson Jay Robison**. Jenkins composed over 800 songs, many of them gospel numbers such as 'If I Could Hear My Mother Pray Again', 'God Put A Rainbow In The Clouds' and 'Church In The Wildwood'. He also had a great talent for writing made-to-order saga or event songs and is especially remembered for the popular train songs, 'Ben Dewberry's Final Run' (popularised by **Jimmie Rodgers**) and 'The Wreck Of The Royal Palm' plus the ballad of the kidnapped and murdered child 'Little Marian Parker'. Other very popular Jenkins songs related the stories of outlaws or gangsters such as 'Kimmie Wagner' and 'Billy The Kid', while 'The Death Of Floyd Collins', told the true story of a youth trapped in a cave. Jenkins wrote the song to order overnight, sold it to Polk Brockman of **OKeh Records** for $25 and it became a big hit for **Vernon Dalhart** in 1925. (Dalhart successfully recorded several of Jenkins' songs). Jenkins made little money from the sale of any of his songs and mainly existed on donations received in respect of his preaching.

Jenkins, Billy

b. 5 July 1956, Bromley, Kent, England. Jenkins started to play the violin when he was seven years old and sang in a Parish church choir until the age of 12, graduating to special choirs at Westminster and St. Paul's Cathedral. Piano and viola lessons started when he was 11, providing a theoretical background to self-taught guitar, which he began the following year. The formation of Burlesque in 1972 began a 10-year partnership with saxophonist Ian Trimmer. Burlesque's derisory attitude - musicians would crowd round drummer Kevin Currie during his solos, gasping with amazement - was not deemed saleable until the birth of punk in 1977, when the band signed to **Arista Records**. The humour did not translate well to record, though it is obvious that Jenkins's guitar is something special. Burlesque folded and Trimmer and Jenkins started working as a duo, performing at the Comic Strip alongside alternative comedians such as Alexei Sayle and Rik Mayall. In 1981 the band toured with maverick master-drummer **Ginger Baker** as his 'Nutters'. Jenkins had the musical training to take his absurdist-punk viewpoint into the web of his music, as was demonstrated by *Greenwich*, the first release with his group Voice Of

God Collective. His prolific ideas demanded more regular release, so he started his own label Wood Wharf (later VOTP Records). *Piano Sketches*, outlined compositions that later became fully fledged suites. Despite his onstage clowning, Jenkins has always managed to attract the best young players, frequently forcing them to produce better playing than they achieved in more self-regarding circumstances. Roy Dodds, drummer with **Fairground Attraction**, provided his music with a firm rhythmic base; **Loose Tubes** members Dai Pritchard (bass clarinet) and **Iain Ballamy** (tenor) provided brilliant solos on *Uncommerciality* and *Motorway At Night*. In 1991 Jenkins formed an alliance with free-improvising drummer **Steve Noble**, releasing *Tumba La Casa!* and engaging him in a sparring match at the 1991 Crawley Outside In Festival (complete with referee and five-minute rounds!). In 1996 he turned to the blues with the Blues Collective and released the excellent *S.A.D.* The unsettling humour and parodic bossa novas of Jenkins' often brilliant music bring life (and audiences) to advanced improvisation: a **Willem Breuker** figure the UK jazz scene badly needs. Like bassist **Danny Thompson** and the late **Frank Zappa** (to whom he is often compared), if Jenkins were unable to play any longer he could become a stand up comedian with natural ease.

● ALBUMS: *Burlesque* (1977)★★★, with Ian Trimmer *Live At The Comic Strip* (1981)★★★, *Sounds Like Bromley* (1982)★★★, *Piano Sketches 1973-1984* (1984)★★★★, *Beyond E Major* (1985)★★★, *Greenwich* (1985)★★, *Uncommerciality* (1986)★★★★, *Scratches Of Spain* (1987)★★★, *In The Nude* (1987)★★★, *Wiesen '87* (1987)★★, *Motorway At Night* (1988)★★★, *Jazz Cafe Concerts Vols 1 & 2* (1989)★★★, *Tumba La Casa!* (1990)★★★, *Blue Moon In a Function Room* (1990)★★★, *First Aural Exhibition* (1992),★★★ *S.A.D.* (Babel 1996)★★★.

Jenkins, Bobo

b. John Pickens Jenkins, 7 January 1916, Forkland, Alabama, USA, d. 14 August 1984, Detroit, Michigan, USA. After hoboing from 1928, and wartime army service, Jenkins settled in Detroit from 1944. In 1954, he recorded for **Chess Records**, singing and playing guitar on a classic record, with both sides notable for the swooping, amplified harmonica of Robert Richard; 'Democrat Blues' was unusual in being politically explicit. In the 50s Jenkins also recorded for Boxer and **Fortune** (the latter session again featuring Richard on excellent versions of 'Baby Don't You Want To Go' and '10 Below Zero'). At this time, Jenkins worked as a photographer in the ghetto bars, and his pictures are a valuable and fascinating record of the musicians and their audience. In the 70s, he founded the Big Star label, and issued three albums.

● ALBUMS: *Detroit Blues - The Early 1950s* (1966)★★★, *The Life Of Bobo Jenkins* (Big Star 1972)★★★, *Here I Am A Fool In Love Again* (Big Star 1975)★★★, *Detroit All Purpose Blues* (Big Star 1978)★★★, *Blues For Big Town* (1989)★★★.

Jenkins, Freddie

b. 10 October 1906, New York City, New York, USA, d. 1978. A student at Wilberforce University, trumpeter Jenkins played in the band directed by **Horace Henderson**, that later turned professional. Jenkins's light, airy style, coupled with an outgoing musical personality, attracted the attention of **Duke Ellington**, who hired him in 1928. Jenkins's health deteriorated, however, and six years later he had to leave the band because of respiratory problems. He continued to play intermittently, recording with his own band and playing in the bands of **Luis Russell** and Ellington again, but retired from music in 1938.

● ALBUMS: *The Indispensable Duke Ellington Vols 1/2 & 3/4* (RCA 1929-34)★★★★.

Jenkins, Gordon

b. 12 May 1910, Webster Groves, Missouri, USA, d. 24 April 1984, Malibu, California, USA. A distinguished songwriter, arranger and conductor, as a child Jenkins occasionally played organ at the Chicago movie theatre where his father was the regular organist. During Prohibition he played piano in a St. Louis speakeasy and was later employed by a radio station in the same city. In 1936 he became chief staff arranger for **Isham Jones**, producing skilful charts for this superior dance orchestra, and later composed and arranged for **Woody Herman**, **Lennie Hayton**, **Vincent Lopez**, **Benny Goodman** and **André Kostalanetz**. He composed Herman's theme, 'Blue Prelude' (with Joe Bishop), and 'Goodbye', which Goodman used as the closing music to hundreds of radio shows. In 1936 he conducted the orchestra for *The Show Is On* on Broadway, and in the following year settled on the west coast, working for Paramount. In 1939 he began a five-year tenure as musical director for NBC in Hollywood. In the mid-40s he worked on the **Dick Haymes** show and in 1945 became staff conductor for **Decca Records**. In the same year Jenkins wrote and recorded a long work, in effect a personal love song to New York City, entitled 'Manhattan Tower'. This piece for orchestra and singers has been performed by the Atlanta Symphony Orchestra, in revues and on television. In 1949 Jenkins was back in New York, working on the score for the Broadway show *Along Fifth Avenue*, and at the Capitol and Paramount theatres. Among his song credits, several of which have attracted the attention of jazz musicians, are 'Homesick - That's All', 'Blue Evening', 'Married I Can Always Get', 'New York's My Home', and 'You Have Taken My Heart', 'P.S. I Love You' and 'When A Woman Loves A Man' (the last three with **Johnny Mercer**). In 1952 Jenkins wrote the score for *Bwana Devil*, the first 3-D feature film, and, through the years, accompanied many top artists on record, such as **Martha Tilton**, **Louis Armstrong** and **Peggy Lee**. His work with **Frank Sinatra** received much critical acclaim, notably the albums *Where Are You?* (1957) and *No One Cares* (1959), and his scores for **Nat 'King' Cole** included the definitive vocal arrangement of 'Stardust' for *Love Is The Thing* (1957). Gordon Jenkins and his Orchestra had their own series of hits from 1942-53, often with various vocalists, which included 'I Don't See Me In Your Eyes Anymore', 'Again', 'Don't Cry Joe', 'My Foolish Heart', 'Bewitched', two with the Weavers, 'Tzena, Tzena, Tzena' and 'Goodnight, Irene' (US number 1 in 1950), 'I'm Forever Blowing Bubbles', and 'So Long (It's Been Good To Know Ya)'. He won a Grammy Award in 1965 for his arrangement of **Frank Sinatra**'s 'It Was A Very Good Year', and served as arranger and conductor on the singer's 1973 television comeback.

● ALBUMS: with Louis Armstrong *Louis Armstrong-Gordon Jenkins* 10-inch album (Decca 1954)★★★, *The Complete Manhattan Tower* (Capitol 1956)★★★, *Dreamer's Holiday* (1958)★★★, *Hawaiian Wedding* (1962)★★, *I Live Alone* (1965)★★★, *Soft Soul* (1966)★★★, *My Heart Sings* (1966)★★★, *Blue Prelude* (1967)★★, *Paris I Wish You Love* (60s)★★, *In The Still Of The Night* (60s)★★★, *P.S. I Love You* (60s)★★.

Jenkins, Gus

b. 24 March 1931, Birmingham, Alabama, USA, d. December 1985, Los Angeles, USA. Like many of his generation, Jenkins drew his influences from 40s blues and spent much of his mature career adapting to the demands of rock 'n' roll and R&B. As his earliest recordings for **Chess** and **Specialty** show, Jenkins, like **Jimmy McCracklin**, modelled himself on St. Louis pianist **Walter Davis**. Both largely unissued sessions took place in 1953 and featured 'Cold Love' and 'Mean And Evil', which along with 'Eight Ball' and 'I Ate The Wrong Part', were based on Davis originals. Thereafter, Jenkins recorded extensively for Combo and Flash, before he started his own Pioneer label in 1959. Most of these recordings were piano or organ instrumentals with his own or Mamie Perry's vocals. He continued this policy through the early 60s with a series of singles on General Artists. Late in the decade, he converted to Islam and assumed the name Jaarone Pharoah.

● ALBUMS: *Cold Love* (Diving Duck 1987)★★★, *Jericho Alley Blues Flash* (Diving Duck 1988)★★★, *Chess Blues* (MCA/Chess 1992)★★★, *Bloodstains On The Wall/Country Blues From Specialty* (Specialty/Ace 1994)★★★, *The Specialty Story* (Specialty/Ace 1994)★★★.

Jenkins, Leroy

b. 11 March 1932, Chicago, Illinois, USA. Jenkins began playing violin as a small child and, although he later tried other instruments, it was as a violinist that he became known in local jazz circles. In the early 60s he taught music in Alabama and back in Chicago, which is where, in 1965, he became involved with **Muhal Richard Abrams** in the AACM. He joined **Anthony Braxton**'s first group with **Leo Smith**, and moved to Paris in 1969. The unit added drummer Steve McColl, recorded several albums, became known as the Creative Construction Company, but then broke up and Jenkins returned to the USA. In 1971, the Creative

Construction played a reunion concert with guests Abrams and **Richard Davis**, which was recorded and later released in two parts by Muse Records. In 1971 Jenkins formed the **Revolutionary Ensemble**, a trio with bassist **Sirone** and drummer **Jerome Cooper**. After the Revolutionary Ensemble folded in the late 70s, Jenkins was associated with the New York-based Composer's Forum and also recorded with both upcoming musicians such as **Anthony Davis**, **George Lewis** and **James Newton** and veterans Muhal Richard Abrams and **Andrew Cyrille**. In his playing style Jenkins ignored the conventions of the European classical violin. Although a jazz predecessor, **Stuff Smith**, had used the instrument in a manner which also ignored preconceptions, scraping the strings and striking the box to create whatever sounds his imagination demanded, Jenkins went much further. In his hands the violin became many instruments; it could be a richly lyrical singer of ballads, it could be used to deliver harsh and sometimes raucous counterpoint, it could be a means to play driving rhythmic patterns. In freeing the instrument from previous constraints, Jenkins has established himself as a major figure in contemporary music. He has also occasionally recorded on viola. The 80s saw him devoting much of his time to composing, though he also led a blues-inspired band, Sting, which featured a front-line of violins and two guitars. In the 90s he recorded with **Joseph Jarman**.

● ALBUMS: with Creative Construction Company *Creative Construction Company, Vols 1 And 2* 1971 recording (1975)★★★, *George Lewis* (Black Saint 1978)★★★★, *For Players Only* (1975)★★★, *Solo Concert* (India Navigation 1977)★★★★, *The Legend Of Ai Glatson* (Black Saint 1978)★★★, *Space Minds, New Worlds, Survival Of America* (Tomato 1979)★★★, with Muhal Richard Abrams *Lifelong Ambitions* 1977 recording (Black Saint 1981)★★★, *Revolutionary Ensemble* (Enja 1982)★★★★, *Mixed Quintet* 1979 recording (1983)★★★, with Sting *Urban Blues* (Black Saint 1984)★★★, *Live!* (Black Saint 1993)★★, with Joseph Jarman *Out Of The Mist* (Ocean 1998)★★★.

Jenkins, Martin

b. 17 July 1946, London, England. A solid, reliable character; an essential component of a successful folk scene. An important member of **Whippersnapper**, Jenkins became interested in acoustic instruments at an early age. Throughout the late 60s and 70s he worked in a number of bands, such as **Dando Shaft**, **Hedgehog Pie**, **Bert Jansch's Conundrum**, **Five Hand Reel** and **Plainsong**. In 1982 he formed an occasional unit, Quiet Riot. The mixture of ex-Dando Shaft personnel and other old friends, resulted in *Carry Your Smile*. Now married to a Bulgarian singer, with whom he occasionally tours, his musical tastes have moved in an Eastern European direction, and he has become a successful record producer.

● ALBUMS: *Carry Your Smile* (1983)★★★.

Jenkins, Snuffy, And Pappy Sherrill

This duo, also known as the Hired Hands, comprised Dewitt Jenkins (b. 27 October 1908, Harris, Rutherford County, North Carolina, USA, d. 30 April 1990; banjo/guitar/washboard/ vocals) and Homer Lee Sherrill (b. 23 March 1915, Sherrill's Ford, near Hickory, North Carolina, USA; fiddle/vocals). Jenkins first played guitar with his fiddle playing brother, Verl, in the late 20s. They later added two other musicians and played for local dances and on WBT Charlotte, as the Jenkins String Band, until 1936. Between 1936 and 1938, he played with **J.E. Mainer**'s Mountaineers and appeared on several of their **Bluebird** recordings. In 1938, when they were resident at WIS Columbia, Mainer decided to leave. Jenkins, his brother and others continued to play WIS, where they were joined by Sherrill late in 1939. Station announcer **Byron Parker**, who always referred to himself as the Old Hired Hand, became leader of the new band, which played radio as the WIS Hillbillies but made recordings as Byron Parker's Mountaineers. Sherrill had learned to play fiddle as a child and played on local radio in his early teens. Prior to joining Jenkins at WIS, he had worked on WBT Charlotte with several units, including the **Blue Sky Boys**, the **Morris Brothers** and Mainer's Mountaineers and also played on Bluebird recordings. Parker's Mountaineers, who included guitarists/vocalists Leonard Stokes and Clyde Robbins, were a versatile band with a repertoire that varied from instrumentals to harmony quartet singing. Parker played no instrument but acted as compere and sang bass in the quartets. They recorded 16 sides for Bluebird in 1940. The band had changes in personnel which saw Julian Medlin, a former medicine show entertainer, Gene Ray and Floyd Lacewell became members by the date of their next recordings for the De Luxe label in 1946. Parker died in 1948 and Jenkins and Sherrill, whose comedy routines as Snuffy And Pappy were increasing, decided to continue to run the band but probably as a tribute to their dead friend, they changed its name to the Hired Hands. Using Medlin's acting skill, Jenkins and Sherrill varied the band's output to include comic sketches as well as their bluegrass and old timey music. It proved very popular and when WIS began television programmes in 1953, the Hired Hands were immediately added to that medium. They made recordings for Folk-Lyric in 1962, which were later reissued by **Arhoolie**, and cut two albums for **Rounder Records** in the 70s. They were popular on the bluegrass festival circuit and continued to play into the late 80s. In the early 70s, Medlin died and Jenkins' health began to prevent him maintaining the hectic schedules. In 1971, guitarist Harold Lucas usually sang lead vocals, while his son, Randy, played banjo and lead guitar. They recorded their last album, in 1989, for Old Homestead. Jenkins' health, which prevented him playing banjo except on two numbers, worsened and he passed away on 30 April 1990. He had begun a three-finger style of bluegrass banjo playing that influenced later players such as **Don Reno** and **Earl Scruggs**. Sherrill, whose fine traditional fiddle playing also influenced others, continued to make appearances at bluegrass and old timey festivals.

● ALBUMS: *Carolina Bluegrass* (Folk-Lyric 1962)★★, *33 Years Of Pickin' And Pluckin'* (Rounder 1971)★★★, *Crazy Water Barn Dance* (Rounder 1977)★★★, *Something Special* (Old Homestead 1989)★★★.

Jenner, Peter

b. c.1944. An economics graduate from Cambridge University, Jenner drifted into the London underground scene in 1966. A jazz fan, he organised **AMM**, an *avant garde* group which made one album for **Elektra**. With former British Airways executive Andrew King, he became manager of **Pink Floyd**, securing them a recording contract with **EMI**. King and Jenner founded Blackhill Enterprises, named after a farm they owned in Wales. Although Pink Floyd moved to another management company in 1968, Blackhill built up a stable of underground artists, including **Edgar Broughton** Band, **Marc Bolan**, **Roy Harper** and **Kevin Ayers**. Blackhill organized free concerts in London's Hyde Park including Floyd, **Rolling Stones** and **Blind Faith**. Jenner also produced a number of albums in the 70s, including most of Roy Harper's output, two records by **Alberto Y Lost Trios Paranoias** and albums by John Gorman and Grimms. He later worked on Philip Rambow's 1979 solo release. In the 80s, King and Jenner split up with the latter managing **Billy Bragg** and running his own label.

Jenney, Jack

b. Truman Elliot Jenney, 12 May 1910, Mason City, Indiana, USA, d. 16 December 1945. After performing in a band directed by his father, a music teacher, Jenney debutted with Austin Wylie but then played trombone in various bands, including one led by Mal Hallett and a junior edition of the high-class **Isham Jones** band. In the late 30s Jenney became a studio musician but also recordedand played with Richard Himber, Phil Harris, Lenny hayton, Andre Kostelanetz, **Freddy Rich**, **Red Norvo**, **Johnny Williams** and **Glenn Miller**. In 1939 he briefly led his own big band, and worked together with vocalists including Louise Tobin, Bonnie Lake and Meredith Blake, but when this band collapsed he joined **Artie Shaw**. In the early 40s he resumed studio work, then tried leading again, including taking over the Bobby Byrne band and recorded with his wife, singer Kay Thompson; soon afterwards he was inducted into the US Navy. On his discharge he returned to the studios after relocating to the west coast and worked in radio (notably with Dick Haymes), but died in a Hollywood hospital during December 1945 after surgery for appendicitis. A polished stylist, Jenney is still highly regarded by musicians for his flawless technique.

● ALBUMS: *Jack Jenney And His Orchestra* (1938-40)★★★.

Jennings, Tommy

b. 8 August 1938, USA. Both his parents and his brother, **Waylon Jennings**, were musical but Tommy only started performing when he left the US Army. He played bass with his brother's group, the Waylors, for five years. He managed Waylon for a time and they adapted 'Delia's Gone' together. Waylon also recorded Tommy's 'Life Goes On'. Jennings has recorded spasmodically, sounding reasonably like his brother, but US country chart placings tell the story - 'Make It Easy On Yourself' (number 96, 1975), 'Don't You Think It's Time' (number 71, 1978) and with Rex Gosdin, 'Just Give Me What You Think Is Fair' (number 51, 1980).

● ALBUMS: *Equal Opportunity Lovin' Man* (1982)★★★.

Jennings, Waylon

b. Wayland Arnold Jennings, 15 June 1937, Littlefield, Texas, USA. Jennings' mother wanted to christen him Tommy but his father, William Alvin, insisted that the family tradition of 'W.A.' should be maintained. His father played guitar in Texas dancehalls and Jennings' childhood hero was **Ernest Tubb**, with whom he later recorded. When only 12 years old, he started as a radio disc jockey and then, in Lubbock, befriended an aspiring **Buddy Holly**. In 1958, Holly produced his debut single 'Jole Blon' and they co-wrote 'You're The One', a Holly demo that surfaced after his death. Jennings played bass on Holly's last tour, relinquishing his seat for that fatal plane journey to the **Big Bopper**. Jennings named his son, Buddy, after Holly and he recalled their friendship in his 1976 song 'Old Friend'. Much later (1996) he contributed a poignant version of 'Learning The Game' with **Mark Knopfler** to the Buddy Holly tribute album *notfadeaway*. After Holly's death, Jennings returned to radio work in Lubbock, before moving to Phoenix and forming his own group, the Waylors. They began a two-year residency at a new Phoenix club, J.D's, in 1964. The album of their stage repertoire has worn well, but less satisfying was *Don't Think Twice*, Jennings' album for **A&M**. '**Herb Alpert** heard me as **Al Martino**,' says Waylon, 'and I was wanting to sound like **Hank Williams**'. Bobby Bare heard the A&M album and recommended Jennings to record producer **Chet Atkins**. Jennings started recording for RCA in 1965 and made the US country charts with his first release, 'That's The Chance I'll Have To Take'. He co-wrote his 1966 country hit, 'Anita, You're Dreaming', and developed a folk-country style with 'For Loving Me'. He and **Johnny Cash** shared two wild years in Nashville, so it was apt that he should star in *Nashville Rebel*, a dire, quickly made film. Jennings continued to have country hits - 'Love Of The Common People', 'Only Daddy That'll Walk The Line' and, with the **Kimberlys**, 'MacArthur Park'. However, he was uncomfortable with session men, feeling that the arrangements were overblown. He did his best, even with the string-saturated 'The Days Of Sand And Shovels', which was along the lines of **Bobby Goldsboro**'s 'Honey'. When Jennings was ill with hepatitis, he considered leaving the business, but his drummer Richie Albright, who has been with him since 1964, talked him into staying on. Jennings recorded some excellent Shel Silverstein songs for the soundtrack of *Ned Kelly*, which starred **Mick Jagger**, and the new Jennings fell into place with his 1971 album, *Singer Of Sad Songs*, which was sympathetically produced by **Lee Hazlewood**. Like the album sleeve, the music was darker and tougher, and the beat was more pronounced. Such singles as 'The Taker', 'Ladies Love Outlaws' and 'Lonesome, On'ry And Mean' showed a defiant, tough image. The cover of *Honky Tonk Heroes* showed the new Jennings and the company he was keeping. His handsome looks were overshadowed by dark clothes, a beard and long hair, which became more straggly and unkempt with each successive album. The new pared-down, bass-driven, no-frills-allowed sound continued on *The Ramblin' Man* and on his best album, *Dreaming My Dreams*. The title track is marvellously romantic, and the album also included 'Are You Sure Hank Done It This Way?', 'Bob Willis Is Still The King', a tribute to his roots, and 'Let's All Help The Cowboys (Sing The Blues)', an incisive look at outlaw country with great phased guitar. *Wanted! The Outlaws* and its hit single, 'Good Hearted Woman', transformed both **Willie Nelson** and Waylon Jennings' careers, making them huge media personalities in the USA (the 1996 Anniversary reissue added nine tracks, plus the brand new **Steve Earle** song 'Nowhere Road', sung by Nelson and Jennings). The first of the four 'Waylon And Willie' albums is the best, including the witty 'Mammas, Don't Let Your Babies Grow Up To Be Cowboys' and 'I Can Get Off On You'. In his autobiography, Nelson subsequently revealed a constant drug habit, while in his own audiobiography, *A Man Called Hoss*, Jennings admitted to 21 years' addiction in an ode bidding farewell to drugs. Jennings was tired of his mean and macho image even before it caught on with the public. He topped the US country charts for six weeks and also made the US Top 30 with a world-weary song for a small township, 'Luckenbach, Texas', which is filled with disillusionment. Further sadness followed on 'I've Always Been Crazy' and 'Don't You Think This Outlaw Bit's Done Got Out Of Hand?'. He aged quickly, acquiring a lined and lived-in face which, ironically, enhanced his image. His voice became gruffer but it was ideally suited to the stinging 'I Ain't Living Long Like This' and 'It's Only Rock & Roll'. His theme for *The Dukes Of Hazzard* made the US Top 30, but the outlaw deserved to be convicted for issuing such banal material as 'The Teddy Bear Song' and an embarrassing piece with **Hank Williams Jnr.**, 'The Conversation'. The latter was included on *Waylon And Company*, which also featured duets with **Emmylou Harris** and actor James Garner. Jennings has often recorded with his wife, **Jessi Colter**, and he and Johnny Cash had a hit with 'There Ain't No Good Chain Gang' and made an underrated album, *Heroes*. His albums with Nelson, Cash and **Kris Kristofferson** as the **Highwaymen** were also highly

successful. Jennings and Cash had major heart surgery at the same time and recuperated in adjoining beds. A change to MCA and to producer Jimmy Bowen in 1985 had improved the consistency of his work, including brilliant reworkings of **Los Lobos**' 'Will The Wolf Survive?' and **Gerry Rafferty**'s 'Baker Street'. His musical autobiography, *A Man Called Hoss* (Waylon refers to everyone as 'hoss'), included the wry humour of 'If Ole Hank Could Only See Us Now'. Despite his poor health, Jennings still looks for challenges and *Waymore's Blues (Part II)* was produced by Don Was. On the *Red Hot And Country* video, his thought-provoking 'I Do Believe' showed him at his best, questioning religious beliefs. Willie and Waylon will be remembered as outlaws and certainly they did shake the Nashville establishment by assuming artistic control and heralding a new era of grittier and more honest songs. Whether they justify the tag 'outlaws' is a moot point - **Jerry Lee Lewis** is more rebellious than all the so-called Nashville outlaws put together. **Bear Family Records** have repackaged Jennings' recordings in a 15-album series, *The Waylon Jennings Files*, which includes many previously unissued titles. In 1996 he signed to Justice Records and released the impressive *Right For The Time*. **Sting**, **Sheryl Crow** and **Mark Knopfler** guested on 1998's hard-rocking *Closing In On The Fire*.

● ALBUMS: *Waylon Jennings At J.D's* (Bat 1964)★★, *Don't Think Twice* (A&M 1965)★★, *Waylon Jennings - Folk/Country* (RCA 1966)★★, *Leaving Town* (RCA 1966)★★, *Nashville Rebel* (RCA 1966)★★★, *Waylon Sings Ol' Harlan* (RCA 1967)★★, *The One And Only Waylon Jennings* (Camden 1967)★★★, *Love Of The Common People* (RCA 1967)★★, *Hangin' On* (RCA 1968)★★, *Only The Greatest* (RCA 1968)★★★, *Jewels* (RCA 1968)★★★, *Waylon Jennings* (Vocalion 1969)★★★, with the Kimberlys *Country Folk* (RCA 1969)★★★, *Just To Satisfy You* (RCA 1969)★★★, *Ned Kelly* film soundtrack (United Artists 1970)★★, *Waylon* (RCA 1970)★★★, *Singer Of Sad Songs* (RCA 1970)★★★, *The Taker/Tulsa* (RCA 1971)★★★, *Cedartown, Georgia* (1971)★★, *Good Hearted Woman* (RCA 1972)★★★, *Ladies Love Outlaws* (RCA 1972)★★★, *Lonesome, On'ry And Mean* (RCA 1973)★★★, *Honky Tonk Heroes* (RCA 1973)★★★★, *Nashville Rebel* film soundtrack (RCA 1973)★★★, *This Time* (RCA 1974)★★★, *The Ramblin' Man* (RCA 1974)★★, *Dreaming My Dreams* (RCA 1975)★★★★, *Mackintosh And T.J.* (RCA 1976)★★★, with Willie Nelson, Jessi Colter, Tompall Glaser *Wanted! The Outlaws* (RCA 1976)★★★★, *Are You Ready For The Country?* (RCA 1976)★★★, *Waylon 'Live'* (RCA 1976)★★, *Ol' Waylon* (RCA 1977)★★★, with Nelson *Waylon And Willie* (RCA 1978)★★★★, with Colter, John Dillon, Steve Cash *White Mansions* (1978)★★★, *I've Always Been Crazy* (RCA 1978)★★★, *The Early Years* (RCA 1979)★★, *What Goes Around Comes Around* (RCA 1979)★★★, *Waylon Music* (RCA 1980)★★★, *Music Man* (RCA 1980)★★, with Colter *Leather And Lace* (RCA 1981)★★, with Nelson *WWII* (RCA 1982)★★★★, with Colter *The Pursuit Of D.B. Cooper* film soundtrack (1982)★★, *Black On Black* (RCA 1982)★★, *It's Only Rock & Roll* (RCA 1983)★★★, *Waylon And Company* (RCA 1983)★★, with

Nelson *Take It To The Limit* (Columbia 1983)★★★, *Never Could Toe The Mark* (RCA 1984)★★, *Turn The Page* (RCA 1985)★★, *Will The Wolf Survive?* (MCA 1985)★★★★, with Nelson, Johnny Cash, Kris Kristofferson, *Highwayman* (Columbia 1985)★★★★, with Cash *Heroes* (Columbia 1986)★★★, *Hangin' Tough* (MCA 1987)★★★, *A Man Called Hoss* (MCA 1987)★★, *Full Circle* (MCA 1988)★★★, with Cash, Kristofferson, Nelson *Highwayman 2* (Columbia 1990)★★★, *The Eagle* (Epic 1990)★★★, with Nelson *Clean Shirt* (Epic 1991)★★, *Too Dumb For New York City - Too Ugly For L.A.* (Epic 1992)★★★, *Cowboys, Sisters, Rascals & Dirt* (Epic 1993)★★★, *Waymore's Blues (Part II)* (Epic 1994)★★, with Nelson, Cash, Kristofferson *The Road Goes On Forever* (Liberty 1995)★★, *Ol' Waylon Sings Ol' Hank* (WJ 1995)★★★, *Right For The Time* (Justice 1996)★★★, with Willie Nelson, Jessi Colter, Tompall Glaser *Wanted! The Outlaws (1976-1996, 20th Anniversary)* (RCA 1996)★★★★, *Closing In On The Fire* (Ark 1998)★★★.

● COMPILATIONS: *Greatest Hits* (RCA 1979)★★★★, *Greatest Hits, Volume 2* (RCA 1985)★★★, *Waylon: Best Of Waylon Jennings* (RCA 1985)★★★, *New Classic Waylon* (MCA 1989)★★★, *Silver Collection* (RCA 1992)★★★, *Only Daddy That'll Walk The Line: The RCA Years* (RCA 1993)★★★, *The Essential Waylon Jennings* (RCA 1996)★★★★, *Super Hits* (RCA 1998)★★★.

● VIDEOS: *Renegade Outlaw Legend* (Prism 1991), *The Lost Outlaw Performance* (1991), *America* (1992).

● FURTHER READING: *Waylon Jennings*, Albert Cunniff. *Waylon - A Biography*, R. Serge Denisoff. *Waylon And Willie*, Bob Allen. *The Waylon Jennings Discography*, John L. Smith (ed.). *Waylon: An Autobiography*, Waylon Jennings with Lenny Kaye.

Jennings, Will

b. 27 June 1944, Kilgore, East Texas, USA. He moved to Tyler when he was 12 and at that time took up the trombone as he had become fascinated with traditional jazz. Jennings is one of the leading lyric writers of the 80s and 90s, best known for his work with the **Crusaders**, **B.B. King**, **Jimmy Buffett** and **Steve Winwood**. As a teenager Jennings played guitar in rock bands, the most notable was Blue Mountain Marriage. He then became a literature teacher at the University of Wisconsin, Eau Claire. He moved to Nashville in 1971 and co-wrote four songs with **Troy Seals** for **Dobie Gray**'s *Drift Away*. During the 70s he composed further material for country artists but had his first pop success co-writing with Richard Kerr. Together they composed 'Somewhere In The Night' for **Barry Manilow** and 'I Know I'll Never Love This Way Again' and 'No Night So Long' for **Dionne Warwick**. Next, Jennings forged a partnership with **Joe Sample** of the **Crusaders** to create the big hits 'Street Life' and 'One Day I'll Fly Away', recorded by **Randy Crawford**. He continued to write with Sample and B.B. King used their songs for three albums, *Midnight Believer*, *Take It Home* and *There's Always One More Time*. One of his biggest selling pop-soul ballads, however, was 'Didn't We Almost Have It All', co-written with Michael Masser for **Whitney Houston**. Jennings' most fruitful long-lasting collaboration has been with Winwood, whom he met in 1981 following an introduction by **Chris Blackwell**. Their first success together was the US hit 'While You See A Chance', from *Arc Of A Diver*. Jennings co-composed a number of tracks from that album. Jennings subsequently wrote the lyrics for many tracks on all further Winwood solo albums, including the hymn-like 'Theres A River', 'Talking Back To The Night', 'And I Go', 'Back In The High Life', 'I Wll Be Here', 'Valerie' and the US hit singles, 'Higher Love' (1986) and 'Roll With It' (1988). He met country star Jimmy Buffett in 1982 and wrote two albums with him *Riddle In The Sand* and *Last Mango In Paris*. The anthem of the movie *An Officer And A Gentleman* 'Up Where We Belong' was written with **Buffy Saint-Marie** and was a worldwide hit for **Joe Cocker** and **Jennifer Warnes** and is Jenning's most lucrative copyright. He received a BMI award with **Eric Clapton** for 'Tears In Heaven' in 1996. He also struck up a friendship and musical partnership with **Roy Orbison**, writing a number of songs including 'Wild Hearts Run Out Of Time' from the Nic Roeg movie *Insignificance*. Hits and Academy and BAFTA awards continued into the 90s as Jennings was commissioned to write songs for movies and established artists. In 1998, he co-wrote (with James Horner) **Celine Dion**'s chart-topping 'My Heart Will Go On', the theme tune to the phenomenally successful film *Titanic*. His success is now self-perpetuating and he is one of the most sought-after writers of the past two decades. Jennings is humble about working with talented musicians like Winwood and Sample and yet he paints their music with colourful romantic lyrics. In 1996 he was collaborating with Winwood again and spent time working in Ireland with **Paul Brady**. Jennings states 'a great piece of (popular) music is so important, it deserves the very best I can write to it'. All this is maintained with a down-to-earth attitude, painful modesty, a love of flat caps, British poetry and literature.

Jensen, Kris

b. Peter Kristian Jensen, 4 April 1942, New Haven, Connecticut, USA. Jensen was a one-hit-wonder whose sole chart entry was the 1962 US Top 20 success, 'Torture', a song written by **John D. Loudermilk** which the **Everly Brothers** had turned down. Jensen recorded singles for the Colpix, Leader and Kapp labels before signing with Hickory Records. 'Torture' was his first release for that label; more than a half-dozen subsequent releases failed to match the debut's success. Jensen later recorded for White Whale and **A&M Records**.

● ALBUMS: *Torture* (1962)★★.

● COMPILATIONS: *Let's Sit Down: A Milestone In Rock 'N' Roll Music, Volume One* (1979)★★, *Torture: A Milestone In Rock 'N' Roll Music, Volume Two* (1979)★★.

Jensen, Papa Bue

b. Arne Jensen, c.1928, Denmark. After becoming hugely popular in his own country during the late 50s and early 60s, trombonist Jensen's reputation spread as his band was used to accompany many visiting American jazz artists. Although these performances were usually restricted to Scandinavian countries, recordings with the visitors helped to give the band and its leader a following elsewhere. In more recent years Jensen has capitalized upon this popularity by travelling the international festival circuit. The mostly traditional musicians with whom he has played, sometimes on record, have included **Wild Bill Davison**, **George Lewis**, **Edmond Hall**, **Wingy Manone** and **Albert Nicholas**.

● ALBUMS: *Papa Bue's Viking Jazz Band: The Anniversary Album* (1956-66)★★★★, *Papa Bue's Viking Jazz Band* (1958)★★★★, *George Lewis With Papa Bue's Viking Jazz Band* (1959)★★★, *Papa Bue's Viking Jazz Band With Wingy Manone And Edmond Hall* (1966)★★★, *Down By The Riverside* (1968)★★★, *Wild Bill Davison With Papa Bue's Viking Jazz Band* (1974-75)★★★★.

Jepson, Tony, And The Whole Truth

While his former colleagues in **Little Angels** made quick headway in 1994 as **b.l.o.w.**, UK vocalist Jepson was more stealthily piecing together the rudiments for his own solo career. At the outset he said: 'I do not want to be a pop star again.' Signing to Cottage Industry Records, Jepson recruited former **Elvis Costello** drummer Pete Thomas, bass player Roger Davis and guitarist Russ Goodwin. The line-up embarked on touring in October 1995 under the name Tony Jepson And The Whole Truth, following the August release of *Ignorance Is Bliss*. Jepson commented: 'I looked long and hard to find the right sort of musicians to work with. The last thing I wanted to do was work with famous people.' The 10-song collection was co-written with guitarist Goodwin, with Jepson taking charge of production in his own barn studio, constructed opposite his home.

● ALBUMS: *Ignorance Is Bliss* (Cottage Industry 1995)★★★.

Jerome, Henry

Henry Jerome formed his dance band orchestra in 1932 in Norwich, Connecticut, USA. Consisting of eight to ten musicians, with vocalists Frank Warren and David Allen, their greatest impact came through frequent radio exposure on the *Dinner At The Green Room* show on the ABC network. This was broadcast remote from the Green Room of the Hotel Edison in New York City. Songs such as 'Homing Pigeon', 'I Love My Mama', 'Nice People', 'Night Is Gone', 'Until Six' and 'Oh, How I Need You, Joe' soon became staples of east coast airwaves. There were also a series of albums titled *Brazen Brass*, a title adapted from their popular 'Theme From Brazen Brass' number. These songs were released on labels including Roulette, **MGM**, **London**, **Coral** and **Decca Records**, building a strong reputation for

the orchestra's **Hal Kemp** derived style. As well as east coast dates the band took engagements at the Chase Hotel in St. Louis, the Claridge and Peabody in Memphis, and the Roosevelt in New Orleans. However, their main income was still derived from the Edison Hotel, where they were booked over several years.

Jerome, Jerry

b. 19 June 1912, New York City, New York, USA. In 1935, after playing tenor saxophone part-time in dance bands as a means of paying his way through medical school, Jerome opted for a career in music. The following year he was in **Glenn Miller**'s short-lived band, then played with **Red Norvo** and **Artie Shaw** and in 1938 became a member of **Benny Goodman**'s highly-popular band. In 1940 he was back with Shaw, but freelanced on record dates with **Lionel Hampton**. Two years later he was mostly working in studios, occasionally playing on record dates and carrying out executive duties with record companies. By the end of the 40s he was fully immersed in broadcasting, as a conductor, composer, arranger and musical director. Highly regarded by the bandleaders for whom he worked, and to whose performances he contributed many fine jazz solos, Jerome eventually retired from his formal work in music, but continued to play for pleasure into the 80s.

● ALBUMS: *The Jerry Jerome Trio* (1985)★★★.

● COMPILATIONS: *The Jerry Jerome Trio* (c.1939-40)★★★, with Lionel Hampton *Historical Recording Sessions* (1939-41)★★★, *Jerry Jerome And His Cats And Jammers* (1944)★★★★.

Jerry Lee's Greatest! - Jerry Lee Lewis

Jerry Lee Lewis's UK tour collapsed when it was revealed that he had married his 13 year old cousin. His sales plummeted but Sun Records persevered, hoping for a single that was so good that rock 'n' rollers would just have to buy it. Unfortunately, Jerry Lee had lost his impetus, so Sam Phillips taunted him by saying, 'You couldn't cover Ray Charles for shit.' Jerry Lee immediately tore into a take-no-prisoners version of 'What'd I Say', which restored him to the charts. The resulting album covered all the periods of his Sun career and included his singles 'Great Balls Of Fire', 'Let's Talk About Us' and Charlie Rich's 'Breakup'. 'Cold Cold Heart', from 1957, shows that Jerry Lee was always a fine country singer. When a researcher asked Jerry Lee who played on his records, he replied: 'I played on them - what the hell else do you need to know?'

● Tracks: *Money; As Long As I Live; Hillbilly Music; Breakup; Hello, Hello Baby; Home; Let's Talk About Us; Great Balls Of Fire; Frankie And Johnny; Cold Cold Heart; What'd I Say; Hello Josephine.*

● First released 1962

● UK peak chart position: 14

● USA peak chart position: did not chart

Jeru The Damaja

His stage name in full reading Jeru The Damaja: D Original Dirty Rotten Scoundrel, Jeru (b. Kendrick Jeru Davis, c.1971) is a native New Yorker, whose name refers to the 'first god', son of Egyptian deities Osiris and Isis (his father was a Rastafarian). Having at one time earned a living changing tyres for Greyhound buses, he made his first demos with his homeboy/DJ PF Cuttin', before meeting up with Guru of **Gang Starr** at their 'Manifest' video shoot. His hardcore, Brooklyn style was thus premiered on Gang Starr's *Daily Operation* album (on 'I'm The Man'). Jeru also worked freestyle on their live shows. In turn **DJ Premier** would produce Jeru's debut cut, 'Come Clean'. This had been originally issued as a promo single entitled 'Gang Starr Doundation Sampler', on Gang Starr's own label, Illkid Records. His approach was resolutely old school: 'A long time ago rhyming was about having some skills, and what I tried to do is say let's bring it back to the skills and forget about the guns, take it to the skills level and then we'll see who the real men are'. His debut album was widely venerated in both the specialist and general music press, not least due to one of Premier's most effective productions and Jeru's clear, heavily enunciated style.

● ALBUMS: *Ths Sun Rises In The East* (Payday/Double Vinyl 1994)★★★, *Wrath Of The Math* (Payday 1996)★★★.

Jerusalem Slim

When **Michael Monroe** began working on the follow-up to his *Not Fakin' It* solo album, songwriting work with ex-**Billy Idol** guitarist Steve Stevens metamorphosed into a full band with the recruitment of drummer Greg Ellis and Monroe's former **Hanoi Rocks** colleague, bassist Sam Yaffa. However, the guitarist's bombastic style never really gelled with Monroe's more straightforward rock 'n' roll approach, and the band dissolved when Stevens joined ex-**Mötley Crüe** vocalist **Vince Neil**'s band; this did little to promote an amicable split, as Neil had been driving in the accident in which Monroe and Yaffa's late bandmate Razzle had died. Monroe and Yaffa formed the more satisfying **Demolition 23**, and publicly disowned the posthumous release of *Jerusalem Slim*, which received universally poor reviews.

● ALBUMS: *Jerusalem Slim* (Mercury 1993)★★★.

Jessie, Obie Donmell 'Young'

b. 28 December 1936, Dallas, Texas, USA. Inspired by **Roy Brown** and **Joe Williams**, Young Jessie teamed up with fellow Jefferson High School alumni - **Johnny Watson**, **Richard Berry** and Cornell Gunter - in the early 50s to set up a vocal group. In 1953, the Debonaires were signed to the Bihari's Flair label and rechristened the Flairs. During 1954-55, Jessie began carving out a solo career on Modern Records, with whom he had his biggest hit, 'Mary Lou' in 1955. The song was later covered successfully by **Ronnie Hawkins** on Roulette. At Modern, Jessie also recorded a classic of black rock 'n' roll, 'Hit Git & Split' before moving on to a brief spell with the **Coasters** and resuming his solo career on **Atlantic/Atco** (1957), **Capitol** (1959), **Mercury** (1961), Vanessa (1962) and Bit (1964). In the early 70s Jessie sang with the group Seeds Of Freedom and toured Europe the following decade as both an R&B performer and a jazz singer. He currently lives with his wife, singer Barbara Prince, near Venice Beach.

● COMPILATIONS: *Hit Git & Split* (Ace 1982)★★★, *Shuffle In The Gravel* (Mr R&B 1986)★★★, *Shufflin' & Jivin'* (Ace 1987)★★★.

Jesters

The Jesters were representative of the classic New York style of doo-wop characterized as 'greasy', in which the vocal harmony was in a rock 'n' roll style, extremely expressive, loaded with exotic flourishes, and usually supporting a falsetto lead. The members of the Jesters were Lenny McKay (lead), Adam Jackson (d. 21 February 1995; lead), Anthony 'Jimmy' Smith (second tenor), Leo Vincent (baritone) and Noel Grant (bass). The group came together in 1955, and was signed by Paul Winley for his Winley label in 1957. They were regularly teamed with another local group, the **Paragons**, in live mock-competitions. Their first release, 'So Strange'/'Love No One But You', was a double-sided hit in the New York area in the summer of 1957. In the autumn they hit again locally with 'Please Let Me Love You'. 'The Plea', a remake of the **Chantels**' hit, made it to number 74 of the **Billboard** pop chart in 1958, but, like the other records, it mainly sold in New York. 'I Laughed'/'Now That You're Gone' from the summer of 1958 was the last record to feature the original group. In 1960 a new line-up of Jackson, Smith, Melvin Lewis and Don Lewis recorded the Jesters' most successful song, 'The Wind', a remake of the 1954 **Diablos** hit.

● COMPILATIONS: *The Paragons Meet The Jesters* (Jubilee 1959)★★★, *The Paragons Meet The Jesters* (Collectables 1990)★★★, *'War': The Paragons Vs The Jesters* (Sting Music Ltd. 1993)★★★, *The Best Of The Jesters* (Collectables 1993)★★★.

Jesus And Mary Chain

Formed in East Kilbride, Scotland, this quartet comprised William Reid (vocals, guitar), Jim Reid (vocals, guitar), Douglas Hart (bass) and Murray Dalglish (drums). In the summer of 1984 they moved to London and signed to **Alan McGee**'s label, **Creation Records**. Their debut, 'Upside Down', complete with trademark feedback, fared well in the independent charts and was backed with a version of **Syd Barrett**'s 'Vegetable Man'. In November 1984, Dalglish was replaced on drums by **Primal Scream** vocalist Bobby Gillespie. By the end of the year, the group was attracting considerable media attention due to the violence at their gigs and a series of bans followed. Early the following year, the group signed to the **WEA/Rough Trade** label Blanco y Negro. The Reid brothers publicly delighted in the charms of amphetamine sulphate, which gave their music a manic edge. Live performances usually lasted 20 minutes, which brought more controversy and truculence from traditional gig habitués, who felt short-changed. 'Never Understand' further underlined comparisons with the anarchic school of 1977 in general and the **Sex Pistols** in particular. For their next release, however, the group surprised many by issuing the more pop-orientated 'Just Like Honey'. By October 1985, Gillespie had grown tired of the Jesus And Mary Chain and returned to his former group, Primal Scream. One month later, the Reid Brothers issued their highly acclaimed debut, *Psychocandy*. Full of multi-tracked guitar distortion, underscored with dark melodies, many critics proclaimed it one of rock's great debuts. The following August the group reached the UK Top 20 with the melodic 'Some Candy Talking', which received curtailed radio play when it was alleged that the subject matter concerned heroin. During the same period, the group found a new drummer, John Moore, and parted from their manager, Alan McGee. Further hits with 'April Skies' and 'Happy When It Rains' preceded their second album, *Darklands*. Again fawned over by the press, though not to quite the same extent as their debut, it was followed by a tempestuous tour of Canada and America, during which one brother was briefly arrested then acquitted on a charge of assaulting a fan. In the spring of 1988 a compilation of the group's various out-takes was issued. This assuaged demand before the arrival of *Automatic* at the turn of the decade. The band was effectively just a duo for this record, with programmed synth drums as backing to the usual barrage of distortion and twisted lyrics (the best example of which was the single, 'Blues From A Gun'). *Honey's Dead* also housed a powerful lead single in 'Reverence', which brought the band back to the charts. After this, the Reid brothers changed tack for *Stoned & Dethroned*, with the feedback all but gone in favour of an acoustic, singer-songwriter approach. Self-produced and recorded at home, its more reflective texture was embossed by the appearance of guest vocalists **Shane MacGowan** and Hope Sandoval (**Mazzy Star**). They rejoined Creation Records at the end of 1997 and issued 'Cracking Up', their debut single of the new era, in March 1998. It was followed by *Munki*, on which the Reid brothers experimented with a motley collection of different styles.

● ALBUMS: *Psychocandy* (Blanco y Negro 1985)★★★★, *Darklands* (Blanco y Negro 1987)★★★, *Automatic* (Blanco y Negro 1989)★★, *Honey's Dead* (Blanco y Negro 1992)★★★, *Stoned & Dethroned* (Blanco y Negro 1994)★★★, *Munki* (Creation 1998)★★★.

● COMPILATIONS: *Barbed Wire Kisses* (Blanco y Negro 1988)★★★, *The Sound Of Speed* (1993)★★★.

● FURTHER READING: *The Jesus and Mary Chain: A Musical Biography*, John Robertson.

Jesus Christ Superstar

Although originating in the UK, the first staging of *Jesus Christ Superstar* was on Broadway, where it opened at the Mark Hellinger Theatre on 17 October 1971. With a book by Tom O'Horgan, which was based on the New Testament, music by **Andrew Lloyd Webber** and lyrics by **Tim Rice**, the show was originally released as an album with a cast that included Murray Head, **Yvonne Elliman**, **Ian Gillan** and **Mike d'Abo**. Record sales were of the spectacular, gold disc variety, and helped counteract the generally unfavourable reviews from the New York critics. Nevertheless, one critic, Otis L. Guernsey Jnr., was far-sighted enough to observe that despite the show's 'indigestible stage imagery' and its 'questionable taste', it was also 'as unstoppable as a circus'. Criticism from religious leaders, who disliked the equating of Christ with a pop star on the decline, helped publicize the show and it ran for 720 performances at the Mark Hellinger Theatre. The London production, which made its debut at the Palace Theatre on 9 August 1972, marked the beginning of Lloyd Webber's unstoppable circus of lavishly-staged, thinly-plotted shows which continue into the 90s. **Paul Nicholas** was among a West End cast which sang songs such as 'Heaven On Their Minds', 'This Jesus Must Die', 'Gethsemane', 'Could We Start Again Please', and 'Everything's Alright'. Another of the numbers, a most appealing ballad, 'I Don't Know How To Love Him', became a hit for Yvonne Elliman and **Helen Reddy**. The show ran until August 1980, a total of 3,358 performances, and reigned as the third-longest-running musical in the history of the London theatre (after *Cats* and *Starlight Express*) until it was overtaken by *Les Misérables* in January 1994.

Over the years it enjoyed phenomenal success throughout the world, and in 1992 a 20th anniversary concert production toured the UK, starring one of the original performers, Paul Nicholas. Also in that year, a highly distinctive Japanese-language version by the Shiki Theatrical Company of Tokyo ('a kabuki-style production') was presented at the Dominion Theatre in London. Critical comments ranged from 'A memorable evening' to 'Seeing this ghastly show once 20 years ago was bad enough, but here it is again, banal and garish as ever.'

In 1994, the show was seen in South Korea, when that country staged the first full-length Japanese theatrical production in Seoul since World War II. A year later, *Jesus Christ Superstar* grossed $3.5 million in two weeks at Madison Square Garden in New York. In November 1996, a major West End revival opened at the Lyceum Theatre, which had undergone a £15 million revamp. In the leading roles were Zubin Varla (Judas), Joanna Ampil (Mary), and unknown Welsh rock singer Steve Balsamo (Jesus), who went on to win the Variety Award for Outstanding New Talent of 1996. Earlier that year, a BBC Radio 2 production starred **Roger Daltry** (Judas), Tony Hadley (ex-**Spandau Ballet**), along with Frances Ruffelle (Mary) and comedian Julian Clary (Herod).

Also in 1996, Ted Neely, who played Jesus in the 1973 film version, reprised his role for a US production at Stamford, Connecticut.

Jesus Jones

Blending the driving force of punk guitar with liberal use of samples and dance rhythms, Jesus Jones made an audacious debut with the single 'Info Freako'. The song was voted into the Top 10 year-end charts of all the UK music papers. Singer and songwriter Mike Edwards (b. 22 June 1964, City of London, England) is supported by Gen (b. Simon Matthews, 23 April 1964, Devizes, Wiltshire, England; drums), Al Jaworski (b. 31 January 1966, Plymouth, Devon, England; bass), Jerry De Borg (b. 30 October 1963, Kentish Town, London, England; guitar) and Barry D (b. Iain Richard Foxwell Baker, 29 September 1965, Carshalton, Surrey, England; keyboards). The group was formed in London, England, early in 1988, and was signed soon afterwards by **Food Records**. *Liquidizer* was an energetic debut that provided further UK hits with 'Never Enough' and 'Bring It On Down'. *Doubt*, produced mainly by Edwards, saw the band inject a stronger commercial element. After six weeks at the top of the US alternative chart it entered the ***Billboard*** chart and in the UK it reached number 1. In the summer of 1991 the band, who had always kept up a busy live schedule, became part of a nucleus of young UK bands enjoying hits in the USA. 'Right Here, Right Now' was a major success and along with **EMF**, who many claim were stylistically indebted to Jesus Jones, they found their abrasive pop suddenly popular within the USA's generally conservative market. However, there was a consequent fall-off in their domestic popularity, highlighted by the poor chart returns afforded *Perverse*. A four-year gap preceded the poorly received *Already*, with the album offering little of interest to attract new fans.
● ALBUMS: *Liquidizer* (Food 1989)★★★, *Doubt* (Food 1991)★★★, *Perverse* (Food 1993)★★, *Already* (Food 1997)★★.
● VIDEOS: *Big In Alaska* (PMI 1991).

Jesus Lizard

Formed in 1989, the Jesus Lizard originally comprised David Yow (vocals), David Sims (bass) - both formerly of the Austin, Texas act **Scratch Acid** - and Duane Denison (guitar), with the help of a drum machine. *Pure*, their abbreviated debut, maintained the uncompromising style of their former incarnation with its ponderous bass lines, growled vocals and crashing guitar. The set was produced by Steve Albini (ex-**Big Black**), with whom Sims had worked in the controversially named **Rapeman**. Albini engineered and coproduced *Head*, on which the Jesus Lizard were joined by drummer Mac McNeilly. The group's sound remained as powerful and compulsive as ever, although some critics detected an artistic impasse. Jesus Lizard would join **Nirvana** on a joint single that broke the UK charts, but *Down* saw the band maintain a ferocity that

deemed them very much a secular concern. They planned to expand their fanbase by signing to Capitol Records in 1995, but *Shot* showed little sign of compromise. The band's strength is as an exciting live act, with frontman Yow as a formidable singer and showman.
● ALBUMS: *Pure* mini-album (Touch & Go 1989)★★★, *Head* (Touch & Go 1990)★★★, *Goat* (Touch & Go 1991)★★★, *Liar* (Touch & Go 1992)★★★, *Show* (Collision Arts/Giant 1994)★★★, *Down* (Touch & Go 1994)★★★, *Shot* (Capitol 1996)★★★, *Blue* (Capitol 1998)★★★.

Jesus Of Cool - Nick Lowe

In America, presumably objecting to the title, they released this record with the title *Pure Pop For Now People*. In 1997, we 'now people' can continue to enjoy this little masterpiece. After serving his apprenticeship in Brinsley Schwarz, Lowe debuted during punk's heyday. He was fêted by the cognoscenti and his face regularly graced the pages of the UK music press. A 'surprise' hit single put Nick on *Top Of The Pops*, and the masses saw him only as the man who sang 'I Love The Sound of Breaking Glass'. It was a pity, because overlooked were gems such as 'So It Goes', 'Little Hitler' and the perceptive 'Music For Money'.
● Tracks: *Music For Money; I Love The Sound Of Breaking Glass; Little Hitler; Shake And Pop; Tonight; So It Goes; No Reason; 36-inches High; Marie Provost; Nutted By Reality; Heart Of The City.*
● First released 1978
● UK peak chart position: 22
● USA peak chart position: 127

Jet

This UK group was formed in 1974 by two former members of the psychedelic pop-orientated **John's Children**, Andy Ellison (vocals) and Chris Townson (drums), alongside Martin Gordon (bass/vocals), David O'List (guitar - erstwhile **Nice** and **Roxy Music** member) and Peter Oxendale (keyboards). They recorded one album that failed to set the music scene alight, despite a rigorous touring schedule. O'List once more demonstrated his inability to remain in a stable group and was later replaced by Ian McLeod. Oxendale soon followed him (to **Gary Glitter**'s **Glitter Band**) supplanted by ex-**Sparks** guitarist Trevor White. After **CBS Records**' unwillingness to finance another album, Jet disintegrated in the summer of 1976. After briefly going their separate ways, the trio of Ellison, Gordon and McLeod (followed later on by White), found a new lease of life in 1977 when they regrouped as the **Radio Stars**.
● ALBUMS: *Jet* (Columbia 1975)★★.

Jet Star

(see **Pama Records**)

Jetboy

This UK glam/sleaze rock quintet featured ex-**Hanoi Rocks** bassist Sam Yaffa, with Mickey Finn (vocals),

Fernie Rod (guitar), Billy Rowe (guitar) and Ron Tostenson (drums) completing the line-up. Applying cosmetic surgery to the riffs of **AC/DC**, **Poison** and **Aerosmith**, they leaned towards the bluesier end of this genre. However, Jetboy failed to add the necessary sparkle to make their material either memorable or commercially accessible. Yaffa quit in 1990 to join forces with former Hanoi Rocks vocalist **Michael Monroe**, and Jetboy have been inactive since.

● ALBUMS: *Feel The Shake* (MCA 1988)★★, *Damned Nation* (MCA 1990)★★.

Jeter-Pillars Orchestra

When the popular **territory band** led by **Alphonso Trent** broke up in 1933, two of the saxophonists decided to form their own small band. These musicians, friends from boyhood, were alto saxophonist James Jeter and tenor saxophonist Hayes Pillars. Taking their example from Trent, they set very high standards of musicianship and owing to careful choice of sidemen and the development of a popular repertoire, they became very successful on the dancehall circuits of the mid and south-western states. Based for many years at the Plantation Club, St. Louis, Missouri, the band played sophisticated danceband charts with considerable elan. Although it was never a jazz orchestra, over the years future jazz stars such as **Art Blakey**, **Jimmy Blanton**, **Sid Catlett**, **Charlie Christian**, **Kenny Clarke**, **Harry Edison**, **Jimmy Forrest**, **Jo Jones** and **Walter Page** were in the ranks. The band played on into the late 40s before disbanding. The Jeter-Pillars Orchestra had only one recording date, cutting four sides in 1937 during a period when none of its future stars was in the band. These records were unexceptional and the band's considerable reputation rests therefore upon the recollections of those who heard it in person or on the air, and for the many fine musicians who graced its ranks.

● ALBUMS: *The Territory Bands* (1937 recordings, one track only)★.

Jethro Tull

Jethro Tull was formed in Luton, England, in 1967 when Ian Anderson (b. 10 August 1947, Edinburgh, Scotland; vocals/flute) and Glenn Cornick (b. 24 April 1947, Barrow-in-Furness, Cumbria, England; bass), members of a visiting Blackpool blues group, John Evan's Smash, became acquainted with **Mick Abrahams** (b. 7 April 1943, Luton, Bedfordshire, England; guitar/vocals) and Clive Bunker (b. 12 December 1946, Blackpool, Lancashire, England; drums), Abrahams' colleague in local attraction, McGregor's Engine, completed the original line-up which made its debut in March the following year with 'Sunshine Day'. This commercially minded single, erroneously credited to Jethro Toe, merely hinted at developments about to unfold. A residency at London's famed Marquee club and a sensational appearance at that summer's Sunbury Blues Festival confirmed a growing reputation, while 'Song For Jeffrey', the quar-

tet's first release for the **Island** label, introduced a more representative sound. Abrahams' rolling blues licks and Anderson's distinctive, stylized voice combined expertly on *This Was* - for many Tull's finest collection. Although the material itself was derivative, the group's approach was highly exciting, with Anderson's propulsive flute playing, modelled on jazzman **Raahsan Roland Kirk**, particularly effective. The album reached the UK Top 10, largely on the strength of Tull's live reputation in which the singer played an ever-increasing role. His exaggerated gestures, long, wiry hair, ragged coat and distinctive, one-legged stance cultivated a compulsive stage personality to the extent that, for many spectators, Jethro Tull was the name of this extrovert frontman and the other musicians merely his underlings.

This impression gained credence through the group's internal ructions. Mick Abrahams left in November 1968 and formed **Blodwyn Pig**. When future **Black Sabbath** guitarist **Tony Iommi** proved incompatible, Martin Barre (b. 17 November 1946) joined Tull for *Stand Up*, their excellent chart-topping second album. The group was then augmented by John Evan (b. 28 March 1948; keyboards), the first of Anderson's Blackpool associates to be invited into the line-up. *Benefit*, the last outwardly blues-based album, duly followed and this period was also marked by the group's three UK Top 10 singles, 'Living In The Past', 'Sweet Dream' (both 1969) and 'The Witch's Promise' (1970). Cornick then quit to form **Wild Turkey** and Jeffrey Hammond-Hammond (b. 30 July 1946), already a legend in Tull's lexicon through their debut single, 'Jeffrey Goes To Leicester Square' and 'For Michael Collins, Jeffrey And Me', was brought in for *Aqualung*. Possibly the group's best-known work, this ambitious concept album featured Anderson's musings on organized religion and contained several tracks that remained long-standing favourites, including 'My God' and 'Locomotive Breath'.

Clive Bunker, the last original member, bar Anderson, left in May 1971. A further John Evan-era acolyte, Barriemore Barlow (b. 10 September 1949), replaced him as Jethro Tull entered its most controversial period. Although *Thick As A Brick* topped the US chart and reached number 5 in the UK, critics began questioning Anderson's reliance on obtuse concepts. However, if muted for this release, the press reviled *A Passion Play*, damning it as pretentious, impenetrable and the product of an egotist and his neophytes. Such rancour obviously hurt. Anderson retorted by announcing an indefinite retirement, but continued success in America, where the album became Tull's second chart-topper, doubtless appeased his anger. *War Child*, a US number 2, failed to chart in the UK, although *Minstrel In The Gallery* proved more popular. *Too Old To Rock 'N' Roll, Too Young To Die* marked the departure of Hammond-Hammond in favour of John Glascock (b. 1953, London, England, d. 17 November 1979), formerly of the Gods, **Toe Fat** and **Chicken**

Shack. Subsequent releases, *Songs From The Wood* and *Heavy Horses*, reflected a more pastoral sound as Anderson abandoned the gauche approach marking many of their predecessors. David Palmer, who orchestrated each Tull album, bar their debut, was added as a second keyboards player as the group embarked on another highly successful phase culminating in November 1978 when a concert at New York's Madison Square Garden was simultaneously broadcast around the world by satellite. However, Glascock's premature death in 1979 during heart surgery ushered in a period of uncertainty, culminating in an internal realignment. In 1980 Anderson began a projected solo album, retaining Barre and new bassist Dave Pegg (ex-**Fairport Convention**), but adding Eddie Jobson (ex-**Curved Air** and **Roxy Music**; keyboards) and Marc Craney (drums). Longtime cohorts Barlow, Evan and Palmer were left to pursue their individual paths. The finished product, *A*, was ultimately issued under the Jethro Tull banner and introduced a productive period that saw two more group selections, plus Anderson's solo effort, *Walk Into Light*, issued within a two-year period. Since then Jethro Tull has continued to record and perform live, albeit on a lesser scale, using a nucleus of Anderson, Barre and Pegg. *Catfish Rising* in 1991, although a disappointing album, was a return to their blues roots. *Roots To Branches* was a return to the standard Tull progressive rock album, full of complicated time changes, and fiddly new age and Arabian intros and codas. Squire Anderson has also become a renowned entrepreneur, owning tracts of land on the west coast of Scotland and the highly successful Strathaird Salmon processing plant.

● ALBUMS: *This Was* (Chrysalis 1968)★★★★, *Stand Up* (Chrysalis 1969)★★★★, *Benefit* (Chrysalis 1970)★★★, *Aqualung* (Chrysalis 1971)★★★★, *Thick As A Brick* (Chrysalis 1972)★★★, *A Passion Play* (Chrysalis 1973)★★, *War Child* (Chrysalis 1974)★★, *Minstrel In The Gallery* (Chrysalis 1975)★★★, *Too Old To Rock 'N' Roll Too Young To Die* (Chrysalis 1976)★★★, *Songs From The Wood* (Chrysalis 1977)★★★★, *Heavy Horses* (Chrysalis 1978)★★★, *Live - Bursting Out* (Chrysalis 1978)★★, *Storm Watch* (Chrysalis 1979)★★, *A* (Chrysalis 1980)★★, *The Broadsword And The Beast* (Chrysalis 1982)★★, *Under Wraps* (Chrysalis 1984)★★, *Crest Of A Knave* (Chrysalis 1987)★★★, *Rock Island* (Chrysalis 1989)★★, as the John Evan Band *Live '66* (A New Day 1990)★★, *Live At Hammersmith* (Raw Fruit 1990)★★, *Catfish Rising* (Chrysalis 1991)★★, *A Little Light Music* (Chrysalis 1992)★★, *Nightcap* (Chrysalis 1993)★★, *In Concert* (Windsong 1995)★★★, *Roots To Branches* (Chrysalis 1995)★★.
Solo: Ian Anderson *Walk Into Light* (Chrysalis 1983)★★, *Divinities: Twelve Dances With God* (EMI 1995)★★.

● COMPILATIONS: *Living In The Past* (Chrysalis 1972)★★★★, *M.U.: Best Of Jethro Tull* (Chrysalis 1976)★★★, *Repeat, The Best Of Jethro Tull - Volume II* (Chrysalis 1977)★★★, *Original Masters* (Chrysalis 1985)★★★, *20 Years Of Jethro Tull* 3-CD box set (Chrysalis 1988)★★★★, *25th Anniversary Box Set* 4-CD box set (Chrysalis 1992)★★★★, *The Anniversary Collection* (Chrysalis 1993)★★★.

● VIDEOS: *Slipstream* (Chrysalis 1981), *20 Years Of Jethro Tull* (Virgin Video 1988), *25th Anniversary Video* (PMI 1993).

Jets

A family act originally from the Polynesian island of Tonga, the Jets are eight of the 14 children of Mike and Vake Wolfgramm. The family moved to Salt Lake City, Utah, USA but eventually settled in Minneapolis, Minnesota. The oldest boy, Leroy (b. 1965), began showing musical interest as a young child and joined a club act including some of his uncles when he was aged 11. Leroy and several of his sisters formed their first group, Quasar, in 1978, performing as a Polynesian act at restaurants in the midwest. In 1984 the group signed with Don Powell, once a manager of the **Jacksons**. They eventually grew to eight, featuring Leroy, Eddie (b. 1966), Rudy (b. 1969), Haini (b. 1968), Kathi (b. 1970), Moana (b. 1973) and Elizabeth Wolfgramm (b. 1972), the last providing lead vocals on many of the group's hits. The eighth member, Eugene, left the group in 1988 to form a duo, Boys Club, earning them a US Top 10 hit that same year with 'I Remember Holding You'. The Jets' first US Top 10 hit, 'Crush On You' in 1986, which was later a 1987 Top 10 hit in the UK, made them teen sensations. The group continued their success in the USA with four further hits, but their albums did not fare as well. By the end of the 80s the appeal of the Jets had lessened considerably.

● ALBUMS: *The Jets* (1986)★★★★, *Christmas With The Jets* (1986)★★★, *Magic* (1987)★★★, *Believe* (1989)★★.

Jett, Joan, And The Blackhearts

b. Joan Larkin, 22 September 1960, Philadelphia, Pennsylvania, USA. Jett was one of the most successful US female singers to emerge from the rock scene of the 70s. She spent most of her childhood in the Baltimore, Maryland area, where she learned guitar as a child, playing along to favourite rock 'n' roll records. In 1972 her family relocated to Los Angeles, where she became enamoured with artists including **David Bowie**, **Suzi Quatro**, **T. Rex** and **Gary Glitter**. At the age of 15 she began infiltrating the Los Angeles rock scene and formed her first band. Producer **Kim Fowley** took the group under his wing and named it the **Runaways**, procuring a record contract with **Mercury Records**. The group recorded three punk-tinged hard rock albums that were unsuccessful in the USA but hits in Japan, where they recorded a live album. Also successful in England, they recorded their swan-song, *And Now ... The Runaways*, in that country in 1979. After the dissolution of the group, Jett moved to New York and teamed up with producer Kenny Laguna, who became her manager. Laguna had previously been involved with a number of 60s bubblegum hits. Laguna produced Jett's first solo album, which was released on the European Ariola label. When no US label picked it up, they issued it themselves and the album sold well, becoming one of the best-selling US independent records of that time. This led to a contract with Neil Bogart's Boardwalk Records, who reissued it as *Bad Reputation* (a title inspired by the less than enthusiastic industry response to Jett after the Runaways), and saw it reach number 51 in the US charts. With her group the Blackhearts (guitarist Ricky Byrd, bassist Gary Ryan and drummer Lee Crystal), Jett recorded *I Love Rock 'N' Roll* in late 1981, produced by Laguna and Ritchie Cordell. The title track, originally an obscure b-side for UK group the **Arrows**, became a major hit, largely owing to a big push from **MTV**, and spent seven weeks at number 1 in the USA in early 1982. The follow-up single, a cover version of **Tommy James And The Shondells**' 'Crimson And Clover', was itself a Top 10 hit, reaching number 7 in 1982. Also on the album was an update of a Jett song from the Runaways era, 'You're Too Possessive'. With Bogart's death, the group signed to MCA, which then distributed Blackheart Records. However, subsequent outings on that label were not nearly as successful as the Boardwalk releases. *Glorious Results Of A Misspent Youth* again retreated to Jett's past with the Runaways, this time on a revision of 'Cherry Bomb'. *Good Music* saw some intriguing collaborations, with members of the **Beach Boys** and **Darlene Love** guesting, and an unlikely rap duet with Scorpio of **Grandmaster Flash** And The Furious Five. The album also saw the departure of Lee Crystal and Gary Ryan, the former permanently replaced by Thommy Price. Jett, meanwhile, found time to make a second film appearance (following *We're All Crazy Now!*), playing Michael J. Fox's sister in *Light Of Day*; she also sang the **Bruce Springsteen**-penned theme. *Up Your Alley* brought another hit with 'I Hate Myself For Loving You', before 1990's *The Hit List*, an album of cover versions, which included a duet with **Ray Davies** on 'Celluloid Heroes'. *Notorious* saw her collaborate with Paul Westerberg of the **Replacements** on the co-written 'Backlash', but by the advent of *Pure And Simple*, Byrd was no longer a permanent member of the band. This set saw a guest appearance from L7 on a track entitled 'Activity Grrrl', emphasizing Jett's influence on a new generation of female rockers (by this time, Jett had also produced **Bikini Kill**, in addition to late 70s LA punk band the **Germs**).

● ALBUMS: *Joan Jett* (Blackheart 1980)★★★, *Bad Reputation* reissue of debut (Boardwalk 1981)★★★, *I Love Rock 'n' Roll* (Boardwalk 1981)★★★★, *Album* (MCA/Blackheart 1983)★★★, *Glorious Results Of A Misspent Youth* (MCA/Blackheart 1984)★★★, *Good Music* (Columbia/Blackheart 1986)★★★, *Up Your Alley* (Columbia/Blackheart 1988)★★★, *The Hit List* (Columbia/Blackheart 1990)★★★, *Notorious* (Epic/Blackheart 1991)★★★, *Pure And Simple* (Blackheart/Warners 1994)★★★.

● COMPILATIONS: *Flashback* (Blackheart 1993)★★★★, *Fit To Be Tied* (Mercury 1997)★★★.

Jeunemann, Margeurite

b. USA. Raised in a musical family, Jeunemann studied classical piano and clarinet, picked up guitar and banjo, and also began singing in folk music groups. Her decision to work within a group rather than as a soloist was prompted by shyness not a lack of belief in her abilities. She gradually branched into jazz while still maintaining a wide interest in many other musical forms. In 1978 she formed the vocal group, Rare Silk, based in Colorado and originally a female trio. In 1979 Rare Silk toured the Far East and the following year achieved considerable prominence touring the USA and Japan with **Benny Goodman**. In 1983 Jeunemann left the group and moved to New York working now as a single. In 1988 she joined the faculty of the University of Maine as Director of the Vocal Jazz department and has continued to successfully mix careers as a teacher and performing artist. She has worked in duos with bassists Ed Schuller, in 1983, and **Richard Davis**, in 1994. She has also sung in reunions with Rare Silk. An exceptionally gifted singer with a thorough understanding of the form and substance of jazz singing, Jeunemann's exceptional skills and talent are worth seeking out.

● ALBUMS: with Benny Goodman, Rare Silk *Live At The Aurex Jazz Festival* (East Wind 1980)★★★, with Rare Silk *New Weave* (Polygram 1982)★★, *By Whose Standards* (Jeunetunes 1994)★★★.

Jewel

b. Jewel Kilcher, 1974, Homer, Alaska, USA. Singer-songwriter Jewel left her home in Alaska at the age of 16 to study opera in Michigan, Illinois. She then joined her mother in her Volkswagen van mobile home in San Diego, California. At that time Jewel first began to sing professionally at the Innerchange coffee shop, an establishment serving the local surfing community. These concerts quickly attracted a strong local following, and inevitably drew the attendance of several major label A&R staff. There were also early indications of her sense of humour - notably a popular on-stage imitation of Dolores O'Riordan of the **Cranberries**. **Warner Brothers Records** won her signature, leading to the release of her February 1995 debut album, *Pieces Of You*. A low-key release, Jewel promoted it with a tour of west coast coffee houses and the release of the album's strongest track, 'Who Will Save Your Soul', as a single. Her first major exposure followed in May with an appearance on the syndicated *Late Night With Conan O'Brien* television show. She subsequently made frequent appearances in the tabloid gossip columns through her on-off relationship with actor Sean Penn (formerly **Madonna**'s husband). Penn, keen to launch himself as a director, later directed the video to Jewel's second single release, 'You Were Meant For Me'. As the album's sales profile began to increase, Jewel was offered the lead in a TNT benefit production of *The Wizard Of Oz*. However, a tour with former **Bauhaus** singer **Peter Murphy** was less well-received ('I wanted to kill myself after every show', she later told *Rolling Stone* magazine). She also performed one show in Detroit where the assembled audience were convinced they were there to see the similarly-named **Death Row Records** rapper, Jewell. Despite this, further television exposure on programmes such as *The Tonight Show With Jay Leno* and *Entertainment Tonight* ensured that *Pieces Of You* eventually achieved gold status. She also signed a $2 million dollar publishing deal with Harper Collins.

● ALBUMS: *Pieces Of You* (Atlantic 1995)★★★★.

Jewels

Formed in 1961 as the Impalas, this Washington, DC, USA-based all-female quartet was comprised of Carrie Mingo, Sandra Bears, Grace Ruffin and Margie Clark. As the Impalas, they came under the wing of **Bo Diddley**, who recorded the group in his personal studio and played guitar on their debut single, 'I Need You So Much'. Diddley secured a recording contract with **Chess Records**, but nothing emerged. They were then taken on by manager/producer Bob Lee, who changed their name to the Four Jewels in 1962. They issued five tracks on Start and then others for Chess, as well as background vocals for **Billy Stewart**, Ruffin's cousin. By 1964, having released another failed single on Tec Records, Mingo left, and was replaced by Martha Harvin. The group shortened its name to the Jewels and recorded a song called 'Opportunity' for **Carole King**'s Dimension label. The record reached number 64 in 1964 and was their only charting release. In 1965 they joined **James Brown**'s revue for a year. They broke up three years later. In the early 80s Mingo sang and recorded with a neo-doo-wop group, the Velons, who released *Moonlight And Music* on the Sold Smoke label in 1984. A year later, Mingo was reunited with the other Jewels - Bears, Ruffin, and Clark - and played in the Washington area. They released an album of re-recorded songs from their Start and Chess singles, *Loaded With Goodies*.

● ALBUMS: *Loaded With Goodies* (BJM 1985)★★★.

Jewels (reggae)

The Jewels were a Kingston, Jamaica-based vocal group formed in the early 70s. The line-up revolved around Glasford Manning, who had until 1975 recorded alongside **Junior Delgado**, Orville Smith and Hugh Marshall in **Time Unlimited**. Manning descended from the revered Jamaican lineage that spawned **Carlton And His Shoes** and, later, the **Abyssinians**. In common with his predecessors, Manning recorded conscientious songs, initially produced by **Winston 'Niney' Holness**. In 1977 the group released 'Jah I', coupled with **Leroy Smart** and **I. Roy**'s performance of 'Jah Is My Light'. The single was one of the first 12-inch vinyl discomixes, at the time referred to as a 'mastermix'. The success of the track resulted in further releases through Holness, including 'One Lick', 'Highest City', 'Prophecy Call' and *Mastermix 5*. The group also recorded 'Mr Big

Man' under the guise of Porti. During the late 70s occasional releases surfaced, including the classic 'Love And Livity' through the combined support of **Gregory Isaac**, **Bunny Wailer**, **Big Youth** and Trevor 'Leggo Beast' Douglas, who formed the Cash & Carry collective. The paean hailed the second coming, appealing for 'Love and livity - A so Jah seh - 'Til I Jah will be forward'. The song provided the foundation to Big Youth's classic 'Political Confusion' which, along with the Jewels' original, has become a prized collector's item. In 1981 the group followed their hit with 'Fountain Of Tears', which, although produced by Bunny Wailer, regrettably faltered.

Jigsaw

Barrie Bernard (b. 27 November 1944, Coventry, Midlands, England; bass), Tony Campbell (b. 24 June 1944, Rugby, Midlands, England; guitar), Des Dyer (b. 22 May 1948, Rugby, Midlands, England; vocals/drums) and Clive Scott (b. 24 February 1945, Coventry, Midlands, England; keyboards/vocals) became Jigsaw in 1966. Bernard came from **Pinkerton's Assorted Colours**, while Campbell had previously played in the **Mighty Avengers**. Scott and Dyer were a successful songwriting team - **Engelbert Humperdinck** covered their material - but it took the band nine years and 13 singles before their big hit, 'Sky High'. It was the theme to *The Man From Hong Kong*, and was the first release on the band's own label Splash. 'Sky High' was a worldwide hit. It was number 1 twice in Japan, thanks to a popular wrestler adopting it as his theme tune. Jigsaw enjoyed continuing success there, but elsewhere their star shone less brightly and in 1977 'If I Have To Go Away' only reached number 36 in the UK.

● ALBUMS: *Leathersdale Farm* (1970), *Sky High* (Splash 1975)★★★, *Jigsaw* (Spalsh 1977)★★★.

Jill Darling

After touring the UK provinces under the title of *Jack And Jill*, the re-named and revised *Jill Darling* opened in the West End at the Saville Theatre on 19 December 1934. The composer **Vivian Ellis** had gone to extreme lengths to bring together his 'dream couple', Frances Day and Arthur Riscoe, in this musical comedy by Marriot Edgar. His story told of a young girl, Jill Sonning (Frances Day), who, for reasons that are not entirely clear, is masquerading as an Hungarian cabaret performer, while Arthur Riscoe has a double role - as Pendleton Brown, who is running for Parliament on an 'anti-booze' ticket, and Jack Crawford, who substitutes for Brown when he gets drunk. Vivian Ellis and Desmond Carter wrote a lovely score which gave the two leading players 'Let's Lay Our Heads Together' and 'I'd Do The Most Extraordinary Thing', and several other charming pieces such as 'Dancing With A Ghost' (Riscoe), along with 'I'm In Budapest' and 'Pardon My English' (Day). The second leads, Louise Brown and John Mills (later to become a celebrated straight actor), had the jolly 'Nonny, Nonny, No', as well as the surprise hit of the show, 'I'm On a See-Saw', which became successful for **Ambrose** And His Orchestra in America, and was subsequently recorded by **Fats Waller**. In a scene reminiscent of a 40s Hollywood movie, the show's backer, a young South African by the name of Jack Eggar, 'suggested' that there might part in *Jill Darling* for his wife, Teddi St. Dennis, and Ellis and Carter obligingly whipped up 'Bats In The Belfrey' for the lady to sing with the young Edward Molloy. The show was a great success, but, after Frances Day had to leave in the early summer of 1935 to fulfil a filming commitment (she was replaced by a *real* Hungarian), business fell off, and the production closed after a run of 242 performances. There was a revival at the Winter Garden Theatre in 1944, with Riscoe in his original role, and Carol Lynne as Jill, but it only lasted for for two months.

Jilted John

Rabid Records, a new wave label based in Manchester, England, received a recording of 'Jilted John', composed and performed by an actor named Graham Fellowes. Rabid released this semi-monologue concerning the woes of a young lover, and were soon so overwhelmed by demand that **EMI** had to take over its marketing in 1978. Fellowes slipped into his Jilted John character in media interviews - a few similarly gormless appearances on BBC Television's *Top Of The Pops* pushed the record to number 4 in the UK chart - and necessitated the issue of an album and an 'answer' single by John's rival, Gordon The Moron. After this episode, however, Fellowes reverted to his acting career, including roles in the UK soap opera *Coronation Street* and a northern stage production of a play about **John Lennon**. Fellowes made a return (of sorts) to music in his new 90s guise - that of John Shuttleworth, a middle-aged showbiz hopeful. Enjoying considerable cult popularity, he has embarked on a series of musical/comedy tours throughout the UK, and makes numerous radio and television appearances, with a set of songs that includes the moving 'Pigeons In Flight' and the philosophical ode 'Up And Down Like A Bride's Nightie'.
● ALBUMS: *True Love Stories* (EMI 1978)★★★.

Jim And Jesse

The McReynolds Brothers, Jim (b. 13 February 1927) and Jesse (b. 9 July 1929, both on a farm at Coeburn, in the Clinch Mountain region of Virginia, USA), came from a musical family; their grandfather was a noted fiddle player, who had recorded for **RCA** Victor. The brothers learned to play several stringed instruments as children and as teenagers played at local dances. They made their radio debut in 1947 on WNVA Norton, by which time Jim usually played guitar and Jesse mandolin. Playing bluegrass/country material, they made their first recordings around 1951 for the small Kentucky label, but in 1952, after moving to WVLK Lexington, they joined **Capitol**. Owing to the Korean

War, Jesse spent two years in the Armed Forces, one in Korea, where he worked as an entertainer with **Charlie Louvin**. In 1954, he rejoined his brother at WNOX Knoxville, where they first worked on the *Tennessee Barn Dance*. Later they moved on to various radio and/or television stations in Alabama, Georgia and North Florida, and with their band, the Virginia Boys, they quickly established a reputation. The brothers' singing, with Jesse taking lead vocals and Jim adding high-pitched tenor harmonies, was obviously influenced by other brother duos such as the **Blue Sky Boys** and the **Louvins**. Jesse's 'crosspicking' mandolin work was a prominent feature in their usual bluegrass instrumental line-up. Their touring show included comedy routines and they performed a variety of material ranging from new songs to old standards and from bluegrass instrumentals to bluegrass versions of country hits. In 1959, some of their broadcasts were sponsored by Martha White Mills, making them that company's number two advertising unit after **Flatt And Scruggs**. They first appeared on the *Grand Ole Opry* in 1961 and became regulars in 1964. Their style of music made them popular at many venues, including a successful appearance at the 1963 Newport Folk Festival. In 1960, they joined **Columbia**, having recorded for Starday during the late 50s and in 1962, the label released their work on their Epic label. Although the recordings were steady sellers, they had limited US country chart success with only minor hits, including 'Cotton Mill Man' (1964). Their only Top 20 hit was 'Diesel On My Tail' (1967). In 1971, after moving to **Capitol**, they recorded an album of modern bluegrass using electrified instruments, but soon resorted back to their preferred acoustic sounds, and by 1972, they were producing their own albums. They have presented their own network television shows and have easily maintained their popularity as top bluegrass performers. They have appeared at all major venues and toured extensively, both in the USA and overseas, including appearances at London's Wembley Festival. They charted in 1982 with 'North Wind' (a trio recording with Charlie Louvin) and again in 1986 with 'Oh Louisiana'.
● ALBUMS: *Sacred Songs* (1961)★★, *Bluegrass Classics* (Epic 1963)★★★, *Bluegrass Special* (Epic 1963)★★★★, *The Old Country Church* (Epic 1964)★★, *Y'All Come: Bluegrass Humour* (Epic 1964)★★★, *Berry (Chuck) Pickin' In The Country* (Epic 1965)★★★, one side is Flatt And Scruggs *Stars Of The Grand Ole Opry* (Starday 1966)★★★, *Sacred Songs We Love* (Epic 1966)★★, *Sing Unto Him A New Song* (Epic 1966)★★★, *Diesel On My Tail* (Epic 1967)★★★, *All-Time Great Country Instrumentals* (Epic 1968)★★★, *Jim And Jesse Salutin' The Louvin Brothers* (Epic 1969)★★★, *Wildwood Flower* (Harmony 1970)★★★, *We Like Trains* (Epic 1970)★★★, *Freight Train* (Capitol 1971)★★★★, *The Jim & Jesse Show* (Capitol 1972)★★★, *Superior Sounds Of Bluegrass* (Capitol 1974)★★★, *Jesus Is The Key To The Kingdom* (1975)★★, *Paradise* (1975)★★★, *Live In Japan* (1975)★★, *Songs About Our Country* (1976)★★★, *Jim & Jesse* (1976)★★★, *Palace Of Songs* (1977)★★★, *Radio Shows*

(1978)★★★, *Early Recordings* (1978)★★★, *Songs Of Inspiration* (1978)★★★, *Jim & Jesse Today* (1980)★★, *Back In Tokyo Again* (1981)★★, *Jim & Jesse & Charlie Louvin* (1982)★★★, *Homeland Harmony* (1983)★★★, *Air Mail Special* (1985)★★★, *Somewhere My Love* (1986)★★★, *In The Tradition* (Rounder 1987)★★★, *Some Old, Some New, Some Borrowed, Some Blue* (1987)★★★, *Music Among Friends* (Rounder 1991)★★★.

By Jesse McReynolds: *Mandolin Workshop* (1972)★★★, *Me And My Fiddles* (1973)★★★, with Marion Sumner *Old Friends* (1979)★★★, *Guitar Pickin' Showcase* (1980)★★★, with Sumner *Fiddle Fantastic* (1986)★★★, *A Mandolin Christmas* (1988)★★, *The Mandolobro* (1991)★★★.

● COMPILATIONS: *Twenty Great Songs* (Capitol 1969)★★★★, *Jim And Jesse Story: 24 Greatest* (CMH 1980)★★★★, *Jim & Jesse: 1952-1955* (Bear Family 1992)★★★★, *Bluegrass And More* (Bear Family 1994)★★★★.

Jiminez, Flaco

b. Leonardo Jiminez, 11 March 1939, San Antonio, Texas, USA. Jiminez's grandfather, Patricio, learned the accordion from German neighbours and played in towns in southern Texas at the turn of the century. Jiminez's father, Santiago, was a noted accordionist and played lively dance music around San Antonio. His best-known composition is the polka 'Viva Seguin', named after a small town near San Antonio. Santiago, who started recording in 1936 and made some records for **RCA**, played the two-button accordion and made no attempt to integrate his music with other American forms. Jiminez, nicknamed El Flaco 'the skinny one', played bajo sexto with his father and made his recording debut in 1955 on 'Los Tecolotes'. He recorded with a group, Los Caminantes, and often had regional successes by considering contemporary lifestyle such as 'El Pantalon Blue Jean' and 'El Bingo'. His albums for **Arhoolie** attracted a following outside Texas, and his appearance alongside **Bob Dylan** on *Doug Sahm And Band* in 1973, brought him to the attention of rock fans. **Ry Cooder** began touring and recording with him, and Jiminez can be heard on Cooder's *Chicken Skin Music*, *Show Time*, *The Border* and *Get Rhythm*. Their key collaborations are the free-flowing 'He'll Have To Go' and the sombre 'Dark End Of The Street'. *Tex-Mex Breakdown* showed that Jiminez was thinking in terms of a wider audience. He has also worked with **Peter Rowan** and a key track is 'Free Mexican Airforce'. Jiminez tours in his own right and is popular at arts centres and folk venues throughout the UK. His father died in 1984 and his younger brother, Santiago Jnr., is also a professional accordionist with several albums to his name.

● ALBUMS: *El Principe Del Acordeon* (1977)★★★, *Flaco Jiminez Y Su Conjunto* (Arhoolie 1978)★★★★, with Santiago Jiminez *El Sonido De San Antonio* (Arhoolie 1980)★★★, *Mis Polkas Favorites* (UK *Viva Seguin*) (1983)★★★, *Tex-Mex Breakdown* (1983)★★★, *On The Move* (1984)★★★, with Los Paisanos, Los Hnos Barron, Los Formales *Augie Meyers*

Presents San Antonio Saturday Night (1986)★★★, *Ay Te Dejo En San Antonio* (Arhoolie 1986)★★★, with Ry Cooder, Fred Ojeda, Peter Rowan *The Accordion Strikes Back* (1987)★★★★, *Flaco's Amigos* (Arhoolie 1988)★★★★, *Partners* (Warners 1992)★★★, *Un Mojada Sin Licencia And Other Hits From The 1960s* (Arhoolie 1993)★★★.

● COMPILATIONS: *Arriba El Norte* (Rounder 1988)★★★, *San Antonio Soul* (Rounder 1991)★★★, *Flaco's First!* 1956-58 recordings (Arhoolie 1996)★★★.

Jiminez, Santiago, Jnr.

b. Texas, USA. In the track 'El Corrido De Santiago Jiminez', the accordionist Santiago Jiminez Jnr. pays tribute to the accomplishments of his father, the accordion player Santiago Jiminez. Santiago Jnr.'s brother, **Flaco Jiminez**, is the better known of the two. Santiago Jnr. is more traditional and has little experience of playing rock music. He favours the two-row button accordion and many of his recordings also feature his impassioned singing.

● ALBUMS: *Familia Y Tradicion* (Rounder 1989)★★★, *El Mero Mero De San Antonio* (Arhoolie 1990)★★★, with Flaco Jiminez *El Gato Negro* (Rounder)★★.

Jimmy Jam And Terry Lewis

Based in Minneapolis, Minnesota, USA, Jimmy 'Jam' Harris and Terry Lewis are prolific producers of contemporary R&B The two first worked together in the early 80s as members of Time (formerly Flyte Time), and subsequently, Harris (keyboards) and Lewis (bass) became black music's most consistently successful production duo. They formed their own record label, Tabu, in 1980, which enjoyed enormous success with artists such as the **S.O.S. Band** throughout the 80s. Among the other early bands and artists to benefit from the duo's writing and production skills were **Change**, **Cherrelle**, the **Force MD's**, **Johnny Gill** and the former Time singer **Alexander O'Neal**. Their greatest success, however, came as the creative catalysts behind **Janet Jackson**'s career. The first album they recorded with her, *Control*, included five hit singles, and the follow-up, *Rhythm Nation 1814*, was similarly successful. In 1990 Jam and Lewis recorded once again with Time, who had re-formed to make *Pandemonium*, which was released on **Prince**'s Paisley Park Records. Though the reunion was not widely regarded as a success, the duo's productions remained in the higher reaches of the charts. Their continued association with Jackson was never surpassed commercially but many others benefited from their expertise, especially with their pioneering work in what would become known as swingbeat, and cross-genre productions with artists ranging from the **Human League** to **Sounds Of Blackness**. In the 90s they also established a new record label, Perspective Records, distributed by **A&M Records**.

Jimmy The Hoover

Simon Barker (b. 22 July 1956, Malta; keyboards), Derek Dunbar (b. 31 August 1958, Aberdeen, Scotland;

vocals), Carla Duplantier (b. Hollywood, Los Angeles, California, USA; drums), Flinto (b. 11 March 1955, Zambia; bass) and Mark Rutherford (b. 14 April 1961, Hackney, London, England; guitar) formed the band in 1982. **Malcolm McLaren** gave them the name and a support tour with **Bow Wow Wow**. Cris Cole stepped in on bass guitar, and in 1983 they signed to **CBS** subsidiary Innervision. That year brought them their one hit, 'Tantalise (Wo Wo Ee Yeh Yeh)', a good pop song with an African influence. Along with Innervision stablemates **Wham!** and **Animal Nightlife**, the group had 'legal' problems that interfered with the promotion of the second single, 'Kill Me Quick', and constrained them for many months.

Jive Bombers

This New York R&B group was formed in 1948 from elements of two earlier acts, the Tinney Brothers (founded during the mid-30s) and the Palmer Brothers (founded late 20s). The group, recording for Coral as the Sparrows in 1949 and as the Jive Bombers after 1952, were from the same era as the **Mills Brothers** and **Ink Spots**. Thus, their age and repertoire of old songs kept them in staid nightclubs during most of their career, and their appearance in the teen rock 'n' roll market was very brief. When the group had a hit with 'Bad Boy' in 1957, the members were Earl Johnson (b. 30 November 1932, New York City, New York, USA; tenor vocals), Al Tinney (b. 28 May 1929, Ansonia, Connecticut, USA; piano), William 'Pee Wee' Tinney (b. 25 September 1930, New York City, New York, USA; drums, guitar) and Clarence Palmer (b. 2 January 1919, Pawtucket, Rhode Island, USA; bass fiddle). 'Bad Boy' went to number 7 on the R&B chart and number 36 on the pop chart. It was written and recorded by **Lillian Armstrong** as 'Brown Gal' in 1936, and had been recorded by the Jive Bombers twice before, in 1949 and 1952, as 'Brown Boy'. The Jive Bombers failed to reach the charts again, despite recording excellent material such as a remake of 'Cherry', a **Don Redman** composition from 1928. Palmer left the group in 1959, but the Jive Bombers stayed together until 1968.

● ALBUMS: *Bad Boy* (Savoy Jazz 1984)★★★★.

Jive Bunny And The Mastermixers

A throwback to the medley craze of the early 80s, with a similarly repetitive disco beat cushioning the samples, Jive Bunny are single handedly responsible for making recent generations believe that rock and pop classics of yesteryear are only 10 seconds long. A UK male production/mixing group comprising John Pickles and disc jockey Ian Morgan, they became UK chart-toppers with their first three singles 'Swing The Mood', 'That's What I Like', and 'Let's Party' during 1989. This equalled the record held by **Gerry And The Pacemakers** (1963) and **Frankie Goes To Hollywood** (1984). The idea was conceived by Pickles, previously the owner of an electrical shop. The concept for 'Swing The Mood' had originally come from an ex-miner

living in Norway called Les Hemstock. John's son Andy Pickles also helped out. They appeared on 'It Takes Two Baby' by Liz Kershaw and Bruno Brookes in December 1989. Subsequent hits scored progressively lower chart placings, doubtless to the relief of many; 'That Sounds Good' (number 4), 'Can Can You Party' (number 8), 'Let's Swing Again' (number 19). More recently they seem to have disappeared up their own bobtails, although Pickles has become highly successful as head of Music Factory, which controls a number of Dance labels such as trax, Defcon and Energize.

● ALBUMS: *Jive Bunny - The Album* (1989)★★★, *It's Party Time* (1990)★★.

● COMPILATIONS: *The Best Of ...* (Music Collection 1995)★★.

Jive Five

From Brooklyn, New York City, New York, USA, the Jive Five were one of the last doo-wop groups to have a national hit and one of the few to make a successful transition to the soul era. The group members were Eugene Pitt (b. 6 November 1937; lead), Jerome Hanna (first tenor), Richard Harris (second tenor), Billy Prophet (baritone) and Norman Johnson (d. 1970; bass). Their biggest hit was 'My True Story' (number 1 R&B, number 3 pop) from 1961, which was something of a neo-doo-wop sound. A particularly outstanding feature of the group's approach was the counterpointing exchanges between lead Pitt and bass Johnson. Continuing with the same sound, the group had lesser hits during the next two years with 'Never Never' (number 74 pop), 'What Time Is It' (number 67 pop) and 'These Golden Rings' (number 27 R&B). By 1964 the group had developed a soul sound and had joined United Artists Records. At this point Pitt and Johnson were supported by new members Casey Spencer (second tenor), Beatrice Best (baritone), and Webster Harris (first tenor). The group found success in 1965 with 'I'm A Happy Man' (number 26 R&B, number 36 pop), and followed with 'A Bench In The Park', which received good airplay in Washington, DC, but nowhere else. The group left United Artists in 1966, and their last chart record was in 1970, for **Decca**. In the 80s Eugene Pitt And The Jive Five made two fine albums for Ambient Sound, who were unable to break the group out of the limited audience for doo-wop harmony.

● ALBUMS: *The Jive Five* (United Artists 1965)★★★, *Here We Are* (Ambient Sound 1982)★★★, *Way Back* (Ambient Sound 1985)★★★.

● COMPILATIONS: *Our True Story* Beltone recordings (Ace 1991)★★★★, *My True Story* Beltone recordings (Relic 1991)★★★, *The Complete United Artists Recordings: I'm A Happy Man* (1992)★★★★.

Jive Records

A subsidiary of the UK Zomba group, founded by chairman Clive Calder, Jive was established in the UK in 1981. In response to the growing base of its US rap roster, Jive Records US was inaugurated three years later, where it has gained a significant market-share. The first rap single to emerge on the label (which also covered sundry other musical styles, including dance and pop) was **Whodini**'s 'Magic Wand'. Whodini also presided over the imprint's first rap album, a self-titled set from 1983. Although steady success continued with artists like **Kool Moe Dee, Boogie Down Productions, Wee Girl Papa Rappers, A Tribe Called Quest** and others, the label's real commercial breakthrough act would be **DJ Jazzy Jeff And The Fresh Prince**. Although already several albums into their career (including a debut set, *He's The Rapper And I'm The DJ*, which would be Jive's biggest seller), 'Boom! Shake The Room' gave the duo a surprise UK number 1. The group had formerly won the first ever Grammy for rap with 'Parent's Just Don't Understand' in 1988.

● ALBUMS: Whodini: *Whodini* (Jive 1983)★★★. DJ Jazzy Jeff And The Fresh Prince: *He's The DJ And I'm The Rapper* (Jive 1988)★★★★. Boogie Down Productions: *By All Means Necessary* (Jive 1988)★★★, *Ghetto Music: The Blueprint Of Hip Hop* (Jive 1989)★★★. A Tribe Called Quest: *People's Instinctive Travels And The Paths Of Rhythm* (Jive 1990)★★.

Jivin' In Bebop

Forget the amateur-night quality of the storyline and concentrate instead on the musical numbers which include a dozen powerful performances by **Dizzy Gillespie**'s big band. Given the relatively short life of this outstanding band, and the fact that it made only a handful of records, this 1946 film thus gains a value far in excess of its other shaky qualities. **Milt Jackson, John Lewis** and **James Moody** are on hand as is the inimitable **Helen Humes**.

JJ Fad

The break dance fad in the USA between 1985 and 1988 was known as the B-Boy period. This Los Angeles female rap trio, comprising M.C.J.B. (b. Juana Burns), Baby D (b. Dania Birks) and Sassy C (b. Michelle Franklin) came into fashion towards the end. Protégés of **Eazy-E**, their collective name stands for 'Just Jammin' Fresh And Def'. Boosted by an eponymous Top 30-peaking single, their debut album made a small dent in the album charts.

● ALBUMS: *Supersonic - The Album* (Ruthless 1988)★★.

Jo Jo Gunne

Formed by **Jay Ferguson** (b. John Ferguson, 10 May 1947, Burbank, California, USA; vocals/piano) and Mark Andes (b. 19 February 1948, Philadelphia, Pennsylvania, USA; bass/vocals), following their departure from **Spirit** in 1971. This hard rock quartet were completed by Matthew Andes (guitar/vocals) and Curly Smith (drums). Their contagious debut single 'Run Run Run' was an instant success, reaching number 6 in the UK. Shortly after, Andes was replaced by Jimmy Randall. Unfortunately, they were unable to progress musically, and their four albums are all a very similar pattern of average hard rock. *Bite Down Hard* is the most powerful album, particularly in 'Rock Around the Symbol' and 'Ready Freddy'. *Jumpin' The Gunne* featured a tacky album cover - with a photo montage depicting the band in bed together watching obese naked females flying through their window. The band broke up in 1974.

● ALBUMS: *Jo Jo Gunne* (Asylum 1972)★★★, *Bite Down Hard* (Asylum 1973)★★★★, *Jumpin' The Gunne* (Asylum 1973)★★, *So ... Where's The Show?* (Asylum 1974)★★.

Jo Jo Zep And The Falcons

This Australian R&B band was formed in Melbourne, Victoria in 1976 and based around talented frontman, **Joe Camilleri**, who shaped the band's musical direction and provided the focal point on stage. Initially the band recorded covers of well-known blues and R&B material, before eventually writing their own songs in the same vein. As a popular live act on the Melbourne circuit, their performances were exciting, their musicianship high and the band were well regarded in the industry. Joe Camilleri gathered quality musicians around him, such as John Power (bass), songwriter Wayne Burt (guitar), Wilbur Wilde (saxophone) and Gary Young (drums). The band continued the tradition of hard work, playing the pubs and smaller venues along the Australian east coast. A contract with the Australian label Mushroom Records started an association with English producer Pete Solley, which led to five hit singles in Australia, and ensured that their records were released in the USA and the UK where the band also toured. The hits dried up and Camilleri shortened the name to Jo Jo Zep in 1982 for a new 11-piece band and a more modern sound. The band continued in a reduced format until the end of 1983, remaining a successful live act. In 1984 Camilleri's next project, the zydeco-influenced Black Sorrows was launched.

● ALBUMS: *Don't Waste It* (1976)★★★★, *Whip It Out* (1977)★★★, *Let's Drip Awhile* (1979)★★★, *Screaming Targets* (1979)★★★★, *Hats Off Step Lively* (1980)★★★, *Sounds Of* (1980)★★★.

Joan Armatrading - Joan Armatrading

The anchor hymn for this album is the gorgeous 'Love And Affection', a song that never fails to captivate the ears when it is played even two decades later. Joan exposes her inner self with a collection of desperately honest tracks that never lapse into sentimentality. Her naturally bass-inflected voice is made in heaven for acoustic guitar - the combination is like gin and tonic, especially on 'Water With The Wine'. This may explain why her rock/guitar-based material of late is of average quality.

● Tracks: *Down To Zero; Help Yourself; Water With The Wine; Love And Affection; Save Me; Join The Boys; People; Somebody Who Loves You; Like Fire; Tall In The Saddle.*

● First released 1976

● UK peak chart position: 12

● USA peak chart position: 67

Joan Baez - Joan Baez

Few debut albums are as assured and self-realized as this impressive set. Folk-singer Baez possessed a voice of unrivalled purity, imbuing these recordings with a moving piquancy. She combined songs drawn from America's rich folk heritage with perceptive readings of Francis Childe ballads, bringing to them a haunting resonance. Her influence on a generation of female singers, including Judy Collins and Joni Mitchell, is immeasurable and two of the selections herein, 'The House Of The Rising Sun' and 'Johnoa', were later taken up, respectively, by Bob Dylan, followed by the Animals, and the Byrds.

● Tracks: *Silver Dagger; East Virginia; Ten Thousand Miles; The House Of The Rising Sun; All My Trails; Wildwood Flower; Donna Donna; John Riley; Rake And The Rambling Boy; Little Moses; Mary Hamilton; Henry Martin; El Preso Numero Nuevo; Johnoa.*
● First released 1962
● UK peak chart position: 9
● USA peak chart position: 15

Joan Baez In Concert - Joan Baez

The 'queen of folk' was an accomplished live performer as this, the first of two *In Concert* albums proved. Accompanying herself on acoustic guitar, Baez brought her pure, virginal soprano to contrasting material. Her interpretations of Childe ballads 'Matty Groves' and 'The House Carpenter' are particularly moving, but an empathy with American folklore, including Woody Guthrie and the Carter Family, is equally apparent. Baez's reading of Malvina Reynolds' protest song, 'What Have They Done To The Rain', is especially arresting and inspired a later pop hit for the Searchers. This album helped take folk music out of the coffee-house circuit and into national consciousness.

● Tracks: *Babe; I'm Gonna Leave You; Geordie; Copper Kettle; Kubaya; What Have They Done To The Rain; Black Is The Colour Of My True Love's Hair; Danger Water; Gospel Ship; The House Carpenter; Pretty Boy Floyd; Lady Mary; Ate Amanha; Matty Groves.*
● First released 1962
● UK peak chart position: did not chart
● USA peak chart position: 10

Joan Baez In Concert Part 2 - Joan Baez

A year had passed between the release of the first *In Concert* album and its successor. Joan Baez continued to draw on Childe ballads, spirituals and Appalachian songs, but the inclusion of Bob Dylan's 'Don't Think Twice, It's Alright' signalled her move from traditional to contemporary styles. The singer's memorable soprano voice ensured the special nature of her interpretations and brought continuity to a seemingly disparate content.

● Tracks: *Once I Had A Sweetheart; Jackaroe; Don't Think Twice, It's Alright; We Shall Overcome; Portland Town; Queen Of Hearts; Manha De Carnaval; Te Ador; Long Black Veil; Fennario; Ne Belle Cardillo; With God On Our Side; Three Fishers; Hush Little Baby; Battle Hymn Of The Republic.*
● First released 1964
● UK peak chart position: 8
● USA peak chart position: 7

Joan Baez/5 - Joan Baez

A gifted interpreter of traditional song, Joan Baez quickly brought that skill to bear on contemporary folk material. Her version of Phil Ochs' cautionary 'There But For Fortune' brought the singer a rare hit single without sacrificing her art. Johnny Richard Farina, Bob Dylan and Johnny Cash were among the others Baez chose to record herein, her pure, virginal soprano investing their songs with a tender beauty. A cello section invests Heitor Villa Lobos's 'Bachianas Brasileiras' with added poignancy, and shows that the singer's grasp of international themes and languages is as sure as that of Francis Childe ballads and broadsides.

● Tracks: *There But For Fortune; Stewball; It Ain't Me Babe; The Death Of Queen Jane; Child Number 170; Bachianas Brasileiras Number 5 - Aria; Go 'Way From My Window; I Still Miss Someone; When You Here Them Cuckoos Hollerin'; Birmingham Sunday; So We'll Go No More A-roving; O'Cangaceiro; The Unquiet Grave; Child Number 78.*
● First released 1965
● UK peak chart position: 3
● USA peak chart position: 12

Jobim, Antonio Carlos

b. Antonio Carlos Brasileiro de Almeida Jobim, 25 January 1927, Rio de Janiero, Brazil, d. 8 December 1994. Jobim can rightfully claim to have started the bossa nova movement when, as director of Odeon Records, he gave his friend **João Gilberto** his own composition 'Chega De Saudade'. The influence of the resulting record soon spread to the USA, where **Stan Getz** and **Charlie Byrd** made his compositions hugely popular. Although Jobim did record, and performed at Carnegie Hall with Getz, Byrd, and **Dizzy Gillespie** in 1962, it is as a composer that Jobim's influence remains huge, with tunes including 'Desafinado', 'How Insensitive', 'The Girl From Ipanema', 'One Note Samba' and 'Wave' still jazz standards. Enigmatic and cruelly underrated, his praises have been sung for many years by **Frank Sinatra**, and in recent times the mantle has fallen to **Lee Ritenour**.

● ALBUMS: *Black Orpheus* soundtrack (1958)★★★, *The Composer Of Desafinado Plays* (Verve 1963)★★★, *Wave* (1967)★★★, *Stone Flower* (1992)★★★, *Compact Jazz* (Verve 1993)★★★★, *A Certain Mr Jobim* (1993)★★★, *Verve Jazz Masters Vol. 13* (Verve 1995)★★★, *The Man From Ipanema* (Verve 1996)★★★★, tribute album *A Twist Of Jobim* (I.E. 1997)★★.

JoBoxers

This pop-soul group achieved minor fame in the early 80s with a sound built on fast beats and imagery from the film *On The Waterfront*. They comprised of Dig Wayne (b. 20 July 1958, USA; vocals), Rob Marche (b.

13 October 1962, Bristol, England; guitar), Dave Collard (b. 17 January 1961, Bristol, England; keyboards), Chris Bostock (b. 23 November 1962, Bristol, England; bass) and Sean McLusky (b. 5 May 1961, Bristol, England; drums). All except Wayne were former members of **Vic Goddard And The Subway Sect** (*c.*1981 onwards), the last incarnation of a punk band who ended their career by backing Goddard's affected crooning. As JoBoxers they first attracted attention after appearing on the BBC television's *Oxford Roadshow* in 1982. Signed to **RCA Records**, in February 1983 they released 'Boxer Beat', which was a Top 5 hit in the UK. The follow-up 'Just Got Lucky' also went into the Top 10 but subsequent singles such as 'Johnny Friendly' did less well. The band split early in 1986, with Wayne going on to a brief solo career (one album, *Square Business*, 1987) with a band that featured Dave Collard of JoBoxers and Mark Reilly (ex-**Matt Bianco**).
● ALBUMS: *Like Gangbusters* (RCA 1983)★★, *Skin And Bone* (RCA 1985)★★.

Jobraith

b. Bruce Campbell, 1949, California, USA, d. 1985, New York, USA. In 1973 Jobraith became the first overtly gay star to be signed, and marketed as such, by a major label. Jobraith was cagey about his past, claiming to have come from Outer Space; he was in fact from California and had initially pursued a career in the theatre - he played the bisexual Woof in the LA and Broadway productions of *Hair*. Manager Jerry Brandt, who ran New York's Electric Circus, discovered Jobraith via an unsolicited demo tape. At the time of glam rock and 'bisexual chic' Brandt felt 'it's gay time and I think the world is ready for a true fairy.' **David Geffen** at **Elektra Records** reportedly paid the singer a £500,000 advance, and spent thousands on promotional stunts which included hiring the Paris Opera House for a three day showcase in December 1973. Journalists mocked this highly theatrical stage debut, and his two albums fared just as badly with press and public alike. Featuring guest appearances from **Peter Frampton** and **Led Zeppelin**'s **John Paul Jones**, the music was a poor pastiche of **David Bowie** circa *The Man Who Sold The World*, and the lyrics, dependent on camp innuendo, rather than explicitly gay, were delivered in a grating fake cockney whine. Brandt dropped the group unceremoniously when they were halfway through an American tour, and Jobraith tried unsuccessfully to return to acting. By the late 70s he had moved into the Chelsea Hotel and performed a regular solo spot at a New York restaurant. He died of an AIDS-related illness in 1985.
● ALBUMS: *Jobraith* (Elektra 1973)★★, *Creatures Of The Street* (1974)★★.

Jobson, Richard

b. 6 October 1960, Dunfermline, Fife, Scotland. Jobson was born the brother of John, a striker for Meadowbank Thistle Football Club, for whom Richard was also on the books. After a four-year tenure with the **Skids** (1977-81), Jobson moved on to join the **Armoury Show**, which failed to repeat the success of any of its illustrious personnel's former bands. With their demise, Jobson toured the UK with Scottish acting company Poines Plough. Turning to poetry, he hit the road once more, falling between two schools in terms of critical reception. On one side, rock critics viewed the move suspiciously, castigating him as pretentious, while the poetry critics reacted with venom to the vulgar intrusion of a rock singer. Placed in its proper context, Jobson was capable of writing good poetry, but was too much at the whim of his own indulgence. The worst example of this was his infamous live rendition of Sylvia Plath's 'Daddy'. He continued to release albums throughout the 80s, the best of which was *16 Years Of Alcohol*, also the title of a book that described his alcohol problems. He also suffers from epilepsy. Meanwhile, Jobson had chanced upon further careers in television and fashion. He appeared variously as the pop correspondent on BBC Television's *The Garden Party*, as presenter of *01 For London*, and most recently in regional arts programmes and the opinion show *Biteback*. On top of this came his highly paid, and some might say unlikely, stint as a fashion model. Most notable was a series of car adverts, for which he also composed the music. His most recent recording, *Badman*, was released on **Parlophone Records** in 1988, produced by Ian Broudie (**Lightning Seeds**, etc.). Although the imagery was typically grandiose, it did include a sprightly cover version of **Everything But The Girl**'s 'Angel'.
● ALBUMS: *The Ballad Of Etiquette* (Cocteau 1981)★★, *An Afternoon In Company* (Crépuscule 1982)★★, *Ten Thirty On A Summer Night* (Crépuscule 1983)★★, *The Right Man* (Crépuscule 1986)★★, *16 Years Of Alcohol* (Crépuscule 1987)★★★, *Badman* (Parlophone 1988)★★★.
● FURTHER READING: *A Man For All Seasons*, Richard Jobson.

Jocasta

Comprising vocalist Tim Arnold, guitarist Jack Reynolds, bass player Andy Lewis and drummer Adrian Meehan, UK indie pop group Jocasta were listed on many industry 'tip sheets' at the end of 1995. The band's history dates back to the time when Arnold, who had spent his youth in London, Yorkshire, France and Spain, was enrolled at the same school as Reynolds. Their first meeting was at a lesson in Greek mythology. Later, they named their band Jocasta, the name of the mother of Oedipus. After Arnold returned to Spain, he renewed his acquaintance with Reynolds as part of a musical relationship. In 1994 he moved to Soho, London, where he was joined by Reynolds. During breaks from their day jobs as chef and doorman at an illegal drinking establishment, they began to write their first songs together. The rhythm section of Lewis and Meehan met them while drinking at the same club. The group's first demos were financed by the delivery of an unmarked envelope through Meehan's door containing 20,000 Yen, the origin of which remains a mystery. The demos instantly secured an American contract, while the group turned down several offers so that they could remain on their own V4 Records in the UK. Their debut single, 'Go', announced a vivacious approach to songwriting - contrasting Britpop harmonies with rhythmic muscle comparable to that of the **Smashing Pumpkins**. With the release of their debut album *No Coincidence*, however, Jocasta were revealed to be a fairly straightforward Britpop band.

● ALBUMS: *No Coincidence* (Epic 1997)★★★.

Jodeci

Among the more eloquent practitioners of New Jack Swing or swingbeat, Jodeci have enjoyed more success in the USA in the genre during the 90s than any other act, with the possible exceptions of **R. Kelly** and **Bobby Brown**. The group consists of two pairs of brothers: Joel 'JoJo' and Gedric 'K-Ci' Hailey, and 'Mr' Dalvin and Donald 'DeVante Swing' DeGrate Jnr. The latter is also responsible for most of the group's writing and production. They began their musical career by harmonizing in their local Tiny Grove, North Carolina church services. They signed to prominent swingbeat stable **Uptown Records** in 1991, and the initial results were impressive. Their silky, soulful vocals were stretched over sparse hip-hop beats to produce a debut album that was at once tough and elegant. It sold two million copies and earned Jodeci numerous accolades. *Diary Of A Mad Band*, much in the vein of their debut, also went multi-platinum, and earned the group an appearance on **MTV**'s *Unplugged* showcase - a rare recognition afforded a band working in their territory. For 1995's third album the group slightly altered their musical backdrop, adopting the G-Funk beats made prevalent by **Dr Dre** and his various acolytes. However, this softer, more resonant sound was once again subordinate to the group's dynamic sense of harmony. They featured on **Tupac** '2Pac' **Shakur**'s number 1 single 'How Do You Want It' in June 1996.

● ALBUMS: *Forever My Lady* (Uptown/MCA 1991)★★★★, *Diary Of A Mad Band* (Uptown/MCA 1993)★★★, *The Show, The After Party, The Hotel* (Uptown/MCA 1995)★★★, as K-Ci & JoJo *Love Always* (MCA 1997)★★★.

Jody Grind

UK-based Jody Grind was formed in 1968 by the late pianist/organist Tim Hinkley. Their name was culled from a **Horace Silver** album title. A veteran of the Bo Street Runners and the Chicago Line Blues Band, he was initially joined by two colleagues, Iav Zagni (guitar) and Barry Wilson (drums). The trio completed an album, *One Step On*, prior to Wilson's departure. He was replaced by Martin Harryman, who in turn made way for Pete Gavin. Guitarist Bernie Holland (who is now an excellent jazz guitarist), meanwhile, took over from Zagni and the restructured line-up recorded *Far*

Canal with the help of bassist Louis Cennamo. Jody Grind broke up in March 1970. Hinkley later became part of the *ad hoc* bands Dick And The Firemen and Hinkley's Heroes, while Gavin joined **Heads, Hands And Feet**. Hinkley produced an album for **Chris Farlowe** in 1992.

● ALBUMS: *One Step On* (Transatlantic 1969)★★★, *Far Canal* (Transatlantic 1970)★★.

Joe

b. Joe Lewis Thomas, c.1972, Cuthbert, Georgia, USA. Raised to sing gospel by his minister father, Joe is another at the cutting edge of the commercial hip-hop/R&B crossover. As a youth he decided to move away from vocal, guitar and piano chores at his father's church and relocated to New Jersey, picking up a whole slew of new jazz, soul, R&B and hip hop influences in the process. He was eventually discovered singing in a Newark church by R&B producer Vincent Henry. He was employed regularly in local studios to add his various musical abilities to records cut in New York studios for swingbeat acts like **SWV** and Hi-Five. Others who used his services included **Toni Braxton**, **TLC** and Vanessa Bell Armstrong. The success of his debut album, and the Top 30 UK single 'I'm In Love', encouraged his new label **Mercury** to employ him in a dual role as staff producer for their black acts.

● ALBUMS: *Everything* (Mercury 1993)★★★, *All That I Am* (Jive 1997)★★★★.

Joe Cocker! - Joe Cocker

Still riding high on the American success of his debut album and a show-stopping appearance at the Woodstock festival, Joe Cocker hastily recorded a follow-up with his Grease Band and guest musicans including Leon Russell and Clarence White. Remarkably, it sustained the quality of his debut, with Cocker barnstorming his way through Russell's instant classic 'Delta Lady' and 'Hitchcock Railway', and reworking two more Beatles songs. As on *With A Little Help From My Friends*, it was the more restrained material that revealed most about Cocker's interpretative talents, with sensitive readings of Leonard Cohen's 'Bird On A Wire' and John Sebastian's 'Darlin Be Home Soon' being particularly impressive.

● Tracks: *Dear Landlord; Bird On The Wire; Lawdy Miss Clawdy; She Came In Through The Bathroom Window; Hitchcock Railway; That's Your Business; Something; Delta Lady; Hello, Little Friend; Darling Be Home Soon.*

● First Released 1969

● UK peak chart position: did not chart

● USA peak chart position: 11

Joe Ely - Joe Ely

Hailing from Lubbock, Texas, Joe Ely had been working with Butch Hancock and Jimmie Dale Gilmore in the Flatlanders. His debut album included their songs ('She Never Spoke Spanish To Me', 'Treat Me Like A Saturday Night') as well as his own ('I Had My Hopes

Up High', 'Mardi Gras Waltz'). The second album, *Honky Tonk Masquerade*, maintained the high standard and for a moment, it looked as though Joe Ely would be the new voice of American country music. He befriended the Clash and developed a hi-res country for his new audience, thereby leaving his country fans behind. Rockin' good stuff.

● Tracks: *I Had My Hopes Up High; Mardi Gras Waltz; She Never Spoke Spanish To Me; Gambler's Bride; Suckin' A Big Bottle Of Gin; Tennessee's Not The State I'm In; If You Were A Bluebird; Treat Me Like A Saturday Night; All My Love; Johnny's Blues.*
● First released 1977
● UK peak chart position: did not chart
● USA peak chart position: did not chart

Joe Popp

A trio formed in Tampa Bay, Florida, USA, in March 1995, Joe Popp comprise ex-Smashmouth members Martin Rice (vocals, bass) and Jeff Wood (drums), plus Joe Popp himself (guitar, vocals), formerly the leader of Dogs On Ice. With their roots in the Tampa Bay alternative rock scene, the group specialize in short snaps of pop/punk, with three-part harmonies and offbeat, youthful lyrics. After formation they were initially heard as support to artists including the **Toadies** and Wayne Kramer.

Their regional following expanded with concerts in several Florida clubs and a prestigious performance at a South-Eastern Music Conference held at the Pantheon Theater. Their debut came with the independently financed and released album *Complex Machine*. Two songs from this, 'Radiance' and 'Me And Van Gogh', were played heavily on local radio, while Popp also contributed original music to two local plays. Their video also featured in the Off Center Theater production of *The Bones Of Danny Winston And Rib Ann Magee.*

● ALBUMS: *Complex Machine* (55 Spec's 1995)★★★.

Joe's Garage - Frank Zappa

The superlative repackaging and remastering undertaken by Ryko has put the original three-part, two-record set of this magnificent nonsense tale together for the first time. This is back to the madness of *Freak Out*, with more pop and doo-wop bursting through all the complicated stuff, letting you know that Zappa could write a hit single, if he could be bothered to do so. *Joe's Garage* is a hoot and harmlessly pornographic. The sleeve-note states that it is 'a stupid story about how the government is trying to do away with music'. It is absolutely no coincidence that throughout, the listener mistakes the 'scrutinizer' as the 'scrotumizer'. Zappa was that rude, and that funny.

● Tracks: *The Central Scrutinizer; Joe's Garage; Catholic Girls; Crew Slut; Fembot In A Wet T-Shirt; On The Bus; Why Does It Hurt When I Pee?; Lucille Has Messed My Mind Up; Scrutinizer Postlude; A Token Of My Extreme; Stick It Out; Sy Borg; Dong Work For Yuda; Keep It Greasy; Outside Now; He Used To Cut*

The Grass; Packard Goose; Watermelon In Easter Hay; A Little Green Rosetta.
● First released 1979
● UK peak chart position: 62 & 75
● USA peak chart position: 27 & 53

Joel, Billy

b. 9 May 1949, Hicksville, Long Island, New York, USA. Joel, a classically-trained pianist, joined his first group, the Echoes, in 1964. Four years later he left them in favour of the Hassels, a popular Long Island act signed to United Artists. Joel appeared on both of their albums, *The Hassels* and *Hour Of The Wolf*, before breaking away with drummer Jon Small to form Attila. The duo completed a self-titled album before moving in separate directions. A demo of Joel's original compositions led to the release of his 1971 debut, *Cold Spring Harbor*, but its progress was marred by insufficient promotion. However, when 'Captain Jack', a new song recorded for a radio broadcast, became an 'underground' hit, **Columbia Records** traced Joel to California and signed him to a long-term contract. The title track to *Piano Man*, became a US Top 30 single in 1973 and sowed the seeds of a highly successful recording career. However, Joel refused to bow to corporate demands for commercially-minded material and despite enjoying hits with two subsequent albums, *Street Life Serenade* and *Turnstiles*, it was not until 1977 that his fortunes flourished with the release of *The Stranger*, which eventually surpassed *Bridge Over Troubled Water* as Columbia's best-selling album. Its best-known track, 'Just The Way You Are' later won two Grammy awards for Song Of The Year and Record Of The Year. This romantic ballad has since become a standard, and was a major UK hit for **Barry White** in 1978.

Joel's 1979 album, *52nd Street*, spawned another smash single, 'My Life' while the singer's first US number 1, 'It's Still Rock 'N' Roll To Me' came from a subsequent release, *Glass Houses*. His image as a popular, uncontroversial figure was shaken with *The Nylon Curtain*, which featured two notable 'protest' compositions, 'Allentown' and 'Goodnight Saigon'. However he returned to simpler matters in 1984 with *An Innocent Man* which included the effervescent best-seller 'Uptown Girl'. This memorable single topped the UK charts and confirmed the artist's status as an international performer. Joel and his wife, model Chrissie Brinkley spend a great deal of their time avoiding the media's fascination with them. Although his recent output has been less prolific, Joel has continued to score the occasional hit single, maintaining his standing in the pop world.

In 1991 he was awarded an honorary doctorate at Fairfield University, Connecticut. Joel's back catalogue continues to sell in thousands and by the mid-90s many had reached multi-platinum status in the USA. A perfectionist by nature, he also indicated a desire to pursue a wider musical style, and in 1997 announced that he would not be writing any pop songs in the fore-seeable future, concentrating instead on classical scores.

● ALBUMS: *Cold Spring Harbor* (Family 1971)★★, *Piano Man* (Columbia 1973)★★, *Street Life Serenade* (Columbia 1975)★★, *Turnstiles* (Columbia 1976)★★★, *The Stranger* (Columbia 1977)★★★★, *52nd Street* (Columbia 1978)★★★, *Glass Houses* (Columbia 1980)★★★, *Songs In The Attic* (Columbia 1981)★★★, *The Nylon Curtain* (Columbia 1982)★★★, *An Innocent Man* (Columbia 1983)★★★, *The Bridge* (Columbia 1986)★★★, *Kohyept - Live In Leningrad* (Columbia 1987)★★, *Storm Front* (Columbia 1989)★★★, *River Of Dreams* (Columbia 1993)★★★★.

● COMPILATIONS: *Greatest Hits Volumes 1 & 2* (Columbia 1985)★★★★, *Greatest Hits 3* (Columbia 1997)★★★, *The Complete Hits Collection 1973-1997* 4-CD box set (Columbia 1997)★★★★.

● VIDEOS: *Video Album Volume 1* (Fox Video1986), *Live At Long Island* (CBS-Fox 1988), *Storm Front* (CMV Enterprises 1990), *Live At Yankee Stadium* (SMV 1992), *Live From Leningrad* (SMV 1992), *A Matter Of Trust* (SMV 1992), *Shades Of Grey* (1994), *Video Album Volume 2* (1994).

● FURTHER READING: *Billy Joel: A Personal File*, Peter Gambaccini.

Joey Negro

b. David Lee, Essex, England. A remixer, producer and artist, and champion of the garage/disco revival, Negro's work on cuts from **Adeva** and **Kym Sims** is among the most representative of his style. The media-labelled 'England's **David Morales**' can trace his heritage back to M-D-Eemm (the chemical formula for acid) in the late 80s. He is a fanatical record collector who often works alongside DJ Andrew 'Doc' Livingstone. Together they have worked on remixes by **Brand New Heavies**, the **Reese Project** and Negro's own album. Negro's career began at the **Republic** label, where he was taught the art of remixing by a friend. Together with Mark Ryder, he produced a number of cuts for the same label, using production team names ranging from Quest For Excellence to Masters Of The Universe. Republic was responsible for classics like Phaze II's 'Reachin'' and Turntable Orchestra's 'You're Gonna Miss Me'. However, Negro ran into trouble when he created the persona Kid Valdez of Mystique. Under that name they mixed the club hit 'Together' for Raven Maize. The track was licensed to an American label, but when the single topped the dance charts journalists tried to hunt down Mr Maize. He was of course, totally fictional, the figure on the cover having been scanned in and adapted from an old rap record. Negro also licensed tracks to Republic, including several house classics, and compiled the *Garage Sound Of New York/Chicago* series. From this point on he picked up the Negro moniker and began to establish an identity as a talented disco remixer. Negro's own material reflects the tastes of his record collection; a penchant for US labels like Prelude and West End, 70s funk (**Brass Construction, Cameo**), jazz fusion and disco (notably the latter's 'syn drums'). His debut album additionally

includes a version of the **Gibson Brothers**' 'Oooh What A Life', featuring **Gwen Guthrie**. Recent mixing work has included **Hue & Cry, Sister Sledge, Fortran 5** ('Look To The Future'), **Soul II Soul** ('Move Me No Mountain') and **Take That** ('Relight My Fire'). In 1994 he teamed up with Andrew 'Doc' Livingstone to become half of the Hedboys.

● ALBUMS: *Universe Of Love* (Virgin 1993)★★★.

Johansen, David

b. 9 January 1950, Staten Island, New York, USA. Johansen gained recognition in the early 70s as lead singer of the **New York Dolls**. A R&B/rock group taking inspiration from the likes of the **Rolling Stones**, the Dolls' street attitude and outrageous sense of dress thrust them into the glitter/glam scene, although their music had little in common with others of that nature. Prior to joining the Dolls, Johansen joined his first band, the Vagabond Missionaries, in high school. At the age of 17 he moved to Manhattan, New York, and briefly worked with a band called Fast Eddie And The Electric Japs. The Dolls came together in late 1971 and quickly built a devoted audience at New York clubs such as the Mercer Arts Center and Max's Kansas City. They recorded two albums for **Mercury Records** and held on until late 1976. After their demise they became an inspiration to numerous artists, from the newly forming punk bands such as the **Sex Pistols**, to **Kiss**, to the **Smiths**. Johansen launched a solo career in 1978, recording for Blue Sky Records. Less flamboyant than the Dolls' records, this was a solid rock effort that stressed Johansen's lyrical acumen. He released three other rock/R&B-oriented solo albums for Blue Sky and one for Passport Records before shifting career directions once again. In 1983 Johansen began booking small cabaret concert dates under the name Buster Poindexter, performing a slick, tightly arranged set of vintage R&B numbers, show tunes, and jump blues. Dressing in a formal tuxedo and playing the lounge lizard, Poindexter built a following of his own, until Johansen the rocker literally ceased to exist; he completely gave up his rock act to pursue the new image full-time. He recorded albums as Buster Poindexter, including *Buster Poindexter* (1987) and *Buster Goes Berserk* (1989), the first yielding a chart and club hit in a cover version of **Arrow**'s 1984 soca dance tune, 'Hot, Hot, Hot'. He was still popular as Poindexter in the early 90s, touring with a 10-piece band and packing clubs, his repertoire now including Caribbean-flavoured music, torch songs and blues, as well as the early R&B. He also launched an acting career in the late 80s, appearing in films including *Scrooged* and *Married To The Mob*.

● ALBUMS: *David Johansen* (Blue Sky 1978)★★★, *In Style* (Blue Sky 1979)★★★, *Here Comes The Night* (Blue Sky 1981)★★, *Live It Up* (Blue Sky 1982)★★★, *Sweet Revenge* (Passport 1984)★★★.

● COMPILATIONS: *Crucial Music: The David Johansen Collection* (Columbia/Relativity 1990)★★★.

Johansson, Jan

b. 16 September 1931, Söderhamn, Sweden, d. 9 November 1968, Stockholm, Sweden. Johansson was a pianist, composer and arranger who became known to European audiences as a member of **Stan Getz**'s quartet touring with **Norman Granz**'s JATP concerts in 1960. The following year he joined **Arne Domnérus**'s band, and also the Swedish Radio Jazz Group, in 1967, composing and arranging for both. Johansson also wrote for film, theatre, ballet (e.g. *Rörelser*) and television (e.g. the Pippi Långströmpa tune). He reached a broad audience with sensitive renditions of Swedish folk songs. His considerable talents as composer and arranger were especially apparent in his experimental writing for the Radio Jazz Group, which fused and reinterpreted European art music, folk and jazz in ways that went beyond the **Count Basie** or **Stan Kenton** formats for big band jazz (*Den Korta Fristen*). As a jazz pianist in a trio context, Johansson adopted a swinging **Wynton Kelly**-like style, but his skill in fully exploring the potentialities of a song far exceeded the American musician (e.g. 'Willow Weep For Me' on *8 Bitar*).

● ALBUMS: *Rörelser* (Megafon, 1963)★★★, *Jazz På Svenska* (Megafon 1964), *Younger Than Springtime* (Artist 1972)★★★★, *8 Bitar/Innertrio* (Megafon 1989)★★★, *Jan Johansson & Radiojazzgruppen: Den Korte Fristen* (Megafon 1991)★★★, *300.000 Km/h* (Heptagon 1994)★★★★, *Musik Genom Fyra Sekler Med Jan Johansson* (Heptagon 1994)★★★, *Jan Johansson Spelar Musik På Sitt Eget Vis* (Heptagon 1995)★★★, *En Resa I Jazz Och Folkton* (Heptagon 1995)★★★, *Jazz På Ungerska/In Pleno* (Heptagon 1996)★★★.

John Barleycorn Must Die - Traffic

This was intended as the first Steve Winwood solo album following the stop-start-stop career of Traffic as a working unit. Capaldi and Wood were drafted in as session musicians. This logic sounds ridiculous now, as of course we always knew they would re-form. *Melody Maker* proclaimed 'TRAFFIC TO ROAR AGAIN'. The rest did them good, both physically and musically with two new Traffic standards added to their catalogue, the instrumental 'Glad' and 'Empty Pages'. The late Chris Wood was an exceptional flute player, never hogging the limelight. The subtlety of his playing excels on the title track. They held it together for four more years after this.

● Tracks: *Glad; Freedom Rider; Empty Pages; Stranger To Himself; John Barleycorn; Every Mother's Son.*
● First released 1970
● UK peak chart position: 11
● USA peak chart position: 5

John Prine - John Prine

Discovered and championed by the unlikely combination of Paul Anka and Kris Kristofferson, John Prine was part of a new wave of singer-songwriters to emerge in the early 70s. Like his friend and contemporary Steve Goodman, Prine was fêted as an ersatz Dylan, a tag that, while flattering, tended to obscure the singer's gifts. An incisive composer and distinctive singer, he showcased his talents to best effect on this, his debut album, which deftly articulated a post-Woodstock, post-Vietnam perspective. Its best-known selection, 'Sam Stone', was recorded by several artists, notably Bonnie Raitt, but each song was strong, resulting in a mature collection that has easily stood the test of time.

● Tracks: *Illegal Smile; Spanish Pipedream; Hello In There; Sam Stone; Paradise; Pretty Good; Your Flag Decal Won't Get You Into Heaven Anymore; Far From Me; Angel From Montgomery; Quiet Man; Donald And Lydia; Six O'clock News; Flashback Blues.*
● First released 1972
● UK peak chart position: did not chart
● USA peak chart position: 154

John Wesley Harding - Bob Dylan

Bob Dylan's eighth album followed a lengthy hibernation in which the singer re-evaluated his art. He emerged with a set of stark simplicity and heartfelt intensity. Neither folk, nor rock, nor country, the selection boasts elements of all three, slipping into consciousness with a mesmerizing power belying its setting. A biblical purity encompasses the collection as Dylan paints graphic portraits of the disenfranchised - hobo, immigrant, drifter, messenger - articulating the uncertainty of the times. The mood lifts for the final track, a beautifully tender love song, suggesting that this is where salvation lies. *John Wesley Harding* repays repeated play with ever-unfolding metaphor and interpretation, including four hidden Beatles on the cover.

● Tracks: *John Wesley Harding; As I Went Out One Morning; I Dreamed I Saw St. Augustine; All Along The Watchtower; The Ballad Of Frankie Lee And Judas Priest; Drifter's Escape; Dear Landlord; I Am A Lonesome Hobo; I Pity The Poor Immigrant; The Wicked Messenger; Down Along The Cove; I'll Be Your Baby Tonight.*
● First released 1968
● UK peak chart position: 1
● USA peak chart position: 2

John's Children

Formed in Leatherhead, Surrey, England, in 1964, John's Children's earliest antecedent was known as the Clockwork Onions. Louie Grooner (vocals), Andy Ellison (harmonica), Geoff McClelland (guitar), Chris Dawsett (bass) and Chris Townson (drums) made up this short-lived ensemble. The following year they emerged under a new name, the Silence, wherein Ellison (now vocalist), McClelland and Townson were joined by bassist John Hewlett. The group became John's Children in 1966 after meeting manager/producer **Simon Napier-Bell**. They made their debut in October with 'The Love I Thought I'd Found', an experimental composition made memorable by a start-stop, staccato tempo. This unusual release was known by its original title, 'Smashed Blocked', in the USA and Europe. A debut album, entitled *Orgasm*, was then readied for release. The set consisted of rudimentary material overdubbed by fake applause, but was withheld until 1970 in deference to its questionable quality and then controversial title. The group's second single, 'Just What You Want, Just What You Get', was a minor UK hit, but marked the departure of McClelland. His replacement was Napier-Bell protégé and budding singer-songwriter, **Marc Bolan**, whose spell in John's Children, although brief, proved contentious. His first offering, 'Desdemona', incurred a BBC ban over the line 'lift up your skirt and fly', and when a second composition, 'A Midsummer Night's Scene', had been recorded unsatisfactorily, Bolan left to form **Tyrannosaurus Rex**. His former colleagues then released the felicitous flower-power anthem, 'Come And Play With Me In The Garden', before exhuming another Bolan song, 'Go Go Girl', from an earlier session. A final John's Children line-up - Ellison, Hewlett, Townson (now guitar) and Chris Colville (drums) completed several outstanding engagements before disbanding. Ellison embarked on a brief solo career, later re-emerging with Townson in 1974 as **Jet** and from there on to **Radio Stars**. John Hewlett became a successful manager with **Sparks**, while also handling Jook, a less celebrated ensemble which also featured Chris Townson.

● ALBUMS: *Orgasm* (1971)★★★.

● COMPILATIONS: *Instant Action* (Hawkeye 1985)★★★, *A Midsummer Night's Scene* (Bam Caruso 1987)★★★, *Legendary Orgasm Album* (Cherry Red 1994)★★★, *Smashed Blocked!* (New Millenium 1997)★★★, *Jagged Time Lapse* (Pilot 1998)★★★.

● FURTHER READING: *John's Children*, Dave Thompson.

John, Elton

b. Reginald Kenneth Dwight, 25 March 1947, Pinner, Middlesex, England. At the age of four, the young Dwight started taking piano lessons. This launched a talent that via the Royal Academy Of Music led him to become the most successful rock pianist in the world, one of the richest men in Britain and one of the world's greatest rock stars. Dwight formed his first band Bluesology in the early 60s and turned professional in 1965 when they secured enough work backing touring American soul artists. **Long John Baldry** joined the band in 1966, which included **Elton Dean** on saxophone and Caleb Quaye on lead guitar. As the forceful Baldry became the leader, John became disillusioned with being a pub pianist and began to explore the possibilities of a music publishing contract. Following a meeting set up by Ray Williams of **Liberty Records** at **Dick James** Music, the shy Dwight first met **Bernie Taupin**, then an unknown writer from Lincolnshire. Realizing they had uncannily similar musical tastes they began to communicate by post only, and their first composition 'Scarecrow' was completed. This undistinguished song was the first to bear the John/Taupin moniker; John had only recently adopted this name, having dispensed with Reg Dwight in favour of the more saleable title borrowed from the first names of his former colleagues Dean and Baldry.

In 1968 John and Taupin were signed by Dick James, formerly of Northern Songs, to be staff writers for his new company **DJM** at a salary of £10 per week. The songs were slow to take off, although **Roger Cook** released their 'Skyline Pigeon' and **Lulu** sang 'I've Been Loving You Too Long' as a potential entry for the Eurovision Song Contest. One hopes that John was not too depressed when he found that 'Boom-Bang-A-Bang' was the song chosen in its place. While the critics liked his own single releases, none were selling. Only 'Lady Samantha' came near to breaking the chart, which is all the more perplexing as it was an excellent, commercial-sounding record. In June 1969 *Empty Sky* was released, and John was still ignored, although the reviews were reasonably favourable. During the next few months he played on sessions with the **Hollies** (notably the piano on 'He Ain't Heavy He's My Brother') and made budget recordings for cover versions released in supermarkets.

Finally, his agonizingly long wait for recognition came the following year when **Gus Dudgeon** produced the outstanding *Elton John*. Among the tracks were 'Border Song' and the classic 'Your Song'. The latter provided Elton John's first UK hit, reaching number 2, and announced the emergence of a major talent. The momentum was maintained with **Tumbleweed Connection** but the following soundtrack, *Friends* and the live *17-11-70* were major disappointments to his fans. These were minor setbacks, as over the next few years Elton John became a superstar. His concerts in America were legendary as he donned ridiculous outfits and outrageous spectacles. At one stage between 1972 and 1975 he had seven consecutive number 1 albums, variously spawning memorable hits including 'Rocket Man', 'Daniel', 'Saturday Night's Alright For Fighting', 'Goodbye Yellow Brick Road', 'Candle In The Wind' and the powerful would-be suicide note, 'Someone Saved My Life Tonight'.

He was partly responsible for bringing **John Lennon** and **Yoko Ono** back together again in 1975, following the Madison Square Garden concert on 28 November 1974, and became Sean Lennon's godfather. In 1976 he topped the UK charts with a joyous duet with **Kiki Dee**, 'Don't Go Breaking My Heart', and released further two million-selling albums, *Here And There* and *Blue Moves*. The phenomenal pattern continued as John courted most of the rock cognoscenti. Magazine articles peeking into his luxury home revealed an astonishing wardrobe, and a record collection so huge that he would never be able to listen to all of it. In 1977 John declared that he was retiring from music, and in 1979 Taupin moved to Los Angeles as the John/Taupin partnership went into abeyance. John started writing with pianist and bandleader **Tony Osborne**'s son, Gary. The partnership produced few outstanding songs, however. The most memorable during that time was the solo instrumental 'Song For Guy', a beautiful tribute to a

Rocket Records motorcycle messenger killed in a road accident.

Elton John then entered an uncomfortable phase in his life; he remained one of pop's most newsworthy figures, openly admitting his bisexuality and personal insecurities about his weight and baldness. It was this vulnerability that made him such a popular personality. His consumerism even extended to rescuing his favourite football team, Watford. He purchased the club and invested money in it, and under his patronage their fortunes changed positively. His albums and sales during the early 80s were patchy, and only when he started working exclusively with Taupin again did his record sales pick up. The first renaissance album was *Too Low For Zero* in 1983, which scaled the charts along with the triumphant single 'I'm Still Standing'. John ended the year in much better shape and married Renate Blauel the following February. During 1985 he appeared at **Wham!**'s farewell concert, and the following month he performed at the historic **Live Aid** concert, giving a particularly strong performance as one of rock's elder statesmen. He completed the year with another massive album, *Ice On Fire*. In January 1986 he and Taupin contested a lengthy court case for back royalties against DJM. However, the costs of the litigation were prohibitive and the victory at best pyrrhic. Towards the end of that year John collapsed onstage in Australia and entered an Australian hospital for throat surgery in January. During this time the UK gutter press were having a field day, speculating on John's possible throat cancer and his rocky marriage. The press had their pound of flesh when it was announced that Renate and John had separated. In 1988 he released the excellent *Reg Strikes Back* and the fast-tempo boogie, 'I Don't Wanna Go On With You Like That'. Meanwhile, the *Sun* newspaper made serious allegations against the singer, which prompted a libel suit. Considering the upheavals in his personal life and regular sniping by the press John sounded in amazingly good form and was performing with the energy of his early 70s extravaganzas. In September, almost as if he were closing a chapter of his life, Elton auctioned at Sotheby's 2000 items of his personal memorabilia including his boa feathers, 'Pinball Wizard' boots and hundreds of pairs of spectacles. In December 1988, John accepted a settlement (reputedly £1 million, although never confirmed) from the *Sun*, thus forestalling one of the most bitter legal disputes in pop history. He appeared a sober figure, now divorced, and concentrated on music, recording two more strong albums (*Sleeping With The Past* and *The One*).

In April 1991 the *Sunday Times* announced that John had entered the list of the top 200 wealthiest people in Britain. He added a further £300,000 to his account when he yet again took on the UK press and won, this time the *Sunday Mirror*, for an alleged incident with regard to bulimia. In 1993 an array of guest musicians appeared on John's *Duets*, including **Bonnie Raitt, Paul Young, k.d. lang, Little Richard** and **George Michael**.

Five new songs by the artist (written with **Tim Rice**) graced the soundtrack to 1994's Disney blockbuster, *The Lion King*, the accompanying album reaching number 1 in the US charts. In 1995 John confronted the media and gave a series of brave and extremely frank confessional interviews with regard to his past. He confessed to sex, drugs, food and rock 'n' roll. Throughout the revelations he maintained a sense of humour and it paid him well. By confessing, his public seemed to warm further to him. He rewarded his fans with one of his best albums, *Made In England*, which scaled the charts throughout the world.

With or without his now substantial wealth Elton John has kept the friendship and admiration of his friends and peers. He remains an outstanding songwriter and an underrated pianist and together with the **Beatles** and **Rolling Stones** is Britain's most successful artist of all time. He has ridden out all intrusions into his private life from the media with considerable dignity and maintained enormous popularity. Above all he is able to mock himself in down-to-earth fashion. His career scaled new heights in September 1997 when, following the tragic death of his friend Diana, Princess Of Wales, he was asked by her family to sing at the funeral. This emotional moment was seen by an estimated 2 billion people. John's faultless performance in Westminster Abbey of a rewritten 'Candle In The Wind' was entirely appropriate. Subsequently released as a charity record, it rapidly became the biggest-selling single of all time, overtaking **Bing Crosby**'s 'White Christmas'. Buoyed by the publicity, John's 1997 album, *The Big Picture*, was another commercial success.

● ALBUMS: *Empty Sky* (DJM 1969)★★, *Elton John* (DJM 1970)★★★★, *Tumbleweed Connection* (DJM 1970)★★★★, *Friends* film soundtrack (Paramount 1971)★, *17-11-70* (DJM 1971)★★, *Madman Across The Water* (DJM 1971)★★★, *Honky Chateau* (DJM 1972)★★★★, *Don't Shoot Me I'm Only The Piano Player* (DJM 1973)★★★, *Goodbye Yellow Brick Road* (DJM 1973)★★★★, *Caribou* (DJM 1974)★★, *Captain Fantastic And The Brown Dirt Cowboy* (DJM 1975)★★★, *Rock Of The Westies* (DJM 1975)★★★★, *Here And There* (DJM 1976)★★, *Blue Moves* (Rocket 1976)★★, *A Single Man* (Rocket 1978)★★★, *London And New York* repressing of *Here And There* (Hallmark 1978)★★, *Victim Of Love* (Rocket 1979)★★, *21 At 33* (Rocket 1980)★★, *Lady Samantha* (Rocket 1980)★★★, *The Fox* (Rocket 1981)★★, *Jump Up* (Rocket 1982)★★, *Too Low For Zero* (Rocket 1983)★★★, *Breaking Hearts* (Rocket 1984)★★, *Ice On Fire* (Rocket 1985)★★★, *Leather Jackets* (Rocket 1986)★★, *Live In Australia* (Rocket 1987)★★, *Reg Strikes Back* (Rocket 1988)★★★, *Sleeping With The Past* (Rocket 1989)★★★, *The One* (Rocket 1992)★★★, *Duets* (MCA 1993)★★, *Made In England* (Rocket/Mercury 1995)★★★★, *The Big Picture* (Rocket/Mercury 1997)★★★.

● COMPILATIONS: *Greatest Hits* (DJM 1974)★★★★, *Greatest Hits Volume 2* (DJM 1977)★★★, *The Elton John Live Collection* (Pickwick 1979)★★, *The Elton John Box Set* (DJM 1979)★★★, *The Very Best Of Elton John* (K-Tel 1980)★★★, *The Album* (Hallmark 1981)★★, *Love Songs* (TV

1982)★★★, *The New Collection* (Everest 1983)★★, *The New Collection Volume 2* (Premier 1984)★★, *The Very Best Of Elton John* (Rocket 1990)★★★★, *Rare Masters* (1992)★★, *Love Songs* (Mercury/Rocket 1995)★★★★.

● VIDEOS: *The Afternoon Concert* (Vestron Music Video 1984), *Night Time Concert* (Vestron Music Video 1984), *The Video Singles* (PolyGram/Spectrum 1984), *Live In Central Park - New York* (VCL 1986), *Live In Australia 1 & 2* (Virgin Vision 1988), *Very Best Of Elton John* (Channel 5 1990), *Single Man In Concert* (4 Front 1991), *Live In Barcelona* (Warner Music Vision 1992), *Live - World Tour 1992* (1993), *Live In Australia* (J2 Communications 1995), *Love Songs* (PolyGram Music Video 1995), *Tantrums And Tiaras* (VVL 1996), *An Audience With . . . Elton John* (1998).

● FURTHER READING: *Bernie Taupin: The One Who Writes The Words For Elton John: Complete Lyrics*, Bernie Taupin. *Elton John*, Cathi Stein. *A Conversation With Elton John And Bernie Taupin*, Paul Gambaccini. *Elton John*, Dick Tatham and Tony Jasper. *Elton John Discography*, Paul Sobieski. *Elton John: A Biography In Words & Pictures*, Greg Shaw. *Elton John: Reginald Dwight & Co*, Linda Jacobs. *Elton: It's A Little Bit Funny*, David Nutter. *The Elton John Tapes: Elton John In Conversation With Andy Peebles*, Elton John. *Elton John: The Illustrated Discography*, Alan Finch. *Elton John 'Only The Piano Player'*, *The Illustrated Elton John Story*, Chris Charlesworth. *Elton John: A Biography*, Barry Toberman. *Two Rooms: A Celebration Of Elton John & Bernie Taupin*, Elton John and Bernie Taupin. *A Visual Documentary*, Nigel Goodall. *Candle In The Wind*, no author listed. *Elton John: The Biography*, Philip Norman. *The Many Lives Of Elton John*, Susan Crimp and Patricia Burstein. *The Complete Lyrics Of Elton John And Bernie Taupin*, no author listed. *Elton John: 25 Years In The Charts*, John Tobler. *Rocket Man: The Encyclopedia Of Elton John*, Claude Bernardin and Tom Stanton.

John, Little Willie

b. William Edgar John, 15 November 1937, Cullendale, Arkansas, USA, d. 26 May 1968. The brother of singer **Mable John**, Willie was one of the most popular 50s R&B performers. His first hit, 'All Around The World', also known as 'Grits Ain't Groceries', was followed by a spectacular double-sided smash, 'Need Your Love So Bad'/'Home At Last' in 1956. The a-side of this successful coupling was later recorded by **Fleetwood Mac** and **Gary Moore**. It was followed by 'Fever'/'Letter From My Darling', both sides of which also reached the US R&B Top 10. 'Fever', written by **Otis Blackwell** (as 'Davenport') and Eddie Cooley, was a million-selling single in its own right, topping that particular chart in May 1956. However, the song is more closely associated with **Peggy Lee**, who took the song into the US and UK charts in 1958. 'Talk To Me, Talk To Me' gave Little Willie John another gold disc that year, while in 1959 he enjoyed further success with 'Leave My Kitten Alone', a favoured song of British beat groups. The singer's professional career faltered during the 60s while his private life ended in tragedy. Convicted of manslaughter in 1966, John died of a heart attack in Washington State Prison in 1968. He was posthu-

mously inducted into the Rock And Roll Hall Of Fame in 1996.

● ALBUMS: *Fever* (King 1956)★★★★, *Talk To Me* (King 1958)★★★★, *Mister Little Willie John* (King 1958)★★★★, *Action* (King 1960)★★★★, *Sure Things* (King 1961)★★★, *The Sweet, The Hot, The Teen Age Beat* (King 1961)★★★, *Come On And Join* (Ling 1962)★★★, *These Are My Favourite Songs* (King 1964)★★, *Little Willie John Sings All Originals* (King 1966)★★.

● COMPILATIONS: *Free At Last* (King 1970)★★★, *Grits And Soul* (Charly 1985)★★★★, *Fever* (Charly 1990)★★★★, *Sure Things* (King 1990)★★★, *Fever - The Best Of ...* (1994)★★★★.

John, Mable

b. 3 November 1930, Bastrop, Louisiana, USA. The elder sister of **Little Willie John**, author of 'Leave My Kitten Alone', Mable John was an early signing to **Berry Gordy**'s Tamla-**Motown** label. She appeared on the first Motortown Revue in 1959, and recorded four singles for the company. After an interlude working in a small Chicago outlet, Four Brothers, she signed to **Stax** in 1966. Here Mable specialized in 'deep' ballads, pitting her emotive pleas against a complementary **Booker T. And The MGs/Mar-Keys** backing. 1966's 'Your Good Thing (Is About To End)', a tale of infidelity and the consequences thereof, which **Lou Rawls** later took into the pop chart, was the first of seven releases. In 1968 she joined **Ray Charles'** Raelettes, and ceased performing as a solo artist. Her distinctive voice is nonetheless audible on several of the group's Tangerine recordings. Mable John subsequently worked as an advisor on *Lady Sings The Blues*, Berry Gordy's film biography of **Billie Holiday**.

● COMPILATIONS: *Stay Out Of The Kitchen* (Stax Sessions 1992)★★★.

John, Monday

b. Monday Olufemi John, *c.*1945, Lagos, Nigeria. John came to music late, having started his professional career as a fine-art illustrator. However, he played guitar intermittently, and in the early 60s opted to make it his profession. He initially joined Roy Gabriel's Highlife Band before moving to Bobby Benson's group. His first solo album followed in the late 60s, on which he was backed by various Benson associates. Abandoning **highlife** music for juju in 1968, he then became Tunde Nightingale's guitarist. They toured widely together, including appearances in the UK that saw him spotted by **Ebenezer Obey**, who recruited him as a sideman in 1971. John appeared on a total of 28 albums recorded with Obey between 1971 and 1978. Afterwards he retired for a number of years, before making his return in 1984 with his own group, the New Wave Juju Band, including musicians such as Sweet Tokunbo, Big Honest Setonji, Willie Bestman and the Genius Jerry. The band then all moved to Chicago, USA.

● ALBUMS: *Emuagbon* (1968)★★★★, *Eyin Terije (The Rich)*

(1984)★★★, *Egbe-Kegbe (Evil Cabal)* (MRVC 1990)★★★.
● VIDEOS: *Egbe Kegbe* (1990).

John, Robert

b. Robert John Pedrick Jnr., 1946, Brooklyn, New York, USA. In 1958, when he was aged 12, Bobby Pedrick (as he was named on record then) charted with his debut 'White Bucks And Saddle Shoes'. He recorded without success on Shell in 1960 and Duel in 1962 and fronted Bobby And The Consoles on Diamond a year later. As a soloist again, this high tenor recorded on **MGM** in 1965 and on their **Verve** subsidiary in 1966. After a name change to Robert John he hit the Hot 100 in 1968 on **Columbia** and 1970 on **A&M**. His first big success was a falsetto revival of 'The Lion Sleeps Tonight' (produced by a member of the **Tokens** whose original of the song also reached the charts), which made number 3 in the US charts in 1972 on **Atlantic**. Yet again he had a period of little activity until 1979 when he scored his biggest success with his own composition 'Sad Eyes' on **EMI**. The record spent six months in the US chart reaching number 1 and was also his only UK Top 40 entry. After a couple of lower chart records, he moved to **Motown** and was last in the Top 100 with a revival of 'Bread And Butter' in 1983, stretching his span of hits to 25 years.
● ALBUMS: *Robert John* (EMI 1979)★★★★.

Johnboy

Comprising Barry Stone (guitar, vocals), Tony Bice (bass, vocals) and Jason Meade (drums), US alternative rock band Johnboy formed in the early 90s and discovered a ready audience for their uncompromising, angular rock 'n' roll. The primary thematic at work on their 1993 **Trance Syndicate Records** debut album, *Pistolswing*, was hate and loathing - a natural antipathy towards conventional rock emanating from the studio that won them admirers in both **Steve Albini** and **Bob Mould**. Albini agreed to engineer their second album, 1994's *Claim Dedications*, after seeing the group play live, while Mould offered them a prestigious support slot on **Sugar**'s 1993 US tour. In the meantime, magazines such as *Magnet* proclaimed Johnboy as one of the most exciting bands to debut in the mid-90s.
● ALBUMS: *Pistolswing* (Trance Syndicate 1993)★★★, *Claim Dedications* (Trance Syndicate 1994)★★★.

Johnnie And Jack

This popular singing duo comprised **Johnnie Wright** (b. John Robert Wright, 13 May 1914, on a farm near Mt. Juliet, Wilson County, Tennessee, USA) and **Jack Anglin** (b. 13 May 1916, on a farm near Columbia, Williamson County, Tennessee, USA, d. 7 March 1963, Madison, Wisconsin, USA). They first worked together as the Dixie Early Birds on WSIX Nashville in 1939. The following year, after forming a band, they became Johnnie And Jack And The Tennessee Hillbillies (soon changing it to the Tennessee Mountain Boys) and between 1940 and Anglin's death in March 1963, they

built themselves a considerable reputation. During the early 40s, they were resident on several radio stations, including WBIG Greensboro (1940) and WCHS Charleston (1941), before moving to WNOX Knoxville in 1942. When Anglin was drafted for military service, Wright's friend, Smilin' Eddie Hill, agreed to deputize. At WNOX, they played on the *Mid-Day Merry-Go-Round*, working for a time with a young fiddle player (but later guitarist) named **Chet Atkins**. At this time, Wright's wife, Muriel Deason, became **Kitty Wells**, and during these years, she only occasionally appeared with the band, as she was raising her first two children, **Ruby** and **Bobby Wright**. However, following Anglin's return when the war ended, the line-up often toured as Johnnie And Jack Featuring Kitty Wells, with appearances on numerous radio stations, including Raleigh, Decatur and Birmingham.

In 1947, Johnnie And Jack returned to Nashville to spend a year on the *Grand Ole Opry* and made their first recordings on the Apollo label. They tended to play gospel songs and old-time ballads, such as 'The Paper Boy' and 'Lord Watch O'er My Daddy'. In 1948, they became regulars on the newly formed *Louisiana Hayride* on KWKH Shreveport, where they remained until December 1951. Late in 1948, with the assistance of their friend Chet Atkins, they joined **RCA** Victor and in January 1949, backed Kitty Wells on her first recordings; further recordings with her followed before she left the label. (The next year she started her highly successful **Decca** career.) In 1951, their repertoire began to include more modern country songs and they registered Top 5 US country chart hits of their own with 'Poison Love' and 'Crying Heart Blues'. They returned as *Opry* regulars in January 1952 and promptly registered a Top 10 hit with 'Three Ways Of Knowing'.

During the 50s, working usually with Kitty Wells, they played their weekly *Opry* commitments and toured extensively, often working the same tours as **Roy Acuff**. In 1954, they had a country number 1 with 'I Get So Lonely' and a number 3 with 'Goodnight Sweetheart Goodnight'. Other Top 10 hits included 'Kiss Crazy Baby' and 'Stop The World (And Let Me Off)'. They are also still remembered for two songs that surprisingly did not chart for them, 'Ashes Of Love' and the rumba-rhythmed 'Down South In New Orleans'. The Tennessee Mountain Boys featured talented musicians including steel guitarist 'Shot' Jackson, fiddler Paul Warren and mandolinist Clyde Baum. Their last chart hit came in 1962, a Top 20 with 'Slow Poison'. At a time when they were one of country music's most popular and respected acts, Anglin died in a car crash on 7 March 1963, on his way to a memorial service for **Patsy Cline**.
● ALBUMS: *Johnnie & Jack And The Tennessee Mountain Boys* (RCA Victor 1958)★★★, *Hits By Johnnie & Jack* (RCA Victor 1959)★★, *Smiles & Tears* (Decca 1962)★★★, *Poison Love & Other Country Favorites* (Camden 1963)★★, *Sincerely* (Camden 1964)★★★, *Here's Johnnie & Jack* (Vocalion

1968)★★, with Kitty Wells *At KWKH* (Bear Family 1994)★★★.
● COMPILATIONS: *All The Best Of Johnnie & Jack* (RCA Victor 1970)★★★, *And The Tennessee Mountain Boys* (Bear Family)★★★.

Johnnie And Joe

This US R&B duo featured Johnnie Louise Richardson (d. 25 October 1988) and Joe Rivers (b. Charleston, South Carolina, USA). Emerging from the Bronx, New York, USA, they were famed for their sublime doo-wop-flavoured ballads, notably 'Over The Mountain, Across The Sea' (number 3 R&B/number 8 pop, 1957), one of the most memorable and enduring early rock 'n' roll hits. Richardson was the daughter of Zelma 'Zell' Sanders, the owner of J&S Records. Sanders teamed her up with Rivers and one of the great blends of voices was born. Most of the duo's records were leased to the Chicago-based **Chess Records**, who were able to distribute the records nationally. Other great Johnnie And Joe singles included their first hit, 'I'll Be Spinning' (number 10 R&B, 1957) and 'My Baby's Gone, On, On' (number 15 R&B, 1957). Johnnie And Joe songs were especially popular in the Hispanic community, particularly 1960's 'Across The Sea'. After a brief association in the Jaynetts girl group in 1964, Richardson resumed her career with Rivers and the pair made records throughout the 60s. During the 70s and 80s they performed in oldies concerts, and made a critically acclaimed album in 1982.
● ALBUMS: *Kingdom Of Love* (1982)★★★.

Johnny And The Hurricanes

Formed by tenor saxophonist Johnny Paris (b. 1940, Walbridge, Ohio, USA), this instrumental group went through a series of line-up changes from 1957-63. With bassist Lionel 'Butch' Mattice and drummer Tony Kaye, the group recorded the single 'Crossfire' under the name the Orbits in 1959. Under the name Johnny And The Hurricanes, they released the rivetting 'Red River Rock', which featured the trademark sound of rasping saxophone, combined with the swirling organ of Paul Tesluk. After enlisting new drummers Don Staczek and Little Bo Savitch along the way, the group continued the hit run in the USA and UK with such instrumentals as 'Reveille Rock', 'Beatnik Fly', 'Down Yonder', 'Rocking Goose' and 'Ja-Da'. In 1963, an entirely new group of Johnny Paris-led Hurricanes toured the UK comprising Eddie Wagenfeald (organ), Billy Marsh (guitar), Bobby Cantrall (bass) and Jay Drake (drums). By this time, however, their instrumental sound was becoming anachronistic and they were soon consumed by the beat boom, which swept the UK and USA. Various line-ups of Hurricanes continued for live performances and cabaret.
● ALBUMS: *Johnny And The Hurricanes* (Warwick 1959)★★★, *Stormsville* (1960)★★★, *Big Sound Of Johnny And The Hurricanes* (Big Top 1960)★★★, *Live At The Star Club* (Attila 1965)★★.

Johnny And The Klugettes

Although little known in the mainstream of rock 'n' roll, Johnny (b. 1914, USA) and his band of sweet-talking vocalists have been delighting fans and their own bank balance for more than five decades. Leader Johnny is still performing at the remarkable age of 84. In fact, it was over six decades ago that Johnny first got the bug for broadcasting by becoming a regional break-out on a radio station in Silver Spring, Maryland. From that moment on he decided that television was the answer and that radio would not give him enough rewards. He set about making a career in both. Over the years the line-up of the Klugettes has changed but one face has been beating the drums with Johnny since 1967. The near-legendary Stu Subotnik (b. 1942, USA) is the **Billy Strayhorn** to Johnny's **Duke Ellington** front-man status. Subotnik, who turned down an offer to join the similarly named **Spotnicks** in the early 60s, has been a key figure. He has collected gig money on behalf of the band for many years and has kept the members clean and on the straight and narrow, without having to resort to dirty laundromats to do their washing. Subotnik (known as 'Scoobydoobie' to his friends) is a keen jazz fan, and it is no secret that his strong **Thelonious Monk** influence has infiltrated the band. Another key member of the Klugettes is the petite, no-nonsense female vocalist Silvia (Miss Moneypenny) Kessel who joined the group in 1984. She is supported by Hilly Walsh and Floy Joy Jackson, the band's 'beautiful backing babes'. The present line-up is completed by Vinnie Santillo, Scotty Gallin and 'Madame Sin' Racine. The quiet-spoken Johnny is one of the most enigmatic characters on the scene, but there is no doubt as to who leads the band, on tour or in the studio. When Johnny takes the stage and Stu rolls out the drums, the Klugettes follow in great style.
● ALBUMS: *Leader Of The Laundromat* (Metro 1959)★★, *Life Is A Cabaret* (Zorba 1962)★★★, *Don't Fiddle On My Roof* (Playbill 1968)★★★.
● COMPILATIONS: *See That My Lawn Is Kept Clean* (Conair 1987)★★, *Steak And Chips* (Metro 1991)★★, *Italian Suits And Huxedos* (Hudson & Spring 1993)★★★★, *I'll Have Square One From You, Baby* (Virgin 1997)★★★★.

Johnny Burnette And The Rock 'N' Roll Trio - Johnny Burnette

Although chiefly recalled for pop hit singles, notably 'Only Sixteen', Johnny Burnette began his career as a rockabilly singer. The genre's speedball crossing of blues and country was brilliantly expressed on this groundbreaking album in which the trio allow themselves unfettered musical expression. 'Train Kept A-Rollin'' is the archetypal selection; Tiny Bradshaw's big band classic is stripped down and supercharged with fervour. Only Elvis Presley's Sun recordings match this collection for exuberance - it is the standard by which all rockabilly is judged.
● Tracks: *Tear It Up; You're Undecided; Oh Baby Babe;*

Midnight Train; Shattered Dreams; Train Kept A Rollin'; Blues Stay Away From Me; All By Myself; Drinkin' Wine Spo-Dee-O-Dee; Chains Of Love; Honey Hush; Lonesome Tears In My Eyes; I Just Found Out; Please Don't Leave Me; Rock Therapy; Rockabilly Boogie; Lonesome Train (On A Lonesome Track); Sweet Love On My Mind; My Love You're A Stranger; I Love You So; Your Baby Blue Eyes; Touch Me; If You Want It Enough; Butterfingers; Eager Beaver Baby.

● First released 1957
● UK peak chart position: did not chart
● USA peak chart position: did not chart

Johnny Cash At Folsom Prison - Johnny Cash

Appearing at Glastonbury in 1994, it was clear that Johnny Cash has become an icon for the current generation. One reason is his alleged background of crime, although, in reality, Cash has only spent three days in jail - one of them for picking flowers. He is more like an old-time preacher, often finding his audiences in prisons. This classic album, which he had wanted to make for some years, brought out the best in his music. There is the gallows humour of 'Twenty-Five Minutes To Go', the whimsy of 'Dirty Old Egg-Sucking Dog', a song written by one of the prisoners, 'Greystone Chapel', and a duet of 'Jackson' with June Carter. But the real star of the record is the audience: Johnny Cash has recorded in other prisons, but this album is special.

● Tracks: *Folsom Prison Blues; Dark As A Dungeon; I Still Miss Someone; Cocaine Blues; 25 Minutes To Go; Orange Blossom Special; The Long Black Veil; Send A Picture Of Mother; The Wall; Dirty Old Egg-Sucking Dog; Flushed From The Bathroom Of Your Heart; Jackson; Give My Love To Rose; I Got Stripes; Green Green Grass Of Home; Greystone Chapel.*
● First released 1968
● UK peak chart position: 8
● USA peak chart position: 13

Johnny Cash At San Quentin - Johnny Cash

A giant of country music, Johnny Cash retained respect for the travails of the audience that elevated him to that position. Recorded live at one of America's most notorious prisons, this album displays an empathy bereft of condescension and captures a performer combining charisma with natural ease. The material is balanced between established favourites and new material, including 'Wanted Man', an unrecorded Bob Dylan song, and the light-hearted hit 'A Boy Named Sue'. It was not the first time Cash had recorded in a penal institution, but this appearance, at a time when American values were being vociferously questioned, suggested the artist's rebelliousness had not diminished.

● Tracks: *Wanted Man; Wreck Of Old 97; I Walk The Line; Darling Companion; Starkville City Jail; San Quentin; A Boy Named Sue; Peace In The Valley; Folsom Prison Blues.*
● First released 1969
● UK peak chart position: 2
● USA peak chart position: 1

Johnny Crash

Following the break-up of Tokyo Blade, vocalist Vicki James Wright became disillusioned with the British rock scene and moved to Los Angeles in search of compatible musicians. After a series of false starts, he finally stabilized a line-up of August Worchell and Christopher Stewart (guitars), Andy Rogers (bass) and Stephen Adamo (drums), under the name Johnny Crash. Blatantly parading traditional metal influences such as **Mötley Crüe**, **AC/DC** and **Kiss**, they delivered a high-energy blast of streetwise, blues-based rock 'n' roll on their Tony Platt-produced debut.

● ALBUMS: *Neighbourhood Threat* (WTG 1990)★★.

Johnny Hates Jazz

Purveyors of super-slick UK pop, the band's line-up featured Calvin Hayes (b. 1963; keyboards/drums), Mike Nocito (b. 5 August 1963, Wiesbaden, Germany; guitar/bass) and Clark Datchler (vocals/keyboards), the son of former **Stargazer** Fred Datchler. Datchler was later replaced by multi-instrumentalist Phil Thornalley (b. 5 January 1964, Worlington, Suffolk, England; vocals/guitar). The connection between all four was **RAK Records**. The label was owned by Hayes' father, **Mickie Most**. Thornalley co-wrote the original single, 'Me And My Foolish Heart' that failed in 1986, but he could not front the band as he was producing Robbie Nevil. Hayes brought in ex-Hot Club team-mate Datchler, and some expensive suits. 'Shattered Dreams' (the Datchler-penned follow-up) was a UK Top 10 hit during 1987 and also fared well in the USA. Three further Top 20 hits followed during the next year: 'I Don't Want To Be A Hero', 'Turn Back The Clock' and 'Heart Of Gold'. The group's first album topped the UK charts, but they were unable to sustain that level of commercial appeal. Datchler would go on to resume a largely unsuccessful solo career (releasing singles like 'Crown Of Thorns' for JHJ stable **Virgin Records**)

● ALBUMS: *Turn Back The Clock* (Virgin 1988)★★, *Tall Stories* (Virgin 1991)★★. Solo: Clark Datchler *Raindance* (Virgin 1990)★★.
● COMPILATIONS: *The Very Best Of* (Virgin 1993)★★.
● VIDEOS: *The Video Singles* (1988).

Johnny Moped

b. Paul Halford, London, England. The bizarre Moped Bands, in their various incarnations, have produced a stream of influential musicians and personalities. The outfit gradually emerged in Croydon, starting off with the Black Witch Climax Blues Band, before switching names to Genetic Breakdown from 1971-75. Some of the key personnel included Ray Burns (later **Captain Sensible**), his brother Phil, the Berk brothers, and the mysterious Xerxes. It was not until 1974 that Moped joined, as the band became known first as Johnny Moped And The 5 Arrogant Superstars, then Johnny Moped's Assault And Buggery. However, it was the birth of punk that saw Moped finding an audience for his 'moronic rock 'n' roll'. Playing support slots with the **Damned** introduced new wave audiences to the strange phenomenon of J. Moped, the performer. After the Berk brothers' stint in the Unusuals (with Chrissie Hynde, soon to be of the Moors Murderers then the **Pretenders**, on vocals), they rejoined the rechristened Captain Sensible in the third Johnny Moped line-up. Having found success with the Damned, the Captain only stayed for three months, his place taken by the hideously titled Slimey Toad. With several singles behind them, notably the charming 'No One'/'Incendiary Device', they recorded the legendary *Cycledelic*, an album acclaimed to this day by both **R.E.M.** and the **Ramones**. The band disappeared after its release, although Dave Berk did replace Rat Scabies in the Damned when the latter stormed off during their European tour. Scabies had previously performed one gig with the Moped band. Against all odds, the Johnny Moped Big Band re-formed in 1991, playing live for the first time in 12 years and recording *The Search For Xerxes*. Live, they were joined on stage by old colleagues **Kirsty MacColl** and the Captain. As former band member Xerxes recently stated: 'It is odd, that such an untalented bunch of people are still held in such affection.'

● ALBUMS: *Cycledelic* (1978)★★★, *The Search For Xerxes* (1991)★★★, *Basically* (Chiswick 1996)★★★.

Johnny Vicious

The proprieter of New York's Vicious Muzik label, Johnny Vicious is one of the most exciting up-and-coming producer/remixers on the circuit. A rock 'n' roller who became bored of rock music after he heard **Tony Humphries** on Kiss FM, he was championed by **Junior Vasquez** in his early days. His career proper began with tunes like 'Liquid Bass' and 'Frozen Bass', before reworking the **Loletta Holloway** standard 'Dreaming' as 'Stand Up' (released in the UK by Six By Six, the label being licensed to the **Network** umbrella organisation). This demonstrated his technique, which was essentially slicing up old disco classics in an alarmingly cavalier fashion and producing a punk disco hybrid. 1994 records like JV verus MFSB's 'TSOP' (another disco chestnut) continued his ascendency and cult status.

Johns, Glyn

b. *c*.1940. Having embarked on a short-lived singing career releasing singles on Pye and Immediate in the 60s, Johns began a concurrent path as an engineer. He assisted **Shel Talmy** on several sessions before establishing his name as a producer through an association with the **Steve Miller** Band. Their fruitful partnership resulted in four exceptional albums (including *Sailor*)which showcased a crafted, timeless sound, which complemented Miller's innovative ideas. Johns was also involved in the recording of the **Beatles'** *Sgt. Pepper's Lonely Hearts Club Band* and *Let It Be*, while **Led Zeppelin**, **Joe Cocker** and **Traffic** also called on his talents. Post-production work on the **Rolling Stones'**

Get Yer Ya Yas Out collection resulted in further collaborations with the group on *Sticky Fingers*, *Exile On Main Street* and *Black And Blue*. During the 70s Johns achieved due respect with his productions for the **Who**, the **Faces**, **Eric Clapton** and **Joan Armatrading**. His connection with the **Eagles**, which spanned the group's first three albums, was fundamental in establishing this highly-successful country-rock group's sound and style. Johns' frantic schedule lessened during the succeeding decade as he embarked on a lower-key approach with newer acts, including Nine Below Zero, Live Wire and, more recently, Helen Watson. Johns' work is now largely determined by artists he respects. In 1992 he was working with **David Crosby** at his studio in Sussex, England.

Johns, Sammy

b. 7 February 1946, Charlotte, North Carolina, USA. Johns was best known for his one hit single, the 1975 hit 'Chevy Van'. Between 1963 and 1973, he performed with a band called the Devilles in his home town, recording a number of singles for the Dixie label, none of which were hits outside of the immediate area. In 1973 he signed as a solo artist with the General Recording Corporation's GRC label and recorded a number of tracks with well-known studio musicians such as Jim Gordon, **James Burton** and Larry Knechtel. The first single from this collaboration resulted in a minor chart placing in 'Early Morning Love' in 1974. 'Chevy Van' followed in 1975, reaching number 5 in the US. Johns had one more chart single, 'Rag Doll', also in 1975, but further recordings for GRC and **Warner Brothers Records** did not fare as well and he disappeared from the music scene.

● ALBUMS: *Sammy Johns* (Warner 1975)★★★.

Johnson Mountain Boys

A popular bluegrass group which, when founded in 1978, consisted of Dudley Connell (b. Dudley Dale Connell, 18 February 1956, Scherr, West Virginia, USA; guitar, banjo, lead vocals), Richard Underwood (b. 14 July 1956, Seabrook, Maryland, USA; banjo, bass, vocals), David McLaughlin (b. David Wallace McLaughlin, 13 February 1958, Washington DC, USA; mandolin, lead vocals), Eddie Stubbs (b. 25 November 1961, Gaithersburg, Maryland, USA; fiddle, vocals) and Larry Robbins (b. 25 April 1945, Montgomery County, Maryland, USA; bass fiddle). When McLaughlin left later that year, his place was taken by Ed D'Zmura (mandolin). They made their first recordings in 1978, which resulted in an album and EP release on Copper Creek and soon gained a following with their appearances in the Washington DC area. In 1981, McLaughlin returned and they established themselves further afield with the help of some fine album releases on **Rounder Records** and some notable concert performances. The personnel remained constant until 1986, when Robbins left and Marshall Willborn replaced him on bass fiddle, while a little later Underwood was replaced by Tom

Adams. They toured extensively in the USA and Canada and also made very popular appearances in the UK. Among special venues were the White House and the **Grand Ole Opry**. In February 1988, with some members tired of the travelling and also a little disappointed that they had not been favoured by network television, the band formally announced their retirement from performing as a full-time unit. A farewell concert was recorded and later released by Rounder. In 1989, they made a welcome appearance at two festivals and in the following two years, they were persuaded to make many more. Earl Yager became the bass player, while past member Underwood played the 1989/90 venues and Adams returned in 1991. In 1993, they released a CD and in 1994, they were still making some appearances.

● ALBUMS: *The Johnson Mountain Boys* (Rounder 1981)★★★, *Walls Of Time* (Rounder 1982)★★★, *Working Close* (Rounder 1983)★★★, *The Johnson Mountain Boys* (Copper Creek 1984)★★★★, *Live At The Birchmere* (Rounder 1984)★★, *We'll Still Sing On* (Rounder 1985)★★★, *Let The Whole World Talk* (Rounder 1987)★★, *Requests* (Rounder 1988)★★, *At The Old Schoolhouse* (Rounder 1989)★★★ *Blue Diamond* (Rounder 1993)★★★.

● COMPILATIONS: *Favorites* (Rounder 1987)★★★.

Johnson, 'Big' Jack

b. 30 July 1940, Lambert, Mississippi, USA. Johnson's father led a local band and at the age of 13 Jack was sitting in on acoustic guitar. He was inspired by **B.B. King**'s records to switch to electric guitar five years later, and in 1962 he sat in with **Frank Frost** and Sam Carr, with whom he continues to work sporadically. This group recorded an album for **Sam Phillips** in 1963 (credited to Frank Frost And The Nighthawks) and another for Jewel in 1966, again under Frost's name. In 1979 they made an album as 'The Jelly Roll Kings', featuring Johnson's first vocals on record, and his first album under his own name, released in 1987, confirmed that he had very strong traditional Mississippi blues roots. His follow-up album in 1989 was more experimental and musically less successful, but a single for Rooster in 1990 found him back on form. *We Got To Stop This Killin'* was an excellent album.

● ALBUMS: *The Oil Man* (1987)★★★, with the Oilers *We Got To Stop This Killin'* (MC Records 1997)★★★★.

Johnson, 'Blind' Willie

b. c.1902, Marlin, Texas, USA, d. c.1949, Beaumont, Texas, USA. Blind Willie Johnson was arguably the greatest and most popular 'sanctified' singer to record in the pre-World War II era. His forceful singing and stunning guitar work ensured that he continued to sell records even into the Depression. His blindness has been attributed to many causes, the most likely being that his stepmother threw lye-water in his face during a jealous fit when he was about seven. That he should turn to music after this is a recurring motif in the

stories of many blind black singers, but even earlier, Johnson had admitted to a desire to preach. Now he combined the two talents to produce outstandingly powerful religious music as he played for tips on the streets. Despite this commitment to the church there seems to have been a secular side to his music, and it remains probable that he recorded two unissued blues under the pseudonym of Blind Texas Marlin at his second session for **Columbia Records**. Johnson began recording for the label in December 1927, by which time he had moved to Dallas; his first release became an instant success, selling in excess of 15,000 copies. Between then and April 1930 he recorded a total of 30 issued tracks (all for the same company), maintaining a level of quality that is amazing even by today's standards. Early research on Johnson's life was done by Sam Charters when he interviewed Johnson's wife Angeline in the late 50s. The picture was fleshed out, 20 years later, by the work of Dan Williams who reported on Johnson's travelling habits, including a spell in the company of **Blind Willie McTell**. Charters also noted the influence exerted on his singing style by an obscure, older singer named Madkin Butler, and his early commitment to the Church Of God In Christ. Many of Johnson's recordings feature a second, female vocalist, and it was long assumed that this was Angeline. Now it seems more likely that this is an early girlfriend (possibly wife) of Johnson's, called Willie B. Harris, whose affiliations were with the 'Sanctified' church. Willie Johnson had returned to the Baptist fold by the time he married Angeline in June 1930. When using a second vocalist Johnson favoured a ragged, antiphonal approach to his singing, in which he usually employed a marked false bass, and when performing alone he used his guitar as the second voice, often leaving it to complete his own vocal lines. He could finger-pick, but is most famous for his outstanding slide technique. Possibly his most well-known piece today is the free-form guitar impersonation of a congregation moaning 'Dark Was The Night And Cold The Ground', which was used in its original form in Pasolini's film *The Gospel According To Saint Mark* and adapted by **Ry Cooder** as the theme music to *Paris, Texas*. Johnson lived his later years in Beaumont, Texas, and it was there that his house caught fire some time in the 40s. Johnson survived the fire but returned to the house and slept on a wet mattress covered by newspapers. This resulted in the pneumonia that killed him.

● COMPILATIONS: *Blind Willie Johnson 1927-1930* (RBF 1965)★★★, *Praise God I'm Satisfied* (Yazoo 1976)★★★, *Sweeter As The Years Go By* (Yazoo 1990)★★★, *Dark Was The Night: The Essential Recordings* (Indigo 1995)★★★.

Johnson, Alfred 'Snuff'

b. 10 August 1913, Cedar Creek, Texas, USA. Recorded for the first time at the age of 75, Johnson's repertoire contains examples from several eras of Texas blues. Unlike **Mance Lipscomb** (also discovered late in life), whom he remembers seeing in the late 20s, Johnson is not a guitar virtuoso, having spent his working life on farms, playing music for recreation and amusement. One of 14 children in a musical family, he learned to play by watching his uncle, Will Tims. After World War II, he joined up with local musicians Teodar Jackson, Edgar Davis and harmonica player Ammie Deaver, who, like him, played for country suppers and house parties and also in church. Johnson never considered making music to be a real profession and thus escaped the notice of succeeding generations of musicologists. While performing songs learned from records such as **John Lee Hooker**'s 'Hobo Blues' and **Muddy Waters**' 'Two Trains Running', he also essays versions of such Texas stalwarts as 'Black Gal', 'Blues In The Bottle' and 'Spend My Money' (learned from his uncle), as well as songs by **Li'l Son Jackson** and **Frankie Lee Sims**. There is a charm to his performances but they reflect the passing of a strong musical tradition rather than its personification.

● ALBUMS: *Will The Circle Be Unbroken* (Black Magic 1994)★★.

Johnson, Alphonzo

b. 2 February 1951, Philadelphia, USA. Johnson learned the double bass and trombone as a child but turned to the bass guitar in 1968. He played with the bands of **Woody Herman**, pianist **Horace Silver** and trumpeters **Chuck Mangione** and **Chet Baker**. It was with **Weather Report** between 1974 and 1976 that Johnson established his reputation. He is a technically accomplished musician whose punchy syncopated ostinatos were a characteristic of the band's playing during that period and contributed much to the wide appeal of Weather Report's music. Since leaving the band he has played with saxophonists **Cannonball Adderly** and **Arthur Blythe**, trumpeter **Eddie Henderson**, drummer **Billy Cobham**, vocalist **Flora Purim**, the **Crusaders**, the band co-led by **Freddie Hubbard** and **Joe Henderson**, and the band of guitarist **Carlos Santana**.

● ALBUMS: with Weather Report *Mysterious Traveller* (1974)★★★★, *Black Market* (1976)★★★.

Johnson, Arnold

Having worked in vaudeville as a pianist and with Rudy Wiedoeft in the New York based Frisco Jazz Band, Johnson became a bandleader in his own right in the mid-20s, after a period dabbling in real estate. His sidemen included Al Cassidy, Nat Natoli, Harold Sturr, Dudley Doe, Bernard Dailey, Ed Shearsby, Johnny Rose, Vic Graffrion, Charlie Dowski, Mickey Bloom, Pete Pumiglio, Chris Killinger, Roy Maxon, Bill Kranz, Roy Henderson, Ken Wittmar, Bobby Burns, Harold Arien, Freddy Martin and Gary Gillis. High calibre dance band songs such as 'Don't Hang Your Dreams On A Rainbow', 'Goodbye Blues', 'Sweetheart', 'Teardrops', 'All For You' and 'The Lovelight In Your Eyes' were released on **Vocalion** and **Brunswick Records**. The orchestra appeared in several Broadway musical pits, including *The George White Scandals*. By the early 30s Johnson switched careers to become a musical director and producer for radio, while members of his band went on to several other significant dance bands.

Johnson, Bessie

A gospel singer from one of the Sanctified sects, Johnson was from Columbus, Mississippi, and was last heard of in Arkansas in 1964. Remembered by Lonnie McIntorsh as 'the singingest woman I've ever known', Johnson possessed a huge contralto voice, with a rasping vibrato as wide as a church door. She was at her best when accompanied by McIntorsh's metronomic guitar, or that of **Will Shade**; her own Sanctified Singers were endearingly ragged, and she had to order them to 'Come on' or 'Get the beat'. The fact that recordings including such *ad libs* were released speaks for their raw authenticity. Two tracks by the Memphis Sanctified Singers (on which Shade played guitar) beautifully contrast her rough style with Melinda Taylor's sweeter voice.

● ALBUMS: *Bessie Johnson* (c.1965)★★★.
● COMPILATIONS: *It Ain't Easy Being Blue* (Marvista 1995)★★★.

Johnson, Bill

b. 10 August 1872, New Orleans, USA, d. unknown. Johnson was the earliest of the first great bass players in jazz. He first took up the harmonica and then the guitar. A member of all the best known bands, Johnson left New Orleans at the beginning of the 20th century. He also helped found the Original Creole Band with which he toured California. A possibly apocryphal story relates how Johnson, who originally used a bowed bass, broke his bow in the course of a gig and had to continue by plucking the strings and thus established the tradition of playing jazz bass pizzicato that has continued ever since. From 1918-24 he worked with **Joe Oliver** and laid the foundation of the style which **Pops Foster** did so much to develop.

● ALBUMS: featured on *The Complete Johnny Dodds* (c.1900)★★★.

Johnson, Bryan

b. 18 July 1926, London, England, d. 18 October 1995. An actor and singer who enjoyed considerable success in the field of popular music on the UK Variety stage, and on records and radio during the late 50s and early 60s. Johnson had acting ambitions from an early age, and as a teenager was noted for his distinctive voice, which invited comparisons with celebrated actors such as Laurence Olivier and Robert Donat. His big break came when, after taking a few minor Shakespearan roles in repertory for Sir Donald Wolfit, the great actor-manager cast him as the Fool in his *King Lear*. In the subsequent period he also appeared at the Old Vic in plays by Ibsen, Rattigan, and Chekov, directed by Tyrone Guthrie. However, Johnson also had a great affection for the world of music hall, and after leaving

Wolfit's company in the early 50s, he played leading roles in numerous regional musicals, appeared in cabaret, and shared Variety bills (including those at the London Palladium) with star names such as **Benny Hill** and Dick Emery. In 1956 he had some initial success with a cover of **Eddie Fisher**'s UK hit, 'Cindy, Oh Cindy', and 'All Of You', one of the hits from **Cole Porter**'s score for the musical *Silk Stockings*. Johnson also frequently appeared on television programmes such as *The Jimmy Logan Show* and *Words And Music*. In 1960 he reached a wider television audience when he sang Britain's entry in the Eurovision Song Contest. 'Looking High, High, High' was placed second and reached the UK Top 20. Ironically, his brother, **Teddy Johnson** (with his wife **Pearl Carr**), had reached the same position in the contest in the previous year with 'Sing Little Birdie'. In 1961 Johnson released *The Million Sellers Sing-Song*, but by this time the beat boom was beginning to burgeon, and ballad singers were becoming *passé*. Later, he diversified into many other areas of showbusiness, and in 1988 a chance meeting with the Irish poet and dramatist, Patrick Galvin, led to Johnson mounting a one-man show about Oscar Wilde. The London production of *The Importance Of Being Oscar* was well received, and critics once again praised his voice with its 'gorgeous antique diction'. In the early 90s, as versatile as ever, he was taking leading roles in traditional Christmas pantomimes.

● ALBUMS: *The Million Sellers Sing-Song* (1961)★★★.

Johnson, Budd

b. Albert J. Johnson, 14 December 1910, Kansas City, Missouri, USA, d. 20 October 1984. Before taking up the tenor saxophone Johnson had earlier played piano and drums. In his teens he performed in a number of **territory bands** in the midwest and in Texas, including those led by **Terrence Holder**, **Jesse Stone** and **George E. Lee**. In the mid-30s he worked in Chicago, playing in several bands, most notably, **Louis Armstrong**'s, but was most often with **Earl Hines**. In the 40s he played in units led by Hines, **Don Redman**, **Al Sears**, **Sy Oliver** and **Dizzy Gillespie**. During these years Johnson was also a busy arranger, providing charts for the bands of **Georgie Auld**, **Woody Herman**, **Buddy Rich** and **Boyd Raeburn**. Johnson was deeply involved in the early days of bebop, writing for numerous small groups and acting as musical director for **Billy Eckstine**'s big band. During the 50s Johnson often led his own small groups for club and record dates, and was also active in music publishing and as a recording company executive. In the late 50s and early 60s he played with **Benny Goodman**, **Count Basie**, **Quincy Jones**, **Gerald Wilson**, Hines and **Jimmy Rushing**. In 1969, after yet another stint with Hines, Johnson formed the JPJ Trio with **Dill Jones**, Bill Pemberton and **Oliver Jackson**. After the dissolution of JPJ in 1975 Johnson worked with the New York Jazz Repertory Orchestra, appeared at numerous international festivals and managed to fit

in time as a teacher. It was as an arranger and contributor to bop that Johnson made his most lasting mark on jazz. Although he never approached the extraordinary improvisational flights of men like Gillespie and **Charlie Parker**, he was one of the musicians who helped give the new form coherence and structure. In his later playing career Johnson's style - on tenor, alto, soprano and clarinet - had thoroughly absorbed the influences of the beboppers with whom he had worked but he remained strongly identified with the jazz mainstream in which he had spent so much of his life. (NB: this artist should not be confused with **Buddy Johnson**.)

● ALBUMS: *Blues A La Mode* (1958)★★★, *Budd Johnson And The Four Brass Giants* (1960)★★★★, *Let's Swing* (1960)★★★, *Ya! Ya!* i (1964)★★★, with Earl Hines, Jimmy Rushing *Blues And Things* (1967)★★★, *Ya! Ya!* ii (1970)★★★, *JPJ Quartet* (1973)★★, *In Memory Of A Very Dear Friend* (1978)★★★★, *The Old Dude And The Fundance Kid* (1984)★★★.

● FURTHER READING: *The Tenor Saxophones Of Budd Johnson, Cecil Scott, Elmer Williams, Dick Wilson*, Jan Evensmo.

Johnson, Buddy

b. Woodrow Johnson, 10 January 1915, Darlington, South Carolina, USA, d. 9 February 1977. Pianist in several dance bands of the 30s, Johnson visited Europe with the Cotton Club Revue and later formed his own big band. Although popular with dancers at Harlem's Savoy Ballroom Johnson's band was not especially jazz-oriented and neither did it become well-known to white audiences. In the mid-40s Johnson adapted his style to suit changes in public taste and had several hit records in the R&B field, notably 'Please, Mr Johnson' which was sung by his wife, **Ella Johnson**. (NB: this artist should not be confused with **Budd Johnson**.)

● ALBUMS: *Buddy Johnson Wails* (1957)★★★, *Go Ahead And Rock* (1958)★★★★.

● COMPILATIONS: *Buddy Johnson And His Orchestra* (1944-52 recordings)★★★, *Buddy Johnson At The Savoy Ballroom* (1945-46 recordings)★★★, *Rock 'N' Roll* (1953-55 recordings)★★★, *Walkin'* (1952-56 recordings)★★★, *Walk Em* (Ace 1996)★★★★.

Johnson, Bunk

b. William Geary Johnson, 27 December 1889, New Orleans, Louisiana, USA, d. 7 July 1949. Johnson's early career has only recently been unravelled, and then only partly, thanks to his own, often inaccurate testimony. Until his enforced retirement from music in 1934 Johnson was certainly an active musician, playing in numerous New Orleans-based bands. He claimed to have worked with **Buddy Bolden** and **Jelly Roll Morton**; however as has been determined by recent researchers such as Christopher Hillman, these associations were unlikely given Johnson's age (he had, for years, claimed to be 10 years older than he was). He certainly played in some of the best New Orleans brass and marching bands, including the Superior and the Eagle bands. Johnson also claimed to have been an important influence upon and teacher of **Louis Armstrong**, but this assertion too should be treated with caution. Undoubtedly, Johnson was an important musician in New Orleans during the early years of jazz; yet he was a somewhat wayward character, whose presence in a band was not always a guarantee of musical excellence. Around 1914 Johnson moved to Alexandria, Louisiana and, from then until the late 20s, he played in scores of bands in many towns and cities of the 'Deep South'. By the early 30s, however, Johnson's career was in disarray and the loss of his front teeth had made playing difficult to the point of impossibility. In 1938 research by jazz writers Frederic Ramsey Jnr. and Charles Edward Smith located Johnson, who was then living at New Iberia, Louisiana. During correspondence with the writers Johnson insisted that, if he could be given money with which to buy false teeth and a trumpet, he could play again. The money was raised and Johnson duly returned to active performing. His return to the jazz public's consciousness came in 1940 and from that point until his death he made a tremendous impact upon that area of the early jazz scene currently enjoying a resurgence of interest. Johnson toured, playing concerts and making broadcasts, and made several records; all the while enhancing his new-found and self-perpetuated reputation as one of the originators of jazz. The quality of the playing which Johnson demonstrated on the records he made in these years shows him to have been a good player of the blues and suggests that in his hey-day he must have been a better-than-average trumpeter. There are also strong hints that he possessed a measure of musical sophistication which, had his career not foundered when he was approaching his prime, would have made him an important figure in the mainstream. As it was, Johnson's reappearance on the jazz scene, which helped to cement the **Revival Movement** of the early 40s, tied him firmly to a musical style that, as his biographer Hillman observes, he had probably outgrown. Instead, Johnson, together with his near contemporary **George Lewis**, was responsible for resurrecting an interest in early jazz that has remained strong until the present day.

● ALBUMS: *Bunk Johnson And His Superior Jazz Band* (Good Time Jazz, 1942 recordings)★★★, *Bunk Johnson In San Francisco* (American Music, 1944 recordings)★★★, *Bunk And Lou* (Good Time Jazz, 1944 recordings)★★★, *Old New Orleans Jazz* (1942)★★★★, *Spicy Advice* (1944)★★★, *The American Music Recordings* (1944)★★★, *Bunk Johnson & Lu Watters* (Contemporary 1983, 1944 recordings)★★★, *The King Of The Blues* (American Music, 1944-45 recordings)★★★, *Bunk Johnson: The Last Testament* (1947)★★★.

● FURTHER READING: *Bunk Johnson: His Life And Times*, Christopher Hillman. *Willie Geary Bunk 'Johnson'*, Austin H. Sonnier.

Johnson, Charlie

b. 21 November 1891, Philadelphia, Pennsylvania, USA, d. 13 December 1959. After playing trombone in the New York area Charlie 'Fess' Johnson switched to piano and moved to Atlantic City around the end of World War I. He led his own small band, at various times, which featured **Benny Carter**, **Sidney De Paris**, **Roy Eldridge** and **Edgar Sampson**. In 1925 Johnson was engaged for a residency at Small's Paradise in New York and remained at the club well into the following decade. By 1938, however, Johnson's bandleading days were over. He continued playing piano in and around New York but his health deteriorated and most of his final years were spent in enforced retirement. Despite the band's long stint at one of Harlem's most important nightspots, they made only few recordings and were poorly promoted.

● ALBUMS: *Jazz Classics In Digital Stereo: New York* (1929)★★★.

Johnson, Denise

b. 31 August 1966, Manchester, Lancashire, England. Former backing vocalist on some of **Primal Scream**'s finest moments, Johnson has also worked with **A Certain Ratio**, **Electronic** and sundry other more minor local projects like the Jam MCs' 'Ironweed'. She had initially been discovered by **Maze**'s Frankie Beverley singing in Fifth Heaven, who supported Maze on their Wembley dates in the UK. She was subsequently enlisted as backing vocalist for Maze. Johnson's solo career began in 1994 with the marvellous 'Rays Of The Rising Sun'. Produced by David Tolan of the **Joy** (for whom she was also a vocalist). Eventually she settled on East West/Magnet, who invited **K Klass** to remix the song. It gave her a sizeable club hit, though this time the version somewhat diminished Johnson's vocal imput. A radio mix also featured Johnny Marr (**Smiths**) on guitar, presumably through his pervious liaisons with K Klass.

Johnson, Edith

b. Edith North, 2 January 1903, St. Louis, Missouri, USA, d. 28 February 1988, St. Louis, Missouri, USA. In 1925, Edith married Jesse Johnson, who was **OKeh Records**' 'race' talent scout in St. Louis, and went to work in his record shop. In 1929, she recorded 18 splendid blues tracks, playing good piano on 'Nickel's Worth Of Liver Blues', and having a hit with 'Honey Dripper Blues'. Her voice was light but tough, sometimes hinting at violence, and making the threat explicit on 'Good Chib Blues'. Her husband's disapproval ended her singing career until 1961, when she made a few recordings that showed her still to be an expressive vocalist, with some interesting compositions. By this time, she had been for many years a successful operator of small businesses, and her elegant appearance belied the toughness of her repertoire.

● ALBUMS: *The Blues In St. Louis* (1984)★★★. *Honey Dripper Blues* (1991)★★★.

Johnson, Ella

b. 22 June 1923, Darlington, North Carolina, USA. Johnson moved to New York City at the age of 17 to be with her brother, bandleader **Buddy Johnson**, who began featuring her unique voice on the most successful of his many fine songs on **Decca Records**. Beginning with 'Please, Mr Johnson' in 1940, she continued with blues and jazz standards-to-be, 'That's The Stuff You Gotta Watch', 'Since I Fell For You' and 'I Still Love You', among dozens of others. She had a solitary release on the small Harlem label in 1946, and moved to **Mercury Records** with Buddy's band in 1953, where she recorded her first album, *Swing Me*. She continued to have strong sellers such as 'I Don't Want Nobody (To Have My Love But You)', and moved on to Roulette in 1958; her final few releases in the early 60s were on Old Town and Mercury. By the mid-60s, Buddy Johnson had disbanded and Ella, still a relatively young woman, retired to be with him in his last few years until his death in 1977. She still lives in New York, but has not resumed her musical career.

● ALBUMS: *Swing Me* (Mercury 1956, reissued Official 1988)★★★, *Say Ella* (Juxebox 1987)★★★.

Johnson, Ellen

b. USA. After studying for a masters' degree in music while at San Diego State University, Johnson decided to sing professionally. She quickly developed an enthusiastic, if localized, following for her work, which ranges across standards and the contemporary popular songbook but generally features a very high proportion of jazz songs. In particular, she favours the music of **Duke Ellington** and **Bill Evans**, while she has also composed lyrics to some of the music of **Charles Mingus**, including 'Peggy Blue Skylight'. Johnson's singing voice is a true, clear soprano and she sings with rare poise and subtle awareness of the music's intrinsic properties.

● ALBUMS: *Too Good To Title* (Nine Winds 1993)★★★.

Johnson, Ernie

b. Winsboro, Georgia, USA. This blues guitarist and singer worked for most of his young life as a truck-driver transporting cotton. Although at this time his musical ambitions were at best unfocused, he idolized blues and soul singers such as **Clyde McPhatter**, **Jackie Wilson** and, in particular, **Bobby Bland**, whom he impersonated in talent competitions. It was only when he was volunteered to deputize at a **Lavelle White** show, performing versions of 'Annie Get Your Yo Yo' and 'You Send Me', that he decided to take music seriously. As he later confessed: 'Next day, I called my day job and quit.' He subsequently formed his own band, the Soul Blenders, who played behind several artists on record (including Fats Washington, later his manager). Johnson made his first record, 'Lovin' You'/'Cold Heart', for Washington's Movin' label in 1968. Washington died two years later, but Johnson followed up his debut with releases for Duplex ('You Got To Be Faithful'/'You Gonna Miss Me') and Steph And Lee

('Drowning In Misery'/'Big Man Cry'). His first album, *Just In Time*, was produced by Al Braggs. Johnson continued to tour widely, before recording a belated second album (his first on CD) for Paula Records in 1993. Self-financed and produced, this featured a suite of distinctive originals in addition to a cover version of **Otis Redding**'s 'I Got Dreams To Remember', which had long proved a live favourite.

● ALBUMS: *Just In Time* (Ronn 70s)★★★, *It's Party Time* (Paula 1993)★★★.

Johnson, Ginger

b. c.1920, Nigeria, d. 1972, Lagos, Nigeria. Percussionist Johnson emigrated to London in the late 40s, where one of his first performances was with the orchestra led by **Edmundo Ros**. As well as being widely respected within the expatriate African community, both as a drummer and herbalist, Johnson was a well-known figure in London's counter culture during the late 60s, as leader of Ginger Johnson's African Drummers (who played alongside the **Rolling Stones** during the famous Hyde Park Concert) and manager of the Iroko Club. He returned to Nigeria in the early 70s, but died of a heart attack within a few months.

Johnson, Gus

b. 15 November 1913, Tyler, Texas, USA. Active in music from about the age of 10, Johnson played piano, bass, drums and sang in a vocal quartet. Choosing drums, he played in a number of **territory bands**, then in 1938 joined the **Jay McShann** band in Kansas City. This was the unit that included the young **Charlie Parker**. Johnson stayed with McShann until entering the US Army in 1943. After the war he played with several bands, including those led by **Earl Hines** and **Cootie Williams**, and in 1949 joined **Count Basie**, with whom he remained until 1954, playing in both the sextet Basie briefly led during hard times and the powerful new-style big band that heralded a change in the leader's fortunes. Later, Johnson worked as a free-lance accompanying singers including **Lena Horne** and **Ella Fitzgerald** and playing on numerous club dates, concert and recording sessions with **Buck Clayton**, **Jimmy Rushing**, **Woody Herman** and the **World's Greatest Jazz Band**. An exemplary drummer, Johnson's style combined fluid grace with skilful dynamics and he was just as happy discreetly supporting singers and soloists as explosively driving a big band. By the early 70s he was living in semi-retirement in Denver, Colorado.

● ALBUMS: with Jay McShann *Early Bird* (1940-43)★★★, *Count Basie Octet* (1950)★★★, with Count Basie *Sixteen Men Swinging* (1953)★★★★, with World's Greatest Jazz Band *Century Plaza* (1971)★★★.

Johnson, Harry 'J'

Harry Johnson started his career in the music business playing in a band whilst still at school. Success failed to materialise however, and he made a living as an insurance salesman until the music bug bit him again in 1968. This time he went into record production, and it paid off. One of his earliest productions, 'No More Heartaches', by the Beltones, was a huge local smash. Other hits from this period included Lloyd Robinson's 'Cuss Cuss', whose rhythm remains one of the most versioned ever, then, in 1969, he released 'Liquidator' by the Harry J All Stars, which became a crossover and international hit, reaching number 9 in the UK charts in November 1969. Further international success came his way with **Bob & Marcia**'s 'Young Gifted & Black', one of the first reggae records to use strings, dubbed on in the UK, where the record reached number 5 in March 1970.

In 1972 Harry sold his record shop and invested the money, and what he had earned from his UK hits, into his sixteen-track studio at 10 Roosevelt Avenue. Later he installed former **Studio One** engineer Sylvan Morris at the controls in place of Sid Bucknor, who moved to England, to ensure that Harry J's became one of the most popular studios for recording live on the island, utilised by such as **Burning Spear**, **Augustus Pablo**, and, prior to the advent of Tuff Gong, **Bob Marley**. Harry's own productions continued to do well, including 'Pied Piper' by **Marcia Griffiths** which reached number 11 in the UK pop charts in July 1971, 'Breakfast In Bed' by Lorna Bennett, and its DJ version, 'Skank In Bed', by **Scotty**. **Island** released an album with the **Heptones** entitled *Night Food* (1976), from which a number of popular singles such as 'Book Of Rules' and 'Mama Say' were plucked. In the late 70s Harry moved down a gear and produced mainly DJ records for the local market. His studio remained popular though, and in 1981 he was tempted back into the production seat to score another international hit with Sheila Hylton's 'The Bed's Too Big Without You', which reached number 35 in February of that year.

● ALBUMS: Heptones: *Night Food* (Island 1976)★★★.

Johnson, Henry

b. 8 December 1908, Union, South Carolina, USA, d. February 1974, Union, South Carolina, USA. Johnson was an elderly man before he became known as a blues singer outside his immediate home area, but he had learned guitar in childhood from his brother, and later taught himself piano. Johnson sang religious material in church in his younger days, and later in quartets, appearing on radio with the West Spring Friendly Four and the Silver Star Quartet in the 30s. His musical career was only ever part-time, but on his retirement, he was discovered by blues enthusiasts and made a number of recordings, as well as personal appearances in South Carolina. He appeared on two albums, exhibiting a strong, distinctive singing voice and a powerful guitar style, especially when playing bottleneck. Oddly, a single was issued in the UK, featuring two fine solo performances.

● ALBUMS: including *Union County Flash* (1973)★★★, *New Beginnings* (1993)★★★.

Johnson, Holly

(see **Frankie Goes To Hollywood**)

● FURTHER READING: *A Bone In My Flute*, Johnson, Holly.

Johnson, Howard

b. 7 August 1941, Montgomery, Alabama, USA. Johnson taught himself baritone saxophone in 1954, then learned tuba a year later. He moved to New York in February 1963 - at a time when the tuba was not a fashionable instrument (outside of dixieland bass-line chores, the only visible player was **Ray Draper**), but **Charles Mingus** welcomed him into his workshop in 1964. In 1965 he toured with soul jazz altoist **Hank Crawford**, playing baritone, but returned to the Workshop for a year from July 1965. In 1966 he played in the **Archie Shepp** band for some months and appeared with him at the Newport Jazz Festival in 1968. **Gil Evans** used his multi-instrumental capacity at various points between 1966 and 1970. Active on the west coast in the mid-60s, Johnson played with **Buddy Rich**, **Gerald Wilson** and **Oliver Nelson**. In 1968 he played on **Michael Mantler**'s *The Jazz Composers Orchestra*, an epic combination of scores and extreme performances from **Cecil Taylor**, **Pharoah Sanders** and **Larry Coryell**. The late 60s also saw him forming a tuba ensemble named Substructure. He supplied the tuba solo on a version of **Jimi Hendrix**'s 'Little Wing' in 1974 (one of **Gil Evans**'s more bizarre inspirations). Johnson's career makes nonsense of the so-called divisions between commercial and *avant garde*: He also arranged for **Taj Mahal**, **B.B. King** and **Paul Butterfield** and played on the **Band**'s *Rock Of Ages*. In 1982 he released the self-deprecatingly titled *When Elephants Dream Of Music* on the Gramavision label. He was reunited with Taj Mahal on 1997's *Right Now!*

● ALBUMS: with Michael Mantler *The Jazz Composers Orchestra* (1968)★★★, with Gil Evans *Svengali* (1973)★★★, *The Gil Evans Orchestra Plays The Music Of Jimi Hendrix* (1974)★★★★, with Bob Moses *Bittersweet In The Ozone* (1975)★★★, with Evans *There Comes A Time* (1976)★★★★, *When Elephants Dream Of Music* (Gramavision 1982)★★★, as Howard Johnson & Gravity *Right Now!* (Verve 1997)★★★.

Johnson, J.J.

b. James Louis Johnson, 22 January 1924, Indianapolis, Indiana, USA. Johnson began playing trombone at the age of 14; by the time he was 18 years old, he had performed professionally with various bands culminating in that led by **Benny Carter**. Johnson was with Carter for three years during which period he also worked with **Jazz At The Philharmonic**. In the mid-40s he was briefly with **Count Basie** and for the rest of the decade was active in small bebop groups in New York. In the early 50s he joined **Oscar Pettiford** but then was forced to earn a living outside music. In 1954 he returned to the jazz scene and immediately attracted widespread attention through the band he co-led with **Kai Winding**. This band, Jay And Kai, remained together for two years, by which time Johnson was re-established and now both leading small jazz groups and composing extended works that encompassed jazz and classical forms. In the early 60s he played with **Miles Davis** and toured with his own groups, and at the end of the decade was also involved in studio work. The 70s saw Johnson writing for films and television but finding time to play too in a variety of settings. In the 80s he began to devote more of his time to playing, demonstrating in the process that his ability had not diminished in the slightest. Tours of Japan with JATP groups led to a brief association on record with another trombone player, **Al Grey**. A major figure in jazz trombone, Johnson was one of very few players of that instrument to succeed in bebop. In his earlier years, especially when playing in bebop groups with artists such as **Charlie Parker**, **Dizzy Gillespie**, **Fats Navarro** and **Max Roach**, his extraordinary technique often dominated the content of his solos; however, in later years the content matured and expanded while his technique showed no signs of faltering. Johnson remains one of the major trombonists in modern mainstream jazz.

● ALBUMS: *Trombone By Three/Looking Back/Early Bones* (1949)★★★, *J.J. Johnson Sextet* (1953)★★★, with Kai Winding *Jay And Kai* i (Savoy 1954)★★★★, *Jay And Kai At Birdland* (1954)★★★, *Jay Jay Johnson, Kai Winding, Bennie Green* (1954)★★★, *The Eminent Jay Jay Johnson Vols 1-3* (Blue Note 1955)★★★★, *Jay And Kai* ii (1955)★★★, *Jay And Kai* iii (1955)★★★, *Jay And Kai Trombone Octet* (1956)★★, *Jay And Kai At Newport* (1956)★★, *Jay And Kai* iv (1956)★★★, *Jay Jay Johnson Quintet* (Savoy 1956)★★★, *Poem For Brass* (1956)★★★, with Stan Getz *At The Opera House* (1957)★★★★, *Live* (1957)★★, *Jay Jay Johnson Quartet* i (1957)★★★, *Live At The Cafe Bohemia* (Fresh Sound 1957)★★★★, *Jay Jay Johnson Sextet* i (1959)★★★, *J.J. Johnson With Frank De Vol's Orchestra* (1960)★★, *Jay Jay Johnson Sextet* ii (1960)★★★, *The Great Kai And J.J.* (1960)★★★, *Jay Jay Johnson Quartet* ii (1960)★★★, with André Previn *Mack The Knife* (1961)★★★, *J.J.'s Broadway* (1963)★★, *Proof Positive* (1964)★★★, *Tribute To Charlie Parker* (1964)★★★, *The Dynamic Sound Of J.J. With Big Band* (1964)★★★, *J.J.!* (1964)★★, *Goodies* (1965)★★★, *J.J. Johnson And His Orchestra* (1965)★★, *J.J. Johnson & Kai Winding* i (1968), *J.J. Johnson & Kai Winding* ii (1968), *J.J. Johnson & Kai Winding* iii (1969)★★★★, *The Yokohama Concert* (Pablo 1977)★★★, *Pinnacles* (Milestone 1979)★★★, *Concepts In Blue* (1980)★★★, with others *All Star Jam At The Aurex Jazz Festival '82, Tokyo* (1982)★★, with Al Grey *Things Are Getting Better All The Time* (Original Jazz Classics 1983)★★★★, *Live At The Village Vanguard* (Emarcy 1988)★★★★, *Standards* (Emarcy 1989)★★★, *Vivian* (Concord 1992)★★★, *Let's Hang Out* (Emarcy 1993)★★★, with the Robert Farnon Orchestra *Tangence* (Verve Gitanes 1994)★★★.

● COMPILATIONS: *Jay Jay Johnson's Quintets/Mad Be Bop* 1949 recordings (Savoy 1985)★★★★, *The Total J.J. Johnson* (RCA 1985)★★★, *The Eminent J. J. Johnson Vols 1 and 2* (Blue Note 1989)★★★★, *Brass Orchestra* (Verve 1997)★★★.

Johnson, James

Johnson was a bass and lead guitarist based in Baton Rouge, Louisiana, USA. He taught himself to play bass from records while at high school and played with a local band called Big Poppa And The Canecutters. It was Big Poppa who introduced him to **Slim Harpo** (James Moore) and Johnson worked with him during the 60s, initially on bass but later replacing Rudi Richard as lead guitarist; Johnson is best-known for playing the lead on Harpo's big hit 'Baby Scratch My Back'. After Harpo's death in 1970, Johnson virtually stopped playing and has a full-time job outside music. However, at the beginning of the 90s he was playing bass with Raful Neal in Baton Rouge on a part-time basis.

Johnson, James 'Stump'

b. 17 January 1902, Clarksville, Tennessee, USA, d. 5 December 1969, St. Louis, Missouri, USA. Called 'Stump' on account of his short stature, Johnson was the brother of Jesse Johnson, and was raised in St. Louis from 1909. He learned piano in pool rooms, his brother's record shop, and Boots' club on the levee. In 1928, he made his first records and enjoyed a success with 'The Duck's Yas-Yas-Yas'. Johnson continued to record until 1933, although gambling seems to have been more important to him than music. He employed a typical St. Louis four-to-the-bar chordal bass, with economical right-hand decoration, and sang in a wistful voice, sometimes delivering remarkably forthright sexual material. He recorded again in 1964, but was, sadly, clearly in decline.

● ALBUMS: *The Duck's Yas-Yas-Yas* (Agram 1988)★★★.

Johnson, James P.

b. 1 February 1894, New Brunswick, New Jersey, USA, d. 17 November 1955. Taught piano by his mother, Johnson assimilated a wide range of musical styles. In the years following his family's relocation to New York, he continued his studies and by his late teens was working in clubs in the Hell's Kitchen district. Johnson was adept in ragtime, blues, and all the popular musical forms of the day. He was also a capable performer of classical music. By the early 20s Johnson was a leading light on New Yorks burgeoning jazz scene and was already known for his compositions, including 'Carolina Shout', which demanded virtuoso technical ability. During this period Johnson became the acknowledged master of stride piano. He also attracted the attention of Broadway producers and in 1923 composed the musical *Runnin' Wild*, in which he introduced his composition 'The Charleston'. He also engaged the admiration of emerging pianists; the young **Fats Waller** was an eager pupil. In the mid-20s and especially during the 30s, Johnson's interest in classical music surfaced in his own work; he composed several long pieces, including 'Yamekraw', a piano rhapsody, 'Harlem Symphony', 'Jassamine', a piano concerto, 'Spirit Of America' a string quartet, and a blues opera,

'De Organizer'. Unfortunately, many of his scores have since been lost. (An album of piano arrangements of some of the surviving pieces, performed by William Albright, was issued in 1983 under the somewhat misleading title, *The Symphonic Jazz Of James P. Johnson.*) Although Johnson continued to play in the 40s, often in small groups with companions such as **Eddie Condon**, **Albert Nicholas** and **Wild Bill Davison**, ill-health damaged his career. A series of strokes culminated in a severe attack in 1951, which left him bedridden and he died in November 1955. As a pianist Johnson was outstanding, not only for his dazzling technique but also for the construction of his solos. However intricate they might be, his solos were logical, non-repetitive and effectively incorporated much of his catholic musical background. Records by Johnson include transcriptions from some early piano rolls and even in this form his music generates excitement. As a composer, the manner in which his work has lasted testifies to its inherent timelessness. Apart from the excitement of 'The Charleston', 'Carolina Shout' and 'Runnin' Wild', there were reflective melodic delights such as 'Old Fashioned Love', 'If I Could Be With You One Hour Tonight' and 'Just Before Daybreak'. Apart from Waller, Johnson influenced most of the pianists working in New York in the 20s and 30s, which means almost everyone of importance. Among the older players were **Count Basie**, **Duke Ellington**, **Art Tatum** and **Teddy Wilson**, while the younger group included **Erroll Garner**, **Johnny Guarnieri** and **Thelonious Monk**. In the history of jazz piano, Johnson's contribution is of paramount importance.

● ALBUMS: *James P. Johnson (1921-26)*★★, *James P. Johnson (1921-39)*★★, *The Original James P. Johnson (1943-45)*★★, *Yamekraw (1962)*★★★, *A Flat Dream 1939-45 recordings (1980)*★★★, *From Ragtime To Jazz: The Complete Piano Solos 1921-1939 (1985)*★★★★, with others *The Complete Edmond Hall/James P. Johnson/Sidney De Paris/Vic Dickenson Blue Note Sessions 1943-44 recordings (1985)*★★★, *Ain'cha Got Music (Pumpkin 1986)*★★★, *Carolina Shout (Biograph 1991)*★★★, *Snowy Morning Blues (GRP 1991)*★★, *The Original James P. Johnson: 1942-1945 Piano Solos (Smithsonian Folkways 1996)*★★★.

● FURTHER READING: *James P. Johnson: A Case Of Mistaken Identity*, Scott E. Brown. *James P. Johnson: Father Of The Stride Piano*, Frank H. Trolle.

Johnson, Jimmy

b. James Thompson, 25 November 1928, Holly Springs, Mississippi, USA. Johnson came from a musical family and was a singer and guitarist with several gospel groups until 1959, nine years after he moved to Chicago. At that time he sat in with **Magic Sam** and **Freddie King**, following the lead of his blues-playing brothers **Syl Johnson** and Mac Thompson (aka Mac Johnson), but in the 60s Jimmy was much more involved in the soul scene. He returned to the blues in the 70s and played second guitar with **Jimmy Dawkins**

and **Otis Rush**, but after recording for MCM in 1975, he has enjoyed a moderately successful solo career. His beautiful, gospel-tinged songs and performances put him in the premier rank of modern blues artists.

● ALBUMS: including *Johnson's Whacks (1979)*★★, *Bar Room Preacher (1983)*★★★, *Heap See* (Blue Phoenix 1985)★★★, *I'm A Jockey* (Verve 1994)★★★.

Johnson, Johnnie

b. 1924, Fairmont, West Virginia, USA. Johnson's name may not be well known but his sound has been heard by millions: he was the piano player on most of **Chuck Berry**'s classic **Chess Records** tracks. Johnson began learning to play piano at the age of seven without the benefit of lessons, influenced by jazz and boogie-woogie musicians such as **Earl Hines**, **Meade 'Lux' Lewis** and **Clarence 'Pinetop' Smith**. After a spell in the US Army Johnson began performing professionally in 1946, and in 1952, leading the Sir John Trio, he hired the young Berry as his guitarist. Berry soon began writing the group's songs and became its leader. Chess artist **Muddy Waters** suggested the group audition for that label and Berry was signed in 1955. Johnson can be heard on Berry hits such as 'Maybellene', 'Roll Over Beethoven' and 'Johnny B. Goode', which Berry has stated was written for Johnson. Johnson also played in Berry's road band but in the 60s left, working with blues guitarist **Albert King**, among others. Johnson led his own band in the 70s but still worked with Berry on occasion. He was featured in the 1986 Berry concert film *Hail! Hail! Rock And Roll* and later appeared as a guest on **Keith Richards**' debut solo album, *Talk Is Cheap*. Johnson has recorded sparingly under his own name, releasing his first solo album in 1987.

● ALBUMS: *Blue Hand Johnnie (1987)*★★★, *Rockin' Eighty-Eights (1991)*★★★, *Johnnie B. Bad* (Elektra 1992)★★★, with the Kentucky Headhunters *That'll Work (1993)*★★★, *Johnnie Be Back* (Music Masters 1995)★★★.

● COMPILATIONS: *Complete Recorded Works Volumes 1-3* (Document 1995)★★★.

Johnson, Johnny, And The Bandwagon

Formed in 1967 and originally known simply as the Bandwagon, this popular soul group consisted of four former solo singers who decided to pool their resources. John Johnson (b. 1945, Florida, USA), Terry Lewis (b. 1946, Baltimore, Ohio, USA), Arthur Fullilove (b. 1947, New York City, USA) and Billy Bradley (b. 1945, Rochester, New York, USA) had a hit with their debut UK release when 'Breaking Down The Walls Of Heartache' reached number 4 in October 1968. This pulsating dance song was the quartet's biggest hit, but two years later they enjoyed further success with 'Sweet Inspiration' and 'Blame It On The Pony Express', both of which reached the UK Top 10. The group was latterly based in Britain where, unlike in America, they had been well received. Johnson assumed leadership as original members dropped out, until the billing eventually read 'Johnny Johnson And His Bandwagon'.

However the singer's frenetic vocal style proved inflexible and as the band's recordings grew increasingly predictable, so their commercial success waned.

● ALBUMS: *Johnny Johnson And The Bandwagon* (Direction 1968)★★, *Soul Survivor* (Bell 1970)★★.

Johnson, Keg

b. Frederic H. Johnson, 19 November 1908, Dallas, Texas, USA, d. 8 November 1967. Born into a musical family (Johnson's father played cornet and his younger brother was tenor saxophonist **Budd Johnson**), he began playing trombone as his principal instrument when in his late teens. With his brother, he performed in local bands before they moved to Kansas City, playing there with **Jesse Stone** and **George E. Lee**, then to Chicago where, in the early 30s, they played with various bands including the Zilner Randolph-organized band fronted by **Louis Armstrong**. In 1933 Johnson moved to New York where he played briefly with **Benny Carter** and **Fletcher Henderson** before joining **Cab Calloway** with whom he remained for almost 15 years. In the early 50s he played with several bands, usually for short periods, sometimes deputizing for regular sidemen, and also sometimes playing guitar. This was mostly on the west coat but he eventually returned to New York where he played with **Gil Evans**, then joined **Ray Charles**' touring band where he remained until his death. A fluid, light-toned player with a great feeling for the blues, Johnson's musicianship was of a very high order and his solos show imagination allied to unforced technique.

Johnson, Ken 'Snakehips'

b. Kenrick Reginald Hymans Johnson, 10 September 1914, Georgetown, British Guiana (now known as Guyana), d. 8 March 1941. Son of a Guyanese doctor and Surinamese mother, Johnson played piano and violin as a child. On completing his schooling in England, he began dancing, making an early appearance in the provinces on the variety circuit. Studying with the African-American choreographer Clarence 'Buddy' Bradley, he gained professional confidence and contacts in the USA. These brought him film work in New York and cabaret in Hollywood, and the chance to observe black American practitioners of jazz and dance at firsthand. On the same trip he made a series of Caribbean appearances; these inspired a host of imitators with the belief that a West Indian could become part of the British showbusiness establishment and were responsible for launching several noteworthy careers. In London he persuaded Jamaican trumpeter Leslie Thompson to form a band for him to front; this, later known as the West Indian Dance Orchestra, was the first regular black band of any size in Britain. It included musicians from the Caribbean, such as clarinettist **Carl Barriteau**, as well as local instrumentalists of African descent, among them Welsh-born guitar-playing brothers Joe and Frank Deniz, and the latter's wife, pianist Clare Deniz. By the start of the war the 'West Indians' were broadcasting regularly and featured artists such as Barbadian trumpeter/vocalist **Dave Wilkins** and Welsh-born vocalist Don Johnson, whose father came from Barbuda, became household names. To many listeners, the Johnson band was the first local unit to 'swing' in the American manner, but the prominence of local black musicians ended when the leader was killed in an air-raid while on stage at London's exclusive Café de Paris in 1941.

● ALBUMS: with others *And The Bands Played On* (1938)★★★, with others *Swing Classics From Europe* (1938)★★★, with others *Al Bowlly - The Big Swoon Of The Thirties* (1940)★★.

Johnson, Kenny

b. 11 December 1939, Liverpool, England. In the early 60s, Johnson was the lead singer/rhythm guitarist of the country Merseybeat band Sonny Webb And The Cascades. They developed into the **Hillsiders**, which for many years was the UK's top country band, recording with **Bobby Bare** and **George Hamilton IV**. Johnson left in 1975 and soon formed his own band, Kenny Johnson And Northwind, which, for many years, has been regarded as one of the best bands on Merseyside. Johnson's passionate vocals are enhanced by Bobby Arnold's driving electric guitar. They play contemporary country music, often written by Johnson, but occasionally perform oldies gigs as Sonny Webb And The Cascades. Johnson's song 'Today' is a favourite on request shows and at Merseyside weddings. Johnson takes his time over his recordings but *Summer Nights* featured 16 of his own compositions with no fillers. **John Fogerty** and **John Anderson** influences are apparent on the album, but there is also much of Johnson's own originality including a touching song about growing up on Merseyside, 'Old Hutte Lane'. Johnson writes for West Virginia and he produced Julie Finney's *Something Called Love*. His weekly programme on BBC Radio Merseyside has the highest listening figures for any regional country show.

● ALBUMS: *Let Me Love You Once* (O.B.M. 1980)★★★, *The Best Of Kenny Johnson* (O.B.M. 1982)★★★, *Summer Nights* (Stox 1991)★★★.

Johnson, Kevin

Australian singer-songwriter Johnson is best remembered for his sole commercial hit, 'Rock 'n' Roll (I Gave You The Best Years Of My Life)'. Originally recorded in 1973 for Mainstream Records in his native territory, it gradually picked up airplay until in 1975 it was covered by **Mac Davis**, who took it into the *Billboard* Top 20 in the US. In consequence **Jonathan King** leased Johnson's original version to his own UK Records label and was rewarded with a Top 30 success (number 23). It proved to be the artist's only success and has not subsequently been anthologised.

Johnson, L.J.

b. Louis Maurice Johnson, 10 December 1950, Chicago, Illinois, USA. This soulful high tenor formed the group Family Affair at the age of 13 with his brother Robert and sister Sherry. Over the next few years the trio evolved into a sextet known as Everyday People. Johnson was conscripted in 1971 and on his return from the army, worked with Chicago group the Mood Mixers, who also included future Hi-NRG star Evelyn Thomas. He and Evelyn were spotted by producer Danny Leake who introduced them to UK producer/writer Ian Levine, who was in Chicago looking for acts. Levine was impressed with Johnson and their first recording together 'Your Magic Put A Spell On Me', which was tailor-made for the UK northern soul scene, jumped straight into the UK Top 40 in its first week of release in 1976. Despite his television and live performances in the UK and some strong releases on **Mercury** and AVI, the singer who remained unknown in his homeland, never managed a chart return.

Johnson, Larry C.

b. 21 February 1952, Charlotte, North Carolina, USA. Johnson grew up in Mountain City, Tennessee, but moved to Chicago in his teens. His mother taught him guitar and, inspired by **Hank Williams**, **George Jones** and **Marty Robbins**, Johnson gained his first professional experience, under an assumed name (he was under-age), singing in the honky tonks of Illinois. He has a fondness for country music with a gospel flavour and early in his career, he privately recorded two volumes called *Songs Of Reality*, the majority of the numbers being self-penned. Operating from Fort Payne, Alabama, he continues to perform and achieved some success with the title track of his first Nashville-recorded album. A recent album of western swing and traditional country songs all composed by Col. Buster Doss also attracted air play on European and Scandinavian country stations. His avowed intention is to preserve traditional country music for future generations and he has plans to develop a country music park on his farm in Mentone, Alabama.
● ALBUMS: *Drinkin' Whisky* (Ye Old Heritage 1992)★★★, *Rainbow Of Roses* (Stardust 1994)★★★.

Johnson, Laurie

b. 7 February 1927, England. A bandleader, musical director, and composer for the stage, television and films, Johnson studied at the Royal College Of Music in London, and spent four years in the Coldstream Guards, before establishing himself on the UK entertainment scene in the late 50s and 60s. One of his first major projects early in 1959, was to write the music, and act as musical director, for *Lock Up Your Daughters*, a musical adaptation of Henry Fielding's *Rape Upon Rape*, which opened Bernard Miles's Mermaid Theatre in the City of London. Johnson's score, in collaboration with lyricist **Lionel Bart**, won an

Ivor Novello Award. The show returned to the Mermaid in 1969 for a 10th anniversary season, and also played around the world, including a spell at the Godspeed Opera House in Connecticut, USA. The film version omitted the songs and featured a score by **Ron Grainer**. Johnson's other work for the West End stage has included music for the Peter Cook revue *Pieces Of Eight* (1959), and the score, with lyrics by **Herbert Kretzmer**, to *The Four Musketeers* (1967), which starred singer-comedian **Harry Secombe**. Despite attracting venomous reviews, *The Four Musketeers* ran for over a year. In 1961 the Laurie Johnson Orchestra had a UK Top 10 chart entry with the Latin-styled 'Sucu Sucu', written by Tarateno Rosa, the theme from the UK television series *Top Secret*. On the b-side was a Johnson composition, the title theme for another television production, *Echo Four-Two*. This is one of over 50 themes and scores that he wrote for television, a list that included *No Hiding Place, When The Kissing Had To Stop, Jason King, Shirley's World, The Adventurers, Thriller, The Avengers, The New Avengers* and *The Professionals*. The latter two were produced by Johnson's company, Avengers (Film And TV) Enterprises, formed with Albert Fennell and Brian Clemens. Johnson has also composed extensively for the cinema, from the late 50s. His film scores include *The Moonraker* (1958), *No Trees In The Street* (1958), *Tiger Bay* (1959), *I Aim At The Stars* (1960), *Spare The Rod* (1961), *Dr Strangelove - Or: How I Learned To Stop Worrying And Love The Bomb* (1964), *The First Men In The Moon* (1964), *The Beauty Jungle* (1966), *East Of Sudan* (1966), *Hot Millions* (1968), *And Soon The Darkness* (1970), *The Belstone Fox* (1976), *Diagnosis: Murder* (1976), *It's Alive II (It Lives Again)* (1978), *It Shouldn't Happen To A Vet* (1979) and *Bitter Harvest* (1981). Among his other works was the music for the television movie *Jericho*, which involved many of the original *Avengers* team, including Patrick MacNee. Late in 1994, Johnson announced the formation of the London Big Band, 'the largest band in Britain', consisting of the 'cream' of the music business, and led by veteran **Jack Parnell**.
● ALBUMS: *Operation Orchestra* (1959)★★★, *Songs Of Three Seasons* (1959)★★, *A Brass Band Swinging* (1961)★★★★, *Top Secret* (1962)★★★, *Two Cities Suite* (1963)★★★, *The Avengers* (1963)★★★★, *The New Big Sound Of Johnson* (1964)★★★, *Something's Coming* (1968)★★★, *Themes And...By Laurie Johnson* (1969)★★★, with Sir Bernard Miles *The Conquistadors* (1971)★★, *Laurie Johnson With The London Philharmonic And London Jazz Orchestras* (1973)★★★★, with the London Studio Orchestra *Music From the Avengers, New Avengers & The Professionals* (KPM 1980)★★★★, *Film Music Of Laurie Johnson* (Unicorn-Kanchana 1981)★★★, *Digital Film Scores Volumes 1-3* (1981)★★★, with the London Studio Symphony Orchestra *Rose And The Gun - The Music Of Laurie Johnson* (Unicorn-Kanchana 1992)★★★, *Laurie Johnson's London Big Band* (1994)★★.

Johnson, Lem

b. Lemuel Charles Johnson, 6 August 1909, Oklahoma City, Oklahoma, USA, d. 1 April 1989. While still at school, Johnson began playing clarinet and worked with local bands. In his late teens he added the tenor saxophone to his instrumental abilities and played with **Walter Page**'s Blue Devils, then with **Sammy Price**. After playing with several other **territory bands** in the Midwest he played with **Earl 'Fatha' Hines** and then moved to New York. There he played in bands led by **Fess Williams**, **Louis Jordan** and others, occasionally led his own small groups, and in the early 40s was with **Buster Harding**, **Edgar Hayes**, **Sidney Bechet** and others. During 1942/3 he frequently played with **Claude Hopkins** on a part-time basis while working in defence industry factories. In the late 40s and on through the 50s he mostly led his own bands in the north-east, occasionally touring overseas, and making record dates with several leaders including **Oran 'Hot Lips' Page**. Gradually, Johnson's musical career became part-time although he continued to perform into the 60s. A relaxed and subtly swinging player, especially on tenor, Johnson's career sometimes seemed to lack direction and drive. On the evidence of his recorded work, this must be seen as a loss to jazz.

● COMPILATIONS: *Sidney Bechet, 1932-43: The Bluebird Sessions* (Bluebird 1932-43)★★★★, *Louis Jordan And His Tympany Five* (MCA/Charly 1939-40),★★★★ *Classics In Swing: Buck Clayton-Jonah Jones-Hot Lips Page* (Commodore 1944)★★★★.

Johnson, Linton Kwesi

b. 1952, Chapelton, Jamaica, West Indies. Johnson's family emigrated to London in 1963, and he quickly developed a keen awareness of both literature and politics, culminating in a degree in sociology at Goldsmith's College, London, in 1973. An interest in poetry manifested itself in two books, *Voices Of The Living And The Dead* (1974) and *Dread Beat And Blood* (1975), both written in a style that put on paper the patois spoken in black Britain, often with a rhythm reminiscent of Jamaican DJs. Johnson also wrote about reggae for *New Musical Express*, *Melody Maker* and *Black Music*, as well as being writer-in-residence for the London Borough of Lambeth and heavily involved in the *Race Today* co-operative newspaper. Experiments with reggae bands at his poetry readings culminated in 1977's *Dread Beat An' Blood*, recorded as Poet And The Roots, an album that virtually defined the 'dub poetry' genre. An intoxicating mixture of Johnson's lucid, plain-spoken commonsense and rhetoric, and **Dennis Bovell**'s intriguing dub rhythms, it sold well. In 1978 Johnson changed labels from **Virgin** to **Island** and issued the strong *Forces Of Victory*, this time under his own name. Johnson became a media face, introducing radio histories of reggae and cropping up on television arts shows, but to his credit he did not exploit his position, preferring instead to remain politically active at grass-roots level in Brixton, London. *Bass Culture* was a more ambitious project that met with a mixed reception, with tracks including the love-chat 'Lorraine' and the title song offering a far broader sweep of subjects than his previous work. *LKJ In Dub* featured Dennis Bovell dub mixes of tracks from his two Island albums. In the same year *Inglan Is A Bitch*, his third book, was published and he also started a record label, LKJ, which introduced Jamaican poet Michael Smith to a UK audience. In the early 80s Johnson seemed to tire of the 'dub poet' tag and became far less active in the music business. In 1986 he issued *In Concert With The Dub Band*, a double live set that consisted chiefly of old material. He finally returned to the studio in 1990 to record *Tings An' Times* for his own label, a more reflective, slightly less brash set. Writing commitments meant another recording hiatus before 1998's *More Time*.

While Johnson has undoubtedly added a notch to reggae's canon in providing a solid focus for the **dub poetry** movement, offering an alternative stance to that of straightforward reggae DJs, he appears to view his musical involvement as secondary to his political and social activities, and is not therefore the 'name' in the media he might have been. However, no other artist would have tackled subjects such as 'Black Petty Booshwah' (petit-bourgeois) or 'Inglan' (England) Is A Bitch', and for that, his place in reggae history is assured.

● ALBUMS: as Poet And The Roots *Dread Beat An' Blood* (Front Line 1977)★★★, *Forces Of Victory* (Island 1979)★★★★, *Bass Culture* (Island 1980)★★★★, *LKJ In Dub* (Island 1980)★★★, *Making History* (Island 1984)★★★★, *Linton Kwesi Johnson Live* (Rough Trade 1985)★★★, *In Concert With The Dub Band* (LKJ 1986)★★★, *Tings An' Times* (LKJ 1990)★★★★, *LKJ In Dub Volume 2* (1992)★★★, *A Cappella Live* (LKJ 1997)★★★, *More Time* (LKJ 1998)★★★.

● COMPILATIONS: *Reggae Greats* (Island 1985)★★★★.

Johnson, Lonnie

b. Alonzo Johnson, 8 February 1889, New Orleans, Louisiana, USA, d. 16 June 1970. A hugely influential and original blues musicians, in the early 1900s Johnson played guitar and violin in saloons in his home-town, performing mainly around the red-light district of Storyville. Shortly before the outbreak of war he visited Europe, returning to New Orleans in 1919. During his absence most of his closest relatives died in an influenza epidemic and upon his return, Johnson soon took to the road. He played guitar and banjo in bands in St. Louis and then Chicago, where he established his reputation as one of the USA's most popular blues singers. For two years the **OKeh Record** Company issued one of his records every six weeks. During this period he became a member of the house band at OKeh, recording with many leading jazz and blues artists, sometimes as accompanist, and at other times as duettist. Among the blues singers with whom he recorded were **Texas Alexander** and **Victoria Spivey**. The jazz musicians with whom he played on 20s sessions included **Duke Ellington**, **Eddie Lang**,

McKinney's Cotton Pickers, **King Oliver** and, most notably, **Louis Armstrong**. During the 30s Johnson divided his time between record sessions, club dates and radio shows. This was not all; like many of his New Orleans compatriots, he seems to have had a deep suspicion that the bubble would one day burst, and consequently he worked regularly outside music, usually at menial and physically demanding jobs. In the 40s Johnson began to gain popularity, adopting the amplified guitar and singing programmes of blues intermingled with many of his own compositions, one of which, 'Tomorrow Night', was a successful record. In the 50s he played in the UK but performed mostly in the USA, living and playing in Chicago and, later, Cincinnati, before settling in Philadelphia. In the 60s he again visited Europe and also appeared in New York and in Canada, where he became resident, eventually owning his own club in Toronto in the last few years before his death in 1970. Johnson's ability to cross over from blues to jazz and back again was unusual among bluesmen of his generation. He brought to his blues guitar playing a level of sophistication that contrasted vividly with the often bitter directness of the lyrics he sang. His mellow singing voice, allied to his excellent diction, helped to make him one of the first rhythm balladeers. He strongly influenced numerous blues and jazz guitarists, among them **T-Bone Walker**, **Lowell Fulson**, **B.B. King**, **Teddy Bunn**, **Eddie Durham** and **Charlie Christian**.

● COMPILATIONS: *Lonesome Road* (King 1958)★★★★, *Blues By Lonnie* (Bluesville 1960)★★★★, *Blues And Ballads* (Bluesville 1960)★★★★, *Losing Game* (Bluesville 1961)★★★★, *Another Night To Cry* (Bluesville 1963)★★★★, *24 Twelve Bar Blues* (King 1966)★★★★, *Tomorrow Night* (King 1970). *The Complete Folkways Recordings* (1993)★★★★, *Stompin' At The Penny* (Columbia Legacy 1994)★★★★, *Playing With The Strings* rec. 1925-1932 (JSP 1995)★★★.

Johnson, Lou

b. 1941, USA. A singer in the mould of **Ben E. King**, Johnson was a former member of the Zionettes. Their single 'Talking About The Man' enjoyed sufficient local interest to prompt his solo ambitions. Signed to the Big Top/Big Hill group of labels, Johnson recorded a series of superb **Burt Bacharach/Hal David** compositions, including 'Reach Out For Me' (1963) and '(There's) Always Something There To Remind Me' (1964). Both reached the lower rungs of the R&B chart. **Sandie Shaw**'s recording of the latter became a UK number 1 while the former song provided **Dionne Warwick** with a US Top 20 hit. Johnson's 'Kentucky Bluebird (Send A Message To Martha)' later became a hit for **Adam Faith** and was subsequently revamped by Dionne Warwick as 'A Message To Michael'. Johnson's last chart record was 'A Time To Love, A Time To Cry' (1965), a vocal version of **Sidney Bechet**'s 'Petite Fleur'.

● ALBUMS: *With You In Mind* (1971)★★★.

Johnson, Luther 'Georgia Snake Boy'

b. Lucius Brinson Johnson, 30 August 1934, Davidsboro, Georgia, USA, d. 18 March 1976. Johnson was a guitarist, bassist and vocalist who formed his first band in Chicago at the age of 19. His boyhood ambition was to play with **Muddy Waters**; he achieved this in the 60s. Johnson played in the raw, urban style of Waters, and was also proficient at older country blues styles. His first recording (as 'Little Luther') was for **Chess Records** and he also recorded with Waters' sideman for the Spivey and Douglas labels. In the 70s he made two albums for the Black And Blue company while touring Europe. Johnson lived in Boston, Massachusetts, from 1970 until his death from cancer in 1976.

● ALBUMS: *Born In Georgia* (Black And Blue 1972)★★★, *On The Road Again* rec. 1972 (1991)★★★.

● COMPILATIONS: *Chicken Shack* (1967/8)★★, *They Call Me The Snake* (1993)★★★.

Johnson, Luther 'Guitar Junior'

b. 11 April 1939, Itta Bena, Mississippi, USA. Johnson's early musical experience was in gospel and he taught himself guitar around 1954, switching to blues before he moved with his family to Chicago's west side in 1955, where he played local clubs and teamed up with **Magic Sam** in the early 60s. Johnson is now regarded as one of the foremost exponents of the guitar-based west side blues style. He spent most of the 70s as a member of **Muddy Waters**' band, with whom he recorded, and also had his own recordings issued on the Big Beat, MCM, Black And Blue, Alligator, Blue Phoenix (the latter also available on Rooster Blues) and Bullseye Blues labels; he was also featured on three albums by the Nighthawks. He has come into his own in the 90s with a series of solo albums which are solid rather than spectacular.

● ALBUMS: *Luther's Blues* (1976)★★★, *I Changed* (1979)★★★, *Doin' The Sugar Too* (1984)★★★, *I Want To Groove With You* (Bullseye Blues 1990)★★★, *It's Good To Me* (1992)★★, *Country Sugar Papa* (Bullseye Blues 1994)★★★, *Slammin' On The West Side* (Telarc 1996)★★, *Live Downstairs At The Rynborn* (Rynborn Blues 1997)★★.

Johnson, Luther 'Houserocker'

Johnson was a blues singer and guitarist based in Atlanta, Georgia, USA, who learned a few rudiments of music from his father but was largely self-taught. His career began around the mid-60s when he worked as a backing musician for major blues artists appearing in Atlanta's clubs, and in the early 80s he began establishing a reputation with his band, the Houserockers. He works regularly at Blind Willie's, Atlanta's best-known blues club, both as a bandleader (his group is now known as the Shadows) in his own right and as backing guitarist for bigger names. He achieved a measure of international prominence in 1990 with the release of a well-received album on Ichiban; the mixture of blues standards and original material revealed a talented modern blues musician with his roots deep in the tradition.

● ALBUMS: *Takin' A Bite Outta The Blues* (Ichiban 1990)★★★.

Johnson, Manzie

b. Manzie Isham Johnson, 19 August 1906, Putnam, Connecticut, USA, d. 9 April 1971. As a very small child Johnson went to New York where he learned to play violin and piano before turning to the drums. While still a teenager and then into his early twenties, he played with bands led by, among many others, Willie Gant, June Clark, **Elmer Snowden** and **Horace Henderson**. In 1931 he joined **Don Redman** for a six-year spell after which he played with **Willie Bryant** before forming his own band, then rejoined Redman. During the 30s he played on numerous record dates with leaders including **Henry 'Red' Allen**, **Lillian Armstrong** and **Mezz Mezzrow**, including an appearance on the famous sessions co-led by Mezzrow and **Tommy Ladnier**. In the 40s Johnson continued to record and play with several bands including **Frankie Newton**, **Fletcher Henderson**, Horace Henderson again, and Ovie Alston; another spell with Redman preceded military service and after the war he was again leading his own groups and playing with Alston. In the 50s Johnson gradually drifted into only occasional playing. He remained a part-time musician for the rest of his life, performing with **Happy Caldwell**, Lem Johnson and others. A sure timekeeper with a good sense of swing overlying a clear understanding of the more traditional role of the drummer in jazz, Johnson's playing was usually discreet and always at the service of the soloist and ensembles with which he performed.

● COMPILATIONS: *The Chronological Don Redman 1931-1933* (Classics 1931-33)★★★★, with Mezz Mezzrow, Tommy Ladnier, Sidney Bechet *The Panassie Sessions* (RCA 1938-39)★★★★, *The Fabulous Sidney Bechet* (Blue Note 1951)★★★★.

Johnson, Marv

b. Marvin Earl Johnson, 15 October 1938, Detroit, Michigan, USA, d. 16 May 1993, Columbia, South Carolina, USA. The gospel training that Johnson received as a teenager in the Junior Serenaders was a major influence on his early R&B releases. In 1958, he formed a partnership with the young **Berry Gordy**, who was then working as a songwriter and producer for **Jackie Wilson**. Gordy produced Johnson's earliest releases on Kudo, and launched his Tamla label with Johnson's single 'Come To Me', which became a hit when it was licensed to United Artists. Johnson remained with the label until 1965, scoring a run of chart entries in the early 60s with 'You Got What It Takes', 'I Love The Way You Move' and 'Move Two Mountains' - all produced by Gordy. Johnson's tracks showcased his delicate tenor vocals against a female gospel chorus, and he maintained this style when he signed to Gordy's **Motown** stable in 1965. His initial

release on the Gordy Records label, the soul favourite 'I Miss You Baby', was a US hit, although it proved to be a false dawn. His subsequent US releases failed, and Johnson eventually abandoned his recording career in 1968. Ironically, the UK Tamla-Motown label chose this moment to revive Johnson's 1966 recording 'I'll Pick A Rose For My Rose', which became an unexpected Top 20 hit amidst a dramatic revival in the label's popularity in Britain. Johnson quickly travelled to the UK to capitalize on this success, before retiring to become a sales executive at Motown. After almost two decades working behind the scenes in the music business, he returned to performing in 1987, touring with the 'Sounds Of Motown' package and re-recording his old hits for the Nightmare label. He was teamed with Carolyn Gill (of the **Velvelettes**) by record producer Ian Levine to release 'Ain't Nothing Like The Real Thing' in 1987. He released *Come To Me* on Levine's Motor City label. Johnson collapsed and died at a concert in South Carolina on 16 May 1993.

● ALBUMS: *Marvellous Marv Johnson* (United Artists 1960)★★★, *More Marv Johnson* (United Artists 1961)★★, *I Believe* (United Artists 1966)★★, *I'll Pick A Rose For My Rose* (Motown 1969)★★, *Come To Me* (Motor City 1990)★★.

● COMPILATIONS: *The Best Of Marv Johnson - You Got What It Takes* (1992)★★★, *The Very Best* (Essential Gold 1996)★★★.

Johnson, Mary

b. *c.*1900, Eden Station, Mississippi, USA. Johnson had six children by **Lonnie Johnson** during their marriage (1925-32). She began her own recording career in 1929 in the company of **Henry Brown**'s piano and **Ike Rodgers**' trombone. Mary continued to appear on the St. Louis music scene at least up until her last recordings as a blues singer in 1936, working with stalwarts such as **Roosevelt Sykes**, **Peetie Wheatstraw**, **Tampa Red** and **Thomas A. Dorsey**. By the 40s she was doing church work and in 1948 she recorded for the Coleman Label with the Mary Johnson Davis Gospel Singers. By the name she employed for these recordings it appears likely that she had remarried. Johnson had been employed as a hospital worker in St. Louis for years before she retired in 1959.

● ALBUMS: *Ike Rodgers' Gut Bucket Trombone* (1968)★★★, *Piano Blues Vol. 19* (1984)★★★, *I Just Can't Take It* (Agram 1989)★★★.

Johnson, Matt

b. 1961, Essex, England. From an early age Johnson turned to music. After beginnings with the school band Road Star, he went on to the electronic trio the Gadgets, who recorded three albums, the last of which was never released. His collaborators were Tom Johnston and Michael O'Shea, both of whom were ex-Plain Characters. While the band were still in progress, Johnson formed **The The** with Keith Laws (keyboards), Tom Johnston (bass) and Peter Ashworth (drums). Following two singles, one each for **4AD Records** and

Some Bizzare, the original formation disintegrated. Some backing tracks were salvaged, however, and these formed the basis of Johnson's solo effort, *Burning Blue Soul*, released in 1981. In cover design it parodied the **Beatles**' *Rubber Soul*-period psychedelia, but in execution it was a very personal affair: 'It is pretty close to the bone. It was one of the most innocent albums made, probably. And very pure, almost virginal in a way. But when I listen to it, its very honest'. Back under The The's moniker, Johnson recorded tracks for a proposed debut album, *Pornography Of Despair*, which never appeared. Essentially a solo album, all of the tracks would eventually surface on subsequent The The albums or related releases.

● ALBUMS: *Burning Blue Soul* (4AD 1981)★★★.

Johnson, Merline

b. *c.*1912, Mississippi, USA. Information on Johnson's early years is sketchy. She began recording in 1937, and enjoyed a successful recording career for several years, making a large number of records before 1941, accompanied by some of the major blues musicians in Chicago at that time, including **Big Bill Broonzy**, **Lonnie Johnson** and **Blind John Davis** (sometimes credited as Her Rhythm Rascals). Her vocals were tough and confident, occasionally reminiscent of **Memphis Minnie**, with an inclination to the sensual as well as the witty. Her nickname, 'The Yas Yas Girl' (a rare American instance of rhyming slang) bears out this image. Some of her records, however, had a jazzier orientation. She recorded again at a single session after the war in 1947, but nothing further is known of her.

● COMPILATIONS: *The Yas Yas Girl* (Best Of Blues 1988)★★★, *The Yas Yas Girl 1937-40 Vols. 1-3* (Document 1995)★★★.

Johnson, Michael

b. 8 August 1944, Alamosa, Colorado, USA. With a taste catholic enough to embrace both **Charlie Byrd** and **Chuck Berry**, Johnson was taught rudimentary guitar by an older brother before spending a year in Barcelona studying flamenco with Graciano Tarrago. After returning to the USA, the 22-year-old toured with the **Chad Mitchell Trio** (with **John Denver**). In 1971, his first solo album was overseen by Peter Yarrow (of **Peter, Paul And Mary**) and Phil Ramone, but he had to wait until 1978 when 'Bluer Than Blue' reached number 12 in the US charts. It was followed by lesser entries with 'Almost Like Being In Love' and 'This Night Won't Last Forever'. Transferring from **EMI**-America to **RCA**, Johnson next addressed himself to the C&W field, beginning well with 'I Love You By Heart', a commercially successful duet with **Sylvia**. He was to top the country chart twice with singles from the movie *Wings* - 'Give Me Wings' (co-written by Rhonda Fleming) and Hugh Prestwick's 'The Moon Is Over My Shoulder' (featuring a galvanizing acoustic guitar solo by Don Potter). Further hits with 'Crying Shame', Randy Vanwarmer's 'I Will Whisper Your Name' and -

another Prestwick opus - 'That's That', established Johnson as a star of the genre by the 90s. However, illness and poor sales of his 1991 album threatened his new-found status.

● ALBUMS: *Michael Johnson* i (1971)★★, *Wings* (RCA 1987)★★★★, *Life's A Bitch* (RCA 1989)★★★, *Michael Johnson* ii (1991)★★, *Departure* (Vanguard 1995)★★.

● COMPILATIONS: *The Best Of Michael Johnson* (RCA 1990)★★★.

Johnson, Mike

b. Grant's Pass, Oregon, USA. Better-known as the bass player with **Dinosaur Jr**, and also as Mark Lanegan's chief collaborator on two solo projects, Johnson had begun his musical apprenticeship in the band George Lane before joining Snakepit, who released two independent singles and featured future members of **Bikini Kill**, Some Velvet Sidewalk and the **Melvins**. He first met Lanegan when Snakepit supported **Screaming Trees** at their performance in Snakepit's home-town of Eugene, Oregon. Following Lanegan to Seattle in 1991 to play on his solo record, he then replaced Lou Barlow in Dinosaur Jr. Johnson's first attempt at a solo album in 1993, *Bon Vivant*, was never issued, though two songs from these sessions later appeared on *Year Of Mondays*. *Where Am I?*, released in 1994, thus became his official debut and announced his melancholic songwriting and doleful baritone singing voice. However, critics were left unsure as to the choice of the material and the conviction of his writing. After producing Seattle band Juned, he secured a new solo contract with TAG/**Atlantic Records** for *Year Of Mondays*. A more defined, focused record, it was better received by critics, though his style remained firmly rooted in folk-styled ballads and melodic rock - two obvious influences being **Nick Drake** and **Tim Buckley**. A star cast of collaborators included a string quartet, as well as Dinosaur Jr colleague J. Mascis (on drums) and Screaming Trees drummer Barrett Martin (on bass). Mark Lanegan provided backing vocals, while other guests included members of Juned (he is married to their bass player Leslie Hardy). Although the album was given an international, high profile release, Johnson insisted he intended to remain a full-time member of Dinosaur Jr.

● ALBUMS: *Where Am I?* (1994)★★, *Year Of Mondays* (TAG/Atlantic 1996)★★★.

Johnson, Money

b. Harold Johnson, 23 February 1918, Tyler, Texas, USA, d. 28 March 1978. He began playing trumpet as a young teenager and in his late teens was living in Oklahoma City where his musical companions included **Charlie Christian**. In 1937 he joined **Nat Towles**' famous **territory band**, remaining there until 1942 when the band effectively transferred to the leadership of **Horace Henderson**. He stayed with Henderson until 1944, then played with various leaders including **Count Basie**, **Cootie Williams** and **Lucky**

Millinder. In the 50s Johnson was with **Louis Jordan**, **Buddy Johnson** and others, continuing into the 60s as a much in-demand session player. In the 60s he played with **Earl Hines**, **Duke Ellington** and others, returning to Ellington in the early 70s where he remained until the leader's death in 1974. He then played in New York, working with **Buck Clayton** and others towards the end of his life. A solid technician with a nice but somewhat underused talent for fluid and interesting solos, Johnson's long career with important bands indicates the high regard in which he was held.

● ALBUMS: *Reuben Phillips And His Orchestra* (Ascot 1961)★★, with Duke Ellington *Second Sacred Concert* (Prestige 1968)★★★, with Houston Person *Houston Express* (Prestige 1971)★★★, with Buck Clayton *Jam Session* (Chiaroscuro 1975)★★★★.

Johnson, Oliver

b. 28 October 1892, Biloxi, Missouri, USA, d. 29 November 1954, Portland, Oregon, USA. Johnson, (aka Dink), played the piano, clarinet and drums. He learned the piano playing around Storyville in the years before World War I. Although he never achieved great technical proficiency he played in a rough and ready way with a great deal of humour. In 1913 he went to California and joined the Original Creole Band playing drums. He only stayed with the band for a year but when he left them he remained in California recording on drums with his brother-in-law, pianist **Jelly Roll Morton** and later on clarinet with **Kid Ory**. During the 20s he led a band called the Five Hounds Of Jazz which became the Los Angeles Six for a residency in Chicago in 1924. He returned to California to play around clubs and eventually settled in Las Vegas playing the piano in his sister's bar. Although he ceased performing in the 40s he continued to record.

Johnson, Pete

b. 25 March 1904, Kansas City, Missouri, USA, d. 23 March 1967. After playing drums when a teenager, Johnson switched to piano in 1926 and swiftly became a leading exponent of the blues. He was also an excellent accompanist to blues singers; especially **Joe Turner**, with whom he established a partnership that lasted for the rest of his life. In 1936 the ubiquitous **John Hammond Jnr.** brought Johnson and Turner to New York where they played at the Famous Door. Two years later Johnson played at one of Hammond's Spirituals To Swing concerts at Carnegie Hall and later performed and recorded with **Albert Ammons** and **Meade 'Lux' Lewis** as the Boogie Woogie Trio. During the 40s, Johnson continued his solo career, interspersed with engagements with Ammons and, often, Joe Turner. In the 50s Johnson toured the USA and Europe and made several records with Turner and with **Jimmy Rushing**. As a blues and boogie-woogie pianist, Johnson was superb and his thunderous left hand was always a joy to hear. In the recordings he made with Turner he invariably rose above himself, delivering both forceful solos

and lifting the singer to some of his best work. Shortly after playing at the Newport Jazz Festival in 1958 Johnson suffered a stroke which incapacitated him. He did venture back to the recording studios in 1960 but did not appear again in public until 1967, when he was helped onstage to receive an ovation from the audience at the Spirituals To Swing 30th Anniversary concert. He took a bow and was being led off when the band swung into his best-known composition, 'Roll 'Em Pete', and his old companion, Joe Turner, prepared to sing. Johnson sat down at the piano alongside **Ray Bryant** and began picking uncertainly at the keys. Then, gradually, with Bryant laying down a solid left hand, Johnson showed that there was still music inside him. It was a long way from great piano playing but given the circumstances it was a highly emotional moment. It was made more so when, two months later, in March 1967, Johnson died.

● ALBUMS: with others *Spirituals To Swing* (1938-39)★★★, with Pete Johnson *8 To The Bar* 10-inch album (RCA Victor 50s)★★★★, *The Essential Jimmy Rushing* (1955)★★★, with Joe Turner *The Boss Of The Blues* (1956)★★★★, with others *Spirituals To Swing 30th Anniversary Concert* (1967)★★★.

● COMPILATIONS: *Master Of Blues And Boogie Woogie Volumes 1-2* (1939-49)★★★, *The Boogie King* (1940-44)★★★, *The Rarest Pete Johnson Volumes 1-2* (1947-54)★★★★, *Classics 1939-41* (Original Jazz Classics 1992)★★★★, *Central Avenue Boogie* 1947 recordings (Delmark 1993)★★★.

● FURTHER READING: *The Pete Johnson Story*, Hans J. Mauerer.

Johnson, Plas

b. 21 July 1931, Donaldsonville, Louisiana, USA. After being taught soprano saxophone by his father, Johnson took up the tenor as well. Resident on the west coast in the 50s he worked in the studios but played jazz dates with artists including **Benny Carter**. His film and television work increased and his work (though not his name) became known to millions when he was featured playing the main title theme on the soundtrack of *The Pink Panther* (1963). He continued to make infrequent jazz appearances, playing on record dates and at clubs and the occasional festival. Among the musicians with whom he worked in the 70s and 80s were **Bill Berry**, **Herb Ellis**, **Carl Fontana**, **Jake Hanna**, **Dave McKenna** and the **Capp-Pierce Juggernaut**. A highly melodic player with an effortlessly graceful ballad style, Johnson's choice of career has meant that he is often overlooked by jazz audiences.

● ALBUMS: *This Must Be Plas* (1959)★★★, under pseudonym Johnny Beecher *Sax Fifth Avenue* (1962)★★★, with Jake Hanna, Carl Fontana *Live At The Concord Festival* (1975)★★, *The Blues* (Concord 1975)★★★, *Positively* (1976)★★★, *Rockin' With The Plas* (Capitol 1983)★★★, *LA 55* (1983)★★, *Hot Blue And Saxy* (Carell 1989)★★★.

Johnson, Robb

An excellent political protest folk singer from south London, who has been compared to a younger **Leon Rosselson**. He commands respect from fellow writers and singers who cover much of his material, although he still seeks a wider audience. *Gentle Men* was a passionate song suite about the First World War, drawing on Johnson's grandfathers' experience of trench warfare at Ypres.

● ALBUMS: *Overnight* (1992)★★★, *Interesting Times* (Irregular 1995)★★★, *The Night Cafe* (Irregular 1996)★★★, *Gentle Men* (Irregular 1997)★★★.

Johnson, Robert

b. Robert Leroy Johnson, 8 May 1911 (sources for this date vary), Hazlehurst, Mississippi, USA, d. 13 August 1938, Greenwood, Mississippi, USA. For a subject upon which it is dangerous to generalize, it hardly strains credulity to suggest that Johnson was the fulcrum upon which post-war Chicago blues turned. The techniques that he had distilled from others' examples, including **Charley Patton**, **Son House** and the unrecorded Ike Zinnerman, in turn became the template for influential musicians such as **Muddy Waters**, **Elmore James** and those that followed them. Credited by some writers with more originality than was in fact the case, it was as an interpreter that Johnson excelled, raising a simple music form to the level of performance art at a time when others were content to iterate the conventions. He was one of the first of his generation to make creative use of others' recorded efforts, adapting and augmenting their ideas to such extent as to impart originality to the compositions they inspired. Tempering hindsight with perspective, it should be noted that only his first record, 'Terraplane Blues', sold in any quantity; even close friends and family remained unaware of his recorded work until decades later, when researchers such as Gayle Dean Wardlow and Mack McCormick contacted them. In all, Johnson recorded 29 compositions at five sessions held between 23 November 1936 and 20 June 1937; a further 'bawdy' song recorded at the engineers' request is as yet unlocated. It has never been established which, if any, of his recordings were specifically created for the studio and what proportion were regularly performed, although associate **Johnny Shines** attested to the effect that 'Come On In My Kitchen' had upon audiences. Similarly, the image of shy, retiring genius has been fabricated out of his habit of turning away from the engineers and singing into the corners of the room, which **Ry Cooder** identifies as 'corner loading', a means of enhancing vocal power. That power and the precision of his guitar playing are evident from the first take of 'Kind-hearted Women Blues', which, like 'I Believe I'll Dust My Broom' and 'Sweet Home Chicago', is performed without bottleneck embellishment. All eight titles from the first session in San Antonio, Texas, exhibit the attenuated rhythm patterns, adapted from a boogie pianist's left-hand 'walking basses', that became synonymous with post-war Chicago blues and **Jimmy Reed** in particular. Several alternate takes survive and reveal how refined Johnson's performances were, only 'Come On In My Kitchen' being played at two contrasting tempos. Eight more titles were recorded over two days, including 'Walkin Blues', learned from **Son House**, and 'Cross Road Blues', the song an echo of the legend that Johnson had sold his soul to the Devil to achieve his musical skill. 'Preachin' Blues' and 'If I Had Possession Over Judgement Day' were both impassioned performances that show his ability was consummate. The balance of his repertoire was recorded over a weekend some seven months later in Dallas. These 11 songs run the gamut of emotions, self-pity, tenderness and frank sexual innuendo giving way to representations of demonic possession, paranoia and despair. Fanciful commentators have taken 'Hellhound On My Trail' and 'Me And The Devil' to be literal statements rather than the dramatic enactment of feeling expressed in the lyrics. Johnson's ability to project emotion, when combined with the considered way in which he lifted melodies and mannerisms from his contemporaries, gainsay a romantic view of his achievements. Nevertheless, the drama in his music surely reflected the drama in his lifestyle, that of an itinerant with a ready facility to impress his female audience. One such dalliance brought about his end a year after his last session, poisoned by a jealous husband while performing in a jook joint at Three Forks, outside Greenwood, Mississippi. At about that time, **Columbia** A&R man **John Hammond** was seeking out Johnson to represent country blues at a concert, entitled 'From Spirituals To Swing', that took place at New York's Carnegie Hall on 23 December 1938. **Big Bill Broonzy** took Johnson's place. Robert Johnson possessed unique abilities, unparalleled among his contemporaries and those that followed him. The importance of his effect on subsequent musical developments cannot be diminished but neither should it be seen in isolation. His name was kept alive in the 80s by a comprehensive reissue project, while in the 90s he was included as part of the US stamp series celebrating the classic blues artists. Even in his absence he managed to provide controversy - when a cigarette was removed from the original painting, the decision was described by tobacco baron Philip Morris as 'an insult to America's 50 million smokers'.

● COMPILATIONS: *King Of The Delta Blues Singers* (Columbia 1961)★★★★, *King Of The Delta Blues Singers, Volume 2* (Columbia 1970)★★★★★, *Robert Johnson Delta Blues Legend* (Charly 1992)★★★★★, *Hellhound On My Trail: The Essential Recordings* (Indigo 1995)★★★★★, *The Complete Recordings* (Columbia Legacy 1996)★★★★★.

● VIDEOS: *The Search For Robert Johnson* (1992).

● FURTHER READING: *Searching For Robert Johnson*, Peter Guralnick. *The Devil's Son-in-Law*, P. Garon. *Love In Vain: Visions Of Robert Johnson*, Alan Greenberg.

Johnson, Ruby

b. 19 April 1936, Elizabeth City, North Carolina, USA. To many soul fans, Johnson is still chiefly remembered for her wonderful deep-soul Volt recording, 'I'll Run Your Hurt Away', released in March 1966, but some of her other material from the same era confirms that she was a high-quality soul singer. Although African-American, Johnson was raised in North Carolina in the quasi-Jewish Temple Beth-El faith. One of nine children, she grew up singing a cappella at the local temple, but aspired to emulate the power-soul style of **Aretha Franklin** and **Etta James**. After singing with Samuel Latham And The Rhythm Makers at Virginia Beach, she moved to Washington, DC, and became show-opener at the popular Spa Club. Never Duncan, manager of **Bobby Parker** (of 'Watch Your Step' fame), signed her first to the Philadelphia-based V-Tone label (for which Parker was also recording), and then to his own Nebs outlet. Subsequently, ex-Washington disc jockey Al Bell signed Johnson to **Stax**/Volt when he moved to Memphis in 1965. For Volt, Johnson cut several excellent cover versions of other artists' soul titles, such as **Theola Kilgore**'s 'The Love Of My Man' and **Ben E. King**'s 'Don't Play That Song'. She also recorded songs by in-house Stax writers, including **Isaac Hayes** and **David Porter**. Porter's 'I'll Run Your Hurt Away' is said to have reduced him to tears as he wrote it; at times it seems that Johnson was so completely immersed in her performance that she might also break down - her rendition of the song represents a mesmerizing masterpiece of soul. Although never a commercial recording artist, Johnson remained a popular club singer until 1974 when she opted out of the 'disco' boom to take a regular government job. In 1993 she was employed in Maryland, recruiting volunteers to work with handicapped children.
● COMPILATIONS: *I'll Run Your Hurt Away* (1993)★★★.

Johnson, Sy

b. 15 April 1930, New Haven, Conneticut, USA. Johnson studied music and the piano while he played jazz in high school bands and in the Air Force. When he was discharged he went to Los Angeles where he earned a living writing arrangements while involved in the *avant garde* jazz scene which centred around musicians such as **Ornette Coleman** and **Paul Bley**. In the 60s Johnson went to New York where he played briefly with **Charles Mingus**, with the **Rod Levitt** Octet and singer **Yolande Bavan** and led his own trio. From the 70s Johnson worked increasingly arranging commercial music but did arrangements for a variety of Mingus groups (1971-78) and for the **Lee Konitz** Nonet among others. In 1984 Johnson was involved in work on the film *The Cotton Club* the score of which sought to recreate the sound of **Duke Ellington**'s classic band of the late 20s and early 30s. Johnson is also an acute jazz journalist and photographer.
● ALBUMS: with Charles Mingus *Let My Children Hear Music* (1971)★★★★.

Johnson, Syl

b. Sylvester Thompson, 1 July 1936, Holly Springs, Mississippi, USA. Johnson was the youngest of three children and his family moved to Chicago during the late 40s. An elder brother, Mac Thompson, played bass with the **Magic Sam Blues Band.** Having learned guitar and harmonica, Johnson began frequenting the city's southside blues clubs, playing alongside **Howlin' Wolf**, **Muddy Waters** and **Junior Wells**. His first recordings were made in 1956 accompanying **Billy Boy Arnold**, after which Johnson appeared on sessions for **Shakey Jake**, Junior Wells and **Jimmy Reed**. In 1959 Federal released Johnson's first solo single, 'Teardrops', and he recorded unsuccessfully for several independents until signing with Twilight (later changed to Twinight) in 1967. His debut there, 'Come On Sock It To Me', reached number 12 in the R&B chart. Johnson's musical activities, however, were not solely confined to performing. He also produced several local acts including **Tyrone Davis** and **Otis Clay**, while the Deacons, his backing group, featuring brother **Jimmy Johnson** on guitar, enjoyed a minor hit on the singer's Shama label. Johnson was then spotted by **Willie Mitchell** and 'Dresses Too Short' (1968) was recorded with the Mitchell's **Hi Records** house band. The remaining Twinight sessions were divided between Memphis and Chicago. Johnson remained with the label until 1971, recording two albums in the process. Free to sign with Hi, he began a series of releases that matched for excellence those of labelmate **Al Green**. Brash, up-tempo topsides, including 'Back For A Taste Of Your Love' and 'We Did It', contrasted with the often-reflective couplings, of which 'Anyway The Wind Blows' and 'I Hear The Love Chimes' were particularly emotive. The third of his exemplary albums for Hi, *Total Explosion*, produced Johnson's only substantial R&B hit when his version of 'Take Me To The River' (1975) reached number 7. However, his final years at Hi were dogged by internal problems and towards the end of the decade he reactivated his Shama label. A contemporary blues/soul collection, *Ms Fine Brown Frame*, was licensed to Boardwalk, while a French album, *Suicide Blues*, followed in 1984. By the mid-80s, he had semi-retired from the music business and opened a string of fast-food fish restaurants. He returned to performing in 1992 and in 1994 with an excellent album *Back In The Game*.
● ALBUMS: *Dresses Too Short* (Twinight 1968)★★★, *Is It Because I'm Black?* i (Twinight 1970)★★★, *Back For A Taste Of Your Love* (Hi 1973)★★★★, *Diamond In The Rough* (Hi 1974)★★★, *Total Explosion* (Hi 1976)★★★★, *Uptown Shakedown* (Shama 1979)★★★, *Brings Out The Blues In Me* (Shama 1980)★★★, *Ms Fine Brown Frame* (Boardwalk 1983)★★★, *Suicide Blues* (1984)★★★, *Foxy Brown* (Shama 1988)★★★, *Back In The Game* (Delmark 1994)★★★.
● COMPILATIONS: *Brings Out The Blues In Me* (Flyright 1986)★★★, *Is It Because I'm Black?* ii (Charly 1986)★★★★, *The Love Chimes* (Hi 1986)★★★, *Stuck In Chicago* (Hi 1989)★★★.

Johnson, Teddy
(see **Carr, Pearl, And Teddy Johnson**)

Johnson, Tex
b. 30 October 1960, St. Vincent, West Indies. Johnson emigrated with his family to the UK in the 60s, completing his education in Stratford, east London. His initial recording was a self-production with David Tyrone of Venture, 'I Wanna Hold You All Night Long'. Encouraged by the sales of his debut he decided to take control of his career with the inauguration of the Discotex label. The project proved encouraging with the release of Johnson's successful follow-up, 'Pillow Talk', which proved a massive hit in 1981. In 1982 he recorded 'Cork Inna Dance' with the UK-based producer Lloyd Cave, which helped to finance further releases under the Discotex banner, including 'Reggae Rhumba' and 'Love To Love You'. His Christmas release was a double a-sided chart buster in the **lovers rock** style, 'Honey', and an exhibition of his DJ style on 'Girls Girls Girls'. By 1983 he released 'Body Snatch' and 'Crowd Of People', both in combination with DJ Ranking Ivan, alongside 'Womaniser' and 'Can't Get By Without You'. The hits continued with 'The Girl Next Door', 'Song Book Of Love', 'Ask For A Dance' and an outstanding combination hit with **Annette Brisset**, 'Eye To Eye'. Throughout his career he has released a number of successful albums but has been unable to emulate the runaway success of 'Pillow Talk' in the singles market. As a producer he carved a considerable niche in the revival market when he enrolled Errol V, Blacksteel and Hector Cross, brother of **Sandra Cross**, to perform as Klearview Harmonix for the phenomenally successful *Happy Memories* compilations. The albums featured faultless cover versions of reggae classics produced by Johnson. *Volume 5* of the series featured Paulette Tajah performing classic lovers rock hits. In the 90s he concentrated on his production skills, although in 1992 he recorded 'That's Life'. He continues to produce and release lovers and roots compilations, asserting his aspirations towards 'Keeping reggae music sweet, clean, loving and conscious'.

● ALBUMS: *Heart Beat* (Discotex 1988)★★★, *Pure Bliss* (Discotex 1989)★★, *The Collection* (Discotex 1989)★★★★, *For Lovers Only* (Discotex 1990)★★★★, *That's Life* (Discotex 1992)★★★, with Klearview Harmonix *Those Were The Days* (Discotex 1993)★★★, with Klearview Harmonix *Happy Memories Volumes 1 - 5* (Discotex 90s)★★★★.

Johnson, Tommy
b. *c.*1896, Mississippi, USA, d. 1 November 1956. Although his recorded output was contained within a mere four sessions, undertaken in February and August 1928, Johnson remains one of the pivotal figures of delta blues. His work includes 'Cool Drink Of Water Blues', which featured the memorable lyric 'I asked her for water and she brought me gasoline', later adopted by **Howlin' Wolf**, while a 60s group comprised of enthusiasts took their name from '**Canned Heat** Blues'. Johnson's haunting falsetto wrought emotion from his excellent compositions which influenced several artists including the **Mississippi Sheiks** and **Robert Nighthawk**. Although Johnson ceased recording prematurely, he remained an active performer until his death from a heart attack in 1956.

● COMPILATIONS: *The Famous 1928 Tommy Johnson/Ishman Bracey Session* (1970)★★★, *The Complete Recordings 1928-1930* (Wolf 1988)★★★★, *Tommy Johnson (1928-29)* (Document 1991)★★★★.

● FURTHER READING: *Tommy Johnson*, David Evans.

Johnson, Wilko
b. John Wilkinson, *c.*1950. A native of Canvey Island, Essex, England, Johnson played in several local groups, including the Roamers and the Heap, prior to a gaining a degree in English Literature at Newcastle-upon-Tyne University. He returned to music with **Dr. Feelgood**, a gritty R&B band, which became one of the leading attractions of the mid-70s 'pub rock' phenomenon. The group's early sound was indebted to Johnson's punchy guitar style, itself inspired by Mick Green of the **Pirates**, while his striking appearance - black suit and pudding-bowl haircut - combined with jerky, mannequin movements, created a magnetic stage persona. Internal friction led to the guitarist's departure in 1976, but the following year he formed the Solid Senders with keyboards player John Potter, a founder member of Dr. Feelgood, Steve Lewins (bass) and Alan Platt (drums). However, despite securing a prestigious deal with **Virgin**, Johnson was unable to regain the success he enjoyed with his erstwhile unit and the band was dissolved following their lone, but excellent, album. Wilko then replaced Chas Jankel in **Ian Dury**'s **Blockheads**, but resumed his solo career having contributed to *Laughter* (1980). A promising act with Canvey Island associate **Lew Lewis** ensued - Johnson's idol Mick Green was also briefly a member - but commercial indifference doomed its potential. Subsequent line-ups appeared on a variety of outlets as the artist became increasingly hidebound to a diminishing pub and club circuit. His 1991 *Don't Let Your Daddy Know*, was recorded live at Putney's Half Moon pub.

● ALBUMS: *Solid Senders* (Virgin 1978)★★★, *Ice On The Motorway* (Nighthawk 1981)★★★, *Watch Out* (Waterfront 1986)★★★, *Barbed Wire Blues* (Jungle 1988)★★★, *Don't Let Your Daddy Know* (1991)★★.

Johnson, Willie
b. Willis Lee Johnson, 4 March 1923, Memphis, Tennessee, USA, d. 26 February 1995, Chicago, Illinois, USA. Johnson was the musical linchpin behind one of the most enduring artists of the twentieth century - **Howlin' Wolf**. He began playing with Wolf as a teenager. He was there at the Memphis Recording Service studios when the former Chester Arthur Burnett cut his first record, 'Moanin' At Midnight', in

the spring of 1951. However, when that record became a huge hit and Wolf moved to Chicago, Johnson initially remained in Memphis, where he accompanied other stellar blues artists including **Bobby Bland**, **Elmore James** and **Sonny Boy Williamson**. He cut his own records alongside harmonica player Little Sammy Lewis for **Sun Records** as well as sessions with **Willie Nix** for RPM and **Checker Records**. Johnson's side of the Lewis single 'So Long Baby Goodbye' remains his only issued vocal. Within three years, however, Wolf returned to Memphis to bring his erstwhile guitarist back with him to Chicago. Johnson remained with Wolf throughout his residencies at clubs such as the 708 Club, the Zanzibar and Silvio's, and also made memorable studio appearances on singles such as 'Who's Been Talkin'?' (1957) and 'Smokestack Lightning' (1956). His performance on the latter was particularly stunning, his easy, evocative style matching tempos beautifully with Wolf's emphatic delivery. However, his relationship with Wolf was precarious, given that Wolf insisted on an alcohol ban for members of his band and Johnson's capacity for drinking was already reaching legendary proportions. There were many disputes, but Johnson finally left Wolf's company for good in 1959 after a show at Theresa's Lounge. That was effectively the end of his creative musical career as alcohol gained increasing control over his life, although he did continue his long service at the 'Mag Wheel' factory. He did, however, continue to make sporadic appearances at local clubs, relying on his versatility and adapting to whatever artist he was supporting. Various blues aficionados tempted him out of semi-retirement during the 80s and 90s, though he would often fail to arrive or be too drunk to play. However, he played one acclaimed set at the Earwig Music's 15th Anniversary Party at **Buddy Guy**'s Legends venue on 2 June 1994, appearing alongside old friends **Sunnyland Slim** and **Homesick James**. Plans to record for Earwig were aborted when he died at home in February 1995. Ironically, his death came at the exact moment that his classic guitar-playing on 'Smokestack Lightning' was being aired daily on a television advert.

Johnston, Bruce

b. c.1943, Los Angeles, California, USA. An early associate of **Sandy Nelson** and **Phil Spector**, whom he often supported on keyboards, Johnston enjoyed a spell backing **Richie Valens** before recording 'Take This Pearl' as half of Bruce And Jerry. He then wrote and played piano on several records by singer Ron Holden, before embracing the surfing craze in 1962 with 'Do The Surfer Stomp'. The following year he began a fruitful partnership with songwriter/producer **Terry Melcher** which not only engendered the excellent *Surfin' 'Round The World*, but a series of well-crafted studio projects. The duo took control of releases by the **Ripchords**, notably 'Three Window Coupe', and the Rogues, as well as completing several singles as Bruce And Terry. In April 1965 Johnston joined the **Beach Boys** as an on-

tour replacement for **Brian Wilson**. He made his recording debut with the group on 'California Girls', but the artist's songwriting skills did not flourish until 1969 when 'The Nearest Faraway Place' surfaced on *20/20*. Johnston's melodramatic approach prevailed on 'Deidre' and 'Tears In The Morning' (*Sunflower*), but 'Disney Girls 1957' (*Surf's Up*) captured the balance between evocation and sentimentality. Johnston also guested on albums by numerous acts, including **Sagittarius**, **(American) Spring** and **Roger McGuinn**. He officially left the Beach Boys in 1972, although his services were still called upon during recording sessions. Johnston then joined former partner Melcher in Equinox Productions, and worked with such disparate acts as **Jack Jones**, the **Hudson Brothers** and **Sailor**. However, this period is best recalled for 'I Write The Songs', his multi-million selling composition, first recorded by the **Captain And Tennille**, which was a hit for both **David Cassidy** and, especially, **Barry Manilow**. Having completed the largely disappointing *Goin' Public*, Bruce returned to the Beach Boys camp in 1978 by producing their *L.A. Light Album*. He has since remained an integral part of the line-up and is often credited as mediator during recurrent internal strife.

● ALBUMS: as Bruce Johnston Surfing Band *Surfer's Pajama Party* (1963)★★★, *Surfin' 'Round The World* (1963)★★★, *Goin' Public* (Columbia 1977)★.

Johnston, Daniel

b. West Virginia, USA. A celebrated figure in the US rock underground through his various activities with small-pressing fanzines and cassette-only releases, Daniel Johnston is the ultimate 'lo-fi' **Syd Barrett**. A number of such cassettes were distributed throughout the early 80s. Featuring cheap keyboards and elementary guitar playing, the real attraction was Johnston's plaintive vocals, capable of conveying an alarming level of honesty and emotional depth. His debut, 1980's *Songs Of Pain*, revealed how close to the edge of sanity he was - hangovers from his fundamentalist background made themselves known through statements against pre-marital sex and humanity's descent into decadence as Johnstone struggled to explain himself, producing both pathos and high comedy. Subsequent efforts have proved just as harrowing, particularly the disorientating *The What Of Whom*. Having moved to Austin, Texas, by 1985 and with *Respect*, he had become something of a cult figure via his exposure on **MTV**'s *Cutting Edge* show, but his new-found fame did little to solidify his state of mind. In 1986 and 1988 his problems resulted in incarceration. In 1988 Homestead Records issued his first recordings on vinyl with the release of *Hi, How Are You*. Another powerful statement, Johnston's songwriting had become more acute and focused, combining resignatory romance narratives with spiteful attacks on former employers. It also included the memorable line: 'I guess I lean toward the excessive/But that's just the way it is when you're a manic depressive', which gave some indication of the artist's state of mind during its recording. The double set *Yip/Jump Music* was performed entirely on chord organ, and included eulogies to the **Beatles**, Danny of **Danny And The Juniors** and cartoon character Caspar The Ghost in addition to God. Both *Retired Boxer* and *Respect* were excellent collections, including typically left-field compositions such as 'I'll Do Anything But Break Dance For Ya, Darling' and 'Just Like A Widow', as well as a cover version of 'Heartbreak Hotel' which managed to sound both offbeat and authentic. *Continued Story* featured contributions from Bill Anderson and Rick Morgan to acidic songs such as 'Ain't No Woman Gonna Make A George Jones Outta Me' and a version of 'I Saw Her Standing There'. Though his collaboration with Jad Fair was not entirely successful, he subsequently secured a new contract with **Kramer**'s Shimmy Disc label. Despite guest appearances with **Sonic Youth** among others, his two albums for the label in the early 90s lacked something of the incisiveness of old. In 1994 former Glass Eye singer K. McCarty recorded an album consisting entirely of Johnston cover versions (*Dead Dog's Eyeball*), as Johnston's profile continued to rise. This was confirmed when he became an unlikely signing to **Atlantic Records** in 1994, for whom his debut major label album, *Fun*, was produced by Paul Leary of the **Butthole Surfers**.

● ALBUMS: *Songs Of Pain* cassette only (Stress 1980)★★★, *Don't Be Scared* cassette only (Stress 1982)★★★, *The What Of Whom* cassette only (Stress 1982)★★★, *More Songs Of Pain* cassette only (Stress 1983)★★★, *Yip/Jump Music* (Homestead 1983)★★★, *Retired Boxer* cassette only (Stress 1984)★★★, *Respect* cassette only (Stress 1985)★★★, *Continued Story* cassette only (Homestead 1985)★★★, *Hi, How Are You* (Homestead 1988)★★★, with Jad Fair *Jad Fair And Daniel Johnston* (50 Skadillion Watts 1989)★★, *Live At SXSW* cassette only (Stress 1990)★★★, *1990* (Shimmy Disc 1990)★★★, *Artistic Vices* (Shimmy Disc 1992)★★★, *Fun* (Atlantic 1994)★★★.

● COMPILATIONS: *The Lost Recordings Volume 1* cassette only (Stress 1983)★★★, *The Lost Recordings Volume 2* cassette only (Stress 1983)★★★.

Johnston, Freedy

b. 1961, Kansas, USA. Johnston, a critically acclaimed singer and songwriter whose music defies easy categorization, made his debut for Bar/None Records in 1990 with the Chris Butler-produced *The Trouble Tree*. An accomplished record, highlighted by the artist's succinct lyrics and able characterization of his subjects, it received positive reviews throughout the US underground. 1992's *Can You Fly* was better still. The opening line: 'Well I sold the dirt to feed the band', was clearly autobiographical, the singer having pawned his family farm to raise money for the studio recording. The results of this investment were impressive, Johnston raising the standard of his still emotive songwriting to produce a succession of neat, charming pop songs. It won him significant praise and a major label

recording contract with **Elektra Records**. *This Perfect World* was produced by **Butch Vig** and, while lacking some of the irreverent exuberance of *Can You Fly*, again won critical plaudits. *Never Home* further consolidated Johnston's reputation as one of the most original singer-songwriters of the 90s.

● ALBUMS: *The Trouble Tree* (Restless/Bar/None 1990)★★★, *Can You Fly* (Bar/None 1992)★★★★, *This Perfect World* (Elektra 1994)★★★, *Never Home* (Elektra 1997)★★★.

Johnston, Jan

b. Manchester, England. Johnston began writing her first songs on the piano in her early teenage years. By the time she was an adult she could be found playing at a wealthy gentlemen's club in her native Manchester: 'Whilst the girls in their cages did their stuff, I was alone at the piano playing **Joni Mitchell** and **Carole King** songs, just occasionally dropping in some of my own material. I thought if I can cope with this, I can cope with anything.' Eventually she teamed up with fellow Mancunian Tony Kirkham to play residencies at clubs such as the Bitter End in New York and the Orange in West London. There the duo managed to find a contract with Sony/**Columbia Records**, scoring a minor UK hit (number 55) with 'If This Is Love', credited to the act's then title, JJ. An album, *Intro*, followed in 1991 but their experience with Columbia proved to be not altogether a happy one, with the artist complaining of a lack of promotion and creative meddling. Putting this down to experience, she elected for a solo career and soon found herself with a new contract at **A&M Records**. The title of her debut album, *Naked But For Lillies*, was dreamed up on a balmy summer evening, and imposed Johnston's maturing instinct for songwriting (still helped musically by Kirkham). The innocence and plaintive songwriting saw critics draw comparisons with **Kate Bush** and Carole King, but it failed to set the charts alive, despite strong reviews in magazines such as **Q**. The first single to be lifted from the collection, 'Paris', was a typically dreamy excerpt produced by Dave Bascombe.

● ALBUMS: *Naked But For Lillies* (A&M 1994)★★★.

Johnston, Tom

(see **Doobie Brothers**)

Johnstone, Clarence Nathaniel

(see **Layton, Turner**)

Johnstons

This mid-60s Irish close harmony group enjoyed immense success in their homeland. The original line-up, which used to play in the family pub in Slane, consisted of Adrienne Johnston (vocals), her sister Luci (vocals), and brother Michael (guitar). Their debut single, a cover of **Ewan MacColl**'s 'Travelling People', reached number 1 in the Irish charts. Michael left the trio, and the sisters were joined by traditionalist Mike

Moloney (b. Co. Limerick, Eire; guitar/banjo/vocals), and shortly after by **Paul Brady** (b. 19 May 1947, Co. Tyrone, Northern Ireland; guitar/vocals). Brady and Moloney had met earlier while at University College, Dublin. While *The Barley Corn* was traditionally based, *Give A Damn* saw the group working with contemporary material, by writers such as **Joni Mitchell**, **Leonard Cohen**, **Jacques Brel**, and **Dave Cousins**. By the time of *Bitter Green* Luci had left the group, which continued as a trio; *If I Sang My Song* was Brady and Adrienne Johnston only, the others having left. The majority of the songs contained on the album came from the pen of Brady and Chris McLoud. The album boasted backing musicians such as **Tim Hart**, Royston Wood, and **Rick Kemp**. Adrienne recorded only one solo album completed in 1975, before her death. Her solo outing, *Adrienne Johnston Of The Johnstons*, had a number of notable musicians in attendance including **Simon Nicol**, Gerry Conway and Pat Donaldson. Brady went on to solo success, outside the limits of the folk arena. Moloney emigrated to the USA in 1973 and studied at the University of Pennsylvania, where he obtained his PhD in Folklore and Folklife Studies in 1992. He contributed to the television series about the history of Irish music, *Bringing It All Back Home*, in 1991. Moloney's expertise in guitar, mandolin and tenor banjo are well known, and he has both produced and played on a great number of recordings by many well established artists. He also writes, and lectures, on folklore at Villa Nova University.

● ALBUMS: *Travelling People* (1966)★★, *The Johnstons* (Transatlantic 1968)★★★, *Give A Damn* (Transatlantic 1969)★★★, *The Barleycorn* (Transatlantic 1969)★★, *Bitter Green* (Transatlantic 1969)★★★, *The Johnstons Sampler* (Transatlantic 1970)★★★, *Colours Of The Dawn* (1971)★★, *If I Sang My Song* (Transatlantic 1972)★★★, *Give A Damn/Bitter Green* (Transatlantic 1997)★★★.
Solo: Mike Moloney *We Have Met Together* (1973)★★.
● COMPILATIONS: *The Johnstons Anthology* (1978)★★★, *Streets Of London - The Johnstons Sampler* (1979)★★★, *The Transatlantic Years Featuring Paul Brady* (1992)★★★.

Joi

Long before the fashion for Asian-influenced dance music took off in the mid- to late 90s, Farook and Haroon Shamsher were fusing the sounds of traditional Bengali music with hip-hop and contemporary dance styles. In the mid-80s they were part of a youth movement in east London called Joi Bangla, which aimed to promote various aspects of Bengali culture. Wishing to concentrate on the music side, the brothers formed a **sound system** with the same name and began playing around local community centres. At the same time they wrote their own material and in 1988 recorded a promo, 'Taj Ma House' (BPM Records), which coincided with the acid house movement. As they continued to write, they produced DATs that they played out on the sound system, with additional live percussion and samples, in the same way as **dub plates**. In 1992

they released 'Desert Storm' on **Rhythm King Records** as Joi, which was also the name of a club night they hosted the following year that ran weekly at London's Bass Clef. Over the next few years they continued to play their own material, and tracks recorded by likeminded artists, as the Joi sound system at various clubs and parties, including Bar Rumba, the Big Chill, Megatripolis, Ministry Of Sound and Return To The Source. They developed a live act and have since performed at such events as Tribal Gathering, Whirl-Y-Gig and WOMAD, as well as others around Europe. In October 1996 the *Bangladesh* EP was released on **Nation Records** to raise awareness of disastrous Western interference in that country's affairs. 'High Times' and 'Nargin' are typical of the group's unique, melodic sound, which blends Asian and Middle Eastern sounds with various styles of dance music without adhering to any one in particular. In 1998 they contributed a remix of **Nusrat Fateh Ali Khan**'s 'Sweet Pain' to the tribute album *Star Rise*, and signed to **Real World Records** with plans to release an album later that year. While they have not had many releases in their own right, they have contributed tracks to a large number of compilations, notably 'Goddess' on Sony's *Eastern Uprising* (1997), 'India' on Zip Dog's *Global Explorer* (1997) and 'Shanti' on Law And Auder's *Further East* (1998). Perhaps more important than the group's releases is their sound system, through which they have promoted their fusion ethic regardless of trends within the music industry. Over the years they have been involved with various other artists and DJs, including **Asian Dub Foundation**, Athletico, **Mixmaster Morris**, Plaid and Spring Heel Jack.

Jojo

This **Toto**-styled, German rock quartet was put together by former **Tokyo** guitarist Robby Musenbilcher and vocalist/guitarist Roko Kohlmeyer after working together as session musicians. Recruiting ex-Tokyo keyboard player Lothar Krell, vocalist George Liszt and ex-Saga drummer Curt Cress, they selected 11 tracks from the 40 they had written for inclusion on their debut album. Produced by **Yes** supremo Eddie Offord, this was a highly polished collection, sophisticated but ultimately clinical. It lacked the necessary gusto to give the band a real identity.
● ALBUMS: *Jojo* (1988)★★★★.

Joker Is Wild, The

One of the first artists that **Frank Sinatra** signed to his own new **Reprise** label in the early 60s was nightclub comedian Joe E. Lewis. Before then, the two had been close friends, so it seemed logical, when Paramount decided in 1957 to make the film biography of a singer with a slick line in patter, that Sinatra's name would be to the fore. Shot in black and white, presumably to heighten the dramatic effect, the film turned out to be a hard-hitting, realistic account as to the likely fate of a young man in the Roaring 20s if he declined to co-operate with men in dark overcoats carrying violin cases. Young Lewis's career is progressing well in one particular nightspot, singing songs such as 'At Sundown' (**Walter Donaldson**) and 'I Cried For You' (**Arthur Freed**-Gus Arnheim-Abe Lyman). After ignoring warnings against moving elsewhere, he manages to impress audiences in the new venue ('where they carry the drunks out - they don't just toss 'em out into the street') with 'If I Could Be With You One Hour Tonight' (Henry Creamer-Jimmy Johnson) and 'All The Way' (**Sammy Cahn-Jimmy Van Heusen**), before his vocals cords are slashed and he finds a new career as a comedian. Subsequent fractured vocalizing is confined to parodies of songs such as 'Out Of Nowhere' (music-**John Green**), 'Swinging On A Star' (music-Van Heusen), and 'Naturally' (music-Flotow), all with new lyrics by Harry Harris. Before he finally kicks the bottle, Lewis has become a physical wreck and ruined the lives of the two women who love him, played by Jeanne Crain and **Mitzi Gaynor**. Eddie Albert plays Lewis's accompanist, whose wife (Beverly Garland) forces him to give up on the comedian, and the cast also included Jackie Coogan, Barry Kelley, Ted de Corsia, Valerie Allen, Hank Henry and **Sophie Tucker**. Oscar Saul's screenplay was adapted from a book by Art Cohn, and the film, which was photographed in VistaVision, was directed by Charles Vidor. The song 'All The Way' won an Academy Award, and gave Frank Sinatra a number 2 hit in the USA.

Joli, France

b. 1963, Montreal, Canada. Joli was only 16-years-old when she recorded the song that would become her first and only chart hit, 'Come To Me'. She had been a singer, dancer and actress from a small child, and had a full-time performing career before she reached her teens. She was discovered by Canadian singer Tony Green, who wrote 'Come To Me' and became her manager. Signed to Prelude Records, she released the maiden recording in the autumn of 1979 and it reached number 15 in the US pop charts. Joli continued to record into the mid-80s, switching to Epic Records, but never made the charts in the USA again.
● ALBUMS: *France Joli* (Prelude 1979)★★★, *Tonight* (1980)★★, *Attitude* (1983)★★★, *Witch Of Love* (1985)★★★.

Jolley, Steve

In 1969, Jolley was guitarist with **Sam Apple Pie**. The following year, he joined **Freedom**, a **Procol Harum** splinter group, in whose ranks he remained until 1972. By the end of the decade, he had become principally a studio functionary. In partnership with **Tony Swain**, he worked on television's *Muppet Show* from 1975. However, it was after the pair's 'Body Talk' smash for Imagination that they emerged as a leading production team from 1982-84. Among their more feted clients were **Truth**, **Bananarama** - notably *Deep Sea Skiving* - **Wang Chung**, Louise Goffin, **Diana Ross**, **Tom Robinson** and **Errol Brown**. Jolley's career peaked

commercially with 1983's *True*, a number 1 album (and title track single) in the UK for **Spandau Ballet**. Advantaged by a huge budget from **CBS Records**, Jolley and Swain also took on the award-winning *Alf*, **Alison Moyet**'s chart-topping solo album debut, for which Jolley contributed co-wrote all but one track. Since a subsequent break with Swain, Steve has continued to thrive in the record industry by forming his own record label.

Jolly, Pete

b. 5 June 1932, New Haven, Connecticut, USA. As a small child Jolly became adept on both accordion and piano. From the early 50s he was resident in Los Angeles, where he became a much in-demand pianist for many of the recording sessions that helped to establish the so-called west coast school of bebop. Among the dates on which Jolly appeared were those for *The Swinging Mr Rogers* with **Shorty Rogers** And His Giants in 1955, when he joined **Jimmy Giuffre**, **Curtis Counce** and **Shelly Manne** and played a fine solo on 'Michele's Meditation'. Also in 1955 he recorded with the Cy Touff Quintet and the following year played with the **Chet Baker-Art Pepper** Sextet on *Playboys*. During the late 50s and most of the 60s Jolly led his own small groups but spent much of his time in film and television studio work. In the 80s he again recorded with Pepper and occasionally deputized with west coast big bands, including that led by **Bill Berry**. Jolly's playing was always of high quality and he made an important contribution to the west coast jazz of the 50s. Some authorities hold his accordion playing in high regard, although this instrument has yet to make a serious impact in the jazz world.
● ALBUMS: *Jolly Jumps In* (1955)★★★, *The Pete Jolly Duo, Trio And Quartet* (Fresh Sounds 1955)★★★★, with Shorty Rogers *The Swinging Mr Rogers* (1955)★★, *Cy Touff, His Octet And Quintet* (1955)★★★, with Chet Baker, Art Pepper *Playboys* (1956)★★★★, *The Pete Jolly Trio* i (1956)★★★, with Ralph Pena *The Pete Jolly Duo* (1959)★★★, with Pepper *Smack Up!* (1960)★★★, *5 O'Clock Shadows* (1962)★★★, *Little Bird* (1963)★★★, *Sweet September* (1963)★★★, *The Sensational Pete Jolly Gasses Everybody* (1963)★★★, *Hello, Jolly* (1964)★★, *The Pete Jolly Trio* ii (1965)★★★, *Pete Jolly With Marty Paich And His Orchestra* (1968)★★, *Give A Damn* (1969)★★★, *Sessions, Live* (1969)★★★, *Strike Up The Band* (1980)★★★, *The Five* (Fresh Sounds 1988)★★★★, *Gems* (1990)★★★.

Jolson - The Musical

After originating at the Theatre Royal in Plymouth in August 1995, and enjoying record-breaking business in the provinces en route to London, the biographical *Jolson* opened at the Victoria Palace on 26 October. The previous tenant of that theatre for almost six years had been another anthology musical, the smash-hit *Buddy* (also begat in Plymouth), which continued to post 'House Full' notices after transferring to the Strand Theatre, nearer to the heart of the West End. Inevitably, comparisons were drawn between the two productions, with many doubting the appeal - in the Politically Correct generation - of a show featuring an egotist with an often turbulent domestic life, who not only appeared regularly in blackface, but actually hit the big time in 1911 singing a song called 'Paris Is A Paradise For Coons'. In the event, Francis Essex and Rob Bettinson's book, which was developed from an original idea by Jolson biographer Michael Freedland, dealt with the blacking-up in a perfunctory manner, and even included 'a mawkishly implausible scene' in which Jolson (superbly portrayed by the popular television personality, Brian Conley), uncharacteristically gives a little encouragement (in the shape of a hug and some cash) to a young black boy, Sammy (Timothy Walker or Sean Parkins), who sings for him. The first act is set in the 20s, and deals with Jolson 'arrogantly steam-rolling his career through the wishes of exasperated managers and agents' on his way to Broadway stardom, replacing obsolete wife number two with nifty hoofer **Ruby Keeler** (Sally Ann Triplett), as well as his involvement in the first talking picture, *The Jazz Singer*. Act II jumps forward to cover his decline in the 40s, and closes with a re-creation of the famous Radio City Concert, thereby providing a good excuse for Conley to belt out the few Jolson blockbusters remaining from the past couple of hours. Triplett's share of the goodies included 'By The Light Of The Silvery Moon', 'You Made Me Love You', 'I'm Just Wild About Harry', and 'I Only Have Eyes For You', and she combined with Conley on the insinuating 'About A Quarter To Nine'. Prominent amongst the cast were John Bennett, who gave a fine performance as Louis Epstein, the singer's long-suffering agent, Brian Greene (Lee Shubert), John Conroy (Frankie Holmes), Craig Stevenson (**Harry Akst**), Chrissy Roberts (Eugenie Besserer), Kit Benjamin (Pat Levin), Gareth Williams (Harry Cohn), Corinna Richards (Henrietta), David Bacon (Sam Warner), and Julie Armstrong, Alison Carter, and Helen McNee as the Rooney Sisters. Tudor Davies was the choreographer, the 'sumptuously contrived period settings' were designed by Robert Jones, and director Rob Bettinson moved the show along at great pace. However, it was Conley, with his brash, swaggering, incandescent performance, accurately incorporating many of Jolson's vocal mannerisms, who kept the coach parties turning up consistently, and it was a good idea to record the Original Cast CD 'live' at the theatre. The versatile Allan Stewart took over when the star was occasionally absent. Overall, *Jolson* was greeted by the critics with grudging admiration, although the general opinion seemed to be that, despite the billboards' claim that 'You truly ain't seen nothing yet', the show was 'not worth walking a million miles to see'. As with **Jerry Herman**'s *Mack And Mabel*, *Jolson* proved once again that it is extremely difficult to mount a successful musical about an unsympathetic central character (except *Evita*?). Even so, it won the 1996 **Laurence Olivier Award** for Best Musical, and was also nominated for

best actor (Conley) and supporting actor (Bennett). After the London run came to an end in March 1997, Conley and the show embarked on a world tour, beginning with a three month stopover in Toronto, Canada. Regarding the controversial question of blacking-up, theatre-watchers pointed out that, ironically, *Jolson* was playing at the same theatre where the renowned (but now redundant) *Black And White Minstrel Show* reigned between 1962 and 1972.

Jolson Sings Again
(see *Jolson Story, The*)

Jolson Story, The
This enormously successful, sanitised film biography of 'The World's Greatest Entertainer', who was actually in at the birth of screen musicals with *The Jazz Singer*, was released by Columbia in 1946. In fact, Stephen Longstreet's screenplay for *The Jolson Story* was very much along the lines of that earlier pioneering film: a cantor's son, Asa Yoelson (**Al Jolson**), breaks his father's heart by leaving home to make a successful career in show business as the black-faced entertainer who had an extraordinary effect on audiences all over the world. After countless actors had been tested for the leading role (Jolson put forward himself [aged 60] and James Cagney), Larry Parks got the part, with Evelyn Keyes as his wife Julie Benson (**Ruby Keeler** would not allow her name to be used). So it was Parks who strutted and gestured in that electrifying manner, but, at his insistence, it was Jolson's own voice that was heard on the carefully selected favourites that he had, over the years, made his own - songs such as 'My Mammy' (**Joe Young-Sam Lewis-Walter Donaldson**), 'California, Here I Come' (**Joseph Meyer-Buddy De Sylva**), 'Let Me Sing And I'm Happy' (**Irving Berlin**), 'Swanee' (**George Gershwin-Irving Caesar**), 'I'm Sitting On Top Of The World' (**Ray Henderson**-Lewis-Young), 'April Showers' (Louis Silvers-De Sylva), 'Toot Toot Tootsie' (Robert King-Ted Fiorito-**Gus Kahn**), 'Avalon' (Jolson-Vincent Rose), 'The Spaniard That Blighted My Life' (Billy Merson), 'Rock-A-Bye Your Baby With A Dixie Melody' (Lewis-Jean Schwartz-Young), 'Liza' George Gershwin-**Ira Gershwin**-Kahn), and the rest. There was also a new number, 'Anniversary Song', which was based on 'Danube Waves' and credited to Jolson, **Saul Chaplin** and Ion Ivanovici. William Demarest played the part of Jolson's mentor, Steve Martin, and the rest of the cast included Tamara Shayne, Ludwig Donath, Bill Goodwin, and Scotty Beckett as the boy Jolson. Jolson himself managed to make a brief appearance, albeit in long shot. Jack Cole staged the dances, and director Alfred E. Green skilfully blended all the various elements into a Technicolor film of blockbuster proportions. It grossed in excess of $7.5 million and was the seventh most popular film of the decade in the USA (after *This Is The Army, The Bells Of St. Mary's* and four **Walt Disney** animated features).
The inevitable sequel, *Jolson Sings Again*, which was

almost, but not quite as successful as the original, came along in 1949 complete with a screenplay by Sidney Buchman in which Jolson (again played by Larry Parks) is seen entertaining US troops during World War II before retiring, initially because of ill-health. Permanently bored with his inactivity, it does not take a lot of persuading for him to agree to appear at a benefit show - which leads to a comeback, which leads to negotiations for a film of his life . . . *The Jolson Story*. Ludwig Donath and Tamara Shayne, who played his parents in that film were in this one too, and so was William Demarest. Barbara Hale was the nurse who helped Jolson to recover after his illness, and then married him, and also featured were Myron McCormick and Bill Goodwin. As before, the score provided a welcome opportunity to wallow in the Jolson songbook. The songs included 'When The Red, Red Robin Comes Bob, Bob Bobbin' Along' (**Harry Woods**), 'Carolina In The Morning' (Gus Kahn-Walter Donaldson), 'I'm Looking Over A Four Leaf Clover' (Woods-**Mort Dixon**), 'Sonny Boy' (**De Sylva, Brown And Henderson**), 'Back In Your Own Back Yard' (**Billy Rose**-Dave Dreyer), and many more. Henry Levin directed, and the film, which would have been known in more contemporary times as *The Jolson Story II*, grossed over $5 million in the US and was another worldwide hit.

Jolson, Al

b. Asa Yoelson, *c.*1885, Snrednicke, Lithuania, d. 23 October 1950. Shortly before the turn of the century, Jolson's father, Moses Yoelson, emigrated to the USA. In a few years he was able to send for his wife and four children, who joined him in Washington DC. Moses Yoelson was cantor at a synagogue and had hopes that his youngest son, Asa, would adopt this profession. After the death of their mother, the two sons, Asa and Hirsch, occasionally sang on street corners for pennies. Following the example of his brother, who had changed his name to Harry, Asa became Al. When family disagreements arose after his father remarried, Al went to New York where his brother had gone to try his luck in show business. For food-money, he sang at McGirk's, a saloon/restaurant in New York's Bowery and later sang with military bands during the time of the Spanish-American War. Back in Washington, he attracted attention when, as a member of the audience at the city's Bijou Theater, he joined in the singing with entertainer Eddie Leonard. The vaudevillian was so impressed he offered the boy a job, singing from the balcony as part of the act. Al refused but ran away to join a theatrical troupe. This venture was short-lived and a week or so later he was back home but had again altered the spelling of his name, this time to Al Joelson. In the audience, again at the Bijou, he sang during the stage act of burlesque queen Aggie Beeler. Once more he was made an offer and this time he did not refuse. This job was also brief, because he was not content to merely sing from the balcony and Beller would not allow him to join her on the stage.

Joelson moved to New York and found work as a singing waiter. He also appeared in the crowd scenes of a play which survived for only three performances. Calling himself Harry Joelson, he formed a double act with Fred E. Moore but abandoned this when his voice broke. Reverting to the name Al he now joined his brother Harry and formed an act during which he whistled songs until his voice matured. The brothers teamed up with Joe Palmer to form the act Joelson, Palmer and Joelson, but again changed the spelling to shorten the space taken on playbills. In 1905 Harry dropped out of the act and the following year Al Jolson was on his own. In San Francisco he established a reputation as an exciting entertainer and coined the phrase which later became an integral part of his performance: 'All right, all right, folks - you ain't heard nothin' yet!' In 1908 Jolson was hired by Lew Dockstader, leader of one of the country's two most famous minstrel shows, and quickly became the top attraction. Around this time he also formed a lifelong association with **Harry Akst**, a song plugger who later wrote songs including 'Dinah', 'Baby Face' and 'Am I Blue?'. Akst was especially useful to Jolson in finding songs suitable for his extrovert style. In 1911 Jolson opened at the Winter Garden in New York City, where he was a huge success. That same year he made his first records, reputedly having to be strapped to a chair as his involuntary movements were too much for the primitive recording equipment. Also in 1911 he suggested that the Winter Garden show be taken on tour, sets and full cast, orchestra and all, something that had never been done before. In 1912 he again did something new, putting on Sunday shows at the Garden so that other show business people could come and see him. Although he sang in blackface for the regular shows, local bylaws on religious observance meant that the Sunday shows had to be put on without sets and make-up. He devised an extended platform so that he could come out in front of the proscenium arch, thus allowing him to be closer to his audience with whom he was already having a remarkable love affair.

Among his song successes at this time were 'The Spaniard That Blighted My Life' and 'You Made Me Love You'. One night, when the show at the Garden was overrunning, he sent the rest of the cast off stage and simply sang to the audience who loved it. From then on, whenever he felt inclined, which was often, he would ask the audience to choose if they wanted to see the rest of the show or just listen to him. Invariably, they chose him. Significantly enough, on such occasions, the dismissed cast rarely went home, happily sitting in the wings to watch him perform. By 1915 Jolson was being billed as 'America's Greatest Entertainer' and even great rivals such as **Eddie Cantor** and George Jessel had to agree with this title. In 1916 Jolson made a silent film but found the experiment an unsatisfactory experience. Jolson's 1918 Broadway show was *Sinbad* and his song successes included 'Rockabye Your Baby With A Dixie Melody', 'Swanee' and 'My Mammy'. In 1919 he again tried something unprecedented for a popular entertainer, a concert at the Boston Opera House where he was accompanied by the city's symphony orchestra. Jolson's 1921 show was *Bombo* which opened at a new theatre which bore his name, Jolson's 59th Street Theater. The songs in the show included 'My Mammy', 'April Showers', 'California Here I Come' and 'Toot, Toot, Tootsie (Goo' Bye)'.

During the mid-20s Jolson tried some more new departures; in 1925 he opened in *Big Boy*, which had a real live horse in the cast, and in 1927 he performed on the radio. Of even more lasting significance, in 1926 he returned to the film studios to participate in an experimental film, a one-reel short entitled *April Showers* in which he sang three songs, his voice recorded on new equipment being tested by Vitaphone, a company which had been acquired by **Warner Brothers Records**. Although this brief film remained only a curio, and was seen by few people, the system stirred the imagination of Sam Warner, who believed that this might be what the company needed if it was to stave off imminent bankruptcy. They decided to incorporate sound into a film currently in pre-production. This was *The Jazz Singer* which, as a stage show, had run for three years with George Jessel in the lead. Jessel wanted more money than the Warners could afford and Eddie Cantor turned them down flat. They approached Jolson, cannily inviting him to put money into the project in return for a piece of the profits. *The Jazz Singer* (1927) was a silent film into which it was planned to interpolate a song or two but Jolson, being Jolson, did it his way, calling out to the orchestra leader, 'Wait a minute, wait a minute. You ain't heard nothin' yet!' before launching into 'Toot, Toot, Tootsie'. The results were sensational and the motion picture industry was revolutionized overnight. The Warner brothers were saved from bankruptcy and Jolson's piece of the action made him even richer than he already was. His follow-up film, *The Singing Fool*, (1928) included a song especially written for him by the team of **De Sylva, Brown And Henderson**. Although they treated the exercise as a joke, the results were a massive hit and Jolson's recording of 'Sonny Boy' became one of the first million sellers.

Although Jolson's films were popular and he was one of the highest paid performers in Hollywood, the cinema proved detrimental to his career. The cameras never fully captured the magic that had made him so successful on Broadway. Additionally, Jolson's love for working with a live audience was not satisfied by the film medium. His need to sing before a live audience was so overpowering that when his third wife, the dancer **Ruby Keeler**, opened on Broadway in *Show Girl*, he stood up in his seat and joined in with her big number, 'Liza'. He completely upstaged Keeler, who would later state that this was one of the things about him that she grew to hate the most. Jolson continued to make films, among them *Mammy* (1930) which included 'Let Me

Sing And I'm Happy', and *Big Boy* (1930), generally cited as the film which came closest to capturing the essence of his live performances. Back on Broadway in 1931 with *The Wonder Bar*, Jolson was still popular and was certainly an extremely rich man, but he was no longer the massive success that he had been in the 20s. For a man who sang for many reasons, of which money was perhaps the least important, this was a very bad time. Fuelling his dissatisfaction was the fact that Keeler, whose film career he had actively encouraged and helped, was a bigger box-office attraction. Despite spreading a thin talent very wide, Keeler rose while Jolson fell. In 1932 he stopped making records and that year there were no shows or films, even though there were still offers. He made a film with Keeler, **Go Into Your Dance** (1935) in which he sang 'About A Quarter To Nine', and participated in an early television pilot. Not surprisingly for a man who had tried many new ventures in show business, Jolson was impressed by the medium and confidently predicted its success, but his enthusiasm was not followed up by producers. He made more films in the late 30s, sometimes cameos, occasionally rating third billing but the great days appeared to be over. Even his return to Broadway, in 1940 in *Hold Onto Your Hats*, was fated to close when he was struck down with pneumonia. The same year Jolson's marriage to Keeler ended acrimoniously.

On 7 December 1941, within hours of learning of the Japanese attack on Pearl Harbor, Jolson volunteered to travel overseas to entertain troops. Appearing before audiences of young men, to whom he was at best only a name, Jolson found and captured a new audience. All the old magic worked and during the next few years he toured endlessly, putting on shows to audiences of thousands or singing songs to a couple of GIs on street corners. With Harry Akst as his accompanist, he visited Europe and the UK, Africa and the Near and Far East theatres of war. Eventually, tired and sick, he returned to the USA where doctors advised him not to resume his overseas travels. Jolson agreed but instead began a punishing round of hospital visits on the mainland. Taken ill again, he was operated on and a part of one lung was removed. The hospital visits had a happier ending when he met Erle Galbraith, a civilian X-ray technician on one of the army bases he visited, who became his fourth wife. The war over, Jolson made a cameo appearance in a film and also performed on a couple of records, but it appeared as though his career, temporarily buoyed by the war, was ended. However, a man named Sidney Skolsky had long wanted to make a film about Jolson's life and, although turned down flat by all the major studios, eventually was given the go-ahead by Harry Cohn, boss of the ailing independent Columbia Pictures, who happened to be a Jolson fan. After surmounting many difficulties, not least that Jolson, despite being over 60 years old, wanted to play himself on the screen, the film was made. Starring Larry Parks as Jolson and with a superb soundtrack on which Jolson sang all his old favourites in exciting new arrangements by Morris Stoloff, *The Jolson Story* (1946) was a hit. Apart from making a great deal of money for Columbia, who thus became the second film company Jolson had saved, it put the singer back in the public eye with a bang. He signed a deal with **Decca Records** for a series of records using the same Stoloff arrangements and orchestral accompaniment. All the old songs became hugely popular as did 'The Anniversary Song' which was written especially for a scene in the film in which his father and mother dance on their wedding anniversary (Hollywood having conveniently overlooked the fact that his real mother had died when he was a boy). The film and the records, particularly 'The Anniversary Song', were especially popular in the UK.

In the USA Jolson's star continued to rise and after a string of performances on radio, where he became a regular guest on **Bing Crosby**'s show, he was given his own series, which ran for four years and helped encourage Columbia to create another Jolson precedent. This was to make a sequel to a bio-pic. *Jolson Sings Again* (1949) recaptured the spirit and energy of the first film and was another huge success. In 1950 Jolson was again talking to television executives and this time it appeared that something would come from the discussions. Before anything could be settled, however, the US Army became involved in the so-called 'police action' in Korea and Jolson immediately volunteered to entertain the troops. With Harry Akst again accompanying him, he visited front-line soldiers during a punishing tour. Exhausted, he returned to the USA where he was booked to appear on Crosby's radio show which was scheduled to be aired from San Francisco. On 23 October 1950, while playing cards with Akst and other long-time friends at the St. Francis hotel, he complained of chest pains and died shortly afterwards.

Throughout the 20s and into the mid-30s, Jolson was the USA's outstanding entertainer and in 1925 his already hyperbolic billing was changed to 'The World's Greatest Entertainer'. Unfortunately, latterday audiences have only his films and records to go on. None of the films can be regarded as offering substantial evidence of his greatness. His best records are those made with Stoloff for the soundtrack of the biographical films, by which time his voice was deeper and, anyway, recordings cannot recapture the stage presence which allowed him to hold audiences in their seats for hours on end. Although it is easy to be carried away by the enthusiasm of others, it would appear to be entirely justified in Jolson's case. Unlike many other instances of fan worship clouding reality, even Jolson's rivals acknowledged that he was the best. In addition, most of those who knew him disliked him as a man, but this never diminished their adulation of him as an entertainer. On the night he died they turned out the lights on Broadway, and traffic in Times Square was halted. It is hard to think of any subsequent superstar who would be granted, or who has earned, such testimonials. There has been only a small handful of entertainers, in any medium, of which it can be truly said, we shall never see their like again. Al Jolson was one of that number.

● ALBUMS: *Jolson Sings Again* soundtrack (Decca 1949)★★★, *In Songs He Made Famous* (Decca 1949)★★★, *Souvenir Album* (Decca/Brunswick 1949)★★★★, *Souvenir Album Vol 2* (Decca 1949)★★★, *Al Jolson* (Decca 1949)★★★, *Souvenir Album Vol 4* (Decca 19490, *Stephen Foster Songs* (Decca 1950)★★★★, *Souvenir Album Vol 5* (Decca 1951)★★★, *Souvenir Album Vol 6* (Decca 1951)★★★, *You Made Me Love You* (Decca 1957)★★★★, *Rock A Bye Your Baby* (Decca 1957)★★★★, *Rainbow Round My Shoulder* (Decca 1957)★★★, *You Ain't Heard Nothing Yet* (Decca 1957)★★★, *Memories* (Decca 1957)★★★, *Among My Souvenirs* (Decca 1957)★★★, *The Immortal Al Jolson* (Decca 1958)★★★★, *Overseas* (Decca 1959)★★★, *The Worlds Greatest Entertainer* (Decca 1959)★★★★, *Al Jolson With Oscar Levant At the Piano* (Decca 1961)★★★, *The Best Of Jolson* (1963)★★★, *Say It With Songs* (1965)★★★, *Jolson Sings Again* (1974)★★★, *You Ain't Heard Nothin' Yet* (1975)★★★, *Immortal Al Jolson* (1975)★★★, *20 Golden Greats* (1981)★★★★, *20 More Golden Greats* (1981)★★★, *The Man And The Legend Vols 1 & 2* (1982)★★★, *The Man And The Legend Vol 3* (1983)★★★, *Al Jolson Collection Vols. 1 & 2* (1983)★★★★, *The World's Greatest Entertainer* (1983)★★★★, *You Ain't Heard Nothin' Yet: Jolie's Finest Columbia Recordings* (Sony 1994)★★★★.

● FURTHER READING: *Jolie: The Story Of Al Jolson*, Michael Freedland. *Jolson: The Legend Comes To Life*, Herbert Goldman.

Jomanda

New Jersey trio who enjoyed chart action in the late 80s and early 90s with sweet vocals embodying what those in dance circles affectionately term 'girlie house', or New Jill Swing. Cheri Williams, who started singing from the age of 14, met Joanne Thomas in 7th grade at college, though they lost contact when each went to high school. They reunited in 1987, when they were joined by Renee Washington, whose youth was spent singing in Baptist church choirs. She had also attended the Newark School Of Performing Arts. Their recording career began in 1988, when they enjoyed hits with 'Make My Body Rock'.and 'Gotta Love For You'. The combination of swing and house with soulful hip hop vocals was instantly popular. 'Make My Body Rock' would also provide the sample around which **Felix**'s huge hit, 'Don't You Want My Love' was built. *Nubia Soul*, referring to the skin pigmentation of 'blackness', was more R&B-based, as Washington explained: 'The reason why we're heading for an R&B market is that we feel club music is very limited and I personally fell we've done all that we could as a group as far as club music is concerned'. That did not stop them from employing **Sasha** for a very well-received remix of 'Never', however. On the album they worked with Buff Love (ex-**Fat Boys**), Dave Hall and Kenny Kornegay of the Untouchables, and the **Band Of Gypsies**.

● ALBUMS: *Nubia Soul* (East West 1993)★★★.

Jon And Robin And The In-Crowd

A husband and wife team from Dallas, Texas, USA, Jon and Robin (Abnor) were known for their 1967 Top 20 single, 'Do It Again A Little Bit Slower'. The song, written by Wayne Thompson, was considered slightly risque for its time, and, released on the duo's own Abnak Records (which had earlier released the **Five Americans**' 'Western Union' hit), made a minor splash. The single was produced by **Dale Hawkins**, the rockabilly artist whose own 'Susie Q' is considered a classic. Collectors, meanwhile, seek the pair's hit because it was pressed on yellow vinyl. Jon And Robin made the singles chart two more times, but never came close to repeating their initial success. Robin then left the act, and Jon continued both with the In-Crowd and as a solo act under several names. Robin also went solo briefly, with no success.
● ALBUMS: *Soul Of A Boy* (1967)★★★, *Elastic Event* (1967)★★.

Jon And The Nightriders

Surf enthusiast John Blair formed this revivalist band in Riverside, California in 1979. It joined a new generation of acts, including the Surf Raiders, the Evasions and the Wedge, devoted to continuing the heritage of 'classic' 60s surf/hot rod attractions. The Nightriders were initially envisaged as a studio-only band, but made their live debut in October 1980, supporting **Dick Dale** And The **Deltones** at the Santa Monica Civic Centre. *Surf Beat 80* captured the Nightriders' grasp of the genre and tours of Europe in support of its release proved successful. Subsequent recordings, including a collaboration with producer **Shel Talmy**, continued in a similar vein which, although entertaining, was of cult interest only.
● ALBUMS: *Surf Beat 80* (1981)★★★★, *Charge Of The Nightriders* (1985)★★★, *Stampede* (1987)★★★.

Jon And Vangelis

(see **Vangelis**; **Anderson, Jon**)

Jon Pleased Wimmin

b. c.1969, London, England. Transvestite DJ who has built his reputation on the dexterity of his deck technique and record selection, rather than his dress sense: 'I get so annoyed by all these bedroom DJ's who say I've done well because I have a gimmick. But my dress doesn't play records'. He began his adult life attending a four-year course in fashion design, eventually running his own shop in Kensington Market. He started out as a DJ at clubs like Glam, Kinky Gerlinky and Camp in the capital, before opening up his own nightspot, Pleased, in Sutton Row, London, in October 1993. The Pleased Wimmin transvestite posse was first sighted as live backing on **Linda Layton** PA's. Their leader's first major appearance on record came with the dancefloor hit 'Passion', released on Southern Fried in 1990. A cover of **Bobby Orlando**'s Hi-NRG classic from 1980, it was produced by **Norman Cook**. He went on to record

further ambivalent gender/genre classics like 'Hammer House Of Handbag'.

Jonathan Fire*eater

The members of Jonathan Fire*eater - Stewart Lupton (b. 1975, Washington DC, USA; vocals), Walter Martin (b. Washington DC, USA; organ), Paul Maroon (b. Washington DC, USA; guitar), Matt Barrick (b. Washington DC, USA; drums) and Tom Frank (b. Washington DC, USA; bass) - began playing together as a punk outfit. In 1995 they transplanted to a one-bedroom apartment in New York City in the hope that the city's atmosphere would be more receptive to their fusion of garage-rock sounds with smart suits and bohemian overtones. Within a year the quintet was playing to thousand-strong houses and comparisons with everyone from **Smokey Robinson** to **Nick Cave** were flying around. A succession of independently released singles, dominated by Lupton's intensity and Martin's atmospheric keyboard lines, attracted major label interest and they were among the first signings to Dreamworks Records in the USA. There was initial suspicion in the UK, where post-Goth 'suit' bands were ten a penny, but the band's live set and debut releases soon won over the critics.
● ALBUMS: *Tremble Under Boom Lights* mini-album (Deceptive 1997)★★★, *Wolf Songs For Lambs* (Deceptive 1997)★★★.

Jones Girls

This US vocal trio comprised Brenda Jones, Shirley Jones and Valerie Jones, and first came to public attention after backing **Diana Ross** on tour. In the past they had opened for artists including **B.B. King**, the **Four Tops** and **Little Richard**. It was through Ross that they gained their first studio session, but it was not until 1977 that they released their debut single, produced by Kenny Gamble of **Gamble And Huff**; 'You Gonna Make Me Love Somebody Else' reached the US Top 40. Surpassing all original criticisms that they were too derivative of the **Emotions**, the trio established their own exquisite style with melodic and soulful vocals, luscious strings, tight horns and slick rhythms. However, owing to bad luck with two record companies that both collapsed, their chart success was wrecked; however, during the early 90s they returned with the release of *Coming Back*.
● ALBUMS: *The Jones Girls* (Philadelphia International 1979)★★★★, *At Peace With Woman* (Philadelphia International 1980)★★★, *Get As Much Love As You Can* (Philadelphia International 1982)★★★, *On Target* (RCA 1983)★★★, *Keep It Comin'* (Philadelphia International 1984)★★★, *Coming Back* (1992)★★★.
● COMPILATIONS: *Artists Showcase: The Jones Girls* (DM Streetsounds 1986)★★★.

Jones, Albennie

b. 29 November 1914, Gulfport, Mississippi, USA, d. 24 June 1989, Bronx, New York, USA. Jones arrived in

New York in 1932, her only singing experience at the Mt. Holy Baptists Church in Gulfport. Her first professional engagement was at the Elk's Rendezvous Club, which proved so successful that she was retained for nine months. Other nightclubs she sang in included the Club Harlem, the Village Vanguard and Murrains Cafe. Her first recordings for National in 1944/5 featured jazz musicians **Dizzy Gillespie**, **Don Byas**, **Edmond Hall**, **Sammy Price** and **Cliff Jackson**. She toured the south and Midwest with Blanche Calloway and **Eddie 'Cleanhead' Vinson**, and worked alongside Gillespie and **Tiny Bradshaw** with the **Erskine Hawkins** Orchestra. After the war, she recorded three sessions for **Decca**, backed by Price's group. In the early 50s she fell over on stage, suffering an injury that forced her to use a crutch at club dates. Because of this, she retired from music shortly afterwards and eventually succumbed to leukemia.
● ALBUMS: *Ladies Sing The Blues* (Savoy 1980)★★★.

Jones, Allan

b. 14 October 1908, Scranton, Pennsylvania, USA. d. 27 June 1992, New York, USA. A popular, romantic tenor star in movies in the late 30s and early 40s, Jones studied singing in Paris, before returning to the USA and working in provincial operettas. He appeared on Broadway in *Roberta* (1933) and the 1934 revival of *Bitter Sweet* before gaining a part in the film *Reckless* (1935). In the same year he made a big impression singing 'Alone' in the Marx Brothers film *A Night At The Opera*. This was followed by leading screen roles in *Rose-Marie*, *Show Boat* (1936), *A Day At The Races*, *The Firefly* (in which he introduced his signature tune 'The Donkey Serenade'), *Everybody Sing*, *The Great Victor Herbert*, *The Boys From Syracuse*, *One Night In The Tropics*, *There's Magic In Music*, *True To The Army*, *Moonlight In Havana*, *When Johnny Comes Marching Home*, *Larceny With Music*, *Rhythm Of The Islands*, *Crazy House*, *You're A Lucky Fellow Mr. Smith*, *The Singing Sheriff*, *Honeymoon Ahead*, and *Senorita From The West* (1945). Jones married actress Irene Hervey and their son, **Jack Jones**, went on to become a popular singer with big hits in the 60s. Allan Jones quit Hollywood in 1945 following a dispute with **MGM** boss Louis B. Mayer, and took to the nightclub circuit. In the 50s he starred in a major US tour of *Guys And Dolls*, and in the 70s he toured with *Man Of La Mancha*. He had recently returned from tour of Australia when he died of lung cancer in June 1992.

Jones, Bessie

b. 8 February 1902, Smithville, Georgia, USA, d. October 1984, USA. Jones became the greatest exponent of the music of the black communities of the Georgia Sea Islands. The islanders' isolation led to the retention of many African cultural elements, and there are also cultural affinities with the Bahamas, where many Royalist slaveholders fled from the Sea Islands during the American Revolution. Jones was the posses-sor of a deep, rich, but very flexible voice, whether singing spirituals, children's songs, slave songs or (very rarely) blues. She was a moving spirit behind the formation of the Sea Islands Singers in the 60s, and continued to tour after the group disbanded owing to the deaths of several members.
● ALBUMS: including *So Glad I'm Here* (Rounder 1975)★★★ *Georgia Sea Island Song* (1977)★★★, *Step It Down* (Rounder 1979)★★★, *Been In The Storm So Long* (1990)★★★.

Jones, Birmingham

b. Wright Birmingham, 9 January 1937, Saginaw, Michigan, USA. Moving to Chicago around 1950, Jones was a saxophonist and guitarist with various blues bands throughout the 50s. By the middle of the decade, when he recorded for Ebony, he was a talented **Little Walter** imitator on harmonica. A 1965 session for Vivid was unissued for many years, and did not live up to the promise of the Ebony 78. Jones returned to club work, but had largely retired from the music business by the mid-70s.
● ALBUMS: *Chills And Fever* (1985)★★★.

Jones, Booker T.

(see **Booker T. And The MG's**)

Jones, Carmell

b. 19 July 1936, Kansas City, Kansas, USA, d. 7 November 1996. After attracting favourable attention for his trumpet playing in bands in the Kansas City area, Jones moved to Los Angeles in 1961, where he joined **Bud Shank** for an engagement at the Drift Inn, Malibu. He recorded with this group and later worked with **Gerald Wilson** and the **Red Mitchell-Harold Land** Quintet with whom he also recorded. Most of 1965 was spent touring with **Horace Silver** and by the end of the year Jones had become resident in Germany. He played regularly as a member of radio and studio orchestras, mainly in Berlin, and also worked with his old high-school friend, **Nathan Davis**. In the music he recorded in the 60s Jones displayed an affinity with **Clifford Brown** and his return to the US jazz scene in the early 80s showed that in maturity he had developed into an accomplished player, who deserved a wide audience.
● ALBUMS: *The Remarkable Carmell Jones* (1961)★★★★, with Bud Shank *New Groove* (1961)★★★, with Red Mitchell, Harold Land *Hear Ye!* (1961)★★★, *Brass Bag* (1962)★★, *Business Meetin'* (1962)★★★, *Jay Hawk Talk* (1965)★★★, *Carmell Jones In Europe* (1965)★★★, with Nathan Davis *Happy Girl* (1965)★★★, *Carmell Jones Returns* (1982)★★★★.

Jones, Casey, And The Engineers

b. Brian Casser, Newcastle, England. Raised in Liverpool, guitarist and vocalist Casser founded the beat group, Cass And The Cassanovas, primarily to play at the local Casanova club. They played Latin-American numbers and rock 'n' roll and performed at the noted Liverpool Stadium concert headed by **Gene Vincent**, in May 1960. They accompanied **Duffy Power** for a tour of Scotland, but the band felt they could do better without Casser. Bass player John Gustafson recalls, 'The rest of us were getting increasingly fed up with him, so we hatched this plot to disband and reform without him.' In 1961, Gustafson, Adrian Barber and Johnny Hutchinson became the **Big Three** while Casser moved to London and formed Casey Jones And The Engineers, who recorded a **Columbia Records** single, 'One Way Ticket'. The band included **Tom McGuinness** on bass and, for a few appearances, **Eric Clapton**. With a Bristol band, he became Casey Jones And The Guvenors and had a successful career in Germany, topping their charts with 'Don't Ha Ha' in 1965.

Jones, Catherine Zeta

b. Wales. Arriving in 1995 in predictable 'I've always loved singing' press interview schlock, and with a stunningly out of date grunge image with para boots and fishnets, this well-known television star (principally of *Darling Buds Of May* fame) turned singer was received by critics with the sort of welcome usually afforded nettles in a nudist colony. Her PR company, meanwhile, contested that she had first made her name in West End musicals, and that her voice had a powerful edge comparable to **Cher**. However, there was little in her debut single, 'In The Arms Of Love', released on **Jeff Wayne**'s Wow! Records in March 1995, to distinguish her from the herd.

Jones, Claude

b. 11 February 1901, Boley, Oklahoma, USA, d. 17 January 1962. After playing various instruments in school, Jones had opted for trombone by the time he attended Wilberforce College. In 1922 he moved to Springfield, Ohio, where he became a member of the band which eventually metamorphosed into **McKinney's Cotton Pickers**. In 1929 he left for a job with the **Fletcher Henderson** band and during the early 30s switched several times between Henderson, **Chick Webb** and **Don Redman**. In 1934 he settled into the **Cab Calloway** band, where he remained until 1940; then moved through a number of bands, working with **Coleman Hawkins**, **Joe Sullivan**, Henderson again, **Benny Carter**, Redman, Calloway, until, in 1944, he joined **Duke Ellington**. He was with Ellington until 1948, when he played briefly with **Machito**, Henderson and Ellington again and then finally his itchy feet led him to leave music and go to sea. He died on board the S.S. *United States*, on which he was a chief steward, in January 1962. An inventive and melodic soloist, Jones was an important influence in the pre-war era for helping to shift perceptions of the trombone's role from a purely rhythmic instrument to one on which melody lines and solos could be played.

● ALBUMS: *McKinney's Cotton Pickers* (1928-29)★★★, with Fletcher Henderson *Swing's The Thing* (1931-34)★★★★.

Jones, Coley

Jones led the Dallas String Band, the sole recorded exemplars of black Texan string band music, although their line-up on record of two mandolins, guitar and bass omits the violin (and sometimes clarinet and trumpet) that was usually included on live dates. Jones was an indifferent guitarist, but a brilliant mandolinist, at his best on the sparkling 'Dallas Rag'. The band also played pop songs and blues (although, like all their repertoire, the blues were played more as entertainment than for personal expression). As a soloist, Jones performed comic songs such as 'Drunkard's Special' and 'Travelling Man', and humorous monologues. In duet with the female singer Bobbie Cadillac, he pandered to more up-to-date tastes, recording four variants of 'Tight Like That', but it is his, and his band's, songster material that is of more enduring value.

● ALBUMS: *Coley Jones & The Dallas String Band* (1983)★★★.

Jones, Curtis

b. 18 August 1906, Naples, Texas, USA, d. 11 September 1971, Munich, Germany. One of a coterie of bluesmen who made Europe their home, pianist Jones began his recording career in 1947 and his debut, 'Lonesome Bedroom Blues', was a major hit. The song remained in **Columbia**'s catalogue until the demise of the 78 rpm record, eventually becoming a blues standard in the repertoire of others. Because of the success, Jones enjoyed a prolific recording career until 1941 whereupon he worked outside of music. In 1958 blues enthusiasts located him living in run-down conditions in Chicago. In the 60s Jones recorded albums for Bluesville, **Delmark**, **Decca** and **Blue Horizon**. He died in penury, his grave in Germany being sold in 1979 because no-one had paid for its upkeep.

● ALBUMS: *Lonesome Bedroom Blues* (1962)★★★.
● COMPILATIONS: *Blues And Trouble 1937-40* (1983)★★★, *In London 1963* (See For Miles 1985)★★, *Curtis Jones (1937-1941)* (Blues Document 1990)★★★, *Complete Recorded Works 1937-53 Vols. 1-4* (Document 1995)★★★★.

Jones, Davey

b. c.1888, Lutcher, Louisiana, USA. Jones was well-known in the early days of jazz and played mainly in St. Louis and on the Mississippi riverboats. It is thought that he played a C tenor saxophone. He was an early inspiration to many musicians including **Gene Sedric** and **Happy Caldwell**. Jones formed the Jones And Collins Astoria Eight with trumpeter **Lee Collins** and recorded four titles for Victor in 1929 including 'Astoria Strut' and 'Damp Weather' both being recognized as classic examples of New Orleans jazz, with fine ensembles receiving the lead from Collins trumpet.

Jones, David Lynn

b. 15 January 1950, Bexar, Arkansas, USA. David Lynn Jones' forefathers lived on the same acres for genera-

tions. His father was the village postmaster and his mother a preacher. His neighbours have also formed the nucleus of his band. His most successful record, 'Bonnie Jean', is about his sister ('She's got a heart of gold and nerves of steel/Little sister rolls them eighteen wheels'). His first album, produced by **Waylon Jennings**' producer Richie Albright, showed the influences of **Bruce Springsteen** alongside country music. Waylon sang with Jones on his US country hit, 'High Ridin' Heroes'. Jones left **Mercury Records**, and moved to Liberty, after he claimed there had been too much interference with the recording of his second album. His best-known song is 'Living In The Promiseland', a US country hit for **Willie Nelson**.
● ALBUMS: *Hard Times On Easy Street* (Mercury 1987)★★★, *Wood, Wind And Stone* (Mercury 1989)★★★, *Mixed Emotions* (Liberty 1992)★★, *Play By Ear* (Liberty 1994)★★★.

Jones, Dill

b. Dillwyn O. Jones, 19 August 1923, Newcastle Emlyn, Wales, England, d. 22 June 1984. After formal studies at London's Trinity College of Music, Jones began associating with the younger jazzmen who were playing bebop. He had already played jazz while serving in the navy and his fluent, inventive style quickly made him a welcome addition to the London scene. In 1948 he performed at the first Nice Jazz Festival and was regularly heard in company with musicians including **Humphrey Lyttelton**, **Ronnie Scott**, **Joe Harriott** and **Bruce Turner**. Jones visited the USA during the 50s while working on a transatlantic liner, and in the early 60s he settled in New York. During the next few years he played with several noted American jazz stars, including **Roy Eldridge** and **Gene Krupa**. In 1969 he became a member of the JPJ Quartet with **Budd Johnson**, Bill Pemberton and **Oliver Jackson**. His fine soloing, whether in subtly developed ballads or on roof-raising spectaculars such as his version of 'Little Rock Getaway', showed his wide stylistic range.
● ALBUMS: *The Dill Jones Trio* i (1955)★★★, *The Dill Jones Trio* ii (1956)★★★, *The Dill Jones Quintet* (1959)★★, *Jones The Jazz* (1961)★★★, with others *Jazz Piano Masters* (1972)★★, *Up Jumped You With Love* (1972)★★★, *The Music Of Bix Beiderbecke* (c.1972)★★★, *The Welsh Connection* (1982)★★★.

Jones, Dolly

b. *c.*1907, USA, d. late 70s. The fact that her mother, **Dyer Jones**, was also a noted jazz trumpeter probably makes Jones unique in jazz. Although she learned initially from her mother, she was largely self-taught. According to musicians who knew her, she was completely dedicated to her instrument, studying and practising when she was not playing. In Chicago in the early 30s she performed in **Irene Eadie**'s band and with **Lillian Armstrong**'s Harlem Harlicans. Jones also played in a trio with saxophonist George James and in **Eddie Durham**'s All-Star Girl Orchestra. In Chicago,

she was often to be found in after-hours clubs jamming with other musicians and earning their respect. **Roy Eldridge** and **Doc Cheatham** were amongst trumpeters who publicly praised her talent. Jones continued to play whenever she could, working intermittently into the 70s. Her role model was **Louis Armstrong** and throughout her career worked hard to maintain the higher-than-high standards needed by any woman trying to succeed in jazz in her era. She made only one record 'Creole Blues', but did appear in the Oscar Micheaux film, *Swing* (1937), playing 'China Boy' and 'I May Be Wrong'. Jones was sometimes billed as Dolly Hutchinson and also as Dolly (Doli) Armenra.

Jones, Dyer

b. *c.*1890, USA, d. unk. Jones played trumpet in pre-jazz and early jazz bands and had already built a reputation before moving to New York in the late 20s. She was presented as a featured attraction with Sammy Stewart and his band at the Arcadia Ballroom. In addition to Jones the band included **Charlie 'Big' Green**, **'Big' Sid Catlett** and Johnny Dunn. Even in distinguished surroundings such as these she more than held her own. Jones appears to have given music lessons and **Valaida Snow** might have studied trumpet with her. And Jones certainly helped her daughter, **Dolly Jones**, when she, too, began playing trumpet. **Tommy Benford** told Sally Placksin, '. . . she was wonderful . . . Man, she was something else . . . and Dolly was right behind her'. Jones appears not to have made records.

Jones, Eddie

b. Edward Jones, 1 March 1929, Red Bank, New Jersey, USA, d. 31 May 1997, Hartford, Connecticut, USA. For 10 years a member of the **Count Basie** band, bass player Eddie Jones grew up in a house just two doors away from Basie's home. As an undergraduate at the local Howard University, Jones studied musical education, and collaborated with **Frank Wess** and Bill Hugham (later members of the Basie band) and composer **Benny Golson**. After graduation he also toured with **Sarah Vaughan** and worked as a teacher. Jones eventually joined Basie's band in 1953, although competition for places was hot: 'You couldn't afford to get sick in that band - if you didn't show up you disappeared.' The bass player's mellifluous style, and deep, resonant tone, proved a perfect accompaniment to drummer **Sonny Payne** in the Basie group, and he soon found himself in demand as a session player. Among the famous band-leaders with whom he recorded were **Milt Jackson**, **Ray Charles**, **Joe Newman**, **Coleman Hawkins**, **Ben Webster** and **Thad Jones**. However, it was his contributions to the 'New Testament' version of Basie's band that made his name. He eventually left Basie in 1963 after a disagreement over wages. He attempted to break into the New York studio scene but was disconcerted by the racism that stood in the way of black musicians attempting to work on commercial projects. Instead, he became an executive with IBM Records. He toured with various jazz aggregations in his holidays, even during his stint as an insurance salesman in Hartford, Connecticut, where he died in 1997.

Jones, Eddie 'Guitar Slim'

b. 10 December 1926, Greenwood, Mississippi, USA, d. 7 February 1959, New York City, New York, USA. Jones took the stage styles of his heroes **T-Bone Walker** and **Gatemouth Brown** and added his own particular flamboyance to become the first truly outrageous blues performer of the modern era. Along the way, he wrote and recorded some blues that remain standards to this day. Raised in Mississippi, he combined the intensity associated with singers from that area with the flair of his Texan models. He sang in church choirs in his home state before forming a trio with pianist **Huey Smith** working around New Orleans. A lean six-footer, he took on the persona of 'Guitar Slim', building a reputation for his extravagant stage antics and offstage drinking problem. One of the first performers to turn to the solid-bodied electric guitar, he began the experimentation with feedback control that reached its apogee with **Jimi Hendrix** in the late 60s. He combined this with garish stage-wear in fantastic colours (including matching dyed hair) and a gymnastic act that would see him leave the stage and prowl the audience - and even the street outside - with the aid of a guitar cable that could extend to 350 feet, and was connected to a PA system rather than to an amplifier, thereby reaching high volume levels. The reputation that he built up in the clubs led Imperial Records to record him, as Eddie Jones, in 1951; although not successful at the time, Imperial later fared better when they recredited the recordings to Guitar Slim. Slim's break came when he recorded in 1952 for the Bullet label in Nashville. The hit 'Feelin' Sad' aroused the interest of **Specialty Records** and sparked off Slim's most productive period. His first release for the new label was to become his anthem, 'The Things That I Used To Do', arranged by his pianist **Ray Charles** and featuring a distinctive guitar signature that has been reproduced almost as often as the **Elmore James** 'Dust My Broom' riff. The record made Slim a blues force across the nation. In 1956 he left Specialty for **Atco** who hoped to sell him to the teenage public as **Chess** had done with **Chuck Berry**. This approach was not a success and before Slim could make a comeback, he died from the combined effects of drinking, fast living and pneumonia.

● COMPILATIONS: *The Things That I Used To Do* (Specialty 1970)★★★, *The Atco Sessions* (Atlantic 1987)★★★, *Sufferin' Mind* (Specialty 1991)★★★★, *The Slaves Eat First* (Mysoundworks 1995)★★★.

Jones, Elvin

b. 9 September 1927, Pontiac, Michigan, USA. The youngest of the remarkable Jones brothers (see also **Thad Jones** and **Hank Jones**), Elvin grew up in a musical atmosphere. He played drums with local bands before and after military service and by the early 50s

was playing regularly with **Billy Mitchell**'s small group. In the middle of the decade Jones relocated in New York, rapidly establishing himself as a leading exponent of bop drumming. He worked with several notable musicians including **J.J. Johnson**, **Donald Byrd** and **Sonny Rollins**, and in 1960 became a member of **John Coltrane**'s quartet. He played with Coltrane for five years during which period he grew into one of the outstanding drummers in jazz history. The role he occupied in this period was of considerable importance in the development of post-bop drumming. Jones's career after Coltrane was mainly as a leader of small groups, where he was able to exercise full control over the musical policy (although he was briefly, in 1966, with **Duke Ellington**). In the late 60s and on through the 70s and 80s Jones toured ceaselessly, playing clubs, concerts and festivals around the world. His sidemen have included **Joe Farrell**, **George Coleman** and Wilbur Little. In 1979 he recorded *Very R.A.R.E.* with **Art Pepper** and that same year saw the release of a documentary film, *Different Drummer: Elvin Jones*. Jones extended the scope of the work done by proto-bop drummers such as **Max Roach** and **Art Blakey**. Although associated with free jazz, in which context his example was an incentive to later occupants of *avant garde* drum chairs, his own playing was always closely linked to what had gone before. Nevertheless, in his expansion of the role of the post-bop jazz drummer, Jones was responsible for a major stylistic shift: he integrated the drums so thoroughly with the improvisations of the front line musicians that the drummer now became their partner on equal terms not merely the accompanist or pulse provider of previous eras. Through his example and his astonishing technical mastery, Jones has become one of the master drummers of jazz and is currently seeing something of a revival in his fortunes with a spate of recently recorded albums.

● ALBUMS: *Thad Jones-Billy Mitchell Quintet* (1953)★★★, with Sonny Rollins *A Night At The Village Vanguard* (Enja 1957)★★★, *Together* (1961)★★★, with John Coltrane *Live At The Village Vanguard* (Impulse 1962)★★★, *Elvin* (Riverside 1962)★★★, with Coltrane *Coltrane Live At Birdland* (Impulse 1963)★★★, with Coltrane *A Love Supreme* (Impulse 1965)★★★★★, *Dear John C* (Impulse 1965)★★★, *And Then Again* (Atlantic 1965)★★★, *Midnight Walk* (Atlantic 1967)★★, *Heavy Sounds* (Impulse 1967)★★, *Puttin' It Together* (Blue Note 1968)★★★, *Poly-Currents* (Blue Note 1969)★★★, *The Ultimate Elvin Jones* (Blue Note 1969)★★★, *Coalition* (1970)★★★, *Genesis* (1971)★★, *Live At The Lighthouse* (1972)★★★, *Mr Thunder* (1974)★★★, *New Agenda* (1975)★★, *Summit Meeting* (1976)★★★, *Time Capsule* (1977)★★★, *Remembrance* (1978)★★★, *Very R.A.R.E.* (1979)★★★, *Brother John* (1982)★★★, *Earth Jones* (1982)★★★, *The Elvin Jones Jazz Machine In Europe* (Enja 1992)★★★, *Live In Japan* (Konnex 1992)★★★, with Takehisa Tanaka *When I Was At Aso-Mountain* (Enja 1993)★★★, *Youngblood* (Enja 1993)★★, *Going Home* (Enja 1994)★★★, as Elvin Jones' 'Special' Quartet *Tribute To John Coltrane: A Love Supreme* (Columbia 1997)★★★.

Jones, Etta

b. 25 November 1928, Aiken, South Carolina, USA. By the time she began singing professionally, she was living in New York. She worked with **Buddy Johnson**, then **Pete Johnson**, J.C. Heard and Earl Hines. From the early 50s she often worked as a single, recording for Prestige and winning an award for *Don't Go With Strangers*. Although her early singing, with Buddy Johnson, had been angled towards the R&B market, by the 70s she was sufficiently eclectic to work with mainstream artists such as **Billy Taylor** and she began a long-running partnership with **Houston Person**, touring and recording extensively. A lively, strong-voiced singer with a rich, bluesy tone, Jones has enjoyed a successful career despite being little known outside the jazz world and even within this arena she is sometimes overlooked in favour of less talented but better hyped singers. On *At Last* her voice sounded richer in texture and her versions of classic popular songs, such as 'God Bless The Child' were a triumph. In particular, pianist **Benny Green** added some exquisite piano.

● ALBUMS: *Don't Go With Strangers* (Prestige 1960)★★★★, with Houston Person *Love Me With All Your Heart* (Muse 1983)★★, *At Last* (Muse 1995)★★★, *My Gentleman Friend* (Muse 1996)★★★.

Jones, Floyd

b. 21 July 1917, Marianna, Arkansas, USA, d. 19 December 1989, Chicago, Illinois, USA. Brought up in the Mississippi Delta, Jones had been playing guitar for some years by the time he settled in Chicago around 1945. He soon became part of a seminal group of musicians that had come up from the south and who were in the process of developing the new electric Chicago blues sound. He played with his guitarist cousin **Moody Jones** and harmonica player **Snooky Pryor** and their first record together, 'Stockyard Blues' and 'Keep What You Got', is a classic of its time and place. Under his own name, he made a number of fine records for JOB, **Chess** and **Vee Jay** in the early 50s, including the atmospheric 'Dark Road' which owed much to the work of **Tommy Johnson**. Rediscovered in the 60s' blues boom, he made records again for Testament and Advent.

● ALBUMS: *Baby Face Leroy & Floyd Jones* (1984)★★★, with Eddie Taylor *Masters Of Modern Blues* (Testament 1994)★★★.

Jones, Frankie

b. Greenwich Farm, Kingston, Jamaica, West Indies. Influenced by local celebrities including Brent Dowe, Tony Brevette, **Tapper Zukie** and Earl 'Chinna' Smith, Jones set his sights on a career as a vocalist. In 1978 he began recording at **Channel One** and enjoyed his first hit with 'Sweeten My Coffee'. During the late 70s and early 80s he performed on the live circuit on the fashionable north coast of Jamaica. By the mid-80s Jones was back in the studio recording with Errol 'Myrie' Lewis and John Marshall. In 1984 he enjoyed hits with

'Settle For Me', 'Best Love', 'Modelling Girl' and with DJ Schreecha Nice, 'Get Out Of My Life'. A collaboration with Triston Palmer, who had enjoyed success as a dancehall vocalist, resulted in recording sessions at Music Mountain and **Harry J.** The sessions were supervised by Keith Wignall with Robbie Lynn and Sylvan Morris. The productions were released in the UK as *The Best Of Frankie Jones Volume One* and included 'Sweet Leoni', 'Mr Bad Boy' and 'Vegetarian'. The compilation confusingly featured a photograph of the legendary drummer and film star **Leroy 'Horsemouth' Wallace** on the cover, with Jones in the background. **Trojan Records** proclaimed that a *Volume Two* would be released in 1988 but it did not appear.

● ALBUMS: with Michael Palmer *Showdown Volume Four* (Empire 1984)★★, with Patrick Andy *Two New Superstars* (Burning Sounds 1985)★★★.

● COMPILATIONS: *The Best Of...* (Trojan 1986)★★★★.

Jones, George

b. George Glenn Jones, 12 September 1931, Saratoga, Texas, USA. Jones is the greatest of honky tonk singers but he has also been a victim of its lifestyle. He learned guitar in his youth, and in 1947, was hired by the husband-and-wife duo Eddie And Pearl. This developed into his own radio programme and a fellow disc jockey, noting his close-set eyes and upturned nose, nicknamed him 'The Possum'. He married at 18 but the couple separated within a year. Jones joined the marines in 1950 and, after being demobbed in November 1953, was signed by Pappy Daily to the new Starday label. He had his first country hit in 1955 with 'Why Baby Why', a pop hit for **Pat Boone**. He recorded some rockabilly tracks including 'Rock It', which Daily released under the name of Thumper Jones. Jones has so strongly disassociated himself from these recordings that he is apt to destroy any copies that he sees. Daily also leased cover versions of well-known songs by Jones and other performers, including **Sleepy La Beef**, to others for budget recordings. Jones's work, for example, was issued under the pseudonyms of Johnny Williams, Hank Davis and Glen Patterson, but collectors should bear in mind that these names were also used for other performers. In 1959 he had his first country number 1 with 'White Lightning', written by his friend the **Big Bopper**. The single made number 73 on the US Top 100 and, despite numerous country hits, it remains his biggest pop hit, perhaps because his voice is too country for pop listeners. (Jones has never reached the UK charts, although he and the Big Bopper supplied the backing vocals for **Johnny Preston**'s 'Running Bear'.) Jones's second US country number 1 was with the sensitive 'Tender Years', which held the top spot for seven weeks. He demonstrated his writing skills on 'The Window Up Above', which was subsequently a hit for **Mickey Gilley**, and 'Seasons Of My Heart', recorded by both **Johnny Cash** and **Jerry Lee Lewis**. His flat-top hairstyle and gaudy clothes may look dated to us now, but he recorded incredibly poignant country music with 'She Thinks I Still Care' and 'You Comb Her Hair', as well as the up-tempo fun of 'Who Shot Sam?'. The American public kept up with the Joneses for 'The Race Is On', but **Jack Jones** was the winner in the charts. George Jones recorded prolifically for the Musicor label, although most of his numerous albums are less than 30 minutes long. He recorded successful duets with other performers; **Gene Pitney** ('I've Got Five Dollars And It's Saturday Night') and **Melba Montgomery** ('We Must Have Been Out Of Our Minds'). In 1970 he recorded the original version of 'A Good Year For The Roses', later a hit for **Elvis Costello**, and 'Tell Me My Lying Eyes Are Wrong', a concert favourite for **Dr. Hook**. His stormy marriage to **Tammy Wynette** (1969-75) included duet albums of lovey-dovey songs and bitter recriminations. A solo success, 'The Grand Tour', is a room-by-room account of what went wrong. His appalling behaviour (beating Wynette, shooting at friends, missing concerts) is largely attributable to his drinking. An album of superstar duets was hampered when he missed the sessions and had to add his voice later. His partners included Elvis Costello ('Stranger In The House'), **James Taylor** ('Bartender's Blues') and **Willie Nelson** ('I Gotta Get Drunk'). His album with **Johnny Paycheck** is a collection of rock 'n' roll classics.

By the late 70s, his drinking and cocaine addiction had made him so unreliable that he was known as 'No Show Jones', although a song he recorded about it suggested he was proud of the name. When he did appear, he sometimes used Donald Duck's voice instead of his own. In 1979 he received medical treatment, and, with support from the music industry, staged a significant comeback with *I Am What I Am*, which included his greatest single, 'He Stopped Loving Her Today', and a further duet album with Wynette. Further trouble ensued when he beat up another fiancée, but a divorcee, Nancy Sepulveda, tolerated his mistreatment and married him in 1983. Jones's behaviour has improved in recent years, although, as he would have it, 'If you're going to sing a country song, you've got to have lived it yourself.' In short, George Jones's major asset is his remarkable voice which can make a drama out of the most mundane lyrics (James O'Gwynn recorded a tribute 'If I Could Sing A Country Song (Exactly Like George Jones)'). Jones has had more records (almost 150) in the US country charts than any other performer, although his comparatively low tally of 13 number 1s is surprising. Undoubtedly, he would have had another with a duet with **Dolly Parton**, 'Rockin' Years', but following an announcement that he was to move to MCA, his voice was replaced by **Ricky Van Shelton**'s.

His first MCA album, *And Along Came Jones*, included a tribute to his deceased mother. In 1995 he renewed his artistic partnership with ex-wife Wynette for *One*. It was as good as anything they had made together, and included an affectionate nod to new country artists: 'I've even heard a few/that sound like me and you'.

Jones may no longer sell records in the quantities he used to, but his albums now show more consistency. He is still regarded by many as the world's leading honky-tonk singer. In April 1996 he released his autobiography, *I Lived To Tell It All*, which was soon followed by a new album of the same title. Two years later he released *It Don't Get Any Better Than This*, one of his most assured and satisfying albums.

Being a George Jones completist is an exhausting task because he has had 450 albums released in the USA and UK alone. The listing concentrates only on albums of new recordings, collections of singles on albums for the first time, and compilations where previously unissued tracks have been added. In addition, in the early 70s, **RCA Records** in America reissued 15 compilations from his Musicor albums, usually with additional tracks, but they are not included below. Jones has recorded such key tracks as 'Ragged But Right' several times. Surprisingly, however, only two live albums have been issued, both in the 80s.

● ALBUMS: *Grand Ole Opry's Newest Star* (Starday 1956)★★★, *Grand Ole Opry's New Star* (Mercury 1957)★★★, *Country Church Time* (Mercury 1958)★★★, *George Jones Sings White Lightning* (Mercury 1959)★★★, *George Jones Salutes Hank Williams* (Mercury 1960)★★★, *The Crown Prince Of Country Music* (Starday 1960)★★★, *Sings His Greatest Hits* (Starday 1962)★★★, *The Fabulous Country Music Sound Of George Jones* (Starday 1962)★★★, *George Jones Sings Country And Western Hits* (Mercury 1962)★★★, *From The Heart* (Mercury 1962)★★★, with Margie Singleton *Duets Country Style* (Mercury 1962)★★★, *The New Favourites Of George Jones* (United Artists 1962)★★★, *The Hits Of His Country Cousins* (United Artists 1962)★★★, *Homecoming In Heaven* (United Artists 1962)★★★, *My Favourites Of Hank Williams* (United Artists 1962)★★★, *George Jones Sings Bob Wills* (United Artists 1962)★★★, *I Wish Tonight Would Never End* (United Artists 1963)★★★, with Melba Montgomery *What's In Our Heart* (United Artists 1963)★★★, *More New Favourites Of George Jones* (United Artists 1963)★★★, *The Novelty Side Of George Jones* (Mercury 1963)★★★, *The Ballad Side Of George Jones* (Mercury 1963)★★★, *Blue And Lonesome* (Mercury 1963)★★★, *C&W No. l Male Singer* (Mercury 1964)★★★, *Heartaches And Tears* (Mercury 1964)★★★, with Montgomery *Bluegrass Hootenanny* (United Artists 1964)★★★, *George Jones Sings Like The Dickens* (United Artists 1964)★★★, *Jones Boys' Country And Western Songbook* (instrumentals) (Musicor 1964)★★★, with Gene Pitney *For The First Time* (Musicor 1965)★★★, *Mr. Country And Western Music* (Musicor 1965)★★★, *New Country Hits* (Musicor 1965)★★★, *Old Brush Arbors* (Musicor 1965), *I Get Lonely In A Hurry* (United Artists 1965)★★★, *Trouble In Mind* (United Artists 1965)★★★, *The Race Is On* (United Artists 1965)★★★, *King Of Broken Hearts* (United Artists 1965)★★★, *The Great George Jones* (United Artists 1965)★★★, *Singing The Blues* (Mercury 1965)★★★, *George Jones* (Starday 1965)★★★, *Long Live King George* (Starday 1966)★★★, with Pitney *It's Country Time Again!* (Musicor 1966)★★★, *Love Bug* (Musicor 1966)★★★, *I'm A People* (Musicor 1966)★★★, *We Found Heaven At 4033* (Musicor

1966)★★★, with Montgomery *Blue Moon Of Kentucky* (United Artists 1966)★★★, with Montgomery *Close Together* (Musicor 1966)★★★, *Walk Through This World With Me* (Musicor 1967)★★★, *Cup Of Loneliness* (Musicor 1967)★★★, with Montgomery *Let's Get Together/Party Pickin'* (Musicor 1967)★★★, *Hits By George* (Musicor 1967)★★★, *The George Jones Story* (Starday 1967)★★★, *The Young George Jones* (United Artists 1967)★★★, *Songbook And Picture Album* (Starday 1968)★★★, with Dolly Parton *George Jones & Dolly Parton* (Starday 1968)★★, *The Songs Of Dallas Frazier* (Musicor 1968)★★★, *If My Heart Had Windows* (Musicor 1968)★★, *The George Jones Story* (Musicor 1969)★★★, with Montgomery *Great Country Duets Of All Time* (Musicor 1969)★★★, *My Country* (Musicor 1969)★★★, *I'll Share My World With You* (Musicor 1969)★★★, *Where Grass Won't Grow* (Musicor 1969)★★★, *My Boys - The Jones Boys* (Musicor 1969)★★★, *Will You Visit Me On Sunday?* (Musicor 1970)★★, *George Jones With Love* (Musicor 1971)★★★, *The Great Songs Of Leon Payne* (Musicor 1971)★★★, with Tammy Wynette *We Go Together* (Epic 1971)★★★, *George Jones (We Can Make It)* (Epic 1972)★★★, with Wynette *Me And The First Lady* (Epic 1972)★★★, *A Picture Of Me* (Epic 1972)★★★, with Wynette *We Love To Sing About Jesus* (Epic 1972)★★, with Wynette *Let's Build A World Together* (Epic 1973)★★★, *Nothing Ever Hurt Me* (Epic 1973)★★★, with Wynette *We're Gonna Hold On* (Epic 1973)★★★, *In A Gospel Way* (Epic 1974)★★★, *The Grand Tour* (Epic 1974)★★★, *George, Tammy And Tina* (Epic 1975)★★★, *Memories Of Us* (Epic 1975)★★★, *The Battle* (Epic 1976)★★, *Alone Again* (Epic 1976)★★★, with Wynette *Golden Ring* (Epic 1976)★★★, *Bartender's Blues* (Epic 1978)★★, *My Very Special Guests* (Epic 1979)★★★, with Johnny Paycheck *Double Trouble* (Epic 1980)★★★, *I Am What I Am* (Epic 1980)★★★★, with Wynette *Together Again* (Epic 1980)★★★, *Still The Same Ole Me* (Epic 1981)★★★, with Merle Haggard *A Taste Of Yesterday's Wine* (Epic 1982)★★★, *Shine On* (Epic 1983)★★★, *You've Still Got A Place In My Heart* (Epic 1984)★★★, *By Request* (1984)★★★, *Ladies Choice* (Epic 1984)★★, *Who's Gonna Fill Their Shoes?* (Epic 1985)★★★, *Wine Coloured Roses* (Epic 1986)★★★, *Salutes Bob Wills & Hank Williams* (Liberty 1986)★★★, *Live At Dancetown USA* (Ace 1987)★★★, *Too Wild Too Long* (Epic 1988)★★★, *One Woman Man* (Epic 1989)★★★, *Hallelujah Weekend* (1990)★★★, *You Oughta Be Here With Me* (Epic 1990)★★★, *Friends In High Places* (Epic 1991)★★★, *And Along Came Jones* (MCA 1991)★★★, *Walls Can Fall* (MCA 1992)★★★, *High Tech Redneck* (MCA 1993)★★★, *The Bradley Barn Sessions* (MCA 1994)★★★, with Wynette *One* (MCA 1995)★★★, *I Lived To Tell It All* (MCA 1996)★★★, *It Don't Get Any Better Than This* (MCA 1998)★★★★.

● COMPILATIONS: *Greatest Hits* (Mercury 1961)★★★, *The Best Of George Jones* (United Artists 1963)★★★, *Greatest Hits, Volume 2* (Mercury 1965)★★★, *Greatest Hits* (Musicor 1967)★★★, *Golden Hits, Volume1* (United Artists 1967)★★★, *Golden Hits, Volume 2* (United Artists 1967)★★★, *Golden Hits, Volume 3* (United Artists 1968)★★★, *The Golden Country Hits Of George Jones* (Starday 1969)★★★, *The Best Of George Jones* (Musicor 1970)★★★, *The Best Of Sacred Music* (Musicor 1971)★★★, with Wynette

Greatest Hits (Epic 1977)★★★, *The Best Of George Jones* (Epic 1978)★★★, with Wynette *Encore: George Jones & Tammy Wynette* (Epic 1981)★★★★, *Anniversary: Ten Years Of Hits* (Epic 1982)★★★★, *White Lightnin'* (Ace 1984)★★★, *The Lone Star Legend* (Ace 1985)★★★, *Burn The Honky Tonk Down* (Rounder 1986)★★★, with Wynette *Super Hits* (Epic 1987)★★★, *Don't Stop The Music* (Ace 1987)★★★, *Greatest Country Hits* (Curb 1990)★★★, *The Best Of George Jones, Volume 1: Hardcore Honky Tonk* (Mercury 1991)★★★★, *The Best Of 1955-1967* (Rhino 1991)★★★★, *Cup Of Loneliness: The Mercury Years* (Mercury 1994)★★★★, *The Spirit Of Country: The Essential George Jones* (Epic/Legacy 1994)★★★★, *All-Time Greatest Hits* (Liberty 1994)★★★, *White Lightning* (Drive Archive 1994)★★, with Gene Pitney *George Jones & Gene Pitney* (Bear Family 1995)★★★, with Melba Montgomery *Vintage Collection Series* (Capitol 1996)★★★, *The Best Of* (Spectrum 1998)★★★.

● VIDEOS: with Tammy Wynette *Country Stars Live* (Platinum Music 1990), *Same Ole Me* (Prism 1990), *Golden Hits* (Beckmann Communications 1994), *Live In Tennessee* (Music Farm Ltd 1994).

● FURTHER READING: *Ragged But Right - The Life And Times Of George Jones*, Dolly Carlisle. *George Jones - The Saga Of An American Singer*, Bob Allen. *I Lived To Tell It All*, George Jones.

Jones, Grace

b. 19 May 1952, Spanishtown, Jamaica, West Indies. Six feet of style, looks and attitude, Jones was raised in New York City, then became a successful Paris model. After a flirtation with acting, she made some unexceptional disco records that sold on the strength of her image and her explicit stage show. Both were carefully crafted by her boyfriend, French artist Jean-Paul Goude. *Warm Leatherette* marked a major stylistic development. Recorded at Compass Point, Nassau, it featured top Jamaican session men **Sly And Robbie**, new wave material and half-spoken delivery that became the Grace Jones trademark. Her first hit was a cover of the **Pretenders**' 'Private Life' which made the UK Top 20. On *Nightclubbing* she turned her hand to writing and producing quality songs including 'Pull Up To The Bumper'. In 1984 she diversified into films, taking on Arnold Schwarzenegger in *Conan The Destroyer*. The following year she played alongside Roger Moore in *A View To A Kill*. A return to the recording studios with writer/producer Trevor Horn provided her most successful single to date, 'Slave To The Rhythm', and the album of extended versions and megamixes sold well. In 1986 the compilation *Island Life* was a big UK success, with 'Pull Up To The Bumper' and 'Love Is The Drug' reaching the charts the second time around. Although Chris Blackwell had faith in her as a musical artist the public always saw her as a personality. Her striking looks, outspoken nature and media coverage buried her musical aspirations and talent.

● ALBUMS: *Portfolio* (Island 1977)★★, *Fame* (Island 1978)★★, *Muse* (1979)★★, *Warm Leatherette* (Island 1980)★★★, *Nightclubbing* (Island 1981)★★★, *Living My Life*

(Island 1982)★★, *Slave To The Rhythm* (ZTT 1985)★★, *Inside Story* (EMI America 1986)★★, *Bullet Proof Heart* (Capitol 1990)★★.

● COMPILATIONS: *Island Life* (Island 1985)★★★, *Private Life: The Compass Point Sessions* 2-CD set (Island 1998)★★★.

● FURTHER READING: Goude, Jean-Paul, *Jungle Fever*. *Grace Jones: Ragged But Right*, Dolly Carlisle.

Jones, Grandpa

b. Louis Marshall Jones, 20 October 1913, Niagara, Henderson County, Kentucky, USA, d. 19 February 1998, Nashville, Tennessee, USA. The youngest of the 10 children of a tobacco farmer, Jones learned guitar and first appeared on radio in 1929, soon after securing his own programme on WJW Akron, where he became known as 'The Young Singer of Old Songs'. He worked on the *Lum and Abner* radio show but in 1935 joined **Bradley Kincaid**'s touring company. Kincaid maintained that he sounded like a grumpy old man on their early morning WBZ Boston show and nicknamed him 'Grandpa'. Jones adopting the name and became a permanent 'Grandpa' at the tender age of 22. He left Kincaid in 1937, readily finding work on many stations including WWVA Wheeling, WCHS Charleston and WMMN Fairmont, before, in 1942, joining the *Boone County Jamboree* on WLW Cincinnati, where he first worked with **Merle Travis**, the **Delmore Brothers** and Ramona Riggins (his future wife). He first recorded for the newly formed King label in 1943, recording two sides with Merle Travis that were released as the Shepherd Brothers. Further recordings were made in 1944 before he joined the army, finally serving in the military police in Germany, where he broadcast daily on AFN radio with his band the Munich Mountaineers. After his discharge in 1946 he returned to Cincinnati, but later that year moved to Nashville and became a *Grand Ole Opry* regular. Between 1947 and 1951 he recorded extensively for King and after changing his style of music from ballads to up-tempo songs and comedy numbers, produced his well-known recordings of 'Eight More Miles To Louisville', 'Mountain Dew' and 'Old Rattler', using the banjo for the first time on record on the latter. He also made some fine recordings with Merle Travis and the Delmores as the gospel group the Brown's Ferry Four. He recorded for **RCA** from 1952-55 and later for several other labels. He entered the US country charts in 1959 with 'The All-American Boy', a pop hit for Bill Parsons, and reached number 5 in 1963 with his recording of the old **Jimmie Rodgers** song, 'T for Texas'. The popularity of his recordings and his *Opry* performances led to him joining the cast of the **CBS** network television show *Hee-Haw* in 1969, where his comedy routines with **Minnie Pearl** became very popular. Grandpa Jones was elected to the **Country Music Hall Of Fame** in 1978 and still performed regularly at the *Opry*. On 3 January 1998, following an *Opry* performance, he suffered a stroke and died a month later.

● ALBUMS: *Grandpa Jones Sings His Greatest Hits* (King 1958)★★★, *Grandpa Jones-Strictly Country Tunes* (King 1959)★★★, *Do You Remember (When Grandpa Jones Sang These Songs)* (King 1962)★★★, *Grandpa Jones Makes The Rafters Ring* (Monument 1962)★★★, *An Evening With Grandpa Jones* (Decca 1963)★★★, *Grandpa Jones Yodeling Hits* (Monument 1963)★★★, *Rolling' Along With Grandpa Jones* (King 1963)★★★, *Grandpa Jones Sings Real Folk Songs* (Monument 1964)★★, *Other Side Of Grandpa Jones (At Home/On Stage)* (King 1964)★★, *Grandpa Jones Remembers The Brown's Ferry Four* (Monument 1966)★★★, *Everybody's Grandpa* (Monument 1968)★★★, *Living Legend Of Country Music* (King 1969)★★★, *Grandpa Jones Sings Hits From Hee-Haw* (Monument 1969)★★★, *Grandpa Jones Live* (Monument 1970)★★★, *What's For Supper?* (1974)★★★, with Ramona And the Brown's Ferry Four *The Grandpa Jones Story* (CMH 1976)★★★, with Ramona Jones *Old Time Country Music Collection* (1978)★★★, with Ramona and their four children *Grandpa Jones' Family Album* (CMH 1979)★★★, *Family Gathering* (1981)★★★, with Roy Clark, Buck Owens, Kenny Price *The Hee-Haw Gospel Quartet* (Songbird 1981)★★★, with Merle Travis *Merle And Grandpa's Farm And Home Hour* (1985)★★★. As a member of the Brown's Ferry Four: *Sacred Songs* (King 1957)★★★, *Sacred Songs Volume 2* (King 1958)★★★, *16 Sacred Gospel Songs* (King 1963)★★★, *Wonderful Sacred Songs* (King 1964)★★★.

● COMPILATIONS: *Good Ole Mountain Dew* (Sony 1995)★★★, *Everybody's Grandpa* 5-CD box set (Bear Family 1996)★★★★.

● FURTHER READING: *Everybody's Grandpa (Fifty Years Behind The Mike)*, Louis M. 'Grandpa' Jones.

Jones, Hank

b. Henry Jones, 31 July 1918, Vicksburg, Mississippi, USA. Eldest of three remarkable brothers in jazz (**Thad Jones** and **Elvin Jones**), Hank Jones was raised in Pontiac, Michigan and by the beginning of his teenage years played piano professionally in local bands. In 1944 he went to New York where he joined the **Oran 'Hot Lips' Page** band. Although Jones had previously been in the mainstream of jazz, he was an eager student and fully aware of the changes currently taking place in the music. He incorporated bebop into his repertoire but remained an eclectic player, happily adapting to suit the needs of the artists he accompanied (who ranged from **Coleman Hawkins** to **Charlie Parker**). Jones freelanced extensively throughout the 50s, working with **Jazz At The Philharmonic**, **Benny Goodman** and **Milt Jackson** among many, and ended the decade by becoming a staff musician at **CBS** where he remained until the mid-70s. During this long period of studio activity, Jones accompanied countless performers outside jazz and continued to record with numerous names in jazz. Since the mid-70s he has continued to work in various jazz contexts, as soloist, as duettist with **Tommy Flanagan**, **George Shearing** and other pianists, as accompanist to singers and instrumentalists, and as leader of his own small groups. A masterly musician, adept in most aspects of the jazz repertoire, Jones

has been an important influence, as much for his professionalism as for the immense sweep of his talent.
● ALBUMS: *Hank Jones Piano* (Mercury 1950)★★★, *The Jazz Trio Of Hank Jones* (Savoy 1955)★★★★, *Bluebird* (Savoy 1955)★★★★, *Have You Met Hank Jones* (Savoy 1956)★★★, *Urbanity - Piano Solos By Hank Jones* (Clef 1956)★★★★, *The Hank Jones Quartet/Quintet* (Savoy 1956)★★★★, *The Trio* (Savoy 1956)★★★, *Relaxin' At Camarillo* (Savoy 1956)★★★, *Hank Jones Swings Songs From Gigi* (Golden Crest 1958)★★, *The Talented Touch Of Hank Jones* (Capitol 1958)★★★, *Porgy And Bess: Swinging Impressions By Hank Jones* (Capitol 1959)★★★, *Arrival Time* (RCA Victor 1962)★★★, *Here's Love* (Argo 1963)★★, *This Is Ragtime Now* (ABC 1964)★★, *The Hank Jones Trio ii* (1964)★★★, with Oliver Nelson *Hank Jones With Oliver Nelson And His Orchestra* (1966)★★★, *Hanky Panky* (1975)★★★, *Satin Doll* (1976)★★★, *Love For Sale* (1976)★★, *Hank* (All Art 1976)★★★, *Jones-Brown-Smith* (Concord 1976)★★★, *Arigato* (1976)★★★, *Bop Redux* (Muse 1977)★★★★, *The Great Jazz Trio At The Village Vanguard Vols 1 & 2* (1977)★★★, *Just For Fun* (Original Jazz Classics 1977)★★★★, *Tiptoe Tapdance* (Original Jazz Classics 1977)★★★, *I Remember You* (Black And Blue 1977)★★★, *Have You Met This Jones?* (1977)★★★, *Kindness, Joy, Love And Happiness* (1977)★★★, *Direct From L.A.* (1977)★★★, *The Trio* (1977)★★★, *Groovin' High* (1978)★★★, *Milestones* (1978),★★★ *Compassion* (1978)★★★, *Ain't Misbehavin'* (1978)★★, with Tommy Flanagan *Our Delights* (1978)★★, *Easy To Love* (1979)★★, *Live In Japan* (Jazz Alliance 1979)★★★, *Piano Playhouse* (1979)★★★, *Bluesette* (Black And Blue 1979)★★★, *The Great Jazz Trio* (1980)★★★, *Chapter II* (1980)★★, *The Incredible Hank Jones* (Stash 1980)★★★, *The Great Jazz Trio Revisited At The Village Vanguard Vols 1 & 2* (1980)★★★★, *The Great Jazz Trio And Friends At The Aurex Jazz Festival, Tokyo '81* (1981)★★★, *Threesome* (1982)★★★, *The Club New Yorker* (1983)★★★, with Flanagan *I'm All Smiles* (MPS 1983)★★★, *Monk's Moods* (1984)★★★, with George Shearing *The Spirit Of 176* (1988)★★, *Duo* (Timeless 1988)★★★, *Lazy Afternoon* (Concord 1989)★★★, *The Oracle* (Emarcy 1990)★★★, *Essence* (DMP 1991)★★★, *Live At the Maybank Recital Hall, Vol 16* (Concord 1991)★★, *Jazzpar 91 Project* (Storyville 1991)★★★, *Handful Of Keys* (Emarcy 1992)★★★, *Upon Reflection* (Verve 1993)★★★, with Charlie Haden *Steal Away* (Verve 1995)★★★★, *Favors* (Verve 1997)★★★.

Jones, Howard

b. John Howard Jones, 23 February 1955, Southampton, Hampshire, England. Coming to prominence as a synthesizer-pop maestro in the mid-80s, Jones had been trying to succeed as a musician for almost 15 years. His childhood saw him on the move from country to country but by the time he reached his teens he was settled in High Wycombe, England. He joined his first band in 1976 and over the next few years played in Warrior, the Bicycle Thieves, and Skin Tight. In 1974 he went to music college in Manchester and after graduation he began performing solo in his home town. He soon introduced dancer Jed Hoile to enliven his act by improvising dance to his songs. Jones was

offered a session by BBC disc jockey **John Peel** which led to tours with **OMD** and **China Crisis**. **WEA Records** signed him in the summer of 1983 and in September he charted with his first single 'New Song'. He won several Best New Artist awards and followed-up with hits like 'What Is Love', 'Hide And Seek', and 'Like To Get To Know You Well'. His debut *Human's Lib* topped the UK charts. Although he performed most of the music on his recordings in 1985 he formed a touring band with his brother Martin on bass, and Trevor Morais on drums. As the 80s drew to a close his singles charted lower and lower but he continues to record sporadically and even joined the unplugged trend with *Live Acoustic America* in 1996.
● ALBUMS: *Human's Lib* (WEA 1984)★★★★, *The 12 Inch Album* (WEA 1984)★★, *Dream Into Action* (WEA 1985)★★★, *One To One* (WEA 1986)★★, *Cross That Line* (WEA 1989)★★★, *In The Running* (1992)★★, *Live Acoustic America* (Plump 1996)★★★.
● COMPILATIONS: *The Best Of Howard Jones* (WEA 1993)★★★.

Jones, Isham

b. 31 January 1894, Coalton, Ohio, USA, d. 19 October 1956. A multi-instrumentalist, Jones was leading his own band by his late teens. He played mostly in the Chicago area until the early 20s, when he moved to New York. After a brief visit to the UK in 1924, he returned to form a new band, which by the end of the decade he had developed into an outstanding dance orchestra. The band enjoyed enormous popularity with audiences. A 1930 recording of **Hoagy Carmichael**'s 'Stardust', arranged as a ballad, was a huge hit and changed perceptions of how this song might be performed. Arrangements were by Jones, together with **Gordon Jenkins** and **Victor Young**, and created a relaxed, melodic style unusual among bands of this type. Fine musicians who played in the band at one time or another included **Jack Jenney** and **Pee Wee Erwin**. In 1936, with the swing era freshly launched and big bands fast becoming popular, Jones went against all logic and decided to fold his band. Some of the more jazz-orientated members decided to go ahead with their own outfit under the leadership of one of the saxophone players, **Woody Herman**. In the late 30s Jones concentrated on composing and arranging, but by the 40s he was working mostly outside music. A possibly apocryphal tale recounts that when his wife bought him a new piano for his 30th birthday, he was so worried at the expense she had incurred, he sat up all night at his birthday gift and by morning had composed three tunes to help restore the family fortunes: 'It Had To Be You', 'Spain' and 'The One I Love Belongs To Somebody Else'.
● ALBUMS: *Isham Jones And His Orchestra* 1920-1924 recordings (Fountain 1979)★★★, *Isham Jones And His Orchestra* (1929-30)★★★, *Isham Jones And His Orchestra Featuring Woody Herman* (1936)★★★★.

Jones, Jack

b. John Allen Jones, 14 January 1938, Los Angeles, California, USA. A popular singer from the early 60s, Jones has one of the finest, and most versatile, light baritone voices in popular music. The son of actress Irene Hervey and actor/vocalist **Allan Jones**, Jack studied singing while still at high school. After graduation in 1957, he joined his father's act, making his first appearance at the Thunderbird Hotel, Las Vegas. He left after eight months, and worked in small clubs and lounges, even bowling alleys, and also appeared in the minor musical film *Juke Box Rhythm*. Jones was spotted, third on the bill in a San Francisco club, by arranger-conductor Pete King, who recommended him to Kapp Records. Shortly afterwards, Jones started a six-month stint in the US Air Force, and, during that time, recorded 'Lollipops And Roses', which won him a Grammy in 1962 for Best Performance By A Male Singer. *Cash Box* magazine voted him Most Promising Vocalist in 1962 and 1963; he had a minor hit with 'Call Me Irresponsible', and won another Grammy for 'Wives And Lovers' (1964), which was also the title of a best-selling album, as was 'Dear Heart', 'The Impossible Dream' and 'Lady'.

Other 60s chart successes, through until 1967, included 'The Race Is On' and *My Kind Of Town*. Jones also sang the title songs for the movies *Where Love Has Gone* and *Love With A Proper Stranger* and the winning entry of the Golden Globe Awards, 'Life Is What You Make It', from the film *Kotch*. In 1967 he switched from Kapp to **RCA Records**, and continued to make highly regarded albums, including *Without Her*, the first for his new label. He also appeared frequently on television with artists such as Jerry Lewis and **Bob Hope**, and was a part of Hope's troupe which entertained the US Forces in Vietnam in December 1965. In concert, Jones is an accomplished performer, skilfully mixing old standards such as 'My Romance' and 'People Will Say We're In Love', with more up-to-date songs like 'Light My Fire', 'I Think It's Gonna Rain Today', 'What Are You Doing The Rest Of Your Life' and 'What I Did for Love'. He also has a slick line in patter, for instance, when rejecting the inevitable request for 'The Donkey Serenade' (his father's most famous number): 'We don't have that one, but I'll sing you another song that has a lot of the same notes in it!'. In fact, he will sometimes sing the song, but at a much greater pace than his father ever did, occasionally prefacing it with lines like: 'I don't know if you know this, but my father recorded 'The Donkey Serenade' on the night that I was born. It's true - he was on a very tight schedule!' Since 1973, Jones has been extremely popular in the UK, and tours regularly. Although to date he has never had a Top 75 single there, he made the charts during the 70s with *A Song For You*, *Breadwinners*, *Together*, *Harbour*, *The Full Life* and *All To Yourself*. *Breadwinners*, with songs by **David Gates**, was typical of the way that Jones selected material from the best writers of the 60s and 70s, including **Michel Legrand**, **Alan And Marilyn Bergman**, **John** **Lennon** and **Paul McCartney**, **Nilsson**, **Leonard Cohen**, **Burt Bacharach** and **Hal David**, **Randy Newman**, **Jimmy Webb**, **Paul Williams**, **Tony Hatch** and **Jackie Trent**. In the 80s and early 90s he continued to thrive in Las Vegas, at venues such as the Golden Nugget and the Desert Inn. During such performances he added contemporary numbers including 'Wind Beneath My Wings' and **Andrew Lloyd Webber**'s 'Music Of The Night' to hoary old favourites such as the *Love Boat* theme. Early in 1991 he played Sky Masterson in a west coast production of *Guys And Dolls*, and continued with his classy singing act at theatres in several countries, including the London Palladium.

● ALBUMS: *Call Me Irresponsible* (Kapp 1963)★★★, *Wives And Lovers* (Kapp 1963)★★★★, *Bewitched* (Kapp 1964)★★★, *Where Love Has Gone* (Kapp 1964)★★★, *Dear Heart* (Kapp 1965)★★★★, *My Kind Of Town* (Kapp 1965)★★★, *There's Love & There's Love & There's Love* (Kapp 1965)★★★, *For The 'In' Crowd* (Kapp 1966)★★★, *The Impossible Dream* (Kapp 1966)★★★★, *Jack Jones Sings* (Kapp 1966)★★★, *Lady* (Kapp 1967)★★★★, *Our Song* (Kapp 1967)★★★, *Without Her* (1967)★★★, *If You Ever Leave Me* (1968)★★★, *Where Is Love?* (RCA 1968)★★, *A Time For Us* (RCA 1969)★★, *A Song For You* (1972)★★★, *Breadwinners* (1972)★★★, *Together* (1973)★★★, *Write Me A Love Song Charlie* (1974)★★★, *In Person, Sands, Las Vegas* (1974)★★★, *Harbour* (1974)★★★, *The Full Life* (1977)★★★, *All To Yourself* (1977)★★★, *Christmas Album* (1978)★★★, *I've Been Here All The Time* (1980)★★★, *Deja Vu* (1982)★★★, *Fire And Rain* (1985)★★★, *I Am A Singer* (1989)★★★, *The Gershwin Album* (1993)★★★, *Live At The London Palladium* (Coolnote 1996)★★★, *New Jack Swing* (Linn 1998).

● COMPILATIONS: *What The World Needs Now Is Love!* (1968)★★★, *Best Of Jack Jones* (1978)★★★, *The Jack Jones Special Collection* (1980)★★★, *The Very Best Of Jack Jones* (1981)★★★, *Magic Moments* (1984)★★★, *Love Songs* (1985)★★★, *Golden Classics* (1986)★★★.

Jones, Janie

b. Marion Mitchell, Seaham, Co. Durham, England. A former Windmill Theatre girl and sister of vocalist Valerie Mitchell, Janie Jones is more renowned for scandal than her brief recording career. Her several 60s singles included 'Witches Brew' (1965), a minor UK Top 50 hit popularized by **pirate radio**, but trials for blackmail, prostitution and payola irrevocably linked the singer with scandal. Imprisoned during the 70s, Janie was immortalized in song by the **Clash** who, as the Lash, provided the requisite backing on her subsequent punk-influenced single, 'House Of The Ju-Ju Queen' (1983).

● COMPILATIONS: *I'm In Love With The World Of Janie Jones: The Complete Singles Collection* (RPM 1997)★★.

Jones, Jimmy (jazz)

b. 30 December 1918, Memphis, Tennessee, USA, d. 29 April 1982. Jones started out on guitar while growing up in Chicago but later switched to piano. In the early and mid-40s he played with several prominent jazzmen including **Stuff Smith**, **Don Byas** and **Coleman Hawkins**. Later in the decade he also played on many recording sessions with such Ellingtonians as **Ben Webster**, **Johnny Hodges** and **Paul Gonsalves**. In 1947 he began accompanying **Sarah Vaughan** with whom he established a great musical rapport. Apart from a two-year break, he remained with Vaughan until 1958. Throughout the 60s Jones was deeply involved with arranging and composing, often working with **Duke Ellington** although he did tour Europe in 1966 as musical director for **Ella Fitzgerald**. An adept and elegant accompanist, Jones chose to follow a musical path which frequently led to his working almost anonymously with brighter stars. For all this apparently deliberate avoidance of the spotlight, his solo work, when heard, displays a musician with orderly thoughts and a lightly swinging touch.

● ALBUMS: *The Jimmy Jones Trio* (1954)★★★, with George Wallington *Trios* (1993)★★★.

Jones, Jimmy (R&B)

b. 2 June 1937, Birmingham, Alabama, USA. Jones, who had spent a long apprenticeship singing in R&B doo-wop groups, became a rock 'n' roll star in the early 60s singing 'Handy Man' and other hits with a dramatic and piercingly high falsetto. He began his career as a tap dancer, and in 1955 joined a vocal group, the Sparks Of Rhythm. In 1956 Jones formed his own group, the Savoys, which were renamed the Pretenders in 1956. With all these groups, tracks were recorded in the prevailing doo-wop manner but with no discernable success beyond a few local radio plays in the New York/New Jersey area. Success finally came when Jones launched a solo career, signing with **MGM**'s Cub subsidiary in 1959 and hitting with his debut, 'Handy Man' (number 3 R&B/number 2 pop chart in 1960). Retaining the same falsetto style, he followed up with 'Good Timin'' (number 8 R&B/number 3 pop chart in 1960), but the decline in sales was considerable for his two other US chart entries, 'That's When I Cried' (number 83 pop chart in 1960) and 'I Told You So' (number 85 pop chart in 1961). In the UK, Jones's chart success was exceptional compared to most of his US contemporaries. In 1960 'Handy Man' reached number 3, 'Good Timin'' number 1, 'I Just Go For You' number 35, 'Ready For Love' number 46 and 'I Told You So' number 33. 'Handy Man' was revived on the charts twice, by **Del Shannon** in 1964 and by **James Taylor** in 1977.

● ALBUMS: *Good Timin'* (MGM 1960)★★★.

Jones, Jo

b. Jonathan Jones, 7 October 1911, Chicago, Illinois, USA, d. 3 September 1985. While he was still a child Jones became adept on several instruments, including trumpet and piano. In his teens he worked as a singer and dancer, taking up drums along the way. By the late 20s he was drumming in **territory bands**, eventually settling in Kansas City in the early 30s. It was here that he met **Count Basie**, at the time still plain Bill Basie, and worked with him on a number of occasions before joining the band full-time in 1936. Here Jones became a member of the magnificent 'All-American Rhythm Section' with Basie, **Freddie Green** and **Walter Page**. The flowing, rhythmic pulse of the band was aided enormously by Jones's changes to previous conceptions of jazz drumming. He shifted the dominant role among the instruments at his disposal from the bass drum to the hi-hat cymbal, thus creating an enviable looseness in which he was free to punctuate the ensemble and 'goose' the soloists with accented bass, snare and tom-tom beats. Although Jones always gave credit for such innovations to others, there is no doubt that he popularized and refined this way of playing himself. After his innovations, the way was open for the further changes in the drummer's role that occurred in bebop. The sleek power of the Basie rhythm section, and Jones's part in its success, made him the envy of and model for numerous other drummers, even if swing era audiences tended to prefer more extrovert, busier and showboating percussionists. Jones left the Basie band when he was inducted into the US Army in 1944; after the war he freelanced with numerous major jazz stars, among them **Lester Young**, **Teddy Wilson** and **Roy Eldridge**, worked with **Jazz At The Philharmonic** and led his own groups on record and for club engagements. In his later years Jones worked the international festival circuits, playing with wit, polish and always that extraordinary subtle swing that had led **Don Lamond** to describe him as the man who played like the wind. A highly perceptive and articulate man, Jones also grew steadily more and more disillusioned with the jazz life, which occasionally created stars out of musical nonentities and lavished attention upon individuals whose talent was minuscule in comparison to his own. His knowledge and understanding of jazz drumming was extensive and, although he preferred to accompany rather than play solo, in his later years he would sometimes enliven his performances by demonstrating the techniques and idiosyncrasies of fellow drummers, often appearing to play even more like them than they did themselves.

● ALBUMS: *Jo Jones Special* (1955)★★★, with Lester Young, Teddy Wilson *Prez And Teddy* (1956)★★★★, *The Jo Jones Special* (Vanguard 1956)★★★, *Jo Jones Plus Two* (Vanguard 1958)★★★, *The Jo Jones Trio* (Fresh Sounds 1959)★★★★, *The Jo Jones Quintet* (1960)★★★, with Milt Hinton *The Jo Jones Duo* (1960)★★★, with Willie 'The Lion' Smith *The Drums* (1973)★★★, *Caravan* (1974)★★★, *The Main Man* (1976)★★, *Papa Jo And His Friends* (1977)★★, *Our Man, Papa Jo* (1977)★★.

● COMPILATIONS: *Count Basie: Complete Recorded Works In Chronological Order* (1937-39)★★★★, *Count Basie At The Chatterbox* (1937)★★★★.

Jones, Joe

b. 12 August 1926, New Orleans, Louisiana, USA. Jones was a pianist and vocalist who made his mark in 1960 with the R&B/novelty single 'You Talk Too Much'. His career began in the mid-40s as a valet and bandleader for **B.B. King**. Jones recorded under his own name as early as 1954 and went on the road as a pianist for **Shirley And Lee**. Jones's big hit was co-written with pianist Reginald Hall, and recorded for the small local label Ric Records. However, as the record began to take off, it was discovered that Jones had already recorded the song for the larger, New York-based Roulette Records. They lodged an injunction and the Ric version was withdrawn. Jones was unable to follow that hit and went into publishing, production and management, his greatest success in that area being with the **Dixie Cups** and, to a lesser degree, **Alvin Robinson**.

● ALBUMS: *You Talk Too Much* (Roulette 1961)★★★.

Jones, John Paul

b. John Baldwin, 3 January 1946, Sidcup, Kent, England. Bassist Jones backed singer Chris Wayne before joining the **Tony Meehan Combo** in 1963. The following year he recorded his lone solo single, 'A Foggy Day In Vietnam', which was co-written by **Andrew Loog Oldham** and Mike Leander. Jones subsequently forged a working relationship with the former, arranging Oldham's orchestral collections and productions for the **Mighty Avengers** and **Del Shannon**, before assisting the **Rolling Stones** during sessions for *Their Satanic Majesties Request*. Jones also collaborated with **Mickie Most** and **Graham Gouldman**, appearing as arranger, musician, or both, on recordings by **Herman's Hermits**, **Jeff Beck**, **Lulu**, **Donovan** and the **Mindbenders**. It was during this frenetic period that Jones became acquainted with session guitarist **Jimmy Page**, a friendship which resulted in the formation of **Led Zeppelin**. Although visually overshadowed by the group's dynamic frontmen, Jones' backroom experience helped shape the quartet's overall sound and progress. His work since the group's demise has been low-key, although in 1985 he completed the film soundtrack to *Scream For Help*. Jones subsequently produced *The First Chapter* for gothic-rock band the **Mission** and later joined the group on several live appearances.

● ALBUMS: *Scream For Help* (1985)★★, with Diamanda Galas *The Sporting Life* (Mute 1994)★★.

● FILMS: *Give My Regards To Broad Street* (1985).

Jones, Johnny

b. 17 August 1936, Edes, Tennessee, USA. Jones is one of the most respected of a clutch of blues artists who have found themselves a niche in the country-dominated musical climate of Nashville, Tennessee. A fixture at local clubs with his band the Imperial Seven, by the 80s his musical ambitions had been subsumed by financial considerations, and he can still be found running his own soul food café in Nashville. Jones travelled to Memphis at the age of 13, witnessing his first live blues performance by **Joe Hill Louis**, before moving with his mother to Chicago in the early 50s when his parents separated. There, he was exposed to all the blues greats of the era, including **Muddy Waters** and **Howling Wolf**, and he shared an apartment with harmonica player Walter McCollum. Together they formed a small group, working regularly with **Junior Wells** and **Freddy King**.

After a brief return to Memphis, Jones moved back to Nashville and became a studio guitarist, working on a number of releases on Bill Beasley's Champion and Cherokee labels. These singles included Jimmy Beck Orchestra's 'Pipe Dreams' instrumental and Larry Birdsong's 'Every Night In The Week'. His band, the Imperial Seven, were formed in the early 60s, and worked regularly at the renowned New Era club in Nashville. **Jimi Hendrix** regularly sat in on these sessions. Jones also played rhythm guitar, alongside **Clarence 'Gatemouth' Brown**, in the backing band for the Dallas television show *The Beat*. Jones recorded his first singles under his own name (including 'Really Part 1') at this time. He formed a new band in 1968, the King Casuals, who cut a number of singles for the Peachtree record label. However, by the late 70s, frustrated with irregular payments, Jones had all but retired, aside from a stint playing guitar for **Bobby Bland**.

Jones, Jonah

b. Robert Elliott Jones, 31 October, 1909, Louisville, Kentucky, USA. As a youth Jones played trumpet with numerous local and **territory bands** before joining **Horace Henderson** in 1928. After drifting through various other minor bands, he joined **Jimmie Lunceford** and then in Buffalo, in 1932, began a highly profitable musical partnership with **Stuff Smith**. Although he found time for excursions with **Lillian Armstrong** and **McKinney's Cotton Pickers**, he was still with Smith when they took their little band into New York and a residency at the Onyx Club in early 1936. For the next four years the band captivated audiences with their hot music, eccentric appearance and crazy clowning. In 1940 Jones left to work with the big bands of **Benny Carter**, **Fletcher Henderson** and then spent a decade with **Cab Calloway**. He next played with **Earl Hines** but from the mid-50s led his own small band, which attained great popularity with the fringe jazz audience. Musically, this and the later bands Jones fronted offered a repertoire that was a long way from the rough and ready excitement of the group he had co-led with Smith. Indeed, as the years passed, it was often seen to be unadventurous, predictable and a little bland, concentrating on straightforward arrangements of show tunes and popular songs of the day. It was easy-listening jazz for the masses, although Jones's playing was always skilful and consistently showed that he had not forgotten the roots of his music. He continued playing throughout the 60s, 70s and into the 80s, proving remarkably durable and, latterly, still to be capable of a few surprises.

● ALBUMS: *Harlem Jump And Swing* (1954)★★★, *The Jonah Jones Quartet* i (1956)★★★, *The Jonah Jones Quartet* ii (1957)★★★, *The Jonah Jones Quartet* iii (1958)★★★, *The Jonah Jones Quartet* iv (1958)★★★, *The Jonah Jones Quartet* v (1958)★★★, *I Dig Chicks* (1958)★★★, *Swingin' 'Round The World* (1958-59)★★★, *An Evening With Fred Astaire* (1959)★★, *The Jonah Jones Quartet* vi (1960)★★★, *The Jonah Jones Quartet* vii (1961)★★★, *The Jonah Jones Quartet* viii (1961)★★★, *The Jonah Jones Quartet* ix (1962)★★★, *A Touch Of Blue* (1962)★★★, *Greatest Instrumental Hits Styled By Jonah Jones* (1962)★★★, *Jonah Jones With Glen Gray And The Casa Loma Orchestra* (1962)★★, *The Jonah Jones Sextet* (1962)★★★, *The Jonah Jones Quartet* x (1963)★★★, *The Jonah Jones Quartet* xi (1963)★★★, *On The Sunny Side Of The Street* (1965)★★, *The Jonah Jones Quartet* xii (1966)★★★, *The Jonah Jones Quartet* xiii (1966), *The Jonah Jones Quartet* xiv (1966)★★★, *The Jonah Jones Quartet* xv (1967)★★★, *The Jonah Jones Quartet* xvi (1968)★★★, *The Jonah Jones Quartet* xvii (c.1969)★★★, *Confessin'* (1978)★★★.

● COMPILATIONS: *Stuff Smith And His Onyx Club Orchestra* (1936),★★ *Sixteen Classics By Cab Calloway* (1939-41)★★★★, *Low Down Blues* (1944)★★★, *Butterflies In The Rain* 1944 recordings (Circle 1987)★★★, with Hot Lips Page *Swing Street Showcase* (1944-45)★★★, *Harlem Jump And Swing* (Affinity 1983)★★★.

Jones, Leroy

b. 20 February 1958, New Orleans, Louisiana, USA. As a small child he began playing guitar and took lessons from veteran jazzman **Danny Barker**. Soon, he became interested in brass instruments, first trying the cornet, then moving on to trumpet and fluegelhorn. He continued studying, taking lessons from a trumpet-playing nun at a Catholic school he attended. Mostly, however, he learned from listening to jazz musicians on record, especially **Louis Armstrong**. His listening was, nevertheless, decidedly eclectic. As he told Derek Ansell in an interview for *Jazz Journal International*, he was influenced also by **Hugh Masakela, Shorty Rogers** and **Freddie Hubbard** amongst several trumpeters of note. Later, he heard records by **Clifford Brown** and **Lee Morgan**. Despite all these influences, Jones steadily matured his own style while still remaining attuned to other young musicians such as **Wynton Marsalis**. His early professional experience included playing in R&B bands and with the Louisiana Repertory Ensemble. In the early 90s he began playing regularly with the band backing popular singer **Harry Connick Jnr.**, an engagement which brought him worldwide exposure. Rich and melodic, his trumpet playing happily blends most of the traditional ingredients of jazz from the blues, through New Orleans and gospel to bop and beyond. His example and dedication should make him one of the keepers of the flame for the 21st century.

● ALBUMS: *Mo' Cream From The Crop* (Columbia 1994)★★★.

Jones, Linda

b. 14 January 1944, Newark, New Jersey, USA, d. 14 March 1972, New York City, New York, USA. This soulful song stylist started in her family's gospel group the Jones Singers at the age of six. Her first recording was 'Lonely Teardrops' under the name Linda Lane, on Cub Records in 1963, and she had unsuccessful singles on **Atco** in 1964 and Blue Cat the following year. In 1967 she worked with writer/producer George Kerr and signed to Russ Regan's Loma label in 1967. This resulted in her biggest hit, 'Hypnotized', which narrowly missed the US Top 20. She later had releases on Warner 7-Arts, Cotique and **Gamble And Huff**'s Neptune label before joining Sylvia Robinson's Turbo Records in 1971. A sufferer of diabetes, Jones collapsed backstage at the **Apollo** in New York on 14 March 1972 and died shortly afterwards in hospital. She was way ahead of her time and made melisma (spreading a syllable over several notes) an art form. This unique singer, who has influenced scores of R&B artists, was aptly described in *Black Music* magazine as 'perhaps the most soulful singer in the history of R&B music'.

● ALBUMS: *Hypnotized* (Loma 1967)★★★.
● COMPILATIONS: *20 Golden Classics* (Collectables 1988)★★★★.

Jones, Little Hat

b. Dennis Jones. Jones was a taut-voiced street singer from San Antonio, Texas, where he recorded 10 blues for ARC Records in 1929 and 1930, also accompanying **Texas Alexander** on one session. His trademark was a fast, rolling guitar introduction, followed by a marked rallentando as he or Alexander began singing. Only on 'Hurry Blues' did he maintain the pace of his introduction throughout, making the record label mistitle (for 'Worried Blues') inadvertently appropriate. An eclectic guitarist, Jones blended fingerpicking, strumming and boogie basses into a style that, while recognizably within the Texas mainstream, was distinctively his own.

● ALBUMS: *Texas Blues Guitar* (Earl Archives 1987)★★★.

Jones, Little Johnny

b. 1 November 1924, Jackson, Mississippi, USA, d. 19 November 1964, Chicago, Illinois, USA. Jones was a key figure in the development of post-war blues piano in Chicago. In the late 40s, he succeeded **Big Maceo** (a major influence on his own playing) as **Tampa Red**'s partner, and helped move Tampa's music towards the amplified ensemble sound. Besides playing on many sessions, Jones made a few splendid recordings under his own name, two with **Muddy Waters** and six with the **Elmore James** band, which he adorned from 1952-60. His extrovert personality is apparent on the rocking 'Sweet Little Woman', but he was also capable of sensitive blues like 'Doin' The Best I Can'. Late in life, he was taped live, both solo and with Billy Boy Arnold on harmonica, on titles that admirably display both his ebullient and introspective sides.

● ALBUMS: *Chicago Piano Plus* (1972)★★★, *Johnny Jones*

With Billy Boy Arnold (Alligator 1979)★★★, with Tampa Red *Tampa Red* (Krazy Kat 1982)★★★, *King Of The Slide Guitar* (1983)★★★, *Midnight Blues* (Cream 1987)★★★, *Knights Of The Keyboard* (1988)★★★, *Trouble Monkey* (Audioquest 1995)★★★.

Jones, Maggie

b. Fae Barnes, *c.*1900, Hillsboro, Texas, USA. Jones worked in black revue from around 1922, first in New York and later in the Dallas/Fort Worth area until her retirement from showbusiness in about 1934. Her history thereafter is unknown. Her **Columbia** recordings, made between 1924 and 1926, besides including some of the most sensitive recorded playing by **Louis Armstrong** and **Charlie Green**, are the work of one of the finest of the female vaudeville blues singers, demonstrating her resonant voice and outstanding technique, powered by a remarkable ability to sustain a note. Never as highly rated as **Bessie Smith** or **Clara Smith**, she easily bears comparison with either.

● COMPILATIONS: *Volume 1* (*c.*1985)★★★, *Volume 2* (*c.*1985)★★★.

Jones, Mazlyn

b. Nigel Maslyn Jones, 26 June 1950, Dudley, Warwickshire, England. Jones started playing guitar, as well as writing poetry and music, when only 14 years old. When he left school, in 1969, he moved to the Channel Islands to work for Gerald Durrell and returned to the mainland in 1971, where he started to teach guitar. It was after moving to Cornwall in 1973 that he bagan to concentrate on performing and writing, and in 1975 toured folk clubs and smaller festivals. Due to confusion, he changed the spelling of his name to Mazlyn, as it was often misspelt or incorrectly pronounced. Jones is a performer who encompasses elements of world music, new age and rock, with a sprinkling of folk, often with environmental themes. He has played with a variety of well-known performers, including **Roy Harper**. Jones toured as support act to **Barclay James Harvest** in 1981, playing every major venue in the UK and Europe. Following the 1981 tour, Mazlyn took a break from live touring to concentrate on the recording of *Breaking Cover*. Live, Mazlyn also presents a show featuring songs accompanied by back projections to highlight the theme of the material. He produced the debut album by new age band Solstice, in 1984. **Johnny Coppin** is featured on Jones's first two albums, while the fourth release, *Water From The Well*, has Nik Turner, of **Hawkwind**, on saxophones and flute on two songs, and Guy Evans, from **Van Der Graff Generator**, on percussion. In 1986, material from *Breaking Cover* was used by independent television for a documentary on the World Surfing Contest, which was held in the UK the same year. Nik Turner again appeared, playing flute, on the 1991 release *Mazlyn Jones*. Jones now performs and records as Mazlyn Jones, having dropped the name prefix.

● ALBUMS: *Ship To Shore* (1976)★★★, *Sentinel* (1979)★★,

Breaking Cover (1981)★★★, *Water From The Well* (1987)★★★, *Mazlyn Jones* (1991)★★.

Jones, Mick

(see **Clash**; **Big Audio Dynamite**)

Jones, Moody

b. 8 April 1908, Earle, Arkansas, USA. From a rural farming background, Jones moved to East St. Louis in the late 20s, by which time he was already making music on home-made instruments. Later, he learned guitar and in 1938, moved to Chicago and joined the blues circuit there. Along with his cousin **Floyd Jones** and harmonica player **Snooky Pryor**, he made some records in the late 40s. Their sound combined a powerful down-home Mississippi/Arkansas style with influences from records by artists such as **Sonny Boy Williamson** - the classic ingredients of post-war Chicago blues. Jones recorded a few tracks under his own name in the early 50s, but these were not issued at the time, despite the emotional quality of his vocals. In later years, he abandoned the blues and became a Christian minister.

● ALBUMS: *Snooky Pryor* (Flyright 1988)★★★.

Jones, Neal

b. 22 March 1922, Scots Hill, Tennessee, USA. He learned guitar as a boy and first worked on WTJS Jackson in 1940 with **Eddy Arnold** And The Johnson Brothers. He relocated to WREC Memphis and played lead guitar with **Curly Fox And Texas Ruby** but later rejoined the Johnson Brothers at WKPT Kingsport. In May 1942, they moved to WDOD Chattanooga, where he also played fiddle within their programme. He could only play three fiddle tunes and was somewhat embarrassed at one show to find Curly Fox in the audience. He was drafted in October 1942 and served as a radar operator during World War II. During these years, he played guitar with a service band. In March 1946, he returned to work with Arnold at WTJS, where he also incorporated comedy into his act. During the late 40s, he also worked with **Billy Walker**. In the early 50s, he became a speciality act at WMPS Memphis and toured with several acts including the **Louvin Brothers**, the **Blackwood Brothers** and **Sonny James**. He also became a regular on the daily *Shindig Show* on WFAA Dallas. Between 1954 and 1958, he worked radio and television at WBAP Fort Worth, Texas, where at times he co-hosted *Barn Dance* with **Pat Boone** and his own daily *The Jones Place*, which at one time had **Willie Nelson** as a regular cast member. His group, at times, included **Johnny Gimble** (fiddle), Paul Buskirk (mandolin), Bill Simmons (piano) and Slim Harbert (bass). In the late 50s, he also hosted *Jones Junction* on KTLA Shreveport, Louisiana and worked with **Jimmie Davis**. In the early 60s, he began to combine his performing with work as a disc jockey and presented radio and television programmes on several California and Texas stations. In 1971, he moved to Nashville presenting syndicated shows, including *Inside Nashville* but throughout the 70s, he also became involved in station management. In 1985, he appeared as a soloist with the Memphis Symphony Orchestra. He first recorded at WFAA Dallas, in 1953, but joined **Columbia Records** in 1954 and recorded several sessions for the label. A compilation of 16 of his recordings, four previously unissued, was released in album form by a German label in 1987, by which time Jones, who had the nickname of 'Tywhop', was living in retirement in Waynesboro, Tennessee.

● COMPILATIONS: *Tywhop's Greatest Country Hits* (Cattle 1987)★★★.

Jones, Nic

b. Nicholas Paul Jones, 9 January 1947, Orpington, Kent, England. The earlier work of this highly-respected guitarist and fiddle player showed great promise, but a tragic accident interrupted his career. In 1967 Jones played guitar and sang on the Halliard's album *It's The Irish In Me*. On 26 February 1982, he was involved in a car crash which left him in a coma for six weeks. He then spent the next six months in hospital while his broken bones were repaired. As a result, Nic has had to try and re-learn his old highly-innovative instrumental technique. *Ballad And Song* contained the folk standards 'Sir Patrick Spens' and 'Little Musgrave'. Jones backed **Maddy Prior** and **June Tabor** on *Silly Sisters* in 1976, and in 1978 recorded *Bandoggs* for **Transatlantic**. The title was also the name of the short-lived titular group which included **Pete** and **Chris Coe** and **Tony Rose**, as well as Jones himself. *Penguin Eggs* became *Melody Maker* folk album of the year, and contained some excellent songs including 'The Humpback Whale'. Jones in the past has been critical of the folk purists who refuse to allow songs to evolve, and on one occasion sang a **Chuck Berry** song at the Nottingham Traditional Music Club, with the inevitable hostile reaction. Nic provided vocals on the 1989 **Gerry Hallom** release *Old Australian Ways*, proving that his voice is still resonant.

● ALBUMS: with the Halliard's *It's The Irish In Me* (1967)★★, *Ballad And Song* (Trailer 1970)★★★, *Nic Jones* (Trailer 1971)★★★★, with Jon Raven, Tony Rose *Songs Of A Changing World* (1973)★★★, *The Noah's Ark Trap* (1977)★★★, *From The Devil To A Stranger* (Transatlantic 1978)★★★, *Bandoggs* (1978)★★★, *Penguin Eggs* (Topic 1980)★★★★.

Jones, Nyles

b. Robert L. Jones, aka **Guitar Gabriel**, 12 October 1924, Atlanta, Georgia, USA, d. 2 April 1996. At the age of five he moved to Winston-Salem, North Carolina, with his bluesman father and began playing guitar when eight years old, meeting many of the area's leading blues artists, including **Rev. Gary Davis** and **Blind Boy Fuller**, both of whom had a great influence on his own music. He left home at the age of 16 and travelled throughout the country, meeting **Lightnin' Hopkins**,

who also left his mark on Jones's music. In 1970 he recorded in Pittsburgh for Gemini, and the resulting album and single were acclaimed for their raw blues passion. However, Jones became disillusioned at the lack of financial reward and returned to Winston-Salem in the mid-70s, assuming the name Guitar Gabriel. He was rediscovered and recorded again in 1991, under the supervision of Tim Duffy.

● ALBUMS: *My South/MyBlues* (1970)★★★, as Guitar Gabriel *Toot Blues* (1991)★★★, as Guitar Gabriel *Guitar Gabriel Volume 1* (Music Maker 1995)★★★.

Jones, Oliver

b. 11 September, 1934, Montreal, Canada. Jones's parents were immigrants from Barbados. As a child he learned classical piano starting at the age of 2. At 5 he played for his local church and later he studied with **Oscar Peterson**'s sister who lived near by. After establishing himself in Canada he began touring internationally in the early 60s as accompanist to pop singers Kenny Hamilton and Terry Malone. In the early 80s he concentrated on playing jazz, initially resident at Biddle's, a club in Montreal. After a succession of eye operations he once again toured but this time in his own right. A highly accomplished technician, Jones's playing style indicates the influences of gifted performers such as Peterson and **Art Tatum**. He has also acknowledged his debt to **Bill Evans**, **Herbie Hancock** and other pianists of a later school. By the late 80s and early 90s, Jones was no longer under the shadow of his mentor even if, inevitably, critics often referred to Peterson in attempting to describe Jones's technical gifts. His work with **Clark Terry**, **Herb Ellis** and **Red Mitchell**, with whom he toured the UK late in 1991, revealed him to be a jazz piano player of considerable stature in his own right. In the mid-90s at the age he decided to ease back from his busy touring schedule and released one of his best ever albums (albeit with Oscar Peterson tracks) *From Lush To Lively*.

● ALBUMS: *Speak Low, Swing Hard* (1985)★★★★, *Requestfully Yours* (1985)★★★, *The Many Moods Of Oliver Jones* (c.1986)★★, *Jazz And Ribs Live At Biddle's* (1986)★★, *Cookin' At Sweet Basil* (1987)★★, with Clark Terry *Just Friends* (1989)★★★, *Northern Summit* (Enya 1990)★★★, *A Class Act* (Enya 1991)★★★, *From Lush To Lively* (Justin Time 1995)★★★★.

Jones, Paul

b. 24 February 1942, Portsmouth, Hampshire, England. Jones began his singing career while studying at Oxford University. One of several aspirants 'sitting in' with the trailblazing Blues Incorporated, he subsequently joined the Mann Hugg Blues Brothers, which evolved into **Manfred Mann** in 1963. This superior R&B act enjoyed several notable hits, including '5-4-3-2-1', 'Do Wah Diddy Diddy' and 'Pretty Flamingo'. The dissatisfied vocalist left the line-up in July 1966, enjoying two UK Top 5 hits with the decidedly poppy 'High Time' (1966) and 'I've Been A Bad, Bad Boy' (1967). The latter was drawn from the soundtrack to *Privilege*, a socio-political film set in the near future in which Jones starred with the fashion model Jean Shrimpton. Subsequent singles, including 'Thinking Ain't For Me', 'It's Getting Better' and 'Aquarius', were minor successes as the artist increased his thespian commitments. Numerous appearances on stage and on celluloid followed, although he maintained a singing career through occasional solo recordings. Jones also contributed to the original recording of the **Tim Rice/Andrew Lloyd Webber** musical *Evita*, but in 1979 he rekindled his first musical love with the formation of the **Blues Band**. He has continued to lead this popular unit whenever acting commitments allow and Jones hosts two weekly blues/gospel radio programmes, demonstrating that his enthusiasm is backed up by a sound knowledge of both genres. In the early 90, Jones suprised a great many people with his polished performances, co-starring with **Elaine Delmar**, in the UK tours of the nostalgia shows *Hooray for Hollywood* and *Let's Do It*.

● ALBUMS: *My Way* (HMV 1966)★★★, *Privilege* film soundtrack (HMV 1967)★★★, *Love Me Love My Friends* (HMV 1968)★★, *Come Into My Music Box* (Columbia 1969)★★, *Crucifix On A Horse* (Vertigo 1971)★★, *Drake's Dream* film soundtrack (President 1974)★★, with Jack Bruce *Alexis Korner Memorial Concert Vol. 1* (Indigo 1995)★★★, *Mule* (Fat Possum 1995)★★★.

● COMPILATIONS: *Hits And Blues* (One-Up 1980)★★, *The Paul Jones Collection: Volume One: My Way* (RPM 1996)★★, *The Paul Jones Collection: Volume Two: Love Me, Love My Friend* (RPM 1996)★★, *The Paul Jones Collection: Volume Three: Come Into My Music Box* (RPM 1998)★★.

Jones, Philly Joe

b. Joseph R. Jones, 15 July 1923, Philadelphia, Pennsylvania, USA, d. 30 August 1985. Jones began his drumming career in his home town, later moving to New York where he worked with many leading bebop musicians. Despite this early exposure to **Charlie Parker**, **Dizzy Gillespie** and other innovators, Jones was able to adapt to the stylistic needs of any group in which he played. Although proficient in bands led by mainstreamers such as **Ben Webster** and **Lionel Hampton** he was happiest in his many fruitful associations with modernists, among whom were **Tadd Dameron**, **John Coltrane** and **Miles Davis**. His tenure with Davis occupied a substantial slice of the 50s; in the following decade he played and recorded with **Gil Evans**, **Bill Evans** and led his own groups. In the late 60s he lived briefly in the UK, playing with musicians such as **Kenny Wheeler** and **Pete King** and also teaching. In the early 80s Jones formed the band Dameronia, with which to play the music of his former associate. Whether subtly encouraging or with sustained power, often working with a minimal, scaled-down drum kit, Jones was able to adjust his playing style to accommodate any group or individual.

● ALBUMS: *Blues For Dracula* (Riverside 1958)★★★, *Drums Around The World* (Riverside 1959)★★★, *Showcase* (Riverside 1959)★★★, *Philly Joe's Beat* (Atlantic 1960)★★★, *Trailways Express* (Black Lion 1968)★★, *'Round Midnight* (1969)★★★, *Mo' Jo* (Black Lion 1969)★★★, *Mean What You Say* (Sonet 1977)★★, *Philly Mignon* (1977)★★★, *Drum Song* (Galaxy 1978)★★, *Advance!* (1978)★★, *To Tadd With Love* (1982)★★★, *Dameronia* (Uptown 1983)★★★, *Look, Stop And Listen* (Uptown 1983)★★★, *Filet De Sole* (Marge 1992)★★★.

Jones, Quincy

b. Quincy Delight Jones Jnr., 14 March 1933, Chicago, Illinois, USA. Jones began playing trumpet as a child and also developed an early interest in arranging, studying at the **Berklee College Of Music**. When he joined **Lionel Hampton** in 1951 it was as both performer and writer. With Hampton he visited Europe in a remarkable group that included rising stars **Clifford Brown**, **Art Farmer**, **Gigi Gryce** and **Alan Dawson**. Leaving Hampton in 1953, Jones wrote arrangements for many musicians, including some of his former colleagues and **Ray Anthony**, **Count Basie** and **Tommy Dorsey**. He mostly worked as a freelance but had a stint in the mid-50s as musical director for **Dizzy Gillespie**, one result of which was the 1956 album *World Statesman*. Later in the 50s and into the 60s Jones wrote charts and directed the orchestras for concerts and record sessions by several singers, including **Frank Sinatra**, **Billy Eckstine**, **Brook Benton**, **Dinah Washington** (an association that included the 1956 album *The Swingin' Miss 'D'*), **Johnny Mathis** and **Ray Charles**, whom he had known since childhood. He continued to write big band charts, composing and arranging albums for Basie, *One More Time* (1958-59) and *Li'l Ol' Groovemaker...Basie* (1963). By this time, Jones was fast becoming a major force in American popular music. In addition to playing he was busy writing and arranging, and was increasingly active as a record producer. In the late 60s and 70s he composed scores for around 40 feature films and hundreds of television shows. Among the former were *The Pawnbroker* (1965), *In Cold Blood* (1967) and *In The Heat Of The Night* (1967), while the latter included the long-running *Ironside* series and *Roots*. Other credits for television programmes include *The Bill Cosby Show*, *NBC Mystery Series*, *The Jesse Jackson Series*, *In The House* and *Mad TV*. He continued to produce records featuring his own music played by specially assembled orchestras. As a record producer Jones had originally worked for **Mercury**'s Paris-based subsidiary Barclay, but later became the first black vice-president of the company's New York division. Later, he spent a dozen years with **A&M Records** before starting up his own label, Qwest. Despite suffering two brain aneurysms in 1974 he showed no signs of reducing his high level of activity. In the 70s and 80s, in addition to many film soundtracks, he produced successful albums for **Aretha Franklin**, **George Benson**, **Michael Jackson**, the **Brothers Johnston** and other popular artists. With Benson he produced *Give Me The Night*, while for Jackson he helped to create *Off The Wall* and *Thriller*, the latter proving to be one of the bestselling albums of all time. He was also producer of the 1985 number 1 charity single 'We Are The World'. Latterly, Jones has been involved in film and television production, not necessarily in a musical context. As a player, Jones was an unexceptional soloist; as an arranger, his attributes are sometimes overlooked by the jazz audience, perhaps because of the manner in which he has consistently sought to create a smooth and wholly sophisticated entity, even at the expense of eliminating the essential characteristics of the artists concerned (as some of his work for Basie exemplifies). Nevertheless, with considerable subtlety he has fused elements of the blues and its many offshoots into mainstream jazz, and has found ways to bring soul to latter-day pop in a manner that adds to the latter without diminishing the former. His example has been followed by many although few have achieved such a level of success. A major film documentary, *Listen Up: The Lives Of Quincy Jones*, was released in 1990, and five years later Jones received the Jean Hersholt Humanitarian Award at the Academy Awards ceremony in Los Angeles. This coincided with *Q's Jook Joint*, a celebration of his 50 years in the music business with re-recordings of selections from his extraordinarily varied catalogue. The album lodged itself at the top of the *Billboard* jazz album chart for over four months. The film *Austin Powers* prompted a release of his 60s classic 'Soul Bossa Nova' in 1998.

● ALBUMS: *Quincy Jones With The Swedish/U.S. All Stars* (Prestige 1953)★★★, *This Is How I Feel About Jazz* (ABC-Paramount 1957)★★★, *Go West Man* (ABC-Paramount 1957)★★★, *The Birth Of A Band* (Mercury 1959)★★★, *The Great Wide World Of Quincy Jones* (Mercury 1960)★★★, *Quincy Jones At Newport '61* (Mercury 1961)★★★, *I Dig Dancers* (Mercury 1961)★★★, *Around The World* (Mercury 1961)★★★, *The Quintessence* (Impulse 1961)★★★, with Billy Eckstine *Billy Eckstine & Quincy Jones At Basin St. East* (Mercury 1962)★★★, *Big Band Bossa Nova* (Mercury 1962)★★★, *Quincy Jones Plays Hip Hits* (Mercury 1963)★★★, *The Boy In The Tree* (1963)★★★, *Quincy's Got A Brand New Bag* (Mercury 1964)★★★, *Quincy Jones Explores The Music Of Henry Mancini* (Mercury 1964)★★★, *Golden Boy* (Mercury 1964)★★★, *The Pawnbroker* (Mercury 1964)★★★, *Quincy Plays For Pussycats* (Mercury 1965)★★★, *Walk Don't Run* (Mainstream 1966)★★★, *The Slender Thread* (Mercury 1966)★★★, *The Deadly Affair* (Verve 1967)★★★, *Enter Laughing* (Liberty 1967)★★★, *In The Heat Of The Night* film soundtrack (United Artists 1967)★★★, *In Cold Blood* film soundtrack (Colgems 1967)★★★, *Banning* (1968)★★★, *For The Love Of Ivy* (ABC 1968)★★★, *The Split* (1968)★★★, *Jigsaw* (1968)★★★, *A Dandy In Aspic* (1968)★★★, *The Hell With Heroes* (1968)★★★, *MacKennas Gold* (RCA 1969)★★★, *The Italian Job* film soundtrack (Paramount 1969)★★★, *The Lost Man* (1969)★★★, *Bob & Carol & Ted & Alice* (Bell 1969)★★★, *John And Mary* (A&M 1969)★★★, *Walking In Space* (A&M 1969)★★★, *Gula Matari* (A&M 1970)★★★, *The Out Of Towners* (United Artists 1970)★★★, *Cactus Flower* (Bell 1970)★★★, *The Last Of The Hot Shots* (1970)★★★, *Sheila* (1970)★★★, *They Call Me Mr Tibbs* (United Artists 1970)★★★, *Smackwater Jack* (A&M 1971)★★★, *The Anderson Tapes* (1971)★★★, *Dollars* (1971)★★★, *Man And Boy* (1971)★★★, *The Hot Rock* (Prophesy 1972)★★★, *Ndeda* (Mercury 1972)★★★, *The New Centurions* (1972)★★★, *Come Back Charleston Blue* (Atco 1972)★★★, *You've Got It Bad Girl* (A&M 1973)★★★, *Body Heat* (A&M 1974)★★★, *This Is How I Feel About Jazz* (Impulse 1974)★★★, *Mellow Madness* (A&M 1975)★★★, *I Heard That!* (A&M 1976)★★★, *Roots* (A&M 1977)★★★, *Sounds ... And Stuff Like That* (A&M 1978)★★★, *The Wiz* (MCA 1978)★★★, *The Dude* (A&M 1981)★★★, *The Color Purple* film soundtrack (Qwest 1985)★★★, *Back On The Block* (Qwest 1989)★★★, *Listen Up, The Lives Of Quincy Jones* (Qwest 1990)★★★, with Miles Davis *Live At Montreux* recorded 1991 (Reprise 1993)★★★★, *Q's Jook Joint* (Qwest 1995)★★★★.

● COMPILATIONS: *Compact Jazz: Quincy Jones* (Phillips/Polygram 1989)★★★★.

● VIDEOS: *Miles Davis And Quincy Jones: Live At Montreux* (1993).

● FURTHER READING: *Quincy Jones*, Raymond Horricks.

● FILMS: *Listen Up: The Lives Of Quincy Jones* (1990).

Jones, Reunald

b. 22 December 1910, Indianapolis, Indiana, USA, d. 1989. Jones came from a musical family; his father and two brothers were professional musicians and he was a cousin of **Roy Eldridge**. Jones played trumpet with various bands around Minneapolis in the late 20s; joined **Speed Webb**'s noted **territory band** in 1930, and thereafter swung through many leading bands of the 30s and early 40s, notably those of **Don Redman**, **Claude Hopkins**, **Chick Webb**, **Jimmie Lunceford** and **Duke Ellington**. In 1952 he joined **Count Basie**, playing lead trumpet until 1957. He subsequently played with **Woody Herman** and spent several years working in studio bands, a period which included stints backing **Nat 'King' Cole** on television and playing with **Gene Ammons**. A strikingly good lead trumpeter, Jones seldom attracted attention, unless it was as a result of a calculatedly casual habit he adopted while with Basie of playing with one hand in his pocket. His few recorded solos included some with Chick Webb, 'Let's Get Together' and 'When Dreams Come True', and 'Swingin' With The Fat Man' with Redman.

● ALBUMS: with Count Basie *Sixteen Men Swinging* (1953)★★★★.

● COMPILATIONS: *The Chronological Chick Webb* (1929-34)★★★★.

Jones, Richard M.

b. 13 June c.1889, Donaldsonville, Louisiana, USA, d. 8 December 1945. Although Jones had learned piano from an early age, as a teenager he played on various wind instruments in dancebands and marching bands in his home town. Later, he reverted to piano, playing solo and as a bandleader. He worked with a number of leading New Orleans musicians before moving to Chicago in 1918. He performed in several bands, but was also active in music publishing and as an executive with **OKeh Records**. During the 20s he recorded with his own pick-up bands and also played with many other recording artists of the day, notably **Louis Armstrong**. He continued playing and occasionally recording during the 30s and early 40s. His compositions include 'Lonesome Nobody Cares', popularized by **Sophie Tucker**, 'Riverside Blues' and, best known of all, 'Trouble In Mind'. He died in 1945.

● COMPILATIONS: included on *Jazz Sounds Of The 20s, Volume 4: The Blues Singers* (1923-31 recordings)★★, *Complete Works 1923-36, Volumes 1 & 2* (RST 1996)★★★★, *Richard M. Jones And The Blues Singers* (Document 1996)★★★.

Jones, Rickie Lee

b. 8 November 1954, Chicago, Illinois, USA. Jones emerged from a thriving Los Angeles bohemian sub-culture in 1979 with a buoyant debut album, peppered with images of streetwise characters and indebted, lyrically, to beat and jazz styles. The set included 'Chuck E.'s In Love', a US Top 5 single, and 'Easy Money', a song covered by **Little Feat** guitarist **Lowell George**. Other selections bore a debt to **Tom Waits** to whom Jones was briefly romantically linked. Although *Rickie Lee Jones* garnered popular success and critical plaudits, the singer refused to be rushed into a follow-up. Two years later, *Pirates*, a less instantaneous, yet more rewarding collection, offered a greater perception and while still depicting low-rent scenarios, Jones revealed a hitherto hidden emotional depth. *Girl At Her Volcano*, a collection of live material and studio out-takes, marked time until the release of *The Magazine* in 1984. The ambitious work confirmed the artist's imagination and blended her accustomed snappy, bop-style ('Juke Box Fury', 'It Must Be Love') with moments of adventurousness, in particular the multi-part 'Rorschachs'. The album also confirmed Jones as an expressive vocalist, at times reminiscent of **Laura Nyro**. However, it was six years before a further album, *Flying Cowboys*, was issued and, while lacking the overall strength of its predecessors, the record maintained its creator's reputation for excellence. The set also marked a fruitful collaboration with the **Blue Nile**. *Naked Songs* was her contribution to the unplugged phenomenon while *Ghostyhead* embraced dance/techno rhythm.

● ALBUMS: *Rickie Lee Jones* (Warners 1979)★★★★, *Pop Pop* (Geffen 1981)★★, *Pirates* (Warners 1981)★★★★, *Girl At Her Volcano* (Warners 1982)★★, *The Magazine* (Warners 1984)★★★, *Flying Cowboys* (Geffen 1990)★★★, *Traffic From Paradise* (1993)★★★, *Naked Songs: Live And Acoustic* (Reprise 1995)★★, *Ghostyhead* (Reprise 1997)★★★.

● VIDEOS: *Naked Songs* (Warner Music Vision 1996).

Jones, Rodney

b. 30 August 1956, New Haven, Conneticut, USA. Jones was raised in a musical family and plays bass and drums as well as guitar. He studied improvization with **John Lewis** at the City College of New York and guitar with a variety of teachers. He became a regular studio musi-

cian before playing with the Music Complex Orchestra led by pianist **Jaki Byard** (1975). In the late 70s Jones worked with the groups of **Chico Hamilton** and **Dizzy Gillespie** as well as forming his own quartet. He toured the world with the Subtle Sounds jazz group in the early 80s before joining vocalist **Lena Horne**. He is a meticulous musician whose aim is 'to make each note have a meaning'. He has won a Certificate of Merit from New Orleans (1977) and a recording grant from the National Endowment for the Arts (1983).

● ALBUMS: *Articulation* (1978)★★★, *When You Feel The Love* (1980)★★★, *Friends* (1981)★★, *My Funny Valentine* (1981)★★★.

Jones, Salena

b. Joan Shaw, 29 January 1944, Newport News, Virginia, USA. After starting to sing in her home-town (which she shares with **Ella Fitzgerald** and **Pearl Bailey**), Jones tried her luck in New York. Like so many other singers of note, she won a talent contest at Harlem's **Apollo** theatre, singing 'September Song', and was soon appearing professionally at the Village Vanguard. In the mid-60s she left the USA for Europe, singing in Paris and London, where she appeared at **Ronnie Scott**'s club attracting considerable praise. She appeared on television and had success with 'A Walk In The Black Forest'. In 1978 she made her first visit to Japan, which proved to be her destiny for almost two decades. Hugely popular in the Far East, she made numerous albums, including 20 for JVC alone. In the mid-90s she renewed her following in the UK with appearances at London's Pizza on the Park and she also appeared at European festivals and in the USA. She worked on the Concord Fujitsu jazz tour in 1995, backed by **Benny Green**, **Ray Brown** and **Scott Hamilton**. The following year she made her first album outside the Far East for 18 years with the Save the Children fund release, *It Amazes Me*. That same year, she began recording in London for Jay/Ter and also toured the USA with a band that included **Alan Barnes**. A distinctive smoky sound lends itself well to Jones's ballad interpretations and when backed by jazz musicians she comfortably accommodates the rhythmic aspects of the music without becoming a full-fledged jazz singer. As a headliner for over 30 years, Jones has a very large following and in the late 90s those of her fans who reside in Europe or the USA were at last able to see and hear her in person and to obtain her records with comparative ease, thus catching up with what the Japanese have been enjoying all along.

● ALBUMS: *It Amazes Me* (HMV 1995)★★, *On Broadway - Only Love* (Ter 1996)★★, *In Hollywood - Making Love* (Ter 1996)★★★, *Salena Jones Meets Kenny Burrell & Richie Cole* (Vinegate 1997)★★★★.

Jones, Sam

b. 12 November 1924, Jacksonville, Florida, USA, d. 15 December 1981. A dependable bass-player, cellist and composer of some fine tunes, Jones never achieved the kind of critical esteem which was accorded other players whose reputations were built during the 50s. The under-estimation of Jones's talent is surprising in view of his contribution to a number of excellent bands, including those of **Cannonball Adderley** (1955-56 and 1959-66), **Oscar Peterson** (1966-69) and **Cedar Walton** from 1971. His partnerships with **Billy Higgins** (in Walton's trio) and **Louis Hayes** (with Adderley and Peterson) were models of the imaginative support that a good modern, mainstream rhythm section should provide. Jones also worked with **Tiny Bradshaw, Illinois Jacquet, Kenny Dorham, Thelonoious Monk, Clark Terry, Bill Evans**, and **Johnny Hodges**. In the 10 years before his death he freelanced and led a big band.

● ALBUMS: *The Soul Society* (1960)★★★, *The Chant* (1961)★★★, *Down Home* (1962)★★★, *Seven Minds* (1974)★★, *Cello Again* (1976)★★, *Changes And Things* (1977)★★★, *Something In Common* (1977)★★★, *Visitation* (1978)★★★, *The Bassist* (1979)★★★, *Something New* (1979)★★.

Jones, Shirley

b. 31 March 1934, Smithton, Pennsylvania, USA. An actress and singer whose film portrayals of sweet and wholesome ingénues in the 50s contrasted sharply with her Academy Award-winning performance as Burt Lancaster's prostitute girlfriend in *Elmer Gantry* (1960). After taking singing lessons from an early age, Jones performed in stage productions before making her film debut opposite **Gordon MacRae** in the excellent film version of **Richard Rodgers** and **Oscar Hammerstein II**'s *Oklahoma!* (1955). So successful was the collaboration that the two stars came together again a year later for another Rodgers and Hammerstein project, *Carousel*. After appearing with **Pat Boone** in *April Love* (1957), Jones turned in an impressive acting performance alongside **James Cagney** in the musical comedy-drama *Never Steal Anything Small*, joined a host of other stars in *Pepe*, and made one or two lacklustre features before partnering **Robert Preston** in another fine screen adaptation of a Broadway show, *The Music Man* (1962). From then on, Shirley Jones eschewed musical films for dramatic roles in big-screen features and on television. She was married for a time to the actor and singer Jack Cassidy, and she co-starred with her step-son, **David Cassidy**, in the top-rated television series *The Partridge Family* in the early 70s. Later in the decade she had her own show entitled *Shirley*. She continued to sing in nightclubs and concerts, and in the late 80s undertook a 14-week tour of the USA in *The King And I* with David Carradine. In the summer of 1994 she appeared with Marty Ingels in a provincial production of A.R. Gurney's two-hander *Love Letters*, and also starred in a Detroit revival of *The King And I*.

Jones, Slick

b. Wilmore Jones, 13 April 1907, Roanoke, Virginia, USA, d. 2 November 1969. Jones began playing drums as a child in Virginia where his father and brother were also musicians. While still in his teens he moved to New York to study and then began playing with **Fletcher Henderson**'s band. In 1936 he began a long association with **Fats Waller**, appearing on numerous recording dates. After Waller's death he played with small bands led by **Stuff Smith, Una Mae Carlisle, Eddie South** and others. He was also with **Claude Hopkins, Don Redman, Gene Sedric, Wilbur De Paris, Doc Cheatham** and **Eddie Durham** through into the early 60s when poor health interfered with his career. Particularly adept with brushes, Jones's drumming had a sprightliness that helped lift the musicians he backed.

● ALBUMS: *Fats Waller Live At the Yacht Club* (Giants of Jazz 1938)★★★.

Jones, Spike

b. Lindley Murray, 14 December 1911, Long Beach, California, USA, d. 1 May 1965. After learning to play the drums while still at high school, Jones began playing professionally in and around Los Angeles. He secured a great deal of work on radio, eventually forming his own band, the City Slickers. With a rag-bag collection of musical instruments and sound effects machines, Jones played novelty songs many of which were send-ups of currently popular recordings. Among his big successes of the 40s and early 50s were 'Der Fuehrer's Face', 'The Sheik Of Araby', 'Oh! By Jingo!', 'Cocktails For Two', 'Chloe', 'Holiday For Strings', 'Hawaiian War Chant', 'William Tell Overture', 'All I Want For Christmas Is My Two Front Teeth' (US number 1 in 1948), 'Dance Of The Hours', 'Rudolph, The Red-Nosed Reindeer', 'I Saw Mommy Kissing Santa Claus', 'I Went To Your Wedding', and 'You Always Hurt The One You Love'. Members of his crazy crew included his wife, Helen Grayco, and **Red Ingle**. Jones appeared in several films of the 40s, including *Thank Your Lucky Stars, Meet The People, Bring On The Girls, Ladies' Man*, and *Variety Girl*, and later made the transfer from radio and records into television. His popularity declined in his later years but in the late 80s a number of his records were re-released.

● ALBUMS: *Spike Jones Plays The Charleston* (RCA Victor 1952)★★★, *Bottoms Up* (RCA Victor 1952)★★★, *Spike Jones Murders Carmen* (RCA Victor 1953)★★★, *Lets Sing A Song For Christmas* (Verve 1956)★★, *Dinner Music for People Who Aren't Very Hungry* (Verve 1957)★★★, *35 Reasons Why Christmas Can Be Fun* (Verve 1958)★★, *Omnibust* (Liberty 1959)★★★, *60 Years Of Music America Hates Best* (Liberty 1959)★★★, *In Hi-Fi* (Warners 1959)★★★, *In Stereo* (Warners 1960)★★★, *Thank You Music Lovers* (RCA Victor 1960)★★, *Washington Square* (Liberty 1963)★★, *Spike Jones New Band* (Liberty 1963)★★, *Plays Hank Williams Hits* (Liberty 1965)★, *Is Murdering the Classics* (RCA Victor 1965)★★.

● COMPILATIONS: *The Best Of Spike Jones* (RCA Victor 1967)★★★, *The Best Of Spike Jones And His City Slickers* (1993)★★★.

● FURTHER READING: *Spike Jones Off The Record: The Man Who Murdered Music*, Jordan R. Young.

Jones, Steve

b. 3 September 1955, London, England. Formerly the provider of the guitar behind Johnny Rotten's sneer in the **Sex Pistols**, Jones's basic but powerful style was then employed as part of the underachieving **Professionals** (with former Sex Pistol member Paul Cook). Prior to that he had worked with the **Avengers** in the USA. He later played a substantial role in the creation of two records: **Iggy Pop**'s *Blah Blah Blah* (1986) and ex-**Duran Duran** member Andy Taylor's *Thunder* (1987). His first solo venture, however, was a lacklustre affair, with Jones's rough Cockney voice spread thinly over a set that mingled rock numbers with, to the horror of old punks, ballads. The worst offender in this category was the comical version of 'Love Letters'. A capable, fluent man with a rhythm guitar, given a microphone Jones came across as forced and inarticulate, a situation not helped by the clumsy moralism of tracks such as 'Drugs Suck'. Undeterred, Jones proceeded to make the same mistakes a second time with *Fire And Gasoline*. Co-produced and co-written with Ian Astbury of the **Cult**, and with a vocal contribution from **Guns N'Roses**' Axl Rose on the Pistols revival track 'Did You No Wrong', it offered further evidence of Jones's decline. Billy Duffy of the Cult even managed to outgun the old stager with his solo on 'Get Ready'. Collectively, the albums offer a sad footnote to the career of one of rock and pop's most influential guitarists. Jones has since worked as part of The Neurotic Outsiders, alongside John Taylor (ex-Duran Duran) and Duff McLagan and Matt Sorum of Guns N'Roses, with the group releasing a self-titled album for **Madonna**'s Maverick label in 1996. The collaboration led to Jones replacing the departed Slash as Guns N'Roses guitarist.

● ALBUMS: *Mercy* (Gold Mountain/MCA 1987)★★, *Fire And Gasoline* (Gold Mountain/MCA 1989)★★.

Jones, Thad

b. Thaddeus J. Jones, 28 March 1923, Pontiac, Michigan, USA, d. 20 August 1986. A self-taught trumpet player, Jones began playing with a band led by his older brother, **Hank Jones**, in his early teens. He developed his technique and advanced his musical knowledge during military service and in several dancebands. In the early 50s he played in a band led by **Billy Mitchell**, which also included his younger brother, **Elvin Jones**. In 1954 Thad was with **Charles Mingus**; the same year he also joined **Count Basie**, an engagement that lasted until 1963. In the mid-60s Jones formed The Jazz Orchestra, which he co-led with **Mel Lewis**. During this period he extended his writing activities, composing and arranging the bulk of this remarkable band's outstanding book. In 1979 Jones quit The Jazz Orchestra and emigrated to Denmark, where he wrote for and performed with the Danish Radio Big Band, often playing valve trombone (which he had taken up following a lip injury). He also appeared with the Swedish Radio Big Band and formed a band of his own, Eclipse. In 1985 he took on the leadership of the Count Basie Orchestra, leaving in February the following year, some six months before his death. A lyrical player, especially on the slightly mellower flügelhorn, Jones was a superbly inventive, bebop-influenced soloist with a crisp tone. Despite such gifts, however, Jones's major contribution to jazz was his extensive library of compositions and arrangements for big bands. In these he ranged widely, experimenting with meters not usually adopted by jazz orchestras, and comfortably incorporating various popular fads and fancies into jazz with a skill that ensured their survival long after fashions had changed.

● ALBUMS: *The Fabulous Thad Jones* (Debut 1954)★★★★, *Jazz Collaborations* (Debut 1954)★★★, *Mad Thad* (Period 1956)★★★, *Detroit New York Junction* (Blue Note 1956)★★★★, *The Magnificent Thad Jones* (Blue Note 1957)★★★, *After Hours* (Blue Note 1957)★★★★, *Motor City Scene* (United Artists 1959)★★★, with Pepper Adams *Mean What You Say* (Milestone 1966)★★★★, with Mel Lewis *The Jazz Orchestra* (1966)★★★, with Lewis *Presenting Joe Williams* (1966)★★★, with Lewis *Live At The Village Vanguard* (Solid State 1967)★★★, with Lewis *Featuring Miss Ruth Brown* (Solid State 1968)★★★, with Lewis *Monday Night* (Solid State 1968)★★★, with Lewis *Central Park North* (Solid State 1969)★★★, with Lewis *Paris-1969* (1969)★★★, with Lewis *Consummation* (1970)★★★, with Lewis *Suite For Pops* (1972)★★★, *Thad Jones, Mel Lewis, Manuel De Sica And The Jazz Orchestra* (1973)★★★, with Lewis *Live In Tokyo* (1974)★★★, with Lewis *Potpourri* (1974)★★★, with Swedish Radio Big Band *Greetings And Salutations* (1975)★★, with Lewis *New Life* (1975)★★, *The Thad Jones-Mel Lewis Jazz Orchestra* (1976)★★★, with Lewis *Live In Munich* (1976)★★★, with Lewis *Thad And Aura Rully* (1977)★★★, *Monica Zetterlund And The Thad Jones-Mel Lewis Jazz Orchestra* (1977)★★★, *The Thad Jones-Mel Lewis Quartet* (1977)★★★, *Thad Jones-Mel Lewis And Umo* (1977)★★, *By Jones, I Think We've Got It* (1978)★★, with Danish Radio Big Band *A Good Time Was Had By All* (1978)★★★, *Live At Monmarte* (Storyville 1978)★★★, *Eclipse* (Storyville 1979)★★★, *Jazzhus Slukefter* (1980)★★, *Three And One* (Steeplechase 1985)★★.

Jones, Tom

b. Thomas Jones Woodward, 7 June 1940, Pontypridd, Mid-Glamorgan, Wales. One of the most famous pop singers of the past three decades, Jones began his musical career in 1963 as vocalist in the group Tommy Scott And The Senators. The following year, he recorded some tracks for **Joe Meek**, which were initially rejected by record companies. He was then discovered by **Decca** A&R producer/scout Peter Sullivan and, following the recommendation of **Dick Rowe**, was placed in the hands of the imperious entrepreneur **Phil Solomon**. That relationship ended sourly, after which Scott returned to Wales. One evening, at the Top Hat Club in Merthyr Tydfil, former **Viscounts** vocalist **Gordon Mills** saw Scott's performance and was impressed. He soon signed the artist and changed his name to Tom

Jones. His first single, 'Chills And Fever', failed to chart but, early in 1965, Jones' second release 'It's Not Unusual', composed by Mills and Les Reed, reached number 1 in the UK. The exuberant arrangement, reinforced by Jones's gutsy vocal and a sexy image, complete with hair ribbon, brought him instant media attention. Jones enjoyed lesser hits that year with the ballads 'Once Upon A Time' and 'With These Hands'. Meanwhile, Mills astutely insured that his star was given first choice for film theme songs, and the **Burt Bacharach/Hal David** composition 'What's New Pussycat?' was a major US/UK hit. By 1966, however, Jones's chart fortunes were in decline and even the title track of a James Bond movie, *Thunderball*, fell outside the UK Top 30. Before long, the former chart topper was back playing working men's clubs and his period of stardom seemed spent. Mills took drastic action by regrooming his protégé for an older market. Out went the sexy clothes in favour of a more mature, tuxedoed image. By Christmas 1966, Jones was effectively relaunched owing to the enormous success of 'Green Green Grass Of Home', which sold over a million copies in the UK alone and topped the charts for seven weeks. Jones retained the country flavour with a revival of **Bobby Bare**'s 'Detroit City' and 'Funny Familiar Forgotten Feelings'. In the summer of 1966, he enjoyed one of his biggest UK hits with the intense 'I'll Never Fall In Love Again', which climbed to number 2. The hit run continued with the restrained 'I'm Coming Home', and the dramatic, swaggering 'Delilah', which added a sense of Victorian melodrama with its macabre line: 'I felt the knife in my hand, and she laughed no more'. In the summer of 1968, Jones again topped the *New Musical Express* charts with 'Help Yourself'.

As the 60s reached their close, Mills took his star to America where he hosted the highly successful television show, *This Is Tom Jones*. Unlike similar series, Jones' show attracted some of the best and most critically acclaimed acts of the era. An unusual feature of the show saw Jones duetting with his guests. Some of the more startling vocal workouts occurred when Jones teamed-up with **David Crosby** during a **Crosby, Stills And Nash** segment, and on another occasion with **Blood, Sweat And Tears**' David Clayton-Thomas. Although Jones logged a handful of hits in the UK during the early 70s, he was now an American-based performer, whose future lay in the lucrative Las Vegas circuit. Jones became enormously wealthy during his supper-club sojourn and had no reason to continue his recording career, which petered out during the 70s. It was not until after the death of Mills, when his son Mark Woodward took over his management, that the star elected to return to recording. His recording of 'The Boy From Nowhere' (from the musical *Matador*) was perceived as a personal anthem and reached number 2 in the UK. It was followed by a re-release of 'It's Not Unusual' which also reached the Top 20. In 1988, a most peculiar collaboration occurred between Jones and the **Art Of Noise** on an appealing kitsch

version of **Prince**'s 'Kiss'. The song reached the UK Top 5 and Jones performed the number at the London Palladium. Soon after, he appeared with a number of other Welsh entertainers on a recording of Dylan Thomas's play for voices *Under Milk Wood*, produced by **George Martin**. Jones's continued credibility was emphasized once more when he was invited to record some songs written by the mercurial **Van Morrison**. After more than a decade on the Las Vegas circuit, Jones could hardly have hoped for a more rapturous welcome in the UK, both from old artists and the new élite. He entered the digital age with a hard dance album produced by various hands including Trevor Horn, **Richard Perry**, **Jeff Lynne** and Youth. Jones clearly demonstrated that his voice felt comfortable with songs written by Lynne, the **Wolfgang Press** and **Diane Warren**.

● ALBUMS: *Along Came Jones* (Decca 1965)★★★, *A-Tom-Ic Jones* (Decca 1966)★★★★, *From The Heart* (Decca 1966)★★★, *Green, Green, Grass Of Home* (Decca 1967)★★★★, *Live At The Talk Of The Town* (Decca 1967)★★★, *Delilah* (Decca 1968)★★★, *Help Yourself* (Decca 1968)★★★★, *Tom Jones Live In Las Vegas* (Decca 1969)★★★, *This Is Tom Jones* (Decca 1969)★★★, *Tom* (1970)★★★, *I, Who Have Nothing* (1970)★★★, *Tom Jones Sings She's A Lady* (1971)★★★, *Tom Jones Live At Caeser's Palace, Las Vegas* (1971)★★★, *Close Up* (1972)★★★, *The Body And Soul Of Tom Jones* (1973)★★★, *Somethin' 'Bout You Baby I Like* (1974)★★★, *Memories Don't Leave Like People* (1975)★★★, *Say You'll Stay Until Tomorrow* (1977)★★★, *Rescue Me* (1980)★★★, *Darlin'* (1981)★★★, *Matador - The Musical Life Of El Cordorbes* (1987)★★★, *At This Moment* (1989)★★★, *After Dark* (1989)★★★, with Engelbert Humperdinck *Back To Back* (1993)★★★, *Velvet Steel Gold* (1993)★★★, *The Lead And How To Swing It* (ZTT 1994)★★★★.

● COMPILATIONS: *13 Smash Hits* (Decca 1967)★★★★, *Tom Jones: Greatest Hits* (1973)★★★★, *Tom Jones: 20 Greatest Hits* (1975)★★★★, *The World Of Tom Jones* (1975)★★★★, *Tom Jones Sings 24 Great Standards* (1976)★★★, *What A Night* (1978)★★★, *I'm Coming Home* (1978)★★★, *Super Disc Of Tom Jones* (1979)★★★, *Tom Jones Sings The Hits* (1979)★★★, *Do You Take This Man* (1979)★★★, *The Very Best Of Tom Jones* (1980)★★★, *Rescue Me* (1980)★★★, *The Golden Hits* (1980)★★★, *16 Love Songs* (1983)★★★, *The Tom Jones Album* (1983)★★★, *The Country Side Of Tom Jones* (1985)★★★, *The Soul Of Tom Jones* (1986)★★★, *Love Songs* (1986)★★★, *The Great Love Songs* (1987)★★★, *Tom Jones - The Greatest Hits* (1987)★★★, *It's Not Unusual - His Greatest Hits* (1987)★★★★, *The Complete Tom Jones* (1993)★★★, *The Ultimate Hit Collection: 1965-1988* (Repertoire 1995)★★★, *Collection* (Spectrum 1996)★★★, *In Nashville* (Spectrum 1996)★★★, *At His Best* (Pulse 1997)★★★, *The Best Of . . . Tom Jones* (Deram 1998)★★★, *The Ultimate Performance* (Reactive 1998)★★.

● VIDEOS: *One Night Only* (Watchmaker Productions 1997).

● FURTHER READING: *Tom Jones: Biography Of A Great Star*, Tom Jones. *Tom Jones*, Stafford Hildred and David Griffen.

Jones, Tom (lyricist)
(see **Schmidt, Harvey**)

Jones, Tutu
b. Johnny Jones Jnr., 9 September 1967, Dallas, Texas, USA. Given his nickname while still a baby by his guitar-playing father, Jones began his musical career at the age of six, playing drums for his uncle's band, L.C. Clark And The Four Deuces. Entering his teenage years, Jones hooked up with local bluesman and club owner R.L. Griffin, which gave him the opportunity to work behind **Barbara Lynn**, **Little Milton**, Little Joe Blue and **Z.Z. Hill**. Through his work with Blue, he took an interest in playing the guitar, which led to him playing drums with one band and guitar with another. In 1989, he formed Tutu Jones And The Right Time Showband, supporting **Clarence Carter** and **Denise LaSalle**, among others. His first album consisted of original material that nevertheless revealed the acknowledged influences of **Freddie King**, **Little Milton** and **Stevie Ray Vaughan**. His guitar playing is clean and fluent, making up in bravura what it lacks in originality. His songwriting is similarly derivative but confident, flirting with blues and soul clichés without entirely succumbing to their temptation. His occasional indulgence in hyperbole, best exemplified in the titles of two proficient instrumentals, 'Too Blues To Be True' and 'Outstanding', may indicate a requisite sense of humour.
● ALBUMS: *I'm For Real* (JSP 1994)★★★, *Blue Texas Soul* (Bullseye Blues 1996)★★★.

Jones, Vince
b. Vincent Hugh Jones, 24 March 1954, Paisley, Scotland. In 1955 Jones's family emigrated to Australia and lived in Wollongong, New South Wales. The son of a musician, he was exposed to the jazz greats at an early age and he began to play trumpet in local bands. As an admirer of cool jazz he was especially influenced by **Chet Baker** and **Miles Davis**. In 1974 Jones began many years of playing and singing on the New South Wales club and jazz circuit. In 1982 he recorded his debut, *Watch What Happens*, which featured standards and some original material. The success of the album enabled him to form a sextet that played and toured extensively. More recordings followed, and Jones became a popular festival and cabaret attraction. In 1990 he accepted an acting role in the ABC period series, *Come In Spinner*. The subsequent album soundtrack of standards, with Jones and **Grace Knight**, became a milestone in the Australian recording industry as the biggest selling Australian jazz album ever, with sales in excess of 200,000. Jones rejected the commercial and celebrity opportunities that beckoned, preferring to concentrate on his own musicality and he released and produced new albums each year. Standards became less obvious in his repertoire and originals, written by himself or band members, became more prominent. In 1992, he toured Europe with his sextet which included **Barney McAll**, Lloyd Swanton and Andrew Gander. There were concerts in The Netherlands, Germany, England and at the **Montreux International Jazz Festival**. An effective concert and cabaret performer, Jones's sensitive, almost tortured persona, complimented the melancholic nature of his music, which became increasingly more introspective. In 1992 after the release of *Trustworthy Little Sweethearts*, the Jones band toured Europe to considerable success. When he returned to Australia Jones retreated to his isolated farm in rural Victoria to compose new material. The 1994 album, *Future Girl*, contained original material, much of it inspired by his passion for the environment and conservation. Jones maintains full control in all aspects of his recordings and performs only when inclined, but his fierce independence and dedication to his art has resulted in a highly original and important body of work. By the mid-90s he had developed more as a vocalist who occasionally played the trumpet. His singing is individual and eloquent, containing sensitive phrasing and sincerity. In 1996 Jones worked on a compilation release with **EMI Records** and once again toured Europe.
● ALBUMS: *Watch What Happens* (EMI 1982)★★★, *Spell* (EMI 1983)★★, *For All Colours* (EMI 1984)★★★, *On The Brink Of It* (EMI 1985)★★★, *It All Ends Up In Tears* (EMI 1987)★★★, *Trustworthy Little Sweethearts* (EMI 1988)★★★★, *One Day Spent* (EMI 1990)★★★, *Come In Spinner* (EMI 1990)★★★★, *Future Girl* (EMI 1993)★★★, *Here's To The Miracles* (EMI 1995)★★★.

Jones, Vivian
Jones has established a long and fruitful career as a reggae vocalist, having initially been regarded as a **lovers rock** performer. He emerged in the late 70s as the lead singer with the Doctor Birds, but by 1980 Jones was pursuing a solo career. 'Good Morning' topped the reggae chart and signalled the beginning of a run of hits for the singer. His popularity spread from the UK to Jamaica where his reputation continued to prosper. In 1988 he was acclaimed as the best reggae performer and won the award for four consecutive years. He released a series of reggae hits, including the chart-topping 'Strong Love', 'Extra Classic', 'I Care', 'A Woman Should Be' and 'Sugar Love'. He also performed on duets with the élite of female UK reggae vocalists, including Sylvia Tella on 'Nu Chat To Me', Debbie Gordon for 'Mr Right' and **Deborahe Glasgow** on the acclaimed 'The First'. By the mid-90s Jones had established his own Imperial House label, and he escaped his lovers rock image when in 1994 he released the rootsy *Iyaman*, an approach that continued with *The King*. In 1994, 'Happiness' reaffirmed his status as one of the UK's top lovers rock performers. In 1995 he recorded his debut for **Fashion Records**, 'Dedicated To His Majesty', which featured an outstanding performance from the contemporary DJ Nico Junior. On his own label he released 'Love Is For Lovers' and an album of the same name, and maintained a high profile through-

out 1996/7 with a series of hits including 'Let's Go Again' and 'Very Thought Of You'. His international notoriety was enhanced when the US-based Wooligan label released 'Jah See Dem A Come', providing the singer with a Top 10 hit in reggae charts worldwide.

● ALBUMS: *Jah Works* (Shaka 1990)★★★, *Strong Love* (Jet Star 1993)★★★, *Iyaman* (Imperial House 1994)★★, *Love Is For Lovers* (Imperial House 1995)★★★, *Reggae Max* (Jet Star 1997)★★★★.

Jones, Wizz

b. Raymond Ronald Jones, 25 April 1939, Croydon, Surrey, England. After seeing **Big Bill Broonzy**, **Jack Elliot** and **Muddy Waters** in 1957, at London's Roundhouse, Wizz Jones took up the guitar. Having learned from the blues licks of **Long John Baldry** and **Davey Graham** whilst playing Soho coffee bars, he busked his way around Europe and Africa throughout the early 60s. On his return to England, together with Pete Stanley (banjo), Jones formed a bluegrass duo and worked on the folk circuit until 1967 (releasing one album for **EMI**). In the 70s Jones was working with the group Lazy Farmer, which included his wife Sandy (b. 23 July 1945, London, England; banjo), John Bidwell (flute/guitar), Don Cogin (banjo) and Jake Walton (hurdy-gurdy/dulcimer). Still playing many of the blues numbers that inspired him, his style transcends the straight 'folk' tag, and he is currently performing, festivals and clubs with his son Simeon (b. 10 March 1964; saxophone/flute/harmonica).

● ALBUMS: with Pete Stanley *Sixteen Tons Of Bluegrass* (EMI 1965)★★★, with Pete Stanley, Mac Wiseman *Folkscene* (1966)★★, *Wizz Jones* (United Artists 1969)★★★★, *The Legendary Me* (Village Thing 1970)★★★★, *Solo Flight* (1971)★★★, *Right Now* (CBS 1971)★★★, *Winter Song* (1972)★★★, *When I Leave Berlin* (Village Thing 1974)★★★, with Lazy Farmer *Lazy Farmer* (1975)★★, *Happiness Was Free* (1976)★★, *Magical Flight* (Plant Life1977)★★★, with Werner Lammerhirt *Roll On River* (1981)★★★, *The Grapes Of Life* (Run River 1988)★★★, with Simeon Jones *Late Nights & Long Days* (Fellside 1993)★★★, *Dazzling Stranger* (Scenescof 1995)★★★.

● COMPILATIONS: *The Village Thing Tapes* (Wandertute 1993)★★★★.

Joneses

An R&B vocal group from Pittsburgh, Pennsylvania, USA, the Joneses were typical of the vocal group renaissance of the early 70s, recording in the soft-soul mode that featured a falsetto lead, pretty harmonies and fully orchestrated arrangements. The original group started in Pittsburgh in 1969, but the recording group arrived at its final line-up after moving to New York to record for V.M.P. Records in the early 70s. The members of the V.M.P. group featured falsetto lead Cy Brooks, Glenn Dorsey, Sam White and brothers Reginald and Wendell Noble, and on that label they had a New York hit with 'Pretty Pretty'. Moving to the Pride label in 1973, they had another local hit, 'Pull My String'.

Mercury Records then took notice and signed them. Brooks left at this point and his lead spot was taken by baritone Harold Taylor (who had earlier been with the group in Pittsburgh). At Mercury the Joneses first hit locally in Baltimore with 'Baby Don't Do It', but in 1974 they began a string of national hits with 'Hey Babe' (number 18 R&B). They then followed with their only crossover hit, 'Sugar Pie Guy' (number 10 R&B, number 47 pop), also in 1974. They also had considerable success with 'I Can't See What You See In Me' (number 28 R&B) in 1975. The Joneses broke up in 1975, but in the following years there were four resurrections of the group, the first in 1977 and the last in 1992, and each time the only constant in the new line-ups was Glenn Dorsey. These new Joneses groups recorded with Epic, Spring, Collectables and **Atlantic Records** with varying success.

● ALBUMS: *Keeping Up With* (Mercury 1974)★★★, *The Joneses* (Epic 1977)★★★, *Hard* (Atlantic 1990)★★.

● COMPILATIONS: *Golden Soul Classics From The Early Years* contains one new track, the rest are their pre-Mercury releases (Collectables 1994)★★★.

Joni Mitchell - Joni Mitchell

Known by the cognoscenti as *Song To A Seagull*, this David Crosby-produced album is a sparse and beautiful folk album. This was her debut, yet already it was apparent that here was an immense lyrical talent. Her great songwriting melodies came later, as these are standard-fare folky items. Few writers had used such a conversational style in song, and for that alone, this was a milestone of a record. The listener was encouraged and welcomed into a stream of dialogue and tales without needing to know what they were all about. However, in the last track, we do know the identity of the man who sails and takes her to his schooner: he has a walrus moustache and is very large.

● Tracks: *I Had A King; Michael From Mountains; Night In The City; Marcie; Nathan La Franeer; Sisotowbell Lane; The Dawntreader; The Pirate Of Pennance; Song To A Seagull; Cactus Tree*.

● First released 1968

● UK peak chart position: did not chart

● USA peak chart position: 189

Jook

Formed in London, England in 1971, Jook was a mod band allied to skinhead aggression. (Ian) Ralph Kimmett (vocals), Trevor White (guitar), Ian Hampton (bass) and Chris Townson (drums) were skilfully managed by John Hewlett who, like Townson, was a former member of **John's Children**. Jook completed five singles for **RCA Records** including 'Oo Oo Rudi', 'King Kapp' (both 1973) and 'Bish Bash Bosh' (1974). Each were tough pop songs, reminiscent of early **Slade** and **Sweet**, with White's jabbing guitar work adding extra excitement. The group split up in 1974 when White and Hampton joined **Sparks**, whom Hewlett also managed. Townson joined Andy Ellison, another ex-member of John's Children, in **Jet**, while Kimmett took up a post at **Warner Brothers Records**.

Joos, Herbert

b. 21 March 1940, Karlsruhe, Germany. Joos studied fluegelhorn, trumpet and bass, but also plays baritone-horn and alphorn. In the first half of the 70s he was a member of **Modern Jazz Quintet**, New Jazz Ensemble and the Fourmenonly group. During this period he also worked with different bands at Free Jazz Meeting in Baden-Baden, Free Jazz Day in Frankfurt and in a fluegelhorn workshop together with **Kenny Wheeler**, **Ian Carr**, **Harry Beckett** and Ack van Rooyen. During the Blow project he collaborated with Bernd Konrad and Wolfgang Czelusta. He had also led his own quartet and orchestra. The most acknowledged of his assignments has been the one with the Vienna Art Orchestra. His warm and big tone and the romantic-impressionistic influences combined with the affinity of free improvisation gives him a strong and personal profile within the European jazz community.

● ALBUMS: *The Philosophy Of The Fluegelhorn* (1973)★★★, *Daybreak* (1976)★★★★, *Blow* (1977)★★★, *Mel-An-Cho* (1981)★★★, *Still Life* (1983)★★★, with Hans Koller And The International Brass Company *The Horses* (1980)★★, *Live At The Jazz Festival Frankfurt* (1981)★★, with Part Of Art *Son Sauvage* (1983)★★★, with Harry Pepl, Jon Christensen *Cracked Mirrors* (1987)★★★, with Vienna Art Choir *Five Old Songs* (1984)★★, with Vienna Art Orchestra *Tango From Obango* (1979)★★★, *Concerto Piccolo* (1981)★★★, *Suite For The Green Eighties* (1982)★★★, *From No Time To Rag Time* (1983)★★★, *Perpetuum Mobile* (1945)★★, *Nightride Of A Lonely Saxophoneplayer* (1985)★★★, *Jazzbuhne Berlin '85* (1985)★★★, *Two Little Animals* (1987)★★★, *Inside Out* (1988)★★★, *Blues For Brahms* (1989)★★★, *Innocence Of Clichés* (1989)★★★, with Eberhard Weber *Eberhard Weber Orchestra* (1988)★★★★.

Joplin, Janis

b. 19 January 1943, Port Arthur, Texas, USA, d. 4 October 1970, Los Angeles, California, USA. Having made her performing debut in December 1961, this expressive singer subsequently enjoyed a tenure at Houston's Purple Onion club. Drawing inspiration from **Bessie Smith** and **Odetta**, Joplin developed a brash, uncompromising vocal style quite unlike accustomed folk madonnas **Joan Baez** and **Judy Collins**. The following year she joined the Waller Creek Boys, an Austin-based act that also featured Powell St. John, later of **Mother Earth**. In 1963 Janis moved to San Francisco where she became a regular attraction at the North Beach Coffee Gallery. This initial spell was blighted by her addiction to amphetamines and in 1965 Joplin returned to Texas in an effort to dry out. She resumed her university studies, but on recovery turned again to singing. The following year Janis was invited back to the Bay Area to front **Big Brother And The Holding Company**. This exceptional improvisational blues act was the ideal foil to her full-throated tech-

nique and although marred by poor production, their debut album effectively captures an early optimism.

Joplin's reputation blossomed following the **Monterey Pop Festival**, of which she was one of the star attractions. The attendant publicity exacerbated growing tensions within the line-up as critics openly declared that the group was holding the singer's potential in check. *Cheap Thrills*, a joyous celebration of true psychedelic soul, contained two Joplin 'standards', 'Piece Of My Heart' and 'Ball And Chain', but the sessions were fraught with difficulties and Joplin left the group in November 1968. **Electric Flag** members **Mike Bloomfield**, **Harvey Brooks** and **Nick Gravenites** helped assemble a new act, initially known as Janis And The Joplinaires, but later as the Kozmic Blues Band. Former Big Brother Sam Andrew (guitar, vocals), plus Terry Clements (saxophone), Marcus Doubleday (trumpet), Bill King (organ), Brad Campbell (bass) and Roy Markowitz (drums) made up the band's initial line-up which was then bedevilled by defections. A disastrous debut concert at the **Stax**/Volt convention in December 1968 was a portent of future problems, but although *I Got Dem Ol' Kozmic Blues Again Mama* was coolly received, the set nonetheless contained several excellent Joplin vocals, notably 'Try', 'Maybe' and 'Little Girl Blue'. However, live shows grew increasingly erratic as her addiction to drugs and alcohol deepened. When a restructured Kozmic Blues Band, also referred to as the Main Squeeze, proved equally uncomfortable, the singer dissolved the band altogether, and undertook medical advice. A slimmed-down group, the Full Tilt Boogie Band, was unveiled in May 1970. Brad Campbell and latecomer John Till (guitar) were retained from the previous group, while the induction of Richard Bell (piano), Ken Pearson (organ) and Clark Pierson (drums) created a tighter, more intimate sound. In July they toured Canada with the **Grateful Dead**, before commencing work on a 'debut' album. The sessions were all but complete when, on 4 October 1970, Joplin died of a heroin overdose at her Hollywood hotel.

The posthumous *Pearl* was thus charged with poignancy, yet it remains her most consistent work. Her love of 'uptown soul' is confirmed by the inclusion of three **Jerry Ragovoy** compositions - 'My Baby', 'Cry Baby' and the suddenly anthemic 'Get It While You Can' - while 'Trust Me' and 'A Woman Left Lonely' show an empathy with its southern counterpart. The highlight, however, is **Kris Kristofferson**'s 'Me And Bobby McGee', which allowed Joplin to be both vulnerable and assertive. The song deservedly topped the US chart when issued as a single and despite numerous interpretations, this remains the definitive version. Although a star at the time of her passing, Janis Joplin has not been accorded the retrospective acclaim afforded other deceased contemporaries. She was, like her idol **Otis Redding**, latterly regarded as one-dimensional, lacking in subtlety or nuance. Yet her impassioned approach was precisely her attraction - Janis knew few boundaries, artistic or personal - and her sadly brief catalogue is marked by bare-nerved honesty.

● ALBUMS: *I Got Dem Ol' Kozmic Blues Again Mama!* (Columbia 1969)★★★, *Pearl* (Columbia 1971)★★★★, *Janis Joplin In Concert* (Columbia 1972)★★★.

● COMPILATIONS: *Greatest Hits* (Columbia 1973)★★★★, *Janis* film soundtrack including live and rare recordings (1975)★★★, *Anthology* (Columbia 1980)★★★, *Farewell Song* (Columbia 1982)★★★, *Janis* 3-CD box-set (Legacy 1995)★★★★, *18 Essential Songs* (Columbia 1995)★★★.

● FURTHER READING: *Janis Joplin: Her Life And Times*, Deborah Landau. *Going Down With Janis*, Peggy Caserta as told to Dan Knapp. *Janis Joplin: Buried Alive*, Myra Friedman. *Janis Joplin: Piece Of My Heart*, David Dalton. *Love, Janis*, Laura Joplin. *Pearl: The Obsessions And Passions Of Janis Joplin*, Ellis Amburn.

● FILMS: *American Pop* (1981).

Joplin, Scott

b. 24 November 1868, Texarkana, Texas, USA, d. 1 April 1917. Joplin's father was born into slavery, becoming a freeman with Emancipation in 1863. A musical individual, he encouraged the musical aspirations of his sons and daughters. Scott Joplin, who was originally self-taught, moved to St. Louis while still in his teens, by which time he was an accomplished pianist. Although adept in various styles, including that of contemporary classicists such as Louis M. Gottschalk, Joplin excelled in the currently popular ragtime music. In 1894 he was in Sedalia and soon afterwards began committing to paper many of the rags he had heard played by ragtime 'professors' and tunes he had himself composed. One of the latter, 'Maple Leaf Rag', was hugely successful and this recognition encouraged him to turn his attention to extended works in a quasi-classical style. His efforts at ragtime ballets and ragtime operas proved disappointingly uncommercial but his straightforward ragtime tunes continued to be very popular. A failed marriage, the death of his child and the fast decline of his health as he succumbed to a debilitating venereal disease, allied to his losing battle to be accepted as a classical composer, created a desperately sad atmosphere for his declining years. Despite his problems, however, Joplin completed another ragtime opera, *Treemonisha*. Unable to interest anyone in staging the opera, he paid for a run-through performance in 1915 only to see it, too, fail. The following year his illness entered its final stages, he was hospitalized and died some months later in April 1917. In the early 70s ragtime suddenly became popular again and its use and success on the soundtrack of a successful film, *The Sting* (1973), brought Joplin to the attention of a new audience. His tunes including 'The Entertainer', 'Elite Syncopations', 'Solace I', 'Solace II' and 'Chrysanthemum' were heard everywhere, often in rather stately recreations by **Joshua Rifkin** and other classically-trained pianists. Such versions would doubtless have pleased their composer as they avoided jazz inflections, but also failed to reflect much of their lively

and sometimes earthy origins. Joplin's belated recognition as a pioneer of Third Stream Music was confirmed by an acclaimed staging and recording of *Treemonisha* by **Gunther Schuller** and the Houston Grand Opera, performed and released in the mid-70s. Unfortunately most of Joplin's other scores for extended compositions have been lost.

● FURTHER READING: *Scott Joplin and the Ragtime Era*, Peter Gammond. *The Life And Works Of Scott Joplin*, A.W. Reed.

Jor The Comeback - Prefab Sprout

Paddy MacAloon is arguably one of England's finest modern songwriters, and this 1990 release was a gloriously overlong mélange of styles, bound together by some of his most inspired melodies. The nineteen tracks cover a typically diverse range of subject matters, including a quartet of songs about the rise and fall of Elvis Presley that provide the album with its thematic core. Elsewhere, on songs such as 'We Let The Stars Go', 'All The World Loves Lovers' and 'Doo Wop In Harlem' MacAloon's songwriting hit new peaks. Never gaining the commercial success it deserved, *Jordan: The Comeback*'s heady brew even appeared to be a step too far for MacAloon, who did not release another album for seven years.

● Tracks: *Looking For Atlantis; Wild Horses; Machine Gun Ibiza; We Let The Stars Go; Carnival 2000; Jordan: The Comeback; Jesse James Symphony; Jesse James Bolero; Moon Dog; All The World Loves Lovers; All Boys Believe Anything; The Ice Maiden; Paris Smith; The Wedding March; One Of The Broken; Michael; Mercy; Scarlet Nights; Doo Wop In Harlem.*

● First released 1990

● UK peak chart position: 7

● USA peak chart position: did not chart

Jordan, Charley

b. *c.*1890, Mabelvale, Arkansas, USA, d. 15 November 1954, St. Louis, Missouri, USA. Jordan arrived in St. Louis in 1925, and became a major figure on the city's blues scene, being closely associated with **Peetie Wheatstraw**, and acting as a talent scout for record companies. In 1928, he was crippled by a shooting incident connected with his bootlegging activities. Jordan recorded extensively from 1930-37, playing light, clean, but often very complex, ragtime-influenced guitar, and singing his wittily original lyrics in a high, taut voice. He accompanied many of his St. Louis contemporaries on disc, notably **'Hi' Henry Brown**, for whom his second guitar work is a dazzling display of improvising skills.

● COMPILATIONS: *It Ain't Clean* (Agram 1980)★★★, *Charley Jordan 1932-1937* (Document 1987)★★★.

Jordan, Clifford

b. 2 September 1931, Chicago, Illinois, USA, d. 27 March 1993, New York City, New York, USA. Jordan began his professional career playing tenor saxophone in R&B bands in the Chicago area. In 1957 he moved to

New York, made the album *Blowin' In From Chicago* with fellow tenor saxophonist **John Gilmore** and then spent time in groups led by **Max Roach** and **Horace Silver**. In the 60s he played with artists including **J.J. Johnson**, **Charles Mingus**, **Kenny Dorham**, **Julian Priester** and also led his own bands, touring extensively. In 1965 he released a tribute to **Leadbelly**, *These Are My Roots*, and in the late 60s began to record for the Strata East label: outstanding releases include *In The World* and *Glass Bead Game*. In the 70s he worked with **Cedar Walton**, often in a quartet context with **Sam Jones** and **Billy Higgins** (known as the Magic Triangle), recording some distinctive large ensemble albums for Muse (*Remembering Me-Me*, *Inward Fire*), and he also established a reputation as a teacher. In the 80s Jordan continued to record regularly, both as a guest with leaders such as **Slide Hampton** (*Roots*) and in various small groups of his own, where his associates have included Walton again (*Half Note*), **Barry Harris** (*Repetition*) and **Junior Cook** (*Two Tenor Winner*). With his roots in blues and the bebop mainstream tempered by work with modernists such as Mingus, **Eric Dolphy** and **Don Cherry**, Jordan was both an accessible, adventurous player and an impressive, underrated composer/arranger.

● ALBUMS: with John Gilmore *Blowing In From Chicago* (1957)★★★, *Clifford Jordan All Stars* (1957)★★★, *Cliff Craft* (1957)★★★, *Spellbound* (1960)★★★, with Sonny Red *A Story Tale* (1961)★★, *Starting Time* (1961)★★★, *Bearcat* (1961-62)★★, *These Are My Roots* (1965)★★★, *Clifford Jordan And His Orchestra* (1966)★★, *In The World* (1969)★★★, *Glass Bead Game* (Strata East 1973)★★★, *The Highest Mountain* (Steeplechase 1975)★★★, *Night Of The Mark VII* (1975)★★★, *On Stage Vols 1-3* (Steeplechase 1975)★★, *Firm Roots* (Steeplechase 1975)★★★, *The Highest Mountain* (1975)★★★, *Remembering Me-Me* (1976)★★, *Inward Fire* (1977)★★★, *The Adventurer* (1978)★★★, *Hello Hank Jones* (1978)★★★, *Adventurer* (Muse 1981)★★, with Jaki Byard *Dr Chicago* (1984)★★★, *Repetition* (Soul Note 1984)★★★, with Junior Cook *Two Tenor Winner!* (Criss Cross 1984)★★★, *Half Note* (1985)★★★, *Royal Ballads* (Criss Cross 1986)★★, *Masters From Different Worlds* (Mapleshade 1990)★★★, *Down Through The Years* (Milestone 1992)★★★.

Jordan, Duke

b. Irving Sidney Jordan, 1 April 1922, New York City, New York, USA. After studying classical music, Jordan played piano in a number of swing era bands, including Al Cooper's **Savoy Sultans**. In the mid-40s, he became involved in bebop, playing with **Charlie Parker** and others. Later in the decade and in the early 50s Jordan played in bands led by **Sonny Stitt** and **Stan Getz** and thereafter led his own units. Also in the early 50s, he married the singer **Sheila Jordan**, but they later split up. Jordan's career drifted for a while in the late 60s, but from 1972 onwards he was very active, playing in many parts of the world, especially in Scandinavia, and since 1978 he has lived in Denmark, recording extensively for the Copenhagen label Steeplechase. A lyrically

inventive player, Jordan has also composed a number of tunes, one of which, 'Jordu', became a bebop classic.

● ALBUMS: *The Duke Jordan Trio* (Savoy 1954)★★★, *Do It Yourself Jazz* (Savoy 1955)★★★, *The Street Swingers* (1955)★★★, *The Duke Jordan Quintet* (1955)★★, *Flight To Jordan* (1955)★★★★, *Les Liaisons Dangereuses* (1962)★★★, *East And West Of Jazz* (1962)★★★, *Brooklyn Brothers* (1973)★★★, *The Murray Hill Caper* (1973)★★★★, *Flight To Denmark* (Steeplechase 1973)★★★, *Two Loves* (Steeplechase 1973)★★★, *Truth* (1975)★★★, *Duke's Delight* (1975)★★, *Misty Thursday* (Steeplechase 1975)★★★, *Lover Man* (1975)★★, *The Duke Jordan Trio Live In Japan* (Steeplechase 1976)★★, *Osaka Concert: Vols 1* and *2* (Steeplechase 1976)★★★, *Flight To Japan* (1976)★★★, *I Remember Bebop* (1977)★★★, with others *They All Played Bebop* (1977)★★, *Duke's Artistry* (Steeplechase 1978)★★, *The Great Session* (Steeplechase 1978)★★★, *Midnight Moonlight* (1979)★★★, *Tivoli One* (Steeplechase 1979)★★★, *Wait And See* (Steeplechase 1979)★★★, *Solo Masterpieces* (Steeplechase 1979)★★, *Lover Man* (1979)★★★, *Change A Pace* (1979)★★★, *Thinking Of You* (Steeplechase 1979)★★★, *Blue Duke* (RCA 1983)★★★, *As Time Goes By* (Steeplechase 1986)★★★★, *Time On My Hands* (Steeplechase 1986)★★★, *Tivoli Two* (Steeplechase 1995)★★★.

Jordan, Fred

b. 5 January 1922, Ludlow, Shropshire, England. In 1952, **Peter Kennedy**, who then worked for the BBC, visited Jordan, a farm labourer, having been told what a good singer he was. Kennedy consequently recorded Jordan for the folk song archive of the BBC. Many of the songs came from his Yorkshire-born father, his mother, and from the travellers. In 1959, he appeared at the English Folk Dance and Song Society Festival wearing his everyday working clothes, but it was his singing that commanded attention. As a result, Jordan increasingly performed in folk clubs and in concerts. *When The Frost Is On The Pumpkin* included versions of such 'standards' as 'Barbara Allen', 'The Bonny Bunch Of Roses', 'The Banks Of Claudy' and 'When Joan's Ale Was New'. *Shropshire Lad* was produced by Peter Kennedy.

● ALBUMS: *Fred Jordan: Traditional Songs* (Eroica Recording Services 60s)★★, *Songs Of A Shropshire Farm Worker* (Topic 1966)★★, *When The Frost Is On The Pumpkin* (Topic 1974)★★★, *Shropshire Lad* (Folktracks 1975)★★★, *'In Course Of Time...': Songs Sung By Fred Jordan* (EFDSS 1991)★★★.

Jordan, Louis

b. Louis Thomas Jordan, 8 July 1908, Brinkley, Arkansas, USA, d. 4 February 1975, Los Angeles, California, USA. Saxophonist and singer, Jordan began touring as a teenager with the Rabbit Foot Minstrels, and supported classic blues singers **Ma Rainey**, **Ida Cox** and **Bessie Smith**. In the 30s, after relocating to New York City, he played in the bands of **Louis Armstrong**, **Clarence Williams**, **Chick Webb** and **Ella Fitzgerald**, appearing with these orchestras on records for RCA

Victor, Vocalion and **Decca**, and making his vocal debut with Webb's band on novelty songs such as 'Gee, But You're Swell' and 'Rusty Hinge'. In 1938 Jordan formed his first combo, the Elks Rendez-Vous Band (after the club at which he had secured a residency), and signed an exclusive deal with Decca. While he had been with Webb, he had often been brought to the front to perform a blues or novelty swing number. These spots had been so well-received that, from the start of his own band, Jordan had decided to promote himself as a wacky musical comedian with a smart line in humorous jive. In early 1939, in line with this image, he changed the band's name to the Tympany Five and enjoyed steady, if unspectacular, success with recordings of 'T-Bone Blues' (1941), 'Knock Me A Kiss' and 'I'm Gonna Move To The Outskirts Of Town' (1942), 'What's The Use Of Gettin' Sober (When You Gonna Get Drunk Again)' and 'Five Guys Named Moe' (1943). After World War II, the Tympany Five really hit their stride with a string of million-selling records, including 'Is You Is Or Is You Ain't My Baby?' (1944), 'Caldonia (Boogie)' (1945), '(Beware, Brother) Beware!', 'Choo Choo Ch'boogie' (1946) and 'Saturday Night Fish Fry' (1949). Other hits which were not so commercially successful, but which are inextricably linked with Jordan's name nevertheless include 'G.I. Jive', 'Buzz Me', 'Ain't Nobody Here But Us Chickens', 'Let The Good Times Roll', 'Reet, Petite And Gone', 'Open The Door, Richard', 'School Days', and 'Blue Light Boogie'. Jordan remained with Decca until 1954, when he switched briefly to Aladdin (1954), **RCA**'s 'X' subsidiary (1955) and **Mercury** (1956-57) but, sadly, his reign was coming to an end; the new generation wanted 'fast and loud' not 'smooth and wry', and Jordan, dogged by ill-health, could not compete against rock 'n' roll artists such as **Little Richard** and **Chuck Berry**, even though his songs were being recycled by these very performers. Chuck Berry ('Run Joe' and 'Ain't That Just Like A Woman') and **B.B. King** 'Do You Call That A Buddy?', 'Early In The Morning', 'Just Like A Woman', 'How Blue Can You Get?', 'Buzz Me', 'Let The Good Times Roll' and 'Jordan For President!' in particular, have been successful with Jordan covers. Surprisingly, his performances were taken to the heart of many Chicago blues artists with songs like 'Somebody Done Hoodooed The Hoodoo Man', 'Never Let Your Left Hand Know What Your Right Hand's Doin'' and 'Blue Light Boogie'; even **Bill Haley** would often admit that his 'revolutionary' musical style was simply a copy of the Tympany Five's shuffles and jumps that had been recorded the previous decade in the same Decca studios.

Owing to his fluctuating health Louis Jordan spent the 60s and 70s working when he could, filling summer season engagements and recording occasionally for small companies owned by old friends including **Ray Charles** (Tangerine Records), **Paul Gayten** (Pzazz) and **Johnny Otis** (Blues Spectrum). His last recordings were as a guest on trumpeter **Wallace Davenport**'s *Sweet Georgia Brown*, after which he suffered eight months of inactivity due to his deteriorating health, and a fatal heart-attack on 4 February 1975. The main factor that set Jordan apart from most of the competition was that he was at once a fine comedian and a superb saxophonist whose novelty value was never allowed to obscure either his musicianship or that of his sidemen, who at one time or another included trumpeters **Idrees Sulieman** and Freddie Webster (both major influences on boppers like **Miles Davis** and **Dizzy Gillespie**), tenor saxophonists Paul Quinichette, **Maxwell Davis** and Count Hastings, drummer Shadow Wilson, and pianists **Wild Bill Davis** and **Bill Doggett**. That Louis Jordan influenced all who came after him, and continues to be a prime source of material for films, theatre, television advertising, R&B bands and bluesmen, 40 or 50 years after his heyday, is a testament to his originality and talent. In 1990 a musical by Clarke Peters entitled *Five Guys Named Moe*, which featured 'music written or originally performed by Louis Jordan', opened in London. Four years later it overtook *Irma La Douce* to become the longest-running musical ever at the Lyric Theatre. After initially lukewarm revues, another production enjoyed a decent run on Broadway.

● ALBUMS: *Go! Blow Your Horn* (Score 1957)★★★★, *Somebody Up There Digs Me* (Mercury 1957)★★★★, *Man, We're Wailin'* (Mercury 1958)★★★★, *Let The Good Times Roll* (Decca 1958)★★★★, *Hallelujah ... Louis Jordan Is Back* (1964)★★★★, *One Sided Love* (1969)★★★★, *Louis Jordan's Greatest Hits* (1969)★★★★, *Louis Jordan* (1971)★★★★, *Great R&B Oldies* (1972)★★★★, *I Believe In Music* (1974)★★★★, *In Memoriam* (1975)★★★★, *Louis Jordan's Greatest Hits Volume 2* (1975)★★★★, *The Best Of Louis Jordan* (1975)★★★★, *Louis Jordan With The Chris Barber Band* (1976)★★★, *Three Hot Big Band Sessions In 1951* (1976)★★★★, *More Stuff* (1976)★★★★, *Some Other Stuff* (1977)★★★★, *Louis Jordan And His Tympany Five* i (1977)★★★★, *Come On ... Get It ...* (1978)★★★★, *Prime Cuts* (1978)★★★★, *Collates* (1979)★★★★, *Good Times* (1980)★★★★, *The Best Of Louis Jordan* (1981)★★★★, with Oran 'Hot Lips' Page *Jumpin' Stuff* (1981)★★★★, *Louis Jordan And His Tympany Five* ii (1982)★★★★, *The Last Swinger, The First Rocker* (1982)★★★★, *Choo Choo Ch'boogie* (1982)★★★★, *G.I. Jive* (1983)★★★★, *Cole Slaw* (1983)★★★★, *Look Out!...It's Louis Jordan And The Tympany Five* (1983)★★★★, *Louis Jordan And His Tympany Five, 1944-1945* (1983)★★★★, *Louis Jordan On Film - Reet, Petite And Gone* (1983)★★★★, *Louis Jordan On Film - Look Out Sister* (1983)★★★★, *Go! Blow Your Horn - Part 2* (1983)★★★★, *Jump 'N' Jive With Louis Jordan* (1984)★★★★, *Louis Jordan And Friends* (1984)★★★★, *Jivin' With Jordan* (1985)★★★★, *Hoodoo Man 1938-1940* (1986)★★★★, *Knock Me Out 1940-1942* (1986)★★★★, *Somebody Done Hoodooed The Hoodoo Man* (1986)★★★★, *Louis Jordan And His Tympany Five, More 1944-1945* (1986)★★★★, *Rock And Roll Call* (1986)★★★★, *Rockin' And Jivin', Volume 1* (1986)★★★★, *Rockin' And Jivin', Volume 2* (1986)★★★★, *Louis Jordan And His Tympany Five* (1986)★★★★, *Out Of Print* (1988)★★★★, *Greatest Hits* (1989)★★★★, *The V-Discs* (1989)★★★★, *Hits*

And Rarities (1989) ★★★★, *More Hits, More Rarities* (1990) ★★★★, *Rock 'N' Roll* (1990) ★★★★, *The Complete Aladdin Sessions* (1991) ★★★★, *The Complete Recordings 1938 - 1941* (1992) ★★★★.
● FURTHER READING: *Let The Good Times Roll: A Biography Of Louis Jordan*, John Chilton.

Jordan, Luke

b. *c.*1890, possibly either Appomattox or Campbell county, Virginia, USA, d. *c.*1945, Lynchburg, Virginia, USA. Post-war research by Bruce Bastin reveals that Luke Jordan was a prime mover in the blues enclave centred around Lynchburg. It seems that he did not work outside music but relied on his talent and local fame. Victor Records discovered him in 1927 and he recorded for them in Charlotte, North Carolina, in August of that year. Jordan's records sold well enough to justify transporting him to New York for a further two sessions in November 1929. Of the total of 10 tracks that he recorded, eight saw release, although only six have been located. The extant sides present a high-pitched singer, given to a fast delivery, backed by a niftily picked Gibson guitar. From the evidence of his records it would seem that a large part of his repertoire was made up from vaudeville songs, although the gambling song 'Pick Poor Robin Clean' may have its roots in the folk tradition. His masterpiece was 'Church Bell Blues', a bravura performance forever associated with him in local tradition, while 'Cocaine Blues' became an early 'crossover' when it was recorded by white bluesman Dick Justice in 1929.
● COMPILATIONS: *The Songster Tradition* (1990) ★★★.

Jordan, Montell

b. Los Angeles, California, USA. Montell Jordan made a huge impact in both the US and UK charts in 1995 with the runaway success of his **Def Jam Records**' single 'This Is How We Do It'. Including a sample from **Slick Rick**, this celebration of life in South Central, Los Angeles, struck a chord with both hip hop fans and modern R&B audiences. Within weeks of release it entered the US R&B Top 10 and then the pop charts, preceding a debut album of the same title. This included several **B.B. King** samples and a guest rap from **Coolio** on the excellent 'Payback'. The lyrics also diverged somewhat from typical Californian swing subjects - 'Daddy's Home' addressing the importance of black fatherhood in the ghettos. He attributes his development in an otherwise hostile environment to the rare presence of both a father and mother as he grew up. Rather than running with the gangs in the 'South Central 'hood', Jordan attended both church and school regularly, eventually graduating from Pepperdine University in Malibu with a degree in Organisational Communication. However, his growing interest in music eventually diverted him from a projected career in law.
● ALBUMS: *This Is How We Do It* (Def Jam 1995) ★★★, *More* (Def Jam 1996) ★★, *Let's Ride* (Def Jam 1998) ★★★.

Jordan, Ronny

b. England. Described by some as 'the quintessential acid-jazz guitarist', Jordan has an intimate and readily accessible musical demeanour which has endeared him to many. By the mid-90s he had begun to disassociate himself with the acid-jazz movement, commenting that 'the way I see acid-jazz, it's more of a fashion statement and I'm not really about that'. Nevertheless, the high profile of the genre had served him well. After signing to **Island Records** subsidiary 4th And Broadway Records in 1991, Jordan released two acclaimed albums and participated in a number of collaborative projects. 1996's *Light To Dark* was a more restrained, mature collection, designed to appeal to jazz purists for the first time. A link with the past was maintained in its rhythms - Jordan favouring pummelling beats informed by a love of good hip hop - while the melodies belonged to an earlier era. 'It's You', the first single to be taken from the album, typified this marriage of the new and the old.
● ALBUMS: *The Antidote* (Island 1991) ★★★, *The Quiet Revolution* (Island 1993) ★★★, *Light To Dark* (Island 1996) ★★.

Jordan, Sheila

b. Sheila Jeanette Dawson, 18 November 1928, Detroit, Michigan, USA. Raised in poverty in Pennsylvania's coal-mining country, Jordan began singing as a child and by the time she was in her early teens was working semi-professionally in Detroit clubs. Her first great influence was **Charlie Parker** and, indeed, most of her influences have been instrumentalists rather than singers. Working chiefly with black musicians, she met with disapproval from the white community but persisted with her career. She was a member of a vocal trio, Skeeter, Mitch And Jean (she was Jean), who sang versions of Parker's solos in a manner akin to that of the later **Lambert, Hendricks And Ross**. After moving to New York in the early 50s, she married Parker's pianist, **Duke Jordan**, and studied with **Charles Mingus** and **Lennie Tristano**, but it was not until the early 60s that she made her first recordings. One of these was under her own name, the other was *The Outer View* with **George Russell**, which featured a famous 10-minute version of 'You Are My Sunshine'. In the mid-60s her work encompassed jazz liturgies sung in churches and extensive club work, but her appeal was narrow even within the confines of jazz. By the late 70s jazz audiences had begun to understand her uncompromising style a little more and her popularity increased - as did her appearances on record, which included albums with pianist **Steve Kuhn**, whose quartet she joined, and an album, *Home*, comprising a selection of Robert Creeley's poems set to music and arranged by **Steve Swallow**. A 1983 duo set with bassist Harvie Swartz, *Old Time Feeling*, comprises several of the standards Jordan regularly features in her live repertoire, while 1990's *Lost And Found* pays tribute to her bebop roots. Both sets display her unique musical trademarks, such as the frequent and unexpected sweeping changes of pitch which still tend to confound an uninitiated audience. Entirely non-derivative, Jordan is one of only a tiny handful of jazz singers who fully deserve the appellation and for whom no other term will do.

● ALBUMS: with George Russell *The Outer View* (1962)★★★, *Portrait Of Sheila* (Blue Note 1962)★★★★, *Confirmation* (1975)vH, *Grapevine Discovery* (1976)★★★, *Sheila* (Steeplechase 1977)★★★, with others *Lennie Tristano Memorial Concert* (1979)★★, *Playground* (1979)★★★, with Harvie Swartz *Old Time Feeling* (Palo Alto 1982)★★, *The Crossing* (Blackhawk 1984)★★★★, *Songs From Within* (MA Recordings 1989)★★★, *Lost And Found* (Muse 1990)★★★, with Mark Murphy *One For Junior* (Muse 1994)★★★★.

Jordan, Stanley

b. 31 July 1959, Chicago, Illinois, USA. Having absorbed a certain amount of theory from an early training on the piano, Jordan taught himself the guitar while in his teens, and performed with the numerous pop and soul groups working around Chicago in the mid-70s. However, winning a prize at the 1976 Reno Jazz Festival inspired Jordan to devote some time to a serious study of music. Studying electronic music, theory, and composition at Princeton University, his reputation quickly spread and he soon found himself playing with **Dizzy Gillespie** and **Benny Carter**. In 1982 he recorded his first album: *Touch Sensitive* was a relatively uninspiring solo collection which registered poor sales. But three years later, Jordan's second album *Magic Touch* was a huge commercial success. Produced by **Al DiMeola**, it featured Onaje Allen Gumbs, Charnett Moffett, and **Omar Hakim**, while retaining some unaccompanied tracks. Since *Magic Touch*, Jordan's band has become a regular feature of the major international jazz festivals. He is commonly known for his development of a complex technique of 'hammering-on' which has enabled him to accompany himself with bass lines and chords.

● ALBUMS: *Touch Sensitive* (1982)★★, *Magic Touch* (Blue Note 1985)★★★, *Standards* (Blue Note 1986)★★★, *Flying Home* (EMI Manhattan 1988)★★★, *Cornucopia* (Blue Note 1990)★★★, *Stolen Moments* (Blue Note 1991)★★★, *Bolero* (Arista 1994)★★★.

Jordan, Steve

b. 15 January 1919, New York, USA, d. 13 September 1993, Alexandria, Virginia, USA. Jordan studied guitar with Allan Reuss who had played with **Benny Goodman**'s band. Steve performed with the big bands of **Will Bradley** and **Artie Shaw** before the war took him off for service in the navy. On his return he played in a series of big bands - the **Casa Loma Orchestra**, **Stan Kenton**, **Jimmy Dorsey** and **Boyd Raeburn**. In the early 50s Jordan became a member of the NBC production staff as well as providing the guitar in the rhythm section on many of the sessions produced by **John Hammond**. Given his role and ability as rhythm

guitarist, he has often been compared to guitarist **Freddie Green** with **Count Basie**'s Orchestra. After completing three years with Benny Goodman in the mid-50s he worked more regularly as a tailor. It was only in 1965 he returned to full-time music with the band of **Tommy Gwaltney** at Blues Alley in Washington.

● ALBUMS: with Vic Dickenson *Showcase* (1953)★★, *Here Comes Mr Jordan* (1972)★★★, *The Many Sounds Of Steve Jordan* (1993)★★★.

Jordan, Taft

b. James Jordan, 15 February 1915, Florence, South Carolina, USA, d. 1 December 1981. Jordan began playing trumpet professionally in 1929 and within four years had achieved such a standard that he was hired by **Chick Webb**. Apart from a few weeks with **Willie Bryant**, Jordan stayed with the band until Webb's death and then continued until 1941 during the period when the band was nominally led by **Ella Fitzgerald**. After briefly leading his own outfit he joined **Duke Ellington** in 1943. From 1947 he worked with various bands, some of which were relatively obscure. In the mid-50s he led his own bands and also played with **Benny Goodman**. In the 60s he was active in the studios and theatre-land, occasionally playing in clubs. In the 70s he worked with the New York Jazz Repertory Company and played with **Earle Warren**. Although the influence of **Louis Armstrong** affected some of his earlier work, both as a trumpeter and a singer, Jordan was a fiery and often inventive player whose solos could ignite a band.

● ALBUMS: *Taft Jordan* (1960)★★★, *Taft Jordan With George Rhodes And His Orchestra* (1960)★★, *Mood Indigo* (1961)★★★.

● COMPILATIONS: *Taft Jordan And The Mob* (1935)★★★, *The Chronological Chick Webb* (1935-39)★★★★, *The Indispensable Duke Ellington Vols 11/12* (1944-46)★★★★.

Jordanaires

This renowned harmony-vocal quartet is best known for their lengthy working relationship with **Elvis Presley**. The group first accompanied the youthful rock 'n' roll star in 1956 during a performance on the pivotal *Louisiana Hayride*. Lead vocalist Gordon Stoker was subsequently featured on Presley's first recordings for **RCA** Victor, notably 'Heartbreak Hotel', while the remaining trio - Neal Matthews (tenor), Hoyt Hawkins (baritone) and Hugh Jarrett (bass) - joined him on the session that produced 'Hound Dog' and 'Don't Be Cruel'. The Jordanaires also supported Presley on the *Steve Allen* and *Milton Berle* television shows, where their clean-cut, conservative appearance contrasted with the impact of the singer's explosive persona. The quartet continued to accompany him throughout the 50s and 60s, although they were noticeably absent from the 'comeback' NBC-TV spectacular, *Elvis* (1968), where their role was taken by girl-group the **Blossoms**. The Jordanaires did not feature on the fruitful sessions spawning 'Suspicious Minds' and 'In The Ghetto', nor the subsequent live appearances, but returned to the fold for recordings undertaken in Nashville during June and September 1970. These marked the end of the Jordanaires' relationship with Presley, but the group remained an integral part of the city's music industry. In 1972 they contributed to *Guitar That Shook The World*, the solo debut by long-time Presley guitarist **Scotty Moore**, and were heavily featured on sessions with **Johnny Cash**, **Kris Kristofferson**, **Don McLean**, **Tracy Nelson** and **Billy Swan**. The Jordanaires - by this point consisting of Stoker, Hawkins, Matthews and new bass player Lovis Nunley - also released several albums in their own right, many of which featured gospel material, but their career remains inextricably linked to that of Elvis Presley. In 1996 they added harmonies to alternative US rock band **Ween**'s album *12 Golden Country Greats*. They continue to tour the world knowing that the audience wants to hear that remarkable smooth harmonic sound, one that has barely changed over five decades.

● ALBUMS: *Beautiful City* 10-inch album (RCA Victor 1953)★★★, *Peace In The Valley* (Decca 1957)★★★★, *Of Rivers And Plants* (Sesac 1958)★★★, *Heavenly Spirit* (Capitol 1958)★★★, *Gloryland* (Capitol 1959)★★★, *Land Of Jordan* (Capitol 1960)★★★★, *To God Be The Glory* (Capitol 1961)★★★, *Spotlight On The Jordanaires* (Capitol 1962)★★★, *We'd Like To Teach The World To Sing* (1972)★★★, *The Jordanaires Sing Elvis' Favourite Spirituals* (Rockhouse 1985)★★★, *The Jordanaires Sing Elvis' Gospel Favourites* (Magnum Force 1986)★★★.

● FILMS: *Jailhouse Rock* (1957), *G.I. Blues* (1960), *Blue Hawaii* (1961), *Girls Girls Girls* (1962), *Fun In Acapulco* (1963), *Elvis - The Movie* (1979).

Jory, Sarah

b. 20 November 1969. Jory's musical talents were quickly recognized and as she loved her parents' country records, she began playing steel guitar since the age of five. She appeared in a club the following year and this was followed by her television debut when she was eight. Her father became her manager and she joined Colorado Country. Her first album, however, *Sarah's Steel Line*, was made with the Warrington band **Poacher**. She worked with Colorado Country for four years, followed by an assortment of gigs while she completed her schooling. She regularly went to the USA and appeared on steel guitar conventions. She made her first vocal tape, *No Time At All*, in 1986 and spent some time developing a new act around the pub circuit in Bristol. She formed a new, fully professional band, and in 1991 she opened for **Eric Clapton** in Dublin and undertook a nationwide tour with **Glen Campbell**. She plays banjo, mandolin, guitar and keyboards as well as steel guitar, but, now signed to Ritz, her main chance of stardom is as a vocalist. One 1994 single was an unremarkable revival of **Jackie DeShannon**'s 'When You Walk In The Room', which had also been recently revived by **Pam Tillis**. She was featured in a major UK television documentary about female country singers

on the *South Bank Show*. *Love With Attitude* was recorded in Nashville with the songs and musicians of Music City USA.

● ALBUMS: *Sarah's Steel Line* (1980)★★, *Cross Country* (Sara 1986)★★★, *No Time At All* (1986)★★★, *Sarah's Dream* (Hitsound 1991)★★★, *New Horizons* (Ritz 1992)★★★★, *The Early Years - 20 Steel Guitar Favourites* (Ritz 1993)★★★, *The Early Years - 20 Classic Songs* (Ritz 1993)★★★, *Web Of Love* (Ritz 1994)★★★★, *Love With Attitude* (Ritz 1995)★★★.

● VIDEOS: *An Evening With* (1992).

José José

b. José Romulo Sosa Ortiz, *c.*1948, Mexico. One of the truly traditional artists working in the Latino music firmament, José José, dubbed The Prince Of Songs by his supporters, has recorded gentle, romantic ballads in his affecting baritone for over four decades. The son of opera tenor José Sosa Esquivel and concert pianist Margarita Ortiz, he grew up listening to the music of **Frank Sinatra** and **Johnny Mathis** in addition to native balladeers. His debut single for Orfeon Records was released in 1965, when he was just 17 years old. Following his first appearance on television, he formed the trio Los Peg. Eventually he was offered a solo contract by composer Rubén Fuentes with **RCA Records**. His first album was credited to his new stage name, José José, adopted in tribute to his father, who had recently died. That album, and practically every subsequent recording bearing his name, became a sizeable national hit. Starting in 1971, he also launched a film career, appearing in *Buscando Una Sonrisa*. Several subsequent appearances culminated in a starring role in his last film, *Perdoname Todo* (1995). Despite his retiring demeanour, in stark contrast to some of his peers in the South American recording industry, conservative estimates of his record sales suggest more than 35 million sales. 1984's *Secretos* alone sold four million copies. In the 90s his success began to transfer increasingly to the American charts, where songs such as 'Como Tu', Amnesia' and 'Llora Corazon' became staples of the ***Billboard*** Latin charts. This fact was acknowledged by his induction into the *Billboard* Latin Music Hall Of Fame in 1997.

● ALBUMS: *Le Nave Del Olvido* (RCA 1969)★★, *Secretos* (BMG 1984)★★★★, *30 Anos De Ser El Principe* (MBG 1993)★★★, *Mujeriego* (BMG 1995)★★★.

Josef K

This Edinburgh, Scotland-based band formed in the ashes of punk as TV Art and were influenced by New York bands such as **Television**, **Talking Heads** and the **Velvet Underground**. The original trio of **Paul Haig** (vocals), Malcolm Ross (guitar) and Ron Torrance (drums) were joined briefly by Gary McCormack (later with the **Exploited**), before a more permanent bassist was found in David Weddell. After a name change inspired by Franz Kafka's 1925 novel *The Trial*, Josef K recorded a 10-track demo before committing 'Chance Meeting' to release on Steven Daly's Absolute label, in late 1979. Daly, who was also the drummer for **Orange Juice**, was the co-founder of **Postcard Records**, and thus signed Josef K to the newly formed label. 'Radio Drill Time' was more frantic than their debut, dominated by hectic, awkward chords and Haig's thin, nasal voice. After numerous support slots, 1980 ended with the more low-key, melodic sound of 'It's Kinda Funny'. The single fared well and Josef K were all set to release their debut, *Sorry For Laughing*, during the early months of 1981. However, unhappy with its production, the band scrapped it at the test pressing stage and moved to a Belgian studio, in conjunction with the Les Disques du Crépuscule label. The 1981 session yielded a re-recorded title track (also the strongest single), which joined tracks from the unreleased album as a session for BBC radio disc jockey **John Peel**, while the band returned to Belgium to work on their album. Back at Postcard, they drafted in Malcolm's brother Alistair to play trumpet on a new version of 'Chance Meeting', issued just two months later, coinciding with a full session for Peel. *The Only Fun In Town* emerged in July to a mixed reception. Its frantic, trebly live sound appeared hurried, and betrayed the fact that it had been recorded in just six days. Josef K announced their demise soon afterwards, prompted by Malcolm Ross's invitation to join Orange Juice. Crépuscule issued Josef K's farewell single, 'The Missionary', in 1982, while other tracks surfaced on various compilations. After Ross had joined Orange Juice, Haig worked with Rhythm Of Life before embarking on a solo career. In 1987, Scottish label Supreme International Editions followed the excellent 'Heaven Sent' with *Young And Stupid*, a collection of Peel session material and tracks from the unreleased *Sorry For Laughing*. Then, in 1990, the entire recorded history of Josef K (plus tracks from their original demo) was compiled onto two definitive CDs by Les Temps Moderne.

● ALBUMS: *The Only Fun In Town* (Postcard 1981)★★.
● COMPILATIONS: *Young And Stupid* (Supreme International 1989)★★★, *The Only Fun In Town/Sorry For Laughing* (Les Temps Moderne 1990)★★★.

Josefus

This band was formed in Houston, Texas, USA, in 1969, and comprised of Pete Bailey (vocals/harmonica), Dave Mitchell (guitar), Ray Turner (bass) and Doug Tull (drums). They had previously worked together as United Gas and were also briefly known as Come, under which name they recorded 'Crazy Man'/'Country Boy', before adopting the above appellation. The self-financed *Dead Man* featured a hard-rock version of the **Rolling Stones** 'Gimme Shelter', but is also notable for its lengthy title track. The heavy-styled follow-up, *Josefus*, was a comparative disappointment, and despite an undoubted popularity in Texas, the group was unable to reach a wider audience. They split up in December 1970, although Bailey and Turner were reunited in Stone Axe. In 1978 the vocalist rejoined Mitchell in a reformed Josefus which completed two

singles - 'Hard Luck' and 'Let Me Move You' - on their reactivated Hookah label before disbanding again.
● ALBUMS: *Dead Man* (1969)★★★, *Josefus* (1970)★★.

Joseph And The Amazing Technicolor Dreamcoat

Andrew Lloyd Webber's eventual domination of musical theatre throughout the world started with this show. It was intitially a 20-minute 'pop cantata' based on the biblical character of Joseph, which he wrote with **Tim Rice** for an end-of-term concert at Colet Court Boys' School in the City of London. That was in March 1968, and, during the next five years, it was gradually revised and expanded during performances in the UK at a variety of venues including the Central Hall Westminster, St. Paul's Cathedral, the Edinburgh Festival, the Roundhouse, and the Young Vic. On 17 September 1973, a production opened at London's Albery Theatre, with Gary Bond as Joseph, and ran for 243 performances. Throughout the 70s, the show was often presented in and around London, generally with pop stars such as **Paul Jones** and **Jess Conrad** in the lead, and in 1976 it had its New York premiere at the Brooklyn Academy of Music. Five years later, in November 1981, *Joseph* opened on Broadway, and ran for 824 performances. However, it was not until Lloyd Webber decided to present it at the London Palladium in June 1991, that the piece was finally developed into its present two-hour, two-act form. A significant factor which contributed to its sensational reception in the 2,271-seater house, was the inspired casting of the teeny-boppers' idol **Jason Donovan**, ex-star of the popular Australian television soap, *Neighbours*. When Donovan went on holiday, Lloyd Webber did it again, and replaced him with **Philip Schofield**, another highly popular television personality. He and Donovan proceeded to alternate during much of the run. While he was associated with the show, Donovan sued a fringe magazine, *The Face*, for inferring that he was homosexual. The High Court heard that the hit song from *Joseph*, 'Any Dream Will Do', which Donovan took the the top of the UK chart, was adapted by gays to become 'Any Queen Will Do'. The whole affair has travelled a long way from its inception in 1968. According to one critic, the simple story of Joseph, son of Jacob, and his brothers, which is narrated in this production by Linzi Hately, is 'a lurid, synthetic Joseph, accompanied by spoofs of sentimental American ballads, calypso, and Presley rock', with 'Joseph's prison cell filled with bopping lovelies', and 'an Elvis lookalike in Tutankhamun gear emerging from a vast sphinx, to sing at inordinate length', while 'Donovan, a macho Goldilocks, makes a climactic entrance in primeval batmobile with lion-heads and wings'. Nevertheless, the score which contained Lloyd Webber's tongue-in-cheek pastiches and some of Rice's deceptively ingenuous lyrics retained its appeal, with songs such as 'One More Angel To Heaven', 'Joseph's Coat', 'Go, Go, Go, Joseph', and 'Pharaoh's Story'. When it closed in

January 1994, *Joseph* had become the longest-running show ever at the London Palladium. In the early 90s, Joseph fever spread quickly, and productions were mounted throughout the world. **Donny Osmond** - who once, just like Joseph, was part of a brother act - played the lead in the Canadian production which toured North American breaking records wherever it went, especially in Chicago and Minneapolis. An American production, with Michael Damien in the leading role, opened on Broadway in November 1993 for a limited season. Joseph was played by Darren Day and ex-boy soprano Aled Jones, amongst others, in 1994 and 1995 UK regional productions.

Joseph And The Amazing Technicolor Dreamcoat - 1991 London Cast

Seventy three minutes of playing time from a show that originally ran for some 15 to 20 minutes, means that this album must be a recording of a contemporary production of Andrew Lloyd Webber and Tim Rice's biblical musical. In fact, it is from the highly successful 1991 London Palladium revival which starred Australian actor and pop star Jason Donovan as Joseph and Linzi Hateley as the Narrator. Donovan had a UK number 1 with 'Any Dream Will Do', and the album itself also topped the chart. Nine months after its release it was reported to have sold 500,000 copies.

● Tracks: *Jacob And Sons; Joseph's Dreams; Poor, Poor Joseph; One More Angel In Heaven; Potiphar; Close Every Door; Go Go Go Joseph; Pharaoh Story; Poor Poor Pharaoh; Pharaoh's Dreams Explained; The Brothers Come To Egypt; Benjamin Calypso; Joseph All The Time; Jacob In Egypt; Stone The Crows; Those Canaan Days; Any Dream Will Do; Grovel Grovel; Song Of The King; Who's The Thief?*.
● First released 1991
● UK peak chart position: 1
● USA peak chart position: did not chart

Joseph, Julian

b. 1967, England. Pianist and bandleader Joseph has been at the forefront of attempts to break down barriers between jazz and classical traditions in the 90s. His 20-piece All Star Big Band certainly includes some of the most prominent musicians in both genres, including Tony Remy, Jean Toussaint and **Andy Sheppard**. His records have received excellent reviews from several quarters, yet Joseph treats them as little more than an adjunct to his live performances: 'Recording is just a documentation of where you are creatively. Live is where you move on and do other things.' His concerts, at venues including the Proms at the Royal Albert Hall and the Barbican in London, the Montreal Jazz Festival and the Wigmore Hall, have captured a wide range of supporters. The successful marriage of disparate forms arose as the result of his studies in classical composition at the **Berklee College Of Music** in Boston, Massachusetts, USA, where he would blend the required listening of Prokofiev and Beethoven with jazz influences such as **Miles Davis** and **Herbie Hancock**.

His third album, meanwhile, documented his set at the Wigmore Hall auditorium, with a set featuring Alec Dankworth, Eddie Daniels, **Jason Rebello** and **Johnny Griffin**. In the same year he also performed Gershwin's Piano Concerto In F, live on BBC television, as well as a duet with **Bheki Mseleku**. Afterwards he began a fourth album, this time a studio affair with the aid of drummer Mark Mondesir and bass player Reginald Veal.
● ALBUMS: *The Language Of Truth* (East West 1991)★★★, *Reality* (East West 1993)★★★, *Julian Joseph In Concert At The Wigmore Hall* (East West 1995)★★★★, *Universal Traveller* (East West 1996)★★★.

Joseph, Margie

b. Margaret Marie Joseph, 1950, Pascagoula, Mississippi, USA. Having recorded unsuccessfully for the **OKeh** label, this excellent singer endured two further flops before an **Aretha Franklin**-influenced ballad, 'Your Sweet Lovin'', reached the R&B chart in 1970. The following year Joseph's ambitious reworking of the **Supremes**' 'Stop! In The Name Of Love' was trimmed down to six minutes to provide her with a second hit. Another interpretation, this time of **Paul McCartney**'s 'My Love', became Margie's best-selling single in 1974. Further releases, including 'Words (Are Impossible)' (1974) and 'What's Come Over Me?' (1975), a duet with the sweet-soul group **Blue Magic**, kept her name alive in the R&B chart.
● ALBUMS: *Margie Joseph Makes A New Impression* (Volt 1971)★★★, *Margie Joseph - Phase Two* (Volt 1971)★★, *Sweet Surrender* (Atlantic 1974)★★★, *Margie* (1975)★★, *Hear The Words, Feel The Feeling* (Cotillion 1976)★★★, *Feeling My Way* (Atco 1978)★★★, *Knockout* (Jive 1983)★★, *Stay* (Ichiban 1988)★★★.
● COMPILATIONS: *In The Name Of Love* (Stax 1988)★★★.

Joseph, Martyn

b. Cardiff, Wales. Martyn Joseph's first abiding passion was golf and it was only when he realised a professional career was not on the cards that he started paying serious attention to the songs he had been writing since the age of 12. He began to build up a loyal following with his sensitive, often spiritual brand of folky AOR, selling 30,000 copies of his self-financed debut, mostly at gigs. Epic Records saw the commercial potential and signed him in 1992. It was an unfashionable move, which Joseph compounded with rather superior sniping about the commercial pop (such as Mr. Blobby) which sold better than his own 'grown-up' music. Joseph was well-received on support slots with artists such as **Celine Dion**, **Joan Armatrading** and **Chris De Burgh** but was unable to make a similar commercial breakthrough and he was dropped by his record company in 1996. Undeterred, Joseph played a number of Christian concerts, including the Greenbelt Festival and then had the last laugh when *Full Colour Black And White* started getting the commercial acclaim that his Epic material had missed.
● ALBUMS: *An Aching And A Longing* (Shark 1989)★★★,

Being There (Epic 1992)★★★, *Martyn Joseph* (Epic 1995), *Full Colour Black And White* (Riff 1996)★★★, *Tangled Souls* (Grapevine 1998)★★★.

Joseph, Nerious

b. Nereus Mwalimu, St. Lucia, West Indies. Mwalimu began his career with UK-based **Fashion Records**, who suggested a name change on the basis that 'Nerious' rhymed with 'serious', and would therefore be easier to pronounce. In 1985 his debut 'Sensi Crisis' was an instant hit, and led to the equally popular 'Let's Play' and the 1990 classic, 'Guidance'. His run of hits resulted in a long association with the A Class Crew. The UK-based DJ **Top Cat** enrolled Joseph to provide the vocals on his combination hit with **Tenor Fly**, 'Hurry Up', while Gussie P and Chris Lane produced the duo for 'My Girl'. In spite of Joseph's ardent following, his adaptability, whether as a **lovers rock**, **dancehall** or roots singer, was not fully recognized, although the critics often suggested that he would be the 'next big thing'. Frustrated by this apparent indifference, Joseph decided to pursue his career with other producers, which led to an amicable break with Fashion and a long sabbatical through to the mid-90s. The critics' predictions came to fruition when in 1996 his return was heralded by the results of sessions with Saxon's Musclehead, who produced 'Giving All My Time', 'Wonderful Feeling', and the sublime 'Shouldn't Touch It'. He became part of reggae's first supergroup, Passion, recording in combination with **Peter Hunningale**, **Mafia And Fluxy** and **Glamma Kid**, and the group enjoyed the smash hit 'Share Your Love'. The single was a dextrous modification of **BLACKstreet**'s 'No Diggity', which crossed over into the UK pop chart and occupied the number 1 position in the reggae charts for two months. Following on from his success with Passion, Joseph released a double a-side, 'Rejoice' and 'I'll Keep Loving You', produced by Gussie P. who had previously engineered most of his Fashion output. The success of the single led to the release of *Rejoice*, featuring contributions from **Frankie Paul**, Tad Hunter, Claudia Fontaine and Ruff Cut, celebrating his long-overdue recognition.

● ALBUMS: *Loves Gotta Take Its Time* (Fashion 1988)★★★, *Yours To Keep* (Fashion 1992)★★, *Guidance* (Fashion 1990)★★★, *Rejoice* (Charm 1997)★★★★.

Josephs, Wilfred

b. 24 July 1927, Newcastle-upon-Tyne, England. Josephs left his career in dentistry and decided to concentrate full-time in the music business, with considerable success. His compositions include 'The Ants' comedy overture, 'Concertante For Viola And Small Orchestra', 'Concerto For Light Orchestra', 'Little Venice Serenade', 'March Glorious', 'Serenade For Small Orchestra' and five symphonies. Josephs' most notable works for television were *The Great War* (BBC, 1964), *Somerset Maugham* (BBC, 1969-70), *Cider With Rosie*, *Sutherland's Law* (BBC, 1973-76), *The Pallisers*

(BBC, 1974), the acclaimed BBC series *I Claudius* (1976), *The Voyage Of Charles Darwin* (BBC, 1978) and *A Voyage Round My Father* (Thames, 1982). He was also commissioned for many film scores, including *Bomb In The High Streeet* (1961), *Cash On Demand* (1963), *Twenty-Four Hours To Kill* (1965), *Fanatic* aka *Die Die My Darling* (1965), *The Deadly Bees* (1967), *Swallows And Amazons* (1973), *All Creatures Great And Small* (1974), *The Hunchback Of Notre Dame* (TVM 1976), *Robinson Crusoe* (TVM 1976) and *Mata Hari* (1984).

● ALBUMS: *TV And Film Themes* (Polydor 1974)★★★★.

Joshua

This American band was formed by Joshua Pehahia (guitar, vocals) in 1981 after he had left **Blind Alley**. In the early days the line-up fluctuated wildly, with the exception of singer Stephen Fontaine, who possessed a vocal range of four octaves. Perahia and Fontaine, with two acquaintances, recorded the mini-album *The Hand Is Quicker Than The Eye*, in 1982. The title was suggested by one of the studio engineers, who noticed Perahia's dexterity on the fretboard. After the album's release, Joshua attempted to tour, but frequent personnel changes made this impracticable, and no more than four dates were completed with the same line-up. In 1984 Joshua were signed to **Polydor** in America with Perahia (guitar, vocals), Ken Tamplin (guitar, vocals), Patrick Bradley (keyboards, vocals), Loren Robinson (bass, vocals), Jo Galletta (drums) and Jeff Fenholt (lead vocals). Perahia produced the album and wrote all the song arrangements. *Surrender* was released in 1985 and offered classy American hard rock, but the European arm of Polydor was not interested, and its European release was handled by FM Revolver. Fenholt was left after the album's completion, while Gregory Valesco joined them as vocalist for touring. Tamplin went on to form his own unit, Shout. Joshua then signed to **RCA** with completely different personnel: Perahia (guitar, vocals), Bob Rock (lead vocals), Greg Schultz (keyboards, vocals), Emil Lech (bass) and Tim Gehrt (drums). This membership recorded *Intense Defence*, which was slightly more restrained. Bob Rock's input helped to raise the standard of the songwriting and their future looked bright. However, Rock, Schultz and Lech left the band after the recording was finished, and formed their own outfit, Driver.

● ALBUMS: *The Hand Is Quicker Than The Eye* (Olympic 1982)★★★, *Surrender* (Polydor 1985)★★★★, *Intense Defense* (RCA 1988)★★★.

Josi, Christian

b. c.1971, Redlands, California, USA. Ballad singer Josi initially rebelled against his mother's preference for **Frank Sinatra** records at his home in favour of drumming in a local heavy metal band. At 17, however, he saw Sinatra in the flesh and his interest sparked. While attending college (studying political science) he was cast in a singing role in two **Cole Porter** musicals, and he soon became fully immersed in the works of torch singers such as **Tony Bennett** and **Bing Crosby**. After graduating from California State University he spent two years touring America as part of the Chris Davis Band. Josi evidently saw this as an integral part of his musical evolution: 'For someone who wants to do this kind of music, you can't do it right unless you've been in front of a big band.' He then moved from west to east coast after sneaking backstage at a **Mel Tormé** concert and passing the singer a copy of his demo tape. The following day his piano player, John Collianni, called, and invited Josi to New York to sing with the new band he was forming. Although the collaboration never came off as planned, while in the metropolis he did find a great deal more opportunity to sing, and also met his wife. A series of high profile concerts accompanied his rapid rise, drawing favourable comments from such as **Grover Washington Jnr.** and **Herb Jeffries**. His debut album, *I Walks With My Feet Off The Ground*, saw him backed by a quartet of Tony Monte (piano), Harry Allen (saxophone), Dave Green (bass) and Trevor Tomkins (drums), with production assistance from Delfeayo Marsalis. This collection of swing and ballad numbers endeared him to many, not least a quantity of young supporters not readily given to appreciating the standards. As Josi commented, 'I think the essence of this music's appeal to the young is that it's finally being presented to them by people they can consider their peers.'

● ALBUMS: *I Walks With My Feet Off The Ground* (MasterMix 1994)★★★.

Jostyn, Mindy

b. San Jose, California, USA. Mindy Jostyn first played the family piano aged two. Inspired by **Judy Garland** in *The Wizard Of Oz*, she attempted to write her first songs just two years later. She had learned accordion, violin, guitar and harmonica by the age of 11, at which time she formed her first band, the Tigers. Her subsequent career at high school was frequently interrupted by musical ambitions, leading to attendance at four different high schools and no diploma. She then moved to New York to form the Cyclone Rangers. Although that band struggled to achieve popularity, Jostyn's career experienced a boost in 1989 when she was called by G.E. Smith, band leader on the American television show *Saturday Night Live*. He needed a female harmonica player for a sketch hosted by **Dolly Parton**, and she was the only such player listed in the New York musician's union book. She was subsequently invited back for a second performance alongside **Billy Joel**, with whom she also toured in 1990. Word of her skills spread, and the following year she joined **Joe Jackson** on his European and Australian dates. 1992 saw her become part of the New York Rock And Soul Revue, led by **Donald Fagen**. She also worked with the **Hooters** and **John Mellencamp**. She featured on **Carly Simon**'s *Live At Grand Central Station* live album and home video in 1994, before deciding the time was right to establish herself as a solo artist. Her debut, *Five Miles From Hope*, also featured Simon on the duet, 'Time Be On My Side'.

● ALBUMS: *Five Miles From Hope* (Demon 1996)★★★.

Journey

This US rock group was formed in 1973 by ex-**Santana** members Neal Schon (b. 27 February 1954, San Mateo, California, USA; guitar) and Gregg Rolie (b. 1948; keyboards), with the assistance of Ross Valory (b. 2 February 1949, San Francisco, USA; bass, ex-**Steve Miller** band) and Prairie Prince (b. 7 May 1950, Charlotte, North Carolina, USA; drums, ex-**Tubes**). George Tickner was later added as rhythm guitarist and lead vocalist. On New Year's Eve the same year, they made their live debut in front of 10,000 people at San Fransisco's Winterland. The following day they played to 100,000 at an open-air festival in Hawaii. In February 1974 Prince returned to the Tubes and was replaced by **Aynsley Dunbar** (b. 10 January 1946, Liverpool, Lancashire, England; ex-**Jeff Beck**; **John Mayall**; **Frank Zappa**, etc.). They initially specialized in jazz-rock, complete with extended and improvised solo spots, a style much in evidence on their first three albums. In 1975 Tickner left (for medical school) and was eventually replaced by ex-Alien Project vocalist **Steve Perry** (b. 22 January 1953, Hanford, California, USA), following a brief tenure by Robert Fleischmann. The switch to highly sophisticated pomp rock occurred with the recording of *Infinity*, when Roy Thomas Baker was brought in as producer to give the band's sound a punchy and dynamic edge. The album was a huge success, reaching number 21 on the *Billboard* charts and gaining a platinum award. Dunbar was unhappy with this new style and left for **Jefferson Starship**, to be replaced by Steve Smith (b. 21 August 1954, Los Angeles, California, USA). *Evolution* followed and brought the band their first Top 20 hit, 'Lovin', Touchin', Squeezin''. *Captured* was a live double album that surprised many critics, being far removed from their technically excellent and clinically produced studio releases; instead, it featured cranked-up guitars and raucous hard rock, eventually peaking at number 9 in the US album chart. Founder-member Rolie departed after its release, to be replaced by Jonathan Cain (b. 26 February 1950, Chicago, Illinois, USA), who had previously played with the **Babys**. Cain's arrival was an important landmark in Journey's career, as his songwriting input added a new dimension to the band's sound. *Escape* represented the pinnacle of the band's success, reaching number 1 and staying in the chart for over a year. It also spawned three US Top 10 hit singles in the form of 'Who's Crying Now', 'Don't Stop Believin'' and 'Open Arms'. The follow-up, *Frontiers*, was also successful, staying at number 2 on the *Billboard* album chart for nine weeks; 'Separate Ways', culled as a single from it, climbed to number 8 in the singles chart. After a series of internal disputes, the band was reduced to a three-man nucleus of Schon,

Cain and Perry to record *Raised On Radio* (though they were joined on live dates by Randy Jackson and Mike Baird on drums and bass). This was Journey's last album before Schon and Cain joined forces with **John Waite**'s **Bad English** in 1988. Smith fronted a fusion band, Vital Information, before teaming up with ex-Journey members Rolie and Valory to form Storm in 1991. Perry concentrated on his long-awaited second solo album. A *Greatest Hits* compilation was posthumously released to mark the band's passing, since which time only a November 1991 reunion to commemorate the death of promoter **Bill Graham** has seen the core members regroup. This continued with new albums in 1996 and 1997 that saw the band religiously refusing to adapt or change from a style of music that now sounds dated.

● ALBUMS: *Journey* (Columbia 1975)★★★, *Look Into The Future* (Columbia 1976)★★★, *Next* (Columbia 1977)★★★, *Infinity* (Columbia 1978)★★★★, *Evolution* (Columbia 1979)★★★, *Departure* (Columbia 1980)★★★, *Dream After Dream* (Columbia 1980)★★, *Captured* (Columbia 1981)★★★, *Escape* (Columbia 1981)★★★★, *Frontiers* (Columbia 1983)★★★, *Raised On Radio* (Columbia 1986)★★★, *Trial By Fire* (Columbia 1996)★★, *Into The Fire* (Columbia 1997)★★, *Greatest Hits Live* (Columbia 1998)★★.
● COMPILATIONS: *In The Beginning* (Columbia 1979)★★, *Greatest Hits/Best Of Journey* (Columbia 1988)★★★★, *Time* 3-CD box set (Columbia 1992)★★★★.

Journey Through The Past

Singer-songwriter **Neil Young** was riding a crest of popularity thanks to his 1972 release, *Harvest*, and his involvement in the supergroup, **Crosby, Stills, Nash And Young**. Mercurial to the end, he confronted the notion of commercial success with this self-indulgent film. 'Every scene meant something to me, though with some of them, I can't say what', he later gave as some kind of explanation about this sprawling 1973 feature. Directed by Young under his 'Bernard Shakey' pseudonym, *Journey Through The Past* is a surreal autobiography, combining elements of Americana with moments drawn from the singer's life as a performer. It included elements from his first successful group, **Buffalo Springfield**, as well as alternative versions of songs from concurrent projects, notably lengthy interpretations of 'Words' and 'Alabama'. The soundtrack also featured 'Ohio', a song inspired by the slaying of four students at Kent State campus, pitted against a reading of 'God Bless America', sung by evangelist Billy Graham and US President Richard Nixon. Variously described as 'pretentious' and 'technically inept', *Journey Through The Past* was withdrawn soon after release. Given public acceptance of Young's now notorious obdurism, it seems ripe for re-appraisal.

Journey Through The Past - Neil Young

Taking its title from one of his most introspective compositions, *Journey Through The Past* is the soundtrack to Neil Young's first foray into film work. This highly personal documentary came hard on the heels of the singer's success with *Harvest*, but in now-customary fashion, he refused to court the easy option. The album included a mesmerizing pot pourri of material, ranging from rough live performances with his first group, Buffalo Springfield, to background sound drawn from the Beach Boys and Handel's Messiah. In-between were some raging in-concert appearances with Crosby, Stills And Nash, notably the lengthy 'Words' and apocalyptic 'Ohio'. Although not an official album *per se*, *Journey Through The Past* is as revealing and intense as anything else in the artist's canon, but not as good.
● Tracks: *For What It's Worth/Mr. Soul; Rock & Roll Woman; Find The Cost Of Freedom; Ohio; Southern Man; Are You Ready For The Country; Let Me Call You Sweetheart; Alabama; Words; Relativity Invitation; Handel's Messiah; King Of Kings; Soldier; Lets's Go Away For Awhile.*
● First released 1972
● UK peak chart position: did not chart
● USA peak chart position: 45

Journey To The Centre Of The Earth - Rick Wakeman

Choosing between this album and the now similarly unlistenable *The Six Wives Of Henry VIII* was a difficult task. This wins because it is that much more grandiose, and a perfect example of 'pomp rock'. The quality of the music is good, the arrangements faultless and Wakeman is (no pun intended) a master of his organ. Rick attempted to put this project on the stage and for ten minutes we all loved it. Wakeman is now producing some fine new age-inspired piano music and appears on television displaying his great sense of humour. Perhaps this was an early practical joke he played on us.
● Tracks: *The Journey; Recollection; The Battle; The Forest.*
● First released 1974
● UK peak chart position: 1
● USA peak chart position: 3

Journeymen

This US folk trio comprising **Scott McKenzie** (guitar/vocals), Dick Weissman (b. Richard Weissman; banjo/guitar/vocals), and **John Phillips** (b. John Edmund Andrew Phillips, 30 August 1935, Parris Island, South Carolina, USA; guitar/vocals). The group were formed, like many others at the time, as a result of the folk revival of the late 50s and 60s, and featured strong harmonies and a commercial sound that made folk such a saleable commodity at the time. The Journeymen made their debut in 1961 at Gerde's Folk City, New York, and shortly afterwards signed to **Capitol Records**, releasing *The Journeymen* later the same year. The group's popularity, and commerciality, waned after a relatively short life span, and the members went their separate ways. John attempted to revive the trio's fortunes with the New Journeymen, which featured his wife **Michelle Phillips** and Marshall Brickman. Phillips went on to form the **Mamas And The Papas**, while McKenzie found fame as the singer of the hit song 'San Francisco'. Weissman continued in the music business, recording *The Things That Trouble My Mind* and *Dick Weissman Sings And Plays Songs Of Protest*.

● ALBUMS: *The Journeymen* (Capitol 1961)★★★, *Coming Attraction-Live* (Capitol 1962)★★★, *New Directions* (Capitol 1963)★★★.

● COMPILATIONS: *The Very Best Of* (Collectables 1998)★★★.

Joy

Built around the production duo of David Tolan (b. 3 May 1967, Dublin, Eire; programming, percussion) and Ali Fletcher (b. Alistair Fletcher, 27 May 1968, Newcastle, England; drums, programming), the Joy additionally number Gavin O'Neill (b. 20 September 1965, Worcester, England; vocals) **Denise Johnson** (b. 31 August 1966, Manchester, Lancashire, England; vocals) and Andy Tracey (b. 11 September 1965, Harehills, Leeds, Yorkshire, England; guitar). Johnson is best known to club-goers for her contributions to **Primal Scream**'s epoch-making *Screamadelica*, but Tolan also produced her debut solo single. He and O'Neill had initially worked together in Perspex Spangles, while Fletcher had been part of the Canoe Club and Tall Americans. The Joy took their name as a revolt against the rejection offered to them by record companies in their early days. They played their first gig at the Buzz Club in Manchester in September 1992, and kicked off their new contract with Compulsion Records in 1994 with a re-release of 'Shine', previously a minor club hit in April 1993 for Playground Records.. As Joy Productions Tolan and Fletcher have also contributed remixes, most notably for the **Dub Disciples**' 'Hyperphoria Parts One And Two'.

Joy Division

Originally known as Warsaw, this Manchester post-punk outfit comprised Ian Curtis (b. July 1956, Macclesfield, Cheshire, England, d. 18 May 1980; vocals), Bernard Dicken/Albrecht (b. 4 January 1956, Salford, Manchester, England; guitar, vocals), Peter Hook (b. 13 February 1956, Manchester, England; bass) and Steven Morris (b. 28 October 1957, Macclesfield, Cheshire, England; drums). Borrowing their name from the prostitution wing of a concentration camp, Joy Division emerged in 1978 as one of the most important groups of their era. After recording a regionally available EP, *An Ideal For Living*, they were signed to Manchester's recently formed **Factory Records** and placed in the hands of producer **Martin Hannett**. Their debut, *Unknown Pleasures*, was a raw, intense affair, with Curtis at his most manically arresting in the insistent 'She's Lost Control'. With its stark, black cover, the album captured a group still coming to terms with the recording process, but displaying a vision that was piercing in its clinical evocation of an unsettling disorder. With Morris's drums employed as a lead instrument, backed by the leaden but compulsive bass lines of

Hook, the sound of Joy Division was distinctive and disturbing. By the time of their single 'Transmission', the quartet had already established a strong cult following, which increased after each gig. Much of the attention centred on the charismatic Curtis, who was renowned for his neurotic choreography, resembling a demented marionette on wires. By the autumn of 1979, however, Curtis's performances were drawing attention for a more serious reason. On more than one occasion he suffered an epileptic seizure and blackouts onstage, and the illness seemed to worsen with the group's increasingly demanding live schedule. On 18 May 1980, the eve of Joy Division's proposed visit to America, Ian Curtis was found hanged. The verdict was suicide. A note was allegedly found bearing the words: 'At this moment I wish I were dead. I just can't cope anymore'. The full impact of the tragedy was underlined shortly afterwards, for it quickly became evident that Curtis had taken his life at the peak of his creativity. While it seemed inevitable that the group's posthumously released work would receive a sympathetic reaction, few could have anticipated the quality of the material that emerged in 1980. The single, 'Love Will Tear Us Apart', was probably the finest of the year, a haunting account of a fragmented relationship, sung by Curtis in a voice that few realized he possessed. The attendant album, *Closer*, was faultless, displaying the group at the zenith of their powers. With spine-tingling cameos such as 'Isolation' and the extraordinary 'Twenty-Four Hours', the album eloquently articulated a sense of despair, yet simultaneously offered a therapeutic release. Instrumentally, the work showed maturity in every area and is deservedly regarded by many critics as the most brilliant rock album of the 80s. The following year, a double album, *Still*, collected the remainder of the group's material, most of it in primitive form. Within months of the Curtis tragedy, the remaining members sought a fresh start as **New Order**. In 1995 Curtis's widow, Deborah, published a book on her former huband and the band, while a compilation album and a re-released version of 'Love Will Tear Us Apart' were back on the shelves on the 15th anniversary of his death.

● ALBUMS: *Unknown Pleasures* (Factory 1979)★★★, *Closer* (Factory 1980)★★★★, *Still* (Factory 1981)★★★.

● COMPILATIONS: *Substance 1977-1980* (Factory 1988)★★★★, *The Peel Sessions* (Strange Fruit 1990)★★★, *Permanent: The Best Of Joy Division* (London 1995)★★★★, *Heart And Soul* 4-CD box set (London 1997)★★★.

● VIDEOS: *Here Are The Young Men* (IKON 1992).

● FURTHER READING: *An Ideal For Living: An History Of Joy Division*, Mark Johnson. *Touching From A Distance*, Deborah Curtis. *New Order & Joy Division*, Claude Flowers.

Joy Of A Toy - Kevin Ayers

Ayers left the Soft Machine for a solo career when his basic pop leanings appeared at odds with the intense jazz/rock of his former colleagues. This album was a cult favourite at the end of the 60s for no reason other than that Ayers was well liked because he was ever so slightly mad. Take a look and listen at the content of this album: 'Song For Insane Times', 'Eleanor's Cake (Which Ate Her)' and 'Stop This Train (Again Doing It)'. Through the haze of quirkiness there is a strong light melodic feel to much of the music, and Ayers did possess a heartbreaker voice that prompted one woman to state, 'he is the sexiest man in the world'.

● Tracks: *Joy Of A Toy Continued; Town Feeling; The Clarietta Rag; Girl On A Swing; Song For Insane Times; Stop This Train (Again Doing It); Eleanor's Cake (Which Ate Her); The Lady Rachel; Oleh Oleh Bandu Bandong; All This Crazy Gift Of Time.*
● First released 1969
● UK peak chart position: did not chart
● USA peak chart position: did not chart

Joy Of Cooking

Formed in Berkeley, California, USA in 1967 as Gourmet's Delight, this individual quintet originally consisted of Terry Garthwaite (b. 11 July 1938, Berkeley, California, USA; guitar/vocals), brother David Garthwaite (bass), Toni Brown (b. 16 November 1938, Madison, Wisconsin, USA; keyboards/guitar/vocals), Ron Wilson (b. 5 February 1933, San Diego, California, USA; percussion) and Fritz Kasten (b. Des Moines, Iowa, USA; drums). David Garthwaite was replaced by Jeff Neighbour (b. 19 March 1942, Grand Coulee, Washington, USA), prior to recording. The group's self-titled debut album was released late in 1970 and yielded a minor hit single in 'Brownsville'. Their easy style, which drew its inspiration from folk, blues and jazz, offered a refreshing spontaneity, although subsequent releases lacked the verve of this first collection. Joy Of Cooking's direction was determined by Brown and Garthwaite and the group was thus a focal point for the Bay Area's women's movement. Toni and Terry carried this support when the group broke up in 1973. They recorded *Cross Country* together before embarking on separate solo careers, but despite excellent releases, were unable to make a significant breakthrough. The two singers put together a new group, known simply as the Joy, in 1977, which released one widely acclaimed album, but resumed their independent work when this new venture failed to generate sufficient commercial interest.

● ALBUMS: as Joy Of Cooking *Joy Of Cooking* (Capitol 1970)★★★★, *Closer To The Ground* (Capitol 1971)★★★, *Castles* (Capitol 1972)★★★, as Toni And Terry *Cross Country* (1973)★★, as the Joy *The Joy* (1977)★★. Solo: Toni Brown *Good For You Too* (1974)★★★, *Angel Of Love* (1980)★★. Terry Garthwaite *Terry* (1975)★★★, *Hand In Glove* (1978)★★★.

Joy, Jimmy

b. Monte Maloney, 1912, USA, d. March 1962, Dallas, Texas, USA. Formed in the mid-20s in Texas, the Jimmy Joy Orchestra took its name after its leader's association with the Joyland Park in Galveston, Texas, where many of their early concerts took place. Maloney later changed his name to Jimmy Joy by deed poll in Kansas City in 1929. His orchestra, which included sidemen Gilbert O'Shaughnessy, Hollis Bradt, Jack Brown, Rex Preis, Lynn Harrell, Clyde Austin, Johnny Cole, Dick Hammell, Amos Ayalisa, Norman Smith, Matty Matlock, Orville Andrews, Ernie Mathias, Al King, Oscar Reed, Elmer Nordgreen and Oscar Miller, was originally formed on campus at the University of Texas. They would find receptive audiences at a variety of Midwest and southern locales, including the Muehlbach, the Peabody, the Baker and Adolphus hotels. Led by Joy himself on saxophone, the group's entertaining stage show was geared directly to the needs of evening dancers, and proved perennially popular. Their theme song was 'Shine On, Harvey Moon', with records released on **OKeh**, **Brunswick** and **Decca Records**. Joy was something of a showman, delighting audiences with his ability to play two clarinets at the same time (an idea borrowed from **Wilbur Sweatman**) and to sing the blues when the occasion demanded. Especially popular in his home state, Joy was made an honorary Texas Ranger in the 30s. He was also made an honorary Kentucky Colonel after his band played three seasons at the race track as the Official Kentucky Derby Orchestra. He remained active as a bandleader through the 40s and 50s, though by then he was not as prolific.

Joy, Ruth

London-born Joy came to prominence as the writer and singer of Sheffield-based **Krush**'s 'House Arrest' crossover success from 1987, at which point she was widely touted as the 'new **Neneh Cherry**'. However, it would take three years of work, and several dumped producers, before her debut solo album finally saw the light of day. Among those involved were **Mantronix** (who produced her debut solo single, 'Don't Push It'), **Loose Ends**' Carl McIntosh and **Aswad**. Singles culled from the set included 'Feel' and 'Pride And Joy'.

● ALBUMS: *Pride And Joy* (MCA 1992)★★★.

Joyce

b. 1949, Rio de Janeiro, Brazil. Joyce began singing professionally in 1968, having previously studied classical guitar. She recorded two albums with little success and then, in 1970, joined the group A Tribo. This band, which also featured **Nana Vasconcelos**, lasted for two years, following which Joyce recorded another solo album and then retired from music. However, in 1975 she accepted an invitation to sing and play the guitar with the band of poet and songwriter Vinicus de Moraes, with whom she embarked on a world tour. During the tour she recorded an album in Rome that featured songs by artists such as Caetano Veloso and Chico Buarque, whose material was banned by the military dictatorship in power in Brazil at the time. In 1977 she moved to New York and recorded an album with local jazz musicians, including **Michael Brecker**, but it was never released and she returned to Brazil to concentrate on songwriting. Following recordings of her songs by artists such as **Milton Nascimento**, Maria Bethania and Elis Regina, she was offered a recording contract by **EMI** (Brazil) and in 1980 released the album *Feminina*. A single taken from the album, 'Clarana', became a national hit. *Aqua E Luz* (1981) and *Tardes Cariocas* (1983) were also successful in Brazil. A track from her next release, *Suedadede Futuro*, was entered for a musical festival in Japan, which led to huge and lasting popularity for Joyce among Japan's Latin-jazz fans. Following this she recorded two albums of the songs of **Antonio Carlos Jobim** and Vinicuis de Moras, and then two albums released by **Verve Records** USA. In 1989 'Aldeia De Ogum', a track from *Feminina*, became hugely popular on London's jazz dance scene, leading to a burst of interest in her elusive Brazilian releases (copies of which were changing hands for £100 or more). Her popularity as a live performer grew as a result of this, while tracks from her albums appeared on various compilations of Brazilian music. *The Essential Joyce*, released in 1997 by Latin dance label Mr Bongo, features a selection of songs from her rare Brazilian releases.

● COMPILATIONS: *The Essential Joyce 1970-1996* (Mr Bongo 1997)★★★★.

Joyce, Archibald

b. 25 May 1873, London, England, d. 22 March 1963, England. Known variously as The English Waltz King or The English Waldteufel, Joyce is mainly remembered for one composition 'Dreaming' which is instantly recognisable around the world, even if not always by its name. Composing was almost secondary, because his main career centred on his ballroom orchestra which, from the 1900's onwards, was greatly in demand at fashionable functions. Dis-satisfied with much of the music available for dancing, he decided to write his own, and 'Dreaming' firmly established his composing credentials. Other works included Acushla', 'Bohemia', 'Love And Life In Holland', 'Passing Of Salome', 'Song Of The River', 'Sweet Williams', 'A Thousand Kisses', 'When The Birds Began To Sing', 'The Prince Of Wales Grand March', 'Songe D'Automne', 'A Thousand Kisses', 'Caravan Suite', 'Dreams Of You' and 'Brighton Hike'. Although he lived to a great age Joyce never shook off the influence of his early years. He disliked the musical scene as it developed from the 30s onwards, and rarely composed any new works.

● ALBUMS: *British Light Music - Archibald Joyce* (Marco Polo 1995)★★★★.

Joye, Col

b. Colin Jacobsen, 13 April 1937, Sydney, New South Wales, Australia. Joye began his career in 1957 singing with his brothers at suburban dances which they organized themselves, becoming popular with teenagers who were anxious to be involved with the 'new' rock 'n' roll emanating from the USA and UK. After recording successfully as Col Joye And The Joy Boys, his success as a solo artist was guaranteed once he had gained

recognition on national television. His good looks and easy-going manner captured the hearts of many teenage girls, even though his vocal talent was not exceptional. From his first record release in 1958 through to 1965 Joye released over 50 singles including 'Oh Yeah, Uh Huh' (1959), 'Bad Man' (1960), 'Goin' Steady' (1961), Sweet Dreams Of You' (1962), 'Whispering Pines' (1964) and 'Can Your Monkey Do The Dog' (1965). Throughout this time, Joye vied with **Johnny O'Keefe** for the title of the most popular teen idol of the rock 'n' roll era in Australia. His material basically consisted of covers of international hits, but later he wrote his own material, or was provided with songs by his backing band the Joy Boys, who also had a successful recording career in their own right. After the initial rock 'n' roll boom died, Joye continued his success with ballads and later resurfaced as a country and MOR artist, recording consistently during the 70s. Joye also became involved in management (having **Andy Gibb** on his books at one time), music publishing, a talent agency and with his brothers Kevin and Keith ran the ATA label. Joye still performs and records today and is popular on the 50s' and 60s' revival circuit.

● ALBUMS: *Jump With Joye* (1959)★★★, *Songs That Rocked The Stadium* (1960)★★★, *Golden Boy* (1960)★★★★, *Joy To The World* (1961)★★★, *Joyride* (1961)★★★, *Col Joye And The Ballad* (1962)★★★, with Judy Stone *Col And Judy* (1962)★★, *Classics Of Rock* (1963)★★, *Stomp Around The Clock* (1964)★★★, *Rock Classics, Number 2* (1964)★★★, *Songs For Swinging Mums And Dads* (1964)★★, *Rockin' And Stompin'* (1964)★★★, *Rhythm And Blues Session* (1965)★★★, *Col Joye Show* (1966)★★★, *For The Good Times* (1972)★★★, *Heaven Is My Woman's Love* (1973)★★★, *Rock Classics Number 4* (1974)★★, *For You* (1975)★★★, with Little Pattie *A Little Bit Country* (1977)★★, *Rocky Road Blues* (1989)★★★.

● COMPILATIONS: *Sings His Solid Gold Hits* (1961)★★★★, *The Best Of Col And Judy* (1963)★★★★, *The Col Joye Story* (1973)★★★, *21 Years Of Rock 'N' Roll* (1978)★★★★.

Joyous Noise

Based in Los Angeles, California, USA, Joyous Noise consisted of Lee Montgomery (vocals), Marc McClure (guitar/keyboards/dobro), Lance Wakely (lead guitar), Happy Smith (bass) and Dennis Dragon (drums). McClure was previously a member of Levitt And McClure, an excellent country-influenced act associated with San Francisco's **Beau Brummels**. A similar style of music was present on both Joyous Noise albums, but an interest in jazz was equally apparent. McClure subsequently embarked on an ill-starred solo career before joining the reformed **Spanky And Our Gang** in 1976. Dennis Dragon, brother of Daryl Dragon of **Captain And Tennille**, later joined the irreverent Surf Punks.

● ALBUMS: *Joyous Noise* (Capitol 1971)★★★, *Wondering Man* (Capitol 1972)★★.

Joyrider

A quartet of Phil Woolsey (vocals, guitar), Cliff Mitchel (guitar), Simon Haddock (bass) and Buck Hamill (drums), bracing alternative rock band Joyrider were formed in Portadown, Northern Ireland, in 1992. Throughout ensuing years they built their reputation on the back of a torturous touring schedule that took them across Europe as support to artists including **Terrorvision**, **Dog Eat Dog** and **Therapy?**. Their hard-drinking but affable outlook immediately won over many critics in the music press, earning them praise that eventually transcended the original criticism that Joyrider were merely 'Therapy? Jnr'. They also made a point of crossing the sectarian divide by bussing both Protestant and Catholic fans to out-of-town gigs, while parodying religious and paramilitary slogans on their record sleeves. They made their debut with two singles, 'Dweeb King' and 'Getting That Joke Now', for Blunt Records, run by Andy Cairns of Therapy?, before signing a contract with **A&M Records** subsidiary Paradox. Three EPs, including the excellent *Fabulae*, endeared them to a growing audience in the UK, but it was their debut album, at which time Hamill had been replaced by Carl Alty, that convinced others of their long-term potential. The lyrics to 'Bible Blackbelt' and 'Another Skunk Song', in particular, were simple but effective, the latter song denouncing the prevalence of a particular brand of marijuana on their fellow musicians ('High every night/And we're all talking shite').
● ALBUMS: *Be Special* (Paradox 1996)★★★, *Skid Solo* (A&M 1997)★★★.

Joystrings

'It's An Open Secret', which entered the UK Top 40 in February 1964, remains one of the most unlikely hits of the beat era. The song was written by Joy Webb, a captain in the Salvation Army. Her eight-piece group, the Joystrings, was drawn from the staff of the Army's Training College in London's Denmark Hill. The sole exception was drummer Wyncliffe Noble, an architect by trade. The octet was signed to **EMI**'s Regal-Zonophone label, following a successful appearance on BBC television's *Tonight* programme, and in December they enjoyed another minor hit with 'A Starry Night'. Despite their seemingly transitory appeal, the Joystrings continued to record for several years, although their novelty aspect quickly waned.
● ALBUMS: *Well Seasoned* (Regal Zonophone 1966)★★★, *Carols Across The World* (Regal Zonophone 1967)★★★.

JSD Band

This Scottish folk-rock act was one of genre's leading attractions during the early 70s. Having made their debut with the low-key *Country Of The Blind*, the group - Des Coffield (guitar/keyboards/vocals), Sean O'Rouke (guitar), Chuck Fleming (violin), Jim Divers (bass) and Colin Finn (drums) - then opted for a more expressive style, echoing that of **Fairport Convention** and **Steeleye Span**, but based on Fleming's showmanship

and dexterity. *JSD Band* encapsulated the quintet's live fire and remains their most popular release, whereas *Travelling Days* was viewed as a disappointment. The loss of several members, including Fleming, proved fatal and although Iain Lyon, formerly of My Dear Watson, bolstered a group latterly known as the New JSD Band, the unit split up in 1974 only to reappear in 1995. Simon Jones writing in *Folk Roots* accurately described O'Rourke's voice as 'like he's been on the Venos, Wild Turkey and Domestos', for those unaware he is referring to cough mixture, whiskey and household bleach. The original line-up reconvened in 1998 on *Pastures Of Plenty*.
● ALBUMS: *Country Of The Blind* (Regal Zonophone 1971)★★★, *JSD Band* (Cube 1972)★★★★, *Travelling Days* (Cube 1973)★★, *For The Record* (Village Music 1995)★★★, *Pastures Of Plenty* (1998)★★★.

Ju Ju Space Jazz

Sydney, Australia-based Daniel Conway and Alexander Nettelbeck worked together in the mid-90s on various projects, including music for contemporary dance and films. Around the beginning of 1996 they began to record material together around the concept of Ju Ju, which is 'about the unexpected, the spooky, the ridiculous, the fantastic - all that makes your hairs stand up and wiggle'. Consequently, their first album, *Head Over Heels In Dub*, released towards the end of 1996 on the Australian label Fluid Records, incorporated a variety of styles without adhering to any particular established genre. In 1997 they signed to **Matsuri Productions** who released 'Pizza' on the *Sympathy In Chaos* compilation and the EP *Mermadium Palladium*, followed by the group's UK debut album, *Shloop*, early the next year. Ju Ju Space Jazz's eccentric, experimental music incorporates unusual combinations of sound with funky, relaxed beats, underpinned by a solid, dubby bass. Familiar electronic noises and effects of dance music sit together with jazz-inspired chords and improvised lines played on various live instruments, including saxophone, trombone and violin, to create the most unusual abstract textures. Some tracks feature guest vocalists including Edwina Blush, Mr Thankyou Very Much, MC Zen, Dr Karshnoofdibah and Miguel Valens. Conway and Nettelbeck often present live performances of their material.

Juan Trip

Versailles-based French team built around mainman Basil, who mortified several commentators with their 1994 *Masterpiece Trilogy* EP. The controversy centred on main track, 'Louis' Cry'. This used a sample of a particularly unhappy one year old of the author's acquaintence who died shortly after the record was made. One of his screams was used, alongside a loop of organist **Jimmy Smith**, to puncuate the track. When the newshounds rang round to confirm the existence of the 'dead baby track' Basil, who had formerly promoted the hugely successful Fantom nights in France, confirmed its origins (though it was conceived more as a tribute to the child's life than anything more exploitative). Released on F Communications in France, many DJ's refused to play it because of the unsettling nature of the scream, including **Darren Emmerson**, who even asked permission to re-record the masterful backing track without it.

Jubilee

The story goes that the celebrated composer **Cole Porter** took librettist **Moss Hart** and director Monty Woolley on a round-the-world cruise to think up ideas for this show. The jaunt lasted for about five months, but the resulting show was unable to stay around for that long. Perhaps the ship docked for a while in England, because the inspiration for the plot is said to have been the Silver Jubilee of Britain's King George V and Queen Mary. The result of the trio's deliberations commenced at the Imperial Theatre in New York on 12 October 1935, and posed the question as to what might happen to an imaginary (Anglicised) royal family, also about to celebrate their jubilee, who have been advised to take off their tiaras for a while, and go incognito to avoid the embarrassment of a left-wing coup. The King (Melville Cooper) and the Queen (Mary Boland), along with their children, welcome this break from conformity, and revel in their new-found freedom which gives the King an opportunity to perfect his rope tricks. In the course of their travels they meet up with several characters bearing a remarkable resemblance to celebrities of the day: there's Charles Rausmiller ('Johnny Weissmuller') played by Mark Plant, and Eric Dare ('**Noël Coward**') as portrayed by Derek Williams (the Queen has a crush on both of those); and Eve Standing ('Elsa Maxwell'), who was played to a 'T' by May Boley. Another famous real-life name in the cast was Montgomery Clift the future cult film actor. Aged only 15, he played the good Prince Peter, and on the first night of the show, out of town in Boston, he received a kidnap threat. It turned out to be from a woman whose son had failed the audition for his part. One more cast member of the Moss Hart's mythical royal family, over 50 years before she became a reality in England, was the prophetically named Princess Diana. However, Mary Boland was the box-office draw, and when she left after four months to resume her film career, her replacement, Laura Hope Crews, was unable to create sufficient impact to prevent the show closing after 169 performances. So, only a limited number of privileged theatre-goers were able to listen to that outstanding Cole Porter score which included 'Mr. And Mrs. Smith', 'Me And Marie', 'When Love Comes Your Way', 'A Picture Of Me Without You', 'The Kling-Kling Bird On The Divi-Divi Tree', and three of the composer's all-time standards, 'Why Shouldn't I?', 'Just One Of Those Things', and 'Begin The Beguine', which became such a big hit for **Artie Shaw** in 1938.

Judas Jump

Formed in 1970, Judas Jump was the confluence of two leading UK 'teenybop' groups. Andy Bown (vocals/piano) and Henry Spinetti (drums) had been members of the **Herd**, while Alan Jones and Mike Smith (both saxophone), were the brass section of **Amen Corner**. Trevor Williams (lead guitar), Adrian Williams (vocals) and Charlie Harrison (bass) completed the line-up. Plans to name the band Septimus were abandoned on Smith's premature departure. Although *Scorch* showed promise, Judas Jump's mixture of pop and progressive styles ultimately proved too unwieldy and they broke up within a year of their inception. Bown, who overdubbed much of the album in deference to what he perceived as incompetence, later embarked on a solo career. Harrison led a chequered career working for **Leo Sayer**, **Frankie Miller**, **Roger McGuinn**, **Al Stewart** and finally ending up in the ranks of **Poco** in 1977.

● ALBUMS: *Scorch* (Parlophone 1970)★★.

Judas Priest

This group was formed in Birmingham, England, in 1969, by guitarist K.K. Downing (b. Kenneth Downing) and close friend, bassist Ian Hill. As another hopeful, struggling young rock band, they played their first gig in Essington in 1971 with a line-up completed by Alan Atkins (vocals) and John Ellis (drums). The name Judas Priest came from Atkins' previous band (who took it from a **Bob Dylan** song, 'The Ballad Of Frankie Lee And Judas Priest') before he joined up with Hill and Downing. Constant gigging continued, with Alan Moore taking over on drums, only to be replaced at the end of 1971 by Chris Campbell. Most of 1972 was spent on the road in the UK, and in 1973 both Atkins and Campbell departed, leaving the nucleus of Hill and Downing (in 1991 Atkins released a debut solo album that included 'Victim Of Changes', a song he co-wrote in Judas Priest's infancy). At this point, their fortunes took a turn for the better. Vocalist and ex-theatrical lighting engineer Rob Halford (b. 25 August 1951, Walsall, England) and drummer John Hinch, both from the band Hiroshima, joined the unit. More UK shows ensued as their following grew steadily, culminating in the addition of second guitarist Glenn Tipton (b. 25 October 1948; ex-Flying Hat Band). In 1974 they toured abroad for the first time in Germany and the Netherlands, and returned home to a record contract with the small UK label Gull. The band made their vinyl debut with *Rocka Rolla* in September 1974. Disappointed with the recording, the band failed to make any impact, and Hinch left to be replaced by the returning Alan Moore.

In 1975 the band's appearance at the Reading Festival brought them to the attention of a much wider audience. *Sad Wings Of Destiny* was an improvement on the debut, with production assistance from Jeffrey Calvert and Max West. However, despite good reviews, their financial situation remained desperate, and Alan Moore left for the second and final time. A worldwide contract with **CBS Records** saved the day, and *Sin After Sin* was a strong collection, with Simon Philips sitting in for Moore. The band then visited America for the first time with drummer Les Binks, who appeared on *Stained Class*, an album that showed Priest at a high watermark in their powers. *Killing Machine* yielded the first UK hit single, 'Take On The World', and featured shorter, punchier, but still familiar, rock songs. *Unleashed In The East* was recorded on the 1979 Japanese tour, and in that year, Binks was replaced on drums by Dave Holland of **Trapeze**. After major tours with both **Kiss** and **AC/DC**, Priest's popularity began to gather momentum. *British Steel* smashed into the UK album charts at number 3, and included the hit singles 'Breaking The Law' and 'Living After Midnight'. After appearing at the 1980 Donington Monsters Of Rock festival, they began recording *Point Of Entry*. It provided the hit single 'Hot Rockin', and was followed by sell-out UK and US tours. The period surrounding *Screaming For Vengeance* was phenomenally successful for the band. The hit single, 'You've Got Another Thing Comin'', was followed by a lucrative six-month US tour, with the album achieving platinum status in the USA. *Defenders Of The Faith* offered a similar potent brand of headstrong metal to *Screaming For Vengeance*. *Turbo*, however, proved slightly more commercial and was poorly received, Judas Priest's traditional metal fans reacting with indifference to innovations that included the use of synthesized guitars. *Ram It Down* saw a return to pure heavy metal by comparison, but by this time their popularity had begun to wane. Dave Holland was replaced by Scott Travis (b. Norfolk, Virginia, USA; ex-**Racer X**) for the return to form that was *Painkiller*. Although no longer universally popular, Priest were still a major live attraction and remained the epitome of heavy metal, with screaming guitars matched by screaming vocalist, and the protagonists clad in studs and black leather. The band were taken to court in 1990 following the suicide attempts of two fans (one successful) in 1985. Both CBS Records and Judas Priest were accused of inciting suicide through the 'backwards messages' in their recording of the **Spooky Tooth** classic, 'Better By You, Better Than Me'. They were found not guilty in June 1993 after a long court battle, Downing admitting: 'It will be another ten years before I can even spell subliminal'. Soon afterwards, Halford became disheartened with the band and decided to quit. He had temporarily fronted an Ozzy-less **Black Sabbath** and recorded 'Light Comes Out Of The Black' with **Pantera** for the *Buffy The Vampire Slayer* soundtrack. He debuted with his new band, Halford, in 1996. With new vocalist Ripper Owens, Judas Priest returned to recording with 1997's *Jugulator*. Halford formed the band Two.

● ALBUMS: *Rocka Rolla* (Gull 1974)★★, *Sad Wings Of Destiny* (Gull 1976)★★, *Sin After Sin* (Columbia 1977)★★★, *Stained Class* (Columbia 1978)★★★, *Killing Machine* (Columbia 1978)★★, *Live - Unleashed In The East* (Columbia 1979)★★★, *British Steel* (Columbia 1980)★★★★, *Point Of Entry* (Columbia 1981)★★★, *Screaming For Vengeance* (Columbia 1982)★★★, *Defenders Of The Faith* (Columbia 1984)★★★, *Turbo* (Columbia 1986)★★, *Priest Live* (Columbia 1987)★★, *Ram It Down* (Columbia 1988)★★★, *Painkiller* (Columbia 1990)★★★, *Jugulator* (SPV 1997)★★★, *Concert Classics* (Ranch Life 1998)★★.

● COMPILATIONS: *Best Of* (Gull 1978)★★, *Hero Hero* (Telaeg 1987)★★, *Collection* (Castle 1989)★★★, *Metal Works '73 - '93* (Columbia 1993)★★★★, *Living After Midnight* (Columbia 1997)★★★.

● VIDEOS: *Fuel Of Life* (Columbia 1986), *Judas Priest Live* (Virgin Vision 1987), *Painkiller* (Sony Music Video 1990), *Metal Works 73-93* (1993).

● FURTHER READING: *Heavy Duty*, Steve Gett.

Judd, Cledus 'T', (No Relation)

b. Barry Poole, Crow Springs, Georgia, USA. A rather unlikely star of the 90s country scene, Cledus 'T' Judd (No Relation) has won many admirers for his cheeky renditions of current hits, and his merciless lampooning of the Nashville hierarchy. After high school, he briefly flirted with a career as a professional basketball player before dropping out of his scholarship to attend the Roffler Hair Design College. Based at the Don Shaw Hairdressers in Atlanta, he began competing in international hairstyling events. At this time he began to write his first 'country-rap' songs, which he would improvise over country records in talent contests. He subsequently moved to Nashville where he continued to work as a hairdresser, but he also sent in his songs to radio for the first time. The first two songs to receive extensive air play were 'Indian In-Laws' (based on **Tim McGraw**'s 'Indian Outlaw') and 'Gone Funky' (based on **Alan Jackson**'s 'Gone Country'). As a result, Judd was signed by the **Walter Yetnikoff**-backed independent label Razor & Tie. Within a few months of his impersonations/parodies airing on radio, being the subject of Judd's humorous attack had become one of the acid tests of an artist's popularity and name recognition. One of his victims, **Shania Twain**, was so charmed by Judd she agreed to appear in the video for his 1996 single, '(She's Got A Butt) Bigger Than The Beatles', a parody of **Joe Diffie**'s hit, 'Bigger Than The Beatles'. Judd also secured a four-night support slot to **Tammy Wynette** in Las Vegas, as many proclaimed him as the '**Weird Al Yankovic** of country'.

● ALBUMS: *Cledus T. Judd (No Relation)* (Razor & Tie 1995)★★★, *I Stoled This Record* (Razor & Tie 1996)★★★.

Judd, Naomi

(see the **Judds**).

Judds

Freshly divorced, Naomi Judd (b. Diana Ellen Judd, 11 January 1946, Ashland, Kentucky, USA) moved with her daughters **Wynonna** (b. Christina Ciminella, 30 May 1964, Ashland, Kentucky, USA) and Ashley (b. 1968) from California back to Morrill, Kentucky, where she worked as a nurse in a local infirmary. Outside working and school hours, she and the children would sing anything from bluegrass to showbiz standards for their own amusement. However, when Wynonna nurtured aspirations to be a professional entertainer, her mother lent her encouragement, to the extent of moving the family to Nashville in 1979. Naomi's contralto subtly underlined Wynonna's tuneful drawl. While tending a hospitalized relation of **RCA Records** producer Brent Maher, Naomi elicited an audition in the company's boardroom. With a hick surname and a past that read like a Judith Krantz novel, the Judds - so the executives considered - would have more than an even chance in the country market. An exploratory mini-album, which contained the show-stopping 'John Deere Tractor', proved the executives correct when, peaking at number 17, 'Had A Dream' was the harbinger of 1984's 'Mama He's Crazy', the first of many country chart-toppers for the duo. The Judds would also be accorded a historical footnote as the earliest commercial manifestation of the form's 'new tradition' - a tag that implied the maintenance of respect for C&W's elder statesmen. This was shown by the Judds' adding their voices to *Homecoming*, a 1985 collaboration by **Jerry Lee Lewis**, **Roy Orbison**, **Johnny Cash** and **Carl Perkins** (who later co-wrote Naomi and Wynonna's 1989 smash, 'Let Me Tell You About Love'). The Judds' repertoire also featured revivals of **Ella Fitzgerald**'s 'Cow Cow Boogie', **Elvis Presley**'s 'Don't Be Cruel' and **Lee Dorsey**'s 'Working In A Coal Mine'. Self-composed songs included Naomi's 1989 composition 'Change Of Heart', dedicated to her future second husband and former Presley backing vocalist, Larry Strickland. Maher too contributed by co-penning hits such as 1984's Grammy-winning 'Why Not Me', 'Turn It Loose', 'Girls Night Out' and the title track of the Judds' second million-selling album, *Rockin' With The Rhythm Of The Rain*. The team relied mainly on songsmiths such as Jamie O'Hara ('Grandpa Tell Me About The Good Old Days'), Kenny O'Dell ('Mama He's Crazy'), **Mickey Jupp**, Graham Lyle and **Troy Seals** ('Maybe Your Baby's Got The Blues') and Paul Kennerley ('Have Mercy', 'Cry Myself To Sleep'). Most Judds records had an acoustic bias - particularly on the sultry ballads selected for *Give A Little Love*. They also have an occasional penchant for star guests that have included the **Jordanaires** ('Don't Be Cruel'), **Emmylou Harris** 'The Sweetest Gift' (*Heartland*), **Mark Knopfler** on his 'Water Of Love' (*River Of Time*) and **Bonnie Raitt** playing slide guitar on *Love Can Build A Bridge*. In 1988, the pair became the first female country act to found their own booking agency (Pro-Tours) but a chronic liver disorder forced Naomi to retire from the concert stage two years later. Naomi and Wynonna toured America in a series of extravagant farewell concerts, before Wynonna was free - conveniently, cynics said - to begin her long-rumoured solo career. This she did in style, with a remarkable album that touched on gospel, soul and R&B, and confirmed her as one of the most distinctive and powerful female vocalists of her generation.

● ALBUMS: *The Judds: Wynonna & Naomi* mini-album (Curb/RCA 1984)★★, *Why Not Me?* (Curb/RCA 1984)★★★, *Rockin' With The Rhythm Of The Rain* (Curb/RCA 1985)★★★, *Give A Little Love* (Curb/RCA 1986)★★★, *Heartland* (Curb/RCA 1987)★★, *Christmas Time With The Judds* (Curb/RCA 1987)★★, *River Of Time* (Curb/RCA 1989)★★★, *Love Can Build A Bridge* (Curb/RCA 1990)★★★.

● COMPILATIONS: *Greatest Hits* (Curb/RCA 1988)★★★★, *Collector's Series* (Curb/RCA 1993)★★★, *Greatest Hits, Volume 2* (Curb/RCA 1991)★★★, *The Judds Collection 1983 - 1990* 3-CD box set (RCA 1991)★★★, *Number One Hits* (Curb 1995)★★★, *The Essential Judds* (RCA 1995)★★★★, *The Judds Collection* (Curb/The Hit 1996)★★★.

● VIDEOS: *Their Final Concert* (1992), *The Farewell Tour* (1994).

● FURTHER READING: *The Judds: Unauthorized Biography*, Bob Millard. *Love Can Build A Bridge*, Naomi Judd.

Judge Dread

b. Alex Hughes, 1942, Kent, England, d. 13 March 1998, Canterbury, Kent, England. Hughes was a bouncer in London clubs at the end of the 60s and became familiar with reggae through his work, where he had become acquainted with the likes of **Derrick Morgan** and **Prince Buster**. In 1969 Buster had a huge underground hit with the obscene 'Big 5', a version of **Brook Benton**'s 'Rainy Night In Georgia'. It was clear there was a yawning gap waiting to be filled when Buster failed to follow up on his hit, so Hughes, aka Judge Dread (a name borrowed from a Prince Buster character), plunged in. His first single, 'Big Six', went to number 11 in 1972, and spent more than six months in the charts. No-one heard it on air: it was a filthy nursery rhyme. 'Big Seven' did better than 'Big Six', and from this point onwards Dread scored hits with 'Big Eight', a ridiculous version of 'Je T'Aime', and a string of other novelty reggae records, often co-penned by his friend and manager, Fred Lemon. Incidentally, 'Big Six' was also a hit in Jamaica. Five years and 11 hits later (including such musical delicacies as 'Y Viva Suspenders' and 'Up With The Cock'), the good-natured Hughes, one of just two acts successfully to combine music-hall with reggae (the other was Count Prince Miller, whose 'Mule Train' rivalled Dread for sheer chutzpah), had finally ground to a halt in chart terms. In later years he was found occasionally working the clubs, and he had also sought employment as a local newspaper columnist in Snodland, Kent. In March 1998 he suffered a fatal heart attack while performing in concert at the Penny Whistle Theatre in Canterbury.

● ALBUMS: *Dreadmania: It's All In The Mind* (Trojan 1972)★★★, *Working Class 'Ero* (Trojan 1974)★★★, *Bedtime Stories* (Creole 1975)★★★, *Last Of The Skinheads* (Cactus 1976)★★★, *40 Big Ones* (Creole 1977)★★★, *Reggae And Ska* (TTR 1980)★★★, *Rub-A-Dub* (Creole 1981)★★★, *Not Guilty* (Creole 1984)★★, *Live And Lewd* (Skank 1988)★★, *Never Mind Up With The Cock, Here's Judge Dread* (Tring 1994)★★,

Ska'd For Life (Magnum 1996)★★, *Dread White And Blue* (Skank 1996)★★★.
● COMPILATIONS: *The Best Of Judge Dread* (Klik 1976)★★★, *The Best Worst Of Judge Dread* (Creole 1978)★★★, *The Legendary Judge Dread Volume 1* (Link 1989)★★★, *The Legendary Judge Dread Volume 2* (Link 1989)★★★, *The Very Worst Of Judge Dread* (Creole 1991)★★★, *The Big 24* (Trojan 1994)★★★, *Big 14* (Hallmark 1995)★★★, *Greatest Hits* (K-Tel 1997)★★★, *Big Hits* (Summit 1997)★★★.

Judge Jules

b. Julius O'Rearden. Together with partner Michael Skins, Jules has become one of the UK's leading remixers. He was originally bedecked with the Judge prefix from Norman Jay during the mid-80s house/rare groove scene, at which time he was studying law. Apparently he proved exceedingly useful when police raided parties, tying the officers up in legal jargon while his friends extinguished their herbal cigarettes. Together with Jay (nicknamed Shake And Finger Pop, while Jules was Family Function) they performed at about thirty warehouse parties between the years 1984 and 1987. He earned a living from buying up rare house records on trips to America and bringing them back to England to sell at exhorbitant prices. As house turned to acid he remained a prominent figure in the rave scene, playing at many of the larger events like Evolution, Sunrise and World Dance, after which he earned his first remixing credits. The clients included Soft House Company, Fat Men, **Big Audio Dynamite** and, bizarrely, the **Stranglers**. In 1991 he re-aquainted himself with an old school-friend, Rolo. They set up a studio together, and learned how to produce and engineer properly, an aspect they'd previously bluffed their way through. A studio was slowly established in the basement of his house, before he teamed up with ex-reggae drummer Michael Skins. By remixing a devastating version of **M People**'s 'Excited' in 1992 the team was established, with guesting musicians like guitarist Miles Kayne adding to the musical melting pot. Having set up Tomahawk Records Jules has gone on record his own work. These have included Datman (licensed to **ffrr**), the All Stars ('Wanna Get Funky', which sampled from **Andrew Lloyd Webber**'s *Jesus Christ Superstar*) and 290 North ('Footsteps'), as well as guest appearances from ex-**KLF** singer Maxine Hardy (Icon's 'I Can Make You Feel So Good') and ex-**O'Jays** singer Ronnie Canada ('Heading For Self-Destruction'). More recent remixes have included **T-Empo**'s handbag house classic 'Saturday Night, Sunday Morning' , Melanie Williams ('Everyday Thing'), BT Express ('Express'), Jeanie Tracy ('Is This Love'), Our Tribe ('Love Come Home'), plus the big money-spinners Doop ('Doop') and **Reel 2 Real** ('I Like To Move It'). Which has ensured he can practically write his own cheque for remixing engagements now, of which he is offered at least ten a week. He also records two radio shows a week for Radio One.

Judy At Carnegie Hall - Judy Garland

The sleeve note begins: 'On the evening of April 23, 1961, 3,165 privileged people packed the world famous Carnegie Hall beyond its capacity, and witnessed what was to be probably the greatest evening in show business history.' This souvenir of that remarkable occasion is said to contain the complete concert, during which Judy Garland sang 26 songs and mesmerized the audience with her sensational all-round performance. The album won Grammys for album of the year, best female vocal performance, best engineering and best cover. It was in the US chart for 73 weeks, 13 of them at number 1.
● Tracks: *When You're Smiling; Almost Like Being In Love (medley); Who Cares?; Puttin' On The Ritz; How Long Has This Been Going On; Just You, Just Me; The Man That Got Away; San Francisco; That's Entertainment; Come Rain Or Come Shine; You're Nearer; A Foggy Day; If Love Were All; Zing Went The Strings Of My Heart; Stormy Weather; You Made Me Love You (medley); Rockabye Your Baby With A Dixie Melody; Over The Rainbow; Swanee; After You've Gone; Chicago; The Trolley Song (overture); Over The Rainbow (overture); The Man That Got Away (overture); Do It Again; You Go To My Head; Alone Together; I Can't Give You Anything But Love.*
● First released 1961
● UK peak chart position: 13
● USA peak chart position: 1

Juggernaut

Formed in Texas, California, USA, in 1985, the band's original line-up consisted of Harlan Glenn (vocals), Eddie Katilius (guitar), Scott Womack (bass) and Bobby Jarzombek (drums). They signed to the Metal Blade Records label and had an early demo track included on the *Metal Massacre VII* compilation album. Their debut long-player, *Baptism Under Fire*, was released in 1986. Their music was as the band's name suggested, traditional heavy metal, with the emphasis on 'heavy'. The outfit received little attention from the media and Glenn left the band to be replaced by Steve Cooper in time for *Trouble Within*. Released in 1987, this similarly made little impact. With any degree of sustained success seemingly beyond them, the band folded in early 1988.
● ALBUMS: *Baptism Under Fire* (Metal Blade 1986)★★★, *Trouble Within* (Metal Blade 1987)★★.

Juicy Lucy

Juicy Lucy was formed in 1969 when three ex-members of the **Misunderstood** - Ray Owen (vocals), Glen 'Ross' Campbell (steel guitar) and Chris Mercer (tenor saxophone) - were augmented by Neil Hubbard (guitar), Keith Ellis (bass) and Pete Dobson (bass). The sextet enjoyed a surprise hit single with their fiery reading of **Bo Diddley**'s 'Who Do You Love', a track featured on the group's first, and best-known, album. The cover became a sexist classmate of **Jimi Hendrix**'s *Electric Ladyland*, and featured a naked busty woman languishing on a banquet table, amid a glut of various sliced and squashed fruits. Owen was later replaced by former **Zoot Money** singer Paul Williams, one of several changes afflicting the group. Their brand of blues-rock became more predictable as one by one the original cast dropped out. A fourth album, *Pieces*, was completed by a reshaped unit of Williams, Mick Moody (guitar), Jean Roussal (keyboards) and ex-**Blodwyn Pig** members Andy Pyle (bass) and Ron Berg (drums), but this was the final line-up of Juicy Lucy, which broke up soon afterwards. A new version of the band appeared in the 90s with Andy Doughty (bass), Mike Jarvis (guitar) and Spencer Blackledge (drums) together with the ever present Owen.

● ALBUMS: *Juicy Lucy* (Vertigo 1969)★★★★, *Lie Back And Enjoy It* (Vertigo 1970)★★, *Get A Whiff A This* (Bronze 1971)★★, *Pieces* (Polydor 1972)★★, *Here She Comes Again* (HTD 1996)★★★.

● COMPILATIONS: *Who Do You Love: The Best Of* (Sequel 1990)★★.

Juju

Juju is guitar-dominated music which started in Lagos, Nigeria, in the 20s. Several historians have attempted to trace the exact date with widely differing results, though usage of the term juju to describe a tambourine-styled instrument was unarguably prevalent as early as the eighteenth century. Juju descended from the native Yoruba tradition as a variant of palm wine music, and was initially pioneered by Irewolede Denge and Tunde Nightingale, but **I.K. Dairo** became its great populariser in the 50s. Through Dairo modern instruments such as the electric bass and accordion were introduced, as well as amplification and the gangan (Yoruba talking drums). A decade later Dairo was joined as the pre-eminent juju spokesman by **Ebenezer Obey**, who strained traditional Yoruba concerns through a conservative, Christian perspective. During the Nigerian Civil War of the late 60s juju supplanted highlife as the most popular native music form. **King Sunny Ade** arrived in the 80s to weld his own 'world beat' style to juju. Competition between Sunny Ade and Obey, at opposite ends of the political, religious and philosophical spectrum, ensured that during this period juju's growth was accelerated. Juju followers had always acknowledged the importance of new 'systems' in the music, which could mean a rhythmic, stylistic or instrumental innovation, but now the will to break new ground was unfettered. Each musician was responsible for a prolific output in the 80s, but it was Sunny Ade who first captured an international market. However, by the end of the decade juju was losing ground to a new variant, **fuji**. Both of juju's giants were confined largely to elder audiences while Nigeria's youth were captivated by the more energetic fuji sound.

Juke Box Jury

Perhaps the least progressive of all pop television programmes of the 60s, BBC Television's *Juke Box Jury* followed a rigid presentational format where four panellists (typically a disc jockey, a celebrity and two musical or theatrical artists) passed verdicts on current releases. Chaired by presenter David Jacobs, they would be encouraged to predict whether the records played would enter the UK Top 20 ('hit') or not ('miss'). Part of the show's problem lay in this formula - its main substance was the panellists' judgement of an item's musical and artistic worth, yet they were forced to vote on entirely different criteria (whether it would be successful as a chart record). Each record was played for only 30 seconds or so before opinions were declared, and even then chairman Jacobs soothed the discourse - extreme negative reactions, for instance, were frowned upon. Richard Mabey caricatured the show's vapidity in his book, *The Pop Process*: 'The comedian made a joke about the title, the disc jockey explained how he had lunch with the recording manager, and the starlet said how lovely it would be "after the party's over, and you're left alone with someone special".' It was not an ideal programme, then, to document the rise of pop music in the 60s, although it did serve the purpose of informing the public about new releases and forming a body of critical opinion - however spurious - about them. The format was revived in the 70s to limited success, with some of its conventions relaxed. Guests even included John Lydon of **PiL**, a panellist guaranteed to mock and sneer his way through any recording that was not his own. In the 90s it was revived for a third time, and presented by **Jools Holland**, but again found limited audience approval. Regardless of the presence of *Juke Boy Jury*, the space for a critical programme on popular music in the UK remains open.

Juluka

(see **Clegg, Johnny**)

July

A quintet of Tony Duhig (guitar), John Field (flute/keyboards), Chris Jackson (drums), Alan James (bass) and Tom Newman (vocals), July began life as a skiffle group based in Ealing, London, originally known as the Playboys. There then followed a brief interlude as an R&B act known as the Tomcats. That group travelled to Spain in 1966 (with the same line-up which would become known as July) and worked the holiday resorts as Los Tomcats. They achieved a minor degree of success there, seeing four EPs reach the domestic charts, including one that was sung entirely in Spanish. On their return to Ealing in 1968 they switched names and recorded a single for Major Minor Records, 'My Clown', with **Spencer Davis** taking over their management. This was followed by what has become one of the most collectible British psychedelic albums of the late 60s. In common with many such obscurities, however, a retrospective CD reissue (on Aftermath Records) has displayed the album's qualities in a harsher light - apart from the eerie psychedelia of the two sides of their debut single, there is little it contains which could in any way be described as essential. One further single emerged in the group's lifetime, 'Hello, Who's There', but there have been a series of retrospective reissues and compilations. Duhig and Field subsequently joined **Jade Warrior**, before Duhig moved on to Assagai. Alan James later played for a number of prominent 70s artists, including **Cat Stevens**, **Duffy Power**, **Neil Innes** and **Kevin Coyne**. Newman later released solo albums for **Virgin** and **Decca Records**. His greatest claim to fame, however, was his involvement with **Mike Oldfield**'s *Tubular Bells* opus, which he engineered. He was also partly responsible for establishing **Richard Branson**'s Manor Studios.

● ALBUMS: *July* (Major Minor 1968)★★★.
● COMPILATIONS: *Dandelion Seeds* (Bam-Caruso 1987)★★★★, *The Second Of July* (Essex 1995)★★★★.

Jumbo

Beset by all kinds of troubles, and undecided for a time whether it was a musical or a circus (it was finally classed as the latter), Jumbo eventually lumbered into the newly renovated Hippodrome in New York, several weeks late, on 16 November 1935. The book, by Ben Hecht and Charles McArthur, told the story of the feuding male figureheads of two circus families who are brought to their senses by the love between the son of one, and the daughter of the other. The show was an extravagant spectacle, and an enormous undertaking, costing upwards of $300,000, with equestrian, acrobatic, and aerial dances, a cast of nearly a hundred, and almost as many animals. Gloria Grafton and Donald Novis played the young lovers, and they shared the three classic songs that emerged from **Richard Rodgers** and **Lorenz Hart**'s lovely score, 'Little Girl Blue', 'My Romance' ('Wide awake, I can make my most fantastic dreams come true/My romance, doesn't need a thing but you'), and 'The Most Beautiful Girl In The World'. The other numbers included 'Over And Over Again' and 'The Circus Is On Parade', both of which were sung by Bob Lawrence and Henderson's Singing Razorbacks. The star of the show was one of the world's greatest clowns - in the widest sense - **Jimmy Durante**, who played the role of press agent Claudius B. Bowers and introduced the lively and amusing 'Laugh' and 'Women'. **Paul Whiteman** And His Orchestra were another big attraction in a magnificent spectacle that ran for just over seven months, 233 performances, but inevitably lost money for its flamboyant producer, **Billy Rose**. The 1962 film version, which is generally known as *Billy Roses's Jumbo*, had a modified storyline, and starred Durante, **Doris Day**, Stephen Boyd, and Martha Raye.

Jumbo (film musical)
(see *Billy Rose's Jumbo*)

Jump 'N The Saddle Band

Jump 'N The Saddle Band had one good idea for a novelty song, recorded it in 1983, took it to the US Top 20 and were never heard from again. Their idea was to record a tribute to Jerome 'Curly' Howard, a long-deceased member of the US comedy troupe the Three Stooges. Mimicking the nonsensical phrases uttered by the comedian in the Stooges' films, and a shuffle-like dance that often accompanied them, the band's vocalist, Peter Quinn, wrote 'The Curly Shuffle' and found a way to immortality. Jump 'N The Saddle Band was a sextet consisting of Quinn, guitarists T.C. Furlong and Barney Schwartz, saxophonist Tom Trinka, bassist Rick Gorley and drummer Vince Dee. They evolved from a Chicago, Illinois, USA-based band called Rio Grande that existed during the mid-70s. The line-up on the hit was the result of several personnel changes. 'The Curly Shuffle' came about during the group's stage show and **Atlantic Records** signed the group on the basis of its popularity at those shows. They were unable to follow that hit with another and an album for Atlantic failed to chart.

● ALBUMS: *Jump 'N The Saddle Band* (1984)★★.

Jumpin' The Gunn

This blues trio were formed in Inverness, Scotland, but it was in Memphis, Tennessee, USA, in the summer of 1992, that the three members, Andy Gunn (guitar), Steve Skelton (keyboards) and Vikki Kitson (vocals), began jamming together in a neighbourhood bar on Beale Street. Their name was taken from an album title of 70s US rock band **Jo Jo Gunne**. They were initially spotted by John Wooler of the Pointblank Records label at a folk festival there, and he recognized in them the talent and potential that merged their own resolute songwriting with US and native blues influences. Highlighted by Kitson's rock-edged delivery (natural comparisons to **Janis Joplin** followed), the group's debut album, *Shades Of Blue*, was recorded in Memphis in 1992. Songs such as 'More And More', 'Green All Over' and 'Crossed Wires' confirmed the promise, with Gunn's songwriting providing Kitson with ample ammunition to produce a range of moods from screaming defiance to emotive resignation.

● ALBUMS: *Shades Of Blue* (Pointblank 1993)★★★.

Jumpleads

Formed in Oxford, England, the Jumpleads, with Caroline Ritson (vocals), Jon Moore (guitars), Dave Townend (melodeon) and Tracy (drums/bass), enjoyed a brief but notorious career. In 1982 they released *The Stag Must Die*, in a blood-splattered cover. The album was called 'loud, noisy, daring and appealing', but its new-wave sensibility, combined with folk songs, (termed 'rogue folk'), appalled and offended many people. Disenchanted with the response, the Jump Leads disbanded. Rogue records released a remix single of 'False Knight On The Road', but the band have only reunited for one-off festival performances. Of the ex-members, Jon Moore has the highest profile with E2.

● ALBUMS: *The Stag Must Die* (1982)★★.

June Brides

This mid-80s UK pop band was built around lyricist, guitarist and singer Phil Wilson. Operating in the independent sector, their sound was characterized by the unusual inclusion of a brass section; Jon Hunter (trumpet), Reg Fish (trumpet) and Frank Sweeney (viola), alongside Simon Beesley (guitar, vocals), Ade Carter (bass) and Dave Bickley (drums; replacing Brian Alexis). Their first release was 'In The Rain', followed by 'Every Conversation', on which **That Petrol Emotion**'s John O'Neill was brought in to help with production. Their only album, however, was disappointing in relation to singles such as 'No Place Called Home'. Sweeney guested on a number of **Creation Records** artefacts (**Peter Astor, Meat Whiplash**), and had another claim to fame in being badly beaten up by skinheads while trying to protect a pregnant woman. Hunter also played with **Marc Riley** for one EP. Press darlings for a couple of months, the June Brides nevertheless quickly departed from the scene because of 'frustration, lack of money, and some of us no longer enjoying being in the band'. Sweeney joined Brick Circus Hour and Wilson moved on to a solo career. A lavishly packaged compilation arrived in 1995, at which point a small-scale but relaxed reunion gig took place.
● ALBUMS: *There Are Eight Million Stories* (Pink 1985)★★.
● COMPILATIONS: *For Better Or Worse (1983-86)* (Overground 1995)★★★.

Jungle

The evolution of jungle is hard to pin down in exactitude. However, the term 'junglist' is Jamaican patois for a native of Trenchtown, the ghetto area of Kingston from whence came **Bob Marley**. Despite this, controversy persists over the use of the name, with some commentators insisting it is a derogatory term. Musically jungle rides on a combination of breakbeats and samples, with ragga's staccato rhythms, and subsonic bass. The tempo is roughly double that of ragga, clocking in at around 160bpm. The use of the hardcore breakbeats neatly completes a circle - they were originally a derivation of hip hop, which in turn leaned heavily on the reggae culture. It is a music widely perceived to be created by and for black people who are disaffected with the sound of 'white techno' (another anomaly considering that all of techno's originators were themselves black). The sound was pioneered in clubs by DJ Ron, Randall, Bobby Konders and on radio by Jumping Jack Frost (on Kiss FM) and pirates like Kool FM, Transmission One and Don FM. The earliest sighting of it outside of the underground came when **SL2**'s 'On A Ragga Tip' broke through in 1993. There had been antecedents, however. Singles like Genaside II's 'Narra Mine', material by **Shut Up And Dance** and even **Rebel MC**'s Comin' On Strong', built on a riot of breakbeats, all predicted the jungle sound. Recent innovations in the sound have arrived from more traditional reggae acts like **General Levy** ('Incredible' on Renk Records) who have begun 'voic-ing' words over the rhythms, where previously sampled chants sufficed. Amongst the better modern proponents, who tend to be anonymous even by dance music's standards, are Blame and Bubbles.
● FURTHER READING: *State Of Bass - Jungle: The Story So Far*, Martin James.

Jungle Book, The
(see **Disney, Walt**)

Jungle Brothers

Rap innovators and precursors to the sound later fine-tuned by **De La Soul**, **PM Dawn** *et al.* Following on from **Afrika Bambaataa**, the Jungle Brothers: Mike G (b. Michael Small, c.1969, Harlem, New York, USA), DJ Sammy B (b. Sammy Burwell, c.1968, Harlem, New York, USA) and Afrika Baby Bambaataa (b. Nathaniel Hall, c.1971, Brooklyn, New York, USA) were unafraid of cross-genre experimentation. The most famous demonstration being their version of **Marvin Gaye**'s 'What's Going On', though their incorporation of house music on 'I'll House You' is another good example. They made their debut for Warlock/Idlers Records in October 1987, before signing to **Gee Street Records**. As part of the **Native Tongues** coalition with **Queen Latifah**, **A Tribe Called Quest** and others, they sought to enhance the living experiences of black men and women by educating them about their role in history and African culture. In many ways traditionalists, the Jungle Brothers carefully traced the lines between R&B and rap, their admiration of **James Brown** going beyond merely sampling his rhythms (including the basis of their name - which shares the godfather of soul's initials). A second album was slightly less funky and more soul-based, particularly effective on cuts like 'Beyond This World'. It has been argued that the Jungle Brothers' failure to break through commercially had something to do with the fact that they were initially signed to a New York dance label, Idlers. More likely is the assertion that audiences for macho skulduggery greatly outnumbered those for which intelligent, discursive hip-hop was a worthwhile phenomenon in the late 80s. By the time of 1993's *J Beez Wit The Remedy*, they had unfortunately succumbed to the former. They suprisingly charted again in 1998 with the **Stereo MCs**' remix of 'Jungle Brother', taken from the one-dimensional *Raw Deluxe*.
● ALBUMS: *Straight Out The Jungle* (Idlers/Warlock 1988)★★★, *Done By The Forces Of Nature* (Warners 1989)★★★★, *J Beez Wit The Remedy* (Warners 1993)★★, *Raw Deluxe* (Gee Street 1997)★★, *Raw Deluxe* with bonus remix album (Gee Street 1998)★★.

Jungr And Parker

Duo, comprising Barbara Jungr (b. Rochdale, Lancashire, England; vocals, harmonica, mandolin, percussion), and Michael Parker (b. 30 December 1958, Kimbolton, Huntingdon, England; guitar, vocals, ukelele, banjo, cornet, piano, bass), who have gradually established themselves as class performers. They met in Fulham, London in the early 80s and worked in a harmony group called the Three Courgettes. It was 1984 before they adopted the name Jungr And Parker. As such, they twice toured nationally as support for comedian/actor Alexei Sayle, and occasionally worked with Julian Clary. They later became known for their regular appearances on the same artist's UK television series, *Sticky Moments*, and *Terry And Julian*, for which they wrote the theme tunes, the latter with Russell Churney. Jungr And Parker won the Perrier Award in 1987 at the Edinburgh Fringe Festival, for the show *Brown Blues*, with comedian Arnold Brown. The following year the duo also won the Swansea Fringe Festival Award. In 1992 they played and gave workshops in Sudan at the Khartoum International Music Festival for the British Council, going on to appear at the Sidmouth, Vancouver, and Winnipeg Folk Festivals, as well as on Canadian national radio. They also featured on BBC Radio 4 in a presentation of *Hell Bent Heaven Bound*, with **Christine Collister** and Helen Watson. Earlier in 1993 Jungr And Parker had travelled to Cameroon, where they performed all over the country, and gave workshops in songwriting, singing, and jazz music. They also played in the *Jazz Sous Les Manguiers* festival in the Cameroon capital Yaounde. Towards the end of 1993, they completed recording of their fifth series of *We Stayed In With Jungr And Parker* for BBC Radio 2, as well as making regular appearances on *Hayes At The Weekend* with Brian Hayes, also on Radio 2. As songwriters, they have provided topical songs for BBC Radio 4's *Stop The Week*, for independent television's *It's Almost Saturday* and the Snarling Beasties Theatre Company production of *The Man Who Cooked Her Husband*, in addition to providing the music for *Deadly Serious*, a radio play by Alan Gilbey. They continue to perform as a duo, having played many of the major festivals in Britain, often with their group the Band Of Gold.

● ALBUMS: *Wicked* (J&P 1986)★★, *Blue Devils* (J&P 1987)★★★, *Day Or Night* (J&P 1988)★★★, *Attitude* (J&P 1989)★★★, *Canada* (Harbourtown 1992)★★★★, *Hell Bent Heaven Bound* (Harbourtown 1993)★★.
● COMPILATIONS: *Off The Peg* (Utility Records 1988)★★★, *Over The Bridge* (Leaping Lizard 1990)★★★. As Band Of Gold: *Smile* (Mo' Love 1994)★★★.

Junior

(see **Giscombe, Junior**)

Junior Boy's Own Records

This label was founded in 1992 by Steven Hall and Terry Farley (who records with Pete Heller and Gary Wilkinson as Fire Island) from the ashes of **Boy's Own Records**, which they had formed in 1990 with **Andrew Weatherall**. Junior Boy's Own became one of the most important independent dance labels of the 90s, with strong releases from the Ballistic Brothers, Black Science Orchestra, the Dust Brothers (who later became

the **Chemical Brothers**), **Underworld**, X-Press 2 and others. Among their first singles were Fire Island's 'In Your Bones' and 'Fire Island', Black Science Orchestra's 'Where Were You', Known Chic's 'Dance' and Outrage's 'That Piano Track'. During the same period Underworld released two early singles, 'Big Mouth' and 'Dirty', as Lemon Interupt. In 1993 the label signed the Dust Brothers on the strength of their track 'Song To The Siren', which, with its reliance on prominent hip-hop beats, helped to kick off the movement that became known as big beat. After more singles from Fire Island ('There But For The Grace Of God'), Roach Motel ('Movin' On' and 'Transatlantic'), Underworld ('Spikee'/'Dogman Go Woof' and 'Dark And Long') and X-Press 2 ('Rock 2 House'/'Hip Housin'), Junior Boy's Own achieved widespread success in 1994 with their first album release, Underworld's *Dubnobasswithmyheadman*. Their compilation *Junior Boy's Own Collection* was followed by the Ballistic Brothers' *London Hooligan School*, Underworld's *Second Toughest In The Infants* and Black Science Orchestra's *Walter's Room*. At the same time they have continued to release a number of hit singles, notably Underworld's 'Born Slippy', Fire Island's 'If I Should Need A Friend' and the **Farley And Heller Project**'s 'Ultra Flava'. In 1998 the label changed their name to JBO Music when they signed a distribution agreement with **Virgin Records**' dance subsidiary V2. With their roots in the Balearic movement, Junior Boy's Own has always had an array of sounds: such artists as the Dust Brothers, Underworld and, more recently, Sycamore have blended a broad range of influences in their music to make what could sometimes only loosely be described as dance music.

Junior MAFIA

Junior MAFIA is a 90s rap collective featuring four acts from the Brooklyn, New York, USA area - Clepto, the Sixes, the Snakes and Lil' Kim. Most attention surrounded the latter artist, widely hailed as a natural successor to **MC Lyte** via her considerable dexterity on the microphone. Their debut single together, 'Player's Anthem', became a major R&B hit in 1995 with sales certified gold. On the album which accompanied it the rhythms were located at a mid-point between hip hop and soul, with 'Backstabbers' proving particularly articulate in this musical climate. The **Notorious B.I.G.** made a guest appearance on the more predictable 'Get Money', though again Lil' Kim earned critical plaudits for her ability to stand shoulder to shoulder with the current favourite son of New York ghetto rap.

● ALBUMS: *Conspiracy* (Undeas/Atlantic 1995)★★★.

Junior's Eyes

This energetic and musically tight UK rock group was formed in 1968 by Mick Wayne (guitar/vocals), one-time member of the Bunch Of Fives, with ex-**Pretty Things**' drummer Viv Prince (b. Loughborough, Leicestershire, England). Tim Renwick (b. 7 August

1949, Cambridge, England; guitar), John 'Honk' Lodge (bass) and John Cambridge (drums) completed the best-known Junior's Eyes line-up which, despite its brevity, was responsible for several excellent records. The group recorded three singles, 'Mr. Golden Trumpet Player', 'Woman Love' and 'Sink Or Swim', as well as the ambitious, uncompromising, *Battersea Power Station*, produced by **Tony Visconti**, whose several other charges included **David Bowie**, whom Junior's Eyes backed on *Man Of Words, Man Of Music* (1969), later known as *Space Oddity*. Cambridge subsequently joined Bowie's short-lived Hype while Renwick and Lodge formed **Quiver**. Mick Wayne later resurfaced in the **Pink Fairies**.

● ALBUMS: *Battersea Power Station* (Regal Zonophone 1969)★★★.

Junkyard

This five-piece US group was comprised of seasoned Los Angeles club circuit musicians. Formed in 1988, the line-up was David Roach (vocals), Chris Gates and Brian Baker (guitars), Clay Anthony (bass) and Patrick Muzingo (drums). Signing to **Geffen Records**, their debut offered 'trashy metallic boogie'. Two years later, *Sixes Sevens And Nines* emerged and the songwriting partnership of Roach and Gates had matured considerably, with the emphasis on the music rather than image. Musically, Junkyard sit somewhere between **Great White**, **Dokken** and **ZZ Top**, dealing in abrasive raunch 'n' roll. On their second album, producer Ed Stasium achieved a harder and bluesier sound (somewhat akin to **Lynyrd Skynyrd**), without pushing the band in a blatantly commercial direction. The group were nevertheless dropped by Geffen in 1992, though they elected to persevere.

● ALBUMS: *Junkyard* (Geffen 1989)★★, *Sixes, Sevens And Nines* (Geffen 1991)★★★.

Juno Reactor

Led by Ben Watkins and Mike MacGuire, who had previously worked with **Youth**, Juno Reactor has at various times included Johann Bley (who records for **Blue Room Released** as Johann), Stephane Holwick (of Total Eclipse) and Jans Waldenback. They grew out of the early Goa vibe in the early 90s, playing at the Full Moon parties on the travellers' circuit around the world, and with their album *Transmissions* (**Mute Records**, 1993) became one of the first trance groups to gain widespread recognition. However they have always stood apart from that sometimes formulaic scene: from an early stage Watkins employed heavy rock guitar in combination with techno ideas for their live shows. After signing to Blue Room, they released the single 'Guardian Angel/Rotorblade' and a second album *Beyond The Infinite* in 1995. The following year 'Conga Fury/Magnetic' gained Juno Reactor widespread praise for its innovative sound. In 1997 the group enjoyed a Top 40 hit with 'God Is God' which featured **Natasha Atlas** on vocals and was taken from their successful album *Bible Of Dreams* (1997). This album perhaps best represents Juno Reactor's varied sound which presents a more melodic slant on the familiar riffs and rhythms of trance in unusual combinations and situations, with live percussion ('Conga Fury' and 'Kaguya Hime'), vocals ('God Is God') and slide guitar and triple time ('Swamp Thing'). Following the policy of Blue Room, the group have been marketed more like a rock band and moved further from the media's perception of how a dance act should function. In an attempt to integrate more live performance and improvisation into their sound Juno Reactor performed with the South African band Amampondo on a tour of the USA in 1997 supporting **Moby**. During the same year they also made a seven-date tour of Japan and played at various festival around the UK and Europe. The group have also provided music for a number of film soundtrack's, notably *Barb Wire*, *Eraser*, *Mortal Kombat*, *Showgirls* and *Virtuosity*.

● ALBUMS: *Transmissions* (Mute 1993)★★★, *Beyond The Infinite* (Blue Room 1995)★★★, *Bible Of Dreams* (Blue Room 1997)★★★.

Jupp, Mickey

b. *c.*1940, Essex, England. Guitarist Jupp began his recording career as a member of the Orioles, a beat group based in Southend, Essex, England. By the end of the 60s he was fronting **Legend**, an act bedeviled by instability, but which anticipated the pub-rock style of **Dr. Feelgood** and **Ducks Deluxe**. The former act recorded one of Jupp's compositions, 'Cheque Book', and the artist in turn became one of the early signings to the nascent **Stiff** label. *Juppanese* enjoyed support from the entire Rockpile line-up. but despite assiduous touring, the guitarist was unable to escape cult status. *Mickey Jupp's Legend* featured Southend contemporaries **Gary Brooker**, Chris Copping and B.J. Wilson, but this newly recorded selection of material drawn from his previous group failed to capture their original informality. Jupp then left Stiff, but subsequent releases failed to expand upon an already well-honed niche.

● ALBUMS: *Juppanese* (Stiff 1978)★★★, *Mickey Jupp's Legend* (Stiff 1978)★★, *Long Distance Romancer* (1979)★★, *Some People Can't Dance* (A&M 1982)★★, *Shampoo, Haircut And Shave* (A&M 1983)★★, *X* (Waterfront 1988)★★, *As The Years Go By* (On The Beach 1991)★★.

Jurgens, Dick

b. 9 November 1911, Sacramento, California, USA. Jurgens, was an accomplished trumpeter by the age of 14. He and his brother Will formed their first band for summer camps at Lake Tahoe, working as rubbish collectors when not playing. Within three years the unit had been booked for a residency local hotel staying until offered a spot at the St. Francis Hotel in San Francisco in 1934. They developed into a polished band with a rich ensemble sound that was ideal for hotel and ballroom work, and vocals by guitarist Eddy Howard, an old friend from Sacramento. Jurgens was resident at the Aragon Ballroom, Chicago, the Elitch Gardens in Denver, and the Avalon Ballroom on Catalina Island, according to the season. He recorded for **Decca**, ARC, Vocalion, **OKeh** and **Columbia** and did many radio transcriptions, issued on Hindsight in the 70s. Jurgens also composed evergreens like 'Careless', 'If I Knew Then', 'Elmer's Tune', 'A Million Dreams Ago' and 'One Dozen Roses', which, as well as being covered by other artists, gave his band hit records without reaching the million-sellers. During World War II service in the US Marine Corps, Dick and Will formed an entertainment unit to tour the South Pacific war areas. Back in civilian life Jurgens returned to the Aragon and Trianon Ballrooms in Chicago until 1956, when he went into business outside the profession. After a break of 13 years he was asked to form a band for the Willowbrook Club outside Chicago, and continued playing there till his retirement in 1976. Singer Don Ring bought the rights to the band's name and library in 1986, and the New Dick Jurgens Orchestra now plays permanently at Ring's Pla Mor Ballroom in Wisconsin.

● ALBUMS: *Radio Years (1937-39)* (1979)★★★, *The Uncollected Dick Jurgens And His Orchestra Vol. 2 (1937-38)* (1979)★★★★.

Jürgens, Udo

b. Udo Jürgen Bockelmann, 30 September 1934, Klagenfurt, Austria. Jürgens grew up in Ottmanach Castle where Napoleon had once resided. His ear for music became evident in his pre-teen mastery of both harmonica and piano-accordion. While attending a local music college, he performed regularly on regional radio and composed 'Je T'Aime', an opus that won a national competition. However, though Jürgens' recording career began in 1954, it only emerged when the self-penned 'Jenny' was a Belgian hit after he had been judged best solo vocalist in 1960's Knokke Song Festival. Three years later, his 'Warum Nur Warum' was voted fifth in the Eurovision Song Contest, and earned considerable royalties in the UK charts when covered (as 'Walk Away') by **Matt Monro**. A celebrity in Europe, through film roles too, Jürgens swept to victory in the 1966 Eurovision Song Contest in Luxembourg with 'Merci Cheri', sung to his own keyboard accompaniment. This ballad was not sufficient to ease him into the English-speaking market in his own right but, from this apogee, his fortunes as an entertainer continued to blossom elsewhere.

Jury

Formed in Winnipeg, Canada in 1964, the Jury became a popular pop-rock group in Canada in the mid-60s. The group's roots are traceable to a unit called the Chord U Roys, formed in Winnipeg in the late 50s and featuring lead guitarist Terry Kenny, vocalist Bruce Walker and drummer Ray Stockwell. After several name and personnel changes the group transformed into the Jury, including Kenny, Walker, Stockwell, bassist Roland Blaquiere and rhythm guitarist George

Johns. They signed to **London Records** in Canada in 1965 and released their first single, 'Until You Do', a regional hit due to heavy local radio airplay. Further London singles increased their national publicity. Stockwell left the group in 1966 and was replaced by Kenny Hordichuk. During that year their fourth single, 'Please Forget Her', marked a switch to the Quality label and was issued in the USA on Port. After its failure to break into the US market the group disbanded.

Just A Gigolo

'My 30 **Elvis Presley** films in one,' was how **David Bowie** once described his starring role in *Just A Gigolo*. Actor David Hemmings directed and played a part in this 1978 feature, which also featured Kim Novak and **Marlene Dietrich** in its cast. Bowie played a disillusioned Prussian, entrenched in Berlin, in this costly West German production. Despite the chameleon qualities he brought to his recordings, the singer is obviously ill-at-ease in the role, undermining any merits the film may have. A glossy soundtrack included material by **Manhattan Transfer** and the Rebels, who perform Bowie's 'Revolutionary Song', but neither it nor the film itself possesses lasting qualities.

Just For Fun

1963 was a pivotal year in British pop. It was the time of **Beatle**mania, the Mersey Boom and beat groups, when a new generation changed the face of music forever. Although one of that period's transitional acts, **Brian Poole And The Tremeloes**, was included in its cast, *Just For Fun* rather reflected the immediate past, one of brylcreem and beehive hairstyles. The plot, in which teenagers try to win the right to vote, is largely irrelevant, hampered by a wooden script and acting. The film is, however, notable for the appearance of a string of acts about to be eclipsed. American stars **Bobby Vee** and the **Crickets** contribute 'The Night Has A Thousand Eyes' and 'My Little One' respectively, **Freddie Cannon** and **Johnny Tillotson** are also on hand, while **Kitty Lester** provides her memorable version of 'Love Letters'. Nevertheless, the cast chiefly comprises of UK performers. These include the **Springfields**, **Mark Wynter**, **Joe Brown** and **Kenny Lynch**, but the highlights are provided by three instrumental groups. Former **Shadows**, **Jet Harris And Tony Meehan**, were captured at their peak; the former's growling basslines offset by the latter's flashy drumming. The **Tornadoes**, protégés of iconoclast producer **Joe Meek**, unleashed a view of science-fiction pop adopted wholesale of Swedish quartet the **Spotniks**. Dressed in space-suits and using guitars linked to amplifiers through radio waves rather than leads, the group took their chosen genre to its limits. *Just For Fun* is worthwhile simply to see this band in action, but it also captures pop in its final innocent moments.

Just Jimmy Reed - **Jimmy Reed**

This was not vintage Reed, but it was one of the first of his albums to fuel the British blues boom. By 1962, the Jimmy Reed boogie groove had not yet become a rut and his accompanists, Lefty Bates, Jimmy Reed Jnr., Phil Upchurch and Al Duncan, knew exactly what was expected of them. They were at their best when they could rock out on something like 'Good Lover'. 'Down In Mississippi' was more bucolic than J.B. Lenoir's song of the same name and bad habits were having a derogatory effect on his already mumbled diction. No one believed it when he sang 'I'll Change My Style', because then it would not have been the Jimmy Reed that everyone liked and no one could imitate.

● Tracks: *Take It Slow; Good Lover; Too Much; I'll Change My Style; In The Morning; You Can't Hide; Back Home At Noon; Kansas City Baby; Oh John; Let's Get Together; Down In Mississippi.*
● First released 1962
● UK peak chart position: did not chart
● USA peak chart position: 103

Just Us

The New York-based team **Chip Taylor** and Al Gorgoni initially began working together as contract songwriters. Their best-known collaboration, 'I Can't Let Go', was originally written for soul-singer Evie Sands, but became an international hit when covered by the **Hollies**. The duo took the name Just Us on beginning a short-lived recording career, and scored a minor US hit in 1966 with 'I Can't Grow Peaches On A Cherry Tree'. Further singles, including 'What Are We Gonna Do' and 'Run Boy Run' duly followed, but these melodic, 'good time' releases were overshadowed by a series of successful Taylor compositions, notably 'Wild Thing' (the **Troggs**/**Jimi Hendrix**), 'Storybook Children' (Billy Vera and **Judy Clay**), 'Any Way That You Want Me' (Troggs) and 'Angel Of The Morning' (**Merilee Rush**). The pair were later joined by a third songwriter, Trade Martin, in Gorgoni, Martin And Taylor, who completed two albums for the Buddah label.

Just-Ice

b. Joseph Williams Jnr., Ft. Greene, Brooklyn, New York, USA. Just Ice (aka Justice) was thrust to prominence in 1987 when his name was attached to the headline 'Murder, Drugs and the Rap Star'. The caption was emblazoned on the cover of the Washington Post. The text revealed that the rapper had been held and questioned in connection with the murder of a drug dealer (at no time were charges laid against him). Members of the Washington black community were so outraged by the implied racism and lack of factual reporting in the story that they picketed the newspaper's offices for several months. This has somewhat overshadowed the artist's recording career for Fresh and **Sleeping Bag**.

● ALBUMS: *Kool & Deadly* (Fresh 1987)★★★, *The Desolate One* (Sleeping Bag 1989)★★★, *Kill The Rhythm (Like A Homicide)* (In A Minute 1996)★★★.

Justice, Jimmy

b. 1940, Carlshalton, Surrey, England. Justice signed to Pye in 1960, owing partly to fellow stable-mate singer, **Emile Ford**, who had spotted Jimmy singing in a coffee-bar. When Justice's first two releases failed in the UK, he relocated to Sweden where his cover of the **Jarmels**' 'Little Lonely One' charted. In 1962 with the help of producer **Tony Hatch**, he strung together three UK Top 20 hits: the remarkably fresh cover of the **Drifters** US hit 'When My Little Girl Is Smiling', 'Ain't That Funny' - an original song penned by Johnny Worth - and 'Spanish Harlem'. Jimmy spent 1962 commuting between England and Sweden (where he had many previous bookings to honour) but managed, together with his group the Excheckers, to join a **Larry Parnes** UK tour headed by **Billy Fury** and **Joe Brown**. This white singer who possessed a mature, soulful voice, was sometimes called 'Britain's **Ben E. King**', and caused some controversy when he covered King's 'Spanish Harlem' with an uncannily similar vocal style. Justice also recorded for **Decca** in 1969, **RCA** in 1968 and B&C in 1972.

● ALBUMS: *Two Sides Of Jimmy Justice* (Pye 1962)★★★, *Smash Hits* (Pye 1962)★★★, *Justice For All* (Kapp 1964)★★★.

Justified Ancients Of Mu Mu

Also known as the JAMS, this coalition saw **Bill Drummond** and Jimmy Cauty engage in some startlingly imaginative methods of undermining the prevailing pop ethos. Drummond had cut his teeth in the Liverpool scene of the early 80s and played a large part in setting up Zoo Records. By 1987 he was working with Cauty and exploiting the techniques of sampling and computers. Their liberal use of other artists' material within the framework of their own songs resulted in a court case with **Abba**, following which all remaining copies of the JAMS' album, *1987 (What The Fuck Is Going On?)*, were legally bound to be destroyed. However, a handful of copies escaped annihilation and ended up on sale for £1,000 each. The following year the duo switched guises to become the **Timelords**, enjoying a worldwide hit with 'Doctorin' The Tardis', with **Gary Glitter**. A manual on how to have a number 1 single was written, to be succeeded by work on their own movie. By this time Drummond and Cauty were calling themselves the **KLF** and enjoying yet more global success with the 'Stadium House' trilogy of singles. In 1991 the JAMS moniker was reactivated for 'It's Grim Up North', a dance single that owed several musical moments to composer William Blake. Subsequently, Drummond and Cauty promptly slipped back into KLF mode to record with country singer **Tammy Wynette**.

● ALBUMS: *1987 (What The Fuck Is Going On?)* (KLF Communications 1987)★★★, *Who Killed The JAMS?* (KLF Communications 1987)★★★.
● COMPILATIONS: *The History Of The JAMS aka The Timelords* (TVT 1989)★★★.

Justis, Bill

b. 14 October 1927, Birmingham, Alabama, USA, d. 15 July 1982. Justis was a saxophonist, arranger and producer who created 'Raunchy', one of the classic rock 'n' roll instrumentals (and, coincidentally, the first song that **George Harrison** learned to play). He grew up in Memphis playing jazz and dance band music before joining **Sam Phillips**' **Sun** label in 1957 as musical director. Phillips liked a tune called 'Backwoods', composed by Justis and guitarist Sid Manker, but renamed it 'Raunchy'. It was issued as a single and Justis' own honking saxophone solo made it a million-seller. Cover versions by **Billy Vaughn** and **Ernie Freeman** also sold well, while there were later recordings by the **Shadows** and **Duane Eddy**. Later singles such as 'College Man' and 'Flea Circus' (written by **Steve Cropper**) were unsuccessful and Justis concentrated on his arrangements for Sun artists. His most important A&R work was with **Charlie Rich**, whom he discovered singing ballads. Urging him to listen to **Jerry Lee Lewis**, Justis produced Rich's biggest rock era hit, 'Lonely Weekends', in 1960 and also co-wrote the answer record 'After The Hop' for Bill Pinky And The Turks. Leaving Sun, Justis recorded rockabilly artist Ray Smith for Sam's brother Judd Phillips and briefly ran his own label (Play Me) before working again with Rich at **RCA**. By 1963 he was with Monument, another significant southern record company, where he produced hits by vocal group the **Dixiebelles**. **Kenny Rogers** was among those for whom he later wrote arrangements. Justis occasionally also made his own instrumental albums. He died in July 1982.

● ALBUMS: *Cloud Nine* (Philips 1958)★★★, *Enchanted Sea* (1972)★★.

JX

Based in south London, JX is the reclusive Jake Williams who established the name with 'Son Of A Gun', a UK Top 20 hit in April 1994 which featured the vocalist Billie Godfrey. This was followed by 'You Belong To Me' and 'Can't Take My Hands Off You'. Each single was originally issued on the cult house label **Hooj Toons** before being licensed either to **London Records** or its subsidiary dance outlet **ffrr Records**. In May 1996 'There's Nothing I Won't Do' entered the UK Top 10 in its first week of release. JX is less prolific than most house artists as Williams insists that 'quality control is very important' in order to gain the respect of his audience.

K - Kula Shaker

Crispin Mills' mother (actress Hayley) must have fed her baby son a balanced diet of **Jimi Hendrix**, **Beatles** and late 60s rock. All these styles are beautifully honed on this stunning debut album. Creamy guitars, crybaby wah-wahs, and chiming sitars are all-pervading. Even the record-cover collage of famous 'K's (Ken Dodd and Lord Kitchener among them) reflects the band's mishmash of influences. The mystical Eastern themes of 'Govinda' and 'Tattva' sit alongside unapologetically retro rockers such as 'Grateful When You're Dead/Jerry Was There' and 'Hey Dude', merely serving to reinforce the atmosphere: you can almost picture the cheesecloth and smell the patchouli from here.

● Tracks: *Hey Dude; Knight On The Town; Temple Of Everlasting Light; Govinda; Smart Dogs; Magic Theatre; Into The Deep; Sleeping Jiva; Tattva; Grateful When You're Dead/Jerry Was There; 303; Start All Over; Hollow Man.*

● First released 1996

● UK peak chart position: 1

● USA peak chart position: did not chart

K Klass

Carl Thomas and Andy Williams, who had previously been part of the band Interstate In Wrexham, met Russ Morgan and Paul Roberts, who were from Chester, at various clubs around Manchester in the late 80s. They began to write music together in 1989 and subsequently sent a demo to Martin Price's Eastern Bloc Records who released the EP *Wildlife* the following year on their label Creed Records. The title track employed the theme to the BBC children's television programme *Animal Magic* and the EP consequently became a hit in the dance charts. At the same time the band gained further exposure when they supported **808 State** on tour during that summer. In April 1991 K Klass released 'Rhythm Is A Mystery' which, with its Italian-style piano lines and singer Bobby Depasois, had more of a commercial edge to hit. This uplifting house track became in popular clubs throughout the north of England and Scotland, as the band gave a series of promotional gigs throughout the summer. However it achieved national success and eventually reached number three in the charts when the band signed to **DeConstruction Records** and released a remix towards the end of 1991. K Klass's popularity was confirmed when 'So Right', 'Don't Stop' (both 1992) and 'Let Me Show You' (1993) continued to sell well. In 1994 they released their debut album *Universal* accompanied by the single 'What You're Missing'. In 1996

DeConstruction released an album of remixes, *Remix and Additional Production*. K Klass have become popular as remix artists and have completed work for a number of artists including **Carleen Anderson**, **Denise Johnson**, **New Order** and Oceanic.

● ALBUMS: *Universal* (DeConstruction 1994)★★★, *Remix And Additional Production* (DeConstruction 1996)★★★.

K Sridhar And K Shivakumar

The two brothers (the family name is given first in India) K Sridhar (b. India; sarod) and K Shivakumar (b. India; violin). are masters of their chosen instruments. They have each perfected Hindustani and Carnatic playing - India's two main musical traditions. Twelve generations of their family were musicians and as children the brothers studied under the renowned Indian artist, Usted Zia Mohiuddin Dagar. Throughout the 80s Sridhar toured the world and played with musicians of other styles, including jazz and flamenco. The brothers' first major performances together were at two WOMAD festivals of 1988 at Toronto, Canada and Bracknell in England. They were joined by percussionist GS Sabri (tabla) and Camilla Hale (tampura). *Shringar* combines two half-hour ragas from each concert.

● ALBUMS: *Shringar* (Earthworks 1989)★★★★.

K-9 Posse

K-9 Posse were the unhappy result of **Arista Records** attempting to gatecrash the hip-hop party in the late 80s. The group were formed at Fairleigh Dickinson University in Teaneck, New Jersey, by Wardell Mahone and Vernon Lynch. The two rappers were in need of a DJ and up to the decks stepped Terrence Sheppard in 1988. Conscious rhymes about 'Someone's Brother' were present on their debut album, but no hit singles were forthcoming and the band soon disappeared from the face of the rap world.

● ALBUMS: *K-9 Posse* (Arista 1989)★★.

K-Ci & Jo Jo

see (**Jodeci**)

K-Doe, Ernie

b. Ernest Kador Jnr., 22 February 1936, New Orleans, Louisiana, USA. Previously a singer with touring gospel groups, K-Doe's earliest non-secular recordings were made in the mid-50s as a member of the Blue Diamonds. His first solo record, 'Do Baby Do', was released on **Specialty** in 1956. The singer's biggest hit came with the **Allen Toussaint** song 'Mother-In-Law'

(1961), which reached number 1 in the US pop charts. This pointed 'novelty' song was followed by 'Te-Ta-Te-Ta-Ta', and a strong double-sided release, 'I Have Cried My Last Tear'/'A Certain Girl'. The latter track proved popular in Britain where it was covered by the **Yardbirds** and the **Paramounts**. Further K-Doe singles included 'Popeye Joe' and 'I'm The Boss', but it was not until 1967 that he returned to the R&B chart with two singles for the Duke label, 'Later For Tomorrow' and 'Until The Real Thing Comes Along'. He remains a popular, energetic performer and occasional recording artist in New Orleans.

● ALBUMS: *Mother-In-Law* (Minit 1961)★★★★.
● COMPILATIONS: *Burn, K-Doe, Burn!* (Charly 1989)★★★★.

K-Passa

Simon Edward's voice, songs and accordion playing are the foundation for **K-Passa**'s position as the favourite live folk-based act in Bristol, England, and for his work with **Richard Thompson**, **Pete Morton** and the **Boothill Foot-Tappers**. Local recognition led to their appearance on the main stage at the 1992 Glastonbury Festival. Their blend of folk, Cajun, dub and reggae are eminently displayed on the live cassette, *2 From The Front*.

● ALBUMS: *2 From The Front* (1992)★★★.

K-Solo

b. Kevin Maddison, Central Islip, New York, USA. K-Solo is a part of the Hit Squad, the **EPMD** clique whose other members include **Das EFX** and **Redman**. Maddison had, in fact, been involved in a pre-EPMD band with Parrish Smith, before making vocal contributions to the group's *Unfinished Business*. Parrish would be on hand to provide production tutelage for K-Solo's debut album, a perfunctory demonstration of his story-telling skills highlighted by the stylish 'Tales From The Crack Side'. K-Solo is an acronym for Kevin Self Organisation Left Others.

● ALBUMS: *Tell The World My Name* (Atlantic 1990)★★★, *Spellbound* (Atlantic 1991)★★, *Times Up* (Atlantic 1992)★★★.

K-Tel Records

This Minneapolis-based company was the pioneer of television-advertised mail-order compilation albums in the early 70s. Among its best sellers were a *Hooked On* (*Country, Rock*, etc.) series and a sequence of nostalgic albums entitled *Back To The 40s, 50s*, and *60s*. K-Tel soon set up foreign branches in Canada, Germany, Holland, Japan, Australia and New Zealand. It moved into the UK in May 1972, revolutionizing music marketing by licensing original versions of hit singles for a *20 Dynamic Hits* album which was heavily promoted on television at a cost of £250,000. Earlier current hits compilations had used soundalike cover versions of chart records. Soon K-Tel was followed by companies such as Arcade, Telstar and Ronco. By the

mid-70s, however, K-Tel had extended into single artist compilations and concept albums (*Great Italian Love Songs, Country Comforts*). Within a couple of years, the major record companies were marketing numerous greatest hits albums although K-Tel's *Chart Hits* series continued to sell in hundreds of thousands. In 1983, **EMI** and **Virgin** launched their *Now That's What I Call Music* series, albums crammed full of recent hits and a direct copy of the original K-Tel concept. The high cost of television advertising and the highly competitive marketplace led to the failure of several companies including **Ronco** (1984) and Stylus (1990). In 1990, K-Tel also closed down its UK record company (but not the video distributor) and sold its Australian label. In the USA, K-Tel narrowly escaped bankruptcy in 1984 but returned with successful rap and breakdance compilations. In the late 80s, it set up new labels, signing jazz organist **Jimmy McGriff**, rapper MC Smooth and purchased the **Marshall Tucker Band**'s catalogue. In 1998 K-Tel announced that they would re-enter the full price album market for the first time since 1990.

K., Leila

b. Leila El Khalifi, *c*.1972, Gothenburg, Sweden. Frequently but somewhat erroneously compared to **Neneh Cherry**, Leila K. comes from an Arabic Muslim background and is one of hip hop's more glamorous rappers. At the age of 16 she ran away from her parents in Gothenburg. On her travels she saw an advert in a newspaper for a rap contest in the capital, Stockholm, and decided to try her luck. Two of the judges, who were impressed enough to reward her with the title, were Rob'N Raz. They were looking for a 'visual front' for their own recordings, and together the trio recorded the single 'Got To Get'. It topped domestic charts and brought a major label contract, the success quickly repeated with the international hit 'Rok The Nation'. Afterwards Leila split from Rob'n Raz to establish a solo career, signing with Swedish label Mega Records. There has been a certain novelty value to this secondary career so far, which began in earnest with a cover version of **Plastic Bertrand**'s 'Ca Plane Pour Moi'. Other singles such as 'Glam', which sampled **Gary Glitter**'s 'Rock & Roll Part 1', with the **Beastie Boys** providing production assistance, did little to dispel this notion. Her debut album did, however, include collaborations with Euro techno wizards Denniz Pop and Douglas Carr (**Ace Of Base, Dr. Alban** etc.).

● ALBUMS: *Carousel* (Polydor/Urban 1993)★★★.

K., Paul

b. USA. Paul Kopasz won a debating scholarship to Kentucky University in 1981. Following a fallow period dominated by an increasing reliance on drugs and crime, Kopasz issued his first songs on cassette in 1983. He has not stopped since - estimating his total output at over 1,000 songs by the mid-90s. However, it was only in the late 80s that the singer/songwriter finally broke his heroin dependency, partially through his

conversion to Christianity. Free from chemicals, his energies were profitably transferred to his muse, as he wrote an incredible five albums' worth of material in a 14-month period. His work for labels including Homestead, Fiasco and MMG Records produced a succession of highly literate albums, many inspired by pulp fiction authors such as Jim Thompson. 1995's *Achilles Heel* was the first Paul K. album to be recorded in a single session, again featured his backing band the Weathermen. The presence of these additional musicians was made financially viable through Kopasz's publishing royalties (several artists including the **Afghan Whigs** have recorded covers of his songs). *Achilles Heel* featured familiar Kopasz subjects such as economic injustice ('Add Up The Bills') as well as a cover version of **Townes Van Zandt**'s 'Tecumseh Valley', an artist with whom he has often been compared.
● ALBUMS: *Blues For Charlie Lucky* (Homestead 1993)★★★, *Garden Of Forking Paths* (Homestead 1993)★★★★, *Achilles Heel* (Thirsty Ear 1995)★★★.

K7

This Latin-flavoured hip-hop unit from Manhattan, New York, USA found chart success in 1993 with the addictive and anthemic 'Come Baby Come'. The quintet combine energetic R&B arrangements with clean raps, a style which has been unkindly referred to as 'The Hispanic Take That'. Led by K7, who gives the group their name, they also feature DJ Non-Stop, Prophet, Tre Duece and LOS. K7's attitude to labelling is unequivocal: 'My music is male bonding on a hip-hop level. It's not rap music'. The party-jam spirit of their debut single was present alongside more of the same on their debut album, which included the bilingual 'Zunga Zeng' cut, as well as a rather embarrassing attempt at 'A Little Help From My Friends'.
● ALBUMS: *Swing Batta Swing* (Tommy Boy 1994)★★.

Kaas, Patricia

b. 1966, Lorraine, France. The top female performer in France in the 90s, the slender waif Kaas had already sold over five million albums by her mid-20s. She was one of seven children to a French coal miner and amateur dancer father, and German mother. The latter was devoted to the world of showbusiness, and as a result Patricia was pushed relentlessly into a singing career. She would perform widely at fairs and country balls, mainly addressing torch singer standards drawn from the songbooks of **Liza Minnelli**, **Joni Mitchell** and even **Eurovision** songs. Her debut release came in 1985, when she recorded a single, 'Jalouse', produced by Gallic film star Gerard Depardieu, which he co-wrote with his wife Elizabeth. Depardieu had seen Kaas on stage in Paris. 'Jalouse' built her a big reputation, and successive singles and albums, initially for **Polygram**, pushed her irrepressibly into the limelight. Touted as the new **Vanessa Paradis**, she enjoyed her first hit with 'Mademoiselle Chante Le Blues'. That, and

other stronger material such as 'Les Hommes Qui Passent', were composed for her by the songwriting team of Francois Bernheim and Didier Barbelivien. She took to the world of celebrity with aplomb, displaying the wherewithal to leave her original record company and management, despite a welter of accusations and counter-accusations. In the process she established her own company, Note de Blues. Like Paradis, she is marketed more on image than talent, and her voice too is noticeably mannered. Conversely, there seems to be no lack of ambition or character beneath the commercial surface. Those who suggest she may be the French **Madonna** gain further credence for their claims with each successive platinum disc she earns.
● ALBUMS: *Je Te Dis Vous* (Columbia 1994)★★★, released in the UK as *Tour De Charme*

Kabulie, Moses

b. 1954, Senegal. Kabulie's father was a popular village singer. Trained in woodcraft, he embarked on a musical apprenticeship at the comparatively late age of 21 after observing visiting musicians at a local festival. As he later told a journalist, 'My father was disappointed that it was not him alone who made me want to become a musician. But I learned a great deal from watching him and I have combined this with modern styles to make what I call the 'old and new' sound of Kabulie.' His first single, 'Asayi', was a modest local hit and eventually led to a series of cassettes recorded in the cheaper local studios. The best of these is probably *Sensi Kabulie*, a profitable merger of East and West African styles with Kabulie's much-admired voice at the forefront.
● ALBUMS: *Sensi Kabulie* (Waka 1985)★★★★.

Kadison, Joshua

Spanning gospel, blues, pop and R&B traditions, US singer/songwriter Joshua Kadison's approach to songwriting is rooted in the art of storytelling. Drama and expansive arrangements introduced his 1994 debut album, and in particular the hit ballad, 'Jessie'. The album was produced by ex-**Zombie** and **Argent** leader **Rod Argent**. Though immediately successful, the approach taken for the follow-up collection, *Delilah Blue*, was radically different. Shunning synthesizers in favour of live instruments, and moving songs away from introspection to what the artist described as 'other people as seen through my eyes', it opened with the quasi-religious 'The Gospel According To My Ol' Man'. As if to confirm this change of direction, Kadison's image changed from one of long blonde hair and denim to a close-crop and goatee beard.
● ALBUMS: *Painted Desert Serenade* (EMI 1994)★★★, *Delilah Blue* (EMI 1995)★★★.

Kaempfert, Bert

b. Berthold Kaempfert, 16 October 1923, Hamburg, Germany, d. 21 June 1980, Majorca, Spain. A conductor, arranger, composer, multi-instrumentalist and record producer. Kaempfert played the piano as a child, and later studied at the Hamburg Conservatory of Music. By the time he joined Hans Bussch and his Orchestra during World War II, he was capable of playing a variety of instruments, including the piano, piano-accordion and all the reeds. After the war he formed his own band, and became a big draw in West Germany before joining **Polydor Records** as a producer, arranger and musical director. In the latter role he had some success with the Yugoslavian Ivor Robic's version of 'Morgen', which made the US Top 20 in 1959, and Freddie Quinn's 'Die Gitarre Und Das Meer'. A year later he made his own global breakthrough when he topped the US charts with his studio orchestra's recording of 'Wonderland By Night'. It was the precursor to a series of similar recordings in which a solo trumpet (usually Fred Moch) and muted brass were set against a cushion of lush strings and wordless choral effects, all emphasized by the insistent rhythm of a two-beat bass guitar. This treatment was effectively applied by Kaempfert to several of his own compositions, which were also successful for other artists, such as 'Spanish Eyes (Moon Over Naples)' (**Al Martino**), 'Danke Schoen' (**Wayne Newton**), 'L-O-V-E' (**Nat 'King' Cole**), 'A Swinging Safari' (**Billy Vaughn**), and 'Wooden Heart', which **Elvis Presley** sang in his film, *G.I. Blues*, and **Joe Dowell** took to the US number 1 spot in 1961. Two other Kaempfert numbers, 'The World We Knew' (Over And Over)' and 'Strangers In The Night' benefited from the **Frank Sinatra** treatment. The latter song, part of Kaempfert's score for the James Garner/Melina Mercouri comedy/thriller, *A Man Could Get Killed*, topped the US and UK charts in 1966. Lyrics for his most successful songs were written by Charles Singleton, Eddie Snyder, Carl Sigman, Kurt Schwabach, **Milt Gabler**, Fred Wise, Ben Weisman and Kay Twomey. Kaempfert himself had easy listening worldwide hits in his own inimitable style with revivals of 'golden oldies' such as 'Tenderly', Red Roses For A Blue Lady', 'Three O'Clock In The Morning' and 'Bye Bye Blues'. In 1961, *Wonderland By Night* spent five weeks at number 1 in the US, and Kaempfert continued to chart in the US and UK throughout the 60s, but his records failed to achieve Top 40 status in the 70s, although he still sold a great many, and continued to tour. Apart from his skill as an arranger and orchestra leader, Bert Kaempfert has another claim to fame in the history of popular music - he was the first person to record the **Beatles**. While they were playing a club in Hamburg in 1961, Kaempfert hired them to back **Tony Sheridan**, a singer who had a large following in Germany. After supplying the additional vocals on 'My Bonnie Lies Over The Ocean' and 'When The Saints Go Marching In', Kaempfert allowed Lennon & Co. to record 'Ain't She Sweet' and 'Cry For A Shadow'. When the beat boom got under way, 'My Bonnie', as it was then called, made the US Top 30 in 1964, and 'Ain't She Sweet' became a minor hit in the UK. By the end of the decade the Beatles had broken up, and Kaempfert's best days were behind him, too. In 1980, after completing a successful series of concerts in the UK, culminating in an appearance at the Royal Albert Hall, he was taken ill while on holiday in Majorca, Spain, and died there on 21 June. The 'New Bert Kaempfert Orchestra' was advertising its availability in UK trade papers in the early 90s.

● ALBUMS: *Wonderland* (1960)★★★, *Wonderland By Night* (1960)★★★, *That Happy Feeling* (1962)★★★, *With A Sound In My Heart* (1962)★★★, *That Latin Feeling* (1963)★★★, *Lights Out, Sweet Dreams* (1963)★★★, *Living It Up* (1963)★★★, *Afrikaan Beat* (1964)★★★, *Blue Midnight* (1965)★★★, *3 O'Clock In The Morning* (1965)★★★, *The Magic Music Of Far Away Places* (1965)★★★, *Strangers In The Night* (1966)★★★, *Bye Bye Blues* (1966)★★★, *A Swinging Safari* (1966)★★★, *Relaxing Sound Of Bert Kaempfert* (1966)★★★, *Bert Kaempfert - Best Seller* (1967)★★★, *Hold Me* (1967)★★★, *The World We Knew* (1967)★★★, *Kaempfert Special* (1967)★★★, *Orange Coloured Sky* (1971)★★★, *A Drop Of Christmas Spirit* (1974)★★★, *Everybody Loves Somebody* (1976)★★★, *Swing* (1978)★★★, *Tropical Sunrise* (1978)★★★, *Sounds Sensational* (1980)★★★, *Springtime* (1981)★★★, *Moods* (1982)★★★, *Now And Forever* (1983)★★★, *Famous Swing Classics* (1984)★★★, *Live In London* (1985)★★★.

Kahn, Gus

b. 6 November 1886, Koblenz, Germany, d. 8 October 1941, Beverly Hills, California, USA. A prolific lyricist during the 20s and 30s for Tin Pan Alley, stage and films. Not particularly well known by the public, but highly regarded in the music business, he was once rated by a trade magazine as the second most popular US songwriter after **Irving Berlin**. After being taken to the USA by his immigrant parents in 1891 when they settled in Chicago, he started writing songs while still at school. However, it was not until 1908 when he collaborated with his future wife, the composer Grace LeBoy, that he had some success with 'I Wish I Had A Girl'. His first big hit came in 1915 with 'Memories', written with composer Egbert van Alstyne. In the following year, Kahn collaborated with him again, and **Tony Jackson**, for 'Pretty Baby', which became one of Kahn's biggest hits, and was featured in the bio-pics *Jolson Sings Again* (1949) and *The Eddie Cantor Story* (1953); two artists who benefited substantially from Kahn's output. 'Pretty Baby' was just one of a series of Kahn 'baby' songs which evoke the 'jazz age' of the 20s. These included 'Yes Sir, That's My Baby', 'There Ain't No Maybe In My Baby's Eyes', 'My Baby Just Cares for Me', 'I Wonder Where My Baby Is Tonight' and 'Sing Me A Baby Song', all written with composer **Walter Donaldson**, Khan's major collaborator. Donaldson, with his playboy image, was the antithesis of Kahn with his sober, family background. Other songs by the team included 'That Certain Party', 'Carolina In The Morning', 'My Buddy' and 'Beside A Babbling Brook'. Some of their best work was contained in the 1928 Broadway show *Whoopee!*. Starring **Ruth Etting** and **Eddie Cantor**, it introduced 'I'm Bringing A Red Red

Rose', 'Love Me Or Leave Me', 'My Baby Just Cares for Me' and 'Makin' Whoopee', the lyric of which is considered to be one of Kahn's best. The show later became an early sound movie in 1930. In 1929, Kahn contributed to another Broadway musical, *Show Girl*. This time his collaborators were **George** and **Ira Gershwin**. The trio produced 'Liza', for the show's star, **Ruby Keeler**. It is said that, during at least one performance, Keeler's husband, **Al Jolson**, stood up in the audience and sang the song *to her*. In 1933, Kahn went to Hollywood to work on various movies, from the Marx Brothers' *A Day At The Races* ('All God's Chillun Got Rhythm'), to *Spring Parade*, starring **Deanna Durbin**, singing 'Waltzing In The Clouds'. In 1933, his first Hollywood project, with composer **Vincent Youmans**, was *Flying Down To Rio*, which featured the title song and 'The Carioca'. It was also the first film to bring together **Fred Astaire** and **Ginger Rogers**. It was Youmans' last original film score before he died in 1946. For the next eight years Kahn's output for films was prolific. They included *Bottoms Up* ('Waiting At The Gate For Katy'), *Caravan* ('Ha-Cha-Cha' and 'Wine Song'), *Hollywood Party* ('I've Had My Moments'), *Kid Millions* ('Okay Toots', 'When My Ship Comes In' and 'Your Head On My Shoulder'), *One Night Of Love*, *The Girl Friend*, *Love Me Forever*, *Thanks A Million* (**Dick Powell** singing the title song), *San Francisco* (**Jeanette MacDonald** singing the title song), *Rose Marie* ('Just For You' and 'Pardon Me, Madame'), *Three Smart Girls* (Deanna Durbin singing 'Someone To Care For Me'), *Everybody Sing* ('The One I Love'), *Girl Of The Golden West* ('Shadows On the Moon' and 'Who Are We To Say'), *Lillian Russell* (a bio-pic of the famous 1890s entertainer) and *Ziegfeld Girl* ('You Stepped Out Of A Dream', written with composer **Nacio Herb Brown**, sung by **Tony Martin**). Kahn's realised a life-long ambition to write with **Jerome Kern** with his last song, 1941's 'Day Dreaming'. Throughout his career Kahn had many different collaborators, including bandleader **Isham Jones** ('I'll See You In My Dreams', 'The One I Love Belongs To Somebody Else', 'Swingin' Down The Lane', and 'It Had To Be You'), **Richard Whiting** ('Ukulele Lady'), Whiting and Ray Egan ('Ain't We Got Fun'), Whiting and Harry Akst ('Guilty'), **Ted Fio Rito** ('I Never Knew', 'Charley My Boy' and 'Sometime'), Ernie Erdman, **Elmer Schoebel** and Billy Meyers ('Nobody's Sweetheart Now'), Erdman and Dan Russo ('Toot Toot Tootsie, Goodbye'), Wilbur Schwandt and Fabian Andre ('Dream A Little Dream Of Me' - a later hit for **'Mama' Cass Elliot**), Charlie Rossoff ('When You And I Were Seventeen'), Carmen Lombardo and **Johnny Green** ('Coquette'), Neil Moret ('Chloe'), Wayne King ('Goofus'), Matty Malneck and Fud Livingston ('I'm Through With Love'), Malneck and Frank Signorelli ('I'll Never Be The Same') and **Victor Schertzinger** ('One Night Of Love'). In the 1951 movie, *I'll See You In My Dreams*, based on his life, Kahn was portrayed by Danny Thomas, and Grace LeBoy by **Doris Day**.

Kahn, John

b. 1948, USA, d. 30 May 1996, Mill Valley, California, USA. Bass player John Kahn was best known for his contributions to the solo work of **Grateful Dead** founder and leader **Jerry Garcia**. Kahn's first mainstream work came in 1969 with his contributions to guitarist **Mike Bloomfield**, including albums such as *The Live Adventures Of Mike Bloomfield And Al Kooper*, *It's Not Killing Me* and *Live At Bill Graham's Fillmore West*. Kahn first linked with Garcia in 1970 as part of a collective of musicians based at San Francisco's Keystone Korner. His first recorded undertaking with Garcia was 1972's *Hooteroll?*, after which he worked on almost every Garcia solo and live project. This included Garcia's multifarious groups with keyboard player **Merl Saunders** as well as the bluegrass group Old (playing double bass) and the Way, which featured Garcia on banjo. His skills were also in demand for many other artists working in the Bay Area, leading to collaborations with **John Lee Hooker**, **Nick Gravenites** and **Maria Muldaur**. On record, he appeared with **Mississippi Fred McDowell**, **Otis Rush**, **Jackie DeShannon** and **Brewer And Shipley**. Kahn was still working regularly with Garcia until his death in 1995. Kahn himself died only a year later, a demise attributed to a narcotic drug overdose (his wife Linda was found in possession of narcotics after having reported the discovery of his body to the emergency services).

Kahn, Roger Wolfe

b. 19 October 1907, Morristown, New Jersey, USA, d. 12 July 1962, New York City, New York, USA. Scion of a very rich New York family, Kahn had money enough to indulge his whims, one of which was to lead a dance-band. For a decade he played exclusive venues frequented by New York's top set and occasionally recorded. Always, Kahn had fun; when the band was playing especially well he used to throw himself onto the floor and wave his legs in the air. For his recording dates he would augment his regular band with renowned jazz artists, including **Jack Teagarden** and **Gene Krupa**. In 1933, he folded his band in order to follow another whim; this time he became a test pilot.
● COMPILATIONS: *Roger Wolfe Kahn* (1925-29 recordings)★★★.

Kahn, Si

b. 23 April 1944, Pennsylvania, USA. With an artist mother and Rabbi father, Si Kahn has been active in the field of civil rights, and labour and community organization in the Southern states for over 25 years. Initially, he was a volunteer with the Student Non-Violent Co-ordinating Committee, but since then, having graduated from Harvard in 1965, Kahn has gone on to become involved in both African-American and white Southern communities. He is also an activist in the Jewish community, and a founder of the Jewish Fund for Justice. Kahn started performing in 1979, at the age of 35, his first appearance being at the Chicago Folk

Festival that year. Apart from his own recordings, Si has recorded with **Pete Seeger** and Jane Sapp, *Carry It On: Songs Of America's Working People*, a collection of civil rights, women's and labour songs. Aside from the USA, Kahn has toured Europe and Britain, playing at festivals, and regularly gives lecture tours to community groups. In 1989, Kahn provided both narration and songs for an accompanying cassette to two children's books, *Goodnight Moon* and *The Runaway Bunny*. A third children's project, this time a recording called *Goodtimes And Bedtimes*, was completed around 1986, but, held up due to a number of problems, is scheduled for release in 1992. The 1993 release, *In My Heart*, was recorded live in Holland in April 1993. Kahn's songs, in particular 'Aragon Mill', and 'What You Do With What You've Got', have been covered by other singers, resulting in an increasing interest in his work.

● ALBUMS: *New Wood* (1975)★★★, *Home* (1980)★★★★, *Doing My Job* (1982)★★★, *Unfinished Portraits* (1985)★★★, with John McCutcheon *Signs Of The Times* (1986)★★★, with Jane Sapp, Pete Seeger *Carry It On: Songs Of America's Working People* (1986)★★★★, *I'll Be There* (1989)★★★, *I Have Seen Freedom* (1992)★★, *In My Heart* (Strictly Country 1993)★★, *Companion* (Appleseed 1997)★★★.

● FURTHER READING: *How People Get Power*, Si Kahn. *The Forest Service And Appalachia*, Si Kahn. *Rural Community Organizing: History And Models*, Si Kahn with Harry Boyte. *Organizing: A Guide For Grassroots Leaders*, Si Kahn. *Si Kahn Songbook*, Si Kahn.

Kahn, Tiny

b. Norman Kahn, c.1923, New York City, New York, USA, d. 19 August 1953. After learning to play drums while in school, Kahn performed with a number of important and progressively-minded big bands of the late 40s - including those of **Boyd Raeburn**, **Georgie Auld** and **Charlie Barnet**. While with these bands Kahn began writing, and his arrangements for **Chubby Jackson**'s band were especially successful. This aspect of his talent was also employed by **Elliot Lawrence** in the early 50s. Kahn's writing was an influence upon other young arrangers of the period, including **Al Cohn** and **Johnny Mandel**. Extremely overweight (his nickname was ironical), Kahn died of cardiac problems in August 1953.

● ALBUMS: with Stan Getz *Jazz At Storyville* (1951)★★★★, *Elliot Lawrence Plays Kahn And Mandel* (1956)★★★.

Kaira Ben

This group was specially formed to record *Singa*, the international debut of Idrissa Magassa (b. 15 August 1952, Kougel, Senegal; vocals, ex-Super Djata Band). The recording sessions for the album took place in Senegal, UK, France and Netherlands. The musicians involved included Zoumana Diarra (b. 1960, Tominian, Mali; guitar) and Abdramane 'Djigui' Fall (b. 29 July 1959, Bamako, Mali; percussion/producer, ex-Super Djata Band). Released in 1996, *Singa* also featured saxophone, trumpet, balafon and keyboards. It was refresh-

ingly low-key and traditional-sounding compared to many of the hi-tec recordings made by West African musicians based in Europe. Magassa, Diarra and Fall also play with Benkadi International.

● ALBUMS: *Singa* (Sterns 1996)★★★.

Kaiser, Henry

b. Oakland, California, USA. Experimental, *avant garde* guitarist Henry Kaiser is a prolific musician whose work has run the gamut from free improvisation, to San Francisco-style 60s psychedelia to country music. Kaiser began playing guitar in 1971, influenced by **Captain Beefheart**'s music, and live concerts by San Francisco groups such as **Quicksilver Messenger Service** and the **Grateful Dead**. He has recorded numerous solo and group albums for labels such as SST Records and his own Metalanguage, and has collaborated on two albums with guitarists **Richard Thompson** and **Fred Frith**, along with former Beefheart drummer John French. The 1990 album, *Heart's Desire*, included keyboards from early Grateful Dead member Tom Constanten and he has recorded with musicians such as **John Zorn**, **Eugene Chadbourne**, the **Golden Palominos** and **Herbie Hancock**. As a session player he had appeared on over 100 hundred albums by the mid-90s.

● ALBUMS: with ROVA *Daredevils* (1979)★★★★, *Protocol* (1979), with Fred Frith *With Friends Like These* (1980)★★★, *Alloha* (1980)★★★, *Outside Pleasure* (1980)★★★★, with others *The Metalanguage Festival Of Improvised Music, Volume One: The Social Set* (1981)★★, *Volume Two: The Science Set* (1981)★★★, as French, Frith, Kaiser And Thompson *Live, Love, Larf And Loaf* (1987)★★★★, *Crazy Backwards Alphabet* (1987)★★★, *Those Who Know History Are Doomed To Repeat It* (1989)★★★, as French, Frith, Kaiser And Thompson *Invisible Means* (1989)★★★, *Heart's Desire* (1990)★★★★, *Hope You Like Our New Direction* (1991)★★★, with Derek Bailey *Wireforks* (Shanachie 1995)★★★★.

Kajagoogoo

Formed in Leighton Buzzard, Hertfordshire, England, this fresh-faced quartet comprised Nick Beggs (b. 15 December 1961; vocals/bass), Steve Askew (guitar), Stuart Crawford (vocals/synthesizer) and lead singer Chris Hamill (b. 19 December 1958), better known as the anagrammatic **Limahl**. Emerging at a time when the 'New Pop' of **Duran Duran**, **Adam Ant**, **Culture Club** and **Spandau Ballet** was in the ascendant, Kajagoogoo was perfectly placed to reap instant chart rewards. Their debut single, 'Too Shy', had an irresistibly hummable, pop melody and reached number 1 in the UK in early 1983. Significantly, the record was co-produced by Nick Rhodes, from their 'rivals' Duran Duran. Both groups relied on a strong visual image, but Kajagoogoo lacked the depth or staying power of their mid-80s contemporaries. They enjoyed two further hits, 'Ooh To Be Ah' and 'Hang On Now', before internal friction prompted Limahl's departure for a solo career. Kajagoogoo struggled on with Beggs taking lead vocals on the hits 'Big

Apple' and 'The Lion's Mouth'. By 1985, however, they were suffering from diminishing chart returns and after briefly abbreviating their name to Kaja, they broke up early the following year. Beggs subsequently formed the Christian folk band **Iona** and more recently, in 1993, joined Phonogram Records UK as A&R manager.

● ALBUMS: *White Feathers* (EMI 1983)★★, *Islands* (EMI 1984)★★.

Kak

Formed in Sacramento, California in 1967, Kak comprised of Dehner C. Patten (guitar/vocals), Gary Yoder (vocals/guitar), Joseph Damrell (bass/guitar/sitar/tambourine) and Christopher Lockhead (drums/keyboards/bass/vocals). The group's sole album, although commercially unsuccessful, has since become a prized collectors' item, showcasing classic West Coast melodies and exciting, but never indulgent, guitar work. The publicity campaign announced 'Get Kak before Kak gets you. Kak split up in 1970, after which Yoder, who had previously managed another aspiring act, the Oxford Circle, joined **Blue Cheer**. Drummer Paul Whaley had been a member of both groups. He participated on their highly-rated releases, *Original Human Being* and *Oh Pleasant Hope*.

● ALBUMS: *Kak* (Epic 1969)★★★.

Kako

b. Francisco Angel Bastar, c.1937, Barrio Obrero, San Juan, Puerto Rico. Percussionist (timbales, bongo-conga) and composer Kako was one of Puerto Rico and New York's most popular bandleaders in the 60s. A shy man by nature, he started as a dancer in Old San Juan. He played with the bands of **Tito Puente**, **Arsenio Rodríguez**, Belisario López, **Mongo Santamaría** and others. He recorded two 78 rpm releases on Gabriel Oller's SMC label. Kako's early albums were on the Alegre Records label, which was founded in 1956 by **Al Santiago**. Kako held the posts of artistic director and general manager with the company. He was a busy studio musician with the label and performed on recordings by artists such as Conjunto Tipico Ladi, Johnny Rodríguez (**Tito Rodríguez**'s older brother), Felipe Rodríguez and **Mon Rivera**. Alegre was the first Latin label to credit accompanists on the sleeves of some of their releases. However, the practice of printing release dates on Latin records was not widely adopted until the early 70s. Kako made his first release on Alegre in 1961 with *Kako y su Combo Vol. 1*. The same year he participated in the first recording by the Alegre All-Stars, directed by **Charlie Palmieri**. In 1962, Chivirico Dávila provided lead vocals to *Kako y su Combo Vol. 2* and Orlando Marín's classic hit *Se Te Quemo La Casa*. Dávila, who is also a composer, worked with **Pérez Prado**, Alegre All-Stars, **Eddie Palmieri**, Joe Cotto, Tito Puente, Pacheco, **Ricardo Ray**, Johnny Sedes, **Rafael Cortijo**, Joey Pastrana, Mark 'Markolino' Dimond and Guarare. He went solo in 1970 and released a series of nine albums up to 1978.

In 1965, Kako organized an 18-piece 'after hours orchestra', which was virtually the Alegre All-Stars, for *Tributo A Noro*, a tribute to his personal friend **Noro Morales**, who had died the year before. This involved Al Santiago, Charlie Palmieri and Héctor Rivera 'kidnapping' musicians after the dances had finished and transporting them to the studio for a session beginning at 5 am. In addition to Kako, Charlie and Héctor, the recording involved **Israel 'Cachao' López** (bass), José 'Chombo' Silva (tenor sax), **Louie Ramírez** (vibes), **Joe Quijano** (bongo), Chivirico (vocals) and Osvaldo 'Chi Hua Hua' Martínez (güiro/gourd scraper). Kako was amongst the personnel on *The Alegre All-Stars Vol. 2 'El Manicero'*. During 1965, Alegre released *Puerto Rican All-Stars Featuring Kako*, which was a jam-session recorded in Puerto Rico in February 1963, and included Rafael Ithier, **Roberto Roena** and other members of El Gran Combo at the time; Chivirico, Paquito Guzmán and Johnny Rodríguez (vocals), **Mario Ortiz** (trumpet) and Charlie Palmieri singing chorus! Kako appeared on the third and fourth volumes by the Alegre All-Stars, and released a further album on Alegre. In 1968, he switched to the Musicor Records label for *Live It Up*, with lead vocals by Panamanian **Camilo Azuquita**. The album was produced by Al Santiago, and in keeping with the fad of the time, it contained several boogaloos. The same year, he appeared on the Santiago produced Latin jam-session album, *The Salsa All Stars*, with Charlie, Cachao, Ramírez, **Pupi Legarreta**, Azuquita and others. He played conga on the now rare, *Cuban Roots* by Mark Weinstein on Musicor. Santiago produced Kako's second Musicor outing, *Sock It To Me, Latino!*, which featured another Panamanian vocalist, Meñique Barcasnegras and as a solo artiste. Kako played timbales on two descarga volumes by the Cesta All-Stars on Joe Quijano's Cesta Records label. Kako teamed up with the Afro Cuban singer/conga player Eugenio Arango 'Totico' for *Siguen Pa'Iante y Pa'Iante*. In 1974, Louie Ramírez produced and arranged *Kako* on the TR Records label, which was founded by Tito Rodríguez. At the time, Ramírez was vice-president of the company. Kako sessioned on Azuquita's *Pura Salsa* (1975). In 1976, the two artists reunited on *Union Dinamica*. In 1977, Kako played on the Alegre All-Stars' 17th anniversary album.

Sadly, Kako was one of a number of bandleaders that '. . . have been relegated to memories because they were not with the "in people" . . .' in the Latin music industry (quote from Max Salazar). He made his last appearances on record (to date) in the late 70s and at the beginning of the 80s, as a guest on albums by other artists and bands, such as **Adalberto Santiago** and **Típica 73**. Kako still performs. He recently put a band together with help from his son, percussionist Richie Bastar, and played in Florida.

● ALBUMS: *Kako y su Combo Vol.I* (1961)★★★, *The Alegre All-Stars* (1961)★★★, *Kako y su Combo Vol.II* (1962)★★★★, *Tributo A Noro* (1965)★★★★, *The Alegre All-Stars Vol.2 'El*

Manicero' (1965)★★★, *Puerto Rican All-Stars Featuring Kako* (c.1965)★★★, *The Alegre All-Stars Vol. 3 'Lost & Found'* (1968)★★★, *The Alegre All-Stars Vol.4 'Way Out'* (1968)★★★, *No Hay Mas Na, Live It Up* (1968)★★★, with various artists *The Salsa All Stars* (1968)★★, *Sock It To Me, Latino!* (1971),★★★ with the Cesta All-Stars *Live Jam Session, Salsa Festival* (1971)★★, with Ismael Rivera *Lo Ultimo En La Avenida* (1971)★★★, with Rafael Cortijo *Ritmos y Cantas Callejeros* (1974)★★★, with Totico *Siguen Pa'Iante y Pa'Iante*; *Kako* (1974)★★, with Azuquita *Union Dinamica* (1976)★★★, *The Alegre All-Stars 'Perdido' (Vol. 5)* (1977)★★★.

Kaleef

After an abortive experience with a major label, Manchester, England hip-hop act Kaleef rose to prominence at the end of 1996 with a UK Top 40 single for an independent label. The group originally signed to **London Records** in 1993 as the Kaliphz (their name translating as 'King' or 'Messenger' in an Arabic tongue). They were pulled together after 2Phaaan (pronounced Du-farn, b. *c.*1967) and Jabba Da Hype (aka The Alien) saw the **Rocksteady Crew** performing at the Runcorn Ideal Homes Exhibition in 1982 and became embroiled in the breakdancing and graffiti movements in their neighbourhood, forming breakdance crew Dizzy Footwork the same year. They were soon joined by Hogweed, and the trio began hanging out together, before finally adding Chokadoodle and SniffaDawg (b. *c.*1974) to complete the line-up.The group were backed by a production team entitled Funk Regulators, a junior back-up rap squad the Underhogs, an all-female troupe the Berserkers, a mixed race group Freaks Of Nature, and a freestyle solo rapper, Paraphinalia. They were paid a great deal of attention by a media fascinated with their predominantly Asian origins, and the deal with London was rumoured to involve a large advance. However, the group's debut album, *Seven Deadly Sins*, stalled commercially, as did a sequence of singles. Their record label having lost interest, the Kaliphz career seemed set to decline until Radio 1 disc jockey Pete Tong (who had been an early supporter of the group) put them in touch with Manchester independent, Unity Records - the label formed by Pete Waterman of **Stock, Aitken And Waterman** fame. They made a demo recording of the **Stranglers'** 1982 hit 'Golden Brown' at Waterman's Manchester studio, The Church. Their revision featured a rap by the group's Twice Born about the dangers of heroin - ironic, given the Stranglers' long-term refusal to admit the song was a paean to the drug.

● ALBUMS: as Kalphiz *Seven Deadly Sins* (Payday 1995)★★★.

Kaleidoscope (UK)

Psychedelic pop band Kaleidoscope were formed in west London, England, in 1964 as the Side Kicks. Comprising Eddie Pumer (guitar), Peter Daltrey (vocals/keyboards), Dan Bridgeman (percussion) and Steve Clarke (bass), they initially worked as an R&B cover band. After changing names to the Key, they switched tempo and style and became Kaleidoscope, and were signed to **Fontana Records** following the intervention of music publisher **Dick Leahy**, who became their producer. Their debut single, September 1967's 'Flight From Ashiya', adopted the in-vogue hippy ethos and terminology. Although it failed to chart the subsequent album, *Tangerine Dream*, became a cult success, a position it sustains to this day among fans of 60s psychedelic rock (with a rarity value in excess of £100). Despite a strong underground following, this proved insufficient to launch subsequent singles 'A Dream For Julie' or 'Jenny Artichoke', nor second album *Faintly Blowing*, into the charts. Two further singles, 'Do It Again For Jeffrey' and 'Balloon' in 1969 were issued, but a projected third album was 'lost' when Fontana dropped the band. It was eventually issued in 1991 on the group's own self-titled label. By 1970 the group had transmuted into progressive rock band **Fairfield Parlour**, whose most vociferous fan was the late UK disc jockey **Kenny Everett**.

● ALBUMS: *Tangerine Dream* (Fontana 1967)★★★, *Faintly Blowing* (Fontana 1969)★★, *White-Faced Lady* (Kaleidoscope 1991)★★.

● COMPILATIONS: *Dive Into Yesterday* (Fontana 1997)★★.

Kaleidoscope (USA)

Formed in 1966, this innovative group owed its origins to California's jugband and bluegrass milieu. Guitarists **David Lindley** and **Chris Darrow** were both former members of the Dry City Scat Band, while Solomon Feldthouse (vocals/oud/caz) had performed in the region's folk clubs. John Vidican (drums) and Charles Chester Crill - aka Connie Crill, Max Buda, Fenrus Epp or Templeton Parceley (violin, organ, harmonic, /vocals) - completed the line-up which, having flirted with the name Bagdhad Blues Band, then settled on Kaleidoscope. *Side Trips* revealed a group of enthralling imagination, offering a music drawn from the individual members' disparate interests. Blues, jazz, folk and ethnic styles abounded as the quintet forged a fascinating collection, but although the album was comprised of short songs, Kaleidoscope's reputation as a superior live attraction was based on lengthy improvised pieces. The group tried to address this contrast with *A Beacon From Mars*, which contrasted six concise performances with two extended compositions, the neo-Eastern 'Taxim' and the feedback-laden title track. The album marked the end of this particular line-up as Darrow then opted to join the **Nitty Gritty Dirt Band**. Vidican also left the group, and thus newcomers Stuart Brotman (bass) and Paul Lagos (drums) were featured on *Incredible Kaleidoscope*, which in turn offered a tougher, less acid-folk perspective. There were, nonetheless, several highlights, including the expanded 'Seven Ate Sweet' and propulsive 'Lie To Me', but the album was not a commercial success, despite the publicity generated by the group's sensational appearance at the 1968 Newport Folk Festival. Further changes in the line-up ensued with the departure of Brotman, who was fired during sessions for a prospective fourth album. His replacement, Ron Johnson, introduced a funk-influenced element to the unit's sound, while a second newcomer, Jeff Kaplan, surprisingly took most of the lead vocals. Kaleidoscope's muse sadly failed to accommodate these changes, and *Bernice* was a marked disappointment. The late-period group did complete two excellent songs for the film soundtrack of *Zabriskie Point*, but the departures of Feldthouse and Crill in 1970 signalled their demise. Despite the addition of Richard Aplan to the line-up, Kaleidoscope dissolved later in the year in the wake of Kaplan's death from a drugs overdose. David Lindley subsequently embarked on a career as a session musician and solo artist, a path Chris Darrow also followed, albeit with less commercial success. The latter subsequently joined Feldthouse, Brotman, Lagos and Crill in the re-formed unit completing *When Scopes Collide* which, although lacking the innovation of old, was nonetheless entertaining. The same line-up reconvened to complete the equally meritorious *Greetings From Kartoonistan ... (We Ain't Dead Yet)*. Such sets simply enhanced the Kaleidoscope legend, which was considerably buoyed by a series of excellent compilations. They remain one of the era's most innovative acts.

● ALBUMS: *Side Trips* (Epic 1967)★★★, *A Beacon From Mars* (Epic 1968)★★★, *Incredible Kaleidoscope* (Epic 1969)★★★, *Bernice* (Epic 1970)★★, *When Scopes Collide* (Island 1976)★★★★★, *Greetings From Kartoonistna ... (We Ain't Dead Yet)* (Curb 1991)★★★.

● COMPILATIONS: *Bacon From Mars* (1983)★★★, *Rampe Rampe* (Edsel 1984)★★★, *Egyptian Candy* (Legacy 1990)★★★, *Blues From Bhagdad - The Very Best Of* (1993)★★★.

Kalin Twins

A classic example of the one-hit-wonder syndrome, the Kalin Twins have a more interesting history than many who fall into that bracket. Herbie and Harold 'Hal' Kalin, who are twins, were born on 16 February 1934 in Port Jervis, New York State, USA (many references give their birth date as 1939 but this was a **Decca Records** diversion, in an attempt to make them appear younger than they in fact were). Their first public performances came at just five years of age at a local Christmas party, and the bug stayed with them. They graduated from Port Jervis High School in June 1952, but plans to break into the music industry were delayed when Hal was drafted into the Air Force as a radio operator. They kept in touch during this period, recording and writing songs on a tape recorder and sending them back and forth. After Hal's discharge in 1956 they set about resurrecting their double act. During these early struggles a demo single was pressed, combining the compositions 'Beggar Of Love' and 'The Spider And The Fly'. The result was an audition for Decca, and their first single proper, 'Jumpin' Jack'/'Walkin' To School'. While searching through piles of writers' demo tapes to find a suitable follow-up the twins discovered a song entitled 'When', written by Paul Evans and Jack Reardon. It became their second single. However, the record company chose to plug its flip side, 'Three O'Clock Thrill', instead. It was not until disc jockeys belatedly began to play 'When' that the single took off. It reached number 5 in the **Billboard** charts but topped the UK charts for no less than five weeks (selling over two million copies worldwide). Coast to coast touring of the US ensued before a two week engagement at the Prince Of Wales Theatre in England (later dates introduced **Cliff Richard** as support artist on his first national tour). The subsequent 'Forget Me Not' and 'Oh My Goodness!' both made reasonable showings in the *Billboard* charts, but neither entered the UK equivalent. Two more minor US hits followed, 'Cool' and 'Sweet Sugarlips', but their remaining Decca sides failed to sell. With the arrival of the **Beatles** there seemed little place in the market for the Kalin Twins' innocent harmonies, although a further single, 'Sometimes It Comes, Sometimes It Goes' for Amy Records, did appear in 1966. Disillusioned with their diminishing rewards, the brothers mutually agreed to return to their day jobs, with each pursuing college degrees. They did not perform again until 1977 when a friend booked them to appear weekly at his new night spot, the River Boat Club. This led to further one-off engagements, in which they were sometimes joined by younger sibling Jack to appear as the Kalin Brothers. A brace of singles appeared for small labels: 'Silver Seagull' and 'American Eagle' both used the same backing track. A 16-track compilation was released by Bear Family Records in 1983. They disappeared again until old support hand Cliff Richard invited them to play at his 30th Anniversary shows in 1989.

● ALBUMS: *The Kalin Twins* (Decca 1958)★★★, *When* (Vocalion 1966)★★★.

● COMPILATIONS: *When* (Bear Family 1983)★★★.

Kaliphz
(see **Kaleef**)

Kalle, Le Grande

b. Joseph Kabasele Tshamala, 1930, Matadi, Zaire, d. 11 February 1983, Paris, France. The father of modern Zairean music, Kalle's earliest musical experiences were as a member of the church choir in his home town of Matadi. Moving to Kinshasa in 1950, he worked with Orchestre De Tendence Congolaise, a band that specialized in acoustic polka and mazurka rhythms, derived from records brought to the country by colonial settlers. In 1953, keen to develop a genuinely Congolese style, he formed **African Jazz**, based on the Afro-Cuban tradition and in particular the rumba, samba and cha cha, all played in a distinctively Congolese fashion. Over the years, the group included many of the future stars of Zairean music, including **Dr Nico** and **Tabu Ley**, and provided a training ground for the next generation of Zairean musicians. By 1960, Kalle and African

Jazz were the top band in the Congo, releasing literally hundreds of 78s each year (mainly on the local **Decca Records** label) and filling dancehalls throughout the country. In 1961, the group embarked on an extensive West African tour, introducing the Congolese Afro-Cuban style to audiences in Ghana, Nigeria, Ivory Coast, Sierra Leone and Guinea and making a huge impact on local musicians. Guinea's **Bembaya Jazz**, for instance, credit Kalle's 1961 tour with the birth of West Africa's Latin American-influenced sub-style, still a popular alternative to highlife, juju and afrobeat. In 1960, Kalle created his own label, Surboum African Jazz, sending musicians like **Franco** and **OK Jazz** to Belgium to record. The same year he composed his still popular hymn to the new independent Congo, 'Independence Cha Cha' (which featured a magnificent guitar solo from Dr Nico, still mimicked by young Zairean guitarists today). Also in 1960, he recorded 'Okuka Lokole', a tribute to **Louis Armstrong**, who visited Zaire on a tour sponsored by the US State Department. Kalle relished composing tribute songs and at the 1967 Organization of African Unity in Kinshasa he presented each of the 30 heads of state with a song praising their own country in the appropriate local melody and rhythm. He also performed satires and lampoons of local politicians, and in 1969, feeling himself to be under surveillance and fearing for his safety - having released a single critical of Kinshasa's Chief of Police - he left the country to settle in Paris, where he formed the Afro-Latin fusion band African Team with **Manu Dibango**, **Jean-Serge Essous** and **Don Gonzalo**. Paris remained his base until his death, though he began to visit Zaire again in the late 70s. Kalle was important not just for the wealth of songs he recorded, but also for the development of the Latin tendency in Zairean music, creating a style whose sweetness and melodic strength is still in evidence in Zaire today.

● ALBUMS: *Joseph Kabaselle Et L'African Jazz Vols 1 & 2* (Sonodisdc 1984)★★★, and *Kalle And The African Team Vols 1 & 2* (Sonodisc 1984)★★★★, consisting of 78s recorded by Kalle and African Jazz in the late 50s and 60s.

Kallen, Kitty
(see **Shaw, Artie**)

Kalmar, Bert
b. 10 February 1884, New York City, New York, USA, d. 18 September 1947, Los Angeles, California, USA. Ill-educated and a runaway before he was in his teens, Kalmar's life was completely immersed in showbusiness. In the years before World War I he wrote lyrics for a number of songs with various composers, among them **Harry Ruby**. For the next few years each wrote with other collaborators, but by the beginning of the 20s they recognized the special qualities of their work together. Throughout the 20s they wrote for Broadway musicals such as *Ladies First, Broadway Brevities Of 1920*, *Ziegfeld Follies* Of 1920, *Midnight Rounders Of 1921*, **Greenwich Village Follies** Of 1922, Helen Of Troy-New York, Puzzles Of 1925, *The Ramblers, Five O'Clock Girl, Lucky, Good Boy,* and *Animal Crackers*. The latter score was written for the Marx Brothers, and contained songs such as 'Who's Been Listening To My Heart?', 'Watching The Clouds Roll By', and 'Hooray For Captain Spaulding'. Other songs from those shows included 'Oh! What A Pal Was Mary', 'So Long, Oo-long', 'Who's Sorry Now?', 'Thinking Of You', 'The Same Old Moon', 'Dancing The Devil Away', 'Some Sweet Someone', and 'I Wanna Be Loved By You'. By the 30s Kalmar and Ruby were writing songs for films and one of their first, and the song by which they are best remembered, was 'Three Little Words' (from *Check And Double Check*). It became the title of the songwriters' 1950 film biography when they were played by **Fred Astaire** and Red Skelton. Their other film work included *The Cuckoos, Horse Feathers, **The Kid From Spain**, Hips Hips Hooray, Kentucky Kernels, Thanks A Million,* aand **The Story Of Vernon And Irene Castle.** They contained numbers such as 'I Love You So Much', 'What A Perfect Combination', 'Only When You're In My Arms', and 'Keep Romance Alive'. Most of their songs were written for either stage or screen but among their great successes were 'Nevertheless' and 'A Kiss To Build A Dream On' - written for neither medium. (The latter did not become popular until the 50s after some rewriting by **Oscar Hammerstein II**.)

Kam
b. Craig Miller, c.1971, Watts, California, USA, before settling in Compton with his mother and brother. With his lyrical worldview drawn from the inter-gang arena of Los Angeles, Kam chose to call for unity rather than glorify the bloodletting of the Crips and Blood brother-hoods. Unfortunately, though his rhymes were deftly weighted tracts against the dissolution of the ghetto, generally arguing for his Muslim beliefs ('So it's hard to keep calm, When I'm accused of being racist, For Loving my people first....'), Kam's delivery lacked the heavyweight impact of Messrs **Ice-T** and **Cube**. The latter was the major influence in his career, picking him up as the first artist on his Street Knowledge empire. He made his debut with 'Every Single Weekend' on the *Boyz N The Hood* soundtrack, before guesting on 'Colorblind', a cut from Cube's *Death Certificate* set. He has also written for **Yo Yo**.

● ALBUMS: *Neva Again* (East West 1992)★★★, *Made In America* (East West 1995)★★★.

Kama Sutra Records
This innovative record label was launched in New York in 1965 as an extension of Kama Sutra Productions, a publishing/production company headed by Artie Ripp and the Koppelman/Rubin team. The latter pair managed the **Lovin' Spoonful** who gave Kama Sutra a Top 10 hit with their first release, 'Do You Believe In Magic'. The group became the label's greatest asset, achieving international success with 'Daydream',

'Summer In The City' and 'Nashville Cats'. Although initially issued under the **Pye International** imprint, Kama Sutra established a UK division with the second of these singles. The Spoonful's melodic blend of folk, blues and pop; dubbed 'good-time music', was heard in several of the company's subsequent releases, notably 'Hello Hello' by **Sopwith Camel** and 'There's Got To Be A Word' by the **Innocence**. The latter act revolved around the songwriting/production team of Pete Anders and Vinnie Poncia. They also recorded for Kama Sutra as the **Tradewinds** and were heavily involved in releases by the Goodtimes, Vincent Edwards and **Bobby Bloom**. Kama Sutra productions enjoyed success with the lyrical **Critters**, who recorded for **Kapp**. However, despite embracing the west coast sound with *Safe As Milk* by **Captain Beefheart And The Magic Band**, the label's star began to wane as the decade progressed. The demise of the Lovin' Spoonful, coupled with the decampment of Anders, Poncia and Bloom, undermined Kama Sutra considerably. In 1970 it sundered its US deal with **MGM Records** to become a subsidiary of **Neil Bogert**'s **Buddah Records**. The Canadian group Ocean reached number 2 in the US charts with 'Put Your Hand In The Hand' in 1971 and followed with three further hits over the next year. Although enjoying success with **Stories**, **Brewer And Shipley**, **Sha Na Na** and **Charlie Daniels**, Kama Sutra was no longer the creative force it had been as an independent concern.

● COMPILATIONS: *Mynd Excursions* (Sequel 1992)★★★.

Kamen, Michael

b. 1948, New York, USA. A former member of the 60s band the New York Rock 'n' Roll Ensemble. A prolific composer, conductor, and arranger, particularly for films, from the 70s through to the 90s. After studying at the Juilliard School Of Music, Kamen contributed some music to the off-beat rock Western film *Zachariah* in 1971. Later in the 70s, he wrote the complete scores for *The Next Man*, *Between The Lines*, and *Stunts* (1977). During the 80s he scored co-composed the music for several films with some of contemporary pop music's most illustrious names, such as **Eric Clapton** (*Lethal Weapon*, *Homeboy*, and *Lethal Weapon II* (also with **David Sanborn**), **George Harrison** (*Shanghai Surprise*), **David A. Stewart** (*Rooftops*), and **Herbie Hancock** (*Action Jackson*). Subsequently, Kamen scored some of the period's most entertaining and diverting UK and US movies, which included *Venom*, *Pink Floyd-The Wall*, *Angleo, My Love*, *The Dead Zone*, *Brazil* (supposedly his favourite score), *Mona Lisa*, *Riot*, *Sue And Bob, Too*, *Someone To Watch Over Me*, *Suspect*, *Die Hard* and *Die Hard II*, *Raggedy Rawney*, *Crusoe*, *For Queen And Country*, *The Adventures Of Baron Munchausen*, *Dead-Bang* (with Gary Chang), *Road House*, *Renegades*, and *Licence To Kill* (1989), Timothy Dalton's second attempt to replace Connery and Moore as James Bond. In the early 90s Kamen composed the music for *The Krays* and *Let Him Have It*, two films that reflected

infamous criminal incidents in the UK, and others such as *Nothing But Trouble*, *Hudson Hawk*, *The Last Boy Scout*, *Company Business*, *Blue Ice*, *Lethal Weapon 3*, *Shining Through* (1992), *Blue Ice*, *Splitting Heirs*, *Last Action Hero*, *The Three Musketeers*, *Circle Of Friends*, and *Don Juan DeMarco* (1995). In several instances, besides scoring the films, Kamen served as musical director, music editor, and played keyboards and other instruments. In 1991, he provided the music for the smash hit Kevin Kostner movie, *Robin Hood: Prince Of Thieves*, and, with lyricists **Bryan Adams** and Robert John 'Mutt' Lange, composed the closing number, '(Everything I Do) I Do For You'. Adams' recording of the song enjoyed phenomenal success, staying at the top of the UK chart for an unprecedented 16 weeks. It was nominated for an Academy Award, and Kamen received two Grammys and a special **Ivor Novello** Award. Three years later the trio of songwriters repeated their success with 'All For Love', which was recorded by Adams, together with **Sting** and **Rod Stewart**, and turned up at the end of *The Three Musketeers* and at the top of the UK chart. Kamen has also composed music for tele-films such as *Liza's Pioneer Diary*, *S*H*E*, *Shoot For The Sun*, and two television mini-series, *The Duty Men* (theme: 'Watching You' (with Sashazoe)), and *Edge Of Darkness*. The theme from the latter, written with Eric Clapton, gained another Ivor Novello Award (1985). He has written a guitar concerto for Clapton, a saxophone concerto for David Sanborn, and composed several scores for the Joffrey Ballet and the La Scala Opera Company.

● ALBUMS: with Orbital *Event Horizon* film soundtrack (London 1997)★★★.

Kaminsky, Max

b. 7 September 1908, Brockton, Massachusetts, USA, d. 6 September 1994, Castle Point, New York, USA. Kaminsky was a trumpet player with a vigorous style, who played briefly with some big bands, including **Tommy Dorsey** and **Artie Shaw**, but was mainly associated with white Chicago-style small groups. Kaminsky started out with bands in Boston around 1924. In the late 20s, he played with **George Wettling** and **Bud Freeman** in New York, and toured with **Red Nichols**. During the 30s and early 40s he worked for several bandleaders, including **Leo Reisman**, **Joe Venuti**, **Pee Wee Russell**, **Tony Pastor**, Tommy Dorsey, **Alvino Rey** and **Joe Marsala**. Between 1942 and 1943, he played for Artie Shaw's famous Navy Band. After his discharge, he led his own popular combo in New York and Boston clubs until 1946, when he resumed freelancing with dixieland groups with artists such as **Eddie Condon** and **Art Hodes**. In 1957, he toured Europe with a **Jack Teagarden-Earl Hines** All Star group, and the following year travelled to Asia with Teagarden. From then on, he was generally based in New York, mainly freelancing, but sometimes leading small groups at venues such as the Gaslight Club, and at Jimmy Ryan's, where he was still appearing occasionally until 1983. He appeared on several US television jazz programmes, including a 1973 Timex Special. His few recordings as leader included 'Love Nest', 'Everybody Loves My Baby', 'Dippermouth Blues', 'Someday Sweetheart' plus the albums *Chicago Style*, *Ambassador Of Jazz* and *Dixieland Horn*. He recorded prolifically with other groups including **George Brunis** ('I Used To Love You', 'I'm Gonna Sit Right Down And Write Myself A Letter' and 'In The Shade Of The Old Apple Tree'); Bud Freeman ('China Boy' and 'The Eel'), Art Hodes ('Sweet Georgia Brown' and 'Sugar Foot Stomp'), **Willie 'The Lion' Smith** ('Muskrat Ramble' and 'Bugle Call Rag'), Tommy Dorsey ('Maple Leaf Rag', 'That's A Plenty' and 'Keepin' Out Of Mischief Now').

● ALBUMS: *Jack Teagarden And Max Kaminsky* (1982)★★★, with various artists *Art Ford's Jazz Party, 1958* (Jazz Connoisseur 1987)★★★★.

● FURTHER READING: *My Life In Jazz*, Max Kaminsky.

Kamissoko, Aminata

b. *c*.1950, Kirina, Mali, d. May 1998. Born into the Jali caste (traditionally musicians), she sang at weddings and baptisms in her local village from an early age, continuing to do so following her marriage at 16. Subsequently singing throughout Mali, as well as with groups in neighbouring Senegal and the Ivory Coast, she worked on developing the traditional Jali music style, adding her own lyrics concerned with contemporary social and personal issues. *Malamine*, her only international release, was recorded in Mali with backing from her multi-instrumentalist son Lamine Soumano. The tapes were then flown to London where overdubs were recorded by producer Abranane Fall and guitarist Zoumana Diarra (both members of **Benkadi International**). In spite of all this travel, *Malamine* is firmly in the West African tradition, with Kamissoko's raw voice backed by sparse hypnotic instrumentation. Aminata Kamissoko died only months after *Malamine* was released, a victim of the hardship and poverty of her environment.

● ALBUMS: *Malamine* (Stern's 1997)★★★.

Kamoze, Ini

b. 9 October 1957, Port Maria, St. Mary, Jamaica, West Indies. In 1981 Kamoze recorded his debut release, 'World Affairs'; other singles followed and he soon became known as the Voice Of Jamaica. His reputation brought him to the attention of the Taxi Gang, led by **Sly Dunbar** and **Robbie Shakespeare**. In 1983 the duo produced a mini-album, *Ini Kamoze*, released through **Island Records**, which earned him international acclaim, but at the same time his local success faltered, as message music was becoming less popular in the **dancehall**. At the 1984 Jamaican Sunsplash, however, Kamoze appeared in the line-up on dancehall night, giving an impressive performance to an audience in the grip of DJ mania. The release of *Statement* followed in the same year, including the track 'Call The Police',

which was included on the soundtrack of *Good To Go*. His debut performance in the UK was at the 1985 Reggae Sunsplash, as part of **Sly And Robbie**'s showcase, which also featured **Gregory Isaacs** and **Sugar Minott**. His performance was greeted with enthusiasm and the tour was equally successful in Europe. In 1986 *Pirate* did not enjoy similar success to its predecessors, despite the inclusion of some notable tracks, including 'Betty Brown's Mother', 'Gunshot', a warning about the dangers of firearms, and 'Queen Of My House'. In the same year he toured with **Yellowman**, **Half Pint** and the Taxi Gang, including a show at the Town & Country Club that was recorded and released as *The Taxi Connection Live In London*. A condensed showcase of the tour was featured on the UK television music show *The Tube*. In 1987 Kamoze left the Taxi Gang and began working with the One Two Crew, where he shared production duties on *Shocking Out*. He won new fans with his single 'Stress', featured on the one rhythm album *Selekta Showcase*. His work remained popular in reggae charts, resulting in a compilation of his earlier Taxi recordings, *Pirate*, and tracks from another two albums on *16 Vibes Of Ini Kamoze*. The ever popular 'Stalag' rhythm found the singer winning dancehall approval when he enjoyed a hit with 'Another Sound'. By the winter of 1994 he had a number 1 in the US charts with 'Here Comes The Hotstepper' from the movie soundtrack of *Prêt A Porter*, which was also a UK Top 5 hit in January 1995. The song was originally recorded for the *Strictly Dancehall* compilation on the Epic label, which also sponsored a tour featuring the artists involved. The success of the single led to a contract with **Elektra Records**.

● ALBUMS: *Ini Kamoze* mini-album (Island 1983)★★★, *Statement* (Island 1984)★★★, *Pirate* (Island 1986)★★★, *Shocking Out* (Greensleeves 1987)★★★, *Here Comes The Hotstepper* (Sony 1995)★★★★, *Lyrical Gangsta* (East West 1995)★★★.

● COMPILATIONS: *16 Vibes Of Ini Kamoze* (Sonic Sounds 1992)★★★.

Kamuca, Richie

b. 23 July 1930, Philadelphia, Pennsylvania, USA, d. 22 July 1977. After working in groups in and around his home town, Kamuca joined the **Stan Kenton** Orchestra on tenor saxophone in 1952. Two years later he was in **Woody Herman**'s band and then settled on the west coast, where he played and recorded with, among others, **Shelly Manne** and **Shorty Rogers**. Kamuca was also on the 1955 Cy Touff Octet and Quintet sessions for Pacific Jazz which featured **Harry Edison** and used charts by **Johnny Mandel**. The following year Kamuca was again on dates for Pacific, as a member of the **Chet Baker-Art Pepper** Sextet and also on a **Bill Perkins** album that included Pepper. In 1959, he again recorded with Pepper and was also featured on the highly successful live recordings made by Manne at the Black Hawk club in San Francisco. In the early 60s, Kamuca moved to New York, where he worked in a small group with **Roy Eldridge** and became a member of the studio orchestra for the Merv Griffin television show. He was a founder member of **Bill Berry**'s rehearsal band, which comprised mostly musicians from the studio orchestra, and when the Griffin show abruptly moved to Los Angeles, Kamuca went too. There, he worked with Berry in his re-formed big band, recording with him and under his own name for the Concord label. A fine player of ballads, with a warm and impassioned style, Kamuca's indebtedness to **Lester Young** is apparent, but he never slavishly followed his idol. One of his last recordings was dedicated to **Charlie Parker**, and throughout his later years he can be heard developing original ideas and gradually changing his style as he matured.

● ALBUMS: with Stan Kenton *Sketches On Standards* (1953)★★★, with Woody Herman *Road Band* (1955)★★★, *Cy Touff, His Octet And Quintet* (1955)★★★★, with Bill Perkins *Just Friends* (1956)★★, *The Richie Kamuca Quartet* (VSOP 1957)★★★, *Jazz Erotica* (Fresh Sound 1958)★★★, with Art Pepper *Modern Jazz Classics* (1959)★★★, *Shelly Manne And His Men At The Black Hawk* (1959)★★, *West Coast Jazz In Hi-Fi* (Original Jazz Classics 1960)★★★, with Roy Eldridge *Comin' Home Baby* (1965-66)★★★, with Bill Berry *Hot & Happy* (1974)★★★, *Drop Me Off In Harlem* (1977)★★★, *Richie* (1977)★★, *Charlie* (1977)★★★.

Kander, John

b. 18 March 1927, Kansas City, Missouri, USA. An important composer for the American musical theatre from the early 60s, Kander studied music as a child, continued at college and was determined to make his way in the musical theatre. He had some successes in the early 50s with various lyricists before meeting Fred Ebb in 1962. Ebb (b. 8 April 1932, New York, USA) had already dabbled with lyric writing, and had collaborated with **Jerry Herman** on some songs for the short-lived musical *From A To Z* (1960). Among Kander and Ebb's first efforts were 'My Coloring Book' and 'I Don't Care Much', both of which were recorded by **Barbra Streisand**. The new team made their Broadway debut in 1965 with the score for *Flora, The Red Menace*, which included an eye-catching, **Tony Award**-winning performance, by **Liza Minnelli**, who would subsequently perform much of their work, and become indelibly associated with them. Although *Flora* was relatively unsuccessful, Kander and Ebb were invited to write the score for *Cabaret* (1966), which starred Joel Grey and Jill Haworth, and won seven Tony Awards including best score. They wrote two additional songs, 'Money, Money' and 'Mein Herr', for the 1972 film version in which Liza Minnelli gave a sensational performance and won an Oscar. The television special produced by Ebb for Minnelli, *Liza With A Z*, also won an Emmy award, with a Grammy later going to the recorded highlights album. Ebb's television work continued with the production of *Ol' Blue Eyes Is Back* (1972) for **Frank Sinatra**. Other Broadway shows followed, including *The Happy Time, Zorba, 70, Girls,*

70, and *Chicago*, which opened in 1975 and ran for 923 performances. In the same year, the duo wrote some songs for the film *Funny Lady*, which starred Barbra Streisand, and followed this with music for two Minnelli films, *A Matter Of Time* (1976) and *New York, New York* (1977). The theme from the latter became an enormous, enduring hit for Frank Sinatra in 1980. Back on Broadway, Kander and Ebb wrote scores for *The Act* (1977) with Minnelli, *Woman Of The Year* (1981), which starred Lauren Bacall, and *The Rink* (1984), yet another Minnelli (and **Chita Rivera**) vehicle. In 1991 they were inducted into the New York Theatre Hall of Fame, and a revue, *And The World Goes 'Round*, which celebrated some 30 of their songs, opened Off Broadway and ran for nearly a year. Another musical anthology, *Sing Happy*, played on the London Fringe in the following year. In 1993 their spectacular musical *Kiss Of The Spider Woman*, starring Chita Rivera, won several Tony Awards in New York following its transfer from the West End. During the 1996/7 Broadway season, a superb concert version of the 20 year old *Chicago* won six Tonys, while *Steel Pier*, a new Kander and Ebb musical about a dance marathon held in Atlantic City in 1933 at the height of the Depression, failed to convert any of its 11 nominations, and closed after only two months. In 1996, the songwriters were among the recipients of the Stage Directors & Choreographers Foundation's 12th annual Mr. Abbott Awards. It was an appropriate gesture, because **George Abbott** directed Kander and Ebb's first Broadway musical, *Flora, The Red Menace*. Apart from their work together, both Kander and Ebb have enjoyed successful independent careers. Kander has written music for film soundtracks, including *Kramer Vs. Kramer* (1980), and Ebb has continued to produce and co-produce numerous television specials, including *Gypsy In My Soul* (1976) and *Baryshnikov On Broadway* (1980).

● ALBUMS: *An Evening With John Kander & Fred Ebb* (DRG 1993)★★.

Kandidate

This expansive UK disco and soul group came together in 1976 comprising members from two previous soul bands: Hot Wax (who went on to become **Hi Tension**) and 70% Proof. They were signed to **Mickie Most**'s **RAK** label and he also produced their recordings. Their debut 'Don't Wanna Say Goodnight' was a minor hit in 1978 and this was followed by three more charting singles, including the number 11 hit, 'I Don't Wanna Lose You' (1979). The line-up of the band was Teeroy (vocals/keyboards), Ferdi (bass), Alex Bruce (percussion), St Lloyd Phillips (drums/vocals), Tamby (guitar/vocals), **Phil Fearon** (guitar) and Bob Collins (percussion/vocals). Of these, only Fearon (b. 30 July 1956, Jamaica) had any further chart success after Kandidate split. He built his own recording studio and had a string of hits in the mid-80s under his own name and the group name Galaxy.

Kane Gang

Martin Brammer (b. 13 May 1957, Easington, Co. Durham, England; songwriter/vocalist) and Dave Brewis (b. 3 June 1957, Sunderland, Tyne And Wear, England; songwriter/multi-instrumentalist) met at school in the northeast town of Seaham, Co. Durham, England. Teaming up with Paul Woods (b. 28 May 1956, Seaham, Co. Durham, England; vocals), the trio developed a liking for 60s/70s soul, funk and R&B which led them through several bands before forming the Kane Gang in late 1982. 'Brother Brother' was planned as their first single on Candle Records, a joint venture with friend Paddy McAloon of **Prefab Sprout**, but both bands were soon signed to new Newcastle label, Kitchenware. In 1984, the company licensed 'Brother Brother' to **London Records**, which signed the group, releasing their attack at the north-south divide, 'Smalltown Creed' (1984), produced by **Pete Wingfield**. In contrast, 'Closest Thing To Heaven' was a smooth ballad, and secured the Kane Gang a Top 20 chart hit. Further success followed that same year with a faithful cover of the **Staple Singers**' 'Respect Yourself', a song which featured soul veteran **P.P. Arnold** on backing vocals. *The Bad And Lowdown World Of The Kane Gang* in early 1985 effectively summarized the band's progress (and featured guest musicians included **Sam Brown**), alongside a single 'Gun Law', before a two-year pause. 'Motortown' (1987) brought another Top 40 hit, preceding a second album. Sporting a slicker, more sophisticated production, *Miracle* also spawned 'What Time Is It', and then a cover of **Dennis Edwards**' Don't Look Any Further' (1988), the latter reaching number 1 in the US dance chart. In 1991, vocalist Paul Woods departed to concentrate on a solo career.
● ALBUMS: *The Bad And Lowdown World Of The Kane Gang* (1985)★★★, *Miracle* (1987)★★★★.

Kane, Big Daddy

Self-styled 'black gentleman vampire' who followed his cousin in to hip-hop by rapping in front of a beatbox for his first shows on Long Island, New York. Aided by his DJ Mr Cee, he has released several albums of laconic, fully-realized songs pitched halfway between soul and rap. His tough but sensual work is best sampled on the hit singles 'Ain't No Stoppin' Us Now' (**McFadden And Whitehead**) and 'Smooth Operator' (**Sade**). Obvious similarities to **Barry White** are given further credence by the duet he shares with that artist on 1991's *Taste Of Chocolate*. He straddled the rap and mainstream R&B markets with his most recent, decidedly mellow album.
● ALBUMS: *Long Live The Kane* (Cold Chillin' 1988)★★★, *It's A Big Daddy Thing* (Cold Chillin' 1989)★★★★, *Taste Of Chocolate* (1991)★★★, *Prince Of Darkness* (1992)★★★, *Looks Like A Job For...* (1993)★★★, *Daddy's Home* (MCA 1994)★★★.

Kane, Eden

b. Richard Sarstedt, 29 March 1942, Delhi, India. When his family returned to England from India during the mid-50s, Kane became involved in music, forming a skiffle group with his brothers. In 1960, he won a talent contest and came under the wing of managers Michael Barclay and Philip Waddilove. They changed his name to Eden Kane, inspired by the movie *Citizen Kane* and the biblical name Cain. Promoted by the chocolate firm, Cadbury's, Kane's first single was 'Hot Chocolate Crazy', which failed to chart. For the follow-up, Kane recorded the catchy, colloquial 'Well I Ask You', which took him to number 1 in the UK during the summer of 1961. Over the next year, three more Top 10 hits followed: 'Get Lost', 'Forget Me Not' and 'I Don't Know Why'. Kane's career suffered a serious setback early in 1963 when Barclay and Waddilove's company Audio Enterprises went into liquidation. The star's management was passed on to **Vic Billings**, who persuaded Fontana's influential A&R manager Jack Baverstock to sign him. In early 1964, Kane returned to the UK Top 10 with 'Boys Cry', which also proved a major hit in Australia. In the autumn of that year, Kane made the momentous decision to emigrate to Australia, later relocating to the USA. Although his chart days were over, his younger brothers **Peter Sarstedt** and Robin Sarstedt both enjoyed hits in their own right. The brothers combined their talents in 1973 for the album, *Worlds Apart Together*. Thereafter, Kane continued to play regularly on the revivalist circuit.
● ALBUMS: *Eden Kane* (Ace Of Clubs 1962)★★, *It's Eden* (Fontana 1964, reissued as *Smoke Gets In Your Eyes* in 1965)★★, with Peter & Robin Sarstedt *Worlds Apart Together* (1973)★★.

Kane, Helen

b. Helen Schroder, 4 August 1904, New York, USA, d. 26 September 1966. Kane is remembered these days as the singer portrayed by **Debbie Reynolds** in *Three Little Words*, the 1950 film biography of songwriters **Bert Kalmar** and **Harry Ruby**. Kane, (who dubbed Reynolds' vocals), was the baby-voiced singer who rose to fame on Broadway in the late 20s. She began her career in vaudeville and night clubs but was much-acclaimed for an appearance with Paul Ash And His Orchestra at New York's Paramount Theatre. She was then featured in such Broadway shows as *A Night In Spain* (1927) and *Good Boy* (1928) in which she sang 'I Wanna Be Loved By You', the 'Boop-Boop-A-Doop' hit that was re-created by Reynolds. After her Broadway success she moved to Hollywood in the late 20s, appearing in several films, including *Nothing But The Truth* (1929), featuring one of her biggest hits, 'Do Something', plus *Sweetie* (1929), *Pointed Heels* (1930), *Dangerous Nan McGrew* (1930), *Heads Up* (1930), and the all-star spectacular, *Paramount On Parade* (1930). Meanwhile, she continued to make hit records such as 'That's My Weakness Now', 'Get Out And Get Under The Moon', 'Me And The Man In The Moon' and

'Button Up Your Overcoat'. Often acknowledged to have been a major influence in the creation of Grim Natwick's cartoon character Betty Boop, Kane continued her career throughout the 30s playing nightclubs. Kane was, for the most part, largely forgotten until the arrival of *Three Little Words*, at which point she became a minor celebrity amid a new generation.

Kane, Kieran

b. 7 October 1949, Queens, New York, USA. The 90s country singer and record company owner Kieran Kane initially enjoyed a certain amount of success as half of the O'Kanes alongside **Jamie O'Hara**. The duo split in 1989 to resume their solo careers, mostly as songwriters. The acoustic *Find My Way Home* did not sell sufficiently well for **Atlantic Records** to want to try again with the artist. This worked to Kane's advantage as, with Mike Henderson, he established his own label, Dead Reckoning, which has already developed into one of the most creative labels in Nashville and whose signings include **Kevin Welch**, Tammy Rogers and Harry Stinson, all of whom work outside of the mainstream. Regarding Kane's own work, the acoustic *Dead Rekoning* cost only $10,000 to make. 'This Dirty Little Town' featured harmony vocals from **Emmylou Harris** and **Lucinda Williams**. Harris also recorded one of his songs, 'If I Could Be There', and **Kathy Mattea** has recorded 'Forgive And Forget'. Kane has much faith in Dead Reckoning, although he is cynical about the industry in general: 'Record companies rarely have anything to do with music.'

● ALBUMS: *Find My Way Home* (Atlantic 1993)★★★, *Dead Rekoning* (Dead Reckoning 1995)★★★, *Six Months, No Sun* (Dead Reckoning 1998)★★★.

Kansas

This US group was formed in 1972 after David Hope (b. *c*.1951, Kansas, USA; bass) and Phil Ehart (b. 1951, Kansas, USA; drums, percussion) changed the name of their band, White Clover, to Kansas, recruiting **Kerry Livgren** (b. 18 September 1949, Kansas, USA; guitar, vocals), Robert Steinhardt (b. *c*.1951, Michigan, USA; violin, strings, vocals), Steve Walsh (b. *c*.1951, St. Joseph, Missouri, USA; keyboards, vocals) and Richard Williams (b. *c*.1951, Kansas, USA; guitars). Although an American band, Kansas were heavily influenced from the outset by British rock of that era, such as **Yes** and **Genesis**, and this was evident in the lyrics of their primary songwriter, Walsh. Kansas released their debut in 1974, and the following two albums attained gold status, guaranteeing the band a high profile in the USA (although no Kansas albums reached the charts in the UK). By 1977 the band had tired of the progressive rock pigeonhole into which the music press was forcing them, and decided to try a more commercial approach. Their popularity was confirmed on 27 June 1978 when they attended a ceremony at Madison Square Gardens in New York, at which the organization UNICEF named the band Deputy Ambassadors of Goodwill. In

the early 80s Walsh decided to leave the band after he became unhappy with their increasingly commercial sound. He released the solo set, *Schemer Dreamer*, which featured other members of Kansas. He was replaced by John Elefante (b. *c*.1958, Levittown, New York, USA; keyboards, vocals), who wrote four of the songs on *Vinyl Confessions*. The band split in 1983 following two unsuccessful albums. Livgren and Hope had become born-again Christians, the former releasing *Seeds Of Change*, a commercially disastrous solo effort based on his religious experiences, and then recorded prolifically with **AD**. In October 1986 Walsh, Ehart and Williams re-formed Kansas with Steve Morse, lately of **Dixie Dregs** (guitar), and Billy Greer (bass). This reunion was celebrated with the release of *Power*, an album that rejected the jazz-rock feel of earlier releases in favour of a heavier sound. Their first studio album in seven years was released in May 1995.

● ALBUMS: *Kansas* (Kirshner 1974)★★★, *Song For America* (Kirshner 1975)★★★, *Masque* (Kirshner 1976)★★★, *Leftoverture* (Kirshner 1977)★★★, *Point Of Know Return* (Kirshner 1977)★★★★, *Two For The Show* (Kirshner 1978)★★★, *Monolith* (Kirshner 1979)★★★, *Audio-Visions* (Kirshner 1980)★★★, *Vinyl Confessions* (Kirshner 1982)★★, *Drastic Measures* (Columbia 1983)★★, *Power* (MCA 1986)★★, *In The Spirit Of Things* (MCA 1988)★★, *Live At The Whisky* (1993)★, *Freaks Of Nature* (Intersound 1995)★★.

● COMPILATIONS: *The Best Of Kansas* (Columbia 1984)★★★.

Kansas City Jazz

During the late 20s and throughout the 30s Kansas City, Missouri, was an important centre for bands touring the southwest and mid-western states. Thanks to the corrupt political machine of city boss Tom Pendergast, with its benign tolerance of the seamier aspects of after-hours drinking and gambling joints, Kansas City became legendary as a place for jam sessions. Musicians with reputations earned elsewhere found themselves up against their peers, likewise passing through, and also confronted by strikingly talented unknowns. In time, these unknowns moved on, some into obscurity, others to become legends of jazz. Amongst the bands based in Kansas City, pride of place is generally granted to **Bennie Moten**'s, although the leader's early death opened the way for others to attain positions of influence. Other leading bands of the region were **Alphonso Trent**, the **Jeter-Pillars Orchestra**, George E. Lee, **Andy Kirk**, Jap Allen, **Harlan Leonard**, Jesse Stone, George Morrison, Thamon Hayes, Clarence Love, **Terrence T. Holder**, **Jay McShann** and **Count Basie**, who took over the reins of the Moten band. Individual musicians who built or consolidated reputations in Kansas City included some who were local while others were from out of town, notably from Texas. These included **Mary Lou Williams, Pete Johnson, Big Joe Turner, Walter Page, Jesse Price**, A.G. Godley, **Jo Jones**, Ben Thigpen, **Gus Johnson, Oran 'Hot Lips' Page, Harry Edison**, Carl

'Tatti' Smith, **Peanuts Holland**, **Buck Clayton**, Buddy Anderson, **Dickie Wells**, **Snub Mosely** and Fred Beckett. The roster of saxophonists is especially notable and includes out-of-towners **Buster Smith**, **Herschel Evans**, **Buddy Tate**, **Budd Johnson**, **Arnett Cobb**, Dick Wilson, **Eddie Barefield**, **Earle Warren**, **Tab Smith**, Henry Bridges and **Lester Young**. Kansas City residents added to the list of saxophonists with **Ben Webster** and **Charlie Parker**. Stylistically, Kansas City jazz differed from the music developing simultaneously elsewhere in the USA. Bands in Kansas City and the southwest drew more heavily upon the blues and used looser arrangements, many of which were 'heads' created in rehearsal or on the stand by the musicians themselves. These arrangements had plenty of solo space and were backed by a subtle, free-flowing rhythmic drive. The music associated with the city, and exemplified by the early Basie band, eventually entered the public's consciousness by way of the swing era. In time, the style and many of its leading exponents became identified with what writer Stanley Dance would later term the 'mainstream' of jazz.

● FURTHER READING: *Jazz Style In Kansas City And The Southwest*, Ross Russell. *Jazz City: The Impact Of Our Cities On The Development Of Jazz*, Leroy Ostransky.

Kansas City Red

b. 7 May 1926, Drew, Mississippi, USA, d. 6 June 1991, Chicago, Illinois, USA. A drummer and blues singer, in the 40s Red worked for **Robert Nighthawk** (who recorded Red's song, 'The Moon Is Rising'), and in the 50s for **Earl Hooker**. He became a club owner in Chicago, and a fixture on the city's blues scene, playing with **Johnny Shines**, **Walter Horton** and **Sunnyland Slim**, and leading his own bands, one of which provided early professional experience for **Jimmy Reed**. Red claimed to have recorded demos for **Chess**, JOB and **Vee Jay Records**, but his debut as a name artist came on a 1975 anthology. Thereafter, he continued to do occasional session drumming for several of his Chicago colleagues, and to combine bar management with live gigs.

● ALBUMS: *Bring Another Half Pint* (1975)★★★.

Kanté, Mory

b. 1951, Kissidougou, Guinea. One of the great preservers and modernizers of the traditional music of west Africa's Mandinka people, Kanté also achieved major recognition in Europe in the 80s, where from his Paris base he fused the ancient sounds of the kora (west African harp) with black American dance music. He was born into a family of famous griots (musician-historians who combine entertainment with tribal history and lore), and at the age of seven, he was sent to Mali to stay with his aunt and learn both the kora technique and the detailed tribal history that he would need if he was to become a professional griot. He stayed with his aunt until he was 15 years old, when he moved to Bamako (also in Mali) and joined the Rail Band, then

Mali's leading group, who for years were resident at the city's Station Hotel, where they entertained both the residents of Bamako and travellers who had completed the long train journey from Dakar in Senegal. During his seven years with the band, he recorded the celebrated album *L'Exil De Soundjata, Le Fondateur De L'Empire Mandingue*, an epic history of the reign of the Malian king and empire builder, Soundjata. As the second singer, he was widely perceived to be chief rival of **Salif Keita** during his time in the Rail Band, and this led directly to Keita's decision to join the Ambassadeurs. In 1977, anxious to broaden his musical horizons, and expand his audience, Kanté left Bamako for the more prosperous and populous city of Abidjan in neighbouring Cote D'Ivoire, where he formed a 35-piece band, Les Milieus Branches, and began introducing elements of black American dance music into his arrangements. He was assisted in these early experiments by the producer Abdouaye Soumare, who had briefly worked with **Stevie Wonder** in the USA. With Soumare, Kanté recorded the album *Courougnegne*, a blueprint for his and other Mandinka musicians' cross-cultural fusions later in the decade. The album was a huge success in Mali, Senegal and Cote D'Ivoire, and also amongst the West African expatriate community in Paris. Encouraged by the French sales, Kante moved to Paris with a slimmed-down version of Les Milieus Branches in 1982, and continued the stylistic innovations set out on *Courougnegne*. In 1984, he released the superb *Mory Kanté A Paris*, which spread his name beyond France and Francophone West Africa to the UK and USA. In 1985, he collaborated with other African musicians on the Tam Tam Pour L'Ethiopie project (a pan-African fund-raising effort for Ethiopia, based on the **Band Aid** principle). Kanté's biggest success to date came in 1988, when his single, 'Ye Ke Ye Ke', an inspired fusion of Mandinka kora and black American house music, enjoyed major chart success throughout Europe and West Africa. In 1990, the similarly inspired and sublime album *Touma* further developed this direction, including input from South African guitarist, and **Paul Simon** collaborator, **Ray Chipika Phiri**, plus **Carlos Santana**.

● ALBUMS: *Mory Kanté & Rail Band* (Syllart 1975)★★, *Courougnegne* (Barclay 1981)★★★, *A Paris* (Barclay 1984)★★★★, *10 Cola Nuts* (Barclay 1986)★★★, *Akwaba Beach* (Barclay 1988)★★★, *Touma* (Barclay 1990)★★★, *Nongo Village* (Barclay 1993)★★★.

Kantner, Paul

b. 17 March 1941, San Francisco, California, USA. Kantner abandoned ambitions of a career in folk music on becoming a founder-member of **Jefferson Airplane** in 1965. Although this revered unit was initially a vehicle for lead singer **Marty Balin**, his influence was gradually eclipsed by those of Kantner and new vocalist **Grace Slick**, particularly when the pair became linked romantically. An early predilection for love songs was replaced by an espousal of hip politics and science fiction; the latter was a particular Kantner favourite. *Volunteers* included 'Wooden Ships', written with **David Crosby** and **Stephen Stills**, and a collaboration reflecting a growing desire among many musicians to break the constraints of a single group. *Blows Against The Empire*, credited to Paul Kantner with **Jefferson Starship**, enshrined this desire by featuring contributions from Slick, Crosby, **Jerry Garcia** and **Graham Nash**. Although the storyline was slight - a group of friends hijack Earth's first starship - it contained several excellent songs, notably 'Have You Seen The Stars Tonite' and 'A Child Is Coming'. The album was nominated for a Hugo science fiction award. Kantner and Slick used several of the same artists on *Sunfighter* and although the duo remained members of Jefferson Airplane, many queried their long-standing commitment in the light of the superior material appearing on 'outside' projects. *Baron Von Tollbooth And The Chrome Nun* emphasized their growing independence and when the parent group disintegrated, Kantner and Slick assembled a permanent Jefferson Starship line-up. Kantner remained at the helm of this highly popular attraction until October 1980 when he suffered a brain haemorrhage, but resumed his role upon making a full recovery. In 1983, he recorded *Planet Earth Rock And Roll Orchestra*, an ambitious sequel to his solo debut which was produced by the **Durocs** team and featured many Bay Area acolytes. The soundtrack to an as yet unrealized science fiction novel, the set appeared as relations within the parent band soured to the extent that Kantner left the following year. In 1985, he rejoined two former Airplane colleagues, Marty Balin and Jack Casady, in **KBC**, but this much heralded unit was a great disappointment. Kantner was a member of the reformed Jefferson Airplane in the late 80s.

● ALBUMS: with Grace Slick *Sunfighter* (Grunt 1971)★★★, with Grace Slick, David Freiberg *Baron Von Tollbooth And The Chrome Nun* (Grunt 1973)★★, *Planet Earth Rock And Roll Orchestra* (RCA 1983)★★★, *A Guide Through The Chaos (A Road To Passion)* spoken word, 2-CD (MonsterSounds 1997)★★.

Kanza, Lokua

b. Zaire. Singer Lokua Kanza moved to Paris, France, from his native Zaire in 1984, and quickly found his vocals employed on a variety of albums by fellow African expatriates such as **Papa Wemba**, **Ray Lema** and **Manu Dibango**. His debut solo album was completed in 1994 and concentrated primarily on his powerful vocal capabilities, supported by a modicum of guitar and percussion. Switching styles between native chants, *a cappella* harmonies and soukous, and employing jazz, blues and soul as well as African rhythms, it delineated a major talent, though his phenomenal range as a performer might have been better served were it harnessed to a more focused musical style.

● ALBUMS: *Lokua Kanza* (Lok 1994)★★★.

Kaper, Bronislaw (Bronislau)

b. 5 February 1902, Warsaw, Poland, d. 26 April 1983, Beverly Hills, California, USA. A composer, arranger and conductor for films, from the mid-30s through to the late 60s. Kaper studied at the Warsaw Conservatory of Music and in Berlin before working as a composer in several European countries, including London and Paris. In 1935, after moving to the USA, he began a collaboration with Walter Jurmann, and sometimes with **Gus Kahn** and **Ned Washington**, on songs for movies such as *A Night At The Opera* ('Cosi Cosa'), *Mutiny On The Bounty* ('Love Song Of Tahiti'), *Escapade* ('You're All I Need'), *San Francisco* (the title song and 'Happy New Year'), *A Day At The Races* ('All God's Chillun Got Rhythm', 'A Message From The Man In The Moon', 'Tomorrow Is Another Day', *Three Smart Girls* ('Someone To Care For Me' and 'My Heart Is Singing'), and *Everybody Sing* ('The One I Love' and 'Swing, Mr. Mendelssohn'). With Kahn, Kaper also wrote 'Blue Lovebird' for the bio-pic, *Lillian Russell* (1940). During the 40s, Kaper composed complete scores for films such as *Johnny Eager, The Chocolate Soldier, Two Faced Woman, Keeper Of The Flame, Somewhere I'll Find You, Gaslight, Mrs. Parkinson, Without Love, Green Dolphin Street* (the song, 'One Green Dolphin Street', became a jazz standard), and contributed 'I Know, I Know I Know', to **Mario Lanza**'s debut movie, *That Midnight Kiss*. In 1953, Kaper won an Academy Award for his score to *Lili*, which also contained the song 'Hi-Lili, Hi-Lo' (lyric by Helen Deutsch). Sung by **Leslie Caron** and Mel Ferrer in the movie, the song later became a hit for both **Richard Chamberlain** and **Alan Price**. In the following year, Kaper, Caron and Deutsch were together again for the film musical *The Glass Slipper*, which included 'Take My Love'. Kaper's other movie music in the 50s and 60s included *A Life Of Her Own, The Red Badge Of Courage, The Wild North, The Naked Spur, Them, Somebody Up There Likes Me, The Swan, Don't Go Near The Water, Auntie Mame, The Brothers Karamazov, Butterfield 8, Green Mansions, The Angel Wore Red, Two Loves, Mutiny On The Bounty* (the 1962 version, containing 'Follow Me', with a lyric by **Paul Francis Webster**, which was nominated for an Oscar), *Kisses For My President, Lord Jim, The Way West, Tobruk, Counterpoint* and *A Flea In Her Ear* (1968). Kaper also composed for television programmes such as *The F.B.I.*, and, in 1945, adapted music by Chopin for the score of the Broadway show *Polonaise*. His collaborators included Herbert Stothart, Bob Russell and Hector Villa-Lobos.

Kaplansky, Lucy

b. Chicago, Illinois, USA. Kaplansky sang backing vocals on albums by **Nanci Griffith**, **John Gorka** and **Shawn Colvin**, but, being a qualified psychologist, she delayed her debut album to work with the homeless in New York. She was part of a duo with Shawn Colvin and Colvin produced *The Tide*. She is a fine singer-

songwriter with folk and country roots and has a good line in cover versions, including **Police**'s 'Secret Journey' and **Richard Thompson**'s 'When I Get To The Border' and 'Don't Renege On Our Love' (from the accomplished follow-up, *Flesh And Bone*). She also sang with **Dar Williams** on 'The Christians And The Pagans'.
● ALBUMS: *The Tide* (Red House 1994)★★★★, *Flesh And Bone* (Red House 1996)★★★★.

Kapp Records

The Kapp label initially served as an MOR outlet. Its first commercial success, Roger Williams, enjoyed a number 1 US hit with the perennial 'Autumn Leaves' in 1955. The singer remained on Kapp for the next 15 years, scoring 22 Hot 100 entries during that period. His singles included 'Hi-Lili Hi-Lo' (1956), 'Near You' (1958), 'Born Free' (1966) and **Jim Webb**'s 'Galveston' (1969), a catalogue reflecting the changing face of popular music, albeit in an uncontroversial manner. This was equally true of an outlet which did not respond to rock 'n' roll, only embracing a teenage perspective in 1960 with **Brian Hyland**'s novelty hit, 'Itsy Bitsy Teeny Weeny Yellow Polkadot Bikini'. Indeed this single was licensed from a minor label, Leader, and the singer quickly changed outlets to **ABC** Paramount. **Lolita**'s number 5 single of the same year, 'Sailor', maintained Kapp's easy-listening image, a fact enhanced with the signing of **Jack Jones**. The son of **Allan Jones**, Jack enjoyed a string of hit singles during the 60s, notably 'Wives And Lovers' (1963) and 'The Race Is On' (1965) which enhanced his standing as one of television's most popular ballad singers. **Johnny Cymbal** and **Ruby And The Romantics** enjoyed smash hits in 1963 with 'Mr Bass Man' and 'Our Day Will Come' respectively but Kapp's most obvious change of perception came upon signing the **Chad Mitchell Trio**. Although offering a clean-cut version of folk music, it did show that the label was becoming aware of prevailing trends. The trio included future star **John Denver** and featured **Byrds** co-founder **Roger McGuinn** as an accompanist. In 1964 Kapp began licensing material from British **Pye**, notably by the **Searchers**. 'Needles And Pins', 'Don't Throw Your Love Away' and 'Love Potion Number Nine' were among the Liverpool group's US chart entries, inspiring Kapp to embrace folk-rock with the New York-based **Critters**, who came to the label via a production deal with **Kama Sutra**. A version of the **Lovin' Spoonful**'s 'Younger Girl' gave this superior group their first hit, although their most popular single was the equally enchanting follow-up, 'Mr. Dieingly Sad'. Composer/arranger **Burt Bacharach** was also associated with Kapp but although his 'solo' recordings failed to emulate the US success of protégé **Dionne Warwick**, Bacharach scored a UK Top 5 entry in 1965 with 'Trains And Boats And Planes', issued on label licensees, **London**/American. Kapp's last significant chart success arrived in 1971 when **Cher** took 'Gypsies, Tramps And Thieves' to the top of the US

chart. By that time the company had been absorbed into the **MCA** group, who latterly dropped the name of this interesting, if lightweight, label.

Karas, Anton

b. 7 July 1906, Vienna, Austria, d. 9 January 1985, Vienna, Austria. The man who arguably did more to popularize the zither than anyone before or after him, is best remembered as the sound behind the famous 'Third Man Theme' (Harry Lime). Carol Reed's classic 1949 film, *The Third Man*, utilized Karas's music throughout, and it was no surprise that film-goers made the song and its accompanying album a number 1 hit in 1951. Although Karas was a virtuoso, he remains one of the more famous one-hit-wonders of our time.
● ALBUMS: *Anton Karas* (Decca 1951)★★★.
● COMPILATIONS: *World Of Anton Karas* (Decca 1971)★★★, *Folk Songs Of Austria* (1974)★★★, *Harry Lime Theme (The Third Man)* (1974)★★★, *Bons Bons De Vienne* (1977)★★★.

Karklins, Ingrid

b. Chicago, Illinois, USA. Singer-songwriter Ingrid Karklins uses words of Latvian, Gaelic and American extraction within her brooding, *avant garde* folk songs, usually accompanied by the thirteen-stringed kokle - an instrument related to the Finnish kantele but exclusive to the Latvian tradition, of which she is an expatriate member. Growing up in the Chicago Latvian community, she later moved to Austin, Texas, from where she currently operates. Though performing opportunities there are limited, with Karklin's unsettling style hardly fitting the new blues and country traditions of the area, she has played regularly with local musicians and travelled to noted *avant garde* club the Knitting Factory in New York and to Latvia in July 1992 for a major concert in Riga. Two cassette only albums led to her debut for Green Linnet Records in 1992, a release which built strong critical reactions with its disturbing lyrical matter and frantic north European rhythms.
● ALBUMS: *Willowbush* cassette only (1988)★★★, *Kas Dimd* cassette only (1990)★★★, *A Darker Passion* (Green Linnet 1992)★★★★.

Karl And Harty

Karl Davis and Hartford Connecticut Taylor (both b. 1905, Mount Vernon, Kentucky, USA). They grew up listening to the musicians who regularly played in their town and learned many songs from their parents and from Brag Thompson, the pianist for the silent films that were shown at the local cinema. By the age of 12, Karl had learned to play the mandolin from Doc Hopkins (a noted local singer) and Harty had taught himself to play the guitar. By 1929, they were regularly appearing with Hopkins as the Kentucky Krazy Kats on WHAS Louisville. The following year, **Bradley Kincaid** was instrumental in their moving to WLS Chicago, where they featured on several programmes including the *National Barn Dance* and appeared with such artists as **Red Foley** in the Cumberland Ridge Runners. In 1933, Karl wrote 'I'm Here To Get My Baby Out Of Jail', which they recorded the following year. It proved so successful that almost every other duet group recorded it and the song went on to become a country standard. The two benefited from the new microphone and broadcasting equipment, which meant that the old mountain shouting style of singing was no longer necessary. During the 30s, their quieter style of close harmony vocal work became the form copied by other acts including the **Blue Sky Boys**, the **Delmore Brothers** and, years later, the **Everly Brothers**. They played on WLS until 1937 and then moved to *Suppertime Frolics* on Chicago WJJD, becoming popular over an even larger area. By the mid-40s, the changing times and the record companies' constant search for jukebox records found the pair forced to record more modern songs aimed at the honky-tonk market. They consequently recorded songs such as 'Seven Beers With The Wrong Woman' and 'Don't Mix Whiskey With Women', while continuing to sing their more usual style of number, such as 'Wreck On The Highway' and 'The Prisoner's Dream', on their radio programmes. They later commented: 'We were like Dr. Jekyll and Mr. Hyde and we didn't much like that either'. In the 50s, they retired from performing when live radio and country music in Chicago declined. Karl remained active as a songwriter and had songs recorded by artists including **Emmylou Harris** and **Linda Ronstadt**. There is little doubt that Karl's best-known song is 'Kentucky'. He wrote it as a tribute to his home state and when it was recorded in January 1941, it became very popular with US servicemen in World War II. However, it was not their own version but that of the Blue Sky Boys, in 1947, that turned the song into a country classic (Karl received the honour of being named a Kentucky Colonel in 1970 by the grateful state). Harty died in 1963 and Karl in 1979.

● COMPILATIONS: *Early Recordings* (1981)★★★.

Karn, Mick

b. Anthony Michaelides, 24 July 1958, London, England. Formerly the bass player with early 80s UK art-pop band **Japan**, Karn released his debut solo album after that band's dissolution in 1982. Featuring several session musicians in addition to Karn on vocals, bass, keyboards and synthesizers, it reached number 74 in the UK charts. In June 1983 he joined **Ultravox**'s **Midge Ure** for a one-off single, 'After A Fashion', which reached number 39 in the UK charts. In the following year he formed **Dali's Car** with former **Bauhaus** singer **Pete Murphy** and Paul Vincent Lawford, before resuming his solo career in 1986. 'Buoy' was credited to Mick Karn featuring **David Sylvian** (his former Japan colleague), and preceded the release of his second album, *Dreams Of Reason Produce Monsters*. Afterwards Karn concentrated on session work, his long list of clients including **Kate Bush** and **Joan Armatrading**,

and his 'secondary' career as a sculptor. His work has been exhibited in galleries in London, as well as Tokyo, Osaka and Sapporo in Japan and Turin in Italy. A long-delayed third collection, 1993's *Bestial Culture*, was followed the next year by *Beginning To Melt*, which paired him with two former Japan members, Steve Jansen and Richard Barbieri, in addition to respected guitarist **David Torn**, to whose solo work Karn had previously contributed.

● ALBUMS: *Titles* (Virgin 1982)★★★, *Dreams Of Reason Produce Monsters* (Virgin 1987)★★★, *Bestial Cluster* (CMP 1993)★★★, with Steve Jansen, Richard Barbieri *Beginning To Melt* (Medium Productions 1994)★★★, with David Torn, Terry Bozzio *Polytown* (CMP 1994)★★★, *Tooth Mother* (CMP 1995)★★★.

Kasenetz-Katz Singing Orchestral Circus

The brainchild of bubblegum pop producers, Jerry Kasenetz and Jeff Katz, the Singing Orchestral Circus was a sprawling aggregation of eight groups on one record: the **Ohio Express**, the **1910 Fruitgum Company**, Music Explosion, Lt. Garcia's Magic Music Box, Teri Nelson Group, Musical Marching Zoo, JCW Rat Finks and the St. Louis Invisible Marching Band. Together, they were responsible for one of bubblegum's more memorable moments with the international hit, 'Quick Joey Small' in 1968. With an attendant array of acrobats, clowns, fire-eaters and scantily-clad girls, the circus played a concert at Carnegie Hall with a repertoire which included such hits as 'Yesterday', 'We Can Work It Out', 'Hey Joe' and 'You've Lost That Lovin' Feelin''. The prestige of this event did not prevent them from taking their place as one-hit-wonders.

Kash, Murray

The Canadian Murray Kash spent many years promoting country music in the UK, working as a radio presenter and compere. He has had series on the BBC and Radio Luxembourg. He worked for promoter **Mervyn Conn** for some years and was the Festival Director for the International Festivals of Country Music at Wembley from 1969-79. He is married to the cabaret entertainer Libby Morris, and he wrote one of the first country books to be published in the UK, *Murray Kash's Book Of Country* (Star Books, 1981). He has recorded narrations for **RCA** ('Sleeping Beauty', 1968) and **Columbia** ('What Is A Boy?', 1974).

Kashmir

This short-lived English folk duo featured Lesley Davies (b. Lesley Anne Davies, 23 March 1959, Stockport, Cheshire, England; vocals/guitar), and her brother Steve Davies (b. Stephen Glyn Davies, 17 February 1964, Romiley, Cheshire, England; piano, synthesizer, vocals). Kashmir was formed in 1985, and performed a combination of contemporary and traditional folk material, touring clubs and festivals. Shortly after the release of *Stay Calm*, which included the vocals of Fiona

Simpson, Steve decided to quit performing full time, and Lesley continued, for only a short while longer as Kashmir, with guitarist Jon Gibbons. Lesley had, by now, also joined **Les Barker**'s Mrs. Ackroyd Band, providing vocals for *Earwigo* in 1987, and for *Oranges And Lemmings* in 1990. She was also touring with the band, as well as playing solo. She can still be seen singing with singer-songwriter **Mike Silver**, and **Paul Metser**'s band, Cave Canem, in addition to a number of local jazz bands. In 1988-89, Davies took the female lead in the Les Barker Folk Opera *The Stones Of Callenish*, performed live at the Sidmouth Folk Festival, and on the recorded work. In 1990, she studied at Leeds College of Music, for a three-year diploma in jazz, contemporary and popular music.
● ALBUMS: *Stay Calm* (1986)★★★.

Kaspersen, Jan

b. 22 April 1948, Copenhagen, Denmark. Composer and pianist Kaspersen's wry, quirky tunes reveal the influences of **Thelonious Monk**, **Horace Silver** and **Abdullah Ibrahim**, who, under the name of Dollar Brand, played regularly at the jazzhouse Montmartre in Copenhagen 1963/4. All have strong roots in Black church music and this may account for Kaspersen's attraction to the funky aspects of American jazz. Kaspersen's composition and playing never descend to mere pastiche or antiquarian seriousness but display a touch of ironic humour that appeals to both head and feet. Kaspersen has written for the Radio Big Band, for theatre, and performed with poets. He regularly records with his own ensemble, large or small.
● ALBUMS: *Bizarre Ballet* (Storyville 1983)★★★, *Puzzle In Four* (Olufsen 1985)★★★★, *Memories Of Monk* (Olufsen 1986)★★★, *Erik Satie-3 Gymnopedies* (Olufsen 1986)★★★★, *Love Eyes* (Olufsen 1987)★★★, *Space And Rhythm Jazz* (Olufsen 1987)★★★, *Ten By Two* (Olufsen 1987)★★★, *Special Occasion* (Olufsen 1990)★★★, *Live In Sofie's Cellar* (Olufsen 1991)★★★, *Heavy Smoke* (Olufsen 1992)★★★, with Horace Parlan *Joinin' Forces* (Olufsen 1993)★★, *Live In Copenhagen Jazzhouse* (Olufsen 1994)★★.

Kassell, Art

Kassell formed his first dance band in 1924 for an appearance at the Midway Gardens in Chicago, Illinois, USA. His full-scale orchestra included, at various times, sidemen Jack Davis, Ponzi Crunz, Ralph Morris, D. Johnson, Floyd Townes, Carl Bertram, Cliff Masterler, Bob Hill, John Jacobs, Ben Bensman, Thal Taylor, Paul Matlow, Emil Elias, Bob McReynolds, Don Gershman, Charlie Amsterdam, George Yadon, Mike Simpson, Lewis Math, Horace Robbins, Fred Benson, Bernie Woods, John Engro, John Gilliland, Larry Hall, Floyd Shaw, Mac Newton, Frank Folmar, Eddie Burbach, Art Waynes, Danny Bridge, James Hefti, Cub Higgins, Roy Henderson, Harvey Crawford, Don Baker, Charlie Kramer, Marty Rogers, Warren Smith, George Winslow, Pete Dudlinger, Milt Samuels, Bob Dayton, Ken Switzer, John Byrne, Tom Taddonic, **Jimmy**

McPartland, **Bud Freeman**, **Dave Tough** and even **Benny Goodman** for a spell. The group's vocalists were Norman Ruvell, Thal Taylor, Billie Leach, Harvey Crawford, Grace Dunn, Marian Holmes, Gloria Hart and the group's own three piece vocal act, the Kassell Trio. Led by Kassell himself on saxophone, the orchestra's engagements after their Midway Gardens bow included the Aragon and Trianon Ballrooms in Chicago, with frequent airplay on the sponsored *Shell Oil Company Show*, *Elgin Watch Show* and *Wildroot Hair Oil Show*. They remained based almost exclusively in the Midwest region, with a fifteen year engagement at the Bismarck Hotel in Chicago, until Kassell relocated to the west coast in the late 50s. This move brought engagements at the Hollywood Palladium and Myron's Ballroom is Los Angeles, then the Golden West Ballroom in Norwalk. They also appeared on television for two seasons on a locally networked show. After Kassell's death in February 1965 his band continued to play the west coast circuit, where their theme song, 'Doodle-Doo-Doo', was now among dance band music's most famous compositions.

Kasseya, Souzy

b. July 1949, Kasseya, Shaba Province, Zaire. A leading light of the mid-80s, Paris-based soukous scene, guitarist and songwriter Kasseya began his career in the Zairean capital, Kinshasa, in the early 70s, as a session musician for vocalists like **Sam Mangwana** and **M'Pongo Love**. He also produced releases by **Bebe Manga** and François Lougha. After moving to Paris in the late 70s, he released his first album, *Princesse Gyonne*, in 1979. This included the track 'Le Telephone Sonne', which as a single went on to become a massive hit in France and throughout central Africa. It was also released in the UK, by specialist label Earthworks, but failed to repeat its European success. In 1984, he toured the UK to coincide with the release of *Le Retour De L'As*, returning the following year as a member of Mangwana's backing band. Later that year, he released his first UK album, *The Phenomenal Souzy Kasseya*, a firmly roots-based soukous set which successfully added hi-tech electronic effects and instrumentation to the mix. During the late 80s, he was most active as a session guitarist, working in Paris studios.
● ALBUMS: *Princesse Gyonne* (Earthworks 1979)★★★, *Le Retour De L'As* (Earthworks 1984)★★, *The Phenomenal Souzy Kasseya* (Earthworks 1985)★★★★.

Kassner, Eddie

b. 1920, Vienna, Austria, d. 19 November 1996, London, England. An 'old school' music publisher, Kassner fled from his native Austria as a child to seek refuge from Nazi expansion. He served in the British Army during World War II, before founding the Edward Kassner Music Co. in the 50s. The catalogue of songs he established provided material for **Frank Sinatra**, **Perry Como**, **Dinah Shore**, **Nat 'King' Cole** and **Vera Lynn**, among others. In 1951 he opened a branch in New York's **Brill Building**, from where his catalogue-acquisition efforts expanded. The group's financial stability was assured by a single song in the mid-50s, 'Rock Around The Clock', acquired for an advance of $250. Other major earners included 'Bobby's Girl' (**Susan Maughan**), 'The White Rose Of Athens' (**Nana Mouskouri**) and 'I Feel So Bad' (**Elvis Presley**). However, by the mid-60s, Kessner had become well aware of the trend towards groups and artists writing their own compositions. As a consequence he established President Records in 1966, releasing hits by the **Equals**, **Symbols** and **KC And The Sunshine Band**. He also signed the **Kinks** to a management deal and began a highly successful 12-year association with **Rick Wakeman**.

Kasuga, Hachirô

b. Minaru Watanabe, 9 October 1924, Fukushima, Japan, d. 1991. Hachirô Kasuga trained himself as a singer of kayôkyoku (formerly the most common and typically Japanese form of popular song) in Tokyo. He was signed by King Records, debuting with a hit single, 'Akai Lampno Shûressha' ('The Last Train With Red Tail Lamps'), in 1952. His popularity increased the following year with 'Otomi-san' ('Miss Tomi'), a convivial song about a character in a well-known kabuki play which was originally intended to be recorded by a senior artist, Haruo Oka. Kasuga's stardom was finally established in 1955 by 'Wakare No Ippon Sugi' ('A Solitary Cedar By Which We Parted'), which led to the emergence of many other 'home-pining' songs in the late 50s, reflecting the increasing influx of population into large cities from rural areas. Many other hits, sung in a well-regulated manner, were produced in his long career, including 'Arekara Jûnen Tattakana' ('Was It Ten Years Ago?') and 'Nagasaki No On'na' ('A Woman In Nagasaki').
● COMPILATIONS: *Zenkyokushû 1* (Complete Works 1) (1990)★★★, *Zenkyokushû 2* (Complete Works 2) (1990)★★★.

Kat

The self-proclaimed 'Great Kat' began her musical career as a classically trained violinist, graduating from the Juilliard School of Music in New York. After six years of solid performance on the instrument, she switched to the guitar and began experimenting with a fusion of classical and rock music. Adopting a high-speed technique, she concentrated on short instrumentals. *Worship Me Or Die* was poorly received, despite Kat's proclamations that it represented 'the first real revolutionary music since Beethoven'. Undaunted, she released *Beethoven On Speed*, which marked a considerable improvement in both musical and production terms. Promoting herself as a grotesque parody of a 'wild woman of rock', this contrivance fell flat with European audiences and, despite her potential to produce an innovative metal/classical crossover album, little has been heard from the artist since.

● ALBUMS: *Worship Me Or Die* (Roadrunner 1987)★★, *Beethoven On Speed* (Roadrunner 1990)★★★★.

Katch 22

British *avant garde* rap troupe headed up by MC Huntkillbury Finn (b. Andrew Ward) and producer Mad Marga (b. Steven Andre), whose additional personnel include DJ Killerman Twice (b. Nicholas Swaby), Cavey (b. Ian Williams; producer), Malika B Poetess (b. Malika Booker) and singer Ann Gray. Their imaginative utilisation of beats and rhythms appropriated from a variety of sources like jazz, dub and ska, place them squarely in the Black British underground tradition. They have also operated in an admirably collective manner, handing the mic over to a number of contributors (including a healthy female ratio) and collaborating with other groups like **Cookie Crew**, **Hijack** and **Son Of Noise**. The mainstays have also given production assistance to several other **Kold Sweat** outfits, including Rude Boy Business, Superb C and Ambassadors Of Swing.
● ALBUMS: *Diary Of A Black Man Living In The Land Of The Lost* (1991)★★★, *Dark Tales From Two Cities* (Kold Sweat 1993)★★★.

Kate & Anna McGarrigle - Kate & Anna McGarrigle

These Canadian sisters unsuspectingly recorded this album, which is a huge critics' favourite yet deserves much wider acceptance. Spotted and recorded by the canny **Joe Boyd** it is an album brimming with melancholy. Kate was formerly the wife of **Loudon Wainwright**, and the excellent 'Swimming Song' was written by him. Elsewhere, the evocative and anthemic '(Talk To Me Of) Mendocino' is a total joy and completely captures a feeling of being resigned to homesickness. Those who have not yet discovered this album will not be disappointed with this strong recommendation. Another quiet classic of great depth.
● Tracks: *Kiss And Say Goodbye; My Town; Blues In D; Heart Like A Wheel; Foolish You; (Talk To Me Of) Mendocino; Complainte Pour Ste-Catherine; Tell My Sister; Swimming Song; Jigsaw Puzzle Of Life; Go Leave; Travellin' On For Jesus.*
● First released 1975
● UK peak chart position: did not chart
● USA peak chart position: did not chart

Katon, Michael

This acclaimed blues rock guitarist/vocalist grew up in Ipsilanti, Michigan, USA, and his musical family background soon inspired him to take up the guitar. Katon began playing with local bands in clubs and roadhouse bars around Detroit from the age of 15, and spent 20 years paying his dues in classic blues fashion, working with a succession of blues and jazz bands. Subsequently based in Hell, Michigan, he released his solo debut, *Boogie All Over Your Head*, on his own Wild Ass label, with Swedish label Garageland picking up the record in Europe. The straightforward R&B boogie style, gravelly vocals and stylish blues guitar of *Proud To Be Loud* endeared Katon to both the blues and heavy metal crowds, and live shows with Ed Phelps (guitar, harmonica), Johnny Arizona (bass) and Gary Rasmussen (drums) proved to be wild affairs, particularly owing to the guitarist's penchant for four- and five-hour sets. Blues label Provogue were suitably impressed, offering Katon a European contract. Katon gave up drinking to concentrate on his guitar playing, resulting in the harder, more focused *Get On The Boogie Train*, and while his lyrics retained their customary humour, he also produced a fine slice of urban blues in 'Cadillac Assembly Line', a lament for Detroit's declining motor industry. *Rip It Hard* continued in the traditional blues-boogie vein, and while, like many bluesmen, major commercial success evades Katon, he remains a respected guitarist in the field.

● ALBUMS: *Boogie All Over Your Head* (Wild Ass 1985)★★★, *Proud To Be Loud* (Wild Ass 1988)★★★, *Get On The Boogie Train* (Wild Ass 1992)★★★★, *Rip It Hard* (Wild Ass 1994)★★★, *Rub* (Provogue 1996)★★★.

Katrina And The Waves

This pop group enjoyed their major hit with 'Walking On Sunshine' in 1985, but were also well-known for their original version of 'Going Down To Liverpool', which was successfully covered by the **Bangles**. The band consisted of Katrina Leskanich (b. 1960, Topeka, Kansas, USA; vocals), Kimberley Rew (guitar), Vince De La Cruz (b. Texas, USA; bass) and Alex Cooper (drums). Leskanich and De La Cruz are Americans, but came to Britain during 1976 when their military fathers served in the UK. Based at Feltwell, Norfolk, the sight of the airforce base, Rew and Cooper were both graduates of Cambridge University. Rew was formerly in the **Soft Boys** and after leaving them released the solo *The Bible Of Pop*, in 1982. Many of the songs he wrote for his solo career were carried over into Katrina And The Waves, where he became the chief songwriter. The band was formed in 1982 but their first two albums were only released in Canada. They followed up 'Walking On Sunshine' with 'Sun Street', which was their last hit, although they remained a popular act on the college circuit for some time thereafter. 1993 brought a series of reunion gigs, at first in their 'adopted city' of Cambridge. Although it caused some surprise, the band were nominated by the British public as the UK entry for the 1997 Eurovision Song Contest. The mantric chorus of 'Love Shine A Light' appealed to the judges and it became the clear winner; obligatory chart success followed.

● ALBUMS: *Walking On Sunshine* (Canada 1983)★★★, *Katrina And The Waves 2* (Canada 1984)★★, *Katrina And The Waves* (Capitol 1985)★★, *Waves* (Capitol 1985)★★, *Break Of Hearts* (SBK 1989)★★.

Katz, Al

Most frequently appearing under the name Al Katz And His Kittens, Katz led dance bands were among the Midwest of America's most prolific performers from the mid-20s onwards. His sidemen included a flexible pool of musicians with George Shechtman, Joe Magliatti, Fred Rollinson, Lewis Story, Jerry Bump, Eddie Kooden, Ray Kleemeyer, Joe Bishop, Greg Brown and **Jess Stacy** among his most regular partners. They recorded for Gennett, **Victor** and **Columbia Records**, with their shows booked by the MCA organisation. Several of these bookings, it later transpired, were contracted without the agency knowing that Katz led the orchestra, such was the profligacy of names he employed. The Kittens also played rare dates along the east coast and in New York, where most of their recording sessions were conducted.

Katz, Jeff

(see **Kasenetz-Katz Singing Orchestral Circus**)

Kaufman, George S.

b. 14 November 1889, Pittsburg, Pennsylvania, USA, d. 2 June 1961, New York, USA. For a man who was supposed to hate music and musicals with considerable fervour, George S. Kaufman made significant contributions as a librettist and director to a variety of productions in the American musical theatre from the 20s through to the 50s. Early in his career he worked as a newpaper columnist for several years in Washington and later in New York where he became one of the brightest young talents in the early 30s, many of whom, including Kaufman, Ring Lardner, Dorothy Parker, Alexander Woollcott, and Robert Benchley, were members of the Algonquin Hotel's Round Table set. After co-writing the book with Marc Connelly in 1923 for *Helen Of Troy, New York*, which had a score by **Bert Kalmar** and **Harry Ruby**, Kaufman contributed sketches or was the librettist or co-librettist on a number of other Broadway musical productions including *The Music Box Revue* (Third Edition), *Be Yourself!*, **The Cocoanuts**, *Animal Crackers*, **The Little Show**, **Strike Up The Band**, *Nine-Fifteen Revue*, and **The Band Wagon** (1931).

By now an established figure, he also directed most of the subsequent productions on which he worked. In the 30s and 40s these included **Of Thee I Sing**, for which he won a Pulitzer Award, **Face The Music** (director only), *Let 'Em Eat Cake*, **I'd Rather Be Right**, *Sing Out The News*, *Seven Lively Arts*, *Hollywood Pinafore*, and *Park Avenue* (1946). In 1950 Kaufman earned a **Tony Award** for his direction of the superb **Guys And Dolls**, and, five years later, collaborated with his second wife, the actress Leueen MacGrath, on the book for the **Cole Porter** musical **Silk Stockings**. His work in the musical theatre was just a part of his wider output. He is credited with 45 plays written in conjunction with some 16 known collaborators who included Edna Furber, Ring Lardner, and his principal later collaborator **Moss Hart**. With Hart he wrote some of the American theatre's most enduring comedies - *Once In A Lifetime*, *You Can't Take It With You* (for which he won his second

Pulitzer Prize), and *The Man Who Came To Dinner*.

● FURTHER READING: *George S. Kaufman: An Intimate Portrait*, Howard Teichmann. *George S. Kaufman And His Friends*, Scott Meredith.

Kaukonen, Jorma

b. 23 December 1940, Washington, DC, USA. The solo career of the former **Jefferson Airplane** lead guitarist started after the demise of the Airplane splinter group **Hot Tuna** in 1978. Kaukonen went back to his roots as a solo acoustic performer in small clubs. Four years earlier, he had released an outstanding recording, *Quah*, joined by Tom Hobson and produced by Jack Casady. The album was well received and although not released in the UK, enough copies were imported to satisfy the small but enthusiastic market. On this album Kaukonen displayed an intensity that had been hidden during his years with the Airplane. The autobiographical 'Song For The North Star' and the emotive 'Genesis' were two outstanding examples. On *Barbeque King* he was joined by Denny DeGorio (bass) and John Stench (drums), otherwise known as Vital Parts, in a not too successful attempt to work again within a rock group. During his solo years Kaukonen's reputation as an acoustic guitarist has grown considerably; his love for ragtime blues continued to find a small and loyal audience fascinated to watch a six-foot, body-tattooed Scandinavian playing such delicate music. In 1989, Kaukonen was cajoled into re-forming the Jefferson Airplane, where once again he sacrificed his love of 'wooden' music for the power of his biting and frantic lead guitar playing. In 1990, he and Casady reconvened as Hot Tuna.

● ALBUMS: *Quah* (Grunt 1975)★★★★, *Jorma* (RCA 1980)★★★, *Barbeque King* (RCA 1980)★★, *Magic* (Relix 1985)★★★, *Too Hot To Handle* (Relix 1987)★★★, with Tom Constanten *Embryonic Journey* (Relix 1995)★★★, *The Land Of Heroes* (American Heritage/Relix 1996)★★★.

Kaukonen, Peter

b. Benson Lee Kaukonen, September 1945, Topeka, Kansas, USA. Guitarist/vocalist Peter Kaukonen is the younger brother of **Jefferson Airplane**'s **Jorma Kaukonen**. He began his career playing blues and folk prior to forming a bluegrass group in 1964 while studying at the University of Stockholm in Sweden. Having moved to California, Kaukonen became member of Petrus. The group recorded an unissued album for **A&M Records** before folding after which Kaukonen moved to San Francisco. He enjoyed close ties with Jefferson Airplane, playing on spin-off releases *Blows Against The Empire* and *Sunfighter*, before recording for the group's Grunt label. Kaukonen's group, Black Kangaroo, formed in 1971, initially comprised of Mario Cipollina (bass) and Bill Gibson (drums), both later of **Huey Lewis And The News**. However, *Peter Kaukonen: Black Kangaroo* featured Larry Knight (b. Larry Weissberg; bass) and Joey Covington (drums; ex-**Hot Tuna**/Jefferson Airplane). Their only album is a hard-edged collection, showing the influence of **Jimi Hendrix** and **Johnny Winter**, with whom Kaukonen worked briefly when Black Kangaroo split up in 1972. Kaukonen was offered the role of bassist in **Jefferson Starship** but opted to work as a solo artist. He recorded *Traveller*, an all-instrumental set, between 1980 and 1984. It did not secure a commercial release, although Kaukonen sold cassette copies at his live appearances. He also revived Black Kangaroo on two occasions. In 1977 he fronted a line-up completed by Stable Brown (bass) and a drummer dubbed 'Stavros'. A third version, featuring Keith Ferguson (bass) and Jimmy Gillen (drums) was active at the end of the 70s, but it folded when Ferguson left. He later helped form the **Fabulous Thunderbirds**.

● ALBUMS: *Peter Kaukonen: Black Kangaroo* (Grunt 1972)★★★★, *Traveller* (private pressing 1985)★★★.

Kavana

b. *c.*1976, Manchester, England. A pop protégé developed by well-known entrepreneur Nigel Martin-Smith, who originally pieced together **Take That**, Kavana made his debut for Martin-Smith's **Virgin Records**-affiliated Nemesis label in 1996. His debut single, 'Crazy Chance', was written by former Take That member Howard Donald, though his second release and all bar one track of his subsequent debut album were self-penned. The smooth soul pop of 'Where Are You' provided typical boy-pop fare, with a quotient of street hipness lent by the production work of Joey Negro on the b-side, 'For The Very First Time'. The a-side was produced by Phil Green, previously a collaborator with **Carleen Anderson** and the **Brand New Heavies**, who also worked on Kavana's album debut. Throughout 1996 Kavana built his profile by appearing on a number of British youth television shows and touring with **Boyzone**.

Kavana, Ron

Kavana spent the 70s and early 80s in an R&B band, Juice On The Loose, before moving in a more traditional direction, inspired by the **Pogues**, and **Shane MacGowan** in particular. He was invited to join MacGowan's band after Ciat O'Riordan left, but the move was blocked by the Pogue's management. After eschewing R&B, he spent several years gigging with his Alias Ron Kavana. The new outfit incorporated African and South American rhythms with Irish sounds, and eagerly sought out further influences. The debut *Think Like A Hero*, emphasised this approach, coupled with an unsuppressable pop energy. Songs such as 'This Is The Night' (a worthy tribute to **Van Morrison**), sit comfortably alongside instrumentals like 'Soweto Trembles'. In the *Folk Roots* readers' poll of 1991, Alias Ron Kavana featured at, or near the top of six of the eight categories. Kavana next assembled the LILT (London Irish Live Trust) album *For The Children*, to promote peace in Northern Ireland, gathering a host of Irish traditional greats. The solo *Home Fires* followed.

Mostly Irish in style, the material has the timbre of the traditional, particularly 'Young Ned Of The Hill' (co-written with Pogue Terry Woods). Of the band album, *Coming Days* (1991), *Folk Roots* stated: 'The man has delivered'. Alias Ron Kavana has since added an Irish piper, and become the Alias Big Band, but the energy and live appeal endures. For the *Coming Days* recording the line-up comprised: Kavana (guitar, slide guitar, mandolin, mandola, keyboards, synthesizers, drum programming, vocals), Les Morgan (drums, percussion), Richie Robertson (bass, vocals), Fran Byrne (button accordion), Mick Molly (guitar, mandolin, mandola, vocals), and all group members played percussion.

● ALBUMS: as Alias Ron Kavana *Think Like A Hero* (1989)★★★★, *Coming Days* (1991)★★★★, *Galway To Graceland* (Alias 1995)★★★; as LILT *For The Children* (1990)★★★; as Ron Kavana *Home Fires* (1991)★★★.

Kavanagh, Niamh

b. Dublin, Eire. Singer Niamh (pronounced 'Neeve') Kavanagh rose to prominence by singing the winning entry in the 1993 Eurovision Song Contest, 'In Your Eyes'. Raised in the family of an Irish showband saxophonist, previously she had worked as a clerk at the Allied Irish Bank, and also contributed three songs to the soundtrack of *The Commitments*. Her primary influence was always **Aretha Franklin** - 'I couldn't believe anybody could sound like that. I nearly fainted when I first heard 'Respect'.' Immediately after the Eurovision Song Contest she was signed to Franklin's former label **Arista Records** by Simon Cowell, with the record label offering her a long-term development deal with the hope of pushing her 'upmarket'. However, internal problems delayed the release of her debut album, which was eventually launched at Dublin Castle early in 1996. It was recorded in Nashville with **Mary-Chapin Carpenter**'s producer John Jennings, with the song selection overseen by Arista's Nigel Grainge and Chris Hill. It included the Shelley Peiken-written single 'Romeo's Twin', on which Carpenter also featured. Tellingly, 'In Your Eyes' was absent as the record label attempted to move Kavanagh away from her perceived image as a 'Eurovision singer'.

● ALBUMS: *Flying Blind* (Arista 1996)★★★.

Kavelin, Al

Formed in New York City, New York, USA, in 1933, the Al Kavelin Orchestra played its first engagement at the Central Park Casino in that year. Kavelin was a graduate of the Royal Verdi Conservatory in Milan, Italy. Before becoming a bandleader he had previously been an associate of **Jean Goldkette**. The decision to form his own orchestra was instigated by **Eddie Duchin**. Duchin had been enormously successful at the Central Park Casino, from where his radio appearances had made him one of the biggest names on the east coast. However, as he was still under contract with the Casino, he was forced to find a replacement for his

bookings there before he could negotiate his own exit. He recommended Kavelin, who organised his band so as to replicate the Duchin sound. The new band's best known member was singer Carmen Cavallaro. Other vocalists to perform with them included **Vivian Blaine**, Bill Darnell, Don Cornell and Virginia Gilcrest. Their initial eight week engagement was extended to 24 weeks, by which time they had secured prestigious airplay through the CBS organisation. Competitors MCA then stepped in to offer the group touring contracts, which took them coast to coast. The 30s and 40s saw the orchestra play most of the major hotels and ballrooms of the dance band circuit, including the Waldorf-Astoria, Essex House and the Biltmore (New York), the Blackstone Hotel (Chicago), the Mark Hopkins (San Francisco), the Baker (Dallas), the Peabody (Memphis) and the Roosevelt (New Orleans). They enjoyed their biggest recording success in 1941 when Kavelin wrote 'I Give You My World'. This topped the Lucky Strike Hit Parade and sold heavily throughout America. By the 50s the dance band boom was fading, and Kavelin chose to set up a new business, the successful Kavelin Tours organisation.

Kawaguchi, George

b. 15 June 1917, Fukakusa, Japan. As a child he was raised in Dairen, Manchuria, returning to Japan after World War II. In the late 40s he first played drums professionally, turning naturally to the newly popular jazz that came with the American occupation. During the 50s and afterwards, Kawaguchi played most often with his own bands, including the Big Four and the Big Two. He also accompanied visiting American musicians including fellow drummers **Art Blakey**, in 1981, and **Elvin Jones**, in the early 90s. His penchant for working with other drummers included recording sessions with countryman **Motohiko Hino**. A very strong player with a commanding technique, Kawaguchi enjoys extended solo excursions often with crowd-pleasing results. In the right company, however, and with his enthusiasm under control, he applies his considerable technique to the services of the band with great effect.

● ALBUMS: *Jazz At The Toris* (King 1957)★★★, *Yesterdays 1: The Original Big Four* (King 1959)★★★, *The Drum Battle: George Kawaguchi vs Motohiko Hino* (Teichiku 1975)★★, *The Original Big Four Live* (Philips 1977)★★★, *Super Drums* (Paddle Wheel 1979)★★★★, *African Hot Dance* (Electric Bird 1980)★★★, with Art Blakey *Killer Joe* (Union 1980)★★★, *Big 2 With Lionel Hampton* (Paddle Wheel 1982)★★.

Kay, Connie

b. Conrad Henry Kirnon, 27 April 1927, Tuckahoe, New York, USA, d. 30 November 1994, New York City, New York, USA. A self-taught drummer, in his late teens Kay played with leading bop musicians, including **Miles Davis**. He gained big band experience with **Cat Anderson** late in the decade. In the early 50s, he was playing R&B in studio backing bands - but was mostly playing in small modern jazz groups with **Lester**

Young, **Stan Getz**, Davis, **Charlie Parker** and others. In 1955, he took over from **Kenny Clarke** in the **Modern Jazz Quartet**, remaining with the group for the next 20 years. During these years he also performed with other artists on record dates, amongst them **Chet Baker**, **Paul Desmond**, **Cannonball Adderley** and fellow MJQ member **John Lewis**. He played on **Van Morrison**'s masterpiece *Astral Weeks*. After the MJQ disbanded in 1974 Kay worked with Lewis and other jazzmen, including **Benny Goodman** in whose band he played at the Carnegie Hall 40th Anniversary Concert. In the late 70s he was mostly working in New York playing jazz-club dates which included several years in the house band at **Eddie Condon**'s. In 1981, he was again a member of the MJQ when the group re-formed. Despite his wide experience in several areas of jazz, Kay was understandably best known for his highly sophisticated work with the MJQ in which context he played with great subtlety and deftly understated swing.

Kay, Herbie

b. 1904, USA, d. 11 May 1944, Dallas, Texas, USA. Formed in the late 20s in Chicago, Illinois, USA, Kay's dance band orchestra concentrated its activities in the Midwest region, enjoying significant but brief success in the process. His musical career had previously begun at Northwestern University, where he was a member of several impromptu campus combos. His professional orchestra included trumpeter Charles 'Bud' Dant, later an executive with Coral and **Decca Records,** in a four saxophone, four brass, three percussion formation. The singers were, at various times, **Dorothy Lamour**, Helen Conner and Ken Nealey. Lamour had joined in 1934, staying with the band for two years before a film career in Hollywood offered more tantalising rewards. This decision resulted in the break up of her marriage to Kay in 1939. The orchestra continued its long stay at the Blackhawk Restaurant in Chicago into the early 40s, by which time several records had been released on **Vocalion** and **Columbia Records**, including the orchestra's theme, 'Violets And Friends'. Shortly afterwards however, Kay gave up the band, and relocated to Dallas.

Kay, Janet

b. Janet Kay Bogle, 17 January 1958, London, England. Kay attended Brondesbury High School, Wembley, and later took up secretarial studies, skills to which she has returned at various junctures in her recording career. Her first recordings came under the aegis of **Alton Ellis** in 1977. This had been brought about by a chance meeting with members of **Aswad** that summer, who recommended her to the reggae stalwart. The first result of the collaboration, 'Loving You', topped the reggae charts. In many ways she was the prototype **lovers rock** singer, with her spirited vocals floating over some of the genre's most inspired basslines. 'That's What Friends Are For' and 'I Do Love You' followed. However, her breakthrough came with 'Silly Games',

produced by **Dennis Bovell** for the Arawak label. It became a huge crossover hit, reaching number 2 in 1979. Kay has returned intermittently to recording, predominantly in the lovers rock style, and has also acted extensively as part of the Black Theatre Co-operative, appearing in several straight acting roles on television. Her work has never lost its popularity with the reggae audience, despite her low profile for much of the 80s and 90s, and she has the talent and personality to be successful on her own terms.

● ALBUMS: *Capricorn Woman* (Solid Groove 1979)★★★, *Silly Games* (Arawak 1980)★★, with Dennis Brown *So Amazing* (Body Work 1987)★★★, *Loving You* (Burning Sounds 1988)★★★, *Sweet Surrender* (Body Music 1989)★★★, with Dennis Bovell *Dub Dem Silly* (Arawak 1994)★★★★.

Kay, Karen

b. 18 July 1947, Blackburn, Lancashire, England. Kay made her UK television debut in 1961 as a gauche 14-year-old in *Search For A Star*. Pursuing a career in showbusiness she subsequently guested on a number of shows with **Des O'Connor** and Paul Daniels. In 1980, she received a 14-month run at London's Palace Theatre and was given a pilot series on BBC television titled *The Vocal Touch*. Her smooth vocal style and bubbly personality eventually led her to receiving her own series for BBC television.

Kaya - Bob Marley & The Wailers

Bob Marley is in a mellow and happy mood as the album opens with 'excuse me while I light my spliff' on 'Easy Skanking' and maintains the feeling throughout. 'Kaya' has one of the best bass riffs of any Marley song (played by the wonderful Aston Family Man Barrett). The hit single 'Is This Love' is included and he sounds upbeat singing 'She's Gone', although the subject is that his lover has just left him. Nothing fazed him; he was able to address political and emotional subjects with the same degree of feeling and his manner was truly saintly. *Kaya* is one of his finest moments.

● Tracks: *Easy Skanking; Kaya; Is This Love; Sun Is Shining; Satisfy My Soul; She's Gone; Misty Morning; Crisis; Running Away; Time Will Tell.*

● First released 1978

● UK peak chart position: 4

● USA peak chart position: 50

Kaye Sisters

This UK pop trio comprised Sheila Jones (b. 21 October 1936, Lewisham, London, England), Shirley 'Shan' Palmer (b. 15 August 1938, Hull, England) and Carole Young (b. 12 April 1930, Oldham, Lancashire, England). Formed in 1954 by Carmen Kaye and originally known as the Three Kayes, their big break came when they appeared on television's *In Town Tonight* in 1956. They followed this with two weeks at the London Palladium and then their debut single, a cover version of the **Charms**' 'Ivory Tower' on **HMV**, made the UK

Top 20. They joined the **Philips** label in 1957 and their first two Top 10 hits, which came in the company of **Frankie Vaughan**, were cover versions of Bob Jaxon's 'Gotta Have Something In The Bank Frank' (their royalties going to the Boys Clubs, an organization with which Vaughan has been involved for many years) and the **Fleetwoods**' 'Come Softly To Me'. Of the many singles they released, their only solo Top 10 hit was their version of **Anita Bryant**'s US hit 'Paper Roses' in 1960. Jones retired in the late 60s and was replaced by Gilly. They continued to work, often supporting **Max Bygraves**. Young left in the late 70s to pursue an acting career, and appeared in the ITV series *Albion Market* and top soap opera *Coronation Street*. 'Shan and Gilly Kaye' appeared at the 1978 Royal Command Performance, and sang together in theatres and cabaret during the 80s. The original three members were reunited in 1992 and 1993, singing numbers made famous by the **Andrews Sisters** in UK tours of *In The Mood*, a tribute to **Glenn Miller**.

● ALBUMS: *Shan, Gill And Carole* (1973)★★.

Kaye, Cab

b. Augustus Kwamlah Nii-lante Quaye, 3 September 1921, London, England. The son of an English music hall artist and Ga (Ghanaian) pianist Caleb Jonas Quaye (who, as 'Mope Desmond', played with **Sidney Bechet** in London in 1921), Kaye began his singing career with **Billy Cotton**. As 'Young Cab', he sang and played percussion with drummer Ivor Kirchin, then in 1940 joined **Ken 'Snakehips' Johnson**, with whom he broadcast on several occasions until the outbreak of World War II. Injuries sustained while serving in the Merchant Navy led to hospitalization in New York, where he later toured clubs in Harlem and Greenwich Village and sat in with **Roy Eldridge** and **Sandy Williams**. Returning to England, Kaye joined clarinettist Harry Parry and accordionist **Tito Burns**, subsequently appearing with the big bands of **Vic Lewis** and **Ted Heath**. In the early 50s, Kaye organized a band to play dances for newly-arrived Caribbean settlers, and with it made two extended trips to Europe. In Holland, he met **Charlie Parker** and renewed his acquaintance with Eldridge. Kaye was a popular figure on the burgeoning London bebop scene, where he worked with Dennis Rose, the music's local *eminence gris*. Kaye found his natural audiences in the 'afterhours' milieu epitomised by the Ringside Club, Paris, where he sang with Americans such as **James Moody**. In 1960, he worked with **Humphrey Lyttelton**, then appeared at **Ronnie Scott**'s Club before moving to West Africa. In 1961, he occupied an entertainments post in Ghana during the Nkrumah regime, then lived briefly in Nigeria before returning to England in 1973. Settling finally in Amsterdam, he opened Cab's Piano Bar. He recorded with clarinettist Keith Bird (1949), arranger Ken Moule (1954), Lyttelton (1960), and several times under his own name (1951, 1952, 1984). Kaye is the father of singer/conga drummer Terri Naa-Koshie

Quaye and ex-Bluesology, **Hookfoot** and **Elton John** guitarist Caleb Quaye.

● ALBUMS: *Cab Meets Humph* (1960)★★★, *Solo Piano* (1984)★★★.

Kaye, Carol

b. Carol Everett, 1935, Washington, USA. Bass guitarist Kaye was one of the few women musicians, as opposed to vocalists, prospering in the enclosed Los Angeles session fraternity. During the 60s she joined, among others, **Glen Campbell**, Tommy Tedesco, Billy Strange (guitars) and Larry Knechtal (piano) as a member of a group affectionately known as **Hal Blaine**'s Wrecking Crew. Kaye contributed to innumerable recordings, the most notable of which were with **Phil Spector** protégées the **Crystals**, the **Ronettes** and **Darlene Love**. Her bass work also appeared on many west coast Tamla/**Motown** sessions and, by contrast, *Freak Out*, the first album by the **Mothers Of Invention**. Her affinity with soul/blues-influenced artists was exemplified in appearances on **Joe Cocker**'s *With A Little Help From My Friends* (1969) and **Robert Palmer**'s *Some People Can Do What They Like* (1976). Classical-styled sessions for David Axelrod contrasted with singer-songwriter work with **Dory Previn** and exemplified the versatility of this talented and prolific musician. The milestone singles on which Kaye claims to have played (there is some dispute that James Jamerson was on the final mix) are: 'River Deep Mountain High' (**Ike And Tina Turner**), 'Theme From Shaft' (**Isaac Hayes**), 'Get Ready' (**Temptations**), 'Reach Out I'll Be There' (**Four Tops**), 'I Was Made To Love Her' (**Stevie Wonder**), 'Everybody's Talkin'' (**Nilsson**), 'Homeward Bound' (**Simon And Garfunkel**), 'Good Vibrations' (**Beach Boys**), 'It's My Party' (**Lesley Gore**), 'Light My Fire' (**Doors**), 'You Can't Hurry Love' (**Supremes**) and 'Young Girl' by **Gary Puckett**.

Kaye, Danny

b. David Daniel Kominsky, 18 January 1913, Brooklyn, New York, USA, d. 3 March 1987, Los Angeles, California, USA. Kaye was an extraordinary entertainer and an apparently inexhaustible comedian, mimic and dancer who seemed to be able to twist his face and body into any shape he wanted. As a singer, he specialized in very fast double talk and tongue-twisters, but could present a gentle ballad equally well. He was also an indefatigable ambassador for numerous charities, especially the United Nations International Children's Emergency Fund (now UNICEF), for which he travelled and worked for many years. A son of Jewish immigrant parents from Russia, Kominsky originally wanted to join the medical profession, but dropped out of high school when he was 14 years old, and hitch-hiked to Florida with his friend, Louis Eilson, where they sang for money. On their return to New York, they formed an act called Red And Blackie, and performed at private functions. During the day, Kominski worked as a soda-jerk, and then as an automobile appraiser with an insurance company. The latter job was terminated after he made a mistake which is said to have cost the company some $40,000. Kominski and Eilson then obtained summer work as 'toomlers', creators of tumult or all-round entertainers, in the Borscht Circuit summer hotels and camps in the Catskill Mountains. After five years, Kominski was earning $1,000 per season.

In 1933, he joined David Harvey and Kathleen Young on the vaudeville circuit in their dancing act, the Three Terpsichoreans, and was billed for the first time as Danny Kaye. An early onstage accident in which he split his trousers, elicited much laughter from the audience and was incorporated into the act. Signed by producer A.B. Marcus, the group toured the USA for five months in the revue *La Vie Paree*, before sailing for the Orient in February 1934. It is often said that this period of playing to non-English speaking audiences in Japan, China and Malaya, was when Kaye first developed his face-making and pantomiming techniques, and his 'gibberish' singing with the occasional recognized word. Back in the USA in 1936, Kaye worked with comedian Nick Long Jnr. and toured with Abe Lyman's Band, before being booked by impresario Henry Sherek, to appear in cabaret at London's Dorchester Hotel. The engagement, in 1938, was not a success. Kaye commented: 'I was too loud for the joint'. (Ten years later in London, it would be an entirely different story.) While appearing in Max Liebman's *Sunday Night Varieties* in New York, Kaye met pianist-songwriter Sylvia Fine (b. 29 August 1913, New York, USA, d. 28 October 1991, New York, USA), who had been raised in the same Brooklyn neighbourhood, and majored in music at Brooklyn College. She became a powerful influence throughout his career, as his director, coach and critic. Working with Liebman's Saturday night revues at Camp Taimiment in the Pennsylvania Hills, during the summer of 1939, they started their collaboration, with Fine accompanying Kaye on the piano, and writing special material that included three of his most famous numbers, 'Stanislavsky', 'Pavlova' and the story of the unstable chapeau designer, 'Anatole Of Paris'. The best of the material was assembled in *The Straw Hat Revue* in which Kaye appeared with Imogene Coca, and which opened on Broadway in September 1939. The show also featured a young dancer named **Jerome Robbins**. After Fine and Kaye were married in January 1940, Kaye appeared in a smash hit engagement at La Martinique nightclub in New York, which led to a part in *Lady In The Dark*, starring **Gertrude Lawrence**. On the first night, Kaye stopped the show with the **Kurt Weill** and **Ira Gershwin** tongue-twister 'Tchaikovsky', in which he reeled off the names of 50 real, or imagined, Russian composers in 38 seconds. After playing a return engagement at La Martinique, and a five-week stint at the Paramount Theatre, Kaye appeared again on Broadway, starring in the **Cole Porter** musical *Let's Face It!*, which opened in October 1941. Porter allowed Sylvia Fine and Max Liebman to

interpolate some special material for Kaye, which included a 'jabberwocky of song, dance, illustration and double-talk' called 'Melody In 4F'. Kaye had to leave the show early in 1942, suffering from nervous exhaustion, but having recovered, he toured on behalf of the war effort and is said to have sold a million dollars' worth of government bonds in six months. Rejected by the US Army because of a back ailment, he entertained troops with his two-hour shows in many theatres of operations including the South Pacific.

In 1944, Kaye made his feature film debut in *Up In Arms*, the first in a series of five pictures for Sam Goldwyn at RKO. His performance as a hypochondriac elevator boy, involving yet another memorable Fine-Liebman piece, 'Manic Depressive Pictures Presents: Lobby Number', moved one critic to hail his introduction as 'the most exciting since Garbo's'. Goldwyn was criticized, however for having Kaye's red hair dyed blonde. His remaining films for the studio included *Wonder Man*, in which he gave his impression of a sneezing Russian baritone with 'Orchi Tchornya'. This was the first of several films in which he played more than one character; *The Kid From Brooklyn* (1946), which featured 'Pavlova', *The Secret Life Of Walter Mitty* (1947), one of his best-remembered roles (six of them), and *A Song Is Born* (1948), one of his least remembered. In 1945, Kaye appeared for a year on his own CBS radio show with **Harry James** and Eve Arden, and during the following year the Kayes' daughter, Dena, was born. When Kaye recorded the old standard 'Dinah', he changed some of the 'i' sounds to 'e', so that the song ran: 'Denah, is there anyone fener? In the State of Carolena . . .', etc. His other hit songs included 'Tubby The Tuba', 'Minnie The Moocher', 'Ballin' The Jack', 'Bloop Bleep', 'Civilization' and 'The Woody Woodpecker Song', both with the **Andrews Sisters**; 'C'est Si Bon'; and 'Blackstrap Molasses', recorded with **Jimmy Durante**, Jane Wyman and Groucho Marx. In 1948, Kaye returned to England to appear at the London Palladium. His enormously successful record-breaking performances began an affectionate and enduring relationship with the British public. He is said to have received over 100,000 letters in a week. His shows were attended by the Royal Family; he met both Winston Churchill and George Bernard Shaw, and was cast in wax for London's Madame Tussaud's Museum. He returned in 1949 for the first of several Royal Command Performances, and also toured provincial music-halls throughout 1952. He endeared himself to the British by singing some of their parochial songs such as the novelty 'I've Got A Lovely Bunch Of Coconuts' and 'Maybe It's Because I'm A Londoner'. During one performance at the Palladium, when a member of the audience enquired after the state of Kaye's ribs following a car accident, he ordered the lights to be lowered while he displayed the actual X-ray plates! Kaye went to Canada in 1950 and became the first solo performer to star at the Canadian National Exhibition, where he sold out the 24,000-seater stadium for each of his 14 performances.

He returned to his multiple roles in films such as *The Inspector General* (1949) and **On The Riviera** (1951), before embarking on the somewhat controversial **Hans Christian Andersen** (1952). After 16 different screenplays over a period of 15 years, and protests in the Danish press about the choice of Kaye to play their national hero, the film, with a final screenplay by **Moss Hart**, became a huge money-spinner. **Frank Loesser**'s score produced several appealing songs, including 'No Two People', 'Anywhere I Wander', 'Inchworm', 'Thumbelina', 'The Ugly Duckling' and 'Wonderful Copenhagen', the latter reaching the UK Top 5. Kaye's other films during the 50s and early 60s included *Knock On Wood* (1954), said to be his favourite, in which he sang two more Fine numbers, the title song, and 'All About Me', **White Christmas** (1954), co-starring with **Bing Crosby**, **Rosemary Clooney** and **Vera-Ellen**, **The Court Jester** (1956), *Me And The Colonel* (1958), *Merry Andrew* (1958), **The Five Pennies** (1959), a biopic of 20s cornet player **Red Nichols** (including a rousing version of 'When The Saints Go Marching In' with **Louis Armstrong**), *On The Double* (1961) and *The Man From The Diners' Club* (1963). After a break, he came back for *The Madwoman Of Challiot* (1969), and the following year, returned to Broadway in the role of Noah, in the **Richard Rodgers** and Martin Charnin musical *Two By Two*. Shortly after the show opened, Kaye tore a ligament in his leg during a performance, and subsequently appeared on crutches or in a wheelchair, in which he tried to run down the other actors, adapting the show to his injury, much to the distaste of producer and composer Richard Rodgers.

During the 70s and 80s, Kaye conducted classical orchestras and appeared on several television shows including *Peter Pan*, *Pinocchio* and *Danny Kaye's Look At The Metropolitan Opera*. He also played dramatic roles on television in *Skokie* and *The Twilight Zone*, but concentrated mainly on his charity work. He had started his association with UNICEF in the early 50s, and in 1955 made a 20-minute documentary, *Assignment Children*. He eventually became the organization's ambassador-at-large for 34 years, travelling worldwide on their behalf, and entering the *Guinness Book Of Records* by visiting 65 US and Canadian cities in five days, piloting himself in his own jet plane. During his career he received many awards including the French Légion d'Honneur, the Jean Hersholt Humanitarian Award, and the Knight's Cross of the First Class of the Order of Danneborg, given by the Danish Government. Other awards included a special Academy Award in 1954, along with Tonys for his stage performances, plus Emmys for his successful 60s television series. He died in 1987, following a heart attack.

● ALBUMS: *Danny Kaye* (Columbia 1949)★★, *Danny Kaye Entertains* (Columbia 1949)★★★, *Gilbert And Sullivan And Danny Kaye* (Decca 1949)★★, *Hans Christian Andersen* film soundtrack (1953)★★★★, *Danny At The Palace* (Decca 1953)★★★, *Mommy, Gimme A Drink Of Water* (Capitol 1958)★★★, *Merry Andrew* film soundtrack (Capitol 1958)★★★, with Louis Armstrong *The Five Pennies* film soundtrack (1958)★★★, *The Court Jester* (Decca 1959)★★★, *For Children* (Decca 1959)★★, with Ivor Moreton *Happy Fingers* (1977)★★★.

● COMPILATIONS: *The Best Of Danny Kaye* (Decca 1962)★★★, *The Very Best Of Danny Kaye - 20 Golden Greats* (MCA 1987)★★★.

● FURTHER READING: *The Danny Kaye Saga*, Kurt Singer. *Nobody's Fool - The Secret Lives Of Danny Kaye*, Martin Gottfried. *The Life Story Of Danny Kaye*, D. Richards. *Fine And Danny*, Sylvia Fine.

● FILMS: *Up In Arms* (1944), *Wonder Man* (1945), *The Kid From Brooklyn* (1946), *The Secret Life Of Walter Mitty* (1947), *A Song Is Born* (1948), *The Inspector General* (1949), *On The Riviera* (1951), *Hans Christian Anderson* (1952), *Knock On Wood* (1953), *White Christmas* (1954), *Assignment Children* (1954), *The Court Jester* (1956), *Me And The Colonel* (1957), *Merry Andrew* (1958), *The Five Pennies* (1959), *On The Double* (1962), *The Man From The Diner's Club* (1963), *The Madwoman Of Chaillot* (1969).

Kaye, Sammy

b. 13 March 1910, Lakewood, Ohio, USA. Kaye began playing in bands while still at college. In the early 30s he led a band at the Statler Hotel in Cleveland and also worked in Pittsburgh. In the later years of the decade he was hired by several top New York hotels, including the Astor and the New Yorker. An adept clarinettist, Kaye also made a name for himself as a bandleader without any help from the critics who unanimously derided his corny arrangements. 'Swing and Sway with Sammy Kaye' ran the billing, but swinging was something beyond the band. Instead, they offered hotel patrons and their later radio audience simple dance music, and becoming enormously successful. The band featured numerous singers, none of them especially memorable, although the musicians Kaye hired were always competent (George T. Simon referred to them as 'magnificently trained and exceedingly unoriginal'). Pianist **Ralph Flanagan** was a member of the band for a while. Kaye survived the collapse of many better dancebands and his career benefited from several popular sponsored radio shows. Replete with gimmicks, including the 'So You Want To Lead A Band' spot, the show transferred to television in the early 50s, in which members of the public were invited to conduct the band. In the late 50s and early 60s Kaye made a number of well-received if uncharacteristic records, including one of dixieland music. He composed a number of popular songs, including 'Hawaiian Sunset' and 'Until Tomorrow'. In 1986, The Sammy Kaye Orchestra, complete with its current vocalist Bob Casper, was reconstituted with a new leader, Roger Thorpe, although Kaye continued as a supervisor of the band's musical activities.

● ALBUMS: *One Night Stand At The Hollywood Palladium* (1946)★★★.

● COMPILATIONS: *One Night Stand With Sammy Kaye*

(1984)★★★, *Sammy Kaye And His Orchestra Play 22 Original Big Band Recordings* (1984)★★★, *Sammy Kaye And His Orchestra, Volume 2 (1944-46)* (1988)★★★, *Sammy Kaye And His Orchestra, Volume 3 (1944-48)* (1988)★★★, *Sammy Kaye* (1993)★★★.

Kaye, Stubby

b. 11 November 1918, New York City, New York, USA, d. 14 December 1997. An actor and singer who carved himself an instant slice of musical history by stopping the show as Nicely-Nicely Johnson in the original Broadway production of *Guys And Dolls* - and then doing it all over again three years later in London. Kaye had his first break when he came first on the Major Bowes Amateur Hour on US radio in 1939. During the late 30s and early 40s he toured as a comedian in vaudeville, and made his London debut in USO shows during World War II. His role in *Guys And Dolls* (1950) was not a leading one, but he was outstanding in numbers such as 'Fugue For Tinhorns', 'The Oldest Established', 'Guys And Dolls', and the rousing 'Sit Down You're Rockin' The Boat'. He had one more big success on Broadway in 1956 as Marryin' Sam in *Li'l Abner*, and subsequently toured in revivals, played nightclubs as a comedian, and appeared on the television series *Love And Marriage* and *My Sister Eileen*. Unlike many stage performers he moved easily into films, and appeared in a variety features including *Guys And Dolls*, *Li'l Abner*, *40 Pounds Of Trouble*, *Cat Ballou* (with **Nat King Cole**), *Sweet Charity*, *The Cockeyed Cowboys Of Calico County*, *The Dirtiest Girl I Ever Met*, *Six Pack Annie* and *Who Framed Roger Rabbit?*. The ample figure and sunny disposition he displayed as Nicely-Nicely in 1953 endeared him to London audiences and he made frequent appearances in the UK, including one in the musical *Man Of Magic* in 1956. Eventually he settled in Britain and married Angela Bracewell, who came to fame in the 50s in her role as the hostess of the audience participation game 'Beat The Clock' in the top-rated television variety show *Sunday Night At The London Palladium*. After appearing in the West End in 1983 in the short-lived musical *Dear Anyone*, Kaye returned to Broadway two years later and won the only good notices in the musical *Grind*, a complete disaster that was described by one critic as 'art slaughter'. He continued to work in the UK and in 1986 starred as Ring Lardner in the radio play *Some Like Them Cold*. His voice also featured in 1988's partly-animated *Who Framed Roger Rabbit?* Kaye died in December 1997.

● ALBUMS: *Music For Chubby Lovers* (1962)★★★, and Original Cast and film soundtrack recordings.

Kayirebwa, Cecile

b. 1946, Kigali, Rwanda. Since 1973, when the first Rwandan civil wars began, Kayirebwa has lived in Belgium. Brought up in the Catholic faith, she had a happy, peaceful childhood in sharp contrast to her nation's later troubles. At school she was exposed to French singers such as **Johnny Hallyday** and **France Gall**, whose songs she would sing with her sister. As part of the school group, the Circle Of Rwandan Song And Dance, she was recorded by Rwandan radio in the 50s, though individuals were not identified as singing was not considered a suitable pursuit for young girls. After school she found work in the north east region of Buganza as a social worker, a period which also saw her explore the origins of Rwandan music. Eventually she began to write her own songs, praising figures such as the benevolent Rwandan Queen Rosali. Soon Kayirebwa would sing such praises to Rosali herself as her reputation grew. However, her happiness was shattered by the outbreak of war in 1973 at which time she and her husband fled for Belgium. Between 1975 and 1980 she worked with Iyange, a troupe of musicians entertaining fellow Rwandan refugees. After studying further her Rwandan heritage at the Royal Museum Of Central Africa in Brussels, in 1984 she joined her second group, Bula Sangoma. They released a solitary album in 1985 and also toured Europe and America. Though her four children were born in Belgium, the tragedies of her homeland have informed most of her subsequent work. When her mother was dying in 1988 she spent a month trying to navigate her way home, only to arrive after she had been buried. Her empathy for Rwanda ('the rivers, the springs, the natural beauty, all the flowers - that you have to buy in the florist here!') gave her the impetus to write again ('the nostalgia welled up and created songs'). For example, the 1988 homecoming resulted in 'Umunerezero' (Happiness), both a lament and a plea of hope for the future of the country. It is said to be enormously popular with the army of the Rwandan Popular Front.

● ALBUMS: *Rwanda* (Globestyle 1994)★★★.

Kayo

b. Kayode Shekoni, Sweden. Of African heritage, Swedish dance music artist Kayo began her musical career at the age of 14. She was signed by the Swedish dance music label **Swemix Records** in 1989, releasing her self-titled debut solo album a year later. *Kayo* featured 'pure dance-orientated pop', while tracks such as 'Another Mother' and 'Change Of Attitude' demonstrated her ability as a songwriter. Both achieved national airplay and confirmed her as one of the most singular talents on a widely acclaimed record label. 'Another Mother' also established her as a successful artist in mainland European countries such as Germany. However, if commercial approbation beckoned, Kayo bucked expectations with her 1993 album, *Karleksland*. Rather than the English-language lyrics which had dominated earlier releases, this record was recorded entirely in the Swedish tongue. The lyrics were written by Swedish pop star **Orup**, while the music, produced by Grammy-winner Dan Sundqvist, largely encompassed a sophisticated blend of pop and soul. Still to the forefront, however, was Kayo's distinctive, uninhibited vocal persona. Throughout 1993 she toured in support of the album, although she also devoted time to her first feature film, *The Pillmaker*. Kayo had previously appeared in the **Creeps**' satiric video for 'Ooh I Like It', which won an award in 1990 as **MTV** viewers' favourite video.

● ALBUMS: *Kayo* (Cheiron 1990)★★, *Karleksland* (Cheiron 1993)★★★.

Kayser, Joe

b. 1895, St. Louis, Missouri, USA. After studying in St. Louis, Kayser moved to New York in 1917 to fill a vacancy as drummer in the **Earl Fuller** Orchestra. Initially based at Rector's Restaurant, his time there saw him make the acquaintance of fellow musician **Ted Lewis**. During World War I Kayser formed a naval base band with violinist Benny Kubelsky (later **Jack Benny**). After his discharge he was appointed as the leader of one of the Meyer Davis organisation's numerous touring bands, stationed predominantly in the Carolinas. He returned to St. Louis in 1921 to form his first dance band under his own name. Initially a quintet, with **Frankie Trumbauer**, **David Rose**, **Muggsy Spanier**, **Jess Stacy** and **Gene Krupa**, the group's ranks swelled as more prestigious bookings came in. They travelled widely, so much so that Kayser would later claim that it was he and **Jan Garber** that initiated the 'one-nighter' circuit which so many dance bands would follow. They negotiated hundreds of miles in a small fleet of Model T Fords, often offering patrons a 'Novelty Orchestra' show themed after the gangster wars. With the central Midwest circuit the most profitable, the group relocated their base of operations first to Rockford, Illinois and then Chicago. Engagements at the Aragon and Trianon Ballrooms followed, before Kayser took up a post as director and master of ceremonies at the Diversey Theater in Chicago in 1929. He then took a similar position at the Midland Theater in Kansas City. The orchestra was kept on the road however, and in 1930 secured long engagements at the Arcadia and Mary Garden Ballrooms. During this time many young musicians, who would later become famous in local dance and jazz bands, passed through the ranks, with the Kayser Orchestra serving as something akin to a finishing school. 1933 saw the group provide the musical backing to **Sally Rand**'s appearance at the World's Fair, before Kayser turned his back on bandleading in 1936 to join the NBC Artists Service. By 1943 he had moved to MCA, taking charge of their Chicago office. He retired in 1955.

Kazebier, Nate

b. Nathan Forrest Kazebier, 13 August 1912, Lawrence, Kansas, USA, d. 22 October 1996. Kazebier began playing trumpet as a small child and became a professional musician while still in his teens. His first name band was **Jan Garber**'s which he joined in 1931, and in the middle of the decade he spent over a year with **Benny Goodman**. Later in the 30s he played in a succession of bands, including those led by **Ray Noble** and **Seger** Ellis, then joined **Gene Krupa** with whom he had recorded in 1935 on some outstanding small group sides. In 1940 he went into the **Jimmy Dorsey** band where he remained for more than three years. After a mid-40s spell in west coast film studios, Kazebier rejoined Goodman for a year, then returned to studio work. He continued to work in the studios with occasional jazz gigs for some years, although **John Chilton** indicates that for a while he worked as a golf professional in Reno. A well-rounded, trained musician, Kazebier often played lead trumpet in the bands with which he worked and was thus less well known than his soloing colleagues. Nevertheless, he played an important role in the success of the bands with which he worked.

Kazee, Buell

b. 29 August 1900, Burton Fork, Magoffin County, Kentucky, USA, d. 31 August 1976. Kazee, a banjo-playing minister, has been described as 'the greatest white male folk singer in the United States'. Charles Wolfe considered him the 'epitome of the Kentucky mountain songster . . . a high, tight, 'lonesome' voice, accompanied only by a banjo 'geared' to unusual tunings'. Kazee started learning songs from his parents and first played banjo at the age of five. During his time at Georgetown College, where he studied for a ministerial career, he developed a keen interest in old English ballads. He also took lessons from a professional tenor and on graduating in 1925, he gave concerts of folk music. Accompanied by a pianist, and dressed in tie and tails, he played banjo and guitar, sang songs and lectured on music at important venues. In 1927, he went to **Brunswick**'s New York studio where, in his trained tenor style, he first sang a mixture of popular ballads and religious numbers. The company were not interested, until they convinced him that he should play his banjo and sing in his natural manner. Between 1927 and 1929, he subsequently recorded over 50 songs of which 46 were issued. These included what has been described as the finest recorded version of 'Lady Gay'. His bestsellers proved to be 'Little Mohee' and 'Roving Cowboy' and some recordings were even released in the UK and Australia. Brunswick wanted him to tour but Kazee had just married and had no wish for a professional career. He became a Baptist minister but sang at revival-style meetings and remained at a church in Morehead for 22 years. He wrote music including a cantata, an operetta ('The Wagoner Lad'), three religious books and a book on banjo playing, as well as an unpublished autobiography. In the 1960s, revived interest among the young devotees to folk music saw Kazee make appearances at the Newport Folk Festival and also give further lectures in spite of failing health. He died in 1976 but his music was continued by his son Philip who, in addition to singing and playing some of his father's material, is also a minister.

● ALBUMS: *Buell Kazee Sings & Plays* (Smithsonian/Folkways 1959)★★★, *Buell Kazee* (June Appal 1976)★★★.

KBC Band

The potential of three ex-**Jefferson Airplane** colleagues joining together once again was enormous. With petty arguing and ego problems behind them the KBC Band announced an album to the world in 1986. **Marty Balin** (b. Martyn Jerel Buchwald, 30 January 1942, Cincinnati, Ohio, USA; vocals), Jack Casady (b. 13 April 1944, Washington DC, USA; bass) and **Paul Kantner** (b. 17 March 1941, San Francisco, California, USA; guitar/vocals) released an album that sounded jaded on release. Somehow, lyrically addressing political themes such as Lebanon and Nicaragua did not work (in 'America') and Marty Balin's old epic ballad's paled against the new ('Mariel'). The addition of Keith Crossan (saxophone, guitar, vocals), Tim Gorman (guitar/vocals), Darrell Verdusco (drums) and Mark 'Slick' Aguilar (lead guitar/vocals) gave the unit a full AOR sound. The album probably charted in the USA on the strength of their names (number 75) and even produced a minor hit single with 'It's Not You, It's Not Me' (number 89). The unit disbanded shortly afterwards.

● ALBUMS: *KBC Band* (Arista 1986)★★.

KC And The Sunshine Band

This racially integrated band was formed in Florida, USA, in 1973 by Harry Wayne (KC) Casey (b. 31 January 1951, Hialeah, Florida, USA; vocals, keyboards) and Richard Finch (b. 25 January 1954, Indianapolis, Indiana, USA; bass). Arguably the cornerstone of the Miami-based TK label, the duo wrote, arranged and produced their own group's successes, as well as those of singer **George McCrae**. The Sunshine Band enjoyed several hits, including 'Queen Of Clubs' (1974, UK Top 10), three consecutive US number 1s with 'Get Down Tonight', 'That's The Way (I Like It)' (both 1975) and '(Shake, Shake, Shake), Shake Your Body' (1976), each of which displayed an enthusiastic grasp of dance-based funk. The style was exaggerated to almost parodic proportions on 'I'm Your Boogie Man' (1977, a US number 1) and 'Boogie Shoes' (1978), but a crafted ballad, 'Please Don't Go', in 1979, not only reversed this bubblegum trend, but was a transatlantic smash in the process (and a UK number 1 in 1992 for K.W.S.). That same year KC duetted with Teri DeSario on the US number 2 hit 'Yes, I'm Ready', on the Casablanca label. Although the group numbered as many as 12 on its live appearances, its core revolved around Jerome Smith (b. 18 June 1953, Hialeah, Florida, USA; guitar), Robert Johnson (b. 21 March 1953, Miami, Florida, USA; drums) and its two songwriters. The team moved to Epic/**CBS Records** after the collapse of the TK organization in 1980. Any benefit this accrued was hampered by a head-on car crash in January 1982 that left Casey paralyzed for several months. Their fortune changed the following year when the group found themselves at the top of the UK charts with 'Give It Up'. It did not reach the US charts until the following year, and was by then credited to 'KC'. Casey and Finch

subsequently seem to have lost the art of penning radio-friendly soul/pop.

● ALBUMS: *Do It Good* (TK 1974)★★, *KC And The Sunshine Band* (TK 1975)★★★, as the Sunshine Band *The Sound Of Sunshine* (TK 1975)★★, *Part 3* (TK 1976)★★★★, *I Like To Do It* (Jay Boy 1977)★★★, *Who Do Ya (Love)* (TK 1978)★★, *Do You Wanna Go Party* (TK 1979)★★, *Painter* (Epic 1981)★★, *All In A Night's Work* (Epic 1983)★★, *Oh Yeah!* (ZYX 1993)★★, *Get Down Live!* (Intersound 1995)★★. Solo: Wayne Casey/KC *Space Cadet* (Epic 1981)★★, *KC Ten* (Meca 1984)★★.

● COMPILATIONS: *Greatest Hits* (TK 1980)★★★, *The Best Of KC And The Sunshine Band* (Rhino 1990)★★★★, *Get Down Tonight: The Very Best Of* (EMI 1998)★★★.

Keane, Dolores

b. 26 September 1953, Caherlistrane, Co. Galway, Eire. Keane was a former member of Irish group folk **De Dannan**. Her first solo album, which received a gold disc, was produced by ex-**Silly Wizard** member Phil Cunningham, and included the **Si Kahn** classic 'Aragon Mill', **Kate And Anna McGarrigle's** much covered 'Heart Like A Wheel' and, most surprisingly, **Marlene Dietrich**'s 'Lili Marlene'. *Farewell To Eirinn*, which included John Faulkner and Eamonn Curran, featured songs describing the story of the Irish emigration to America from 1845 to 1855, when nearly two million people (or 25 per cent of the population), left Ireland. *Lion In A Cage* remained in the contemporary setting, with songs by **Chris Rea**, **Paul Brady** and **Kieran Halpin**. The title track was a reference to Nelson Mandela, who was still a political prisoner in South Africa at the time. As with many songs of social statement, political changes often render them out of date very quickly. However, despite the freeing of Mandela, 'Lion In A Cage' remains a powerful song, and one of the better of the genre. Dolores participated in the television series *Bringing It All Back Home*, in 1991, performing with **Mary Black** and **Emmylou Harris**. In June 1993, Keane set out on an extensive UK tour, backed by a band comprising John Faulkner (guitar/bouzouki/vocals), Ted Ponsonby (guitar/dobro), Daragh Connelly (keyboards), Liam Bradley (drums/vocals), and Eddie Lee (bass).

● ALBUMS: *There Was A Maid* (1978)★★, with John Faulkner *Broken Hearted I'll Wander* (1979)★★★, *Farewell To Eirinn* (1980)★★★★, with Faulkner *Sail Og Rua* (1983)★★★, *Dolores Keane* (1988)★★★★, *Lion In A Cage* (1990)★★★, *A Woman's Heart* (1992)★★★, *Solid Ground* (1993)★★★.

● COMPILATIONS: *The Best Of Dolores Keane* (Dara 1997)★★★.

Keane, Ellsworth 'Shake'

b. Ellsworth McGranahan Keane, 30 May 1927, St. Vincent, West Indies, d. 10 November 1997. Although taught music by his father as a child, Keane did not turn to the trumpet as a career until the mid-50s. Originally a teacher in St. Vincent, he came to England in 1952 to study English literature. He was already an accomplished poet - his nickname is short for 'Shakespeare' - with two collections of verse published, but could find no work in London except as a musician. For several years he played as a sideman in nightclubs and on recording sessions, performing calypso and Latin music as well as blues and jazz. One regular employer was calypso king Lord Kitchener, while a selection of tracks Keane originally made for the west African market with Guyanese pianist Mick McKenzie was reissued on the compilation *Caribbean Connections: Black Music In Britain In The Early 50s, Volume 2*. From 1959-65, Keane was a member of the **Joe Harriott** Quintet, which pioneered freeform and abstract jazz in the UK. Keane played on all their classic recordings, notably *Free Form, Abstract* and *Movement*. When the group disbanded in the mid-60s he moved to Germany, becoming a featured soloist with **Kurt Edelhagen**'s Radio Band. In the 70s he returned to St. Vincent where he was Minister of Culture for several years, and published prize-winning books of poetry. In the early 80s, he settled in New York, where he occasionally played reggae and soca but spent most of his time writing poetry. In 1989, however, he toured the UK with the Joe Harriott Memorial Quintet, which also included original members **Coleridge Goode** and Bobby Orr. A documentary film was made in 1992 covering his early years in London at the Sunset Club. Equipped with flawless technique and brilliant invention, Keane - equally adept at calypso and bebop, freeform and classical - was recognized as one of the outstanding trumpeters of his generation. He died of cancer in November 1997. His son Roland Ramanan is a trumpeter and writer on jazz.

● ALBUMS: with Joe Harriott *Free Form* (1960)★★★, *In My Condition* (1961)★★★, with Harriott *Abstract* (1962)★★★, *Shake Keane And The Boss Men* (1962)★★, *The Shake Keane And Michael Garrick Quartet* (1963)★★, with Harriott *Movement* (1963)★★★, with Harriott *High Spirits* (1964)★★★, *Shake Keane And The Keating Sound* (1965)★★★, with Harriott *Indo-Jazz Fusions* (1966)★★★★, *Shake Keane And His Orchestra* i (1966)★★★, *Shake Keane And His Orchestra* ii (1968)★★★.

● FURTHER READING: *The Volcano Suite* (1979), *One A Week With Water*.

Keane, Sean

b. *c*.1960, Caherlistrane, County Galway, Eire. The Galway-based singer-songwriter Sean Keane comes from three generations of musicans. He is the brother of **Dolores Keane**, and with his three brothers and three sisters he recorded an album called *Muintir Ui Chathain*. Previously Keane had played the whistle and flute in Segui, a traditional Celtic band, but, after touring for two years, the group had their equipment stolen and Keane joined Delores's band, Reel Union. When that too fell apart Keane earned money as a welder, but also appeared at dozens of fleadhs and joined the band Arcady. He starred in **Sean Tyrell**'s theatrical adoption of the bawdy eighteenth-century poem, *The Midnight Court* and finally made his solo recorded debut in 1993 on *All Heart, No Roses* on which he was accompanied by Alec Finn (**De Dannan**), Johnny 'Ringo' McDonaugh (Arcady), Dermot Byrne (**Altan**) and others. Three years later Keane released *Turn A Phrase*, on which he covered tracks by **Richard Thompson** ('Galway To Graceland') and **Ewan McColl** ('The Tunnel Tigers'), and demonstrated his own songwriting skill on 'Green Among The Gold', which dealt with Irish emigration to Australia.

● ALBUMS: *All Heart No Roses* (CBM 1993)★★★, *Turn A Phrase* (Direct 1996)★★★★.

Keb' Mo'

b. Kevin Moore, Los Angeles, California, USA. Although he was born on the west coast of America, Kevin Moore's parents came from Texas and Louisiana and so instilled in him an appreciation of blues and gospel. At 21, he and his band were hired by violinist **Papa John Creach** as his backing band. Three years later, he was employed by **A&M**'s Almo Music as contractor and arranger of the company's demo sessions. In 1980, he made an album for Chocolate City, a subsidiary of Casablanca Records, just before the label's collapse. He met veteran bandleader **Monk Higgins** in 1983, joining the saxophonist's Whodunit Band on guitar and playing a residency at Marla's Memory Lane. In 1990, he was contacted by the Los Angeles Theater Center to play a blues guitarist in a play called *Rabbit Foot*, and he continued this line of work by becoming understudy to Chick Streetman in *Spunk*, adapted from the writings of Zora Neale Hurston. The nickname for his blues persona was given to him by drummer Quentin Dennard when Moore sat in with his jazz band. Dennard also backs him on *Keb' Mo'*, an album that tempers its blues bias. It includes good reworkings of **Robert Johnson**'s 'Come On In My Kitchen' and 'Kind Hearted Woman', with elements of folk and soul music. Moore is adept at electric and acoustic guitar styles, with a tasteful approach to the use of slide. These skills stood him in good stead when he portrayed Robert Johnson in *Can't You Hear The Wind Howl?*, a documentary-drama narrated by Danny Glover and including interviews with musicians and acquaintances who knew or were influenced by Johnson. On *Just Like You* the material is even more varied, from the beautiful, feel-good pop/soul of 'More Than One Way Home' to the raw acoustic blues of 'Momma, Where's My Daddy', and some singer-songwriter pop featuring **Bonnie Raitt** and **Jackson Browne** ('Just Like You'). Keb is an exciting new talent with a voice that can melt hearts and make you shiver.

● ALBUMS: *Rainmaker* (Chocolate City 1981)★★, *Keb' Mo'* (OKeh 1994)★★★, *Just Like You* (OKeh 1996)★★★★.

Kebnekaise

A Swedish communal 70s folk/rock band, characterised by ringing strings, spacey guitar and an ability to bring a fresh approach to old dance tunes. The music was pioneering, but the group remained little-known outside Sweden. Had they enjoyed greater exposure they could easily have been more widely influential.

● ALBUMS: *Kebnekaise* (1990)★★★.

Kee, Rev. John P., And The New Life Community Choir

The 30-member New Life Community Choir was assembled in 1981 by its leader, the Rev. John P. Kee. A former drug addict, Kee had found redemption through Christianity, and was keen to put something back into the Charlotte community. Many members of the New Life Community were also rescued from violent or criminal backgrounds, the choir serving as a rehabilitation process for many. The group began its career by supporting several renowned gospel acts, before releasing their first record, *Yes Lord*, in 1987. A succession of devout albums for Verity Records established the group as residents in the gospel charts, while Kee also used the group's standing and finances to organise social programmes, local businesses and work opportunities for the community.

● ALBUMS: *Yes Lord* (Tyscot 1987)★★★, *Wait On Him* (Verity 1989)★★★, *Wash Me* (Verity 1991)★★★, *We Walk By Faith* (Verity 1993)★★★★, *Show Up!* (Verity 1995)★★★.

Keel

US-born vocalist Ron Keel started his career in 1983 with **Steeler**, who also temporarily featured future guitar hero **Yngwie Malmsteen**. After one self-titled album on Shrapnel Records, he dissolved the band to go solo. Forming a typical **Kiss/Aerosmith**-styled band with musicians Brian Jay (guitar), Marc Ferrari (guitar), Kenny Chaisson (bass) and Dwain Miller (drums), Keel obtained the production services of **Gene Simmons** (**Kiss**) for a second album that won them many fans. The follow-up, 1986's *The Final Frontier*, featured an all-star line-up including **Joan Jett, Michael Des Barres** (**Silverhead/Detective**) and Simmons. The album also spawned a hit single with a cover version of **Patti Smith**'s 'Because The Night'. Moving to **MCA** in 1987 proved less fruitful and after one album, they switched to an indie label and sundered shortly afterwards. In 1991 Keel talked in depth about forming a new act with an all-female band. This has, so far, proved wishful thinking. Ferrari sped off and formed Marc Ferrari And Friends in 1996.

● ALBUMS: *Lay Down The Law* (Shrapnel 1984)★★, *The Right To Rock* (Vertigo 1985)★★★, *The Final Frontier* (Vertigo 1986)★★★, *Keel* (MCA 1987)★★, *Larger Than Live* (Mountain Castle 1989)★★★.

Keel, Howard

b. Harry Clifford Leek, 13 April 1917, Gillespie, Illinois, USA. A popular singer in films and on the musical stage, with a rich, powerful baritone voice and commanding presence. After starting his career as a singing waiter in Los Angeles, Keel became an 'in-house entertainer' for the huge Douglas aircraft manufacturing company. In 1945, he appeared in *Carousel* on the west coast and then travelled to the UK to appear in the London production of *Oklahoma!*. At this time he was known as Harold Keel, having reversed the spelling of his last name. He subsequently changed his first name and after making a non-singing appearance in the film *The Small Voice* (1948), he returned to the USA where he landed the role of Frank Butler in the film *Annie Get Your Gun* (1950). He continued to make films, mostly musicals, including *Show Boat* (1951), *Kiss Me Kate* and *Calamity Jane* (both 1953), *Rose Marie* and *Seven Brides For Seven Brothers* (both 1954) and *Kismet* (1955). By the 60s he was touring the USA in revivals of popular shows, and appearing in non-musical low-budget western movies. In 1981 his acting career received a boost when he started to appear in the long-running television soap opera *Dallas*. This revived interest in his singing, particularly in the UK, and in 1984 he recorded his first solo album. In 1993, with tongue firmly in his cheek, he announced his farewell tour of the UK, but subsequently returned 'by public demand' for encores.

● ALBUMS: *And I Love You So* (Warwick 1984)★★★★, *Reminiscing* (Telstar 1985)★★★, *Live In Concert* (BBC 1989)★★★, *The Collection* (Castle 1989)★★★, *The Great MGM Stars* (MGM 1991)★★★, *An Enchanted Evening With Howard Keel* (Music Club 1991)★★★, *Close To My Heart* (Premier 1991)★★★, and the soundtrack albums from the above musicals.

● VIDEOS: *Close To My Heart* (PMI 1991).

● FURTHER READING: *A Bio-Bibliography*, Bruce R. Leiby.

● FILMS: *The Small Voice* (1948), *Pagan Love Song* (1950), *Annie Get Your Gun* (1950), *Texas Carnival* (1951), *Three Guys Named Mike* (1951), *Show Boat* (1951), *Lovely To Look At* (1952), *Desperate Search* (1952), *Callaway Went Thataway* (1952), *Calamity Jane* (1953), *Fast Company* (1953), *I Love Melvin* (1953), *Kiss Me Kate* (1953), *Ride Vaquero!* (1953), *Deep In My Heart* (1954), *Seven Brides For Seven Brothers* (1954), *Rose Marie* (1954), *Jupiter's Darling* (1955), *Kismet* (1955), *Floods Of Fear* (1958), *The Big Fisherman* (1959), *Armoured Command* (1961), *Day Of The Triffids* (1963), *The Man From Button Willow* voice only (1965), *Waco* (1966), *Red Tomahawk* (1967), *The War Wagon* (1967), *Arizona Bushwackers* (1968).

Keeler, Ruby

b. Ethel Keeler, 25 August 1909, Halifax, Nova Scotia, Canada, d. 28 February 1993, Rancho Mirage, California, USA. A charming and petite actress and singer renowned for the **Busby Berkeley** 'Depression-era' musicals she made with **Dick Powell** in the 30s, particularly for *42nd Street* in which Warner Baxter barked at her: 'You're going out a youngster but you've got to come back a star.' That is exactly what she did do, some time after taking dance lessons as a child and tap-dancing in the speakeasies of New York while she was still a teenager. In 1927 she danced her way into three Broadway musicals *Bye, Bye Bonnie, Lucky*, and

The Sidewalks Of New York, and **Florenz Ziegfeld** offered her an important role with **Eddie Cantor** and **Ruth Etting** in *Whoopee!*. While the show was being cast she travelled to Hollywood to make a short film, and there met **Al Jolson**. He followed her back to New York, and they were married in September 1928. At her husband's request, Keeler left *Whoopee!* before it reached Broadway, and for the same reason she only spent a few weeks in *Show Girl* (in which she was billed as Ruby Keeler Jolson). While she was performing in the latter show, Jolson rose from his seat in the stalls and serenaded his wife with a song. For the next few years she stepped out of the spotlight and concentrated on being just Mrs. Jolson. That is, until 1933, when Darryl F. Zanuck at Warner Brothers saw a film test she had made some years before, and signed her for the ingenue role *42nd Street*. All her years of training paid off as she and Dick Powell and those marvellous Busby Berkeley dance routines (coupled with a tremendous **Harry Warren** and **Al Dubin** score) made the film a smash hit. Keeler's most memorable moment came with a soft shoe number, 'Shuffle Off To Buffalo', but her demure, sincere personality and fancy footwork delighted audiences throughout the picture. *42nd Street* was followed by more of the same in the form of *Gold Diggers Of 1933*, *Footlight Parade*, *Flirtation Walk*, *Shipmates Forever*, and *Colleen*. In 1934 she and Jolson starred in their only film together, *Go Into Your Dance*. Keeler made her last film for Warners, *Ready Willing And Able* in 1937. It contained what is supposed to be one of her favourite sequences in which she dances with co-star Lee Dixon on the keys of a giant typewriter. After playing a straight dramatic role in *Mother Carey's Chickens* (1938) and appearing in one more musical, *Sweetheart Of The Campus* (1941), she retired from the screen. In between making those two films, she had divorced Jolson in 1940, and, a year later, married John Homer Lowe, a wealthy broker from California, and they raised four children. Apart from making some guest appearances on television during the 50s and 60s, and playing in a brief revival tour of the play *Bell, Book And Candle*, Keeler stayed well away from the public eye until 1970, a year after Lowe died. She was tempted back to Broadway for a revival of the 1925 musical *No, No Nanette*, partly because she was assured that it would not ridicule the old musicals, and also because Busby Berkeley was to be the production supervisor. The show was a triumph, running for 871 performances and winning several **Tony Awards**. US television viewers were reminded of her prowess in 1986 when Ruby Keeler made her last major public appearance in the ABC special *Happy Birthday Hollywood*.

Keen, Robert Earl

b. 11 January 1956, Houston, Texas, USA. In the mid-70s, Keen befriended **Lyle Lovett** at Texas A&M University, an establishment that combined academic and military activities. They often sang and played guitar together and they wrote 'This Old Porch', which appeared on Lovett's first album. Keen also formed a bluegrass band, the Front Porch Boys. In 1981, he moved to Austin and worked as the Incredible Robert Keen and Some Other Guys Band. He financed an album on loans of $4,500, *No Kinda Dancer*, which has twice been reissued. *The Austin Chronicle* nominated him Songwriter of the Year, an honour that invariably went to **Butch Hancock**. On **Steve Earle**'s advice that there were too many distractions in Austin - namely, pretty women and drugs - Keen moved to Nashville, although he returned to Texas in 1987. He was a backing singer on **Nanci Griffith**'s 'St. Olav's Gate' and she recorded his songs 'Sing One For Sister' and 'I Would Change My Life'. He appeared on the recording of the 1986 Kerrville Folk Festival and then recorded a live album for Sugar Hill. In 1989, he made a spirited album about Texas life, *West Textures*. His rough-hewn voice suited the bittersweet songs, which included a country music parody worthy of **David Allan Coe**, 'It's The Little Things (That Piss Me Off)'. The stand-out track, ironically, was a song he did not write - Kevin Farrell's western tale of 'Sonora's Death Row'. Although Keen is a frequent performer, he prefers to write at home: 'I'm not a very good writer on the road because I only come up with lonely hotel songs.' *Gringo Honeymoon* was another excellent album, full of narratives and the telling observation that 'there are just two ways to go - dyin' fast or livin' slow'. *Number 2 Live Dinner* was a raucous live album recorded in Texas. His major label debut was a typically uncompromising collection comprised largely of Keen originals, and featuring Margo Timmins of **Cowboy Junkies** on the duet 'Then Came Lo Mein'.

● ALBUMS: *No Kinda Dancer* (Philo 1984)★★★★, *The Live Album* (Sugar Hill 1988)★★, *West Textures* (Sugar Hill 1989)★★★, *A Bigger Piece Of Sky* (Sugar Hill 1993)★★★, *Gringo Honeymoon* (Special Delivery 1994)★★★★, *Number 2 Live Dinner* (Sugar Hill 1996)★★★, *Picnic* (Arista 1997)★★★★.

Keen, Speedy

b. John Keen, 29 March 1945, Ealing, London, England. A former member of several struggling beat groups, Keen garnered considerable acclaim for his composition 'Armenia City In The Sky', which opened the **Who**'s third album, *The Who Sell Out*. The group's guitarist, **Pete Townshend**, nurtured this emergent talent and helped assemble **Thunderclap Newman**, which scored an international hit with Keen's portentous 'Something In The Air'. The artist's first solo album, *Previous Convictions*, continued the promise of his early work, but a second selection, *Y'Know Wot I Mean?*, although of interest, was less incisive. An affinity with malcontents resurfaced during the punk era when Keen produced several sessions for the influential **Heartbreakers**, since when he has kept a much lower profile.

● ALBUMS: *Previous Convictions* (Track 1973)★★★★, *Y'Know Wot I Mean?* (1975)★★.

Keene, Nelson

b. Malcolm Holland, 1942, Farnborough, Hampshire, England. This early 60s photogenic pop-rocker was one of 10 children. He formed a quartet called the Raiders and sent a dem to top impresario **Larry Parnes**. Parnes signed him and put him in *Idols On Parade*, a summer show at Blackpool in 1960, which starred **Joe Brown**, **Tommy Bruce** and **Lance Fortune**. Keene made the UK Top 40 with his first single 'Image Of A Girl', a cover of the US hit by the **Safaris** (it was another cover by **Mark Wynter** which won the chart race in Britain). He recorded two other singles for **HMV** which fell by the wayside for this would-be teen idol.

Keene, Steven

b. Brooklyn, New York, USA. Contemporary folk/blues artist Steven Keene began his travels under the guidance of his uncle Tex as part of a circus troupe operating in the southern regions of the USA. Learning to play guitar and harmonica, he eventually left the circus to take up more regular employment at a lumber mill in Austin, Texas. Spending his evenings playing on the local blues scene, he subsequently moved to Memphis to form his own band. After touring throughout the region, he left for New York's Greenwich Village and solo performances in small folk clubs. Returning to a band format, he secured more lucrative gigs at venues such as the Lonestar Roadhouse and **CBGB's**. The New York independent label Moo Records invited him to record a debut album at this time. *No Alternative*, released in 1996, consisted of songs whittled down from an original tally of 50 compositions. The musicians involved included **Bob Dylan** collaborators John Jackson, Tony Garrier and Bucky Baxter, as well as guitarist Danny Kalb from the **Blues Project**. It featured a mélange of folk, blues and rock songs, with declamatory titles such as 'Far Better Friend Than Lover' and Before You Save The World, Save Yourself'. Three obscure Dylan songs, 'Never Say Goodbye', 'Walkin' Down The Line' and 'Sign On The Window', were also included.
● ALBUMS: *No Alternative* (Moo 1996)★★★.

Keep On Rockin'

Released in 1972, *Keep On Rockin'* was an abridged version of an earlier release, *Sweet Toronto* (1970), which chronicled a rock 'n' roll festival from the previous year. The performance by the **Plastic Ono Band**, featuring **John Lennon**, **Yoko Ono** and **Eric Clapton** was dropped from the first draft at the former **Beatle**'s behest. (Lennon's first on-stage appearance since 1966 was nonetheless immortalised on the album *Live Peace In Toronto*.) Despite this loss, *Keep On Rockin'* is a sometimes dazzling film, partly through the skilled direction D.A. Pennebaker, famed for his work on **Bob Dylan**'s *Don't Look Back*, but principally for sensational sets rock 'n' roll veterans **Bo Diddley**, **Jerry Lee Lewis**, **Little Richard** and **Chuck Berry**. Their years as creative forces had ebbed, but they invested their best-known material with passion and urgency. Doubtlessly fired by sharing a bill together, each claimed the spotlight with rekindled vigour. **Janis Joplin** and **Jimi Hendrix** also appeared, but their individual personal problems undermined their performances. Indeed the latter was arrested for drugs' possession during his visit to Canada. *Keep On Rockin'* is thus a testament to rock 'n' roll's origins and the enduring power of some of its early acts and songs.

Kefford, Ace, Stand

This short-lived group was led by Chris 'Ace' Kefford, formerly of the **Move**. In April 1968 he joined forces with Dave Ball (guitar), Dennis Ball (bass) and **Cozy Powell** (drums), previously members of Cirencester, England, act the Sorcerers. The Ace Kefford Stand recorded one single for **Atlantic Records**. The a-side was a slow rendition of the **Yardbirds**' hit, 'For Your Love', whereas the flipside, 'Gravy Booby Jamm', was a loud, hard-rocking instrumental. Kefford, who suffered from nervous breakdowns, left the group in 1969, and remaining musicians then formed **Big Bertha**.

Keineg, Katell

b. France. The child of a Breton father and Welsh mother who were active in the Breton independence movement, Katell Keineg (pronounced Cat-Ell-Kay-Neck) listened to both Welsh and French folk music in her youth. When the family moved to Wales, Keineg immersed herself in local choirs, appearing at several *eisteddfods* and exposing herself to the pop sounds of the day. By the age of 16 she was busking on the streets of Cardiff, before professional engagements took her throughout Britain, before making her home in Dublin. Her first release was the haunting 'Hestia', a 7-inch single released on **Bob Mould**'s Singles Only Label. Fred Maher, a veteran of work with **Lou Reed** and **Scritti Politti**, helped out on the production of her debut album, recorded in New York. Also present were her long-standing musical collaborators, Paul Tiernan (guitar) and Garvan Gallagher (double bass) on a collection of songs which spanned jazz, unaffected Celtic folk, raw blues and passages of spoken word narration.
● ALBUMS: *O Seasons O Castles* (Elektra 1994)★★★★, *Jet* (Elektra 1997)★★★, *Mother's Map* (Elektra 1997)★★★.

Keisker, Marion

b. 23 September 1917, Memphis, Tennessee, USA, d. 29 December 1989. Marion Keisker was **Sam Phillips**' assistant at **Sun Records** in the 50s, and as such was the employee who first recorded the young **Elvis Presley** in 1953. In 1946, she began working for radio station WREC. Phillips joined as an announcer a year later and when he launched the Memphis Recording Service in 1950, Keisker went along as his assistant, continuing to work part-time for the station until 1955. Phillips started Sun in 1952 and Keisker arranged sessions for the blues musicians who recorded there. She kept a log of all activities at the company, which provided future historians with interesting details. Keisker was on duty in 1953 when Presley arrived at Memphis Recording Service to record two songs as a gift for his mother. She took his fee, ran the recording machines and made a note of the boy's potential. It was she who suggested to Phillips that he record Presley on Sun the following year and she who took Presley around to visit disc jockeys and the press. Presley called her his 'first fan'. As Sun grew, Keisker performed such duties as handling accounts with distributors and pressing plants. All of the aspiring artists who wanted to record for Sun had to speak to Keisker before they were accepted or rejected by Phillips. Keisker left Sun in 1957 to join the US Air Force, with which she worked until 1969. She died of cancer in December 1989.

Keita, Salif

b. 25 August 1949, Djoliba, Mali. Born into one of Mali's most distinguished families, albino vocalist/composer Keita can trace his descent directly back to Soundjata Keita, who founded the Mali empire in 1240. He originally wished to become a teacher, but unemployment at the time was high, so he switched to music. In the west, musicians are often thought of as dissolute and irresponsible; in Mali, for the son of a royal family to go into a job that was traditionally the preserve of lower castes was virtually unthinkable. Keita's decision caused a storm - he was dismissed from school, and formed a trio with his brother, playing in Bamako nightclubs. In 1970, he was invited to join the Rail Band, playing in the buffet of the Station Hotel in Bamako. Three years later he switched to the Rail Band's main rivals, Les Ambassadeurs, who were playing what he considered to be a more modern music, with a greater range of outside influences. With the help of guitarist Kante Manfila, he further extended the band's range by incorporating traditional Malian rhythms and melodies into their existing repertoire of Afro-Cuban material. Fortunately for today's African music audience, these early experiments were captured on three superb 1977 albums - *Les Ambassadeurs Du Motel* (Son Afrique 1977), *Les Ambassadeurs De Bamako Vol. 1* (Son Afrique 1977) and *Les Ambassadeurs De Bamako Vol. 2* (Son Afrique 1977). By 1978, the reputation of Les Ambassadeurs had spread beyond Mali throughout Francophone West Africa, and that year Keita was made an Officer of the National Order of Guinea by President Sekou Toure, one of the few African statesmen of that time to give real encouragement and support to African musicians working to preserve and develop traditional music and culture. In response, Keita composed the hugely successful 'Mandjou', which told the history of the Malian people and paid tribute to Sekou Toure. Following the song's success, Keita took Les Ambassadeurs to Abidjan, capital of the Cote D'Ivoire (Ivory Coast), the then music centre of Francophone West Africa. From Abidjan, Keita was determined to forge an international career,

and duly renamed the band Les Ambassadeurs Internationaux/Internationales. In 1980, he took three members of the new line-up to the USA, where he recorded *Wassolon-Foli*, blending electric reggae with acoustic Malian folksong. In 1986, following a dispute between Keita and Manfila, Les Ambassadeurs split, with Keita going on to lead a new outfit, Super Ambassadeurs. In 1987, he effectively disbanded Super Ambassadeurs to pursue a solo career, debuting with the astonishing rock-flavoured album *Soro*, recorded in Paris and successfully fusing traditional Malian music with hi-tech electronics and western instrumentation. The marriage of influences, which all but the most hidebound traditionalists welcomed as a positive step forward for Malian music, was further developed on the 1990 album, *Ko-Yan*. Its successor, *Amen*, was recorded the following year with the aid of jazz musicians **Wayne Shorter** and **Joe Zawinul**, with guitar work by **Carlos Santana**. However, the reception afforded both was lukewarm, and his live performances of this period were judged to be wildly erratic. *Folon*, produced by **Wally Badarou**, represented something of a return to form, with the title track and a revised version of 'Mandjou' his most outstanding songs since 1987's *Soro*.

● ALBUMS: *Soro* (Stern's 1987)★★★★, *Ko-Yan* (Mango 1990)★★, *Amen* (Mango 1991)★★, *Folon* (Mango 1995)★★★★, *Sosie* (MSS 1997)★★★.

● COMPILATIONS: *The Mansa Of Mali* (Mango 1993)★★★.

● VIDEOS: *Salif Keita Live* (1991).

Keith

b. James Barry Keefer, 7 May 1949, Philadelphia, Pennsylvania, USA. Keith was best known for his Top 10 folk rock single '98.6' in January 1967. Keefer started with a band called the Admirations in the early 60s, recording one single for **Columbia Records**, 'Caravan Of Lonely Men'. He was then discovered by journalist Kal Rudman, who took Keefer to **Mercury Records** executive Jerry Ross. Signed to that label, and renamed Keith, he recorded his first solo single, 'Ain't Gonna Lie', which narrowly made the US Top 40. '98.6' followed and was his biggest hit, although Keith charted twice in 1967 with lesser hits, 'Tell Me To My Face' and 'Daylight Savin' Time'. He recorded a few more singles for Mercury and two albums, only the first of which made the charts. After spending time in the armed forces, he returned to a changed musical direction, recording a single, 'In And Out Of Love', for **Frank Zappa**'s Discreet label, and singing briefly with Zappa's band (he did not record with them). Keefer recorded one last album, for **RCA Records**, with no luck, and then left the music business until 1986, when an attempted comeback under his real name proved unsuccessful.

● ALBUMS: *98.6/Ain't Gonna Lie* (Mercury 1967)★★, *Out Of Crank* (Mercury 1968)★★, *The Adventures Of Keith* (RCA 1969)★★.

Keith And Enid

In Jamaica Keith Stewart and Enid Cumberland recorded as a duo throughout the early 60s. In 1961 they notched up a number of hits, 'Only A Pity', 'Never Leave Me Throne' and 'What Have I Done'. In 1964 the duo recorded 'Lost My Love', an early example of the new ska beat, produced by D Darling. Many of the singles were released in the UK, albeit marketed within the Jamaican community. By the mid-60s Cumberland found a new partner, Roy Richards, who joined her on 'He'll Have To Go'. The single curiously featured an all-time ska classic, 'Love Me Forever' by **Carlton And His Shoes**, on the b-side when released in the UK on the Coxsone label. Working with Richards and producer **Coxsone Dodd** at **Studio One** she also recorded the up-tempo 'Rocking Time'. Both Stewart and Cumberland have faded into obscurity, while Richards was last seen entertaining tourists by playing his harmonica at a hotel in Kingston.
● ALBUMS: *Keith And Enid Sing* (Island 1963)★★★.

Keith And Rooney

Bill Keith (b. October 1939, Boston, Massachusetts, USA; banjo/vocals) and Jim Rooney (guitar/vocals) forged one of the lynchpin acts active during the folk revival of the early 60s. They were based in Cambridge, Massachusetts, USA and, along with the Charles Valley River Boys, helped inspire the New England folk scene. *Livin' On The Mountain* was produced by **Paul A. Rothchild**, at that point a director of the famed Club 47. Bob Weinstock, owner of **Prestige Records**, was so impressed with the results that he released the results and employed Rothchild. The album is an excellent old-time/bluegrass selection. Keith and Rooney are aided by Joe Val (mandolin/vocals), Herb Hooven (fiddle), Herb Applin (guitar) and Fritz Richmond (washtub bass). Richmond later became a founder member of the **Jim Kweskin Jug Band**. Keith and Rooney made a highly successful appearance at the 1962 Philadelphia Folk Festival during which Keith won the five-string banjo contest. They parted company in 1963 after which Keith joined **Bill Monroe** and Red Allen before moving to the west coast. There he became associated with a new generation of blue-grass band, including **Muleskinner** and **Old And In The Way**. Jim Rooney temporarily abandoned music to study classics in Greece, before settling in Nashville where he has become a highly-respected producer, notably with **Nancy Griffith**. He also continues to tour and play with Rooney.
● ALBUMS: *Livin' On The Mountain* (Prestige/International 1960)★★★★.

Keith And Tex

Texas Dixon and Keith Rowe first auditioned for **Derrick Harriott** in the late 60s, and the producer was so enamoured with their voices that he immediately took them under his wing and into his studio. Backed by musicians of the calibre of **Lynn Tait** and Hux Brown, they recorded two of reggae's most enduring and versioned staples, 'Tonight' and 'Stop That Train'. However, they faded into obscurity soon after these releases, although 'Hypnotizing Eyes' and a cover version of the **Temptations**' 'Don't Look Back' prolonged their career. Rowe went on to release 'Groovy Situation' for **Lee Perry**, but afterwards emigrated to the USA and joined the army, while Dixon relocated to Canada. The duo might well have languished in obscurity had it not been for rapper **Vanilla Ice**'s version of 'Stop That Train' in the early 90s. In its wake, Crystal Records put together an admirable retrospective package of early recordings, which, rather than bursting the bubble, served to reaffirm their legendary status.
● COMPILATIONS: *Stop That Train* (Crystal 1992)★★★.

Keith, Bill

b. October 1939, Boston, Massachusetts, USA. Keith is known for his innovative banjo style, and is credited with helping the development of the progressive blue-grass mode of playing, partly attributed to his chromatic technique. Having started out learning the piano, Keith moved on to tenor banjo. In 1957, after seeing **Pete Seeger** of the **Weavers**, Keith bought a five-string banjo and gradually worked his way round the folk clubs and bars of New England with his partner Jim Rooney. In September 1962, Keith won the Philadelphia Folk Festival banjo contest. His first professional job was playing with Red Allen and mandolin player Frank Wakefield from Tennessee, eventually joining **Bill Monroe**'s Blue Grass Boys and also the **Country Gentlemen**. In 1964, Keith recorded with Wakefield and Allen for the **Folkways** label, and the same year, joined the **Jim Kweskin Jug Band**, which featured **Geoff** and **Maria Muldaur** and **Richard Greene**. When the group split up in 1968, Keith joined **Ian And Sylvia Tyson**'s Great Speckled Bird, a country rock outfit, in which he also played steel guitar. After approximately a year, he went on tour with **Jonathan Edwards**, and later **Judy Collins**. From his work with the **Blue Velvet Band**, he then formed Muleskinner with **David Grisman**, **Clarence White**, Richard Greene and **Peter Rowan**. Keith spent much of the following period in session work and touring with Rooney, both in Europe and the UK. For *Something Auld, Something Newgrass, Something Borrowed, Something Bluegrass* he is backed by **Vassar Clements** (fiddle), Tony Rice (guitar) and **David Grisman** (mandolin). The album includes a cover version of a **Mick Jagger/Keith Richard** composition, 'No Expectations', as well as **Duke Ellington**'s 'Caravan'. During the 80s, he toured a number of British clubs along with long-time colleague Jim Rooney as **Keith And Rooney**, before forming the New Blue Velvet Band with Rooney, Eric Weissberg and Kenny Koseck.
● ALBUMS: *Sweet Moments With The Blue Velvet Band* (1969)★★★, *Something Auld, Something Newgrass, Something Borrowed, Something Bluegrass* (Rounder 1976)★★★★, *Bill*

Keith And Jim Collier (Hexagone 1979)★★, *Banjoistics* (Rounder 1984)★★★, with Rooney *Collection* (Waterfront 1984)★★★.
● VIDEOS: *Muleskinner - Live Video* (1991).

Keith, Toby

b. 8 July 1961, Elk Town, Clinton, Oklahoma, USA. The 90s country singer Toby Keith grew up on an Oklahoma farm listening to his father's favourite, **Bob Wills**, and finding his own hero in **Merle Haggard**. He tested broncs and bulls for a rodeo during his summers in high school. Oil was found in Elk Town and Keith worked as a roughneck and then an operational manager. This experience inspired 'Boomtown', of which he says, 'The wells ran dry. The rich people got rich by saving their money. The fools who spent it were broke.' Keith himself had formed the Easy Money Band, originally playing **Alabama**'s hits but then widening the repertoire as they accumulated new and better equipment. He was signed by Harold Shedd, who produced his first album, *Toby Keith*. It included a tribute to the film stars of yesteryear, 'Should've Been A Cowboy', a number 1 country record that also became the anthem of the Dallas Cowboys football team. The album included further hits with 'Wish I Didn't Know Now', 'Ain't Worth Missing' and 'A Little Less Talk (And A Lot More Action)'. *Billboard* named him the Top New Country Artist of 1993. His number 1 country song 'Who's That Man' started as a joke: 'You know the old one that goes, "What do you get if you play country music backwards? Answer: your wife back, your dog back, your house back and your car back." I was kicking that idea round as a fun song when I hit upon the line, "Who's that man running my life?" It dawned on me that it would work better as a serious song.' In 1995 he released a sentimental seasonal album, *Christmas To Christmas*, which featured songs from the cream of Nashville's songwriters. In 1996 he appeared in the film *Burning Bridges*, with **Tanya Tucker** and **Vanessa Williams**. The same year he had a major country hit with 'Does That Blue Moon Ever Shine On You' and a huge hit album with *Blue Moon*. He followed up with 1997's superior *Dream Walkin'*, featuring the hit single 'We Were In Love'.
● ALBUMS: *Toby Keith* (Polygram 1993)★★★, *Boomtown* (Polygram 1995)★★★, *Christmas To Christmas* (Polygram 1995)★★★, *Blue Moon* (A&M 1996)★★★★, *Dream Walkin'* (Mercury 1997)★★★★.
● VIDEOS: *Who's That Man* (1994).

Kellaway, Roger

b. 1 November 1939, Waban, Massachusetts, USA. Kellaway was initially attracted to jazz by the piano playing of **George Shearing**. He switched from piano to double bass and studied at the New England Conservatory (1957-59). He played the bass with **Jimmy McPartland** before returning to work full-time at the piano. In the mid-60s he played with the bands of Kai Winding, **Al Cohn** and **Zoot Sims**, and Clark

Terry/Bob Brookmeyer, as well as working in the studios with musicians as varied as **Ben Webster**, **Wes Montgomery** and **Sonny Rollins**. In 1966, he moved to Los Angeles and played with the **Don Ellis** band. Since the late 60s he has worked as musical director for **Bobby Darin** (1967-69) and concentrated on studio work with musicians as diverse as **Joni Mitchell** and **Jimmy Knepper**. He has written numerous film scores including *The Paper Lion* (1968), *A Star Is Born* (1976) and *Breathless* (1983), as well as writing a ballet *PAMTGG* (1971), commissioned by George Balanchine and *Portraits Of Time* (1983), commissioned by the Los Angeles Philharmonic Orchestra. In 1984, he returned to New York to studio work and a duo with **Dick Hyman**. In the mid-90s he recorded an interestin album with cornetist **Ruby Braff**.
● ALBUMS: *Portrait Of Roger Kellaway* (Fresh Sound 1963)★★★★, *Roger Kellaway Trio* (1965)★★★★, *Spirit Feel* (1967)★★★, *Cello Quartet* (1971)★★★, *Come To The Meadow* (1974)★★★, *Nostalgia Suite* (1978)★★★, *Say That Again* (1978)★★, *Fifty-Fifty* (Natasha 1987)★★★, with Red Mitchell *Alone Together* (Dragon 1989)★★, *In Japan* (All Art Jazz 1987)★★, with Red Mitchell *Life's A Take* (Concord 1982)★★★, *Live At the Maybank Recital Hall Vol II* (Concord 1991)★★★, with Ruby Braff *Inside And Out* (Concord 1996)★★★.

Keller, Jerry

b. 20 June 1938, Fort Smith, Arkansas, USA. After moving to Tulsa in 1944 Keller formed the Lads Of Note Quartet in the 50s before joining the Tulsa Boy Singers. He won a talent contest organized by bandleader **Horace Heidt** which earned him the vocalist job with Jack Dalton's Orchestra. He then spent nine months as a disc jockey in Tulsa before moving to New York in 1956. He recorded a series of demos for record companies before fellow performer **Pat Boone** introduced him to Marty Mills who became his manager. Keller recorded the self-penned 'Here Comes Summer' for the Kapp record label, and it became a US summer hit in 1959. Ironically it only entered the UK charts in late August as the warmer months lapsed into autumn, but it still went to number 1. Follow-ups such as 'If I Had A Girl', and 'Now Now Now' failed to repeat the success. In 1960, he toured the UK replacing **Eddie Cochran** in a package tour engagement after Cochran had died in a car crash. Despite the lack of subsequent hits as a singer, his songs charted handsomely for artists such as **Andy Williams** and the **Cyrkle**. In 1977, he appeared in the film *You Light Up My Life* and the following year in *If I Ever See You Again*.
● ALBUMS: *Here Comes Jerry Keller* (Kapp 1960)★★.

Kelley, Eileen

b. Eileen Kelly, Cork, Eire. A part-time photographic model, she joined the Music Makers showband in 1964, replacing Della Heslin. After a year, she moved on to the more prestigious Nevada. During the mid-60s, the blonde Kelley specialized in ballads, particularly those recorded by **Dusty Springfield**. The Nevada continued to tour Eire and abroad up until the early 70s. Kelley alternated the lead spot on records with the talented Red Hurley and enjoyed hits with such songs as 'How Great Thou Art' and 'The Wedding Song'. In 1974, she joined **Brendan Bowyer** (formerly of the **Royal Showband**) in the showband supergroup, the Big 8. Kelley lasted a year, but soon grew tired of the monotony of playing identical sets night after night in Las Vegas. Thereafter, she formed Kelley With Klass, before returning to solo work in cabaret.

Kelley, Peck

b. John Dickson Kelley, 1898, Houston, Texas, USA, d. 26 December 1980. In the early 20s pianist Kelley led a band, Peck's Bad Boys, which featured several excellent musicians who were then beginning their careers. They included **Jack Teagarden** and **Pee Wee Russell**. Although he made occasional trips to mid-western cities and also to New Orleans, Kelley concentrated his career on his home town. He resisted offers to join important bands such as those of **Paul Whiteman** and both **Tommy** and **Jimmy Dorsey**, and continued playing in self-imposed obscurity. His reputation among fellow musicians was very high, but his first formal recordings were not made until he was almost 60 and partially blind. Even allowing for the ravages of time and health, these records support the view that in his prime he must have been a formidable talent. Further evidence emerged with the release, in 1987, of an album containing earlier recordings. Home-made and with some reminiscing by Kelley, but with astonishing bursts of bravura piano-playing, they go a long way to proving that this time, at least, the legend was right. Kelley eventually became totally blind and died in December 1980, in the obscurity he had sought during his lifetime.

● ALBUMS: with the Dick Shannon Quartet *Peck Kelley Jam, Volumes 1 & 2 (1957)* (1987)★★★.

Kellin, Orange

b. Örjan Kjellin, 21 July 1944, Ljungby, Sweden. Kellin began playing clarinet at the age of 15 and two years later formed his first band in partnership with pianist Lars Edegran. The band played music in the New Orleans manner. Kellin made his first records in his native Sweden at the age of 17. In 1966, he moved to New Orleans where he became a regular performer at several leading jazz venues including the Preservation Hall. In 1968 he was a founder member of the New Orleans Ragtime Orchestra. He also led his own bands in the city including, in 1970, a band which held a residency at the Maison Bourbon Club. Two years later he formed the New Orleans Joymakers. Kellin recorded with several veteran New Orleans musicians including **Josiah 'Cié' Frazier**, **Preston Jackson**, **Jim Robinson**, **Jabbo Smith**, **Zutty Singleton** and **Kid Thomas Valentine**. In 1978, Kellin played with the NORO for the soundtrack of the film *Pretty Baby*. The following year he appeared in New York with the stage musical

One Mo' Time for which he was musical director and co-arranger in addition to playing in the onstage band. In the early 80s he appeared with the same show during its long and successful run in London's West End. Kellin has toured extensively with his own bands and with bands formed largely from New Orleans veterans. In 1992 he made his first solo tour of the UK. A gifted and highly musicianly clarinettist, Kellin's dedication to the music of New Orleans has contributed greatly to the preservation of the style. He has an excellent technique and solos with flair and eloquence. As an admirable ensemble player, he lends authority to any group of which he is a member.

● ALBUMS: *Orange Kellin In New Orleans* i (1967)★★★, *Orange Kellin In New Orleans* ii (1967)★★, *Scandanavians In New Orleans* (c.1971)★★★, *New Orleans Ragtime Orchestra* (1971)★★★, *Pretty Baby* film soundtrack (1978)★★.

Kelly Blue - Wynton Kelly Trio & Sextet

From the opening flute played by **Bobby Jasper**, the listener is immediately hooked and welcomed; Kelly's piano floats in, his fingers landing like a butterfly. The title track opens this album, and although all the other tracks are excellent, the album is worth the price of this one piece. The cool support in addition to Jasper comes from **Nat Adderley** (cornet), Benny Golson (tenor), **Paul Chambers** (bass) and **Jimmy Cobb** (drums). This is an amaxingly relaxed album with Kelly at times seemingly only breathing on the keys. The CD reissue has the bonus of the third take of 'Keep It Moving': only serious buffs will notice the difference. An essential album, often overlooked by the populist vote.

● Tracks: *Kelly Blue; Soflty, As In A Morning Sunrise; Do Nothin' Till You Hear From Me; On Green Dolphin Street; Willow Weep For Me; Keep It Moving (take four); Keep It Moving (take three); Old Clothes*.

● First released 1960
● UK peak chart position: did not chart
● USA peak chart position: did not chart

Kelly Brothers

(see **King Pins**)

Kelly Family

The phenomenal popularity of Irish Americans the Kelly Family, a nine-piece aggregation of siblings specialising in simple folk, pop and rock tunes, has occurred incredibly swiftly. But their appeal should not be underestimated: they have achieved platinum status in Germany, Switzerland and Austria, where their concert appearances regularly draw crowds of 20,000 plus. The family father and mentor is Dan Kelly, who started the band after years working as a street musician. This first version of the group specialised in traditional folk singing, but found it difficult to progress beyond cult status in the video dominated era of the early 80s. After leaving **Polydor Records** Dan Kelly retired the family to a house in Spain and formed the group's own label, Kel-Life Records. Their own publishing company, Kel-Fam, was also established, which now licenses their recordings to various companies worldwide. The Kellys then returned to street busking in Paris, France, then the USA and Germany, slowly building an audience through their dedicated, high energy performances. The ranks were systematically swelled by Dan's younger children, with each member invited to interchange instruments to keep the act fresh (a tradition maintained to this day in their spectacular stage show). The Kelly Family age range spans Angelo (b. c.1984) to Kathy (b. c.1963), though Joey (b. c.1973) appears to be the group's main subject of idol worship. His description of the Kelly's sound: 'Clean, honest rock, and good enough to be on stage with anyone from **Metallica** to the **Rolling Stones**', goes some way to justifying their international status, though it is hard to equate a group who are regularly showered in cuddly toys while on stage with either of those bands.

● ALBUMS: *Over The Hump* (Kel-Life 1995)★★★.

Kelly, Arthur Lee 'Guitar'

b. 14 November 1924, Clinton, Louisiana, USA. Like many blues singers, Kelly learned to play religious songs first, but his main interest was in the blues. In the 40s, he was living near Baton Rouge and beginning to develop his own guitar style, under the influence of local artist **Lightning Slim**, as well as copying records by artists such as **Muddy Waters** and **Lightnin' Hopkins**. Although active on the blues scene through the boom in Baton Rouge blues in the 50s, he never made any records during this time. In the 60s, he formed a small group along with **Silas Hogan** and at last in 1970, he appeared on a couple of albums of Louisiana blues artists, as well as a single on Excello. He continued his partnership with Hogan for many years, and joined that artist in his residency at **Tabby Thomas**'s Blues Box club, but he has also toured widely, including visits to Europe.

● COMPILATIONS: *Louisiana Blues* (1970)★★★.

Kelly, Chris

b. 18 October c.1890, Deer Range Plantation, Louisiana, USA, d. 19 August 1929. Resident in New Orleans from around 1915, Kelly began playing cornet and eventually led his own bands. His reputation rests entirely upon hearsay for he never recorded. Reports suggest that he was an exciting player who could, when occasion demanded, play with deep feeling. His most popular number was 'Careless Love'. Kelly led a riotous life, drank heavily, and died young. Amongst the musicians with whom he worked, and from whom stem most of what is known of this legendary character of early jazz, were **George Lewis** and **Kid Howard**. The latter reputedly adopted many facets of Kelly's style.

Kelly, Dave

b. 1948, London, England. Kelly's first instrument was trombone, but he became a bottleneck slide guitar specialist, sitting in with **John Lee Hooker** and **Muddy Waters** during a 1966 visit to the USA. On his return, Kelly joined his first R&B band which evolved into the **John Dummer Blues Band**, with whom he recorded in 1968-69. Leaving the group, he performed as a solo artist on the folk club circuit, and played on numerous recording sessions involving a loose-knit circle of London blues musicians that included his sister **Jo Ann Kelly** (guitar/vocals), Bob Hall (piano) and Bob Brunning (bass). They recorded together as Tramp and as Firefall, while Kelly also played on albums by visiting US blues singers **Son House** and **Arthur Crudup** (*Roebuck Man*, 1974). Around this time Kelly made his first two solo albums for **Mercury** with accompaniment from **Peter Green**, Jo Ann, Brunning and Steve Rye (harmonica). Kelly also led an early 70s group called Rocksalt and in 1974 rejoined John Dummer in the Ooblee Dooblee Band. In the late 70s he became a founder-member of the **Blues Band** and when the group temporarily split up, he formed his own band with fellow Blues Band members Rob Townshend (drums) and Gary Fletcher (bass), plus Mick Rogers (guitar), Lou Stonebridge (keyboards) and John 'Irish' Earle (saxophone). With numerous personnel changes (including the addition of Peter Filleul on keyboards and Tex Comer on bass), the group continued for several years, touring Europe and recording occasionally for the German label Metronome and Apoloosa, owned by Italian blues fan Franco Ratti. During the 80s, Kelly developed a parallel career in writing jingles and film and television soundtrack music. He rejoined the Blues Band when it re-formed in 1989.

● ALBUMS: *Keep It In The Family* (Mercury 1969)★★★, *Dave Kelly* (Mercury 1971)★★★, with Bob Hall *Survivors* (Appaloosa 1979)★★★, *Willin'* (Appaloosa 1979)★★★, *Feels Right* (Cool King 1981)★★★, *Dave Kelly Band Live* (Appaloosa 1983)★★, *Heart Of The City* (Line 1987)★★★, *...When The Blues Come To Call ...* (Hypertension 1994)★★★.

● COMPILATIONS: *Making Whoopee 1979/1982* (RPM 1993)★★★.

Kelly, Dave 'Rude Boy'

Kelly worked with **Donovan Germain** in the late 80s, and was employed as the resident engineer at the Penthouse studio in Slipe Road, Kingston, Jamaica. In 1990 he was introduced to **Buju Banton**, and together they wrote many of the songs that helped to earn the DJ an award as the Most Exciting Newcomer Of 1991. Kelly continued to work at Penthouse while he set up his own Mad House label, which was eventually launched with Buju Banton's 'Big It Up', featured on the DJ's Penthouse debut *Mr Mention*. Kelly is widely regarded as an innovator, contriving distinctive rhythms including the 'Pepperseed', 'Joyride', 'Arab', 'Stink' and 'Medicine'. He has worked with many top performers in the 90s, including **Beenie Man** ('Old Dawg' and 'Slam'), **Frisco Kid** ('Rubbers'), **Lady Saw** ('Sycamore Tree') and **Nadine Sutherland** with **Terror Fabulous** ('Action'). In 1997 Kelly embarked on an adventurous musical project known as Alias, electing to avoid any media hype; he refused to be photographed and formed a co-operative with **Wayne Wonder**, Frisco Kid, **Spragga Benz**, Alley Cat, Baby Cham, Textra and Mr. Easy. Working on a totally non-hierarchical basis, the enterprise featured Kelly as producer, writer, musician and even performing as a DJ (hiding behind an alias). He courted controversy when he produced Beenie Man's 'Nuff Slam' jingle to promote a new condom known as 'the Slam'. The sheath's packaging featured Carlene the **dancehall** queen in an alluring pose and the proclamation 'Slam Country' over the Jamaican flag, which led to protests in Gordon House.

● ALBUMS: *Pepperseed* (Mad House 1996)★★★, *Joyride* (Mad House 1997)★★★.

Kelly, Gene

b. Eugene Curran Kelly, 23 August 1912, Pittsburgh, Pennsylvania, USA, d. 1 February 1996, Los Angeles, California, USA. An actor, dancer, singer, choreographer, director, producer, and one of the most innovative and respected figures in the history of the screen musical. Kelly took dance lessons at the age of eight - albeit against his will - and excelled at sports when he was at high school. During the Depression he had a variety of jobs, including gymnastics instructor, and, with his brother Fred, performed a song-and-dance act at local nightclubs. In the early 30s, he spent a few months at law school before opening the Gene Kelly Studios of the Dance, and discovering that he had a real aptitude for teaching, which would manifest itself throughout his career in some of the most creative choreography ever seen on the big screen. In 1937 Kelly moved to New York, and gained a small part as a dancer in the musical comedy *Leave It To Me!*, in which **Mary Martin** also made her Broadway debut. A larger role followed in the revue *One For The Money*, and he also played Harry, the 'good natured hoofer', in the Pulitzer prize-winning comedy, *The Time Of Your Life*. In 1940, after working in summer stock, and serving as a dance director at **Billy Rose**'s Diamond Horseshoe club, Kelly won the title role in the new **Richard Rodgers** and **Lorenz Hart** musical, *Pal Joey*. His portrayal of the devious, unscrupulous nightclub entertainer made him a star overnight in New York, but, after choreographing another Broadway hit show, *Best Foot Forward*, he moved to Hollywood in 1942, and made his screen debut with **Judy Garland** in *For Me And My Gal*. He appeared in two more musicals for MGM, *DuBarry Was A Lady* and *Thousands Cheer*, before the company loaned him to **Columbia** for *Cover Girl* (1944). Co-starring with **Rita Hayworth** and Phil Silvers, the film was a major landmark in Kelly's career, and an indication of the heights he would achieve during the next 10 years. It was memorable in many respects, particularly for Kelly's sensitive rendering of **Jerome Kern** and **Ira Gershwin**'s 'Long Ago And Far Away', and the 'Alter Ego' dance, during which Kelly danced with his own reflection in a shop window. Back at MGM, he was called upon to play several dramatic roles as well as appearing in *Anchors Aweigh* (1945), for which he received an Oscar nomination for best actor. In the film, as a couple of sailors on leave, Kelly and **Frank Sinatra** were accompanied by **Kathryn Grayson**, a **Sammy Cahn** and **Jule Styne** score - and Jerry - an animated mouse, who joined Kelly in a live-action/cartoon sequence that is still regarded as a classic of its kind.

After spending two years in the real US Navy during World War II, supervising training films, Kelly resumed at MGM with *Ziegfeld Follies* (1946), in which he sang and danced with **Fred Astaire** for the first time on screen, in 'The Babbitt And The Bromide'. Two years later he was reunited with Judy Garland for *The Pirate*, a somewhat underrated film, with a score by **Cole Porter** that included 'Be A Clown'. He then choreographed the 'Slaughter On Tenth Avenue' sequence in the Rodgers and Hart biopic *Words And Music*, in which he danced with **Vera-Ellen**, before joining Sinatra and Jules Munshin, first for the lively *Take Me Out To The Ball Game* (1949), and again for *On The Town*, 'the most inventive and effervescent movie musical Hollywood had thus far produced'. Although criticized for its truncation of the original Broadway score, *On The Town*, with its integrated music and plot, and the athletic dance sequences on the streets of New York, was acclaimed from all sides. After his triumph in *On The Town*, Kelly went on to *Summer Stock*, with Judy Garland again, before turning to what many consider to be the jewel in MGM's musical crown - *An American In Paris* (1951). Directed by **Vincente Minnelli**, and set in an idealized version of Paris, Kelly and his partner, **Leslie Caron**, danced exquisitely to a **Gershwin** score that included 'I Got Rhythm', 'Our Love Is Here To Stay', ''S Wonderful' and 'I'll Build A Stairway To Paradise'. The film ended with a 17-minute ballet sequence, a 'summation of Gene Kelly's work as a film dancer and choreographer, allowing him his full range of style - classical ballet, modern ballet, Cohanesque hoofing, tapping, jitterbugging, and sheer athletic expressionism'. It won eight Academy Awards, including one for best picture. Kelly received a special Oscar 'in appreciation of his versatility as an actor, singer, director, and dancer, and specifically for his brilliant achievements in the art of choreography on film'. If *An American In Paris* was MGM's jewel, then *Singin' In The Rain* (1952), was probably its financial plum - arguably the most popular Hollywood musical of them all. Produced by **Arthur Freed**, who also wrote the songs with **Nacio Herb Brown**, the film's witty screenplay, by **Betty Comden** and **Adolph Green**, dealt with the Hollywood silent movie industry trying to come to terms with talking pictures. **Debbie Reynolds** and **Donald O'Connor** joined Kelly in the joyous spoof, and sang and danced to a score that included 'You Were Meant For Me', 'Make 'Em Laugh', 'Good Mornin'' and 'Moses Supposes'. The scene in which Kelly sings the title song, while getting completely drenched, is probably the most requested film clip in the history of the musical cinema.

For *Deep In My Heart* (1955), the **Sigmund Romberg** biopic, Kelly went back to his roots and danced with his younger brother, Fred, in one of the film's high spots, 'I Love To Go Swimmin' With Wimmen'. Kelly's final major musical projects for MGM were *Brigadoon* (1954) and *It's Always Fair Weather* (1955). In the former, 'the magical story of a Scottish village long lost to history and coming to life once every hundred years for a single day', Kelly co-starred with **Cyd Charisse** and Van Johnson in a production that was criticized for being shot in Cinemascope, and in the studio, rather than on location. For the latter film in 1955, Kelly co-starred with **Dan Dailey** and **Michael Kidd** for what was essentially a satirical swipe at the cynical commercialism of the US television industry - with music. His next project, *Invitation To The Dance* (1956), with script, choreography, and direction by Kelly, consisted of three unrelated episodes, all entirely danced, with Kelly accompanied by a classically trained troupe. A commercial failure in the USA, it was acclaimed in some parts of Europe, and awarded the grand prize at the West Berlin film festival in 1958. Following its success there, Kelly choreographed a new ballet for the Paris Opera's resident company, and was made a Chevalier of the Legion of Honor by the French government. *Les Girls* (1957) was Kelly's final MGM musical, and Cole Porter's last Hollywood score - the golden era of screen musicals was over. Subsequently, Kelly played several straight roles in films such as *Marjorie Morningstar* and *Inherit The Wind*, but spent much of his time as a director on projects such as Richard Rodgers and **Oscar Hammerstein**'s Broadway musical *Flower Drum Song*, and 20th Century Fox's $24,000,000 extravaganza, *Hello, Dolly!* (1969), which starred **Barbra Streisand**, Walter Matthau and a young **Michael Crawford**. In 1974, he was back on the screen in *That's Entertainment!*, 'a nostalgia bash, featuring scenes from nearly 100 MGM musicals'. It became a surprise hit, and two years later, Kelly and Fred Astaire hosted the inevitable sequel, *That's Entertainment, Part 2*. After viewing all that vintage footage, it would be interesting to know Kelly's real opinions on a more modern musical film, such as *Xanadu* (1980), in which he appeared with **Olivia Newton-John**. By then, together with director **Stanley Donen**, the complete Arthur Freed Unit, and the rest of the talented personnel who produced most of his musicals at MGM, Kelly, with his athletic performance, choreography and direction, had completed a body of work that was only equalled by the other master of dance on film, Fred Astaire - but in a very different style. Whereas Astaire purveyed the image of a smooth man about town, with top hat, white tie and tails, Kelly's preferred to appear casual in sports shirt, slacks and white socks. As he said himself: 'Astaire represents the aristocracy when he dances - I represent the proletariat!'.

● ALBUMS: *Song And Dance Man* (1954)★★★★, *Singin' In The Rain Again* (Decca 1978)★★, *Best Of Gene Kelly - From MGM Films* (MCA 1988)★★★, *Great MGM Stars* (MGM 1991)★★★, *Gotta Dance! The Best Of Gene Kelly* (1994)★★★, and film soundtracks.

● FURTHER READING: *Gene Kelly: A Biography*, Clive Hirschhorn. *The Films Of Gene Kelly*, Tony Thomas. *Gene Kelly*, J. Basinger.

● FILMS: *For Me And My Gal* (1942), *Pilot No. 5* (1943), *Du Barry Was A Lady* (1943), *Thousands Cheer* (1943), *The Cross Of Lorraine* (1943), *Cover Girl* (1944), *Christmas Holiday* (1944), *Anchors Aweigh* (1945), *Ziegfeld Follies* (1946), *Living In A Big Way* (1947), *The Pirate* (1948), *The Three Musketeers* (1948), *Words And Music* (1948), *Take Me Out To The Ball Game* (1949), *On The Town* (1949), *The Black Hand* (1950), *Summer Stock* (1950), *An American In Paris* (1951), *It's A Big Country* (1952), *Singin' In The Rain* (1952), *The Devil Makes Three* (1952), *Brigadoon* (1954), *Crest Of The Wave* (1954), *Deep In My Heart* (1955), *It's Always Fair Weather* (1955), *Invitation To The Dance* (1956), *The Happy Road* (1957), *Les Girls* (1957), *Marjorie Morningstar* (1958), *The Tunnel Of Love* as director (1958), *Inherit The Wind* (1960), *Gigot* as director (1962), *Let's Make Love* (1960), *What A Way To Go* (1964), *The Young Girls Of Rochefort* (1968) *A Guide For The Married Man* as director (1967), *Hello, Dolly!* as director (1969), *The Cheyenne Social Club* as director and producer (1970), *40 Carats* (1973), *That's Entertainment!* as narrator (1974), *That's Entertainment, Part 2* as narrator (1976), *Viva Knievel!* (1977), *Xanadu* (1980), *Reporters* (1981), *That's Dancing!* (1985).

Kelly, George

b. 31 July 1915, Miami, Florida, USA, 24 May 1998. Kelly began playing tenor saxophone in childhood and was a bandleader in his home state while still in his teenage years. After playing with several **territory bands** during the late 30s he joined Al Cooper's **Savoy Sultans** in New York. After leaving the Sultans, he played in and around New York for the rest of the 40s and on through the 50s. He also worked as a commercial arranger and songwriter, with his songs covered by artists including **Sarah Vaughan**. After playing with drummer **William 'Cozy' Cole**'s quintet for a lengthy period, Kelly switched to piano as accompanist for the **Ink Spots** from 1970 to 1976. Occasional visits further afield attracted a small amount of attention, but it was not until the late 70s that he made an impact on the jazz world's consciousness. In 1979, **David 'Panama' Francis**, who had played in Kelly's Florida band, formed a new version of the Savoy Sultans and invited Kelly into the group. Thanks to successful records and hugely popular appearances at festivals around the world, Kelly's qualities were widely recognized. During the 80s and into the early 90s he worked with Francis and led his own bands for tours and record dates, amongst which was a set paying tribute to **Don Redman** on which Kelly was joined by **Glenn Zottola**. A fine tenor saxophonist with a relaxed style, Kelly was also an accomplished arranger and entertaining singer.

● ALBUMS: *Stealin' Apples* (1976)★★★, *George Kelly In Cimiez* (1979)★★★, with David 'Panama' Francis *Gettin' In*

The Groove (1979)★★, *Fine And Dandy* (1982)★★★, *Live At The West End Cafe* (1982)★★, *The Cotton Club* (1983)★★★, *George Kelly Plays The Music Of Don Redman* (Stash 1984)★★★.

Kelly, Jack

b. *c.*1905, Mississippi, USA, d. *c.*1960, Memphis, Tennessee, USA. Kelly's first jug band, formed in 1925, included Frank Stokes, Dan Sane and **Will Batts**. Kelly, Batts, Sane and juggist D.M. Higgs recorded as the South Memphis Jug Band in 1933. (Kelly, Batts and a guitarist, possibly Ernest Lawlars, recorded again in 1939.) Their sound was characterized by Kelly's vibrant singing, the broad, bluesy tones of Batts' fiddle and the complex interplay of twin guitars. Kelly's penchant for re-recording the tune of 'Highway No. 61 Blues' is offset by a talent for striking lyrics. After the band broke up in 1934, Kelly worked either solo, with Stokes, or in *ad hoc* bands. In 1953, he recorded for **Sun**, playing piano with **Walter 'Shakey' Horton** and Joe Hill Louis. A 78 rpm record was scheduled, but never released; part of one side was issued many years later.
● COMPILATIONS: *Sun Records The Blues Years* (1985)★★★, *Jack Kelly & His South Memphis Jug Band 1933-1939* (Blues Document 1991)★★★.

Kelly, Jo Ann

b. 5 January 1944, Streatham, London, England, d. 21 October 1990. This expressive blues singer, sister of **Blues Band** guitarist **Dave Kelly**, was renowned as one of the finest of the genre. She made her recording debut in 1964 on a privately pressed EP and appeared on several specialist labels before contributing a series of excellent performances to guitarist Tony McPhee's **Groundhogs** recordings, issued under the aegis of United Artists. Her self-titled solo album displayed a hard, gritty vocal delivery evocative of **Memphis Minnie** and confirmed the arrival of a major talent. In 1969, the singer appeared live with **Mississippi Fred McDowell** and later made several tours of the USA. Kelly became a constituent part of the British blues circuit, recording with the **John Dummer Blues Band**, **Chilli Willi And The Red Hot Peppers** and **Stefan Grossman**. In 1972, she completed an album with Woody Mann, John Miller and acoustic guitarist **John Fahey**, before forming a group, Spare Rib, which performed extensively throughout the UK. Kelly recorded a second solo album, *Do It*, in 1976 and maintained her popularity throughout the 70s and 80s with appearances at European blues festivals and judicious live work in Britain. Her last performance was at a festival in Lancashire in August 1990, when she was given the award for Female Singer of the Year by the British Blues Federation. Having apparently recovered from an operation in 1989 to remove a malignant brain tumour, she died in October 1990.
● ALBUMS: *Jo Ann Kelly* (Columbia 1969)★★★, *Jo Ann Kelly, With Fahey, Mann And Miller* (1972)★★★, with Pete Emery *Do It* (Red Rag 1976)★★★, *It's Whoopie* (1978)★★,

with Mississippi Fred McDowell *Standing At The Burying Ground* (Red Lightnin' 1984)★★, *Just Restless* (Appaloosa 1984)★★★, *Women In (E)Motion* rec. 1988 (Indigo/Traditon & Moderne 1995)★★★.
● COMPILATIONS: with Tony McPhee *Same Thing On Our Minds* (Sunset 1969)★★, *Retrospect 1964-1972* (Connoisseur 1990)★★★.

Kelly, Keith

b. 1937, Selby, Yorkshire, England. This pop/rock, singer/guitarist was an original member of the **John Barry** Seven, who he had joined after spending three years in the Royal Air Force. He left Barry's group in 1959 and sang at the renowned 2Is coffee bar in Soho, London, where he was spotted by producer **George Martin**. Martin signed him to **Parlophone** and his first recording 'Tease Me' made the UK Top 20. The bespectacled singer (who reputedly wrote his hit on a London Underground train on the way to his flat in Shepherds Bush), managed to put the follow-up 'Listen Little Girl' into the lower reaches of the chart, but it was to be his last success. Kelly, one of the earliest UK rock singer-songwriters, briefly re-appeared with a single 'Save Your Love For Me' on **CBS** in 1965.

Kelly, Pat

b. 1949, Kingston, Jamaica, West Indies. Kelly spent a year in Springfield, Massachusetts, USA, during 1966, studying electronics, before returning to Jamaica. In 1967 he replaced **Slim Smith** as lead singer of the **Techniques**, who along with **Alton Ellis**, the **Paragons** and the **Melodians** were spearheading **Duke Reid**'s campaign to dominate Jamaican music via his epochal **rocksteady** productions. With Kelly's wholly distinctive and utterly beautiful falsetto soaring over the impeccable harmonies of **Winston Riley** and **Bruce Ruffin**, the trio easily maintained the flow of hits they had begun when Smith had been lead singer. Their first record, an adaptation of a **Curtis Mayfield** tune, 'You'll Want Me Back', retitled 'You Don't Care' in Jamaica, held the number 1 position in the local chart for six weeks. Their next, another Mayfield cover version, this time adapted from the **Impressions**' 'Minstrel And Queen' and retitled 'Queen Majesty', enjoyed similar hit status, as did the subsequent 'My Girl' and 'Love Is Not A Gamble'. All are *bona fide* classics of Jamaican vocal harmony, rocksteady style. In 1968 Kelly went solo, joining the roster of artists under the wing of the leading producer **Bunny Lee**. His first effort for Lee was another Mayfield cover version, 'Little Boy Blue'. Subsequently, he provided Lee with the biggest-selling Jamaican hit of 1969, 'How Long Will It Take', a landmark recording in that it was the first Jamaican record to feature a string arrangement, overdubbed when the song was released in the UK by the Palmer Brothers on their Unity label. Other hits and an album for Lee soon followed, and Kelly's superb, **Sam Cooke**-derived falsetto even came to the attention of the **Beatles**' **Apple** label, who reputedly offered Kelly a £25,000 contract. Unable to act on this offer because of prior contractual commitments, he returned to Jamaica disillusioned, where he recorded sporadically, enjoying a huge local hit for producer Phill Pratt in 1972, 'Talk About Love', as well as recording songs at Treasure Isle studios in the same period with former **Gaylad, B.B. Seaton**. He then returned to engineering, principally for the **Channel One** studios owned by the Hookim brothers. Throughout the late 70s and early 80s he continued recording, for Winston Riley, Phill Pratt, Bunny Lee and the London-based sound system owner Fatman. He still records occasionally, and his contribution as one of the great Jamaican soul voices cannot be underestimated.

● ALBUMS: *Pat Kelly Sings* (Pama 1969)★★★, *Talk About Love* (Terminal 1975)★★★★, *Lonely Man* (Burning Sounds 1978)★★, *One Man Stand* (Third World 1979)★★, *From Both Sides* (Ital 1980)★★★, *I Wish It Would Rain* (Joe Gibbs 1980)★★★, *Pat Kelly And Friends* (Chanan-Jah 1984)★★★, *One In A Million* (Sky Note 1984)★★, *Ordinary Man* (Body Music 1987)★★★, *Cry For You No More* (Blue Moon 1988)★★★.

● COMPILATIONS: *The Best Of Pat Kelly* (Vista Sounds 1983)★★★★.

Kelly, Paul

b. 1955, Adelaide, South Australia, Australia. Regarded as one of Australia's foremost lyricists, guitarist and singer Kelly began performing in the coffee shops in Adelaide, but moved to Melbourne and formed the High Rise Bombers in 1977. That band gave way in 1978 to Paul Kelly And The Dots who managed to record two albums and scored a minor Australian hit single with 'Billy Baxter'. The Dots suffered constant line-up changes which saw 15 musicians from various Melbourne bands pass through the ranks. The Paul Kelly Band followed in 1983, but the line-up changes continued and the group barely lasted a year. Kelly resurfaced with a solo acoustic album, *Post* which showcased his observations of the inner-city area of Melbourne. Encouraged by the response to *Post*, Kelly gathered together a band of high quality musicians, the Coloured Girls, who comprised Michael Armiger (bass), Michael Barclay (drums), Pedro Bull (keyboards), Steve Connolly (guitar) and Chris Coyne (saxophone). Subsequent albums have garnered more success and hit singles in Australia. The Coloured Girls were renamed the Messengers for tours and album releases in the USA and Europe, because of worries that the name had racist connotations. Ironically, Kelly is noted in Australia for his support of Aboriginal rights; indeed his 'Bicentennial' was a scathing attack on the Australian Bicentennial celebrations as seen from an Aboriginal viewpoint. He is in the vanguard of singer-songwriters in Australia, his contemporaries such as James Griffin, John Dowler, Steve Hoy, John Kennedy and Billy Baxter have not achieved his level of success.

● ALBUMS: with the Dots *Talk* (1981)★★★, *Manilla* (1982)★★★, *Post* (1985)★★★★, with the Coloured Girls/Messengers *Gossip* (1986)★★★, with the Coloured Girls/Messengers *Under The Sun* (1988)★★, with the Coloured Girls/Messengers *So Much Water Close To Home* (1989)★★★, with the Coloured Girls/Messengers *Comedy* (1991)★★, with the Messengers *Hidden Things* (1991)★★★, *Live, May 1992* (1992)★★, *Wanted Man* (1994)★★★.

● FURTHER READING: *Paul Kelly Lyrics*, Paul Kelly.

Kelly, Paula

b. 1920, USA, d. 2 April 1992, Costa Mesa, California, USA. An excellent band and ensemble singer with a vivacious personality, Kelly began her career in 1937 with top saxophonist **Dick Stabile**'s band, and then spent two years with **Al Donahue**. She joined **Glenn Miller** in 1941 as a featured singer with the Modernaires vocal group; her husband, Hal Dickinson, was founder-leader. Early in 1941 Kelly appeared in the first Glenn Miller movie, *Sun Valley Serenade*, in which the Modernaires sang classics such as 'Chattanooga Choo Choo' and 'I Know Why'. Later in the year she left Miller when former vocalist **Marion Hutton** rejoined the band. For a while Kelly sang with **Artie Shaw**, and then for **Bob Allen**'s band. In the mid-40s she rejoined the Modernaires when the group expanded to five. In the 50s they appeared in clubs and theatres, toured with **Bob Crosby**, and sang on his radio and television shows. They also featured with Crosby, **Frankie Laine** and **Billy Daniels** in the movie *When You're Smiling* (1950), and in *The Glenn Miller Story* (1954). After Dickinson died on 18 November 1970, Kelly and the Modernaires worked with ex-Miller sideman **Tex Beneke**'s band and Miller's original boy vocalist, **Ray Eberle**, riding on the nostalgia boom of the 70s. Kelly's records with the Modernaires included 'Jukebox Saturday Night', 'There, I've Said It Again', 'You Belong To My Heart', 'Goody Goody', 'Margie' and 'Stop, Look And Listen'. With Dick Stabile she recorded 'Lost And Found' and 'My Heart Is Taking Lessons'; with Al Donahue, 'Jeepers Creepers', 'Moon Love', 'The Lambeth Walk', 'Stairway To The Stars' and 'South American Way'; and with Artie Shaw, 'Someone's Rocking My Dreamboat' and 'I Don't Want To Walk Without You'. Kelly retired in 1978, and in the late 80s her daughter, Paula Kelly Jnr., was reported to be singing an updated version of 'Jukebox Saturday Night' with the Modernaires, accompanied by a 15-piece band led by the same Tex Beneke.

Kelly, R.

b. Robert Kelly, *c.*1969, Chicago, Illinois, USA. Dance/R&B artist who made his first impact with the release of a debut album in 1991, with his band, Public Announcement. Kelly grew up in the housing projects of Chicago's South Side, but channelled his energies away from fast money-making schemes and into long-term musicianship. He had a natural flair for most instruments, eventually becoming, more by accident than design, a useful busking act. It earned the young Kelly a living, until constant police disruptions forced him to reconsider his employment. He put together the R&B group MGM, and went on to win a national talent contest on the *Big Break* television show, hosted by **Natalie Cole**. Unfortunately, that group's energy dissipated, and his next major break came when manager Barry Hankerson spotted him while auditioning for a play at the Regal Theatre in Chicago. He soon had Kelly acting as musical co-ordinator/producer for a slew of acts, including **Gladys Knight**, David Peaston, **Aaliyah** (who Kelly married in August 1994) and the **Hi-Five** (who had a number 1 single, 'Quality Time', with Kelly at the controls). His diversity was confirmed with his work with the **Winans** gospel family, notably a duet with Ronald Winans on 'That Extra Mile'. However, all this would be surpassed by the success of his second album, *12 Play*, which stayed on top of the R&B charts for nine weeks. Two huge singles were included on the set, 'Sex Me (Parts I & II)' and 'Bump 'N Grind' (US number 1/UK number 8). As if from nowhere, despite a long apprenticeship, Kelly seemed to have acquired the Midas touch. 'I Believe I Can Fly' became another massive hit when it was featured as the theme for the 1997 movie *Space Jam*.

● ALBUMS: *Born Into The '90s* (Jive 1991)★★★, *12 Play* (Jive 1993)★★★★, *R. Kelly* (Jive 1995)★★★.

● VIDEOS: *12 Play-The Hit Videos Vol. 1* (Jive 1994), *Top Secret Down Low Videos* (6 West 1996).

Kelly, Sandy

b. 27 February 1954, Ballintogher, Co. Sligo, Eire, but raised in Wales. Kelly became a professional in her teens, singing with the Fairways Showband in Ireland and then with her younger sister Barbara and two cousins as the Duskeys. They represented Ireland in the 1982 Eurovision Song Contest. After developing a successful solo career in Ireland as a middle-of-the-road country singer, Kelly decided to promote the songs of her favourite performer, **Patsy Cline**. In her 1992 K-Tel video *The Voice Of Sandy Kelly - The Songs Of Patsy Clyne* (sic), she sang 13 songs by her musical hero, backed by the **Jordanaires**. Kelly was teamed with **George Hamilton IV** in the stage show *Patsy Cline - A Musical Tribute*, which toured the UK and Ireland for a year, including a three-month West End run. Sandy's husband, Michael, plays bass and acts as musical director while her sister, Barbara Ellis (b. 8 October 1961, Mohill, Co. Leitrim, Eire) records for K-Tel (Ireland), releasing an album, *Breakin' Ground*, in 1994. Kelly's 1994 album *Kelly's Heroes* includes duets with **Willie Nelson**, **Johnny Cash** and both George Hamilton IV and V.

● ALBUMS: *Paradise Tonight* (CBS Ireland 1986)★★★, *I Need To Be In Love* (K-Tel Ireland 1989)★★★★, *An Evening With Sandy Kelly* (K-Tel Ireland 1990)★★, *The Voice Of Sandy Kelly - The Songs Of Patsy Cline* subsequently repackaged as *A Musical Tribute To Patsy Cline* (K-Tel Ireland 1991)★★★, *Everytime You Need A Friend* (K-Tel Ireland 1992)★★★, *Kelly's Heroes* (K-Tel Ireland 1994)★★★.

● VIDEOS: *An Evening With Sandy Kelly* (Prism 1990).

Kelly, Vance

b. 24 January 1954, Chicago, Illinois, USA. Kelly's urban soul-blues came to prominence in 1995 when his debut album, *Call Me*, won a *Living Blues* magazine award in 1995. Rooted in the music of the Windy City from birth, Kelly was born on Maxwell Street, where musicians played impromptu open-air sets every Sunday. His father was a gospel musician, while his uncle was an occasional blues player. By the age of seven Kelly was already playing guitar, and began sitting in at blues clubs in his early teens, backing the West-Side singer Mary Lane. His musical education was broadened in the late seventies by work in the disco field, but it was an invitation to join saxman **A.C. Reed**'s band in 1987 that provided Kelly with an opportunity to gain valuable experience on the road. After playing with Reed for three years Kelly moved on to develop his own sound, which not only reflected his diversity by mixing blues, R&B, funk and disco, but also catered to the demands of the club audiences: 'If the older folks come in, I want to take them back to the Delta blues. When the middle-aged folks come in, they just want to hear regular-type blues. If a younger crowd comes in, they want to hear up-to-date type blues.' Though hardly known outside Chicago before the release of *Call Me*, that album's critical reception saw Kelly reaping the rewards of his long apprenticeship. The follow-up, *Joyriding In The Subway*, featured John Primer repeating his co-guitar and production duties from the debut album, and was another fine mix of cover versions and originals (co-written by Kelly and his daughter, Vivian), covering a variety of styles from traditional blues to contemporary R&B. An excellent guitarist and singer, Kelly has established himself as one of the leading exponents of modern Chicago blues.

● ALBUMS: *Call Me* (Wolf 1994)★★★★, *Joyriding In The Subway* (Wolf 1995)★★★.

Kelly, Wynton

b. 2 December 1931, Jamaica, West Indies, d. 12 April 1971. Raised in New York, Kelly first played piano professionally with various R&B bands, where his musical associates included **Eddie 'Lockjaw' Davis**. In the early 50s, he played with **Dizzy Gillespie**, **Dinah Washington** and **Lester Young**. In 1954, after military service, he rejoined both Gillespie and Washington for brief stints and later played with many important contemporary musicians, notably **Charles Mingus** and **Miles Davis**, with whom he worked from 1959-63. Kelly also led his own trio, using the bass (**Paul Chambers**) and drums (**Jimmy Cobb**) from Davis' band, and also recorded successfully with a variety of artists such as **Wes Montgomery**, **Freddie Hubbard** and **George Coleman**. A subtle and inventive player, Kelly's style was individual even if his work denotes his awareness both of his contemporaries and the piano masters of an earlier generation. Throughout his records there is a constant sense of freshness and an expanding maturity of talent, which made his death, in

1971, following an epileptic fit, all the more tragic.

● ALBUMS: *New Faces, New Sounds* (1951)★★★, *Piano Interpretations By Wynton Kelly* (Blue Note 1951)★★★, *The Big Band Sound Of Dizzy Gillespie* (1957)★★★, *Wynton Kelly Piano* (Riverside 1957)★★★, *Wynton Kelly i* (1958)★★★, *Autumn Leaves* (1959)★★★, *Kelly Blue* (Riverside 1959)★★★★★, *Kelly Great!* (Vee Jay 1959)★★★, *Kelly At Midnight* (Vee Jay 1960)★★★, *Wynton Kelly ii* (Vee Jay 1961)★★★, with Miles Davis *Some Day My Prince Will Come* (Columbia 1961)★★★★, *Miles Davis At Carnegie Hall* (1961)★★★★, *The Wynton Kelly Trio With Claus Ogermann And His Orchestra i* (1963)★★★, *The Wynton Kelly Trio With Claus Ogermann And His Orchestra ii* (1964)★★★, *Comin' In The Back Door* (Verve 1964)★★★, *It's All Right* (Verve 1964)★★★, *Undiluted* (Verve 1965)★★★, with Wes Montgomery *Smokin' At The Half Note* (Verve 1965)★★★, *Blues On Purpose* (Xanadu 1965)★★★, *Wynton Kelly And Wes Montgomery* (1965)★★★, *Full View* (1967)★★★, *Wynton Kelly And George Coleman In Concert* (1968)★★★, *In Concert* (Affinity 1981)★★★, *Live In Baltimore* (Affinity 1984)★★★, *Wrinkles* (Affinity 1986)★★★, *Last Trio Session* (Delmark 1988)★★★, *Takin' Charge* (Le Jazz 1993)★★★.

Kemp, Hal

b. James Harold Kemp, 27 March 1904, Marion, Alabama, USA, d. 21 December 1940, near Madera, California, USA. One of the greatest bandleaders of his generation, Kemp's early death robbed the dance band world of one of its most innovative talents. Long after his demise the memory of his orchestra's distinctive, staccato rhythms would be kept alive by numerous artists, particularly **Henry Jerome**. Kemp formed his first orchestra, a quintet dubbed the Merrymakers, while still attending high school in Charlotte, North Carolina. He also played in various campus bands while a student at the University of North Carolina. By his senior year he had found the core musicians with which he would form his first professional version of the Hal Kemp Orchestra in the mid-20s. The nucleus of this band was John Scott Trotter (piano and arranger), Saxie Dowell (saxophone) and **Skinnay Ennis** (drums, and later the band's featured vocalist). Strong shows in the North Carolina region brought them to the attention of **Paul Specht** and through him **Fred Waring**. Waring brought the group to New York, but a dispute with the manager of the ballroom they had been booked to play left them unemployed and without any funds of their own. But with Waring backing them, they survived until he was able to find replacement bookings for them. They gradually found a foothold in New York first at the Strand Roof, then the Hotel Manger and New Yorker Hotel. Their biggest break, however, came when Otto Roth booked them at his Blackhawk Restaurant in Chicago in 1932. A long engagement here ensured radio play over the WGN and Mutual Networks, quickly establishing them as a top drawer dance band attraction. They were only able to break their contract with the Blackhawk's management to cash in on this new found fame when Kemp discov-

ered **Kay Kyser**, whose band replaced him. Engagements at premier venues followed, including the Waldorf-Astoria, Pennsylvania, the Drake and the Palmer House, while a series of sponsored radio spots, including the *Chesterfield Program*, *The Quaker Oats Program*, and *The Gulf Gas Program*, secured national exposure. Their records too, released on **RCA-Victor** at this time, were selling in large quantities. The Cocoanut Grove (Los Angeles) and the Mark Hopkins Hotel (San Francisco) were booked for the band as their Californian debut. While commuting between those two venues Kemp was involved in an automobile accident caused by a heavy morning fog. He died in hospital two days later on 21 December 1940. The band played the Mark Hopkins' engagement without him, with vocalist **Bob Allen** eventually taking over as the leader. He then turned over that responsibility to **Art Jarrett**. A memorial album was issued on Victor Records. Twenty years after Kemp's death old friend and colleague Skinnay Ennis recorded a tribute album for **Philips**, which included such Kemp standards as 'How I'll Miss You When The Summer Is Gone'.

● ALBUMS: *This Is Hal Kemp* (RCA Victor 50s)★★★, *Hal Kemp & His Orchestra 1927-31* (RCA 50s)★★★, *Great Dance Bands* (RCA Victor 1960)★★★★, *Hal Kemp Volume 1* (Hindsight 1988)★★★, *On The Air 1940* (Aircheck 1988)★★★★, *Hal Kemp Volume 2* (Hindsight 1989)★★★.

● FILMS: *Radio City Revels* (1938).

Kemp, Wayne

b. 1 June 1941, Greenwood, Arkansas, USA. Kemp's father was a motor mechanic and as a teenager Kemp drove racing cars. His interest changed to music and, forming his own band, he toured the south-west. In 1963, he gained fame as a songwriter when **George Jones** had a big hit with 'Love Bug'. After his own recording of 'The Image Of Me' had made little impression, **Conway Twitty**'s version became a number 5 country hit. Twitty had further major success with Kemp's songs 'Next In Line', 'Darling You Know I Wouldn't Lie' and 'That's When She Started To Stop Loving You'. Kemp's own first hit came in 1969 with his **Decca** recording of 'Won't You Come Home'. Between then and 1982, also recording on MCA, United Artists and **Mercury**, he charted 20 more hits, the only Top 20 entrant being 'Honky Tonk Wine' (1973). In 1983, he had a minor hit on Door Knob with his song 'Don't Send Me No Angels' (the song was later successfully recorded by both **Ricky Van Shelton** and George Jones). Kemp remains active as a writer but his last chart hit was a duet with **Bobby G. Rice**, 'Red Neck And Over Thirty', in 1986.

● ALBUMS: *Wayne Kemp* (1972)★★★, *Kentucky Sunshine* (1974)★★.

Kemper, Ronnie

When USA-born Kemper turned to bandleading in 1942, he had already made his name with **Dick Jergen**'s Orchestra, playing on their massive hit, 'Cecilia'. He also appeared frequently in **Horace Heidt**'s *Pot Of Gold* radio show, and the film of similar title. He used this reputation to piece together his first dance band in San Francisco with vocalist Ruth Russell. The most notable musical sideman was **Claude Gordon**, who would later form a dance band in his own right. Original compositions were written for the purpose, including 'It's A Hundred To One I'm In Love', 'Knit One - Purl Two', 'The Doodlebug Song' and 'What You Gonna Do With Somebody Else', though their theme tune remained 'Cecilia', which always garnered a rapturous reception from audiences. However, Horace Heidt was reluctant to free Kemper from his contract with him, which stipulated that his musicians could only be released if America was attacked during World War II. Luckily for Kemper, a Japanese submarine made a token effort at bombarding Brookings, Oregon, in the summer of 1942 and thus facilitated Kemper's freedom. Kemper took up the cudgels and began touring in earnest, but his career ended prematurely when he was, ironically, called into the services himself. After the war ended he chose not to pursue his bandleading career.

Kendalls

Royce Kendall (b. 25 September 1934, St. Louis, Missouri, USA) and Jeannie Kendall (b. 30 November 1954, St. Louis, Missouri, USA). Royce learned guitar from the age of five and formed a duo, the Austin Brothers, with his brother Floyce. After serving in the US Army, Royce and his wife Melba started a hairdressing business in St. Louis. Their only child, Jeannie, began harmonizing with her father on old-time country songs, and they were soon entertaining family and friends. Their first record, for a small local label, was 'Round Round Round', and their talents were recognized in Nashville by **Pete Drake**, although they simply recorded country versions of pop hits such as 'Leavin' On A Jet Plane', 'Proud Mary' and 'You've Lost That Lovin' Feelin''. Jeannie Kendall was among the backing singers on **Ringo Starr**'s Nashville album *Beaucoups Of Blues*. The family moved to Hendersonville, just outside Nashville, and the Kendalls had success with **Dot Records**, notably 'Two Divided By Love' and 'Everything I Own'. In the mid-70s, Ovation Records started a country division and the Kendalls, who had a contemporary sound with traditional overtones, were to test the market. When a single of 'Live And Let Live' was released, Ovation found that country disc jockeys preferred the b-side, 'Heaven's Just A Sin Away'. It topped the US country charts and became the Country Single of the Year. The father and daughter followed the record with other 'cheating' songs, notably 'It Don't Feel Like Sinnin' To Me' and 'Pittsburg Stealers'. They had a further US country number 1 with the double-sided 'Sweet Desire'/'Old Fashioned Love', plus further Top 10 hits with 'I'm Already Blue' and **Dolly Parton**'s 'Put It Off Until Tomorrow'. In 1981, they moved to **Mercury** and continued their success with 'Teach Me How To Cheat' and 'If You're Waiting On Me (You're

Backing Up)'. They had their third chart-topper in 1984 with 'Thank God For The Radio'. Jeannie, who takes most of the lead vocals, married band member Mack Watkins. The Kendalls' chart success has deserted them, but they continue to tour.

● ALBUMS: *Meet The Kendalls* (Stop 1970)★★★, *Two Divided By Love* (Dot 1972)★★★, *Leavin' On A Jet Plane* (1974)★★★, *Let The Music Play* aka *Heaven's Just A Sin Away* (1977)★★★, *Old Fashioned Love* (1978)★★★, *1978 Grammy Awards Winners: Best Country Duo* (Gusto 1978)★★, *Just Like Real People* (1979)★★★, *Heart Of The Matter* (1979)★★★, *Lettin' You On A Feelin'* (Mercury 1981)★★, *Stickin' Together* (Mercury 1982)★★★, *Moving Train* (Mercury 1983)★★, *Two Heart Harmony* (Mercury 1985)★★★, *Fire At First Sight* (MCA 1986)★★★, *Break The Routine* (Step One 1987)★★★, *Make A Dance* (Branson 1995)★★★.

● COMPILATIONS: *16 Greatest Hits* (Deluxe 1988)★★★.

Kendricks, Eddie

b. 17 December 1939, Union Springs, Alabama, USA, d. 5 October 1992, Alabama, USA. Kendricks was a founder-member of the **Primes** in the late 50s, an R&B vocal group that moved to Detroit in 1960 and formed the basis of the **Temptations**. His wavering falsetto vocals were an essential part of the group's sound throughout their first decade on **Motown Records**. He was singled out as lead vocalist on their first major hit, 'The Way You Do The Things You Do', and was also given a starring role on the 1966 US number 29 'Get Ready'. **David Ruffin** gradually assumed the leadership of the group, but in 1971 Kendricks was showcased on 'Just My Imagination', one of their most affecting love ballads. Kendricks chose this moment to announce that he was leaving the Temptations, weary of the production extravaganzas that **Norman Whitfield** was creating for the group. His initial solo albums failed to establish a distinctive style, and it was 1973 before he enjoyed his first hit, with an edited version of the disco classic 'Keep On Truckin''. The accompanying album, *Eddie Kendricks*, was in more traditional style, while *Boogie Down!* had Kendricks displaying emotion over a succession of dance-oriented backing tracks. Rather than repeat a winning formula, Kendricks bravely chose to revise his sound on *For You* in 1974. The first side of the album was a masterful arrangement of vocal harmonies, with Kendricks submerged by the backing. 'Shoeshine Boy' was extracted as a single, and followed 'Keep On Truckin'' and 'Boogie Down' to the summit of the soul charts. *The Hit Man* and *He's A Friend* repeated the experiment with less conviction, and by the time he left Motown for **Arista** in 1978, Kendricks had been forced to submit to the prevailing disco current. After a run of uninspiring efforts, *Love Keys* on **Atlantic** in 1981 was a welcome return to form, teaming the singer with the **Muscle Shoals** horns and the **Holland/Dozier/Holland** production team. Poor sales brought this liaison to an end, and Kendricks returned to the Temptations fold for a reunion tour and album in 1982. When this venture was completed, he formed a duo with fellow ex-Temptation David Ruffin, and the pair were showcased at **Live Aid** as well as on a live album by **Hall And Oates**. This exposure allowed them to secure a contract as a duo, and *Ruffin And Kendricks* in 1988 represented the most successful blending of their distinctive vocal styles since the mid-60s. Kendricks died of lung cancer in 1992, after having already had his right lung removed the previous year.

● ALBUMS: *All By Myself* (Tamla 1971)★★★, *People...Hold On* (Tamla 1972)★★★, *Eddie Kendricks* (Tamla 1973)★★★, *Boogie Down!* (Tamla 1974)★★★, *For You* (Tamla 1974)★★★, *The Hit Man* (Tamla 1975)★★★, *He's A Friend* (Tamla 1976)★★★, *Goin' Up In Smoke* (Tamla 1976)★★★, *Slick* (Tamla 1977)★★★, *Vintage '78* (Arista 1978)★★, *Something More* (Arista 1979)★★, *Love Keys* (Atlantic 1981)★★★, with David Ruffin *Ruffin And Kendricks* (RCA 1988)★★★.

● COMPILATIONS: *At His Best* (Motown 1990)★★★.

Kenickie

One of a number of UK 'lo-fi' indie groups heavily tipped to make inroads into the charts following the success of **Bis**, Kenickie, named after the character in *Grease*, were formed in August 1994 after Lauren Le Laverne (vocals), Marie Du Santiago (guitar) and Emmy-Kate Montrose (bass) left their convent school in Tyne And Wear, Sunderland. Drafting in Le Laverne's brother, Johnny Le Laverne, nicknamed X, as their drummer, they established the group as a means of staying in touch while they pursued courses in further education. By the mid-90s their demo tapes were receiving airplay from **John Peel**, leading to the release of their debut single, 'Cat Suit', on Newcastle independent Slampt Records in April 1995. Their second release, the *Skillex* EP, followed for journalist Simon Reynold's hip Fierce Panda Records. By 1996 they had been signed to Emidisc, the new major-backed label launched by Bob Stanley and Pete Wiggs of **Saint Etienne** with **EMI Records** A&R director, Tris Penna. The first single to result from the new contract was 'Punka', but the group showed a commendable indifference to music industry manners, turning down a cover feature for *Melody Maker* before its release because of fear of 'over-exposure'. *Kenickie At The Club* was a confident and punchy debut containing short, sharp, power-pop songs.

● ALBUMS: *Kenickie At The Club* (EMI 1997)★★★.

Kennedy Rose

Mary Ann Kennedy and Pam Rose, who together form 90s country duo Kennedy Rose, are session singers who decided to work together. Pam Rose had a few minor entries on the US country charts in the late 70s, the most notable being 'It's Not Supposed To Be That Way', which featured **Willie Nelson**'s vocals. Mary Ann Kennedy wrote 'Ring On Her Finger, Time On Her Hands' (**Lee Greenwood**) and 'I'll Still Be Loving You' (**Restless Heart**). Together they provided backing vocals for **Emmylou Harris** and **Sting**, who signed

them to his company, Pangaea. Their songs have been covered by **Reba McEntire**, **Art Garfunkel** and Restless Heart, and they wrote **Martina McBride**'s 1995 country hit 'Safe In The Arms Of Love'. They feature a driving, acoustic-based country rock sound, playing many of the instruments themselves and, unusually for Nashville, including instrumentals. Their first album, *Hai Ku*, featured 'Love Like This'. *Walk The Line* features guest appearances by Emmylou Harris and Sting and owes as much to rock as to country.

● ALBUMS: *Hai Ku* (IRS 1989)★★, *Walk The Line* (IRS 1994)★★★★.

Kennedy, Brian

b. Belfast, Northern Ireland. Having grown up in the notorious Falls Road district of Belfast, Kennedy relocated to London at the age of 18. Now hugely popular in his home country and beginning to make a serious impact throughout the rest of Europe, singer/songwriter Brian Kennedy originally launched his career with much less fanfare. Two albums, one solo, the other with ex-**Fairground Attraction** songwriter Mark Nevin, had been released to negligible interest in the early 90s. After being released from his contract, Kennedy flew to New Orleans and began travelling around the USA, employing his unusual, somewhat feminine vocals at bar-singing sessions. On his return, he became a regular associate and duettist with **Van Morrison**. This led to a recording contract, ironically with the same record label, **RCA Records**, which had dropped him a few years previously. As well as its Irish success, *A Better Man* also reached number 19 in the UK charts, his previous poor fortunes seemingly permanently reversed.

● ALBUMS: *The Great War Of Words* (1991)★★★★, as Sweetmouth *Sweetmouth* (1992)★★★, *A Better Man* (BMG 1996)★★★★.

Kennedy, Jerry

b. Jerry Glenn Kennedy, 10 August 1940, Caddo Parish, Shreveport, Louisiana, USA. Kennedy has been a featured session guitarist for many top Nashville country stars and in the early 60s, he played lead guitar on some of **Elvis Presley**'s recordings. He also worked with guitarist Charlie Tomlinson and recorded several guitar albums with him under the name of Tom And Jerry. After he became a record producer with **Mercury**/Phonogram, he produced the recordings of many artists including **Roy Orbison**, **Bobby Bare**, **Charlie Rich**, **Patti Page**, **Roger Miller**, the **Statler Brothers**, **Reba McEntire** and **Becky Hobbs**. He was responsible for **Jerry Lee Lewis**'s commercial renaissance in the late 60s, when he steered him back towards the country market. He has also worked in several administration posts within the music industry, including that of Vice-President of A&R of the Country Division of Mercury.

● ALBUMS: *Jerry Kennedy's Dancing Guitars (Rock Elvis' Hits)* (1962)★★ *Jerry Kennedy's Guitars & Strings Play The Golden*

Standards (Smash 1963)★★, *From Nashville To Soulville* (Smash 1965)★★, *Jerry Kennedy Plays With All Due Respect To Kris Kristofferson* (Mercury 1971)★★★, *Jerry Kennedy & Friends* (1974)★★★; as Tom And Jerry *Guitar's Greatest Hits Volume 1* (Mercury 1961)★★, *Guitar's Greatest Hits Volume 2* (Mercury 1962)★★, *Guitars Play The Sound Of Ray Charles* (Mercury 1962)★★, *Surfin' Hootenanny* (Mercury 1963)★★.

Kennedy, Jesse 'Tiny'

b. 20 December 1925, probably Chattanooga, Tennessee, USA. Blues shouter Kennedy first came to prominence in Kansas City in November 1949, where he recorded a session for **Capitol Records** with **Jay McShann**'s Quintet. In 1951, he joined **Tiny Bradshaw**'s Orchestra as vocalist, recording two unusual tracks with Bradshaw's band for King Records; the tracks were curious in that the two risqué blues feature Kennedy duetting with himself as both deep-voiced macho male and shrill female! While touring with the orchestra in the south in 1951-52, Kennedy made some recordings under his own name with local musicians for Trumpet Records at **Sam Phillips**' Sun studio in Memphis, including the successful 'Strange Kind Of Feelin'', which was later covered by **Elmore James**. Gotham Records' 20th Century subsidiary leased the hit for the northern market, and Trumpet Records tried unsuccessfully to record another hit by Kennedy in New York City in 1953. Nevertheless, he recorded a fine session for **RCA**-Victor's Groove subsidiary in April 1955 as the contradictory 'Big Tiny Kennedy'; the recordings included a remake of his Trumpet hit, after which he seems to have drifted into obscurity.
● ALBUMS: with Clayton Love, Jerry 'Boogie' McCain *Strange Kind Of Feelin'* (1990)★★★.

Kennedy, Jimmy

b. 20 July 1902, Omagh, Co. Tyrone, Northern Ireland, d. 6 April 1984, Cheltenham, England. One of Britain's leading songwriters from the mid-30s through to the 50s, Kennedy's collaboration with Michael Carr, in particular, produced some of the most popular songs of the day. After graduating from Trinity College, Dublin, Kennedy spent brief periods as a teacher and a civil servant before deciding to concentrate on songwriting. His first big break came when he signed a contract with music publisher Bert Feldman, which led to him writing lyrics for songs such as 'Oh, Donna Clara' (music by J. Petersburski, 1930), 'The Teddy Bear's Picnic' (a new lyric to John Bratton's 1907 melody), 'My Song Goes Round The World' (Hans May, Ernst Neubach), 'Beside My Caravan' (Karel Vacek), 'Café In Vienna' (Vacek), 'Little Valley In The Mountains' (J. Dvoracek, K. Zeleny), 'Play To Me, Gypsy' (Vacek) and 'Isle Of Capri' (Will Grosz). The latter number has proved to be an enduring all-time standard: **Gracie Fields'** version, in particular, is fondly remembered. In 1934 Kennedy began his five-year association with Michael Carr, which resulted in several mostly memorable

compositions, including 'Ole Faithful', 'Misty Islands Of The Highlands', 'The General's Fast Asleep', 'Did Your Mother Come From Ireland?', 'The Sunset Trail', 'Why Did She Fall For The Leader Of The Band?', 'Waltz Of The Gypsies', 'Cinderella, Stay In My Arms', 'A Handsome Territorial', 'Two Bouquets', and probably their best-known song, 'South Of The Border'. Kennedy and Carr also contributed to films, and London Palladium shows such as *O-Kay For Sound* ('There's A New World'), *The Little Dog Laughed* ('There's Danger In The Waltz'), and the **Flanagan And Allen** revue *London Rhapsody* ('Home Town' and 'Sing A Song Of London'). Towards the end of their partnership, they wrote one of the biggest morale-boosting hits of World War II, 'We're Gonna Hang Out The Washing On The Siegfried Line'. During this comparatively brief but highly productive period, Kennedy continued to collaborate with other composers on songs such as 'Red Sails In The Sunset' (Hugh Williams, 1935), 'At The Café Continental', 'Bird On The Wing' and 'Ten Pretty Girls' (all three: Will Grosz), 'Serenade In The Night' (C.A. Bixio, B. Cherubini), 'Harbour Lights' (Hugh Williams), 'The Chestnut Tree' (**Tommie Connor**, Hamilton Kennedy), 'My Prayer' (Georges Boulanger) and 'Oh Nicholas, Don't Be So Ridiculous' (Harry Castling, 1939). He also wrote both words and music for 'Roll Along Covered Wagon' (1935), 'The Coronation Waltz', 'There's A Boy Coming Home On Leave', 'Saint Mary's In The Twilight', 'All Our Tomorrows', and 'An Hour Never Passes' (1944), among many others, and his lyrical addition to a traditional tune resulted in 'The Cokey Cokey' (often called 'The Hokey Cokey') becoming one of the most popular party dances of all time. After serving in the army during the war, in the late 40s and early 50s Kennedy's prolific and varied output continued with songs such as 'An Apple Blossom Wedding' (Nat Simon), 'Down The Old Spanish Trail' (Kenneth Leslie Smith), 'And Mimi' (Simon), 'Pigalle' (George Ulmer, George Koger), 'French Can-Can Polka' (Jacques Offenbach), 'Down The Trail Of Aching Hearts' (Simon), 'April In Portugal (Coimbra)' (Raul Ferrao, Jose Galhardo) and 'Istanbul (Not Constantinople)' (Simon, 1953). Later, although he was still able to come up with occasional hits such as 'Love Is Like A Violin (Mon Coeur Est Un Violin)' (Miarka Laparcerie) and 'Romeo' (Robert Stolz) for **Ken Dodd** and **Petula Clark**, respectively, like so many others, Kennedy's style of songs were swamped by the rock 'n' roll revolution. In the early 60s he retreated to Switzerland, but eventually moved back home to Ireland where he devoted much of his time to writing music for dramatic plays. During his long and distinguished career, his honours included two **ASCAP** Awards, and **Ivor Novello** Awards - for Outstanding Services To British Music (1971) and Life Achievement (1980). He was also awarded an honorary doctorate by the University of Ulster (1978), and an OBE (1983). In 1984, the year of his death, the British Academy of Songwriters,

Composers and Authors (BASCA) inaugurated a special annual Jimmy Kennedy Award. Further recognition came in 1997, when Kennedy was inducted into the American Songwriters' Hall Of Fame.

Like his sometime partner, Michael Carr (b. 1904, Leeds, England, d. 16 September 1968) was one of Tin Pan Alley's great characters. He spent much of his early life in Dublin before moving to America where he worked at a variety of jobs. Soon after he returned to the UK he was introduced to Jimmy Kennedy and their historic partnership began. Over the years, Carr also collaborated with others on songs such as 'Fonso My Hot Spanish (K)Night' (Leo Tower, Will Haines, 1930), 'Getting Around And About' and 'Old Timer' (both Lewis Ilda), 'The Girl With The Dreamy Eyes' (Eddie Pola), 'The Wheel Of The Wagon Is Broken' (Elton Box, Desmond Cox), 'The Little Boy That Santa Claus Forgot' (Tommie Connor, Jimmy Leach), 'Merrily We Roll Along' (Raymond Wallace), 'A Pair Of Silver Wings' (**Eric Maschwitz**), 'The First Lullaby' (Jack Popplewell), 'I Love To Sing' (Tommie Connor, Paul Misraki) and 'Lonely Ballerina' (Paul Lambrecht). Early in his career, he wrote, unaided, 'Dinner For One Please, James', 'Cowboy' and 'On The Outside Looking In', and in the early 60s provided the **Shadows** with the highly successful 'Man Of Mystery' and 'Kon-Tiki'. Just before he died in 1968, Carr wrote **Des O'Connor**'s Top 5 hit 'One-Two-Three O'Leary' with Barry Mason, and **Jackie Lee**'s first chart entry, 'White Horses', with Ben Nisbet.

Kennedy, Nigel

b. England. Cited as one of the most gifted violinists in contemporary classical music, before the mid-90s Kennedy was best known within the popular music field for his on-off relationship with Brix Smith of the **Fall**, a strong lisp and his affection for Aston Villa football club. His reputation was originally built on his interpretation of Vivaldi's *Four Seasons*, which sold more than a million copies in 1989. Some critics suggested this was enough to make him 'the first classical music pop star'. However, he retired from classical performance in 1992 owing to a combination of artistic stagnation and a painful neck condition which required surgery. He finally returned to action in 1996 after moving from **EMI Records**' classical division to the main label. *Kafka* witnessed his debut as a contemporary composer, with its genesis partially indebted to Kennedy's obsession with **Jimi Hendrix**. Though projected cover versions of Hendrix's songs had to be abandoned owing to disputes with the Hendrix estate, *Kafka* also featured collaborations with **Robert Plant** and **Kate Bush**. The album was recorded over two years with **Peter Gabriel** producer Dave Bottrill, with musicians including **Jane Siberry**, **Duffy**, **Stéphane Grappelli** and old flame Brix Smith. Of some amusement to critics was the fact that the album was recorded at Rockfield Studios in Wales at the same time as **Oasis** were preparing their second album. While Oasis's

patronage of Manchester City Football club was regularly making headlines, Kennedy's *Kafka* included 'I Believe In God', with terrace chants of 'Ooh-aah Paul McGrath' sampled from Aston Villa's Holte End.

● ALBUMS: *The Four Seasons* (EMI Classics 1989)★★★★, *Kafka* (EMI 1996)★★★.

Kennedy, Peter

b. 18 November 1922, London, England. Kennedy joined BBC Bristol in 1949, and also freelanced with his own 'Haymakers' Folk Dance Band for Village Barn Dance broadcasts from 1950. These broadcasts featured Kennedy on melodeon, with the band featured in monthly radio programmes. It was whilst doing these that a number of 'local characters' who still remembered many of the traditional tunes and songs were 'discovered'. The same year he recorded folk singers and musicians in the various republics of Yugoslavia: Bosnia, Hercegovina, Croatia, Macedonia, Montenegro, and Slovenia. The following year he was recording groups in the Basque Country. In 1952, with the help of American ethno-musicologist **Alan Lomax**, the BBC was persuaded to start a National Folk Music Dialect Recording Scheme, which was run by Kennedy and the Irish singer **Seamus Ennis** Ennis and Kennedy presented a weekly Sunday morning radio programme *As I Roved Out*. Kennedy then started working with Margaret Davies and **George Martin** of The Gramophone Company, Abbey Road, London, publishing the first field recordings of traditional singers. Their first album, *Folk Song Today*, featured, among others, Harry Cox, Jeannie Robertson, and the **Copper Family**. He then convinced commercial record companies of the value of releasing recordings some of the first 'revival' performers, including Dominic Behan, **Steve Benbow**, **Shirley Collins**, **Isla Cameron**, the **Dubliners**, **Robin Hall And Jimmy McGregor**, **Stan Hugill**, the **Watersons**, and many others. In 1964, Kennedy organized the first National Folk Festival, held at Keele University, featuring local musicians, as well as American Blues and Bluegrass. He also set up the National Federation, launched in 1965, by **Pete Seeger**, at an Irish Bingo Hall in Camden Town, London. Along with Roy Guest, he ran a Folkclub and Performers Booking Agency. He also edited the first International Folk Film Directory, in 1970, and the International Folk Directory in 1973. Kennedy's book *The Folksongs Of Britain And Ireland*, received the Library Association McColvin Award for the most outstanding reference book of 1975. In addition to the many self- produced recordings he has also published over 300 cassettes, since 1975, of original field recordings.

● ALBUMS: Selected list of recordings produced by Peter Kennedy and therefore are not rated: *World Library Of Folk & Primitive Music: England* (Columbia 1950), *World Library Of Folk & Primitive Music: Yugoslavia* (Columbia 1951), *Folk Song Today: Ballads Of England And Scotland* (His Masters Voice 1956), Guy Carawan, Peggy Seeger *America At Play* (His

Masters Voice 1958), *Rocket Along: New Ballads On Old Lines* (His Masters Voice 1960), Rory McEwen, Isla Cameron *Folksong Jubilee:* (His Masters Voice 1960), *Jug Of Punch: Broadside Ballads* (His Masters Voice 1960), *A Pinch Of Salt: British Sea Songs* (His Masters Voice 1960), *English Folksongs Miss Pringle Never Taught Us* (Dobells 1960), with Alan Lomax *Folksongs Of Britain* (Caedmon 1961, 10 album set), Cyril Tawney *Songs Of The West Country* (His Masters Voice 1962), The Liverpool Spinners *Quayside Songs* (His Masters Voice 1962), Stan Hugill *Shanties From The Seven Seas* (His Masters Voice 1962), *William Kimber: Documentary Of A Morris Musician* (EFDSS 1963), Cyril Tawney *Between Decks: Songs Of A Sub-Mariner* (DTS Records 1963), *Bob & Ron Copper: Country Singers From Sussex* (EFDSS 1963), *Johnny Doherty: Donegal Fiddler, Singer and Storyteller* (EFDSS 1964), *Harry Cox: English Folksinger From Norfolk* (EFDSS 1965), *Folksounds Of Britain: Festival Hall Concert Introduced By Dominic Behan* (His Masters Voice 1965), *All Around England And Back Again: English Folk Customs* (Saydisc 1982), Jim Couza *The Enchanted Valley* (Saydisc 1983), *Children's Singing Games Of Britain And Ireland* (Saydisc 1983), *Songs Of The Travelling People* (Saydisc 1994), *Traditional Songs Of Ireland* (Saydisc 1995).

● FURTHER READING: *The Fiddlers Tune Book Volume 1. The Fiddlers Tune Book Volume 2. Everybody Swing: Square Dances With Calls And Parts. The Folksongs Of Britain And Ireland.*

Kennedy, Ray

b. 13 May 1954, Buffalo, New York, USA. Kennedy's father worked as a credit manager for Sears, and his demanding career kept the family on the move. Kennedy dropped out of college in the mid-70s and lived in a cabin in the woods of Oregon. After a year developing his style, he began performing in the Pacific Northwest. In 1980 he took his songs to Nashville and 'The Purple Heart' and 'The Same Old Girl' were recorded by **David Allan Coe** and **John Anderson**, respectively. Kennedy built his own 24-track studio, and in 1990 he wrote, produced, engineered, sang and played all the instruments except steel guitar on his debut *What A Way To Go*. He made the US country charts with the title track, 'Scars' and 'I Like The Way It Feels', and his highly danceable music is described as 'hi-tech hillbilly'. The second album was equally strong but featured other musicians and only one song was self-penned.

● ALBUMS: *What A Way To Go* (Atlantic 1990)★★★, *Guitar Man* (Atlantic 1993)★★★.

Kennedys

A husband and wife team of Maura (b. Maura Boudreau, Syracuse, New York, USA) and Pete Kennedy (b. Washington, D.C., USA), the Kennedys play jangly folk-pop shot through with the influences of the **Byrds** and **Beatles**. The couple's first date came at **Buddy Holly**'s grave in Lubbock, Texas, while their first gig was held in Liverpool as part of **Nanci Griffith**'s Blue Moon Orchestra. Working in tandem, they discovered a shared love for American roots rock 'n' roll and British pop and folk rock. The Kennedys made a strong impression in 1995 with the release of their **Green Linnet Records** debut, *River Of Fallen Stars*. Pete Kennedy's exquisite Rickenbacker guitar tones gelled easily with his partner's sweet voice and her own rhythmic guitar playing. The album was largely written in Ireland while the duo toured as part of Nanci Griffith's band. Pete Kennedy had also formerly worked with **Mary-Chapin Carpenter** and before that with **Kate Wolf**, while his numerous solo albums have achieved massive local success in Washington, including the award of Artist Of The Year in 1992. Maura had formerly been a member of the Austin country group, the Delta Rays. *River Of Fallen Stars* drew excellent reviews - *Goldmine* magazine recommended the record as a 'nearly flawless amalgamation of the sort of ringing Byrdsy guitars and gorgeous floating harmonies that make a pure pop fan swoon'. For the follow-up collection, the duo envisaged a more 'straightforward record, a live band, with different musical personalities bouncing off each other'. *Life Is Large* succeeded in this goal with the help of a star-studded cast, including **Roger McGuinn**, **Steve Earle**, **Nils Logfren**, **Charlie Sexton**, **John Gorka**, the **Dixie Hummingbirds**, Peter Holsapple (formerly of the **dB's**) and Susan Cowsill. Despite this impressive cast, reviewers were not as sympathetic to the duo's efforts as had previously been the case, **Q** magazine noting that the record 'never really gets into orbit and the cast of thousands can't add the weight of their experience'.

● ALBUMS: *River Of Fallen Stars* (Green Linnet/Redbird 1995)★★★★, *Life Is Large* (Green Linnet 1996)★★★.

Kenner, Chris

b. 25 December 1929, Kenner, Louisiana, USA, d. 25 January 1976. This New Orleans-based artist had a US Top 20 R&B hit in 1957 on the **Imperial** label with his own composition, 'Sick And Tired', a song later revived by **Fats Domino**. Kenner was one of the first signings to the Instant label, on which he recorded his three best-known songs. In 1961, a song co-written with Fats Domino, 'I Like It Like That, Part 1', reached number 2 in the US pop charts. Kenner later received a Grammy nomination for the song. This was followed by 'Something You Got' and 'Land Of A 1,000 Dances' (1963). The latter, based on a gospel song, 'Children Go Where I Send You', later became a hit for **Cannibal And The Headhunters** (1965) and **Wilson Pickett** (1966 - US Top 10/UK Top 30). Although Kenner was beset throughout much of his career by alcohol problems, received a prison sentence in 1968 for statutory rape of a minor, and to a lesser degree, had a reputation as a poor live performer, he managed to record some of the best R&B to emanate from the Crescent City. He died of a heart attack in January 1976.

● ALBUMS: *Land Of 1,000 Dances* (Atlantic 1966)★★★.
● COMPILATIONS: *I Like It Like That* (Charly 1987)★★★.
● FILMS: *Be My Guest* (1965).

Kennerley, Paul

b. 1948, Hoylake, Wirral, England. Kennerley moved to London and worked in advertising, ran a small pub-rock booking agency and managed the Winkies. He was drawn to country music after hearing **Waylon Jennings** sing 'Let's All Help The Cowboys Sing The Blues' on the radio. His knowledge of American history was apparent on *White Mansions*, a concept album about the Civil War, atmospherically produced by **Glyn Johns** and featuring Waylon and his wife, **Jessi Colter**. This was followed by *The Legend Of Jesse James*, which included **Levon Helm** and **Johnny Cash** as Jesse and Frank James, respectively, as well as **Emmylou Harris** and **Albert Lee**. The album was coincidentally released at the same time as *The Long Riders*, a film about the James brothers. One song, 'The Death Of Me', was later recorded by Emmylou Harris with the lyric altered to 'Born To Run'. In 1981 the eight-piece Paul Kennerley Band had success at the Wembley Festival. He moved to America, wrote a concept album with Harris, *The Ballad Of Sally Rose*, and subsequently married her. Kennerley wrote several songs for her and played on her albums. He also wrote for the **Judds** including 'Have Mercy', 'Cry Myself To Sleep', both country number 1s, and 'Give A Little Love'. On her first solo album, **Wynonna** sang 'Live With Jesus' simply by recording her voice over Paul Kennerley's demo. He has also written 'Everybody Knows' (Prairie Oyster) and 'World Without You' (Kelly Willis). Kennerley's marriage to Harris ended, but both he and Albert Lee have been the most successful Brits in country music, and both have found success through Emmylou Harris.
● ALBUMS: *White Mansions* (A&M 1978)★★★★, *The Legend Of Jesse James* (A&M 1981)★★★.

Kenney, Mart

One of the more prominent Canadian bandleaders, Kenney formed his first professional orchestra in 1931 in Vancouver, British Columbia. Previously he had worked with Len Chamberlain and Sam Silverman. The group's featured vocalists included Art Hallman, Roy Roberts, Wally Koster, Georgia Dey, Judy Richards and Norma Locke, as Kenney strived hard to carve out a market by playing regularly in British Columbia and Alberta. A season at Penley's Academy and Chestermere Lake in Calgary was followed by his first network radio show, broadcast remote from a performance at Waterton park, Alberta, in 1934. Through the auspices of the CPR management organisation, he was recruited to play at their Hotel Saskatchewan complex in Regina and the Lake Louise Hotel in the summer of 1935. They returned to Vancouver for further shows at the Hotel Vancouver and Banff Springs Hotel, followed by their longest run at the Royal York Hotel. Sponsored radio appearances of this time included the *Home Oil Company*, *Union Oil Company* and *Borden's Canadian Cavalcade* shows, as well as many programmes originating from CBC's studio. During World War II Kenney continued to tour widely, returning to the Royal York

immediately after the war's close. After that he retired from bandleading to concentrate on other activities, but made a popular return in the mid-60s with a new recording contract with **RCA-Victor Records**.

Kenny

Former employees at a banana warehouse in Enfield, Middlesex, England, Richard Driscoll (vocals), Yan Style (guitar), Christopher Lacklison (keyboards), Chris Redburn (bass) and Andy Walton (drums) were collectively known as Chufff (sic), a group of glam-rock late-comers who, after a 1974 showcase at London's exclusive Speakeasy, signed with manager **Peter Walsh**. In doing so, they acquired a new name - and a producer in **Mickie Most** who, with the highest calibre of session musicians, arrangers and songwriters at his disposal, guided them with mathematical precision to transient success. This was despite the confusion of an Irish singer called Kenny who was also signed to Most's **Rak Records** at this time. **Chris Spedding** and **Clem Cattini** were among those heard anonymously on the group Kenny's four UK smashes. All inconsequentially catchy and topped with a trademark falsetto in unison with Driscoll, these were 'The Bump' (a dance craze ditty that fought off competition from a b-side version by the **Bay City Rollers**) 'Fancy Pants', 'Baby I Love You OK' and autumn 1975's Top 20 swansong, Bill Martin and **Phil Coulter**'s 'Julie Ann'. This chart run was rounded off neatly when the hits and some makeweight tracks were lumped together on a collection which bubbled under the album Top 50 in January 1976. They later provided the backing to the theme tune for UK Television's popular *Minder* series, sung by Dennis Waterman. Redburn is now a successful road haulage businessman and still gigs with Andy Walton as the Legendary Old Brown Growlers. Style runs his own PA hire company.
● ALBUMS: *The Sound Of Super K* (RAK 1975)★★.
● COMPILATIONS: *The Best Of ...* (Repertoire 1995)★★.

Kenny And The Kasuals

Formed in Dallas, Texas, USA in 1965, and previously known as the Ken Daniel Combo. Kenny Daniel (vocals), Tommy Nichols (lead guitar), Paul Roach (keyboards), Lee Lightfoot (bass) and David Blackley (drums) completed three singles for their manager Mark Lee's Mark label, prior to becoming a fixture at a local nightclub. *Live At The Studio Club*, which comprised of cover versions, including 'Gloria' (**Them**) and 'All Day And All Of The Night' (the **Kinks**), was intended solely as a promotional tool for the venue. A mere 500 copies were pressed, but the set quickly achieved legendary status, establishing the Kasuals' name in Texas garage-band circles. Jerry Smith replaced Nichols for 'Raindrops To Teardrops' and 'Journey To Tyme', the latter of which was a superior pop/psyche-delic original. However, the group began to fragment following 'Sea Saw Ride' (1967) and the following year Daniels was drafted into the armed forces. The remaining members redubbed themselves the Truth, but the new act fell apart following the release of 'Chimes On 42nd Street'. In 1977, Mark Lee re-pressed *Live At The Studio Club*, inspiring Daniels and Smith to reform their group with Dan Green (guitar), Greg Daniels (bass) and Ron Mason (drums). However, neither subsequent albums, nor the EP *The Kasuals Are Back*, recaptured the fire of the original unit and the quintet was disbanded during the early 80s.

● ALBUMS: *The Impact Sound* (1966)★★★, *Live At The Studio Club* (1966)★★★, *Garage Kings* (1979)★★, *4* (1981)★★.

● COMPILATIONS: *Teen Dreams* (1978)★★★.

Kensit, Patsy
(see **Eighth Wonder**)

Kent, Stacey
b. *c.*1967, USA. Starting to sing as a child, Kent never thought of singing as a career, treating it only as a hobby. She took a degree in comparative literature, also studying languages. After graduation she visited England, 'just to get away', and while in London decided to take a post-graduate course in jazz. This brought her into contact with musicians and she began singing and soon found offers of work coming in. She was soon working at prestigious venues including **Ronnie Scott**'s, the Purcell Room, Pizza On The Park, the 100 Club and the Barbican, appearing with the Vile Bodies Swing Orchestra, resident at London's Ritz Hotel from 1991-95, and also with her own group which features saxophonist Jim Tomlinson to whom she is married. Kent has toured the UK and appeared in and sung on the soundtrack of the 1995 film, *Richard III*. A self-taught singer, 'I just listened a lot', Kent was influenced before she knew she would be a singer by a wide range of artists including **Louis Armstrong**, **Ella Fitzgerald**, **Frank Sinatra** and **Billie Holiday**, together with instrumentalists **Stan Getz**, **Duke Ellington**, **Ben Webster**, **Charlie Christian** and **Django Reinhardt**. Her repertoire is eclectic but draws heavily upon the Great American Song Book to which she is devoted. Kent sings expressively, displays great understanding of and emotional involvement with her material, and she swings. Casual though her drift into jazz singing was, she is clearly a serious talent.

● ALBUMS: *Stacey Kent Sings* (SK 1995)★★★.

Kent, Walter
b. 29 November 1911, New York City, New York, d. 1 March 1994, Los Angeles, California, USA. A composer of numerous songs, mainly for movies in the 30s and 40s. After attending Juilliard, where he studied the violin, Kent led an orchestra which played on radio and in theatres. He began his career as an architect, writing music in his spare time. In 1932 he had his first success with the novelty 'Pu-leeze, Mr. Hemingway' (written with Milton Drake and Abner Silver), which was a hit in the US for **Guy Lombardo**, and in the UK for **Gracie**

Fields. Kent's best-known song, '(There'll Be Bluebirds Over) The White Cliffs Of Dover' (1942, lyric: Nat Burton), was popular on record for many bands and singers, including **Kay Kyser** (vocal: **Harry Babbitt**), **Glenn Miller** (vocal: **Ray Eberle**), **Sammy Kaye** (vocal: Arthur Wright), **Jimmy Dorsey** (vocal: **Bob Eberly**), **Ambrose** (vocal: **Denny Dennis**), **Vera Lynn** and **Kate Smith**. 'I'll Be Home For Christmas' (with Kim Gannon and Buck Ram), became yet another festive song to be associated with **Bing Crosby**, and among Kent's other numbers were 'Mama, I Wanna Make Rhythm', 'Love Is Like A Cigarette', 'Apple Blossoms And Chapel Bells', 'Once And For All', 'When The Roses Bloom Again', 'Ah, But It Happens', 'The Last Mile Home', and 'I'm Gonna Live Till I Die', which received a powerful rendering from **Frankie Laine**. Kent contributed several songs to films such as *Manhattan Merry-Go-Round* (1937), *My Best Gal* (1943), *Casanova In Burlesque* (1944), *Beautiful But Broke* (1944), *Meet Miss Bobby Socks* (1944), *Bowery To Broadway* (1944), *Hitchhike To Happiness* (1945), *Senorita From The West* (1945), *That's My Gal* (1947), *April Showers* (1948), *Melody Time* (1948), *Sunny Side Of The Street* (1951), *This Could Be The Night* (1957), and *Swingin' Along* (1962). Two of his songs, 'Too Much In Love' (from *Song Of The Open Road*, 1944) and 'Endlessly' (from *Earl Carroll's Vanities*, 1945), were nominated for Academy Awards. His other collaborators included **Al Hoffman**, Mann Curtis, Jerome Jerome, Richard Byron, and Milton Drake. In 1951, Kent worked again with Kim Gannon on the score for the Broadway musical *Seventeen* ('I Could Get Married Today', 'After All, It's Spring'), which ran for five months. However, nothing he did could top 'The White Cliffs Of Dover', the number that was so special to many people during the dark years of World War II, and in 1989 Kent finally visited the section of coastline that he immortalised.

Kent, Willie
b. 24 February 1936, Sunflower, Mississippi, USA. Kent was brought up in Shelby, Mississippi, and was influenced by the blues he heard on the radio. He settled in Chicago in 1952 and was soon able to hear the top blues artists live in the clubs, although he was under-age. Kent began working as a singer in 1957 and started to play guitar the following year. He quickly switched to bass and formed his own group around 1959. As a bass player, Kent worked in the 60s with **Hip Linkchain**, **Jimmy Dawkins**, and **Luther 'Guitar Junior' Johnson**. In 1975, he shared a live album with **Willie James Lyons** for the MCM label, and he has subsequently had his intense, powerful vocals and bass playing issued on various labels.

● ALBUMS: with Willie James Lyons *Ghetto* (MCM 1975)★★★, *I'm What You Need* (Big Boy 1989)★★★, *Ain't It Nice* (1991)★★★.

Kente

The term Kente is associated with a hand-woven cloth made up of radiant and dynamic shades of striped material, the strips being assembled to symbolize unity in diversity. This theme inspired the name of the popular Ghanaian group Kente, who have played their brand of roots reggae promoting black awareness since their formation in the early 90s. They are among several Ghanaian performers, including Felix Bell and Swapo, to have embraced and been inspired by Jamaican music. In 1992 the group hosted and successfully supported **Ziggy Marley And The Melody Makers** on a tour of Ghana. They also played at both the 1992 and 1994 Panafest festivals, where they performed with **Stevie Wonder**, **Jermaine Jackson**, **Public Enemy**, and the **Sounds Of Blackness**, alongside African reggae stars **Lucky Dube** and **Alpha Blondy**. In 1995 the group came to the attention of the German-based African Dance Records organization, who produced and released their debut, *Keep On Moving*. The album led to a successful winter tour of Germany. In their early years the band had provided support to **Jah Shaka** during a tour of West Africa, and in 1997 they were reunited with him on an acclaimed UK tour celebrating Ghana's 40 years of independence. The tour included a stunning performance by the group at the Essential Festival.

● ALBUMS: *Keep On Moving* (African Dance 1995)★★★.

Kenton, Stan

b. 15 December 1911, Wichita, Kansas, USA, d. 25 August 1979. After playing piano in various dance bands, including those of Everett Hoagland and **Vido Musso**, mostly on the west coast, Kenton decided to form his own band in 1941. Although geared partially to the commercial needs of the dancehall circuit of the time, Kenton's band, which he termed the 'Artistry In Rhythm' orchestra, also featured powerful brass section work and imaginative saxophone voicings, unlike those of his more orthodox competitors. The band developed a substantial following among the younger elements of the audience who liked their music brash and loud. During the remainder of the 40s Kenton's popularity increased dramatically, seemingly immune to the declining fortunes that affected other bands. A succession of exciting young jazz musicians came into the band, among them **Buddy Childers**, **Art Pepper**, **Kai Winding**, **Shelly Manne**, **Bob Cooper** and **Laurindo Almeida**, playing arrangements by Kenton, **Gene Roland** and **Pete Rugolo**. His singers included **Anita O'Day**, **June Christy** and **Chris Connor**. In the 50s, his enthusiasm undimmed, Kenton introduced a 43-piece band, his 'Innovations In Modern Music' orchestra, again featuring Pepper and Manne as well as newcomers such as **Maynard Ferguson** and **Bud Shank**. Complex, quasi-classical arrangements by **Bob Graettinger** and others proved less appealing, but a 1953 tour of Europe ensured Kenton's international reputation. Reduced to a more manageable 19-piece, his New Concepts In Artistry In Rhythm band contin-

ued playing concerts and recording, using arrangements by Roland, **Gerry Mulligan** and **Johnny Richards**. Always eager to try new ideas, and to clearly label them, in the 60s Kenton introduced his 'New Era In Modern Music' orchestra, a 23-piece band using mellophoniums, and the 'Neophonic' orchestra, five pieces larger and tempting fate with neo-classical music. In the 70s, he embraced rock rhythms and looked as if he might go on forever. By 1977, however, his health had begun to deteriorate and although he returned from hospitalization to lead his band until August 1978, his bandleading days were almost over. He died in August 1979.

More than most bandleaders, Kenton polarized jazz fans, inspiring either love or hatred and only rarely meeting with indifference. Almost half a century after the event it is hard to understand what all the fuss was about. Certainly the band did not swing with the grace of, for example, the **Jimmie Lunceford** band, but it was equally wrong to declare, as many critics did, that Kenton never swung at all. Although some of the arrangements were too monolithic for effective jazz performances, the abilities of his key soloists were seldom buried for long. Kenton's band was important in bringing together many excellent musicians and for allowing arrangers free rein to experiment in big band concepts, a practice that few other leaders of the period would tolerate.

● ALBUMS: *Stan Kenton At The Hollywood Palladium* (1945)★★★, *Progressive Jazz* (1946-47)★★★, *One Night Stand With Nat 'King' Cole And Stan Kenton* (1947)★★★, *One Night Stand At The Commodore* (1947)★★★, *Stan Kenton And His Orchestra With June Christy* (1949)★★★, *Encores* 10-inch album (Capitol 1950)★★★, *Innovations In Modern Music* 10-inch album (Capitol 1950)★★★★, *Milestones* 10-inch album (Capitol 1950)★★★, *Artistry In Rhythm* 10-inch album (Capitol 1950)★★★★, *A Presentation Of Progressive Jazz* 10-inch album (Capitol 1950)★★★, *One Night Stand With Stan Kenton* i (1950)★★★, *Stan Kenton Presents* 10-inch album (Capitol 1950)★★★★, *Nineteen Fifty-One* (1951)★★★, *One Night Stand With Stan Kenton* ii (1951)★★★, *Carnegie* (1951)★★★★, with Charlie Parker *Kenton And Bird* (1951-54)★★★, *Artistry In Tango* (1951-52)★★★, *Concert In Miniature* (1952)★★★, *Classics* 10-inch album (Capitol 1952)★★★, *City Of Glass* 10-inch album (Capitol 1952)★★★, *Concert In Miniature No 9 And 10* (1952)★★★, *Concert In Miniature No 11 And 12* (1952)★★★, *Concert In Miniature No 13 And 14* (1952)★★★, *New Concepts Of Artistry In Rhythm* (Capitol 1953)★★★★, *Concert Encores* (1953)★★★, *Prologue This Is An Orchestra* 10-inch album (Capitol 1953)★★★, *Popular Favorites* 10-inch album (Capitol 1953)★★★, *The Definitive Stan Kenton With Charlie Parker And Dizzy Gillespie* (1953-54)★★★, *Stan Kenton In Berlin* (1953)★★★, *Europe Fifty Three Part One and Two* (1953)★★★, *Paris, 1953* (1953)★★★, *Sketches On Standards* 10-inch album (Capitol 1953)★★★, *This Modern World* 10-inch album (Capitol 1953)★★★, *Stan Kenton Radio Transcriptions* 10-inch album (MacGregor 1953)★★★, *Portraits Of Standards* 10-inch album (Capitol 1953)★★★,

Artistry In Kenton (1954)★★★, *Kenton Showcase - The Music Of Bill Russo* 10-inch album (Capitol 1954)★★★, *Kenton Showcase - The Music Of Bill Holman* 10-inch album (Capitol 1954)★★★, *Stan Kenton Festival* (1954)★★★, with June Christy *Duet* (Capitol 1955)★★★★, *Contemporary Concepts* (Capitol 1955)★★★, *Stan Kenton In Hi-Fi* (Capitol 1956)★★★★, *Kenton In Concert* (1956)★★★, *Kenton In Stereo* (1956)★★★, *In Stockholm* (1956)★★★, *Cuban Fire!* (Capitol 1956)★★★★, *Kenton '56* (1956)★★★, *Rendez-vous With Kenton/At The Rendezvous Volume 1* (Capitol 1957)★★★, *Kenton With Voices* (Capitol 1957)★★★, *Back To Balboa* (Capitol 1958)★★★, *Lush Interlude* (Capitol 1958)★★★, *The Stage Door Swings* (Capitol 1958)★★★, *On The Road* (1958)★★★, *The Kenton Touch* (Capitol 1958)★★★, *The Ballad Style Of Stan Kenton* (Capitol 1958)★★★, *Stan Kenton At The Tropicana* (Capitol 1959)★★★, *In New Jersey* (1959)★★★, *At Ukiah* (1959)★★★, *Viva Kenton* (Capitol 1959)★★★, with Christy *The Road Show, Volumes 1 & 2* (Capitol 1960)★★★, with Ann Richards *Two Much* (1960)★★★, with Christy *Together Again* (Capitol 1960)★★★, *Standards In Silhouette* (Capitol 1960)★★★, *Stan Kenton's Christmas* (1961)★★★, *The Romantic Approach* (Capitol 1961)★★★, *Stan Kenton's West Side Story* (Capitol 1961)★★★★, *Mellophonium Magic* (1961)★★★, *Sophisticated Approach* (1961)★★★, *Adventures In Standards* (1961)★★★, *Adventures In Blues* (Capitol 1961)★★★, *Adventures In Jazz* (Capitol 1961)★★★, *The Sound Of Sixty-Two* (1962)★★★, *Adventures In Time* (Capitol 1962)★★★, *Stan Kenton's Mellophonium Band* (Capitol 1962)★★★, *Artistry In Bossa Nova* (Capitol 1963)★★★, *Artistry In Voices And Brass* (Capitol 1963)★★★, *The Best Of Brant Inn* (1963)★★, *Kenton In England* (1963)★★★, *Wagner* (1964)★★★, *Stan Kenton Conducts The Los Angeles Neophonic Orchestra* (Capitol 1965)★★★, *Rhapsody In Blue* (1965)★★★, *Stan Kenton Conducts The Jazz Compositions Of Dee Barton* (Capitol 1968)★★★, *Live At Redlands University* (Creative World 1970)★★, *Live At Brigham Young University* (Creative World 1971)★★, *Live At Fairfield Hall, Croydon* (1972)★★, *Live At Butler University* (Creative World 1972)★★, *National Anthems Of The World* (1972)★★, *Stan Kenton Today* (London Philharmonic 1972)★★★, *Birthday In Britain* (Creative World 1973)★★, *7.5 On The Richter Scale* (Creative World 1973)★★, *Solo: Stan Kenton Without His Orchestra* (1973)★★, *Stan Kenton Plays Chicago* (Creative World 1974)★★, *Fire, Fury And Fun* (Creative World 1974)★★, *Kenton 1976* (Creative World 1976)★★, *Journey Into Capricorn* (Creative World 1976)★★, *Stan(dard) Kenton: Stan Kenton In Warsaw* (1976)★★★, *Stan Kenton In Europe* (1976)★★★, *Live At Sunset Ridge Country Club Chicago* (Magic 1977)★★, *Live In Cologne 1976 Vols. 1 and 2* (Magic 1977)★★, *Street Of Dreams* (Creative World 1977)★★.

● COMPILATIONS: *The Kenton Era (1940-53)* (Capitol 1955)★★★★, *Stan Kenton's Greatest Hits* (Capitol 1965)★★★★, *Stan Kenton's Greatest Hits (1943-51)* (1983)★★★★, *The Christy Years (1945-47)* (Creative World 1985)★★★★, *The Fabulous Alumni Of Stan Kenton (1945-56)* (Creative World 1985)★★★★, *Collection: 20 Golden Greats* (Deja Vu 1986)★★★★, *Retrospective 1943-1968* 4-CD box set (Capitol 1992)★★★★, *Best Of* (Capitol 1995)★★★★.

● VIDEOS: *Stan Kenton And Frank Rosolino* (Kay Jazz 1988), *Stan Kenton And His Orchestra* (Kay Jazz 1988).

● FURTHER READING: *Straight Ahead: The Story Of Stan Kenton*, Carol Easton. *Stan Kenton: Artistry In Rhythm*, William F. Lee. *Stan Kenton: The Man And His Music*, Lillian Arganian.

Kentucky Colonels

Fêted as one of the finest ever bluegrass groups, the Kentucky Colonels evolved out of a family-based ensemble, the Three Little Country Boys. The White brothers (born Le Blanc), Roland (mandolin, vocals), **Clarence White** (b. 6 June 1944, Lewiston, Maine, USA, d. 14 July 1973; guitar, vocals) and Eric (bass, vocals), began performing during the mid-50s, but Billy Ray Latham (banjo) and Leroy Mack (dobro) later joined the founding trio. The unit was then renamed the Country Boys. Roger Bush replaced Eric White in 1961, after which the quintet became known as the Kentucky Colonels. Their progress was undermined following Roland White's induction into the army, although the group completed its debut album, *New Sounds Of Bluegrass America*, in his absence. The Colonels enjoyed their most prolific spell on his return. Fiddler Bobby Slone replaced Leroy Mack and the revitalized quintet recorded the classic *Appalachian Swing*. However, Clarence White grew increasingly unhappy with the music's confines and harboured ambitions towards a more electric style. The group attempted an awkward compromise, offering sets both traditional and contemporary, but this forlorn balance failed to satisfy either party. A new fiddler, Scotty Stoneman, joined, but by April 1966, the Colonels had all but collapsed. Roland and Eric White did attempt to revive the group the following year, adding Dennis Morris (guitar) and Bob Warford (banjo), but although this proved short-term, numerous other reunions have taken place. Latham and Bush, meanwhile, joined **Dillard And Clark**, while Clarence White was drafted into the **Byrds**.

● ALBUMS: *New Sounds Of Bluegrass America* (Briar 1963)★★★, *Appalachian Swing* (World Pacific 1964)★★★, *Kentucky Colonels* (United Artists 1974)★★★, *The White Brothers Live In Sweden* (Rounder 1979)★★★.

● COMPILATIONS: *Livin' In The Past* (Briar 1975)★★★, *The Kentucky Colonels With Scotty Stoneman* (1975)★★★, *Kentucky Colonels 1966* (Shiloh 1978)★★★, *Kentucky Colonels 1965-1966* (Rounder 1979)★★★, *Clarence White And The Kentucky Colonels* (Rounder 1980)★★★, *On Stage* (Rounder 1984)★★★.

Kentucky Headhunters

The Kentucky Headhunters come, naturally enough, from Kentucky. Ricky Lee Phelps (lead vocal) and his brother, Doug, played in various groups around Kentucky before meeting Greg Martin (lead guitar) in 1984. He introduced them to his cousins, the brothers Richard Young (rhythm guitar) and Fred Young (bass). Previously, the Young brothers and Martin had been in a group together, Itchy Brother, which was almost signed to **Led Zeppelin**'s own label Swan Song. Since then, Fred Young had played **Patsy Cline**'s drummer in the film, *Sweet Dreams*. This time, taking their name from **Muddy Waters**' band, the Headchoppers, the five musicians financed their own album, *Pink*, in 1988, and the tracks were subsequently released by **Mercury**, with additional material, on *Pickin' On Nashville*. Their first US country hit was with a revival of **Bill Monroe**'s 'Walk Softly On This Heart Of Mine'. This was followed by their anthemic tribute to a 74-year-old marbles champion, Dumas Walker, and then by a revival of **Don Gibson**'s 'Oh Lonesome Me'. Their boisterous stage act included some magic from Ricky Lee Phelps. The Kentucky Headhunters, like **Lynyrd Skynyrd** before them, are a controversial band who bring heavy metal influences to country music, and vice versa: on *Electric Barnyard*, they thrash through 'The Ballad Of Davy Crockett'. The decision of the two Phelps brothers to quit the Headhunters in 1992 delayed the release of their third album, *Rave On*. Replaced by Anthony Kenney and Mark Orr the band concentrated on the heavier side of their sound. Doug Phelps rejoined in 1996 before the release of *Stompin' Grounds*.

● ALBUMS: *Pickin' On Nashville* (Mercury 1989)★★★, *Electric Barnyard* (Mercury 1991)★★★, *Rave On!* (Mercury 1993)★★, with Johnnie Johnson *That'll Work* (Elektra 1993)★★★, *Stompin' Grounds* (BNA 1997)★★★.

● COMPILATIONS: *Best Of The Kentucky Headhunters: Still Pickin'* (Mercury 1994)★★★★.

Kenyon, Carol

b. *c.*1960, London, England. As a child Kenyon was encouraged to sing and dance, taking lessons and entering arts festival contests; she also played piano and listened to her father's collection of jazz records. While singing with a school choir at a music festival in Harrow she was heard by **Guy Barker**, a young musician who was also appearing there. With his encouragement she began moving towards a serious and focused interest in singing. With Barker, she joined Steam Heat, a local jazz-rock band, and was then encouraged by him to attend an engagement by the **National Youth Jazz Orchestra**. There, she sang 'Summertime' with the band and to such good effect that NYJO took her on as its first regular band singer, at the age of only 14. With a repertoire of quality songs, many of them written especially for her by **Bill Ashton** and others, Kenyon quickly became an integral part of the band's performances, singing with the ensemble in addition to performing solos. With NYJO she toured extensively, appeared on television and record, and at the Royal Command Variety Performance in 1978. On leaving NYJO, Kenyon sang with Car Park, an outfit formed from NYJO members, with the band led by **Dick Morrissey** and **Jim Mullen**, and frequently appeared on television in support of better-known artists. She also toured internationally with some of them, including

Mick Jagger. She then joined **Heaven 17**, who in 1983 charted at number 2 in the UK with 'Temptation'. Signed to **A&M Records** and relaunched as the 'Warrior Woman', complete with gimmicky black leather gear and a live hawk, she made more records. She was then with **Go West**, and in 1986 teamed with **Paul Hardcastle** for further chart successes, particularly with 'Don't Waste My Time', which reached number 5. She continued to work on television and also sang on motion picture soundtracks, and in 1995 appeared again at the Royal Command Variety Performance, this time opening the show. Always singing with superb control and great flair, Kenyon's stylistic range appears unlimited. In addition to straight pop and the jazz-inflected ballads she sang with NYJO, she has also sung in a classical vein, performing memorably on NYJO's 'The Sherwood Forest Suite', composed by Paul Hart, and a 1996 album aimed at the elusive classical crossover market. An enormously versatile singer with a secure musical foundation, Kenyon seems well-placed to continue expanding her growing audience well into the twenty-first century.

● ALBUMS: with NYJO *Return Trip* (NYJO 1976)★★★, with NYJO *To Russia With Jazz* (NYJO 1977)★★★, *Go West* (Chrysalis 1986)★★.

Kepone

Alternative US rock/punk band Kepone are Michael Bishop (bass, vocals), Tim Harris (guitar, vocals) and former Honor Role drummer Seth Harris (later replaced by Ed Trask). Formed in the early 90s, they took their name from the pesticide that was manufactured by the Allied Signal Corporation of Hopewell, Virginia, in the 70s, and caused the company's employees severe neurological damage (this incident was also the subject of a **Dead Kennedys** song, 'Kepone Factory'). The group's deliberate, anthemic rock style was unveiled with the 1994 release of *Ugly Dance* for Quarterstick Records. A potent collision of punk-pop with the distinctive employment of dual lead vocals, it followed on from the group's excellent 1993 singles, 'Henry' and '295'. The latter single was released on **Jello Biafra**'s (ex-Dead Kennedys) Alternative Tentacles Records - supplying ample evidence of Kepone's original inspiration. *Skin* and *Kepone* were further slices of the band's endearingly offbeat alternative rock.

● ALBUMS: *Ugly Dance* (Quarterstick 1994)★★★, *Skin* (Quarterstick 1995)★★★, *Kepone* (Quarterstick 1997)★★★.

Keppard, Freddie

b. 27 February 1890, New Orleans, Louisiana, USA, d. 15 July 1933. Before choosing to play the cornet, Keppard experimented with various other instruments, none of which was especially suitable for performing jazz. In the years before World War I he played with the Olympia Orchestra in New Orleans and several other parade and concert bands. He was leader of the Original Creole Orchestra which toured California and the east coast, and also worked in Chicago. After the war Keppard settled in Chicago, where he worked with **Joe 'King' Oliver**, **Jimmie Noone** and other luminaries of the city's jazz scene. In the early 20s he played in various bands, sometimes leading his own, almost always in or around Chicago. Among the last bands with which he worked were those of Erskine Tate and Charlie Elgar. He seldom played after 1928 and died in July 1933. Keppard's few recordings barely support his status as a leading hornman of early jazz and a direct link to the legendary playing of **Buddy Bolden**. Nevertheless, there are suggestions of his qualities and it is hard to question the reputation he enjoyed among fellow musicians such as **Sidney Bechet** and **Milt Hinton**. Along with **Edward 'Kid' Ory**, Keppard was important in helping to spread jazz into areas of the west coast not previously familiar with the music.

● ALBUMS: *Carol Kidd* (1984)★★★, *All My Tomorrows* (1985)★★★, *Nice Work* (1987)★★★, *Night We Called It A Day* (1990)★★★, *I'm Glad We Met* (1991)★★★.

● COMPILATIONS: *The Legend Of Freddie Keppard (1923-27)* (1973)★★★, *Freddie Keppard (1923-28)* (Jazz Treasury 1988)★★★★★, *Complete Freddie Keppard* (King Jazz 1993)★★★★.

Kerbdog

Irish alternative rock band Kerbdog enjoyed their biggest success to date in 1994 when 'Dummy Crusher' took them into the UK Top 40. Heavily influenced by the more abrasive US bands (**Smashing Pumpkins**, **Helmet**, **Hüsker Dü**, etc.), they received excellent press within the UK hard rock press for their efforts. However, shortly after this initial success they lost original guitarist Billy Dalton, slimming down to a trio led by bassist Colin Fenelley, vocalist/guitarist Cormac Battle and drummer Butler. They re-emerged two years later with an intensive work schedule aimed at recapturing their previous high profile within the hard rock media. New material was initially unveiled on the four-track 1996 EP *JJ's Song*, recorded at the same sessions that produced their follow-up album, *On The Turn*. Garth Richardson, best known for his work with **Rage Against The Machine**, and partner Joe Barresi, who assisted Richardson on his production work with **Jesus Lizard**, oversaw production.

● ALBUMS: *Totally Switched* (Vertigo 1994)★★★, *On The Turn* (Fontana 1996)★★.

Kern, Jerome

b. 27 January 1885, New York City, New York, USA, d. 11 November 1945, New York, USA. One of the most important composers in the history of American popular music, Kern was taught to play the piano by his mother, and proved to be a gifted musician with a remarkable ear. While still at junior school he was dabbling with composition, and by his mid-teens was simultaneously studying classical music and writing songs in the popular vein. He became a song plugger in New York's Tin Pan Alley and occasionally accompanied leading entertainers of the day. Some of his early songs were picked up by producers of Broadway shows and were also used in London, a city Kern visited first in 1902/3 and thereafter held in great affection. During the next few years Kern became a familiar figure at theatres in London and New York, working on scores and acting as a rehearsal pianist. He had his first hit in 1905 with 'How'd You Like To Spoon With Me?' (lyric: Edward Laska), which was interpolated in the score for *The Earl And The Girl*. Throughout this period, Kern continued to contribute songs to various shows, and in 1912 wrote his first complete score, with lyrics by Paul West, for *The Red Petticoat*. Two years later, his most accomplished work so far, *The Girl From Utah*, contained the delightful 'They Didn't Believe Me' (lyric: Herbert Reynolds), and in 1915 Kern had his second song hit, 'Babes In The Wood' (lyric: Kern and Schuyler Greene), from *Very Good Eddie*. In 1916, Kern contributed a few songs to *Miss Springtime*, an operetta, with lyrics by **P.G. Wodehouse**, and a book by **Guy Bolton**. This marked the beginning of the partnership which, with its witty books and lyrics, and songs cleverly integrated, into the story, is credited with helping to create America's own indigenous musical comedy format, as opposed to the imported European operetta. Kern, Bolton and Wodehouse's first complete show together, *Have A Heart* (January 1917), ran for only 76 performances, but *Oh, Boy!* (February 1917), the first and most successful of their renowned **Princess Theatre Musicals**, stayed at the tiny 299-seater house for more than a year. It's charming score included 'Words Are Not Needed', 'An Old Fashioned Wife', 'A Pal Like You', 'You Never Knew About Me,' 'Nesting Time In Flatbush', and 'Till The Clouds Roll By' (lyric: Kern and Wodehouse). The latter song was a tremendous hit for Anna Wheaton, one of the stars of the show, and James Harrod. The success of *Oh, Boy!* meant that the trio's *Leave It To Jane* ('The Crickets Are Calling', 'The Siren's Song', 'Wait Till Tomorrow', 'Leave It To Jane', 'Cleopatterer'), which opened in August 1917, had to be accommodated in the much larger Longacre Theatre. After *Oh Lady! Lady!!* ('Do Look At Him', 'Before I Met You', 'Not Yet', 'It's A Hard Hard World'), which made its debut at the Princess Theatre in February 1918, Kern, Bolton and Wodehouse, went their separate ways, reuniting briefly in 1924 for the disappointing *Sitting Pretty*. During the early 20s Kern was perhaps the most prolific composer on Broadway, with numerous show scores to his credit. These included *The Night Boat* (1920), *Sally* (1920, 'Look For The Silver Lining', lyric: **Buddy De Sylva**), *The Cabaret Girl* (London 1921), *Good Morning Dearie* (1921), *The Beauty Prize* (London 1923), *The Stepping Stones* (1923, 'Raggedy Ann', lyric: Anne Caldwell), and *Sunny* (1925, 'Who?', lyric: **Oscar Hammerstein II**). In 1927, Kern composed his masterpiece, *Show Boat*, which ran on Broadway for 575 performances. Oscar Hammerstein wrote the lyrics for the magnificent score which included 'Ol' Man River', 'Make Believe', 'Why Do I Love You?', and 'Can't Help Lovin' Dat Man'.

Also present was 'Bill' (lyric: Wodehouse and Hammerstein), which had been cut from *Oh Lady! Lady!!* nearly 10 years previously. Naturally enough, Kern's subsequent Broadway shows were unable to match the enormous success of *Show Boat*, but fine songs were invariably found in the scores for most of them, such as *Sweet Adeline* (1929, 'Why Was I Born?', lyric: Hammerstein), *The Cat And The Fiddle* (1931, 'She Didn't Say "Yes"', lyric: **Otto Harbach**), *Music In The Air* (1932, 'I've Told Ev'ry Little Star', 'The Song Is You', lyrics: Hammerstein), *Roberta* (1933, 'The Touch Of Your Hand', Yesterdays', 'Smoke Gets In Your Eyes', lyrics: Harbach), and *Very Warm For May* (1939, the exquisite 'All The Things You Are' [lyric: Hammerstein]). Four years before the latter show drew a line under Kern's prolific and distinguished Broadway career, the composer had begun to compose the music for a number of extremely popular film musicals. These included *Roberta* (1935), for which 'Lovely To Look At' (lyric: **Dorothy Fields** and **Jimmy McHugh**) and 'I Won't Dance' (lyric: Harbach and Hammerstein) were added to the original stage score), *Swing Time* (1936, 'The Way You Look Tonight' [Academy Award], 'A Fine Romance', 'Pick Yourself Up', 'Bojangles Of Harlem', lyrics: Fields), *High, Wide And Handsome* (1937, 'The Folks Who Live On The Hill', 'Can I Forget You?', lyrics: Hammerstein), *Joy Of Living* (1938, 'You Couldn't Be Cuter', 'Just Let Me Look At You', lyrics: Fields), *One Night In The Tropics* (1940, 'Remind Me', lyric: Fields), *Lady Be Good* (1941, 'The Last Time I Saw Paris' [Academy Award], lyric: Hammerstein), *You Were Never Lovelier* (1942, 'Dearly Beloved', 'I'm Old Fashioned', 'You Were Never Lovelier', lyrics: **Johnny Mercer**), *Cover Girl* (1944, 'Long Ago And Far Away', lyric: **Ira Gershwin**), Can't Help Singing (1944, 'Califor-ni-ay', 'More And More', 'Any Moment Now', 'Can't Help Singing', lyrics: **E.Y. 'Yip' Harburg**), and *Centennial Summer* (1946, 'In Love In Vain', 'The Right Romance', lyrics: **Leo Robin**). Kern and Hammerstein also wrote some new numbers, including 'I Have The Room Above' and 'Ah Still Suits Me', for the 1936 film version of *Show Boat*. That show, along with many of Kern's other marvellous songs, was showcased in the 1946 biopic *Till The Clouds Roll By*, in which the composer was portrayed by Robert Walker. Having conquered Broadway and Hollywood, Kern turned to writing music for the concert platform, composing a classical suite based upon his music for *Show Boat*, and another suite entitled 'Mark Twain: A Portrait For Orchestra'. He had agreed to write the music, with Hammerstein's lyrics, for a new Broadway show entitled *Annie Get Your Gun*, when he collapsed and died in November 1945. An outstanding songwriter with an ability to find beautiful, lilting and emotional melodies with deceptive ease while At the same time incorporating elements of ragtime and syncopation into his lively dance tunes, Kern's work has remained popular with singers and jazz musicians. More than half a century after his last great songs were written, the music remains fresh and undated. In 1994, a highly acclaimed revival of *Show Boat*, directed by **Harold Prince**, opened on Broadway and won five **Tony Awards**. Several leading artists such as **Ella Fitzgerald** have recorded albums in tribute to him, and there are compilations of Kern's music including *Capitol Sings Jerome Kern* (1992), currently available.

● FURTHER READING: *The World Of Jerome Kern*, David Ewen. *Jerome Kern: A Biography*, Michael Freedland. *Jerome Kern: His Life And Music*, Gerald Bordman. *Bolton And Wodehouse And Kern*, Lee Davis.

Kernaghan, Lee

b. 1965, Australia. The 90s country singer Lee Kernaghan is the son of country music performer Ray Kernaghan, best known for his album *Me And Louis On The Road*. Lee joined his father on the road from an early age and won a recording contract with **RCA Records**. He appeared with his father at the International Fan Fair show in Nashville in 1986, and spent time writing with Nashville songwriters. Returning to Australia, he was invited to record again by songwriter/producer Garth Porter. They wrote songs that celebrated their Australian roots and *The Outback Club* became a top-selling country album in Australia. The follow-up, *Three Chain Road*, is regarded as a high point of New Country, perhaps the Australian equivalent of **Garth Brooks** and selling 100,000 copies. It included a song about a man's love for his 4WD truck, 'She's My Ute', and a duet with **Slim Dusty** about a much-loved horse, 'Leave Him In The Longyard'. There is also a plea for Australia to become a republic, 'Southern Son'. His 1995 album included the sentimental '1959' and a version of **Porter Wagoner**'s 'This Cowboy's Hat', rewritten to reflect Australian life. Lee's sisters, Tania and Fiona, are also country performers, respectively releasing the albums *December Moon* and *Cypress Grove* in 1995.

● ALBUMS: *The Outback Club* (ABC 1992)★★★, *Three Chain Road* (ABC 1994)★★★★, *1959* (ABC 1995)★★★, *1959* reissue with bonus CD featuring new solo material and duets (ABC 1997)★★★.

Kerr, Anita

b. Anita Jean Grob, 31 October 1927, Memphis, Tennessee, USA. Kerr took piano lessons from the age of four and she was soon appearing on her mother's radio show in Memphis. By the age of 14, she was the staff pianist and was making vocal arrangements of church music for the station. In 1949, she formed the Anita Kerr Quartet (later Singers) with Gil Wright (tenor), Dorothy Ann 'Dottie' Dillard (alto) and Louis D. Nunley (baritone). They established themselves as session singers, particularly in Nashville. By the early 60s, they were featured on, it is estimated or alleged, a quarter of all the country records being made there, including records by **Chet Atkins**, **Floyd Cramer**, **Jim Reeves** and **Hank Snow** as well as pop records by **Brook Benton**, **Perry Como**, **Connie Francis**, **Brenda**

Lee and **Roy Orbison**. Kerr also produced **Skeeter Davis**'s 'The End Of The World'. In 1960, the quartet made the US Top 10 with 'Forever' under the name of the **Little Dippers**. In 1962, this time as the Anita And Th' So-And-So's, they had a minor US hit with 'Joey Baby'. From the mid-60s, the Anita Kerr Singers made several easy-listening albums and also accompanied Rod McKuen on his best-selling poetry albums as the San Sebastian Strings And Singers.

● ALBUMS: *Voices In Hi-Fi* (1958)★★★, *Georgia On My Mind* (1965)★★★, *We Dig Mancini* (1966)★★, *Slightly Baroque* (1967)★★★, *The Anita Kerr Singers Reflect On The Hits Of Burt Bacharach And Hal David* (Dot 1969)★★, *Velvet Voices And Bold Brass* (Dot 1969)★★★, *The Look Of Love* (1970)★★★, *The Simon And Garfunkel Songbook* (Bainbridge 1971)★★, *Grow To Know Me* (1972)★★★, *Anita Kerr's Christmas Story* (1972)★★, *Daytime, Nighttime* (1973)★★★, *Precious Memories* (1974)★★★, *Grow To Know Me* (1974)★★★, *Halleluhah Brass* (1975)★★, *Gentle As Morning* (1975)★★★, *Halleluhah Guitarists* (1976)★★★, *Walk A Little Slower* (1976)★★★, *Anita Kerr & The French Connection* (RCA 1977)★★.

Kersh, David

b. 1970, Texas, USA. Kersh is another anonymous, good-looking country newcomer, but his debut album has been well received. The album is mostly up-tempo but the key track is the slow dance tune 'Goodnight Sweetheart', which made the US country Top 10 in 1996. On *If I Never Stop Loving You* he attempted a cover of **Eric Clapton**'s 'Wonderful Tonight' in addition to a credible version of **Willie Nelson**'s 'Hello Walls'.

● ALBUMS: *Goodnight Sweetheart* (Curb 1996)★★★, *If I Never Stop Loving You* (Curb 1998)★★★.

Kershaw, Doug

b. 24 January 1936, Tiel Ridge, Louisiana, USA. This renowned fiddle player and vocalist is a major figure in Cajun, or acadian circles, the traditional music of Louisiana's French-speaking minority. He was introduced to music by 'Daddy Jack' and 'Mama Rita', who subsequently appeared on many of the artist's compositions, and joined a family-based band, the Continental Playboys, on leaving high school. When Kershaw's songwriting talent resulted in a publishing and recording contract, he formed a duo with one of his brothers, and as **Rusty And Doug** quickly became popular throughout the southern USA. By 1956, they were a regular attraction on *The World's Original Jamboree*, a weekly showcase for local talent, and the following year enjoyed a residency on the famed *Grand Ole Opry*. Three of Kershaw's original compositions, 'Louisiana Man', 'Joli Blon' and 'Diddy Liggy Lo', not only became Cajun standards, but have been the subject of numerous cover versions by both pop and country acts. The brothers embarked on separate careers in 1964, but despite the approbation of their peers, Kershaw did not secure a larger audience until 1968, when he guested on

The Johnny Cash Show. This appearance coincided with the release of *The Cajun Way*, the artist's debut for **Warner Brothers Records**, which affirmed his new-found popularity. Cameos on albums by **Bob Dylan** and **John Stewart** endeared Kershaw to the rock fraternity, while a series of stellar 70s recordings confirmed his talent as a flamboyant musician and gifted composer. He signed with Scotti Bros. in 1981, and achieved his highest chart position (number 29) with 'Hello Woman' the same year. After an enforced absence through substance abuse, he returned to the charts in 1988 with 'Cajun Baby', on which he duetted with **Hank Williams Jr**.

● ALBUMS: *The Cajun Way* (Warners 1969)★★★, *Spanish Moss* (Warners 1970)★★★, *Swamp Grass* (Warners 1971)★★★, *Doug Kershaw* (Warners 1972)★★★★, *Devil's Elbow* (Warners 1972)★★★, *Douglas James Kershaw* (Warners 1973)★★★, *Mama Kershaw's Boy* (Warners 1974)★★★, *Alive & Pickin'* (Warners 1975)★★★★, *Ragin' Cajun* (Warners 1976)★★★, *Flip, Flop & Fly* (Warners 1977)★★★, *Louisiana Man* (Warners 1978)★★★, *Hot Diggity Doug* (BMG 1989)★★★.

● COMPILATIONS: *The Best Of Doug Kershaw* (Warners 1989)★★★★. As Rusty And Doug *Louisiana Man And Other Favorites* (Warners 1971)★★★★, *Cajun Country Rockers* (Bear Family 1979)★★★★, *Cajun Country Rockers 2* (Bear Family 1981)★★★★, *Instant Hero* (Scotti Bros 1981)★★★, *Cajun Country Rockers 3* (Bear Family 1984)★★★, *More Cajun Country Rock* (Bear Family 1984)★★★, *Jay Miller Sessions Volume 22* (Flyright 1986)★★★, *Rusty, Doug, Wiley And Friends* (Flyright 1989)★★★, *The Best Of Doug And Rusty Kershaw* (Curb 1991)★★★.

Kershaw, Nik

b. Nicolas David Kershaw, 1 March 1958, Bristol, Somerset, England. Diminutive singer, guitarist, songwriter Kershaw shone brightly for a couple of years in the mid-80s UK charts before taking a more behind the scenes role in the 90s. Son of a flautist father and opera singing mother, Kershaw's first foray into the arts was as a 13-year-old student actor planning to go into repertory when he finished training. However, around 1974 he learned guitar and played **Deep Purple** covers in a school band called Half Pint Hogg (the name doubtless related to Kershaw's stature). Leaving school in 1976, he started work at the Department of Employment (and later the Co-op) but spent his evenings performing in the jazz-funk outfit Fusion. Fellow members were Reg Webb (keyboards), Ken Elson (bass), and Alan Clarke (drums). Signed to Plastic Fantastic Records and later to Telephone Records, they released one single and an album respectively. The album, *'Til I Hear From You*, contained an early version of the track 'Human Racing', which Kershaw later re-recorded. When Fusion folded, Kershaw linked with **Nine Below Zero**'s manager Micky Modern, who helped him sign to MCA Records. The UK chart hits started to come in 1983 when his debut - 'I Won't Let The Sun Go Down On Me' -

reached a modest number 47. However, early the next year the follow-up 'Wouldn't It Be Good' reached the Top 5. This perfect pop song justifiably gave Kershaw a high profile. That summer a reissue of his debut gave him his biggest success (number 2) and for the next 12 months a succession of his pleasant, simple tunes paraded through the upper reaches of the UK chart. Kershaw was backed by the Krew whose nucleus was Dennis Smith, Keiffer Airey (brother of **Rainbow**'s **Don Airey**), Tim Moore, Mark Price and Kershaw's wife, Sheri. The first two albums featured guest appearances from Don Snow (ex-**Squeeze**; Sinceroes) and Mark King of **Level 42**. In 1985, **Elton John** - a big Kershaw fan - asked him to play guitar on his single 'Nikita'. Although the first two albums had been successes, the third proved a relative failure, and despite regular comebacks Kershaw's performing career declined. In recent years he has returned as a songwriter of note behind other hit acts, notably **Chesney Hawkes**' massive hit 'The One And Only'.

● ALBUMS: *Human Racing* (MCA 1984)★★★, *The Riddle* (MCA 1984)★★★, *Radio Musicola* (MCA 1986)★★, *The Works* (MCA 1990)★★.

● COMPILATIONS: *The Collection* (MCA 1991)★★★.

Kershaw, Sammy

b 24 February 1958, Kaplan, Louisiana, USA. He is related to **Doug Kershaw** and hence there is a strong Cajun feel to his work. Among his other influences are **Cal Smith** and **Mel Street**. Sammy Kershaw started playing country clubs when he was 12 years old, working with local musician J.B. Perry. During his eight years with Perry, they opened for **George Jones** and **Ray Charles** (years later he would duet with Jones on 'Never Bit A Bullet Like This'). He joined a local band, Blackwater, but after a few years, decided to leave the industry and help design shops for the Wal-Mart Corporation. Some of his early tracks were released in the USA in 1993 on a MTE album, *Sammy Kershaw*, that was designed to look like his current product. He was encouraged back into music by a contract with **Mercury Records** in 1990. Kershaw had his first country hit with 'Cadillac Style' and ended up as spokesman for their 1992 sales campaign. He courted controversy when he recorded 'National Working Women's Holiday' but he is well able to deal with hecklers, having once been a stand-up comic. He topped the US country charts with 'She Don't Know She's Beautiful' in 1993. He has been married three times and says, 'I'm a ballad-singing fool and I've lived all those songs at one time or another.' Following a greatest hits compilation, Kershaw released the disappointing *Politics, Religion And Her*, but bounced back with *Labor Of Love*.

● ALBUMS: *Don't Go Near The Water* (Mercury 1991)★★★, *Haunted Heart* (Mercury 1993)★★★, *Sammy Kershaw* (MTE 1993)★★, *Feelin' Good Train* (Mercury 1994)★★★, *Christmas Time's A Comin'* (Mercury 1994)★★, *Politics, Religion And Her* (Mercury 1996)★★, *Labor Of Love* (Mercury 1997)★★★.

● COMPILATIONS: *The Hits Chapter 1* (Mercury 1995)★★★.

● VIDEOS: *The Hit Video Collection* (1994).

Kessel, Barney

b. 17 October 1923, Muskogee, Oklahoma, USA. After playing in various bands (including one led by Chico, the piano-playing Marx brother), Kessel began to establish a name for himself on the west coast. He appeared in the **Norman Granz**-produced short film *Jammin' The Blues* (1944), then played in various big bands of the late swing era. From the mid-40s he was in great demand for studio work, jazz record sessions, club and concert dates, and on tours with **Jazz At The Philharmonic**. Among the artists with whom he performed and recorded over the next 20 years were **Charlie Parker**, **Oscar Peterson**, **Billie Holiday** and **Harry Edison**. By the mid-60s he was one of the best-known and most-recorded guitarists in jazz. He continued to tour and record in groups and as a solo artist. In the early 70s, he teamed up with **Herb Ellis** and **Charlie Byrd** to perform as the group Great Guitars. This project continued to tour into the 80s, which saw Kessel as active as ever. An exceptionally gifted musician with a very wide range, Kessel's versatility has ensured that he is always in demand. In a jazz context he plays in a boppish, post-**Charlie Christian** style, but has his own distinctive flavour. In the context of Great Guitars, he ably fills the mid-ground between Byrd's latent classicism and Ellis's blues-tinged swing. In person, Kessel has a swift and waspish sense of humour, a characteristic which often appears in his music. He was incapacitated by a stroke in 1992.

● ALBUMS: *Barney Kessel Vol 1* (Contemporary 1953)★★★, *Barney Kessel Vol 2* (Contemporary 1954)★★★, *To Swing Or Not To Swing* (Contemporary 1955)★★★, *Plays Standards* (Contemporary 1955)★★★★, *Easy Like* (1956)★★★, *Sessions, Live* (1956)★★★, *Let's Cook* (1957)★★★, *Music To Listen To Barney Kessel By* (Contemporary 1957)★★★, with Holiday *Body And Soul* (1957)★★★★, *The Poll Winners* (Contemporary 1958)★★★★, *The Poll Winners Ride Again* (Contemporary (1959)★★★, *Some Like It Hot* (Contemporary 1959)★★★, *Plays Carmen* (Contemporary 1959)★★, *Workin' Out* (Contemporary 1961)★★★, *Breakfast At Tiffany's* (Reprise 1961)★★★, *Bossa Nova Plus Big Band* (Reprise 1962)★★★, *Let's Cook* (Contemporary 1962)★★★, *Swingin' Party* (Contemporary 1963)★★★, *Kessel Jazz* (Reprise 1963)★★, *Feelin' Free* (Contemporary 1965)★★★, *On Fire* (Emerald 1965)★★★, *Swinging Easy* (1968)★★★, *Kessel's Kit* (1969)★★, with others *Limehouse Blues* (Black Lion 1969)★★★, *Autumn Leaves* (Black Lion 1970)★★★, *Just Friends* (Sonet 1973)★★★, with Ken Baldcock *Summertime In Montreux* (1973)★★★, *Yesterday* (Black Lion 1974)★★★, *Two-Way Conversation* (1975)★★★, *Three Guitars* (Concord 1975)★★★, *Plays Barney Kessel* (Concord 1975)★★★, *Soaring* (Concord 1977)★★★, *Great Guitars: Straight Tracks* (c.1978)★★★, *Live At Sometime* (Storyville 1978)★★★, *Great Guitars At The Winery* (Concord 1980)★★★, *Jelly Beans* (Concord 1981)★★★, *Great Guitars At Charlie's, Georgetown*

(Concord 1982)★★★, *Solo* (Concord 1983)★★★, *Spontaneous Combustion* (JVC 1987)★★★, *Kessel Plays Standards* (Contemporary 1989)★★★.
● COMPILATIONS: *The Artistry Of Barney Kessel* (Fantasy 1987)★★★.

Kessinger Brothers

Clark Kessinger (b. 27 July 1896, South Hills, Kanawha County, West Virginia, USA, d. 4 June 1975) spent most of his life in the county either at St. Albans or South Charleston. He learned to play the banjo as a very young child and was playing the fiddle at the age of five. He made his professional debut when seven years old (earning more than his father's foundry wage), playing in the local saloons and later, as a teenager, also for country dances and on radio WOBU Charleston. He served in the US Army during World War I and on discharge started to play regularly with his nephew Luches (b. 1906, Kanawha County, West Virginia, USA, d. 1944; guitar). The record company believed that they would market better if classed as brothers and so they became known primarily as the Kessinger Brothers, but also recorded as the Wright Brothers, the Arnold Brothers and the Birmingham Entertainers. They made their first recordings for **Brunswick**-Vocalion in 1928 and by 1930, they were instrumental stars with some 29 single records released on Brunswick's *Songs From Dixie* series. Clark Kessinger recorded additional fiddle tunes for Vocalion releases with the material varying from old-time traditional fiddle tunes such as 'Sally Goodin' and 'Turkey In The Straw' to local tunes such as 'Kanawha March' and 'Going Up Bushy Fork'. He has been described by noted authority Ivan M. Tribe as 'an outstanding breakdown fiddler, but he was probably unexcelled in his ability to play slower and more difficult waltzes and marches with almost equal dexterity'. During the 30s, Clark met and discussed playing styles with world-famous classical violinist Fritz Kreisler, when he appeared in Charleston. The Kessingers played together around the Charleston area until 1944, when Luches died. After his nephew's death, Clark continued to play at local dances and worked as a painter during the day. In 1964, he won a state fiddling contest in Virginia, which led to new successes and publicity. He played various folk festivals including Newport, the Smithsonian Folklife Society, appeared at the *Grand Ole Opry* and on network television and recorded four albums. In July 1971, he suffered a stroke soon after he had recorded an album for Rounder. He died four years later in June 1975, on his way to hospital following a further stroke.
● ALBUMS: *The Legend Of Clark Kessinger (Sweet Bunch Of Daisies)* (1965)★★★, *Old Time Music With Fiddle And Guitar* (Rounder 1971)★★★, *The Kessinger Brothers (1928-1930 Recordings)* (1975)★★★, *The Legend Of Clark Kessinger* (1975)★★★, *Memorial Album* (1976)★★★, *Live At Union Grove* (Smithsonian/Folkways 1977)★★★, *Old-Time Country Music* (70s)★★★, *Old-Time Country Music Volume 2* (70s)★★★.

Ketchum, Hal

b. Hal Michael Ketchum, 9 April 1953, Greenwich, New York, USA. Ketchum credits his early influences as **Buck Owens**, **Merle Haggard** and **Marty Robbins**, but he was equally inspired by John Steinbeck's novels. His early musical career included playing drums for an R&B band and guitar in a blues band. He then began to establish himself as a singer and songwriter at the Kerrville Folk Festival. In 1987, he recorded his self-produced, first album as Hal Michael Ketchum, which was initially only released in cassette form. In 1989, it was reissued on CD by the German Sawdust label. In 1991, Ketchum joined Curb Records and, with his grey hair, he could hardly be marketed as a New Country act. *Past The Point Of Rescue*, however, produced US country chart singles: 'Small Town Saturday Night' was a US country number 1 and he followed it with 'Past The Point Of Rescue' and 'Somebody's Love'. His producer, **Allen Reynolds**, had written the **Vogues**' 1965 US hit 'Five O'Clock World', and Ketchum worked up a new version of the song. *Sure Love* was a confident second album, including tributes to his working-class roots in 'Mama Knows The Highway' and 'Daddy's Oldsmobile'. He made a cameo appearance in the movie *Maverick* singing 'Amazing Grace', and became a member of the *Grand Ole Opry* in 1994. Ketchum tours with his band, the Alibis, and is touted by many to develop into a major country star. He says, 'I have a two hundred song catalogue which is, by Nashville standards, not a lot.' Ketchum also paints and writes children's stories, should his two-hundred song catalogue prove insufficient. His most recent release, *Hal Yes*, was produced by Stephen Bruton (ex-**Kris Kristofferson** guitarist) and proved to be one of his finest albums.
● ALBUMS: *Threadbare Alibi* (Watermelon 1989)★★★, *Past The Point Of Rescue* (Curb 1991)★★★, *Sure Love* (Curb 1992)★★★, *Every Little Word* (Curb/Hit 1994)★★★, *Hal Yes* (Curb/Hit 1997)★★★★, *I Saw The Light* (Curb 1998)★★★.
● COMPILATIONS: *Hal Ketchum The Hits* (Curb 1996)★★★★.
● FILMS: *Maverick*.

Ketelbey, Albert William

b. William Aston, 4 August 1875, Birmingham, England, d. 26 November 1959, Isle of Wight, England. His early career mainly involved arranging musical comedy selections, but his composition 'In A Monastery Garden' (1915) brought instant recognition. It was played by every kind of ensemble, and 40 years later it gained a new lease of life when whistled by Ronnie Ronalde. Another great success was 'In A Persian Market' (1920), beloved of comedy acts especially the revered British trio of sand dancers Wilson, Keppel And Betty. Both these works achieved substantial record sales on a famous 30s HMV 78 by organist Reginald Foort. Ketelbey's other works included 'Chal Romano' (1924), 'Suite Romantique' (1924), 'The Clock And The Dresden Figures', 'Cockney Suite'

(1924), 'In The Mystic Land Of Egypt', 'Wedgwood Blue' (1920), 'Bells Across The Meadows' (1921), 'The Sanctuary Of The Heart', 'With Honour Crowned', 'In A Chinese Temple Garden' and 'The Phantom Melody' (1912). Ketelbey made numerous recordings (often anonymously) and was musical director and adviser to **Columbia Records** (UK).

● ALBUMS: *The Immortal Works Of Ketelbey* (Decca)★★★, *Albert Ketelbey* remastered 78s (Pearl 1992)★★★, *British Light Music - Albert Ketelbey* (Marco Polo 1994)★★★★.

Kewley, Ian

b. c.1950, England. A highly experienced British instrumentalist and songwriter, he achieved his greatest success in partnership with **Paul Young**. In the late 60s he played keyboard for Samson, recording an album for Instant Records. Kewley moved on to Strider, a well-respected early 70s band which featured Gary Grainger, later **Rod Stewart**'s guitarist. Kewley next recorded with Limey, a hard rock group aimed at the USA market. The group also included Brian Engel (guitar/vocals) and guitarist Garth Watt-Roy. Signed to **RCA**, Limey made two albums in 1976-77. With Watt-Roy, Kewley joined **Q-Tips** in 1979. This soul band was formed from the remnants of **Streetband**, and Kewley formed a songwriting partnership with the lead singer, **Paul Young**. When Young was signed to a solo contract with **CBS**, Kewley joined him as musical director of the touring group, the Royal Family. He co-wrote eight of the songs on Young's *Between Two Fires* and co-produced the record.

Key, Troyce

b. 1937, Jordon Plantation (70m from Monroe), Louisiana, USA, d. 9 November 1992, Oakland, California, USA. In the early 50s Key became interested in blues after hearing a record by **Lightnin' Hopkins** and he began playing guitar following a serious illness that resulted in hospitalization. During this time he was greatly influenced by the records of **Fats Domino**, **Johnny Otis**, **Muddy Waters**, and others. He was signed by **Warner Brothers Records** in 1958 and had three singles released. Key teamed up with **J.J. Malone** in 1961 and they recorded together around three years later; they also had two albums released by Red Lightnin' and enjoyed a near-hit in Britain in 1980 with the single 'I Gotta New Car (I Was Framed)'. He continued, until his death from leukaemia, to present his good-natured, rocking blues in Oakland, California, at his own club called Eli Mile High, which was also the name of his blues record label.

● ALBUMS: with J.J. Malone *I've Gotta New Car* (Red Lightnin' 1980)★★★, with Malone *Younger Than Yesterday* (Red Lightnin' 1982)★★★.

Keyes, Jimmy

b. c.30s, Kentucky, USA, d. 22 July 1995, New York City, New York, USA. After growing up in Kentucky, Keyes moved to the Bronx, New York, in 1947, where he formed his first vocal group, the Four Notes. This band eventually evolved into the Tunestoppers, with Carl Feaster, Claude Feaster, Floyd McCrae, James Edwards and Rupert Branker appearing alongside him. They signed to the **Atlantic Records** subsidiary label Cat, and in March 1954, now billed as the **Chords**, recorded 'Sh-Boom', co-written by Keyes. An R&B/doo-wop song that also crossed over into the pop charts, it was considered by many as one of the first rock 'n' roll hits. It reached number 5 on the *Billboard* charts, while a cover version by the **Crewcuts** made number 1. However, the Chords never enjoyed another hit single, and in the late 60s Keyes joined soul band the Popular Five. Again, success eluded him, despite several singles for Mr Chand and **Minit Records**. However, recurrent interest in 'Sh-Boom' led to Keyes re-forming the Chords with Carl Feaster in the late 70s. When Feaster died in 1981 Keyes opted to keep the group on the oldies circuit, employing various sidemen. He suffered a brain aneurysm in 1995, and died following an operation in New York.

KGB

This ill-starred supergroup was formed in 1976 around the talents of former **Electric Flag** colleagues **Barry Goldberg** (keyboards) and **Mike Bloomfield** (guitar). Ray Kennedy (vocals), **Ric Gretch** (bass, ex-**Family**, **Blind Faith** and **Traffic**) and **Carmine Appice** (drums, ex-**Vanilla Fudge** and **Beck, Bogert And Appice**) completed a stellar line-up, drawing its punning appellation from the initials of the prime participants. The enterprise was doomed at its inception when Bloomfield refused to fly to Los Angeles to record - his contributions were overdubbed in a Sausalito studio - and subsequently greeted the album's release with an interview to the *Los Angeles Times* in which he disowned the project, admitting his motivations were purely financial. KGB, not unnaturally, imploded, leaving behind an unspectacular set notable for the inclusion of 'Sail On Sailor' and originally recorded by the **Beach Boys** on *Holland*.

● ALBUMS: *KGB* (MCA 1976)★★.

Khac Chi Ensemble

Based in Vancouver, Canada, married partners Khac Chi and Ngoc Bich have steadily built a reputation for introducing authentic Vietnamese instrumentation and musical cadences to the west. Chi began to play the dan bau (a single-string zither) when he was eight years old. By his mid-twenties he was made deputy head of the Traditional Music department at the Conservatory Of Music in Hanoi. He met Bich there in 1979, both playing dan bau in the school orchestra. Chi was also an orchestra conductor. Marrying in 1988, they formed their own ensemble in order to export indigenous Vietnamese music abroad. Although they performed extensive international touring dates, they elected to settle in Canada after playing at the 1992 Vancouver Folk Festival. With assistance from the city's expatriate

Vietnamese community, they found regular work playing in schools and as guest soloists for symphony orchestras. In the summer of 1996 the Khac Chi Ensemble came to Europe for the first time, performing at three festivals in France at which the duo played over a dozen Vietnamese instruments (including the t'rung zylophone, the ko ni stick fiddle and the k'longput bamboo pan-pipes in addition to the dan bau). Their repertoire ranges from classical Vietnamese compositions and folk songs to western film themes.

Khaled

b. Khaled Hadj Brahim, 29 February 1960, Sidi-el-Houri, Algeria. Singing and playing accordion from an early age, Khaled dropped out of school to pursue a musical career in spite of the disapproval of his father (a policeman). From 1976 he released a series of singles that revolutionized Algerian music by introducing drum machines, synthesizers and lyrics celebrating alcohol, sex and partying (some of these early releases are collected on *Young Khaled*). Khaled was also a popular local live attraction, performing at weddings and circumcisions as well as nightclubs. His highly charged and physical onstage persona had much the same effect on Algeria's youth as **Elvis Presley**'s live shows had on teenage Americans in the 50s. By the early 80s Cheb Khaled (Cheb, meaning 'young', was the name given to Khaled and the singers who followed him in order to differentiate him from older, more traditional performers) was banned from Algerian television and radio. However, a performance at Algeria's first National Rai Festival took the country by storm, leading to a lifting of the ban. He moved to France in 1986, soon becoming a star among the large immigrant North African population. *Hada Raykoum* (1987) had originally appeared in Algeria two years earlier and was the first rai album to be released internationally. *Kutche* was Khaled's first European recording. Produced in collaboration with Safy Boutella, it introduced a more sophisticated sound, incorporating elements of funk, jazz and reggae. Dropping the 'Cheb' from his name, he released *Khaled* in 1992. Co-produced by **Don Was** and **Michael Brook**, the album's rai/rock/electro funk fusion was best exemplified by the single 'Didi', a huge hit in many countries throughout the world (including India where a Hindi version was released). By now unable to return to Algeria, where the growing Islamic Fundamentalist movement attacked him for his outspokenly hedonistic stance, Khaled released *N'ssi N'ssi* in 1993. Again featuring some songs produced by Don Was, this time co-producer Philippe Eidel added sweeping middle Eastern strings to the other tracks. *Sahra*, released in 1996, embraced an even wider range of influences. Some of the tracks were recorded in Jamaica with producer **Clive Hunt** and local musicians such as **Dean Fraser** and the **I-Threes**. Eidel and Was both contributed tracks, while the single 'Aicha' was produced by Jean Jack Goldman and became a huge hit throughout mainland Europe and beyond. In 1997

Khaled toured extensively to promote *Sahra*. *Hafla* (meaning 'party'); he was recorded at concerts in Belgium and France during this tour, backed by a slick, multicultural band and, on some songs, accompanied by enthusiastic mass singing from the audience.
● ALBUMS: *Hada Raykoum* (Triple Earth 1987)★★★★, *Kutche* (Stern's 1989)★★★, *Khaled* (Barclay 1992)★★★, *N'ssi N'ssi* (Mango 1993)★★★, *Young Khaled* (CMM 1996)★★★, *Sahra* (Mango 1996)★★★★, *Hafla* (Barclay 1998)★★★.

Khan

Formed in London, England, in 1971, Khan was founded by guitarist **Steve Hillage**. In 1967 he had been a member of the flower-power influenced Uriel with **Dave Stewart** (organ), Mont Campbell (bass) and Clive Brooks (drums). When Hillage opted for university, his erstwhile colleagues formed **Egg**. Khan was completed by Dick Henn (organ), Nick Greenwood (bass) - both ex-Crazy World Of **Arthur Brown** - and Eric Peachy (drums). *Space Shanty*, a blend of jazz rock and lengthy improvised passages, was recorded with the aid of Stewart, who then replaced Henn in June 1972. Khan split up, almost penniless, four months later. Stewart then formed **Hatfield And The North**, while Hillage found fame in **Gong** and as a solo artist and producer.
● ALBUMS: *Space Shanty* (Deram 1971)★★.

Khan, Ali Akbar

b. Ustad Ali Akbar Khan, 14 April 1922, Shivpur, East Bengal (Bangladesh since 1971). Ali Akbar Khan is acknowledged throughout the continent of his birth as the master of the sarod, an elongated steel lute. He follows in the tradition established by his father and teacher, Allauddin Khan, who himself did much to popularise the instrument. His sister, Annapurna Devi, also studied music with his father, and later married another of his students, **Ravi Shankar**. Together with Shankar, Ali Akbar performed celebrated duets (or jugalbandis in the classical Hindustan tradition), which established their reputation. Both survived the days when Hindustani music was subject to court patronage to a modern age where each was free to perform in their own right. Ali Akbar worked at the court of Maharajah Hanumantha Singh, before finding his first radio commissions at a station in Rajasthan. However, it took the intervention of **Yehudi Menuhin** to bring him to foreign shores. Enraptured by Hindustan (Northern Indian) music and culture, the violinist visited Delhi in 1955 and intended to bring Shankar back to America with him. When Shankar was reluctant, Ali Akbar took his place. Thus he played the first American concert of Hindustan music in New York, also appearing on a television programme, *Omnibus*, and recording with Shirish Gor (tanpura) and Chatur Lal (tabla). *Piloo, Music Of India - Morning And Evening Ragas*, was the world's first album of Indian classical music. On its 30th anniversary it was re-released on AMMP Records as part of a double CD collection, the second CD comprising a 1994 concert performance at the Palace

Of Fine Arts in San Francisco. By 1960 Ali Akbar's music had accompanied several 'Bollywood' films, including Satyajit Ray's *Devi*, Chetan Anand's *Aandhiyan* and *Ham Safar*, Dilip Nag's *Nupur* and *Necklace*, and he also recorded with arguably India's most popular singer, Asha Bhosle. He reunited with Shankar to appear at the August 1971 Concerts For Bangladesh. He had already done much for his country's evolution, including the founding of a college of Indian classical music (in 1967 a similar enterprise was started in California, and another in Switzerland in 1985). He reunited with Bhosle for 1996's *Legacy*, with the meeting between two of India's greatest musical talents generating the expected praise. Though never sharing the international fame afforded his brother-in-law Shankar, Ali Akbar is judged by many to be the greatest living exponent not only of his instrument, but of classical Indian music in its entirety.

● ALBUMS: *Music Of India - Morning And Evening Ragas* (EMI 1955)★★, *Signature Series Volumes 1 & 2* (Connoisseur Society 1967, re-released by AMMP in 1991)★★★, with Ravi Shankar *Raga Mishra Piloo* (EMI India 60s)★★★, *Live In San Francisco* (AMMP 1979)★★, *Ali Akbar Khan Plays Alap* (AMMP 1993)★★★, *Morning Visions* (AMMP 1994)★★★, *Then And Now* (AMMP 1995)★★★★, *Legacy* (AMMP 1996)★★★★, *Passing On The Tradition* (AMMP 1996)★★★.

Khan, Chaka

b. Yvette Marie Stevens, 23 March 1953, Great Lakes Naval Training Station, Illinois, USA. Having sung with several Chicago club bands, including Lyfe, Lock And Chains and Baby Huey And The Babysitters, Chaka Khan became acquainted with Ask Rufus, a group formed from the remnants of hit group the **American Breed**. When Khan replaced original singer Paulette McWilliams, the line-up truncated its name to **Rufus** and as such released a succession of superior funk singles. Khan's stylish voice was the group's obvious attraction and in 1978 she began recording as a solo act. 'I'm Every Woman' topped the US R&B chart that year while subsequent releases, 'What Cha' Gonna Do For Me' (1981) and 'Got To Be There' (1982), consolidated this position. However, a 1984 release, 'I Feel For You', established the singer as an international act when it reached number 2 in the USA and number 1 in the UK pop charts. This exceptional performance was written by **Prince** and featured contributions from **Stevie Wonder** and **Melle Mel**. It not only led to a platinum-selling album, but won a Grammy for Best R&B Female Performance. Khan has since continued to forge a successful career, working with **David Bowie** and **Robert Palmer**, and duetting with **Steve Winwood** on his international smash, 'Higher Love'. In 1985 she enjoyed two Top 20 UK chart entries with 'This Is My Night' and 'Eye To Eye', while four years later a remix of 'I'm Every Woman' reached the Top 10 in the UK. She collaborated with **Gladys Knight**, **Brandy** and Tamia on the minor hit single 'Missing You' in 1996, taken from the **Queen Latifah** film *Set It Off*. She formed her own label Earth Song, in 1998.

● ALBUMS: *Chaka* (Warners 1978)★★★, *Naughty* (Warners 1980)★★★, *What Cha' Gonna Do For Me* (Warners 1981)★★★, *Echoes Of An Era* (Elektra 1982)★★★, *Chaka Khan* (Warners 1982)★★★, *I Feel For You* (Warners 1984)★★★, *Destiny* (Warners 1986)★★, *CK* (Warners 1988)★★★, *Life Is A Dance - The Remix Project* (Warners 1989)★★, *The Woman I Am* (Warners 1992)★★★, *Come 2 My House* (Earth Song 1998)★★★.

● COMPILATIONS: *Epiphany: The Best Of ... Volume 1* (Reprise 1996)★★★★.

● FILMS: *Breakdance - The Movie* (1984).

Khan, Nusrat Fateh Ali

b. 12 July 1948, Lyallpur (later renamed Faisalabad), Pakistan, d. 16 August 1997. One of the most popular singers in the Indian subcontinent, Khan predominantly sang qawwali, the music of devotional Sufism, but incorporated other forms including Khyal (traditional classical) to produce a unique style that appealed to followers of all religions. He performed with the Party, a group of highly trained Pakistani musicians which included several family members. In 1971, Nusrat took over from his father (Ustad Fateh Ali Khan) as leader of the Party after experiencing recurring dreams that he was singing at the famous Muslim shrine of Hazratja Khawaja Moid-Ud-Din Christie in Ajmer, India. This dream became reality eight years later. Through the 70s and 80s Khan's music began to become increasingly synonymous with India and Pakistan's vibrant film industry. Such was his popularity with the stars of the movies that in 1979 he was invited to sing at the wedding of Rishi, son of actor/director Raj Kapoor, in front of the most prominent members of the Bombay film industry. **Peter Gabriel**'s admiration of Nusrat's singing led to him working with WOMAD on projects including a compilation album, many festival appearances and releases on the **Virgin**/Real World Records label, recorded in England. The first of these, *Shahen-Shah* was named after Nusrat's Pakistani nickname, Shahen-Shah-e-Qawwali (The Brightest Star In Qawwali). For *Mustt Mustt*, Nusrat worked with experimental composer **Michael Brook** in an attempt to give his sound a western orientation. On all but two tracks, traditional songs were replaced by classical vocal exercises which were edited around western rhythms. Brook said of the project 'everyone was excited, although it wasn't painless - it worked'. A remix of the title track by **Massive Attack** led to a surprise UK club hit. Khan returned to his roots with *Shahbaaz*, four traditional qawwali songs all praising the Devine Beloved. Successive albums for Real World continued to see cross-experimentation between qawwali and Western influences, though none were as integrationist as *Mustt Mustt*. Despite this, the vibrancy of the artist's deeply spiritual performances, on record and stage, militated against the suspicion that he had forgotten his roots. His sudden death robbed the world of one of it's finest voices.

● ALBUMS: *Shahen-Shah* (Real World 1989)★★, *Mustt Mustt* (Real World 1990)★★★★, *En Concert A Paris, Volumes 1 & 2* (Ocoro 1990)★★★, *En Concert A Paris, Volumes 3-5* (Ocoro 1990)★★★, *Shahbaaz* (Real World 1991)★★★, with Jan Garbarek *Ragas And Sagas* (1992)★★★, *Revelation* (Real World 1993)★★, *The Last Prophet* (Real World 1994)★★★, *Night Song* (Real World 1995)★★★, with Jaed Akhtar *Sangam* (EMI India 1997)★★★, with Michael Brook *Star Rise* (Real World 1997)★★★★.

Khan, Steve

b. 28 April 1947, Los Angeles, California, USA. Khan is the son of lyricist **Sammy Cahn** and learned to play the piano and drums as a child. He was the drummer with the surf group the **Chantays** (1962-63) and only turned to the guitar when he was 20. After graduating in music from UCLA in 1969, he settled in New York where he became a prolific session musician recording with artists as varied as **George Benson**, **Hubert Laws**, **Maynard Ferguson**, **Billy Joel** and **Steely Dan**. In 1977, he worked with **Larry Coryell** and **Randy** and **Michael Brecker** before touring Japan with the **CBS** All Stars. In 1978, he published a transcription of solos by **Wes Montgomery**. He has continued to develop his skills as a composer as can be seen in his tribute to pianist **Thelonious Monk** on *Evidence*. In 1981, he formed Eyewitness with Manolo Badrena, Anthony Jackson and **Steve Jordan**.

● ALBUMS: with Larry Coryell *Two For The Road* (1977)★★★★, *Tightrope* (1977)★★★★, *Evidence* (Arista 1980),★★★★ with Eyewitness *Eyewitness* (Antilles 1981)★★, with Eyewitness *Casa Loco* (1983)★★, *Local Colour* (Denon 1988)★★★, *Public Access* (GRP 1990)★★★, *Let's Call This* (Polydor 1991)★★★, *Headline* (Polydor 1993)★★, *Crossings* (Verve 1994)★★★, *Got My Mental* (Evidence 1997)★★★.

● COMPILATIONS: *Best Of Steve Khan* (CBS 1980)★★★.

Kiani, Mary

Prior to the start of her solo career 90s UK pop-dance vocalist Mary Kiani was the singer with Glasgow, Scotland-based techno/house group the Time Frequency (often abbreviated to **TTF**). That group was enormously successful in Scotland, reaching number 1 in the charts with 'Real Love', which also peaked at number 8 in the main UK charts. Their other successful singles included 'New Emotion' and 'The Ultimate High', both of which also charted in the UK Top 40. She made her debut *Top Of The Pops* appearance with T.T.F. and also supported **Prince** at Edinburgh's Meadowbank Stadium. Later she worked with the Welsh band Waterfront, who toured the USA to strong acclaim and reached number 6 in the *Billboard* charts with 'Cry'. She signed a solo deal in 1995 with the management team behind **Dina Carroll**, MN8 and **Eternal**, and released her first single, 'When I Call Your Name', in August. It reached number 18 in the UK charts in its first week of release. The follow-up single, 'I Give It All To You'/'I Imagine', followed in December. This was a double a-side release, featuring a ballad and a rhythmic techno-house number, with remixes from producers including Tony de Vit and Eddie Fingers. Once again it was a hit.

● ALBUMS: *Long Hard Funky Dreams* (Mercury 1997)★★★.

Kibbey, Sue

b. England. Singing as a child in school opened her mind to the joys of music. Although Kibbey sang in a school choir, she really wanted to be in the Music and Movement class and she had herself deliberately relegated there by singing out of tune: 'I knew enough at that age to know how to sing out of tune on purpose'. As a teenager she sang in choirs and at folk festivals. She also spent many years training as a dancer and became a qualified teacher of dance. As an adult she continued to sing, mostly pop with some jazz, but was diverted into marriage and children. After her fourth child and a divorce she sang on, gradually dropping all but jazz from her repertoire and gaining a reputation. In 1987 she studied jazz and rock at the Guildhall School of Music and Drama and in the 90s was teaching at the Royal Academy of Music. Kibbey has worked with many noted jazz musicians ranging stylistically from **Acker Bilk** and **Bud Freeman** to **Harry Beckett** and **Tony Coe**. In 1991 she was featured singer in a jazz suite composed by **Michael Garrick**. She has played jazz festivals in the USA, Europe and in the UK, including appearance at Sacramento, Köln and Ascona. Kibbey has also been featured at arts festivals including those at Bradford on Avon and Bath where, in 1994, she performed a one-woman show. She has also held residencies in Sweden and Japan. Kibbey's repertoire ranges widely across traditional and modern jazz and encompasses the best of popular songs. Her vocal range is similarly wide and she sings with great dramatic flair and has a commanding stage presence.

Kick Out The Jams - The MC5

A true explosion of a record. Unfeasibly heady in its approach and delivery, it still stands today as one of the great, unabashed roars of bare, musical energy. Vocalist Rob Tyner crawls from a whisper to a scream, the tunnel of sound constructed around him both desperate and admirable. The title track is a manifestation of sound threatening to stumble and fall in on itself, and on the simply great 'Motor City Is Burning', the appropriately monikered guitarist, Fred 'Sonic' Smith, proves the power of his well-chosen nickname. Meanwhile, the eager sentiment of 'I Want You Right Now' speaks volumes about the tone of the album. One that will blow away your speaker covers, if you have not already removed them by now.

● Tracks: *Ramblin' Rose; Kick Out The Jams; Come Together; Rocket Reducer No. 62 (Rama Lama Fa Fa Fa); Borderline; Motor City Is Burning; I Want You Right Now; Starship.*

● First released 1969

● UK peak chart position: did not chart

● USA peak chart position: 30

Kickin' Records

Record label originally established in 1988, at that time under the name GTI Music (the Great Techno Institution), based in Notting Hill Gate in West London (still its current home). At first the label supplied a demand for tough street soul, with April 1988's 'Good Living' from Dave Collins their first release. However, there was an immediate musical shift afterwards, with label boss Peter Harris signing **Shut Up And Dance** after hearing a demo track (eventually releasing '5678'). The Kickin' Records name was first invoked in 1990 when the Scientist's 'The Exorcist' arrived. This, claimed to be the first record with a BPM above 130, became a *de rigeur* accessory among followers of the burgeoning rave scene. The follow-up, 'The Bee', also sold strongly, and the Scientist would go on to join Kickin' at 1991's 'first ever Russian rave'. 1991 saw the label signing a second, hugely successful rave act, **Messiah**. Two years later the label began its popular *Hard Leaders* compilation series, which has become a favourite among hardcore fans. In the meantime a new roster of artists had been assembled, including Wishdokta, Xenophobia (a front for former members of **Rubella Ballet**), PMA, Kicksquad (Scientist with DJ Hype), Flat 47, Noodles & Wonder, Giro Kid and Green Budha. Kickin' also set up two subsidiary operations, **Slip 'n' Slide** (house/garage) and Pandemonium (indie guitar), as well as liaising with **Colin Dale** for his *The Outer Limits* series.
● COMPILATIONS: Various: *Hard Leaders 1-4* (Kickin' 1994)★★★.

Kid 'N Play

Among rap's most innocuous outfits, Kid 'N Play came to light in 1988 through an album that to date represents their best work; and typified their happy-go-lucky, cartoon style. So much so that the group were offered their own cartoon series, following their appearance in *House Party* (*Kid 'N Play's Funhouse* is a spin-off from the film, including actual dialogue). Kid (b. Christopher Reid) and Play (b. Christopher Martin) concentrate heartily on a youthful style of braggadocio, typified on their debut album by the two-timing morality sequence, 'Undercover' (which featured guest vocals by the **Real Roxanne**), or the self-explanatory 'Rollin' With Kid 'N Play'. Their music is underpinned by the production of mentor **Hurby Luv Bug**, while their practical messages like 'Don't do drugs' and 'Stay in school' are unlikely to offend middle-class American sentiments.
● ALBUMS: *2 Hype* (Select 1988)★★, *Kid 'N Play's Funhouse* (Select 1990)★★★, *Face The Nation* (Select 1991)★★★.

Kid Creole And The Coconuts

b. August Darnell, 1951, Haiti. A relatively exciting entry into the UK charts at the height of New Romanticism in the early 80s, Kid Creole And The Coconuts introduced many to the dynamic pulse of Latin pop. Creole originally formed Dr. Buzzard's Original Savannah Band in the 70s with his brother Stoney Darnell. They would go on to create the Coconuts with the aid of 'Sugar Coated' Andy Hernandez (aka Coati Mundi), plus several multi-instrumentalists and a singing/dancing troupe. The group's fusion of salsa with disco pop was conducted with immense flair on their 1980 debut, *Off The Coast Of Me*. The follow-up album introduced a concept also pursued by three subsequent collections - namely a search by Kid and the Coconuts for Mimi, with nods to the various geographical stop-off points on the journey. The theme was not laboured, however, and proved entirely secondary to the bristling musical energy and zest beneath the surface. The Coconuts then hit a rich commercial vein with *Tropical Gangsters* (known as *Wise Guy* outside the UK). Three Top 10 chart placings followed for the album's singles; 'I'm A Wonderful Thing, Baby', 'Stool Pigeon' and 'Annie, I'm Not Your Daddy', the latter missing the top spot by just one place. Their live shows at this time were among the most propulsive and enchanting of the period, with outlandish dancing and cod theatricals garnishing the Latin beats. Afterwards the band's commercial profile declined, but there was no similar qualitative discount. *Doppelganger* returned to the grand theme as its premise - this time the cloning of Kid Creole by evil scientist King Nignat. Again such considerations proved secondary to the gripping music, particularly effective on 'The Lifeboat Party', which crept inside the UK Top 50. Elsewhere the selections spanned reggae, soul, scat jazz and funk, all flavoured by the familiar salsa rumble. The Coconuts also released an album of their own at this time, based on the dynamics of their powerful stage revue, while Hernandez released a solo album under his assumed title Coati Mundi. Kid Creole had become King Creole by the advent of *In Praise Of Older Women*, but this was another full-bodied work, and certainly far superior to 1987's *I, Too, Have Seen The Woods*. This introduced female vocalist Haitia Fuller on shared lead vocals, but the more laboured material made it a disappointing chapter. More promising was *Private Waters*, a return to form with inspired lyrics and buckets of the type of sexual innuendo which Creole had made his own.
● ALBUMS: *Off The Coast Of Me* (Ze 1980)★★, *Fresh Fruit In Foreign Places* (Ze 1981)★★★, *Tropical Gangsters* aka *Wise Guy* (Ze 1982)★★★, *Doppelganger* (Ze 1983)★★★, *In Praise Of Older Women And Other Crimes* (Sire 1985)★★★, *I, Too, Have Seen The Woods* (Sire 1987)★★, *Private Waters In The Great Divide* (Columbia 1990)★★, *You Shoulda Told Me You Were . . .* (Columbia 1991)★★.
● COMPILATIONS: *Cre-Ole: Best Of Kid Creole And The Coconuts* (Island 1984)★★★, *The Best Of ...* (Island 1996)★★★.
● VIDEOS: *Live At Hammersmith* (1984).

Kid From Spain, The

One of the most lavish and successful musicals of the early 30s, and 'the kid' in question was, of course, the irrepressible **Eddie Cantor**. On this hilarious occasion, while on the run from the US Federal authorities, he winds up in Spain where, through no fault of his own, he is somehow mistaken for a famous bullfighter. His efforts to justify this exalted position - actually in the bullring - are delightful to see. Robert Young and Lyda Roberti gave him all the support they could, and the rest of the cast included Ruth Hall, John Miljan, Noah Beery, and J. Carrol Naish. Soon-to-be-familiar faces in the chorus were those of **Betty Grable** and Paulette Goddard. Cantor's most engaging vocal moment came with 'What a Perfect Combination' (**Bert Kalmar-Irving Caesar** [lyric]; **Harry Ruby**-Harry Askst [music]), and Ruby and Kalmar also contributed 'The College Song', 'Look What You've Done', and 'In The Moonlight'. The two songwriters also wrote the screenplay in collaboration with William Anthony McGuire. **Busby Berkeley** was the choreographer so the dance sequences were imaginative and high-class, and Samuel Goldwyn produced the film so the Goldwyn Girls were present - and pretty. Leon McCarey was responsible for directing a kind of musical and comedy masterpiece.

Kid Frost

b. Arturo Molina Jnr., 31 May 1964, Los Angeles, California, USA. Mexican-descended rapper who was raised on military bases in Guam and Germany, but did most of his growing up in East Los Angeles, where he began delivering rhymes in 1982. He was inducted into the ranks of Uncle Jam's Army, as the west coast began to accomodate the innovations of the Bronx. A major force in the establishment of Latin hip-hop, Frost brought together several other Hispanic rappers for the **Latin Alliance** project in 1991. Before then he had made strides with his 1990 solo set, another important signpost in the sub-genre's development. His blend of Chicano social observation and pulsing rap breakbeats provided him with a considerable audience outside of his own socio-genetic bracket. Now signed to **Virgin**, Kid Frost deploys the intelligence to sample not only from funk's back-catalogue, but also that of the salsa tradition of his own people.

● ALBUMS: *Hispanic Causing Panic* (Virgin 1990)★★, *East Side Story* (Virgin 1992)★★★.

Kid Galahad

Elvis Presley starred in this 1962 film, which was a remake of Edward G. Robinson's 1937 vehicle. In a plot later echoed by the *Rocky* series, an unfancied fighter rises from obscurity to become a boxing champion. It was not an artistic success, although Presley's popularity ensured greater box-office returns than the action merited. Six songs, including 'King Of The Whole Wide World' and 'I Got Lucky', were completed for the soundtrack. These were compiled on the *Kid Galahad* EP, which remained on the US singles chart for seven weeks.

Kid Millions

In fact, all of $77 millions - that is the sum the naive kid from Brooklyn (**Eddie Cantor**) inherits from his archaeologist father early on in this 1934 Samuel Goldwyn picture (released by United Artists). Naturally, as soon as the word gets around regarding his windfall, several unsavoury individuals come crawling out of the woodwork - or rather, the stonework, as in this case the loot is hidden somewhere in Egypt. Arthur Sheekman, Nat Perrin, and Nunnally Johnson wrote the screenplay, but it was all academic anyway, because, as usual with a Cantor vehicle, it is Eddie's infectious humour and a batch of peppy numbers that propel the film along. A talented supporting cast helps as well, and in this case, Ann Sothern, **Ethel Merman**, George Murphy, Jesse Block, Warren Hymer, the **Nicholas Brothers** and Eve Sully, along with Goldwyn girls Lucille Ball and Paulette Goddard, more than filled the bill. Cantor managed to don his traditional blackface for some of the time, and he had four splendid songs, 'When My Ship Comes In' and 'Okay Toots' (both **Walter Donaldson-Gus Kahn**), 'I Want To Be A Minstrel Man' (**Burton Lane-Harold Adamson**) featuring the marvellous dancing Nicholas Brothers, and 'Mandy' (**Irving Berlin**). Merman was thrilling on 'An Earful Of Music' (Donaldson-Kahn), and Murphy and Sothern tender on 'Your Head On My Shoulder' (Lane-Adamson). Cantor, Merman, Hymer, and the Goldwyn Girls were all involved in the spectacular 'Ice Cream Fantasy' finale which was filmed in Technicolor. Seymour Felix was the choreographer, and *Kid Millions* was directed by Roy Del Routh.

Kid Sensation

b. Steven Spence, Seattle, Washington, USA. Rapper who first came to fame as **Sir Mix-A-Lot**'s DJ and keyboardist, before scoring a minor success with his own debut album. After graduating in 1988, he became part of the Sir Mix-A-Lot posse behind 1988's platinum-selling *Swass* set. It encouraged him to embark on his own career, which was soon rewarded when his debut album provided three hit singles, 'Back To Boom', 'Seatown Ballers' and 'Prisoner Of Ignorance'. His self-aggrandising title was reflected in the cool braggadocio of much of the material on offer, but by the advent of a follow-up album there was a message behind the rhymes. 'I'm trying to show I'm a down to earth guy, it's more of what I'm all about'. The b-side of the album's promotional single, 'Ride The Rhythm', was 'The Way I Swing'. This was a duet with the Seattle Mariner's all-star centerfielder, and Sensation's sporting idol, Ken Friggy Jnr.

● ALBUMS: *Rollin' With Number One* (Nastymix 1990)★★★, *The Power Of Rhyme* (Nastymix 1992)★★★.

Kidd, Carol

b. 19 October 1945, Glasgow, Scotland. Kidd began her career singing in and around Glasgow in the early 60s, entering numerous talent shows where one of her regular fellow contestants was Marie McDonald, later to find fame as pop singer **Lulu**. At the age of 15, Kidd was singing with a traditional jazz band; two years later she married the trombone player and started a family, then spent a further five years with another trad band. By this time she was developing an appreciation of the finer aspects of popular music. Unfortunately, her options were limited, trad and rock being the only commercially viable choices. Frustrated at not being able to sing how and what she wanted, she retired from the music scene for four years, returning only when a Glasgow-based quartet asked her to join them for a Saturday morning session. She stayed for 11 years, the quartet evolving into a trio with which she worked regularly until early 1990. This long relationship proved invaluable in allowing Kidd to develop an extensive and well-honed repertoire that has at its centre a fine selection of standards. Her record albums, appearances at **Ronnie Scott**'s and an annual engagement at the prestigious Edinburgh Festival helped to expand her audience. A series of concert appearances in 1989 and 1990 with **Humphrey Lyttelton**'s band also opened new doors. Midway through 1990, with different accompanists, including the excellent pianist **David Newton**, and a wholesale change in her repertoire, Kidd relaunched her career. An invitation to open at a **Frank Sinatra** concert and an appearance at London's Queen Elizabeth Hall, in November 1990, helped to raise her career profile. Although she has still to achieve her ambition to appeal to more than a specialist jazz audience, there seems little chance that her rich talent will go unrecognized in the larger public arena through another decade. She was awarded an MBE in the Queen's Birthday Honours List in 1998.

● ALBUMS: *Carol Kidd* (Linn 1984)★★, *All My Tomorrows* (Linn 1985)★★★, *Nice Work (If You Can Get It)* (Linn 1987)★★★★, *Night We Called It A Day* (Linn 1990)★★★, *I'm Glad We Met* (Linn 1992)★★★, *When I Dream* (1992)★★★.

Kidd, Johnny, And The Pirates

Kidd (b. Frederick Heath, 23 December 1939, Willesden, London, England, d. 7 October 1966), is now rightly revered as an influential figure in the birth of British rock. Although his backing group fluctuated, this enigmatic figure presided over several seminal pre-**Beatles** releases. Formed in January 1959, the original line-up consisted of two former members of the Five Nutters skiffle group, Kidd (lead vocals) and Alan Caddy (b. 2 February 1940, London, England; lead guitar), joined by Tony Docherty (rhythm guitar), Johnny Gordon (bass) and Ken McKay (drums), plus backing singers Mike West and Tom Brown. Their compulsive debut single, 'Please Don't Touch' barely scraped into the UK Top 20, but it remains one of the few authentic home-grown rock 'n' roll performances to emerge from the 50s. Its immediate successors were less original and although they featured session men, most of Kidd's group were then dropped in favour of

experienced hands. By 1960, Kidd and Caddy were fronting a new rhythm section consisting of Brian Gregg (bass) and **Clem Cattini** (drums). Their first single, 'Shakin' All Over', was another remarkable achievement, marked by its radical stop/start tempo, Kidd's feverish delivery and an incisive lead guitar solo from session man Joe Moretti. The song deservedly topped the charts, but its inspiration to other musicians was equally vital. Defections resulted in the formation of a third line-up - Kidd, Johnny Spence (bass), Frank Farley (drums) and Johnny Patto (guitar) - although the last was replaced by Mick Green. Onstage, the group continued to wear full pirate regalia while the singer sported a distinctive eye-patch, but they were under increasing competition from the emergent Liverpool sound. Two 1963 hits, 'I'll Never Get Over You' and 'Hungry For Love', although memorable, owed a substantial debt to Merseybeat at the expense of the unit's own identity. The following year, Green left to join the **Dakotas**, precipitating a succession of replacements, and although he continued to record, a depressed leader talked openly of retirement. However, the singer re-emerged in 1966, fronting the New Pirates, but Kidd's renewed optimism ended in tragedy when, on 7 October, he was killed in a car crash. This pivotal figure is remembered both as an innovator and for the many musicians who passed through his ranks. John Weider (the **Animals** and **Family**), Nick Simper (**Deep Purple**) and Jon Morshead (**Aynsley Dunbar Retaliation**) are a few of those who donned the requisite costume, while the best-known line-up, Green, Spence and Farley, successfully re-established the **Pirates**' name during the late 70s.

● COMPILATIONS: *Shakin' All Over* (Regal Starline 1971)★★★, *Johnny Kidd - Rocker* (EMI France 1978)★★★, *The Best Of Johnny Kidd And The Pirates* (EMI 1987)★★★, *Rarities* (See For Miles 1987)★★★, *The Classic And The Rare* (See For Miles 1990)★★★, *The Complete Johnny Kidd* (EMI 1992)★★★★.

● FURTHER READING: *Shaking All Over*, Keith Hunt.

Kidd, Kenneth

b. 1935, Newton, Mississippi, USA, d. June 1995. Aka Prez Kenneth, as a youngster Kidd sang in the church choir but was also attracted to the blues. He settled in Chicago in 1956 and soon tried to learn guitar, switching to bass because he found it easier. In the 60s, Kidd recorded in a **Jimmy Reed** vein for the Biscayne label. His track 'Devil Dealing' was the prototype for **G.L. Crockett**'s hit 'It's A Man Down There', but he received no credit. Towards the end of the decade he formed his own label, Kenneth Records, and although he recorded on a **Hip Linkchain** session in 1976, little was heard of him subsequently. He continued to work occasionally in west side Chicago clubs until his death in 1995.

Kidd, Michael

b. Milton Greenwald, 12 August 1919, New York City, New York, USA. An important choreographer and director who pioneered a joyful and energetic style of dancing. Kidd was a soloist with the Ballet Theatre (later called the American Ballet Theatre) before making his Broadway debut as choreographer with *Finian's Rainbow* in 1947. He won a **Tony Award** for his work on that show, and earned four more during the 50s for *Guys And Dolls* (1950), *Can-Can* (1953), *Li'l Abner* (1956) and *Destry Rides Again* (1959). His other shows around that time were *Hold It*, *Love Life* and *Arms And The Girl*. From *Li'l Abner* onwards he also directed, and sometimes produced, most of the shows on which he worked, but it was as a choreographer of apparently limitless invention that he dominated the Broadway musical during the 50s. In the 60s and early 70s he worked on productions such as *Wildcat*, *Subways Are For Sleeping*, *Here's Love*, *Ben Franklin In Paris*, *Skyscraper*, *Breakfast At Tiffany's* (which closed during previews), *The Rothschilds* (1970), *Cyrano*, and a revival of *Good News* (1974). Kidd also filled the big screen with his brilliant and exuberant dance sequences in classic Hollywood musicals such as *The Band Wagon*, *Seven Brides For Seven Brothers*, *It's Always Fair Weather* and *Hello, Dolly!* He co-starred with **Gene Kelly** and **Dan Dailey** in *It's Always Fair Weather*, and appeared in several other films, including *Movie Movie*, an affectionate parody of a typical 30s double-feature that went largely unappreciated in 1979. However, recognition of his immense contribution to the screen musical came in 1997 when he received a special Honorary Academy Award.

● FILMS: *It's Always Fair Weather* (1955), *Movie Movie* (1979).

Kidjo, Angelique

b. Ouidah, Benin, West Africa. Angelique Kidjo's family background provided her with both the impetus and platform to launch her singing career. Her mother, the director of Benin's first professional theatre/dance company, travelled widely to research different dances and rhythms for the company's ballets. Angelique was part of the company from the age of six, and progressed from dancing to learning French *variété* songs, gradually adding material from the **Beatles** and **Miriam Makeba**. The local music most popular in Ouidah was based on the gobahon rhythm, a percussion effect achieved by slapping different parts of the body in a steady pulse similar to that of reggae. Traditional singers, who rooted their storytelling in an anecdotal, blues-based style, also influenced Kidjo's technique. Although the market for her marriage of cool jazz and soul has long since extended beyond her native continent, there is plenty in her work that militates against Western values. The title-track of *Mogozo*, for example, attacks the lack of community in France, which she discovered on her arrival in Paris in 1983. At that time she spent two fruitless years studying classical voice technique, before enrolling at the C.I.M.S. jazz school. There she discovered old masters such as **Billie Holiday**, **Sarah Vaughan** and **Duke Ellington**, who

were much more to her taste. Playing with jazz groups around Paris, she eventually teamed up with Dutch pianist **Jasper Van't Hof** and his group, Pili-Pili. After six albums and five years as vocalist and co-songwriter, Kidjo decided it was time to move on, and her debut solo album was signed up by **Island Records** subsidiary Mango. Despite lyrics delivered predominantly in her native tongue, Fon, a language not well appointed to a traditional harmonic approach to singing, there was a universality to the melodies and rhythms of *Parakou*. Produced by **Miami Sound Machine**'s Joe Galdo, *Logozo* saw her dabbling in other African dialects such as Yoruba (on 'Eledjire'). The album acknowledged the position of artists like herself as emissaries from the third world, with songs such as 'We We' attacking the continuing torture and denial of human rights. She is married to French musician Jean Hebrail, who guested on *Logozo* alongside other African stars, **Manu Dibango** and **Ray Lema**. *Ayé* (which means 'life') was produced by **Prince/Fine Young Cannibals** associate David Z and Will Mowat (**Soul II Soul**). Recorded at the Paisley Park studio complex, it comprised a selection of new compositions about love, and maintained its political edge on tracks such as 'Houngbati' and 'Azan Nan Kpé'. *Fifa* and *Oremi* were her most contemporary-sounding albums to date, although on both Kidjo's soulful vocals were forced to struggle against bland production.

● ALBUMS: *Pretty* (1980)★★, *Parakou* (Mango 1992)★★★, *Logozo* (Mango 1993)★★★, *Ayé* (Mango 1994)★★★★, *Fifa* (Mango 1996)★★★, *Oremi* (Mango 1998)★★★.
● VIDEOS: *Angelique Kidjo, The Video* (1994).

Kids Are Alright, The

Taking its title from one of guitarist/composer **Pete Townshend**'s early songs, this 1978 documentary of the **Who** is a fine resume of one of rock's most fascinating acts. Having begun life in 1964 as an aspiring R&B group, the quartet fell under the influence of Peter Meadon who turned them into a leading exponent of the Mod subculture. The film charts their innovative pop-art period, smashing instruments in auto-destructive manner to the strains of early hits 'I Can't Explain' and 'My Generation'. Townshend's rise as a distinctly English songwriter is shown in period television appearances, drawn from UK, USA and European sources. (Mild controversy arose when the compiler allegedly failed to return these archive shots.) The Who's rise from pop to rock attraction is shown through their appearance at the **Monterey Pop Festival** and part of their set on the hitherto unscreened *Rolling Stones' Rock 'n' Roll Circus* is also exhumed. Their pounding performance of 'A Quick One While He's Away' sets the scene for the rock opera *Tommy*, which was at the core of their live shows during the late 60s/early 70s. By that point the Who had become one of the world's most popular live attractions, as footage drawn from albums, notably *Who's Next*, attests. Promotional shorts for concurrent singles, including

'Joined Together' are spliced with interview material, such as a memorable appearance on UK television's *Russell Harty Show* during which **Keith Moon** removed his clothes. The drummer's eccentric behaviour became the stuff of legend, but the road of excess brought his life to a premature end. Film shot during the recording of his last album with the group, *Who Are You*, adds poignancy to this resume. *The Kids Are Alright* is dedicated to the memory of the person who lay at the heart of this leading rock attraction.

Kids From Fame

In 1980, British film director Alan Parker made his Hollywood debut with a movie about the New York City High School for Performing Arts called *Fame*. The movie did not make that much of an impression at the box office, but American television network NBC bought the rights and developed the original idea into a weekly serial. The series was originally dropped in the USA, but subsequently hit the top of the ratings in the UK and further episodes were produced. In the UK, the success crossed over to the record industry where a soundtrack album of songs from the first series was compiled. Written by top writers such as **Rick Springfield**, Gary Portnoy and **Carole Bayer Sager**, the series produced five top-selling albums, and three Top 20 singles, including the US number 4/UK number 1 hit, 'Fame' for **Irene Cara**. Each song was sung by a different cast member and backed by top session musicians. The series ran for a couple of years before UK interest declined. The series turned out to be a showcase for many aspiring young actors.

● ALBUMS: *Kids From Fame* (1982)★★★, *Kids From Fame, Again* (1982)★★, *Kids From Fame, Live* (1983)★, *Kids From Fame, Songs* (1983)★★★, *Kids From Fame, Sing For You* (1983)★★.

● COMPILATIONS: *Best Of Fame* (1984)★★★.

Kihn, Greg

b. 1952, Baltimore, USA. Kihn was a singer-songwriter who started out as a folk singer but switched to rock. He moved to Berkeley, California in 1974, and the following year provided two solo songs for a compilation album on Matthew Kaufman's **Beserkley Records**. Afterwards, he became one of the first four acts signed to the label, adding backing vocals on label-mate **Jonathan Richman**'s classic 'Road Runner'. Influenced by 60s pop such as the **Yardbirds**, he initially used another Beserkley signing **Earth Quake** to back him but then formed his own band in 1976 based initially around Earth Quake guitarist Ronnie Dunbar (brother of the **Rubinoos**' founder Tommy Dunbar). The initial line-up was Greg Kihn (vocals/guitar), Robbie Dunbar (lead guitar), Steve Wright (bass), and Larry Lynch (drums). They were based in the San Francisco Bay area from 1976, playing local clubs and bars. Dunbar left after the first album to concentrate on Earth Quake and was replaced by Dave Carpender. The second album, *Greg Kihn Again*, included covers of **Bruce**

Springsteen's 'For You' and **Buddy Holly**'s 'Love's Made A Fool Of You'. This line-up came closest to a hit with 'Moulin Rouge', before Gary Phillips (again ex-Earth Quake) joined on guitar in 1981. The change brought about a more commercial direction which found quick reward. 'The Breakup Song (They Don't Write 'Em)' reached the US Top 20 and *Kihntinued*, which housed it, became their biggest selling album, making number 4, after which Carpender was replaced by Greg Douglas (ex-**Steve Miller** Band). They managed a US number 2 in 1983 with the disco-styled 'Jeopardy', before Kihn dropped the band title and recorded solely as Greg Kihn. He continues to collaborate with bubblegum pop writer Kenny Laguna, and has become renowned for his punning album titles. In recent years he has additionally become a rock radio presenter, written a novel and still records.

● ALBUMS: *Greg Kihn* (Beserkley 1975)★★, *Greg Kihn Again* (Beserkley 1977)★★★, *Next Of Kihn* (Beserkley 1978)★★, *With The Naked Eye* (Beserkley 1979)★★★, *Glass House Rock* (Beserkley 1980)★★, *Rockihnroll* (Beserkley 1981)★★★★, *Kihntinued* (Beserkley 1982)★★★, *Kihnspiracy* (Beserkley 1983)★★★★, *Kihntageous* (Beserkley 1984)★★★, *Citizen Kihn* (EMI 1985)★★, *Love And Rock And Roll* (EMI 1986)★★, *Unkihntrollable* (Rhino 1989)★★★, *Kihn Of Hearts* (FR 1992)★★★, *Mutiny* (Clean Cuts 1994)★★★, *Horror Show* (Clean Cuts 1996)★★★.

● COMPILATIONS: *Kihnsolidation: The Best Of Greg Kihn* (Rhino 1989)★★★★.

● FURTHER READING: *Horror Show*, Greg Kihn.

Kik Tracee

This US hard rock quintet was formed in 1990 by Stephen Shareux (vocals) and Michael Marquis (guitar). The line-up was completed by the addition of Rob Grad (bass), Gregory Hex (rhythm guitar) and Johnny Douglas (drums). Signed by **RCA Records**, they debuted in 1991 with *No Rules*, a varied and uncompromising collection of mature rock numbers that included, in an unusual choice of cover material, a version of **Simon And Garfunkel**'s 'Mrs. Robinson'.

● ALBUMS: *No Rules* (RCA 1991)★★★.

Kikuchi, Masabumi

b. 19 October 1939, Tokyo, Japan. Kikuchi took piano lessons from the age of five and studied music at Tokyo University (1955-58). He led his own trio in the early 60s when his playing displayed the influence of **Thelonious Monk**. He toured Japan with **Lionel Hampton**, recorded with **Charlie Mariano** and then toured with **Sonny Rollins**. In 1968 he went to the **Berklee College Of Music** in Boston, Massachusetts on a *Downbeat* magazine scholarship. The following year he returned to Japan where he led a trio with **Gary Peacock** and worked with visiting American musicians. He recorded an album with **Gil Evans** conducting a band of Japanese musicians. In the early 70s, he worked with **Elvin Jones** and, briefly, with **McCoy Tyner**. After 1974, he again worked regularly with Sonny Rollins as well as with the trumpet player, **Terumasa Hino**.

● ALBUMS: *Masabumi Kikuchi/Gil Evans* (1972)★★★, with Terumasa Hino *East Wind* (1974)★★★★, *Reconfirmation* (1970),★★★ *Doo Sun* (1970)★★★, *Dancing Mist* (1970)★★★★, *But Not For Me* (1978),★★★ *Susoto* (1980)★★★, *One Way Traveller* (1980)★★★.

Kila

Instantly acclaimed as the revelation at the 1993 Festival Interceltique in Lorient, France, Irish folk ensemble Kila comprise Colm O'Snodaigh (flute), Ronan O'Snodaigh (vocals/congos), Rossa O'Snodaigh (pipes), Dee Armstrong (violin), Eoin O'Brien (guitar) and Ed Kelly (bass). All brought diverse former band experience to bear on the new venture, ranging from jazz to R&B and classical music. Kila was started as a school band in Dublin in 1988, as a result of being offered the chance to play a youth music festival in Germany. From then on they elected to stay together, making their recording debut with a 10-strong Gaelic language collection in 1990. A summary of their live set followed a year later, by which time they had decided to put other careers on hold to pursue Kila as a full-time occupation. Their self-titled debut album proper followed in 1992, including a version of a W.B. Yeats' poem which was their only concession to the English language. A new album, *Mind The Gap*, was completed by 1995, though some of the material was drawn from an extensive songwriting arsenal which dated back to much earlier in the decade. Again all the songs were written in the Irish tongue, but the ferocity of the musicianship, and their willingness to experiment with tempos and rhythms as well as ethnic instruments (bodhran, darabuka), won them fans outside of the traditional Irish folk community.

● ALBUMS: *Kila* (Kila 1992)★★★, *Mind The Gap* (Kila 1995)★★★, *Tóg É Go Bog É* (Key 1998)★★★★.

Kilbey, Steven

b. England, although his parents emigrated to Australia when he was a child. As leader and main writer in the **Church**, Kilbey led the resurgence of interest in Australia for 60s music. His performances on the 12-string guitar evoked the sound of the **Byrds** and their ilk of the psychedelic era. The band enjoyed considerable success on the college radio network in the USA and on the European live circuit. This enabled Kilbey to enjoy a prolific output outside the confines of the band with the publication of a book of poetry and the release of several solo albums on the small independent Red Eye label. This solo work often proved a little more adventurous than that of the Church. A 1991 collaboration with **Grant McLennan** of the **Go-Betweens** resulted in the album *Jack Frost*, although otherwise his most important partnership was that with Donnette Thayer (ex-**Game Theory**) under the title Hex (his only other project to see release outside of Australia). In 1996 **Jack Frost** released an accomplished follow-up, *Snow Job*.

● ALBUMS: *Unearthed* (Enigma 1987)★★, *Earthed* (Rykodisc 1988)★★★, *The Slow Crack* (Red Eye 1988)★★, *Remindlessness* (Red Eye 1990)★★★. As Hex: *Hex* (1989)★★★, *Vast Halos* (1990)★★★.

Kilburn And The High Roads

An important link between 'pub rock' and punk, Kilburn And The High Roads were formed in November 1970 by art lecturer **Ian Dury** (b. 12 May 1942, Upminster, Essex, England; vocals) and Russell Hardy (b. 9 September 1941, Huntingdon, Cambridgeshire, England; piano). As a frontman, Dury cut an almost Dickensian figure, with his growling, half-spoken vocals, squat figure, polio-stricken leg and a withered hand, encased in a black leather glove. In fact, throughout the band's entire history their visual image was the antithesis of the prevalent glitter and glam-pop fashion. The initial line-up included Ted Speight (guitar), Terry Day (drums) and two former members of the Battered Ornaments, George Khan (saxophone) and Charlie Hart (bass). By 1973, despite a series of fluctuating line-ups, Dury and Russell had eventually settled down with a collection of musicians comprising: Keith Lucas (b. 6 May 1950, Gosport, Hampshire, England; guitar - a former art-school pupil of Dury's), Davey Payne (b. 11 August 1944, Willesden, London, England; saxophone), David Newton-Rohoman (b. 21 April 1948, Guyana, South America; drums) and Humphrey Ocean (bass). The last subsequently left the Kilburns to concentrate on a successful career as an artist and was replaced by Charlie Sinclair in January 1974. The group's early repertoire consisted of rock 'n' roll favourites mixed with early 50s Tin Pan Alley pop, but this was later supplemented and supplanted by original material utilizing Dury's poetry, mostly depicting the loves and lives of everyday east London folk. The Kilburns were, by this point, enshrined on London's 'pub rock' circuit. Managed by **Charlie Gillett**, they completed an album for the Raft label. This good fortune suffered a setback when the album's release was cancelled after the label went bankrupt. **Warner Brothers Records**, the parent company, chose to drop the group from its roster (but later released the sessions as *Wotabunch* in the wake of Dury's solo success). By late spring 1974, Gillett had left the scene, as had Hardy, who was replaced by Rod Melvin. Later that year they signed to the Dawn label, and released two superb singles, 'Rough Kids'/'Billy Bentley (Promenades Himself In London)' and 'Crippled With Nerves'/'Huffety Puff'. The subsequent album, *Handsome*, released the following year, was a huge disappointment, largely due to the bland production, which captured little of the excitement and irreverence of a Kilburns gig. The album marked the end of this particular era as the group then disintegrated. Keith Lucas embraced punk with the formation of **999**, performing under the name of Nick Cash, while Dury, Melvin and Payne became founder members of a revitalized unit, Ian Dury And The Kilburns. Ted Speight was also involved in this transitional band, during which time the singer introduced 'What A Waste' and 'England's Glory', two songs better associated with Ian Dury And The Blockheads, the group with which he found greater, long-deserved success.

● ALBUMS: *Handsome* (Dawn 1975)★★, *Wotabunch* (Warners 1978)★★.

● COMPILATIONS: *The Best Of Kilburn And The High Roads* (Warners 1977)★★★.

Kiley, Richard

b. 31 March 1922, Chicago, Illinois, USA. An actor and singer, with an imposing bearing and inimitable voice, Kiley studied at Loyala University and spent more than three years in the US Navy, before moving to New York in 1947. Although he appeared out of town with Nancy Walker in the musical *A Month Of Sundays*, during the late 40s and early 50s Kiley worked mostly in dramatic parts off-Broadway and in first-class televisions productions such as *Patterns* (*Kraft Television Theatre*) and *P.O.W.* (*United States Steel Hour*). His career in the musical theatre really began in 1953 when he created the role of Caliph in **Kismet**, in which he introduced, with others, several memorable numbers, including 'Stranger In Paradise' and 'And This Is My Beloved'. Following a gap of six years, Kiley returned to Broadway in the murder mystery musical **Redhead** (1959), for which he and his co-star **Gwen Verdon** won **Tony Awards**. *No Strings* followed in 1962, and with Diahann Carroll he sang the lovely 'The Sweetest Sounds'. After taking over from Craig Stevens in **Meredith Willson**'s *Here's Love*, Kiley played pitchman Sam the Shpieler in *I Had A Ball* (1964) - and then came the role of a lifetime. Kiley won a second Tony Award for his memorable portrayal of Don Quixote in **Man Of La Mancha** (1965), and introduced **Mitch Leigh** and Joe Darion's 'The Impossible Dream', a song with which he is always identified. He reprised the part on several occasions, including the 1969 London revival, two further New York productions, and on tour. Since his triumph in *Man Of La Mancha*, Kiley's appearances in musical productions have been limited. He played Julius Caesar in *Her First Roman* (1968), an adaptation of Bernard Shaw's *Caesar And Cleopatra*; took part in the one-night tribute, *A Celebration Of Richard Rodgers* (1972); played an aviator in **Alan Jay Lerner** and **Frederick Loewe**'s poorly received fantasy movie, *The Little Prince* (1974); appeared in a brief revival of **Knickerbocker Holiday** (1977) at Town Hall, New York; and starred out of town in a musical version of *A Christmas Carol* (1981), with music and lyrics by **Michel Legrand** and **Sheldon Harnick**. However, he has continued to appear in dramatic roles in the theatre and on television, and won an Emmy in 1984 for his performance in *The Thorn Birds*.

● ALBUMS: *The Rodgers And Hammerstein Songbook* (RCA Camden 1960)★★★, and Original Cast and spoken word recordings.

● FILMS: *The Mob* (1951), *Eight Iron Men* (1952), *The Sniper* (1952), *Pickup On South Street* (1953), *The Blackboard Jungle* (1955), *The Phenix City Story* (1955), *Spanish Affair* (1958), *Pendulum* (1969), *AKA Cassius Clay* (1970), *The Little Prince* (1974), *Looking For Mr. Goodbar* (1977), *Endless Love* (1981), *Howard The Duck* voice only (1986).

Kilgore, Merle

b. Merle Wyatt Kilgore, 9 August 1934, Chickasha, Oklahoma, USA. Kilgore was raised in Louisiana when the family moved to Shreveport. He learned to play guitar as a boy and started working on the radio station KENT as a disc jockey at the age of 16. By the time he was 18, he was the leading guitarist on the *Louisiana Hayride* and had also appeared on the *Grand Ole Opry* in Nashville and the *Big D Jamboree* in Dallas. Between 1952 and 1954 he was also a regular on KFAZ-TV in Monroe, Louisiana. His songwriting ability soon became apparent. In 1954, his song 'More And More' became a hit for both **Webb Pierce** and **Guy Lombardo** and in 1959, 'Johnny Reb' was a country and pop hit for **Johnny Horton**. Throughout the 50s, Kilgore was very active as a disc jockey, club performer and regular member of the *Hayride*, and had his own first US country chart hits on the Starday label in 1960 with 'Dear Mama' and 'Love Has Made You Beautiful' and although it never charted, his song '42 in Chicago' is something of a country standard. In 1962, he teamed with **Claude King** to write 'Wolverton Mountain'. King's subsequent recording sold a million copies and became a US country and pop hit. It later transpired that the trigger-happy old mountain man in the song, Clifton Clowers, was Kilgore's uncle. (Kilgore had originally offered the song to **Johnny Horton**, who believed it to be the worst song Kilgore had written, and when he offered it to **George Jones**, the latter told Kilgore that he hated mountain songs.) The following year, Kilgore teamed up with **June Carter** to write 'Ring Of Fire', which repeated the million-selling success when recorded by Carter's future husband, **Johnny Cash**. Kilgore recorded for several labels but his releases never proved great sellers. Through the 60s and 70s, he worked steadily, including film appearances in *Country Music On Broadway*, *Nevada Smith* (for which he wrote and recorded the title song) and *Five Card Stud*. He starred in shows in Las Vegas, played Carnegie Hall, New York, but gradually became more involved with music publishing, production and management. He was the opening act for **Hank Williams Jnr.** for 21 years and later became his manager and the vice-president of Hank Williams Jnr. Enterprises. Kilgore portrayed himself in the television movie *Living Proof: The Hank Williams Jnr. Story* in 1983.

● ALBUMS: *There's Gold In Them Thar Hills* (Starday 1963)★★★★, *Ring Of Fire* (1965)★★★, *Merle Kilgore, The Tall Texan* (Mercury/Wing 1966)★★, *Big Merle Kilgore* (Starday 1973)★★.

● COMPILATIONS: *Teenager's Holiday* (1991)★★★.

Kilgore, Rebecca

b. USA. Raised in New England, Kilgore played guitar and sang as a child. In 1979 she moved to Portland, Oregon, where she sang with a wide range of groups in many different musical styles, including a big band, a western swing group, and her own sextet, Beck-a-Roo. This group mostly performed country music hits from the 60s. Her jazz credentials were greatly enhanced through engagements with **Dave Frishberg** with whom she worked as a duo. She has also recorded with a mainstream band, **Dan Barrett**'s Celestial Six. Kilgore sings with lithe swing and has a breathily engaging tone. Her repertoire ranges through the great song standards which she interprets with charm and felicity.

● ALBUMS: *I Saw Stars* (Arbors Jazz 1994)★★★.

Kilimanjaro - The Teardrop Explodes

The **Teardrop Explodes** evolved from a nucleus of Liverpool musicians that also spawned **Echo And The Bunnymen**. Where the latter group explored a darker psyche, this particular unit, led by the eccentric **Julian Cope**, offered a brash brand of pop psychedelia. Cope's grand vision encompassed a range of mentors from **Scott Walker** to the **Turtles**, bound together by a grasp of strong, exciting melodies. *Kilimanjaro* contains a succession of brilliant songs - several of which were re-recorded from early singles - marked either by ebullient passion or melancholic reflection. Cope's quirky sense of humour adds another perspective to a highly inventive album.

● Tracks: *Ha Ha I'm Drowning; Sleeping Gas; Treason; Second Head; Reward Poppies; Went Crazy; Brave Boys Keep Their Promises; Bouncing Babies; Books; The Thief Of Baghdad; When I Dream.*

● First released 1980

● UK peak chart position: 24

● USA peak chart position: 156

Kill 'Em All - Metallica

Occasionally one album can be pinpointed as the turning point in a musical genre. *Kill 'Em All* is one such album and, boy, did the heavy metal genre need a transfusion of new blood. Herein trad metal was stripped of its late-70s pomposity and reduced to its base element of brutal sonic force. The rhythm section of Burton and Ulrich do a masterful job, as does rhythm guitar ace and vocalist James Hetfield, on a set that owes a debt to punk as much as to **Iron Maiden** and **Judas Priest**. The phantasmagorical allusions are still there in the lyrics, as are some long-winded guitar solos, but otherwise *Kill 'Em All* promised a creative rebirth for hard rock.

● Tracks: *Hit The Lights; The Four Horsemen; Motorbreath; Jump In The Fire; (Anesthesia) - Pulling Teeth; Whiplash; Phantom Lord; No Remorse; Seek & Destroy; Metal Militia.*

● First released 1983

● UK peak chart position: did not chart

● USA peak chart position: 155

Kill For Thrills

Formed in Los Angeles, California, USA, this group delivered a trademark sound best described as 'sleaze rock'. Featuring the talents of Gilby Clarke (vocals, guitar), Jason Nesmith (guitar), Todd Muscat (bass) and David Scott (drums), their 1990 debut, *Dynamite From Nightmare Land*, was a prime example of no-nonsense standard-chord hard rock. The album was produced by Vic Maile and Ric Browde who are renowned, respectively, for their work with **Motörhead** and **Poison**.

● ALBUMS: *Dynamite From Nightmare Land* (MCA 1990)★★★.

Killah Priest

(see **Wu-Tang Clan**)

Killdozer

Killdozer were formed in Madison, Wisconsin, USA, and the music of the area was regularly celebrated in their primal country blues. The original line-up featured Michael Gerald (bass, vocals), plus the brothers Dan (guitar) and Bill Hobson (drums). From their formation the trio released a steady stream of albums that often highlighted their distaste at what they saw as the social and political malaise of their native country. They were just as likely to turn the spotlight on small-town weirdness, however, or their singer's rampant confusion about the state of the world. In a respite from this angst, *For Ladies Only* was a project dedicated to cover versions of classic songs of the 70s, including 'One Tin Soldier' and 'Good Lovin' Gone Bad'. Guitarist Paul Zagoras was recruited during the 90s in place of Dan Hobson, during which time Killdozer's formidable output was restrained somewhat due to Gerald sitting accountancy exams (he is a former mathematics teacher). However, the band bounced straight back to form with albums in 1994 and 1995, both featuring further bizarre anecdotes. The band broke up at the end of 1996 with the aptly named 'fuck you we quit tour'.

● ALBUMS: *Intellectuals Are The Shoeshine Boys Of The Ruling Elite* (Bone Air 1984)★★★, *Snakeboy* (Touch & Go 1985)★★★, *Burl* mini-album (Touch & Go 1986)★★★, *Little Baby Buntin'* (Touch & Go 1987)★★★, *Twelve Point Buck* (Touch & Go 1988)★★★, *For Ladies Only* (Touch & Go 1989)★★★, *Uncompromising War On Art Under The Dictatorship Of The Proletariat* (Touch & Go 1994)★★★, *God Hears Pleas Of The Innocent* (Touch & Go 1995)★★★, *The Last Waltz* 1996 recording (Man's Ruin 1997).

● VIDEOS: *Little Baby Buntin' Live* (Jettisoundz 1990).

Killen, Buddy

b. 13 November, Florence, Alabama, USA. Little appears to be known of Killen's early life or where he gained his first musical experience. However, after arriving in Nashville, he became a regular session musician playing stand-up bass, and also regularly appeared as a sidesman on the *Grand Ole Opry*. In the early 50s,

Jack Stapp, the President of Tree Publishing, employed Killen to work with the company. Killen proved to be a very talented independent record producer and was instrumental in helping many artists on the way to stardom, including **Bill Anderson**, **Dottie West**, **Mel Tillis** and **Roger Miller**. He also signed up a young singer-songwriter named **Dolly Parton**, when she first arrived in Nashville. Killen proved so successful in his work and promotion of the company that, in 1975, when Stapp moved on to become the chairman of the company's many enterprises, he promoted Killen to the position of co-owner and president. When Stapp died in 1980, Killen became sole owner and as such, one of the music industry's most powerful businessmen. Everyone has their failures, and Killen certainly had one in 1957 when, after listening to an unknown folk/country singer called **Jimmie Driftwood** sing two verses of a song called 'Battle Of New Orleans', he told him: 'Son, if that's the kind of stuff you've got, you'd better go home. We couldn't sell one record of that.' Two years later, after Driftwood's own recording had charted and Johnny Horton's had become a country and pop number 1, Driftwood met Killen again; on seeing Driftwood approach, Killen bent over and said, 'Kick me'. Over the years, Killen has held many executive posts in Nashville and the music industry, including President of the National Academy Of Recording Arts And Sciences (NARAS). Although never noted as a recording artist, in 1969 he actually made the *Billboard* country charts singing a duet with **Bonnie Guitar** called 'A Truer Love You'll Never Find Than Mine'.

● FURTHER READING: *By The Seat Of My Pants: My Life In Country Music*, Buddy Killen with Tom Carter.

Killen, Ked

b. 10 May 1911, Jenkins, Kentucky, USA, d. 1986. Killen learned to play guitar as a teenager and influenced by recordings of **Jimmie Rodgers**, he began performing in the late 20s, both as a solo artist and with local groups. He eventually formed his Western All Stars and played for many years at venues in Kentucky and Virginia. Killen's raw traditional country singing, in styles that bore touches, without ever being imitations, of **Hank Williams** and **Mac Wiseman**, with proper country backing may well have led him to great success had he recorded in the late 40s or early 50s. He made no recordings until he was 55, then between 1966 and 1969, following their newspaper advertisement for singers, he recorded 20 sides for Western Ranch Music in Clintwood, Virginia. He gained some local success with material that ranged from 'Crying Blues' and 'Worried Blues', through to country weepies such as 'The Little Blind Boy' asking God for his sight, 'Will The Pardon Arrive Too Late' and a crippled boy making excuses for his drunken father in 'They Call Him A Bum'. He retired from public performances in 1969, but years later was persuaded to make further recordings. However, before they were made, depression, caused by his wife's sudden death, saw his own

health deteriorate. He died in 1986 and is buried at Clintwood. In 1989, his recordings were reissued in album form by the German label, Binge. It is no fault of the artist that even their remastering failed to completely improve the poor tonal quality of some of the originals but for containing the only Killen recordings available, the album obviously is collectable.

● COMPILATIONS: *Ked Killen And His Western All Stars* (Binge 1989)★★★

Killen, Louis

b. January 1934, Gateshead, County Durham, England. This English folk singer is known for his a cappella vocals and occasional use of whistle and concertina. Following his time in the Oxford University Folk Song Club, he concentrated on this style exclusively. He formed one of Britain's first folk clubs, the 'Folk Song & Ballad Club' in Newcastle, in 1958. Finding himself unemployed in 1961, he pursued a professional singing career thereafter. One of his major influences in the early 60s, was **Ewan MacColl** which led Killen to concentrate on British, rather than American material. In 1962, Killen recorded two EPs for **Topic Records**, *The Colliers Rant* (with **Johnny Handle**), and *Northumberland Garland. Along The Coaly Tyne* included the material from these recordings, as well as Handle's *Stottin' Doon The Waall* EP. Killen emigrated to the USA in 1967, where he performed solo on the college and coffee house circuit. A move to the west coast in 1968 as an unknown artist, left Killen looking for extra work, occasionally finding employment in the shipyards. The following year, he headed back east, joining the crew of the Clearwater, the Hudson River Sloop that had been built for an ecological and educational restoration project. The crew included such luminaries as **Pete Seeger** and **Gordon Bok**. In addition, for two years from late 1970 he joined the **Clancy Brothers**, taking the place of **Tommy Makem**. Killen also recorded and performed with **Peter Bellamy** and **Robin Williamson**. Killen's career continued with concerts and lecture tours, often in collaboration with his wife Sally. *The Rose In June* was Killen's first album since *Gallant Lads Are We*. Still based in the USA, Killen set out, in 1991, on his first British tour for 10 years and recommenced recording in 1990.

● ALBUMS: *Ballads And Broadsides* (1965)★★★, *Sea Shanties* (1968)★★★★, with Johnny Handle *Along The Coaly Tyne* (1971)★★★★, *50 South To 50 South* (1972)★★★, with Sally Killen *Bright Shining Morning* (1975)★★★, *Old Songs, Old Friends* (1978)★★, *Gallant Lads Are We* (1980)★★★, *The Rose In June* (1990)★★★, *A Bonny Bunch* (Knock Out 1996)★★★, *Sailors, Ships & Chanteys* (Knock Out 1996)★★★.

Killers

This UK quintet was founded in 1991 by former **Iron Maiden** vocalist **Paul Di'Anno**. Recruiting Steve Hopgood (drums), Cliff Evans (guitar), Gavin Cooper (bass) and Nick Burr (guitar), their approach was firmly rooted in the **New Wave Of British Heavy Metal** movement of the early 80s. *Murder One*, released in early 1992, was rather anachronistic, sounding virtually identical to early Iron Maiden, though the calibre of the protagonists guaranteed press and public interest.

● ALBUMS: *Murder One* (RCA 1992)★★.

Killian, Al

b. Albert Killian, 15 October 1916, Birmingham, Alabama, USA, d. 5 September 1950. Killian began playing trumpet as a child and in his late teens was regularly in New York. He worked with several bands in the late 30s including those of **Teddy Hill** and **Don Redman** and in 1940 joined **Count Basie**. During the 40s he had spells with **Lionel Hampton**, **Charlie Barnet**, Basie, **Billy Eckstine**, and also led his own band. He was also with **Jazz At The Philharmonic** and in the closing years of the decade was briefly with **Boyd Raeburn** and **Duke Ellington**, visiting Europe with the latter. A strong player with a distinctively aggressive style, he was alert to bop but was rooted in swing era concepts. He was murdered in 1950.

● ALBUMS: *Lester Young And Charlie Christian 1939-1940* (Jazz Archives 1939-40)★★★, *Jazz Concert West Coast* (Regent 1947)★★★, *Duke Ellington Carnegie Hall Concert, December 1947* (Prestige 1947)★★★.

Killin' Time - Clint Black

Although *Killin' Time* was **Clint Black**'s debut album, many country fans thought they had been listening to him for years, as his solid, honky tonk style was modelled on **Merle Haggard**'s. The title track, a drinking song, was a US country number 1 as was 'A Better Man', written about a broken romance he had experienced. His second album, *Put Yourself In My Shoes*, was another million-seller but managerial disputes halted his career just as he was beginning to rival **Garth Brooks**.

● Tracks: *Straight From The Factory; Nobody's Home; You're Gonna Leave Me Again; Winding Down; Live And Learn; A Better Man; Walkin' Away; I'll Be Gone; Killin' Time.*

● First released 1988
● UK peak chart position: did not chart
● USA peak chart position: 31

Killing Joke

This immensely powerful post-punk UK band combined a furious rhythm section with near-psychotic performances from Jaz Coleman (b. Jeremy Coleman, Cheltenham, England; vocals, keyboards). The band came about when Coleman, of Egyptian descent, was introduced to Paul Ferguson, then drumming for the Matt Stagger Band. Coleman joined as a keyboard player, before they both left to form their own group. This first incarnation added 'Geordie' (b. K. Walker, Newcastle, England; guitar) and Youth (b. Martin Glover Youth, 27 December 1960, Africa; bass), who had made his first public appearance at the Vortex in 1977 with forgotten punk band the Rage. After relocat-

ing to Notting Hill Gate they paid for a rehearsal studio and borrowed money from Coleman's girlfriend to release the *Turn To Red* EP. Picked up by UK disc jockey **John Peel**, the band provided a session that would become the most frequently requested of the thousands he has commissioned. Via **Island Records** the band were able to set up their own Malicious Damage label, on which they released 'Wardance' in February 1980, notable for its remarkably savage b-side, 'Psyche'. A succession of fine, aggressive singles followed, alongside live appearances with **Joy Division**. They were in a strong enough position to negotiate a three-album contract with EG, which allowed them to keep the name Malicious Damage for their records. After the release of a typically harsh debut album, the band were banned from a Glasgow gig when council officials took exception to posters depicting Pope Pius giving his blessing to two columns of Hitler's Brown Shirts (a genuine photograph). It was typical of the black humour that pervaded the band, especially on their record sleeves and graphics. After the recording of the third album was completed the band disintegrated when Coleman's fascination with the occult led him to the conclusion that the apocalypse was imminent, and he fled to Iceland. He was followed later by Youth. When Youth returned it was to begin work with Ferguson on a new project, **Brilliant**. However, having second thoughts, Ferguson became the third Joker to flee to Iceland, taking bass player Paul Raven (ex-Neon Hearts) with him. Brilliant continued with Youth as the only original member. The Killing Joke output from then on lacks something of the menace that had made them so vital. However, *Night Time* combined commercial elements better than most, proffering the hit single 'Love Like Blood'. While *Outside The Gate* was basically a Coleman solo album wrongly credited to the band, they returned with their best album for years with 1990's *Extremities, Dirt And Various Repressed Emotions*, which saw the drumming debut of Martin Atkins (ex-**Public Image Limited**). Regardless, the band broke up once more with bitter acrimony flying across the pages of the press the same year. While his former co-conspirators pronounced Killing Joke dead, Coleman pledged to continue under the name. He did just that after a brief sojourn into classical/ethnic music via a collaborative project with **Anne Dudley** which resulted in *Songs From The Victorious City* released on China Records in 1990. *Pandemonium* saw Youth return to join Geordie and Coleman, with the addition of new drummer Geoff Dugmore. This saw a revitalized Killing Joke, notably on 'Exorcism', recorded in the King's Chamber of the Great Pyramid in Cairo. They were welcomed back by a wide cross-section of critics (or at least, those whom Coleman had not physically assaulted at some point) and friends. Indeed, bands claiming Killing Joke as a direct influence ranged from the **Cult, Ministry** and **Skinny Puppy** to **Metallica** and **Soundgarden**, while many noticed an uncanny similarity between the band's 'Eighties' and **Nirvana**'s 'Come

As You Are'. *Pandemonium* yielded two UK Top 20 singles, 'Millennium' and the title track, and sold in excess of 100,000 copies in the USA where they signed to Zoo Records. Meanwhile, Coleman's secondary career had evolved. In addition to scoring a second symphony alongside Youth and arranging classical interpretations of the music of **Pink Floyd**, **Led Zeppelin** and the **Who**, he became composer in residence for the New Zealand Symphony Orchestra (the country where he spends most of his time). It led to him being hailed by conductor Klaus Tennstedt as 'the new Mahler'. For his part Youth had become one of the UK's top dance remixers, also recording with acts as diverse as **Bananarama** and **Crowded House**. He returned to Killing Joke in 1996 for *Democracy* - a cynical snipe at the build-up to election year in the UK.

● ALBUMS: *Killing Joke* (EG 1980)★★★, *What's THIS For ...!* (EG 1981)★★★, *Revelations* (Malicious Damage/EG 1982)★★★, *Ha! Killing Joke Live* (Malicious Damage/EG 1982)★★★, *Fire Dances* (EG 1983)★★★★, *Night Time* (EG 1985)★★★, *Brighter Than A Thousand Suns* (EG/Virgin 1986)★★★, *Outside The Gate* (EG/Virgin 1988)★★★, *Extremities, Dirt And Various Repressed Emotions* (RCA 1990)★★★, *Pandemonium* (Butterfly/Big Life 1994)★★★, *BBC In Concert* (Strange Fruit 1995)★★★, *Democracy* (Big Life 1996)★★★.

● COMPILATIONS: *An Incomplete Collection* (EG 1990)★★★, *Laugh? I Nearly Bought One* (EG 1992)★★★, *Wilful Days* (Virgin 1995)★★★.

Killjoys

The Killjoys were among the first musical enterprises of **Dexys Midnight Runners**' leader Kevin Rowland (b. 17 August 1953, Wolverhampton, West Midlands, England). Having formerly played guitar and sang in the Birmingham, England group Lucy And The Lovers, Rowland recruited Gill Weston (bass), Mark Phillips (guitar), Heather Tonge (vocals) and Joe 45/Trevor (drums) as punk took hold in 1977. Their first single, 'Johnny Won't Go To Heaven', was released on Raw Records in July of that year. No further records were issued, and in November Rowland formed Dexys Midnight Runners with Al Archer, who had also worked as part of the Killjoys and would later join the Bureau. Both sides of the 'Johnny Won't Go To Heaven' single and various demo tracks were subsequently reissued on compilations documenting the notorious Raw Records. The best example being 'Naive', issued by Damaged Goods Records in the early 90s, and featuring interviews and out-takes, where Rowland's unreconstructed 'Brum' accent and the band's raucous playing sound quite unlike his subsequent incarnation. Weston also enjoyed success in a new project, as bass player for **Girlschool** during their most productive years.

Kilo

b. *c.*1972, Atlanta, Georgia, USA. Prolific young artist who was raised by his grandparents in the north-west

projects of Atlanta, known as Bowen Homes. Turned on to hip-hop, he recorded his first demos at the age of 15 with the help of his DJ Red Money. These recordings eventually crystallised into a debut set that was released on the local Arvis imprint. The album would sell over 40,000 copies in the South East region, its sales profile buoyed by the attendant hit single, 'Cocaine'. *A-Town Rush* was similarly successful, again almost entirely on the back of local sales. Kilo went on to win Atlanta's Coca Cola Music Awards for the best Rap Artist in March 1992, prompting a bidding war within the rap label community. Wrap/**Ichiban** won out, and promptly re-released and re-promoted the artist's first and second albums. The duo returned to the studio in 1993 with a less commercial approach making the resultant album less airplay-friendly, but it was again highly regarded by critics (and spawned the hit single 'Tick Tock'). Kilo's second album from the same year was granted the production expertise of Carl Cooley, 'C' Dorsey and Craze, and was another ample demonstration of his resonant, high-pitched delivery and lyrical skill. As Kilo Ali he released *Organized Bass* in 1997.

● ALBUMS: *America Has A Problem...Cocaine* (Arvis Records 1991)★★★, *A-Town Rush* (Arvis Records 1992)★★★, *Bluntly Speaking* (Wrap/Ichiban 1993)★★★★, *Git Wit Da Program* (Wrap/Ichiban 1993)★★★, as Kilo Ali *Organized Bass* (Interscope 1997)★★★.

● COMPILATIONS: *The Best And The Bass* (Wrap/Ichiban 1994)★★★★.

Kimbrough, James

b. 1926, on a cotton farm near Florence, Alabama, USA. He was attracted to country music by recordings he heard as a child, first by the **Carter Family** and then in the late 30s, the recordings of **Roy Acuff**. He was particularly drawn to the sound of the dobro on Acuff's recordings and was totally impressed by the playing of **Pete Kirby**. During service in the US Navy during World War II, Kimbrough met Kirby and bought one of his old dobro guitars. He recalled years later that 'By the time I got it, it was the most beat up dobro you ever saw but it still had the sound and I was the happiest person in the world'. After the war, Kimbrough returned to the farm and although he never became a full time musician, he played and sang with various groups. A dedicated traditionalist, his vocal work was reminiscent of Acuff's. He also wrote many songs such as the biographical 'Sundown At Our Old Home Place' and dobro instrumentals but did not record until 1973. During the 80s, he formed his own Kimbro Records and also had releases on Cattle, a German label.

● ALBUMS: *Country Music Is Still Alive* (Cattle 1980)★★★, *The Pure Dobro Country Sound* (Cattle 1982)★★★, *Country Songs For Country Folks* (Cattle 1983)★★★, *Sings Saturday Night Favorites Of The 30s And 40s* (Kimbro 80s)★★★.

Kimbrough, Junior

b. David Kimbrough, 28 July 1930, Hudsonville, Mississippi, USA, d. 17 January 1998, Holly Springs,

USA. Kimbrough described his music as 'cottonpatch blues' but commentators preferred to see it as the resurgence of the 'juke joint' style, once synonymous with **Frank Frost**, of which Kimbrough and **R.L. Burnside** are the finest recent exponents. His synthesis of the North Mississippi hill country musical tradition relied upon minimal instrumentation, mesmeric repetition and the seemingly random but instinctive orchestration of basic blues disciplines. Picking up his brother's guitar at the age of eight, Kimbrough absorbed the music of neighbours **Mississippi Fred McDowell** and Eli Green, became part of their circle and played for parties and jukes until his untimely death in 1998. Cited by rockabilly artist **Charlie Feathers** and others as a major influence and thus, by inference, vital to the creation of the '**Sun** sound', Kimbrough organized his own parties in and around Holly Springs from the mid-60s, backed by the Soul Blues Boys, a band that consisted of members of his and Burnside's families. He was filmed at the Chewalla Rib Shack for Robert Palmer's film documentary *Deep Blues* and 'Jr. Blues' was featured on the soundtrack album. Both subsequent albums predominantly featured his own songs, which relied heavily upon the recognizable 'floating' verses associated with the area.

● ALBUMS: *Deep Blues* (Atlantic/Anxious 1992)★★★, *All Night Long* (Fat Possum/Demon 1993)★★★, *Sad Days, Lonely Nights* (Fat Possum/Capricorn 1994)★★★, *Most Things Haven't Worked Out* (Fat Possum 1997)★★★.

Kimono My House - Sparks

Somewhere between art and glam rock, **Sparks** and **Roxy Music** were the doyens of whatever label this music is called. The familiar hit single 'This Town Ain't Big Enough For Both Of Us' is on this album, and worthy of owning simply to find out what on earth Russell Mael was singing about; for example, 'Zoo time is she and you time'. Without the lyric sheet, the lyrics are obliterated by the catchiness of the song. Their finest album containing some wonderful arty pop.

● Tracks: *This Town Ain't Big Enough For Both Of Us; Amateur Hour; Falling In Love With Myself Again; Here In Heaven; Thank God It's Not Christmas; Hasta Manana Monsieur; Talents Is An Asset; Complaints; In My Family; Equator; Barbecutie; Lost And Found.*

● First released 1974
● UK peak chart position: 4
● USA peak chart position: 101

Kimono, Ras

b. Nigeria. Kimono served a long apprenticeship on the Nigerian music circuit, experimenting with a number of styles, before making his late 80s breakthrough as a reggae singer. Together with his Massive Dread Reggae Band, Kimono released his debut album, *Under Pressure*, in 1989. Accompanied by the popular single, 'Rum-Bar Stylee', this revealed both a Jamaican and native African influence (the latter particularly evident in his 'patois' delivery, as frequently employed by **Fela Kuti** to communicate with the urban underclass). His strongly polemical lyrics produced album sales of over 100,000 copies, and a fervent following for his advocacy of social change. *What's Gwan* proved even more successful, with the topics selected including legalisation of marijuana, and the need for Africans to intellectually repel colonialism and its arbitrary boundaries between tribes. Most controversially, he was not averse to naming directly those in power he saw as synonymous with backdoor imperialism.

● ALBUMS: *Under Pressure* (1989)★★★★, *What's Gwan* (Polydor Nigeria 1990)★★★.

Kincaid, Bradley

b. 13 July 1895, near Lancaster, Garrard County, Kentucky, USA, d. 23 September 1989. Kincaid grew up strumming folk tunes, mountain ballads and vaudeville songs on an old 'hound dog' guitar, so-called because his father had swapped a hunting dog for it. He gained a college education in Chicago and lectured on folk music to learned societies. Kincaid described himself as a folk-singer rather than a hillbilly (a term he hated), and he became known as the Kentucky Mountain Boy. In 1926, he gained a regular spot on WLS Chicago and became the star of its *National Barn Dance*. Kincaid began recording in 1927 and his pseudonyms included Dan Hughey, John Carpenter and Harley Stratton. His best-known records are 'Barbara Allen', 'The Fatal Derby Day', 'The Legend Of The Robin's Red Breast' and 'The Letter Edged In Black'. Like A.P. Carter of the **Carter Family**, he collected songs, and the individual sales of his 12 folios, *My Favourite Mountain Ballads And Old Time Songs*, were as many as 100,000. Sears manufactured a replica of his 'hound dog' guitar. Kincaid toured extensively, and in 1936, he discovered Lewis Marshall Jones, whom he renamed **Grandpa Jones**. Between 1944 and 1947, Kincaid was a regular on the *Grand Ole Opry* and he then bought his own radio station, WWSO Springfield. He retired in 1953, although he still performed at folk festivals. In 1963, he recorded 162 songs in four days, but only six albums from that session were ever released. He died in September 1989 in Springfield, Ohio, USA.

● ALBUMS: *American Ballads* 10-inch album (Varsity 1955)★★★★, *Bradley Kincaid Sings American Ballads And Folk Songs* (Varsity 1957)★★★★, *Bradley Kincaid - Mountain Ballads And Old Time Songs* 6 volumes (mid-60s)★★★★, *Family Gospel Album* (1971)★★, *Bradley Kincaid - The Kentucky Mountain Boy* (1973)★★, *Mountain Ballads And Old Time Songs* (1976)★★★, *Favourite Old Time Songs* (1984)★★★, *Old Time Songs And Hymns* (1984)★★★, *Mountain Ballads And Old Time Songs, Volume 7* (1989)★★★.

● FURTHER READING: *Radio's Kentucky Mountain Boy - Bradley Kincaid*, Loyal Jones.

Kincaide, Deane

b. 18 March 1911, Houston, Texas, USA, d. 14 August 1992, St. Cloud, Florida, USA. Although he played saxophone in the **Ben Pollack** band of the early 30s and its successor, the highly successful **Bob Crosby** band, Kincaide's main talent was his arranging. Indeed, his charts were a principal factor in creating the distinctive two-beat style of the Crosby band. He later worked for **Woody Herman** and **Tommy Dorsey** as both arranger and musician. In the 40s Kincaide freelanced, his arrangements finding their way into the repertoire of several bands, including **Glenn Miller**'s. After World War II, Kincaide continued much as before, writing for the Glenn Miller Orchestra and for films and television.

● ALBUMS: *The Solid South* (1959)★★.

Kinchen, Mark

In 1988, together with **Terrence Parker**, Mark 'MK' Kinchen was part of the US duo Separate Minds for the techno/soul cut, 'We Need Somebody'. Kinchen went on to engineer on many of the early **Inner City** Records, and most of **Kevin Saunderson**'s associated **KMS** label product, having been adopted as 'studio mascot' by Saunderson from the age of 17 onwards. He began to make records on his own as MK - like 'Mirror Mirror'. However, he was still eclipsed by his boss, and he elected to relocate to New York, recording songs like 'Play The World'. This was somewhat removed from the traditional Detroit sound, confounding expectations. A good example was the 'Burnin'' single (featuring vocal support from Alana Simon), given a UK release after success as an import on Kinchen's own Area 10 label in 1992. He returned to the Separate Minds name for '2nd Bass' in 1992, a full three and a half years since recording '1st Bass'. Among other *nom de plumes* he also records as 4th Measure Men. He has also remixed for **Bizarre Inc** and **Masters At Work** ('Can't Stop The Rhythm').

Kind Of Blue - Miles Davis

Advocates from the many corners of jazz will argue their points, some with bigoted passion and self righteousness - a trait that has been known to follow some jazz buffs. When you find jazzers, rock and popular music followers unanimously united over one record, then you know something must be right. This album contains only five tracks, with musicians Julian Adderley (alto), **John Coltrane** (tenor), **Bill Evans** (piano), **Paul Chambers** (bass), **James Cobb** (drums) and Miles on trumpet. It is played with absolute cool perfection, not a drop of sweat or cigarette ash. There can be no debate, this is the greatest jazz album in the world ever; so what, just accept it.

● Tracks: *So What; Freddie Freeloader; Blue In Green; Al Blues; Flamenco Sketches.*

● First released 1960

● UK peak chart position: did not chart

● USA peak chart position: did not chart

King

This Coventry-based group was formed in 1983 after the break-up of the Reluctant Stereotypes of which Paul King (vocals) was a member. The remainder of King comprised Tony Wall (bass), Mick Roberts (keyboards), James Jackel Lantsbery (guitar) and ex-**Members** Adrian Lillywhite (drums). They made their debut supporting the **Mighty Wah!** and signed to **CBS Records**. Despite extensive touring and a sizeable following, their first three singles and *Steps In Time* sold poorly. The break came late in 1984 when they supported **Culture Club** and reached a whole new teen audience. 'Love And Pride' was released early next year, and made number 2 in the UK chart, while the album went to number 6. The hits continued throughout the year, most notably with the Top 10 hit, 'Alone Without You', and King abruptly disbanded in 1986. Paul King pursued a solo career, which at best gave him a minor hit with 'I Know' which reached number 59. The group will probably be remembered as much for their trademark spray-painted Dr. Martens boots and Paul King's affable personality than for their engaging pop songs. Paul King later became a video jockey for **MTV**.

● ALBUMS: *Steps In Time* (Columbia 1984)★★, *Bitter Sweet* (Columbia 1985)★★.

King & Queen - Otis Redding And Carla Thomas

The **Stax** label 'crowned' their leading male and female singers following the pair's charming version of **Lowell Fulson**'s 'Tramp'. Taking a cue from 50s 'sweethearts' **Shirley And Lee**, the duo's verbal sparrings were lighthearted, but accomplished, playing on both vocalists' strengths. 'Ooh Carla, Ooh Otis' and 'Lovey Dovey' rock with an engaging innocence, while the pair bring an emotive resonance to **Aaron Neville**'s 'Tell It Like It Is'. **Otis Redding**'s premature death ended any prospects of a reprise, and **Carla Thomas** sadly failed to retain her regal position. *King & Queen* is a beguiling snapshot in time.

● Tracks: *Knock On Wood; Let Me Be Good To You; Tramp; Tell It Like It Is; When Something Is Wrong With My Baby; Lovey Dovey; New Year's Resolution; It Takes Two; Are You Lovely For Me Baby; Bring It On Home To Me; Ooh Carla, Ooh Otis.*

● First released 1967

● UK peak chart position: 18

● USA peak chart position: 36

King (stage musical)

'The road to opening night, now shifted to April 18, has been the bloodiest of any musical in recent memory. Writers, directors, a producer, and even a leading actor, have either walked out or been fired after rows over racial politics and money.' That was the kind of advance publicity that this show received prior to its first performance which eventually took place at the Piccadilly Theatre in London on 23 April 1990. The £2.5 million production, which was directed by Clarke Peters, and based on the life of the controversial civil rights leader, Martin Luther King Jnr., had a book by Lonnie Elder III, music by Richard Blackford, and lyrics by Maya Angelou and Alistair Beaton. Just prior to the opening, Angelou left in a huff, and demanded that her name be removed from the credits, but that was refused, and although Elder is credited with the final libretto, the completed work was the product of many hands. Apparently, one of Angelou's objections was that 'it takes a black man to write about a black man and there hasn't been a single black man in the writing of this show.' That was also the reported attitude of King's widow, Coretta Scott King, who initially with-held her approval from the project. Most critics savagely dismissed the book and the production in general as 'an insignificant little offering' . . . 'of such banality it is in itself a crime against humanity' . . . 'evoking a pocket history of bloody protest marches, political intrigue, factionalism, melodramatic Jim Crowism, and character defamation, but with little dramatic flair and less depth'. American opera singers Simon Estes (King) and Cynthia Haymon (Coretta) were absolved from the blame - in the singing depart-ment, at least. The score, 'a mix of jazz, gospel, and showbiz pizzazz', consisted of some 24 numbers, along the lines of 'Cotton's My Momma', 'Bus Boycott', 'Welcome To Atlanta', 'Equal Rights', 'No More Sorrow', 'The Price Of Freedom'. 'They're After You're Vote', 'Sacrifice', 'For I Am An American', 'Safe In Your Arms', and one inspired by King's immortal words, 'I Have A Dream' ('so did I,' said one cynic, 'but I fought against temptation and stayed awake.'). More money was ploughed in, but to no avail. Not many shows could withstand that sort of battering, and *King* closed after six weeks, with losses estimated at between £2.6 million and £3.3 million.

King And I, The (film musical)

Yul Brynner became a legend in the 1951 Broadway show, and no other actor could even have been consid-ered for the leading role in this 1956 screen version. Brynner's stage partner, **Gertrude Lawrence**, died during the Broadway run, and his co-star for this film, the British actress Deborah Kerr, proved to be an ideal replacement. She plays Anna, the widowed English governess, who is engaged by King Mongkut of Siam (Brynner) to educate his many children. In spite of their fundamental differences and principles, they fall in love, but are parted by the King's death. The film's other love story is that between one of the King's daughter's, Tuptim (**Rita Moreno**) and Lun Tha (Carlos Rivas), but that romance, too, is destined to end unhappily. Other parts were taken by Martin Balsam, Rex Thompson, Terry Saunders, Alan Mowbray, Patrick Adiarte, Yuriko, Michiko, Geoffrey Toone, and Charles Irwin. The highly emotional story was complemented by **Richard Rodgers** and **Oscar Hammerstein II**'s magnificent score, which included 'I Whistle A Happy Tune' (Kerr), 'March Of The Siamese Children' (instrumental), 'Hello, Young Lovers' (Kerr), 'A Puzzlement' (Brynner), 'Getting To Know You' (Kerr with the children), 'We Kiss In A Shadow' (Moreno-Rivas), 'Something Wonderful' (Saunders),

'The Small House Of Uncle Thomas' (ballet) and 'Song Of The King' (Brynner). Perhaps the film's most memorable moment comes when Anna tries to teach the King how to dance, and they - awkwardly at first - and then exuberantly, whirl around the floor to the sublime 'Shall We Dance?'. Deborah Kerr's singing voice was dubbed by Marni Nixon. Ernest Lehman's screenplay was based on Hammerstein's original libretto and Margaret Landon's novel *Anna And The King Of Siam*. **Jerome Robbins** was the choreographer and the film, which was directed by Walter Land, was superbly photographed by Leon Shamroy in DeLuxe Color and CinemaScope. It won Oscars for best actor (Brynner), its sumptuous costumes (Irene Shariff), sound recording, art-set decoration and scoring of a musical picture (**Alfred Newman** and Ken Darby), and went on to gross well over $8 million in the USA, rank-ing high in the Top 10 musical films of the 50s.

King And I, The (stage musical)

With music by **Richard Rodgers** and book and lyrics by **Oscar Hammerstein II**, *The King And I* opened at the St. James Theatre in New York on 29 March 1951. It starred **Yul Brynner** as the King of Siam and **Gertrude Lawrence** as Anna Leonowens, a schoolteacher engaged to educate the royal children. Set in the 1860s, the story of *The King And I* was based on Anna Leonowens' book *The English Governess At The Siamese Court* (Margaret Landon's novel *Anna And The King Of Siam* was also based upon the same source material). The project was Lawrence's brainchild and once she had set the wheels in motion and Rodgers and Hammerstein were hired to write it, the show was scheduled to become one of the greatest money-spinners in Broadway history. The strong storyline highlighted an Oriental nation's attempts to advance towards the progressive ideologies of the west, while still being shackled to the concept of a slave-owning, male-dominated society. With settings of Oriental opulence, a masterly score and superb central performances, *The King And I* was a great success, and ran for 1,246 performances. Among the songs were 'I Whistle A Happy Tune', 'Hello, Young Lovers', 'Getting To Know You', 'My Lord And Master', 'Shall We Dance?', 'I Have Dreamed', 'A Puzzlement', 'We Kiss In A Shadow' and 'Something Wonderful', which was sung by Dorothy Sarnoff in the role of Lady Thiang. Additionally, there was the engaging 'March Of The Siamese Children', in which Rodgers effectively captured an Oriental flavour while using orthodox western musical forms. Fittingly, given her involvement in its creation, *The King And I* was a triumph for Lawrence. It was also her swan-song; she died 18 months after the show's opening, to be succeeded by Constance Carpenter. A London production opened in 1953, starring Herbert Lom and Valerie Hobson. Brynner reprised the greatest role of his career for Broadway in 1977 and London two years later. He was touring the show in the USA in 1983 when he first discovered that he had cancer. Over the years, the show has proved to be a convenient vehicle for artists from different branches of showbusiness. In 1989 a Baltimore production starred **Alan Jay Lerner**'s widow, Liz Robertson, and the ballet superstar Rudolph Nureyev, and in the same year Stacy Keach and Mary Beth Pell starred in an acclaimed Pittsburgh production. In 1990 and 1991 Susan Hampshire was teamed with David Yip and Koshiro Matsumoto IX at Sadlers Wells for limited seasons, and a 1991/92 tour with Hayley Mills and Tony Marinyo grossed $13.5 million in 35 weeks. Liz Robertson and ballet star Irek Mukhamedov brought the show back to London as part of the Covent Garden Festival in 1995. In the following year, a ravishing Broadway revival, starring **Donna Murphy** and Lou Diamond Phillips (who came to prominence in the 1987 film *La Bamba*), won four **Tony Awards** for best musical revival, leading actress (Murphy), scenic design (Brian Thompson) and costume design (Roger Kirk). In 1992, **Julie Andrews**, whom many consider would have been the perfect Anna, sang the role for a studio cast CD, with British actor Ben Kingsley as the King. The 1956 film version starred Yul Brynner and Deborah Kerr.

King Brothers

Brothers Michael (b. 25 April 1935, Barking, Essex, England; guitar), Tony (b. 31 January 1937, Barking, Essex, England; bass and bass guitar) and **Denis King** (b. 25 July 1939, Hornchurch, Essex, England; piano, guitar) were one of Britain's top groups in the 50s. The trio, fronted by Denis, made their television debut in 1953 on *Shop Window* and were often seen on mid-50s children's programmes. In 1954, they appeared at London's famous Astor and Embassy clubs, played a season at the Windmill Theatre and performed at the Palladium in 1955. After recording unsuccessfully for World Record Club and Conquest, the old-styled young trio, who were mistakenly tagged 'Britain's Rock 'n' Roll Kids', joined **Parlophone**. In 1957, they charted with cover versions of 'A White Sport Coat', 'In The Middle Of An Island' and even the **Everly Brothers**' 'Wake Up Little Susie' and were voted Britain's Top Vocal Group by *New Musical Express* readers. They had four more Top 40 hits in 1960-61, again with **Norman Newell**-produced cover versions of songs popular in the USA. The biggest of these was 'Standing On The Corner', from the musical *The Most Happy Fella*, which reached number 4 in 1960. Their final chart hit came a year later with '76 Trombones'. In those days, when UK vocal groups were rare, these successes helped them to regain the *NME* Vocal Group award in 1960 and collect *Melody Maker*'s similar award a year later. When they decided to record their own compositions, the hits stopped for the trio, who disliked being associated with rock 'n' roll. They were the last of the old-school vocal groups to be successful in the UK, and were perhaps fortunate to be on the scene when Britain badly needed a vocal group to call its own. They recorded for Pye in 1963, Oriole in 1964

and **CBS** and Page One in 1966. Denis King has since become one of the best-known television music writers in the UK, composing the themes for such successful television series as *Bouquet Of Barbed Wire*, *The Fenn St. Gang*, *Within These Walls* and *Black Beauty*, among many others.

● ALBUMS: with Geoff Love *Three Kings And An Ace* (Decca 1959)★★★, *Kings Of Song* (1962)★★★.

King Creole

This 1958 film is, for many, the best of **Elvis Presley**'s Hollywood career. Based on the Harold Robbins novel *A Stone For Danny Fisher*, it afforded him a first-rate plot - that of a singer performing in a New Orleans club owned by mobsters - providing Presley with a dramatic role equal to the memorable soundtrack. 'Trouble', 'Crawfish' and the title track itself rank among the finest tracks he recorded and the content ranged from compulsive rock 'n' roll numbers to melodic ballads. Presley's singing is self-assured yet unmannered and only his induction into the US Army thwarted the direction both his acting and music were taking.

King Creole - Elvis Presley

King Creole was one of the very few **Elvis Presley** films with good songs, recorded when he was first and foremost a rock 'n' roll singer. Although crudely recorded, the dated sound gives the album great bounce - thin guitar recorded in the bathroom, pudding drums and soggy stand-up bass - but the instrumentation complement the King's quite magnificent voice. 'Hard Headed Woman' remains one of his liveliest tracks and the title track still has incredible moodiness, and even with 50s dance band brass it still works. The CD reissue announces a playing time of only 21.12, the only negative thing about the record.

● Tracks: *King Creole; As Long As I Have You; Hard Headed Woman; Trouble; Dixieland Rock; Don't Ask Me Why; Lover Doll; Crawfish; Young Dreams; Steadfast, Loyal And True; New Orleans.*

● First released 1958

● UK peak chart position: 4

● USA peak chart position: 2

King Crimson

Arguably progressive rock's definitive exponents, King Crimson was formed in January 1969 out of the ashes of the eccentric Giles, Giles And Fripp. **Robert Fripp** (b. 1946, Wimbourne, Dorset, England; guitar) and Mike Giles (b. 1 March 1942; Bournemouth, Dorset, England; drums) were joined by Ian McDonald (b. 25 June 1946, London, England; keyboards), before former Gods member **Greg Lake** (b. 10 November 1948, Bournemouth, Dorset, England; vocals/bass), completed the first official line-up. A fifth addition to the circle, Pete Sinfield, supplied lyrics to the guitarist's compositions. The group's debut album, *In The Court Of The Crimson King*, drew ecstatic praise from critics and a glowing, well-publicized testimonial from the

Who's **Pete Townshend**. An expansive use of mellotron suggested a kinship with the **Moody Blues**, but Fripp's complex chord progressions, and the collection's fierce introduction '21st Century Schizoid Man', revealed a rare imagination. This brief courtship with critical popularity ended with *In The Wake Of Poseidon*. Damned as a repeat of its predecessor, the album masked internal strife which saw **McDonald And Giles** depart to work as a duo and Greg Lake leave to found **Emerson, Lake And Palmer**. Having resisted invitations to join **Yes**, Fripp completed the album with various available musicians including Gordon Haskell (b. 27 April 1946, Bournemouth, Dorset, England; bass/vocals) and Mel Collins (saxophone), both of whom remained in the group for *Lizard*. Drummer Andy McCullough completed this particular line-up, but both he and Haskell left the group when the sessions terminated. Boz Burrell (bass/vocals - Fripp taught Burrell how to play the instrument) and Ian Wallace (drums) replaced them before the reshaped quartet embarked on a punishing touring schedule. One studio album, *Islands*, and a live selection, *Earthbound*, emanated from this particular version of King Crimson which collapsed in April 1972. Collins, Wallace and Burrell then pursued studio-based careers although the bassist later found fame with **Bad Company**. With Sinfield also ousted from the ranks, Fripp began fashioning a new, more radical line-up. John Wetton (b. 12 June 1950, Derby, England), formerly of **Family**, assumed the role of bassist/vocalist while **Bill Bruford** left the more lucrative ranks of **Yes** to become King Crimson's fourth drummer. Percussionist Jamie Muir and violinist David Cross (b. 23 April 1949, Plymouth, Devon, England) completed the innovative unit unveiled on *Larks Tongues In Aspic*, but were discarded over the next two years until only Fripp, Wetton and Bruford remained for the exemplary *Red*. 'King Crimson is completely over for ever and ever', Fripp declared in October 1974 as he embarked on an idiosyncratic solo career. However, in 1981 the guitarist took a surprisingly retrograde step, resurrecting the name for a unit comprising himself, Bruford, Tony Levin (bass) and Adrian Belew (guitar). The albums which followed, *Discipline*, *Beat* and *Three Of A Perfect Pair*, showed both adventure and purpose, belying the suspicion that the group would rest on previous laurels. It was, however, a temporary interlude and Fripp subsequently resumed his individual pursuits and established a new unit, the League Of Gentlemen. King Crimson, a group that married invention and ambition while avoiding the trappings prevailing in rock's experimental arena, may nonetheless prove Fripp's crowning achievement. Fripp reconvened King Crimson in 1994 with the line-up of Belew, Trey Gunn (stick and backing vocals), Levin, Bruford and Pat Mastelotto (acoustic/electric percussion) and a new album *Thrak* appeared the following year.

● ALBUMS: *In The Court Of The Crimson King* (Island 1969)★★★★, *In The Wake Of Poseidon* (Island 1970)★★★, *Lizard* (Island 1970)★★★, *Islands* (Island 1971)★★, *Earthbound* (Island 1972)★★, *Larks Tongues In Aspic* (Island 1973)★★★★, *Starless And Bible Black* (Island 1974)★★★, *Red* (Island 1974)★★★★, *USA* (Island 1975)★★★, *Discipline* (EG 1981)★★★, *Beat* (EG 1982)★★★, *Three Of A Perfect Pair* (EG 1984)★★★, *Thrak* (Virgin 1995)★★★, *Vroom* (Discipline 1995)★★★, *B'Boom* (Discipline 1995)★★, *THRaKaTTak* (Discipline 1996)★★★.

● COMPILATIONS: *A Young Person's Guide To King Crimson* (Island 1976)★★★, *The Compact King Crimson* (EG 1986)★★★, *The Essential King Crimson - Frame By Frame* (EG 1991)★★★★, *The Great Deceiver* (1992)★★★, *Epitaph: Live In 1969* (Discipline 1997)★★★.

King Curtis

b. Curtis Ousley, 7 February 1934, Fort Worth, Texas, USA, d. 13 August 1971. A respected saxophonist and session musician, Curtis appeared on countless releases, including those as disparate as **Buddy Holly** and **Andy Williams**. He is, however, best recalled for his work on the **Atlantic** label. A former member of **Lionel Hampton**'s band, Curtis moved to New York and quickly became an integral part of its studio system. He also scored a number 1 US R&B single, 'Soul Twist', billed as King Curtis And The Noble Knights. The same group switched to **Capitol Records**, but the leader took a solo credit on later hits 'The Monkey' (1963) and 'Soul Serenade' (1964). Curtis continued his session work with the **Coasters**, the **Shirelles** and **Herbie Mann**, while releases on Atco, backed by the Kingpins, progressively established his own career. Several were simply funky instrumental versions of current hits, but his strongest release was 'Memphis Soul Stew' (1967). The saxophonist had meanwhile put together a superb studio group: **Richard Tee**, Cornell Dupree, Jerry Jemmott and **Bernard 'Pretty' Purdie**, all of whom contributed to several of **Aretha Franklin**'s finest records. Curtis guested on **John Lennon**'s *Imagine* and was capable of attracting the best session musicians to put in appearances for his own albums, including guitarist **Duane Allman** on *Instant Groove* and organist **Billy Preston** on *Live At Fillmore West*. Curtis did venture to the Fame and American studios, but he preferred to work in New York. 'In the south you have to restrain yourself to make sure you come back alive', Ousley said to writer **Charlie Gillett**. Six months later, in August 1971, he was stabbed to death outside his West 86th Street apartment.

● ALBUMS: *Have Tenor Sax, Will Blow* (Atco 1959)★★★, *The New Scene Of King Curtis* (New Jazz 1960)★★★, *Azure* (Everest 1961)★★★, *Trouble In Mind* (Tru-Sound 1961)★★★, *Doin' The Dixie Twist* (Tru-Sound 1962)★★★, *It's Party Time* (Tru-Sound 1962)★★★★, *Soul Meeting* (Prestige 1962)★★★, *Arthur Murray's Music For Dancing: The Twist* (RCA Victor 1962)★★, *Soul Twist* (Enjoy 1962)★★★, *Country Soul* (Capitol 1963)★★, *The Great King Curtis* (Clarion 1964)★★, *Soul Serenade* (Capitol 1964)★★★, *King Curtis Plays The Hits Made Famous By Sam Cooke* (Capitol 1965)★★★, *That Lovin' Feelin'* (Atco 1966)★★★, *Live At*

Small's Paradise (Atco 1966)★★★, *Plays The The Great Memphis Hits* (Atco 1967)★★★, *King Size Soul* (Atco 1967)★★, *Sax In Motion* (1968)★★, *Sweet Soul* (Atco 1968)★★★, *Instant Groove* (1969)★★, *Eternally Soul* (1970)★★★, *Get Ready* (1970)★★★, *Blues At Montreux* (1970)★★★, *Live At Fillmore West* (1971)★★, *Mr. Soul* (1972)★★★, *Everybody's Talkin'* (1972)★★, *Jazz Groove* (1974)★★★.

● COMPILATIONS: *Best Of King Curtis* (Capitol 1968)★★★★, *20 Golden Pieces* (1982)★★★, *Didn't He Play!* (1988)★★★, *It's Partytime With King Curtis* (1989)★★★, *Instant Groove* (1990)★★★★, *The Capitol Years 1962-65* (1993)★★★★, *Instant Soul - The Legendary King Curtis* (1994)★★★★.

King Diamond

When popular metal act **Mercyful Fate** split into two separate factions in March 1985, vocalist King Diamond (b. Kim Bendix Petersen, 14 June 1956, Copenhagen, Denmark), Michael Denner (guitar) and Timi Hansen (bass) decided to pursue their obsession with Satanic heavy metal and the occult, while the others sought a more mainstream direction. King Diamond's music was characterized by supernatural storylines, high-pitched, banshee-like vocals and meandering guitarwork. On live performances, their leader specialized in amateurish theatrical stunts to bring the songs to life. This included face make-up not dissimilar to that worn by **Alice Cooper**. Since 1985 there have been numerous line-up changes, but the most enduring personnel have included Andy Larocque (guitar, who joined **Death**, replaced by ex-**Madison** guitarist Mikael Myllynen, aka Mikael Moon), Pete Blakk (guitar), Hal Patino (bass) and Snowy Shaw (drums). Each successive album has offered ever more complex themes and subplots, resulting in the musical equivalent of a sinister version of Dungeons and Dragons. After the failure of *The Eye*, Diamond resurrected Mercyful Fate in 1993, but returned to his solo career two years later to record *Spider's Lullaby*. His current intention seems to be to keep both careers separate but ongoing.

● ALBUMS: *Fatal Portrait* (Roadrunner 1986)★★★, *Abigail* (Roadrunner 1987)★★★, *Them* (Roadrunner 1988)★★★, *The Dark Sides* (Roadrunner 1988)★★, *Conspiracy* (Roadrunner 1989)★★★, *The Eye* (Roadrunner 1990)★★★, *Spider's Lullaby* (Massacre 1995)★★★, *The Graveyard* (Massacre 1996)★★, *Voodoo* (Massacre 1998)★★★.

King Floyd

b. 13 February 1945, New Orleans, Louisiana, USA. This itinerant singer first began performing at the age of 11, but his reputation was established by several mid-60s recordings produced by **Harold Battiste**. Floyd's first major hit came in 1970 with the excellent 'Groove Me', which reached the US Top 10, and he enjoyed two further Top 5 R&B singles with 'Baby Let Me Kiss You' (1971) and 'Woman Don't Go Astray' (1972). He continued to enjoy limited success throughout the first half of that decade, but 'Body English', released in 1976,

was his last chart entry to date.

● ALBUMS: *King Floyd - A Man In Love* (1967)★★★, *King Floyd* (1971)★★★, *Think About It* (1973)★★, *Well Done* (1974)★★★, *Body English* (1976)★★.

King Harvest

Formed in New York City c.1972, King Harvest was best known for its one US hit single, 'Dancing In The Moonlight', in 1973. The group consisted of three keyboardists, Ron Altback, Sherman Kelly and Davy 'Doc' Robinson, plus Ed Tuleja (guitar), Tony Cahill (bass), Rod Novack (saxophone) and David Montgomery (drums). All had been involved previously with other bands and done session work. In 1972, they signed to the small Perception label. Their first single was Altback's 'Dancing In The Moonlight', a soulful pop song that he and Robinson had performed with their earlier group, Boffalongo. It reached number 13 in the US in early 1973 but King Harvest's future singles were unable to match its success. Only one other, 'A Little Bit Like Magic', charted, reaching number 91 in 1973. The original line-up recorded one album titled after the hit single, which reached number 136 in the US. The group made other singles, but by the mid-70s had disbanded. A new version of the group was formed in 1976, and included four original members. With support from **Beach Boys** members **Carl Wilson** and **Mike Love**, they were signed to **A&M Records** and made another album, but, failing to achieve any hits, they subsequently broke up. Tuleja played on **Dennis Wilson**'s 1977 solo *Pacific Ocean Blue* while Altback and Robinson performed with Love in his band **Celebration**.

● ALBUMS: *Dancing In The Moonlight* (1973)★★★, *King Harvest* (1976)★★★.

King Jammy

b. Lloyd James, Kingston, Jamaica, West Indies. Jammy, the undisputed king of computerized, digital reggae music for the 80s, was interested in little else but the **sound system** business from a very early age. He began by building amplifiers and repairing electrical equipment from his mother's house in the Waterhouse area of downtown Kingston, and was soon playing live with his own sound system. His prowess earned him a deserved local reputation and as Prince Jammy, he built equipment for many Waterhouse sounds - he was even acknowledged by the legendary **King Tubby**, another Waterhouse resident, with whom Jammy often worked. In the early 70s Jammy left Jamaica to work in Canada, where his reputation had preceded him, and he was soon working in live stage shows, and employed in various studio activities and sound system work. He stayed for a few years but returned to Kingston and set up his first studio (with extremely limited facilities) at his in-laws' home in Waterhouse. At the same time Tubby's top engineer, Phillip Smart, left for New York and Jammy joined Tubby's team. It was during his time with Tubby that Jammy met the most influential people in reggae; he acknowledges, in particular, the inspiration provided by **Bunny Lee** and **Yabby You**. Jammy was continually expanding his own studio and sound system and in the late 70s he began to release his own productions, including the debut **Black Uhuru** album, coming into contact with many rising **dancehall** artists such as **Half Pint**, **Junior Reid** and **Echo Minott**.

His constant involvement with the grass-roots side of the business gave Jammy a keen sense of what was currently happening in the music, and also allowed him to anticipate new trends. In 1985 he recorded a youth singer called **Wayne Smith** with a tune called 'Under Me Sleng Teng', which was to alter irrevocably the nature, and revolutionize the sound, of reggae music. The basis for 'Sleng Teng' was a Casio 'Music Box' and one of the 'rock' rhythms from the box was adapted and slowed down to become a 'reggae' rhythm. The shockwaves were scarcely believable and before long there were over two hundred different versions of the rhythm available, as every producer and artist jumped on the bandwagon. More than anything else, it opened the music to young independent producers and artists, since expensive studio time and 'real' musicians were no longer a prerequisite for recording. **Digital** reggae ruled, and Jammy, the originator, rode the crest of the wave. His records and sound system dominated and controlled reggae music for the remainder of the decade and on into the 90s. **Bobby Digital**, now an established producer in his own right, was brought into Jammy's camp and he soon became right-hand man in the set-up, with **Steely And Clevie** providing the rhythms. Both were established musicians with a real feeling for the new sound, and a bewildering array of 7-inch and 12-inch singles and albums were released every month. Most were massive Jamaican hits and with the help of long-time associate Count Shelly, the records were released simultaneously in New York and London while Jammy administered the business in Jamaica. Countless artists made their debut on the Jammys label, but veteran singers and vocal groups were all keen to play their part in the new sound. There was no one to rival him and in 1987, Jammy won the coveted Rockers Award for best producer. Jammy's 90s output is not as prolific (by his standards), but he still continues to lead while others follow. In 1995, he revived his most innovative tune on *Sleng Teng Extravaganza '95*, featuring the modish stars updating the rhythm with their own interpretations. It is impossible to overstate his contribution to Jamaican music, because, as the top producer throughout the digital era, he has altered the sound of reggae music without ever losing touch with its foundation - the **sound system**.

● COMPILATIONS: Various Artists: *Superstar Hit Parade Volumes 1 - 7* (Greensleeves 1984-1992)★★★, *Ten To One* (Jammys 1985)★★★★, *Sleng Teng Extravaganza Volumes 1 & 2* (Jammys 1986)★★★, *A Man And His Music Volumes 1, 2 & 3* (RAS 1991)★★★★, *Sleng Teng Extravaganza '95* (Greensleeves 1995)★★★.

● FURTHER READING: *King Jammy's*, Beth Lesser.

King Just

b. *c.*1974. Another of the new crop of Staten Island (aka Shaolin), New York, USA, rappers, whose appropriation of the 'Shaolin' martial arts ethos saw him compared to neighbours the **Wu-Tang Clan**. He made his debut with the 'Warrior's Drum' 12-inch, which became a huge underground hit in 1994. Backed by his crew/gang, Blackfist (also the title of his label, operated through Select), it was competent hardcore but seemed somewhat unoriginal in the context.

King Kobra

After departing as the drummer of **Ozzy Osbourne**'s band in 1984, **Carmen Appice** (b. 15 December 1946, Staten Island, New York, USA) decided to form his own group under the King Kobra moniker. Enlisting the services of four relative unknowns, Mark Free (vocals), David Michael-Phillips (guitar), Mike Sweda (guitar) and Johnny Rod (bass), he negotiated a contract with **EMI Records**, which eventually resulted in *Ready To Strike* in 1985, a hard rock album full of infectious hooks and pyrotechnic guitar breaks. On the strength of this release they were offered the chance to write the theme music for the film *Iron Eagle*. They changed styles at this juncture, switching to a more sophisticated and lightweight AOR approach. As a result, album sales dried up and they were dropped by their label. Johnny Rod left to join **W.A.S.P.** and the band disintegrated. A few months later, the nucleus of Appice and Michael-Phillips rebuilt the band with ex-**Montrose** vocalist Johnny Edwards, Jeff Northrup (guitar) and Larry Hart (bass). They returned to their hard rock origins and released *King Kobra III* on Music For Nations, but it was again poorly received. The band finally became obsolete when Appice joined John Sykes' **Blue Murder** project in 1989.

● ALBUMS: *Ready To Strike* (Capitol 1985)★★★★, *Thrill Of A Lifetime* (EMI 1987)★★★, *King Kobra III* (Music For Nations 1988)★★★.

King Kong

b. Dennis Anthony Thomas, Kingston, Jamaica, West Indies. First named Junior Kong after his father, he started out as a DJ at Tuff Gong, releasing his debut, 'Pink Eye', in 1982. After stints with GT and his own Love Bunch **sound system**, he went on to record for **King Tubby**'s Firehouse label, using a powerful, gospel-tinged wail not dissimilar to that of **Tenor Saw**. The gravity and realism of early songs such as 'Aids' and 'Babylon', when matched to Tubby's prototype **digital** 'riddims' in 1985, quickly established his reputation alongside **Anthony Red Rose**, with whom Tubby teamed him for their debut album, *Two Big Bull Inna One Pen*. By the following year he was voicing for **King Jammy**, with 'Trouble Again', 'Mix Up' and 'Legal We Legal' becoming notable hits and leading to his first solo album release in the UK via **Greensleeves Records**. Jammy was one of many producers in both the UK and Jamaica to record him throughout 1986/7. Others included Black Scorpio, **Harry J.** ('Musical Terrorist'), Errol T., Ossie Hibbert, **Prince Jazzbo**, Java ('Toots Boops') and Jah Life. Albums for **Bunny Lee**, Black Solidarity and King Jammy ensued before he took up residency first in New York, then Canada, as the 80s drew to a close, recording only intermittently on his own short-lived Conscious Music label. 'He Was A Friend' was prompted by the death of Tenor Saw in 1988. The following year he relocated to England and attempted a comeback with strong work for **Mafia And Fluxy** and Gussie P. in 1991/2, since which time he has been inactive.

● ALBUMS: *Legal We Legal* UK title *Trouble Again* (King Jammys 1986/Greensleeves 1986)★★★, with Anthony Red Rose *Two Big Bull Inna One Pen* (Firehouse 1986)★★★, *Dancehall Session* (Striker Lee 1986)★★★★, with Nitty Gritty *Musical Confrontation* (Jammys 1986)★★★, *Big Heavy Load* (Striker Lee 1987)★★★, *Identify Me* (Black Solidarity 1987)★★★.

King Kurt

This UK 'psychobilly' band consisted of Bert, Rory Lyons, Maggit, John Reddington, Smeg and Thwack. Formed at the beginning of 1983, they rose to fame in the autumn of that year with the UK Top 40 single 'Destination Zululand'. A riotous *Top Of The Pops* television appearance gave some clues as to the nature of their live shows, in which audiences would be regularly doused in flour, water, and less savoury items. Produced by **Dave Edmund**s, the band's debut album *Ooh Wallah Wallah* combined raw rockabilly with punk energy. Two minor UK hit singles emerged in 1984 with a captivating version of the Brecht/**Kurt Weill** composition 'Mack The Knife' and the decidedly less challenging 'Banana Banana'. By 1985, Bert and Reddington had been replaced by bassist Dick Crippen and guitarist Jim Piper.

● ALBUMS: *King Kurt* (1983)★★★, *Big Cock* (1986)★★, *Last Will And Testicle* (1988)★★.

● VIDEOS: *Zulu Land* (Visionary 1994).

King Missile

One of the more arresting crop of underground bands drawn from New York, USA, in recent years, King Missile are led by vocalist and spoken word/poetry maverick John S. Hall. His early albums (credited to King Missile (Dog Fly Religion)) for Kramer's **Shimmy Disc** label were expanded in sound by the latter's auxiliary musicianship and production, as well as the efforts of guitarist Dogbowl. When the latter left, he took the parenthesized portion of the name with him, though Hall's instinct for black humour and caustic commentary remained. Dogbowl would go on to his own erratic solo career, while *Mystical Shit* saw Hall joined by **Bongwater** guitarist Dave Rick and multi-instrumentalist Chris Xefos (from **When People Were Shorter**). This included notable, gilt-edged cuts such as 'Jesus Is Way Cool', which no doubt helped to entice **Atlantic Records** in the group's direction. King Missile began to

break into the US college charts with *Happy Hour*, notably via the single 'Detachable Penis', which was released a year before the John Wayne Bobbit case came to light. A self-titled album released in 1994, meanwhile, saw production expertise from Daniel Rey (**Ramones**, **White Zombie**, etc.), but Hall decided to fold the band.

● ALBUMS: as King Missile (Dog Fly Religion) *Fluting On The Hump* (Shimmy Disc 1987)★★★, *Mystical Shit* (Shimmy Disc 1990)★★★, as John S. Hall with Kramer *Real Men* (Shimmy Disc 1991)★★★, *The Way To Salvation* (Atlantic 1991)★★★, *Happy Hour* (Atlantic 1992)★★★, *King Missile* (Atlantic 1994)★★★.

Solo: Dogbowl *Tit! An Opera* (Shimmy Disc 1989)★★, *Cyclops Nuclear Submarine Captain* (Shimmy Disc 1991)★★.

● COMPILATIONS: as King Missile (Dog Fly Religion) *They* (Shimmy Disc 1988)★★★.

King Of America - Elvis Costello

Elvis Costello's first album without the **Attractions** in tow also proved to be his best since 1980's *Get Happy*. A varied selection of musicians appear on the album, including legendary session veterans **James Burton** and **Jerry Scheff**, lending Costello's songs a distinctly American roots-rock feel. The songs, in turn, were some of the strongest he had ever written, from the finely observed character studies of 'American Without Tears' and 'Sleep Of The Just', to the scathing rants of 'Glitter Gulch' and 'Little Palaces'. On 'Our Little Angel', Costello sings about 'a chainsaw running through a dictionary', an apt description of the endlessly inventive lyricism that characterizes *King Of America*.

● Tracks: *Brilliant Mistake; Lovable; Our Little Angel; Don't Let Me Be Understood; Glitter Gulch; Indoor Fireworks; Little Palaces; I'll Wear It Proudly; American Without Tears; Eisenhower Blues; Poisoned Rose; The Big Light; Jack Of All Parades; Suit Of Lights; Sleep Of The Just.*

● First released 1986

● UK peak chart position: 11

● USA peak chart position: 39

King Of Jazz

The title of this lavish and spectacular musical revue which was released by Universal in 1930 refers, of course, to **Paul Whiteman**, who led the most popular orchestra of his time. Although not a jazzman himself, he did promote that brand of music by employing many fine jazz musicians over the years, such as **Joe Venuti**, **Eddie Lang**, and **Frankie Trumbauer**. That trio are all featured prominently in this film along with Whiteman's most famous vocalist, **Bing Crosby** and his fellow Rhythm Boys Harry Barris and Al Rinker, plus a host of other artists including John Boles, Jeannie Lang, the Brox Sisters, William Kent, Grace Hayes, Stanley Smith, Jeanette Loff, **Walter Brennan**, Laura La Plante, and Slim Summerville. Inevitably the spotlight is very firmly on Paul Whiteman And His Orchestra throughout, from the opening 'Rhapsody In Blue' (**George**

Gershwin), during which the entire orchestra seated inside - and at the keyboard - of a gigantic grand piano, through to the breathtaking finalé when, beginning with 'D'Ye Ken John Peel' and 'Santa Lucia', the music from various countries around the world is symbolically blended together in 'The Melting Pot Of Music'. In between those two amazing sequences, and introduced every time by a caption card giving song title and performer details, were well over 50 musical items ranging from folk and classical pieces to popular songs such as 'Mississippi Mud' (Harry Barris-James Cavanaugh), 'It Happened In Monterey' (**Mabel Wayne**-**Billy Rose**), 'So The Bluebirds And The Blackbirds Got Together' (Barris-Billy Moll), 'Ragamuffin Romeo' (Wayne-Harry DeCosta); and 'A Bench In The Park', 'Happy Feet', 'Music Hath Charms', and 'Song Of The Dawn' (all by **Milton Ager** and **Jack Yellen**). As well as conducting the orchestra, Whiteman appeared at other times in a variety of costumes (including baby clothes, complete with feeding bottle), mugging to the camera and looking not unlike Oliver Hardy *sans* Stan Laurel. Russell Markert staged the dances, and the sketches were written by John Murray Anderson who had enjoyed a great deal of success on Broadway with several editions of the *Greenwich Village Follies*, and his own *John Murray Anderson's Almanac*. He was also the director, the man responsible for assembling this whole marvellously original concept, parts of which eventually influenced many a future screen musical. Hal Mohr, Jerome Ash and Ray Rennahan photographed the film in two-colour Technicolor which gave the film a charm of its own, and contributed to the desire to watch it over again, if only to catch some of the details and bits of business missed the first time around.

King Of The Delta Blues Singers - Robert Johnson

If you are a mountain climber you tackle Everest; if you are a blues lover you get to know this album very well. Very few had heard **Robert Johnson**'s music when this milestone album was first released in 1962, but it was evident that this was a body of work of fundamental importance to the development of postwar Chicago blues and blues in general. Little known in his lifetime, Johnson synthesized traditions represented by men like **Charley Patton**, **Son House**, **Lonnie Johnson** and **Leroy Carr**, and refined them through his unique interpretative skills. An accomplished guitarist with finger and slide, Johnson matched his virtuosity with a tortured vocal style that added deeper resonance to his words.

● Tracks: *Crossroads Blues; Terraplane Blues; Come On In My Kitchen; Walking Blues; Last Fair Deal Gone Down; 32-20 Blues; Kindhearted Woman Blues; If I Had Possession Over Judgment Day; Preaching Blues; When You Got A Good Friend; Rambling On My Mind; Stones In My Passway; Traveling Riverside Blues; Milkcow's Calf Blues; Me And The Devil Blues; Hellhound On My Trail*

● First released 1962
● UK peak chart position: did not chart
● USA peak chart position: did not chart

King Of The Hill

This St. Louis, Missouri-based four-piece heavy metal outfit began life on the local club circuit as a covers band, with the line-up settling when bassist George Potsos joined Frankie Muriel (vocals), Vito Bono (drums) and Jimmy Griffin (guitar). Initially known as Broken Toyz, the band gradually introduced original material into their set, until the demand for their own songs allowed them to drop the cover versions entirely. They signed a recording contract in 1990, and, having adopted the name King Of The Hill, recorded their self-titled debut with **Bang Tango** producer Howard Benson. The album mixed party metal in the grand **Van Halen** style with funk influences, while also touching on AOR, with vocal harmonies that echoed **Bon Jovi**. The opening single, 'I Do U', did well on MTV, and with major backing from their record label the band spent much of 1991 on the road, touring with **White Lion**, **Trixter**, **Lynch Mob** and **Steelheart** in the USA, and received a rapturous reception as **Extreme**'s guests on their autumn UK tour. This, the band's first live work outside their own country, served to sharpen their performing abilities, with the charismatic Muriel becoming the visual focus of the band, drawing comparisons to both **David Lee Roth** and **Prince**, not least for his multiple costume changes throughout each show. However, despite the fact that King Of The Hill were due to record a second album in early 1992, they seemed to disappear almost overnight.

● ALBUMS: *King Of The Hill* (SBK 1991)★★★.

King Of The Slums

Formed near Manchester, England, by vocalist Charley Keigher (vocals) and Sarah Curtis (electric violin), Salford's King Of The Slums first surfaced with the amateurish 'Spider Psychiatry' on SLR Records in 1986. The single went unnoticed and the band spent nearly two years refining their sound, before issuing the impressive EP *England's Finest Hopes*, on the local Play Hard label in February 1988. Curtis's scratchy, **John Cale**-like violin playing and Keigher's vehement polemic were augmented by Jon Chandler (bass) although over the next few years the band used a succession of drummers - Trevor Rising, Ross Cain and Ged O'Brian, before eventually settling with Stuart Owen. 'Bombs Away! On Harpurhey' and the controversial 'Vicious British Boyfriend' (with its Enoch Powell/Union Jack sleeve) followed in quick succession early in 1989. A live appearance on BBC Television's *Snub TV* helped both singles into the independent charts, capturing one of the band's most electrifying moments, 'Fanciable Headcase'. *Barbarous English Fayre* compiled the group's Play Hard recordings, as the band moved to Midnight Music, acquiring a new bassist, James Cashan, along the way. Another indepen-

dent hit, 'Once A Prefect', preceded King Of The Slums' first proper album, *Dandelions*. Titles such as 'Up The Empire/Balls To The Bulldog Breed' and 'Barbarous Superiors' continued Keigher's fork-tongued lyrical attacks on racism and the establishment. By the time 'It's Dead Smart' arrived in 1990, Pete Mason had replaced previous guitarist Gary Sparkes, but the sound was just as razor-sharp, and the rhetoric no less poignant. *Blowzy Weirdos* followed a move to **Cherry Red Records** in 1991, and also saw the group catch a little of the spotlight that had fallen on Manchester in the wake of the **Happy Mondays**' arrival. Sadly, it was not enough to ensure the survival of this talented act.
● ALBUMS: *Dandelions* (Midnight 1990)★★★, *Blowzy Weirdos* (Cherry Red 1991)★★★.
● COMPILATIONS: *Barbarous English Fayre* (Play Hard 1989)★★★.

King Pins

An R&B vocal group from Clarksdale, Mississippi, USA, the King Pins were essentially a secularized gospel group, and thus their early 60s records display some of the incipient sounds of the soul revolution. Members were three Kelly brothers - Andrew, Curtis and Robert - Charles Lee and Offee Reece. Curtis and Robert were the two leads in the group. They had one hit as the King Pins, 'It Won't Be This Way Always' (number 13 R&B, number 89 pop), from 1963, and one as the Kelly Brothers, 'Falling In Love Again' (number 39 R&B), from 1966. The group returned to their gospel roots in the 70s.
● ALBUMS: *It Won't Be This Way Always* (King 1963)★★★, as the Kelly Brothers *Sweet Soul* (President 1968)★★★.
● COMPILATIONS: as the Kelly Brothers *Sanctified Southern Soul* (Kent 1996)★★★.

King Pleasure And The Biscuit Boys

One of several UK groups devoted to reviving the jump-jive music pioneered in the 40s by **Louis Jordan**, they gathered a strong following across Europe in the late 80s. The group was formed in the Birmingham area in 1986 by ex-rockabilly bassist King Pleasure (b. 13 March 1966, Wednesbury, West Midlands, England; vocals, saxophone) and Bullmoose K. Shirley (b. 6 December 1967, Bilston, West Midlands, England; guitar). Other founder-members were P. Popps Martin (b. 23 February 1968, Wednesfield, West Midlands, England; saxophone), Piano-Man Skan (b. 22 March 1962, Birmingham, West Midlands, England; keyboards), Slap Happy (b. 5 November 1970, Rugby, Warwickshire, England; double bass), 'Bam Bam' Beresford (b. 25 March 1968; drums) and Lisa 'Sugar' Lee (vocals). They signed to local label Big Bear in 1988, following their debut album with a cover version of Jordan's 'Ain't Nobody Here But Us Chickens'. The band played support gigs to **B.B. King** and **Cab Calloway** as well as appearing in 10 European countries. In 1991, Lee and Skan left to be replaced by Ivory Dan McCormack (b. 1974, Norton, Cleveland,

England; piano), ex-Big Town Playboy Big Al Nichols (b. 1964, Wrexham, North Wales; tenor saxophone) and Cootie Alexander (b. 6 September 1969, Birmingham, West Midlands, England; trumpet). They are one of the most exciting live bands and are leaders in waving the flag for 40s jump R&B.
● ALBUMS: *King Pleasure And The Biscuit Boys* (Big Bear 1988)★★★, *This Is It!* (Big Bear 1990)★★★, *Better Beware!* (Big Bear 1991)★★★, *Blues And Rhythm Revue, Volume 1* (Big Bear 1995)★★★.

King Sisters

b. Salt Lake City, Utah, USA. Alyce, Donna, Louise and Yvonne King were arguably one of the most technically accomplished vocal groups to emerge from the big band era. They took their stage name from their father, William King Driggs, who was a college voice trainer. Together with another sister and a friend, they appeared with **Horace Heidt**'s band in Chicago in 1935, billed as the Six King Sisters. After singing on Heidt's Alemite radio show in 1936-38, they became a quartet in the late 30s, and appeared on radio with Al Pearce. When **Alvino Rey**, Louise's husband, who played electric guitar with Heidt, left to form his own band, the Kings went with him, and performed with the band, and as individual soloists, until 1943. Yvonne King sang on several Rey hits, including the band's theme song, 'Nighty Night', 'I Said No' and 'Idaho'. The sisters also featured on 'Tiger Rag' and 'Strip Polka'. In addition they had successful records under their own name, through to 1945, including 'The Hut-Sut Song', 'Rose O'Day', 'My Devotion', 'I'll Get By', 'It's Love-Love-Love', 'Milkman, Keep Those Bottles Quiet', 'The Trolley Song', 'Candy' and 'Saturday Night (Is The Loneliest Night Of The Week)'. They also appeared in several movies including *Sing Your Worries Away* (1942), *Meet The People* (1944), *The Thrill Of A Romance* (1945), *On Stage Everybody* (1945) and *Cuban Pete* (1945). Rey broke up the band when he went into the US Navy, and when it re-formed after the war, it was without the Sisters. They had been resident on **Kay Kyser**'s radio show during 1944, but in the late 40s, and beyond, were only making occasional personal appearances and recordings. In the mid-60s, they were once again in demand with the advent of the enormously popular *The King Family* television show, in which they featured, together with a vast cast of relatives. Their 60s television series spawned several albums and they continued to record into the 70s covering popular standards such as 'Nina Never Knew', 'Too Late Now', 'Street Of Dreams' and 'Don't Get Around Much Anymore'.
● ALBUMS: *The King Family Show!* (1965)★★★, *The King Family Album* (1965)★★★.

King Solomon Hill

b. Joe Holmes, 1897, McComb, Mississippi, USA, d. 1949, Sibley, Louisiana, USA. Controversy long surrounded the identity of this itinerant blues singer.

He fused the styles of his friends Sam Collins and Ramblin' Thomas (respectively, south Mississippi and east Texas/Louisiana musicians), and elements from **Blind Lemon Jefferson**, into the eerie bottleneck guitar sound that accompanied his chilling falsetto on his 1932 recordings. His stage-name was derived from his address in Louisiana King Solomon Hill Baptist Church, having given its name to the community of Yellow Pines. Holmes's masterpieces are 'The Gone Dead Train' and 'Whoopee Blues', the former a hobo's lament that is made all the more impressive by his near impenetrable diction. 'Whoopee Blues' transforms an anodyne **Lonnie Johnson** song, imbuing it with the brimstone reek of hell with which the singer threatens his wayward girlfriend.

● COMPILATIONS: *Backwoods Blues* (1991)★★★.

King Sounds

b. *c.*1948, St. Elizabeth, Jamaica, West Indies. King Sounds emigrated to the UK in 1974 , but his first foray into the music business was back in Jamaica, where he danced to **ska** music in talent shows. His friend **Alton Ellis** asked him to compere a show, which led to further bookings showcasing his ability to work crowds into a frenzy before an artist's stage appearance ; a cameo as an MC in *Babylon* captured an early performance in this role. In 1975 he recorded 'Rock & Roll Lullaby', which was a minor hit, before jointly founding the Grove Music collective based in Ladbroke Grove, London. Together with Mikey Campbell, he introduced **Aswad**, **Delroy Washington** and the Sons Of Jah as well as distributing **Yabby You**'s productions from Jamaica. His debut recording was re-released by the label, but his 'Spend One Night In A Babylon', featuring DJ **Trinity**, captivated the market. Sharing the production with Yabby You, the duo gained a number of hits as the Prophets, including a remake of **Slim Smith**'s 'Blessed Are The Meek'. He was frequently involved in performances at the annual Notting Hill Carnival where, with the Israelites, he proved a popular live act. King Sounds often performed as a support to Aswad, and the energetic Israelites, including Clifton 'Bigga' Morrison, Eddie 'Tan Tan' Thornton and Michael 'Bammi' Rose, provided the horns and keyboards for both acts. *Forward To Africa*, a 1981 release featuring the title track, a version of **Clarence Carter**'s 'Patches' and 'Batman', was successful in Europe. Sounds also made successful appearances at the British Invasion to Reggae Sunsplash, performing alongside Winston Reedy and **Steel Pulse**. His success was followed by a hit in Jamaica when he covered the **Heptones**' 'Book Of Rules', released through his own King & I label. The track was lifted from *There Is A Reward* which featured some of the top session musicians in Jamaica, including **Sly Dunbar, Pam Hall, J.C. Lodge** and **Dean Fraser**. King Sounds 'bubbled under' the UK charts when he worked with **Lloyd Charmers** and **B.B. Seaton** for the singles 'Black & White', 'I Really Don't Want To Hurt You' and 'Would You Like

To Be Happy'. King Sounds' membership of the Twelve Tribes Of Israel, alongside **Freddie McGregor, Dennis Brown** and **Bob Marley**, has influenced much of his work. His desire to educate the youth has not always been popular, but he is regarded with 'nuff respect'. Now seen as an elder statesman of British Reggae he was one of the representatives in the House Of Parliament for the launch of COBRA, aiming to look after the interests of performers who had previously suffered exploitation in the music industry. In 1996 he performed and toured with Freddie McGregor.

● ALBUMS: *Come Zion Side* (Grove 1979)★★★, *Forward To Africa* (Island 1981)★★★★, *Moving Forward* (King & I 1983)★★★, *There Is A Reward* (King & I 1985)★★★, *Strength To Strength* (King & I 1988)★★★, *I Shall Sing* (King & I 1992)★★★.

King Sporty

b. Noel Williams, *c.*1945, Kingston, Jamaica, West Indies. King Sporty was one of the first DJs to record with **Coxsone Dodd** at **Studio One**, where he chanted over **Delroy Wilson**'s 'Feel Good All Over' and 'I'm Not A King', the latter of which enjoyed an enormous revival through **Cocoa Tea**'s 1997 remake of the song. King Sporty also provided the DJ version of the **Heptones**' classic 'Choice Of Music', which has since become a much sought-after collector's item. By the early 70s King Sporty had relocated to Miami where he continued to be involved in the music. He linked up with the TK organization, working with **KC And The Sunshine Band**, who in 1975 played on sessions for King Sporty's production of *The Chosen Few In Miami*. His songwriting skills were to prove advantageous when **Bob Marley** recorded 'Buffalo Soldier', a posthumous hit; King Sporty was involved in the original production. As well as producing, King Sporty continued to perform in Florida where in 1983, backed by the Ex-tras he enjoyed the disco hits 'Do You Wanna Dance' and 'Meet Me At The Disco', the latter of which led to an album of the same name. With the Ex-tras he also released '(The) Boomerang', 'Haven't Been Funked Enough' and 'I Can't Keep Still'. By the early 90s the disco-orientated albums were marketed by Receiver who also controlled **Trojan Records**' vast back catalogue. In 1995 he had set up Sporty's Studio in Miami, patronized by a number of top reggae performers including the **Wailers** Band. He is married to the US singer **Betty Wright**, noted for her R&B hits 'Clean Up Woman' and 'Shoorah Shoorah', as well as for her tour with the **Bob Marley** And The Wailers in the 70s.

● ALBUMS: *Meet Me At The Disco* (Dancefloor 1983)★★, with the Ex-tras *Extra Funky* (Dancefloor 1983)★, with the Ex-tras *Can't Keep Still* (Dancefloor 1984)★★★.

King Stitt

The 'Ugly One', apparently born Winston Spark, never let his seriously disfigured facial features inhibit his progress in the highly competitive Kingston music world. By 1969 he was the regular DJ for **Coxsone**

Dodd's Number One Set. His success paved the way for U-Roy, I. Roy and Big Youth, but unfortunately, their new style and approach soon superseded Stitt. His style was firmly rooted in the older tradition of Jamaican DJing, influenced by American radio DJs - shouted introductions and interjections as opposed to 'riding the rhythm' and filling out the entire length of the record. Stitt's contributions were fragmentary and explosive as hit followed hit for Clancy Eccles in the early 70s - 'Herbman', 'Fire Corner', 'The Ugly One' and, possibly the most interesting of all, 'Dance Beat', where Eccles and Stitt reminisce about the old ska days, the dances and the dancehalls. Sadly, there is no album of strictly King Stitt material, although *Fire Corner*, credited to the Dynamites (Clancy's Studio band), features a fairly representative cross-section of his work. His few recordings at Studio One failed to match the quality of his Clancy's output, but he has continued to work there in a non-recording capacity. In 1997 the DJ recorded 'Small Axe' alongside Buju Banton.

● ALBUMS: with The Dynamites *Fire Corner* (Trojan/Clandisc 1969)★★★★, various artists *Dance Hall '63* (Studio One 1994)★★★.

● COMPILATIONS: *Reggae Fire Beat* (Jamaican Gold 1997)★★★★.

King Sun

Mediocre artist whose records contain the over-familiar self-deifying advocacy of a rash of other rappers, alongside Afrocentric/Islamic concerns. Matters began more promisingly in 1987 when he teamed up with D Moe for the 'Hey Love' minor hit, which borrowed liberally from 'Moments In Love' by the Art Of Noise. Nothing in his more recent work has proved other than dispensable, however, and he remains best known for his bravery in dissing Ice Cube while the latter was peforming.

● ALBUMS: *XI* (Profile 1989)★★, *Righteous But Ruthless* (Profile 1990)★★, *King Sun With The Sword* (Profile 1991)★★.

King Tee

b. Los Angeles, California, USA. Based in Compton, King Tee made his first entrance into music as a mixer for Houston's KTSU and KYOK radio stations. Through his radio connections he recorded his first record, 'Payback's A Mother', for Greg Mack's Mackdaddy Records. A contract with Capitol brought two albums together with producer DJ Pooh, but negligible success. However, he did have his moments. The first album was distinguished by jokey cuts like 'I Got A Cold', on which he delivered a remarkable impression of a vexed sinus. The follow-up was harder, tracks like 'Skanless' extolling the joys of bedding his friend's wife. 'Time To Get Out' was a rare flash of insight, and by far the best track on show. Tee did at least introduce the world to the potentially far more interesting Tha Alkaholics.

● ALBUMS: *Act A Fool* (Capitol 1989)★★★, *At Your Own Risk* (Capitol 1990)★★★.

King Tubby

b. Osbourne Ruddock, 28 January 1941, Kingston, Jamaica, West Indies, d. 6 February 1989. King Tubby grew up around High Holborn Street in Central Kingston before moving to Waterhouse in 1955. He started repairing radios and by the late 50s had begun to experiment with sound system amplifiers. By 1968 he was operating his own Tubby's Home Town Hi-Fi, where he later incorporated a custom reverb and echo facility into his system. At the same time he was working as disc-cutter for Duke Reid and it was here that he discovered that he could make special versions of well-known rocksteady tunes. By cutting out most of the vocal track, fading it in at suitable points, reducing the mix down to the bass only, and dropping other instrumental tracks in or out, Tubby invented dub. Initially the technique was used for 'specials' or dub plates - custom acetates made exclusively for sound system use. The spaces left in the mix allowed sound system DJs to stretch out lyrically, predating the emergence of US rappers by some years. Record producers soon began to see the potential of these versions. Joe Gibbs' engineer, Errol Thompson, working at Randy's Studio 17, had started employing rhythm versions as b-sides by 1971. To keep ahead of the competition, Tubby acquired an old four-track mixing console from Dynamic Studios. He then introduced further refinements - delay echo, slide faders, and phasing. By late 1971 he was working with producers such as Bunny Lee, Lee Perry, Glen Brown, Augustus Pablo and 'Prince' Tony Robinson. The latter issued records that credited Tubby as mixer, including 'Tubby's In Full Swing', the b-side to a DJ track by Winston Scotland.

Throughout the 70s Tubby mixed dubs for all the aforementioned producers, in addition to Roy Cousins, Yabby You, Winston Riley, Carlton Patterson and Bertram Brown's Freedom Sounds. His most important work, in terms of sheer quantity, was with Bunny Lee. Lee used Tubby for dub and voicing on rhythms he had built elsewhere with the Aggrovators session band. All the singers who worked with Lee at this time - Johnny Clarke, Cornell Campbell, Linval Thompson, Jackie Edwards, Derrick Morgan, Delroy Wilson, Horace Andy, John Holt and Owen Grey - made records with Aggrovators rhythms, voiced and mixed at King Tubby's. Lee began to issue dub albums featuring Tubby's mixes, and other producers soon followed that lead. Tubby's name as mixer soon appeared on well over 100 albums. A generation of engineers trained under Tubby's supervision, including King Jammy and 'Prince' Phillip Smart, both subsequently finding success on their own terms. Throughout this period Tubby planned to build his own studio, and by 1988 he had begun to issue computer-generated digital music, featuring many of the new-wave ragga singers and DJs, including Pad Anthony, Courtney Melody, Anthony Red Rose, Pliers and Ninjaman, as well as established talents such as Cornell Campbell. Just when it seemed Tubby was poised to challenge top producers such as

Jammy and **Gussie Clarke**, tragedy struck. On 6 February 1989, a lone gunman murdered King Tubby outside his home, the motive apparently robbery. The loss shocked Jamaican music fans and artists. Many innovations, not only in Jamaican music but in other 'dance' forms as well - the 'dub mix', the practice of DJing extended lyrics over rhythm tracks, the prominence of bass and drums in the mix - were developed by King Tubby, both on his sound system and in the studio during the period 1969-74. His place as a seminal figure in the music's development through three decades is assured.

● ALBUMS: *Black Board Jungle* (Upsetter 1974)★★★, *Dub From The Roots* (Total Sounds 1974)★★★, *The Roots Of Dub* (Grounation 1975)★★★★, *Shalom Dub* (Klik 1975)★★★, *King Tubby Meets the Aggrovators At Dub Station* (Live & Love 1975)★★★★, *King Tubby Meets The Upsetter At The Grass Roots Of Dub* (Fay Music 1975)★★★, *Harry Mudie Meets King Tubby In Dub Conference Volumes 1, 2 & 3* (Mudies 1975/76/77)★★★★, *Dubbing With The Observer* (Trojan 1975)★★★, *King Tubby Meets Rockers Uptown* (Clocktower 1976)★★★★, *King Tubby's Prophecy Of Dub* (Prophet 1976)★★★★, *Ital Dub* (Trojan 1976)★★★, *Beware Dub* (Grove Music 1978)★★★, *Rockers Meets King Tubby In A Firehouse* (Yard Music 1980)★★★, *Dangerous Dub: King Tubby Meets Roots Radics* (Copasetic 1981)★★★★, *King Tubby's Presents Soundclash Dubplate Style* (Taurus 1989)★★★, *King Tubby's Special 1973-1976* (Trojan 1989)★★★, *Dub Gone Crazy: The Evolution Of Dub At King Tubby's 1975-79* (Blood & Fire 1994)★★★★, *Creation Dub* (Roir 1995)★★★, *King Tubby & Friends* (Trojan 1996)★★★★, *Dub Gone 2* (Blood & Fire 1996)★★★.

King Tubby's Meets Rockers Uptown - Augustus Pablo

Augustus Pablo's 'Far East' melodies and approach to building rhythms were hugely influential on the whole of reggae music in the early and mid-70s. This set features the mixing talents of **King Tubby** let loose on some of Pablo's finest rhythms. Tubby, ostensibly a studio engineer but so much more, not only transformed reggae but the sound of popular music as we know it, and his work here brings out the depth and mystery of Pablo's music without ever sacrificing its inherent qualities. This album is a timeless showcase of his mixing skills and Pablo's singular musicianship.

● Tracks: *Keep On Dubbing; Stop Them Jah; Young Generation Dub; Each One Dub; Braces Tower Dub; King Tubby's Meets Rockers Uptown; Corner Crew Dub; Say So; Skanking Dub; Frozen Dub; Satta.*

● First released 1975

● UK peak chart position: did not chart

● USA peak chart position: did not chart

King's Rhapsody

With the stage musical *King's Rhapsody*, **Ivor Novello** maintained the successful formula of the Ruritanian-based fantasy that had stood him in such good stead for the past decade. Opening at the Palace Theatre in London on 15 September 1949, the production was replete with gypsy dances, unrequited love and hugely sentimental music, lyrics and concept. Critics were almost unanimous in their disdain, having gratefully adjusted to the new style of musical coming into London from the USA. However, by this stage of his career, Novello had built up a massive following and audiences flocked to see the show. The songs included 'Someday My Heart Will Awake', 'The Violin Began To Play', 'If This Were Love', 'Fly Home, Little Heart', 'The Gates Of Paradise', and 'Take Your Girl'. The cast was virtually a roll-call of Novello's private repertory company which included Olive Gilbert, Zena Dare, Phylis Dare and Vanessa Lee. *King's Rhapsody* was still playing to packed houses when Novello died suddenly on 5 March 1951. The show closed later in the year following a run of 881 performances. A 1955 film version starred Errol Flynn and **Anna Neagle**, and Vanessa Lee recreated her original role when the show appeared on BBC Television in 1957. To commemorate the 100th anniversary of Ivor Novello's birth, in 1993 BBC Radio 2 transmitted a complete performance.

King, Al

b. Alvin Smith, 8 August 1926, Monroe, Louisiana, USA. Anything other than church music was forbidden in the Smith household, so it was not until Alvin Smith sang with USO bands while serving in the World War II that he discovered his taste for the musical life. Moving to San Francisco and then Los Angeles, he made his recording debut, 'Homesick Blues', for Recorded In Hollywood in 1951. Two years later he led the Savoys, who recorded 'Chop Chop Boom' with saxophonist **Jack McVea** for Combo. Returning north to Oakland, he recorded 'On My Way' for Music City, on which he was accompanied by the guitarist **Johnny Heartsman**, and then joined **Jimmy McCracklin**'s touring band, which led to two singles on which he was teamed with a female singer (their records were released under the collective name of Al And Nettie). One of the singles, 'Now You Know', was an answer record to McCracklin's 'Just Got To Know'. In 1964, now calling himself Al King, he made 'Reconsider Baby', the record most closely associated with his name. Recorded for Triad and later leased to the **Atlantic** subsidiary Shirley, it remains one of the best versions of **Lowell Fulson**'s composition, not least for Heartsman's contribution. King made further records for Flag, Sahara, Modern and Kent during the 60s and a final session for Ronn in 1970, but failed to repeat the successful formula.

● COMPILATIONS: *West Coast Winners* (Moonshine 1985)★★★, *On My Way* (Diving Duck 1986)★★★, *More West Coast Winners* (Moonshine 1989)★★, *Cruisin' And Bluesin'* (Ace 1990)★★★.

King, Albert

b. Albert Nelson, 23 April 1923 (although three other dates have also been published), Indianola, Mississippi, USA, d. 21 December 1992, Memphis, Tennessee, USA.

Despite the fact that his work has been overshadowed by that of his regal namesake **B.B. King**, this exceptional performer was one of the finest in the entire blues/soul canon. King's first solo recording, 'Bad Luck Blues', was released in 1953, but it was not until the end of the decade that he embarked on a full-time career. His early work fused his already distinctive fretwork to big band-influenced arrangements and included his first successful single, 'Don't Throw Your Love On Me Too Strong'. However, his style was not fully defined until 1966 when, signed to the **Stax** label, he began working with **Booker T. And The MGs**. This tightly knit quartet supplied the perfect rhythmic punch, a facet enhanced by a judicious use of horns. 'Cold Feet', which included wry references to several Stax stablemates, and 'I Love Lucy', a homage to King's distinctive 'Flying V' guitar, stand among his finest recordings. However, this period is best remembered for 'Born Under A Bad Sign' (1967) and 'The Hunter' (1968), two performances that became an essential part of many repertoires including those of **Free** and **Cream**. King became a central part of the late 60s 'blues boom', touring the college and concert circuit. His classic album, *Live Wire/Blues Power*, recorded at San Francisco's Fillmore Auditorium in 1968, introduced his music to the white rock audience. More excellent albums followed in its wake, including *King Does The King's Thing*, a tribute collection of **Elvis Presley** material, and *Years Gone By*. His work during the 70s was largely unaffected by prevailing trends. 'That's What The Blues Is All About' borrowed just enough from contemporary styles to provide King with a Top 20 R&B single, but the bankruptcy of two outlets dealt a blow to King's career. A five-year recording famine ended in 1983, and an astute programme of new material and careful reissues kept the master's catalogue alive. King remained a commanding live performer and an influential figure. A new generation of musicians, including **Robert Cray** and the late **Stevie Ray Vaughan** continued to acknowledge his timeless appeal, a factor reinforced in 1990 when King guested on guitarist **Gary Moore**'s 'back-to-the-roots' collection, *Still Got The Blues*. King died late in 1992.

● ALBUMS: *The Big Blues* (King 1962)★★★, *Born Under A Bad Sign* (Atlantic 1967)★★★★, *King Of The Blues Guitar* (Atlantic 1968)★★★★, *Live Wire/Blues Power* (King 1968)★★★★, with Steve Cropper, 'Pops' Staples *Jammed Together* (Stax 1969)★★★, *Years Gone By* (Stax 1969)★★★★, *King, Does The King's Thing* (Stax 1970)★★★, *Lovejoy* (Stax 1971)★★★, *The Lost Session* (1971)★★★, *I'll Play The Blues For You* (Stax 1972)★★★, *Live At Montreux/Blues At Sunrise* (Stax 1973)★★★, *I Wanna Get Funky* (Stax 1974)★★, *The Pinch* (Stax 1976)★★, *Albert* (Utopia 1976)★★★, *Truckload Of Lovin'* (Utopia 1976)★★, *Albert Live* (Utopia 1977)★★★, *King Albert* (1977)★★★, *New Orleans Heat* (Tomato 1978)★★★, *San Francisco '83* (Stax 1983)★★★, *I'm In A 'Phone Booth, Baby* (Stax 1984)★★★, with John Mayall *The Lost Session* recorded 1971 (Stax 1986)★★, *Red House* (Essential 1991)★★★, *Blues At Sunset* (Stax 1996)★★★.

● COMPILATIONS: shared with Otis Rush *Door To Door* (Chess 1969)★★★, *Laundromat Blues* (Edsel 1984)★★★, *The Best Of Albert King* (Stax 1986)★★★, *I'll Play The Blues For You: The Best Of Albert King* (Stax 1988)★★★, *Let's Have A Natural Ball* recorded 1959-63 (Modern Blues Recordings 1989)★★★, *Wednesday Night In San Francisco (Live At The Fillmore)* and *Thursday Night In San Francisco (Live At The Fillmore)* (Stax 1990)★★, *Live On Memory Lane* (Monad 1995)★★★, *Hard Bargain* (Stax 1996)★★★★.

King, B.B.

b. Riley B. King, 16 September 1925, Indianola, Mississippi, USA. The son of a sharecropper, King went to work on the plantation like any other young black in Mississippi, but he had sung in amateur gospel groups from childhood. By the age of 16, he was also playing blues guitar and singing on street corners. When he was 20 years old, he temporarily quit sharecropping and went to Memphis, where he busked, and shared a room for almost a year with his second cousin, **Bukka White**. However, it was not until 1948 that he managed to pay off his debts to his former plantation boss. After leaving farming, he returned to Memphis, determined to become a star. He secured work with radio station KWEM, and then with WDIA, fronting a show sponsored by the health-tonic Pepticon, which led to disc jockeying on the *Sepia Swing Show*. Here he was billed as 'The Beale Street Blues Boy', later amended to 'Blues Boy King', and then to 'B.B. King'. Radio exposure promoted King's live career, and he performed with a band whose personnel varied according to availability. At this stage, he was still musically untutored, and liable to play against his backing musicians, but it was evident from his first recordings made for Bullet Records in 1949, that his talent was striking.

The Bullet recordings brought King to the attention of Modern Records, with whom he recorded for the next 10 years. As he began to tour beyond the area around Memphis, his first marriage, already under strain, ended in divorce in 1952. By that time, he was a national figure, having held the number 1 spot in the **Billboard** R&B chart for 15 weeks with 'Three O'Clock Blues'. He had embarked on the gruelling trail of one-nighters that has continued ever since. Through the 50s, King toured with a 13-piece band, adopting a patriarchal attitude to his musicians that has been compared to that of a kindly plantation boss. Briefly, he operated his own Blues Boy's Kingdom label, but had no success. Modern, however, were steadily producing hits for him, although their approach to copyright-standard practice in its day was less ethical, with the label owners taking fictitious credit on many titles. B.B. King's blues singing was heavily mellifluent, influenced by **Peter J. 'Doctor' Clayton** and gospel singer Sam McCrary of the Fairfield Four. However, his true revolutionary importance was as an electric guitarist. He admired **Charlie Christian** and **Django Reinhardt** as well as **Lonnie Johnson**, **Blind Lemon Jefferson**, and also saxophonist **Lester Young**. He derived ideas about phrasing and harmony from all these musicians. His extensive use of sixths clearly derived from jazz. His sound, however, consisted chiefly of a synthesis of the bottleneck styles of the delta blues (including that of **Bukka White**) with the jazzy electric guitar of '**T-Bone' Walker**. To Walker's flowing, crackling music, King added finger vibrato, his own substitute for the slide, which he had never managed to master. The result was a fluid guitar sound, in which almost every note was bent and/or sustained. This, together with King's penchant for playing off the beat, gave his solos the pattern of speech, and the personification of his beautiful black, gold plated, pearl inlaid Gibson 335 (or 355) guitar as 'Lucille' seemed highly appropriate.

In 1960, King switched labels, moving to **ABC** in the hope of emulating **Ray Charles**'s success. The times were against him, however, for black tastes were moving towards soul music and spectacular stage presentation. King had always felt a need to make the blues respectable, removing sexual boasting and references to violence and drugs. As a result of these endeavours his lyrics were, ironically, closer to those of soul, with their emphasis on love, respect and security in relationships. He remained popular, as his interplay with the audience on a live album recorded in Chicago in 1964 illustrates, but by the mid-60s, his career seemed in decline, with the hits coming from Modern's back catalogue rather than his new company. Revitalization came with the discovery of the blues by young whites - initially musicians, and then the wider audience. In 1968, King played the Fillmore West with **Johnny Winter** and **Mike Bloomfield**, who introduced him as 'the greatest living blues guitarist', provoking a standing ovation before he had even played a note. His revival of **Roy Hawkins**' 'The Thrill Is Gone', which made innovatory use of strings, provided the crucial pop crossover. Consequently, in 1969, King paid his first visit to Europe, where the way had been prepared by **Eric Clapton** (and where an ignorant reviewer called him an 'up-and-coming guitarist of the Clapton-**Peter Green** school'). In 1970, he recorded his first collaboration with rock musicians, produced by **Leon Russell**, who played on and composed some numbers, as did **Carole King**. King's career has been smooth sailing ever since, and he has been in demand for commercials, movie soundtracks, television show theme tunes, and guest appearances (e.g., with **U2** on 1989's 'When Love Comes To Town'). His workaholic schedule probably results, in part, from a need to finance his compulsive gambling, but he has also worked unobtrusively to provide entertainment for prisoners (co-founding the Foundation for the Advancement of Inmate Rehabilitation and Recreation in 1972).

His professional life is marked by a sense of mission, coupled with a desire to give the blues status and acceptability. This he has achieved, bringing the blues into the mainstream of entertainment, although he has done so by removing much of the sense of otherness that first brought many whites to it. Sometimes his live performances can be disappointingly bland, with singalong segments and misplaced attempts to ingratiate, as when he proudly told a Scottish audience of his meeting with **Sheena Easton**. His recordings since the 70s have been of inconsistent quality. King has deliberately kept in touch with his roots, returning to Mississippi each year to play, but the adulation of rock musicians has been a mixed blessing. Recordings made in London with, among others, **Alexis Korner**, **Steve Winwood** and **Ringo Starr** proved particularly disappointing. Equally, his collaboration with jazz-funk band the **Crusaders**, who produced and played on two albums, stifled his invention, and it has often seemed that King's creativity has run into the sands of MOR pop in a 12-bar format. These are the times when he is most likely to return with a brilliant, vital album that goes back to his roots in jazz, jump and the Delta. At the end of 1995 King announced that, as he had turned 70 years of age, he would be drastically reducing his performing schedule which he had maintained for many decades. Instead of a regular 300 or more gigs a year, he would be winding down in his old age, to a modest 200!

B.B. King has achieved the blues singer's dream - to live in Las Vegas and to have full access to the material benefits that the American way of life still withholds from so many black Americans. Without a doubt, though, things have changed for him; the teenager playing in the 40s streets became a man with whom the chairman of the Republican Party in the 80s considered it an honour to play guitar. B.B. King was a great influence on the sound of the blues, the sincerity of his singing and the fluency of his guitar spawning a flock of imitators as well as having a more general effect on the music's development, as reflected in the playing of **Buddy Guy**, his namesakes **Freddie** and **Albert King**, '**Little' Joe Blue** and innumerable others. Arguably, his most far-reaching effect has been on rock music. King's limitations include an inability to play guitar behind his own singing. This has led him to make a strict demarcation between the two, and has encouraged rock guitarists to regard extended solos as the mark of authentic blues playing. In lesser hands, this has all too easily become bloated excess or meaningless note-spinning. B.B. King has always aspired to elegance, logic and purpose in his guitar playing; it is ironic that his success has spawned so many imitators possessing so little of those very qualities. B.B. King's career, like that of other black musicians in America, has been circumscribed by the dictates of the industry. Like **Louis Armstrong**, he has nevertheless achieved great art through a combination of prodigious technical gifts and the placing of his instinctive improvisatory skills at the service of emotional expression. Also like Armstrong, he stayed firmly within the compass of showbusiness, attempting to give the public what he perceives it to want. His greatest music, however, testifies to his standing as a titanic figure in popular music.

● ALBUMS: *Singin' The Blues* (Crown 1957)★★★, *The Blues* (Crown 1958)★★★, *B.B. King Wails* (Crown 1959)★★★,

B.B. King Sings Spirituals (Crown 1960)★★, *The Great B.B. King* (Crown 1961)★★★, *King Of The Blues* (Crown 1961)★★★, *My Kind Of Blues* (Crown 1961)★★★, *More B.B. King* (Crown 1962)★★★, *Twist With B.B. King* (Crown 1962)★★, *Easy Listening Blues* (Crown 1962)★★★, *Blues In My Heart* (Crown 1962)★★★, *B.B. King* (Crown 1963)★★★, *Mr. Blues* (ABC 1963)★★★, *Rock Me Baby* (1964)★★★★, *Live At The Regal* (ABC 1965)★★★★★, *Confessin' The Blues* (ABC 1965)★★★, *Let Me Love You* (1965)★★★, *B.B. King Live On Stage* (1965)★★★, *The Soul Of B.B. King* (1966)★★★, *The Jungle* (1967)★★★, *Blues Is King* (Bluesway 1967)★★★★, *Blues On Top Of Blues* (Bluesway 1968)★★★, *Lucille* (Bluesway 1968)★★★★, *Live And Well* (1969)★★★★, *Completely Well* (MCA 1969)★★★, *Back In The Alley* (MCA 1970)★★★, *Indianola Mississippi Seeds* (MCA 1970)★★★★, *Live In Cook County Jail* (MCA 1971)★★★★, *In London* (MCA 1971)★★★, *L.A. Midnight* (ABC 1972)★★★, *Guess Who* (ABC 1972)★★★, *To Know You Is To Love You* (ABC 1973)★★★, with Bobby Bland *Together For The First Time ... Live* (MCA 1974)★★★★, *Friends* (ABC 1974)★★★, *Lucille Talks Back* (MCA 1975)★★★★, with Bland *Together Again ... Live* (MCA 1976)★★★, *King Size* (MCA 1977)★★★, *Midnight Believer* (MCA 1978)★★★, *Take It Home* (MCA 1979)★★★, *Now Appearing At Ole Miss* (MCA 1980)★★, *There Must Be A Better World Somewhere* (MCA 1981)★★★★, *Love Me Tender* (MCA 1982)★★, *Blues 'N' Jazz* (MCA 1983)★★, *Six Silver Strings* (MCA 1985)★★, *Do The Boogie* (Ace 1988)★★★, *Lucille Had A Baby* (Ace 1989)★★, *Live At San Quentin* (MCA 1990)★★★★, *Live At The Apollo* (GRP 1991)★★★, *Singin' The Blues & The Blues* (Ace 1991)★★★, *There's Always One More Time* (MCA 1992)★★★★, *Blues Summit* (MCA 1993)★★★★, with Diane Schuur *Heart To Heart* (GRP 1994)★★, *Lucille And Friends* (MCA 1995)★★★, *Deuces Wild* (MCA 1997)★★★★.

● CD-ROM: *On The Road With B.B. King* (MCA 1996)★★★★.

● COMPILATIONS: *The Best Of B.B. King* (Galaxy 1962)★★, *His Best - The Electric B.B. King* (Kent 1968)★★★, *The Incredible Soul Of B.B. King* (Kent 1970)★★★, *The Best Of B.B. King* (MCA 1973)★★★★, *The Rarest King* (Blues Boy 1980)★★★, *The Memphis Master* (Ace 1982)★★★, *B.B. King - 20 Blues Greats* (Déjà Vu 1985)★★★, *Introducing (1969-85)* (MCA 1987)★★★, *Across The Tracks* (Ace 1988)★★★, *My Sweet Little Angel* (Ace 1992)★★★, *King Of The Blues* 4-CD box set (MCA 1993)★★★★, *Gold Collection* (1993)★★★, *King Of The Blues* (Pickwick 1994)★★★, *Heart & Soul: A Collection Of Blues Ballads* (Pointblank Classic 1995)★★★, *The Collection: 20 Master Recordings* (Castle 1995)★★★, *How Blue Can You Get Classic Live Performances 1964-1994* (MCA 1996)★★★★.

● VIDEOS: *Live At Nick's* (Hendring Video 1987), *A Blues Session* (Video Collection 1988), *Live In Africa* (BMG Video 1991), *Blues Master, Highlights* (Warner Music Video 1995), *The Blues Summit Concert* (MCA 1995).

● FURTHER READING: *The Arrival Of B.B. King: The Authorized Biography*, Charles Sawyer. *B.B. King*, Sebastian Danchin. *Blues All Around Me, The Autobiography Of B.B. King*, B.B. King and David Ritz.

King, Ben E.

b. Benjamin Earl Nelson, 28 September 1938, Henderson, North Carolina, USA. King began his career while still a high-school student singing in a doo-wop group, the Four B's. He later joined the Five Crowns who, in 1959, assumed the name the **Drifters**. King was the featured lead vocalist and occasional composer on several of their recordings including 'There Goes My Baby' and 'Save The Last Dance For Me' (written by **Doc Pomus** and **Mort Shuman**). After leaving the group in 1960, he recorded the classic single 'Spanish Harlem' (1961), which maintained the Latin quality of the Drifters' work and deservedly reached the US Top 10. The follow-up, 'Stand By Me' (1961), was even more successful and was followed by further hits including 'Amor' (1961) and 'Don't Play That Song (You Lied)' (1962). Throughout this period, King's work was aimed increasingly at the pop audience. 'I (Who Have Nothing)' and 'I Could Have Danced All Night' (both 1963) suggested showbusiness rather than innovation, although **Bert Berns'** 'It's All Over' (1964) was a superb song. 'Seven Letters' and 'The Record (Baby I Love You)' (both 1965) prepared the way for the rhetorical 'What Is Soul?' (1967), which effectively placed King alongside such soul contemporaries as **Otis Redding**, **Wilson Pickett** and **Joe Tex**. Unfortunately, King's commercial standing declined towards the end of the 60s when he left the **Atlantic/Atco** group of labels. Unable to reclaim his former standing elsewhere, King later re-signed with his former company and secured a US Top 5 hit in 1975 with 'Supernatural Thing Part 1'. In 1977, a collaboration with the **Average White Band** resulted in two R&B chart entries and an excellent album, *Benny And Us*. King's later recordings, including *Music Trance* (1980) and *Street Tough* (1981), proved less successful. In 1986, 'Stand By Me' was included in a film of the same name, reaching the US Top 10 and number 1 in the UK, thereby briefly revitalizing the singer's autumnal career.

● ALBUMS: *Spanish Harlem* (Atco 1961)★★★, *Ben E. King Sings For Soulful Lovers* (Atco 1962)★★★, *Don't Play That Song* (Atco 1962)★★★, *Young Boy Blues* (Clarion 1964), *Seven Letters* (Atco 1965)★★★, *What Is Soul* (Atco 1967)★★★, *Rough Edges* (1970)★★★, *Beginning Of It All* (1971)★★★, *Supernatural* (Atco 1975)★★★, *I Had A Love* (Atco 1976)★★, with the Average White Band *Benny And Us* (Atlantic 1977)★★★, *Let Me Live In Your Life* (Atco 1978)★★, *Music Trance* (Atlantic 1980)★★, *Street Tough* (Atlantic 1981)★★, *Save The Last Dance For Me* (EMI 1988)★★★.

● COMPILATIONS: *Greatest Hits* (1964)★★★, *Here Comes The Night* (Edsel 1984)★★★, *The Ultimate Collection: Ben E. King* (Atlantic 1987)★★★★, *Anthology One: Spanish Harlem* (RSA 1996)★★★, *Anthology Two: For Soulful Lovers* (RSA 1996)★★★, *Anthology Three: Don't Play That Song* (RSA 1996)★★★, *Anthology Four: Seven Letters* (RSA 1997)★★★, *Anthology Five: What Is Soul?* (RSA 1997)★★★, *Anthology Six: Supernatural* (RSA 1997)★★★, *Anthology Seven: Benny And Us* (RSA 1997)★★, *The Very Best Of Ben E. King* (Rhino 1998)★★★★.

King, Carole

b. Carole Klein, 9 February 1942, Brooklyn, New York, USA. A proficient pianist from the age of four, King was a prolific songwriter by her early teens. When friend and neighbour **Neil Sedaka** embarked on his recording career, she followed him into the New York milieu, recording demos, singing back-up and even helping arrange occasional sessions. As a student at Queen's College, New York, she met future partner and husband **Gerry Goffin** whose lyrical gifts matched King's grasp of melody. She completed a handful of singles, including 'The Right Girl' (1958), 'Baby Sittin'', 'Queen Of The Beach' (1959), prior to recording 'Oh Neil' (1960), a riposte to Sedaka's 'Oh Carol'. Although not a hit, her record impressed publishing magnate **Don Kirshner**, who signed the Goffin/King team to his Aldon Music empire. They scored notable early success with the **Shirelles** ('Will You Still Love Me Tomorrow'), **Bobby Vee** ('Take Good Care Of My Baby') and the **Drifters** ('Up On The Roof') and were later responsible for much of the early output on Dimension, the company's in-house label. The duo wrote, arranged and produced hits for **Little Eva** ('The Locomotion') and the **Cookies** ('Chains' and 'Don't Say Nothin' Bad About My Baby') while a song written with Bobby Vee in mind, 'It Might As Well Rain Until September', provided King with a solo hit in 1962. Although this memorable and highly evocative song barely reached the US Top 30, it climbed to number 3 in the UK. However, two follow-up singles fared less well. The Goffin/King oeuvre matured as the 60s progressed, resulting in several sophisticated, personalized compositions, including 'A Natural Woman' (**Aretha Franklin**), 'Goin' Back' (**Dusty Springfield** and the **Byrds**) and 'Pleasant Valley Sunday' (the **Monkees**). The couple also established the short-lived Tomorrow label, but their disintegrating marriage was chronicled on King's 1967 single, 'The Road To Nowhere', the year they dissolved their partnership. King then moved to Los Angeles and having signed to **Lou Adler**'s Ode label, formed the **City** with ex-**Fugs** duo **Danny Kortchmar** (guitar) and Charles Larkey (bass). (The latter became King's second husband.) The trio's lone album included the artist's versions of 'I Wasn't Born To Follow' and 'That Old Sweet Roll (Hi De Ho)', covered, respectively, by the **Byrds** and **Blood, Sweat And Tears**. King began a solo career in 1970 with *Writer*, before fully asserting her independence with *Tapestry*. This radiant selection contained several of the singer's most incisive compositions, notably 'You've Got A Friend', a US number 1 for **James Taylor**, 'It's Too Late', a US chart-topper for King, and 'So Far Away'. Unlike many of her former production-line contemporaries, King was able to shrug off teen preoccupations and use her skills to address adult doubts and emotions. *Tapestry* has now sold in excess of 15 million copies worldwide and established its creator as a major figure in the singer-songwriter movement. However, the delicate balance it struck between perception and

self-delusion became blurred on *Music* and *Rhymes And Reasons*, which were regarded as relative disappointments. Each set nonetheless achieved gold disc status, as did *Fantasy*, *Wrap Around Joy* (which contained her second US number 1, 'Jazzman') and *Thoroughbred*. The last marked the end of King's tenure at Ode and she has since failed to reap the same commercial success. Her first release of the 80s, *Pearls*, comprised 'classic' Goffin/King songs, a release which many interpreted as an artistic impasse. Certainly King subsequently pursued a less frenetic professional life, largely restricting her live appearances to fund-raising concerns. In the early 90s she had relocated to Ireland. Her recordings also became more measured and if *Speeding Time* or *City Streets* lacked the cultural synchronization *Tapestry* enjoyed with the post-**Woodstock** audience, her songwriting skills were still in evidence. In the USA *Tapestry* exceeded 10 million copies sold in July 1995.

● ALBUMS: *Writer* (Ode 1970)★★, *Tapestry* (Ode 1971)★★★★, *Music* (Ode 1971)★★★, *Rhymes And Reasons* (Ode 1972)★★★, *Fantasy* (Ode 1973)★★★★, *Wrap Around Joy* (Ode 1974)★★★, *Really Rosie* (Ode 1975)★★★, *Thoroughbred* (Ode 1976)★★★, *Simple Things* (Capitol 1977)★★, *Welcome Home* (Avatar 1978)★★, *Touch The Sky* (Capitol 1979)★★, *Pearls (Songs Of Goffin And King)* (Capitol 1980)★★, *One To One* (Atlantic 1982)★★, *Speeding Time* (Atlantic 1984)★★★, *City Streets* (Capitol 1989)★★, *In Concert* (Quality 1994)★★.

● COMPILATIONS: *Her Greatest Hits* (Ode 1973)★★★, *Carole King, A Natural Woman - The Ode Collection 1968-1976* (Legacy 1995)★★★★.

● VIDEOS: *In Concert* (Wienerworld 1994).

● FURTHER READING: *Carole King*, Paula Taylor. *Carole King: A Biography In Words & Pictures*, Mitchell S. Cohen.

King, Claude

b. 5 February 1923, on a farm near Keithville, Shreveport, Louisiana, USA. His date of birth has, since 1961, frequently been cited incorrectly owing to promotional material released by his then manager, Tillman Franks, who at the time thought it tactful to lose a decade from his new client's age. King showed an early interest in music and was a proficient guitarist by the age of 12. He won a sports scholarship to the University of Idaho, intending to pursue an athletic career, but changed his mind and returned to Shreveport to work on the *Louisiana Hayride*. During the 50s, he played various local venues and took to writing songs. He first recorded for Gotham in 1952, but it was in 1961, after he signed for **Columbia**, that he achieved his first US country and pop chart hits with 'Big River, Big Man' and 'The Comancheros'. In 1962, he teamed with **Merle Kilgore** to write 'Wolverton Mountain'. After the song was rejected by **Johnny Horton** and **George Jones**, King decided to record it himself and promptly found that he had a million-selling country and pop hit on his hands. During the 60s, King had an impressive list of 23 country chart hits.

They included Top 10 successes with 'The Burning Of Atlanta', 'Tiger Woman' and his version of Johnny Horton's song 'All For The Love Of A Girl'. (In 1969, King recorded a tribute album to his great friend Horton.) In the early 70s, he found things more difficult, and his only Top 20 hit came with 'Mary's Vineyard'. The total of King's country chart hits stands at 30, the last being 'Cotton Dan' in 1977. During his career he made appearances in several films including *Swamp Girl*, and in 1982, he also acted in the television mini-series *The Blue And The Grey*.

● ALBUMS: *Meet Claude King* (Columbia 1962)★★★, *Tiger Woman* (Columbia 1965)★★★, *I Remember Johnny Horton* (Columbia 1969)★★, *Friend, Lover, Woman, Wife* (Columbia 1970)★★★, *Chip 'N' Dales Place* (Columbia 1971)★★★.

● COMPILATIONS: *The Best Of Claude King* (Harmony 1968)★★★, *Greatest Hits* (True 1977)★★★, *Claude King's Best* (Gusto 1980)★★★, *American Originals* (Columbia 1990)★★★, *Claude King More Than Climbing That Mountain, Wolverton Mountain That Is* 5-CD box set (Bear Family 1994)★★★★.

King, Dave

b. Twickenham, Middlesex, England. A very popular comedian and singer in the UK during the 50s and 60s, at the age of 15 King was a stooge and washboard player in the bill-topping variety act, Morton Fraser's Harmonica Gang. He joined the Royal Air Force in 1950 and returned to the Gang afterwards. His big solo break came with appearances on UK television's *Showcase* and *Television Music Hall*. These resulted in West End appearances and his own television variety series. King first recorded in 1955 with producer **George Martin** for **Parlophone** and his debut hit came in 1956, with a cover of 'Memories Are Made Of This' on **Decca**, which gave the **Dean Martin** original strong competition in the UK charts. He also enjoyed success with 'You Can't Be True To Two' in 1956 and 'Story Of My Life', which was one of three versions of the **Burt Bacharach** song to make the UK Top 20 in 1958. King was one of the rare UK comedians to make any impact in the USA having his own summer television series there in the late 50s. He joined Pye in 1959 but no more hits came the way of this easy-going, relaxed ballad singer whose television appearances also eventually dried up. In later years King became a respected character actor in UK films and television.

● ALBUMS: *Memories Are Made Of This* (Ace Of Hearts 1962)★★★.

King, Denis

b. 25 July 1939, Hornchurch, Essex, England. In 1945, at the age of six, King (piano) and his elder brothers Tony (double and electric bass) and Michael (guitar), played local shows in Hornchurch. Five years later they were appearing professionally as a vocal-instrumental trio, the King III, but when they supported **Max Bygraves** at the London Palladium in 1955, their billing had changed to the **King Brothers**. After recording some tracks for the minor label Conquest, they had several hits on **Parlophone Records** in the late 50s, including 'A White Sports Coat', 'In The Middle Of An Island', 'Standing On The Corner', 'Mais Oui' and '76 Trombones'. In the 60s, their appeal waned, and they split up. Denis carved out a new career for himself as a composer of commercial jingles, television themes, film music and stage musicals. The possessor of a light touch, his best known music for television was probably 'Galloping Home', the theme for the successful BBC production of *The Adventures Of Black Beauty*. Other themes included *Lovejoy*, *Hannay* and *Taking The Floor*. He also composed the film music for *Sweeney!*, *Not Tonight Darling*, *The Spy's Wife*, *The Chairman's Wife* and *Holiday On The Buses*. In 1977, King provided the music, and served as musical director, for *Privates On Parade*, Peter Nicholls' hit vaudeville play about 'camp and colonialism in 1948 Malaya', which starred Denis Quilley, and eventually made it to New York, off-Broadway, in 1989, with **Jim Dale** in the leading role. During the 80s, King combined with Keith Waterhouse and Willis Hall for *Worzel Gummidge*, a theatrical spin-off from the popular television series, starring Jon Pertwee. King also collaborated with **Benny Green** for *Bashville*, adapted from a play by George Bernard Shaw, and wrote the music for two other Hall projects, *Wind In The Willows* and *Treasure Island*. In 1988, he was involved in the West End revue, *Re: Joyce*, an anecdotal biography of the British comedienne-actress, Joyce Grenfell, which starred Maureen Lipman. He served as her accompanist, comic foil, narrator of much of the biographical material, and impersonated several of the individuals in Grenfell's life, such as composer Richard Addinsell and Dame Myra Hess. King returned to the West End twice with *Re: Joyce*, and featured in the US production, plus the 1991 UK television version. Earlier that year, he had re-joined Benny Green for another attempt to set Bernard Shaw to music. For *Valentine's Day*, adapted from Shaw's *You Never Can Tell*, King's music 'reflected a move towards sweetness: slow waltz, quick waltz, here a touch of minuet', all of which was enhanced by the virtuoso performance of Edward Petherbridge.

King, Diana

b. *c*.1972, Spanish Town, Jamaica, West Indies. As a child King lived in the Hope Road neighbourhood, Kingston, famous for number 56, the Jamaican home of **Bob Marley** and his family. She often played with his children Cedella and Sharon, who in the early 80s continued their father's work as the Melody Makers. King began her singing career performing on the tourism circuit in the north of Jamaica at hotels between Negril and Ocho Rios. She soon found work in the studios; in 1990 she recorded with **Junior Tucker**, the child prodigy-turned-ragga star, for 'Stop To Start', included on his album *Don't Test*. The track was featured on two single releases, 'Sixteen' and the 'Junior Tucker EP'. In 1993 an album of Bob Marley cover

versions, *Stir It Up*, by a variety of Jamaican performers included a version of the title track by King which bought her to the attention of major label Sony. Her initial release, 'Shy Guy', crossed over into the pop charts in 1995 which led to the release of *Tougher Than Love*, which showcased her skills both as a singer and DJ. The album included a version of **Alton Ellis**'s 'I'm Still In Love' produced by **Sugar Minott** and **Coxsone Dodd**. The follow-up single, 'Ain't Nobody', failed to match its predecessor's performance. *Think Like A Girl* featured King's version of 'I Say A Little Prayer', and was included on the soundtrack for the film *My Best Friend's Wedding*.
● ALBUMS: *Tougher Than Love* (Columbia 1995)★★★, *Think Like A Girl* (Work 1997)★★★.

King, Don

b. Donald Alan King, 1 May 1954, Omaha, Nebraska, USA. A singer/songwriter, he first played trumpet in the school band before teaching himself to play electric guitar and in his teens, he studied acoustic classical guitar. After first playing around the clubs in Omaha, he relocated to Nashville in 1974. He played a residency in a hotel for two years and in 1976, he began recording for Con Brio. He first charted with 'Cabin High In The Blue Ridge Mountains' and in 1977, he registered two Top 20 hits with co-wrote numbers 'I've Got You To Come Home To' and 'She's The Girl Of My Dreams'. By 1979, he had registered 10 country hits, these successes leading to him joining **CBS**, who recorded him on their Epic label. He gained an immediate chart hit with 'Lonely Hotel' and he became a popular touring act working on shows with many stars including **Reba McEntire**, **Conway Twitty**, **Alabama** and **Tammy Wynette**. In 1981, he recorded a Top 40 with his fine version of **Johnny Cash**'s 'I Still Miss Someone', which included **Rosanne Cash** on harmony vocal. In 1982, he left Epic, his final chart entry for the label being 'Maximum Security (To Minimum Wage)'. In all, King who sang in a similar style to **John Denver**, registered 19 chart hits, the last being 'Can't Stop The Music', a Top 90, on the minor 615 1015 label. King also wrote with other writers, especially Dave Woodward with whom he wrote the superb ballads 'Old Nebraska Memories' and 'Drinkin' In Texas' and the amusing 'If I'da Known That I Was Gonna Live This Long'. In 1983, in partnership with his father, he formed the Don King Music Group publishing company and built a recording studio and in 1992, they also became involved in video production. In 1987, King recorded a concept album about the State of Tennessee, much of which was recorded in the State. The songs covered various Tennessee locations including Nashville and also presented historic facts in the self-penned 'The Civil War Song'.
● ALBUMS: *Dreams'N Things* (Con Brio 1977)★★★★, *The Feelings So Right* (Con Brio 1978)★★★, *Lonely Hotel* (Epic 1980)★★, *Whirlwind* (Epic 1981)★★, *Tennessee Souvenirs* (Kings X Music 1987)★★★.

King, Earl

b. Earl Silas Johnson IV, 7 February 1934, New Orleans, Louisiana, USA. The son of a blues pianist, King became an accomplished guitarist and singer with local bands before making his first recordings in 1953 for Savoy ('Have You Gone Crazy') and **Specialty** ('A Mother's Love'). Strongly influenced by **Guitar Slim** (Eddie Jones), during the mid-50s he worked with **Huey Smith**'s band and recorded his biggest hit, 'Those Lonely Lonely Nights', with Smith on piano; this was on **Johnny Vincent**'s Ace label, for whom King was house guitarist. In 1958, he made a version of 'Everyone Has To Cry Sometime' as Handsome Earl. He went on to record for Rex and Imperial where he made 'Come On' and the R&B hit 'Trick Bag' (1962) which featured King's influential guitar figures. He was also starting to enjoy success as a songwriter, composing the **Lee Dorsey** hit 'Do Re Mi', 'He's Mine' for Bernadine Washington, 'Big Chief' recorded by **Professor Longhair** and 'Teasin' You', Willie Tee's 1965 R&B hit. **Jimmy Clanton**, **Dr. John** and **Fats Domino** were others who recorded King compositions. During the 60s and early 70s, King himself made recordings for Amy, **Wand**, **Atlantic** and **Motown**, although the **Allen Toussaint**-produced Atlantic session was not released until 1981 and the Motown tracks remain unissued. King remained active into the 80s, recording with Roomfull Of Blues for Black Top. His Imperial tracks were reissued by **EMI** in 1987.
● ALBUMS: *New Orleans Rock 'N' Roll* (Sonet 1977)★★★, *Street Parade* (Charly 1981)★★★, with Roomfull Of Blues *Glazed* (Black Top 1988)★★★, *Sexual Telepathy* (Black Top 1990)★★★, *Hard River To Cross* (1993)★★★.
● COMPILATIONS: *Soul Bag* (Stateside 1987)★★★, *Earl's Pearls* (Westside 1997)★★★.

King, Eddie

b. 21 April 1938, Talledega, Alabama, USA. King was orphaned in 1950 and eventually settled in Chicago, where he played in various blues clubs. He worked as a guitarist with **Muddy Waters**, **Howlin' Wolf**, and **Willie Dixon** in the 50s before he began a long association with **'Little' Mack Simmons** at the end of the decade. He recorded with Simmons and **Detroit Junior** and also released singles under his own name in the early 60s. He worked briefly with **Willie Cobbs** and he recorded further singles (sometimes in the company of his sister Mae Bee May) and in 1987 he and his sister released an album on Double Trouble. In the early 90s he was to be found working as lead guitarist for **Koko Taylor**. Eddie Taylor was a member of the Burning Chicago Blues Machine that recorded *Boogie Blues* on GBW label in 1992. He sang four songs. His second solo album was on drummer Joe Roesch's record label and received excellent reviews.
● ALBUMS: *The Blues Has Got Me* (Double Trouble 1987)★★★, *Another Cow's Dead* (Roesch 1997)★★★★.

King, Evelyn 'Champagne'

b 1 July 1960, Bronx, New York, USA. A former office cleaner at **Gamble And Huff**'s Sigma Sound studios, King was nurtured by T. Life, a member of the company's writing and production staff. He coached the aspiring singer on recording technique and was instrumental in preparing King's career. Her debut single, 'Shame', was released in 1977 and after considerable success on the dance/club circuit - since regarded as a classic of its kind - it finally broke into the national pop charts the following year, reaching the US Top 10/UK Top 40. Evelyn's second hit, 'I Don't Know If It's Right', became the artist's second gold disc and she later enjoyed international hits with 'I'm In Love' (1981) and a UK Top 10, 'Love Come Down' (1982). After a disappointing period during the mid-80s, her 1988 album *Flirt* was generally considered to be a return to form. King has remained a popular performer on the soul/dance music charts.

● ALBUMS: *Smooth Talk* (RCA 1977)★★★, *Music Box* (RCA 1979)★★★, *Call On Me* (RCA 1980)★★★, *I'm In Love* (RCA 1981)★★★, *Get Loose* (RCA 1982)★★★, *Face To Face* (RCA 1983)★★, *So Romantic* (RCA 1984)★★, *A Long Time Coming* (RCA 1985)★★, *Flirt* (EMI 1988)★★★.

● COMPILATIONS: *The Best Of Evelyn 'Champagne' King* (RCA 1990)★★★, *The Essential Works Of* (1992)★★★, *Let's Get Funky* (Camden 1997)★★★.

King, Freddie

b. Billy Myles, 30 September 1934, Gilmer, Texas, USA, d. 28 December 1976, Dallas, Texas. Freddie (aka Freddy) was one of the triumvirate of Kings (the others being **B.B.** and **Albert**) who ruled the blues throughout the 60s. He was the possessor of a light, laid-back, but not unemotional voice and a facile fast-fingered guitar technique that made him the hero of many young disciples. He learned to play guitar at an early age, being influenced by his mother, Ella Mae King, and her brother Leon. Although forever associated with Texas and admitting a debt to such artists as **T-Bone Walker** he moved north to Chicago in his mid-teens. In 1950, he became influenced by local blues guitarists **Eddie 'Playboy' Taylor** and **Robert Lockwood**. King absorbed elements from each of their styles, before encompassing the more strident approaches of **Magic Sam** and **Otis Rush**. Here, he began to sit in with various groups and slowly built up the reputation that was to make him a star. After teaming up with **'Lonesome' Jimmy Lee Robinson** to form the Every Hour Blues Boys he worked and recorded with Little Sonny Cooper's band, Earlee Payton's Blues Cats and Smokey Smothers. These last recordings were made in Cincinnati, Ohio, in August 1960 for **Sydney Nathan**'s King/Federal organization, and on the same day, King recorded six titles under his own name, including the influential instrumental hit 'Hideaway'. He formed his own band and began touring, bolstering his success with further hits, many of them guitar showpieces, some trivialized by titles such as 'The Bossa Nova

Watusi Twist', but others showing off his 'crying' vocal delivery. Many, such as '(I'm) Tore Down', 'Have You Ever Loved A Woman' and particularly 'The Welfare (Turns Its Back On You)', became classics of the (then) modern blues. He continued to record for King Federal up until 1966, his career on record being masterminded by pianist **Sonny Thompson**. He left King Federal in 1966 and took up a short tenure (1968-69) on the **Atlantic** subsidiary label Cotillion.

Ironically, the subsequent white blues-boom provided a new-found impetus. **Eric Clapton** was a declared King aficionado, while **Chicken Shack**'s Stan Webb indicated his debt by including three of his mentor's compositions on his group's debut album. The albums that followed failed to capture the artist at his best. This was not a particularly successful move, although the work he did on that label has increased in value with the passage of time. The same could be said for his next musical liaison, which saw him working with **Leon Russell** on his **Shelter** label. Much of his work for Russell was over-produced, but King made many outstanding recordings during this period and a re-evaluation of that work is overdue. There was no denying the excitement it generated, particularly on *Getting Ready*, which was recorded at the famous **Chess** studio. This excellent set included the original version of the much-covered 'Going Down'. Live recordings made during his last few years indicate that King was still a force to be reckoned with as he continued his good-natured guitar battles with allcomers, and usually left them far behind. *Burglar* featured a duet with Eric Clapton on 'Sugar Sweet', but the potential of this new relationship was tragically cut short in December 1976 when King died of heart failure at the early age of 43. His last stage appearance had taken place three days earlier in his home-town of Dallas.

● ALBUMS: *Freddie King Sings The Blues* (King 1961)★★★, *Let's Hideaway And Dance Away* (King 1961)★★★★, *Boy-Girl-Boy* (King 1962)★★★, *Bossa Nova And Blues* (King 1962)★★, *Freddie King Goes Surfing* (King 1963)★★, *Freddie King Gives You A Bonanza Of Instrumentals* (King 1965)★★★, *24 Vocals And Instrumentals* (King 1966)★★★, *Hide Away* (King 1969)★★★★, *Freddie King Is A Blues Master* (Atlantic 1969)★★★, *My Feeling For The Blues* (Atlantic 1970)★★★, *Getting Ready* (Shelter 1971)★★★★, *Texas Cannonball* (Shelter 1972)★★★, *Woman Across The Water* (Shelter 1973)★★★, *Burglar* (RSO 1974)★★★, *Larger Than Life* (RSO 1975)★★★, *Live At The Electric Ballroom 1974* (Black Top 1996)★★★.

● COMPILATIONS: *King Of R&B Volume 2* (1969)★★★, *The Best Of Freddie King* (Shelter 1974)★★★★, *Original Hits* (1977)★★★, *Rockin' The Blues - Live* (Crosscut 1983)★★★, *Takin' Care Of Business* (Charly 1985)★★★, *Live In Antibes, 1974* (Concert 1988)★★★, *Live In Nancy, 1975 Volume 1* (Concert 1989)★★★, *Blues Guitar Hero: The Influential Early Sessions* (1993)★★★, *King Of The Blues* (EMI/Shelter 1996)★★★★, *Key To The Highway* (Wolf 1995)★★★, *Stayin' Home With The Blues* RSO material (Spectrum 1998)★★★.

● VIDEOS: *Freddie King Jan 20 1973* (Vestapol Music Video

1995), *Freddie King In Concert* (Vestapol Music Video 1995), *Freddie King: The !!!!Beat 1966* (Vestapol Music Video 1995).

King, Henry

b. 1906, USA, d. August 1974. King initially chose classical music as his profession, being the son of a renowned concert pianist. However, early in the 30s he found the allure of popular big band dance music irresistible, and formed his own group in New York City, New York, USA. His musicians included Jack Diamond, George Tudor, Joseph Sudy, Leo Arends, John Porpora, Neil De Luca, Jules Losch, Sidney Sudy, William Weems, Al Wallack, Phil Hart, Tubby Mertz, Vince Raff, Tom Enos, Eddie Bergman, Bobby Yacoubian, Johnny Paliso, Russ Michaels, Henry Jaworski, Charlie Enright, Harold Dohrman and Bill Jabionski. At various times the group featured vocalists such as Dick Robertson, Ray Hunkel, Don Reid, Sidney Study, Sonny Schuyler, Carmina Calhoun, Don Raymond, Bob Carroll, Phil Hanna and Eugenie Marvin. The firm orientation for this group was evening society dances and ballroom functions, with smooth tempos originated from Henry's piano, and an accent on violins rather than brass. They travelled to venues including the Mark Hopkins Hotel (San Francisco), the Cosmopolitan (Denver), the Claridge and Peabody (Memphis), the Roosevelt (New Orleans) and the Shamrock (Houston). Their longest engagement came at the Biltmore in Los Angeles, but most of their popularity could be ascribed to radio. King claimed to have recorded over 5,000 remote broadcasts for numerous networks during the group's career, lending enormous popularity to their theme, 'A Blues Serenade'. By the late 50s King had retired to Houston, though he did make occasional appearances on demand.

King, Jigsy

b. Errol King, *c.*1970, Kingston, Jamaica, West Indies. In 1993, King developed his DJ skills chanting on various **sound systems**. He voiced a number of hits at various studios with a number of producers in Jamaica and gained a reputation as the youths' DJ. His vocal style and delivery was similar to **Buju Banton**, whose gritty delivery over popular rhythms guaranteed a hit. An early example of his style can be found on 'Cock Up And Ride'; the tune was produced by **King Jammy**'s son John John and was a **dancehall** smash. The lyrics ('Push out your foot and do the bogle dance') and the 'bogle' rhythm inspired a provocative dancing style and led to an adult rating for dancehall videos! In 1994 a combination with **Barrington Levy**, 'Work', was an international hit that 'bubbled' under the pop chart. The single crossed many barriers and proved especially popular among the East Indian population. Ragga had influenced many Asian performers, notably **Apache Indian**, and the tune was a guaranteed floor filler at bhangra dances. King's other 1994 hits, 'Have What It Takes' and 'Kick Up', were unable to generate similar

enthusiasm. In 1995, he recorded 'God Never Fail Me' and 'Give Me The Weed' with Courtney Cole at Roof International. Other recordings have maintained his profile in the reggae charts, including 'Judge The Book', 'Mr Bate' and 'Ragga Ragga'. In 1996 he topped the Jamaican chart in combination with an English singer known as Jamie Irie, for an ode to marijuana, 'Sweet Sensimella'.
● ALBUMS: *Load It Back* (VP 1994)★★★, *Have To Get You* (Jet Star 1995)★★, *Ashes To Ashes* (VP 1995)★★★.

King, Jonathan

b. 6 December 1944, London, England. While studying for his finals at Cambridge University, King hit the charts in 1965 with his plaintive protest song 'Everyone's Gone To The Moon'. That song has been a radio hit ever since. Although the catchy follow-up 'Green Is The Grass' failed, the English student was already revealing his entrepreneurial talents by discovering and writing for others. **Hedgehopper's Anonymous** gave him his second protest hit with 'It's Good News Week', while King next took on **Manfred Mann** with an unsuccessful cover of **Bob Dylan**'s 'Just Like A Woman'. A perennial pop columnist and socialite, he impressed **Decca Records'** managing director Sir Edward Lewis who took on his talent-spotting services. King discovered, named and produced **Genesis**' first album, but the group soon moved to **Tony Stratton-Smith**'s **Charisma** label. King, meanwhile, was releasing occasionally quirky singles like 'Let It All Hang Out' and another Dylan cover 'Million Dollar Bash'. He was also an inveterate pseudonymous hit maker, heavily involved in such studio novelty numbers as the **Piglets**' 'Johnny Reggae', Sakkarin's 'Sugar Sugar', the Weathermen's 'The Same Old Song' and St. Cecilia's 'Leap Up And Down (Wave Your Knickers In The Air)'. In 1972, King launched UK Records, best remembered for its hits courtesy of **10cc** rather than the label boss's latest wealth of pseudonyms, which included Shag ('Loop Di Love'), Bubblerock ('Satisfaction'), 53rd And 3rd ('Chick-A-Boom'), 100 Ton And A Feather ('It Only Takes A Minute') and Sound 9418 ('In The Mood'). He also scored a major hit in his own name during 1975 with the summer smash 'Una Paloma Blanca'. Despite his array of unlikely hits, King had many failures and as a label manager could do little with the careers of either Ricky Wilde or the **Kursaal Flyers**. Apart from the odd witty parody such as his reading of **Cat Stevens'** 'Wild World', juxtaposed to the provocative tune of the **Pet Shop Boys'** 'It's A Sin', King has worked hard maintaining a high-media profile via newspaper columns, radio appearances and his BBC television programme, *Entertainment USA*. He established his own music business newpaper in 1993, the *Tip Sheet*. Always controversial, King thrives on conflict and remains a lively and vocal member of the music business.
● ALBUMS: *Or Then Again* (Decca 1965)★★, *Try Something Different* (Decca 1972)★★, *A Rose In A Fisted Glove* (UK

1975)★★, *JK All The Way* (UK 1976)★★, *Anticloning* mini-album (Revolution 1992)★★.
● COMPILATIONS: *King Size King* (PRT 1982)★★, *The Butterfly That Stamped* (Castle 1989)★★, *The Many Faces Of Jonathan King* (1993)★★.

King, Little Jimmy
b. Manuel Gales, 4 December 1964, Memphis, Tennessee, USA. Citing **Albert King** and **Jimi Hendrix** as influences, King's guitar style exhibits an uneasy amalgam of both disparate elements, which as yet, he has been unable to mould into a recognizably individual sound. He and twin brother Daniel received acoustic guitars for Christmas when they were six. Being left-handed like his mentors, he learned to play 'upside-down-and-backwards' and graduated to an electric model soon afterwards. As a teenager, he played in whichever Beale Street clubs would let him in. In 1984 he was seen by Albert King and worked with his band for four years, at the end of which he changed his name legally to King and was 'adopted' as a grandson by his bandleader. After King's death, he took over the band and renamed it the Memphis Soul Survivors, with whom his first album was made. For his second, King recruited the **Hi** Rhythm Section, calling them the King James Version Band, and also cut several tracks with Double Trouble, the late **Stevie Ray Vaughan**'s band. More noticeably than his debut album, this was caught between traditional blues and its rock equivalent, a problem that artists like King have not yet resolved.
● ALBUMS: *Little Jimmy King And The Memphis Soul Survivors* (Bullseye Blues 1991)★★★, *Something Inside Of Me* (Bullseye Blues 1994)★★, *Soldier For The Blues* (Bullseye Blues 1997)★★.

King, Morgan
Alongside Nick E, the London-based King was responsible for over 90% of Sweden's B-Tech label output in the 90s. Some of his flags of convenience include Clubland (soulful garage), Soundsource ('Take Me Up' and other Balearic moments), Al Hambra ('Al Hambra'), Maniac Tackle ('Bass FU'), Technoir ('Logic And Knowledge'), Control E ('The Power Of Freedom'), Bassrace ('Futurama'), Full On Sound ('Mayhem') - all housed on B-Tech. King also remixed **Moodswings**' 'Spiritual High' for **Arista Records** and played a part in establishing London label, **Om Records**.

King, Morgana
b. 4 June 1930, Pleasantville, New York, USA. Although classically trained, King made the shift to singing jazz-inflected standards with surprising ease. Her appeal embraced both the popular audience and many jazz musicians, who hold her work in high regard. Despite her successes as a singer, King had ambitions in other fields and in the early 70s played Don Corleone's wife in *The Godfather* and *The Godfather II*, opposite Marlon Brando. She later continued with her singing career, making occasional records which emphasized her commercial leanings.
● ALBUMS: *For You, For Me, Forever More* (1956)★★★, *Morgana King Sings For You* (1956)★★, *Morgana King Sings The Blues* (1958)★★★, *The Greatest Songs Ever Swung* (1959)★★★, *Let Me Love You* (1960)★★★, *Folk Songs Ala King* (1960)★★, *A Taste Of Honey* (1964)★★, *The Winter Of My Discontent* (1965)★★★, *The End Of A Love Affair* (1965)★★★, *Everybody Loves Saturday Night* (1965)★★★, *Wild Is Love* (1966)★★★, *Gemini Changes* (1967)v, *I Know How It Feels* (1968)★★, *New Beginnings* (1973)★★★, *Stretchin' Out* (1977)★★, *Everything Must Change* (1978)★★★, *Higher Ground* (1979)★★★, *Looking Through The Eyes Of Love* (1981)★★★, *Portraits* (1983)★★★, *Simply Eloquent* (1986)★★★.

King, Norah Lee
b. USA. King became quite well known in the 30s and early 40s, mostly singing the blues with flair, and developed an easy-going rapport with audiences. In the mid-40s she recorded with **Mary Lou Williams** but most of her later records found her in harness with her husband, Lawrence Lucie. In her early years, King performed and often recorded under a bewildering array of pseudonyms, including Lenore King, Lenore Kinsey, Susan King and Susan Lenore King.
● ALBUMS: all with Lawrence Lucie *Travellin' Guitars* (Request 50s)★★★, *Cool And Warm Guitar* (Toy 50s)★★★, *Mixed Emotions* (Toy 50s)★★★, *Sophisticated Lady/After Sundown* (Toy 50s)★★.
● COMPILATIONS: with Mary Lou Williams *The Asch Recordings, 1944-47* (Folkways 1944-47)★★★★.

King, Pee Wee
b. Julius Frank Anthony Kuczynski, 18 February 1914, Milwaukee, Wisconsin, USA. His parents, whose families had been Polish immigrants, relocated to Abrams when he was a child and he grew up in the Polish community there. His father, who played fiddle and concertina, ran a polka band and the boy was encouraged to play instruments from an early age. He first played concertina and then fiddle, but at the age of 14, he changed to accordion. He made appearances with his father's band but while still at high school and calling himself Frankie King, he formed a five-piece band that played on radio at Racine, Wisconsin. After graduating in 1932, he fronted a band he called the King's Jesters and played various radio stations and venues in Wisconsin, Michigan and Illinois. In 1934, he was given the chance to tour with **Gene Autry** as the accordionist with his group. In 1935, he moved to WHAS Louisville, where Autry headed a band called the Log Cabin Boys. Here he found three members of the band called Frank, and, being a mere 5 feet 6 inches tall, he was given the nickname of Pee Wee, a name he later took legally. When Autry left for Hollywood in 1936, King took over the band and renamed it the Golden West Cowboys. In 1937, he moved to Nashville and became a member of the ***Grand Ole Opry***, where he remained until 1947.

His band included, at different times, such noted country music performers as **Ernest Tubb**, **Eddy Arnold**, **Cowboy Copas**, Redd Stewart and Clell Summey. In 1941, he and his band, with other Opry acts including **Minnie Pearl**, toured extensively with *The Grand Ole Opry Camel Caravan*. In 1938, he made his film debut with Autry in *Goldmine In The Sky* and later appeared in other B-movie westerns, not only with Autry, but other cowboy stars including Johnny Mack Brown and Charles Starrett. In 1947-57, he had his own radio and television series on WAVE, Louisville. He recorded for RCA-Victor and in 1948, he achieved his first US country and pop chart hit with 'Tennessee Waltz'. Inspired by **Bill Monroe's** 'Kentucky Waltz', King and Redd Stewart merely added lyrics to Monroe's theme song, the 'No Name Waltz'. King quickly followed with his other 'state' song hits, 'Tennessee Tears' and 'Tennessee Polka', as well as his co-written 'Bonaparte's Retreat'. In 1951, he had a US country and pop number 1 with his song 'Slowpoke', which topped the country charts for 15 weeks and went on to sell a million (it was also a Top 10 hit for **Hawkshaw Hawkins**). When released in Britain, it was for some reason called 'Slow Coach'. Other King songs to become Top 10 country hits for him were 'Silver And Gold', 'Busybody', 'Changing Partners' (a UK hit for both **Kay Starr** and **Bing Crosby**) and 'Bimbo' (later recorded successfully by **Jim Reeves**). In all cases, the vocals were performed by Redd Stewart. In the late 50s and early 60s, King had four television shows in different venues but in 1962, work pressure forced him to abandon them. Between 1952 and 1956, he won every available award for western bands. Noted country authority Colin Escott once wrote that **Bill Haley** and rock 'n' roll owed a great debt to Pee Wee King, as far as instrumentation was concerned. By 1959, King found that this very genre badly affected his music and he broke up his band. For the next four years, he worked with Redd Stewart in Minnie Pearl's Roadshow. In 1963, she gave up touring but King continued to run the show until, in 1968, he once again disbanded the group. He later relied on local musicians to back him on his appearances. In 1969, he retired from performing to concentrate on the business side of the music industry and through the 70s spent much time on promotional work. He was one of the first members elected to the Nashville Songwriters' International Hall Of Fame when it was founded in 1970 and his many varied services to the country music industry also earned him the honour of election to the Country Music Hall Of Fame in 1974. He later became a director of the Country Music Foundation in Nashville. In 1986, he appeared on the *Opry*'s 60th Anniversary Show. He suffered two strokes in the 90s.

● ALBUMS: *Pee Wee King* 10-inch album (RCA Victor 1954)★★★, *Pee Wee King* 10-inch album (RCA Victor 1955)★★★, *Waltzes* 10-inch album (RCA Victor 1955)★★★, *Swing West* 10-inch album (RCA Victor 1955)★★★★, *Swing West* (RCA Victor 1956)★★★, with the New Golden West Cowboys *Back Again (With The Songs That Made Them Famous)* (Starday 1964)★★, *Country Barn Dance* (Camden 1965)★★★, *The Legendary (Live Transcriptions)* (Longhorn 1967)★★, *Golden Olde Tyme Dances* (Briar 1975)★★★, *Ballroom King* (Detour 1982)★★★, *Hog Wild Too!* (Zu Zazz 1990).

● COMPILATIONS: *Biggest Hits* (Capitol 1966)★★★, *Best Of Pee Wee King And Redd Stewart* (Starday 1975)★★★, *Rompin', Stompin', Singin', Swingin'* (Bear Family 1983)★★★, *Pee Wee King And His Golden West Cowboys* 6-CD box set (Bear Family 1995)★★★★.

● FURTHER READING: *Hell-Bent For Music: The Life Of Pee Wee King*, Wade Hall.

King, Peter (jazz)

b. 11 August 1940, Kingston-upon-Thames, Surrey, England. Self-taught on several reed instruments, by the late 50s King had established himself as an important and exciting alto saxophonist on the UK jazz scene. Over the next few years he worked with **John Dankworth**, **Tubby Hayes**, **Stan Tracey** and other leading British musicians. He also worked with numerous visiting American artists, ranging stylistically from **Ray Charles** to **Red Rodney**, from **Jimmy Witherspoon** to **Hampton Hawes**. By the 70s King's stature had grown until he was on the verge of becoming a major international figure. During the 80s he consolidated his gains and amply fulfilled his potential. In the early 90s King was one of the world's outstanding hard bop alto saxophonists. Playing with a hard-edged brilliant tone, his remarkable agility and technical virtuosity are at the command of an exceptionally fast mind. Although his remarkable imagination and improvisational ability are best displayed on up-tempo tunes he is also a lyrical balladeer. His latest release, an attempt to reach a wider audience, was co-produced by **Everything But The Girl's** Ben Watt.

● ALBUMS: *My Kind Of Country* (Tank 1977)★★, *New Beginning* (Spotlite 1982)★★★, *East 34th Street* (Spotlite 1983)★★★, *Hi Fly* (Spotlite 1984)★★★, *90% Of 1%* (Spotlite 1985)★★★, *Live At The Bull* (1987)★★, with Guy Barker *Brother Bernard* (Miles 1988)★★★, *Blues For Buddy* (1988)★★★, *Crusade* (Blanco Y Negro 1989)★★★, *New Years' Morning '89* (1989)★★★.

King, Peter (reggae)

In 1976 a **sound system** known as Imperial Rockers, based in Lewisham, London, surfaced through Lloyd 'Musclehead' Francis and Dennis Rowe. By the early 80s the sound had evolved into the phenomenally successful Saxon sound. Many of the UK's top performers served their apprenticeships there, including **Maxi Priest**, **Tippa Irie** and **Phillip Papa Levi**. In 1981 King regularly performed with the posse alongside Papa Levi and is acknowledged as the DJ who conceived the 'fast style mic chat'. At the Dick Shepherd Youth Club in 1982, King unleashed his spectacular speed rap, which instantly caught on and a number of other DJs immediately emulated his style. His unique, rapid-fire lyricism earned him a reputation as the originator, although the foundation of the style was soon forgotten when a myriad of fast-style tunes surfaced; Papa Levi's 'Mi God Mi King' builds up to a speed rap in the closing verses and Tippa Irie's 'All The Time The Lyric A Rhyme' is also modelled around the style. While his cohorts have reaped the rewards, King's recorded output is not as abundant, but he is still respected in the reggae world. On the **Fashion** label, notable releases include 'Me Neat Me Sweet' and 'Step On The Gas'. Fellow Saxon crew members **Smiley Culture** and Asher Senator recorded both in combination and as soloists and acknowledged King's influence. When Smiley Culture crossed over into the mainstream King and Senator joined forces and gave a memorable performance on the television show *Club X*. The programme, hosted by Smiley, featured some of Jamaica's best musicians, including Ernest Wilson, **Bloodfire Posse**, **Delroy Wilson** and **Freddie McGregor**. King and Senator performed 'You Too Lie Fib Fib'. King has remained a popular MC on the dancehall circuit and should not be confused with the UK-based mellow saxophonist who records sentimental **lovers rock**.

● ALBUMS: various artists *Live At DSYC Volume One* (Raiders 1984)★★★.

King, Reg

b. England. King pursued a brief and largely unsuccessful solo career in the early 70s after having earlier sung in the mid-60s R&B group the **Action**. He left that group prior to their evolution into **Mighty Baby**. However, several members of the Action/Mighty Baby contributed to his sole, self-titled album, released in 1971. This collection included 'Little Boy', which was originally intended to be the Action's final a-side. Despite the presence of King's winning vocals, among the best the UK R&B movement had ever offered, the album failed to sell and King disappeared from the music industry thereafter.

● ALBUMS: *Reg King* (United Artists 1971)★★.

King, Sandra

b. 12 October 1950, London, England. King's family background included singers and other performing artists and by the age of nine she knew that she was to be a singer. At 16 years old she was heard by **Mark Murphy** who recommended her to **Ronnie Scott** who in turn booked her into his club. In the late 60s she sang with the **National Youth Jazz Orchestra**, touring eastern Europe. She continued to work in the UK and Europe for some years, receiving accolades from many distinguished musicians including **Henry Mancini** ('an extraordinary artist for her age, in fact, for any age'). In 1981 while at Ronnie Scott's she was asked by **Stan Getz** to sing with him. For many years her musical mentor was **Pat Smythe** who accompanied her in 1985 when she sang at the Corcoran Gallery of Art in Washington, DC, performing a concert of songs by **Vernon Duke**. The concert won a rave review from John S. Wilson in the New York *Times* and the subsequent release of an

album recorded at the concert was a major breakthrough. She made more dates, for Audiophile Records including a set of **Jimmy Van Heusen** songs with Richard Rodney Bennett, and continued to work in the USA, where she was based mostly from 1986-93. Nevertheless, she found time during this period for appearances in Copenhagen in 1988 with the **Thad Jones** big band and in 1994 in The Netherlands with **Robert Farnon**. In the mid-90s King has worked in the UK and Europe, with more US visits and albums planned for the late 90s. Quite clearly, her career is still on an upward curve. King has a deep, richly expressive voice and sings with enormous charm, skill and integrity.

● ALBUMS: *Warm And Swingin: The Songs Of Henry Mancini* (Avenue 1970)★★★, *The Sentimental Touch Of Albert Van Dam* (RCA 1984)★★, *Sandra King In A Concert Of Vernon Duke* (Audiophile 1985)★★★, *Magic Window: The Songs Of Jimmy Van Heusen* (Audiophile 1988)★★★★.

King, Saunders

b. 13 March 1909, Staple, Louisiana, USA. Starting out as a singer, and obtaining a job with the NBC network, King took up the electric guitar in 1938 after hearing **Charlie Christian**. King formed his own band in 1942, and became popular around the San Francisco area; he then began recording for the small Rhythm Records and the first session produced his biggest hit, 'Saunders Blues'. The song achieved more fame under the title 'S.K. Blues' and became a staple in the repertoires of many blues shouters, such as **Jimmy Witherspoon** and **Big Joe Turner**. Later recordings for Modern/RPM/Flair (who bought the Rhythm masters and cheekily reissued 'S.K. Blues' as 'New S.K. Blues'!), Cavatone and Aladdin failed to emulate the success of 'S.K. Blues', and his final recordings were made in 1961 for Galaxy, after which he retired from professional music, although he was brought back in 1979 when asked to guest on Carlos Devadip **Santana**'s *Oneness* album. Over the years, Saunders King has taken a back seat to the mighty **'T-Bone' Walker**, but it is often overlooked that he, in fact, was recorded playing electrified blues guitar before Walker made his recording debut on that instrument.

● COMPILATIONS: *What's Your Story, Morning Glory* (Blues Boy 1987)★★★, *The First King Of The Blues* (Ace 1988)★★★.

King, Sid

b. Sidney Erwin, 1936, Denton, Texas, USA. King was one of the foremost rockabilly singers of the 50s. As a teenager he formed the Western Melodymakers, which became Sid King And The Five Strings when he signed to Starday in 1954. Among the group's earliest recordings was 'Who Put The Turtle In Myrtle's Girdle', but after joining **Columbia**, King concentrated on more hard-rocking material. Recording in Dallas, he released a version of **Roy Orbison**'s 'Ooby Dooby' in 1955 but though King's record was issued first, Orbison himself had the hit. He also recorded 'Sag, Drag And Fall' as

well as versions of R&B hits including 'Drinkin' Wine Spoo-De-O-Dee'.
● COMPILATIONS: *Gonna Shake This Shack Tonight* (Bear Family 1984)★★★, *Rockin' On The Radio* (Rollercoaster 1984)★★, *Let's Get Loose* (Rockhouse 1987)★★★.

King, Solomon

This US singer came to prominence in 1968 with the powerful hit ballad 'She Wears My Ring'. It was based on a classical piece of music called *Golandrina (The Swallow)*. King was signed by manager/entrepreneur **Gordon Mills** but failed to emulate the phenomenal success of his stablemates **Tom Jones** and **Engelbert Humperdinck**. He continued to record well into the 70s, and his version of 'Say A Little Prayer' (1970) is a prized rarity among soul fans.
● ALBUMS: *She Wears My Ring* (Columbia 1968)★★★, *You'll Never Walk Alone* (Columbia 1971)★★.

King, Stan

b. 1900, Hartford, Connecticut, USA, d. 19 November 1949. King played drums part-time for a number of years before heading for New York and a full-time career in music. He worked with several leading dance bands, including those led by **Roger Wolfe Kahn** and **Paul Whiteman** and he also played jazz with the **California Ramblers**. By the early 30s he had become a respected and sought-after studio musician in New York and he also played in the bands of **Benny Goodman** and **Joe Haymes**. King performed in jazz groups supporting leading artists such as **Jack Teagarden** and **Louis Armstrong**. He was an exceptionally good dance band drummer with meticulous time; however, his jazz work always left something to be desired. Listening to, for example, Goodman's recordings in late 1934 will reveal how King's playing never lifts the band in the way **Gene Krupa** did when he took over as drummer in December that year. In his own field, however, that of dance music, King was always a very good drummer.

King, Teddi

b. Theodora King, 18 September 1929, Boston, Massachusetts, USA, d. 18 November 1977. Teddi King was a jazz-pop singer who enjoyed some crossover success on the 50s pop charts. Her singing career began upon graduation from high school. After working with the bands of Jack Edwards and George Graham she joined **Nat Pierce**'s band in 1951, with which she made her recording debut. She also recorded with **George Shearing** during this period before going solo in 1953. After setting out on her own, King was signed to **RCA Records**, who had her recording pop songs, much to the artist's own dismay. Nevertheless, 'Mr. Wonderful', a 1956 single, reached the US Top 20, and two subsequent singles also charted. She then returned to pure jazz singing. Albums she recorded during the 50s for RCA, Storyville and **Coral Records** all became collectors' items in later years.

● ALBUMS: *'Round Midnight* (1954)★★★★, *Storyville Presents* (1954)★★★, *Now In Vogue* (1956)★★★, *Bidin' My Time* (1956)★★★, *To You From Teddi King* (1957)★★★★, *A Girl And Her Songs* (1957)★★.

King, Wayne

b. unknown, d. 16 July 1985. Dubbed 'the Waltz King', before establishing his first dance band King had served as featured saxophonist in the **Del Lampe** Orchestra operating out of the Trianon Ballroom in Chicago, Illinois, USA. However, he soon dropped the primarily jazz influenced sound of this combo in favour of a smooth, highly stylised sound when his own orchestra made their debut at the nearby Aragon Ballroom in 1927. His large band comprised sidemen Tony Hillis, Lee Keller, Burke Bibens, Louis Henderson, Andy Hansen, Ernie Birchill, Bill Heller, Paul Mack, Bill Egner, Johnny Kozel, Roger Wilson, Harry Waidley, Dick Harry, Sugar Harold, G. Belogh, Wayne Barclay, Oscar Kobelk, Herbert Miska, Wayne Alexander, Art Ellefsen, Bay Bluett, Louis Kastler, Emil Vanda, George Bay, Earl Schwaller, Kenneth La Bohn, Ray Johnson, Bill Kleeb and Jerry Vaughan. The featured vocalists included Elmo Tanner, Charles Farrell, **Buddy Clark**, the Barry Sisters, Linda Barrie and the Aragon vocal trio. That first engagement at the Aragon lasted for eight years as radio shows such as *The Lady Esther Serenade*, *The Elgin-American Watch Company Show* and, later, his own *Wayne King Show*, sponsored by the United Drug Company, made him a household name throughout America. The group's recordings for **Victor Records** were also very popular, especially 'Josephine', a major hit in 1937. 1942 saw King enlist in the army, but at the end of World War II he returned to bandleading and renewed his popularity with dates throughout the best American venues. He continued to tour, though now mainly in the Midwest, during the 50s, before entering semi-retirement in Scottsdale, Arizona. He was invited back to the Aragon Ballroom in February 1964 to play on its final nights just before closure. He returned to Arizona afterwards but died on 16 July 1985.

King, Yvonne

(see **King Sisters**)

Kingbees

New York-based contemporaries of the Vagrants and the Myddle Class, this superior R&B group comprised of **Danny Kortchmar** aka Danny Kootch (guitar), John McDuffy (organ/vocals), Dickie Frank (bass) and Joel 'Bishop' O'Brien (drums). The quartet completed three excellent singles during its brief existence, which included notable versions of 'Four In The Morning' and 'Lost In The Shuffle', also recorded, respectively, by the **Youngbloods** and **Blues Project**. McDuffy replaced **Al Kooper** in the latter act following the Kingbees' disintegration in autumn 1966. Kortchmar and O'Brien resurfaced in the Flying Machine, a group which also featured **James Taylor**, and were eventually reunited in Jo Mama in the wake of the guitarist's spells in the **Fugs**, Clear Light and **City**.

Kingdom Come (70s)

This UK group was formed in 1971 by the eccentric **Arthur Brown**, a vocalist who had achieved momentary commercial fame three years earlier with his memorable single, 'Fire'. This new venture was completed by Andy Dalby (guitar), Michael Harris (keyboards), Phil Shutt (bass) and Martin Steer (drums), a line-up immortalized in the film *Glastonbury Fayre*. Their debut album, *Galactic Zoo Dossier*, was a radical, experimental set, and featured an extended version of 'Space Plucks', a piece the singer had written for his previous group with organist Vincent Crane. This high standard was sadly not maintained on its follow-up, *Kingdom Come*, which relied on contemporary progressive styles. Harris and Steer were dropped from the group for *Journey*, on which Brown employed a drum machine. The group broke up completely when their founder embarked on an erratic solo career.
● ALBUMS: *Galactic Zoo Dossier* (Polydor 1971)★★★★, *Kingdom Come* (Polydor 1972)★★★, *Journey* (Polydor 1973)★★.
● COMPILATIONS: *The Lost Ears* (1977)★★★.

Kingdom Come (80s)

In 1984 German vocalist Lenny Wolf fronted the **Led Zeppelin**-inspired **Stone Fury**, who released *Burns Like A Star*. After they disbanded he returned to Germany and had a rethink. He moved back to America in 1987 with a new plan and found like-minded musicians Danny Stag (guitar), Rick Stier (guitar), Johnny Frank (bass) and James Kottak (drums). He then took his idea to ex-**Gentle Giant** vocalist Derek Shulman, now working in A&R, who ensured that the new group signed to **Polydor Records**. Their 1988 album revealed Wolf's great plan: the band had not so much been influenced by, but had totally reproduced Led Zeppelin, from the drum sound of **John Bonham** to the vocals of **Robert Plant**. It was a complete facsimile, yet such was the interest in America that the album went gold on advance orders alone. The rock world soon fell into two factions - those who hated it and those who did not. Of their detractors, Robert Plant and **John Paul Jones** made less than flattering remarks and guitarist **Gary Moore** was prompted to write the song 'Led Clones' on his *After The War* album later that same year. Wolf lacked the ability to argue his case convincingly and even those who chose to support them began to change sides. Realizing that all was not well, they attempted to be a little more original for the second album, *In Your Face*. This produced a classic rock track in 'Do You Like It', a highly charged song that managed to avoid previous comparisons. However, the title of their final single, 'Overrated', summarized the whole project, and they summarily disbanded. Lenny Wolf later returned as a solo artist and produced a fine single, 'Shouldn't I', but the ghost of *Kingdom Come* haunted his every move.
● ALBUMS: *Kingdom Come* (Polydor 1988)★★★, *In Your Face* (Polydor 1989)★★.

Kingfish

Formed in 1974 in San Francisco, California, USA, Kingfish were one of the city's most popular live attractions during the late 70s. Founder-members Matt Kelly (guitar/vocals) and Chris Herold (drums) first worked together in the 60s in the New Delhi River Band. In 1968 they formed Horses who recorded an album for White Whale Records. This group's lead guitarist Bobby Hoddinot joined Kelly and Herold in 1973 in Lonesome Janet, along with Nick Ward (keyboards). When Dave Torbert (bass, ex-**New Riders Of The Purple Sage** and New Delhi Blues Band) was added to the line-up in 1974, Lonesome Janet became known as Kingfish. Ward died in 1974, after which **Grateful Dead** guitarist/vocalist **Bob Weir** joined the remaining musicians, boosting their popularity overnight. *Kingfish* captures their relaxed, bar band style, but it disguised internal disharmony. Weir left soon after its completion and *Live'N'Kicking* featured a four-piece group. Dave Perber replaced Herold for *Trident*, which also introduced newcomers Mike O'Neil (guitar) and Barry Flast (keyboards). Perber then left, and Mark Neilson became the group's third drummer for *Two For The Sun*. Kingfish disbanded officially in 1979, although Kelly and Flast subsequently revived the name during the 80s. *Kingfish* (1985) featured assistance from **John Lee Hooker** and **Mike Bloomfield**, as well as Bob Weir, who resumed his association with the group, albeit on a part-time basis. *Live From The Sweetwater* proved their in-concert sparkle had not disappeared.
● ALBUMS: *Kingfish* (Round 1976)★★★, *Live'N'Kicking* (Jet 1977)★★★, *Trident* (Jet 1978)★★, *Two For The Sun* (Krishner 1979)★★, *Kingfish* (Relix 1985)★★, *Live From The Sweetwater* (Relix 1986)★★★.

Kinghorse

Based in Louisville, Kentucky, USA, Kinghorse are a four-piece rock band featuring Sean Garrison (vocals), Kevin Brownstein (drums), Mark Abromavage (guitar) and Mike Bucayu (bass). They attracted a good deal of critical interest after their debut release, not least because they had secured cover artwork from legendary heavy metal artist Pushead (singer for **Septic Death**, but best known for his work with **Metallica**), and had Glenn Danzig (of **Misfits** and **Danzig** fame) on production duties. The resultant album was an exercise in heated nihilism and aggressive angst. Potent, painfully gritty and, at times, oddly poignant, Kinghorse were perhaps too unremittingly bleak for most tastes.
● ALBUMS: *Kinghorse* (Caroline 1990)★★★.

Kingmaker

Indie rock band founded in Hull, North Humberside, England, by Loz Hardy (b. Lawrence Paul Hardy, 14

September 1970, Manchester, Lancashire, England; vocals, guitar) with Myles Howell (b. 23 January 1971, Rugby, Warwickshire, England; bass) and John Andrew (b. John Ricardo Andrew, 27 May 1963, Hull, North Humberside, England; drums). The group was formed by Hardy and Howell during their year off after school, eventually recruiting the significantly older Andrew, an ex-travelling puppeteer, to complete the unit. The band made their debut with *The Celebrated Working Man* EP, after which they signed to **Chrysalis Records** for a second EP, *Idiots At The Wheel*. They were immediately courted by the press, who invented a niche category for the group: New Cool Rock. At one time tipped by many as a potential next big thing, Kingmaker rapidly fell out of favour with the fashionable climate of their genre. Paul Heaton of local stars the **Beautiful South** went so far as to accuse them of being middle-class pretenders, living in castles on the outskirts of Hull. Nevertheless, Hardy's songwriting prowess seems to have grown in inverse proportion to their stature. The songs on 1992's *Sleepwalking*, primarily located in Hardy's bitter world view, far surpassed anything on the debut album and the early singles that won them most attention. Tucked away on the b-side to the BRIT Awards-baiting 'Armchair Anarchist', 'Everything's Changed Since You've Been To London' and 'Kissing Under Anaesthetic' stood head and shoulders above many of their peers. The band's lyrical austerity, much ridiculed by some critics, was matched by strong musical craft (particularly Andrew's forceful, accomplished drumming) and an emotive resonance not confined to the young audience the band seemed to attract. *In The Best Possible Taste* emerged, in 1995, within one month of the death of disc jockey **Kenny Everett**, who had popularized the phrase, adding an unconscious irony to its use. Tracks such as 'One False Move' revealed a shift towards urban rockabilly.

● ALBUMS: *Eat Yourself Whole* (Chrysalis 1991)★★★, *Sleepwalking* (Chrysalis 1992)★★★, *To Hell With Humdrum* mini-album (Chrysalis 1993)★★, *In The Best Possible Taste* (Chrysalis 1995)★★★.
● COMPILATIONS: *The Best And The Rest Of* (Chrysalis 1997)★★★.

Kings Of The Wild Frontier - Adam And The Ants

Adam Ant succeeded in the pop charts as a result of style as much as music. He rode the crest of post-punk new wave, with his brand of pop leaning heavily on the drumming and chanting of African artists such as Barundi Black. 'Dog Eat Dog' and 'Antmusic' are two good examples of his sound. A track such as 'Feed Me To The Lions' attempts a more regular sound and, as such, falls short. The title track was the main hit, but spare a thought for 'The Magnificent Five', with its opening lyric: 'long ago in London town, a man called Ant sat deeply sighing'.

● Tracks: *Dog Eat Dog; Antmusic; Feed Me To The Lions; Los Rancheros; Ants Invasion; Killer In The Home; Kings Of The Wild Frontier; The Magnificent Five; Don't Be Square (Be There); Jolly Roger; Making History; The Human Beings.*
● First released 1980
● UK peak chart position: 1
● USA peak chart position: 44

Kings X

Initially known as the Edge and specializing in Top 40 cover versions, Doug Pinnick (bass, vocals), Ty Tabor (guitar) and Jerry Gaskell (drums) relocated to Houston, Texas, USA, in 1985, and were taken under the wing of **ZZ Top** video producer, Sam Taylor. Under Taylor's guidance, they concentrated on their own material and changed their name to Kings X. After recording demos and being turned down by several major record companies in the USA, they finally secured a contract with the independent Megaforce label. *Out Of The Silent Planet*, with its unique sound and offbeat approach, emerged in 1988 to widespread critical acclaim. Fusing **Beatles**-style harmonies with hard rock and blues riffs, they encompassed a variety of genres that defied simple pigeonholing. *Gretchen Goes To Nebraska* was an even greater triumph, building on previous strengths, but adding depth in both a technical and lyrical sense. Preferring the 'positive' tag to that of Christian rockers, *Faith, Hope, Love*, released in 1990, scaled even greater heights with its state-of-the-art production and inspired compositions. After a long gap from recording, *Ear Candy* was a pleasant surprise, both in quality and in the fact that their fans had not deserted them.

● ALBUMS: *Out Of The Silent Planet* (Megaforce 1987)★★★, *Gretchen Goes To Nebraska* (Megaforce 1989)★★★★, *Faith, Hope, Love* (Megaforce 1990)★★★★, *King's X* (Atlantic 1992)★★★★, *Dogman* (Atlantic 1994)★★★, *Ear Candy* (Atlantic 1996)★★★.
● COMPILATIONS: *Best Of Kings X* (Atlantic 1998)★★★★.

Kingsmen

Jack Ely (vocals/guitar), Mike Mitchell (guitar) Bob Nordby (bass) and Lynn Easton (drums) began working as the Kingsmen in 1958. Based in Portland, Oregon, USA, they became a staple part of the region's thriving circuit prior to the arrival of Don Gallucci (keyboards) in 1962. The group's debut single, 'Louie Louie', was released the following year. The song was composed and originally recorded by **Richard Berry** in 1956, and its primitive, churning rhythm was later adopted by several northwest state bands, including the **Wailers** and **Paul Revere And The Raiders**. However, it was the Kingsmen who popularized this endearing composition when it rose to number 2 in the US chart. Its classic C-F-G chord progression, as simple as it was effective, was absorbed by countless 'garage bands', and 'Louie Louie' has subsequently become one of rock's best-known and most influential creations. Indeed, a whole album's worth of recordings of the song by various artists, including the Kingsmen and Richard Berry, was issued by **Rhino Records** entitled, *The Best Of*

Louie Louie. Relations between the individual Kingsmen were sundered on the single's success. Easton informed Ely that he now wished to sing lead, and furthered his argument by declaring himself the sole proprietor of the group's name, having judiciously registered the moniker at their inception. Ely and Norby walked out, although the former won a victory of sorts when a judgement declared that every pressing of the Kingsmen's greatest hit must include the words 'lead vocals by Jack Ely'. His former cohorts added Norm Sundholm (bass) and Gary Abbot (drums), but despite a succession of dance-related releases including 'The Climb', 'Little Latin Lupe Lu' and 'The Jolly Green Giant', the group was unable to maintain a long-term livelihood. Gallucci formed **Don And The Goodtimes**, Kerry Magnus and Dick Petersen replaced Sundholm and Abbot, but the crucial alteration came in 1967 when Easton left the group. Numerous half-hearted reincarnations aside, his departure brought the Kingsmen to an end.

● ALBUMS: *The Kingsmen In Person* (Wand 1963)★★, *The Kingsmen, Volume 2 (More Great Sounds)* (Wand 1964)★★, *The Kingsmen, Volume 3* (Wand 1965)★★, *The Kingsmen On Campus* (Wand 1965)★★, *How To Stuff A Wild Bikini* film soundtrack (1965)★, *Up Up And Away* (Wand 1966)★★.

● COMPILATIONS: *15 Great Hits* (Wand 1966)★★, *The Kingsmen's Greatest Hits* (Wand 1967)★★, *Louie Louie/Greatest Hits* (Charly 1986)★★.

● FILMS: *How To Stuff A Wild Bikini* (1965).

Kingston Trio

An influential part of America's folk revival, the Kingston Trio was formed in San Francisco in 1957 and was popular in the late 50s. The group consisted of Bob Shane (b. 1 February 1934, Hilo, Hawaii), Nick Reynolds (b. 27 July 1933, Coronado, California, USA) and Dave Guard (b. 19 October 1934, San Francisco, California, USA, d. 22 March 1991). The Kingston Trio had limited singles successes and are most often remembered for 'Tom Dooley' which reached number 5 in the UK charts, and number 1 in the US chart in 1958. The song, written by Guard, was based on an old folk tune from the 1800s called 'Tom Dula'. *The Kingston Trio*, from which 'Tom Dooley' came, also reached number 1 in the USA. The group had a run of successful albums in 1959, with *From The Hungry i*, a live recording, reaching number 2, and *The Kingston Trio At Large* and *Here We Go Again* both achieving top placings. Further chart-toppers followed with *Sold Out* and *String Along*. Their fresh harmonies and boyish enthusiasm endeared the trio to an America suspicious of the genre's New Left sympathies, but in the process paved the way for a generation of more committed performers. Guard was replaced by **John Stewart** (b. 5 September 1939, San Diego, California, USA) in May 1961, having left to pursue a solo career and form the **Whiskeyhill Singers**. *Close-Up* was the first release featuring Stewart, who had previously been with the **Cumberland Three**, and it reached number 3 in the US

charts. 'San Miguel', the follow-up to 'Tom Dooley', only just managed to reach the Top 30 in the UK the following year. 'The Reverend Mr Black' achieved a Top 10 placing in the US chart in 1963. The line-up with Stewart continued until 1967. Shane later re-formed the group, as the New Kingston Trio, with Roger Gamble and George Grove. The group continued to enjoy widespread popularity and their output, if stylistically moribund, was certainly prolific. However, the success of more exciting folk and folk-rock acts rendered them increasingly old-fashioned, and the Trio was disbanded in 1968. A group reunion was hosted on television, by Tom Smothers in 1981, when all six members were brought together for the first time. Stewart went on to achieve a cult following as a soloist, and continues to record and perform. In 1987 the Trio was on the road again, with Shane, Grove, and new member Bob Haworth.

● ALBUMS: *The Kingston Trio* (Capitol 1958)★★★, *From The Hungry i* (Capitol 1959)★★★, *The Kingston Trio At Large* (Capitol 1959)★★★★, *Here We Go Again!* (Capitol 1959)★★★★, *Sold Out* (Capitol 1960)★★★, *String Along* (Capitol 1960)★★★, *Stereo Concert* (Capitol 1960)★★★, *The Last Month Of The Year* (Capitol 1960)★★★, *Make Way!* (Capitol 1961)★★★, *Goin' Places* (Capitol 1961)★★★, *Close-Up* (Capitol 1961)★★★, *College Concert* (Capitol 1962)★★★, *Something Special* (Capitol 1962)★★★, *New Frontier* (Capitol 1962)★★★, *The Kingston Trio No. 16* (Capitol 1963)★★, *Sunny Side!* (Capitol 1963)★★, *Sing A Song With The Kingston Trio* (Capitol 1963)★★, *Time To Think* (Capitol 1963)★★★, *Back In Town* (Capitol 1964)★★★, *Nick-Bob-John* (Decca 1965)★★, *Stay Awhile* (Decca 1965)★★, *Somethin' Else* (Decca 1965)★★, *Children Of The Morning* (Decca 1966)★★, *Once Upon A Time* 1966 live recording (Tetragrammaton 1969)★★, *American Gold* (Longines 1973)★★★★, *The World Needs A Melody* (1973)★★★, *Aspen Gold* (1979)★★★, *Best Of The Best* (Proarté 1986)★★.

● COMPILATIONS: *Encores* (Capitol 1961)★★★★, *The Best Of The Kingston Trio* (Capitol 1962)★★★★, *The Folk Era* 3-LP box set (Capitol 1964)★★★, *The Best Of The Kingston Trio Volume 2* (Capitol 1965)★★★★, *The Best Of The Kingston Trio Volume 3* (Capitol 1966)★★★, *The Kingston Trio* (1972)★★★, *Where Have All The Flowers Gone* (1972)★★★★, *The Historic Recordings Of The Kingston Trio* (1975)★★★★, *The Very Best Of The Kingston Trio* (Capitol 1987)★★★★, *Capitol Collectors Series* (Capitol 1991)★★★, *Greatest Hits* (Curb 1991)★★★, *The EP Collection* (See For Miles 1997)★★★★.

● FURTHER READING: *The Kingston Trio On Record*, Kingston Korner.

Kinks

It is ironic that one of Britain's most enduring and respected groups spawned from the beat boom of the early 60s, received, for the best part of two decades, success, adulation and financial reward in the USA. This most 'English' institution were able to fill stadiums in any part of the USA, while in Britain, a few thousand devotees watched their heroes perform in comparatively small clubs or halls. The Kinks is the continuing obsession of one of Britain's premier songwriting talents, **Raymond Douglas Davies** (b. 21 June 1944, Muswell Hill, London, England; vocals/guitar/piano). Originally known as the Ravens, the Kinks formed at the end of 1963 with a line-up comprising: **Dave Davies** (b. 3 February 1947, Muswell Hill, London; guitar/vocals) and Peter Quaife (b. 31 December 1943, Tavistock, Devon, England; bass), and were finally joined by Mick Avory (b. 15 February 1944, London; drums). Their first single 'Long Tall Sally' failed to sell, although they did receive a lot of publicity through the efforts of their shrewd managers Robert Wace, Grenville Collins and **Larry Page**. Their third single, 'You Really Got Me', rocketed to the UK number 1 spot, boosted by an astonishing performance on the UK television show *Ready Steady Go*. This and its successor, 'All Day And All Of The Night', provided a blueprint for hard rock guitar playing, with the simple but powerful riffs supplied by the younger Davies. Over the next two years Ray Davies emerged as a songwriter of startling originality and his band were rarely out of the best-sellers list. Early in 1965, the group returned to number 1 with the languid 'Tired Of Waiting For You'. They enjoyed a further string of hits that year, including 'Everybody's Gonna Be Happy', 'Set Me Free', 'See My Friend' and 'Till The End Of The Day'. Despite the humanity of his lyrics, Davies was occasionally a problematical character, renowned for his eccentric behaviour. The Kinks were equally tempestuous and frequently violent. Earlier in 1965, events had reached a head when the normally placid drummer, Mick Avory, attacked Dave Davies on stage with the hi-hat of his drum kit, having been goaded beyond endurance. Remarkably, the group survived such contretemps and soldiered on. A disastrous US tour saw them banned from that country, amid further disputes.

Throughout all the drama, Davies the songwriter remained supreme. He combined his own introspection with humour and pathos. The ordinary and the obvious were spelled out in his lyrics, but, contrastingly, never in a manner that was either. 'Dedicated Follower Of Fashion' brilliantly satirized Carnaby Street narcissism while 'Sunny Afternoon' (another UK number 1) dealt with capitalism and class. 'Dead End Street' at the end of 1966 highlighted the plight of the working class poor: 'Out of work and got no money, a Sunday joint of bread and honey', while later in that same song Davies comments 'What are we living for, two-roomed apartment on the second floor, no money coming in, the rent collector knocks and tries to get in'. All these were embraced with Davies' resigned laconic music-hall style. Their albums prior to *Face To Face* had contained a staple diet of R&B standards and comparatively harmless Davies originals. With *Face To Face* and *Something Else*, however, he set about redefining the English character, with sparkling wit and steely nerve. One of Davies' greatest songs was the final track on the latter; 'Waterloo Sunset' was a simple but

emotional *tour de force* with the melancholic singer observing two lovers (many have suggested actor Terence Stamp and actress Julie Christie, but Davies denies this) meeting and crossing over Hungerford Bridge in London. It narrowly missed the top of the charts, as did the follow-up, 'Autumn Almanac', with its gentle chorus, summing up the English working class of the 50s and 60s: 'I like my football on a Saturday, roast beef on Sunday is all right, I go to Blackpool for my holiday, sit in the autumn sunlight'. Throughout this fertile period, Ray Davies, along with **John Lennon/Paul McCartney** and **Pete Townshend**, was among Britain's finest writers. But by 1968 the Kinks had fallen from public grace in the UK, despite remaining well respected by the critics. Two superb concept albums, *The Kinks Are The Village Green Preservation Society* and *Arthur Or The Decline And Fall Of The British Empire*, failed to sell. This inexplicable quirk was all the harder to take as they contained some of Davies' finest songs. Writing honestly about everyday events seemingly no longer appealed to Davies' public. The former was likened to Dylan Thomas's *Under Milk Wood*, while *Arthur* had to compete with **Pete Townshend**'s *Tommy*. Both were writing rock operas without each other's knowledge, but as Johnny Rogan states in his biography of the Kinks: 'Davies' celebration of the mundane was far removed from the studious iconoclasm of *Tommy* and its successors'. The last hit single during this 'first' age of the Kinks was the glorious 'Days'. This lilting and timeless ballad is another of Davies' many classics and was a major hit for **Kirsty MacColl** in 1989.

Pete Quaife permanently departed in 1969 and was replaced by ex-**Creation** member John Dalton. The Kinks returned to the UK best-sellers lists in July 1970 with 'Lola', an irresistible fable of transvestism, which marked the beginning of their breakthrough in the USA by reaching the US Top 10. The resulting *Lola Vs Powerman And The Moneygoround Part One* was also a success there. On this record Davies attacked the music industry and in one track, 'The Moneygoround', openly slated his former managers and publishers, while alluding to the lengthy high court action in which he had been embroiled. The group now embarked on a series of huge US tours and rarely performed in Britain, although their business operation centre and recording studio, Konk, was based close to the Davies' childhood home in north London. Having signed a new contract with **RCA** in 1971 the band had now enlarged to incorporate a brass section, amalgamating with the **Mike Cotton** Sound. Following the interesting country-influenced *Muswell Hillbillies*, however, they suffered a barren period. Ray Davies experienced drug and marital problems and their ragged half-hearted live performances revealed a man bereft of his driving, creative enthusiasm. Throughout the early 70s a series of average, over-ambitious concept albums appeared as Davies' main outlet. *Preservation Act I*, *Preservation Act II*, *Soap Opera* and *Schoolboys In Disgrace* were all thematic, and *Soap Opera* was adapted for British television as *Starmaker*. At the end of 1976 John Dalton departed, as their unhappy and comparatively unsuccessful years with RCA ended. A new contract with **Arista Records** engendered a remarkable change in fortunes. Both *Sleepwalker* (1977) and *Misfits* (1978) were excellent and successful albums; Ray had rediscovered the knack of writing short, punchy rock songs with quality lyrics. The musicianship of the band improved, in particular, Dave Davies, who after years in his elder brother's shadow, came into his own with a more fluid style.

Although still spending most of their time playing to vast audiences in the USA, the Kinks were adopted by the British new wave, and were cited by many punk bands as a major influence. Both the **Jam** ('David Watts') and the **Pretenders** ('Stop Your Sobbing') provided reminders of Davies' 60s songwriting skill. The British music press, then normally harsh on 60s dinosaurs, constantly praised the Kinks and helped to regenerate a market for them in Europe. Their following albums continued the pattern started with *Sleepwalker*, hard-rock numbers with sharp lyrics. Although continuing to be a huge attraction in the USA they have so far never reappeared in the UK album charts, although they are regular victims of ruthless 'Greatest Hits' packages. As Ray Davies' stormy three-year relationship with Chrissie Hynde of the Pretenders drew to its close, so the Kinks appeared unexpectedly back in the UK singles chart with the charming 'Come Dancing'. The accompanying video and high publicity profile prompted the reissue of their entire and considerable back catalogue. Towards the end of the 80s the band toured sporadically amid rumours of a final break-up. In 1990 the Kinks were inducted into the **Rock And Roll Hall of Fame**, at the time only the fourth UK group to take the honour behind the **Beatles**, **Rolling Stones** and the **Who**. During the ceremony both Pete Quaife and Mick Avory were present. Later that year they received the **Ivor Novello** award for 'outstanding services to British music'. After the comparative failure of *UK Jive* the band left London Records, and after being without a recording contract for some time signed with Sony in 1991. Their debut for that label was *Phobia*, a good album that suffered from lack of promotion (the public still perceiving the Kinks as a 60s band). A prime example was in 'Scattered', as good a song as Davies has ever written, which when released was totally ignored apart from a few pro-Kinks radio broadcasters. Following the commercial failure of *Phobia* the band were released from their contract and put out *To The Bone*, an interesting album on their own Konk label, which satisfied long-standing fans. This unplugged session was recorded in front of a small audience at their own headquarters in Crouch End, north London, and contained semi-acoustic versions of some of Davies' classic songs. Both brothers had autobiographies published in the 90s. Ray came first with the cleverly constructed *X-Ray*

and Dave responded with *Kink*, a pedestrian, though revealing, book in 1996. Whether or not they can maintain their reputation as a going concern beyond the mid-90s, Ray Davies has made his mark under the Kinks' banner as one of the most perceptive and prolific popular songwriters of our time. His catalogue of songs observing ordinary life is one of the finest available. A long-awaited reissue programme was undertaken by **Castle Communications** in 1998; this was particularly significant as the Kinks' catalogue has been mercilessly and often badly reissued for many years. The additions of many bonus tracks for each CD make their first five albums essential listening. Much of the Britpop movement from the mid-90s acknowledged a considerable debt to Davies as one of the key influences. Bands such as **Supergrass**, **Oasis**, **Cast** and especially Damon Albarn of **Blur** are some of the Kinks' most admiring students.

● ALBUMS: *Kinks* (Pye 1964)★★★, *Kinda Kinks* (Pye 1965)★★★, *The Kink Kontroversy* (Pye 1966)★★★★, *Face To Face* (Pye 1966)★★★★, *Live At The Kelvin Hall* (Pye 1967)★, *Something Else* (Pye 1967)★★★★★, *The Kinks Are The Village Green Preservation Society* (Pye 1968)★★★★★, *Arthur Or The Decline And Fall Of The British Empire* (Pye 1969)★★★★, *Lola Versus Powerman And The Moneygoround, Part One* (Pye 1970)★★★, *Percy* film soundtrack (Pye 1971)★★, *Muswell Hillbillies* (RCA 1971)★★★★, *Everybody's In Showbiz, Everybody's A Star* (RCA 1972)★★★ *Preservation Act 1* (RCA 1973)★★, *Preservation Act 2* (RCA 1974)★★, *Soap Opera* (RCA 1975)★★, *Schoolboys In Disgrace* (RCA 1975)★★★, *Sleepwalker* (Arista 1977)★★★, *Misfits* (Arista 1978)★★★★, *Low Budget* (Arista 1979)★★★, *One For The Road* (Arista 1980)★★★, *Give The People What They Want* (Arista 1982)★★★, *State Of Confusion* (Arista 1983)★★★, *Word Of Mouth* (Arista 1984)★★, *Think Visual* (London 1986)★★, *The Road* (London 1988)★★, *UK Jive* (London 1989)★★, *Phobia* (Columbia 1993)★★★, *To The Bone* (Konk 1994)★★★, *To The Bone (USA)* (Guardian 1996)★★★★, *Kinks* reissue (Castle 1998)★★★, *Kinda Kinks* reissue (Castle 1998)★★★, *The Kink Kontroversy* reissue (Castle 1998)★★★★, *Face To Face* reissue (Castle 1998)★★★★, *Something Else* reissue (Castle 1998)★★★★★

● COMPILATIONS: *Well Respected Kinks* (Marble Arch 1966)★★★★, *The Kinks* double CD (Pye 1970)★★★★, *A Golden Hour Of The Kinks* (Golden Hour 1973)★★★★, *All The Good Times* 4-LP box set (Pye 1973)★★★★, *The Kinks File* (Pye 1977)★★★★, *Greatest Hits* (PRT 1983)★★★, *The Ultimate Collection* (Castle 1989)★★★★, *The EP Collection* (See For Miles 1990)★★★★, *Fab Forty: The Singles Collection, 1964-70* (Decal 1991)★★★★, *Tired Of Waiting For You* (Rhino 1995)★★★, *The Singles Collection/Waterloo Sunset* (Essential/Castle 1997)★★★★★.

● FURTHER READING: *The Kinks: The Sound And The Fury*, Johnny Rogan. *The Kinks: The Official Biography*, Jon Savage. *You Really Got Me: The Kinks Part One*, Doug Hinman. *X-Ray*, Ray Davies. *Kink: An Autobiography*, Dave Davies. *The Kinks: Well Respected Men*, Neville Marten and Jeffrey Hudson. *Waterloo Sunset*, Ray Davies.

Kinky Machine

Kinky Machine were initially categorized as a mod/glam quartet by the UK music press after they formed at the end of 1991. Comprising Louis Elliot (vocals, guitar), Julian Fenton (drums) and John Bull (guitar), they were signed to Lemon Records in April 1992. Two Top 10 independent chart singles followed. Initial support slots to **Ned's Atomic Dustbin** and **Manic Street Preachers** led to press observations that they offered a halfway house between the **Only Ones** and **Mott the Hoople**. They built a substantial live following at this time, with swaggering singles such as 'Going Out With God', 'Swivelhead', 'Supernatural Giver' and 'Shockaholic'. They also appeared at the 1992 Phoenix Festival. All four of the singles were included on their debut album, by which time they had enlisted new bass player Nick Powell. Although it received a warm critical reaction, the group were then overtaken by the New Wave of the New Wave - in particular, bands such as S*M*A*S*H and **Elastica** who had begun their careers as support acts to Kinky Machine. A second album, *Bent*, followed in 1995. As Elliot told the press at this time: 'We write about what we know about - bad sex, cheap drugs'. It featured the excellent single '10 Second Bionic Man'. Afterwards, however, the group began to suffer from problems at their new record label, MCA Records. By the end of the year Kinky Machine had moved to a new label, EastWest Records, and recruited a new drummer, Anthony (Fenton went on to work with the **Lightning Seeds**). After releasing a final single, Elliot and Bull reinvented themselves as **Rialto**.

● ALBUMS: *Kinky Machine* (Oxygen 1993)★★★, *Bent* (MCA 1995)★★★.

Kinnaird, Alison, And Christine Primrose

Kinnaird (b. 30 April 1949, Edinburgh, Scotland) and Primrose (b. 17 February 1952, Carloway, Isle Of Lewis, Scotland), were known for their Gaelic-influenced folk music. Kinnaird studied the cello from the age of seven, and the Scottish harp from the age of 14, and has since gone on to win numerous competitions and awards. These include the Clarsach Trophy at the National Mod and the Harp competition at the Pan Celtic festival in Killarney. Having studied archaeology and Celtic studies at university, Alison recorded *The Harp Key*, the first record of the Scottish harp, after researching old manuscripts. This came out when fiddle music was particularly popular in folk circles, and the harp was often employed more as an instrument purely for accompaniment. A meeting with Ann Heymann, exponent of the wire-strung harp, in 1982, led to the follow-up *The Harper's Land*. By comparison, Christine Primrose has been singing since early childhood, with Gaelic as her first language. She too won the National Mod in 1974, and the Pan Celtic Festival in Killarney in 1978. As a result of the success of *Aite Mo Ghaoil*, Primrose has toured both Canada and the USA, as well as Europe,

taking her voice and Gaelic language to a wide audience. The two together complement one another perfectly, with the purity of Primrose's voice combining with the equally pure harp sound of Kinnaird.

● ALBUMS: *The Quiet Tradition* (1990)★★★.
Solo: Alison Kinnaird *The Harp Key* (1978)★★★, *The Harper's Gallery* (1980)★★★★, with Ann Heymann *The Harper's Land* (1983)★★★. Christine Primrose *Aite Mo Ghaoil* (1982)★★★, *S Tu Nam Chuimhne* (1987)★★★.

Kinney, Fern

b. Jackson, Mississippi, USA. In the late 60s, Kinney replaced Patsy McClune in the Poppies, a female pop/R&B trio whose 'Lullabye Of Love' on Epic had been a minor US hit in 1966. Together with Rosemary Taylor and **Dorothy Moore** (also a successful solo artist later), she remained in the group for two years. In the 70s, she worked as a session singer for two local studios, **Malaco** and North American. During this time she backed singers including **Jean Knight**, **King Floyd**, **Frederick Knight** and her old friend Dorothy Moore. Kinney's first solo recording was 'Your Love's Not Reliable' on **Atlantic** in 1968, but it was not until 1979 that she had her only US success, which came with a revival of King Floyd's 'Groove Me', an R&B chart-topper from 1970. It reached the R&B Top 30, number 54 on the US pop chart and was a club hit in the UK. In 1980, her revival of UK singer-songwriter Ken Leray's 1977 recording 'Together We Are Beautiful' gave the singer, with her thin, high voice, a surprise UK number 1 hit. The record had no impact in her homeland and, after various follow-ups failed to restore her to the UK chart, she returned to session singing and family life.

● ALBUMS: *Groove Me* (Warners 1980)★★★, *Fern* (Warners 1981)★★.

Kinsey Report

A family blues group formed in Gary, Indiana, USA, in the late 60s, the Kinsey brothers were taught by their father, **Big Daddy Kinsey**, a blues harpist and slide guitarist. As well as the delta tradition he also introduced them to gospel and soul, and it is the marriage of these influences which has dominated their output. Donald Kinsey (b. 12 May 1953, Gary, Indiana, USA; vocals/guitar) and Ralph 'Woody' Kinsey (drums) were inspired by receiving their first instruments before either were five years old. Later they joined their father in the family act and toured with another blues maestro on the 'Big Daddy and B.B. King Jnr' package. They also joined with another famous musical family from Gary, Indiana, the **Jacksons**, on US touring dates. However, in 1972 the group broke up as Ralph joined the armed forces. Donald played with **Albert King**, before his brother's return, at which point the duo formed White Lightnin'. Signed to **Island Records**, this blues-rock based experiment released one album and toured with **Uriah Heep**, **Average White Band**, **Crosby Stills And Nash** and **Aerosmith**. Afterwards Donald relocated to Jamaica to tour with **Peter Tosh**, playing on Tosh's albums *Legalize It*, *Bush Doctor* and *Mama Africa*. He also contributed to **Bob Marley**'s *Rastaman Vibration* and *Babylon By Bus*. However, when he was nearly killed in an attempt on Marley's life, Donald returned to the US. There he wrote and arranged tracks for **Betty Wright**'s *Wright Back At You* album, toured with the **Staple Singers** and added rhythm guitar to two **Roy Buchanan** albums. The Kinsey Report was then reunited in 1974 when Donald rejoined Ralph, finding further family accompaniment in younger brother Kenneth Kinsey (bass). Their father also combined with his offspring for *Big Daddy Kinsey And The Kinsey Report*. Produced by Donald, it traded the delta influences of Kinsey senior with his sons' eclectic marriage of modern influences. The resulting album won them a contract with Bruce Iglauer of **Alligator Records**, with two albums ensuing. Both *Edge Of The City* and *Midnight Drive* spread their influence in the US blues market, though the albums were not initially released elsewhere. The latter collection included a duet (a cover version of **Sam And Dave**'s 'I Take What I Want') with Chris Robinson of the **Black Crowes**. There was also an unrecorded **Prince** composition, '5 Women', which Donald described as a 'soap opera all in one song'. *Powerhouse*, as the title implied, belonged more firmly in the hard rock tradition, and saw them move to a major record label, **Atlantic Records**.

● ALBUMS: *Big Daddy Kinsey And The Kinsey Report* (1984)★★★★, *Edge Of The City* (Alligator 1990)★★★, *Midnight Drive* (Alligator 1990)★★★, *Powerhouse* (Atlantic 1991)★★.

Kinsey, Big Daddy

b. Lester Kinsey, 18 March 1927, Pleasant Grove, Mississippi, USA. An acknowledged disciple of **Muddy Waters**, Kinsey owned his first guitar at the age of six. Before travelling north in 1944, he had seen both Waters (then still McKinley Morganfield) and pianist **Pinetop Perkins** play at local parties and juke houses. Moving to Gary, Indiana, he played harmonica in a local band, the Soul Brothers. As his own family grew, he trained each of his sons, Ralph, Donald and Kenneth, to play an instrument and perform as a family unit. By the late 60s, the band was working the Ramada Inn circuit, the first black unit to do so. For much of the 70s, Daddy Kinsey worked local clubs with non-family musicians while his sons worked with **Albert King** and **Bob Marley**. In 1984, they were reunited as the **Kinsey Report** and the following year made their debut album. The following year, the sons signed to Alligator and their father toured with them as their opening act. They also backed him on 'Can't Let Go', assisted by Lucky Peterson on keyboards. Kinsey's albums on **Verve**/Gitanes benefit from superlative accompaniment from musicians such as **Buddy Guy**, **John Primer**, **James Cotton**, Pinetop Perkins, **Johnnie Johnson** and **Willie Smith**. *I Am The Blues* is dedicated to Muddy Waters and Kinsey is plainly content to continue in his shadow.

● ALBUMS: as the Kinsey Report *Bad Situation* (Rooster Blues 1985)★★★, *Can't Let Go* (Blind Pig 1989)★★★, *I Am The Blues* (Verve/Gitanes 1993)★★, *Ramblin' Man* (Verve/Gitanes 1994)★★★.

Kinsey, Tony

b. 11 October 1927, Sutton Coldfield, West Midlands, England. Kinsey was a key drummer in the London jazz scene of the 50s, having studied formally in the UK and USA before joining the **John Dankworth** Seven in 1950. He later formed his own groups, working with many leading jazz musicians, including **Joe Harriott**, **Peter King** and a succession of visiting American stars. Kinsey's early musical studies had extended into composition, and he has written many longer works for jazz orchestra and for classical groups. He has also written for films and television, but in the late 80s was still leading his small jazz groups around London clubs. As a skilful technician, Kinsey is comfortable playing in bebop or mainstream settings and is an outstanding jazz drummer.

● ALBUMS: *Starboard Bow* (1955)★★★, *Jazz At The Flamingo* (1956)★★★★, *The Tony Kinsey Quartet* (1957)★★★★, *The Tony Kinsey Quintet* i (1957)★★★, *The Tony Kinsey Quintet* ii (1958)★★★, *The Tony Kinsey Quintet* iii (1959)★★, *Foursome* (1959)★★, *The Tony Kinsey Quintet* iv (1961)★★★, *How To Succeed In Business* (1963)★★, *The Thames Suite* (Spotlite 1976)★★★.

Kipper Family

Discovered in 1978 by Norfolk singers Chris Sugden and Dick Nudds, the Kipper Family were originally founded by Ephraim Kipper in 1837. After a number of personnel changes over the years, the remaining duo of Henry Kipper (b. 4 August 1914, St. Just-near-Trunch, Norfolk, England; vocals, tremelodeon) and Sid Kipper (b. 3 September 1939, St. Just-near-Trunch, Norfolk, England; vocals, accordion, Trunch blow-pipes, walnut shells) continued the family tradition of keeping alive the songs from their native village. It is interesting to note that while Henry was born on the day that World War I began, so Sid was brought into the world the day that the World War II commenced. *The Ever Decreasing Circle* featured classic songs such as 'Spencer The Wild Rover', 'The Wild Mountain Thyme' and 'Joan Sugarbeet'. Active on the British folk scene from 1982, Henry decided to retire in 1991, while Sid continued in a solo capacity. *Broadside*, a compilation album of various artists, featured two songs by the Kipper Family, 'When I'm Abroad On The Broads' and 'Dicky Riding'. In 1994 Sid Kipper toured with Dave Burland.

● ALBUMS: *Since Time Immoral* (1984)★★, *Ever Decreasing Circle* (1985)★★★, *The Crab Wars* (1986)★★★, *Fresh Yesterday* (1988)★★★, *Arrest These Merry Gentlemen* (1989)★★, *In The Family Way* (1991)★★★.
Solo: Sid Kipper *Like A Rhinestone Ploughboy* (1993)★★★.
● COMPILATIONS: *Broadside* (1989)★★★.

Kippington Lodge

Best remembered as the vehicle for the earliest **Nick Lowe** (b. 24 March 1949, Walton-On-Thames, Surrey, England.) recordings, Kippington Lodge stemmed from Lowe's first band, Sounds 4+1, which he formed with school pal, **Brinsley Schwarz**. On leaving school, Lowe, already used to a nomadic existence as his father was in the Royal Air Force, decided to go and see some more of the world leaving, Schwarz to return to his native Tunbridge Wells in Kent. Here Schwarz formed Three's A Crowd who were signed to **EMI** in 1967. Changing their name to Kippington Lodge they released their debut 'Shy Boy' in October. This effective pop song was accompanied by the equally good 'Lady On A Bicycle'. At this point, Lowe returned to England and joined his friends in time for the second single 'Rumours' which was produced by Mark Wirtz. Lowe's arrival fixed the line-up as Schwarz (guitar/vocals), Lowe (bass/vocals), Barry Landerman (organ) and Pete Whale (drums). Landerman soon departed - later resurfacing in **Vanity Fare** - and was replaced by Bob Andrews (b. 20 June 1949). To supplement their lack of income from record sales, Kippington Lodge became Billie Davies' backing group and released three further singles during 1968-69. These releases were produced by EMI stalwarts such as Mike Collier, Roger Easterby and Des Champ. The last single, a version of the **Beatles**' 'In My Life', came out in April 1969 and, after doing as poorly as previous efforts, left the group at a loose end. In September they replaced Pete Whale with the American drummer Billy Rankin and the name Kippington Lodge was dropped in favour of that of lead guitarist Brinsley Schwarz.

Kirby, John

b. 31 December 1908, Baltimore, Maryland, USA, d. 14 June 1952. Kirby's career began in New York but suffered a hiatus when his first instrument, a trombone, was stolen. Replacing this with a tuba, he resumed his musical career, joining **Fletcher Henderson** in 1930. Soon after this he began using a string bass, at first alternating between the two instruments. He spent about two years with **Chick Webb**, then rejoined Henderson, but in 1937 decided to form his own band. Securing a residency at New York's Onyx Club, Kirby set about melding his group into a smooth, thoroughly rehearsed and musicianly outfit. Although this was the height of the big band-dominated swing era, he settled on a six-piece band and within a year saw his judgement pay off. The John Kirby Sextet, billed as 'The Biggest Little Band In The Land', became the yardstick by which nearly all sophisticated small jazz groups were measured. For most of the band's four-year existence the personnel was stable; **Charlie Shavers, Buster Bailey, Russell Procope, Billy Kyle** and drummer O'Neill Spencer. The addition of Kirby's wife, **Maxine Sullivan**, did the group's popularity no harm at all. The group disbanded with the onset of World War II and, although Kirby re-formed after the war, he never again achieved either the quality or the popularity of his first band. He was planning a comeback when he died in June 1952.

● ALBUMS: *John Kirby* (Atlantic 1986)★★★, *The Biggest Little Band In The Land (1938-41)* (Giants Of Jazz 1987)★★★, *John Kirby And His Orchestra, With Maxine Sullivan* (1988)★★★, *More* (Circle 1988)★★, *John Kirby And Onyx Club Boys Volumes 1-4* (Collectors Classics 1988)★★★, *John Kirby And His Orchestra* (Circle 1988), *Biggest Little Band* (Columbia 1993)★★★★.

Kirby, Kathy

b. 20 October 1940, Ilford, Essex, England. Her *bel canto* eloquence when in a convent school choir had her earmarked for a career in opera until 1956, when an unscheduled performance with **Ambrose** And His Orchestra at a local dancehall precipitated three years as the outfit's featured singer - with Ambrose as her mentor until his death in 1971. After stints with the big bands of Denny Boyle and Nat Allen, she headlined seasons in Madrid and London nightspots, and won recording contracts on Pye and then **Decca** - but it was only when her strawberry blonde, moist-lipped appeal was transferred to UK television in 1963, as a regular on the *Stars And Garters* variety show, that her records started selling. Her biggest UK smashes were with consecutive revivals of **Doris Day**'s 'Secret Love' and **Teresa Brewer**'s 'Let Me Go Lover', but these were adjuncts to her earnings for personal appearances and two BBC series (*Kathy Kirby Sings*). After a spot on 1965's Royal Command Performance - the apogee of British showbusiness - signs of danger were not yet perceptible. However, with that year's Eurovision Song Contest entry ('I Belong') her Top 40 farewell, and her aspirations to be a film actress frustrated, Ambrose's managerial arrogance and old-fashioned values upset BBC (and ITV) executives, thus consigning his cocooned client to a cabaret ghost-kingdom. Confused by post-Ambrose administrative chaos, Kirby's prima donna tantrums and failure to honour contracts made her a booker's risk. The 70s were further underscored by a disastrous marriage, bankruptcy, failed comebacks and, in 1979, a spell in a mental hospital following her arrest for an unpaid hotel bill (of which she was innocent). Just as unwelcome was publicity concerning her cohabitation with another woman. When the latter was jailed, the affair ended, and Kirby returned to the stage as an intermission act in a Kent bingo hall. Since then, she has played one-nighters, nostalgia revues and has sold the story of her tragic downfall to a Sunday newspaper. In more recent years Kirby has become a recluse, and speculation as to her whereabouts is constantly being expressed in the UK media. In 1994, 'an exciting new play' entitled *Whatever Happened To Kathy Kirby?*, was presented in the London provinces, while a year later, an unauthorized biography was published.

● ALBUMS: *16 Hits From Stars And Garters* (1964)★★, *Make Someone Happy* (Decca 1967)★★★, *My Thanks To You* (Columbia 1968)★★.

● COMPILATIONS: *The Best Of Kathy Kirby* (Ace of Clubs 1968)★★★, *The World Of Kathy Kirby* (Decca 1970)★★★, *Let Me Sing And I'm Happy* (1983)★★★, *Secret Love* (1989)★★★.
● FURTHER READING: *Kathy Kirby: Is That All There Is?*, James Harman.

Kirby, Pete

b. Beecher Kirby, c.1915, near Gatlinburg, Sevier County, Tennessee, USA. The Kirbys were a musical family with all 10 siblings playing some instrument, though not professionally. Kirby learned guitar and banjo but worked in mills and on a farm before finding work as a guitarist in an Illinois club. After hearing a dobro, he also mastered that instrument. In 1939, he became a member of **Roy Acuff**'s Smoky Mountain Boys, starting an association that lasted to Acuff's death in 1992. Kirby's dobro became a distinctive feature of the Acuff sound and he has become known as one of the instrument's finest exponents. He was also a fine harmony vocalist. He figured in the comedy routines that were part of Acuff's show and, wearing his bib and brace overalls and playing a banjo for his solo spots, he became known as Bashful Brother Oswald and a great favourite of the *Grand Ole Opry* audiences. He played on many of Acuff's recordings but recorded in his own right for Starday in 1962 and for Rounder in the 70s, including two fine albums with fellow Acuff band member Charlie Collins. He was also one of the stars chosen to play on the **Nitty Gritty Dirt Band**'s famous *Will The Circle Be Unbroken* project in 1972.
● ALBUMS: *Bashful Brother Oswald* (Starday 1962)★★, *Brother Oswald* (Rounder 1972)★★★, *Banjo & Dobro* (Rounder 1974)★★★, with Charlie Collins *That's Country* (Rounder 1975)★★★, with Collins *Os & Charlie* (Rounder 1976)★★★, *Don't Say Aloha* (1978)★★★.

Kirk

b. c.1964, USA. This teetotal, drug-free rapper, who recorded his debut album for East West Records in 1994, reminded many critics of the old school rappers of the Bronx, New York. Concentrating on the African-American experience as postulated by **Afrika Bambaataa** and others, his 1994 debut album, *Makin' Moves*, was marred by inferior production and a lack of musical dexterity. Many of his melancholy raps, which included subjects such as the difficulty of getting started in the rap business (though he was still only 19), were effective narratives reminiscent of the work of **Leaders Of The New School** and other rappers retreating to rap's 70s beginnings for inspiration.
● ALBUMS: *Makin' Moves* (East West 1994)★★.

Kirk, Andy

b. 28 May 1898, Newport, Kentucky, USA, d. 11 December 1992, New York, USA. Raised in Colorado, Kirk dabbled in music as a child, learning to play several instruments. He studied assiduously, one of his tutors being Wilberforce Whiteman, father of **Paul Whiteman**. Kirk played in several bands in and around Denver, in particular that led by George Morrison which played popular music of the day mixed with a smattering of light classics. It was a solid musical apprenticeship for the young man, but he was cautious about his career and all the while kept other regular employment. In 1927, he moved to Dallas, Texas, where he joined **Terrence Holder**'s band, the Dark Clouds Of Joy. By this time Kirk was mostly playing tuba, doubling on baritone and bass saxophones. In 1929, Holder, an erratic individual with his own ideas on how to run the band's finances, was persuaded to quit and Kirk took over leadership. The band's name underwent various minor changes but thereafter was mostly known as Andy Kirk And His **Clouds Of Joy**. At the instigation of **George E. Lee**, the band auditioned for and obtained an engagement at Kansas City's prestigious Pla-Mor Restaurant. During their stay at the Pla-Mor the band auditioned again, this time for a recording contract. When Marion Jackson, the regular pianist, could not make the date, Kirk brought in **Mary Lou Williams**. In addition to playing on the date, Williams also supplied several arrangements, some of which were of her own compositions. She so impressed the record company's executives, Jack Kapp and Dick Voynow, that they insisted she appear on all the band's record dates. Soon afterwards, Jackson tired of this implied slur, quit the band. Williams joined the band full-time and quickly became one of its most important and influential members. The band's personnel was relatively stable over the years and included many excellent musicians such as **Buddy Tate** (tenor saxophone), **Edgar Battle** (trumpet), **Claude Williams** (violin), Ben Thigpen (drums), Pha Terrell (vocals) and Mary Lou's husband, John Williams (alto saxophone). A subtly swinging band, epitomizing the best of the more commercial end of the **Kansas City Jazz** sound, the Clouds Of Joy enjoyed several years of success. There were difficult moments, not least in early 1931 when the band had to take engagements and record dates under the nominal leadership of Blanche Calloway, but they survived into the late 40s. The size of the band, usually ranging between 11-13 pieces, meant that it was smaller than the average swing era big band and this, allied to Mary Lou Williams's skilful charts, gave it an enviable cohesion. Mary Lou Williams left in 1942 to develop her remarkable career. Williams apart, the band's outstanding soloist was tenor saxophonist Dick Wilson. A light-toned player with a sound, if not style, akin to that of **Lester Young**, he contributed many memorable moments to the band's recorded output. Wilson's death, in 1941 at the age of 30, was a great loss. For all the enormous talents of Williams and Wilson as far as the non-jazz public was concerned, the band's greatest asset for many years was singer Pha Terrell. He had a light tenor voice with little or no jazz feeling but had several hit records, of which the best known was 'Until The Real Thing Comes Along'. One of the few **territory bands** to gain a national reputation, the Clouds Of Joy folded in 1948. Thereafter, Kirk played only occasionally but eventually left of music to take up hotel management. In the 60s, he was occasionally active in music, then dabbled in real estate. In the 80s he took a further job with the local New York American Federation of Musicians, where he continued to put in appearances until long after retirement age.

● COMPILATIONS: *Walking And Swinging (1936-42)* (Affinity 1983)★★★★, *Andy's Jive (1944-45)* (Swing House 1984)★★★, *Cloudy (1929)* (Hep Jazz 1984)★★★, *All Out For Hicksville (1931)* (Hep Jazz 1988)★★★, with Mary Lou Williams *Mary's Idea* (GRP 1993), *Mellow Bit Of Rhythm* (RCA 1993)★★★, *Kansas City Bounce* 1936-1940 recordings (Black And Blue 1993).

● FURTHER READING: *Twenty Years On Wheels*, Andy Kirk as told to Amy Lee.

Kirk, Eddie

b. Edward Merle Kirk, 21 March 1919, on a ranch near Greeley, Colorado. The ranch hands taught him cowboy songs and he was singing and tap-dancing with a small band at the age of nine. In 1934, he relocated to California where, for a time, he worked with the Beverly Hill Billies. He was National Yodelling Champion in 1935 and 1936 and between 1933 and 1937, he earned a reputation as an amateur boxer. He worked in films and made personal appearances until 1943, when he joined the navy. He returned to California in 1945, appearing in films, and directed the Hollywood Barn Dance choir. In the late 40s, he appeared on **Gene Autry**'s radio show and also on the *Town Hall Party* in Compton. He made his recording debut for Capitol in 1947 and in 1948/9, he registered Top 10 country hits with 'The Gods Were Angry With Me' (which included a recitation by **Tex Ritter**) and 'Candy Kisses'. He later developed a fondness for flying.

Kirk, Mary

b. Mary Colston, *c*.1900, Denver, Colorado, USA. As a child at school, Kirk had the good fortune to grow up in a region which benefited from a progressive outlook on musical education. Head of the schools' music department was Wilberforce Whiteman, father of **Paul Whiteman**, through whose hands passed many future professional musicians. Kirk had begun playing piano at home, copying lessons being given to her sister until she excelled and was actively encouraged by her parents. At school she extended her studies and also took private lessons. Taught classical music and the popular music of the early years of the twentieth century, her repertoire was extremely wide. In the early 20s she was hired as one of two pianists in a show band led by George Morrison which was extremely popular in the mid-western states. Another member of the band was **Andy Kirk** who greatly admired her playing. The couple were married in 1925 and for a time both played in bands directed by Morrison until Kirk moved on, eventually to lead his own band. His wife played less after this time, instead bringing up a child. Her profes-

sional career was over although she continued to take an interest in music and would still play either privately or in church.

Kirk, Rahsaan Roland

b. 7 August 1936, Columbus, Ohio, USA, d. 5 December 1977. Originally named 'Ronald', Kirk changed it to 'Roland' and added 'Rahsaan' after a dream visitation by spirits who 'told him to'. Blinded soon after his birth, Kirk became one of the most prodigious multi-instrumentalists to work in jazz, with a career that spanned R&B, bop and the 'New Thing' jazz style. According to Joe Goldberg's sleevenotes for *Kirk's Works* (1961), Kirk took up trumpet at the age of nine after hearing the bugle boy at a summer camp where his parents acted as counsellors. He played trumpet in the school band, but a doctor advised against the strain trumpet-playing imposes on the eyes. At the Ohio State School for the Blind, he took up saxophone and clarinet from 1948. By 1951 he was well-known as a player and was leading his own dance band in the locality. Kirk's ability to play three instruments simultaneously gained him notoriety. Looking through the 'scraps' in the basement of a music store, Kirk found two horns believed to have been put together from different instruments, but which possibly dated from late 19th century Spanish military bands. The manzello was basically an alto sax with a 'large, fat, ungainly' bell. The strich resembled 'a larger, more cumbersome soprano'. He found a method of playing both, plus his tenor, producing a wild, untempered 'ethnic' sound ideal for late-60s radical jazz. He also soloed on all three separately and added flute, siren and clavietta (similar to the melodica used by **Augustus Pablo** and the **Gang Of Four**) to his armoury. With all three horns strung around his neck, and sporting dark glasses and a battered top hat, Kirk made quite a spectacle. The real point was that, although he loved to dally with simple R&B and ballads, he could unleash break-neck solos that sounded like a bridge between bebop dexterity and *avant garde* 'outness'. His debut for a properly distributed label - recorded for Cadet Records in Chicago in June 1960 at the behest of **Ramsey Lewis** - provoked controversy, some deriding the three-horn-trick as a gimmick, others applauding the fire of his playing. In 1961, he joined the **Charles Mingus** Workshop for four months, toured California and played on *Oh Yeah!*. He also played the Essen Jazz Festival in Germany. In 1963, he began the first of several historic residencies at **Ronnie Scott**'s club in London. Despite later guest recordings with **Jaki Byard** (who had played on his *Rip Rig & Panic*) and Mingus (at the 1974 Carnegie Hall concert), Kirk's main focus of activity was his own group, the Vibration Society, with whom he toured the world until he suffered his first stroke in November 1975, which paralysed his right side. With characteristic single-mindedness, he taught himself to play with his left hand only and started touring again. A second stroke in 1977 caused his death. Long before the 80s 'consolidation' period for jazz, Kirk presented a music fully cognizant of black American music, from **Jelly Roll Morton** and **Louis Armstrong** on through **Duke Ellington** and **John Coltrane**; he also paid tribute to the gospel and soul heritage, notably on *Blacknuss*, which featured songs by **Marvin Gaye**, **Smokey Robinson** and **Bill Withers**. Several of his tunes - 'The Inflated Tear', 'Bright Moments', 'Let Me Shake Your Tree', 'No Tonic Pres' - have become jazz standards. His recorded legacy is uneven, but it contains some of the most fiery and exciting music to be heard.

● ALBUMS: *Triple Threat* (King 1956)★★★, with Booker Ervin *Soulful Saxes* (Affinity 1957)★★★, *Introducing Roland Kirk* (Argo 1960)★★★, with Jack McDuff *Kirk's Work* (Prestige 1961)★★★★, *We Free Kings* (Emarcy 1962)★★★★, *Domino* (Mercury 1962)★★★, *Roland Kirk In Copenhagen* (Mercury 1963)★★★, *Meets the Benny Golson Orchestra* (Mercury 1963)★★★, *Reeds And Deeds* (Mercury 1963)★★★, *Gifts & Messages* (Mercury 1964)★★★, *I Talk To The Spirits* (Limelight 1964)★★★, *Rip Rig & Panic* (Limelight 1965)★★★★, *Now Please Don't You Cry, Beautiful Edith* (Verve 1967)★★★, *Funk Underneath* (Prestige 1967)★★★, *Here Comes The Whistle Man* (Atlantic 1967)★★★, *The Inflated Tear* (Atlantic 1968)★★★★, *The Case Of The Three Sided Dream In Audio Colour* (Atlantic 1969)★★★, *Left And Right* (Atlantic 1969)★★★, *Volunteered Slavery* (Atlantic 1969)★★★★, *Rahsaan, Rahsaan* (1970)★★★, *Roller Coaster* (Bandstand 1971)★★★, *Blacknuss* (Rhino 1972)★★★★, *Bright Moments* (Rhino 1973)★★★, *The Return Of The 5000 lb Man* (Atlantic 1975)★★★, *Other Folks' Music* (1976)★★★, *Boogie-Woogie String Along For Real* (1977)★★★, *Prepare To Deal With A Miracle* (Atlantic 1978)★★★, *Vibration Society* (Stash 1987)★★★, *Paris 1976* (1990), *Soul Station* (Affinity 1993)★★★.

● COMPILATIONS: *The Art Of Rahsaan Roland Kirk (1966-71)* (1973)★★★★, *The Man Who Cried Fire (60s/70s)* (Virgin 1990)★★★★, *Complete Mercury Recordings* (Mercury 1991)★★★★, *Rahsaan* 11-CD box set (Mercury 1992)★★★★.

Kirk, Red

b. 24 May 1925, Knoxville, Tennessee, USA. Kirk started playing steel guitar at seven but changed to ordinary guitar and began singing at 10. He served in the US Army during World War II and on discharge played on WNOX Knoxville's *Mid Day Merry-Go-Round* and *Tennessee Barn Dance*. He spent three years as a member of **Archie Campbell**'s touring show but later his fine vocals, reminiscent of **Eddy Arnold**, saw him tour and work radio and television at numerous venues including Dayton, Lexington and Louisville. He also played on WLS *National Barn Dance* in Chicago, the *Big "D" Jamboree* in Dallas and the *Louisiana Hayride* in Shreveport and made guest appearances on the *Grand Ole Opry* in Nashville. He made his first recordings for **Mercury** in 1949, on some being accompanied by noted session musicians that included **Jerry Byrd** (steel guitar) and **Tommy Jackson** (fiddle). He later recorded for **ABC** Paramount, Starday, Dewitt and

Great. A compilation of **Mercury** recordings were reissued on an album by a German label in 1988.

● COMPILATIONS: *The Voice Of Country* (Cattle 1988)★★★.

Kirk, Richard H.

Founding member of **Cabaret Voltaire** whose releases under his own name in the 90s have seen him increasingly accommodated by the rave generation. Kirk released his first solo set in 1981, following it with the double album, *Time High Fiction* two years later. His taste for dance music was probably most obviously previewed by the release of Cabaret Voltaire's 'James Brown', before further solo work in 1986 with *Black Jesus Voice*, a mini-album, and *Ugly Spirit*. This was followed a year later by a collaborative project, *Hoodoo Talk*, with the **Box**'s Peter Hope. Further expansions in Cabaret Voltaire's dance sound were refined by the 1989 single 'Hypnotised', after the duo had visited Chicago. A year later Kirk released 'Test One', an excellent example of the acid house style, under the guise of Sweet Exorcist. It launched what became known as the 'bleep' sound, which was widely imitated and dominated clubs for almost a year. A second hugely popular 12-inch arrived with 'Clonk'. Kirk currently enjoys his own Western Works studio in Sheffield, and looks to be one of the true survivors of the late 70s industrial scene centred in that town.

● ALBUMS: *Disposable Half Truths* (Rough Trade 1981)★★★, *Time High Fiction* (Rough Trade 1983)★★★★, *Black Jesus Voice* (Rough Trade 1986)★★★, *Ugly Spirit* (Rough Trade 1986)★★★, with Peter Hope *Hoodoo Talk* (Native 1987)★★, as Sweet Exorcist *Clonk's Coming* (Warp 1991)★★★, *Virtual State* (Warp 1994)★★★, *The Number Of Magic* (Warp 1995)★★★.

Kirkland, Eddie

b. 16 August 1928, Kingston, Jamaica, West Indies. The career of guitarist Eddie Kirkland spans 40 years and a variety of musical styles. Soon after his birth the family relocated to the southern states of America and at the age of 15 he took a day job at the Ford Motor Company in Detroit. He met **John Lee Hooker** and became his regular accompanist both on the club circuit and on record, proving to be one of the few who could follow Hooker's erratic style. Kirkland's first recordings were made in 1952 and throughout the decade he recorded for RPM, King, Cobra, Fortune and Lupine. In 1961 he made his first deviation from 'down-home' blues when he recorded with **King Curtis** and **Oliver Nelson** for Prestige. In the mid-60s he moved to Macon, Georgia, where he turned to soul music, eventually signing to **Otis Redding**'s enterprise Volt, in 1965. Redding used Kirkland in his touring band, but Kirkland's role as a soul artist was never more than minor. In the 70s, he returned to his blues roots, recording for Pete Lowery's Trix label, both solo and with small bands, and has since maintained a heavy touring schedule at home and in Europe.

● ALBUMS: *The Devil And Other Blues Demons* (Trix 1972)★★★, *Pickin' Up The Pieces* (GRP 1981)★★★, *The Way It Was* (Red Lightnin' 1983)★★★, *Have Mercy* (Pulsar 1993)★★★, *All Around The World* (Deluge 1993)★★★, *Some Like It Raw* (Deluge 1994)★★★, *Where You Get Your Sugar?* (Deluge 1995)★★★, *Front And Center* (Trix 1995)★★★.

Kirkland, Kenny

b. 28 September 1957, New York City, New York, USA. After graduating from the Manhattan School of Music in 1977, Kirkland toured with **Michal Urbaniak**, and joined **Miroslav Vitous** in 1979. But it was with **Wynton Marsalis** (1981-85) that he gained his reputation as a skilful **Herbie Hancock**-influenced pianist, and he has since been in demand from a host of band-leaders including **Branford Marsalis** and **Chico Freeman**. His work with **Sting**, and the resulting 1985 *The Dream Of The Blue Turtles*, helped widen Kirkland's audience.
● ALBUMS: with Miroslav Vitous *Miroslav Vitous Group* (1980)★★★★, with Wynton Marsalis *Black Codes From The Underground* (1985)★★★, *Kenny Kirkland* (GRP 1991)★★★.

Kirkland, Leroy

b. 10 February 1906, South Carolina, USA, d. 6 April 1988, New York, USA. Raised in Jacksonville, Florida, Kirkland was a butcher before he moved to New York in 1942. He became an arranger whose career spanned the eras of big band jazz, R&B, rock 'n' roll and soul. Kirkland played guitar in southern jazz bands in the 20s and during the 30s worked as arranger and songwriter for **Erskine Hawkins**. He joined **Tommy** and **Jimmy Dorsey** in the 40s and later in that decade began arranging music at Savoy Records in New York. He continued to arrange R&B artists for **OKeh Records**, **Mercury Records** and other companies, working with such groups as the **Five Satins**, the Ravens and the **Everly Brothers**. He managed **Ruby And The Romantics** during the 60s, and in the last few years of his life concentrated on gospel music.

Kirkpatrick, Anne

b. 4 July 1952, Sydney, Australia. **Slim Dusty**, that is David Kirkpatrick, is Australia's best-loved country performer and his wife, Joy McKean, is the 'Queen of Aussie Cowgirls'. Their daughter, Anne Kirkpatrick, allegedly gave her first performance at the age of two when she strayed onto the stage in her nightdress while her father was singing and subsequently stole the show. She also presented her father with a gold disc for 'A Pub With No Beer'. By the time she was 12, she was working regularly with the Slim Dusty Show and doing her studying by correspondence courses. She sang and played bass on many of his recordings and her first solo album was released while she was at university. After graduating, she formed the Anne Kirkpatrick Band and built up a reputation in Sydney. The first phase of her career is neatly summarized in the aptly titled *Annie's Songs*, and she can also be heard to good advantage on

the live double album *Slim Dusty - The Entertainer*. After taking time off to raise a family, she remodelled herself as a contemporary country music performer. She often records US country hits ('Sight For Sore Eyes', 'A Bottle Of Wine And Patsy Cline') but is also a fine songwriter in her own right. She has won several awards in Australia but so far she has not toured Europe or the USA.
● ALBUMS: *Shoot The Moon* (EMI 1979)★★, *Merry Go Round Of Love* (Nulla 1986)★★★★, *Come Back Again* (1988)★★★, with Slim Dusty *Two Singers, One Song* (EMI 1990)★★★, *Out Of The Blue* (ABC 1992)★★★, *The Game Of Love* (ABC 1994)★★★, *Live - 21st Anniversary Concert* (ABC 1995)★★. All the record labels are Australian.

Kirkpatrick, Don

b. 17 June 1905, Charlotte, North Carolina, USA, d. 13 May 1956. After playing piano with bands in and around Baltimore, Kirkpatrick journeyed to New York in 1926 and the following year began a long association with **Chick Webb**. He played piano in Webb's band and also wrote arrangements during its early years. In the early 30s he worked with **Don Redman** and also played piano in bands led by **Henry 'Red' Allen** and **Coleman Hawkins**. During these and succeeding years Kirkpatrick was very active as a freelance arranger, writing charts for Webb, **Count Basie**, **Benny Goodman**, **Alvino Rey** and **'Cootie' Williams**. In the mid-40s he was once again to be found playing piano, generally working in amongst traditional musicians, including **Mezz Mezzrow** and **Bunk Johnson**, although stylistically he was more attuned to swing. In the 50s, he played with **Sidney Bechet** and **Wilbur De Paris**, and also worked as a solo artist up to his death in 1956.
● COMPILATIONS: *The Chronological Chick Webb And His Orchestra* (1929-34)★★★★, *The Fabulous Sidney Bechet And His Hot Six With Sidney De Paris* (1951)★★★★, *Wilbur De Paris And His Rampart Street Paraders* (1952)★★★.

Kirkpatrick, John

b. 8 August 1947, Chiswick, London, England. Kirkpatrick is often held to be the master player of the accordion, melodeon and the concertina. Having spent some time in the early **Steeleye Span** line-up, he went on to be involved with folk-rock recordings of the 70s. He has toured and recorded with a veritable who's who of the folk-rock establishment, in particular **Ashley Hutchings**, **Richard Thompson** and **Martin Carthy**. Kirkpatrick also performed with **Brass Monkey**. *A Really High Class Band* included 'The Cherry Tree Carol' and Sir John Betjeman's 'A Shropshire Lad'. Kirkpatrick regularly records and performs with Sue Harris (b. 17 May 1949, Coventry, Warwickshire, England), who is known for her hammer dulcimer and oboe playing. They first started working together in 1971. Harris was, for a time, a member of the English Country Blues Band, and has contributed incidental music for television, theatre and radio, including *The Canterbury Tales* on BBC Radio 4. Kirkpatrick, Harris and Carthy were in one of the early line-ups of the **Albion Band**. Kirkpatrick also played on *Night Owl* by **Gerry Rafferty** in 1979, and, in 1988, on **Pere Ubu**'s *The Tenement Year*. By complete contrast, and highlighting Kirkpatrick's wide diversity, he also formed the Shropshire Bedlams Morris Dance team. In recent years, Kirkpatrick has toured as a trio with the two fine melodeon players Riccardo Tesi from Italy and Marc Perrone from France. Harris and Kirkpatrick also performed and recorded with Umps And Dumps, which included Derek Pearce (percussion), Tufty Swift (melodeon) and Alan Harris (banjo). Other commitments, such as performing with the Richard Thompson Band and his involvement with the National Theatre production of *Lark Rise To Candleford* have reduced Kirkpatrick's solo touring. In 1991, he presented a six-week radio series for the BBC, *Squeezing Around The World*, which featured many of the world's leading squeezebox players. Harris and Kirkpatrick have now started working, as a trio with Dave Whetstone (melodeon/guitar).

● ALBUMS: *Jump At The Sun* (1972)★★★, with Sue Harris *The Rose Of Britain's Isle* (1974)★★★, with Ashley Hutchings *The Compleat Dancing Master* (1974)★★★★, with Harris *Among The Many Attractions At The Show Will Be A Really High Class Band* (1976)★★★, *Plain Capers* (1976)★★, with Harris *Shreds And Patches* (1977)★★, *Going Spare* (1978)★★★, with Harris *Facing The Music* (1980)★★★, with Umps And Dumps *The Moon's In A Fit* (1980)★★★, *Three In A Row - The English Melodeon* (1984)★★★, *Blue Balloon* (1987)★★★, *Sheepskins* (1988)★★★, with Harris *Stolen Ground* (1989)★★★, with Kepa Junkera, Ricardo Tesi *Trans-Diatonique* (1993)★★★, *Earthling* (Music & Words 1994)★★, *Force Of Habit* (Fledg'ling 1996)★★★. Solo: Sue Harris *Hammers And Tongues* (1978)★★★.

Kirkwood, Pat

b. 24 February 1921, Manchester, England. An actress and singer; one of the premier leading ladies of 40s and 50s West End musicals, British films, and Christmas pantomimes. Her frequent appearances in the latter medium earned her the title of 'the greatest principal boy of the Century', and the critic Kenneth Tynan called her legs 'the eighth wonder of the world'. She started her career at the age of 14 at the Salford Hippodrome, and a year later appeared in pantomime in Cardiff. When she was 16 she made her West End debut as Dandini in **Cinderella** at London's Princes' Theatre. In 1939 at the age of only 18, Pat Kirkwood headlined the revue *Black Velvet* at the London Hippodrome and sang a sizzling version of 'My Heart Belongs To Daddy', a song that is forever identified with her. Further West End successes followed, including *Top Of The World* (1940), *Lady Behave* (1941), *Let's Face It!* (1942), *Starlight Roof* (1947), *Ace Of Clubs* (1950) (in which she introduced **Noël Coward**'s witty song 'Chase Me Charlie'), *Fancy Free* (1951), **Wonderful Town** (1955), and *Chrysanthemum* (1956). It was while she appearing in *Starlight Roof* (in which

the 12-years-old **Julie Andrews** made her West End debut) that Kirkwood was introduced to Prince Philip, consort of Queen Elizabeth, by her boyfriend, the fashion photographer Baron. Rumours that they had an affair - always strenuously denied by the actress - continue to surface even in the 90s. Her film career began in 1938 with *Save A Little Sunshine*, and continued with *Me And My Pal* (1939), **Band Waggon** (with Arthur Askey and Richard Murdoch) (1939), *Come On George* (with **George Formby**) (1939), *Flight From Folly* (1944), *No Leave, No Love* (made in America with Van Johnson) (1946), *Once A Sinner* (1950), *Stars In Your Eyes* (1956), and *After The Ball* (1957). Miss Kirkwood also appeared in several Royal Command Performances, in cabaret, and on radio and television. On the small screen during the 50s she portrayed the renowned musical hall performers Marie Loyd in *All Our Yesterdays* and *Our Marie*; and Vesta Tilley in *The Great Little Tilley*. Two years after her second husband wealthy Greek-Russian ship-owner Spiro de Spero died in 1954, she married the actor-broadcaster-songwriter ('Maybe It's Because I'm A Londoner', 'I'm Going To Get Lit Up') Hubert Gregg. They were divorced in 1976, and Kirkwood went to live in Portugal for four years where she met the solicitor Peter Knight who subsequently became her fourth husband. They retired to Yorkshire, where Pat Kirkwood consistently turned down offers to return to the stage. Even **Cameron Mackintosh** was unable to tempt her with the prime role of Carlotta Campion in the 1987 London production of **Follies**. Eventually, however, she did emerge into the spotlight again with her own show, *Glamorous Nights Of Music*, which opened to excellent reviews at the Wimbledon Theatre on the outskirts of London in April 1993. In the following year, she stole the show when making a rare guest appearance in a revue which celebrated the music and lyrics of **Cole Porter** and Noël Coward entitled *Let's Do It!*, which was presented at Chichester and beyond.

Kirshner, Don

b. 17 April 1934, The Bronx, New York, USA. An aspiring songwriter while still in his teens, Kirshner gained early experience penning several naive, and unsuccessful, tracks for **Bobby Darin**. In an effort to subsidize their careers, the duo composed advertising jingles, one of which was sung by **Connie Francis**, whom Kirshner later managed. In 1958, he founded Aldon Music with publisher Al Nevins, having convinced the latter of the potential of the burgeoning teen market. The partnership attracted several stellar songwriting teams, including **Neil Sedaka** and Howard Greenfield, **Gerry Goffin** and **Carole King**, and **Barry Mann** and **Cynthia Weil**, who composed hits for the **Shirelles**, **Bobby Vee** and the **Drifters**. Kirshner then established Dimension Records as an outlet for his proteges, scored major successes with **Little Eva** ('The Loco-Motion'), the **Cookies** ('Chains') and Carole King ('It Might As Well Rain Until September') which was issued on the short-lived Companion subsidiary. In 1963, the Aldon empire was sold to Screen-Gems/**Columbia**, of which Kirshner later rose to president. Work for the in-house Colpix label was artistically less satisfying, but established the groundwork for the executive's greatest coup, the **Monkees**. His ambitious plan to marry a recording group with a weekly television series was initially a great success, fuelled by material provided by the entrepreneur's staff songwriters, notably **Boyce And Hart**. However, disputes with the band over royalties, material and the right to perform on record inspired a legal wrangle which ended with Kirshner's departure from the Screen-Gems board. In riposte, he embarked on a similar project, the **Archies**, but with cartoon characters, rather than temperamental musicians, promoting the songs on the attendant series. New composers, including Andy Kim and **Ron Dante**, provided a succession of hit songs, including the multi-million selling 'Sugar Sugar'. In 1972, Kirshner began an association with ABC-Television which in turn inspired *Don Kirshner's Rock Concert*, a widely syndicated weekly show which became an integral part of that decade's music presentation. This astute controller successfully guided the career of **Kansas** under the aegis of his Kirshner record label and has also maintained considerable publishing interests.

Kirwan, Dominic

b. Omagh, County Tyrone, Northern Ireland. Kirwan's mother was a talented pianist who played in local theatres, but his first connections with the stage came when, at the age of five, he joined a school to learn Irish dancing. He toured as a dancer appearing at festivals in the UK and at the age of 12, as the Ulster minor champion, he appeared at a major Norwegian festival. He began singing semi-professionally in the late 70s and worked with several groups while supporting himself through his daytime occupation as a car salesman. He formed his own band in 1988 and, after winning two major talent competitions, recorded his debut album. These recordings proved popular enough to attract the attention of Ritz Records and he subsequently signed to that label. His career received a boost in 1990, when he toured the UK with **Charley Pride**. This led to appearances as a guest on a UK tour by **Tammy Wynette**. His music ranges from modern easy listening to country standards, as well as the expected Irish ballads such as 'My Wild Irish Rose'. In 1993, a duet, 'I'll Walk Beside You', with fellow Ritz artist Tracey Elsdon, proved very popular. In his stage act, Kirwan incorporates a routine that shows that he can still compete with the best when it comes to Irish dancing.

● ALBUMS: *The Green Fields Of Ireland* (Music Box 1988)★★, *Try A Little Kindness* (Ritz 1989)★★★ *Love Without End* (Ritz 1990)★★★ *Evergreen* (Ritz 1991)★★★★, *Today* (Ritz 1993), *Irish Favourites* (Ritz 1994)★★★★, *On The Way To A Dream* (Ritz 1995)★★★.

● VIDEOS: *Live In Concert* (Ritz 1990), *Christmas Party* (1994).

Kismet (film musical)

This opulent but rather unsatisfying adaptation of the hit Broadway musical reached the screen in 1955, courtesy of **Arthur Freed**'s renowned MGM production unit. Although the show's librettists, Charles Lederer and Luther Davis, were entrusted with the screenplay, much of the magic in this Arabian Nights saga was somehow lost in the transfer. For some strange reason, **Alfred Drake**, who had enjoyed such a triumph in the stage production, was replaced by **Howard Keel**. He plays the public poet-turned-beggar Hajj, who lives on the streets of old Baghdad, and embarks on a hectic day-long adventure during which his daughter (Ann Blyth) is married to the young Caliph (**Vic Damone**), while he elopes with the lovely Lalume (**Dolores Gray**) after getting rid of her husband, the evil Wazir (Sebastian Cabot). **Robert Wright** and **George Forrest**'s majestic score was based on themes by Alexander Borodin, and there were several memorable songs in the score, including 'Baubles, Bangles, And Beads', 'The Olive Tree', 'Stranger In Paradise', 'And This Is My Beloved', 'Not Since Ninevah', 'Fate', 'Bored', 'Sands Of Time', 'Night Of My Nights', 'Rhymes Have I' and 'Gesticulate'. While perhaps regretting the absence of Drake (he only ever made one film), there is no doubt that Keel was in fine voice and he made an adequate substitute. Also taking part were Jay C. Flippen, Monty Woolley, Jack Elam, Ted De Corsia and Aaron Spelling. Jack Cole was the choreographer, and the film was directed by **Vincente Minnelli**. Whatever its faults, the film did at least look beautiful, owing in no small part to the Eastman Color and Cinemascope photography of Joseph Ruttenberg. The source of *Kismet* - the 1911 play by Edward Knoblock - has also been adapted into three other, non-musical films, in 1920, 1930 and 1944.

Kismet (stage musical)

This was by no means the first time **George Forrest** and **Robert Wright** had raided the world of classical music in an effort to devise a hit Broadway musical. They had 'borrowed' elements of Grieg for their highly successful *Song Of Norway* (1944), and for *Kismet* they turned to the work of Alexander Borodin. Forrest and Wright adapted the music and wrote the lyrics, and the book was by Charles Lederer and Luther Davis. When *Kismet* opened at the Ziegfeld Theatre in New York on 3 December 1953, it was met with a measure of indifference from the critics. However, by a fortuitous quirk of fate, there was a newspaper strike at the time and before the reviews were printed, the show had already become a success. Audiences liked this lavish production, and *Kismet*, with its Arabian Nights setting, ran for 583 performances. Several of the songs became popular, including 'Stranger In Paradise', 'Baubles, Bangles And Beads' and 'And This Is My Beloved', but there were other attractive numbers too, such as 'Not Since Nineveh', 'Rhymes Have I', 'Fate', 'Gesticulate', 'The Olive Tree', 'He's In Love', 'Sands Of Time' and 'Night

Of My Nights'. Original cast members included **Alfred Drake**, Richard Kiley and Doretta Morrow. The show won **Tony Awards** for best musical, actor (Drake) and musical conductor (Louis Adrian). Drake and Morrow recreated their roles for the 1955 London production which ran for 648 performances. In the same year, a film version was released starring **Howard Keel**, Ann Blyth, **Dolores Gray** and **Vic Damone**. A 1978 version of the show, retitled *Timbuktu*, featured an all-black cast.

Kiss

Following the demise of Wicked Lester, Kiss was formed in 1972 by Paul Stanley (b. Paul Eisen, 20 January 1950, Queens, New York, USA; rhythm guitar, vocals) and **Gene Simmons** (b. Chaim Witz, 25 August 1949, Haifa, Israel; bass, vocals), who went on to recruit **Peter Criss** (b. Peter Crisscoula, 27 December 1947, Brooklyn, New York, USA; drums, vocals) and **Ace Frehley** (b. Paul Frehley, 22 April 1951, Bronx, New York, USA; lead guitar, vocals). At their second show at the Hotel Diplomat, Manhattan, in 1973, Flipside producer Bill Aucoin offered the band a management contract, and within two weeks they were signed to Neil Bogart's recently established Casablanca Records. In just over a year, Kiss had released their first three albums with a modicum of success. In the summer of 1975 their fortunes changed with the release of *Alive*, which spawned their first US hit single, 'Rock 'N' Roll All Nite'. The appeal of Kiss has always been based on their live shows: the garish greasepaint make-up, outrageous costumes and pyrotechnic stage effects, along with their hard-rocking anthems, combined to create what was billed as 'The Greatest Rock 'n' Roll Show On Earth'. Their live reputation engendered a dramatic upsurge in record sales, and *Alive* became their first certified platinum album in the USA. *Destroyer* proved just as successful, and also gave them their first US Top 10 single, earning Peter Criss a major songwriting award for the uncharacteristic ballad, 'Beth'. Subsequent releases, *Rock And Roll Over*, *Love Gun* and *Alive II*, each certified platinum, confirmed the arrival of Kiss as major recording artists. By 1977 Kiss had topped the prestigious Gallup poll as the most popular act in the USA. They had become a marketing dream: Kiss merchandise included make-up kits, masks, board games, and pinball machines. *Marvel Comics* produced two super-hero cartoon books, and a full-length science-fiction film, *Kiss Meet The Phantom Of The Park*, was even produced. The ranks of their fan club, the Kiss Army, had swollen to a six-figure number. In 1978 all four group members each produced solo albums released on the same day, a feat never before envisaged, let alone matched. At the time, this represented the biggest shipment of albums from one 'unit' to record stores in the history of recorded music. The albums enjoyed varying degrees of success; Ace Frehley's record came out on top and included the US hit single, 'New York Groove'. Gene Simmons, whose album featured an impressive line-up of guests including **Cher**, **Donna Summer**, **Bob Seger** and **Janis Ian**, had a hit single in the UK with 'Radioactive', which reached number 41 in 1978. After the release of *Dynasty* in 1979, which featured the worldwide hit single, 'I Was Made For Lovin' You', cracks appeared in the ranks. Peter Criss left to be replaced by session player Anton Fig, who had previously appeared on Frehley's solo album. Fig played drums on the 1980 release *Unmasked* until a permanent replacement was found in the form of New Yorker Eric Carr (b. 12 July 1950, d. 24 November 1991), who made his first appearance during the world tour of 1980. A fuller introduction came on *Music From The Elder*, an album that represented a radical departure from traditional Kiss music and included several ballads, an orchestra and a choir. It was a brave attempt to break new ground but failed to capture the imagination of the record-buying public. Frehley, increasingly disenchanted with the musical direction of the band, finally left in 1983. The two albums prior to his departure had featured outside musicians. Bruce Kulick, who had contributed to the studio side of *Alive II* and played on Stanley's solo album, supplied the lead work to the four previously unreleased tracks on the *Killers* compilation of 1982, and Vincent Cusano (later to become **Vinnie Vincent**) was responsible for lead guitar on the 1982 release, *Creatures Of The Night*. By 1983 the popularity of the band was waning and drastic measures were called for. The legendary make-up that had concealed their true identities for almost 10 years was removed on **MTV** in the USA. Vinnie Vincent made his first official appearance on *Lick It Up*, an album that provided Kiss with their first Top 10 hit in the UK. The resurgence of the band continued with *Animalize*. Vincent had been replaced by Mark St. John (b. Mark Norton), a seasoned session player and guitar tutor. His association with the band was short-lived, however, as he was struck down by Reiters Syndrome. Bruce Kulick, the brother of long-time Kiss cohort Bob, was enlisted as a temporary replacement on the 1984 European Tour, and subsequently became a permanent member when it became apparent that St. John would not be able to continue as a band member. Further commercial success was achieved with *Asylum* and *Crazy Nights*, the latter featuring their biggest UK hit single, 'Crazy, Crazy Nights', which peaked at number 4 in 1987 and was followed by two more Top 40 hit singles, 'Reason To Live' and 'Turn On The Night'. *Hot In The Shade* succeeded their third compilation album, *Smashes, Thrashes And Hits*, and included their highest-charting hit single in the USA, 'Forever', which reached number 4 in 1990. Work on a new Kiss album with producer Bob Ezrin was delayed following Eric Carr's illness due to complications from cancer. He died on 24 November 1991, in New York, at the age of 41. Despite this setback, Kiss contributed a cover version of **Argent**'s classic 'God Gave Rock 'N' Roll To You' to the soundtrack of the film *Bill And Ted's Bogus Journey*, and brought in replacement drummer Eric Singer (ex-**Black Sabbath**; **Badlands**). 1994, meanwhile, brought the *Kiss My Ass* tribute album, with contributions from **Lenny Kravitz**, **Stevie Wonder**, **Garth Brooks**, **Lemonheads**, **Faith No More**, **Dinosaur Jr**, **Rage Against The Machine** and others. The interest in *Kiss My Ass* led to a historic reunion for *MTV Unplugged*. A stable unit with Bruce Kulick (guitar) and Eric Singer (drums), together with Simmons and Stanley, appeared to be on the cards, but Frehley and Criss returned for a reunion tour. So successful was the tour that Kulick and Singer were naturally somewhat annoyed and both quit. Their irritation was further exacerbated by the fact that a new studio album, *Carnival Of Souls*, featured both of them. In 1997 Vincent sued the band, alleging that they owed him royalties. With a history spanning three decades, Kiss's impact on the consciousness of a generation of music fans, particularly in the USA, remains enormous.

● ALBUMS: *Kiss* (Casablanca 1974)★★★, *Hotter Than Hell* (Casablanca 1974)★★, *Dressed To Kill* (Casablanca 1975)★★★, *Alive* (Casablanca 1975)★★★, *Destroyer* (Casablanca 1976)★★★★, *Rock And Roll Over* (Casablanca 1976)★★, *Love Gun* (Casablanca 1977)★★★, *Alive II* (Casablanca 1977)★★★, *Dynasty* (Casablanca 1979)★★, *Unmasked* (Casablanca 1980)★★, *Music From The Elder* (Casablanca 1981)★★, *Creatures Of The Night* (Casablanca 1982)★★, *Lick It Up* (Vertigo 1983)★★, *Animalize* (Vertigo 1984)★★, *Asylum* (Vertigo 1985)★★, *Crazy Nights* (Vertigo 1987)★★, *Hot In The Shade* (Vertigo 1989)★★, *Revenge* (Mercury 1992)★★★, *Alive III* (Mercury 1993)★★, *MTV Unplugged* (Mercury 1996)★★★, *Carnival Of Souls The Final Sessions* (Mercury 1997)★★.

● COMPILATIONS: *The Originals* (Casablanca 1976)★★★, *Double Platinum* (Casablanca 1978)★★★, *Killers* (Casablanca 1982)★★★, *Smashes, Thrashes And Hits* (Vertigo 1988)★★★, *Revenge* (Mercury 1992)★★, *You Wanted The Best, You Got The Best* (Mercury 1996)★★★★, *Greatest Kiss* (Mercury 1996)★★★.

● VIDEOS: *Animalize* (Embassy Home Video 1986), *The Phantom Of The Park* (IVS 1987), *Exposed* (PolyGram 1987), *Crazy Crazy Nights* (Channel 5 1988), *Age Of Chance* (Virgin Vision 1988), *X-Treme Close Up* (1992), *Konfidential* (1993), *Kiss My A*** (PolyGram 1994), *Unplugged* (PolyGram 1996).

● FURTHER READING: *Kiss*, Robert Duncan. *Still On Fire*, Dave Thomas. *Kiss: The Greatest Rock Show On Earth*, John Swenson. *Kiss: The Real Story Authorized*, Peggy Tomarkin. *Kiss Live*, Mick St. Michael. *Black Diamond: The Unauthorised Biography Of Kiss*, Dale Sherman. *Kiss And Sell: The Making Of A Supergroup*, CK Lendt.

Kiss Me Kate (film musical)

This film had most of the elements of a great screen musical - an outstanding score, a witty screenplay, and a fine cast. The original Broadway show from which it was adapted is generally considered to be **Cole Porter**'s masterpiece, and this 1953 version only served to emphasize and reaffirm that view. The story of thespians Fred Graham (**Howard Keel**) and his ex-wife, Lilli

Vanessi (**Kathryn Grayson**), who allow their onstage conflict in an out-of-town production of *The Taming Of The Shrew* to spill over into their own tempestuous private lives, was both hilarious and musically thrilling. The dance sequences, which were choreographed by **Hermes Pan** and his assistant **Bob Fosse**, were stunning, involving high-class hoofers such as **Ann Miller**, Bobby Van, Tommy Rall and Carol Haney. Most observers cite Miller's scintillating 'Too Darn Hot' as the film's high spot, but all the songs were performed memorably, including 'I Hate Men' (Grayson), 'So In Love', 'Wunderbar' and 'Kiss Me Kate' (Grayson-Keel), 'I've Come To Wive It Wealthily In Padua', 'Were Thine That Special Face' and 'Where Is The Life That Late I Led?' (Keel), 'Always True To You In My Fashion' and 'Why Can't You Behave? (Miller-Rall), 'We Open In Venice' (Keel-Grayson-Miller-Rall), and 'From This Moment On' (Miller-Rall-Haney-Van-Fosse-Jeannie Coyne). One other item, which would have stopped the show every night if it had been performed in a similar fashion on stage, was 'Brush Up Your Shakespeare', in which James Whitmore and Keenan Wynn, as a couple of affable debt-collecting gangsters, mangle the Bard, courtesy of Porter, in lines such as 'If your blonde won't respond when you flatter 'er/Tell her what Tony told Cleopaterer'. George Sidney directed, and the film was photographed in Ansco Color. Dorothy Kingsley's screenplay was based on Bella and Sam Spewack's original libretto. Some sequences appear slightly puzzling and unnerving - even unnatural - until one realizes that certain effects, such as characters throwing items towards the camera, were inserted to take advantage of the 3-D process in which the film was originally shot.

Kiss Me, Kate (stage musical)

Even before its 30 December 1948 opening at the New Century Theatre in New York, the word was out that the stage musical *Kiss Me, Kate* would be a hit. Whatever purists might think, it is hard to imagine any songwriter better suited than **Cole Porter** to blend words, wit and music with the work of Shakespeare. Using the device of a show-within-a-show, Bella and Sam Spewack's book deftly shifts back and forth between Shakespeare's Padua and present-day Baltimore, as a touring theatrical troupe put on performances of the Bard's work while simultaneously engaging in back-stage rivalries and love affairs. As the warring Fred and Lilli, who are 'acting' Petruchio and Kate in *The Taming Of The Shrew*, the show starred **Alfred Drake** and Patricia Morison. Despite their first-rate performances, however, the real stars of *Kiss Me, Kate* were Porter's songs which included 'So In Love', 'Always True To You In My Fashion', 'Wunderbar', 'I Hate Men', 'Another Openin', Another Show', 'Brush Up Your Shakespeare', 'We Open In Venice', 'Why Can't You Behave?', 'Were Thine That Special Face', 'Where Is The Life That Late I Led?' and 'Too Darn Hot'. *Kiss Me, Kate* ran for over 1,007 performances, and won a **Tony Award** for best musical. Patricia Morison recreated her role, opposite Bill Johnson, in the London production which stayed at the Coliseum for 501 performances. West End revivals were presented in 1970, with Emile Belcourt and Ann Howard, and in 1987 with **Paul Jones**, Nichola McAuliffe, Tim Flavin and Fiona Hendley. The 1953 film version, which captured much of the sparkle of the original (especially after its non-3-D reissue), starred **Howard Keel** and Kathryn Grayson as Fred and Lilli, and benefited from the vibrant dancing of Ann Miller. The film also included 'From This Moment On', a song not used in the stage version. *Kiss Me, Kate* was produced in several European and Far-Eastern countries and was revived in New York in 1956 and 1965 at the City Centre.

Kiss Me Kiss Me Kiss Me - The Cure

This hefty double album often sounds more like a compilation than a coherent whole, with musical ideas bouncing frantically back and forth. Nevertheless, in typical **Cure** style, *Kiss Me Kiss Me Kiss Me* successfully combined catchy pop with bitter despair. Through 17 immensely sensual songs, Robert Smith is at his most poetic ('strange as angels, dancing in the deepest ocean, twisting in the water, you're just like a dream') and vitriolic ('get your fucking voice out of my head . . . I never wanted any of this, I wish you were dead'). The joyous pop of 'Just Like Heaven' and 'The Perfect Girl' still delights, and the frisson provided by 'Shiver And Shake' reinforces the physical nature of this collection.

● Tracks: *The Kiss; Catch; Torture; If Only Tonight We Could Sleep; Why Can't I Be You?; How Beautiful You Are; The Snakepit; Just Like Heaven; All I Want; Hot Hot Hot!!!; One More Time; Like Cockatoos; Icing Sugar; The Perfect Girl; A Thousand Hours; Shiver And Shake; Fight.*

● First released 1987
● UK peak chart position: 6
● USA peak chart position: 35

Kiss Of Life

UK band Kiss Of Life comprise Mike Benn (b. c.1963; keyboards) and Victoria Maxwell (b. 1970; vocals). Formed in 1991, their jazz, soul and R&B mix, with soothing female vocals and a leaning towards the club scene, soon attracted the attention of **Virgin Records**. The duo had met in Hamburg, where Victoria, classically trained, was a dancer, while Benn was working on session tracks. Back in London, Benn hooked up with **Acid Jazz** man Chris Bangs, for whom Benn had co-written one track on the *Totally Wired 9* album. It was through Bangs that **Paul Weller** got involved with Kiss Of Life, guesting on the track 'Fiction In My Mind'. Singles so far have included 'Love Has Put A Spell On Me' and 'Holding On To A Dream'. Virgin Records had high hopes for their investment, but there has been little evidence of a breakthrough so far.

● ALBUMS: *Reaching For The Sun* (Circa 1993)★★★.

Kiss Of The Gypsy

This melodic hard-rock quintet (formerly known as Fantasia) was formed in Blackpool, Lancashire, England, in 1990, by Tony Mitchell (vocals, guitar) and Martin Talbot (bass). With the addition of Darren Rice (guitar), George Williams (keyboards) and Scott Elliot (drums), they signed to **Atlantic** the following year. The band's music is blues-rock-based, with a sense of energetic songwriting not dissimilar to that of **Bad Company** or **Whitesnake**. Following successful support slots to **Winger**, **Magnum** and **Great White**, the band released their self-titled debut album on the **WEA**/East West label in 1992, which saw them widely hailed as one of the most promising commercial British groups to emerge since **Def Leppard**.

● ALBUMS: *Kiss Of The Gypsy* (East West 1992)★★★.

Kiss Of The Spider Woman

'And the curtain will shake, and the fire will hiss, here comes her kiss' - read the cobwebbed publicity handouts prior to the show's debut at London's Shaftesbury Theatre on 20 October 1992. Extensively revised following its New York/Purchase workshop in 1990, this production of *Kiss Of The Spider Woman* had received its world premiere in June 1992 in Toronto, Canada. Considered by many to be an unlikely - even unsuitable - choice for a musical - it was adapted by Terrence McNally from Manuel Puig's 1976 novel, which was also made into an acclaimed film in 1984. The story concerns two cellmates in a prison somewhere in Latin America, the gay window dresser, Molina (Brent Carver), and the single-minded Marxist revolutionary, Valentin (Anthony Crivello). The two men are gradually drawn together and eventually become lovers. For some of the time, Molina lives in a fantasy world in which his childhood idol, film star, Aurora (**Chita Rivera**), frequently comes to life in a series of gaudy routines from her tacky 40s B-movies. Rivera is also the black-clad Spider Woman, the temptress who lures men to their death. In this way, the grim reality of the torture and persecution of life in the jail (almost too realistically created) is contrasted effectively with the unreal world outside. **John Kander** and **Fred Ebb**'s score switched from 'serious' numbers such as 'The Day After That' and 'You Could Never Shame Me', to the spectacular 'Gimme Love', and more conventional and good-humoured songs which included the lovely 'Dear One', along with 'Dressing Them Up', 'Russian Movie', 'Morphine Tango', 'Gimme Love', and 'Only In The Movies'. Critical reaction was mixed, although both Brent Carver and Chita Rivera, making her first appearance in London for 30 years, were both highly acclaimed. **Harold Prince**'s 'triumphant' direction and Jerome Sirlin's 'staggering scenic design, with the steel bars of the cells fading into fanciful projections of tropical jungles and glittering palaces of pleasure' were also applauded. Although it was voted best musical in the *Evening Standard* Drama Awards, *Kiss Of The Spider Woman* had a disappointingly short West End stay of nine months. In May 1993, a Broadway production, with Chita Rivera and Brent Carver, began its run at the Broadhurst Theatre, and scooped the **Tony Awards**, winning for best musical, score (tied with the *The Who's Tommy*), book, actress (Chita Rivera), actor (Brent Carver), and featured actor (Anthony Crivello). It also gained the New York Critics' prize for Best Musical, ran for 906 performances, and became a popular touring attraction.

Kiss The Boys Goodbye

Screen adaptations of Broadway plays and musicals generally make alterations to the story which are considered to be desirable. In this case one of the changes at least was essential, because the central topic of Clare Booth's 1938 play *Kiss The Boys Goodbye* was the all-consuming question of who was going to play the role of Scarlett in the film of *Gone With The Wind*. So, three years later, that had to go, and along with it went a lot of the play's bite and satire. What was left turned out to be a more or less conventional backstage story in which Broadway producer **Don Ameche** falls for chorus girl **Mary Martin**. She introduced most of **Frank Loesser** and **Victor Schertzinger**'s songs, including 'I'll Never Let A Day Pass By', 'That's How I Got My Start', and the lively title song, but **Connee Boswell** provided the film's musical highlight with her sultry rendering of 'Sand In My Shoes'. **Oscar Levant**, who invariably raised the laughter (and musical) quota of any film in which he appeared, was in the supporting cast, along with Eddie (Rochester) Anderson, Raymond Walburn, Virginia Dale, Barbara Jo Allen, and Elizabeth Patterson. Harry Tugend and Dwight Taylor wrote the amusing screenplay, and the film was directed by Victor Schertzinger.

Kissin' Cousins

Trusting that two would prove more popular than one, director Gene Nelson cast **Elvis Presley** in a dual role for this 1964 feature. The singer played a GI and also a dim-witted hillbilly (donning a wig for the latter) in a plot involving plans to build an ICBM base in the backwoods. The title song reached number 10 (UK) and number 12 (US) when issued as a single; an alternate version, 'Kissin' Cousins (Number Two)', was one of 11 songs from the film featured on an attendant soundtrack album. Fearful, for once, of seeming parsimonious, **RCA** added 'Echoes Of Love' and 'Long Lonely Highway', two tracks from an earlier session, to enhance the playing time. Sadly, little was being done to halt the artistic decline in Presley's films.

Kissing Bandit, The

Frank Sinatra himself is among the many (including his friend **Dean Martin**) who have been known to mock this 1948 MGM release in which he co-starred (yet again) with **Kathryn Grayson**. At least on this occasion Grayson was not trying to make it to the top as an operatic singer - that would have been rather

difficult anyway because the setting for Isobel Lennart and John Briard Harding's screenplay was way out west in old California. Sinatra, with long hair and even longer sideburns, was in the middle of his early 'shy' period (*Anchors Aweigh*, *Step Lively*, *It Happened In Brooklyn*, *On The Town*). He played the young and retiring son of an infamous womanizing bandit who is reluctantly forced to follow in his father's footsteps. Two of the screen's favourite dancing ladies, **Ann Miller** and **Cyd Charisse**, were also in the cast, along with Ricardo Montalban, J. Carrol Naish, Mildred Natwick, Billy Gilbert, Mikhail Rasumny, and Clinton Sundberg. Most of the songs, by **Nacio Herb Brown**, Earl K. Brent and Edward Heyman were romantic ballads tailored for Sinatra, such as 'Siesta', 'If I Steal A Kiss', 'Senorita', 'What's Wrong With Me?', but things livened up a lot when Charisse, Miller and Montalban got together for the scintillating 'Dance Of Fury'. Grayson had the best song, 'Love Is Where You Find It' (Brown-Brent). Laszlo Benedek directed this Technicolor flop which gave no indication whatsoever that Sinatra was just a few years away from the sophisticated comedy of *The Tender Trap*, and an Oscar-winning performance in *From Here To Eternity*.

Kissoon, Mac And Katie

Brother and sister Gerald (Mac) and Kathleen Kissoon were both born in Port Of Spain, Trinidad and later raised in Great Britain. In 1965, they formed half of the Marionettes, a two man/two woman singing group produced by 50s pop star **Marty Wilde**. The siblings were later part of the Rag Dolls, while Kathleen also recorded under the name Peanut. As a duo, Mac And Katie Kissoon caused a minor stir in 1971 with the veiled anti-war song, 'Chirpy Chirpy Cheep Cheep', which despite losing out to the more successful version by **Middle Of The Road** in the UK charts, it did reach the US Top 20. The Kissoons then embarked on a Euro-soul direction which resulted in two UK Top 10 singles, 'Sugar Candy Kisses' and 'Don't Do It Baby' (both 1975), but despite further, lesser hits, their sweetened charm ultimately faded. Katie Kissoon continues to perform and record in her own right and guests with luminaries such as **Van Morrison** and **Roger Waters**.
● ALBUMS: *Sugar Candy Kisses* (1975)★★, *The Two Of Us* (1976)★★★.
● COMPILATIONS: *The Mac & Katie Kissoon Story* (1978)★★★.

Kitamura, Eiji

b. 8 April 1929, Tokyo, Japan. Kitamura began playing clarinet while still a student and was a professional musician from his twenties onwards. He often played with visiting American jazzmen, including **Benny Goodman** (never renowned for his eagerness to share the bandstand with another clarinettist) in the 50s, and **Teddy Wilson** and **Woody Herman** in the 70s. From the late 70s Kitamura began making regular appearances in the USA, mostly on the west coast. Through the late 80s and into the mid-90s he was frequently associated with **Bill Berry**, sharing stages and bandleading duties in festivals such as the Pacific International Jazz Party. Kitamura is a highly accomplished technician with a subtle sense of swing. He has helped inspire a succeeding generation of Japanese musicians with his skill and dedication to his craft and art.

● ALBUMS: *Kitamura Eiji vs Suzuki Shoji* (Teichiku 1976)★★★, *Because Of You* (Audio Lab 1976)★★★★, *My Monday Date* (Victor 1977)★★★, *Memories Of You* (RCA 1978)★★★★, *April Date* (CBS/Sony 1979),★★★ *3 Degrees North* (CBS/Sony 1980)★★★, *Seven Stars* (Toshiba/EMI 1981),★★★ *We With Woody Herman* (Toshiba/EMI 1983)★★★.

Kitarô

b. Masanori Takahashi, 4 February 1953, Toyohashi, Japan. Soon after graduating from high school, Takahashi formed a rock band to perform in discos. He was converted to synthesizer music while visiting Asian countries including, in particular, India and the remoter reaches of his Japanese homeland. His debut, *Tenkai (The Heavens)*, a suite for synthesizer, prompted NHK (the Japanese broadcasting company) to commission Kitarô to write a score for the lengthy television documentary, *Silk Road*. This atmospheric, meditative piece full of simple melodies and unhurried tempos earned the composer national and international recognition. A resident of a small village in the Nagano prefecture in central Japan, Kitarô is able to pursue his work in contemplative surroundings, as reflected in his music. For much of the 80s Kitarô's distribution outlet in the west was handled by **Polydor Records** and the Kuckuck (Line) labels. However, in 1986 Kitarô signed a major deal with **Geffen Records** confirming his status as one of the world's leading 'new age' artists.

● ALBUMS: *Tenkai (The Heavens)* (Polydor 1978)★★, *Oasis* (Polydor 1979)★★★, *Silk Road I* (Polydor 1980)★★★★, *Silk Road II* (Polydor 1980)★★★, *Tonkô* (Polydor 1981)★★★, *Tenjiku (India, Or The Heavens)* (Polydor 1983)★★★, *Huin (Flying Clouds)* (Polydor 1983)★★, *From The Full Moon Story* (Polydor 1985)★★★, *Tanhaung* (Polydor 1986)★★★, *Towards The West* (Polydor 1986)★★★, *Tenkû (The Sky)* (Geffen 1986)★★★, *Silver Cloud* (Polydor 1986)★★★, *Ki* (Polydor 1986)★★★, *Live In Asia* (Geffen 1986)★★, *The Light Of The Spirit* (Geffen 1987)★★★, with the London Symphony Orchestra *Silk Road Suite* (Geffen 1987)★★★★, *Kojiki (The Legendary Stories Of Ancient Japan)* (Geffen 1990)★★★, *Music From The Motion Picture Soundtrack Heaven And Earth* (Geffen 1994)★★, *An Enchanted Evening* (Domo 1995)★★★, *Peace On Earth* (Domo 1996)★★★, *Kitarô's World Of Music Featuring Yu-Xiao Guang* (Domo 1996)★★★, *Cirque Ingenieux* (Domo 1997)★★★.

● COMPILATIONS: *Best Of Silk Road* (Polydor 1983)★★★, *Best Of Kitarô* (Kuckuck 1987)★★★, *Ten Years* (1988)★★★.

Kitchens Of Distinction

Formed in Tooting, London, England, in 1986 by Patrick Fitzgerald (b. 7 April 1964, Basel, Switzerland), Julian Swales (b. 23 March 1964, Gwent, Wales) and Daniel Goodwin (b. 22 July 1964, Salamanca, Spain), Kitchens Of Distinction took their name from a Hygena advertisement and pursued a precarious path through the UK independent record industry. A debut single on their own Gold Rush Records in 1987, 'Last Gasp Death Shuffle', brought them a *New Musical Express* Single Of The Week award, and after signing to **One Little Indian Records** there were hints at an upturn in fortunes. Marrying a melodic sensibility with a stunning array of guitar effects, slight problems only appeared when the critical success of their first album, *Love Is Hell*, was not matched in commercial terms. The most popular theories for the band's slow rise centred upon their peculiar moniker and singer Patrick Fitzgerald's unwillingness to disguise or avoid the subject of his homosexuality, but whatever the reasons, the threesome struggled to break away from the threat of cult status. The battle seemed to pay dividends when the second album, *Strange Free World*, entered the UK charts at number 36, although the full-blown crossover their powerful, emotive songs so richly deserved was still not forthcoming. A nationwide tour with the **Popinjays** led to a friendship between the two groups, with the Kitchens often appearing under the pseudonym the Toilets Of Destruction. Meanwhile, the band found a more willing audience through college radio in the USA. They returned in 1994 with *Cowboys And Aliens*, and a full-blown UK headlining tour to re-establish their credentials, but were subsequently dropped by their record company. They shortened their name to Kitchens OD and signed to Fierce Panda.

● ALBUMS: *Love Is Hell* (One Little Indian 1989)★★★★, *Strange Free World* (One Little Indian 1991)★★, *The Death Of Cool* (One Little Indian 1992)★★★, *Cowboys And Aliens* (One Little Indian 1994)★★★.

Kitchings, Irene

b. Irene Eadie, c.1910, Marietta, Ohio, USA, d. c.1975. After taking piano lessons from her piano-teacher mother, Kitchings moved to Chicago and in her late teens was working as a solo pianist in jazz clubs and sitting-in at after-hours sessions. She formed her own jazz groups, mostly with all-male personnel, and was very popular especially with the club-owning gangsters of late-20s Chicago. In addition to playing piano, she also wrote music but at this time playing came first. At the start of the 30s she met and married **Teddy Wilson** and for a while their careers ran in parallel. When Wilson moved to New York, however, she went with him, abandoning her playing career. In the mid-30s, Wilson was a highly popular member of the **Benny Goodman** organization and the marriage foundered. She was encouraged by **Benny Carter** to turn to her composing as a means of lifting her from the depression the breakdown in her marriage had caused. **Billie Holiday**, who had become friendly with her when recording with Wilson, effected an introduction to lyricist Arthur Herzog Jnr. Their first collaboration, 'Some

Other Spring', was recorded by Holiday, and for the next few years the partnership produced some fine songs, the last of which was 'I'm Pulling Through', also recorded by Holiday. At this time, the early 40s, Kitchings was unwell and had gone to Cleveland where she was cared for by an aunt. Here she met and married Elden Kitchings. Her later years were largely inactive in musical terms, although happy ones. Such musical activity as there was centred upon the church where she sang and played the organ. She suffered from an eye disease which made her final years difficult. Kitchings' reputation as a pianist was restricted largely to musicians with whom she played in Chicago but within this group she was highly praised. As a composer her reputation is even higher. Sally Placksin quotes her collaborator Herzog as saying, 'Anything she wrote, I could put words to, and that doesn't happen very often'. Helen Oakley Dance said, 'Her musical streak came out in composition'. Kitchings and Dance were good friends and another of their group, who was encouraged by both, was **Carmen McRae**, then a teenager starting out. But for the hiatus in her career during her marriage to Wilson, there seems little doubt that Kitchings would be remembered today as an exceptionally good pianist and leader. As it is, her name lives on with her songs, some of which became standards and paradigms of the songwriter's art.

Kitsyke Will

This UK three-piece folk group included Peadar Long (clarinet/whistles/flute/saxophones/vocals), Patrick Gundry-White (French horn/harmonium/vocals), and John Burge (guitar/bouzouki/fiddle/banjo/vocals). *Devil's Ride*, their only release, was a crossover jazz and folk recording, combining original material with traditional numbers. Peadar Long has since performed and recorded with other artists.
● ALBUMS: *Devil's Ride* (1982)★★★.

Kitt, Eartha

b. 26 January 1928, Columbia, South Carolina, USA. Raised in New York's Harlem, Kitt attended the High School for Performing Arts before joining Katharine Dunham's famed dancing troupe. At the end of a European tour Kitt decided to stay behind, taking up residence in Paris. Having added singing to her repertoire, she was a success and on her return to New York appeared at several leading nightclubs. She appeared on Broadway in *New Faces Of 1952* introducing 'Monotonous', and was later seen more widely in the film version of the show. Her other Broadway shows around this time included *Mrs. Patterson* (1954) and *Shinbone Alley* (1957). She continued to work in cabaret, theatre and television, singing in her uniquely accented manner and slinkily draping herself across any available object, animate or otherwise. She made a few more films over the years, playing a leading role in *St Louis Blues* (1958), with **Nat 'King' Cole**, and in an all-black version of *Anna Lucasta* (1959), opposite **Sammy**

Davis Jnr. Although her highly mannered presentation of songs is best seen rather than merely heard, Kitt has made some songs virtually her own property, among them 'I Want To Be Evil', 'An Englishman Needs Time', 'Santa Baby' and 'I'm Just An Old-Fashioned Girl', a claim which is patently untrue. Her other record successes over the years have included 'Uska Dara - A Turkish Tale', 'C'est Si Bon', 'Somebody Bad Stole De Wedding Bell', 'Lovin' Spree', 'Under The Bridges Of Paris', 'Where Is My Man', 'I Love Men' and 'This Is My Life'. In 1978 Kitt appeared on Broadway with Gilbert Wright and **Melba Moore** in an all-black version of *Kismet* entitled *Timbuktu*. Her career has continued along similar lines on both sides of the Atlantic throughout the 80s and into the 90s, although she was courted by a much younger audience (witness her collaboration on 'Cha Cha Heels' with **Bronski Beat** in 1989) who were suitably impressed by her irreverent coolness. In 1988 Kitt played the role of Carlotta Campion in the London production of *Follies* and sang **Stephen Sondheim**'s legendary anthem to survival, 'I'm Still Here', which, appropriately, became the title of her second volume of autobiography. In the early 90s she performed her one-woman show in London and New York and appeared as a witch in the comedy/horror movie *Ernest Scared Stupid*. She also toured Britain with the **Ink Spots** in the revue *A Night At The Cotton Club*. In 1993 Kitt appeared in cabaret at several international venues, including London's Café Royal, and in the following year she played the role of Molly Bloom, the heroine of James Joyce's novel *Ulysses*, in 'an erotic monologue punctuated with songs by the French crooner, **Charles Aznavour**', which proved to be a cult hit at the Edinburgh Festival.
● ALBUMS: *New Faces Of 1952* original cast (RCA Victor 1952)★★★, *Songs* 10-inch album (RCA Victor 1953)★★★, *That Bad Eartha* 10-inch album (RCA Victor 1953)★★★★, *Down To Eartha* (RCA Victor 1955)★★★, *Thursday's Child* (RCA Victor 1956)★★★, *St. Louis Blues* (RCA Victor 1958)★★★, *The Fabulous Eartha Kitt* (Kapp 1959)★★★, *Eartha Kitt Revisited* (Kapp 1960)★★★, *Bad But Beautiful* (MGM 1962)★★★, *At The Plaza* (1965)★★★, *Eartha Kitt Sings In Spanish* (Decca 1965)★★★, *C'est Si Bon* (IMS 1983)★★★, *I Love Men* (Record Shack 1984)★★★, *Love For Sale* (Capitol 1984)★★, *The Romantic Eartha Kitt* (Pathe Marconi 1984)★★, *St. Louis Blues* (RCA Germany 1985)★★★, *That Bad Eartha* (RCA Germany 1985)★★★, *Eartha Kitt In Person At The Plaza* (GNP 1988)★★★★, *I'm A Funny Dame* (Official 1988)★★★, *My Way* (Caravan 1988)★★★, *I'm Still Here* (Arista 1989)★★★, *Live In London* (Arista 1990)★★★★, *Thinking Jazz* (1992)★★★, *Back In Business* (1994)★★★.
● COMPILATIONS: *At Her Very Best* (RCA 1982)★★★, *Songs* (RCA 1983)★★★, *Diamond Series: Eartha Kitt* (Diamond 1988)★★★, *Best Of Eartha Kitt* (MCA 1990)★★★.
● FURTHER READING: *Thursday's Child*, Eartha Kitt. *Alone With Me: A New Biography*, Eartha Kitt. *I'm Still Here*, Eartha Kitt.

Kittrell, Christine

b. 11 August 1929, Nashville, Tennessee, USA. Kittrell made a number of attractive and moderately successful records for local labels during the 50s. A choir member as a child, her voice lacked the distinctive nuance that might have brought her more durable success. Her first record, 'Old Man You're Slipping' (Tennessee 117), was backed by tenor saxophonist Louis Brooks and his band, with whom she had made her professional debut six years earlier in 1945. **Fats Domino** sidemen Buddy Hagans and Wendell Duconge played on her first and biggest hit, 'Sittin' Here Drinking' (Tennessee 128), which brought her a six-week engagement at the Pelican Club in New Orleans. Kittrell had toured with the **Joe Turner** band in 1951 but she preferred to work around Nashville, at clubs such as the New Era and the Elks. Engaged as singer with Paul 'Hucklebuck' Williams' band in December 1952, *Billboard* noted that the 'five-foot-six chirp' was the 'blues find of the decade'. She made her west coast debut in 1954 with **Earl Bostic** and later **Johnny Otis**. Several releases on the Republic label at this time led to only regional success. One session, which included 'Lord Have Mercy' (Republic 7096), is reputed to feature **Little Richard** on piano. In August 1954, *Billboard* announced her departure from the R&B field to sing with the Simmons Akers spiritual singers. In the early 60s she recorded for **Vee Jay** but her original version of 'I'm A Woman' was covered by **Peggy Lee**. She re-recorded an old Republic song, 'Call His Name' (Federal 12540), in 1965, and spent the next few years touring army bases in south-east Asia entertaining US troops. Subsequently, she retired to her Ohio home.
● COMPILATIONS: *Nashville R&B, Vol 2* (1986)★★★.

Kix

This US group was formed by Donnie Purnell (bass) and Ronnie Younkins (guitar) in 1980. After experimenting with a number of line-ups, Steve Whiteman (vocals), Brian Forsythe (guitar) and Jimmy Chalfant (drums) were drafted in on a permanent basis. Their style was typical of America's east coast, a brash amalgam of influences that included **Mötley Crüe**, **AC/DC** and **Kiss**, while their live reputation within their native West Virginia was second to none. Securing a contract with **Atlantic Records** in 1981, their first two albums were rather derivative and poorly promoted. *Midnight Dynamite*, however, produced by Beau Hill (who had previously worked with **Ratt**), attracted some attention, and the band were given the support slot on **Aerosmith**'s 1985 USA tour. *Blow My Fuse* and *Hot Wire* received a good reception on both sides of the Atlantic, with the band maturing as songwriters and starting to develop an identity of their own.
● ALBUMS: *Atomic Bomb* (Atlantic 1981)★★, *Cool Kids* (Atlantic 1983)★★, *Midnight Dynamite* (Atlantic 1985)★★★, *Blow My Fuse* (Atlantic 1988)★★★★, *Hot Wire* (Atlantic 1991)★★★.

Klaatu

Klaatu was a Canadian rock trio led by vocalist, songwriter and drummer Terry Draper, who formed the group c.1975 along with John Woloschuk and Dee Long. The group's main claim to fame was that for a brief period a rumour circulated that Klaatu might actually be the **Beatles** in disguise. The first single by Klaatu - whose name was that of the robot alien in the 1951 film *The Day The Earth Stood Still* - was 'Doctor Marvello/California Jam', a minor hit in Canada on Daffodil Records and picked up in the USA by **Island Records**. Switching to **Capitol Records** in 1976, the group released a single titled 'Calling Occupants Of Interplanetary Craft'. Along with its b-side 'Sub Rosa Subway' and the accompanying album, *Klaatu* (titled *3:47 E.S.T.* in Canada), the band's sound closely resembled that of the latter-day Beatles, and when the group included no biographical material with its recordings, and supplied its record company with no information about themselves, a US journalist surmised that it might very well *be* the Beatles. The group did nothing to stem the rumours and ***Rolling Stone*** named Klaatu 'hype of the year' for 1977. While the story aided sales of the group's debut album, when it was revealed that Klaatu was indeed just Klaatu, sales of their future recordings diminished. The song 'Calling Occupants...' did eventually attain chart status in the hands of the **Carpenters** when, in 1977, it reached the US Top 40 and UK Top 10. Klaatu meanwhile, carried on working until 1981 when, after releasing four further albums, the group eventually disbanded. Dee Long is very successful in software animation technology, Draper has his own roofing business and Woloschuk is an accountant.
● ALBUMS: *Klaatu* (Capitol 1976)★★★, *Hope* (Capitol 1977)★★, *Sir Army Suit* (Capitol 1978)★★, *Endangered Species* (Capitol 1980)★★, *Magentalane* (1981)★★.

Klark Kent

Whether this Klark Kent is the same man who works as a reporter for the *Daily Planet* is unclear. His close friend **Stewart Copeland** (b. 16 July 1952, Alexandria, Egypt), drummer with the **Police**, tells us that Kent 'dabbles in politics, religion and anthropology'. He owns a huge multinational company called the Kent Foundation, whose sinister influence is behind many world events. Kent is unable to tour because an unpleasant odour emitted from his body makes him intolerable to other musicians . . . The truth is, of course, that Kent and Copeland are one and the same. In 1978 when the Police were still waiting for their major breakthrough, Copeland was looking for some extra-curricular activities, having previously been cited as a member of the unrealized group the Moors Murderers. Creating the *alter ego* of Kent, his first single 'Don't Care' was released on Kryptone in 1978 and later reissued on **A&M** when it was a minor hit. The follow-up, 'Too Kool To Kalypso' (back on the Krypton label), was pressed in lurid Kryptonite green; two more singles and a solitary mini-album followed, before Kent disappeared allowing Copeland to write film music and continue drumming with the Police.

● ALBUMS: *Klark Kent* (A&M 1980)★★.

Klaudt Indian Family

The Klaudts are Arikari Native Americans, initially from the Fort Bethold Indian Reservation in North Dakota but they later relocated to Norcross, Georgia. They were originally formed in the 30s by Ronald Klaudt, his wife Lillian and their children Vernon, Ken, Ray and Melvin. Later Vernon's wife, Betty, joined the group and Ronald gave up singing to become the group's manager. Dressed in traditional costumes, they have toured extensively singing country gospel music in countless venues that range from churches and small halls to major concert halls. They have also appeared regularly on networked television and radio shows especially those of **Wally Fowler**. Their show varied from family-style close harmony quartet singing to solos and their talented instrumentation varied from guitar, piano, organ and bass through to saxophone and trombone. The only non-family members to have played with the Klaudts over the years have been pianists Mal Stewart and Ralph Seibel. They have recorded numerous albums on their own Klaudt Family label.

● ALBUMS: *Coast To Coast Television* (Klaudt 70s)★★, *Traveling On* (Klaudt 80s)★★★, *Gospel Favorites* (Klaudt 80s)★★, *Whispering Hope* (Klaudt 80s)★★★, *At The End Of The Trail* (Klaudt 80s)★★★★, *The Klaudt Indian Family* (Klaudt 80s)★★★, *The Highest Hill* (Klaudt 80s)★★★, *Where He Leads Me* (Klaudt 80s)★★, *Christmas Peace On Earth* (Klaudt 80s)★★★, *Mom Klaudt Sings Peace Like A River* (Klaudt 80s)★★, *Gospel War Whoops* (Klaudt 80s)★★, *Gospel Moods Of Ralph Seibel* (Klaudt 80s)★★★.

Kleenex

Widely regarded (especially by American critic Greil Marcus) Swiss punk band, whose two releases on the fledgling **Rough Trade Records** label, 'Ain't You' and 'You', attracted many admirers. Unfortunately they also attracted the attention of the tissue company of the same name, who took objection to the use of their patent. From 1980 onwards they consequently became **Lilliput**, going to to release two further singles and an album. The band included Marlene Marder (guitar), Klaudi Schiff (bass), Crigele Freund (vocals) and Lislot Ha (drums).

● COMPILATIONS: *Lilliput* also comprises Kleenex material (Off Course 1993)★★★.

Klein, Allen

b. 1932, Newark, New Jersey, USA. A name synonymous with 'notorious', Allen Klein has a reputation as one of the most litigious, and thus feared, entrepreneurs in the music business. He spent his formative years at a Hebrew orphanage, then studied accountancy, paying for his own tuition along the way. During the early 60s, he took over the affairs of singer **Buddy Knox** and claimed to discover irregularities in the royalties he was due from his record company. The technique was habitual. Again and again, Klein would accost record companies, insist on audits, and produce writs at a moment's notice. His client roster soon extended to include **Steve Lawrence**, **Eydie Gorme**, **Bobby Darin**, **Bobby Vinton** and **Sam Cooke**. Always an over-reacher, Klein's grand ambition was to win the management of the **Beatles**. During the mid-60s, he infiltrated the British music scene with the notable acquisition of **Donovan**. His greatest coup, however, was effectively ousting first Eric Easton, then the charismatic **Andrew Loog Oldham**, as managers of the **Rolling Stones**. Klein and Oldham had originally formed a partnership in 1965, cemented by the American's success in securing a million-dollar advance from Sir Edward Lewis at **Decca Records**. Klein's history with the Rolling Stones and Andrew Loog Oldham ended in protracted litigation during the late 60s. In the meantime, Klein had bought the **Cameo-Parkway Record** label, an acquisition that prompted an investigation from the Securities and Exchange Commission. As his reputation grew, he reiterated his dream of managing the Beatles and, following the death of **Brian Epstein** in 1967, that ambition at last seemed feasible. In early 1969, Klein had a meeting with **John Lennon** and **Yoko Ono** and won them over. Both **George Harrison** and **Ringo Starr** also accepted Klein, but **Paul McCartney** preferred to place his future in the hands of his father-in-law, Lee Eastman. Just as he had done with the Rolling Stones, Klein renegotiated the Beatles contract to spectacular effect and also reorganized their business empire Apple, firing many personnel along the way. Although he boasted that he would win Epstein's company NEMS, he was thwarted when the company was sold to the Triumph Investment Trust. Music publisher **Dick James** had similar reservations about the American and, wary of provoking a legal battle, he sold the lucrative Beatles catalogue Northern Songs to Lew Grade's ATV network. Klein's hopes of reuniting the Beatles onstage also proved chimerical. Indeed, he seemed to represent a wedge between McCartney and the others and in 1971 the High Court ordered the dissolution of the Beatles' partnership. Klein's career in the echelons of pop was more prosaic during the late 70s, and in 1979 he suffered the indignity of a prison sentence after the US Internal Revenue Service indicted him on charges of tax evasion. By the 80s, Klein had switched his attention from rock music to feature films and the Broadway stage with varying degrees of success.

Klein, Manny

b. Emmanuel Klein, 4 February 1908, New York City, New York, USA. Although he spent most of his long working life as a studio musician, Klein played the trumpet in many of the leading white bands of the late 20s and 30s, making countless records. At one time or another, his powerful lead trumpet sparked the bands of **Benny Goodman**, **Jimmy** and **Tommy Dorsey**, **Frank Trumbauer** and **Red Nichols**. His studio work included soundtrack appearances in many feature films, most notably ghosting for Montgomery Clift in the 1953 film *From Here To Eternity*. He also played most of the trumpet solos in *The Benny Goodman Story* (1955), regardless of who might be seen performing on the screen. A stroke in 1973 barely made him pause, and he continued to play with enormous skill and enthusiasm.

● ALBUMS: *Manny Klein And His Sextet* (1956)★★★, with Tutti Camarata *Tutti's Trumpets* (1957)★★★.

● COMPILATIONS: with Benny Goodman *Breakfast Ball* (1934) (1988)★★★★.

Klemmer, John

b. 3 July 1946, Chicago, Illinois, USA. After trying guitar and alto saxophone in early childhood, Klemmer settled on tenor saxophone in his early teens. He studied extensively, playing in school and other youth bands, then played professionally with several name dancebands of the early 60s, including those led by **Les Elgart** and **Ralph Marterie**. In the late 60s he made his first records and then joined **Don Ellis**'s formidable big band. During these years he also played in small groups led by **Oliver Nelson** and **Alice Coltrane**. During this time he led his own groups, making jazz and jazz-fusion records. He experimented with electronics and fusion and some of his 1969 recordings slightly pre-date **Miles Davis**'s *Bitches Brew*. Sometimes Klemmer used electronic enhancements to allow him to record complex solo saxophone albums. He continued to develop these electronic concepts throughout the 70s and into the 80s. Playing with a diamond-hard tone, Klemmer's solos are filled with daring lines and imaginative ideas, often tossed out almost casually. On ballads, at which he excels, he introduces a breathy quality which aids the sometimes light and airy feeling he imparts. Many of his recordings feature his own compositions. Musically, his interest in areas on the fringes of jazz has tended to keep him from acceptance by the jazz world at large.

● ALBUMS: with Don Ellis *Autumn* (CBS 1968)★★★★, with Oliver Nelson *Black, Brown And Beautiful* (1969)★★★, *Eruptions* (1969)★★★, *All The Children Cried* (1969)★★★, *Blowin' Gold (Eruptions/All The Children Cried)* (Chess 1969)★★★, *Constant Throb* (1971)★★★, *Solo Saxophone I: Cry* (1975)★★★, *Arabesque* (1977)★★★, *Nexus For Duo And Trio* (1978)★★★, *Nexus One (For Trane)* (1979)★★★, *Straight From The Heart* (1979)★★★, *Hush* (Elektra 1981)★★★, *Finesse* (Elektra 1983)★★, *Solo Saxophone II: Life* (1985)★★, *Barefoot Ballet* (MCA 1987)★★, *Music* (MCA 1989)★★★, *Waterfalls* (Impulse 1990)★★★, with Oscar Castro-Neves *Simpatico* (JVC 1997)★★★.

Klezmatics

Lorin Sklamberg (b. 6 March 1956, Los Angeles, California, USA; vocals, accordion, keyboards), Frank

London (b. 29 March 1958, New York City, USA; trumpet, cornet, keyboards, vocals), Alicia Svigals (b. 8 January 1963, New York City, New York, USA; violin, vocals), Paul Morrissett (b. 19 October 1956, Indianapolis, Indiana, USA; bass, vocals), David Licht (b. 13 September 1954, Detroit, Michigan, USA; drums) and Matt Darriau (b. 21 February 1960, Colorado Springs, Colorado, USA; clarinet, saxophone, flute). Formed by London (who had previously played with **David Byrne** and the **Art Ensemble Of Chicago**, among many others), in New York in 1986, the Klezmatics set out to play the traditional Klezmer music of the Jewish communities of Eastern and Central Europe. However, the group instinctively added their own contemporary influences, (rock, funk, *avant garde* jazz), creating an old world/new world fusion of hard-edged, modern Yiddish dance music. In 1988 the group played at the anti-Fascist Heimatklinge festival in Berlin. Performing a set of tunes traditional to both the Yiddish and German cultures. These songs subsequently formed the basis of the Klezmatics' debut, *Shvaygn=Toyt* (Silence=Death), released the following year. Subsequent releases *Rhythm And Jews* (1992) and *Jews With Horns* (1995) featured the group's mix of fast-paced, mournful ballads, improvised experimentation and overtly political sentiments. The group have toured extensively throughout the world and have collaborated with a number of other artists, including **Allen Ginsberg**, the **Master Musicians Of Joujouka**, **John Zorn** and classical violinist Itzhak Perlman (whom they backed on two award-winning albums and a number of well-received tour dates). The Klezmatics have also produced the music for various films, dance productions and plays, including 'The Third Seder' (their own 'multimedia Passover production') and playwright Tony Kushner's 'A Dybbuk: Between Two Worlds', the score of which subsequently made up half of *Possessed*, their fourth release and the first to feature predominantly contemporary material.

● ALBUMS: *Shvaygn=Toyt* (Piranha 1989)★★★, *Rhythm And Jews* (Piranha 1992)★★★★, *Jews With Horns* (Piranha 1995)★★★★, *Possessed* (Piranha 1997)★★★.

KLF

Since 1987 the KLF have operated under a series of guises, only gradually revealing their true nature to the public at large. The band's principal spokesman is **Bill Drummond** (b. William Butterworth, 29 April 1953, South Africa), who had already enjoyed a chequered music industry career. As co-founder of the influential **Zoo** label in the late 70s, he introduced and later managed **Echo And The Bunnymen** and the **Teardrop Explodes**. Later he joined forces with Jimmy Cauty (b. 1954), an artist of various persuasions and a member of **Brilliant** in the mid-80s. Their first project was undertaken under the title JAMS (**Justified Ancients Of Mu Mu** - a title lifted from Robert Shea and Robert Anton Wilson's conspiracy novels dealing with the *Illuminati*). An early version of 'All You Need Is Love' caused little reaction compared to the provocatively titled LP that followed - *1987 - What The Fuck Is Going On?* Released under the KLF moniker (standing for Kopyright Liberation Front), it liberally disposed of the works of the **Beatles**, **Led Zeppelin** *et al* with the careless abandon the duo had picked up from the heyday of punk. One of the disfigured supergroups, **Abba**, promptly took action to ensure the offending article was withdrawn. In the wake of the emerging house scene the next move was to compromise the theme tune to well-loved British television show *Dr Who*, adding a strong disco beat and **Gary Glitter** yelps to secure an instant number 1 with 'Doctorin' The Tardis'. Working under the title Timelords, this one-off coup was achieved with such simplicity that its originators took the step of writing a book; *How To Have A Number One The Easy Way*. Returning as the KLF, they enjoyed a big hit with the more legitimate cult dance hit 'What Time Is Love'. After the throwaway send-up of Australian pop, 'Kylie Said To Jason', they hit big again with the soulful techno of '3 A.M. Eternal'. There would be further releases from the myriad of names employed by the duo (JAMS - 'Down Town', 'Its Grim Up North'; Space - *Space*; Disco 2000 - 'Uptight'), while Cauty, alongside Alex Paterson, played a significant part in creating the **Orb**. Of the band's later work, perhaps the most startling was their luxurious video for the KLF's 'Justified And Ancient', featuring the unmistakable voice of **Tammy Wynette**. The song revealed the KLF at the peak of their creative powers, selling millions of records worldwide while effectively taking the michael. They were voted the Top British Group by the BPI. Instead of lapping up the acclaim, the KLF, typically, rejected the comfort of a music biz career, and deliberately imploded at the BRITS award ceremony. There they performed an 'upbeat' version of '3AM Eternal', backed by breakneck-speed punk band **Extreme Noise Terror**, amid press speculation that they would be bathing the ceremony's assembled masses with pig's blood. They contented themselves instead with (allegedly) dumping the carcass of a dead sheep in the foyer of the hotel staging the post-ceremony party, and Drummond mock machine-gunning the assembled dignitaries. They then announced that the proud tradition of musical anarchy they had brought to a nation was at a close: the KLF were no more. Their only 'release' in 1992 came with a version of 'Que Sera Sera' (naturally rechristened 'K Sera Sera', and recorded with the Soviet Army Chorale), which, they insisted, would only see the light of day on the advent of world peace. The KLF returned to their rightful throne, that of England's foremost musical pranksters, with a stinging art terrorist racket staged under the K Foundation banner. In late 1993, a series of advertisements began to appear in the quality press concerning the Turner Prize art awards. While that body was responsible for granting £20,000 to a piece of non-mainstream art, the K Foundation (a new vehicle for messrs Drummond and Cauty) promised double that for the worst piece of art

displayed. The Turner shortlist was identical to that of the KLF's. More bizarre still, exactly £1,000,000 was withdrawn from the National Westminster bank (the biggest cash withdrawal in the institution's history), nailed to a board, and paraded in front of a select gathering of press and art luminaries. The money was eventually returned to their bank accounts (although members of the press pocketed a substantial portion), while the £40,000 was awarded to one Rachel Whiteread, who also won the 'proper' prize. The K Foundation later cemented its notoriety by burning the aforementioned one million pounds, an event captured on home video. Since that time, Drummond and Cauty have made several pseudonymous returns to the singles charts, including the 1996 tribute to footballer Eric Cantona, 'Ooh! Aah! Cantona', as 1300 Drums Featuring The Unjustified Ancients Of Mu, and in 1997 as 2K for the charmingly titled 'Fuck The Millenium'. Urban guerrillas specializing in highly original shock tactics, the KLF offer the prospect of a brighter decade should their various disguises continue to prosper.

● ALBUMS: *Towards The Trance* (KLF Communications 1988)★★★★, *The What Time Is Love Story* (KLF Communications 1989)★★★, *The White Room* (KLF Communications 1990)★★★, *Chill Out* (KLF Communications 1990)★★★.
● VIDEOS: *Stadium House* (PMI 1991).
● FURTHER READING: *Justified And Ancient: The Unfolding Story Of The KLF*, Pete Robinson. *Bad Wisdom*, Mark Manning and Bill Drummond.

Klink, Al

b. 28 December 1915, Danbury, Connecticut, USA, d. 8 March 1991. One of the many unsung heroes of the swing era, Klink's career took him through the bands of **Benny Goodman** and **Tommy Dorsey** and he was a mainstay of the **Glenn Miller** Orchestra during its most successful period. Although an excellent soloist on both saxophones and clarinet, Klink was usually overshadowed either by soloing leaders or other more favoured sidemen. After World War II he worked mostly in the studios, recording with **Billie Holiday**, the **Sauter-Finegan Orchestra** and **Ruby Braff**. In the late 70s and early 80s he joined fellow veterans **Bob Haggart** and **Yank Lawson** in their **World's Greatest Jazz Band** and also freelanced with several other jazz groups.
● ALBUMS: *The Al Klink Quintet* one side only (1955)★★, *The World's Greatest Jazz Band Of Yank Lawson And Bob Haggart On Tour* (1975)★★★★.

Kluger, Irving

b. 9 July 1921, New York City, New York, USA. In the early 40s, after studying music at high school and while still at university, Kluger drifted into New York's bebop scene. He played drums in **Georgie Auld**'s modernistic band and also worked with **Dizzy Gillespie**, appearing with him on a 1945 recording date which produced the hugely popular 'Salt Peanuts' and 'Good Bait'. Kluger then moved on to the adventurous **Boyd Raeburn** band

and also worked with **Stan Kenton** and **Artie Shaw** in the late 40s. In the 50s and subsequently, Kluger played in studio, as well as in theatre and casino orchestras, across the country, eventually settling on the west coast. In the early 80s he was an executive of the American Federation of Musicians in Las Vegas and talked of returning to drumming in his 'retirement', and, time permitting, also of writing his memoirs.

● ALBUMS: *Boyd Raeburn: On The Air Vol. 2* (1945-47)★★★, with Milt Bernhardt *Modern Brass* (1955)★★★.

● COMPILATIONS: with Stan Kenton *The Kenton Era* (1940-55 recordings)★★★★.

Klugh, Earl

b. 16 September 1953, Detroit, Michigan, USA. Jazz guitarist Klugh has an unorthodox style in that when he sits down he rests the guitar on his right knee instead of the left. After studying piano and nylon string guitar as a child, Klugh settled on the latter instrument. While still in his mid-teens he recorded with **Yusef Lateef** and **George Benson**, with whom he also toured. He continued to work with Benson and briefly with **Return To Forever** and, in the mid-70s, he also led his own groups for a solo career. Influenced by a wide range of guitarists including Benson (jazz), **Chet Atkins** (country) and folk, Klugh's style contains elements of all, yet is presented with a strong feeling for the great tradition of post-**Charlie Christian** jazz guitar through which his own personality constantly shines.

● ALBUMS: with Yusef Lateef *Suite 16* (1970)★★★★, with George Benson *White Rabbit* (1971)★★★, *Earl Klugh* (1976)★★, *Living Inside Your Love* (Liberty 1976)★★★, *Finger Paintings* (Liberty 1977)★★★, *Magic In Your Eyes* (United Artists 1978)★★★, *Heart String* (United Artists 1979)★★★, with Bob James *One On One* (1979)★★★, *Dream Come True* (EMI 1980)★★, with Hubert Laws *How To Beat The High Cost Of Living* soundtrack (1980)★★, *Late Night Guitar* (United Artists 1980)★★★, *Crazy For You* (Liberty 1981)★★★, with Bob James *Two Of A Kind* (Capitol 1982)★★★, *Low Ride* (Capitol 1983)★★★, with Hiroki Miyano *Hotel California* (Mercury 1984)★★, *Wishful Thinking* (Capitol 1984)★★★, *Nightsongs* (Capitol 1983)★★★, *Soda Fountain Shuffle* (WEA 1985)★★★, *Life Stories* (WEA 1986)★★★, with Benson *Collaboration* (1987)★★★★, *A Time For Love* (Capitol 1988)★★★, *Solo Guitar* (WEA 1989)★★★, *Sounds And Visions* (1993)★★★, *Sudden Burst Of Energy* (Warners 1996)★★★, *The Journey* (Warners 1997)★★★.

● COMPILATIONS: *The Best Of Earl Klugh (1977-84)* (Blue Note 1985)★★★★, *World Star* (1985)★★★, *The Best Of Earl Klugh Volume 2* (Blue Note 1993)★★★★.

KMD

Long Beach, Long Island, New York-based rap outfit who have allied their breakbeats to a strong moral and political stance. This was made evident by their commitment to be a 'positive Kause (sic) in a Much Damaged Society', on their 'Rap The Vote' college tour of the US, an attempt to encourage young people to vote. They were a key element in **3rd Bass**'s RIF production roster, whose **MC Serch** (who discovered them) and **Pete Nice** handled executive production duties on *Mr Hood*. The fluid sound of the latter featured twisted riffs and hip hop holding together a barrage of samples. However, the following years would not prove easy ones for the band. Their DJ, Subroc, brother to lead rapper Zevlove X, was killed in a car accident in 1993. The band were just readying themselves for the release of a promotional single ('What A Niggy Know'), when they were called into a meeting with label bosses on April 8 1994, where chairman Bob Krasnow informed them that they were not happy with the artwork for *Black Bastards*. This featured a 'Sambo' character being hung by the noose. The thinking, on KMD's part, was to 'execute the stereotype'. However, R&B *Billboard* columnist Terri Rossi had already taken issue with the image, without really understanding the statement. It was a classic case of Time Warner paranoia in the wake of the 'Cop Killer' issue, dropping the band even though they were prepared to discuss changes, and hardly the tonic a recovering Zevlove needed. Ironically, the music on the second long playing venutre was a more sober affair, in a more reflective mode ala **A Tribe Called Quest**. It was lyrically informed by **Last Poet** Gylan Kain's spoken jazz (notably the *Blue Geurilla* set).

● ALBUMS: *Mr Hood* (Elektra 1991)★★★, *Black Bastards* (Elektra 1994; withdrawn).

KMS Records

One of the original Detroit techno stables, and home to **Kevin Saunderson**'s **Inner City/Resse Project** family, with its title taken from the proprieter's ful name (Kevin Maurice Saunderson). Its important releases during the late 80s included Inner City's 'Big Fun' and Reese & Santonio's 'Truth Of Self Evidence'. However, by the 90s, in tandem with the Reese Project's more soulful approach to techno/house, Saunderson was using the label for more vocal-based tracks. A new subsidiary imprint, Transfusion, was planned to house any idiosyncratic excursions into techno. Just to confirm what he has always said: 'If its dance music, I do it all'. The label was also home to Saunderson projects like E-Dancer's 'Pump The Move', which was remixed by **Joey Beltram** and Tronik House ('Straight Outta Hell') while guest artists included Chez Damier ('Can You Feel It', which also featured **Mark 'MK' Kinchen**). In 1994 the label unveiled a triple compilation set featuring tracks from Inner City, Esser'ay, Members Of The House, Chez Damier and Ron Trent. KMS product is licensed in the UK through **Network**.

Knack

Formed in Los Angeles in 1978, the Knack comprised Doug Fieger (vocals, guitar), Prescott Niles (bass), Berton Averre (guitar) and Bruce Gary (drums). Taking their name from a cult British movie of the 60s, they attempted to revive the spirit of the beat-boom with matching suits, and short songs boasting solid, easily memorable riffs. After garnering considerable media attention for their club appearances on the Californian coastline in early 1979, they became the fortuitous objects of a record company bidding war, which ended in their signing to **Capitol Records**. The fact that this was the **Beatles'** US label was no coincidence, for the Knack consistently employed imagery borrowed from the 'Fab Four', both in their visual appearance and record sleeves. Their prospects were improved by the recruitment of renowned pop producer **Mike Chapman**, who had previously worked with **Blondie**. During the summer of 1979, the Knack's well-publicized debut single 'My Sharona' promptly topped the US charts for six weeks, as well as reaching the UK Top 10 and selling a million copies. The first album, *The Knack*, was a scintillating pop portfolio, full of clever hooks and driving rhythms and proved an instant hit, selling five million copies in its year of release. Implicit in the Knack's abrupt rise were the seeds of their imminent destruction. In adapting 60s pop to snappy 70s production, they had also spiced up the standard boy/girl love songs with slightly more risqué lyrics for their modern audience. Critics, already suspicious of the powerful record company push and presumptuous Beatles comparisons, pilloried the group for their overt sexism in such songs as 'Good Girls Don't', as well as reacting harshly to Fieger's arrogance during interviews. At the height of the critical backlash, the Knack issued the apologetically titled *But The Little Girls Understand*, a sentiment that proved over-optimistic. Both the sales and the songs were less impressive and by the time of their third album, *Round Trip*, their power-pop style seemed decidedly outmoded. By the end of 1981, they voluntarily disbanded with Fieger attempting unsuccessfully to rekindle recent fame with Taking Chances, while the others fared little better with the ill-fated Gama. A reunion in 1991 resulted in the forgettable *Serious Fun*.

● ALBUMS: *The Knack* (Capitol 1979)★★★, *But The Little Girls Understand* (Capitol 1980)★★, *Round Trip* (Capitol 1981)★★, *Serious Fun* (Charisma 1991)★★.

● COMPILATIONS: *The Best Of ...* (1993)★★.

Knapp, Orville

Formed in 1934 in Los Angeles, California, USA, the Orville Knapp Orchestra included sidemen Michael Paige, George Mays, Jack Miller, Chick Floyd, Clarence Nelson, Jess Randall, Wally Rutan, Bill Echolstone, Guy Dick, Donald Swihart, Charlie Broad and Leighton Noble. The featured singers were, at one time or another, Virginia Verrill, Edith Caldwell, Don Raymond, Ray Hendricks, Dave Marshall and Leighton Noble. Their longest professional engagement came at the Beverly Wilshire Hotel between 1934 and 1935, but they also played other top venues including the Aragon Ballroom in Chicago. 'Indigo' and 'Accent On Youth' were the band's theme tunes, and these and other songs were released on **Decca** and **Brunswick Records** to strong popular support. However, Knapp's steady rise was thwarted in 1936 when a light plane he was piloting crashed with no survivors. His band was then taken over by **George Olsen**, who had worked briefly with Knapp. He renamed it 'The Music Of Tomorrow Orchestra'.

Knepper, Jimmy

b. 22 November 1927, Los Angeles, California, USA. Knepper learned to play trombone as a small child, later studying intensively. In the early 40s he played in local dance bands, playing jazz with various small groups. From the late 40s and into the early 50s he played with numerous name bands, including those led by **Freddie Slack**, Roy Porter, **Charlie Spivak**, **Charlie Barnet**, **Woody Herman** and **Claude Thornhill**. Later in the 50s Knepper worked extensively with **Charles Mingus** and also with **Art Pepper** and **Stan Kenton**. During the 60s he was with Mingus again, **Benny Goodman** and he also began a long-lasting if intermittent association with **Gil Evans**. Towards the end of the 60s he began another long-term musical relationship, this time with the **Thad Jones-Mel Lewis** Jazz Orchestra. In the 70s he was a member of the nine-piece band led by **Lee Konitz** and also worked with Mingus Dynasty. He made several records under his own name, including *Cunningbird* which featured such distinguished jazz musicians as **Al Cohn**, **Roland Hanna** and **Richard Davis**. A virtuoso performer, Knepper's bop-influenced style is technically on a par with that of **J.J. Johnson**, one of the few other trombonists to adapt wholly to bop. Nevertheless, Knepper's style is very much his own, with few obvious direct influences. His remarkable technical dexterity allows him to develop solo lines of startling ingenuity and imagination. In the 80s, Knepper was active on both sides of the Atlantic, renewing interest among older fans and finding a new audience for his exceptional skills and talent.

● ALBUMS: with Charles Mingus *Tijuana Moods* (1957)★★★★, with Mingus *East Coasting* (1957)★★★★, *A Swinging Introduction To Jimmy Knepper* (1957)★★★, *The Pepper-Knepper Quintet* (Metrojazz 1958)★★★, with Mingus *Blues And Roots* (1959)★★★★, *Mingus Dynasty* (1959),★★★★ *Cunningbird* (Steeplechase 1976)★★★, *JK In LA* (1977)★★★, *Just Friends* (1978)★★★, *Tell Me...* (1979)★★★, *Primrose Path* (1980)★★★, with Bobby Wellins *Primrose Path* (Hep Jazz 1982)★★★★, *Idol Of The Flies* (Affinity 1982)★★★, *I Dream Too Much* (Soul Note 1984)★★★, *Dream Dancing* (Criss Cross 1987)★★★, *Muted Joys* (Affinity 1989)★★★.

Knickerbocker Holiday

Not a particularly successful show, but notable for the the participation of two much-admired American citizens, the distinguished character actor Walter Huston, and the celebrated playwright Maxwell Anderson; and the introduction of one the most cherished songs in the history of popular music, 'September Song'.

Knickerbocker Holiday opened on 12 October 1938 at the Ethel Barrymore Theatre in New York, with a book by Anderson which was based on Washington Irving's *Knickerbocker History Of New York*. The show begins as Irving, played by Ray Middleton, is beginning to write his book, and then flashes back to New Amsterdam in 1647. The author himself is also transported back in time, and actually takes part in, and occasionally comments on certain aspects of the story that he is supposed to be writing. The piece, in which an all-powerful town council select the knife-sharpener Brom Breck (Richard Kollmar), as the candidate for their 'hanging day', only to see him reprieved by the incoming governor, Peter Stuyvesant (Walter Huston), was considered by many at the time to be a bitter attack on the US President, Franklin D. Roosevelt and his cabinet. *Knickerbocker Holiday* was the first production by the Playwrights Company, an organization which was made up of five distinguished (and sometimes, disillusioned) American dramatists, which included Maxwell Anderson. The show's score, with Anderson's lyrics and music by **Kurt Weill**, was different in many respects from conventional Broadway show music. The songs were completely integrated into the plot, and included 'How Can You Tell An American?', 'Will You Remember Me?', 'The One Indispensable Man', ''You People Think About Love', 'There's Nowhere To Go But Up', 'Sitting In Jail', 'Our Ancient Liberties', 'No Ve Vould'nt Gonnto To Do It' (much of the dialogue is spoken in a strong Dutch accent), and a lovely ballad, 'It Never Was You'. Walter Huston sang the poignant 'September Song', and his recorded version became widely popular. The show itself was unable to sustain a long run, and closed after only 168 performances. After Huston's death in 1950, his version of 'September Song' was played in the film, *September Affair*, and was acclaimed all over again. It was also selected for the US National Academy of Recording Arts and Sciences (NARAS) Hall of Fame. In the 1944 film version of *Knickerbocker Holiday* the song was sung by Charles Coburn.

Knickerbockers

The Knickerbockers was formed in 1964 by Buddy Randell (saxophone), a former member of the **Royal Teens** and Jimmy Walker (drums/vocals). The line-up was completed by the Charles brothers, John (bass) and Beau (lead guitar). Originally known as the Castle Kings, the group took its name from an avenue in their hometown of Bergenfield, New Jersey, USA. Signed to the Challenge label, owned by singing cowboy **Gene Autry**, the quartet initially forged its reputation recording cover versions, but in 1965 they scored a US Top 20 hit with 'Lies', a ferocious rocker which many listeners assumed was the **Beatles** in disguise. However, the Knickerbockers were more than mere copyists and later releases, which featured the instrumental muscle of experienced studio hands, established an energetic style which crossed folk rock and the **Four Seasons**. The

group broke up in 1968, unable to rekindle that first flame of success. Randell and Walker both attempted solo careers and for a short time the latter replaced **Bill Medley** in the **Righteous Brothers**.

● ALBUMS: *Sing And Sync-Along With Lloyd: Lloyd Thaxton Presents The Knickerbockers* (Challenge 1965)★★, *Jerk And Twine Time* (Challenge 1966)★★★, *Lies* (Challenge 1966)★★★.

● COMPILATIONS: *The Fabulous Knickerbockers* (1988)★★★, *A Rave-Up With The Knickerbockers* (Big Beat 1993)★★★, *Hits, Rarities, Unissued Cuts And More ...* (Sundazed 1997)★★★.

Knight Brothers

An R&B duo from Washington, DC, USA, consisting of Richard Dunbar (b. 31 May 1939) and Jimmy Diggs (b. 1937), the Knight Brothers reflected the emergence of a new entity in R&B music in the early 60s - the impassioned gospel duos - the most significant being the **Righteous Brothers** and **Sam And Dave**. Their one hit was 'Temptation 'Bout To Get Me' (number 12 R&B, number 70 pop) from 1965, for **Chess Records**. The Knight Brothers never managed to reach the charts again, however, and after an unsuccessful stay at **Mercury Records**, the duo broke up in 1969. Dunbar went on to sing with a revived **Orioles** group during the 70s and 80s. Dunbar's joining of the placid-sounding Orioles was not entirely anomalous, as the singer had started his career as a member of a doo-wop group, the Starfires, who recorded on several labels from 1958-61.

Knight, Bob, Four

Formed in 1956 in Brooklyn, New York, USA, this doo-wop vocal group featured Bob Bovino (aka Bob Knight; lead), Paul Ferrigno (first tenor), Ralph Garone (baritone) and John Ropers (bass). They initially started working as the Bobby Dells (a quintet additionally featuring second tenor Charlie Licarta) and practising standards of the day by the **Heartbeats** and **Flamingos**. They recorded one single under this guise, but 'Hymn Of Love' remained unreleased. Their debut record, 'Good Goodbye', was released on Laurel Records in 1961. Following a second Laurel effort, 'For Sale', the Bob Knight Four appeared as uncredited backing vocalists for rock 'n' roll artist **Eddie Delmar**. This engagement, 'Love Bells', was the first of four singles to combine group and singer, but the quartet received little recognition for their efforts. After Knight's vocals were replaced by the female lead of Sandy Lynn on the Taurus Records single 'So So Long', which in ever other respect was the group's debut, 'Good Goodbye', the quartet moved to Josie Records in 1962. However, neither the heavily orchestrated 'Memories' nor 'Two Friends' revived their fortunes. With line-up changes including the replacement of Bovino/Knight by Frank Iovino, and a returning Charlie Licarta replacing Paul Ferrigno, the group signed off with a final effort for Goal Records. 'Tomorrow We'll Be Married' featured both the **Angels** and **Tokens** providing studio accompaniment, but its sentimental lyric and construction failed to win new supporters. The group disbanded in 1964, but like so many doo-wop groups found an opportunity to reform in the early 70s on the wave of a nostalgia boom. Versions of the group have continued to perform in the New York area into the 90s.

Knight, Curtis

b. 1945, Fort Scott, Kansas, USA. Having completed his national service, Knight settled in California where he hoped to pursue a career in music. He appeared in a low-budget film, *Pop Girl*, before relocating to New York during the early 60s. Knight then recorded for several minor labels, but these releases have been eclipsed by the singer's collaborations with **Jimi Hendrix**, who joined Curtis's group, the Squires, in 1965. Hendrix's tenure there was brief, but the contract he signed with Knight's manager, Ed Chalpin, had unfortunate repercussions, particularly as the guitarist ill-advisedly undertook another recording session in 1967. His spells with Knight yielded 61 songs, 26 studio and 35 live, which have since been the subject of numerous exploitative compilations. Although some of this material is, in isolation, worthwhile, such practices have undermined its value. As Curtis Knight continued to pursue his career throughout the 60s using whatever musicians were available, he increasingly relied on his Hendrix association, and in 1974 published *Jimi*, 'an intimate biography'. By this point Knight was based in London where he led a new group, Curtis Knight - Zeus. This band comprised Eddie Clarke (guitar; later in **Motörhead**), Nicky Hogarth (keyboards), John Weir (bass) and Chris Perry (drums). They completed two albums, but only one was issued in the UK. The singer undertook a European tour and an unremarkable album before returning to the USA.
● ALBUMS: *Down The Village* (1972)★★, *Second Coming* (1974)★★, *Live In Europe* (1989)★★. Selected recordings with Jimi Hendrix *Get That Feeling* (Capitol 1967)★, *Strange Things* (1968)★★, *Flashing/Jimi Hendrix Plays Curtis Knight Sings* (1968)★★, *The Great Jimi Hendrix In New York* (1968)★★, *In The Beginning* (1973)★, *Looking Back With Jimi Hendrix* (1975)★, *My Best Friend* (1981)★, *Second Time Around* (1981)★★, *Hush Now* (1981)★ *Last Night* (1981)★, *Mr. Pitiful* (1981)★★, *Welcome Home* (1981)★.
● FURTHER READING: *Jimi*, Curtis Knight.

Knight, Evelyn

b. Washington, DC, USA. A popular singer in the US during the 40s, Knight turned professional by singing on a local radio show, followed by a spell at the King Cole Room in Washington. She was particularly effective with the perky novelty songs which were so prevalent in the 40s. Her first hit came in 1944 with 'Dance With A Dolly (With A Hole In Her Stocking)', backed by trumpeter **Tutti Camarata**'s Orchestra. This was followed by Sidney Lippman and Sylvia Dee's 'nonsense' song, 'Chickery Chick'. After 'Brush Those Tears From Your Eyes' (1948), she had a US number 1,

and million-seller, with 'A Little Bird Told Me'. This was followed during the next two years by 'Buttons And Bows', 'Powder Your Face With Sunshine' (another number 1), 'It's Too Late Now', 'You're So Understanding', 'Candy And Cake' and 'All Dressed Up To Smile'. On her last hit, 'My Heart Cries For You', she duetted with country singer **Red Foley**. After the hits dried up she continued to be a popular nightclub attraction.

Knight, Frederick

b. 15 August 1944, Alabama, USA. Knight had a Top 30 hit in both the USA and UK with 'I've Been Lonely For So Long', a light, but deceptively memorable single. This 1972 release on the **Stax** label was the singer's only major success, although 'I Betcha Didn't Know That' (1975) and 'The Old Songs' (1981) reached the minor R&B placings. In the interim, however, the artist had written and produced singles for **Anita Ward**, including her international smash 'Ring My Bell', and had formed his own Junta and Park Place labels in the late 70s and mid-80s, respectively. Knight continues to pursue an active career.
● ALBUMS: *I've Been Lonely For So Long* (Stax 1972)★★★, *Let The Sunshine In* (1979)★★★, *Knight Time* (Timeless 1981)★★, *Knight Rap* (Timeless 1987)★★.
● COMPILATIONS: *Timeless Soul Collection* (Timeless 1987)★★★, *I've Been Lonely For So Long* (Stax 1992)★★★.

Knight, Gladys, And The Pips

Gladys Knight (b. 28 May 1944, Atlanta, Georgia, USA), her brother Merald 'Bubba' (b. 4 September 1942, Atlanta, Georgia, USA), sister Brenda and cousins Elenor Guest and William Guest (b. 2 June 1941, Atlanta, Georgia, USA) formed their first vocal group in their native Atlanta in 1952. Calling themselves the Pips, the youngsters sang supper-club material in the week, and gospel music on Sundays. They first recorded for **Brunswick** in 1958, with another cousin of the Knights, Edward Patten (b. 2 August 1939), and Langston George making changes to the group line-up the following year when Brenda and Elenor left to get married. Three years elapsed before their next sessions, which produced a version of **Johnny Otis**'s 'Every Beat Of My Heart' for the small Huntom label. This song, which highlighted Knight's bluesy, compelling vocal style, was leased to **Vee Jay Records** when it began attracting national attention, and went on to top the US R&B charts. By this time, the group, now credited as Gladys Knight And The Pips, had signed a long-term contract with Fury Records, where they issued a re-recording of 'Every Beat Of My Heart' which competed for sales with the original release. Subsequent singles such as 'Letter Full Of Tears' and 'Operator' sealed the group's R&B credentials, but a switch to the Maxx label in 1964 - where they worked with producer **Van McCoy** - brought their run of successes to a halt. Langston George retired from the group in the early 60s, leaving the line-up that survived into the 80s.

In 1966, Gladys Knight and the Pips were signed to **Motown**'s Soul subsidiary, where they were teamed up with producer/songwriter **Norman Whitfield**. Knight's tough vocals left them slightly out of the Motown mainstream, and throughout their stay with the label the group were regarded as a second-string act. In 1967, they had a major hit single with the original release of 'I Heard It Through The Grapevine', an uncompromisingly tough performance of a song that became a Motown standard in the hands of its author **Marvin Gaye** in 1969. 'The Nitty Gritty' (1968) and 'Friendship Train' (1969) proved equally successful, while the poignant 'If I Were Your Woman' was one of the label's biggest-selling releases of 1970. In the early 70s, the group slowly moved away from their original blues-influenced sound towards a more middle-of-the-road harmony blend. Their new approach brought them success in 1972 with 'Neither One Of Us (Wants To Say Goodbye)'. Later that year, Knight and The Pips elected to leave Motown for **Buddah**, unhappy at the label's shift of operations from Detroit to Hollywood. At Buddah, the group found immediate success with the US chart-topper 'Midnight Train To Georgia', an arresting soul ballad, while major hits such as 'I've Got To Use My Imagination' and 'The Best Thing That Ever Happened To Me' mined a similar vein. In 1974, they performed **Curtis Mayfield**'s soundtrack songs for the film *Claudine*; the following year, the title track of *I Feel A Song* gave them another soul number 1. Their smoother approach was epitomized by the medley of 'The Way We Were/Try To Remember' which was the centrepiece of *Second Anniversary* in 1975 - the same year that saw Gladys and the group host their own US television series. Gladys made her acting debut in *Pipedream* in 1976, for which the group recorded a soundtrack album. Legal problems then dogged their career until the end of the decade, forcing Knight and the Pips to record separately until they could sign a new contract with **CBS**. *About Love* in 1980 teamed them with the **Ashford And Simpson** writing/production partnership, and produced a strident piece of R&B social comment in 'Bourgie Bourgie'. Subsequent releases alternated between the group's R&B and MOR modes, and hits such as 'Save The Overtime (For Me)' and 'You're Number One In My Book' (1983) and, after a move to MCA Records, 'Love Overboard' (1988), demonstrated that they could work equally well in either genre. The latter song earned them a Grammy award for the Best R&B performance in early 1989. Following this, Knight and the Pips split. Merald remained with Gladys Knight when she achieved a UK Top 10 that year with the James Bond movie song 'Licence To Kill', and released *A Good Woman* the following year. She collaborated with **Chaka Khan**, **Brandy** and Tamia on the minor hit 'Missing You' in 1996, taken from the **Queen Latifah** film *Set It Off*.

● ALBUMS: *Letter Full Of Tears* (Fury 1961)★★, *Gladys Knight And The Pips* (Maxx 1964)★★, *Everybody Needs Love* (Soul 1967)★★★, *Feelin' Bluesy* (Soul 1968)★★★, *Silk 'N' Soul* (Soul 1969)★★★, *Nitty Gritty* (Soul 1969)★★★, *All In A Knight's Work* (Soul 1970)★★★, *If I Were Your Woman* (Soul 1971)★★★, *Standing Ovation* (Soul 1972)★★★, *Neither One Of Us* (Soul 1973)★★★★, *All I Need Is Time* (Soul 1973)★★★, *Imagination* (Buddah 1973)★★★★, *Knight Time* (Soul 1974)★★, *Claudine* (Buddah 1974)★★★, *I Feel A Song* (Buddah 1974)★★★, *A Little Knight Music* (Soul 1975)★★★, *Second Anniversary* (Buddah 1975)★★★, *Bless This House* (Buddah 1976)★★, *Pipe Dreams* film soundtrack (Buddah 1976)★★, *Still Together* (Buddah 1977)★★★, *The One And Only* (Buddah 1978)★★★, *About Love* (Columbia 1980)★★, *Touch* (Columbia 1981)★★★, *That Special Time Of Year* (Columbia 1982)★★, *Visions* (Columbia 1983)★★★, *Life* (Columbia 1985)★★★, *All Our Love* (MCA 1987)★★★. Solo: Gladys Knight *Miss Gladys Knight* (Buddah 1979)★★, *Good Woman* (MCA 1991)★★★. The Pips *At Last - The Pips* (Casablanca 1979)★★, *Callin'* (Casablanca 1979)★★.

● COMPILATIONS: *Gladys Knight And The Pips Greatest Hits* (Soul 1970)★★★★, *Anthology* (Motown 1974)★★★★, *The Best Of Gladys Knight And The Pips* (Buddah 1976)★★★★, *30 Greatest* (K-Tel 1977)★★★, *The Collection - 20 Greatest Hits* (1984)★★★, *The Best Of Gladys Knight And The Pips: The Columbia Years* (Columbia 1988)★★★, *Every Beat Of My Heart: The Greatest Hits* (Chameleon 1989)★★★, *The Singles Album* (PolyGram 1989)★★★, *Soul Survivors: The Best Of Gladys Knight And The Pips* (Rhino 1990)★★★★, *17 Greatest Hits* (1992)★★★, *The Greatest Hits* (Camden 1998)★★★.

● FURTHER READING: *Between Each Line Of Pain And Glory - My Life Story*, Gladys Knight.

Knight, Grace

b. 1958, Glasgow, Scotland. Knight was raised in Hertfordshire, England, and her father was a professional opera singer. Music became a part of family life and she began singing in folk clubs and talent contests. Keen to start a career in music Knight sang her passage on a cruise ship to Perth, Australia. There she met musician Bernie Lynch, who became her musical mentor and the co-founder of the rock band **Eurogliders**. The group recorded several albums including *Pink Suit Blue Lady* (1982), *Absolutely* (1985) and *Come In Spinner* (ABC 1989), and national and international tours led to a filmed concert - *Eurogliders Live At Sydney's Horden Pavilion*. The talented Knight also pursued non-musical activities including recording albums for children and publishing a book, *Dragons, Flies, Monsters And Spies*. Her career changed direction when she appeared in the ABC period series, *Come In Spinner*. The resulting album, which she shared with **Vince Jones**, became a huge seller and she found herself singing jazz and torch standards. In 1991 her first solo venture, *Stormy Weather*, sold over 100,000 copies in Australia and she was awarded the title of the Most Popular Australian Jazz Artist the following year. Knight became popular on the jazz and cabaret circuit, usually appearing with a big band under the direction of Roy Alldridge (b. 12 October 1944, Brisbane, Queensland, Australia). In 1996 ABC Music released, *Grace Knight Live*, a double album containing highlights from three performances at the Basement Club in Sydney. Grace Knight is an excellent live performer and her ability to reach an audience emotionally and musically makes her one of the most popular Australian cabaret singers of the 90s.

● ALBUMS: *Stormy Weather* (EMI 1991)★★★, *Gracious* (EMI 1993)★★★★, *Grace Knight Live* (ABC 1996)★★★★.

Knight, Jean

b. 26 June 1943, New Orleans, Louisiana, USA. Knight's early releases with producer **Huey P. Meaux** were overshadowed by 'Mr. Big Stuff' in 1971, one of soul's most popular releases. Released on **Stax** and produced by Wardell Quezerque at the same session that yielded the **King Floyd** hit 'Groove Me', Knight's performance was rewarded with a US number 2 pop hit and R&B number 1. The combination of the irresistible rhythms of southern and New Orleans dance styles indicated the emergence of a new-found style; however, despite several excellent follow-up singles, including 'You Think You're Hot Stuff' and 'Carry On', the studio team were unable to develop this style further. The singer did re-emerge during the 80s with 'You Got The Papers (But I Got The Man)' (1981) and a version of the perennial, if suggestive, favourite, 'My Toot Toot' (1985).

● ALBUMS: *Mr. Big Stuff* (Stax 1971)★★★, *Keep It Comin'* (1981)★★★, *My Toot Toot* (Mirage 1985)★★.

● COMPILATIONS: *Mr. Big Stuff* (Ace 1990)★★★.

Knight, Marion 'Suge'

(see **Death Row Records**)

Knight, Peter

b. 23 June 1917, Exmouth, Devon, England, d. 30 July 1985. An arranger, composer and musical director, Knight played the piano by ear as a young child, and studied piano, harmony and counterpoint privately before making his first broadcast on BBC Radio's *Children's Hour* in 1924. After working in semi-professional bands at venues such as London's Gig club, he won the individual piano award with Al Morter's Rhythm Kings in the 1937 *Melody Maker* All London Dance Band Championship. Three years later he played with the **Ambrose** Orchestra at the Mayfair Hotel before joining the Royal Air Force for service in World War II. On his discharge, he worked with **Sydney Lipton** at the Grosvenor House in London for four years before forming a vocal group, the Peter Knight Singers, which became popular on stage and radio. His wife Babs was a founder member and remained with the group for over 30 years. Besides operating the Singers, Knight also worked for **Geraldo** for a year before becoming a musical director for London West End shows such as *Cockles And Champagne* and *The Jazz Train*, a revue which gave American actress Bertice Reading her first London success. In the late 50s, Knight became musical director for Granada Television, and worked on popular programmes such

as *Spot The Tune* and *Chelsea At Nine*. When he resumed freelance work, he arranged and conducted records by artists such as **Harry Secombe**, **Petula Clark**, **Sammy Davis Jnr.** and the **Moody Blues** (*Days Of Future Passed*). Knight was musical director for a 1964 touring version of **Leslie Bricusse** and **Anthony Newley**'s show, *The Roar Of The Greasepaint - The Smell Of The Crowd*, and for several series of the extremely popular *Morecambe And Wise Show* on television. In the late 70s, Knight spent some time in Hollywood, and conducted the Los Angeles Philharmonic Orchestra in concerts by the **Carpenters**. In 1979, he scored and conducted the music for Roman Polanski's Oscar-nominated film *Tess*. His other film credits include the scores for *Sunstruck* (1972) and *Curse Of The Crimson Altar* (1968). Shortly after his death in 1985, Yorkshire television inaugurated the annual Peter Knight Award which 'celebrates and rewards the craft of musical arranging'. Knight rarely put a foot wrong throughout his career and is remembered still with the utmost respect and affection.

● ALBUMS: with the Peter Knight Singers *Vocal Gems From My Fair Lady* (1959)★★★, with his orchestra *A Knight Of Merrie England* (1960)★★★, with two pianos and orchestra *The Best Of Ivor Novello And Noël Coward* (1961)★★★, with the Peter Knight Singers *Voices In The Night* (Deram 1967)★★★, *Sgt Pepper* (Mercury 1967)★★, with the Moody Blues *Days Of Future Passed* (Deram 1967)★★★★, with Bob Johnson *The King Of Elfland's Daughter* (1977)★★★.

Knight, Robert

b. 24 April 1945, Franklin, Tennessee, USA. Knight made his professional vocal debut with the Paramounts, a harmony quintet consisting of schoolfriends. Signed to **Dot Records**, they recorded 'Free Me' in 1961, a US R&B hit, outselling the cover version by **Johnny Preston**. After this initial success their subsequent releases flopped and resulted in the group breaking up. Unfortunately, they also broke their contract with Dot and were prevented from recording for four-and-a-half years. Knight continued his studies in chemistry at the Tennessee State University where he formed vocal trio the Fairlanes. In 1967, Knight was spotted performing with the Fairlanes in Nashville, and was offered a contract as a solo artist by the Rising Sons label. His first recording, 'Everlasting Love', written by label owners Buzz Cason and Mac Gayden, was an immediate success and earned him a US Top 20 hit. This enduring song was an even bigger success in Britain the following year where a cover version by **Love Affair** reached number 1, and in doing so, kept the singer from progressing further than a Top 40 position. Knight scored two further pop hits at home, 'Blessed Are The Lonely' and 'Isn't It Lonely Together'. In 1973, he overshadowed his previous chart entry in the UK when 'Love On A Mountain Top' reached the Top 10. However, the reissued 'Everlasting Love' went some way to making amends the following year, this time achieving Top 20 status. He continues, perhaps wisely, to advance his career in chemical research, while occasionally performing and recording.

● ALBUMS: *Everlasting Love* (Monument 1967)★★★, *Love On A Mountain Top* (Monument 1968)★★★.

Knight, Sonny

b. Joseph C. Smith, 1934, Maywood, Illinois, USA. Sonny Knight succeeded with one beautiful R&B ballad, 'Confidential', in the *Billboard* charts in 1956 before fading from the scene. Smith's family moved to Los Angeles in the early 50s, where he not only sang but wrote a novel. Encouraged to seek a recording contract by a girlfriend, Smith looked in the telephone book and called the first label listed, Aladdin Records. He changed his professional name to Sonny Knight and recorded unsuccessfully for Aladdin, then switching to **Specialty Records**. Specialty producer **Robert 'Bumps' Blackwell** partnered him with songwriter Dorinda Morgan, who penned 'Confidential' for Knight. The single reached number 17 in the USA, but Knight was unable to follow it up. He had two less successful singles in the mid-60s before retiring from singing.

● ALBUMS: *If You Want This Love* (1964)★★★.
● COMPILATIONS: *Confidential* (1985)★★★.
● FURTHER READING: *The Day The Music Died*, Sonny Knight.

Knight, Terry

b. Terry Knapp, 9 April 1943, Flint, Michigan, USA. Knight first achieved fame as a disc jockey on Detroit's influential station CKLW. Fired for his controversial views, he formed Terry Knight And The Pack who debuted in 1966 with a sympathetic interpretation of the **Yardbirds**' 'You're A Better Man Than I'. The group then scored a US Top 50 hit with a dramatic version of '(I) Who Have Nothin'', but split when later releases flopped. While his former colleagues continued as the Fabulous Pack, Knight pursued a lacklustre and unsuccessful, solo career. Never more than adequate as a vocalist, his acumen lay in business and promotion, which flourished when Mel Schacher (ex-**? And The Mysterians**) joined Mark Farner and Don Brewer, (both ex-members of the Pack), in **Grand Funk Railroad**. Under Knight's ruthless direction this musically pedestrian trio became one of America's biggest-selling acts during the early 70s. Their mentor later represented Bloodrock, but his empire crumbled in 1972 when both attractions entered protracted legal suits to sever their management relationships. Knight lost both cases, but re-emerged with a new label, Brown Bag, which featured Mom's Apple Pie and **Wild Cherry**. However, his entrepreneurial skills had now deserted him, Brown Bag was a commercial failure, and a disillusioned Knight abandoned music altogether in favour of other business interests.

● ALBUMS: *Terry Knight And The Pack* (Cameo Parkway 1966)★★.

Knights Of The Occasional Table

South-east London multiracial dance band, comprising Steve, Nygell, Moose, Andrew and vocalist Aquamanda. Their debut album was initially released on their own label before being picked up by **Club Dog**. Its title - *Knees Up Mother Earth* - offered a big clue to their sound, wherein modern technological means (programmes, drum machines, samplers) were employed to deliver a primal beat with varied ethnic stylings. The Knights have not been as immediately successful as stylistic counterparts **Fun-Da-Mental** or **Trans-Global Underground**, ensuring Steve and Andy continue their day-time jobs as psychiatric nurse and journalist for *Stage And Television Today* respectively.

● ALBUMS: *Knees Up Mother Earth* (Club Dog 1993)★★★.

Knobloch, Fred

b. Jackson, Mississippi, USA. Fred Knobloch enjoyed one brief brush with pop success before an equally brief solo run on the country charts. Knobloch had been a member of the rock band Let's Eat in the 70s. When that effort ran its course after six years, Knobloch signed as a country-rock artist to the Scotti Brothers Records label. 'Why Not Me' was the most visible result, a number 18 hit in 1980. That same year and the following he made number 10 on the US country charts with two successive singles, 'Killin' Time' (a duet with actress Susan Anton which also made number 26 pop) and a cover of **Chuck Berry**'s 'Memphis'. One final country chart single, 'I Had It All', came in 1982, after which Knobloch teamed up with Thom Schuyler Jnr. and Paul Overstreet as the successful trio Schuyler, Knobloch And Overstreet (SKO). That outfit became SKB when Craig Bickhardt replaced Overstreet in 1987.

● ALBUMS: *Why Not Me* (1980)★★★.

Knock On Wood - Eddie Floyd

Eddie Floyd began his career as a member of gospel act the **Falcons**, before embarking on a solo career which was initially ill-starred. Having joined the **Stax** label as a songwriter and performer, he struck gold with 'Knock On Wood', one of soul music's immutable anthems. The album it inspired is equally strong, with its judicious cross-section of original songs and cover versions. Floyd reclaims '634-5789', which he wrote for **Wilson Pickett** and breathes new life into material first recorded by **James Ray**, **Tommy Tucker** and **Jerry Butler**. The label's brilliant house band provides supple, rhythmic support to an underrated singer, whose strengths are displayed on this excellent album.

● Tracks: *Knock On Wood; Something You Got; But It's Alright; I Stand Accused; If You Gotta Make A Fool Of Somebody; I Don't Want To Cry; Raise Your Hand; Got To Make A Comeback; 634-5789; I've Just Been Feeling Bad; High Heel Sneakers; Warm And Tender Love.*
● First released 1967
● UK peak chart position: 36
● USA peak chart position: did not chart

Knopfler, David

b. 27 December 1951, Glasgow, Scotland. David cemented elder brother Mark's lead vocals and fretboard solos with subordinate guitar chords until the heated complications of their relationship forced **Dire Straits** to replace David with Hal Lindes (keyboards) in September 1982. Within a year came David Knopfler's first effort as a solo recording artist, *Release* (and its single, 'Soul Kissing'), a one-off project for Peach River Records. Despite a similar commercial failure with 1984's 'Madonna's Daughter' for Fast Alley, a third independent label, Making Waves, issued *Behind The Lines* and *Cut The Wire* plus attendant singles like 'Heart To Heart' and 'Shock Waves'. The continued success of Dire Straits ensured that these sold enough by association to warrant release on CD. Nevertheless, the winding up of Making Waves' affairs in 1988 left Knopfler still overshadowed by his brother's more evident commercial talent. His 1994 album *The Giver* had some beautiful touches but was ultimately a sombre afair. Knopfler has gone some way to achieving his 'dream of success without fame, happiness without hype or glory'. Certainly he has stayed away from the usual pitfulls of the rock world and should be applauded for remaining sane. Now if only he could allow his contentment and happiness permeate his records.

● ALBUMS: *Release* (Peach River 1983)★★★, *Behind The Lines* (1985)★★★, *Cut The Wire* (1987)★★★, *Lips Against The Steel* (1988)★★, *Lifelines* (1990)★★, *The Giver* (Permanent 1994)★★★.

Knopfler, Mark

b. 12 August 1949, Glasgow, Scotland. This homely ex-teacher is **Dire Straits'** main asset through his skill as a composer, a tuneful if detached vocal style - and a terse, resonant fretboard dexterity admired by **Eric Clapton** and **Chet Atkins**, both of whom sought his services for studio and concert projects in the 80s. Courted also by movie directors to score incidental music, he inaugurated a parallel solo career in 1983 with David Puttnam's film *Local Hero* from which an atmospheric tie-in album sold moderately well with its single 'Going Home' (the main title theme) a minor UK hit (which was incorporated into the band's stage act). Further film work included soundtracks to *Cal*, Bill Forsyth's *Comfort And Joy* and with Dire Straits' Guy Fletcher, *The Princess Bride*. After he and the group's Pick Withers played on **Bob Dylan**'s *Slow Train Coming*, Knopfler was asked to produce the enigmatic American's *Infidels* in 1983. Further commissions included diverse acts such as **Randy Newman**, Willy (**Mink**) DeVille (*Miracle*), **Aztec Camera** (*Knife*) and **Tina Turner**, for whom he composed the title track of *Private Dancer*. Knopfler was also in demand as a session guitarist, counting **Steely Dan** (*Gaucho*), **Phil Lynott** (*Solo In Soho*), **Van Morrison** (*Beautiful Vision*) and **Bryan Ferry** (*Boys And Girls*) among his clients. By no means confining such assistance to the illustrious,

he was also heard on albums by Sandy McLelland And The Backline and **Kate And Anna McGarrigle** (*Love Over And Over*). For much of the later 80s, he was preoccupied with domestic commitments and, in 1986, he was incapacitated by a fractured collar bone following an accident at a celebrity motor race during the Australian Grand Prix. In 1989, however, he and old friends **Brendan Croker** and **Steve Phillips** formed the **Notting Hillbillies** for an album and attendant tour, but neither this venture nor several nights backing Clapton during a 1990 Albert Hall season indicated an impending schism in Dire Straits' ranks. Throughout the first half of the 90s Knopfler sessioned on countless albums and it was only in 1996 that his 'official' solo career was announced. The debut *Golden Heart* featured support from slide blues guitarist **Sonny Landreth**, singer songwriter **Paul Brady**, the **Chieftains** and **Vince Gill**.

● ALBUMS: *Music From 'Local Hero'* film soundtrack (Vertigo 1983)★★★, *Cal - Music From The Film* film soundtrack (Vertigo 1984)★★★, *The Princess Bride* film soundtrack (Warners 1987)★★, *Last Exit To Brooklyn* film soundtrack (Warners 1989)★★, with Chet Atkins *Neck And Neck* (Columbia 1990)★★★, *Golden Heart* (Mercury 1996)★★★, *Wag The Dog* mini-album soundtrack (Vertigo 1998)★★.

● FURTHER READING: *Mark Knopfler: An Unathorised Biography*, Myles Palmer.

Knowledge

Knowledge were based in the Rema area of Kingston, Jamaica, West Indies, where they established a solid reputation. The group began their career in the late 70s under the guidance of DJ **Tapper Zukie**. The line-up included Anthony Doyley, Delroy Folding, Earl MacFarlane, Michael Smith, Michael Samuels, and later, Paul Freeman. The group's debut, 'Make Faith', featured Zukie introducing the band as his protégés, and proved a winning combination. They released a number of hits through Zukie's Stars label, which culminated in a major label signing in 1978. The contract was short-lived and in the early 80s the group went through a period of anonymity. During this unproductive time, Freeman, under the pseudonym of Jah Showie, linked up with Trevor 'Leggo Beast' Douglas to set up his own Sunshine label. In 1981 Samuels, under the guise of Michael Knowledge, attempted a solo career with the release of 'Dreadlock Time'. In the early 90s the band began recording for **Roy Cousins**, resulting in the hits 'Na Buy Apartheid', 'Chant Rasta Man' and 'Fire Burn', for his Tamoki-Wambesi label. The group avoided the **digital** sound, preferring to use real musicians, and enlisted some of Jamaica's top players including Pablove Black, **Winston Wright, Leroy 'Horsemouth' Wallace** and **Sowell Radics**. After a lengthy delay, the sessions eventually appeared on a CD compilation in 1995.

● ALBUMS: *Hail Dread* (A&M 1978)★★★.

● COMPILATIONS: *Stumbling Block* (Tamoki-Wambesi 1995)★★★★.

Knowles, Pamela

b. c.1950, Australia. After studying drama at the American Conservatory Theater and at London's Academy of Music and Dramatic Art, Knowles spent some time working in the theatre in New York before deciding to concentrate on singing. She played clubs in New York, Paris, where she worked with **Claude Bolling**'s big band, and London, appearing at **Ronnie Scott**'s club. She has also sung in her native Australia and in New Zealand, sometimes with classical orchestras such as the Christchurch Symphony, and at jazz festivals. Her rich, contralto voice lends itself admirably to ballads and show tunes but her repertoire extends beyond these to incorporate Latin and contemporary pop. Her dramatic flair and big voice, allied to a great stage presence, have considerable audience appeal and she is at her best in live settings that allow her to develop this enviable rapport.

● ALBUMS: *Love Dance* (Larrikin 1993)★★★.

Knowling, Ransom

b. 24 June 1912. Knowling played bass, and was best known for his extensive work as a session player, used by producer Lester Melrose on hundreds of blues records in Chicago in the 30s and 40s, by artists such as **Big Bill Broonzy**, **Tampa Red** and **Sonny Boy** 'Rice Miller' **Williamson**. His rock-solid bass work was also used to add a more urban sound to the work of country blues singers such as **Tommy McClennan**. In later years he claimed never to have liked the blues, preferring more sophisticated sounds, but he owes virtually all his fame to that idiom. Although known to have died, details of Knowling's death are scant.

Knox, Buddy

b. Buddy Wayne Knox, 14 April 1933, Happy, Texas, USA. Knox was one of the first 'pop-abilly' hit-makers in the 50s. With bassist **Jimmy Bowen**, he formed the country band the Rhythm Orchids in 1956, adding Don Lanier (guitar) and Dave Alldred (drums). The following year Knox sang lead vocals on 'Party Doll', recorded at **Norman Petty**'s Oklahoma studio. First issued locally on the Triple-D label, it became the first release on Roulette, formed by New York nightclub owner Maurice Levy. 'Party Doll' went to number 1 in the USA. At the same session Bowen recorded another hit, 'I'm Stickin' With You'. With his light voice skimming over the insistent rhythms, Knox was the first in a line of Texan rockers that included **Buddy Holly** and **Roy Orbison**. Both 'Rock Your Little Baby To Sleep' and the gimmicky 'Hula Love' were Top 20 hits later in 1957, when he also appeared in the film *Disc Jockey Jamboree*. Although he toured frequently with **Alan Freed**'s package shows, 'Somebody Touched Me' (1958) was his only later hit and in 1960, Knox and Bowen moved to Los Angeles. There, Knox turned to 'teenbeat' material such as 'Lovey Dovey', 'Ling Ting Tong' and 'She's Gone' (a minor UK hit in 1962) with producer **Snuff Garrett**. During the mid-60s he returned to country music, recording in Nashville for **Reprise** and had a hit with 'Gypsy Man', composed by ex-**Crickets**' Sonny Curtis. This led to film appearances in *Travellin' Light* (with **Waylon Jennings**) and *Sweet Country Music* (with **Boots Randolph** and **Johnny Paycheck**). Knox was now based in Canada, where he set up his own Sunnyhill label. He also visited Europe with rockabilly revival shows during the 70s and early 80s. Jimmy Bowen became one of Nashville's most powerful A&R men, working for **Dot**, MCA and latterly **Capitol**.

● ALBUMS: *Buddy Knox* (Roulette 1958)★★★, with Jim Bowen *Buddy Knox And Jimmy Bowen* (Roulette 1959)★★★, *Buddy Knox In Nashville* (1967)★★★, *Gypsy Man* (United Artists 1969)★★★, *Four Rock Legends* (1978)★★, *Sweet Country Music* (Rockstar 1981)★★, *Texas Rockabilly Man* (Rockstar 1987)★★, *Travellin' Light* (Rundell 1988)★★.

● COMPILATIONS: *Buddy Knox's Golden Hits* (Liberty 1962)★★★, *Rock Reflections* (Sunset 1971)★★★, *Party Doll* (Pye 1978)★★★, *Greatest Hits* (Rockhouse 1985)★★★, *Liberty Takes* (Charly 1986)★★★, *Party Doll And Other Hits* (Capitol 1988)★★★, *The Best Of Buddy Knox* (Rhino 1990)★★★★, with Jim Bowen *The Complete Roulette Recordings* (Sequel 1996)★★★★.

● FILMS: *Jamboree* aka *Disc Jockey Jamboree* (1957).

Knox, Chris

b. New Zealand. A prolific singer, producer and songwriter, particularly in the 90s, Knox first rose to prominence as part of the New Zealand punk band the **Enemy**. From there he moved to **Toy Love**, who were briefly signed to a major record label, before forming a more permanent partnership with Alec Bathgate as the **Tall Dwarfs**. His solo career began in 1983 with *Songs For Cleaning Guppies*, which stayed close to the musical territory explored by the Tall Dwarfs - short songs dependent on Knox's celebrated instinct for pop hooks. There was also humour in abundance - notably on the bristling 'Jesus Loves You', which followed Marx's tenet about religion as 'the opiate of the masses'. Subsequent albums have continued to explore the possibilities of pop acoustics. Songs such as 'Haze' sardonically parodied New Zealand's sesquicentennial celebrations of 1990, at which time his solo output increased. In keeping with his work for the Tall Dwarfs, none of his numerous albums offer a definitive statement, but taken as a whole his discography is a strong legacy, his best songs a peerless combination of humbling humour and acute observation.

● ALBUMS: *Songs For Cleaning Guppies* (Flying Nun 1983)★★★, *Monk III* cassette only (Walking Monk 1987)★★★, *Seizure* (Flying Nun 1989)★★★, *Not Given Lightly/Guppiplus* (Flying Nun 1989)★★★, *Song For 1990* (Flying Nun 1990)★★★, *Croaker* (Flying Nun 1991)★★★, *Meat* (Communion 1993)★★★, *Polyfoto, Duck Shaped Pain & Gum* (Flying Nun 1993)★★★.

Knuckles, Frankie

b. c.1955, New York, USA. Knuckles is often credited with 'creating' house music while a Chicago DJ at venues like the Warehouse and Powerplant. As a child he was inspired by his sister's jazz records, and took up the double bass. He attended the Dwyer School Of Art in the Bronx and F.I.T. in Manhattan to study textile design. However, he was soon lured into DJing at $50 a night at the Better Days emporium. Eventually Larry Levan of the Paradise Garage asked him to work at the Continental Baths club, and he was subsequently invited to travel to Chicago for the opening of the Warehouse. At the time he played mainly Philadelphia soul and R&B, bringing back hot records from New York for his shows. According to Knuckles, the term 'house' had not yet been coined. 'One day I was driving in the South Side and passed a club that had a sign outside that read 'We Play House Music'. I asked them what it meant and he told me that they played the same music as I did'. Into the 90s he was still to be found orchestrating the dancefloor until 10am at New York's Sound Factory on a Saturday night. The Powerplant, which he set up after the Warehouse, lasted for three years before outbreaks of violence and the criminal fraternity appeared on the fringes. Knuckles moved into production and recording work with **DJ International**, recording 'Tears' with the help of **Robert Owens** and also producing 'Baby Wants To Ride' for **Jamie Principle** on **Trax** and. About which DJ International's Rocky Jones was singularly unimpressed, obtaining a tape of the record and pressing it up in competition, though Knuckles reasoned he was only signed to DJI as an artist. He had first started to remix records for his own DJing purposes, and later would go on to become an in-demand remixer for everyone from **Chaka Khan** to the **Pet Shop Boys** and **Kenny Thomas** following his unofficial peerage by dance cognoscenti. He even remixed **Nu Colours** version of his own classic, 'Tears'. He also recorded as a solo artist for Ten/**Virgin**. Knuckles became the partner of **David Morales** in Def-Mix Productions, one of the most high profile remix and production teams ever. Morales was present on Knuckles' 1991 album, along with frequent co-conspirators Satoshi Tomiie, Ed Kupper (who wrote the hit single, 'The Whistle Song') and Danny Madden. Brave attempts to tackle ballads proved misguided, although back in the familiar territory of house Knuckles can usually be relied upon to at least pull muster, and at best pull the foundations down. His collaboration with **Adeva** on *Welcome To The Real World* enhanced and spread his reputation.

● ALBUMS: *Frankie Knuckles Presents: The Album* (Westside 1990)★★★★, *Beyond The Mix* (Ten 1991),★★★ *Welcome To The Real World* (Virgin America 1995)★★★.

Knudsen, Kenneth

b. 28 September 1946, Copenhagen, Denmark. Knudsen is a keyboardist and composer who during the 70s co-led, with alto saxophonist and composer Karsten Vogel, two of the best Danish jazz-rock groups, Secret Oyster and Birds Of Beauty. In 1976 Knudsen joined **Palle Mikkelborg**'s Entrance band inspired by **Weather Report**. Knudsen's keyboards provides an ambience of tonal colouration that works best in slow, sparse minimalist settings. Close to **ECM Records**'s sound Knudsen's music successfully avoids any new age saccharine mellowness.

● ALBUMS: with Karsten Vogel *Birds Of Beauty* (1976)★★★, with Niels-Henning Ørsted Pedersen *Pictures* (1977)★★★, *Anima* (Kong Pære 1979)★★★, with Ørsted Pedersen, Palle Mikkelborg *Heart To Heart* (1986)★★★, *I Me Him* (1987)★★★★, *Bombay Hotel* (1989),★★ *Sounds And Silence* (1993)★★★, *Nordic Frames* (1994)★★★.

Koda, Cub

b. Michael Koda, 1 August 1948, Detroit, Michigan, USA. Guitarist Michael 'Cub' Koda led the hard-rock/soul trio **Brownsville Station** during the 70s and later released a string of roots-oriented solo albums for various labels. Koda took his nickname from a character on television's *Mickey Mouse Club*, Cubby. Raised listening to jazz records as a child, he began playing drums at the age of five, switching to guitar at the age of 13. His first high-school band, the Del-Tinos, recorded three singles and a number of unreleased tracks later collected on an album. In 1969, he formed Brownsville Station, at first a 50s-rock-orientated group, with Mike Lutz (guitar), Tony Diggins (bass) and T.J. Cronley (drums). Their claim to fame was the 1973/4 US number 3/UK Top 30 single 'Smokin' In The Boys' Room' (successfully covered by **Mötley Crüe** in 1985). When Brownsville Station disbanded, Koda formed the Points and later the Bone Gods, as well as releasing solo albums spotlighting rockabilly music, blues, **Chuck Berry** and **Bo Diddley**, and one on which he acted as a disc jockey, playing his favourite records and providing between-song patter. He also penned a regular record review column for the US record collector magazine *Goldmine*.

● ALBUMS: *Cub Koda And The Points* (1980)★★★, *It's The Blues, Volume 1* (1981)★★, *That's What I Like About The South* (1984)★★★, *Go! Go! With The Del-Tinos* (1984)★★★, *The Cub Koda Crazy Show* (1984)★★★, *Let's Get Funky* (1985)★★, *Cub Digs Chuck* (1989)★★★, *Cub Digs Bo* (1991)★★★.

Kodaks

An R&B vocal group from Newark, New Jersey, USA, the original members were lead Pearl McKinnon, first tenor James Patrick, second tenor William Franklin, baritone Larry Davis and bass William Miller. The Kodaks were representative of the pre-teen lead sound, featuring a girlish and innocent, pre-pubescent male voice. When the pre-teen leads first became popular, it was assumed that they were all male, but research conducted in the 70s into the history of many such groups discovered that some were led by females, notably Pearl McKinnon of the Kodaks and Faith Taylor of the Sweet Teens. The Kodaks came together in 1957 and signed with **Bobby Robinson**'s Fury label. The first release paired a terrific jump, 'Little Boy And

Girl', with the touching ballad 'Teenager's Dream', and received significant local airplay. The second release, in the spring of 1958, the exhilarating 'Oh Gee, Oh Gosh', was their most sizeable hit, winning air time on the entire east coast and some in the Midwest. The b-side, 'Make Believe World', was especially appealing, with creatively harmonized choruses. At this time, Davis and Franklin left to form the Sonics, who would later record 'This Broken Heart'. They were replaced with Richard Dixon and Harold Jenkins. Two more singles followed, the last one being the excellent jump 'Runaround Baby' (1958), but it did not attract the public who were evidently tiring of the **Frankie Lymon** sound. McKinnon left the group around 1959 and a reorganized Kodaks recorded some more singles for first J&S and then Wink before finally disbanding in 1961. Meanwhile, McKinnon became lead of a new group, Pearl And The Deltars, who released a fine single on Fury in 1961 that met with little success. McKinnon in the 70s was the amazing 'Frankie Lymon' lead in the reunited Teenagers group, and those who heard her Kodaks tracks in the 50s could easily understand how she managed the deception.

● COMPILATIONS: *The Kodaks Versus The Starlites* (Sphere Sound 1965)★★★, *Oh Gee Oh Gosh* (Relic 1992)★★★.

Kodo

An ensemble specializing in traditional Japanese drumming techniques, Kodo became a successful international export during the mid-90s. *Ibuki*, released in 1997, was their tenth album, and was promoted with appearances on syndicated US television, including the *David Letterman Show*. The group also appeared live at Carnegie Hall, New York, and became one of the most popular world music acts to emerge from the Orient. Indeed, from their base on Sado Island in the Sea of Japan, the group now divides its time into three parts - the first part of the year touring America and Europe, the second in Japan, and the remainder at home, working on new material. Comprising 19 members, Kodo practise 'taiko', the ancient Japanese martial drumming style, with the ritualistic percussion accentuated by the use of chanting and flute. Since forming in 1981 the group has performed over 2,000 concerts in five continents, collaborating with artists including **Grateful Dead** drummer **Mickey Hart**, fusion maestro **Bill Laswell** (who produced *Ibuki*) and jazz drummer **Max Roach**. Group member Eiichi Saito explained the meaning of the term 'Kodo' to *Billboard* magazine in 1997: 'The drum is a primordial expression of the human spirit - and it's in all cultures. When I play, I can feel a connection with people from Minneapolis or London.'

● ALBUMS: including *Heartbeat Drummers Of Japan* (Sheffield Lab 1985)★★★, with Isao Tomia *Nasca Fantasy* (Tristar/Sony 1991)★★★★, *The Hunted* (Tristar/Sony 1992)★★★, *The Best Of Kodo* (Tristar/Sony 1993)★★★, *Ibuki* (Tristar/Sony 1997)★★★.

● VIDEOS: *Live At The Acropolis* (Sony 1995).

Koehler, Ted

b. 14 July 1894, Washington DC, USA, d. 17 December 1973, Santa Monica, California, USA. A lyricist for several of the most appealing songs of the 30s and early 40s, Koehler was educated in New York, and Newark, New Jersey. As a young man, he worked as a photo-engraver, a theatre pianist, and a song plugger in silent movie cinemas, as well as writing special material for vaudeville performers. After writing 'When Lights Are Low' with **Ted Fio Rito** and **Gus Kahn** in 1923, he produced night club floor shows for a time, and when he began writing songs consistently in the early 30s, many of them were introduced in Cotton Club shows and revues such as *Earl Carroll's Vanities*, Rhythmania, and *Brown Sugar*. His chief collaborator was **Harold Arlen**, and in 1930 their future standard, 'Get Happy', was introduced by **Ruth Etting** in the *9:15 Revue*. During the next few years, Koehler and Arlen wrote several other superior and enduring numbers in a list that included 'Hittin' The Bottle', 'Linda', 'Between The Devil And The Deep Blue Sea', 'I Love A Parade', 'Kickin' The Gong Around', 'Wrap Your Troubles In Dreams', 'I Gotta Right To Sing The Blues', (theme song of trombonist and bandleader **Jack Teagarden**), 'I've Got The World On A String', 'Minnie The Moocher's Wedding Day', 'Calico Days', 'Happy As The Day Is Long', 'Stormy Weather', 'As Long As I Live', 'Here Goes (A Fool),' and 'Ill Wind' (1934). These songs were popularized by artists such as **Lena Horne**, **Cab Calloway**, Aida Ward, **Bing Crosby**, and the **Jimmy Lunceford** Orchestra. Arlen and Koehler's 'Let's Fall In Love' was the title number for a 1934 movie starring Gregory Ratoff, with Edmund Lowe and Ann Sothern, and it also contained their 'Breakfast Ball', 'This Is Only The Beginning', and 'Love Is Love Anywhere'. In the late 30s and 40s, Koehler wrote extensively for films such as *Curly Top* ('Animal Crackers In My Soup' and 'It's All So New To Me', both with **Irving Caesar** and **Ray Henderson**; 'Curly Top', with Henderson), *King Of Burlesque* ('I'm Shooting High', 'I've Got My Fingers Crossed', 'Lovely Lady', with **Jimmy McHugh**), *Dimples* ('Picture Me Without You', 'Hey, What Did The Bluebird Say?', with McHugh), the 1937 version of *Artists And Models* ('Public Melody Number One', with Arlen), *Up In Arms* ('Now I Know', 'All Out For Freedom', 'Tess's Torch Song', with Arlen), and *Hollywood Canteen* ('What Are You Doing the Rest Of Your Life?', with **Burton Lane**), and *My Wild Irish Rose* ('Wee Rose Of Killarney', 'Miss Lindy Lou', 'The Natchez And The Robert E. Lee', 'There's Room In My Heart For Them All', M.K. Jerome, 1947). Among Koehler's other best known songs were 'When The Sun Comes Out' (Arlen), 'Ev'ry Night About This Time' (**James V. Monaco**), and several collaborations with **Rube Bloom**, including two Ruth Etting hits, 'Stay On The Right Side Sister' and 'Out In The Cold Again'; and the lovely ballad 'Don't Worry 'Bout Me'. Koehler and Bloom also wrote the catchy 'Truckin'', which was sung by

Cora La Redd and her Ensemble in a Cotton Club Revue of 1935. Nearly 30 years later, a new version which was retitled 'Everybody's Twistin'' in order to cash in on the early 60s dance fad, was taken into the UK chart by **Frank Sinatra**.

Koerner, 'Spider' John

b. 31 August 1938, Rochester, New York, USA. Koerner, who earned his nickname due to his previous employment at an automobile shop where he climbed shelves to reach parts, studied aeronautical engineering at the University of Minnesota. He was into his second year as a student before he picked up a guitar for the first time. Bitten by the folk bug, he left college and drove aimlessly around America, enlisting in the US Mariness at one point. When he eventually returned to Minneapolis he met **Bob Dylan** and, more importantly, **Dave Ray**. On a visit to Rochester he also met Tony Glover - and with him and Ray formed an acoustic blues trio, **Koerner, Ray And Glover**. They played the coffee-house circuit together before eventually securing a recording contract with Audiophile Records through contacts at the influential *Little Sandy Review* magazine. However, the liaison with Ray and Glover was never intended to be a permanent one, and after the success of his debut *Spider's Blues* set he concentrated on a solo career. In 1969 he recorded a more pop-orientated album with pianist Willie Murphy, *Running, Jumping, Standing Still*. This included 'I Ain't Blue', a song later covered by **Bonnie Raitt**. *Music Is Just A Bunch Of Notes* was recorded for Ray's new Sweet Jane imprint in 1972, but afterwards Koerner left the USA for **Denmark**. There his interest in blues faded in favour of folk; he formed another trio in Denmark, accompanied by washboard and harmonica, but issued only one further recording, *Some American Folk Songs Like They Used To Be*. He returned to the USA in 1977 and spent a long period out of music. He did tour the UK, however, appearing at the **Cambridge Folk Festival** and a series of club dates. He has continued recording into the 90s, often linking up with old friends Ray and Glover in a resurrected version of the trio that first established him as one of the most talented songwriters of his generation.

● ALBUMS: *Spider's Blues* (Elektra 1965)★★★, with Willie Murphy *Running, Jumping, Standing Still* (1968)★★★, *Music Is Just A Bunch Of Notes* (Sweet Jane 1972)★★★, *Some American Folk Songs Like They Used To Be* (Sweet Jane 1974)★★★, *Nobody Knows The Trouble I've Been* (Red House 1986)★★★, *Raised By Humans* (Red House 1992)★★★, *Star Geezer* (Red House 1996)★★★.

Koerner, Ray And Glover

This US trio, who were a pivotal influence on the **Beatles**, among many others, were among the first to authenticate the notion that 'white men *can* play the blues'. Tony 'Little Sun' Glover, **Dave Ray** and **John 'Spider' Koerner** first began to play together in the early 60s. Koerner had previously been a contemporary of **Bob Dylan** at the University of Minnesota. By the time he linked up with Ray and Glover, he had perfected a unique take on country blues, employing a customized seven-string guitar and rack harmonica while writing new blues songs rather than relying on standards. The trio released their first album for Audiophile Records in 1963, which eventually brought them to the attention of **Elektra Records**. They reissued the album (minus four tracks on the original to ensure a better pressing quality), and also hosted the follow-up collection. Koerner was still clearly the artistic force behind each of these sets - a situation exemplified by the fact that Ray (guitar) and Glover (harmonica) rarely appeared on the same track. Unlike Koerner, who launched his solo career in 1965 with *Spider Blues*, they never toured Europe. Although they reunited sporadically, each member of the trio subsequently took a solo path, primarily because the basis of their collaboration had never been formalized. As Dave Ray told *Folk Roots* in 1996: 'It was travel arrangements primarily. We were often in the same town, so we all showed up in the same place at the same time. We didn't really do that many turns together.' However, there were further reunions over ensuing years, the most notable being a support to the **Who** at the Guthrie Theater in 1968 and a performance at the Winnipeg Festival in 1995. In the early 70s Ray also founded Sweet Jane Records, a label that issued recordings by Koerner as well as **Bonnie Raitt** and **Junior Wells**. Ray And Glover also released three albums in the late 80s and early 90s, which were issued on the punk labels Treehouse and Tim Kerr Records.

● ALBUMS: *Blues, Rags & Hollers* (Audiophile/Elektra 1963)★★★, *Lots More Blues, Rags & Hollers* (Elektra 1964)★★★, *The Return Of Koerner, Ray & Glover* (Elektra 1965)★★★, *Live At St. Olaf Festival* (Elektra 1968)★★★, *One Foot In The Groove* (Tim Kerr 1996)★★★.

● VIDEOS: *Blues, Rags & Hollers: The Koerner, Ray & Glover Story* (Latch Lake 1986).

Kofi

b. Carol Simms. Formerly with female **lovers rock** trio **Brown Sugar**, Simms pursued an equally prolific career as **Kofi** following the former's demise in the mid-80s. She worked with the **Mad Professor**, revisiting Brown Sugar's past glories on 'I Am So Proud' and 'I'm In Love With A Dreadlocks', alongside versions of 'Place In The Sun' and 'Didn't I'. She also recorded a duet with John McLean on 'I'm Still In Love With You'. Kofi released three albums on **Ariwa Sounds** and one on **Atlantic Records**. In 1990 her remake of the Brown Sugar songs, 'Proud Of Mandella' and 'Dread A Who She Love', were also used as the basis for combination hits with DJ **Macka B**. In the 90s she released the popular 'Coming Down To See Me' and continued to maintain a high profile as a lovers rock performer.

● ALBUMS *Black With Sugar* (Ariwa 1989)★★★, *Wishing Well* (Ariwa 1992)★★, *Fridays Child* (Ariwa 1994)★★, *A Very Reggae Christmas* (Atlantic 1994)★.

Koglmann, Franz

b. 22 May 1947, Vienna, Austria. Koglmann took up the trumpet after seeing a **Louis Armstrong** concert at the age of 13. Despite this epiphany, he studied exclusively classical trumpet at the Vienna Conservatory and his interest in jazz was reawakened only in 1968, this time by an encounter with **Miles Davis**. Koglmann, trumpeter, flügelhorn player and composer, is serious about 'roots' and the influence of countrymen Schubert, Berg and Krenek is to be discerned in his music, tempering and shaping the nature of the jazz, and giving new credence to the maligned ideas of Third Stream Music. Though *A White Line*, specifically setting out to celebrate the (under-recognized) achievements of white jazz musicians, prompted predictable sermonizing from (white) critics, other Koglmann recordings draw upon the music of **Thelonious Monk** and **Dizzy Gillespie**, and the list of distinguished soloists who have played with Koglmann's band includes **Bill Dixon** and **Alan Silva**, as well as **Paul Bley**, **Ran Blake** and **Steve Lacy**. Most of Koglmann's music is written for his 10-12 piece band, the Pipetet, launched in 1973. The prevalent mood is one of melancholy, the compositional structures are labyrinthine, the execution is consistently brilliant.

● ALBUMS: *Flaps* (1973)★★★, *Opium/For Franz* (1976)★★★, *Schlaf Schlemmer, Schlaf Magritte* (Hat Art 1984)★★★★, *Good Night* (1985)★★★, *Ich, Franz Koglmann* (Hat Art 1986)★★★★, *About Yesterday's Ezzthetics* (Hat Art 1987)★★★, *Orte Der Geometrie* (Hat Art 1988)★★★, *A White Line* (Hat Art 1989)★★★, *The Use Of Memory* (Hat Art 1990)★★★, *L'Heure Bleue* (Hat Art 1991)★★★, *Canto I-IV* (Hat Art 1993)★★★, with Paul Bley, Gary Peacock *Annette* (1993)★★.

Koite, Sourokata

b. 1955, Tambacouda, Gambia. As has been the case with many famous Gambian musicians, Sourokata Koite was born into a family of griots (or folklorists). As a child he was instructed in both the kora and balafon, before travelling to Dakar in 1975 to join the staff of a tourist hotel band. After securing a contract with a French company in 1977 he relocated to northern France, performing at another hotel for six months. With his indenture completed he sought employment in Paris in 1978. Throughout the late 70s and early 80s he made his precarious living playing restaurant and club dates in the metropolis, gradually building momentum as a 'name' African artist. This translated into several prestigious festival slots around Europe, and the release of his first album, recorded in Holland. A second album followed in 1987, recorded with fellow griot Diombe Kouyate as accompanying balafon player.

● ALBUMS: *En Hollande* (1985)★★★, with Diombe Kouyate *Les Griots* (JND 1987)★★★.

Kojak And Liza

Kojak (b. Floyd Anthony Perch, 30 September 1959, Kingston, Jamaica, West Indies) began his career chant-ing on various **sound systems** under the guise of Pretty Boy Floyd. He adopted the gangster image that had proved successful for **Dennis Alcapone** and **Dillinger**, but was unable to emulate the fortunes of his role models and changed his stage name to Nigger Kojak in response to a title given to him by his followers. Inspired by the 70s television series *Kojak*, he emulated the show's star with a shaved head and often appeared with the obligatory lollipop. His debut, 'Massacre', proved a local hit and led on to many others. In 1978 **Dennis Brown** had an international hit with the remake of 'Money In My Pocket', which was followed by 'Ain't That Loving You', featuring Kojak And Liza performing 'Hole In De Bucket'. The hit proved a success in the dancehall, which resulted in the inauguration of a popular winning combination. The partnership led to conflicting reports as to the identity of Kojak's fellow artist, as there were in fact two Mama Lizas, Beverly Brown and Jacqueline Boland. His female partner was always labelled simply as Liza, which hindered the women's careers, making it impossible to judge them on their individual merits. The duo performed 'Fist To Fist Rub A Dub', a tribute to the soft drink Sky Juice, the modest 'One Thousand Gal' and the festive 'Christmas Stylee'. By 1981 Kojak And Liza had become well established and the unprecedented success of 'Nice Up Jamaica' was endorsed by the Jamaican tourist board. The song, although on some pressings credited to the duo, was actually a solo from Floyd Perch that verged on the surreal. By 1982 he became known as Papa Kojak and was a featured DJ at the acclaimed Skateland show, recorded live as *A Dee Jay Explosion*. By 1996, his resurgence as a singer, performing 'What Time Is It', was met with enthusiasm. The song was included on his distinguished comeback album of soul cover versions, which featured backing vocals from **Nadine Sutherland**, **J.C. Lodge**, **Marcia Griffiths** and **Judy Mowatt**. The paucity of female DJ performers has often been criticized, along with the fact that early performances were only in a supporting role. The pioneering efforts of the two Lizas have since been acknowledged on record as influencing the likes of **Sister Nancy** and **Lady Saw**.

● ALBUMS: *Kojak And Liza Showcase* (Gorgon 1981)★★★, *Floyd Perch A/K/A Papa Kojak* (Mouthpiece 1996)★★.

Kokane

Kokane was previously premiered as the dancehall DJ featured on **NWA**'s *Efil4Zaggin*'. He moved over to more traditional rapping for his solo debut, which featured guest appearances from **Above The Law**'s Cold 187um (who also produced, and was responsible for giving **Kokane** his nickname), **Tha Alkaholics** (on 'All Bark And No Bite'), while 'Don't Bite The Phunk' continued **Ruthless**' 'house policy' of lambasting **Dr Dre**. Like much of the rest of the album's tired G-funk formula, it was a somewhat misplaced and unoriginal move.

● ALBUMS: *Funk Upon A Rhyme* (Ruthless 1994)★★.

Kokomo (UK)

Formed in 1973, this blue-eyed soul band was made up from the remnants of several British groups. Vocalists Dyan Birch (b. 25 January 1949), Paddie McHugh (b. 28 August 1946) and Frank Collins (b. 25 October 1947) were ex-members of **Arrival**, a superior pop harmony band, while Neil Hubbard (guitar) and Alan Spenner (bass) had previously worked with **Joe Cocker**'s **Grease Band**. The line-up was completed by further formidable musicians, Tony O'Malley (piano), **Jim Mullen** (guitar), Terry Stannard (drums), Joan Linscott (congas) and journeyman saxophonist Mel Collins. A popular live attraction, Kokomo's acclaimed debut album suggested a future akin to that of the **Average White Band**. However, the group failed to sustain its promise and quickly ran out of inspiration, possibly because of the conflict of so many strong musical ideas and styles. This line-up split in January 1977, but a reconstituted version of the band appeared on the London gig circuit in the early 80s and recorded one album. The fluctuating activity of the group saw yet another reunion in the latter part of the 80s. This incarnation faltered when Spenner died in August 1991.
● ALBUMS: *Kokomo* (Columbia 1975)★★★, *Rise And Shine!* (Columbia 1976)★★, *Kokomo* (Columbia 1982)★★. Solo: Tony O'Malley *Naked Flame* (Jazz House 1995)★★★.
● COMPILATIONS: *The Collection* (1992)★★★.

Kokomo (USA)

b. Jimmy Wisner, 8 December 1931, Philadelphia, Pennsylvania, USA. Kokomo's 'Asia Minor', which merged a melody from Greig's Piano Concerto In A Minor with a rock 'n' roll beat, was a pop sensation in 1961, hitting number 8 on the US pop chart. (In the UK, 'Asia Minor' went to number 35.) Part of the record's appeal was that classically-trained Wisner purposefully used a cheap stand-up piano to give the record a honky-tonk flavour. He adopted the Kokomo pseudonym fearing that making a rock 'n' roll disc would tarnish his reputation as a well-respected jazz musician (ironically, his jazz friends liked the record). After graduating from Temple University as a psychology major in 1959, Wisner formed the Jimmy Wisner Trio with Chick Kenney (drums) and Ace Tsome (bass). With the trio he made two albums and as Kokomo he made an album and two further singles. 'Asia Minor' launched Wisner's career in pop music as a composer of television and film scores and as a session musician, working with such artists as **Freddy Cannon**, **Judy Collins**, and **Miriam Makeba**.
● ALBUMS: *Asia Minor* (1961)★★★, as the Jimmy Wisner Trio *Blues For Harvey* (1961)★★★, *Apperception* (1962)★★.

Kold Sweat

Innovative and highly regarded UK hip hop operation, who initially made their name by staking over £6,000 of studio time in the embryonic **Katch 22**, allowing them to spend a month recording their *Diary Of A Blackman*. Their other artists include the **F9s**, SL Trooper's (who began the catalogue with 'Knowledge...Put Your Brain in Gear'), Rude Boy Business, **Unanimous Decision**, **Korperayshun**, Black Prophets and **Son Of Noise**.
● ALBUMS: Various: *Raw Flavours Volume 1* (Kold Sweat 1994)★★.

Kolderie And Slade

One of the 90s most impressive new USA rock production teams, Paul Q. Kolderie and Sean Slade were pronounced 'rulers of the underground' by *Billboard* magazine in 1995. They had earned this description with a remorseless working schedule, which had seen them allied to **Hole**, **Dinosaur Jr.**, **Big Dipper**, **Radiohead**, **Juliana Hatfield**, **Uncle Tupelo**, **Tripmaster Monkey**, **Paw**, **Family Cat**, **Buffalo Tom**, **Atom Seed** and others. Individually, Kolderie was responsible for production on work by **Morphine**, **Connells**, **firehose**, **Lemonheads**, **Pixies**, **10,000 Maniacs** and **Throwing Muses**; while Slade has worked with **Buffalo Tom**, **360's** and **Cold Water Flat**. The latter were the first act signed in a new production deal between **MCA Records** and Fort Apache, the well-known label and studio complex in Boston, Massachusetts, founded by Kolderie and Slade in an abandoned laundry in 1986. They had met in the mid-70s when students at Yale University and formed the punk band Sexexecs, before drifting to Boston because of its music scene. There they soon became the only studio outlet for alternative bands, gradually attracting an increasing number of high profile clients. The secret of the duo's success would seem to lie in their teamwork, as both are able to handle either the producer or engineer's role. 'The French word for producer is "réalisateur", and that's a pretty good definition of what we do. We "realize" artist's songs.' Another important aspect of their approach is the use of vintage studio equipment. The complex is jointly owned nowadays by Juliana Hatfield's manager Gary Smith and **Billy Bragg**, who obtained his stake from original proprietor Joe Harvard. Having sold their concern Kolderie & Slade are instead directors of a company entitled Prodco.
● ALBUMS: *This Is Fort Apache* (Fort Apache/MCA 1994)★★★.

Koller, Fred

b. Chicago, Illinois, USA. Fred Koller has been a professional songwriter since he was 23. He hitchhiked to Nashville and his first songs were recorded by the **Sons Of The Pioneers**, **Tex Williams** and **Rosemary Clooney**. He befriended **Shel Silverstein** and they wrote many songs together, notably 'Jennifer Johnson And Me' (**Mac Davis**), ' This Guitar Is For Sale' (**Bobby Bare**) and 'Rock Star's Lament' (Bobby Bare). He co-wrote the country standard 'Lonestar State Of Mind' (**Nanci Griffith**) with **Pat Alger** and Gene Levine. Another song first recorded by Nanci Griffith, 'Goin' Gone', written by Koller, Alger and Bill Dale, was a US country number 1 for **Kathy Mattea**. Mattea has also recorded 'Life As We Knew It' and 'She Came From

Fort Worth'. The **Jeff Healey** Band had a pop hit with another of Koller's songs, 'Angel Eyes', and other songs include 'Boom Town' (**Lacy J. Dalton**), 'The TV Tells Me So' (Smothers Brothers), 'Lord, I Want My Rib Back' (**Gene Watson**) and 'Circumstantial Evidence' (**Jerry Lee Lewis**). Koller makes his own eccentric records in a corncrake voice, as though **Dave Van Ronk** were recording novelty songs. The best-known of his novelty songs are 'Let's Talk Dirty In Hawaiian', which he wrote with **John Prine**, and 'Juanita', which was recorded by **David Allan Coe** and **Burl Ives**. Koller has done much to encourage other songwriters by writing magazine columns and the book *How To Pitch And Promote Your Songs*.

● ALBUMS: *Songs From The Night Before* (Alcazar 1988)★★★, *Night Of The Living Fred* (Alcazar 1989)★★★ *Where The Fast Lane Ends* (Alcazar 1990)★★★.

● FURTHER READING: *How To Pitch And Promote Your Songs*, Fred Koller.

Koller, Hans

b. 12 February 1921, Vienna, Austria. Koller studied clarinet at the Academy of Music in Vienna (1936-39) before doing wartime service in the army. After the war he played in the group of the Hot Club of Vienna and became its leader in 1947. He moved to Germany in 1950 and formed an influential modern group with **Albert Mangelsdorff**. He played with many visiting Americans including **Dizzy Gillespie**, **Lee Konitz** and **Benny Goodman**. Koller continued to lead a quartet in the late 50s while he was working in Hamburg as musical director of Norddeutscher Rundfunk jazz workshops (1958-65) and at Deutsches Schauspielhaus (1968). In 1970, he returned to Vienna where he founded the band Free Sounds and in the late 70s occasionally led the International Brass Company. He has a duo with Fritz Pauer. Koller has also performed with **Warne Marsh** who had been a member of pianist **Lennie Tristano**'s group which had been the biggest influence on the young Koller, though he later tried to absorb the music of **John Coltrane**. Since the late 50s he has been an exhibiting abstract painter.

● ALBUMS: *Hans Is Hip* (1952)★★★, *Exclusive* (1963)★★, *Zoller-Koller-Solal* (1965)★★★, *Relax With My Horns* (1966)★★★, *New York City* (1968)★★, *Phoenix* (1972)★★.

Kollington

b. Anyila Kollington, 1952, Ibadan, Nigeria. Between the mid-70s and late 80s, Kollington ranked with **Barrister** as the leading star of Nigerian **fuji** music - like apala and waka, a Muslim-dominated relation of **juju**, retaining that style's vocal and percussion ingredients but abandoning its use of electric guitars in order to obtain a more traditional, roots-based sound. He began recording for Nigerian **EMI** in 1974, and in 1978 achieved a pronounced, but temporary, lead over Barrister when his introduction of the powerful bata drum (fuji had until that time relied almost exclusively on talking, or 'squeeze', drums) caught the imagination

of record buyers. In 1982, when fuji was beginning to seriously rival juju as Nigeria's most popular contemporary roots music, he set up his own label, Kollington Records, through which he released no less than 30 albums over the next five years. As the popularity of fuji grew, and the market became big enough to support both artists, Kollington and Barrister's enmity diminished, though not before Kollington released an album accusing Barrister of being responsible for the death of fellow bandleader Ayinla Omowura during a 1982 bar brawl. By 1983, both men were able to stand side by side as mourners at the funeral of apala star **Haruna Ishola**. A new and equally public rivalry emerged in the mid-80s, this time with waka star **Queen Salawah Abeni**, who exchanged bitter personal insults with Kollington over a series of album releases and counterreleases. Sadly, for non-Yoruba speakers, the verbal fisticuffs remain unintelligible, though the drum-heavy, hypnotic music was universal in its appeal.

● ALBUMS: *Ibi Eri Kigbe Mi Lo* (EMI Nigeria 1976)★★★, *Ebami Dupe* (EMI Nigeria 1977)★★★★, *Se Boti Mo* (Kollington 1986),★★★★ *Oki Mi Gbe Mi* (Kollington 1986)★★★, *E Ba Mi Dupe* (Kollington 1986)★★★, *Second Tier* (Kollington 1987)★★★, *I Kilo* (Kollington 1987)★★★, *Late Obafemi Awlowo* (Kollington 1987)★★★, *American Yankee* (Kollington 1988)★★, *Message* (Kollington 1988)★★, *Quality* (Kollington 1988)★★, *Blessing* (Kollington 1989)★★★, *Nigeria* (Kollington 1989)★★★, *Megastar* (Kollington 1989)★★★, *Fuji Ropopo* (Kollington 1990)★★★, *Iji Yoyo* (Kollington 1991)★★.

Komeda, Krzysztof

Long before western Europe enthused over **Zbigniew Namyslowski** and the **Ganelin Trio**, pianist and composer Komeda showed that Warsaw Pact countries, especially Poland, were capable of producing fine jazz. He composed the music for Roman Polanski's films *Two Men And A Wardrobe*, *When Angels Fall*, *The Fat And The Lean*, *Knife In The Water*, *Cul-De-Sac*, *Dance Of The Vampires* and *Rosemary's Baby*. The score for *Knife In The Water*, featuring fast and freewheeling themes for saxophone and rhythm, demonstrated that he had kept abreast of modern jazz developments, and his album *Astigmatism*, taking up the directions pointed out by **Miles Davis**'s mid-60s Quintet and featuring Namyslowski, has just been re-issued by the Polish state record label. His band included tenor saxist **Bernt Rosengren** and trumpeter **Tomasz Stanko**. His last work was on Buzz Kulik's film *Riot* in 1968. In April 1969, he died from an illness resulting from a head injury sustained in November 1968.

● ALBUMS: *Knife In The Water* (1962)★★★, *Polish Jazz Volume 3* (Polskie Nagrania Muza 1960, 1961, (1965)★★★, *Live In Copenhagen* (Polonia 1965)★★, *Astigmatism* (1967)★★★, *Rosemary's Baby* (1968)★★★.

Komuro, Tetsuya

b. Japan. The pre-eminent Japanese pop producer of the 90s, Tetsuya Komuro began his musical career in the early 80s with the techno pop trio TMN, alongside Takashi Utsunomiya and Naoto Kine. That group enjoyed a great deal of success in the Japanese pop market, but by 1992 they were on the verge of collapse. At that time Komuro established trf (Tetsuya Rave Factory), a five member group signed to Tokyo dance label Avex Trax. Since making their debut in 1993, the group has gone on to sell over 21 million records. In 1995 the group sold more records than any other Japanese group. That year Komuro was also announced to be the country's top songwriter in terms of royalties collected. His 'Survival Dance' helped substantially, becoming a huge hit when performed by trf and winning JASRAC's annual Gold Prize. By 1996 Komuro had his own weekend television show and own record label, named Orumok (his surname spelt backwards). All trf releases feature Komuro's lyrics and music, and he also plays synthesiser and handles all the programming. Many of his songs are very similar and there is an established pattern to his writing - usually a pulsing techno beat overlaid with a catchy female vocal hook. This ensures that his popularity extends to the karaoke booths as well as pop charts. He has also produced extensively for others, working on recordings such as 'Don't Wanna Cry' by Okinawan singer Namie Amuro, and 'I'm Proud' by Tomomi Kahala. Indeed, at one point in 1996 Komuro could boast of having written and produced all the top five songs in the local Dempa Publications chart list.

Konadu, Alex

b. Kumasi, Asante, Ghana. Billed variously as 'One Man Thousand' or 'The One Man Battalion', those nicknames attest to Konadu's phenomenal musical abilities. A purist in his dedication to Ghanaian traditional musics above outside influences, he sings still in the Twi language of the Asantes, offering personal observations on the fibre of his country and his complicated love life. He is not only a gifted guitarist, songwriter and stage performer, but also a prodigious musical entity, conducting shows in practically every village, town and city throughout Ghana. This has ensured enormous local popularity, which has latterly transferred abroad. In 1987 he played his first concerts in London, England (a well-received event documented by a live album on World Circuit Records). By this time he had taken over **E.K. Nyame**'s mantle as Ghana's most popular exponent of palm-wine guitar **highlife**.

● ALBUMS: *Abiba Nagoodey* (Mayala 1972)★★★, *Kunkonuhunu* (Mayala 1974)★★★, *Odo Ma Yenka Nkam* (Mayala 1975)★★★, *Okafo Didi* (Mayala 1976)★★, *Assasse Ase* (Mayala 1977)★★★, *Odo Beko Ma Obi Aba* (Mayala 1978)★★★, *Obi Aba Wuo* (Mayala 1978)★★★, *Konadu's Dance Band Of Ghana* (KBL 1980)★★★, *Yere Wo Ato Mu Ate Ebi Awe* (KBL 1983)★★★, *One Man Thousand: Live In London* (World Circuit 1988)★★, *One Man Thousand In Toronto* (RTP 1990)★★★.

Konders, Bobby

b. *c.*1962. New York DJ whose mixture of dancehall reggae with house and hip hop breakbeats is widely acknowledged as a harbinger of the nascent jungle scene. Konders is a white boy from Philadelphia who ended up mixing it up for WBLS and living in the Bronx. He started DJing at the age of 15 at house parties, playing funk and reggae back to back. By 1986 he had started the Saturday Lunch Mix for WBLS. With singles like 'Mack Daddy' he successfully combined the new rap language with dance stylings. Konders also worked on mixes for **Maxi Priest**, **Shabba Ranks**, **Papa Dee** and **Shinehead** and used dancehall vocalists like Mikey Jarrett on his own recordings. His *Massive Sounds* set saw him teamed with artists like Connie Harvey, Monyaka's Raphael and soulstress Lisa Makeda.

● ALBUMS: *Cool Calm And Collective* (Desire 1990)★★★, *Massive Sounds* (Mercury 1992)★★.

Köner, Thomas

b. Dortmund, Germany. A minimalist *avant garde* composer with a distinctive ethos, Köner bases much of his output on the concept of cold - and the gradual acceleration of global warming. More precisely he has described it as 'Asthetik Der Untergang', a term originally coined by **Einsturzende Neubaten**, meaning the 'aesthetic of decline'. He claims that no picture exists of him in the company of another human being. Though his music would be anathema to creators of dance records, he feels a kinship with techno and ambient artists working in that field. His debut, *Nunatak Gonamur*, took as its theme the final moments of Scott's polar expedition. Its sources included gongs scraped and rubbed, before electronic 'layering'. Its successor, *Teimo*, explored the process of cooling which takes place in the molecular structure of humans and animals after death. This time the musical imagery was dominated by circular movements frequently ending in silence. *Permafrost*, as the title suggested, took the permanently frozen Arctic subsoil as its text. As Köner explained, 'In a cold environment, everything slows down, and everything is going towards a stop event. And that is my favourite area in sound - just before it stops. It's an interesting border.' 1996's *Aubrite*, which explored other concepts, still maintained the link to his previous albums with the track 'Nuuk', titled after the capital of Greenland.

● ALBUMS: *Nunatak Gonamur* (Barooni 1990)★★★, *Teimo* (Barooni 1992)★★, *Permafrost* (Barooni 1994)★★, *Aubrite* (Barooni 1996)★★★.

Kong, Leslie

b. 1933, Kingston, Jamaica, West Indies, d. 1971. In partnership with his three brothers, Chinese Jamaican Kong ran a combination ice-cream parlour and record shop called **Beverley's**, on Orange Street in Kingston. He became a record producer in 1961 after hearing **Jimmy Cliff** sing 'Dearest Beverley' outside his establishment, which he subsequently recorded and released on the Beverley's label. The following year he recorded **Bob Marley**'s first records, 'Judge Not' and 'One Cup Of Coffee', and had huge hits with Cliff's 'Miss Jamaica' and Derrick and Patsy's 'Housewives Choice'. For the rest of the decade he worked with nearly all of the top names in Jamaican music, including **John Holt**, **Joe Higgs**, **Derrick Morgan**, **Stranger Cole**, **Desmond Dekker**, the **Maytals**, the **Melodians** and the **Pioneers**, and many of these recordings were licensed for release in the UK on **Chris Blackwell**'s **Island Records**.

In 1967 Kong achieved a big international hit with Desmond Dekker's '007', and a massive worldwide smash with the same artist in 1969 with 'Israelites'. In late 1969 Kong again recorded Bob Marley, this time with the **Wailers**, and he released these sessions as *The Best Of The Wailers*. He crossed over again into the UK national charts with the Pioneers' 'Long Shot Kick The Bucket', the Melodians' 'Rivers Of Babylon' (the blueprint for **Boney M**'s hit version a decade later) and 'Sweet Sensation', and the Maytals' 'Monkey Man' - only one of a long series of hits that he enjoyed with the group. Kong's work has for too long been viewed as 'unfashionable' by reggae's self-appointed experts. Much of this is owing to professional jealousy - few producers ever came near to matching Beverley's in terms of hit records, and many of Beverley's releases were also huge international successes - Kong was one of the first producers to popularize Jamaican music outside of its immediate target audience. His productions were always clean and sharp and he used the best available musicians. His reputation has sadly never matched these achievements - a highly unusual situation in the reggae field - but time will, hopefully, redress the balance, and allow his work to be appreciated on its true merits.

● COMPILATIONS: various artists *Reggae Party* (MFP 1970)★★★, *The Best Of Beverley's* (Trojan 1981)★★★★, *The King Kong Compilation* (Island 1981)★★★★.

Kongos, John

This singing multi-instrumentalist left his native South Africa for London in 1966. After leading a group called Scrub through several unsuccessful singles, he was signed as a solo artist by Dawn Records who released 1969's *Confusions About Goldfish*. A transfer to Fly two years later and the services of producer **Gus Dudgeon** and engineer Roy Thomas Baker gave Kongos a fleeting taste of pop fame when 'He's Gonna Step On You Again' and 'Tokoloshe Man' each bounded to number four in the UK charts. These highly inventive singles and their associated album were blessed with studio assistance from a cast that included **Lol Coxhill**, Mike Moran, Ray Cooper, **Caleb Quaye** and **Ralph McTell**. Kongos' uncompromising lyrics were born of the socio-political state back home paralleling a flavour of the Transvaal in backing tracks that anticipated the fusions of **Johnny Clegg** in the 80s. Kongos received some unexpected publicity in 1990, when the **Happy**

Mondays covered 'Tokoloshe Man' (as 'Step On'), reaching the UK Top 5.

● ALBUMS: *Kongos* (Fly 1971)★★★.
● COMPILATIONS: *Tokoloshe Man Plus ...* (See For Miles 1990)★★★.

Konimo

b. Daniel Amponsah, 1935, Fuase, Ghana. Born in the Ashante region of Ghana, vocalist and acoustic guitarist Konimo has devoted his career to preserving Ghana's rich heritage of traditional guitar-based music. His training began at an early age from his father, who was a trumpeter and guitarist, and his mother, who was a chorister in the local Methodist church. At high school, he additionally learned to play the church organ. In 1954, he joined I.E.'s Band, who that year enjoyed a big local hit with 'Go Inside'. The following year, he was with the Antobre Guitar Band in Kumasi and began playing in the traditional single-string, rather than chordal, style that he has remained with throughout subsequent decades. In 1962, he left for the UK, where he studied science technology and took guitar lessons from the father of the classical guitarist **John Williams**. Returning to Ghana in 1965, he recorded with Dr. K. Gyasi And His Noble Kings. In 1968, Konimo released his first album, *Asante Ballads*, a collection of traditional Ashante folk songs with the lyrics translated into English. In 1969, he returned to the UK for further study, attending the Manchester School of Music and developing an interest in jazz. Back in Ghana in 1977, he released the classic album *Odonsan Nkoro*. With the massive import of Western music into Ghana, Konimo's crusade to keep the younger generation in touch with their roots had added urgency. He continues to perform regularly with his percussion and choral group Adadam Agormomma ('roots ensemble') at festivals and concerts featuring younger, electric bands. He also trained the highlife guitarist **George Darko**, who was brought to his house to learn the traditions of Ghanaian roots music by his parents. In the 80s Konimo travelled abroad for live performances with his band (now including his son, Little Noah as well as long-standing accompanist Kofi Twumasi), playing a prestigious Broadway show. Despite this, his recorded output remains disappointingly sparse.

● ALBUMS: *Asante Ballads* (EBL 1968)★★★, *Part Time With Ceekay* (EBL 1973)★★★, *Funky Highlife* (EBL 1975)★★★, *Odonsan Nkoro* (EBL 1977)★★★★, *Osabarima* (1987)★★★.

Konitz, Lee

b. 13 October 1927, Chicago, Illinois, USA. Konitz began on clarinet, studying in the classical form, later switching to alto saxophone. In the mid-late 40s he played in the bands of Jerry Wald and **Claude Thornhill**, appeared on jazz dates with **Miles Davis** and was simultaneously studying with **Lennie Tristano**, with whom he also recorded. In the early 50s he worked for a while with **Stan Kenton** and although he left the band before the end of 1953, he had established his name and an international reputation. From the mid-50s onwards Konitz generally led his own bands, recording and playing publicly, and made a brief return visit to work with Tristano. He also became involved in teaching. During the following years Konitz's interest in teaching developed and soon he was running clinics and workshops, giving private tuition and also conducting worldwide correspondence courses. In the mid-70s he recorded several albums with **Warne Marsh**, all finding immediate critical and commercial popularity. He also formed a nine-piece band modelled upon the one led by Davis in which he had played 30 years earlier. One of very few alto saxophonists of his generation not to have been influenced by **Charlie Parker**, Konitz managed to avoid being cast in any mould other than that which he created himself. Unlike many of his peers, he has proved to be flexible and capable of continually growing to accommodate new concepts. In performance his sound has changed over the years. Originally he played with a deliberately thin sound but he thickened this during his time with Kenton, a necessity to avoid being drowned by the volume of the band. ('It was not easy playing alto in that band. Next time around, I'd rather be the drummer.') Deeply interested in and committed to jazz education, Konitz encourages his students to respect their material and through his courses strives to teach solo improvisation, something he regards as being just as much a measurable discipline as ensemble playing. His own playing remains exemplary of that strain of contemporary music which emphasizes thoughtfulness rather than instinctive responses.

● ALBUMS: *Subconscious Lee* 1949-50 recordings (Original Jazz Classics)★★★★, *Lee Konitz Meets Gerry Mulligan* (Pacific 1953),★★★ *Jazz At Storyville* (Black Lion 1954)★★★★, *Konitz* (Black Lion 1954),★★★ *Quintets* (Vogue 1954)★★★, *Swingtime* (1956)★★★, *Very Cool* (Verve 1957)★★★★, *Motion* (1961),★★★ *Timespan* 1954-61 recordings (Wave 1977)★★★, *Together Again* (Moon 1966)★★★, *The Lee Konitz Duets* (Original Jazz Classics 1967)★★★★, *Spirits* (1971),★★★ *Satori* (1974), *Lone-Lee* (Steeplechase 1974)★★★, *Oleo* (Sonet 1975)★★★, *Jazz A Juan* (Steeplechase 1975)★★★★, *Chicago 'N' All That Jazz* (LRC 1976),★★★ *The Nonet* (1976)★★★, *Windows* (Steeplechase 1977)★★★, *Pyramid* (Improvising Artists 1977)★★★, *Yes, Yes, Nonet* (Steeplechase 1979)★★★, *Live At The Berlin Jazz Days* (1980)★★, *Live At Laren* (Soul Note 1980)★★, *Toot Sweet* (Owl 1982)★★★, *Dovetail* (1984)★★★, *Wild As Springtime* (1984)★★★, *Stereokonitz* (RCA 1985)★★★, *Ideal Scene* (Soul Note 1986)★★★, *Medium Rare* (Label Blue 1986)★★, *Wild As Springtime* (GFM 1987)★★, *Blew* (Philology 1988)★★★, *Round And Round* (Limelight 1988)★★★, *Shades Of Kenton* (Hep Jazz 1988)★★★, *Songs Of The Stars* (1988)★★★, *The New York Album* (Soul Note 1988)★★★★, *Spirits* (Milestone 1988)★★★, *12 Gershwin In 12 Keys* (Philology 1989)★★★, *Frank-Lee Speaking* (West Wind 1990)★★★, *In Rio* (MA Music 1990)★★, *Once Upon A Live* (Musidisc 1991)★★★, *Zounds* (Soul Note 1991)★★★, *S'Nice* (Nabel 1991)★★★, with Peggy Stern *Lunasea* (Soul Note 1992)★★, *From Newport To Nice* 1955-80 recordings (Philology 1992)★★★★, *So Many Stars* (Philology 1993)★★★, *A Venezia* (Philology 1994)★★★, *Rhapsody II* (Evidence 1996)★★★, *Strings For Holiday* (Enja 1997)★★★, *Dig Dug Dog* (Sony Jazz 1997)★★★, with Charlie Haden and Brad Meldau Alone Together (Blue Note 1998), with Charlie Haden and Brad Meldau *Alone Together* (Blue Note 1998)★★★★.

Konte, Dembo

b. 1942, Banjul, Gambia. A son of the late Alhaji Bai Konte, regarded by many as the greatest master of the kora (west African harp) of recent times, and certainly the musician who did most to introduce it to an international audience, Dembo Konte is maintaining both the family tradition and the detailed tribal histories that are contained within the Konte canon of songs. Tours of the UK in the late 80s alongside Senegal-born Kausu Kouyate, with whom he has recorded a number of albums, brought major acclaim, throwing off some of the critical baggage associated with his family ties. The best of these was arguably *Simbomba*, which featured the presence of **3 Mustaphas 3** in addition to Kouyate on a pleasing collection of duets and songs conducted in the familiar casamance style.

● ALBUMS: with Malamini Jobarteh *Jaliyah* (Stern's 1985)★★★, with Kausu Kouyate *Tanante* (Rogue 1988)★★★★, with Malamini Jobarteh *Baa Toto* (Stern's 1987)★★★, with Kouyate *Simbomba* (Rogue 1987)★★, with Kouyate *Jali Roll* (Rogue 1990)★★, *Jaliology* (Xenophile 1995)★★★.

Konte, Lamine

b. c.1940, Kolda, Casamance, Senegal. A distant relation of the Gambian Konte family of kora (west African harp) players, Lamine Konte first studied under his father, Dialy Keba Konte, then Souldiou Cissoko. After attending the School of Arts in Dakar, he began to develop his own unique style. Rather than traditional music he was more inclined towards a fusionist direction, employing both kora and guitar. The style saw fruition with the formation of his first band in 1960, which quickly established a national reputation for their live performances. In 1965 they were the Senegalese representatives at the Black Arts Festival in Dakar. However, the group was disbanded in 1972 when Konte relocated to Paris for a solo career. His most enduring collection of songs following in 1977 with the *Tinque Rinque* album, which blended kora, rock and folk musics - if not seamlessly then at least convincingly. It was the first of a series of albums for French labels, but despite the quality of his musicianship, Konte has not been able to build or maintain a Western audience. This should not rob him, however, of his standing in the Senegalese kora community, where he is acknowledged as a true master.

● ALBUMS: *Tinque Rinque* (Son Afrique 1977)★★★, *Bako L'Autre Rime* (Son Afrique 1978)★★★, *Baara* (Les Disques Esperance 1979)★★★, *La Kora Du Senegal* (1987)★★★,

Chant Du Negre - Chant Du Monde (1987)★★, *Afrique, Mon Afrique (Kora Chants Of Senegal)* (1987)★★★, *Senegal, Volume 2 - La Kora* (1987)★★.

Koobas

Formed in Liverpool, England, in 1962 and initially known as the Kubas, this superior beat group was comprised of two ex-members of the Midnighters - guitarists Stu Leatherwood and Roy Morris - alongside Keith Ellis (bass) and Tony O'Riley (drums), formerly of the Thunderbeats. The Koobas enjoyed a role in *Ferry Across The Mersey* and in 1965 supported the **Beatles** on a national tour. The group secured a deal with **Pye Records** and their debut, 'Take Me For A Little While' (1965), showed considerable promise. Following 'You'd Better Make Up Your Mind' (1966) the Koobas switched to **Columbia Records** for the exceptional 'Sweet Music'. A misguided version of **Gracie Fields**' 'Sally' (1967) undermined the group's growing reputation, as did the equally insubstantial 'Gypsy Fred'. However, they closed their singles career with a superb rendition of **Cat Stevens**' 'The First Cut Is The Deepest', before completing *The Koobas*. The content of this excellent album ranges from a rendition of **Erma Franklin**'s 'Piece Of My Heart' to the musically complex 'Barricades', one of the finest songs of its era. The group had actually disbanded prior to its release, after which Ellis joined **Van Der Graaf Generator**.

● ALBUMS: *The Koobas* (Columbia 1969)★★★.

Kool And The Gang

Originally formed as a quartet, the Jazziacs, by Robert 'Kool' Bell (b. 8 October 1950, Youngstown, Ohio, USA; bass), Robert 'Spike' Mickens (b. Jersey City, New Jersey, USA; trumpet), Robert 'The Captain' Bell - later known by his Muslim name Amir Bayyan (b. 1 November 1951, Youngstown, Ohio, USA; saxophone, keyboards) and Dennis 'D.T.' Thomas (b. 9 February 1951, Jersey City, New Jersey, USA; saxophone). Based in Jersey City, this aspiring jazz group opened for acts such as **Pharoah Sanders** and **Leone Thomas**. They were later joined by Charles 'Claydes' Smith (b. 6 September 1948, Jersey City, New Jersey, USA; guitar) and 'Funky' George Brown (b. 5 January 1949, Jersey City, New Jersey, USA; drums), and as the Soul Town Band, moderated their early direction by blending soul and funk, a transition completed by 1969 when they settled on the name Kool And The Gang. The group crossed over into the US pop chart in 1973 and initiated a run of 19 stateside Top 40 hits on their own De-Lite label starting with 'Funky Stuff', a feat consolidated the following year with a couple of Top 10 hits, 'Jungle Boogie' and 'Hollywood Swinging'. They continued to enjoy success although their popularity momentarily wavered in the latter half of the 70s as the prominence of disco strengthened. In 1979 the Gang added vocalists James 'J.T.' Taylor (b. 16 August 1953, Laurens, South Carolina, USA) and Earl Toon Jnr., with Taylor emerg-

ing as the key member in a new era of success for the group, which coincided with their employment of an outside producer. Eumire **Deodato** refined the qualities already inherent in the group's eclectic style and together they embarked on a series of highly successful international hits including 'Ladies Night' (1979), 'Too Hot' (1980) and the bubbling 'Celebration', a 1980 platinum disc and US pop number 1 - later used by the media as the home-coming theme for the returning American hostages from Iran. Outside the USA they achieved parallel success and proved similarly popular in the UK where 'Get Down On It' (1981), 'Joanna' (1984) and 'Cherish' (1985) each reached the Top 5. The arrival of Taylor also saw the group's albums achieving Top 30 status in their homeland for the first time, with *Celebrate!* reaching the Top 10 in 1980. Their longevity was due, in part, to a settled line-up. The original six members remained with the group into the 80s and although newcomer Toon left, Taylor blossomed into an ideal frontman. This core was later supplemented by several auxiliaries, Clifford Adams (trombone) and Michael Ray (trumpet). This idyllic situation was finally undermined by Taylor's departure in 1988 and he was replaced by three singers, former **Dazz Band** member Skip Martin plus Odeen Mays and Gary Brown. Taylor released a solo album in 1989, *Sister Rosa*, while the same year the group continued recording with the album *Sweat*. The compilation set *The Singles Collection* shows that Taylor left behind him one of the most engaging and successful of soul/funk catalogues.

● ALBUMS: *Kool And The Gang* (1969)★★, *Live At The Sex Machine* (De-Lite 1971)★★, *Live At P.J.s* (De-Lite 1971)★★, *Music Is The Message* (1972)★★, *Good Times* (De-Lite 1973)★★★, *Wild And Peaceful* (De-Lite 1973)★★★, *Light Of Worlds* (De-Lite 1974)★★★, *Spirit Of The Boogie* (De-Lite 1975)★★, *Love And Understanding* (De-Lite 1976)★★, *Open Sesame* (De-Lite 1976)★★, *The Force* (De-Lite 1977)★★, *Everbody's Dancin'* (1978)★★, *Ladies' Night* (De-Lite 1979)★★★, *Celebrate!* (De-Lite 1980)★★★, *Something Special* (De-Lite 1981)★★, *As One* (De-Lite 1982)★★, *In The Heart* (De-Lite 1983)★★★★, *Emergency* (De-Lite 1984)★★, *Victory* (Curb 1986)★★, *Forever* (Mercury 1986)★★, *Sweat* (Mercury 1989)★★, *Kool Love* (Telstar 1990)★★, *State Of Affairs* (Curb 1996)★★.

● COMPILATIONS: *The Best Of Kool And The Gang* (De-Lite 1971)★★, *Kool Jazz* (De-Lite 1974)★★, *Kool And The Gang Greatest Hits!* (De-Lite 1975)★★★, *Spin Their Top Hits* (De-Lite 1978)★★★★, *Kool Kuts* (De-Lite 1982)★★★, *Twice As Kool* (De-Lite 1983)★★★★, *The Singles Collection* (De-Lite 1988)★★★★, *Everything's Kool And The Gang: Greatest Hits And More* (Mercury 1988)★★★★, *Great And Remixed 91* (Mercury 1992)★★★, *The Collection* (Spectrum 1996)★★★.

Kool G Rap And DJ Polo

New York-based protégés of the omnipresent **Marley Marl**, Kool G (b. Nathaniel Wilson, 20 July 1968, Elmhurst, Queens, New York), so called to infer 'Kool Genius Of Rap', has yet to build a commensurate profile following three rich, undervalued albums. This despite hardcore benchmarks like 'Streets Of New York', and a marvellous debut single, 'It's A Demo'. 'Streets Of New York' was housed on a second album produced by **Eric B** and **Large Professor** and featuring guest appearances from **Big Daddy Kane** and **Biz Markie**. Their third album was passed over by **Warners** when they saw the sleeve - which merrily depicted the duo in baraclavas feeding steak to a pair of Rottweilers, while in the background stand two white males on chairs with nooses around their necks. As if to send the censorship lobby into further frenzy there was a guest appearance for **Ice Cube**, one of their oldest enemies, on the enclosed record. The best of their admittedly patchy first three albums were pieced together for *Killer Kuts*.

● ALBUMS: *Road To The Riches* (Cold Chillin' 1989)★★, *Wanted: Dead Or Alive* (Cold Chillin' 1990)★★, *Live And Let Die* (Cold Chillin' 1992)★★, *Kool G Rap 4,5,6* (Epic 1995)★★★.

● COMPILATIONS: *Killer Kuts* (Cold Chillin' 1994)★★★.

Kool Gents

The Kool Gents were one of the numerous underexposed doo-wop groups that never had a hit, but who, decades later, became appreciated as great disseminators of R&B harmony. The group was formed in Chicago, Illinois, USA, in 1952, by Cicero Blake from among his classmates at Marshall High School, and after a number of changes in personnel, including the loss of Blake, the recording group consisted of lead **Dee Clark**, John McCall (first tenor), Doug Brown (second tenor), Teddy Long (baritone) and Johnny Carter (bass). They signed with **Vee Jay Records** and the first releases in 1954 featured John McCall as lead and lacked distinctiveness. A switch to Clark proved most dramatic, as the group produced three beautiful ethereal ballads during 1956, namely 'I Just Can't Help Myself', 'Just Like A Fool' and 'When I Call On You'. Also in 1956, the Kool Gents recorded a novelty number called 'The Convention', on which they were billed as the Delegates. Vee Jay were alerted to Clark's talents, pulled him out of the Kool Gents, and launched him as one of the company's most successful recording acts (on most Dee Clark albums there are songs he recorded as a member of the Kool Gents). The remaining Kool Gents joined Pirkle Lee Moses (who had just lost his group, the **El Dorados**) and formed a new El Dorados group that made a few records for Vee Jay. Cicero Blake, who started the ball rolling, became a moderately successful soul-blues singer.

Kool Herc

b. Clive Campbell, 1955, Kingston, Jamaica, West Indies, moving to New York in 1967. Kool Herc (aka Kool DJ Herc) owns the rights to the accolade 'first hip hop DJ', though his talent was never captured on record. Illustrating the connections between reggae and rap which have largely been buried by successive hip

hop generations, Herc brought his sound system to block parties in the Bronx from 1969 onwards. By 1975 he was playing the brief rhythmic sections of records which would come to be termed 'breaks', at venues like the Hevalo in the Bronx. His influence was pivotal, with **Grandmaster Flash** building on his innovations to customise the modern hip hop DJ approach. Herc's methods also pre-dated, and partially introduced, sampling. By adapting pieces of funk, soul, jazz and other musics into the melting pot, he would be able to keep a party buzzing. With his **sound system** the Herculords, he would tailor his sets to the participants, most of whom he knew by name. He would call these out over improvised sets: 'As I scan the place, I see the very familiar face...Of my mellow: Wallace Dee in the house! Wallace Dee! Freak For Me!'. Grandmaster Flash himself admits he would often be so embarassed when Herc picked him out of the crowd and offered him elementary lessons in the art of DJing that he would have to leave. Nevertheless, the pack eventually caught up and his influence was dying down when his career was effectively aborted by a knife fight. He was an innocent bystander when three youths attempted to push past his house security and he was stabbed three times, twice in the side and once across his hands. After that his club burned down and, as he himself recalls: 'Papa couldn't find no good ranch, so his herd scattered'. As one of hip hop's founding fathers, Kool Herc's reputation and influence has outlasted the vaguaries of musical fashion. A status no doubt boosted by the fact that he has not attempted to launch a spurious recording career on the back of it. A shame though, that he has never seen the commercial rewards of his innovations, though he was the subject of celebration at the Rapmania Festival in 1990.

Kool Moe Dee

Once of original rap pioneers **Treacherous 3**, Kool Moe Dee (b. Mohandas DeWese, Harlem, New York, USA) has carved a solo career bracing his old school style against the more urbane concerns of the new wave. He originally started rapping in his native Harlem by grabbing the mic at house parties, soon hooking up with his Treacherous colleagues L.A. Sunshine and Special K. However, with intrest failing in the group following the arrival of **Run DMC** *et al*, he elected to leave the group: 'Rap is repetitous. It gets to the pont where you wana hear hard beats, then it goes back to where you wanna hear melodies. You just gotta be on the right vibe at the right time'. He would go on to graduate from SUNY at Old Westbury, before his solo CV started in earnest when he joined up with **Teddy Riley** for the crossover hit, 'Go See The Doctor', a cautionary account of the dangers of AIDS. Released on Rooftop Records, it won him a fresh contract with **Jive**. Much of his notoriety as the 80s progressed involved a long-running duel on record with **LL Cool J**, the first flowering of which was the title-track to his second, platinum-selling album. A succession of minor hit singles has ensued, including

'Wild, Wild West', 'They Want Money' and 'Rise And Shine', the latter featuring Chuck D (**Public Enemy**) and **KRS-1** on complementary vocals. He also became the first rap artist to perform at the Grammy Awards (following the success of *Knowledge Is King*), and continued to fight back against gangsta rap's misogynist vocabulary: 'When you get funke funke wisdom, then you'll understand, The woman is the driving force for any powerful man, From birth to earth to earth to rebirth, it ain't a curse, Put your thoughts in reverse'. This from a man who has already written over half a dozen screenplays.

● ALBUMS: *Kool Moe Dee* (Jive 1986)★★★, *How Ya Like Me Now* (Jive 1987)★★★, *Knowledge Is King* (Jive 1989)★★, *Funke, Funke Wisdom* (Jive 1991)★★★.

● COMPILATIONS: *Greatest Hits* (Jive 1993)★★★★.

Kool Rock Jay

b. Leo Dupree Ramsey Jnr., Oakland, California, USA. A rapper whose depictions of urban reality were addressed with a detached, almost resigned air. He began to freestyle at the age of 10, when his radio first picked up rap on the Californian airwaves. He adopted the style, and wrote his own words to the beats he heard, competing with the neighbourhood boys to perfect his delivery. His principal influences were the political heavyweights **Public Enemy** and **KRS-1**. He hooked up with his DJ, Slice (b. Michael Brown, though he was known in Oakland circles as the 'Beat Fixer'), at a party in Fresno, adding Nate The Great (b. Jonathon Matthews) and Chuck Nice (b. Charles Johnson). As they built a strong local reputation the final jigsaw piece arrived in the shape of producer Lionel 'The Super Duper Dope Hook Man' Bea. Through him the group won a contract with **Jive** Records. Their debut album was premiered by their best-known cut, 'It's A Black Thing', released as a single. Decidedly on the Afrocentricity theme, it was critically well received but afterwards their camp remained comparatively quiet.

● ALBUMS: *Tales From The Dope Side* (Jive 1990)★★★.

Kooper, Al

b. 5 February 1944, Brooklyn, New York, USA. Kooper embarked upon a professional music career in 1959 as guitarist in the **Royal Teens**, who had enjoyed a novelty hit the previous year with 'Short Shorts'. He became a noted New York session musician and later forged a successful songwriting partnership with Bobby Brass and Irwin Levine. Their collaborations included 'This Diamond Ring', a chart-topper for **Gary Lewis And The Playboys**, 'I Must Be Seeing Things' (**Gene Pitney**) and 'The Water Is Over My Head' (the **Rockin' Berries**). In 1965, producer Tom Wilson asked Kooper to attend a **Bob Dylan** session. With **Mike Bloomfield** already installed on guitar, the eager musician opted for organ, an instrument with which he was barely conversant. Dylan nonetheless loved his instinctive touch which breathed fire into 'Like A Rolling Stone' and its

attendant *Highway 61 Revisited* album. Kooper maintained his links with Dylan over the years, guesting on *Blonde On Blonde* (1966), *New Morning* (1970) and *Under The Red Sky* (1990).

Kooper became involved in several electric folk sessions, notably for **Tom Rush** (*Take A Little Walk With Me*) and **Peter, Paul And Mary** (*Album*). His solo version of 'I Can't Keep From Crying Sometimes' appeared on an **Elektra** label sampler, *What's Shakin'*, and his reading of 'Parchman Farm' was issued as a single in 1966. The organist was then invited to join the **Blues Project**, which became one of America's leading urban R&B acts. Kooper left the group in 1967 to found **Blood, Sweat And Tears**, one of the originals of US jazz-rock, with whom he remained for one album before internal unrest resulted in his dismissal. He accepted a production post at **Columbia Records**, before recording the influential *Super Session* with Mike Bloomfield and **Stephen Stills**. This successful informal jam inspired several inferior imitations, not the least of which was the indulgent *Live Adventures Of Al Kooper And Mike Bloomfield*, which featured cameos by **Elvin Bishop** and the then relatively unknown Carlos **Santana** when Bloomfield was unable to finish the schedule. Kooper's solo career was effectively relaunched with *I Stand Alone*, but in keeping with many of his albums, this promising set was marred by inconsistency. A limited vocalist, his best work relied on his imaginative arrangements, which drew on the big band jazz of **Maynard Ferguson** and **Don Ellis** (whom he produced), and the strength of the supporting cast. *You Never Know Who Your Friends Are* and *New York City (You're A Woman)* were among his most popular releases. His double set *Easy Does It* contained a superb slowed-down version of **Ray Charles**' 'I Got A Woman', resplendent with an exquisite jazz-piano solo introduction. Kooper, however, remained best-known for his role as a catalyst. He appeared on *Electric Ladyland* (**Jimi Hendrix**) and *Let It Bleed* (**Rolling Stones**) and produced the debut albums by **Nils Lofgren** and the **Tubes**. He established his own label, Sounds Of The South, in Atlanta, Georgia, and secured international success with early protégés **Lynyrd Skynyrd**.

During the 70s, Kooper became involved in several Blues Project reunions and the following decade he formed Sweet Magnolia, an *ad hoc* group comprising several studio musicians. In 1982, he completed *Championship Wrestling*, his first solo album for five years, which featured contributions from guitarist Jeff 'Skunk' Baxter (**Steely Dan** and **Doobie Brothers**). Al Kooper has since pursued an active career recording computerized soundtrack music, but in 1991 produced *Scapegoats* for **Green On Red**. After a spell when he relocated to Nashville he is back in New York, 'the cold-hearted bitch' he referred to in his song 'New York City'. Kooper has been a major background personality in American rock for more than 30 years and has made a considerable contribution.

● ALBUMS: with Mike Bloomfield, Stephen Stills *Super Session* (Columbia 1968)★★★, *The Live Adventures Of Al Kooper And Mike Bloomfield* (Columbia 1969)★★, *I Stand Alone* (Columbia 1969)★★★, *You Never Know Who Your Friends Are* (Columbia 1969)★★, with Shuggie Otis *Kooper Session* (Columbia 1970)★★, *Easy Does It* (Columbia 1970)★★★★, *Landlord* soundtrack (1971)★★, *New York City (You're A Woman)* (Columbia 1971)★★★, *A Possible Projection Of The Future/Childhood's End* (Columbia 1972)★, *Naked Songs* (1973)★★, *Unclaimed Freight* (Columbia 1975)★★, *Act Like Nothing's Wrong* (United Artists 1977)★★, *Championship Wrestling* (1982)★★, *Live: Soul Of A Man* (Music Masters 1995)★★★.

● COMPILATIONS: *Al's Big Deal* (Columbia 1989)★★★.

● FURTHER READING: *Backstage Pass*, Al Kooper with Ben Edmonds.

Korgis

The Korgis comprised two former members of **Stackridge**, James Warren (bass/guitar/vocals) and Andy Davis (drums/guitar), plus Phil Harrison (keyboards/percussion), and Stuart Gordon (guitar/violin). This UK group reached the Top 20 with their debut record 'If I Had You', but had problems when their next two singles failed. When their self-titled album also failed to make an impact it seemed they would end up as one-hit-wonders. However, 'Everybody's Gotta Learn Sometime' a classy love song, reached the UK Top 5 and was followed by a minor hit with 'If It's Alright With You Baby'. By 1983, the group had been dropped by their label Rialto and were basically down to a core of just Warren, who carried the name on for a few more years and a number of one-off record deals. European success continued on a limited basis but at home the Korgis' success had ended. The unit of Warren and Davis reformed in 1990 with the addition of John Baker (b. 2 April 1961, Bath, Avon, England; guitar, keyboards, vocals; ex-Graduate). They recorded an album of new material together with a new version of 'Everybody's Gotta Learn Sometime'. During their career the band never performed live, so it came as a surprise when they announced their first tour, due for the summer of 1993.

● ALBUMS: *The Korgis* (Rialto 1979)★★★, *Dumb Waiters* (Rialto 1980)★★★, *Sticky George* (Rialto 1981)★★, *Burning Questions* (Sonet 1986)★★, *This World's For Everyone* (Dureco 1992)★★.

● COMPILATIONS: *The Best Of The Korgis* (1983)★★★.

Kormoran

A long-running Hungarian group that performs ancient folk tunes in a rock style. They had a hit single in their homeland, but very few of their releases can be obtained outside of Hungary.

● ALBUMS: *Live In Holland* (1986)★★★.

Korn

Hardcore rock band Korn formed in the early 90s in Bakersfield, California, USA, and toured widely, playing over 200 shows before releasing their self-titled debut album for EastWest Records in 1994. Subsequently based in Huntington Beach in California, the quintet, whose members are Jonathan Davis (vocals), Reggie Fieldy Arvizu (bass), James Munky Shaffer (guitar), Brian Welch (guitar, vocals) and David Silveria (drums), released their first single, 'Blind', which was widely shown on late-night **MTV** shows. The album gave them their commercial breakthrough and saw them cited in *Billboard* magazine as 'the first debut hardcore rock act to top the Heatseekers chart and one of the first to crack the upper half of the *Billboard* 200 in the last two years.' Much of this success arose from the reputation garnered by their live work, which was bolstered by tours alongside **House Of Pain**, **Biohazard**, 311, **Sick Of It All**, **Danzig**, **Marilyn Manson** and **Megadeth**. A second single, 'Shoots And Ladders', featured Davis playing the bagpipes. The Ross Robinson-produced *Life Is Peachy* continued the anger, although further breakthrough success was limited by the explicit lyrics liberally laced throughout. In late 1997 Korn established their own label, Elementree. They also made the news by serving a cease-and-desist order to the assistant principal of a Michigan high school, who had suspended a student for wearing a T-shirt featuring the band's name.

● ALBUMS: *Korn* (Immortal 1995)★★★, *Life Is Peachy* (Epic 1996)★★★, *Follow The Leader* (Epic 1998)★★★.

● VIDEOS: *Who Then Now?* (SMV 1997).

Korner, Alexis

b. 19 April 1928, Paris, France, d. 1 January 1984. An inspirational figure in British music circles, Korner was already versed in black music when he met **Cyril Davies** at the London Skiffle Club. Both musicians were frustrated by the limitations of the genre and transformed the venue into the London Blues And Barrelhouse Club, where they not only performed together but also showcased visiting US bluesmen. When jazz trombonist **Chris Barber** introduced an R&B segment into his live repertoire, he employed Korner (guitar) and Davies (harmonica) to back singer Ottilie Patterson. Inspired, the pair formed Blues Incorporated in 1961 and the following year established the Ealing Rhythm And Blues Club in a basement beneath a local cinema. The group's early personnel included Charlie Watts (drums), Art Wood (vocals) and Keith Scott (piano), but later featured **Long John Baldry**, **Jack Bruce**, **Graham Bond** and **Ginger Baker** in its ever-changing line-up. **Mick Jagger** and **Paul Jones** were also briefly associated with Korner, whose continued advice and encouragement proved crucial to a generation of aspiring musicians. However, disagreements over direction led to Davies' defection following the release of *R&B From The Marquee*, leaving Korner free to pursue a jazz-based path. While former colleagues later found success with the **Rolling Stones**, **Manfred Mann** and **Cream**, Korner's excellent group went largely unnoticed by the general public, although he did enjoy a residency on a children's television show backed by his rhythm section of **Danny Thompson** (bass) and Terry Cox (drums). The name 'Blues Incorporated' was dropped when Korner embarked on a solo career, punctuated by the formation of several temporary groups, including Free At Last (1967), New Church (1969) and Snape (1972). While the supporting cast on such ventures remained fluid, including for a short time singer **Robert Plant**, the last two units featured Peter Thorup who also collaborated with Korner on **CCS**, a pop-based big band that scored notable hits with 'Whole Lotta Love' (1970), 'Walkin'' and 'Tap Turns On The Water' (both 1971). Korner also derived success from his BBC Radio 1 show that offered a highly individual choice of material. He also broadcast on a long-running programme for the BBC World Service. Korner continued to perform live, often accompanied by former **Back Door** virtuoso bassist Colin Hodgkinson, and remained a highly respected figure in the music fraternity. He joined Charlie Watts, Ian Stewart, Jack Bruce and **Dick Heckstall-Smith** in the informal **Rocket 88**, and Korner's 50th birthday party, which featured appearances by **Eric Clapton**, **Chris Farlowe** and **Zoot Money**, was both filmed and recorded. In 1981, Korner began an ambitious 13-part television documentary on the history of rock, but his premature death from cancer in January 1984 left this and other projects unfulfilled. However, his stature as a vital catalyst in British R&B was already assured.

● ALBUMS: by Alexis Korner's Blues Incorporated *R&B From The Marquee* (Ace Of Clubs 1962)★★★★, *Alexis Korner's Blues Incorporated* (Ace Of Clubs 1964)★★★, *Red Hot From Alex* aka *Alexis Korner's All Star Blues Incorporated* (Transatlantic 1964)★★★★, *At The Cavern* (Oriole 1964)★★★, *Sky High* (Spot 1966)★★, *Blues Incorporated (Wednesday Night Prayer Meeting)* (Polydor 1967)★★★; by Alexis Korner *I Wonder Who* (Fontana 1967)★★★, *A New Generation Of Blues* aka *What's That Sound I Hear* (Transatlantic 1968)★★★, *Both Sides Of Alexis Korner* (Metronome 1969)★★★, *Alexis* (Rak 1971)★★★, *Mr. Blues* (Toadstool 1974)★★★, *Alexis Korner* (Polydor 1974)★★★, *Get Off My Cloud* (Columbia 1975)★★★, *Just Easy* (Intercord 1978)★★★, *Me* (Jeton 1979)★★★, *The Party Album* (Intercord 1980)★★★, *Juvenile Delinquent* (1984)★★, *Live In Paris: Alexis Korner* (Magnum 1988)★★★; by New Church *The New Church* (Metronome 1970); by Snape *Accidentally Born In New Orleans* (Transatlantic 1973)★★★, *Snape Live On Tour* (Brain 1974)★★★.

● COMPILATIONS: *Bootleg Him* (Rak 1972)★★★, *Profile* (Teldec 1981)★★★, with Cyril Davies *Alexis 1957* (Krazy Kat 1984)★★★, with Colin Hodgkinson *Testament* (Thunderbolt 1985)★★★, *Alexis Korner 1961-1972* (Castle 1986)★★★, *Hammer And Nails* (Thunderbolt 1987)★★★, *The Alexis Korner Collection* (Castle 1988)★★★, *And ....* (Castle 1994)★★, *On The Move* (Castle 1996)★★.

● VIDEOS: *Eat A Little Rhythm And Blues* (BBC Video 1988).

● FURTHER READING: *Alexis Korner: The Biography*, Harry Shapiro.

Korngold, Erich Wolfgang

b. 29 May 1897, Brno (Brunn), Czechoslovakia, d. 29 November 1957, Hollywood, California, USA. An important composer, conductor and arranger for films, from the mid-30s into the 50s. Korngold was a child prodigy, and, in his teens, wrote short operas, such as *The Ring Of Polycrates* and *Violant*. He performed as a pianist in concerts, and was the resident conductor at the Hamburg Opera House for several years. He also re-scored vintage operetta classics, giving them a new lease of life. During the 20s, his own operatic compositions, including *Die Tote Stadt (The Dead City)*, and *The Miracle Of Heliane*, played European opera houses, and his enormous popularity on that continent led him to move to the USA in 1934, where he subsequently became an American citizen in 1943. In 1935, he worked on the first of a series of films for Warner Brothers Studio, when he adapted Mendelssohn's music for the highly regarded film *A Midsummer Night's Dream*, starring **Dick Powell** and **James Cagney**. In the same year, he composed the score for *Captain Blood*, the movie that made Errol Flynn a star. Such was his prestige, Korngold was able to pick and choose which movies he cared to work on. During the 30s, his film scores included *Give Us This Night*, *Anthony Adverse*, for which Korngold won his first Academy Award (1936), *The Green Pastures*, *The Prince And The Pauper*, *Another Dawn*, *Of Human Bondage*, *The Adventure Of Robin Hood*, (another Oscar for Korngold), *Juarez* and *The Private Lives Of Elizabeth And Essex*. In 1940, Korngold composed some of his most stirring music for *Sea Hawk*, his last for an historical adventure, and was nominated for another Academy Award. His other scores during the 40s included *Sea Wolf*, *King's Row*, *The Constant Nymph*, *Between Two Worlds*, *Devotion*, *Deception* and *Escape Me Never* (1947). In 1944, he conducted and adapted Offenbach's music for the Broadway show, *Helen Goes To Troy*, and added a few things of his own. In the late 40s, Korngold became disenamoured with movies, and turned again to classical composing. These included 'Piano Sonata In E', 'Violin Concerto In D', 'Piano Trio', and 'Piano Concerto For The Left Hand', and the opera, *Die Kathrin*, which flopped in Vienna in 1950. He returned to films in 1955 with his score for the 'uninspired' Richard Wagner bio-pic, *The Magic Fire*, but died two years later in 1957. In spite of his relatively small output, he is still regarded as the leader of his craft. Recordings include: *Elizabeth And Essex* and *The Sea Hawk*, both played by the National Philharmonic Orchestra, and *Music Of Erich Wolfgang Korngold*, conducted by **Lionel Newman**.

● FURTHER READING: *Erich Wolfgang Korngold* by R.S. Hoffman. *Erich Wolfgang Korngold: Ein Lebensbild* by L. Korngold.

Kortchmar, Danny

b. New York City, USA. This talented guitarist, also known as Danny Kootch and 'Kootch', was a member of several aspiring New York 60s groups, including the **Kingbees** and Flying Machine, the latter of which featured **James Taylor**. In 1967, Kootch joined ex-Myddle Class bassist Charles Larkey in the **Fugs**, where they added considerable musical dexterity to a once-anarchic act. The pair then moved to California, and having joined songwriter **Carole King** in the **City**, remained part of her studio back-up group during her subsequent, highly-successful solo career. Kootch was also reunited with James Taylor on *Sweet Baby James* (1970), and their rekindled relationship was to prove equally enduring. The guitarist continued his association with Larkey in Jo Mama, before completing *Kootch* in 1973. He remained a stellar member of the west coast session fraternity, playing on dozens of major albums in the 70s, but, despite completing the accomplished *Innuendo*, he was always better known for his contributions to other artists' recordings. Kootch co-wrote several songs for *I Can't Stand Still*, the debut solo album by former **Eagles** drummer/vocalist, **Don Henley**. The most notable of these was 'Dirty Laundry', a US Top 5 single in 1982.

● ALBUMS: *Kootch* (1973)★★, *Innuendo* (70s)★★★.

Kossoff, Kirke, Tetsu And Rabbit

This instrumental studio band formed in 1971 after what was to be a brief split in the ranks of **Free** by guitarist **Paul Kossoff** and drummer Simon Kirke. The duo had struck up a relationship with Tetsu Yamauchi while on tour with Free in Japan and were joined by former **Johnny Nash** keyboardist, **John 'Rabbit' Bundrick**. The ensemble recorded one album for **Island Records** in late 1971. After Free reunited in early 1972, its troubled history continued, resulting in Bundrick and Tetsu joining their ranks the following year for a tour of Japan and carrying on until the demise of the popular blues group in 1973.

● ALBUMS: *Kossoff, Kirke, Tetsu And Rabbit* (Island 1971)★★★.

Kossoff, Paul

b. 14 September 1950, Hampstead, London, England, d. 19 March 1976. The son of English actor David Kossoff, Paul was an inventive, impassioned guitar player who was initially a member of **Black Cat Bones**, a late 60s blues band that included drummer Simon Kirke. In 1968, both musicians became founder-members of **Free** and later worked together in **Kossoff, Kirke, Tetsu And Rabbit**, a spin-off project that completed a lone album in 1971 during a hiatus in the parent group's career. Free was reactivated in 1972, but Kossoff's tenure during this second phase was blighted by recurring drug and health problems. Absent on portions of several tours, Kossoff finally left the group to pursue a solo career. *Back Street Crawler* contained several excellent performances, notably 'Molten Gold', but it was two years before the guitarist was well enough to resume live work. He accompanied **John Martyn** on a 1975 tour before assembling a new group,

also entitled **Back Street Crawler**. The quintet completed one album but projected concerts were cancelled when Kossoff suffered a near-fatal heart attack. Specialists forbade an immediate return, but plans were hatched for a series of concerts the following year. However, in March 1976, Paul Kossoff died in his sleep during a flight from Los Angeles to New York. On **Jim Capaldi**'s 1975 solo album, *Short Cut Draw Blood*, two songs were reputedly written in tribute to Kossoff: 'Seagull' and 'Boy With A Problem'; Kossoff had played lead guitar on the latter.

● ALBUMS: *Back Street Crawler* (Island 1973)★★★, *Live In Croydon, June 15th 1975* (Repertoire 1995)★★.

● COMPILATIONS: *Koss* (DJM 1977)★★★, *The Hunter* (Street Tunes 1983)★★, *Leaves In The Wind* (Street Tunes 1983)★★, *Blue Soul* (Island 1986)★★★, *The Collection* (Hit Label 1995)★★★, *Stone Free* (Carlton Sounds 1997)★★★.

Kostelanetz, André

b, 22 December 1901, St. Petersburg, Russia, d. 13 January 1980, Port-au-Prince, Haiti. A distinguished conductor, composer, arranger and pianist who was instrumental in bridging the divide between classical and popular music. The son of wealthy parents, Kostelanetz is said to have been able to play the piano by the age of five. While in his teens he studied at the St. Petersburg Conservatory of Music, and then served as an assistant conductor for the Imperial Grand Opera in Petrograd, before emigrating to the USA with his family in 1922. In America he worked in various capacities for a number of opera companies, and in 1928 became a naturalized American. In the same year he began his association with the Atlantic Broadcasting System (later **CBS**) which resulted in an enormously popular series of radio programmes which lasted from the early 30s through to the 50s. As a conductor, arranger and musical advisor, Kostelanetz presented popular music in a large orchestral setting, while tailoring serious works to suit the tastes of the ever-growing radio audiences. He also pioneered various significant advances in sound reproduction, and his recordings in the **Columbia Records** Masterworks series are superb examples of their kind. In 1938 Kostelanetz married the operatic soprano Lily Pons, and their concerts together were a major attraction. They also entertained US troops abroad during World War II. The marriage ended in divorce in 1958, and Pons died in 1976. Over the years, Kostelanetz served as guest conductor with various symphony orchestras, and in 1952 he began an association with the New York Philharmonic which lasted for a remarkable 27 seasons. In 1953 he inaugurated a renowned series of non-subscription concerts, and from 1963-79 served as Artistic Director and Principal Conductor of Promenade Concerts. With the Promenades, Kostelanetz once again succeeded in his ambition to provide an entertaining and satisfying mix of elements from a wide range of the performing arts. He conducted the music for several films, and accompanied **Perry Como** on his 1946 US number 1 hit,

'Prisoner Of Love'. He made the US chart himself in 1955 with *Meet André Kostelanetz*, and released several excellent albums featuring the work of celebrated theatre composers such as **Cole Porter**, **Richard Rodgers**, **Jerome Kern**, **George Gershwin** and **Vincent Youmans**. For many years his distinctive recording of 'With A Song In My Heart' was used to introduce *Family Favourites* on BBC radio. Although two of his best-remembered compositions, 'Moon Love' (written with **Mack David** and Mack Davis, and a US number 1 for **Glenn Miller**) and 'On The Isle Of May' (lyric: Mack David), were adapted from Tchaikovsky themes, Kostelanetz was involved in the whole musical spectrum, including jazz. Among his lifetime honours was the US Army Asiatic-Pacific campaign ribbon which he received for his work in organizing and conducting bands consisting of military personnel in Europe, the Middle East and North Africa during World War II. He loved to travel to various parts of the world, and died from a heart attack while on holiday in Haiti.

● ALBUMS: *Romantic Music Of Tchaikovsky* (1958)★★★★, *Encore!* (1958)★★★, *Lure Of France* (1958)★★★, *Theatre Party* (1958)★★★, *Lure Of Paradise* (1959)★★, *Flower Drum Song* (1959)★★★, *Romantic Arias For Orchestras* (1959)★★★, *Tender Is The Night* (50s)★★★, *Musical Comedy Favourites* (50s)★★, *You And The Night And The Music* (50s)★★★, *Gypsy Passion* (1960)★★★★, *Wonderland Of Sound* (1961)★★★, *Kostelanetz Festival* (1961)★★, *The Unsinkable Molly Brown* (1961)★★, *Fire And Jealousy* (1962)★★★, *Broadway Hits* (1962)★★★, *Star Spangled Marches* (1962)★★, *Wonderland Of Hits* (1963)★★★, *The World's Great Waltzes* (1963)★★★, *Wonderland Of Opera* (1963)★★★, *I Wish You Love* (1964)★★★, *Thunderer-Strauss* (1965)★★★, *Romantic Strings* (1965)★★★, *Showstoppers* (1965)★★★, *Great Movie Themes* (1966)★★, *Today's Golden Hits* (1966)★★★, *Promenade Favourites* (1966)★★, *Concert In The Park* (1967)★★★, *Sound Of Today* (Columbia1967)★★★, *Favourite Romantic Concertos* (Columbia 60s)★★, *Plays Charlie Chaplin And Duke Ellington* (Columbia 1981)★★★, *That's Entertainment* (Columbia 1981)★★★, with narration by Johnny Cash *Grand Canyon Suite* (Columbia 1981)★★★.

● FURTHER READING: *Echoes: Memoirs Of André Kostelanetz*, André Kostelanetz and G. Hammond.

Kota, Tera

b. Gboyega Femi, Nigeria. Kota took his stage name from 'terra cotta', meaning an ancient artefact preserved today for the purposes of tomorrow. In advance of both **Majek Fashek** and **Ras Kimono**, Kota was the first Nigerian to successfully integrate **reggae** into the Nigerian songbook. Further, he would publically claim that the music itself was of Nigerian descent, derived from the ancient form of praise song, ere-ege. Despite such proclamations, he only switched musical style to reggae in the early 80s. He recorded his first album in 1982 and watched it top the Nigerian charts, remaining there for a period of four months and selling over half a million copies in the process. His second

album was part-dedicated to **Fela Kuti**, at that time serving a jail sentence, which mirrored the social consciousness which now dominated his lyrics. That collection and the subsequent *Peasant Child* have continued to push his desire to attract Nigerian youth to the 'righteous' sounds of roots reggae.

● ALBUMS: *Lamentation In Sodom* (1982)★★★, *Solitude And Shackles* (1985)★★, *Peasant Child* (1987)★★★.

Kotch

Kotch have been in existence since 1981, although only drummer Steven Lee and his guitarist uncle Pablo Stewart have remained constant. First called Psalms, the band offered straightforward roots reggae at a time when **dancehall** was starting to become popular. Their first single, 'In The Hills', produced by themselves and **Third World**'s Willie Stewart, flopped, but it was followed by the better-received 'Ska-ba', produced by Ibo Cooper, also from Third World. By that time, in 1982, their lead singer, Parry Hinds, had been replaced by the distinctive, soulful baritone of Rueben 'Norman' Espuet and the line-up settled to Espuet, Lee, Pablo Stewart, Ian Heard (saxophone), Al Wilson (trombone), Earl Thorpe (bass) and Herbie Harris (keyboards). Four singles arrived in 1983, the last two, 'Head Over Heels' and 'Jean', charting in Jamaica. Their first album, *Sticks And Stones*, was also issued that year. Steven Lee's other job, at his father's Sonic Sounds record distribution company in Kingston, gave Kotch an important connection. Upstairs at Sonic Sounds was a tiny computerized studio, Megabyte, that **Sly Dunbar** rented. Kotch's keyboard player, Herbie Harris, became resident programmer and, with reggae changing in 1986 to a fully digital sound, Sly was looking for his Taxi label to follow suit. In 1988 it arrived: a rocking, woodblock snare, a subsonic, growling bass, and a simple keyboard and guitar arrangement that owed something to **rocksteady**. When Dunbar needed a voice, he simply called on the band downstairs, but Kotch's first new hit, 'Cruising', caused confusion. Many believed that it was the work of a girl group, as Espuet's baritone had been sidelined for a falsetto worthy of the **Stylistics**. An appearance at the Reggae Sunsplash festival in 1988 confirmed that it was Espuet with the high-rise larynx. 'Cruising' hit number 1 in Jamaica, and it was quickly followed by 'Tears' (a Top 10 hit) and a cover version of **Smokey Robinson**'s 'Ooh Baby Baby', which Mango issued in England to considerable reggae chart success. 'Heartbreak', a cover version of **Eric Clapton**'s 'Wonderful Tonight', and 'Tracks Of My Tears' have all since sold well. The album *Kotch* was released internationally and to support it they toured Africa, South America and Europe and played extensively, backing singers and DJs in Jamaica - a facet of their work that success forced them to abandon. 'Don't Take Away' with **U-Roy**, and 'Clock' maintained their profile into the 90s.

● ALBUMS: *Sticks And Stones* (Sonic Sounds 1983)★★★, *Kotch* (Mango/Island 1989)★★★★.

KOUYATÉ, KANDIA

Kotick, Teddy

b. 4 June 1928, Haverill, Massachusetts, USA, d. 17 April 1986. Kotick started playing the guitar when he was six years old and only took up the double bass in high school. He moved to New York in 1948 and played with **Buddy Rich**, **Buddy De Franco** and **Artie Shaw**. Throughout his career Kotick played interesting lines with perfect timing, secure pitch and a full tone. In the early 50s he played with **Charlie Parker** and **Stan Getz**. Later Kotick played on **Bill Evans**' debut album and then toured with the **Horace Silver** Quintet (1957-58). After a break in his career he settled in Massachusetts and recorded again with **Allen Eager** and **J.R. Monterose**.

● ALBUMS: with Stan Getz *Jazz At Storyville* (1951)★★★, *Charlie Parker Plays Cole Porter* (1954)★★★★, with Bill Evans *New Jazz Conceptions* (1956)★★★★, with Horace Silver *Further Explorations* (1958)★★★★, with J.R. Monterose *Live In Albany* (1979)★★★★.

Kottke, Leo

b. 11 September 1945, Athens, Georgia, USA. This inventive guitarist drew inspiration from the country-blues style of **Mississippi John Hurt**, and having taken up the instrument as an adolescent, joined several aspiring mid-60s groups. Induction into the US Navy interrupted his progress, but the artist was discharged following an accident that permanently damaged his hearing. Kottke subsequently ventured to Minneapolis where a spell performing in the city's folk clubs led to a recording contract. *Circle Round The Sun* received limited exposure via two independent outlets, but his career did not fully flourish until 1971 when **John Fahey** invited Kottke to record for his company, Takoma. *Six And Twelve String Guitar* established the artist as an exciting new talent, with a style blending dazzling dexterity with moments of introspection. Kottke's desire to expand his repertoire led to a break with Fahey and a major contract with **Capitol Records**. *Mudlark* included instrumental and vocal tracks, notably a version of the **Byrds**' 'Eight Miles High', and while purists bore misgivings about Kottke's languid, sonorous voice, his talent as a guitarist remained unchallenged. Several excellent albums in a similar vein ensued, including *Greenhouse*, which boasted an interpretation of Fahey's 'Last Steam Engine Train', and the in-concert *My Feet Are Smiling*. Prodigious touring enhanced Kottke's reputation as one of America's finest acoustic 12-string guitarists, although he was unable to convert this standing into commercial success. He later switched labels to **Chrysalis**, but by the 80s had returned to independent outlets on which his crafted approach has continued to flourish.

● ALBUMS: *12-String Blues: Live At The Scholar Coffee House* (Oblivion 1968)★★★, *Six And Twelve String Guitar* (Takoma/Sonet 1971)★★★, *Circle Round The Sun* (Symposium 1970)★★★, *Mudlark* (Capitol 1971)★★★, *Greenhouse* (Capitol 1972)★★★★, *My Feet Are Smiling* (Capitol 1973)★★★, *Ice Water* (Capitol 1974)★★★★, *Dreams And All That Stuff* (Capitol 1975)★★, *Chewing Pine* (Capitol 1975)★★★, *Leo Kottke* (Chrysalis 1976)★★★★, *Burnt Lips* (Chrysalis 1979)★★★, *Balance* (Chrysalis 1979)★★, *Leo Kottke Live In Europe* (Chrysalis 1980), *Guitar Music* (Chrysalis 1981)★★★, *Time Step* (Chrysalis 1983)★★★★, *A Shout Towards Noon* (Private Music 1986)★★★, *Regards From Chuck Pink* (Private Music 1988)★★★★, *My Father's Face* (Private Music 1989)★★★, *That's What* (Private Music 1990)★★★, *Great Big Boy* (Private Music 1991)★★★, *Peculiaroso* (Private Music 1994)★★★, *Live* (Private Music 1995)★★★, *Standing In My Shoes* (Private Music 1997)★★★★.

● COMPILATIONS: *Leo Kottke 1971-1976 - Did You Hear Me?* (Capitol 1976)★★★, *The Best Of Leo Kottke* (Capitol 1977)★★★, *The Best Of Leo Kottke* (EMI 1979)★★★, *Essential Leo Kottke* (Chrysalis 1991)★★★★.

Kotzen, Richie

This highly gifted, US-born new-age rock guitar god is very much in the **Joe Satriani** mould. By the time Kotzen had reached his seventh birthday, he had moved from piano to guitar lessons, and was playing live with his own band, Arthur's Museum, when he entered his teens. Taken under the wing of Mike Varney, he was introduced to bassist Stuart Hamm and ex-**Journey** drummer Steve Smith, with whom he recorded a solo instrumental album. This showcased Kotzen's inherent ability and feel for the electric guitar, but also highlighted the limitations of rock music without vocals. Realizing this, he formed Fever Dream, a power trio comprising Danny Thompson (bass), Atma Anur (drums) and himself on guitar and vocals. Although the guitar breaks were excellent, there was a paucity of hooks and a scarcity of real tunes. Kotzen went on to replace C.C. Deville in **Poison**'s ranks in 1991.

● ALBUMS: *Richie Kotzen* (Roadrunner 1989)★★★, *Fever Dream* (Roadrunner 1990)★★★, *Electric Joy* (Roadrunner 1993)★★.

Kouyaté, Kandia

b. 1958, Kita, Mali. With origins in a highly musical family, Kouyaté became a distinctive solo artist in her own right from the mid-80s onwards. Her main attribute has always been a voice which can convey both beauty and strength in equal measure, and when matched with appropriate material, the results can be spectacular. Her professional career began with the Mali National Ensemble, but she soon formed her own band in the early 80s. This included two notable participants, kora star **Toumani Diabate** and **Bouba Sacko** on guitar. She drew on various traditions for her musical accompaniment, from the kora of Senegal and Gambia to traditional Kita songs taught to her as a child. She travelled to Abidjan in 1985 to record her debut cassette album, which featured a major domestic hit in 'Maimouna Sarama'. This brought her to the attention not only of the Malian populace in general, but also businessman Baba Cissoko, who became her patron (as he had been with her namesake, **Tata Bambo Kouyaté**,

3069

before her). Much of her output from then onwards was concerned with the singing of his praises. This served to diminish the impact of an otherwise superb singer, though she has become one of the wealthiest African singers in the process.

● ALBUMS: *Amary Dou Présente K. Kouyaté* cassette only (1985)★★★, *Project Dabia* (BM 1987)★★★★.

Kouyaté, Ousmane

b. 1952, Dabola, Guinea. A member of Les Ambassadeurs in the late 80s, guitarist Kouyaté was also a frequent member of **Salif Keita**'s other bands. In common with so many African artists, Kouyaté was born into a musical family, his mother a singer and dancer, his father an accordionist and ngoini player. After experimenting with the balafon he started to learn the guitar and formed his first band with friends in 1966. A career break was enforced by his attendance at university (studying agriculture), but he left shortly before graduation to return to music. He moved to Bamako and met Manfila Kante, leader of Les Ambassadeurs. He joined in 1977, remaining with the band for many years and becoming a close confidant of Keita. When he left the band so did Kouyaté, the pair teaming up once more on Keita's albums *Soro* and *Ko-Yan*. His own solo career had begun in 1982 with *Beni Haminanko*, before *Kefimba* was recorded with members of **Bembaya Jazz** in 1985 to international critical acclaim. It announced Kouyaté as a major player in wassoulou music, a style with origins in south Bamako which utilises five note melodies and is based on the local tradition for hunting songs. He resurfaced in 1990 with a three album contract with London-based label Stern's Records, but despite a significant budget *Domba* failed to produce major sales. Kouyaté's reputation has never really recovered, though he continues to record, but is now less willing to sacrifice musical traditions at the altar of crossover success.

● ALBUMS: *Beni Haminanko* (SACO 1982)★★★, *Kefimba* (OK 1985)★★★, *Domba* (Stern's 1990)★★★, *In Paris* (VSSF 1993)★★.

Kouyaté, Tata Bambo

b. c.1948, Bamako, Mali. Kouyaté is part of an extended family of celebrated Jalis, the hereditary stream of Manding musicians dedicated to preserving tradition and religious service. After being taught vocal technique almost from the cradle she joined the Mali National Ensemble in the early 60s, staying with them for several years and appearing with them on their trip to the 1967 Pan-African Music Festival in Algiers. Her first solo hit came with 'Bamba', a title which, in slightly altered form, became her nickname. Her extensive tours of Africa and later Europe were largely conducted at the behest of various expatriate Malian communities, for whom she acted as a metaphor for national identity. On one such journey she was spotted by Babani Cissoko, a wealthy businessman who became her patron. He joined her in Paris, France, where she recorded her biggest hit, 'Hommage A Baba Cissoko', which featured Keletigui Diabate on violin and balafon. As well as such tribute songs her recordings focused on traditional Manding hearth songs, though until 1988 none of her numerous cassette albums reached Western ears. *Jatigui*, released in 1989, helped rectify that problem, and received universally strong reviews (it is actually a re-release of her 1984 Paris recording sessions). *Djely Mousso*, on the other hand, featured a more modern approach, with synthesizers and electric guitars and bass. The traditional mainstay of her music, the ngoni (fiddle), was still present however, with Boncana Magia's production shaping the elements into a fine, cohesive whole.

● ALBUMS: *Ejely Mousoo* (Syllart 1988)★★★, *Jatigui* (Globestyle 1989)★★.

Kowald, Peter

b. 21 April 1944, Masserberg, Germany. Kowald, who plays bass, tuba and alphorn, is one of the key figures in the development of European improvisation. Before he became a professional musician he was a translator, and his multilingual abilities have stood him in good stead on his travels. Kowald opened up the contacts between the German free-jazzers and their British counterparts, and played with the **Spontaneous Music Ensemble** in London in 1967. He was responsible for bringing **Peter Brötzmann** and Dutch drummer **Han Bennink** together, and that there exists a Greek free-jazz scene at all has much to do with his endeavours. Kowald was also one of the first of his generation of players to journey to the USA and Japan. He was also instrumental in the revival of **Globe Unity** in 1973 and for five years co-led this free orchestra with **Alexander Von Schlippenbach**. Globe Unity's *Jahrmarkt/Local Fair* (1977), on which the improvisers encounter a Greek folk group and 25 Wuppertal accordion players, is a typically Utopian Kowald project.

● ALBUMS: *Peter Kowald Quintet* (1972)★★★, with Michel Pilz, Paul Lovens *Carpathes* (1976)★★★, with Barre Phillips *Die Jungen: Random Generators* (1979)★★, with Leo Smith, Günter Sommer *Touch The Earth* (1980)★★★, with Smith, Sommer *Break The Shells* (1981)★★★, with Barry Guy *Paintings* (1982)★★★, with Maarten Altena *Two Making A Triangle* (1982)★★★, with Frank Wright, A.R. Penck *Run With The Cowboys* (1987)★★★, with Danny Davis, Takehisa Kosugi *Global Village Suite* (1988)★★★★, *Open Secrets* (1988)★★★★, *Duos Europa/USA/Japan* 1984-1990 recording (FMP 1992)★★★.

Koz, Dave

b. Los Angeles, California, USA. Saxophonist Dave Koz is one of a small number of modern jazz players to have found significant contemporary success without necessarily obtaining critical approval for their efforts. His repertoire, like that of both **Kenny G.** and **Najee**, incorporates instrumental treatments of familiar pop fare, as well as extended solo spots. His technique may not bear comparison with the greats of jazz, but within his limitations he is an accomplished performer. His debut album was a continual presence on the *Billboard* Contemporary Jazz charts in that year (charting for 25 weeks). Singles drawn from it included 'Nothing But The Radio On' and 'Castle Of Dreams', both of which also sold well. He secured widespread fame by appearing regularly on the *Arsenio Hall* television show as part of the 'Posse', and also appeared and performed on *Family Matters* and *General Hospital*. The latter chose his song, 'Faces Of The Heart', as their new theme song - the first such revision in 30 years of transmission. 1993's *Lucky Man* was similarly successful and led to him being hailed as 'a prince of multi-media'. It was promoted with widespread television and concert appearances alongside artists such as **Michael Bolton** and **Kenny Loggins**. Spending over two years in the Contemporary Jazz chart, by 1995 the album had earned a gold award for sales of over half a million. Further prestige bookings followed, including one for the Inaugural Celebration at the Lincoln Memorial alongside **Grover Washington Jnr.**, **David Sanborn** and **Gerry Mulligan**. He also began to host his own radio show - *Personal Notes With Dave Koz* - a two hour contemporary jazz programme. While continuing to work as a session musician with artists including **Jonathon Butler**, **Stevie Nicks** and **Julio Iglesias**, Koz also composed themes for television shows *Late Night With Greg Kinnear* and *Jones Vs. Jury*. He also regularly hosts the United Cerebral Palsy telethon.

● ALBUMS: *Dave Koz* (Capitol 1990)★★, *Lucky Man* (Capitol 1993)★★★★, *Off The Beaten Path* (Capitol 1996)★★★, *December Makes Me Feel That Way* (Capitol 1997)★★.

Kpiaye, John

b. John Ogetti Kpiaye, 1948, London, England. Kpiaye was born to an English mother and Nigerian father, spending his formative years in the English countryside. He left school in London at the age of 15 and, emulating luminaries such as **Bob Marley** and **Desmond Dekker**, he embarked on an apprenticeship in welding. In 1966 his mother bought him his first guitar, and he joined a band called the Hustling Kind, who later changed their name to the Cats. In 1968 Kpiaye encouraged the band to record a reggae rendition of Tchaikovsky's 'Swan Lake', working out the piano melody line on his sister's piano at home, and the Cats secured their first British reggae UK Top 50 chart hit. The success of the single resulted in a European tour, but by 1971 the group disbanded. Kpiaye soon found work playing for the In Brackets, who provided backing for a number of top performers including **Dandy**, **Ginger Williams**, **Owen Gray**, **Winston Groovy** and Joy White. In 1973 the band was dissolved and Kpiaye became immersed in production work, initially for **Dennis Harris**, and provided direction for notable lovers rock performers **Brown Sugar** and **15-16-17**. In the latter half of the 70s he became an in-demand guitarist, playing for **Ijahman Levi**, **Aswad**, **Dennis Brown**, **Janet Kay** and **Linton Kwesi Johnson**, **Eddy Grant** and **Georgie Fame**. In 1982 Kpiaye became the resident guitarist in **Dennis Bovell**'s Dub Band, touring the globe and providing backing to Linton Kwesi Johnson's acclaimed appearances. In 1997 Kpiaye released *Red, Gold And Blues*, a reggae instrumental album drawing from his many influences.

● ALBUMS: *Red, Gold And Blues* (LKJ 1997)★★★★.

Kraftwerk

The word 'unique' is over-used in rock music, but Kraftwerk have a stronger claim than most to the tag. Ralf Hutter (b. 1946, Krefeld, Germany; organ) and woodwind student Florian Schneider-Esleben (b. 1947, Düsseldorf, Germany; woodwind) met while they were studying improvised music in Düsseldorf, Germany. They drew on the influence of experimental electronic forces such as composer Karlheinz Stockhausen and **Tangerine Dream** to create minimalist music on synthesizers, drum machines and tape recorders. Having previously recorded an album with Organisation (*Tone Float*), Hutter and Schneider formed Kraftwerk with Klaus Dinger and Thomas Homann and issued *Highrail*, after which Dinger and Homann left to form **Neu**. Their first two albums, released in Germany, were later released in the UK as an edited compilaton in 1972. Produced by Conny Plank (later to work with **Ultravox** and the **Eurythmics**), the bleak, spartan music provoked little response. After releasing a duo set, *Ralf And Florian*, Wolfgang Flur (electronic drums) and Klaus Roeder (guitar/violin/keyboards) join the group. *Autobahn* marked Kraftwerk's breakthrough and established them as purveyors of hi-tech, computerized music. The title track, running at more than 22 minutes, was an attempt to relate the monotony and tedium of a long road journey. An edited version reached the Top 10 in the US and UK charts. In 1975, Roeder was replaced by Karl Bartos, who played on *Radioactivity*, a concept album based on the sounds to be found on the airwaves. *Trans-Europe Express* and *The Man-Machine* were pioneering electronic works which strongly influenced a generation of English new-wave groups like the **Human League**, Tubeway Army (**Gary Numan**), **Depeche Mode** and OMD, while **David Bowie** claimed to be have long been an admirer. The *New Musical Express* said of *The Man-Machine*: 'It is the only completely successful visual/aural fusion rock has produced so far'. Kraftwerk spent three years building their own Kling Klang studios in the late 70s, complete with, inevitably, scores of computers. The single 'The Model', from *The Man-Machine*, gave the band a surprise hit when it topped the UK charts in 1982, and it led to a trio of hits, including 'Showroom Dummies' and 'Tour De France', a song that was featured in the film *Breakdance* and became the theme for the cycling event of the same name in 1983. *Electric Cafe* was a disappointment, but the group were now cited as a major influence on a host of dance artists from **Afrika**

Bambaataa to the respected producer **Arthur Baker**. Bambaattaa and Baker's pioneering 1982 'Planet Rock' single was built around samples of both 'Trans-Europe Express' and 'Numbers' (from 1981's *Computer World*).

Hutter and Schneider have remained enigmatically quiet ever since *Electric Cafe*. In 1990, a frustrated Flur departed to be replaced by Fritz Hijbert (Flur later collaborated with **Mouse On Mars** under the name of Yamo). Kraftwerk's best known songs were collected together in 1991 on the double, *The Mix*, aimed chiefly at the dance market by **EMI Records**. 'I think our music has to do with emotions. Technology and emotion can join hands . . .' said Hutter in 1991. They made a surprise return to live performance with a headline appearance at the UK's Tribal Gathering in the summer of 1997.

● ALBUMS: *Highrail* (1971)★★, *Var* (1972)★★, *Ralf & Florian* (Philips 1973)★★★, *Autobahn* (Vertigo 1974)★★★★, *Radioactivity* (Capitol 1975)★★★, *Trans-Europe Express* (Capitol 1977)★★★★, *The Man-Machine* (Capitol 1978)★★★★, *Computer World* (EMI 1981)★★★★, *Electric Cafe* (EMI 1986)★★★.

● COMPILATIONS: *Kraftwerk* a UK compilation of the first two releases (Vertigo 1973)★★, *The Mix* (EMI 1991)★★★★.

● FURTHER READING: *Kraftwerk: Man, Machine & Music*, Pacal Bussy.

Kral, Irene

b. 18 January 1932, Chicago, Illinois, USA, d. 15 August 1978. Taking heed of the success of her older brother, **Roy Kral**, she began singing while still a teenager. She gained valuable on-the-road experience with bands led by **Woody Herman** and former Herman bassist **Chubby Jackson** before spending some time with a vocal group. In the late 50s she was with **Maynard Ferguson**'s band and during the next few years sang with units led by **Stan Kenton** and ex-Kenton drummer **Shelly Manne**. Kral then took off on a solo career which lasted until shortly before her early death. An elegantly poised ballad singer, she acknowledged **Carmen McRae** as one of her musical guides. Not surprisingly, given the time in which she was an up-and-coming singer, Kral was comfortable in a boppish setting and her up-tempo work was free-flowing and distinctive. She also had a jaunty way with Latin-flavoured songs.

● ALBUMS: with Maynard Ferguson *Boy With Lots Of Brass* (EmArcy 1957)★★★, with Herb Pomeroy *Detour Ahead* (UA 1958)★★★, *Steveireneo* (UA 1959)★★★, *Better Than Anything* (DRG 1963)★↝★★, with Laurindo Almeida *Guitar From Ipanema* (Capitol 1964)★★★, *Wonderful Life* (Mainstream 1965)★★★.

Kral, Roy

b. 10 October 1921, Chicago, Illinois, USA. Kral played piano and sang alone and in small groups until, in the mid-40s, he met singer Jackie Cain (b. 22 May 1928, Milwaukee, Wisconsin, USA). Together, Kral and Cain became very popular, working as Jackie And Roy. They joined **Charlie Ventura**'s 'Bop for the People' band for which Kral also played piano and contributed arrangements. In 1949, Kral and Cain quit Ventura, were married, and continued to perform as a duo throughout the 50s. In the 60s Kral was active in the studios but they frequently performed together, recording on into the late 80s. Apart from interesting and duly deferential interpretations of the great standards, Kral and Cain are noted for their vibrant enthusiasm, the sparkling audacity of their bop styling and their use of vocalese. Kral also performs with his sister, the singer Irene Kral.

● ALBUMS: *Jackie Cain And Roy Kral* (1954)★★★, *Spring Can Really Hang You Up The Most* (1955)★★★★, *Free And Easy* (1957)★★★, *Like Sing* (1962)★★★, *Lovesick* (1966)★★★, *Time And Love* (1972)★★, *Concerts By The Sea* (1976)★★★, *Star Sounds* (1979)★★★, *East Of Suez* (1980)★★, *High Standards* (1982)★★★, *A Stephen Sondheim Collection* (1982)★★, *We've Got It: The Music Of Cy Coleman* (1984)★★★, *Bogie* (1986)★★★, *One More Rose* (1987)★★★, *Full Circle* (1988)★★★.

● COMPILATIONS: *Jackie & Roy With Charlie Ventura And His Orchestra* (1948)★★★, as Jackie And Roy *Forever* (Music Masters 1995)★★.

Krall, Diana

b. Nanaimo, British Columbia, Canada. Raised in a musical family, and hearing in particular **Fats Waller** records, as a child Krall tried to learn all his tunes and to play and sing at the same time. She studied classical piano at school but played jazz piano in a school band. Her first professional gig was at the age of 15 and she has not stopped since. She won a Vancouver Jazz Festival scholarship to **Berklee College Of Music** in the USA but later returned to her hometown where she continued to play professionally. Amongst her musical associates were visiting Americans **Ray Brown** and **Jeff Hamilton**. The visitors were deeply impressed and convinced Krall to go to Los Angeles which she did with help from a Canadian Arts Council grant. In Los Angeles, she studied with **Jimmy Rowles** who persuaded her to sing more. Although she had sung from the start she had always entertained reservations about this aspect of her work. Nevertheless, the inclusion of singing into her performances led to more engagements than had been the case as a pianist. In 1984 she returned to Canada from Los Angeles, this time settling in Toronto and she appeared in New York in 1990. She continued to attract respectful admiration from other musicians, including **John Clayton** and he and Hamilton accompanied her on her first album. By the mid-90s Krall was also attracting the attention of jazz fans and even featured in articles in the non-jazz media. Her accompanists on later records have included Brown, **Stanley Turrentine** and Christian McBride, and her regular working band colleagues, Russell Malone, guitar, and Paul Keller, bass. Krall's piano playing is crisp, deft and swinging. Her singing style is relaxed and intimate and she interprets ballads with warmth and persuasive charm. Although forward thinking and alert to contemporary musical thought in jazz, Krall's heritage is such that she brings echoes of earlier swinging simplicity to her work. The fact that her first album for **Impulse! Records**, in 1995, was a tribute to **Nat 'King' Cole** seems highly appropriate to the direction she appears to be taking.

● ALBUMS: *Only Trust Your Heart* (GRP 1994)★★★, *All For You (A Dedication To The Nat King Cole Trio)* (Impulse! 1995)★★★, *Love Scenes* (Impulse! 1997)★★★★.

Kramer

Maverick producer/recording artist (Mark) Kramer became directly involved in music as the live sound engineer for several 70s New York bands, including the **Waitresses** and Pulsallama. He moved to Woodstock at the end of the decade where he became acquainted with **Carla Bley** and **Anthony Braxton**. Writing orchestral scores for the latter financed a trip to Europe, following which Kramer formed **Shockabilly** with **Eugene Chadbourne** and David Licht. This exceptional trio deconstructed 60s classic songs, fusing them with Chadbourne's crazed perception of roots music. Five unique albums were completed before inner tensions forced them apart. Kramer then joined the **Butthole Surfers** in a touring, but not recording, capacity, before returning to New York to found a studio (Noise New York) and record label (**Shimmy Disc**). He was also a member of two groups recording for his label, **B.A.L.L.** and **Bongwater**, the latter of which featured former Pulsallama singer Ann Magnuson. Kramer's eclectic taste was reflected by the acts he chose to sign/produce, including **John Zorn**, **Tuli Kuperberg**, **Galaxie 500** and the **Walkingseeds**. Shimmy Disc afforded Kramer the luxury of self-indulgence, as evinced by collaborations with Jad Fair from **Half Japanese** (*Roll Out The Barrell, The Sound Of Music*), **King Missile**'s John S. Hall (*Real Men*) and *Happiness Finally Came To Them* with Ralph Carney and Daved Hild. Bongwater remained Kramer's most intriguing outlet, a commitment that delayed his inevitable solo debut, but *The Guilt Trip* was finally unleashed following an acrimonious split Magnuson. This expansive three-record set, housed in a pastiche of **George Harrison**'s *All Things Must Pass*, was a musical triumph, crammed with wonderful songs and textured guitarwork. The artist undertook a rare British tour to promote its release, accompanied by associate guitarist Dogbowl. With Shimmy Disc's future in jeopardy, Kramer set up new outlets, Kokopop and See Eye, the former of which specialized in 'one-off' singles. The high standard of their releases confirms its founder's continued creative gifts.

● ALBUMS: with Ralph Carney and Daved Hild *Happiness Finally Came To Them* (Shimmy Disc 1987)★★, with Jad Fair *Roll Out The Barrel* (Shimmy-Disc 1988)★★, with Jad Fair *The Sound Of Music* (Shimmy-Disc 1990)★★, with John S. Hall *Real Men* (Shimmy Disc 1991)★★★, *The Guilt Trip* (1994)★★★★, *The Secret Of Comedy* (Shimmy Disc 1995)★★★.

Kramer, Alex

b. 30 May 1903, Montreal, Canada, d. 10 February 1998. A songwriter with a small, but important catalogue, Kramer studied at the McGill Conservatory of Music in Montreal and led orchestras on local radio stations, before moving to the USA in the late 30s. There, he met and married Joan Whitney (b. 26 June 1914, Pittsburgh, Pennsylvania, USA, d. 1990), who had been making a name for herself, singing in clubs and on radio. During the 40s and 50s, they wrote a string of popular songs, among which were some of the biggest hits of the day. Their first success came in 1941 with 'It All Comes Back To Me Now' and 'My Sister And I' (both written with Hy Zaret), and 'High On A Windy Hill'. **Gene Krupa** and **Hal Kemp** made best-selling records of the former, while **Jimmy Dorsey** And His Orchestra (with vocals by **Bob Eberly**) took the last two songs to number 1 in the US. In 1944 Whitney and Kramer collaborated with lyricist **Mack David** on the lively 'It's Love, Love, Love!', which was featured in the Larry Parks movie *Stars On Parade*, and became extremely popular on record for **Guy Lombardo**. They worked with David again on 'Candy', one of their most engaging songs, and another number 1, this time in a duet by **Jo Stafford** and **Johnny Mercer** in 1945. After enjoying further success with the jivey 'Money Is The Root Of All Evil' (the **Andrews Sisters**, and later a big hit for the **Viscounts**), the couple formed their own publishing company in 1947. From then on the hits continued to flow with such as 'Ain't Nobody Here But Us Chickens' (**Louis Jordan**), 'Love Somebody' (a number 1 for **Doris Day** with **Buddy Clark**), 'Comme Ci, Comme Ca' (English words by Kramer and Whitney, music by Bruno Coquatrix), 'Far Away Places (with Strange Sounding Names)' (popular for **Bing Crosby** and **Margaret Whiting** in 1949, and for **Perry Como**), 'You'll Never Get Away' (with Zaret), and 'No Other Arms, No Other Lips' (with Zaret). The **Chordettes**' version of the latter song was Whitney and Kramer's last US Top 40 hit (to date) in 1959. Between 1954 and 1959 Kramer was the director of the American Society of Composers, Authors and Publishers. He also wrote scores for several films including *The Second Greatest Sex*, *Meet Miss Bobby Socks*, *Far Away Places* and *Come With Me My Honey*. In 1991, the Canadian Broadcasting Company paid tribute to Whitney and Kramer in an interview which was illustrated by some of their best-known songs. One of the featured numbers, 'Candy', was also used in the same year on the soundtrack of the hit movie *Bugsy*, sung as it was originally, more than 45 years ago, by Jo Stafford and Johnny Mercer.

Lyricist Hy Zaret (b. 21 August 1907, New York, USA), sometime collaborator of Whitney and Kramer, practised as a lawyer before concentrating on writing songs. His varied output has included numbers such as 'Young, Warm and Wonderful', 'The Lass With The Delicate Air', 'What Makes A Good American?', 'So Long For A While', 'Song Of The Army Nurses Corps', as well as a radio operetta and an opera. In 1945, his novelty, 'One Meat Ball' (with Lou Singer), became popular for **Josh White** and the Andrews Sisters, and 10 years later his dramatic ballad, 'Unchained Melody' (music by **Alex North**), was an international hit for **Les Baxter** and **Al Hibbler**, and gave British balladeer **Jimmy Young** his first UK chart-topper. The **Righteous Brothers** revived 'Unchained Melody' in 1964, and their version became enormously popular all over again in 1990 after it was extensively featured in the Patrick Swayze movie *Ghost*. Five years later the song returned to number 1 in the UK in a version by Robson Green and Jerome Flynn, two actors from the popular UK television series *Soldier, Soldier*.

Kramer, Billy J., And The Dakotas

b. William Howard Ashton, 19 August 1943, Bootle, Merseyside, England. Kramer originally fronted Merseybeat combo the Coasters, but was teamed with the Manchester-based **Dakotas** - Mike Maxfield (b. 23 February 1944; lead guitar), Robin McDonald (b. 18 July 1943; rhythm guitar), Ray Jones (bass) and Tony Mansfield (b. 28 May 1943; drums) - upon signing to **Brian Epstein**'s management agency. Having topped the UK charts with the **Beatles**' 'Do You Want To Know A Secret' (1963), Kramer's UK chart success was maintained with a run of exclusive **John Lennon/Paul McCartney** songs, including the chart-topping 'Bad To Me', 'I'll Keep You Satisfied' (number 4) and 'From A Window' (number 10). 'Little Children' (1964), penned by US writers **Mort Shuman** and John McFarland, gave the group a third number 1 and their first taste of success in the USA, reaching number 7. This was quickly followed by the reissued 'Bad To Me' which also reached the Top 10. Their chart reign ended the following year with the **Burt Bacharach**-composed 'Trains And Boats And Planes' peaking at number 12 in the UK. Although subsequent efforts, most notably the lyrical 'Neon City', proved effective, Kramer's career was firmly in the descendent. He embarked on a solo career in January 1967, but having failed to find a new audience, sought solace on the cabaret and nostalgia circuit.

● ALBUMS: *Listen - To Billy J. Kramer* (Parlophone 1963)★★★, *Little Children* (Imperial 1964)★★★, *I'll Keep You Satisfied* (Imperial 1964)★★★, *Trains And Boats And Planes* (Imperial 1965)★★, *Kramer Versus Kramer* (1986)★★.
● COMPILATIONS: *The Best Of Billy J. Kramer* (1984)★★★, *The EMI Years* (1991)★★★, *The EP Collection* (See For Miles 1995)★★★, *... At Abbey Road* (EMI 1998)★★★.

Kramer, Wayne

b. c.1949, USA. The rise of **Epitaph Records** in the 90s was built largely on the success of bands such as the **Offspring** and **Rancid**, yet the label also signed a solo artist whose early involvement in Detroit's **MC5** had laid the foundations for the whole punk movement. The MC5 played their final gig on 31 December 1972, Kramer subsequently forming Gang War. In the late

80s he began work on an off-Broadway musical, *The Last Words Of Dutch Schultz*, before performing with former members of MC5 in 1992 at a tribute to their recently departed vocalist, Rob Tyner. At the same he recorded his first solo album, *Wayne Kramer's Deathtongue*. However, it was only when he signed with Epitaph that his career once again hit an upswing. Brett Gurevitz, head of Epitaph, told *Music Week* how he managed to recruit Kramer. 'One day the phone rang and a voice said, "This is Wayne Kramer from the MC5, I've got a new record, will you put it out?"' The album concerned, *The Hard Stuff*, became a major critical hit both in Europe and the USA. A follow-up collection, *Dangerous Madness*, saw Kramer indulging further in the loose, raucous guitar technique copied by so many. However, it also included a series of reflective, considered lyrics, especially the sanguine 'God's Worst Nightmare'. *Citizen Wayne* featured more involvement from producer **Don Was**, but was still an effective and powerful hard rock record.

● ALBUMS: *Wayne Kramer's Deathtongue* (1992)★★, *The Hard Stuff* (Epitaph 1995)★★★, *Dangerous Madness* (Epitaph 1996)★★★, *Citizen Wayne* (Epitaph 1997)★★★.

Krause, Dagmar

b. Germany. Vocalist Krause began performing in Hamburg's thriving underground scene during the late 60s. She subsequently joined **Peter Blegvad** and **Anthony Moore** in **Slapp Happy**, a 70s *avant garde* attraction which drew heavily on European musical traditions. Dagmar's dispassionate vocals were among the group's many attributes and her intonation proved ideal when the trio joined forces with the politically-orientated **Henry Cow**. Moore and Blegvad took Slapp Happy out of the collective in 1975, but Krause opted to remain with the former act until its disintegration later in the decade. The singer recorded *Babble* with **Kevin Coyne** in 1979 and subsequently embarked on a solo career with *Supply And Demand*, a collection of playwright Bertold Brecht's theatrical songs. *Angebot Und Nachfrage* was the same selection, sung in German, while *Tank Battles: The Songs Of Hanns Eisler* revealed the artist's continued infatuation with the cabaret of Germany's Weimar Republic. She rejoined Blegvad and Moore in 1997 to record a new Slapp Happy album.

● ALBUMS: *Supply And Demand* (1986)★★★, *Angebot Und Nachfrage* (1987)★★★★, *Tank Battles: The Songs Of Hanns Eisler* (1988)★★.

Krauss, Alison

b. 23 July 1971, Decatur, Illinois, USA. Krauss is unique in the 90s crop of female country singers in that she leans strongly towards more traditional forms of country music, especially bluegrass. She began learning classical music on violin at the age of five and won her first fiddle contest at the age of eight when she took the honours in the Western Longbow competition. In 1983 at the age of 12, she met singer-songwriter John Pennell, who introduced her to old bluegrass cassettes.

By the end of the same year she had been awarded the Most Promising Fiddle Player (Mid West) accolade by the Society For The Preservation of Bluegrass Music. Pennell encouraged her to join his group Silver Rail when she was 14 years old. After two years with them she spent a year playing in Indiana group Classified Grass, with whom she recorded the demo tape that successfully attracted the attention of **Rounder Records**' head, Ken Irwin. Krauss then returned to Pennell's group, who had changed their name to Union Station, replacing their fiddler Andrea Zonn. In 1987 she recorded *Too Late To Cry* with them; it included the fiddle classic 'Dusty Miller', alongside six originals by Pennell. The album also included noted acoustic musicians such as Sam Bush and **Jerry Douglas**. Union Station again joined her for the Grammy-nominated follow-up album, which included a duet of 'Wild Bill Jones' with her lead guitarist, Jeff White. Inspired by **Ricky Skaggs**, who had brought bluegrass back into contemporary country music's mainstream, she worked hard to achieve similar acclaim. Though *I've Got That Old Feeling* was subsequently awarded a Grammy as best bluegrass recording of 1990, she insisted on maintaining her links with Union Station and remained with the independent Rounder label despite offers from several major labels. Her popularity was furthered in 1993 as opening act on a major **Garth Brooks** tour. Her video for 'Steel Rails' topped the CMT video chart and she made a successful debut in London in 1994. She has recorded albums of gospel songs with the Cox Family from Louisiana and her harmony vocals and fiddle playing can be heard to good advantage on **Dolly Parton**'s *Eagle When She Flies* and *Heartsongs* and **Michelle Shocked**'s *Arkansas Traveller*. She contributed 'When You Say Nothing At All' with Union Station to the tribute album to **Keith Whitley** and also performed 'Teach Your Children' with **Crosby, Stills And Nash** on *Red Hot + Country*. She subsequently became the youngest member of the *Grand Old Opry*. On inducting her, **Bill Monroe** opined, 'Alison Krauss is a fine singer and she really knows how to play bluegrass music like it should be played.' In 1995 she received five nominations at the annual **Country Music Association** awards, though one had to be withdrawn when the organizers realized that the platinum-selling compilation *Now That I've Found You* did not meet the criteria for Album Of The Year, which requires 60% new material. She did, however, win all other sections for which she was nominated, including Female Vocalist, Horizon Award, Single Of The Year (for 'When You Say Nothing At All') and Vocal Event (her collaboration with **Shenandoah**). *So Long So Wrong*, her first new album with Union Station in five years, proved to be an outstanding collection of songs that justified all the accolades.

● ALBUMS: with Union Station *Too Late To Cry* (Rounder 1987)★★★, with Union Station *Two Highways* (Rounder 1989)★★★, with Union Station *I've Got That Old Feeling* (Rounder 1990)★★★, with Union Station *Every Time You Say Goodbye* (Rounder 1992)★★★, with the Cox Family *Everybody's Reaching Out For Someone* (Rounder 1993)★★★, with the Cox Family *I Know Who Holds Tomorrow* (Rounder 1994)★★★, with the Cox Family *Beyond The City* (Rounder 1995)★★★, with Union Station *So Long So Wrong* (Rounder 1997)★★★★.

● COMPILATIONS: *Now That I've Found You: A Collection* (Rounder 1995)★★★★.

Kravitz, Lenny

b. 26 May 1964, New York, USA. Kravitz' family ties - his Jewish father was a top television producer; his Bahamian mother an actress - suggested a future in showbusiness. As a teenager he attended the Beverly Hills High School where his contemporaries included Slash, later of **Guns N' Roses**, and **Maria McKee** of **Lone Justice**. Kravitz's interest in music flourished in 1987 with the completion of the first of several demos which concluded with an early version of *Let Love Rule*. These recordings engendered a contract with **Virgin America**, but the company was initially wary of Kravitz' insistence that the finished product should only feature 'real' instruments - guitar, bass, keyboards and drums - rather than digital and computerized passages. Although denigrated in some quarters as merely retrogressive, notably in its indebtedness to **Jimi Hendrix**, *Let Love Rule* proved highly popular. Kravitz then gained greater success when **Madonna** recorded 'Justify My Love', a new, rap-influenced composition quite unlike his previous work. In 1991, the artist continued his unconventional path by writing a new arrangement to **John Lennon**'s 'Give Peace A Chance' as a comment on the impending Gulf War. The resultant recording, credited to the Peace Choir, featured several contemporaries, including **Yoko Ono** and Sean Lennon. The latter also appeared on *Mama Said*, wherein Kravitz' flirtation with 60s and early 70s rock was even more apparent. The set spawned the hit 'It Ain't Over 'Til It's Over'. *Circus* was a stripped down version of his overall sound and one that displayed his talent as a writer of more contemporary songs, rather than the 60s hybrid flavour of his past work. The belated follow-up, *5*, saw Kravitz embracing digital recording and attempting a more relaxed fusion of soul and hip-hop styles.

● ALBUMS: *Let Love Rule* (Virgin 1989)★★★, *Mama Said* (Virgin 1991)★★★, *Are You Gonna Go My Way?* (Virgin 1993)★★★, *Circus* (Virgin 1995)★★, *5* (Virgin 1998)★★★.

● VIDEOS: *Alive From Planet Earth* (1994)★★★.

Kreator

Formed in Essen, Germany, in 1984, originally under the name Tormentor, this heavy metal band originally comprised Mille Petroza (guitar, vocals), Rob (bass) and Ventor (drums). Their vicious thrash style was inspired by the filth and industrial pollution problem that Essen, on the River Ruhr, was experiencing. After changing their name to Kreator, they signed with the German-based Noise Records label, and their debut album, *Endless Pain*, appeared in 1985. Despite roughshod production, it was eagerly purchased by fans of the then fast-growing thrash metal scene. After *Pleasure To Kill*, Kreator grew to become one of the most popular bands of the genre, especially in Europe. Lyrically, they have always dealt with the dark side of life, a theme encapsulated in their slogan, 'Flag Of Hate'. Only in the 90s did they even slightly waver from their established musical path, endearing them to fans who have helped to maintain their place in the crowded and highly competitive field of thrash and death metal. After employing a number of second guitarists, they eventually settled on Frank 'Blackfire' Gosdzik, once with fellow German thrash metallers **Sodom**. Together with Petrozza, Andreas Herz (bass) and Jürgen 'Jüille' Reil (drums), they toured South America supported by **Sick Of It All** in 1994. However, by the following year when they signed a new contract with Gun Records, Herz had been replaced by Christian Giesler and Reil by Joe Canglosi (ex-Whiplash). A new album, *Cause For Conflict*, was released in 1995.

● ALBUMS: *Endless Pain* (Noise 1985)★★, *Pleasure To Kill* (Noise 1986)★★★★, *Terrible Certainty* (Noise 1988)★★★, *Out Of The Dark Into The Light* (Noise 1989)★★★, *Extreme Aggression* (Noise 1989)★★★, *Coma Of Souls* (Noise 1990)★★★, *Renewal* (Noise 1992)★★★, *Cause For Conflict* (Gun 1995)★★, *Outcast* (Gun 1997)★★★.

Kress, Carl

b. 20 October 1907, Newark, New Jersey, USA, d. 10 June 1965. An outstanding and highly-respected guitarist, Kress was active throughout the 20s and 30s, making numerous recordings. Often he worked in company with other guitarists, including **Eddie Lang** and **Dick McDonough**, with whom he recorded duets. In the 40s and 50s Kress retained his earlier unusual chordal style and preference for the acoustic instrument, despite changes generated by **Charlie Christian** and others. He continued to work into the 60s, frequently in partnership with **George Barnes**, and was performing with him in Reno, Nevada, when he collapsed and died in June 1965.

● ALBUMS: *Carl Kress* (1958)★★, with George Barnes *Two Guitars* (Stash 1962)★★★, with Barnes *Guitars Anyone?* (1963)★★★, with Barnes *Town Hall Concert* (1963)★★.

Kretzmer, Herbert

b. 5 October 1925, Kroonstad, South Africa. A distinguished journalist and lyricist, Kretzmer left his home country in the late 40s, and drifted for a few years. He lived in Paris for a time, playing the piano in a bar on the Left Bank, before settling in London in 1954. Pursuing twin careers, he served as drama critic for the *Daily Express* and television critic for the *Daily Mail*, as well as collaborating with Dave Lee on two novelty hits for **Peter Sellers** and **Sophia Loren**, 'Goodness Gracious Me' and 'Bangers And Mash'. The former went to number 4 in the UK chart, and won an **Ivor Novello** Award. Kretzmer and Lee were commissioned to write a topical song each week for BBC television's

satirical *That Was The Week That Was*, and their 'In The Summer Of His Years', which was performed by Millicent Martin within hours of the assassination of President Kennedy, was swiftly covered in America by **Mahalia Jackson**, **Kate Smith**, and **Connie Francis**. Kretzmer then wrote the book and lyrics for the West End musical *Our Man Crichton* (1964), and contributed lyrics only to **The Four Musketeers** (1967) and **Anthony Newley**'s cult musical film *Can Heironymus Merkin Ever Forget Mercy Humppe And Find True Happiness?* From the latter, 'When You Gotta Go' has become a closing song for many cabaret singers, while 'On The Boards', performed in the film by Bruce Forsyth, is a skilfully-worded tribute to music hall. Kretzmer's English lyrics for the **Charles Aznavour** songs, 'Yesterday When I Was Young', 'Happy Anniversary' and 'She' (from the ITV series *The Seven Faces Of Woman*), were brought to the attention of **Cameron Mackintosh**, who invited Kretzmer to write the lyrics for the London production of the French musical **Les Misérables**. This was done by adapting into English the original text by **Alain Boublil** and Jean-Marc Natel, and involved expanding the two-hour piece into a three-hour show. The all-sung musical has been a West End success since 1985, and includes the witty and ingenious rhymes of 'Master Of The House' as well as the familiar ballads, 'I Dreamed A Dream', 'On My Own' and 'Bring Him Home'. In 1988 Kretzmer was made a Chevalier of the Order of Arts and Letters by the French Government. His lyrics have been translated into several languages to enable *Les Misérables* to be performed with enormous success throughout the world.

Kreuger, Bernie

b. USA. Big band leader Bernie Kreuger established his first orchestra in the early 20s in Chicago, Illinois, USA. The group, which appeared mainly in theatres rather than ballrooms, included musicians Hymie Farberman, Benny Bloom, Fred Schilling, Herman Kaplan, Perry Billitzer, Lester Morris, Bill Arenburg, Dick Cherwin, Happy Reis, Harry Reser and, at one time, **Benny Goodman**. The vocalists were Al Bernard, Billie Jones, Ernest Hare, Scrappy Lambert, Dick Robertson and Fran Frey. They became one of the first bands to be signed to the MCA label when it established its base of operations in Chicago, and enjoyed some success with releases such as 'It's Getting Dark On Old Broadway, Honey' on **Brunswick Records**.

Kreuz

Hailed as the future of UK swingbeat when they first appeared in 1992, Kreuz were the first artists to be signed to **Motown**'s new UK division. The trio of Sean Cummings (vocals), Wayne Lawes (bass) and Ricardo Reid (keyboards, vocals) based themselves in London, with their initial demos being funded by a local community arts project. Hardly new to the music scene, Lawes had undertaken production work for **Mica**

Paris, **Loose Ends** and the **Jones Girls** among others, Reid was an in-demand session keyboardist, and all three had contributed to Vanessa Simon's 1992 release *Family Madness*. Already signed to ARP, Kreuz released the popular club track 'Hush Hush' and finalized a contract with Motown to release their debut *New Generation*. The album featured a statement of intent with 'UK Swing', but there was actually little to differentiate their sound from American swingbeat acts such as **Boyz II Men**.

● ALBUMS: *New Generation* (Motown 1992)★★★.

Kriegel, Volker

b. 24 December 1943, Darmstadt, Germany. Kriegel taught himself guitar at the age of 15 and started his own trio when he was 18. Both he and the trio won awards at the 1963 German Amateur Jazz Festival. While studying social science and psychology at Frankfurt University he met Emil and **Albert Mangelsdorff** and continued to develop his jazz interests. An offer to join the new band being set up by American expatriate vibes-player **Dave Pike** led him to give up his studies to become a full-time musician. He stayed with the Dave Pike Set until the leader returned to the USA, at which point Kriegel and **Eberhard Weber** founded Spectrum. When Weber left in 1976 Kriegel started the Mild Maniac Orchestra. In the meantime, in 1975, he had been a co-founder of the **United Jazz And Rock Ensemble**. In 1977 he co-founded Mood Records. As well as his musical activities, he is a distinguished cartoonist (both for journals and record sleeves), animator and broadcaster.

● ALBUMS: *Spectrum* (1971)★★★, *Missing Link* (1972)★★★, *Topical Harvest* (1975)★★★, *Octember Variations* (1976)★★★, *Elastic Menu* (1977)★★★, *Houseboat* (MPS 1978)★★★, *Long Distance* (MPS 1979)★★★, *Missing Link* (MPS 1981)★★, *Journal* (1981)★★★, *Star Edition* (MPS 1981)★★, *Schone Aussichten* (1983)★★★, *Palazzo Blue* (1987)★★★; with the United Jazz And Rock Ensemble: *Live In Schutzenhaus* (1977)★★, *Teamwork* (1978)★★★, *The Break Even Point* (1980)★★★, *Live In Berlin* (1981)★★, *United Live Opus Sechs* (1984)★★★.

Krispy 3

Chorley, Lancashire, England-trio comprising Mr Wiz, Sonic G and Microphone Don, who made their reputation with two strong 1991 cuts, 'Destroy All The Stereotypes' and 'Don't Be Misled', both of which showcased their jazz/rap leanings. Their debut album, however, only included three tracks not released on their initial brace of 12-inches, which lessened its impact. Much more representative was a subsequent set for **Kold Sweat**, which included an attack on music business nepotism in 'Who Ya Know' while the title-track argued against the virtual ending of the vinyl format (ironic given that their debut was on CD only).

● ALBUMS: *Krispy 3* (Gumh 1992)★★★, *Can't Melt The Wax* (Kold Sweat 1993)★★, *Head Out Da Gate* mini-album (Kold Sweat 1993)★★★.

Kriss Kross

Two youths from Atlanta, Georgia, USA, who topped the *Billboard* charts with 'Jump', a song anchored by the bass line to the **Jackson 5**'s 'I Want You Back'. Chris 'Mack Daddy' Kelly (b. 1978) and Chris 'Daddy Mack' Smith (b. 10 January 1979) were both just 13 years old when they scored with 'Jump', the fastest-selling single the USA had seen for 15 years. In the process they instigated a batch of 'kiddie rap' clones. They were discovered in 1991 by writer/producer Jermaine Dupree, himself only 19, when he was shopping for shoes in Atlanta. Influenced by the likes of **Run DMC** and **Eric B And Rakim**, their visual character was enhanced by their determination to wear all their clothes backwards. Strangely enough, considering their natural teen appeal, they were signed up to the genuinely hardcore New York label **Ruffhouse**, home of **Tim Dog** and others. *Totally Krossed Out* sold over four million copies and spawned another hit, 'Warm It Up'. *Young Rich & Dangerous* stalled, and fell far short of its predecessor's success and critical acclaim.

● ALBUMS: *Totally Krossed Out* (Ruffhouse 1992)★★★, *Da Bomb* (Ruffhouse 1993)★★★, *Young Rich & Dangerous* (Sony 1996)★★★.

Kristina, Sonja

b. 14 April 1949, Brentwood, Essex, England. Former **Curved Air** vocalist, Kristina, released a solo album in 1988 on the Chopper Records label. A few 1977 tracks were produced by Roy Thomas Baker but remain unreleased. Marriage to her old group's drummer Stewart Copeland, (who had since joined the **Police**) and the rearing of two children delayed a resumption of an acting career that had been suspended since she resigned from the London cast of *Hair* in 1970. A role in the *Curriculum Curricula* musical and the lead in *Romeo And Juliet* were followed in 1988 by a spell performing in Britain's arts centres and more adventurous folk clubs. Later, she was the brains behind a UK tour of acts from this circuit, before forming her own 'psychedelic acoustic acid folk' combo whose personnel included a violinist and cellist. Subsequent album and live reviews have indicated an upturn in this artist's fortunes in the 90s.

● ALBUMS: *Sonja Kristina* (Chopper 1980)★★★, *Songs From The Acid Folk* (1991)★★★, *Harmonics Of Love* (HTD 1995)★★.

Kristofferson, Kris

b. 22 June 1936, Brownsville, Texas, USA. Kristofferson, a key figure in the 'New Nashville' of the 70s, began his singing career in Europe. While studying at Oxford University in 1958 he briefly performed for impresario **Larry Parnes** as Kris Carson, while for five years he sang and played at US Army bases in Germany. As Captain Kristofferson, he left the army in 1965 to concentrate on songwriting. After piloting helicopters part-time he worked as a cleaner at the **CBS** studios in Nashville, until **Jerry Lee Lewis** became the first to record one of his songs, 'Once More With Feeling'. **Johnny Cash** soon became a champion of Kristofferson's work and it was he who persuaded **Roger Miller** to record 'Me And Bobby McGee' (co-written with Fred Foster) in 1969. With its atmospheric opening ('Busted flat in Baton Rouge, waiting for a train/feeling nearly faded as my jeans'), the bluesy song was a country hit and became a rock standard in the melodramatic style of **Janis Joplin** and the **Grateful Dead**. Another classic among Kristofferson's early songs was 'Sunday Morning Coming Down', which Cash recorded. In 1970, Kristofferson appeared at the Isle of Wight pop festival while **Sammi Smith** was charting with the second of his major compositions, the passionate 'Help Me Make It Through The Night', which later crossed over to the pop and R&B audiences in **Gladys Knight**'s version. Knight was also among the numerous artists who covered the tender 'For The Good Times', a huge country hit for **Ray Price**, while 'One Day At A Time' was a UK number 1 for **Lena Martell** in 1979. Kristofferson's own hits began with 'Loving Her Was Easier (Than Anything I'll Ever Do Again)' and 'Why Me', a ballad that was frequently performed in concert by **Elvis Presley**. In 1973, Kristofferson married singer **Rita Coolidge** and recorded three albums with her before their divorce six years later. Kristofferson had made his film debut in *Cisco Pike* (1971) and also appeared with **Bob Dylan** in *Pat Garrett And Billy The Kid*, but he achieved movie stardom when he acted opposite **Barbra Streisand** in a 1976 remake of the 1937 picture *A Star Is Born*. For the next few years he concentrated on his film career (until the 1979 disaster *Heaven's Gate*, the same year he split from Coolidge), but returned to country music with *The Winning Hand*, which featured duets with **Brenda Lee**, **Dolly Parton** and **Willie Nelson**. A further collaboration, *Highwaymen* (with Nelson, Cash and **Waylon Jennings**), headed the country chart in 1985. The four musicians subsequently toured as the Highwaymen and issued two further collaborative albums. A campaigner for radical causes, Kristofferson starred in the post-nuclear television drama *Amerika* (1987) and came up with hard-hitting political commentaries on *Third World Warrior*. Kristofferson compered and performed at the Bob Dylan Tribute Concert in 1992, during which he gave **Sinead O'Conner** a sympathetic shoulder to cry on after she was booed off stage. His recording career took an upturn with the release of *A Moment Of Forever* in 1995.

● ALBUMS: *Kristofferson* (Monument 1970)★★, *The Silver-Tongued Devil And I* (Monument 1971)★★★, *Me And Bobby McGee* (Monument 1971)★★★, *Border Lord* (Monument 1972)★★★, *Jesus Was A Capricorn* (Monument 1972)★★★, with Rita Coolidge *Full Moon* (A&M 1973)★★★, *Spooky Lady's Sideshow* (Monument 1974)★★, with Coolidge *Breakaway* (A&M 1974)★, *Who's To Bless ... And Who's To Blame* (Monument 1975)★★, *Surreal Thing* (Monument 1976)★★, five tracks on *A Star Is Born* film soundtrack (Monument 1976)★★★, *Easter Island* (Monument 1977)★★,

with Coolidge *Natural Act* (A&M 1979)★★, *Shake Hands With The Devil* (Monument 1979)★★★, *To The Bone* (Monument 1981)★★, with Dolly Parton, Brenda Lee, Willie Nelson *The Winning Hand* (Monument 1983)★★★, with Willie Nelson *Music From Songwriter* film soundtrack (Columbia 1984)★★★, with Nelson, Johnny Cash, Waylon Jennings *Highwayman* (Columbia 1985)★★★★, *Repossessed* (Mercury 1986)★★, *Third World Warrior* (Mercury 1990)★★, with Nelson, Cash, Jennings *Highwayman 2* (Columbia 1990)★★★, *Live At The Philharmonic* (Monument 1992)★★★, with Nelson, Cash, Jennings *The Road Goes On Forever* (Liberty 1995)★★, *A Moment Of Forever* (Justice 1995)★★★.

● COMPILATIONS: *The Songs Of Kristofferson* (Monument 1977)★★★, *Country Store* (Starblend 1988)★★★, *The Legendary Years* (Connoisseur Collection 1990)★★★, *Singer/Songwriter* (Monument 1991)★★★, *The Best Of Kristofferson* (Sony 1995)★★★★.

● FURTHER READING: *Kris Kristofferson*, Beth Kalet.

● FILMS: *The Last Movie* (1970), *Cisco Pike* (1972), *Blume In Love* (1973), *Pat Garrett And Billy The Kid* (1973), *Bring Me The Head Of Alfredo Garcia* (1974), *Alice Doesn't Live Here Any More* (1975), *The Sailor Who Fell From Grace With The Sea* (1976), *A Star Is Born* (1976), *Vigilante Force* (1976), *Semi-Tough* (1978), *Convoy* (1978), *Heaven's Gate* (1980), *Rollover* (1981), *Flashpoint* (1984), *Songwriter* (1984), *Trouble In Mind* (1985), *Blood And Orchids* television movie (1986).

Krivda, Ernie

b. c.1945, Cleveland, Ohio, USA. Having turned down an offer to play in **Miles Davis**'s band in the mid-70s, tenor saxophonist Ernie Krivda spent the early part of his career performing around the Cleveland area before moving to New York in his mid-thirties. By then he was a veteran of work with **Quincy Jones**, but he had left that band due to dissatisfaction with Jones' increasing orientation towards pop music. However, Krivda found the pace of life in New York unsatisfying, and subsequently returned to Cleveland to concentrate on his own more idiosyncratic and jazz-based compositions. Throughout this period he recorded and collaborated widely, though it was not until he signed a new deal with Koch Records in the 90s that he began to attract more widespread attention. In 1995 he released an album with pianist Bill Dobbins, director of the West German Radio Orchestra in Cologne. This highlighted Krivda's unusual style, of which Harvey Pekar noted in *Down Beat* magazine that 'he tongues faster and more often than the vast majority of tenor players, and, like trumpeters, makes wide interval leaps into the upper register. And sometimes he uses a fast, violin-like vibrato'.

● ALBUMS: with Bill Dobbins *The Art Of The Ballad* (Koch 1995)★★★★.

Krog, Karin

b. 15 May 1937, Oslo, Norway. Although she had already worked extensively in Scandinavia with players such as **Jan Garbarek** and **Arild Andersen**, vocalist

Krog's first impact on the international jazz scene came in 1964 with her appearance at the Antibes Jazz Festival. She subsequently toured Europe and the USA, frequently working with some of the more progressive musicians. In the late 60s she performed, and sometimes recorded, with **Don Ellis** and **Clare Fischer** and during the following decade she extended her reputation through sessions with **Warne Marsh, Dexter Gordon, Archie Shepp, Red Mitchell** and **Bengt Hallberg**. In the 80s and 90s she recorded and toured with **John Surman**, with whom she had first performed in the early 70s. An effortless singer, with a good vocal range and excellent taste in material, Krog's penchant for more modern music has tended to restrict her popularity to the hardcore jazz audience, although her repertoire does incorporate the sophisticated songs of **Dave Frishberg** alongside standards and jazz classics. By the mid-80s her repertoire had extended still further to encompass African click rhythms and Indian Alap music, which she performs with absolute confidence and considerable charm. She is also an experienced television producer and has made several programmes on jazz, which have been broadcast in Norway.

● ALBUMS: *By Myself* (1964)★★★, *Jazz Moments* (1966)★★★, *Eleven Around Karin* (1967)★★★★, with Jan Garbarek, Arild Andersen *Joy* (1968)★★★★, *Blue Eyes* (1969)★★★, with others *Gittin' To Know Y'all* (1969)★★★, *Different Days, Different Ways* (1970)★★★, with Dexter Gordon *Some Other Spring* (Storyville 1970)★★★★, *My Workshop Songbook* (1970)★★★, *Karin Krog* (1973)★★★★, *You Must Believe In Spring* (1974)★★★, *Jazz Jamboree '75 Vol. 2* (1975)★★★, with Archie Shepp *Hi-Fly* (Meantime 1976)★★, *The Malmö Sessions* (1976)★★★, with Bengt Hallberg *A Song For You* (Phontastic 1977)★★★, with Red Mitchell *Three's A Crowd* (1977)★★★, with John Surman *Cloud Line Blue* (1978)★★★, *With Malice Toward None* (1980)★★, with Warne Marsh, Mitchell *I Remember You* (Spotlite 1980)★★★, *Swingin' Arrival* (1980)★★, with Hallberg *Two Of A Kind* (1982)★★★, with Surman *Such Winters Of Memory* (ECM 1983)★★★★, *Freestyle* (Odin 1985)★★★, *Something Borrowed...Something New* (Meantime 1989)★★★, *Krog Sings Gershwin* (Meantime 1993)★★★★, *Jubilee: The Best Of 30 Years* (Verve 1994)★★★, with Surman, Terje Rypdal *Nordic Quartet* (ECM 1995)★★★.

Krokus

Formed in Soluthurn, Switzerland, Krokus appeared in 1974 playing symphonic rock similar to **Yes, Genesis** and **Emerson, Lake And Palmer**. After four years and two rather lacklustre albums, they switched to a hard rock style and dropped the frills in favour of a back-to-basics approach in the mode of **AC/DC**. The group originally comprised Chris Von Rohr (vocals), Fernando Von Arb (guitar), Jurg Naegeli (bass), Tommy Kiefer (guitar) and Freddy Steady (drums). The songs were formulaic numbers based on simple riffs and predictable choruses that were chanted repeatedly. With Von Rohr's voice lacking the necessary vocal range, he stepped down to became the bass player in

favour of new arrival 'Maltezer' Marc (b. Marc Storace, Malta; ex-Tea). Naegeli occasionally played keyboards and subsequently took over the technical side of the band. *Metal Rendez-vous* was the turning point in the band's career; released in 1980, it was heavier than anything they had done before and coincided with the resurgence of heavy metal in Britain. They played the Reading Festival in 1980 and were well received, and their next two albums continued with an aggressive approach, though they streamlined their sound to make it more radio-friendly. *Hardware* and *One Vice At A Time* both reached the UK album charts, at numbers 44 and 28, respectively. Before *Headhunter* materialized, a series of personnel changes took place. The most important of these was the replacement of Kiefer with ex-roadie Mark Kohler (guitar), while Steve Pace stepped in on drums. Kiefer subsequently returned to replace Rohr. Produced by Tom Allom, *Headhunter*'s high-speed, heavy-duty approach propelled it to number 25 in the ***Billboard*** album charts. Further line-up changes (the temporary addition of ex-Crown guitarist Patrick Mason and the exit, then return of Pace) delayed the release of *The Blitz*, an erratic album that reached number 31 on the US chart mainly on the strength of its predecessor. Since 1985 there has been a continuing downward trend in the band's fortunes, with their personnel in a constant state of flux (Kesier committed suicide in 1986 and guitarist Mandy Meyer joined). Their music has progressed little during the last decade and still relies heavily on the legacy of AC/DC and the **Scorpions**. In 1995 the band were touring with a line-up of Storace (vocals), Fernando Von Arb (bass), Maurer (guitar), Kohler (guitar) and Steady (drums), and recording sessions followed.

● ALBUMS: *Krokus* (Schmontz 1975)★★, *To You All* (Schmontz 1977)★★, *Painkiller* (Mercury 1978)★★, *Pay It In Metal* (Mercury 1979)★★, *Metal Rendez-vous* (Ariola 1980)★★★, *Hardware* (Ariola 1981)★★★, *One Vice At A Time* (Ariola 1982)★★★, *Headhunter* (Arista 1983)★★★, *The Blitz* (Arista 1984)★★, *Change Of Address* (Arista 1985)★★, *Alive And Screamin'* (Arista 1986)★★, *Heart Attack* (MCA 1987)★★, *Stampede* (Ariola 1990)★★.

Kroner, Erling

b. 16 April 1943, Copenhagen, Denmark. Composer and trombonist who began playing dixieland music in the early 60s, but soon also participated in 'free' jazz groups with **John Tchicai** and others. Kroner participated in **George Russell**'s 'Electronic Sonata For Souls Loved By Nature' performed by Russell with the Danish Radio Big Band in 1969. At the end of that year a *Down Beat* stipend enabled him to study at the **Berklee College Of Music**. A gifted composer and arranger Kroner has successfully adopted **Charles Mingus**'s improvisational method of writing and arranging in changing moods, metres and tempos for soloists in a 10-piece band that employs unusual textures and voicings, e.g. a tuba in the brass section. In the 80s Kroner co-led with drummer Leif Johansson a band, which with similar music and orchestration, extended complex compositions for quasi-operatic or dramatic stagings. Kroner's long-standing fascination with Argentinian culture and music, in particular the tango, is reflected in several compositions dedicated to **Astor Piazzolla** and **Dino Saluzzi**. Kroner has also visited and worked with musicians in Argentina.

● ALBUMS: *Music Book* (Spectator 1970)★★★, *The Forgotten Art* (Storyville 1977)★★★, with Leif Johansson *Jo-Jo* (Metronome 1979)★★★★, *Entre Dos Cielos* (Music Mecca 1983)★★★, *Vølvens Spådom* (Olufsen 1985)★★★, *Beowulf Suite/Nijinsky Suite* (Music Mecca 1985-86)★★, *From The Dark Side* (Music Mecca 1987)★★★, *The Erling Kroner Dark Side Orchestra* (Olufsen 1992)★★★, with Lars Beijbom *Live In Copenhagen* (Four Leaf Clover 1996)★★.

Kronos Quartet

David Harrington (first violin), John Sherba (second violin), Joan Jeanrenaud (cello) and Hank Dutt (viola) formed Kronos in San Francisco, California, USA, in 1978. Although classically trained, all of the members had catholic musical upbringings and felt that the gap between classical and popular music was becoming increasingly irrelevant. Led by the charismatic Harrington, whose idols are **Bessie Smith** and Beethoven, they crossed musical barriers by performing chamber music with the spirit and energy of rock, and refused to dress in the formal garb of the classical establishment. They also established a unique musical identity in several ways: by commissioning new works for the group by modern composers (**Philip Glass**, **Terry Riley**, Alfred Schnittke and **John Zorn**); by working with musicians form other cultures, notably on *Pieces Of Africa*, where every cut is written by African musicians; by transforming popular music (**Jimi Hendrix**, **Willie Dixon**, **Ornette Coleman**) into string quartet arrangements. Their weekly US Public Radio show, *Radio Kronos*, ensured that they reached the widest possible audience on a regular basis.

● ALBUMS: *White Man Sleeps* (1985)★★★, *Kronos* (1987)★★★, *Music Of Sculthorpe, Hendrix, Sallinen, Glass And Nancarrow* (Nonesuch 1987)★★★★, *Winter Was Hard* (1988)★★★, *Black Angels* (1991)★★★, *Information* (Reference 1991)★★★, *Pieces Of Africa* (Nonesuch 1992)★★★, *Short Stories* (Nonesuch 1993)★★★, *Monk Suite* (Landmark 1993)★★★, *Kronos Quartet Performs Phillip Glass* (Nonesuch 1995)★★★★, *Howl, USA* (Nonesuch 1996)★★★, *Early Music* (Nonesuch 1997)★★★.

● COMPILATIONS: *Released 1985-1995* (Nonesuch 1996)★★★.

KRS-1

b. Lawrence Krisna Parker, 20 August 1965, New York, USA. The kingpin of **Boogie Down Productions** and a genuine hip-hop pioneer, KRS-1's standing is reflected not only in terms of his music, but also his lecture tours of the US, appearing at Yale, Harvard, and countless other institutions to the dismay of some members of those establishments. His list of achievements is hardly limited to this, however. He has been given the keys to Kansas City, Philadelphia and Compton, California. He was nominated for the NACA 1992 Harry Chapman Humanitarian Award, and holds the Reebok Humanitarian Award, and three Ampex Golden Reel Awards. He inaugurated the **Stop The Violence Movement**, and recorded 'Self-Destruction', which raised over $600,000 for the National Urban League, and the human awareness single, 'Heal Yourself'. He has collaborated with **REM** (rapping on 'Radio Song', Michael Stipe returning the favour by assisting on the HEAL project), **Sly And Robbie**, **Shelley Thunder**, **Shabba Ranks**, **Ziggy Marley**, **Billy Bragg**, the **Neville Brothers**, **Kool Moe Dee**, Chuck D of **Public Enemy** and **Tim Dog**, among many others, and taken part in several important benefit shows for Nelson Mandela, Earth Day etc., as well as attending rallies with Jesse Jackson. Following the death of his erstwhile partner, Scott La Rock (whose violent exit played a significant role in KRS-1's anti-violence tracts), he has been joined on recent recordings by **DJ Premier** and Kid Capri. His post-BDP work combines hints of ragga with strong, bass driven funk and beatbox samples. He remains one of the philosophically more enlightened rappers: in particular fighting against the use of the terms 'ho' and 'bitch' when discussing women. His first album to be released outside of the Boggie Down Productions banner was *Return Of Da Boom Bap*, though many references to his past remained. 'KRS-One Attacks', for instance, looped part of the *Criminal Minded* title-track, and 'P Is Still Free' updated his 1986 anti-crack opus, 'P Is Free'. KRS-1 remained as arrogant as they come: 'I'm not a rapper. I am rap. I am the embodiment of what a lot of MCs are trying to be and do. I'm not doing hip-hop, I am hip-hop'. The early 90s also saw some words and actions that would seem to contradict earlier statements, notably his physical attack on Prince B of **PM Dawn**. 'The way I stop the violence is with a baseball bat and beat the shit out of you . . . If negativity comes with a .22, positivity comes with a .45. If negativity comes with .45, positivity comes with an Uzi: The light has got to be stronger than darkness'. An adequate rebuttal, but apparently all PM Dawn had done to diss KRS-1 was to suggest in a copy of *Details* magazine that: 'KRS-1 wants to be a teacher, but a teacher of what?'. In retaliation KRS-1 and his posse invaded the stage during the following night's PM Dawn gig at the Sound Factory Club in New York, throwing Prince Be offstage and commandeering the microphone for his own set. The whole event was filmed live by *Yo! MTV Raps*. Though he later apologised publicly, in private KRS-1 was telling the world that he was tired of MCs and hip-hop crews disrespecting him. That he felt it necessary so piously to protect it is the only real blemish on his reputation.

● ALBUMS: *HEAL: Civilization Versus Technology* various artists (Elektra 1991)★★★, *Return Of Da Boom Bap* (Jive 1993)★★★, *KRS-One* (Jive 1995)★★★, *I Got Next* (Jive 1997)★★.

Kruger, Jeffrey

b. England. Kruger has enjoyed a long and distinguished career in the music and entertainment industry. Under his management, the Kruger Organisation (TKO) grew from its ownership of the Flamingo Club, one of the most prominent early 50s London jazz clubs, to an international entertainment corporation with interests in film, video, music publishing, recording and concerts, spanning musical genres from classical to country, blues, pop and jazz. In that time Kruger has amassed an impressive list of musical firsts. He established Ember Records, the UK's first independent label, produced **Tony Crombie** And The Rockets, the first British rock 'n' roll group to make the UK charts, and co-produced *Rock You Sinners*, the first English rock 'n' roll film. His involvement in the music industry began in the 50s. During this time he was employed selling *Batman* and *Superman* serials for Columbia Pictures, while playing piano by night for various pick-up bands. Finally he formed his own band, Sonny Kruger And The Music Makers. His business career began when he sensed that London's thriving jazz scene required a more 'upmarket' venue. Hence, he established the Flamingo club, where artists such as **Billie Holiday** and **Sarah Vaughan** made their British debuts. Kruger then formed his own talent and management agencies in the late 50s. The new decade saw him introduce **Glen Campbell** to the UK market for the first time, and he also organized his first tour in the territory. The Flamingo club, meanwhile, continued to prove its popularity with all manner of musicians, offering period entertainment that included such stellar acts as **Jimi Hendrix**, **Black Sabbath**, **Yes**, the **Moody Blues** and **Genesis**. As well as opening the door to European tours by **Marvin Gaye**, Kruger also invited **Gladys Knight And The Pips** to perform before they had made their name in the USA. This paved the way for tours by **Barry White**, the **Jacksons**, **Temptations**, **Supremes**, **Isaac Hayes** and black country star **Charlie Pride**. His involvement with country music increased throughout the 70s and 80s. This period saw him working with **Johnny Cash**, **Nanci Griffiths**, **Kris Kristofferson** and **Tammy Wynette**, as well as the promotion of festivals including the Country Music Festival in Peterborough. TKO went public in the USA in 1986, the expansion including the purchase of music publishing companies (Full Armor Music and Whole Armor Music, two Nashville Christian concerns), adding film and video properties to its film library and launching a marketing campaign to raise the company profile and awareness of its product. TKO has also continued to promote tours, including dance and theatre productions (Bolshoi and Kirov ballets, Rudolph Nureyev, **Placido Domingo**, Harlem Globe Trotters) plus a backbone of musical works (**Chuck Berry**, **Julio Iglesias**). Among many other awards, Kruger has subsequently been made an Honorary Citizen of the State of Tennessee by the Governor for services to country music, and received a similar honour from the governor of Kansas. He is a member of the Academy Of Motion Pictures and Arts and Sciences, and the Performing Rights Society.

Krupa, Gene

b. 15 January 1909, Chicago, Illinois, USA, d. 16 October 1973. Krupa began playing drums as a child and after his mother failed to persuade him to become a priest, most of his large family actively encouraged his career in music. He studied formally, his most important teacher being Roy C. Knapp. However, growing up in Chicago in the 20s meant that he was inevitably drawn to jazz. He listened to relocated New Orleans masters such as **Baby Dodds**, **Zutty Singleton** and Tubby Hall. In his teens he played in several local dancebands, among them those led by Al Gale, Joe Kayser, Thelma Terry and **Mezz Mezzrow** and the **Benson Orchestra**. In 1927, Krupa made his first records in a band nominally fronted by visitor **Red McKenzie** but actually organized by **Eddie Condon** whose record debut this also was. This date is reputed to be the first on which a drummer used a bass drum and tom-toms (engineers feared the resonance would cause the needle to lift off the wax). The records were successful and when, in 1929, Krupa and Condon decided to move to New York, their reputation had preceded them. Although highly regarded in the jazz world the new arrivals found the going tough. Mostly, Krupa worked in theatre pit bands, including some directed by **Red Nichols**, in which he played alongside **Benny Goodman** and **Glenn Miller**. In the early 30s, Krupa played in dance bands led by **Russ Columbo**, Mal Hallett and Buddy Rogers. Late in 1934, he joined Goodman's recently-formed big band. Krupa was the most enthusiastic of sidemen, urging the band along as if it were his own and helping to establish the distinctive sound of the Goodman band. After the band's breakthrough in August 1935 Krupa quickly became a household name. His fame and popularity with the fans built upon his highly visual playing style and film-star good looks, eventually irritated Goodman, although Krupa's frequent alteration of the tempos the leader set did not help their relationship. Soon after the band's Carnegie Hall concert in 1938 Krupa and Goodman had a public quarrel and Krupa quit. He formed his own band, which swiftly became one of the most popular of the swing era.

In 1941, after he had hired **Roy Eldridge** and **Anita O'Day**, the band also became one of the best. Success was short-lived, however, and in 1943 it folded after Krupa was jailed following a drugs bust in San Francisco. By the time that he was released on bail pending an appeal against his 1-6 years sentence, he believed his career was over. He returned to New York, planning to spend his time studying and writing music, but was persuaded by Goodman to join a band with which he was touring east coast US Army bases. When Goodman prepared to extend the tour across the USA, Krupa opted to stay behind. He was convinced that audiences would react against him and instead joined **Tommy Dorsey**, believing that the comparative anonymity of working in a band based at a New York movie theatre would be best for him. In fact, his appearance, unannounced, at the Paramount Theatre was greeted with rapturous applause and proved to be a remarkably emotional milestone in his rehabilitation. He went on tour with Dorsey and when the charges against him were deemed to have been improper, he decided to form a new band of his own. He maintained a band throughout the rest of the 40s, adapting to bop by incorporating musicians such as **Charlie Ventura**, **Red Rodney** and **Don Fagerquist** and playing charts by **Gerry Mulligan**, even though Krupa himself was never able to adapt his own playing style which, since his arrival in New York at the end of the 20s, had been closely modelled upon that of **Chick Webb**. Krupa managed to keep the band working until 1951 and thereafter continued playing with a small group, usually a quartet, touring with **Jazz At The Philharmonic** and, for a while, operating a drum school with **William 'Cozy' Cole**. During the 60s he began to appear at occasional reunions of the Benny Goodman Quartet (with **Teddy Wilson** and **Lionel Hampton**). The 60s also saw his health deteriorate, first with heart trouble and later with leukaemia. By the early 70s, he was limited to working around New York and most public performances, usually now with Goodman, Wilson and Hampton, had to be preceded by a blood transfusion. He died in October 1973.

Stylistically, Krupa was usually a heavier-handed version of Webb, the man he always acknowledged as his greatest influence and for whom he had genuine admiration and respect. There can be little doubt that Krupa was a major contributor to the powerful attack of the pre-1939 Goodman band. Apart from the 1943 stint with Goodman, when he came close to the standards set by Webb, his big band playing never had the subtlety and swing of his mentor or other contemporaries such as **Jo Jones**. His spectacular visual style, adored by the fans, tended to alienate critics, though another great contemporary, **'Big' Sid Catlett**, was even more flamboyant. Krupa's best playing came in his performances with the Goodman trio and quartet. On these recordings, usually playing only with brushes, he performs with subtlety, skill and great verve. Krupa made the jazz drummer into a highly visible and extremely well-paid member of the band. His countless imitators usually supplied the flash and spectacle without the content, but thanks to his example and encouragement many fine swing style drummers continued to play in the decades following his death. Even in the 90s echoes of his work can still be heard.

● ALBUMS: *Gene Krupa* (Columbia 1949)★★★, *Dance Parade* (Columbia 1949)★★★★, *Drum Boogie* (1952)★★★★, *The Exciting Gene Krupa* (1953)★★★★, *The Gene Krupa Sextet/Driving Gene* (1953)★★★, *Gene Krupa Trio* (Mercury 1953)★★★, *Sing, Sing, Sing* (Clef 1953)★★★★, *The Gene Krupa Trio At JATP* (Mercury 1953)★★★, *The Jazz Rhythms Of Gene Krupa* (1954)★★★, *Gene Krupa Sextet Number 1* (Clef 1954)★★★★, *Gene Krupa Sextet Number 2* (Clef 1954)★★★★, *Gene Krupa's Sidekicks* (Columbia 1955)★★★, *Drummin' Man* (Columbia 1955)★★★, *Selections From The Benny Goodman Story* (Clef 1956)★★★★, with Buddy Rich *Krupa And Rich* (Clef 1955)★★★★, *The Big Band Sound Of Gene Krupa* (1956)★★★★, *Hey, Here's Gene Krupa* (1957)★★★, *Gene Krupa Plays Gerry Mulligan* (Verve 1958)★★★★, *Krupa Rocks* (Verve 1958)★★★★, *The Gene Krupa Story/Drum Crazy* (1959)★★★★, *Hey Here's Gene Krupa* (Verve 1959)★★★, *Big Noise From Winnetka: Gene Krupa At The London House* (Verve 1959)★★★, *The Gene Krupa Sory In Music* (Harmony 1960)★★★, with Buddy Rich *Drum Battle* (Verve 1960)★★★★, *Percussion King* (1961)★★★, *Drummer Man: Gene Krupa In Highest-Fi* (Verve 1961)★★★, *Gene Krupa Trio* (Verve 1961)★★★, *Classics In Percussion* (1961)★★★, *Drum Boogie* (Verve 1961)★★★★, *The Driving Gene Krupa* (Verve 1961)★★★, *The Jazz Rhythms Of Gene Krupa* (Verve 1961)★★★, *Percussion King* (Verve 1961)★★★, *Gene Krupa Meets Buddy Rich/The Burning Beat* (1962)★★★★, *Perdido* (1962)★★★★, with Louie Bellson *The Mighty Two* (Roulette 1963)★★★, with Goodman *Together Again!* (1963)★★★★, *The Great New Gene Krupa Quartet Featuring Charlie Ventura* (Verve 1964)★★★, *The Swingin' Gene Krupa Quartet* (1965)★★★, *That Drummer's Band* (Verve 1966)★★★, with Eddie Condon *Jazz At The New School* (Chiaroscuro 1971)★★★.

● COMPILATIONS: *The Essential Gene Krupa: Let Me Off Uptown* (Verve 1964)★★★★, *Gene Krupa, Volumes 1-14 (1935-41)* (Ajax 1979)★★★★, *The Gene Krupa Collection - 20 Golden Greats* (1987)★★★★, *Gene Krupa - On The Air (1944-46)* (1988)★★★, *The Drummer* (Flapper 1993)★★★.

● FURTHER READING: *Gene Krupa: His Life & Times*, Bruce Crowther.

Krush

Commercial house artists from Sheffield who scored a big breakthrough hit with 'House Arrest', which rose to UK number 3 in 1988, featuring the vocals of later **Definition Of Sound** member Kevwon (Kevin Clark). The band comprise Mark Gamble and Cassius Campbell, who lace their standard house/disco rhythms with a quicksilver backbeat which was actually less obtrusive than many similar outfits. The unobscured vocals belonged to Ruth Joy, the veteran house diva. The follow-up material was less effective largely because it lacked the hypnotic, catchy tone of 'House Arrest'. Following record company problems Gamble would go on to work with **Rhythmatic**. The Krush name was revived in 1992 with a cover of **Rockers Revenge**'s 'Walking On Sunshine', by which time they had moved from Fon to **Network** records.

Kryztal

b. Henry Buckley, 1972, Jamaica, West Indies. Chicago-based Pancho Kryztal was working as a desktop publishing consultant before an inspirational return trip to Jamaica convinced him to pursue a career in music. Returning to Chicago, he was introduced to

Jeremy Freeman, who was setting up the Scratchie label with James Iha and D'arcy Wretzky of **Smashing Pumpkins**, and Adam Schlesinger of **Fountains Of Wayne**. Kryztal signed to Scratchie, but retained Caribbean rights for his own label, Skinny Bway. An initial 12-inch DJ promo, 'Girl A Chat'/'I Need You Badly', gained extensive airplay in Jamaica and the USA. Subsequent singles, 'Lethal Weapon' and 'Sweet Gal', generated further interest in Krystal's 'dancehall R&B', which blended the contrasting styles of R&B balladeer and macho toaster. His self-titled debut was released in October 1997 on Scratchie/**Mercury**, drawing favourable comparisons with both the current crop of urban R&B singers and established ragga artists such as **Shaggy** and **Chaka Demus And Pliers**. The album's diverse production credits included **dancehall** stalwart Tony Kelly and rapper DJ Spinner.

● ALBUMS: *Kryztal* (Scratchie/Mercury 1997)★★★.

Kuban, Bob, And The In-Men

This eight-piece rock 'n' roll band came from St. Louis, Missouri, USA. The members were Bob Kuban (b. August 1940, St. Louis, Missouri, USA; drums), Walter Scott (b. Walter S. Notheis, Jnr., 7 February 1943; lead vocals), John Michael Krenski (bass), Greg Hoeltzel, (keyboards), Roy Schult (guitar), Skip Weisser (trombone), Harry Simon (saxophone), and Pat Hixon (trumpet). Bob Kuban And The In-Man were a classic one-hit-wonder Top 40 group, with 'The Cheater', which reached number 12 in the US pop charts in 1966. Also in 1966, the group scraped the bottom of the charts with two follow-ups, 'The Teaser' (number 70) and a cover of the **Beatles**' 'Drive My Car' (number 93). 'The Cheater' had something of a blue-eyed soul flavour with the vibrant horn arrangements and Scott's almost black vocal approach. The In-Men were formed in 1964 and made their first record in 1965. Scott left the group in 1967. He had planned to rejoin the In-Men in 1983, but he was murdered by his wife and her lover, which rendered ironical his success with 'The Cheater' and its hook-line 'look out for the cheater'. Kuban continued to perform in St. Louis for weddings and other social affairs with his band, the Bob Kuban Brass.

● ALBUMS: featuring various Bob Kuban groups *Look Out For The Cheater* (1966)★★★, *The Bob Kuban Explosion* (1966)★★★, *Get Ready For Some Rock & Soul* (1975)★★.

● COMPILATIONS: *Look Out For The Cheater* (Collectables 1996)★★★. Solo: Walter Scott *Great Scott* (1967)★★★, *Walter Scott* (1970)★★.

Kubek, Smokin' Joe

b. 30 November 1956, Grove City, Pennsylvania, USA. Having grown up in Irving, Texas, Kubek was playing in Dallas clubs at the age of 14. Three years later, he took a deeper interest in blues, prompted by **Eric Clapton** and **Peter Green**, and formed his first band. Shortly afterwards, he played rhythm guitar behind **Freddie King** until King's death in December 1976.

After a short spell with Robert Whitfield's Last Combo, he joined Al Braggs' band. Examples of his work can be heard on Braggs' 1979 production of tracks by R.L. Griffin. He also recorded with Charlie Robinson, Big Ray Anderson and Ernie Johnson, and on Little Joe Blue's album, *It's My Turn Now*. In 1989, he teamed up with singer/guitarist B'Nois King, from Monroe, Louisiana, whose soul-tinged vocals and jazz-orientated style contrasted well with Kubek's more strident finger and slide techniques. *The Axe Man* is an album of covers recorded before their Bullseye Blues debut. Subsequent releases have consolidated their reputation as a solid, entertaining band.

● ALBUMS: *The Axe Man* (Double Trouble 1991)★★★, *Steppin' Out Texas Style* (Bullseye Blues 1991)★★★, *Chain Smokin' Texas Style* (Bullseye Blues 1992)★★★, *Texas Cadillac* (Bullseye Blues 1994)★★★, *Cryin' For The Moon* (Bullseye Blues 1995)★★★, *Got My Mind Back* (Bullseye Blues 1996)★★★, with Bnois King *Take Your Best Shot* (Bullseye 1998)★★★★.

Kubis, Tom

b. 1951, Los Angeles, California, USA. After studying, Kubis began playing also, tenor and soprano saxophones with various bands. He also played piano for **Bobby Vinton**. However, Kubis's chief interest was in writing and his arrangements were in much demand, especially from big band leaders. He formed his own big band expressly to play his charts and this attracted the attention of **Jack Sheldon** who became an informal co-leader of the band. Apart from writing for the band, Kubis continues to provide charts for others, including **Bill Watrous**, the BBC Radio Big Band, and his work is also performed by youth and college bands in the USA and UK. His writing is always lively and entertaining, often difficult but never simply for the sake of being hard to play. His own recording career has been relatively meagre, beginning with Dimitri Pagalidis and only relatively recently has his own big band been heard and appreciated by fans of contemporary big band music around the world.

● ALBUMS: with Dimitri Pagalidis *Silverware* (Mark 56 70s)★★, with Pagalidis *Another Place Setting* (Mark 56 1970)★★★, *Slightly Off The Ground* (Seabreeze 90s)★★★★, *At Last* (Cexton 90s)★★★★.

Kubota, Toshi

b. c.1962, Japan. Arguably the most successful Japanese artist to transfer American-styled soul and urban R&B into an Oriental vernacular, in 1995 Toshi made a serious push to gain international acceptance. *Sunshine Moonlight* featured noted collaborators such as **Nile Rodgers**, **Omar Hakim** and **Caron Wheeler**, with whom he performed a duet cover version of **Bill Withers**' 'Just The Two Of Us'. The lead-off single, 'Funk It Up', was remixed for the US market by leading house music producer **David Morales**, and also featured on a mini-album of remixes of previously Japanese-only singles. Resident in New York since 1993, the album was recorded there with Toshi as producer, along with three tracks completed in Los Angeles sessions with Christian Warren. Describing the results as 'pop, but with a black flavour', Toshi was coached in the presentation of lyrics to make them more accessible to native English speakers.

● ALBUMS: *Sunshine Moonlight* (Sony/Columbia 1995)★★.

Kuepper, Ed

b. Edmund Kuepper, Germany. Guitarist Kuepper began his musical career in 1975 as co-founder of the **Saints**, sharing songwriting duties with Chris Bailey. After leaving the band before its zenith he formed the **Laughing Clowns**, leading this group from 1979-85. As leader he directed the group into a more jazzy, brassy, almost experimental vein, recording prolifically although not 'commercially' viable. However, with the release of his debut solo album, his work has taken a decidedly more positive approach and he has thus endeared himself to radio programmers. Signed to **Capitol**, the 1988 album *Everybody's Got To* presented Kuepper's strongest set to date, consisting of powerful, brass-enhanced songs, typified by 'Burned My Fingers' and 'Not A Soul Around'. The group consisted of Mark Dawson (drums), Paul Smith (bass), Rebecca Hancock (brass/vocals), Jim Bowman (keyboards). In 1990 he pared down the instrumentation, now know as The Yard Goes On Forever, even further to record an acoustic album, *Today Wonder* with Mark Dawson accompanying. That same year, Kuepper formed the retaliationary **Aints** as a riposte to Chris Bailey's continued usage of the Saints name, eventually releasing *Ascension* on the UFO label. The habit of winning good reviews that were not translated into sales continued in 1992 with the release of *Honey Steel's Gold*. A tongue in cheek titled *Sings His Greatest Hits For You* was issued in 1995; among his numerous recent releases, *Cloudland* was an all-instrumental affair.

● ALBUMS: *Electrical Storm* (Hot 1986)★★, *Rooms Of The Magnificent* (Hot 1987)★★, *Everybody's Got To* (True Tone/Capitol 1988)★★★★, *Today Wonder* (Rattlesnake 1990)★★★, *Honey Steel's Gold* (Hot 1992)★★, *Black Ticket Day* (Hot 1992)★★★, *Serene Machine* (Hot 1993)★★★, *The Butterfly Net* (Restless 1994)★★★, *A King In The Kindness Room* (Hot 1995)★★★, *Frontierland* (Hot 1996)★★★, *I Was A Mail Order Bridegroom* (Hot 1995)★★, *Exotic Mail Order Moods* (Hot 1995)★★, *Starstruck: Music For Films & Adverts* (Hot 1997)★★★, *With A Knapsack On My Back* (Hot 1997)★★★, *Cloudland* (Hot 1998)★★★.

● COMPILATIONS: *Legendary Bully* (Castle 1993)★★★, *Sings His Greatest Hits For You* (Hot 1995)★★★★, *The Wheelie Bin Affair* (Hot 1997)★★★.

Kühn, Joachim

b. 15 March 1944, Leipzig, Germany. Between the ages of five to his mid-teens, Kühn took lessons in classical piano and composing, then became a professional jazz musician. He set up his own trio in 1962, which lasted until 1966, when he established a quartet with his brother, clarinettist Rolf Kühn. When this band ended in 1969 he led his own group in Paris, until joining the **Jean-Luc Ponty** Experience in 1971. He left Ponty in 1972 to co-lead a group with **Eje Thelin**. Since then he has frequently worked solo, but has also been a member of the acclaimed **Tony Oxley** Quintet. While he has done work which might be categorized as 'new age' in the late 80s, recent concerts have shown that he can still play in tougher fashion.

● ALBUMS: *Boldmusic* (1969)★★★, *Piano* (1971)★★★★, *Solos* (Futura 1971)★★★★, *This Way Out* (1973),★★★ with Rolf Kuhn *Connection 74* (1973)★★, with Rolf Kuhn *Transfiguration* (70s)★★★, *Open Strings* (70s)★★★, *Spring Fever* (Atlantic 1977)★★★, Distance (CMP 1984)★★★★, *Wandlungen Transformations* (CMP 1987)★★★, *Ambiance* (AMB 1988)★★★, *Get Up Early* (AMB 1991)★★★,.with Ray Lema *Euro African Suite* (1993)★★★.

Kühn, Rolf

b. 29 September 1929, Cologne, Germany. After playing piano, Kühn turned to the clarinet and during the 40s and early 50s worked with numerous dance bands. His frequent broadcasts, often as leader, led to widespread popularity. In the mid-50s he was encouraged to visit the USA where he attracted attention, not least when he deputized for an incapacitated **Benny Goodman** in the latter's own band. He played with several other bands, including those led by **Urbie Green** and **Toshiko Akiyoshi**. Back in Germany from the early 60s, he resumed regular broadcasting and also played concerts and recording dates with various bands and in a star-tlingly wide range of styles including bop, free jazz, and jazz-rock fusion. Technically, Kühn is wholly assured and in complete command of his instrument and repertoire. A virtuoso player, unafraid to explore beyond the artificial limitations imposed upon clarinet-tists in the jazz world since the arrival of bop, Kühn has done much to liberate other players of this instrument. His younger brother is pianist **Joachim Kühn**.

● ALBUMS: *Streamline* (Vanguard 1956)★★★, *Impressions Of New York* (Impulse! 1967)★★★★, *The Day After* (MPS 1972),★★ *Cinemascope* (MPS 1974)★★★, *Total Space* (MPS 1975)★★, *Symphonic Swampfire* (MPS 1978)★★, *Don't Split* (L+R 1982)★★★.

Kuhn, Steve

b. 24 March 1938, New York, USA. Kuhn began playing the piano when he was five and was studying with **Serge Chaloff**'s mother when he was 12. He first played professionally at the age of 13. He graduated from Harvard in 1959 and worked with **Kenny Dorham** before spending two months with **John Coltrane**. He joined **Stan Getz** in 1961 and stayed right through the bossa nova craze. After two years with trumpeter **Art Farmer**, he settled in Stockholm, Sweden in 1966, working with his own trio throughout Europe. Since his return to New York in 1971, he has worked extensively in the world of commercial music. He has also performed with his own quartet which includes **Sheila Jordan** and has become an **ECM Records** solo artist. Kuhn is an accomplished musician whose playing and compositions have developed from standard post-bop to include increasingly dissonant harmony and unusual time signatures and phrase lengths. Kuhn's favourites range from **Fats Waller** to **Bill Evans**.

● ALBUMS: *Stan Getz/Bob Brookmeyer* (1961)★★★, *Ecstasy* (1974),★★★ *Trance* (1974)★★★, *Mobility* (1977)★★, *Non Fiction* (1978)★★★, *Last Year's Waltz* (ECM 1981)★★★, *Life's Magic* (Blackhawk 1986)★★, *The Vanguard Date* (Owl 1986)★★, *Mostly Ballads* (New World 1987)★★★, *Raindrops Live In My* (Muse 1988)★★★, *Porgy* (Jazz City 1988)★★, *Oceans In The Sky* (Owl 1990)★★★, *Looking Back* (Concord 1991)★★★, *Live At The Maybank Recital Hall Vol 13* (Concord 1991)★★★, *Years Later* (Concord 1993)★★★, *Seasons Of Romance* (Postcards 1995)★★★.

Kula Shaker

North London, England retro-rockers Kula Shaker (named after an Indian emperor) formed originally as the Kays then the Lovely Lads in 1994. Despite regular live work, that group was abandoned when the singer left. Ex-Objects Of Desire Crispian Mills (b. 18 January 1963; vocals), Jay Darlington (keyboards), Paul Winter-Hart (b. Somerset; drums) and Alonzo Bevin (bass) then regrouped under a new name and embarked on a support tour with **Reef** that resulted in a contract with **Columbia Records**. Columbia were evidently impressed by Kula Shaker's commitment to recreating the 'authenticity' of 60s groups the **Beatles** and **Small Faces**. Their debut single, 'Grateful When You're Dead' (a reference to the recent death of **Jerry Garcia**), immediately entered the UK Top 40 as critics feverishly scrambled to interview them. Mills, the son of 60s actress Hayley Mills and grandson of venerated actor Sir John Mills, did his best not to disappoint them: 'By the end of the century we're gonna be the biggest band in the world, and to celebrate we'll play a gig at the Pyramids on the last day of 1999. That's where we're headed.' Further singles proved no fluke; 'Tattva' and 'Hey Dude' were sparkling slices of intelligent guitar pop, with its heart in the sounds of the late 60s. Their debut album entered the UK chart at number 1. The band crowned an extraordinary first year by winning a BRIT award in February 1997 and released a frenetic cover version of **Joe South**'s 'Hush', previously a hit for **Deep Purple**. Mills' reputation was subsequently tarnished by some ill-advised remarks about the Nazi swastika, provoking a hostile reaction from the music press. They returned in 1998 with the UK Top 10 single, 'The Sound Of Drums'.

● ALBUMS: *K* (Columbia 1996)★★★★.
● FURTHER READING: *Kula Shaker*, Nigel Cross.

Kulka, Leo de Gar

b. Czechoslovakia. Kulka arrived in California with his family in 1939. He developed an interest in recording techniques while serving in the US Army and in 1957 co-founded Sound Enterprises in Los Angeles. This company was a pioneer in stereo recording and over the ensuing seven years Kulka worked with **Frank Sinatra**, **Sam Cooke**, **Little Richard** and **Nat 'King' Cole**. In 1964 computer expert George Bahrs invited Kulka to move to San Francisco. The partners opened Golden State Records in the city's warehouse district in September 1965. It quickly attracted custom from local acts and labels, notably **Autumn Records**, but Autumn's subsequent collapse briefly put Kulka's new venture into jeopardy. However, in 1966 Golden State produced its first major hit with the **Syndicate Of Sound**'s 'Little Girl'. Other acts attracted to the studio included the **Vejtables**, **Mourning Reign** and **E-Types**. Several groups opted to issue their recordings on Golden State's self-titled in-house label. Kulka eventually found production partners in Larry Goldberg and Hank Levine, two Los Angeles-based entrepreneurs, who sold finished master tapes to major companies, including **Dot**, **Capitol** and **Liberty**. **Mad River** was one such group to secure a recording deal in this manner. Kulka's eminent position waned during the 70s, but he has remained a fixture within San Francisco's music industry. During the 90s Kulka prepared master tapes and unissued material for release by Britain's **Ace Records**.

Kunene, Madala

b. 1951, Kwa-Mashu, South Africa. Kunene began busking on the guitar while still at school. As a teenager he played soccer for African Wanderers FC and considered making this his career. However, friends convinced him that his talents lay in music and he became a regular performer in the clubs of nearby Durban. He briefly lived in Cape Town but returned to Durban and worked on developing his own musical style (a mixture of South African folk with blues and soul influences). Nevertheless, he still worked mostly as a sideman and only started to play solo in 1988. He participated in B&W Music's 'Outernational Meltdown' recording sessions in 1994 and two years later, the same label released *King Of The Zulu Guitar - Vol. 1* as part of their Bootleg Net series, which was only available via the Internet and mail order. A field recording made on a portable DAT player, it showcased Kunene's intense and hypnotic vocal and guitar style. *Kon'ke Man*, his first generally available recording as a leader, was released in the same year. Closer to the African/jazz/funk fusion of the 'Outernational Meltdown' sessions, it featured co-production from **Airto Moreira** and **Pops Mohamed**.

● ALBUMS: *King Of The Zulu Guitar - Vol. 1* (B&W Music 1996)★★★★, *Kon'ke Man* (MELT 2000 1996)★★★.

Kunkel, Leah

b. Leah Cohen, 1948, Baltimore, Maryland, USA. The younger sister of '**Mama**' **Cass Elliot** of the **Mamas And The Papas**, Cohen married session player Russ Kunkel in 1968. After recording some demonstration record-

ings of her own songs, Kunkel was signed to Dunhill Records. Her first record, 'Billy', was issued under the name Cotton Candy, but failed to sell. Kunkel then returned to the LA City Music College after which she played with a band from Phoenix, Arizona - Chicken Train. That group soon folded and Leah continued her apprenticeship in the music business, learning about singing, songwriting and recording techniques. Always wary of being compared to her more famous sister, she was reluctant to record until the time was right. However, she did appear as guest vocalist on **Jackson Browne**'s first album. This was followed by appearances on albums by **James Taylor** and **Art Garfunkel**. The latter became something of a mentor and encouraged **Columbia** to sign her to a recording deal. Her self-titled debut album was issued in 1979 and as well as featuring her own songs, included covers of material by **Jules Shear**, the **Bee Gees** and **Marvin Gaye** & **Tammi Terrell**. Interestingly, there was also a revival of an old Mamas And The Papas song, 'Step Out'. Garfunkel contributed some liner notes, effusively describing Kunkel 'along the lines of truly great singers: **Billie Holiday**, the **Everly Brothers**, **Aretha Franklin**, James Taylor, **Linda Ronstadt** . . . listen to Leah Kunkel'. Unfortunately, Kunkel failed to cross over to the mainstream as effectively as many hoped.
● ALBUMS: *Leah Kunkel* (1979)★★.

Kunz, Charlie

b. 18 August 1896, Allentown, Pennsylvania, USA, d. 17 March 1958. After playing brass instruments and piano in various bands, Kunz led his own band while still in his early teens. He visited the UK in 1922 and decided to make his home there. He led bands through the late 20s and into the early 30s, enjoying residencies at several leading West End nightclubs. From one of these he was broadcast by the BBC and this helped spread his popularity. Later in his career he toured variety theatres and made many records, favouring medleys of popular tunes from present and past. Kunz played in a diluted form of stride and if he possessed a great technique, he skilfully concealed it from his many fans. Ill-health dogged him in his later years and for some time he suffered from a form of arthritis which affected his hands and threatened to cut short his career. Having won that battle he finally succumbed to respiratory complaints and died in his sleep in March 1958.
● COMPILATIONS: *The World Of Charlie Kunz* (1969)★★★, *Focus On Charlie Kunz* (1977)★★★, *Clap Hands, Here Comes Charlie* (1983)★★★, *Charlie Kunz And His Casani Club Orchestra* (1983)★★★, *Dance Your Way Through The Thirties* (1987)★★★, *A Pretty Girl Is Like A Melody* (1988)★★★, *The Music Goes Round* (1989)★★★, *The Very Best Of* (1993)★★★.

Kunze, Heinz Rudolf

A talented singer-songwriter, composer and lyricist, Kunze is perhaps Germany's best-known musical writer. Hermann Van Veen and Milva are just two of

the artists to have taken his songs to the top of the domestic charts. His career breakthrough came in 1980 when he won the German Pop-Nachwuchs Festival in Wurzburg for 'newcomers to the pop scene'. Since then he has released over 15 albums for **WEA Records** Germany, usually produced by Kunze himself alongside long-standing collaborators Peter Miklis and Heiner Lurig. These have brought an avalanche of platinum records and awards, including the Willy Dehmel-Preis, the Berliner Wecker Cabaret Prize, the Deutscher Schallplattenpreis (German Record Prize) and the RTL Sonderlowe Award, all in 1982. His 1995 album, *Der Golem Aus Lemgo*, continued to concentrate on his natural melodic ability and sentimental lyrics. Kunze also wrote the German translation libretto for the Berlin production of **Miss Saigon**.
● ALBUMS: *Eine Form Von Gewalt* (WEA 1982)★★★★, *Der Golem Aus Lemgo* (WEA 1995)★★★★.

Kupferberg, Tuli

An active member of New York's 60s bohemian milieu, Kupferberg joined fellow poet **Ed Sanders** in the **Fugs**, a musically crude ensemble which blended political comment and songs about sex and drugs to material drawn from William Blake. Tuli composed some of the group's best-known songs, including 'Kill For Peace' and 'Coca Cola Douche', while his lyrical 'Morning, Morning' was later recorded by **Richie Havens**. The artist also completed a rare solo album, *No Deposit, No Return*, which drew its material from published advertisements and popular poetry. Kupferberg retired from active involvement in music following the Fugs' demise, but rejoined Sanders in a revived line-up which emerged during the 80s. He then enjoyed a fruitful association with the maverick New York label, **Shimmy Disc**, appearing on their first release, *The 20th Anniversary Of The Summer Of Love*. *Tuli And Friends* showed his idiosyncratic skills remained intact. Its highlight was 'Way Down South In Greenwich Village', where he updated the 20s classic, replete with ukulele impressions.
● ALBUMS: *No Deposit, No Return* (1967)★★★, *Tuli And Friends* (1989)★★★.

Kurious

b. Jorge Antonio Alvarez, *c.*1969. Of Puerto Rican descent, Kurious broke big in late 1992 with the underground smash, 'Walk Like A Duck'. Based in uptown Manhattan (as described in the single, 'Uptown Shit'), Jorge and his Constipated Monkey crew won their reputation as talented freestylers, Jorge himself earning the title 'Freestyle King'. Despite the kudos his name inspired in the early 90s, by 1994 he was making a staunch bid to crossover with the radio-friendly 'I'm Kurious', originally written as long ago as 1991. His debut album, too, was three years in the making, eventually emerging as the debut platter on **Prime Minister Pete Nice**'s Hoppoh Records. It was titled *Constipated Monkey* because of protracted negotiations between

Hoppoh and **Def Jam**, who he had originally signed a contract with. He had worked as a messenger for Def Jam Records in 1988, before **Russell Simmons** offerred him a contract. However, after he rose to prominence because of his open mic dexterity, he decided to honour a verbal arrangment with Nice instead. His debut album was produced in conjunction with the Stimulated Dummies and the **Beatnuts**. It featured excellent, thoughtful rhymes of the ilk of 'Spell It With J (Yes, Yes Jorge): 'Malt liquor got me trapped so my rap is controversial, Might drink the brew but I won't do the commercial'. It revealed the depth of the education his single parent mother had encouraged him to pursue at Farleigh Dickinson University.
● ALBUMS: *A Constipated Monkey* (Hoppoh 1994)★★★.

Kursaal Flyers

Formed in Southend, Essex, England, the Kursaal Flyers - Paul Shuttleworth (vocals), Graeme Douglas (guitar), Vic Collins (guitar/steel guitar/vocals), Richie Bull (bass/vocals), and Will Birch (drums) - secured the approbation of producer **Jonathan King** who signed the quintet to his label, UK. *Chocs Away* and *The Great Artiste* enjoyed considerable praise for their grasp of melodic pop, and the group also became a popular live attraction, with Shuttleworth's 'spiv' persona an undoubted focal point. The Kursaals attained commercial success after joining **CBS**. 'Little Does She Know' reached the Top 20 in 1975 although the group struggled to find a suitable follow-up. Barry Martin replaced Douglas when the latter joined **Eddie And The Hot Rods**, but the unit disintegrated following *Five Live Kursaals*. Will Birch subsequently formed the **Records**, but having compiled the commemorative *In For A Spin*, reunited the Flyers for *Former Tour De Force Is Forced To Tour*.
● ALBUMS: *Chocs Away* (UK 1975)★★★, *The Great Artiste* (UK 1975)★★★, *Golden Mile* (Columbia 1976)★★★, *Five Live Kursaals* (Columbia 1977)★★, *Former Tour De Force Is Forced To Tour* (Waterfront 1988)★★.
● COMPILATIONS: *The Best Of The Kursaal Flyers* (Teldec 1983)★★★, *In For A Spin* (Edsel 1985)★★★.

Kuryokhin, Sergey

b. 16 June 1954, Murmansk, Russia. Kuryokhin started to play piano at the age of four and when his family settled in Leningrad in 1971 he attended the Leningrad Conservatory and later the Institute of Culture, but was expelled from both for failing to attend classes. After playing in rock groups at school, he was attracted to jazz by **McCoy Tyner**'s playing on the **John Coltrane** records he heard broadcast on 'Voice Of America' radio programmes. Later piano influences have included **Cecil Taylor**, **Muhal Richard Abrams** and **Alex Von Schlippenbach**, though he has said that his chief inspirations have been contemporary saxophonists such as **Anthony Braxton**, **Evan Parker** and, particularly, his compatriots **Vladimir Chekasin** and **Anatoly Vapirov**. He first came to notice playing with Vapirov in 1977

and later worked in groups with Chekasin and **Boris Grebenshikov** (with whom he co-led the rock group Aquarium) as well as forming his own Crazy Music Orchestra. The tapes of his first record, the solo *The Ways Of Freedom*, were smuggled out of the USSR and released by the London-based **Leo Records** in 1981. The album established him as a virtuoso technician, but many critics considered there was more style than substance to his music. Later releases on Leo included sessions with Chekasin (*Exercises*), Vapirov (*Sentenced To Silence, Invocations, De Profundis*) and Grebenshchikov (*Subway Culture* and the minimalist organ/guitar duo, *Mad Nightingales In The Russian Forest*) as well as further solos (*Popular Zoological Elements, Some Combinations Of Fingers And Passion*) and concerts with Pop Mechanics, the name he has given to all his ensembles since 1984. Increasingly eclectic in style and anarchic in spirit, Pop Mechanics became a major presence in the Russian musical underground; their one UK appearance, in Liverpool in 1989, featured massed electric guitars, bagpipes, African drummers, gospel singers, the Bootle Concertina Band and the brass section of the Liverpool Philharmonic, as well as theatrical elements such as onstage karate fights, Kuryokhin eating flowers and brief appearances by assorted cows and goats! The same year he toured the USA, playing with a range of musicians from **John Zorn** to **Henry Kaiser** to **Boz Scaggs** and recording for the Nonesuch label. The first international celebrity to emerge from the Russian jazz scene, Kuryokhin is now as much a performance artist as a pianist and is also in demand as a composer, collaborating on recent projects with both Alfred Schnittke and the Kronos String Quartet.
● ALBUMS: *The Ways Of Freedom* (Leo 1981)★★★, with Anatoly Vapirov *Sentenced To Silence* 1981 recording (1983)★★★, with Boris Grebenshchikov *Subway Culture* (Leo 1986)★★★★, *Introduction In Pop Mechanics* (Leo 1987)★★★★, *Popular Zoological Elements* (Leo 1987),★★★ *Pop Mechanics No 17 Live In Novosibirsk 1983* (Leo 1988)★★★, with Grebenshchikov *Mad Nightingales In The Russian Forest* (Leo 1989)★★★, with others *Document* (1990, 8-CD box-set)★★★★, *Some Combinations Of Fingers And Passion* (Leo 1992)★★★★.

Kut Klose

Formed in Atlanta, Georgia, USA, by the female trio of Tabitha Duncan, Athena Cage and LaVonn Battle, Kut Klose specialize in a sassy brand of urban R&B pop, primarily mounted on their smooth harmonies. Their debut album, *Surrender*, was the second to be released on **Keith Sweat**'s Keia Records label (the first being **Silk**'s platinum-selling debut), and merged pop sensibilities with hip-hop beats and simplistic but effective lyrics - as Battle puts it: 'A little hip-hop, a little rhythm and blues, a little soulful and a little youthful.' Comprising ballads such as 'I Like' and 'Giving You My Love' alongside the New Jill Swing of 'Don't Change', the opening single was 'Get Up On It', a duet with

Sweat himself. The album was written and produced by Sweat, Eric McCaine (of Entouch) and the group themselves, and recorded at the Sweat Shop, the state-of-the-art studio built by Sweat in his Atlanta home.

● ALBUMS: *Surrender* (Keia 1995)★★★.

Kuti, Fela

b. Fela Anikulapo Kuti, 15 October 1938, Abeokuta, Nigeria, d. 2 August 1997. Kuti was a primary influence behind the invention and development of afrobeat, the west African fusion of agit-prop lyrics and dance rhythms which has been a major medium of social protest for the urban poor since the late 60s. Kuti was born to middle-class parents and enjoyed a relatively privileged childhood and adolescence before breaking with family wishes and becoming a bandleader and political catalyst. In 1958, he was sent to London, England by his parents, who had agreed to support him there while he studied to become a doctor. Within weeks of arriving, however, he had enrolled at Trinity College of Music, where he spent the next four years studying piano, composition and theory and leading his highlife-meets-jazz group Koola Lobitos. By 1961, the band was a regular fixture on London's growing R&B club scene, drawing substantial audiences to influential clubs like the Marquee and Birdland. In 1962, Kuti left Trinity and moved back to Nigeria, basing himself in Lagos, where he became a trainee radio producer with Nigerian Broadcasting. His after-hours activities with a re-formed Koola Lobitos interfered with his work, however, and he was fired after a few months. From this point on, he devoted himself entirely to a career as a bandleader. By 1968, Kuti was calling the music Koola Lobitos played afrobeat - as a retort to the slavish relationship most other local bandleaders had with black American music. His ambition to reverse the one-way tide of musical influence led him to take Koola Lobitos to the USA in 1969, where the group struggled to survive playing small clubs on the west coast. Although financially unsuccessful, the visit did much to awaken Kuti's political sensibilities, and he forged important friendships with radical black activists such as Angela Davis, Stokley Carmichael and the **Last Poets**. Back in Nigeria, Kuti changed the name of Koola Lobitos to Afrika 70, and in 1971 enjoyed a big local hit with 'Jeun Ko'ku' (Yoruba for 'eat and die'). He also founded the Shrine Club in Lagos, which was to become the focus for his music and political activity. By 1972, Kuti had become one of the biggest stars in west Africa; because he sang in 'broken English' rather than one of the tribal languages, his lyrics were understandable in all Anglophone countries. He also rejected the traditional African bandleader stance of promoting local politicians and their policies, choosing instead to articulate the anger and aspirations of the urban poor. In the process he became a figurehead and hero for street people throughout Nigeria, Ghana and neighbouring countries. A typical early swipe at the ruling elite was contained in the 1973 album *Gentleman*, in which Kuti

lampooned the black middle-class fetish for wearing western clothing in a tropical climate: 'him put him socks him put him shoes, him put him pants him put him singlet, him put him trouser him put him shirt, him put him tie him put him coat, him come cover all with him hat; him be gentleman; him go sweat all over, him go faint right down, him go smell like shit'. Not surprisingly, the Nigerian establishment did not enjoy hearing songs like these - nor did they approve of Kuti's high-profile propaganda on behalf of igbo (Nigerian marijuana). The drug squad attempted to clamp down on him on several occasions, all of them unsuccessful, but these attempts provided plenty of substance for a string of hilarious album releases. Enraged, the army was sent to arrest him at his home, Alagbon Close, in late 1974. The house was practically razed to the ground, and Kuti delighted his fans by telling the tale in gory detail on the album *Alagbon Close*, questioning the right of uniformed public servants to go around breaking heads and property at will. The attack only confirmed Kuti's political aspirations and also cemented his total embrace of African mores and customs. In 1975, he changed his middle name from Ransome (which he regarded as a slave name) to Anikulapo. His full name, Fela Anikulapo Kuti, now meant 'He Who Emanates Greatness (Fela), Having Control Over Death (Anikulapo), Death Cannot Be Caused By Human Entity (Kuti)'. Kuti needed all this ceremonial power on 18 February 1977, when the army mounted a second all-out attack on his new home, a walled compound of houses called Kalakuta Republic. Some 1,000 soldiers cordoned off the area, set fire to the premises and viciously attacked the occupants - Kuti suffered a fractured skull, arm and leg, while his 82-year-old mother was thrown out of a first-floor window, narrowly escaping death. The army then prevented the fire brigade reaching the compound, and for good measure beat up and arrested anyone they identified as a journalist among the onlookers. Although Kuti won the war of words which followed, he sensibly decided to leave Nigeria for a while, and in October 1977 went into voluntary exile in Ghana. Unfortunately, his Accra recordings (such as *Zombie*, a virulent satire on the military mentality), did not endear him to the Ghanaian authorities either, and in 1978 he was deported back to Lagos. On arrival, to mark the anniversary of the previous year's pillage of Kalakuta and to reaffirm his embrace of African culture, he married 27 women simultaneously in a traditional ceremony (he divorced them all in 1986, stating 'no man has the right to own a woman's vagina'). Kuti did not drop his revolutionary profile in subsequent years. With albums such as *Coffin For Head Of State*, *International Thief Thief*, *VIP Vagabonds In Power* and *Authority Stealing* (all attacking government corruption and abuse of human rights), he continued to keep himself and his band (renamed Egypt 80 in 1979) at the forefront of west African roots culture, while also acquiring a substantial international profile.

In 1984, Kuti was jailed in Nigeria on what were widely regarded as trumped-up currency smuggling charges. During his 27-month incarceration, leading New York funk producer **Bill Laswell** was brought in to complete the production of the outstanding *Army Arrangement* album. On release from prison in 1987, Kuti issued the **Wally Badarou**-produced *Teacher Don't Teach Me Nonsense* - a rich, dense, at times almost orchestral work which showed him recharged, rather than weakened, by his latest persecution. In 1996 Kuti was arrested, and later released for an alleged drugs charge. The National Drug-Law Enforcement Agency got him to agree to some counselling for his alleged drug abuse. In 1997 he sued the Nigerian government for the previous incident. He died before this was resolved of an AIDS related complication.

● ALBUMS: *Fela's London Scene* (HNLX 1970)★★★, *Open And Close* (HNLX 1971)★★★, with Ginger Baker *Live With Ginger Baker* (Regal Zonophone 1972)★★★, *Shakara* (EMI 1972)★★★, *Gentleman* (NEMI 1973)★★★★, *Alagbon Close* (JILP 1974)★★★★, *Expensive Shit* (SWS 1975)★★★, *Yellow Fever* (Decca West Africa 1976)★★★, *Zombie* (CRLP 1977)★★★, *Kalakuta Show* (CRLP 1978)★★★★, *Coffin For Head Of State* (KALP 1979)★★★★, *VIP Vagabonds In Power* (KILP 1979)★★★, with Roy Ayers *Africa, Center Of The World* (Polydor 1981)★★★, with Lester Bowie *Perambulator* (LIR 1983)★★★, *Army Arrangement* (Celluloid 1985)★★★, *Teacher Don't Teach Me Nonsense* (London 1987)★★★★, *I Go Shout Plenty* (Decca 1987)★★★★, with Roy Ayers *2000 Blacks* (Justin 1988)★★★, *Beasts Of No Nation* (JDEUR 1988)★★★, *Us* (Stern's 1992)★★★, *Underground System* (Stern's 1993)★★★, *The '69 Los Angeles Sessions* (Stern's 1993)★★★, with Africa 70 *He Miss Road* (Stern's 1995)★★★.

● COMPILATIONS: *Fela Kuti Volumes 1 & 2* (EMI 1977)★★★★.

● VIDEOS: *Teacher Don't Teach Me Nonsense* (1984), *Fela Live* (1984).

Kwamé

b. Kwamé Holland, East Elmhurst, Queens, New York, USA. Mild-mannered rapper whose relatively sunny disposition enshrines his recording profile. Something of a welcome change to the OG's and their attendant posturing, he is supported on stage and record by his backing band A New Beginning, variously credited in the titles of his first three releases. Growing up in and around the New York jazz set, he mingled happily with musicians of the order of **Stevie Wonder** and **Lionel Hampton**, the latter giving Kwamé his first set of drums. His debut album was produced by **Hurby Luv Bug Azor**, while the second was something of a 'concept' affair. This and his third set, *Nastee*, brought a string of hit singles in 'Only You', 'The Rhythm', 'The Man We All Know And Love', 'One Of The Big Boys', 'Nastee' and 'Sweet Thing'. He moved to Wrap/**Ichiban** in 1994 for *Incognito*, recorded alongside partners DJ Tat Money and A-Sharp in Atlanta, Georgia. 'This record is growth', he eulogised, 'It's my reincarnation, and I return Incognito'.

● ALBUMS: *The Boy Genius* (Atlantic 1989)★★★, *A Day In The Life - A Pokadelic Adventure* (Atlantic 1990)★★★, *Nastee* (Atlantic 1991)★★, *Incognito* (Wrap/Ichiban 1993)★★★.

Kweskin, Jim, Jug Band

b. 18 July 1940, Stamford, Connecticut, USA. Kweskin began to forge a ragtime/jugband style in the New England folk haunts during the early 60s. His early groups were largely informal and it was not until 1963, when he secured a recording deal, that this singer and guitarist began piecing together a more stable line-up. **Geoff Muldaur** (guitar, washboard, kazoo, vocals), Bob Siggins, Bruno Wolf and Fritz Richmond (jug/washtub bass) joined Kweskin on his enthusiastic, infectious debut. Siggins dropped out of the group prior to a second album, *Jug Band Music*. **Bill Keith** (banjo, pedal steel guitar) and Maria D'Amato (vocals, kazoo, tambourine) were now enlisted, while Kweskin's extended family also included several other individuals, the most notorious of whom was Mel Lyman, who added harmonica on *Relax Your Mind*, the leader's 'solo' album. D'Amato married Geoff Muldaur and later became better known for her solo career as **Maria Muldaur**. *See Reverse Side For Title*, arguably the Jug Band's finest album, featured versions of 'Blues In The Bottle' and 'Fishing Blues', both of which were recorded by the **Lovin' Spoonful**. 'Chevrolet', a magnificent duet between Muldaur and D'Amato, was another highlight and the entire selection balanced humour with a newfound purpose. Fiddler **Richard Greene** worked with the line-up for what was the group's final album, *Garden Of Joy*. He subsequently joined Keith on several projects, including the excellent bluegrass quintet, Muleskinner, while Geoff and Maria commenced work as a duo. Kweskin's own progress was rather overshadowed by his immersion in Lyman's dark, quasi-religious, Charles Manson-like commune, but he emerged as a solo performer in the early 70s and has since continued to forge an idiosyncratic, traditional musical-based path.

● ALBUMS: *Jim Kweskin And The Jug Band* i (Vanguard 1965)★★★, *Jug Band Music* (Vanguard 1965)★★★★, *Relax Your Mind* (Vanguard 1966)★★★, *Jim Kewskin And The Jug Band* ii (1966)★★★★, *See Reverse Side For Title* (Vanguard 1967)★★★, *Jump For Joy* (Vanguard 1967)★★★, *Garden Of Joy* (Reprise 1967)★★★, *Whatever Happened To Those Good Old Days* (Vanguard 1968)★★★, *American Aviator* (1969)★★★, *Jim Kweskin's America* (1971)★★★, *Jim Kweskin* (1978)★★★, *Jim Kweskin Lives Again* (1978)★★★, *Side By Side* (1980)★★★, *Swing On A Star* (1980)★★★.

● COMPILATIONS: *Best Of Jim Kweskin And The Jug Band* (Vanguard 1968)★★★★, *Greatest Hits* (1990)★★★★, *Strange Things Happening* (Rounder 1994)★★★.

KWS

This dance team from Nottingham, who originally signed to **Network Records** as B-Line, featured Chris King and Winnie Williams with a series of guest vocalists. They had a big commercial hit with the **KC And**

The **Sunshine Band** cover 'Please Don't Go', following the success in Europe of a dance version by **Double You?** (on **ZYX Records**). KWS's version which featured Delroy Joseph on vocals and supposedly took only a couple of hours to complete, stayed at number 1 for five weeks. The follow-up 'Rock Your Baby' was a another KC composition and once again it jumped in front of a proposed ZYX label release, a Baby Roots version of the same track. Following the release of the album *Please Don't Go (The Album)* the members of KWS left Network in 1994 to form X-Clusive.
● ALBUMS: *Please Don't Go (The Album)* (Network 1992)★★.

Ky-mani

b. *c.*1975, Jamaica, West Indies. In addition to **Bob Marley**'s musical legacy, his lifestyle was evidently irresistible to the media, who considered his consumption of ganja and his siring of many offspring newsworthy. Following Bob's demise many of his relatives have entered the music business, notably **Ziggy Marley And The Melody Makers**, Julian Marley, Damien 'Jr Gong' Marley and Ky-mani Marley. Critics tended to approach releases by members of the Marley family with accusations of nepotism, and to avoid this Ky-mani refused to capitalize on his father's name, in spite of the title of his debut, *Like Father Like Son*. The album featured cover versions of his father's hits complete with their respective dub versions, which gave the singer the opportunity to establish his recording career. He relocated to the USA with his mother when he was eight years old. He initially followed in **Bunny Wailer**'s footsteps as a percussionist, although he was attracted by the **dancehall** style, and by the early 90s emerged as a DJ. In common with his siblings, Ky-mani's vocal styling is very reminiscent of his father, particularly on 'Thank You Lord', the 1997 combination hit with DJ **Shaggy**. The single, lifted from *Midnite Lover*, was originally recorded with **Brian And Tony Gold** until Clifton 'Specialist' Dillon suggested adding Ky-mani's vocals. The project resulted in commercial success, topping a number of specialist charts worldwide. Further hits included 'Judge Not' with **Patra**, the stimulating 'Sensimella' and the stirring 'Dear Dad'. In late 1997 Ky-mani joined forces with **Tito Puente** Jnr., fulfilling the Bronx-born singer's desire to record in combination with a reggae artist. Puente, a notable salsa performer, dabbled with the Jamaican sound, having recorded a version of **Musical Youth**'s 'Pass The Dutchie'. The duo appeared at the annual MIDEM seminar in Miami, where both artists achieved critical acclaim for their performance.
● ALBUMS: *Like Father Like Son* (Rhino 1997)★★.

Kyle, Billy

b. 14 July 1914, Philadelphia, Pennsylvania, USA, d. 23 February 1966. Kyle began playing piano semi-professionally while still at school and in the mid-30s was accompanying the popular singer **Bon Bon Tunnell**.

Later in the decade he played with **Tiny Bradshaw** and **Lucky Millinder** and in 1938 joined **John Kirby**'s band, where he remained until drafted for military service in 1942. After the war, Kyle rejoined Kirby for a while, then worked with **Sy Oliver** and also led his own small groups. Studio and theatre work occupied him for the next few years until, in 1953, he joined **Louis Armstrong**'s All Stars. He remained with the All Stars until his death in February 1966. Although a highly-accomplished technician, Kyle preferred the accompanist's role, content to lend rhythmic support to his front-line colleagues. His delicate touch fitted superbly into the Kirby band and, although somewhat at odds with the flamboyance of the Armstrong band (he succeeded **Earl 'Fatha' Hines**), there were times when he appeared to be its most musicianly member.
● ALBUMS: *Louis Armstrong Plays W.C. Handy* (1954)★★★★.
● COMPILATIONS: with John Kirby *The Greatest Little Band In The Land (1939-42)* (1987)★★★★, *Finishing Up A Date 1939-46* (Collectors Item 1988)★★★.

Kyoung, Park Mi

b. 1965, South Korea. One of Asia's rising pop performers, Park Mi Kyoung enjoyed her first substantial hit in 1985 with the gentle pop ballad, 'When A Dandelion Becomes A Spore'. Previously she had attended art school. By the 90s she had abandoned her previous musical platform for a more rhythmic, dance-based style. Typical of this approach was 1995's *Jungle*, where stripped-down rhythm tracks accompanied Park's husky voice. Among the best tracks were the African-influenced 'Warning Of Eve' and a version of **Roberta Flack**'s 'Killing Me Softly'. The majority of her domestic audience is composed of women, who respond well to the feminist content of many of her lyrics.
● ALBUMS: *Jungle* (Line 1995)★★★.

Kyper

b. Randall Kyper, Baton Rouge, Louisiana, USA. This rapper achieved a one-off hit single in 1990 when his appealing 'Tic-Tac-Toe' peaked at number 14 in the *Billboard* charts. His debut album was also titled after that track, but disappointed many who had expected some variation on the single's formula. The impetus behind Kyper disappeared and **Atlantic Records** did not renew his contract.
● ALBUMS: *Tic-Tac-Toe* (Atlantic 1990)★★.

Kyser, Kay

b. James King Kern Kyser, 18 June 1906, Rocky Mount, North Carolina, USA, d. 23 July 1985, Chapel Hill, North Carolina, USA. A popular bandleader in the USA during the 30s and 40s, Kyser was born into an academically excellent family, and he too became a 'professor', though hardly in the conventional sense. Whilst at high school he developed a flair for showmanship, and entered the University of North Carolina in 1924 with the intention of studying law. The subject was soon discarded in favour of music, and Kyser took over the leadership of the campus band from Hal Kemp when Kemp departed to form one of the most popular 'sweet' bands of the 30s. Kyser was soon on the road himself, and in 1927 he recruited **George Duning**, a graduate of the Cincinnati Conservatory of Music, as the chief arranger of what was originally a jazz unit. This turned out to be a smart move, because Kyser could not read or write a note of music. Duning stayed with the Kyser band for most of its life, before going on to write films scores as diverse as *Jolson Sings Again* and *Picnic*. By 1933, when Kyser played the Miramar Hotel in Santa Monica, California, the band had developed a 'sweeter' style, and had become a major attraction. Kyser, the showman, also injected several gimmicks. For example, instead of a having a spoken introduction to a song, the vocalist would *sing* the title at the beginning of each number; and later, just before the vocal chorus, the band would play a few bars of its theme, **Walter Donaldson**'s 'Thinking Of You', while Kyser announced the singer's name. It was simple, but highly effective. In the following year, Kyser took over from Hal Kemp yet again, this time at the Blackhawk Restaurant in Chicago. The band's sell-out performances at the venue were supplemented by regular radio broadcasts, and so the renowned *Kay Kyser's Kollege Of Musical Knowledge* was born. It was a zany, comedy quiz programme in which the Blackhawk's patrons' skill in identifying song titles was rewarded with prizes (there were rarely any losers). NBC's networked airings brought Kyser (by then known as the 'old perfesser'), national recognition, and in the late 30s he and the band had several hit records, including 'Did You Mean It?', 'Cry, Baby, Cry', 'Music, Maestro, Please!', 'Ya Got Me', 'Two Sleepy People', 'I Promise You', 'Cuckoo In The Clock', 'The Tinkle Song', 'The Little Red Fox', 'The Umbrella Man', 'Three Little Fishies', and 'Stairway To The Stars'. Throughout its life, Kyser's band had a string of popular vocalists, including **Harry Babbitt**, Ginny Simms (d. 4 April 1994, Palm Springs, California, USA, aged 81), Sully Mason, Gloria Wood, Julie Conway, Trudy Erwin, Dorothy Dunn, Lucy Ann Polk, and Ish Kabibble. The latter name was a pseudonym for trumpeter Merwyn Bogue (d. 5 June 1994, Joshua Tree, California, USA, aged 86), and he featured on most of the band's many novelty numbers, and in their series of comedy films which included *That's Right, You're Wrong* (1939), *You'll Find Out, Playmates, My Favorite Spy, Around The World, Swing Fever*, and *Carolina Blues* (1944). **Mike Douglas**, who later became a popular television talk show host, also sang with the band in the 40s, and for a few months in the 50s. In the early 40s, the recruitment of **Van Alexander**, who had arranged the **Chick Webb**-**Ella Fitzgerald** recording of 'A-Tisket A-Tasket', coincided with a critical reappraisal of Kyser's musical output. As well as winning polls in the 'corn' category, the band came to be regarded as a genuine swing unit that also had a way with a ballad. During World War II, Kyser toured extensively for the USO, entertaining troops in over 500 service camps and hospitals over a wide area. In 1944, he married the blonde Hollywood model, Georgia Carroll, who had decorated such movies as *Ziegfeld Girl* and *Du Barry Was A Lady*. She was a singer, too, and provided the vocals on one of the band's 1945 hits, 'There Goes That Song Again'. Throughout the decade the Kyser band was almost permanently in the US Top 20 with a variety of titles such as 'You, You, Darlin'', 'Playmates', 'With The Wind And The Rain In Your Hair', 'Friendship', 'Blue Love Bird', 'Tennessee Fish Fry', 'Who's Yehoodi?', 'Blueberry Hill', 'Ferryboat Serenade', 'You Got Me This Way'. 'Alexander The Swoose (Half Swan, Half Goose)', '(Lights Out) 'Til Reveille', 'Why Don't We Do This More Often?', '(There'll Be Bluebirds Over) The White Cliffs Of Dover', 'A Zoot Suit (For My Sunday Girl)', 'Who Wouldn't Love You', 'Johnny Doughboy Found A Rose In Ireland', 'Got The Moon In My Pocket', 'Jingle, Jangle, Jingle', 'He Wears A Pair Of Silver Wings', 'Strip Polka', 'Ev'ry Night About This Time', 'Praise The Lord And Pass The Ammunition' (the band's biggest hit), 'Can't Get Of This Mood', 'Let's Get Lost', 'Bell Bottom Trousers', 'One-Zy, Two-Zy (I Love You-Zy)', 'Ole Buttermilk Sky', 'The Old Lamp-Lighter', 'Huggin' And Chalkin'', 'Managua, Nicaragua', 'Woody Woodpecker', and 'Slow Boat To China' (1948). During that period *The Kollege Of Musical Knowlege* continued to delight and amuse American radio audiences who knew that when Kyser welcomed them with: 'Evenin' Folks. How y'all?', in that strong southern accent, he was dressed in his professor's white gown and mortarboard, 'jumping, cavorting, mugging, and waving his arms like a dervish', just for the benefit of the few in the studio. In 1949, while the show was still high in the ratings, it was unexpectedly cancelled by the sponsors, and Kyser switched the concept to television, but it made little impact. By 1951 he had lost interest, and retired to North Carolina a wealthy man. He devoted the rest of his life to Christian Science, a subject in which he was an authorised practitioner.

● ALBUMS: *Greatest Hits* (50s)★★★, *Dance Date* (80s)★★, *The Songs Of World War II* (1993)★★★★.

Kyuss

Formed in Palm Springs, California, USA, this quartet of schoolfriends mixed their differing tastes to provide a blues-based retro rock sound of stunning heaviness charged with a spiritual air. Vocalist John Garcia's mainstream tastes and bassist Nick Oliveri's metal background blended with guitarist Josh Homme and drummer Brant Bjork's penchant for **Black Flag**, the **Misfits** and the **Ramones**, to produce music with the groove of classic **Black Sabbath** but with a modern intensity and their own definite identity. Although their early efforts were unpopular in the hardcore-oriented late 80s, the band stuck doggedly with their music and were accepted as tastes broadened in the post-grunge

90s. *Wretch* was a decent debut, but the band found a kindred spirit in **Master Of Reality** leader Chris Goss, who produced *Blues For The Red Sun*. On the latter, the looser atmosphere and mature material were given extra ambience as Goss captured the band's live power in the studio. Kyuss were suddenly hot property, touring the USA with **Danzig** and **Faith No More**, and in Australia with **Metallica**, although Oliveri departed to be replaced by Scott Reeder from old touring partners the **Obsessed**. When their label collapsed, distributors **Elektra** offered Kyuss a contract, and the band collaborated with Goss again on the pounding sludge-rock of *Sky Valley*, with new drummer Alfredo Hernandez replacing the tour-weary Bjork. Goss was again producer for the group's fourth album, which further enhanced their reputation, although the band decided to call it a day later that year. Garcia formed Slo-Burn and Homme formed Gamma Ray. Bjork later joined **Fu Manchu** in 1996. Homme released a solo album at the end of 1997, *Instrumental Driving Music For Felons*, amid rumours of a Kyuss reunion. *Queens Of The Stone Age* was a collection of their last studio recordings.

● ALBUMS: *Wretch* (Dali-Chameleon 1991)★★★, *Blues For The Red Sun* (Dali-Chameleon 1992)★★★★, *Sky Valley* (Elektra 1994)★★★, *...And The Circus Leaves Town* (Elektra 1995)★★★, *Queens Of The Stone Age* (Man's Ruin 1998)★★.

L'Aventure Du Jazz

An outstanding documentary produced and directed in 1969 by Louis and Claudine Panassie, this film features numerous leading mainstream musicians. Amongst the artists on view are **Eddie Barefield**, **Buck Clayton**, **William 'Cozy' Cole**, **Jimmy Crawford**, **Vic Dickenson**, **Sister Rosetta Tharpe**, **Milt Hinton**, Pat Jenkins, **Budd Johnson**, **Jo Jones**, Eli Robinson, **Zutty Singleton**, **Willie 'The Lion' Smith**, **Tiny Grimes**, **Buddy Tate** and Dick Vance. Also on hand are blues singers **John Lee Hooker** and **Memphis Slim** and the exciting dance team, Lou Parks' Lindy Hoppers. Rarely seen, this film is a major achievement and worth a place on the shelf of any collector lucky enough to come across a copy. Soundtrack excerpts were issued as a double album on the Jazz Odyssey label.

L'Trimm

Cutesy rappers whose 'Grab It!' was a literal answer to **Salt 'N' Pepa**'s 'Push It'. As the pun might suggest, their records were dominated by a locker-room approach to sexuality, and anatomical revelry of the old school. The duo are Tigra (b. 1970, New York, USA) and Bunny D. (b. Chicago, Illinois, USA).
● ALBUMS: *Grab It!* (Time X/Atlantic 1988)★★★, *Drop That Bottom* (Atlantic 1989)★★, *Groovy* (Atlantic 1991)★★.

L.A. And Babyface

US songwriters and producers who have become the **Chinn And Chapman** of black pop/dance in the 90s. Sharing a knack for knowing what is palatable both on radio and in clubland, L.A. Reid (also of the Deele) and **Babyface** (b. Kenneth Edmonds, 10 April 1959, Indianapolis, Indiana, USA, ex-Manchild and the Deele, originally nicknamed Babyface by **Bootsy Collins**) began a glittering career when helming **Pebbles**' instant smash, 'Girlfriend', in 1988. Reid would later marry the San Franciscan diva, while Babyface boasts kinship with Kevon and Melvin Edmonds of After 7. Their output is typified by hard, fast rhythms, and an up-tempo approach enhanced by the strong melodic abilities of their chosen vocalists. These have included such prestigious names as **Bobby Brown**, **Paula Abdul**, the **Boys**, **Midnight Star**, **Toni Braxton** and the **Jacksons**. Babyface, meanwhile, has also released a succession of smooth, lovers' rock albums. His 1991 set included duets recorded for albums by Pebbles and Karyn White. Babyface won a Grammy award for Producer of the Year in 1995.

L.A. Guns

This US group was formed by ex-**Guns N'Roses** guitarist Tracii Guns and Paul Black in Los Angeles in 1987, though the latter was soon replaced by ex-**Girl/Bernie Torme** vocalist Phil Lewis. Working on material that was a hybrid of metal, glam and blues-based rock 'n' roll, they signed with **PolyGram Records** in the USA the following year. With the addition of Mick Cripps (guitar), Kelly Nickels (bass) and Steve Riley (drums, ex-**W.A.S.P.**) the line-up was complete. However, with Riley arriving too late to appear on their self-titled debut, the group used the services of Nickey Alexander (formerly 'Nicky Beat' of punk legends the **Weirdos**). *Cocked And Loaded* was a marked improvement on its predecessor; the band had matured as songwriters and Lewis's vocals were stronger and more convincing. *Hollywood Vampires* saw them diversifying musically, but retaining the essential energy and rough edges for which they had become renowned. Touring as support to **Skid Row** in Europe, it at last looked as though Guns would no longer have to look longingly at the phenomenal success his former band had achieved in his absence. However, it was not to be. As the group disintegrated, Guns went on to form a new outfit, Killing Machine, while Lewis formed Filthy Lucre. However, L.A. Guns were soon re-formed when both these bands failed. *Vicious Circle* continued the vampiric metaphors of the group's previous album with the track 'Crystal Eyes', a song also included on *Hollywood Vampires*. Greeted as a strong return from a group still held in high regard, it was arguably the best recorded work to date by either Guns or Lewis.
● ALBUMS: *L.A. Guns* (PolyGram 1988)★★, *Cocked And Loaded* (PolyGram 1989)★★★, *Hollywood Vampires* (PolyGram 1991)★★★, *Vicious Circle* (PolyGram 1994)★★★.
● VIDEOS: *One More Reason* (1989), *Love, Peace & Geese* (1990).

L.A. Mix

Despite the title this is a British concern, L.A. standing for frontman Les Adams, a long-term disco mixer and club DJ, and his production partner and wife, Emma Freilich. Adams has earned a weighty crust in the late 80s/early 90s releasing pop-house singles like 'Check This Out' (UK number 6) and 'Get Loose', a hit after the team had been diagnosed by **Stock, Aitken And Waterman** as being 'unlikely to score another hit'. They were not without their detractors but, as Adams insisted: 'We never said we set out to break new ground or deliver a message. We just want to make dance records that people will enjoy and buy'. He had already taken Maurice Joshua's 'This Is Acid' to the top of the US club charts in 1988. However, chart placings for subsequent singles, 'Love Together', 'Coming Back For More', 'Mysteries' etc. were comparatively poor. His 1991 album for **A&M** was a familiar blend of old school British soul dance, including **Juliet Roberts** on 'All Mine' and Beverley Brown on 'Mysteries Of Love'. Another of his sometime vocalists, Jazzie P, would embark on a solo career for the same record label. Adams continued to concentrate on production work, including 'Baby Love' for **Dannii Minogue**.

● ALBUMS: *On The Side* (A&M 1989)★★★, *Coming Back For More* (A&M 1991)★★.

L.A. Woman - The Doors

The final **Doors** album to feature vocalist Jim Morrison reaffirmed the quartet's grasp of blues/rock. Beset by personal and professional problems, they retreated to a rehearsal room, cast such pressures aside and recorded several of their most memorable compositions. The musicianship is uniformly excellent, the interplay between guitarist Robbie Krieger and keyboard player Ray Manzarek exudes confidence and empathy, while the strength and nuances of Morrison's voice add an unmistakable resonance. His death within weeks of the album's completion inevitably casts a pall over its content, especially the eerie rain and the funereal electric piano of 'Riders On The Storm'.

● Tracks: *The Changeling; Love Her Madly; Been Down So Long; Cars Hiss By My Window; L.A. Woman; L'America; Hyacinth House; Crawling King Snake; The W.A.S.P. (Texas Radio And The Big Beat); Riders On The Storm.*
● First released 1971
● UK peak chart position: 28
● USA peak chart position: 9

L.A.M.F. - The Heartbreakers

The **Heartbreakers** revolved around two former members of the **New York Dolls**, **Johnny Thunders** and Jerry Nolan. Having decamped to London in 1976, they became an integral part of the early punk circuit, before their solitary studio album. Although hampered by an insubstantial mix, the set contains some of the era's most expressive songs, notably 'Born Too Loose' and 'Chinese Rocks', the latter a chilling account of heroin addiction, co-written with Dee Dee Ramone. Tight, unfussy playing emphasizes the power of material that proved pivotal in the development of the new music in both the UK and USA. Sadly, the featured line-up disintegrated soon afterwards and numerous permutations failed to recreate its strengths.

● Tracks: *Born Too Loose; Baby Talk; All By Myself; I Wanna Be Loved; It's Not Enough; Chinese Rocks; Get Off The Phone; Pirate Love; One Track Mind; I Love You; Goin' Steady; Let Go.*
● First released 1977
● UK peak chart position: 55
● USA peak chart position: did not chart

L.V.

b. Larry Sanders, Los Angeles, California, USA. His stage name an acronym for Large Variety, engaging gospel/soul singer L.V. first came to prominence through his contribution to the huge international success of rapper **Coolio**'s 'Gangsta's Paradise'. For many, it was L.V.'s soaring vocal refrain that made the song so memorable, as much as Coolio's bleak, understated narrative. L.V. grew up the youngest of six brothers, his interest in music fired by his father's skills in singing gospel and R&B, while still working as a carpenter. He sang in talent shows throughout his high school years, usually covering classic soul material. When he attended college he majored in music and joined the gospel group Voices Of South Central. However, in the mid-80s he became the innocent victim of a mistaken identity shooting, and was shot nine times at close range outside his home in South Central, Los Angeles. Hospitalized for two months, he spent the next two years in a wheelchair. Although already religious, the event hardened his spiritual resolve. When 'Gangsta's Paradise' became a major hit, it was due in no small part to **Stevie Wonder**'s allowing L.V. and Coolio to adapt the song from his 'Pastime Paradise'. All three later appeared on stage together to sing the song at the 1995 *Billboard* Awards ceremony. He followed up this collaborative success with the release of his own single, 'Throw Your Hands Up', featuring **Naughty By Nature**, and his debut album.

● ALBUMS: *I Am L.V.* (Tommy Boy 1996)★★★.

L7

Guitarist/vocalists Donita Sparks (b. 8 April 1963, Chicago, Illinois, USA) and Suzi Gardner (b. 1 August 1960, Sacramento, California, USA) formed L7 in the mid-80s, linking with Jennifer Finch (b. 5 August 1966, Los Angeles, California, USA; bass, vocals) and trying several drummers, finally finding Dee Plakas (b. 9 November 1960, Chicago, Illinois, USA) after domestic touring to promote *L7*, supporting **Bad Religion** (drummer on their debut album was Roy Kolltsky). The band's raw punk-metal caught the interest of **Sup Pop Records**, who released *Smell The Magic*, a raucous, grunge-flavoured blast that further enhanced the band's growing underground reputation. *Bricks Are Heavy* brought major success, with the surprisingly poppy 'Pretend We're Dead' becoming a major hit on both sides of the Atlantic. Subsequently, the band became darlings of the music press with their multi-coloured hair and shock-tactic humour - at 1992's Reading Festival, Sparks retaliated against missile throwers by removing her tampon on stage and throwing it into the crowd, and later dropped her shorts during a live television performance on *The Word* - but the band's serious side led them to form Rock For Choice, a pro-abortion women's rights organization that has gathered supporters from **Pearl Jam** to **Corrosion Of Conformity** for fund-raising concerts. L7 went on to appear as a band named Camel Lips in a

John Waters film, *Serial Mom*, before *Hungry For Stink* picked up where *Bricks Are Heavy* left off, blending serious and humorous lyrics against a still-thunderous musical backdrop. Jennifer Finch departed in the summer of 1996 and formed Lyme. Her replacement was Gail Greenwood from **Belly**, who provided greater musical diversity on 1997's *The Beauty Process: Triple Platinum*.

● ALBUMS: *L7* (Epitaph 1988)★★★, *Smell The Magic* mini-album (Sup Pop 1990)★★★, *Bricks Are Heavy* (Slash/London 1992)★★★★, *Hungry For Stink* (Slash/London 1994)★★★, *The Beauty Process: Triple Platinum* (Slash/Reprise 1997)★★★.

La Bouche

A duo of D. Lane McCray Jnr. and Melanie Thompson, German pop/dance act La Bouche achieved instant success when their debut single, 'Sweet Dreams', became a European best-seller and topped the German charts, selling over half a million copies in the process. An accompanying album of the same title was also released in 1995, and rose to number 5 in the German charts. A second single, 'Fallin' In Love', was then released in the USA in an attempt to breach international markets. The group is produced by Uli Brenner and Amir Saraf, who have also enjoyed considerable success and international acclaim as the creative force behind Le Click.

● ALBUMS: *Sweet Dreams* (Hansa 1995)★★★★, *S.O.S.* (RCA 1998)★★★.

La Cage Aux Folles

After experiencing his biggest hits with the all-frills and femininity of *Hello, Dolly!* and *Mame*, composer and lyricist **Jerry Herman** gave Broadway a dose of effeminacy in 1983 with its first homosexual musical, *La Cage Aux Folles*. It opened at the Palace Theatre on 21 August with a book by Harvey Fierstein based on the play by Jean Poiret and the cult 1978 French-Italian movie, which itself was inspired by the real-life Les Allonges by the harbour in St. Tropez. The La Cage Aux Folles nightclub is owned by Georges (Gene Barry), whose cosy 20 years 'marriage' to his transvestite star Albin (George Hearn), is disturbed when Jean-Michel (John Weiner), Georges' son from his 'closet days', announces that he is to be married to the daughter of a family who would just not understand or appreciate his father's long-standing domestic relationship. Albin (stage name Zaza) has to fade into the background for a time, but returns to the scene masquerading as Georges' wife. Despite the show's highly contemporary theme, Herman's score was good old-fashioned musical comedy with a couple of beautifully poignant ballads, 'Song On The Sand (La Da Da Da)' and 'Look Over There', the jaunty 'With You On My Arm', the defiant 'I Am What I Am', a rousing 'The Best Of Times', plus 'A Little More Mascara', 'Masculinity', and an hilarious tour of 'La Cage Aux Folles': 'It's slightly bawdy and a little bit 'new wave'/You may be dancing with a girl

who needs a shave . . . Eccentric couples always punctuate the scene/A pair of eunuchs and a nun with a marine.' The show was a tremendous success, and stayed on Broadway for 1,176 performances and toured throughout the USA. Gene Barry, who has a reputation in America as a song-and-dance man but whose main claim to fame internationally is due to television programmes such as *Burke's Law*, was a revelation. He was nominated for a Tony for best actor but the award went to George Hearn, and the show also won for best musical, score, book, director (Arthur Laurents), and costumes. Hearn recreated his role for the London production, which co-starred British actor Denis Quilley and ran for nine months. In 1994, a new US national touring company starred Walter Charles as Georges and Lee Roy Reams as Albin.

La Costa

b. LaCosta Tucker, 6 April 1951, Seminole, Texas, USA. The elder sister of **Tanya Tucker**. During the 60s, she worked briefly with her sister in a group called the Country Westerners in Phoenix, but became disenchanted with a musical career and left to work in a hospital in Toltrec, Arizona. After sister Tanya's chart hit with 'Delta Dawn' in 1972, she returned to music and between 1974 and 1978, recording as La Costa for **Capitol**, she registered 12 country chart hits. These included Top 20 successes with 'Get On My Love Train', 'He Took Me For A Ride', 'This House Runs On Sunshine' and 'Western Man'. Since then, in spite of a change of label to Elektra, only two further hits (both minor) have followed; the last, 'Love Take It Easy On Me', released under her full name of LaCosta Tucker, was in 1982.

● ALBUMS: *Get On My Love Train* (Capitol 1974)★★★, *With All My Love* (Capitol 1975)★★, *Lovin' Somebody* (Capitol 1976)★★★, *Changing All The Time* (Elektra 1980)★★.

La Cucina

Likened to everyone from **Les Negresses Vertes** to **Madness**, La Cucina were a fun and fundamental plank in the development of UK roots music of the early 90s. They were formed in Southampton, England, in 1988, from the ashes of indie band Who's In The Kitchen?. Originally a trio of Owain Clarke (vocals, guitar, keyboards), Dylan Clarke (bass/vocals) and Eliseo D'Agostino (accordion), they concentrated on recreating Neopolitan-styled songs. However, after performing as a seven piece at a Southampton pub, with Scott Tobin (drums, once a part-time member of the **Levellers**), Jock Tyldesley (fiddle) and a Sikh priest on tablas, they decided that the band needed to have a more eclectic musical foothold. Enthusiastic audience receptions confirmed that the more dance-orientated their sound was, the better. Tobin joined on a permanent basis, with Rob Greenstock (conga; ex-Steam Kings) completing the line-up in October 1991 (Tyldesley and Dylan Clarke also played with local friends the **Flatville Aces**, but Clarke opted for La Cucina because of the greater opportunities for song-writing). They side-stepped musical categorisation by employing Cajun fiddle alongside the percussive force of rave music, Latin American piano and skewed, highly original songs roughly in the spirit of Neopolitan standards. There were some who now accused them of not being authentic Italians. (D'Agostino, a second-generation Neopolitan capable of perfectly fluent English, sometimes used to adopt an Italian accent to help get bookings.) However, this is hardly of concern to the band themselves, nor should it be to audiences: 'The way that we see it is that we play good dance music, people come along and have a good time, a dance. We see it as a bit of a show really, a spectacle.' Their liberal adoption of Latin traditions to their own ends is more of an asset than a disclaimer, as can be demonstrated by playing their early cassettes, *La Luna Spinosa* and *Morte Accidentale De Musiciste*, alongside their 1994 CD release, *Chucheria*. Self-produced and promoted, *Chucheria* offered new listeners a thrilling introduction to the band's vibrant stage show, but also demonstrated their increasing instrumental sophistica-tion and ability to write songs that borrow from a number of traditions without compromising the group's identity. *Nabúmla* was even better, a seamless collection of songs drawing on a bewildering range of musical styles.

● ALBUMS: *La Luna Spinosa* cassette only (1989)★★★, *Morte Accidentale De Musiciste* cassette only (1990)★★★, *Kemado* cassette only (1992)★★★, *Chucheria* (1994)★★★★, *Nabúmla* (Osmosys 1996)★★★★.

La De Das

Formed in 1965 in New Zealand, the La De Das initially comprised **Kevin Borich** (guitar/vocals), Howard Bruce (organ), Phil Key (vocals/slide guitar), Trevor Wilson (bass) and Nelson Brett (drums). The group were heav-ily influenced by the R&B style of the fledgling **Rolling Stones** and achieved local success in New Zealand with chart singles and an album. The band journeyed to Sydney, Australia in 1967, as did so many other successful New Zealand bands. During this period, drummer Nelson Brett was replaced by Brian Harris, and in turn, by Keith Barber. After taking a while to consolidate, the band adopted a more psychedelic, adventurous approach recording a concept album, *The Happy Prince*, with sophisticated recording techniques and a narration blending the songs together. The band went to the UK in 1969 and recorded at London's Abbey Road studios. Further line-up changes occurred and with the group now performing as a quartet with Barber, Borich, Key and new bassist Peter Roberts, the band emerged with a more hard rock sound. By 1971-72 the band had become one of the biggest in Australia, but by late 1972 Borich was the sole survivor from the early days, and the band now largely a vehicle for his guitar playing. Phil Key went on to lead Band Of Light, but died in 1985.

● ALBUMS: *La De Das* (1966)★★, *Find Us A Way* (1967)★★, *The Happy Prince* (1969)★★★★, *Rock And Roll Sandwich* (1973)★★★, *Legend* (1975)★★★, *Rock And Roll Decade* (1981)★★.

La Dusseldorf

This cult German group was founded by guitarist/vocalist Klaus Dinger, formerly of **Neu**. Comprising Thomas Dinger (percussion/vocals), Hans Lampe (percussion/synthesizer/keyboards), Nikolaus Van Rhein (keyboards), Harald Konietzo (bass) and Andreas Schell (piano), they completed *La Dusseldorf*, originally issued in 1976, but it was denied a UK release until 1978, when it was licensed to the **WEA**/Radar label. The group maintained the insistent pulsebeat of Neu, but offered a much fuller sound, shown to great effect on *Viva*. With Schell now musically superfluous, the set acknowledged the concurrent punk movement without deflecting from La Dusseldorf's individuality, but it failed to reap due commercial rewards. *Individuellos* maintained the Dingers brothers' capacity for surprise and inventiveness, but their unique version of German rock was increasingly obscured by the elec-tro-dance styles of **Kraftwerk** and **D.A.F.** and the unit was subsequently dissolved.

● ALBUMS: *La Dusseldorf* (1976)★★★★, *Viva* (1978),★★★ *Individuellos* (1981)★★★.

La Faro, Scott

b. 3 April 1936, Newark, New Jersey, USA, d. 6 July 1961. After playing clarinet and saxophones in his early teens, La Faro switched to bass when he was 17 years old. Despite this late start, it was only a couple of years before he was good enough to join the **Buddy Morrow** band. Alerted to contemporary developments in jazz bass playing by listening to **Percy Heath** and **Paul Chambers** on records, La Faro quit Morrow late in 1956 while the band was in Los Angeles. During the next two years he played with several prominent west coast musicians, including **Chet Baker**, **Buddy De Franco**, **Sonny Rollins** and **Herb Geller**. In 1958, La Faro recorded with **Harold Land** and **Hampton Hawes**, and the following year joined **Paul Motian** and **Bill Evans** to form the Bill Evans Trio. This group played an important role in reshaping ideas on how the bass should function in a piano/bass/drums line-up. From being merely a supportive instrument which had only briefly enjoyed front-line status, after La Faro's work with Evans the bass became a major instrumental voice in its own right with considerable harmonic freedom. In 1959, La Faro worked with **Thelonious Monk** and the following year recorded with **Ornette Coleman**. La Faro's exceptional technique was facilitated by modifi-cations he made to his instrument to accommodate his remarkably fast fingering. La Faro's death, in a road accident, came when he was just turned 25 years of age. His influence on bass playing in jazz was akin to that of **Jimmy Blanton** who, with sad coincidence, also died in his early twenties.

● ALBUMS: *Joe Gordon And Scott La Faro* reissue (1993)★★, with Joe Gordon *West Coast Days* (Fresh Sounds 1994)★★★.

La Lugh

From Balymaskellet, Ravensdale, near Dundalk, Eire, Irish folk quintet La Lugh's name translates as 'the day of Lugh', and refers to the ancient pagan god Lugh, patron of arts and crafts and father of Cuchulainn in Gaelic mythology. The group is led by Gerry O'Connor (b. Dundalk, Eire; fiddle), a fiddle teacher and also a member of Skylark and **Four Men And A Dog**, and his partner Eithne Ni Uallachain (flute, vocals). Together they preside over an arsenal of songs drawn from Irish border folk lore as well as Scottish, English and Shetland traditions, with the aid of Seanie McPhail (guitar), classically trained musician Clare O'Donoghue (cello) and, occasionally, Martin O'Hare (flute/bodhran; also a member of Ashplant). Their debut album was released in 1993 and confirmed the charm of their ensemble playing, with the self-titled collection comprising original compositions as well as rarely heard traditional County Louth songs. *Brighid's Kiss* featured Breton guitarist Gilles LeBigot and Angolan percussionist Mario N'Gomo, and was another outstanding collection reminiscent of **Clannad** at their peak.

● ALBUMS: *La Lugh* (Claddagh 1993)★★★, *Brighid's Kiss* (Lughnasa 1996)★★★★.

La Lupe

b. Lupe Victoria Yoli Raymond, 23 December c.1940, Santiago de Cuba, Oriente Province, Cuba. Notorious for her frenzied stage performances and admired by some as the epitome of camp, La Lupe (aka La Yi Yi Yi) peaked in popularity in the second half of the 60s. La Lupe came from a poor background. She played truant from school to enter a singing competition on the radio and won first prize. At her father's insistence, she finished a course of teacher training. While working as a schoolteacher in Havana, La Lupe joined the Trio Los Tropicales and appeared with them at the El Roco nightspot, but was later thrown out of the group for her undisciplined behaviour. Her 1959 solo debut at another Havana nightclub, La Red, coincided with the period of the Cuban revolution. La Lupe's combination of rock 'n' roll numbers sung in Spanish and anarchical stage antics became a great success and she made several hit albums. However, her outrageousness became too unpalatable for the increasingly puritanical post-revolutionary regime, which eventually compelled her to leave Cuba at the beginning of 1962. She moved to Mexico, but failed to gain acceptance there.

La Lupe relocated to New York and her flagging career was given a boost when compatriot **Mongo Santamaría** teamed up with her to make *Mongo Introduces La Lupe* in 1963. The album, which marked her transition to typical Latin music, featured percussionists **Kako** and Osvaldo 'Chi Hua Hua' Martínez and trumpeter **Alfredo 'Chocolate' Armenteros**. She also performed on Mongo's 1963 Latin Top 10 crossover hit 'Watermelon Man'. She signed with Tico Records and was paired with **Tito Puente** and his big band for *Tito Puente Swings, The Exciting Lupe Sings* in 1965. She shot to stardom and the album went gold. The Latin press in New York named her singer of the year in 1965 and 1966. La Lupe recorded three more collaborations with Puente in the 60s and worked with prominent Latin names, such as producer **Al Santiago**, Cuban arranger/musical director **Arturo 'Chico' O'Farrill**, arranger/pianist Héctor Rivera and Puerto Rican composer C. Curet Alonso.

Various scandals started to rock her career. In Puerto Rico for example, where she had earlier won an award for unprecedented record sales, she was banned from appearing on television because she had torn off her clothing during a live broadcast. Her already precarious career was said to have suffered a major blow in the mid-70s when Fania Records absorbed Tico. Label boss Jerry Masucci was keen to develop the career of another woman singer on Tico's roster, the 'safer' **Celia Cruz**, and La Lupe was neglected as a consequence. Despite releasing further albums between 1977 and 1980, including another collaboration with Puente, she failed to recapture her former success, and her career went into further decline. La Lupe retired from performing in the early 80s amidst an escalation of personal problems. Massive bills for her husband's mental health care and large donations to the African-derived Santaria religion had forced her into destitution, and she and her family were repeatedly made homeless. She became paralysed following a domestic accident and was healed by an evangelical preacher. She converted to evangelicalism and recorded Christian orientated material in the late 80s.

● ALBUMS: *Con El Diablo En El Cuerpo . . .* (1960)★★★, *La Lupe Is Back, Es Lupe*, with Mongo Santamaría *Mongo Introduces La Lupe* (1963, reissued as *Mongo y La Lupe* in 1973)★★★★, with Tito Puente *La Excitante Lupe Canta Con El Maestro Tito Puente/Tito Puente Swings, The Exciting Lupe Sings* (1965)★★★★, with Puente *Tú y Yo/You 'N' Me* (c.1965)★★★, with Puente *Homenaje A Rafael Hernández* (1966)★★★, *La Lupe y su Alma Venezolana* (1966)★★★★, with Puente *The King And I/El Rey y Yo* (1967)★★★, *Two Sides Of La Lupe/Dos Lados De La Lupe* (1968)★★★, *Queen Of Latin Soul/Reina De La Canción Latina* (1968)★★★★, *La Lupe's Era/La Era De La Lupe* (1968),★★★ *La Lupe Es La Reina/La Lupe The Queen* (1969)★★★, *Definitely La Yi Yi Yi/Definitivamente La Yi Yi Yi* (1969)★★★, *That Genius Called The Queen . . .* (1970)★★★★, *La Lupe In Madrid Vol. 17* (1971)★★★, *La Lupe, The Queen, Stop! I'm Free Again* (1972)★★★, *Pero Como Va Ser?* (1973)★★★, with C. Curet Alonso *Un Encuentro Con La Lupe* (1974)★★★, with various artists *Tico - Alegre All Stars Recorded Live At Carnegie Hall, Vol. I* (1974)★★★★, *Unica En Su Clase* (1977)★★★, with Puente *La Pareja* (1979)★★, *En Algo Nuevo* (1980)★★.

● COMPILATIONS: *Lo Mejor de La Lupe* (1974)★★★, *Apasionada* (1978)★★★, *Too Much* (1989)★★★★.

La Momposina, Toto

b. Columbia. A cantadora singer from Bogota, Columbia, Toto La Momposina was born into a family of musicians, who put her on stage at a tender age as part of their dance troupe. By the age of 12 she began singing professionally with other members of her family, inheriting the position once held by her mother. Cantadoras are, according to the artist herself, 'supposed to be very wise, to know about medicine, cooking, spiritual things . . . we become channels for many things.' Her songbook encompasses much of the folklore of Columbia, including such traditional forms as bailes cantados (sung dances), gaitas (cumbia dances) and sesetos (saloon dances). This richness of texture reflects Columbian history, and the influences of native peoples, Africans and their mixed race offspring following slavery, and nearby Cuban music. To this La Momposina added her experiences of voice training and dance tuition in France. Her current band continues the family thread, featuring her son as musical director, one of her daughters as backing vocalist and her granddaughter, who was only three years old when she first took the stage. A long waiting list of cousins and non-family members audition every two years in an attempt to join what is among Columbia's most popular bands. Her debut international release was recorded for **Real World Records** in separate sessions in 1991 and 1992, and finally released to support a European tour in 1993.

● ALBUMS: *Toto La Momposina* (Real World 1993)★★★★, *Carmelina* (Yard High 1997)★★★.

La Roca, Pete

b. Peter Sims, 7 April 1938, New York City, New York, USA. Although classically trained, drummer La Roca's early professional work was with Latin bands (hence his adopted name). Before he was out of his teens he was playing jazz with some of the music's leading exponents, including **Sonny Rollins** with whom he worked for two years. In the late 50s and early 60s La Roca played with **Jackie McLean**, **Slide Hampton** and **John Coltrane**. Later, he worked with, among others, **Art Farmer** and **Freddie Hubbard**, but, disenchanted with the music scene of the mid-60s, he retired in 1968 to practice law. Subsequent returns to music have proved only fleeting. He was a vigorous exponent of the complex free-time school of jazz, a concept that defies all preconceptions of the drummer's role.

● ALBUMS: *Basra* (1965)★★★, *Bliss!/Turkish Women At The Baths* (1967)★★.

La Vallee

Barbet Schroeder directed this 1972 film in which the French cast travels to New Guinea seeking the lost valley of its title. Its idealistic view of back-to-nature hippie lifestyles proved some five years out-of-date and *La Vallee* would have inspired little interest but for the involvement of **Pink Floyd**. The group had already scored a previous Schroeder feature, *More* (1969) and

he invited them to contribute to this project. The results were issued on *Obscured By Clouds*, a release sandwiched between ground-breaking albums **Meddle** and **Dark Side Of The Moon**. Although worthwhile in its own right, *Obscured By Clouds* contained several short pieces of mood music ideally suited for airplay on US FM stations. This facilitated acceptance of its successor's lengthier, more complex, compositions.

La Velle

b. La Velle McKinnie, 22 May 1944, Kankakee, Illinois, USA. Born into a musical family, McKinnie was a child prodigy, singing at the age of three, taking piano lessons from four, and at five was a member of the Little Black Angels gospel group with whom she appeared on *The Ed Sullivan Show*. Six years later she was studying at Chicago's American Conservatory of Music. As a young teenager, she sang classical music including oratorios and opera, appearing in productions of Handel's *Messiah*, Verdi's *Tosca*, Puccini's *Madame Butterfly*, and Bizet's *Carmen*. Earning a living in music, however, thrust her onto the nightclub and hotel lounge circuit with engagements in Chicago, Dallas and Las Vegas. She visited Europe, becoming very popular in France and decided to base herself in Paris. Her repertoire had by now encompassed the great standards of popular song with touches of jazz, the blues and gospel. She ventured into a rock-funk mode for a time, but her career faltered a little, reviving in the late 80s by which time she was based in Geneva, Switzerland. She recorded with **Ray Brown**, **Guy Lafitte**, and others, and returned to Paris for a 1992 engagement with **Archie Shepp**, playing in *Black Ballad* at the Casino de Paris. She also made a hit at the 1994 Marciac jazz festival. She has worked extensively on radio and television both on-screen and on advertising jingles. Among her single recordings have been winners of the Disques D'or Européen (1980 and 1983) while her album appearances include guest spots on the rock operas *Deamonia* and *Nostradamus*, and backing to **Dee Dee Bridgewater** and **Ray Charles**. Her albums under her own name clearly demonstrate her highly developed sense of style. Always musical, she ranges through her repertoire with flair and great zest. Her piano-playing is sure and sound as befits one with her background. Although her name remains little known outside France and Switzerland, her reputation is gradually spreading throughout Europe.

● ALBUMS: with Bessie Griffin *Gospel* (1974)★★★, *Right Now* (1980)★★★, *Brand New Start* (1983)★★★, with Psalms *Psalms* (1987)★★, with Steve Lacy *Festival De Jazz De Besançon* (1989)★★★, *Hot Brass Club* (1989)★★, *Straight Singing'* (OMD 1991)★★★.

La's

The La's were originally formed by artist/musician Mike Badger (b. 18 March 1962) in 1984 in Liverpool, Merseyside, England, but his departure in 1986 left a line-up comprising songwriter Lee Mavers (b. 2 August

1962, Huyton, Liverpool, England; guitar, vocals), John Power (b. 14 September 1967; bass), Paul Hemmings (guitar) and John Timson (drums). Early demo tapes resulted in their signing with **Go! Discs** in 1987. After a well-received debut single, 'Way Out', which hallmarked the group's effortless, 60s-inspired pop, they took a year out before issuing the wonderfully melodic 'There She Goes'. When this too eluded the charts, the La's, far from disillusioned, returned to the studio for two years to perfect tracks for their debut album. The line-up also changed, with Lee's brother Neil (b. 8 July 1971, Huyton, Liverpool, England) taking up drums and ex-Marshmellow Overcoats guitarist Cammy (b. Peter James Camell, 30 June 1967, Huyton, Liverpool, England) joining the line-up. In the meantime, 'There She Goes' became a massive underground favourite, prompting a reissue two years on (after another single, 'Timeless Melody'). In October 1990 it reached the UK Top 20. *The La's* followed that same month, an invigorating and highly musical collection of tunes that matched, and some would argue outstripped, the **Stone Roses**' more garlanded debut. Its comparative lack of impact could be put down to Mavers' truculence in the press, verbally abusing Go! Discs for insisting on releasing the record and disowning its contents: 'That's the worst LP I've ever heard by anyone.' Comparisons with the best of the 60s, notably the **Byrds** and **Beach Boys**, stemmed from the band's obsession with real instruments, creating a rootsy, authentic air. After 'Feelin'' was drawn from the album, the La's set about recording tracks for a new work and spent much of summer 1991 touring America and Japan. Little was then heard of the band for the next four years, which took few acquainted with Mavers' studio perfectionism by surprise. The delays proved too much for Power, however, who departed to set up **Cast**. Back in the notoriously insular La's camp, rumours continued to circulate of madness and drug addiction. A collaboration with Edgar Summertyme of the **Stairs** was vaunted, but no public assignments were forthcoming. Mavers finally performed a solo acoustic set in 1995, in support of **Paul Weller**, which went so badly awry that he had the plug pulled on him. In April he spoke to the *New Musical Express* about a 'second' La's album. Sessions were undertaken in the west London studio owned by Rat Scabies of the **Damned**, with Mavers playing all the instruments.

● ALBUMS: *The La's* (Go! Discs 1990)★★★★, *Strange Things Happening* (Rounder 1994)★★.

LaBarbera, Joe

b. 22 February 1948, Mount Morris, New York, USA. The youngest of three musically active brothers, LaBarbera was taught to play drums by his father before moving on to **Berklee College Of Music**. In the late 60s he worked and recorded with a number of jazz musicians, including his brother **Pat LaBarbera**, and also showed a special aptitude for accompanying singers. After a brief stint with **Woody Herman** in the 70s he

joined **Chuck Mangione** with whom he remained for four years. He then joined **Bill Evans** for two years and for much of the 80s was with singer **Tony Bennett**. A highly sophisticated, stylish and subtle player, his work with singers is light, uncluttered and always propulsive. As an accompanist to instrumentalists, he is similarly swinging and supportive.

● ALBUMS: with Chuck Mangione *Land Of Make Believe* (Mercury 1973)★★★, with Bill Evans *The Paris Concert: Edition One* (Elektra 1979)★★★★, with Norma Winstone *Well Kept Secret* (Hot House 1993)★★★.

LaBarbera, Pat

b. Pascel LaBarbera, 7 April 1944, Warsaw, New York, USA. Older brother of John and **Joe LaBarbera**, he, too, was first taught by his father. He later studied at **Berklee College Of Music** from where he went into **Buddy Rich**'s band as featured tenor saxophone soloist. In the mid-70s he moved to Canada and then joined **Elvin Jones**. A powerful player with a style rooted in post-**John Coltrane** tenor thinking, his talent is such that he has not fallen into the self-induced trap which befell so many others. His energy and improvisational skills are linked to an engaging romantic flavour which he displays on several other instruments in the saxophone family and also the flute.

● ALBUMS: with Buddy Rich *Buddy And Soul* (Pacific Jazz 1969)★★★, *Pass It On* (Pausa 1976)★★★, with Elvin Jones *The Main Force* (Vanguard 1976)★★.

LaBeef, Sleepy

b. Thomas Paulsey LaBeff, 20 July 1935, near Smackover, Arkansas, USA. (The family name was originally LaBoeuf). The tenth of 10 children, his early years were spent on the small family farm, where his father taught him to play guitar. He gained the nickname of Sleepy on his first day at school owing to heavy-lidded eyes that gave the impression that he was half asleep. In 1953, he relocated to Houston, where he worked a land surveyor and briefly to earn extra income as a wrestler - a pastime probably encouraged by his 6 feet 7 inches. After first singing gospel country on local radio and greatly inspired by the singing and guitar playing of **Sister Rosetta Thorpe** and **Martha Lou Carson**, he formed his own country/rockabilly band and played regularly on the *Houston Jamboree*. He first recorded as Sleepy La Beff for Starday in 1956, but later recorded, sometimes as Tommy LaBeff, for various others including **Mercury** and obscure labels such as Wayside and Dixie, before moving to Nashville in 1964. In 1968, after recording for **Columbia**, he gained a minor hit with 'Every Day'. The following year he joined **Shelby Singleton**'s Plantation label, where he gained his second and surprisingly his final chart hit (at writing) with his version of **Frankie Miller**'s 1959 hit 'Black Land Farmer'. In 1974, when Singleton took over **Sun Records**, LaBeef moved to the label and recorded rockabilly and country. In 1978, a compilation of tracks from *The Bulls Night Out* and *1977 Rockabilly* were released in the UK as *Beefy Rockabilly* on the Charly label. He toured extensively in America and was well received on European tours, including appearances in London at the 1979 and 1987 Wembley Festivals. On the former visit he also recorded *Rockabilly Heavyweight* with backing from British musicians. Some critic's claim that LaBeef's recordings never seemed to match his stage performances, where he captivated audiences with his loud deep voiced vocals and his brilliant guitar playing. In 1981, he moved to **Rounder Records** where his first album gained good reviews and featured one of his idols, Martha Lou Carson, singing harmonies on two of her gospel numbers 'Wonderful Time Up There' and 'Satisfied'. The label also later captured some of his dazzling stage delivery by recording *Nothin' But The Truth* live on stage in a smoky honky tonk. In 1979, author Peter Guralnick featured LaBeef in his informative work *Lost Highway* and in 1994, Guralnick and his son Jake produced *Strange Things Happening* for Rounder. He continued to record for the label into the 90s. His repertoire is believed to run to 6,000 songs and it has been claimed that he never forgets the words to any of them. They cover all forms of country music, blues, rockabilly, gospel, bluegrass and R&B, which led him to once describe his act's content as 'goosebump' music. One reviewer describing his act once wrote 'the music comes out in guitar driven torrents, often in extended stream-of-consciousness medleys that leave the listeners gaping in astonishment'. He has been termed one of the last of the rockabilly greats and the *New York Times* called him 'a national treasure'. In spite of such glowing praise, it seems true that his popularity and stardom has never quite matched up to his undisputed talents.

● ALBUMS: *Black Land Farmer* (Plantation 1971)★★★, *The Bulls Night Out* (Sun 1974)★★★, *Western Gold* (Sun 1976)★★★, *1977 Rockabilly* gold vinyl (Sun 1977)★★★, *Down Home Rockabilly* gold vinyl (Sun 1979)★★★, *Electricity* (1979)★★★, *It Ain't What You Eat It's The Way That You Chew It* (Rounder 1981)★★★, *Nothin' But The Truth* (Rounder 1987)★★★, *Strange Things Happening* (Rounder 1994)★★★, *I'll Never Lay My Guitar Down* (Rounder 1996)★★★.

● COMPILATIONS: *Beefy Rockabilly* (Charly 1978), *Early Rare And Rockin' Sides* (Baron 1979)★★★, *Larger Than Life* 6-CD box set (Bear Family 1997)★★★.

LaBelle

This popular soul act evolved from two friends, **Patti LaBelle** (b. Patricia Holte, 24 May 1944, Philadelphia, Pennsylvania, USA) and Cindy Birdsong (b. 15 December 1939, Camden, New Jersey, USA), who sang together in a high school group, the Ordettes. In 1962, they teamed up with two girls from another local attraction, the Del Capris - **Nona Hendryx** (b. 18 August 1945, Trenton, New Jersey, USA) and Sarah Dash (b. 24 May 1942, Trenton, New Jersey, USA). Philadelphia producer Bobby Martin named the quartet after a local label, Bluebell Records, and the group

became Patti LaBelle And The Blue-Belles. Infamous for their emotional recordings of 'You'll Never Walk Alone', 'Over The Rainbow' and 'Danny Boy', the quartet also wrung a fitting melodrama from 'I Sold My Heart To The Junkman' and 'Down The Aisle (Wedding Song)'. This almost kitchen-sink facet has obscured their more lasting work, of which 'Groovy Kind Of Love' (later a hit for the **Mindbenders**) is a fine example. Cindy Birdsong left the group in 1967 to replace **Florence Ballard** in the **Supremes**, but the remaining trio stayed together despite failing commercial fortunes. Expatriate Briton Vicki Wickham, a former producer on UK television's pop show *Ready Steady Go!*, became their manager and suggested the trio drop their anachronistic name and image and embrace a rock-orientated direction. Having supported the **Who** on a late 60s concert tour, LaBelle then accompanied **Laura Nyro** on *Gonna Take A Miracle*, a session that inspired their album debut. One of the few female groups to emerge from the passive 60s to embrace the radical styles of the next decade, their album releases won critical praise, but the trio did not gain commercial success until the release of *Nightbirds*. The 1975 single 'Lady Marmalade (Voulez-Vous Coucher Avec Moi Ce Soir?)' was an international hit single produced by **Allen Toussaint** and composed by **Bob Crewe** and Kenny Nolan. Subsequent singles, however, failed to emulate this achievement. *Phoenix* and *Chameleon* were less consistent, although the group continued to court attention for their outlandish, highly visual stage costumes. LaBelle owed much of its individuality to Nona Hendryx, who emerged as an inventive and distinctive composer. Her sudden departure in 1976 was a fatal blow and the group broke apart. Patti LaBelle embarked on a solo career and has since enjoyed considerable success.

● ALBUMS: as Patti LaBelle And The Blue-Belles *Sweethearts Of The Apollo* (Atlantic 1963)★★★, *Sleigh Bells, Jingle Belles* (Atlantic 1963)★★, *On Stage* (Atlantic 1964)★★, *Over The Rainbow* (Atlantic 1966)★★; as LaBelle *LaBelle* (Warners 1971)★★★, *Moonshadow* (Warners 1972)★★★, *Pressure Cookin'* (1973)★★★★, *Nightbirds* (Epic 1974)★★★★, *Phoenix* (Epic 1975)★★, *Chameleon* (Epic 1976)★★.

● COMPILATIONS: *The Early Years* (1993)★★★, *Over The Rainbow - The Atlantic Years* (1994)★★★, *Something Silver* (Warners 1997)★★★.

LaBelle, Patti

b. Patricia Holte, 24 May 1944, Philadelphia, Pennsylvania, USA. The former leader of **LaBelle** began her solo career in 1976. Although her first releases showed promise, she was unable to regain the profile enjoyed by her former group and at the beginning of the 80s, Patti agreed to tour with a revival of the stage play *Your Arms Are Too Short To Box With God*. The production reached Broadway in 1982 and, with **Al Green** as a co-star, became one of the year's hits. Having made her film debut as a blues singer in *A Soldier's Story* (1984), Patti LaBelle resumed recording with 'Love Has Finally Come At Last', a magnificent duet with **Bobby Womack**. Two tracks from 1984's box-office smash *Beverly Hills Cop*, 'New Attitude' (US Top 20) and 'Stir It Up', also proved popular. 'On My Own', a sentimental duet with **Michael McDonald**, was a spectacular hit in 1986. This million-selling single confirmed LaBelle's return and although some commentators criticize her almost operatic delivery, she remains a powerful and imposing performer. She made a return to the US stage in 1989, performing in various states with the 'lost' **Duke Ellington** musical *Queenie Pie*, and has continued to release strong albums throughout the 90s.

● ALBUMS: *Patti LaBelle* (Epic 1977)★★★, *Tasty* (Epic 1978)★★★, *It's Alright With Me* (Epic 1979)★★★, *Released* (Epic 1980)★★★, *The Spirit's In It* (Philadelphia International 1981)★★★, *I'm In Love Again* (Philadelphia International 1983)★★★, *Patti* (Philadelphia International 1985)★★★, *The Winner In You* (MCA 1986)★★★, *Be Yourself* (MCA 1989)★★, *Starlight Christmas* (MCA 1990)★★★, *Burnin'* (MCA 1991)★★★, *Live!* (MCA 1992)★★, *Gems* (MCA 1994)★★★, *Flame* (MCA 1997)★★★.

● COMPILATIONS: *Best Of ...* (Epic 1986)★★★, *Greatest Hits* (MCA 1996)★★★.

Labour Of Love - UB40

Playing reggae and supporting the UK Labour Party during a decade of Thatcherism and racism demonstrated that these chaps had morals and guts. They eventually prospered (good ultimately conquers bad) and they can now look back and taste their achievement. In the UK, **UB40** have done as much to popularize reggae as **Bob Marley** did for the rest of the world. This is their most refined album and contains some of their major hits. They make a point in the sleeve-notes of informing the listener that all these songs had been recorded by Jamaican artists. No apology is needed - their 'Cherry Oh Baby' and 'Red Red Wine' have become classics for this band. Much respect, irie.

● Tracks: *Cherry Oh Baby; Keep On Moving; Please Don't Make Me Cry; Sweet Sensation; Johnny Too Bad; Red Red Wine; Guilty; She Caught The Train; Version Girl; Many Rivers To Cross.*

● First released 1983

● UK peak chart position: 1

● USA peak chart position: 14

Labradford

A duo of Carter Brown (keyboards) and Mark Nelson (guitar/vocals) from Virginia, USA, Labradford made an immediate impact with their 1995 debut album, *A Stable Reference*. Informed by Brown's studies into early and medieval music, it offered listeners an entirely new take on conventional music semantics, in keeping with their stated intention to 'move beyond pop'. Many critics were enraptured by the group's ability to balance improvised ambient, almost ecclesiastical textures with more accessible passages. *A Stable Reference* was duly voted among the best albums of the year by *Melody*

Maker. Its successor, *Prazision*, was similarly inventive, this time with a greater exploration of Moog synthesizers. The claustrophobic nature of several songs, 'Accelerating On A Smoother Road' in particular, recalled the dense atmospherics of **Joy Division**. The band's recent albums have become successively more experimental and minimal, with *Mi Medea Naranja* reducing song titles down to bare initials ('S', 'G', 'WR' etc.). In the influential post-rock music scene Labradford have established themselves as vital innovators. Nelson also records as Pan-American, releasing a self-titled debut in 1998.

● ALBUMS: *A Stable Reference* (Flying Nun 1995)★★★★, *Prazision* (Flying Nun 1996)★★★, *Labradford* (Blast First 1996)★★★, *Mi Medea Naranja* (Blast First 1997)★★★★.

Lace, Bobbi

Model, actress and singer from Florida, USA. She had a minor role in the 1984 film *Scarface*, and then, as Bobbi Lace, she had several minor US country hits including 'It's Gonna Be Love' with Mark Gray and a revival of **Dusty Springfield**'s 'Son Of A Preacher Man'. She has now dropped the name and performs as Lori Smith.

Lacey, Rubin, Rev.

b. 2 January 1901, Pelahatchie, Mississippi, USA, d. *c.*1972, Bakersfield, California, USA. Learning guitar and mandolin from the unrecorded George Hendrix as a young man, Lacey moved to Jackson, where he contributed to the musical ideas of **Tommy Johnson** and **Ishman Bracey**. In 1927, he recorded a solitary, but outstanding 78 rpm record. Lacey's secular career ended when he became a preacher in 1932, but when rediscovered in 1966 he was a mine of information about both his blues and his preaching careers, and became the chief subject of Alfred Rosenberg's book *The Art Of The American Folk Preacher*.

● COMPILATIONS: *Sorrow Come Pass Me Around* (1975)★★★, *Son House And The Great Delta Blues Singers* (1990)★★★★, *Best Kept Secret* (Lady Bianca 1995)★★★.

Lacy, Steve

b. Steven Lackritz, 23 July 1934, New York City, New York, USA. Few modern jazzmen have chosen the soprano saxophone as their main instrument; Steve Lacy is probably unique in choosing it as his only one. Reputed to be the player who inspired **John Coltrane** to take up the soprano (after which, thousands followed!), he is ultimately responsible for the renaissance and current popularity of the straight horn. He may also be unique for a career that has taken him through virtually every genre of jazz, from dixieland to bebop, free-form and total improvisation. As a child he started piano lessons, then changed to clarinet and finally soprano saxophone. Inspired initially by **Sidney Bechet**, he began his career playing dixieland (two 1954 dates led by trumpeter Dick Sutton were reissued under Lacy's name as *The Complete Jaguar Sessions* in 1986). Then, in an extraordinary switch, he spent the mid-50s working with *avant garde* pioneer **Cecil Taylor** (*In Transition*) and by the end of the decade had also played with **Gil Evans** (*Pacific Standard Time*), **Jimmy Giuffre** and **Sonny Rollins**. His own 1957 debut, *Soprano Saxophone*, featured **Wynton Kelly** and the follow-up, *Steve Lacy Plays The Music Of Thelonious Monk*, marked the beginning of a long, and continuing association with **Mal Waldron**. Both albums also included several tracks by **Thelonious Monk**, by whose music Lacy had become increasingly beguiled. In 1960, he persuaded Monk to hire him as a sideman for 16 weeks, and between 1961 and 1965 he and **Roswell Rudd** co-led a group that played only Monk tunes - 'to find out why they were so beautiful'. (This fascination has remained with him - *School Days*, *Epistrophy*, *Eronel*, *Only Monk* and *More Monk* are all devoted to further exploring, in group and solo context, the great man's compositions.) In 1965, Lacy moved to Europe, where he worked with **Carla Bley** in the Jazz Realities project and co-led a group with **Enrico Rava**, with whom he also toured South America in 1966. In this period, influenced in part by earlier collaborations with **Don Cherry**, Lacy was playing mostly free jazz (*Sortie* and *The Forest And The Zoo*). The focus of his attention would later shift back towards jazz compositions, especially after the mid-60s when he completed his first major piece, 'The Way', a suite based on text from the ancient Chinese *Tao Te Ching*; he has maintained an occasional involvement with total improvisation, most notably on records with **Derek Bailey** (*Company 4*) and **Evan Parker** (*Chirps*). In 1966, he revisited New York and played in a quintet with **Karl Berger** and **Paul Motian** but, finding work scarce, he returned to Europe in 1967, settling in Rome with his Swiss wife, Irene Aebi, who sings and plays cello and violin on many of his albums. Three years later, he relocated to Paris, which has since been his home base. Leading his own group (usually a sextet), he has in the last two decades built up one of the most impressive and diverse recording catalogues in jazz, hitting a peak in the 80s with a series of albums - *Prospectus*, *Furturities*, *The Gleam* and *Momentum* - which show the group honing to perfection the intricate dialogues and seamless blends of invention and discipline so typical of their music. Important group members over the years have included Steve Potts (saxophone), Kent Carter and Jean-Jacques Avenal (both bass), Bobby Few (piano), Oliver Johnson (drums), guest **George Lewis** (trombone) and - perhaps most crucially - Aebi, for whose severe, lieder-style vocals Lacy created what is virtually a new concept of jazz songwriting. He has often set texts by modern writers - *Sons* is a collaboration with Brion Gysin, *Futurities* a series of poems by Robert Creely - but *Tips* is more unusual still, with Lacy shaping his tunes around extracts from the notebooks of painter Georges Braque. Outside of his regular group (currently one of the most adventurous in jazz), Lacy's recent projects have included duos with Potts, **Ran Blake**, Mal Waldron and Gil Evans; plus tributes to Monk and

Herbie Nichols (*Regenerations*, *Change Of Season* and *The ICP Orchestra Performs Nichols - Monk*) in the company of **Misha Mengelberg** and **Han Bennink**, who also collaborated on the *Dutch Masters* recording. Lacy is also one of today's outstanding practitioners of solo saxophone music. Inspired by hearing the solo work of **Anthony Braxton**, he began to develop his own soprano saxophone repertoire in the early 70s and has since developed this over a succession of solo concerts and recordings, the latter including such notable examples of the genre as *Hocus Pocus*, *The Kiss* and *Remains*. Incredibly prolific, Lacy has released over 80 albums under his own name and probably appeared on as many again as a sideman: paradoxically, 1991's *Itinerary* was his first-ever release as leader of a big band. A brilliant composer and improviser, Lacy can be counted one of the most significant jazz figures of the era, his music sure to stand as an enduring treasure. He is, as well, simply an enchanting player. To quote Graham Lock's 1983 comment: 'There are few sounds as distinctive or as lovely as Lacy's soprano, with its comet-trails of bare bones lyricism.'

● ALBUMS: *Soprano Saxophone* aka *Soprano Today* (Original Jazz Classics 1957)★★★★, reissued as *With Wynton Kelly*) *Steve Lacy Plays The Music Of Thelonious Monk* (Original Jazz Classics 1958)★★★★, reissued as *Reflections*, *The Straight Horn Of Steve Lacy* (Candid 1960)★★★, with Don Cherry *Evidence* (Original Jazz Classics 1962)★★★★, *Disposability* (1965)★★★, *Sortie* (1966)★★, *The Forest And The Zoo* (1967)★★, *Epistrophy* (1970)★★★, reissued as *Steve Lacy Plays Monk*, *Moon* (1970)★★★, *Roba* (1971)★★★, *Wordless* (1971)★★★, *Lapis* (1971)★★★★, *Solo* (In Situ 1972)★★★, *The Gap* (1972)★★, *Mal Waldron With The Steve Lacy Quarter* (1972)★★, *Estilhaços (Chips) - Live In Lisbon* (1972)★★★, *The Crust* (1973)★★★, *Flaps* (1973)★★★, *Scraps* (1974)★★, *Saxophone Special* (1974)★★, *Flakes* (1974)★★★, *School Days* 1963 recordings (Hat Art 1975)★★★★, *Dreams* (1975)★★★, *Lumps* (1975)★★★, *Trickles* (Black Saint 1976)★★★, *Solo At Mandara* (1976)★★, *Torments (Solo In Kyoto)* (1976)★★★, with Andrea Centazzo *Clangs* (1976)★★★, *Stabs* (1976)★★★, *Stalks* (1976)★★, *The Wire* (1976)★★★, *Distant Voices* (1976)★★★, with Michael Smith *Sidelines* (Improvising Artists 1977)★★★, with Centazzo, Kent Carter *Trio Live*, (1977)★★★★, *Threads* (1977)★★, *Raps* (1977)★★★, *Straws* (1977)★★, *Clinkers* (1977)★★, with Derek Bailey *Company 4* (Incus 1977)★★★, *Axieme 1 & 2* 1975 recording (Red 1978)★★★, *Follies* (1978)★★★, *Points* (1978)★★, *Catch* (1978)★★★, *Crops/The Woe* 1973/76 recordings (1979)★★★, *Troubles* (Black Saint 1979)★★★, *The Owl* (1979)★★, with Maarten Altena *High, Low And Order* (Hat Art 1979)★★★, *Stamps* (1979)★★, *Eronel* (1979)★★★, *Tao* 1976 recording (1980)★★★, *Shots* (1980)★★, *The Way* (1980)★★★★, with Walter Zuber Armstrong *Alter Ego* (1980)★★★, with Armstrong *Call Notes* (1980)★★★, with Steve Potts, Irene Aebi *Tips* 1979 recordings (1981)★★★, *NY Capers* (1981)★★★, with Brion Gysin *Songs* (Hat Art 1981)★★★★, *Ballets* (1982),★★★ *The Flame* (Soul Note 1982)★★★, with Mal Waldron *Snake Out* (1982)★★, with Waldron *Herbe D'Oublie* 1981 recordings (1983)★★★,

Prospectus (1983)★★, with Roswell Rudd, Misha Mengelberg and others *Regeneration* (1983)★★★, *Blinks* (1984)★★, *Futurities* (Hat Art 1985)★★★, with Evan Parker *Chirps* (1985)★★★, with Mengelberg and others *Change Of Season* (1985)★★★★, *The Complete Jaguar Sessions* 1954 recordings (1986),★★★ *Hocus Pocus* (1986)★★★, *Morning Joy: Live At Sunset Paris* (Hat Art 1986)★★★, with Waldron *Let's Call This* 1981 recordings (1986)★★★, *The Condor* (Soul Note 1986)★★★, *Outings* (1986)★★★, *Only Monk* (Soul Note 1987)★★★, with Ulrich Gumpert *Deadline* 1985 recordings (Sound Aspects 1987)★★, *This Kiss* (1987)★★★, *Momentum* (1987)★★, with Waldron *Sempre Amore* (Soul Note 1987)★★, *The Gleam* (1987)★★★, *One Fell Swoop* (1987)★★★, with Potts *Live In Budapest* (West Wind 1988)★★, with Helen Merrill *Music Makes* (1988)★★, with Gil Evans *Paris Blues* (1988)★★★★, *The Window* (Soul Note 1988)★★★, *The Door* (Novus 1989)★★★, with Steve Argüelles *Image* (Ah-Um 1989)★★★, *Morning Joy* 1986 recording (1989)★★★★, with Eric Watson *Your Tonight Is My Tomorrow* (1989),★★ *Anthem* (Novus 1990)★★, with Waldron *Hot House* (Novus 1991)★★★, *In Situ* 1985 recording (1991)★★★, *Rushes: 10 Songs From Russia* (Nuerva 1990)★★★★, *More Monk* 1989 recordings (Soul Note 1991)★★★, with Potts *Flim-Flam* 1986 recordings (Hat Art 1991), *Itinerary* (Hat Art 1991), with Mengelberg and others *Dutch Masters* 1987 recording (1992)★★, *Remains* (Hat Art 1992)★★★, *Live At Sweet Basil* (1992)★★★, *Spirit Of Mingus* (Freelance 1992)★★★, *We See* (Hat Art 1993)★★★★, *Vespers* (Soul Note 1994)★★★, *Lets Call This Esteem* (Slam 1994)★★★, *Bye-Ya* (Free Lance 1997)★★★, with Mal Waldron *Communiqué* (Soul Note 1997)★★★.

Ladies And Gentlemen...The Rolling Stones

The **Rolling Stones**' 1972 US tour has assumed legendary proportions. Undertaken in the wake of two acclaimed albums, *Sticky Fingers* and *Exile On Main Street*, it captured the band at the height of its creative and performing powers. The offstage hedonism that accompanied life on the road was graphically described in Robert Greenfield's book *Stones Touring Party* and Robert Frank's rarely seen documentary *Cocksucker's Blues*. The warts-and-all premise of the latter was not apparent on *Ladies And Gentlemen*, released in 1974. This straightforward film focused on the Rolling Stones' music, showcasing 15 of their best-known and most popular numbers. Executive producer Marshall Chess, then head of Rolling Stones' Records' ensured that the film celebrated music and not lifestyle excess. *Ladies And Gentlemen* confirmed that the sobriquet 'the world's greatest rock 'n' roll band' was not misplaced during this era.

Ladies Of The Canyon - Joni Mitchell

No longer the wistful folkie, **Joni Mitchell** had by now joined the late 60s rock fraternity through her association with **Graham Nash**. Her lyrics had acquired an originality, which she expanded on *Blue* and *For The Roses*, but it was the quality of the songs that made them classics of the era. 'For Free' was recorded by **David Crosby** and the re-formed **Byrds**, and **Crosby, Stills, Nash And Young** turned 'Woodstock' into a full-blown rock number. Mitchell's own definitive stamp remains on the much-covered 'The Circle Game', the ecology-conscious 'Big Yellow Taxi' and 'Willy', her song for her then 'old man' Nash.

● Tracks: *Morning Morgan Town; For Free; Conversation; Ladies Of The Canyon; Willy; The Arrangement; Rainy Night House; The Priest; Blue Boy; Big Yellow Taxi; My Old Man; Woodstock; The Circle Game.*
● First released 1970
● UK peak chart position: 8
● USA peak chart position: 27

Ladnier, Tommy

b. 28 May 1900, Florenceville, Louisiana, USA, d. 4 June 1939. As a child Ladnier played trumpet locally, as well as in nearby Mandeville where he was heard by **George Lewis** and **Bunk Johnson**. Later, during Johnson's renaissance, he claimed to have taught Ladnier. In 1917, Ladnier travelled to Chicago where he played in several bands, culminating, in 1924, with the band led by his idol, **Joe 'King' Oliver**. Early in 1925, Ladnier was hired by **Sam Wooding** with whom he visited Europe. During the next few years Ladnier played in Germany, Poland, France and other European countries with, among others, Wooding, Benny Peyton, Louis Douglas, **Noble Sissle** and also played engagements back in the USA, mainly with **Fletcher Henderson**. In the early 30s, Ladnier teamed up with **Sidney Bechet** to co-lead a band they named the New Orleans Feetwarmers. In 1933, Ladnier and Bechet continued their partnership but on a non-musical basis, jointly running a tailor's shop in New York. In the mid-30s, Ladnier led his own small groups in comparative obscurity, but in 1938 he played with Bechet on recording dates for the French jazz writer Hugues Panassie. The two musical partners also played at a Carnegie Hall concert, *Spirituals To Swing*, organized by **John Hammond Jnr**. Ladnier's playing style was a simple and direct exposition of the blues and as an accompanist to blues singers, like **Ma Rainey**, he displayed considerable empathy.

Lady And The Tramp
(see **Disney, Walt**)

Lady Anne

b. Anne Smith, *c*. 1960, Jamaica, West Indies. In the late 70s a new wave of DJs including **Charlie Chaplin**, **Josie Wales** and **Brigadier Jerry** were plying their trade in the dancehalls. The number of female performers in the same area was small, and when they rendered a chant it was mainly in a supporting role, as in Liza's assistance to Papa Kojak. The situation was rectified when **Sister Nancy** began performing, and ushered in a new dimension to dancehall entertainment. Lady Anne was one of the first, alongside Nancy, who won the support of the crowds and her popularity led to studio sessions. Lady Anne's debut was with Roots Tradition, where she recorded an answer to 'Shine Eye Girl' as 'Shine Eye Boy'. Other hits included 'Take A Set', 'Heroes Connection', 'Talk Talk Talk' and 'Lady Anne You're Sweet', as well as combinations with **Peter Metro** ('Bossanova') and reggae's Santana ('Love Life'). She continued to record and appear on various **sound systems** and in 1982 her hit 'Informer', for **Joe Gibbs**, enjoyed a lengthy spell in the Jamaican Top 10. She was known for her cheerful disposition and sense of humour, but the song revealed another side of her character in her condemnation of ghetto informants. Plans for an international tour were thwarted owing to problems with the immigration authorities, and this undermined her chance of wider recognition. The trailblazing spirit of Nancy and Anne has since inspired many performers, including **Sister Carol**, Lady Shabba, **Lady Saw**, **Lady G** and **Patra**.

● ALBUMS: *Informer* limited pressing (Joe Gibbs 1983)★★★★, with Peter Metro And Friends *Dedicated To You* (CSA 1984)★★★, *Vanity* (Pre 1984)★★★.

Lady B

Lady B's debut single was originally released in the mid-80s on the Tec label, based in Philadelphia, USA. Afterwards it was picked up by **Sugarhill**, who re-packaged it in a slightly re-recorded version. Entitled 'To The Beat Y'All', it told of Jill (from the nursery rhyme scenario of Jack and Jill fame) falling pregnant, rather than just down the hill, and advising her of her stupidity in not using contraception. Fellow Sugarhill act **Sequence** would come back at her with the answer record 'Simon Says', extending the onus of responsibility to the man.

Lady Flash

This vocal trio was originally formed as a nucleus of career backing singers who first met when invited to work with **Barry Manilow** in the early stages of his career. Comprising Lorraine 'Reparata' Mazzola (b. Brooklyn, New York, USA), Debra Byrd (b. Cleveland, Ohio, USA) and Ramona Brooks (b. Akron, Ohio, USA), the three singers brought varied and prolific professional experience to bear on their new vocation. Mazzola had previously sung with the Brooklyn College Chorus and teenage group **Reparata And The Dolrons**. In the latter guise she scored a surprise UK hit (number 13) in March 1968 with 'Captain Of Your Ship', and toured England in the same year. It was while stationed in London she first began to work as a backing singer, before starting a television career upon her return to the USA (as producer to Pat Collins's news bulletin on CBS). Byrd was the daughter of a member of the Harlem Globetrotters, and had first performed as part of the 50 member Community Voices Of Faith Choir (which she formed) while at high school. She studied music theory at Kent State University before becoming the musical director of the Black Theatre Workshop.

After recording with gospel group the Jean Austin Singers she entered the world of secular music as part of **Columbia Records**' artists the Interpreters. Brooks, meanwhile, had mainly played the night-club circuit as a solo singer before she became a part of Lady Flash. The trio were brought together by Manilow just as he was about to launch the tour which would break him in the US. He first contacted Mazzola, who quit her television job to give singing another go, but his suggestion to put the Delrons back together was declined by her erstwhile partners. So auditions brought together Byrd and Brooks to cement the trio. They began rehearsing immediately, taking the name Flashy Ladies. The three vocalists, resplendent in black glitter, became intrinsic to Manilow's subsequent breakthrough, as he promoted the release of 'Mandy' with a nationwide tour. By 1976 Brooks had returned to her solo career, and was replaced by Monica Burruss. The revamped trio continued with Manilow, singing on his second major hit, 'Could It Be Magic', the first of nine collaborations which made the charts (both 'I Write The Songs' and 'Looks Like We Made It' became US number 1's). Manilow had already shown his willingness to repay his debt to the trio, and arranged a deal with **Polydor Records** for them. The resulting album spanned several genres with a mix of originals and standards. It housed one notable single, 'Street Singin'', a tribute to the early vocal groups, which reached number 27 in the *Billboard* charts in 1976. Afterwards they returned to working with Manilow, until Burruss left in 1977 to be replaced by Muffy Hendricks. By the following year Lady Flash had ground to a halt with Manilow touring much less frequently. Mazzola went on to start an acting career, appearing in the movie *Dark Before Dawn*, before writing a bestselling book, *Mafia Kingpin*. Byrd stayed as a back-up singer, working with the **Eurythmics** and **Bob Dylan**. Burruss did likewise, with **Melanie**, **Joan Baez** and many others, becoming the first female vocalist to win the *Star Search* television programme.

● ALBUMS: *Beauties In The Night* (Polydor 1976)★★★.

Lady G

b. Janice Fyffe, c.1974, Kingston, Jamaica, West Indies. Fyffe began DJing with the Black Scorpio **sound system** and her reputation soon spread. Her initial recording came in 1988 with producer **Gussie Clarke** who utilized **J.C. Lodge**'s hit 'Telephone Love' for Lady G's 'Nuff Respect'. The song was a warning to all chauvinists and has since become an anthem among ragga girls. Championed as the sisters' DJ, she recorded in combination with **Papa San** the hit 'Round Table Talk', which topped the Jamaican charts. The duo performed a comical altercation, in which Lady G won the squabble. Other hits prior to a temporary sabbatical included 'Rock Back' and 'Is It Me Or The Gun'. The lapse in her career allowed Lady G as a single mother to spend more time with her two children. In 1994 she returned to the stage, performing a stunning presentation at the annual

Fresh concert. In the spring of 1995 she performed in combination with **Chevelle Franklin** 'The Real Slam', in response to the many male DJ records on that theme initiated by **Beenie Man**. Lady G and Franklin also recorded with **Exterminator** the conscientious 'Thank You', riding the 'No Woman No Cry' rhythm, and also 'Love And Hate' at **Donovan Germain**'s Penthouse studio, reaffirming the success of the duo.

● ALBUMS: *God Daughter* (Pre 1995)★★★★.

Lady In Autumn - Billie Holiday

Without question the greatest jazz singer there has ever been (or will ever be), **Billie Holiday**'s unmistakable sound, her inimitable phrasing, her faultless sense of what was right, helped mould an artist unique in the history of popular music. In the early years her joyous, youthful voice was backed by soloists of the calibre of **Buck Clayton**, her close friend **Lester Young**, and her ideal arranger, pianist **Teddy Wilson**. Towards the end of her life her voice was a flaking, fractured caricature of itself but her commanding artistry and musical integrity lent dignity and poignancy to her recordings.

● Tracks: *Body And Soul; Strange Fruit; Trav'lin' Light; All Of Me; (There Is) No Greater Love; I Cover The Waterfront; These Foolish Things (Remind Me Of You); Tenderly; Autumn In New York; My Man; Stormy Weather; Yesterdays; (I Got A Man, Crazy For Me) He's Funny That Way; What A Little Moonlight Can Do; I Cried For You (Now It's Your Turn To Cry Over Me); Too Marvelous For Words; I Wished On The Moon; I Don't Want To Cry Anymore; Prelude To A Kiss; Nice Work If You Can Get It; Come Rain Or Come Shine; What's New?; God Bless The Child; Do Nothin' Till You Hear From Me; April In Paris; Lady Sings The Blues; Don't Explain; Fine And Mellow; I Didn't Know What Time It Was; Stars Fell On Alabama; One For My Baby (And One More For The Road); Gee Baby, Ain't I Good To You; Lover Man (Oh, Where Can You Be?); All The Way; Don't Worry 'bout Me.*

● First released 1973
● UK peak chart position: did not chart
● USA peak chart position: did not chart

Lady In Satin - Billie Holiday

This was her penultimate album, recorded when her body was telling her enough was enough. During the sessions with arranger Ray Ellis she was drinking vodka neat, as if it were tap water. Yet, for all her ravaged voice (the sweetness had long gone) she was still an incredible singer. The feeling and tension she manages to put into almost every track sets this album as one of her finest achievements. 'You've Changed' and 'I Get Along Without You Very Well' are high art performances from the singer who saw life from the bottom upwards. The CD reissue masterminded by Phil Shaap is absolutely indispensable.

● Tracks: *I'm A Fool To Want You; For Heaven's Sake; You Don't Know What Love Is; I Get Along Without You Very Well; For All We Know; Violets For Your Furs; You've Changed; It's Easy To Remember; But Beautiful; Glad To Be Unhappy; I'll Be Around; The End Of A Love Affair; I'm A Fool To Want You* (Alternate tracks); *The End Of A Love Affair* (Alternate tracks).; *Pause Track.*

● First released 1958
● UK peak chart position: did not chart
● USA peak chart position: did not chart

Lady In The Dark

For his first Broadway book musical following his brother **George**'s death in 1937, **Ira Gershwin** teamed with composer **Kurt Weill** for this show which arrived in New York at the Alvin Theatre on 23 January 1941. Moss Hart's book had started out as a straight play, *I Am Listening*, and when it became obvious that the piece would work better as a musical, Katherine Cornell, the original choice for leading lady, was replaced by **Gertrude Lawrence**. She played Liza Elliott, the editor of a highly successful fashion magazine who seeks psychiatric help in an effort to allay her feelings of insecurity, and to explain the extraordinary dreams that she is constantly experiencing. These generally concern four men: Kendall Nesbitt (Bert Lytell) her lover and professional patron; Randy Curtis, a Hollywood star played by Victor Mature, who was on the brink of a lucrative movie career himself, during which he became known as 'The Hunk'; Randall Paxton, the magazine's photographer (**Danny Kaye** making his Broadway musical comedy debut), and Charley Johnson (Macdonald Carey), Liza's cantankerous advertising manager, and the man she eventually falls for. All the songs, except one, are presented in four dream sequences, linked together with Gershwin and Weill's beautifully ethereal ballad, 'My Ship', a song which subsequently received sensitive readings over the years from popular singers such as **Tony Bennett** and **Buddy Greco**. *Lady In The Dark* contained at least two more memorable songs, 'The Saga Of Jenny' and 'Tschaikowsky'. The former, performed in the 'Circus Dream' by Gertrude Lawrence, stopped the show every night, and concerned a lady who, throughout her life, just could not make up her mind: 'Jenny made her mind up when she was twelve/That into foreign languages she would delve/But at seventeen to Vassar it was quite a blow/That in twenty-seven languages she couldn't say no.' The number has been described as 'a sort of blues bordello', and, it is said, was written especially so that Lawrence could 'follow' the immense impact made by Danny Kaye with the tongue-twisting 'Tschaikowsky', in which he listed the names of 49 Russian composers in 39 seconds, the last few of which went thus: 'And Glazounoff and Caesar Cui, Kalinikoff, Rachmaninoff, Stravinsky and Gretchaninoff/I really have to stop, the subject has been dwelt upon enough!'. The remaining songs in what was a classy score included 'One Life To Live', 'Girl Of The Moment', 'This Is New', 'The Princess Of Pure Delight', and 'Tributes To Liza Elliott'. Following several cast changes in June 1941, *Lady In The Dark* completed a run of 467 performances, and then toured before returning to Broadway for another two and half months in 1943. A year later, a film version was released starring **Ginger Rogers** and Ray Milland, but minus several of the songs. Ten years after that, there was a US television production with Anne Sothern and Carleton Carpenter. The show endured in various presentations, including a tour of the UK provinces in 1981, and an appearance at the Edinburgh Festival in 1988. In 1992, a CD was released of Gertrude Lawrence recreating her original role for a 1950 *Theatre Guild Of The Air* broadcast.

Lady Is A Square, The

This was Britain's high-kicking 50s heart-throb **Frankie Vaughan**'s third picture - and his first musical. He played Johnny Burns, a pop singer who poses as a butler in the service of a hard-up society lady, Frances Baring (**Anna Neagle**), and secretly helps her to prolong the life of her husband's symphony orchestra. Janette Scott plays the dutiful daughter, and other roles went to **Anthony Newley**, Wilfred Hyde White, Ted Lune, Christopher Rhodes, Kenneth Cope, and Josephine Fitzgerald. Vaughan sang the lovely **Ray Noble** ballad, 'Love Is The Sweetest Thing', as well as the more contemporary 'The Lady Is A Square' (Raymond Dutch-**Johnny Franz**), 'That's My Doll' (Dick Glasser-Ann Hall), and 'Honey Bunny Baby'. The last number is credited to 'Frank Able', which sounds suspiciously like an abridged version of Vaughan's real name of Frank Abelson. Harold Purcell, Pamela Bower and Nicholas Phipps adapted the screenplay from a story by Purcell, and the director was **Herbert Wilcox**. He and his wife, Anna Neagle, produced the picture in 1959 for Everest Films in the UK.

Lady Of Rage

Coming to prominence via her engaging support/crowd-warmer spot on tours with **Snoop Doggy Dogg** and mentor **Dr Dre**, the Lady Of Rage also part-times as hairdresser to the stars of the Dogg Pound. She was living in New York when Dre called her at her job at Chung King Studios, where she was the receptionist. He had heard her guesting on the **LA Posse** album, having also performed with **Chubb Rock** and **Branford Marsalis**. She did not believe it was Dre until he sent her an air ticket in the post, but Rage has remained in Los Angeles since she arrived there in 1990. Part of the Dogg Pound alongside luminaries like Snoop Doggy Dogg, and signed to Dre's **Death Row Records**, her debut release was the ruffhouse 'Afro Puffs' cut, also featured on the basketball movie, *Above The Rim*.

● ALBUMS: *Necessary Roughness* (Death Row 1997)★★★.

Lady Saw

b. Marion Hall, 1969, St. Mary, Jamaica, West Indies. Lady Saw began chatting on the microphone at the age of 15. Being located some distance from the recording studios, she served an apprenticeship on local **sound systems** before appearing on vinyl. Inspired by the popularity of the slackness style, she performed lewd songs, which earned her a reputation as an X-rated DJ. Her earliest tunes, 'Stab Up De Meat' and 'Just Anuddah Day', reinforced her bad girl image which she eloquently defended on the controversial television documentary *Yardies*. In 1994 her shows were banned in certain Jamaican parishes, to which she responded with 'Freedom Of Speech'. She complained that many male performers had performed slack lyrics without having to endure the censorship to which she was exposed. Her grievance faltered when she performed 'Peanut Punch Mek Man Shit Up Gal Bed' on her video *The Legend Returns* with **Lady G**, Shamara, Michelle and Lo Lo. In spite of the controversies, she maintained a high musical profile with the hits 'Me Naw Lock Mi Mouth', 'Lonely Without You' and the popular 'Good Wuk'. Other releases followed, including the celebratory 'Glory Be To God' and 'Ask God For A Miracle'. She enjoyed her biggest hit in 1995 with 'Hardcore', while with **King Jammy**'s son John John, her rendition of 'Welding Torch' left little doubt as to the subject matter. The controversy surrounding the AIDS virus resulted in **Buju Banton**'s recording of 'Don't Be Silly (Put A Rubber On Your Willy)'. The tune and a television report inspired Lady Saw to advise girls of the dangers of unprotected sex with her recording of 'Condom'. By the autumn of 1995, the continued drive towards conscientious lyrics found Lady Saw being drawn into the roots and culture style, though her audiences demanded to see the more notorious raunchy performances. In 1996 she enjoyed hits with 'Give Me A Reason' and 'You Yuh Husband Of Mine'. The same year, *Give Me The Reason* was released and included 'Condom' and 'Saturday Night At The Movies' in combination with Brian and Tony Gold.

● ALBUMS: *Bare As You Dare* (VP 1994)★★★, *Lover Girl* (Pre 1995)★★★★, *Give Me The Reason* (VP 1996)★★★, *Passion* (VP 1997)★★★.

● COMPILATIONS: *The Collection* (Diamond Rush 1997)★★★.

Lady Sings The Blues

Roundly criticized at the time of its release in 1972 (in some instances before it was even seen), this bio-pic purports to tell the life story of **Billie Holiday**. Loosely based upon Lady Day's autobiography, which was itself only linked tenuously with reality (though this is an assertion contested by research in the 90s), the film misses the essential tragedy while simultaneously failing to establish the young Holiday's often over-exuberant love of life. Instead, the film settles for gloomy melodrama. One of the men in Holiday's later life was on hand in an advisory capacity and, predictably, the plot line suffered as axes were ground and excuses made. In the end the film offers a sanitised version of the singer's life, adding a sheen to her heroin addiction and troubled personal relationships. Most of the initial critical flak came from the casting of **Diana Ross** in the lead (the production originated with **Motown** to whom Ross was contracted). In fact, Ross's performance was excellent and she was nominated for an Oscar in this, her first acting role. Ross also drastically altered her singing style to leave behind her Tamla/Motown origins and move towards jazz. Of course, she did not sound at all like Holiday but that was never her intention.

Lady Soul - Aretha Franklin

Aretha's Franklin's position as soul music's premier female vocalist was consolidated by this album. Her strident reading of **Don Covay**'s 'Chain Of Fools' set the tone for a collection on which the singer unveiled several original compositions and reinterpreted a batch of classic songs. Franklin's gospel roots were clearly displayed on the anthem-like 'People Get Ready' while her interpretation of 'Natural Woman' showed both vulnerable and assertive qualities. *Lady Soul* captures a performer at the peak of her power, restating her ability to take material and make it uniquely her own.
- Tracks: *Chain Of Fools; Money Won't Change You; People Get Ready; Niki Hoeky; (You Make Me Feel Like) A Natural Woman; Since You've Been Gone (Sweet Sweet Baby); Good To Me As I Am To You; Come Back Baby; Groovin'; Ain't No Way.*
- First released 1968
- UK peak chart position: 25
- USA peak chart position: 2

Lady, Be Good!

Although he had already achieved international success, thanks to his popular songs and 'Rhapsody In Blue', **George Gershwin** was eager to continue to write for Broadway and his stage show, *Lady, Be Good!*, opened there at the Liberty Theatre on 1 December 1924. With a book by **Guy Bolton** and Fred Thompson and lyrics by **Ira Gershwin**, the show ran for 330 performances. *Lady, Be Good!* had several excellent production numbers and starred Adele and **Fred Astaire**. The plot, such as it was, centred upon a sister and brother dance team who, unavoidably 'resting' between jobs, survived by crashing parties as a pair of Spanish aristocrats. Amongst the show's songs were two of the Gershwins' all-time standards, 'Oh, Lady, Be Good!' and 'Fascinating Rhythm', along with other delightful numbers such as 'Little Jazz Bird' 'The Half Of It Dearie Blues', 'Juanita', 'Swiss Miss', and 'So Am I'. Another song, 'The Man I Love', which had been written especially for Adele Astaire, was dropped during pre-Broadway tryouts but was rescued by Gershwin and used in **Strike Up The Band** (1927) before gaining a life of its own as one of the masterpieces of the Great American Song Book. The Astaires also starred in the show's 1926 London production which ran for 326 performances and contained three different George Gershwin songs, 'I'd Rather Charleston' (lyric by Desmond Carter), 'Swiss Miss' (lyric by Ira Gershwin and Arthur Jackson), and 'Something About Love' (lyric by Lou Paley). *Lady, Be Good!* was revived in London in 1968 with Lionel Blair and Aimi Macdonald, and was seen again in 1992 at the Open Air Theatre in Regent's Park, starring Bernard Cribbins, Joanna

Riding, and Simon Green. A 1941 film entitled *Lady, Be Good!*, starring Ann Sothern and Robert Young, had a different storyline and many of the songs came from other sources.

Ladysmith Black Mambazo

The success of **Paul Simon**'s album *Graceland* did much to give the music of black South Africa international recognition in the mid-80s, and in particular gave a high profile to the choral group Mambazo, who had sung on it. Founded by Joseph Shabalala in 1960, the group's name referred to Shabalala's home town of Ladysmith, while also paying tribute to the seminal 50s' choral group Black Mambazo (black axe) led by Aaron Lerole (composer of the 1958 UK hit 'Tom Hark' by his brother **Elias** [Lerole] **And His Zig Zag Flutes**). The group began working professionally in 1971, with a version of ingoma ebusukuk ('night music'), which Shabalala dubbed 'cothoza mfana' ('walking on tiptoe', an accurate description of Mambazo's ability to follow choruses of thundering intensity with split-second changes into passages of delicate, whisper-like intimacy). Until 1975, most of Mambazo's album output concentrated on traditional folk songs, some of them with new lyrics that offered necessarily coded, metaphorical criticisms of the apartheid regime. After 1975, and Shabalala's conversion to Christianity, religious songs were added to the repertoire - although, to non-Zulu speakers, the dividing line will not be apparent. In 1987, following the success of *Graceland*, the group's **Warner Brothers Records** debut album *Shaka Zulu*, produced by Paul Simon, reached the UK Top 40, and also sold substantially in the USA and Europe. In 1990, *Two Worlds One Heart* marked a radical stylistic departure for the group through its inclusion of tracks recorded in collaboration with **George Clinton** and the **Winans**. On 10 December 1991, as the result of what was described as a 'roadside incident' in Durban, South Africa, founder member Shabalala was shot dead. The group were back on a major label for 1997's *Heavenly*, which featured **Dolly Parton** singing lead vocals on a cover version of 'Knockin' On Heaven's Door'.
- ALBUMS: *Amabutho* (BL 1973)★★★, *Isitimela* (BL 1974)★★★, *Amaqhawe* (BL 1976)★★★, *Ulwandle Olunggewele* (BL 1977)★★★, *Umthombo Wamanzi* (BL 1982)★★★, *Ibhayibheli Liyindlela* (BL 1984)★★★, *Unduku Zethu* (Shanachie 1984)★★★, *Inala* (Shanachie 1986)★★★, *Ezulwini Siyakhona* (1986)★★★, *Shaka Zulu* (Warners 1987)★★★★, *Journey Of Dreams* (Warners 1988)★★★★, with Danny Glover *How The Leopard Got His Spots* (Windham Hill 1989)★★★, *Two Worlds One Heart* (Warners 1990)★★★★, *Inkanyezi Nezazi* (1992)★★★, *Liph'Iqiniso* (Flame Tree 1994)★★★, *Gift Of The Tortoise* (Flame Tree 1995)★★★, *Heavenly* (A&M 1997)★★.
- COMPILATIONS: *Classic Tracks* (Shanachie 1991)★★★★, *Best Of* (Shanachie 1992)★★★★, *Spirit Of South Africa* (Nascente 1997)★★★★.

LaFarge, Pete

b. 1931, Fountain, Colorado, USA, d. 27 October 1964, New York City, New York, USA. The son of a Pulitzer Prize-winning author, LaFarge was a noted dramatist and painter, as well as an accomplished performer. Folksinger **Cisco Houston** first guided the aspiring musician's skills, which flourished in the 50s following Peter's active service in the Korean War. Of Pima-Indian heritage, LaFarge became a tireless champion of the oppressed, although his most famous composition, 'The Ballad Of Ira Hayes', a forthright indictment of the plight of the native American, achieved popularity through a sympathetic cover version by **Johnny Cash**. Pete also acted as a contributing editor to the radical *Broadside* magazine, and recorded for the **Folkways** and **Columbia** labels. However, he grew increasingly unhappy with his performing role and planned to abandon music in favour of writing and painting. Pete LaFarge died officially from a stroke, despite persistent rumours of suicide.

● ALBUMS: *On The Warpath* (1961)★★★, *As Long As The Grass Shall Grow* (1962)★★★, *Songs Of The Cowboys* (1964)★★★★, *Iron Mountain And Other Songs* (1965)★★.

Lafitte, Guy

b. 12 January 1927, St. Gaudens, France, d. 10 June 1998. Lafitte took up the tenor saxophone in his early 20s, having earlier played clarinet with gypsy bands in the Toulouse area. He later led his own bands in Paris and worked extensively with visiting American jazz and blues artists, including **Big Bill Broonzy**, **Mezz Mezzrow**, **Bill Coleman** and **Buck Clayton**. This was in the early 50s and by the end of the decade he had also played with **Lionel Hampton** and **Arnett Cobb**, and appeared in the film *Paris Blues* (1961), in which **Louis Armstrong** and **Duke Ellington** also featured. Although capable of powerful, earthy playing, Lafitte is at his best as a balladeer where the early influence of **Coleman Hawkins** gleams through his solos.

● ALBUMS: *Club Sessions No. 2* (1954)★★★, *Blue And Sentimental* (1954)★★★, *Guy Lafitte Et Son Orchestre* (1954)★★★, *Guy Lafitte, Son Saxo-ténor Et Son Orchestre* (1954)★★★★, *Guy Lafitte Et Son Quartette* (1955)★★★, *Guy Lafitte Avec Frank Pourcel Et Son Orchestre* (1955)★★★, *Les Classiques Du Jazz Vol. 1* (1955)★★★, *Do Not Disturb* (1956)★★★, *Guy Lafitte Quartet* i (1956)★★★, *Guy Lafitte Et Son Grand Orchestre* (1957)★★, *Classiques Du Jazz Vol. 2* (1957)★★★, *Guy Lafitte Et Son Grand Orchestre, Sextet Et Quartet* (1959)★★★, *Guy Lafitte Quartet* ii (1960)★★★, *10 Sax Succes* (1960)★★★, *Guy Lafitte* (1961)★★★, *Guy Lafitte Jazz Sextet* (1962)★★, *Love In Hi-Fi* (1962)★★★, *Jambo!* (1963)★★, *Guy Lafitte Quintet* (1964)★★★, *Blues* (1969)★★★★, *Blues In Summertime* (1970)★★★, *Sugar And Spice* (1972)★★★, with Bill Coleman *Mainstream At Montreux* (1973)★★★, *Guy Lafitte Joue Charles Trenet* (1977-84)★★★, *Corps Et Ame* (1978)★★, *Happy!* (1979)★★★, *Three Men On A Beat* (1983)★★★, with Wild Bill Davis *Lotus Blossom* (Black And Blue 1983)★★★★, *The Things We Did Last Summer* (Black And Blue 1990)★★★.

LaForet, Marie

b. 1940, Perigord, France. When supplying moral support at her sister's audition for a part in a play, La Foret's fragile beauty was noted by director Rene Clement who secured her a female lead opposite Alain Delon in the 1959 movie *Plein Soleil*. Further films such as *Le Rat Amerique* (1963), established her as a star of the genre with the nickname 'The Girl With The Golden Eyes'. A parallel career as a *chanteuse* began in 1964 when occupational therapy during a long illness included learning the guitar chords that accompanied her singing of mostly folk and Latin American material. She was also a fan of **Bob Dylan**. Her first single, 'Les Vendages De L'Amour' (composed by **Danyel Gerard**), was *the* hit song in France that summer before she was back on the silver screen with *Marie Chantel Contra Docteur Kha*. Prior to 1967's *Le Treizieme Caprice*, she gave birth to a daughter, had her own nose remodelled and returned to the recording studio. She continued to plug gaps between her celluloid dramas with many European hits, including 'Viens Sur La Montagne', the topical 'Manchester Et Liverpool' and 'Marie Colere Marie Douceur'. Athough she was willing to promote these in concert, acting remained her chief vocation.

● COMPILATIONS: *Portrait* (1975)★★★, *Greatest Hits* (1977)★★★.

Lagbaja

b. Bisade Ologunde, Lagos, Nigeria. Now based in Manhattan, New York, USA, Nigerian singer Ologunde adopted the name Lagbaja (meaning 'anonymous' or 'faceless one' in Yoruba) as he embarked on his career in the early 90s. His name was reflected in his choice of stage attire - a slitted textile and rubber mask adopted so that the artist represented the 'common man' in keeping with the carnival tradition of his Yoruba tribe. He formed his first small band in 1991 in Lagos after he had taught himself to play the saxophone. With a high quotient of percussion instruments including congas and talking drums, this group drew its principal inspiration from the traditional highlife music of the 60s, as well as western jazz. Following regular performances at the Sea Garden venue in Lagos (an aquarium), they soon built up enough local support to acquire bookings at the French Institute. Their debut album was released in 1992. *Colours - The Colour Of Rhythm* included versions of stage classics such as 'My Favourite Things' and 'Lilli Bolero', in addition to the **Beatles**' 'Yesterday', reflecting Ologunde's long-standing fascination with English culture and music. Despite this, his attempts to have the album pressed on compact disc in England in 1993 were aborted when the British Embassy in Lagos refused him a work permit. America proved to be more welcoming. A further cassette followed in 1994, a self-titled collection which included songs such as 'Naija Must Sweet Again', which many took to be an attack on Nigeria's military rulers. This theme was continued on sessions for Lagbaja's 1996 album. Songs such as 'Bad Leadership' concerned what

Ologunde views as the biggest problem afflicting contemporary Africa. He was then invited by the International Red Cross Committee to join **Youssou N'Dour**, **Papa Wemba** and **Lucky Dube** on a Pan-African project to promote awareness of humanitarian abuses. Each member of Ologunde's band was sent to selected troubled areas of Africa and invited to submit two songs each documenting their experiences. The other participants joined together in Senegal to compose and record two of these songs at N'Dour's Xippi studios. The project was also the subject of a film documentary by Cameroonian director Bassek Bakhobio.

● ALBUMS: *Colours - The Colour Of Rhythm* (1992)★★★, *Lagbaja* cassette (1994)★★.

Lagrene, Bireli

b. 4 September 1966. Saverne, Alsace, France. The son of Fiso Lagrene, a popular guitarist in pre-war France, Lagrene displayed a prodigious talent as a very young child. Born into a gypsy community, his origins and his fleet, inventive playing style inevitably generated comparisons with **Django Reinhardt**. In 1978, he won a prize at a festival at Strasbourg and subsequently made a big impact during a televised gypsy festival. In his early teenage years Lagrene toured extensively playing concerts and festivals across Europe, often accompanied by distinguished jazz artists such as **Benny Carter**, **Benny Goodman**, **Stéphane Grappelli** and **Niels-Henning Ørsted Pedersen**. He also made his first record *Routes To Django*, which helped to prove that early estimates of his capabilities were not excessive. An outstanding technician, Lagrene has revealed influences other than Reinhardt, happily incorporating bebop phraseology, rock rhythms and Brazilian music into his work. By the late 80s he had moved substantially from his early Reinhardt-style to fully embrace jazz-rock and other electronically-aided fusions, a shift which, while extending his popularity to a wider audience, tended to lower his standing among jazz purists. In mid-summer 1991, he was one of several leading guitarists featured at the International Guitar Festival in Seville, Spain.

● ALBUMS: *Routes To Django: Live At The Krokodil* (Jazzpoint 1980)★★★★, *Bireli Swing '81* (Jazzpoint 1981)★★★, with Joseph Bowie Concert *And Space* (Sackville 1981)★★, *15* (Antilles 1982)★★★, *Down In Town* (Antilles 1983)★★★, *Musique Tzigane/Manouch* (1984)★★, *Erster Tango* (1985)★★★, *Bireli Lagrene Ensemble Live Featuring Vic Juris* (1985)★★★, *Stuttgart Aria* (Jazzpoint 1986)★★★, *Special Guests Freitag 2 Mai, Samstag 3 Mai, Mühle Hunziken* (1986)★★★, *Foreign Affairs* (1986)★★, *Inferno* (Blue Note 1987)★★★★, with Larry Coryell, Miroslav Vitous *Bireli Lagrene* (1988)★★★, *Acoustic Moments* (Blue Note 1990)★★★, *Standards* (Blue Note 1992)★★★.

Lahr, Bert

b. Irving Lahrheim, 13 August 1895, d. 4 December 1967, New York, USA. An actor, comedian and singer, with his rubber-faced expression and noisy antics -

which included his trademark expression 'gnong-gnong' - Lahr was one of the all-time great clowns of the American musical theatre. After working for a good many years in vaudeville and burlesque - some of the time with his first wife in an act called Lahr And Mercedes - he appeared on Broadway in the revue *Harry Delmar's Revels* (1927), before making an immediate impact as an erratic prize fighter in the musical comedy **Hold Everything!** in 1928. He repeated his success, this time as airport mechanic who accidentally sets an endurance flying record because he cannot land the plane, in *Flying High* (1930). During the remainder of the 30s, Lahr spent most of his time in revues, such as *Hot-Cha!* (1932), **George White**'s *Music Hall Varieties* (1932), **Life Begins At 8:40** (1934), *George White's Scandals* (1935), and **The Show Is On** (1936), in which he introduced the hilarious 'Song Of The Woodman' (**E.Y. 'Yip' Harburg-Harold Arlen**). In 1939, he played a nightclub washroom attendant who dreams that he is Louis XV, in the **Cole Porter** book musical, **Du Barry Was A Lady**, and duetted with co-star **Ethel Merman** on 'But In The Morning, No!' and the lively 'Friendship'. By this time Lahr had modified his raucous image somewhat, and he brought his new, softer - but often satirical - personality to the character of the Cowardly Lion, in the classic 1939 movie, **The Wizard Of Oz**. He had two solo numbers, 'Lions And Tigers And Bears' and the splendid 'King Of The Forest', as well as ensemble pieces with **Judy Garland**, **Ray Bolger** and Jack Haley. Throughout the 40s and 50s he continued to appear in revues, including *Seven Lively Arts* (1944), *Meet The People* (1944), *Make Mine Manhattan* (1948), *Two On The Aisle* (1950), and *The Boys Against The Girls* (1959), as well as starring on radio, television and in films. Towards the end of his career, he also worked extensively in the straight theatre in highly regarded productions such as *Waiting For Godot*, *Hotel Paradiso*, and *The Beauty Part*. Lahr made his final Broadway appearance in *Foxy* (1964), a musical comedy adaptation of Ben Jonson's *Volpone*, in which the action was switched from Venice to the Klondike gold rush. His film career, which had begun with the screen version of one his first stage hits, *Flying High*, and peaked with *The Wizard Of Oz*, ended, appropriately enough, with a movie in which he played a burlesque comic, *The Night They Raided Minsky's*. Lahr died during the filming. Two years after his death, he was the subject of a biography written by his son.

● FURTHER READING: *Notes On A Cowardly Lion*, John Lahr.

● FILMS: *Flying High* (1931), *Mr. Broadway* (1933), *Merry-Go-Round Of 1938* (1937), *Love And Hisses* (1937), *Just Around The Corner* (1938), *Josette* (1938), *Zaza* (1939), *The Wizard Of Oz* (1939), *Sing Your Worries Away* (1942), *Ship Ahoy* (1942), *Meet The People* (1944), *Always Leave Them Laughing* (1949), *Mr. Universe* (1951), *Rose-Marie* (1954), *The Second Greatest Sex* (1955), *The Night They Raided Minsky's* (1968).

Lai, Francis

b. 1932, Nice, France. A composer and conductor for films from the early 60s. After scoring *Circle Of Love*, Roger Vadim's re-make of Ophuls' classic *La Ronde*, starring Jane Fonda, Lai won an Academy Award for his music to director Claud Lelouch's classic love story *A Man And A Woman* (1966). He also scored Lelouch's follow-up, *Live For Life*, before going on to something lighter with the comedy-drama, *I'll Never Forget What's 'Is Name*; followed by others in the late 60s such as *Three Into Two Won't Go*, *Mayerling* and *Hannibal Brooks*. In 1970, Lai won his second Oscar for *Love Story*, one of the most popular movies of the decade. The soundtrack album stayed at number 2 in the US album chart for six weeks, and the film's theme, 'Where Do I Begin?' (lyric by Carl Sigman), was a singles hit in the USA for **Andy Williams**, **Henry Mancini** and Lai himself; and in the UK for Williams and **Shirley Bassey**. In the same year, Lai, with his Orchestra, had a big hit in Japan with the title music for the film *Le Passager De La Pluie (Rider Of The Rain)*. During the 70s, Lai's cosmopolitan career included several more films for Lelouch, such as *The Crook*, *Money, Money, Money*, *Happy New Year*, *Cat And Mouse*, *Child Under A Leaf*, *Emmanuelle II* and *Another Man, Another Chance*; and others, such as . . . *And Hope To Die*, *Visit To A Chief's Son*, *And Now My Love*, *International Velvet* and the sequel to *Love Story*, *Oliver's Story* (1979) (music written with Lee Holdridge). In the 80s and early 90s the majority of Lai's music continued to be for French productions, and the Lelouch connection was maintained through films such as *Bolero* (in conjunction with **Michel LeGrand**), *Edith And Marcel*, *Bandits*, *La Belle Histoire (The Beautiful Story)* (co-composer Philippe Servain) and *Les Cles Du Paradis (The Keys To Paradise)* (1992). His work for other directors included *Beyond The Reef*, *Marie*; *A Man And A Woman: 20 Years Later* and *My New Partner II*. Besides his scores for feature films, Lai also contributed music to television programmes such as *Berlin Affair* and *Sins* (miniseries). Recordings include: *Great Film Themes*; *A Man, A Woman And A Love Story*; and the soundtracks, *Bilitis* and *Dark Eyes*.

Laibach

With origins in Trbovlje, Slovenia, Northern Yugoslavia, Laibach's powerful imagery has long been confused with the fascist icons they have tried to deconstruct. They were formed in 1980 by members of the Yugoslavian army, including Tomaz Hostnik (b. 1961, d. 1982; vocals) and Miran Mohar. They acted as the musical arm of the political art movement NSK (Neue Slowenische Kunst - New Slovian Art), conceived in 1980 and formulated in 1984. Laibach form one of three sections of the movement, the others being Irwin (painters) and Scipion Nasice (theatre). Laibach themselves have a constantly fluctuating line-up. However, the nucleus can be identified as Milan Frez, Dejan Knez, Ervin Markosek and Ivan Novak, the latter acting

as spokesman after Hostnik had committed suicide. In 1982 they toured outside of their native country for the first time, releasing their first UK single, 'Boji', in 1984. In the mid-80s they recorded Teutonic reworkings of rock classics such as 'Sympathy For The Devil', and appeared on *The South Bank Show*. The 1987 release 'Life Is Life', later covered by Opus, had the unfortunate effect of becoming an anthem for neo-Nazis. Other notable pursuits included the commissioning of a soundtrack to *Macbeth* performed by the German theatre company Deutsches Schauspielhaus. It was played live during performances. In 1988 the band also covered the **Beatles**' *Let It Be*, bar the title track, in its entirety, in Wagnerian military style. They also released the German-only single '3 Oktober', to celebrate reunification in 1990. Although they have achieved some degree of prominence, any realistic study of Laibach should focus on them as merely one component in a larger and more important artistic movement.

● ALBUMS: *Through Occupied Europe Tour* (Staal 1984)★★, *Laibach* (Skuc 1985)★★★, *Nova Arkopola* (Cherry Red 1985)★★★, *Krst Pod Triglavom-Baptism* (Walter Ulbricht 1986)★★★, *Opus Dei* (Mute 1987)★★★, *Let It Be* (Mute 1988)★★★, *Sympathy For The Devil* mini-album (Mute 1990)★★★, *Macbeth* (Mute 1990)★★★, *Kapital* (Mute 1992)★★★, *Ljubljana Zagreb Beograd* (1993)★★★, *Trans-Slovenia Express* (1994)★★★, *Sarajevo - Occupied Europe NATO Tour 1994-1995* (Mute 1996)★★★, *Jesus Christ Superstars* (Mute 1996)★★★, *MB December 21, 1984* (Mute 1997)★★★.

● COMPILATIONS: *Rekapitulacija 1980 - 1984* (Walter Ulbricht 1985)★★★.

● VIDEOS: *Nato* (Mute 1996).

Laine, Cleo

b. Clementina Dinah Campbell, 28 October 1927, Southall, Middlesex, England. Her earliest performance was as an extra in the film, *The Thief Of Bagdad* (1940). Laine's singing career started with husband **John Dankworth**'s big band in the early 50s working with some of the best modern jazz musicians available. She married Dankworth in 1958 and since then they have become one of the UK's best-known partnerships, although they have clearly developed additional separate careers. Throughout the 60s, Laine began extending her repertoire adding to the usual items like 'Riding High', 'I Got Rhythm' and 'Happiness Is Just A Thing Called Joe', arrangements of lyrics by literary figures like Eliot, Hardy, Auden and Shakespeare (*Word Songs*). Her varied repertoire also includes **Kurt Weill** and Schoenberg's 'Pierrot Lunaire'. She possesses a quite unique voice which spans a number of octaves from a smokey, husky deep whisper to a shrill but incredibly delicate high register. Her scat-singing matches the all time greats including **Ella Fitzgerald** and **Sarah Vaughan**. In 1976, she recorded 'Porgy And Bess' with **Ray Charles** in a non-classical version, which is in the same vein as the earlier Ella Fitzgerald and **Louis Armstrong** interpretation. She has recorded, with great success, duets with flautist **James Galway** and guitarist **John Williams**. Additionally, Laine is an accomplished actress having appeared in a number of films and stage productions. In addition to her incredible vocal range and technique she has done much, through her numerous television appearances, to broaden the public's acceptance of different styles of music in a jazz setting, and in doing so she has broken many barriers.

● ALBUMS: *Cleo Laine* (Esquire 1955)★★★, *Cleo's Choice* (Pye 1958)★★★, *She's The Tops* (MGM 1958)★★★, *All About Me* (Fontana 1962)★★★, *Woman Talk* (Fontana 1966)★★★, *Cleo Laine Live At Carnegie Hall*, (RCA 1973)★★★★, *Day By Day* (Buddah 1974)★★★, *A Beautiful Thing* (RCA 1974)★★★, *Born On A Friday* (RCA 1976)★★★, with Ray Charles *Porgy And Bess* (RCA 1976)★★★★, *A Lover And His Lass* (1976)★★★★, *Feel The Warm* (1976)★★★, with John Williams *Best Friends* (RCA 1978)★★★★, *Cleo* (Arcade 1978)★★★, *Word Songs* (1978)★★★, *Return To Carnegie* (RCA 1979)★★★★, *I Am A Song* (RCA 1979)★★★, with James Galway *Sometimes When We Touch* (RCA 1980)★★★, *The Incomparable Cleo Laine* (1980)★★★, *Gonna Get Through* (1980)★★★, *This Is Cleo Laine* (1981)★★★, *Smilin' Through* (1982)★★★, *Let The Music Take You* (1983)★★★, *Off The Record* (1984)★★★, *Themes* (1985)★★★, *That Old Feeling* (Music Collection 1987)★★★, *Cleo Sings Sondheim* (1987)★★★★, *Shakespeare And All That Jazz* (Affinity 1988)★★★★, *Woman To Woman* (RCA 1989)★★★, with Mel Tormé *Nothing Without You* (1993)★★★, *Blue And Sentimental* (1993)★★★.

● COMPILATIONS: *Platinum Collection* (Cube 1981)★★★★, *The Essential Collection* (1987)★★★★, *Cleo's Choice* (1988)★★★★, *Unforgettable Cleo Laine* (PRT 1988)★★★★, *Portrait Of A Song Stylist* (Masterpiece 1989)★★★★, *The Very Best Of ...* (RCA Victor 1997)★★★★.

● FURTHER READING: *Cleo*, Cleo Laine. *Cleo And John*, Graham Collier (ed.).

Laine, Denny

b. Brian Hines, 29 October 1944, Jersey, Channel Islands. An integral part of the Birmingham beat scene, this vocalist/guitarist formed his own group, Denny Laine And The Diplomats, in 1962. Two years later, he became a founder-member of the **Moody Blues**, and was the featured singer on the group's international hit, 'Go Now'. Later recordings were less successful and, in November 1966, Laine abandoned the group to embark on an ill-starred solo career. Although his debut release, 'Say You Don't Mind', failed to chart, the single garnered considerable critical plaudits. **Colin Blunstone**'s sympathetic cover version later became a UK Top 20 hit in 1972. Laine's experimental ensemble, the Electric String Band, collapsed prematurely, and he spent much of the late 60s drifting between several short-lived groups, including **Balls** and **Ginger Baker**'s **Airforce**. He also completed a solo album, but this remained unissued for several years. Between 1971 and 1980, Laine was an integral member of **Wings**, co-writing the multi-million selling 'Mull Of Kintyre'. His

departure followed adverse publicity in the wake of leader **Paul McCartney**'s arrest on drugs charges. An intermittently talented individual, Denny Laine has since pursued a solo path, which has failed to match its original promise.

● ALBUMS: *Aah Laine* (Wizard 1973)★★, with Paul McCartney *Holly Days* (EMI 1976)★★, *Japanese Tears* (Scratch 1980)★★, *In Flight* (Breakaway 1984)★★, *Weep For Love* (1985)★★, *Hometown Girls* (1985)★★, *Wings On My Feet* (1987)★★, *Master Suite* (1988), *Lonely Road* (1988)★★, *Blue Nights* (President 1993)★★★, *The Rock Survivor* (WCP 1994)★★★.

Laine, Frankie

b. Frank Paul LoVecchio, 30 March 1913, Chicago, Illinois, USA. Laine had been a chorister at the Immaculate Conception Church in his city's Sicilian quarter before entering showbusiness proper on leaving school. For nearly a decade he travelled as a singing waiter, dancing instructor (with a victory in a 1932 dance marathon as his principal qualification) and other lowly jobs, but it was as a member of a New Jersey nightclub quartet that he was given his first big break - replacing **Perry Como** in Freddie Carlone's touring band in 1937. This was a springboard to a post as house vocalist with a New York radio station until migration to Los Angeles, where he was 'discovered' entertaining in a Hollywood spa by **Hoagy Carmichael**. The songwriter persuaded him to adopt an Anglicized *nom de theatre*, and funded the 1947 session that resulted in 'That's My Desire', Laine's first smash. This was followed by 'Shine' (written in 1924) and a revival again in **Louis Armstrong**'s 'When You're Smiling'. This was the title song for a 1950 movie starring Laine, the **Mills Brothers**, **Kay Starr** and other contributors of musical interludes to its 'backstage' plot. His later career on celluloid focused largely on his disembodied voice carrying main themes of cowboy movies such as *Man With A Star*, the celebrated *High Noon*, *Gunfight At The OK Corral* and the *Rawhide* television series. Each enhanced the dramatic, heavily masculine style favoured by Laine's producer, **Mitch Miller**, who also spiced the artist's output with generous pinches of C&W. This was best exemplified in the extraordinary 1949 hit 'Mule Train', one of the most dramatic and impassioned recordings of its era. Other early successes included 'Jezebel', 'Jalousie' and 'Rose Rose, I Love You', an adaptation by Wilfred Thomas of Hue Lin's Chinese melody 'Mei Kuei'.

Laine proved a formidable international star, particularly in the UK, where his long chart run began in 1952 with 'High Noon'. The following year he made chart history when his version of 'I Believe' topped the charts for a staggering 18 weeks, a record that has never been eclipsed since, despite a valiant run of 16 weeks by **Bryan Adams** 28 years later. Laine enjoyed two further UK chart-toppers in 1953 with 'Hey Joe' and 'Answer Me'. Incredibly, he was number 1 for 27 weeks that year, another feat of chart domination that it is difficult to envisage ever being equalled. No less than 22 UK Top 20 hits during the 50s emphasized Laine's popularity, including such memorable songs as 'Blowing Wild', 'Granada', 'The Kid's Last Fight', 'My Friend', 'Rain Rain Rain', 'Cool Water', 'Hawkeye', 'Sixteen Tons', 'A Woman In Love' and 'Rawhide'. Laine was also a consummate duettist and enjoyed additional hits with **Johnnie Ray**, **Doris Day** and **Jimmy Boyd**. After his hit-parade farewell with 1961's 'Gunslinger', he pursued a full-time career commuting around the world as a highly paid cabaret performer, with a repertoire built around selections from hit compilations, one of which (*The Very Best Of Frankie Laine*) climbed into international charts as late as 1977. New material tended to be of a sacred nature - though in the more familiar 'clippetty-clop' character was 'Blazing Saddles', featured in Mel Brooks' (the lyricist) 1974 spoof-western of the same name. By the mid-80s, he was in virtual semi-retirement in an opulent ocean-front dwelling in San Diego, California, with his wife, former actress Nanette Gray. With sales in excess of 100 million copies, Laine was a giant of his time and one of the most important solo singers of the immediate pre-rock 'n' roll period.

● ALBUMS: *Favorites* (Mercury 1949)★★★, *Songs From The Heart* (Mercury 1949)★★, *Frankie Laine* (Mercury 1950)★★★, *Mr Rhythm Sings* (Mercury 1951)★★★, *Christmas Favorites* (Mercury 1951)★★, *Listen To Laine* (Mercury 1952)★★★, *One For My Baby* (Columbia 1952)★★★★, with Jo Stafford *Musical Portrait Of New Orleans* (Columbia 1954)★★, *Mr Rhythm* (Columbia 1954)★★★, *Songs By Frankie Laine* (Mercury 1955)★★★★, *That's My Desire* (Mercury 1955)★★★★, *Lovers Laine* (Columbia 1955)★★★, *Frankie Laine Sings For Us* (Mercury 1955)★★★, *Concert Date* (Mercury 1955)★★★, *With All My Heart* (Mercury 1955)★★★, *Command Performance* (Columbia 1956)★★★, *Jazz Spectacular* (Columbia 1956)★★, *Rockin'* (Columbia 1957)★★, *Foreign Affair* (Columbia 1958)★★★, *Torchin'* (Columbia 1960)★★★, *Reunion In Rhythm* (Columbia 1961)★★★, *You Are My Love* (Columbia 1961)★★★, *Frankie Laine, Balladeer* (Columbia 1961)★★★, *Hell Bent For Leather!* (Columbia 1961)★★★, *Deuces Wild* (Columbia 1962)★★★, *Call Of The Wild* (1962)★★★, *Wanderlust* (1963)★★, *I'll Take Care Of Your Cares* (ABC 1967)★★★, *I Wanted Someone To Love* (ABC 1967)★★★, *To Each His Own* (ABC 1968)★★, *You Gave Me A Mountain* (ABC 1969)★★★, with Erich Kunzel And The Cincinnati Pops Orchestra *Round Up* (1987)★★★.

● COMPILATIONS: *Greatest Hits* (Columbia 1959)★★★★, *Golden Hits* (Mercury 1960)★★★★, *Golden Memories* (Polydor 1974)★★★, *The Very Best Of Frankie Laine* (Warwick 1977)★★★★, *American Legend* (Columbia 1978)★★★, *Songbook* (World Records 1981)★★★★, *All Of Me* (Bulldog 1982)★★★, *Golden Greats* (Polydor 1983)★★★, *The Golden Years* (Phillips 1984)★★★, *His Greatest Hits* (Warwick 1986)★★★, *The Uncollected* (Hindsight 1986)★★★, *Rawhide* (Castle 1986)★★★, *20 Of His Best* (The Collection 1987)★★★, *Sixteen Evergreens* (Joker 1988)★★★, *Country Store: Frankie Laine* (Country Store 1988)★★★, *Portrait Of A Song Stylist* (Masterpiece 1989)★★★, *21 Greatest Hits* (Westmoor 1989)★★★, *Memories In Gold* (Prestige 1990)★★★, *All Time Hits* (MFP 1991)★★★, with Jo Stafford *Goin' Like Wildfire* (Bear Family 1992)★★★, *On The Trail Again* (1993)★★★.

● FURTHER READING: *That Lucky Old Son*, Frankie Laine and Joseph F. Laredo.

Laine, Papa Jack

b. 21 September 1873, New Orleans, Louisiana, USA, d. 1 June 1966. Towards the end of the 19th century, drummer and alto horn player Laine formed ragtime and marching bands in his home town. The marching band, which Laine named the Reliance Brass Band, became very popular and he continued to lead it, and also to run other bands under the same banner up until his retirement in 1917. Many of the best-known white musicians in New Orleans played in one or another of Laine's bands, among them Nick La Rocca and **Joseph 'Sharkey' Bonano**. Although he did not record as a musician, Laine did record his reminiscences while some of his former sidemen recorded as Papa Laine's Children.

Lair, John

b. 1 July 1894, on a farm near Livingston, Kentucky, USA, d. 13 November 1985, Lexington, Kentucky, USA. Lair developed a childhood interest to become a respected authority on and a collector of old-time music. After military service in World War I, he ran the family farm until, concerned by the threatened over-development of Renfro Valley, he moved to Battle Creek, Michigan. Here, he worked as a teacher and an insurance agent, before becoming a programme director at WLS Chicago in 1927. He immediately began to organize the station's *National Barn Dance* programme and formed a band of musicians and singers that he called the **Cumberland Ridge Runners**. He occasionally played harmonica and jug, but, being no great musician himself, he usually confined himself to narrations, writing material and announcing duties. In 1937, Lair left WLS for WLW Cincinnati, where he helped create the *Boone County Jamboree* and soon afterwards the *Renfro Valley Barn Dance*, which, through his business acumen and some help from others, including **Red Foley** and Slim Miller, Lair moved to his own home in Renfro Valley, Kentucky, in 1939. The programme, which took place in a barn, was soon carried by WHAS Louisville, whose transmissions in turn were carried by other stations, even, eventually, by the NBC Network. The programme helped to launch the careers of many artists including the **Coon Creek Girls** and on its 25th anniversary in 1962, the State Governor proudly declared Lair's show 'a Kentucky institution'. The Barn Dance was only one of the many folk music activities that Lair organized and his beloved Valley eventually became a noted tourist attraction with its festivals, museum and shops.

Laird, Rick

b. 5 February 1941, Dublin, Eire. Laird started playing the piano when he was aged five and turned to the double bass when he was 18. The family had moved to New Zealand but he went on to Australia where he played with **Mike Nock** before coming to England where he studied at the Guildhall School of Music in the early 60s. He accompanied vocalists **Lambert, Hendricks And Ross**, joined the house band at **Ronnie Scott**'s club (1964-66) and played with **Sonny Rollins** on the soundtrack of the film *Alfie* (1965). In 1966, he went to the **Berklee College Of Music** in Boston, USA and in 1968 started playing bass guitar. He toured with **Buddy Rich** (1969-71) and then played with the **Mahivishnu Orchestra** (1971-73). While the double bass remains his favourite instrument it was on bass guitar that he played with the Orchestra combining with drummer **Billy Cobham** to provide its massive rhythmic punch. Since leaving the Orchestra he has worked primarily in the New York studios with artists such as **Chick Corea** and tenor saxophonists **Stan Getz** and **Joe Henderson**.

Lake

This multi-national rock band was formed in Hamburg, Germany, in 1973. Initial members included Ian Cussick (b. Scotland; vocals), Geoff Pacey (b. England; keyboards), Bernie Whelan (b. Ireland; trumpet), plus four European partners (three German, one Italian). Despite innumerable line-up shuffles Lake's harmonic, neo-orchestral approach to rock music remained intact, which led to a glowing and growing international reputation. Their self-titled 1976 debut album enhanced this impression further, and sold over 400,000 copies in Germany. A fierce retinue of gigs included several open air concerts throughout mainland Europe, dates at the London Marquee in England and a 40-concert tour of the US (where the album charted). After a live album they returned to the studio in 1978 for *Lake II*, which was promoted by an appearance on the UK's **Old Grey Whistle Test** television programme and support slots with **Genesis** and **Bob Dylan**. They were also voted the best rock band in several German music polls. The constantly revolving line-ups continued to make their history confusing, and by the late 70s the group's personnel included James Hopkins-Harrison (d. May 1991; vocals), Alex Conti (guitar) and Detlef Petersen (keyboards). By 1981 the band decided that, having failed to capitalize on their initial success, it was time to go their separate ways. Conti went on to a solo career, while other members became embroiled in session work. There was subsequently a brief and successful reunion of various former members in 1983.

● ALBUMS: *Lake* (Columbia 1976)★★, *Live* (Columbia 1977)★★, *Lake II* (Columbia 1978)★★, *Paradise Island* (Columbia 1979)★★, *Ouch* (1980)★★, *Hot Day* (1981)★, *Live/On The Run* (1982)★★.

Lake, Greg

b. 10 November 1948, Bournemouth, Dorset, England. Lake is a vocalist and bass guitarist of great ability. He started to play the guitar at the age of 12, earning small amounts of money by entertaining customers at his local bingo hall. At 15, he left school to pursue a career as a draughtsman, but by the age of 17 had played as a full-time musician with both Shame and the Gods. In 1968, he was contacted by **Robert Fripp** and Michael Giles, who had heard of his musical abilities and peculiar choir-like tone of his voice, and was invited to form **King Crimson** with them. With King Crimson, Lake played at the **Rolling Stones**' Hyde Park, free concert on 5 July 1969, and the high profile of this occasion guaranteed the band almost overnight fame. However, during the recording of *In The Wake Of Poseidon*, he left to join **Emerson, Lake And Palmer**. This trio quickly gained a reputation for being one of the most technically skilled bands of the 70s. **Keith Emerson** (b. 1 November 1944, Todmorden, England; keyboards) and Carl Palmer (b. 20 March 1951, Birmingham, England; drums/percussion) made up the outfit which first played at the Isle of Wight festival in 1970. The band set up their own record label, Manticore, but despite considerable commercial success, they temporarily disbanded in 1974. Lake resurfaced around Christmas time 1975 when he released what was to become one of the most perennially-popular Christmas singles with 'I Believe In Father Christmas' (co-written with King Crimson/ELP lyricist Pete Sinfield) - the song carried on the ELP tradition of including a passage of popular classical music with Prokofiev's 'Sleigh Bell Ride'. This single, which reached number 2 in the UK, was so successful that it was re-released in both 1982 and 1983. In 1977 Lake collaborated with Sinfield again to write blues-oriented songs such as 'Closer To Believing' on *Works, Volumes 1 And 2* by the reformed Emerson, Lake And Palmer. A huge tour followed this project, during the course of which the trio were accompanied by a full symphony orchestra. They disbanded for a second time in 1980, and Lake released the solo *Greg Lake* the following year. The album peaked at number 62 in both UK and US charts. The Greg Lake Band, which lasted from June 1981 to April 1982 included **Gary Moore** (guitar), Tommy Eyre (keyboards), Tristram Margetts (bass) and Ted McKenna (drums, former **Rory Gallagher** group and later **MSG**). Another solo album was released in 1983 for **Chrysalis Records**, but this time failed completely. In September 1983, Lake briefly replaced **John Wetton** in **Asia**. In 1984, he renewed his relationship with Emerson, and in 1985 *Emerson, Lake And Powell* was released, the latter name belonging to experienced drummer **Cozy Powell**. A new drummer, Richard Berry, was recruited for the release of the unsuccessful 1988 *To The Power Of Three*. By 1992, the original trio were performing and recording together again.

● ALBUMS: *Greg Lake* (Chrysalis 1981)★★, *Manoeuvres* (Chrysalis 1983)★★.

Lake, Oliver

b. 14 September 1942, Marianna, Arkansas, USA. Lake's family moved to St. Louis, Missouri in 1943. He played in high school, but only applied himself seriously to alto saxophone at the age of 20. Lake worked in R&B and soul bands with **Lester Bowie**, then formed his own group with Floyd LeFlore (trumpet) and Leonard Smith (drums). In 1968, he received a BA in music education from Lincoln University and taught music in St. Louis schools for three years. During this time he became a founder member of the **Black Artists Group** (BAG) and co-ordinated exchange concerts with Chicago's **AACM**. He studied arrangement and composition with **Oliver Nelson** and bassist **Ron Carter**. In 1972, he joined other BAG members in Paris, played with **Anthony Braxton** and explored electronic music. He relocated to New York in September 1973, but returned to Paris to record *Passing Thru*, a solo alto saxophone record with a sax/synthesizer dialogue called 'Whap', in May 1974. Braxton used his position at **Arista Records** to get Lake a record contract and wrote a sleevenote for *Heavy Spirits* (1975). The album was a masterpiece of chilled modernity, including three tracks of improvised alto against scored strings. Lake subsequently lightened his approach, to mixed results. A band with Michael Gregory Jackson (guitar) and Paul Maddox (drums, later Pheeroan akLaff) played startlingly original music (1976-8), spiky *avant garde* classical sonorities threaded with pliant saxophone. *Prophet*, recorded in 1980 for the Black Saint label, was a tribute to Lake's idol **Eric Dolphy**, while the next year's *Clevont Fitzhubert*, was classic free-bop. Later signed to Gramavision, Lake attempted to come on as a pop band (*Jump Up*), but despite spirited playing they never seemed to quite get the hang of the reggae rhythms they attempted to use. Lake had played in a saxophone quartet brought together by Braxton for his *New York, Fall 1974* and in 1977, with **David Murray** replacing Braxton, they called themselves the **World Saxophone Quartet**. By the mid-80s the group were firm favourites at international jazz festivals. Lake meanwhile led small groups that often included **Geri Allen**, akLaff and Fred Hopkins, producing shining, incisive music that brought together all the diverse threads of his career. In the late 80s he was also playing with **Reggie Workman** in the bassist's own Ensemble and in the collective Trio Transition, and he can also be heard in electrifying form on **Marilyn Crispell**'s live 1991 *Circles*.

● ALBUMS: *Passing Thru* (1974)★★★, *Heavy Spirits* (1975)★★★★, *NTU: Point From Which Creation Begins* 1971 recording (1976)★★★★, *Holding Together* (Back Saint 1976)★★★, *Life Dance Of Is* (1978)★★★, *Shine* (1978)★★★, *Prophet* (Black Saint 1981)★★★★, *Clevont Fitzhubert* (Black Saint 1981)★★★★, *Jump Up* (Gramavision 1982)★★, *Plug It* (Gramavision 1983)★★★, *Expandable Language* (1985)★★★, *Gallery* (Gramavision 1986)★★★, *Impala* (1987)★★★, *Otherside* (Gramavision 1988)★★★, *Trio Transition With Oliver Lake* (1989)★★★, *Again And Again* (Gramavision 1991)★★★, *Zaki* (Hat Art 1992)★★★★, *Prophet* 1980 recording (1993)★★★, with Donai Leonellis Fox *Boston Duets* (Music And Arts 1992)★★, *Virtual Reality (Total Escapism)* (1993)★★★.

● COMPILATIONS: *Compilation 1982-1988 recordings* (1990).

Lakeman Brothers

Sean (b. *c*.1973; guitar), Sam (b. *c*.1975; keyboards) and Seth Lakeman (b. *c*.1977; violin) were responsible for one of the best roots music releases of 1994. From the unfortunately named Crapstone town, near Yelverton, Devon, England, they had a strong musical thread inherited from their parents. They originally formed their own group as teenagers, appearing on BBC television's *Saturday Superstore*. Over a period of years they proved popular attractions on the jazz and folk circuits throughout their native South West England. During this time they became acquainted with similarly inclined groups such as the **Battlefield Band** and **Oyster Band**, who regularly stayed at their home during visits to the area. They produced *3 Piece Suite* themselves, and it received excellent reviews in the folk music press. As well as a cover of **Billy Joel**'s 'And So It Goes' there were fine renditions of traditional and original compositions, all of which were honed with an impressive ear for construction and arrangement. It featured contributions from **Kathryn Roberts**, with whom the brothers later in **Equation**.

● ALBUMS: *3 Piece Suite* (Crapstone Music 1994)★★★.

Lakeside

Formed in 1969, US vocalists Tiemeyer McCain, Thomas Oliver Shelby, Otis Stokes and Mark Woods were augmented by an instrumental unit consisting of Steve Shockley (guitar), Norman Beavers (keyboards), Marvin Craig (bass), Fred Alexander (drums) and Fred Lewis (percussion). Originally based in Dayton, Ohio, USA, this funk group secured its first hit in 1978 with 'It's All The Way Live'. Released on the **Solar** label, it was the first of a series of popular singles including 'Fantastic Voyage' (1980), 'I Want To Hold Your Hand' (1982) and 'Outrageous' (1984), all of which reached the US R&B Top 10. Although guitarist Shockley was an integral part of the Solar house band, Lakeside lacked the profile of labelmates **Shalamar**. A three-year chart hiatus ended in 1987, but that year's 'Bullseye' remains the group's last chart entry to date.

● ALBUMS: *Shot Of Love* (Solar 1978)★★★, *Rough Riders* (Solar 1979)★★★, *Fantastic Voyage* (Solar 1980)★★★, *Keep On Moving Straight Ahead* (Solar 1981)★★, *Your Wish Is My Command* (Solar 1982)★★, *Untouchables* (Solar 1983)★★★, *Outrageous* (Solar 1984)★★.

Lalor, Trudi

b. 23 March 1972, Portlaoise, County Laoise, Eire. She grew up with an interest in music and in her teens sang with local musical societies. Successful appearances at local concerts led to her joining Hazel records where her first release, a four-track EP, *Money Talks*, gained her considerable air play. Lalor's break came in September 1993, when the very popular **Louise Morrissey** was incapacitated by a serious car crash. During Morrissey's absence, the talented Lalor fronted her band, fulfilled all her Irish and UK commitments and quickly established herself as one of the best young singers on the British and Irish country scene. She has since fronted her own Country Band and has created a considerable impression at concerts all over Ireland and the UK. At one concert, she even greatly impressed **Garth Brooks**, who unexpectedly arrived at the show during his visit to Ireland. Her debut album, produced by Ray Lynam, clearly demonstrates her ability to handle new country material such as Jamie O'Hara's 'For Reasons I've Forgotten' and Eurovision composer Teresa O'Donnell's 'If This World Could Love', as well as old-time favourites, all interspersed with the expected country and Irish, especially her stunning rendition of 'Lovely Laoise'.

● ALBUMS: *Next Time 'Round* (Hazel 1995)★★★.

Lamare, Hilton 'Nappy'

b. Hilton Napoleon Lamare, 14 June 1907, New Orleans, Louisiana, USA, d. 9 May 1988. Guitarist and banjo player Lamare's early career was spent in his home town where he played with a number of leading bands of the 20s including those of Johnny Bayersdorffer, Johnny Wiggs and **Sharkey Bonano**. In 1930, he joined **Ben Pollack**'s nationally-popular band and stayed in the group when it evolved into the **Bob Crosby** band. As a member of Crosby's sprightly rhythm section Lamare, who also sang occasionally, became a well-known performer on record, on the dancehall circuit and in films. In 1942, he left Crosby with other sidemen for the **Eddie Miller** Orchestra. During the 40s he regularly led his own bands and helped run the Club 47 in Los Angeles of which he was co-owner. In subsequent decades he worked with various like-minded musicians, including **Joe Darensbourg**. Lamare also appeared in a number of Crosby reunion bands and led his own band, the Straw Hat Strutters, on a television show, *Dixie Showboat*, and, with **Ray Bauduc**, another old comrade from the Crosby band, he co-led the Riverboat Dandies.

● ALBUMS: with Ray Bauduc *Riverboat Dandies* (Capitol 1957)★★★, with Bauduc *On A Swinging Date* (Mercury 1960)★★★.

● COMPILATIONS: *Masters Of Dixieland, Volume 4* (1975).

Lamb (UK)

A Manchester, Lancashire, England based duo of Louise Rhodes (songwriting/vocals) and Andrew Barlow (production), Lamb were signed to **Fontana Records** in 1995 before A&R manager Richard O'Donovan had heard any proper demo recordings. Instead he was impressed by Rhodes' vision and personality, and the four songs they played him at a hastily arranged meeting in Manchester convinced him of their star qualities. The group were formed in 1994 shortly after Barlow's

return from a three and a half year spell attending high school in Philadelphia. He had come back to attend a sound engineering course, eventually becoming in-house remixer for the So What management stable. He met Rhodes, the daughter of a folk singer, through a mutual friend. They set about working on songs together almost immediately. Their debut for Fontana, 'Cotton Wool', proved popular on the underground club scene with its dextrous employment of jazz and drum 'n' bass textures. It was followed by the similarly impressive 'Gold'. Remixers involved in these two singles included Fila Brazilia, Mr Scruff and **Autechre**. Their own remix work includes collaborations with UK indie band **Space**.

● ALBUMS: *Lamb* (Mercury 1996)★★★.

Lamb (USA)

Formed in San Francisco, California, USA, Lamb was formed as a folk-based duo by Barbara Mauritz (vocals) and Bob Swanson (vocals/guitar). **Bill Graham** signed them to his Fillmore label where by 1970 they had developed into a rock act with the addition of Mark Springer (guitar), Tom Salisbury (keyboards), David Hayes (bass) and Rick Schlosser (drums). Now managed by Graham, the sextet were heavily promoted around the Bay Area, securing a slot on the closing bills at the **Fillmore** West and on the resultant film and soundtrack album. However, although Mauritz's vocals were strong, the material played was unexceptional. Mauritz then had an unsuccessful solo career while Hayes and Schlosser joined **Van Morrison**'s band. Schlosser then played with **Boz Scaggs**' band, playing once again with Tom Salisbury.

● ALBUMS: *A Sign Of Change* (Fillmore 1970)★★★, *Cross Between* (Warners 1971)★★, *Bring Out The Sun* (Warners 1971)★★★.

Lamb, Annabel

Although this UK pop vocalist is relegated to the one-hit wonder category, her unusual vocal delivery of the **Doors**' hit 'Riders On The Storm' created considerable interest and made the UK Top 30. The brooding, breathy vocal style was used to great effect on this and subsequent releases. Her backing musicians comprised: Robin Langridge (keyboards), Steve Greetham (bass), Chris Jarrett (guitar) and Jim Dvorak (trumpet). The hybrid of jazz, rock and reggae consistently produced by Wally Brill found only a loyal coterie of fans. Little has been heard of Lamb since 1988.

● ALBUMS: *Once Bitten* (A&M 1983)★★★, *The Flame* (A&M 1984)★★★, *Brides* (RCA 1987)★★★, *Justice* (1988)★★★.

● COMPILATIONS: *Heartland* (1988)★★★.

Lamb, Paul, And The Kingsnakes

b. 9 July 1955, Blyth, Northumberland, England. Lamb's initial interest in blues came from listening to **John Mayall**'s records; he then discovered the music of **Sonny Terry**, in whose style he thoroughly immersed himself for 12 years. He played in folk clubs and in 1975 was successful in a harmonica championship held in Germany. Around 1980, he began playing amplified harmonica, initially in **Walter 'Shakey' Horton**'s style, and as a member of the Blues Burglars he recorded for Red Lightnin' in 1986. Shortly afterwards, Lamb moved to London and formed his own band. In 1990, 1991 and 1992 Paul Lamb And The Kingsnakes were voted UK Blues Band of the Year, and Lamb himself received the Instrumentalist of the Year award which he won for a further five years, well into the 90s. The line-up of the King Snakes is Martin Deegan (drums), Chad Strentz (vocals), Jim Mercer (bass), and the weathered-looking but highly accomplished guitarist John Whitehill (b. 11 February 1952, Newcastle-upon-Tyne, England). Lamb may never receive mass acceptance, but they are one of the most exciting bands playing white-boy Chicago blues to have appeared for many years. Lamb's playing has been heard in the stage musical *Tommy*, in television advertisements for Nissan cars, and in television drama, *Spender* and *Crocodile Shoes*. He recorded a top 40 single 'Harmonica Man' for **PWL** (Pete Waterman) in 1995 under the name Bravado (UK number 37). The many awards in magazines such as *Blueprint* represent a worthy recognition of Lamb's unrivalled position as a brilliant harmonica player at the forefront of British blues. *Blues & Rhythm* described the band as 'lazily cocksure and coolly aggressive'.

● ALBUMS: *Paul Lamb And The Kingsnakes* (Ace 1991)★★, *Shifting Into Gear* (Tight & Juicy 1993)★★★, *Fine Condition* (Indigo 1995)★★★★, *She's A Killer* (Indigo 1996)★★★, *John Henry Jumps In* (Indigo 1998)★★★.
Solo: John Whitehill *Guitar Slinger* (Indigo 1997)★★★.

Lambchop

Led by singer and guitarist Kurt Wagner, Lambchop are a large, Nashville, Tennessee-based ensemble whose instrumentation is highly unique within the popular music tradition. Wagner's world-weary vocals (which in an earlier age would have delineated him as a 'crooner') are backed by an eight-piece orchestra featuring clarinet, lap steel guitar, saxophone, trombone, organ, cello and 'open-end wrenches'. While the group appear immaculately dressed in suits for their live appearances, Wagner's urbane, often seedy narratives offer a highly contrary proposition, describing such delights as suicide and romantic allure on their highly praised alternative country debut, *I Hope You're Sitting Down*. For 1996's *How I Quit Smoking*, Lambchop employed the services of arranger John Mock, previously best known for his work with **Kathy Mattea**, to embellish the lush orchestral backdrop. This was aided by the presence of a string quartet. The results were excellent, allowing Wagner to indulge himself in the sort of grandiose country melodramas not heard since the heyday of **Jim Reeves**.

● ALBUMS: *I Hope You're Sitting Down* (Merge 1994)★★★, *How I Quit Smoking* (Merge 1996)★★★, *Thriller* (City Slang 1996)★★★★.

Lambe, Jeanie

b. c.1949, Scotland. Lambe sang at the age of 17 with the Clyde Valley Stompers and then for many years she worked in the London area with a variety of bands including **Kenny Ball**, **Chris Barber**, **Acker Bilk** and **Alex Welsh**. Gradually, her fame spread, partly owing to appearances at many international jazz festivals where she often sang with small groups led by her husband **Danny Moss**. With him, she spent time in Australia, residing there at the start of the 90s but continuing to tour annually either in America or Europe. During her career Lambe has sung with modern and mainstream jazz musicians including **Monty Alexander**, **Ben Webster**, **Budd Johnson**, **Oscar Peterson**, **Wild Bill Davison**, **Kenny Davern**, **Joe Pass** and **Buddy Tate**. Over the years, Lambe's voice has subtly darkened, adding greater texture to an already fluid musical instrument.

● ALBUMS: *Jeanie Lambe With The Danny Moss Quartet* (Flyright 1980)★★★, *Blues And All That Jazz* (Zodiac 1982)★★★, *The Midnight Sun* (Zodiac 1983)★★★★, *My Man* (Zodiac 1988)★★★, *Happy Birthday Jazz Welle Plus* (Nagel-Heyer 1994)★★★, *Three Great Concerts Jeanie Lambe And The Danny Moss Quartet Live In Hamburg* (Nagel-Heyer 1996)★★★★.

Lambert, Dave
(see **Lambert, Hendricks And Ross**)

Lambert, Donald

b. c.1904, Princeton, New Jersey, USA, d. 8 May 1962. Taught initially by his mother, Lambert developed into a leading exponent of the stride piano style. During the late 20s he was much in demand as a solo pianist in clubs and at 'rent parties' in Harlem. From the early 30s he worked mostly in and around New York, spending many years in long residencies at a small number of clubs. Consequently, Lambert's fame was largely localized although he was highly-regarded by fellow pianists. He made a handful of well-received records in the early 40s and a few more in the years just prior to his death in 1962.

● COMPILATIONS: *Harlem Stride Classics 1960-62* (1979)★★★★, *Piano Giant - Stride* (1979)★★★★, *Classics In Stride* (1988)★★★★.

Lambert, Hendricks And Ross

In the late 50s a group of singers began informal 'vocalese' jam sessions at the New York apartment of Dave Lambert (b. 19 June 1917, Boston, Massachusetts, USA, d. 3 October 1966). At these sessions singers would improvise vocal lines in much the same manner as jazz instrumentalists. Ten years previously, Lambert had worked as arranger and singer in **Gene Krupa**'s band, recording 'What's This?', an early example of a bop vocal. In 1955, Lambert teamed up with **Jon Hendricks** (b. 16 September 1921, Newark, Ohio, USA) to record a vocalized version of 'Four Brothers'. In 1958, Lambert and Hendricks added to their duo the highly distinctive singer **Annie Ross** (b. Annabelle Short Lynch, 25 July 1930, Mitcham, Surrey, England) to record the album *Sing A Song Of Basie*. The concept of the Lambert, Hendricks And Ross recordings was simple, although highly complex in execution. The singers performed wordless vocal lines, matching the brass and reed section parts of the **Count Basie** band's popular recordings. With this formula they enjoyed great success in the late 50s and early 60s. In 1962, Ross left the trio and was replaced by Yolande Bavan (b. 1 June 1940, Colombo, Ceylon). Two years later Lambert also left and soon thereafter the trio concept was abandoned. Subsequently, Lambert worked briefly as a studio arranger before his death in 1966.

● ALBUMS: *Sing A Song Of Basie* (ABC 1957)★★★, *Sing Along With Basie* (Roulette 1958)★★★, *The Swingers* (Affinity 1959)★★★, *The Hottest Group In Jazz* (Columbia 1959)★★★, *Lambert, Hendricks And Ross Sing Ellington* (Columbia 1960)★★★, *High Flying* (Columbia 1960)★★★★. As Lambert, Hendricks And Bavan *Lambert, Hendricks And Bavan: Having A Ball At The Village Gate* (RCA 1963)★★★, *Live At Basin Street East* (RCA Victor 1963)★★★, *At Newport* (RCA Victor 1963)★★★, *At The Village Gate* (RCA Victor 1964)★★★.

● COMPILATIONS: *Twisted: The Best Of Lambert , Hendricks And Ross* (Rhino 1992)★★★★.

Lambert, Kit

Initially a budding film-maker, Lambert became involved with music when he and partner Chris Stamp sought a group to star in a short feature film. They discovered the **Who** - then known as the High Numbers - in September 1964, but having abandoned their initial intention, assumed management duties within a week. A mutual acquaintance brought Lambert together with producer **Shel Talmy** and although a recording deal ensued, the former quickly grew disillusioned with its terms. He broke the deal in 1966 by producing the Who's fourth single, 'Substitute', but although an out-of-court settlement awarded Talmy substantial damages, the group was free to record elsewhere. The following year Lambert and Stamp created Track Records, the roster of which included not only the Who, but **Jimi Hendrix, Arthur Brown, Thunderclap Newman** and **John's Children**. Lambert played an important role in the conception of the Who's pop-opera *Tommy* - he was the son of noted composer/arranger Constant Lambert - and his suggestions and inspiration were later acknowledged by its creator, **Pete Townshend**. The resultant album, however, was the last to bear Lambert's production credit and during the ensuing decade, relations between the group and management gradually deteriorated. Two years of legal wrangling were finally settled in 1975. The Who adopted a new manager, Bill Curbishley, and label, **Polydor**, while the subsequent collapse of Track effectively ended Lambert's active tenure in the music business. Whereas Stamp resumed his interest in film work, his former partner embarked

on a life of excess which ended tragically on 7 April 1981 when he died of a brain haemorrhage following a fall at his mother's home.

Lambert, Lloyd

b. 4 June 1928, Thilbodaux, Louisiana, USA, d. 31 October 1995. Blues bassist Lloyd Lambert was best known as the bandleader of **Guitar Slim**'s band, who enjoyed significant national popularity in the 50s. After initially training as a trumpet player, he had his first break with Hosea Hill's Serenaders. He then formed a touring band, largely consisting of former members of the Serenaders, for Guitar Slim, after the latter had secured a contract with **Specialty Records**. Lambert's electric bass (at that time an innovation) was present on all the recordings made by Slim for Specialty and **Atlantic Records**, and he also backed **Little Richard** and **Ray Charles**. He recorded his own solo record for Specialty, an instrumental entitled 'Heavy Sugar'. Following Slim's death in 1959, Lambert toured for a time with **Nappy Brown**, then settled in Houston. For most of the 60s he was employed in session work for the Duke and Peacock labels. Eventually, he returned to New Orleans, and in 1981 formed his own Dixieland band, playing at the Maison Bourbon for the remainder of the decade. In later years he helped to resurrect the career of **James 'Thunderbird' Davis**, who had formerly opened for Guitar Slim. Lambert died of cancer in 1995.

Lambrettas

This English, Brighton-based band comprised Jez Bird (vocals, guitar), Doug Saunders (guitar, vocals), Mark Ellis (bass, vocals) and Paul Wincer (drums). Together with **Secret Affair**, the **Merton Parkas** and the **Chords**, they were part of the UK's short-lived mod revival of 1979-80. After securing a contract with **Elton John**'s Rocket Records, they had 'Go Steady' included on the label's compilation *499 2139*, alongside fellow mod hopefuls the **Act**, the Escalators, Les Elite and the Vye. A month later, in November 1979, the same version of 'Go Steady' was released as a single, with little success, but drew much attention from the growing mod audiences. Success arrived with 'Poison Ivy', a catchy remake of the **Leiber And Stoller**-penned classic, reaching number 7 in the UK charts during 1980, eight places higher than the **Coasters**' original version of 1959. Their popularity continued with follow-up singles entering the charts, 'D-a-a-ance' climbed to number 12, and 'Another Day (Another Girl)' just managed to scrape into the UK Top 50, reaching number 49. The latter was originally called 'Page Three', but threatened legal action by *The Sun* newspaper persuaded the band to rethink the title. Their debut, *Beat Boys In The Jet Age*, peaked at number 28 and was also their last glimpse of the charts. Successive releases, 'Steppin' Out', 'Good Times', 'Anything You Want', 'Decent Town' and 'Somebody To Love', had little impact on either critics or record-buying public, and by the time they issued *Ambience* in 1981, the mod revival was dead and buried and the band quickly folded. In 1985, Razor Records unearthed the Lambrettas' back catalogue, releasing a compilation of their singles, entitled *Kick Start*.

● ALBUMS: *Beat Boys In The Jet Age* (Rocket 1980)★★★, *Ambience* (Rocket 1981)★★.

● COMPILATIONS: *Kick Start* (Razor 1985)★★★.

Lamond, Don

b. 18 August 1920, Oklahoma City, Oklahoma, USA. Lamond's early drumming career was spent in and around Washington, DC, where he was raised, and later in Baltimore, Maryland. In the early 40s he played in **Sonny Dunham**'s dance band and in the forward-looking big band of **Boyd Raeburn**. In 1945, he joined **Woody Herman**'s First Herd where he had the unenviable task of replacing the excellent if unstable **Dave Tough**. Lamond stood up well to the test and became an important member of Herman's band, playing in the Second Herd in the late 40s. Lamond also made records with several small bebop groups of the period, including those led by **Charlie Parker** and by fellow Herdsman **Serge Chaloff**. Lamond's abilities are such that he proved a welcome addition to bands covering a wide range of jazz, from bebop to dixieland by way of big and small mainstream groups. Always swinging, he played with **Benny Goodman**, **Zoot Sims**, **Sonny Stitt**, **Quincy Jones**, **Johnny Guarnieri** and the **Sauter-Finegan Orchestra**. In the 60s, Lamond toured extensively, visiting Europe and the following decade began leading a big band formed from eager young musicians in Florida where he had become resident.

● ALBUMS: as Don Lamond And His Big Band *Extraordinary* (Progressive 1983)★★★.

Lamour, Dorothy

b. Mary Leta Dorothy Stanton (or Kaumeyer), 10 December 1914, New Orleans, Louisiana, USA, d. 22 September 1996, Los Angeles, California, USA. An actress and singer particularly remembered for the series of 'Road' films with **Bing Crosby** and **Bob Hope** in which she invariably wore her trademark sarong. Crowned Miss Orleans at the age of 14, she moved to Chicago in the early 30s and worked in clubs and on radio, becoming known as the 'Sultry Songstress of the Airwaves' even though the listeners were unaware that she had 'a stunning statuesque figure'. She married bandleader Herbie Kay in 1934 and they were divorced in 1939. A subsequent marriage to millionaire business William Ross Howard survived for 35 years until his death in 1978. She made her breakthrough into films in 1936 with *The Jungle Princess*, the first of what she calls 'those silly, but wonderful jungle pictures', which included *Her Jungle Love* and *Moon Over Burma*. In the late 30s she appeared in several musical films, including *Swing High Swing Low*, *College Holiday*, **High Wide And Handsome**, *Thrill Of A Lifetime*, *The Big Broadcast Of 1938*, and *Tropic Holiday*. One of her best roles came

in **St. Louis Blues** (1939), in which she played an ex-Broadway star and sang several appealing numbers such as 'Blue Nightfall', 'I Go For That', 'Let's Dream In The Moonlight', and the title song. She joined Crosby and Hope on **The Road To Singapore** in 1940, and continued to travel with them along other 'Roads' to Zanzibar (1941), Morocco (1942), Utopia (1946), Rio (1947), and Bali (1953). Rumour has it that she nearly did not make the trip to Hong Kong in 1962, but Hope is said to have insisted on her presence in the picture, although Joan Collins played the main female role. Over the years, in between the 'Roads', she made several other mostly entertaining musicals including **The Fleet's In**, *Star Spangled Rhythm*, *Dixie*, *Riding High, And The Angels Sing*, *Rainbow Island*, *Duffy's Tavern*, *Variety Girl*, *Lulu Belle*, *Slightly French*, and *The Greatest Show On Earth* (1952). This was in addition to films in which she played straight roles - a total of more than 60 in all. She was still making the occasional feature film and television appearance into the 80s. In her one-woman show she poked fun at her image - the sarongs and all that - and told of the occasion when she received a standing ovation from 5,000 people while heading a touring company of **Hello, Dolly!** in the late 60s. All the sarongs have been auctioned off for charity, and there is a rumour that one resides in the Smithsonian Museum.

● COMPILATIONS: *The Moon Of Manakoora* (ASV 1997)★★★.

● FURTHER READING: *My Side Of The Road*, Dorothy Lamour and D. McInnes.

● FILMS: *The Jungle Princess* (1936), *Swing High Swing Low* (1937), *The Last Train From Madrid* (1937), *College Holiday* (1937), *High Wide And Handsome* (1937), *Thrill Of A Lifetime* (1937), *The Hurricane* (1937), *The Big Broadcast Of 1938* (1938), *Spawn Of The North* (1938), *Her Jungle Love* (1938), *Tropic Holiday* (1938), *Man About Town* (1939), *St. Louis Blues* (1939), *Disputed Pasage* (1939), *Johnny Apollo* (1940), *Road To Singapore* (1940), *Typhoon* (1940), *Moon Over Burma* (19440), *Chad Hanna* (1940), *Caught In The Draft* (1941), *Road To Zanzibar* (1941), *Aloma Of The South Seas* (1941), *The Fleet's In* (1942), *Beyond The Blue Horizon* (1942), *Road To Morocco* (1942), *They Got Me Covered* (1943), *Star Spangled Rhythm* (1943), *Dixie* (1943), *Riding High* (1943), *And The Angels Sing* (1944), *Rainbow Island* (1944), *Duffy's Tavern* (1945), *Masquerade In Mexico* (1945), *A Medal For Benny* (1945), *Road To Utopia* (1946), *Road To Rio* (1947), *My Favourite Brunette* (1947), *Wild Harvest* (1947), *Variety Girl* (1947), *On Our Merry Way* (aka *A Miracle Can Happen*, 1948), *The Girl From Manhattan* (1948), *Lulu Belle* (1948), *Slightly French* (1949), *Manhandled* (1949), *Lucky Stiff* (1949), *Here Comes The Groom* (1951, cameo), *The Greatest Show On Earth* (1952), *Road To Bali* (1953), *The Road To Hong Kong* (1962), *Donovan's Reef* (1963), *Pajama Party* (1964), *The Phynx* (1970, cameo), *Creepshow 2* (1987).

Lamplighters

This vocal R&B outfit was formed in 1952 at Jordan High School in Los Angeles, California, USA, but was always too erratic and plagued with personal problems to be destined for success in the long haul. Leon Hughes, Matthew Nelson and Willie Ray Rockwell comprised the initial trio, who entered a talent show at **Johnny Otis**'s Barrell House but came second to singer **Thurston Harris** (b. 11 July 1931, Indianapolis, Indiana, USA, d. 1990, California, USA). They set about convincing him to join forces with them, and he eventually agreed. Al Frazier, formerly vocalist with the Mellomoods, helped to choreograph their rough stage act. Their performances soon evolved into some of the most exciting and wild events on the west coast R&B circuit, with acrobatics and audience participation that predated the rock 'n' roll boom. Frazier, too, was persuaded to join the group. After losing Leon Hughes, the unit secured a contract at Federal Records, having been once more reduced to a quartet. Their debut single, a powerful ballad titled 'Part Of Me', failed to garner its just reward, though it did introduce them as the Lamplighters (Federal boss Ralph Bass had chosen the name in the absence of any band decision). A second single emerged, 'Bee Bop Wino', but its title ironically mirrored the slide of several members of the band into alcoholism. Indeed, Rockwell later died after drunkenly crashing his car into a telephone pole. In 1954, following the release of 'Sad Life', 'Smoothie', 'I Used To Cry Mercy, Mercy' and 'Salty Dog', the group embarked on a major tour, with Eddie Jones and Harold Lewis deputizing for Rockwell and Nelson. Harris quit halfway through the tour because of a disagreement over money, and that appeared to be the end of the story. However, back in Los Angeles, Frazier put together a new version of the band with Carl White, Sonny Harris and a returning Matthew Nelson. The new formation christened itself the Tenderfoots. Four singles, beginning with 'Kissing Bug' in March 1955, failed to bring any success, and they returned to the Lamplighters name after renewing their friendship with Thurston Harris. Three final singles emerged on Federal between 1955 and 1956. However, Thurston Harris's old behaviour problems resurfaced and he was soon replaced by Turner Wilson III. After this, the group changed names again to become the Sharps, while Thurston Harris enjoyed one major solo single, 'Little Bitty Pretty One' (which ironically featured the Sharps as uncredited backing band).

Lancaster, Byard

b. 1942, Philadelphia, Pennsylvania, USA. Multi-instrumentalist Lancaster (alto, tenor and soprano saxophones/flutes/clarinets/piano) was, with **Sonny Sharrock**, **Dave Burrell** and Eric Gravatt, part of a second generation of African-American 'new jazz' players who viewed themselves as **John Coltrane**'s spiritual heirs or 'John's Children' as the title of an early Lancaster band song (written by Sharrock) insisted, committed to the same 'healing' energies inherent in the jubilant scream. Lancaster identified with secular screams, hence the motto on his business cards: *From A*

Love Supreme To The Sex Machine And All In Between. In the 80s, following the demise of the French Palm label, which had championed his solo work, Lancaster was heard often as a star guest musician, playing loud and proud with **Ronald Shannon Jackson**'s Decoding Society, Kip Hanrahan and Garrett List.

● ALBUMS: *It's Not Up To Us* (1967)★★, *Live At McAlester College '72* (1972)★★★, *Sounds Of Liberation - New Horizons* (1972)★★★, *Us* (1974)★★★, *Exactement* (1974)★★★, with Clint Jackson *Mother Africa* (1974)★★, *Funny Funky* (1975)★★★, *Exodus* (1977)★★★, *Documentation: The End Of A Decade* (1980)★★, *Personal Testimony* (1980)★★★.

Lancastrians

The Lancastrians made their recording debut in 1964 with a version of **Gale Garnett**'s million-seller 'We'll Sing In The Sunshine' but, despite a crafted production by **Shel Talmy**, this personable cover version barely scraped the UK Top 50. The UK group's breezy, if anonymous style was later captured on 'Let's Lock The Door' (1965), first recorded by **Jay And The Americans**, and 'The World Keeps Going Round' (1966), donated by fellow-Talmy proteges the **Kinks**. The producer's interest in the Lancastrians waned as their singles proved increasingly unsuccessful and they subsequently disbanded.

Lance, Major

b. 4 April 1939, Winterville, Mississippi, USA, d. 3 September 1994, Decatur, Georgia, USA. A former amateur boxer and a dancer on the Jim Lounsbury record-hop television show, Lance also sang with the Five Gospel Harmonaires and for a brief period with **Otis Leavill** and Barbara Tyson in the Floats. His 1959 **Mercury** release, 'I Got A Girl', was written and produced by **Curtis Mayfield**, a high school contemporary, but Lance's career was not truly launched until he signed with **OKeh Records** three years later. 'Delilah' opened his account there, while a further Mayfield song, the stylish 'The Monkey Time' in 1963, gave the singer a US Top 10 hit. The partnership between singer and songwriter continued through 1963-64 with a string of US pop chart hits: 'Hey Little Girl', 'Um Um Um Um Um Um', 'The Matador' and 'Rhythm'. Although Lance's range was more limited than that of his associate, the texture and phrasing mirrored that of Mayfield's work with his own group, the **Impressions**. 'Ain't That A Shame', in 1965, marked a pause in their relationship as its commercial success waned. Although further vibrant singles followed, notably 'Investigate' and 'Ain't No Soul (In These Rock 'N' Roll Shoes)', Lance left OKeh for Dakar Records in 1968 where 'Follow The Leader' was a minor R&B hit. Two 1970 releases on Curtom, 'Stay Away From Me' and 'Must Be Love Coming Down', marked a reunion with Mayfield. From there, Lance moved to Volt, Playboy and Osiris, the last of which he co-owned with Al Jackson, a former member of **Booker T. And The MGs**. These spells were punctuated by a two-year stay in

Britain (1972-74), during which Lance recorded for Contempo and **Warner Brothers**. Convicted of selling cocaine in 1978, the singer emerged from prison to find his OKeh recordings in demand as part of America's 'beach music' craze, where aficionados in Virginia and the Carolinas maintained a love of vintage soul. A heart attack in September 1994 proved fatal for Lance.

● ALBUMS: *Monkey Time* (OKeh 1963)★★★, *Major Lance's Greatest Hits - Recorded 'Live' At The Torch* (OKeh 1973)★★, *Now Arriving* (Motown 1978)★★, *The Major's Back* (1983)★★, *Live At Hinkley* (1986)★★.

● COMPILATIONS: *Um Um Um Um Um - The Best Of Major Lance* (OKeh 1964)★★★, *Major's Greatest Hits* (OKeh 1965)★★★, *The Best Of Major Lance* (Epic 1976)★★★, *Monkey Time recorded 60s* (Edsel 1983)★★★, *Swing'est Hits Of ...* (1984)★★★, *The Best Of Major Lance* (Beat Goes On 1998)★★★.

Land, Harold

b. 18 December 1928, Houston, Texas, USA. Resident in California from early childhood, tenor saxophonist Land practised extensively with **Eric Dolphy**, holding informal, all-day sessions at Dolphy's home. Arising from the local fame these sessions engendered, Land was hired as replacement for **Teddy Edwards** in the **Max Roach-Clifford Brown** Sextet. This was in 1954, and by the time he left the band in November of the following year, Land's name and reputation were thoroughly established. In 1956, he became a member of **Curtis Counce**'s influential group, made numerous important record dates with many leading west coast musicians, led his own groups and also co-led a fine band with **Red Mitchell**. An exceptionally gifted player, Land developed his own distinctive style early in his career although he later acknowledged **John Coltrane** by incorporating some of the latter's stylistic patterns into his own highly original work.

● ALBUMS: *The Harold Land All Stars* (1949)★★★, *Clifford Brown And Max Roach* (1954)★★★★, *The Curtis Counce Group/Landslide* (1956)★★★, *You Get More Bounce With Curtis Counce* (1957)★★★, with Curtis Counce *Carl's Blues* (1958)★★, *Harold In The Land Of Jazz* (Original Jazz Classics 1958)★★★★, *Grooveyard* (Contemporary 1958)★★★, *The Fox* (Contemporary 1959)★★★, *West Coast Blues!* (1960)★★★, *Eastward Ho! Harold Land In New York* (Original Jazz Classics 1960)★★★★, *Take Aim* (1960)★★★, with Red Mitchell *Hear Ye!* (1961)★★★, *The Harold Land Quintet* (1963)★★★, *The Harold Land-Carmell Jones Quintet* (1963)★★★, *The Pace-maker* (1968)★★, *Choma* (1971)★★★, *Damisi* (1974)★★★, with Blue Mitchell *Mapanzi* (Concord 1977)★★★, *Live At Junk* (1980)★★, *Xocia's Dance (Sue-sha)* (Muse 1981)★★★.

Land, Jon

b. Nicholas Febland, 6 October 1960, London, England. This keyboard player and ex-orchestral trumpeter began composing in the 'new age' vein when a student at London's Royal Academy of Music. He continued to do so on becoming a full-time teacher. He has since

emerged as one of the genre's leading lights, over many instrumental albums that have charted the evolution of an unpredictably exotic style. *Nicholas Land Plays The Classics* was a change of style as an affectionate amble down 'memory lane'. From 1984, much of his output has been produced, arranged and co-written by **Clifford White**, a former pupil. Released on the Audio Art label, 1991's ground-breaking *Beyond The Sky*, a work in 10 movements, was, arguably, Land's strongest offering with respectable sales.

● ALBUMS: *The Seasons* (1978)★★, *The Wonders Of The World* (1979)★★, *Nicholas Land Plays The Classics* (1980)★★★, *Night Echoes* (1982)★★★, *Shimmering Moon* (1983)★★★, *Ionospheres* (1985)★★★, *The Speed Of Sound* (1987)★★★, *Legacy* (1989)★★★, *Beyond The Sky* (1991)★★★★.

Landers, Jake

b. Jacob Landers, 14 August 1938, Lawrence County, Alabama, USA. Landers is well respected in bluegrass music not only as a performer but also as a songwriter. He learned guitar and during the 60s, along with Herschel Sizemore and Rual Yarborough, he played for several years as a member of the Dixie Gentlemen. During this time they recorded five albums which contained almost 20 songs either wrote or co-wrote by Landers including 'Soldier's Return' and 'Your Heart Tells The Truth'. When Sizemore and Yarborough moved to other groups, Landers played with other combinations but concentrated more on his songwriting. This received a boost, in 1969, when **Bill Monroe** recorded 'Walk Softly On My Heart' and 'Beyond The Gate'. In 1970, he and banjoist Tom McKinney each recorded one side of an album on Tune, a label owned by Yarborough. In the early 70s, he and Yarborough formed the Dixiemen, with whom they recorded four albums. Landers' song 'Down By The Waterfall' became very popular and was covered with considerable success by the **Country Gentlemen**. After they disbanded, in 1976, he began to record albums for Old Homestead, including one that consisted of all gospel material but all contained several self-penned numbers. In the 80s, Landers' daughters became involved in the music when he formed the Jake Landers Family Band and recorded for Old Homestead. He also appeared in a reunion of the Dixie Gentlemen which resulted in an album release on Rutabaga. In 1989, the **Kentucky Headhunters**, charted at number 25, with their rock country version of his song 'Walk Softly On My Heart', retitled 'Walk Softly On This Heart Of Mine'.

● ALBUMS: *Jake Landers & Tom McKinney Present Original Songs & New Banjo Sounds Of The 70s* one side each (Tune 1971)★★★, *Singer/Writer* (Old Homestead 1978)★★★★; as the Jake Landers Family Band *The Old Folks Don't Live Here* (Old Homestead 1981)★★★, *The River Is Deep* (Old Homestead 1983)★★★, *I'd Like To Ride That Big Train Again* (Old Homestead 1992)★★.

Landreth, Sonny

Being born in Canton, Mississippi, USA, birthplace or thereabouts of **Elmore James**, did not mean that Sonny Landreth had to play slide guitar, but it certainly makes good copy. In fact, after five years in Jackson, Mississippi, the family moved to Lafayette, Louisiana, and Landreth grew up surrounded by Cajun music and its lifestyle. At the age of 10, he began studying trumpet in school, and three years later took up the guitar. At 20, he left college and, with his band Brer Rabbit, moved to Colorado. There he met **Robben Ford**, and worked in Michael Murphy's band. He also developed his unique slide technique, chording behind the steel at the 12th fret. Returning to Louisiana, he became involved with several Cajun bands, including Zachary Richard, Beausoleil, Red Beans & Rice, and in 1979 became the first white musician in **Clifton Chenier**'s band. His first recordings were made for **Huey Meaux** in 1973. Then, in 1981, he made *Blues Attack*, the first of two albums for **Jay Miller**'s Blues Unlimited label. *Way Down In Louisiana* was issued in 1985. When not playing sessions, Landreth toured with his band, Bayou Rhythm. In 1988, he and the band backed **John Hiatt** on his *Slow Turning* album, touring America and Europe as 'The Goners'. Landreth spent the next two years preparing his *Outward Bound* album, eventually released in 1992. Landreth has been compared to **Ry Cooder** and **David Lindley** but his distinctive blend of rock, blues and Cajun music gives him prominence in the hierarchy of slide guitarists.

● ALBUMS: *Blues Attack* (Blues Unlimited 1981)★★★, *Way Down In Louisiana* (Blues Unlimited 1985)★★★, with John Hiatt *Slow Turning* (A&M 1988)★★, with John Mayall *A Sense Of Place* (Island 1990)★★★★, *Outward Bound* (1992)★★★★, *South Of I-10* (Zoo Entertainment 1995)★★★,.

Landry, Art

One of the earliest dance orchestras, the Art Landry Band (also known as Art Landry's Call Of The North Orchestra) formed in the early 20s and recorded widely on the east coast of America. Led by Landry on clarinet, the usual formation featured bass, piano, drums, guitar, trombone, two trumpets and three saxophones. Musicians included John Maitland, Dean Duel, George De Kay, Hal Sorensen, Joe Smith, Ted Mack, Sam Carr, Wilbur Edwards, Howard Emerson, Jimmie Greco, Boyce Cullen, Carl Gauper, Red Thomas, Dick Humphrey, Al Marineau and Henry Burr. Their records for Gennett and **Victor Records** were primarily recorded in either New York or Camden, New Jersey, but failed to produce enough popular support to ensure their longevity. The band retired in the 30s, a short time before the dance band boom took off.

Landsborough, Charlie

b. Charles Alexander Landsborough, 26 October 1941, Wrexham, Clywd, Wales. Landsborough's family come from Birkenhead and he has spent his life on Merseyside. After several jobs, he trained as a teacher, but music has been the mainstay of his life. He was part of a local beat group, the Top Spots, but developed his own style by writing gentle, melodic, romantic ballads, albeit influenced by the American singer-songwriter **Mickey Newbury**. Because of his teaching commitments and transport problems with 'unreliable cars', he is little known outside Merseyside. His main strength is as a songwriter. Foster And Allen entered the UK charts with the astute reflections of 'I Will Love You All My Life', and Roly Daniels put 'Part Of Me' into the Irish charts. The repertoire of many Irish country artists includes 'The Green Hills Are Rolling Still', while 'Heaven Knows', which suggests that people should be colour-coded according to their deeds, has been recorded by **George Hamilton IV**. Landsborough does not stray from his niche of astute social or romantic observations, and, sooner or later, a big-name artist will convert one of his songs into a standard. The most likely contenders are 'No Time At All' and 'I Will Love You All My Life'.

● ALBUMS: *Heaven Knows* (1989)★★★ *Songs From The Heart* (1992)★★★, *What Colour Is The Wind?* (Ritz 1994)★★★, *With You In Mind* (Ritz 1996)★★★, *Further Down The Road* (Ritz 1997)★★★.

● VIDEOS: *An Evening With Charlie Landsborough* (1995).

Landscape

Formed in 1975, this English jazz-funk instrumental group comprised Richard James Burgess (vocals/computer/drums), Andy Pask (bass), Christopher Heaton (keyboards), Peter Thomas (trombone/synthesizer) and John Walters (computer programming/wind synthesizers). They built up a loyal following by continuously touring and after a couple of years formed their own independent record label. Their album debut came in 1979 when they signed to **RCA**. However, the record sold badly, this was a surprise considering the reputation they had gained as a live act. In 1980, 'European Man' revealed the band going in a new direction. The easy-going jazz-funk had been replaced by advanced technology, computer programming, synthesizers and vocals. The single became a dancefloor favourite and just missed a national chart position. In 1981, the group finally made an impact with the commercial 'anti-war' track 'Einstein A Go-Go'. Complete with a simple catchy hookline, it reached number 5 in the UK and Top 10s all over Europe. The follow-up, 'Norman Bates', a tribute to the classic Hitchcock movie *Psycho*, also reached the UK Top 40. The line-up survived another album and a handful of singles, but by 1983 they had been reduced to a trio renamed Landscape 3. By the time the final split came in 1984 Burgess was already making a name for himself by producing acts including **Spandau Ballet** and **Living In A Box**.

● ALBUMS: *Landscape* (1979)★★★, *From The Tea Rooms Of Mars...To The Hell Holes Of Uranus* (1981)★★★, *Manhattan Boogie Woogie* (1982)★★.

Lane, Burton

b. 2 February 1912, New York City, New York, USA, 5 January 1997. Lane was a distinguished composer for films and the stage. After studying piano as a child, he later played stringed instruments in school orchestras. Some early compositions written for the school band attracted attention, and while still in his early teens he was commissioned to write songs for a projected off-Broadway revue, which never came to fruition. In his mid-teens Lane joined the staff of the Remick Music Company where he was encouraged in his songwriting career by **George Gershwin**. In 1929 he worked with **Howard Dietz** on some songs for the Broadway revue *Three's A Crowd*, and with **Harold Adamson** on *Earl Carroll's Vanities Of 1931*. When the effects of the Depression hit Broadway, Lane went to Hollywood and wrote for numerous musical films, often with Adamson. During the 30s his screen songs included 'Heigh Ho, The Gang's All Here', 'You're My Thrill', 'Stop, You're Breaking My Heart', 'Says My Heart' and his first major hit, 'Everything I Have Is Yours'. Perhaps the most popular of his songs of this period were 'The Lady's In Love With You' (**Frank Loesser**), from the film *Some Like It Hot*, 'I Hear Music' (Loesser) and 'How About You?' (Ralph Freed). The latter was sung by **Judy Garland** and **Mickey Rooney** in *Babes On Broadway* (1940). Lane also contributed scores or single songs to other movies such as *Dancing Lady*, *Bottoms Up*, *Her Husband Lies*, *Love On Toast*, *Artists And Models*, *Champagne Waltz*, *College Holiday*, *Swing High, Swing Low*, *Cocoanut Grove*, *College Swing*, **St. Louis Blues**, *Spawn Of The North*, *She Married A Cop*, *Dancing On A Dime*, *Ship Ahoy*, *Du Barry Was A Lady*, *Hollywood Canteen*, **Royal Wedding**, and *Give A Girl A Break* (1952). *Royal Wedding* contained one of the longest song titles ever - 'How Could You Believe Me When I Said I Love You When You Know I've Been A Liar All My Life?', as well as the lovely 'Too Late Now' and 'Open Your Eyes' (all **Alan Jay Lerner**). Among the other songs in those aforementioned pictures were 'I Hear Music', 'Poor You', 'Last Call For Love', 'I'll Take Tallulah', 'Tampico', 'Moonlight Bay', 'Madame, I Love Your Crepe Suzettes', 'You Can Always Tell A Yank', 'What Are You Doing The Rest Of Your Life?', and 'I Dig A Witch In Witchita'.

In the 40s Lane wrote the score for the Broadway musicals *Hold On To Your Hats* (with **E.Y. 'Yip' Harburg**), *Laffing Room Only* (with **Al Dubin**), and the whimsical **Finian's Rainbow** (Harburg). The latter show, which opened in 1947 and ran for more than 700 performances, contained a fine set of songs including 'That Great Come-And-Get-It Day', 'Old Devil Moon', 'How Are Things In Glocca Morra?', 'When I'm Not Near The Girl I Love', 'If This Isn't Love', and 'Look To The Rainbow'. It was 18 years before Lane was back on Broadway with **On A Clear Day You Can See Forever** (Lerner) from which came 'Come Back To Me', 'Hurry! It's Lovely Up Here!', 'Melinda', and several other fine numbers. Lane and Lerner were teamed again in 1978 for *Carmelina*, which, despite the engaging 'One More Walk Around The Garden', 'Someone In April', 'I'm A Woman', and 'It's Time for A Love Song', was a resounding flop.

Throughout his long career Lane worked with many partners. As well as the men already mentioned, these included Ted Koehler, Sam Coslow, **Ira Gershwin**, and **Sammy Cahn** with whom he collaborated on songs such as 'Can You Imagine?' and 'That's What Friends Are For' for the Hanna-Barbera animated film *Heidi's Song* in 1982. Ten years after that, at the age of 80, Burton Lane was inducted into the US Theatre Hall Of Fame and was presented with the Berkshire Festival Theatre's fourth American Theatre Award at a benefit performance appropriately entitled *Hold On To Your Hats*. One of the stars of the show, singer and music archivist Michael Feinstein, released two CDs of Lane's songs in the early 90s. On each one he was accompanied by the composer himself on the piano. A long-time member of the Songwriters Hall of Fame, Burton was honoured in the Lyrics and Lyricists series at New York's 92nd Street 'Y' in April 1995.

Lane, Cristy

b. Eleanor Johnston, 8 January 1940, Peoria, Illinois, USA. Lane was the eighth of 12 children brought up in a economically depressed area. In 1959, she married country music fan Lee Stoller, who encouraged her to sing country, and, after many local performances, she made her first single, 'Janie Took My Place', in Nashville in 1968. She and her husband sold their Peoria nightclub, Cristy's Inc., and moved to Nashville in 1972. Stoller formed LS Records, chiefly to release his wife's product. Her first entry on the US country charts was with 'Tryin' To Forget About You' in 1977. She then had Top 10 country hits with 'Let Me Down Easy', 'I'm Gonna Love You Anyway', 'Penny Arcade' and 'I Just Can't Stay Married To You'. Further country hits followed but Stoller was jailed for financial irregularities. She moved to United Artists and had a US country number 1 in 1980 with a gospel song written by Marijohn Wilkin and **Kris Kristofferson**, 'One Day At A Time'. Her husband, released from jail and inspired by **Slim Whitman**'s album sales through television advertising, took over her career and started marketing her in a similar way. He did it so well that he was able to write about his success in a book, *One Day At A Time*. Cristy Lane has continued performing into the 90s, basing herself in Branson, Missouri.

● ALBUMS: *Cristy Lane...Is The Name* (LS Records 1977)★★, *Love Lies* (LS Records 1978)★★★, *Simple Little Words* (United Artists 1979)★★★, *I Have A Dream* (United Artists 1980)★★, *Ask Me To Dance* (United Artists 1980)★★★, *Fragile - Handle With Care* (United Artists 1981)★★★, *Amazing Grace* (United Artists 1982)★★★, *Here's To Us* (United Artists 1983)★★★, *Christmas Is The Man From Galilee* (United Artists 1983)★★, *Amazing Grace, Vol. 2* (Arrival 1986)★★, *All In His Hands* (Heartwarming 1989).

● COMPILATIONS: *Footprints In The Sand* (United Artists

1983)★★★, *My Best To You* (Arrival 1992)★★★.
● FURTHER READING: *Cristy Lane: One Day At A Time*, Lee Stoller with Pete Chaney.

Lane, Lois

b. Lois Wilkinson, 3 April 1944, Sleaford, Lincolnshire, England. As half of female singing duo the **Caravelles**, Lois enjoyed a major hit in 1963 with 'You Don't Have To Be A Baby To Cry'. Their light, breathy vocal style quickly found favour, but by 1966 Lane had left the duo to pursue an alternative career. Dubbing herself 'Lois Lane' after the *Superman* comic character, she recorded a handful of MOR-styled singles but became better known as a fixture of BBC Light Programme and Radio 2 sessions, singing versions of popular hits of the day when 'needletime' restrictions precluded the use of original records.
● ALBUMS: *Lois Lane* (Mercury 1968)★★★.

Lane, Lupino

b. Henry George Lupino, 16 June 1892, London, England, d. 10 November 1959, London, England. An actor, singer, dancer, choreographer, author, and director. Lane was born into a theatrical family which could trace its connections with the stage back to 1632 - one of his famous ancestors was the clown Grimaldi. At the age of four he was performing in theatres, and soon earned the nickname 'Nipper'. He developed his own individual style of extremely skilful, and sometimes dangerous comic acrobatic dancing, and appeared in many English and American two-reelers. However, his greatest impact was made in stage musicals where his trademark bowler hat and Cockney persona endeared him to audiences, especially those in London. From 1915 through to 1934 he appeared in the West End in musical productions such as *Watch Your Step*, *Follow The Crowd*, *Extra Special*, *Afgar*, *League Of Notions*, *Puss-Puss* (1920), *Brighter London*, *Turned Up*, *Silver Wings* (1930), *The One Girl*, and *The Golden Toy*. In 1935, *Twenty To One*, a musical with a plot about horse racing, was Lane's first show as director and producer as well as actor. Two years later he had the biggest hit of his career with *Me And My Girl* (1937) in which he introduced the enormously popular 'Lambeth Walk'. In the 40s Lane continued on the London stage with *La-Di-Da-Di-Da*, *Meet Me Victoria*, and *Sweetheart Mine* (1946). Although he had enjoyed success in silent films during the 20s, he was unable to recreate his later stage appeal in talkies. However, he and Lillian Roth were acclaimed for their performances as second leads in *The Love Parade* (1929), which starred **Maurice Chevalier** and **Jeanette MacDonald**. Another well-known member of Lane's show business family was Stanley Lupino (b. 15 May 1894, London, England, d. 10 June 1942, London England), who was also an athletic dancer and a talented all-round performer. He appeared in a number of London musical productions from 1917 until 1941, and introduced several amusing songs including Leslie Sarony's 'I Lift Up My Finger And I Say 'Tweet Tweet'' in *Love Lies* (1929). Among his other shows were *Suzette*, *Arlette*, *Hullo, America!*, *Cinderella*, *Jig-Saw*, *The Peep Show*, *Phi-Phi*, *Dover Street To Dixie*, *Puppets*, *Better Days*, *So This Is Love*, *The Love Race*, *Hold My Hand*, *Sporting Love*, *Over She Goes*, *Crazy Days*, *The Fleet's Lit Up*, *Funny Side Up*, *Lady Behave*. He also made nearly 20 films. Stanley Lupino was the father of the actress Ida Lupino, who went to Hollywood and starred in numerous films from the 30s through to the 80s, including *They Drive By Night*, *High Sierra*, and *Roadhouse*. Lupino Lane's only child, Lauri Lupino Lane, who appeared with his father in *Me And My Girl*, was a regular performer in UK variety theatres until television closed them down in the early 60s. He died at the age of 64 in 1986, and is reckoned to be the last in the line of the celebrated family of entertainers.
● FURTHER READING: *Born To Star - The Lupino Lane Story*, J.D. White. *From The Stocks To The Stars*, Stanley Lupino.

Lane, Red

b. Hollis R. DeLaughter, 9 February 1939, near Bogalusa, Louisiana, USA. A singer-songwriter who learned guitar as a child, Lane moved to Nashville in the early 60s, where he worked with **Justin Tubb** and as a session musician. In 1967, he became frontman for **Dottie West**'s band and co-wrote with West her 1968 hit 'Country Girl'. In the early 70s, he recorded for **RCA** and charted four minor hits, the biggest being 'The World Needs A Melody' and the last, 'It Was Love While It Lasted', in 1972. Since then he has remained active as a session musician and toured as a guitarist with **Merle Haggard**. Some of his songs have been recorded by top artists but he has failed to achieve further chart successes of his own.
● ALBUMS: *The World Needs A Melody* (RCA 1971)★★.

Lane, Ronnie

b. 1 April 1946, Plaistow, London, England, d. 4 June 1997, Trinidad, Colorado, USA. A founder-member of the **Small Faces** and **Faces**, Lane left for a highly stylized solo career in 1973. He formed a backing group, Slim Chance, which included (Benny) **Gallagher And** (Graham) **Lyle**, and had a UK Top 20 hit with the effervescent 'How Come?', in 1974. In the same year 'The Poacher' was a UK Top 40 hit, but the group were unable to maintain their chart success. Ronnie's debut, *Anymore For Anymore*, was a finely honed mixture of good-time original songs and folksy cover versions, the most impressive of which was Lane's reading of **Derroll Adams**' 'Roll On Babe'. Lane's progress, however, faltered on an ambitious tour, the Passing Show, with its attendant fire-eaters and jugglers. Financial burdens caused its abandonment and the original Slim Chance broke up in disarray. A new line-up was later convened around Brian Belshaw (bass - formerly of **Blossom Toes**), Steve Simpson (guitar/mandolin), Ruan O'Lochlainn (keyboards/saxophone), Charlie Hart (keyboards/accordion) and Colin Davey (drums). Two excellent albums, *Ronnie Lane's Slim Chance* and *One For The Road*, confirmed the promise of that first collection. The singer disbanded his group in 1977, although several ex-members, including Gallagher, Lyle and Hart, appeared on *Rough Mix*, Ronnie's excellent collaboration with **Who** guitarist **Pete Townshend**. This critically acclaimed release was preceded by *Mahoney's Last Stand*, a less satisfying venture with former Faces member **Ron Wood**. Although Lane completed another stylish collection, *See Me* in 1979, his progress was blighted by the debilitating disease, multiple sclerosis. Over the years Lane's condition deteriorated considerably and he lived in comparative poverty, although efforts were made to raise money for him through various rock benefits. Despite his illness, he still managed to tour in the USA and embarked on a tour in Japan during 1990. A financial settlement of past royalties made in 1996 from **Castle Communications** helped immensely with his medical bills. He finally lost his battle against the disease in 1997, dying at his adopted home in Trinidad, Colorado, where he lived with his wife and stepchildren. Lane's collaborations with Steve Marriott in the 60s produced some of the best songs of the decade.

● ALBUMS: *Anymore For Anymore* (GM 1973)★★★, *Ronnie Lane's Slim Chance* (GM 1974)★★★★, *One For The Road* (GM 1975)★★★★, with Ron Wood *Mahoney's Last Stand* (Atlantic 1976)★★★, with Pete Townshend *Rough Mix* (Polydor 1977)★★★★, *See Me* (Gem 1979)★★★.

Lang, Don

b. Gordon Langhorn, 19 January 1925, Halifax, Yorkshire, England, d. 3 August 1992, London, England. Lang started as a dance band trombonist working with the bands of Peter Rose, **Teddy Foster** and **Vic Lewis**. It was with Lewis that he made his first recordings. He began singing with **Ken Mackintosh**'s Band and is credited under his real name on some of their records and also one recording with the **Cyril Stapleton** Orchestra. Lang went solo in the mid-50s and after a couple of singles on **Decca** he made the UK Top 20 with a 'vocalese' (scat jazz) version of 'Cloudburst' in 1956/56 on **HMV Records**. Together with his Frantic Five (which included the late saxophonist Red Price) he was one of the first UK acts to get involved with rock 'n' roll and skiffle, although his jazz roots were always audible. The group appeared regularly on UK television's seminal *6.5 Special* and sang the theme song over the credits. After many unsuccessful singles he charted with a cover of **Chuck Berry**'s 'School Day' and reached the Top 10 with a version of **David Seville**'s 'Witch Doctor' (with the curious lyric, 'ooh ee ooh aha bing bang walla walla bing bang'). When the hits dried up for this elder statesman of UK pop, he formed a new band and played the dancehall and club circuit for many years. At times he sang alongside such notable acts as the **Mike Sammes** and **Cliff Adams** Singers and played on records like the **Beatles**'

'white album' (*The Beatles*). Alongside 50s acts like **Wee Willie Harris** and **Tommy Bruce**, he could still be seen on the UK rock 'n' roll circuit. For a time he returned to his first love - jazz, but for the last few years of his life he was in virtual retirement, emerging for the occasional rock 'n' roll revival show or recording session. He died of cancer in the Royal Marsden Hospital in August 1992. His son Brad has played bass for **ABC** and **Toyah**.

● ALBUMS: *Skiffle Special* (HMV 1957)★★★, *Introducing The Hand Jive* (HMV 1958)★★★, *Twenty Top 20 Twists* (HMV 1962)★★.

● COMPILATIONS: *Rock Rock Rock* (1983)★★★, with the Twisters *20 Rock 'n' Roll Twists* (1988)★★★.

Lang, Eddie (blues)

b. Edward Langlois, 15 January 1936, New Orleans, Louisiana, USA, d. 10 May 1985, New Orleans, Louisiana, USA. Lang grew up liking country and hillbilly music, so much so that when he became a member of **Jessie Hill**'s House Rockers, he would often regale audiences with a **Hank Williams** song. In 1952 he joined **Guitar Slim**'s band and his diminutive stature earned him the nickname Little Eddie. It was the artist credit used when both artists recorded for Nashville's Bullet label, although Eddie's 'My Baby Left Me' did less well than Slim's 'Feelin' Sad'. Apart from a solitary title for Savoy that was not released for 27 years, Lang next recorded for RPM in 1956, and 'Come On Home' became a regional hit. 'Troubles, Troubles' and three other titles, although recorded by **Johnny Vincent** for Ace with a band that included **Mac Rebennack** on guitar, were released on the new Ron label. In 1966 he signed with Seven-B Records and again, two singles were released, although a second session, including 'I'm Gonna Make You Eat Those Words' and 'The Fooler', remained unissued until 1987. Lang's greatest success came in 1973, when his SuperDome single, 'Food Stamp Blues', sold some 80,000 copies. His career was ended in 1979 by a stroke and he died from a second seizure in 1985.

● ALBUMS: *Southern Blues* (Savoy 1981)★★★, *Rough Dried Blues* (Charly 1987)★★★, *Loaded Down With The Blues* (Charly 1987)★★★, *Troubles, Troubles* (Rounder 1988)★★★, *Good To The Last Drop* (Charly 1989)★★★.

Lang, Eddie (jazz)

b. Salvatore Massaro, 25 October 1902, Philadelphia, Pennsylvania, USA, d. 26 March 1933. The first truly significant guitarist in jazz, Lang began his career playing violin but was familiar with what was to become his main instrument through his father's work as a guitar maker. As a youth, Lang became acquainted with **Joe Venuti**, forming a musical partnership of exceptional quality. After working in bands in his home town and Atlantic City he joined the **Mound City Blue Blowers**, visiting London with the band in 1924. Later, Lang played in a band led by Venuti and then the pair joined **Roger Wolfe Kahn**, **Adrian Rollini**, led their own band, then were hired by **Paul Whiteman**. During their stint with Whiteman, Lang recorded with **Bing Crosby** and appeared in the films, *King Of Jazz* (1930) and *The Big Broadcast* (1932). After leaving Whiteman, Lang accompanied Crosby, who had a clause in his recording contract stipulating that the guitarist should always be present on his record dates. During this time, Lang continued to record with Venuti. Lang's playing was notable for his single-string solos and his deft accompaniments. Until his emergence the guitar had been thought of as little more than a rhythm instrument, but his work opened the way for it as an effective solo voice. During his brief career he made numerous records including superb duets with **Lonnie Johnson** and sessions with Crosby and **Joe 'King' Oliver**, but is best-remembered for those with Venuti which remain classics of their kind. Lang died in March 1933 while undergoing a tonsillectomy.

● COMPILATIONS: with Venuti *The Golden Days Of Jazz: Stringing The Blues* (1976)★★★, *Joe Venuti And Eddie Lang (1926-28)* (1983), *Jazz Guitar Virtuoso* (Yazoo 1988)★★★, with Lonnie Johnson, King Oliver *A Handful Of Riffs (1927-29)* (Living Era 1989)★★★, *Jazz Guitar Rarities* (Recording Arts 1993)★★★.

Lang, Jonny

b. 29 January 1981, Fargo, North Dakota, USA. Blues guitarist/singer Jonny Lang was signed to **A&M Records** as a child prodigy before his sixteenth birthday - having only received his first guitar at the age of 13. By this time he had already earned a strong regional reputation as an interpreter of the blues, eventually moving from Fargo to Minneapolis to become leader of Kid Jonny Lang And The Big Bang. That group's independently released *Smokin'* album underscored Lang's growing reputation, selling an impressive 25,000 copies without the aid of national distribution. By the time A&M stepped in for his signature, he had also played alongside such blues greats as **Luther Allison, Lonnie Brooks** and **Buddy Guy**. *Lie To Me*, produced by David Z (**Janet Jackson, Collective Soul, Fine Young Cannibals**), was an impressive major label debut. Although more mainstream in its combination of blues and soul textures than the raw *Smokin'*, it confirmed Lang as a guitarist of impressive range and astonishing maturity. It included songs written by David Z, Lang's keyboard player, Bruce McCabe, Dennis Morgan and Lang himself, alongside cover versions of material by **Sonny Boy Williamson** ('Good Morning Little School Girl') and **Ike Turner** ('Matchbox').

● ALBUMS: *Smokin'* (Own Label 1996)★★, *Lie To Me* (A&M 1997)★★★.

lang, k.d.

b. Kathryn Dawn Lang, 2 November 1961, Consort, Alberta, Canada. She prefers the lower case appearance of her name because 'it's generic and unlike Cherry Bomb, it's a name, not a sexuality'. This farmer's daughter had become a skilled pianist and guitarist by

adolescence and, on leaving school, scratched a living in the performing arts, classical and *avant garde* music, before choosing to sing country - a genre that she had once despised as the corniest in pop. She forsook much of its rhinestoned tackiness for a leaner, more abandoned approach on *A Truly Western Experience*. She was known for her slightly skewered sensibility and a tough backing combo consisting in 1983 of Gordon Matthews (guitar), Ben Mink (violin, mandolin), Mike Creber (piano), John Dymond (bass) and Michel Pouliot (drums). She named them the Reclines - a genuflexion towards **Patsy Cline**. Overseen by **Dave Edmunds**, *Angel With A Lariat* was favoured by influential rock journals such as *Rolling Stone* (who voted lang Female Vocalist of the Year), but many country radio stations refused to play it, prejudiced as they were by lang's spiky haircut, vegetarian stance and ambiguous sexuality (she would only go public on the latter subject in a June 1992 interview with *Advocate* magazine). Nevertheless, she charted via 'Cryin'', a duet with **Roy Orbison** for 1987's *Hiding Out* comedy movie soundtrack. The following year, she gained a breakthrough with the lush *Shadowland*, which was rendered agreeable to country consumers through a Nashville production by **Owen Bradley** and the presence of the **Jordanaires, Brenda Lee, Loretta Lynn, Kitty Wells**. Tracks such as the tear-jerking 'I Wish I Didn't Love You So' and **Chris Isaak**'s 'Western Stars' exemplified what lang described as 'torch and twang' - an expression incorporated into the title of her next collection. Mostly self-composed with Mink, it set the seal on the grudging acceptance of her by bigots and, more to the point, confirmed her as a behemoth of country's New Tradition. In 1992, she became newsworthy and featured in dozens of magazines in Europe and the USA, who finally picked up on the considerable talent of k.d. lang when the acclaimed *Ingenue* was released. This excellent release was, however, far removed from country, C&W or new country; it was a sensual and deep collection firmly putting her in sight of major honours. The same year showed lang to possess a promising acting ability when she made her film debut in *Salmonberries*. Since *Ingenue*, her commercial profile has waned, although she has continued to produce interesting albums. *Drag* included a highly original interpretation of **Steve Miller**'s 'The Joker'.

● ALBUMS: *A Truly Western Experience* (Bumstead 1984)★★, *Angel With A Lariat* (Sire 1987)★★★, *Shadowland* (Sire 1988)★★★, *Absolute Torch And Twang* (Sire 1989)★★★, *Ingenue* (Sire/Warners 1992)★★★★, *Even Cowgirls Get The Blues* film soundtrack (Sire/Warners 1993)★★, *All You Can Eat* (Sire/Warners 1995)★★★, *Drag* (Warners 1997)★★★.

● VIDEOS: *Harvest Of Seven Years* (Warner Music Video 1992), *Live In Sydney* (Warner Music Video 1998).

● FURTHER READING: *Carrying The Torch*, William Robertson. *k.d. lang*, David Bennahum. *All You Get Is Me*, Victoria Starr.

● FILMS: *Salmonberries* (1992).

Langa Langa Stars

Formed in 1981, Langa Langa Stars are one of the many splinter groups from Zaire's revolutionary ensemble **Zaiko Langa Langa**, playing in the same raw-edged, streetwise vein. Keeping track of the various members of the group is complicated by their propensity for solo and group collaborations with other zaiko groups, including Choc Choc Stars. In the mid-80s they were joined by Evoloko 'Joker', the original vocalist with Zaiko Langa Langa. The mainstay of the band, however, is Bozi, with whom they have perfected a rough-toned Zaiko style without ever threatening to establish its native popularity on foreign shores.

● ALBUMS: *Requiem* (Vercky's 1983)★★★, *Likombe* (Vercky's 1984)★★★★, *Eliyo* (Vercky's 1985)★★★, *Done Bis* (Vercky's 1987)★★★.

Langford, Frances

b. 4 April 1913, Lakeland, Florida, USA. Langford began singing as a child and after some stage work, mostly in vaudeville, she established a reputation as a nightclub singer. By the mid-30s her light, sweet singing voice had made her a popular recording and broadcasting star and she was invited to Hollywood. Some of her films were merely vehicles in which she played supporting roles and sang a couple of songs, such as in *Hollywood Hotel* (1937) and *Follow The Band* (1943), the latter an early Robert Mitchum film. Occasionally, she was the female lead as in *Palm Springs* (1936), where she played opposite David Niven in his first leading role in Hollywood, and *Girl Rush* (1944), a Wally Brown-Alan Carney comedy, in which she worked again with Mitchum. In the late 30s she had several hit records, including 'I Feel A Song Comin' On', 'I'm In The Mood For Love', 'Easy To Love', 'Was It Rain?', 'Harbour Lights', 'So Many Memories', and 'Falling In Love With Love'. During World War II she toured extensively, entertaining US troops with **Bob Hope** and Jerry Colonna, continuing her commitment later in Korea. For several years she was a regular on Hope's popular radio show. By the end of the 40s Langford's film career was virtually over but she continued to broadcast on the radio and make records, often teaming up with major stars such as **Louis Armstrong**. In 1954, she played herself in *The Glenn Miller Story*. Subsequently, her career has drifted quietly away.

● COMPILATIONS: *Gettin' Sentimental* (1988).

Lanier, Jaron

b. *c.*1960, USA. One of the more surprising musical artists of the 90s, Jaron Lanier is much better known as a computer scientist - wherein he is widely described as the 'father of virtual reality', having been the first to coin the term. Despite his interests in cyber-technology, in 1994 he recorded a debut album, *Instruments Of Change*, which was dominated by analogue recording techniques. As he told the press, '*Instruments Of Change* was intended to make a statement that music is primary, culture is primary and that we can't get lost in machines.' Including medieval bowed harp and musical patterns drawn from India and the Far East, Lanier confessed the real imperative behind the project was that music was his first love. Further, his most famous invention, the Data Glove (an instrument allowing the user to control various aspects of the virtual reality environment) was based on his desire to play 'air guitar'. He combined both his interests for 'The Sound Of One Hand', a live improvisational performance piece which featured him performing musical instruments in a virtual reality environment. 1996's *Music From Inside Virtual Reality* pushed the boundaries back further, featuring such elements as a rhythm generated by dancers inside a virtual world and virtual instruments such as flutes 'bent and twisted inside virtual reality by my motions while I play them, which definitely does make new sounds'.

● ALBUMS: *Instruments Of Change* (Point 1994)★★★★, *Music From Inside Virtual Reality* (Sony 1996)★★★.

Lanin, Sam

b. Philadelphia, Pennsylvania, USA, d. 5 May 1977. Lanin studied clarinet formally with composer **Victor Herbert** before deciding to form a dance band. Shortly after the end of World War I he took a band into New York's popular Roseland Ballroom where he was resident for 13 years. His band included many future stars of jazz and the swing era, amongst them **Tommy** and **Jimmy Dorsey**, **Frank Teschemacher**, **Bix Beiderbecke** and **Artie Shaw**. For several years in the 20s Lanin's band was featured on a radio show sponsored by Ipana Toothpaste and his band, known as the Ipana Troubadours, had a substantial following. By the late 30s he had opted to leave centre stage and moved to Florida. Lanin's brothers, Howard and Lester, have also led bands: although Howard achieved little distinction, Lester's brand of blandly inoffensive dance music has brought him many prestigious engagements at US presidential functions and British royal family parties.

● COMPILATIONS: *It's Fun To Fox-Trot* (1981)★★★.

Lanois, Daniel

b. 1951, Hull, Canada. This esteemed producer rose to fame during the late 80s through his contribution to major releases by **Peter Gabriel** (*So*) and U2 (*The Unforgettable Fire* and *The Joshua Tree*). He subsequently produced *Robbie Robertson*, the widely-acclaimed 'comeback' album by the former leader of the **Band**, and in 1989 undertook a similar role on **Bob Dylan**'s *Oh Mercy*, widely-regarded as the artist's finest work in several years. Lanois's love of expansive, yet subtle, sound, reminiscent of 'new age' styles, combines effectively with mature, traditional rock, as evinced on the artist's own album, *Acadie*. Drawing inspiration from French-Canadian heritage - Lanois used both his native country's languages, sometimes within the same song - he created a haunting tapestry combining the jauntiness of New Orleans' music with soundscaped instrumentals. Contributions by **Brian Eno** and the **Neville Brothers**, the latter of whom Lanois also produced, added further weight to this impressive collection. Lanois and Eno co-produced U2's two aforementioned multi-million-selling studio albums and their combined influence has given the band's sound new dimensions. He was instrumental in re-directing **Emmylou Harris**'s career with *Wrecking Ball* in 1995 and toured with her, leading his own band during the autumn of that year. He produced Dylan's excellent *Time Out Of Mind* in 1997.

● ALBUMS: *Acadie* (Opal 1989)★★★★, *For The Beauty Of Wynona* (1993)★★★.

Lanor Records

Lanor Records is the brainchild of famed Cajun producer Lee Lavergne, a native of rural town Church Point, near Crowley in Louisiana, USA. He formed the label in 1960 as an adjunct to his day job as a cleric in a wholesale grocery. Influenced by **Hank Williams** and other country artists as a child, Lavergne began to record local artists after being demobbed from the army. The first release on which he worked was with Shirley Bergeron, a local artist popular in Lafeyette. 'J'ai Fait Mon Edée' sold out of its pressing of 2,000 copies and established the Lanor Records label in the area. Although inexperienced with the production process, he knew enough to supervise his musicians on direction and sound, gradually accumulating knowledge as the label grew. Booking studios such as J.D. Miller's in Crowley or Cosimo's in New Orleans, he engaged a number of prominent Cajun artists. Eventually, with studio rates escalating, he built his own studio with a cheap mixing board and reel-to-reel recorder. By 1972 he was also running his own music store, which would help finance his activities with the label. His first big hit came with Elton Anderson, after that artist was dropped by **Mercury Records**. 'Life Problem' became a major local seller and was picked up for national distribution by **Capitol Records**. Later, Billy Matte and Charles Mann ('Red Red Wine') furthered the label's reputation with sustained singles success. However, despite some 150 singles by the turn of the 90s, it is only relatively recently that Lanor has issued cassette albums and compact discs. Despite its sporadic recording activity and limited discography, Lanor has become a Mecca for fans of Cajun and zydeco music passing through Louisiana.

Lanphere, Don

b. 26 June 1928, Wenatchee, Washington, USA. Lanphere first played tenor saxophone professionally at 13, having already played in public as a guest with visiting bands. At the age of 17 he guested with the **Jimmie Lunceford** Orchestra when they played a gig in his home town. After studying music at Northwestern University, Illinois, Lanphere recorded in New York under his own name with, among others, **Fats Navarro** and **Max Roach**. In 1949, he joined **Woody Herman**

and the following year was with **Artie Shaw**. In 1951, he was in **Sonny Dunham**'s band which was touring with Bob Hope. It was then that addiction to narcotics interrupted his career but he straightened out and made brief appearances in bands led by Herman, **Charlie Barnet**, **Billy May**, **Herb Pomeroy** and others during the period 1958-61. Further personal problems, with alcohol and drugs, then arose and little was heard of him until the early 80s. Thoroughly straight this time, actively supported by his wife, Midge, and encouraged by UK record producer Alastair Robertson, Lanphere subsequently toured extensively and made many fine records. Originally a **Coleman Hawkins** disciple, Lanphere later absorbed the work of **Lester Young** and **Charlie Parker**, but was able to retain his own strikingly individual approach to jazz. In addition to tenor, Lanphere also plays alto and, since his return, has proved to be an especially adept and interesting player on soprano saxophone and, in turn, exhilaratingly inventive on fast numbers and lyrical on ballads.

● ALBUMS: *Don Lanphere Quartet With Fats Navarro* (1949)★★, *Woody Herman's Big New Herd* (1959)★★★★, *Out Of Nowhere* (Hep Jazz 1982)★★★, *Into Somewhere* (Hep Jazz 1983)★★★, *Stop* (Hep Jazz 1983)★★★, *Don Loves Midge* (Hep Jazz 1984)★★, *Go Again* (Hep Jazz 1988)★★★, with Larry Coryell *Lanphere/Coryell* (Hep Jazz 1990)★★★★, *Jazz Worship: A Closer Walk* (1993)★★★.

Lansbury, Angela

b. Angela Brigid Lansbury, 16 October 1925, London, England. An actress and singer who enjoyed a prolific career in Hollywood before blossoming into a star of Broadway musicals in the 60s. Angela Lansbury's grandfather was George Lansbury, the legendary social reformer, and leader of the British Labour Party for a time during the 30s. She was taken to America in 1942 by her widowed mother, a popular actress named Moyna MacGill. After attending drama school in New York, Lansbury received an Oscar nomination for her first film performance in *Gaslight* (1944). It was the beginning of a long career in Hollywood during which she appeared in several musicals including *The Harvey Girls* (1946), *Till The Clouds Roll By* (1947), *The Court Jester* (1956), *Blue Hawaii* (1961, as **Elvis Presley**'s mother), and *Bedknobs And Broomsticks* (1971). For much of the time she played characters a good deal older than herself. From 1957 onwards, Lansbury played several straight roles on Broadway, but it was not until 1964 that she appeared in her first musical, *Anyone Can Whistle*, which had a score by **Stephen Sondheim**. It only ran for nine performances, but Lansbury's subsequent excursions into the musical theatre proved far more successful. She won wide acclaim, and Tony Awards, for her roles in *Mame* (1966), *Dear World* (1969), *Gypsy* (1974 revival), and *Sweeney Todd* (1979). She also took *Gypsy* to London in 1973. In the 80s, Lansbury began to work more in television and created the part of the writer-come-supersleuth, Jessica Fletcher, in the US series *Murder,*

She Wrote. The programme's long-term success resulted in her being rated as one of the highest-paid actresses in the world by the early 90s. In 1991 she received a Lifetime Achievement Award from the British Academy of Film and Television Arts (BAFTA), and, in the same, year, she lent her voice to Mrs Potts, the character that sang the Academy Award-winning title song in the highly acclaimed **Walt Disney** animated feature ***Beauty And The Beast***. In 1992 Angela Lansbury was back to her Cockney roots playing a charlady in the film *Mrs 'Arris Goes To Paris*, and two years later she was awarded a CBE in the Queen's Birthday Honours List.

● FURTHER READING: *Angela Lansbury - A Biography*, Margaret Wander Bonanno.

Lanson, Snooky

b. Roy Landman, 1914, d. 2 July 1990, Nashville, Tennessee, USA. Snooky Lanson was a singer on the popular US television musical variety programme *Your Hit Parade* during the 50s. His career began in 1934 as a singer on WSM radio in Nashville, Tennessee. Lanson then sang with the **Ray Noble** Orchestra and, during World War II, in **Ted Weems**' big band, which also included pianist **Owen Bradley**, later one of Nashville's most successful record producers. *Your Hit Parade*, a syndicated television programme, featured its own cast of singers interpreting the current Top 12 songs of each week; Lanson appeared as a regular on the show from its inception in 1950 until 1957. He hosted his own 15-minute television variety show in the summer of 1956 and in the 70s he hosted his own syndicated big band show. Lanson died in 1990 of lung cancer.

Lanza, Mario

b. Alfredo Arnold Cocozza, 31 January 1921, Philadelphia, Pennsylvania, USA, d. 7 October 1959. An enormously popular star in film musicals and on records during the 50s, with a magnificent operatic tenor voice. The son of Italian immigrants, he took his stage name from the masculine version of his mother's maiden name, Maria Lanza. From the age of 15, Lanza studied singing with several teachers, and was introduced into society circles with the object of gaining a patron. He was signed to **Columbia** Artistes Management as a concert singer, but their plans to send him on an introductory tour were quashed when Lanza was drafted into the US Army in 1943. He appeared in shows, billed as 'the Service Caruso', and sang in the chorus of the celebratory Forces show *Winged Victory*. After release, he lived in New York, gave concerts and worked on radio shows. One of the audition recordings that he made for **RCA** found its way to the MGM Film Studios, and when he deputized for another tenor at the Hollywood Bowl, MGM chief Louis B. Mayer was in the audience. Soon afterwards Lanza was signed to a seven-year MGM contract by Hungarian producer Joe Pasternak, who was quoted as saying: 'It was the most beautiful voice I had ever heard - but his bushy hair made him look like a caveman!' Lanza's contract allowed him to continue with his concert career, and in April 1948 he made his first, and last, appearance on the professional operatic stage, in two performances of *Madame Butterfly*, with the New Orleans Opera. In Lanza's first film in 1949 for MGM, *That Midnight Kiss*, he co-starred with **Kathryn Grayson** and pianist Jose Iturbi; the musical contained a mixture of popular standards as diverse as 'They Didn't Believe Me' and 'Down Among The Sheltering Palms', and classical pieces, including 'Celeste Aida' (from Verdi's *Aida*), which gave Lanza one of his first record hits. The film was a big box-office success, and was followed by *The Toast Of New Orleans*, also with Grayson, which, along with the operatic excerpts, contained some songs by **Sammy Cahn** and **Nicholas Brodszky**, including one of Lanza's all-time smash hits, the million-seller, 'Be My Love'. Lanza starred in the biopic ***The Great Caruso*** (1951), performing several arias associated with his idol. He also introduced 'The Loveliest Night Of The Year', a song adapted by **Irving Aaronson** from 'Over the Waves', by Juventino Rosas, with a new lyric by **Paul Francis Webster**; it gave Lanza his second million-selling record.

By this point, he was one of Hollywood's hottest properties, and as his career blossomed, so did his waistline. There were rumours of breakfasts consisting of four steaks and six eggs, washed down with a gallon of milk, which caused his weight to soar to 20 stone. He claimed that 'nervousness' made him eat. In 1951, Lanza embarked on a country-wide tour of 22 cities, and also appeared on his own CBS radio series. Back in Hollywood, he initially rejected MGM's next project, *Because You're Mine*, because of its 'singer-becomes-a-GI' storyline. After some difficulties, the film was eventually completed, and was chosen for the 1952 Royal Film Premiere in the UK. The title song, by Cahn and Brodszky, was nominated for an Academy Award in 1952, and became Lanza's third, and last, million-selling single. He had already recorded the songs for his next MGM project, *The Student Prince*, when he walked out on the studio following a disagreement with the director. He avoided damaging breach of contract lawsuits by allowing MGM to retain the rights to his recordings for the film. British actor Edmund Purdom took his place, miming to Lanza's singing voice. Ironically, Lanza's vocal performances for the film were considered to be among his best, and *Songs From The Student Prince And Other Great Musical Comedies* (containing 'The Drinking Song'), was number 1 in the USA for several weeks. Beset by problems with alcohol, food, tranquillizers and the US tax authorities, Lanza became a virtual recluse, not performing for over a year, before appearing on CBS Television with **Betty Grable** and **Harry James**. He was criticized in the press for miming to his old recordings on the show, but proved the voice was still intact by resuming his recording career soon afterwards. In 1956, Lanza returned to filming, this time for Warner Brothers. *Serenade*, adapted from the novel by James M. Cain, in which Lanza co-starred with Joan Fontaine, was considered by the critics to be one of his best movies. Once again, the operatic excerpts were interspersed with some romantic songs by Cahn and Brodszky, including 'Serenade' and 'My Destiny'. In 1957, tired of all the crash diets, and disillusioned by life in the USA, Lanza moved to Italy, and settled in Rome. He made one film there, *The Seven Hills Of Rome* (1958). Apart from the sight of Lanza playing an American entertainer doing impersonations of **Dean Martin**, **Frankie Laine** and **Louis Armstrong**, the film is probably best remembered for the inclusion of the 1955 hit song 'Arrivederci, Roma', written by Renato Rascel (Ranucci) and Carl Sigman, impressively sung in the film by Lanza, and which has become the accompaniment to many a backward glance by tourists ever since. In 1958, Lanza visited the UK, making his first stage appearances for six years, in concert at London's Royal Albert Hall and on the Royal Variety Show. From there, he embarked on a European tour. While on the Continent, he made *For The First Time* (1959), which was the last time he was seen on film. He appeared relatively slim, and was still in excellent voice. In the autumn of 1959 he went into a Rome clinic; a week later, he died of a heart attack. Much later it was alleged that he was murdered by the Mafia because he refused to appear at a concert organized by mobster Lucky Luciano. The city of Philadelphia officially proclaimed 7 October as 'Mario Lanza Day', and subsequently established a museum that still preserves his memory in the 90s. Opinions of his voice, and its potential, vary. José Carreras is quoted as saying that he was 'turned on' to opera at the age of 16 by seeing Lanza in *The Great Caruso*, and he emphasized the singer's influence by presenting his *Homage To Mario Lanza* concert at London's Royal Albert Hall in March 1994. Arturo Toscannini allegedly described it as the greatest voice of the twentieth century. On the other hand, one critic, perhaps representing the majority, said: 'He just concentrated on the big "lollipops" of the opera repertoire, he had a poor musical memory, and would never have been an opera star.' Ironically, it was one of the world's leading contemporary opera singers, **Placido Domingo**, who narrated the 1981 television biography *Mario Lanza-The American Caruso*.

● ALBUMS: *The Great Caruso* (HMV 1953)★★★★, *Operatic Arias* (HMV 1954)★★★, *Songs Of Romance* (HMV 1955)★★★, *Serenade* (HMV 1956)★★★★, *Songs From The Student Prince* film soundtrack (RCA 1956)★★★★, *Lanza On Broadway* (HMV 1957)★★★★, *The Touch Of Your Hand* (HMV 1957)★★★, *In A Cavalcade Of Show Tunes* (RCA 1957)★★★, *Seven Hills Of Rome* film soundtrack (RCA 1958)★★★, *Songs From The Student Prince/The Great Caruso* (1958)★★★★, *Sings A Kiss And Other Love Songs* (RCA 1959)★★★, *For The First Time* film soundtrack (RCA 1959)★★★, *Lanza Sings Christmas Carols* (RCA 1959)★★★, *Mario Lanza Sings Caruso Favourites/The Great Caruso* (RCA 1960)★★★★, *You Do Something To Me* (RCA 1969)★★★.

● COMPILATIONS: *I'll Walk With God* (1962)★★, *His Greatest Hits, Volume 1* (RCA 1971)★★★, *Art And Voice Of Mario Lanza* (RCA 1973)★★★, *Pure Gold* (RCA 1980)★★★, *His Greatest Hits From Operettas And Musicals, Volumes One, Two & Three* (RCA Classics 1981)★★★★, *The Legendary Mario Lanza* (K-Tel 1981)★★★★, *Collection* (RCA Red Seal 1982)★★★, *20 Golden Favourites* (RCA 1984)★★★★, *Magic Moments With Mario Lanza* (RCA 1985)★★★, *Forever* (RCA 1986)★★★, *A Portrait Of Mario Lanza* (Stylus 1987)★★★★, *Diamond Series: Mario Lanza* (Diamond Series 1988)★★★★, *Be My Love* (RCA 1991)★★★, *The Ultimate Collection* (1994)★★★★, *With A Song In My Heart: The Love: Collection* (Camden 1997)★★★★.

● FURTHER READING: *Mario Lanza*, Matt Bernard. *Mario Lanza*, Michael Burrows. *Lanza - His Tragic Life*, R. Strait and T. Robinson. *Mario Lanza*, Derek Mannering.

Laquan

b. *c*.1975, Los Angeles, California, USA. Rapper whose debut set was surprisingly mature, especially in its grasp of social issues, considering he was barely 16 when he recorded it. Though the harmonies were gentle, Laquan's words were not, accusing President Bush of 'Living large while others starve', among other charges. His debut album featured a live band and backing singers, orchestrated by **Bell Biv Devoe** studio crew Richard Wolf and Bret Mazur, adding a soulful sheen to proceedings.

● ALBUMS: *Notes Of A Native Son* (4th & Broadway 1990)★★★.

Lara, Jennifer

b. *c*.1959, Kingston, Jamaica, West Indies. In 1974 she recorded her debut album with **Coxsone Dodd** at **Studio One** in Brentford Road. The results of the sessions appeared on *Studio One Presents Jennifer Lara*, which was an instant success. She also enjoyed a massive hit with the single 'Where Have All The Good Men Gone', which has since become an anthem. Other Downbeat-produced hits followed, including 'Consider Me' and 'Do That To Me One More Time'. While working in Brentford Road she was also employed as a backing singer and is recognized for her notable contribution on **Freddie McGregor**'s *I Am Ready*. She has toured in Europe and her appearances in the UK were greeted with enthusiasm by both media and audiences. In the autumn of 1980 she recorded three tracks on the six-track compilation *Sir Coxsone's Family Christmas Album*. Her contributions included 'Lonely Christmas', 'Hands Of The Lord' and a duet with **Johnny Osbourne** and the family group, 'Christmas Medley'. The success of her Studio One output has overshadowed her later work, although she enjoyed minor hits with 'All My Love For You' and 'Mark My Words'. By the mid-80s she had recorded with **Prince Far I**, Henry 'Junjo' Lawes and Tristan Palmer. Her work with Palmer included a duet, 'Midnight Confession'. Into the 90s she worked with **King Jammy**, lending her vocal skills to 'I Wanna Sex You Up' with **Thriller U**, 'You Turn Me On', with a host of Jamaica's top DJs includ-

ing **Bounty Killer**, and 'Stop' with Major Mackerel.
● ALBUMS: *Studio One Presents* (Studio One 1974)★★★★, *Across The Line* (Sonic Sounds 1980)★★★, *Dancehall Roots And Lovers* (Rads 1994)★★★.

Larkin, Kenny

b. c.1968, USA. A popular DJ through his European travels, Larkin began his musical career in 1989 after having served two years in the US Airforce. Returning back home to his native Detroit, he discovered the underground techno scene by attending the Magic Institute and Shelter clubs. He subsequently met **Plus 8** proprieters **Richie Hawtin** and John Aquiviva, for whose label he recorded his debut 12-inch, 'We Shall Overcome', in 1990. A year later he returned with the *Integration* EP. He formed his own label, Art Of Dance, in June 1992, going on to record 'War Of The Worlds', as Dark Comedy, on **Transmat**/Art Of Dance in the US, and on Belgium label Buzz Records in Europe. He also provided the latter with the *Serena* EP, under the guise of Yennek, and the *Vanguard* EP, as Pod.

Larkin, Patty

b. Wisconsin, USA. Expert guitarist and singer-songwriter Patty Larkin has described her style as 'folk music meets the beat generation meets rock 'n' roll.' In the meantime critics have described her acoustic, electric and slide guitar technique and presentation as 'comparable to the best of **Bonnie Raitt**'. Larkin studied classical piano for four years before she took up slide guitar as her primary instrument during her seventh grade. Her first songs were written a year later. She enrolled at **Berklee College Of Music** in the 70s after first attending the University Of Oregon and studying jazz guitar privately. Her time at Berklee saw her researching composition skills and music theory and history, also playing mandolin and guitar in a Celtic band that busked on the streets of Cambridge, Massachusetts. It was during this time that she developed her distinctive playing style, a highly percussive and melodic framework derived from her education in Irish folk tunes by **John Martyn** and jazz by various local musicians. In the early 80s Larkin formed a rock band as rhythm and lead guitarist, before electing to embark on her own solo career, influenced by **Ry Cooder** and **Richard Thompson**. Regularly playing about 150 shows a year, Larkin made her album debut in 1985 with *Step Into The Light*. Though well received, the subsequent *I'm Fine* collection was the more enduring, with fine compositions including the feisty 'If I Was Made Of Metal'. After a lively recording of her potent stage show (*In The Square*), she moved over to High Street Records. *Tango* added more studio polish, and included guest appearances by fellow High Street/Windham Hill associates Darol Anger and **John Gorka**. By this time she was well into her record run of nine Boston Music Awards (she lives in Cape Cod, Massachusetts), and she had also gained the Distinguished Alumnae Award from Berklee College.

Angels Running was another highly acclaimed release, placing Larkin in the Top 10 of the AAA (Adult Album Alternative) charts. *Strangers World* united her with multi-instrumentalist producer John Leventhal (a veteran of work with **Shawn Colvin**, **Marc Cohn** and **Rosanne Cash**), and was described by the artist as a 'song cycle'. Certainly it evaded the dichotomy of old, where Larkin would often craft either instrumentals or comedic pieces. The effect was startling and confirmed a talent that seems capable of sustaining itself for many years to come.
● ALBUMS: *Step Into The Light* (Philo 1985)★★, *I'm Fine* (Philo 1988)★★★, *In The Square* (Philo 1990)★★★, *Tango* (High Street 1990)★★, *Angels Running* (High Street 1993)★★★, *Strangers World* (High Street 1994)★★★, *Perishable Fruit* (High Street 1997)★★.

Larkins, Ellis

b. 15 May 1923, Baltimore, Maryland, USA. A child prodigy, Larkins performed on the piano in public at the age of seven, playing Mozart. He attended the Paebody Conservatory of Music in Baltimore, then the Juilliard School of Music where he was one of only a few black musicians at that time. To support himself while studying he played clubs in New York and was heard by **John Hammond** while with the Billy Moore Trio. Hammond booked the trio for the Cafe Society Uptown, with the proviso that Larkins was in the group. During the next two decades Larkins became a regular on the New York club and recording scene, but remained discreetly in the background as he developed into one of the finest accompanists to singers. Among those who have enjoyed his supportive playing are **Mildred Bailey**, **Georgia Gibbs** and **Ella Fitzgerald**. His recordings with Fitzgerald, reputedly unrehearsed, remain among the best the First Lady made. Larkins also played on record in numerous pick-up groups, but made only occasional albums as soloist or as leader of his own trio. In the 70s, during a period when he was accompanist to Rod McKuen, a series of records corrected this imbalance in Larkins's recorded output. He appeared on record again with **Ruby Braff**, with whom he had first recorded in the mid-50s. One of the most musicianly pianists to grace jazz, Larkins has been content to remain in the shadows, unobtrusively using his enormous yet delicate gifts to the benefit of others.
● ALBUMS: *The Ellis Larkins Trio* i (c.1949)★★★, with Ella Fitzgerald *Ella Sings Gershwin* (1950)★★★, *Blues In The Night* (1951)★★★, *Ellis Larkins* i (1954)★★★, *Ellis Larkins Duo* (1955)★★★★, with Ruby Braff *Holiday In Braff* (1955)★★★★, *Manhattan At Midnight* (1956),★★★ *Ellis Larkins* ii (1957)★★, *Ellis Larkins* iii (1958)★★★, *Ellis Larkins* iv (1958)★★★, *Ellis Larkins* v (1959)★★★, *Ellis Larkins Plays The Bacharach & McKuen Songbook* (1972)★★, with Braff *The Grand Reunion* (1972)★★★, *Concert In Argentina* (1974)★★, *A Smooth One* (1977)★★★, *Swingin' For Hamp* (1979)★★★, *The Ellis Larkins Trio* ii (1980)★★★.

Larks

Originally known as Don Julian And The Meadowlarks, and formed in 1953, this US group consisted of Julian (lead), Ronald Barrett, (tenor) Earl Jones (baritone) and Randy Jones (bass). Barrett was replaced with Glen Reagan by the time the group recorded its first single, 'Heaven And Paradise', for the Dootone label. That record failed to make the R&B charts and Julian went on to record under various names for the next decade. In 1965, Julian wrote a dance song, 'The Jerk', after seeing a group of children doing a new dance by that name. He assembled a new group, consisting of Charles Morrison, Ted Waters and himself, and called it the Larks; the group's back-up band assumed the Meadowlarks name. Released on the Money label, the single climbed to number 7 in early 1965. The group was unable to follow it with another hit, although other bands, such as the **Capitols** and the **Miracles**, capitalized on the new dance craze by recording, respectively, 'Cool Jerk' and 'Come On And Do The Jerk'.

● ALBUMS: *The Jerk* (Money 1965)★★★, *Soul Kaleidoscope* (Money 1966)★★★, *Superslick* (Money 1967)★★★.

Larks (Apollo)

An R&B vocal group from Raleigh, North Carolina, USA. The members were Eugene Mumford (tenor, lead), Thurmon Ruth (baritone, lead), Alden Bunn (baritone, lead, guitar), Raymond Barnes (tenor), Hadie Rowe Jnr. (baritone) and David McNeil (bass). The group began as a gospel ensemble, the Jubilators, who were formed in 1950 by Ruth and Bunn after they had withdrawn from the Selah Jubilee Singers (a New York City gospel group that Ruth had formed and led since 1927). The Jubilators went to New York City and to obtain seed money, immediately recorded gospel with four different companies under four different names; the Selah Singers for Jubilee, Jubilators for Regal, Four Barons for Savoy and Southern Harmonaires for Apollo. The latter wanted the group to record some secular tracks and so the group became the Larks to record R&B. It was with the Larks' tracks that the group obtained lasting success and fame. They made their first impact with romantic ballads, using as lead the beautiful voice of Mumford, and initial hits in early 1951 were 'Hopefully Yours' (backed with the masterful 'When I Leave These Prison Walls') and 'My Reverie'. The blues side of the group, with Bunn as lead and on guitar, came to the forefront on their next tracks, when in the last half of 1951 they had hits with a **Sonny Boy Williamson** song, 'Eyesight To The Blind' (number 5 R&B), and 'Little Side Car' (number 10 R&B). These were the group's last hits, and in 1952 the Larks disbanded. Mumford joined the **Golden Gate Quartet**, and in 1954 formed a new Larks group, but the magic was gone and the records they made were poor. The new Larks disbanded in 1955, and Mumford joined **Billy Ward And The Dominoes** and sang lead on their 'Stardust' and 'Deep Purple' hits. Alden Bunn organized the Wheels ('My Heart's Desire') before later

carving out a career as blues singer **Tarhill Slim**. He also made some successful duet recordings with Little Ann.

● COMPILATIONS: *My Reverie* (Relic 1988)★★★, *When I Leave These Prison Walls* (Relic 1988)★★★.

Larson, Nicolette

b. 1952, Helena, Montana, USA, d. 16 December 1997, Los Angeles, California, USA. Larson moved to California where she became a member of touring roadbands with **Hoyt Axton** and **Commander Cody**. By the 70s she had become established as a session singer and appeared on albums by **Emmylou Harris** (*Luxury Liner*), **Linda Rondstadt** (*Mad Love*) and **Neil Young** (*American Stars And Bars, Comes A Time*). She began her solo career in 1978 with *Nicolette*, which featured support from **James Burton** and **Klaus Voorman** as well as members of **Little Feat** and the **Doobie Brothers**. Despite the all-star cast, the singer's voice retained its individuality and she was rewarded when the track 'Lotta Love' reached the US Top 10. After three strong albums she moved to Nashville and recorded *Say When* which showed her to be equally adept at country music, which was well-suited to her high, clear intonation. Larson nonetheless retained contact with her associates from the past, singing backing vocals on Neil Young's *Harvest Moon* and *Unplugged* albums. *Sleep, Baby, Sleep* was a collection of lullabies and a difficult album to market. The duets with **Graham Nash**, **David Crosby** and Linda Ronstadt made it an album for adults, presumably to send children to sleep. The effect was paradoxical! Larson died in December 1997 of complications arsing from cerebral edema.

● ALBUMS: *Nicolette* (Warners 1978)★★★, *In The Nick Of Time* (Warners 1979)★★, *Radioland* (Warners 1981)★★★, *All Dressed Up With No Place To Go* (Warners 1982)★★★, *Say When* (MCA 1985)★★★, *Sleep, Baby, Sleep* (Sony 1994)★★★.

LaSalle, Denise

b. Denise Craig, 16 July 1939, LeFlore County, Mississippi, USA. Having moved to Chicago in 1954 to pursue a career as a fiction writer, LaSalle turned to songwriting and by the late 60s had begun to record for Billy 'The Kid' Emerson's Tarpon label, on which she achieved a sizeable local hit, 'A Love Reputation', in 1967. In 1969, she formed Crajon productions with her husband, Bill Jones, and also began working with producer **Willie Mitchell** in Memphis. After a period writing and producing for other artists, LaSalle returned to recording her own compositions, and one of the first results, 'Trapped By A Thing Called Love', released not on her own label but on Westbound in 1971, reached number 1 in the US R&B charts and climbed to the US pop Top 20. Several excellent, sometimes uncompromising, singles followed, including 'Man Sized Job' (1972), 'Married, But Not To Each Other' (1976) and 'What It Takes To Get A Good

Woman' (1973). A stylist in the mould of **Laura Lee**, **Ann Peebles** and **Millie Jackson**, LaSalle continued to enjoy hits during the late 70s, but is now better known for her 1985 UK Top 10 novelty hit, 'My Toot Toot'. Her 1997 album *Smokin' In Bed* was an unexpected commercial success.

● ALBUMS: *Trapped By A Thing Called Love* (Westbound 1972)★★★, *On The Loose* (Westbound 1973)★★★, *Here I Am Again* (Westbound 1975)★★★, *Second Breath* (ABC/Dot 1976)★★★, *The Bitch Is Bad* (ABC 1977)★★, *Under The Influence* (ABC 1978)★★, *Unwrapped* (MCA 1979)★★★, *I'm So Hot* (MCA 1980)★★, *And Satisfaction Guaranteed* (MCA 1981)★★★, *A Lady In The Streets* (Malaco 1983)★★★, *Right Place, Right Time* (Malaco 1984)★★★, *Love Talkin'* (Malaco 1985)★★★, *My Toot Toot* (Malaco 1985)★★★, *Rain And Fire* (Malaco 1986)★★★, *It's Lying Time Again* (Malaco 1987)★★★, *Hittin' Where It Hurts* (Malaco 1988)★★★, *Holding Hands With The Blues* (Malaco 1989)★★★, *Still Trapped* (Malaco 1990)★★★, *Smokin' In Bed* (Malaco 1997)★★★.

● COMPILATIONS: *Doin' It Right* (Malaco 1973)★★★★.

Lashley, Barbara

b. *c.*1938, New York City, New York, USA. Lashley grew up in a musical family (in their youth her parents danced at the Savoy Ballroom in Harlem) and was constantly hearing singers on record. While still a child, she moved to Washington, DC, and with her brother and parents she sang to records, often R&B hits of the day. Although her brother began singing semi-professionally with a group, Lashley did not and eventually married, had four children, was divorced; which made a career in music out of the question. It was not until 1974, when she moved to San Francisco, that she began to consider the possibility. She was working as a freelance film editor and decided to study part-time at the University of California, Berkeley, reading for a degree in Afro-American Studies. This focused her interest in black music and eventually she began visiting local jazz clubs, encouraged in this by the director of the chorus of the Berkeley Community Chorus and orchestra of which she was a member. She began singing with local jazz groups, sitting in at jam sessions and the like, and was coached in this by bass player Billy Cayou. Gradually, her confidence grew and her reputation spread as her talent blossomed. She sang with several bands including those led by Manny Funk, Rex Allen and a big band she helped organize for **Earl Hines** in 1981, during a lecturing engagement the veteran pianist had undertaken at Berkeley. Later in the 80s, Lashley moved further afield, singing at international festivals, including those at Rimini, where she worked with Merrill Hoover, and Breda, where she sang with **Dick Hyman** and also met and was encouraged by **Maxine Sullivan**. She also visited Japan with the Royal Street Jazz Members Band. In the USA, she has worked at the Walnut Creek Jazz Festival both singing and organizing concerts. Much influenced by singers of the 30s and 40s, such as **Ivie Anderson**, **Billie Holiday**, **Lee Wiley**,

Mildred Bailey and, especially, **Ethel Waters**, Lashley has developed a wide-ranging repertoire and a good, if so far limited, following. Considering that she began singing professionally at the age of 40, her ability and reputation are remarkable. Her voice and style are finely crafted and her love for the music she performs gleams through every song.

● ALBUMS: *How Long Has This Been Going On?* (Shoestring 1983)★★★★, *Sweet And Lowdown* (Stomp Off 1986)★★★.

Last Crack

Last Crack, from Wisconsin, USA, specialized in schizophrenic 'acid-metal', a truly unique aural experience that revelled in the desecration of musical boundaries from thrash to blues, then back through funk, psychedelia and rock 'n' roll. Lead vocalist Buddo Buddo conveyed a mixture of gut-wrenching passion, flamboyance and deranged eccentricity in his caterwauling (his other claim to fame being his penchant for posing naked at photo sessions). The backbeat was equally unpredictable, with guitarists Pablo Schuter and Don Bakken switching and blending styles with consummate ease. Phil Buerstate (drums) and Todd Winger (bass) provided the necessary power in the rhythm section. The latter was replaced by Dave Truehardt in 1990.

● ALBUMS: *Sinister Funkhouse #17* (Roadracer 1989)★★★, *Burning Time* (Roadrunner 1991)★★★.

Last Exit

Last Exit is a high-power, high-intensity band that came together by chance when its members happened to be playing in the same city (Zurich) in early 1986 and has since become something of a cult institution. Comprising **Peter Brötzmann** (b. 6 March 1941, Remscheid, Germany; reeds), **Sonny Sharrock** (b. 27 August 1940, Ossining, New York, USA; guitar), **Bill Laswell** (bass) and **Ronald Shannon Jackson** (b. 12 January 1940, Fort Worth, Texas, USA; drums/vocals), their music is passionate and visceral, mixing elements of free jazz, blues, metal, hardcore, R&B and even the occasional quote from Wordsworth surreally interjected by Jackson. Last Exit, though largely a musical law unto itself, is flexible enough to have incorporated other musicians in live sessions, including **Diamanda Galas**, Akira Sakata and **Herbie Hancock**, who Laswell worked with on his *Future Shock* album which produced the hit single 'Rockit'. Their earliest (and probably wildest) recording, a tape of a concert in Cologne, was held up by legal difficulties until 1990, when it became available on compact disc in some European countries. It is now on general issue.

● ALBUMS: *Last Exit* (1986)★★★, *The Noise Of Trouble* (1987)★★★, *Cassette Recordings 1987* (1988)★★, *Iron Path* (1989)★★★, *Koln 1986* recording (1990)★★★★, *Live In Europe - Headfirst Into The Flames* (1993)★★★.

Last Of The Blue Devils, The

A superior USA documentary, worth its place in any collection, this film celebrates the remarkable contribution to jazz provided by Kansas City-based musicians. Extensive interviews and live performances filmed especially for the documentary mingle effectively with archive film clips. Amongst the artists displaying their considerable talents are **Count Basie**, **Jimmy Forrest**, **Dizzy Gillespie**, **Budd Johnson**, **Gus Johnson**, **Jo Jones**, **Jay McShann**, **Charlie Parker**, **Jesse Price**, **Buster Smith**, **Joe Turner** and **Lester Young**.

Last Poets

Coming out of the poverty-stricken ghetto of Harlem, New York, in the mid-60s, there are many who claim the Last Poets to be the first hip hop group proper. Comprising Suliaman El Hadi, Alafia Pudim, Nilijah, Umar Bin Hassan (aka Omar Ben Hassan - as with other personnel name alterations occurred frequently) and Abio Dun Oyewole, the Last Poets formed on 19 May 1968 (Malcolm X's birthday). Hassan was not actually an original member, joining the band after seeing them perform on campus and insisting on membership. Together, the Last Poets recorded powerful protest gems like 'Niggas Are Scared Of Revolution' and 'White Man's Got A God Complex'. Their legacy, that of the innovative use of rap/talk over musical backing, has born obvious fruit in subsequent generations of hip-hop acts. Oyewole left after their debut album. They re-formed in 1984, with two 12-inch singles, 'Super Horror Show' and 'Long Enough', although the group was still split into two separate camps. Hassan released a solo LP featuring **Bootsy Collins**, **Buddy Miles** and others, after a period of seclusion, and drug and family problems. He also kept company with rap stars like **Arrested Development** and **Flavor Flav**, and starred in John Singleton's *Poetic Justice* film. While not bitter about failing to reap the financial rewards that subsequent rappers have done, Hassan remained philosophical: 'As far as I'm concerned we made a market, for those young boys to have their careers . . . I understand that some brothers are still trying to find their manhood. But it ain't about drive-by shootings. That's madness. Self-destruction. Real gangsters don't go around shooting everybody'. Another former Last Poet, Jalal Nuridin, who released an album alongside **Kool And The Gang** and Eric Gale under the title Lightnin' Rod, went on to become mentor to UK acid jazzers **Galliano**. Incidentally, this is a different Last Poets to the one comprising David Nelson, Felipe, Luciano and Gylan Kain who titled themselves the Original Last Poets and recorded an album for Juggernaut in 1971.

● ALBUMS: *The Last Poets* (Douglas 1970)★★★, *This Is Madness* (Douglas 1971)★★★, *Oh My People* (Celluloid 1985)★★★, *Freedom Express* (Acid Jazz 1989)★★★, *Scattarap/Home* (Bond Age 1994)★★★, *Holy Terror* (Ryko 1995)★★★.
Solo: Umar Bin Hassan *Be Bop Or Be Dead* (Axiom 1993)★★★. Jalal Nuridin As Lightnin' Rod *Hustlers Convention* (Douglas 1973)★★★. Oyewole *25 Years* (Rykodisk 1995)★★★.
● COMPILATIONS: *Right On!* (Collectables 1986)★★★.

Last Time Around - Buffalo Springfield

Although this album is effectively the potato peelings of a delicious meal, the fragmentation of the band is no longer apparent thirty years later. Reappraising this record puts it still behind *Buffalo Springfield Again*, but there is a gentle quality about the whole record. As **Jim Messina** and **Richie Furay** took control, the album develops a country rock feel. **Neil Young**'s premier contribution is 'I Am A Child' and the prolific **Stephen Stills** hits the button with four gems: the plea for world unity, 'Uno Mundo', the song of a fugitive, 'Four Days Gone', 'Special Care' and the original 'Questions'. A much better album than we could have expected from this outstanding group.

● Tracks: On The Way Home; It's So Hard To Wait; Pretty Girl Why; Four Days Gone; Carefree Country Day; Special Care; The Hour Of Not Quite Rain; Questions; I Am A Child; Merry-Go-Round; Uno Mundo; Kind Woman.
● First released 1968
● UK peak chart position: did not chart
● USA peak chart position: 42

Last Waltz, The

By 1976, years of road life coupled with personal excess had taken its toll of the **Band**. Famed as **Bob Dylan**'s backing group and creators of milestone albums, *Music From Big Pink* and *The Band*, the group was beset by internal problems. They decided to host a farewell Thanksgiving Day concert at San Francisco's Winterland Ballroom which would be filmed for posterity by Martin Scorsese. The extravaganza not only featured some of the Band's best-known material, including 'The Night They Drove Old Dixie Down' and 'The Weight', the group was clearly inspired to invest the songs with renewed vigour. *The Last Waltz* was also a showcase for acts with whom they associated themselves. One of their early inspirations, **Muddy Waters**, provided a searing rendition of 'Mannish Boy' and **Ronnie Hawkins**, whom the Band backed in an earlier incarnation, the Hawks, offered an explosive 'Who Do You Love'. San Francisco-based poet Lawrence Ferlingetti brought a literary air to the proceedings - much to Band drummer **Levon Helm**'s chagrin - whereas contributions from **Joni Mitchell**, **Neil Young**, **Eric Clapton** and **Van Morrison** were more in keeping with the notion of a rock concert. The arrival of Bob Dylan wrought images of his tours with the Band in 1966 and 1972, and the event closed with an all-cast version of the hymnal 'I Shall Be Released'. A commemorative three-album set formed a précis of the evening's proceedings. *The Last Waltz* film also featured newly recorded material, shot in a studio some months following the concert. Interview footage with Band members was also included, much of which reflected a jaded perception of their history and the project itself. Only guitarist/composer **Robbie Robertson**, the prime mover of the film, showed real enthusiasm. Nonetheless, *The Last Waltz* is an endearing tribute to one of rock's most fascinating groups and, given the advent of punk the following year, acts as a eulogy to an entire generation of musicians.

● ALBUMS: *The Last Waltz* 3-LP set (Warners 1977)★★★.
● VIDEOS: *The Last Waltz* (Warner Home Video 1988).

Last, James

b. Hans Last, 17 April 1929, Bremen, Germany. This phenomenally successful bandleader and arranger brought up to date the tradition of big band arrangements for current pop hits. By the end of the 80s, Last had released over 50 albums and had sold 50 million copies worldwide. Trained as a bass player, in 1946 he joined Hans-Gunther Oesterreich's Radio Bremen Dance Orchestra. Two years later he was leading the Becker-Last Ensemble. When that folded in 1955 Last worked as an arranger for radio stations and for **Polydor Records**. There he worked with **Caterina Valente**, **Freddy Quinn** and bandleader **Helmut Zacharias**, and in 1965 released *Non-Stop Dancing*. Blending together well-known tunes with a jaunty dance beat, this was the first of 20 volumes that helped make Last a star across Europe by the mid-80s. Hansi, as he was known to his fans, varied the formula in several other ways. He took material from different musical genres (classics, country, **Beatles**, Latin, from various countries (Ireland, Russia, Switzerland, Scotland) and he added guest artists. Among these were bossa nova singer **Astrud Gilberto** (*Plus* 1987) and pianist **Richard Clayderman** (*Together At Last* 1991). One 'added attraction' to his party sets is the technique Last employs of 'non-stop' atmosphere by incorporating claps, cheers and laughter between each segueing track. Relying on albums and tours for his success, Last had only one hit single in the USA and the UK, 'The Seduction', the theme from the 1980 Richard Gere film, *American Gigolo*.

● ALBUMS: *Non Stop Dancing Volume 1* (Polydor 1965)★★★, *This Is James Last* (Polydor 1967)★★★, *Hammond A-Go Go* (Polydor 1967)★★★, *Dancing '68 Volume 1* (Polydor 1968)★★★, *James Last Goes Pop* (Polydor 1968)★★★, *Classics Up To Date Volumes 1-6* (Polydor 1970-84)★★★, *Non Stop Dancing Volume 12* (Polydor 1971)★★★, *Beach Party 2* (Polydor 1971)★★★, *Non Stop Dancing Volume 13* (Polydor 1972)★★★, *Voodoo Party* (Polydor 1972)★★★, *Non Stop Dancing Volume 14* (Polydor 1973)★★★, *Non Stop Dancing Volume 15* (Polydor 1973)★★★, *Ole* (Polydor 1973)★★★, *Non Stop Dancing Volume 16* (Polydor 1974)★★★, *Country & Square Dance Party* (Polydor 1974)★★★, *Ten Years Non Stop Party Album* (Polydor 1975)★★★, *Make The Party Last* (Polydor 1975)★★★, *Christmas James Last* (Polydor 1976)★★★, *In London* (Polydor 1978)★★★, *East To West* (Polydor 1978)★★★, *Last The Whole Night Long* (Polydor 1979)★★★, *Christmas Classics* (Polydor 1979)★★★, *Caribbean Nights* (Polydor 1980)★★★, *Seduction* (Polydor 1980)★★★, *Classics For Dreaming* (Polydor 1980)★★★, *Hansimania* (Polydor 1981)★★★, *Roses From The South - The Music Of Johann Strauss* (Polydor 1981)★★★, *Bluebird* (Polydor 1982)★★★, *Biscaya* (Polydor 1982)★★★, *Tango* (Polydor 1983)★★★,

Christmas Dancing (Polydor 1983)★★★, *Greatest Songs Of The Beatles* (Polydor 1983)★★★, *Games That Lovers Play* (Polydor 1984)★★★, *Rose Of Tralee And Other Irish Favourites* (Polydor 1984)★★★, *All Aboard With Cap'n James* (Polydor 1984)★★★, *In Russia* (Polydor 1984)★★★, *At St. Patrick's Cathedral, Dublin* (Polydor 1984)★★★, *Im Allgau (In The Alps)* (Polydor 1984)★★★, *In Scotland* (Polydor 1985)★★★, *In Holland* (Polydor 1987)★★★, *Everything Comes To An End, Only A Sausage Has Two* (Polydor 1987)★★★, with Astrud Gilberto *Plus* (Polydor 1987)★★★, *The Berlin Concert* (Polydor 1987)★★★, *Dance, Dance, Dance* (Polydor 1987)★★★, *Flute Fiesta* (Polydor 1988)★★★, *Plays Bach* (Polydor 1988)★★★, *Happy Heart* (Polydor 1989)★★★, *Classics By Moonlight* (Polydor 1990)★★★, with Richard Clayderman *Together At Last* (Polydor 1991)★★★.

● COMPILATIONS: *The Best From 150 Gold* (Polydor 1980)★★★, *By Request* (Polydor 1988)★★★.
● VIDEOS: *Berlin Concert* (PolyGram Music Video 1988).
● FURTHER READING: *James Last Story*, James Last. *James Last*, Bob Willcox, *James Last*, Howard Elson.

Laswell, Bill

b. 14 February 1950. Laswell started playing guitar but later switched to bass. He was, he has said, more interested in being in a band than in playing music, but in the 70s he became more committed and has since organized some of the most challenging bands in recent popular music, including **Material**, Curlew (with Tom Cora, Nicky Skopelitis and George Cartwright) and **Last Exit** (with **Sonny Sharrock**, **Peter Brötzmann** and **Ronald Shannon Jackson**). He also established OAO and Celluloid, two adventurous record labels. For the latest Material album, *Third Power*, he assembled a band including **Shabba Ranks**, the **Jungle Brothers**, **Herbie Hancock**, **Sly And Robbie** and **Fred Wesley**. Laswell and Hancock had already worked together, in Last Exit (on *The Noise Of Trouble*) and on two Hancock albums which he produced: on *Future Shock* in particular the 'backing band' was effectively Material. In the late 90s, Laswell has begun to explore drum 'n' bass. The list of albums below includes only those that Laswell has made under his own name; in addition he has produced for a wide range of people, including **Iggy Pop**, **Motörhead**, **Laurie Anderson**, **Fela Kuti**, **Gil Scott-Heron**, **Yellowman**, **Afrika Bambaataa**, **Yoko Ono**, **Public Image Limited**, **Mick Jagger**, **Nona Hendryx**, **James 'Blood' Ulmer** and **Manu Dibango**.

● ALBUMS: *Baselines* (Rough Trade 1984)★★★, with John Zorn *Points Blank/Metlable Snaps* (No Mans Land 1986),★★★ with Peter Brötzmann *Low Life* (1987)★★★, *Hear No Evil* (Venture 1988)★★★, *Outer Dark* (Fax 1994)★★★, with Pete Namlook *Outland* (Fax 1994)★★★, with Klaus Schulze, Pete Namlook *Dark Side Of The Moog IV* (Fax 1996)★★, *Oscillations 2* (Sub Rose 1998)★★★.
● COMPILATIONS: *The Best Of Bill Laswell* (Celluloid 1985)★★★, *Panthalassa: The Music Of Miles Davis 1969-1974* (Columbia 1998)★★★★.

Late For The Sky - Jackson Browne

Jackson Browne's early career was inextricably linked to the singer-songwriter movement of the 70s, and *Late For The Sky* has proved to be one of the era's strongest and most enduring albums. Browne's reflective songwriting style attained a new level of maturity on songs such as 'Fountain Of Sorrow' and 'For A Dancer', the latter a strikingly literate meditation on death. *Late For The Sky* is overshadowed by the title track and 'Before The Deluge', two brooding songs of personal and social apocalypse that book-end the album and serve as a textbook definition of the Californian mindset of the 70s.

● Tracks: *Late For The Sky; Fountain Of Sorrow; Farther On; The Late Show; The Road And The Sky; For A Dancer; Walking Slow; Before The Deluge.*

● First released 1974

● UK peak chart position: did not chart

● USA peak chart position: 14

Lateef, Yusef

b. William Evans, 9 October 1920, Chattanooga, Tennessee, USA. Raised in Detroit, Michigan, Lateef began playing tenor saxophone in his late teens. In New York in the mid-40s he played in bands led by **Lucky Millinder**, **Roy Eldridge** and other leading jazz musicians of the swing era, but later in the decade, in Chicago, he played with **Dizzy Gillespie**. Thereafter, his work was consciously modern in style. In the mid-50s he adopted the Muslim faith and took the name by which he is now known. He led several small bands during this period and also began to play flute. At the end of the decade he was again in New York, this time working with leading modernists amongst whom were **Charles Mingus** and **Cannonball Adderley**. He also led his own groups for public performance and record dates. In the 70s and 80s Lateef extended the number of instruments upon which he performed, now including the oboe and bassoon and also a wide range of similar Asian and African reeds. He revealed himself as a gifted performer on all these instruments and later recordings showed an increasing interest in various ethnic musical forms, sometimes - not always - fused with jazz. In addition to his performing career in music he has also taught music and has lately become proficient as a writer and painter.

● ALBUMS: *Jazz And The Sounds Of Nature* (1957)★★★, *Jazz Moods* (Savoy 1957)★★★, *Prayer To The East* (1957)★★★★, *Yusef Lateef At Cranbrook* (1958)★★, *The Dreamer* (1959)★★★, *Contemplation* (1960)★★, *Cry! Tender* (Original Jazz Classics 1960)★★★★, *The Centaur And The Phoenix* (Original Jazz Classics 1961)★★★★, *Into Something* (1961)★★, *Eastern Sounds* (Original Jazz Classics 1961)★★★, *Live At Pep's Music Lounge* (Impulse 1965)★★★, *The Golden Flute* (1966)★★★★, *The Blue Yusef Lateef* (Atlantic 1968)★★★, *The Gentle Giant* (Atlantic 1974)★★★, *The Doctor Is In...And Out* (1976)★★★, *Sax Masters* (Vogue 1976)★★★★, *In A Temple Garden* (1979)★★★, *In Nigeria* (1985)★★, *Yusuf Lateef's Little Symphony* (Atlantic 1988)★★★, *Concerto For Yusef Lateef* (Atlantic 1988)★★★, *Nocturnes* (Atlantic 1990)★★★, *Yusek Lateef's Encounters* (Atlantic 1991)★★, *Heart Vision* (YAL 1992)★★★, *Tenors i* (YAL 1992)★★★, *Plays Ballads* (YAL 1993)★★, *Tenors ii* (YAL 1994)★★★.

● COMPILATIONS: *The Live Session* 1964 recording (1978).

● FURTHER READING: *The Pleasures of Jazz: Leading Performers On Their Lives, Their Music, Their Contemporaries,* Leonard Feather.

Later With Jools Holland

The format of an experienced musician hosting a 'jam' session may not be entirely new to UK television, but in the hands of compere **Jools Holland** it has been revived as one of the most successful televisual media of the 90s. BBC2's *Later With Jools Holland* began its broadcast run on 8 October 1992 with guests including the **Neville Brothers**, the **Christians**, **D-Influence** and **Nu Colours**. The gospel/soul-themed show was followed by one concerned with country, featuring **k.d. lang**, the **Rockingbirds** and **Dwight Yoakam**. A third programme featured world artists **Baaba Maal** and **Oumou Sangare**, alongside **Was (Not Was)** and **Tasmin Archer**. As that cast indicated, the programme was already being broken down from a thematic format to a more eclectic programming policy, with many of the acts selected by Holland himself. By the end of the show's first run in December 1992, other artists featured had included **Mary-Chapin Carpenter**, **John Martyn**, **Joan Baez**, **Nick Cave**, **En Vogue**, **Simply Red**, **Mary Coughlan**, **Sonic Youth**, **Shabba Ranks**, **Morrissey** and **Tori Amos**. By the time the series returned in May 1993 the format had been established - a series of name and newer artists playing live in the studio, their equipment set up in different locations, allowing the cameras to track between them - with one or two numbers conducted with Holland sitting in at the piano, with informal interviews. In keeping with Holland's affable and relaxed television persona, artists were given the necessary space to perform with a more minimal approach to camera angles and rehearsal than was deemed necessary by other programmes. In turn Holland was rewarded with appearances by legends such as **Leonard Cohen**, **Robert Plant**, **Buddy Guy**, **Bryan Ferry**, the **Kinks**, **Al Green** and **Richard Thompson** on the second series, as well as more contemporary notables such as **PJ Harvey**, **Björk** and **Paul Weller**. Holland's old friend **Elvis Costello** introduced a third series in May 1994, which also included appearances by **Otis Rush**, **Traffic**, **Nick Cave**, **Angelique Kidjo**, **Jonathan Richman**, **David Byrne**, **Ali Farka Touré**, **Bonnie Raitt**, **Crowded House**, the **Cranberries** and **Johnny Cash**. A 'hootenanny' special on New Year's Eve 1993 additionally featured **Sting** and **Freddie McGregor** - a similarly themed 1994 transmission included **Steve Winwood**, **Shane McGowan** and **Blur**. By the fourth and fifth series in 1994 and 1995 guests, including PJ Harvey, Robert Plant and Elvis Costello, had begun to make return appearances. Among the highlights was Paul Weller singing with cousins **Carleen** and **Jhelisa Anderson** and a rare view of **Scott Walker**, both on the same show broadcast in June 1995. **Van Morrison** and **David Bowie** were among the debutants on the sixth series.

Latimore

b. Benjamin Latimore, 7 September 1939, Charleston, Tennessee, USA. This singer, who performed under his surname only, brought a blues feeling to 70s soul music. His passionate vocal delivery and keyboard-dominated style was particularly popular with his female audience. Latimore sang gospel music as a child in his family's Baptist church but did not sing professionally until his first year of college, where he worked with a group called the Hi-Toppers. The group had already recorded for Excello Records when Latimore took over the piano position; he never recorded with the group but remained with them until 1962. At that time he joined **Joe Henderson**'s revue as pianist, and with that group backed artists such as **Ben E. King**, **Slim Harpo** and **Jimmy Reed** in concert. Latimore left Henderson in 1964 and worked as an opening act for teen-idol **Steve Alaimo**. He also recorded some unsuccessful singles for the Dade label at this time, but finally achieved a hit in 1973 for the related Glades label, with a remake of **'T-Bone' Walker**'s 'Stormy Monday'. The following year Latimore reached his commercial height with a number 1 R&B single, 'Let's Straighten It Out'. He charted with 13 singles in total for Glades during the 70s, reaching the R&B Top 10 twice more. In 1982, he switched to **Malaco Records**, for whom he continues to record.

● ALBUMS: *Latimore* (Glades 1973)★★★, *More, More, More* (Glades 1974)★★★, *Latimore III* (Glades 1975)★★★★, *It Ain't Where You Been . . .* (Glades 1977)★★★, *Dig A Little Deeper* (Glades 1978)★★★, *Singing In The Key Of Love* (Malaco 1982)★★★, *Good Time Man* (Malaco 1985)★★★, *Every Way But Wrong* (Malaco 1988)★★★, *I'll Do Anything For You* (Malaco 1988)★★★, *Slow Down* (Malaco 1989)★★★, *The Only Way Is Up* (1992)★★★, *Catchin' Up* (1994)★★★.

● COMPILATIONS: *Sweet Vibrations - The Best Of . . .* (Sequel 1991)★★★★.

Latin Alliance

A consortium of Latin and Hispanic hip-hop artists formed by **Kid Frost** in October 1989, which included other luminaries such as **Mellow Man Ace** and **A.L.T.** Topics such as slavery in Puerto Rico and other ethnocentric concerns such as exploitation and alienation dominated. The most effective track was 'Latinos Unidos', which celebrated the cultural and social identity of the race. It produced one Top 60 single, 'Low Rider (On The Boulevard)'.

● ALBUMS: *The Latin Alliance* (Virgin 1991)★★★.

Latour

b. William LaTour, Chicago, Illinois, USA. House producer made famous by his US crossover success,

'People Are Still Having Sex'. Unfortunately he was never able to quite follow this up, despite further wacky song titles like 'Allen's Got A New Hi-Fi'. The harsher critics described him as 'a poor man's **Baby Ford**, without the stylings or passion for the music'.

● ALBUMS: *Latour* (Smash 1991)★★★.

Lattimore, Kenny

b. USA. Lattimore first entered the music industry at the age of 14 when he joined the R&B vocal group Maniquin, who recorded briefly for Epic Records in the 80s. When that group broke up, Lattimore remained in the industry as a songwriter for artists including Glenn Jones and Jon Lucien. As a solo artist, Lattimore and new label **Columbia Records** were keen to project a more mature, sophisticated image, though one still rooted in a traditional R&B style. The reward was substantial sales for his solo debut, which marked him out as a strong male R&B voice, sympathetic towards but stylistically opposed to the hold hip-hop had taken on the genre. As he told the press: 'I have an appreciation for hip-hop and what it's about, but that's not the life I live. I grew up listening to **Earth, Wind And Fire** albums, and that's what I know.' He also stressed his wish to address the negative portrayal of African-American males in the media, and the music industry in particular. Columbia's marketing of Lattimore was certainly targeted at the mainstream, with support slots for R&B/soul traditionalists such as **Chaka Khan** and **Barry White**. In the meantime, Lattimore achieved his biggest singles success in the autumn of 1997 with 'For You'.

● ALBUMS: *Kenny Lattimore* (Columbia 1997)★★★.

Lattisaw, Stacy

b. 25 November 1966, Washington, DC, USA. Lattisaw emerged as a child prodigy in the late 70s, touring with **Ramsey Lewis** at the age of 11 and recording her first album for Cotillion Records a year later. Her light and breezy pop-disco style was epitomized by her 1980 US hits, 'Dynamite' and 'Let Me Be Your Angel', produced by **Van McCoy** and Narada Michael Walden, respectively. She enjoyed success in 1982 with the novelty record 'Attack Of The Name Game', but her subsequent Cotillion releases failed to match the sparkle of her early work. An album of duets with fellow teenager **Johnny Gill** in 1984 was well received in the disco market, but her solo career was only revived after she signed to **Motown** in 1986 and enjoyed a major dance hit with 'Nail It To The Wall'.

● ALBUMS: *Young And In Love* (Cotillion 1979)★★★, *Let Me Be Your Angel* (Cotillion 1980)★★★, *With You* (Cotillion 1981)★★★, *Sneakin' Out* (Cotillion 1982)★★★, *16* (Cotillion 1983)★★★, with Johnny Gill *Perfect Combination* (Cotillion 1984)★★, *I'm Not The Same Girl* (1985)★★, *Take Me All The Way* (Motown 1986)★★★, *Personal Attention* (Motown 1988)★★★.

● COMPILATIONS: *The Very Best Of Stacy Lattisaw* (Rhino 1998)★★★.

Lauder, Harry

b. 4 August 1870, Portobello, near Edinburgh, Scotland, d. 26 February 1950, Strathaven, Scotland. This popular singer, comedian and composer was a minstrel of the British music halls. The son of a potter, Lauder worked in a flax mill, and for 10 years in a coal mine. He made his first stage appearance in 1882, and continued to perform as an amateur, before turning professional in 1894. After touring Scotland in concert parties, he ventured to England, first with appearances in the Newcastle area, and then London, where he made his debut at Gatti's, Westminster in 1900. A short, stocky, bandy-legged figure, dressed in the tartan kilt complete with sporran, and carrying his 'crummock' (a stick with a curved head), Lauder exuded vitality and good humour. He sang his own songs, such as 'Tobermory' and 'The Lass Of Killiecrankie', and performed a sketch about an Irish tailor named 'Callaghan'. Despite his Scottish burr amid what was basically a Cockney form of entertainment, Lauder soon became one of the leading figures and highest paid entertainers in such London music halls as the Oxford, Royal Holborn and London Pavilion. In 1908 he performed for King Edward VII at Rufford Abbey. He toured abroad, including the USA, and had his first record hit there in 1907 with his theme song, 'I Love A Lassie', followed (through until 1916) with 'The Wedding Of Sandy McNab', 'When I Get Back To Bonnie Scotland', 'She Is My Daisy', 'He Was Very Kind To Me', 'Stop Your Tickling Jock', 'The Bounding Bounder', 'We Parted On the Shore', 'The Blarney Stone', 'Roamin' In The Gloamin'', 'The Picnic (Every Laddy Loves A Lassie)', 'She's The Lass For Me' and 'My Bonnie, Bonnie Jean'. Several of those were his own songs, written mostly in collaboration with Gerald Grafton. Others included 'Early In The Morning', 'The Last Of The Sandies', 'The Saftest O' The Family', 'Bonnie Hielan Mary', 'Glasgow Belongs To Me', 'That's The Reason Noo I Wear A Kilt', 'A Wee Deoch-An-Doris', 'It's Nice To Get Up In The Morning' and the rousing 'End Of The Road'.

During World War I, Lauder raised large sums of money for charity through his concerts, entertained the troops on the French front and, in 1919, received a knighthood for his services. He lost his only son in the conflict. In 1916 he starred in Harry Gratton's revue, *Three Cheers*, at London's Shaftesbury Theatre, and during the 20s and 30s continued to appear in variety theatres in London and the provinces, as well as touring South Africa, New Zealand, Australia and the Dominions. In 1932 he made his 25th tour of the USA. Lauder also made several films, including *Huntingtower* (1927), *Auld Lang Syne* (1929) and the musical, *The End Of The Road* (1936). He wrote several novels and collected his own reminiscences in *Harry Lauder: At Home And On Tour*. Other books included *Roamin' In The Gloamin'*, *A Minstrel In France* and *Wee Drappies*. His biographies included *Great Scot: The Life Of Sir Harry Lauder* by G. Irving. Vocal evidence of his pre-eminence in the music hall era, rivalled only, perhaps,

by Dan Leno, has been preserved on several recent compilations. After his death, the Harry Lauder Society continued to flourish, with members throughout the world. In 1991, over 40 years later, the Society became affiliated to the Clyde Valley Tourist Board.

● COMPILATIONS: *Sir Harry Lauder Sings Scottish Songs* (1974)★★★, *The Very Best Of Sir Harry Lauder* (1976)★★★★, *I Love A Lassie* (1980)★★★, *The Golden Age Of Sir Harry Lauder* (1983)★★★★, *We Parted On The Shore* (1988)★★★, *Roamin' In The Gloamin'* (1990)★★★.

● FURTHER READING: *Great Scot: The Life Of Harry Lauder*, G. Irving.

Lauderdale, Jim

b. 11 April 1957, Statesville, North Carolina, USA. His father was a minister and his mother a music teacher and choir director. Lauderdale played drums in the school band and after graduation decided to become a solo performer in New York. He impressed record producer Pete Anderson while in the Los Angeles production of *Pump Boys And Dinettes* and was recorded for the compilation *A Town South Of Bakersfield, Volume 2*. He then sang backing vocals for various artists including **Carlene Carter** and **Dwight Yoakam**, and had his songs recorded by **Vince Gill** and **George Strait**. *Planet Of Love* is an impressive album that was co-produced by **Rodney Crowell** and John Leventhal and included **Marc Cohn** and Shawn Colvin among the musicians. Lauderdale himself wrote all the songs and performs them in a variety of styles ranging from western swing to **Jerry Lee Lewis**. He has also written several songs for Kelly Willis and he appears on the chorus of Carlene Carter's 'Little Love Letters'. *Persimmons* was another accomplished album sprinkled with classy country rock and ballads with a formidable list of helpers - **Emmylou Harris**, Dan Dugmore (guitar), Al Perkins (guitar), Pat Buchanan (guitar) and Larry Knechel (piano).

● ALBUMS: *Planet Of Love* (Reprise 1991)★★★★, *Pretty Close To The Truth* (Atlantic 1993)★★★, *Every Second Counts* (Atlantic 1995)★★★, *Persimmons* (Upstart 1996)★★★★, *Whisper* (BNA 1998)★★★.

Laugh

This UK, Manchester-based group first appeared with the punchy, guitar-dominated 'Take Your Time, Yeah!', featured on a flexi-disc given away free with the city's *Debris* magazine in 1986. In November of the same year the track fronted their first vinyl single on the Remorse label, but although it was well received, Laugh had to wait until August the following year before their second offering appeared, a decidedly poppy effort entitled 'Paul McCartney'. This had been previewed on a 1986 session for disc jockey **John Peel**, and also featured the assistance of **Smiths** guitarist Craig Gannon. After 'Time To Lose' in 1988, which reached the UK Independent Top 30, the band moved to the short-lived Sub Aqua label for *Sensation No. 1*, the title of both the album and a single. Neither made any significant

impact and Martin Mittler (bass), Spencer Birtwhistle (drums), Ian Bendelow (guitar) and Martin Wright (guitar, vocals) rethought their strategy, later emerging as a dance outfit.
● ALBUMS: *Sensation No.1* (Sub Aqua 1988)★★.

Laughing Buddha
(see **Cosmosis**)

Laughing Clowns
Based in Sydney, Australia, the Laughing Clowns were led by **Ed Kuepper**, who formed the band in 1979 after leaving the **Saints**. The group rehearsed for six months before gigging, and the music that emerged was complex. As the members: Louise Elliot (saxophone), Peter Doyle (trumpet), the Wallace-Crabbe brothers Ben and Dan (bass and keyboards, respectively), Peter Walsh (bass) and Jeffrey Wegener (drums), came from different disciplines such as jazz, many of Kuepper's fans had difficulty appreciating what the band was attempting. The media found difficulties in pigeonholing the Laughing Clowns as easily as their contemporaries. Representative of their style, and an in-concert favourite, was 'Eternally Yours'. Despite this lack of acceptance the band recorded regularly on independent labels (including their own, called Prince Melon). The band toured the UK and Europe from 1982 onwards, releasing several records there, but to no great success. Undaunted, Kuepper continued solo, and formed a new outfit called the Yard Goes On Forever. Walsh went on to form the highly-praised Apartments.
● ALBUMS: *Mr Uddich Schmuddich Goes To Town* (Prince Melon 1981)★★★, *Laughter Around The Table* (Red Flame 1983)★★★, *Law Of Nature* (Hot 1984)★★, *Ghost Of An Ideal Wife* (Hot 1985)★★.
● COMPILATIONS: *Laughing Clowns* (Red Flame 1982)★★★, *History Of Rock 'N' Roll, Volume 1* early 80s recordings (Hot 1985)★★★, *The Butterfly Net* (Hot 1993)★★★.

Laughner, Peter
b. Cleveland, Ohio, USA, d. 22 June 1977, Cleveland, Ohio, USA. Guitarist/vocalist Peter Laughner was an integral part of Cleveland's punk scene of the mid-70s. Having established, then left, two struggling bands, Cinderella's Revenge and the Finns, he joined **Rocket From The Tombs** in 1975. In 1976 he formed **Pere Ubu** with Rocket From The Tombs' founder, **David Thomas**. Laughner remained with Pere Ubu for their first two singles, 'Heart Of Darkness' and 'Life Stinks', before conflict with the other members resulted in his departure. In 1976 Laughner formed Friction with Tony Maimone (also ex-Pere Ubu) and Anton Fier of the **Styrenes**. This short-lived group, the repertoire of which was largely cover versions, was succeeded by Peter And The Wolves, another temporary affair brought to ground by Laughner's increasingly erratic personality and drug addiction. On 21 June 1977 he recorded a tape mixing new material with favourite

songs from writers such as **Tom Verlaine**, **Richard Thompson**, **Lou Reed** and **Robert Johnson**. Laughner died the following day. A talented poet and songwriter and a perceptive record reviewer, he fell foul to the life of excess perceived as integral to rock 'n' roll. Posthumous releases are gleaned from live appearances and demo tapes from throughout the singer's career.
● COMPILATIONS: *Peter Laughner* (Koolie 1982)★★★, *Take The Guitar For A Ride* (TK 1993)★★★.

Laula, Carol
b. 12 December 1963, Johnstone, Paisley, Renfrewshire, Scotland. Scottish singer-songwriter, descended from Romany Gypsies. Her parents bought Carol her first guitar when she was just 12. She later joined local bands, Playing For Time and This Perfect Heart. In 1989 she recorded her first solo single, 'Gypsy'. This was followed, in 1990, by 'Standing Proud', a song officially adopted by the City Of Glasgow as the theme for its Year Of Culture. After a spell of busking on the continent, Carol returned to Scotland, during the summer of 1990, this time adding to the solo guitar/vocal format, by forming the Carol Laula Band. The group comprised a number of top Scottish musicians, namely Martin Hanlin (drums), Alan Hosie (bass), and Johnny Cameron (guitars, mandolin, vocals), and the resultant 1991 Scottish tour was highly successful. On 5 October 1992, *Still* was released, on Iona Records, and for the recording, the group were augmented by James Prime (Hammond organ, accordion), Ewan Vernal (bass), and Dougie Vipond (from **Deacon Blue**; drums), Anne Wood (from the Cauld Blast Orchestra; fiddle), and Mark Duff (from **Capercaillie**; whistle). All the songs were composed by Laula, apart from the classic 'White Dress' written by **Dave Swarbrick**. For the subsequent Scottish tour, she was supported by former **Go-Go**, **Jane Wiedlin**. She then went out to Louisiana, USA, to work on songs for the follow-up album with a new line-up which included Gavin McComb (bass), Martin Hanlin (drums), and Johnny Cameron (guitars). *Precious Little Victories* moved into soft-rock, but still had an acoustic feel. Again, apart from one track co-written with Wiedlin, the songs were composed by Laula.
● ALBUMS: *Still* (Iona 1992)★★★, *Precious Little Victories* (Iona 1993)★★★★, *Naked* (CL 1996)★★★.

Lauper, Cyndi
b. Cynthia Anne Stephanie Lauper, 22 June 1953, Queens, New York, USA. Starting her career as a singer in Manhattan's clubs, Lauper began writing her own material when she met pianist John Turi in 1977. They formed Blue Angel and released a self-titled album in 1980 which included raucous versions of rock classics as well as their own numbers. She split with Turi and in 1983 began working on what was to become her multi-million-selling solo debut, *She's So Unusual*. It made number 4 in the USA and provided four hit singles - the exuberant 'Girls Just Want To Have Fun' (UK/US

number 2), which became a cult anthem for independent young women; 'Time After Time' (US number 1/UK number 3, later covered by **Miles Davis** on *You're Under Arrest* and by the jazz duo **Tuck And Patti**), 'She Bop' (US number 3, which broached the unusual subject of female masturbation) and 'All Through The Night' (US number 4, written by **Jules Shear**). The album also contained **Prince**'s 'When You Were Mine'. At the end of 1984 *Billboard* magazine placed her first in the Top Female Album Artists and she was awarded a Grammy as Best New Artist. Her image was one that adapted, for the American market, something of a colourful 'punk' image that would not offend parents too much but at the same time still retain a sense of humour and rebelliousness that would appeal the youth. Pundits in the UK claimed to have seen through this straight away, yet they acknowledged Lauper's talent nonetheless. *True Colors* did not have the same commercial edge as its predecessor, yet the title track still provided her with an US number 1 and a Top 20 hit in the UK. The follow-up, 'Change Of Heart' (written by **Essra Mohawk** and featuring the **Bangles**), reached US number 3 in November 1986. In 1987, she took a role as a beautician in the poorly received film, *Vibes*. She made a brief return to the charts in 1990 with the single 'I Drove All Night' (US number 6, UK number 9) from *A Night To Remember*. Another lacklustre film appearance in *Off And Running* was not seen in the UK until two years later. Seen in some quarters as little more than a visual and vocal oddity, Lauper has nevertheless written several magnificent pop tunes ('Time After Time' is destined to become a classic) and, in 1985, boosted her credibility as a singer when she performed a stirring duet with **Patti LaBelle** at LaBelle's show at the Greek Theater in Los Angeles. Lauper was joined by her former writing partners Ron Hyman and Eric Bazilian for *Hat Full Of Stars*, a successful mix of soul/pop/hip-hop with a smattering of ethnic/folk. A reworked version of her biggest hit, retitled 'Hey Now (Girls Just Want To Have Fun)', reached number 4 in the UK charts in September 1994.

● ALBUMS: as Blue Angel *Blue Angel* (Polydor 1980)★★★, *She's So Unusual* (Portrait 1984)★★★★, *True Colors* (Portrait 1986)★★★, *A Night To Remember* (Epic 1989)★★, *Hat Full Of Stars* (Epic 1993)★★, *Sisters Of Avalon* (Epic 1997)★★★.

● COMPILATIONS: *12 Deadly Cyns* (Epic 1994)★★★★.

● VIDEOS: *Twelve Deadly Cyns ... And Then Some* (Epic 1994).

Laurel And Hardy

Laurel (b. Paul Dawkins, October 1962, London, England) and Hardy (b. Anthony Robinson, April 1962, London, England). Before entering the reggae scene in 1978 the duo tried their luck at performing soul but found the DJ style more absorbing. The pair followed the **sound systems** of the day, such as Neville King, Moa Ambassa and Sufferer. They began performing with a young girl known as the Virgin Mary, while they were known as Reverend T and Pope Paul.

Following in the combination style of **Clint Eastwood And General Saint**, **Yellowman** And Fathead, and Michigan And Smiley they became known as the Holy Two. Located in Battersea, London, it was not long before their debut single appeared on the locally based **Fashion** label, and they became known as Laurel And Hardy. Emulating Stan and Ollie, they would appear in bowler hats, bow ties, white gloves and suits, to the delight of the audience. The release of 'You're Nicked' surfaced on a 10-inch disc, a popular fad at the time, and the success of the single brought them to the attention of **CBS Records**. The signing led to a tour of universities supporting the funk fusion group **Pigbag**. Following the rave reviews on campus another tour of universities was arranged, using a band as opposed to backing tapes, and supported by the dub poet **Benjamin Zephaniah**. The pair were also featured in the national press and appeared on Saturday morning television shows promoting the release of 'Clunk Click' in 1983. However, major label contracts frequently prompted the demise of reggae performers' careers, and the duo were no exception. Following the second release, 'Lots Of Loving And She's Gone', Laurel And Hardy returned to an independent label and recorded with Papa Face. Sadly, the duo's credibility was already low and they were unable to recapture the popularity that they had previously enjoyed. Other outings followed, notably 'Dangerous Shoes', but they were unable to maintain a high profile in the reggae chart. During a quiet spell they set up their own recording studio and worked in the background, although an appearance on the television series *Black On Black* was met with enthusiasm.

● ALBUMS: *What A Bargain* (Upright 1983)★★★.

Lauren, Rod

b. 26 March 1940, Fresno, California, USA. This photogenic pop/rock singer was launched in 1959 by **RCA Records** with an all-encompassing promotional campaign. The label saw him as their answer to the clean-cut, good looking Philadelphia school of late 50s pop stars. Lauren, who previously attended acting school, had studied trombone for nine years and his only musical experience till then had been playing in local jazz bands. He reached the US Top 40 with his first single, a Tepper and Bennett composition 'If I Had A Girl'. It beat a rival version by erstwhile hit-maker **Jerry Keller**, partly thanks to being seen on labelmate **Perry Como**'s top-rated television show. Lauren, who in truth was just an average singer, did not return to the charts. After he was dropped by RCA in 1962 he joined Chancellor Records, the same label that had launched **Frankie Avalon** and **Fabian**, the teen idols whom Lauren was anticipated to emulate. As it happened, none of them reached the Top 40 again.

● ALBUMS: *I'm Rod Lauren* (1961)★★★.

Laurence Olivier Awards

These awards are presented by the Society of West End Theatre in recognition of distinguished artistic achievement in West End Theatre, London, England. They were established in 1976 as the Society of West End Theatre Awards. Lord Olivier agreed to have his name associated with them in 1984 and they are now regarded as the highlight of the British theatrical year. The Awards are judged by three separate panels; for theatre, opera, and dance. The Theatre Panel comprises seven people chosen for their specialist knowledge and professional experience, plus six members of the theatre-going public. Anyone who applies to be included in the latter group should be prepared to see some 80 productions during the Awards year. The musical categories consist of: best director choreographer, actress, actor, supporting performance, revival, and the American Express Award for Best Musical. A musical production, or those associated with it, can also conceivably win in other sections such as best entertainment, costume design, lighting design, set design, outstanding achievement, and lifetime achievement. The bronze Laurence Olivier Award itself was specially commissioned by the Society from the sculptor Harry Franchetti and represents the young Laurence Olivier as Henry V at the Old Vic in 1937.

Laurence, Chris

b. 6 January 1949, London, England. Laurence was born into a musical family and studied at the Royal Junior College of Music and the Guildhall School of Music. He started playing the bass professionally at the end of the 60s as one of a remarkable wave of new British jazz musicians. He worked with the bands of **Mike Westbrook**, **Mike Pyne**, **John Surman**, **John Taylor** and **Kenny Wheeler**. The breadth of his musicianship has made him one of the most dependable bass players in any rhythm section. During the 80s he played in the Orchestra of the Academy of St. Martins in the Fields and the London Bach Orchestra as well as in trios with **Tony Oxley**, **Alan Skidmore** and **Tony Coe** as well as continuing to appear in the various bands of John Surman.

● ALBUMS: with Frank Ricotti *Our Point Of View* (1969)★★★, with the London Jazz Composers Orchestra *Ode* (1972)★★★, with John Surman *Morning Glory* (1973)★★★, with Tony Coe, Tony Oxley *Nutty On Willisau* (1983)★★, *Aspects Of Paragonne* (1985)★★★★.

Laurents, Arthur

b. 14 July 1918, New York, USA. A distinguished stage director, author and screenwriter, Laurents has enjoyed equal success in both the musical and legitimate theatre. His parents did not approve of his early ambitions to be a playwright, and young Laurents went alone to New York theatres in the Depression-hit early 30s. He made his name as the author of plays such as *Home Of The Brave* (1945) and *The Time Of The Cuckoo* (1952), before writing the libretto for the landmark musical *West Side Story* (1957). The 50s were troubled times for Laurents: blacklisted during the McCarthy witch hunts, he was nearly bankrupted by the lawyers fees incurred in securing the return of his passport. He and composer **Leonard Bernstein** auditioned **Stephen Sondheim** as lyricist for *West Side Story*, enabling him to make his Broadway debut. Laurents and Sondheim collaborated again in 1959 on *Gypsy* (music: **Jule Styne**), *Anyone Can Whistle* (1964, Laurents also directed) and *Do I Hear A Waltz?* (1965). Laurents made his debut as the director of a musical in 1962 with *I Can Get It For You Wholesale*, in which **Barbra Streisand** made an enormous impact, stopping the show every night with the comic 'Miss Marmelstein'. Since then, Laurents has experienced mixed fortunes. *Hallelujah, Baby!* (1967), with his libretto and a score by Jule Styne, **Betty Comden** and **Adolph Green**, was considered a failure in New York, but the first West End production of *Gypsy* in 1973, starring **Angela Lansbury**, which Laurents directed, was acclaimed, and subsequently transferred to Broadway. Laurents also directed another New York revival of his favourite musical in 1989, with Tyne Daly. In 1979, *The Madwoman Of Central Park West*, a one-woman entertainment that Laurents wrote with and for Phyllis Newman, played off-Broadway at the 22 Steps Theatre. After being nominated for a **Tony Award** for his direction of the original *Gypsy*, Laurents' staging of *La Cage Aux Folles* finally won him an Award in 1983. However, there were no Tonys awarded to *Nick And Nora* (1991); Laurents was associated with this colossal flop as author and director, but ironically, for him personally, some good came from it. Disillusioned with musical productions, he immediately launched into the creation of a series of plays, their content spanning four decades: *Jolson Sings Again*, a piece about politics and principles set in Hollywood during the McCarthy era, a comedy of manners entitled *The Radical Mystique*, *My Good Name*, and *Two Lives*. He also settled on two venues sympathetic to his work, Seattle Rep and the Manhattan Theatre Club. Laurents' other notable contributions to the straight theatre over the years have included *Invitation To A March* (1960), which had incidental music by Sondheim, *The Way We Were*, *Scream*, *A Clearing In The Woods*, and the homosexually themed *The Enclave* (1973). One of his earliest efforts, *The Time Of The Cuckoo*, had already provided the basis for the musical *Do I Hear A Waltz?*, before it was filmed in 1955 as *Summertime*, starring Katharine Hepburn, while *The Way We Were* came to the big screen in 1973, with Barbra Streisand and Robert Redford in the leading roles. Laurents wrote the screenplay for the latter, and he also scripted *The Snake Pit* (1948), *Rope* (1948), *Caught* (1948), *Anna Lucasta* (1949, with Philp Yordan), *Anastasia* (1956), *Bonjour Tristesse* (1958) and *The Turning Point* (1977). In 1995, the York Theatre Company presented Laurents with its sixth annual **Oscar Hammerstein II** Award, and his many other honours have included Golden Globe,

Drama Desk, National Board of Review, Writers Guild of America, National Institute of Arts and Letters, Screen Writers Guild, Sydney Drama Critics awards. He has been inducted into the Theatre Hall of Fame.

Laurie, Annie

Rumoured to be **Dinah Washington**'s favourite singer and a big influence on **Joe Williams**, Annie Laurie sang professionally with the **territory bands** led by Snookum Russell and Dallas Bartley (the latter with whom she made her recording debut - 'St. Louis Blues' - in 1945), before arriving in New Orleans where she was hired by **Paul Gayten**. With Gayten's band she had a string of successful records between 1947 and 1950, such as her covers of **Buddy Johnson**'s 'Since I Fell For You' on DeLuxe Records and **Lucky Millinder**'s 'I'll Never Be Free' on Regal - both of which spawned numerous cover versions. Following Regal's demise in 1951, Annie Laurie commenced her solo career on **Columbia**'s reactivated **OKeh** subsidiary, subsequently recording for Savoy (1956), DeLuxe again (1956-59 - where she had her biggest hit in 1957 with 'It Hurts To Be In Love'), and Ritz (1962). In the 60s she gave up secular singing and has devoted her voice to the church ever since.

Laurie, Cy

b. 20 April 1926, London, England. A leading figure in the post-war traditional jazz boom in the UK, clarinettist Laurie led his own band in the late 40s and early 50s. He also played with the band led by **Mike Daniels**. Dividing his time between playing and running a popular London jazz club, Laurie became a seemingly immovable fixture on the scene but in 1960 dropped out of music. In the early 70s he was back and by the end of the decade had re-established his following. In the 80s he was a very popular figure on the UK traditional jazz scene, recording and playing concerts with fellow-veteran performers **Ken Colyer** and **Max Collie**. Although rooted in the playing of **Johnny Dodds**, Laurie's performances display an acute ear for changing musical fashions and there are often hints that his range could in fact be much wider than either he or his fans have ever allowed.
● ALBUMS: *Cy Laurie Blows Blue-Hot* (1956)★★★, *Cy Laurie And Les Jowett* (1957)★★, *Shades Of Cy* (Suntan 1984)★★★, with Max Collie, Ken Colyer *New Orleans Mardi Gras* (1985)★★★, *That Rhythm Man* (1989)★★, *Delving Back With Cy* (Esquire 1986)★★★.

Laurin, Anna-Lena

b. Sweden. Laurin began playing piano as a child, studying classical music. Then she played alto saxophone before finally settling on singing. Her first musical experience as a professional was in rock and she also sang Irish folk and Balkan music amongst many other forms. Declaring herself to be unsatisfied at the time with what she was singing, she moved to Malmö in 1987 and discovered that jazz was her métier. She sings with several Malmö-based groups including Con Brio

and, especially Fee-Fi-Fo-Fum, a band comprising Anders Bergcrantz (trumpet, flügelhorn), Rolf Nilsson (guitar), Hans Andersson (bass), Kristofer Johansson (drums). While including standards in her jazz repertoire, Laurin writes a great deal of her own material, words and music, and writes her own arrangements. In performance, she sings as an ensemble member rather than as a featured singer. She is also interested in Brazilian music and some of her own work reflects this with its Latin nuances.
● ALBUMS: *Dance In Music* (Dragon 1994)★★★.

Laury, Lawrence 'Booker T'

b. 1914, USA, d. 23 September 1995, Memphis, Tennessee, USA. One of the true originals in the field of boogie-woogie and barrelhouse blues piano, Laury's period of greatest activity stretched from the 20s to the 50s. Laury, a Memphis blues pianist active in the 20s, went unrecorded until the late 70s, but even in 1990 was still a vigorous survivor from the barrelhouse tradition. He was dismissed from playing during the intermission spot at the tourist-orientated Blues Alley club because he was 'too old-fashioned'. He learned piano from **Mose Vinson** and **Memphis Slim**, whom he claimed to be a cousin; however, Laury's rough, energetic playing and powerful vocals were much less polished than Slim's. Following the death of his wife in the mid-50s he retired from the music business, but was persuaded by Slim to make his return to performing in the 70s. Laury supported Slim on his European tour, and also accompanied him on treks through Africa and Asia in the 70s and 80s. In 1989 he featured in the **Jerry Lee Lewis** biopic *Great Balls Of Fire*, and his version of the sexually explicit 'Big Leg Woman' is based on Lewis's adaptation of the original recording by **Johnny Temple**. Heralded as one of the last great authentic blues pianists, he recorded his debut album in 1994 at the age of 80. Sadly he died of cancer within a year of its release, just as his contribution to the development of blues piano was being widely acknowledged.
● ALBUMS: *Nothing But The Blues* (1980)★★★, *Memphis Piano Blues Today* (1991)★★★, *Blues On The Prowl* (Wolf 1994)★★★.

Lavelle, Caroline

b. England. Cellist Caroline Lavelle was first heard by the public on **De Dannan**'s album, *Ballroom*. Lavelle attended classical music college in London, where she would often also busk in Covent Garden playing jigs and reels. It was here that members of De Dannan, a group whose music already had its place in her record collection, first approached her. She was a member of the band for just over two years and still occasionally returns as a guest musician. Lavelle then collaborated with the **Waterboys, June Tabor, Siouxsie And The Banshees, Peter Gabriel** and the **Pogues**. In 1994 she took part in the Real World Records' recording week, both with her own string trio, Elektra, and as singer and cellist on 'She Moved Through The Fair', released on the *Jam Nation* compilation. She also became a fan of experimental dance music (**Portishead**, etc.) after playing cello on a song by **Massive Attack**, for whom she also sang and co-produced the track 'Home Of The Whale'. This was heard by the dance music producer **William Orbit**, who was then brought in to work with her on *Spirit*. Lavelle wrote much of the material, and arranged it too, while Orbit produced the rhythm tracks and mixed the sessions.

● ALBUMS: *Spirit* (Warners 1995)★★★.

LaVere, Charles

b. Charles LaVere Johnson, 18 July 1910, Salina, Kansas, USA, d. 28 April 1983. A talented multi-instrumentalist, he mostly played piano, working with an array of fine early jazzmen, including **Wingy Manon**, **Jack Teagarden** and **Zutty Singleton**. LaVere worked with several bandleaders, among them **Paul Whiteman** and **Ben Pollack** and was for a while with the **Casa Loma Orchestra**. During the 40s he began regularly to lead his own bands, often hiring top-flight jazz musicians especially for recording dates, such as **Joe Venuti** and Matty Matlock. He had a hit record as a singer in 1947, 'Maybe You'll Be There', accompanied by **Gordon Jenkins**. He also made many recording dates, including a 1950 session with Jenkins to accompany **Billie Holiday**. During the second half of the 50s LaVere was resident at Disneyland playing a somewhat denaturalized Dixieland for the mass audience. He continued to lead bands through the 60s, 70s and into the 80s. He composed several pieces including 'Cuban Boogie Woogie', which he recorded with **Charlie Barnet** in 1939. LaVere was an accomplished player with an abiding enthusiasm for music. Many of his bands, although often overlooked, were solid jazz groups with very good soloists.

Lavette, Betty

b. Betty Haskin, 1946, Muskegon, Michigan, USA. She gained her first professional experience as part of the touring review run by soul singers **Don Gardner** and **Dee Dee Ford** in the early 60s. Her passionate vocal style won her a solo contract with **Atlantic Records**, where she adopted her stage name for the 1962 R&B hit 'My Man - He's A Loving Man', one of the finest early examples of southern soul. However, she was unable to build on this success, and only made sporadic recordings with small labels during the rest of the decade. Her torch ballad 'Let Me Down Easy' was an R&B hit in 1965, written by country 'rebels' Jim and **Tompall Glaser**, the song was later covered by the **Spencer Davis Group**. Lavette recorded material by other country writers, and her version of **Mickey Newbury**'s 'Just Dropped In (To See What Condition My Condition Is In)' in 1969 was later picked up by **Kenny Rogers**. She enjoyed two further chart successes in 1969-70 with country/soul recordings on Lelan Rogers' Silver Fox label, most notably with the superb, if risqué, 'He Made A Woman Out Of Me', turned into a pop release for

Bobbie Gentry. After singles for SSS-International and TCI, LaVette next returned to the Atlantic fold to record two 1971/2 singles for their **Atco** label. Of these, her searing version of **Joe Simon**'s 'Your Time To Cry' (retitled 'Your Turn To Cry') became yet another high point in a career of little-known but aesthetically sublime recordings. The mid- to late 70s saw singles on Epic and a disco-influenced outing for West End, while LaVette also starred in the Broadway musical *Bubbling Brown Sugar*. In the early 80s, renewed interest in her early recordings led to her being offered a contract with **Motown**. There she recorded the acclaimed *Tell Me A Lie*, one of the label's few ventures into southern soul. Besides the R&B hit 'Right In The Middle (Of Falling in Love)', the album included impressive remakes of 'I Heard It Through The Grapevine' and 'If I Were Your Woman'. Lavette remains a cult figure among soul fans in the UK, and many of her 60s recordings have been reissued in recent years. In 1992 she recorded two singles and *Not Gonna Happen Twice* on Ian Levine's Motor City label.

● ALBUMS: *Tell Me A Lie* credited as Bettye Lavette (Motown 1980)★★★, *Not Gonna Happen Twice* (Motor City 1992)★★★.

● COMPILATIONS: *Easier To Say* (Charly 1980)★★★, *I'm In Love* (Charly 1985, reissued in 1991 as *Nearer To You* with extra tracks)★★★.

Lavoe, Héctor

b. Héctor Pérez, 30 September 1946, Ponce, Puerto Rico, d. 29 June 1993. Lavoe is known as 'El Cantante' (*The* Singer), after the title of the biographical song **Rubén Blades** composed for his 1978 *Comedia*. Lavoe's high-nasal voice and style of phrasing are unmistakable, and his often witty, sometimes risqué, ad-libbed anecdotes became renowned. Héctor was heavily influenced by his father, Luis Pérez, who sang and played guitar with local bands and trios. When he was six-years-old, Lavoe stood by the radio and sang along with Chuíto el de Bayamón (Jesús Sanchez Erazo), who was one of the greats of jibaro music, the country music of Puerto Rico. He received tuition from his father and attended the Free School of Music in Ponce, where he met **Papo Lucca** and began his longstanding friendship with José Febles. At the age of 14, Héctor sang professionally with a 10-piece band in a local club. After arriving in New York in May 1963, he was hired to perform with a sextet. This was followed by stints with Orchestra New Yorker and **Kako**. Lavoe met **Willie Colón** in June 1966 and became the lead singer with his two trombone band. Their partnership was highly successful, and between 1967 and 1975, Lavoe sang on twelve of Colón's albums.

Colón handed his band over to Lavoe in 1974. With two trumpets added, Héctor made his solo debut on the Colón-produced *La Voz* in 1975. The album went gold. José Febles arranged Héctor's composition 'Paraiso de Dulzura' and the outstanding 'Rompe Saragüey', which featured an elegant and ingenious piano solo by Mark

'Markolino' Dimond. Febles arranged the title track, a romantic bolero, of Lavoe's follow-up *De Ti Depende/It's Up To You*, again produced by Colón. The album also went gold and contained the smash hit single 'Periodico de Ayer' (Yesterday's Newspaper). The song's title became a household phrase. The Colón produced-*Recordando A Felipe Pirela*, was a tribute to the great bolero singer Felipe Pirela (b. Felipe Antonio Pirela Morón, El Empedrado, Venezuela; d. 5 July 1972). In 1980, Febles played trumpet and wrote over half the arrangements on *El Sabio*, which was another Colón production job. The title track was an interpretation of the **Tito Rodríguez** classic. Febles and **Louie Ramírez** were co-musical directors on *Que Sentimiento!*, Héctor's first and only self-production. 1985's *Revento* did not get the recognition it deserved, being released at a time when New York salsa was in the doldrums, Dominican merengue was peaking and Lavoe's career was at a low ebb commercially. In 1987, He reunited with Colón and reverted to a two-trombone front-line for *Strikes Back*.

In 1988 his son was murdered and shortly afterwards he was the victim of an arson attack in which he jumped from his apartment window to save his life, breaking both his legs. Lavoe's career had been dogged by drug problems. He became critically ill and rumours circulated about his medical condition. It was later confirmed he had Aids. His pathetic 90lb frame had to be carried on and off the stage, when he gave a moving performance at the first part of the 1990 New York Salsa Festival at Meadowlands Arena, New Jersey. It was reported that his medical bills had reduced his families financial situation to near destitution. Héctor was a founder member of the Fania All Stars and recorded with them between 1968 and 1988. He was seen performing at his peak with the All Stars in the 1991 UK video release, *Salsa Madness*, which contains 1974 concert footage filmed in Zaire. He made his second UK appearance with them in 1976. In November 1984, he gave a memorable concert at a church hall in Pimlico, London, with some of **Angel Canales**' accompanists. Lavoe appeared on the second and third volumes (1979 and 1985) of **Tito Puente**'s three-album tribute to **Beny Moré**.

● ALBUMS: with Willie Colón *El Malo* (1967)★★★, *The Hustler* (1968)★★★★, *Guisando - Doing A Job* (1969)★★★, *Costa Nuestra* (1970)★★★★, *Asalto Navideño* (1971)★★★, *The Big Break - La Gran Fuga* (1971)★★★, *El Juicio* (1972)★★★, *Lo Mato* (1973)★★★, *Asalto Navideño Vol.2* (1973)★★, *The Good, The Bad, The Ugly* (1975)★★, with Colón *Vigilante* (1983)★★★; with Daniel Santos, Yomo Toro *Feliz Navidad* (1979)★★★; solo *La Voz* (1975)★★★, *De Ti Depende/It's Up to You* (1976)★★★, *Comedia* (1978)★★★, *Recordando A Felipe Pirela* (1979)★★★, *El Sabio* (1980)★★★★, *Que Sentimiento!* (1981)★★★, *Revento* (1985)★★★★, *Hector Strikes Back* (1987)★★★.
● COMPILATIONS: *Héctor's Gold* (1980)★★★★, *El Cantante (The Singer)* (1990)★★★★.

Lavoy, Fernando

b. 1950, Havana, Cuba. Salsa singer and composer Lavoy, arrived in the USA in 1980 and was introduced on *y sigo con mi son* by **Alfredo 'Chocolate' Armenteros**. He sang lead vocals and wrote half the tracks on *Los Soneros*, the 1981 debut by the band of the same name. In 1981, Lavoy appeared on two albums by SAR All Stars. In 1982, he took star billing on *Fernando Lavoy y Los Soneros* and composed half the songs. Apart from sessioning as a chorus singer in Miami, Lavoy disappeared from the scene during the remainder of the 80s. He returned with *Fernando Lavoy Con El Conjunto Dinastiadiez*, which was recorded in Bogotá, Colombia and Miami, Florida. Musically, the album was one of the strongest salsa releases of 1990.
● ALBUMS: with Chocolate *y sigo con mi son* (1980)★★; with Los Soneros *Los Soneros* (1981)★★★★; with SAR All Stars *SAR All Stars Recorded Live In Club Ochentas, Album 1* (1981)★★★, *SAR All Stars Interpretan A Rafael Hernández* (1981)★★★; solo *Fernando Lavoy y Los Soneros* (1982)★★★, *Fernando Lavoy Con El Conjunto Dinastiadiez* (1989)★★★.

Lawal, Gasper

b. 23 September 1948, Ijebu-Ode, Nigeria. A percussionist and bandleader, Lawal left Nigeria to settle in the UK in the mid-60s. Basing himself in London, he became rapidly established in the session scene, and over the next 10 years recorded with a large number of local and visiting musicians, covering a wide variety of styles, including **Ginger Baker**'s **Airforce**, **Stephen Stills**, the **Rolling Stones**, **George Clinton**'s **Funkadelic** and **Barbra Streisand**. In 1975, he joined London-based rock band Clancy, leaving in 1977 to return to Nigeria. Moving back to London in 1978, Lawal formed his own group, Afriki Sound (later renamed the Drum Oro Band), creating a highly individual style which succeeded in marrying traditional West African roots music and instrumentation with elements of experimental rock and jazz. A fervent believer in the value of traditional African music, Lawal was also convinced that it needed to develop and could benefit from the incorporation of certain western ideas and influences. With Afriki Sound he released two superb albums on his own Cap label, *Ajomase* (which in Yoruba means 'We all have to do it together'), which spawned two dancefloor hit singles in 'Kita Kita' and 'Oromoro', and *Abiosunni* (Yoruba for 'Are you sleeping or what?!'). Both albums featured the cream of expatriate African musicians living in London, notably Olalekan Babolola (percussion), Tunji Omoshebi (trumpet), Abdul Salongo (guitar), Don Amaechi (guitar, percussion, kora, keyboards), Ray Allen (saxophones) and **Osibisa**'s Mac Tontoh (trumpet). In the mid-80s, Lawal was a founder member of Britain's Black Music Association, a pressure group which worked to achieve greater exposure and better working conditions for black musicians. In the late 80s he once again embraced a wide range of session work, including spells alongside the **Pogues**, **UB40** and **Robert Palmer**. In 1989 he toured with Zairean superstar **Papa Wemba** and appeared in a Royal Command Performance before the Queen and President Babangida. In 1990 sessions began on his third album, the critically acclaimed *Kodara*, effectively a masterclass in traditional percussion.

● ALBUMS: *Ajomase* (Cap 1980)★★★, *Abiosunni* (Cap 1985)★★, *Kadara* (Globestye 1991)★★★★.

Lawes, Henry 'Junjo'

b. Henry Lawes, Kingston, Jamaica, West Indies. One of the most prolific and influential producers of the 80s, Lawes was born and raised in Olympic Way, West Kingston. In 1978 he made his musical debut singing in the trio Grooving Locks. The following year, he took **Barrington Levy** to **Channel One**. Subsequently, 'Collie Weed', 'Looking My Love' and 'Shine Eye Gal' all reached number 1 on the Jamaican charts, and the resulting *Bounty Hunter* album is generally considered to be the first of the new **dancehall** era. With the **Roots Radics** and **Scientist** working on the majority of his releases, Lawes began voicing a dazzling array of talent. **Michael Prophet** ('Gun Man'), Papa Tullo, **General Echo**, Ranking Toyan ('How The West Was Won'), Billy Boyo, Little Harry, **Little John** ('Dancehall Style'), Barry Brown ('Give Another Israel A Try'), Anthony Johnson and **Eek A Mouse** ('Wa Do Dem') were among those who recorded for his Arrival and Volcano labels throughout 1980-82.

Apart from pioneering the concept of two artist 'clash' albums and presenting dubmixer Scientist as an artist in his own right, his next step was to instigate albums of live dancehall sessions, often featuring **Yellowman**, whose rapid rise owed much to the many hit singles and albums recorded for Lawes. Early B, **Josey Wales** ('Outlaw Josey Wales'), **Nicodemus**, **Buru Banton**, **Michigan And Smiley** ('Diseases'), **Peter Metro**, **Charlie Chaplin**, Audie Murphy and Lord Sassafras all recorded over his rhythm tracks, which began to dominate the dancehall market. Quick to spot new talent, he also revived the careers of several established acts who had slipped into decline. Under his direction, **John Holt** enjoyed a revival, voicing hits such as 'Sweetie Come Brush Me' and then 'Police In Helicopter'; **Alton Ellis**, **Ken Boothe**, **Johnny Osbourne** ('Fally Lover'/'Ice Cream Love'), **Al Campbell**, the **Wailing Souls** and **Earl Sixteen** similarly benefited from his winning touch. In 1983 he formed his own Volcano **sound system**. With access to unlimited **dub plates** and using state-of-the-art equipment, Volcano soon became the top sound in Jamaica. By the following year, Yellowman ('Zungguzungguguzungguzeng'), Barrington Levy ('Prison Oval Rock') and Eek A Mouse ('Anaxerol') were vying for the top slot, and he had already added new talents such as **Cocoa Tea** ('Rocking Dolly'/'Lost My Sonia') and **Frankie Paul** ('Pass The Tushenpeng') to his roster, co-writing an ever-increasing number of hit songs himself. In 1985 he took Volcano to New York, where he remained for six years. He had missed out on the **digital** revolution that had

swept through Jamaican music during those years, but worked with several of his former artists on his return, including John Holt, Linval Thompson, Cocoa Tea ('Kingston Hot') and Yellowman, to varying degrees of success. By 1994 he had recorded albums with **Ninjaman**, General TK and Shaka Shamba, voiced an increasing number of younger artists and had plans for his own studio in Kingston. With his uncanny eye for new talent, his lyrical ability and shrewd marketing sense, few would bet against him making further significant contributions to reggae music in the future. Productions include: Barrington Levy *Bounty Hunter* (1979), *Englishman* (1980), *Robin Hood* (1980); Scientist *Heavyweight Dub Champion* (1980), *Scientist Wins The World Cup* (1983); Ranking Toyan *How The West Was Won* (1982); Eek A Mouse *Wa Do Dem* (1981), *The Mouse And The Man* (1983), *Mouseketeer* (1984); Yellowman *Mr Yellowman* (1982), *Zungguzungguguzungguzeng* (1983); Yellowman with Josey Wales *Two Giants Clash* (1984); Josey Wales *The Outlaw Josey Wales* (1983); John Holt *Police In Helicopter* (1983); Johnny Osbourne *Fally Lover* (1980); Don Carlos *Day To Day Living* (1983); Wailing Souls *Inch Pinchers* (1983); Frankie Paul *Pass The Tu-Sheng Peng* (1984); Cocoa Tea *Wha Dem A Go Do, Can't Stop Cocoa Tea* (1985), *Kingston Hot* (1992); Ninjaman *Booyakka! Booyakka!* (1994).

● COMPILATIONS: various artists *Live At Aces International* (1983)★★★, *Total Recall* (VP 1991)★★★, *Total Recall Volume 2* (VP 1992)★★★.

● FURTHER READING: *Reggae Inna Dancehall Style*, Tero Kaski and Pekka Vuorinen.

Lawhorn, Sammy

b. Samuel David Lawhorn, 12 July 1935, Little Rock, Arkansas, USA, d. 29 April 1990, Chicago, Illinois, USA. Soon after Sammy Lawhorn's birth, his mother and stepfather moved to Chicago, leaving him to be brought up by his grandparents. By the time he was 12, his mother had bought him a Stella and soon after that a Supro electric guitar. Three years later, he was gigging around Helena with Elmon (**Drifting Slim**) Mickle. He also became a King Biscuit Boy, backing **Sonny Boy Williamson** (Rice Miller) and Houston Stackhouse, who taught him to play slide. From 1953, Lawhorn spent five years in the navy and was wounded while serving in Korea as an aerial photographer. On his return, he linked up with harmonica player **Willie Cobbs** and played on the original recording of 'You Don't Love Me'. After appearing in Chicago with Cobbs, he decided to remain in the city and backed **Junior Wells** at Theresa's Club. After jamming with **Muddy Waters** at Pepper's Lounge, he joined Muddy's band in 1964, touring and recording with him for some 10 years until his excessive drinking habits made him an unreliable character. Thereafter, alcohol and the onset of arthritis sent him into a decline from which he never recovered. His only solo album suffered from a lack of rehearsal and commitment, and remains a less

than fitting memorial to such a talented and once-strong musician.
● ALBUMS: *After Hours* (Isabel 1986)★★, with the Teardrops and Little Mac Simmons *My Little Girl* (Wolf 1995)★★★.

Lawnmower Deth

Lawnmower Deth were a thrash metal parody band from the north of England. Founded in 1987, the combined forces of Qualcast Mutilator (vocals), Mr Flymo (drums), Concorde Faceripper (guitars), Mightymo Destructimo (bass) and Scitzophrenic Sprintmaster (guitar) proved a timely antidote to the more ridiculous excesses of banal bloodlust and po-faced pretension in the thrash and death metal genres. With songs including 'Satan's Trampoline' and 'Can I Cultivate Your Groinal Garden', Lawnmower Deth were characterized by their schoolboy sense of humour. This same infantile sense of fun, stretched to their live shows, with 'gimmicks' such as throwing around buckets of baked beans or dressing in third-rate Robin Hood costumes (a direct satire of the pagan Medieval thrash band **Skyclad**). Eventually, the joke began to lose its edge, and Lawnmower Deth expanded musically by including snatches of ska and funk in their repertoire, but wound up the band over Christmas 1994.
● ALBUMS: *Quack Em All* (Earache 1988)★★★, *Ooh Crikey Its...* (Earache 1990)★★★, *Return of The Fabulous Metal Bozo Clowns* (Earache 1992)★★, *Billy* (Earache 1994)★★★.

Lawrence, Denise

b. England. An established singer on the British jazz and jazz-fringe scene for many years, Lawrence has a wide-ranging repertoire. Comfortably at home with standards, blues and gospel, she has a warm, clear voice and always presents her material with an easy-flowing swing. She often works with the Storeyville Tickle Bands, based in Reading, Berkshire, and led by her husband, pianist Tony Lawrence.
● ALBUMS: *Let It Shine* (Lake 1994)★★, *Can't Help Lovin' Those Men Of Mine* (Lake 1995)★★★.

Lawrence, Derek

One of Britain's leading rock producers, Lawrence worked briefly with **Joe Meek** and **Ronan O'Rahilly** (of Radio Caroline) from 1964-65 before becoming a freelance producer. Often creating tracks for US release, Lawrence worked in the late 60s with artists such as **Jethro Tull**, **Kim Fowley**, **Garnet Mimms**, the V.I.Ps (later **Spooky Tooth**) and **Tony Wilson** (later of Hot Chocolate). His first chart success came in 1968 when he supervised the first recordings of **Deep Purple**, including the US hits 'Hush' and *Shades Of Deep Purple*. He went on to work with **Wishbone Ash**, recording four albums with the group from 1970-74. During the early 70s he also produced Flash and Green Bullfrog, the shortlived studio group led by **Ritchie Blackmore**. Among Lawrence's regular studio group were **Big Jim Sullivan** (guitar), Chas Hodges (piano) and Dave Peacock (guitar). When the producer set up

his own label, Retreat, in 1973, among the first acts to be recorded was Sullivan's band Tiger and **Chas And Dave**, the Hodges-Peacock partnership singing rock standards and 'cockney' originals. The Retreat roster also included female singer Theo Scherman and rock bands Dragonfly and Strange Days. After the label folded in 1976, Lawrence moved to Los Angeles where he produced heavy metal bands Angel and **Fist**. Returning to England in 1979, Lawrence was less active in the 80s, recording occasionally with Carl Wayne, Tony Wilson and others.

Lawrence, Elliot

b. Elliot Lawrence Broza, 14 February 1925, Philadelphia, Pennsylvania, USA. A precociously talented pianist, at the age of four Lawrence participated in his father's children's shows on the radio and in his teens he led an orchestra of children for a local broadcast. He continued to be active in music during his university days, and his early professional work was in dance bands and with radio orchestras, some of which he led himself. Lawrence wrote many arrangements for his own bands, accommodating, but without wholly embracing, contemporary shifts in jazz. He also used arrangements by other young men who were testing the boundaries of big band music, notably **Gerry Mulligan**, **Al Cohn** and **Tiny Kahn**. As times became harder for big bands, Lawrence eventually abandoned his full-time bandleading career, but occasionally reformed the group for special engagements and record dates. On such sessions his choice of musicians reflected his determination to look ahead, and soloists included Cohn, **Red Rodney**, **Zoot Sims** and **Urbie Green**. Subsequently, Lawrence's career took him into television and theatrical work.
● ALBUMS: *One Night Stand With Elliot Lawrence* (1947)★★, *Elevation* (1947)★★, *College Prom* 10-inch album (Decca 1950)★★, *Moonlight On The Campus* 10-inch album (Decca 1950)★★, *Elliot Lawrence Plays Tiny Kahn And Johnny Mandel Arrangements* (Fantasy 1956)★★★, *Dream* (Fantasy 1956)★★★, *Swinging At The Steel Pier* (Fantasy 1956)★★★, *The Four Brothers Together Again!* (Fantasy 1957)★★★, *Elliot Lawrence And His Orchestra* i (Fantasy 1957)★★★, *Elliot Lawrence And His Orchestra* ii (Fantasy 1957)★★, *Elliot Lawrence And His Orchestra* iii (Fantasy 1958)★★★, *Elliot Lawrence And His Orchestra* iv (Fantasy 1958)★★★, *Elliot Lawrence And His Orchestra* v (Fantasy 1958)★★★, *Elliot Lawrence And His Orchestra* vi (Fantasy 1959)★★, *Elliot Lawrence And His Orchestra* vii (Fantasy 1960)★★.

Lawrence, Gertrude

b. Gertrud Alexandra Dagmar Lawrence Klasen, 4 July 1898, London, England, d. 6 September 1952. An actress, singer, dancer, comedienne, one of the most vivacious and elegant performers in the history of West End and Broadway theatre. Coming from a showbusiness family, her mother was an actress and her father a singer, Lawrence studied dancing under Madame Espinosa. She made her first proper stage appearance at the age of 12, as a child dancer in the pantomime *Babes In The Wood* at the south London, Brixton Theatre. In 1913, while studying acting and elocution under Italia Conte, where her cockney accent was obliterated, she met the 12-year-old **Noël Coward** who was to have such an important influence on her later career. After appearing in various provincial theatres in shows such as *Miss Lamb Of Canterbury* and *Miss Plaster Of Paris,* Lawrence made her West End debut in 1916 at the Vaudeville Theatre as principal dancer and understudy in Andre Charlot's revue, *Some.* In 1920, after taking a variety of roles in other revues such as *Cheep, Tabs* and *Buzz-Buzz,* she appeared as leading lady at Murray's Club, London's first cabaret entertainment. Later, she toured variety theatres with Walter Williams, before taking the lead, with **Jack Buchanan**, in *A-To-Z* (1921), followed by *De-De, Rats* and Noël Coward's ***London's Calling!*** (1923), in which she introduced his bitter-sweet 'Parisian Pierrot'. She then co-starred on Broadway with Beatrice Lillie in the successful *Andre Charlot's Revue of 1924,* giving America its first taste of 'Limehouse Blues'.

In 1926, after more Charlot associations, including his *Revue Of 1926,* in which she sang 'A Cup of Coffee, A Sandwich And You', Lawrence became the first English actress to originate a role on Broadway before playing it in London, when she took the lead in her first 'book' musical, ***Oh, Kay***, with a score by **George** and **Ira Gershwin**, which included 'Someone To Watch Over Me', 'Maybe', and 'Do-Do-Do'. After repeating her triumph in the West End, Lawrence appeared in several other musicals productions in the late 20s, although none were as lavish as the *International Revue* (1930) in New York, in which she sang **Jimmy McHugh** and **Dorothy Fields**'s catchy 'Exactly Like You' with **Harry Richman**. In the same year she was back in London, co-starring with Coward in his sophisticated light comedy *Private Lives,* fondly remembered for lines such as 'Strange how potent cheap music is', and the waltz, 'Someday I'll Find You'. During the 30s Lawrence appeared in a number of successful straight plays, including *Can The Leopard?, Behold We Live, This Inconsistancy, Heavy House, Susan And God* and *Skylark.* One musical highlight of the decade was ***Nymph Errant*** (1933), in which she sang the title song 'Experiment', 'How Could We Be Wrong?', 'It's Bad For Me' and one of **Cole Porter**'s most amusing 'list songs', 'The Physician' ('He said my epidermis was darling/And found my blood as blue as could be/He went through wild ecstatics when I showed him my lymphatics/But he never said he loved me'). Another, ***Tonight At 8.30*** (1936), saw her re-united with Coward in his series of one-act plays, two of which, *Shadowplay,* ('Then', 'Play Orchestra Play' and 'You Were There') and *Red Peppers* ('Has Anybody Seen Our Ship?' and 'Men About Town'), are particularly celebrated. That was the last time Lawrence was seen in a musical production in London. She and Coward took *Tonight At 8.30* to New York in 1936, and, five years later,

Lawrence had her biggest Broadway success to date when she appeared in ***Lady In The Dark***, with a score by **Kurt Weill** and Ira Gershwin, which gave her the droll 'Jenny' and the haunting 'My Ship'.

For much of the 40s she toured countries such as Belgium, France, Holland and the Pacific Ocean Area, on behalf of the USO and ENSA, entertaining the Allied Troops. At the end of World War II, Lawrence began a three-year engagement as Eliza in a revival of *Pygmalion,* which played New York and toured the USA. She also appeared in various other straight plays in the UK and the USA, including *September Tide* (1949), and completed *The Glass Menagerie,* the last in a series of films she made, beginning with *The Battle Of Paris* (1929). In March 1951, she opened on Broadway in 'the most satisfying role of my career', **Richard Rodgers** and **Oscar Hammerstein II**'s spectacular musical ***The King And I***, playing the part of the children's Governess, Anna for well over a year before being taken ill with a rare form of cancer. She died in September 1952, within a week of being admitted into hospital. Rodgers subscribed to the view, widely held throughout her lifetime, that Lawrence sang flat. 'Just the same', he said, 'whenever I think of Anna, I think of Gertie'.

In 1968, the movie ***Star!***, purported to relate her life story. Starring **Julie Andrews** and Daniel Massey as Noël Coward, it ran for almost three hours ('cost $14 million and took four'), and was subsequently trimmed to two and re-titled *Those Were The Happy Times.* In the early 80s, UK critic and author Sheridan Morley devised the after-dinner entertainment *Noel And Gertie,* which, revised and expanded, toured abroad and played in the West End in 1989 with Patricia Hodge as Gertie and Simon Cadell as Coward. Subsequently, the leading roles were played by Susan Hampshire and Edward Petherbridge, amongst others, and - Off-Broadway in 1992 - by Jane Summerhays and Michael Zaslow.

● ALBUMS: *A Souvenir Album* (Decca 1952)★★★, *Noël And Gertie* (1955)★★★, *A Remembrance* (Decca 1958)★★★, *The Incomparable Gertrude Lawrence* (1964)★★★.

● FURTHER READING: *Gertrude Lawrence: A Bright Particular Star,* Sheridan Morley.

Lawrence, Jack

b. 7 April 1912, New York, USA. Although mainly a lyricist, as well as a singer and conductor, Lawrence wrote both words and music for some of his most popular songs. He studied at Long Island University, and sang on various radio stations, before having his first efforts published in the early 30s. One of these, 'Play, Fiddle, Play' (1932, written with Emery Deutsch and Arthur Altman), was made popular in the USA by the bands of **George Olsen** and **Ted Lewis**, and in the UK by **Al Bowlly** with the New Mayfair Dance Orchestra. During the remainder of the 30s, Lawrence's output resulted in record success for artists such as **Glen Gray** and the **Casa Loma Orchestra** and **Glenn Miller** ('Sunrise Serenade', 1938, with **Frankie Carle**),

Ella Fitzgerald ('All Over Nothing At All', 1937), Ella Fitzgerald with the **Mills Brothers** ('Big Boy Blue', 1937), **Andy Kirk** And His **Clouds Of Joy** and **Bing Crosby** ('What's Your Story, Morning Glory?', 1938, with **Paul Francis Webster**-**Mary Lou Williams**), **Horace Heidt** and Crosby with **Jimmy Dorsey** ('What Will I Tell My Heart?' (1937, with Peter Tinturin-Irving Gordon), Heidt, the **Andrews Sisters** and Dick Barrie ('Tu-li-Tulip Time', 1938, with Maria Grever), **Raymond Scott** ('Huckleberry Duck', with Scott), and **Guy Lombardo** ('In An Eighteenth Century Drawing Room', 1939, with Scott). One of the songs for which Lawrence composed both words and music was the enduring ballad 'If I Didn't Care', which was a big hit in 1939 for the **Ink Spots**, and later revived by the **Hilltoppers** (1954), **Connie Francis** (1961), the **Platters** (1970), and **David Cassidy** (UK 1974). Lawrence was also solely responsible for 'It's Funny To Everyone But Me', and collaborated with Arthur Altman on 'All Or Nothing At All'. Both of those numbers were recorded by **Frank Sinatra** in 1939 when he was with the **Harry James** band, but they only entered the US Hit Parade in the early 40s after the singer began to attract a lot of attention during his stint with **Tommy Dorsey**.

Glenn Miller made the bestseller lists in 1940 with two Lawrence numbers, 'Vagabond Dreams' (with **Hoagy Carmichael**) and 'Handful Of Stars' (**Ted Shapiro**), while in the same year **Larry Clinton** had a hit with 'Johnson Rag' (Guy H. Hall-Henry Kleinkauf), and **Kay Kyser** and Bob Chester, did well with 'With The Wind And Rain In Your Hair' (Clara Edwards). In the following year Lawrence wrote 'Yes, My Darling Daughter', which was introduced in the revue *Crazy With The Heat* by **Gracie Barrie**. It subsequently became popular for **Dinah Shore** and Glenn Miller, and was revived by **Eydie Gorme** in 1962. Also in 1941, Lawrence adapted Tchaikovsky's 'Piano Concerto Number 1' for 'Concerto For Two', and wrote the English lyric for Toots Camarata and Isaac Albeniz's adaptation of Albeniz's 'Tango In D', which was entitled 'Moonlight Masquerade'. He also provided a lyric for the old **Eric Coates** composition '(By The) Sleepy Lagoon', which was then recorded by Harry James and Dinah Shore, and became the title number of a 1943 movie starring Judy Canova and Ruth Donnelly. During World War II, Lawrence served in the US Coastguard and the US Navy-US Maritime Service. He wrote the official song for the latter organization, 'Heave Ho, My Lads, Heave Ho', which subsequently appeared in the 1944 film *Moonlight And Cactus*. Lawrence also organized various service bands, welfare and morale units, and worked overseas for a time. After the war, he provided the English lyrics for European numbers such as 'Symphony' (1945, music: Alex Alstone), 'Beyond The Sea' (1947, adapted from **Charles Trenet**'s 'La Mer', and a big hit in 1960 for **Bobby Darin**), 'Choo Choo Train' (1953, music: Marc Fontenoy), and 'The Poor People Of Paris' (1954, music: Marguerite Monnet). In 1946, with composer Walter Gross, Lawrence produced what is arguably his most enduring song, the lovely ballad 'Tenderly', which **Rosemary Clooney** adopted as her signature number. There were also many other popular items, such as 'Hand In Hand' (1947), 'Linda' (1947), 'Hold My Hand' (1950, with **Richard Myers**, sung in the film *Susan Slept Here* by **Don Cornell**, and nominated for an Academy Award), 'Delicado' (1952, Waldyr Azevado, a US number 1 for **Percy Faith**), and 'No One But You', written with **Nicholas Brodszky** for the 1954 Lana Turner movie *The Flame And The Flesh*, and given a memorable recording by **Billy Eckstine**. Lawrence's work was featured in several other films, including *Outside Of Paradise* (1938, 'A Little Bit Of Everything', 'All For One', 'Outside Of Paradise', 'A Sweet Irish Sweetheart Of Mine', 'Doing Shenanigans', with Peter Tinturin), *Hullabaloo* (1940, 'A Handful Of Stars', with **Ted Shapiro**), *The Great American Broadcast* (1941), *Doughboys In Ireland* (1943), *Stars On Parade* (1944, 'My Heart Isn't In It'), *Weekend Pass* (1944), *This Is The Life* (1944), *Peter Pan* (1953, 'Never Smile At A Crocodile', with Frank Churchill), *So This Is Love* (1953, 'Ciribiribin', with Harry James), and *Sleeping Beauty* ('Once Upon A Dream', with **Sammy Fain**). He was also represented on Broadway with the musicals *Courtin' Time* (1951, 'Heart In Hand', with Don Walker), *Torch Song* (1953), and *I Had A Ball* (1964, 'The Fickle Finger Of Fate', 'The Other Half Of Me', with Stan Freeman), starring Buddy Hackett, as well as the aforementioned *Crazy With The Heat*. Among his other collaborators have been John Green, **John Barry** and **Victor Young**.

● ALBUMS: *Come To The Circus* (50s) ★★★.

Lawrence, Lee

b. Leon Siroto, c.1921, Salford, Lancashire, England, d. February 1961. This former ENSA entertainer's quasi-operatic tenor was similar to that of **Ronnie Hilton**, whom he rivalled as the BBC Light Programme's most featured vocalist in the early 50s. Both of his parents were members of the Carl Rosa Opera Company, and, at the age of 16, Lawrence went to Italy to study opera. After service in World War II he sang with various bands, and made his broadcasting debut on *Beginners Please*. After his 1953 cover version of **Rex Allen**'s 'Crying In The Chapel' peaked at number 7 in the UK Top 10, Lawrence's chart career slumped until a transfer from **Decca** to **EMI** in 1955 brought a second - and final - entry with a version of 'Suddenly There's A Valley' (1955). This, like many other of his recordings, was produced by **Ray Martin**, and followed a false dawn with an arrangement of **Tennessee Ernie Ford**'s 'Give Me Your Word'. He is fondly remembered for his powerful versions of songs such as 'Fascination', 'The Story Of Tina', 'Lonely Ballerina', 'Falling In Love With Love' and his theme, 'The World Is Mine Tonight'. In the late 50s he moved to the USA and played in cabaret and appeared on television. Before his death in February 1961, among the more interesting of

Lawrence's later releases were **Anisteen Allen**'s 'Don't Nobody Move' and 1956's opportunist 'Rock 'N' Roll Opera', a spoof that mentioned **Elvis Presley**, **Gene Vincent**, **Tommy Steele** and other newcomers who were lessening the chances of Lawrence ever returning to the charts.

● ALBUMS: *Presenting Lee Lawrence* (Decca 1953)★★★, *Fascination* (President 1983)★★★.

Lawrence, Steve

b. Stephen Leibowitz, 8 July 1935, Brooklyn, New York, USA. The son of a cantor in a Brooklyn synagogue, Lawrence was in the Glee club at Thomas Jefferson High School, where he began studying piano, saxophone, composition and arranging. He made his recording debut for King Records at the age of 16. The record, 'Mine And Mine Alone', based on 'Softly Awakes My Heart' from *Samson & Delilah*, revealed an amazingly mature voice and style. Influenced by **Frank Sinatra**, but never merely a copyist, he was an individual singer of great range and warmth. He got his first break on Steve Allen's *Tonight* television show, where he met, sang with and later married **Eydie Gorme**. He recorded for Coral Records and had his first hit in 1957 with 'The Banana Boat Song'. It was the infectious 'Party Doll' which gave him a Top 5 hit in 1957 and he followed that same year with four further, although lesser successes, namely 'Pum-Pa-Lum', 'Can't Wait For Summer', 'Fabulous' and 'Fraulein'. During his US Army service (1958-60) he sang with military bands on recruiting drives and bond rallies. Back home he and Eydie embarked on a double act, their most memorable hit being 'I Want To Stay Here' in 1963. As Steve And Eydie they made albums for **CBS**, **ABC** and **United Artists**, including *Steve And Eydie At The Movies*, *Together On Broadway*, *We Got Us*, *Steve And Eydie Sing The Golden Hits* and *Our Love Is Here To Stay*, the latter a double album of great **George Gershwin** songs, which was the soundtrack of a well-received television special. Lawrence, on his own, continued to have regular hits with 'Portrait Of My Love' and 'Go Away Little Girl' in 1961/2, and enjoyed critical success with albums such as *Academy Award Losers* and *Portrait Of My Love*. As an actor he starred on Broadway in *What Makes Sammy Run?*, took the lead in *Pal Joey* in summer stock, and has acted in a crime series on US television. During the 70s and 80s he continued to record and make television appearances with Gorme, with the couple gaining a record-breaking seven Emmys for their *Steve And Eydie Celebrate Irving Berlin* special. The couple also joined Frank Sinatra on his *Diamond Jubilee Tour* in 1991.

● ALBUMS: *About That Girl* (Coral 1956)★★★, *Songs By Steve Lawrence* (Coral 1957)★★★, *Here's Steve Lawrence* (Coral 1958)★★★, *All About Love* (Coral 1959)★★★, *Steve Lawrence* (King 1959)★★★, *Swing Softly With Me* (ABC-Paramount 1960)★★★★, *The Steve Lawrence Sound* (United Artists 1960)★★★★, *Steve Lawrence Goes Latin* (United Artists 1960)★★, *Portrait Of My Love* (United Artists 1961)★★★★, *Winners!* (Columbia 1963)★★★, *Come Waltz With Me* (Columbia 1963)★★★, *People Will Say We're In Love* (United Artists 1963)★★★, *Steve Lawrence Conquers Broadway* (United Artists 1963)★★★, *Songs Everybody Knows* (Coral 1963)★★★, *Academy Award Losers* (Columbia 1964)★★★★,*What Makes Sammy Run* film soundtrack (Columbia 1964)★★, *The Steve Lawrence Show* (Columbia 1965)★★★, *We're All Alone* (President 1985)★★★.

With Eydie Gorme *We Got Us* (ABC-Paramount 1960)★★★★, *Steve And Eydie Sing The Golden Hits* (ABC-Paramount 1960)★★★, *Cozy* (United Artists 1961)★★★, *Two On The Aisle* (United Artists 1963)★★★, *Our Best To You* (ABC-Paramount 1964)★★★, *Together On Broadway* (Columbia 1967)★★★, *What It Was, Was Love* (RCA 1969)★★★, *Real True Lovin'* (RCA 1969)★★★, *Tonight I'll Say A Prayer* (RCA 1970)★★★, *We Can Make It Together* (Ember 1975)★★★, *Our Love Is Here To Stay* (United Artists 1977)★★★, *I Still Believe In Love* (President 1985)★★★, *Alone Together* (GL 1989)★★★, *Since I Fell For You* (1993)★★★.

● COMPILATIONS: *The Best Of Steve Lawrence* (ABC-Paramount 1960)★★★, *The Very Best Of Steve Lawrence* (United Artists 1962)★★★,*The Best Of Steve Lawrence* (Taragon 1995)★★★.

With Eydie Gorme *The Very Best Of Eydie And Steve* (United Artists 1962)★★★, *The Golden Hits Of Eydie And Steve* (United Artists 1962)★★★, *The Best Of Steve And Eydie* (Columbia 1977)★★★, *20 Golden Performances* (1977)★★★.

Lawrence, Syd

b. 26 June 1923, Shotton, Flintshire, Wales, d. 5 May 1998, Wilmslow, Cheshire, England. As a child Lawrence studied violin but began playing cornet with a brass band. In 1941, he became a professional musician, playing dance music but then entered the Royal Air Force. During his military service he became a member of the RAF Middle East Command Dance Orchestra. After the war, he played with, among others, **Ken Mackintosh** and **Geraldo**. In 1953, he joined the BBC Northern Dance Orchestra, where he remained for 15 years. Towards the end of his stint with the orchestra Lawrence formed a rehearsal band, playing the kind of dance music and swing popularized in the late 30s and 40s by American bands, especially that led by **Glenn Miller**. Over the next few months Lawrence found that his rehearsal band was attracting a growing audience which was especially appreciative of the Miller music he had transcribed from records. In 1969, he made the decision to form a full-time professional band. Although in its original concept the band played highly derivative music, it was done with such spirit and enthusiasm that he successfully retained an audience for concerts and records.

● ALBUMS: *Syd Lawrence And The Glenn Miller Sound* (1971)★★★, *Something Old, Something New* (Philips 1972)★★★, *My Favourite Things* (Philips 1973)★★★, *Singin' 'N' Swingin'* (Philips 1975)★★★, *Great Hits Of The 30s, Volume 1* (Philips 1975)★★★, *Ritual Fire Dance* (1975)★★★, *Band Beat* (BBC 1976)★★★, *Disco Swing* (1976)★★★, *Swing Classics* (Philips 1982)★★★, *Remember Glenn Miller* (Ditto

1983)★★★, *Holland Special* (Philips 1986)★★★, *Big Band Swing* (Philips 1988).
● COMPILATIONS: *The Syd Lawrence Collection* (1976)★★★, *Spotlight On The Syd Lawrence Orchestra* (1977)★★★.

Lawrence, Tracy

b. 27 January 1968, Atlanta, Texas, USA. The son of a banker, Lawrence was raised in Foreman, Arkansas, and sang in the church choir. He started working in honky tonks when he was 17 years old and moved to Nashville in 1990. He recorded his first album and the future looked bright until he and his girlfriend were accosted by four thugs in a hotel parking lot. He suffered gunshot wounds and his album was put on hold for five months while he recovered. *Sticks And Stones* sold 500,000 copies and he had country hits with 'Today's Lonely Fool', 'Runnin' Behind' and 'Somebody Paints The Wall'. In 1993, he had a hat trick of number 1s, 'Alibis', 'Can't Break It To My Heart' and 'My Second Home'. He recorded 'Hillbilly With A Heartache' as a duet with **John Anderson** and his video for 'My Second Home' is a who's who of New Country music. In 1996 he reached number 1 again with 'Time Marches On'. His road band is called Little Elvis, even though the most likely crown he could steal would be **Garth Brooks'** and not Presley's.
● ALBUMS: *Sticks And Stones* (Atlantic 1991)★★★, *Alibis* (Atlantic 1993)★★★, *I See It Now* (Atlantic 1994)★★★★, *Tracy Lawrence Live* (Atlantic 1995)★★, *Time Marches On* (Atlantic 1996)★★★, *The Coast Is Clear* (Atlantic 1997)★★★.
● VIDEOS: *I See It Now* (A*Vision 1994), *In The Round* (Warner Vision 1996).

Lawrence, Vicki

b. 26 March 1949, Inglewood, California, USA. Lawrence was a well-known actress in 1973 when she recorded 'The Night The Lights Went Out In Georgia'. Lawrence studied dance and played piano and guitar as a child. By the time she attended college she had joined folk groups, including the Young Americans. Due to her resemblance to comic actress Carol Burnett, a meeting between the two was arranged and, following an audition, Lawrence was awarded a role in Burnett's television programme which lasted from 1967-78. She married songwriter Bobby Russell in 1969. He wrote 'The Night The Lights Went Out In Georgia' for Lawrence and it reached the top of the US charts. Lawrence charted twice more, for Bell and Private Stock Records, but never managed to emulate her initial success. She starred in the television show *Mama's Family* in the early 80s.
● ALBUMS: *The Night The Lights Went Out In Georgia* (1973)★★★.

Laws, Hubert

b. 10 November 1939, Houston, Texas, USA. The brother of saxophonist **Ronnie Laws**, flautist Hubert has enjoyed successful careers in both classical and jazz

contexts. In the 60s and 70s he recorded for **Atlantic Records** and CTI and played in the New York Jazz Sextet, while retaining a place in the New York Metropolitan Opera House and the New York Philharmonic Orchestra. Still making jazz records in the 80s, Laws also undertook a series of concerts with classical flautist Jean-Pierre Rampal. Having played with **Gunther Schuller**, **James Moody**, **Clark Terry** and many others, Laws' virtuosity has done much to increase the flute's credibility in the jazz world.
● ALBUMS: *The Laws Of Jazz* (1964)★★, *Crying Song* (1970)★★★, *At Carnegie Hall* (1973)★★, with Ronnie Laws *In The Beginning* (1974)★★★, *The Rite Of Spring* (1988)★★★, *Family* (1989)★★★.

Laws, Ronnie

b. 3 October 1950, Houston, Texas, USA. Laws played the saxophone from the age of 12, growing up with the musicians who were to become the **Crusaders** - the band with which his brother Hubert played. Ronnie studied flute at the Stephen F. Austin State University and then at Texas Southern University. When he was 21 he moved to Los Angeles, where he worked with Von Ryan's Express, **Quincy Jones**, pianist **Walter Bishop Jnr.** and **Kenny Burrell**. After playing with **Earth, Wind And Fire** for 18 months, during the period when they recorded *Last Days In Time* (1972), he worked with **Hugh Masekela** and Ujima. His solo career in the late 70s and early 80s saw him achieve popularity with a smooth jazz style similar to that of **Bob James**, **Earl Klugh**, **Lonnie Liston Smith** and **Grover Washington**.
● ALBUMS: with Hubert Laws *In The Beginning* (1974)★★★, with Pressure *Pressure Sensitive* (EMI 1975)★★★, *Fever* (Blue Note 1976)★★★★, *Friends And Strangers* (EMI 1977)★★, *Flame* (United Artists 1978)★★★, *Every Generation* (United Artists 1980)★★★, *Solid Ground* (Liberty 1981)★★★, *Mr. Nice Guy* (Capitol 1983)★★★, *Mirror Town* (CBS 1986)★★★, *All Day Rhythm* (CBS 1987)★★, *Identity* (New Note 1992)★★★, *Deep Soul* (1993)★★★, *True Spirit* (Par 1993)★★★, *Brotherhood* (101 South 1993)★★★, *Fever* (Blue Note 1993)★★★, *Natural Laws* (Capitol 1995)★★.
● COMPILATIONS: *Ronnie Laws* (1987)★★★, *Classic Masters* (1988)★★★★, *The Best Of Ronnie Laws* (Blue Note 1992)★★★★.

Lawson, Doyle

b. Doyle Wayne Lawson, 20 April 1944, Fordtown, near Kingsport, Tennessee, USA. His father sang in a gospel quartet and he was attracted to both gospel and bluegrass music as a child. By the time he reached his teens, he could play mandolin, banjo and guitar but captivated by **Bill Monroe**'s playing, he specialized in the former. He began his professional career in 1963, playing banjo with **Jimmy Martin**'s Sunny Mountain Boys. In 1966, he began an association with **J.D. Crowe**, first playing guitar but soon becoming the mandolinist with Crowe's Kentucky Mountain Boys and, in the late 60s, he played on two albums with Crowe and also recorded with **Red Allen** for Rebel. He joined the **Country**

Gentlemen in 1971, and remained a member until 1979. During this time, he toured to Japan and Europe, recorded 10 albums with the group and also recorded a solo mandolin instrumental album. In 1979, he left the Gentlemen and formed his own group, Quicksilver. The group initially comprised Lawson, Terry Baucom (banjo), Jimmy Haley (guitar) and Lou Reid (bass), but over the years, there have been several changes of personnel. In 1979, they recorded *Doyle Lawson & Quicksilver* on **Sugar Hill Records** and followed it, throughout the 80s, with a series of albums, some gospel, some bluegrass, but eventually the albums were a mixture of both genres. Guest musicians on recordings have included Sam Bush, **Mike Auldridge** and **Jerry Douglas**. The group were noted for their harmonies and a cappella singing and on *Heaven's Joy Awaits*, they included no musical accompaniment. During the 80s, Lawson also recorded a series of five albums for Rounder with J.D. Crowe, Tony Rice and Bobby Hicks as the **Bluegrass Album Band**. In 1990, Lawson moved his recording work to Brentwood Music and in the mid-90s, was still a very active and respected figure in bluegrass and gospel music.

● ALBUMS: *Tennessee Dream* (County 1977)★★★, *Doyle Lawson & Quicksilver* (Sugar Hill 1980)★★★, *Rock My Soul* (Sugar Hill 1981)★★★, *Quicksilver Rides Again* (Sugar Hill 1982)★★, *Heavenly Treasures* (Sugar Hill 1983)★★★, *Once And For Always* (Sugar Hill 1985)★★★, *Beyond The Shadows* (Sugar Hill 1986)★★★, *The News Is Out* (Sugar Hill 1987)★★★, *Heaven's Joy Awaits* (Sugar Hill 1987)★★★, *Hymn Time In The Country* (Sugar Hill 1988)★★, *I'll Wander Back Someday* (Sugar Hill 1988)★★★, *I Heard The Angels Singing* (Sugar Hill 1989)★★★, *My Heart Is Yours* (Sugar Hill 1990)★★★, *Treasures Money Can't Buy* (Brentwood Music 1992)★★, *Pressing On Regardless* (Brentwood Music 1992)★★, *Never Walk Away* (Sugar Hill 1995)★★★, *There's A Light Guiding Me* (Sugar Hill 1996)★★★.

Lawson, Rex

b. 1932, Ijebu, Nigeria, d. 1976, Lagos, Nigeria. Vocalist and trumpeter Lawson was one of the most popular Nigerian bandleaders of the 60s and early 70s, playing a style of big band **highlife** informed by African-American jazz, which crossed tribal boundaries and was enjoyed by all Nigeria's ethnic groups (a process he encouraged by singing in a wide variety of tribal languages as well as English). He joined Port Harcourt's leading band the Starlite Melody Orchestra as a bandboy at the age of 12, and four years later, when the band were playing in the capital, Lagos, left the group - with a battered old trumpet that had been bequeathed to him by an uncle - to find work in the city's nightclubs. During the 50s he played at various times with Bobby Benson, Roy Chicago, Chris Ajiko and **Victor Olaiya**. In 1960, he formed his first band, originally known as the Nigeraphone Studio Orchestra and later renamed the Mayor's Dance Band. Inspired by the 'Dukes', 'Counts' and 'Ladies' populating American jazz, Lawson dubbed himself Pastor, later promoting himself

to Cardinal, and with the 11-piece Mayor's Dance Band quickly took the Lagos club scene by storm. He enjoyed massive West African hits with 'Oko', 'Yellow Sisi', 'Jolly Papa' and 'Gowon Special' before dying at the early age of 44, still at the peak of his popularity. His band continued without him, as the **Professional Seagulls**, led by Prince David Bull. They are still active and enjoyed a major Nigerian hit in 1981 with 'Soko Soko'.

● ALBUMS: *Dancing Time* (African Sonodisc 1964)★★★, *Rex Lawson's Victories* (PRL 1976)★★★, *The Highlife King In London* (AGB 1982)★★★, *Love M'Adure Special* (AGB 1984)★★★.

● COMPILATIONS: *Greatest Hits* (Polydor Nigeria 1973)★★★★.

Lawson, Tim

b. 1953, London, Ontario, Canada. Lawson played guitar as a child, but he went into business when he left school. In the early 90s, he began to write songs and his debut album, *The Quiet Canadian*, was full of thoughtful work. The title track was a tribute to Canada's wartime intelligence expert, Sir William Stephenson, the man called Intrepid. 'Wartime Letters' was inspired by correspondence between his parents (the multimedia version has considerable background information).

● ALBUMS: *The Quiet Canadian* (Timberholme 1995)★★★.

Lawson, Yank

b. John Rhea Lawson, 3 May 1911, Trenton, Missouri, USA, d. 18 February 1995. After playing the trumpet in various local bands, in 1933 Lawson joined **Ben Pollack**'s popular band. When this group developed into the co-operative **Bob Crosby** band Lawson was one of its dominant musical voices. He later played in the bands of **Tommy Dorsey** and **Benny Goodman** and then spent a quarter of a century, on and off, in the studios, making occasional jazz club and record dates. Reunions with other veterans of the Crosby band eventually led to a partnership with **Bob Haggart**. Their co-led band eventually evolved into the **World's Greatest Jazz Band** and when this group folded in the late 70s Lawson and Haggart continued to perform together well into the 80s. A striking and aggressive player, Lawson dominated any of the dixieland-orientated jazz bands with which he played and drew admiration from such leading jazz artists as **Louis Armstrong**, with whom he appeared on record.

● ALBUMS: *Lawson-Haggart Jazz Band* (1952)★★★, with Bob Haggart *South Of The Mason-Dixon Line* (1953)★★, with Louis Armstrong *Satchmo: A Musical Autobiography* (1957)★★★★, with Bob Crosby *Porgy And Bess* (1958)★★★, *The Best Of Broadway* (1959)★★★★, *Ole Dixie* (1966)★★★, with Haggart *The Best Of Dixieland (1952-53)* (1975)★★★★, *Live At Louisiana Jazz Club* (1979)★★, *Century Plaza* (World Jazz 1979)★★★, with Haggart *Best Of Jazz At The Troc* (World Jazz 1981)★★★, *Plays Mostly Blues* (Audiophile 1987)★★★, *Something Old, Something New, Something Borrowed, Something Blue* (1988)★★★, *Easy To Remember*

(Flyright 1989)★★★, with Haggart *Yank Lawson And Bob Haggart* (Jazzology 1992)★★★★.

Lawton, Jimmy

Lawton was born in the USA but he is mainly known as a country artist in Europe. He settled in the Netherlands and built himself a reputation in various European venues, but although he made tours in the UK, he was unable to match his level of support in mainland Europe. He has recorded with European musicians, including an excellent version of **Merle Haggard**'s song 'Somewhere Between' with Dutch country girl Ine Masseurs.
● ALBUMS: *Arizona Sunday* UK release (Westwood 1978)★★★, *Jimmy Lawton* European release (Arcade 1986)★★★.

Lay, Rodney

b. Coffeyville, Kansas, USA. Lay worked as a DJ and singer on KGGF Coffeyville, and in the mid-60s, toured with **Wanda Jackson**. In 1973, he gained a small acting role in *Pat Garrett And Billy The Kid* which starred **Kris Kristofferson**. Lay became musical director and leader of **Roy Clark**'s band. When not working with Clark, he fronted his own band, the Wild West. Recording with them, he enjoyed six minor hits during the 80s, including 'Happy Country Birthday Darling', and his version of the 1973 **Mel Street** hit 'Walk Softly On The Bridges', but his fondness for rock and rockabilly material did little to attract the traditionalists.
● ALBUMS: *Desert Rock* (Sun 1979)★★★, *Rockabilly Nuggets* (Sun 1980)★★★, *Silent Partners* (Sun 1981)★★★.

Lay, Sam

b. 20 March 1935, Birmingham, Alabama, USA. The drummer Fred Below put the backbeat into the blues and elevated the records of **Muddy Waters** and **Little Walter**, among a host of others, into defining statements. Close behind him is Sam Lay, the inventor of the 'double shuffle'. Lay began playing drums at 14 and joined his first band, the Moon Dog Combo, in 1956. The following year he joined the Thunderbirds, before spending 1959 in **Little Walter**'s band. He then became the backbone of **Howlin' Wolf**'s band, where he stayed from 1960 to 1966. He was the driving force behind 'Down In The Bottom', 'The Red Rooster', 'Goin' Down Slow', 'Built For Comfort' and 'Killing Floor'. He then joined the **Paul Butterfield** Blues Band, played on the group's first two influential albums and also backed **Bob Dylan** on his controversial electric debut at the 1965 Newport Folk Festival. In the ensuing years, he worked with most of the best-known names in the blues world, having a particular regard for his work on Muddy Waters' *Fathers And Sons* album. Lay leads his own band, which features former **Commander Cody** harmonica player Billy C. Farlowe and guitarist Chris James, as well as freelancing when the opportunity arises. *Shuffle Master* combines original material with a number of cover versions, while *Live*, recorded at Nashville's Boardwalk Cafe, relies upon more traditional material.
● ALBUMS: *The Paul Butterfield Blues Band* (Elektra 1966)★★★★, with Muddy Waters *Fathers And Sons* (Chess 1969)★★★, *Shuffle Master* (Appaloosa 1993)★★★, *Live* (Appaloosa 1995)★★★, *Stone Blues* (Evidence 1996)★★★.

Laycock, Tim

b. 20 February 1952, Malmesbury, Wiltshire, England. At the age of four, Laycock's family moved to Fontwell Magna, Dorset, and he later became interested in folk music through learning guitar chords from school friends. Leaving school in 1970, Laycock went to the University of East Anglia in Norwich, and he met singers and musicians in folk clubs who converted him to British traditional music. He started playing regularly in 1971 as part of a folk group at university, which included Terry Fisher and Dave Bordeway, who later played with the Crows. In 1974, after moving to London, Tim became a resident at Dingle's Folk Club and the Engineer Folk Club. In 1976, he joined Magic Lantern for a Christmas tour, and was later asked to join full-time when Mike Frost (Major Mustard), left to get married. *Lydlinch Bells*, produced by Laycock, was a strong collection of dialect poems by William Barnes, read by Laycock, David Strawbridge, Ethel Gumbleton, Charlie Andrews and Frank Hilliar. Since then Laycock has worked continuously as a singer, concertina player and actor, collaborating for three years from, 1979, with **Peter Bond** and **Bill Caddick**. Dividing his time between the theatre, folk clubs and festivals, Laycock occasionally works with Taffy Thomas and appears in a local Dorset group, the Hambledon Hopstep Band.
● ALBUMS: *Lydlinch Bells* (Forest Tracks 1977)★★, *Capers And Rhymes* (Greenwich Village 1980)★★★, with Peter Bond, Bill Caddick *A Duck On His Head* (Highway 1984)★★★, *Giant At Cerne* (Dingle's 1985)★★★, *Blackmore By The Stour* (Forest Tracks 1985)★★★★, with Sneaks Noyse *Christmas Now Is Drawing Near* (Saydisc 1988)★★, *Shillingstone Moss* (Laycock 1989)★★★.

Laye, Evelyn

b. Elsie Evelyn Lay, 10 July 1900, London, England, d. February 1996. An actress and singer - one of the most celebrated leading ladies of the English musical stage. Her father was the actor and composer Gilbert Laye (he added the 'e' on to the family name for stage appearances) and her mother the actress Evelyn Stewart. Known as 'Boo' from when she was a baby, Evelyn Laye was constantly performing as a child, and made her professional stage debut at the age of 15 as a Chinese servant in a production entitled *Mr. Wu*. After appearing in *The Beauty Spot*, *Going Up*, and *The Kiss Call*, she had her first West End success in 1920 with *The Shop Girl*, in which she was backed by a chorus of real guardsmen as she sang 'The Guards' Parade'. In the early 20s she delighted London audiences in shows such as *Phi-Phi*, and ***The Merry Widow***. *Madame Pompadour* (1923), her first show for **C. B. Cochran**, was a significant landmark in her career, and was followed by more good roles in stylish productions such as *Cleopatra*, *Betty In Mayfair*, *Merely Molly*, and *Blue Eyes*. By 1929, when Evelyn Laye introduced Drury Lane audiences to 'Lover, Come Back To Me' in **Sigmund Romberg**'s musical *The New Moon*, she had become the brightest star on the London theatre scene; Cochran called her 'the fairest prima donna this side of heaven' ('I think he must have had a little too much champagne', says Miss Laye). Around this time she was separated from her husband, the comedian **Sonnie Hale**, and he later married one of her main 'rivals', the enchanting **Jessie Matthews**. She turned down the leading role in the London production of **Noël Coward**'s *Bitter Sweet*, but triumphed in the 1929 Broadway production, and later succeeded Peggy Wood in the West End version. Her success on Broadway resulted in a trip to Hollywood and appearances in *One Heavenly Night* with John Boles, and *The Night Is Young*, in which she co-starred with Ramon Novarro and sang Sigmund Romberg and **Oscar Hammerstein II**'s enduring 'When I Grow Too Old To Dream'. While in America she married the British actor, Frank Lawton, and they were together until he died in 1969. On her return to England she made more film musicals, including *Princess Charming*, *Waltz Time*, and *Evensong* (1934). The latter is regarded as perhaps the most accomplished of her relatively few screen appearances. Even in the 90s it continues to be re-shown in cinema retrospective seasons, and on television, providing a tantalising glimpse of an artist who lit up the screen whenever she chose to neglect her beloved stage for a while. During the remainder of the 30s, Evelyn Laye was a 'ravishing' Helen of Troy in *Helen!*, appeared with the embryonic John Mills in *Give Me A Ring*, co-starred with the far more mature Viennese tenor Richard Tauber in *Paganini*, and returned to Broadway in 1937 with **Jack Buchanan** and Adele Dixon for *Between The Devil*. The show made history when it was presented for one night at the National Theatre in New York on the occasion of President Roosevelt's birthday, thereby becoming the first American Command Performance. In 1940 she sang 'You've Done Something To My Heart', 'Only A Glass Of Champagne', and 'Let The People Sing' in Ronald Jeans' revue, *Lights Up*. During the remainder of World War II she appeared in the 1942 revival of **The Belle Of New York** and another Romberg/Hammerstein show, *Sunny River*. She also served as Entertainments Director for the Royal Navy, and led the first-ever concert party for the troops based in the remote Scapa Flow in the Orkneys. In 1945 Evelyn Laye returned to the London stage in *Three Waltzes*. Immediately after the war, when suitable parts in the musical theatre were few and far between, she played straight roles in plays throughout the UK and on a 1951 tour of Australia, but made a triumphant comeback to the London musical stage in *Wedding In Paris* in 1954. More straight plays followed before she starred in the musical, *Strike A Light* (1966),

and replaced **Anna Neagle** for a time in the long-running **Charley Girl**. In her last West End musical (to date), **Phil The Fluter** (1969), she reflected on a better, more civilised age, in the memorable 'They Don't Make Them Like That Any More', a number that was so perfectly suited to her. In 1971 she appeared with **Michael Crawford** in the comedy, *No Sex, Please - We're British*, and two years later was awarded the CBE. During the rest of the 70s and 80s she made several more films, including *Say Hello To Yesterday* with Jean Simmons, and *Never Never Land* with **Petula Clark**. She also did a good deal of television work, and appeared in the provinces in *A Little Night Music* with Honor Blackman in 1979/80. In 1992, at the age of 92, she toured parts of the UK with the nostalgia show *Glamorous Nights At Drury Lane*, and received standing ovations. In July of that year, in *A Glamorous Night With Evelyn Laye At The London Palladium*, the élite of British show-business gathered to pay tribute and nod in agreement as she sang 'They Don't Make Them Like That Any More'.

● ALBUMS: *Golden Age Of Evelyn Laye* (1985)★★★★, *When I Grow Too Old To Dream* (1991)★★★, *Gaiety Girl* (ASW Living Era 1996)★★★★.
● FURTHER READING: *Boo To My Friends*, Evelyn Laye.

Layla And Other Assorted Love Songs - Derek And The Dominos

Studying the photographs inside the fold-out sleeve makes you question how such a wrecked bunch of musos could make such a great record. Excess was obviously the order of the day, yet excel was what they did. Everybody knows that 'Layla' is one of the best rock songs ever written, but here is the chance to strike a blow for **Duane Allman**'s consistent guitar, especially on lost gems such as 'Anyday' and 'Key To The Highway'. Did anybody also notice how good Jim Gordon's drumming was? And the CD age means we can skip past the dreadful 'Thorn Tree In The Garden'.

● Tracks: *I Looked Away; Bell Bottom Blues; Keep On Growing; Nobody Knows You; I Am Yours; Anyday; Key To The Highway; Tell The Truth; Why Does Love Got To Be So Sad; Have You Ever Loved A Woman; Little Sing; It's Too Late; Thorn Tree In The Garden; Layla.*
● First released 1970
● UK peak chart position: did not chart
● USA peak chart position: 16

Layne, Joy

b. 1939, Chicago, Illinois, USA. Layne had only one US Top 20 single in 1957, 'Your Wild Heart', and never returned to the charts. Managed by her mother, she auditioned for **Mercury** in Chicago. Given a song that had already been recorded by the **Poni-Tails**, 'Your Wild Heart' was released in early 1957 and reached number 20. With a dynamic voice comparable to **Brenda Lee**'s, great things were predicted for Layne, but her mother would not let her tour or promote her recordings, and by 1961 her career was over.

Layton And Johnstone

(see **Layton, Turner**)

Layton, Linda

b. Belinda Kimberley Layton, 7 December 1970, Chiswick, London, England. Renowned for her vocal contribution to **Beats International**'s 'Dub Be Good To Me', Layton's mother was a professional dancer, responsible for choreographing West End productions of *The King And I* and *The Sound Of Music*. Layton's solo album was a disappointment, with a limp cover of **Janet Kay**'s 'Silly Game' notwithstanding. An MOR club sound was engaged which did little to bolster the flimsy song structures, even though **Norman Cook** from her old band and Jolly Harris Jolly were still on hand as part of the backroom set-up.

● ALBUMS: *Pressure* (Arista 1991)★★★.

Layton, Turner

b. 1894, Washington, DC, USA, d. 2 February 1978. Although born into a musical family, Layton studied medicine for a few years before becoming a professional pianist. He appeared in New York where he teamed up with Henry Creamer, forming a duo to play in vaude-ville and in several musical shows and revues. Creamer also wrote lyrics for many songs composed by Layton, one of which, 'Dear Old Southland', became **Louis Armstrong**'s signature tune. Amongst their other songs, several of which also became very popular with jazz musicians, were 'Everybody's Crazy About The Doggone Blues', 'After You've Gone', 'Way Down Yonder In New Orleans' (popularized by Blossom Seeley) and '(If I Could Be With You) One Hour Tonight'. In 1922, Layton formed another partnership, this time with Clarence Nathaniel Johnstone. They settled in London the following year and quickly became popular with audiences at theatres and the hotels, restaurants and nightclubs frequented by the elite. They also appealed to a wider audience thanks to broadcasts on the radio. Although Layton had recorded in New York in the early 20s, the collaboration with Johnstone was hugely successful and their records, especially 'Alabamy Bound', 'Bye Bye Blackbird' and 'The Song Is Ended', sold extremely well. In 1935, when their combined record sales were running into several millions, Johnstone was named as co-respondent in the divorce of a well-known classical musician. Despite Johnstone's popularity, London society of that era could not sanction an affair between a black man and a white woman. Bookings plummeted and the partner-ship of Layton and Johnstone was forced to end. Johnstone returned to the USA where he died in obscu-rity and poverty in 1953. Layton continued to perform, this time as a solo artist, into the late 40s. He retained his popularity and was very successful, but never quite recaptured the glory of earlier days.

● ALBUMS: by Layton And Johnstone *Alabamy Bound (1920-30)* (1980)★★★, *The Song Is Ended (1920-30)* (1983)★★★, *When You're Smiling* (1986)★★.

Lazarus, Ken

Lazarus began his career from the inception of ska in the early 60s. He performed lead vocals for **Byron Lee And The Dragonaires**, playing on tours of the West Indies and North America. In 1965, credited as performing with the Byron Lee Orchestra, he relished his first taste of international fame when 'Funny' was released through **Island Records** in the UK. He also performed as part of an idiosyncratic, neglected Jamaican rock band, Tomorrow's Children. His sporadic output resulted in a few releases of note, although in 1971 he maintained a high profile with 'Girl' and the bewildering 'Tomorrow's Children'. Although Lazarus's releases were erratic he worked in the studios as an arranger, producer and songwriter. In 1972, as a performer, he secured a one-single contract with a major label for the release of 'Hail The Man', but failed to satisfy the company's expectations. By the 90s, having relocated to California, he joined Pluto and **Ernie Smith** on a small island tour. The jaunt was to promote his solo release, *Reflections*, which featured Lazarus's unique renditions of reggae classics including the **Maytals**' 'Peeping Tom', **Ken Boothe**'s 'Freedom Street' and **Jimmy Cliff**'s 'Wonderful World Beautiful People'.

● ALBUMS: *Reflections* (Laz Rec 1997)★★.

Lazer Guided Melodies - Spiritualized

Since *Lazer Guided Melodies* **Spiritualized** have had to endure the vagaries of indie credibility, but their musi-cal blueprint has altered little from this powerful debut. Picking up where his former band **Spaceman 3** had left off, Jason Pierce refined his exploration of trance-rock with elaborate arrangements and more sympathetic production values. The uptempo 'Run' and 'Angel Sigh' hinted at the band's awesome live sound, but the album's true heart is found in the blissed-out nirvana of tracks such as 'Symphony Space', 'Sway' and '200 Bars'. This record virtually requires the listener be in a tran-scendental state while it is being played.

● Tracks: *You Know It's True; If I Were With Her Now; I Want You; Run; Smiles; Step Into The Breeze; Symphony Space; Take Your Time; Shine A Light; Angel Sigh; Sway; 200 Bars.*
● First released 1992
● UK peak chart position: 27
● USA peak chart position: did not chart

Lazy Lester

b. Leslie Johnson, 20 June 1933 (or 1923), Torras, Louisiana, USA. Blues harmonica player and vocalist Lazy Lester recorded numerous singles for Excello Records in the late 50s and early 60s. Forming his first band in 1952, the musician's first significant job was as a sideman for bluesman **Lightnin' Slim**. Owing to his slow-moving, laid-back approach, Johnson received his performing name during this period from record producer J.D. Miller, who was known for his 'swamp pop' sound. Miller recorded Lester and placed him with the Nashville-based Excello in 1958. Lester's first solo single was 'Go Ahead' (1956), and his first local hit was 'Sugar Coated Love'/'I'm A Lover Not A Fighter'. The latter was covered in the UK by the **Kinks**. Lester continued to record as a leader until 1965. He also played harmonica for such artists as the blues-rock guitarist **Johnny Winter** (an early recording in 1961) and **Lonesome Sundown**. At the end of the 60s, Lester moved around the country and did not record again until 1987, for the UK Blues 'N' Trouble label. The following year he recorded *Harp & Soul* for Alligator Records, and was back touring the USA in the late 80s and early 90s, enjoying new-found acclaim.

● ALBUMS: *True Blues* (Excello 1966)★★★★, *Lazy Lester Rides Again* (Blue Horizon 1987)★★★, *Harp & Soul* (Alligator 1988)★★★, *I'm A Lover Not A Fighter* (Ace 1994)★★★.

● COMPILATIONS: *They Call Me Lazy* (Flyright 1977)★★★★, *Poor Boy Blues - Jay Miller Sessions* (Flyright 1987)★★★★.

Lazy, Doug

More widely known for his production work, Lazy's own recorded output betrays not only a love of hip-hop energy, but also an eye for house music's pulsing rhythms. As a producer he is one of the more credible exponents of the hip house movement, while his solo hits include 'Let It Roll' and 'Let The Rhythm Pump', the latter based on **Funkadelic**'s 'One Nation Under A Groove'. He also appeared on **Raze**'s 1991 single, 'Bass Power'.

● ALBUMS: *Doug Lazy Gettin' Crazy* (Atlantic 1990)★★★.

Le Gop

French folk rock band Le Gop were originally formed in 1989 to play at a festival in the suburbs of Paris. The original line up featured no less than 10 musicians. It was from their greatness of number they derived their name - Le Grand Orchestra Parisien, or Le Gop in shorthand. However, as their numbers decreased they moved from concentrating on authentic traditional dances to improvising their own material, albeit usually based still on elements of those same dances. The group, led by guitarist and founder Michel Le Cam, feature hurdy gurdy and fiddle in addition to more familiar rock elements, and include former members of both **Malicorne** and Ti Jaz. Their 1994 debut album confirmed the promise shown on several European tours, with original songs such as 'Nuit De Gala' and 'Rendezvous' encouraging a positive critical response.

● ALBUMS: *Le Gop* (Silex 1994)★★★.

Le Griffe

Despite using the French moniker Le Griffe (meaning 'The Claw'), this band was formed in Stoke-on-Trent, Staffordshire, England, in 1980. Le Griffe's original line-up consisted of Chris Hatton (vocals, guitar), Paul Wood (guitar), Tim Blackwood (guitar), Kevin Collier (bass) and Martin Allen (drums). Quickly becoming popular on their local live circuit, the band signed to the (now defunct) Bullet Records label, who released a

three-track EP entitled *Fast Bikes* in 1981. The EP was a worthy debut, featuring melodic rockers reminiscent of early **Def Leppard** coupled with 12-bar **Status Quo**-style boogie. The band gigged extensively throughout the UK and released a mini-album, *Breaking Strain*, again on the Bullet Records label, in 1984. At the time of its release guitarist Tim Blackwood left the band to be replaced by Amos Sanfillipo, but the band dissolved early in 1985. Collier went on to join **Rogue Male**.

● ALBUMS: *Breaking Strain* mini-album (Bullet 1984)★★.

Le Mystère Des Voix Bulgares

The State Radio and Television choir from Bulgaria was founded in 1952, in Sofia, and included 15 singers and instrumentalists. This number has gradually increased as new voices have ben selected from various folk festivals and song contests. As well as traditional pieces, the choir also performs the work of modern composers. The choir was brought to the attention of the British music press and public by the esoteric **4AD** label who released their UK debut set in 1986. The ethereal nature of their singing drew some comparisons with that of 4AD's own **Cocteau Twins** - a connection with attracted a young audience. *A Cathedral Concert* (released on the Jaro label), was recorded in a church in Bremen, Germany, on 6 December 1987, during one of the choir's first trips to the West. Subsequent releases have shown the powerful vocals of the choir to good effect. The general interest shown in world music has opened up Eastern Europe and shown it to contain a wealth of musical heritage hitherto unheard. Choir member Eva Georgeiva appeared as one of the Trio Bulgarka's *The Forest Is Crying* (1988) on **Hannibal Records**.

● ALBUMS: *Le Mystère Des Voix Bulgares* (4AD 1986)★★★★, *Le Mystère Des Voix Bulgares Volume 2* (1988)★★, *A Cathedral Concert* (Jaro 1988)★★★★, *Le Mystère Des Voix Bulgares Volume 3* (1990)★★, *From Bulgaria With Love* (1993)★★★, *Melody Rhythm Harmony* (Jara 1993)★★★, *Ritual* (Elektra Nonesuch 1995)★★★.

Le Roux

Formed in the mid-70s in Louisiana, USA, Le Roux was originally called Louisiana's Le Roux and consisted of Jeff Pollard (guitar, vocals), Tony Haselden (guitar), Rod Roddy (keyboard), Bobby Campo (horn), Leon Medica (bass) and David Peters (drums). They were originally session musicians backing blues, folk and Cajun artists, and took the name Le Roux from the Cajun word for the gravy used in gumbo, a traditional Louisiana dish. Discovered by William McEuen, manager of the **Nitty Gritty Dirt Band**, they signed to **Capitol Records**, and released their debut, *Louisiana's Le Roux*, in 1978. Their first three albums only glanced the charts and they signed to **RCA Records** in 1982 (having shortened their name to Le Roux). The single 'Nobody Said It Was Easy (Lookin' For The Lights)' became their only major hit, reaching US number 18 that year. *Last Safe Place* became their biggest album, making number 64. They had two further chart singles after the hit, but by 1983 there were personnel changes and the group disappeared from the music scene.

● ALBUMS: *Louisiana's Le Roux* (Capitol 1978)★★, *Keep The Fire Burnin'* (Capitol 1979)★★★, *Up* (Capitol 1980)★★, *Last Safe Place* (RCA 1982)★★★★, *So Fired Up* (1983)★★.

Le Sage, Bill

b. 20 January 1927, London, England. From the mid-40s Le Sage was a popular figure on the London jazz scene, leading his own group and also playing in the **John Dankworth** Seven. At this point in his career Le Sage played piano, on which he was self-taught. In the early 50s he began playing vibraphone, the instrument he later became associated with. During the 50s and 60s he played with bands led by **Tony Kinsey**, Ronnie Ross and also led his own groups. In 1970, he formed his Bebop Preservation Society band which remained in existence until midway through the following decade. During this period he also worked with many of the UK's leading contemporary jazz artists including **Barbara Thompson** and **Martin Drew**. Alongside his playing career, Le Sage has also written music for a number of television shows.

● ALBUMS: *The Bill Le Sage-Ronnie Ross Quartet* (1963)★★★, *Directions In Jazz* (1964)★★★, *Road To Ellingtonia* (1965)★★, *Martin Drew And His Band* (1977)★★★, with John Dankworth *Gone Hitchin'* (1983)★★.

Lea, Barbara

b. Barbara LeCoq, 4 October 1929, Detroit, Michigan, USA. Her family name was changed to Leacock and she shortened this when she took up a career as a singer. Her higher education took place at Wellesley College where she majored in Music Theory. She sang in the college choir and in the late 40s sang jazz and with dance bands in the north eastern states. She also worked as a jazz disc jockey, wrote a jazz column for the college newspaper, sang and taught classical music and jazz. When Lea graduated she began working professionally as a singer almost at once, singing mostly in Boston and in New Jersey but occasionally picked up engagements at swish New York venues. During the 50s she worked extensively in the north-east and in Canada and also made records, including sets with trumpeter **Johnny Windhurst**. Her early recordings were very well received and in 1956 was voted *Down Beat*'s Best New Singer. She then moved into acting, mostly on the stage, performing in musical and straight drama. Her theatrical life, which included supporting and leading roles in works from William Shakespeare to **Stephen Sondheim**, extended from off-Broadway productions to touring companies. In the late 70s she was invited to join the radio series, *American Popular Music With Alex Wilder And Friends*. Lea then returned to performing in clubs, in New York, Washington, Los Angeles, sang at festivals and jazz parties and also recorded for Audiophile from 1978 into the mid-90s. She is a great admirer of **Lee Wiley** and is highly knowledgeable

about her work. In 1996 she was showing no signs of slowing up, having been booked to appear at the Kool-JVC Jazz Festival in New York and had just recorded her latest album. she sings in a deep, rich-toned voice with a pleasingly astringent sound which is especially effective in her meaningful interpretation of ballads.

● ALBUMS: *A Woman In Love* (Riverside/Audiophile 1955)★★★, *Barbara Lea* (Prestige/Fantasy/OJC 1956)★★★★, *Lea In Love* (Prestige/Fantasy/OJC 1957)★★★, *The Devil Is Afraid Of Music* (Audiophile 1979)★★★, *Remembering Lee Wiley* (Audiophile 1979)★★★, *Do It Again* (Audiophile 1983)★★★, *Hoagy's Children* (Audiophile 1983)★★★★, *You're The Cats* (Audiophile 1989)★★★, *Sweet And Slow* (Audiophile 1990)★★★, *At The Atlanta Jazz Party* (Jazzology 1993)★★★, *Pousse Cafe* (Audiophile 1993)★★, *Hoagy's Children Vols 1* and *2* (Audiophile 1994)★★★★, *Fine And Dandy* (Challenge 1996)★★★.

Leach, Lillian, And The Mellows

The original members of the line-up were lead Lillian Leach, first tenor Johnny Wilson, second tenor Harold Johnson and bass Norman Brown. This 50s vocal harmony group from the Bronx, New York, USA, never had a national R&B hit, but enjoyed a number of regional hits on the east coast on the strength of the lead voice of Leach, who possessed one of the warmest and most sensual voices in the history of doo-wop. The group was formed in 1954 and soon signed a contract with veteran Joe Davis on his Jay Dee label. They made their biggest impact with their second release, the exquisitely romantic 'Smoke From A Cigarette', from early 1955. It achieved substantial local success, and during the neo-doo-wop renaissance of the early 60s became one of the most requested oldies. The next release, another remarkable ballad, 'I Still Care' (1955), received modest airplay. Its b-side featured another wonderful ballad, 'I Was A Fool To Care'. The last release for Jay Dee was 'Yesterday's Memories', another underappreciated masterpiece of its time. In 1956 the Mellows moved to the Celeste label, and at this point Norman Brown left and vocal group veterans Arthur Crier and Gary Morrison were added. Commercial success at Celeste was not forthcoming, even for the outstanding 'My Darling'. The group left the company in 1957, and completed one more recording session for Apollo in 1958 (which was left in the can) before disbanding. Johnson and Crier went on to form the Halos, who backed Curtis Lee on 'Pretty Little Angel Eyes'. Lillian Leach And The Mellows probably attained greater fame after the record collecting community rediscovered the group's recordings during the 60s and lionized them, making them perennials on oldies shows for decades afterwards.

● COMPILATIONS: *Yesterday's Memories* (Relic 1992)★★★.

Lead Belly

b. Huddie William Ledbetter, 20 January 1889, Jeder Plantation, Mooringsport, Louisiana, USA, d. 6 December 1949, New York City, New York, USA. Lead

Belly's music offers an incredible vista of American traditions, white as well as black, through his enormous repertoire of songs and tunes. He learned many of them in his youth when he lived and worked in western Louisiana and eastern Texas, but to them he added material from many different sources, including his own compositions, throughout the rest of his life. He played several instruments, including mandolin, accordion, piano and harmonica, but was best known for his mastery of the 12-string guitar. In his early 20s, he met and played with **Blind Lemon Jefferson**, but the encounter was to leave little if any lasting impression on his music. His sound remained distinctive and individual, with his powerful, yet deeply expressive, vocals and his 12-string guitar lines, which could be booming and blindingly fast or slow and delicate as appropriate. His style and approach to music developed as he played the red-light districts of towns such as Shreveport and Dallas - a tough, often violent background that was reflected in songs like 'Fannin Street' and 'Mr Tom Hughes Town'. Although he built up a substantial local reputation for his music as a young man, he served a number of prison sentences, including two stretches of hard labour for murder and attempted murder, respectively. While serving the last of these sentences at the Louisiana State Penitentiary at Angola, he was discovered by the folklorist **John A. Lomax**, then travelling throughout the south with his son Alan, recording traditional songs and music - frequently in prisons - for the Folk Song Archive of the Library of Congress. On his release (which he claimed was due to his having composed a song pleading with the governor to set him free), Lead Belly worked for Lomax as a chauffeur, assistant and guide, also recording prolifically for the Archive. His complete Library of Congress recordings, made over a period of several years, were issued in 1990 on 12 albums. Through Lomax, he was given the opportunity of a new life, as he moved to New York to continue to work for the folklorist. He also embarked on a reborn musical career with a new and very different audience, playing university concerts, clubs and political events, appearing on radio and even on film. He also made many records, mainly aimed at folk music enthusiasts. However, he did have the chance to make some 'race' recordings which were marketed to the black listener, but these enjoyed little commercial success, probably because Lead Belly's music would have seemed somewhat old-fashioned and rural to the increasingly sophisticated black record buyer of the 30s; although 50 songs were recorded, only six were issued. The New York folk scene, however, kept him active to some extent, and he played and recorded with artists such as **Josh White**, **Woody Guthrie**, **Sonny Terry** and **Brownie McGhee**. There was also a series of recordings in which he was accompanied by the voices of the Golden Gate Quartet, although this was an odd pairing and seemed rather contrived. Newly composed songs, such as 'New York City' and the pointed 'Bourgeois Blues', which described the racial prejudice he encoun-

tered in Washington DC, show how his perspectives were being altered by his new circumstances. It was his apparently inexhaustible collection of older songs and tunes, however, that most fascinated the northern audience, embracing as it did everything from versions of old European ballads ('Gallis Pole'), through Cajun-influenced dance tunes ('Sukey Jump') and sentimental pop ('Daddy, I'm Coming Home'), to dozens of black work songs and field hollers ('Whoa Back Buck'), southern ballads ('John Hardy'), gospel ('Mary Don't You Weep'), prison songs ('Shorty George'), many tough blues ('Pigmeat Papa') and even cowboy songs ('Out On The Western Plains'). His best-known and most frequently covered songs are probably the gentle C&W-influenced 'Goodnight Irene', later to be a hit record for the **Weavers** (one of whose members was **Pete Seeger**, who was also to write an instruction book on Lead Belly's unique 12-string guitar style) and 'Rock Island Line', which was a hit for **Lonnie Donegan** in the UK a few years later. His classic 'Cottonfields' was a success for the **Beach Boys**. In 1949, he travelled to Europe, appearing at jazz events in Paris, but the promise of wider appreciation of the man and his music was sadly curtailed when he died later that same year.

Note: In keeping with the Lead Belly Society in the USA we have adopted the correct spelling, and not the more commonly used Leadbelly.

● COMPILATIONS: *Take This Hammer* (Folkways 1950)★★★, *Rock Island Line* (Folkways 1950)★★★, *Lead Belly's Legacy Volume 3* (Folkways 1951)★★★, *Easy Rider: Lead Belly's Legacy Volume 4* (Folkways 1951)★★★, *Lead Belly Memorial Volumes 1 &2* (Stinson 1951)★★★, *Play-Party Songs* (Stinson 1951)★★★, *More Play-Party Songs* (Stinson 1951)★★★, *Lead Belly Memorial Volumes 3 & 4* (Stinson 1951)★★★, *Sinful Songs* (Allegro 1952)★★★, *Last Sessions Volumes 1 & 2* (Folkways 1958)★★★, *Sings Folk Songs* (Folkways 1959)★★★, *Lead Belly: Huddie Ledbetter's Best . . . His Guitar-His Voice-His Piano* (Capitol 1962)★★★, *Midnight Special* (RCA Victor 1964)★★★, *Keep Your Hands Off Her* (Verve/Folkways 1965)★★★, *The Library Of Congress Recordings* (Elektra 1966)★★★, *From The Last Sessions* (Verve/Folkways 1967)★★★, *Bourgeois Blues* (Collectables 1989)★★★, *Alabama Bound* (Bluebird 1989)★★★, *Lead Belly Sings Folk Songs* (Smithsonian/Folkways 1990)★★★, *Complete Library Of Congress Sessions* (1990)★★★, *King Of The 12 String Guitar* (Columbia/Legacy 1991)★★★, *Midnight Special* (Rounder 1991)★★★★, *Gwine Dig A Hole To Put The Devil In* (Rounder 1991)★★★★, *Let It Shine On Me* (Rounder 1991)★★★★, *Storyteller Blues* (Drive Archive 1995)★★★, *Lead Belly In Concert* (Magnum 1996)★★★, *In The Shadow Of Gallows Pole* (Tradition 1996)★★★, *Where Did You Sleep Last Night - Lead Belly Legacy Volume 1* (Smithsonian/Folkways 1996)★★★★.

● FURTHER READING: *Negro Folk Songs As Sung By Lead Belly*, John Lomax. *The Midnight Special: The Legend Of Lead Belly*, Richard M. Garvin and Edmond G. Addeo. *The Life And Legend Of Lead Belly: A Revisionist Look*, Charles Wolfe and Kip Lornell.

Leaders Of The New School

Uniondale, New York-based hip-hop troupe, combining aggressive vocals with loping bass beats, who like many of the newer rap artists of the 90s deployed lyrics which extolled the joys of marijuana. However, they retained an experimental edge - particularly in their complex rhythmic structures and 'mysticism'. Fronted by the giant **Busta Rhymes** (b. 1972, Brooklyn, New York, USA), an impressive rapper who served a long apprenticeship freestyling before cutting his first record. Backed by Charlie 'The Freestyle Wizard' Brown, Dinco 'The Rhyme Scientist' D and Milo In De Dance (aka The Cut Monitor), the Leaders concerned themselves not only with the current problems facing black culture in general and hip-hop in particular, but also its immediate past: 'Leaders Of The New School learnt from the old school and groups like the **Cold Crush Brothers**. We then developed our own unique style which a lot of people have started to copy'. It was certainly true that the band had etched a real impression with their debut, with three tracks produced by Eric Sadler of the **Bomb Squad**. The temptation to make their second set a facsimile of the winning formula was avoided, subtitling the album 'The Inner Mind's Eye - The Endless Dispute With Reality'. The group broke up in 1994, with Rhymes going on to a successful solo career.

● ALBUMS: *A Future Without A Past* (Elektra 1991)★★★, *T.I.M.E.* (Elektra 1993)★★★.

Leadon, Bernie

b. 19 July 1947, Minneapolis, Minnesota, USA. A guitarist and singer, Leadon was a member of the **Flying Burrito Brothers** and a founder member of the **Eagles**. After leaving the group in 1976, he linked up with session guitarist/singer Michael Georgiades to cut *Natural Progression* - which had Eagles' manager Irving Azoff on backing vocals. The album was a minor hit and contained the single 'You're The Singer'. Throughout the 70s, Leadon worked on numerous recording sessions with such artists as **Emmylou Harris**, **Danny O'Keefe**, **Dory Previn** and **Paul Kennerley**, to whose excellent concept album *White Mansions* Leadon added guitar solos. In the UK, his instrumental 'Journey Of The Sorcerer' (recorded originally for the Eagles' *One Of These Nights*) was used as the theme for the UK cult radio series, *The Hitchhiker's Guide To The Galaxy*. During the 80s Leadon remained a sought after session player and he briefly joined the **Nitty Gritty Dirt Band**, playing on their 1988 album, *Workin' Band*. In 1992 Leadon was a member of the Remington's, a band in the style of all his previous conglomerations. In 1993 he appeared as part of the spoof country supergroup **Run C&W** as Crashen Burns.

● ALBUMS: with Michael Georgiades *Natural Progression* (Asylum 1977)★★★★.

League Of Gentlemen

(see **Fripp, Robert**)

Leahy, Dick

b. 1937, London, England. Leahy first came to the fore in the music business during the late 60s when he was appointed A&R manager of Philips Records. Their artists during that period included **Dusty Springfield**, **Dave Dee, Dozy, Beaky, Mick And Tich** and the **Walker Brothers**. From 1970-74, Leahy worked as managing director of Bell Records, a company that dominated the UK market with a string of hit singles from such artists as **Dawn**, **David Cassidy**, **Gary Glitter**, the **Drifters**, the **Delfonics**, **Barry Blue**, **Showaddywaddy** and **Slik**. Leahy was directly responsible for the label's signing of the hugely successful **Bay City Rollers** and he showed a keen ability to recognize hit potential. During the late 70s, he moved to GTO Records, whose roster included **Donna Summer** and, coincidentally, the Walker Brothers. With his considerable experience of the music business, Leahy branched out into music publishing in the 80s, teaming up with former **Pretty Things**' manager Bryan Morrison. The new company, Morrison/Leahy, missed the opportunity to sign the **Smiths**, but secured the songwriting catalogue of **Wham!** Leahy was instrumental in advising the young star **George Michael** and is generally regarded as his most powerful ally in the music business. Although Michael dispensed with most of his working colleagues over the years, Leahy was retained as music publisher when the star left Wham! for a successful solo career.

Leake County Revellers

One of the best and most respected of the old-time string bands. They were formed in 1926, when the members began to play together for relaxation in the evenings or for local dances at Sebastopol, Scott County, Mississippi, USA. The band comprised Will Gilmer (b. William Bryant Gilmer, 27 February 1897, Leake County, USA, d. 28 December 1960; fiddle), R.O. Mosley (b. R. Oscar Mosley, 1885, Sebastopol, Scott County, Mississippi, USA, d. early 30s; mandolin), Jim Wolverton (b. 1895, Leake County, USA, d. 50s; banjo) and Dallas Jones (b.17 December 1889, Sebastopol, Scott County, Mississippi, USA; guitar). Their local popularity grew and led to them making their first four recordings for **Columbia Records** in 1927. Their recording of 'Wednesday Night Waltz', for which they are best remembered, proved so successful that it became one of the bestselling records of old-time music. In the late 20s, further Columbia sessions led to over 20 releases and their popularity saw them tour and gain their own programmes on WJDX Jackson. Their repertoire, much at variance with most of the early string bands, consisted mainly of waltzes or slow numbers and experts in the music have attributed much of their success to Gilmer's gentle fiddle playing. After Mosley's death, in the early 30s, the Revellers disbanded (arguably, they should have been the Scott and not Leake County Revellers - geographically Sebastopol was in the former county; they were actually named by Columbia). Gilmer and Jones both continued to play for some years, although with different bands.

● COMPILATIONS: *The Leake County Revellers 1927-1930* (County 1975)★★★.

Leake, Lafayette

b. 1 June 1920, Wynomie, Mississippi, USA, d. 14 August 1990, Chicago, Illinois, USA. Lafayette Leake was a blues pianist whose prime contribution was his collaboration with **Chess Records** producer **Willie Dixon**. After moving to Chicago, Leake first worked with Dixon in 1951, replacing **Leonard 'Baby Doo' Caston** in Dixon's group the Big Three Trio. Leake performed on many Chess sessions during the 50s and 60s, playing on recordings by **Howlin' Wolf**, **Chuck Berry**, **Sonny Boy** 'Rice Miller' **Williamson**, **Bo Diddley**, **Junior Wells** and **Otis Rush**. Leake joined Dixon's Chicago Blues All Stars, appearing on the 1969 *I Am The Blues*. He also recorded for the Cobra, Ovation and Spivey labels. Leake died after suffering a diabetic coma.

Leander, Mike

b. 30 June 1941, England, d. 18 April 1996, Spain. Leander, a respected composer and songwriter, will best be remembered by rock and pop fans for his contribution to the ascendancy of **Gary Glitter** in the 70s. Leander played drums, piano and guitar as a child before giving up legal studies to pursue a music career in composition at the Trinity College Of Music in London. He joined **Decca Records** as musical director at the age of 20, after studio work with artists including the **Rolling Stones** and **Phil Spector**. While at Decca his achievements included arranging the string section for the **Beatles**' 'She's Leaving Home' (from *Sgt. Pepper's Lonely Hearts Club Band*). Other production, composition and arranging credits included **Joe Cocker**, **Marianne Faithfull**, **Alan Price**, **Shirley Bassey**, **Gene Pitney** and **Roy Orbison**. In the USA the **Drifters** took Leander's version of 'Under The Boardwalk' to number 1. It was his work with Gary Glitter, however, which gave him his most high-profile success in the UK. As well as writing most of Glitter's successful songs, Leander also discovered the then Paul Raven in 1965 when he was working as a warm-up act. They chose the stage name Gary Glitter together and developed the high camp persona with which the artist would take the stage. Leander also came up with the visual image of shoulder pads, high stack-heeled boots, outlandish hair and garish costumes with which Glitter would be associated long into the 90s. Leander and Glitter wrote their first song together, the enduring 'Rock And Roll', then a sequence of successful singles including 'I Didn't Know I Loved You (Till I Saw You Rock And Roll)', 'Oh Yes, You're Beautiful' and 'I Love

You Love Me Love'. They also worked together on Glitter's signature tune, the hugely successful 'I'm The Leader Of The Gang (I Am)' - remaining unconcerned about clumsy parentheses getting in the way of otherwise snappy song titles. Leander married model Penny Carter in 1974, and continued to win awards for his compositions outside of his work with Glitter, including one for the role of executive producer on **Andrew Lloyd Webber** and **Tim Rice**'s *Jesus Christ Superstar*. Leander was also a member of the MCC and a keen cricket supporter, but he retired to Majorca at the end of the 70s. A musical for the West End, *Matador*, was considered a relative failure in 1991. He returned again three years later with a series of cassettes featuring actors reading the work of Henry Miller and extracts from the *Kama Sutra*.

Léandre, Joëlle

b. 12 September 1951, Aix-en-Provence, France. One of Europe's most gifted and versatile young bassists, Léandre is equally at home performing scores by *avant garde* composers such as Giacinto Scelsi or playing total improvisation with the likes of **Maggie Nicols** and **Irène Schweizer**. She studied both double bass and piano as a child; later graduated from the Conservatoire National Superieur de Musique de Paris; played with Pierre Boulez's Ensemble Intercontemporain and studied in the USA with **John Cage**. Her 1981 debut, *Contrebassiste*, featured mostly her own composed music, but also included vocals, overdubbing and pre-recorded tapes (of taxi-drivers refusing to take her bass in their cabs!) - intimations of the invention and droll humour that have become hallmarks of her improvisations (along with her *bravura* technique). The recording of *Live At The Bastille* in 1982, with Nicols and **Lindsay Cooper**, was completely improvised and this has been the dominant mode on most of her subsequent recordings (the exceptions being *Contrebasse Et Voix*, which includes pieces by Scelsi and Cage and the recent *All Scelsi*). *Sincerely* was another solo, while other releases feature duos and trios with leading European improvizers, such as Schweizer, **Derek Bailey**, **Barre Phillips**, **Peter Kowald**, the Portuguese violinist Carlos Zingaro, plus US trombonist **George Lewis** and violinist Jon Rose; the latter of whom she recorded a duo album of 'domestic' noises, including pieces for television set, fridge, bathroom, creaking door and pet dog! In 1983, Léandre joined Schweizer's European Women's Improvising Group and played with her at the 1986 Canaille Festival of Women's Improvised Music in Zurich, as well as appearing on the pianist's *Live At Taktlos* and *The Storming Of The Winter Palace*, and recording the duo *Cordial Gratin* with her. In 1988, Léandre played at Canada's Victoriaville Festival, recording with **Anthony Braxton** on his *Ensemble (Victoriaville) 1988*: a duo project with Braxton released in late 1992 as is an album by her current Canvas Trio with Zingaro and reedman/accordionist Rüdiger Carl.

● ALBUMS: *Contrabassiste* 1981 recording (1983)★★★, with

Maggie Nicols, Lindsay Cooper *Live At The Bastille* 1982 recording (1984)★★★, *Les Douze Sons* (Nato 1984)★★★, *Sincerely* (1985)★★★, with Irène Schweizer *Cordial Gratin* (1987)★★★★, *Paris Quartet* 1985 recording (1989)★★★★, *Contrebasse Et Voix* 1987 recording (1989)★★★, *Urban Bass* (Adda 1990)★★★, with Jon Rose *Les Domestiques* 1987 recording (1990)★★★, with Carlos Zingaro *Ecritures* (Adda 1990)★★★, with others *Unlike* (1990)★★★, with Eric Watson *Palimpeste* (Hat Art 1992)★★★, *Canvas Trio* (1992)★★★, *All Scelsi* (1992)★★★, *L'Histoire De Mme Tasco* (Hat Art 1993)★★, *Blue Goo Park* (FMP 1993)★★★, with Giacinto Scelsi *Okanagon* (1993)★★.

Leandros, Vicky

b. 23 August 1948, Greece. Leandros was raised in Hamburg, Germany, and groomed for showbusiness with a disciplined regime of vocal, classical guitar and ballet lessons. Managed by her songwriting father Leo, she recorded her first single (as 'Vicky') in 1965 and had become quite well known in northern Europe by 1967 when she was chosen to perform Luxembourg's entry in the Eurovision Song Contest. 'L'Amour Est Bleu' (Love Is Blue) finished 4th and was a massive hit in 19 countries, but the Leandros original fell behind instrumental versions by **Jeff Beck** and **Paul Mauriat** in the UK and the USA. Vicky emerged as a huge attraction in such diverse territories as Canada and Japan - where she received 1968's *Prix Du Disque* - and any disappointment over 'L'Amour Est Bleu' was mitigated when her 'Apres Toi' was the winning Eurovision song for Luxembourg in 1972. Translated as 'Come What May', it almost topped the UK chart. In its afterglow, 'The Love In Your Eyes' and 1973's 'When Bouzoukis Played' were minor UK hits. The most far-reaching benefit of this episode, however, was the broadening of Vicky's concert itinerary and fame.
● ALBUMS: *Apres Toi* (1974)★★★★, *My Favourite Songs In Greek* (1975)★★★★, with Nana Mouskouri, Demis Roussos *Greek Songs* (1979)★★, *Love Is Alive* (1981)★★★.

Lear, Amanda

b. Amanda Tapp, 1941. This tall, blonde jet-setter of Russian descent performed in burlesque as 'Peki d'Oslo' in her teens prior to a short marriage to Alain-Philippe Malignac, a French record producer. In the 70s, she was linked romantically to **Bryan Ferry**, Oliver Tobias, John Bentley - and, especially, surrealist Salvadore Dali for whom she modelled. She secured a recording contract after an introduction by **Marianne Faithfull** to **David Bowie** resulted in Bowie insisting that his Mainman management sign her. After singing lessons from his former teacher, Florence Wiese-Norberg, she was launched as a 'White Disco Queen' (in competition with **Grace Jones**), amid publicity that cast unfounded doubts about her gender and provocative photographs portraying her in cutaway black leotards and high leather boots. Another trademark was her husky vocals likened to 'gargling with rusty nails' on singles such as 'Follow Me', which earned her one of

four gold discs awarded her for chart success in continental Europe. Propositions that she star in a film based on the anti-Soviet *Oktobriana* cartoon were not pursued, and despite occasional recording sessions she re-launched herself in the 80s as a painter.
● ALBUMS: *I Am A Photograph* (1978)★★★★, *Sweet Revenge* (1978)★★★, *Never Trust A Pretty Face* (1979)★★★, *Diamonds For Breakfast* (1980)★★, *Tam Tam* (1984)★★, *Secret Passion* (1987)★★.
● COMPILATIONS: *The Collection* (1993)★★★.

Leather Nun

This post-punk group was founded in Goreburg, Sweden. In the mid-70s, disc jockey, fanzine editor, and **Iggy Pop/Ramones** enthusiast Jonas Almqvist made frequent trips to London to see bands and while there he formed a friendship with Genesis P. Orridge of **Throbbing Gristle**. Almqvist played him a demo of a song he had written - 'Death Threat' - and Orridge agreed to issue it on his own Industrial Records. Returning to Sweden, Almqvist recruited Bengt Aronsson (guitar), Freddie (bass) and Gert Claesson (drums) from what was regarded as Sweden's finest punk band, Strait Jacket. This was the first line-up of Leather Nun and later in 1979 they released the EP *Slow Death* on Industrial Records. Their use of hardcore gay pornographic films to illustrate their material provoked allegations of obscenity. This led to Freddie eventually leaving the band, though not before recording the seminal 'Prime Mover' in 1983. His replacement was Haken, a singer-songwriter rapidly trained to play the bass. The band also added Nils Wohlrabe as second guitarist. They recorded for five different labels by 1985 and enjoyed cult attention in the UK with their cover version of **Abba**'s 'Gimme Gimme Gimme (A Man After Midnight)'. Anders Olsen replaced Haken on bass soon afterwards.
● ALBUMS: *Slow Death* (Wire 1984)★★, *Alive* (Wire 1985)★★★, *Lust Games* (Wire 1986)★★★, *Steel Construction* (Wire 1987)★★★, *Force Of Habit* (Wire 1988)★★★, *International Heroes* (Wire 1990)★★★.

Leatherwolf

The origins of this Californian quintet date back to 1983 when Michael Olivieri (vocals, guitar), Geoff Gayer (guitar), Carey Howe (guitar), Matt Hurich (bass) and Dean Roberts (drums) were at high school together. Influenced by a range of styles, from hard rock to jazz, they recorded a self-titled, five-track mini-album that attracted the attention of **Island Records**. Matt Hurich was replaced by Paul Carman before they left to record their second album in the Bahamas, under the guidance of **REO Speedwagon** producer Kevin Beamish. *Street Ready* avoided the pitfalls of their previous release, and saw the band developing their own identity, as they gingerly ventured into the pop-metal crossover market. Beamish achieved a harder and more powerful sound this time, but with an added dimension of accessibility and the potential for commercial success. Ultimately, however, this remained unrealized, with Leatherwolf disintegrating before the start of the new decade.

● ALBUMS: *Leatherwolf I* (Tropical 1986)★★, *Leatherwolf II* (Island 1987)★★, *Street Ready* (Island 1989)★★★.

Leave Home - Ramones

Basic chords, furious tempos and moronic intensity had defined the **Ramones**' debut album. On their second, they simply repeated that mix. Despite appearances to the contrary, the quartet understood the attraction of primeval pop, grafting urgency to exciting hooklines that snapped shut when their appeal peaked. **Brill Building** ghosts hover around the commercial twists of 'Swallow My Pride', whereas gore films and cartoons inspired 'Gimme Gimme Shock Treatment' and 'Pinhead'. The latter's 'gabba gabba' refrain comes directly from Tod Browning's shocker, *Freaks*. *Leave Home* shows the Ramones fully aware of their strengths and the result is another unqualified classic.

● Tracks: *Glad To See You Go; Gimme Gimme Shock Treatment; I Remember You; Oh, Oh I Love Her So; Carbona Not Glue; Suzy Is A Headbanger; Pinhead; Now I Wanna Be A Good Boy; Swallow My Pride; What's Your Game; California Sun; Commando; You're Gonna Kill That Girl; You Should Never Have Opened That Door.*
● First released 1977
● UK peak chart position: 45
● USA peak chart position: 148

Leave It To Jane

One of the five engaging and tuneful musicals that the team of **Jerome Kern** (music), **Guy Bolton** (book), and **P.G. Wodehouse** (book and lyrics) turned out in 1917, this particular production could not get into their favourite 499-seater Princess Theatre, situated on the corner of Broadway and 48th Street, because their *Oh, Boy!*, was still playing to packed houses for an incredible (in those days) 467 performances. So, *Leave It Jane* made its debut at the Longacre Theatre on 28 August 1917. Based on George Ade's play, *The College Widow*, and set in the football-mad Atwater College, the story concerns Jane Witherspoon (Edith Hallor), the daughter of the college president. When the highly talented and extremely supple Billy Bolton (Robert Pitkin) announces that he intends to devote his footballing talents to Atwater's deadly rivals, Bingham, Jane persuades Billy to play for Atwater under an assumed name - and inevitably, she eventually changes hers to Bolton. The breezy, optimistic score included 'The Crickets Are Calling', 'I'm Going To Find A Girl', 'It's A Great Big Land', 'Just You Watch My Step', 'A Peach Of A Life', 'Poor Prune', 'Sir Galahad', 'The Siren's Song', 'The Sun Shines Brighter', 'There It Is Again', 'Wait Till Tomorrow', 'What I'm Longing To Say', and 'Why?'. The novelty number that usually stopped the show was a highly amusing mock-Egyptian piece called 'Cleopatterer', which was sung by Georgia O'Ramey, and had a typical Wodehouse lyric. He had the knack of

noticing and using the current fad phrases, like 'ginks' and 'Oh, you kid!': 'She gave those poor Egyptian ginks/Something else to watch beside the Sphinx . . . They'd take her hand and squeeze it, and murmer, "Oh, you kid!"/But you bet they never started to feed, till Cleopatterer did'. That song, and 'Leave It To Jane', were sung by **June Allyson** in the Jerome Kern biopic *Till The Clouds Roll By* (1946). *Leave It To Jane* ran for 167 performances in 1917, and was revived, over 40 years later in May 1959, when it remained Off Broadway at the Sheridan Square Playhouse for over two years, a remarkable 928 performances. The show was presented again at the Goodspeed Opera House, Connecticut, in 1985, and at the Guildhall School of Music and Drama in London 10 years later.

Leave It To Me!

Just a year after his riding accident, during which both his legs were very badly injured, **Cole Porter** came up with a terrific score for this funny and satirical show which opened at the Imperial Theatre in New York on 9 November 1938. With a book by Bella and Sam Spewack which was based on their play, *Clear All Wires*, it heralded the Broadway debut of **Mary Martin**, who went on to become one of the American musical theatre's cherished leading ladies. Her big moment came as she sat on a trunk at a Siberian railway station clad in furs which she slowly and deliberately removed during Porter's wonderful 'My Heart Belongs To Daddy'. Closely in attendance were five male dancers, and the one visible over Martin's right shoulder in the publicity shots is **Gene Kelly**. After the show had been running for three months she received feature billing. Her saucy first impression is interesting because, it is said, that in subsequent shows she was extremely reluctant to be involved with material that was anywhere 'near the knuckle'. The Spewacks' story for *Leave It To Me!* told of the meek and mild Alonzo P. Goodhue (Victor Moore), whose wife, played by **Sophie Tucker**, raised such a big bundle of cash for President Roosevelt's re-election campaign, that Alonzo is made the American ambassador to the Soviet Union. This is precisely what he does not want, and he sets out make a real hash of things so that he will be recalled. Unfortunately for him, everything he touches turns out right - until he gets together with foreign correspondent Buckley Joyce Thomas (William Gaxton) to inaugurate a plan that will guarantee world peace. This, of course, is in nobody's interest, and he is immediately removed, and returned to the USA. Gaxton and Tamara, who played his girlfriend, Colette, combined in two romantic duets, 'From Now On' and 'Far, Far Away', and she sang one of Porter's most potent love songs, 'Get Out Of Town'. The composer gave Sophie Tucker, appearing in her only Broadway book musical, one of her early 'advice to young ladies' numbers with the clever 'Most Gentlemen Don't Like Love', and she and the chorus also had 'Tomorrow'. There was lots of larking about in Red Square, and other appropriate locations, particularly by funny-men Gaxton and Moore who teamed in several other Broadway musicals. After its initial run of 291 performances, *Leave It To Me!* returned to New York for another two weeks in September 1939 when Mary Martin was succeeded by Mildred Fenton. During the subsequent tour, the character of Stalin was removed from the piece following the Russian dictator's signing of non-aggression pact with Hitler. Many years later, the show still retained some interest, and it was revived as recently as 1991 at the Arts Theatre in Cambridge, England.

Leavell, Chuck

An in-demand session player, Leavell (b. 1950, Tuscaloosa, Alabama, USA) has played piano and keyboards for some of the most famous artists in rock music. Growing up in the south, he was first influenced by the music being played on the local R&B and gospel radio stations , and in particular by **Ray Charles**. By the age of 15 he was working with a black vocal group called the Jades, and looking to develop a career in music. Moving to Macon, Georgia, he worked as a session musician for Capricorn Records, and released an album on the Ampex label as part of the group Sundown. After working on the **Allman Brothers Band**'s *Brothers And Sisters*, Leavell was invited to join the group, and stayed on as their keyboard player until 1976. He then fronted Sea Level, a boogie/jazz-style group who released seven albums between 1976 and 1981, before striking up a long-term partnership with the **Rolling Stones**, appearing on every tour and record by the group from 1982 onwards. He has also recently toured and recorded with **Eric Clapton** (*24 Nights*, *Unplugged*), **George Harrison** (*Live In Japan*), **Richie Sambora** and **Iris DeMent**.

Leaves

Formed in Northridge, California, USA, in 1964, this folk rock group began its career as the Rockwells, a college-based 'frat' band. Founder-members Robert Lee Reiner (guitar) and Jim Pons (bass) were joined by Bill Rinehart (guitar) and Jimmy Kern (drums) in an attraction offering a diet of surf tunes and R&B-styled oldies. By the end of the year vocalist John Beck had been added to the line-up, while Kern was replaced by Tom Ray early in 1965. Having branched into the Los Angeles club circuit, the Rockwells were among the finalists auditioning to replace the **Byrds** at the fabled Ciro's on Sunset Strip. They duly won the residency whereupon the group took a more contemporary name, the Leaves. Having secured a recording contract with Mira Records via a production deal with singer **Pat Boone**'s Penhouse production company, the Leaves made their recording debut with 'Too Many People' in September 1965. For a follow-up the quintet opted to record 'Hey Joe', a song popularized by the aforementioned Byrds, **Love** and **Music Machine** and a subsequent hit for **Jimi Hendrix**. Their initial recording was not a success, prompting the departure of Rinehart in

February 1966. He later surfaced in the **Gene Clark** Group and, later, **Merry Go Round**. Bobby Arlin, veteran of the Catalinas with **Leon Russell** and **Bruce Johnson**, took his place. A second version of 'Hey Joe' was released, then withdrawn, before the group proclaimed themselves happy with a third interpretation, which featured fuzz guitar and a vibrant instrumental break. It reached the US Top 40 in May that year, much to the chagrin of those initially playing the song. However, ensuing releases were not well received, placing a strain on the group. Reiner left the line-up, but although the remaining quartet were signed to **Capitol Records**, further ructions ensued. Pons joined the **Turtles** during sessions for *All The Good That's Happening*, Ray was fired by the producer, and Beck quit in disgust leaving Arlin to tidy the proceedings. The last-named pair did reunite in 1967 to record a handful of songs, but plans to work as the New Leaves, with the aid of Buddy Sklar (bass) and Craig Boyd (drums), were abandoned when Beck quit. The remaining trio took a new name, Hook. Of the remaining ex-members only Pons retained a high profile as a member of **Flo And Eddie** and the **Mothers Of Invention**.

● ALBUMS: *Hey Hoe* (Mira 1966)★★, *All The Good That's Happening* (Capitol 1967)★★.
● COMPILATIONS: *The Leaves 1966* (Panda 1985)★★.
● FILMS: *The Cool Ones* (1967).

Leavill, Otis

b. Otis Leavill Cobb, 8 February 1941, Atlanta, Georgia, USA. Brought up on Chicago's west side, Leavill came to music through his family's gospel group, the Cobb Quartet. He later formed the short-lived Floats with a childhood friend, **Major Lance**, and Barbara Tyson. Leavill's first solo single was issued in 1963 and coupled 'Rise Sally Rise' with 'I Gotta Right To Cry', an early **Curtis Mayfield** song. The singer's reputation was secured with a 1964 release, 'Let Her Love Me', written by **Billy Butler** and produced by Major. Although he continued to record for several companies, Leavill's principal task was undertaken at **OKeh** where he assisted producer **Carl Davis**. The partners would subsequently form the Dakar label in 1967. Leavill recorded four singles for the company, two of which, 'I Love You' and 'Love Uprising', were written by Eugene Record of the **Chi-Lites**. Leavill later returned to a backroom role working with Davis at **Brunswick**, and later Chi-Sound, which folded in 1984.

Leavitt, Raphy

b. 17 September 1948, Puerta De Tierra, San Juan, Puerto Rico. All rounder Salsa bandleader, pianist, arranger, composer, producer Raphy Leavitt formed his first band, called Los Señoriales, when he was in his early teens. In 1966, he organized another group, named La Banda Latina. At this stage of his career, Raphy only performed cover versions of hits by other bands. After graduating from the University of Puerto Rico, where he studied commercial administration, he worked as a teacher/lecturer of commerce at the San Agustin College in Puerta De Tierra, which was the same educational institution from which he received his own elementary, intermediate and secondary education. In 1971, the prolific Raphy formed La Selecta, an orquesta with a line-up of trombones and trumpets, rhythm section (conga, bongo, timbales, cowbell, güiro, bass, piano) and voices (lead and chorus). They signed a contract with Borinquen Records and released 10 albums (including a compilation) on the label between 1971-79. His first composition, a bolero montuno called 'Payaso' (clown), was a best seller. The single, and La Selecta's self-titled debut album, both went gold. The following year, the band had a huge international hit with 'Jibaro Soy'. Leavitt and the band were involved in a motor vehicle accident on the Connecticut Turnpike in the USA. Trumpeter Luisito Maisonet was killed and Leavitt nearly died from a cerebral contusion. He had to spend six months recovering in hospital and three other band members were also hospitalized.

Leavitt composed 'La Cuna Blanca' as a posthumous tribute to the memory of Maisonet and the song topped the charts in Puerto Rico, Dominican Republic, Panamá, Venezuela, Colombia and the latin charts in the USA. This composition caused Leavitt to receive his second gold disc for the sales of *Jibaro Soy*. He was awarded the prize of 'Composer of the Year' for 'Jibaro Soy' and 'La Cuna Blanca', and received the 'Golden Bust of Rafael Hernández'. Hernández (b. 1891, Aguadilla, Puerto Rico, d. 11 December 1965) is regarded as one of Puerto Rico's greatest composers. La Selecta made their first public appearance after the accident at New York's Madison Square Garden. At the end of the concert they were awarded the 'Bronze Plaque of Madison Square Garden'. In 1976, the single 'El Buen Pastor' from *De Frente A La Vida . . . Facing Life*, was another international hit and went gold. On *Raphy Leavitt La Selecta Orchestra* in 1978, Sammy Marrero, lead singer with La Selecta since their formation, was joined by **Tony Vega**, who sang lead vocals on half the tracks. Vega left to join **Willie Rosario**'s band before Leavitt's next album. Raphy signed to T H (Top Hits) Records and released three albums on the label between 1981 and 1983. Carlitos Ramírez joined La Selecta as co-lead singer on their 10th anniversary album. Leavitt and the band switched to **Bobby Valentín**'s Bronco Records for two albums. In 1986, he hired talented Puerto Rican arranger/pianist Isidro Infante to write half the tracks on their Bronco debut, *Somos El Son*. In 1987, La Selecta received the Puerto Rican music industries Diplo award for 'Band of the Year'. Young, subtle-voiced Osvaldo Díaz, born in the Puerto Rican coastal town of Arecibo, joined Marrero and Ramírez to form a trio of lead vocalists on *Se Solicita Un Cariño* in 1988. Infante wrote all the arrangements for the album.

Leavitt commenced the 90s with the launch of his own R L Records label. The first release was his own *Provócame!*, which charted in the **Billboard**

tropical/salsa list. The salsa romántica single of the same title, sung by Díaz, was a Top 5 hit in Puerto Rico. Infante arranged 'Provócame' and six other tracks on the album.

● ALBUMS: *Payaso* (1971)★★★, *Herido* (1974)★★★★, *A Recorded Inferno* (1975)★★★, *De Frente A La Vida - Facing Life* (1976)★★★, *Con Sabor A Tierra Adentro* (1977)★★★, *Soledad* (1979)★★★, *Raphy Leavitt y La Selecta* (1981)★★, *10 Años* (1982)★★★, *Siempre Alegre* (1983)★★★, *Se Solicita Un Cariño* (1988)★★★, *Provócame!* (1990)★★.

Leavy, Calvin

b. 1942, Scott, Arkansas, USA. Leavy began his musical career in the gospel field at the age of 16, but in 1969 he recorded, singing and playing rhythm guitar, a strong southern blues entitled 'Cummins Prison Farm'. The song featured an excellent guitar break from Robert Tanner. The recording was released by Calvin C. Brown, owner of Soul Beat Records and became a surprise hit about a year after it was made; it was subsequently picked up by **Shelby Singleton** Enterprises. Leavy made several more records for Soul Beat (and associate label Acquarian), often in the company of his bass-playing brother Hosea. Soon afterwards, however, he dropped into obscurity and little has been heard of him, although his hit has become a blues standard. Last reports seem to indicate he was playing bass guitar with a gospel group.

● ALBUMS: *Cummins Prison Farm* (1977)★★★.

LeBlanc And Carr

A duo consisting of Lenny LeBlanc (b. 17 June 1951, Leominster, Massachusetts, USA) and Pete Carr (b. 22 April 1950, Daytona Beach, Florida, USA), this act enjoyed one chart album and a handful of singles in the late 70s, including the US Top 20 single 'Falling'. Carr had formerly been a member of **Hourglass** the pre-**Allman Brothers Band**, featuring **Duane** and **Gregg Allman**. He later became a session musician and met LeBlanc in **Muscle Shoals**, Alabama, USA while recording sessions. Both musicians released solo albums with no success, and in 1978 they teamed up for *Midnight Light*, on the Big Tree label. From that album, three singles were released, each making the charts. 'Falling' was the second one, ascending to number 18. When the album's title track failed to follow its predecessor up the charts, the duo split up, each returning to session work. LeBlanc later turned to Christian music.

● ALBUMS: *Midnight Light* (1978)★★★★.

LeBlanc, Keith

LeBlanc was previously an anonymous drummer and keyboard player as part of the **Sugarhill Gang**'s house band in New Jersey, New York, USA, but cut himself a slice of the action in 1983 when he recorded the before-its-time Malcolm X anthem, 'No Sell Out', for **Tommy Boy** Records. This fused sections of the black leader's speeches with a cut-up dance groove. It led to disputes between Tommy Boy and **Sugarhill Records** over ownership of the speeches (LeBlanc had defected when he learned that Sugarhill were not going to pay any royalties to the Malcolm X estate), while LeBlanc was also questioned on his part in the process - he was, after all, white. However, the record was sanctioned by Betty Shabazz, Malcolm X's widow, and the song played no small part in pushing the name of the black leader back into the political firmament. It was also released a year later, intended as a tribute to the UK's striking miners. By 1986 LeBlanc had assembled an album, *Major Malfunction*, which included contributions from his old and future sparring partners Doug Wimbush and Skip McDonald. They too had been part of Sugarhill's house band, and would go on to join LeBlanc as **Tackhead** took shape. They were also present for LeBlanc's second 'solo' album *Stranger Than Fiction*, which again spanned boundless experimentation and styles, but maintained a strong political edge. By 1991 Leblanc had joined with Tim Simenon (**Bomb The Bass**) in a new project, entitled Interference (singles included 'Global Game').

● ALBUMS: *Major Malfunction* (World 1986)★★★, *Stranger Than Fiction* (Nettwerk/Enigma 1989)★★★, *Time Traveller* (Blanc 1992)★★.

Lebrón Brothers

Now into their third decade, the Lebrón Brothers are one of New York salsa's most original and distinctive sounding bands. They were formed in the mid-60s and co-led by José Lebrón (piano/arranger/composer/lead and chorus singer) and Angel Lebrón (bass/arranger/composer/lead and chorus singer/cuatro - which is a small 10-string guitar). The brothers were born in Aguadilla, Puerto Rico, and grew up in Brooklyn, New York City, USA. The band made their recording debut in 1967 when the R&B/Latin-fusion style called boogaloo was at the height of its popularity, and the bands of **Ricardo Ray**, **Joe Cuba**, Pete Rodríguez, Johnny Colón and others, were having hits with their recordings. The Lebrón's repertoire continued to feature a mixture of Latin numbers and R&B/soul oriented tunes with English lyrics. Pablo sang Spanish lead vocals with the band until 1988, when unfortunately he suffered a heart attack. In addition to 'Mala Suerte', their debut album contained the hit boogaloos 'Summertime Blues' (aka 'Funky Blues') and 'Tall Tale'. Goldner, who co-owned Cotique, produced the Lebrón's first five albums on the label.

In an interview with Max Salazar, Angel made this comment about the demise of boogaloo: 'The boogaloo era came to an end when we threatened to rebel against the package deals'. On the same theme, another star of the period, King Nando (Fernando Rivera) recounted: ' . . . It was killed off by envious old bandleaders, a few dance promoters and a popular Latin music disc jockey. We were the hottest bands and we drew the crowds. But we were never given top billing or top dollar. The boogaloo bandleaders were forced to accept package deals which had us hopping all over town . . . one hour

here, one hour there . . . for small change. When word got out that we were going to unite and no longer accept the package deals, our records were no longer played over the radio. The boogaloo era was over and so were the careers of most of the boogaloo bandleaders'. However, the Lebrón Brothers managed to outlive the brief late 60s craze for boogaloo, which many Latin musicians detested and only recorded to keep in fashion. The Lebrón's fourth release, *Brother*, marked a 'promotion in the ranks' for brother Carlos (bongo/tres - which is a six or nine-string Cuban guitar/vocals/trap drums/timbales/composer), who was pictured alongside José and Angel on the front cover of the record sleeve. The classic hit title-track of *Salsa y Control*, was cited by Venezuelan salsa authority, César Miguel Rondon, as being one of the factors contributing to the use of the word 'salsa' (sauce) as a descriptive term for Latin music. The expression 'salsa y control' also designates the swinging, yet restrained style the Lebron's have made their speciality. Ironically, the song was not representative of this. José arranged and conducted Pablo's solo release *Pablo*, which mainly contined slow romantic numbers.

Cotique was taken over by **Fania Records**, and one of the top stars on their roster at the time, Larry Harlow, produced the Lebrón Brothers *Asunto de Familia* in 1973. Conga playing brother Frank, was 'promoted' to the front cover of this album. Fania's co-founder, **Johnny Pacheco**, produced the band's three albums between 1975 and 1978. This included one of their best, *10th Anniversary*, which contained the smash hit 'Disco Bailable'. The story goes that this song was a 'filler-track' composed by José in a subway train on the way to the studio. The Lebrón's final release on Cotique, *Criollo*, was another fine album. After a gap of three years, the Lebrón Brothers switched to Sergio Bofill and Humberto Corredor's Caimán Records label for their recording comeback *Salsa Lebrón* in 1986. Pablo was replaced on this album by young lead vocalist Frankie Morales, who was an ex-member of Los Amigos And The Bad Street Boys. The record was even more of a family affair than usual. Young Adrian and Angel Jnr. joined the band on trombone and percussion, respectively. Angel's daughter Nadine played piano on her father's composition 'La Niña'. Regular **Conjunto Libre** and **Ray Barretto**, trombonist Jimmy Bosch, joined the horn section. **Bobby Rodríguez**, on the Caimán roster at the time, played flute on 'Amores de Ayer'. The title track featured a medley of the Lebron's earlier hits. Morales split acrimoniously with the band and went on to perform with his own outfit. His albums include: *En Su Punto* (1987) on Caimán, and *Sobresaliendo/Standing Out* (1989) on Corredor's El Abuelo label.

Pablo returned in 1988 for his last appearance on *El Boso*, which was the first release on the new El Abuelo label. Bosch was back in the brass section joined by veteran trumpeter **Alfredo 'Chocolate' Armenteros**. For their second release in 1988, *Loco Por Ti*, the lead vocals were shared by Angel, José, Carlos and Enrique Estupiñan, who was one of the album's four executive producers. In 1990, Estupiñan was joined by José Luis 'Luisito' Ayala as co-lead singer on *Salsa en el Paraiso con los Lebrón*, which was recorded in Cali, Colombia. Vocalist/composer Ayala was a former member of the band Saoco (see **Fiol, Henry**) and recorded with **Eddie Palmieri** and **Alfredo Rodríguez**.

● ALBUMS: *Psychedelic Goes Latin* (1967)★★★, *The Brooklyn Bums, I Believe, Brother* (1969)★★★, *Llegamos/We're Here* (1969)★★★, *Salsa y Control* (1970)★★★★, *Picadillo a la Criolla* (1971)★★★, *En La Union Esta La Fuerza* (1972)★★★, *Asunto de Familia* (1973)★★★, *4 + 1 = The Lebrón Brothers* (1975)★★, *Distinto y Diferente* (1976)★★, *10th Anniversary* (1977)★★★, *The New Horizon* (1978)★★★, *La Ley* (1980)★★, *Hot Stuff* (1981)★★★, *Criollo* (1982)★★★, *Salsa Lebrón* (1986)★★★, *El Boso* (1988)★★★, *Loco Por Ti* (1988)★★★, *Salsa en el paraiso con los Lebrón* (1990)★★★.

● COMPILATIONS: *Lo Mejor de/The Best of the Lebrón Brothers* (1975)★★★★.

Lecuona, Ernesto

b. August 1896, Guanabacoa, Cuba, d. 1963. Pianist Ernesto Lecuona was one of the most internationally famous composers to come out of Cuba. His two brothers and two sisters all became musicians. One brother was a violinist, the rest played piano. Ernesto received his first piano lessons from his elder sister and became a prodigy. He gave his first public performance at the age of five and had his first composition published at 11. He graduated from Havana's National Conservatory of Music at the age of 15 and taught piano and voice. At 17, he played in concert at the Aeolian Hall, New York City. In the early 20s, Lecuona continued his musical studies in France, where he studied under Maurice Ravel.

Lecuona has composed over 400 Cuban tunes. His composition 'Siboney' - published in the USA by Leo Feist in 1929 - became a Latin standard, covered by numerous artists. His other popular compositions, included: 'Maria La O' (Maria My Own), c.1931; 'Para Vigo Me Voy' ('Say Si Si'), 1933; and 'La Comparsa'. He also attempted classical type pieces like 'Malagueña' (1927) and 'Andalucia'/'The Breeze And I' (1930).

Lecuona had his own band, originally called his Orquesta Cubana, that performed popular Cuban music. Curiously, he was not the pianist with the band. This slot was filled by the classically trained Armando 'Fichin' Oréfiche (b. 1911, Havana, Cuba), who was also a composer and arranger. Their concerts comprised of Ernesto performing his own pieces for solo piano and the band playing material from their repertoire of popular Cuban numbers, many of which were written by Lecuona and Oréfiche. In 1934, he was medically advised to return to Cuba after suffering from severe pneumonia while touring in Spain with the band. The band was renamed the Lecuona Cuban Boys, and under the musical leadership of Oréfiche and trumpeter/guitarist/composer/arranger Ernesto 'Jaruco'

Vázquez, they continued to tour Europe extensively with considerable success until the outbreak of World War II. Collections of recordings they made in Europe during this period have been issued. During the war the band toured Latin America. In 1946, Armando Oréfiche and his tenor saxophone and bongo playing brother, Adalberto 'Chiquito' Oréfiche, left after a leadership dispute and formed the Havana Cuban Boys. Albums by Armando Oréfiche and his Havana Cuban Boys were released in the UK on the **Decca** and Felsted labels. Their *Rumba Colora* on the Panart label, featured Afro Cuban Bola de Nieve or Snow Ball (b. Ignacio Villa, 1913, Cuba, d. 1971, Cuba) on piano and lead vocal, who, in addition to being a popular cabaret artist with Cuban cafe society, was a Professor of Mathematics. Ten years after Bola's death, the Cuban state label, Areito, released *Bola de Nieve In Memoriam*, a collection of recordings made for Radio Havana that included four of his own compositions and a version of 'Babalú', written by Ernesto's niece, Margarita Lecuona. Margarita was a mezzo soprano and a prolific composer. Her two most famous compositions, 'Babalú' and 'Tabu', have been covered by numerous Latin artists and bands. The legendary Cuban vocalist, Miguelito Valdés, came to be known as 'Mr Babalú' because he sang and recorded the song so many times. Ernesto's daughter, Ernestina Lecuona, sang with the Lecuona Cuban Boys for a while and also with Armando Oréfiche and his Havana Cuban Boys.

● COMPILATIONS: with the Lecuona Cuban Boys *A Cuban Night With The Lecuona Cuban Boys* (1935-37)★★★, *Lecuona Cuban Boys* 1939-40 recordings (1989)★★★.

Led Zeppelin

This pivotal quartet was formed in October 1968 by British guitarist **Jimmy Page** (b. James Patrick Page, 9 January 1944, Heston, Middlesex, England) following the demise of his former band, the **Yardbirds**. **John Paul Jones** (b. John Baldwin, 3 June 1946, Sidcup, Kent, England; bass, keyboards), a respected arranger and session musician, replaced original member Chris Dreja, but hopes to incorporate vocalist **Terry Reid** floundered on a contractual impasse. The singer unselfishly recommended **Robert Plant** (b. 20 August 1948, West Bromwich, West Midlands, England), then frontman of struggling Midlands act Hobbstweedle, who in turn introduced drummer John Bonham (b. 31 May 1948, Birmingham, England, d. 25 September 1980), when first choice B.J. Wilson opted to remain with **Procol Harum**. The quartet gelled immediately and having completed outstanding commitments under the name 'New Yardbirds', became Led Zeppelin following a quip by the **Who**'s **Keith Moon**, who, when assessing their prospects, remarked that they would probably 'go down like a lead Zeppelin'. Armed with a prestigious contract with **Atlantic Records**, the group toured the USA supporting **Vanilla Fudge** prior to the release of their explosive debut, *Led Zeppelin*, which included several exceptional original songs, including

'Good Times, Bad Times', 'Communication Breakdown', 'Dazed And Confused' - a hangover from the Yardbirds' era - and skilled interpretations of R&B standards 'How Many More Times?' and 'You Shook Me'. The set vied with **Jeff Beck**'s *Truth* as the definitive statement of English heavy blues/rock, but Page's meticulous production showed a greater grasp of basic pop dynamics, resulting in a clarity redolent of 50s rock 'n' roll. His staggering dexterity was matched by Plant's expressive, beseeching voice, a combination that flourished on *Led Zeppelin II*. The group was already a headline act, drawing sell-out crowds across the USA, when this propulsive collection confirmed an almost peerless position. The introductory track, 'Whole Lotta Love', a thinly veiled rewrite of **Willie Dixon**'s 'You Need Love', has since become a classic, while 'Livin' Lovin' Maid' and 'Moby Dick', Bonham's exhibition piece, were a staple part of the quartet's early repertoire. Elsewhere, 'Thank You' and 'What Is And What Should Never Be' revealed a greater subtlety, a factor emphasized more fully on *Led Zeppelin III*. Preparation for this set had been undertaken at Bron-Y-Aur cottage in Snowdonia (immortalized in 'Bron-Y-Aur Stomp'), and a resultant pastoral atmosphere permeated the acoustic-based selections 'That's The Way' and 'Tangerine'. 'The Immigrant Song' and 'Gallow's Pole' reasserted the group's traditional fire and the album's release confirmed Led Zeppelin's position as one of the world's leading attractions. In concert, Plant's sexuality and Adonis-like persona provided the perfect foil to Page's more mercurial character, yet both individuals took full command of the stage, the guitarist's versatility matched by his singer's unfettered roar.

Confirmation of the group's ever-burgeoning strengths appeared on *Led Zeppelin IV*, also known as 'Four Symbols', the 'Runes Album' or 'Zoso', in deference to the fact that the set bore no official title. It included the anthemic 'Stairway To Heaven', a group *tour de force*. Arguably the definitive heavy-rock song, it continues to win polls, and the memorable introduction remains every guitar novice's first hurdle. The approbation granted this ambitious piece initially obscured other tracks, but the energetic 'When The Levee Breaks' is now also lauded as a masterpiece, particularly for Bonham's drumming. 'Black Dog' and 'Rock 'N' Roll' saw Zeppelin at their immediate best, while 'The Battle Of Evermore' was marked by a vocal contribution from **Sandy Denny**. *IV* was certified as having sold 16 million copies in the USA by March 1996. However, the effusive praise this album generated was notably more muted for *Houses Of The Holy*. Critics queried its musically diverse selection - the set embraced folk ballads, reggae and soul - yet when the accustomed power was unleashed, notably on 'No Quarter', the effect was inspiring. A concurrent US tour broke all previous attendance records, the proceeds from which helped to finance an in-concert film, issued in 1976 as *The Song Remains The Same*, and the formation of the group's own record label, Swan Song. **Bad Company**,

the **Pretty Things** and **Maggie Bell** were also signed to the company, which served to provide Led Zeppelin with total creative freedom. *Physical Graffiti*, a double set, gave full rein to the quartet's diverse interests, with material ranging from compulsive hard rock ('Custard Pie' and 'Sick Again') to pseudo-mystical experimentation ('Kashmir'). The irrepressible 'Trampled Underfoot' joined an ever-growing lexicon of peerless performances, while 'In My Time Of Dying' showed an undiminished grasp of progressive blues. Sell-out appearances in the UK followed the release, but rehearsals for a projected world tour were abandoned in August 1975 when Plant sustained multiple injuries in a car crash. A new album was prepared during his period of convalescence, although problems over artwork delayed its release. Advance orders alone assured *Presence* platinum status, yet the set was regarded as a disappointment and UK sales were noticeably weaker. The 10-minute maelstrom 'Achilles Last Stand' was indeed a remarkable performance, but the remaining tracks were competent rather than fiery and lacked the accustomed sense of grandeur. In 1977 Led Zeppelin began its rescheduled US tour, but on 26 July news reached Robert Plant that his six-year-old son, Karac, had died of a viral infection. The remaining dates were cancelled amid speculation that the group would break up.

They remained largely inactive for over a year, but late in 1978 they flew to **Abba**'s Polar recording complex in Stockholm. Although lacking the definition of earlier work, *In Through The Out Door* was a strong collection on which John Paul Jones emerged as the unifying factor. Two concerts at Britain's Knebworth Festival were the prelude to a short European tour on which the group unveiled a stripped-down act, inspired, in part, by the punk explosion. Rehearsals were then undertaken for another US tour, but in September 1980, Bonham was found dead following a lengthy drinking bout. On 4 December, Swansong announced that the group had officially retired, although a collection of archive material, *Coda*, was subsequently issued. Jones later became a successful producer, notably with the **Mission**, while Plant embarked on a highly successful solo career, launched with *Pictures At Eleven*. Page scored the film *Death Wish 2* and, after a brief reunion with Plant and the **Honeydrippers** project in 1984, he inaugurated the short-lived **Firm** with **Paul Rogers**. He then formed the Jimmy Page Band with John Bonham's son, Jason, who in turn drummed with Led Zeppelin on their appearance at **Atlantic**'s 25th Anniversary Concert in 1988. Despite renewed interest in the group's career, particularly in the wake of the retrospective *Remasters*, entreaties to make this a permanent reunion were resisted. However, in 1994 Page and Plant went two-thirds of the way to a re-formation with their ironically titled *Unledded* project, though John Paul Jones was conspicuous by his absence (for want of an invitation). The duo cemented the relationship with an album of new Page And Plant material in 1998.

Although their commercial success is unquestionable, Led Zeppelin are now rightly recognized as one of the most influential bands of the rock era and their catalogue continues to provide inspiration to successive generations of musicians.

- ALBUMS: *Led Zeppelin* (Atlantic 1969)★★★★, *Led Zeppelin II* (Atlantic 1969)★★★★, *Led Zeppelin III* (Atlantic 1970)★★★★, *Led Zeppelin IV* (Atlantic 1971)★★★★★, *Houses Of The Holy* (Atlantic 1973)★★★★, *Physical Graffiti* (Swan Song 1975)★★★★, *Presence* (Swan Song 1976)★★★, *The Song Remains The Same* film soundtrack (Swan Song 1976)★★, *In Through The Out Door* (Swan Song 1979)★★★, *Coda* (Swan Song 1982)★★, *BBC Sessions* (Atlantic 1997)★★★★.
- COMPILATIONS: *Led Zeppelin* 4-CD box set (Swan Song 1991)★★★★, *Remasters* (Swan Song 1991)★★★★, *Remasters II* (Swan Song 1993)★★★.
- VIDEOS: *The Song Remains The Same* (Warner Home Video 1986).
- FURTHER READING: *Led Zeppelin*, Michael Gross and Robert Plant. *The Led Zeppelin Biography*, Ritchie Yorke. *Led Zeppelin*, Howard Mylett. *Led Zeppelin: In The Light 1968-1980*, Howard Mylett and Richard Bunton. *Led Zeppelin: A Celebration*, Dave Lewis. *Led Zeppelin In Their Own Words*, Paul Kendall. *Led Zeppelin: A Visual Documentary*, Paul Kendall. *Led Zeppelin: The Book*, Jeremy Burston. *Jimmy Page: Tangents Within A Framework*, Howard Mylett. *Led Zeppelin: The Final Acclaim*, Dave Lewis. *Hammer Of The Gods: The Led Zeppelin Saga*, Stephen Davis. *Illustrated Collector's Guide To Led Zeppelin*, Robert Godwin. *Led Zeppelin: Heaven & Hell*, Charles Cross and Erik Flannigan. *Stairway To Heaven*, Richard Cole with Richard Trubo. *Led Zeppelin: Breaking And Making Records*, Ross Clarke. *Led Zeppelin: The Definitive Biography*, Ritchie Yorke. *On Tour With Led Zeppelin*, Howard Mylett (ed.). *Led Zeppelin*, Chris Welch. *The Complete Guide To The Music Of . . .*, Dave Lewis. *Led Zeppelin Live: An Illustrated Exploration Of Underground Tapes*, Luis Rey. *The Making Of: Led Zeppelin IV*, Robert Godwin. *The Photographer's Led Zeppelin*, Ross Halfin (ed.). *The Led Zeppelin Concert File*, Dave Lewis and Simon Pallett. *Led Zeppelin - Dazed And Confused*, Chris Welch.

Led Zeppelin - Led Zeppelin

Led Zeppelin emerged from the ashes of the **Yardbirds**, but their self-assured debut album immediately established them in their own right. Faultless musicianship combined with strong material to create an emphatic statement of purpose. Blues standards are extensively reworked and original songs either acknowledge pop/rock structures or allow the quartet to extend itself musically. Guitarist **Jimmy Page** explored the instrument's potential with dazzling runs of sonic inventiveness, while **Robert Plant** took the notion of vocalist into new realms of expression. *Led Zeppelin* announced the arrival of one of the most important groups of our time.

- Tracks: *Good Times Bad Times; Babe I'm Gonna Leave You; You Shook Me; Dazed And Confused; Your Time Is Gonna Come; Black Mountain Side; Communication Breakdown; I Can't Quit You Baby; How Many More Times.*
- First released 1969
- UK peak chart position: 6
- USA peak chart position: 10

Led Zeppelin II - Led Zeppelin

Having declared an individual brand of blues rock on their debut album, **Led Zeppelin** significantly expanded musical horizons on its successor. The opening riff to 'Whole Lotta Love' declared a strength of purpose and excitement and the song quickly achieved anthem-like proportions. *Led Zeppelin II* personifies the entire heavy metal spectrum, from guitar hero to virile vocalist. Sexual metaphor ('The Lemon Song') collides with musical dexterity ('Moby Dick') and the faintest whiff of sword and sorcery to create one of the most emphatic and celebratory heavy rock albums.

- Tracks: *Whole Lotta Love; What Is And What Should Never Be; The Lemon Song; Thank You; Heartbreaker; Livin' Lovin' Maid (She's Just A Woman); Ramble On; Moby Dick; Bring It On Home.*
- First released 1969
- UK peak chart position: 1
- USA peak chart position: 1

Led Zeppelin III - Led Zeppelin

They could do no wrong for many years, both in Britain and America. At the point of this album they were massive, and, therefore, if they had gone into a recording studio and recited Enid Blyton stories, they would have topped the charts. *Led Zeppelin III* was only a good album by their standards, great by most of their imitators. It was a forerunner to the peerless *IV*, and remains overshadowed by it. Hints of acoustic material to follow came with 'Gallows Pole', first rehearsed with others at Bron-Y-Aur Stomp, the idyllic 'cottage in the country'. This is followed by the fat 12-string opening sound of 'Hats Off To - Harper', a composition by the mysterious Charles Obscure.

- Tracks: *Immigrant Song; Friends; Celebration Day; Since I've Been Loving You; Out On The Tiles; Gallows Pole; Tangerine; That's The Way; Bron-Y-Aur Stomp; Hats Off To - Harper.*
- First released 1970
- UK peak chart position: 1
- USA peak chart position: 1

Led Zeppelin IV - Led Zeppelin

Its unscripted sleeve design suggested anonymity, but nothing was left to question over this album's content. **Led Zeppelin** were never so strident as on 'Rock 'n' Roll' and 'Black Dog', two selections of undiluted urgency. Blues standard 'When The Levee Breaks' is recast as a piece of unremitting power, particularly through John Bonham's expansive drumming, and the group's love of folk forms surfaces on the graceful 'Battle Of Evermore', complete with a cameo from **Fairport Convention**'s **Sandy Denny**. 'Stairway To Heaven' has, of course, become the album's best-known track, but the anthem-like stature it has since

assumed should not obscure its groundbreaking companion selections. *Led Zeppelin IV* left much of heavy metal, and indeed rock itself, trailing in its wake.
● Tracks: *Black Dog; Rock 'n' Roll; The Battle Of Evermore; Stairway To Heaven; Misty Mountain Hop; Four Sticks; Going To California; When The Levee Breaks.*
● First released 1971
● UK peak chart position: 1
● USA peak chart position: 2

Ledford, Steve

b. Steven Walter Ledford, 2 June 1906, Bakersville, Mitchell County, North Carolina, USA, d. 19 September 1980. One of 12 children, with help from his father, he started playing fiddle aged seven and won a competition two years later. His first professional work came as a member, with two siblings, of the Carolina Ramblers String Band. In 1931, the band travelled to New York, where they played on radio and in February 1932, they recorded 20 sides for ARC, eight of which gained release on various labels including Perfect. Soon afterwards, they disbanded and Ledford returned to North Carolina, where he married and became a farmer. He returned to music in the late 30s, working with **J.E. Mainer**, **Wade Mainer** and **Zeke Morris** on various radio stations and tours, during which time he also made several recordings with Mainer's Mountaineers, including a version of 'Little Maggie', that has since led to the song always being associated with him. Ledford also recorded with Jay Hugh Hall and **Clyde Moody** as the Happy-Go-Lucky Boys and in the early 40s, he worked for some time at WDBJ Roanoke, Virginia, with Jay Hugh and **Roy Hall**. The bands played a mixture of old-time and modern music and undoubtedly were an influence on later bluegrass bands. In 1942, Ledford retired to work his farm but several years later, he, with his brother Wayne and James Gardner, re-formed a version of the Carolina Ramblers, which played a long residency in Maggie Valley. In 1971, as the Ledford String Band, they recorded for Rounder Records. Ledford continued to play at some venues until shortly before his death in September 1980.
● ALBUMS: *Ledford String Band* (Rounder 1971)★★★.

Ledin, Tomas

At one time a 'roadie' for **Jimi Hendrix**, Tomas Ledin has subsequently established a reputation for his own rock and pop ballads in his native Sweden. His other previous experiences included stints as a backing musician for **Abba**. In the 90s, he has been acclaimed as 'Sweden's most consistent singer-songwriter'. His albums have consistently topped the Scandinavian charts, and by the mid-90s he could claim to have sold nearly one million records. Among his earliest successes was the 'Never Again' duet sung with Abba's **Agentha Fältskog**, which became a major European success in 1982. Two years earlier he had represented Sweden in the Eurovision Song Contest, finishing tenth. In the

mid-80s he married Marie Andersson, becoming a multi-millionaire in the process. He ducked the limelight from then on, but returned to his previous stature in the 90s with a series of number 1 albums. *Tillfälligheternas Spel* (Game Of Chance), *Du Kan Lita Pa Mig* (You Can Rely On Me) and *Släpp Hästerna Fria* (Set The Horses Free) demonstrated his affinity with the sophisticated rock ballad - each album presented with his familiar professionalism and natural energy.
● ALBUMS: *Tillfälligheternas Spel* (Record Station 1990)★★★★, *Du Kan Lita Pa Mig* (Record Station 1992)★★★, *Släpp Hästerna Fria* (Record Station 1993)★★★★.

LeDoux, Chris

b. 2 October 1948, Biloxi, Mississippi, USA. LeDoux's father was an airforce pilot who was posted to various parts of the USA. His grandfather, who had served in the US cavalry and fought against Pancho Villa, encouraged LeDoux to ride horses on his Wyoming farm. LeDoux attended high school at Cheyenne, Wyoming, and, while still at school, he twice won the state's bareback title. In 1967, after graduating, he won a rodeo scholarship and received a national title in his third year. In 1976, he became the Professional Rodeo Cowboys Association's world champion in bareback riding. LeDoux has been playing guitar and harmonica and writing songs since his teens, and he used his musical ability as a means of paying his way from one rodeo to another. Since 1971, he has been recording songs about 'real cowboys', although his voice would not win world championships and he has never had a substantial US country hit. His albums combine his own compositions about rodeo life with old and new cowboy songs. He describes his music as 'a combination of western soul, sagebrush blues, cowboy folk and rodeo rock 'n' roll'. For all his tough image, his music has a soft centre ('God Must Be A Cowboy At Heart' and the narration 'This Cowboy's Hat'), but one of his love songs is titled 'If You Loved Me, You'd Do It'. **Charlie Daniels**, **Johnny Gimble** and **Janie Frickie** are among the musicians on his records and **Garth Brooks** pays tribute to him in 'Much Too Young (To Feel This Damn Old)'. LeDoux lives with his family on a ranch in Wyoming and farms sheep. He is a popular entertainer with his band, Western Underground, particularly on the rodeo circuit. All his albums are released on his own label, American Cowboy Songs, but only *Rodeo's Singing Bronc Rider* has been released in the UK. Garth Brooks' testimony, together with the success of a single, 'Ridin' For A Fall', brought him to the attention of **Liberty Records**, who signed LeDoux for new recordings and have reissued his earlier work. He moved to **Capitol Records** in 1995.
● ALBUMS: *Songs Of Rodeo Life* (American Cowboy Songs 1971)★★★, *Chris LeDoux Sings His Rodeo Songs* (American Cowboy Songs 1972)★★★, *Rodeo Songs - Old And New* (American Cowboy Songs 1973)★★★, *Songs Of Rodeo And Country* (American Cowboy Songs 1974)★★★, *Songs Of*

Rodeo And Living Free (American Cowboy Songs 1974)★★★, *Life As A Rodeo Man* (American Cowboy Songs 1975)★★★, *Songbook Of The American West* (American Cowboy Songs 1976)★★★, *Sing Me A Song, Mr. Rodeo Man* (American Cowboy Songs 1977)★★, *Songs Of Rodeo Life* a re-recording of the 1971 album (American Cowboy Songs 1977)★★★, *Western-Country (Cowboys Ain't Easy To Love)* (American Cowboy Songs 1978)★★★, *Paint Me Back Home In Wyoming* (American Cowboy Songs 1979)★★★, *Rodeo's Singing Bronc Rider* (American Cowboy Songs 1979)★★, *Western Tunesmith* (American Cowboy Songs 1980)★★★, *Sounds Of The Western Country* (American Cowboy Songs 1980)★★★, *Old Cowboy Heroes* (American Cowboy Songs 1980)★★★, *He Rides The Wild Horses* (American Cowboy Songs 1981)★★★, *Used To Want To Be A Cowboy* (American Cowboy Songs 1982)★★★, *Thirty Dollar Cowboy* (American Cowboy Songs 1983)★★★, *Old Cowboy Classics* (American Cowboy Songs 1983)★★★, *Wild And Wooly* (American Cowboy Songs 1986)★★★, *Melodies And Memories* (American Cowboy Songs 1984)★★★, *Powder River* (American Cowboy Songs 1990)★★★, *Western Underground* (Liberty 1991)★★★, *What Ya Gonna Do With A Cowboy* (Liberty 1992)★★★, *Under This Old Hat* (Liberty 1993)★★★, *Haywire* (Liberty 1994)★★★, *Stampede* (Capitol 1996)★★★★, *Live* (Capitol 1997)★★, *One Road Man* (Capitol 1998)★★★.

● COMPILATIONS: *Best Of Chris Le Doux* (Liberty 1994)★★★, *Rodeo Rock And Roll Collection* (Liberty 1995)★★★.

● FURTHER READING: *Gold Buckle, The Rodeo Life Of Chris LeDoux*, David G. Brown.

Lee Davis, Janet

b. 1966, London, England. Lee Davis moved to Jamaica at the age of three and was raised in the Old Harbour Bay area of St. Catherine. Following the customary path of many Jamaican singers, her vocals were nurtured singing in the local church choir. Although a competent chorister, she was influenced by the country, R&B, pop and reggae hits that she performed in neighbourhood shows. In 1981 she progressed into the **sound system** circuit, forming an allegiance with the St. Catherine-based Ghetto Sound, performing both as a vocalist and in the DJ style. Her versatility gained her notoriety and she proved that she was equally proficient at performing in stage shows. Lee Davis relocated to the UK and her initial recording session came when she met up with DJ Jah Walton through soundman Vego Wales. She was asked to chat on the massive number 1 hit for **Fashion Records**, 'No Touch The Style', with the DJ performing as **Joseph Cotton**. Although Lee Davis was not credited for her performance on the hit, she quickly gained recognition with her solo hit for Flash, 'Never Gonna Let You Go'. In 1987 she returned to Fashion for 'Two Timing Lover', while the b-side, 'Call Me An Angel', featured her DJ skills, recorded under the name of Shako Lee. The song was written by Philip Leo who also worked with her for the vocal/DJ release 'I'm Gonna Make You Happy Again' and 'I'm In Love'. She also worked with High Power, resulting in the concur-

rent release of 'Prisoner Of Love'. In 1990 she topped the reggae charts in combination with CJ Lewis, performing a version of the 60s hit from **Keith And Enid**, 'Worried Over You'. Lee Davis's success led to a four-album contract with **Island Records**, and although no album surfaced, the label released 'Spoilt By Your Love' and 'Pleasure Seekers'. The Island sessions were supervised by **Barry Boom**, who released 'Just The Lonely Talking Again', 'Love Is Alive', 'Never Say Never' and the classic 'Hello Stranger'. Following from his success with the late **Deborahe Glasgow**, **Gussie Clarke** recruited Lee Davis to perform backing vocals on **Cocoa Tea**'s *Authorised* and released her solo hit, 'Oops There Goes My Heart'. Following from her disappointing brush with the majors she returned to Fashion, secure in the knowledge that she could compete on the wider market while maintaining her credibility within the reggae community. By 1992 she dominated the UK **lovers rock** scene with a continuous profile on the reggae chart, including the hits 'Ooh Baby Baby', 'Big Mistake', 'Ready To Learn' and another chart-topper, in combination with **Tippa Irie**, 'Baby I've Been Missing You'. Another DJ combination came with **General Levy** for a version of the Joya Landis Treasure Isle hit, 'Moonlight Lover'. In 1994 her series of Fashion hits surfaced on *Missing You*, alongside an array of self-composed new tracks and has proved to be an all-time classic in the lovers rock genre. In 1995 she was awarded a number of accolades including Best Female Singer and Best UK Album by the British Reggae Industry and the **Bob Marley** Award for Best Female Singer by the Black Arts, Sports And Enterprise Awards. By 1997 her quest for international recognition was almost complete, having been described as the 'queen' of contemporary lovers rock. Her collaboration with Mr. G Spot, **Wayne Marshall** and Barry Boom highlighted her songwriting, singing and DJ skills, as well as consolidating her reputation for sheer hard work and professionalism.

● ALBUMS: *Missing You* (Fashion 1994)★★★.

Lee, 'Little' Frankie

b. 29 April 1941, Mart, Texas, USA. Lee began singing as a child, encouraged by his grandmother and, after leaving school, he sang blues around the clubs in Houston, Texas, turning professional at the age of 22. He began recording in 1963 and had singles released on the Houston labels Great Scott and Peacock. After settling in the San Francisco bay area in 1973, he made singles for Elka and California Gold. Lee had tracks issued on several anthologies but had to wait until 1984 for the first complete album under his own name, recorded for the Hightone label. Lee admits to varied influences, including Reverend Claude Jeter, **Sam Cooke**, **Roy Acuff** and the **Everly Brothers**, although he has infused these elements into a strong southern soul/blues style.

● ALBUMS: *Face It!* (Hightone 1984)★★★.

Lee, Albert

b. 21 December 1943, Leominster, Herefordshire, England. Lee is a country rock guitarist of breathtaking ability. If a poll of polls were taken from leading guitarists in the field, Lee would be the likely winner. During the early 60s he was the guitarist in the R&B-influenced **Chris Farlowe** And The Thunderbirds. He departed in 1967, as by then offers of session work were pouring in. During that time he joined Country Fever, playing straight honky-tonk country music, before recording as **Poet And The One Man Band** with Chas Hodges (later of **Chas And Dave**). The unit evolved into **Heads Hands And Feet**, a highly respected band, playing country rock. It was during this stage in his career that Lee became a 'guitar hero'; he was able to play his Fender Telecaster at breakneck speed and emulate and outshine his American counterparts. Lee played with the **Crickets** in 1973-74 and spent an increasing amount of time in America, eventually moving out there. After appearing on a reunion album with Chris Farlowe in 1975, he joined **Emmylou Harris**'s Hot Band, replacing one of his heroes, the legendary **James Burton**. During the late 70s and early 80s Lee performed in touring bands with **Eric Clapton**, **Jackson Browne**, **Jerry Lee Lewis** and **Dave Edmunds**. His solo on 'Sweet Little Lisa' on Edmund's *Repeat When Necessary* is a superb example of the man's skill. Lee played a major part in the historic reunion of the **Everly Brothers** at London's Royal Albert Hall in 1983, and he continues to be a member of their regular touring band. He has made several solo albums which are impressive showcases for one of Britain's finest guitarists.

● ALBUMS: *Hiding* (A&M 1979)★★★★, *Albert Lee* (Polydor 1982)★★★, *Speechless* (MCA 1987)★★★, *Gagged But Not Bound* (MCA 1988)★★, *Black Claw And Country Fever* (Line 1991)★★, with Hogan's Heroes *Live At Montreux 1992* recording (Round Tower 1994)★★, *Undiscovered - The Early Years* (Diamond 1998)★★★.

● COMPILATIONS: *Country Guitar Man* (Magnum 1986)★★★.

Lee, Alvin

b. 19 December 1944, Nottingham, England. Guitarist Lee began his professional career in the Jaybirds, a beat trio popular both locally and in Hamburg, Germany. In 1966, an expanded line-up took a new name, **Ten Years After**, and in turn became one of Britain's leading blues/rock attractions with Lee's virtuoso solos its main attraction. His outside aspirations surfaced in 1973 with *On The Road To Freedom*, a collaboration with American Mylon Lefevre, which included support from **George Harrison**, **Steve Winwood** and **Mick Fleetwood**. When Ten Years After disbanded the following year, the guitarist formed Alvin Lee & Co. with Neil Hubbard (guitar), Tim Hinkley (keyboards), Mel Collins (saxophone), Alan Spenner (bass) and Ian Wallace (drums). Having recorded the live *In Flight*, Lee made the first of several changes in personnel, but

although he and Hinkley were joined by Andy Pyle (bass, ex-**Blodwyn Pig**) and Bryson Graham (drums) for *Pump Iron!*, the group struggled to find its niche with the advent of punk. Lee toured Europe fronting Ten Years Later (1978-80) and the Alvin Lee Band (1980-81), before founding a new quartet, known simply as Alvin Lee, with **Mick Taylor** (guitar, ex-**John Mayall; Rolling Stones**), Fuzzy Samuels (bass, ex-**Crosby, Stills, Nash And Young**) and Tom Compton (drums). This promising combination promoted *RX-5*, but later disbanded. In 1989, Lee reconvened the original line-up of Ten Years After to record *About Time*. Lee released *Zoom* in 1992 with Sequel Records, after finding the major companies were not interested. Although offering nothing new, it was a fresh and well-produced record, and featured George Harrison on backing vocals.

● ALBUMS: with Mylon Lefevre *On The Road To Freedom* (Columbia 1973)★★★, *In Flight* (Columbia 1975)★★★, *Pump Iron!* (Columbia 1975)★★, *Rocket Fuel* (Polydor 1978)★★, *Ride On* (Polydor 1979)★★★, *Free Fall* (Avatar 1980)★★, *RX-5* (Avatar 1981)★★★, *Detroit Diesel* (21 Records 1986)★★★, *Zoom* (Sequel 1992)★★, *Nineteen Ninety Four* (Magnum Music 1994)★★, *I Hear You Rockin'* (Viceroy 1994)★★★, *Going Back Home* (Blind Pig 1994)★★★, *Pure Blues* (Chrysalis 1995)★★★, *Sweetheart Of The Blues* (Delmark 1995)★★★, *Braille Blues Daddy* (Justin Time 1995)★★★.

Lee, Arthur

b. 1944, Memphis, Tennessee, USA. Lee's musical career began in Los Angeles with Arthur Lee And The LAGs. This instrumental group - Lee (organ), Johnny Echols (guitar), Alan Talbot (saxophone), Roland Davis (drums) - was inspired by **Booker T. And The MGs** as demonstrated by their lone single, 'The Ninth Wave' (1963). Lee also pursued a career as a songwriter, composing two surfing songs, 'White Caps' and 'Ski Surfin' Sanctuary', and 'My Diary', a local R&B hit for singer Rosa Lee Brooks which featured **Jimi Hendrix** on guitar. Lee then began an association with producer **Bob Keene**'s group of labels, writing 'I've Been Trying' for protégé Little Ray and performing 'Luci Baines' - 'Twist And Shout' clone, with a new group, the American Four. Lee also composed 'Everybody Jerk' and 'Slow Jerk' for a thriving bar-band, Ronnie And The Pomona Casuals. Both songs appeared on the unit's lone album and featured Lee on lead vocals. The all-pervasive success of the **Byrds** inspired Lee to form a folk rock band, initially dubbed the Grass Roots, but later known as **Love**. He led this erratically brilliant group throughout its tempestuous history, but temporarily abandoned the name in 1972 for his solo album, *Vindicator*. This energized set featured support from Band-Aid, which included Frank Fayad (bass), Don Poncher (drums) and guitarists Craig Tarwarter (Ex-**Daily Flash** and Jeff Simmons) and Charles Karp. The collection polarized opinion; some bemoaned its unsubtle approach, while others praised its exciting aggression. Lee then joined **Paul A. Rothschild**'s Buffalo label, but a completed album was shelved when the company folded. Lee subsequently resurrected Love. The singer resumed his solo career in 1977 with a four-track EP, which included the haunting 'I Do Wonder'. These tracks later formed the basis of a second album, *Arthur Lee*, but its newer material showed a sad lack of direction. The singer undertook another comeback in 1992 with *Arthur Lee And Love*, issued on the independent French outlet, New Rose. It included the captivating 'Five String Serenade', later covered by **Mazzy Star**, but the overall set was again marred by baffling inconsistancy. An attendent promotional tour provided flashes of Lee's former genius, particularly his appearance at the **Creation** label's 10th anniversary concert. In 1994 he formed yet another incarnation of Love, releasing 'Girl On Fire'/'Midnight Sun' on the independent Distortions label. He remains an enigmatic figure on America's West Coast and both he and his groups have retained their cult following. Any stable musical unions are unlikely as Lee now suffers from Parkinson's Disease. In 1996 he was imprisoned with an eight year sentence for threatening his neighbours with a gun.

● ALBUMS: *Vindicator* (A&M 1972)★★, *Arthur Lee* (Beggars Banquet 1981)★★, as Arthur Lee And Love *Arthur Lee And Love* (New Rose 1992)★★.

● FURTHER READING: *Arthur Lee: Love Story*, Ken Brooks.

Lee, Brenda

b. Brenda Mae Tarpley, 11 December 1944, Lithonia, Georgia, USA. Even in early adolescence, Lee had an adult husk of a voice that could slip from anguished intimacy through sleepy insinuation to raucous lust, even during 'Let's Jump The Broomstick', 'Speak To Me Pretty' and other jaunty classics that kept her in the hit parade from the mid-50s to 1965. Through local radio and, by 1956, wider exposure on **Red Foley**'s Ozark Jubilee broadcasts, 'Little Brenda Lee' was ensured enough airplay for her first single, a revival of **Hank Williams**' 'Jambalaya', to crack the US country chart before her *Billboard* Hot 100 debut with 1957's 'One Step At A Time'. The novelty of her extreme youth facilitated bigger triumphs for 'Little Miss Dynamite' with the million-selling 'Rockin' Around The Christmas Tree' and later bouncy rockers, before the next decade brought a greater proportion of heartbreak ballads, such as 'I'm Sorry' and 'Too Many Rivers' - plus an acting role in the children's fantasy movie *The Two Little Bears*. 1963 was another successful year - especially in the UK with the title song of *All Alone Am I*, 'Losing You' (a French translation), 'I Wonder' and 'As Usual' each entering the Top 20. While 1964 finished well with 'Is It True' and 'Christmas Will Be Just Another Lonely Day', only minor hits followed. Although she may have weathered prevailing fads, family commitments caused Lee to cut back on touring and record only intermittently after 1966's appositely titled *Bye Bye Blues*. Lee resurfaced in

1971 with a huge country hit in **Kris Kristofferson**'s 'Nobody Wins'; this and later recordings established her as a star of what was then one of the squarest seams of pop. When country gained a younger audience in the mid-80s, respect for its older practitioners found her guesting with **Loretta Lynn** and **Kitty Wells** on **k.d. lang**'s *Shadowland*. - produced in 1988 by **Owen Bradley** (who had also supervised many early Lee records). In Europe, Brenda Lee remained mostly a memory - albeit a pleasing one as shown by Coast To Coast's hit revival of 'Let's Jump The Broomstick', a high UK placing for 1980's *Little Miss Dynamite* greatest hits collection and Mel Smith And **Kim Wilde**'s 'Rockin' Around The Christmas Tree'. Lee is fortunate in having a large rock 'n' roll catalogue destined for immortality, in addition to her now high standing in the country music world. In 1993, billed as 'the biggest-selling female star in pop history', Brenda Lee toured the UK and played the London Palladium, headlining a nostalgia package that included **Chris Montez**, **Len Barry** and **Johnny Tillotson**. From her opening 'I'm So Excited', through to the closing 'Rockin' All Over The World', she fulfilled all expectations, and won standing ovations from packed houses. In keeping with many of their packages, the **Bear Family** box set is a superb retrospective.

● ALBUMS: *Grandma, What Great Songs You Sang* (Decca 1959)★★, *Brenda Lee* (Decca 1960)★★★★, *This Is ... Brenda* (Decca 1960)★★★★, *Miss Dynamite* (Brunswick 1961)★★★★, *Emotions* (Decca 1961)★★★, *All The Way* (Decca 1961)★★★, *Sincerely Brenda Lee* (Decca 1962)★★★★, *Brenda, That's All* (Decca 1962)★★★★, *All Alone Am I* (Decca 1963)★★★, *Let Me Sing* (Decca 1963)★★★, *Sings Songs Everybody Knows* (Decca 1964)★★★, *By Request* (Decca 1964)★★★, *Merry Christmas From Brenda Lee* (Decca 1964)★★★, *Top Teen Hits* (Decca 1964)★★★, *The Versatile Brenda Lee* (Decca 1965)★★★, *Too Many Rivers* (Decca 1965)★★★, *Bye Bye Blues* (Decca 1965)★★★, *Coming On Strong* (Decca 1966)★★★, *Call Me Brenda* (Decca 1967)★★★, *Reflections In Blue* (Decca 1967)★★★, *Good Life* (Decca 1967)★★★, with Tennessee Ernie Ford *The Show For Christmas Seals* (Decca 1968)★★★, with Pete Fountain *For The First Time* (Decca 1968)★★★, *Johnny One Time* (Decca 1969)★★★, *Memphis Portrait* (Decca 1970)★★★, *Let It Be Me* (Vocalion 1970)★★★, *A Whole Lotta* (MCA 1972)★★★, *Brenda* (MCA 1973)★★★, *New Sunrise* (MCA 1974)★★★, *Brenda Lee Now* (MCA 1975)★★★, *The LA Sessions* (MCA 1977)★★★, *Even Better* (MCA 1980)★★★, *Take Me Back* (MCA 1981)★★★, *Only When I Laugh* (MCA 1982)★★★, with Dolly Parton, Kris Kristofferson, Willie Nelson *The Winning Hand* (Monument 1983)★★★, *Feels So Right* (MCA 1985)★★★, *Brenda Lee* (Warners 1991)★★★, *A Brenda Lee Christmas* (Warners 1991)★★★, *Greatest Hits Live* (MCA 1992)★★★, *Coming On Strong* (Muskateer 1995)★★★.

● COMPILATIONS: *10 Golden Years* (Decca 1966)★★★, *The Brenda Lee Story - Her Greatest Hits* (MCA 1973)★★★★, *Little Miss Dynamite* (MCA 1976)★★★★, *Greatest Country Hits* (MCA 1982)★★★, *25th Anniversary* (MCA 1984)★★★★, *The Early Years* (MCA 1984)★★★, *The Golden*

Decade (Charly 1985)★★★★, *The Best Of Brenda Lee* (MCA 1986)★★★★, *Love Songs* (MCA 1986)★★★, *Brenda's Best* (Ce De 1989)★★★★, *Very Best Of Brenda Lee Volume 1* (MCA 1990)★★★★, *Very Best Of Brenda Lee Volume 2* (MCA 1990)★★★, *The Brenda Lee Anthology Volume One, 1956-1961* (MCA 1991)★★★★, *The Brenda Lee Anthology Volume Two, 1962-1980* (MCA 1991)★★★, *Little Miss Dynamite* 4-CD box set (Bear Family 1996)★★★★, *The EP Collection* (See For Miles 1996)★★★★.

Lee, Bunny

b. Edward O'Sullivan Lee, 23 August 1941, Jamaica, West Indies. Bunny Lee, aka Bunny and Striker, was introduced to the music business by vocalist **Derrick Morgan** in 1962. Morgan, at that time one of Jamaica's most prolific and successful performers, took Lee to producer/**sound system** operator **Duke Reid**, who gave him a job as record plugger for his Treasure Isle label. Following his stay with Reid, Lee began working with Ken Lack, erstwhile road manager for the **Skatalites** band. By 1966, Lack had started releasing records by **Ken Boothe**, the **Clarendonians**, **Max Romeo**, the Tartans, the **Heptones** and others. Lee's first production, 'Listen To The Beat' by Lloyd Jackson And The Groovers, was released on Lack's Caltone label in 1967. His first hit was 'Music Field' by **Roy Shirley** (1967), on the WIRL label. He then began releasing his productions on his own label, Lee's. He enjoyed local hits during 1967-68 with Derrick Morgan's 'Hold You Jack', **Slim Smith** And The **Uniques**' 'My Conversation', Lester Sterling and **Stranger Cole**'s 'Bangarang', **Pat Kelly**'s 'Little Boy Blue' and the Sensation's 'Long Time Me No See You Girl'. Lee's talent for producing music that was commercially and artistically satisfying ensured his position as the leading hitmaker in Jamaica by 1969. During the following four years Lee enjoyed hits with Slim Smith's 'Everybody Needs Love' (1969), Pat Kelly's 'How Long?' (1970), Delroy Wilson's 'Better Must Come' (1971) and the Jamaica Song Festival winner, **Eric Donaldson**'s 'Cherry Oh Baby' (1971), later a UK hit for **UB40**, and **John Holt**'s 'Stick By Me' (1972). By 1974 he was producing **Johnny Clarke** on a string of local hits, beginning with 'None Shall Escape The Judgement' and 'Move Out Of Babylon'. **Owen Grey** had showcased 'Bongo Natty' that same year, while 1975 saw **Cornell Campbell** release a series of strong-selling tunes, beginning with 'The Gorgon'. Lee, along with producer **Lee Perry** and engineer **King Tubby**, had changed the face of Jamaican music, breaking the dominance of the big producers such as **Coxsone Dodd** and Duke Reid. Bunny Lee's contribution had been to grasp the commercial opportunities created by technological innovations such as the multi-track studio. A rhythm track could be made that could then be used as the backing for many songs or 'versions', often remixed or 'dubbed'. In addition to King Tubby, engineers such as **King Jammy** and Philip Smith developed their talents on Bunny Lee productions. During the period 1969-77, Lee produced literally thousands of tracks - vocals, DJ records and dubs - with a wide range of artists. As well as those already mentioned, he produced music for singers, including **Jackie Edwards**, **Leroy Smart**, Linval Thompson, David Isaacs, **Alton Ellis**, Dave Barker, Ken Boothe and Frankie Jones, and for DJs such as **Dennis Alcapone**, **U-Roy**, **I. Roy**, **Prince Jazzbo**, U Brown, Big Joe, **Trinity**, **Dr. Alimantado**, Jah Stitch and **Tapper Zukie**, most with additional corresponding dub versions. The early 80s saw a reduction in output; Lee was hampered because he did not control his own studio, although he continued to release music through his connection with Count Shelley in London and New York. He bought **Joe Gibbs**' old studio in North Parade, Kingston, and released material in the late 80s using computer-generated rhythms, but seems content to hire his studio to newer producers.

● ALBUMS: *Leaping With Mr. Lee* (1968)★★★.
● COMPILATIONS: *Jumping With Mr Lee 1967-68* (Trojan 1989)★★★★.

Lee, Byron, And The Dragonaires

b. 27 June 1935, Jamaica, West Indies. Lee and his manager, Ronnie Nasralla, first put together the Dragonaires in 1956 and worked as a support act for touring singers including **Harry Belafonte**, and their debut single 'Dumplins' in 1960 was the first release on the UK's Blue Beat label (although it originally came out on his own Dragons Breath label in Jamaica). The 14-piece Dragonaires featured an ever fluctuating line-up and are often cited as one of Jamaica's first **ska** bands, although they were firmly an 'establishment' band and their success was largely due to Lee's business and political connections. They toured extensively in the West Indies, North America and Canada and did much to popularize the ska sound. In 1969 Lee bought out the old WIRL set-up and established Dynamic Sounds as the best equipped and most popular studio in the Caribbean. As well as supporting home-grown talent, visiting stars such as the **Rolling Stones**, **Eric Clapton** and **Paul Simon** recorded at Dynamic hoping for a piece of the reggae action. Lee still records occasionally but concentrates on the soca style these days.

● ALBUMS: *Rocksteady Explosion* (Trojan 1968; reissued as *Reggay Eyes*, Jamaican Gold 1993)★★★, *Reggae With Byron Lee* (Trojan 1969)★★★★, *Sparrow Meets The Dragon* (1970)★★★, *Reggae Roun' The World* (Dragon 1973)★★★, *Reggae Fever* (Polydor 1974)★★★★, *The Midas Touch* (Dragon 1975)★★★, *Mighty Sparrow* (Dynamic 1976)★★★, *Reggae International* (Dynamic 1976)★★★, *Six Million Dollar Man* (Dynamic 1976)★★★, *This Is Carnival* (Dynamic 1976)★★★, *Art Of Mas* (Dynamic 1977)★★★, *Jamaica's Golden Hits* (Stylus 1977)★★★, *More Carnival* (Dynamic 1978)★★★, *Carnival Experience* (Dynamic 1979)★★★, *Jamaican Ska* (Rhino 1980)★★★★, *Soft Lee Volume 3* (Vista 1983)★★★, *Soul-Ska* (Vista 1983)★★★★, *Best Of Carnival* (Dynamic 1984)★★★, *Jamaica's Golden Hits Volume 2* (Dynamic 1984)★★★, *Wine Miss Tiny* (Creole 1985)★★★, *Soca Girl* (Dynamic 1986)★★★, *Soca Thunder* (Dynamic

1987)★★★, *De Music Hot Mama* (Dynamic 1988)★★★, *Reggae Blast Off* (Trojan 1988)★★★, *Soca Bachannal* (Dynamic 1989)★★★, *Play Dynamite Ska* (Dr Buster Dynamite 1992)★★★, *Wine Down* (Dynamic 1992)★★★, *Play Dynamite Ska With The Jamaican Allstars* (Jamaican Gold 1994)★★★.

Lee, Coco

b. *c*.1974, USA. Pop singer Coco Lee entered the music industry within a year of leaving high school in Taiwan, discovering immediate commercial rewards in the process. Her break came during a graduation trip to Hong Kong, where he was entered in a local singing concert by her mother. Her rendition of **Whitney Houston**'s 'Run To You' won second place in the contest (there were 30,000 applicants) and a recording contract in 1994. Within a year and a half she had released some five albums for Fancy Pie, becoming one of a growing number of American-born Chinese to find success in the Asian music industry. The success of these endeavours produced an eight-album contract with Sony Music Taiwan in the summer of 1996.
● ALBUMS: *Brave Enough To Love* (Fancy Pie 1996)★★★★.

Lee, Curtis

b. 28 October 1941, Yuma, Arizona, USA. Lee was the beneficiary of two great 1961 productions by **Phil Spector**, 'Pretty Little Angel Eyes' (US Top 10) and 'Under The Moon Of Love' (US Top 50). In the UK, 'Pretty Little Angel Eyes' was a minor hit record, going no higher than 47 in 1961. Lee began his recording career in 1959, and the following year was signed by Dunes Records. Handsome and photogenic, Lee had a vocal approach close to the teen idols of the period. Spector's genius with the productions, besides his deft handling of the instrumental support, was to provide fills with strong doo-wop riffing from an R&B vocal group, the Halos, to produce two classic rock 'n' roll tunes. After Spector fell out with Dunes in 1961, Lee never had another hit although he made some highly regarded 'blue-eyed soul' records in the late 60s.

Lee, Dave

b. 12 August 1930, London, England. After winning a *Melody Maker* poll for his jazz piano playing while still in his mid-teens, Lee joined **Johnny Dankworth**'s band, later winning another poll in the same magazine. From the mid-50s and throughout the 60s, Lee was active in jazz, the musical theatre, television and films, contributing scores for several well-known films. In the early 80s Lee was sufficiently active on the jazz scene to be elected BBC Jazz Society Musician of the year, but begun to plan a 'jazz-only' radio station which, while not unusual in the USA, was unheard of in the UK. Against the odds and all expectations, Lee was successful, and in 1990, Jazz FM was on the air. Broadcasting to the Greater London area, Jazz FM made an important contribution to the hopes and aspirations of jazz musicians and broadcasters until financial pressures forced policy and other changes, after which Lee moved on to other ventures.
● ALBUMS: *Jazz Improvisations Of 'Our Man Crichton'* (1965)★★★.

Lee, Dickey

b. Richard Lipscombe, 21 September 1941, Memphis, Tennessee, USA. Lee was a country singer and composer whose most recorded composition was 'She Thinks I Still Care', made famous by **George Jones**. At high school in Memphis, he sang rock 'n' roll and recorded the **Elvis Presley**-influenced 'Dreamy Nights' and 'Good Lovin'' with the Collegiates for the local **Sun** label. When producer **Jack Clement** left Sun to set up his own studio in Beaumont, Texas, Lee went with him. There he concentrated on pop material, releasing an unsuccessful revival of the 1953 hit tune 'Oh Mein Papa', before recording his biggest success, the million-selling 'Patches' (1961). Produced by Clement, this lachrymose death-ballad was composed by **Barry Mann** and Larry Kolber. The follow-up, 'I Saw Linda Yesterday', was also a hit but Lee's later teen-ballads made little impact until another song about a deceased girlfriend, 'Laurie (Strange Things Happening)', reached the US Top 20 in 1965. By now, however, Lee was based in Nashville and had established himself as a successful country songwriter following Jones's 1962 hit version of 'She Thinks I Still Care'. Among the numerous artists who later recorded the song were Elvis Presley, **Michael Nesmith** and **Anne Murray**. During the late 60s and 70s Lee himself recorded for **RCA** and had a country number 1 with 'Never Ending Song Of Love' in 1971. In Britain, the song was a Top 10 hit for the **New Seekers**. Nearly 30 more singles by Lee were US country hits over the next decade. They included 'Rocky' (1975), 'Ashes Of Love' (1976), '9,999,999 Tears' (1976), 'It's Not Easy' (1978) and 'Lost In Love' (1980). Among those who successfully recorded Lee's compositions were **Don Williams**, **Glen Campbell** and **Brenda Lee**. He moved to **Mercury Records** in 1979.
● ALBUMS: *The Tale Of Patches* (Smash 1962)★★★, *Dickey Lee Sings Laurie And The Girl From Peyton Place* (TCF Hall 1965)★★, *Never Ending Song of Love* (RCA 1971)★★, *Crying Over You* (RCA 1972)★★★★, *Sparklin' Brown Eyes* (RCA 1973)★★★, *Rocky* (1975)★★★, *Ashes Of Love* (RCA 1976) *Angels, Roses And Rain* (RCA 1976)★★★, *Baby Bye Bye* (RCA 1977)★★★, *Dickey Lee* (Mercury 1980)★★★, *Everybody Loves A Winner* (Mercury 1981)★★★.

Lee, Ernie

b. Ernest Eli Cornelison, 12 April 1916, Berea, Kentucky, USA, d. 23 May 1991. His father was the jailer at Madison County jail and Lee was taught to play guitar by one of the convicts. He completed high school in 1934 and began to play local venues on a part-time basis, while maintaining a day-time job, until 1940. **John Lair**, the producer of *Renfro Valley Barn Dance*, heard him singing and when **Red Foley** (who also came from Berea) was unable to present a show, Lee, who was in the audience, was chosen to deputise. Lair was impressed and changing his name to Ernie Lee, he linked him with steel guitarist **Jerry Byrd** and gave them a regular spot on the programme as the Happy Valley Boys. They recorded eight sides for **RCA Bluebird** and stayed in Renfro Valley for four years. In 1944, they relocated to WJR Detroit, a more powerful station, and spent two years on the popular *Goodwill Frolic Gang*. In 1947, the duo split when Lee moved to WLW Cincinnati, where he appeared on several shows but most notably as a singer and compere of the station's noted *Midwestern Hayride*. He also worked on a series of networked programmes with Judy Perkins, Louis Innis and the Turner Brothers for the Mutual Broadcasting System. In 1951/2, when NBC networked the *Hayride* show, Lee was always a very popular performer. Between 1947 and 1950, he recorded for RCA Bluebird as Ernie Lee And His Midwesterners, gaining local success with such numbers as 'Headin' Home To Old Kentucky' and 'Hominy Grits'. In 1950, he recorded for **Mercury** being joined on some recordings by Byrd and the Turner Brothers. One Mercury single 'One Little Candle', even gained later release on the German Austroton label. In 1951, he made recordings for **MGM**. Lee was a keen angler and always wanted to live in Florida, where he could pursue this sport and enjoy the warm climate. When in 1954, he was offered a daily radio and television show on WSUN St. Peterburg, he relocated to that State. In 1958, he moved to WTVT Tampa. For over 30 years, he became the major country music figure in Florida. He invited acts from the *Hayride* days to appear with him, played venues all over the State and was always the expected headline act at the annual State Fair. In 1961, he recorded an album on his own label for sale at his shows. In 1965 and 1979, he suffered serious health problems but recovered each time sufficiently to continue performing until 23 May 1991, when he died following a stroke. He left a widow, Jean and three sons, Gordon, Sam and Stephen. Lee was a talented performer who avoided the problems encountered by many of his contemporaries. He was unfortunate to never find the one record that would have started to turn his local into national success. He sang as well, arguably better, than Foley and possessed an equal ability to host radio and television shows but somehow national stardom sadly eluded him. In 1997, a compilation of 20 of his Bluebird, Mercury and MGM recordings were issued on CD by a German label.

● ALBUMS: *Ernie Lee's Big Thirteen* (Ernie Lee 1961)★★★.

● COMPILATIONS: *Ernie Lee - The Kentucky Balladeer* (Bronco Buster 1997)★★★.

Lee, George E.

(see **Lee, Julia**; **Kansas City Jazz**)

Lee, Jackie (Eire)

b. 29 May 1936, Dublin, Eire. A great lover of pseudonyms, Lee began her career touring Ireland under the billing 'Child Star'. In 1956, she made her recording debut with 'The Outskirts Of Paris' and by the end of the decade had joined the Squadronaires showband. After several years on the road, she married musician Len Beadle in 1963 and together they formed Jackie And The Raindrops. Two years later, she went solo again for the tear-jerker, 'I Cry Alone'. In 1967, she was relaunched as Emma Rede but failed with 'Just Like A Man'. By now, she had recorded for **Columbia**, **Decca**, **Polydor** and **CBS**, but it was with Philips that she finally found chart success courtesy of 'White Horses', the theme from a UK children's television series. The single was recorded under the name Jacky and its success coincided with a serious assault on the US market via film soundtrack recordings. Most notable among these was Lee's contribution to the 1968 film *Barbarella*, in which she sang over the credits. Dismissed as a 60s one-hit-wonder, she defied the odds by signing to her umpteenth label, Pye, reverting to her real name and winning through with yet another children's song, 'Rupert', in 1971.

Lee, Jackie (USA)

b. Earl Nelson, 8 September 1928, Lake Charles, Louisiana, USA. Lee had an impressive success in 1965 with the dance hit 'The Duck' (number 4 R&B, number 14 pop), but his presence in the R&B scene was far more ubiquitous than was indicated by that one hit. He sang lead on the **Hollywood Flames**' hit, 'Buzz Buzz Buzz', and was part of the duo of **Bob And Earl** that had a hit with 'Harlem Shuffle' (number 3 R&B, number 44 pop) in 1964. After 'The Duck', a follow-up, 'Would You Believe', did not make any of the national charts but was highly successful in regional markets across the USA. Lee had a minor success with 'African Boo-Ga-Loo' in 1968 and his last chart record was 'The Chicken' in 1970.

● ALBUMS: *The Duck* (Mirwood 1965)★★.

Lee, Jeanne

b. 29 January 1939, New York City, New York, USA. Lee studied modern dance at Bard College (1956-60), where she met **Ran Blake**. They began to work as a duo, with Lee improvising on vocals, recording together in 1961 (*The Newest Sound Around*) and toured Europe in 1963. In 1964, she moved to California and married the sound-poet David Hazelton. Returning to Europe in 1967, she began a long association with **Gunter Hampel**, recording with him on his Birth label on numerous occasions over the next two decades (*The 9th July 1969*, *Spirits* in 1971, *Journey To The Song Within* in 1974, *Fresh Heat* in 1985), including one entirely improvised session with him and **Anthony Braxton** in 1972. Although a striking singer in conventional terms, with a strong, husky voice, Lee developed a new, inventive approach to vocals, often improvising wordlessly and using lip, throat and mouth sounds rather than standard pitches. In the 60s and 70s she was a prominent member of the jazz *avant garde*, working with fellow pioneers **Archie Shepp** (*Blasé*), **Marion Brown** (*Afternoon Of A Georgia Faun*), Braxton again (*Town Hall 1972*) and **Enrico Rava**, as well as recording her own *Conspiracy* and, later, in a trio with **Andrew Cyrille** and **Jimmy Lyons**. In the 80s and 90s she has worked with the group Vocal Summit (with **Bobby McFerrin**, Lauren Newton, **Urszula Dudziak** and Jay Clayton) and with the **Reggie Workman** Ensemble (*Images*), but has concentrated more on writing her own material. Her works include a five-part suite, *Emergence*, and a ten-act oratorio, *A Prayer For Our Time*. In 1990, she again recorded a duo album with Blake, with whom she has been teaching in the Third Stream department of the New England Conservatory of Music since 1976.

● ALBUMS: with Ran Blake *The Newest Sound Around* (1961)★★★, *The Gunter Hampel Group Und Jeanne Lee* (1969)★★★★, with Hampel, Anthony Braxton *Familie* (1972)★★★★, *Conspiracy* (1974)★★★, with Andrew Cyrille, Jimmy Lyons *Nuba* (1979)★★★, with Vocal Summit *Sorrow Is Not Forever - Love Is* (1983)★★★, with Blake *You Stepped Out Of A Cloud* (1990)★★★, *Natural Affinities* (Owl 1992)★★★.

Lee, Joe, And Jimmy Strothers

Lee was 71 years old when he and Strothers recorded for the Library of Congress in 1936; both men were inmates of the Virginia State Farm at Lynn. Lee sang 11 unaccompanied spirituals with great intensity, and duetted with Strothers on 'Do Lord Remember Me', on which he also played the fingerboard of Strothers' guitar with two straws, while the latter played in the orthodox fashion. Strothers, who also played banjo, was a street and medicine show entertainer who had been blinded in an explosion (and was serving time for killing his wife with an axe). His repertoire of blues, work songs, dance tunes, gospel, humorous songs (including obscenity) and a protest song about the contract labour system, forms a most important body of black music.

● ALBUMS: *Negro Religious Songs and Services* (1960)★★★, *Red River Runs* (1979)★★★.

Lee, John

b. John Arthur Lee, 24 May 1915, Mt. Willing, Alabama, USA. Few post-war country blues tracks merit the description 'masterpiece', but John Lee's July 1951 recording of 'Down At The Depot' deserves the accolade. In essence a standard train blues, it is elevated by his propulsive slide guitar playing and keening vocal. Lee came from a musical family, in which all seven brothers, a sister and both parents played guitar. However, the significant influence on his playing was Uncle Ellie Lee, renowned in Evergreen, Alabama, as its finest exponent of slide technique, using a knife rather than a bottleneck. Both 'Down At The Depot' and the equally impressive 'Blind Blues' bear witness to his tutelage. Lee was also influenced by Brewton musician Levi Kelley. He supplemented practical instruction with

the records of **Blind Blake**, **Blind Lemon Jefferson** and **Leroy Carr**. Moving to Montgomery in 1945, he soon had, by his own estimation, 'the town sewed up' when it came to playing at house parties and suppers. In 1951 he heard talent scout **Ralph Bass** advertise for talent on WMGY radio; four of the six songs he recorded were released on two Federal singles, representing some of the last instances of country blues being issued on a major label. Lee retired from active performance in 1960. He was rediscovered in 1973 after a three-year search and recorded sessions in Montgomery and Cambridge, Massachusetts, at which he revealed an equally individual piano style.

● ALBUMS: *Down At The Depot* (Rounder 1974)★★★.

Lee, Johnny

b. John Lee Ham, 3 July 1946, Texas City, Texas, USA. Lee was raised on a dairy farm in Alta Loma, Texas, but his main interest was rock 'n' roll and he led a high school band, Johnny Lee And the Roadrunners. He worked through the 60s by playing popular hits in Texas clubs and bars. In 1968, he began a 10-year working relationship with **Mickey Gilley**, both on the road and at his club Gilley's in Pasadena. He had moderate US country successes in the mid-70s with 'Sometimes', 'Red Sails In The Sunset' and 'Country Party', and appeared in the 1979 television movie *The Girls In The Office*. Lee was featured in the film *Urban Cowboy*, which was shot at Gilley's, and in 1980, he had a US number 1 country single and US Top 5 pop hit with a song from the film, 'Lookin' For Love', which had previously been turned down by 20 different performers. Further number 1 country hits came with 'One In A Million' and 'Bet Your Heart On Me'. Another US country hit, 'Cherokee Fiddle', featured **Michael Martin Murphey** and **Charlie Daniels**. Lee married actress Charlene Tilton (who played Lucy in the television series *Dallas*) on St. Valentine's Day 1982 in a much-publicized wedding at **Tony Orlando**'s house, with Gilley as best man. Lee contributed a track, 'Lucy's Eyes', to an album by the stars of *Dallas*. However, their stormy marriage only lasted three years and Lee remarried in 1987. He had a further number 1 country single with a theme from a short-lived television soap opera, *The Yellow Rose*, with actress-singer Lane Brody, who was in the country music film *Tender Mercies*. His final solo number 1 country single was with 'You Could've Heard A Heart Break' in 1984. Lee was in the right place at the right time, but unfortunately for him, a stringent management contract meant that he enjoyed very few financial rewards. Setting up a rival club to Gilley's, called Johnny Lee's, was not a wise career move. He reappeared in 1991 with a country version of **Chris De Burgh**'s 'Lady in Red'.

● ALBUMS: *For Lovers Only* (JMS 1977)★★, *Lookin' For Love* (Asylum 1980)★★★, *Bet Your Heart On Me* (Full Moon 1981)★★, *Party Time* (Full Moon 1981)★★, *Sounds Like Love* (Full Moon 1982)★★★, *Country Party* (Full Moon 1983)★★★, *Hey Bartender* (Full Moon 1983)★★★, *Till The*

Bars Burn Down (Full Moon 1983)★★★, *Workin' For A Livin'* (1984)★★★, with Willie Nelson *Johnny Lee And Willie Nelson* (Astan 1984)★★★, *Keep Me Hangin' On* (1985)★★★, *New Directions* (Curb 1989)★★.

● COMPILATIONS: *Greatest Hits* (Full Moon 1983)★★★.

● FURTHER READING: *Looking For Love*, Johnny Lee with Randy Wiles.

Lee, Julia

b. 13 October 1903, Booneville, Missouri, USA, d. 8 December 1958. Beginning her career as a pianist and singer while in her early teens, Lee joined a band led by her brother, George E. Lee (1896-1958), a popular vocalist whose 'Novelty Singing Orchestra' played extensively in and around Kansas City. Despite the musical advances being made by other **Kansas City Jazz** bands of the time, notably the Lees' great rival, **Bennie Moten**, they retained their popularity into the mid-30s. After her brother's retirement, Julia Lee continued her career as a solo artist, enjoying a resurgence of popularity during the blues revival of the early and mid-40s. Her recordings of these and the following few years feature leading jazz musicians, including **Benny Carter** and **Red Norvo**. An effective if sometimes unprofound performer of the blues, and a disarming singer of popular songs of the day, Lee was well-placed to adapt to the growing public interest in R&B. However, her decision to spend most of her career in Kansas City rather than New York or Los Angeles, where R&B really took off, meant that she was far more unfamiliar to the wider public than many less talented singer-pianists of her generation.

● COMPILATIONS: *Tonight's The Night (1944-52)* (1982)★★★★, *Party Time (1946-52)* (1983)★★★★, *Ugly Papa (1945-52)* (1987)★★★★, *Snatch And Grab It* (1987)★★★, *A Porter's Love Songs* (1988)★★★, *Of Lions And Lambs* (1988)★★★.

Lee, Laura

b. Laura Lee Newton, 9 March 1945, Chicago, Illinois, USA. A member of her adopted mother's, Ernestine Rundless's, gospel group the Meditation Singers, Lee's first secular recording was made for the Detroit-based Ric-Tic label. She was signed to **Chess Records** in 1966, who, after failing to find success with a Chicago-recorded single, sent her to Rick Hall's Fame Studio in Muscle Shoals where 'Dirty Man' and the Fame-cut 'Uptight Good Man' became two 1967 R&B hits. She recorded many fine, assertive sides for Chess, before beginning her most prolific period when she joined Hot Wax, one of the companies founded by the **Holland/Dozier/Holland** songwriting team. 'Wedlock Is A Padlock', 'Women's Love Rights' (both 1970), 'Rip Off' and 'If You Can Beat Me Rockin' (You Can Have My Chair)' (both 1972), continued the singer's uncompromising demands, but such declarations were inverted on 'I'll Catch You When You Fall' (1973) and 'I Can't Make It Alone' (1974) as Lee broadened her canvas. The singer left the HDH stable in 1975, but

despite enjoying an R&B hit with 'You're Barking Up The Wrong Tree' (1976), her later output was largely unsuccessful. Laura Lee returned to the gospel field in 1983 with *Jesus Is The Light Of My Life*, which she co-produced with singer **Al Green**.

● ALBUMS: *Women's Love Rights* (Hot Wax 1971)★★★, *The Two Sides Of Laura Lee* (Hot Wax 1972)★★★, *I Can't Make It Alone* (Invictus 1974)★★★, *Jesus Is The Light Of My Life* (1983)★★★.

● COMPILATIONS: *Best Of ...* (1972)★★★, *Love More Than Pride* (1972)★★★, *The Rip Off* (HDH 1984)★★★, *Uptight Good Woman* (1984)★★★, *That's How It Is - The Chess Years* (Chess/MCA 1990)★★★, *Greatest Hits* (HDH/Fantasy 1991)★★★, *Love Rights And Wrongs* (Deep Beats 1997)★★★.

Lee, Leapy

b. Lee Graham, 2 July 1942, Eastbourne, England. One of the troubled stars of British 60s pop, Lee's career took a surprise upswing when he moved from **Kinks** co-manager Robert Wace to the charismatic **Gordon Mills**. The latter produced the catchy 'Little Arrows', which narrowly failed to reach the UK number 1 spot. A minor hit with 'Good Morning' and a suitably broad showbusiness repertoire should have served Leapy well, but his waywardness proved his undoing. He began drinking with East End villains and befriended starlet Diana Dors and her husband Alan Lake. One evening at a pub in Sunnydale, Lake and Lee were involved in a fracas during which a publican was slashed across the wrist with a flick knife. Leapy was arrested, charged and suffered the indignity of a jail sentence which seriously put back his career, although Mills occasionally employed him as a producer. Lee eventually left the UK to sing in bars in Majorca, Spain.

Lee, Lovie

b. Edward Lee Watson, 17 March 1909, Chattanooga, Tennessee, USA, d. 23 May 1997, Chicago, Illinois, USA. A nickname bestowed in infancy has its drawbacks in later life, especially if you're a member of **Muddy Waters**' band. With his seven brothers and sisters, Lee moved to Meridian, Mississippi, when he was 12 years old. There he learned to play the piano in his grandfather Henry Austin's restaurant, coming under the influence of Cap King, the area's principal barrelhouse musician. From 1940-57, Lee worked at a woodworking factory and led Lovie's Swinging Cats, playing at fairs and clubs around Meridian. In 1951, he took in **Carey Bell**, then a 14-year-old runaway, whom he coached in his harmonica playing. In 1957 Lee brought Bell to Chicago, where they discovered that work was not as plentiful as they had expected. Lee took a job at the Brody Seating Company and formed a band called the Sensationals, using guitarists **Lee Jackson** and Byther Smith at different times. They played west and south side clubs, including Cinderella's, Florence's and Porter's Lounge. He had retired from his day job when he received a phone call from Muddy Waters asking him to join what would prove to be his last band, along with 'Mojo' George Buford, John Primer, Earnest Johnson and Jesse Clay. In the late 70s, he began to release cassettes of his own music, and had a session released on Alligator's Living Chicago Blues series. Tracks from his own releases formed part of *Good Candy*, along with a 1992 session featuring Carey and Lurrie Bell, and offered an engaging portrait of a minor talent.

● ALBUMS: *Lovie's Music* cassette (Blues On Blues 1978)★★★, *Living Chicago Blues Volume 3* (Alligator 1978/1991)★★★, *Lovie's Music 2* cassette (Blues On Blues 1979)★★★, *Lovie Lee* cassette (Blues On Blues 1992)★★★, *Good Candy* (Earwig 1994)★★★.

Lee, Peggy

b. Norma Deloris Egstrom, 26 May 1920, Jamestown, North Dakota, USA. Lee is of Scandinavian descent, her grandparents being Swedish and Norwegian immigrants. She endured a difficult childhood and her mother died when she was four; when her father remarried she experienced a decidedly unpleasant relationship with her stepmother. Her father took to drink, and at the age of 14 she found herself carrying out his duties at the local railroad depot. Despite these and other hardships, she sang frequently and appeared on a local radio station. She took a job as a waitress in Fargo, where the manager of the radio station changed her name to Peggy Lee. In 1937, she took a trip to California to try her luck there but soon returned to Fargo. Another California visit was equally unsuccessful and she then tried Chicago where, in 1941, as a member of a vocal group, The Four Of Us, she was hired to sing at the Ambassador West Hotel. During this engagement she was heard by Mel Powell, who invited Benny Goodman to hear her. Goodman's regular singer, Helen Forrest, was about to leave and Lee was hired as her replacement. She joined the band for an engagement at the College Inn and within a few days sang on a record date. A song from this period, 'Elmer's Tune', was a huge success. Among other popular recordings she made with Goodman were 'How Deep Is The Ocean?', 'How Long Has This Been Going On?', 'My Old Flame' and 'Why Don't You Do Right?'. Later, Lee married Goodman's guitarist, Dave Barbour. After she left Goodman's band in 1943, she had more successful records, including 'That Old Feeling' and three songs of which she was co-composer with Barbour, 'It's A Good Day', 'Don't Know Enough About You' and 'Mañana'. She also performed on radio with Bing Crosby. In the 50s she made several popular recordings for Capitol, the orchestral backings for many of which were arranged and conducted by Barbour, with whom she maintained a good relationship despite their divorce in 1952. Her 1958 hit single 'Fever' was also a collaboration with Barbour. Her *Black Coffee* album of 1953 was particularly successful, as was *Beauty And The Beat* a few years later. On these and other albums of the period, Lee was often accompanied by jazz musicians, including Jimmy Rowles, Marty Paich and George

Shearing. During the 50s Lee was also active in films, performing the title song of *Johnny Guitar* (1954), and writing songs for others including *Tom Thumb* (1958). She also made a number of on-screen appearances in acting roles, including *The Jazz Singer* (1953), and for one, *Pete Kelly's Blues* (1955), she was nominated for an Academy Award as Best Supporting Actress. However, her most lasting fame in films lies in her off-screen work on Walt Disney's *Lady And The Tramp* (1955), for which Lee wrote the song 'He's A Tramp' and provided the voice for the characters of 'Peg', the Siamese cats, and one other screen feline. Her recording successes continued throughout this period even if, on some occasions, she had to fight to persuade Capitol to record them. One such argument surrounded 'Lover', which executives felt would compete directly with the label's then popular version by Les Paul. Lee won out and her performance of her own arrangement, played by a studio orchestra under the direction of Gordon Jenkins, was a sensation. Towards the end of the 50s, the intense level of work began to take its toll and she suffered a period of illness. Throughout the 60s and succeeding decades Lee performed extensively, singing at concerts and on television and, of course, making records, despite being frequently plagued with poor health. Her voice is light with a delicate huskiness, offering intriguing contrasts with the large orchestral accompaniment that is usually a part of a Lee performance. Over the years her repeated use of previously successful settings for songs has tended to make her shows predictable but she remains a dedicated perfectionist in everything that she does. In the early 80s she attempted a stage show, *Peg*, but it proved unpopular and closed quickly. In the late 80s she again suffered ill health and on some of her live performances her voice was starting to betray the ravages of time. For her many fans, it did not seem to matter: to paraphrase the title of one of her songs, they just loved being there with Peg. In 1992, wheelchair-bound for the previous two years, Lee was persisting in a lawsuit, begun in 1987, against the Walt Disney Corporation for her share of the video profits from *Lady And The Tramp*. A year later, dissatisfied with the 'paltry' £2 million settlement for her six songs (written with Sonny Burke) and character voices, she was preparing to write a book about the whole affair. Meanwhile, she continued to make occasional cabaret appearances at New York venues such as Club 53. In 1993 she recorded a duet with Gilbert O'Sullivan for his album *Sounds Of The Loop*. Lee is one of the greatest 'classy' vocalists of the century, alongside such stellar artists such as Ella Fitzgerald, Billie Holiday, Sarah Vaughan and Betty Carter.

● ALBUMS: with Benny Goodman *Benny Goodman And Peggy Lee* (Columbia 1949)★★★, *Rendezvous* (Capitol 1952)★★★, *My Best To You* (Capitol 1952)★★★, *Song In Intimate Style* (Decca 1953)★★★, *Black Coffee* (Decca 1953)★★★★★, *White Christmas* film soundtrack (Decca 1954)★★★★, *The Lady And The Tramp* film soundtrack (Decca 1955)★★★★, with Ella Fitzgerald *Songs From Pete*

Kelly's Blues film soundtrack (Decca 1955)★★★, *Dream Street* (Decca 1956)★★★, *The Man I Love* (Capitol 1957)★★★★, *Jump For Joy* (Capitol 1958)★★★, *Sea Shells* (Decca 1958)★★★, *Things Are Swingin'* (Capitol 1958)★★★★, with George Shearing *Beauty And The Beat* (Capitol 1959)★★★★, *I Like Men* (Capitol 1959)★★★, *Miss Wonderful* (Capitol 1959)★★★, *Pretty Eyes* (Capitol 1960)★★★, *Alright, Okay, You Win* (Capitol 1960)★★★, *Latin A La Lee!* (Capitol 1960)★★★, *All Aglow Again* (Capitol 1960)★★★, *Olé A La Lee* (Capitol 1960)★★★, *Christmas Carousel* (Capitol 1960)★★★, *At Basin Street East* (Capitol 1960)★★★, *Blues Cross Country* (Capitol 1961)★★★, *If You Go* (Capitol 1961)★★★, *Sugar 'N' Spice* (Capitol 1962)★★★, *I'm A Woman* (Capitol 1963)★★★, *Mink Jazz* (Capitol 1963)★★★, *In Love Again* (Capitol 1963)★★★, *Lover* (Decca 1964)★★★, *In The Name Of Love* (Capitol 1964)★★★, *Pass Me By* (Capitol 1965)★★★, *That Was Then, This Is Now* (Capitol 1965)★★★, *Big Spender* (Capitol 1966)★★★, *Extra Special* (Capitol 1967)★★★, *Guitars A La Lee* (Capitol 1967)★★★, *Is That All There Is?* (Capitol 1969)★★★, *Bridge Over Troubled Water* (Capitol 1970)★★★, *Make It With You* (Capitol 1970)★★★, *Let's Love* (Atlantic 1974)★★★, *Mirrors* (A&M 1976)★★★, *Close Enough For Love* (DRG 1979)★★★, *Miss Peggy Lee Sings The Blues* (Music Masters 1988)★★★, *The Peggy Lee Songbook: There'll Be Another Spring* (Musicmasters 1990)★★★, with Quincy Jones *P'S & Q'S* (1992)★★★, *Love Held Lightly* (1993)★★★, *Moments Like This* (1993)★★★, *If I Could Be With You* 1951-52 recordings (1993)★★★.

● COMPILATIONS: *Bewitching-Lee!* (Capitol 1962)★★★★, *The Best Of Peggy Lee* (MCA 1980)★★★★, *Peggy Lee Sings With Benny Goodman (1941-43)* (Columbia 1984)★★★★, *The Peggy Lee Collection - 20 Golden Greats* (MCA 1985)★★★★, *Unforgettable: Peggy Lee* (Unforgettable/Castle 1987)★★★, *The Capitol Years* (Capitol 1988)★★★★, *Capitol Collectors Series: The Early Years* (Capitol 1990)★★★, *All-Time Greatest Hits* (Curb 1990)★★★, *Peggy Lee - Fever* (1992)★★★★, *The Best Of* (1993)★★★★, with Bing Crosby *It's A Good Day* (1993)★★★, *The Best Of Peggy Lee, 1952-1956* (Music Club 1994)★★★★, *EMI Presents The Magic Of Peggy Lee* (EMI 1997)★★★★, *Black Coffee: The Best Of The Decca Years* (Half Moon 1998)★★★★, *Miss Peggy Lee* 4-CD box set (Capitol 1998)★★★★.

● VIDEOS: *Quintessential* (Hendring 1989).

● FURTHER READING: *Miss Peggy Lee*, Peggy Lee.

Lee, Phil

b. 8 April 1943, London, England. Lee's parents were musical, but he is a self-taught guitarist. He was a member of the group that Ivor Mairants (guitar) took to the Antibes Jazz Festival in the mid-60s, and worked with the John Williams Big Band. He first came to prominence with the **Graham Collier** Septet. He became co-leader with **Tony Coe** (reeds) of Axel while freelancing with musicians like **Henry Thomas Lowther**, **Michael Garrick** and **Jeff Clyne**. He played in and wrote for the band **Paz** formed by Dick Crouch (vibes) in 1972. Later he toured with **Michel Legrand**'s Quartet (1979) and **Gordon Beck**'s Nonet (1983). In 1991, he played with Michael Garrick's Big Band in performances of Garrick's suite Hardy Country.

● ALBUMS: with Graham Collier *Deep Dark Blue Centre* (1967)★★, with Tony Coe *Zeitgeist* (1976)★★★★, with Gilgamesh *Gilgamesh* (1975)★★★, *Another Fine Tune I've Got You Into* (1978)★★★, with Andres Boiarsky *Play South Of The Border* (1980)★★★.

Lee, Ranee

b. Canada. A gifted singer with a growing maturity of style and purpose, Lee first attracted international attention when she played the 1992 Nice Jazz Festival. Until that time, her performances were sometimes overly energetic with a deliberately tough and raunchy manner. That same year, she appeared in the Canadian film *Giant Steps*. During the early 90s, Lee's style displayed much greater subtlety and an acute awareness of the needs of the music. Her voice is full and mellow, with delicate shadings on ballads and an easy sense of swing on mid- and up-tempo songs. She has recorded with a number of leading jazzmen including **Ray Brown**, **Pat LaBarbera** and **Ed Thigpen**.

● ALBUMS: *Live At Le Bijou* (Justin Time 1983)★★★, *You Must Believe In Swing* (Justin Time 1996)★★★★, *Seasons Of Love* (Justin Time 1997)★★★.

Lee, Robin

b. Robin Lee Irwin, 7 November 1953, Nashville, Tennessee, USA. In spite of early glowing praise for her vocal abilities from some critics, Lee has so far failed to establish herself as a top country singer. Between 1983 and 1988, she charted 13 minor *Billboard* country chart hits, one, 'Paint The Town Blue', being a duet with **Lobo**. Most were on the Evergreen label, but in 1990, her **Atlantic** recording of 'Black Velvet' (a song about **Elvis Presley** that was a 1990 number 1 hit for **Alannah Myles**), peaked at number 10. However, she failed to maintain that standard and by the mid-90s she had only managed three more minor chart entries, the last, 'Nothin' But You', a modest number 51 in 1991.

● ALBUMS: *Evergreen* (Atlantic 1986)★★★, *Black Velvet* (Atlantic 1990)★★★, *Heart On A Chain* (Atlantic 1991)★★, *This Old Flame* (Atlantic 1994)★★.

Lee, Will

b. 8 September 1950, San Antonio, Texas, USA. Lee studied jazz at the University of Miami before coming to New York. He played bass with **Randy** and **Michael Brecker** in **Billy Cobham**'s band Dreams (1971). From 1973 he has worked in the studios with an enormous variety of musicians including **Larry Coryell**, **David Sanborn**, **Herbie Mann**, **George Benson** and **Maynard Ferguson**.

Leecan, Bobby, And Robert Cooksey

Both b. USA. Bobby Leecan was a fine and fluent single string guitarist, banjoist and an occasional kazooist and vocalist. He made most of his recordings in the company of Robert Cooksey, whose rather sweet, warbling harmonica favoured clear tone production rather than the slurs and bends of most blues players. Their output lies in the borderland between blues, vaudeville and jazz, ranging from 'Dirty Guitar Blues' to 'Ain't She Sweet', and blending easily with the jazz cornet of Tom Morris. Some sources suggest that they were based in Philadelphia.

● ALBUMS: *The Remaining Titles* (Matchbox 1986)★★★, *The Blues Of Bobbie Leecan & Robert Cooksey* (Collector's Classics 1988)★★★.

Leeman, Cliff

b. 10 September 1913, Portland, Maine, USA, d. 26 April 1986. After playing in the percussion section of a local symphony orchestra, Leeman turned to dance-band and jazz drumming as a career. In 1936, he joined **Artie Shaw**, playing an important role in the band's swing era success story. After leaving Shaw, he played in several leading big bands, including those led by **Tommy Dorsey**, **Charlie Barnet** and **Woody Herman**. In the late 40s, as the big bands became fewer, Leeman played in many small groups along New York's 52nd Street, returning briefly to big band work whenever opportunities were offered. In the 50s he worked in the studios but continued to play in jazz groups, usually those with a traditional bent. During this and the following decade he worked with **Big Joe Turner**, (appearing on the singer's classic *Boss Of The Blues*), **Eddie Condon**, **Ralph Sutton** (with whom he recorded a duo album, *I Got Rhythm*), **Wild Bill Davison**, **Yank Lawson** and **Bob Haggart**. In the 70s he toured extensively, including a trip to Japan with Condon and an all-star band that featured **Buck Clayton**, **Pee Wee Russell** and **Jimmy Rushing**. Leeman also recorded with **Bobby Hackett**, **Bud Freeman**, **Don Ewell**, **Joe Venuti**, **Zoot Sims** and Lawson and Haggart's group, the **World's Greatest Jazz Band**. A powerful yet self-effacing big band drummer and a subtly encouraging small group player, Leeman's work was always exemplary. In the dixieland bands, with which he spent many of his later years, he played with zesty enthusiasm. In all of these settings his playing maintained a standard which should have eclipsed many of his better-known contemporaries. Sadly, he was the one who was often overshadowed and he remains one of the unsung heroes of jazz drumming.

● ALBUMS: *I Got Rhythm* (1953),★★★ with Joe Turner *The Boss Of The Blues* (1956)★★★★, *Eddie Condon In Japan* (1964)★★★, with Bobby Hackett *String Of Pearls* (1970)★★★★, with Hackett *Live At The Roosevelt Grill Vols. 1-4* (1970)★★★, with Joe Venuti, Zoot Sims *Joe And Zoot* (1974★★★, with Bud Freeman *The Joy Of Sax* (1974)★★★.

● COMPILATIONS: *The Indispensable Artie Shaw Vols. 1/2 (1938-39)* (RCA 1986)★★★.

Leeman, Mark, Five

A popular attraction in London's clubs, the Mark Leeman Five made their debut in January 1965 with the **Manfred Mann**-produced 'Portland Town'. Mark Leeman (vocals/guitar), Alan Roskams (lead guitar),

Terry Goldberg (keyboards), David Hyde (bass) and Brian 'Blinky' Davidson (drums) showed an impressive, almost 'progressive' grasp of R&B, a feature confirmed on their next release 'Blow My Blues Away'. Leeman was killed in a car crash in June 1965 and his place was taken by former Cheynes frontman Roger Peacock. Thomas Parker then replaced Goldberg, but despite two further excellent singles, the quintet was unable to achieve chart success. Peacock left for a solo career in July 1966 and although the remaining musicians were augmented by Pete Hodges (vocals) and Pat 'Rave' Sandy (saxophone), the group subsequently split up. Drummer Davidson later found fame in the **Nice**.

● COMPILATIONS: *The Mark Leeman Five Memorial Album* (1991)★★.

Lees, Gene

b. 8 February 1928, Hamilton, Ontario, Canada. After studying music at Hamilton and the **Berklee College Of Music** in Boston, Massachusetts, Lees developed his writing talent, working in journalism, often as music critic, in both Canada and the USA. Lees has also written many song lyrics, some, like 'Quiet Nights On Quiet Stars' and 'Yesterday I Heard The Rain', were originals while others, for bossa nova songs by **Antonio Carlos Jobim**, he translated from Portuguese. In addition to his work as journalist and lyricist, Lees has also been active in musical education. His journal, *Jazzletter*, is widely read and respected and such books as *Singers And The Song* reveal an abiding interest in lyric writing and such diverse jazz artists as **Sarah Vaughan** and the **Clarke-Boland Big Band**, all of which is communicated with an able command of language.

● FURTHER READING: *Waiting For Dizzy*, Gene Lees.

Lefevre, Raymond

The most famous of a long line of musical Lefevres, Raymond rivalled **Franck Pourcel** and **Paul Mauriat** as France's 'answer' to **Mantovani** after leading his orchestra beyond national celebrity into the US Top 40 in spring 1958 with a string-laden arrangement of **Gilbert Becaud**'s 'The Day The Rains Came (La Jour Ou La Pluie Viendra)'. Judging by a prolific output licensed from Barclay Records, Lefevre's records continued to sell well in the interim preceding another international smash with 1968's uptempo 'Soul Coaxing (Ame Caline)' (from *Raymond Lefevre Volume Two*). Singles chart windfalls were, however, secondary to trans-continental concert tours and the regular release of themed albums demonstrating the wonders of stereo. Often augmented with chorale, these consisted mainly of light classics (eg *Operamania*), film material, tributes to other artists, standards, Gaelic chansons - and trademark easy-listening versions of the hits of others, exemplified by 1977's *Rock And Rhythm In Hi-Fi* in which he reconciled with ease works originated by the **Coasters**, **Beatles**, **Simon And Garfunkel**, **Silver Convention** and further disparate acts. A show-business institution, he was able to risk occasional stylistic tangents such as 1985's *Sheep In Wolves' Clothing*, attributed to Raymond Lefevre And The Broken Hearts, which was not as lush as his fans might have expected.

● ALBUMS: *Raymond Lefevre* (Major Minor 1967),★★★★ *Raymond Lefevre Volume Two* aka *Soul Coaxing (Ame Caline)* (Major Minor 1968)★★★★, *Le Premier Pas* (1976)★★★, *Rock And Rhythm In Hi-Fi* (1977)★★★, *Love In Stereo* (1978)★★★, *French Love In Hi-Fi* (1978)★★★, *Disco Symphonies* (1979)★★, *Film Symphonies* (1979)★★, *Love Symphonies* (1980)★★★, *Rock Symphonies* (1980)★★, *French Love Songs* (1980)★★★★, *Operamania* (1981)★★★, *Interprets Julio Iglesias* (1982)★★★, *Sheep In Wolves' Clothing* (1985)★★★, *Demonstration* (1988)★★★.

Left Banke

Formed in 1966, the Left Banke was the brainchild of pianist/composer Michael Brown (b. Michael Lookofsky, 25 April 1949, New York City, New York, USA). The son of a noted arranger and producer, Brown's early work appeared on releases by **Reparata And The Delrons** and Christopher And The Chaps, prior to the founding of the Left Banke. Steve Martin (vocals), Jeff Winfield (guitar), Tom Finn (bass) and George Cameron (drums) completed the original Left Banke line-up, which scored a US Top 5 hit with 'Walk Away Renee'. This gorgeous song adeptly combined elements drawn from the **Beatles** and baroque, and became a major hit the following year when covered by the **Four Tops**. The Left Banke enjoyed further success with 'Pretty Ballerina', but underwent the first of several changes when Rick Brand replaced Winfield during sessions for an attendant album. Internal ructions led to Brown completing a third release, 'Ivy Ivy', with the aid of session musicians, but the band was reunited for 'Desiree', their final chart entry. Michael then abandoned his creation - he later formed **Stories** - and when Brand also departed, Finn, Cameron and Martin completed *The Left Banke Too* as a trio. Although bereft of their principal songwriter, the group still captured the spirit of earlier recordings, but broke up in 1969 in the wake of a final single, 'Myrah', which was issued in an unfinished state. However, a New York independent, Camerica, coaxed the final line-up back into the studio in 1978. Although initially shelved, the set, which successfully echoed the group's glory days, was belatedly issued eight years later as *Voices Calling* (UK title)/*Strangers On A Train* (US). Several excellent compilations have been released since.

● ALBUMS: *Walk Away Renee/Pretty Ballerina* (Smash 1967)★★★, *The Left Banke, Too* (Smash 1968)★★, *Voices Calling* aka *Strangers On A Train* (1986)★★★.

● COMPILATIONS: *And Suddenly It's ... The Left Banke* (Bam Caruso 1984)★★★★, *The History Of The Left Banke* (Rhino 1985)★★★★, *Walk Away Renee* (1986)★★★.

Left Hand Frank

b. Frank Craig, 5 October 1935, Greenville, Mississippi, USA. Frank had a rocking good-time approach to the traditional sound of 50s Chicago blues, although his distinctive guitar and vocals were only captured on record for the first time in 1978. At the end of the 70s he enjoyed some international acclaim, but remains one of the blues' lesser-known figures. He received his first guitar for his fourth birthday and quickly learned to play blues and country. He moved to Chicago at the age of 14 and was inspired to play blues by listening to the sounds he could hear emanating from the doors of the clubs. He played behind many of the city's blues musicians, including **Junior Wells**, **Theodore 'Hound Dog' Taylor** and **Willie Cobbs**, and recorded on several occasions as a bass player. He is now based in California.

● ALBUMS: *Living Chicago Blues Volume One* four tracks only (1978)★★★★, with Jimmy Rogers *The Dirty Dozens* (JSP 1985)★★★.

Leftfield

Leftfield originally comprised just Neil Barnes, formerly of Elephant Stampede and, bizarrely, the London School Of Samba. He released a solo track, 'Not Forgotten', on **Outer Rhythm**, before Leftfield were expanded to a duo with the addition of former **A Man Called Adam** contributor Paul Daley. Barnes first met him through a poetry group who wanted live backing. However, as 'Not Forgotten', a deeply resonant song, broke big, disputes with Outer Rhythm followed. Unable to record due to contractual restraints, they embarked instead on a career as remixers to the stars. This first batch included **React 2 Rhythm**, **Ultra Nate** and **Inner City**. They were profligate in order to keep the Leftfield name prominent in the absence of their own brand material. Later remixes for **David Bowie**, **Renegade Soundwave** and **Yothu Yindi** would follow, but by now the duo had already established their Hard Hands imprint. This debuted with the reggae-tinted 'Release The Pressure' (featuring **Earl Sixteen**), then the more trance-based 'Song Of Life', which gave them a minor chart success in 1992. They subsequently teamed up with John Lydon (**Sex Pistols/PiL**) for what *Q Magazine* described as the unofficial single of 1993, 'Open Up'. Remixed in turn by **Andy Weatherall** and the **Dust Brothers**, it was an enormous cross-party success - especially for Barnes, whose primary musical influence had always been PiL. It might have risen higher in the charts had it not been pulled from ITV's *The Chart Show* at the last minute because of the line 'Burn Hollywood, burn' embedded in its fade, as parts of Los Angeles were by coincidence affected by fire. They also produced a soundtrack for the film *Shallow Grave*, and recorded as Herbal Infusion ('The Hunter'), alongside **Zoom Records** boss Dave Wesson. Gaining favour with a mainstream audience, 1995's *Leftism* paved the way for the later crossover success of the **Chemical Brothers** and the **Prodigy**.

● ALBUMS: *Backlog* (Outer Rhythm 1992)★★★, *Leftism* (Hard Hands/Columbia 1995)★★★★.

Leftism - Leftfield

With *Leftism*, Leftfield made the crossover of techno into the pop mainstream two years before the likes of the **Chemical Brothers**. Embarking on a series of high-profile collaborations, they introduced to the charts a musical manifesto that had been popular in the clubs for years - including ambient ('Song Of Life'), pure techno, ragga, African tribal chants ('Afro-Left') and the all-important remix. The pumping, snarling 'Open Up', featuring John Lydon, predated the **Prodigy** in its blend of punk and dance, and 'Original', with **Curve's** Toni Halliday, ironically inspired a multitude of imitators. Most of these tracks have become ubiquitous through mainstream television and film, and it is easy to forget that, before Leftfield, techno music had only rarely stepped outside clubland.

● Tracks: *Release The Pressure; Afro-Left; Melt; Song Of Life; Original; Black Flute; Space Shanty; Inspection (Check One); Storm 3000; Open Up; 21st Century Poem.*
● First released 1995
● UK peak position: 3
● USA peak position: did not chart

Lefty Dizz

b. Walter Williams, 29 April 1937, Osceola, Arkansas, USA, d. 7 September 1993. Dizz was taught the rudiments of music by his father, after the family had moved north to Kankakee, Illinois, and he has been a stalwart of the Chicago blues scene since the late 50s, having accompanied numerous blues artists as rhythm or lead guitarist. He reportedly made his first record (credited to the 'Wallets') for the King label in 1960, and he recorded with **Junior Wells** in the mid-60s. For many years he was based at the Checkerboard Lounge in Chicago. Records under his own name have appeared on the CJ, JSP, Black And Blue, and Isabel labels. He can also be heard on a bootleg of the **Rolling Stones**. His stage name referred to his left-handed playing and his youthful habit of imitating **Dizzy Gillespie**. Lefty's forte was tough, gritty guitar blues.
● ALBUMS: *Ain't It Nice To Be Loved* (1989)★★★.
● COMPILATIONS: *Chicago Blues At Burnley* (JSP 1991)★★★.

LeGarde Twins

This popular duo, also on occasions referred to as Australia, comprises identical twins Tom (the eldest by 30 minutes) and Ted Legarde (b. 15 March 1931, Mackay, Queensland, Australia), the youngest members of a family of nine. They were raised on the family farm, both becoming expert horsemen. At the age of 15, clutching an old guitar and influenced by cowboy films and the recordings of **Wilf Carter**, they left home. They worked on Queensland's largest cattle ranch, took part in cattle drives and rode in rodeos, and they began singing at a Victoria rodeo, when they failed to win any prize money but needed to eat. They joined **Buddy Williams'** touring rodeo and circus and, at the age of 17, became Australia's youngest professional rodeo riders. They soon found singing to be less painful than rodeo work and concentrated on it. In 1950, they made their first recordings for Rodeo, but between 1952 and 1957, they had several single releases on **Regal Zonophone**. In 1954, they toured Australia with their boyhood idol Hopalong Cassidy (William Boyd), but in 1957, they decided to seek success in America. They first played shows in Canada but later hosted their own television series in Los Angeles. Between 1958 and 1963, they relocated to Nashville, where they recorded singles for **Dot** and **Liberty Records** and made appearances on the *Grand Ole Opry*, debuting with their own song, 'Cooee Call'. They returned to Australia, where they briefly ran a country show from a Paddington, Sydney theatre, recorded albums for **Columbia Records** and compered two local country shows. In 1965, they returned to the USA where, under **'Colonel' Tom Parker's** management, they worked in Las Vegas and even appeared in television's *Star Trek*. They recorded for numerous labels and in 1978, as the Le Gardes, they achieved a minor hit with 'True Love' (a cover of the 1956 **Bing Crosby**/Grace Kelly pop hit) on Raindrop. A further minor hit came in 1978, with 'I Can Almost Touch The Feeling' on 4 Star. In 1980, as the Legarde Twins, they achieved a minor hit, 'Daddy's Making Records In Nashville', for Invitation 101. In 1987, they were awarded Hall Of Fame status at Australia's prestigious Tamworth Country Festival and during the 80s, they launched their own Boomerang label and made several appearances in the UK, including at the Wembley Festival. Their last US country chart entry reached number 92, 'Crocodile Man From Walk-About-Creek', in 1988. During the 90s, they have operated their own theatre near Nashville's Music Row.
● ALBUMS: *Ballads Of The Bushland* (Columbia 1964)★★★, *Twincerely Yours* (Columbia 1964)★★★, *Songs Of Slim & Buddy* (Columbia 1964)★★, *Australia Down Under Country Volume 1* (Boomerang 1983)★★★, *Australia - Down Under Country Volume 2* (Boomerang 1984)★★.

Legarreta, Félix 'Pupi'

Innovative Cuban violinist, flautist, singer, bandleader, arranger, composer Legarreta was a key participant in the early 60s pachanga/charanga craze, mid-70s to early 80s charanga revival and New York descarga movement. As a boy he paid for violin tuition by working as a barber, which his father urged him to abandon. Pupi left Cuba in 1959 and joined the USA's second charanga band, Orquesta Nuevo Ritmo, (the first was a short-lived outfit founded by Gilberto Valdés in 1952) organized in the mid-50s by Cuban conguero Armando Sánchez in Chicago. Nuevo Ritmo's personnel included other prominent Latin music names, such as vocalists Rudy Calzado and Pellín Rodríguez, flautist Rolando Lozano, pianist René 'El Latigo' Hernández and bassist Victor Venegas. With Nuevo Ritmo, Pupi made the single 'Tumba La Caña', the New York recorded *The Heart Of Cuba* (1960) on GNP and performed at New York's legendary Palladium Ballroom. **Mongo**

Santamaría took over the reins of leadership after Sánchez's departure, adding violinist/tenor saxophonist Jose 'Chombo' Silva and timbalero **Willie Bobo**. Based on the USA west coast, Pupi performed on six Fantasy label recordings by Santamaría's charanga (including one with pianist/leader Joe Loco) between 1961 and 1962, and wrote all the arrangements on *Ay Que Rico!* (late 1962) by the Benny Velarde Orchestra for the same company.

Pupi's recording debut as bandleader was 1963's *Salsa Nova* on Tico Records; the title was one of first uses on record in New York of the term 'salsa'. The album featured an impressive line-up, including Chombo, violin; 'El Latigo' Hernández, piano; Osvaldo 'Chi Hua Hua' Martínez, güiro; Carlos 'Patato' Valdez, conga; Totico and Elliot Romero, vocals; Pupi played violin, sang in the chorus and wrote all the arrangements and **Tito Puente** handled the musical direction. He switched to Remo Records and issued a string of six albums on the label from the mid to late 60s; particularly outstanding was the Latin jam orientated *Pupi En Venezuela* (late 60s), which was reissued with three tracks from another Remo release *Pupi: Jala Jala* under the title *Pupy* (sic) *y su Charanga* on the UK Tumi label in 1993. 'Superb, long descarga jams of classic folk numbers show how the flute/violin charanga orchestras had progressed from the elegant to the electrifying,' was DJ Tomek's comment about *Pupy y su Charanga* in *Jazz On CD*, June 1993. Pupi's second Remo release, *Jala Jala Con Boog - A - Loo* (mid-60s, aka *Salsa*), contained his self-penned 'Salsa'; on another track, the guaracha 'Cada Quien', a vocalist describes him as 'El Rey de la Salsa y la Sabor' (The King of Sauce and Flavour).

He performed on the noteworthy descarga sets *Pacheco His Flute And Latin Jam* (1965) led by **Johnny Pacheco** and *Descarga Cubana Vol. 1* (1966) led by Osvaldo 'Chi Hua Hua' Martínez (this album was coupled with its successor *Latin Cuban Session Vol. 2*, c. 1967, on the Palladium label CD reissue *Descarga Cubana* (1991). A decade later he took part the classics *Cachao y su Descarga '77 Vol. 1* (1976) and *Dos* (1977) by descarga pioneer Cachao (see **López, Israel**).

He signed with Fania Records and released a series of four albums between 1975 and 1980 on their Vaya Records offshoot, starting with the highly regarded *Pupi y su Charanga* (1975), with Cuban flautist Don Gonzalo Fernández. In 1976 he performed on Fernández's weighty *Super Típica de Estrellas*, virtually a summit meeting of most of New York's leading charanga stars at the time. Pupi's 1977 collaboration with Johnny Pacheco, *Los Dos Mosqueteros - The Two Musketeers*, included a remake of his composition 'Salsa'.

Pupi became a member of the **Fania All Stars**, with whom he appeared in the movie *Live In Africa* (1974; UK title *Salsa Madness*, 1991), and made his UK debut in 1976. He played on three Fania All Stars' albums between 1978 and 1980, including *Habana Jam* (1979), recorded in his home land of Cuba; plus their 1986 20th anniversary releases *Live In Africa* and *Live In*

Japan 1976. In the second half of the 70s he regularly guested on **Larry Harlow**'s albums, including *El Judio Maravilloso* (1975); *Con Mi Viejo Amigo* (1976); *El Jardinero Del Amor* (1976); *La Raza Latina* (1977; nominated for a Grammy Award); and *El Albino Divino* (1978). *Pupi Pa' Bailar* was his last album as a leader in 1980; and by that time the 70s New York charanga explosion had begun to run out of steam. Thereafter, his recording activity diminished to session and arranging work for other bands and artists, including **Roberto Torres**, **Papaíto**, Orquesta Sublime, Israel 'Kantor' Sardiñas, Rudy Calzado and Orquesta Son Primero.

● ALBUMS: with Orquesta Nuevo Ritmo *The Heart Of Cuba* (1960)★★★; with Mongo Santamaría y su Orquesta *'Sabrosa' Sabroso!* (1961)★★★, *Pachanga con Joe Loco* (1961)★★★★, reissued as half of the CD *Loco Lotion*, 1994, *Arriba! La Pachanga* (1962)★★★★, *Más Sabroso* (1962)★★★, *Viva Mongo!* (1962)★★★; with Benny Velarde Orchestra *Ay Que Rico!* (1962)★★★, reissued as half of the CD *Ay Que Rico!*, 1993)★★★; with Mongo Santamaría *Mighty Mongo* (1962)★★★★, reissued with *Viva Mongo!* on the CD *At The Blackhawk*, 1994, *Salsa Nova* (1963)★★★★, reissued as *Toda La Verdad*, 1976; with Johnny Pacheco *Pacheco His Flute And Latin Jam* (1965)★★★★, *Pupi And His Charanga* (1965)★★★, *Jala Jala Con Boog - A - Loo* aka *Salsa* (1965)★★, *Pupi: Jala Jala* (1966)★★, *Soy Campesino* (1968)★★, *Pupi En Venezuela* (1969)★★, reissued with three tracks from *Pupi: Jala Jala* as *Pupy y su Charanga* on UK Tumi label, 1993, *Que Lío!* (1969)★★★, *Pupi y su Charanga* (1975)★★★, directed by Gonzalo Fernández *Super Típica de Estrellas* (1976)★★★; with Cachao *Cachao y su Descarga '77 Vol. 1* (1976)★★★, *Dos* (1977)★★★; with Johnny Pacheco *Los Dos Mosqueteros - The Two Musketeers* (1977)★★★★, *El Fugitivo* (1979)★★★, co-arranger on *Charanga de la 4* (1979)★★★, *Pupi Pa' Bailar* (1980)★★★; with Javier Vázquez y su Charanga *Las Tres Flautas* (1980)★★★; with Roberto Torres *Roberto Torres Presenta: Ritmo de Estrellas* (1980)★★★; with Papaíto *Papaíto Rinde Homenaje A Abelardo Barroso* (1980)★★★; co-arranger on Orquesta Sublime's *Simplemente Sublime* (1981)★★★; with Rudy Calzado *Rica Charanga* (1986)★★★; with Orquesta Son Primero *Charanga - Tradición Cubana En Nueva York* (1987)★★★.

Legend

This popular English, Essex-based act evolved from the ashes of beat attraction the Orioles. Guitarist **Mickey Jupp** was initially accompanied by Chris East (guitar/vocals), Steve Geare (bass/vocals) and Nigel Dunbar (drums), but this line-up was dissolved following the release *Legend*. Mo Witham (guitar), John Bobin (bass) and former lettering artist Bill Fifield (b. Dagenham, Essex, 1946; drums) joined Jupp for *Red Boot*, released on the renowned **Vertigo** label. Although another commercial flop, the album helped inspire the back-to-basics 'pub rock' genre, influencing such acts as **Dr. Feelgood** and **Ducks DeLuxe**. The former later covered one of its tracks, 'Cheque Book'. Fifield left in December 1970 to join **T. Rex** - where he was known as 'Bill Legend' - and was replaced by Bob Clouter.

However, their final album *Moonshine* lacked the verve of its predecessor and the now-moribund group disbanded. Jupp subsequently achieved a degree of success as a solo act but acknowledged his former act with *Mickey Jupp's Legend* (1978). Ex-members of Southend contemporaries the **Paramounts** were among those backing the artist as he re-recorded some of Legend's most popular songs.

● ALBUMS: *Legend* (Bell 1969)★★★, *Red Boot* (Vertigo 1970)★★★, *Moonshine* (Vertigo 1971)★.

Legend - Bob Marley

Although reggae is still perceived as a minor specialist genre, when it hits the button right, the music captures the hearts of the masses. **Bob Marley** is a giant similar to **Elvis Presley**: both continue to sell vast numbers of records long after their deaths, and both are clear leaders of their respective genres. This album is the most perfect selection of hits. The running order is unbeatable, each track is made for the next. There is a superb four-CD box set available for serious collectors, but for those who want to put on a CD at any time of the day this will always hit the spot.

● Tracks: *Is This Love; Jamming; No Woman No Cry; Stir It Up; Get Up And Stand Up; Satisfy My Soul; I Shot The Sheriff; One Love; People Get Ready; Buffalo Soldier; Exodus; Redemption Song; Could You Be Loved; Want More.*

● First released 1984

● UK peak chart position: 1

● USA peak chart position: 54

Legend Of American Folk Blues - Woody Guthrie

Folk-singer is too small a term to describe **Woody Guthrie**. Political activist, rambler, poet and commentator, he encapsulated the aura of Roosevelt's New Deal America. Guthrie spoke for the okie underclass in song the way Steinbeck chronicled their lives in novels and this superb selection compiles the best of his expansive output. The topical song was Guthrie's métier and his simple melodies and pungent lyrics left a huge impression on the 60s folk revival. **Bob Dylan**, **Phil Ochs** and **Tom Paxton** owe him a considerable debt, but Guthrie's importance lies in the lasting quality of his own work. This CD has replaced *This Land Is Your Land* as the definitive Guthrie album.

● Tracks: *This Land Is Your Land; Pastures Of Plenty; Pretty Boy Floyd; Take A Whiff On Me; Do Re Mi; Put My Little Shoes Away; Washington Talkin' Blues; Hard Travelin'; Jesus Christ; Whoopee Ti Yi Yo, Get Along Little Dogies; Grand Coulee Dam; A Picture From Life's Other Side; Talkin' Hard Luck Blues; Philadelphia Lawyer; I Ain't Got No Home; The Wreck Of The Old '97; Keep Your Skillet Good And Greasy; Dust Pneumonia Blues; Going Down That Road Feeling Bad; Goodnight Little Arlo (Goodnight Little Darlin'); So Long It's Been Good To Know You.*

● First released 1992

● UK peak chart position: did not chart

● USA peak chart position: did not chart

Legendary Blues Band

Formed in June 1980, the Legendary Blues Band emerged from the **Muddy Waters** band of the mid to late 70s. The original line-up consisted of Jerry Portnoy (harmonica), **Louis Myers** (guitar, harmonica), **Pinetop Perkins** (piano), Calvin Jones (bass) and Willie Smith (drums), with the vocals shared among all the members. There were numerous personnel changes over the subsequent years and Smith and Jones are the only remaining original members. The sound remains solidly in the Chicago blues vein. They recorded two albums for the **Rounder** label in the early 80s and signed with **Ichiban** in 1989.

● ALBUMS: *Life Of Ease* (Rounder 1981)★★★, *Red Hot 'N' Blue* (Rounder 1983)★★★, *Woke Up With The Blues* (Ichiban 1989)★★★, *Keeping The Blues Alive* (Ichiban 1990)★★★, *U B Da Judge* (Ichiban 1991)★★★, *Blue Devil Blues* (Amazing 1991)★★★, *No Beginner* (Amazing 1993)★★★.

Legendary Pink Dots

This east London experimental group was formed in 1981, based around lyricist and singer Edward Ka-spel and keyboard player Phillip Knight, who emerged as part of the burgeoning do-it-yourself scene of the late 70s. Performing what they described as 'psychedelic' music - in an 'exploratory sense, rather than nostalgia' - they released their first album, *Brighter Now*, on the small Birmingham independent label Phaze Records, eventually running through two other homes before settling with Play It Again Sam. The band emigrated to the Netherlands in 1985, after Ka-spel had become disenchanted with his native country's reaction to *The Tower* ('a really important album to me'). A series of recordings continued to fare better on the continent than in the UK, while Ka-spel recorded the latest of several solo albums with Steve Stapleton of **Nurse With Wound**. He has also branched out with a side project, the Maria Dimension, and worked with **Skinny Puppy** (as Teargarden for the 1987 album, *Tired Eyes Slowly Burning*) The latest incarnation of Legendary Pink Dots, meanwhile, has added Nils Van Hoorne (saxophones, flute, bass, clarinet) and Bob Pisteer (guitars, bass, sitar). Ka-Spel's prolific recording schedule continues apace, despite the market for his marginalized electronic pop songs having barely enlarged since the early 80s.

● ALBUMS: *Brighter Now* (Terminal Kaleidoscope 1982)★★★, *Curse* (Terminal Kaleidoscope 1983)★★★, *Faces In The Fire* (Terminal Kaleidoscope 1984)★★★, *The Tower* (Terminal Kaleidoscope 1984)★★★, *Greeting 9* (Materiali Sonori 1984)★★, *The Lovers* (Ding Dong 1985)★★★, *Asylum* (Play It Again Sam 1985)★★★, *Island Of Jewels* (Play It Again Sam 1987)★★★, *Any Day Now* (Play It Again Sam 1987)★★★, *The Golden Age* (Play It Again Sam 1988)★★★, *The Crushed Velvet Apocalypse* (Play It Again Sam 1990)★★★, *The Maria Dimension* (Play It Again Sam 1991)★★★, *Shadow Weaver* (Play It Again Sam 1992)★★★.

Solo: Edward Ka-spel *Laugh China Doll* (Torso 1984)★★★, *Eyes! China Doll* (Scarface 1985)★★★, *Chyekk, China Doll*

(Torso 1986)★★★, *Perhaps We'll Only See A Thin Blue Line* (Play It Again Sam 1989)★★★.

● COMPILATIONS: *Stone Circles: A Legendary Pink Dots Anthology* (Play It Again Sam 1987)★★★, *Legendary Pink Box* 3-album box set (Play It Again Sam 1989)★★★.

Legg, Adrian

b. 16 May 1948, Hackney, London, England. Although a highly respected guitarist, Legg actually played oboe as a child, both for the school orchestra and the Cheltenham Young People's Orchestra. He left home at the age of 15, and stopped playing oboe. Three or four years later he took up the guitar, joining a country band in Liverpool, and turning professional a year later. After a period of working with Irish and UK country bands, he turned solo during 1973. By 1974, Legg had won both the composition and performance categories in the folk guitar competition run by *Guitar* magazine. From 1978, he stopped all performing, moving instead, in 1979, into the musical instrument industry, working in research, development and repairs. He also held instrument clinics and demonstrations. Legg resumed his playing during 1982, having produced the book, *Customising Your Electric Guitar*, the previous year. After recording *Technopicker*, for Making Waves, he left the musical instrument industry. He then followed up with *Fretmelt* and *Lost For Words*, again for Making Waves, who, unfortunately, were soon to go out of business. *Guitar For Mortals*, released on Relativity Records, was recorded in May 1991, in Los Angeles, and produced by Bobby Cochran. Legg also recorded a teaching video, *Beyond Acoustic Guitar*, for Arlen Roth's Hot Licks series, which was released in the autumn of 1991. Legg is still involved with the industry, with the final research and development, and subsequent launch, of the Trace Elliot acoustic guitar amplifier, as well as work for Ovation guitars. In addition to this, he still holds regular teaching clinics in the USA for Kaman Corporation, Ovation's parent company. Legg regularly contributes to magazines, on matters legal and technical, and has also been doing shows and clinics for the Dean Markley String Corporation, as well as fitting in a UK tour at least once a year.

● ALBUMS: *Requiem For A Hick* (1977)★★★, *Technopicker* (Making Waves 1983)★★★, *Fretmelt* (Making Waves 1984)★★★, *Lost For Words* (Making Waves 1986)★★★, *Guitars And Other Cathedrals* (MMC 1990)★★★, *Guitar For Mortals* (Relativity 1992)★★★, *Mrs Crowes's Blue Waltz* (1993)★★★★, *Wine, Women And Waltz* (1993)★★★, *Waiting For A Dancer* (Red House 1997)★★★.

● FURTHER READING: *The All Round Gigster*, Adrian Legg. *Acoustic Guitars-A Musician's Manual*, Adrian Legg with Paul Colbert.

Legrand, Michel

b. 24 February 1932, Paris, France. Legrand grew up in a musical environment - his father was an orchestra leader and film composer - and studied formally at the Paris Conservatoire. In the 50s he was an active pianist but was most successful as an arranger. Later in the decade he moved to New York and continued to arrange, but now with a strong orientation towards the contemporary jazz scene, for leading artists such as **Miles Davis** and **John Coltrane**. In France he had occasionally led his own bands and did so again in the USA. In these years he was also a prolific composer, writing material performed by **Stan Getz**, **Phil Woods** and others, and occasionally playing with jazzmen such as **Shelly Manne**. He had begun to compose music for French films in 1953, and, in the 60s, developed this area of his work on productions such as *Lola*; *Cleo From 5 To 7*, which he also appeared in, and *My Life To Live*. In 1964 he received the first of his many Academy Award nominations, for the score to *The Umbrellas Of Cherbourg*, which contained 'I Will Wait For You' and 'Watch What Happens' (English lyrics by Norman Gimbel). His second Oscar came for his work on the follow-up, *The Young Ladies Of Rochefort* (1968). In the late 60s he began to compose for US and British films. His score for one of the first of these, *The Thomas Crown Affair*, included 'The Windmills Of Your Mind' (lyric by **Alan** and **Marilyn Bergman**), which became popular for **Noel Harrison** (son of actor Rex) and **Dusty Springfield**, and won an Academy Award in 1968. Another collaboration with Alan and Marilyn Bergman produced 'What Are You Doing The Rest Of Your Life?', from *The Happy Ending* (1969). Throughout the 70s, Legrand continued to write prolifically for films such as *The Go-Between*, *Wuthering Heights*, *Summer Of 42* (another Oscar), *Lady Sings The Blues*, *One Is A Lonely Number* and *The Three Musketeers*. He teamed with the Bergmans yet again for **Barbra Streisand**'s film *Yentl* (1983). Two of their 12 songs, 'Papa, Can You Hear Me?' and 'The Way He Makes Me Feel' were nominated, and the complete score won an Academy Award. Legrand's other film music included *Never Say Never Again*, Sean Connery's eagerly awaited return to the role of James Bond; *Secret Places* (title song written with **Alan Jay Lerner**); the amusing *Switching Channels* (theme written with **Neil Diamond**), *Fate* and *The Burning Shore*, and *Pret-A-Porter* (1994). In 1991 Legrand was back to his jazz roots for the score to *Dingo*, which he wrote with **Miles Davis**. Davis also gave an impressive performance in the movie. At his best with lyrical and sometimes sentimental themes, Legrand's writing for films remains his major contribution to popular music. Besides his feature film credits, Legrand also worked extensively in television, contributing music to *Brian's Song*, *The Adventures Of Don Quixote*, *It's Good To Be Alive*, *Cage Without A Key*, *A Woman Called Golda*, *The Jesse Owens Story*, *Promises To Keep*, *Sins* (mini-series), *Crossings*, *Casanova* and *Not A Penny More, Not A Penny Less*.

● ALBUMS: *Legrand Jazz* (1958)★★★★, *At Shelly's Manne Hole* (1968)★★★★, *Michel Legrand Recorded Live At Jimmy's* (1973)★★, *Themes And Variations* (1973)★★★, *After The Rain* (1982)★★★, and film soundtracks.

Legs Diamond

Deriving their name from an infamous 1920s gangster, Legs Diamond were formed by Michael Diamond (bass) and Jeff Poole (drums) in San Francisco, California, during 1977. Moving to Los Angeles, they recruited Rick Sanford (vocals), Michael Prince (guitar, keyboards) and Roger Romeo (guitar) to consolidate the line-up. Signed by **Mercury Records**, their debut release was a classy hard rock album influenced by the traditions of **Led Zeppelin** and **Deep Purple**. The songs were well constructed, but the album was let down by a weak production. The follow-up was every bit as strong, with the band alternating between brooding and intense power ballads and unabashed rockers. They toured as support to **Ted Nugent**, **Kiss** and **Styx**, but, to their surprise, were dropped by their label shortly afterwards. They subsequently negotiated a contract with the independent Cream label, releasing *Fire Power* in 1978. This marked a change in style to a more AOR-orientated approach, but it was poorly received. The band members, disillusioned, decided to go their separate ways. Six years later, Rick Sanford resurrected Legs Diamond, and after several personnel changes stabilized the line-up with Romeo and Prince joined by new members Dusty Watson (drums) and Mike Christie (bass). Signing to the independent metal specialists **Music For Nations**, they have delivered several albums of sophisticated hard rock and captured much of the excitement and promise that was not fulfilled the first time around.

● ALBUMS: *Legs Diamond* (Mercury 1977)★★★★, *A Diamond Is A Hard Rock* (Mercruy 1977)★★★★, *Fire Power* (Cream 1978)★★★, *Out On Bail* (Music For Nations 1984)★★★, *Land Of The Gun* (Music For Nations 1986)★★★, *Town Bad Girl* (Music For Nations 1990)★★★, *Captured Live* (Music For Nations 1992)★★, *The Wish* (Music For Nations 1994)★★★.

Lehár, Franz

b. Ferencz Lehár, 30 April 1870, Komorn, Hungary, d. 24 October 1948, Bad Ischl, Austria. An important figure in the world of Viennese operetta, from an early age Lehár exhibited a prodigious musical talent, and by the time he was six, was composing simple tunes on the piano. At the age of 12, he embarked on a six-year course at the renowned Prague Conservatorium of Music, studying principally violin, as well as piano and composition. His father was a multi-instrumentalist and a Band Sergeant-Major in the 5th Austrian Regiment of Infantry.

After graduating with honours in 1888, Lehár became a violinist with the orchestra at the Vereinigte Theatre (Allied Municipal Theatres) of Barmen-Elberfeld in Germany's Rhineland. A year later, he joined his father as first violinist with the 50th Regiment in Vienna. At the age of 20 he was promoted to Bandmaster of the 25th Infantry Regiment at Losoncz, in the northern part of Hungary, the first of several military appointments he undertook before leaving to become a theatre

conductor. For some years Lehár had been writing orchestral works, popular songs, and the opera *Kukushka*, which was produced in 1896, with the composer conducting, and subsequently revised under the title of *Tatjana* in 1905. In 1902 he composed the waltz, 'Gold And Silver', which helped to launch his career in the light musical theatre. In the same year, he wrote the music for two operettas, *Wiener Frauen* and *Der Rastelbinder*. These were followed by *Der Göttergatte* and *Die Juxheirat*, before Lehár composed the music for his masterpiece, *Die Lustige Witwe*. This operetta in three acts by Victor Léon and Leo Stein, became known the world over as **The Merry Widow**. After opening in Vienna in 1905, it was presented by George Edwardes two years later at Daly's Theatre in London, and on Broadway. With an English adaptation by Edward Morton, and lyrics by Adrian Ross, the London production ran for 778 performances, and launched the young Lily Elsie to stardom. Also among the cast were Joseph Coyne as Prince Danilo, and George Graves in the role of Ambassador Baron Popoff. Its magnificent score included 'Maxim's', 'Vilia', 'Girls, Girls, Girls', 'Love In My Heart', and 'I Love You So' (also known as 'Merry Widow Waltz'). The show has since been presented on numerous occasions in many countries, even in Nazi Germany where it rivalled the popularity of Wagner's music. Several film versions have been released, including some early shorts, and in 1925 a silent directed by Erich von Stroheim. **Ernst Lubitsch** shot his *Merry Widow* in 1934 with **Jeanette MacDonald** and **Maurice Chevalier**, for whom **Lorenz Hart** contributed new words to 'Vilia'.

After the phenomenal success of *The Merry Widow*, Lehár's output during the next few years proved to be variable. However, in a remarkably short period between October 1909 and January 1910, he pulled off an unparalleled feat when three works containing his music opened in Vienna. These shows, which are among the best known of all operettas, were *Das Fürstenkind* (*The Prince's Child*), *Der Graf Von Luxemburg* (*The Count Of Luxembourg*) and *Zigeunerliebe* (*Gypsy Love*). The latter, with an English book by Basil Hood, and lyrics by Adrian Ross, played at Daly's in London in 1912, with a cast which included Robert Michaelis, W.H. Berry and the musical comedy star, Gertie Millar, in the role of Lady Babby. Amongst the score were two charming numbers, 'A Little Maiden' and 'Love And Wine'. *The Count Of Luxembourg*, another in that particular trio of operettas, proved popular in London, and was seen by Broadway audiences in 1912 at the New Amsterdam Theatre. This was the same house where *The Merry Widow* had enjoyed its one year run. As in Vienna, it was again one of three Lehár operettas - this time in company with *Eva* (*Das Fabriksmädel*) and *The Man With Three Wives* (*Der Mann Smit Den Drei Frauen*)- to be presented in quick succession, from September 1912 to January 1913. It was also the only one of the trio to achieve any degree of success.

As an ex-soldier Lehár found himself unable to write for long periods during World War I, and some of the work he did manage to complete, such as *Der Sterngucker* (*The Star Gazer*) (1916), was poorly received. In the USA it proved to be the fastest flop of the 1917/18 season, being withdrawn after only eight performances. However, when hostilities ceased, Lehár experienced a surge of creativity. He had been following closely the developments in world music, particularly the gradual evolvement of jazz in America. This and many other influences would be reflected in his future scores. In 1920, together with librettists Leo Stein and Béla Jenbach, he celebrated his 50th birthday by devising a contemporary musical comedy, *Die Blaue Mazur* (*The Blue Mazurka*), which made its debut in Vienna four weeks after the special day, and stayed at the Theater an der Wien in Vienna for 11 months, but was not seen in London until 1927. Five years before that, Lehár collaborated with A.M. Willner and Heinz Reichart on an unusual piece - a Spanish operetta - entitled *Frasquita*. This show is especially significant because it was at one of the early performances in Vienna that the great operatic singer, Richard Tauber, became 'wildly excited' by Lehár's music. One song in particular thrilled him - 'Farewell My Love, Farewell', which is also known as 'Serenade'. He sang the number, and the major part of the dance-orientated score, when he took over the leading role in the summer of 1923. Tauber went on to become indelibly associated with Lehár's work, and introduced another of the composer's best-known songs, 'Girls Were Made To Love And Kiss', to London audiences in 1937. *Paganini* marked a return to critical approval after his series of early 20s shows, such as *The Blue Mazurka* and *Cloclo*, had been compared unfavourably with his pre-war productions. In addition, whereas Lehár's early works had been distinguished by feelings of gaiety and elation, his current operettas and musical plays were profoundly romantic, and usually had unhappy endings. After opening in Vienna in 1925, *Paganini* had received much acclaim when it moved to Berlin, and from then on, Lehár decided to preview his work in the German capital. *Friederike* (*Frederica*) made its debut there in 1928. It was a daring notion of librettists Dr. Ludwig Herzer and Dr. Fritz Löhner to create a musical based on the early love life of Johann Wolfgang Goethe, Germany's greatest poet, but the result, which contained such attractive melodies as 'Oh Maiden, My Maiden', 'I Love Him So' and 'A Heart As Pure As Gold', was regarded by Lehár biographers W. Macqueen Pope and D.L. Murray, as the show 'which perhaps discloses more of the intimate soul of its composer than any other of his works'. *Das Land Des Lächelns*, a revised version of Victor Léon's earlier *Die Gelbe Jacke* (*The Yellow Jacket*), by L. Herzer and Fritz Löhner, was the most successful of Lehár's romantic operettas. Berlin audiences saw it in 1929, two years before it came to London's Drury Lane in a version by Harry Graham entitled *The Land Of Smiles*. Its engaging score includes 'Appleblossoms', 'Patiently Smiling', and 'You Are My Heart's Delight' (known in the USA as 'Yours Is My Heart Alone'). *Das Land Des Lächelns* was virtually Lehár's swan song, although there were more revisions and another original piece, *Guiditta*, in 1934. Lehár considered that to be his best work, although it was more opera than operetta. During World War II he hardly composed at all, and eventually, in failing health, retired to his villa at Bad Ischl in Austria where he died in 1948.

● FURTHER READING: *Franz Lehár*, E. Decsey. *Franz Lehar: Sein Weg Und Sein Werk*, S. Czech. *Fortune's Favourite: The Life And Times Of Franz Lehár*, W. Macqueen Pope and D.L. Murray. *Gold And Silver: The Life And Times Of Franz Lehár*, B. Grun. *Franz Lehár: Eine Biographie In Zitaten*, O. Schneiderheit.

Lehr, Zella

b. 14 March 1941, Burbank, California, USA. At the age of six, adept at juggling and riding a unicycle, she was already performing as a member of the Crazy Lehrs Family, a vaudeville act started by her father some years earlier. (When big enough, she also added displays with a bull whip to her act). When vaudeville was badly affected by television competition in the USA, the act toured extensively in Europe and the Far East. When her parents retired, she continued to perform with her two brothers and a sister-in-law as the Young Lehrs, until the act ended on the death of her father. She took singing and dancing lessons and appeared on television commercials before applying for an audition for the popular **Hee Haw** television programme. She made quite an impression when she arrived on a large unicycle and impressed the producer enough to get a job. After two years with *Hee Haw*, she also began appearing as a solo act on the Las Vegas-Lake Tahoe casino circuit. In 1977, she relocated to Nashville, where she recorded for **RCA** and gained her first chart hit, a Top 10, with her version of **Dolly Parton**'s 'Two Doors Down'. By 1980, when she left the label, she had eight further hits, the biggest being 'Danger Heartbreak Ahead', a number 20 and 'Rodeo Eyes', a number 25. RCA surprisingly never released an album of her recordings. Between 1981 and 1983, recording for **Columbia**, she added four more hits, including a Top 16 with 'Feedin' The Fire'. In 1984/5, she had moved to the Compleat label, where she registered her final two chart entries. During the 80s, she toured with her band the Gypsy Riders, making visits to Australia in 1988 and 1989. In later years, she shortened her name to Zella.

● ALBUMS: *Feedin' The Fire* (Columbia 1982)★★★.

Lehrer, Tom

b. Thomas Andrew Lehrer, 9 April 1928, New York City, New York, USA. Lehrer was a song satirist who also recorded a number of albums during the 50s and 60s. Having graduated from Harvard University, Lehrer then taught mathematics there. Having trained on piano, he began to perform song satires of his own for colleagues at the college. They enjoyed his songs, so Lehrer recorded a dozen of them in 1953 and had 400 copies pressed on a 10-inch album, on his own Lehrer label. An instant success on campus, Lehrer was forced to press more copies to meet the demand. He then began entertaining in clubs and writing songs for television programmes. Before the end of the 50s he had recorded three more albums on his own label and had begun to tour extensively, even gaining a following in Europe. His sense of black humour is encapsulated in the titles 'Poisoning Pigeons In The Park', 'The Old Dope Peddler' and 'The Masochism Tango' - which could be described as falling somewhere between *Mad* magazine and Lenny Bruce. He stopped making live appearances in 1960 but continued to record, signing with **Reprise Records** in 1965. He also wrote for the US editions of the television programme *That Was The Week That Was* in 1964-65, lampooning current news events. His album *That Was The Year That Was* collected songs that had featured on the programme. He largely stopped writing in the late 60s and returned to teaching, but contributed songs to the television show *The Electric Company* in 1972. In 1980, Robin Ray and **Cameron Mackintosh** adapted some of his songs for the revue, *Tomfoolery*, which was still visiting the London Fringe in the early 90s. In 1998, BBC Radio 2 celebrated his 70th birthday with a special programme entitled *An Evening Wasted With Tom Lehrer*.

● ALBUMS: *Songs By Tom Lehrer* 10-inch album (Lehrer 1953)★★★★, *More Of Tom Lehrer* (Lehrer 1959)★★★★, *An Evening Wasted With Tom Lehrer* (Lehrer 1959)★★★★, *Tom Lehrer Revisited* (Lehrer 1960)★★, *That Was The Year That Was* (Reprise 1965)★★★, *Songs By Tom Lehrer* re-recorded versions of first album's songs (Reprise 1966)★★.

● COMPILATIONS: *Too Many Songs By Tom Lehrer* (1981)★★★★, *Songs & More Songs By Tom Lehrer* (Rhino 1997)★★★.

Leiber And Stoller

Jerry Leiber (b. 25 April 1933, Baltimore, Maryland, USA) and Mike Stoller (b. 13 March 1933, New York City, New York, USA) began their extraordinary songwriting and production partnership at the age of 17. Leiber was a blues enthusiast and record store assistant, while Stoller played jazz piano. Based in Los Angeles, they provided numerous songs for the city's R&B artists during the early 50s. 'Hard Times' by **Charles Brown** was the first Leiber and Stoller hit, but their biggest songs of the era were 'Hound Dog' and 'K.C. Lovin'' (later renamed 'Kansas City'). Originally recorded by **Big Mama Thornton**, 'Hound Dog' was one of the songs that came to define rock 'n' roll after **Elvis Presley** performed it. 'Kansas City' had its greatest success in a version by **Wilbert Harrison**, and went on to become part of every UK beat group's repertoire. In 1954, the duo set up their own Spark label to release material by the Robins, a vocal group they had discovered. Renamed the **Coasters** a year later, when Leiber and Stoller moved to New York, the group was given

some of the songwriters' most clever and witty compositions. Songs such as 'Smokey Joe's Cafe', 'Searchin'', 'Yakety Yak' and 'Charlie Brown' bridged the gap between R&B and rock 'n' roll, selling millions in the mid to late 50s, while Leiber And Stoller's innovative production techniques widened the scope of the R&B record, prompting hosts of imitators. In New York, Leiber and Stoller had a production contract with **Atlantic Records**, where they created hits for numerous artists. They wrote 'Lucky Lips' for **Ruth Brown** and 'Saved' for **LaVern Baker**, but their most notable productions were for the **Drifters** and the group's lead singer **Ben E. King**. Among these were 'On Broadway', 'Spanish Harlem', 'There Goes My Baby', 'I (Who Have Nothing)' and 'Stand By Me', which was an international hit when reissued in 1986. Away from Atlantic, Leiber and Stoller supplied Elvis Presley with songs including 'Jailhouse Rock', 'Baby I Don't Care', 'Loving You', 'Treat Me Nice' and 'His Latest Flame'. They also wrote hits for **Perry Como**, **Peggy Lee** ('I'm A Woman') and **Dion**. In 1964, the duo set up the **Red Bird** and Blue Cat record labels with George Goldner. Despite the quality of many of the releases (**Alvin Robinson**'s 'Down Home Girl' was later covered by the **Rolling Stones**), the only big hits came from the **Shangri-Las**, who were produced by **George 'Shadow' Morton** rather than Leiber and Stoller. Subsequently, the duo took several years away from production, purchasing the King Records group and creating the *Cabaret*-like songs for **Peggy Lee**'s album *Mirrors* (1976). They returned to the pop world briefly in 1972, producing albums for UK acts including **Stealer's Wheel** and **Elkie Brooks**, for whom they part-wrote 'Pearl's A Singer'. During the 70s, they were in semi-retirement, developing *Only In America*, a stage show involving 30 of their compositions. Another musical based on their work - *Yakety Yak* - was presented in London with oldies band **Darts**. During the 80s Leiber and Stoller's songs were featured in the cartoon film *Hound Dog* and they were reported to be working on a musical. However, their public appearances seemed to be confined to awards ceremonies where they were made members of several Halls of Fame, including that of the **Rock And Roll Hall Of Fame** in 1987. In 1979, US critic Robert Palmer wrote a highly praised biography of the duo. The stage musical *Smokey Joe's Cafe: The Songs Of Leiber And Stoller*, which opened to rave reviews in March 1995 at New York's Virginia Theatre, featured nearly 40 songs by the duo.

● FURTHER READING: *Baby, That Was Rock & Roll: The Legendary Leiber And Stoller*, Robert Palmer.

Leigh, Carolyn

b. Carolyn Paula Rosenthal, 21 August 1926, New York, USA, d. 19 November 1983, New York, USA. An important lyricist in the late 50s and 60s, Leigh began writing verse and doggerel when she was only nine. She later studied at Queens College and New York University. She began her career by writing announcements for radio station WQXR and working as a copy-writer. By the time she was 25 years old Leigh is reputed to have written about 200 songs, although none had been published. In 1951, she wrote 'I'm Waiting Just For You' (with **Lucky Millinder** and Henry Glover), which was modestly successful for Millinder, **Rosemary Clooney**, and later, **Pat Boone**. Her first big hit came in 1954, when **Frank Sinatra** took 'Young At Heart', written with **Johnny Richards**, to number 2 in the USA, and it became the title and theme of a film in which he co-starred with **Doris Day**. This led to Leigh being offered the chance to write most of the songs, with composer Mark 'Moose' Charlap, for the Broadway show *Peter Pan* (1954, 'I'm Flying', 'I've Gotta Crow' and 'I Won't Grow Up'). She also contributed to the off-Broadway revue *Shoestring '57*. Leigh's other work around this time included 'The Day The Circus Left Town' (with E.D. Thomas), which was recorded by **Eartha Kitt**, 'Stowaway' (with **Jerry Livingston**, a UK Top 20 entry for Barbara Lyon), '(How Little It Matters) How Little We Know' (Philip Springer) and 'Witchcraft' (**Cy Coleman**). The last two songs were chart hits for Frank Sinatra. Leigh's fruitful - and, apparently, stormy - collaboration with the composer Cy Coleman lasted from the late 50s into the early 60s. During that time they wrote the scores for the Broadway musicals *Wildcat*, a Lucille Ball vehicle (1960, 'Hey, Look Me Over', 'Give A Little Whistle', 'You've Come Home', 'What Takes My Fancy'), and the marvellous *Little Me* (1962, 'I've Got Your Number', 'Real Live Girl', 'On The Other Side Of The Tracks', 'Deep Down Inside'). Another number intended for *Little Me*, 'When In Rome', was recorded by **Barbra Streisand** and **Vikki Carr**. The team also worked on an abortive musical adaptation of the memoirs of stripper Gypsy Rose Lee (later immortalized as *Gypsy* with a score by **Jule Styne** and **Stephen Sondheim**), from which came 'Firefly'. It gave **Tony Bennett** a bestselling record, and he included the song, along with Leigh and Coleman's sensitive ballad 'It Amazes Me', on *Tony Bennett At Carnegie Hall*. After they split up, Leigh and Coleman worked together again on the charming 'Pass Me By', which was sung over the titles of the 1964 Cary Grant movie *Father Goose*; and 'A Doodlin' Song', which was recorded by **Peggy Lee**. In 1967, Leigh teamed with composer **Elmer Bernstein** on the score for *How Now, Dow Jones* ('Live A Little', 'Walk Away', 'He's Here!' and 'Step To The Rear'), and in later years continued to write occasionally for the stage, television and films. She wrote the lyrics for the Bicentennial show *Something To Do*, and for the television special *Heidi*. Her other songs included 'Stay With Me', 'Love Is A Melody (Short And Sweet)', 'Disenchanted Castle', 'Playboy Theme', 'On Second Thought', 'In The Barrio', 'Westport' and 'Bouncing Back For More'. Among her collaborators were **Morton Gould**, Lee Pockriss and **Marvin Hamlisch**. She was working on a musical adaptation of *Smiles* with Hamlisch when she died from a heart attack in 1983.

Leigh, Mitch

b. Irwin Mitchnick, 30 January 1928, Brooklyn, New York, USA. A composer, producer and director for the musical theatre and television, Leigh studied music at Yale, graduating with a B.A. and M.A. In the late 50s he formed Music Makers, a company which eventually became the prime source of television and radio jingles in the USA. In the early 60s, Leigh wrote the incidental music for two plays, *Too Good To Be True* and *Never Live Over A Pretzel Factory*, before collaborating with lyricist Joe Darion (b. 30 January 1917, New York, USA.) on the musical *Man Of La Mancha* in 1965. It ran for 2,328 performances in New York and won five Tony Awards, and one of its songs, 'The Impossible Dream', was awarded the Contemporary Classic Award by the Songwriters Hall of Fame. Since then, Leigh has been unable to attain anywhere near that degree of success with Broadway shows such as *Cry For Us All* (1970), *Home Sweet Homer* (one performance in 1976), *Sarava* (1979), *Chu Chem* (1989), and *Ain't Broadway Grand* (1993). Indeed, they were all flops, and one or two more of Leigh's efforts closed out of town. A 25th anniversary production of *Man Of La Mancha*, starring Raul Julia and **Sheena Easton**, toured the US, and played 108 performances on Broadway in 1992.

Leigh, Richard

b. Virginia, USA. In 1974, immediately following his graduation, the songwriter Richard Leigh went to Nashville. Within a year he had written **Crystal Gayle**'s first country number 1, 'I'll Get Over You', and shortly after that he also wrote her third, 'Don't It Make My Brown Eyes Blue'. He had initially believed that 'Don't It Make My Brown Eyes Blue' would suit **Shirley Bassey**, but Gayle took the song, for which Leigh won a Grammy, and made it a worldwide hit (it reached number 5 in the UK). Leigh also co-wrote the following country number 1 singles: 'That's The Thing About Love' by **Don Williams** (co-written with Gary Nicholson), 'Put Your Dreams Away' by **Mickey Gilley** (co-written with Wayland Holyfield) and 'Life's Highway' by **Steve Wariner** (co-written with Roger Murrah). Other songs he has written include 'The Greatest Man I Never Knew' (**Reba McEntire**), 'I Wouldn't Have It Any Other Way' (**Aaron Tippin**), 'It's All I Can Do' (**Anne Murray**) and 'It Ain't Gonna Worry My Mind' (**Ray Charles** and Mickey Gilley). He has said of his songwriting talent: 'I work from my own experiences because that makes it possible to put details in and make it believable. Without details, people are tipped off that it's just fiction.'
● ALBUMS: *Richard Leigh* (United Artists 1980)★★.

Leiner, Robert

b. c.1966, Gothenburg, Sweden. One of the first techno artists to actually appear, in soft focus, on his album sleeves, robbing the genre of its usual anonymity. Leiner was formerly the in-house engineer for the Belgian-based **R&S** Label. He himself has relocated to

Ghent after establishing himself as a DJ in Gothenburg. His own output reflects his prolific nature: 'I have ideas all the time, it never ends. I just wish I could put something into my head and record direct from there'. He started making music at the age of 14, and keeps a stock of old tapes, sounds or sequences that he constantly returns to in the way of samples. Hence his second album was titled *Visions Of The Past*, as it included snapshots from several eras of his life. His first dance-floor manoeuvres were conducted under the name the Source, and included two double-pack 12-inches, 'Organised Noise' and 'Source Experience'. Both showcased Leiner's trippy, engaging work, redolent in tribal, spacey rhythms which have also characterised his work under his own name.

● ALBUMS: *Organised Noise* (R&S 1993)★★★, *Visions Of The Past* (Apollo 1994)★★★.

Lema, Ray

b. 20 July 1946, Lufu-Toto, Zaire. At the age of 11, vocalist, keyboard player, composer and bandleader Lema was placed in a seminary by his parents, who intended him to become a priest. Introduced to the church organ by one of his teachers, it soon became apparent that the boy had an immense musical talent, and during the five years he spent at the seminary, ecclesiastical studies increasingly gave way to the theory and practice of music. At the age of 15, he gave a solo concert of Beethoven's 'Moonlight Sonata' in the cathedral of Kinshasa, the capital of Zaire. Leaving the seminary, Lema began attending Kinshasa's University of Lovanium, where he studied chemistry by day and performed with a wide variety of soukous musicians by night, including such major figures as **Tabu Ley** and **M'Pongo Love**. In 1974, he was appointed musical director of the National Ballet of Zaire, and began to travel widely around Zaire studying the traditional music of the nearly 250 different ethnic groups. In 1978, with his group Ya Tupas, he won the Maracas D'Or, the first time a Zairean musician had acquired this prestigious French award. The following year he was given a grant by the Rockefeller Foundation to work and study in the USA. Returning from the USA in 1982, Lema moved from Kinshasa to Paris - then emerging as a major centre for African music in Europe - where he signed to the new African music label, Celluloid Records. He rapidly established himself as one of the most innovative stylists in expatriate Zairean music, with the self-chosen, and highly controversial, mission of reinterpreting traditional Zairean music through the use of synthesizers and electronics. In 1985, he collaborated with **Stewart Copeland** of the **Police** on the single, 'Koteja', a marriage of electronic keyboards with a heavy-funk drumtrack and synthesized percussion, creating a sound that went far beyond what was then normally thought of as Zairean music. In 1990, he signed to the **Island Records** subsidiary Mango, and produced his most commercially successful album to date. *Nangadeef* was typically adventurous and icono-

clastic, still solidly based in Zairean rhythm and melody but also including contributions from British jazz saxophonist **Courtney Pine** and South African vocal group the **Mahotella Queens**. Now dividing his time between Paris, Zaire and the USA, Lema continues to expand the boundaries of Zairean music, drawing enthusiasm and condemnation in roughly equal proportions. Albums such as *Gaia*, which married synthesized keyboard work to soukous in a daring manner, outraged the purists.

● ALBUMS: *Koteja-Koluto* (Celluloid 1979)★★★, *Paris-Kinshasa-Washington DC* (Celuloid 1984)★★★, *Medicine* (Celuloid 1986)★★★, *Nangadeef* (Mango 1990)★★★★, *Gaia* (Mango 1991)★★★, *Ray Lema/Les Voix Bulgaires* (1992)★★★, *Ray Lema/Professor Stefanov* (1992)★★, with Joachim Kuhn *Euro African Suite* (1993)★★★, *Green Light* (Buda-Melodie 1996)★★★★.

LeMarc, Peter

b. Sweden. LeMarc, who is arguably Sweden's most popular male vocalist/singer-songwriter, began his musical career in 1982 when he moved to the country's capital, Stockholm. Since then he has recorded prolifically, securing enormous popular appeal as well as critical support. The best of his 80s recordings was undoubtedly the self-titled 1987 collection which, with strong marketing support, became a gold seller and earned a Grammy award for LeMarc as Best Male Artist. Both *Nämare Gränsen* (Closer To The Edge) and *Välkommen Hem!* (Welcome Home) also achieved gold status. His popularity still rising, *Sangen Dom Spelar När Filmen Är Slut* (The Song They Play At The End Of The Film) and *Hittegods* (Lost Luggage) bettered this feat by achieving platinum status. Although covering a wide emotional spectrum, part of LeMarc's appeal as a writer can be attributed to the lack of sentiment in his lyrics. Instead his songs radiate an earnestness of approach which has seen him compared to artists such as **Bruce Springsteen**.

● ALBUMS: *Buick* (MNW 1982)★★★, *Circus Circus* (MNW 1983)★★★, *Efter Tusen Timmar* (MNW 1984)★★★, *Marmor* (MNW 1986)★★★, *Peter LeMarc* (MNW 1987)★★★, *Nämare Gränsen* (MNW 1988)★★★, *Välkommen Hem!* (MNW 1990)★★★, *Sangen Dom Spelar När Filmen Är Slut* (MNW 1991)★★★★, *Hittegods* (MNW 1992)★★★, *Det Finns Inget Bättre* (MNW 1992)★★★, *Bueno Sera* (MNW 1993)★★★.

Lemer, Pepi

b. 25 May 1944, Ilfracombe, Devon, England. Lemer was born into a musical family and had classical singing lessons from the age of five. She went on to stage school and has worked in cabaret and the theatre both in the UK and abroad. Lemer was able to cover all sorts of singing styles from the most abstract improvisation to popular song and has done session work with **Alan Price** and **Mike Oldfield**. In the 60s and early 70s she worked with **John Stevens' Spontaneous Music Ensemble**, Pete Lemer's E, **Keith Tippett**'s Centipede,

Mike Gibbs and Barbara Thompson's Paraphernalia. Then with Jeff Clyne she led the band Turning Point, which undertook an Arts Council UK tour in 1971 with guests Allan Holdsworth and Neil Ardley, who later wrote 'The Harmony Of The Spheres' for a 9-piece ensemble with her voice and that of Norma Winstone.

● ALBUMS: *Will Power* (1974)★★★★, with Turning Point *Creatures Of The Night* (1977)★★★, with Neil Ardley *The Harmony Of The Spheres* (1978)★★★★, *Silent Promise* (1979)★★★.

Lemon Kittens
(see Dax, Danielle)

Lemon Pipers
This New York-based quintet - Ivan Browne (vocals/rhythm guitar), Bill Bartlett (lead guitar), R.G. (Reg) Nave (organ), Steve Walmsley (bass) and Bill Albuagh (drums) - made its debut in 1967 with 'Turn Around And Take A Look'. Its rudimentary style was then replaced by the measured approach of aspiring songwriting/production team, Paul Leka and Shelly Pinz. Together they created a distinctive Lemon Pipers sound, a sparkling mélange of sweeping strings and percussive vibraslaps exemplified on the group's million-selling hit, 'Green Tambourine'. The attendant album contained several songs - 'Rice Is Nice', 'Shoeshine Boy' - which were recorded in a similar style, but the set also contained the startling 'Through With You', an extended *tour de force* for Bartlett's rampaging guitarwork and a surprise for those anticipating easy-on-the-ear fare. Subsequent recordings failed to match their early success, and although a second album, *Jungle Marmalade*, offered several inventive moments, the Lemon Pipers were tarred as a bubblegum attraction on the strength of that first hit. The group broke up in 1969, although Bartlett later found success as a member of Ram Jam.

● ALBUMS: *Green Tambourine* (Buddah 1967)★★★, *Jungle Marmalade* (1968)★★.
● COMPILATIONS: *The Lemon Pipers* (1990)★★★, *Best Of The Lemon Pipers* (Camden 1998)★★★.

Lemon Popsicle
Released in 1977, but set 20 years earlier, *Lemon Popsicle* has been described as an Israeli *American Graffiti*, as its plot revolves around the lives of a group of teenagers. Sadly, the film provided little insight into the participants' experience of Israeli life, grafting instead impressions from American movies of that period gained by director Boaz Davidson. The soundtrack, although exemplary, was too often anachronistic and critics have often commented that too often a song replaced the on-screen narrative. Briefly popular, it inspired an even poorer sequel, *Going Steady*.

Lemon Tree
Comprising Derek Arnold (bass), Mike Hopkins (guitar), Keith Smart (drums), Mick Taylor (vocals) and Gary Wortley (organ), Lemon Tree formed in Birmingham, Midlands, England, in the mid-60s. Smart was formerly a member of Danny King And The Mayfair Set, while Hopkins had worked with Denny Laine in the Diplomats. After signing a contract with Parlophone Records in 1968 the group released its debut single, 'William Chaulker's Time Machine'. A quasi-psychedelic pop single, it was written by Ace Kefford, formerly of the Move. His fellow Move colleague Trevor Burton produced it in association with Andy Fairweather-Low. The partnership arose because both Burton and Kefford had also been members of Danny King And The Mayfair Set alongside Smart. A second single produced by the same team, 'It's So Nice To Come Home', followed in 1969. However, this too proved unsuccessful, leading to the band's dissolution. Smart later worked with bands including the Uglys, Balls, Wizzard and Mongrel, while Hopkins spent a short time in the Idle Race.

Lemon, Brian
b. 11 February 1937, Nottingham, England. After playing piano in and around his home town, Lemon moved to London in the mid-50s where he joined the Freddy Randall band. During the late 50s and early 60s he played with several bands ranging from those of a traditional bent through to the mainstream and into post-bop. Amongst the leaders with whom he has worked are Betty Smith, Al Fairweather, Sandy Brown, Dave Shepherd, Danny Moss, George Chisholm and Alex Welsh. A regular member of the house band at leading London venues such as the Pizza Express and Ronnie Scott's, he has also backed several visiting American jazz musicians, including Benny Goodman, Ben Webster, Milt Jackson and Buddy Tate. Always displaying considerable flair and switching styles with rare ease, by the 70s Lemon had become a familiar and popular figure on the UK jazz scene, a role he maintained throughout the 80s and into the early 90s. He is also in demand as a session musician on radio, performing and writing music within and beyond the framework of jazz.

● ALBUMS: *Our Kind Of Music* (Hep Jazz 1970)★★★, *Piano Summit* (1975)★★★★, with Warren Vache . . . *Play Harry Warren: An Affair To Remember* (Zephyr 1997)★★★★.

Lemonheads
From their origins in the Boston, USA hardcore scene, the Lemonheads and their photogenic singer/guitarist Evan Dando (b. Evan Griffith Dando, 4 March 1967, Boston, Massachusetts, USA) have come full circle; from sweaty back-street punk clubs to teen-pop magazines such as *Smash Hits*. The group first formed as the Whelps in 1985, with Jesse Peretz on bass and Dando and Ben Deily sharing guitar and drum duties. Enthused by DJ Curtis W. Casella's radio show, they pestered him into releasing their debut EP, *Laughing All The Way To The Cleaners*, in a pressing of 1,000 copies, on his newly activated Taang! label. It featured a cover

version of Proud Scum's 'I Am A Rabbit', an obscure New Zealand punk disc often aired by the DJ. By January 1987, Dando had recruited the group's first regular drummer, Doug Trachten, but he stayed permanent only for their debut album, *Hate Your Friends*, allegedly pressed in over seventy different versions by Taang! with an eye on the collector's market. This was a more balanced effort than the follow-up, which this time boasted the services of **Blake Babies** drummer John Strohm. *Creator* (reissued in 1996 with extra tracks) revealed Dando's frustration at marrying commercial punk-pop with a darker lyrical perspective, evident in the cover version of Charles Manson's 'Your Home Is Where You're Happy' (the first of several references to the 60s figurehead). The band split shortly afterwards, following a disastrous Cambridge, Massachusetts gig, where Dando insisted on playing sections of **Guns N'Roses'** 'Sweet Child O Mine' during every guitar solo. However, the offer of a European tour encouraged him to reunite the band, this time with himself as drummer, adding second guitarist Coorey Loog Brennan (ex-Italian band Superfetazione; Bullet Lavolta). After *Lick* was issued in 1989, Deily, Dando's long-time associate and co-writer, decided to leave to continue his studies. He would subsequently assemble his own band, Pods. However, for the second time Dando dissolved the Lemonheads, immediately following their acclaimed major label debut, *Lovey*. Peretz moved to New York to pursue his interests in photography and film, while new recruit David Ryan (b. 20 October 1964, Fort Wayne, Indiana, USA) vacated the drum-stool. The new line-up featured Ben Daughtry (bass) and Byron Hoagland (drums, ex-**Squirrel Bait**). However, the new rhythm section was deemed untenable because Daughtry 'had a beard', so Peretz and Ryan (both Harvard graduates) returned to the fold. The band, for some time hovering on the verge of a commercial breakthrough, finally achieved it by embarking on a series of cover versions; 'Luka' (**Suzanne Vega**) and 'Different Drum' (**Michael Nesmith**) were both *Melody Maker* singles of the week. There were also two cover versions on their *Patience And Prudence* EP, the old 50s chestnut 'Gonna Get Along Without You Now', plus a humorous reading of **New Kids On The Block**'s 'Step By Step' - wherein Dando imitated each of the five vocal parts. Other choices have included **Gram Parsons**, hardcore legends the **Misfits**, and even a track from the musical *Hair*. However, the cover version that made them cover stars proper was an affectionate reading of **Simon And Garfunkel**'s 'Mrs Robinson'. By 1992 Nic Dalton (b. 6 June 1966, Canberra, Australia; ex-Hummingbirds, and several other less famous Antipodean bands) had stepped in on bass to help out with touring commitments, his place eventually becoming permanent. Dando had met him while he was in Australia, where he discovered Tom Morgan (ex-Sneeze, who had also included Dalton in their ranks), who would co-write several songs for the forthcoming *It's A Shame About*

Ray set. Dando's 'girlfriend' **Juliana Hatfield** (bass, ex-Blake Babies) also helped out at various points, notably on 'Bit Part'. She was the subject of 'It's About Time' on the follow-up, *Come On Feel The Lemonheads*, on which she also sang backing vocals. Other guests included **Belinda Carlisle**. The success of *It's A Shame About Ray* offered a double-edged sword: the more pressure increased on Dando to write another hit album, the more he turned to hard drugs. Sessions were delayed as he took time out to repair a badly damaged voice, allegedly caused through smoking crack cocaine. That *Come On Feel The Lemonheads* emerged at the tail-end of 1993 was surprise enough, but to hear Dando's songwriting continue in its purple patch was even more gratifying. *Car Button Cloth* came in the wake of Dando attempting to clean himself up. It was generally well received and contained some of his most mellow (some would say broody) songs to date. The band were dropped by **Atlantic** after its release.

● ALBUMS: *Hate Your Friends* (Taang! 1987)★★, *Creator* (Taang! 1988)★★, *Lick* (Taang! 1989)★★★, *Lovey* (Atlantic 1990)★★, *Favourite Spanish Dishes* mini-album (Atlantic 1990)★★, *It's A Shame About Ray* (Atlantic 1992)★★★★, *Come On Feel The Lemonheads* (Atlantic 1993)★★★★, *Car Button Cloth* (Atlantic 1996)★★★.

● VIDEOS: *Two Weeks In Australia* (1993).

● FURTHER READING: *The Illustrated Story*, Everett True. *The Lemonheads*, Mick St. Michael.

Lena Horne At The Waldorf Astoria - Lena Horne

This album, which was made when on-site recording was very much in its infancy, has become a classic of its kind. It gives a tantalizing insight into the ritzy world of New York cabaret and one of the supreme exponents of that art. The risqué 'New-Fangled Tango' received much air play at the time, but **Lena Horne** ran the gamut of musical emotions in a perfectly balanced programme that ranged from the witty 'How You Say It', through a storming version of 'Day In Day Out', to a medley of what she herself calls 'the surprising Cole Porter tunes'. Still as fresh as ever after 40 years.

● Tracks: *Today I Love Everybody; Let Me Love You; Come Running; How's Your Romance; After You; Love Of My Life; It's Alright With Me; Mood Indigo; I'm Beginning To See The Light; How You Say It; Honeysuckle Rose; Day In, Day Out; New-Fangled Tango; I Love To Love; From This Moment On.*

● First released 1957

● UK peak chart position: did not chart

● USA peak chart position: 24

Lend An Ear

Notable mainly for the Broadway debut of **Carol Channing**, the blonde comedienne with a the wide-eyed look and a voice that no-one has ever described satisfactorily, this revue opened at the National Theatre in New York on 16 December 1948, after stop-overs during the previous few years in Pittsburgh and Los Angeles. *Lend An Ear* was also the first Broadway musical to be directed and choreographed by the former dancer, **Gower Champion**, and Charles Gaynor, another new boy in the 'back-stage' department, contributed the witty music, lyrics, and sketches. Gaynor went through the card, pointing-up and lampooning a variety of targets, but some of the funniest moments came when he concentrated on a pair of celebrities who lived their lives according to the columnists, the effect on society by the growing influence of psychoanalysts, an opera company that just reads the librettos because it cannot afford an orchestra, and a wicked 20s spoof concerning a theatrical touring company that has sent out several versions of *The Gladioli Girl* over the years, none of which has returned. The songs, too, were affectionate parodies of the kind from days gone by, and included 'Give Your Heart A Chance To Sing', 'Doin' The Old Yahoo Step', 'Molly O'Reilly', 'Who Hit Me?', 'In Our Teeny Weeny Little Nest', 'Where Is The She For Me?'. The lively, young and talented cast consisted of William Eythe, Yvonne Adair, Jennie Lou Law, Gloria Hamilton, Bob Scheerer, and **Gene Nelson**, the song-and-dance man who had had begun his film career in 1947, and will be affectionately remembered for his performances in musicals such as *Lullaby Of Broadway*, *Tea For Two*, and especially *Oklahoma!*. In some ways, a suprising and gratifying production for its time, *Lend An Ear* enjoyed a good run of 460 performances.

Lennon Sisters

In 1955, the Lennon sisters, Dianne (b. 1939, Los Angeles, California, USA), Peggy (b. 1941, Los Angeles, California, USA), Kathy (b. 1944, Santa Monica, California, USA) and Janet (b. 1939, Culver City, California, USA) came to national attention in the USA as a featured vocal group - all scripted grinning and harmless fun - on light orchestral supremo **Lawrence Welk**'s weekly television show. It was through his influence that they were contracted by Coral Records. Catchy tunes with jaunty rhythms were the sisters' speciality - as demonstrated in their cover (with accompaniment by Welk musicians) of the Patience And Prudence novelty, 'Tonight You Belong To Me', which reached number 15 in the *Billboard* Hot 100 in 1956. The Lennons' second - and final - chart success was with the atypically downbeat choice of Sue Thompson's 'Sad Movies (Make Me Cry)' in 1961.

● ALBUMS: *Christmas With The Lennon Sisters* (1961),★★ *Somethin' Stupid* (1967)★★★.

Lennon, John

b. 9 October 1940, Liverpool, England, d. 8 December 1980, New York, USA. John Winston Ono Lennon has been exhumed in print more than any other popular musical figure, including the late **Elvis Presley**, of whom Lennon said that he 'died when he went into the army'. Such was the cutting wit of a deeply loved and sadly missed giant of the 20th century. As a member of the world's most successful group ever, he changed lives

for the better. Following the painful collapse of the **Beatles**, he came out a wiser but angrier person. Together with his wife **Yoko Ono**, he attempted to transform the world through non-musical means. To many they appeared as naïve crackpots; Ono in particular has been victim of some appalling insults in the press. One example shown in the film *Imagine* depicts the cartoonist Al Capp being both hostile and dangerously abusive. Their bed-in in Amsterdam and Montreal, their black bag appearances on stage, their innocent flirting with political activists and radicals, all received massive media attention. These events were in search of world peace, which regrettably was unachievable. What Lennon did achieve, however, was to educate us all to the idea of world peace. During the Gulf War of 1991, time and time again various representatives of those countries who were initially opposed to war (and then asked for a ceasefire), unconsciously used Lennon's words; 'Give Peace A Chance'. The importance of that lyric could never have been contemplated, when a bunch of mostly stoned members of the **Plastic Ono Band** sat on the floor of the Hotel La Reine and recorded 'Give Peace A Chance', a song that has grown in stature since its release in 1969.

Lennon's solo career began a year earlier with *Unfinished Music No 1 - Two Virgins*. The sleeve depicted him and Ono standing naked, and the cover became better known than the disjointed sound effects contained within. Three months later Lennon continued his marvellous joke on us, with *Unfinished Music No 2 - Life With The Lions*. One side consisted of John and Yoko calling out to each other during her stay in a London hospital while pregnant. Lennon camped by the side of her bed during her confinement and subsequent miscarriage. Four months after 'Give Peace a Chance', 'Cold Turkey' arrived via the Plastic Ono Band, consisting of Lennon, Ono, **Eric Clapton**, **Klaus Voorman** and drummer Alan White. This raw rock song about heroin withdrawal was also a hit, although it failed to make the Top 10. Again, Lennon's incorrigible wit worked when he sent back his MBE to the Queen, protesting about the Biafran war, Britain supporting the American involvement in Vietnam and 'Cold Turkey' slipping down the charts. In February 1970, a cropped-headed Lennon was seen performing 'Instant Karma' on the BBC Television programme *Top Of The Pops*; this drastic action was another anti-war protest. This **Phil Spector**-produced offering was his most melodic post-Beatles song to date and was his biggest hit thus far in the UK and the USA. The release of *John Lennon - Plastic Ono Band* in January 1971 was a shock to the system for most Beatles' fans. This stark 'primal scream' album was recorded following treatment with Dr. Arthur Janov. It is as brilliant as it is disturbing. Lennon poured out much of his bitterness from his childhood and adolescence, neat and undiluted. The screaming 'Mother' finds Lennon grieving for her loss and begging for his father. Lennon's Dylanesque 'Working Class Hero' is another stand-out track; in less vitriolic tone he croons: 'A working class hero is something to be, if you want to be a hero then just follow me'. The irony is that Lennon was textbook middle-class and his agony stemmed from the fact that he *wanted* to be working-class. The work was a cathartic exorcism for Lennon, most revealing on 'God', in which he voiced the heretical, 'I don't believe in the Beatles . . .', before adding, 'I just believe in me, Yoko and me, and that's reality.' More than any other work in the Lennon canon, this was a farewell to the past. The album was brilliant, and 20 or more years later, it is regarded as his finest complete work.

His most creative year was 1971. Following the album Lennon released another strong single, 'Power To The People'. After his move to New York, the follow-up *Imagine* was released in October. Whilst the album immediately went to number 1 internationally, it was a patchy collection. The attack on **Paul McCartney** in 'How Do You Sleep?' was laboured over in the press and it took two decades before another track, 'Jealous Guy', was accepted as a classic, and only then after **Bryan Ferry**'s masterly cover became a number 1 hit. Lennon's resentment towards politicians was superbly documented in 'Gimme Some Truth' when he spat out, 'I'm sick and tired of hearing things from uptight, short-sighted, narrow-minded hypocrites'. The title track, however, remains as one of his greatest songs. Musically 'Imagine' is extraordinarily simple, but the combination of that simplicity and the timeless lyrics make it one of the finest songs of the century. A Christmas single came in December, 'Happy Christmas (War Is Over)', another song destined for immortality and annual reissue. Again, an embarrassingly simple message: 'War is over if you want it'. The following year *Sometime In New York City* was issued; this double set contained a number of political songs, and was written during the peak of Lennon's involvement with hippie-radical, Jerry Rubin. Lennon addresses numerous problems with angry lyrics over deceptively melodic songs. The lilting and seemingly innocent 'Luck Of The Irish' is one example of melody with scathing comment. The album's strongest track is yet another song with one of Lennon's statement-like titles: 'Woman Is The Nigger Of The World'. Once again he was ahead of the game, making a bold plea for women's rights a decade before it became fashionable. The following year he embarked on his struggle against deportation and the fight for his famous 'green card'. At the end of a comparatively quiet 1973, Lennon released *Mind Games*, an album that highlighted problems between him and Yoko. Shortly afterwards, Lennon left for his 'lost weekend' and spent many months in Los Angeles in a haze of drugs and alcohol. During a brief sober moment he produced **Nilsson**'s *Pussycats*. At the end of a dreadful year, Lennon released *Walls And Bridges*, which contained more marital material and a surprise US number 1, 'Whatever Gets You Through The Night', a powerful rocker with Lennon sounding in complete control. That month (November 1974), he made his last ever concert appearance when he appeared onstage at Madison Square Garden with **Elton John**. That night Lennon was reunited with Ono and, in his words, 'the separation failed'.

Rock 'N' Roll was released the next year; it was a tight and energetic celebration of many of his favourite songs, including 'Slippin' And Slidin'', 'Peggy Sue' and a superb 'Stand By Me'. The critics and public loved it and it reached number 6 on both sides of the Atlantic. Following the birth of their son Sean, Lennon became a house husband, while Ono looked after their not inconsiderable business interests. Five years later, a new album was released to a relieved public and went straight to number 1 virtually worldwide. The following month, with fans still jubilant at Lennon's return, he was suddenly brutally murdered by a gunman outside his apartment building in Manhattan. Almost from the moment that Lennon's heart stopped in the Roosevelt Hospital the whole world reacted in unprecedented mourning, with scenes usually reserved for royalty and world leaders. His records were re-released and experienced similar sales and chart positions to that of the Beatles' heyday. While all this happened, one could 'imagine' John Lennon calmly looking down on us, watching the world's reaction, and having a celestial laugh. Lennon could be cruel and unbelievably kind; he could love you one minute and destroy you with his tongue a few minutes later. Opinions as to his character are subjective. What is undeniable, is that the body of songs he created with Paul McCartney is the finest popular music catalogue ever known.

● ALBUMS: *Unfinished Music No 1 - Two Virgins* (Apple 1968)★, *Unfinished Music No 2 - Life With The Lions* (Zapple 1969)★, *The Wedding Album* (Apple 1969)★, *The Plastic Ono Band; Live Peace In Toronto 1969* (Apple 1970)★★★, *John Lennon Plastic Ono Band* (Apple 1971)★★★★★, *Imagine* (Apple 1971)★★★★, *Sometime In New York City* (Apple 1972)★★★, *Mind Games* (Apple 1973)★★★, *Walls And Bridges* (Apple 1974)★★★, *Rock 'N' Roll* (Apple 1975)★★★★, *Double Fantasy* (Geffen 1980)★★★, *Heartplay - Unfinished Dialogue* (Polydor 1983)★, *Milk And Honey* (Polydor 1984)★★, *Live In New York City* (Capitol 1986)★★, *Menlove Ave* (Capitol 1986)★★, *The Last Word* (Baktabak 1988)★, *Imagine - Music From The Motion Picture* (Parlophone 1988)★★, *John & Yoko: The Interview* (BBC 1990)★.

● COMPILATIONS: *Shaved Fish* (Apple 1975)★★★★, *The John Lennon Collection* (Parlophone 1982)★★★★★, *The Ultimate John Lennon Collection* (Parlophone 1990)★★★★, *Lennon Legend* (Parlophone 1997)★★★★.

● VIDEOS: *The Bed-In* (PMI 1991), *The John Lennon Video Collection* (PMI 1992), *One To One* (BMG 1993), *John Lennon: Imagine* (PMI 1997).

● FURTHER READING: many books have been written about Lennon, many are mediocre. The essential three are Ray Coleman's biography, Lennon's own *Spaniard In The Works/In His Own Write* and *The Ballad Of John And Yoko*, from *Rolling Stone*.

The full list: *In His Own Write*, John Lennon. *The Penguin*

John Lennon, John Lennon. *Lennon Remembers: The Rolling Stone Interviews*, Jann Wenner. *The Lennon Factor*, Paul Young. *The John Lennon Story*, George Tremlett. *John Lennon: One Day At A Time: A Personal Biography Of The Seventies*, Anthony Fawcett. *A Twist Of Lennon*, Cynthia Lennon. *John Lennon: The Life & Legend*, editors of Sunday Times. *John Lennon In His Own Words*, Miles. *A Spaniard In The Works*, John Lennon. *Lennon: What Happened!*, Timothy Green (ed.). *Strawberry Fields Forever: John Lennon Remembered*, Vic Garbarini and Brian Cullman with Barbara Graustark. *John Lennon: Death Of A Dream*, George Carpozi. *The Lennon Tapes: Andy Peebles In Conversation With John Lennon And Yoko Ono*, Andy Peebles. *The Ballad Of John And Yoko*, Rolling Stone Editors. *The Playboy Interviews With John Lennon And Yoko Ono*, John Lennon. *John Lennon: In My Life*, Peter Shotton and Nicholas Schaffner. *Loving John*, May Pang. *Dakota Days: The Untold Story Of John Lennon's Final Years*, John Green. *The Book Of Lennon*, Bill Harry. *John Ono Lennon 1967-1980*, Ray Coleman. *John Winston Lennon 1940-1966*, Ray Coleman. *Come Together: John Lennon In His Own Time*, Jon Wiener. *John Lennon: For The Record*, Peter McCabe and Robert D. Schonfeld. *The Lennon Companion: 25 Years Of Comment*, Elizabeth M. Thomson and David Gutman. *Imagine John Lennon*, Andrew Solt and Sam Egan. *Skywriting By Word Of Mouth*, John Lennon. *The Lives Of John Lennon*, Albert Goldman. *John Lennon My Brother*, Julia Baird. *The Other Side Of Lennon*, Sandra Shevey. *Days In The Life: John Lennon Remembered*, Philip Norman. *The Murder Of John Lennon*, Fenton Bresler. *The Art & Music Of John Lennon*, John Robertson. *In My Life: John Lennon Remembered*, Kevin Howless and Mark Lewisohn. *John Lennon: Living On Borrowed Time*, Frederic Seaman. *Let Me Take You Down: Inside The Mind Of Mark Chapman*, Jack Jones. *The Immortal John Lennon 1940-1980*, Michael Heatley. *John Lennon*, William Ruhlmann. *AI: Japan Through John Lennon's Eyes (A Personal Sketchbook)*, John Lennon. *Lennon*, John Robertson. *We All Shine On*, Paul Du Noyer.

● FILMS: *A Hard Day's Night* (1964), *Help* (1965), *Magical Mystery Tour* (1968), *Let It Be* (1971).

Lennon, Julian

b. John Charles Julian Lennon, 8 April 1963, Liverpool, England. To embark on a musical career in the same sphere as his late father was a bold and courageous move. The universal fame of **John Lennon** brought the inevitable comparisons, which quickly became more a source of irritation than pride. This awful paradox must have hampered the now low-profile career of a young star who began by releasing a commendable debut album in 1984. At times, Julian's voice uncannily and uncomfortably mirrored that of John's, nevertheless he was soon scaling the pop charts with excellent compositions like 'Valotte' and the reggae-influenced 'Too Late For Goodbyes'. The album was produced by **Phil Ramone** and showed a healthy mix of styles. Lennon was nominated for a Grammy in 1985 as the Best New Act. Success may have come too soon, and Julian indulged in the usual excesses and was hounded by the press, merely to find out what club he frequented

and whom he was dating. *The Secret Value Of Daydreaming* was a poor album of overdone rock themes and was critically ignored. Lennon licked his wounds and returned in 1989 with *Mr. Jordan* and a change of style. The soul/disco 'Now You're In Heaven' was a lively comeback single, and the album showed promise. 1991 saw Julian return to the conventional activities of recording and promotion with the release of a single embracing 'green' issues, 'Salt Water' supported by an imaginative video and a heavy promotion schedule. With his last album Lennon seemed to be making a career on his own terms, rather than those dictated by the memories of his father. By 1995, following the poor sales of his previous album, Virgin released Lennon from his contract, and he joined a touring production of the play *Mr Holland's Opus* for which he sang the title song. After many years of legal wrangles Lennon received a financial settlement from his father's estate and the executor **Yoko Ono**. The sum of £20 million was alleged to have been agreed. Lennon was quoted as saying he needed the money to relaunch his rock career. He subsequently broke a seven-year silence with *Photograph Smile*. The album was on his own label and was issued on the same day as his half-brother Sean's debut. The first single 'Day After Day' was a fabulous song but was virtually ignored by the media as they fawned over young Sean. The album was varied and much more like his father's mid-period Beatles' work. Sadly, due to his past overindulgence, Julian needs to court the media favourably before his recent work is listened to. *Photograph Smile* is an outstanding record of great maturity.

● ALBUMS: *Valotte* (Virgin 1984)★★★, *The Secret Value Of Daydreaming* (Virgin 1986)★★, *Mr Jordan* (Virgin 1989)★★, *Help Yourself* (Virgin 1991)★★, *Photograph Smile* (Music From Another Room 1998)★★★★.

Lennox, Annie

b. 25 December 1954, Aberdeen, Scotland. Following the amicable dissolution of the **Eurythmics** in 1991, the component parts of that band have gone on to widely varying degrees of success. Both of Lennox's first two solo efforts would reach number 1 in the UK charts, the second of which doing so while fellow **Dave Stewart** was underachieving with *Greetings From The Gutter*, which failed to break the UK Top 75. In fairness to Stewart, this may have more to do with the public's perceptions of the artists than any measure of their individual talents; Lennox was always the visual focus of their records, while her vocal presence defined their musical charm. However, in 1990 after winning her fourth Best British Female Artist award at the BRITS ceremony, she returned backstage to tell reporters that she intended to take a two-year sabbatical, and to concentrate on her family life. While pregnant she worked with computer expert Marius de Vries on songs she had recorded as rough demos, a process happily interrupted by the birth of Lennox's first child, Lola, in December 1990. Her debut solo album was produced

with Steve Lipson (**Simple Minds**, etc.) at her home and at Mayfair Studios in London, with co-writing collaborations with the **Blue Nile** and **Jeff Lynne**. *Diva* was released in February 1992 and its number 1 status confirmed that Lennox was still the subject of considerable affection among the British public. Released three years later, *Medusa* offered a wide-ranging selection of covers, mainly of songs which had previously been aired by a male vocalist. The classics included 'Whiter Shade Of Pale' ('the first serious record I bought', according to Lennox) and 'Take Me To The River', though others were drawn from less familiar sources, including the **Lover Speaks**' 'No More I Love You's, the **Clash**'s 'Train In Vain' and Blue Nile's 'Downtown Lights'. Aided by **Anne Dudley**'s string arrangements, harmonica, tabla and accordion, it allowed the artist to escape the rigours of lyric writing which had proved such a strain on the previous album. Further delay in hearing new material was created by the release of the limited edition live album *Live In Central Park*.
● ALBUMS: *Diva* (RCA 1992)★★★★, *Medusa* (RCA 1995)★★★, *Live In Central Park* (Arista 1996)★★★.
● VIDEOS: *In The Park* (BMG 1996).
● FURTHER READING: *Annie Lennox*, Lucy O'Brien.

Lenoir, J.B.

b. 5 March 1929, Monticello, Mississippi, USA, d. 29 April 1967, Champaign, Illinois, USA. Christened with initials, Lenoir was taught to play the guitar by his father, Dewitt. Other acknowledged influences were **Blind Lemon Jefferson**, **Arthur 'Big Boy' Crudup** and **Lightnin' Hopkins**, with the latter's single-string runs and verse tags becoming an integral part of the mature Lenoir style. He relocated to Chicago in 1949, and was befriended by **Big Bill Broonzy** and **Memphis Minnie**. Having leased his first recordings to **Chess** in 1952, label owner Joe Brown issued Lenoir's first success, 'The Mojo Boogie', on JOB Records in 1953. A propulsive dance piece sung in a high, keening tenor, it typified an important element of Lenoir's repertoire. The second main element was exhibited the following year with the release on **Parrot** of 'Eisenhower Blues', an uncompromising comment upon economic hardship, which the singer laid at the President's door. Also released that year, 'Mama Talk To Your Daughter' was another light-hearted boogie that became his signature tune, its ebullience mirrored by Lenoir's penchant for wearing zebra-striped jackets on stage. Subsequent records for Chess neglected the serious side of his writing, attempts at emulating previous successes taking preference over more sober themes such as 'We Can't Go On This Way' and 'Laid Off Blues'. Lenoir revealed that seriousness in an interview with Paul Oliver in 1960; this mood was in turn reflected in a series of recordings initiated by **Willie Dixon** and released to coincide with his appearance at the 1965 American Folk Blues Festival tour of Europe. *Alabama Blues* perfectly reconciled the two extremes of his style, remakes of 'The Mojo Boogie' and 'Talk To Your Daughter'

tempering the stark reality of the title song, 'Born Dead' and 'Down In Mississippi', in which Lenoir, with both passion and dignity, evoked America's civil rights struggle of the time. The great benefit that might have accrued from what, in hindsight, was the master work of his career, was prevented by his tragic death in a car crash.
● ALBUMS: *Alabama Blues* (Chess 1965)★★★, *Natural Man* (Chess 1968)★★★, *Chess Blues Masters* (Chess 1976)★★★★, *The Parrot Sessions 1954-55* (Relic 1989)★★★★, *His J.O.B. Recordings 1951-1954* (Flyright 1989)★★★★, *Mama Watch Your Daughter* (1993)★★★, *Vietnam Blues: The Complete L + R Recordings* (Evidence 1995)★★★★, with Geoffrey Richardson *Follow Your Heart* (Mouse 1995)★★★.

Leo Records

Founded in London, England, in 1980 by Russian expatriate Leo Feigin (b. 1 February 1938, St. Petersburg, Russia), Leo Records is the label that brought new Russian jazz to the west. Several of its first releases were of tapes smuggled out of Russia (formerly the USSR) and the sleeves bore the dramatic disclaimer: 'The musicians do not bear any responsibility for publishing these tapes.' Sometimes (of necessity) poorly recorded, these early albums met with a decidedly mixed critical reception, but Feigin proved an indefatigable champion of Russian jazz, gradually building up an impressive catalogue on only minimal resources. In addition to the **Ganelin Trio**, the first and best-known of the Russian groups on Leo, the label introduced numerous other artists from the then-USSR, including **Sergey Kuryokhin**, **Anatoly Vapirov**, Valentina Ponomareva, Jazz Group Archangelsk and the Siberian **Homo Liber**. Feigin also released many albums of west European and American jazz, usually from the more *avant garde* end of the spectrum: notable among these are releases by **Anthony Braxton**, **Marilyn Crispell**, **Amina Claudine Myers**, **Sun Ra** and **Cecil Taylor**, whose sound-poetry was first released on the Leo album *Chinampas* and whose *Live In Bologna* on Leo was voted record of the year in the 1988 *Wire* magazine critics' poll. Nevertheless, it is for its stalwart support of Russian new music that the label is best known - arguably its finest achievement. The realization of a dream for Feigin - who still runs the label on a shoestring from his front room - was the 1990 *Document*, a lavishly-presented eight-CD boxed-set that traced the development of Russia's contemporary jazz through the 80s. (This label should not be confused with the Finnish Leo label, run by **Edward Vesala**.)
● COMPILATIONS: *Document* 8-CD box set (Leo 1990)★★★★.
● FURTHER READING: *Russian Jazz New Identity*, Leo Feigin (ed.).

Leo, Philip

b. Philip Pottinger, Greenwich, London, England. Leo is widely known for his work with **C.J. Lewis**, who enjoyed crossover success in the early 90s. Leo and Lewis shared a love of music from childhood and both pursued careers within the music industry. Leo's first musical experience was at the Roger Manwood school, playing in the institute's steel band, which led to his mastering of both kit drums and keyboards. He began his professional involvement in the music business as a songwriter, following the presentation of his initial 90-minute demo to **Fashion Records**. The latter were suitably impressed and stated that when they asked whether Leo could provide any more, 'two further tapes arrived within the week!'. Some of the songs on the introductory demos provided hits for a number of the UK's top singers, including **Janet Lee Davis** ('Two Timing Lover'), Peter Spence ('Crazy Feeling') and **Nerious Joseph** ('Show The World' and 'She Gone And Left Me'). Leo's long-time cohort Lewis was enrolled to provide the DJ skills on the 1989 reggae chart-topper 'Why Do Fools Fall In Love', and in 1990, 'Good Thing Going'. In 1993 Leo recorded the entrancing 'Hypnotic Love', which featured his sparring partner on the ragga mix. Shortly after the hit, Lewis secured a major label contract that included Leo as the DJ's co-producer, and the duo subsequently released a succession of crossover hits. Following his success with Lewis, Leo diversified into an R&B style for the 1994 release of 'Second Chance', which sadly faltered. He had always demonstrated a willingness to expand his repertoire regardless of genre, but his enthusiasm was not greeted sympathetically; he continues to work within the industry and is a much-loved character.

● ALBUMS: *Today* (1991)★★★, *Down To Earth* (1997)★★, *Space Dub* (1997)★★★.

Leon, Craig

Producer Craig Leon has for nearly two decades busied himself with 'alternative' music. He began his career as a keyboard player and arranger with his own studio in Miami, Florida, USA, before transferring to New York. In the 70s he held an A&R post at **Sire Records**, where he was responsible for the development of pivotal acts including the **Ramones** and **Talking Heads**. He produced the Ramones first album and **Richard Hell And The Voidoids'** *Blank Generation* EP. He became an independent producer in 1976, moving to Europe a decade later. In the interim his name had been linked with high profile work with the **Bangles** and **Blondie**, two female-fronted bands who influenced UK bands such as the **Primitives** and **Adult Net**, whom Leon would also later produce. The Adult Net in turn connect with the **Fall**, and some of Leon's most pleasing work can be found on that band's early 90s trilogy; *Extricate*, *Shiftwork* and *Code Selfish*. He has also found time to partner **New Fast Automatic Daffodils, Front 242, Jesus Jones, Suicide, Pogues** and **Go-Betweens**.

Leonard, Deke

b. Roger Leonard, Wales. A veteran of a small, but thriving, Welsh beat group scene, Leonard was a member of Lucifer And The Corncrakers, the Jets, the Blackjacks, the Jets (again), the Smokeless Zone and the Dream prior to replacing Vic Oakley in the **Bystanders** in 1968. Concurrently, this close-harmony group had decided to pursue a more progressive direction and became **Man** on the newcomer's arrival. Influenced by Mickey Green of the **Pirates** and **Bo Diddley**, Leonard's guitar work and compositional skill was crucial in their evolution from concept album acolytes to free-flowing improvisers. He left the group in 1972, following the release of *Live At The Padgett Rooms, Penarth* and immediately recorded an impressive solo album, *Iceberg*. This inspired the formation of a permanent group which coincidentally supported Man on tour, but a disappointing second album, *Kamikaze*, doomed the project. Leonard subsequently rejoined his former colleagues, where he remained until their break-up in 1976. He completed a third album in 1981 and has continued to pursue a career in less fashionable enclaves, both as a solo attraction, and as a member of the reformed Man. In the early 90s, he turned his hand to music journalism.

● ALBUMS: *Iceberg* (1973)★★★★, *Kamikaze* (1974)★★, *Before Your Very Eyes* (1981)★★★.

Leonard, Harlan

b. 2 July 1905, Kansas City, Missouri, USA, d. 1983. After working in various bands in and around Kansas City, including that led by **George E. Lee**, in 1923, saxophonist Leonard joined **Bennie Moten** for a lengthy stay. In 1931, he co-led a band with Thamon Hayes that they named the Kansas City Skyrockets, which, by 1934, had relocated to Chicago, becoming Harlan Leonard And His Rockets. In 1937, the band folded, but Leonard reformed it in 1938, this time keeping the band together until the mid-40s. Despite some important engagements at such venues as the Savoy Ballroom in Harlem and the Hollywood Club in Los Angeles, the Rockets remained relatively little known among jazz fans. Thanks to the handful of records they made it is possible to see that the band had many important qualities. Notably, it was an early testing ground for arranger **Tadd Dameron** whose arrangements for 'A La Bridges' and 'Dameron Stomp', recorded in 1940, were ahead of their time. There were also some sidemen of merit; in addition to drummer **Jesse Price**, tenor saxophonists Jimmy Keith and Henry Bridges stood out, both composing and soloing on 'A La Bridges'. This same track also features the band's outstanding soloist, trombonist Fred Beckett, who later joined **Lionel Hampton**. In the mid-40s Leonard left music to work for the US Internal Revenue Service.

● COMPILATIONS: *Harlan Leonard Volumes1/2* (1939-40 recordings)★★★★, *Harlan Leonard And His Rockets 1940* (Original Jazz Classics 1992)★★★★.

Leonard, Jack

(see **Dorsey, Tommy**)

Leonardo

Early in 1993, residents of the UK could have been forgiven for consulting their calendars to see if the date was April 1 after reading reports that the Republic of Nauro, a small island in the Pacific (population 8,000), was financing a West End musical show with the proceeds from its major export - bird droppings (they are high in phosphates). *LEONARDO - THE MUSICAL - A PORTRAIT OF LOVE*, which opened at the Strand Theatre in London on 3 June 1993, was the brainchild of Duke Minks, an advisor to the Nauruan government, and a former road manager with the 60s pop group, **Unit Four Plus Two**, which had a UK number 1 in 1965 with 'Concrete And Clay'. Tommy Moeller, the co-writer of 'Concrete And Clay', is credited with *Leonardo*'s music and lyrics, along with Greg Moeller, Russell Dunlop, and Minks, who also produced the piece. John Kane's book ('half fact-half guesswork') begins and ends with the hero, Leonardo da Vinci (Paul Collis), on his deathbed - his masterpiece, the Mona Lisa, by his side. In Kane's scenario, Leonardo is commissioned by nobleman Francesco Del Giocondo (James Barron) to paint a portrait of his fiancé, Lisa (Jane Arden), but the artist falls in love with his model, and makes her pregnant. She cannot marry him, but must pretend that the child is Del Giocondo's or he will have them both killed. Eventually, she returns to the by now successful Leonardo, and begs his forgiveness, but he is accidentally killed by her husband in a jealous rage. Kane also hints at a homosexual relationship between the painter and his devoted friend, Melzi (Hal Fowler). Some 20 musical numbers accompanied this sad tale, and they included 'Who The Hell Are You?', 'Firenza Mia', 'Part Of Your Life', 'Just A Dream Away', 'Her Heart Beats', 'Endless As My Love', 'Just One More Time', 'Goodbye And No One Said A Word', 'Forever Child', 'Portrait Of Love', and 'She Lives With Me'. The President of Nauru hosted a first night party while the critics polished their prose: 'A great deal of risible tosh' . . . 'Only six months to Christmas and the first turkey has arrived', were typical tabloid comments. In addition, bearing in mind the source of the show's reported £2 million investment, there was a good deal of talk about fertiliser, and 'dropping us all in it'. *Leonardo* folded on 10 July after a run of just over four weeks. From his house in Cannes, Duke Minks, the instigator of it all, was quoted as saying: 'Leonardo died in Italy in 1519, and again in the Strand in 1993.'

Lerner, Alan Jay

b. 31 August 1918, New York, USA, d. June 1986. A lyricist and librettist, and one of the most eminent and literate personalities in the history of the Broadway musical theatre, Lerner played the piano as a child, and studied at the Juilliard School of Music, the Bedales public school in England, and Harvard University, where he took a Bachelor of Science degree in the late 30s. After working as a journalist and radio scriptwriter, he met composer **Frederick Loewe** at the Lamb's Club

in 1942. Also a pianist, Loewe had moved to the USA in 1924, and had previously been involved in some unsuccessful musical shows. The new team's first efforts, *What's Up?* and *The Day Before Spring* (1945; 'A Jug Of Wine', 'I Love You This Morning'), did not exactly set Broadway alight, but two years later, they had their first hit with *Brigadoon*. Lerner's whimsical fantasy about a Scottish village that only comes to life every 100 years, contained 'Waitin' For My Dearie', 'I'll Go Home To Bonnie Jean', 'The Heather On The Hill', 'Come To Me, Bend To Me', 'From This Day On', and the future standard, 'Almost Like Being In Love'. A film version was made in 1954, starring **Gene Kelly**, **Cyd Charisse** and Van Johnson.

After *Brigadoon*, Lerner collaborated with **Kurt Weill** on the vaudeville-style *Love Life* (1948), and then spent some time in Hollywood writing the songs, with **Burton Lane**, for *Royal Wedding* (1951). Among them was one of the longest-ever titles, 'How Could You Believe Me When I Said I Loved You (When You Know I've Been A Liar All My Life?)', expertly manipulated by **Fred Astaire** and **Jane Powell**. Another of the numbers, 'Too Late Now', sung by Powell, was nominated for an Academy Award. In the same year, Lerner picked up an Oscar for his story and screenplay for **George** and **Ira Gershwin**'s musical film *An American In Paris* (1951). Also in 1951, Lerner reunited with Loewe for the 'Gold Rush' Musical, *Paint Your Wagon*. The colourful score included 'They Call The Wind Maria', 'I Talk To The Trees', 'I Still See Elisa', 'I'm On My Way' and 'Wand'rin' Star', which, in the 1969 movie, received a lugubrious reading from Lee Marvin. Precisely the opposite sentiments prevailed in *My Fair Lady* (1956), Lerner's adaptation of *Pygmalion* by George Bernard Shaw, which starred **Rex Harrison** as the irascible Higgins, and **Julie Andrews** as Eliza ('I'm a good girl, I am'). Sometimes called 'the most perfect musical', Lerner and Loewe's memorable score included 'Why Can't The English?', 'Wouldn't It Be Loverly?', 'The Rain In Spain', 'I Could Have Danced All Night', 'On The Street Where You Live', 'Show Me', 'Get Me To The Church On Time', 'A Hymn To Him', 'Without You' and 'I've Grown Accustomed To Her Face'. 'Come To The Ball', originally written for the show, but discarded before the opening, was, subsequently, often performed, particularly by Lerner himself. After a run of 2,717 performances on Broadway, and 2,281 in London, the show was filmed in 1964, when Andrews was replaced by Audrey Hepburn (dubbed by Marni Nixon). The Broadway Cast album went to number 1 in the US charts, sold over five million copies, and stayed in the Top 40 for 311 weeks. In 1958 Lerner was back in Hollywood, with a somewhat reluctant Loewe, for one of the last original screen musicals, the charming *Gigi*. Lerner's stylish treatment of Colette's turn-of-the-century novella, directed by **Vincente Minnelli**, starred **Maurice Chevalier**, **Leslie Caron**, Louis Jourdan and Hermione Gingold, and boasted a delightful score that included 'The Night They Invented

Champagne', 'Say A Prayer For Me Tonight', 'I'm Glad I'm Not Young Anymore', 'Thank Heaven For Little Girls', 'Waltz At Maxim's', 'She Is Not Thinking Of Me' and the touching 'I Remember It Well', memorably performed by Chevalier and Gingold. Lerner won one of the film's nine Oscars for his screenplay, and another, with Loewe, for the title song.

Two years later, Lerner and Loewe returned to Broadway with **Camelot**, a musical version of the Arthurian legend, based on T.H. White's *The Once And Future King*. With Julie Andrews, Richard Burton and **Robert Goulet**, plus a fine score that included 'C'Est Moi', 'The Lusty Month Of May', 'If Ever I Would Leave You', 'Follow Me', 'How To Handle A Woman' and the title song, the show ran on Broadway for two years. During that time it became indelibly connected with the Kennedy presidency: 'for one brief shining moment, that was known as Camelot'. The 1967 movie version was poorly received. In the early 60s, partly because of the composer's ill health, Lerner and Loewe ended their partnership, coming together again briefly in 1973 to write some new songs for a stage presentation of *Gigi*, and, a year later, for the score to the film *The Little Prince*. Lerner's subsequent collaborators included Burton Lane for *On A Clear Day You Can See Forever* (1965) ('Come Back To Me', 'On The S.S. Bernard Cohn', and others). Lerner won a Grammy award for the title song, and maintained that it was his most frequently recorded number. He wrote with Lane again in 1979 for *Carmelina*. In the interim he collaborated with **André Previn** for *Coco* (1969), which had a respectable run of 332 performances, mainly due to its star, Katherine Hepburn, and with **Leonard Bernstein** for *1600 Pennsylvania Avenue* (1976). Lerner's last musical, **Dance A Little Closer** (1983), which starred his eighth wife, English actress Liz Robertson, closed after one performance. They had met in 1979 when he directed her, as Eliza, in a major London revival of *My Fair Lady*. Shortly before he died of lung cancer in June 1986, he was still working on various projects, including a musical treatment of the 30s film comedy *My Man Godfrey*, in collaboration with pianist-singer Gerard Kenny, and *Yerma*, based on the play by Federico Garcia Lorca. Frederick Loewe, who shared in Lerner's triumphs, and had been semi-retired since the 60s, died in February 1988. In 1993, New Yorkers celebrated the 75th anniversary of Lerner's birth, and his remarkable and fruitful partnership with Loewe, with *The Night They Invented Champagne: The Lerner And Loewe Revue*, which played for a season at the Rainbow and Stars.

● ALBUMS: *An Evening With Alan Jay Lerner* (Laureate 1977)★★★.

● FURTHER READING: *The Musical Theatre: A Celebration*, Alan Jay Lerner. *The Street Where I Live: The Story Of My Fair Lady, Gigi And Camelot*, Alan Jay Lerner. *A Hymn To Him: The Lyrics Of Alan Jay Lerner*, Benny Green (ed.). *The Wordsmiths: Oscar Hammerstein & Alan Jay Lerner*, Stephen Citron.

Lerner, Sammy

b. 1904, USA, d. 13 December 1990, Los Angeles, California, USA. A popular songwriter from the 20s through to the 50s, Lerner wrote mostly lyrics, but sometimes composed the music as well. He wrote special material for vaudeville performers, and contributed lyrics and scripts to early musical shorts for Paramount Pictures. Later, several of his songs were interpolated into minor movie musicals such as *Laugh It Off* (1939), *Ma, He's Making Eyes At Me, Margie, La Conga Nights, A Little Bit Of Heaven, Larceny With Music, His Butler's Sister*, and *Golden Girl* (1951). He was the sole author of 'I'm Popeye The Sailor Man', which was introduced in the 1934 cartoon *Popeye The Sailor*, and his other best known songs include '(Oh Suzanna) Dust Off That Old Pianna', 'Is It True What They Say About Dixie?' (both with Gerald Marks and **Irving Caesar**), and 'Judy' (with **Hoagy Carmichael**). Lerner also wrote the English words for 'Falling In Love Again' (music Frederick Hollander), which was introduced by **Marlene Dietrich** in the classic 1930 move *The Blue Angel*. Lerner teamed with Al Goodhart and **Al Hoffman** on the scores for several British stage shows in the 30s, including *Going Greek* and *Hide And Seek*, and contributed to some Broadway productions. Among his other collaborators were **Burton Lane**, George Jessel, **Richard Whiting**, Charles Previn, Ben Oakland, and Frank Skinner.

LeRoi Brothers

Formed in Austin Texas in 1980 by Steve Doerr (guitar/vocals), Don Leady (guitar/vocals) and Mike Buck (drums; ex-**Fabulous Thunderbirds**). Keith Ferguson, bassist with the latter group, augmented the trio on *Check This Action*, where vibrant readings of 'Ain't I'm A Dog' and 'Big Time Operator' confirmed their grasp of rockabilly/rock. Jackie Newhouse (bass) and Joe Doerr (vocals) were then added to the line-up on *Forget About The Action, Think Of The Fun*, but progress was undermined in 1985 when Leady left to join Ferguson in the Tailgators. Evan Johns (guitar) brought a cajun flavour to *Protection From Enemies*, but the newcomer subsequently left to re-establish his own act, Evan Johns And The H-Bombs. Joe Doerr was also absent from *Open All Night* which featured new guitarist Rick Rawls. Although turbulent, the LeRoi Brothers remain a highly-popular live attraction.

● ALBUMS: *Check This Action* (1981)★★★★, *Forget About The Danger, Think Of The Fun* (1984)★★★, *Lucky Lucky Me* (1985)★★★, *Protection From Enemies* (1985)★★★, *Open All Night* (1987)★★.

Lerole, Elias, And His Zig Zag Jive Flutes

This studio band was one of the most popular pennywhistle jive outfits in South Africa in the mid-50s, and released the first version of the evergreen and hypnotic 'Tom Hark' in 1956. Although a massive international hit for the group - spawning countless cover versions from **Ted Heath** in the 50s through to the present day - the members of the Zig Zag Jive Flutes are reputed to have received only $10 each for their efforts, while composer Aaron Lerole, Elias's brother, received the princely sum of $15 and the added accolade of having his song credited to producer Ernest Bopape. However, that was showbusiness, 50s-style, in South Africa.

Les Aiglons

A five-piece instrumental group in 1963 and 1964, Les Aiglons were briefly France's answer to the **Tornadoes**, whose 'Telstar' was a number 1 hit in that country early in 1963. Signed to Barclay's trendy new Golfe-Drouot label, named after Paris' Hippest disco club of the time, Les Aiglons recorded five EPs of tunes composed principally by their organist Jean-Marc Blanc and lead guitarist Leon Francioli. It was, however, Ken Lean's vivid production, with its echo, space effects and percussiveness, which gave 'Stalactite' its impact and turned it into a hit record. Perhaps the group's (and Lean's) pinnacle was 'Dans Le Vent' on the second EP, with deep, swirling guitar taking the slow melody while the organ emerges ominously to haunt it. The advent of the 'Mersey sound' spelt the end of instrumental beat groups as a commercial force, and by 1966 the group had disbanded.
● COMPILATIONS: *Bohm La* (1989)★★★.

Les Amazones

Formed by Keletigui Traore in Guinea in 1961, the all-female Amazones has a 15-piece line-up drawn entirely from officers serving in the Guinea Police Force. Something of a rarity in Africa, the band plays a mixture of traditional Guinean music and Zairean rumba, and tours widely throughout the continent. On its 1987 tour of the UK, Les Amazones were taken up by the feminist movement as the standard bearers of a new African women's music - an accolade that the members deeply resented when it was brought to their attention. Throughout their three decades of existence (and into the 1990s) only one collective album was released, though several members have embarked on solo projects after or during their tenure with Les Amazones.
● ALBUMS: *Au Coeur De Paris* (SLP 1983)★★★★.

Les Bantous De La Capitale

Formed by saxophonists Nino Maslapet and Jean-Serge Essous in Brazzaville, Congo in the late 50s, Les Bantous were one of central Africa's most popular interpreters of the Cuban rumba. Still active in the 90s, the peak of their popularity stretched from the early 60s to the mid-70s, during which time they employed several notable musicians including Kosmos, **Pamelo Mounka**, Tchico and guitarists Papa Noel and Master Mwana Congo. They are widely credited with being the first band to record in the soukous style (in 1966), a genre that became hugely popular throughout central and west Africa in the 70s, and overseas in the 80s. In

1974 the band were able to pay tribute to their original Cuban roots when Fidel Castro invited them to tour the island. 1989's 'comeback' studio album, *Monument*, featured Essous, Mounka and newcomer Mick Jeager.
● ALBUMS: *Les Merveilles Du Passe* (African Sonodisc 1964)★★★, *El Manicero* (Soul Posters 1970)★★★, *Marie Jeanne* (Safari Afrique 1976)★★★, *Special 20ème Anniversaire* (BAE 1980)★★★★, *L'Amour Et La Danse* (VME 1987)★★, *Monument* (VME 1989)★★★.

Les Fleur De Lys

Formed in Southampton, England in 1964, (Les) Fleur De Lys was initially comprised of Frank Smith (guitar/vocals), Alex Chamberlain (keyboards), Gary Churchill (bass) and Keith Guster (drums). They secured a deal with **Andrew Loog Oldham**'s **Immediate Records** in 1965. **Jimmy Page** produced their debut, a version of **Buddy Holly**'s 'Moondreams', and wrote the b-side, 'Wait For Me'. Chamberlain and Churchill were replaced by Phil Sawyer (guitar) and Gordon Haskell (bass) for 'Circles', a **Pete Townshend** song also known as 'Instant Party'. (Les) Fleur De Lys performed it in creditable pop art fashion. The line-up then underwent further changes when Smith was replaced by Chris Andrews and Bryn Hayworth came in for Phil Sawyer. The group switched labels to **Atlantic Records**, where they embraced rock/soul style of music. 'Mud In Your Eye' (1966) was a highly accomplished single and the group was invited to back **Donnie Elbert** and Sharon Tandy. In 1967 (Les) Fleur De Lys assumed an alias, Rupert's People, for 'Reflections Of Charles Brown', a dreamy single modelled on **Procol Harum**'s 'A Whiter Shade Of Pale'. Its composer, Rod Lynton, formed a 'new' Rupert's People, (Les) Fleur De Lys reverted to their original name. Andrews left for a solo career (as **Tim Andrews**) in 1967, leaving Hayworth, Haskell and Guster to work as a trio. Two marvellous singles followed: the haunting 'I Can See A Light' (1967) and hard-rocking 'Gong With The Luminous Nose' (1968), before Haskell was replaced by Tago Byers (bass) and Tony Head (vocals). 'Stop Crossing The Bridge' (1968) and 'Liar' (1969) followed but (Les) Fleur De Lys folded in the wake of the latter release. Hayworth became a solo artist during the 70s, while Haskell joined **King Crimson**.

Les Girls

To many it must have seemed like the end of an era when **Gene Kelly** completed his very last MGM musical. The string of hits he left behind are firmly registered in the vaults of film musical history. His last project, *Les Girls*, released in October 1957, and adapted by John Patrick from a Vera Caspery story, struggles to live up to Kelly's own high standards, but there are enough entertaining sequences to maintain the momentum. Directed by George Cukor and produced by Sol C Siegel, the film is set in Paris 1949. It follows the adventures of Kelly, a musical performer, and his female trio, Les Girls, played by **Mitzi Gaynor**,

Kay Kendall and Taina Elg. The unusual story is revealed in a series of flashbacks. The first of them concerns the courtroom battle between two of the girls that opens the film. Lady Wren (Kay Kendall) has included an account of her experiences with Les Girls in her memoirs, and stands in the dock defending her words, while furious Taina Elg refuses to accept any of the book as the truth. As the film continues, the viewer begins to wonder who is really telling the truth, and with which one of the girls Kelly is in love. Or did he have flings with all of them? It is only towards the conclusion of the movie that it is revealed that Mitzi Gaynor is the girl he truly desires. Indeed, during one of the flashbacks he reveals a whole wall of photos of Gaynor, and pretends he is terribly ill in order to win his way into her affections. In the aftermath of the court case, she demands Kelly's assurance that his flings with the other girls were purely fictional. With all these complications, it is hardly surprising that the film becomes rather weighed down, but one or two individual performances and the words and music of **Cole Porter** save the day (*Les Girls* was his last original score for the big screen). The musical highlights included Kelly and Gaynor's tongue-in-cheek send-up of Marlon Brando in 'Why Am I So Gone About That Gal?' and Kendall's almost music-hall routine with Kelly, 'You're Just Too, Too'. Other songs were 'Ladies In Waiting' and 'Ca, C'est L'Amour'. Among the supporting cast, which had a definite European flavour, were Leslie Phillips, Jacques Bergerac, Henry Daniell and Patrick MacNee. Jack Cole was the choreographer, and it was photographed in Metrocolor and CinemaScope. Not an MGM classic for Kelly and Porter to end with, but amusing and enjoyable all the same.

Les Misérables

Opening in Paris in 1980, in the seemingly unlikely setting of a sports arena, *Les Misérables* brought light to the darkness of the European musical theatre. Taking as its improbable text, Victor Hugo's grim novel of one man's determined survival in the face of another's vengeful persecution, *Les Misérables* became a musical jewel. With music by **Claude-Michel Schönberg**, who also wrote the book with **Alain Boublil**, and lyrics by **Herbert Kretzmer** adapted into English from the French text by Boublil and Jean-Marc Natel, the show was originally staged at the Barbican in London on 30 September 1985 by **Trevor Nunn** and John Caird of the Royal Shakespeare Company. It subsequently transferred to the Palace Theatre and, after initially mixed reviews, settled in for a long run. Set in nineteenth-century France, the show was an impressive drama of political and social comment brimming with stirring music all impressively staged. The dramatic and memorable score included numbers such as 'I Dreamed A Dream', 'On My Own', 'Who Am I?', 'Come To Me', 'Do You Hear The People Sing?', 'Drink With Me To Days Gone By', and the grieving 'Empty Chairs At Empty Tables'. Starring **Patti LuPone**, Colm Wilkinson

and Alun Armstrong, *Les Misérables* became the musical highlight of London's West End and ran on into the 90s as vivid proof that audiences were not deterred by musical shows with depth and that the musical theatre need not depend upon escapism for its continued existence. In January 1994, it overtook *Jesus Christ Superstar* as the third-longest-running musical (after *Cats* and *Starlight Express*) in the history of the London musical theatre. At that time it was estimated that *Les Misérables* had played to 30 million people in more than 35 cities around the world, and taken £600 million at the box office, including £60 million in London alone. The American production, which opened at the Broadway Theatre in New York on 12 March 1987, soon became one of the hottest tickets in town, and won Tony Awards for best musical, score, book, featured actress (Frances Ruffelle), directors (Nunn and Caird), scenic design (John Napier), costumes (Andreane Neofitou), and lighting (David Hersey).
● VIDEOS: *10th Anniversary Concert* (VCI Columbia 1996), *Les Miserables In Concert* (Video Collection 1996).
● FURTHER READING: *The Complete Book Of Les Misérables*, Edward Behr.

Les Quatre Étoiles

Les Quatre Étoiles (Four Stars) is a Paris, France-based supergroup that features four top Zairean musicians: Nyboma and **Wuta May** (vocals), and Bopol and Syran Mbenza (guitars). Apart from Wuta May, they all worked with the **African All Stars** in the late 70s, with Bopol and Syran in the original line-up and Nyboma joining in 1979. The quartet came together as a studio band in Paris - a centre of expatriate Zairean musical activity since the 60s - in 1982. Their first album, *Mayi*, contained one lengthy track from each musician. Nyboma's contribution, 'Mama Iye Ye', was a re-recorded song that he had written in the 70s when he was singing with Orchestre Bella Bella in Zaire. The new version, replacing the sweetness of the original with a solid beat and faint reggae-inflection in the guitar rhythms, showed the Étoiles' willingness to adapt their music for western ears. The name of the band is no idle boast. In Zaire, the individual members of Les Quatre Étoiles had made their names with many of the country's best musicians. Wuta May started his career in 1967 and played with Jamel Natinal, Bambala and Rock-A-Mambo before joining Orchestre Continentale, one of the bands who brought in the new youth music in the later 60s. In 1974, he joined **Franco** in **OK Jazz**. Wuta May's vocal brilliance is matched only by that of Nyboma, who has one of the classic voices in Zaire - high, pure and controlled even at the top of his range. Nyboma cut his teeth with Baby National in 1969 and moved to Negreo Succes before joining Zaire's biggest bands, Orchestre Bella Bella and then Orchestre Lipua Lipua. By the late 70s he had left, to join African All Stars, later forming Orchestre Du Zaire. Syran worked as a guitarist with Orchestre Abanite and Orchestre

Lovy Du Zaire, while Bopol, who released a series of his own albums in the early 80s under the title *Innovations,* worked as a bass guitarist with **Dr Nico**'s African Fiesta and Afrisa before creating his distinctive, needle-sharp rhythm lines for **Sam Mangwana**. Together, Les Quatre Étoiles produce an infectious brand of rumba saccade, a fast dance music which blows fresh heat on to the rumba of Zaire. Their second album, *Enfant Bamileke,* released in 1984, offered further tracks from each of the musicians. Their 1985 outing, *Dance,* introduced electronic drums into the mix to underscore their new dance, the kinsenengoma, or 'cricket' (the insect, not the game). The rhythm remained the same: the group's own blend of pure vocal melody, over a hot-rumba saccade base. In the meantime, Les Quatre Étoiles had also released a succession of solo albums, Npoma's 1981 *Double Double* proving an early classic, while later ones, including Bopol's *Helena,* drew on the service of Jean-Claude Maimro and Jacob Desvarieux, from Kassav, to create a strong Afro-Zouk fusion. Nyboma followed suit in 1986 with an album co-recorded with Pepe Kalle, from **Empire Bakuba**, which used zouk rhythms and guitar patterns, but little of the electronic technology so beloved of zouk musicians. The following year, Syran Mbenza formed his own zouk-flavoured outfit, Kass Kass, and joined Les Quatre Étoiles for their epic of hi-tech and elaborate arrangement, *6 Tubes.* In the late 80s and early 90s the individual members concentrated on their solo careers, though they did reunite sporadically for studio sessions.
● ALBUMS: *Mayi* (1983)★★★, *Enfant Bamileke* (Syllart 1984)★★★★, *Dance* (Tangent 1985)★★★, *6 Tubes* (Syllart 1987)★★★★, *Quatre Grandes Vedettes De La Musicque Africaine* (1989)★★★, *Souffrance* (1991)★★★.

Lesberg, Jack

b. 14 February 1920, Boston, Massachusetts, USA. After playing bass in a number of jazz clubs in and around his home town in his late teens, Lesberg moved to New York. From 1945, he spent three years doubling with the New York Symphony Orchestra and at **Eddie Condon**'s club. During the 50s and 60s Lesberg concentrated on playing jazz, working with numerous top-flight traditional and mainstream musicians including **Sarah Vaughan**, **Benny Goodman**, **Louis Armstrong**, **Jack Teagarden**, **Earl Hines**, **Sidney Bechet**, **Tommy Dorsey**, **Billy Butterfield**, **Ruby Braff** and **Joe Venuti**. Solid, reliable and obviously highly respected by his fellow musicians, in the early 70s Lesberg was resident in Australia and later in the decade resumed his extensive gigging with artists such as **Kenny Davern**, **Howard Alden**, **Yank Lawson** and **Keith Ingham**.
● ALBUMS: *Hollywood Swing* (1977)★★★, with Howard Alden *No Amps Allowed* (1990)★★.

Lesh, Phil

b. Philip Chapman, 15 March 1940, Berkeley, California, USA. A formally trained trumpeter from an academic and classically trained background, Phil Lesh began playing bass guitar on joining the Warlocks in 1965. An R&B act formed around disaffected folk musicians, the group later evolved into the **Grateful Dead**. Lesh quickly became an intrinsic part of the group as an improviser and composer, although this latter role has decreased over the years. He was also responsible for editing and remixing the original tapes of the band's *Anthem Of The Sun* and *Aoxomoxoa* when they were re-released during the 70s. In 1975, Lesh completed *Seastones,* an experimental collaboration with electronics wizard Ned Lagin. Described as 'cybernetic biomusic' by a contemporary newsletter, the set used a battery of technological gadgets and computers to create impressionistic patterns of sound. **Jerry Garcia**, **Grace Slick** and **David Crosby** appeared on the project, but their contributions were masked by layers of treated effects. Lesh and Lagin also made live appearances showcasing similar material, but the bassist pursued a more orthodox sideline with Too Loose To Truck, a bar-band specializing in cover versions. Despite these outside activities, Lesh's strongest work has been made within the core of the parent group and he remains a remarkably inventive, meandering bassist with occasional breathtaking bursts, none better highlighted than on 'Dark Star' from *Live/Dead.*
● ALBUMS: as Seastones with Phil Lesh *Seastones* (Round 1975)★★★★.

LeShaun

b. c.1973. US female rapper whose debut album was an acclaimed, thoughtful variant on the gangsta rap trip. LeShaun had become a single mother at the age of 18, experiences recalled in tracks like 'Young Girlz', and brought maternal widom to bear on a number of her better cuts. The influence of **Queen Latifah**, her stated idol, was undeniably strong. She also collaborated on the **Lords Of The Underground** cut, 'Flow On'.
● ALBUMS: *Ain't No Shame In My Game* (Tommy Boy 1993)★★★.

Leslie, Edgar

b. 31 December 1885, Stamford, Connecticut, USA, d. 1976. An important lyricist of the 20s and 30s who had a penchant for writing 'place-name' titles, such as 'That Italian Rag', 'America, I Love You', 'In The Gold Fields Of Nevada', 'When Kentucky Bids The World Good Morning', 'The Dixieland Volunteers', 'Rose Of The Rio Grande', 'Kansas City Kitty', 'California And You', 'Moon Over Miami', 'Ashby De La Zouch (Castle Abbey)' (in the UK) and '(Home In) Pasadena' (co-written with **Harry Warren** and Grant Clarke). Leslie was brought up in New York, and wrote material for vaudeville performers such as Billy B. Van, Joe Welch, and Nat Wills. His first published songs, in 1909, included 'Lonesome', 'I Didn't Go Home At All' and 'Sadie Salome', with music by the young **Irving Berlin**. Leslie's other early songs included 'He'd Have To Get Under - Get Out And Get Under' (with Clarke and

Maurice Abrahams), 'For Me And My Gal' (with Ray Goetz and **George W. Meyer**), 'Oh! What A Pal Was Mary' (with Pete Wendling), 'Blue And Broken Hearted', 'Dirty Hands, Dirty Face' and 'Me And The Man In The Moon'. In 1927 Leslie moved to England and wrote 'Among My Souvenirs', the first of several songs on which he collaborated with Horatio Nicholls (the pseudonym for song publisher **Lawrence Wright**). The song became one of his most enduring titles and was a big hit all over again in 1959 for **Connie Francis**. Other Leslie-Nicholls numbers included 'Mistakes' (a UK hit for **Vera Lynn**) and 'Shepherd Of The Hills' (successful for **Jack Hylton** And His Orchestra). Leslie's output during the 30s included ''Taint No Sin', 'And I Still Do', 'The Moon Was Yellow', 'Were You Foolin'?', 'In A Little Gypsy Tea Room', 'The Girl I Left Behind Me', 'Midnight Blue' (from *Ziegfeld Follies Of 1936*), 'Cling To Me', 'Robins And Roses', 'It Looks Like Rain In Cherry Blossom Lane', 'At A Perfume Counter' and 'Rainbow Valley'. As well as the 'place-name' titles, his catalogue included some other amusing captions such as 'When Ragtime Rosie Ragged The Rosary', 'Where Was Moses When The Light Went Out?', 'All The Quakers Are Shoulder Shakers' and 'Lord, Have Mercy On The Married Man'. His other collaborators included **Fred Ahlert**, **Harry Ruby**, **Joe Burke**, **Jimmy Monaco** and **Walter Donaldson**. In the 40s he retired from songwriting and concentrated on his publishing interests.

Lester, Ketty

b. Revoyda Frierson, 16 August 1934, Hope, Arkansas, USA. Ketty Lester began her singing career on completing a music course at San Francisco State College. A residency at the city's Purple Onion club was followed by a successful tour of Europe before she joined bandleader **Cab Calloway**'s revue. Later domiciled in New York, Lester's popular nightclub act engendered a recording contract, of which 'Love Letters' was the first fruit. The singer's cool-styled interpretation of this highly popular standard, originally recorded by **Dick Haymes**, reached the Top 5 in both the USA and UK in 1962, eventually selling in excess of one million copies. The song has been covered many times, with notable successes for **Elvis Presley** and **Alison Moyet**. Its attractiveness was enhanced by a memorable piano figure but Lester was sadly unable to repeat the single's accomplished balance between song, interpretation and arrangement. She later abandoned singing in favour of a career as a film and television actress, with appearances in *Marcus Welby MD*, *Little House On The Prairie*, *The Terminal Man* and *The Prisoner Of Second Avenue*, to name but a few. She was later coaxed back into the studio, but only on her stipulation that it would be exclusively to perform sacred music.
● ALBUMS: *Love Letters* (Era 1962)★★, *Soul Of Me* (RCA Victor 1964)★★, *Where Is Love* (RCA Victor 1965)★★, *When A Woman Loves A Man* (1967)★★, *I Saw Him* (1985)★★.

Lesurf, Cathy

A vocalist on the Fiddler's Dram folk flavoured UK hit, 'Daytrip To Bangor', Lesurf went on to sing for nearly eight years with the **Albion Band**, and in 1985 with **Fairport Convention**. Consequently, her solo album contained many well known electric folk musicians. She has since retired from music altogether.
● ALBUMS: *Surface* (1985)★★.

Let George Do It

In the early years of World War II, **George Formby**'s comedy-musical films raised the spirits of millions of people in the Britain. This one was typical of the genre: George is about to join his fellow members of the Dinkie Doo Concert Party when he is whisked off to Bergen in Norway to replace a ukulele player (a member of British Intelligence) who has died in mysterious circumstances while playing in a hotel band. George discovers that its leader, Mark Mendez (Garry Marsh), is a German spy who is transmitting shipping information by code in his band's broadcasts. With the help of Mary Wilson (Phyllis Calvert), George breaks the code, warns the Admiralty, and as a result five U-Boats are sunk. Not surprisingly, he flees the country - in a German submarine! In the midst of all that derring-doo, he found the time to introduce two of his best-known novelty numbers, 'Grandad's Flannelette Nightshirt' and 'Mr Wu's A Window Cleaner Now', as well as the cheery 'Count Your Blessings And Smile' and 'Oh, Don't The Wind Blow Cold' (Formby-Fred E. Cliffe-Harry Gifford). Ronald Shiner, a leading star of the famous Whitehall farces after the war, had a minor role as a clarinettist in this picture, and other parts went to Romney Brent, Bernard Lee (he played 'M' in the James Bond films), Ian Fleming (an Australian character, not the Bond author), Coral Browne, Percy Walsh, Diana Beaumont, Donald Calthrop, Torin Thatcher, Hal Gordon, Jack Hobbs, and Alec Clunes. The screenplay was written by John Dighton, Austin Melford, Angus Macphail, and Basil Dearden. The latter was also the Associated Producer for Ealing-Associated Talking Pictures. The director was Marcel Varnel, and this invaluable little morale booster was released in 1940.

Let It Be

The concept for *Let It Be* was, on paper, simple. The **Beatles**, who were about to record a new album, would have a feature film of the proceedings to show them at work, 'warts and all'. Michael Lindsay-Hogg, who had previously worked on television's seminal *Ready, Steady, Go!*, was brought in as director and on 2 January 1969, the group convened in a cold studio in Twickenham to begin recording. Unfortunately, relations between the individual members were strained and, despite bonhomie when jamming and playing 'oldies' from their Hamburg days, it seemed the camera was chronicling a wake rather than a celebration. **Paul McCartney**'s attempts at marshalling proceedings alienated the others, in particular **George Harrison**, who walked out when instructed on how to play a solo. Within weeks the Beatles opted to move to the basement of their **Apple** offices, where they hoped to create a better atmosphere. Such events make watching *Let It Be* a sad experience, although circumstances do brighten up when pianist/organist **Billy Preston** joins their ranks. The infamous live rooftop scene, where they perform 'Don't Let Me Down' and 'Get Back', is a glorious moment, both musically and emotionally and although it closes the film on a positive note, in reality further sessions for the album followed. However, all work was suspended at the end of January and the following month the Beatles began work on what became *Abbey Road*. The *Let It Be* film was released in 1970, by which time the relevant recording had been 'post-produced' by **Phil Spector** to create a corresponding album, which initially came complete with a lavish book of photographs from the recording session.

Let It Be - Replacements

The **Replacements** were one of America's greatest bands of the 80s, irrespective of genre, though they received thin acknowledgement outside of informed critics during their lifetime. *Let It Be* demonstrates why they drove fans to devotion and critics to supplication. It was 1984, and the Replacements had left behind their sonic links to the Minneapolis punk scene. In particular, **Paul Westerberg**'s songs had lost the timerity of old and he was increasingly willing to tackle subjects head on - 'Unsatisfied' is arguably the best song he ever wrote. However profundity aside, there is also a huge sense of fun about *Let It Be*, and even throwaway material like 'Gary's Got A Boner', and their cover of **Kiss**'s 'Black Diamond', is enormous fun.

● Tracks: *I Will Dare; Favorite Thing; We're Comin' Out; Tommy Gets His Tonsils Out; Androgynous; Black Diamond; Unsatisfied; Seen Your Video; Gary's Got A Boner; Sixteen Blue; Answering Machine.*
● First released 1984
● UK peak chart position: did not chart
● USA peak chart position: did not chart

Let It Be - The Beatles

On the back of the sleeve is the ironic note: 'This is a new phase Beatles album'. The new phase being, here are four maturing men growing apart and desperately needing a break from each other. The accompanying film is too painful to watch, as tempers fray and tension is in the air. In addition to the title track, only 'Get Back' and maybe 'Long And Winding Road' rate as great **Beatles** songs. The others are all brief entertainments and scraps of tunes. Lennon and Harrison had already moved on in their heads and McCartney was left to paste it together. The overwhelming feeling of this album is one of incredible sadness.

● Tracks: *Two Of Us; Dig A Pony; Across The Universe; I Me Mine; Dig It; Let It Be; Maggie Mae; I've Got A Feeling; One After 909; The Long And Winding Road; For You Blue; Get Back.*

● First released 1970
● UK peak chart position: 1
● USA peak chart position: 1

Let It Bleed - The Rolling Stones

The last **Rolling Stones** album to feature the presence of the band's creator, Brian Jones, was a brilliant culmination of all their musical influences over the previous monumental decade. The power of the opening track, 'Gimme Shelter', will haunt many of us forever with the memory of the **Altamont** murder, **Mick Jagger**'s top hat and scarf and the death of the 60s. The repeated line, 'It's just a shot away', complements the repetition of the naïvely profound lyric of the album's last track: 'you can't always get what you want'. The filling in-between, like the layered cake on the cover, is equally delectable.

● Tracks: *Gimme Shelter; Love In Vain; Country Honk; Live With Me; Let It Bleed; Midnight Rambler; You Got The Silver; Monkey Man; You Can't Always Get What You Want.*
● First released 1969
● UK peak chart position: 1
● USA peak chart position: 3

Let Loose

One of a gamut of 'boy bands' to dominate the UK charts in the mid-90s, Let Loose formed in 1987 when Richie Wermerling (b. *c.*1968, England; vocals/keyboards) recruited Rob Jeffery (b. *c.*1968, England; guitar) and Lee Murray (b. *c.*1970, England; drums) via an advertisement in *Melody Maker*. However, their early efforts were rather different to the clean-cut incarnation of Let Loose which would grace the charts of the mid-90s. As Jeffrey told the press 'In the early days of Let Loose we always used to wear black, and the music was a lot more bikery, more metally. We didn't dance on stage - it wasn't dance music - we'd stand there and perform real music with guitars.' They toured widely, and, gradually changing style, signed a **Virgin Records** deal at the end of the 80s. However, they were one of several artists displaced when the company sold out to **EMI Records**. **Mercury Records** were keen to offer them a new contract and enjoyed minor chart returns in 1993 and 1994 when both 'Crazy For You' and 'Seventeen' peaked at number 44 in the UK charts. When 'Crazy For You' was re-released and re-promoted it spent 10 weeks in the UK Top 10, peaking at number 2 and earning a gold disc. When 'Seventeen' was also reissued and became another major hit it gave the band total sales of 700,000 singles in 1994, though their debut album's chart placing was a more modest number 33. The band started 1995 with 'One Night Stand', another accessible slice of 'boy group' pop without offering anything too distinctive. 'Best In Me' suffered the ultimate indignity when a member of **2 Unlimited** criticised the lyrics for being 'corny' while guest reviewing the single.

● ALBUMS: *Let Loose* (Mercury 1995)★★, *Rollercoaster* (Mercury 1996)★★★.

Let The Good Times Roll

Perhaps one of the finest paeans to classic rock 'n' roll, *Let The Good Times Roll* is a sumptuous amalgamation of documentary footage and memorable concert performances. At its core was a 1972 marathon, hosted at Madison Square Gardens by New York impresario Richard Nader. Directors Sid Levin and Robert Abel blended footage from that event with television appearances, newsreels, interviews and demonstration films. Scenes from 50s genre movies *The Wild One* and *I Was A Teenage Werewolf* help to place the music in a broader cultural context, while intelligent use of split-screen techniques facilitated then-and-now scenarios. One particular clip of **Little Richard**, in monochrome from the 50s and in colour from the 70s, is particularly memorable. 'Good Golly Miss Molly', 'Rip It Up' and 'Lucille' are among the songs he performs as part of a cast that also includes **Fats Domino**, **Chuck Berry**, the **Coasters**, **Danny And The Juniors**, the **Five Satins**, **Shirley And Lee**, **Bo Diddley**, the **Shirelles**, **Chubby Checker** and **Bill Haley And His Comets**. 'Blueberry Hill', 'Reelin' And Rockin'', 'At The Hop', 'Poison Ivy', 'I'm A Man' and, of course, 'Rock Around The Clock', are among the songs featured in this endearing tribute to rock's first golden era.

Let There Be Drums - Sandy Nelson

The rock 'n' roll drummer **Sandy Nelson** made numerous albums, but the best-known is the one riding on his hit single, 'Let There Be Drums'. Nelson, who lives in the Mohave Desert, says, '"Let There Be Drums" was done with a lot of love and sincerity. When it was a hit, we had to put out an album and some of the sessions were dreadful because they were done after a night's drinking with Bruce Johnston in Tijuana. I got to bed at five in the morning and I had to get up at nine. I was hungover and the producer did some terrible arrangements for "My Girl Josephine", "Slippin' And Sliding" and "Tequila". He never even finished the phrase on "Tequila"! I am ashamed of those sessions but I messed up my own career. I was often drunk when I made my records.'
● Tracks: *Slippin' And Sliding; Tequila; My Girl Josephine; The Big Noise From Winnetka; Let There Be Drums; Bouncy; The Birth Of The Beat; Quite A Beat; Get With It.*
● First released 1962
● UK peak chart position: did not chart
● USA peak chart position: 6

Let's Active

Ostensibly the vehicle for veteran US all-rounder Mitch Easter, Let's Active issued three melodic albums during the mid-80s. Easter previously played alongside various members of the **dB's** in the Sneakers in the late 70s, and also worked with the H-Bombs and the Cosmopolitans. His first solo outing graced *Shake To Date*, a UK compilation of material from the US Shake label, in 1981. In-between 'discovering' **R.E.M.** and then producing their early work, Easter eventually set up Let's Active. *Cypress* did not emerge until 1984, and featured Easter joined by Faye Hunter (bass) and Sam Romweber (drums). The songwriting skills were evident (and the debt to **John Lennon** and **Paul McCartney** was clear), but the album lacked bite, and despite the band supporting **Echo And The Bunnymen** on tour it did not sell. Almost two years later, Let's Active found that bite with *Big Plans For Everybody*, aided by drummers Eric Marshall and Rob Ladd, and Angie Carlson (guitar, keyboards, vocals). Promoted by 'In Little Ways', the album seemed the perfect encapsulation of Easter's aims: superb production, an ingenious blend of instrumentation and, above all, strong songs. Easter's commitments elsewhere delayed the third Let's Active album for nearly three years, and as such, *Every Dog Has His Day* (with John Heames now in the ranks) was slightly disappointing.
● ALBUMS: *Cypress* (IRS 1984)★★, *Big Plans For Everybody* (IRS 1986)★★★★, *Every Dog Has His Day* (IRS 1988)★★★.

Let's Dance - David Bowie

David Bowie's best work since *Heroes* at that time, and the critics responded with relief as much as anything else. The Nile Rodgers production was an inspired partnership as Bowie entered another phase in his chameleon-like career - this time rock/disco. Even **Stevie Ray Vaughan** was added to sharpen the guitar parts, although the overall impression is that this is not a guitar album. Had that been the case then surely **Mick Ronson** would have been hired. Rarely has an album opened with three similarly blockbusting tracks, 'Modern Love', 'China Girl' and the title track.
● Tracks: *Modern Love; China Girl; Let's Dance; Without You; Ricochet; Criminal World; Cat People (Putting Out Fire); Shake It.*
● First released 1983
● UK peak chart position: 1
● USA peak chart position: 4

Let's Face It!

Danny Kaye confirmed the star qualities he had shown earlier in the year in *Lady In The Dark* when he played his first leading role on Broadway in this show which opened at the Imperial Theatre in New York on 29 October 1941. In *Lady In The Dark*, Kaye had been called upon to sing a song, listing 49 Russian composers, in 39 seconds; in *Let's Face It!*, he stopped the show with 'Melody In 4-F', which encapsulated a rookie soldier's first few weeks in the army - this time in 90 seconds. That particular piece of special material was written by Kaye's wife, Sylvia Fine and Max Liebman. Herbert and **Dorothy Fields**'s book, which was based on the 1925 hit comedy, *The Cradle Snatchers*, deals with three wives who suspect that their husbands' sporting activities may be of the indoor, rather the outdoor variety, so they enlist the help of three soldiers from the local army camp to assist them in their own night-time manoeuvres. However, serious complications arise when the husbands return - with the girlfriends of the soldiers on their arms. With Kaye in the cast, were Eve Arden, Benny Baker, Edith Meiser, Vivan Vance, Mary Jane Walsh, and, in a minor role, Nanette Fabray, who later had success in other Broadway musicals such as *High Button Shoes*, and in several films, particularly *The Band Wagon* (1953) with **Fred Astaire** and **Jack Buchanan**. **Cole Porter**'s score was smart and witty as usual, and included 'Ace In The Hole', 'Farming', 'Ev'rything I Love', 'A Little Rhumba Numba', 'A Lady Needs A Rest', and 'I Hate You Darling'. The composer's riposte to Kaye's 'Melody In 4-F' that he (Porter) allowed to be interpolated from another source, was another equally vocally taxing piece which Kaye shared with Eve Arden: 'Let's Not Talk About Love' ('Why not discuss, my dee-arie, the life of Wallace Bee-ery/Or bring a jeroboam on, and write a drunken poem on/Astrology, mythology, geology, philology/ Pathology, psychology, electro-physiology/Spermology, phrenology/I owe you an apology/But let's not talk about love.'). During the show's New York run of 547 performances, Danny Kaye was succeeded by José Ferrer, and, when *Let's Face* it began its 10 months' stay at the London Hippodrome, it starred **Bobby Howes**, Joyce Barbour, Jack Stamford, and **Pat Kirkwood**. The 1943 film version featured **Bob Hope**, **Betty Hutton**, and Eve Arden.

Let's Get It On - Marvin Gaye

Relishing the artistic freedom afforded by the success of *What's Goin' On*, **Marvin Gaye** recorded this sultry paean to sex. Where its predecessor relied on complex arrangements, the straightforward sound of *Let's Get It On* focused attention on its tight rhythms, strong melodies and Gaye's expressive singing. Either celebratory, as on the explicit title track, or reflective ('Distant Lover'), he explores a range of emotions with equal ease and intensity. Seductive sound matches seductive lyrics and attitudes at a time when **Al Green**, **Barry White** and **Isaac Hayes** laid claim to the 'lover man' sobriquet. *Let's Get It On* showed Marvin Gaye to be its undoubted master.

● Tracks: *Let's Get It On; Please Don't Stay (Once You Go Away); If I Should Die Tonight; Keep Gettin' It On; Come Get To This; Distant Lover; You Sure Know How To Ball; Just To Keep You Satisfied.*
● First released 1973
● UK peak chart position: 39
● USA peak chart position: 2

Let's Make Love

The story worked well in *On The Avenue* (1937), so screenwriter Norman Krasna adapted it slightly for this 20th Century-Fox release some 23 years later. A seriously wealthy businessman (Yves Montand) discovers that he is going to be lampooned in a satirical off-Broadway revue, so, after honing his almost non-existent performing skills with the help of **Gene Kelly** (dancing), **Bing Crosby** (singing), and Milton Berle (comedy), he joins the show as a lookalike of himself

and immediately falls for the leading lady (**Marilyn Monroe**). Her boyfriend-in-residence is British singer **Frankie Vaughan**, but after Montand turns on the Gallic charm he does not stand a chance and might as well go home. (In fact that is what Vaughan did shortly after filming was finished - Mrs Vaughan had explained that when Monroe offered to help him with his lines that was not really what she meant). **Sammy Cahn** and **Jimmy Van Heusen**'s were pleasant but uninspired, and included 'Let's Make Love', 'Incurably Romantic' (which Monroe sang with both Vaughan and Montand), 'Latin One', 'Specialization', 'Hey You With The Crazy Eyes', and 'Strip City'. However, the film's musical highlight was Monroe's sizzling version of **Cole Porter**'s 'My Heart Belongs To Daddy'. Tony Randall was his usual amusing self as Montand's long-suffering personal assistant, and other parts went to Wilfred Hyde White, David Burns, Michael David, and Mara Lynn. Jack Cole staged the smart and contemporary dances, and the director was George Cukor. This good-looking picture was photographed in De Luxe Color and CinemaScope by Daniel L. Fapp.

Let's Stay Together - Al Green

The evocative title track that opens this glorious record sets a paradox. **Al Green**'s remarkable voice, one that is hidden in the back of his throat, makes you constantly feel good. The subject matter of many of the songs on this album, however, is of sadness, lost love, frustration and confusion. Green was to popular soul in the 70s what **Otis Redding** was in the 60s; it was refreshing to see him performing and recording again in the early 90s. Perhaps the good reverend already knew in 1972 that he would be called to the church, because this collection has amazing healing powers.

● Tracks: *Let's Stay Together; La-La For You; So You're Leaving; What Is This Feeling; Old Time Lovin'; I've Never Found A Girl; How Can You Mend A Broken Heart; Judy; It Ain't No Fun To Me.*
● First released 1972
● UK peak chart position: did not chart
● USA peak chart position: 8

Let's Twist-Her - Bill Black

By 1962 everyone (**Elvis Presley**, **Frank Sinatra**, Zsa Zsa Gabor) wanted to cash in on the twist, but for the Bill Black Combo, the sound was pretty much the same as before. The *Let's Twist Her* album included rock 'n' roll standards and his first US hit, 'Smokie (Part 2)', from 1959. Of the new material, 'Twist-Her' was a US Top 30 single. **Bill Black** died of a brain tumour in 1965, but the group continued playing. His double-bass was bought by **Paul McCartney**, who later played it on 'Baby's Request'.

● Tracks: *Twist Her; High Train; Corrine Corrina; The Hucklebuck; Royal Twist; Yogi; My Girl Josephine; Twistaroo; Johnny B. Goode; Twist With Me Baby; Slippin' And Slidin'; Smokey (Part 2).*
● First released 1962

- UK peak chart position: did not chart
- USA peak chart position: 35

Letman, Johnny

b. 6 September 1917, McCormick, South Carolina, USA. Growing up in Chicago, Letman played trumpet in various youth bands including the first band organized by **Nat 'King' Cole**. After leaving Cole in 1934 he continued to play in the Chicago area, appearing with leaders such as 'Scat Man' Carruthers, Delbert Bright, **Horace Henderson** and Red Saunders. In the early 40s he moved to New York and during the rest of the decade played in numerous bands including those of **Cab Calloway** and **Lucky Millinder**. In the 50s he was active in the studios and also played in theatre bands along Broadway, but found time for gigs with **Count Basie**, **Stuff Smith**, **Chubby Jackson** and many others, as well as leading his own bands for club and record dates. In the 60s and 70s he continued much as before but also visited Europe, playing with **Milt Buckner**, **Tiny Grimes**, **Lionel Hampton** and **Earl Hines**. In the 80s he was often on tour, playing festivals throughout Europe. Infrequently recorded, Letman has many sterling qualities which appear to have passed largely unnoticed by the jazz world.
- ALBUMS: *Cascade Of Quartets* (50s)★★★, *The Many Angles Of Johnny Letman* (1960)★★.

Lettermen

This very successful US close-harmony pop trio comprised Bob Engemann (b. 19 February 1936, Highland Park, Michigan, USA), Tony Butala (b. 20 November 1940, Sharon, Pennsylvania, USA), Jim Pike (b. 6 November 1938, St. Louis, Missouri, USA). Pike, a letterman at Utah's Brigham Young University, released an unsuccessful single on **Warner Brothers Records** in 1959. In 1960, he and fellow student and ex-Mormon missionary Engemann formed a trio with supper-club singer Butala, who had recorded previously on Topic and Lute. After two unsuccessful singles, they joined **Capitol Records** and struck gold immediately with 'The Way You Look Tonight'. The smooth ballad singers put an impressive 24 albums in the US chart in the 60s, with 10 of them reaching the Top 40. The popular live act also had another 19 chart singles including the Top 10 hits 'When I Fall In Love' in 1961 and the medley 'Goin' Out Of My Head/Can't Take My Eyes Off You' in 1967. In 1968, Jim's brother Gary replaced Engemann and six years later their brother Donny replaced Jim. In the 70s they were a top-earning club act and were much in demand for television commercial work. The group recorded on their own Alfa Omega label in 1979 and signed with Applause in 1982. In all, the distinctive harmonic vocal group, who have never charted in the UK, have earned nine gold albums and sold over $25 million worth of records.
- ALBUMS: *A Song For Young Love* (1962)★★★, *Once Upon A Time* (1962)★★★, *Jim, Tony And Bob* (1962)★★★, *College Standards* (1963)★★★, *The Lettermen In Concert* (1963)★★★, *A Lettermen Kind Of Love* (Capitol 1964)★★★, *The Lettermen Look At Love* (1964)★★★, *She Cried* (1964)★★★, *Portrait Of My Love* (1965)★★★, *The Hit Sounds Of The Lettermen* (1965)★★★, *You'll Never Walk Alone* (1965)★★★, *More Hit Sounds Of The Lettermen!* (1966)★★★, *A New Song For Young Love* (1966)★★★, *For Christmas This Year* (1966)★★★, *Warm* (1967)★★★, *Spring!* (1967)★★★, *The Lettermen!!! ... And Live!* (1967)★★★, *Goin' Out Of My Head* (1968)★★★, *Special Request* (1968)★★★, *Put Your Head On My Shoulder* (1968)★★★, *I Have Dreamed* (1969)★★★, *Hurt So Bad* (1969)★★★, *Traces/Memories* (1970)★★★, *Reflections* (1970)★★★, *Everything's Good About You* (1971)★★★, *Feelings* (1971)★★★, *Love Book* (1971)★★★, *Lettermen 1* (1972)★★★, *Alive Again ... Naturally* (1973)★★★, *Evergreen* (1985).
- COMPILATIONS: *The Best Of The Lettermen* (1966)★★★, *The Best Of The Lettermen, Vol. 2* (1969)★★★, *All Time Greatest Hits* (1974)★★★.

Letters To Cleo

The debut release by New England, US band Letters To Cleo, 1993's *Aurora Glory Alice*, caused an immediate impact, leading to a major label contract with Giant Records. They repackaged and re-released the album in October 1994, including the song 'Here And Now'. This featured on the soundtrack to the syndicated television show *Melrose Place*, giving the group, originally featuring Kay Hanley (vocals), Scott Riebling (bass), Michael Eisenstein (guitar), Greg McKenna (guitar) and Stacy Jones (drums), its first mainstream exposure. However, the rushed release of *Wholesale Meats And Fish* failed to consolidate on the group's initial breakthrough. It spent just one week in the ***Billboard*** charts in the summer of 1995. The whole experience left Hanley sceptical about the true impact of the single's success: 'the crowds got bigger and people actually cared about our music, which was awesome. But when you have that type of success, people automatically assume that there is nothing more to you.' By the advent of a third album, 1997's *Go!*, Giant had changed its name to Revolution Records and Letters To Cleo's personnel had shifted. Jones departed to join **Veruca Salt**, and was replaced by Tom Polce. The producer was Peter Collins (**Jewel**, **Indigo Girls**, **Sneaker Pimps**). **Cars** keyboard player Greg Hawkes also made a guest appearance on *Go!* Between albums, Hanley had expanded her horizons by appearing as Mary Magdalene in the Boston Rock Opera's production of ***Jesus Christ Superstar*** (her co-star was Gary Cherone, the voice of **Van Halen** and ex-**Extreme**).
- ALBUMS: *Aurora Glory Alice* (CherryDisc 1993)★★★, *Wholesale Meats And Fish* (Giant 1995)★★, *Go!* (Revolution 1997)★★★.

Levallet, Didier

b. 19 July 1944, Arcy sur Cure, France. Levallet is largely a self-taught bass player who studied journalism at L'Ecole Superieure de Journalisme de Lille (1963-66) and went on for a short time to study bass at Lille

Conservatory. He moved to Paris in 1969 and played with a wide range of local and visiting musicians including **Ted Curson**, **Hank Mobley**, **Mal Waldron** and **Johnny Griffin**. He worked with the free-jazz quartet Perception through the 70s and worked in the USA with tenor saxophonist **Byard Lancaster** (1974-76). He also led Confluence, a group based on strings and percussion only. In the early 80s he played with **Frank Lowe**, **Archie Shepp**, **Mike Westbrook**'s Concert Band and **Chris McGregor**'s Brotherhood Of Breath as well as the Double Quartet with **Tony Oxley**. Levallet is a prolific composer who can combine free-improvisation and structure coherently. He works within four bands - the Quintet, a 12-piece band, Swing Strings System (which utilises seven string players plus drums) and a trio with Pifarely (violin) and Marais (guitar). In 1976, he founded ADMI (Association pour le Developement de la Musique Improvise) which acts as a pressure group and concert organizer. He teaches jazz at L'Ecole National de Musique in Angouleme.

● ALBUMS: *Perception* (1976)★★★, *Swing String System* (1978)★★★★, *Ostinato* (1981)★★★, *Instants Cavires* (1982)★★, *Scoop* (1983)★★★, *Quiet Days* (1985)★★★.

Levant, Oscar

b. 27 December 1906, Pittsburg, Pennsylvania, USA, d. 14 August 1972, Beverly Hills, California, USA. Hypochondriacal, witty, neurotic, grouchy, melancholic, acidic, and eccentric, are just a few of the adjectives that have been used over the years in a desperate attempt to accurately describe one of the most original characters in films, radio, and popular and light classical music. All the above definitions apparently apply to his personal as well as his public image. After graduating from high school, Levant struggled to make a living as pianist before moving to New York where he studied with Sigismund Stojovskis and Arnold Schoenberg. He also played in clubs, and appeared on Broadway in the play, *Burlesque* (1927), and in the movie version entitled *The Dance Of Life*, two years later. In 1930 Levant worked with **Irving Caesar**, Graham John and Albert Sirmay on the score for another Broadway show, the Charles B. Dillingham production of *Ripples*, which starred Fred and Dorothy Stone and included songs such as 'Is It Love?', 'There's Nothing Wrong With A Kiss', and 'I'm A Little Bit Fonder Of You'. In the same year Levant collaborated with Irving Caesar again on 'Lady, Play Your Mandolin' which was successful for **Nick Lucas** and the Havana Novelty Orchestra, amongst others. He wrote his best-known song, 'Blame It On My Youth', with Edward Heyman in 1934, and it is still being played and sung 60 years later. Levant spent much of the late 20s and 30s in Hollywood writing songs and scores for movies such as *My Man* (**Fanny Brice**'s film debut in 1928), *Street Girl*, *Tanned Legs*, *Leathernecking*, *In Person*, *Music Is Magic*, and *The Goldwyn Follies* (1938). Out of those came several appealing songs, including 'If You Want A Rainbow (You Must Have Rain)', 'Lovable And Sweet', 'Don't

Mention Love To Me', 'Honey Chile', and 'Out Of Sight Out Of Mind'. His collaborators included Ray Heindorf, **Mort Dixon**, Billy Rose, **Sam M. Lewis**, **Vernon Duke**, Sidney Clare, **Dorothy Fields**, Stanley Adams, and **Joe Young**. Beginning in the late 30s, Levant also demonstrated his quick wit on the long-running radio series *Information Please*, and brought his grumpy irascible self to the screen in films such as *In Person* (1935), *Rhythm On The River*, *Kiss The Boys Goodbye*, *Rhapsody In Blue* (in which he played himself), *Humoresque*, *Romance On The High Seas*, *You Were Meant For Me*, *The Barkleys Of Broadway*, *An American In Paris*, and *The Band Wagon* (1953). In the last two pictures, both directed by **Vincente Minnelli**, he seemed to be at the peak of his powers, especially in the former which has a famous dream sequence in which Levant imagines he is conducting part of **George Gershwin**'s Concert In F and every member of the orchestra is himself. Levant was a lifelong friend and accomplished exponent of Gershwin's works. His final musical, *The 'I Don't Care Girl'*, was a fairly dull affair, and his last picture of all, *The Cobweb* (1955), was set in a mental hospital. That was both sad and ironic, because for the last 20 years of his life Levant suffered from failing mental and physical health, emerging only occasionally to appear on television talk shows. In 1989 a one-man play based on the works of Oscar Levant entitled *At Wit's End* ('An Irreverent Evening'), opened to critical acclaim in Los Angeles.

● ALBUMS: *Plays Levant And Gershwin* (1994)★★★, and other soundtrack and classical recordings.

● FURTHER READING: *A Smattering Of Ignorance. Memoirs Of An Amnesiac. The Unimportance Of Being Oscar* all by Oscar Levant. *A Talent For Genius: The Life And Times Of Oscar Levant*, Sam Kashner and Nancy Schoenberger.

Level 42

Formed in 1980 as an instrumental jazz/funk unit, heavily influenced by the music of **Stanley Clarke**. The band comprised Mark King (b. 20 October 1958, England; bass/vocals), Phil Gould (b. 28 February 1957, England; drums), Boon Gould (b. 4 March 1955, England; guitar) and Mark Lindup (b. 17 March 1959; keyboards). By the release of their debut single, 'Love Meeting Love', King was urged to add vocals to give the band a more commercial sound. Their **Mike Vernon**-produced album was an exciting collection of dance and modern soul orientated numbers that made the UK Top 20. Cashing in on this unexpected success, their previous record company issued a limited edition album of early material, which their new record company **Polydor Records** re-packaged the following year. Word had now got round that Level 42 were one of the most exciting new bands of the 80s, the focal point being Mark King's extraordinary bass-slapping/thumb technique, which even impressed the master of the style, Stanley Clarke. Most of their early singles were minor hits until 'The Sun Goes Down (Living It Up)' in 1984 made the UK Top 10. Their worldwide breakthrough came with **World Machine**, a faultless record that pushed their style towards straight, quality pop. King's vocals were mixed up-front and the group entered a new phase in their career as their fans left the dance floor for the football stadiums. This also coincided with a run of high-quality hit singles between 1985 and 1987, notably, 'Something About You', 'Leaving Me Now', 'Lessons In Love', the autobiographical 'Running In The Family' and the immaculate tear-jerker 'It's Over'. Both *Running In The Family* and *Staring At The Sun* were major successes, although the latter had no significant hit singles. At the end of 1987 the band had changed its line-up drastically with only King and Lindup remaining as the nucleus of the group. Jakko Jakszyk joined the band as lead guitarist in 1991 an added a stronger sound to their live performances. Their career had faltered by the mid-90s as both their recording and public activity took a lower profile. Mark King was taking life easy from his base in the Isle Of Wight. Nevertheless, Level 42 have done much to bring quality jazz/funk music to the foreground by blending it with catchy pop melodies.

● ALBUMS: *Level 42* (Polydor 1981)★★★, *Strategy* (Elite 1981)★★★, *The Early Tapes: July-August 1980* (Polydor 1981)★★, *The Pursuit Of Accidents* (Polydor 1982)★★★, *Standing In The Light* (Polydor 1983)★★★, *True Colours* (Polydor 1983)★★★, *A Physical Presence* (Polydor 1985)★★, *World Machine* (Polydor 1985)★★★★, *Running In The Family* (Polydor 1987)★★★, *Staring At The Sun* (Polydor 1988)★★, *Guaranteed* (RCA 1991)★★, *Forever Now* (RCA 1994)★★.

Solo: Mark King *Influences* (Polydor 1993)★★.

● COMPILATIONS: *Level Best* (Polydor 1989)★★★★, *The Remixes* (1992)★★★.

● VIDEOS: *Live At Wembley* (Channel 5 1987), *Family Of Five* (Channel 5 1988), *Level Best* (Channel 5 1989), *Fait Accompli* (1994).

● FURTHER READING: *Level 42: The Definitive Biography*, Michael Cowton.

Levellers

This five-piece unit from Brighton, Sussex, England, combined folk instrumentation with rock and punk ethics: 'We draw on some Celtic influences because it's a powerful source, but we're a very English band - this country does have roots worth using.' They took their name, and much of their ideology, from the Puritans active at the time of the English Civil War between 1647 and 1649, whose agenda advocated republicanism, a written constitution and abolition of the monarchy. Their original line-up featured songwriter Mark Chadwick (lead vocals, guitar, banjo), Jonathan Sevink (fiddle), Alan Miles (vocals, guitars, mandolin, harmonica), Jeremy Cunningham (bass, bouzouki) and Charlie Heather (drums). Sevink's violin, like many of their instruments, was typically unconventional and ecologically sound, 'recycled' from three different broken violin bodies. Chadwick, meanwhile, used a guitar that had an old record player arm acting as pick-ups, as well as an amplifier acquired from the **Revillos**. The *Carry Me* EP was released on Brighton's Hag Records in May 1989, after label boss Phil Nelson had taken over their management. They signed to French label Musidisc Records in 1989, and **Waterboys** producer Phil Tennant recorded their debut album. When their guitarist left during a tour of Belgium in April 1990, they recruited Simon Friend, a singer-songwriter and guitarist from the north of England, and set off on a typically extensive UK tour. Distribution problems with their debut led to a new contract with China Records, with whom they made a breakthrough into the national charts with the minor 1991 hits 'One Way' and 'Far From Home'. Their second album, *Levelling The Land*, reached the UK Top 20. A mixture of English and Celtic folk with powerful guitar-driven rock, it was acclaimed throughout Europe where the band toured before performing sell-out domestic concerts. May 1992 saw the *Fifteen Years* EP enter the UK chart at number 11, confirming that their widespread popularity had not been diminished by their almost total absence from the mainstream press. Signed to **Elektra Records** in the USA, the Levellers made their initial impact touring small venues there before returning to the UK to stage three Christmas Freakshows, which combined music and circus acts at the Brighton Centre and Birmingham NEC. They also continued to play benefits for the environmental and social causes that remain the subject of many of their songs. In 1993 they again toured Europe, released a compilation of singles and live tracks, *See Nothing, Hear Nothing, Do Something*, and recorded songs for a new album at **Peter Gabriel**'s **Real World** studios. In the summer of that year 'Belaruse' registered high in the UK Top 20. The accompanying self-titled album also rose to number 2 in the UK charts, and followed the familiar formula of rousing, agit-prop folk rock. In truth, the band themselves were disappointed with the lack of progress *The Levellers* demonstrated, and it would be a full two years before the next studio album. It sold well, however, and their popularity, particularly in live appearances, made them regulars in the underground music press, wherein they took to criticizing **The Men They Couldn't Hang** and **New Model Army**, who, paradoxically, appeared to be their biggest influences. By 1994 the band had purchased their own disused factory, the Metway, a base for various activities including the running of a fan club and pressure groups as well as an integral studio complex. The first album to be constructed in these surrounds, *Zeitgeist*, was recorded over a leisurely nine-month period which gave the songs, notably 'Fantasy', time to develop and breathe. The Levellers' affinity with the neo-hippie/new-age travellers initially seemed likely to prevent them from achieving mass appeal, but the success of their records and their huge following continues to surprise the cynics, of which there are many. This new-found appeal was confirmed when 'What A Beautiful Day' reached the UK charts, and new album *Mouth To Mouth* recorded impressive sales.

● ALBUMS: *A Weapon Called The Word* (Musidisc 1990)★★★, *Levelling The Land* (China 1991)★★★, *The Levellers* (China 1993)★★★★, *Zeitgeist* (China 1995)★★★, *Best Live: Headlights, White Lines, Black Tar Rivers* (China 1996)★★, *Mouth To Mouth* (China 1997)★★★.

● COMPILATIONS: *See Nothing, Hear Nothing, Do Something* (China 1993)★★★.

● VIDEOS: *The Great Video Swindle (Live At Glasgow Barrowlands)* (1992), *Best Live: Headlights, White Lines, Black Tar Rivers* (Warner Video 1996).

Leven, Jackie

b. Fife, Scotland. Former **Doll By Doll** singer Jackie Leven saw that band fall apart in 1983, without any of the commercial recognition to match the warmth with which UK critics greeted them. If he thought that signalled the zenith of his misery, he was wrong. Attacked in a London street shortly afterwards, he received several broken ribs and a badly damaged larynx. Unable to sing, his doctor prescribed anabolic steroids which only exacerbated matters. Down on his luck and utterly despondent about his prospects, Leven turned to heroin as a prop. Eventually, together with his partner Carol, he devised a new, holistic approach to his problems, which proved so successful that their new doctor urged them to spread news of the system. Together they set up the C.O.R.E. (Courage to stop, Order in life, Release from addiction, Entry into new life) charity. This organization has since become highly successful in treating those with substance abuse problems. Another effect of this rebirth was to reawaken Leven's interest in music. Concrete Bulletproof Invisible was a short-lived band put together with two former bandmates and ex-**Sex Pistols** bass player Glen Matlock. However, when he came to record again, it was as a solo artist. *The Argyll Cycle*, a mini-album, was a Scotland-only release on **Cooking Vinyl Records**, comprising five tracks Leven had written while relaxing in his beloved West Scotland (shortly after his partner had left him). It was followed almost immediately by a second collection, completed with American poet Robert Bly and featuring readings from **Mike Scott** of the **Waterboys**. Leven had read Bly's work (Bly is the nominal head of the US 'men's movement') while at school, and his interest was reawakened by hearing recent tapes. Leven has gone on to become the UK representative/organizer of the men's movement, appearing on Gloria Hunniford's television show and other outlets in that capacity. As if that was not enough to make him a media personality on a par with another Scots refugee from the punk wars, **Richard Jobson**, he also markets his own brand of single malt whisky, 'Leven's Lament' (his father had once written an encyclopedia on whiskeys). *Forbidden Songs Of The Dying West* mined the same rich vein of Celtic soul, and served to emphasize what a powerful and distinctive voice Leven possesses. Following the CD reissue of *The Argyll Cycle* he released 1997's *Fairytales For Hard Men*

which, aptly, had a harder-edged sound than the previous records.

● ALBUMS: *The Argyll Cycle* mini-album (Cooking Vinyl 1994)★★★, *The Mystery Of Love Is Greater Than The Mystery Of Death* (Cooking Vinyl 1994)★★★★, *The Forbidden Songs Of The Dying West* (Cooking Vinyl 1995)★★★★, *Songs From The Argyll Cycle* (Cooking Vinyl 1994)★★★, *Fairy Tales For Hard Men* (Cooking Vinyl 1997)★★★, *Control* recorded 1971 (1997)★★★.

Levene, Sam

b. 28 August 1905, Russia, d. 28 December 1980, New York, USA. Some sources suggest that this popular stage and screen character actor was born in New York. However, it seems more likely that he was taken to the USA in 1907, and became a naturalized citizen some 30 years later. After graduating from high school, Levene attended the American Academy of Dramatic Art in New York from 1925-27, and made his Broadway debut almost immediately in *Wall Street* (1927). The Depression made work scarce, but Levene persevered, and after making an impression in *Dinner At Eight* (1932), he established himself as a fine actor with *Three Men On A Horse* (1935). His hustling, fast-talking, streetwise style meant he was a natural choice for the role of Nathan Detroit, the operator of 'the oldest established permanent floating crap game in New York', in **Guys And Dolls** (1950). Levene reprised his role for London audiences in 1953, but was overlooked by producers of the film version, who preferred **Frank Sinatra** in the part. Although the remainder of his career was mostly spent in Hollywood film studios and the straight theatre, where he is particularly remembered for his performances in *The Devil's Advocate* (1961, **Tony Awards** nomination) and Neil Simon's 1972 hit, *The Sunshine Boys*, Levene did star in two more Broadway musicals, *Let It Ride* (1961, as Patsy) and *Café Crown* (1964, as Hymie). He continued to sigh and shrug in projects of variable quality on stage and screen until shortly before his death.

● FILMS: *Three Men On A Horse* (1936), *After The Thin Man* (1936), *Yellow Jack* (1938), *The Mad Miss Manton* (1938), *The Shopworn Angel* (1938), *Golden Boy* (1939), *Married Bachelor* (1941), *Shadow Of The Thin Man* (1941), *Grand Central Murder* (1942), *Sunday Punch* (1942), *Sing Your Worries Away* (1942), *The Big Street* (1942), *I Dood It* (1943), *Action In the North Atlantic* (1943), *Whistling In Brooklyn* (1943), *Gung Ho!* (1943), *The Purple Heart* (1944), *The Killers* (1946), *Brute Force* (1947), *Boomerang!* (1947), *Killer McCoy* (1947), *The Babe Ruth Story* (1948), *Leather Gloves* (1948), *Dial 1119* (1950), *Guilty Bystander* (1950), *Three Sailors And A Girl* (1953), *The Opposite Sex* (1956), *Sweet Smell Of Success* (1957), *A Farewell To Arms* (1957), *Designing Woman* (1957), *Slaughter On Tenth Avenue* (1957), *Kathy O* (1958), *Act One* (1963), *A Dream Of Kings* (1969), *Such Good Friends* (1971), *The Money* (1976), *God Told Me So* (1976), *Demon* (1977), *Last Embrace* (1979), *And Justice For All* (1979).

LeVert

From Philadelphia, USA, contemporary R&B band LeVert derived their name from the surname of brothers Sean and **Gerald Levert**, the offspring of **O'Jays** founder **Eddie Levert**. The predominantly vocal trio additionally included schoolfriend Marc Gordon. Their debut album, *I Get Hot*, produced the US R&B hit 'I'm Still', but marketing at the small independent Tempre Records failed to satisfy their ambitions. A year later they signed to **Atlantic Records** and struck number 1 in the US R&B charts with '(Pop, Pop, Pop) Goes My Mind', taken from *Bloodline*. The similarity of Gerald's voice to that of his father's was unmistakable, yet LeVert were undoubtedly a product of the 80s with their advanced production techniques and layered rhythms. The follow-up album, *Bloodline*, went gold and yielded a further substantial crossover pop hit with 'Cassanova'. *Just Coolin'*, accompanied by a successful single of the same title, kept up the commercial momentum, but failed to match the impact of the group's earlier work. With Gerald freelancing as a producer for several other R&B acts, *Rope-A-Dope* again achieved gold status, despite apparent creative stagnation. The group was put on temporary hold when Gerald announced the launch of a solo career in 1991, but he returned in time for *For Real Tho'*. However, with their lead singer's busy schedule taking centrestage, it appeared for some time that LeVert's absence would become permanent, until the release of *The Whole Scenario* in 1997.

● ALBUMS: *I Get Hot* (Tempre 1985)★★★, *Bloodline* (Atlantic 1986)★★★, *The Big Throwdown* (Atlantic 1987)★★★, *Just Coolin'* (Atlantic 1988)★★★, *Rope-A-Dope* (Atlantic 1990)★★, *For Real Tho'* (Atlantic 1992)★★, *The Whole Scenario* (Atlantic 1997)★★★.

Levert, Gerald

b. Philadelphia, USA. Bridging the gap between traditional and contemporary R&B, Gerald Levert has a fine vocal technique first heard in 1985 with the release of the debut album by the group **LeVert**. By the time that group's *Just Coolin'* had become a major US success, Gerald had already taken time off from the parent group to produce a number of artists with Marc Gordon, including **Stephanie Mills**, **James Ingram**, **Miki Howard**, the **O'Jays** and Troop. He also wrote 'Whatever It Takes' for **Anita Baker**'s platinum-selling *Compositions* album. *Rope-A-Dope* also went gold for the group, while as head of **Atlantic Record**'s Trevel Productions, Gerald worked with new vocal groups Rude Boy and Men At Large. All these endeavours preceded the announcement of his solo career in 1991. The timing had been carefully planned, and paid huge rewards when 'School Me', 'Can You Handle It', 'Baby Hold On To Me' (featuring his father, Eddie Levert of the O'Jays) and the title track of the parent album *Private Line* achieved major success. The songs, written in conjunction with new partner Tony Nicholas, established him as a major force in contemporary R&B and

soul, with an equal emphasis on up-tempo dance numbers and balladeering. Afterwards, Gerald returned to work with LeVert (the band), and their fifth album, *For Real Tho*, earned another gold disc. Further production work with **Barry White**, Little Joe (lead singer of Rude Boy), Drama and Men At Large interrupted preparations for a second solo set, which finally followed in 1994. *Groove On* was envisaged by the artist as 'a 90s version of a 60s soul show, with a band, a whole horn section, the works'. Once more working with Nicholas, this time the ballads included 'I'd Give Anything', which became the album's first hit single, produced by the Grammy award-winning David Foster, and the 'issue' song 'How Many Times', which dealt with a woman suffering physical and emotional abuse. The reconstruction of a traditional soul dynamic was enshrined by the presence of his father as co-producer on 'Same Time, Same Place', while 'Can't Help Myself' was originally written for the Forest Whitaker film *Strapped*. In 1995 he enjoyed further international success with 'Answering Service', confirming Levert as one of the leading lights of modern soul and vocal R&B. The same year also produced a well-received collection of duets performed with his father, titled *Father And Son* (see **Levert, Gerald And Eddie**). In 1997 he joined with **Keith Sweat** and **Johnny Gill** for the 'soul supergroup' album, *Levert Sweat Gill*.

● ALBUMS: *Private Line* (Atlantic 1991)★★★★, *Groove On* (Atlantic 1994)★★★, as Levert Sweat Gill *Levert Sweat Gill* (East West 1997)★★.

Levert, Gerald And Eddie

The 1995 release of *Father And Son* paired two legends of soul music, singer and producer **Gerald Levert** (of **LeVert**) and his father Eddie, lead singer and founding member of the **O'Jays**. The album featured a combination of original songs written expressly for the purpose by the duo and a selection of cover versions, including several O'Jays remakes. Produced by Gerald and Tony Nicholas, a co-writer on the project who had worked extensively with Gerald in the past, the album was prompted by requests from fans after the father and son team had performed together in concert on several occasions. With 10 gold and four platinum albums between them, it was a partnership bound to appeal to fans of soul and R&B. The pair had first recorded a duet, 'Baby Hold On To Me', for Gerald's 1991 debut solo album, *Private Line*. It reached the top of the US R&B singles chart in January 1992. In addition to the customary accompanying promotional tour for *Father And Son*, the duo also announced details of a new national scholarship fund overseen by Eddie's 100 Black Men collective.

● ALBUMS: *Father And Son* (East West 1995)★★★.

Levey, Stan

b. 5 April 1925, Philadelphia, Pennsylvania, USA. After working as a professional heavyweight boxer and part-time drummer in his home town, Levey moved to New

York while still in his teens. Abandoning boxing and concentrating on drumming, he was soon in great demand. He had already gigged with **Dizzy Gillespie** in Philadelphia and worked with him again, also playing in bebop bands such as those led by **Oscar Pettiford**, **Charlie Parker**, **Coleman Hawkins** and **George Shearing**. In 1945, he was a member of the remarkable band co-led by Gillespie and Parker, of which the other members were **Al Haig** and **Ray Brown** (and sometimes **Milt Jackson** and **Eli 'Lucky' Thompson**), which took the bebop message around the USA. Perhaps the most notable point on the tour was Billy Berg's nightclub in Los Angeles, an engagement which proved to be the catalyst for the creation of the west coast school of bebop. In the late 40s Levey played in a number of big bands including those of **Georgie Auld** and **Woody Herman** and in 1952 joined **Stan Kenton**. After leaving Kenton in 1954, Levey became resident in Los Angeles, working with **Howard Rumsey**'s Lighthouse All Stars, where he replaced **Max Roach**, and recording extensively, often under his own name, with musicians such as **Conte Candoli**, **Frank Rosolino**, **Lou Levy**, **Richie Kamuca**, **Art Pepper** and **Dexter Gordon**. In such company, Levey appeared on several of the best albums made by the west coast beboppers. He also played in the **Shorty Rogers** big band assembled for a record date in 1956. Subsequently, Levey worked in film and television studio bands and appeared on many recording dates, occasionally playing jazz gigs. One of the best of the early bebop drummers, Levey's playing was marked by his clean, precise attack which was at its most striking at fast tempos.
● ALBUMS: with Dizzy Gillespie *The Development Of An American Artist* (1945)★★★, *Stan Levey Plays Bill Holman, Jimmy Giuffre* (1954)★★★★, *This Time The Drum's On Me/Stanley The Steamer* (1955)★★★, *Grand Stan* (1956)★★★, with Shorty Rogers *Blues Express* (1956)★★★, with the Lighthouse All Stars *Double Or Nothin'* (1957)★★, *The Stan Levey Quintet* (VSOP 1957)★★★, with Max Roach *Drummin' The Blues* (1957)★★★.

Levi Roots

b. K. Graham, 1958, Clarendon, Jamaica, West Indies. Levi is an affable man who has softened the industry's hardest critics with his charismatic personality. By the age of 12 Levi relocated in the UK with his family. He soon became involved in the local music scene, initially with the legendary Sir Coxsone Outernational **Sound System**. He primarily performed as a DJ on the sound before becoming one of England's leading exponents of the Roots and Culture movement. His recording debut, 'Poor Man Story', was produced by **Lloyd Coxsone** and adroitly mixed by **Dennis Bovell**. The song was an instant success and became regarded as an anthem, being highly sought after in the 90s. The song was later covered by a dance duo who enjoyed crossover chart success. In the early 80s Levi followed his solo success by forming the band Matic 16. The group released the favoured 'Jahoviah', another prized rarity, especially the

initial pressings, which surfaced on green vinyl through **Jimmy Lindsay**'s Music Hive label. The song was regularly featured on **Jah Shaka**'s Sound System, acknowledging the roots appeal. Levi embarked on a series of live performances with two principal members of the Matics, Patrick and Henry Tenyue. The singer also formed his own Conqueror label, releasing the group's second single - the sadly neglected 'Say You Want Me'. In addition to their hectic live schedule, the group provided support for a number of Jamaican stars, including **Sugar Minott**, **Junior Reid**, **Half Pint** and **Yammie Bolo**, who also released hits through the Matics' label. Conqueror was also responsible for launching the career of **Jack Radics**, whose release of 'Walk On By' enabled the singer to relinquish his job as a cab driver. By 1985 the Matics parted company, which led Levi to pursue a solo career. Recording in Jamaica, Levi worked with **Philip 'Fatis' Burrell** alongside **Sly And Robbie**, which resulted in the hits, 'It A Fi Burn', 'Sweet Africa' and 'Shashamane City'. Levi concentrated on writing and producing for his Conqueror label. Having earned respect for the label's earlier releases, his production skills were in demand and he promoted the careers of a number of new artists. The singer **Mikey General** recorded his debut, 'Baby Mother', with Levi building a solid foundation before his eventual return to Jamaica, where he joined the **Exterminator** Crew. In 1996 Levi and the Tenyue brothers were reunited and began working on *Free Your Mind*. The album featured a host of top musicians, including **Mafia And Fluxy**, the Ruff Cut Crew, Gussie P, **Jah Shaka** and Speedy. In 1998 the release was critically acclaimed and has enjoyed a favourable response in the marketplace. Levi's dexterity resulted in him writing a book, *Dreadlock Holiday*, drawn from his own experiences at Her Majesty's pleasure on the Isle Of Sheppey. The novel echoed *Free Your Mind*, which tied in nicely with the album, although, regrettably, the releases were not simultaneous.
● ALBUMS: *Free Your Mind* (Soundbox 1998)★★★★.

Levi Smiths Clefs

Formed Adelaide, Australia in 1966. The Levi Smiths Clefs were Barrie McAskill. McAskill formed the band and has presided over its history and destiny during its subsequent phases. McAskill, possessing one of the country's most distinct and raspy voices, led the troupe through two decades of change, with many talented members, his main love being soul and R&B-based material. The band held residencies at popular discos and clubs in both Melbourne and Sydney, and provided the music at a consistently high level. Perhaps the band's failing was that they did not record more often, nor did they write much original material. Their one album did contain several originals, but the strongest song was a **Beatles** cover. The list of musicians that passed through the ranks is considerable. Of these, one of the most notable was the 1968 line-up which became Fraternity with the addition of Bon Scott in his pre-

AC/DC days, and which recorded two albums. The 1969 band became Tully and the 1971 big band provided members for SCRA - an 11-piece **Chicago/Blood Sweat And Tears**-styled band that released two albums. The 1972 line-up became Mighty Mouse briefly before assuming the name **Chain**. McAskill still performs in Sydney, bringing the band together as required by various promoters.

● ALBUMS: *Empty Monkey* (1970)★★★.

Levi, Ijahman

b. Trevor Sutherland, 1946, Manchester, Jamaica, West Indies. Levi received his earliest musical tutoring as a youth living in Trenchtown from **Joe Higgs**, eventually becoming proficient enough to appear on Vere John's 'Opportunity Hour', the launching pad for many a reggae career. He made his first recording, 'Red Eyed People', under the name Youth for producer **Duke Reid** in 1961. Levi emigrated to England in 1963, settling in Harlesden, London, and formed a short-lived group called the Vibrations. Once the Vibrations folded, he and another singer, Carl Simmons, formed a stage act called Youth And Rudie And The Shell Shock Show, performing a **Tamla-Motown** and **Stax**-style soul revue at the famous London niterie the Q Club, as well as touring Europe. He recorded a number of obscure singles at this time for various labels including **Polydor**, **Pama** and **Deram**, for whom he cut a reggae version of **P.P. Arnold**'s 'Angel Of The Morning', as well as a reggae version of 'White Christmas' for **Trojan Records**, under the unlikely name of Nyah And The Snowflakes. None of these recordings made any impact, and Levi put his career on hold while he settled down to pursue a normal family life.

His career was resuscitated in 1972 when he was reborn as Ijahman Levi, after turning to the Bible. In 1976 he recorded three excellent singles for Dennis 'Dip' Harris: 'Chariot Of Love', 'I'm A Levi' and 'Jah Heavy Load'. At this time he also contributed some vocal harmonies to **Rico Rodriguez**'s 'Man From Warieka'. This brought him to the attention of **Island Records** boss **Chris Blackwell**, who set about producing his 1978 debut, *Haile I Hymn*. Hampered by Blackwell's stated intention of creating a reggae *Astral Weeks*, the album contained only four extended tracks, including new versions of 'Jah Heavy Load' and 'I'm A Levi', and garnered mixed reviews. Nevertheless, despite accusations of self-indulgence and pretension, *Haile I Hymn* remains Levi's most important and popular album. After the follow-up, *Are We A Warrior*, Levi parted company with Island. He set up his own labels, Tree Roots and Jahmani, releasing several Jamaican pressed singles in the early 80s including 'Thank You', another version of 'Jah Heavy Load' and 'Tradesman', as well as a new, more conventional album, *Tell It To The Children*. During the 80s Levi's style of roots Rasta reggae fared less well, in common with many of his contemporaries. Nevertheless, in 1985 he enjoyed perhaps his biggest reggae hit with the sentimental 'I

Do', a duet with his wife Madge, a radical departure from his usual militant spiritual style.

● ALBUMS: *Haile I Hymn (Chapter 1)* (Island 1978)★★★★, *Are We A Warrior* (Mango/Island 1979)★★★, *Tell It To The Children* (Jahmani/Tree Roots 1982)★★, *Africa* (Jahmani/Tree Roots 1984)★★★, *Lily Of My Valley* (Jahmani 1985)★★, with Maj *I Do* (Jahmani 1986)★★, *Culture Country* (Tree Roots 1987)★★★, *Forward Rastaman* (Fat Shadow 1987)★★, *Ijahman & Friends* (Tree Roots 1988)★★★, *Inside Out* (Tree Roots 1989)★★★, *Live Over Europe* (Jamaica Sound 1989)★★, *Love Smiles* (Jahmani 1991)★★★, *On Track* (Jahmani 1991)★★.

Leviathan (60s)

Although inaugurated in December 1968, Leviathan evolved out of a UK, Brighton-based pop group, the Mike Stuart Span. Four singles had been completed under this early appellation before Stuart Michael Hobday (vocals), Brian Bennett (guitar), Roger McCabe (bass) and Roscoe Murphy (drums) embarked on a progressive rock direction. Signed to the **Elektra** label, the renamed quartet's first two singles were issued as a package in April 1969. Dubbed 'The Four Faces Of Leviathan', each song deliberately showed contrasting musical styles, but this ambitious idea failed to generate the anticipated enthusiasm. The group completed an entire album, but broke up when it was rejected by their label. Leviathan did return to the studio to record a final single, 'Flames', before finally disintegrating. Stuart Hobday is now a respected free-lance producer for BBC Radio.

Leviathan (90s)

US hard rock quintet Leviathan comprises Jack Aragon (vocals), Ron Skeen (guitar), John Lutzow (guitar), James Escobedo (bass) and Ty Tameus (drums). Formed in Colorado in 1992, they rose to public prominence in the same year with the release of a self-titled, self-financed five-song debut CD. Afterwards, the group accepted a contract with European label Rock The Nation and recorded its first full-length album, *Deepest Secrets Beneath*. Aided by producer Jim Morris (**Savatage**, **Crimson Glory**), the group offered a technically precise demonstration of their songwriting skills and power riffs, with an emphasis on textual, neo-progressive structures.

● ALBUMS: *Deepest Secrets Beneath* (RTN 1994).

Leviev, Milcho

b. 19 December 1937, Plovdiv, Bulgaria. Leviev studied formally at the Bulgarian State Music Academy, and by the early 60s was playing piano and directing orchestras on radio and television. He was also active as a composer, experimenting with music to be played by classical and jazz ensembles. In the early 70s he was in Germany and soon moved to the USA, where he began a fruitful association with **Don Ellis**. In addition to playing with Ellis he also composed and arranged, finding considerable rapport with Ellis's imaginative use of complex time signatures and incorporation of ethnic concepts. Also in the 70s, Leviev played in small groups led by, amongst others, **John Klemmer** and **Billy Cobham**. In the early 80s, Leviev worked with **Art Pepper**, with whom he appeared at **Ronnie Scott**'s, an occasion recorded on *Blues For The Fisherman* and *True Blues*. He also worked with **Al Jarreau** and led his own small band, Free Flight. Although Free Flight was a jazz-rock fusion band, Leviev continued to associate with big bands, working with **Gerald Wilson** and others. In the mid-80s he formed a duo with **Charlie Haden** and later in the decade was involved in a number of US west coast-based small groups. In addition to the valuable contribution he has made through his writing, Leviev consistently demonstrates his skills as a keyboard player, bringing his classical training to bear upon the complexities of the advanced musical style in which he frequently chooses to work.

● ALBUMS: *Jazz Focus 65* (1967)★★★, *Piano Lesson* (1977)★★★, *Music For Big Band And Symphony Orchestra* (1981)★★★★, *Blues For The Fisherman* (1981)★★★★, *What's New?* (1980)★★★, *True Blues* (1982)★★★, *Milcho Leviev Plays The Music Of Irving Berlin* (1983)★★★.

Levine, Henry 'Hot Lips'

b. 26 November 1907, London, England. Levine's family emigrated to the USA early in 1908. In 1917, Levine heard Nick La Rocca playing with the **Original Dixieland Jazz Band**, an event which determined his future career. He learned to play trumpet and turned professional in 1925; by extraordinary coincidence his first job was with the ODJB, by then much-changed from the line-up Levine had seen as a child. Levine played in several studio bands of the mid-20s, recording with **Nat Shilkret**, **Vincent Lopez** and others, but in 1927 was hired by British bandleader Bert **Ambrose**. He opened with Ambrose at the Mayfair Hotel in London in March and in June made records with the band. The following month he recorded under the leadership of **Fred Elizalde**. Towards the end of the year, he returned to New York where, for the next few years, he played in bands led by Cass Hagan, **Rudy Vallee** and other popular entertainers of the period. He then returned to studio work, among other things leading NBC's Chamber Music Society of Lower Basin Street jazz group. After World War II Levine directed radio, television and hotel orchestras in various parts of the USA, settling in Las Vegas in 1961 where he played in numerous hotel and casino bands. He retired in 1982. A fine lead trumpeter and an effective soloist, Levine remains little known among jazz fans despite his long and active career.

● ALBUMS: *Chamber Music Society Of Lower Basin Street* (1940-41 recordings)★★★.

Levitation

This rock-pop combo featured several experienced UK musicians, and was formed by Terry Bickers (vocals, guitar, ex-**Colenso Parade**) and Dave Francollini (drums, ex-Something Pretty Beautiful) after an altercation between the former and his ex-group leader, Guy Chadwick of the **House Of Love**, in 1989. Levitation's line-up was completed by Christian Hayes (guitar, ex-**Cardiacs**), Robert White (keyboards) and Laurence O'Keefe (bass, ex-**Jazz Butcher**). Their pedigree was enough to see them shoot to prominence in the UK press, and two EPs, *Coppelia* and *After Ever*, revealed a band with no lack of enthusiasm or ideas. They were ousted from an early **Transvision Vamp** support officially because there was not enough room on stage for their equipment. Another story suggests that singer Wendy James was concerned that Levitation's growing live reputation might overshadow her own group. Bickers certainly enjoyed a reputation for being something of an eccentric, but initially seemed to have found a happier home for his obvious talents. Levitation's debut album featured John McGeoch of **PiL** guesting on guitar, and the critical response was strong. However, Bickers found himself moving on once more in 1993 following their debut single for **Chrysalis**, making the following announcement live on stage at the Tufnell Park Dome in London: 'Oh dear. We've completely lost it, haven't we?'. While Levitation attempted to soldier on in his absence, Bickers disappeared to write songs, using the name Cradle to cover these exploits, though this was no band as such. An album was eventually recorded in 1994 with the help of various friends in a 'collective' set up (including new vocalist Steven Ludwin), while Bickers also contributed guitar to the debut album by Oedipussy (who include Phil Parfitt, ex-**Perfect Disaster**). He also contributed to and produced Vex's 1997 debut, *Frontiers And New Technologies*.

● ALBUMS: *Coterie* mini-album (Rough Trade 1992)★★★, *Need For Not* (Rough Trade 1992)★★★, *Meanwhile Gardens* (Festival 1994)★★.

Levitt, Rod

b. 16 September 1929, Portland, Oregon, USA. A regular trombone player in studio orchestras, Levitt first attracted attention in the jazz world through a job with **Dizzy Gillespie**, with whose big band he played in 1956. Apart from Gillespie, he also recorded with big bands led by **Ernie Wilkins**, **Sy Oliver** and **Gil Evans**. In the early 60s, he recorded with his own octet which included **Bill Berry** and **Rolf Ericson** but was most often heard on big band sessions under leaders such as **Quincy Jones**, **Oliver Nelson** and the **Chuck Israels**'s National Jazz Ensemble. Apart from his sound playing ability, Levitt is also a gifted arranger.

● ALBUMS: *Dynamic Sound Patterns* (1963)★★★, *Insight* (1964)★★, *Solid Ground* (1965)★★★, *42nd Street* (1966)★★★.

Levy, Barrington

b. 1964, Kingston, Jamaica, West Indies. Barrington Levy was one of the first singers to challenge the dominance of DJs in 80s **dancehall** reggae, although his earliest recording, under the name of the Mighty Multitude ('My Black Girl' in 1977), predated that era. Another early single, 'A Long Long Time Since We Don't Have No Love' in 1978, followed the first into obscurity, but Barrington, undaunted, went into the dancehalls. By 1981 Levy's effortlessly buoyant voice had spread his fame to the point where **Henry 'Junjo' Lawes**, at the time the most in-demand producer in Jamaica, pursued him. His first Junjo single was 'Ah Yah We Deh', which sold moderately well, as did two further releases. His fourth single, 'Collie Weed', was a great success. Levy did not sound like anyone else: he perhaps revealed some of **Jacob Miller**'s style, and a little of **Bob Andy**'s influence, but his phrasing evoked the raw energy of the dancehalls. While other singers were struggling, Levy was slugging it out at the top. His debut, *Bounty Hunter*, sold well and a string of singles consolidated his position: 'Robber Man', 'Black Rose', 'Like A Soldier', the massive hits 'Money Move' and 'Shine Eye Gal', and the stunning 'Prison Oval Rock', and a series of albums were released between 1982-85 to capitalize on his success. He later denounced many of these as 'joke business', being packaged with old singles, out-takes and one-off private **sound system** recordings. He performed his first UK gigs in 1984, including an appearance as a winner at the UK Reggae Awards. He then linked with young producer Jah Screw and enjoyed a big hit with the anthemic 'Under Me Sensi'. He followed it with 'Here I Come', which was a hit in the soul clubs and scraped the UK charts when licensed by **London Records**, who also issued an album of the same title. However, Screw and Levy made the mistake of courting crossover success and he sounded lost on subsequent rocky singles. Levy travelled between Jamaica, London and New York, and although he lost momentum at the end of the 80s, he still had all the talent of his peak period, as *Love The Life You Live* made clear. Two Bob Andy cover versions, 'Too Experienced' and 'My Time', brought him back to the forefront of reggae, and he signed to **Island Records** in 1991 for the fine *Divine* set. While it remains to be seen whether he can ever achieve the broader success that seemed to be his in the mid-80s, he remains one of reggae's most powerful and original voices.

● ALBUMS: *Bounty Hunter* (Jah Life 1979)★★★, *Shine Eye Gal* (Burning Sounds 1979)★★★, *Englishman* (Greensleeves 1980)★★★, *Robin Hood* (Greensleeves 1980)★★★, *21 Girls Salute* (Jah Life 1983)★★★, *Poor Man Style* (Trojan 1983)★★★, *Run Come Yah* (1983)★★★, *Lifestyle* (GG's 1983)★★★, *Teach Me Culture* (Live & Learn 1983)★★★, with Frankie Paul *Barrington Levy Meets Frankie Paul* (Ariwa 1984)★★★, *Barrington Levy* (Clock Tower 1984)★★★★, *Here I Come* (Time/London 1985)★★★★, *Hunter Man* (Burning Sounds 1988)★★★, *Love The Life You Live* (Time/London 1988)★★★★, *Open Book* (Tuff Gong 1988)★★, *Prison Oval Rock* (Volcano 1989)★★, *Divine* (Mango/Island 1991)★★★, *Turning Point* (Greensleeves 1992)★★★, *D.J. Counteraction* ragga mixes (Greensleeves 1995)★★★.

● COMPILATIONS: *The Collection* (Time/London 1991)★★★★, *20 Vintage Hits* (Sonic Sounds 1992)★★★★.

Levy, Hank

b. Henry J. Levy, 27 September 1927, Baltimore, Maryland, USA. After an extensive period of formal study, baritone saxophonist Levy joined **Stan Kenton** in 1953. By the 60s Levy was mostly writing, arranging and, in many instances, composing original material for Kenton, **Don Ellis** and other bands. Towards the end of the decade Levy entered musical education on a full-time basis. His work with students at Towson State University has generated considerable interest and enthusiasm, and many of his graduates found work in latter-day 'name' bands.

● ALBUMS: by Don Ellis *Live At Monterey* (1966)★★★★, by Ellis *Connection* (1972)★★★, by Stan Kenton *Journey To Capricorn* (1976)★★★.

Levy, Lou

b. 5 March 1928, Chicago, Illinois, USA. Among Levy's early piano jobs were stints in the late 40s with the big bands of **Georgie Auld** and **Woody Herman**. He also accompanied **Sarah Vaughan** in 1947, the first of many singers with whom he worked over the years. Others included **Ella Fitzgerald**, **Anita O'Day**, **Nancy Wilson** and **Peggy Lee**, whom he accompanied sporadically for 18 years from 1955. Among the bands with which he has played are those led by **Terry Gibbs**, **Benny Goodman** and **Stan Getz**. He also worked with **Supersax**, **Conte Candoli**, **Shelly Manne**, **Zoot Sims** and **Al Cohn**. Influenced by **Bud Powell** but with his own forthright style and a distinctive soloist and superb accompanist, Levy remains an important if sometimes overlooked jazz pianist.

● ALBUMS: *The Lou Levy Trio* (1954)★★, with Conte Candoli *West Coast Wailers* (1955)★★★, *Solo Scene* (1956)★★★, *Jazz In Four Colors* (1956)★★★★, *A Most Musical Fella* (1956)★★, *Award Winner: Stan Getz* (1957)★★★★, *Piano Playhouse* (1957)★★★, *Lou Levy Plays Baby Grand Jazz* (1958)★★, with Ella Fitzgerald *Ella Swings Lightly* (1958)★★★★, *The Hymn* (1963)★★★, with Candoli *Tempus Fugue-It* (1977)★★★, with Supersax *Chasin' The Bird* (1977)★★★★, *Touch Of Class* (1978)★★★, with Anita O'Day *Mello' Day* (1979)★★★, with Getz *The Dolphin* (1982)★★★, *The Kid's Got Ears* (1982)★★★.

Levy, Ron

b. Reuvain Zev ben Yehoshua Ha Levi, 29 May 1951, Cambridge, Massachusetts, USA. Ron Levy played clarinet during his childhood and, inspired by a **Ray Charles** concert, started playing piano at the age of 13. He soon took up organ too, and, influenced by **Booker T**, **Billy Preston** and **Jimmy Smith**, was a quick learner. Two years later he was backing up blues artists performing in the Boston area. At 17 the young musician was discovered and hired by blues legend **Albert King**. Still in high school, Levy worked with King, who had become his legal guardian, for 18 months. From

December 1969 to February 1976 he played piano and organ in **B.B. King**'s band. The period from that time until 1980 saw him work with the Rhythm Rockers, led by 'Guitar' Johnny Nicholas and featuring the young **Ronnie Earl** on lead guitar. As the house band of the Speakeasy in Cambridge they honed their skills backing up great blues musicians, among them Walter Horton, Johnny Shines and Roosevelt Sykes. After working with Luther 'Guitar Jnr' Johnson for three years, Levy played with **Roomful Of Blues** from 1983 to 1987. In addition to recording with his own band, Ron Levy's Wild Kingdom, he has played on numerous recordings by other artists, and since 1985, has produced a steady stream of albums for labels such as Black Top, **Rounder** and Bullseye.
● ALBUMS: *Ron Levy's Wild Kingdom* (Black Top 1986)★★★, *Safari To New Orleans* (Black Top 1988)★★★, *B-3 Blues & Grooves* (1992)★★★, *It's Getting Harder* (Miss Butch 1995)★★★, *Zim Zam Zoom* (Bullseye 1996)★★★.

Lewie, Jona

b. *c.*1943, England. A former member of **Brett Marvin And The Thunderbolts** and **Terry Dactyl And The Dinosaurs**, Lewie was one of several unconventional artists signed to the **Stiff** label. *On The Other Hand There's A Fist* maintained the quirky approach of earlier acts, but despite an appearance on the highly publicized *Be Stiff* tour, the artist remained largely unknown until 1980 when 'You'll Always Find Me In The Kitchen At Parties' broached the UK Top 20. A follow-up release, 'Stop The Cavalry', reached number 3 later that year when its nostalgic brass arrangement proved popular in the Christmas market. However, a subsequent album, *Heart Skips Beat*, failed to consolidate this success. 'Stop The Cavalry' continues to be an annual favourite during the Christmas season, thanks to its inclusion on compilation albums.
● ALBUMS: *On The Other Hand There's A Fist* (Stiff 1980)★★★, *Heart Skips Beat* (Stiff 1982)★★★.
● COMPILATIONS: *Gatecrasher* (Sonet 1979)★★★.

Lewis And Clarke Expedition

Formed in 1967, this short-lived group featured **Michael Murphey** (guitar/vocals) and Owen Castleman (guitar/vocals), who had already performed together as the Texas Twosome. Having adopted the respective roles of Travis Lewis and Boomer Clarke, they were augmented by Ken Bloom (guitar), John London (bass) and John Raines (bass). The quintet was signed by Colgems, the label which launched the **Monkees**, in part because London was a friend and ex-colleague of the latter group's **Michael Nesmith**. *The Lewis And Clarke Expedition* was a promising pop/country collection but although it contained a minor hit single, 'I Feel Good (I Feel Bad)', sales were far from encouraging and the group split up in 1968. Murphey remained signed to Screen Gems as a contract songwriter, penning 'What Am I Doing Hanging 'Round?' for the Monkees, and 'Calico Silver' for **Kenny Rogers** And The First

Edition. He returned to Texas in the early 70s and subsequently forged a highly successful solo career.
● ALBUMS: *The Lewis And Clarke Expedition* (1967)★★★.

Lewis, Barbara

b. 9 February 1943, Salem, Michigan, USA. Signed to **Atlantic Records** in 1961, Lewis enjoyed several regional hits before the sensual 'Hello Stranger' established her light but enthralling style. Recorded in Chicago, the performance was enhanced by the vocal support of the **Dells**. Further singles included the vibrant 'Someday We're Gonna Love Again' (1965), while 'Baby I'm Yours' and 'Make Me Your Baby' (both 1966) maintained her smooth, individual approach. Barbara remained with the label until 1968, but the following year moved to the **Stax** subsidiary Enterprise. Internal problems sadly doomed the album she made there, and having completed a handful of singles, Lewis withdrew from music altogether.
● ALBUMS: *Hello Stranger* (Atlantic 1963)★★★, *Snap Your Fingers* (Atlantic 1964)★★★, *Baby I'm Yours* (Atlantic 1965)★★★, *It's Magic* (Atlantic 1966)★★★, *Workin' On A Groovy Thing* (Atlantic 1968)★★★, *The Many Grooves Of Barbara Lewis* (Enterprise 1970)★★★.
● COMPILATIONS: *The Best Of ...* (Atlantic 1971)★★★, *Hello Stranger* (Solid Smoke 1981)★★★, *Golden Classics* (Collectables 1987)★★★, *The Many Grooves Of Barbara Lewis* (1992)★★★, *Hello Stranger: The Best Of ...* (Rhino/Atlantic 1994)★★★.

Lewis, Bobby (country)

b. 9 May 1946, Hodgenville, Hardin County, Kentucky, USA. Lewis, who comes from the birthplace of Abraham Lincoln, began to play the guitar at the age of nine and made his television debut at 13. He joined *The Old Kentucky Barn Dance* on WHAS Louisville, where he also appeared on the CBS-networked *Saturday Night Country Style*, before joining the WHAS-TV weekly *Hayloft Hoedown*. Being only 5 feet 4 inches tall, he found his Gibson J-200 guitar heavy and cumbersome and took to playing a lute (he had bought the instrument under the inital impression that it was a strange-shaped, but much lighter, guitar when he saw it in a music shop window). After stringing it with steel guitar strings, he began to use it in his act. He is, in all probability, the first and only person in country music to use a lute as his main instrument. Influenced and helped by **Ernest Tubb**, he moved to Nashville in 1964 and recorded for **United Artists**. In 1966, he gained his first US country chart entry with 'How Long Has It Been?', which peaked at number 6. Further Top 20 country hits included 'Love Me And Make It All Better', 'From Heaven To Heartache' and in 1970, his version of 'Hello Mary Lou' (a pop hit for **Rick Nelson** in 1961). He guested on the *Grand Ole Opry*, played venues all across the USA and made tours to both Europe and the Far East. After 1973, he recorded for various labels and achieved some minor chart entries, the best being 'Too Many Memories', a number 21 country hit in 1973. His last chart entry came in 1985, with a song called 'Love Is An Overload', after which he seems to have disappeared from the music scene.

● ALBUMS: *Tossin' And Turnin'* (Beltone 1961)★★★, *Little Man With A Big Heart* (United Artists 1966)★★, *How Long Has It Been* (United Artists 1967)★★, *A World Of Love* (United Artists 1967)★★★, *An Ordinary Miracle* (United Artists 1968)★★★, *From Heaven To Heartache* (United Artists 1969)★★★, *Things For You And I* (United Artists 1969)★★★, *Too Many Memories* (1973)★★★, *Portrait In Love* (1977)★★★, *Soul Full Of Music* (1977)★★.

● COMPILATIONS: *The Best Of Bobby Lewis* (United Artists 1970)★★★.

Lewis, Bobby (rock 'n' roll)

b. 17 February 1933, Indianapolis, Indiana, USA. Lewis grew up in an orphanage before being adopted by a Detroit family at the age of 12. He reportedly worked with jazz greats **Duke Ellington** and **Wes Montgomery** during his youth and befriended a young **Jackie Wilson** in the mid-50s. Lewis's first single, for the Parrot label, was released in 1956. Three years later he met the doo-wop group the **Fireflies**, whose lead singer, Richie Adams, went on to write songs for the New York Beltone label. Lewis signed to Beltone and recorded 'Tossin' And Turnin'', a danceable rock 'n' roll song Adams had co-written with Joe Rene. The record stayed at number 1 for seven weeks in 1961, becoming one of the year's biggest-sellers (in the UK it was covered by the **Ivy League**). Lewis followed it up with 'One Track Mind' another Top 10 hit, but subsequent efforts were commercially disappointing. He still performed at oldies concerts in the early 90s.

● ALBUMS: *Tossin' And Turnin'* (Beltone 1961)★★★.

● COMPILATIONS: *Tossin' N Turnin'* (Relic 1992)★★★.

Lewis, C.J.

b. Stephen Lewis, London, England. Lewis shadowed the **sound systems** around London with his childhood friend Philip 'Leo' Pottinger, and soon established himself as a respected DJ. **Philip Leo** himself began a recording career as a singer-songwriter with two successful releases for **Fashion Records**. For his third release, 'Why Do Fools Fall In Love', a reworking of **Frankie Lymon And The Teenagers**' 1956 chart-topper, he introduced Lewis to a wider audience. The single had considerable exposure through **ffrr Records**, and narrowly missed reaching the UK pop chart. In 1990 Lewis appeared on a number of releases, notably in combination with **Janet Lee Davis** for a version of **Keith And Enid**'s 'Worried Over You', while with Pottinger he recorded a version of the **Michael Jackson/Sugar Minott** hit, 'Good Thing Going'. In 1993 the duo recorded the reggae chart-topper 'Hypnotic Love', which was number 1 for seven weeks. This success resulted in Lewis signing with Black Market/MCA, with Pottinger as co-producer. The arrangement led to crossover success when 'Sweets For My Sweet' peaked at number 3 in the UK Top 10. He

followed the hit with a version of **Stevie Wonder**'s 'Everything Is Alright (Uptight)', **Earth, Wind And Fire**'s 'Best Of My Love' and an original composition, 'Dollars', utilizing **Prince Buster**'s 'Ten Commandments' rhythm. In 1994 he toured Europe, Asia and the Far East and began working on his second album for the label. He continued to play the live circuit on a 28-day tour of the UK, resulting in an award for Best P.A. Of The Year In Britain. His popularity in Japan resulted in his second album selling 150,000 copies in one day, increasing to 250,000 in the first two weeks of its release. In September 1995 he played seven sell-out dates in the Far East, and had a UK Top 40 summer hit with 'R To The A'. By the beginning of 1996, he had returned to the UK to promote the release of 'Can't Take It (Street Life)'. The release of 'Phat Ting' went some way towards soothing the disaffected hardcore reggae fans, who had become somewhat disillusioned by Lewis's crossover success.

● ALBUMS: *Dollars* (MCA 1993)★, *Rough And Smooth* (MCA 1995)★★.

Lewis, Darlene

Garage diva from the USA in the early 90s whose original 'Let The Music (Lift You Up)', licensed in England through the London-based duo **Network**, started a strange, and influential chain of events in dance music. Manchester band Loveland (affiliated to the **Eastern Bloc** record shop/label) released their own version of the record without obtaining sample clearance. A major war of legal attrition looked sure to ensue, until both parties agreed to release a joint version, performing together on *Top Of The Pops*. The case was hailed in turn as a perfect example of inter-artist co-operation and goodwill. Lewis herself is a former music student who was spotted as a waitress 'humming' by producer Hassan Watkins. Asking her to put words to the tune, a few minutes later she received a standing ovation from the clients of the restaurant. Not surprising, perhaps, as she was already engaged in the process of winning more than 40 awards for her opera singing. Although she also loves country, rock and opera, she has an instinct for club music that was honed in the Chicago house party scene. Following the success of 'Let The Music (Lift You Up)', she was signed to Kevin Saunderson's KMS label.

Lewis, Donna

b. Cardiff, Wales. Despite her initial inability to secure a UK recording contract, Lewis's career was galvanized meteorically when her debut single, 'I Love You Always Forever', climbed straight to the top of the US *Billboard* charts in 1996. The singer-songwriter was commendably relaxed about this turn of events, that reaction a testament to the fact that she had been involved in making music from the age of 14. At that time, influenced by jazz, **Motown Records** and **Rickie Lee Jones**, she began writing her first songs. She then attended the Welsh College of Music and Drama, before spending four years playing in European piano bars as a cabaret singer. When she returned to the UK she took a residency at the Belfry Hotel in Birmingham, at which time she began sending out her first demo tapes to record companies. By a strange set of coincidences, one such tape was passed to Jennifer Stark of **Atlantic Records** by Jerry Marreta, the drummer with **Peter Gabriel**. Atlantic paired her with Kevin Killen, who had previously worked with **U2**, **Kate Bush** and **Elvis Costello**. She was marketed in similar terms to **Enya**, whose 'ethereal' singing technique is close to her own, but the success of 'I Love You Always Forever' took everybody by surprise, not least UK record label executives who had passed on her demo tapes.

● ALBUMS: *Now In A Minute* (East West 1996)★★★★, *Blue Planet* (Atlantic 1998)★★★.

Lewis, Ed

b. Edwards Lewis, 22 January 1909, Eagle City, Oklahoma, USA, d. 18 September 1985. After briefly playing baritone horn in a marching band in Kansas City, where he was raised, Lewis switched to trumpet. He worked with a number of **territory bands**, notably **Bennie Moten**'s, during the 20s and early 30s. Other leaders included Thamon Hayes, **Harlan Leonard** and **Jay 'Hootie' McShann**. In 1937 he joined **Count Basie**, coincidentally auditioning on the same day as **Billie Holiday**. After spending more than a decade with Basie he dropped out of music for a while, returning in the mid-50s to lead his own band. He continued to play for the rest of his life, visiting Europe with the Countsmen the year before his death. Although best known as a capable and often inspiring lead trumpet, Lewis was a good soloist and played with a light, airy sound. He also composed several tunes.

Lewis, Gary, And The Playboys

One of the most commercially successful US pop groups of the mid-60s, the original Playboys comprised Gary Lewis (b. Gary Levital, 31 July 1946, New York, USA; vocals/drums), Alan Ramsey (b. 27 July 1943, New Jersey, USA; guitar), John West (b. 31 July 1939, Unrichville, Ohio, USA; guitar), David Costell (b. 15 March 1944, Pittsburgh, Pennsylvania, USA; bass) and David Walker (b. 12 May 1943, Montgomery, Alabama, USA; keyboards). Group leader Gary Lewis was the son of comedian Jerry Lewis and had been playing drums since the age of 14. After appearing at selected Hollywood parties, the ensemble was offered a residency at the Disneyland Park and soon after was signed by **Liberty Records** and producer **Leon Russell**. Their debut single, 'This Diamond Ring' (co-written by **Al Kooper** and originally intended for former idol, **Bobby Vee**), topped the American charts in February 1965 and spearheaded an remarkable run of Top 10 hits that included 'Count Me In', 'Save Your Heart For Me', 'Everybody Loves A Clown', 'She's Just My Style', 'She's Gonna Miss Her' and 'Green Grass'. The latter, although written by UK composers **Cook And**

Greenaway (alias **David And Jonathan**), predictably failed to make any impact in the UK market where the group remained virtually unknown. Undoubtedly the best-selling US group of the mid-60s without a UK hit to their name, they nevertheless enjoyed healthy record sales all over the world, appeared regularly on television, and even participated in a couple of low-budget movies, *A Swingin' Summer* and *Out Of Sight*. Their relative decline in 1967 probably had less to do with changing musical fashions than the induction of Gary Lewis to the US Armed Forces. By the time of his discharge in 1968, a set of Playboys were ready to return him to the charts with a remake of **Brian Hyland**'s 'Sealed With A Kiss'. A revival of the **Cascades**' 'Rhythm Of The Rain' pointed to the fact that the group were running short of ideas while also indicating their future on the revivalist circuit. After disbanding the group at the end of the 60s, Lewis was unsuccessfully relaunched as a singer/songwriter but later assembled a new version of the Playboys for cabaret and festival dates.

● ALBUMS: *This Diamond Ring* (Liberty 1965)★★★, *Everybody Loves A Clown* (1965)★★★, *Out Of Sight* soundtrack (1966)★★★, *She's Just My Style* (1966)★★★★, *Gary Lewis Hits Again!* (1966)★★★, *You Don't Have To Paint Me A Picture* (Liberty 1967)★★, *New Directions* (1967)★★, *Gary Lewis Now!* (1968)★★, *Close Cover Before Playing* (1968)★★, *Rhythm Of The Rain* (1969)★★, *I'm On The Road Now* (1969)★★.

● COMPILATIONS: *Golden Greats* (1966)★★★, *More Golden Greats* (1968)★★, *Twenty Golden Greats* (1979)★★★, *Greatest Hits: Gary Lewis And The Playboys* (1986)★★★.

Lewis, George (clarinet)

b. George Louis Francis Zeno, 13 July 1900, New Orleans, Louisiana, USA, d. 31 December 1968, New Orleans, Louisiana, USA. Lewis began playing clarinet in his early teens and between 1917 and the early 20s had worked alongside many leading New Orleans musicians including **Buddy Petit** and **Edward 'Kid' Ory**. Through the 20s and 30s, Lewis chose to play mostly in and around his home town, thus missing the attention paid to many early jazz musicians who visited Chicago, New York and other urban centres outside the south. In the early 40s Lewis benefited from the resurgence of interest in New Orleans jazz and began recording extensively, sometimes in partnership with **Bunk Johnson**. By the middle of the decade, however, Lewis was back in New Orleans, but the 50s found him touring all over the USA and to Europe. Although he lacked the sophisticated grace of, say, an **Edmond Hall**, Lewis's playing was marked by an often delightful simplicity and his fans were happy to overlook occasional musical inconsistencies in order to enjoy what they regarded as his authentic style. At his best, especially on some of the records made by William Russell in his American Music series, Lewis played with a charming distinction, which went a long way to deter criticism of his occasionally out-of-tune performances.

On those records cited, and others where he was in complete control of the style in which his accompanists played, Lewis's work gives a taste of how some facets of early jazz might well have been and, as such, should be heard by anyone interested in the origins of the music. Plagued by ill-health during the 60s, Lewis continued playing almost to the end of his life.

● ALBUMS: *George Lewis At Herbert Otto's Party* (1949)★★★, *A Very Good Year* (1957)★★, *The Perennial George Lewis* (1959)★★★, *George Lewis In Japan, 1 In Osaka* (1963)★★, *George Lewis In Japan, 2 In Tokyo* (1965)★★, *George Lewis In Japan, 3 In Kokura* (1965)★★, *George Lewis And The Moustache Stompers* (1965)★★★.

● COMPILATIONS: *The Oxford Series Volume 1* (1952)★★★★, *On Parade* (1953)★★★, *George Lewis Memorial Album* (1953)★★★, *New Orleans Stompers, Volumes 1 & 2* (1974)★★★★, *Pied Piper, Volumes 1-3 (1959)* (1981)★★★, *George Lewis Authentic New Orleans Ragtime Jazz Band* (1981)★★★, *Live At The Club Hangover (1953-54)* (1986)★★★, *In Japan Volumes 1-3* (GHB 1986)★★, *In New Orleans* (Ace 1993)★★★.

● FURTHER READING: *Call Him George*, Jay Alison Stuart (Dorothy Tait). *George Lewis: A Jazzman from New Orleans*, Tom Bethell.

Lewis, George (trombone)

b. 14 July 1952, Chicago, Illinois, USA. By chance George Lewis went to school with **Ray Anderson**, the other leading trombonist to emerge in the late 70s. Lewis took up trombone at the age of nine and taught himself by copying **Lester Young**'s tenor saxophone solos from records. He studied philosophy at Yale, playing there with pianist **Anthony Davis** and percussionist **Gerry Hemingway**. In 1971, he returned to Chicago where the **AACM** was active: he studied with **Muhal Richard Abrams** and began a long association with reeds player **Douglas Ewart**. He developed a virtuoso technique, combining tailgate bluster with bebop agility - something he attributes to listening to saxophonists and practising from **Eddie Harris**'s exercise books. He then studied music at Yale, graduating with a BA in 1974. In 1976, he spent two months with **Count Basie**. In 1976, he started working with **Anthony Braxton**, recording duo, quartet and orchestra pieces with him (*Elements Of Surprise, Quartet (Dortmund) 1976, Creative Orchestra Music 1976*); later he became an international figure of the *avant garde*, playing with Richard Teitelbaum of Musica Elettronica Viva and free-improvisers **Derek Bailey** and **Dave Holland**. He also played in the **Gil Evans** Orchestra, with pianist **Randy Weston**, recorded regularly with Abrams and worked with **Steve Lacy** (*Prospectus, Futurities* and the **Herbie Nichols** tribute *Change Of Season*). Lewis appeared in several of Bailey's **Company** line-ups and with leading European improvisers such as **Joëlle Léandre** and **Irène Schweizer**. He also recorded again with Braxton, both on the saxophonist's own *Four Compositions (Quartet) 1983* and with him on Teitelbaum's extraordinary *Concerto Grosso*. In 1987, he

recorded *News For Lulu*, a retrospective of hard bop tunes, with **John Zorn** and **Bill Frisell**, showing a stunning combination of bebop chops and free-improvising imagination. From the early 80s Lewis began to develop an interest in electronics, amazing people with improvised duets with programmed computers, and in recent years much of his time has been devoted to this project. From 1980-82 he was also the director of the New York radical theatre and music venue, The Kitchen.

● ALBUMS: with Anthony Braxton *Elements Of Surprise* (1976)★★★★, *Jazz At Ohio Union* (1976)★★★, *The George Lewis Solo Trombone Record* (1977)★★, *Shadowgraph 5* (Black Saint 1978)★★★, *Chicago Slow Dance* recorded 1977(1979)★★★, *George Lewis - Douglas Ewart* (1979)★★★, *Homage To Charles Parker* (Black Saint 1979)★★★★, with Evan Parker *From Saxophone & Trombone* (1980)★★★★, with Company *Fables* (1980)★★★, with Derek Bailey, John Zorn *Yankees* (Celluloid 1983)★★★★, with Parker *Hook, Drift & Shuffle* (1985)★★★, with various *Change Of Season* (1985)★★★, with Zorn, Bill Frisell *News For Lulu* (1987)★★★★, with Zorn, Frisell *More News For Lulu* (1992)★★★.

Lewis, Hopeton

Lewis began recording in the mid-60s, and found fame with 'Take It Easy'. The song was an instant hit and heralded the arrival of the less frenzied **rocksteady** beat. The song has frequently been reworked, notably on versions by **Johnny Clarke** ('Rockers Time Now') and Joyce Bond ('Do The Teasy'). He continued to record a number of hits through to the early 70s, including 'Sound And Pressure' and 'Music Got Soul'. In 1970 he entered and won the Jamaican Song Festival with 'Boom Shaka Lacka' and began working as a vocalist with **Byron Lee And The Dragonaires**. In 1971 he released 'Grooving Out On Life', supported by the Dragonaires, which led to an album of the same name. The songs proved to be too lightweight for the reggae audience and he similarly failed to cross over into the mainstream. In 1973 he released 'Good Together' and 'City Of New Orleans', neither of which made an impression on the charts.

● ALBUMS: *Take It Easy* (Island 1968)★★, *Grooving Out On Life* (Trojan 1973)★★, *Dynamic Hopeton Lewis* (Dragon 1974)★★.

Lewis, Huey, And The News

The group was formed in Marin Country, California, USA in 1980 by ex-**Clover** members singer and harmonica player Huey Lewis (b. Hugh Anthony Cregg III, 5 July 1951, New York, USA) and keyboards player Sean Hopper. They recruited guitarist and saxophonist Johnny Colla, Mario Cipollina (bass), Bill Gibson (drums) and Chris Hayes (lead guitar), all fellow performers at a regular jam session at local club Uncle Charlie's. A debut album produced by Bill Schnee was released by **Chrysalis Records** and a single from it, 'Do You Believe In Love' reached the US Top 10 aided by a tongue-in-cheek video. The band's easy-going rock/soul fusion reached its peak with *Sports*, which provided five US Top 20 hits. Among them were the **Chinn And Chapman** and song 'Heart & Soul', 'The Heart Of Rock & Roll', 'If This Is It' and 'I Want A New Drug'. Lewis sued **Ray Parker Jnr.** over the latter song, claiming it had been plagiarised for the *Ghostbusters* theme. From 1985-86, three Lewis singles headed the US charts. They were 'The Power Of Love' (chosen as theme tune for Robert Zemeckis's film *Back To The Future*), the Hayes-Lewis composition 'Stuck With You' and 'Jacob's Ladder', written by **Bruce Hornsby**. 'Perfect World' (1988) from the fifth album was also a success although *Hard At Play* did less well. Huey Lewis' status with AOR audiences was underlined when he was chosen to sing the national anthem at the American Bowl in the 80s. Although Lewis has had a much lower profile so far in the 90s, he did return with a beautiful a cappella version of **Curtis Mayfield**'s 'Its All Right' in June 1993, followed by *Four Chords And Several Years Ago*, a tour of Lewis's musical mentors.

● ALBUMS: *Huey Lewis & The News* (Chrysalis 1980)★★, *Picture This* (Chrysalis 1982)★★★★, *Sports* (Chrysalis 1983)★★★★, *Fore!* (Chrysalis 1986)★★, *Small World* (Chrysalis 1988)★★, *Hard At Play* (Chrysalis 1991)★★, *Four Chords And Several Years Ago* (Elektra 1994)★★★.

● COMPILATIONS: *The Heart Of Rock & Roll: The Best Of* (Chrysalis 1992)★★★, *Time Flies: The Best Of Huey Lewis And The News* (East West 1996)★★★.

Lewis, Hugh X

b. Hugh Brad Lewis, 7 December 1932, Yeaddiss, Kentucky, USA. He learned to play guitar and began writing songs in his early teens. After completing his education, he played small local venues in his spare time. Around 1956, he began to make weekly appearances on television in Johnson City, Tennessee and on the *Tennessee Barn Dance* in Knoxville, but during the week worked as foreman at a mine in Lynch, Kentucky. In the early 60s, he made regular appearances on the *Saturday Night Jubilee* on WSAZ Huntingdon and on the **Ernest Tubb** *Show* in Nashville. He finally quit the mine and relocated to Nashville, where he became a songwriter for **Jim Denny**'s publishing company. Lewis gained his first success as a writer, in 1963, when **Stonewall Jackson**'s recording of 'B.J. The D.J.' became a country number 1. The following year Jackson scored again with another Lewis song 'Not My Kind Of People' and Lewis began to appear on the **Grand Ole Opry** but also maintained appearances on the *Tennessee Barn Dance*. Between 1964 and 1969, he recorded for Kapp, registering 11 chart hits including 'What I Need Most', 'You're So Cold I'm Turning Blue' and 'Wish Me A Rainbow' (from the Robert Redford film *This Property Is Condemned*). Other artists began to take his songs into the charts, including **Carl Smith** ('Take My Ring Off Your Finger', a number 15 in 1964) and **Carl And Pearl Butler** ('Just Thought I'd Let You Know', a number 22 in 1965). Jackson later recorded several more Lewis songs, including 'Have Your Next Affair

With Me' and 'My Favorite Sin'. In 1966/7 Lewis' acting talent saw him make appearances in three films namely *Forty Acre Feud*, *Gold Guitar* and *Cotton-Pickin' Chicken-Pickers*. During the 70s, he made further recordings for **Columbia**, GRT, and Little Darlin' gaining four minor hits including the prophetic 'Blues Sells A Lot Of Booze' and 'What Can I Do' - equally prophetic since it proved to be his last chart entry. Many of Lewis' songs, apart from those mentioned previously had predictable subjects for country songs, such as divorce ('If It Wasn't For The Kids'), illicit love ('I'm Thinking Of You Thinking Of Him'), mother ('Meanest Mother In The World') and the expected gospel song ('God Is Making House Calls'). During the 80s, Lewis continued to write and make personal appearances before semi-retiring to live in Donelson, Tennessee.

● ALBUMS: *The Hugh X Lewis Album* (Kapp 1966)★★★, *Just Before The Dawn* (Kapp 1966)★★, *My Kind Of Country* (Kapp 1967)★★★, *Just A Prayer Away* (Kapp 1968)★★★, *Country Fever* (Kapp 1968)★★, *Goodwill Ambassador* (President 1980)★★★.

Lewis, Jeannine

One of Australia's finest women singers, Lewis has had a varied career. Performing initially in blues bands and at folk festivals, she then took to the theatre stage. Lewis also displayed her left-wing political affiliations openly, particularly during an extended visit to South America for three years. She has also covered an album of songs by **Edith Piaf**, after portraying her life in a 1982 stage production. However, some of her strongest work are covers of the little-known Australian singer/songwriter, Graham Lowndes, particularly on *Till Time Brings Change*. She continues to work mainly in women's theatre, both in production and performance.

● ALBUMS: *Free Fall Through Featherless Flight* (1973)★★★★, *Looking Backwards Towards Yesterday* (1974)★★★★, *Tears Of Steel And The Clowns Of Calaveras* (1976)★★★, *Piaf, The Songs & The Story* (1982)★★, *Till Time Brings Change* (1983)★★★, *So U Want Blood* (1983)★★★.

Lewis, Jerry Lee

b. 29 September 1935, Ferriday, Louisiana, USA. The 'Killer' is the personification of 50s rock 'n' roll at its best. He is rowdy, raw, rebellious and uncompromising. The outrageous piano-pounder has a voice that exudes excitement and an aura of arrogance that becomes understandable after witnessing the seething hysteria and mass excitement at his concerts. As a southern boy, Lewis was brought up listening to many musical styles in a home where religion was as important as breathing. In 1950, he attended a fundamentalist bible school in Waxahachie, Texas, but was expelled. The clash between the secular and the religious would govern Lewis's life and art for the remainder of his career. He first recorded on the **Louisiana Hayride** in 1954 and decided that **Elvis Presley**'s label, **Sun Records**, was where he wanted to be. His distinctive version of country star **Ray Price**'s 'Crazy Arms' was his Sun debut, but it was his second single, a revival of **Roy Hall**'s 'Whole Lotta Shakin' Goin' On' in 1957 that propelled him to international fame. The record, which was initially banned as obscene, narrowly missed the top of the US chart, went on to hit number 1 on the R&B and country charts and introduced the fair-haired, one-man piano wrecker to a world ready for a good shaking up. He stole the show from many other stars in the film *Jamboree* in which he sang the classic 'Great Balls Of Fire', which became his biggest hit and topped the UK chart and made number 2 in the USA. He kept up the barrage of rowdy and unadulterated rock with the US/UK Top 10 single 'Breathless', which, like its predecessor, had been written by **Otis Blackwell**.

Problems started for the flamboyant 'god of the glissando' when he arrived in Britain for a tour in 1958, accompanied by his third wife, Myra, who was also his 13-year-old second cousin. The UK media stirred up a hornet's nest and the tour had to be cancelled after only three concerts, even though the majority of the audience loved him. The furore followed Lewis home and support for him in his homeland also waned; he never returned to the Top 20 pop chart in the USA. His last big hit of the 50s was the title song from his film *High School Confidential*, which made the UK Top 20 in 1959 and number 21 in the USA. Despite a continued high standard of output, his records either only made the lower chart rungs or missed altogether. When his version of **Ray Charles**' 'What'd I Say' hit the UK Top 10 in 1960 (US number 30) it looked like a record revival was on the way, but it was not to be. The fickle general public may have disowned the hard-living, hell-raiser, but his hardcore fans remained loyal and his tours were sell-outs during the 60s. He joined Smash Records in 1963 and although the material he recorded with the company was generally unimaginative, there were some excellent live recordings, most notably *The Greatest Live Show On Earth* (1964).

In 1966, Lewis made an unexpected entry into rock music theatre when he was signed to play Iago in **Jack Good**'s *Catch My Soul*, inspired by *Othello*. After a decade playing rock 'n' roll, Lewis decided to concentrate on country material in 1968. He had often featured country songs in his repertoire, so his new policy did not represent an about-face. This changeover was an instant success - country fans welcomed back their prodigal son with open arms. Over the next 13 years Lewis was one of country's top-selling artists and was a main attraction wherever he put on his 'Greatest Show On Earth'. He first appeared at the **Grand Ole Opry** in 1973, playing an unprecedented 50-minute set. He topped the country chart with records such as 'There Must Be More To Love Than This' in 1970, 'Would You Take Another Chance On Me?' in 1971 and a revival of 'Chantilly Lace' a year later. The latter also returned him briefly to the transatlantic Top 40. However, he also kept the rock 'n' roll flag flying by playing revival shows around the world and by always including his old 50s hits in his stage shows. In fact, long-time fans have always been well catered for - numerous compilations of top-class out-takes and never previously issued tracks from the 50s have regularly been released over the last 20 years. On the personal front, his life has never been short of tragedies, often compounded by his alcohol and drug problems. His family has been equally prone to tragedy. In November 1973, his 19-year-old son, Jerry Lee Jnr., was killed in a road accident following a period of drug abuse and treatment for mental illness. Lewis's own behaviour during the mid-70s was increasingly erratic. He accidentally shot his bass player in the chest - the musician survived and sued him. Late in 1976, Lewis was arrested for waving a gun outside Elvis Presley's Gracelands home. Two years later, Lewis signed to **Elektra Records** for the appropriately titled *Rockin' My Life Away*. Unfortunately, his association with the company ended with much-publicized lawsuits. In 1981, Lewis was hospitalized and allegedly close to death from a haemorrhaged ulcer. He survived that ordeal and was soon back on the road. In 1982, his fourth wife drowned in a swimming pool. The following year, his fifth wife was found dead at his home following a methodone overdose. The deaths brought fresh scandal to Lewis's troubled life. Meanwhile, the IRS were challenging his earnings from the late 70s in another elongated dispute. A sixth marriage followed, along with more bleeding ulcers and a period in the Betty Ford Clinic for treatment for his pain-killer addiction. Remarkably, Lewis's body and spirit have remained intact, despite these harrowing experiences. During his career he has released dozens of albums, the most successful being *The Session* in 1973, his sole US Top 40 album, on which many pop names of the period backed him, including **Peter Frampton** and **Rory Gallagher**. Lewis was one of the first people inducted into the **Rock And Roll Hall Of Fame** in 1986. In 1989, a biopic of his early career, *Great Balls Of Fire*, starring Dennis Quaid, brought him briefly back into the public eye. In 1990, a much-awaited UK tour had to be cancelled when Lewis and his sixth wife (who was not even born at the time of his fateful first tour) failed to appear. He moved to Dublin, Eire, to avoid the US taxman, but eventually returned to Memphis. In 1995, he jammed with **Bruce Springsteen** at the opening of the Rock And Roll Hall Of Fame building in Cleveland. His cousin **Mickey Gilley** is an accomplished country artist, while another cousin, Jimmy Lee Swaggart, has emerged as one of America's premier television evangelists. Any understanding of the career of Jerry Lee Lewis is inextricably linked with the parallel rise and fall of Swaggart. They were both excellent piano players, but whereas Lewis devoted his energies to the 'devil's music', Swaggart damned rock 'n' roll from the pulpit and played gospel music. Lewis has often described his career as a flight from God, with Swaggart cast in the role of his conscience and indefatigable redeemer. The relationship, however, was more complex than that, and the spirits of these two American institutions were latterly revealed as more complementary than antithetical. When Swaggart was discovered with a prostitute in a motel, the evangelist created a scandal that surpassed even his cousin's series of dramas. Tragedy, scandal and, above all, rock 'n' roll have seldom played such an intrinsic role in one musician's life.

● ALBUMS: *Jerry Lee Lewis* (Sun 1957)★★★★, *Jerry Lee Lewis And His Pumping Piano* (London 1958)★★★, *Jerry Lee's Greatest* (Sun 1961)★★★★, *Rockin' With Jerry Lee Lewis* (Design 1963)★★★, *The Greatest Live Show On Earth* (Smash 1964)★★★, with the Nashville Teens *Live At The Star Club, Hamburg* (Philips 1965)★★, *The Return Of Rock* (Smash 1965)★★★, *Country Songs For City Folks* (Smash 1965)★★★, *Whole Lotta Shakin' Goin' On* (London 1965)★★★★, *Memphis Beat* (Smash 1966)★★★, *By Request - More Greatest Live Show On Earth* (Smash 1966)★★★, *Breathless* (London 1967)★★★, *Soul My Way* (Smash 1967)★★★, *Got You On My Mind* (Fontana 1968)★★★, *Another Time, Another Place* (Mercury 1969)★★★, *She Still Comes Around* (Mercury 1969)★★★, *I'm On Fire* (Mercury 1969)★★★, *Jerry Lee Lewis' Rockin' Rhythm And Blues* (Sun 1969)★★★, with Linda Gail Lewis *Together* (Mercury 1970)★★★, *She Even Woke Me Up To Say Goodbye* (Mercury 1970)★★★, *A Taste Of Country* (Sun 1970)★★★, *There Must Be More To Love Than This* (Mercury 1970)★★★, *Johnny Cash And Jerry Lee Lewis Sing Hank Williams* (Sun 1971)★★★, *Touching Home* (Mercury 1971)★★★, *In Loving Memories* (Mercury 1971)★★★, *Would You Take Another Chance On Me* (Mercury 1972)★★★, *The Killer Rocks On* (Mercury 1972)★★★, *Old Tyme Country Music* (Sun 1972)★★★, with Johnny Cash *Sunday Down South* (Sun 1972)★★, *The Session* (Mercury 1973)★★★, *Live At The International, Las Vegas* (Mercury 1973)★★★, *Great Balls of Fire* (Hallmark 1973)★★★, *Southern Roots* (Mercury 1974)★★★, *Rockin' Up A Storm* (Sun 1974)★★★, *Rockin' And Free* (Sun 1974)★★★, *I'm A Rocker* (Mercury 1975)★★★, *Odd Man In* (Mercury 1975)★★★, *Jerry Lee Lewis* (Elektra 1979)★★★, *Killer Country* (Elektra 1980)★★★, *When Two Worlds Collide* (Elektra 1980)★★★, with Johnny Cash, Carl Perkins *The Survivors* (Columbia 1982)★★★, *My Fingers Do The Talking* (MCA 1983)★★★, *I Am What I Am* (MCA 1984)★★★, with Webb Pierce, Mel Tillis, Faron Young *Four Legends* (1985)★★★, with Johnny Cash, Carl Perkins, Roy Orbison *Class Of '55* (America 1986)★★★, *Interviews From The Class Of '55 Recording Sessions* (America 1986)★★, *Keep Your Hands Off It* (Zu Zazz 1987)★★★, *Don't Drop It* (Zu Zazz 1988)★★★, *Live In Italy* (Magnum Force 1989)★★, *Great Balls Of Fire!* film soundtrack (Polydor 1989)★★★, with Carl Perkins and Elvis Presley *The Million Dollar Quartet* (RCA 1990)★★★, *Rocket* (Instant 1990)★★★, *Live At The Vapors Club* (Ace 1991)★★★, *Young Blood* (Sire/Elektra 1995)★★★, *Jerry Lee Lewis At Hank Cochran's* recorded 1987 (Trend 1996)★★★.

● COMPILATIONS: *Golden Hits* (Smash 1964)★★★★, *Country Music Hall Of Fame Hits Volume 1* (Smash 1969)★★★★, *Country Music Hall Of Fame Hits Volume 2* (Smash 1969)★★★★, *Original Golden Hits Volume 1* (Sun 1969)★★★★, *Original Golden Hits Volume 2* (Sun 1969)★★★, *The Best Of Jerry Lee Lewis* (Smash 1970)★★★★, *Original Golden Hits Volume 3* (Sun 1971)★★★, *Monsters* (Sun 1971)★★★, *Rockin' With Jerry Lee Lewis* (Mercury 1972)★★★★, *Fan Club Choice* (Mercury 1974)★★★, *Whole Lotta Shakin' Goin' On* (Hallmark 1974)★★★★, *Good Rockin' Tonight* (Hallmark 1975)★★★, *Jerry Lee Lewis And His Pumping Piano* (Charly 1975)★★★, *Rare Jerry Lee Lewis Volume 1* (Charly 1975)★★★, *Rare Jerry Lee Lewis Volume 2* (Charly 1975)★★★, *The Jerry Lee Lewis Collection* (Hallmark 1976)★★★★, *Golden Hits* (Mercury 1976)★★★★, *The Original Jerry Lee Lewis* (Charly 1976)★★★★, *Nuggets* (Charly 1977)★★★★, *Nuggets Volume 2* (Charly 1977)★★★, *The Essential Jerry Lee Lewis* (Charly 1978)★★★★, *Shakin' Jerry Lee* (Arcade 1978)★★★, *Back To Back* (Mercury 1978)★★★, *Duets* (Sun 1979)★★★, *Jerry Lee Lewis* (Hammer 1979)★★★, *Good Golly Miss Molly* (Bravo 1980)★★★, *Trio Plus* (Sun 1980)★★★, *Jerry Lee's Greatest* (Charly 1981)★★★★, *Killer Country* i (Elektra 1981)★★★★, *Jerry Lee Lewis* (Mercury 1981)★★★, *The Sun Years* 12-LP box set (Sun 1984)★★★★, *18 Original Sun Greatest Hits* (Rhino 1984)★★★★, *Milestones* (Rhino 1985)★★★★, *The Collection* (Deja Vu 1986)★★★★, *The Pumpin' Piano Cat* (Sun 1986)★★★, *Great Balls Of Fire* (Sun 1986)★★★★, *The Wild One* (Sun 1986)★★★, *At The Country Store* (Starblend 1987)★★★, *The Very Best Of Jerry Lee Lewis* (Philips 1987)★★★★, *The Country Sound Of Jerry Lee Lewis* (Pickwick 1988)★★, *The Classic Jerry Lee Lewis* 8-CD box set (Bear Family 1989)★★★★, *The Classic Jerry Lee Lewis* (Ocean 1989)★★★, *Killer's Birthday Cake* (Sun 1989)★★★, *Killer's Rhythm And Blues* (Sun 1989)★★★★, *Killer: The Mercury Years, Volume One, 1963-1968* (Mercury 1989)★★★, *Killer: The Mercury Years, Volume Two, 1969-1972* (Mercury 1989)★★★, *Killer: The Mercury Years, Volume Three, 1973-1977* (Mercury 1989)★★★, *Great Balls Of Fire* (Pickwick 1989)★★, *The EP Collection* (See For Miles 1990)★★★★, *The Jerry Lee Lewis Collection* (Castle 1990)★★★, *The Best Of Jerry Lee Lewis* (Curb 1991)★★★, *Pretty Much Country* (Ace 1992)★★★, *All Killer, No Filler: The Anthology* (Rhino 1993)★★★★, *The Complete Palamino Club Recordings* (1993)★★★, *The EP Collection Volume 2 ... Plus* (See For Miles 1994)★★★★, *The Locust Years . . . And The Return To The Promised Land* 8-CD box set (Bear Family 1995)★★★★, *Sun Classics* (Charly 1995)★★★★, *Killer Country* ii (Mercury 1995)★★★, *The Country Collection* (Eagle 1997)★★★, *Sings The Rock 'N' Roll Classics* (Eagle 1997)★★★.

● VIDEOS: *Carl Perkins & Jerry Lee Lewis Live* (BBC Video 1987), *Jerry Lee Lewis* (Fox Video 1989), *I Am What I Am* (Charly Video 1990), *The Killer* (Telstar Video 1991), *Killer Performance* (Virgin Vision 1991), *The Jerry Lee Lewis Show* (MMG Video 1991).

● FURTHER READING: *Jerry Lee Lewis: The Ball Of Fire*, Allan Clark. *Jerry Lee Lewis*, Robert Palmer. *Whole Lotta Shakin' Goin' On: Jerry Lee Lewis*, Robert Cain. *Hellfire: The Jerry Lee Lewis Story*, Nick Tosches. *Great Balls Of Fire: The True Story Of Jerry Lee Lewis*, Myra Lewis. *Rockin' My Life Away: Listening To Jerry Lee Lewis*, Jimmy Guteman. *Killer!*, Jerry Lee Lewis And Charles White.

● FILMS: *Jamboree* aka *Disc Jockey Jamboree* (1957), *Beach Ball* (1964), *Be My Guest* (1965), *American Hot Wax* (1976).

Lewis, John

b. 3 May 1920, LaGrange, Illinois, USA. A formally trained pianist from a very early age, Lewis first took an interest in jazz after meeting **Kenny Clarke**. In 1946, both men joined **Dizzy Gillespie**'s big band with Lewis writing charts in addition to his rhythm section duties. In the late 40s and early 50s, Lewis continued his musical studies and also accompanied numerous important jazz artists including **Charlie Parker, Miles Davis** and **Milt Jackson**. His association with Jackson continued with their group taking the name, the **Modern Jazz Quartet**. The MJQ stayed in existence until 1974 after which Lewis turned to teaching. In the 80s the MJQ reformed and Lewis also worked with his own sextet and as musical director of the American Jazz Orchestra, a group especially dedicated to the performance of big band music and which played and recorded such important pieces as **Benny Carter**'s 'Central City Sketches'. Although he began his jazz career in bebop, a style that is always apparent in his playing, Lewis's classical training and extensive musical studies emerge in many of his compositions, which use 18th and 19th century European musical forms. In the 80s Lewis was also musical director of the **Monterey Jazz Festival**, a role he gave up as his long-lived playing career continued to blossom.

● ALBUMS: *Modern Jazz Quartet* (1955)★★★, with MJQ *Fontessa* (1956)★★★, *2 Degrees East, 3 Degrees West* (1956)★★★★, *Grand Encounter* (Blue Note 1956)★★★, *The John Lewis Piano* (1956)★★★★, *Afternoon In Paris* (1956)★★★, *European Windows* (1958)★★★, *Improvised Meditations And Excursions* (1959)★★★, *Odds Against Tomorrow* (1959)★★★, *The Modern Jazz Quartet And Orchestra* (1960)★★★, with MJQ *The Golden Striker* (1960)★★★, *The Wonderful World Of Jazz* (Atlantic 1960)★★★★, *Jazz Abstractions: John Lewis Presents Contemporary Music* (1960)★★★★, *Original Sin* (1962)★★★, *A Milanese Story* (1962)★★★, *Essence* (1962), with Svend Asmussen *European Encounter* (1962)★★★, *John Lewis-Albert Mangelsdorff* (1962), *John Lewis-Helen Merrill* (1976)★★, *John Lewis Solo/Duo With Hank Jones* (1976)★★★, *I Remember Bebop* (1977)★★★, *Mirjana* (1978)★★, with Hank Jones *An Evening With Two Grand Pianos* (1979)★★★, with Jones *Piano Playhouse* (1979)★★★, *Piano, Paris 1979* (1979)★★, *The John Lewis Album With Putte Wickman And Red Mitchell* (1981)★★★, *Kansas City Breaks* (DRG 1982)★★★, *Slavic Smile* (1982)★★, *J.S. Bach Preludes And Fugues From The Well-Tempered Clavier, Book 1* (1984)★★, *The Bridge Game* (Philips 1984)★★★, with the American Jazz Orchestra *Central City Sketches* (1987)★★★, *Private Concert* (Emarcy 1991)★★★.

Lewis, Lew

This R&B harmonica player extraordinaire was originally an asphalter by trade. He grew up amid the Southend/Canvey Island, Essex, UK musical scene, and made his first ventures with the Southside Jug Band in 1969, which featured Lee Brilleaux and Sparko of **Dr. Feelgood**, before transferring to the Fix which also included Dave Higgs. After they broke up, Lewis became a busker but later reunited with Higgs in 1973 when he formed **Eddie And The Hot Rods**. Lewis stayed with them until 1976, when a solo single emerged on **Stiff Records**. Although credited to Lewis, it featured the backing of Dr. Feelgood under a pseudonym. The a-side was 'Boogie On The Street', recorded in one take. April 1977 saw 'Out For A Lark' on United Artists, once more with the aid of Brilleaux and Sparko, and soon afterwards, he formed the Lew Lewis Reformer, consisting of Lewis (vocals, harp), Rick Taylor (guitar), Johnny Squirell (bass) and Buzz Barwell (drums). They recorded the unreleased **Status Quo** song 'Win Or Lose', before setting out on a tour supporting **Dave Edmunds**' **Rockpile** in 1979. *Save The Wail* was recorded with the basic Reformer band and Gavin Povey from the **Edge** on keyboards. Lewis went on to guest on several albums of the time, including **Kirsty MacColl**'s *Desperate Character* in 1981. A year later he formed a short-lived band with **Wilko Johnson**. However, his musical career hit a low and in 1987 he held up a post office with a fake pistol (erroneously reported as a shotgun) and was sentenced to seven years' imprisonment for armed robbery. He has since been released. Coincidentally, Epic released his single 'Shame Shame Shame' in August 1987.

● ALBUMS: *Save The Wail* (Stiff 1980)★★★.

Lewis, Linda

b. *c.* 1950, London, England. Linda's first steps in the entertainment business were made as a pre-teen actress. In the 60s she had bit-parts in the films *Help!* and *A Taste Of Honey*. She quit acting and school to play in bands, and soon formed her own, White Rabbit. In 1967, she first achieved recognition in Europe with Ferris Wheel, before becoming a leading session singer in the early 70s. She had an exceptionally good range (five octaves), and had already recorded for **David Bowie, Al Kooper** and **Cat Stevens** when she had her first UK Top 20 hit. 'Rock-A-Doodle-Doo' was a self-penned pop song, with the gimmick of a deep **Helen Shapiro**-style verse and a leap to a petulant little girl voice in the chorus. *Lark* offered a good example of her brand of soft soul. Any momentum gained was stalled when the Raft label went out of business. Her highest UK chart position came in 1975 with a cover of the **Betty Everett** hit, 'It's In His Kiss (Shoop Shoop Song)' reaching number 6. The accompanying album, *Not A Little Girl Anymore*, reached the Top 40. The remainder of the 70s saw her achieve two minor hits with 'Baby I'm Yours' (1976) and 'I'd Be Surprisingly Good For You' (1979), but she continued her session work, and put in appearances for **Steve Harley, Chris Spedding, Mike Batt, Rod Stewart** and **Rick Wakeman** in the late 70s. She married Jim Cregan (ex-**Family**) for some time, but her career floundered with personal problems. She relocated to the USA in the early 80s and retired from music. In June 1995 Lewis returned to the UK and completed a new album of her own sparse pop songs with strong, semi-autobiographical lyrics. During recent years her old material has found a new audience with the UK dance scene.

● ALBUMS: *Hacienda View* (Raft 1970)★★, *Say No More* (1971)★★, *Lark* (Reprise 1972)★★★★, *Fathoms Deep* (1973)★★★, *Heart Strings* (1974)★★★, *Not A Little Girl Anymore* (1975)★★★★, *Woman Overboard* (1977)★★, *A Tear And A Smile* (1983)★★, *Second Nature* (Turpin 1995)★★.

Lewis, Linda Gail

b. 18 July 1947, Ferriday, Louisiana, USA. The youngest sister of **Jerry Lee Lewis**. Encouraged by his success, she was only 13 when, with sister Frankie Jean, she recorded a single for **Sun Records** on 13 December 1960. It was not released but it sparked her desire to be a singer. She quit school in the early 60s and took to the road as a backing vocalist with her brother's show. She gained no preferential treatment from the unpredictable star, on one occasion being embarrassed when, after missing her cue, her brother stopped singing to ask through the microphone 'Are you watching this show or are you in it?' She was not so backward regarding marriage since she first married at 14 and divorced to marry a sailor, after a three day romance, when she was 15. He went back to sea and she never saw him again but soon married Jerry Lee Lewis's best friend Cecil Harrelson. They had two children, Cecil Jnr. and Mary Jean, then divorced but after a brief marriage to husband number four, Jerry Lee Lewis's guitarist Kenneth Lovelace, she remarried Cecil in 1971. In March 1963, she duetted with her brother on 'Seasons Of My Heart' and at the same Sun session, she cut two solo numbers 'Nothin' Shakin'' and 'Sittin' And Thinkin''. They were set for release on Sun 385 but for some reason were not issued. When Jerry Lee Lewis moved to Smash in 1964, she duetted on 'We Live In Two Different Worlds', which appeared on *Another Place Another Time*, his first album for the label. The success of this record led to a duet album, which contained fine versions of 'Milwaukee Here I Come' and two chart hits, 'Don't Let Me Cross Over' (number 9) and the less popular 'Roll Over Beethoven' (number 71). She recorded several singles for the label (some were later reissued by **Mercury Records**), including 'Turn Back The Hands Of Time', a superb version of 'Paper Roses' and 'Before The Snow Flies'. She also gained her first solo album and registered her only solo chart hit, in 1972, with a Mercury release 'Smile, Somebody Loves You'. In the early 70s, the whirlwind life style, as a member of her brother's touring show, finally showed she did not have the stamina or resilience of her sibling. Her health began to cause concern, she suffered from drug addiction and underwent a nervous breakdown. While confined to hospital in 1976, she almost died but after a long period of convalescence, she regained her health and broke the drug addiction. In 1977, she married husband number six, Brent Dolan and retired from show business for 10

years, during which time she had two more children Oliver and Annie. In 1987, she re-emerged as a rockabilly revivalist. She again began to appear with her brother and accompanied him on his European tour that included an appearance at London's Wembley Festival. However differences with her brother's sixth wife, Kerrie McCarver, who had vocal aspirations of her own, soon saw Linda Gail leave to pursue a solo career. In this, she was initially helped by husband number seven, a nightclub singer Bobby Memphis (b. Robert Stefanow). With a backing group that included her daughter, Mary Jean, singing backing harmonies and mainly featuring rockabilly material, she began to tour with her own show. She played piano (standing up) in a similar pounding style to her brother and cousin **Mickey Gilley** and recorded a second album. Her first tour to the UK, in June 1991, proved so popular (one critic described her as 'the hottest rockabilly act in Europe at this time who served up piano playing rock 'n' roll that was not a million miles away from the style of her illustrious brother') that she made two further European tours in 1991/2. One London show (backed by Sonny West And The Rhythm Kings) was recorded live and released on CD by Deep Elem. In the USA, she also released a cassette album on her own label, which contained her much requested self-penned 'I'll Take Memphis' and a mixture of country and rock. In December 1991, she married husband number eight Eddie Braddock. She continued to perform into the 90s, including to Europe where she enjoyed considerable success in the Scandinavian countries. By 1998, (she was married to husband number nine) but was becoming more respected for her fine singing of material other than rock. Frankie Jean never had her sister's desire to be a singer. She made record rockabilly duets with **Jesse Lee Turner** for Sun, in 1958, that attracted **Chet Atkins**. She claimed she wanted to sing **Patsy Cline** material not rockabilly and turned down a **Decca** contract. She toured with Jerry Lee Lewis for some years and later became involved with the Jerry Lee Lewis Museum at Ferriday.

● ALBUMS: *Two Sides Of Linda Gail Lewis* (Smash 1969)★★★, *Jerry Lee Lewis & Linda Gail Lewis Together* (Smash 1969)★★★★, *International Affair* (New Rose Records 1990)★★★, *Rockin' With Linda* (Deep Elem 1992)★★★, *Do You Know* cassette (Lewis 1992)★★, *I'll Take Memphis* (Fox 1992)★★★, *Love Makes The Difference* (Ice House 1997)★★★.

Lewis, Little Roy

b. 24 February 1942, Lincolnton, Georgia, USA. The youngest member of the popular gospel and bluegrass singing group, the Lewis Family. He played banjo at the age of six and gained his nickname by playing full-time with the family group at the age of nine, when an elder brother, Esley, who usually played the instrument for the group, was called for military service. When Esley returned, he found himself upstaged by his young sibling and happily moved to playing bass until he left the group. In 1954, when the Lewis Family started a long residency on WJBF-TV Augusta, Roy played with them. He subsequently played on all the family's recordings but during the 60s, he also made solo recordings for Starday, the first, in 1962, being an EP release. Over the years, he has also played guitar, bass and autoharp as well as adding vocals to his input to the family show. Lewis has also become very popular for the comedy that he brings to the proceedings, which takes the form of constant chatter, good-natured badinage aimed at the other members and the amusing sound effects he adds to some of the songs. During the 70s and 80s, he may no longer have been little but he remained very much the focal point of the Lewis Family, both live and on record.

● ALBUMS: *Golden Gospel Banjo* (Starday 1962)★★★, *Gospel Banjo* (Canaan 1972)★★★, *The Entertainer* (Canaan 1977)★★★, *Super Pickin'* (Canaan 1981)★★, *In The Heart Of Dixie* (Canaan 1984)★★.

● COMPILATIONS: *The Best Of Little Roy Lewis* (Canaan 1985)★★★.

Lewis, Meade 'Lux'

b. 4 September 1905, Chicago, Illinois, USA, d. 7 June 1964. Although he was popular in Chicago bars in the 20s, Lewis was little known elsewhere and made his living running a taxicab firm with fellow-pianist **Albert Ammons**. A record he made in 1927, 'Honky Tonk Train Blues', but which was not released until 1929, eventually came to the attention of **John Hammond Jnr.** some half-dozen years later. Encouraged by Hammond and the enormous success of 'Honky Tonk Train Blues', which he re-recorded in 1936 (and later), Lewis became one of the most popular and successful of the pianists to enjoy fleeting fame during the boogie-woogie craze. With Ammons and **Pete Johnson**, billed as the 'Boogie Woogie Trio', he played at Hammond's Carnegie Hall 'Spirituals to Swing' concert and at many top New York clubs. Later resident in Los Angeles, Lewis continued to tour and make records. From the mid-30s onwards, Lewis often played celeste and records such as those he made in the early 40s with **Edmond Hall**'s Celeste Quartet, where the remaining members of the group were **Israel Crosby** and **Charlie Christian**, showed him to be much more versatile than his mass audience appeared to assume. Lewis died following a road accident in 1964.

● ALBUMS: *Yancey's Last Ride* (1954)★★★, *Cat House Piano* (1955)★★★★, *Barrel House Piano* (1956)★★★★, *The Meade 'Lux' Lewis Trio* (1956)★★★, *The Blues Artistry Of Meade 'Lux' Lewis* (Original Jazz Classics 1961)★★★★, *Boogie Woogie House Party* (1962)★★★★.

● COMPILATIONS: with Albert Ammons *The Complete Blue Note Recordings Of Albert Ammons And Meade Lux Lewis* (Mosaic 1983)★★★★, *Honky Tonk Piano* (Classic Jazz Masters 1988)★★★, with others *Meade Lux Lewis Volume 1 (1927-39)* (1988)★★★★, *Tell Your Story* (1989)★★★, *Meade Lux Lewis 1927-1939* (Original Jazz Classics 1993)★★★★.

Lewis, Mel

b. 10 May 1929, Buffalo, New York, USA, d. 3 February 1990. Following in the footsteps of his father, Lewis took up drumming as a child and was playing professionally by his early teens. In 1948, he joined **Boyd Raeburn**'s modern big band, then played in a number of well-known dance bands of the late swing era, including those of **Ray Anthony** and **Tex Beneke**. In 1954, he was hired by **Stan Kenton** and then worked in the west coast film studios, with the big bands of **Bill Holman** and **Woody Herman**, later performing with various small jazz groups until the end of the decade. In the 60s, he played with numerous bands, including those led by **Gerry Mulligan**, **Benny Goodman** and **Dizzy Gillespie**. Settling in New York, Lewis established a musical partnership with **Thad Jones**, which in 1965 resulted in the formation of the Jazz Orchestra, a big band formed from the many fine jazz players living in the city and earning their living in non-jazz work in radio and television orchestras. The Thad Jones-**Mel Lewis** Jazz Orchestra, with a regular weekly gig at the Village Vanguard and a series of fine recordings, became a byword for the best in contemporary big band music. National and international tours helped spread the word and by the time the Jones-Lewis partnership was dissolved, in 1978, there were few comparable units left in existence. With Jones gone, Lewis decided to continue with the band (as someone was to remark, 'Mel and Thad got divorced, Mel got the kids') and with **Bob Brookmeyer** providing new arrangements to augment the magnificent library Jones had created, the band was still a big attraction. A skilled and always swinging drummer, equally at home subtly urging a small group or punching along a powerful big band, Lewis was a master of his craft and greatly respected among his peers.

● ALBUMS: *The Mel Lewis Septet* (1956),★★★ with Stan Kenton *Cuban Fire* (1956)★★★★, *Woody Herman's New Big Band At The Monterey Jazz Festival* (1959)★★★★, with Gerry Mulligan *A Concert In Jazz* (1961)★★★★, with Thad Jones And The Jazz Orchestra (TJO)★★★, *Live At The Village Vanguard* (Red Baron 1967)★★★★, with TJO *Central Park North* (1969)★★★, with TJO *Paris 1969 Volume 1* (1969)★★★, with TJO *Consummation* (1970)★★★, with TJO *Suite For Pops* (1972)★★, *Mel Lewis And Friends* (1976)★★, *Thad Jones-Mel Lewis Quartet* (1977)★★★★, *The Mel Lewis Quintet Live* (1978)★★★, *Naturally* (Telarc 1979)★★★, *The New Mel Lewis Quintet Live* (1979)★★, *Live At The Village Vanguard* (1980)★★★★, *Mel Lewis Plays Herbie Hancock: Live In Montreux* (1980)★★★, *Mellofluous* (1982)★★★, *Make Me Smile And Other New Works By Bob Brookmeyer* (1982)★★★, *Twenty Years At The Village Vanguard* (Atlantic 1985)★★★, *The Definitive Thad Jones* (1988)★★★, *Soft Lights And Hot Music* (1988)★★, *Got Cha* (Fresh Sounds 1988)★★★, *The Lost Art* (Limelight 1989)★★★.

● COMPILATIONS:, *Jazz At The Smithsonian Volume 3* (Parkfield 1990)★★★.

Lewis, Noah

b. 3 September 1895, Henning, Tennessee, USA, d. 7 February 1961, Ripley, Tennessee, USA. Lewis's ability to play two harmonicas at once, one with his nose, secured him work on the travelling medicine shows, but his recorded music is notable more for its melancholy expressiveness than showmanship - a descriptive train imitation ('Chickasaw Special') apart. He combined technical accomplishment with exceptional breath control and a very subtle, sensitive handling of emotional nuance, whether on his 1927 solos, leading his own jug band in 1930, or as a member of **Cannon's Jug Stompers**, with whom he recorded from 1928-30. His singing had the same emotional depth as his harmonica playing, most notably on 'Viola Lee Blues' (recorded by the **Grateful Dead** in the 60s). Lewis lived in poverty, and died of gangrene as a consequence of frostbite.

● ALBUMS: *Gus Cannon & Noah Lewis* (1991)★★★.

Lewis, Ramsey

b. 27 May 1935, Chicago, Illinois, USA. Lewis started playing piano at the age of six. He graduated from school in 1948, after winning both the American Legion Award as an outstanding scholar and a special award for piano services at the Edward Jenner Elementary School. He began his career as an accompanist at the Zion Hill Baptist Church, an experience of gospel that never left him. He later studied music at Chicago Music College with the idea of becoming a concert pianist, but left at the age of 18 to marry. He found a job working in a record shop and joined the Clefs, a seven-piece dance band. In 1956, he formed a jazz trio with the Clefs' rhythm section (whom he had known since high school) - bassist Eldee Young and drummer Isaac 'Red' Holt. Lewis made his debut recordings with the Argo record label, which later became **Chess**. He also had record dates with prestigious names such as **Sonny Stitt**, **Clark Terry** and **Max Roach**. In 1959, he played at Birdland in New York City and at the Randall's Island Festival. In 1964, 'Something You Got' was a minor hit, but it was 'The In Crowd', an instrumental cover version of **Dobie Gray**'s hit, that made him famous, reaching number 5 in the US charts and selling over a million copies by the end of 1965. Lewis insisted on a live sound, complete with handclaps and exclamations, an infectious translation of a black church feel into pop. His follow-up, 'Hang On Sloopy', reached number 11 and sold another million. These hits set the agenda for his career. Earnings for club dates increased tenfold. His classic 'Wade In The Water' was a major hit in 1966, and became a long-standing encore number for **Graham Bond**. The rhythm section left and resurfaced as a funk outfit in the mid-70s, variously known as Redd Holt Unlimited and **Young-Holt Unlimited**. Lewis had an astute ear for hip, commercial sounds: his replacement drummer **Maurice White** left in 1971 to found the platinum mega-sellers **Earth, Wind And Fire**. Lewis never recaptured this commer-cial peak; he attempted to woo his audience by using synthesizers and disco rhythms, and continued securing *Billboard* Top 100 hits well into the 70s. His album success was a remarkable achievement, with over 30 of his albums making the *Billboard* Top 200 listings. *The In Crowd* stayed on the list for almost a year, narrowly missing the top spot. *Mother Nature's Son* was a tribute to the **Beatles**, while the *Newly Recorded Hits* in 1973 was a dreadful mistake: the originals were far superior. By the 80s he was producing middle-of-the-road instrumental albums and accompanying singers, most notably **Nancy Wilson**. Nevertheless, it is his 60s hits - simple, infectious and funky - that will long endure.

● ALBUMS: *Down To Earth* (EmArcy 1958)★★★, *Gentleman Of Swing* (Argo 1958)★★★, *Gentlemen Of Jazz* (Argo 1958)★★★, *An Hour With The Ramsey Lewis Trio* (Argo 1959)★★★, *Stretching Out* (Argo 1960)★★★, *The Ramsey Lewis Trio In Chicago* (Argo 1961)★★★, *More Music From The Soil* (Argo 1961)★★★, *Sound Of Christmas* (Argo 1961)★★★, *The Sound Of Spring* (Argo 1962)★★★, *Country Meets The Blues* (Argo 1962)★★★, *Bossa Nova* (Argo 1962)★★★, *Pot Luck* (Argo 1962)★★★, *Barefoot Sunday Blues* (Argo 1963)★★★, *The Ramsey Lewis Trio At The Bohemian Caverns* (Argo 1964)★★★, *Bach To The Blues* (Argo 1964)★★★, *More Sounds Of Christmas* (Argo 1964)★★★, *You Better Believe It* (Argo 1965)★★★★, *The In Crowd* (Argo 1965)★★★★, *Hang On Ramsey!* (Cadet 1965)★★★★, *Swingin'* (Cadet 1966)★★★★, *Wade In The Water* (Cadet 1966)★★★★, *Goin' Latin* (Cadet 1967)★★, *The Movie Album* (Cadet 1967)★★, *Dancing In The Street* (Cadet 1967)★★★, *Up Pops Ramsey Lewis* (Cadet 1968)★★★, *Maiden Voyage* (Cadet 1968)★★★, *Mother Nature's Son* (Cadet 1969)★★, *Another Voyage* (Cadet 1969)★★, *Ramsey Lewis: The Piano Player* (Cadet 1970)★★★, *Them Changes* (Cadet 1970)★★★, *Back To The Roots* (Cadet 1971)★★★, *Upendo Ni Pamoja* (Columbia 1972)★★★, *Funky Serenity* (Columbia 1973)★★, *Sun Goddess* (Columbia 1974)★★★, *Don't It Feel Good* (Columbia 1975)★★★, *Salongo* (Columbia 1976)★★★, *Love Notes* (Columbia 1977)★★★, *Tequila Mockingbird* (Columbia 1977)★★★, *Legacy* (Columbia 1978)★★★, *Routes* (Columbia 1980)★★★, *Three Piece Suite* (Columbia 1981)★★★, *Live At The Savoy* (Columbia 1982)★★★, *Les Fleurs* (1983)★★, *Chance Encounter* (Columbia 1983)★★, with Nancy Wilson *The Two Of Us* (Columbia 1984)★★★, *Reunion* (Columbia 1984)★★★, *Fantasy* (1986)★★, *Keys To The City* (Columbia 1987)★★, *Classic Encounter* (Columbia 1988)★★, with Billy Taylor *We Meet Again* (Columbia 1989)★★★, *Urban Renewal* (Columbia 1989)★★★, *Electric Collection* (Columbia 1991)★★★, *Ivory Pyramid* (GRP 1992)★★, with King Curtis *Instrumental Soul Hits* (1993)★★, *Between The Keys* (GRP 1996)★★, *Dance Of the Soul* (GRP 1998)★★★.

● COMPILATIONS: *Choice! The Best Of The Ramsey Lewis Trio* (Cadet 1965)★★★, *The Best Of Ramsey Lewis* (Cadet 1970)★★★, *Ramsey Lewis' Newly Recorded All-Time, Non-Stop Golden Hits* (Columbia 1973)★★★, *The Greatest Hits Of Ramsey Lewis* (Chess 1988)★★★, *20 Greatest Hits* (1992)★★★, *Collection* (More Music 1995)★★★, *Priceless Jazz Collection* (GRP 1998)★★★.

● FILMS: *Gonks Go Beat* (1965).

Lewis, Sabby

b. William Sebastien Lewis, 1 November 1914, Middleburg, North Carolina, USA. Pianist Sabby Lewis entered the jazz world in the early 30s in Boston, Massachusetts, becoming leader of his own band in 1936. Although he rarely strayed far from Boston during the rest of his career, Lewis's small groups and big bands were highly regarded among musicians. Many visiting bandleaders, among them **Woody Herman**, **Benny Goodman** and **Stan Kenton**, were eager to sit in with Lewis at such Boston nightspots as the Savoy Cafe whenever they were in town. Lewis's bands were proving grounds for a number of youngsters who went on to become big names in their own right. Saxophonists **Paul Gonsalves** and **Sonny Stitt**, trumpeters **Cat Anderson**, Joe Gordon and Freddie Webster, drummers **Alan Dawson**, **Jimmy Crawford** and **Roy Haynes** are just a few who played for Lewis, usually early in their careers. Despite a hit record with 'Bottoms Up', which reworked **Illinois Jacquet**'s version of 'Flying Home', Lewis never made the national big-time, nor appeared to feel the need to do so. He continued to lead a big band well into the 50s and thereafter led smaller groups until the late 70s.

● COMPILATIONS: *Sabby Lewis Orchestra And Quartet (1946)* (1981)★★★, *Boston Bounce (1944-47)* (1988)★★★.

Lewis, Sam M.

b. 25 October 1885, New York, USA, d. 22 November 1959, New York, USA. A prolific lyricist who began writing around 1912, producing songs such as 'That Mellow Melody', 'When You're A Long Long Way From Home', 'My Little Girl' and 'There's A Little Lane Without A Turning'. From 1916-30, he collaborated with fellow lyricst **Joe Young**, and various composers. His period with Lewis produced 'Where Did Robinson Crusoe Go With Friday On Saturday Night?' (with **George W. Meyer** for the **Al Jolson** Broadway musical *Robinson Crusoe Jr.*), 'Rock-A-Bye-Your-Baby With A Dixie Melody' (with Jean Schwartz), 'My Mammy' and 'How Ya Gonna Keep 'Em Down On The Farm?' (both with **Walter Donaldson**), 'I'm Sitting On Top Of The World' (**Ray Henderson**), 'In A Little Spanish Town' (**Mabel Wayne**), 'I Kiss Your Hand, Madame' (Ralph Irwin), and 'Then You've Never Been Blue' (Ted Fiorito), and 'King For A Day'. In 1930, Young and Lewis worked with **Harry Warren** on one of their last projects together, the early talkie, *Spring Is Here*, which included 'Cryin' For The Carolines', 'Have A Little Faith In Me', 'Bad Baby' and 'How Shall I Tell?'. The final Young-Lewis song appears to have been 'Absence Makes The Heart Grow Fonder'. Lewis subsequently wrote lyrics for 'Song Of The Fool', 'Just Friends', 'Too Late', 'For All We Know', 'Lawd, You Made The Night Too Long', 'Street Of Dreams', 'I Believe In Miracles', 'Close To Me', 'I'm A Fool For Loving You', 'Now Or Never', 'Don't Wake Up My Heart', and 'The Last Two Weeks In July', amongst others. Among his collaborators were **J. Fred Coots**, **Victor Young**, Ted Snyder, M.K.

Jerome and **Oscar Levant**. Lewis was also responsible for the English translation to 'Gloomy Sunday', a Hungarian song originally written by Laszio Javor and Rezso Seress, and considered to be one of the most mournful songs ever written ('The black coach of sorrow has taken you. . .'). Sometimes known as the 'Budapest Suicide Song', it has been recorded by Hal Kemp, **Mel Tormé**, **Artie Shaw** and **Paul Robeson**. In the UK, the BBC banned it from broadcasts for some time. Lewis retired from writing in the early 40s.

Lewis, Smiley

b. Overton Amos Lemons, 5 July 1913, DeQuincy, Louisiana, USA, d. 7 October 1966. While failing to gain the commercial plaudits his work deserved, this New Orleans-based artist was responsible for some of that city's finest music. He made his recording debut, as Smiling Lewis, in 1947, but his strongest work appeared during the 50s. 'The Bells Are Ringing' (1952) took him into the US R&B chart, and his biggest hit came three years later with 'I Hear You Knocking'. This seminal slice of Crescent City blues featured pianist **Huey 'Piano' Smith** and bandleader **Dave Bartholomew**, and was revived successfully in 1970 by **Dave Edmunds**. Smiley's career was dogged by ill luck. His original version of 'Blue Monday' was a hit in the hands of **Fats Domino**, while **Elvis Presley** took another song, 'One Night', and by altering its risqué lyric, secured a massive pop hit in the process. A further powerful Lewis performance, 'Shame, Shame, Shame', has subsequently become an R&B standard and it was even covered by the **Merseybeats** on their EP *On Stage* in 1964. This underrated artist continued recording into the 60s, but died of cancer in 1966.

● ALBUMS: *I Hear You Knocking* (Imperial 1961)★★★.
● COMPILATIONS: *Shame Shame Shame* (1970)★★★, *The Bells Are Ringing* (1978)★★★, *Caledonia's Party* (KC 1986)★★★, *New Orleans Bounce - 30 Of His Best* (Sequel 1991)★★★.

Lewis, Ted

b. 6 June 1892, Circleville, Ohio, USA, d. 25 August 1971, New York, USA. An experienced performer in vaudeville, Lewis formed his first band in 1917 and within a few years was one of the most popular entertainers in the USA. He made many appearances on radio, records and in several Broadway revues, including *Greenwich Village Follies*, *Ziegfeld Midnight Frolics*, *Ted Lewis Frolic*, and *Artists And Models* (1927). In 1925, he visited the UK, appearing at London's Kit Kat Club and at the Hippodrome Theatre. In his clarinet playing, Lewis often used the gimmicky techniques of farmyard-animal imitations while his 'singing' usually amounted to little more than a doleful recitation of the lyric. His best-known routine was to the song 'Me And My Shadow', while his singing of the phrase 'Is everybody happy?', was used whenever appropriate - and frequently when it was not. For all his schmaltzy performing style, over the years Lewis was admired by almost as many jazz musicians as criticized him. Indeed, he employed many promising names of the jazz world in his bands. Among these stars were **Jimmy Dorsey**, **Jack Teagarden** and **Benny Goodman**. Whatever Goodman might have thought privately about Lewis's style, it made a big enough impression for him to drop into cod take-offs at odd times in his later career. He co-wrote several popular songs, including 'When My Baby Smiles At Me', 'While We Danced 'Til Dawn', 'Bees Knees', and 'Is Everybody Happy Now?'. From 1929 he was also in several films: *Is Everybody Happy*, *Show Of Shows*, *Here Comes The Band*, *Manhattan Merry-Go-Round*, *Hold That Ghost*, *Is Everybody Happy?* (his 1943 biopic), and *Follow The Boys* (1944). Lewis continued to appear in theatres and on television well into the 60s.

● ALBUMS: *Ted Lewis And His Orchestra* (1949)★★★.

● COMPILATIONS: *A Jazz Holiday* (1981)★★★★, *Is Everybody Happy* (1986)★★★, *Ted's Highlights, Volumes 1-3* (1988)★★★★.

Lewis, Texas Jim

b. James Lewis Jnr., 15 October 1909, Meigs, Georgia, USA, d. 23 January 1990. His mother died when he was five and his father remarried and raised two more children. In 1919, the family relocated to Fort Myers, Florida, where Lewis stayed until 1928, when he relocated to Texas. Here, he began singing and also acquired his nickname. By 1930, the family were in Detroit and he returned home and played local bars with 14-year-old Jack Rivers (in reality his half-brother Rivers Lewis). In 1932, he returned to Texas where, until 1934, he played with the Swift Jewel Cowboys in Houston. Returning to Detroit, he joined Jack West's Circle Star Cowboys and also worked on WJR. He then formed his own Lone Star Cowboys, which included Jack Rivers and **Smokey Rogers**, and moved to New York, where they remained for five years. With a repertoire of western swing and popular numbers, they played a residency at the Village Barn, various theatres and clubs and made regular radio appearances. They recorded for **Vocalion Records** and between August 1940 and February 1944 cut almost 40 sides for **Decca Records**. They ranged from the gentle 'Molly Darling', to the comedy of 'When There's Tears In The Eye Of A Potato (Then I'll Be Crying For You)'. They also recorded numerous transcription discs and toured as far as California. Lewis became noted for the strange musical instrument that he called Hootenanny. It consisted of washboards, motor horns, cowbells, sirens and guns that actually fired. When Lewis was drafted in 1942, **Spade Cooley** became leader of the band. When he returned to the music in 1944, he formed a new band, opened a club and toured until 1950, when he relocated to Seattle. Here he presented a radio show and then established his *Rainier Ranch* and his very popular *Sheriff Tex's Safety Junction* children's show on KING-TV, which lasted for seven years. He also appeared on Canadian television with the programme.

Most of his recordings at this time were children's records. After his children's show ended, he continued to play around the Seattle clubs and over the years, he has been afforded many tributes for his dedicated work in promoting western swing music. He appeared in several films including *Badmen From Red Butte* (1940), *Pardon My Gun* (1942), *Law Of The Canyon* and *The Stranger From Ponca City* (both 1947). He also successfully recorded 'Squaws Along The Yukon', several years before the **Hank Thompson** version and had a number 3 US country hit, 'Too Late To Worry Too Blue To Cry', on **Decca Records**, in 1944. Although few of his recordings are available on US labels, in the 80s Cattle Records of Germany issued several albums of his early work and also one, *Just Plain Old Ordinary Me* (1985), by Jack Rivers.

● COMPILATIONS: *Texas Jim Lewis & His Lone Star Cowboys Volume 1 & 2* (Cattle 1981)★★★, *Squaws Along The Yukon* (Cattle 1985)★★★, *Rootin' Tootin, Hootenanny* (Cattle 1985)★★★ *The King Of North Western Swing* (Cattle 1985)★★★.

Lewis, Vic

b. 29 July 1919, London, England. Lewis began playing a four-string banjo while still a child, later switching to guitar. In his teens he formed his own quartet, having developed an interest in jazz through listening to records. His quartet appeared on a talent show and soon obtained radio work on the BBC and Radio Luxembourg and also in London theatres. In the London jazz clubs Lewis met and played with artists such as **Django Reinhardt**, **Stéphane Grappelli**, **George Shearing** and **George Chisholm**. In 1938, he visited New York where he played with **Joe Marsala**, Marty Marsala, **Joe Bushkin**, **Buddy Rich**, **Pee Wee Russell**, **Bobby Hackett** and other noted jazzmen, even sitting in with **Tommy Dorsey**, **Jack Teagarden** and **Louis Armstrong**. He also made a handful of records during this trip with Hackett, **Eddie Condon** and **Zutty Singleton** in the band. He returned to England and with the outbreak of war served in the RAF where he played in a band whenever the opportunity presented itself. After the war, Lewis formed a new unit, teaming up with **Jack Parnell** to co-lead a small group. When Parnell moved on, Lewis continued to lead the band, which proved very popular and broadcast frequently on the BBC. In the late 40s Lewis formed a big band, employing musicians such as Ronnie Chamberlain, **Bob Efford** and Gordon Langhorn, that emulated the music of **Stan Kenton**. He also formed an orchestra that backed visiting American artists including Armstrong and **Johnny Ray**. On occasion, Lewis sat in with Armstrong and Kenton, playing trombone. In the 60s, Lewis switched tracks, becoming a manager and agent, handling tours by **Count Basie**, whom he had met in New York in 1938, **Dudley Moore** (his first client), **Judy Garland**, **Carmen McRae**, **Johnny Mathis**, **Andy Williams** and **Nina Simone**. Lewis was also deeply involved with NEMS Enterprises, working with

Brian Epstein, the Beatles and Cilla Black. Lewis's activities in these areas continued through the 70s when he organized tours for Shirley Bassey and Elton John. He retained his jazz links, however, recording a bossa nova album in 1963, half in the USA with several Kenton alumni and half in London with a band featuring Tubby Hayes and Ronnie Scott. In the early 80s he began to form occasional big bands for jazz dates. He recruited visiting American stars such as Shorty Rogers and Bud Shank to perform on a series of records. As a bandleader and promoter, Lewis has been active for many decades and has brought to the UK jazz scene a great deal of enthusiasm; his activities on the pop scene were also of much value. For all that, as his autobiography hints, he would probably have given away his entire musical career for a chance to play cricket for England.

● ALBUMS: *Mulligan's Music And At The Royal Festival Hall* (1955)★★★, *Vic Lewis And His Bossa Nova All Stars* (1963)★★★★, *Vic Lewis At The Beaulieu Jazz Festival* (1965)★★★, *Vic Lewis Plays The Music Of Donovan Leith* (1968)★★, *Vic Lewis With Maynard Ferguson* (1969)★★★, *Don't Cry For Me Argentina* (1974)★★, *Vic Lewis And R.P.O.* (RCA 1977)★★★, *Back Again* (1984)★★★, *Vic Lewis Big Bands* (1985)★★★, *Tea Break* (1985)★★★, *Vic Lewis And The West Coast All Stars* (1989)★★★★, *Know It Today, Know It Tomorrow* (1993)★★★, *Shake Down The Stars* (Candid 1993)★★★, *Play Bill Holman* (Candid 1994)★★★.

● COMPILATIONS: *My Life, My Way* 4-LP box set (1975)★★★, *New York, 1938* (Esquire 1986)★★★, *Vic Lewis Jam Sessions, Volumes 1-6 (1938-49)* (Harlequin 1986)★★★, *Vic Lewis Plays Stan Kenton (1948-54)* (Harlequin 1987)★★★★, *The EMI Years* (EMI 1991)★★★★.

● FURTHER READING: *Music And Maiden Overs: My Show Business Life*, Vic Lewis with Tony Barrow.

Lewis, Walter 'Furry'

b. 6 March 1893, Greenwood, Mississippi, USA, d. 14 September 1981, Memphis, Tennessee, USA. Furry Lewis was a songster, a blues musician, a humorist and an all-round entertainer. Raised in the country, he picked up the guitar at an early age and moved into Memphis around 1900 where he busked on the streets. After he ran away from home, he had experience working on travelling medicine shows under the influence of Jim Jackson. He worked with W.C. Handy and claimed that Handy presented him with his first good guitar. Hoboing across country in 1916, he had an accident while hopping a train and consequently lost a leg. After this he moved to Memphis and, while performing and recording, he supplemented his income by sweeping the streets. Apart from periods working on riverboats and with medicine shows in the 20s, this remained the style of his life for approximately the next 40 or more years. He recorded 11 titles for Vocalion in 1927, eight for Victor in 1928 and four more for Vocalion in 1929. He had a guitar style that incorporated aspects of both the Mississippi county style and the lighter, more ragged Memphis sound, supplemented by some impressive slide work. His voice was clear and his

approach to lyrics often self-mockingly humorous. Several of his recordings were ballads and his treatment of these was equally original. Well known around the city, he sometimes appeared as part of the Memphis Jug Band. He was one of the first pre-war blues artists to be 'rediscovered', and from 1959 he pursued a second successful career on the college circuit and played in several movies, including an unlikely appearance with Burt Reynolds in *W.W. And The Dixie Dance Kings*. Still an able performer he made many recordings during this period and was confirmed an Honorary Colonel of the State of Tennessee in 1973. Highly regarded by many performers, he received a touching tribute from Joni Mitchell on 'Furry Sings The Blues', which was featured on her 1976 album *Heijera*.

● ALBUMS: *Furry Lewis Blues* (Folkways 1959)★★★, *Back On My Feet Again* (Prestige 1961)★★★, *Done Changed My Mind* (1962★★), *Presenting The Country Blues* (1969)★★★, *In Memphis* (1970)★★, *On The Road Again* (1970)★★, *When I Lay My Burden Down* (1970)★★★, *Live At The Gaslight* (1971)★★★.

● COMPILATIONS: *Furry Lewis In His Prime 1927-29* (Yazoo 1988)★★★, *Shake 'Em On Down* (Ace/Fantasy 1994)★★★.

Lewis, Willie

b. 10 June 1905, Cleburne, Texas, USA, d. 13 January 1971. Lewis's first important job was as a clarinettist and saxophonist in the band led by Will Marion Cook, one of the leading black musicians in New York in the first quarter of the century. In the mid-20s Lewis joined another popular New York-based bandleader, Sam Wooding, with whom he toured Europe. In 1931, Lewis decided to stay in Europe and formed his own band for a residency at a Parisian nightclub. By the end of the decade, Lewis had built-up a big name for himself and his band, which featured a number of visiting American jazz musicians including Benny Carter and Bill Coleman. In 1941, Lewis was forced to fold the band and left Europe for his homeland. Back in New York, he drifted on the edges of music for a while but then worked outside the business for the rest of his life.

● COMPILATIONS: *Willie Lewis In Paris (1925-37)* (1988)★★★.

Ley, Eggy

b. Derek Ley, 4 November 1928, London, England, d. 20 December 1995. Beginning as a drummer and pianist when he was 13 years old, Ley took up soprano saxophone and by the early 50s was playing professionally. Among the bands with which he played were those led by Eric Silk, Mick Mulligan and Ron Simpson. In 1955, Ley took his own band to Germany for a two-week tour but stayed seven years, visiting Scandinavia and building a formidable reputation as a powerful exponent of latter-day dixieland jazz. Throughout the 60s he led bands in the UK and Europe, but at the end of the decade began working in radio as a producer, first with Radio Luxembourg and then the British Forces Broadcasting Service. He continued performing, however, and in 1980 began playing alto saxophone. In 1983, he returned to bandleading, once again dividing his time between the UK and engagements in Europe. Enormously popular on the continent, even if he is much less known in his homeland, Ley appeared at many festivals including those at Frankfurt, Breda and Cork. Stylistically, Ley is rooted in the great tradition of soprano saxophonists of which **Sidney Bechet** is the grand master while Ley's work on alto recalls **Pete Brown**. His singing may have been something of an acquired taste, but it is always rhythmically infectious.

● ALBUMS: with Benny Waters *Live At The Esplanade* (1981)★★★, *Come And Get It* (1985)★★★, *Eggy Ley's Hotshots* (1986)★★.

Ley, Tabu

b. Tabu Pascal, 1940, Bandoundou, Zaire. Alongside **Franco**, Ley (aka Rochereau) is one of the most influential and prolific musicians in contemporary Zairean music, with a catalogue of recordings - some 160 albums - almost as vast as Franco's. But there the similarity ends. Where Franco played a rootsier version of Zairean rumba, Ley has based his career on a tuneful, sweet-voiced ballad style that has inspired many of the new generation of Zairean artists, including **Empire Bakuba**, **Kanda Bongo Man**, **Langa Langa Stars** and **Victoria Eleison**. Born to middle-class parents, Ley attended one of Kinshasa's most prestigious schools, and outraged his father when he announced that he wished to make a career as a dancehall star. His first public appearance on stage was at the enormous Stadium Du 20 Mai in 1955, guesting with a long-forgotten rhumba band, when his performance of his own composition 'Besame Muchacha' (later recorded by **Le Grand Kalle**) turned him into an overnight star. The next year he met Kalle and began writing songs for the latter's African Jazz (all of which would be released with composing credits given to Kalle). In 1959, he joined African Jazz as a full-time vocalist, also assisting **Manu Dibango** and **Dr. Nico** with arrangements. Three years later, rivalry split the band and Ley founded a shortlived breakaway group, also called African Jazz, along with Nico. Ley and Nico then formed African Fiesta. Two years later, a further split took place. Nico left to form African Fiesta, while Ley's band took the suffix National, later to be renamed Afrisa International. It was this band that was to establish Ley as a major figure in Zairean music. In 1968, Ley embarked on a six-month tour of the Congo, Cameroon and Ivory Coast, then set the seal on his African success with a legendary concert at the Paris Olympia, playing to a capacity audience of wildly enthusiastic expatriate Congolese. His ambition for an international reputation had been apparent since the mid-60s: he made a practice of singing in French and Spanish as well as Lingala. He made further innovations: the first was to do with the drum kit, which was initially dismissed in Zaire as a 'white' instrument. Ley used the instrument in an entirely novel and African

way, supporting rather than replacing traditional percussion, and so achieved its acceptance. His second major innovation lay in the way he presented his performances. While most bands of the time remained fairly static on stage, Ley introduced energetic and infectious choreography, and performed with an accompanying dance troupe, the Leyettes. By 1969, Ley had become a leading exponent of the soukous rhythm that was sweeping Kinshasa. By the late 80s, the name was used to describe a whole genre of fast Zairean rhythms. In Kinshasa in the late 60s it referred to a single, well-defined sound, an attempt to accelerate the rumba and mix it with an urgent disco feel. Ley's adoption of soukous won him a new generation of younger, more westernized Zairean fans, alongside his existing rumba-based audience. A second new rhythm, the soumdjoum, and a new guitar sound, the soum, came from of a tour of Senegal in 1972. Since then, Ley has continued to mix old and new forms, harnessing new technology to re-create traditional rhythms. 'Cadence Mundanda', recorded in 1984 with his co-singer and lover **M'Bilia Bel**, used synthesized keyboards to pick out the centuries-old likembe rhythm. Although Franco is usually pointed to as the main lyrical spokesman on life and politics in Zaire, Ley has also made his mark. Tracks like 'Congo Nouveau, Afrique Nouvelle', 'Salongo' and a host of later pro-Mobutu numbers made him into a leading government praise singer. But he has also voiced criticisms of the state: in 1969, the government interpreted 'Kashama Nkoi' as a defence of an anti-Mobutu rebel who was later executed. Another song of the late 60s supposedly took the side of three other government opponents who had just been executed by firing squad. Unlike Franco, who was jailed for perceived anti-government lyrics on two occasions, Ley managed to keep out of the courts and prison. Ley's relationship with Franco had its ups and downs, and in the 60s and 70s both frequently attacked the other in their lyrics. By the 80s, such rivalries had been left behind, and a new era of co-operation between the two musicians culminated with their working together on a series of joint albums, sharing musicians, contributing their own songs and creating a new, muscular, disco-flavoured sound. Notable examples are *L'Evenement* and *Choc Choc Choc* (both 1983).

● ALBUMS: *Mokrano* (1963)★★★, *Tabu Ley* (1963)★★★, *Rochereau/Sam Mangwana Vols 3 & 4* (1965)★★★★, *Tango Ya Ba* (1969)★★★★, *Seigneur Rochereau Presentment* (1969)★★★, *La Musique Congolais* (1970)★★★, *A L'Olympia Vols. 1 & 2* (1971), *Pitie* (1973)★★★, with Franco *Omana Wapi* (Shanachie 1976)★★, *Festac 77* (1978)★★★, *Dernieres Nouveautes* (1979)★★★, *A Abidjan Vols 1 - 4* (1982)★★★★, with Franco *L'Evenement* (1983)★★, *Choc Choc Choc* (1983)★★★, *In America* (1984)★★, *Mobutu* (1985)★★★, *La Beauté D'Une Savage* (1986)★★★, *Entente Zaire* (1989)★★★, *Man From Kinshasa* (Shanachie 1991)★★★, *Africa Worldwide* (Rounder 1996)★★★.

Leyton Buzzards

This new wave/pop group was formed by Geoffrey Deanne (b. 10 December 1954, London, England; vocals) and David Jaymes (b. 28 December 1954, Woodford, Essex, England; bass). They recruited Kevin Steptoe (drums) and Dave Monk (guitar). From playing R&B cover versions on the pub circuit, they changed direction in 1976 after witnessing the new punk movement at the Roxy Club in London. By the following year they had secured a recording contract with Small Wonder Records, releasing the single '19 & Mad', and changing surnames to the likes of Nick Nayme (Deanne) to reinforce their new image. After the single, Monk was replaced by Vernon Austin. After entering The Band Of Hope And Glory contest, jointly sponsored by the *Sun* newspaper and BBC Radio 1, they won the final at the London Palladium. Their prize was a recording contract with **Chrysalis**. The result was the band's best-remembered moment, as 'Saturday Night (Beneath The Plastic Palm Trees)' saw them appearing on *Top Of The Pops*, celebrating band members' former weekend drinking and fighting antics. Shortening their name to the Buzzards, they were unable to capitalize on their early success, though their last Chrysalis single, 'We Make A Noise', featured a cover designed by Monty Python's Terry Gilliam. The contract-fulfilling *Jellied Eels To Record Deals* compiled early singles, demos, and radio session tracks. Their final recording was a one-off single for **WEA Records** titled 'Can't Get Used To Losing You', before Deane and Jaymes set up the more successful, salsa-flavoured **Modern Romance**.

● ALBUMS: *Jellied Eels to Record Deals* (Chrysalis 1979)★★.

Leyton, John

b. 17 February 1939, Frinton-on-Sea, Essex, England. Originally a small-time actor in the television series *Biggles*, Leyton's good looks won him a recording contract with Top Rank Records. Backed by the strong management of **Robert Stigwood** and talented producer **Joe Meek**, he recorded 'Tell Laura I Love Her', but lost out to the chart-topping **Ricky Valence**. A second flop with 'Girl On The Floor Above' was followed by the timely intervention of songwriter Geoff Goddard with the haunting 'Johnny Remember Me'. Stigwood ensured that the song was incorporated into Leyton's latest television role as pop singer Johnny St. Cyr in *Harpers, West One*. The nationwide exposure focused attention on the record and its otherworldly ambience and elaborate production were enough to bring Leyton a UK number 1. The Goddard-composed follow-up 'Wild Wind' reached number 2, and there were further minor hits with 'Son This Is She', 'Lone Rider' and 'Lonely City'. Avoiding the ravages of the beat boom, Leyton continued his acting career in such films as *The Great Escape* (1963), *Von Ryan's Express* (1965) and *Krakatoa* (1968). After a 10-year recording hiatus, he made a brief comeback in 1974 with an album written entirely by **Kenny Young**. Thereafter, Leyton concentrated on television work and related business interests.

● ALBUMS: *The Two Sides Of John Leyton* (HMV 1961)★★, *Always Yours* (HMV 1963)★★, *John Leyton* (York 1974)★★.

● COMPILATIONS: *Rarities* (1984)★★, *The Best Of John Leyton* (1988)★★★, *The EP Collection ... Plus* (See For Miles 1994)★★★.

● FILMS: *It's Trad, Dad* aka *Ring-A-Ding Rhythm* (1962), *Every Day's A Holiday* aka *Seaside Swingers* (1965).

LFO

Among the most unrelenting and popular exponents of hard techno, LFO's output on **Warp Records** represents everything an outsider might fear of the music: harsh, crashing, thumping 'bleep' music. When forced to play their debut single 'LFO' on Radio 1, Steve Wright described it as the worst record in the world. Gez Varley and Mark Bell are the mainstays, though extra keyboard players Simon Hartley and Richie Brook were drafted in for occasional live outings. The pair met at college in Leeds, where they discovered mutual interests in music and technology as well as partying in the city's clubs, where **Nightmares On Wax** worked. The duo gave the DJs a demo of a track they had recorded on a Casio SKI keyboard called 'LFO' which proved a success in the Leeds clubland. Among the audience were the fledgling Warp team who decided to release 'LFO' and were rewarded when it became a Top 20 hit in the summer of 1990. Along with NOW and the Forgemasters, LFO helped pioneer the sound that became known as 'bleep'. Almost a year later the single 'We Are Back' heralded their first album, *Frequencies* (Warp 1992), and 'What Is House' followed in early 1992. Their next album, *Advance*, did not arrive until the beginning of 1996 with only 'Tied Up' in November 1994 in between. However, during this time the duo had remixed and collaborated with a number of other artists notably **Kraftwerk** (for their *Elektrik Music* recordings), **Afrika Bambaataa**, the **Yello Magic Orchestra** and the **Art Of Noise**. Bell also teamed up with Simon Hartley of Wild Planet, releasing the acid techno EP *I'm For Real* under the name Feedback. Since *Advance* the group have split up to concentrate on individual projects, with Bell retaining the name and a contract with Warp. In 1997 he was involved in the production of **Björk**'s album *Homogenic* and later toured with the singer around Europe. He also remixed tracks by **Radiohead**, Gus Gus and **Sabres Of Paradise** among others.

● ALBUMS: *Frequencies* (Warp 1991)★★★★, *Advance* (Warp 1996)★★★.

Li Kôlan (Li Xianglan)

b. Yoshika Ôtaka, 12 February 1920, Fushun, China. A daughter of Japanese residents in China, Ôtaka first performed as an singing actress in 1938 soon after the Sino-Japanese war began, and was forced to pass herself off as a Chinese with the name of Li Xianglan (pronounced as Li Kôlan in Japan) in the late 30s in

Manchuria, which had been politically manoeuvered into declaring independence by the Japanese government. Fluent both in Chinese and Japanese and with attractive looks, Li had her stardom secured when she made her appearance in Japan, playing and singing in such movies as *Byakuranno Uta* (*Song Of White Orchids*) (1939) and *Shinano Yoru* (*A Night In China*) (1940), the stories of which tried to strengthen the ties of friendship between Japan and China. The theme song of *Shinano Yoru* was tremendously popular. After World War II, she was summoned to a Chinese military court under suspicion of co-operating with the Japanese government in its policy of aggression, but she won an acquittal by proving that her nationality was Japanese. Renaming herself Yoshiko Yamaguchi, she continued her active career as a singer and film actress, and became internationally known after moving to the USA in 1954, appearing in Hollywood films and getting married to a renowned visual artist, Isamau Noguchi. Yamaguchi retired in 1958 to remarry Hirshi Ôtaka, a diplomatic official, and later became involved in sociopolitical affairs, especially regarding the Palestinian/Israeli problem. In 1974, she successfully ran for the Upper House of the Japanese parliament, and is still an active Member of the House.

● ALBUMS: *Yogirino Basha* (*A Wagon In A Night Fog*) (1989)★★★, *Watashino Uguisu* (*My Nightingale*) (1989)★★★, *Yelaishang* (1989)★★★.

● FURTHER READING: *Daremo Kakanakatta Arab* (*Arabia No One Has Written About*), Yoshiko Yamaguchi. *Li Kôlan: Watashino Hansei* (*Li Kôlan: My Life*), Yoshiko Yamaguchi and Sakuya Fujiwara.

Li'l Abner (film musical)

Probably because most of the original cast of the 1956 hit Broadway show recreated their roles, this 1959 screen version was a satisfying and entertaining affair. Norman Panama and Melvin Frank adapted their libretto, which was based on Al Capp's popular cartoon character, and the community of Dogpatch - one of the most underrated areas in the whole of the USA - was up there on the screen in Technicolor and VistaVision. When they learn that their town has been earmarked as a testing site for atom bombs, the residents, Daisy Mae (Leslie Parrish), Abner Yokum (Peter Palmer), Pappy and Mammy Yokum (Joe E. Marks and Billie Hayes), Marryin' Sam (**Stubby Kaye**), Earthquake McGoon (Bernie Hoffman), Stupifyin' Jones (Julie Newmar) and the rest, discover that, many years ago, their beloved Dogpatch was designated a national shrine. **Johnny Mercer** and **Gene De Paul**'s witty score sounded as good as ever and included 'If I Had My Druthers', 'Jubilation T. Cornpone', 'The Country's In The Very Best Of Hands', 'Put 'Em Back', 'Namely You', 'Room Enuff For Us', 'A Typical Day', 'Don't Take That Rag Off'n The Bush', 'I'm Past My Prime', 'Unnecessary Town', and 'I Wish It Could Be Otherwise'. Dee Dee Wood and **Michael Kidd**'s exuberant and exhilarating choreography, coupled with Panama and Frank's skilful and sympathetic direction, made this a film to savour and remember. Another, non-musical, version of Al Capp's tale was released in 1940.

Li'l Abner (stage musical)

The wonderful world of Dogpatch, a rural community somewhere in the south of the USA, came to The St. James Theatre on Broadway in November 1956 when librettists Norman Panama and Melvin Frank adapted Al Capp's famous comic strip, *Li'l Abner*, for the musical stage. All the familiar characters made the trip, including Daisy Mae (Edith Adams) who is still trying to catch Abner Yokum (Peter Palmer) in the annual Sadie Hawkins' Day Chase (if you catch 'em, Marryin' Sam [**Stubby Kaye**] will do the rest). Then there is Appassionata von Climax (Tina Louise) - she's after Li'l Abner as well - Earthquake McGoon (Bern Hoffman - *he's* after Ellie Mae), General Bullmoose (Howard St. John), Mammy Yokum (Charlotte Rae), Stupefyin' Jones (Julie Newmar), Romeo Scragg (Mark Breaux), Clem Scragg (James Hurst), Moonbeam McSwine (Carmen Alvarez), and many more. All of them are shocked when they hear that the US Goverment has such a low opinion of Dogpatch that they want to test an atom bomb there. Fortune smiles on the town and its amiable inhabitants when they discover that, back in Abraham Lincoln's time, the town was designated a national shrine. The lively and exhilarating score, by **Johnny Mercer** and **Gene De Paul**, was full of good things, including what could be said to be the community's theme song, 'Progress Is The Root Of All Evil', along with 'Past My Prime', 'Put 'Em Back', 'Oh Happy Day', 'Unnecessary Town', the rousing 'The Country's In The Very Best Of Hands', and a hymn to the founder of Dogpatch, the incompetent 'Jubilation T. Cornpone', which was sung by Stubby Kaye who was oustanding throughout, as usual. There was also the tender ballad, 'Love In A Home', and 'Namely You', which achieved some popularity through recordings by **Lawrence Welk** and **Carmen McRae**. Another of the songs, 'If I Had My Druthers', was included by Johnny Mercer on *Two Of A Kind*, an album he made with **Bobby Darin** in 1961. **Michael Kidd** won a Tony Award for his spirited choreography (just two years after his tremendous work in Hollywood on *Seven Brides For Seven Brothers*) and *Li'l Abner* enjoyed a run of 693 performances. The 1959 film version starred Peter Palmer, Leslie Parrish, Stubby Kaye, and some of the other actors from the show.

Liberace

b. Wladziu Valentino Liberace, 16 May 1919, West Allis, Wisconsin, USA, d. 4 February 1987, Palm Springs, Florida, USA. This larger-than-life pianist had no major chart hits - but had an indefinable charm and talent that gave delight to multitudes of fans across the globe. Of Polish-Italian extraction, he was raised in a household where there was always music - particularly from father Salvatore who played French horn in both

John Philip Sousa's Concert Band and the Milwaukee Symphony Orchestra. George and the younger Wladziu were, likewise, both eager to become professional players. Wladziu's piano skills were praised by no less than Paderewski, and he won a place at Wisconsin College of Music at the age of seven. During his 17-year scholarship - the longest ever awarded by the academy - he made his concert debut as a soloist at the age of 11 and was fronting renowned symphony orchestras while still an adolescent. A fulfilling career of classical recitals and university master classes might have beckoned but for the artist's innate sense of humour and flair for self-promotion. In 1934, he had elocution lessons to dilute his Polish accent. After service in an overseas entertainments unit during World War II, he played and sang in club dance bands and it was during a residency at the Wunderbar in Warsaw, Wisconsin, that he was first introduced as 'Liberace'. At New York's Persian Rooms, an experiment whereby he performed counterpoints to records - including his own one-shot single for the Signature label - played on the venue's sound system, was curtailed by a Musicians Union ban. A happier season in a Californian hotel resulted in a **Decca** contract, for which he was visualized as a second **Frankie Carle**. However, wishing to develop a more personal style, he moved to **Columbia Records** where, supervised by **Mitch Miller**, he recorded a flamboyant version of 'September Song' which, supplemented by an in-concert album, brought Liberace to the attention of a national audience.

By the early 50s, his repertoire embraced **George Gershwin** favourites, cocktail jazz, film themes ('Unchained Melody'), boogie-woogie and self-composed pieces ('Rhapsody By Candlelight'), as well as adaptations of light classics such as 'Story Of Three Loves' - borrowed from a Rachmaninov variation on a tune by Paganini. Nevertheless, Liberace struck the most popular chord with his encores, in which doggerel such as 'Maizy Doats' or 'Three Little Fishes' were dressed in arrangements littered with twee arpeggios and trills. He also started garbing himself from a wardrobe that stretched to rhinestone, white mink, sequins, gold lamé and similar razzle-dazzle. Crowned with a carefully waved coiffeur, he oozed charm and extravagant gesture, with a candelabra-lit piano as the focal point of the epic vulgarity that was *The Liberace Show*, televised coast-to-coast from Los Angeles; the show established a public image that he later tried in vain to modify. His fame was such that he was name-checked in 'Mr. Sandman', a 1954 million-seller by the **Chordettes**, and a year later, starred (as a deaf concert pianist) in a film, *Sincerely Yours*, with brother George (future administrator of the Liberace Museum in Las Vegas) as musical director. Another spin-off was the publication of a Liberace cookbook. Following the celebration of his quarter century in showbusiness with a Hollywood Bowl spectacular in 1956, Liberace crossed to England (where a vocal outing, 'I Don't Care', was lodged in the Top 30) for the first of three Royal

Command Performances. While in the UK, he instigated a High Court action, successfully suing the *Daily Mirror*, whose waspish columnist Cassandra had written an article on the star laced with sexual innuendo. During the next decade, a cameo in the film satire *The Loved One* was reviewed not unfavourably, as was one of his early albums for **RCA Records** in which he aimed more directly at the contemporary market. This, however, was a rare excursion, as his work generally maintained a certain steady consistency - or 'squareness', in the words of his detractors - that deviated little from the commercial blueprint wrought in the 50s. Nonetheless, Liberace's mode of presentation left its mark on stars such as **Gary Glitter**, **Elton John** and **Queen**. Although attendant publicity boosted box office takings on a world tour, embarrassing tabloid newspaper allegations by a former employee placed his career in a darker perspective. When the singer died on 4 February 1987 at his Palm Springs mansion, the words 'kidney complaint' were assumed to be a euphemism for an AIDS-related illness. For a 75th Birthday Celebration in 1994, fans from all over America gathered to pay their respects at Liberace Plaza in Las Vegas.

● ALBUMS: *Piano* (Advance 1951)★★★, *Liberace At the Piano* (Columbia 1952)★★★, *An Evening With Liberace* (Columbia 1953)★★★★, *Liberace By Candlelight* (Columbia 1953)★★★, *Concertos For You* (Columbia 1953)★★★, *Concertos For You Volume 2* (Columbia 1954)★★★, *Plays Chopin* (Columbia 1954)★★★, *Plays Chopin Volume 2* (Columbia 1954)★★★, *Sincerely Yours* film soundtrack (Columbia 1953)★★★, *Piano Reverie* (Columbia 1955)★★★, *Kiddin' On The Keys* (Columbia 1956)★★★, *My Inspiration* (Coral 1960)★★★, *Liberace At The Palladium* (Coral 1961)★★★, *My Parade Of Golden Favourites* (Coral 1961)★★★, *As Time Goes By* (Coral 1962)★★★, *Rhapsody By Candlelight* (Coral 1962)★★★, *Mr. Showmanship* (1963)★★★, *Christmas* (1963)★★, *My Most Requested* (1964)★★★, *Liberace At The American* (1964)★★★, *Golden Hits Of Hollywood* (Coral 1965)★★★, *Liberace Now* (1967)★★★, *A Brand New Me* (Warners 1970)★★, *Candlelight Classics* (Ember 1973)★★★, *Piano Gems* (Pye 1976)★★★, *Mr. Showmanship - Live* (Pye 1978)★★★, *New Sounds* (Dot 1979)★★★.

● COMPILATIONS: *Just For You* (PRT 1976)★★★, *Best Of Liberace* (MCA 1983)★★★, *The Collection* (Castle 1988)★★★.

● VIDEOS: *Liberace In Las Vegas* (Virgin Vision 1988), *Liberace Live* (Vestron Music 1988).

● FURTHER READING: *Liberace*, Liberace. *Liberace: The True Story*, B. Thomas.

Liberty Cage

Based in Brighton, Sussex, England, Liberty Cage were formed as the career of celebrated indie/roots band **Men They Couldn't Hang** stalled in 1991. From that group, songwriters Phil 'Swill' Odgers (vocals, guitar) and Paul Simmonds (guitar) recruited Paul's brother Neil Simmonds (bass) and 'just decided to go into a

studio in Brighton and see what happened'. After multi-instrumentalist Dave Kent and former Tender Trap drummer Simon Lomond joined, Liberty Cage quickly established a strong reputation for their live shows - an aptitude they shared with their former incarnation. In Paul Simmonds and Odgers they similarly possessed two talented lyricists, capable of combining folky humanism with caustic political tracts. This was confirmed by the May 1994 release of *Sleep Of The Just*, a self-produced and financed album recorded during 'studio down-time'. Though strong early demo material such as 'This Side Of The Street' had been jettisoned, new songs such as 'Mercy Of The Guards' and 'Fire Below' ably compensated. Though the songs were played with punk ferocity, the album indelibly cast Liberty Cage as a folk band, just as the Men They Couldn't Hang had been before them. As Paul Simmonds conceded: 'The best folk music will have something to say in 100 years when pop fads become sociologist's footnotes and clothes to laugh at.'
● ALBUMS: *Sleep Of The Just* (Cage 1994)★★★.

Liberty Grooves

Notable UK record label/shop run in Tooting, South London by Johnny F, a long time collector and fan of hip-hop music, which opened in May 1992. Liberty Grooves began by releasing breakbeat albums and material from UK artists including the Gutter Snypes and Sniper, and also signed a licensing deal with American label Dolo. The first fruits of this marriage have been two acclaimed albums, *Freestyle Frenzy 1* and *2*, which showcased artists such as **Nas**, **Large Professor**, Q-Tip (**A Tribe Called Quest**), **Wu Tang Clan** and more, freestyling on DJ Stretch Armstrong's New York radio show.
● ALBUMS: *Freestyle Frenzy 1 & 2* (Liberty Grooves/Dolo 1993/94)★★★★.

Liberty Records

Founded in Los Angeles in 1955 by Simon (Si) Waronker and Jack Ames, Liberty became one of the most successful post-rock 'n' roll independent labels. Other key figures in their development were Alvin S. Bennett (president and latterday owner) and Ted Keep (chief engineer). Their most notable early signing was **Eddie Cochran**, whose short, but influential, career included such seminal recordings as 'Summertime Blues' (1958) and 'C'mon Everybody' (1959). The finely-honed commercial productions of **Snuff Garrett** proved successful for early 60s signings **Johnny Burnette** and **Bobby Vee**, while the acquisition of the **Imperial** label in 1963 brought **Fats Domino**, **Ricky Nelson**, **Sandy Nelson** and discotheque star **Johnny Rivers** to the label. Aware of the success of New York's Aldon publishing house, Waronker supervised Liberty's Metric Music subsidiary, which introduced the talents of contract songwriters **Jackie DeShannon**, **Randy Newman**, **David Gates** and Russ Titleman to the company. Liberty enjoyed considerable commercial

success with **Jan And Dean** and **Gary Lewis And The Playboys**, while an association with the **Ventures**, through their distribution of the Dolton label, also proved fruitful. Despite the acquisition of leading blues group **Canned Heat**, Liberty was generally unable to sustain its eminent position in the face of underground rock, although its UK office, under the aegis of A&R director Andrew Lauder, made several astute signings, including the **Groundhogs**, **Brinsley Schwarz** and **Hawkwind**. By 1972, the label's roster and back catalogue had been absorbed by the **United Artists** conglomerate and Liberty's brief tenure was ended
● FURTHER READING: *Liberty Records*, Michael 'Doc Rock' Kelly.

Libre, Conjunto

Libre, aka Manny Oquendo's Libre, was co-founded in October 1974 by Manny Oquendo (b. 1931, Brooklyn, New York, USA, of Puerto Rican parentage; leader, timbales, bongo, güiro, other percussion, chorus, arrangements) and Andy González (b. 1951, Manhattan, New York, USA; bass, claves, other percussion, chorus, arrangements). They met while working with **Eddie Palmieri**'s band and decided to organize Libre after having 'irreconcilable problems' with the bandleader. Their founding principle was that Libre ('free') should be based on Afro-Cuban roots, not just copying them, but allowing a freer, jazzier, more urban sound which broke away from what they perceived as the 'cold, unemotional and mechanical sound' of most recorded salsa. Libre adopted a trombones and flute 'trombanga' frontline, a combination that Oquendo had helped Palmieri develop when he was a member of his group, La Perfecta, in the 60s. Oquendo literally grew up on Latin music. In the 30s his family lived above Almacenes Hernández, then one of the leading record stores in El Barrio (Spanish Harlem). As a youngster he listened to **Machito**'s original Afro-Cubans and began collecting 78 rpm discs of Cuban music. He started playing timbales at the age of 13 and worked with various bands, including Charlie Valero (1946), Los Hermanos Mercado and El Boy. He played with the legendary **Chano Pozo** in 1947 and replaced **Tito Puente** in José Curbelo's band in 1948. During the 50s mambo era, he performed with both of the great Titos: **Rodríguez** and Puente. He informed Eddie Palmieri about the music coming out of Cuba while they were both accompanists in the Vicentico Valdés band in the late 50s, and became a founder member of Palmieri's Conjunto La Perfecta in 1962, remaining with the group until 1967. Afterwards he continued to work with Palmieri until Libre's formation. In addition, he worked with, among others, Pupi Campo, **Noro Morales**, Miguelito Valdés, **Johnny Pacheco**'s charanga band, **Charlie Palmieri**, **Larry Harlow** and Israel 'Cachao' López.

González started violin tuition when he was at grade school. He switched to bass at junior high school and organized a Latin jazz quintet with his older brother,

Jerry. He began gigging with dance bands when he was 13-years of age. In 1967, he made his recording debut with the band of Monguito Santamaría (**Mongo Santamaría**'s son) on *On Top*. After two years and a further album with Santamaría, González did a stint with **Ray Barretto**'s band between 1969 and 1971, taking six months out to work with **Dizzy Gillespie**. From 1971-74, he performed with Eddie Palmieri. González has sessioned with an impressive list of Latin artists, including **Justo Betancourt**, Johnny Pacheco, Tito Rodríguez, **Willie Colón**, Machito, **Arturo 'Chico' O'Farrill**, Charlie Palmieri, **Roberto Torres**, Don Gonzalo Fernández, Virgilio Marti and **Rubén Blades**. In the jazz and fusion contexts, he has worked with **Kenny Dorham**, Clifford Thornton, **Hank Jones**, **Jazz Composers Orchestra**, Kip Hanrahan, **Jaco Pastorius**, **Astor Piazzolla**, **J.C. Heard**, **Paul Simon** and brother Jerry's Fort Apache Band, amongst others. González appeared with the latter in London in November 1990. Like Oquendo, he has steeped himself in the Afro-Cuban tradition: 'I've studied the whole history of Cuban music through recordings', he explained to Larry Birnbaum in 1989, 'and I've talked to quite a few people who are knowledgeable about that music and those periods . . . Afro Cuban music history has a line to it, just like jazz . . . Things change over the years, but I think you've got to keep the link to the past.'

Jerry González (b. New York, USA; conga, trumpet, fluegelhorn, chorus, bandleader) was a founder member of Libre. He co-founded the Latin Jazz Quintet in 1964; performed with Monguito Santamaría; toured with the **Beach Boys** (playing trumpet), and worked with Kenny Dorham, Dizzy Gillespie (six months), Orquesta Flamboyán (two years), Clifford Thornton Quintet, **Tony Williams**' Lifetime, Eddie Palmieri (playing conga for two-and-a-half years), Jeremy Steig, Larry Young, **George Benson**, Justo Betancourt, Totico and Kip Hanrahan, among others. Jerry made his solo debut with the notable *Ya Yo Me Cure* in 1980. He formed his own Latin jazz outfit, the Fort Apache Band, and made his album debut with them on *The River Is Deep*, which was recorded at the Berlin Jazz Festival in November 1982 (Libre also appeared). He left Libre at the end of the 80s to devote his energies to band leading. In 1989, he released *Obatalá* and *Rumba Para Monk*. In November 1990, the Fort Apache Band made their UK debut with an outstanding gig at London's Empire Ballroom.

Oquendo and the González brothers all performed with the short-lived Grupo Folklorico y Experimental Nuevayorquino on the pioneering *Concepts In Unity* (1975) and *Lo Dice Todo* (1977), both on Salsoul Records. Shortly after the first Grupo Folklorico record, Libre signed with Salsoul and released four albums on the label between 1976 and 1981.

On their debut, *Con Salsa . . . Con Ritmo Vol. 1*, Libre gave 'Bamboleate' and 'No Critiques' - two songs Oquendo had originally recorded with Eddie Palmieri in the 60s - a rugged and jazzy interpretation. Also featured was a moving version of the 1929 classic 'Lamento Borincano (El Jibarito)' by the great Puerto Rican composer Rafael Hernández (1891-1965). Another classic, 1928's 'Suavecito' by Cuban Ignacio Piñeiro (1888 -1969; composer and leader of Septeto Nacional) was given a charanga-style treatment on the band's follow-up *Tiene Calidad - Con Salsa . . . Con Ritmo Vol. 2* in 1978. *Los Lideres De La Salsa* in 1979 compiled a track each from Libre's first two albums, 'La Salsa' performed by Grupo Folklorico (with lead vocals by former big band leader Marcelino Guerra), plus three new tracks, two of which featured Cuban violinist **Alfredo de la Fé**. Young and talented singer, Herman Olivera, made his recording debut with Libre, sharing lead vocals with Tony 'Pupy Cantor' Torres (a band member since 1975) on *Increible* in 1981. Olivera was the replacement for Libre's other co-lead singer, Héctor 'Tempo' Alomar, who also joined in 1975 and went on to record with Nestor Torres, Charanga América, Johnny 'Dandy' Rodríguez and Grupo ABC. Libre switched to the Montuno label for *Ritmo, Sonido y Estilo* in 1983. The album featured an outstanding version of the plena 'Elena, Elena' composed by Manuel 'Canario' Jiménez (b. 1895, Manatí, Puerto Rico, d. 1975), a master of Puerto Rican jibaro (country) music, and a swinging interpretation of the classic 'Que Humanidad', co-written by the incredibly prolific Cuban composer Ñico Saquito (1901-1982). Torres departed and became a co-lead vocalist with **Willie Rosario**'s band for a brief stint.

Olivera left in 1991 to sing with Cruz Control, a swinging new outfit co-led by percussionist Ray Cruz and pianist Sergio Rivera. He was replaced on lead vocals by Frankie Vásquez (b. 6 January 1958, Guayama, Puerto Rico), who in addition to doing stints with Fuego '77, Sonido Taibori, Orquesta Calidad, Chi Hua Hua's Orquesta Metropolitana, Wayne Gorbea (b. 22 October 1950, Manhattan, New York, USA; bandleader, pianist, percussionist, vocalist, composer, producer) and Javier Vázquez, has performed with **Henry Fiol**, Junior González, Frankie Morales and others. Libre's trombone section has included such luminaries as the late Barry Rogers and Jose Rodrigues (both longstanding Eddie Palmieri accompanists); Angel 'Papo' Vásquez, Jimmy Bosch (a long-time Ray Barretto compatriot) and Reinaldo Jorge; and jazz musicians Ed Byrne, Dan Reagan and Steve Turre (who also plays conch shell). Jazz fusioneer **Dave Valentín** played flute on all but one of Libre's first five albums. New York born pianist, Oscar Hernández, performed on the band's first four releases and guested on one track of *Ritmo, Sonido y Estilo* (ex-**Típica 73** and Los Kimbos member, Joe Mannozzi, played on the remainder). Hernández worked with Joey Pastrana, **Ismael Miranda**, **Alfredo 'Chocolate' Armenteros**, Roberto Torres, **Pupi Legaretta**, **Pete 'El Conde' Rodríguez**, Ray Barretto and Rubén Blades, among others. He has been working increasingly as a producer in recent years, and albums to his credit include: *Azucar A Granel!* (1988) by

Camilo Azuquita, *Twice As Good!* (1988) by Rafael de Jesús and *Carabalí* (1988) and *Carabalí II* (1991) by the septet of the same name. The impact of the salsa cum Latin jazz formular of Carabalí's first release on the London Latin scene led to a five-night residency at London's Bass Clef club followed by a nine-date UK tour, returning to the Bass Clef for the final gig (all in April, 1989). Hernández was with them as keyboardist and musical director.

Libre still gig frequently, touring the States, Latin America, Africa and Europe, and appeared in Leon Ichaso's movie *Crossover Dreams* (1985) starring Rubén Blades. In May 1989, Carlos Agudelo wrote in his *Billboard* 'Latin Notas' column: 'The fact that Libre has been without a recording contract for several years calls attention to the intelligence and priorities of the Latin recording business in this country'. In 1991, the band returned to the studio and Libre's personnel performed on 'Descarga de Turre', a track on Steve Turre's *Right There*.

● ALBUMS: *Con Salsa . . . Con Ritmo Vol. 1* (1976)★★★★, *Tiene Calidad - Con Salsa . . . Con Ritmo Vol. 2* (1978)★★★, *Los Lideres De La Salsa* (1979)★★★, *Increible* (1981)★★★, *Ritmo, Sonido y Estilo* (1983)★★★.

Licensed To Ill - The Beastie Boys

Wholly original, the first and the best rap group to make the genre universally palatable. These Brooklyn boys succeeded with a combination of tremendously exciting backgrounds, from straight riff metal (on 'Rhymin' & Stealin'' and 'She's Crafty') to sample ('The New Style'). Having learnt their art by observing rather than participating while at NYU, they sounded street-cred, even though they were positively middle-class. The Volkswagen badge-stealing craze was unknowingly started by the band, who wore the pendant merely in order to mock the hippies who had worn the ban-the-bomb medallion. The rap album for people who think they don't like rap.

● Tracks: *Rhymin' & Stealin'*; *The New Style*; *She's Crafty*; *Posse In Effect*; *Slow Ride*; *Girls*; *Fight For Your Right*; *No Sleep Till Brooklyn*; *Paul Revere*; *Hold It Now, Hit It*; *Brass Monkey*; *Slow And Low*; *Time To Get Ill*.

● First released 1986
● UK peak chart position: 7
● USA peak chart position: 1

Lick My Decals Off, Baby - Captain Beefheart And The Magic Band

Captain Beefheart's second recording for **Frank Zappa**'s Straight label consolidated the artistic freedom expressed on its predecessor *Trout Mask Replica*. *Avant garde* rock and free jazz melt into a seamless whole, jagged guitars and ravaged saxophone splinter through the mix while ex-**Mothers Of Invention** drummer Artie Tryp, herein renamed Ed Marimba, brings new rhythmic possibilities to the Captain's heady brew. Beefheart prowls around the proceedings with consummate ease, his expressive voice, which echoes bluesman

Howlin' Wolf, emphasizing the adventurism of both music and lyrics. By demolishing previous notions of tonality and structure, Captain Beefheart inspired a whole generation of post-punk disciples, from **Pere Ubu** to **Sonic Youth**.

● Tracks: *Lick My Decals Off, Baby*; *Doctor Dark*; *I Love You, You Big Dummy*; *Peon*; *Bellerin' Plain*; *Woe-Is-Uh-Me-Bop*; *Japan In A Dishpan*; *I Wanna Find A Women That'll Hold My Big Toe Till I Have To Go*; *Petrified Forest*; *One Rose That I Mean*; *The Buggy Boogie Woogie*; *The Smithsonian Institute Blues (Or The Big Dig)*; *Space-Age Couple*; *The Clouds Are Full Of Wine (Not Whiskey Or Rye)*; *Flash Gordon's Ape*.

● First released 1970
● UK peak chart position: 20
● USA peak chart position: did not chart

Lick The Tins

Well-crafted UK folk/pop group who became turntable favourites with a Celtified version of 'Can't Help Falling In Love'. Their excellent repertoire was characterized by a bustling energy. 'Accept no substitutes', ran their press blurb, but they disbanded soon afterwards.

● ALBUMS: *Blind Man On A Flying Horse* (Sedition 1987)★★★.

Lieb, Oliver

b. *c.*1970, Frankfurt, West Germany. A well-known and highly regarded member of **Sven Vath**'s **Eye Q/Harthouse** stable and Omen Club, Lieb's most popular work thus far came out under the Spicelab moniker, which varied between hard house, acid and trance cuts. Contrastingly he utilized the name Mirage for the more spacey, transcendental theme of 'Airborn'. Other *nom de plumes* employed include Ambush, whose debut album was an enchanting collection of 'world techno' tracks, dominated by a thorough exploration of drums and rhythm: 'I programmed it in the way that I would lay the drums, the way I would feel them, and then I took vocals from CDs and old records'. Lieb also works as Superspy, Infinite Aura, LSG, Psilocybin and Azid Force. He is half of Paragliders with Torsten Stenzl ('Paragliders (The Remixes)'), and has remixed for Sven Vath, **Vapourspace** and **Messiah** among others. Together with Dr Atmo he recorded *Music For Films*, for **Peter Namlook**'s Fax label, an alternative score to **Philip Glass**'s ambient documentary *Koyaanisquatsi*.

● ALBUMS: as Ambush *The Ambush* (Harthouse 1994)★★★★, with Dr Atmo *Music For Films* (Fax 1994)★★★.

Lieberson, Goddard

b. 5 April 1911, Hanley, Staffordshire, England, d. 29 May 1977, New York City, New York, USA. A record company executive, composer, author, and musician, Lieberson was four years old when his family moved to Seattle, Washington, USA. After graduating from the local university, he studied at the Eastman School of Music in New York, and originally intended to pursue a career as a composer. Financial reality intervened, and in 1939, he became the assistant director of the Masterworks division of **Columbia Records**, part of the **CBS** group. During the 40s he recorded plays, operas, and other classical works, while at the same time rising to the position of executive vice-president of Columbia. In the late 40s, he was influential in the decision to select the 33 1/3 speed as the standard for the new long-playing record. The development also contributed directly towards his greatest success as a pioneering producer of original cast recordings of hit Broadway shows. He began in 1949 with *South Pacific*, for which he won the first of seven Gold Discs. The other award winners were *Flower Drum Song, Camelot, West Side Story, Mame, The Sound Of Music* and *My Fair Lady*. He was so impressed by the score for the latter show that he persuaded CBS to become the sole investor - and, with sales of over six million units, they made a fortune. His 'amazing ear, his enthusiasm for theatre music, and his respect for the work he was doing' made him a legendary figure in the industry. Lieberson also recorded many shows when they had closed after only a few performances, convinced, quite rightly in most cases, that the scores were worth preserving. He was responsible for recording the vast majority of the shows that have been re-released in CD form on the **Sony Broadway** label. During a long and distinguished career, Lieberson is credited with having signed many important artists, including **Simon And Garfunkel** and **Bob Dylan**. He rose to become the president of Columbia Records (1955-56), of the CBS/Columbia Group (1966-71 and 1973-75), but he will be remembered mainly for his sensitive and brilliant work in preserving so much wonderful Broadway music. His final recordings, in the early 70s, were *A Little Night Music, Billy* and the record-breaking *A Chorus Line.*

Liebert, Ottmar

b. 1963, Cologne, Germany. On being given a guitar at the age of 11, Liebert found his emotional release. Classically trained at the Rheinische Musikhockschule, he later travelled Europe absorbing musical influences from Russia to Spain, where Flamenco first fired his imagination. Even so, his early bands were in a jazz/funk groove, first in Cologne, then in Boston, Massachusetts in the early 80s. A move to Santa Fe, New Mexico in 1986, found him working in restaurants, simplifying Flamenco styles to forge a dynamic contemporary instrumental sound, which he developed further in 1988 when he formed the group Luna Negra. His 1989 limited edition CD, *Marita: Shadows And Storms*, brought exposure on the west coast New Age radio network, and was picked up by the Higher Octave Records label who reissued it as *Nouveau Flamenco*. Reaching large audiences as support to **Basia** on her 1989/90 tour helped it peak at number 3 on *Billboard*'s Adult Alternative chart. A move to the major Epic label brought *Solo Para Ti* in 1992, with guest appearances by **Carlos Santana**. Another valuable support on **Natalie**

Cole's Unforgettable tour in 1992 broadened his profile, and in 1993/4 Luna Negra toured extensively in Europe and South America. *The Hours Between Night And Day* found him interpreting soul and blues standards, while the subsequent *Euphoria* featured remixes by **Steve Hillage** and others, aimed at the ambient-ethnic-dance crowd.
● ALBUMS: *Poets And Angels* (Higher Octave 1990)★★★, *Nouveau Flamenco* (Higher Octave 1991)★★★★, *Borrasca* (Higher Octave 1991)★★★, *Solo Para Ti* (Epic 1992)★★★, *The Hours Between Night And Day* (Epic 1994)★★★, *Euphoria* (Epic 1995)★★★, with Luna Negra *Viva!* (Epic 1995)★★★, *Opium* (Epic 1996)★★★.

Liebman, Dave

b. 4 September 1946, New York City, New York, USA. After studying theory and composition with **Lennie Tristano**, and saxophone and flute with **Charles Lloyd**, Liebman's first important job was with **Elvin Jones** in 1971. When he joined **Miles Davis** in 1974, he was simultaneously running Lookout Farm, one of many groups that have tried to fuse jazz and Indian music. Touring with **Chick Corea** and leading a highly successful quintet in the late 70s, featuring **Terumass Hino, John Scofield**, Ron McLure and **Adam Nussbaum**. Liebman was already one of the leading saxophonists playing improvised fusion. In the 80s he co-led **Quest**, and is today very active in jazz education. His recent output has been extraordinary, over a dozen albums so far this decade, including the smooth (by his standards) *Setting The Standard*.
● ALBUMS: *Doin' It Again* (Timeless 1980),★★★ *If They Only Knew* (Timeless 1980)★★★★, *Pendulum* (Artists House 1981)★★★, *Quest* (1981)★★★, *Opal Heart* (Enja 1982)★★★, *Spirit Renewed* (Owl 1983)★★★, *The Loneliness Of The Long Distance Runner* (CMP 1985)★★, *One Of A Kind* (Core 1985)★★★★, *Double Edge* (Storyville 1985)★★★, *Homage To John Coltrane* (Owl 1987)★★, *Quest II* (Storyville 1987)★★★, *Trio + One* (Owl 1989)★★★, *The Tree* (Soul Note 1990)★★★, *Time Line* (Owl 1990)★★★, *Chant* (CMP 1990)★★★★, *Nine Again* (Red 1990)★★, *The Blessing Of The Old Long Sound* (Neuva 1991)★★★, *Dedications* (CMP 1991)★★★, *First Visit* (West Wind 1991)★★, *West Side Story* (Today) (Owl 1991)★★, *Classic Ballads* (Candid 1992)★★★, *Classique* (Owl 1992)★★★, *Joy* (Candid 1993)★★★, *Setting The Standard* (Red 1993)★★★.

Liebrand, Ben

b. The Netherlands. A well-known Dutch house remixer (though he claims his work is more geared to genuine cover versions because of the re-recording process he embarks on), Liebrand recorded in his own right in the 90s with 'Eve Of The War' and 'Black Belly'. His remixes include high-profile work for **Phil Collins** and **Hot Chocolate**. Within a more conventional dance format he also produced the Crystal Palace featuring CP's 'Son Of Godzilla'. His solo album featured British vocalist Carol Kenyon (of **Heaven 17**'s 'Temptation' fame) and rapper Toni Scott. 'I've always enjoyed being a bit in the background', he maintained. His chart successes include **Jeff Lynne**'s 'Eve Of The War', **Bill Withers**' 'Lovely Day', Phil Collins' 'In The Air Tonight', **Vangelis**'s 'Puls(t)ar' and the Ram Jam Band's 'Black Berry'. All were created originally for his own radio show on Radio Veronica in Holland.

Liege And Lief - Fairport Convention

Where so much began. The advertisements ran: 'the first (literally) British folk rock LP ever.' It also represented a catharsis for the band, reconvening after a traumatic road accident that killed drummer Martin Lamble. Once again focused and with redoubtable folk fiddler **Dave Swarbrick** now permanently involved, they threw themselves into the electrification of ballads, myths and rollickin' jigs. The results were both innovative and stimulating. The union was blessed. If you sat down and tried to imagine a dream folk rock band, it still would not match the potential here. From the lusting pace of 'Matty Groves' to the tender cooing of 'Crazy Man Michael', **Sandy Denny**'s voice is the perfect vehicle for this milestone. Imitated a thousand times, but never equalled.

● Tracks: *Come All Ye; Reynardine; Matty Groves; Farewell Farewell; The Deserter; The Lark In The Morning; Tamlin; Crazy Man Michael; Rakish Paddy; Foxhunters Jigs; Toss The Feathers.*

● First released 1970

● UK peak chart position: 17

● USA peak chart position: did not chart

Lien, Annbjorg

b. *c.*1970, Alesund, Norway. Fiddler Annbjorg Lien first recorded at the age of 12, but made her greatest impact at the age of 18 with the release of her 1988 collaboration with arranger Helge Forde. *Annbjorg* saw Lien meld her traditional playing of the hardingfele (Handanger fiddle), conventional fiddle and nyckelharpa in a variety of settings - including jazz, rock and classical, with accompanying musicians drawn from each genre. It sold well in Norway but attracted some criticism for overstepping geographical boundaries (most Norwegian fiddlers concentrate on the individual traditions of the valley or area they were born in). As Lien elaborated: 'People don't go around so much, so we have Setesdal, Telemark, the west coast and the north, each with a different way of playing; the dynamic is very different.' She is additionally a member of Bukkene Bruse, a trio featuring singer and fiddle player Arve Moen Bergset and flute/strings musician Steinar Ofsdal, who in 1994 were sponsored by the Winter Olympics committee and also collaborated with a bluegrass group from Atlanta, with whom they toured the USA. In 1994 Lien began performing as a duo with Shetland fiddler Catriona MacDonald, touring the UK, before beginning sessions on a second solo album. *Felefeber* duly featured Roger Tallroth on guitar, octave mandolin and bass balalaika, Ofsdal on flute and Iver Kleive on church organ, but the main spotlight fell on

Lien herself. Comprising traditional and self-written material, the relaxed timbre of her voice was well matched with Celtic as well as Nordic influences, resulting in an affecting, understated album. Energetic and fluent, 1997's *Prisme* was predominantly self-composed and Lien's best album to date.

● ALBUMS: *Annbjorg* (Kirkelig Kulturverksted 1988)★★★, with Bukkene Bruse *Bukkene Bruse* (Grappa 1994)★★★★, *Felefeber* (Grappa 1994)★★★, with Bruse *Åre* (Grappa 1995)★★★, *Prisme* (Grappa 1997)★★★.

Lieutenant Pigeon

From Coventry, England, this 'novelty' group evolved from the minor local band, Stavely Makepiece. Lieutenant Pigeon's line-up comprised Robert Woodward (piano), Stephen Johnson (bass) and Nigel Fletcher (drums). Their single, 'Mouldy Old Dough', an instrumental occasionally punctuated by the deadpan refrain of the title, was issued in January 1972. It was revived the following autumn and topped the UK charts for four weeks. The single had actually been recorded in Woodward's front room and featured his 60-year-old mother, Hilda, on piano. Although strong candidates for one-hit-wonder status, the group managed one more UK Top 20 hit, 'Desperate Dan'. An attempt to incorporate disco music on 'And The Fun Goes On' failed to reach the charts and afterwards Lieutenant Pigeon returned to obscurity as a genuine chart curio, at least in the UK. However, the group enjoyed further success abroad, with 1974's 'I'll Take You Home' becoming their third Australian number 1 single. The group finally broke up in 1978, with Fletcher joining two unsuccessful groups, Tasty and Oakie. He subsequently worked for British Rail before reuniting with former bandmate Steve Johnson (also of Tasty) on his Mediatrax documentary video production unit. Johnson also recorded as Class 50, while Woodward still works on freelance studio projects.

● ALBUMS: *Mouldy Old Music* (Decca 1973)★★, *Pigeon Pie* (Decca 1974)★, *Pigeon Party* (Decca 1974)★.

● COMPILATIONS: *Mouldy Old Dough* (Emporio 1998)★★.

Lieutenant Stitchie

b. Cleveland Laing, 29 September 1962, Spanish Town, Jamaica, West Indies. In 1979 the young Stitchie was a singer, eventually joining the Django **sound system** as the DJ Ranking Noseworthy in 1983, while still working as a biology teacher in a Spanish Town school. Within two years he had graduated from City Lights Disco and Lightning Super Mix to **Stereo One**, adapting the name Citchie from his love of citrus fruit. His first tune was 'If I Don't Care' for Nonsul as Ranking Citrus. By his second ('Two Is Better Than Too Many'), he was Stitchie thanks to a label misspelling. Hits for Stereo One ('Nice Girl', 'Story Time' and 'Natty Dread') followed before he visited **King Jammy** in 1986. Immediately, his perfectly observed and humorous lyrics caught the popular imagination, with 'Wear Yuh Size' and 'Broad Hips' attaining instant success. In 1987 he was voted DJ Of The Year in Jamaica and celebrated with a debut album, *Great Ambition*. **Atlantic** signed him in 1988, releasing *The Governor* album but failing to retain his **dancehall** audience with the next (*Wild Jamaican Romances*). In 1993 he returned to the Kingston studios eager to recapture lost ground, recording a spate of local hits for Danny Browne, **Penthouse**, **Digital B**, King Jammy's ('Hot Like The Sun'), Shocking Vibes ('Bun It Down'), Carib ('Bandy Leg'), John John and his own Drum And Bass label, on which he produced emergent talents such as the late **Pan Head**. His third Atlantic album, *Rude Boy*, was released that year and he made successful tours of both Europe and America. Always entertaining on stage or record, he is currently enjoying his most popular spell since his 1987 heyday.

● ALBUMS: *Great Ambition* (King Jammys 1987)★★★, *The Governor* (Atlantic 1989)★★, *Wild Jamaican Romances* (Atlantic 1991)★★, *Rude Boy* (Atlantic 1993)★★★, with Beenie Man, Mad Cobra *Mad Cobra Meets Lt Stitchie And Beenie Man* (VP 1995)★★★★.

Life - Inspiral Carpets

The **Inspiral Carpets** emerged from Manchester's rave/club scene alongside the **Stone Roses** and **Happy Mondays**. Each of these groups fused a dance groove to 60s-styled pop, the Inspiral's brand of psychedelia fashioned by Clint Boon's Vox-styled organ work. Taking inspiration from garage bands and the **Doors**, he added a distinctive flourish to the band's grasp of simple, commercial melodies. *Life* is the unit's first full-length album, following three EPs and a selection drawn from **John Peel** sessions. It captures their enthusiastic slant on a genre briefly in vogue, and one to which they brought humour and a refreshing eclecticism.

● Tracks: *Real Thing; Song For A Family; This Is How It Feels; Directing Traffik; Besides Me; Many Happy Returns; Memories Of You; She Comes In The Fall; Monkey On My Back; Sun Don't Shine; Inside My Head; Move; Sackville*.

● First released 1990

● UK peak chart position: 2

● USA peak chart position: did not chart

Life After Death - The Notorious B.I.G.

Fabulous arrangements, thoughtful samples and production by **Sean 'Puffy' Combs** make this ambitious double CD easy on the ear. **Notorious B.I.G.** had a hip-hop voice that never grated; in fact, he had the ability to lapse into smooth soul so easily, he could have been **Luther Vandross**. Rap has come a long way since the angry shouters, and this takes the genre to a peak of perfection; listeners who feel that rap is not for them should start with this as a sampler. The sermonizing is there, and much of it is relevant, but there is so much cool soul that the record is easy on the ear. Tragically, in the light of his later murder, B.I.G. posed for the album cover standing beside a hearse.

● Tracks: *Life After Death Intro; Somebody's Gotta Die; Hypnotize; Kick In The Door; !@ You Tonight; Last Day; I Love*

The Dough; What's Beef; B.I.G. Interlude; Mo Money Mo Problems; Niggas Bleed; I Got A Story To Tell; Notorious Thugs; Miss U; Another; Going Back To Cali; Ten Crack Commandments; Playa Hater; Nasty Boy; Sky's The Limit; The World Is Filled; My Downfall; Long Kiss Goodnight; You're Nobody (Til Somebody Kills You).

● First released 1997

● UK peak chart position: 23

● USA peak chart position: 1

Life And Times

This English duo features Graeme Meek (b. 7 September 1954, Luton, Bedfordshire, England; guitar/vocals), and Barry Goodman (b. 3 December 1950, Sutton, Surrey, England; melodeon/vocals). Life And Times were formed in 1983, and originally included Gregg Lindsay (flute). Meek had earlier been working in various rock bands, including one from his schooldays which included singer **Paul Young**. Subsequently, Meek worked as one half of a duo called Midas with Debra Arthurs, from 1977-80, playing folk clubs and festivals. The duo only recorded one single, in 1977. Meanwhile, Goodman had spent four years in folk duo Mead, with Steve Rackstraw, then Vermin with Gadfan Edwards, and later Gregg Lindsay, as well as solo work. Luton Museum and Art Gallery published *Strawplait And Bonelace* in 1983, and the following year, the Eastern Arts Association agreed to help fund Life And Time's recording of the songbook. *Strawplait And Bonelace,* was eventually released on Fellside Records, and featured song and music of Bedfordshire life over the past 200 years. During 1986, *Shropshire Iron* was made into a radio documentary and broadcast by local radio stations around the UK, and during the following year the duo represented Bedfordshire at the English Folk Dance And Song Society National Gathering in London. *Shropshire Iron*, featuring songs and music of the early industrial revolution, was also released on Fellside. From 1985, until February 1991, Meek also presented *Three Counties Folk* on BBC Radio Bedfordshire. The duo continue to play festivals and clubs, sometimes in the guise of dance band Time Of Your Life, with Brian Scowcroft (caller/bass), but currently no recordings are imminent.

● ALBUMS: *Strawplait And Bonelace* (1985)★★★, *Shropshire Iron* (1989)★★★★.

Life Begins At 8:40

One of the outstanding revues of the 30s, *Life Begins At 8:40* opened at the Winter Garden Theatre in New York on 27 August 1934. There was high quality throughout, in every department. The backstage team included directors Philip Loeb and John Murray Anderson who was renowned for his work on several editions of the **Greenwich Village Follies**, and his own John Murray Anderson's Almanac, and much else; the sketches were mainly written by David Freedman, and the songs provided by the classy trio of **Harold Arlen** (music) with **Ira Gershwin** and **E.Y. 'Yip' Harburg** (lyrics).

They included 'Let's Take A Walk Around The Block', 'What Can You Say In A Love Song?', 'Things', 'Fun To Be Fooled', 'Shoein' the Mare', 'I Couldn't Hold My Man', and 'You're A Builder-Upper', which had some success via recordings by Leo Reisman (with Arlen), Henry King, and Glen Gray. Two of America's funniest song-and-dance men, Bert Lahr and **Ray Bolger**, led the cast, which included Luella Gear, Frances Williams, Dixie Dunbar, Earl Oxford, and Brian Donlevy, the Irish-American actor who went on to become one of Hollywood's top tough guys. The combination of good songs and a series of sometimes hilarious sketches ensured a decent run of 237 performances.

Life Of Agony

Formed in Brooklyn, New York, USA, this quartet was formed in 1989 by Alan Robert Goldstein (b. *c.*1972; bass, vocals) and cousins Keith Caputo (b. *c.*1974; vocals, keyboards) and Joseph Zampella (b. *c.*1972; guitar, vocals), otherwise known as Joey Z. They initially recruited Sal Abruscato on drums, but he was later replaced by Daniel Joseph Richardson (b. *c.*1969). Together, they began Life Of Agony as a simple hardcore act, propelled by flaring nostrils and flying sweat, until diminutive lead singer Caputo had singing lessons from vocal coach Don Lawrence (who had previously worked with **Mick Jagger**, Sebastian Bach from **Skid Row** and **Jon Bon Jovi**). The result was a much greater level of dexterity employed in both songwriting and execution by the band, with Goldstein operating as chief lyricist behind Caputo's powerful delivery. Playing on the road in support of **Agnostic Front**, **Biohazard**, **Fear Factory**, **Motörhead**, **Corrosion Of Conformity** and **Obituary**, their debut set for Roadrunner Records represented a conscious attempt to appeal to fans of more melodic metal (comparisons with **Stone Temple Pilots** were a feature of the critical response). Their second album was released in October 1995, an 11-track selection produced by Steve Thompson. Following the release of their third album, Life Of Agony abandoned plans for a tour of the UK and Europe in autumn 1997, as vocalist Caputo was 'suffering from mental exhaustion and fatigue'. Caputo later announced that he was leaving the band permanently; he was replaced by former **Ugly Kid Joe** vocalist Whitfield Crane.
● ALBUMS: *River Runs Red* (Roadrunner 1994)★★★, *Ugly* (Roadrunner 1995)★★★, *Soul Searching Sun* (Roadrunner 1997)★★★.

Life's Too Good - The Sugarcubes

The album with an exclamation mark for a spine gave more credence to Icelandic music in a moment than all the unfortunate musical history that had gone before. Fronted by the now near-legendary **Björk**, and befuddled as a band by the whole thing, they were highly inconsistent. They once wandered on to the Astoria stage a full two hours late, Björk taking a bite from an apple before telling the audience to stop complaining.

Their droll logic endured in this musical cavalcade of wonder and high jinks, and if it was not for Björk's *Debut*, they would still be sorely missed.
● Tracks: *Traitor; Motorcrash; Birthday; Delicious Demon; Mama; Coldsweat; Blue Eyed Pop; Deus; Sick For Toys; F***ing In Rhythm And Sorrow.*
● First released 1988
● UK peak chart position: 14
● USA peak chart position: 54

Life, Sex And Death

This trio was formed in Los Angeles, USA, during 1991 by demented vocalist and ex-Chicago street hobo Stanley. LSD, as they are often known, are completed by drummer Brian Michael Horak and ex-**Enuff Z'Nuff** guitarist Alex Kane. Signing to **Warner Brothers**, they debuted in July 1992 with *The Silent Majority*, which met with a mixed reception. Influences as diverse as **Cheap Trick**, **Sex Pistols**, **Beatles** and **Guns N'Roses** manifested themselves clearly, but Stanley's rasping yet inherently melodic vocal style gave the band some identity. LSD were certain to earn a degree of notoriety with their provocative album cover and Stanley's outrageous claim to not having washed for over a year, but their critical reception was hardly gleaming either.
● ALBUMS: *The Silent Majority* (Warners 1992)★★.

Life, The

Having been workshopped almost seven years previously, announced for Broadway on several occasions, and had more than half its score performed on a concept album by a wide variety of artists, *The Life* finally surfaced at the Ethel Barrymore Theatre on 26 April 1997. It was set in the pre-AIDS awareness late 70s, in and around 42nd Street, when that whole area of New York had become a neon-lit haven of porn parlours, whores and pimps. This is the *milieu* of *The Life*, where hooker Queen (Pamela Isaacs) works flat out (literally) in order to service the drug habit of her husband (and pimp) Fleetwood (Kevin Ramsey). Fleetwood is attempting to block out the memories of his time in Vietnam, but the arrival in town of pretty, fresh-faced blonde Mary (Bellamy Young) also provides some relief from those horrors. After he has given Mary the benefit of his personal attention, Queen, consoled by her best friend, the ageing prostitute Sonja (Lillias White), jumps ship and lands up with Memphis (Chuck Cooper), the nastiest pimp of them all. Mary, on the other hand, turns out to be a surprisingly shrewd, hard-headed career woman, intent on a Hollywood career as a porn star, by way of go-go dancing. Also involved in this compelling mixture of sleaze, violence and incongruity ('The Hookers' Ball', for example) were Carmen (Lynn Sterling), Chichi (Sharon Wilkins), Frenchie (Katy Grenfell), Tracy (Judine Richard), Bobby (Mark Bove), Oddjob (Michael Gregory Gong), Silky (Rudy Roberson), Slick (Mark Anthony Taylor), April (Felicia Finlay), Snickers (Gordon Joseph Weiss), Lacy (Vernel Bagneris), Lou

(Rich Herbert) and Doll House Dancer (Stephanie Michels). It was written by **David Newman**, Ira Gasman, and **Cy Coleman**, and augmented by a melodic, jazzy, dynamic score, composed by Coleman (music) and Gasman (lyrics), which lifted the piece out of the gutter into a world of sheer entertainment. As well as Sonja's hilarious 'The Oldest Profession', there were numerous other highlights in a fine set of songs that included 'Check It Out!', 'Use What You Got', 'A Lovely Day To Be Out Of Jail', 'A Piece Of The Action', 'Don't Take Much', 'Go Home', 'You Can't Get To Heaven', 'My Body', 'Why Don't They Leave Us Alone', 'Easy Money', 'He's No Good', 'Was That A Smile', 'I'm Leaving You', 'Step Right Up', 'Mr. Greed', 'My Way Or The Highway', 'People Magazine', 'We Had A Dream', 'Someday Is For Suckers', 'My Friend', and 'We Gotta Go'. The director was Michael Blakemore, choreographer Joey McKneely, and set designer Robin Wagner. *The Life* won **Tony Awards** for featured actor (Chuck Cooper) and featured actress (Lillias White), and was voted best musical in the Drama Desk, Outer Critics Circle and Drama League awards. The aforementioned concept album featured artists such as **Liza Minnelli, Jennifer Holliday, Jack Jones, Lou Rawls** and **Billy Preston**, as well as comedian George Burns in his final recording.

Lifers Group

A rap troupe culled from the bowels of the US criminal underworld, namely Rahway State Pennitentiary in East Jersey. Put together by the thinking of inmate 660604 (Maxwell Melvins), this was an intriguing project that gathered together the incarcerated 'lifers' to discourage those who still had their freedom from living the gangsta rap lifestyle to the full. The nightmare vision of prison life was revealed in intimate, gory detail on tracks like 'The Real Deal', while the cover rammed home the message with pictures of the criminals and the cells they were forced to occupy. The set was recorded in three months after the Disney-funded Hollywood Basic Records, ever sensitive to a good cause, had heard of the scheme.
● ALBUMS: *Belly Of The Beast* (Hollywood Basic 1991)★★.

Lifes Rich Pageant - R.E.M.

For the first time in four albums, Michael Stipe evidently wanted the 'happy throngs' of listeners to hear and absorb his lyrics. On *Lifes Rich Pageant*, the band confidently tackled political and environmental issues, a direction more fully explored on the later *Document* and *Green*. Defiant and celebratory returns to their punk influences ('Just A Touch', 'These Days') were balanced by laments about US environmental policy and the folk tradition of the American South ('Swan Swan H'). Mills' and Berry's harmonies shone through, particularly on 'Fall On Me', still one of the best songs in the vast R.E.M. catalogue. A curiously sensitive and affecting album, packed with crafted pop songs, it marked a watershed for a group on the brink of unimagined worldwide success.
● Tracks: *Begin The Begin; These Days; Fall On Me; Cuyahoga; Hyena; Underneath The Bunker; The Flowers Of Guatemala; I Believe; What If We Give It Away?; Just A Touch; Swan Swan H; Superman.*
● First released 1986
● UK peak chart position: 43
● USA peak chart position: 21

Lifetime

Led by former **Miles Davis** drummer **Tony Williams** and named after his 1965 solo debut, the Lifetime appellation has been used and abandoned at the whim of its creator. It was first applied with reference to a group on the pulsating *Emergency*, but is best recalled for the exciting jazz-rock quartet formed in 1970. Here Williams was joined by guitarist **John McLaughlin**, keyboard player **Larry Young** and former **Cream** bassist **Jack Bruce** in what was, potentially, one of the genre's most impressive line-ups. *Turn It Over* showcased its loud, dexterous talents, but personality clashes doomed the group to a premature end. Bruce resumed his solo career and while Young joined McLaughlin for the latter's propulsive *Devotion*, Williams forged a less intensive musical path. In 1976, the drummer resurrected the Lifetime name for *Believe It*, but the new unit lacked the purpose and commitment of its predecessor.
● ALBUMS: as Lifetime *Emergency* (1969)★★★★, *One Word/Two Worlds* (Polydor 1970)★★★, *Turn It Over* (1970)★★, *Ego* (Polydor 1971)★★.
● COMPILATIONS: *Lifetime* (1975)★★★. As Tony Williams' New Lifetime *Believe It* (1976)★★★, *Million Dollar Legs* (1976)★★.

Ligabue

b. Italy. Rated as his country's most pre-eminent contemporary mainstream rock artist, the gravel-voiced Ligabue has become a fixture of Italian charts and magazine covers since beginning his career in the 80s. *Buon Compleanno Elvis* (*Happy Birthday Elvis*) was a collection of songs inspired by **Elvis Presley**'s 60th Birthday celebrations, and dedicated to him. After the album was released it quickly amassed sales figures of over 500,000 copies (equivalent to quadruple platinum status in Italy). It was voted Album Of The Year by the radio network Radio Deejay and readers of the country's most successful music magazine, *Musica!* Typical of its contents was the hugely successful romantic ballad 'Certi Notti' ('Certain Nights'), where any notion of art was swamped by sentiment.
● ALBUMS: *Buon Compleanno Elvis* (WEA 1995)★★★.

Liggins, Jimmy

b. 14 October 1922, Newby, Oklahoma, USA, d. 18 July 1983, Durham, North Carolina, USA. Starting out as a disc jockey and boxer before becoming the driver for his brother Joe's band, the Honeydrippers, Jimmy Liggins taught himself guitar and formed his own band in 1947. Signing for Art Rupe's **Specialty** label, he immediately had major hits with 'I Can't Stop It', 'Cadillac Boogie' and, notably, 'Teardrop Blues'. Following a serious accident in 1948 when he was shot in the mouth, he continued with big sellers for **Specialty Records**, including his most successful release, 1953's 'Drunk'. Like Joe, he left Specialty in 1954, and recorded for Aladdin, before becoming a record distributor and forming his own Duplex Records which survived on few releases from 1958-78, financed from a diverse musical business, ranging from teach-yourself-piano charts to artist management.

● ALBUMS: including with Joe Liggins *Saturday Night Boogie Woogie Man* (1974)★★★, *I Can't Stop It* (1981)★★★, *Jimmy Liggins & His Drops Of Joy* (Ace 1989)★★★, *Vol. 2: Rough Weather Blues* (1993)★★★.

Liggins, Joe

b. 9 July 1916, Guthrie, Oklahoma, USA, d. 26 July 1987, Los Angeles, California, USA. After attempting to learn various brass instruments, Joe Liggins settled down to study musical composition and piano arrangement. After moving to California, he began writing for and playing with local bands, graduating in the 40s to the respected units of Cee Pee Johnson and Sammy Franklin; he was working with the latter when, in 1945, he left to form his own group, the Honeydrippers. Joe Liggins And His Honeydrippers first recorded for Exclusive, with whom they had 10 hits between 1945 and 1949 - including the huge crossover hits 'The Honeydripper' and 'I've Got A Right To Cry'; he followed his brother Jimmy to **Specialty Records** in 1950 where the hits continued with 'Rag Mop' and the hugely successful 'Pink Champagne' (**Billboard**'s number 1 blues record of the year). Leaving Specialty in 1954, Liggins went briefly to **Mercury** (1954) and **Aladdin Records** (1956) before returning to Mercury to record an album in 1962. Later singles appeared on tiny independents such as his own Honeydripper label and Jimmy Liggins' Duplex Records, and he was enjoying something of a renaissance at the time of his death in 1987.

● ALBUMS: *Honeydripper* (Mercury 1962)★★★★, *Great R&B Oldies* (1972)★★★, with Jimmy Liggins *Saturday Night Boogie Woogie Man* (Sonet 1974)★★★.

● COMPILATIONS: *Darktown Strutters' Ball* (Jukebox Lil 1981)★★★, *The Honeydripper* (Jukebox Lil 1988)★★★, *Joe Liggins & The Honeydrippers* (Ace 1989)★★★★, *Vol. 2: Drippers Boogie* (Ace 1993)★★★★.

Light Crust Doughboys

A western swing group that originally featured **Bob Wills** (fiddle), Herman Arnspiger (guitar) and Milton Brown (vocals), who were then performing as the Aladdin Laddies (sponsored by the Aladdin Mantle Lamp Company) on WBAP Fort Worth, Texas. When Burrus Mill and Elevator Company, the makers of Light Crust flour, sponsored a show on KFJZ in 1931, their general manager Wilbert Lee O'Daniel decided to use them for his show. During their first broadcast for the

new sponsors, after originally being named the Fort Worth Doughboys, the station announcer referred to them as the Light Crust Doughboys. The public wrote in for more, although the group did not get paid. O'Daniel actually sacked them two weeks later, claiming to dislike 'their hillbilly music'. The station continued to use them without a sponsor and O'Daniel relented, later appearing on the programme himself. Arnspiger had left (being replaced by Sleepy Johnson) and Brown's brother Durwood had joined, when the group made their first recordings for Victor on 9 February 1932. In 1932, Milton Brown left to follow a very successful career with his own swing band, the Musical Brownies, until his untimely death in a car crash in 1936. In 1933, Wills, after an acrimonious association with O'Daniel, left to form his famed Texas Playboys. The Doughboys, although undergoing many changes of personnel, remained with Burrus Mills until 1942 and made many popular recordings. After a short spell as the Coffee Grinders (due to sponsorship by Duncan Coffee) and without Burrus Mill's sponsorship, they once again became the Light Crust Doughboys. Throughout the 50s and 60s, they worked on radio and television, played live shows and recorded for several labels, but never managed to recapture their original popularity.

● ALBUMS: *The Light Crust Doughboys* (Audio Lab 1959)★★★.

● COMPILATIONS: *String Band Swing Volumes 1 & 2* (Longhorn 1981)★★★, *We're The Light Crust Doughboys From Burrus Mills*, *The Light Crust Doughboys Original Hit Songs*, *The Light Crust Doughboys 1936-1939* (Texas Rose 1982)★★★, *Live 1936* (Jambalaya 1990)★★★.

Light Of The World

Pioneering Brit funk band Light Of The World were formed in London in 1978, the original line-up comprising Jean Paul 'Bluey' Maunick (guitar), Neville 'Breeze' McKreith (guitar), Everton McCalla (drums), Chris Etienne (percussion), Paul 'Tubs' Williams (bass), Peter Hinds (keyboards), Canute Wellington (trumpet) and David 'Baps' Baptiste (trumpet). Taking their name from a **Kool And The Gang** album, they signed to Ensign Records in 1979, achieving an immediate dancefloor hit with their debut single 'Swingin''. The release of their self-titled debut album was marred by the death of Etienne during a promotional tour. Nigel Martinez, Nat Augustin and Ganitu 'Gee' Bello were added to the line-up for *Round Trip* (produced by Augie Johnson), but following further minor hits the band split up in 1981. Wellington, Baptiste and McKreith became Beggar & Co., while Maunick, Hinds and Williams formed Incognito. There was a brief Light Of The World reunion when Augustin, Bello and Tubs collaborated on an album for **EMI** in 1982. Hinds went on to become a respected R&B/soul producer, including work with the **Chimes**. Light Of The World reformed in 1990, recording for **Chrysalis Records**.

● ALBUMS: *Light Of The World* (Ensign 1979)★★★, *Round*

Trip (Ensign 1980)★★★, *Check Us Out* (EMI 1982)★★.
● COMPILATIONS: *Best Of Light Of The World* (Ensign 1985)★★★.

Light, Enoch

b. 1907, Canton, Ohio, USA, d. 31 July 1978, New York, USA. Tagged Enoch Light And His Light Brigade, Light's dance band recorded a number of original compositions for Bluebird, Vocalion and **RCA Records** during their lifetime. These included 'Rio Junction', 'The Daddy Of Them All', 'Big Band Bossa', 'Private Eye Suite', 'Cinderella' and 'Daniel Boone', as well as their theme tune, 'You Are My Lucky Star'. Many of these were novelty affairs themed after popular characters and occupations of the day, but all were performed with skill and verve. Light had originally attended Johns Hopkins University before establishing the band in the late 20s, with the intention of playing the hotel and ballroom circuit with their sweet, highly commercial music. In the early 30s the band toured Europe, before returning to the US for dates at the Taft Hotel in New York. Light also enjoyed enormous popularity on radio during this period. The early 40s saw the Light Brigade switch direction to swing, shortly before their leader retired from bandleading to concentrate on a career as a producer and conductor. Many of these recordings were revisions of staples of the big band era.

Lightfoot, Alexander 'Papa George'

b. 2 March 1924, Natchez, Mississippi, USA, d. 28 November 1971, Natchez, Mississippi, USA. A self-taught harmonica player, Papa Lightfoot first recorded in 1949 for Peacock Records as part of the Gondoliers vocal group. He had a sporadic recording career in New Orleans in the early 50s (and accompanied **Champion Jack Dupree** on the King label). The majority of his 50s recordings remained unreleased until Bob Hite, famed blues collector and lead singer with **Canned Heat**, persuaded **Liberty Records** to issue them in their 1968 *Legendary Masters* series. This resulted in Lightfoot being rediscovered in 1969 and recording for the Los Angeles-based Vault Records. He was unable to capitalize on this new-found fame: the following year he fell ill and in 1971 died from a heart attack in his home-town.
● ALBUMS: *Natchez Trace* (Vault 1969)★★★.
● COMPILATIONS: *Goin' Back To The Natchez Trace* (Ace 1995)★★★.

Lightfoot, Gordon

b. 17 November 1938, Orillia, Ontario, Canada. Lightfoot moved to Los Angeles during the 50s where he studied at Hollywood's Westlake College of Music. Having pursued a short-lived career composing jingles for television, the singer began recording demos of his own compositions which, by 1960, owed a considerable debt to folk singers **Pete Seeger** and **Bob Gibson**. Lightfoot then returned to Canada and began performing in Toronto's Yorktown coffeehouses. His work was championed by several acts, notably **Ian And Sylvia**

and **Peter, Paul And Mary**. Both recorded the enduring 'Early Morning Rain', which has since become a standard, while the latter group also enjoyed a hit with his 'For Lovin' Me'. Other successful compositions included 'Ribbon Of Darkness', which **Marty Robbins** took to the top of the US country chart, while such renowned artists as **Bob Dylan**, **Johnny Cash**, **Elvis Presley** and **Jerry Lee Lewis** have all covered Lightfoot's songs. Having joined the **Albert Grossman** management stable, the singer made his debut in 1966 with the promising *Lightfoot*. *The Way I Feel* and *Did She Mention My Name* consolidated the artist's undoubted promise, but it was not until 1970 that he made a significant commercial breakthrough with *Sit Down Young Stranger*. Producer **Lenny Waronker** added an edge to Lightfoot's approach which reaped an immediate benefit with a US Top 5 hit, 'If You Could Read My Mind'. The album also included the first recording of **Kris Kristofferson**'s 'Me And Bobbie McGee'. A series of crafted albums enhanced his new-found position and in 1974 the singer secured a US number 1 with the excellent 'Sundown'. Two years later 'The Wreck Of The Edmund Fitzgerald' peaked at number 2, but although Lightfoot continued to record mature singer-songwriter-styled material, his increasing reliance on safer, easy-listening perspectives proved unattractive to a changing rock audience. He nonetheless retains the respect of his contemporaries, although, recording infrequently, his profile has lessened quite considerably during the 80s and 90s.
● ALBUMS: *Lightfoot* (United Artists 1966)★★★, *Early Lightfoot* (United Artists 1966)★★★, *The Way I Feel* (United Artists 1967)★★★, *Did She Mention My Name* (United Artists 1968)★★★, *Back Here On Earth* (United Artists 1969)★★, *Sunday Concert* (United Artists 1969)★★★, *Sit Down Young Stranger* aka *If You Could Read My Mind* (Reprise 1970)★★★★, *Summer Side Of Life* (Reprise 1971)★★, *Don Quixote* (Reprise 1972)★★★, *Old Dan's Records* (Reprise 1972)★★, *Sundown* (Reprise 1974)★★★, *Cold On The Shoulder* (Reprise 1975)★★, *Summertime Dream* (Reprise 1976)★★★, *Endless Wire* (Warners 1978)★★, *Dream Street Rose* (Warners 1980)★★, *Shadows* (Warners 1982)★★, *Salute* (Warners 1983)★★★, *East Of Midnight* (Warners 1986)★★★, *Waiting For You* (1993)★★★.
● COMPILATIONS: *The Very Best Of Gordon Lightfoot* (United Artists 1974)★★★, *Gord's Gold* (Reprise 1975)★★★, *The Best Of Gordon Lightfoot* (Warners 1981)★★★, *Gord's Gold, Volume 2* (Warners 1988)★★.
● FURTHER READING: *Gordon Lightfoot*, Alfrieda Gabiou. *If You Could Read My Mind*, Maynard Collins.

Lightfoot, Terry

b. 21 May 1935, Potters Bar, Middlesex, England. Lightfoot made his first appearance on the UK jazz scene as a clarinettist in the early 50s. After leading his own band throughout the 50s, he maintained a band into the next decade, having established a reputation strong enough to shrug off the decline in popularity of his brand of music. During the trad boom of the early

60s he appeared in the film *It's Trad Dad*. Apart from a brief spell in **Kenny Ball**'s band he continued to lead into the 70s only stepping sideways into hotel management towards the end of the decade. He continued to play however, and by the mid-80s was back in full-time music. Amongst the most polished of British traditional clarinettists, Lightfoot achieved and maintained high standards of performance not only from himself but also from the many fine musicians he employed over the years.

● ALBUMS: *Jazz Gumbo Volume 1* (Nixa 1956)★★★★, *Tradition In Colour* (Columbia 1958)★★★★, *Trad Parade* (Columbia 1961)★★★, *King Kong* (1961)★★★, *Lightfoot At Lansdowne* (Columbia 1962)★★★★, *Alleycat* (Columbia 1965)★★★, *Personal Appearance* (1975)★★★, *Terry Lightfoot In Concert* (Black Lion 1979)★★, *Clear Round* (Plant Life 1981)★★★, *As Time Goes By* (PRT 1986)★★★, *At The Jazzband Ball* (Bold Reprive 1988)★★, *Stardust* (Upbeat 1990)★★★, *New Orleans Jazzmen* (Hanover 1990)★★★, *When The Saints* (See For Miles 1991)★★★★.

Lighthouse

Lighthouse was formed in the USA by Skip Prokop, one-time drummer in the **Paupers**, a respected Canadian rock band. His subsequent association with the **Al Kooper/Mike Bloomfield** *Super Session* project secured Prokop's reputation and inspired the inception of this new group. Lighthouse also featured guitarist Ralph Cole, a veteran of several Michigan-based units, and an ambitious string and horn section. Initially compared favourably with **Chicago**, a series of personnel changes undermined what potential Lighthouse offered and consequently later albums lacked direction. Al Wilmot, the one-time bassist with **SRC**, joined the act towards the close of its career, but the group had folded by the end of 70s.

● ALBUMS: *Lighthouse* (1969)★★, *Peacing It All Together* (RCA 1970)★★★, *Suite Feeling* (RCA 1970)★★★, *One Fine Morning* (Evolution/Vertigo 1971)★★★, *Thoughts Of Moving On* (Evolution/Vertigo 1972)★★, *Live* (Evolution 1972)★★, *Sunny Days* (Evolution 1972)★★, *Can Feel It* (1974)★★, *Good Day* (1974)★★.

Solo: Skip Prokop *All Growed Up* (1977)★★.

Lighthouse Family

UK soul band the Lighthouse Family consists of the Newcastle-based duo of Tunde Baiyewu (b. 1969), a vocalist of Nigerian descent, and London-born songwriter and musician Paul Tucker (b. 1969, England). They met while working at nightclub bars in the northeast of England, at which time Tucker was also recording his own compositions at home in his spare time. They formed a partnership in early 1993 after being introduced by a local soul DJ. After hearing a tape of the group's 'Ocean Drive' played down the phone, **Polydor Records** A&R director Colin Barlow recognized their potential, particularly in the mainstream album market, and signed them to a long-term development contract. Influenced by artists such as **Bob Marley**, **Stevie Wonder** and **Marvin Gaye**, the duo made their debut in June 1995 with 'Lifted', which entered the lower reaches of the UK chart. This, like their debut album, was produced by Mike Peden, formerly of UK soul band the **Chimes** and producer for **Shara Nelson** and **Darryl Hall**. 'Ocean Drive', also the title of the debut album, was placed on the soundtrack to the Richard E. Grant film *Jack And Sarah* before being released as their second single. Determined not to see a good song die, 'Lifted' was reissued in 1996 and this time caught the mood of the public by becoming a major hit. 'Goodbye Heartbreak' and 'Loving Every Minute' completed the duo's impressive run of hit singles. The 1997 follow-up, *Postcards From Heaven*, confirmed Lighthouse Family's status as one of Britain's biggest new bands, and featured the huge-selling singles 'Raincloud' and 'High'.

● ALBUMS: *Ocean Drive* (Polydor 1995)★★★★, *Postcards From Heaven* (Polydor 1997)★★★.

Lightnin' Slim

b. Otis Hicks, 13 March 1913, St. Louis, Missouri, USA, d. 27 July 1974, Detroit, Michigan, USA. It is as a Louisiana blues stylist that Hicks is best known, having settled in that state in his early teens. He learned guitar from his father and his brother, and made a name for himself on the Baton Rouge blues circuit during the 40s. In 1954, he recorded for **J.D. 'Jay' Miller**'s Feature label, and began that producer's long and fruitful relationship with the blues. These early recordings had a tough, spare sound that helps to place them alongside the very finest down-home blues of the 50s, and the quality was largely maintained over much of the next decade, with many singles leased to Excello Records. His partnership with harmonica player **Lazy Lester** was particularly effective and releases such as 'Mean Old Lonesome Train', 'Hoodoo Blues' and, especially, 'Rooster Blues', provided him with commercial success and kept him in demand for tours both locally and further afield. Many of his releases demonstrate his particular facility for taking raw material from the work of other popular bluesmen, such as **Muddy Waters** and **Lightnin' Hopkins**, and turning it into something entirely his own. The relationship with Miller finally came to an end in 1965, but within a few years, Slim found a wider forum for his music when he became a regular visitor to Europe.

● ALBUMS: *Rooster Blues* (Excello 1960)★★★★, *Lightnin' Slim's Bell Ringer* (Excello 1965)★★★★, *High And Lowdown* (Excello 1971)★★★, *Over Easy* (Excello 1971)★★.

● COMPILATIONS: *The Early Years* (1976)★★★, *London Gumbo* (Sonet 1978)★★, *The Feature Sides* (Flyright 1981)★★★, *We Gotta Rock Tonight* (Flyright 1986)★★★, *Blue Lightnin'* (Indigo 1992)★★★, *King Of The Swamp Blues* 1954 recording (Flyright 1992)★★★, *It's Mighty Crazy* 1954-58 recordings (Ace 1995)★★★★, *Nothing But The Devil* (Ace 1996)★★★★, *Winter Time Blues* (Ace 1998)★★★★.

Lightning Seeds

Contrary to the multiples suggested by the moniker, Lightning Seeds was the brainchild of one man, **Ian Broudie** (b. 4 August 1958, Liverpool, England), who had gouged a significant niche in the Merseyside music scene during the 80s. Originally a member of **Big In Japan** - a forerunner of the likes of **Echo And The Bunnymen** and **Teardrop Explodes**, not to mention a breeding ground for future **Frankie Goes To Hollywood** singer **Holly Johnson** and drummer Budgie, who was later to join **Siouxsie And The Banshees** - Broudie eventually ended up playing in the Original Mirrors and developed an appetite for production work. His efforts on the first two Bunnymen albums acted as a springboard from which he was catapulted into the studio with numerous acts, including the **Fall**, **Wah!**, the **Icicle Works** and **Frazier Chorus**. On the creative front, Broudie collaborated with **Wild Swans** singer Paul Simpson under the name Care, releasing three immaculate singles and preparing the blueprint for his own pop-obsessed project. Thus, Lightning Seeds was born as an opportunity for Broudie to expand his own songwriting ideas. The project had an immediate impact when his first single, 'Pure', fuelled everyone's interest by virtue of being a deliberately low-key release, and went on to reach number 16 in the UK chart. *Cloudcuckooland* followed, encapsulating Broudie's notion of the perfect, sweet pop song, whereupon he put his producer's hat back on to work with contemporary bands such as **Northside**, the **Primitives**, **Frank And Walters**, **Alison Moyet** and **Sleeper**, among many others. He continued his work under the Lightning Seeds moniker in 1992 with *Sense*, another collection of perfect pop, but he would have to wait until 1994's *Jollification* for a further commercial breakthrough. This time he put together a full touring band, playing live for the first time since the Original Mirrors folded. The assembled line-up; Martin Campbell (bass, ex-**Rain**), Chris Sharrock (drums, ex-**Icicle Works**; **La's**) and Paul Hemmings (guitar, ex-La's) drew on his Liverpool connections, but Broudie remained very much the nucleus. In 1996, Broudie composed England's anthem for football's European championships, 'Three Lions' (recorded with comedians David Baddiel and Frank Skinner), which reached number 1 in the UK chart. Later in the year his songwriting reached a creative peak with the gloriously melodic *Dizzy Heights*. The compilation *Like You Do* included two new tracks.

● ALBUMS: *Cloudcuckooland* (Epic 1990)★★★, *Sense* (Epic 1992)★★★, *Jollification* (Epic 1994)★★★, *Dizzy Heights* (Epic 1996)★★★★.

● COMPILATIONS: *Pure Lightning Seeds* (Virgin 1996)★★★, *Like You Do* (Epic 1997)★★★★.

● VIDEOS: *Like You Do - The Greatest Hits* (SMV 1997).

Lightsey, Kirk

b. 15 February 1937, Detroit, Michigan, USA. A gifted modern jazz pianist, and a competent if occasional singer, Lightsey has not yet received the attention his talents deserve, despite a career that has included sessions with some of America's finest modern jazz instrumentalists, and a series of enjoyable recordings under his own name. He began working in jazz in the mid-50s, largely accompanying vocalists, first in New York and then, in the early 60s, on the west coast. He recorded with the great bebop saxophonist **Sonny Stitt** in 1965, and began an association with the subtle west coast singer/trumpeter **Chet Baker**, that resulted in five fine album recordings. At the beginning of the 80s, his career received a boost when he joined the popular saxophonist **Dexter Gordon**'s band for four years. He has since worked with individualistic trumpeter **Don Cherry**, guitarist **Jimmy Raney** and brilliant tenor saxophonists **Clifford Jordan** and **James Moody**, as well as touring and recording with the Leaders, a daring, Chicago-orientated group featuring trumpeter **Lester Bowie** and saxophonists **Arthur Blythe** and **Chico Freeman**. He has earned a reputation as a fine solo performer, visiting the UK regularly. Recommended recordings include *Isotope*, a lively trio plus percussion date from 1983, and *Everything Happens To Me*, a subtle date under Chet Baker's deft, romantic leadership.

● ALBUMS: with Chet Baker *Groovin' With The Chet Baker Quintet* (1965)★★★★, with Harold Land *Mapanzi* (1977)★★★, *Lightsey* (1982)★★, with Dexter Gordon *American Classic* (1982)★★★, with Jimmy Raney *The Master* (1983)★★, with Baker *Everything Happens To Me* (1983)★★★★, *Shorter By Two* (1983)★★★, *Isotope* (1983)★★★, with Clifford Jordan *Two Tenor Winner* (1984)★★★, *Lightsey Live* (1985)★★, *First Affairs* (1986)★★★, *Everything Is Changed* (1986)★★★, *Kirk'n'Marcus* (1986)★★★, with James Moody *Something Special* (1986)★★★, with the Leaders *Out Here Like This* (1986/87)★★, with Ricky Ford *Saxotic Stomp* (1987)★★, with Woody Shaw *Imagination* (1987)★★★, with the Leaders Trio *Heaven Dance* (1988)★★★, *From Kirk To Nat* (1990)★★★, *Goodbye Mr Evans* (Evidence 1997)★★★.

Lijadu Sisters

Sisters Kehinde and Taiwo Lijadu began working as session vocalists in Nigerian recording studios in the late 60s, and recorded their first own-name album, *Iya Mi Jowo*, in 1969, going on to release an average of one new album every two years until the mid-80s. Their style, a catholic mixture of Afrobeat, funk and straightforward pop, was pleasant enough, but would have fared much better in the international marketplace towards which their label, West African **Decca Records**, strove to place them, given strong and individual production. In 1990 they supported General Prince Adekunle on his *Evil Cabal* album.

● ALBUMS: *Iya Mi Jowo* (Decca West Africa 1969),★★ *Danger* (Decca West Africa 1973)★★★, *Lijadu Sisters* (Decca West Africa 1975)★★★★, *Double Trouble* (Shanachie 1984)★★★★.

Like A Prayer - Madonna

Madonna's exquisite sense of the pop song, and suitably stylish aesthetic to match, was pushed to the hilt for 1989's *Like A Prayer*. Sporting a bare midriff and a stylishly dark bob, she immediately set the Moral Majority up in arms with the title track's video, depicting, among other things, a negro Christ and a hillside of burning crosses. The song, however, was as strong and as dazzling as the images. Before deciding on utilizing a constant barrage of public sexuality over songs, Madonna made great records. Highlights here include the sexy bubble-gum of 'Cherish' and the delightful 'Express Yourself'. Great pop to go.

● Tracks: *Like A Prayer; Express Yourself; Love Song; Till Death Us Do Part; Promise To Try; Cherish; Dear Jessie; Oh Father; Keep It Together; Spanish Eyes; Act Of Contrition.*
● First released 1989
● UK peak chart position: 1
● USA peak chart position: 1

Like A Virgin - Madonna

The title track, which, combined with her overt sexuality, caused waves of controversy at the time, has now become part of movie folklore, with director Quentin Tarantino letting his brutish cast mull over the meaning of its lyrics for the opening sequence of the film *Reservoir Dogs*. It is somehow gratifying that the **Madonna** album that unleashed her on the world should have become a cultural icon and reference point for the 80s. A telling blend of lush pop songs and street suss - the snappy come-on of 'Into The Groove', the **Marilyn Monroe** pastiche of 'Material Girl' - the dancing went on all through the night.

● Tracks: *Material Girl; Shoo-bee-doo; Pretender; Stay; Angel; Like A Virgin; Over And Over; Love Don't Live Here Anymore; Into The Groove; Dress You Up.*
● First released 1984
● UK peak chart position: 6
● USA peak chart position: 1

Like Someone In Love - Ella Fitzgerald

An album of sensitive arrangements by the underrated Frank DeVol, this collection was staple diet for 50s lounge romantics. Perched with a martini and a cherry in one of those triangular glasses, this is immaculate music. **Ella Fitzgerald** stepped outside the pattern of recording the *Songbook* series and used some lesser-known writers. Both 'Hurry Home', by Meyer, Emmerick and Bernier, and 'Night Wind', by Rothberg and Pollock, are strong tracks. She later re-recorded 'How Long Has This Been Going On', while the title track is so perfect it could never be done again. The CD reissue has four bonus tracks to make this a collection by which to propose marriage.

● Tracks: *There's A Lull In My Life; More Than You Know; What Will I Tell My Heart; I Never Had A Chance; Close Your Eyes; We'll Be Together Again; Then I'll Be Tired Of You; Like Someone In Love; Midnight Sun; I Thought About You; You're Blase; Night Wind; What's New; Hurry Home; How Long Has*

This Been Going On; I'll Never Be The Same; Lost In A Fog; Everything Happens To Me; So Rare.
● First released 1958
● UK peak chart position: did not chart
● USA peak chart position: did not chart

Lil' Ed And The Blues Imperials

b. Ed Williams, Lil' Ed learned slide guitar from his uncle **J.B. Hutto**. Singing his own compositions, he formed the Blues Imperials in 1975 and built up a reputation on the Chicago club scene. In 1986 Lil' Ed recorded for **Alligator** with Dave Weld (guitar), James Young (bass) and Louis Henderson (drums). In 1989 Mike Garrett and Kelly Littleton replaced Weld and Henderson.

● ALBUMS: *Roughhousin'* (Alligator 1986)★★★, *Chicken, Gravy & Biscuits* (Alligator 1989)★★★, *What You See Is What You Get* (1993)★★★.

Lil' Kim

b. Brooklyn, New York, USA. Having survived some time on the streets as a teenager, Lil' Kim was aided by Biggie Smalls (**Notorious B.I.G.**) who helped her team up with the New York rap collective **Junior MAFIA**. A strong response to her contributions to their 1995 debut single, 'Player's Anthem', and the ensuing *Conspiracy*, earned her comparisons with **MC Lyte** for her adept microphone skills. She then worked on albums by artists including Skin Deep and Total, before launching her own career in 1996 with *Hard Core*. This sexually explicit hardcore rap album came as something of a shock in the male-dominated world of hip-hop, but an aggressive marketing campaign and strong reviews helped *Hard Core* reach number 11 in the **Billboard** charts. The album featured an array of star producers, including **Sean 'Puffy' Combs**, with whom Lil' Kim dueted on the number 1 rap single 'No Time'.

● ALBUMS: *Hard Core* (Undeas/Big Beat 1996)★★★.

Lil' Louis

b. Louis Sims. Lil' Louis is the son of Bobby Sims, one of Chicago's premier blues guitarists who has played with **BB King** and **Bobby 'Blue' Bland**. The most notable moment in his son's career came with 'French Kiss' in 1989, peaking at number 2 in the UK charts, reportedly having been licensed from Diamond Records to **ffrr** for a figure in the region of £30,000. It was banned by the BBC because of its female 'vocal' (heavy breathing) being too near the knuckle. The censorship was not merely a British invention, however. New York DJ **Frankie Bones** was sacked for playing it at his club night in breach of prior warnings. Other hits in the piano-house mould followed, notably 'I Called U But You Weren't There'. Again this was no ephemeral dance tune, concerning instead a disastrous relationship with an ex-girlfriend which got so out of hand he was forced to take out a restraining order. His debut album was a surprisingly pleasing and varied selection, with tracks spanning soul and jazz (and including contributions from his father). Louis was responsible for singing, producing and much of the instrumentation. He returned after a long break in 1992 with 'The Club Lonely' and 'Saved My Life', having relocated from Chicago to New York, and taken time out to update his keyboard skills and reaquaint himself with the jazz records of his youth. Another long break preceded 1997's R&B-orientated 'Clap Your Hands' single.

● ALBUMS: *From The Mind Of Lil' Louis* (London 1989)★★★, *Journey With The Lonely* (London 1992)★★★.

Lilac Time

Turning his back on pop stardom as a solo performer, Stephen 'Tin Tin' **Duffy** dropped the 'Tin Tin' part of his name (after legal action by lawyers representing Hergé), and formed the Lilac Time with his brother Nick (guitar) in 1987. Deliberately low-profile, the group's debut, *The Lilac Time*, was released by the tiny Birmingham label Swordfish. The other group members were Michael Giri (bass) and Micky Harris (drums). The subtle blend of pop harmonies and folk instrumentation was well received and Phonogram signed the band and re-released the debut. *Paradise Circus* was more commercial, with pop gems such as 'The Girl Who Waves At Trains'. *And Love For All*, produced jointly by Duffy, Andy Partridge of **XTC** and John Leckie, was more introspective, and despite strong efforts by Phonogram the group failed to record a hit in the singles chart, mainly because of a general unwillingness to forget Duffy's rather twee past as a pop idol (he was also in the early line-up of **Duran Duran**). In 1991, the group signed with the leading independent label **Creation** and released *Astronauts*. In the week of its release it was announced that the group had split and that Duffy would revert once again to solo status.

● ALBUMS: *The Lilac Time* (Swordfish 1987)★★★, *Paradise Circus* (Fontana 1989)★★★, *And Love For All* (Fontana 1990)★★★, *Astronauts* (Creation 1991)★★★.

Lilac Time (stage musical)

(see *Blossom Time*)

Lili

Just two years after she made her Hollywood debut in **Vincente Minnelli**'s *An American In Paris* (1951), **Leslie Caron** delighted cinema audiences once again with this enchanting film which was also released by MGM. She plays a 16-year-old French orphan who joins a carnival and falls madly in love with a handsome magician (Jean-Pierre Aumont). After she is fired for devoting too much her time to him and his illusions, she finds consolation in talking to a group of puppets operated by a disillusioned cripple (Mel Ferrer), and their subsequent, touching relationship makes this a rather special film. One of the highlights came when Caron danced a dream ballet with the puppets to the lovely, haunting music of Bronislau Kaper for which he won an Oscar. He and lyricist Helen Deutsch also wrote the song 'Hi-Lili, Hi-Lo', which was performed in captivating fashion by the puppets, and later became quite a hit. Helen Deutsch was also responsible for the screenplay which she adapted from a novel by Paul Gallico. **Charles Walters** and Dorothy Jarnac were responsible for the imaginative choreography, and Walters also directed. Zsa Zsa Gabor led a strong supporting cast which also included Kurt Kasznar, Alex Gerry, Amanda Blake, and Wilton Graff. The film was produced by Edwin H. Knopf and photographed in Technicolor. In 1961 the magic of *Lili* was transferred to the stage in *Carnival*, the first Broadway musical show to be adapted from a screen musical. With a score by **Bob Merrill**, and starring Anna Maria Alberghetti, it became a popular hit and ran for 719 performances.

Lilith Fair

Founded by Canadian singer-songwriter **Sarah McLachlan** in 1997, the Lilith Fair concert tour proved to be one of the year's major surprises. Naming the all-female travelling festival after Adam's first wife (in Hebrew folklore), McLachlan's aim was to raise the profile of female musicians within an industry that has traditionally remained male-dominated. Based around a rotating roster of 61 artists and bands, the tour boasted a veritable who's who of women's music in the 90s, including **Jewel, Sheryl Crow, Shawn Colvin, Fiona Apple, Paula Cole, Meredith Brooks, Abra Moore, Suzanne Vega, Victoria Williams, Lisa Loeb, Tracy Bonham, Joan Osborne, Cassandra Wilson, Emmylou Harris, Dar Williams, Susanna Hoffs**, the **Indigo Girls** and McLachlan herself. Reflecting the increasingly dominant chart positions in America of female artists, the tour proved to be an astounding success, becoming the summer's highest grossing tour ($16.7m) at a time when other package tours were struggling to survive. Sponsorship of the tour eschewed the blatant consumerism of rival packages such as **Ozzy Osbourne**'s Ozzfest, with the emphasis placed on the sponsor's charitable impulses. A double CD compiling highlights of the 1997 tour was released in mid-1998, generating increased interest in that year's tour. Playing at 57 sold-out venues, the tour added **Erykah Badu, Missy Elliott, Bonnie Raitt, Neneh Cherry, Liz Phair, Me'Shell Ndegé Ocello, Heather Nova, Natalie Merchant** and **Sinead O'Connor** to the bill.

● COMPILATIONS: *Lilith Fair: A Celebration Of Women In Music* (Arista 1998)★★★.

Lillian Axe

This melodic rock quintet, originally from Michigan, USA, comprised Ron Taylor (vocals), Steve Blaze (guitar), Jon Ster (guitar, keyboards), Rob Stratton (bass) and Danny King (drums). Initially known as Stiff, the band were taken under the wing of **Ratt** guitarist Robbin Crosby before changing their name to Lillian Axe. Produced by Crosby, their debut was a fine amalgam of infectious rockers and hard-edged pop tunes. *Love And War* was even more impressive, featuring extended atmospheric compositions that were both anthemic and memorable. However, the record sold poorly and **MCA** dropped the band from their roster. In 1990 Danny King and Rob Stratton were replaced by Gene Barnett and Darren DeLatta, respectively, after which the Music For Nations independent became their home during the early 90s.

● ALBUMS: *Lillian Axe* (MCA 1988)★★★, *Love And War* (MCA 1989)★★★★, *Poetic Justice* (Music For Nations 1992)★★★, *Psychoschizophrenia* (Music For Nations 1994)★★★.

Lillie, Beatrice

b. 29 May 1894, Toronto, Canada, d. 20 January 1989, Henley-On-Thames, England. An incomparable artist - a comedienne, actress, and singer - who was known in the 20s and 30s as 'the funniest woman in the world.' After leaving school at the age of 15 to form a singing trio with her mother and sister, Lillie moved to England just prior to World War I. From 1914-1922, she starred in a series of West End revues, mostly produced by André Charlot. These included *Not Likely!* (1914), *5064 Gerrard* (1915), *Samples* (1916), *Some* (1916), *Cheep* (1917), *Tabs* (1918), *Bran Pie* (1919), *Now And Then* (1921), *Pot Luck* (1921), and *The Nine O'Clock Revue* (1922). She also took the comic lead in the **Jerome Kern-Guy Bolton-P.G. Wodehouse** musical comedy, *Oh, Joy!* (1919), which had played at the **Princess Theatre** in New York under the title of *Oh, Boy!* In 1920 Lillie married Robert Peel, a descendant of the founder of the Metropolitan Police, and became Lady Peel five years later when his baronet father died. Two years later she made her Broadway debut, with **Gertrude Lawrence** and **Jack Buchanan**, in the smash hit *André Charlot's Revue*, and almost stopped the show every night with the splendidly chaotic 'March With Me' number. After more Charlot revues in London and New York, Lillie appeared in two musical comedies. She duetted with Charles Purcell on Anne Caldwell and **Vincent Youmans**' 'I Know That You Know' in *Oh, Please!* (New York 1926), and brought the house down every night with her rendering of **Richard Rodgers** and **Lorenz Hart**'s 'A Baby's Best Friend' (is his mother) in *She's My Baby* (New York 1928). Returning to revue, she co-starred with **Noël Coward**, and sang the enduring 'World Weary', in his immensely successful *This Year Of Grace!* (New York 1928). A brief foray into the West End with *Charlot's Masquerade* (1930), was followed by *The Third Little Show* (New York 1931), in which she introduced American audiences to another Coward classic, 'Mad Dogs And Englishmen'. During the 30s Lillie was one of the most sought after of celebrities, the darling of the social set, and the toast of two continents. She continued to excite and delight theatregoers on both sides of the Atlantic in productions such as *Walk A Little Faster* (New York 1932), *Please* (London 1933), *At Home Abroad* (New York 1935), *The Show Is On* (New York 1936), *Happy Returns* (London 1938), and *All Clear* (London 1939).

It is said that **Cole Porter** wrote his 'story of a nightmare weekend', 'Thank You So Much, Mrs. Lowsborough-Goodby', for Lillie, and Coward gave her his delightfully gossipy 'I've Been To A Marvellous Party' in *Set To Music* (1939). She made her cabaret debut in 1939 at London's Café Royal, and then - apart from appearing in Herbert Farjeon's revue, *Big Top* (London 1942), and some straight theatre - spent most of World War II entertaining the troops at home and abroad. She was decorated by General de Gaulle with the French Liberation Medal, and throughout the 40s continued to criss-cross the Atlantic, appearing in revues such as *Seven Lively Arts* (New York 1944), *Better Late* (London 1946), and *Inside USA* (New York 1948), as well as working regularly on radio and in cabaret. In 1953 she won a **Tony Award** for the New York production of *An Evening With Beatrice Lillie*, which was also presented at the Globe Theatre in London a year later. Among the West End cast then was composer/librettist **Leslie Bricusse**, who retained his association with her for some years. In fact, he and **Anthony Newley** wrote their smash hit musical, *Stop The World-I Want To Get Off*, early in 1961, while Bricusse was working with Lillie in New York. Before that, she was the best thing in a generally disappointing Golden Jubilee edition of the *Ziegfeld Follies* (1957), a superbly eccentric aunt in *Auntie Mame* in London (1958), as well as being her anarchic self in *Late Evening With Beatrice Lillie* at the 1960 Edinburgh Festival. She made her final Broadway appearance, as Madame Arcati, in *High Spirits*, the 1964 musical based on Noël Coward's play *Blithe Spirit*. Although her career spanned the period from silent features to *The Sound Of Music*, Lillie made only a few films - she needed a live audience to inspire her. Probably her most telling screen appearance was as an hilarious oriental white slave trader in *Thoroughly Modern Millie* (1967). Shortly after suffering a stroke in 1975 which left her partly paralysed, she returned to England and spent the remainder of her life in poor health at her home in Henley. After her death, Sir John Gielgud paid a touching tribute, and said that he regarded her as The Mistress of the Absurd, recalling her in performance at the Winter Garden Theatre, in New York, 'standing dramatically against a pillar dressed in a flowing gown which she lifted suddenly to reveal her feet shod in roller skates on which she gravely skidded across the stage'. With her trademark Eton crop topped with a smart cap, and bearing a long cigarette holder, she was a true original - the enemy of pomposity, and a murderer of the sentimental - much to the delight of her audience. Fortunately, many of her satirical and surrealistic comic numbers and skits, such as 'There Are Fairies At The Bottom Of My Garden', 'Double Damask', 'Weary Of It All', 'Wind Round My Heart', and 'This Is My First Affair' ('so please be kind' - which during the course of her version, became 'please be quick'), are preserved on record.

● ALBUMS: *Auntie Bea* (Decca 1959)★★★, *Queen Bea*

(1970)★★★, *The Unique! The Incomparable!* (Pavilion 1995)★★★★.

● FILMS: *Exit Smiling* (1926), *The Show Of Shows* (1929), *Are You There?* (1929), *Dr. Rhythm* (1938), *On Approval* (1943), *Around The World In 80 Days* (1956), *Thoroughly Modern Millie* (1967).

● FURTHER READING: *Every Other Inch A Lady*, Beatrice Lillie. *Beatrice Lillie: The Funniest Woman In The World*, B. Laffey.

Lilliput

Formed from **Rough Trade Records** aspirants **Kleenex**, when the company was presented with legal pressure from the tissue manufacturer of the same name, Lilliput took their new moniker in 1980 and included the same line-up; Marlene Marder (guitar), Klaudi Schiff (bass), Crigele Freund (vocals) and Lislot Ha (drums). Their first release as Lilliput was 'Die Matrosen', followed by 'Eisgerwind' and a debut album, all housed on Rough Trade. However, by the time the album was released Lilliput were no more. Marder went on to form Danger Mice (two singles, 'I Have Got You' and 'Broken New Heart') during the mid-80s. She now runs a record shop in her native Zurich. Schiff, contrastingly, has become one of Switzerland's most celebrated painters.

● ALBUMS: *Lilliput* (Rough Trade 1983)★★★, *Some Songs* Germany only (Rough Trade 1983)★★.

● COMPILATIONS: *Lilliput* comprises Kleenex/ Lilliput material (Off Course 1993)★★★.

Lilly Brothers

Mitchell B. Lilly (b. 15 December 1921) and Charles Everett Lilly (b. 1 July 1923) were both born at Clear Creek, near Beckley, West Virginia, USA. Always known as Bea and Everett, the two brothers began performing in the mid-30s, being especially influenced by **Bill Monroe** and the **Blue Sky Boys**. In the late 30s, using mandolin and guitar to back their high harmony vocals, they began their professional career. In 1939, they played the *Old Farm Hour*, at the radio station WCHS Charleston, as the Lonesome Holler Boys. They sometimes played three radio shows a day as well as evening dances, and in late 1939 and 1940, they were a very popular act on WJLS Beckley. When America became involved in World War II, Everett joined the armed forces. In 1945, they played with Molly O'Day at Beckley and also at KRLD Dallas and WNOX Knoxville. They next formed the Smiling Mountain Boys, which included Paul Taylor, Burk Barbour (fiddle) and Lonnie Glosson (harmonica), but surprisingly, they refused the opportunity to record for the King label. Between 1948 and 1950, they were a featured duet with Red Belcher And His Kentucky Ridge Runners and played WWVA Wheeling with him. The brothers split up in 1950 when Everett joined **Lester Flatt** and **Earl Scruggs**, playing mandolin and taking tenor vocals. In 1951, he appeared on the classic Flatt and Scruggs **Columbia** recordings of such numbers as 'Somehow

Tonight', ''Tis Sweet To Be Remembered' and 'Over The Hills To The Poorhouse' (he was the only sidesman of their band to receive a billing on a record label). Late in 1952, the brothers reunited and relocated to Boston, where with Don Stover (banjo) and Tex Logan (fiddle), and initially calling themselves the Confederate Mountaineers, they played local radio, television and clubs for several years until for a short time in 1958. Everett again joined Flatt And Scruggs. In 1959, the Lillys and Stover began to play at Boston's *Hillbilly Ranch*, where they stayed for approximately 16 years. In 1960, they were recorded live at this venue by Robert Tainaka and a tape of their act gained album release in Japan, with the result that the Lilly Brothers became the most popular act of its kind in that country. Everett Lilly retired, heartbroken, back to West Virginia following the death in a car crash of his son, Giles, in 1970. Bea stayed in Boston and Stover went on to form his own band. In 1973, the brothers and Stover were persuaded to re-form and not only recorded an album for the County label but actually made two tours of Japan. Their success was described as 'nothing less than phenomenal' and the live recording of one concert resulted in the release of three albums. Everett later worked for a Japanese company and arranged further tours for American bluegrass groups to tour Japan. They continued to play their mountain, folk and old-time music on occasions at folk festivals and colleges. In 1979, they featured as the subjects of an educational film, *True Facts In A Country Song*. There were many brother harmony acts in West Virginia but it seems that only the Lillys, along with the **Bailes Brothers**, really gained a reputation of any significance outside their own state.

● ALBUMS: with Don Stover *Live At Hillbilly Ranch* (1960)★★, with Stover *Folk Songs Of The Southern Mountains* (Folkways 1961)★★★ *Bluegrass Breakdown* (Folkways 1963)★★★★ *Country Songs Of The Lilly Brothers* (Folkways 1964)★★★ with Stover *Early Recordings* (Rebel 1971)★★★, *What Will I Leave Behind* (County 1973)★★★, *Holiday In Japan (Volumes 1-3)* (1973)★★.

Lillywhite, Steve

b. 1955, England. Lillywhite is a leading contemporary UK record producer, best known for his work with the **Pogues** and U2. He started out as a tape operator for Phonogram in 1972. After producing the demo tapes which won **Ultravox** a contract with **Island Records**, he joined the company as a staff producer. Lillywhite specialised in producing new wave bands such as **Eddie And the Hot Rods**, **Siouxsie And the Banshees** (the hit 'Hong Kong Garden'), the **Members**, Penetration, **XTC** and the Buzzards before he was approached to supervise **Peter Gabriel**'s third solo album. By the early 80s, Lillywhite was widely recognised as one of the most accomplished of younger producers. Now a freelance, Island brought him in to work on U2's debut *Boy*. He also produced the group's next two albums. In addition he worked with artists as varied as singer-songwriter

Joan Armatrading, stadium rockers Simple Minds, art-punks Psychedelic Furs and the Rolling Stones (*Dirty Work*, 1987). In 1987, Lillywhite produced contrasting albums by the Pogues and Talking Heads (*Naked*), continuing with the Pogues' follow-up *Peace And Love* (1988) and with David Byrne's solo effort *Rei Momo*. Among Lillywhite's other productions was *Kite* by Kirsty MacColl whom he had married in 1984.

Limahl

b. Christopher Hamill, 19 December 1958. Limahl (an anagram of his surname) came to prominence as lead vocalist with Kajagoogoo. His rancorous exit from the group in 1983 was caused partly by guitarist Nick Beggs' increasing control over the outfit's destiny. However, a flamboyant performer and a friend of BBC pop presenter Paul Gambaccini, Limahl was well placed for solo success which began with 'Only For Love' in the UK Top 20. After a relative flop with 1984's 'Too Much Trouble', he touched number 4 with the movie title theme, 'Never Ending Story'. This Giorgio Moroder opus was also Limahl's only US chart entry. Other than *Don't Suppose* flitting briefly into the UK charts, he has since been absent from charts in nearly all territories.

● ALBUMS: *Don't Suppose* (EMI 1984)★★.

Limbo Records

Emergent record label based in Bath Street, Glasgow, Scotland. Since the release of Havanna's 'Schtoom' in August 1992 Limbo has built an enviable profile as a home to underground house. The label was inaugurated by Billy Kiltie (b. *c*.1973) and Davey Mackenzie through the auspices of their 23rd Precinct shop. Both had been involved in DJing and running clubs in the area over several years. Originally titled 23rd Precinct, the label was launched in early 1992, at which point dozens of demo tapes flooded in through the doors (not least due to the fact that a dance newsletter was distributed to Scotland from the premises). One was passed to Kiltie by local act Q-Tex, and their *Equator* EP consequently became the first release. By the time of Q-Tex's second, *Natural High* EP, they had national distribution through Revolver. Soon Limbo emerged, with most of the tracks released in its short history centring on funky, accessible house with distinctive breakbeats. Their success is founded, according to the label's proprietors, on the fact that every record features the involvement of DJs: so that each is geared to ensuring a strong club reaction. Other staples in its schedule have included Gipsy ('I Trance You'), Mukkaa, Deep Piece (Kiltie himself with releases like 'Bup, Bup, Birri, Birri' and 'Torwart', in association with Stuart Crichton) and Sublime ('Sublime'). They have also added the experimental Out On A Limb subsidiary for material like Space Buggy's eponymous debut (a side project from one of the Havanna team).

● ALBUMS: Various: *House Of Limbo Vol. 1 & 2* (Limbo 1993/94)★★★★.

Limelight

This UK heavy metal trio, based in Mansfield, Nottinghamshire, was formed by the Scrimshaw brothers - Glen (guitar, keyboards) and Mike (bass, vocals) - with Pat Coleman occupying the drum-stool. Limelight specialized in extended melodic compositions of a progressive nature, featuring complex time changes and individual virtuoso sections (similar to Yes, yet also incorporating the contemporary style of the New Wave Of British Heavy Metal). Their one and only album contained strong material, but was let down by low-budget production and weak vocals. The Scrimshaw brothers returned to the pub rock scene, playing mainly pop-rock cover versions.

● ALBUMS: *Limelight* (Future Earth 1980)★★★, *Limited Limelight* remix/reissue of debut (Avatar 1981)★★★.

Limeliters

The Limeliters were one of the popular forces behind the 50s folk revival in America. The group comprised Lou Gottlieb (b. 10 October 1923, Los Angeles, California, USA, d. 11 July 1996, Sebastopol, California, USA; bass), Alex Hassilev (b. 11 July 1932, Paris, France; guitar/banjo/vocals) and Glenn Yarbrough (b. 12 January 1930, Milwaukee, Wisconsin, USA; guitar/vocals). They formed in Los Angeles in 1959 and took their name from a club, run by Hassilev and Yarbrough, called The Limelite in Aspen, Colorado, USA. Gottlieb was a Doctor of Musicology, having studied under the Austrian composer Arnold Schoenberg, and had previously sung with the Gateway Singers. The group had a minor hit with 'A Dollar Down' in April 1961 on RCA Records, but their albums sold better than singles. Many of their albums were live recordings, including the popular *Tonight: In Person*, which reached number 5 in the US charts in 1961. The follow-up, *The Limeliters*, narrowly reached the Top 40 the same year. A third release, *The Slightly Fabulous Limeliters* made the US Top 10, also in 1961. A series of albums followed, with *Sing Out!* making the US Top 20 in 1962. Gradually their popularity waned, and when Yarbrough left in November 1963 to pursue a solo career, the group replaced him with Ernie Sheldon. In 1965, Yarbrough, also with RCA, reached the Top 40 in the US album charts with 'Baby The Rain Must Fall'. The title track, taken from a film of the same title, made the Top 20 the same year. In the late 80s Yarbrough re-formed the Limeliters with new members

● ALBUMS: *The Limeliters* (RCA Victor 1960)★★★★, *Tonight: In Person* (RCA Victor 1961)★★★, *The Slightly Fabulous Limeliters* (RCA Victor 1961)★★★, *Sing Out!* (RCA Victor 1962)★★★★, *Through Children's Eyes* (RCA Victor 1962)★★, *Folk Matinee* (RCA Victor 1962)★★★, *Our Men In San Francisco* (RCA Victor 1963)★★★, *Makin' A Joyful Noise* (RCA Victor 1963)★★★, *Fourteen 14K Folk Songs* (RCA Victor 1963)★★★, *More Of Everything!* (RCA Victor 1964)★★★, *London Concert* (RCA Victor 1965)★★★, *The Limeliters Look At Love In Depth* (RCA Victor 1965)★★★, *The Original 'Those Were The Days'* (RCA Victor 1968)★★, *Time*

To Gather Seeds (RCA Victor 1970)★★★, *Their First Historic Album* (RCA Victor 1986)★★★★, *Alive In Concert* (RCA Victor 1988)★★★.
● COMPILATIONS: *The Best Of The Limeliters* (RCA Victor 1964)★★★.

Limerick, Alison

b. *c*.1959, London, England. The first part of Limerick's entertainment career was spent on roller skates in the stage production of **Starlight Express** in London's West End. Her recording work, predictably, kicked off with sumptuous garage tunes, notably 'Where Love Lives (Come On In)', which showcased a simplistic but well executed musical approach, and was voted dance record of 1991 by *Billboard* magazine. This despite the fact that it was never released in the US. Alongside fellow Top 20 singles, 'Make It On My Own' (co-written and produced by Steve Anderson of **Brothers In Rhythm**, and featuring Limerick's boyfriend jazzman Roger Beaujolais) and 'Come Back (For Real Love)', it was housed on an impressive debut album. The presence of **David Morales** and **Frankie Knuckles** on her second album, *With A Twist*, added further spice to the formula.
● ALBUMS: *And Still I Rise* (Arista 1992)★★★, *With A Twist* (Arista 1994)★★★.

Limit

A Dutch duo known only by their pseudonyms Oattes and Van Shaik, the Limit reached number 17 in the UK charts in January 1985 with 'Say Yeah'. It was to be their sole hit - a problem exacerbated by their subsequent name change. Within weeks the Limit had become Oattes And Van Shaik - though their debut album for Portrait Records was actually titled *The Limit*. Unsurprisingly given the conditions of its release, the album's sales were minimal and the duo disappeared from the charts.
● ALBUMS: *The Limit* (Portrait 1985)★★.

Limmie And The Family Cooking

Led by Limmie Snell (b. Dalton, Alabama, USA), this vocal trio was hugely popular on the UK disco scene in the mid-70s. Snell's first musical influence was gospel but at the age of 11 he made a series of novelty records as Lemmie B. Good. He next formed a singing group with his sisters Jimmy and Martha. After an initial recording for **Phil Spector**'s Scepter label, they were signed to Avco, where Steve Metz and Sandy Linzer produced the catchy 'You Can Do Magic', a UK Top 10 hit in 1973. This was followed by the less successful 'Dreamboat', but the next year the trio had another UK bestseller with a revival of the **Essex**'s 1963 hit 'A Walking Miracle'. More pop than soul, Limmie And the Family Cooking next recorded a version of the 50s hit 'Lollipop'. Despite its failure, the group remained a favourite with British disco audiences and appeared on soul revival bills in the UK over the next decade.

Lin Que

Previously known as Isis, Lin Que is a tough-talking New York rapper who rose to fame as part of Blackwatch, the militant consciousness movement that also spawned **X-Clan**. She was joined on several tracks of her debut album by Professor X of the former outfit, who offered priceless interjections of a religious/moral nature. However, not everyone found the production values to be up to scratch, and she became vulnerable to the 'Blackwatch hype' backlash that has also affected the career of X-Clan. She has since joined **MC Lyte**'s Duke The Moon management where she works in an A&R capacity.
● ALBUMS: *Rebel Soul* (Island 1990)★★★.

Lincoln, Abbey

b. Gaby Wooldridge, 6 August 1930, Chicago, Illinois, USA. Lincoln began singing publicly in the early 50s, working in Chicago nightclubs and using a variety of pseudonyms, including Anna Marie and Gaby Lee, as well as her real name. By the middle of the decade she was using the name by which she has since been largely known. She appeared successfully at the Moulin Rouge in Los Angeles and also made her first records, with **Benny Carter**, but was soon associating with bop musicians including **Thelonious Monk**, **Mal Waldron** and **Max Roach**. Her style changed during these years and following her marriage to Roach in 1962 she also became more politically aware. She wrote some of her own material, much of it stressing the rising tide of black consciousness in the USA. She collaborated with Roach on some important works, including *We Insist!*, *Freedom Now Suite* and *Straight Ahead*. In the 60s Lincoln had a simultaneous career as an actress, co-starring in the films *Nothing But A Man* (1964) and *For Love Of Ivy* (1968), for both of which she received excellent notices. Following a tour of Africa in the mid-70s, she adopted the name Aminata Moseka (her marriage to Roach had ended in 1970) and subsequent albums have been released, generally, under this name while reissues of early albums still use that of Abbey Lincoln. With a deeply emotional singing voice, she has always made a close connection with her audiences. Her style veers between powerful versions of ballads from her early years and the sometimes bitter polemic of her middle period. By the late 80s her repertoire was once again featuring love songs and more accessible material akin to that of her youth. Nevertheless, it is probable that her politically motivated material will prove to be her most lasting contribution to black American culture.
● ALBUMS: *Affair* (EMI 1956)★★★, *That's Him!* (Original Jazz Classics 1957)★★★★, *It's Magic* (Original Jazz Classics 1958)★★★★, *Abbey Is Blue* (Original Jazz Classics 1959)★★★★, *Straight Ahead* (Candid 1961)★★★, *People In Me* (1973)★★★, *Golden Lady* (1980)★★, *Talking To The Sun* (Enja 1983)★★★, *Thats Him* (Riverside 1984)★★★, *A Tribute To Billie Holiday* (Enja 1987)★★, with Dave Liebman *People In Me* (ITM 1990)★★, *Abbey Sings Billie Vol 2* (Enja

1992)★★, *The World Is Falling Down* (Verve 1991)★★★, *Devil's Got Your Tongue* (Verve 1992)★★★, with Stan Getz *You Gotta Pay The Band* (Verve 1992)★★★, *Painted Lady* (1993)★★★, *When There Is Love* (Verve 1993)★★★, *Turtle's Dream* (Verve 1995)★★★.

● FILMS: *The Girl Can't Help It* (1956).

Lincoln, Abe

b. Abraham Lincoln, 29 March 1907, Lancaster, Pennsylvania, USA. Lincoln took up the trombone as a small child and by his late teens was proficient enough to follow **Tommy Dorsey** into the **California Ramblers**. He played in various other bands and in the 20s was with those led by **Roger Wolfe Kahn** and **Paul Whiteman**. During the late 30s he was with **Ozzie Nelson**'s popular dance band. During the 40s he was active in film studio work but made occasional record dates with singers and a handful of jazz musicians. In the 50s he made rather more jazz dates, including sessions with the Rampart Street Paraders, **Pete Fountain**, **Matty Matlock** and **Bob Scobey**. In the 60s, he played club and festival dates with several bands including brief stints with **Wild Bill Davison** and Fountain. Although Lincoln was capable of playing in the legato style achieved by such notable contemporaries as Dorsey and **Jack Teagarden**, it is as a bristling dixieland player that he has made his greatest mark.

● ALBUMS: with the Rampant Street Preachers, *Jam Session Coast To Coast* (1953)★★★.

Lincoln, Charley

b. Charley Hicks, 11 March 1900, Lithonia, Georgia, USA, d. 28 September 1963, Cairo, Georgia, USA. Like his younger brother, Robert '**Barbecue Bob**' Hicks, Lincoln learned guitar from **Curley Weaver**'s mother, but was less accomplished than Bob. He recorded from 1927-30, probably thanks to his brother's hit-making status, and his blues are a mix of the sad and the mildly risqué, backed by a simple 12-string guitar. Despite being billed as 'Laughing Charley' on a duet with Bob, Lincoln was prone to extreme mood swings under the influence of drink, from introverted to choleric; this trait was exacerbated by the alcoholism that followed various family tragedies, notably the premature death of his brother in 1929. On Christmas Day 1955, he senselessly murdered a man, and spent the rest of his life in prison, repentant and performing only religious songs.

● COMPILATIONS: *Charley Lincoln* (Matchbox 1983)★★★, *Complete Recordings 1927-1930* (1984)★★★.

Lind, Bob

b. 25 November 1944, Baltimore, Maryland, USA. Lind is best known for writing and recording the Top 5 folk rock song 'Elusive Butterfly' in 1966. He moved around frequently with his family, and while settled in Denver, Colorado, he began singing folk music in clubs. He moved to the west coast and was signed to World Pacific Records, a division of the larger **Liberty**

Records. Produced by **Jack Nitzsche**, Lind played guitar on his recordings for the label, while piano was handled by **Leon Russell**. His first single, 'Cheryl's Goin' Home', failed to catch on but was later covered by **Cher** and the **Blues Project**. 'Elusive Butterfly' was its b-side and became an international Top 10 hit. Lind was widely touted as 'the new **Bob Dylan**' and the latest spokesperson for youth during 1966. Despite his pop star looks and sensitive lyrics, however, his subsequent singles failed to reach the charts. *Don't Be Concerned* contained a number of sentimental, but attractive songs. His compositions continued to find interpreters, among them the **Turtles**, **Noel Harrison**, **Nancy Sinatra** and **Bobby Sherman**. Lind continued to record into the early 70s, switching to **Capitol Records** without a revival of his commercial fortunes. He was still performing in folk and country music circles in the early 80s.

● ALBUMS: *Don't Be Concerned* (World Pacific 1966)★★, *The Elusive Bob Lind* (Verve/Forecast 1966)★★, *Photographs Of Feeling* (World Pacific 1966)★★, *Since There Were Circles* (Capitol 1971)★★.

Lind, Ove

b. 29 June 1926, Stockholm, Sweden, d. 16 April 1991. After playing clarinet for some years he became a professional musician in the mid-40s, quickly becoming well known in his homeland. He was co-leader of the co-operative band the Swinging Swedes, and of a quartet which also featured **Bengt Hallberg**. In the early 60s Lind worked in popular music but retained his interest in swing era jazz and was therefore in a good position to capitalize on a revival of interest in this form in Sweden in the late 60s. An accomplished technician, Lind plays with a clean flowing and swinging style, delivering inventive solos with great aplomb.

● ALBUMS: *Who's Harry Warren? Evergreen!* (Phontastic 1975)★★★★, *Swinging Down The Lane* (Phontastic 1977)★★★★.

Linde, Dennis

b. 13 March 1943, Abilene, Texas, USA. Dennis Linde (pronounced Lin-dy) played in a group called the Starlighters in the 60s and by the 70s he occasionally played bass guitar on **Elvis Presley**'s recordings. His song 'Burning Love' was originally recorded by **Arthur Alexander**, but became a worldwide hit for Presley, who also recorded Linde's ballad 'For The Heart'. Linde has played in **Kris Kristofferson**'s band and produced his album *Jesus Was A Capricorn*. Kristofferson said about him, 'Dennis Linde may be a genius, he certainly is weird, possibly the most creative and prolific songwriter in the business.' He wrote several songs for **Roy Orbison**'s *Regeneration* and his compositions include 'Long Long Texas Road' (**Roy Drusky**), 'The Love She Found In Me' (**Gary Morris**), 'Vanessa' (**Shakin' Stevens**), 'Walkin' A Broken Heart' (**Don Williams**) and 'Cast Iron Heart' (**Blackhawk**). He wrote US country number 1 hits for **Eddy Raven**, 'I'm Gonna Get You' and 'In A Letter To You'; when Raven heard 'In A Letter To You', he told the publishers that it sounded like Don Williams' 'Then It's Love' - it transpired that Linde had written that song too. From time to time he makes his own records, including the 1973 single 'Hello, I Am Your Heart'.

● ALBUMS: *Linde Manor* (Intrepid 1968)★★★, *Dennis Linde* (Elektra 1973)★★★, *Trapped In The Suburbs* (Elektra 1974)★★★, *Surface Noise* (Monument 1976)★★★, *Under The Eye* (Monument 1977)★★★.

Lindenberg, Udo

b. 17 May 1946, Gronau, Germany. From the 70's *Lindenberg* to the aiming of his output more directly at the English-speaking market in the late 80s, Lindenberg had sales of over 15 million albums in Germany alone. His early career included a spell as drummer in a local jazz group playing mainstream standards such as 'The Shadow Of Your Smile' that later found a place in his vocal repertoire. 'Lover Man (Where Can You Be)' would be performed with no lyrical alterations to reflect what he called his 'flexible' sexuality. Further aspects of **David Bowie**'s artistic presentation were noted in Lindenberg's multi-media concerts which featured wrestlers, trampolinists and similar non-musical support acts. Another influence was a less famous friend, Jean-Jacques Kravetz, whom Udo assisted willingly on three 70s albums. His interest in national left-wing politics manifested itself in active membership of the Green party and its peace movement - with compositions like 'Father You Should Have Killed Hitler' and 'They Don't Need Another Fuehrer' expressing concern over the renaissance of Nazism. This was balanced with the pride apparent in 1984's 'Germans' which lauded Goethe, Kafka, Mozart, Schumann and other cultural icons. Though this single - buttressed by a promotional visit - made ripples in Britain, a duet with Leata Galloway ('Gesang'), 'Berlin', the lighter 'Special Train To Pankow' (portraying a prominent East German leader 'as a closet rock 'n' roller') and other worthy singles together made less worldwide impact than his characteristically controversial appearance, backed by the Panik Orchestra, as his country's representative on **Live Aid**. Nevertheless, though not neglecting a still huge home following, releases such as 1987's *All Clear!* (which embraced a revival of **Steppenwolf**'s 'Born To Be Wild') demonstrated a continued attempt to woo a wider audience.

● ALBUMS: *Lindenberg* (1971)★★★★, *Daumen Im Wind* (1972)★★★, *Alles Klar Auf Der Andrea Doria* (1973)★★★, *Ball Pompos* (1974)★★★, *Votan Wahnwitz* (1975)★★★, *Das Sind Die Herrn Vom Andern Stern* (1976)★★★, *Galaxo Gang* (1976)★★★, *Sister King Kong* (1977)★★★, *No Panic* (Decca 1977)★★★, *Lindenbergs Rock Revue* (1978)★★, *Droehnland Symphonie* (1978)★★★, *Odyssee* (1979)★★★, *Livehaftig* (1979)★★★, *Der Detektiv* (1979)★★★, *Panische Zeiten* (1980)★★★, *Udopia* (1981)★★★, *Intensivstationen* (1982)★★★, *Keule* (1982)★★★, *Lindstarke 10* (1983)★★★, *Gottewrhammerung* (1984)★★★, *Udo Lindenberg Und Das Panik Orchestra* (Teldec 1985)★★, *Feuerlamnd* (1987)★★★, *All Clear! aka Alles Klar!* (Teldec 1987)★★★, *Lieder Statt Briefe* (1988)★★★, *CasaNova* (1988)★★★, *Hermine* (1988)★★★, *Bunte Republik Deutschland* (1989)★★★, *Niemandsland* (1990)★★★, *Ich Will Dich Haben* (1991)★★★, *Gustav* (1991)★★★, *Panik-Panther* (1992).

Lindisfarne

This Newcastle, UK-based quintet - **Alan Hull** (b. 20 February 1945, Newcastle-upon-Tyne, Tyne And Wear, England, d. 18 November 1995; vocals/guitar/piano), Simon Cowe (b. 1 April 1948, Jesmond Dene, Tyne And Wear, England; guitar), Ray Jackson (b. 12 December 1948, Wallsend, Tyne And Wear, England; harmonica/mandolin), Rod Clements (b. 17 November 1947, North Shields, Tyne And Wear, England; bass/violin) and Ray Laidlaw (b. 28 May 1948, North Shields, Tyne And Wear, England; drums) - was originally known as the Downtown Faction, but took the name Lindisfarne in 1968. Their debut *Nicely Out Of Tune*, was issued the following year and this brash mixture of folk rock and optimistic harmonies is arguably the group's most satisfying set. The album contained the wistful and lyrically complex 'Lady Eleanor'. Their popularity flourished with the release of *Fog On The Tyne* the humorous title track celebrating life in Newcastle and containing such verses as; 'Sitting in a sleazy snack-bar sucking sickly sausage rolls'. The number 1 album's attendant single, 'Meet Me On The Corner', reached the UK Top 5 in 1972 where it was followed by a re-released 'Lady Eleanor'. *Fog On The Tyne* was produced by Bob Johnston, and although they pursued this relationship on a third selection, *Dingly Dell*, the group was unhappy with his work and remixed the set prior to release. The final results were still disappointing, creatively and commercially, and tensions within the line-up were exposed during an ill-fated tour of the USA. In 1973, Laidlaw, Cowe and Clements left for a new venture, **Jack The Lad**. Kenny Craddock (keyboards), Charlie Harcourt (guitar), Tommy Duffy (bass) and Paul Nichols (drums) were brought in as replacements but this reconstituted line-up lacked the charm of its predecessor and was overshadowed by Alan Hull's concurrent solo career. A 1974 release, *Happy Daze*, offered some promise, but Lindisfarne was disbanded the following year. The break, however, was temporary and the original quintet later resumed working together. They secured a recording deal with **Mercury Records** and in 1978 enjoyed a UK Top 10 single with 'Run For Home'. Despite further releases, Lindisfarne was unable to repeat this success and subsequently reached an artistic nadir with *C'mon Everybody*, a medley of rock 'n' roll party favourites with six of the group's own best-known songs saved for the finale. In November 1990, Lindisfarne were back in the UK charts, joined together with the England international footballer, and fellow Geordie, Paul Gascoigne. Their reworked, and inferior, version of 'Fog On The Tyne' reached number 2.

Although they are now restricted to only the occasional chart success, the group's following remains strong, particularly in the north-east of England, and is manifested in their annual Christmas concerts. Until his sudden death Hull maintained an independent solo career although he still performed Lindisfarne classics, as heard on his *Back To Basics* in 1994.

● ALBUMS: *Nicely Out Of Tune* (Charisma 1970)★★★★, *Fog On The Tyne* (Charisma 1971)★★★★, *Dingly Dell* (Charisma 1972)★★★, *Lindisfarne Live* (Charisma 1973)★★, *Roll On Ruby* (Charisma 1973)★★, *Happy Daze* (Warners 1974)★★★, *Back And Fourth* (Mercury 1978)★★★, *Magic In The Air* (Mercury 1978)★★, *The News* (Mercury 1979)★★, *Sleepless Night* (LMP 1982)★★, *LindisfarneTastic Live* (LMP 1984)★★, *LindisfarneTastic Volume 2* (LMP 1984)★★, *Dance Your Life Away* (River City 1986)★★, *C'mon Everybody* (Stylus 1987)★★, *Peel Sessions* (Strange Fruit 1988)★★★, *Amigos* (Black Crow 1989)★★, *Elvis Lives On The Moon* (Essential 1993)★★, *Another Fine Mess* (Grapevine 1995)★★.
Solo: Ray Jackson *In The Night* (Mercury 1980)★★. Rod Clements with Bert Jansch *Leather Launderette* (Black Crow 1988)★★.

● COMPILATIONS: *Take Off Your Head* (Rubber 1974)★★, *Finest Hour* (Charisma 1975)★★★, *Singles Album* (1981)★★★, *The Best Of Lindisfarne* (Virgin 1989)★★★, *Buried Treasures Volume 1* (Virgin 1993)★★, *Buried Treasures Volume 2* (Virgin 1993)★★, *On Tap* (Essential 1994)★★, *City Songs* (New Millenium 1998)★★★.

Lindley, David

Guitarist Lindley first attracted attention for his work in a multitude of traditional USA groups, including the Smog City Trestle Hangers, the Mad Mountain Ramblers and the Dry City Scat Band. Having embraced rock music in the short-lived Rodents, he became a founder member of **Kaleidoscope (USA)**, one of the 60s most enduring, and enigmatic, acts. Lindley's skills as a guitarist, violinist and banjo player were crucial to the eclectic approach of the group, which he led until its demise in 1970. During the 70s his talents were much in demand and David appeared as an accompanist for such diverse acts as **Terry Reid**, **David Blue**, **Linda Ronstadt**, **James Taylor** and **Crosby And Nash**. However, Lindley is best-recalled for his association with **Jackson Browne** which spanned seminal releases such as *Late For The Sky*, *The Pretender* and *Running On Empty*. His wailing falsetto on Browne's version of 'Stay' (1978) brought an unlikely UK/US Top 20 hit. In 1981, the guitarist released his first solo album, *El Rayo-X*. The set featured a mixture of New Orleans, Latin and reggae styles and included versions of 'Mercury Blues', 'Twist And Shout' and 'Petit Fleur', the last of which he also recorded with Kaleidoscope. Although several writers criticized its unadventurous content, there was no denying the infectious enthusiasm which Lindley clearly delighted in. Having formed a group around Bernie Larsen (guitar), Jorge Calderon (bass), Ian Wallace (drums) and Ras 'Baboo' Pierre (percussion), David began extensive touring. The

excitement they generated was captured on *El Rayo-X Live* while further studio selections continued the eclectic mix of his debut. Lindley remains a consummate and skilled musician, never more apparent than in the 90s when he undertook live dates with **Ry Cooder**. He appeared on **Rory Block**'s *Tornado* in 1996.

● ALBUMS: *El Rayo-X* (1981)★★★★, *Win This Record* (1982)★★★, *El Rayo-X Live* (1983)★★★★★, *Mr. Dave* (1985)★★, *Very Greasy* (1988)★★, with Hani Naser *Official Bootleg* (Pleemhead 1994)★★.

Lindner, Patrick

b. *c.*1961, Munich, Germany. One of the most popular MOR singers in central Europe, Lindner made his breakthrough in 1990 at the Grand Prix der Volksmusik. Since then he has earned a number of awards in recognition of his inoffensive, highly melodic German-language songs. These include the German 'Bambi', the Edelweis and Hermann-Lous-Preis awards - and the Goldene Stimmgabel award three times. His 1995 album, *Meine Lieder Streicheln Dich*, underlined his motto ('My Songs Caress You'). It was helmed by noted production team Jean Frankfurther and Irma Holder and collected yet another platinum sales award.

● ALBUMS: *Meine Lieder Streicheln Dich* (BMG Ariola 1995)★★★.

Lindo, Kashief

b. *c.*1978, Kingston, Jamaica, West Indies. The Lindo dynasty has featured heavily in the reggae industry: Earl 'Wire' Lindo played keyboards for **Bob Marley**, the singer Hopeton Lindo has enjoyed many hits, the producer Jack Ruby was born Laurence Lindo and Willie Lindo played guitar for the Hi Times Band. Kashief spent his childhood years surrounded by music - his father is Willie Lindo, who formed his own production stable. Although Willie produced **dancehall** hits, including 'Girlie Girlie' for **Sophia George**, he is celebrated for his tender ballads, including UK chart-topping hits for **Boris Gardiner** in the mid-80s. In 1992 Willie produced his son's recording debut, which surfaced on the one rhythm *Rougher Yet* compilation. Kashief's earliest success came in late 1993 with 'Hard Times', performed over the evergreen 'Satta A Massa Gana' rhythm. In 1996, inspired by the **Fugees**' success with their cover version of **Roberta Flack**'s 'Killing Me Softly With His Song', Kashief recorded his own version, which was enthusiastically received within the contemporary market. As a youthful performer, he remains unperturbed by the fact that he has yet to produce a commercially successful dancehall hit.

● ALBUMS: *Trouble Free* (Heavy Beat 1994)★★★, *Sings Christmas* (Heavy Beat 1995)★, *Soul And Inspiration* (Heavy Beat 1996)★★.

Lindsay, Arto

b. Brazil. Musician and writer Arto Lindsay has a distinguished track record on the fringes of rock history. Founder and leader of the New York 'no wave' group **DNA**, he was venerated by cognoscenti as, alternatively, high priest of the musical intelligentsia or 'the sultan of skronk'. One other famous description of Lindsay analogized his musical stature as that of '**James Brown** trapped in Don Knotts' body.' He was born in Brazil the son of a missionary, only returning to take up American citizenship in order to attend college in the 70s. After DNA's dissolution he became half of the critically championed Ambitious Lovers over the course of three albums, which saw him work with artists of the stature of **Vernon Reid** and **John Zorn** in addition to regular partner Peter Scherer. His first solo record was put together as a response to an approach by **Ryuichi Sakamoto**. *The Subtle Body* was initially conceived of as a bossa nova record, but in typical Lindsay fashion, a single genre proved too limiting for his oeuvre. As well as English language songs, Portuguese language numbers such as 'Este Seu Olhar' were in evidence, as they had been on previous Ambitious Lovers albums. Guests included Marc Ribot, **Bill Frisell**, **Brian Eno** and Amadeo Pace of **Blonde Redhead**. The album, which once again attracted glowing reviews, was released outside of Japan on the cult indie label Bar/None Records. Following its release Lindsay moved on to work on a new set for the Knitting Factory Works label, and also produced albums by Brazilian artists Marisa Monte and Caetano Veloso. *Noon Chill/Re Entry* was a startling collection that fused the rhythms of samba with layers of avant-garde noise.

● ALBUMS: *The Subtle Body* (Güt 1995)★★★★, *O Corpo Sutil* (1996)★★★, *Mundo Civilzado* (Bar/None 1997)★★★, *Noon Chill/Re Entry* (Rykodisc 1998)★★★★.

Lindsay, Erica

b. 5 June 1955, San Francisco, California, USA. Lindsay spent her childhood in Europe, her parents being teachers in American schools there. She took up clarinet at high school, then alto and tenor saxophones. At this time she was studying with **Mal Waldron**. In 1973, she went to the **Berklee College Of Music** in Boston for a year, then returned to Europe to tour with her own quartet and to freelance as soloist, composer and arranger. She came back to New York in 1980, composing for television, video and ballet, and playing with **Melba Liston**, **Clifford Jordan**, **Ted Curson** and **McCoy Tyner**. As a composer of well-crafted and atmospheric tunes, her influences include Waldron, **Gene Ammons**, **Johnny Griffin**, **Dexter Gordon**, **Wayne Shorter**, **John Coltrane** and **Miles Davis**.

● ALBUMS: *Dreamer* (1989)★★★.

Lindsay, Jimmy

b. 1950, Kingston, Jamaica, West Indies. At the age of nine Lindsay and his family relocated to the UK. His first venture into music began in 1965 with a soul group named the Healers, followed by a short term with the Nighthawks. Other ventures included a spell with the rock band Pure Medicine, back to soul with the Garments, and notably as a member of the more

successful group Cymande. In the early 70s his first recordings surfaced, 'Tribute To Jimi Hendrix', and on the Cymande album, *Promised Heights*. By 1976 he began concentrating on reggae and recorded lead vocals on the **sound system** hit, 'What You Gonna Do'. This encouraged **Lloyd Coxsone** to produce him as a soloist. The first release, 'Motion', surfaced through Cactus, followed by 'Easy', a cover version of the **Commodores** hit, on Lloyd's own Tribesman label. The latter was picked up for release by **Island Records**, appearing on the revived Black Swan logo. The single's success led Lindsay to put his energies into his own Music Hive label and, sharing lead vocals with Larry Walker under the collective name of Dambala, they enjoyed a big hit with 'Zimbabwe'. The song, featuring the lyrics, 'Crucify Smith and take back Zimbabwe, crucify Smith and take back Namibia, crucify Vorster and take back Anzania', was released shortly before **Bob Marley**'s plea for the country then known as Rhodesia. The group consisted of a multiracial line-up including members from Nigeria, Guyana, St. Lucia, Barbados and the UK. The group were commissioned by the BBC to record a theme to a six-part current affairs programme, *Babylon*. Lindsay began to concentrate on his solo career when he signed a contract with the Gem label, and in the autumn of 1979 he released *Where Is Your Love*, produced by Lloyd Coxsone. To promote the album he toured with his new band Rasuji, including members from Dambala in the line-up. In 1980 he released *Children Of Rastafari*, which conveyed a more spiritual message, notably on the track 'It's Hard (For A Dread To Live In Babylon)'. It was lifted for single release and promoted on a tour of the UK when Lindsay supported **Steel Pulse**.

● ALBUMS: *Where Is Your Love* (Gem 1979)★★★, *Children Of Rastafari* (Gem 1980)★★.

Lindsay, Mark

b. 9 March 1942, Cambridge, Idaho, USA. Lindsay first achieved recognition as the lead vocalist of the US rock group **Paul Revere And The Raiders**. While with that group he launched a solo career. He first sang publicly in 1956 at a high school talent contest. Receiving a favourable response, he started a rock band. In 1958, he moved to Caldwell, Idaho, he sat in with an early band of Revere's, and was soon asked to replace singer Red Hughes. Lindsay also became the band's saxophonist. In the early 60s the group became one of the most popular in its region and ultimately one of the most popular in the USA. Lindsay made three singles in 1966 with Keith Allison and **Steve Alaimo**, as the Unknowns, but these were recorded as side projects; he was still very much at the helm of the Raiders. Lindsay announced his decision to begin an official solo career in April 1969 and for some time worked both as a soloist and the Raiders' singer. Lindsay's first solo single for **Columbia Records** was a **Jimmy Webb** composition, 'First Hymn From Grand Terrace' (1969), but it failed to make any impression upon the charts. His next, 'Arizona', signalled the true start of his solo success by reaching number 10 in the USA, remaining his most successful solo single. At that point, Columbia opted to shorten the group's name simply to the Raiders, to denigrate Revere's involvement (Revere was primarily the keyboardist and bandleader, while Lindsay sang all of their material.) Despite that action, Lindsay's *Arizona* outperformed the Raiders' own *Collage* in early 1970, the former reaching number 36 on the US charts while the latter stalled at number 154. This pattern continued, with Lindsay's single 'Silver Bird' reaching number 25 that year and the album of the same title hitting number 82. Oddly, in 1971, the Raiders' career received a great boost with the success of the single 'Indian Reservation (The Lament Of The Cherokee Reservation Indian)', a cover of a song which English singer **Don Fardon** had taken to number 20 in 1968. It became the Raiders' only number 1 single and sparked a Top 20 album of the same title. But that was to be a last gasp for both the Raiders and Lindsay. Although Lindsay returned to working with the group, neither party scored another major hit record. Lindsay failed to make either the singles or albums charts after 1971, and the Raiders' own run ended in 1973. Lindsay finally left the group in early 1975, making two unsuccessful singles for **Warner Brothers Records** in 1977. He quit performing and recording altogether when that contract expired, and did not make another appearance until the late 80s. In 1990, he began work on what would be his first solo album in 18 years.

● ALBUMS: *Arizona* (1970)★★★★, *Silverbird* (1970)★★★, *You've Got A Friend* (1971)★★★.

Lindsay, Reg

b. 7 July 1930, Parkes, New South Wales, Australia. The family's ancestors had arrived from the UK to seek gold but found only hard work, which led ultimately to the boy growing up in an inland farming area known as the Golden West. He learned to play fiddle and mandolin from his father and is reputed to have played 'The Wheel Of The Wagon Is Broken' on the harmonica at the age of four. He developed a great interest in country music from the recordings of such singers as **Wilf Carter** and **Tex Morton**. The family relocated to Adelaide but whenever possible, Lindsay spent his free time out of town, working on farms and learning the life of a cowboy. During this time, he mastered the banjo and guitar and worked hard on his singing and yodelling. After leaving school, he worked in the shearing sheds and as a fencing contractor before being hurt in a rodeo accident. In 1951, while confined to bed recuperating, he heard of a major talent show being held in Sydney that was organized by top country singer **Tim McNamara**. He made the long trip to Sydney and, singing 'Streamlined Yodel Song', won the contest, pushing **Shorty Ranger** into second place. The prize was a recording contract with Rodeo Records, but the win also led to demands for personal appearances and considerable radio work. Throughout the 50s and 60s,

he had popular radio shows on major Australian stations including 2CH, 2SM and 2KY. In the mid-60s, he also added television work to his busy schedule, which included touring with his own show. In 1954, he married Heather McKean (**Slim Dusty**'s sister-in-law) and worked some tours with his brother-in-law (the marriage produced three daughters but the couple later divorced). The same year, Lindsay was booked to accompany his idol, Wilf Carter, on his Australasian tour and when (after a week) Carter was forced through throat problems to quit, Lindsay continued the tour with his own show. He proved so popular that the 'tour' went on for over five years. In 1968, he made his first visit to the USA, where he appeared on the ***Grand Ole Opry***. A later appearance saw him become the first Australian country artist to play the networked Saturday Night *Opry* segment. He has since made many trips to the USA and has made several recordings in Nashville and even worked on record production there. Over the years, he has released a steady stream of records, on **EMI** (after Rodeo) until the late 60s, then the Festival label, another spell with EMI, and subsequently the Seven label, which led to his recordings being released in America on Con Brio. He is probably the first Australian artist to use an electric lead guitar and he even used a didgeridoo on records (on 'Walkabout Rock 'n' Roll'). His many recordings have included rockabilly, bluegrass, boogie and on occasions, he has used orchestral backings. Though rated by many to be one of the best exponents around, he dropped the yodel during the late 50s, citing overkill of the technique, but in more recent times, he has used it again to great effect. In a career now lasting over four decades, he has become one of Australia's most popular and versatile entertainers. He has won many awards, including being made an honorary citizen of Tennessee for his promotion of country music worldwide. He also starred on the first ever country music show at the Sydney Opera House. In 1984, he became the ninth artist to be elected to the Country Music Roll Of Renown (Australia's equivalent to Nashville's Country Music Hall Of Fame). Surprisingly, although he is a major star in his own hemisphere and well known in the USA, he is still relatively unknown in the UK and Europe, except to the devout band of followers of Australian country music.

● ALBUMS: *Country Music Comes To Town* (EMI 1961)★★★★, *Reg Lindsay Favourites* (EMI 1962)★★★, *Country And Western Singalong* (EMI 1963)★★★, *Songs For Country Folk* (EMI 1964)★★★, *Another Country And Western Singalong* (EMI 1964)★★★, *Reg Lindsay Encores* (EMI 1964)★★★, *Reg Lindsay's National Country & Western Hour* (Festival 1965)★★★, *Country & Western Million Sellers* (Festival 1966)★★★, *Glory Land Way* (Festival 1967)★★★, with Heather McKean *Country Duets From Reg And Heather* (Festival 1968)★★★, *TV Requests* (Festival 60s)★★★, *Roadside Mail Box* (Festival 60s)★★★, *Reg Lindsay On Tour* (Festival 60s)★★, *Australia's Country Music Man* (Festival 60s)★★★★, *Hot Shot Country* (Festival 60s)★★★, *She*

Taught Me To Yodel (Festival 1970)★★★, *Armstrong* (Festival 1970)★★★, *Out On The Lone Prairie* (Columbia 70s)★★★, *Country & Western Greats* (WRC 1972)★★★, *Country Music Jamboree* (Summit 1973)★★★, *Australia's King Of The Road* (Summit 1973)★★★, *21st Anniversary Album* (Festival 1973)★★★, *Country Favourites* (Summit 1974)★★★, *Country Classics* (Summit 1974)★★★, *Reg Lindsay* (Festival 1974)★★★, *Country And Western Greats* (Calendar 1974)★★★, *Reg Lindsay In Nashville* (Festival 1975)★★★, *The Travellin' Man* (Festival 1976)★★★, *Silence On The Line* (EMI 1977)★★★, *Play Me A Simple Song* (EMI 1978)★★★, *The World Of Rodeo* (EMI 1978)★★★, *Some Of The Best* (EMI 1978)★★★, *Standing Tall* (Brook 1979)★★★, *Ten Ten Two And A Quarter* (Brook 1980)★★★, *If You Could See Me Now* (Telmak 1981)★★★, *Will The Real Reg Lindsay* (Powderworks 1982)★★, *I've Always Wanted To Do That* (RCA 1985)★★★, *Lifetime Of Country Music* (Hammard 1987)★★★.

● COMPILATIONS: *20 Golden Country Greats* (Festival 1965)★★★★, *Classics* (EMI 1981)★★★★

Lindsey, Judy

b. Austin, Texas, USA. The country singer Judy Lindsey attended North Texas State University and then took a job at the Bauder Fashion College where she taught modelling and psychology. She had her own modelling career and took part in a long-running campaign for Dodge cars. She wanted to be a singer and when she met **Johnny Carroll** in 1977, she encouraged Carroll to start performing again; they formed the Judy And Johnny Band, which had a residency at the Hilton Hotel in Fort Worth. By 1983, Lindsey had added **Wanda Jackson**'s rock 'n' roll hits to her repertoire, which proved popular with audiences. She released 'Fujiyama Mama' as a single and as time went on, she recorded more and more on her own. She had a minor hit in 1989 with 'Wrong Train'.

Lindsey, LaWanda

b. 12 January 1953, Tampa, Florida, USA. Lindsey's family moved to Savannah, Georgia, soon after her birth; her father was the manager of a local country music radio station and played on air with his group the Dixie Showboys. From the age of five, Lindsey was featured with the band. **Conway Twitty** was impressed by her talent and, through his help, she signed with Chart Records in 1967. Her first singles included 'Beggars Can't Be Choosers', 'Wave Bye Bye To The Man' and two duets with Kenny Vernon, 'Eye To Eye' and 'Pickin' Wild Mountain Berries', which was her biggest-selling record. In 1970, she had a solo hit on the US country charts with 'Partly Bill'. Although she continued to record and had several minor successes, she did not manage to establish herself as an adult country artist.

● ALBUMS: *Swingin' And Singin' My Songs* (Chart 1969)★★★, *We'll Sing In The Sunshine* (Chart 1970)★★★, with Kenny Vernon *Pickin' Wild Mountain Berries* (Chart 1970)★★★, *This Is LaWanda Lindsey* (Capitol 1974)★★.

● COMPILATIONS: *Greatest Hits* (Chart 1971)★★★.

Line Records

Germany's leading independent label, Line Records was founded in Hamburg in 1979 by Uwe Tessnow, a former A&R representative of **Decca Records**' German branch. Initially the label was launched as an outlet for long-deleted gems licensed by Anglo-American companies, featuring artists including **Link Wray**, **Terry And The Pirates**, Jon Lord, **Moby Grape**, **Mike Bloomfield**, **Randy California**, Jon Mark and others. Tessnow specialised in re-activating yesterday's heroes, relaunching the careers of **Family** singer **Roger Chapman**, **Mickey Jupp**, Chris Youlden (ex-**Savoy Brown**) and **Mitch Ryder**, the latter still contracted to the label into the 90s. One of Line's outstanding landmarks was the highly recommended 50 CD series, *Rock File*, comprising 800 rare classics from the American Top 40 of the 50s and early 60s. In the second half of the 80s Line concentrated on acquiring rights to new material, having signed **Iain Matthews**, **Plainsong** and **Richard Barone** since.

Linkchain, Hip

b. Willie Richard, 10 November 1936, near Jackson, Mississippi, USA, d. 13 February 1989, Chicago, Illinois, USA. As a baby, Linkchain was known as Long Linkchain. He heard the blues at home and learned to play acoustic guitar, switching to electric after settling in Chicago in the early 50s. He formed his first band in 1959 and recorded singles in the 60s for the Lola and Sann labels under the name 'Hip Lanchan'. In the 70s he had a single issued by Blues King, and on the JSP label, an album featuring further titles from this session plus earlier tracks. Albums also appeared on MCM, Rumble (with **Jimmy Dawkins**), Teardrop (including a collaboration with Jimmy Rogers) and a highly acclaimed set for Black Magic. He died of cancer in 1989. Linkchain's guitar style was unique in the west side Chicago tradition, and he was a talented songwriter and singer.

● ALBUMS: *Airbuster* (Black Magic 1987)★★★★.

Linn County

Formed in Chicago, Illinois, USA, this powerful, blues-based quintet - Stephen Miller (organ, vocals), Fred Walk (guitar, sitar), Larry Easter (saxophones, flute), Dino Long (bass) and Jerome 'Snake' McAndrew (drums) - subsequently moved to San Francisco. Their impressive debut, *Proud Flesh Soothsayer*, included the lengthy 'Protect And Serve/Bad Things' which showcased the exhilarating interplay between the unit's instrumental protagonists. A more orthodox collection, *Fever Shot*, nonetheless featured several hard-edged, disciplined performances, while a final release, *Till The Break Of Dawn*, offered a vibrant reading of **John Lee Hooker**'s 'Boogie Chillun' as its highlight. By this point McAndrew had been replaced by Clark Pierson, but the group was unable to capitalize upon their cult status and broke up soon afterwards. Miller completed a solo album, which featured the entire Linn County line-up,

before joining the **Elvin Bishop** group. Pierson drummed in **Janis Joplin**'s Full Tilt Boogie Band.
● ALBUMS: *Proud Flesh Soothsayer* (1968)★★★, *Fever Shot* (1969)★★★, *Till The Break Of Dawn* (1970)★★★.

Linus

Linus consist of two American sisters, Jennifer (bass, guitar, vocals) and Tammy Denitto (vocals), now based in the UK, who formed the band in 1989 in London along with Peter (drums) and Andy Roberts (guitar). In 1992, their performances began to attract attention and their debut EP, issued on Bone Records, aroused further interest. Their music, ranging from wiry, cutting pop to restrained, reflective laments, was more forcefully promoted the following year. The single, 'Super Golgotha Crucifixion Scene', and album, *Yougli*, won them new fans. The single was BBC Radio One's *Evening Session*'s Single Of The Week. Its title was typical of their intriguing but often obscure lyrics. Steve Hughes was brought in on drums before a UK tour to promote the album. In 1995 two EPs were released by Elemental Records, *Supercool* and *Better Genes*.
● ALBUMS: *Yougli* (Elemental 1994)★★★.

Linx

One of the leading lights in the brief but high-profile Brit-funk movement of the early 80s (with **Light Of The World**, its spin-offs Beggar And Co, **Imagination** and **Freeez**), Linx were based around the duo of **David Grant** (b. 8 August, 1956, Kingston, Jamaica, West Indies; vocals) and Sketch Martin (b. 1954, Antigua, West Indies; bass), and completed by Bob Carter (keyboards) and Andy Duncan (drums). Grant's family moved to the UK in the late 50s and he grew up in north London. Sketch was taken to the UK when he was four, and was based in West Ham, east London. They met while working in a hi-fi shop. Grant later opened a record shop with his cousin, and became a junior reporter on a local paper, before working at **Island Records**' press office. Martin worked for the civil service, a film company, and the Performing Rights Society. They had their debut single, 'You're Lying', released as a private pressing (1,000 copies) and sold through a specialist funk shop before **Chrysalis Records** picked up on it and enabled it to be a hit. They were the first of the Brit Funk bands to make an impression in the USA, when 'You're Lying' made the R&B charts. Further singles included 'Intuition' and 'So This Is Romance'. The video for 'Intuition' featured the late Bertice Reading, while their stage performances harked back to the best traditions of the **Glitter Band** and **Adam And The Ants** by employing twin drummers. Grant moved on to a solo career with Chrysalis and had hit duets with **Jaki Graham**. He moved to **Polydor** in 1987 then Fourth and Broadway in 1990.
● ALBUMS: *Intuition* (Chrysalis 1981)★★★, *Go Ahead* (Chrysalis 1981)★★.
● COMPILATIONS: *The Best Of David Grant And Linx* (Chrysalis 1993)★★★.

Lion

After the demise of the largely overlooked UK hard rock band **Tytan**, vocalist Kal Swan left England for Los Angeles to assemble his own band. Formed in 1983, Lion consisted of Swan (vocals), Doug Aldrich (guitar), Jerry Best (bass) and ex-**Steeler** drummer Mark Edwards. The band quickly produced a self-financed EP, *Powerlove* (only available as a Japanese release), which gained them a strong following in the Far East. Owing to the interest being shown in them, primarily through their contributions to the soundtracks of two films, *The Wraith* and *Transformers*, they attracted the attention of the Scotti Brothers label. This resulted in the band's debut, *Dangerous Attraction*, released in 1987. This proved to be a strong, melodic hard rock effort, on which Swan's soaring vocals came to the fore. However, Scotti Brothers failed adequately to promote the record and album sales suffered. The band signed a new recording agreement with Grand Slam Records after disentangling themselves from their former employers, resulting in *Trouble At Angel City* being released in 1989. Unfortunately, soon after the record's release, the band folded owing to drummer Mark Edwards experiencing a debilitating accident and guitarist Doug Aldrich leaving to join **Hurricane**.
● ALBUMS: *Power Love* Japan only (Lion 1985)★★★★, *Dangerous Attraction* (Scotti Bros 1987)★★★, *Trouble At Angel City* (Grand Slam 1989)★★.

Lion King, The

'Prepare to be awed', was *Time* magazine's warning when the latest **Walt Disney** blockbuster was preparing to dominate the world's cinema screens in 1994. Unlike the Studio's previous feature length animated triumphs, *The Lion King* is not based on an established fairy tale or children's book. Instead, the witty screenplay, by Irene Mecchi, Jonathan Roberts and Linda Woolverton, weaves a timeless tale of 'monarchical principal, family unity and male supremacy', and has 'lions dancing with zebras, monkeys aping around with warthogs and ostriches, and giraffes performing as in the *Folies Bergère*'. With a soundtrack full of perfectly selected, familiar voices, the Hamlet-style hero, Simba the lion cub (Jonathan Taylor Thomas), is cheated out of his inheritance by his wicked Uncle Scar (Jeremy Irons), after he has seen his regal father, Mufasa (James Earl Jones), killed while trying to rescue him from a stampeding herd of hyenas and wildebeests. It takes a long period in the wilderness, where he meets up with Pumbaa, the weird and wonderful warthog (Ernie Sabella) and Timon, the marvellous meercat (Nathan Lane), before the grown Simba (now voiced by Matthew Broderick), urged by the ghost of his dead father, returns to dispose of his murdering uncle and take his rightful place in the scheme of things. Also contributing their vocal talents to a heartwarming range of characters, are Rowan Atkinson (as Zazu the hornbill) and Whoopi Goldberg, Cheech Marin (ex-**Cheech And Chong**) and Jim Cummings as a trio of a leering hyenas. The critics were unanimous in their praise of the film's 'technical wizardry and rich imagery, the late 20th century sophistication', and 'the lurid colours, that are so right for the African subject matter', although some of them had reservations about the degree of violence involved in some scenes, and the lack of political correctness. The general feeling seemed to be that the film's music was not in the same class as that which graced two of Disney's other recent animated successes, *The Little Mermaid* and *Beauty And The Beast*. Even so, **Hans Zimmer**'s score, and one of **Elton John** and **Tim Rice**'s songs, 'Can You Feel The Love Tonight', won Oscars, and the soundtrack was awarded two Grammys. With forecasts in the order of 'this will be the most successful film of the century', *The Lion King*, which was directed by Roger Allers and Rob Minkoff, grossed £21 million over the first weekend of its release.

Lioness

Founded by lead singer and songwriter Teri Owens, and largely inspired by her staunch Rastafarian beliefs and morals, Lioness's sound is rendered unique by the employment of instrumentation drawn from outside of reggae's normal canon, notably Janet Irvine's flute. Their 'cultural' lyrics are equally refreshing, a return to the roots flavour that has been overshadowed by modern **dancehall** tastes.
● ALBUMS: *Jah Works* (1989)★★★, *Jah Victory* (Dawter 1991)★★★.

Lionheart

Formed in 1980 by Dennis Stratton (guitar) on his exit from **Iron Maiden**, he was joined in this crusade by vocalist Jess Cox (**Tygers Of Pan Tang**), Frank Noon (Next Band/**Def Leppard**) on drums, Steve Mann (Liar) on guitar and Rocky Newton (**Wildfire**) on bass. They made their highly impressive debut one Saturday night at the Marquee, London, but suffered from bad press thanks to criticism of Cox. This led to the cancellation of the next two appearances and saw Cox replaced by Reuben Archer (Lautrec). Noon quit in 1981 to join **Paul Di'Anno**'s band before setting off for **Waysted**. The nucleus of Stratton, Mann and Newton continued with various line-ups that included drummers Les Binks (**Judas Priest**) and Clive Edwards (**Grand Prix**). In 1982 they signed to Heavy Metal Records but only managed to release one track, on the *Heavy Metal Heroes Vol 2* compilation. That track, 'Lionheart', remains the only representative recording of their early sound, as they later changed their style significantly. With the addition of Chad Brown on vocals and session drummer Robert Jenkins, they went on to record an album with producer Kevin Beamish (**REO Speedwagon**). This was a slick, Americanized effort that failed to capture the old fans' interest or that of their target audience in the USA. In 1985 they continued with drummer Andy Bierne and Phil Lanzon (keyboards), who had been playing with re-formed glam rockers **Sweet**. After a while, Lanzon also left and was replaced by Steve Mann from Stratus and new vocalist Keith Murrell. They eventually split up in 1986, with Bierne going into management, Murrell to **Mama's Boys** and Newton and Mann joining **MSG**. Stratton later found fame in Japan as part of the British All Stars/**Praying Mantis** line-up, which featured a number of ex-**N.W.O.B.H.M.** musicians.
● ALBUMS: *Die For Love* (Epic 1984)★★★.

Lionrock

Lionrock is one of the many vehicles used by Manchester disc jockey/remixer/artist **Justin Robertson** (b. *c.*1968, England). Robertson had risen to prominence in 1990 by launching the Spice club session, a meeting place for like-minds such as the **Chemical Brothers** (at that time the Dust Brothers). Alongside **Andy Weatherall**, Robertson subsequently became among the most prominent of a new wave of DJs, with his sets as Manchester's Heavenly club making him well-known within the dance community. This impression was confirmed by remixing credits for **Björk**, **New Order**, the **Shamen**, **Sugarcubes**, **Inspiral Carpets**, **Stereo MC's**, **Erasure** and many others. Lionrock, a name synonymous with uplifting house music and originally featuring keyboard player Mark Stagg, was formed in 1992 for the release of a self-titled 12-inch single on Robertson's own MERC Records. The following year's 'Packet Of Peace' included a rap from **MC Buzz B** and saw the group transfer to **DeConstruction Records**. It entered the UK charts and became a staple of house clubs throughout the UK. 'Carnival', which sampled from the **MC5**, again secured several Single Of The Week awards, from both dance magazines and more mainstream publications. 'Tripwire' was released in 1994 and again reached the UK Top 40. Robertson described the contents of Lionrock's 1996 debut album as '**Coxsone Dodd** meets **Ennio Morricone**', a statement which indicated that earlier experiments with reggae and dub were continuing. MC Buzz B again guested, with samples of dialogue taken from old Sherlock Holmes films. Lionrock's line-up now included Roger Lyons (keyboards/electronics), Paddy (bass), Mandy Whigby (keyboards) and Buzz B (vocals) as the album was promoted with a full-scale national tour. Release of the follow-up was delayed, allowing Robertson the opportunity to record new tracks and rework the album, which was finally released in early 1998. *City Delirious* eschewed the guitar riffing of the debut to return to Robertson's dance roots on tracks such as 'Push Button Cocktail' and 'Best Foot Forward'.
● ALBUMS: *An Instinct For Detection* (DeConstruction 1996)★★★★, *City Delirious* (DeConstruction 1998)★★★★.

Lionsheart

Following his departure from UK heavy metal thrashers **Onslaught**, ex-**Grim Reaper** vocalist Steve Grimmett set about forming a more melodic band to suit his vocal abilities and musical inclinations, enlisting twin brothers Mark (guitar) and Steve Owers (bass), Graham Collet (keyboards) and Anthony Christmas (drums). Lionsheart signed to Music For Nations, but the Owers brothers departed before the release of their self-titled debut, with illness leaving Mark Owers unable to tour, and they were replaced by Nick Burr (guitar, ex-**Killers**; Idol Rich) and Zak Bajjon (bass). Lionsheart ignored grunge trends in favour of guitar-driven melodic hard rock with high-quality songwriting, and despite minimal reaction at home and in the USA, the band achieved deserved success in Europe and major status in Japan. *Pride In Tact* saw Lionsheart extending their approach from near-AOR balladry to harder blues-rock, with Burr proving equal to the task of following Mark Owers' performance on the debut.

● ALBUMS: *Lionsheart* (Music For Nation 1993)★★★, *Pride In Tact* (Music For Nations 1994)★★★.

Lipscomb, Mance

b. 9 April 1895, Navasota, Texas, USA, d. 30 January 1976, Navasota, Texas, USA. The son of a former slave and professional fiddle player, Lipscomb initially learned that instrument and later the guitar. For many years he played on a solely local basis, while working as a farmer, and only made his first recordings at the age of 65, in 1960. Over the following 15 years, he made a series of highly regarded albums, mainly for Chris Strachwitz's **Arhoolie** label. On the strength of these and his frequent live performances, he built up a very strong reputation for his skills as a singer of a wide range of material. His remarkably extensive repertoire encompassed gospel, rags, ballads and other traditional songs, as well as Texas-style blues. He also appeared in several films, including one biopic, *A Well Spent Life*.

● ALBUMS: *Texas Songster, Volumes 1 - 6* (1960, 1964, 1964, 1967, 1970, 1974)★★★, *You'll Never Find Another Man Like Mance* (Arhoolie 1964), *Texas Songster In A Live Performance* (Arhoolie 1966)★★★.

● COMPILATIONS: *Texas Songster* CD compilation of the *Texas Songster* series (Arhoolie 1989)★★★★, *You Got To Reap What You Sow* (Arhoolie 1993)★★★, *Right On Time* (Bullseye 1995)★★★.

● FURTHER READING: *I Say Me For A Parable: The Oral Autobiography*, Mance Lipscomb with Glen Alyn.

● FILMS: *A Well Spent Life*.

Lipton, Sydney

b. 4 January 1906, London, England. A popular and stylish dance band leader, Lipton learned to play the violin as a child, and was a member of cinema ensembles accompanying silent films in his early teens. His interest in dance band music led him to work in the 20s with Murray Hedges and **Billy Cotton**, before forming his own band in the early 30s. His first recordings to be released were made in 1932, and from then, until 1941, Sydney Lipton And His Orchestra were resident at the Grosvenor House in London, from where they broadcasted regularly. In the early days Lipton's signature tune was 'I'll See You In My Dreams', but in later years

he used two others, 'Just Dance And Leave The Music To Me' and 'Sweet Harmony'. After service in the Royal Artillery and the Royal Signals during World War II, Lipton returned to the Grosvenor House, and continued to purvey his particular brand of sophisticated dance music until 1967. He then formed his own successful entertainment agency, as well as serving as musical director for various prestige venues and cruise ships. Top sidemen who played in his bands over the years included **Ted Heath**, Harry Hayes, **Bill McGuffie**, Freddy Gardner, George Evans, Max Goldberg, Billy Munn and many more, along with vocalists such as Anona Wynn, Primrose Hayes, Les Allen, Chips Chippindall, and Lipton's daughter, Celia. An accomplished dancer and singer, Celia appeared in London shows such as *Get A Load Of This* and *The Quaker Girl,* and was a notable Peter Pan at the Scala Theatre, before moving to America while in her 20s. After appearing in cabaret, on television and starring in straight roles on Broadway, she retired from show business and settled in California, living the life of a society hostess, raising millions of dollars for charity. After her husband died in 1985 (leaving her a reported $200 million), Celia recorded two albums for her Independent label, *The London I Love* and *The Best Of Times*, and appeared in her own television special. In the late 80s she was joined in America by Sydney Lipton.

● ALBUMS: *Sweet Harmony* (Decca 1959),★★★★ *Dancing At The Grosvenor House Volumes 1, 2 and 3* (Decca 1960-61)★★★★, *Sydney Lipton And His Orchestra 1932-3* (Retrospect 1977)★★★★, *Just Dance* (Decca 1982)★★★, *Beautiful Melodies From Around The World* (Horatio Nelson 1985)★★★★.

LiPuma, Tommy

b. Cleveland, Ohio, USA. It is likely that any music fan with even a rudimentary record collection will be able to find Tommy LiPuma's name on the credits of at least one of their albums. By 1995 the president of **GRP Records**, a subsidiary of the MCA Entertainment Group, LiPuma has worked on sessions with **Miles Davis**, **George Benson**, **Barbra Streisand**, **Al Jarreau**, **Bill Evans**, **Dave Sanborn**, **Dave Mason**, **Michael Franks**, **Dan Hicks**, **Randy Crawford**, **Anita Baker** and **Natalie Cole**. Although a gifted business executive, it is his deeds in and around studios that have endeared him to so many in the USA's music industry, with his provinces including jazz, soul, R&B, pop and rock. His original interest in music sprung from playing the saxophone in Cleveland, where he was a regular purchaser of records by **Coleman Hawkins** and **Stan Getz**. His first industry post came as local promoter for M.S. Distribution, subsequently transferring to **Liberty Records** in Los Angeles, then New York. As a junior publisher he supervised demos for **Randy Newman**, **Jackie DeShannon** and others. His first single production was the **O'Jays'** 'Lipstick Traces'. He became the first A&R staff producer for **A&M Records** in 1966, securing his first gold record with the **Sandpipers**

(*Guantanamera*). He joined the **Blue Thumb Records** label in 1970, signing **Tina Turner** and the **Pointer Sisters**, and producing for Dan Hicks and Dave Mason. His first platinum-rated production was Barbra Streisand's 1973 **Columbia Records** release, *The Way We Were*. In 1974 he switched to **Warner Brothers Records**, producing Al Jarreau, Michael Franks and George Benson. His work on the latter's *Breezin'* album and 'This Masquerade' single won him 1976 Grammies for both Record and Album Of The Year. After a brief return to A&M (their Horizon label) he became vice president, jazz and progressive music, for Warners in 1979. His tenure there saw him work alongside Jarreau, **Earl Klugh**, **Patti Austin**, **Jennifer Holiday**, **Aztec Camera**, **Everything But The Girl** and Miles Davis, several of these projects producing platinum, gold or Grammy awards. He became executive vice president at **Elektra Records** in 1990, where his most notable achievement was his Grammy award-winning co-production of **Natalie Cole**'s *Unforgettable*. Although embroiled in the day-to-day running of GPR he still finds time to work with his artists, many of whom (**Dr. John**, George Benson) turn to him again and again for treatment sympathetic to their aims.

● ALBUMS as producer, therefore no ratings are given: O'Jays *Comin' Through* (Imperial 1965), Dan Hicks And His Hot Licks *Where's The Money* (Blue Thumb 1971), Barbra Streisand *The Way We Were* (Columbia 1974), George Benson *Breezin'* (Warners 1976), Al Jarreau *Glow* (Warners 1976), Dr. John *City Lights* (Horizon 1978), Randy Crawford *Secret Combination* (Warners 1981), Patti Austin *Getting Away With Murder* (Warners 1985), Miles Davis *TuTu* (Warners 1986), Aztec Camera *Love* (Warners 1987), Everything But The Girl *The Language Of Life* (Atlantic 1990), Natalie Cole *Unforgettable* (Elektra 1991), Anita Baker *Rhythm Of Love* (Elektra 1994), Dr. John *Afterglow* (Blue Thumb 1995).

Liquid

Group who originally comprised Eamon Downes and Shane Honegan, until the latter party left. They had become one of the first progressive house acts in the Top 20, with 1992's 'Sweet Harmony', recorded while they were still a duo, as a reaction to the 'louder faster' rules of hardcore techno. It cost only £200 to record yet saw them grace UK television's *Top Of The Pops* stage. Downes re-emerged in 1993 on the **XL** roster, after a period in the shadows with the *Time To Get Up* EP. He maintains that he calls himself Liquid because he 'likes the odd drink'. Early influences were dub maestros such as **Barrington Levy** and **Scientist**.

Liquid Jesus

This experimental Los Angeles-based quintet was formed in 1990 by bassist Johnny Lonely and guitarist Scott Tracey. Adding Todd Rigione (guitar), Buck Murphy (vocals) and John Molo (drums), they gigged incessantly on the LA bar and club circuit. Fusing psychedelic, blues, jazz and metal influences to bizarre extremes, they debuted with an independently released live album. Tipped by some as the next **Jane's Addiction**, they were signed by **Geffen Records** in 1991 and delivered *Pour In The Sky*. This pooled their influences of **Jimi Hendrix**, **Led Zeppelin**, the **Red Hot Chili Peppers** and **Queen**, but accusations of plagiarism were sidestepped by virtue of their totally deranged and unpredictable delivery.

● ALBUMS: *Liquid Jesus Live* (Liquid Jesus 1990)★★★, *Pour In The Sky* (Geffen 1991)★★★.

Liroy

b. Kielce, Poland. Proof of the increasing globalization of rap and hip-hop culture, Liroy is Poland's most prominent rapper. According to his self-aggrandizing record company biography, his youth was spent in a constant maelstrom of drunkenness, fights and reform schools, claims made to substantiate his billing as a gangsta rapper comparable with his heroes **Ice-T** and **LL Cool J**. He had originally joined several rock bands in the mid-80s before becoming a local DJ, making his live debut as a rapper in the late 80s. In 1991 he moved to France and founded Leeroy And The Western Posse with French and English friends, the group performing widely on the burgeoning French hip hop scene. After his return to Poland he secured a contract with BMG Ariola in 1994, leading to the release of the mini-album *Scyzoryk* (literally 'pocketknife') in 1995. The brutal themes included street violence and hardcore sex, with backing rhythms drawn from rock, pop and jazz.

● ALBUMS: *Scyzoryk* mini-album (BMG Ariola 1995)★★★.

Lisa Lisa And Cult Jam

Formed in Brooklyn, New York, USA, consisting of Lisa Velez (b. 1967, New York City, USA), the youngest of 10 children in her family, plus Mike Hughes (b. 1963) and Alex 'Spanador' Mosely (b. 1962). The two men in the group were members of the New York funk/soul group **Full Force**. Lisa Lisa And Cult Jam were signed to **Columbia Records** in 1985 and recorded their debut single, 'I Wonder If I Take You Home', only a week after forming. The single, which rose to the Top 10 in the R&B charts in the USA and the national UK Top 20, was produced, written and recorded with the complete Full Force aggregation - only in concert did Lisa Lisa work strictly in the reduced trio format. Lisa Lisa And Cult Jam continued to achieve US Top 10 singles in the national and dance charts throughout the late 80s, including two US number 1 hits in 1987, 'Head To Toe' and 'Lost In Emotion', as well as 'All Cried Out', 'Someone To Love Me For Me' and 'Everything Will B-Fine'. Their 1985, self-titled debut album was only moderately successful but 1987's *Spanish Fly* reached the US Top 10. In 1989, their third album, *Straight To The Sky*, stalled at number 77 and produced no hit singles.

● ALBUMS: *Lisa Lisa And Cult Jam With Full Force* (1985)★★★★, *Spanish Fly* (1987)★★★★, *Straight To The Sky* (1989)★★★.

Solo: Lisa Lisa *LL-77* (Pendulum 1994)★★★.

Lisberg, Harvey

b. 1940, Manchester, England. A chartered accountant turned pop manager, Lisberg entered the music business in 1964 after signing the Heartbeats (better known as **Herman's Hermits**). He took them to producer **Mickie Most** and by the end of the year they were number 1 in the UK with 'I'm Into Something Good'. Lisberg later teamed-up with the renowned agent **Danny Betesh** and became involved in his Kennedy Street Enterprises. During one week in early 1965, agent and manager found themselves on the top of the world when three of their acts, **Freddie And The Dreamers**, **Wayne Fontana And The Mindbenders** and Herman's Hermits held the first three places in the US chart. As manager of Herman's Hermits, Lisberg took full advantage of singer **Peter Noone**'s stardom in America, and supervised his entry into films by negotiating with the renowned producer, Sam Katzman. Lisberg was also responsible for directly selecting three of Herman's Hermits biggest world hits: 'Mrs Brown You've Got A Lovely Daughter', 'I'm Henry VIII, I Am' and 'Listen People'. While enjoying amazing success with Noone, Lisberg was less lucky with another Manchester group, the **Mockingbirds**, who failed to chart despite the presence of top songwriter **Graham Gouldman**. After briefly managing the **Herd**, Lisberg signed songwriters **Andrew Lloyd Webber** and **Tim Rice**, but abandoned them just before they completed the astonishingly successful musical, *Jesus Christ Superstar*. A brief association with vocalist **Tony Christie** was followed by another spectacular run of hits with **10cc**. Lisberg managed them from their early days as **Hotlegs** right through to the emergence of **Godley And Creme**. Along the way, he entered the 'progressive' market with acts such as **Julie Driscoll** and **Barclay James Harvest**, before finding another major hit act with **Sad Cafe**. For a time, Lisberg abandoned pop management in favour of looking after the careers of various snooker players, but sought new pop acts in the late 80s.

Lisbon Story, The (film musical)

Released by British National in 1946, this war-time story of intrigue set in Lisbon and Paris in 1940, was adapted by Jack Whittingham from Harold Purcell's long-running musical which opened in London in 1943. The delightful Patricia Burke recreated her stage role as Gabrielle Gerard, a French actress and singer, who risks accusations of collaborating with the invading Germans to assist a member of British Intelligence, David Warren (David Farrar), in his successful efforts to smuggle atom scientist Pierre Sargon (John Ruddock) back to England. David returns to Gabrielle after Paris has been liberated by the Allies, and they are married. The celebrated tenor, Richard Tauber, played Andre Joubert, Gabrielle's singing partner, and Walter Rilla was suitably evil as Karl von Schriner, Director of German Propaganda in Paris. Other roles went to Lawrence O'Madden, Austin Trevor, Harry Welchman, Paul Bonifas, Esme Percy, Noele Gordon, John Ruddock, and Joan Seton. Violin virtuoso **Stéphane Grappelli** was in it too, and so were two of the original show's hit songs, 'Pedro the Fisherman', 'Never Say Goodbye' (music Harry Parr-Davies, lyrics Harold Purcell). The former song was enormously popular during and after the war, especially in a recording by **Gracie Fields**. The picture itself, which was directed by Paul Stein, was pretty popular as well.

Lisbon Story, The (stage musical)

One of the most popular West End musicals during World War II, *The Lisbon Story* opened at the London Hippodrome on 17 June 1943. Fifty years on, it is still recalled fondly because of the inclusion of the jaunty 'Pedro The Fisherman', which almost immediately became an enormous hit. The song was part of a score written by composer Harry Parr-Davies and lyricist Harold Purcell, who also provided a book in which wartime drama was mixed with sentimental music and lavish dance sequences in a spectacular and entertaining fashion. The story concerns a Parisian prima ballerina, Gabrielle Gerard (Patricia Burke), who colludes with the Nazis in an effort to secure the release of an important French scientist. When her deceit is discovered, she is executed. Albert Lieven played her German go-between, Carl von Shriner, and the cast also included Arséne Kiriloff, Zulia, Noele Gordon, Jack Livesey, Margaret McGrath, Reginald Long, and Joseph Dollinger. There were two major dance scenes and a lovely operetta sequence. The score contained several attractive numbers, including the waltz, 'Someday We Shall Meet Again', 'Never Say Goodbye', 'For The First Time (I've Fallen In Love)', 'Follow The Drum', 'Happy Days', and 'A Serenade For Sale', but it was 'Pedro The Fisherman', which was sung in the show by Vincent Tildsley's Master Singers, in sailor rig, that audiences were whistling when they left the theatre. Patricia Burke made a successful recording of the song, as did the distinguished tenor, Richard Tauber, who appeared with her in the 1946 film of *The Lisbon Story*. Probably the version that endured the most, and which received consistent exposure on BBC Radio's *Family Favourites* programme, was that by **Gracie Fields**.

Lismor Records

This Glasgow, Scotland folk label was originally to have been named Lismore, after the region, until the Registrar Of Companies informed founder Peter Hamilton that a land mass could not be used to register a new company. He promptly dropped the vowel and Lismor Records, based at his music store in Argyll Street, Glasgow, was established with the 1973 release of *The Dark Island* by Gaelic tenor, David Solley. Hamilton had owned the store since the early 60s, and the record label became the fruition of his dream to offer Scottish folk talent an outlet that previous generations had been forced to travel south to London to enjoy. Artists such as Peter Morrison, Jim Johnstone and the Tartan Lads became house stars, while Scottish pipe bands such as the Shotts And Dykehead Caledonia and Dysart And Dundonald also recorded extensively for the label. This connection led to Lismor being invited to document successive World Championship Pipe Winners, culminating in a trip to Toronto, Canada, to record a tattoo led by the 78th Fraser Highlanders - the first 'foreign' winners. The series is maintained to this day. In the 80s the label was taken over by Ronnie Simpson, former deputy to Frank Lynch at the famed Glasgow Apollo Centre, alongside accountant Andrew Harvey. They sought to expand the label further and managed to sign the **Alexander Brothers**, among Scottish traditional music's most popular practitioners, on their return from London-based recording arrangements in 1981. **Andy Stewart** and **Kenneth McKellar** followed in 1983 and 1985. When **Moira Anderson** also signed in 1988 it meant that Lismor had a near monopoly of the major Scottish traditional artists of the period. In 1990 the label took over the running of Iona Records, adding a contemporary roster of groups such as **Rock, Salt And Nails, Avalon** and **Wolfstone**. The main imprint itself had also established a dialogue with rock/pop based artists, including the first recordings issued by the subsequently hugely popular **Runrig**. Lismor's foresight in allowing Scottish voices a platform in their own country and context has paid rich rewards, and the label's part in the resurgence of tartan music in the 90s (through bands such as **Capercaillie** and the aforementioned Runrig) is equally significant.

Liston, Melba

b. 13 January 1926, Kansas City, Missouri, USA. Although she was born and spent her childhood in Kansas City during its hottest jazz years, Liston's entry into music began in Los Angeles where her family moved when she was 11 years old. At the age of 16, she joined the pit band, playing trombone, at the Lincoln Theatre and the following year, 1943, joined **Gerald Wilson**'s orchestra. With Wilson's guidance and encouragement, she began arranging but remained an active performer, appearing on record with an old school friend, **Dexter Gordon**. When the Wilson band folded while on a tour of the east coast, Liston was hired by **Dizzy Gillespie**. This was in 1948 and the following year she toured briefly with Wilson who was leading a band accompanying **Billie Holiday**. The tour was a disaster and the experience led to Liston quitting music for a while. She worked as an educational administrator in California, played occasionally in clubs, and also worked as an extra in films. In 1956, and again in 1957, she returned to Gillespie for his State Department tours of the Middle East, Asia and South America. She then began a musical association with **Quincy Jones**, writing scores for his band and working on the show *Free And Easy* with which they toured Europe. In the 60s, she wrote extensively for **Randy Weston** and occasionally for **Duke Ellington**, **Solomon Burke** and **Tony Bennett**. Her arrangements were used on **Johnny**

Griffin's *White Gardenia*. In the 70s she was involved in a number of jazz educational projects, especially in Jamaica where, for almost six years, she ran the pop and jazz division of the country's School of Music. She continued to write charts for the bands of Ellington and **Count Basie** and singers such as **Abbey Lincoln** and **Diana Ross**. At the end of the 70s she was persuaded to return to the USA as the headline attraction at the first Kansas City Women's Jazz Festival. There, she led her own band, with an all-woman line-up, and made a great impact. Her successful return to playing led to a revitalisation of her performing career and although her band later developed into a 'mixed' group, she has continued to play an important role in furthering the role of women in jazz. A sound section player whose ballad solos are particularly effective, Liston is one of the best latter-day arrangers in jazz. Unfortunately, the male domination of so many aspects of the jazz life has resulted in this enormously talented artist remaining little-known, even within the jazz community itself.

● ALBUMS: with Dexter Gordon *The Chase* (1947)★★★, *Dizzy Gillespie At Newport* (1957)★★★★, *Melba Liston And Her Orchestra* (1958)★★★, with Randy Weston *Uhuru Afrika* (1960)★★, with Weston *Volcano Blues* (1993)★★★.

Lisztomania

In his early career the maverick British film director Ken Russell made several controversial biographies of revered classic composers. These early films were notable for introducing previously unknown aspects of the composers' private lives. This reached a peak with the Tchaikovsky feature, *The Music Lovers*. Russell's later work was often criticised as excessive, particularly in the wake of his film of the **Who**'s rock-opera, *Tommy* (1975). The group's lead singer, **Roger Daltrey**, starred in *Lisztomania*, which was released that same year. However, the director's attempt to portray the composer as a hedonistic rock star was artistically unsatisfying, and did much to undermine Russell's reputation. **Ringo Starr** and **Paul Nicholas** were part of an uninspired cast while ex-**Yes** keyboard player **Rick Wakeman** provided a score comprised of heavy-handed treatments of Liszt and Wagner compositions. *Lisztomania* played upon the artistic flaws of all the participants.

Litherland, Harry

b. Lancashire, England. Litherland is an excellent example of England's street busking tradition, an important arena for young musicians to learn their craft but also a viable occupation in its own right. Playing his concertina (a McCann Duet model which was originally owned by his father) in northern market towns, Litherland formerly earned his living working on the railways. However, now he considers his redundancy to be a 'blessing'. His repertoire is predominantly drawn from the earlier half of the twentieth century, and includes popular standards such as 'Daisy, Daisy' and 'I Do Like To Be Beside The Seaside'. He occasionally travels to Europe, and despite his advancing years still relishes the busker's life: 'You're meeting people all the time, different people.'

Litter

Based in Minneapolis, Minnesota, USA, Denny Waite (vocals/organ), Tom Kaplan (lead guitar), Dan Rinaldi (rhythm guitar/vocals), Jim Kane (bass) and Tom Murray (drums) won cult acclaim for the impressive *Distortions*. Inspired by British favourites the **Who**, **Spencer Davis Group** and **Yardbirds**, the Litter drew material from such mentors, infusing it with garage band simplicity and a penchant for feedback. The same style prevailed on *$100 Fine*, on which the quintet's own songwriting flourished, although the set lacked the naive charm of its predecessor. This artistic demise was confirmed with *Emerge*, the group's first recording for a major label. With a new lead vocalist in Mark Gallagher, the brand of progressive hard rock on offer here was indistinguishable from a myriad of contemporaries and Litter ceased recording with its release.

● ALBUMS: *Distortions* (1968)★★★, *$100 Fine* (1969)★★, *Emerge* (1969)★★, *Distortions/$100 Fine* (Eura 1997)★★★.

Little Angels

This UK heavy rock quintet was formed in Scarborough, Yorkshire, during 1985, originally under the title Mr Thrud. Comprising Tony Jepson (vocals), Bruce John Dickinson (b. 10 May 1968, Berwick-upon-Tweed, Scotland; guitar), Mark Plunkett (bass), Jimmy Dickinson (keyboards) and Dave Hopper (drums), they were a youthful outfit, whose energy and enthusiasm in the live setting won them a loyal fanbase in their native north-east. Following a series of independent releases, notably the seven-track *Too Posh To Mosh*, they attracted the attention of **Polydor Records**. *Don't Prey For Me*, which featured new drummer Michael Lee, included a dozen gems of melodic, but roughshod, rock 'n' roll, characterized by Jepson's raucous and charismatic vocals. The big-budget follow-up, mixed by the Steve Thompson/Michael Barbiero partnership, was a disappointment. Abandoning their roots, this set saw them make a concerted attempt to break into the American FM radio market. Internal disputes began to manifest themselves in 1991. Drummer Michael Lee secretly auditioned for the **Cult**, and was ejected from the band as a result. His replacement was Mark Richardson. *Jam* regained much of the lost ground in 1993, entering the UK charts at number 1 and winning them the support slot on **Van Halen**'s European tour. However, having found their niche, they nevertheless elected to go their separate ways in 1994. The Dickinsons moved on to **b.l.o.w.**

● ALBUMS: *Too Posh To Mosh* (Powerstation 1987)★★★★, *Don't Prey For Me* (Polydor 1989)★★★★, *Young Gods* (Polydor 1991)★, *Jam* (Polydor 1993)★★★, *Little Of The Past* (Polydor 1994)★★★.

● COMPILATIONS: *Too Posh To Nosh* (Castle 1994)★★★.

● VIDEOS: *Big Bad Video* (1991).

Little Anthony And The Imperials

Formed in Brooklyn, New York, USA, in 1957, and originally called the Chesters, the group comprised 'Little' Anthony Gourdine (b. 8 January 1940, Brooklyn, New York, USA), Ernest Wright Jnr. (b. 24 August 1941, Brooklyn, New York, USA), Clarence Collins (b. 17 March 1941, Brooklyn, New York, USA), Tracy Lord and Glouster Rogers (b. 1940). A vital link between doo-wop and sweet soul, the Imperials were the prototype for the **Delfonics** and **Stylistics**. Gourdine first recorded in 1956 as a member of the Duponts. From there he helped form the Chesters, who became the Imperials on signing to the End label. The 'Little Anthony' prefix was subsequently added at the suggestion of the influential disc jockey **Alan Freed**. The group's first hit, the haunting 'Tears On My Pillow' (1958), encapsulated the essence of street-corner harmony. Further success came with 'So Much' (1959) and 'Shimmy Shimmy Ko-Ko-Bop' (1960), before Gourdine was persuaded to embark on an ill-fated solo career. In 1964, he formed a 'new' Imperials around Wright, Collins and Sammy Strain (b. 9 December 1940). Their first hit, 'I'm On The Outside (Looking In)', showcased Gourdine's dazzling falsetto, a style continued on 'Goin' Out Of My Head' and 'Hurt So Bad' (both of which reached the US pop Top 10). Complementing these graceful releases were such up-tempo offerings as 'Better Use Your Head' and 'Gonna Fix You Good' (both 1966). The line-up later drifted apart and in 1974 Sammy Strain replaced William Powell in the **O'Jays**. Three years later, Collins formed his own 'Imperials', touring Britain on the strength of two hit singles, a reissued 'Better Use Your Head', and a new recording, 'Who's Gonna Love Me'. In the 80s Gourdine released *Daylight* on the religious outlet Songbird.

● ALBUMS: *We Are Little Anthony And The Imperials* (End 1959)★★★, *Shades Of The 40's* (End 1961)★★★, *I'm On The Outside Looking In* (DCP 1964)★★★, *Goin' Out Of My Head* (DCP 1965)★★★, *Paying Our Dues* (Veep 1967)★★★, *Reflections* (Veep 1967)★★, *Movie Grabbers* (Veep 1968)★★, *Out Of Sight, Out Of Mind* (United Artists 1969)★★, *On A New Street* (Avco 1974)★★.

Solo: Anthony Gourdine *Daylight* (Songbird 1980)★★.

● COMPILATIONS: *Little Anthony And The Imperials Greatest Hits* (Roulette 1965)★★★, *The Best Of Little Anthony And The Imperials* (DCP 1966)★★★, *The Best Of Little Anthony And The Imperials* (Rhino 1989)★★★.

Little Beaver

b. William Hale, 15 August 1945, Forest City, Arkansas, USA. Little Beaver, a singer and guitarist, made his mark on the tail-end of the soul era in the early 70s, with a typical southern-style body of work that included both blues and soul traditions. Little Beaver grew up in Arkansas but as a teenager moved to Florida. He recorded some local hits for various labels, with a **Bobby Bland**-style gospel-blues voice. He then joined Henry Stone's TK complex of labels in 1971, and penned some hits for **Betty Wright** as well as playing on innumerable sessions. By the time Little Beaver first recorded on his own for TK's Cat subsidiary in 1972, he had found his own voice and style and had a national hit with 'Joey' (number 48 R&B). His biggest hit was 'Party Down' (number 2 R&B) from 1974. His deep southern sound was not all that compatible with the emerging disco and funk trends and Beaver had his last chart record in 1976.

● ALBUMS: *Joey* (Cat 1972)★★★★, *Black Rhapsody* (Cat 1973)★★★, *Little Beaver* (Cat 1974)★★★, *Party Down* (Cat 1975)★★, *When Was The Last Time* (Cat 1977)★★.

● COMPILATIONS: *Party Down* (Collectables 1994)★★★, *The Very Best Of ...* (Sequel 1997)★★.

Little Big Band
A pseudonym for the talented folk/blues musician, Rob Gray, from Manchester, England. Between high level gigs, he busks in city centre shopping arcades.

● ALBUMS: *Little Big Band* (1989)★★★.

Little Caesar
A highly underrated R&B-influenced rock band from Los Angeles, Little Caesar made their recorded debut with one track, 'Down To The Wire', on *Street Survivors*, a compilation showcasing the best unsigned local bands. With a line-up of Ron Young (vocals), Apache (guitar, steel guitar), Louren Molinaire (guitar), Fidel Paniagua (bass) and Tom Morris (drums), an EP, *Name Your Poison*, was recorded, helping the band to secure a major contract with **Geffen**. The self-titled debut, produced by Bob Rock, deservedly received excellent reviews. Packed with good material, from the basic rock 'n' roll of 'Down-N-Dirty' to the more soulful R&B of 'In Your Arms', plus two **Motown** cover versions in 'Chain Of Fools' and 'I Wish It Would Rain', the album displayed the band's strong songwriting talents and sense of melody, coupled with an emotive performance from the smoky-voiced Young. Despite praise in the press, the album failed to take off. As it was released, **Guns N'Roses** were gaining enormous mass popularity, and the band's tattooed biker image, unpremeditated though it may have been, allowed many to dismiss them as yet another Guns N'Roses clone band without hearing the evidence. Little was heard from the group for some time, although Young made a cameo appearance in *Terminator 2: Judgement Day*, and 'Down To The Wire' featured on the *Point Break* soundtrack, until they reappeared with ex-**David Bowie/Dirty White Boy** guitarist Earl Slick replacing the departed Apache for some live shows prior to recording *Influence*. Boasting a harder sound than the debut, the album was another high-quality outing, but despite further good press, sales were again disappointing. When Geffen failed to take up a third-album option, the band split up, with Young going on to front the similarly ill-fated Manic Eden.

● ALBUMS: *Little Caesar* (Geffen 1990)★★★, *Influence* (Geffen 1992)★★★.

Little Caesar And The Romans
The roots of doo-wop group Little Caesar And The Romans are found in a 50s vocal group from Los Angeles called the Cubans, featuring David Caesar Johnson (b. 16 June 1934, Chicago, Illinois, USA), Leroy Sanders (bass), Johnny O'Simmons and Early Harris (both tenors). The group first recorded in 1959. When Cuba underwent a political revolution that year the group became the Upfronts. Two years later they met songwriter Paul Politi, who had penned a song called 'Those Oldies But Goodies (Remind Me Of You)'. After personnel changes they became Little Caesar And The Romans with a faintly ludicrous gimmick of dressing up in togas and sandals and recorded Politi's ballad for **Del-Fi Records**. It reached the US Top 10 and they followed with one other minor hit single, 'Hully Gully Again', before disbanding in 1962. In 1975, Johnson put together a new Little Caesar And The Romans and recorded a single called 'Disco Hully Gully'. For a while they toured as **Marvin Gaye**'s opening act and in the late 70s, one of the backing singers for the group was **Rickie Lee Jones**. Little Caesar And The Romans were still active in the early 90s.

● ALBUMS: *Memories Of Those Oldies But Goodies, Volume 1* (1961)★★★.

● COMPILATIONS: *Toga! Toga! Toga!* (Del-Fi 1998)★★★.

Little Charlie And The Nightcats
The line-up comprises Rick Estrin (b. 5 October 1950, San Francisco, California, USA; vocal, harmonica), Charlie Baty (b. 10 July 1953, Birmingham, Alabama, USA; guitar), Brad Lee Sexton (b. 11 November 1948, South Carolina, USA; bass) and Dobie Strange (b. 15 November 1948, Red Bluff, California, USA; drums). One of the most popular bands performing in the west coast Chicago blues style, the Nightcats grew out of a 1973 meeting between Estrin and Baty, at that time a harmonica player himself. Estrin had been professional since 1968, when a jam with **Lowell Fulson** turned into a three-week booking. By 1975, he had turned down the opportunity to join **Muddy Waters**' band. When Estrin tired of San Francisco a year later, he contacted Baty with the idea of putting together a group. In 1982, the band pressed a single which they then sold at gigs, and began to put together a tape, which in 1986 they submitted to Bruce Iglauer at **Alligator**. A year later, *All The Way Crazy* was released. With their succeeding albums, the band established a reputation for hard driving music with a humorous edge to the lyrics. Estrin is their principal composer; **Robert Cray** recorded his 'I'm Just Lucky That Way', while 'My Next Ex-Wife' won the 1993 **W.C. Handy** award for Best Blues Song Of The Year.

● ALBUMS: *All The Way Crazy* (Alligator 1987)★★★, *Disturbing The Peace* (Alligator 1988)★★★, *The Big Break* (Alligator 1989)★★★, *Captured Live* (Alligator 1991)★★★, *Night Vision* (Alligator 1993)★★★, *Straight Up!* (Alligator 1995)★★★.

● COMPILATIONS: *Deluxe Edition* (Alligator 1997)★★★.

Little Criminals - Randy Newman

Randy Newman's most commercially successful album opens with his misunderstood masterpiece, 'Short People'. Of course he is not being derogatory towards people of restricted growth, that's just the way it seems. Those who understand Newman's brilliant pathos and irony know he has a heart of gold. After all, what heart of stone could write evocative material such as 'Baltimore' and 'I'll Be Home'. It is widely known that Newman is one of America's greatest ever songwriters - if only his music could be more widely known and appreciated, and not have to rely on the 'helping hands' of the **Eagles** to escalate its US sales and chart position.
- Tracks: *Short People; You Can't Fool The Fat Man; Little Criminals; Texas Girl At The Funeral Of Her Father; Jolly Coppers On Parade; In Germany Before The War; Sigmund Freud's Impersonation Of Albert Einstein In America; Baltimore; I'll Be Home; Rider In The Rain; Kathleen (Catholicism Made Easier); Old Man On The Farm.*
- First released 1977
- UK peak chart position: did not chart
- USA peak chart position: 9

Little Dippers

One of several groups of singers formed by successful backup vocalist/group leader/producer **Anita Kerr**, the Little Dippers had one US Top 10 single, 'Forever', in 1960, before disappearing forever themselves. The quartet consisted of Delores Dinning, Emily Gilmore, Darrell McCall and Hurshel Wigintin. Written by popular Nashville writer/producer Buddy Killen, 'Forever' was released on University Records. Although it reached number 9 in 1960, no other record by that particular aggregation ever charted.

Little Earthquakes - Tori Amos

With this debut, **Tori Amos** rose above the inevitable **Kate Bush** comparisons, producing a stunning set of brutally honest songs. A skilled and imaginative pianist, Amos also proved a versatile vocalist, moving from whisper to scream in an instant. She concentrates on intimate stories of her religious upbringing, childhood traumas, and predominantly, sex, self-discovery and unhappy relationships. 'Silent All These Years' was the first to hit a nerve with the public on single release, but all the tracks - memories of her father in 'Winter', the bittersweet 'Happy Phantom', the harrowing account of her own rape, 'Me And A Gun' - combine to make this inspiring, if rarely comfortable, listening.
- Tracks: *Crucify; Girl; Silent All These Years; Precious Things; Winter; Happy Phantom; China; Leather; Mother; Tear In Your Hand; Me And A Gun; Little Earthquakes.*
- First released 1992
- UK peak position: 14
- USA peak position: 54

Little Egypt

Claiming their initial notoriety from the fact that lead guitarist and vocalist Nick Rossi is the son of Francis Rossi of **Status Quo**, Little Egypt formed in the early 90s as a similarly inclined metal/boogie affair. The nepotism extended further: the group supported Quo on their 1993 tour, while Francis, who wrote several of their early songs, also co-produced their debut album. Bob Young, famed for his harmonica contributions to the denim warriors, is their manager. The other members of Little Egypt include Duncan Turmain (guitar, vocals), Dan Eames (drums) and 'Flying' Dave Conti (bass).
- ALBUMS: *Little Egypt* (1994)★★.

Little Esther

(see **Phillips, Esther**)

Little Eva

b. Eva Narcissus Boyd, 29 June 1943, Bellhaven, North Carolina, USA. Discovered by songwriters **Carole King** and **Gerry Goffin**, Little Eva shot to fame in 1962 with the international hit 'The Loco-Motion', a driving, dance-based song. Its ebullient, adolescent approach was muted on a follow-up single, 'Keep Your Hands Off My Baby', but although further releases from the following year, 'Let's Turkey Trot' and 'Old Smokey Locomotion', revived its novelty appeal, they lacked its basic excitement. Eva continued to record until 1965, but her only other substantial hit came with 'Swinging On A Star', a duet with **Big Dee Irwin**, on which she was, unfortunately, uncredited. She made a UK chart comeback in 1972 with a reissue of 'The Loco-Motion', which peaked at number 11, and the song's lasting appeal was reaffirmed in 1988 when **Kylie Minogue** emulated Eva's original UK chart position.
- ALBUMS: *L-L-L-L-Loco-Motion* (Dimension 1962)★★.
- COMPILATIONS: *Lil' Loco'Motion* (Rock Echoes 1982)★★, *The Best Of Little Eva* (1988)★★★, *Back On Track* (1989)★★★, *L L L L Little Eva: The Complete Dimension Recordings* (Westside 1998)★★★.

Little Feat

The compact rock 'n' roll funk displayed by Little Feat put them out of step with other Californian rock bands of the early 70s. By combining elements of country, folk, blues, soul and boogie they unwittingly created a sound that became their own, and has to date never been replicated or bettered. The band comprised Lowell George (b. 13 April 1945, Hollywood, California, USA, d. 29 June 1979), who had already had experience with the earthy garage band the **Standells** and with the **Mothers Of Invention**, plus, Roy Estrada (b. Santa Ana, California, USA; bass), Bill Payne (b. 12 March 1949, Waco, Texas, USA; keyboards) and Richie Haywood (drums). Although they signed to the mighty **Warner Brothers Records** in 1970, no promotional push was given to the band until their second album in 1972. The public later latched on to the debut, *Little Feat*. It remains a mystery as to why the band were given such a low profile. George had already been noticed as a potentially major songwriter; two of his songs, 'Truck Stop Girl' and 'Willin'', were taken by the **Byrds**. The debut sold poorly and, quite inexplicably, so did their second and third albums. The band were understandably depressed and began to fragment. Lowell began writing songs with **John Sebastian** amid rumours of a planned supergroup featuring Phil Everly. Fortunately, their record company made a further advance to finance *Feats Don't Fail Me Now*, with the revised band now comprising **Paul Barrere** (b. 3 July 1948, Burbank, California, USA; guitar), Kenny Gradney (b. New Orleans, Louisiana, USA; bass) and Sam Clayton (b. New Orleans, Louisiana, USA; percussion). Deservedly, they made the album charts in the USA, although the excellent material was no better than their three previous albums. *Feats Don't Fail Me Now* marked the development of other members as credible songwriters and George's role began to diminish. The European critics were unanimous in praising the band in 1975 on the 'Warner Brothers Music Show'. This impressive package tour featured **Graham Central Station**, **Bonaroo**, **Tower Of Power**, **Montrose**, Little Feat and the headliners, the **Doobie Brothers**, who were then enjoying unprecedented acclaim and success. Without exaggeration, Little Feat blew everyone off the stage with a series of outstanding concerts, and, from that moment onwards, they could do no wrong. *The Last Record Album* in 1975 contained George's finest (albeit short) winsome love song, 'Long Distance Love'; the sparseness of the guitar playing and the superb change of tempo with drum and bass, created a song that evoked melancholy and tenderness. The opening question and answer line: 'Ah Hello, give me missing persons, tell me what is it that you need, I said oh, I need her so, you've got to stop your teasing' - is full of emotional pleading. George, meanwhile, was overindulging with drugs, and his contribution to *Time Loves A Hero* was minimal. Once again they delivered a great album, featuring the by now familiar and distinctive cover artwork by Neon Park. Following the double live *Waiting For Columbus*, the band disintegrated and George started work on his solo album, *Thanks, I'll Eat It Here* (which sounded like a Little Feat album); two notable tracks were 'Missing You', and '20 Million Things To Do'. During a solo concert tour George had a heart attack and died, the years of abuse having taken their toll. The remaining band re-formed for a benefit concert for his widow and at the end of a turbulent year, the barrel was scraped to release *Down On The Farm*. The record became a considerable success, as did the compilation *Hoy-Hoy*.

In 1988, almost a decade after they broke up, the band re-formed and *Let It Roll* became their most successful album to date. The band had ex-**Pure Prairie League** Craig Fuller taking Lowell's place, and the musical direction was guided by the faultless keyboard playing of Bill Payne. A second set from the re-formed band came in 1990, and although it disappointed many, it added fuel to the theory that this time they intended to stay together. *Shake Me Up* finally buried the ghost of

George, as the critics accepted that the band was a credible force once again and could claim rightful ownership of both its name and history, without forgetting Lowell George's gigantic contribution. Fuller was not present on *Ain't Had Enough Fun*, the band recruiting a female lead singer, Shaun Murphy, instead.

● ALBUMS: *Little Feat* (Warners 1971)★★★★, *Sailin' Shoes* (Warners 1972)★★★★, *Dixie Chicken* (Warners 1973)★★★★, *Feats Don't Fail Me Now* (Warners 1974)★★★★, *The Last Record Album* (Warners 1975)★★★★, *Time Loves A Hero* (Warners 1977)★★★, *Waiting For Columbus* (Warners 1978)★★★, *Down On The Farm* (Warners 1979)★★★, *Let It Roll* (Warners 1988)★★, *Representing The Mambo* (Warnera 1990)★★, *Shake Me Up* (Polydor 1991)★★, *Ain't Had Enough Fun* (Zoo 1995)★★. Solo: Lowell George *Thanks I'll Eat It Here* (Warners 1979)★★★.

● COMPILATIONS: *Hoy Hoy* (Warners 1981)★★★★, *As Time Goes By - The Best Of Little Feat* (Warners 1986)★★★★.

Little Hatch

b. Provine Hatch Jnr., 25 October 1921, Sledge, Mississippi, USA. Though some 10 years older than **Little Walter Jacobs**, Hatch was one of many harmonica players to be tagged 'Little Walter Jnr.' The seventh of nine sons who all played harmonica, he was seven when he owned his first harp. The family moved to Helena, Arkansas, in the mid-30s, where Hatch first encountered **Howlin' Wolf**, **Johnny Shines**, **Robert Lockwood** and **Sonny Boy 'Rice Miller' Williamson**. After serving in the Navy during the war, on his return he moved to Kansas City, where he has since remained. While running his own business and then working for the Hallmark Company by day, he played in KC clubs such as Cotton-Eyed Joe's and Nightingales'. In 1962 he played with guitarist **George Jackson** before forming his own band, the Houserockers. His first album, as *The Little Hatchet Band*, was recorded live by a German student during June and July 1970 with a band that included Troy Banks, Bill Wells and Lewis Patties. At the end of the decade, he retired from music for nearly 10 years before resuming in 1987. *Well, All Right!* was also recorded live, at The Grand Emporium in Kansas City, with guitarist Bill Dye, Joe Whitfeld on bass and drummer C. Jaisson H. Taylor. All the material is claimed to be original, but songs by **Albert King** and **Little Walter** are little more than barely disguised.

● ALBUMS: *The Little Hatchet Band* (M&M 1974)★★, *Well, All Right!* (Modern Blues 1993)★★★.

● COMPILATIONS: *Texas Harmonica Rumble, Vol. 2* (Fan Club 1992)★★★.

Little Joe And The Thrillers

This R&B vocal group came from Philadelphia, Pennsylvania, USA. The group was formed in 1956 by Joe Cook (b. 29 December 1922, Philadelphia, Pennsylvania, USA), who had made his first record in 1949 as lead of a gospel group, the Joe Cook Quartet. While recording as a member of a later gospel group, the Evening Star Quartet, Cook formed the Thrillers, which besides Cook consisted of Farris Hill (tenor), Richard Frazier (tenor), Donald Burnett (baritone) and Harry Pascle (bass). Their only real claim to fame was 'Peanuts', which entered the US Top 30 in 1957 on the **OKeh** label. Cook's piercing falsetto lead became the standard for many R&B doo-wop groups from the late 50s through the 70s. The first release by the group was a dance number called 'The Slop', which achieved some local east coast recognition in 1956. The Thrillers never hit the charts after 'Peanuts' and they broke up, Little Joe continued recording up to 1966 on various small Philadelphia labels. In 1964, Cook organized an all-girl group, the **Sherrys**, two of whom were his daughters, and enjoyed a Top 40 hit with 'Pop Pop Pop-Pie'.

● ALBUMS: *Little Joe Cook-In* (1981)★★★.

Little Joey And The Flips

This US vocal group from Philadelphia, Pennsylvania, comprised Joey Hall (b. 1943; lead), Fred Garace (b. 1947; first tenor), James Meagher (b. 1946; second tenor), John Smith (b. 1946; baritone) and Jeff Leonard (b. 1946; bass). Hall, the lone black member, was from west Philadelphia, while the remainder of the group was from the Philadelphia suburb of Upper Darby. The group's only chart record was 'Bongo Stomp', which went to number 33 in 1962, a classic in the teen-lead genre made famous by **Frankie Lymon And The Teenagers**. Amazingly, Hall who sounded as though he was a 13-year-old, was actually a diminutive 19-year-old when he made the record. The group came together in 1959 as the Elads, but after the group was signed by their manager he replaced their original lead, Jimmy Dilks, with Joey Hall and renamed the group Little Joey And The Flips. Two more releases followed - 'Bongo Gully' (1962) and 'Fool, Fool, Fool' (1964) - but the group could not repeat the magic and broke up in 1967. Joey Hall died in 1974.

Little John

b. John McMorris, *c.*1970, Kingston, Jamaica, West Indies. McMorris first recorded with **Captain Sinbad** for the Youth In Progress label at the tender age of nine, where his piping interjections contrasted neatly with Sinbad's gruff style, and throughout the 80s he was seldom out of the reggae charts. Claimed by many to be the first **dancehall** singer, his ability to fit lyrics over any rhythm or backing track became something of a legend in a business that has scant regard for second takes and 'dropping in'. Little John did it every time - and he rode on the crest of the 80s' dancehall music explosion, becoming a superstar by the age of 17. He began his career on Romantic Hi Fi, moving up through Killimanjaro, Gemini and Volcano Hi Power, where he honed and perfected his craft with a lengthy string of live appearances. Simultaneously, he was recording for virtually every producer in Jamaica, notably **Henry 'Junjo' Lawes**, **Joseph 'Joe Joe' Hookim**, George Phang, Jah Thomas and Jammys, and he has

released countless records on a bewildering string of labels. He no longer records as extensively as he once did, and limits his live appearances to a minimum. Hits for **Exterminator** proved that he was not relying on his past glories, and his talent, warm personality and skill as a raconteur remained.

● ALBUMS: *True Confession* (Power House 1984)★★★, *Unite* (Vista Sounds 1984)★★★★, with Frankie Paul *Showdown Volume 6* (Empire 1984)★★, *Clark's Booty* (Live & Love/Jammys 1985)★★★, *River To The Bank* (Power House 1985)★★★, *Warriors & Trouble* (World Enterprise 1986)★★★, *Youth Of Today* (Skengdon 1987)★★★, *Reggae Dance* (Midnight Rock 1989)★★★.

● COMPILATIONS: *Best Of Little John* (R&M 1985)★★★★, *Junjo Presents A Live Session With Aces International* includes Little John (Volcano/Greensleeves)★★★.

Little Johnny Jones

George M. Cohan's first Broadway hit, and the beginning of his long association with producer Sam H. Harris. The show opened at the Liberty Theatre in New York on 7 November 1904, and, as was to become the norm throughout his career, Cohan provided the book, music and lyrics, as well directing and appearing in the piece. He is said to have got the idea for the plot from a newspaper account about an American jockey, Tod Sloane, who rode in the English Derby race in 1903. In Cohan's version, Johnny Jones refuses to be bribed to throw the race, but he loses anyway. When he arrives at Southampton docks to board a ship for his return to America, he is besieged by an angry crowd. Eventually they disperse and he is left alone waiting for a signal from his friend on the ship, now some way out at sea, to indicate that his innocence has been proved. The moment when the rocket soars into the sky and Jones goes into an exuberant rendering of 'Give My Regards To Broadway', is one of the most memorable sequences in musical comedy history. It was recreated superbly by **James Cagney** when he starred in the George M. Cohan biopic, *Yankee Doodle Dandy*, in 1942. The latter film got it's title from 'The Yankee Doodle Boy', which Cohan introduced in *Little Johnny Jones*, along with other numbers such as 'Life's A Funny Proposition After All', 'If Mr. Boston Lawson Got His Way', and 'I'm Might Glad I'm Living And That's All'. Cohan's wife, Ethel Levy, had a leading role, and so did his mother and father, Helen and Jerry Cohan. Also in the cast was Donald Brian, the actor, singer, and dancer who was to appear in Cohan's next Broadway musical, *Forty-Five Minutes From Broadway*, before going on to star in other important shows such as *The Merry Widow* and *The Girl From Utah*, in which he introduced **Jerome Kern** and Herbert Reynolds' lovely song, 'They Didn't Believe Me'. Although Cohan is often criticized for his sentimental, flag-waving approach, *Little Johnny Jones*, with its strong score and solid, believable book is considered to a be significant landmark in development of the indigenous American musical. It ran for only 52 performances in its first outing on

Broadway, but Cohan brought it back twice during 1905, and toured it extensively. The 1930 film version starred Alice Day and Eddie Buzzell. A 1981 revival of the show which began its life at the Goodspeed Opera House, Connecticut, amended the original plot and introduced some other Cohan songs. After using several actors in the lead role during its pre-Broadway tour, **Donny Osmond** was chosen to play the part at the Alvin Theatre in New York - but for the one-night run only.

Little Louie Vega

A New York-based DJ, Vega's career began at high school at the age of 18, after watching his friends spin records. He played high school parties before eventually establishing his own label. He went on to DJ at the Devil's Nest (regarded as the birthplace of the New York 'freestyle' approach, alongside TKA and Sa-Fire), then Hearthrob and 1018. By the time he had reached the 4,000 capacity Studio 54 **Todd Terry** would pass Vega his new mixes to try out on the crowd. His first remix job was 'Running' by Information Society, then Noel's 'Silent Morning'. He even worked **Debbie Gibson**'s first record. He began his own-name productions with the instrumental 'Don't Tell Me' for SBK in 1989 and 'Keep On Pumpin' It Up' (as Freestyle Orchestra), before signing to **CBS** subsidiary WTG Records with singer Mark Anthony. He had previously been commissioned to write songs for the movie *East Side Story*, where he first met the singer. Together they hooked up for a Latin R&B flavoured album and single, 'Ride On The Rhythm'. He also worked with his girlfriend, 'India', and Todd Terry for the latter's 'Todd's Message'. Together with **Barbara Tucker**, Vega runs the Underground Network Club in New York, and he has also produced 'Beautiful People' for that artist. Despite this background as an established house star, he is probably best known now for his work alongside **Kenny 'Dope' Gonzalez** as half of the **Masters At Work** remix team. He is not to be confused with Chicago house veteran **Lil' Louis**, or, for that matter, with the Louie Vega who remixed for **Lakim Shabazz**, despite the fact that both shared the same management. Vega's most recent remix clients include **Juliet Roberts** and **Urban Species**.

Little Mary Sunshine

On first sight a show with a title like that, and characters with names such as Mme. Ernestine Von Liebedich and General Oscar Fairfax, plus songs with titles like 'Do You Ever Dream Of Vienna?', the casual observer could be forgiven for thinking that this is an operetta. It is the date that gives the game away: *Little Mary Sunshine* opened Off Broadway (another clue) at the Orpheum Theatre on 19 November 1959. With rock 'n' roll already into its stride, there was not much of an audience in those days for genuinely new operetta, and, sure enough, this show turned out to be an elaborate spoof of the real thing. Sub titled A New Musical About

An Old Operetta, *Little Mary Sunshine* unmercifully sends up prime examples of the genre such as **Rose Marie** and **Naughty Marietta**. Set in the upper reaches of the Colorado Rockies, Rick Besoyan's book tells the hot-blooded story of Mary Potts (Eileen Brennan), the hostess of the local hostelry, who makes it quite clear to the Rangers' Captain Big Jim Warrington (William Graham), that there is always plenty of room at her inn, for him. However, Big Jim is more interested in capturing the despicable Indian, Yellow Feather (Ray James), who has indicated on more than one occasion that he would like to get Mary into his wigwam. Fortunately for our heroine, she and Big Jim give out with the 'Colorado Love Call', which proves to have more of a deterrent effect on amorous, ambitious Indians than a whole company of cavalry. The sub-plot involves another young loving couple Nancy Twinkle (Elmarie Wendel) and Corporal Billy Jester (John McMartin), who promise to be true to each other 'Once In A Blue Moon'. The remainder of Rick Besoyan's score was in that same mocking vein, and included 'Look For Sky Of Blue', 'Playing Croquet', 'Tell A Handsome Stranger', 'Every Little Nothing', 'Naughty Naughty, Nancy', and 'Such A Merry Party', and 'In Izzenschnooken On The Lovely Ezzenzook Zee', which is 'authentically' rendered by a visiting opera star of yesterday (or the day before), Mme. Ernestine Von Liebedich (Elizabeth Parrish). It all must have touched the right nerve, because *Little Mary Sunshine* became one of the longest-running Off Broadway musicals ever, during its run of 1,143 performances. Londoners did not seem to see the joke, and, despite the presence in the cast of comedy stalwarts such as Patricia Routledge and Bernard Cribbins, the show folded after five weeks.

Little Me

Conceived as a vehicle for one of US television's favourite performers, Sid Caesar, the versatile comedian needed all his skills and ingenuity to cope with a scenario that called upon him to play seven different characters. The leading female role, on the other hand, is shared by two different actresses. *Little Me* opened at the Lunt-Fontanne Theatre in New York on 17 November 1962. Neil Simon's book, which was based on the play by Patrick Dennis, opens with the older Belle Poitrine (Nancy Andrews), 'queen of the silver screen', dictating her memoirs ('The Truth'). The young, ambitious Belle Schlumpfort (Virginia Martin) then relives the scenes as they actually occurred, and in each one she is accompanied by a male admirer played by Caesar. These range from her first love, the snobby 16-years-old Noble Eggleston, from whom she gets a taste for the high-life ('Rich Kids Rag') and yearns to be 'On The Other Side Of The Tracks', to the geriatric banker Amos Pinchley, who is surely a good person 'Deep Down Inside', the 'great French entertainer', Val du Val, ('Boom-Boom'), her temporary husband, Fred Poitrine a World War I sad soldier who yearns for a 'Real Live Girl', a dominating film director, ('Poor

Little Hollywood Star'), and Prince Cherney 'the expiring regent of Rosenzweig' ('Goodbye'). George Musgrove, a childhood admire of Belle's, and now a big-time gambler, comes back into her life at one point and tries to seduce her with the sensuous 'I've Got Your Number'. This was the only major male role not played by Sid Caesar. At the end, the two Belles get together to try and make sense of it all and unite in 'Little Me'. The older Belle is then left alone, seated in her Beverly Hill mansion, realising that she has achieved her aims of 'wealth, culture and social position' - but not, unfortunately, Noble Eggleston. **Cy Coleman** and **Carolyn Leigh**'s score was, in turn, witty and tender, especially in numbers such as 'Real Live Girl' ('Speaking of miracles, this must be it/Just when I started to learn how to knit/I'm all in stitches from finding what riches a waltz, can reveal/With a real, live girl'), and 'The Other Side Of The Tracks', which became popular through a recording by **Tony Bennett**. **Bob Fosse** won a **Tony Award** for his ingenious choreography, and the Broadway run of only 257 performances was followed by a much better reception in London, where the show stayed at the Cambridge Theatre for 10 months. It proved to be a personal triumph for Bruce Forsyth, the young comedian and television compere. In 1982, a Broadway revival, starring James Coco and Victor Garber, lasted for only a month, but, two years later, London audiences approved of the show again, with Russ Abbott, Lynda Baron, and Sheila White. In 1993, another, more 'intimate' musical entitled *Little Me*, with a score by Brad Ross, Ellen Greenfield, Hal Hackady, *et al*, played at Steve McGraw's in New York.

Little Mermaid, The

Based on the Hans Christian Andersen fairytale, this 1989 **Walt Disney** release was the Studio's 28th animated feature, and a reminder of that golden era during which cinema audiences of all ages all over the world were enchanted with the immortal stories of **Snow White And The Seven Dwarfs**, **Peter Pan**, **Cinderella**, and **Sleeping Beauty**. This particular tale concerns the 16-year-old mermaid Ariel, who, after a series of exciting watery adventures, takes on a human form and marries the handsome and heroic Prince Eric. The action is enhanced by the 'contemporary songs and score ranging from English folk to French cabaret, from lively Caribbean to showstopping Broadway'. The composer **Alan Menken** won an Academy Award for his original score, and he and lyricist **Howard Ashman** gained another Oscar for the song, 'Under The Sea'. 'Kiss The Girl' was also nominated, and there were other attractive numbers such as 'Poor Unfortunate Souls' and 'Part Of Your World'. All these contributed to a soundtrack album which won a Grammy for the 'Best Recording For Children'. The film's spectacular animation, particularly in the underwater sequences, was widely applauded, and as usual the Disney organization selected appropriate voices for characters such as Ariel (Jodi Benson), her father King Triton (Kenneth

Mars), Ursula (Pat Caroll), Prince Eric (Christopher Daniel Barnes), and Flotsam/Jetsam (Paddi Edwards). No one could mistake the distinctive tones of Ariel's friend Scuttle the seagull, which were provided by comedian Buddy Hackett. He has also made several impressive on-screen performances in movies such as **The Music Man** and *It's A Mad Mad Mad Mad World*. *The Little Mermaid*, which was directed by John Musker and Ron Clements who also wrote the screenplay, enjoyed substantial success in the US and abroad, and set up audiences nicely for Disney's sensational early 90s trio of **Beauty And The Beast**, **Aladdin** and **The Lion King**.

Little Milton

b. James Milton Campbell Jnr., 7 September 1934, Inverness, Mississippi, USA. Having played guitar from the age of 12, Little Milton (he legally dropped the James when he discovered that he had a brother of the same name on his father's side) made his first public appearances as a teenager in the blues bars and cafés on Greenville's celebrated Nelson Street. He first appeared on record accompanying pianist **Willie Love** in the early 50s, then appeared under his own name on three singles issued on **Sam Phillips**' **Sun** label under the guidance of **Ike Turner**. Although their working relationship continued throughout the decade, it was on signing to Chicago's **Chess**/Checker outlet that Milton's career flourished. An R&B-styled vocalist in the mould of **Bobby Bland** and **'T-Bone' Walker**, his work incorporated sufficient soul themes to maintain a success denied to less flexible contemporaries. Propelled by an imaginative production, Milton had a substantial hit in 1965 with the optimistic 'We're Gonna Make It', and followed it with other expressive performances, including 'Who's Cheating Who?' (1965), plus the wry 'Grits Ain't Groceries' (1968). Campbell remained with Chess until 1971, whereupon he switched to **Stax**. 'That's What Love Will Do' returned the singer to the R&B chart after a two-year absence, but despite his appearance in the pivotal *Wattstax* film, Little Milton was unable to maintain a consistent recording career. A series of ill-fitting funk releases from the late 70s reinforced the perception that the artist was at his peak with blues-edged material, something proved by his excellent contemporary work for **Malaco Records**. In the 90s he was with **Delmark** and experienced something of a resurgence during the most recent blues boom.
● ALBUMS: *We're Gonna Make It* (Checker 1965)★★★, *Little Milton Sings Big Blues* (Checker 1966)★★★, *Grits Ain't Groceries* (Chess 1969)★★★, *If Walls Could Talk* (Chess 1970)★★★, *Waiting For Little Milton* (Stax 1973)★★★, *Blues 'N' Soul* (Stax 1974)★★★, *Montreux Festival* (Stax 1974)★★★, *Me For You, You For Me* (Glades 1976)★★★, *Friend Of Mine* (Glades 1976)★★★, shared with Jackie Ross *In Perspective* (1981)★★★, *I Need Your Love So Bad* (MCA 1982)★★★, *Age Ain't Nothing But A Number* (MCA 1983)★★★, *Playin' For Keeps* (Malaco 1984)★★★, *Annie Mae's Cafe* (Malaco 1987)★★★, *Movin' To The Country*

(Malaco 1987)★★★, *I Will Survive* (Malaco 1988)★★★, *Too Much Pain* (Malaco 1990)★★★, *Reality* (1992)★★★, *I'm A Gambler* (Malaco 1994)★★★, *Live At Westville Prison* (Delmark 1995)★★★, *Cheatin' Habit* (Malaco 1996)★★★, *For Real* (Malaco 1998)★★★★.

● COMPILATIONS: *Little Milton's Greatest Hits* (Chess 1972)★★★★, *Little Milton* (1976)★★★, *Sam's Blues* (Charly 1976)★★★, *Walkin' The Back Streets* (1981)★★★, *Raise A Little Sand* (Red Lightnin' 1982)★★★, *Little Milton Sings Big Blues* (Chess 1987)★★★, *His Greatest Hits* (Chess 1987)★★★, *Chicago Golden Years* (Vogue 1988)★★★, *Hittin' The Boogie (Memphis Days 1953-1954)* (Zu Zazz 1988)★★★, *We're Gonna Make It* (Charly 1990)★★★★, *The Sun Masters* (Rounder 1990)★★★, *Blues In The Night* (Dillon 1992)★★★★, *Welcome To The Club: The Essential Chess Recordings* (MCA 1994)★★★★, *Little Milton's Greatest Hits* (Malaco 1995)★★★★, *The Complete Stax Singles* (Ace 1995)★★★★.

Little Miss Marker

That old show-biz maxim about not working with animals or children must have crossed Adolphe Menjou's mind more than once during the filming of this Paramount musical which was released in 1934. He was top-billed, but, although she was only six years old, **Shirley Temple** dominated this Damon Runyon story in which she is adopted by bookmaker Sorrowful Jones (Menjou), after being used as security for a losing bet. Shirley then proceeds to look after Jones while having a far more beneficial effect on the New York gambling fraternity than any government commission could hope for. Shell-shocked as he must have been, Menjou gave a creditable performance under heavy fire. Also suffering from the tremendous impact of this little blonde bombshell were Charles Bickford, Dorothy Dell, Lynne Overman, Willie Best, and Frank McGlynn Snr. **Leo Robin** and **Ralph Rainger** wrote the songs which included 'Low Down Lullaby', 'I'm A Black Sheep Who Is Blue', and 'Laugh, You Son-Of-A-Gun'. William R. Lipman, Sam Hellman and Gladys Lehman were responsible for the neat screenplay, and the director was Alexander Hall. The 'marker' of the title being an indigenous American term for IOU, the name of the film was changed to *The Girl In Pawn* for UK distribution. *Little Miss Marker* was remade in 1949 as *Sorrowful Jones*, in 1963 as *40 Pounds Of Trouble*, and again in 1980 under its original title, but none of them made anything like the impact of the 1934 version.

Little Night Music, A

Suggested by Ingmar Bergman's film, *Smiles Of A Summer Night*, *A Little Night Music* opened at the Shubert Theatre in New York on 25 February 1973. The music and lyrics were by **Stephen Sondheim**, and Hugh Wheeler's book followed an intricate series of love affairs set in turn-of-the-century Sweden. Mature lawyer Fredrik Egerman (Len Cariou) has a young wife, Anne (Victoria Mallory), who has so far shown no inclination to consummate their relationship. Fredrik's former mistress, the actress Desirée Armfeldt (Glynis Johns), is in the neighbourhood with her touring show. Her daughter Fredrika (Judy Kahan), the fruit of an earlier Fredrik-Desirée dalliance, is back home with grandmother Madame Armfeldt (**Hermione Gingold**). Desirée's current companion is the hustling hussar, Count Carl-Magnus Malcolm (Laurence Guittard). He and his wife, Countess Charlotte (Patricia Elliott), join Desirée and various other family members and friends - including Fredrik's teenage son, Henrik (Mark Lambert) - for a weekend at Madame Armfeldt's country estate. Attended by their host and the often bemused servants, Petra (D. Jamin-Bartlett) and Frid (George Lee Andrews), the resulting *ménage* finds Anne inclined towards Henrik, Carl-Magnus attempting a reconciliation with Charlotte, while Desirée and Fredrik lie back and think of the old days. The show was elegantly staged by **Harold Prince** (choreography by Patricia Birch), and filled with Sondheim's delightful, waltz-time tunes. The superb score included 'Liaisons', 'The Miller's Son', 'Night Waltz', 'Now', 'Later', 'Soon', 'In Praise Of Women', 'A Weekend In The Country', 'The Sun Won't Set', 'Perpetual Anticipation', 'Every Day A Little Death', 'Remember?', 'It Would Have Been Wonderful', 'You Must Meet My Wife' and 'The Glamorous Life'. There was also a rarity - a Sondheim number that became popular outside the context of its show setting. 'Send In The Clowns', which was sung in a quiet, touching, contemplative manner by Desirée at the house party, soon entered the repertoires of both accomplished and mediocre vocalists around the world, notably those of **Judy Collins** and **Frank Sinatra**.

A Little Night Music ran on Broadway for 601 performances and won **Tony Awards** for best musical, score, book, leading actress (Johns), supporting actress (Elliott), and costumes (Florence Klotz), along with the New York Critics' Circle Award for Best Musical. Gingold reprised her role as the aged dowager who manipulates happy endings for the various love affairs, for the 1975 London production, with a cast that also included Jean Simmons (Desirée), Joss Ackland (Fredrik), Terry Mitchell (Henrik), Maria Aitken (Charlotte), Veronica Page (Anne), Christine McKenna (Fredrika), David Kernan (Carl-Magnus), Diane Langton (Petra), and Michael Harbour (Frid). A 1989 West End revival starred Susan Hampshire (Charlotte), Lila Kedrova (Mme. Arnfeldt), Peter McEnery (Fredrik), Eric Flynn (Carl-Magnus), and Dorothy Tutin (Desirée), and in 1991, Glynis Johns, the original Desirée, portrayed Mme. Armfeldt in Los Angeles. In 1995, **Betty Buckley** gave her rendition of 'Send In The Clowns' when she led the cast of a BBC Radio 2 concert version of *A Little Night Music*, and Judi Dench was acclaimed for a highly individual reading of the number in a splendid 1995 Royal National Theatre repertory production. Among the rest of the distinguished cast were Patricia Hodge (Charlotte), Siân Phillips (Madame Armfeldt), Brenda O'Hea (Henrik), Joanna Riding (Anne), Lambert Wilson (Carl-Magnus), Paul

Kynman (Frid), and Issy van Randwyck (Petra). Laurence Guittard, who created the role of Carl-Magnus in the original Broadway production, played Fredrik. The score was supplemented by one additional song, Charlotte's 'My Husband The Pig'.

Ironically, although *A Little Night Music* has been produced successfully by theatre companies throughout the world, a 1978 film version, which starred Elizabeth Taylor, vanished from public gaze before it could do any lasting harm to Sondheim's reputation.

Little Richard

b. Richard Wayne Penniman, 5 December 1935, Macon, Georgia, USA. The wildest and arguably the greatest and most influential of the 50s rock 'n' roll singers and songwriters. He first recorded in late 1951 in Atlanta for **RCA**, cutting eight urban blues tracks with his mentor **Billy Wright**'s Orchestra, 'Taxi Blues' being the first of four unsuccessful single releases on the label. He moved to Houston, Texas, in 1953, and with the Tempo Toppers (vocals) and the Duces of Rhythm (backing), he recorded four R&B tracks including 'Ain't That Good News'. Eight months later he recorded another four with **Johnny Otis**'s Orchestra but none of these were released at the time. In February 1955, at the suggestion of **Lloyd Price**, he sent a demo to **Specialty Records** who realized his potential, and in September, under the guidance of producer **Robert 'Bumps' Blackwell**, recorded a dozen tracks in New Orleans. The classic 'Tutti Frutti', which was among them, gave him his first R&B and pop hit in the USA. The follow-up, 'Long Tall Sally', topped the R&B chart and was the first of his three US Top 10 hits, despite being covered by **Pat Boone**, whose previous record, a cover version of 'Tutti Frutti', was still charting. Richard's string of Top 20 hits continued with the double-sider 'Rip It Up'/'Ready Teddy', the former being his first UK release and chart entry in late 1956. Richard's frantic, unrestrained performance of his first two hits, 'Long Tall Sally' and 'Tutti Frutti', in the film *Don't Knock The Rock*, undoubtedly helped to push his subsequent UK single, which coupled the tracks, into the Top 3.

His next film and single was *The Girl Can't Help It*, the title song of which missed the US Top 40 but together with its b-side, 'She's Got It' (a reworking of his earlier track 'I Got It'), gave him two more UK Top 20 hits. The remainder of 1957 saw him notch up three more huge transatlantic hits with the rock 'n' roll classics 'Lucille', 'Keep A Knockin'' (he featured both in the movie *Mr. Rock & Roll*) and 'Jenny Jenny' and a Top 20 album with *Here's Little Richard*. At the very height of his career, the man with the highest pompadour in the business shocked the rock world by announcing, during an Australian tour, that he was quitting music to go into a theological college. In 1958, previously recorded material such as the transatlantic Top 10 hit 'Good Golly Miss Molly' kept his name on the chart, and a year later he had his biggest UK hit with a 1956 record-ing of the oldie 'Baby Face', which reached number 2.

Between 1958 and 1962 Richard recorded only gospel music for Gone, **Mercury** (with producer **Quincy Jones**) and **Atlantic**. In late 1962, Richard toured the UK for the first time and the now short-haired wild man who pounded pianos and pierced eardrums with his manic falsetto was a huge success. In 1963, he worked in Europe with the **Beatles** and the **Rolling Stones**, who were both great admirers of his music. His first rock recordings in the 60s were made back at Specialty and resulted in the UK Top 20 hit 'Bama Lama Bama Loo'. In 1964, he signed with **Vee Jay** where he re-recorded all his hits, revived a few oldies and cut some new rockers - but the sales were unimpressive. In the mid-60s, soul music was taking hold worldwide and Richard's soulful Vee Jay tracks, 'I Don't Know What You've Got But It's Got Me' (which featured **Jimi Hendrix** on guitar) and 'Without Love', although not pop hits, were among the best recordings of the genre. For the rest of the 60s he continued to draw the crowds, singing his old hits, and in the studios he mixed 50s rock and 60s soul for Modern in 1965, **OKeh** a year later and **Brunswick** in 1967. The best of these were his OKeh tracks, which included 'Poor Dog', 'Hurry Sundown' and the UK-recorded 'Get Down With It' (which gave **Slade** their first hit in the 70s).

Reprise Records, whom he joined in 1970, tried very hard to return him to the top, and under the expertise of producer **Richard Perry** he managed minor US hits 'Freedom Blues' and 'Greenwood, Mississippi', but his three albums sold poorly. The rest of the 70s was spent jumping from label to label, recording in supergroup-type projects and playing oldies shows. When he desired, he could still 'out-rock' anyone, but there was often too much Las Vegas glitter, excessive posturing and an element of self-parody. In 1976, he rejoined the church and for the next decade preached throughout America. In 1986, Richard was one of the first artists inducted into the **Rock And Roll Hall of Fame** and he successfully acted in the film *Down And Out In Beverly Hills*, which included the rocking 'Great Gosh A'Mighty', which narrowly missed the US Top 40. Renewed interest spurred **WEA** to sign him and release *Lifetime Friend*, which included the chart record 'Operator'. Since the mid-80s he has become a frequent visitor on chat shows, an in-demand guest on other artist's records and a familiar face in videos (by acts ranging from **Hank Williams Jnr.** to **Living Colour** to **Cinderella**). He even has his own star on the Hollywood Walk of Fame and a boulevard named after him in his home-town. Nowadays a regular presenter of music awards, he has also been the star of **Jive Bunny** hits. The leader of rebellious 50s rock 'n' roll, and the man who shook up the music business and the parents of the period, is now a much-loved personality accepted by all age groups.

● ALBUMS: *Little Richard* (Camden 1956)★★★, *Here's Little Richard* (Specialty 1957)★★★★★, *Little Richard Volume 2* (Specialty 1957)★★★★★, *The Fabulous Little Richard* (Specialty 1958)★★★★★, *Sings Gospel* (20th Century

1959)★★, *It's Real* (Mercury 1961)★★, *Little Richard Sings Freedom Songs* (Crown 1963)★★, *Coming Home* (Coral 1963)★★, *King Of The Gospel Singers* (Wing 1964)★, *Little Richard Is Back* (Vee Jay 1965)★★, *The Explosive Little Richard* (Columbia 1967)★★★, *Good Golly Miss Molly* (Specialty 1969)★★★, *The Little Richard Story* (Joy 1970)★★★, *Well Alright* (Specialty 1970)★★★, *Rock Hard Rock Heavy* (Specialty 1970)★★, *You Can't Keep A Good Man Down* (Union Pacific 1970)★★, *The Rill Thing* (Reprise 1970)★★, *Mr Big* (Joy 1971)★★, *Cast A Long Shadow* (Epic 1971)★★, *King Of Rock 'n' Roll* (Reprise 1971)★★★, *The Original Little Richard* (Specialty 1972)★★★, *The Second Coming* (Warners 1973)★★★, *Rip It Up* (Joy 1973)★★, *Slippin' And Slidin'* (Joy 1973)★★, *Good Golly Miss Molly* (Hallmark 1974)★★★, *Greatest Hits Recorded Live* (Embassy 1974)★★★, *Keep A Knockin'* (Rhapsody 1975)★★, *Dollars Dollars* (Charly 1975)★★, *The Great Ones* (MFP 1976)★★, *Little Richard And Jimi Hendrix Together* (Ember 1977)★, *Whole Lotta Shakin' Goin' On* (DJM 1977)★★★, *Little Richard Now* (Creole 1977)★★, *The Georgia Peach* (Charly 1980)★★★, *Little Richard And His Band* (Specialty 1980)★★, *Ooh! My Soul* (Charly 1982)★★★, *Whole Lotta Shakin'* (Bulldog 1982)★★★, *Get Down With It* (Edsel 1982)★★, *The Real Thing* (Magnum Force 1983)★★★, *Little Richard* (Cambra 1983)★★★, *He's Got It* (Topline 1984)★★, *Lifetime Friend* (Warners 1986)★★★.

● COMPILATIONS: *His Biggest Hits* (Specialty 1963)★★★★, *Little Richard's Greatest Hits* (Vee Jay 1965)★★★★, *Little Richard's Greatest Hits* (OKeh 1967)★★★★, *Little Richard's Greatest Hits* (Joy 1968)★★★, *Little Richard's Grooviest 17 Original Hits* (Specialty 1968)★★★★, *20 Original Greatest Hits* (Specialty 1976)★★★★, *The Essential Little Richard* (Specialty 1985)★★★★, *18 Greatest Hits* (Rhino 1985)★★★★, *20 Classic Cuts* (Ace 1986)★★★★, *Shut Up! A Collection Of Rare Tracks (1951 - 1964)* (Rhino 1988)★★★, *The Collection* (Castle 1989)★★★★, *The Specialty Sessions* 6-CD box set (Specialty 1990)★★★★★, *The Formative Years, 1951-53* (Bear Family 1989)★★★, *The EP Collection* (See For Miles 1993)★★★★★.

● FURTHER READING: *The Life And Times Of Little Richard: The Quasar Of Rock*, Charles White.

● FILMS: *The Girl Can't Help It* (1956), *Don't Knock The Rock* (1956), *Catalina Caper* (1967).

Little River Band

Prior to the success of **AC/DC**, **Air Supply**, **Men At Work** and **INXS**, the Little River Band were probably Australia's most successful international rock band. Evolving out of the group Mississippi, who had previously spent much time working in London, former members Graham Goble (b. 15 May 1947, Adelaide, South Australia, Australia; guitar), Beeb Birtles (b. Gerard Birtlekamp, 28 November 1948, Amsterdam, Netherlands; guitar) and Derek Pellicci (drums) met up with Glen Shorrock (b. 30 June 1944, Rochester, Kent, England; vocals) in Melbourne in 1975. With a name change to the Little River Band and the addition of Rick Formosa (guitar) and Roger McLachlan (bass) the band boasted years of experience and chose the US west coast

harmony and guitar sound as their major influence. They had immediate success in Australia with their first single and album. Under the guidance of Glen Wheatley (ex-**Masters Apprentices**), the band was soon aiming for the overseas market, the USA in particular, and by the end of 1976 they had enjoyed their first appearance in the US charts. With Formosa and McLachlan being replaced, respectively, by David Briggs (b. 26 January 1951, Melbourne, Victoria, Australia) and George McArdle (b. 30 November 1954, Melbourne, Victoria, Australia), the second album *Diamantina Cocktail* went gold in the USA in 1977, the first time an Australian act had managed this. The band followed this with another hugely successful album in 1978, *Sleeper Catcher*, and they found themselves also selling well in Latin-America and Europe, especially France. The band's popularity waned a little in Australia but continued unabated in the USA. In 1983, lead vocalist Glen Shorrock left to pursue a solo career and was replaced by **John Farnham**, one of Australia's most popular singers. By 1986 Farnham had left to pursue his solo career and the band continued with a low profile, playing live occasionally at upmarket venues but still releasing records. In 1988, with the return of Shorrock, the group signed to MCA Records, releasing *Get Lucky* two years later.

● ALBUMS: *Little River Band* (Harvest 1976)★★★, *Diamantina Cocktail* (Harvest 1977)★★★, *Sleeper Catcher* (Harvest 1978)★★, *First Under The Wire* (Capitol 1979)★★, *Backstage Pass* (Capitol 1980)★★, *Time Exposure* (Capitol 1981)★★, *The Net* (Capitol 1983)★★, *Playing To Win* (Capitol 1985)★★, *No Reins* (Capitol 1986)★★, *Monsoon* (MCA 1988)★★, *Too Late To Load* (1989)★, *Get Lucky* (MCA 1990)★★, *Worldwide Love* (Curb 1991)★★.

● COMPILATIONS: *Greatest Hits* (Capitol 1984)★★★, *The Best Of ...* (EMI 1997)★★★.

● VIDEOS: *Live Exposure* (PMI 1981).

Little Roy

b. Earl Lowe, *c.*1950, Jamaica, West Indies. Little Roy began his career at **Studio One**, with **Jackie Mittoo** as the producer, initially recording 'Cool It'. He retired for a time but returned and pursued his career performing as a member of an unsigned vocal group alongside **Bunny Maloney** and George Thompson. Following his departure from Studio One and the group, Little Roy recorded as a soloist with **Prince Buster** the singles 'It's You I Love' and 'Reggae Soul'. In the late 60s Little Roy achieved immense popularity with **Lloyd Daley** with the classic 'Bongo Nyah', and alongside Joy Lindsay as Roy And Joy, notably with 'Keep On Trying' and 'Righteous Man'. From the outset he wrote about Rasta themes - slavery, the wearing of dreadlocks and exile. By 1972 he had formed the Tafari label with the help of **Lloyd Barnes** and Munchie Jackson, and his records soon received simultaneous release in New York through Barnes' Aries label. Often part of a trio alongside two mysterious characters, Ian and Rock, he recorded some alluring and atmospheric tracks: 'Tribal

War', 'Blackbird' and 'Prophecy'. Barnes put them together to form an album, *Tribal War*, which had a decidedly limited pressing. In 1978 he recorded *Columbus Ship*, a far less artistically successful set, and then dropped below reggae's horizon altogether, though there were occasional sightings of him in New York. His business associate Munchie Jackson was shot by his own son in a bizarre Brooklyn domestic killing in 1977. However, in one of those twists unique to reggae, ragga rulers **Steely And Clevie** decided to remake the 'Prophecy' rhythm in 1990, and it was an instant hit for **Freddie McGregor**. Not slow to spot an opportunity, Little Roy emerged from nowhere with a 10-track compilation of his now in-demand old material, *Prophecy*, and then recorded the excellent *Live On* the following year. In 1994 he began residing in the UK and he was invited to record with **On-U-Sound**, releasing the results of the sessions in 1996.

● ALBUMS: *Tribal War* (Tafari 1975)★★★, *Free For All Dub* (1975)★★★, *Columbus Ship* (Copasetic 1978)★★, *Live On* (1991)★★★★, *Long Time* (On-U-Sound 1996)★★★.

● COMPILATIONS: *Prophecy* (1990)★★★, *Tafari Earth Uprising* (Pressure Sounds 1996)★★★★.

Little Shop Of Horrors (film musical)

As a film to put audiences off gardening for life, *Little Shop Of Horrors*, released in December 1986, is top of the heap. It tells the story of Seymour (Rick Moranis), a rather sweet but accident-prone character - a sort of **Norman Wisdom** of the 80s - whose working life at Mushnik's Skid Row flower shop just is not going to plan. On to the scene comes Audrey II, named after the girl Seymour adores, who changes from a tiny shrub to a sinister blood sucking flytrap. When Seymour has bled his fingers dry in an attempt to feed it, the plant forces him to find some human meat to satisfy its hunger. In return Seymour is to have as much success in love and life as he can handle. Eventually, realizing that the man-eating plant really wants to take over the world, Seymour faces up to its menace and, with the help of a few volts of electricity, blows Audrey II into oblivion. *Little Shop Of Horrors* was first seen off-Broadway in 1982, and that production itself was based on Roger Corman's 60s low-budget horror movie. Directed by Frank Oz, and produced by **David Geffen** for the Geffen Company, the show's author and lyricist, **Howard Ashman**, also wrote the movie's screenplay. It is interesting to note that the film's ending is distinctly different in tone to its stage predecessor, when Seymour and Audrey are both eaten and Audrey II succeeds. It appears the preview audiences preferred a happy ending and so it was changed. Ashman was joined by **Alan Menken** to write the quirky, clever and often extremely funny score. Highlights included 'Skid Row', the film's only real production number of any sorts, involving most of the cast, and 'Suddenly Seymour', by no means an average love song. A host of guest stars joined in the fun, among them Steve Martin, James Belushi, John Candy, and Bill Murray. Ellen Greene

recreated her stage role as Audrey. Martin plays Audrey's sadistic dentist boyfriend (in 'Somewhere That's Green', she sings 'I know Seymour's the greatest, but I'm dating a semi-sadist'). Consequently, it is not surprising that Martin becomes Audrey II's first human victim. The plant's big number is 'Mean Green Mother From Outer Space' (the voice is that of the **Four Tops**' Levi Stubbs). The song was written especially for the film, and is quite a treat, especially its flower bud chorus. The rest of the score included 'Little Shop Of Horrors', 'Grow For Me', 'Dentist', 'Feed Me', and 'Suppertime'. Pat Garrett was the choreographer, and the film was photographed in Technicolor and Panavision by Robert Paynter.

Little Shop Of Horrors (stage musical)

After making its debut at the tiny WPA Theatre in New York, *Little Shop Of Horrors* moved to the Orpheum Theatre on the Lower East Side on 27 July 1982. The book, by **Howard Ashman**, was based on Charles Griffith's screenplay for the 1960 spoof of the horror movie genre, which had become a cult classic. Hardly the usual Broadway - or off-Broadway - fare, the grisly tale tells of Seymour Krelbourn (Lee Wilkof), an assistant at Mushnik's florist shop on Skid Row, who decides to boost sales by producing a strange houseplant. He names it Audrey II, because of his love for sales assistant Audrey (Ellen Greene), and finds that it grow faster if it is fed with a few drops of blood - and subsequently, human flesh. Things rapidly get out of hand as the monster - and the business - thrives, eventually devouring just about everything and everyone in sight. The amusing and imaginative score by Ashman and composer **Alan Menken** had some 'good rock in the **Phil Spector** Wall of Sound idiom', and included 'Grow For Me', 'Suddenly Seymour', 'Skid Row', 'Somewhere That's Green', and 'Little Shop Of Horrors'. The show's bizarre humour caught on in a big way, as Audrey II and *Little Shop Of Horrors* became a sort of phenomenon. It continued to amaze and delight off-Broadway audiences for 2,209 performances, and was awarded the New York Drama Critics Circle Award for best musical. The 1984 London production, which ran for over a year, also received the Evening Standard prize for outstanding musical. Ellen Greene reprised her role in London, and for the 1986 film version, which also starred Rick Moranis, Vincent Gardenia and Steve Martin. In 1994, a 'gorgeously funny' revival toured the UK starring Sue Pollard, better know for her role as Peggy, the zany chalet maid, in the popular television comedy series *Hi-Di-Hi*.

Little Show, The

Composer **Arthur Schwartz** and lyricist **Howard Dietz**, one of the top Broadway songwriting teams of the 30s, got together for the first time to write several songs for this smart, classy revue which opened at the Music Box Theatre on 30 April 1929. Dietz also wrote most of the sketches, along with **George S. Kaufman** and others. He and Schwartz contributed 'I've Made A Habit Of You', 'Hammacher-Schlemmer, I Love You', and 'I Guess I'll Have To Change My Plan', ('I should have realized there'd be another man/Why did I buy those blue paja-mas/Before the big affair began?'), which, for obvious reasons became known as 'The Blue Pajama Song', and, while never becoming a big hit, was one of the song-writers' hardy standards. It was very effectively sung by a couple of song-and-dance-men, **Fred Astaire** and **Jack Buchanan** in the film of *The Band Wagon* in 1953. It was introduced in *The Little Show* by Clifton Webb, who finally became recognized as a star in this revue, as did the resident funny man, 'dead-pan' Fred Allen. The third leading player, Libby Holman, had 'Can't We Be Friends?' (written by **Kay Swift** and Paul James - a pseudonym for her husband, James P. Warburg), which was quite a jolly little song for many years until **Frank Sinatra** turned it into a lonely ballad on his *In The Wee Small Hours*. Holman also sang the show's big hit, 'Moanin' Low', which had music and lyric by **Ralph Rainger** and Dietz. One of the other songs, 'A Little Hut In Hoboken', was one of a the rela-tively few numbers written by **Herman Hupfield** in his career; two years later he produced another, 'As Time Goes By', which was later immortalised in the film, *Casablanca*. *The Little Show* ran for 321 performances. Without Holman, Webb, and Allen neither of the sequels did well. *The Second Little Show* (1929), again had some songs by Schwartz and Dietz ('You're The Sunshine', 'What A Case I've Got On You', and 'Lucky Seven') and one by Hupfield ('Sing Something Simple'), but only ran for 63 performances; and *The Third Little Show* (1930), starred Beatrice Lillie who introduced **Noël Coward**'s 'Mad Dogs And Englishmen' to the American public. The show also contained another rare Hupfield number, 'When Yuba Plays The Rhumba On His Tuba', and stayed at Music Box Theatre for four months.

Little Son Joe

b. Ernest Lawlars, 18 May 1900, Hughes, Arkansas, USA, d. 14 November 1961, Memphis, Tennessee, USA. Lawlars is best known for his musical partnership with his wife, **Memphis Minnie**, but he had been playing guitar and singing blues for some years around Memphis before they collaborated, including a period with **Rev. Robert Wilkins**, whom he accompanied on record in 1935. He teamed up with Minnie in the late 30s, replacing her previous husband and partner, **Joe McCoy**. Like McCoy, Lawlars also made records under his own name, including the well-known 'Black Rat Swing', but he mainly appeared in the supporting role, on a large number of sides covering most of the 40s and the early years of the following decade. As their popu-larity in Chicago waned, they settled back in Memphis and retired from music in the 50s.
● ALBUMS: *Memphis Minnie* (1964)★★★, *Chicago Blues* (1982)★★, *World Of Trouble* (1982)★★★.

Little Sonny

b. Aaron Willis, 6 October 1932, Greensboro, Alabama, USA. Despite the claims of his first album, its evidence shows that Little Sonny Willis is an adequate harmon-ica player and reluctant singer whose music career has been, at best, intermittent. With little experience in music apart from singing in church choirs, Willis moved to Detroit in 1954. Working as a photographer in the bars of the Hastings Street area, he also picked up the rudiments of the harmonica. His first gig was in the Good Time Bar with **Washboard Willie**'s band. Willis gained some harmonica tuition from **Sonny Boy 'Rice Miller' Williamson**, from whom he adopted his nick-name. In March 1956, he formed his own band with pianist Chuck Smith, guitarist Louis (Big Bo) Collins and drummer Jim Due Crawford. Two years later Smith, Crawford and **Eddie Burns** backed Willis on his debut record, 'I Gotta Find My Baby', for Duke Records. Another record, 'Love Shock', recorded by **Joe Von Battle**, was leased to Excello. An unissued 1961 session for **Chess Records** presaged a five-year record-ing silence, followed by singles for Speedway, Revilot (including the instrumental 'The Creeper') and Wheel City at the end of the decade. In 1969 he recorded his first album for the **Stax** subsidiary Enterprise. *New King Of The Blues Harmonica*, an album of mostly uninven-tive instrumentals, evoked Hans Christian Andersen fairy tales. A second album, *Hard Goin' Up*, released in 1973, was a more honest, balanced exercise. **Albert King** recorded Willis's 'Love Shock' and 'Love Mechanic' for Tomato in 1978. *King Albert* was recorded in Detroit and used Willis's sons, Aaron Jnr., Anthony and Eddie, in the back-up band. Perhaps their father had read *King Lear*.
● ALBUMS: *New King Of The Blues Harmonica* (Stax 1969)★★, *Hard Goin' Up* (Stax 1973)★★★, *New Orleans Rhythm And Blues* (Black Magic 1994)★★★, *Sonny Side Up* (Sequel 1995)★★★, *Blues With A Feeling* (Sequel 1996)★★★★.

Little Steven And The Disciples Of Soul
(see **Van Zandt, 'Miami' Steven**)

Little Texas

Following their 1992 debut album, *First Time For Everything*, Little Texas emerged as one of America's biggest 'new country' phenomena. The band comprised Tim Rushlow (vocals), Del Gray (drums), Porter Howell (guitar, bass), Duane Propes (bass, backing vocals), Jeff Huskins and Brady Seals (keyboards, guitar, backing vocals), and they were rewarded soon after their debut with the American Country Music award for Top Vocal Group. With sales of the album achieving gold status, Little Texas toured the USA with artists including **Travis Tritt** and **Trisha Yearwood**. *First Time For Everything* produced a run of successful singles, as did its follow-up, *Big Time*, whose sales figures would reach platinum status. They promptly recorded a third set, *Kick A Little* (their first to be released outside the USA), which contained more strong material including 'Your Days Are Numbered', 'A Night I'll Never Remember' and 'Southern Grace'. The band's self-titled fourth album was released in 1996, but poor sales and diverging interests led to their split the following year.

● ALBUMS: *First Time For Everything* (Warners 1992)★★★, *Big Time* (Warners 1993)★★★, *Kick A Little* (Warners 1994)★★★, *Little Texas* (Warners 1996)★★.

● COMPILATIONS: *Greatest Hits* (Warners 1995)★★★.

● VIDEOS: *Kick A Little* (Warner Reprise 1994), *Greatest Hits* (Warner Reprise 1995).

Little Tony

b. Antonio Ciacci, 1940, San Marino, Italy. Little Tony and his two brothers formed a vocal group and were 'discovered' by **Jack Good** in 1959. Despite profound language difficulties, the trio - as Little Tony And His Brothers - won female hearts with their Latinate charm on UK television; toured with **Cliff Richard**, and recorded 'Foxy Little Mama', **Chan Romero**'s 'Hippy Hippy Shake' and other singles under Good's supervision in London. However, it was without his siblings that Ciacci grazed the UK Top 20 with 1960's 'So Good'. With the withdrawal of Good's support, he returned to Italy where he was runner-up in 1961's San Remo Song Festival with a song translated as '42,000 Kisses' when covered by Liverpudlian vocalist Paul Rogers. Little Tony became a regular performer at this event - even after 1967 brought a million-seller in 'Cuore Matto' (composed by Ambrosino and Tito Savio). Nevertheless, this was covered in the English-speaking market, where the song appeared as **Tony Hatch** and **Jackie Trent**'s 'Long Is The Lonely Night'.

● COMPILATIONS: *Little Tony Volume 1* (Big Beat 1996)★★★★, *Little Tony Volume 2* (Big Beat 1996)★★.

Little Village

(see **Cooder, Ry**; **Lowe, Nick** and **Hiatt, John**)

Little Walter

b. Marion Walter Jacobs, 1 May 1930, Marksville, Louisiana, USA, d. 15 February 1968. A major figure of post-war blues, Little Walter is credited for bringing the harmonica, or 'French harp', out from its rural setting and into an urban context. His career began at the age of 12 when he left home for New Orleans, but by 1946 Jacobs was working in Chicago's famed Maxwell Street. Early recordings for the Ora Nelle label were the prelude to his joining the **Muddy Waters** band, where he helped to forge what became the definitive electric Chicago blues group. The harmonica player emerged as a performer in his own right in 1952 when 'Juke', an instrumental recorded at the end of a Waters session, topped the R&B chart, where it remained for eight consecutive weeks. Little Walter And The Night Caps - David Myers (guitar), Louis Myers (guitar) and Fred Below (drums) - enjoyed further success when 'Sad Hours' and 'Mean Old World' reached the Top 10 in

the same chart. The group then became known as Little Walter And The Jukes and, although obliged to fulfil recording agreements with Waters, Jacobs actively pursued his own career. He enjoyed further R&B hits with 'Blues With A Feeling' (1953), 'Last Night' (1954) and the infectious 'My Babe' (1955). The last song, patterned on a spiritual tune, 'This Train', was a second number 1 single and became much covered during later years. Other notable releases included 'Mellow Down Easy' and 'Boom Boom (Out Go The Lights)' which were later recorded, respectively, by **Paul Butterfield** and the **Blues Band**. A haunting version of 'Key To The Highway' (1958), previously recorded by **Big Bill Broonzy**, gave Walter his final Top 10 entry. He nonetheless remained a pivotal figure, undertaking several tours, including one of Britain in 1964. His career, however, was undermined by personal problems. A pugnacious man with a quick temper and a reputation for heavy drinking, he died on 15 February 1968 as a result of injuries sustained in a street brawl. This ignominious end should not detract from Little Walter's status as an innovative figure. The first musician to amplify the harmonica, his heavy, swooping style became the lynchpin for all who followed him, including Norton Buffalo, Butterfield and **Charlie Musselwhite**.

● ALBUMS: *The Best Of Little Walter* (Checker 1958)★★★★, *Little Walter* (Pye International 1964)★★★★, *Hate To See You Go* (Chess 1969)★★★, *Thunderbird* (Syndicate Chapter 1971)★★★, *On The Road Again* (Xtra 1979)★★★, *Quarter To Twelve* (Red Lightnin' 1982)★★★.

● COMPILATIONS: *Chess Masters* (Charly 1983)★★★★, *Boss Blues Harmonica* (Vogue 1986)★★★★, *Confessin' The Blues* (Chess 1986)★★★★, *Windy City Blues* (Blue Moon 1986)★★★, *Collection: Little Walter 20 Blues Greats* (Deja Vu 1987)★★★, *The Blues World Of Little Walter* (Delmark 1988)★★★★, *The Best Of Little Walter Volume 2* (Chess 1989)★★★, *The Chess Years 1952 - '63* 4-CD box set (Chess 1993)★★★★, *Blues With A Feeling* (MCA/Chess 1995)★★★★.

Little Whitt And Big Bo

Based in Tuscaloosa, Alabama, USA, the blues talents of 'Little Whitt' Wells (b. 19 February 1931, Ralph, Alabama, USA) and 'Big Bo' McGhee (b. 1928, Alabama, USA) remained largely undiscovered until the mid-90s, despite the fact that Wells had previously turned down offers to play guitar with **Freddie King**, **Howlin' Wolf** and **'Little' Junior Parker**. Harmonica player McGhee boasts a similarly intriguing past - having previously worked as a long-distance lorry driver shipping explosives and at one time having died on an operating table. He was revived several hours later after morgue technicians noticed a heartbeat. Wells was first turned on to the blues by the records of **Blind Boy Fuller** and **Blind Lemon Jefferson**, his father buying him his first guitar when he was 11. He originally met McGhee prior to forming his own band, Little Whitt And The Downbeats. For his part, McGhee started playing harmonica at the age of six. They began playing together full-time at the turn of the 80s, forming the Kokomo Blues Band. In 1995 the duo travelled to the UK, helped by sponsorship from Debbie Bond and Mike McCracken of the Alabama Blues Project, who also helped out by playing on stage.

● ALBUMS: various *Moody Swamp Blues* (Alabama Blues Project 1995)★★★.

Little, Booker

b. 2 April 1938, Memphis, Tennessee, USA, d. 5 October, 1961. One of the most promising of all trumpeters in the second bebop wave of the 50s, Booker Little was equipped with a superb technique, crystal clarity of intonation and rhythmic originality. His imagination extended beyond the strict harmonic disciplines of bop however, and hinted at the vision of **Ornette Coleman** or **Miles Davis**, but an early death from uraemia consigned such promise to the realm of speculation. Little was born into a musical family, and played clarinet before taking up the trumpet at the age of 12. He was involved in Memphis jam sessions with local pianist **Phineas Newborn Jnr.** in his teens, but moved to Chicago in 1957 to enrol at the city's Conservatory. During this period Little worked with **Johnny Griffin**'s band, but his most significant engagement of the period was with **Max Roach**, replacing another gifted trumpeter, **Clifford Brown**. His recordings with Roach include *Deeds Not Words*, *We Insist!*, *Freedom Now Suite* and *Percussion Bitter Sweet*. Little's originality quickly marked him out, as did his flexibility about non-bop settings, and he collaborated with **Eric Dolphy** on *Far Cry* and *Live At The Five Spot* (reissued as *The Great Concert Of Eric Dolphy*) and **John Coltrane** on the *Africa/Brass* recording. Little's own recordings featured some outstanding players, including Roach, Dolphy (*Out Front*), **Booker Ervin** and the 'legendary quartet' of **Scott La Faro**, **Roy Haynes** and both **Wynton Kelly** and **Tommy Flanagan** taking turns on piano. He worked too with **Donald Byrd** (*The Third World*), **Abbey Lincoln** (*Straight Ahead*) and **Frank Strozier**. By the time of his death Little was balancing tonality and dissonance with an insight that suggested his influence on jazz directions in general might have been even more substantial.

● ALBUMS: *Booker Little 4 And Max Roach* (Blue Note 1959)★★★★, *Booker Little* (Time 1960)★★★, *In New York* (Jazz View 1960)★★★, *The Legendary Quartet Album* (1960)★★★★, *Out Front* (Candid 1961)★★★, with Booker Ervin *Sounds Of The Inner City* (1961)★★★, *Victory And Sorrow* (Affinity 1961)★★★.

Littlefield, 'Little' Willie

b. 16 September 1931, El Campo, Texas, USA. By the age of 16, Littlefield was emulating his hero **Amos Milburn**, shouting the blues and hammering the pianos of nearby Houston's Dowling Street clubs. He made his recording debut the following year for the local Eddie's Records and for the Freedom label. In August 1949,

Littlefield was discovered by the Bihari brothers, who had flown to Houston to find their own version of Aladdin's Amos Milburn, and signed him to their Los Angeles-based Modern label. Littlefield's first Modern session, recorded in Houston, resulted in the huge hit 'It's Midnight', which featured his schoolfriend, Don Wilkerson, on tenor saxophone. From October 1949, Littlefield was recording in Los Angeles, but subsequent releases did not match the promise of the debut single, in spite of bands that included **Jimmy 'Maxwell Street' Davis**, Chuck Norris and **Johnny Moore**. In 1952, Littlefield signed with Federal Records and continued to make fine records in his own right and in duets with Lil Greenwood and **Little Esther Phillips**. His first Federal session resulted in his best-known recording, 'K.C. Lovin'' which was later altered slightly by **Leiber And Stoller** and recorded by **Wilbert Harrison** as 'Kansas City'. By 1957, Littlefield had moved to northern California, where he recorded for the Rhythm label. He stayed in San José throughout the 60s and 70s, making occasional club appearances, but in the early 80s he moved with his family to the Netherlands, and has since experienced a minor comeback with new material on various European labels and frequent appearances at jazz and blues festivals.

● ALBUMS: *K.C. Loving* (1977)★★★, *It's Midnight* (Route 66 1980)★★★, *Little Willie Littlefield - Volume One* (1980)★★★, *Little Willie Littlefield - Volume Two* (1981)★★★, *I'm In The Mood* (Oldie Blues 1984)★★★, *Jump With Little Willie Littlefield* (Ace 1984)★★★, *Happy Pay Day* (Ace 1985)★★★, *House Party* (Oldie Blues 1988)★★★, *Plays Boogie Woogie* (Schubert 1988)★★★.

● COMPILATIONS: *Yellow Boogie & Blues* (Oldie Blues 1995)★★★, *Going Back To Kay Cee* (Ace 1995)★★★.

Littlejohn, Johnny

b. John Wesley Funchess, 16 April 1931, Learned, Mississippi, USA, d. 1 February 1994, Chicago, Illinois, USA. Littlejohn taught himself to play guitar and was inspired by Henry Martin, a blues guitarist friend of his father. In 1946, he left home and was an itinerant worker before settling in Gary, Indiana, in 1951 and taking up the guitar seriously. He quickly became a popular attraction and later relocated to Chicago. A chronically underrated slide guitarist and singer, Littlejohn recorded for numerous labels, including Ace, Margaret, Bluesway, and Wolf, but his best work is to be found on **Arhoolie** and Rooster. Although often categorized as an **Elmore James**-influenced player, he could also recall the smooth approach of **B.B. King** with his picking and singing.

● ALBUMS: *John Littlejohn's Chicago Blues Stars* (Arhoolie 1968)★★★, *So-Called Friends* (Rooster 1985)★★★.

Live

A US alternative rock band from York, Pennsylvania, Live comprise Ed Kowalczyk (vocals), with Patrick Dahlheimer, Chad Taylor and Chad Gracey. The group was formed from blue-collar friends attending high school because 'we share the same ignorance'. The group's dynamic is one of fraught pop that occasionally expands into full-blown rock mode - with lyrics striking an idealistic tone. This was particularly true of the group's 1991 debut, the largely ignored *Mental Jewelery*, where spiritual overtones were also present. No less intense was the subsequent *Throwing Copper*, however, by this point Kowalczyk's lyrics had developed in a less literal direction: 'I'm more into letting my subconscious write, I want to let go completely, without becoming addicted to anything - which is a danger'. Another danger was a track such as 'Shit Towne', which addressed the populace of home-town York, and did little to ingratiate the band to their old community. The band's unexpected success continued into 1996 when *Throwing Copper* was certified as selling six million copies in the USA alone. *Secret Samadhi* looked set to be equally successful, even though it was an altogether bleaker-sounding record.

● ALBUMS: *Mental Jewelery* (Radioactive 1991)★★, *Throwing Copper* (Radioactive 1994)★★★★, *Secret Samadhi* (Radioactive 1997)★★★.

Live (X Cert) - The Stranglers

It may not even be the definitive **Stranglers** live album - in that *X-Cert* draws on just three studio sets; yet it conveys the character and the colour (black) of the punk movement's most undesirables. From its dramatic cover, in itself more in keeping with the early 70s than the cut and paste of the **Sex Pistols**, the Stranglers combined the movement's venom with an aggressive musicality and narcotic lyricism. This set also became legendary for **Hugh Cornwall**'s onstage patter, deriding his audience for spitting ('I know you like spitting but I don't particularly like being spat at while I'm playing') and remonstrating with an audience member audacious enough to call him a wanker (anybody who did the same at subsequent gigs was hoisted up on stage and spanked).

● Tracks: *Get A Grip On Yourself; Dagenham Dave; Burning Up Time; Dead Ringer; Hanging Around; Feel Like A Wog; Straight Out; Do You Wanna - Death And Night And Blood; Five Minutes; Go Buddy Go.*
● First released 1979
● UK peak chart position: 7
● USA peak chart position: did not chart

Live Aid

Millions saw the 1984 BBC television news report, by newscaster Michael Buerk, showing devastating images from the famine in Ethiopia. **Bob Geldof** was so moved that he organized, promoted and produced a fund-raising enterprise like the world had never before seen. His likeable bullying and eloquently cheeky publicity ultimately endeared him to millions. The song 'Do They Know It's Christmas?', co-written with **Midge Ure**, brought together a cavalcade of rock and pop stars under the name Band Aid, and included members of **Status Quo**, **Culture Club**, **Bananarama**, Style

Council, **Duran Duran**, **Spandau Ballet**, **Heaven 17** and **U2**. Solo stars included **Phil Collins**, **Sting**, **George Michael**, and **Paul Young**. Geldof bludgeoned artists, record companies, pressing plants, distributors and record shops into forgoing their profits. The record scaled the UK charts and stayed at the top for five weeks, eventually selling millions of copies. Geldof topped this masterstroke in July 1985 by organizing the twin Live Aid concerts in London and Philadelphia. This spectacular rock and pop event was televised worldwide, and the stellar cast included **Sade**, **Queen**, **Bob Dylan**, **Neil Young**, the **Cars**, **Beach Boys**, **Pat Metheny**, **Santana**, **Madonna**, **Kenny Loggins**, **Bryan Adams**, **Crosby, Stills And Nash**, **Eric Clapton**, Phil Collins (who, via Concorde, appeared at both venues), **Judas Priest**, **REO Speedwagon**, **Jimmy Page**, **Robert Plant**, Status Quo, **Elvis Costello**, **Bryan Ferry**, Sting, Paul Young, **Adam Ant**, **Simple Minds**, U2, the **Who**, **Paul McCartney**, **Mick Jagger**, **Tina Turner**, **Elton John**, Spandau Ballet and **David Bowie**. The huge worldwide television audience raised over £50 million through pledged donations. Geldof carried through his sincere wish to help starving children with integrity, passion and a sense of humour. The Live Aid concert remains one of the greatest musical events of all time. Geldof received an honorary knighthood in 1986 for his humanitarian activities.

● VIDEOS: *Do They Know It's Christmas?* (PolyGram Music Video 1986).
● FURTHER READING: *Live Aid: The Greatest Show On Earth*, Peter Hillmore.

Live And Dangerous - Thin Lizzy

Phil Lynott's glorious call to arms; a heady mix of wry humour and wonderfully constructed vignettes of youthful indulgence and an intricate weave of Celtic moods. This soulful and stirring double album evocatively captured the real show-stopping energy that **Thin Lizzy** displayed. Riding roughshod over a variety of styles - the woeful 'I'm Still In Love With You', the frantic enthusiasm of 'Boys Are Back In Town', or the clever knitting of styles with 'Rosalie/Cowgirl's Song', complete with giant mirror ball - Thin Lizzy were a band blessed with grace and a fistful of ideas. All the evidence you need is here.

● Tracks: *Boys Are Back In Town; Dancing In The Moonlight; Massacre; I'm Still In Love With You; Me And The Boys...; Don't Believe A Word; Warriors; Are You Ready?; Sha-la-la-la; Baby Drives Me Crazy; Rosalie/Cowgirl's Song.*
● First released 1978
● UK peak chart position: 2
● USA peak chart position: 84

Live At Fillmore East/The Fillmore Concerts - The Allman Brothers Band

The original *Fillmore East* album is one of the finest live documents of the rock era, capturing the original line-up of one of the 70s' tightest outfits before they were cruelly robbed of **Duane Allman** and Berry Oakley.

Taken from five 1971 performances at New York's fabled Fillmore East, the extended and effortlessly melodic workouts of 'In Memory Of Elizabeth Reed' and 'Whipping Post' remain definitive recordings. The dual guitar interplay of Duane Allman and **Dickey Betts** glides effortlessly over the propulsive rhythm section of Oakley and twin drummers Jaimoe and Butch Trucks, while **Greg Allman**'s powerful blues voice and melodic keyboard work provides the icing on the cake. The expanded *Fillmore Concerts* CD adds more tracks and digital clarity.

● Tracks: *Statesboro Blues; Trouble No More; Don't Keep Me Wonderin'; In Memory Of Elizabeth Reed; One Way Out; Done Somebody Wrong; Stormy Monday; You Don't Love Me; Hot 'Lanta; Whipping Post; Mountain Jam; Drunken Hearted Boy.*
● First Released 1971
● UK peak chart position: did not chart
● USA peak chart position: 13

Live At Leeds - The Who

The **Who** forged their reputation as an exciting live attraction and elected to issue this set in the wake of the highly successful *Tommy*. Selections from that ground-breaking rock opera formed the core of this concert, but the group used the opportunity equally to restate past glories and acknowledge influences. Rock 'n' roll star **Eddie Cochran** had inspired the Who's **Pete Townshend**; the former's 'Summertime Blues' exploded with new fury within. 'Young Man Blues', first recorded by jazz singer **Mose Allison**, was given a new dimension through power chords, pulsating drumming and **Roger Daltrey**'s expressive vocal. The CD reissue with bonus tracks is outstanding.

● Tracks: *Magic Bus; My Generation; Shakin' All Over; Substitute; Summertime Blues; Young Man Blues.*
● First released 1970
● UK peak chart position: 3
● USA peak chart position: 4

Live At Max's Kansas City - The Velvet Underground

'Excuse me can I have a Pernod, get me a Pernod'. Whoever he is, wherever he is, he must realize by now that his boorish demands for a bloody Pernod ruined the illegal cassette taping of this ramshackle gig. Had it been professionally recorded, the sound would be much better, although the guitars would still be out of tune and the drums would be playing a different song. Wonderful but unlistenable because every time it is played, the desire to punch the Pernod character on the nose manifests itself. Will the offender please own up.

● Tracks: *I'm Waiting For The Man; Sweet Jane; Lonesome Cowboy Bill; Beginning To See The Light; I'll Be Your Mirror; Pale Blue Eyes; Sunday Morning; New Age; Femme Fatale; After Hours.*
● First released 1974
● UK peak chart position: did not chart
● USA peak chart position: did not chart

Live At San Quentin - B.B. King

Much gutsier than *Live At The Regal*, this is in harmony with the patrons as **B.B. King** plays to a different audience: the inmates of one of America's toughest prisons. King devotes much of his time every year to performing to prisoners, and he communicates on this album without patronizing them. This is a fairly predictable set but the high level recording (presumably to block out any obscenities) makes it one of his most exciting live albums. Songs he has played a thousand times sound fresh and energetic, notably 'Everyday I Have The Blues and 'Let The Good Times Roll'.

● Tracks: *BB King Intro; Let The Good Times Roll; Everyday I Have The Blues; Whole Lotta Lovein'; Sweet Little Angel; Never Make A Move Too Soon; Into The Night; Ain't Nobody's Bizness If I Do; The Thrill Is Gone; Peace To The World; Nobody Loves Me But My Mother; Sweet Sixteen; Rock Me Baby.*
● First released 1990 rec.70s
● UK peak chart position: did not chart
● USA peak chart position: did not chart

Live At The Apollo Vol. 1 - James Brown

Superlatives abound when considering this seminal set. It has been called 'the greatest live album of all time' while **James Brown**'s position as the Godfather of Soul is almost indisputable. The singer was largely unknown outside black music circles prior to the release of this million-seller which fully captured the power and intensity of Brown in concert. It contains the cream of his releases, each of which is injected with a passionate fervour. Brilliantly paced, the set grows in stature, as the famed **Apollo** audience responds to and, indeed, adds to the excitement. Brown towers majestically over the proceedings; pleading, extolling, proving himself not just the finest R&B singer of his generation, but one of the most distinctive in the history of popular music.

● Tracks: *I'll Go Crazy; Try Me; Think; I Don't Mind; Lost Someone (Part 1); Lost Someone (Part 2); Please, Please, Please; You've Got The Power; I Found Someone; Why Do You Do Me Like You Do; I Want You So Bad; I Love You Yes I Do; Why Does Everything Happen To Me; Bewildered; Please Don't Go; Night Train.*
● First released 1963
● UK peak chart position: did not chart
● USA peak chart position: 2

Live At The Budokan - Cheap Trick

A richly coloured bubble-gum wrapper of a record that took **Cheap Trick**'s reputation, not to mention their commercial appeal, to a much more exalted level. Probably, in retrospect, their greatest record, *Live At Budokan* set their majestic ear for four-minute pop nuggets against the backdrop of more than a thousand screaming Japanese teens. Robin Zander's pin-up, suave playboy and Nielsen's and Carlos's endearingly wacked out images sat alongside the truly great 'I Want You To Want Me', 'Surrender', 'Need Your Love', the occasional well groomed cover version, and a handful of roof down, summertime blow-outs, all of which ensured them a place in live album legend.

● Tracks: *Hello There; Come On, Come On; Lookout; Big Eyes; Need Your Love; Ain't That A Shame; I Want You To Want Me; Surrender; Goodnight Now; Clock Strikes Ten.*

● First released 1979

● UK peak chart position: 29

● USA peak chart position: 4

Live At The Regal - B.B. King

No matter how good the studio sessions were, **B.B. King** was at his best on stage in front of an appreciative, if not ecstatic, crowd. This set, recorded at Chicago's premier black theatre on 21 November 1964, delivered just that. Despite the less than perfect recording conditions, at a time when technology had yet to catch up with the demands placed upon it, the King of the Blues delivers a definitive performance in a programme that includes his then most recent single, 'Help The Poor', and a clutch of songs that were responsible for much of his success, 'Everyday I Have The Blues', 'Sweet Little Angel', 'It's My Own Fault', 'You Upset Me Baby' and 'Woke Up This Morning', among them. The band, including tenorman Johnny Board and organist Duke Jethro, is lean but tight, providing King with a springboard from which to leap into flights of immaculate guitar playing and singing.

● Tracks: *Everyday I Have The Blues; Sweet Little Angel; It's My Own Fault; How Blue Can You Get; Please Love Me; You Upset Me Baby; Worry, Worry; Woke Up This Morning; You Done Lost Your Good Thing Now; Help The Poor.*

● First released 1965

● UK peak chart position: did not chart

● USA peak chart position: 78

Live At The Witch Trials - The Fall

One of rock's most original and distinctive acts, the **Fall** have consistently refused to brook compromise. Led by the irascible Mark E. Smith, they declared a pungent individuality on a debut indebted to punk's freedom, but which rejected its trappings. Smith's bitter wit is crucial to their métier; half speaking, half singing, he savages insincerity, implying political statements without overtly expressing them. The group supports his rant with rudimentary dissonance, creating scratchy pulses of sound that are invigorating and exciting. Terse and combative, *Live At The Witch Trials* is a radical statement, the power of which remains undiminished.

● Tracks: *Frightened; Crap Rap 2 - Like To Blow; Rebellious Jukebox; No Xmas For John Quays; Mother-Sister?; Industrial Estate; Underground Medicin; Two Steps Back; Live At The Witch Trials; Futures And Pasts; Music Scene.*

● First released 1979

● UK peak chart position: did not chart

● USA peak chart position: did not chart

Live Bullet - Bob Seger And The Silver Bullet Band

The double live album that, not unlike **Kiss**'s experience, truly opened the floodgates for **Bob Seger**'s real

commercial success in the USA. This full-blown gatefold sleeve affair, recorded at two sold-out and enthusiastic shows in Detroit, highlighted Seger's unpretentious and sometimes quietly profound take on small town living and its consequences. The sublime 'Jody Girl' acts as a strong indication of his storytelling abilities. However, it is on nefarious blow-outs such as the indulgent, crowd-pleasing 'Heavy Music' and the stomping honky tonk of 'Katmandu', that this record really comes to life.

● Tracks: *Nutbush City Limits; Travellin' Man; Beautiful Loser; Jody Girl; Looking Back; Get Out Of Denver; Let It Rock; I've Been Working; Turn The Page; UMC; Bo Diddley; Ramblin' Gamblin' Man; Heavy Music; Katmandu.*

● First released 1976

● UK peak chart position: did not chart

● USA peak chart position: 34

Live Dead - The Grateful Dead

As the archetypal west coast band, famed for lengthy improvisation, the **Grateful Dead** found it difficult to translate their in-concert fire onto record. The group addressed this dilemma by recording *Live Dead* live in the studio, allowing free rein for guitarist **Jerry Garcia**'s liquid flights. The twin drumming of Mickey Hart and Bill Kreutzman provides an imaginative platform, bassist **Phil Lesh** takes his instrument into new dimensions, while organist Pigpen provides a distinctive swirling sound that envelops and enhances his colleagues' interplay. The last-named takes a vocal cameo on 'Turn On Your Lovelight', a performance showing the Dead's R&B roots, while 'Dark Star' exposes new levels of musical empathy. Such factors ensure this album's prominence in the group's canon.

● Tracks: *Dark Star; Death Don't Have No Mercy; Feedback; And We Bid You Goodnight; St. Stephen; Eleven; Turn On Your Lovelight.*

● First released 1970

● UK peak chart position: did not chart

● USA peak chart position: 64

Live Through This - Hole

With the world and its dog besotted with the latest hybrid of punk rock (grunge) and its finest exponents (**Nirvana**), *Live Through This* almost slipped through the net. With Kurt Cobain dead a week before its release, journalists were more interested in his widow's reactions than her music. Little wonder - it was hard to overlook lyrics such as 'With a bullet, number one/Kill the family, save the son' ('Jennifer's Boy'). Courtney Love had just released the best album of her career. *Live Through This* saw her songwriting develop accessibility and personality. Most songs provided a happy halfway house between brash pop and blazing guitar workouts. There are some truly startling lyrical images that make *Live Through This* a thrilling experience.

● Tracks: *Violet; Miss World; Plump; Asking For It; Jennifer's Body; Doll Parts; Credit In The Straight World; Softer, Softest; She Walks On Me; I Think That I Would Die; Gutless; Rock Star.*

- First released 1994
- UK peak chart position: 13
- USA peak chart position: 52

Live Wire/Blues Power - Albert King

Albert King had been recording for **Stax** for two years, releasing a series of epochal contemporary blues records - 'Oh Pretty Woman', 'Crosscut Saw', 'Born Under A Bad Sign' and 'The Hunter' - when his label decided to record him live at San Francisco's Fillmore Auditorium. Later issues of material from the two nights that were recorded show that he performed most of his recent successes to his new-found hippie audience. By contrast, on *Live Wire/Blues Power*, King's torturously convoluted guitar style was given full and free rein. Despite his tetchy reputation, King responded gratefully to his new fans, but made no concessions to their initial ignorance of his music. The resulting record underlined his musical strengths and the vitality of the blues itself.

- Tracks: *Watermelon Man; Blues Power; Night Stomp; Blues At Sunrise; Please Love Me; Lookout.*
- First released 1968
- UK peak chart position: did not chart
- USA peak chart position: 150

Live! - Bob Marley

Nobody who likes music could fail to be emotionally moved by this album, and not just because **Bob Marley** is no longer with us. It was a special live treat before he died. The great thing about this record is the feeling that this is what it was like every night, unlike other live recordings which capture one or two gigs of a tour. Marley was extra special and a giant of popular music. Wallow in this vital record and listen to a man who had something to say and yet had fun while he said it. Most of the tracks you would want to be on the record are here, including the definitive version of 'No Woman No Cry' and a funky 'Lively Up Yourself'.

- Tracks: *Trenchtown Rock; Burnin' And Lootin'; Them Belly Full (But We Hungry); Lively Up Yourself; No Woman No Cry; I Shot The Sheriff; Get Up, Stand Up.*
- First released 1975
- UK peak chart position: 38
- USA peak chart position: 90

Liver Birds

There had been all-female musical groups before such as the 17 strong **Vernons Girls** Choir and the **Ivy Benson** Band, but in 1962, an all-female rock 'n' roll group was something new. They started as the Debutones and became the Liver Birds with the line-up settling to Pam Birch (guitar, vocal), Mary McGlory (bass, vocal), Valerie Gill (guitar, vocal) and Sylvia Saunders (drums). One of the founder members, Irene Green, became Tiffany of **Tiffany's Thoughts**. Saunders recalls, 'We started off in Liverpool and played the **Cavern** doing the usual songs like 'Roll Over Beethoven' and 'Johnny B. Goode'. The fans were

mostly girls and they never really accepted us.' Nevertheless, **Brian Epstein** offered them a management contract, provided they were patient and waited until he had launched **Cilla Black** and **Billy J. Kramer**. Instead they relocated to Hamburg and were managed by the owner of the Star-Club in Hamburg, Manfred Weissleder. They also recorded for Star-Club Records and their single, 'Diddley Daddy', made the German Top 5. The group split up in 1967. Saunders returned to the UK and married John Wiggins from the **Bobby Patrick's Big Six**. In 1997 they bought a bar in the Costa Del Sol and plan to play there.

Liverpool Express

Liverpool Express centred on singer/guitarist Billy Kinsley (b. 28 November 1946, Liverpool, England), veteran of 60s groups the **Merseybeats**, the **Merseys** and the **Swinging Blue Jeans.** He later formed Rockin' Horse with songwriter **Jimmy Campbell**, before embarking on a solo career in 1973 with 'Annabella'. Liverpool Express evolved out of the club group Kinsley had been working with and this new venture made its debut in 1975 with 'Smile (My Smiler's Smile)'. The quartet scored four chart hits between 1976-77, two of which, 'You Are My Love' and 'Every Man Must Have A Dream', reached the UK Top 20. The resulting touring schedule brought success in South America and on the European continent. *Dreamin'* was issued only in South America and *ELX* was only released in Europe A brief hiatus was followed by a modest UK chart position for 'So What?' in 1983. Liverpool Express have continued to perform and record into the 90s.

- ALBUMS: *Tracks* (1977)★★, *Dreamin'* (1977)★★★, *ELX* (1978)★★★.

Liverpool Scene

The name 'Liverpool Scene' was derived from a poetry anthology which featured Roger McGough, Adrian Henri and Brian Patten. The writers subsequently appeared on UK television's *Look Of The Week*, where their readings were accompanied by guitarist **Andy Roberts**. McGough and Henri then recorded *The Incredible New Liverpool Scene*, which included definitive performances of their best-known work, including 'Let Me Die A Young Man's Death' (McGough) and 'Tonight At Noon' (Henri). While McGough pursued a career within **Scaffold**, Henri and Roberts added Mike Hart (guitar/vocals), Mike Evans (saxophone/vocals), Percy Jones (bass) and Brian Dodson (drums) to create an explicitly rock-based ensemble. UK disc jockey **John Peel** was an early patron and the group quickly found itself an integral part of music's underground circuit, culminating in their impressive appearance at the 1969 **Isle Of Wight Festival**. *The Amazing Adventures Of ...* captured the sextet at their most potent, but successive albums, although worthwhile, failed to match the crucial balance between musical and lyrical content and the group broke up in 1970. Hart embarked on a solo career, but while Roberts initially found fame in

Plainsong, he was later reunited with both Henri and McGough in **Grimms**.

● ALBUMS: *The Incredible New Liverpool Scene* (Columbia 1967)★★, *The Amazing Adventures Of ...* (RCA 1968)★★★★, *Bread On The Night* (RCA 1969)★★★, *Saint Adrian Co. Broadway And 3rd* (RCA 1970)★★★, *Heirloom* (RCA 1970)★★★.

● COMPILATIONS: *Recollections* (1972)★★★.

Livgren, Kerry

The former **Kansas** guitarist (b. 18 September 1949, Kansas, USA) departed the fold in the early 80s to put on record his new-found religious beliefs as a born-again Christian. His debut solo effort saw him keeping a nucleus of Kansas personnel in support, adding the vocals of **Ronnie James Dio** on a competent set. Afterwards, Livgren indulged in some tepid AOR albums, often allied to grandiose orchestral concepts, both solo and with his spin-off project, **AD**.

● ALBUMS: *Seeds Of Change* (Kirshner 1980)★★.

Livin' Joy

At a time when the simple joys of Eurodisco had been reduced to the MOR noodling of **Robert Miles** and the naff behemoth that was 'Macarena', Livin' Joy provided some hope for the much-maligned form. This was mainly due to the efforts of singer/lyricist Tameka Star, a US forces brat and a fan of **Natalie Cole**. After a childhood spent on numerous army bases throughout Europe, Tameka met the Visnadi brothers, Paulo and Gianni, major Italo-house producers, and the trio began to work together as Livin' Joy. The anthem 'Dreamer' was a decent club hit but it was 'Don't Stop Movin'' that dominated the airwaves. Tameka's soulful vocals gave guts to the brothers' infectious backing, creating a major UK hit in the second half of 1996, although the act's Continental origin has so far denied them the critical credibility that US and British dance outfits can command.

● ALBUMS: *Don't Stop Movin'* (MCA 1996)★★★.

Living Colour

This US rock band was originally formed by **Vernon Reid** (b. 22 August 1958, London, England; guitar), Muzz Skillings (bass) and William Calhoun (b. 22 July 1964, Brooklyn, New York, USA; drums). Reid had studied performing arts at Manhattan Community College, having moved to New York at the age of two. His first forays were in experimental electric jazz with Defunk, before he formed Living Colour as a trio in 1984. Both Skillings and Calhoun were experienced academic musicians, having studied and received acclaim at City College and **Berklee College Of Music**, respectively. The line-up was completed by the induction of vocalist Corey Glover (b. 6 November 1964, Brooklyn, New York, USA), who had just finished a role in Oliver Stone's film *Platoon*, and whom Reid had originally encountered at a friend's birthday party. Their first major engagement came when **Mick Jagger** saw them performing at **CBGB's** and invited them to the studio for his forthcoming solo album. Jagger's patronage continued as he produced two demos for the band, which secured them a contract with Epic Records. Their debut, *Vivid*, earned them early critical acclaim and rose to number 6 in the US charts. Fusing disparate black musical formats such as jazz, blues and soul, alongside commercial hard rock, its diversity was reflected in the support slots the band acquired to promote it, **Cheap Trick**, **Robert Palmer** and **Billy Bragg** among them. Musically, the band is most closely aligned to the first of that trio, although their political edge mirrors the concerns of Bragg. In 1985 Reid formed the *Black Rock Coalition* pressure movement alongside journalist Greg Tate, and Living Colour grew to be perceived as their nation's most articulate black rock band. Two subsequent singles, 'Cult Of Personality' (which included samples of John F. Kennedy's speeches and won a Grammy award) and 'Open Letter (To A Landlord)', were both provocative but intelligent expressions of urban concerns. The ties with the **Rolling Stones** remained strong, with Reid collaborating on **Keith Richards**' solo album. They also joined the Stones on their *Steel Wheels* tour. After sweeping the boards in several Best New Band awards in such magazines as *Rolling Stone*, *Time's Up* was released in 1990, and afforded another Grammy Award. Notable contributions, apart from the omnipresent Jagger, included **Little Richard** on the controversial 'Elvis Is Dead'. In 1991 worldwide touring established them as a highly potent force in mainstream rock. Following Skillings' departure, bassist Doug Wimbush (b. 22 September 1956, Hartford, Connecticut, USA) from **Tackhead** joined them for *Stain* which added a sprinkling of studio gimmickry on a number of tracks. The band announced its dissolution early in 1995; Vernon Reid stated: '. . . Living Colour's sense of unity and purpose was growing weaker and fuzzier, I was finding more and more creative satisfaction in my solo projects. Finally it became obvious that I had to give up the band and move on'. An excellent retrospective, *Pride*, was released following their demise. Reid released an impressive solo debut album in 1996.

● ALBUMS: *Vivid* (Epic 1988)★★★★, *Time's Up* (Epic 1990)★★★★, *Stain* (Epic 1993)★★★, *Dread* Japanese live release (Epic 1993)★★★.

● COMPILATIONS: *Pride* (Epic 1995)★★★★.

Living In A Box

This Sheffield, UK-based pop group comprised Richard Darbyshire (b. 8 March 1960, Stockport, Cheshire, England; vocal/guitars), Marcus Vere (b. 29 January 1962; keyboards) and Anthony Critchlow (drums). Their first single, the self-referential, 'Living In A Box' was a UK Top 10 hit in the spring of 1987 and further successes followed over the next two years, most notably, 'Blow The House Down' and 'Room In Your Heart'. Meanwhile, vocalist Richard Darbyshire guested on **Jellybean**'s *Jellybean Rocks The House*. Having enjoyed a hit album with their self-titled debut, the group consolidated their success with *Gatecrashing*. However, the group sundered in 1990 as their chart fortunes declined. Darbyshire subsequently launched a solo career with **Virgin Records**.

● ALBUMS: *Living In A Box* (Chrysalis 1987)★★★, *Gatecrashing* (Chrysalis 1989)★★★.

Living It Up

One of the best films that **Dean Martin** and Jerry Lewis made together in the mid-50s, this 1954 Paramount release was twice blessed - with an amusing story and a set of good songs. Jack Rose and Melville Shavelson's screenplay was based on James Street's story *Letter To The Editor* and the 1937 movie *Nothing Sacred*, which starred Fredric March and Carole Lombard. Proving that nothing *is* sacred in Hollywood, Lombard's role was played this time by Jerry Lewis, who gave a typically zany performance as a man who thinks he has had a hefty dose of radiation poisoning. Encouraged by his doctor (Martin), who knows very well it is only a sinus condition, and a newspaper reporter (Janet Leigh), who believes he is going to die and knows a good story when she sees one, Lewis takes a press-sponsored trip to New York for one final all-out binge. It was all very entertaining, but much of the original film's bite and satire seemed to be lost on the way. Two of **Jule Styne** and **Bob Hilliard**'s songs, 'How Do You Speak To An Angel?' and 'Money Burns A Hole In My Pocket', became popular record hits, and Martin's relaxed and easy manner was ideal for the engaging 'That's What I Like' and a duet with Lewis, 'Ev'ry Street's A Boulevard (In Old New York)'. The other songs were 'Champagne And Wedding Cake' and 'You're Gonna Dance With Me, Baby'. Also featured were Edward Arnold, Fred Clark, Sheree North, Sig Ruman and Sammy White. Norman Taurog was the director and the film was shot in Technicolor. Styne and Hilliard also wrote the score for a 1953 Broadway musical based on this story. It was called *Hazel Flagg*, and ran for just 190 performances.

Livingston, Fud

b. Joseph Anthony Livingston, Charleston, South Carolina, USA, d. 25 March 1957. After learning to play piano, Livingston turned to tenor saxophone and clarinet and while still in his teens was working regularly with several bands including that led by **Ben Pollack**. He also played with the **California Ramblers**, **Jean Goldkette**, **Nat Shilkret**, **Jan Garber** and others. In demand as a studio sideman on record dates, he also arranged, and by the 30s was active in this field for **Paul Whiteman** and Pollack. In the late 30s he joined **Jimmy Dorsey**'s reed section, then turned again to arranging. Later in his career he was working in film studios in California but his career gradually went awry through personal problems, and he eked a living playing barroom piano. Livingston's playing, especially on clarinet, sets him apart from most of his contemporaries. He played with a quirky distinctiveness and his thinking often appears to have been far ahead of his more orthodox musical companions.

● COMPILATIONS: *Ben Pollack* (RCA 1926)★★★, *Benny Goodman's Boys And The Whoopee Makers* (Sunbeam 1928)★★★.

Livingston, Jay

b. 28 March 1915, Pittsburgh, Pennsylvania, USA. After studying music at school, Livingston attended the University of Pennsylvania where he met and formed a lasting friendship with Ray Evans (b. 4 February 1915, Salamanca, New York, USA) with whom he worked in shipboard bands on transatlantic and cruise liners. Their joint careers as songwriters were barely under way when they were interrupted by World War II. In the post-war years Livingston and Evans worked in Hollywood, writing songs for films. Their major success during this period was the title song from *To Each His Own* (1946). Other films they contributed to included *The Cat And The Canary*, *On Stage Everybody*, *The Stork Club*, *My Favourite Brunette*, *Dream Girl*, *Whispering Smith*, *Samson And Delilah*, *Bitter Victory*, *The Great Lover*, *Sorrowful Jones*, *My Friend Irma*, *Fancy Pants*, *The Lemon Drop Kid*, *Here Comes The Groom*, *Aaron Slick From Punkin Crick*, *Thunder In The East*, *Here Come The Girls*, and *Red Garters*. While continuing their partnership, in which Livingston usually wrote the music and Evans the words, both men occasionally worked with other composers. Their joint successes included the Oscar-winning songs 'Buttons And Bows' (*The Paleface* 1948) and 'Mona Lisa' (*Capt. Carey, USA* 1950). Among their other movie songs were 'Golden Earrings' (music by **Victor Young**), 'My Love Loves Me', 'Silver Bells', 'I'll Always Love You', 'Home Cookin'', 'A Place In The Sun' (music by **Franz Waxman**), 'Never Let Me Go', and another Oscar winner and **Doris Day** hit, 'Whatever Will Be, Will Be (Que Sera, Sera)'. Throughout the 50s Livingston and Evans continued to turn out film songs such as 'Tammy' and 'Almost In Your Arms'. In 1958 they wrote the score for a Broadway show *Oh, Captain!*, which included 'Femininity'. In the 60s came 'The Arms Of Love' and 'Wait Until Dark', and the duo also wrote the themes for the television series *Bonanza* and *Mr. Ed*. In the 70s Livingston and Evans continued to write occasional material for films and television, and contributed to the Broadway musical *Sugar Babies*.

Livingston, Ulysses

b. 29 January 1912, Bristol, Tennessee, USA. As a young man Livingston played guitar in a college band and also gained on-the-road experience with **Horace Henderson**, although in a non-musical capacity. After working around the country as a guitarist, he went to New York in the mid-30s where he played with several leaders of small bands including **Lillian Armstrong**, **Stuff Smith** and **Frankie Newton**. He then spent some time in **Benny Carter**'s band before joining **Ella Fitzgerald**. After military service during World War II, he played with a number of west coast bands including the **Spirits Of Rhythm**, **Illinois Jacquet** and **Rex Stewart**. He also appeared with **Norman Granz**'s **Jazz At The Philharmonic**. From the 50s onwards, Livingston worked mostly outside music but continued to make occasional record dates and club appearances. A fluid player with imagination and rhythmic solidity, Livingston had much more talent than his relatively short full-time career would suggest.

● ALBUMS: with JATP *The Beginning* (Charly 1945)★★, with Jack McVea *Nothin' But Jazz* (77 Records 1962)★★★.

Livingstone, Dandy

b. Robert Livingstone Thompson, 1944, Kingston, Jamaica, West Indies. Livingstone was at one time a member of the 60s duo Sugar And Dandy with Sugar Simone, and he became a very popular performer in the UK as a solo artist after he relocated there at the age of 15. His records appeared on a variety of different labels under different names and he was responsible for many of the UK's **rocksteady** and reggae hits throughout the 60s, 'Reggae In Your Jeggae' proving particularly popular in 1969. His first UK chart entry was 'Suzanne Beware of the Devil' in 1972, when reggae was briefly enjoying great popularity in the charts due to the skinhead connection. The follow-up, 'Big City', was a smaller hit the following year. His name was revered by many ska/2-Tone fans who recalled his 60s heyday, and the **Specials** recorded a cover version of his 'A Message To You Rudy'.

● ALBUMS: *Your Musical Doctor* (Downtown 1965)★★★, *Dandy Livingstone* (Trojan 1972)★★★★, *South African Experience* (Night Owl 1978)★★★.

Livingstone, John Graeme

b. 21 February 1951, Nelson, Lancashire, England. Livingstone is a singer-songwriter mostly working around his home in the Lake District. 'Wings Of Fire' was a powerful single, influenced by his love of **John Stewart**. 'Ship Of The Sky' is about the courage of the Archbishop of Canterbury's envoy, Terry Waite. A new album, *Innocent Bystander*, featuring **Wes McGhee** and Cathryn Craig, was set for release in 1997. Livingstone also completed a series of songs about soldiers fighting Napoleon's forces in Spain, 'Just A Little War'. Livingstone owns Stillwater Records and Fair Oaks Entertainer. He has brought singer-songwriter **Dave Mallett** and Don-Oja Dunaway to the UK as well as promoting concerts by Bill Zorn, now with the **Limeliters**.

● ALBUMS: *House Full Of Strangers* (Stillwater 1988)★★★.

Lizzie

b. Sweden. Swedish soul singer Lizzie earned immediate comparisons to **Kate Bush** with her sultry debut single 'Impossible'. Released by MNW Records in 1993, it was not her first attempt to make a career in the music industry. In the mid-80s she had sung with Houses And Gardens - a briefly successful band noted for its exuber-ant live performances. She was also previously half of the Master Twins duo, who worked with some of London's top producers.

Lizzy

The DJ phenomenon began in the early 60s, but it was the unprecedented success of **U-Roy** that signalled the turning point in the development of Jamaican music. By 1970 there was a considerable number of new DJs, including **Dennis Alcapone**, **I. Roy**, **Big Youth** and Lizzy. The young DJs were inspired by the scat toasting of **Count Matchuki**, **Sir Lord Comic** and **King Stitt**, but the newcomers took the art to a different level. Lizzy recorded in the innovative 'sing talk' style for **Duke Reid**, initially enjoying hits with 'Love Is A Treasure', which employed **Freddie McKay**'s original **rocksteady** hit, and 'I See Your Face (Version)', which utilized the **John Holt** hit. Inspired by this success, Duke Reid encouraged Lizzy to join forces with his sparring partner, Dennis Alcapone, for a string of classic combination hits, notably 'Baba Riba Skank' (based on **Ken Parker**'s 'I Can't Hide'), 'The Right Song' (the **Paragons**' 'Same Song') and the excellent 'Cry Tough', which further embellished the **Alton Ellis** classic. By 1973 Lizzy's association with Alcapone ended when the El Paso DJ relocated to the UK. Lizzy remained in Jamaica where he embarked on sessions with **Joe Gibbs**, who produced the hit 'Aquarius' and a remake of the Paragons' 'Wear You To The Ball' aka 'Harmony Hall'. Lizzy continued to release sporadic hits, including 'Double Attack' with **Delroy Wilson**. Although he was often considered as a sidekick of Dennis Alcapone, his individual efforts were recognized in the mid-90s. He savoured a revival and interest in his early work resulted in the release of two similar compilations.

● ALBUMS: with Dennis Alcapone *Soul To Soul DJ's Choice* reissued 1996 (Trojan 1973)★★★, *Baba Riba Skank* (Esoldun 1996)★★★★.

Lizzy Borden

This theatrical heavy rock band formed in Los Angeles in 1983, and took their name from the infamous axe murderess. Utilizing strong sexual and horror imagery, their visual style owed much to **Alice Cooper**. The group featured Lizzy Borden (vocals), his brother Joey Scott Harges (drums), Mike Kenny (bass) and Tony Matuzak (guitar). Their contribution to the *Metal Massacre IV* compilation impressed **Metal Blade** boss Brian Slagel enough to offer them a contract. The mini-album *Give 'Em The Axe* emerged in the summer of 1984, followed a year later by *Love You To Pieces*, their official full-length debut. Both were highly derivative of **Rainbow/Iron Maiden**, with Lizzy's vocals sounding similar to Geoff Tate's of **Queensrÿche**. Alex Nelson replaced Matuzak on guitar before the recording of *The Murderess Metal Roadshow*. This was a double live collection whose low-tech origins did little to flatter the band. Two more studio albums followed, including the abbreviated *Terror Rising*, which saw Betsy from **Bitch** duetting on a cover version of the **Tubes**' kitsch classic, 'Don't Touch Me There'. Gene Allen was added as a second guitarist and Jesse Holmes and Mychal Davis replaced Nelson and Kenny, respectively, before the recording of what is arguably the band's most enduring set, *Visual Lies*. Loosely based around a central theme of illusions, the album was varied and hard-hitting, characterized by infectious hooks, anthemic choruses and smouldering guitar breaks. They played the Reading Festival in 1987 to an indifferent reaction and Lizzy disbanded the group shortly afterwards (Holmes and Allen having already departed, with guitarist Ron Cerito replacing Mike Davis). Concentrating on a solo career, he released the ambitious concept album, *Master Of Disguise*.

● ALBUMS: *Give 'Em The Axe* mini-album (Metal Blade 1984)★★★, *Love You To Pieces* (Metal Blade 1985)★★★, *The Murderess Metal Roadshow* (Roadrunner 1986)★★, *Menace To Society* (Roadrunner 1986)★★★, *Terror Rising* mini-album (Metal Blade 1987)★★★, *Visual Lies* (Roadrunner 1987)★★★★.
Solo: Lizzy Borden *Master Of Disguise* (Roadrunner 1989)★★★.

● COMPILATIONS: *Best Of* (Metal Blade 1994)★★★.

● VIDEOS: *Murdress Metal Roadshow* (1986).

LL Cool J

b. James Todd Smith, 16 August 1969, St. Albans, Queens, New York, USA. Long-running star of the rap scene, LL Cool J found fame at the age of 16, his pseudonym standing for 'Ladies Love Cool James'. As might be inferred by this, LL is a self-professed ladykiller in the vein of **Luther Vandross** or **Barry White**, yet he retains a superior rapping agility. Smith started rapping at the age of nine, after his grandfather bought him his first DJ equipment. From the age of 13 he was processing his first demos. The first to respond to his mail-outs was Rick Rubin of **Def Jam Records**, then a senior at New York University, who signed him to his fledgling label. The first sighting of LL Cool J came in 1984 on a 12-inch, 'I Need A Beat', which was the label's first such release. However, it was 'I Just Can't Live Without My Radio', which established his gold-chained, barechested B-boy persona. The song was featured in the *Krush Groove* film, on which the rapper also performed. In its wake he embarked on a 50-city US tour alongside the **Fat Boys**, **Whodini**, **Grandmaster Flash** and **Run DMC**. The latter were crucial to LL Cool J's development: his *modus operandi* was to combine their beatbox cruise control with streetwise B-boy raps, instantly making him a hero to a new generation of black youth. As well as continuing to tour with the trio, he would also contribute a song, 'Can You Rock It Like This', to Run DMC's *King Of Rock*. His debut album too, would see Rubin dose the grooves with heavy metal guitar breaks first introduced by Run DMC. LL Cool J's other early singles included 'I'm Bad', 'Go Cut Creator Go', 'Jack The Ripper' and 'I Need Love' (the first ballad rap, recorded with the Los Angeles Posse), which brought

him a UK Top 10 score. Subsequent releases offered a fine array of machismo funk-rap, textured with personable charm and humour. Like many of his bretheren, LL Cool J's career has not been without incident. Live appearances in particular have been beset by many problems. Three people were shot at a date in Baltimore in December 1985, followed by an accusation of 'public lewdness' after a 1987 show in Columbus, Ohio. While playing rap's first concert in Cote d'Ivoire, Africa, fights broke out and the stage was stormed. Most serious, however, was an incident in 1989 when singer David Parker, bodyguard Christopher Tsipouras and technician Gary Saunders were accused of raping a 15-year-old girl who attended a backstage party after winning a radio competition in Minneapolis. Though LL Cool J's personal involvement in all these cases was incidental, they have undoubtedly tarnished his reputation. He has done much to make amends, including appearances at benefits including Farm Aid, recording with the Peace Choir, and launching his *Cool School Video Program*, in an attempt to encourage children to stay at school. Even Nancy Reagan invited him to headline a 'Just Say No' concert at Radio City Music Hall. Musically, Cool is probably best sampled on his 1990 set, *Mama Said Knock You Out*, produced by the omnipresent **Marley Marl**, which as well as the familiar sexual braggadocio included his thoughts on the state of rap past, present and future. The album went triple platinum, though the follow-up, *14 Shots To The Dome*, was a less effective attempt to recycle the formula. Some tracks stood out: 'A Little Something', anchored by a sample of **King Floyd**'s soul standard 'Groove Me', being a good example. Like many of rap's senior players, he has also sustained an acting career, with film appearances in *The Hard Way* and *Toys*, playing a cop in the former and a military man in the latter. *Phenomenon* celebrated Cool's remarkable longevity on the rap scene, and featured guest appearances from **Keith Sweat** and **Ralph Tresvant**.

● ALBUMS: *Radio* (Columbia 1985)★★★, *Bigger And Deffer* (Def Jam 1987)★★, *Walking With A Panther* (Def Jam 1989)★★★, *Mama Said Knock You Out* (Def Jam 1990)★★★★, *14 Shots To The Dome* (Def Jam 1992)★★★, *Mr. Smith* (Def Jam 1995)★★★, *Phenomenon* (Def Jam 1997)★★★★.

● COMPILATIONS: *Greatest Hits All World* (Def Jam 1996)★★★.

Lloyd Webber, Andrew

b. 22 March 1948, London, England. The 'Sir Arthur Sullivan' of the rock age was born the son of a Royal College of Music professor and a piano teacher. His inbred musical strength manifested itself in a command of piano, violin and French horn by the time he had spent a year at Magdalen College, Oxford, where he penned *The Likes Of Us* with lyricist (and law student) **Tim Rice**. As well as his liking for such modern composers as Hindemith, Ligeti and Penderecki, this first musical also revealed a captivation with pop music that surfaced even more when he and Rice collaborated in 1967 on *Joseph And The Amazing Technicolor Dreamcoat*, a liberal adaptation of the scriptures. Mixing elements of psychedelia, country and French *chanson*, it was first performed at a London school in 1968 before reaching a more adult audience, via fringe events, the West End theatre (starring **Paul Jones**, **Jess Conrad** and Maynard Williams), an album, and, in 1972, national television.

In the early 70s, Lloyd Webber strayed from the stage, writing the music scores for two British films, *Gumshoe* and *The Odessa File*. His next major project with Rice was the audacious *Jesus Christ Superstar* which provoked much protest from religious groups. Among the studio cast were guest vocalists **Michael D'Abo**, **Yvonne Elliman**, **Ian Gillan** and Paul Raven (later **Gary Glitter**), accompanied by a symphony orchestra under the baton of **André Previn** - as well as members of **Quatermass** and the **Grease Band**. Issued well before its New York opening in 1971, the tunes were already familiar to an audience that took to their seats night after night as the show ran for 711 performances. A less than successful film version was released in 1976. After the failure of *Jeeves* in 1975 (with Alan Ayckbourn replacing Rice) Lloyd Webber returned to form with *Evita*, an approximate musical biography of Eva Peron, self-styled 'political leader' of Argentina. It was preceded by high chart placings for its album's much-covered singles, most notably **Julie Covington**'s 'Don't Cry For Me Argentina' and 'Oh! What A Circus' from **David Essex**. *Evita* was still on Broadway in 1981 when *Cats*, based on T.S. Eliot's *Old Possum's Book Of Practical Cats*, emerged as Lloyd Webber's most commercially satisfying work so far. It was also the composer's second musical without Rice, and included what is arguably his best-known song, 'Memory', with words by Eliot and the show's director, **Trevor Nunn**. **Elaine Paige**, previously the star of *Evita*, and substituting for the injured Judi Dench in the feline role of Grizabella, took the song into the UK Top 10. Subsequently, it became popular for **Barbra Streisand**, amongst others. With *Song And Dance* (1982), which consisted of an earlier piece, *Tell Me On Sunday* (lyrics by **Don Black**), and *Variations* composed on a theme by Paganini for his cellist brother, Julian, Lloyd Webber became the only theatrical composer to have three works performed simultaneously in both the West End and Broadway. Two items from *Song And Dance*, 'Take That Look Off Your Face' and 'Tell Me On Sunday' became hit singles for one of its stars, **Marti Webb**. Produced by **Cameron Mackintosh** and Lloyd Webber's Really Useful Company, it was joined two years later by *Starlight Express* (lyrics by **Richard Stilgoe**), a train epic with music which was nicknamed 'Squeals On Wheels' because the cast dashed around on roller skates pretending to be locomotives. Diversifying further into production, Lloyd Webber presented the 1983 comedy *Daisy Pulls It Off*, followed by *The Hired Man*, *Lend Me A Tenor* and **Richard Rodgers** and

Lorenz Hart's *On Your Toes* at London's Palace Theatre - of which he had become the new owner.

Like Sullivan before him, Lloyd Webber indulged more personal if lucrative artistic whims in such as *Requiem*, written for his father, which, along with *Variations*, became a best-selling album. A later set, *Premiere Collection*, went triple platinum. A spin-off from *Requiem*, 'Pie Jesu' (1985), was a hit single for Paul Miles-Kington and **Sarah Brightman**, the composer's second wife. She made the UK Top 10 again in the following year, with two numbers from Lloyd Webber's *The Phantom Of The Opera* (adapted from the Gaston Leroux novel), duetting with **Steve Harley** on the title theme, and later with **Cliff Richard** on 'All I Ask Of You'. The original 'Phantom', **Michael Crawford**, had great success with his recording of another song hit from the show, 'The Music Of The Night'. Controversy followed, with Lloyd Webber's battle to ensure that Brightman re-created her role of Christine in the Broadway production in 1988. His US investors capitulated, reasoning that future Lloyd Webber creations were guaranteed box office smashes before their very conception. Ironically, *Aspects Of Love* (lyrics by Charles Hart and Don Black), which also starred Brightman (by now Lloyd Webber's ex-wife), was rated as one of the failures (it did not recoup its investment) of the 1990/1 Broadway season, although it eventually ran for over 300 performances. In London, the show, which closed in 1992 after a three year run, launched the career of **Michael Ball**, who had a UK number 2 with its big number, 'Love Changes Everything'. In April 1992, he intervened in the Tate Gallery's attempt to purchase a Canaletto. Anxious, that it should remain in Britain, he bought the picture for £10 million. He was reported as commenting 'I'll have to write another musical before I do this again'. That turned out to be *Sunset Boulevard*, a stage adaptation of Billy Wilder's 1950 Hollywood classic, with Lloyd Webber's music, and book and lyrics by Don Black and Christopher Hampton. It opened in London on 12 July 1993 with **Patti LuPone** in the leading role of Norma Desmond, and had its American premiere in Los Angeles five months later, where Desmond was played by Glenn Close. Legal wrangles ensued when Lloyd Webber chose Close to star in the 1994 Broadway production instead of LuPone (the latter is said to have received 'somewhere in the region of $1 million compensation'), and there was further controversy when he closed down the Los Angeles production after having reservations about the vocal talents of its prospective new star, Faye Dunaway. She too, is said to have received a 'substantial settlement'. Meanwhile, *Sunset Boulevard* opened at the Minskoff Theatre in New York on November 17 with a record box office advance of $37.5 million. Like *Cats* and *The Phantom Of The Opera* before it, the show won several **Tony Awards**, including best musical, score and book. Lloyd Webber was living up to his rating as the most powerful person in the American theatre in a list compiled by *TheaterWeek* magazine. His knighthood in

1992 was awarded for services to the theatre, not only in the US and UK, but throughout the world - at any one time there are dozens of his productions touring, and resident in main cities. Among his other show/song honours have been Drama Desk, Grammy, **Laurence Olivier**, and **Ivor Novello** Awards. *Cats*, together with *Starlight Express* and *Jesus Christ Superstar*, gave Lloyd Webber the three longest-running musicals in British theatre history for a time, before the latter show was overtaken by *Les Misérables.*. He is also the first person to have a trio of musicals running in London and New York. *Jesus Christ Superstar* celebrated its 20th anniversary in 1992 with a UK concert tour, and other Lloyd Webber highlights of that year included a series of concerts entitled *The Music Of Andrew Lloyd Webber* (special guest star Michael Crawford), a smash hit revival of *Joseph And The Amazing Technicolor Dreamcoat* at the London Palladium, and the recording, by Sarah Brightman and José Carreras, of Lloyd Webber and Don Black's Barcelona Olympic Games anthem 'Friends For Life' ('Amigos Para Siempre').

Since those heady days, Lloyd Webber admirers have waited in vain for another successful theatrical project, although there has been no shortage of personal kudos. He was inducted into the Songwriters Hall of Fame, presented with the Praemium Imperiale Award for Music, became the first recipient of the **ASCAP** Triple Play Award, and in 1996 received the **Richard Rodgers** Award for Excellence in the Musical Theatre. In the same year a revised version of his 1975 flop, *Jeeves*, entitled *By Jeeves*, was well received during its extended West End season, but a new work, *Whistle Down The Wind* (lyrics: Jim Steinman, book: Patricia Knop), failed to transfer to Broadway following its Washington premiere. A revival of *Jesus Christ Superstar* re-opened the old Lyceum, just off the Strand, and a film version of *Evita*, starring **Madonna**, was released, containing a new Lloyd Webber-Rice song, 'You Must Love Me', for which they won Academy Awards. Elevated to the peerage in 1997, Baron Lloyd-Webber of Sydmonton disclosed that the New York and London productions of *Sunset Boulevard*, which both closed early in that year, 'lost money massively overall', and that his Really Useful Group had reduced its staff and suffered substantial financial setbacks. On the brighter side, in January 1996 the West End production of his most enduring show, *Cats*, took over from *A Chorus Line* as the longest-running musical of all time, and in June 1997, the show's New York production replaced *A Chorus Line* as the longest-running show (musical or play) in Broadway history. Early in 1998, Lloyd Webber was honoured with *Variety*'s first British Entertainment Personality Of The Year Award.

● COMPILATIONS: *The Very Best Of ... Broadway Collection* (Polydor 1996)★★★.

● FURTHER READING: *Andrew Lloyd Webber*, G. McKnight. *Fanfare: The Unauthorized Biography Of Andrew Lloyd Webber*, J. Mantle. *Andrew Lloyd Webber: His Life And Works*, M. Walsh.

Lloyd, A.L.

b. February 1908, London, England. Bert Lloyd was one of the prime movers of the 50s folk song revival in Britain. He had collected some 500 songs by 1935 and was determined to study and conduct research into folk music. In 1937, he sailed to Antarctica with a whaling fleet, adding further songs to his repertoire. On his return he joined BBC Radio as a scriptwriter. During the 40s he wrote *The Singing Englishman*, the first general book on folk song since **Cecil Sharp**'s in 1909. He also compiled the *Penguin Book Of English Folk Song* with the composer Ralph Vaughan Williams. By the 50s, Lloyd was a full-time folklorist, making several field trips to record material in Bulgaria and Albania as well as publishing a selection of coalfield ballads, which provided repertoire for young singers in the growing number of folk song clubs. At this time he met **Ewan MacColl**, with whom he made his own first recordings, as part of the *Radio Ballads* series. During the 60s he made a series of solo albums for **Topic Records**, with accompanists including singers **Anne Briggs** and **Frankie Armstrong**, Alf Edwards (accordion), **Martin Carthy** (guitar, mandolin), **Dave Swarbrick** (fiddle) and actor and singer Harry H. Corbett. They covered drinking songs, industrial songs and selections from his sheep-shearing and whaling exploits. Lloyd also arranged compilation albums of sea shanties, industrial songs (*The Iron Muse*) and recordings from the Balkan field trips.

● ALBUMS: *Selections From The Penguin Book Of English Folk Songs* (Topic 1960)★★★, *The Iron Muse* (Topic 1963)★★★, with Ewan MacColl *English And Scottish Popular Ballads* (Topic 1964)★★★★, *All For Me Grog* (Topic 1964)★★★, *The Bird In The Bush* (Topic 1964)★★★, *First Person* (Topic 1966)★★★, *Leviathan* (Topic 1968)★★★, *The Great Australian Legend* (Topic 1969)★★★, *Sea Songs And Shanties* (1981)★★★★.

● COMPILATIONS: *Classic A.L. Lloyd* (Fellside 1995)★★★★.

● FURTHER READING: *The Singing Englishman*, A.L. Lloyd.

Lloyd, Charles

b. 15 March 1939, Memphis, Tennessee. Lloyd was self-taught on tenor saxophone, which he played in his high school band. He gained a Masters Degree at the University of Southern California and became a music teacher at Dorsey High in Los Angeles. In October 1960, he joined the **Chico Hamilton** Quintet, where he played flute, alto and clarinet as well as tenor, and soon became the band's musical director. In January 1964, he joined the **Cannonball Adderley** Sextet, where he stayed until forming his own quartet with guitarist **Gabor Szabo**, bassist **Ron Carter** and drummer **Tony Williams** in July 1965. Soon Szabo was replaced by pianist **Keith Jarrett** and Carter and Williams returned to the **Miles Davis** group. At the start of 1966 **Cecil McBee** came in on bass (he was replaced by **Ron McClure** in 1967), **Jack DeJohnette** took the drum chair and the stage was set for a jazz phenomenon.

Manager George Avakian decided to market the band in the same way he would a rock group, and the tactic paid off. In modern jazz terms the Quartet was hugely successful, playing to massive rock audiences at the Fillmore Stadium in San Francisco and becoming the first American band to appear in a Soviet festival. While the public and musicians such as Miles Davis and **Ian Carr** admired the band, the critics were predictably cynical, criticizing the musicians' clothes, hair styles and hippy attitudes but ignoring the basic virtues of the music itself, which included rhythmic vitality, a sound foundation in bop and the blues, and Lloyd's surging and emotionally affecting tenor sound. In due course his public looked elsewhere and, eventually, Lloyd left music to pursue his interest in philosophy and meditation, although during this period he did work and record with the **Beach Boys** (*Surf's Up*) as a result of his friendship with Mike Love. His solo on 'Feel Flows' is particul;arly memorable. In the early 80s he edged back onto the jazz scene, notably with a **Montreux Festival** performance featuring **Michel Petrucciani**, and he began to tour again with a quartet containing Palle Danielson and **Jon Christensen**. In the 90s he hit another peak with some excellent recordings for **ECM Records**. During his semi-retirement his flute playing had become stronger whilst his tenor took on some of the ethereal quality his flute formerly had.

● ALBUMS: *Discovery!* (Columbia 1964)★★★, *Of Course Of Course* (Columbia 1965)★★★, *Dream Weaver* (Atlantic 1966)★★★★, *Live At Antibes* (1966)★★★, *Forest Flower* (Atlantic 1966)★★★★, *Charles Lloyd In Europe* (Atlantic 1967)★★★, *Love-In At The Fillmore* (Atlantic 1967)★★★, *Live In The Soviet Union* (Atlantic 1967)★★★, *Nirvana* (Columbia 1968)★★★, *Journey Within* (Atlantic 1968)★★★, *Moon Man* (1970)★★★, *The Flowering Of The Original Charles Lloyd Quartet* (1971)★★★, *Warm Waters* (1971)★★★, *Geeta* (1972)★★★, *Waves* (1972)★★★, *Weavings* (1978)★★★, *Big Sur Tapestry* (1979)★★★, *Montreux '82* (1982)★★★, *A Night In Copenhagen* (Blue Note 1989)★★★, *Fish Out Of Water* (ECM 1990)★★★★, *Notes From Big Sur* (ECM 1992)★★★★, *The Call* (ECM 1994)★★, *All My Relations* (ECM 1995)★★★★.

Lloyd, Jon

b. 20 October 1958, Stratford-upon-Avon, Warwickshire, England. Lloyd dabbled with piano at the age of 12, and then taught himself tenor saxophone at 23. His first public appearances were with a pop/soul band in the mid-80s and with an **ECM**-inspired duo, Confluence. His first professional job was with a duo playing standards on the restaurant/wine-bar/pub circuit. Despite his relatively late start on saxophone he has developed an individual style of music that is exhibited to especially good advantage on his first, privately-produced recording. His influences include **Jan Garbarek**, **John Surman**, **Trevor Charles Watts** and, 'more for affirmation than emulation', **Eric Dolphy**, **Evan Parker**, **Jimmy Lyons**, **Anthony Braxton** and **Arthur Blythe**. He has also been inspired by composers

Olivier Messiaen (who has influenced several non-classical figures, notably Mike Ratledge of the **Soft Machine** and **Mike Gibbs**) and Benjamin Britten. He has organized several worthy attempts at regular venues for improvised music, including the 'Sun Sessions' in Clapham, south London. Apart from his own trio and quartet he has worked with Dave Fowler and in duos with **Evan Shaw Parker** and **Phil Wachsmann**, and organizes Anacrusis, a nine-piece improvising group containing several major names.

● ALBUMS: *Pentimento* (1988)★★, *Syzygy* (Leo 1990)★★★, with Dave Fowler *As It Was* (1990)★★★, *Head* (Leo 1993)★★★★.

Lloyd, Richard

Having established himself as a rhythm guitarist of standing in **Television**, Lloyd embarked on a solo career in 1979, releasing an album whose quality rivalled the efforts of his more illustrious ex-partners, **Tom Verlaine** and **Richard Hell**. *Alchemy* should have projected Lloyd towards a bigger audience but its reviews were not matched by its sales and Lloyd failed to exploit the work due to an alarming slump into drug addiction. It was five years before a chemical-free Lloyd returned with a new album, *Field Of Fire*, but from the mid-80s his output remained decidedly low. By 1991, he had joined Verlaine, Ficca and Smith in a re-formed Television, spending much of the first part of 1992 rehearsing and recording.

● ALBUMS: *Alchemy* (Elektra 1979)★★★★, *Field Of Fire* (Mistlur/Moving Target 1985)★★★, *Real Time* (Celluloid 1987)★★★.

Lloyd, Robert

Inspired by **T. Rex** and the fact that girls tended to pin posters of pop stars on their walls and not pictures of the professional footballers that Robert Lloyd (b. 1959, Cannock, Staffordshire, England) aspired to emulate, the teenager switched his allegiance from the football field to concert hall. Between 1974 and 1976 he played in several bands that never escaped the rehearsal room. He left school at the age of 16 and in 1976 attended a concert by the **Sex Pistols**. He started to follow the Pistols around on the Anarchy Tour and at one of the gigs, he persuaded a promoter to offer him some gigs. The result was the hurriedly assembled Prefects in February 1977, consisting of Lloyd, Alan and Paul Appelby, and Joe Crow. After one performance at a private party and one at the famous Barbarella's club in Birmingham, the Prefects were offered the chance of standing in for the **Slits** at a **Clash** concert. When the **Buzzcocks** dropped out of the subsequent tour, the Prefects were offered a permanent place. Although the band recorded two **John Peel** BBC radio sessions, no records were released until after the band's split in 1979. Lloyd's next move was to form the **Nightingales** and his own Vindaloo label. When the Nightingales fell apart in the mid-80s he concentrated on the label and songwriting, the results of which surfaced in further

Peel sessions (he holds the record for the most sessions for Peel in his various forms) under the name Robert Lloyd And The New Four Seasons. This led to a single with the In-Tape label and in 1989 he signed to **Virgin Records**. After a few false starts, the album emerged in 1990 and featured Steve Nieve and Pete Thomas (the **Attractions**), Andy Scott (the **Sweet**) and Craig Gannon (formerly of the **Bluebells**, **Aztec Camera**, the **Colourfield** and the **Smiths**), among others. However, when it came to promoting the album, Lloyd had to assemble a new band centred around former Nightingales guitarist, The Tank.

● ALBUMS: *Me And My Mouth* (Virgin 1990)★★★.

Lo, Cheikh

b. 12 September 1955, Bobo Dioulassa, Burkina Faso. The son of Senegalese parents, Lo became interested in music, especially Congolese rumba and the Cuban 'son' style from which it derived, at an early age. He frequently played truant from school in order to practice on a borrowed guitar and drum-kit. He made his professional debut in 1976, playing percussion with a local group called Orchestra Volta Jazz. Lo then moved to Senegal where he played drums with Ouza, and in 1984, he became drummer and vocalist with the house band of the Hotel Savana. The following year he moved to Paris, where he spent three years working as a session musician; he played on a wide variety of recording sessions, including work with **Papa Wemba**. On his return to Senegal in 1987, Lo tried to rejoin the Hotel Savana band, only to be turned away because of the flowing dreadlocks he now sported. He decided to concentrate on developing his own material and in 1990 'Doxandem', his debut cassette for the Senegalese market, was released. It became a big local hit and a follow-up was recorded, but owing to business complications, it was never released. In 1995 he gave a demo tape of his material to **Youssou N'Dour**, who was impressed by Lo's warm voice, spiritual lyrics and multicultural sound, and he offered to produce an album with him. The recording session took place at N'Dour's Xippi Studio in Dakar in August of that year and featured Lo with support from N'Dour, along with members of his Super Etoile band. Released in Senegal in early 1996, *Ne La Thaiss* was a collection of strong, haunting melodies with light, predominantly acoustic, backing. Reflecting Lo's varied musical influences, the album incorporated elements of reggae, salsa, jazz and rumba, while retaining a firm base of Senegal's 'mbalax' sound. A huge success in Senegal (one track was even used by the Senegalese government as part of a campaign to clean up the streets), *Ne La Thaiss* was released internationally in November 1996 and was immediately hailed as a major world music recording. Lo toured internationally with N'Dour's Jololi Review at the time of the album's release and subsequently with his own band.

● ALBUMS: *Ne La Thaiss* (World Circuit 1996)★★★★.

Lo, Ismaël

b. Niger. Ismaël 'Iso' Lo has widely been appraised as the '**Bob Dylan** of Senegal music', referring to the country he made his home in as a child in Rufisque, near Dakar. That description arguably does little justice to his voice, which is fixed in a tradition more redolent of 60s America's classic soul singers. By the time he was 15, Lo was performing on television shows, and by the late 70s had joined **Super Diamono**. He combined this with his second love, painting, which he studied at art college. He left the group for Spain in order to pursue this further, but returned to Senegal in 1984 to release the first of a succession of cassette albums. *Diawar*, produced by Sylla, was licensed to Stern's Records as his first international album. Recorded in Paris, it saw him joined by Manu Lima (keyboards), Guy Lobe (drums) and Ndjock (rhythm guitar). Lo himself handled vocals, lyrics, rhythm guitar and arrangements. By 1994 he had switched to **Island Records**' subsidiary Mango, recording an epic of high-energy mblax fusion music in *Iso*. His lush, densely crafted music accompanies lyrics which adopt a righteous, reflective tone. The combination has ensured his status as the latest Senegalese superstar behind **Youssou N'Dour** and **Baaba Maal**.

● ALBUMS: *Xalat* (Syllart 1986)★★★, *Xiff* (Celluloid 1986),★★★★ *Diawar* (Stern's 1989)★★★, *Tajabone* (Barclay 1992)★★★, *Iso* (Mango 1994)★★★★.

Lo-Fidelity Allstars

Formed in 1996, the Lo-Fidelity Allstars combine indie and dance influences in a manner reminiscent of the late 80s' 'Madchester' or 'baggy' scene. From Brighton, Sussex, England, the quintet released their debut single, 'Kool Roc Bass', for local record label Skint Records in 1997. The band, who all employ impenetrable surnames, are led by songwriter Phil the Albino Priest. Originally from Leeds, he formed the group while working at Tower Records in London's Piccadilly Circus. He originally intended the Lo-Fidelity All Stars to be an instrumental-only group, until meeting with vocalist Dave, whose alcohol-fuelled ramblings neatly complemented the group's loose, funky sound. The band achieved further exposure with a series of 1997 support slots to **18 Wheeler**, a remix of **Cast**'s 'History' and two further singles, 'Disco Machine Gun' and 'Vision Incision'. Their swaggering debut album was widely touted as one of 1998's key releases.

● ALBUMS: *How To Operate With A Blown Mind* (Skint 1998)★★★★.

Loaded - The Velvet Underground

The **Velvet Underground** were never ones to follow the crowd. In 1966, when catchy, lucid, three-minute pop tunes were the rule, they recorded their first album, which was dominated by dark celebrations of drug use. By 1970, when they recorded their fourth album, the vogue was for unwieldy drug anthems. Therefore, they made *Loaded*, an album dominated by catchy, lucid three-minute pop tunes. Their record label, expecting a wild, Warholesque romp, did not know what to make of the album, and it died a commercial death. Since then, it has gained respect from both fans and critics as the source of many of **Lou Reed**'s best compositions, including bona fide classics such as 'Rock And Roll' and 'Sweet Jane'.

● Tracks: *Who Loves The Sun; Sweet Jane; Rock And Roll; Cool It Down; New Age; Head Held High; Lonesome Cowboy Bill; I Found A Reason; Train Round The Bend; Oh! Sweet Nuthin'.*

● First released 1970.

● UK peak chart position: did not chart

● USA peak chart position: did not chart

Loaded Records

Record label which is also the home of the Brighton-based remix team of JC Reid and Tim Jeffreys (also a *Record Mirror* journalist), who operate under the name Play Boys. Their first production work together was for the London Community Gospel Choir in 1992 with 'I'll Take You There' and 'Ball Of Confusion', before they set up the Loaded imprint. Titles like 'Ransom' and 'Suggestive', co-produced with Pizzaman, aka **Norman Cook**, emerged. Their next work was on a hot re-activated version of 'Love So Strong' by **Secret Life** which proved more than merely a remix, with re-recorded Paul Bryant vocals. Other remix projects included Brother Love Dub's 'Ming's Incredible Disco Machine', **PM Dawn**'s 'When Midnight Says' and Talizman. As the Play Boys they also released in their own right, included 'Mindgames' from 1992. They also returned the compliment to Norman Cook by remixing his Freak Power track, 'Turn On, Tune In, Cop Out'. The Loaded release schedule continued apace too, with records like those from Key Largo (Eddie Richards) and the garage house of Wildchild Experience (the *Wildtrax* EP, which ran to several volumes, created by Southampton-born DJ Roger McKenzie). Other artists included Jason Nevins ('The Upper Room').

Loading Zone

The Loading Zone - Linda Tillery (vocals), Paul Fauerso (keyboards), Steve Dowler (guitar), Patrick O'Hara (trombone), Todd Anderson (wind instruments), Bob Kridle (bass) and George Newcom (drums) - were one of several R&B-based US groups popular in San Francisco's ballrooms during the late 60s. Although signed to **RCA Records** in 1968, their jazz/blues debut album failed to capture an onstage verve. Tillery's powerful voice provided much of the unit's identity, but their potential was undermined by several changes in personnel and the band collapsed following the release of a second album on the Umbrella label. The singer has remained a popular figure on the Bay Area circuit.

● ALBUMS: *The Loading Zone* (RCA 1968)★★★, *One For All* (Umbrella 1970)★★.

Lobo

b. Roland Kent Lavoie, 31 July 1943, Tallahassee, Florida, USA. Lobo was the pseudonym of Roland Lavoie, a singer-songwriter who was successful in the early 70s. He was raised in the town of Winter Haven, Florida, where he began his musical career as a member of the Rumors. He apprenticed in several other groups during the 60s as well, notably, the Legends from Tampa, Florida, which included **Gram Parsons** and **Jim Stafford**, who would also enjoy success in the early 70s with two US Top 10 hits, produced by Lavoie. (Other members of the Legends included Gerald Chambers and Jon Corneal, the latter remaining an associate of Parsons for many years.) Lavoie also performed with bands called the Sugar Beats and Me And The Other Guys, neither of which had any success outside of their region. In 1971, former Sugar Beats member Phil Gernhard signed Lavoie, calling himself Lobo (Spanish for wolf) to Big Tree Records, where he was an executive, and released their first single, 'Me And You And A Dog Named Boo'. It reached number 5 in the US and launched a successful series of singles. The song became his only hit in the UK, where it reached number 4. Back-to-back Top 10 hits in 1972, 'I'd Love You To Want Me' and 'Don't Expect Me To Be Your Friend', were the last major hits for Lobo. However, he continued to chart with Big Tree until 1975 (six albums also charted, but only the second, *Of A Simple Man*, in 1972, made the Top 40). In 1979, Lobo resurfaced on MCA Records, 'Where Were You When I Was Falling In Love', reached number 23. After the end of that decade his recording career ended.

● ALBUMS: *Introducing Lobo* (Big Tree/Philips 1971)★★★, *Of A Simple Man* (Big Tree 1972)★★★★, *Calumet* (Big Tree 1973)★★★, *Just A Singer* (Big Tree 1974)★★★, *A Cowboy Afraid Of Horses* (Big Tree/Philips 1975)★★★, *Come With Me* (Power Exchange 1977)★★, *Lobo* (1979)★★.

● COMPILATIONS: *The Best Of Lobo* (Big Tree 1975)★★★★, *I'd Love You To Love Me* (Rhino 1996)★★★★.

Lock Up Your Daughters

This show was the first to be presented at the new Mermaid Theatre in the City of London, on 28 May 1959, and was, appropriately enough, the brainchild of the Mermaid's founder, Bernard (later, Sir Bernard) Miles. His adaptation of Henry Fielding's *Rape Upon Rape* was an extremely bawdy tale in which a gentle maiden, Hilaret (Stephanie Voss), and her would-be rapist, Ramble (Frederick Jaeger), appear before the lecherous Justice Squeezum (Richard Wordsworth). Squeezum's efforts to inflict his own individual brand of custodial sentence on Hilaret lead to highly complicated manoeuvres that involve the far-from-innocent Mrs Squeezum (Hy Hazell), and result in the Justice himself going to prison. The object of his affections is then reunited with her true love, Captain Constant (Terence Cooper). The score, by two young newcomers, composer **Laurie Johnson** and lyricist **Lionel Bart** (Bart's ***Fings Ain't Wot They Used T'Be*** was just starting out at the Theatre Royal Stratford), complemented perfectly the lusty outrages of the story, in songs such as 'Lock Up Your Daughters' ('Here comes a rake!'), 'When Does The Ravishing Begin?', 'Red Wine And A Wench' and 'I'll Be There'. Hilaret *almost* seduces Squeezum in 'On A Sunny Sunday Morning', and the other delights included 'Lovely Lover', 'Kind Fate', 'A Proper Man', 'It Must Be True', ''Tis Plain To See' and 'Mr. Jones'. The show ran for 330 performances, and subsequently had its US premiere in New Haven in April 1960. *Lock Up Your Daughters* returned to the Mermaid two years later before transferring to the Her Majesty's theatre in the West End for a stay of some 16 months; it returned to the Mermaid in 1969 for a brief stay. Another American production, with 50s film star Carleton Carpenter as Squeezum, was presented at the Goodspeed Opera House in 1982.

Locke, Josef

b. Joseph McLaughlin, 23 March 1917, Londonderry, Northern Ireland. A extremely popular ballad singer in the UK from the 40s through to the 60s, with an impressive tenor voice and substantial stage presence, Locke sang in local churches as a child, and, when he was 16, added two years to his age in order to enlist in the Irish Guards. Later, he served abroad with the Palestine Police before returning to Ireland in the late 30s to join the Royal Ulster Constabulary. Nicknamed the 'Singing Bobby', he became a local celebrity in the early 40s, and then toured the UK variety circuit. In the following year, he played the first of 19 seasons at the popular northern seaside resort of Blackpool. He made his first radio broadcast in 1949 on the famous *Happydrome*, which starred the trio of 'Ramsbottom, Enoch and Me', and subsequently appeared on television programmes such as *Rooftop Rendezvous*, *Top Of The Town*, *All-Star Bill* and the *Frankie Howerd Show*. In 1947, Locke released 'Hear My Song, Violetta', which became forever associated with him. His other records were mostly a mixture of Irish ballads such as 'I'll Take You Home Again Kathleen', 'Dear Old Donegal' and 'Galway Bay'; excerpts from operettas, including 'The Drinking Song', 'My Heart And I' and 'Goodbye'; along with familiar Italian favourites such as 'Come Back To Sorrento' and 'Cara Mia'. He also made several films, including the comedy, *Holidays With Pay*. In 1958, after appearing in five Royal Command Performances, and while still at the peak of his career, the Inland Revenue began to make substantial demands that Locke declined to meet. Eventually he 'fled from public view to avoid tax-evasion charges'. Meanwhile, on the television talent show, *Opportunity Knocks*, the host, Hughie Green introduced 'Mr. X', a Locke look-alike, as a 'is-he-or-isn't-he' gimmick. He was in reality, Eric Lieson, who carved a long and lucrative career out of the impersonation. When Locke's differences with the tax authorities were settled, he retired to County Kildare, emerging for the occasional charity concert. He attracted some attention in 1984 when he was the

subject of a two-hour birthday tribute on Gay Bryne's talk show, *The Late, Late Show*, on Irish television, but faded into the background once more until 1992, when the Peter Chelsom film *Hear My Song*, was released in the UK. It was an 'unabashed romantic fantasy based on the exuberant notion of Locke returning to Britain to complete an old love affair and save a Liverpool-based Irish night-club from collapse'. Locke was flown to London for the royal premiere, which was attended by Princess Diana, and became the 'victim' of television's *This Is Your Life*. In the movie, the songs are dubbed by the operatic tenor Vernon Midgely. Although determined not to become a celebrity all over again, during the spring of 1992, Locke found himself in the UK Top 10 album chart with *Hear My Song*.

● ALBUMS: *My Many Requests* (1964)★★★★, *I'll Sing It My Way* (1974)★★★, *Josef Locke Sings Favourite Irish Songs* (1978)★★★, *Let There Be Peace* (1980)★★, *In Concert* (1989)★★.

● COMPILATIONS: *The World Of Josef Locke Today* (1969)★★★, *Hear My Song* (1983)★★★, *34 Great Singalong Songs* (1988)★★★, *Hear My Song: The Best Of* (1992)★★★, *Take A Pair Of Sparkling Eyes* (1992)★★★, *A Tear, A Kiss, A Smile* (1993)★★★.

Locklin, Hank

b. Lawrence Hankins Locklin, 15 February 1918, McLellan, Florida, USA. A farm boy, Locklin worked in the cottonfields as a child and on the roads during the Depression of the 30s. He learned to play the guitar at the age of 10 and was soon performing on local radio and at dances. His professional career started in 1938 and after an interruption for military service, he worked various local radio stations, including WALA Mobile and KLEE Houston. In 1949, he joined the *Louisiana Hayride* on KWKH Shreveport and achieved his first country chart entry with his Four Star recording of his self-penned 'The Same Sweet One'. In 1953, 'Let Me Be The One' became his first country number 1. After moving to **RCA Records** in the mid-50s, he had Top 10 US country hits with 'Geisha Girl', his own 'Send Me The Pillow You Dream On', both also making the US pop charts, and 'It's A Little More Like Heaven'. His biggest chart success came in 1960, when his million-selling recording of 'Please Help Me I'm Falling' topped the US country charts for 14 successive weeks and also reached number 8 in the pop charts. It also became one of the first modern country songs to make the British pop charts, peaking at number 9 in a 19-week chart stay. (An answer version by **Skeeter Davis** called '(I Can't Help You) I'm Falling Too' also became a US country and pop hit the same year.) Locklin became a member of the *Grand Ole Opry* in 1960 and during the next decade, his fine tenor voice and ability to handle country material saw him become one of the most popular country artists. He registered over 20 US chart entries including 'We're Gonna Go Fishing' and a number 8 hit with what is now a country standard, 'The Country Hall Of Fame', in 1967. He hosted his own television series in Houston and Dallas in the 1970s and during his career has toured extensively in the USA, Canada and in Europe. He is particularly popular in Ireland, where he has toured many times, and in 1964, he recorded an album of Irish songs. Although a popular artist in Nashville, he always resisted settling there. In the early 60s, he returned to his native Florida and built his home, the Singing L, on the same cottonfield where he had once worked as a boy. After becoming interested in local affairs, his popularity saw him elected mayor of his home-town of McLellan. Although Locklin's last chart success was a minor hit in 1971, he remained a firm favourite with the fans and still regularly appeared on the *Opry*. He is now retired from the music business.

● ALBUMS: *Foreign Love* (RCA Victor 1958)★★★, *Please Help Me I'm Falling* (RCA Victor 1960)★★★, *Encores* (King 1961)★★, *Hank Locklin* (Wrangler 1962)★★, *10 Songs* (Design 1962)★★, *A Tribute To Roy Acuff, The King Of Country Music* (RCA Victor 1962)★★★, *This Song Is Just For You* (Camden 1963)★★★, *The Ways Of Life* (RCA Victor 1963)★★★, *Happy Journey* (RCA Victor 1964)★★★, *Irish Songs, Country Style* (RCA Victor 1964)★★★, *Hank Locklin Sings Hank Williams* (RCA Victor 1964)★★★, *Born To Ramble* (Hilltop 1965)★★★, *My Kind Of Country Music* (Camden 1965)★★★, *Down Texas Way* (Metro 1965)★★★, *Hank Locklin Sings Eddy Arnold* (RCA Victor 1965)★★★, *Once Over Lightly* (RCA Victor 1965)★★★, with the Jordanaires *The Girls Get Prettier* (RCA Victor 1966)★★★, *The Gloryland Way* (RCA Victor 1966)★★★, *Bummin' Around* (Camden 1967)★★, *Send Me The Pillow You Dream On* (RCA Victor 1967)★★★, *Sings Hank Locklin* (1967)★★★, *Nashville Women* (RCA Victor 1967)★★★, *Queen Of Hearts* (Hilltop 1968)★★★, *My Love Song For You* (RCA Victor 1968)★★★, *Softly - Hank Locklin* (RCA Victor 1969)★★★, *That's How Much I Love You* (Camden 1969)★★★, *Wabash Cannonball* (Camden 1969)★★★, *Best Of Today's Country Hits* (RCA Victor 1969)★★★, *Lookin' Back* (RCA Victor 1969)★★★, *Bless Her Heart - I Love Her* (RCA Victor 1970)★★, *Candy Kisses* (Camden 1970)★★★, *Hank Locklin & Danny Davis & The Nashville Brass* (RCA Victor 1970)★★, *The Mayor Of McLellan, Florida* (RCA Victor 1972)★★★, *There Never Was A Time* (1977)★★★, with various artists *Carol Channing & Her Country Friends* (1977)★★, *All Kinds Of Everything* (Topspin 1979)★★★, *Please Help Me I'm Falling* (Topline 1986)★★★.

● COMPILATIONS: *The Best Of Hank Locklin* (King 1961)★★, *The Best Of Hank Locklin* (RCA Victor 1966)★★★, *Country Hall Of Fame* (RCA Victor 1968)★★★★, *The First Fifteen Years* (RCA Victor 1971)★★★, *Famous Country Music Makers* (RCA 1975)★★, *The Golden Hits* (1977)★★★, *The Best Of Hank Locklin* (RCA 1979)★★★, *20 Of The Best* (RCA 1982)★★★, *Please Help Me I'm Falling* 4-CD box set (Bear Family 1995)★★★★, *Send Me The Pillow That You Dream On* 3-CD box set (Bear Family 1997)★★★★.

Lockran, Gerry

b. Gerald Loughran, 19 July 1942, Yeotmal, Central Province, India, d. 17 November 1987. Born to an Irish father and an Indian mother, Lockran and his family moved to England in 1953. Two years later, aged just 13, Lockran was playing guitar in a skiffle band called the Hornets. However, it was not until he heard **Elvis Presley**'s guitarist **Scotty Moore** that Lockran really took interest in the instrument. What clinched it for Lockran was hearing **Big Bill Broonzy** and **Brownie McGhee**. They, he claimed, were his greatest influences. He regularly played in clubs in Europe through the early 60s, and the latter half of the period saw him consolidate his popularity in the UK and on the continent. In 1974 Lockran toured the US with **Joe Cocker**, and at one stage was offered the chance of replacing the headlining artist, who had fallen ill, but declined saying that he 'didn't want to be Joe Cocker' as he had his own loyal following. Lockran also supported artists such as **Stevie Wonder**, the **Eagles**, **Rod Stewart**, and at one time the American press likened Lockran to another great blues man, **Taj Mahal**. Lockran gradually moved away from the British folk scene, finding himself able to make a better living playing in the US. This decision was also prompted by the fact that the British folk scene had largely scorned blues through the early 70s, preferring to retain its traditional image. It was while returning from a German tour in October 1981 that Lockran suffered a heart attack, and not long after this, a stroke left him partially paralyzed down the left side. In 1982 another heart attack left him unable to perform, cruelly ensuring that his legacy of country-blues and rag-time were confined to his recorded works. Lockran's albums featured a veritable who's who of the music business, notably **Cliff Aungier**, **Henry McCullough**, **Pete Wingfield**, and **Neil Hubbard**. A collection of Lockran's poems were published in 1983 under the title *Smiles And Tears*. Lockran died in November 1987 following another heart attack. Such was the respect that he was held in that a benefit night held for his family on 24 January 1988 at the Half Moon, Putney, London, saw artists such as Cliff Aungier, **Gordon Giltrap**, **Wizz Jones**, **Bert Jansch**, **Dave Kelly**, **Alexis Korner** and Henry McCullough turn out to play.

● ALBUMS: *Hold On I'm Coming* (Philips 1963)★★★, *The Essential Gerry Lockran* (Pye 1966)★★★★, *Blues Vendetta* (EMI 1967)★★★, *Wun* (Polydor 1968)★★★, *Rags To Glad Rags* (Decca 1970)★★★, *Blues Blast Off* (Autogram 1972)★★★, *Live/Rally Round The Flag* (Autogram 1973)★★, *No More Cane On The Brazos* (Munich 1976)★★, *The Shattered Eye* (Autogram 1977)★★, *Total* (Autogram 1978)★★, *Across The Tracks* (BML 1981),★★★ with Hans Theesink *Cushioned For A Soft Ride* (Autogram 1981)★★★.

● FURTHER READING: *Smiles And Tears*, Gerry Lockran.

Locks, Fred

b. Stafford Elliot, *c.*1955, Kingston, Jamaica, West Indies. Locks began his sporadic recording career as a member of the Lyrics, who recorded tracks such as 'A Get It', 'Girls Like Dirt', and 'Hear What The Old Man Say' for **Coxsone Dodd** in the late 60s, 'Give Praises' for Randy's, and the self-financed 'Sing A Long', both in

1971. The Lyrics disbanded shortly afterwards, and Locks, discouraged by the lack of financial reward endemic to the Jamaican music business, immersed himself in the Rasta faith, which was at the time gaining significant ground amongst Jamaica's ghetto youth, and he retired to live a spartan existence on the beach at Harbour View. During this time, Locks allowed his dreads to grow to a formidable length - hence his nickname - and continued to write songs, one of which, a prophetic Garveyite vision of repatriation entitled 'Black Star Liners', he was persuaded to record by producer Hugh Boothe.

Released in 1975 on the Jahmikmusic label in Jamaica, and on Grounation in the UK, 'Black Star Liners' struck a resounding chord with the new generation of Rastafarian youth on both islands, propelling Locks to cult status in the process. Two years later Grounation offshoot Vulcan officially released the long-awaited *Black Star Liners/True Rastaman*, a classic example of 70s roots Rasta reggae, packed with fine songs including former singles 'Last Days' (retitled 'Time To Change') and 'Wolf Wolf', and raw, guileless vocals. Throughout this time Locks had also been a member of the vocal trio Creation Steppers with Eric Griffiths and Willy Stepper, who had been releasing singles on their Star Of The East label in Jamaica, achieving considerable local success with 'Stormy Night' - later covered at **Channel One** by the Rolands. A various artists album entitled *Love & Harmony* featured the title track (also a 12-inch in Jamaica) credited to Fred Locks, and 'Kill Nebuchadnezzar' by the Creation Steppers also emerged, in 1979. In 1980 Locks and the Creation Steppers went to the UK for several shows and linked up with the legendary **sound system** operator and record producer **Lloyd Coxsone**, who released a number of discs by both the group and Locks, including the classic 'steppers' 'Homeward Bound', 'Love And Only Love' and 'Voice Of The Poor'. These and other tracks were eventually released on *Love And Only Love*. Locks moved to the USA in 1982, effectively halting his and the Steppers' career. Settling in Philadelphia, he immersed himself in the local Twelve Tribes organization, after which he recorded only sporadically. He reappeared in 1998 on the **Exterminator** label with the excellent 'conscious' album, *Never Give Up*, featuring a rootsy production from **Philip 'Fatis' Burrell**. The album included a updated version of 'Black Star Liners'.
● ALBUMS: *Black Star Liners/True Rastaman* (Vulcan 1977)★★★★, *Love And Only Love* (Tribesman 1981)★★★, *Never Give Up* (Exterminator 1998)★★★.

Lockwood, Didier

b. 11 February 1956, Calais, France. Lockwood studied classical violin at the Conservatoire de Musique de Paris, but exposure to the blues of **Johnny Winter** and **John Mayall** persuaded him to cut short formal study in 1972 and form a jazz-rock group with his brother, Francis. A three-year stint with **Magma** followed, but Lockwood was more excited by the improvising of **Jean-Luc Ponty**, whom he heard on **Frank Zappa**'s 'King Kong'. He listened to other jazz violinists, particularly the Pole, **Zbigniew Seifert** and the veteran **Stéphane Grappelli**. The latter quickly realised the talent in Lockwood and played with him whenever possible. During the late 70s Lockwood played and recorded with many major European and American artists including **Tony Williams**, **Gordon Beck**, **John Etheridge**, **Daniel Humair** and **Michal Urbaniak**. In 1981, Lockwood recorded *Fusion*, which typified the approach he followed throughout the 80s: a solid rock-based rhythm with plenty of soloing room for lightning improvisations on his 160-year-old violin.
● ALBUMS: with Magma *New World* (MPS 1979)★★★★, *Fusion* (1981)★★★, *New World* (1984)★★★★, *1,2,3,4* (JMS 1987)★★★, *Pheonix 90* (1990)★★, *DLG* (JMS 1993)★★, *Martial Solal* (JMS 1993)★★★.

Lockwood, Robert, Jr.

b. 27 March 1915, Marvell, Arkansas, USA. In his youth, Lockwood learned some guitar from **Robert Johnson**, who was evidently a major influence. Lockwood's earliest recordings emphasize that debt. He worked the Mississippi Delta area throughout the 30s, playing with musicians such as **Sonny Boy 'Rice Miller' Williamson** and **Howlin' Wolf**. In 1941, he was in Chicago, Illinois, making his first records as a solo artist, as well as some accompaniments to **Peter J. 'Doctor' Clayton**. Lockwood spent some time as one of the resident musicians on the famous *King Biscuit Time* radio programme, broadcast from Helena, Arkansas. In the early 50s he settled in Chicago where he recorded with **Sunnyland Slim**. Johnson's influence was detectable, but the style was becoming distinctly urban in orientation. Throughout that decade Lockwood played the blues clubs, and often accompanied **Little Walter** on record. As his status as one of Chicago's master guitarists grew, he also contributed to material from **Muddy Waters**, **Eddie Boyd** and others. In 1960, he made some classic recordings with **Otis Spann**, his delicate runs and big, chunky chords betraying a more sophisticated, jazzy direction. Indeed, these sessions are considered by many to be among the greatest piano/guitar duo recordings of all time. He has continued to be very active in music through the ensuing years, working with **Willie Mabon**, among others. In the late 70s he formed a touring and recording partnership with **John Ed 'Johnny' Shines**, and into the 90s he was still producing high-calibre work, notably on an album with **Ronnie Earl**. In 1995 he received a National Heritage Award at the White House. His 12-string guitar album is particularly noteworthy, recorded in 1975 and reissued in 1996.
● ALBUMS: *Steady Rolling Man* (Delmark 1973)★★★, *Contrasts* (Trix 1973)★★★★, *Windy City Blues* (1976)★★★, *Does 12* (Trix 1977)★★★, *Johnny Shines & Robert Lockwood - Dust My Broom* recorded 50s (Flyright 1980)★★★, *Hangin' On* (Rounder 1980)★★★, *Johnny Shines & Robert Lockwood: Mr Blues Is Back To Stay* (Rounder 1981)★★★, *Robert &*

Robert (Black & Blue 1982)★★★, *What's The Score* (1990)★★★, *Plays Robert Johnson & Robert Lockwood Jr.* (1992)★★★, *Contrasts* (Trix 1995)★★★, *I Got To Find Me A Woman* (Verve 1997)★★★.

Lockyer, Malcolm

b. Malcolm Neville Lockyer, 5 October 1923, Greenwich, London, England, d. 28 June 1976, England. Trained as an architect, Lockyer's interest in dance music dated from the age of 12, and he played semi-professionally until called up for war service as a musician in the Royal Air Force at the age of 19. He played with Sid Phillips And His Quintet, and in 1944 he joined the Buddy Featherstonehaugh Sextet and recorded with them for Radion and HMV. After leaving the RAF, Lockyer worked as pianist with **Ambrose**, **Cyril Stapleton** and **Robert Farnon**. He started with BBC radio in 1945, and during his career he worked on almost 6,000 broadcasts. He formed his own orchestra in 1951. A prolific composer (often under the pseudonym Howard Shaw), his biggest successes were 'Friends And Neighbours' (for the 1954 BBC television series), 'Fiddler's Boogie' and 'The Big Guitar' (for the BBC television series *Stranger Than Fiction* - 1955). Lockyer scored over 30 feature films and also the television series *The Pursuers* and *The Pathfinders*. Together with **Reg Owen** he made a collection of albums for Top Rank with the Knightsbridge Strings and the Cambridge Strings. He succeeded **Harry Rabinowitz** as conductor of the BBC Revue Orchestra in 1960, and was associated with many radio shows, among them *Mid-day Music Hall*, *Take It From Here* and *Beyond Our Ken*. When the Revue and Variety orchestras were amalgamated in 1966 to form the new Radio Orchestra, Lockyer became associate conductor. His connection with **Glenn Miller** began in 1944, when he was stationed in Bedford at the same time as the famous American band leader. He was able to study at first-hand how that unmistakeable sound was achieved. Shortly before his death in 1976 he conducted the Million Airs Orchestra in 26 highly-successful Glenn Miller Tribute Concerts.

Locomotive

Formed in Birmingham, England, Locomotive initially achieved fame as a ska/bluebeat band and by the fact that one of their early members, Chris Wood had departed in 1967 to join the fledgling **Traffic**. Having made their debut with 'Broken Heart' on the dance-oriented Direction label, they switched to **Parlophone** for 'Rudi's In Love'. This enchanting rock-steady ballad reached the UK Top 30 in 1968, but by the following year the group had completely changed its musical direction. Norman Haines (guitar/vocals) took control of the band on 'Mr. Armageddon', a haunting progressive rock piece drawing an air of mystery from its pulsating, yet distant, horn section. Mick Taylor (trumpet), Bill Madge (saxophone), Mick Hincks (bass) and Bob Lamb (drums) completed the line-up featured on

We Are Everything You See which, despite contemporary commercial indifference, has become one of the era's most fêted releases. Locomotive split up soon after its release, with Haines founding the Norman Haines Band. Lamb, Hincks and associate member Keith Millar formed the Dog That Bit People. The drummer then went on to join the **Steve Gibbons** Band.
● ALBUMS: *We Are Everything You See* (Parlophone 1969)★★★★.

Locust

In the accelerating flurry of ambient dance releases following the **Orb**'s breakthrough, at least the work of Mark Van Hoen contained a snatch of humour. The track 'Xenophobia', for example: 'I started with this Japanese vocal sample, and began thinking I'd have to surround it with five-note Japanese pentatonik scales. Then I gave up and called myself xenophobic'. Elsewhere the musical territory on his debut album was mapped out in traditional genre style, eerie mood pieces with more than a passing nod to composers like **Steve Reich**. Diverting enough, but hardly a substantial listening experience. He originally came to prominence through the heavily-imported *Skyline* EP, before a contract with **R&S Records** subsidiary Apollo for six albums. Unlike many similar artists, however, Van Hoen has no ambitions to remix other people's music, preferring instead to concentrate on his own music.
● ALBUMS: *Weathered Well* (R&S 1994)★★★, *Truth Is Born Of Argument* (R&S 1995)★★★, *Morning Light* (R&S 1997)★★★.

Lodestar

A group forged after disagreements in the **Senser** camp over musical direction, Lodestar feature three former members of that 'crustoid, pan-cultural fusioneering' group - Heitham Al-Sayed (vocals), Haggis (bass) and John Morgan (drums). Their line-up completed with the addition of Jules Hodgson (guitar), Lodestar were unequivocally a hard rock band. As Al-Sayed told the press, '. . . a lot of it's a lot less accessible than the Senser stuff. I started to hear music for the melody much more. Our sound is influenced by a lot of old British rock bands and really old American blues stuff.' Their debut album was released by Ultimate Records at the end of 1996 and certainly came as a surprise to old Senser fans, though reviews, particularly in the metal press, were generally good. The one obvious continuity from the past was Al-Sayed's distinctive vocals - whether rapping or singing, his approach remained one of absolute personal conviction.
● ALBUMS: *Lodestar* (Ultimate 1996)★★★.

Lodge, J.C.

b. June Carol Lodge. Lodge's entrance into the reggae world came courtesy of an audition for **Joe Gibbs**. Their first recording together was a version of **Charley Pride**'s 'Someone Loves You, Honey', which went to the top of the Jamaican charts. Ironically, the result for

Gibbs was bankruptcy, after he failed to pay royalties to the songwriter. In 1988 she recorded 'Telephone Love' for **Gussie Clarke**, which subsequently became a big hit in Jamaica and America, where, after being housed on the Pow Wow label, it achieved crossover status. Its success brought her to the attention of the predominantly hip-hop-focused, **Warners**-owned Tommy Boy subsidiary. In the process she became the first female reggae star to secure a major label contract. Her debut for Tommy Boy played safe by revisiting 'Telephone Love', and branching out musically to encompass soul and rock. Also a talented painter, Lodge has exhibited in Kingston art galleries, and acted in several theatrical productions.

● ALBUMS: *I Believe In You* (Greensleeves 1987)★★★, *Revealed* (RAS 1988)★★★, *Tropic Of Love* (Tommy Boy 1992)★★.

Loeb, Lisa

US singer-songwriter Loeb sprang to fame in 1994 when her friend, actor Ethan Hawke, persuaded the producers of the film *Reality Bites* to use her song 'Stay (I Missed You)' as its theme. The result was a US number 1 despite Loeb not yet having a recording contract. That situation was quickly rectified with the intervention of **Geffen Records**, who are alleged to have offered over $1 million for her signature. Some of the furore then died down while Loeb set about crafting her debut album, the first evidence of which arrived with the release of 'Do You Sleep' in September 1995. The accompanying album was co-produced with long-standing colleague Juan Patino and the help of her band, Nine Stories. The songs were drawn from over ten years' writing, notably the very early composition 'Garden Of Delights'. In press interviews of the time she was keen to salute rock influences as diverse as **Jimi Hendrix**, **Led Zeppelin** and **Fugazi**, rather than the acoustic singer-songwriters with whom she has been most readily identified in the press. Tracks such as 'Alone' and 'It's Over' bore this out, though even the quieter selections were imbued with sarcasm and Loeb's confrontational instincts.

● ALBUMS: *Tails* (Geffen/MCA 1995)★★★, *Firecracker* (Geffen 1997)★★★.

Loesser, Frank

b. Frank Henry Loesser, 29 June 1910, New York City, New York, USA, d. 28 July 1969. A leading songwriter for the stage, films and Tin Pan Alley from the 30s through to the 60s. Initially, he only wrote lyrics, but later in his career he provided both words and music, and sometimes co-produced through his Frank Productions. Born into a musical family (his father was a music teacher, and his brother a music critic and pianist), Loesser rejected a formal musical education, and trained himself. During the Depression years of the early 30s, following a brief spell at City College, New York, Loesser worked in a variety of jobs including city editor for a local newspaper, jewellery salesman and

waiter. His first published song, written with William Schuman in 1931, was 'In Love With A Memory Of You'. Loesser also wrote for vaudeville performers and played piano in nightclubs around New York's 52nd Street. In 1936, he contributed some lyrics to *The Illustrators Show*, with music by Irving Actman, including 'Bang-The Bell Rang!' and 'If You Didn't Love Me', but the show closed after only five Broadway performances. In 1937, Loesser went to Hollywood and spent the next few years writing lyrics for movies such as *Cocoanut Grove* ('Says My Heart'), *College Swing* ('Moments Like This' and 'How'dja Like To Make Love To Me?'), *Sing You Sinners* (**Bing Crosby** singing 'Small Fry'), *Thanks For The Memory* (**Bob Hope** and Shirley Ross singing 'Two Sleepy People'), *The Hurricane* (**Dorothy Lamour** singing 'Moon Of Manakoora'), *Man About Town* ('Fidgety Joe' and 'Strange Enchantment'), *Some Like It Hot* (1939 film starring Bob Hope and Shirley Ross singing 'The Lady's In Love With You'), *Destry Rides Again* (**Marlene Dietrich** with a memorable version of 'See What The Boys In The Backroom Will Have'), *Dancing On A Dime* ('I Hear Music'), *Las Vegas Nights* ('Dolores'), *Kiss The Boys Goodbye* ('I'll Never Let A Day Pass By', 'Sand In My Shoes' and the title song), *Sweater Girl* ('I Don't Want To Walk Without You' and 'I Said No'), *Forest Rangers* ('Jingle Jangle Jingle'), *Happy-Go-Lucky* ('Let's Get Lost' and ''Murder' She Says'), *Seven Days Leave* ('Can't Get Out Of This Mood') and *Thank Your Lucky Stars* ('They're Either Too Young Or Too Old', sung by Bette Davis, and featuring one of Loesser's most amusing lyrics, including the couplet: 'I either get a fossil, or an adolescent pup/I either have to hold him off, or have to hold him up!'). These songs were written in collaboration with composers **Burton Lane**, **Hoagy Carmichael**, **Alfred Newman**, Matty Malneck, Frederick Hollander, Louis Alter, **Victor Schertzinger**, **Jule Styne**, Joseph Lilley, **Jimmy McHugh** and **Arthur Schwartz**. The first song for which Loesser wrote both music and lyrics is said to be 'Praise The Lord And Pass The Ammunition', and when he left Hollywood for military service during World War II he added some more service songs to his catalogue, including 'First Class Private Mary Brown', 'The Ballad Of Roger Young', 'What Do You Do In The Infantry?' and 'Salute To The Army Service Forces'. He also continued to write for films such as *Christmas Holiday* (1944, 'Spring Will Be A Little Late This Year') and *The Perils Of Pauline* (1947), the biopic of silent-movie queen Pearl White, with Loesser's songs 'Poppa Don't Preach To Me' and 'I Wish I Didn't Love You So', the latter of which was nominated for an Academy Award. Loesser finally received his Oscar in 1949 for 'Baby It's Cold Outside', from the **Esther Williams**/Red Skelton movie *Neptune's Daughter*. In 1948, Loesser wrote 'On A Slow Boat To China', which became a hit for several US artists including **Kay Kyser**, **Freddy Martin**, **Eddy Howard** and **Benny Goodman**. In the same year he again turned his attention to the Broadway stage, writing the score for a musical adaptation of Brandon Thomas's classic English farce, *Charley's Aunt*. **Where's Charley?**, starring **Ray Bolger**, included the songs 'My Darling, My Darling', 'Once In Love With Amy', 'The New Ashmoleon Marching Society And Student Conservatory Band' and 'Make A Miracle'. The show ran for a creditable 792 performances.

Far more successful, two years later, was **Guys And Dolls**, a musical setting of a Damon Runyon fable, starring Robert Alda, **Vivian Blaine**, Sam Levene, Isabel Bigley and **Stubby Kaye**. It ran for 1,200 performances, and is generally considered to be Loesser's masterpiece. As with *Where's Charley?*, he was now writing both music and lyrics, and the show is such a legend that it is worth listing the principal songs: 'Fugue For Tinhorns', 'The Oldest Established', 'I'll Know', 'A Bushel And A Peck', 'Adelaide's Lament', 'Guys And Dolls', 'If I Were A Bell', 'My Time Of Day', 'I've Never Been In Love Before', 'Take Back Your Mink', 'More I Cannot Wish You', 'Luck Be A Lady', 'Sue Me', 'Sit Down, You're Rockin' The Boat' and 'Marry The Man Today'. The original cast album is still available in the 90s, and among the other associated issues was an all-black cast album, released on the **Motown** label, and *Guys And Dolls: The Kirby Stone Four*. A film adaptation of *Guys And Dolls* was released in 1955, starring **Frank Sinatra**, Marlon Brando, Jean Simmons and **Vivian Blaine**. The movie version left out some of the original songs, and Loesser replaced them with 'A Woman In Love' and 'Adelaide'. In 1952, *Where's Charley?* was released as a film version, and the same year saw a movie of **Hans Christian Andersen**, starring **Danny Kaye** in the title role, and featuring a Loesser score that included 'Wonderful Copenhagen', 'No Two People', 'Anywhere I Wander', 'Inchworm' and 'Thumbelina'. Loesser's next Broadway project was *The Most Happy Fella*, for which he also wrote the libretto. The show was adapted from the original story *They Knew What They Wanted*, by Sidney Howard, which told the tale of an elderly Italian winegrower living in California, who falls in love at first sight with a waitress. Loesser created what has been called 'one of the most ambitiously operatic works ever written for the Broadway musical theatre'. Arias such as 'Rosabella' and 'My Heart Is So Full Of You' contrast with more familiar Broadway fare such as 'Standing On the Corner', 'Big D' and 'Happy To Make Your Acquaintance'. The show ran for 676 performances, far more than Loesser's 1960 production of the folksy *Greenwillow*, which closed after less than three months. It starred Anthony Perkins in his first musical, and contained a religious hymn, the baptism of a cow, and wistful ballads such as 'Faraway Boy' and 'Walking Away Whistling', along with 'Never Will I Marry' and 'Summertime Love', both sung by Perkins. A three-album set was issued, containing the complete score. In terms of number of performances (1,417), Loesser's last Broadway show, which opened in 1961, was his most successful. *How To Succeed In Business Without Really Trying* was a satire on big business that starred Robert Morse as the aspiring executive J. Pierpont Finch, and **Rudy Vallee** as his stuffy boss, J.B. Biggley. The songs, which, most critics agreed, fitted the plot neatly, included 'The Company Way', 'A Secretary Is Not A Toy', 'Grand Old Ivy', 'Been A Long Day', 'I Believe In You' and 'Brotherhood Of Man'. The show became one of the select band of American musicals to be awarded a Pulitzer Prize; a film version was released in 1967. Loesser died of lung cancer on 28 July 1969, with cigarettes by his side. A lifelong smoker, with a contentious, volatile temperament, he is regarded as one of the most original, innovative men of the musical theatre. In the early 90s *The Most Happy Fella*, *Guys And Dolls* and *How To Succeed In Business Without Really Trying*, were all revived on Broadway, and Loesser's second wife, Jo Sullivan, and one of his daughters, Emily Loesser, appeared in a provincial production of *Where's Charley?* In 1993, the two ladies also featured on the album *An Evening With Frank Loesser*, singing medleys of songs from his shows. Of even more interest, in the same year a fascinating album consisting of demo recordings by Loesser himself was released.

● ALBUMS: *An Evening With Frank Loesser* (1993)★★★, *Loesser By Loesser* (DRG 1993)★★★★.
● FURTHER READING: *A Most Remarkable Fella*, Susan Loesser.

Loewe, Frederick

b. 10 June 1901, Vienna, Austria, d. 14 February 1988, Palm Springs, Florida, USA. A distinguished composer for the musical theatre, Loewe was born into a musical family (his father was a professional singer). He studied piano as a child, appearing with the Berlin Symphony Orchestra in 1917. In 1924, he visited the USA, but was unable to find work in a classical enviroment. Instead, he eked out a living playing piano in restaurants and bars, then roamed throughout the USA, tackling a variety of jobs, including boxing, prospecting and cowpunching. As a young teenager he had written songs and he resumed this activity in New York in the early 30s. Later in the decade he contributed to various musical shows, and in 1942 began to collaborate with lyricist **Alan Jay Lerner**. Their first Broadway score was for *What's Up?* in 1943, which was followed two year later with *The Day Before Spring*. From that point onwards, they wrote the music and lyrics (Lerner also contributed the librettos) for some of the most memorable productions in the history of the American musical theatre. They had their first hit in 1947 with **Brigadoon**, from which came 'The Heather On The Hill', 'From This Day On' and 'Almost Like Being In Love', and the association was renewed in 1951 with **Paint Your Wagon**, containing such lovely songs as 'They Call The Wind Maria', 'I Talk To The Trees' and 'Wand'rin' Star'. In 1956, the team had a major triumph with the legendary **My Fair Lady**, which ran on Broadway for 2,717 performances. The score included such lasting favourites as 'On The Street

Where You Live', 'Get Me To The Church On Time', 'With A Little Bit Of Luck', 'Wouldn't It Be Loverly?', 'The Rain In Spain', 'Why Can't The English?', 'I'm An Ordinary Man' and 'I Could Have Danced All Night'. After the huge success of *My Fair Lady*, Lerner and Loewe were invited to write the script, music and lyrics for a musical film, and while Lerner was enthusiastic about the idea, Loewe was somewhat reluctant. Eventually he agreed, and together they created the incomparable *Gigi* (1958), one of the final flourishes of the old-style Hollywood musical. The magnificent score included 'Thank Heaven For Little Girls', 'I'm Glad I'm Not Young Anymore', 'I Remember It Well', 'The Night They Invented Champagne', and the charming title song. After being hospitalized with serious heart trouble, Loewe collaborated with Lerner on *Camelot*, which opened in 1960, and ran for over two years. Although the show's pre-production was marred with problems, the result was another success, with such outstanding songs as 'If Ever I Would Leave You' and 'How To Handle A Woman'. Afterwards, Loewe decided to retire, emerging briefly in the early 70s to work with Lerner on two unsucessful projects - a stage adaptation of *Gigi* and the film *The Little Prince*.

Lofgren, Nils

b. 21 June 1951, Chicago, Illinois, USA. In the late 60s, Lofgren first recorded as Paul Dowell And The Dolphin before forming Grin. The latter made several excellent albums during the early 70s and although a critics' favourite they never quite managed to receive the recognition they deserved. Lofgren, meanwhile, was already branching out into other ventures after making a guest appearance on **Neil Young**'s *After The Goldrush*. He briefly teamed up with Young's backing group **Crazy Horse** for their critically acclaimed debut album. Lofgren's association with Young continued in 1973 when he was invited to join the *Tonight's The Night* tour. By now, Lofgren was a highly respected guitarist and it was widely speculated that he might be joining the **Rolling Stones** as **Mick Taylor**'s replacement. Instead, he signed to **A&M Records** as a solo artist and recorded a self-titled album, which included the tribute 'Keith Don't Go (Ode To The Glimmer Twin)'. The album was applauded on its release, as were Lofgren's solo tours during which he astounded audiences with his acrobatic skills, often propelling himself in the air from a trampoline. An 'official bootleg' from the tour, *Back It Up*, captured some of the excitement. Lofgren's *Cry Tough* displayed his power as a writer, arranger and musician. It was a best seller on both sides of the Atlantic and momentarily placed Lofgren on a level with the other acclaimed new guitar-playing artists such as **Bruce Springsteen**. With *I Came To Dance* and *Nils*, the singer/guitarist consolidated his position without breaking any new ground. The latter included some lyrics from **Lou Reed** which added some bite to the proceedings. By the end of the 70s, Lofgren left A&M and found himself recording for the MCA

subsidiary, Backstreet. By the early 80s, his reputation as a solo artist had declined and it was generally accepted that his real genius lay as a 'right-hand man' to other artists. In early 1983 he embarked on Neil Young's *Trans* tour and the following year joined Bruce Springsteen's E Street Band. By this point, his solo standing was such that he was recording for an independent label, Towerbell. During the late 80s, he continued to work with Springsteen, but also undertook occasional low-key solo tours. In 1991, he ended a six-year hiatus from recording with *Silver Lining*, which included guest appearances from Springsteen and various members of **Ringo Starr**'s All Starr Band. *Damaged Goods* was a surprisingly good album on which Lofgren reinvented his voice. Taking his range down one or two octaves to give him a sexy growl, Lofgren had either been drinking whiskey by the gallon, smoking ten thousand cigarettes a day, or simply his voice had at last broken. Even better was *Acoustic Live*, obviously an arena in which Lofgren comes into his own with some sensitive guitar playing.

● ALBUMS: *Nils Lofgren* (A&M 1975)★★★, *Back It Up (Official Bootleg)* (A&M 1976)★★★, *Cry Tough* (A&M 1976)★★★, *I Came To Dance* (A&M 1977)★★★, *Night After Night* (A&M 1977)★★, *Nils* (A&M 1979)★★★, *Night Fades Away* (Backstreet 1981)★★, *Wonderland* (MCA 1983)★★★, *Flip* (Towerbell 1985)★★★, *Code Of The Road* (Towerbell 1986)★★★, *Silver Lining* (Essential 1991)★★★, *Crooked Line* (Essential 1992)★★, *Live On The Test* (Windsong 1994)★★★, *Everybreath* (Permanent 1994)★★, *Damaged Goods* (Essential 1995)★★★★, *Acoustic Live* (Demon 1997)★★★★.

● COMPILATIONS: *A Rhythm Romance* (A&M 1982)★★★, *Classics Volume 13* (A&M 1987)★★★, *Don't Walk, Rock* (Connoisseur 1990)★★, *The Best Of Nils Lofgren* (A&M 1992)★★★, *Shine Silently* (Spectrum 1995)★★, *Soft Fun, Tough Tears 1971-1979* (Raven 1995)★★★, *Steal Your Heart* (A&M 1996)★★★.

● VIDEOS: *Nils Lofgren* (Castle 1991).

Loft

The Loft were formed in 1980 when Bill Prince (b. 19 July 1962, Devon, England) and Andy Strickland (b. 16 July 1959, Isle Of Wight, England; guitar, vocals) met with **Peter Astor** (b. 1959, Colchester, Essex, England), then singing in the group News Of Birds. Later joined by drummer Dave Morgan (drums), the band's first gig was under the name the Living Room which, by sheer coincidence, was also the banner of a small but significant London venue set up by Scottish entrepreneur Alan McGee. Fortunately, the freshly named Loft linked up with McGee's nascent **Creation Records** label to release the single, 'Why Does The Rain?', which encapsulated their stylishly downbeat driving guitar sound. A year later, the follow-up, 'Up The Hill And Down The Slope', furthered the Loft's cause and strengthened their cult status, bolstered by championing from BBC disc jockey Janice Long. As their reputation grew, so did tensions within the band, causing them to split just as their career appeared to be in full flow. As Astor recalled: 'We split for the same reason all bands do - people's feet smell.' Both Strickland and Prince pursued journalistic vocations and started up the **Caretaker Race** and the Wishing Stones, respectively. Astor and Morgan formed the marginally successful **Weather Prophets** until they disbanded at the end of the 80s, allowing Astor to embark upon a solo career while Morgan went on to join the country-flavoured **Rockingbirds**. He would leave that band in 1994 to concentrate on a B.Sc. in psychology, managing Bingo Salad, and playing sessions with several artists. After the demise of the Wishing Stones Prince recorded a 1992 solo album for **Heavenly Records**. He became production editor for **Q** magazine in 1993.

● COMPILATIONS: *Once Around The Fair* (Creation 1989)★★★.

Lofton, Cripple Clarence

b. 28 March 1887, Kingsport, Tennessee, USA, d. 9 January 1957. Living and playing in Chicago from the age of 20, pianist and vocalist Lofton became a popular accompanist to visiting blues singers, in many instances appearing in this role on record. He worked steadily through the 30s, proving very popular in the Windy City, and enjoyed the fleeting benefits of the boogie-woogie craze. Influenced by **Charles 'Cow Cow' Davenport** and **Jimmy Yancey**, he in turn influenced a number of other pianists, notably **Meade 'Lux' Lewis**.

● COMPILATIONS: *Clarence's Blues (1930s)* (Oldie Blues 1988)★★★.

Logan, Ella

b. *c*.1913, Glasgow, Scotland, d. 1 May 1969. A member of a well-known theatrical family, Logan first appeared on the stage at the age of three, singing 'The End Of A Perfect Day' at the Grand Theatre in Paisley, Scotland. She became a popular singer during the 20s, performing with various bands and at many theatres in the UK and Europe. In 1932 she went to the USA to appear with **Fred Waring**'s band and worked on radio, the stage and in films. Accompanying her to Hollywood was her three-year-old niece, **Annie Ross**. Logan appeared in a small number of musical films, including *Top Of The Town* (1937), *52nd Street* (1937) and *The Goldwyn Follies* (1938). Her stage appearances were more successful and included *Calling All Stars*, *George White's Scandals* and *Sons O'Fun*. During World War II Logan entertained troops in Africa, Italy and various other parts of the European campaign and then returned to the USA. In 1947 she appeared on Broadway, playing the role of Sharon McLonergan (Finian's daughter) in ***Finian's Rainbow*** at the 46th St Theatre, running for more than 500 performances. In the 50s and 60s she appeared at clubs and on television. A dynamic singer with great flair, Logan's varied career perhaps prevented her from attaining stardom in any one area. Apart from Ross, another famous relative is her nephew, Scottish comedian Jimmy Logan.

Logan, Jack

b. *c*.1958, Greenville, Mississippi, USA. It was only in his late thirties, at which time his main income still derived from his job as a mechanic repairing swimming pool pumps, that Jack Logan's songs began to make an impression on the mainstream. Indeed, when 1996's *Mood Elevator* produced a rash of good reviews, his long-standing place of employment, Doraville Electric Motor Service in Georgia, became a regular stopping point for music journalists and camera crews. The establishment is key to Logan's development, as it is there he writes songs with his co-worker and fellow member of Liquor Cabinet, pianist and guitarist Kelly Keneipp. Together they wrote more than 1,000 songs together between, and sometimes during, shifts, from 1979 onwards. Collaborators include former members of Athens, Georgia band, Dashboard Saviours, as well as guitarist Dave Philips, bass player Eric Sales and drummer Aaron Phillips (all members of Liquor Cabinet) and **Vic Chesnutt**. They finally made their debut in 1994 with *Bulk*, a sprawling 42-track package compiled in tandem with producer Peter Jesperson of Medium Cool Records from more than 600 demos. Conversely, for Logan's breakthrough album, *Mood Elevator*, most of the 36 compositions were entirely new, and many were improvised live in the studio. With lyrics indebted to the southern dankness of author Flannery O'Connor's literature, his pithy, compressed narratives won over critics from ***Rolling Stone*** magazine to the *Today* television programme. There is also a great deal of small-town observation, which never descends into mawkishness, behind songs such as '75 Years In Indiana'. He first met partner Keneipp in an English class and discovered a shared appreciation of the **Rolling Stones** and **Neil Young**. It was only when he moved to Georgia with Keneipp in 1984 that his ambition to record music was fuelled. They played together in a band called Lava Treatment, who self-released 200 copies of a 1987 album, *Lake Eerie*. After that Logan returned to kitchen table songwriting with Keneipp until he was recommended to Jesperson by **R.E.M.**'s Peter Buck. In May 1993 he offered Logan a recording deal. However, success has changed him little - he remains committed to his job and his hobby of rebuilding dragsters and collecting model cars. Between times he still manages to write six or seven songs in a single burst of inspiration.

● ALBUMS: *Bulk* (Medium Cool 1994)★★★, *Mood Elevator* (Medium Cool 1996)★★★.

Logan, Josh

b. Richmond, Kentucky, USA. One of the New Country's hat brigade with a difference - his hat is of the Humphrey Bogart variety. Logan's favourite country performer was **Mel Street** and his own vocals were very close to the latter's. He had the misfortune of having his single, 'I Made You A Woman For Somebody Else', covered by **Conway Twitty**, and thereby lost any possible success. He eventually made the US charts with 'Everytime I Get To Dreamin''. His debut album included Street's 'Easy Lovin' Kind' and the good-natured 'Somebody Paints The Wall': 'Everytime I make my mark, somebody paints the wall.' There was an excellent cover by **George Jones** under the title, 'Somebody Always Paints The Wall', but Logan disappeared for several years before bouncing back with 1996's *Something Strange*.

● ALBUMS: *Somebody Paints The Wall* (Curb 1989)★★★, *Something Strange* (Bob Grady 1996)★★★.

Loggins And Messina

This duo featured **Kenny Loggins** and Jim Messina (b. 5 December 1947, Maywood, California, USA). Following his premature departure from **Poco**, Messina intended to resume his career as a record producer, a role he had previously carried out by producing the final **Buffalo Springfield** album, *Last Time Around*. Songwriter Loggins, who had recently experienced success when the **Nitty Gritty Dirt Band** took his whimsical song 'House At Pooh Corner' into the US charts, was signed by **CBS** and was introduced to Messina who was now a staff producer. This started a partnership that lasted six years and produced numerous gold albums. By combining country rock with hints of Latin, Mexican and R&B, the duo hit upon a strong formula. All nine albums reached high US chart positions and spawned a number of hit singles including 'Your Mama Don't Dance' and 'My Music'. As seasoned performers, their regular tours of North America made them a major attraction during the first half of the 70s. Following an amicable split, Loggins embarked on a solo career. Messina, following three moderately successful albums, instigated the reformation of the much-loved Poco in 1989 to considerable acclaim and a successful album *Legacy*. A surprisingly fresh album was issued in 1996 covering Messina's entire career. Reworkings and new recordings of his back catalogue demonstrated a relaxed and mature voice, that has clearly improved with age.

● ALBUMS: *Kenny Loggins With Jim Messina Sittin' In* (Columbia 1972)★★★★, *Loggins And Messina* (Columbia 1972)★★★★, *Full Sail* (Columbia 1973)★★, *On Stage* (Columbia 1974)★★★, *Mother Lode* (Columbia 1974)★★, *So Fine* (Columbia 1975)★★, *Native Sons* (Columbia 1976)★★, *Finale* (Columbia 1977)★★.

● COMPILATIONS: *The Best Of Friends* (Columbia 1976)★★★.

Loggins, Kenny

b. 7 January 1948, Everett, Washington, USA. Loggins came to prominence as a member of **Loggins And Messina** from 1972-77. After separating from Jim Messina, he set out on a solo recording career, specialising in rock ballads such as 'Whenever I Call You Friend', a 1978 Top 10 hit in the US which was co-written by **Melissa Manchester** and had harmony vocals by **Stevie Nicks**. There was subsequent success with 'This Is It' and Loggins co-wrote with **Michael McDonald**

'What A Fool Believes', a million-seller and a US number 1 for the **Doobie Brothers**. Don't Fight It' (1982) was a collaboration with **Journey** singer Steve Ferry. During the 80s, Loggins came to prominence as a writer and performer of theme songs for the new breed of Hollywood action movies. Beginning with 'I'm Alright' (from *Caddyshack*, 1980) and the chart-topping title song from *Footloose* (1984), he reached his commercial peak with the soundtrack of *Top Gun* (1986). As well as co-writing several of the songs used in the film, Loggins recorded the best-selling 'Danger Zone'. This was followed by music for *Caddyshack II*, including another hit single, 'Nobody's Fool'. He had a minor hit with 'Convictions Of The Heart' in 1991, but his most successful outlet remains his soundtrack work.

● ALBUMS: *Celebrate Me Home* (Columbia 1977)★★★, *Nightwatch* (Columbia 1978)★★★, *Keep The Fire* (Columbia 1979)★★★★, *Alive* (Columbia 1980)★★★, *High Adventure* (Columbia 1982)★★★, *Footloose* (1984)★★, *Vox Humana* (Columbia 1985)★★, *Top Gun* film soundtrack (1986)★★, *Back To Avalon* (Columbia 1988)★★, *Leap Of Faith* (Columbia 1991)★★, *Outside From The Redwoods - An Acoustic Afternoon* (Columbia 1993)★★★, *The Unimaginable Fire* (Columbia 1997)★★★.

● COMPILATIONS: *At His Best* (Hollywood 1992)★★★, *Yesterday, Today, Tomorrow: The Greatest Hits Of Kenny Loggins* (Columbia 1997)★★★.

● VIDEOS: *Return To Pooh Corner* (Sony Wonder 1996).

● FILMS: *Footloose* (1984).

Logic Records

Founded in Frankfurt, Germany, in the early 90s by Luca Anzilotti and Michael Munzing, Logic Records provided the original home for their enormously successful Euro-techno creations, notably **Snap!**'s 'Exterminate'. The label was set up because: 'With Logic we have total creative control over every aspect of a record: the mixes, the artwork, the promotion, everything'. They operate Logic in addition to their interests in the highly popular Omen club in Frankfurt. Mark Spoon of **Jam And Spoon** held an A&R post at Logic for a number of years, before choosing to concentrate fully on his own music. In addition to high profile Euro techno, the label has also released high profile techno material from **Blake Baxter** ('One More Time') and Rapination featuring **Kym Mazelle** ('Love Me The Right Way'). Other successes included Pressure Drop's 'Release Me' and Durga McBroom (ex-**Blue Pearl**)'s solo debut. Logic is just as well known for its impressive compilations which include *Logic Trance 1 & 2*. A subsidiary imprint, Save The Vinyl, which produces work on vinyl only, was established in 1993. It was then overhauled and relaunched at the end of 1995 at which time it was run by Logic's senior product manager, Wendy 'K'. The release schedule of one 12-inch per month began with material by artists such as High Stepper, the Angel and Anacoeic Void.

Logsdon, Jimmy

b. James Lloyd Logsdon, 1 April 1922, Panther, Kentucky, USA. The son of a Methodist minister, he began singing in his father's church choir at the age of 12 and first played clarinet at school before changing to guitar. Between 1944 and 1946, he served in the Air Force and on release opened a record shop in LeGrange, Kentucky. By 1948, he was performing locally and received a break in 1950, when he won his own 15-minute country radio show, first on WLOU but later on WINN Louisville. In October 1952, **Decca Records** heard him singing on his own show and signed him to the label. He was also helped by his friendship with **Hank Williams**, by whom he was greatly influenced (at times his style was very similar) and with whom he toured in 1952. In January 1953, his double-side tribute release, 'The Death Of Hank Williams' and 'Hank Williams Sings The Blues No More', gained him considerable acclaim, although it failed to make the national country charts. Soon afterwards, together with his band, the Golden Harvest Boys, he began his live *Country & Western Music Show* on WHAS-TV, as well as maintaining a country radio show on WKLO. During the late 50s, after three further Decca singles, he also recorded singles for **Dot** and Starday and two more rockabilly-type numbers as Jimmy Lloyd for Roulette. In the early 60s, he appeared on various major NBC and CBS radio shows, the *Louisiana Hayride* and the *Grand Ole Opry*. In July 1962, Logsdon was chosen to replace **Wayne Raney** as the presenter on WCKY Cincinnati's major night-time country music show and that same year, he recorded an album for the King label. In the late 60s, he presented major shows on WTVF Mobile and WCLU Louisville. He remained fairly active as a performer and as a radio presenter on various stations until around 1976, when he took up a post with the Kentucky Labour Department. During his career, he wrote many songs, some of which were recorded by other artists including **Johnny Horton**, **Carl Perkins** and even **Woody Herman**, who recorded Logsdon's 'No True Love'.

● ALBUMS: *Howdy Neighbors* (King 1963)★★★, *Doin' It Hank's Way* (Castle 1980)★★★.
● COMPILATIONS *I Got A Rocket In My Pocket* (Bear Family 1993)★★★★.

Lohan, Sinéad

b. *c.*1971, Cork, Eire. One of the most successful commercial artists based in Ireland in the mid-90s, singer-songwriter Sinéad Lohan made a huge impact with the release of her debut album. Initially released on the small independent label Dara Records, *Who Do You Think I Am*, which featured **Mary Black** collaborator and former **Moving Hearts** member Declan Sinott as producer and principal musician, received rave reviews from publications stretching across several musical genres. It was re-packaged and re-released by Grapevine Records in the summer of 1995 and quickly achieved double platinum status in Ireland. The album's contents revealed a maturity in stark contrast to the fact that most of the songs it contained were written when Lohan was a teenager. She had risen to prominence initially by featuring on the Irish album, *A Woman's Heart 2*, alongside Mary Black, **Mary Coughlan** and **Sinead O'Connor**. It was through this project that she came to the attention of Sinott, a fellow Cork native. Lohan had originally come to music via her parents, who were both active in the local music community, though she loved the **Jam** and **Madness** more than ethnic Irish music, and these influences continue to inform her own songwriting.

● ALBUMS: *Who Do You Think I Am* (Dara/Grapevine 1995)★★★.

Loïs Lane

Taking their name from *Superman*'s female foil, this eclectic Dutch dance music band added an umlaut to their moniker to reinstate their European origins. Led by sisters Monique and Suzanne Klemann, they were originally signed to a publishing contract in 1985 by Andre de Raaff, at that time working at **Warner Brothers Records** but now the head of their present label, CNR Records. They gained an international profile in 1992 with their album for **Polydor Records**, *Precious*, which featured a collaboration with **Prince** and entered several European Top 30s. However, they were not able to build on this impact, and had to wait until 1995 for their next major hit, 'Tonight'.

● ALBUMS: *Precious* (Polydor 1992)★★★★.

Lolita

b. Ditta Zuza Einzinger, 17 January 1931, St. Poelten, Austria. Lolita Ditta was not expected to enter show-business by her civil servant father. She worked as a children's nurse and then a secretary. Yet her soloing in a local church choir earned her a regular spot on Radio Linz, which prompted Lolita to take her chances as a full-time cabaret singer. Subsequent recordings for **Polydor** made her a star in German-speaking Europe. A grander destiny awaited her in 1960 when 'Seeman' (composed by Werner Scharfenberger and Fini Busch) managed the hitherto impossible as the first German-made single by a female artist to reach the US Hot 100 - climbing to number 5. This triumph was dampened slightly when simultaneous covers (translated as 'Sailor (Your Home Is The Sea)' by lyricist Norman Newell) by **Anne Shelton** and **Petula Clark** stole her thunder in the UK chart. Indeed, Lolita was to enjoy no more big hits in English-speaking regions while remaining a top domestic attraction - epitomized when her detailing of a 'Gateau a la Lolita' recipe on Danish television was headlined in a national newspaper.

Lollapalooza

The first modern 'travelling festival', America's Lollapalooza, a rolling convoy of packaged bands, became something of a cultural phenomenon on a par with the rise of **MTV** since its inception in 1990. The original idea came from Perry Farrell, the singer with **Jane's Addiction** (who co-headlined the first Lollapalooza) and **Porno For Pyros**. Inspired by the atmosphere of the UK's **Glastonbury Festival**, Farrell hoped to replicate that event's cosmopolitan, philanthropic nature with a roster of varied bands as well as various other activities and sideshows, including environmental and political stalls, world arts and body-piercing. The first line-up reflected Farrell's desire to provide a broad range of alternative rock music and featured the **Butthole Surfers**, **Ice-T**, **Nine Inch Nails**, **Living Colour**, **Henry Rollins** (the Rollins Band) and **Siouxsie And The Banshees** each taking turns to headline and support. It was an immediate success at a time when most US rock promoters were struggling to fill auditoriums. 1991's line-up included **Pearl Jam**, **Ice Cube**, **Ministry** and the **Red Hot Chili Peppers**, with an expansion of non-musical events. Another major success, the festival nevertheless suffered a decline in 1993 when Farrell, more concerned with launching Porno For Pyros, was less instrumental in picking the lacklustre line up. He returned to direct 1994's Lollapalooza (alongside former Jane's Addiction manager and festival organiser Ted Gardner), however, promising to restore the festival's original intention of offering 'something special, excellent or exceptional'. However, **Nirvana** were forced to cancel (shortly before Kurt Cobain's suicide in April), leaving many of the participants with the hangover of filling the void he had left behind in alternative music. **L7**, Japan's **Boredoms**, **A Tribe Called Quest**, the **Breeders**, **Verve**, **Nick Cave**, the **Beastie Boys** and **George Clinton** were all on the extended bill, though this time **Smashing Pumpkins** were awarded a 'headlining' role. While some, including Cave, complained of the 'fast food' nature of the event, Lollapalooza undoubtedly went at least some way towards satisfying Farrell's original vision. The festival struggled to attract big names in later years, however, and was wound up in 1998.

Lollipop Shoppe

Based in Los Angeles, California, USA, the Lollipop Shoppe revolved around the talents of vocalist/songwriter Fred Cole. A native of Portland, Oregon, USA, Cole was leader of a local act, Deel Cole Six, in 1964. The group recorded one track, 'Poverty Shack', for **MGM Records**, which was pressed as an acetate, but never officially released. Cole subsequently moved to Los Angeles, where he formed the Weeds and issued 'It's Your Time' on Teen Beat Records in 1966. A further Weeds single, 'No Good News' was released in 1969. In 1967 Cole formed the Lollipop Shoppe with Ed Bowen (lead guitar/vocals), Ron Buzzell (rhythm guitar/vocals), Bob Atkins (bass) and Tim Rockson (drums). They came under the wing of DJ/scenemaker **Lord Tim Hudson**, who also managed the **Seeds**. The Lollipop Shoppe recorded two tracks, 'Mr. Madison Avenue' and 'Who's It Gonna Be' for the soundtrack to *Angels From Hell* (1967) before securing a recording

deal with UNI Records subsidiary, Shamley. *Just Colour* bears the influence of the Seeds and **Love**, particularly through Cole's stylistic vocals, but it contains several excellent garage band-cum-flower power songs, notably 'She Must Be A Witch' and 'Underground Railroad'. A heavily orchestrated single, 'Someone I Know', closed the Lollipop Shoppe's career in 1968. In 1974 Cole re-emerged as leader of Zipper, who issued *Zipper* on Cole's own label, Waizeagle. The same outlet released recordings by his subsequent groups, King Bee, ('Hot Pistol', 1978) and Rats (*Rats*, 1980, *Intermittent Signals*, 1981).

● ALBUMS: *Just Colour* (Shamley 1968)★★★, reissued Big Beat 1985 with extra tracks.

Lomax, Alan And John A.

A well-known and well-read folklorist, Alan Lomax (b. 15 January 1915, Austin, Texas, USA) travelled with his father, John A. Lomax (b. John Avery Lomax, 23 September 1875, Goodman, Mississippi, USA, d. 26 January 1948, Greenville, Mississippi, USA), on field recording trips during the 30s, collecting folk songs and tunes from various states in the USA. They collected songs for the Library of Congress Archive, for which **Woody Guthrie** was later recorded. Until that time, John Lomax had been an administrator at a college, and had collected cowboy songs, including 'Home On The Range', as a hobby. As a result of the Depression and economic crash of the 30s, John Lomax became jobless, and started collecting folk songs and related material on a full-time basis. By the time Alan was 23 years old he was assistant director of the Archive of Folk Song at the Library of Congress. The Lomaxes met a number of singers who later became almost household names, including **Lead Belly** and **Muddy Waters**. Lead Belly was discovered in a Louisiana prison, but John Lomax managed to secure his release, employing him as a chauffeur. Lomax later took him to New York where he performed to college audiences. In 1934, John Lomax became honorary consultant and head of the Library of Congress archive of folk song. Alan Lomax travelled to Britain during the 50s and collaborated with **Ewan MacColl** on the radio series *Ballads And Blues*. He later returned to the USA to conduct field recordings in the southern states. The results were subsequently released on **Atlantic Records** as part of a series called 'Southern Folk Heritage'. John and Alan Lomax were also responsible for collecting a number of the songs of the Ritchie family of Kentucky. In addition to his many other activities, Alan Lomax was a fine performer in his own right, as can be heard on *Texas Folk Songs*, which contains the standards 'Ain't No More Cane On The Brazo's' and 'Billy Barlow'. *Alan Lomax Sings Great American Ballads*, on **HMV**, included **Guy Carawan** (banjo) and Nick Wheatstraw (guitar). It featured such classics as 'Frankie', 'Darlin' Corey' and 'Git Along Little Doggies'. The latter song had been recorded by John Lomax in 1908, and originates from an Irish ballad, converted and adapted by cowboys. After World

War II, Alan was the Director of Folk Music for **Decca**, subsequently working for the Office of War Information from 1943-44, and then for the army's Special Services Section until 1945. As a singer, Alan performed both in the USA and Britain. Twelve years of research culminated in *Cantometrics*, a set of seven cassettes with a book.

● ALBUMS: John A. Lomax *The Ballad Hunter, Lectures On American Folk Music* 10-LP box set (Folkways 50s)★★★, Alan Lomax *Alan Lomax Sings Great American Ballads* (HMV 1958)★★★, *Texas Folk Songs* (1958)★★★, *Folk Song Saturday Night* (60s)★★★, *Murderer Is Home* (1976)★★★, various artists *The Alan Lomax Collection Sampler* (Rounder 1997)★★★★.

● FURTHER READING: Alan Lomax *American Folk Song And Folk Lore*, with Sidney Robertson Cowell. *Mister Jelly Roll - The Fortunes Of Jelly Roll Morton, New Orleans, Creole And Inventor Of Jazz, The Folksongs Of North America, The Land Where The Blues Began*. Editor of *Folk Songs Of North America In The English Language, Folk Song Style And Culture, Cantometrics - An Approach To The Anthropology Of Music*. John A. Lomax *Cowboy Songs, Adventures Of A Ballad Hunter, Cowboy Songs And Other Frontier Ballads, Songs Of The Cattle Trail And Cow Camp*. John And Alan Lomax *American Ballads And Folk Songs, Cowboy Songs And Other Frontier Ballads, Negro Folk Songs As Sung By Lead Belly, Folksong USA, Our Singing Country, The Penguin Book Of American Folk Songs*. *Last Cavalier: The Life & Times Of John A. Lomax*, Nolan Porterfield.

Lomax, Jackie

b. 10 May 1944, Wallasey, Merseyside, England. A former vocalist with the 60s beat group the **Undertakers**, Lomax began a new career in America when this respected Liverpool unit disbanded. Spells with two short-lived bands, the Mersey Lads and the Lost Souls, preceded a return to England where the singer worked with his own group, the Lomax Alliance, and as a solo act. Two strong, but unsuccessful, singles followed before he was signed to the fledgling Apple label but his opening release, 'Sour Milk Sea', written for him by **George Harrison**, was unfortunately overshadowed by hits for stablemates the **Beatles** and **Mary Hopkin**. Lomax's debut, *Is This What You Want*, featured contributions from a host of star names including Harrison, **Paul McCartney**, **Ringo Starr** and **Eric Clapton**. The artist's stylish compositions and superb voice were equal to such esteemed company. Sadly, Apple's internal problems doomed his undoubted potential and following an interlude as part of the elusive **Heavy Jelly**, Lomax returned to America where he completed two more excellent albums, *Home Is In My Head* and *Three*. In 1973, the singer joined the British-based Badger, a group formed by ex-**Yes** organist, Tony Kaye. Lomax helped transform them from a progressive rock band into a more soulful aggregation, exemplified on *White Lady*, which was produced by **Allen Toussaint** and consisted solely of Lomax's songs. Badger then split into two factions, with Lomax and

bassist Kim Gardner instigating an offshoot unit named after the album. Lomax subsequently resumed his solo career, but the releases that followed were disappointing and the bad luck which had often dogged this worthwhile performer further undermined his career. Lomax did resurface in 1990 as one of several acts contributing to the 'tribute' album *True Voices*, wherein he sang a version of **Tim Buckley**'s 'Devil Eyes'.

● ALBUMS: *Is This What You Want* (Apple 1969)★★★, *Home Is In My Head* (1971)★★★, *Three* (1972)★★, with Badger *White Lady* (1974)★★, *Livin' For Lovin'* (1976)★★★, *Did You Ever* (1977)★★.

Lombardo, Guy

b. 19 June 1902, London, Ontario, Canada, d. 5 November 1977, Houston, Texas, USA. A celebrated bandleader and impresario, early in the 20s, Lombardo formed a dance band in collaboration with his brothers Carmen and Lebert (a fourth brother, Victor, joined later). After some limited success in their own country they travelled across the border and secured a regular radio engagement in Cleveland, Ohio, where they adopted the name 'Guy Lombardo And His Royal Canadians'. The band played in Chicago before moving to New York where they remained, mostly enjoying very long residencies, until 1963. Frequent broadcasts and their immaculately played dance music, which was billed as 'the sweetest music this side of heaven', appealed to a huge audience. He is probably best remembered for his theme tune, 'Auld Lang Syne', and 'Boo-Hoo' which was written by Carmen Lombardo, Edward Heyman and John Jacob Loeb. However, from 1927-54, he had an enormous number of hits, including 'Charmaine', 'Sweethearts On Parade', 'You're Driving Me Crazy', 'By the River St. Marie', '(There Ought To Be) A Moonlight Saving Time', 'Too Many Tears', 'Paradise', 'We Just Couldn't Say Goodbye', 'The Last Roundup', 'Stars Fell On Alabama', 'What's The Reason (I'm Not Pleasin' You')', 'Red Sails In The Sunset', 'Lost', 'When Did You Leave Heaven?', 'September In The Rain', 'It Looks Like Rain In Cherry Blossom Lane', 'So Rare', 'Penny Serenade', 'The Band Played On', 'It's Love-Love-Love', 'Managua, Nicaragua', and 'The Third Man Theme'. The band's worldwide record sales were extraordinary - published estimates vary between 100 and 300 million copies. Lombardo also appeared in several films such as *Many Happy Returns* (1934), *Stage Door Canteen* (1943), and *No Leave, No Love* (1946). From 1954 Lombardo took over the operation of the Marine Theatre at New York's Jones Beach, and continued to produce all manner of spectacular musical extravaganzas adaptations for successive seasons until shortly before his death. He also had extensive business interests, and was a long-time speedboat racing enthusiast, a pastime which brought him many awards, including that of National Champion in the late 40s.

● ALBUMS: *Your Guy Lombardo Medley* (1957)★★★, *Berlin By Lombardo* (1958)★★★, *The Sounds Of The Swing Years*

(1960)★★★★, *Sweetest Music This Side Of Heaven* (Ace Of Hearts 1962)★★★, *Every Night Is New Year's Eve* (1973)★★★, *Guy Lombardo And The Royal Canadians, 1950* (1988)★★★★.

● COMPILATIONS: *Guy Lombardo In Hi-Fi* (*c*.1955)★★★, *The Uncollected* (1986)★★★, *All Time Favourites* (1988)★★★.

● FURTHER READING: *Auld Acquaintance: An Autobiography*, Guy Lombardo and J. Altschue.

Londin, Larrie

b. 15 October 1943, Norfolk, Virginia, USA, d. 24 August 1992, Nashville, USA. Londin, who grew up in the Miami/Fort Lauderdale area of Florida, began to play drums as a boy and went on to become one of the most respected drummers to play in several genres of music. He first played professionally with a pop group, the Headliners, at 15. He had aspirations to be a singer commenting 'I was going to be the next **Elvis Presley** but it paid more to play drums than wash dishes. They liked my drumming so I told them I'd play if they let me sing a couple of tunes a night'. When the group found they were under investigation for playing in bars under age, they quickly left Florida and relocated to Detroit. Londin and the Headliners then spent nine years working as staff musicians for **Motown Records**, playing on recordings by the **Supremes** and **Marvin Gaye**. He was offered a recording contract by **Atlantic** but declined as he did not want to leave the group. In 1969, after Motown decided to move to Los Angeles, Londin relocated to Nashville, where he quickly adapted his style to country music. He worked with **Jerry Reed** and **Glen Campbell** on *Goodtime Hour* and played nights at the Carousel Club for three years, where he sang and did comedy and impressions as part of his act. He soon became a popular session musician recording with such stars as **Waylon Jennings**, Reed and others and went on to play on hundreds of recordings by numerous country singers. He was the first musician to use electronic synthesized drums on Nashville studio recordings. He spent five years working with **Rodney Crowell** and **Rosanne Cash** as a member of their Cherry Bomb Band. In 1976, he also toured with **Elvis Presley** and played on Presley's last concert. He later worked with and produced recordings by the **Everly Brothers**. During the 80s, he worked in Nashville, New York and California, where he recorded with **Merle Haggard.** At times he even accepted invitations to record with rock musicians, crediting his ability to switch genres without problems to his days with the Headliners. Londin was his own worst critic and drove himself on relentlessly. 'I'm never happy with what I do. I listen to things I've done and realise it's as good as I could do at that moment. But I've got to keep striving to be better on every project. I just play whatever fits the song because the song is what's important'. He travelled around the USA giving instructional lectures and demonstrations to introduce young musicians to the art of playing drums. It was on one of these trips that he suffered a severe heart attack while lecturing in Denton, Texas on 24 April 1992. He was taken by ambulance back to Nashville, where he remained in a diabetic coma in hospital, until he died on 24 August.

London

As punk sent an electric shock through a complacent late 70s UK music scene, major labels were to be found hurriedly signing acts regardless of ability. London, like many other second division new wavers, were scooped up only to disappear after all the fuss had died down. Two releases in 1977, 'Everyone's A Winner' and 'No Time', were both of their time - punchy and urgent but ultimately lacking in substance. *Animal Games*, London's one and only album (and accompanying single) in 1978 followed suit, its power-pop feel lacking the true bite of punk's pioneers. Lead singer Riff Regan later attempted a solo career, while drummer Jon Moss joined the **Edge** before making his name in the early 80s with **Culture Club**.

● ALBUMS: *Animal Games* (MCA 1978)★★.

London Calling - The Clash

If punk rejected pop history, *London Calling* reclaimed it, albeit with a knowing perspective. The scope of this double set is breaktaking, encompassing reggae, rockabilly and the group's own furious mettle. Where such a combination might have proved over-ambitious, the **Clash** accomplish it with swaggering panache. **Guy Stevens**, who produced the group's first demos, returns to the helm to provide a confident, cohesive sound equal to the set's brilliant array of material. Boldly assertive and superbly focused, *London Calling* contains many of the quartet's finest songs and is, by extension, virtually faultless.

● Tracks: *London Calling; Brand New Cadillac; Jimmy Jazz; Hateful; Rudie Can't Fail; Spanish Bombs; The Right Profile; Lost In The Supermarket; Clampdown; The Guns Of Brixton; Wrong 'Em Boyo; Death Or Glory; Koka Kola; The Card Cheat; Lover's Rock; Four Horsemen; I'm Not Down; Revolution Rock; Train In Vain.*

● First released 1979

● UK peak chart position: 9

● USA peak chart position: 27

London Calling!

The name '**Noël Coward**' went up in West End lights for the first time when this André Charlot revue opened at the Duke of York's Theatre on 4 September 1923. Coward also co-wrote the book, with Ronald Jeans, and the music and lyrics with Philip Braham. Also in the cast was Coward's favourite leading lady, **Gertrude Lawrence**, along with Maisie Gay, Eileen Molyneux, and comedian Tubby Edlin. **Fred Astaire**, who was appearing with his sister Adele in *Stop Flirting* at the Shaftesbury Theatre, arranged some of the dances. The songs included 'What Love Means To Girls Like Me', 'Carrie', 'Life In The Old Girl Yet', 'Sentiment', and 'Other Girls'. Gertrude Lawrence introduced one of

Coward's most enduring numbers, 'Parisian Pierrot', and together they sang 'You Were Meant For Me', another future standard, written by **Arthur Freed** and **Nacio Herb Brown**. The show was a great success until Charlot decided to transfer Gertrude Lawrence and several other members of the company to the Broadway production of *André Charlot's London Revue Of 1924* which opened in January. After Joyce Barbour replaced Lawrence, *London Calling!* soon ran out of steam.

London Jazz Composers Orchestra
(see **Guy, Barry**)

London Posse
One of Britain's first credible rap acts, utilising rhymes built over expertly executed ragamuffin breaks, with cockney accents thrown in for good measure. Unfortunately, London Posse were not free of the misogyny made more explicit by the gangsta rappers (tracks like 'Sexy Gal' and 'Living' implied that the entire female gender was out *en masse* to rob them of their money). London Posse at least possessed wit and a nose for rhythm to dilute their urban warnings. Stylistically, the album was notable for its **Eric B And Rakim**-styled delivery.
● ALBUMS: *Gangster Chronicles* (Mango/Island 1990)★★★★.

London Records
Founded in 1947, this renowned label was established in the USA by British **Decca** to provide an outlet for its domestic releases. The UK counterpart was introduced in 1949 when the parent company began recording American acts, including **Teresa Brewer** and **Josh White**. London began licensing material from other US outlets in October 1951 and within two years had acquired the rights to Essex and **Imperial**, with which it laid the foundations of its impressive rock 'n' roll catalogue. **Bill Haley And His Comets** and **Fats Domino** were an important part of its early roster, but the label enjoyed commercial success with releases by **Slim Whitman** and the bright pop of **Pat Boone**. The addition of **Atlantic Records** (1955), **Chess**, **Specialty** (both 1956) and **Sun** (1957) ensured a virtually peerless position. **Little Richard**, **Chuck Berry**, **Bo Diddley**, **Jerry Lee Lewis**, the **Everly Brothers**, **Rick Nelson** and the **Coasters** were among the many artists introduced to British audiences by this cogent outlet whose reputation flourished as the 50s progressed. London's eminent position continued into the 60s. Success with **Duane Eddy**, **Del Shannon** and **Roy Orbison** was derived by distributing the Jamie, Big Top and Monument labels and the girl-group genre was satisfied through releases drawn from **Phil Spector**'s Philles label. However, several other licencees felt the wide roster jeopardized their individuality. **Berry Gordy** removed his fledgling Tamla/**Motown** empire after a mere handful of releases, **EMI** acquired the rights to **Liberty**, United Artists, Imperial and Minit, while the defection of Chess to Pye International was particularly ill-timed, given that the emergent British R&B movement brought renewed interest to a catalogue London had failed to exploit fully. Another crucial loss was that of Atlantic and although London had secured a measure of success with **Otis Redding**, the US company took its catalogue to **Polydor** in 1966, just as the soul style it contained began a commercial ascendancy. **Elektra** made a similar move, thus depriving London of a prime outlet for folk-rock and the emergent US underground scene, and by 1967 releases on this once-prolific outlet had lessened dramatically. Minor labels - White Whale, Bang and Laurie - provided occasional hits, but London's sole remaining jewel was the Memphis-based **Hi Records**, home of **Al Green**, **Ann Peebles** and **Willie Mitchell**. Releases by these artists provided commercial and artistic success, but the company's decline during the 70s mirrored that of Decca itself. This once-mighty concern had failed to adapt to the changing face of pop and was sold to Phonogram in 1980 upon the death of its patriarch, Sir Edward Lewis. Although initially reserved - two singles were released bearing the London imprint between 1980 and 1981 - the new owners resurrected the name fully in 1982 for a new generation of British-based acts. Hits for the **Bluebells**, **New Edition**, **Blancmange**, **Bronksi Beat**, **Communards** and Glenn Medeiros ensued, but **Bananarama** enjoyed the most comprehensive success with a run of 17 Top 40 hits for the label between 1982-1988.
● COMPILATIONS: *London American Legend, Part One* (1975)★★★★, *London American Legend, Part Two* (1976)★★★★.

London SS
Historically, London SS were one of the most important British bands of the punk era, despite never playing in front of a paying audience, nor releasing any recordings. Musically they were either 'raw rock 'n' roll' or 'pretty crap' depending on which of their many members you cared to ask. An *ad hoc* combo of London youth (or migrants drifting in from elsewhere), they were started around March 1975 by Tony James and Mick Jones. They spent the entire 10 months or so of the group's life auditioning musicians and rehearsing 60s beat and R&B classics. The only other semi-permanent member they found was guitarist Bryan James but among the others who traded licks and rimshots were: Terry Chimes (drums), who was rejected; Paul Simenon (vocals), rejected as well; Nicky Headon (drums) turned the gig down; Tony James tried out for bass; Rat Scabies (b. Chris Miller) had a bash at drums despite being in his own proto-punk group - Rot; Matt Dangerfield and Casino Steel of the **Hollywood Brats** popped in for two rehearsals on their way to forming the **Boys**; Roland Hot played drums briefly as did Andy (whose surname has been lost to the mists of time; and another long-forgotten soul called George had a spell on the guitar). The only recording they ever made was a

demo featuring the James/Jones/James/Hot line-up which was the penultimate assembly. In January 1976 they kicked out Hot, and Bryan James went off with Rat Scabies to join the Subterraneans and then form the **Damned**. That left the two originators on their own again, but James eventually went off to find a job before running into **Billy Idol** and joining **Chelsea** with him. They soon split Chelsea to form **Generation X**. Messrs Jones, Simenon and Chimes teamed up with **101ers** vocalist Joe Strummer to form the **Clash**, and when Chimes left to form Jem, another London SSer, Nicky 'Topper' Headon, replaced him.

London Town

This 1946 release, the first picture be made at 'Sound City Studios', Shepperton, England, after World War II, was an attempt to mount a lavish Technicolor British musical to rival the legendary Hollywood productions. It failed dismally, even though the American producer-director Wesley Ruggles was joined by several of his fellow countrymen including highly experienced song-writers **Johnny Burke** and **Jimmy Van Heusen**, and musical director-arranger **Salvador 'Tutti' Camarata**. The dreary and overly sentimental screenplay by Elliot Paul and Siegfried Herzig concerns ambitious comedian Jerry Ruggles (Sid Field), who is merely the understudy for star Charlie DeHaven (Sonnie Hale) in the West End production of *London Town*, until his fawning daughter, Peggy (14-years-old **Petula Clark**), gets to work. She persuades Charlie's dresser, Belgrave (Claude Hulbert), to feed him a potion which makes his face go green. Naturally, he cannot go on stage like that, so, step forward Jerry, the world of show business is at your feet. The delectable Kay Kendall rose above it all, and also trying their best were Greta Gynt, **Tessie O'Shea**, **Sonnie Hale**, and Mary Clare. Jerry Desmonde, Sid Field's regular straight man, was also on hand to assist him in several of the celebrated comedian's classic routines, including his famous golfing sketch. 'My Heart Goes Crazy' was the big number, and it was reprised several times. Burke and Van Heusen's other songs consisted of an appealing ballad, 'So Would I' (introduced by Beryl Davis) 'You Can't Keep A Good Dreamer Down', and 'Any Way The Wind Blows'. Drummer-singer **Jack Parnell** turned up in 'The 'Amstead Way' production number which topped and tailed a knees-up medley of Cockney favourites such as 'Don't Dilly Dally On The Way' (Fred W. Leigh-Charles Collins), 'Any Old Iron' (Collins-Fred Terry-E.A. Sheppard), and 'Wot Cher' ('Knock 'Em In The Old Kent Road') (Albert Chevalier-Charles Ingle). The finalé, which featured an enormous grand piano with 10 men seated at the keyboard, reminded many of previous films in which the instrument was featured in a visually effective fashion, such as *King Of Jazz* and *Gold Diggers Of 1935*. Unfortunately, *London Town* was just not in the same class as either of those pictures. In America it was re-titled *My Heart Goes Crazy*.

London, Jimmy

b. *c*.1953, Kingston, Jamaica, West Indies. In the late 60s London recorded, with the Inspirations, the **Joe Gibbs**-directed hits 'Take Back Your Duck', 'La La' and 'The Train Is Coming'. He achieved international renown in the early 70s with the Impact All Stars at Randy's studios. His version of **Simon And Garfunkel**'s 'Bridge Over Troubled Waters' topped the Jamaican chart and was equally successful in the UK reggae charts. This was swiftly followed by 'A Little Love', and both songs were featured on *Bridge Over Troubled Waters*. Versions of the **Temptations**' 'Just My Imagination' and 'It's Now Or Never' were also lifted from the album for release as singles. In 1974 'Rock And Roll Lullaby' made a significant impression on the reggae chart with its infectious 'Na Na Na It'll Be Alright' chorus. He then topped the reggae chart for two consecutive months with 'No Letter Today', which was released on the Dragon label. With a variety of producers, the hits 'Together', 'Jim Say Hello' and 'Don't Keep The Kids', sustained his high profile in the specialist charts. In 1975 London toured the UK, making his debut at the Lyceum in London supporting soul artist **George McCrae**. London joined forces with **Pat Rhoden**, releasing the first single on the newly formed Jama label, 'What Good Am I', which was soon followed by 'I'm Your Puppet' and 'Am I That Easy To Forget'. By 1976 he had recorded 'Thank The Lord', featured on *Welcome To My World*, which included a remake of his earlier hit 'A Little Love', a version of the **Drifters**' 'Kissing At The Back Row Of The Movies' and the particularly popular 'Hold On'. Jimmy London continued to record throughout the 70s and 80s.
● ALBUMS: *Bridge Over Troubled Waters* (Trojan 1972)★★★★, *Welcome To My World* (Burning Sounds 1977)★★★, *Crying In The Ghetto* (Imp 1977)★★, *Hold On* (Lagoon 1996)★★★.

London, Julie

b. June Webb, 26 September 1926, Santa Rosa, California, USA. Actress-singer London is inextricably linked to the sultry Andy Hamilton song 'Cry Me A River', which gave the artist her sole million-seller in 1955. Her memorable performance of the song in the film *The Girl Can't Help It*, showcased a lachrymose delivery best exemplified on *Julie Is Her Name*, which also featured the talent of jazz guitarist **Barney Kessel**. London continued to record prodigiously throughout the late 50s to the mid-60s, but this aspect of her career vied with roles in films, notably *The Great Man* and *A Question Of Adultery*. She later appeared in several television series, often alongside her second husband and long-time producer and songwriter **Bobby Troup**. Her popularity underwent a revival in the UK in the early 80s after **Mari Wilson** gained a hit with London's classic lament. London's looks were stunning, she oozed style, but unfortunately she did not possess the vocal range or expression to make her a truly great singer.
● ALBUMS: *Julie Is Her Name* (Liberty 1956)★★★, *Lonely*

Girl (Liberty 1956)★★★, *Calendar Girl* (Liberty 1956)★★★, *About The Blues* (Liberty 1957)★★, *Make Love To Me* (Liberty 1957)★★, *Julie* (Liberty 1957)★★, *Julie Is Her Name, Volume 2* (Liberty 1958)★★, *London By Night* (Liberty 1958)★★, *Swing Me An Old Song* (Liberty 1959)★★, *Your Number Please* (Liberty 1959)★★, *Julie London At Home* (Liberty 1959)★★, *Around Midnight* (Liberty 1960)★★, *Send For Me* (Liberty 1960)★★, *Whatever Julie Wants* (Liberty 1961)★★, *Sophisticated Lady* (Liberty 1962)★★, *Love Letters* (Liberty 1962)★★, *Latin In A Satin Mood* (Liberty 1963)★★, *The End Of The World* (Liberty 1963)★★, *Love On The Rocks* (Liberty 1963)★★, *The Wonderful World Of Julie London* (Liberty 1963)★★, *Julie London* (Liberty 1964)★★, *In Person At The Americana* (Liberty 1964)★★, *Our Fair Lady* (Liberty 1965)★★, *Feelin' Good* (Liberty 1965)★★, *All Through The Night* (Liberty 1965)★★, *For The Night People* (Liberty 1966)★★, *Nice Girls Don't Stay For Breakfast* (Liberty 1967)★★, *With Body And Soul* (Liberty 1967)★★, *Easy Does It* (Liberty 1968)★★, *Yummy Yummy Yummy* (Liberty 1969)★★, *By Myself* (Liberty 1969)★★.

● COMPILATIONS: *The Best Of* (Liberty 1962)★★★, *Julie's Golden Greats* (Liberty 1963)★★★, *Great Performances* (Liberty 1968)★★★, *The Best Of Julie London* (Liberty 1984)★★★, *The Best Of Julie London: The Liberty Years* (Liberty 1988)★★★.

● FILMS: *The Girl Can't Help It* (1956).

London, Laurie

b. 19 January 1944, London, England. At the age of 13, this pop singer, who had the confidence and showmanship of a veteran, appeared in a closed circuit transmission of *6.5 Special* at the BBC stand at the 1958 Radio Show. He so impressed producer John Warrinton that he was invited back every day and thereby came to the attention of **EMI**, who put him in the studio with producer Norman Newell. The result was a **Geoff Love**-arranged revival of the spiritual 'He's Got The Whole World In His Hands'. The record climbed to number 12 in the UK and went on to become the most successful record by a British male in the 50s in the USA, topping the *Billboard* chart. Fame forced London to leave school and his father Will gave up his sales management job to manage him, but he refused the chance of a US tour in 1958 for the 14-year-old. London recorded a handful of other pop/gospel singles including 'Joshua', 'The Gospel Train' and 'I Gotta Robe', but the adolescent, who for all too brief a time had the whole world in his hands, never charted again. He released one album for **Capitol Records**. He was later reported to be successfully working in the clothing industry in London.

● ALBUMS: *Laurie London* (Parlophone 1958)★★.
● COMPILATIONS: *He's Got The Whole World In His Hands* (Bear Family 1984)★★.

Londonbeat

This group featured a white English guitarist and three black American singers. Their line-up comprises Jimmy Chambers (b. 20 January 1946), **Jimmy Helms** (b.

Florida, USA) and George Chandler (b. Atlanta, Georgia, USA), plus Willy M, (b. William Henshall, London, England). Helms was best known for his UK Top 10 hit in 1973 with 'Gonna Make You An Offer You Can't Refuse'. He released several other singles at the time, including 'Jack Horner's Holiday'. Chandler was in 60s soul group the Four Kents who were American but based in northern Italy as servicemen. He too had released solo singles in the 70s. They came together and settled in London where they signed to **David A. Stewart**'s AnXious label. Much of their material was close to a cappella though they used session musicians when necessary. Their debut '9am (The Comfort Zone)' reached UK number 21 in 1988, but it was 1990's 'I've Been Thinking About You' that gave the band their biggest hit, rising to number 2. They also appeared with BBC Radio 1 disc jockeys, Liz Kershaw and Bruno Brooks on the Christmas 1989 charity record 'It Takes Two Baby'.

● ALBUMS: *Speak* (AnXious 1987)★★★, *In The Blood* (AnXious 1990)★★★, *Harmony* (1992)★★★.

Lone Justice

This group of US country-rockers were fronted by **Maria McKee** (b. 17 August 1964, Los Angeles, California, USA) who is the half-sister of **Love**'s Bryan Maclean. When she was just three years old, her brother would take her to the various clubs along Los Angeles' Sunset Strip and she was befriended by the likes of **Frank Zappa** and the **Doors**. When she grew up, she and MacLean formed a duo initially called the Maria McKee Band, but later changed to the Bryan MacLean Band to cash in on *his* slightly higher profile. Heavily immersed in country music, McKee formed the first incarnation of Lone Justice with Ryan Hedgecock (guitar), Don Heffington (drums), Marvin Etzioni (bass) and Benmont Tench (keyboards, ex-**Tom Petty And The Heartbreakers**). The group were signed to the **Geffen** label at the recommendation of **Linda Ronstadt**. McKee's talents were also admired by artists such as **Bob Dylan**, U2's Bono, who offered them a support slot on tour, and Tom Petty, who donated songs to the first album. One of these, 'Ways To Be Wicked', while not achieving any notable chart status, was responsible for bringing the group to the attention of the UK audience via an imaginative black-and-white, cut-up-and-scratched video. The band's more established line-up transmuted to that of expatriate Brit Shayne Fontayne (guitar), Bruce Brody (keyboards, ex-**Patti Smith**; **John Cale**), Greg Sutton (bass) and Rudy Richardson (drums). They were managed by the respected producer **Jimmy Iovine**. In 1985, former **Undertones** singer **Feargal Sharkey** had a UK number 1 hit with McKee's 'A Good Heart'. Lone Justice split suddenly in 1987 with McKee going on to a solo career, taking only Brody with her from Lone Justice.

● ALBUMS: *Lone Justice* (Geffen 1985)★★★, *Shelter* (Geffen 1987)★★, *Radio One Live In Concert* 1986 recording (Windsong 1993)★★.

Lone Pine, Hal, And Betty Cody

Harold John Breau (b. 5 June 1916, Pea Cove, Maine, USA, d. 26 March 1977; guitar, vocals) and Rita M. Coté (b. 17 August 1921, Sherbrooke, Quebec, Canada; guitar, vocals). In the mid-30s, Breau sang on radio in his native state and became the leader of the Lone Pine Mountaineers. He first met Coté in 1938, after her family had relocated to Auboorn, Maine, where, greatly influenced by **Patsy Montana**, she started her singing career as the vocalist with Curly And The Country Boys on WCOU Lewiston. They were married in June 1940 and, changing her name from the French to the English spelling, they worked together for over 10 years with the Lone Pine Mountaineers, on radio and shows in the New England area and over the border to Canada's Maritime Provinces. In the early 50s, they recorded both solo and duet numbers for **RCA Records**, achieving particular success with their duets 'It's Goodbye And So Long To You' and 'Trail Of The Lonesome Pine'. In 1953, Cody's 'Tom Tom Yodel' was a Canadian hit, while 'I Found Out More Than You Ever Knew' reached number 10 in the US country chart (the song was the 'answer' version of the **Davis Sisters**' hit 'I Forgot More Than You'll Ever Know'). In June 1953, the couple became regulars on the *Wheeling Jamboree*, where they remained for several years. After relocating to Manitoba in the late 50s, they divorced. Breau, usually only known then as Hal Lone Pine, later recorded for Arc Records, including duets with Jean Ward. He eventually returned to Maine, where he remarried and continued to play in the area where he had started his career years earlier, until his death in 1977. Cody retired for a time to look after her family, but in the early 70s, she toured with **Dick Curless** and between 1972 and 1982, she played a residency. She eventually returned to Lisbon Falls, Maine, where she made occasional appearances with her son, Dennis. The Breaus' eldest son, Leonard, was the noted jazz guitarist Lenny Breau, who was sadly murdered in 1984. Lone Pine is remembered as the writer of two very popular Canadian country songs, 'When It's Apple Blossom Time In Annapolis Valley' and 'Prince Edward Island Is Heaven To Me', both of which have been recorded by many artists, including **Wilf Carter** and **George Hamilton IV**. In the 80s, Cattle Records of Germany released albums of their recordings.

● ALBUMS: *Lone Pine & His Mountaineers* (RCA 60s)★★★, *Hal Lone Pine* (Arc 60s)★★★, *More Show Stoppers* (Arc 60s)★★, *Songs Everyone Remembers* (Arc 60s)★★, *Coast Of Maine* (Arc 60s)★★★, *Betty Cody Sings Again* (1979)★★★, *Hal Lone Pine & His Mountaineers* i (Cattle 1979)★★★, *Betty Cody's Country Souvenir Album* (Cattle 1985)★★★, *Duets & Memories* (Elmwood Station 1992)★★★, *Hal Lone Pine & His Mountaineers* ii (Castle 1995)★★★.

Lone Ranger

b. Anthony Waldron, the Lone Ranger was one of the late 70s' most lyrically inventive DJs, with a considerable influence on the British school of MCing. Waldron spent a large proportion of his formative years in the UK, which perhaps accounted for his radically different stance, and, like so many others, he began his own recording career at **Studio One**. Welton Irie partnered him at first, but he soon graduated to working solo, tackling several classic Studio One rhythms, after which he became virtually unstoppable. His version of **Slim Smith**'s seminal 'Rougher Yet', retitled 'Love Bump', was a major success. So too was his reading of Smith's 'Never Let Go', a version known as 'The Answer', which has become more famous than the original. As top DJ for Kingston's Virgo Sound, he kept up appearances in the dancehalls and Virgo Hi Fi were voted the top sound of 1980. His recordings for Alvin 'GG' Ranglin assured his legendary status. 'Barnabas Collins' (about a vampire show on television) included the classic line, 'chew ya neck like a Wrigley's', and was a UK reggae chart number 1 in 1980. His additional work for **Winston Riley** and **Channel One**, which included the memorable 'M16', proved almost as popular. His tour of the UK that year reiterated that he could perform on stage as well as on record and for the **sound systems**. His repertoire of strange voices, 'oinks' and 'ribbits', was widely imitated. Lone Ranger recorded sparingly, sometimes branching out into self-production, like many other DJs, and his catalogue has always been assembled with style, class and a dash of great humour.

● ALBUMS: *Barnabas Collins* (GG's 1980)★★★, *On The Other Side Of Dub* (Studio One 1981)★★★, *M16* (Channel One 1982)★★★, *Hi-Yo Silver Away!* (Greensleeves 1982)★★★★, *Badda Dan Dem* (Studio One 1982)★★★, *Dee Jay Daddy* (Techniques 1984)★★★, *Learn To Drive* (Bebo's Music 1985)★★★.

● COMPILATIONS: *Collection* (Grapevine)★★★★.

Lone Star

This traditional UK hard rock quintet was formed in 1975 by Kenny Driscoll (lead vocals), Tony Smith (guitar), Paul 'Tonka' Chapman (guitar), Pete Hurley (bass) and Dixie Lee (drums). Specializing in dynamic heavy rock, they attracted considerable attention with their Roy Thomas Baker-produced debut, offering an approach and sound not dissimilar to early **Queen**'s pomp/hard rock formula. Driscoll was replaced by John Sloman in 1977 before the release of *Firing On All Six*. This album pushed the dual guitars of Chapman and Smith to the forefront and concentrated on heavier material. Shortly after its release the band disintegrated, with Sloman joining **Uriah Heep**, Chapman replacing **Michael Schenker** in UFO and Dixie Lee teaming up with **Wild Horses**.

● ALBUMS: *Lone Star* (Columbia 1976)★★★, *Firing On All Six* (Columbia 1977)★★★★, *BBC Radio 1 Live* (Windsong 1994)★★★.

Lonely At The Top - Randy Newman

A criminally underrated man who has been writing poetical songs about American life for four decades. This is **Randy Newman**'s greatest hits offering with the reality being that he only hit once with the misunderstood 'Short People'. Many of his early songs recorded by the likes of **Dusty Springfield** and **Gene Pitney** are still overlooked on this compilation, but we do have heartfelt ramblings and powerful understatements. To think that Newman can move us to tears of emotion with a lyric that merely states 'I think it's going to rain today' is remarkable. Please note the section 'did not chart'! Perhaps the next century will discover this man's genius.

● Tracks: *Love Story; Living Without You; I Think It's Going To Rain Today; Mama Told Me Not To Come; Sail Away; Simon Smith And The Amazing Dancing Bear; Political Science; God's Song; Rednecks; Birmingham; Louisiana 1927; Marie; Baltimore; Jolly Coppers On Parade; Rider In The Rain; Short People; I Love L.A.; Lonely At The Top.*

● First released 1987

● UK peak chart position: did not chart

● USA peak chart position: did not chart

Lonesome Pine Fiddlers

This noted early bluegrass band, whose input did much to help popularize the music, was initially formed at WHIS Bluefield, West Virginia, in 1938, by Ezra Cline (b. 13 January 1907, Baisden, West Virginia, USA, d. 11 July 1984; bass fiddle, vocals) and his cousins/brothers-in-law, **Curly Ray Cline** and Ned Cline and Gordon Jennings (singer, guitarist). World War II hindered the band's career and Ned Cline, serving in the US Army, died in the Normandy landings. When the band re-formed at WHIS, **Charlie Cline** joined his relatives. In 1949, Charlie and Curly Ray both left, although the latter rejoined in 1951. The early 50s saw various personnel changes, and among contributing musicians were Ray Morgan, Bob Osborne, Larry Richardson, Jimmy and Paul Williams and Ray and Melvin Goins. In 1952, the band relocated, first to WOAY Oak Hill, then WJR Detroit, but in 1953, they moved to WLSI Pikeville, where they played daily radio shows for several years. In the late 50s, other musicians who played with the band included James Carson, Billy Edwards and Udell McPeak. In 1957, the band was comprised of Ezra, Curly Ray, Charlie and his wife Lee, and for two years, they varied their output, even electrifying some instruments. They played a regular television show on WSAZ Huntington, and in 1961, also WCYB Bristol, Virginia. Ezra, Curly Ray and the Goins brothers eventually returned to their normal bluegrass style and even recorded with **Hylo Brown**. In 1964, the Fiddlers ceased full-time playing but a unit consisting of Ezra (bass), Curly Ray (fiddle), Lowell Verney (banjo) and Landon Messer (guitar) played bluegrass shows, until Curly Ray left to join the **Stanley Brothers**, after which the Fiddlers basically ceased to exist. Over the years, they recorded for several labels including Cozy, **RCA/Victor** and Starday. Ezra continued to run his Pikeville restaurant for a time but eventually retired to Gilbert, West Virginia, where he made some appearances at purely local events, before he died on 11 July 1984. There is little doubt that the Lonesome Pine Fiddlers made a major contribution to bluegrass music. It has even been suggested that the only reason that they are not ranked with **Bill Monroe** and other bluegrass legends is because, for some reason, Ezra refused the opportunity for the band to star in the *Martha White Flour* segment on the **Grand Ole Opry**, on WSM Nashville. The programme was then offered to **Flatt And Scruggs**. In 1988, Curly Ray, Charlie and Ray and Melvin Goins recorded a reunion album on which Curly Ray's son, Timmy, took Ezra's place. In 1992 **Bear Family Records** issued a CD containing all of the Cozy and **RCA** masters.

● ALBUMS: *The Lonesome Pine Fiddlers* (Starday 1961)★★★, *14 Mountain Songs With 5-String Banjo* (Starday 1962)★★★, *Bluegrass* (Starday 1962)★★★, *More Bluegrass* (Starday 1963)★★★, *Hylo Brown Meets The Lonesome Pine Fiddlers* (Starday 1963)★★★, *Kentucky Bluegrass* (Nashville 1966)★★★, *Bluegrass Music '52 & '53* (London 1969)★★★, *Lonesome Pine Fiddlers Reunion* (Riverside 1988)★★★. As Charlie Cline And The Lonesome Pine Fiddlers: with Lee Cline *Shalom (Peace)* (Atteiram 1977)★★★, *Bluegrass Gospel* (Shiloh 1977)★★★, *Lonesome Pines* (Old Homestead 1978)★★★, *Strictly Cline* (Atteiram 1978)★★★, *Why Ray Ralph* (Old Homestead 1979)★★★, *Brushy Creek Bluegrass* (Old Homestead 1981)★★★, *Sunset Is Coming* (Old Homestead 1983)★★★.

● COMPILATIONS: *The Best Of The Lonesome Pine Fiddlers* (London 1971)★★★, *Lonesome Pine Fiddlers* (Collectors Classic 1974)★★★, *Early & Great Bluegrass Volume 1* (Old Homestead 1979)★★★★, *Early & Great Bluegrass Volume 2* (Old Homestead 1983)★★★★, *Windy Mountain* (Bear Family 1992)★★★★.

Lonesome Strangers

Lonesome Strangers is a Los Angeles-based country band formed during the cowpunk explosion of the 80s. Their lead vocalist, Jeff Rhymes, writes most of their material, while other members include Randy Weeks, Lorne Rall and Mike McLean. Opening regularly for **Dwight Yoakam**, they built up a strong reputation that led to them being signed by Hightone Records in 1988. Their debut album was released to great acclaim, and they had minor US country hits with 'Goodbye Lonesome, Hello Baby Doll' and 'Just Can't Cry No More'. McLean and Rall left the band, before the follow-up finally appeared in 1997. The new line-up included Greg Perry (drums) and Jeff Roberts (bass).

● ALBUMS: *The Lonesome Strangers* (Hightone 1989)★★★★, *Land Of Opportunity* (Little Dog 1997)★★★.

Lonesome Sundown

b. Cornelious Green, 12 December 1928, Donaldsonville, Louisiana, USA, d. 23 April 1995, Gonzales, Louisiana. Green taught himself piano while growing up, then took guitar lessons in his early 20s. He joined **Clifton Chenier**'s band in 1955, and can be heard on several of that artist's recordings on the **Specialty** label. The following year he recorded for the first time in his own right and 16 singles were issued over the next nine years under the name given to him by producer **Jay Miller** - Lonesome Sundown. Many of these, such as 'My Home Is A Prison' and 'Lonesome Lonely Blues', were classic examples of the unique Louisiana sound - swamp blues - with a resonant production, featuring a strong, booming rhythm section, rippling piano and support from **Lazy Lester** or John Gradnigo on harmonica and Lionel Prevost on tenor saxophone. Green's vocals and biting lead guitar invariably provided just the right gritty edge. A religious conversion towards the end of this period led to his withdrawal from the music scene, but he returned, if only briefly, to record an excellent album for the Joliet label in the late 70s. He was severely debilitated in later years following two strokes, and died in 1995.

● ALBUMS: *Been Gone Too Long* (Alligator 1980)★★★, *Lonesome Whistler* (Flyright 1986)★★★,

● COMPILATIONS: *If Anybody Asks You (My Home Ain' t Here* (Flyright 1988)★★★, *I'm A Mojo Man: The Best Of The Excello Singles* (Ace 1995)★★★★.

Lonestar

This US country rock band signed to **RCA Records** in the 90s after establishing their reputation through a touring schedule that regularly encompassed over 200 performances a year. Comprising Richie McDonald (lead vocals, guitar), John Rich (lead vocals, bass), Michael Britt (guitar), Keech Rainwater (drums) and Sean Sams (keyboards), the group formed in Nashville, Tennessee, though all the members are natives of Texas. They made their debut in January 1995 when BNA Records released the *Lonestar Live* EP, recorded at Nashville's renowned Wildhorse Saloon. The group's superb harmonies and deep-rooted affection for the country tradition soon won supporters, and the highly successful singles 'Tequila Talkin'' and 'No News', made them a hot property in contemporary country circles. When the latter release made number 1 on the *Billboard* Hot Country Singles & Tracks chart, it built interest for the release of the group's self-titled debut album in 1995. This was promoted by a typically rigorous touring schedule, which had given Lonestar much of their fanbase in the first place. As a result the group were invited to perform at the annual ACM telecast, where five years previously, McDonald had heard a Miller Lite beer jingle he had sung air during the commercial break. 'Come Cryin' To Me' was another number 1 single taken from 1997's *Crazy Nights*, the slick but enjoyable follow-up. Rich left the band shortly afterwards.

● ALBUMS: *Lonestar* (BNA 1995)★★★, *Crazy Nights* (BNA 1997)★★★.

Loney, Roy, And The Phantom Movers

b. San Francisco, California, USA. Forsaking an early experience as an actor, Loney turned to music during the folk boom of the early 60s. Impressed by the **Beatles** and the **Rolling Stones**, he later formed the Chosen Few, a high school band which evolved into the **Flamin' Groovies**. Loney's voice and compositions provided the focal point for this cult-favourite act during its early history, but internal tension led to his departure in 1971. Roy then retired from professional music until 1977 when various ex-colleagues backed him on *Artistic As Hell*, an EP invoking the artist's love of classic rockabilly. The following year he formed the Phantom Movers with James Ferrall (guitar) and Danny Mihm (drums), plus two further ex-Groovies' alumni, Larry Lea (guitar) and Maurice Tani (bass). *Out After Dark* fully captured the spirit and style of the singer's former group and was the subject of critical acclaim. Despite innumerable changes in personnel, Loney continued to pursue his unique blend of 50s rock 'n' roll and tongue-in-cheek humour through successive, often excellent albums and a powerful stage show. The singer disbanded his backing group in 1981 following the artistic failure of *Contents Under Pressure*, a flawed 'power-pop' experiment. A second period of retirement ended with the release of *Scientific Bombs Away*, which also marked the reinstatement of the 'Phantom Movers' name. Although denied widespread popularity, Loney has nonetheless retained a small, but highly loyal, following.

● ALBUMS: *Out After Dark* (1979)★★★★, *Phantom Tracks* (1980)★★★, *Contents Under Pressure* (1981)★★★★, *Rock 'N' Roll Dance Party With Roy Loney*, (1982)★★, *Fast And Loose* (1983)★★★, *Scientific Bombs Away* (1988)★★★.

Long And The Short

The Long And The Short enjoyed a brief spell in the UK pop spotlight when 'The Letter' reached number 30 in September 1964. The song was originally recorded by R&B act **Don And Dewey**, but was revived by its composer, **Sonny Bono**, as the debut release by Caesar And Cleo, the duo he had formed with his wife, **Cher**. The Long And The Short, meanwhile, broached the UK Top 50 in December with a follow-up single, 'Choc Ice', but their perky, 'beat' intonations were quickly overtaken by newer, more exciting styles of music

● FILMS: *Gonks Go Beat* (1965).

Long Ryders

Formed in November 1981, the Long Riders (as they were then known) initially included three ex-members of the Unclaimed - **Sid Griffin** (guitar, vocals), Barry Shank (bass, vocals) and Matt Roberts (drums). **Steve Wynn** completed this early line-up, but the guitarist was replaced by Stephen McCarthy on leaving to form the **Dream Syndicate**. Griffin and McCarthy remained at the helm throughout the group's turbulent history. As part of Los Angeles' 'paisley underground' movement, the Long Ryders' history is linked with not only that of the Dream Syndicate, but also that of other guitar-orientated bands such as **Rain Parade**, (early) **Bangles**, **Green On Red** and **Blood On The Saddle**. A mini-album, *The Long Ryders*, was completed with Des Brewer (bass) and Greg Sowders (drums), although by the time the quartet secured a permanent contract, Tom Stevens had joined in place of Brewer. *Native Sons*, an excellent set influenced by **Buffalo Springfield** and **Gram Parsons**, suggested a promising future, but the Long Ryders were unable to repeat its balance of melody and purpose. They withered on record company indecision and, unable to secure a release from their contract, the group broke up in 1987. Griffin moved on to a dual career leading the **Coal Porters** and working as a music journalist.

● ALBUMS: *The Long Ryders* aka *10.5.60* mini-album (PVC 1983)★★★, *Native Sons* (Frontier/Zippo 1984)★★★★, *State Of Our Union* (Island 1985)★★★, *Two-Fisted Tales* (Island 1987)★★, *BBC Radio One In Concert* (Windsong 1994)★★★.

● COMPILATIONS: *Metallic B.O.* early recordings (Overground 1990)★★.

Long, George

b. George Long, 8 May 1921, Kansas City, Kansas, USA. He learned guitar and began his musical career at the age of 10. In his early teens, with his brothers Harry and Jimmy, he toured playing rodeos and fairs with Roy Knapp's Rough Riders. He gained radio work at KITE Kansas City, Missouri, eventually fronting the popular daily *Heart Of America Hoedown*. During this time, he became leader and lead vocalist with the **101 Ranch Boys** and throughout the late 30s, they became a popular act on several other stations playing coast to coast network on WSBA York and WCMB Harrisburg. Later on the advise of **Smiley Burnette**, they appeared on WLS Chicago. They toured with **Gene Autry** and were the first C&W band to play Constitution Hall in Washington, DC. During World War II, Long served in the US Naval Air Corps. After the war, he and the 101 Ranch Boys were reunited and during the late 40s and early 50s continued to entertain. In 1946, they recorded for Security and Rich and in 1948, for **Columbia**. When the band broke up around 1955, Long, a qualified pilot, settled in Meza, Arizona and made solo appearances on local radio and television. Long was a fine vocalist but seemingly few of the band's recordings remain except for a 1985 German compilation of 20 Security, Rich or Columbia recordings.

● COMPILATIONS: *George Long And The 101 Ranch Boys* (Cattle 1985)★★★.

Long, Hubert

b. 3 December 1923, Poteet, Texas, USA, d. 7 September 1982, Nashville, Tennessee, USA. Long grew up in Freer, Texas, and after completing high school in 1942, he joined the US Navy. In 1945, he returned to Texas, working in a record store until 1946, when he worked briefly with both **Decca** and **RCA Records**. After meeting **'Colonel' Tom Parker**, he became involved in promotional work, initially with **Eddy Arnold**, whom Parker was then managing, and relocated to Nashville. Around 1950, he became the manager of the *Louisiana Hayride* in Shreveport, where he first became involved with the booking and

management of artists. In 1952, he formed the Hubert Long Agency, and in 1955, he created Nashville's first country music management company, the Stable Of The Stars, which represented many of the music's major artists. In 1959, he formed his first music publishing business, Moss Rose, and was responsible for the construction of Nashville's SESAC building. By 1960, his business interests were numerous, involving advertising, publishing and publications, not only in the USA but in many overseas locations, including England, Australia, Japan, South Africa and several European countries. He was also involved in real estate and owned many prestigious properties, including some on Nashville's Music Row. He was the first person to be elected both Chairman and President of the **Country Music Association** and was involved with the formation of both the CMA and the CMA Foundation. Long had to undergo surgery for a brain tumour in March 1982, but the operation failed to effect a long-term cure, and on 7 September, he died in Nashville's Baptist Hospital. Long's services to country music saw him win many awards, not least his induction to the **Country Music Hall Of Fame** in 1979.

Long, Johnny

b. North Carolina, USA, d. January 1972. A talented left-handed violinist, Long established his 11-piece orchestra at the Duke University campus in 1932. Originally titled 'the Freshmen', upon graduation the same line-up remained intact and entered the professional world in 1935. Their vocalists included Paul Harman, Helen Young, Bob Houston, Julie Wilson and 'the Beachcombers'. They continued to play college proms as well as major hotel venues throughout the Midwest and west coast, including the Hollywood Palladium. The group's 1940 recording of 'In Old Shanty Town' provided them with their first major success, and sold over a million copies. Further records, including theme tune 'The White Star Of Sigma Nu', were released on record labels including King, Signature, Forum, Roulette, **Coral**, **Mercury** and **Decca Records**. Radio play on *The Teen-Timers Show* and *Judy, Joe And Johnny* also spread their appeal. Despite the slim opportunities available to dance bands in postwar years, Long kept his band on the road, though by the 50s he had been forced to cut its size. He still found bookings, including the Fremont Hotel in Las Vegas, but later retired to take up a teaching post. He enrolled at Marshall University in the 70s, but died of a heart attack in 1972 before completing his course.

Long, Shorty

b. Frederick Earl Long, 20 May 1940, Birmingham, Alabama, USA, d. 29 June 1969, Detroit, Michigan, USA. Multi-instrumentalist Long received tutelage from **W.C. Handy** and **Alvin Robinson** before joining **Harvey Fuqua**'s Tri-Phi label in 1961. This Detroit-based company was later acquired by Tamla/**Motown** and Long acted as master of ceremonies on his new outlet's touring revues before recording 'Devil With The Blue Dress On' in 1964 for the Motown subsidiary Soul. The singer's slow, blues-based interpretation was not a hit, but the song became successful in the hands of **Mitch Ryder** and **Bruce Springsteen**. Long enjoyed minor chart entries with 'Function At The Junction' (1966) and 'Night Fo' Last' (1968), before reaching the US Top 5 in 1968 with a version of 'Here Comes The Judge'. His premature death as a result of a boating accident on the Detroit River robbed Motown of an ebullient talent.

● ALBUMS: *Here Comes The Judge* (Soul 1968)★★, *The Prime Of Shorty Long* (Soul 1969)★★.

Longbranch Pennywhistle

This Los Angeles-based duo is better recalled for the member's subsequent escapades. **Glenn Frey** (b. 6 November 1948, Detroit, Michigan, USA; guitar/vocals) arrived in California in 1968 where he met **J.D. Souther**, an aspiring singer-songwriter. The pair then began performing together as Longbranch Pennywhistle. They secured a record deal with the Amos label, but although pleasant, the resultant album lacked identity and distinctiveness. A contract dispute then ensued, preventing the duo from further recording and they broke up in 1971. Frey subsequently joined **Linda Ronstadt**'s backing group, from which the **Eagles** evolved, while Souther forged a successful solo career as both singer/songwriter and with the Souther-Hillman-Furay Band.

● ALBUMS: *Longbranch Pennywhistle* (Amos 1969)★★★.

Longdancer

A short-lived English folk-rock band, Longdancer were best remembered as the first professional band to feature **David A. Stewart** (b. 9 September 1952, Sunderland, England). The group grew out of a folk duo comprising Stewart and Brian Harrison, formerly with the London-based band Ball Of Yarn. The pair played clubs and support gigs in the north east of England and in 1971 recorded an EP for the local Multichord label. Soon afterwards they added further singer/guitarists Steve Sproxton and Kai Olsson and became Longdancer. In 1973, they became the first artists to sign to **Elton John**'s Rocket label, touring with John before Olsson left to be replaced by Matt Irving (keyboards) and Charlie Smith (drums). The new line-up made a second album and released an unsuccessful single, 'Puppet Man' in 1974. Shortly afterwards, Longdancer split up. Kai Olsson made a 1979 solo album for **Chrysalis** (*Crazy Love*) while Harrison and Smithplayed with folk singers **Robin** and **Barry Dransfield** before Smith joined **Blue**. Irving recorded with Philip Rambow before joining the **Lords Of The New Church** in the 80s. In 1977, Stewart would form the **Tourists** and in 1981, with **Annie Lennox**, the highly successful **Eurythmics**.

● ALBUMS: *If It Was So Simple* (Rocket 1973)★★★, *Trailer For A Good Life* (Rocket 1974)★★.

Longo, Pat

b. 11 September 1929, Passaic, New Jersey, USA. Adept on several reed instruments, Longo concentrated on alto saxophone and clarinet. During military service he played in the band of the 2nd Marine Airwing and following his discharge studied music full-time. Although intent on a career in music, throughout the 60s and into the early 70s Longo found it necessary to support himself by working in a bank. However, in 1974 and resident in Los Angeles, he decided the time was right to give up banking and just play music. He joined the **Harry James** band but had ambitions to lead his own big band. In 1979, he achieved his goal and formed a big band which quickly gained regular bookings in and around LA. In the late 70s and early 80s Longo's Super Big Band successfully blended the more traditional aspects of big band music with currently popular jazz-rock funkiness. His line-ups usually featured many of the best west coast session men and a useful handful of talented jazzmen, including **Gordon Brisker**, **Lanny Morgan**, **Bob Efford**, **Buddy Childers**, Frank Szabo and **Nick Ceroli**. Intent on developing other areas of exposure for the band, Longo has recently been involved in a television series.

● ALBUMS: *Crocodile Tears* (1980)★★★, *Billy May For President* (1982)★★★, *Chain Reaction* (1983)★★.

Longpigs

Comprising Crispin Hunt (b. London, England; vocals, guitar), Richard Hawley (guitar), Simon Stafford (bass) and Dee Boyle (b. Rotherham, Yorkshire, England; bass), Longpigs formed in Sheffield, Yorkshire, England, in 1993. Their extended gravitation towards the mainstream since that time was hindered by a series of corrupt band managers and soured recording contracts, but by 1996 the Longpigs were standing on the threshold of a national breakthrough. Chief songwriter and lyricist Hunt moved to Bradford from his native London at the age of 10, his hippie parents keen to 'commune with nature'. After a dalliance with the Catholic church and dropping out of his university philosophy studies, he moved to Amsterdam as the first stage in his plan to busk around Europe. He soon returned, and by that time had written enough material to furnish the Longpigs' debut album. It was his explicit intention to return to the rock 'n' roll grandeur of artists such as **Lou Reed**, **Iggy Pop** and the **Beatles**. He recruited former **Cabaret Voltaire** drummer Boyle, Stafford and Hawley, the group making its performance debut at local venue The Owl. An album was recorded with Gil Norton but it was then that the group had its first setback. The label in question closed its UK offices and demanded a £500,000 'release-fee', and while lawyers fought over the group's contract Hunt 'went off experimenting with drugs'. Eventually Longpigs were free to sign a new contract with **U2**'s Mother Records and re-recorded their debut album. Tours with **Echobelly**, **Supergrass** and **Radiohead** followed, while the extracted single, 'Far', reached the UK Top 40 in

February 1996. 'On And On' became another success, this time reaching the UK Top 20, before *The Sun Is Often Out* was finally released. Songs such as 'She Said' (an unlikely meeting point between the Beatles and **Nirvana**, and another chart hit), 'Lost Myself' and 'Sally Dances' confirmed the promise of the earlier singles, while the Longpigs' breakthrough was celebrated by a partisan media keen to present Hunt as a major new songwriting talent.

● ALBUMS: *The Sun Is Often Out* (Mother 1996)★★★.

Lonzo and Oscar

A vocal and instrumental comedy duo that for many years consisted of John Sullivan (b. 7 July 1917, Edmonton, Kentucky, USA, d. 5 June 1967, Nashville, Tennessee, USA; bass fiddle, guitar) and his brother Rollin Sullivan (b. 19 January 1919, Edmonton, Kentucky, USA; mandolin, guitar). The brothers toured the south as a duo in the late 30s and appeared on WTJS Jackson, Tennessee, where they worked with **Eddy Arnold**. In 1942, Rollin played on the *Grand Ole Opry* as a member of **Paul Howard**'s band, but the following year, he joined that of Eddy Arnold. A fellow band member was Ken Marvin (b. Lloyd George, 27 June 1924, Haleyville, Alabama, USA; bass fiddle, guitar) and the two men immediately resumed a comedy act that they had started at WTJS. Initially known as Cicero (Marvin) And Oscar (Rollin), they were soon renamed Lonzo And Oscar by Arnold. Dressed in ill-fitting costumes and singing novelty songs in country harmony, interspersed by inane banter (John Sullivan wrote material for them), they were a well-established act when war service intervened. After their discharge, they resumed as part of Arnold's touring show and played with him at WAVE Louisville but in 1946, Marvin retired. John Sullivan assumed the role of Lonzo and they remained as part of Arnold's group until they became regular *Opry* members in their own right in 1947. In January 1948, an **RCA**-Victor recording of 'I'm My Own Grandpa' charted to give them a major Top 5 hit on both juke-box and country charts (the song, attributed to Dwight Latham and Moe Jaffe, was based on a humorous Mark Twain anecdote). The original single was made by Ken Marvin and Rollin but the brothers later made their own version. Their partnership lasted two decades until John's death following a heart attack in 1967. During this period they maintained their *Opry* status, proved a very popular touring act and appeared frequently on network television. They recorded for several other labels including Starday, **Decca** and their own Nugget label but only achieved one further chart hit, 'Country Music Time'. Their songs varied from the sublime 'Ole Buttermilk Sky' to the ridiculous 'You Blacked My Blue Eyes Once Too Often' and 'There's A Hole In The Bottom Of The Sea'. Late in 1967, the act was re-formed when David Hooten (b. St. Claire, Missouri, USA) took over the role of Lonzo. They resumed the touring and the *Opry* shows and, recording for **Columbia**, they found some

success with 'Did You Have To Bring That Up While I Was Eating?'. The comedy continued but surprisingly, on a 1974 GRC album, the hillbilly harmony is completely missing. Some of the material may almost be classed as gospel and their fine harmony work saw them chart with the title track 'Traces Of Life'. Further recordings appeared in the early 80s on the Brylen label. The original 'I'm My Own Grandpa' appears on RCA's mid-60s compilation *Stars Of The Grand Ole Opry*.

● ALBUMS: *America's Greatest Country Comedians* (Starday 1960)★★★, *Lonzo & Oscar* i (Starday 1961)★★★, *Country Comedy Time* (Decca 1963)★★★, *Country Music Time* (Starday 1963)★★★, *Lonzo & Oscar* ii (Hilltop 1965)★★, *Mountain Dew* (Columbia 1968)★★★, *Hole In The Bottom Of The Sea* (Nugget 1969)★★★, *Traces Of Life* (GRC 1974)★★★, *Old & New Songs* (Brylen 1982)★★.

Look Twice

This Swedish hip-hop duo comprised Wincent (aka Vinny) and Crazy G., backed by their friend, writer and producer Håkan Libdo. Look Twice formed in 1992 to offer the Scandinavian world their 'positive' brand of rap music, promoting strong humane messages in their lyrics rather than self-aggrandisement or the chastising of rap peers common to American hip-hop. They specialised in a fast verbal delivery reminiscent of the UK reggae MC 'chatting' style. This was highlighted on their initial two singles for the Swedish MNW dance label, 'Shake That Rump' and 'Good Thing'. Released in 1993, both failed to secure an international audience.

Look What The Cat Dragged In - Poison

A roving party waiting to happen on eight spindly legs was this album, **Poison**'s first and finest moment. It was this record that set the standard for 80s west coast trash pop and big hair - no mean achievement for a band who valued eyeliner prices over devotion to their musical duties. At the end of the day, however, it made no difference. 'Cry Tough', 'I Want Action' and 'Talk Dirty To Me' helped them to create a truly great glam album, partly because they were obviously enjoying themselves as much as we were. These days, however, they keep talking about being taken seriously, and unsurprisingly, the magic has all gone.

● Tracks: *Cry Tough; I Want Action; I Won't Forget You; Play Dirty; Look What The Cat Dragged In; Talk Dirty To Me; Want Some, Need Some; Blame It On You; No.1 Bad Boy ; Let Me Go To The Show.*

● First released 1986

● UK peak chart position: did not chart

● USA peak chart position: 3

Looking Glass

This New Jersey, USA-based quartet was led by vocalist/guitarist Elliot Lurie (b. 19 August 1948, Brooklyn, New York, USA) with backing from Larry Gonsky (keyboards), Pieter Swerval (bass) and Jeffrey Grob (drums). Initially as a mid-heavy rock band, they played the east coast bar circuit for many months before refining their act for record company consumption. An audition for **CBS Records**' president **Clive Davis** proved successful and in 1972 the group recorded Lurie's melodic 'Brandy (You're A Fine Girl)' for the CBS subsidiary, Epic. Within a few weeks it had topped the US charts, but the group was unprepared for what was to follow. Bracketed as a soft rock act, their live act was confusingly guitar heavy and drew only lukewarm support. They continued to adopt a lighter approach on record, but their follow-up 'Jimmy Loves Mary-Anne' proved only a minor hit. Bereft of ideas, the group split and Lurie went on to pursue an unsuccessful solo career.

● ALBUMS: *Looking Glass* (Epic 1972)★★.

Looking Through A Glass Onion

Subtitled 'John Lennon In Word And Music', this one-man show consisted of 'a series of wry monologues spliced with the singer's songs, which attempted to unearth the man beneath the mythology'. It was written by the Australian-based, British-born actor John Waters, and toured successfully for two years in Australia before opening at the 600-seater newly-refurbished subterranean Criterion Theatre in London on 18 October 1993. Waters himself starred in the piece, backed by a band which included Stewart D'Arrietta on keyboards and Hamish Stewart on drums. The title image, from the song 'Glass Onion', 'seems to promise a peeling away of the layers of a crystal ball', but what actually transpires is a non-chronological narrative framework around the songs, beginning at the end with Lennon at the door of his New York apartment block watching an autograph hound coming towards him. Waters' 'exaggerated Liverpudlian twang' in the spoken passages, supplemented by a 'good bluesy voice' for the classic **Beatles** and later, subtler songs, brought him some critical appreciation, but the concept as a whole was generally considered to be 'charmless and depressing - a fraction of the real thing'. Reportedly capitalised at £160,000 and expected to make a profit after three months, closure on 1 January 1994 presumably resulted in a small loss.

Loop

Along with **Spacemen 3**, Loop, from Croydon, London, England, proved to be the UK's answer to the onslaught of harsh, guitar-wielding acts that dominated the late 80s independent scene. Like the Spacemen, Loop refined fuzz-laden, pulsing guitar riffs, monotonous vocals and distinctive drum patterns to build bruised and intimidating soundscapes. An uncompromising blend of late 60s Detroit rock (**Stooges** and **MC5**) and Germany's early 70s *avant garde* (**Can** and **Faust**), the result was a dense, brooding mantra-like noise, not unlike early **Hawkwind**. Loop have always revolved around singer and guitarist Robert Wills (b. Robert Hampson), who formed the band with his wife, drummer Bex, and bassist Glen Ray in 1986. After the garage-like feedback on '16 Dreams' began their

recording legacy in 1987, Bex was replaced by John Wills, who introduced a harder, rhythmic sound. This was further strengthened when James Endicott joined as second guitarist, after the reverberating psychedelia of 'Spinning' set the scene for Loop's impressive debut, *Heavens End*, in November. Alongside a cover version of **Suicide**'s 'Rocket USA' came a barrage of layered guitar noise, awash with distortion and wah-wah. With a new bassist, Neil McKay, Loop moved to Midlands label Chapter 22 for April 1988's dynamic 'Collision', backed by a cover version of the **Pop Group**'s 'Thief Of Fire'. After the departure of Endicott, and the Head label's compilation of their singles on *The World In Your Eyes* in August, Loop released *Fade Out* in November. Its sparser, more discordant sound pushed the Can influence to the fore. A cover version of Can's hypnotic magnum opus, 'Mother Sky', appeared on the b-side of 'Black Sun' the following month. After a quiet year, Loop ended 1989 with the powerful 'Arc-Lite', their first single for Situation Two and with new guitarist Scott Dawson. Chapter 22 signalled their departure with another collection of two 12-inch singles, but this time, Loop publicly denounced the set. *A Gilded Eternity*, in 1990, again fared well commercially, and moved further towards ethereal soundscapes and away from the aggression of *Fade Out*. With only *Wolf Flow*, a double set of sessions for BBC disc jockey **John Peel**, appearing in 1991, it was announced that the band had split. Hampson and Scott formed Main, while McKay and John Wills started the Hair And Skin Trading Company.

● ALBUMS: *Heavens End* (Head 1987)★★★, *Fade Out* (Chapter 22 1988)★★★, *A Gilded Eternity* (Beggars Banquet 1990)★★★★.

● COMPILATIONS: *The World In Your Eyes* (Head 1988)★★★, *Eternal - The Singles 1988* (Chapter 22 1989)★★★, *Wolf Flow* 1987-90 recordings (Reactor 1991)★★★.

Loop Guru

The listening tastes of spokesman Jal Muud (South American pipe music, Morrocan indigenous sounds) has informed the career of Nation Records' Loop Guru. Together with Salman Gita he forms the core of the band, aided by up to 10 guest musicians for various events (who include former **Pigbag** drummer Chip Carpenter and percussionist Mad Jym). The duo have been involved in music since 1980 when they were early members of the Megadog enclave, meeting through mutual friend Alex Kasiek (**Trans-Global Underground**). It was at this time that Jamuud: '. . . stopped listening to Western music altogether. I found that the wealth of sound and mood in Asian and African music was vastly more alive than its Western counterparts.' Offering their listeners 'total enlightenment through music', Loop Guru have perfected a package of chants, laments, tablas, Eastern religion and ethnic samples, which was first brought to the public's attention via their *Sus-San-Tics* EP, which featured the guest vocals of Sussan Deheim (b. Iran). A debut album was recorded, its title, *Duniya*, translating from Urdu as 'The World'. Part of the methodology evolved from **Brian Eno**'s 'Choice Cards' ethos, wherein different instructions on musical structure are carried out via the turn of a set of cards. It placed them at the forefront of the 'world dance' movement. Arguably their most effective and popular single to date has proved to be 'Paradigm Shuffle', which included at its core Martin Luther King's 'I Have A Dream' speech.

● ALBUMS: *Duniya* (Nation 1994)★★★, *Amrita ... All These And The Japanese Soup Warriors* (North South 1995)★★★, *Catalogue Of Desires Volume 3* (North South 1996)★★★, *Peel To Reveal* (Strange Fruit 1996)★★★, *Loop Bites Dog* (North South 1997).

Loose Ends

Formed in 1982 by Jane Eugene, Steve Nichol and Carl McIntosh, Loose End (as they were originally known) were the first all-black British band to be signed to the **Virgin** label. After several unsuccessful singles they changed their name to Loose Ends, enlisted producer Nick Martinelli, and started to make an impression on the soul/dance scene with a series of excellent releases. Their major breakthrough came with the Top 20 singles 'Hangin' On A String (Contemplating)' and 'Magic Touch', and their second album *So Where Are You*, featuring backing vocals by American singer Joanna Gardner. Subsequent singles and albums were not as successful, but they developed a busy sideline as songwriters and producers (**Juliet Roberts**, **Five Star**, Lavine Hudson). Following the disbandment of the original line-up, McIntosh returned in 1990 with new members Linda Carriere and Sunay Suleyman, breaking into the Top 20 with 'Don't Be A Fool'.

● ALBUMS: *A Little Spice* (Virgin 1984)★★★, *So Where Are You* (Virgin 1985)★★★, *Zagora* (Virgin 1986)★★★, *The Real Chuckeeboo* (Virgin 1988)★★★, *Look How Long* (Ten 1990)★★.

Loose Gravel

Loose Gravel were formed in San Francisco, California, USA, in the early-70s by Mike Wilhelm (guitar/vocals; ex-**Charlatans**), Kenny Sreight (bass) and Gene Rymer (drums). The line-up also sometimes featured Chris Wilson, later of the **Flamin' Groovies**. Several tracks they recorded between 1971 and 1972 were later released on Wilhelm's self-titled debut, eventually issued in 1976. These included a searing version of 'Styrofoam', later popularised by pub-rockers **Ducks DeLuxe**. Michael Deryckx (bass) and Rol Gjano (drums) then joined Wilhelm and together they recorded two privately-pressed singles, 'Frisco Band' and 'Gravel Rash'. However, Wilhelm folded the band in 1976 when he joined the Flamin' Groovies. He remained in the line-up for seven years, after which he resumed a low-key solo career that included the album *Mean Ol' Frisco* in the late 80s. Loose Gravel's *Thanks For The Memories* meanwhile combines three studio

tracks with a live set recorded at the Coffee House, Long Beach, California, in 1976.

● ALBUMS: *Wilhelm* (United Artists/ZigZag 1976)★★★, *Thanks For The Memories* (Bucketfull Of Brains 1992)★★★.

Loose Tubes

Appearing on the London scene in 1984 this big (20-piece plus) band appealed to (and reflected) the new, smart young audience jazz was attracting at the time, and seemed likely to prove a considerable 'crossover' success. It was run as a collective, although trombonist Ashley Slater acted as 'frontman' and **Django Bates** (b. Leon Bates, 2 October 1960, Beckenham, Kent, England) emerged as a main writer for the band. Characterized by clever arrangements, technically slick soloing and an urbane stage-presence, Loose Tubes was acclaimed by many critics and created interest in jazz among sections of the public which had not previously paid the genre any attention. It spawned several other successful units, which indulged in various styles (funk, African, soca, bebop and so on), including Human Chain, Pig Head Son, Lift, the **Iain Ballamy** Quartet, the Steve Berry Trio, the **Tim Whitehead** Band, Parker Bates Stubbs and the **Julian Argüelles** Quartet. By the early 90s the parent group had disbanded - although reunions should never be ruled out.

● ALBUMS: *Loose Tubes* (Loose Tubes 1986)★★★★, *Delightful Precipice* (Loose Tubes 1986)★★★, *Open Letter* (Editions EG 1988)★★★.

Loosegroove Records

US record label Loosegroove was formed in 1995 by two celebrated musicians and a producer. Stone Gossard, guitarist with **Pearl Jam**, was already well known, while Regan Hagar had performed in the underground band **Satchel**. The third member of the founding trio was Dennis Herring, a veteran producer with previous credits including **Throwing Muses** and **Cracker**. The intention was to provide a base for some of America's more innovative acts, who might not be able to find a recording contract elsewhere. The roster included Gossard's own side project outside of Pearl Jam, **Brad**. Brad also featured Satchel's Shawn Smith, and their debut album, *Shame*, earned early critical plaudits. Weapon Of Choice provided wild rock 'n' roll, while Prose And Concepts provided the label with some hip-hop. Critters Buggin' (featuring former Pearl Jam drummer Matt Chamberlain and three former members of **Edie Brickell And The New Bohemians**) and Devilhead were the two other primary acts at the label's launch, though more interest was focused on an album by the defunct Malfunkshun. This 10-year-old recording was by the band who later became **Mother Love Bone**, and then Pearl Jam.

Loot

Formed in Andover, Hampshire, England, the Loot began their career in the mid-60s and featured a line-up of Chris Bates (vocals), Jeff Glover (bass), Roger Pope (drums), Bruce Turner (lead guitar) and Dave Wright (guitar). Glover and Pope had formerly played in the Soul Agents, while Wright had previously been an early member of his town's most famous exports, the **Troggs**. Through Wright the group were signed to Troggs' manager **Larry Page**'s Page One label in 1966. Their debut single and most enduring song, 'Baby Come Closer', failed to excite critics and missed out on the charts. The same fate befell 'Whenever You're Ready', 'You Need Someone To Love', 'She's A Winner' (produced by Ronnie Bond of the Troggs), 'Don't Turn Around' and 'Radio City'. Lacking the rustic charm of the Troggs, but with a similarly unsophisticated approach to songwriting, by this time the group were beginning to accept that their slow progress was becoming a terminal decline. They broke up with only Glover and Pope remaining in the music industry as members of **Hookfoot**.

López, Israel 'Cachao'

b. 14 September 1918, Havana, Cuba. The name of revered bassist Cachao (who also arranges, composes and plays piano, tres, bongo, trumpet and trombone) is linked with the origins of mambo and is virtually synonymous with descarga, which was defined by pianist/bandleader **Charlie Palmieri** as having '. . . no music written. It's a soloists freedom of expression, ad-libs, an improvisation of the melody . . . whatever he (she) feels at the moment . . .' (quoted by Latin music historian Max Salazar). Leading Cuban bandleader of the 50s, Bebo Valdés said in 1991: '. . . if Cachao and **Arsenio Rodríguez** had not been born, the Cuban music of the 50s and perhaps the last 30 years, would have sounded like the music of the 30s'.

López was born to a musical family and started learning guitar when he was six years of age. When he was about eight he played guitar and bongo with Conjunto Miguel De Seste. This was followed by a stint with Ignacio Villa (who later became popular as Bola de Nieve; also see **Ernesto Lecuona**), whose band provided the music for silent films at a movie house in Guanabacoa, Havana. In 1931, he joined the Havana Symphonic Orchestra and remained a member for over 30 years. Meanwhile, López performed with the dance band of violinist Marcelino González, turning out exciting bass solos that earned him the nickname 'Cachao' (derived from 'cachandeo', meaning 'lively with joy'). Between 1934 and 1936 he worked with Ernesto Muñoz, Antonio Maria Cruz and Orquesta Antillana. In 1937, he joined La Maravilla del Siglo, a flute, strings and rhythm section band led by singer Fernando Collazo. The following year, the musicians mutinied after a row with Collazo and formed themselves into a co-operative directed by Antonio Arcaño Betancourt, which became known as Arcaño y sus Maravillas. Besides Cachao and Arcaño, membership of the band included Orestes López (Cachao's brother; b. 29 August 1908, Havana, Cuba; cello/bass/piano/composer/arranger); Enrique Jorrín (b. 1926, Cuba, d. 1988, Cuba; violin; he later joined Orquesta América, developed the cha cha chá rhythm and became a bandleader in his own right); Félix Reina (violin; he went on to work with Orquesta América, **José Fajardo** and lead Estrellas Cubanas); Elizardo Aroche (violin); Jesús López (piano); Ulpiano Díaz (timbales) and Oscar Pelegrin (güiro). The band, along with other flute and strings outfits of the era, specialized in performing the Cuban ballroom dance form called the danzón, which was descended from 17th and 18th century French contradanza.

Amid the ongoing controversy about the creation of the mambo, Orestes López's 1938 danzón composition called 'Mambo', which had its debut performance on the radio station Mil Diez, has been cited as one of the earliest examples of the rhythm. In a 1979 interview with Erena Hernández, Orestes said: '. . . I must give Arcaño credit in the development of my mambo. When I played it for him, he blew flute montunos (improvisations) I had never heard before. His floreos (ad-libs) are what enhanced my mambo'. In addition to Orestes and Arcaño, two leading contenders for the title of likely inventor of the mambo are regarded to be **Pérez Prado** and Arsenio Rodríguez. Cachao stated his position in the debate to Max Salazar: 'Prado's mambo is different to my brother's mambo . . . he's deserved all the fame and wealth with his new sound . . . we Cubans are proud of him . . . Arcaño y su Maravillas were the first to play the mambo . . . we played it before Arsenio's diablo (his initial name for the rhythm) and we did it over the radio.' The new danzón-mambo sound took a while to gain acceptance. Inspired by Arsenio, who was the first bandleader to incorporate the conga into a trumpet-led conjunto (group/band), Arcaño added the conga of Eliseo El Colorao to his line-up in 1939. By 1943, Arcaño's band rivalled Arsenio as the top orchestra in Cuba. However, working with a popular dance band eventually took its toll on Cachao. 'In 1943, I couldn't take the pressure of arranging music, playing every day, and being on the move all day long. I was on the verge of a nervous breakdown' (quote from 'El Gran Cachao', 1991). After a break in Miami, he returned to the arduous routine. In 1948, Cachao suffered a further stress-related bout of depression and despite another respite, which included a period in New York and a stint with an American ice follies orchestra back in Cuba, he eventually quit Arcaño's band on amicable terms in 1949. Stints with Mariano Mercerón and José Fajardo followed; with the latter he played at New York's famed Palladium Ballroom in 1954.

The earliest pieces that could be described as Latin jam or descarga (which literally means 'discharge') were recorded in New York in the 40s. It is currently believed that the first descarga to be recorded in Cuba was probably 'Con Coco Poco' in 1952 by Bebo Valdés and members of the Tropicana nightclub orchestra, performing under the name of the Andres All Stars. The number was later included on the 10-inch album *Cubano* released on the Panart label. In 1956, Panart used the bait of a well-advertised 'party' to attract some of Cuba's leading musicians to a jam session for which they received a nominal payment. The participants were told that the recording being made was for private use but shortly afterwards Panart released *Cuban Jam Session Vol. 1*. The album was a huge success and was closely followed by volume two. Popular musician Julio Gutiérrez was credited as the director on both volumes. However, the extent of his involvement later became the subject of speculation. Panart continued with *Cuban Jam Session Vol. 3* directed by Niño Rivera. In 1957, Cachao organized a group to record *Cuban Jam Session In Miniature 'Descargas'* for Panart. The album, which sold well over a million copies, achieved the status of a classic and acted as the launch-pad for Cachao's widespread acclaim. Cachao followed up with further descarga releases: *Jam Sessions With Feeling* on the Maype label and *Cuban Music In Jam Session* on the Bonita label. The final volume in the Panart *Cuban Jam Session* series was provided by José Fajardo and his All-Stars. In the late 50s, Cachao reassembled the disbanded members of Arcaño y sus Maravillas for two albums of danzones on the Kubaney label. Cachao performed with **Chico O'Farill**'s Cuban All Stars on 'Descarga Numero Uno' and 'Descarga Numero Dos' for the Gema label, which were included on the various artists collection *Los Mejores Musicas de Cuba* (c.1960, reissued by Palladium Records in 1988). He played bass on *Cuban Jazz* (c.1961, aka *Sabor Cubano*) on Gema (reissued by Palladium in 1988) by percussionist Walfredo de los Reyes, who appeared on the first two Panart *Cuban Jam Session* volumes. The album also featured pianist Paquito Echavarría. Meanwhile in New York, the *Cuban Jam Session* releases inspired the first in a series of Latin jam albums by the Alegre All-Stars in 1961. Descarga recordings by other New York-based artists and bands followed, including albums by **Kako**, **Johnny Pacheco**, percussionist Osvaldo 'Chi Hua Hua' Martínez, Tico All-Stars, Cesta All-Stars, Salsa All-Stars, Fania All Stars and SAR All Stars.

In 1963, Cachao took up residence in New York and was initially desperate for work. Charlie Palmieri persuaded his regular bassist to stand down for a while (he had gigs with other bands available) so that Cachao could step-in to earn some money. Stints with various bandleaders followed, including Johnny Pacheco, **Tito Rodríguez**, **Candido**, **Eddie Palmieri**, Julio Gutiérrez, Lou Pérez, George Hernández and Pupi Campo (he worked with the latter two in Las Vegas), before he relocated to Miami. Rodríguez paid tribute to him with the track 'Descarga Cachao' on his 1964 release *Tito Tito Tito*. Cachao received the opportunity to record with the Alegre All-Stars in 1965. **Al Santiago** explained: '. . . we decided to do a tribute to **Noro Morales** and we called it the Kako After Hours Orchestra; picking up the musicians at five in the morning after everyone was done with their regular gigs. We had Cachao there, and Bobby Rodríguez, one played one side of the record and one played the other! . . .' (quote from 1990 interview with Nancy

Rodríguez). He appeared on recordings by the Tico All-Stars in 1966, at New York's Village Gate, and in 1974 at Carnegie Hall. Cachao again shared bass playing chores with Bobby Rodríguez on 1968's *Salsa All-Stars* produced by Al Santiago.

Cachao appeared at the memorable March 1977 *Lo Dice Todo* (*This Says It All*) concert at the Avery Fisher Hall, New York. Shortly afterwards, some of the musicians who participated in the concert, such as Charlie Palmieri; Don Gonzalo Fernández (flute); **Pupi Legarreta**, **Alfredo de la Fé** and Eddie Drennon (violins); and Chi Hua Hua and Rolando Valdés (percussionists), were amongst the personnel on Cachao's *Cachao y su Descarga '77 Vol. 1* and *Dos, Vol. 2* on Salsoul Records. In 1981, Cachao collaborated with Walfredo de los Reyes, Paquito Echavarría and Cuban percussionist Tany Gil on the Latin jam oriented *Walpataca* on the Miami-based Tania Records label. In 1986, he led a descarga group on *Maestro de Maestros/Israel López 'Cachao' y su Descarga '86* also on the Tania label, which included José Fajardo, de los Reyes and Echavarría. In November 1987, Cachao journeyed to New York to perform at a tribute to him at Hunter College Auditorium, which featured **Tito Puente**, Charlie Palmieri, Pupi, José Fajardo, **Alfredo 'Chocolate' Armenteros**, saxophonist/violinist José 'Chombo' Silva, trombonist Barry Rogers and others. During his years in New York and Miami, Cachao sessioned on albums by a string of artists and bands, including Carlos 'Patato' Valdez and Eugenio Arango 'Totico', Candido, **Hubert Laws**, Eddie Palmieri, **Mongo Santamaría**, Lou Pérez, Pedro Rafael Chaparro, Héctor Rivera, Charlie Palmieri, Chano Montes, Pepe Mora, Hernán Gutiérrez, Ñico Rojas, La India de Oriente, **Roberto Torres**, Hansel And Raúl and **Grupo Niche**. He also performed with the Miami Symphony Orchestra.

● ALBUMS: *Cuban Jam Sessions In Miniature 'Descargas'* (1957)★★★, *Jam Session With Feeling* (1958)★★★, *Con El Ritmo De Cachao* (1959)★★★, aka *Cachao y su Típica*, *El Gran Cachao* (1959)★★★★, aka *Cachao y su Típica Vol. 2*, *Cuban Music In Jam Session* (1961)★★★, with Arcaño y sus Maravillas *Danzón Mambo* (1974),★★★ *Arcaño y sus Maravillas 1944-47/La Radiofonica* (1976)★★★★; *Cachao y su Descarga '77 Vol. 1* (1977)★★★, *Dos, Vol. 2* (1977)★★★, *Walpataca* (1981)★★★, *Maestro de Maestros/Israel López 'Cachao' y su Descarga '86* (1986)★★.

Lopez, Trini

b. Trinidad Lopez III, 15 May 1937, Dallas, Texas, USA. Trini Lopez took folk songs and rocked them up into Latin rhythms, recording 14 chart albums and 13 chart singles between 1963 and 1968. Propelled by a strong R&B-influenced backbeat (usually provided by bassist Dave Shriver and drummer Gene Riggio) and his own incessantly rhythmic guitar, Lopez was at his best when playing live. A number of his nightclub performances were recorded and released as albums. Lopez listened to R&B music while growing up, and formed his first band in Wichita Falls, Texas, at the age of 15. At the recommendation of **Buddy Holly**, Lopez went to the producer **Norman Petty** in Clovis, New Mexico, but Lopez did not record with him as Petty wanted to record only instrumental music. In 1958, however, Petty did secure Lopez and his group the Big Beats a contract with **Columbia Records**, which released the single 'Clark's Expedition'/'Big Boy', ironically, an instrumental. Lopez made his first solo recording, his own composition 'The Right To Rock', for the Dallas-based Volk Records, and then signed with King Records in 1959, recording more than a dozen singles for that label, none of which charted. In late 1962, after the King contract expired, Lopez followed up on an offer by producer **Snuff Garrett** to join the post-Holly **Crickets** as vocalist. After a couple of weeks of auditions in Los Angeles that idea did not bear fruit and Lopez formed his own group.

He landed a steady engagement at the nightclub PJ's, where his audience soon grew. He was heard there by **Frank Sinatra**, who had started his own label, **Reprise Records**, and who subsequently signed Lopez. He was placed with arranger/producer **Don Costa**, who wisely chose to record Lopez in concert at the club. His first album, *Trini Lopez At PJ's*, rose to number 2 in the summer of 1963 and stayed in the US charts for nearly two years. The first single from the album, an uptempo party-like version of **Pete Seeger**'s 'If I Had A Hammer', reached number 3 (number 4 in the UK), out-performing **Peter, Paul And Mary**'s more sedate rendering a year earlier. Lopez's subsequent recordings for Reprise displayed a musical eclecticism - he recorded a folk album, an R&B album, two Latin albums, country, in foreign languages (Spanish and German) and even Broadway show tunes, all in his infectiously simple singalong style. Only one other Top 20 single resulted, 'Lemon Tree' in 1965, and he appeared in a number of films, including *The Dirty Dozen* and *Marriage On The Rocks*, but by the end of the 60s Lopez had largely disappeared from public view. He recorded sporadically in the 70s, including *Viva* and a number of singles for **Capitol Records** in 1971-72, and *Transformed By Time* for Roulette Records in 1978, and although he continued to sing in Las Vegas during the 80s little has been heard from Lopez since his heyday. There are numerous budget-label album releases of his music available, and several anthologies on European labels.

● ALBUMS: *Teenage Love Songs* (King 1963)★★, *Trini Lopez At PJ's* (1963)★★★★, *More Of Trini Lopez* (King 1964)★★, *More Trini Lopez At PJ's* (1963)★★★, *On The Move* (1964)★★★, *The Latin Album* (1964)★★★, *Live At Basin St. East* (1964)★★★, *The Folk Album* (1965)★★, *The Love Album* (1965)★★★, *The Rhythm & Blues Album* (1965)★★, *The Sing-Along World Of Trini Lopez* (1965)★★★, *Trini* (1966)★★★, *24 Songs By The Great Trini Lopez* (King 1966)★★, *The Second Latin Album* (1966)★★★, *Trini Lopez In London* (1967)★★★, *Now!* (1967)★★★, *It's A Great Life* (1968)★★★, *Trini Country* (1968)★, *Viva* (1972)★★,

Transformed By Time (Roulette 1978)★★.
● COMPILATIONS: *Greatest Hits!* (1966)★★★, *La Bamba - 28 Greatest Hits* (1988)★★★.

Lopez, Vincent

b. 30 December 1898, New York City, New York, USA, d. 20 September 1975, North Miami, Florida, USA. The celebrated pianist and leader of a highly popular 'sweet style' danceband, Lopez originally intended to go into the church, and also tried his hand as a businessman. However, his father was a bandsman in the US Navy, and urged his son into a musical career, apparently forcing him to practice incessantly. He had his first professional job when he was 17-years-old and by 1916 was leading his own band at the prestigious Pekin Restaurant. By 1921, he was bandleading at the Statler Hotel where his was among the first dance bands to receive national fame through remote radio link-ups (outside broadcasts). Lopez became a national name, his opening remark, 'Hello everybody, Lopez speaking,' appealing to the public. During the 20s the band appeared in the Broadway musicals *Love Birds*, **Greenwich Village Follies** *Of 1924*, and **Earl Carroll's Vanities** *Of 1928*, and the early movie musical **The Big Broadcast** *Of 1932*. Among his many record hits, from 1922 to 1939, were 'Nola' (his theme tune), 'Teasin'', 'I'm Just Wild About Harry', 'I Want To Be Happy', 'Show Me The Way To Go Home', 'Always', 'Hello, Bluebird', 'My Angel (Angela Mia)', and 'There's Honey On The Moon Tonight'. He and his band appeared at the Hippodrome in London but it was as a stalwart of radio and the plush hotel circuit in America that he was best noted. In 1941, he took the band into New York's Hotel Taft where he remained for 25 years. From 1949, he appeared regularly on television. Among the well known musicians and vocalists who played and sang with the Lopez band at various stages of their careers were **Glenn Miller**, **Artie Shaw** and **Xaviar Cugat**, and **Betty** and **Marion Hutton**. Defying the radical changes that took place in popular music over the years, Lopez led his band into the 70s
● FURTHER READING: *Lopez Speaking*, V. Lopez.

Lora Logic

London art student Susan Whitby originally adopted the pseudonym Lora Logic during her stint as saxophonist in **X-Ray Spex**. After leaving that group following their debut single, she soon re-emerged in 1978 with her own outfit, **Essential Logic**, who quickly recorded a couple of hard-edged EPs, *Aerosol Burns* and *Wake Up*. One album was recorded, *Beat Rhythm News* (1979), before Lora commenced on a series of solo recordings in 1981. Her quirky, occasionally arresting, vocals were in evidence on her sole album, *Pedigree Charm*, and she can also be heard on a number of recordings by other artists including the **Raincoats**, **Stranglers**, **Swell Maps** and **Red Crayola**.
● ALBUMS: *Pedigree Charm* (Rough Trade 1982)★★.

Lorber, Jeff

b. 4 November 1952, Philadelphia, USA. Lorber started playing the piano when he was four and played in local R&B bands while he was still at school. While studying at the **Berklee College Of Music** in Boston he came under the influence of **Herbie Hancock** and his contemporaries. When he left Berklee he studied privately with **Ran Blake**. In 1979, he moved to Portland, Oregon and taught improvisation at Lewis and Clark College. In 1977, he had recorded *Jeff Lorber Fusion* and in 1979 he was able to form a band of the same name. Lorber's compositions are characterized by syncopated, chromatic melody and modal writing which facilitated a funk style. In the early 80s he started singing on record and playing the guitar and his music incorporated increasing pop elements.

● ALBUMS: *Jeff Lorber Fusion* (1977)★★★★, *Soft Space* (1978)★★★, *Water Sign* (1978)★★★, *Jeff Lorber Fusion* (1979)★★★★, *Wizard Island* (1979)★★★, *Galaxian* (1980)★★★, *Its A Fact* (1981)★★, *In The Heat Of The Night* (1983)★★, *Step By Step* (1984)★★, *Worth Waiting For* (1993)★★★, *State Of Grace* (Verve 1996)★★★.

Lord Creator

b. Kentrick Patrick, *c*.1940, San Fernando, Trinidad, West Indies. As his imperious name suggests, Lord Creator began his career as a calypso singer. Some time in the mid- to late 50s he arrived in Jamaica, just as the music scene was starting to take off. Lord Creator's smooth, honeyed tones were not ideal for the raucous jump to R&B soon to emerge from **ska**, but as a big band crooner in Jamaica, he had no equal. 'Evening News' (1959) was his first huge hit, and it was a song to which he returned at several points during his career. The narrative of a barefoot child feeding his siblings by selling newspapers he could not even read, had greater resonance at a time when Jamaica was struggling for its independence. In 1962 his 'Independent Jamaica' was the first single on the **Island** label in the UK, although legend has it that **Owen Gray**'s 'Twist Baby', scheduled as Island 002, reached the shops first. 'Don't Stay Out Late' (1963) was a major Jamaican hit, and made Lord Creator the island's biggest star at the time. 'Little Princess' (1964) helped to maintain his status. He also released a calypso album for the **Studio One** label. However, he was overtaken by other smooth voices such as **Ken Boothe** and **Bob Andy**, both of whom offered more contemporary songs. In 1969, he teamed up with producer **Clancy Eccles** and recorded the single 'Kingston Town', perhaps the finest sentimental reggae record ever released. By this time, Creator was in financial trouble and a week after recording the record, he borrowed $30 from Eccles. A couple of months later, Eccles spotted Creator in a Kingston street and the singer ran off. Eventually, Eccles caught him, and Creator immediately began to make excuses for not paying back the money he owed; Eccles explained that he owed Creator $1,000 in royalties for 'Kingston Town'. The record sold thousands of copies in Britain

without ever making the charts. During the 70s, Lord Creator's croon became obsolete in a reggae music obsessed with roots, Rasta and heavy dub. He did record one powerful single in 1977, 'Life', a new version of a 1967 single, 'Such Is Life'. During the 80s rumour had it that Lord Creator had succumbed to a life as a homeless rum-drinker on the streets of Kingston, and eventually Eccles helped to organize enough money for Creator to be returned to his family in Trinidad. In 1989 **UB40** covered 'Kingston Town', and Clancy Eccles and Creator were recruited to give their seal of approval in the accompanying video. While it seems sadly ironic that he never had the hit he deserved with his own version, at least UB40's success meant that a royalty cheque would go to the song's creator.

● ALBUMS: *Songs My Mother Never Taught Me* (Port O Jam 1964)★★★★, *Big Bamboo* (Dynamic 1974)★★★★.

Lord Rockingham's XI

Scottish bandleader Harry Robinson and his band assumed the pseudonym of Lord Rockingham's XI (after a genuine historical character) to appear on the **Jack Good** UK television pop programme *Oh Boy*, playing 'novelty' rock instrumentals. Other key members were Chery Wainer (organ), and Red Price (saxophone) as well as renowned British rock 'n' roll drummer Rory Blackwell, the former two of which would feature in their own spots on *Oh Boy*. The first release was 'Fried Onions' in May 1958, but in September **Decca** released the Robinson-penned 'Hoots Mon', complete with Scottish cries of 'Hoots mon, there's a moose in the hoose!'. It was a UK number 1 hit but the follow-up, 'Wee Tom', only made number 16. They featured on an *Oh Boy* EP but after a further attempt to have a hit with 'Ra Ra Rockingham' failed, Robinson reverted to more straightforward orchestra names such as Harry Robinson's XV and the Robinson Crew. He later revived the Lord Rockingham moniker in an attempt to cash in on the 1962 Twist phenomenon with 'Newcastle Twist'/'Rockingham Twist'. **Benny Green** played tenor sax with Rockingham before he realized he could make more money writing and talking about jazz than performing. He is now a respected author and broadcaster, but still plays saxophone semi-professionally. Robinson was later involved with another UK number 1 when he provided the musical accompaniment to **Millie**'s 'My Boy Lollipop'.

Lord, Bobby

b. 6 January 1934, Sanford, Florida, USA. Lord's singing career began in his teens, singing jazz on **Paul Whiteman**'s New York television show. With the intention of pursuing a medical career, he returned to Florida to study at the University of Tampa, but a casual appearance on television prompted a change of mind, and in 1953, he was hosting *Bobby Lord's Homefolks Show* on television. He moved to Springfield, Mississippi, in the late 50s, as a member of **Red Foley**'s *Jubilee USA*. He gained a number 10 US country hit in

1956, with his **Columbia** recording, 'Without Your Love'. In 1960, he became a member of the *Grand Ole Opry* in Nashville and began to appear on other major televised country shows. In the early 60s, he recorded for Hickory, achieving a number 21 in 1964 with his self-penned 'Life Can Have Meaning'. In 1965, he was given his own syndicated televised *Bobby Lord Show*, which ran for some years. Between 1968 and 1971, he scored seven further chart hits when recording for **Decca Records**. The biggest was 'You And Me Against The World', a number 15 in 1970, and the last was the prophetically titled 'Goodbye Jukebox', a number 75 and his only 1971 hit. In 1969, he wrote *Hit The Glory Road*, a book that looked at religion and country music. He eventually returned to Florida and supervised his business enterprises, including property. He continued to make limited appearances at local venues and sometimes, when in Nashville, even played on the *Opry*.

● ALBUMS: *The Bobby Lord Show* (Hickory 1965)★★, *Bobby Lord* (Decca 1970)★★.

● COMPILATIONS: *Bobby Lord's Best* (Harmony 1964)★★★.

● FURTHER READING: *Hit The Glory Road!*, Bobby Lord.

Lord, Mary Lou

b. Salem, Massachusetts, USA. Singer/ songwriter Lord began her career by toiling as a busker in the public parks and subways of London, Boston and San Francisco, befriending **Shawn Colvin** in the process. Having attended the **Berklee College Of Music** for one year, she then studied sound engineering in England. Her debut single, 'About A Boy', on Kill Rock Stars Records, was seen by many as a reference to Kurt Cobain of **Nirvana**. Cobain's widow, Courtney Love of **Hole**, used the press to slam Lord for cashing in her musical career on the back of an alleged 'affair' with Cobain. The slanging match continued in both the US and UK press for some time thereafter. Undeterred, Lord's debut album included contributions from **Juliana Hatfield** and members of **Helium** on 'The Lights Are Changing', plus a version of the **Bevis Frond**'s 'He'd Be A Diamond'. Many wondered if the lyrics to 'That Kind Of Girl': 'All of her ex's, they could form a band', were a direct rebuff to Love. However, the words were actually written by Matt Keating. Of more interest was her own composition, 'His Indie World', in which she berated her boyfriend for spending too many hours listening to deliberately obscure indie bands (many of which are mentioned by name) instead of paying her attention. The final pay-off line came when she pledged her personal allegiance to 'Joni, Nick, Neil and Bob', an obvious if slightly optimistic summation of her own style.

● ALBUMS: *Mary Lou Lord* (Kill Rock Stars 1995)★★★, *Got No Shadow* (Work 1998)★★★.

Lordan, Jerry

b. Jeremiah Patrick Lordan, 30 April 1934, London, England, d. 24 July 1995. After leaving the Royal Air Force in 1955, Lordan sought work as a comedian before forming a short-lived duo, Lee And Jerry Elvin. During this unsatisfying time he was busy writing songs, and one of his demos, 'A Home, A Car And A Wedding Ring', with **Emile Ford** guesting on piano, became a minor US hit for **Mike Preston**. When **Anthony Newley** took Lordan's 'I've Waited So Long' to number 3 in the UK, the composer was signed as a soloist by **Parlophone**. Five low-ranking Top 50 hits in the first six months of 1960 confirmed Lordan's promise but it was as a songwriter for other people that he shone. His biggest solo hit was 'Who Could Be Bluer?' The shimmering 'Apache' gave the **Shadows** a momentous UK number 1, while Jorgen Ingmann almost achieved the same position in the USA. Thereafter, Lordan was lauded as the great composer of many instrumentals, enjoying chart toppers with the Shadows' 'Wonderful Land', and **Jet Harris And Tony Meehan**'s 'Diamonds'. He still wrote lyrics for artists including **Cleo Laine**, **Petula Clark**, **Matt Monro**, **Shane Fenton** ('I'm A Moody Guy' and 'Walk Away') and one-hit-wonder Louise Cordet ('I'm Just A Baby'). At the end of the 60s, two more Lordan hits were high in the charts, courtesy of **Cilla Black** ('Conversations') and **Cliff Richard** ('Good Times'). After an all too brief recording comeback in 1970 with 'Old Man And The Sea', which was rumoured to have sold only two hundred copies, Lordan's musical career ended and he ceased writing altogether. Following a spell as an alcoholic he suffered serious mental problems. During the 70s his financial problems prompted him to sell the copyrights to most of his major songs. In the 80s his personal life improved and he started to write songs once again as a hobby. The Shadows recognized his massive contribution to their career and **Bruce Welch** participated during the memorial service.

● ALBUMS: *All My Own Work* (Parlophone 1960)★★.

Lords

Formed in 1959 as the Skiffle Lords, this German act dropped the prefix four years later, upon adopting a style more in keeping with British beat. In September 1964 they won a 'Battle Of The Bands' contest at Hamburg's famed *Star Club*, the prize for which was a recording contract. Although their debut single, 'Hey Baby, Lass Den Ander'n', was sung in German, subsequent releases featured their highly stylized version of English. However, despite a lack of subtlety, 'Shakin' All Over', 'Poor Boy' and 'Boom Boom' were highly accomplished. The Lords - Ulrich Gunther (vocals), Rainer Petry (guitar), Klaus-Peter Lietz (guitar), Knud Kuntze (bass) and Peter Donath (drums) - were later viewed as Germany's leading group and successful tours of other European countries ensued. In 1965, Kuntze was replaced by Bernd Zamulo, but the promise of their early work was undermined by increasingly substandard fair, including 'Have A Drink On Me' (1966), 'John Brown's Body' and 'Gloryland' (both 1967). The Lords nonetheless embraced psychedelia with *Ulleogmamaxbe*, but having failed to revive their reputation, were supplanted by newer, progressive rock acts. The group has been revived on several occasions to exploit the nostalgia market.

● ALBUMS: *In Black And White, In Beat In Sweet* aka *Deutschland's Beatband Nr. 1* (1965)★★, *2 - Shakin' All Over* (1966)★★★, *Some Folks By The Lords* (1967)★★★, *Good Side Of June* (1967)★★★, *Ulleogmamaxbe* (1968)★★, *Shakin' All Over '70* (1970)★★.

Lords Of The New Church

This rock band was made up of several well-known personalities, and was often described as a punk 'super-group'. The personnel was: Brian James (b. 18 February 1961; guitar, ex-**Damned**), **Stiv Bators** (b. 22 October 1956, Cleveland, Ohio, USA; vocals, ex-**Dead Boys**; Wanderers), Dave Treganna (b. 1954, Derby, England; bass, ex-**Sham 69**; Wanderers) and drummer Nicky Turner (b. 4 May 1959; ex-**Barracudas**). When **Jimmy Pursey** left Sham 69, the rest of the band had continued in the Wanderers, drafting in Stiv Bators. It was at this point that James contacted Bators with a view to setting up a group. Miles Copeland took on their management, their name coming from his original suggestion, Lords Of Discipline. They made their live debut in Paris in 1981. Their debut vinyl, 'New Church', helped to increase criticisms about the band's apparent blasphemy, hardly dispelled when the album appeared with lines such as: 'Greed and murder is forgiven when in the name of the Church'. The self-titled debut premiered an authentic rock band with dark shades, flirting with apocalyptic and religious imagery. The single, 'Dance With Me', from *Is Nothing Sacred?*, gained several **MTV** plays with a video directed by Derek Jarman. Unfortunately its success was scuppered after mistaken allegations about paedophilia saw it taken off air. Their final studio album, *Method To Our Madness*, revealed a band treading water with stifled heavy rock routines. They did not split officially until 1989, but before that Treganna had departed for Cherry Bombz, while Alistair Ward contributed some guitar.

● ALBUMS: *Lords Of The New Church* (IRS 1982)★★, *Is Nothing Sacred?* (IRS 1983)★★★, *Method To Our Madness* (IRS 1984)★★, *Live At The Spit* 1982 recording (Illegal 1988)★★.

● COMPILATIONS: *Killer Lords* (IRS 1985)★★★.

● VIDEOS: *Holy War* (JE 1994).

Lords Of The Underground

Based in Newark, New Jersey, USA, Lords Of The Underground came to prominence via tours with **Cypress Hill** and **Funkdoobiest**, with whom their music shares more than a passing acquaintance. The group first met at college where all the band were majoring in radio communication. The frontmen are Doitall and Mr Funke (aka Mr Funky). The former also has acting interests, taking his first role in the film *The School Game*. They are backed by their DJ, Lord Jazz. Doitall and Mr Funke were originally solo artists,

collaborating for the first time on a cut called 'Psycho'. 'Flow On' was eventually issued as a single, remixed by **Pete Rock**, while the debut collection was produced by **Marley Marl**. They have also been responsible for fostering the career of Rated R.

● ALBUMS: *Here Come The Lords* (Pendulum/Elektra 1993)★★★.

Lords, Traci

US actor Traci Lords made her recording debut as guest vocalist on the **Manic Street Preachers**' 'Little Baby Nothing'. For her solo career she signed to the Los Angeles, California-based Radioactive Records label, enlisting some high-profile musical personnel to back her on her debut album, *1000 Fires*. The participants included Mike Edwards (**Jesus Jones**), Tom Bailey and Alannah Currie (**Thompson Twins**) and Ben Watkins (**Juno Reactor**). The latter penned 'Control', which reached number 2 in the *Billboard* Dance Charts before the album's release. Lords' peculiar story began in the late 80s with an under-age porn career that ended in a well-publicized drug overdose. She emerged from the wreckage with the help of therapy and began to attend acting and vocal classes. Appearances in a variety of film and television shows, including *Roseanne* and *Melrose Place*, saw her re-establish herself, though journalists were reluctant to let her escape the shadow of her past completely. Rather than pursue the mainstream direction that her standing now warranted, Lords and her A&R director, Brendan Bourke, opted for a techno-dance slant for *1000 Fires*. This decision followed the artist's own conversion to dance music when she came to London in 1992 on a modelling assignment.

● ALBUMS: *1000 Fires* (Radioactive 1995)★★★.

Lordz Of Brooklyn

With an obvious stylistic debt to fellow New York, USA white rappers the **Beastie Boys**, the Lordz Of Brooklyn emerged in 1995 with an impressive debut album, *All In The Family*. There were several features to distinguish the group - their Italian heritage and lyrics which betrayed a passion for the 50s rather than 90s gang culture. Their name was chosen deliberately to reflect their territorial devotion to Brooklyn, with nearly all their songs offering everyday narratives attributed to growing up in the area. A quintet of lead rapper Kaves, brother and producer Admoney, Scotty Edge, Dino Bottz and Paulie Two Times, their debut single, 'Saturday Nite Fever', typified the album's approach. Borrowing from both the Robert De Niro and Quentin Tarantino school of urban cinema, 'Saturday Nite Fever' used a sample of the **Bee Gees**' 'Staying Alive' (as well as a more traditional rap staple, **Schoolly D**'s similarly named 'Saturday Night'). The gritty simplicity of their collages of second-generation immigrant working class life were bolstered by a rough but effective musical delivery akin to DJ Muggs' work with **Cypress Hill** or **House Of Pain**. Kaves, a renowned graffiti artist, had

previously acted as warm up man for the latter group.
● ALBUMS: *All In The Family* (American 1995)★★★★.

Lore And The Legends

Lore Cayote Orion (b. Ramona, California, USA) developed an esoteric form of country music by combining Spanish influences with his love of rock music. He wrote 'That's What Made Me Love You', a US country hit for **Bill Anderson** and Mary Lou Turner. He worked as part of Bandera in the early 80s and then built up a UK following as Lore And The Legends. One UK single was released as a picture disc. Lore currently manages a dude ranch.
● ALBUMS: *One Step Ahead Of The Law* (Colt 1987)★★★, *Lore Cayote Orion* (PT 1988)★★.

Lori And The Chameleons

Formed in 1979 in Liverpool, England, the group was a vehicle for the evocative teenage singer Lori Larty. With backing, production and songwriting provided by former **Big In Japan** alumni David Balfe and **Bill Drummond**, Lori emerged with an appealing, almost spoken-word tribute to Japan (the country), entitled 'Touch'. A sparkling arrangement, the disc entered the bottom of the UK charts and appeared to signal the emergence of a new talent. The concept of the group appeared to revolve vaguely around exotic, travelogue pop, with each song title referring to a specific geographical location: Japan, Peru, Russia and the Ganges River in India. The second single, 'The Lonely Spy', boasted another impressive, atmospheric vocal from Lori and an astonishing backing that emulated the bombastic scores associated with *James Bond* films. After four superb tracks, which represented some of the best UK pop of the period, the group ceased operating. The journeyman Troy Tate reappeared in the **Teardrop Explodes**, while Drummond turned to management and was later the brains behind a series of pseudonymous groups including the **Justified Ancients Of Mu Mu** (JAMS) and the **Timelords** who later emerged as the very successful **KLF**. Lori, meanwhile, spurned imminent pop success by returning to art college and effectively retiring from the music business. Her fleeting career provided as much mystery and instant appeal as the extraordinary discs on which she appeared.

Los Bravos

Originally known as Los Sonor, Mike Kogel (b. 25 April 1945, Beuliu, Germany; vocals), Antonio Martinez (b. 3 October 1945, Madrid, Spain; guitar), Manolo 'Manuel' Fernandez (b. 29 September 1943, Seville, Spain; organ), Miguel Vicens Danus (b. 21 June 1944, Palma de Mallona, Spain; bass) and Pablo 'Gomez' Samllehi (b. 5 November 1943, Barcelona, Spain; drums) were voted Spain's top beat group following two Top 10 hits in their own country. They achieved international recognition in 1966 when 'Black Is Black', a song composed by two Englishmen, Tony Hayes and Steve Wadey, rose to number 2 in the UK charts in the wake of heavy promotion on pirate radio. The song's compulsive hookline proved equally popular in the USA where it reached number 4, but the quintet was sadly unable to repeat this success. Despite a series of superior pop performances, including an effervescent reading of an **Easybeats** composition, 'Bring A Little Lovin'', 'I Don't Care' (1966) was the group's last UK Top 20 entry.
● ALBUMS: *Black Is Black* (Press 1966)★★, *Los Bravos* aka *Bring A Little Lovin'* (Parrott 1968)★★.

Los Del Rio

By the time long-standing musical partners Raphael Ruiz and Antonio Romero reached the top of *Billboard*'s Hot 100 chart for seven weeks in the summer of 1996, they had recorded over 30 albums of traditional Spanish music. The song which produced their breakthrough was 'Macarena', which they originally released on the independent label Zafiro Records in 1994. After gaining popularity on Latin radio stations and appearing on a number of Spanish compilations it was transferred to BMG Latin for national distribution. Of the song, Romero commented: '[it] is a revelation of happiness, and that happiness is captured in the rhythm of the song. It puts the world in agreement to dance and celebrate.' It was included on the group's debut major label album, *Macarena Non Stop*, and was recorded in several languages for release in different international markets. It also served to launch the 'Macarena dance craze', culminating in a packed-house festival at the Dodger Stadium in Los Angeles.
● ALBUMS: *A Mi Me Gusta* (Zafiro 1994)★★★, *Macarena Non Stop* (BMG Latin 1996)★★★★.

Los Indios Tabajaras

Musiperi and Herundy (b. Ceara, Brazil) were sons of a Tabajaras Indian chieftain of an isolated jungle tribe. The story circulated by their publicist stated that they found guitars mislaid by European explorers, and taught themselves to play. Next, they travelled to Rio de Janiero to perform South American folk in the city's clubland where they were noticed by an agent who polished both their act and cultural education. As 'Natalicio and Antenor Lima', they toured other South American regions including Mexico before a trip to Europe where they proved particularly popular in Italy and Spain. It was, therefore, hardly surprising that, as Los Indios Tabajaras, they began recording principally for the Latin market in 1943. After 20 years, however, their instrumental revival of **Jimmy Dorsey**'s 'Maria Elena' - dedicated to the wife of a Mexican president - was issued in the USA on **RCA Records** where, with no obvious precedent, it was a huge hit. In Britain and Australia too, it reached the Top 10, but its ear-catching sound was regarded as a one-off novelty and the duo made no further impact on charts in English-speaking territories.
● ALBUMS: *Maria Elena* (RCA 1963)★★★★, *Always In My Heart* (RCA 1964)★★★.

Los Lobos

This group were leaders of the Tex-Mex brand of rock 'n' roll, which is Latin-based Chicano music built around accordion and guitar. They were formed in 1974 in Los Angeles by Cesar Rosas (b. 1954, Los Angeles, California, USA; vocals/guitar/mandolin), David Hidalgo (b. c.1954, Los Angeles, California, USA; vocals/guitar/accordion), Luis (Louie) Perez (b. c.1953, Los Angeles, California, USA; drums/guitar/quinto), Conrad Lozano (b. c.1952, Los Angeles, California, USA; vocals/bass/guitarron) and Steve Berlin (b. c.1957, Philadelphia, Pennsylvania, USA). Their mixture of **Clifton Chenier** zydeco and **Richie Valens** rock was a totally refreshing new sound. Their debut album came in 1978 with the self-financed *Just Another Band From East LA*, and although not a hit it was a critical success. The reviewers welcomed their second **How Will The Wolf Survive?** with open arms, but still it only made moderate sales. The superb title track vocal has an uncanny resemblance to **Steve Winwood**. The band continued to receive excellent reviews of their stage act, but it was not until 1987 that they found commercial success. Following their major contribution to the film soundtrack *La Bamba* the title single was released. It became an international number 1 and the first song in Spanish to top the pop charts. *La Pistola Y El Corazon* was a deliberate attempt to go back to their roots following their recent overwhelming profile. *Kiko* in 1992 was an excellent record, moving them back to a varied rock approach with delightful hints of Cajun, straight rock and even soul music. *Colossal Head* in 1996 featured ex-**Attractions** drummer Pete Thomas.

● ALBUMS: *Si Se Puede!* (Pan American 1976)★★★, *Just Another Band From East LA* (New Vista 1978)★★★, *. . . And A Time To Dance* (Slash 1983)★★★, *How Will The Wolf Survive?* (Slash 1984)★★★★, *By The Light Of The Moon* (Slash 1987)★★★★, *La Bamba* (Slash 1987)★★★, *La Pistola Y El Corazon* (Slash 1988)★★★, *The Neighbourhood* (Slash 1990)★★★★, *Kiko* (Slash 1992)★★★★, *Papa's Dream* (Warners 1995)★★★, *Colossal Head* (Warners 1996)★★★.

● COMPILATIONS: *Just Another Band From East L.A: A Collection* (Warners 1993)★★★★.

Loss, Joe

b. Joshua Alexander Loss, 22 June 1909, Spitalfields, London, England, d. 6 June 1990, London, England. One of the most popular bandleaders in the UK over a period of many years, Loss was taught to play the violin with a view to pursuing a classical career. He won a scholarship to the Trinity College of Music, and later studied at the London School of Music before forming his own band at the age of 16, playing local halls and accompanying silent movies. In 1930 he moved into London's Astoria Ballroom, and played at the Kit-Kat Club a year later. His band made its broadcasting debut in 1933, and, early in 1934, topped the variety bill at the Holborn Empire. Later that year, he returned to the Astoria for a long residency, and while there adopted 'Let's Dance At The Make Believe Ballroom' as his first proper signature tune. Also in 1934, he started recording for the Regal-Zonophone label, later part of **EMI**, and stayed with the company for over 50 years. A large part of the Loss band's popularity during the 30s was due to the many featured vocalists including Paula Greene, Betty Dale, **Adelaide Hall**, Shirley Lenner, Elizabeth Batey, Marjorie Kingsley, Monte Rey (with his big hit 'The Donkey Serenade') and especially Chick Henderson, later killed while in the Royal Navy, who recorded the very popular 'Begin The Beguine'. Some of the band's other successes were 'Woodchopper's Ball' and 'Honky Tonk Train Blues'. Loss also gave **Vera Lynn** her first broadcasting opportunity in 1935, when she sang 'Red Sails In The Sunset'. In 1940, Loss left the Astoria and went to France to play for the British Expeditionary Forces before returning to the UK, and spending the rest of World War II successfully touring the UK's ballrooms. After the war he was resident at the Hammersmith Palais, and later, during the 50s, survived the onslaught of rock 'n' roll. By this time, he also had a successful band agency. In the early 60s he had chart hits with 'Wheels Cha Cha', 'Sucu Sucu', 'The Maigret Theme', 'Must Be Madison', 'The March Of The Mods', and many bestselling albums. During the war Loss had adopted the **Glenn Miller** favourite 'In The Mood' as his theme tune, and it was his recording that featured on the Jive Bunny And The Mastermixers novelty single in 1989. His series of *World Championship Ballroom Dances* albums reflected his many appearances on BBC Television's *Come Dancing*, and the 14 Carl Alan Awards presented by the industry. During one of his annual working holidays on the QE2 in 1978, he became the first dance bandleader to play in communist China. His post-war singers included Howard Jones (the vocalist on the 1948 Loss US hit 'A Tree In A Meadow'), Larry Gretton, **Rose Brennan** (who stayed with the band for over 15 years) and Ross McManus (father of **Elvis Costello**). (McManus and Costello sang together for the first time on stage in a charity tribute to Joe Loss that was presented at the Barbican Theatre in London in 1994.) Loss played at many royal functions, including the Queen's 50th birthday celebrations and the Queen Mother's 80th birthday. The most energetic and mobile of bandleaders officially retired in 1989 after 60 years at the top. Among his many awards were an OBE in 1978, Her Majesty's Silver Medal in 1977 and a Lieutenant in the Royal Victorian Order in 1984.

● ALBUMS: *Dancing Time For Dancers, Number 11* (HMV 1957)★★★, *Dancing Time For Dancers, Number 12* (HMV 1957)★★★, *Dancing Time For Dancers, Number 13* (HMV 1958)★★★, *Dancing Time For Dancers, Number 14* (HMV 1958)★★★, *36 All-Time Hits* (HMV 1960)★★★, *Come Dancing* (HMV 1960)★★★, *Party Dance Time - Another 36 All-Time Hits* (HMV 1961)★★★, *Dancing Party* (HMV 1962)★★★, *Must Be Madison - Must Be Twist* (HMV 1963)★★★★, *Go Latin With Loss* (HMV 1964)★★★, *Latin A La Loss* (Columbia 1968)★★★, *Joe Loss Plays Glenn Miller* (MFP 1969)★★★, *Latin Like Loss* (Columbia 1970)★★★,

Play It Latin (Starline 1971)★★, *All-Time Party Hits* (MFP 1971)★★, *The Loss Concertium* (1972)★★, *Dances For The World Ballroom Championship* (Columbia 1972)★★, *Non-Stop Latin Lovelies* (EMI 1973)★★, *Joe Loss Hits The Road To Songland* (EMI 1974)★★, *Dance At Your Party* (Columbia 1975)★★, *Top Pop Party Time* (Columbia 1975)★★, *Jitterbug And Jive With Joe Loss* (EMI 1976)★★, *Swing Is The Thing* (MFP 1976)★★, *World Ballroom Championship Dances* (Note 1977)★★, *Championship Dances For The World Ballroom* (Columbia 1978)★★, *New World Championship Ballroom Dances* (Columbia 1979)★★.
● COMPILATIONS: *The Very Best Of Joe Loss And His Big Band* (Studio 2 1976)★★, *Let's Dance At The Make-Believe Ballroom 1934-40* (Retrospect 1977)★★, *50 Fabulous Years* (Note 1980)★★, *The Golden Age Of Joe Loss* (Golden Age 1985)★★, *Isn't It Heavenly* (Happy Days 1986)★★, *In A Romantic Mood* (EMI 1987)★★, *The Joe Loss Story* (EMI 1990)★★.

Lost

Formed in 1964 at Goddard College, Vermont, USA, the Lost comprised of **Willie Alexander**, Walter Powers, Ted Myers, Lee Mason and Kyle Garrahan. They subsequently moved to Boston, Massachusetts, USA, where they became part of a small, but thriving, garage band scene, headed by the **Remains**. The Remains' leader Barry Tashain produced a demo tape for the Lost which secured them a contract with **Capitol Records**. The confident punk rock-styled 'Maybe More Than You' was issued in 1965 but it was almost a year before a follow-up, 'Violet Gown', was released. Although endearing in its own right, this ballad was unrepresentative of the Lost's live sound and the disillusioned group split up in 1967. Ted Myers joined the **Ultimate Spinach** before being reunited with Garrahan in Chameleon Church. Powers and Alexander joined the **Velvet Underground** following **Lou Reed**'s departure.

Lost And Found (country)

A bluegrass group founded, in 1973, by Allen Mills (b. Allen Herman Mills, 4 November 1937, Danville, Virginia, USA; bass fiddle, guitar, vocals, MC), Gene Parker (b. 28 April 1942; banjo, guitar, vocals), Dempsey Young (b. 1 July 1954, Richmond, Virginia, USA; mandolin, guitar, banjo, bass, vocals) and Roger Handy (guitar, vocals). They soon established a reputation on the bluegrass festival circuit with their repertoire of old standards and new numbers, some penned by Mills. They recorded three albums for Outlet before moving to Rebel in 1980, where they recorded a steady series of albums until they moved to Copper Creek in 1994. There have been changes in personnel over the years which, after Handy left, led to appearances on guitar and vocals by several other musicians, in order of membership, Bubba Chandler, Steve Wilson and Ronnie Bowman. Founder-member Parker remained with the group until 1987, when Jody King became the banjoist for a time. In 1991, Barry Berrier (b. 10

October 1960, Mount Airy, North Carolina, USA; guitar, vocals) and Lynwood Lunsford (b. 31 January 1962, Roxboro, North Carolina, USA; banjo, vocals) joined founder-members Mills and Young, and continued to uphold the expected high standard of this popular bluegrass band. In 1995, Mills, Young and Parker were together again with Wilson or Steve Thomas on fiddle for another Rebel album. Mills' song 'Sweet Rosie By The River', which they recorded on *The Deal*, has become a very popular number in bluegrass music.
● ALBUMS: *First Time Around* (Outlet 1975)★★, *The Second Time Around* (Outlet 1976)★★, *The Third Time Around* (Outlet 1978)★★, *The Lost & Found* (Rebel 1980)★★, *Endless Highway* (Rebel 1982)★★, *The Sun's Gonna Shine* (Rebel 1985)★★, *The Deal* (Rebel 1987)★★, *Hymn Time* (Rebel 1988)★★, *New Day* (Rebel 1989)★★, *Bluegrass Classics* (Rebel 1991)★★★, *January Rain* (Rebel 1992)★★, *Just Pickin'* (Copper Creek 1994)★★.
● COMPILATIONS: *The Best Of Lost & Found* Outlet material (Rebel 1984)★★★, *Across The Blue Ridge Mountains* 1984-87 recordings (Rebel 1995)★★.

Lost And Found (rock)

This US group was formed in Houston, Texas in 1965 and originally known as the Misfits. The quartet - Jimmy Frost (lead guitar), Peter Black (guitar/vocals), James Harrell (bass), and Steve Webb (drums) - enjoyed a residency at the city's Living Eye Club and became friendly with the **Thirteenth Floor Elevators** following frequent trips to Austin. The latter's guitarist, **Roky Erickson**, introduced Lost And Found to the International Artists label, a debt they repaid by including the Elevator's 'Don't Fall Down' on *Everybody's Here*. Although pleasant, the album lacked incisiveness, but a later single, 'When Will You Come Through?'/'Professor Black', showed a greater sense of purpose. Lost And Found split up in 1968, although Black and Harrell resurfaced in stablemates Endle (latter Potter) St. Cloud.
● ALBUMS: *Everybody's Here* (1968)★★.
● COMPILATIONS: *Forever Lasting Plastic Words* (1988)★★.

Lost And Found - Sheila Jordan

Sheila Jordan is commonly regarded as the finest contemporary singer working within the jazz field. With a musical grounding in the bebop language of the late 40s, she single-mindedly developed her own demanding and complex style of improvisation, based on what she learned from **Charlie Parker**, but with a freer and more dramatic edge that suits the vocalist's art. This highly acclaimed 1990 date features the fabulous piano of **Kenny Barron**, her long-standing musical partner Harvie Swartz on bass and ex-**Thelonious Monk** drummer Ben Riley, and helped put Jordan back firmly in the limelight.
● Tracks: *Good Morning Heartache; Anthropology; I Concentrate On You; The Water Is Wide; Alone Together; The Very Thought Of You; Lost In The Stars; My Shining Hour/We'll Be Together Again*

- First released 1990
- UK peak chart position: did not chart
- USA peak chart position: did not chart

Lost Generation

An R&B vocal group from Chicago, Illinois, USA. The Lost Generation bucked the early 70s major trend in sweet falsetto-led vocal groups by providing a fresh sound of a dry, hard lead. The members were Lowrell Simon (lead), his brother Fred Simon, Larry Brownlee (d. 1978; ex-**CODs**) and Jesse Dean. Lowrell and Dean had previously been members of the Vondells, who had a local Chicago hit in 1964 with 'Lenore'. The Lost Generation established themselves with the 'The Sly, Slick, And The Wicked' (number 14 R&B, number 30 pop) in 1970, and although they were never able to penetrate the national pop charts again, they managed to sustain themselves on R&B hits for the next several years, notably with 'Wait A Minute' (number 25 R&B) in 1970, and 'Talking The Teenage Language' (number 35 R&B) in 1971. The group broke up after their last chart record in 1974. Lowrell Simon, under the name of 'Lowrell', went on to establish a solo career, having a solid hit with 'Mellow Mellow Right On' (number 32 R&B) in 1979. AVI released his self-titled debut the same year.

- ALBUMS: *The Sly, Slick And The Wicked* (Brunswick 1970)★★★, *Young, Tough And Terrible* (Brunswick 1971)★★.

Lost Gonzo Band

In the early 70s many country and rock musicians settled in Austin, Texas, and a key venue was the Armadillo World Headquarters. Here **Jerry Jeff Walker** recruited the musicians to back him on an album to made in Luckenbach, Texas. The album, recorded in August 1973, was called *Viva Terlingua* and the musicians were named the Lost Gonzo Band. The mainstays were **Gary P. Nunn** (keyboards, vocals) and Bob Livingston (bass, vocals), along with Michael McGeary, Herb Steiner, Craig Hillis and Kelly Dunn. The band toured with Walker for five years and cut solo albums. The line-up changed but an important addition was John Inmon (lead guitar). They did session work individually and also worked with **Ray Wylie Hubbard**. In 1990 Jerry Jeff Walker re-formed the band (Inmon, Livingston and drummer Freddie Krc) for the Gonzo Compadres. The Lost Gonzo Band has now recorded two more albums, the current personnel being Inmon, Livingston, Riley Osborne (keyboards), Tomas Ramirez (saxophone), Paul Pearcy (drums) and producer Lloyd Maines (steel guitar). They describe themselves quite accurately as 'a rock 'n' roll jazz country reggae R&B Texas roadhouse band.'

- ALBUMS: *The Lost Gonzo Band* (MCA 1975)★★★, *Thrills* (MCA 1976)★★★★, *Signs Of Life* (Capitol 1979)★★, *Rendezvous* (Amazing 1992)★★★★, *Hands Of Time* (Vireo 1995)★★★.

Lost In The Stars

Following their collaboration on *Knickerbocker Holiday* in 1938, composer **Kurt Weill** and librettist and lyricist Maxwell Anderson renewed their association more than a decade later for this show which opened at the Music Box Theatre in New York on 30 October 1949. It was a musical adaptation of Alan Paton's novel, *Cry, The Beloved Country*, which was set in apartheid South Africa, and told the powerful story of a black Anglican minister, Stephen Kumalo (Todd Duncan), whose son, Absalom (Julian Mayfield), is sentenced to hang after accidentally killing a young white man - a liberal - during an attempted robbery in Johannesburg. A few minutes before Absalom is due to die, the victim's father, James Jarvis (Leslie Banks), who is a supporter of apartheid, calls at Stephen Kumalo's house, and the two men unite in their grief. The music score reflected the show's brooding, tragic mood, and included "Thousands Of Miles', 'Cry, The Beloved Country', 'The Hills Of Ixipo', 'Train To Johannesburg', 'Stay Well', 'The Little Gray House', 'Trouble Man', 'Big Mole', 'A Bird Of Passage', 'The Wild Justice, 'Who Will Buy', and the haunting ballad, 'Lost In The Stars', which was sung in the piece by Todd Duncan, and has been recorded many times over the years by artists such as **Tony Bennett**, **Vic Damone**, **Dick Haymes**, **Frank Sinatra**, Lotte Lenya, and Singers Unlimited. It was to be Kurt Weill's last Broadway show - he died during the run of 273 performances, on 3 April 1950. Eight years later, *Lost In The Stars* entered the repertory of the New York City Opera, and, in 1972, it returned to Broadway for a month, starring Brock Peters as Stephen Kumalo. He also appeared in the 1974 film version, along with **Melba Moore**, Raymond St. Jacques, Clifton Davis, and Paula Kelly. The Long Wharf Theatre, New Haven, Connecticut, presented a 'chamber version' of the show in 1986, and the work received its UK professional premiere in a production by the New Sussex Opera at the Gardner Centre, Brighton, in 1991. Three years later, a new musical adaptation of Alan Paton's novel, by Frank Galati, was presented by the Goodman Theatre in Chicago. It used the book's title, *Cry, The Beloved Country*, and re-arranged the original score to such an extent that the Kurt Weill Foundation demanded that an apology be included in the showbill. Also in 1993, a 'fine new recording' of the score was issued, with a cast which included Arthur Woodley, Gregory Hopkins, Cynthia Clarey, Reginald Pindell, and Carol Woods, who had impressed in recent years in *Blues In The Night* and *The Goodbye Girl*.

Lost Tribe

This group from New York City, New York, USA, escape easy categorization, their armoury spanning funk, soul, hardcore punk and hip-hop. 'Our music is a reflection of who we are, where we live, and what we've been through. That has an effect on the kind of music we play. It's a very intense environment.' Comprising

David Benney (alto saxophone), Fima Ephron (bass), David Gilmore (guitar), Ben Perowsky (drums) and Adam Rogers (guitar), each contributes to the group's songwriting platform, bringing diverse personal influences to bear. Lost Tribe began by jamming in local New York clubs and Central Park, with members involved in sundry side projects. It was not until 1988 that the core of the group was cemented when Ephron, Perowsky and Rogers decided to put previous collaborations on a more permanent footing. By 1989 Binney and Gilmore had cemented the line-up. By this time members had amassed considerable and varying experience playing with **John Cale, George Russell, Me'shell NdegéOcello, Roy Ayers, Steve Coleman, Rickie Lee Jones** and **Walter Becker**, among others. The latter produced their self-titled debut album at his Maui studio. This mesh of contrasting influences was quickly followed by *Soulfish* a year later. This time working with Joseph Marciano at Brooklyn's Systems Two enclave, guests included Benny Nitze and Joe Mendelson of Rise Robots Rise, with whom Ephron, Rogers and Gilmore had formerly participated. *Soulfish* duly included several memorable songs, not least Perowsky's 'Daze Of Ol' and Rogers' 'Steel Orchards'.

● ALBUMS: *Lost Tribe* (High Street 1994)★★, *Soulfish* (High Street 1995)★★★.

Lothar And The Hand People

Although this splendidly named quintet became fixtures of New York's underground circuit, they were formed in Denver, Colorado, USA, in 1965. College drop-out John Arthur Emelin (vocals/theremin) was initially joined by Richard Lewis (rhythm guitar), Russell 'Rusty' Ford (bass) and Tom Lyle (drums), before William C. Wright (lead guitar) completed the line-up. Lewis and Wright were later replaced by Kim King (guitar) and Paul Conly (keyboards). Much attention to the group was given due to Emelin's use of the theremin, an instrument capable of eerie electronic 'cries' similar to those used in horror movies and previously heard on the **Beach Boys**' 'Good Vibrations'. Lothar headed east at the behest of the **Lovin' Spoonful** whom they supported on a provincial tour. The new arrivals quickly secured a recording deal, but the apathy that greeted their first three singles delayed a debut album. *Presenting Lothar And The Hand People* was not issued until late 1968, although its simple, folksy atmosphere recalled a more innocent era. The album was produced by Robert Margouleff who went on to form the experimental **Tonto's Expanding Headband**. A second collection, *Space Hymn*, followed within a matter of months and showed a group embracing synthesized technology. The set maintained a love of melody, but despite positive reviews, the album was not a commercial success and Lothar And The Hand People broke up in 1971.

● ALBUMS: *Presenting Lothar And The Hand People* (Capitol 1968)★★, *Space Hymn* (Capitol 1969)★★.

● COMPILATIONS: *This Is It ... Machines* (1986)★★.

Lotion

With a line-up comprising Tony Zajkowski (vocals, guitar), Bill Ferguson (bass), Rob Youngberg (drums) and Jim Ferguson (guitar), New York, USA guitar band Lotion displayed initial musical similarities to both **R.E.M.** and, particularly, the **Stone Roses**. With Lotion licensed to the UK indie label Big Cat Records from Spin-Art in the USA, their sound was more Anglophile than their typically noise-obsessed New York peers. This helped them escape accusations of being just another American guitar band, a fate that befell many other imported records of the period. *Full Isaac* received substantial attention in Britain during 1994, particularly in the small press, and preceded an appearance at that year's Reading Festival stage. The group consolidated their European reputation with touring commitments throughout 1995, leading to the release of a second album in September. This featured sleeve notes penned by reclusive author Thomas Pynchon, and a full, mature guitar sound tied to Zajkowski's world-weary lyrics. Once again, the reviews were strong, with Lotion becoming the latest in a long tradition of Americans to use Europe in general and the UK in particular to attempt to launch their careers in the face of domestic apathy. By 1997's excellent *The Telephone Album* the band must have been wondering what they had to do to sell records.

● ALBUMS: *Full Isaac* (Spin-Art/Big Cat 1994)★★★, *Nobody's Cool* (Spin-Art/Big Cat 1995)★★★, *The Telephone Album* (Spin-Art 1997)★★★.

Lotis, Dennis

b. 8 March 1925, Johannesburg, South Africa. An extremely popular singer in the UK, particularly in the 50s, with a sophisticated style that was particularly attractive to the young female population. Lotis trained for four years as a boy soprano, and won several cups and medals. He made his first stage appearance at the age of seven, and his first broadcast when he was nine. After leaving school, he worked as a bus conductor and electrician, and sang in cinemas and nightclubs in Johannesburg. When he moved to the UK in the early 50s, he carried with him a letter of introduction to **Ted Heath** from the former London saxophonist and bandleader Don Barrigo. Following a couple of broadcasts with **Henry Hall**, Lotis joined the Heath band, and, together with the other resident vocalists **Lita Roza** and **Dickie Valentine**, became one of the most popular singers on the circuit. Lotis's vocal talents were evident on such records as 'Sam's Song', 'Goodnight Irene', 'Nevertheless' and 'She's A Lady' (with Roza and Valentine). After enjoying a hit with 'Cuddle Me', he went solo, and during the late 50s toured the UK variety circuit, appeared in his first Royal Command Performances, and rejoined the Heath band for a tour of the USA, including an appearance at Carnegie Hall. He was also voted Top Male Singer in the 1957 *Melody Maker* poll. In 1956 he appeared in a touring production of the stage musical *Harmony Close* and, two years later, starred in John Osborne's *The World Of Paul Slickey*, a 'musical comedy of manners' that was poorly received in Britain. Lotis also made several films, a mixture of drama, comedy, musicals and horror, including *The Extra Day*, *It's A Wonderful World*, *City Of The Dead* and *She'll Have To Go*. Among his other stage roles was an appearance as Lucio in John Neville's Playhouse Production of Shakespeare's *Measure For Measure*. Adversely affected by the changing face of popular music, he played the working men's clubs, and ran his own antiques and restaurant businesses for a time. Eventually, in the 80s and 90s, he returned to the theatres, singing in nostalgia shows with contemporaries such as **Joan Regan** and **Russ Conway**.

● ALBUMS: *How About You?* (1958)★★★, *Bidin' My Time* (1959)★★★, *Night And Day* (1983)★★, *Get Happy* (1994)★★★.

Lottin, Eboa

b. Emanuel Eboa Lotti, 1942, Douala, Cameroon. A gifted guitarist, bass player, keyboardist and harmonica player, Lottin was a popular, albeit second division, makossa bandleader of the 70s and early 80s. He was born into a celebrated family - his father was a Cameroonian national hero and martyr of the Native Church. He also founded the African version of the musical 'Godspeil'. Lottin recorded his first single for Phillips Records in 1962, 'Mulema Mwam, Elimba Dikalo', the first of several dozen releases. As the 80s progressed he found acclaim among knowledgeable followers of African music for the dexterity of his playing and arrangements. Several international stars confirmed this standing by appearing on his 1988 album, *Musique Anti-Crise Vol. 1*, including **Nyanka Bell**, **James Brown**, **Manu Dibango** and Cameroon football star, Thomas Nkono. The subsequent *Sodome Et Gomorho* served as a tribute album to one of Cameroon's legendary music figures, **Francis Bebey**.

● ALBUMS: *Bessombe I* (1975)★★★, *Tete Youngo* (1979)★★★, *Les Trois Visages* (TG 1983)★★, *Disque D'Or* (TSI 1986)★★★, *Musique Anti-Cris Volume 1* (1988)★★★, *Sodome Et Gomorho* (1988)★★★.

Lotus Eaters

Rising from the ashes of the **Wild Swans**, Liverpool's Lotus Eaters enjoyed instant commercial success with a fragrant pop song, 'The First Picture Of You', their debut single in June 1983. Revolving around Peter Coyle (vocals) and Jeremy Kelly (guitar), plus Alan Wills (drums), Gerard Quinn (keyboards) and Phil (bass), the rhythm section was later replaced by Michael Dempsey (bass) and Steve Creese (drums). However, the band never managed to regain their Top 20 status, despite four catchy follow-ups; 'You Don't Need Someone New' later in 1983, 'Set Me Apart' and 'Out On Your Own' (both 1984) and a final attempt, 'It Hurts' (1985). Those who appreciate well-crafted, quality melodic pop should look no further than their only album, *No Sense Of Sin*, from 1984. Coyle and Kelly

later reactivated the Wild Swans but were again unable to sustain significant interest.

● ALBUMS: *No Sense Of Sin* (Sylvan 1984)★★★.

Louchie Lou And Michie One

Female duo Louchie Lou and Michie One met at a **Rebel MC** gig in 1991, and quickly found the backing of independent label **Fashion Records** for their debut single 'Rich Girl'. Switching to London Records in 1993, they released an exuberant version of **Lulu**'s 'Shout' which stayed in the UK Top 10 for eight weeks. After protracted legal wranglings they eventually signed to China Records in 1994, working on their delayed debut album in Jamaica with **Sly & Robbie**, and then in Los Angeles, California with **Quincy Jones**' son QDIII (**Ice Cube**, **Tupac Shakur**). A diverse blend of reggae rhythms with elements of dancehall, pop, R&B and hip-hop, *I'll Be Free*'s material did not always do justice to the production talent on show, although the club hit 'Champagne And Wine' and the funky 'Free' were notable highlights. The video for the Top 40 'Good Sweet Lovin'' included a cameo appearance from **Suggs**, resulting in the duo guesting on the ex-**Madness** singer's hit single 'Cecilia'. They also went on to headline the Japansplash Festival alongside **Shaggy**, **Snow** and **Barrington Levy**, performing to audiences of over 100,000, while further tours of Japan and the Far East served to strengthen their popularity in the Asian market. *Danger-Us* was released in September 1997, and featured a more mature and full sound. Ranging from the reggae/dancehall workouts 'Before The Night Is Over' and 'Kingman', through an excursion into salsa ('The Crickets Sing For Ana Maria'), to the modern urban soul of 'You'll Never Know' and 'I Knew I Blew It', the album again featured QDIII and Sly & Robbie, with additional production work by the in-demand Jazzwad (**Buju Banton**, **Shabba Ranks**) and Buzz Productions (**Maxi Priest**, Barrington Levy).

● ALBUMS: *I'll Be Free* (China 1995)★★★, *Danger-Us* (IndoChina 1997)★★★.

Loudermilk, John D.

b. 31 March 1934, Durham, North Carolina, USA. Loudermilk's first musical experience was banging a drum for the Salvation Army; he played various instruments as a child and appeared regularly on the radio from the age of 11. In 1956, **George Hamilton IV** recorded his song 'A Rose And A Baby Ruth', which went from the local to the national charts, reaching number 6. A few months later, **Eddie Cochran** made his debut in the US Top 20 with 'Sittin' In The Balcony', another Loudermilk song that he had recorded himself under the pseudonym Johnny D. When Loudermilk moved to Nashville, a stream of hits followed, the UK chart successes being 'Waterloo' (**Stonewall Jackson**, 1959), 'Angela Jones' (**Michael Cox**, 1960), 'Tobacco Road' (**Nashville Teens**, 1964), 'Google Eye' (which was a catfish, Nashville Teens, 1964), 'This Little Bird' (**Marianne Faithfull**, 1965, and subsequently parodied by the **Barron Knights**), 'Then You Can Tell Me Goodbye' (**Casinos**, 1967, and a US country number 1 for **Eddy Arnold**), 'It's My Time' (the **Everly Brothers**, 1968), 'Indian Reservation (The Lament Of The Cherokee Reservation Indian)' (**Don Fardon**, 1970 and a US number 1 for the **Raiders**, 1971) and 'Sunglasses' (a revival of a **Skeeter Davis** record by **Tracey Ullman**, 1984). His controversial 'death' song, 'Ebony Eyes', was the b-side of the **Everly Brothers**' 1961 number 1, 'Walk Right Back'. Other successful b-sides include 'Weep No More My Baby' (**Brenda Lee**'s 'Sweet Nuthins'), 'Stayin' In' (**Bobby Vee**'s 'More Than I Can Say'), 'Heaven Fell Last Night' (the **Browns**' 'The Three Bells') and 'In A Matter Of Moments' (**Louise Cordet**'s 'I'm Just A Baby'). Near misses include 'All Of This For Sally' (**Mark Dinning**), 'The Guitar Player (Him And Her)' for **Jimmy Justice** and 'To Hell With Love' for **Adam Faith**. He arranged an old song, 'Abilene', for George Hamilton IV, which made the US charts in 1963 and became a country standard. His other country music successes include 'Talk Back Trembling Lips' (**Ernest Ashworth** and **Johnny Tillotson**), 'Bad News' (**Johnny Cash** and **Boxcar Willie**), 'Break My Mind' (George Hamilton IV, **Gram Parsons** and the **Hillsiders**), 'You're Ruinin' My Life' (**Hank Williams Jnr.**) and 'Half-Breed' (**Marvin Rainwater**). He wrote clever novelty songs for **Bob Luman** ('The Great Snowman' and 'The File') and for **Sue Thompson** ('Sad Movies (Make Me Cry)', 'Norman', 'James (Hold The Ladder Steady)' and 'Paper Tiger', all US Top 30 hits). Loudermilk had his own hit with 'The Language Of Love', which made number 13 in the UK in 1962. He made several albums of his own material and they have been collected on two Bear Family compilations, *Blue Train* and *It's My Time*, which contain two previously unreleased tracks in 'The Little Wind Up Doll' and 'Giving You All My Love'. He has often worked in the UK and performs his songs in a similar manner to Burl Ives. He produced Pete Sayers' best album, *Bogalusa Gumbo*, in 1979, but an album that he recorded at the same sessions has not been released. He now spends his time studying ethnomusicology.

● ALBUMS: *The Language Of Love* (RCA Victor 1961)★★★, *Twelve Sides Of Loudermilk* (RCA Victor 1962)★★★, *John D. Loudermilk Sings A Bizarre Collection Of Unusual Songs* (RCA Victor 1965)★★★, *Suburban Attitudes In Country Verse* (RCA Victor 1967)★★, *Country Love Songs* (RCA Victor 1968)★★, *The Open Mind Of John D. Loudermilk* (RCA Victor 1969)★★, *Elloree* (1975)★★, *Just Passing Through* (1977)★★.

● COMPILATIONS: *The Best Of John D. Loudermilk* (RCA 1970)★★★, *Encores* (RCA 1975)★★★, *Blue Train* (Bear Family 1989)★★★, *It's My Time* (Bear Family 1989)★★★, *Sittin' In The Balcony* (Bear Family 1995)★★★.

Louis, Big Joe, And His Blues Kings

b. Jamaica. Moving to England when he was 12, Jamaican-born Louis did not start playing guitar until he was over 20, having learnt to play music on the clar-inet. Living in Kent, Louis played in a duo with guitarist David Purdy while avidly building up his collection of obscure blues records, before moving to London in 1984. After initially performing with harmonica player Shakey Vick, Louis played low-key sets around the capital with various personnel who gradually became known as 'Big' Joe Louis And His Band (the 'Big' was there simply 'to get further up the listings'). With a strong live reputation built up over ten years of touring, and some well-received studio sets, Louis and his band (now known as Big Joe Louis And His Blues Kings) are an important force in modern British blues. The current line-up, comprising George Sueref (guitar, harmonica, piano), Brian Nevill (drums) and Matt Radford (bass), recorded 1996's *Big Sixteen*, which was nominated for a British Blues Connection award. Louis also researches blues music for the Mechanical Copyright Protection Society.

● ALBUMS: *Big Joe Louis And His Blues Kings* (Blue Horizon 1988)★★★, *Big Sixteen* (Ace 1996)★★★★.

Louis, Joe Hill

b. Lester Hill, 23 September 1921, Whitehaven Tennessee, USA, d. 5 August 1957, Memphis, USA. Hill learned blues harmonica from **Will Shade** as a teenager and was given the name Joe Hill Louis after victory in a boxing match. He performed in Memphis in the late 40s, where he became known as 'The Be-Bop Boy', and developed a one-man band act with guitar, foot-drum and harmonica. Louis's first recordings were made for **Columbia** in 1949 before he took over **B.B. King**'s radio spot as the Pepticon Boy on WDIA in Memphis. This led to 'Boogie in the Park', a single produced by **Sam Phillips** for his short-lived Phillips label in 1950. Next, Phillips signed Louis to the **Bihari Brothers**' Modern label, for which 'I Feel Like A Million' was a local hit. By 1952, Phillips was recording him with a backing group on tracks such as 'We All Gotta Go Sometime', and also used Louis to accompany such artists as the **Prisonaires** and **Rufus Thomas**, for whose 'Tiger Man' (1953) he supplied a scintillating guitar solo. There were other tracks for Checker, Meteor and Ace. His final records were made for House Of Sound shortly before his death from tetanus in Memphis in August 1957.

● COMPILATIONS: *Blues In The Morning* reissue (1972)★★★, *The One Man Band 1949-56* reissue (Muskadine 1979)★★★.

Louise

b. Louise Nurding, 4 November 1974, Croydon, Surrey, UK. After two successful years with **Eternal**, Nurding (now billed simply as Louise) took the risky step of embarking on a solo career when Eternal were at their chart-topping peak. Remaining at **EMI**, the gamble paid off when her debut single 'Light Of My Life' reached number 8 in the UK in October 1995. Although 'In Walked Love' stalled at number 17, her next three singles, 'Naked' (number 5 in June 1996),

'Undivided Love' (number 5 in August 1996) and 'One Kiss From Heaven' (number 9 in November 1996), all reached the UK Top Ten. On the back of widespread media coverage, her debut album *Naked* went on to sell over 400,000 units. Belying the perceived image of the beautiful but vacuous glamour girl voted 'sexiest woman in the world', Louise contributed to the writing and production of her follow-up album, *Woman In Me*, recorded with producers Steve Levine (**Culture Club**), Simon Climie (**Climie Fisher**) and Nigel Lowis (Eternal). Buoyed by the success of the album's first two singles, 'Arms Around The World' and a cover version of the **Average White Band**'s 'Let's Go Round Again', Louise set off on her first UK solo tour. She kept in the spotlight by marrying her soccer player boyfriend Jamie Redknapp, shortly before the World Cup began in June 1998.
● ALBUMS: *Naked* (EMI 1996)★★★, *Woman In Me* (EMI 1997)★★★.

Louisiana Hayride, The

This popular radio show was first broadcast on station KWKH Shreveport on 3 April 1948, the brainchild of the manager Henry Clay, the programme director Horace Logan and the commercial manager Dean Upson (a former member of the **Grand Ole Opry** singing trio, the **Vagabonds**). The programme, a three-hour Saturday night show broadcast live from Shreveport's Municipal Auditorium, quickly attracted the public's attention. It was soon rated by many to be second only to Nashville's *Opry* as the important venue for would-be country stars to reach. The *Opry* had already been established for over 20 years but the *Hayride* did not have the budget to compete with the mighty WSM, and consequently, it became the practice that artists first established themselves on the *Hayride* and then moved up to the *Opry*. In its way, therefore, if only as a final grooming place for stardom, the show became a very important part of country music and soon acquired the nickname of 'the cradle of the stars'. The first *Hayride* show actually featured some established acts, including the **Bailes Brothers** and **Johnny And Jack** (plus Johnny's then unknown wife, **Kitty Wells**), but within four months, under the careful management of its director and compere Horace Logan, the show had its own new star in **Hank Williams** (Hank would later return to play the *Hayride* in November 1952, after he was dropped by the *Opry*). From that point, the country music side of KWKH's programming saw a steady progression of future stars, including **Red Sovine**, **Webb Pierce**, **George Jones**, **Faron Young**, **Johnny Horton**, **Jimmy C. Newman**, **Floyd Cramer**, **Hank Locklin**, **Slim Whitman** and **Elvis Presley** (Whitman recorded two of his biggest hits, 'Indian Love Call' and 'Love Song Of The Waterfall', for **Imperial Records** in the studio of KWKH). **Jim Reeves** launched his career with KWKH, first as an announcer and DJ before being given the chance to sing one night on the *Hayride* in 1952, when Hank Williams failed to arrive. **Johnny Cash** also started on the road to stardom as a member of the *Hayride* in 1955. In its heyday, the *Hayride* show was broadcast over CBS national network and also carried internationally on the Armed Forces Network. Recordings of performances on the show by some artists, including one by Presley, have been issued on CD. When the show finally ended, after undergoing various formats, in the early 90s, it marked the end of a piece of country music history.

Louisiana Purchase

This show, which made its debut at the Imperial Theatre in New York on 28 May 1940, was **Irving Berlin**'s first Broadway score since his successful revue *As Thousands Cheer* brightened up America's gradual emergence from the Depression in 1933. In the intervening years, the prolific songwriter had scored several Hollywood films, including the classic **Fred Astaire-Ginger Rogers** musicals, *Top Hat*, *Follow The Fleet*, and *Carefree*. Morrie Riskin's humorous and satirical book was based on a story by **B.G. 'Buddy' De Sylva**, and was said to have been influenced by a recent political scandal involving Huey Long, a well-known Louisiana politician. The upstanding and incorruptible Senator Oliver P. Loganberry (Victor Moore), travels to New Orleans in an effort to disentangle the somewhat unconventional business methods practised by the Louisiana Purchase Company. The firm's lawyer, Jim Taylor (William Gaxton), tries to deflect the heat by putting the Senator in a series of compromising situations with the titillating trio of Marina Van Linden (Vera Zorina), Mme. Boredelaise (Irene Bordoni), and Beatrice (Carol Bruce). Happily, Loganberry emerges with his honour intact. As usual, Berlin's score complemented the story perfectly. Two of the numbers, 'It's A Lovely Day Tomorrow', sung by Bordoni, and 'You're Lonely And I'm Lonely', which served as a duet for Moore and Zorina, became quite popular - the latter for **Tommy Dorsey**'s Orchestra, with a vocal by the young **Frank Sinatra**. Carol Bruce made a memorable musical comedy debut, and sang the chirpy title song. The rest of the score included 'Outside Of That I Love You', 'Latins Know How', 'The Lord Done Fixed Up My Soul', 'Fools Fall In Love', 'What Chance Have I?', and 'You Can't Brush Me Off'. Chorus members, Hugh Martin and Ralph Blane, later went on to write the scores for *Best Foot Forward* on Broadway, and *Meet Me In St. Louis* in Hollywood. The presence of the familiar team of Gaxton and Moore ensured that *Louisiana Purchase* had a lot of laughs, and a successful run of 444 performances.

Louisiana Red

b. Iverson Minter, 23 March 1936, Vicksburg, Mississippi, USA. Although beginning as a sincere imitator of his various heroes, including **Muddy Waters**, **Lightnin' Hopkins** and **John Lee Hooker**, **Louisiana Red** has gained stature of his own as an instinctive and creative blues singer and guitarist. Red spent his earliest years in a variety of orphanages, his mother having died a week after his birth, and his estranged father a victim of Ku Klux Klan violence. Raised in Pittsburg by an aunt, Corrine Driver, he owned his first guitar at the age of 11 and had instruction from the veteran Crit Walters. At the age of 16, he joined the army and served in Korea. On his return, although claiming to have recorded with Waters and **Little Walter**, his first known record, 'Gonna Play My Guitar', was released under the name of Playboy Fuller on his own Fuller label. Another session for Checker as Rocky Fuller yielded a single, 'Soon One Morning'; further titles were reissued during the 80s. Working alongside Hooker and **Eddie Kirkland**, he gained a reputation as 'a guitar fiend'. Much of the 50s was spent travelling throughout the south. In 1960 he moved to New Jersey and made his first record as Louisiana Red for Atlas; 'I Done Woke Up' was backed by James Wayne & The Nighthawks. After recording an unissued session for **Bobby Robinson**'s Fury label, Red was signed to Roulette in 1962 by veteran producer Henry Glover, and the subsequent album, *The Lowdown Backporch Blues*, brought him much critical praise. During 1965 he was comprehensively recorded for Festival Records by **Herb Abramson**, from which the **Atco** album *Louisiana Red Sings The Blues* was assembled. Further titles appeared on the Red Lightnin' *Hot Sauce* album. Other sessions took place in 1967, 1971 and 1973. He recorded a number of sessions in 1975 for Blue Labor, from which two volumes of *The Blues Purity Of Louisiana Red* were issued; he also participated on albums by **Peg Leg Sam**, **Johnny Shines**, **Roosevelt Sykes** and **Brownie McGhee**. In 1976 he moved to Germany, where he has remained, touring Europe extensively and recording for several labels including Black Panther, JSP, L+R, Orchid, MMG and Blues Beacon. He is a dependable if mercurial performer, his spontaneity sometimes a brick wall but often a springboard.

● ALBUMS: *The Lowdown Backporch Blues* (Vogue 1984)★★★, *Midnight Rambler* (Tomato 1988)★★★, *Live At 55* (1991)★★★, *Sings The Blues ...* (Blue Sting 1994)★★★, *Sittin' Here Wonderin'* early 50s recording (Earwig 1995)★★★★.

● COMPILATIONS: *The Best Of Louisiana Red* (Evidence 1995)★★★★, *Midnight Rambler* (Charly 1996)★★★.

Louiss, Eddy

b. Edouard Louise, 2 May 1941, Paris, France. Born into a musical family, his father was a trumpet player, and he studied several musical instruments, including trumpet and piano. In his early teenage years Louiss played in his father's band. In the early 60s he was playing piano in various Paris nightclubs and continuing with his studies. He also sang with the French vocal group Double Six, other members of which included **Roger Guérin**, Ward Swingle and Christiane Legrand, the sister of **Michel Legrand**. Adding the organ to his

array of instrumental ability, Louiss played with various jazzmen in the 60s, among them **Johnny Griffin**, **Art Taylor**, **Dizzy Gillespie**, **Jean-Luc Ponty** and **Stan Getz**. In the late 60s he was with a trio led by **Kenny Clarke** and he also recorded with **Barney Kessell**. Louiss continued to play extensively throughout Europe during the 70s and into the 80s when he formed an adventurous big band, Multicolor Feeling. In the 90s he was also heard in duo with **Michel Petrucciani**. A very melodic player on both piano and organ, Louiss also has an intense rhythmic undercurrent to his work which adds excitement especially on mid- and up-tempo numbers.

● ALBUMS: *Our Kind Of Sabi* (Verve 1958)★★★, *Les Double-six* (Columbia 1961-62)★★, *Dizzy Gillespie Et Les Double Six* (Philips 1963)★★★, with Jean-Luc Ponty *Jazz Long Playing* (Philips 1964)★★★★, with Ponty, Daniel Humair Trio *HLP* (Columbia 1968)★★★, *Barney Kessel* (Mercury 1969)★★★, with Stéphane Grappelli *Satin Doll* (Festival 1972)★★★, *Eddy Louiss Orgue* (America 1972)★★, with Michel Petrucciani *Conference De Presse* (Dreyfus 1994)★★★.

Loup Garou

Pronounced 'Loo Ga Roo', which translates from the Creole word for 'folkloric werewolves', this New York, USA based group mine musical territory in the classic Cajun tradition, updated through their fierce employment of traditional instruments and contemporary technology: 'Our music is about celebration', is how they themselves surmise their method, which has thus far ingratiated them to an ever expanding audience. The group comprises Jimmy Macdonell (b. Lafayette, Louisiana, USA; accordion/vocals), Jim Gregory (b. West Virginia, USA; bass), George G. Recile (b. New Orleans, Louisiana, USA; drums), Mark Dufault (b. New York, USA; guitar), Neil Thomas (b. Philadelphia, USA; keyboards; ex-Surreal McCoys) and Ronin (b. Brooklyn, New York, USA; vocals/washboard). Their early shows quickly attracted several famous name advocates. **David Byrne** was one, going on to recruit Macdonell on his 'Don't Fence Me' cut for the *Red, Hot And Blue* **Cole Porter** charity tribute. **Bryan Ferry** booked the group to open his American tour after witnessing just one show, and other celebrity fans include Tina Weymouth and Chris Frantz (**Talking Heads**, **Tom Tom Club**), **Robert Palmer**, Bob Weir of the **Grateful Dead** and **Paul Simon**, who employed the group on his *Rhythm Of The Saints* tour and invited Macdonell to contribute to that album. The band also made its soundtrack debut in John Sayles' film *Passion Fish*, which the permanently in-demand Macdonell helped to score.

● ALBUMS: *Loup Garou* (Sky Ranch/Virgin 1993)★★★.

Loussier, Jacques

b. 26 October 1934, Angers, France. A classically taught pianist, he found a career in commercial popular music more lucrative. Then, in 1959, he hit upon the idea of performing the classical piano works of Johann Sebastian Bach in a quasi-jazz style. Together with **Pierre Michelot** and Christian Garros, the trio had enormous international success with the wider public. The concept, the low-key detached style, and possibly the huge commercial success, failed to endear the group to the hardcore jazz audience.

● ALBUMS: *Play Bach* i (Decca 1960)★★★, *Play Bach* ii (Decca 1961)★★★, *Play Bach* iii (Decca 1962)★★★, *Play Bach* iv (London 1963)★★★, *The World Of Jacques Loussier - Live* (Decca 70s)★★★★, *Bach To The Future* (State Of The Art 70s)★★★, *The Jacques Loussier Trio In Concert At The Royal Festival Hall* (Philips 70s)★★★, *The Four Seasons* (Telarc 1997)★★★.

Louvin Brothers

Brothers Lonnie Ira Loudermilk (b. 21 April 1924, d. 20 June 1965) and Charlie Elzer Loudermilk (b. 7 July 1927) were both born in Rainesville, Alabama, USA. They were raised on a 40-acre farm in Henegar, Alabama, but only half of it could be cultivated. Despite their poverty, their parents sang gospel songs and encouraged their sons' musical talents. Ira took up the mandolin and Charlie the guitar, and they created perfect harmonies for country and gospel music, inspired, in particular, by the **Blue Sky Boys**. In 1943, after winning a talent contest in Chattanooga, they began broadcasting regularly, leading to three shows a day for WMPS in Memphis. They recorded for **Decca**, **MGM** and **Capitol**, but they found it hard to make ends meet and worked night shifts in the Post Office. Some radio broadcasts to promote a songbook, *Songs That Tell A Story*, have been released and show the Louvin Brothers at their best, with no additional instruments. Their career was also interrupted by Charlie's military service in Korea (their 'Weapon Of Prayer' was an emotional plea for peace). They performed as the Louvin Brothers because the family name was considered too long for stage work, although their cousin, **John D. Loudermilk**, was to have no such qualms. Capitol Records re-signed the brothers as gospel artists but a tobacco company sponsoring a portion of the *Grand Ole Opry* told them to sing secular songs as 'you can't sell tobacco with gospel music'. They crossed over to the country market with their own composition 'When I Stop Dreaming', which is now a standard. Their secular US country hits included 'I Don't Believe You've Met My Baby' (their only number 1), 'Hoping That That You're Hoping', 'You're Running Wild' and 'My Baby's Gone', but Charlie says, 'I don't think we ever did a show without some gospel music. Our mother would have thrashed us if we hadn't done that!'

By the late 50s, their sound was old-fashioned and their songs too melodramatic for the rock 'n' roll era. The **Everly Brothers**, who acknowledged their debt to the Louvins, may also have contributed unwittingly to their downfall. Charlie says, 'Ken Nelson told Ira, in 1958, that the mandolin was hindering the sales of our music, so my brother lost total interest in the mandolin and

never picked another note on it on a record. He had put 25 years of his life into mastering that instrument, and it messed his head to hear a good friend whose opinion he respected say, "You're the problem, you've got to throw that thing away".' Ira's drink problem worsened, their own relationship deteriorated and their last success together was, ironically, 'Must You Throw Dirt In My Face?'. Charlie broke up the partnership on 18 August 1963: '*He* had said a lot of times he was going to quit, but it was the first time *I* had ever said it.' Charlie went on to have solo hits with 'I Don't Love You Anymore' and 'See The Big Man Cry, Mama'. Ira started his solo career with 'Yodel Sweet Molly' but he was shot and badly injured by his wife, Faye, whom he then divorced. He then married Florence, who sang on his shows as Anne Young, but soon afterwards they both perished in a car crash in Jefferson City, Missouri, USA, on 20 June 1965. Ira and **Bill Monroe** had pledged that whoever lived the longest would sing at the other's funeral, and Monroe sang 'Where No One Stands Alone'. **Gram Parsons** introduced their songs to a new audience, recording 'The Christian Life' with the **Byrds**, and 'Cash On The Barrelhead' and 'The Angels Rejoiced In Heaven Last Night' with **Emmylou Harris**. After Parsons' death, Harris continued recording their songs: 'If I Could Only Win Your Love', 'When I Stop Dreaming', 'You're Learning' and, with Don Everly, 'Everytime You Leave'. Charlie Louvin had a country hit with 'You're My Wife, She's My Woman' and made two successful albums with **Melba Montgomery**. A single, 'Love Don't Care' with Emmylou Harris, made the US country charts.

● ALBUMS: by the Louvin Brothers *Tragic Songs Of Life* (Capitol 1956)★★★★, *Nearer My God To Thee* (Capitol 1957)★★★, *The Louvin Brothers* (MGM 1957)★★★★, *Ira And Charlie* (Capitol 1958)★★★, *The Family Who Prays* (Capitol 1958)★★★★, *Country Love Ballads* (Capitol 1959)★★★, *Satan Is Real* (Capitol 1960)★★★, *Those Louvin Brothers Sing The Songs Of The Delmores* (Capitol 1960)★★★, *My Baby's Gone* (Capitol 1960)★★★, *Encore* (Capitol 1961)★★★, *Country Christmas With The Louvin Brothers* (Capitol 1961)★★★, *Weapon Of Prayer* (Capitol 1962)★★★, *Keep Your Eyes On Jesus* (Capitol 1963)★★★, *The Louvin Brothers Sing And Play Their Current Hits* (Capitol 1964)★★★, *Thank God For My Christian Home* (Capitol 1965)★★★, *Two Different Worlds* (Capitol 1966)★★★, *The Louvin Brothers Sing The Great Roy Acuff Songs* (Capitol 1967)★★★, *Country Heart And Soul* (Tower 1968)★★★, *Live At The New River Ranch* recorded 1956 (Copper Creek 1989)★★★, *Running Wild* (1992)★★★.
Solo: Ira Louvin *The Unforgettable Ira Louvin* (Capitol 1965)★★★.

● COMPILATIONS: *The Great Gospel Singing Of The Louvin Brothers* (1973)★★★, *Songs That Tell A Story* (Rounder 1981)★★★, *Radio Favourites 1951-1957* (CMF 1987)★★★, *Close Harmony* 8-CD box set (Bear Family 1992)★★★★, *Capitol Country Music Classics* (1993)★★★, *When I Stop Dreaming: The Best Of The Louvin Brothers* (Razor & Tie 1995)★★★★.